THE SEVENTH MENTAL MEASUREMENTS YEARBOOK

Volume I

THE SEVENTH
MENTAL
MEASUREMENTS
YEARBOOK

Edited by

OSCAR KRISEN BUROS
Director, The Institute of Mental Measurements

VOLUME I

THE GRYPHON PRESS
HIGHLAND PARK · NEW JERSEY
1972

DESIGNED BY LUELLA BUROS

LIBRARY OF CONGRESS CATALOG CARD NUMBER 39-3422
ISBN 910674-11-6

MANUFACTURED BY QUINN & BODEN COMPANY, INC., RAHWAY, NEW JERSEY
PRINTED IN THE UNITED STATES OF AMERICA

To Luella

Table of Contents

Contributing Test Reviewers

IRA E. AARON, Professor of Education and Head of the Reading Department, The University of Georgia, Athens, Georgia

GEORGIA S. ADAMS, Professor of Education, California State College, Los Angeles, California

C. J. ADCOCK, Retired Professor of Psychology, Victoria University of Wellington, Wellington, New Zealand

DOROTHY C. ADKINS, Professor and Researcher, College of Education, University of Hawaii, Honolulu, Hawaii

J. STANLEY AHMANN, Professor of Psychology, Colorado State University, Fort Collins, Colorado

LEWIS E. ALBRIGHT, Director, Organization and Management Development, Kaiser Aluminum and Chemical Corporation, Oakland, California

HENRY A. ALKER, Assistant Professor of Psychology and Sociology, Cornell University, Ithaca, New York

ANNE ANASTASI, Professor of Psychology and Chairman of the Department, Fordham University, New York, New York

NICHOLAS ANASTASIOW, Director, Institute for Child Study, Indiana University, Bloomington, Indiana

O. F. ANDERHALTER, Professor of Education, Saint Louis University, Saint Louis, Missouri; and Director of Research and Service, Scholastic Testing Service, Inc., Bensenville, Illinois

HOWARD R. ANDERSON, Senior Consulting Editor, Social Studies, Houghton Mifflin Company, Boston, Massachusetts

ALEXANDER W. ASTIN, Director, Office of Research, American Council on Education, Washington, D.C.

J. DOUGLAS AYERS, Professor of Education, University of Victoria, Victoria, British Columbia, Canada

LEONARD L. BAIRD, Research Psychologist, Educational Testing Service, Princeton, New Jersey

THOMAS S. BALDWIN, Associate Professor of Education, University of North Carolina, Chapel Hill, North Carolina

ALLAN G. BARCLAY, Professor of Psychology, Saint Louis University, Saint Louis, Missouri

REBECCA C. BARR, Director, The Reading Clinic, The University of Chicago, Chicago, Illinois

W. L. BASHAW, Professor of Educational Psychology, The University of Georgia, Athens, Georgia

ROBERT H. BAUERNFEIND, Professor of Educational Psychology, Northern Illinois University, DeKalb, Illinois

HAROLD P. BECHTOLDT, Professor of Psychology, The University of Iowa, Iowa City, Iowa

E. G. BEGLE, Professor of Mathematics Education, Stanford University, Stanford, California

GEORGE K. BENNETT, Formerly President, The Psychological Corporation, New York, New York

PETER M. BENTLER, Associate Professor of Psychology, University of California, Los Angeles, California

ARTHUR L. BENTON, Professor of Neurology and Psychology, The University of Iowa, Iowa City, Iowa

RALPH F. BERDIE, Professor of Psychology and Director, Student Life Studies, University of Minnesota, Minneapolis, Minnesota

HARRY D. BERG, Professor, Office of Evaluation Services, Michigan State University, East Lansing, Michigan

PAUL CONRAD BERG, Professor of Education and Director, Reading Clinic, University of South Carolina, Columbia, South Carolina

ALLEN BERGER, Associate Professor of Reading Education, The University of Alberta, Edmonton, Alberta, Canada

L. B. BIRCH, Macdonald Professor of Education and Director of Graduate Studies, Faculty of Education, McGill University, Montreal, Quebec, Canada

DONALD B. BLACK, Professor of Educational Psychology, The University of Calgary, Calgary, Alberta, Canada

BENJAMIN S. BLOOM, Charles H. Swift Distinguished Service Professor of Education, The University of Chicago, Chicago, Illinois

BRUCE BLOXOM, Assistant Professor of Psychology, Vanderbilt University, Nashville, Tennessee

JACK L. BODDEN, Assistant Professor of Psychology, Texas Tech University, Lubbock, Texas

DANIEL R. BOONE, Professor of Speech Pathology, University of Denver, Denver, Colorado

FRED H. BORGEN, Research Psychologist, National Merit Scholarship Corporation, Evanston, Illinois

HAROLD BORKO, Professor of Psychology, School of Library Service, University of California, Los Angeles, California

JOHN R. BORMUTH, Associate Professor of Education, The University of Chicago, Chicago, Illinois

THOMAS J. BOUCHARD, JR., Associate Professor of Psychology, University of Minnesota, Minneapolis, Minnesota

JAMES BRASWELL, Associate Examiner in Mathematics, Educational Testing Service, Princeton, New Jersey

JOHN R. BRAUN, Professor of Psychology and Chairman of the Department, University of Bridgeport, Bridgeport, Connecticut

ANN BRICKNER, Editor in Chief, EDL/McGraw-Hill, Huntington, New York

ROBERT G. BRIDGHAM, Assistant Professor of Education, Stanford University, Stanford, California

M. A. BRIMER, Head of Research Unit, School of Education, University of Bristol, Bristol, England

FREDERICK G. BROWN, Professor of Psychology, Iowa State University, Ames, Iowa

JAMES E. BRYAN, Education Specialist, Department of Health, Education, and Welfare, Health Services and Mental Health Administration, Public Health Service, Center for Disease Control, Atlanta, Georgia

MIRIAM M. BRYAN, Consultant, Cooperative Tests and Services, Educational Testing Service, Princeton, New Jersey

N. DALE BRYANT, Professor of Psychology and Education, Teachers College, Columbia University, New York, New York

CAROLYN L. BURKE, Assistant Professor of Education and Associate Director, Reading Miscue Research, Wayne State University, Detroit, Michigan

ALVIN G. BURSTEIN, Professor of Psychology and Chief of the Division, The University of Texas Medical School at San Antonio, San Antonio, Texas

NANCY W. BURTON, Fellow, Laboratory of Educational Research, University of Colorado, Boulder, Colorado

H. J. BUTCHER, Professor of Educational Psychology, University of Sussex, Brighton, Sussex, England

KATHARINE G. BUTLER, Professor of Speech Pathology and Audiology, San Jose State College, San Jose, California

MARGARET C. BYRNE, Professor of Speech Pathology and Audiology, University of Kansas, Lawrence, Kansas

LEONARD S. CAHEN, Research Psychologist, Educational Testing Service, Princeton, New Jersey

JAMES R. CALDWELL, Counselor, Alhambra High School, Alhambra, California

DAVID P. CAMPBELL, Professor of Psychology and Director, Center for Interest Measurement Research, University of Minnesota, Minneapolis, Minnesota

JOEL T. CAMPBELL, Senior Research Psychologist, Educational Testing Service, Princeton, New Jersey

VINCENT N. CAMPBELL, Associate Program Director, Social and Educational Research Program, American Institutes for Research, Palo Alto, California

THORSTEN R. CARLSON, Professor of Education, Sonoma State College, Rohnert Park, California

JOHN B. CARROLL, Senior Research Psychologist, Educational Testing Service, Princeton, New Jersey

L. RAY CARRY, Assistant Professor of Mathematics Education and Mathematics, The University of Texas, Austin, Texas

COURTNEY B. CAZDEN, Associate Professor of Education, Harvard University, Cambridge, Massachusetts

ROBERT C. CHALLMAN, Clinical Psychologist, 301 Kenwood Parkway, Minneapolis, Minnesota

CLINTON I. CHASE, Professor of Educational Psychology and Chairman of the Department; and Director, Bureau of Educational Studies and Testing; Indiana University, Bloomington, Indiana

MAURICE CHAZAN, Senior Lecturer, Department of Education, University College of Swansea, Swansea, Wales

BRAD S. CHISSOM, Assistant Professor of Educational Research, Georgia Southern College, Statesboro, Georgia

D. F. CLARK, Consultant Clinical Psychologist, North-East Regional Hospital Board, Ladysbridge Hospital, Banff, Scotland

JOHN L. D. CLARK, Examiner in Foreign Languages, Test Development Division, Educational Testing Service, Princeton, New Jersey

DOROTHY M. CLENDENEN, Formerly Assistant Director, Test Division, The Psychological Corporation, New York, New York

VICTOR B. CLINE, Professor of Psychology, The University of Utah, Salt Lake City, Utah

RICHARD W. COAN, Professor of Psychology, The University of Arizona, Tucson, Arizona

WILLIAM E. COFFMAN, E. F. Lindquist Professor of Educational Measurement, The University of Iowa, Iowa City, Iowa

JACOB COHEN, Professor of Psychology and Chairman, Quantitative Psychology Area, New York University, New York, New York

S. ALAN COHEN, Associate Professor of Education and Director, Reading and Language Arts Center, Yeshiva University, New York, New York

NANCY S. COLE, Research Psychologist, The American College Testing Program, Iowa City, Iowa

ROBERTA R. COLLARD, Assistant Professor of Human Development, University of Massachusetts, Amherst, Massachusetts

RICHARD COLWELL, Professor of Secondary and Continuing Education and Music, University of Illinois, Urbana, Illinois

ANDREW L. COMREY, Professor of Psychology, University of California, Los Angeles, California

JOHN COOK, Educational Psychologist, Buryfields Clinic, Guildford, Surrey, England

WILLIAM R. CRAWFORD, Assistant Professor of Medical Education and Educational Psychology, University of Illinois at the Medical Center, Chicago, Illinois

JOHN O. CRITES, Professor of Psychology, University of Maryland, College Park, Maryland

LEE J. CRONBACH, Vida Jacks Professor of Education, Stanford University, Stanford, California

RICHARD H. DANA, Professor of Psychology, University of Arkansas, Fayetteville, Arkansas

FREDERICK B. DAVIS, Professor of Education, University of Pennsylvania, Philadelphia, Pennsylvania; and Director, Test Research Service, Bronxville, New York

DENNIS J. DELORIA, Vice President for Research, High/Scope Educational Research Foundation, Ypsilanti, Michigan

R. G. DEMAREE, Professor of Psychology and Research Scientist, Institute of Behavioral Research, Texas Christian University, Fort Worth, Texas

EVELYN DENO, Director, Psycho-Educational Center, University of Minnesota, Minneapolis, Minnesota

CLARENCE DERRICK, Professor of Humanities, University of Florida, Gainesville, Florida

M. VERE DEVAULT, Professor of Education, The University of Wisconsin, Madison, Wisconsin

PAUL B. DIEDERICH, Senior Research Associate, Educational Testing Service, Princeton, New Jersey

RICHARD F. DOCTER, Professor of Psychology, San Fernando Valley State College, Northridge, California

ROBERT H. DOLLIVER, Associate Professor of Psychology and Counseling Psychologist, University of Missouri, Columbia, Missouri

GEORGE DOMINO, Associate Professor of Psychology and Director, Counseling Center, Fordham University, New York, New York

JEROME E. DOPPELT, Associate Director, Test Division, The Psychological Corporation, New York, New York

VINCENT R. D'OYLEY, Professor of Education, The Ontario Institute for Studies in Education, Toronto, Ontario, Canada

PAUL L. DRESSEL, Assistant Provost and Director, Institutional Research, Michigan State University, East Lansing, Michigan

ROBERT C. DROEGE, Research Psychologist, Manpower Administration, United States Department of Labor, Washington, D.C.

PHILIP H. DUBOIS, Professor of Psychology, Washington University, Saint Louis, Missouri

GERALD G. DUFFY, Associate Professor of Education, Michigan State University, East Lansing, Michigan

JAMES A. DUNN, Director, Developmental Systems Division, American Institutes for Research, Palo Alto, California

WALTER N. DUROST, Adjunct Professor of Education, University of New Hampshire, Durham, New Hampshire

RALPH D. DUTCH, Principal Lecturer in Educational Psychology, Aberdeen College of Education, Aberdeen, Scotland

ROBERT DYKSTRA, Professor of Education, University of Minnesota, Minneapolis, Minnesota

NORMAN EAGLE, Coordinator of Institutional Research, Bronx Community College, The City University of New York, Bronx, New York

ROBERT L. EBEL, Professor of Education and Psychology, Michigan State University, East Lansing, Michigan

WILLIAM J. EICHMAN, Associate Professor of Psychology, The University of North Carolina; and Director of Psychology Service, John Umstead Hospital; Chapel Hill, North Carolina

DOROTHY H. EICHORN, Research Psychologist and Administrator, Child Study Center, Institute of Human Development, University of California, Berkeley, California

ALBERT ELLIS, Executive Director, Institute for Advanced Study in Rational Psychotherapy, New York, New York

GERALD L. ERICKSEN, Professor of Psychology and Head of the Department, St. Olaf College, Northfield, Minnesota

LAWRENCE W. ERICKSON, Professor of Education and Assistant Dean, Graduate School of Education, University of California, Los Angeles, California

LEONARD D. ERON, Professor of Psychology, University of Illinois at Chicago Circle, Chicago, Illinois

BARBARA F. ESSER, Associate Director, National Board of Medical Examiners, Philadelphia, Pennsylvania

ALEXANDER EVEN, Assistant Professor of Education, The Ontario Institute for Studies in Education, Toronto, Ontario, Canada

H. J. EYSENCK, Professor of Psychology and Director of the Department, Institute of Psychiatry, University of London, London, England

ROGER FARR, Associate Professor of Education and Director, Reading Clinic, Indiana University, Bloomington, Indiana

LEONARD S. FELDT, Professor of Education, The University of Iowa, Iowa City, Iowa

WARREN G. FINDLEY, Professor of Education and Psychology, The University of Georgia, Athens, Georgia

ROBERT FITZPATRICK, Principal Research Scientist, American Institutes for Research, Pittsburgh, Pennsylvania

JOHN P. FOLEY, JR., President, J. P. Foley and Company, Inc., New York, New York

MARY O. FOLSOM, Professor of Education, University of Miami, Coral Gables, Florida

ROBERT A. FORSYTH, Assistant Professor of Education, The University of Iowa, Iowa City, Iowa

RAYMOND D. FOWLER, JR., Professor of Psychology and Chairman of the Department, University of Alabama, University, Alabama

THOMAS T. FRANTZ, Associate Professor of Counselor Education, State University of New York at Buffalo, Buffalo, New York

NORMAN FREDERIKSEN, Director, Division of Psychological Studies, Educational Testing Service, Princeton, New Jersey

DAVID FREIDES, Associate Professor of Psychology, Emory University, Atlanta, Georgia

JOHN W. FRENCH, Research Consultant, 800 Ben Franklin Drive, Sarasota, Florida

JOSEPH L. FRENCH, Professor of Special Education and Educational Psychology and Head of the Department of Special Education, The Pennsylvania State University, University Park, Pennsylvania

EDWARD B. FRY, Professor of Education and Director, Reading Center, Rutgers, The State University, New Brunswick, New Jersey

EDWARD J. FURST, Professor of Education, University of Arkansas, Fayetteville, Arkansas

ROSSLYN GAINES, Associate Research Psychologist and Project Director, Institute of Human Development, University of California, Berkeley, California

ERIC F. GARDNER, Margaret O. Slocum Professor of Education and Psychology and Chairman, Department of Psychology; and Director, Psychological Services and Research Center; Syracuse University, Syracuse, New York

SOL L. GARFIELD, Professor of Psychology and Director, Clinical Psychology Program, Washington University, Saint Louis, Missouri

EDGAR R. GARRETT, Professor of Speech and Head of the Department, New Mexico State University, Las Cruces, New Mexico

JOHN J. GEYER, Associate Professor of Education, Rutgers, The State University, New Brunswick, New Jersey

CECIL A. GIBB, Professor of Psychology, Australian National University, Canberra City, Australia

GENE V GLASS, Professor of Education and Co-Director, Laboratory of Educational Research, University of Colorado, Boulder, Colorado

GOLDINE C. GLESER, Professor of Psychology and Director, Psychology Division, University of Cincinnati College of Medicine, Cincinnati, Ohio

MARVIN D. GLOCK, Professor of Educational Psychology, Cornell University, Ithaca, New York

LEWIS R. GOLDBERG, Professor of Psychology, University of Oregon; and Research Associate, Orgeon Research Institute; Eugene, Oregon

BERT A. GOLDMAN, Dean of Academic Advising, The University of North Carolina at Greensboro, Greensboro, North Carolina

MARCEL L. GOLDSCHMID, Associate Professor of Psychology and Director, Centre for Learning and Development, McGill University, Montreal, Quebec, Canada

ELIZABETH J. GOODACRE, Lecturer, Institute of Education, University of London, London, England

CLARENCE J. GOODNIGHT, Professor of Biology and Head of the Department, Western Michigan University, Kalmazoo, Michigan

LEONARD D. GOODSTEIN, Professor of Psychology and Director of Professional Training in Psychology, University of Cincinnati, Cincinnati, Ohio

EDWIN GORDON, Professor of Music and Education, The University of Iowa, Iowa City, Iowa

LEONARD V. GORDON, Professor of Educational Psychology and Statistics, State University of New York at Albany, Albany, New York

HARRISON G. GOUGH, Professor of Psychology, University of California, Berkeley, California

RUSSEL F. GREEN, Research Consultant in Psychology and Education, Henrietta, New York

ARNOLD B. GROBMAN, Professor of Zoology and Dean of Rutgers College, Rutgers, The State University, New Brunswick, New Jersey

HULDA GROBMAN, Professor of Education, New York University, New York, New York

RICHARD E. GROSS, Professor of Education, Stanford University, Stanford, California

ARLEN R. GULLICKSON, Research Assistant, College of Education, University of Minnesota, Minneapolis, Minnesota

R. GULLIFORD, Senior Lecturer in Education, The University of Birmingham, Birmingham, England

JOHN T. GUTHRIE, Assistant Professor of Education, The Johns Hopkins University, Baltimore, Maryland

MALCOLM D. GYNTHER, Professor of Psychology, Saint Louis University, Saint Louis, Missouri

ELIZABETH HAGEN, Professor of Psychology and Education, Teachers College, Columbia University, New York, New York

MICHIO PETER HAGIWARA, Associate Professor of French, University of Michigan, Ann Arbor, Michigan

A. RALPH HAKSTIAN, Associate Professor of Educational Psychology, University of Alberta, Edmonton, Alberta, Canada

RAPHAEL M. HALLER, Associate Professor of Special Education, Newark State College, Union, New Jersey

GARY R. HANSON, Research Psychologist, The American College Testing Program, Iowa City, Iowa

ROBERT A. HARPER, Consulting Psychologist, 3000 Connecticut Avenue N.W., Washington, D.C.

ALBERT J. HARRIS, Emeritus Professor of Education, The City University of New York, New York, New York

DALE B. HARRIS, Professor of Psychology, The Pennsylvania State University, University Park, Pennsylvania

DAVID P. HARRIS, Professor of Linguistics and Director, The American Language Institute, Georgetown University, Washington, D.C.

LARRY A. HARRIS, Associate Professor of Education, The University of North Dakota, Grand Forks, North Dakota

ROBERT C. HARRIS, Assistant Professor of Vocational Education, Indiana University, Bloomington, Indiana

MARY T. HARRISON, Supervisor, Personnel Services Division 3255, Sandia Laboratories, Albuquerque, New Mexico

DAVID G. HAWKRIDGE, Director, Institute of Educational Technology, The Open University, Bletchley, Bucks, England

ALFRED B. HEILBRUN, JR., Professor of Psychology and Director of Clinical Training, Emory University, Atlanta, Georgia

A. W. HEIM, The Psychological Laboratory, University of Cambridge, Cambridge, England

G. C. HELMSTADTER, Director, University Testing Services, Arizona State University, Tempe, Arizona

JOHN K. HEMPHILL, Laboratory Director, Far West Laboratory for Educational Research and Development, Berkeley, California

DAVID O. HERMAN, Assistant Director, Test Division, The Psychological Corporation, New York, New York

A. N. HIERONYMUS, Professor of Education and Psychology, The University of Iowa, Iowa City, Iowa

JOHN R. HILLS, Professor in Educational Research and Testing, The Florida State University, Tallahassee, Florida

PHILIP HIMELSTEIN, Professor of Psychology and Head of the Department, The University of Texas at El Paso, El Paso, Texas

MARSHALL S. HISKEY, Professor of Educational Psychology and Measurements and Director, Educational-Psychological Clinic, University of Nebraska, Lincoln, Nebraska

ROBERT HOGAN, Assistant Professor of Psychology, The Johns Hopkins University, Baltimore, Maryland

RAYMOND H. HOLDEN, Professor of Psychology and Coordinator, Learning Center, Rhode Island College, Providence, Rhode Island

WAYNE H. HOLTZMAN, President, Hogg Foundation for Mental Health; and Hogg Professor of Psychology and Education, The University of Texas; Austin, Texas

MARJORIE P. HONZIK, Lecturer in Psychology and Research Psychologist, Institute of Human Development, University of California, Berkeley, California

KENNETH D. HOPKINS, Professor of Education and Director, Laboratory of Educational Research, University of Colorado, Boulder, Colorado

JOHN L. HORN, Professor of Psychology, University of Denver, Denver, Colorado

THOMAS D. HORN, Professor of Curriculum and Instruction and Chairman of the Department, The University of Texas, Austin, Texas

CYRIL J. HOYT, Professor of Educational Psychology, University of Minnesota, Minneapolis, Minnesota

CARL J. HUBERTY, Assistant Professor of Education, The University of Georgia, Athens, Georgia

MILDRED H. HUEBNER, Professor of Education and Director, Reading Center, Southern Connecticut State College, New Haven, Connecticut

JANE V. HUNT, Assistant Research Psychologist, Institute of Human Development, University of California, Berkeley, California

DOUGLAS N. JACKSON, Senior Professor of Psychology, The University of Western Ontario, London, Ontario, Canada

COLLEEN B. JAMISON, Associate Professor of Education, California State College, Los Angeles, California

ARTHUR R. JENSEN, Professor of Educational Psychology and Research Psychologist, Institute of Human Learning, University of California, Berkeley, California

CARL F. JESNESS, Senior Behavioral Research Analyst, California Youth Authority, Sacramento, California

RICHARD T. JOHNSON, Senior Research Scientist, American Institutes for Research, Limbe, Malawi

JOSEPH A. JOHNSTON, Associate Professor of Education, University of Missouri, Columbia, Missouri

CLIVE JONES, Consultant, Management Selection Ltd., London, England

DAVID JONES, Lecturer in Psychology, Birkbeck College, University of London, London, England

DOROTHY L. JONES, Assistant Professor of Education, University of Pennsylvania, Philadelphia, Pennsylvania

LAWRENCE M. KASDON, Associate Professor of Education, Ferkauf Graduate School, Yeshiva University, New York, New York

MARTIN R. KATZ, Senior Research Psychologist, Educational Testing Service, Princeton, New Jersey

RAYMOND A. KATZELL, Professor of Psychology and Head of the Department, New York University, New York, New York

WALTER V. KAULFERS, Professor of Foreign Language Education, University of Illinois, Urbana, Illinois

E. LOWELL KELLY, Professor of Psychology, The University of Michigan, Ann Arbor, Michigan

JAMES E. KENNEDY, Professor of Psychology, The University of Wisconsin, Madison, Wisconsin

NEWELL C. KEPHART, Director, Glen Haven Achievement Center, Fort Collins, Colorado

WILLARD A. KERR, Professor of Psychology and Head of the Department, Middle Tennessee State University, Murfreesboro, Tennessee

JEREMY KILPATRICK, Associate Professor of Mathematics, Teachers College, Columbia University, New York, New York

ALBERT J. KINGSTON, Professor of Educational Psychology, The University of Georgia, Athens, Georgia

BARBARA A. KIRK, Director, Counseling Center, University of California, Berkeley, California

PHILIP M. KITAY, Professor of Psychology, Adelphi University, Garden City, New York

BENJAMIN KLEINMUNTZ, Professor of Psychology, Carnegie-Mellon University, Pittsburgh, Pennsylvania

PAUL KLINE, Lecturer in Psychology, University of Exeter, Exeter, Devon, England

WILLIAM E. KLINE, Director of Test Development, CTB/McGraw-Hill, Monterey, California

MARTIN KLING, Associate Professor of Education, Rutgers, The State University, New Brunswick, New Jersey

ROBERT R. KNAPP, Director, Educational and Industrial Testing Service, San Diego, California

JOHN F. KNUTSON, Assistant Professor of Psychology, The University of Iowa, Iowa City, Iowa

CHARLES J. KRAUSKOPF, Professor of Psychology and Associate Director of Testing and Counseling, University of Missouri, Columbia, Missouri

ROY A. KRESS, Professor of Psychology and Educational Psychology, Temple University, Philadelphia, Pennsylvania

DANA G. KURFMAN, Supervisor of Social Studies, Prince George's County Public Schools, Upper Marlboro, Maryland

ROBERT LADO, Dean, School of Languages and Linguistics, Georgetown University, Washington, D.C.

DANIEL LANDIS, Social Systems Division, Riverside Research Institute, New York, New York

RICHARD I. LANYON, Associate Professor of Psychology, Northeastern University, Boston, Massachusetts

PETER A. LAPPAN, JR., Professor of Mathematics, Michigan State University, East Lansing, Michigan

JULIAN J. LASKY, Clinical Research Branch, National Institute of Mental Health, Chevy Chase, Maryland

ROBERT L. LATHROP, Assistant Dean for Resident Instruction, The Pennsylvania State University, University Park, Pennsylvania

J. S. LAWES, Principal Lecturer in Education, Westminster College, North Hinksey, Oxford, England

WILBUR L. LAYTON, Vice President for Student Affairs and Professor of Psychology, Iowa State University, Ames, Iowa

S. G. LEE, Professor of Psychology and Head of the Department, The University of Leicester, Leicester, England

PAUL R. LEHMAN, Professor of Music Education, Eastman School of Music, The University of Rochester, Rochester, New York

IRVIN J. LEHMANN, Professor, Office of Evaluation Services, Michigan State University, East Lansing, Michigan

DONALD A. LETON, Professor of Educational Psychology, University of Hawaii, Honolulu, Hawaii

EUGENE E. LEVITT, Professor of Clinical Psychology and Director, Section of Psychology, Indiana University School of Medicine, Indianapolis, Indiana

LESTER M. LIBO, Professor of Psychiatry (Psychology), University of New Mexico School of Medicine, Albuquerque, New Mexico

C. M. LINDVALL, Professor of Education, Learning Research and Development Center, University of Pittsburgh, Pittsburgh, Pennsylvania

WILLIAM M. LITTELL, Professor of Psychology, San Francisco State College, San Francisco, California

AILEENE S. LOCKHART, Professor of Physical Education, Movement and Motor Learning Laboratory, University of Southern California, Los Angeles, California

PAUL R. LOHNES, Professor of Education, State University of New York at Buffalo, Buffalo, New York

WALTER F. W. LOHNES, Professor of German, Stanford University, Stanford, California

JOHN W. LOMBARD, Director, Guidance Department, Science Research Associates, Inc., Chicago, Illinois

MAURICE LORR, Professor of Psychology, Catholic University of America, Washington, D.C.

KENNETH LOVELL, Professor of Educational Psychology, The Institute of Education, The University, Leeds, England

ROBERT W. LUNDIN, Professor of Psychology and Chairman of the Department, The University of the South, Sewanee, Tennessee

CLIFFORD E. LUNNEBORG, Associate Professor of Psychology and Director, Bureau of Testing, University of Washington, Seattle, Washington

DAVID T. LYKKEN, Professor of Psychiatry and Psychology, University of Minnesota, Minneapolis, Minnesota

HOWARD B. LYMAN, Associate Professor of Psychology, University of Cincinnati, Cincinnati, Ohio

CHARLES C. MCARTHUR, Psychologist to the University Health Services, Harvard University, Cambridge, Massachusetts

JOHN N. MCCALL, Associate Professor of Psychology, Southern Illinois University, Edwardsville, Illinois

BOYD R. MCCANDLESS, Professor of Education and Psychology and Director, Educational Psychology, Emory University, Atlanta, Georgia

JAMES J. MCCARTHY, Professor of Education, The University of Wisconsin, Madison, Wisconsin

CONSTANCE M. MCCULLOUGH, Professor of Education, San Francisco State College, San Francisco, California

CHRISTINE H. MCGUIRE, Professor of Medical Education; Assistant Director and Chief of the Evaluation Studies Section, Center for Educational Development; College of Medicine, University of Illinois, Chicago, Illinois

MICHAEL G. MCKEE, Psychologist, Department of Psychiatry, Cleveland Clinic, Cleveland, Ohio

ARTHUR C. MACKINNEY, Dean of Graduate Studies, Wright State University, Dayton, Ohio

JOHN MCLEISH, Professor of Educational Psychology, The University of Alberta, Edmonton, Alberta, Canada

DOUGLAS M. MCNAIR, Professor of Psychiatry, Boston University School of Medicine, Boston, Massachusetts

PAUL MCREYNOLDS, Professor of Psychology, University of Nevada, Reno, Nevada

GEORGE G. MALLINSON, Dean of the Graduate College, Western Michigan University, Kalamazoo, Michigan

JACQUELINE V. MALLINSON, Associate Professor of Science Education, Western Michigan University, Kalamazoo, Michigan

LESTER MANN, Director, Special Education, Montgomery County Intermediate Unit, Blue Bell, Pennsylvania

JOHN MANNING, Professor, Department of Humanities and the Office of Evaluation Services, Michigan State University, East Lansing, Michigan

SAMUEL T. MAYO, Professor of Educational Psychology, Loyola University of Chicago, Chicago, Illinois

EDWIN I. MEGARGEE, Professor of Psychology, Florida State University, Tallahassee, Florida

HOWARD D. MEHLINGER, Associate Professor and Director, Social Studies Development Center, Indiana University, Bloomington, Indiana

WILLIAM A. MEHRENS, Professor of Education, Michigan State University, East Lansing, Michigan

MANFRED J. MEIER, Professor of Psychology and Director, Neuropsychology Laboratory, University of Minnesota Medical School, Minneapolis, Minnesota

GERALD M. MEREDITH, Evaluation Officer, Office of the Dean for Academic Development, University of Hawaii, Honolulu, Hawaii

JACK C. MERWIN, Professor of Educational Psychology and Dean, College of Education, University of Minnesota, Minneapolis, Minnesota

JOAN J. MICHAEL, Associate Professor of Educational Psychology, California State College at Long Beach, Long Beach, California

WILLIAM B. MICHAEL, Professor of Educational Psychology and Psychology, University of Southern California, Los Angeles, California

JOHN E. MILHOLLAND, Professor of Psychology, The University of Michigan, Ann Arbor, Michigan

LOVICK C. MILLER, Director of Research, Child Psychiatry Research Center, Louisville, Kentucky

JASON MILLMAN, Professor of Educational Research Methodology, Cornell University, Ithaca, New York

JAMES V. MITCHELL, JR., Associate Dean for Graduate Studies, College of Education, The University of Rochester, Rochester, New York

RONALD W. MITCHELL, Assistant Executive Secretary, International Reading Association, Newark, Delaware

ARTHUR MITTMAN, Professor of Education and Chairman, Department of Educational Psychology, University of Oregon, Eugene, Oregon

FLOYD V. MONAGHAN, Professor of Natural Science, Michigan State University, East Lansing, Michigan

WALTER J. MOORE, Professor of Elementary Education, University of Illinois, Urbana, Illinois

G. A. V. MORGAN, Staff Inspector, Primary and Special Education, Education Office for Wales, Cardiff, Wales

ALICE E. MORIARTY, Senior Psychologist, The Menninger Foundation, Topeka, Kansas

DONALD L. MOSHER, Professor of Psychology, The University of Connecticut, Storrs, Connecticut

LEO A. MUNDAY, Vice President, Research and Development Division, The American College Testing Program, Iowa City, Iowa

JOSEPH A. MURPHY, Professor of French, Lycoming College, Williamsport, Pennsylvania

BERNARD I. MURSTEIN, Professor of Psychology, Connecticut College, New London, Connecticut

SHELDON S. MYERS, Chairman, Mathematics Department, Educational Testing Service, Princeton, New Jersey

T. F. NAUMANN, Professor of Psychology, Central Washington State College, Ellensburg, Washington

CLARENCE H. NELSON, Professor, Office of Evaluation Services, Michigan State University, East Lansing, Michigan

T. ERNEST NEWLAND, Professor of Educational Psychology, University of Illinois, Urbana, Illinois

BERNARD H. NEWMAN, Professor of Business and Business Division Director, Essex County College, Newark, New Jersey

JOHN NISBET, Professor of Education, University of Aberdeen, Aberdeen, Scotland

STANLEY NISBET, Professor of Education, University of Glasgow, Glasgow, Scotland

VICTOR H. NOLL, Emeritus Professor of Education, Michigan State University, East Lansing, Michigan

WARREN T. NORMAN, Professor of Psychology, The University of Michigan, Ann Arbor, Michigan

ROBERT D. NORTH, Associate Director, Professional Examinations Division, The Psychological Corporation, New York, New York

JUM C. NUNNALLY, Professor of Psychology, Vanderbilt University, Nashville, Tennessee

THOMAS C. O'BRIEN, Associate Professor of Education, Southern Illinois University, Edwardsville, Illinois

MARY ELLEN OLIVERIO, Professor of Economic Education, Teachers College, Columbia University, New York, New York

CARL J. OLSON, Assistant Professor of Medical Education, University of Illinois at the Medical Center, Chicago, Illinois

DAVID B. ORR, President, Scientific Educational Systems, Inc., Washington, D.C.

ALAN R. OSBORNE, Associate Professor of Mathematics Education, The Ohio State University, Columbus, Ohio

R. T. OSBORNE, Professor of Psychology and Director, Testing and Evaluation Center, The University of Georgia, Athens, Georgia

STUART OSKAMP, Professor of Psychology, Claremont Graduate School, Claremont, California

C. ROBERT PACE, Professor of Education, University of California, Los Angeles, California

ELLIS BATTEN PAGE, Professor of Educational Psychology, The University of Connecticut, Storrs, Connecticut

OSMOND E. PALMER, Professor, Office of Evaluation Services, Michigan State University, East Lansing, Michigan

JOSEPHINE BRUNO PANE, Associate Professor of Foreign Language Education, Rutgers, The State University, New Brunswick, New Jersey

GINO PARISI, Assistant Professor of Spanish and Head of the Department, Georgetown University, Washington, D.C.

WALTER PAUK, Professor of Education and Director, Cornell Reading-Study Center, Cornell University, Ithaca, New York

JEROME D. PAUKER, Associate Professor of Psychiatry (Medical Psychology) and Psychology, University of Missouri, Columbia, Missouri

DAVID A. PAYNE, Professor of Educational Psychology and Curriculum and Supervision, The University of Georgia, Athens, Georgia

R. W. PAYNE, Professor of Psychology and Chairman, Department of Behavioral Science, Temple University School of Medicine, Philadelphia, Pennsylvania

WILLIAM H. PERKINS, Professor in Communicative Disorders, University of Southern California, Los Angeles, California

HAROLD A. PETERSON, Associate Professor of Audiology and Speech Pathology, The University of Tennessee, Knoxville, Tennessee

ROGER P. PHELPS, Professor of Music Education, New York University, New York, New York

THEODORE G. PHILLIPS, President, Amundsen-Mayfair College, Chicago, Illinois

DOUGLAS A. PIDGEON, Deputy Director, National Foundation for Educational Research, Slough, Bucks, England

LEN PIKAART, Professor of Mathematics Education, The University of Georgia, Athens, Georgia

A. E. G. PILLINER, Director, Godfrey Thomson Unit for Academic Assessment, University of Edinburgh, Edinburgh, Scotland

GUS P. PLESSAS, Professor of Education and Chairman of the Department of Teacher Education, Sacramento State College, Sacramento, California

LYNNETTE B. PLUMLEE, Formerly Director of Test Development, Educational Testing Service, Princeton, New Jersey

ROBERT C. POOLEY, Professor Emeritus of English, The University of Wisconsin, Madison, Wisconsin

JOAN PRESTON, Assistant Professor of Education, The Ontario Institute for Studies in Education, Toronto, Ontario, Canada

JACK PRICE, Director, Curriculum Coordination Section, Department of Education, San Diego County, San Diego, California

RAY G. PRICE, Professor of Business Education, University of Minnesota, Minneapolis, Minnesota

HUGH F. PRIEST, Senior Lecturer in Psychology, University of Canterbury, Christchurch, New Zealand

M. L. KELLMER PRINGLE, Director, National Children's Bureau, London, England

GLEN W. PROBST, Professor of Spanish, Michigan State University, East Lansing, Michigan

ALAN C. PURVES, Professor of English, University of Illinois, Urbana, Illinois

M. Y. QURESHI, Professor of Psychology, Marquette University, Milwaukee, Wisconsin

ALBERT I. RABIN, Professor of Psychology, Michigan State University, East Lansing, Michigan

EARL F. RANKIN, Professor of Education, University of Kentucky, Lexington, Kentucky

JAMES C. REED, Associate Professor of Psychology, Tufts University School of Medicine, Boston, Massachusetts

RALPH M. REITAN, Professor of Neurological Surgery and Psychology, University of Washington, Seattle, Washington

WILLARD E. REITZ, Associate Professor of Psychology, The University of Western Ontario, London, Ontario, Canada

MARVIN REZNIKOFF, Professor of Psychology and Director of Clinical Training, Fordham University, New York, New York

JAMES M. RICHARDS, JR., Professor of Psychology, University of Missouri, Kansas City, Missouri

ROGER A. RICHARDS, Professor of English and Chairman of the Humanities Division, North Shore Community College, Beverly, Massachusetts

C. ALAN RIEDESEL, Professor of Education, Georgia State University, Atlanta, Georgia

SEYMOUR RIGRODSKY, Professor of Speech Pathology, Teachers College, Columbia University, New York, New York

A. OSCAR H. ROBERTS, Senior Research Scientist, American Institutes for Research, Palo Alto, California

G. EDITH ROBINSON, Associate Professor of Mathematics, The University of Georgia, Athens, Georgia

H. ALAN ROBINSON, Professor of Reading, Hofstra University, Hempstead, New York

HELEN M. ROBINSON, Professor Emeritus, Department of Education, The University of Chicago, Chicago, Illinois

DAVID A. RODGERS, Head, Section of Psychology and Research, Department of Psychiatry, Cleveland Clinic, Cleveland, Ohio

VIRGINIA M. ROGERS, Assistant Professor of Education, University of Kentucky, Lexington, Kentucky

W. TODD ROGERS, Fellow, Laboratory of Educational Research, University of Colorado, Boulder, Colorado

THOMAS A. ROMBERG, Associate Professor of Education and Associate Director, Wisconsin Research and Development Center for Cognitive Learning, The University of Wisconsin, Madison, Wisconsin

LEONARD G. RORER, Research Associate, Oregon Research Institute, Eugene, Oregon

CARL L. ROSEN, Professor of Education and Director, Educational Child Study Center, Kent State University, Kent, Ohio

JOHN H. ROSENBACH, Professor of Educational Psychology and Head of the Department, State University of New York at Albany, Albany, New York

BENJAMIN ROSNER, University Dean, Teacher Education, The City University of New York, New York, New York

JEROME ROSNER, Research Associate, Learning Research and Development Center, University of Pittsburgh, Pittsburgh, Pennsylvania

JOHN W. M. ROTHNEY, Professor of Counseling and Guidance, The University of Wisconsin, Madison, Wisconsin

ROGER A. RUTH, Assistant Professor of Education, University of Victoria, Victoria, British Columbia, Canada

RICHARD RYSTROM, Associate Professor of Reading, The University of Georgia, Athens, Georgia

H. BRADLEY SAGEN, Associate Professor of Education, The University of Iowa, Iowa City, Iowa

JEAN-GUY SAVARD, Research Officer, International Center for Research on Bilingualism; and Assistant Professor of Linguistics, Université Laval; Quebec, Canada

LYLE F. SCHOENFELDT, Associate Professor of Psychology, The University of Georgia, Athens, Georgia

DOUGLAS G. SCHULTZ, Associate Professor of Psychology, Case Western Reserve University, Cleveland, Ohio

DONALD H. SCHUSTER, Professor of Psychology and Computer Science, Iowa State University, Ames, Iowa

RICHARD E. SCHUTZ, Director, Southwest Regional Laboratory for Educational Research and Development, Los Alamitos, California

S. B. SELLS, Research Professor of Psychology and Director, Institute of Behavioral Research, Texas Christian University, Fort Worth, Texas

MELVIN I. SEMMEL, Professor of Special Education, Indiana University, Bloomington, Indiana

CARLETON B. SHAY, Professor of Education and Associate Dean, School of Education, California State College, Los Angeles, California

EUGENE C. SHEELEY, Associate Professor of Speech, University of Alabama, Tuscaloosa, Alabama

RALPH L. SHELTON, Professor of Speech, The University of Arizona, Tucson, Arizona

JOHN C. SHERWOOD, Professor of English, University of Oregon, Eugene, Oregon

BENJAMIN SHIMBERG, Senior Program Director, Vocational-Technical Education Projects, Educational Testing Service, Princeton, New Jersey

RICHARD E. SHINE, Assistant Professor of Speech Pathology, The Pennsylvania State University, University Park, Pennsylvania

EVAN D. SHULL, Coordinator of Mathematics, Township High School District 214, Mount Prospect, Illinois

A. B. SILVERSTEIN, Research Specialist, Pacific State Hospital, Pomona, California

HARRY SINGER, Professor of Education, University of California, Riverside, California

EDWARD R. SIPAY, Professor of Education and Director of Reading Clinics, State University of New York at Albany, Albany, New York

RODNEY W. SKAGER, Associate Professor of Education, University of California, Los Angeles, California

FRED M. SMITH, Professor of Education and Director, Bureau of Educational Research, Louisiana State University, Baton Rouge, Louisiana

JANE E. SMITH, Professor and Assistant Dean of Lyman Briggs College, Michigan State University, East Lansing, Michigan

KENNETH J. SMITH, Professor of Education and Head, Department of Reading, The University of Arizona, Tucson, Arizona

LYMAN J. SMITH, Director, Assessment Operations, Science Research Associates, Inc., Chicago, Illinois

CHARLES D. SMOCK, Professor of Psychology, The University of Georgia, Athens, Georgia

GEORGE D. SPACHE, Professor Emeritus, University of Florida, Gainesville, Florida

JOEL STARK, Professor of Communication Arts and Sciences, Queens College of the City University of New York, Flushing, New York

LESLIE P. STEFFE, Associate Professor of Mathematics Education, The University of Georgia, Athens, Georgia

JACK M. STEIN, Professor of German, Harvard University, Cambridge, Massachusetts

HANS H. STRUPP, Professor of Psychology, Vanderbilt University, Nashville, Tennessee

ALAN R. SUESS, Associate Professor of Industrial Education, Purdue University, Lafayette, Indiana

RICHARD M. SUINN, Professor of Psychology and Associate Head of the Department, Colorado State University, Fort Collins, Colorado

NORMAN D. SUNDBERG, Dean, The Wallace School of Community Service and Public Affairs, University of Oregon, Eugene, Oregon

MARILYN N. SUYDAM, Associate Professor of Education, The Pennsylvania State University, University Park, Pennsylvania

RICHARD A. SWANSON, Associate Professor and Director, Graduate Studies in Industrial Education, Bowling Green State University, Bowling Green, Ohio

ERWIN K. TAYLOR, President, Personnel Research and Development Corporation, Cleveland, Ohio

HUGH TAYLOR, Assistant Professor of Education, University of Victoria, Victoria, British Columbia, Canada

ROBERT L. THORNDIKE, Professor of Psychology and Education, Teachers College, Columbia University, New York, New York

DAVID V. TIEDEMAN, Professor of Education, Harvard University, Cambridge, Massachusetts

CAROL K. TITTLE, Assistant Professor of Teacher Education, City University of New York, New York, New York

KENNETH J. TRAVERS, Associate Professor of Mathematics Education, University of Illinois, Urbana, Illinois

ARTHUR E. TRAXLER, Adjunct Lecturer in Education, University of Miami, Coral Gables, Florida

HAROLD C. TRIMBLE, Professor of Mathematics Education, The Ohio State University, Columbus, Ohio

LAWRENCE J. TURTON, Program Director for Speech and Language Pathology, Institute for the Study of Mental Retardation, The University of Michigan, Ann Arbor, Michigan

LEONA E. TYLER, Professor of Psychology and Dean of the Graduate School, University of Oregon, Eugene, Oregon

PAOLO VALESIO, Associate Professor of Romance Languages and Literatures, Harvard University, Cambridge, Massachusetts

ROBERT E. VALETT, Professor of Education, Fresno State College, Fresno, California

FORREST L. VANCE, Professor of Psychology and Director of Counseling and Special Services, The University of Rochester, Rochester, New York

BYRON H. VAN ROEKEL, Professor of Teacher Education, Michigan State University, East Lansing, Michigan

DONALD J. VELDMAN, Professor of Educational Psychology, The University of Texas, Austin, Texas

PHILIP E. VERNON, Professor of Educational Psychology, the University of Calgary, Calgary, Alberta, Canada

J. R. JEFFERSON WADKINS, Associate Examiner in Mathematics, Educational Testing Service, Princeton, New Jersey

JOHN WAGNER, Professor of Mathematics, Michigan State University, East Lansing, Michigan

DAVID A. WALKER, Formerly Director, The Scottish Council for Research in Education, Edinburgh, Scotland

WIMBURN L. WALLACE, Director, Professional Examinations Division, The Psychological Corporation, New York, New York

JAMES A. WALSH, Professor of Psychology and Statistics, Iowa State University, Ames, Iowa

W. BRUCE WALSH, Associate Professor of Psychology, The Ohio State University, Columbus, Ohio

EDWIN WANDT, Professor of Education and Chairman, Department of Educational Foundations, California State College, Los Angeles, California

CHARLES F. WARD, Assistant Professor of Occupational Education and Research Associate, Center for Occupational Education, North Carolina State University, Raleigh, North Carolina

WILLIAM C. WARD, Research Psychologist, Educational Testing Service, Princeton, New Jersey

DAVID M. WARK, Professor of Psychology, University of Minnesota, Minneapolis, Minnesota

WILLARD G. WARRINGTON, Director, Office of Evaluation Services, Michigan State University, East Lansing, Michigan

RICHARD W. WATKINS, Associate Laboratory Director for Programs, Far West Laboratory for Educational Research and Development, Berkeley, California

WILLIAM J. WEBSTER, Director, System-Wide Evaluation, Dallas Independent School District, Dallas, Texas

DAVID P. WEIKART, President, High/Scope Educational Research Foundation, Ypsilanti, Michigan

SHELDON A. WEINTRAUB, Assistant Professor of Psychology, State University of New York at Stony Brook, Stony Brook, New York

DAVID J. WEISS, Associate Professor of Psychology, University of Minnesota, Minneapolis, Minnesota

HENRY WEITZ, Professor of Education and Director, Counseling Center, Duke University, Durham, North Carolina

JOSEPH M. WEPMAN, Professor of Psychology, Surgery and Education, The University of Chicago, Chicago, Illinois

EMMY E. WERNER, Professor of Child Development and Research Child Psychologist, University of California, Davis, California

ALEXANDER G. WESMAN, Director, Test Division, The Psychological Corporation, New York, New York

LEONARD J. WEST, Professor of Education, Office of Teacher Education, The City University of New York, New York, New York

BERT W. WESTBROOK, Associate Professor of Psychology, North Carolina State University, Raleigh, North Carolina

JERRY S. WIGGINS, Professor of Psychology, University of Illinois, Champaign, Illinois

CARL G. WILLIS, Assistant Director, University Testing and Counseling Service, University of Missouri, Columbia, Missouri

JAMES W. WILSON, Associate Professor of Mathematics Education and Head of the Department, The University of Georgia, Athens, Georgia

WILLIAM L. WINNETT, Professor of Business Education, San Francisco State College, San Francisco, California

GEORGE P. WINSHIP, JR.,Professor of English and Chairman of the Department, King College, Bristol, Tennessee

ROBERT D. WIRT, Professor of Psychology, Child Development, and Psychiatry and Director, Graduate Education in Clinical Psychology, University of Minnesota, Minneapolis, Minnesota

EMORY E. WISEMAN, Assistant Professor of Automotive and Power Technology, Illinois State University, Normal, Illinois

FRANK B. WOMER, Professor of Education, The University of Michigan, Ann Arbor, Michigan

BLAINE R. WORTHEN, Co-director, Laboratory of Educational Research, University of Colorado, Boulder, Colorado

ROBERT L. WRIGHT, Professor of American Thought and Language and Comparative Literature, Michigan State University, East Lansing, Michigan

AUBREY J. YATES, Professor of Psychology, University of Western Australia, Nedlands, Australia

ALBERT H. YEE, Professor of Curriculum and Instruction, The University of Wisconsin, Madison, Wisconsin

WAYNE S. ZIMMERMAN, Test Officer and Professor of Counseling and Testing, California State College at Los Angeles, Los Angeles, California

DONALD G. ZYTOWSKI, Associate Professor of Psychology and Assistant Director, Student Counseling Service, Iowa State University, Ames, Iowa

Preface

FOLLOWING publication of *The Sixth Mental Measurements Yearbook* and my early retirement from Rutgers University, we gave serious consideration to discontinuing the MMY series. We actually made plans in 1966 for disposing of our huge test collection, bibliographic files, and books. However, unable to reconcile ourselves to seeing this service to test users die out, we began to explore the possibilities of getting a university or some other organization to take over the project, with me phasing out over a period of a few years. Although two institutions indicated an interest in continuing the MMY series, we finally concluded that we would do it alone, at least for another yearbook, in order to preserve its present form and standards.

In this age of widespread financial grants for research and information clearinghouses in education and psychology, it may come as somewhat of a surprise to readers to learn that *The Seventh Yearbook* was prepared without any outside support whatsoever. This has been both a strength and a weakness. We have been strengthened because we are independent to do what we think best in the way we think best. On the other hand, we have been weakened because of our dependence on income from yearbook sales to finance the preparation of new publications. The losses probably offset the gains, since we could have provided additional services had financial support been available.

It probably is not generally known that The Gryphon Press, the publisher of the MMY's

and related volumes, consists of my wife and myself. We have published eight of the ten major publications in the MMY series—*The 1938 Mental Measurements Yearbook* and *The Third Mental Measurements Yearbook* were originally published by Rutgers University Press. We became publishers only after we were convinced that this held the greatest promise for the continuance of the yearbook series.

A new edition of *Tests in Print* will be published early in 1973. The new TIP will be expanded to include specific test bibliographies for all tests in print. I cannot speak with confidence regarding other publication plans. Much depends upon the sales of the MMY's, TIP 2, and the monographs on personality and reading. In the meantime, work is proceeding on the preparation of another yearbook and two or three additional monographs. The target date for the publication of *The Eighth Mental Measurements Yearbook* is 1975.

I have enjoyed the active assistance and cooperation of many individuals and organizations in the preparation of this yearbook. Their combined efforts have helped to make this huge project possible. It has been particularly gratifying to me that so many educators and psychologists have given us their cooperation and assistance.

There are many to whom I wish to give special thanks: (*a*) The testing and subject specialists who gave generously of their time to review tests; their contributions constitute the heart of this yearbook. I wish to extend very special thanks to the five contributors who have reviewed for all seven yearbooks: Anne Anastasi, Howard R. Anderson, Walter V. Kaulfers, Victor H. Noll, and Arthur E. Traxler. Their continuous cooperation has been most heartwarming. (*b*) The testing and subject specialists who helped us to identify competent reviewers have played an important though anonymous role. (*c*) With very few exceptions, test publishers have been cooperative and helpful. They have generously given or loaned us specimen sets of their tests for the use of reviewers and our own editorial staff. (*d*) Thanks are also due to the many journal editors who gave us permission to reprint excerpts from their reviews of tests and books on testing. By excerpting the journal reviews, we are, in a sense, sharing our editorial responsibilities with the journal editors.

Dozens of libraries, both in this country and abroad, have been used to locate and check references for specific tests. Special acknowledgment and thanks should be given to the Rutgers University Libraries for the extensive use which we have made of their facilities and services.

I have been fortunate in having a dedicated and efficient staff. Miss Ethel Kersting, the only full-time member of the editorial staff, has done outstanding work in every phase of manuscript preparation and in seeing the book through the press. I am most happy to have had the services of Professor Roger A. Richards, the only member of the editorial staff who has worked on earlier yearbooks, both as an editorial associate and test reviewer. Professor Richards has had a major responsibility in the editing of reviews; he is also a contributing reviewer. I cannot speak too highly of the quality of his work. The third editorial associate, Mrs. Joan S. Paszamant, has competently performed a variety of editorial responsibilities—the writing of test entries, editing of reviews, and proofreading. I also wish to point out the valuable services provided by two editorial assistants, Mrs. Shirle M. Hartley and Mrs. Shirley Johnes. Mrs. Hartley prepared test entries in the early stages of the yearbook's preparation.

She was succeeded by Mrs. Johnes who devoted most of her time to editing reviews and proofreading.

The preparation of this yearbook placed heavy demands upon the production and secretarial staff. They not only performed the usual clerical duties, but also did copyreading, index making, and proofreading. Special mention should be made of the staff members who served at least one year: Miss Alice B. Heinlein, Mrs. Doris G. McCan, Miss Susan S. Montegna, Miss Mary T. Mooney, and Miss Natalie J. Rosenthal. Special recognition should be given to the two veterans of earlier yearbooks. Mrs. McCan, who has worked on the last five yearbooks, has had a major responsibility for preparing indexes and proofreading of references. Miss Mooney assisted in the preparation of the first yearbook and three earlier publications. We are pleased that she has rejoined our staff following her early retirement from Rutgers University.

Professor Henry Weitz rendered valuable assistance as an editorial associate during the summer of 1970 and also contributed two reviews. During the same period, Mr. Gary D. Novak served as an editorial assistant.

Thirty-four years ago, we delivered the manuscript for *The 1938 Mental Measurements Yearbook* to Quinn and Boden Company, the manufacturer of this yearbook. Since then, they have printed seven of our major publications. We wish to express our gratitude for the magnificent job they have done in printing and binding this yearbook.

Finally, my greatest indebtedness is to my wife for the constant support and active assistance she has given me in preparing the yearbooks over these many years. Her participation has ranged over the whole gamut of activities involved in the preparation, production, and distribution of the yearbooks. It gives me great happiness to dedicate this yearbook to my wife.

OSCAR KRISEN BUROS

Highland Park, New Jersey
January 21, 1972

Introduction

THIS MMY, like the six earlier year-books [1] in the series, is designed to assist test users in education, psychology, and industry to make more intelligent use of standardized tests of every description.

Since initiated in 1938, the objectives of the *Mental Measurements Yearbooks* have been essentially the same: (*a*) to provide information about tests published as separates throughout the English-speaking world; (*b*) to present frankly critical test reviews written by testing and subject specialists representing various viewpoints; (*c*) to provide extensive bibliographies of verified references on the construction, use, and validity of specific tests; (*d*) to make readily available the critical portions of test reviews appearing in professional journals; and (*e*) to present fairly exhaustive listings of new and revised books on testing, along with evaluative excerpts from representative reviews which these books receive in professional journals.

The implementation of the above five objectives has depended not only on the work of

---

1 BUROS, OSCAR KRISEN, EDITOR. *The Nineteen Thirty-Eight Mental Measurements Yearbook*. Highland Park, N.J.: Gryphon Press, 1938 (reissued 1972). Pp. xv, 415. $15.00. * For reviews, see 2:B858. (This volume is sometimes referred to as *The First Mental Measurements Yearbook*.)
BUROS, OSCAR KRISEN, EDITOR. *The Nineteen Forty Mental Measurements Yearbook*. Highland Park, N.J.: Gryphon Press, 1941 (reissued 1972). Pp. xxv, 674. $17.50. * For reviews, see 3:788 and 4:B70. (This volume is sometimes referred to as *The Second Mental Measurements Yearbook*.)
BUROS, OSCAR KRISEN, EDITOR. *The Third Mental Measurements Yearbook*. Highland Park, N.J.: Gryphon Press, 1949. Pp. xv, 1047. $20.50. * For reviews, see 4:B71.
BUROS, OSCAR KRISEN, EDITOR. *The Fourth Mental Measurements Yearbook*. Highland Park, N.J.: Gryphon Press, 1953. Pp. xxv, 1163. $22.50. * For reviews, see 5:B84.
BUROS, OSCAR KRISEN, EDITOR. *The Fifth Mental Measurements Yearbook*. Highland Park, N.J.: Gryphon Press, 1959. Pp. xxix, 1292. $25.00. * For reviews, see 6:B104.
BUROS, OSCAR KRISEN, EDITOR. *The Sixth Mental Measurements Yearbook*. Highland Park, N.J.: Gryphon Press, 1965. Pp. xxxvii, 1714. $35.00. * For reviews, see B122.

myself and the MMY staff, but also on the contributions of cooperating reviewers, the willingness of journal editors to permit us to reprint excerpts from their reviews, and the cooperation of publishers in providing us with information and review copies. Because of the important contributions of hundreds of cooperating reviewers and the cooperation of editors and publishers, we feel that we have been reasonably successful in fulfilling the above five objectives.

Concomitantly, we attach considerable importance to other objectives of a crusading nature: (*f*) to impel test authors and publishers to publish better tests and to provide test users with detailed information on the validity and limitations of their tests; (*g*) to inculcate test users with a keener awareness of the values and limitations of standardized tests; (*h*) to stimulate contributing reviewers to think through more carefully their own beliefs and values relevant to testing; (*i*) to suggest to test users better methods of appraising tests in light of their own particular needs; and (*j*) to impress test users with the need to suspect all tests unaccompanied by detailed data on their construction, validity, uses, and limitations—even when products of distinguished authors and reputable publishers.

Our success in attaining the last five missionary objectives has been disappointingly modest. Test publishers continue to market tests which do not begin to meet the standards of the rank and file of MMY and journal reviewers. At least half of the tests currently on the market should never have been published. Exaggerated, false, or unsubstantiated claims are the rule rather than the exception. Test users are becoming more discriminating, but not nearly fast enough. It is still true, as I said over ten years ago in *Tests in Print*,[2] that "At present, no matter how poor a test may be, if it is nicely packaged and if it promises to do all sorts of things which no test can do, the test will find many gullible buyers." Nevertheless, we are continuing in our efforts to influence practices of constructing, distributing, and using tests. If it were not for the conviction that our project is primarily a crusade, we would never have had the zeal to keep on preparing these MMY's.

THE FIRST SIX MMY's

Since the *Mental Measurements Yearbooks* are fairly well known, we shall not describe the six earlier volumes. Readers wishing further information should consult the book review section in Volume II.[3] Since each MMY supplements preceding volumes, it is necessary to consult all seven *Mental Measurements Yearbooks* for complete coverage of tests, test reviews, and bibliographies on specific tests. The latest volumes are, of course, of greatest value. But even the yearbooks published in 1938 and 1941 have some current as well as historical value. Because of this, The Gryphon Press reissued in 1972 both *The 1938 Mental Measurements Yearbook* and *The 1940 Mental Measurements Yearbook*. Consequently, all seven yearbooks are now in print.

TESTS IN PRINT

Tests in Print, a comprehensive bibliography of standardized tests and a master index to the contents of the first five yearbooks, was published in 1961. This volume lists 2,967 tests, 2,126 of which were in print early in 1961. TIP indicates which of the first five MMY's presents the most recent listing of a test along with information regarding its in print status, the number of reviews it received, the names of the reviewers, the number of references on

its construction, use, and validity, and the number of excerpts reprinted from reviews in journals. In addition, TIP also presents similar information for all tests published since 1933 but out of print as of 1961.

Tests in Print, Volume 2 is now in preparation for publication early in 1973. Until it becomes available, the first edition of *Tests in Print* will remain an indispensable tool for all who wish to derive the maximum benefit from the MMY's in the shortest possible time. Even after the publication of TIP 2, the first edition of *Tests in Print* will still need to be consulted for information about many tests which are out of print.

The scope of *Tests in Print, Volume 2* will be expanded to include for the first time bibliographies of references on the construction, use, and validity of specific tests. These bibliographies will cover references published through 1971 and will supplement those given in the MMY's and *Personality Tests and Reviews*.[4] The simultaneous publication of specific test bibliographies for all tests in print will be somewhat of a landmark in the history of the MMY's and related publications.

MMY MONOGRAPHS

In 1968, the first Mental Measurements Yearbook monograph, *Reading Tests and Reviews*,[5] was published to meet the needs of reading specialists and teachers. This 542-page monograph includes a comprehensive bibliography of reading tests as of early 1968, a reprinting of all reading test reviews in the first six MMY's, and a master classified index to all other tests and reviews in the first six MMY's. Even if a person interested in reading tests has at hand a complete set of MMY's, the reading monograph will still be more convenient to use than the yearbooks. Furthermore, RTR includes information about 33 reading tests—new, revised, or supplemented since *The Sixth Yearbook*—which are not listed in *The Seventh Yearbook* (see Table 1). The 349 original reviews and 38 excerpted reviews of reading tests in RTR and the 104

2 BUROS, OSCAR KRISEN, EDITOR. *Tests in Print: A Comprehensive Bibliography of Tests for Use in Education, Psychology, and Industry.* Highland Park, N.J.: Gryphon Press, 1961. Pp. xxix, 479. $10.00. * For reviews, see 6:B105.
3 See B122. For an informal discussion of the early history, read "The Story Behind the Mental Measurements Yearbooks" in the Summer 1968 issue of *Measurement and Evaluation in Guidance.* Reprints are available without charge from The Institute of Mental Measurements.

4 BUROS, OSCAR KRISEN, EDITOR. *Personality Tests and Reviews: Including an Index to The Mental Measurements Yearbooks.* Highland Park, N.J.: Gryphon Press, 1970. Pp. xxxi, 1659. $35.00. * For reviews, see B120.
5 BUROS, OSCAR KRISEN, EDITOR. *Reading Tests and Reviews: Including a Classified Index to The Mental Measurements Yearbooks.* Highland Park, N.J.: Gryphon Press, 1968. Pp. xxii, 520. $15.00. * For reviews, see B121.

TABLE 1

Tests New, Revised, or Supplemented
Since The Sixth Yearbook but Presented
Only in Reading Tests and Reviews

Test	RTR Entry Number
★A.C.E.R. Lower Grades Reading Test	1
*American School Reading Readiness Test	180
*Buffalo Reading Test for Speed and Comprehension	8
*Canadian English Achievement Test	11
★Comprehensive Primary Reading Scales	14
★Comprehensive Reading Scales	15
*Cooperative Reading Comprehension Test, Form Y	16
*Cooperative Reading Comprehension Test, Forms L and M	17
*Diagnostic Reading Tests	121
*Doren Diagnostic Reading Test of Word Recognition Skills	122
*Elementary Reading: Every Pupil Achievement Test	23
*Gray Oral Reading Test	167
★Group Reading Assessment	32
★Keystone Ready to Read Tests	186.1
*Learning Methods Test	153
*OC Diagnostic Syllabizing Test	128
★Ohio Diagnostic Reading Test	129
*Primary Reading: Every Pupil Achievement Test	52
*Primary Reading Profiles	132
★Primary Reading Test 2	54
*Reader Rater With Self-Scoring Profile	154
★Reading: Adult Basic Education Student Survey	217
★Reading Comprehension Test	57
★Reading for Understanding Placement Test	61
★Reading Skills Diagnostic Test	133
★SRA Reading Checklist	158
★Secondary Reading Tests 1–3	68
★Steinbach Test of Reading Readiness	198
★Study Habits Checklist	244.1
*Tests of Reading: Cooperative Inter-American Tests	80
★Van Wagenen Analytical Reading Scales	84
*Van Wagenen Reading Readiness Scales	200
*W.A.L. English Comprehension Test	85

original reviews and the 16 excerpted reviews in this yearbook provide the reading specialist with a wealth of information about reading tests and yet require him to consult only two volumes.

The second monograph, *Personality Tests and Reviews,* was published early in 1970. The major purpose of this monograph is to make readily available to users of personality tests the vast amount of information—original test reviews, excerpted test reviews, and specific test bibliographies—to be found in the first six *Mental Measurements Yearbooks.* PTR also includes a great deal of new material on personality testing: a comprehensive bibliography of 513 personality tests; 7,116 new references dealing with the construction, use, and validity of specific tests; separate author indexes for all tests having 25 or more references; and a scanning index to all personality tests in that

volume. In addition to information on personality tests, PTR includes several other useful features: the MMY Test Index, a master index to the nonpersonality tests, reviews, and references in the first six MMY's; the MMY Book Review Index, an index to all reviews of measurement books excerpted in the first six MMY's; a reprinting of the APA-AERA-NCME *Standards for Educational and Psychological Tests and Manuals;* a title index which includes every test listed in an MMY, TIP, or RTR; and an analytical name index which includes the authors of all reviews and excerpts in the six MMY's.

Personality Tests and Reviews is a must for all MMY users interested in personality assessment. It contains a great deal of material which will not be found in any of the yearbooks. Eighty tests, new, revised, or supplemented since *The Sixth Yearbook,* are listed in PTR but not in this yearbook (see Table 2). Up-

TABLE 2

Tests New, Revised, or Supplemented
Since The Sixth Yearbook but Presented
Only in Personality Tests and Reviews

Test (Number of References in PTR)	PTR Entry Number
★Addiction Research Center Inventory (15)	3
★Anxiety Scale for the Blind (3)	8
*Blacky Pictures (39)	416
★Braverman-Chevigny Auditory Projective Test (2)	417
*Bristol Social Adjustment Guides (6)	20
★CYR Youth Survey (2)	22
★Cardiac Adjustment Scale (1)	30
*Children's Apperception Test (18)	419
*Children's Personality Questionnaire (14)	38
★Clinical Behavior Check List and Rating Scale	40
*Courtship Analysis	52
*Curtis Completion Form (3)	421
*Draw-A-Person Quality Scale (3)	423
*Embedded Figures Test (47)	71
★Getting Along (2)	89
★Graphoscopic Scale (8)	433
*Grassi Block Substitution Test (13)	94
★Group Psychotherapy Suitability Evaluation Scale (1)	99
*H-T-P: House-Tree-Person Projective Technique (24)	437
*Hand Test (12)	438
★Hartman Value Inventory (2)	106
★Hellenic Affiliation Scale	108
★Hill Interaction Matrix	109
*Hoffer-Osmond Diagnostic Test (22)	110
★[Re Holtzman Inkblot Technique.] Computer Scoring Service for the Holtzman Inkblot Technique (5)	440
*Hooper Visual Organization Test (7)	111
*IPAT Humor Test of Personality (8)	119
★Independent Activities Questionnaire (2)	122
*Institute of Child Study Security Test (4)	125
★Integration Level Test Series (12)	125A
★JIM Scale	132
★Katz Adjustment Scales (10)	138
*Kuder Preference Record—Personal (9)	139

Test (Number of References in PTR)	PTR Entry Number
★Kundu's Neurotic Personality Inventory (5)	140
★Level of Aspiration Board (9)	144
*Lowenfeld Kaleidoblocs	449
★M-Scale	146
*M-B History Record (3)	148
★Mandel Social Adjustment Scale (2)	151
*Marriage Adjustment Sentence Completion Survey	453
★Maryland Parent Attitude Survey (6)	160
★Measurement of Self Concept in Kindergarten Children	454
*Minnesota Percepto-Diagnostic Test (19)	457
*Object Relations Technique (5)	458
★Object Sorting Scales	181
★Ohio College Association Rating Scale	183
*Opinion, Attitude, and Interest Survey (19)	185
★PRADI Autobiographical Form	190
★PRADI Draw-A-Person Test	459
★Percept and Concept Cognition Test	460
★Personnel Reaction Blank	202
★Picture Identification Test (17)	463
★Picture Story Test Blank	465
*Picture World Test (1)	466
★Polarity Scale (1)	205
★Preschool Self-Concept Picture Test (1)	212
*Press Test (1)	213
★Psychological Audit for Interpersonal Relations	218
★Richardson Emergency Psychodiagnostic Summary	228
★Russell Sage Social Relations Test (3)	230
*STS Junior Inventory (4)	232A
*STS Youth Inventory (2)	233
★Scale of Socio-Egocentrism	234
*Scale to Measure Attitudes Toward Disabled Persons (14)	235
*Social Competence Inventories for Adults and for Older Persons	249
★Social Relations Test (1)	473B
★Sound-Apperception Test (3)	474
★Stamp Behaviour Study Technique	252
*Stanford Profile Scales of Hypnotic Susceptibility (4)	254
★Stockton Geriatric Rating Scale (2)	257
★Student Description Form	258
★Study of Values: British Edition	259A
*Szondi Test (24)	480
★Tasks of Emotional Development Test (1)	481
*Test of Basic Assumptions	268
★Test of Subjective and Objective Factors in Relationship to Communication Skills	483
*Theological School Inventory (5)	273
★Thorman Family Relations Conference Situation Questionnaire	275
*Vineland Social Maturity Scale (21)	281
★Ward Behavior Inventory (14)	285

dated information will be found for 408 other personality tests (276 in print, 132 out of print) not listed in *The Seventh Yearbook*. The 7,116 new references in the bibliographies for specific tests supplement the references given in the yearbooks. Finally, the name indexes for specific tests are extremely useful.

MMY readers would, no doubt, have found it more convenient if all personality tests and references were presented in the *Mental Measurements Yearbooks*. The diversion of some material to the personality monograph has been dictated by the tremendous expansion of the literature on personality assessment. Had this channeling of over 7,000 test references to PTR not been done, we would have had to omit references altogether in this yearbook.

THE SEVENTH YEARBOOK

Like other yearbooks in the series, *The Seventh Mental Measurements Yearbook* is a completely new publication, supplementing rather than supplanting earlier volumes. Although the major coverage is for the seven year period 1964–70, some earlier material is also included. For example, many older tests which generate a great deal of literature (e.g., MMPI, Rorschach, EPPS, 16PF, CPI, WAIS, TAT, and WISC) are listed and reviewed.

The Seventh Yearbook, the first yearbook in two volumes, consists of three main parts: a 1,532-page section Tests and Reviews; a 314-page section Books and Reviews; and a 140-page section of indexes—Periodical Directory and Index, Publishers Directory and Index, Index of Book Titles, Index of Test Titles, Index of Names, and Classified Index of Tests.

TESTS AND REVIEWS

The heart of an MMY is the section Tests and Reviews. This section presents extensive listings for 1,157 tests, 798 test reviews by 439 reviewers, 181 excerpted test reviews from 39 journals, and 12,372 references for specific tests.

TESTS

Table 3 presents statistics on the number and percentage of tests in each of the 15 major classifications. Three classes—intelligence, personality, and vocations—account for 38.8 percent of all tests in this volume. The total number of tests is 1,157, 5.1 percent less than the number in *The Sixth Yearbook*. When, however, the new, revised, and supplemented tests listed only in *Reading Tests and Reviews* and in *Personality Tests and Reviews* are also included, the total number of tests is 1,270, 4.2 percent more than in *The Sixth Yearbook*.

Two minor changes have been made in the classification of tests. A new section, Speech and Hearing, has been introduced. The tests in this section were formerly scattered under several headings: Character and Personality, English—Speech, and Sensory-Motor—Hearing. Tests formerly classified under the main heading Business Education have been shifted to Miscellaneous—Business Education or to Vocations—Clerical.

TABLE 3

Tests by Major Classifications †

Classification	Number	Percentage
Vocations	181	15.6
Personality	147	12.7
Miscellaneous	129	11.1
Intelligence	121	10.5
Reading	102	8.8
Mathematics	96	8.3
Science	80	6.9
Foreign Languages	75	6.5
English	55	4.8
Social Studies	53	4.6
Speech and Hearing	38	3.3
Achievement Batteries	36	3.1
Sensory-Motor	20	1.7
Fine Arts	14	1.2
Multi-Aptitude	10	0.9
Total	1,157	100.0

† This table does not include the following tests new or revised since the publication of the 6th MMY: 76 personality tests (45 new, 31 revised) and 4 courtship and marriage tests (2 new, 2 revised) presented only in *Personality Tests and Reviews* and 33 reading tests (16 new, 17 revised) presented only in *Reading Tests and Reviews*. For references to these tests, see Tables 1 and 2.

The percentages of new and revised or supplemented tests in each classification are shown in Table 4. More than half of the tests, 55.6 percent, are new tests not previously listed in a *Mental Measurements Yearbook*; 38.9 percent are tests which have been revised or supplemented since they were last in an MMY; and only 5.5 percent are old tests. Throughout this volume, stars (★) are used to indicate new

TABLE 4

New and Revised or Supplemented Tests by Major Classifications ‡

Classification	Number of Tests	Percentage		
		New	Revised	Total
Achievement Batteries	36	61.1	38.9	100.0
English	55	47.3	49.1	96.4
Fine Arts	14	64.3	28.6	92.9
Foreign Languages	75	28.0	72.0	100.0
Intelligence	121	45.5	46.3	91.8
Mathematics	96	47.9	46.9	94.8
Miscellaneous	129	58.1	39.5	97.6
Multi-Aptitude	10	40.0	50.0	90.0
Personality	147	67.3	20.4	87.7
Reading	102	63.7	27.5	91.2
Science	80	33.8	65.0	98.8
Sensory-Motor	20	70.0	25.0	95.0
Social Studies	53	47.2	52.8	100.0
Speech and Hearing	38	81.6	7.9	89.5
Vocations	181	68.5	26.5	95.0
Total	1,157	55.6	38.9	94.5

‡ This table does not include the following tests new or revised since the publication of the 6th MMY: 76 personality tests (45 new, 31 revised) and 4 courtship and marriage tests (2 new, 2 revised) presented only in *Personality Tests and Reviews* and 33 reading tests (16 new, 17 revised) presented only in *Reading Tests and Reviews*. For references to these tests, see Tables 1 and 2.

tests and asterisks (*) to indicate tests revised or supplemented since last listed in an MMY. The percentage of new tests ranges from 28.0 for foreign language tests to 81.6 for speech and hearing tests. Earlier yearbooks, TIP, and the MMY monographs on personality and reading should be consulted for information about other tests.[6]

Except for the 113 tests listed only in the personality and reading monographs, *The Seventh Yearbook* includes: (*a*) all tests—new, revised, or supplemented—known to have been published in English-speaking countries during the period mid-1964 through 1970; (*b*) tests published earlier but not previously included in an MMY; and (*c*) older tests selected for review. This last category includes tests listed but not reviewed in earlier yearbooks, tests which received only one review in previous volumes, and older tests which are generating a great deal of literature on their construction, use, and validity.

ORIGINAL TEST REVIEWS

The Seventh Yearbook contains 798 original reviews of 546 tests. Table 5 presents statistics on the review coverage in the various classifications of tests. Over half (56.0 percent) of the reviews are of tests classified as personality (21.9 percent), reading (13.0 percent), intelligence (10.9 percent), and vocations (10.2 percent). Nearly half (47.2 percent) of the 1,157 tests listed have at least one review,

TABLE 5

Original Test Reviews in the 7th MMY

Classification	Number of Reviews	Number of Tests Reviewed	Percentage of Tests	
			1 or More Reviews	2 or More Reviews
Achievement Batteries	30	20	55.6	27.8
English	41	27	49.1	23.6
Fine Arts	10	6	42.9	28.6
Foreign Languages	27	23	30.7	5.3
Intelligence	87	57	47.1	23.1
Mathematics	71	50	52.1	21.9
Miscellaneous	60	43	33.3	11.6
Multi-Aptitude	4	3	30.0	10.0
Personality	175	110	74.8	40.8
Reading	104	72	70.6	30.4
Science	32	26	32.5	7.5
Sensory-Motor	18	14	70.0	15.0
Social Studies	22	19	35.8	5.7
Speech and Hearing	36	22	57.9	36.8
Vocations	81	54	29.8	14.4
Total	798	546	47.2	20.7

6 A single listing of standardized tests published throughout the English-speaking world will be presented in *Tests in Print, Volume 2*, to be published in the spring of 1973.

about a fifth (20.7 percent) have two or more reviews. The percentage of tests reviewed in each category ranges from 29.8 for vocations to 74.8 for personality.

Since the test output is too great to permit us to review all tests, it has been necessary to give some tests priority over others. The highest priority has been given to tests sold commercially in the United States. Even in this category, however, some tests have not been reviewed because: (*a*) tests may have been published too late; (*b*) we may have been unable to locate competent reviewers; (*c*) persons who agreed to review may have failed to fulfill their commitment; or (*d*) reviews may have been rejected as not meeting minimum MMY standards.

We have given only partial review coverage of the 193 secure and semi-secure tests such as the Advanced Placement Examinations, College Board Achievement Tests, CLEP Subject Examinations, Graduate Record Examinations, and the National Teacher Examinations. Except for some tests published in Canada and England, no attempt has been made to review tests published outside the United States.

The most crucial editorial decisions have been made in the selection of reviewers. Our objective has been to secure reviewers who are representative of various viewpoints among subject and testing specialists. We are constantly on the search for persons who will write frankly critical reviews competently and judiciously. Over 400 specialists in a great variety of fields assisted us in our search by recommending promising reviewers.

In order to make sure that persons invited to review would know what was expected of them, the following "Suggestions to MMY Reviewers" was enclosed with each letter of invitation:

1) Reviews should be written with the following major objectives in mind:
   a) To provide test users with carefully prepared appraisals of tests for their guidance in selecting and using tests.
   b) To stimulate progress toward higher professional standards in the construction of tests by commending good work, by censuring poor work, and by suggesting improvements.
   c) To impel test authors and publishers to present more detailed information on the construction, validity, reliability, uses, and possible misuses of their tests.
2) Reviews should be concise, the average review running from 600 to 1,200 words in length. The average length of the reviews written by one person generally should not exceed 1,000 words. Except for reviews of achievement batteries, multi-factor batteries, and tests for which a literature review is made, longer reviews should be prepared only with the approval of the Editor.

3) Reviews should be frankly critical, with both strengths and weaknesses pointed out in a judicious manner. Descriptive comments should be kept to the minimum necessary to support the critical portions of the review. Criticism should be as specific as possible; implied criticisms meaningful only to testing specialists should be avoided. Reviews should be written primarily for the rank and file of test users. An indication of the relative importance and value of a test with respect to competing tests should be presented whenever possible. If a reviewer considers a competing test better than the one being reviewed, the competing test should be specifically named.

4) If a test manual gives insufficient, contradictory, or ambiguous information regarding the construction, validity, and use of a test, reviewers are urged to write directly to authors and publishers for further information. Test authors and publishers should, however, be held responsible for presenting adequate data in test manuals—failure to do so should be pointed out. For comments made by reviewers based upon unpublished information received personally from test authors or publishers, the source of the unpublished information should be clearly indicated.

5) Reviewers will be furnished with the test entries which will precede their reviews. Information presented in the entry should not be repeated in reviews unless needed for evaluative purposes.

6) The use of sideheads is optional with reviewers.

7) Each review should conclude with a paragraph presenting a concise summary of the reviewer's overall evaluation of the test. The summary should be as explicit as possible. Is the test the best of its kind? Is it recommended for use? If other tests are better, which of the competing tests is best?

8) A separate review should be prepared for each test. Each review should begin on a new sheet. The test and forms reviewed should be clearly indicated. Your name, title, position, and address should precede each review, e.g.: John Doe, Professor of Education and Psychology, University of Maryland, College Park, Maryland. The review should begin a new paragraph immediately after the address.

9) All reviews should be typed double spaced and in triplicate. Two copies of each review should be submitted to the Editor; one copy should be retained by the reviewer.

10) If for any reason a reviewer thinks he is not in a position to write a frankly critical review in a scholarly and unbiased manner, he should request the Editor to substitute other tests for review.

11) Reviewers may not invite others to collaborate with them in writing reviews unless permission is secured from the Editor.

12) Most tests will be reviewed by two or more persons in order to secure better representation of various viewpoints. Noncritical content which excessively overlaps similar materials presented by another re-

viewer may be deleted. Reviews will be carefully edited, but no important changes will be made without the consent of the reviewer. Galley proofs (unaccompanied by copy) will be submitted to reviewers for checking.

13) The Editor reserves the right to reject any review which does not meet the minimum standards of the MMY series.

14) Each reviewer will receive a complimentary copy of *The Seventh Mental Measurements Yearbook.*

The 439 contributing reviewers represent an extremely wide range in age, interests, and specialities. Over half the reviewers, 249 or 56.7 percent, are new reviewers. Of the 190 old reviewers, 5 have reviewed for all seven yearbooks, 4 for six yearbooks, 18 for five yearbooks, 24 for four yearbooks, 48 for three yearbooks, and 91 for two yearbooks. For the 248 for whom dates of birth are available, their ages range from 30 to 72, with quartiles 42, 48, and 55. The quartiles for the new reviewers are 38, 42, and 48; for old reviewers, 47, 53, and 58.

Most contributors were asked to review two tests: 9.6 percent reviewed three or more tests; 70.4 percent, two or more tests; and 29.6 percent reviewed only one test.

The distribution of reviewers by countries follows: United States, 394; United Kingdom, 24; Canada, 16; Australia, 2; New Zealand, 2; and Malawi, 1. States represented by 10 or more reviewers are: California, 51; New York, 49; Michigan, 31; Illinois, 26; New Jersey, 22; Georgia, 20; Iowa, 17; Minnesota, 16; Pennsylvania, 16; Ohio, 13; Massachusetts, 11; Missouri, 11; Colorado, 10; and Texas, 10. Altogether, 40 states and 5 foreign countries are represented by the 439 test reviewers.

EXCERPTED TEST REVIEWS

In addition to the 798 reviews written specifically for *The Seventh Yearbook,* the section Tests and Reviews includes excerpts from 181 test reviews originally published in 39 journals. Table 6 gives a distribution by journals. The *Journal of Educational Measurement,* a new journal which began publishing test reviews in 1965, ranks first with 59 (32.6 percent) excerpted reviews. The *Journal of Counseling Psychology* ranks second with 29 (16.0 percent).

Journal editors sometimes request a person to evaluate several tests in the same review. This always creates a problem for us since our listings and reviews are for single tests. Some-

TABLE 6

JOURNALS REPRESENTED BY THREE OR MORE TEST REVIEW EXCERPTS

Journal	Number	Percentage
Journal of Educational Measurement	59	32.6
Journal of Counseling Psychology	29	16.0
Contemporary Psychology	9	5.0
Perceptual and Motor Skills	9	5.0
Professional Psychology	7	3.9
British Journal of Psychology	6	3.3
Journal of Projective Techniques and Personality Assessment	6	3.3
American Educational Research Journal	5	2.8
British Journal of Psychiatry	5	2.8
Educational and Psychological Measurement	5	2.8
British Journal of Social and Clinical Psychology	3	1.7
Journal of Special Education	3	1.7
Personnel and Guidance Journal	3	1.7
Psychological Reports	3	1.7
25 other journals	29	16.0
Total	181	100.3

times we are able to disentangle the critical remarks for each test reviewed. In the case of a review of a series of tests (e.g., the Pimsleur Modern Foreign Language Proficiency Tests), we have placed the excerpt under a dummy series entry with cross references from the entries for the individual tests. In the few cases where neither of these expediencies proved practicable, the review was not excerpted. A few other reviews have been omitted because they are purely descriptive or are of extremely poor quality.

Table 7 presents statistics on the review coverage which journals have been giving to tests. Only 9.9 percent of the tests in *The Seventh Yearbook* have review excerpts from one

TABLE 7

EXCERPTED TEST REVIEWS IN THE 7TH MMY

Classification	Number of Review Excerpts	Number of Tests Reviewed	Percentage of Tests	
			1 or More Reviews	2 or More Reviews
Achievement Batteries	10	6	16.7	8.3
English	3	2	3.6	1.8
Fine Arts	3	2	14.3	7.1
Foreign Languages	7	7	9.3	
Intelligence	42	20	16.5	9.1
Mathematics	9	7	7.3	2.1
Miscellaneous	6	4	3.1	0.8
Multi-Aptitude	2	2	20.0	
Personality	47	26	17.7	10.2
Reading	16	11	10.8	4.9
Science	6	5	6.2	1.2
Sensory-Motor	5	4	20.0	5.0
Social Studies	1	1	1.9	
Speech and Hearing	4	4	10.5	
Vocations	20	14	7.7	2.8
Total	181	115	9.9	4.0

or more journals; only 4.0 percent from two or more journals. The corresponding percentages for our MMY reviews are 47.2 and 20.7, respectively. Sixty-nine percent of the journal reviews, compared to 56 percent of the original MMY reviews, are of tests in the areas of intelligence, personality, reading, and vocations. The MMY's are currently producing between four and five times as many test reviews as all other reviewing publications combined.

The 181 excerpted reviews were authored by 157 persons. Unlike the original MMY reviews, some of the excerpted reviews have joint authors. About a quarter (24.2 percent) of the journal reviewers also reviewed for *The Seventh Yearbook*. Of the 558 authors of original or excerpted reviews, 71.9 percent reviewed only for the yearbook, 21.3 percent reviewed only for journals, and 6.8 percent reviewed for both the yearbook and one or more journals.

TEST BIBLIOGRAPHIES

This volume lists 12,372 references on the construction, use, and validity of specific tests —55.2 percent more references than were in *The Sixth Yearbook*. A more accurate picture of the literature explosion may be obtained by combining the reference counts for both the 7th MMY and PTR to get the total number of references published since the 6th MMY. Table 8 presents these statistics. The combined total, 19,488 references, is 144.6 percent greater than the 7,967 references reported in *The Sixth Yearbook!* The number of references in the 7th MMY and PTR together is greater than the total number of references in the 4th, 5th, and 6th yearbooks combined.

Because of the tremendous expansion in the literature being published on specific tests, we

TABLE 8

REFERENCES IN THE MMY'S AND PTR

Volume	Personality	Intelligence	Other Tests	Total
7th	4,933	4,058	3,381	12,372
PTR	7,116			7,116
7th & PTR	12,049	4,058	3,381	19,488
6th	4,187	1,623	2,157	7,967
5th	3,454	1,393	1,629	6,476
4th	2,024	1,036	1,375	4,435
3rd	1,117	939	1,376	3,432
2nd	473	380	661	1,514
Total	23,304	9,429	10,579	43,312

would have been overwhelmed had we attempted to continue our practice of listing all references in the MMY's. The task of handling references has been made manageable, at least for the present, by running 7,116 references in the MMY monograph *Personality Tests and Reviews*. References will also be given in *Tests in Print, Volume 2*, to be published early in 1973, in order to make easier the task of preparing *The Eighth Mental Measurements Yearbook*.

Although not exhaustive, the bibliographies for specific tests are extraordinary because of their accuracy, relevancy, and scope. Our objective has been to cover (*a*) the published literature in the English-speaking world, (*b*) references written in English but published in non-English-speaking countries, and (*c*) unpublished theses.

All published references reported in the MMY's have been examined by us to make sure that they meet our criteria for inclusion as references to specific tests and to enable us to prepare accurate bibliographic entries. References from more than 600 journals have been gathered firsthand. Secondary sources are used to provide leads but they are never used as the basis for listing a reference. If a reference could not be located in one of the numerous libraries used by us in this country and abroad, the reference has not been listed. The number of not-seen (and consequently not reported) references—usually in foreign publications—is probably less than one percent of all references in the yearbooks.

Research reports prepared for internal use within an organization and prepublication reports are not listed as references. Doctoral theses abstracted in *Dissertation Abstracts International* are listed along with a reference to DAI without further checking on our part. Other theses references, gathered from secondary sources, are always submitted to the graduate office of the institution issuing the degree for checking before being used in an MMY.

Bibliographies prepared by authors for their own tests are rarely worth checking for references we may have missed, since test authors usually have less restrictive standards for listing a publication as a reference.

Fifty-three tests in this volume have generated bibliographies of 100 or more references in the seven MMY's and PTR (see Table 9).

TABLE 9

7TH MMY TESTS WITH 100 OR MORE REFERENCES
IN THE SEVEN MENTAL MEASUREMENTS YEARBOOKS
AND PERSONALITY TESTS AND REVIEWS

Test (Rank)	References	
	Cumulative Total	7th MMY and PTR
Rorschach (1)	4,202	1,174
Minnesota Multiphasic Personality Inventory (2)	3,306	1,897
Thematic Apperception Test (3)	1,534	636
Strong Vocational Interest Blank for Men (4)	1,098	485
Edwards Personal Preference Schedule (5)	1,088	754
Stanford-Binet Intelligence Scale (6)	988	258
Wechsler Intelligence Scale for Children (7)	806	518
California Psychological Inventory (8)	769	620
Wechsler Adult Intelligence Scale (9)	761	539
Study of Values (10)	687	407
Sixteen Personality Factor Questionnaire (11)	654	544
Bender-Gestalt Test (12)	621	362
College Board Scholastic Aptitude Test (13)	419	298
General Aptitude Test Battery (14)	402	138
Progressive Matrices (15)	387	194
SRA Primary Mental Abilities (16)	312	98
Goodenough-Harris Drawing Test (17)	295	158
ACT Test Battery (18)	279	265
Differential Aptitude Tests (19)	268	139
Illinois Test of Psycholinguistic Abilities (20)	261	239
Cooperative School and College Ability Tests (21)	257	186
Torrance Tests of Creative Thinking (22)	243	243
Adjective Check List (23)	233	233
Peabody Picture Vocabulary Test (24)	223	202
Holtzman Inkblot Technique (25)	218	196
California Test of Mental Maturity (26)	205	102
Porteus Maze Test (27)	189	67
Eysenck Personality Inventory (28)	174	173
Strong Vocational Interest Blank for Women (29)	171	92
Revised Minnesota Paper Form Board Test (30)	159	19
Omnibus Personality Inventory (31)	153	142
Stern Environment Indexes (32)	143	124
Metropolitan Readiness Tests (33)	142	124
College and University Environment Scales (34)	139	139
Bennett Mechanical Comprehension Test (35)	130	22
Stanford Achievement Test (36.5)	129	44
Stern Activities Index (36.5)	129	102
Miller Analogies Test (38)	127	57
AAHPER Youth Fitness Test (39)	125	104
Marianne Frostig Developmental Test of Visual Perception (40)	124	117
Personal Orientation Inventory (41)	123	123
Shipley-Institute of Living Scale for Measuring Intellectual Impairment (42)	121	59
Tennessee Self Concept Scale (43)	118	118
FIRO Scales (44.5)	115	100
Medical College Admission Test (44.5)	115	57
Inpatient Multidimensional Psychiatric Scale (46)	114	88
Wonderlic Personnel Test (47)	113	28
Lorge-Thorndike Intelligence Tests (48)	112	95
Cornell Medical Index—Health Questionnaire (49.5)	109	109
Watson-Glaser Critical Thinking Appraisal (49.5)	109	74

Test (Rank)	References	
	Cumulative Total	7th MMY and PTR
Leader Behavior Description Questionnaire (51)	108	108
Jr.–Sr. High School Personality Questionnaire (52)	104	83
Remote Associates Test (53)	100	100
Total for the 53 tests	24,011	13,353
Total for all other tests in the 7th MMY	4,830	3,512
Grand total	28,841	16,865

The Rorschach continues to lead with a total of 4,202 references, 27.1 percent more than the MMPI with its 3,306 references. Three other tests are represented by bibliographies with over 1,000 references: TAT, 1,534; SVIB, 1,098; and EPPS, 1,088.

Table 10 presents statistics on the current output of literature for the 46 tests averaging

TABLE 10

7TH MMY TESTS WITH 50 OR MORE REFERENCES
IN THE SEVEN MENTAL MEASUREMENTS YEARBOOKS
AND PERSONALITY TESTS AND REVIEWS FOR THE
FIVE-YEAR PERIOD 1965–69

Test (Rank)	References 1965–69	Yearly Average
Minnesota Multiphasic Personality Inventory (1)	1,199	240
Rorschach (2)	650	130
Edwards Personal Preference Schedule (3)	483	97
Sixteen Personality Factor Questionnaire (4)	401	80
California Psychological Inventory (5)	388	78
Wechsler Adult Intelligence Scale (6)	373	75
Thematic Apperception Test (7)	369	74
Wechsler Intelligence Scale for Children (8)	349	70
Strong Vocational Interest Blank for Men (9)	318	64
Study of Values (10)	255	51
Bender-Gestalt Test (11)	233	47
ACT Test Battery (12)	211	42
College Board Scholastic Aptitude Test (13)	205	41
Torrance Tests of Creative Thinking (14)	169	34
Illinois Test of Psycholinguistic Abilities (15)	166	33
Stanford-Binet Intelligence Scale (16)	165	33
Peabody Picture Vocabulary Test (17)	152	30
Adjective Check List (18)	139	28
Holtzman Inkblot Technique (19)	134	27
Progressive Matrices (20)	132	26
Eysenck Personality Inventory (21)	128	26
Cooperative School and College Ability Tests (22)	120	24
College and University Environment Scales (23)	108	22
Omnibus Personality Inventory (24)	107	21
Goodenough-Harris Drawing Test (25)	104	21
Personal Orientation Inventory (26)	95	19
General Aptitude Test Battery (27)	94	19
Stern Environment Indexes (28)	92	18
Differential Aptitude Tests (29.5)	88	18

Test (Rank)	References 1965–69	Yearly Average
Marianne Frostig Developmental Test of Visual Perception (29.5)	88	18
Tennessee Self Concept Scale (31)	82	16
Metropolitan Readiness Tests (32)	77	15
Stern Activities Index (33)	68	14
AAHPER Youth Fitness Test (34)	67	13
Remote Associates Test (35)	65	13
FIRO Scales (37)	61	12
Multiple Affect Adjective Check List (37)	61	12
Strong Vocational Interest Blank for Women (37)	61	12
Lorge-Thorndike Intelligence Tests (39.5)	60	12
SRA Primary Mental Abilities (39.5)	60	12
Inpatient Multidimensional Psychiatric Scale (41)	58	12
Jr.–Sr. High School Personality Questionnaire (42)	57	11
California Test of Mental Maturity (43)	56	11
Vocational Preference Inventory (44)	55	11
Leader Behavior Description Questionnaire (45)	52	10
Cornell Medical Index · (46)	51	10
Total for the 46 tests	8,506	1,701
Total for all other tests in the 7th MMY	2,401	480
Grand total	10,907	2,181

10 or more references per year over the five-year period 1965–69. The MMPI leads with a staggering total output of 240 references annually—20 references per month! It takes 4.3 MMY pages of 6-point type to list the MMPI references published in a single year! And the trend is still upwards. The Rorschach, second with 130 references per year, has been producing fewer and fewer references since it reached its peak record of 205 references per year during the five-year period 1950–54. Of the 10 tests averaging 50 or more references per year, 7 are personality tests, 2 are intelligence tests, and 1 is a vocational interest inventory. For all tests in this volume, the current output of references is averaging 2,181 per year or 182 per month.[7]

BOOKS AND REVIEWS

The section Books and Reviews has been a regular feature of the MMY's following the introduction of the section in *Educational, Psychological, and Personality Tests of 1936*.[8] This monograph and the seven *Mental Measurements Yearbooks* together list practically all books on testing and assessment techniques written in English and published over the 38-year period 1933–70. Excerpts from representative reviews these books received in professional journals have been reprinted.

The MMY Book Review Index[9] is a useful index to the book reviews excerpted through *The Sixth Yearbook*. "The primary purpose of the Index is to facilitate, for historical purposes, the retrieval of comments, criticisms, and viewpoints from among the thousands of review excerpts which have been published in the six MMY's and related publications."[10]

This MMY lists 664 books on testing, most of which were published in the years 1964 through 1970 with a few older and a few more recent titles. Five hundred and eighty-seven (88.4 percent) are new books not previously listed in an MMY; 45 (6.8 percent) are revised books; and 32 (4.8 percent) are books which were in *The Sixth Yearbook*.

We have attempted to include practically all measurements books written in English, regardless of the country of origin, with a few exceptions. Practice books have been excluded unless reviewed in a professional journal. Research monographs intended primarily for use within an organization have not been included. Finally, we omitted a few books which we learned about from secondary sources but could not locate for firsthand examination.

Hundreds of journals were searched for reviews of books on testing. The critical portions of the reviews located were excerpted for possible inclusion in *The Seventh Yearbook*. About two-thirds of these review excerpts were selected for reprinting. However, unused reviews were not necessarily poorer than those finally chosen. For books receiving numerous reviews, we tried to pick two to four reviews which would be fairly representative of the better reviews. Since only the evaluative portions of each review were selected, the excerpts range from a few sentences to an entire review.

The Seventh Yearbook includes 555 excerpted book reviews from 86 journals. No reviews (or reviews worth excerpting) were found for 55.0 percent of the books. Of the 299 books with reviews in this yearbook, 51.8 percent have two or more reviews; 20.4 percent, three or more reviews; and 6.7 percent, four or more reviews.

7 The average number of references per year for *all* tests in print will be reported in *Tests in Print, Volume 2*.
8 BUROS, OSCAR K. *Educational, Psychological, and Personality Tests of 1936: Including a Bibliography and Book Review Digest of Measurement Books and Monographs of 1933–36*. Rutgers University Bulletin, Vol. 14, No. 2A; Studies in Education, No. 11. [Highland Park, N.J.: Gryphon Press], August 1937. Pp. 141. * Out of print. For reviews, see 1:B326 and 2:B857.

9 BUROS, OSCAR KRISEN, EDITOR. *Personality Tests and Reviews*, pp. 1428–77.
10 *Ibid.*, p. 1428.

INDEXES

One hundred and forty pages are devoted to the six indexes presented in Volume II: the Periodical Directory and Index (6 pages), Publishers Directory and Index (9 pages), the Index of Book Titles (9 pages), Index of Test Titles (24 pages), Index of Names (73 pages), and the Classified Index of Tests (19 pages).

The Periodical Directory and Index lists the 99 journals which cooperated by giving us permission to reprint excerpts from their book and test reviews. The journals represented by 10 or more excerpted reviews are as follows: *Contemporary Psychology,* 117 reviews; *Educational and Psychological Measurement,* 90 reviews; *Journal of Educational Measurement,* 76 reviews; *British Journal of Educational Psychology,* 30 reviews; *Journal of Counseling Psychology,* 30 reviews; *Journal of Projective Techniques and Personality Assessment,* 29 reviews; *Personnel and Guidance Journal,* 25 reviews; *British Journal of Psychology,* 24 reviews; *American Educational Research Journal,* 19 reviews; *British Journal of Psychiatry,* 16 reviews; *British Journal of Social and Clinical Psychology,* 16 reviews; *Personnel Psychology,* 14 reviews; *Perceptual and Motor Skills,* 11 reviews; and *British Journal of Educational Studies,* 10 reviews. Over two-thirds of the 736 reviews excerpted are from these 14 journals. The geographical distribution of the 99 journals is as follows: United States, 69 journals; England, 16; Australia, 4; India, 4; Canada, 2; Germany, 2; New Zealand, 1; and South Africa, 1.

The Publishers Directory and Index presents up-to-date information on the addresses of 440 publishers of tests and books on testing. One hundred and ninety-eight of these publishers publish books only. The remaining 242 publishers have one or more tests in this yearbook.

Test publishing is characterized by two extremes. On the one hand, a few publishers are in a dominating position; the top three percent of the publishers by number of tests listed in this yearbook account for 37.2 percent of the 1,157 tests. On the other hand, the number of small publishers is extremely large; 55 percent of the publishers are one-test publishers accounting for only 11.5 percent of the tests.

The heavy concentration of test production among a few test publishers is more obvious when we examine the list of publishers represented by 25 or more tests: Educational Testing Service, 96 tests; College Entrance Examination Board, 87 tests; Harcourt Brace Jovanovich, Inc., 63 tests; Psychological Corporation, 47 tests; Cooperative Tests and Services, 46 tests; Western Psychological Services, 46 tests; Science Research Associates, Inc., 45 tests; Data Processing and Educational Measurement Center, 40 tests; CTB/McGraw-Hill, 30 tests; and Houghton Mifflin Co., 25 tests.

The top five publishers are not independent; they may be divided into two conglomerates of interlocking companies. Since Cooperative Tests and Services is a subdivision of Educational Testing Service and since CEEB tests are constructed by ETS under contract, these three publishers may be considered as a single testing conglomerate. Together, this giant test publishing combination is responsible for 229 tests (19.8 percent). The other conglomerate consists of Harcourt Brace Jovanovich, Inc. and its two subsidiaries, Psychological Corporation and Grune and Stratton, Inc. This combination accounts for 120 tests (10.4 percent). Together these two giant conglomerates account for 349 tests, 30.2 percent of the tests in *The Seventh Yearbook.* The number of their tests in this yearbook is very nearly the same as the total number accounted for by the 217 smallest test publishers—publishers with 9 or fewer tests in this yearbook.

Among the 25 publishers with 10 or more tests are five foreign publishers: Ginn and Co. Ltd. (England), 22 tests; NFER Publishing Co. Ltd. (England), 16 tests; Australian Council for Educational Research (Australia), 13 tests; National Institute for Personnel Research (South Africa), 11 tests; and Human Sciences Research Council (South Africa), 10 tests.

The Index of Book Titles appears for the first time in this yearbook. Book titles were formerly listed with test titles in a single Index of Titles.

The Index of Test Titles includes more than the usual alphabetical listing of titles. Many titles have been inverted so as to bring together in the alphabetical sequence keywords such as "algebra," "diagnostic," "interest," and "nursing," to provide a keyword-in-title subject index. Test titles consisting of two parts separated by a colon have been entered twice so that each part may be listed first; for example, there are entries for both *Cooperative Mathematics Tests: Algebra* and *Algebra: Cooperative Mathematics Tests*. Superseded and non-preferred titles are also listed, followed by the correct or preferred title and its entry number. Acronyms are presented for tests having a combined total of 25 or more references since the publication of *The Sixth Yearbook*. Numbers preceded by P or R refer to tests which are new, revised, or supplemented since *The Sixth Yearbook,* but the entries are to be found only in *Personality Tests and Reviews* or in *Reading Tests and Reviews.*

The Index of Names is an analytical index which indicates whether a citation refers to authorship of a test review (*rev*), a test (*test*), a measurements book (*bk*), an excerpted review (*exc*), or a reference dealing with a specific test (*ref*). Names mentioned in cross references (*cross ref*), footnotes (*f*), and otherwise (*other*) are also indexed.

Forenames have been reduced to initials to lower the cost of indexing. Since authors are not always consistent in the way they list their names on publications, two or more listings may refer to the same person. On the other hand, the use of initials instead of forenames increases the probability that the citations for two or more persons will be listed together. Reference to the cited material in the text will resolve these ambiguities in most all cases, since it is our policy to list authors' names exactly as reported in an article, book, or test.

The Classified Index of Tests is an expanded table of contents for the section Tests and Reviews. It is a compact presentation of the titles of all tests in each classification used in the yearbook along with the following information for each test: (*a*) whether or not the test is new, revised, or unchanged since last listed in an MMY; (*b*) names of the authors who wrote original reviews of the test; and (*c*) the number of excerpted reviews.

HOW TO USE THIS YEARBOOK

The reader who wishes to get the maximum help in as brief a time as possible from *The Seventh Mental Measurements Yearbook* should read the following suggestions and explanations. This should be done even though the reader has had experience using earlier volumes.

1) *Table of Contents.* The Table of Contents should be consulted first to get an overall picture of the yearbook's contents and the classification plan used. The Table of Contents lists all the main headings, subheadings, and sub-subheadings under which tests are classified in the section Tests and Reviews. The numbers referred to in the Table of Contents are page numbers, not entry numbers. Elsewhere in the yearbook, all references are to entry numbers.

2) *Classified Index of Tests.* After examining the Table of Contents, the reader may find it profitable to turn to the Classified Index of Tests at the end of Volume II. The Classified Index, an expanded table of contents of the section Tests and Reviews, presents a complete list of all tests and reviewers in this yearbook.

3) *Page and Entry Numbers.* Confusion of page and entry numbers is probably responsible for more difficulty in using the MMY's than is any other characteristic of the volumes. Readers are urged, therefore, to keep in mind that page numbers appear in the running heads next to the *inside* margins; entry numbers (i.e., the numbers assigned to specific tests and books) appear in the running heads next to the *outside* margins. The entry numbers on facing pages represent the first and last tests or books listed on the facing pages. The Table of Contents refers to page numbers—the numbers next to the inside margins. Cross references and indexes refer to entry numbers—the numbers next to the outside margins. Except when using the Table of Contents, the reader will have no need to use page numbers.

4) *Stars, Asterisks, and Ellipses.* A star (★) preceding a title indicates a new test or book not previously listed in an MMY. An asterisk (*) preceding a title indicates a test or book which has been revised or supplemented in some way since last listed in an MMY. An asterisk following an entry for a test, book, or reference indicates that the entry was prepared from a first-hand examination of the publication in question. Asterisks and ellipses in quotations and excerpts indicate omissions; asterisks indicate a break in the continuity of reading, and ellipses indicate continuity of reading.

5) *Test Entries.* For each test, an attempt has been made to present the following information in the order given:

a) TITLE. Test titles are printed in boldface type. Secondary or series titles are set off from main titles by a colon. Titles are always presented exactly as reported in the test materials. When the titles on the test booklet and manual differ, the better known title is given in boldface; the second title is generally given in italic type within the entry. Entry titles which differ from those reported in the test materials (generally because no definitive title is used) are enclosed in brackets. Stars (★) precede titles of tests which have not been listed before in an MMY; asterisks (*) precede titles of tests which have been revised or supplemented since their last MMY listing.

b) DESCRIPTION OF THE GROUPS FOR WHICH THE TEST IS INTENDED. The grade, chronological age, or semester range, or the employment category is usually given. "Grades 1.5-2.5, 2-3, 4-12, 13-17" means that there are four test booklets: a booklet for the middle of the first grade through the middle of the second grade, a booklet for the beginning of the second grade through the end of the third grade, a booklet for grades 4 through 12 inclusive, and a booklet for undergraduate and graduate students in colleges and universities. "First, second semester" means that there are two test booklets: one covering the work of the first semester, the other covering the work of the second semester. "1, 2 semesters" indicates that the second booklet covers the work of the two semesters. "Ages 10-2 to 11-11" means ages 10 years 2 months to 11 years 11 months; and "grades 4-6 to 5-9" means the sixth month in the fourth grade through the ninth month in the fifth grade. Commas are used to separate levels. "High school and college" denotes a single test booklet for both levels; "High school, college" denotes two test booklets, one for high school and one for college.

c) DATE OF COPYRIGHT OR PUBLICATION. The inclusive range of copyright dates (or publication dates if not copyrighted) for the various forms, accessories, and editions of a test is reported. When the publication date differs from the copyright date, both dates are sometimes given; e.g., "1971, c1965-68" means that the test was copyrighted both in 1965 and 1968 (and possibly in between) but was not published until 1971. When publication or copyright dates do not appear on the materials and the date has been secured through correspondence with the publisher, it is enclosed in brackets.

d) ACRONYM. An acronym is given for many tests. The Index of Test Titles, however, lists acronyms only for tests with 25 or more references since *The Sixth Yearbook*.

e) PART SCORES. The number of part scores is presented along with their titles or descriptions of what they presumably represent.

f) INDIVIDUAL OR GROUP TEST. All tests are group tests unless otherwise indicated.

g) FORMS, PARTS, AND LEVELS. All available forms, parts, and levels are listed.

h) PAGES. The number of pages on which print occurs is reported for test booklets, manuals, technical reports, profiles, and other nonapparatus accessories. Blank pages and pages containing only material not related to the test (e.g., advertising pages and pages containing only printer's marks) have not been counted. Self-covers have been counted only when the cover is not duplicated by a title page inside.

i) FACTUAL STATEMENTS IMPLYING CRITICISM. Some of the test entries include factual statements which imply criticism of the test. Examples of such statements follow: no data on reliability, no data on validity, no data on predictive validity, no norms, norms for grade 5 only, no description of the normative population, no norms for difference scores, test copyrighted in 1970 identical with test copyrighted in 1960, statistical data based on earlier forms, no manual, and scoring stencils (answer pattern must be punched out locally).

j) MACHINE SCORABLE ANSWER SHEETS. All types of machine scorable answer sheets available for use with a specific test are reported: Digitek (OpScan Test Scoring and Document Scanning System, see 656), IBM 805 (IBM Test Scoring Machine, see 6:669), IBM 1230 (IBM Optical Mark Reader, see 6:668), MRC (MRC Scoring and Reporting Service, see 653), NCS (NCS Scoring and Reporting Service, see 654, and NCS Sentry/70, see 655), and a few other answer sheets not widely used.

k) COST. Price information is reported for test packages (usually 20 to 35 tests), answer sheets, all other accessories, and specimen sets. The statement "$5.20 per 35 tests" means that all accessories are included unless otherwise indicated by the reporting of separate prices for accessories. The statement also means 35 tests of one level, one edition, or one part unless stated otherwise. Quantity discounts and special discounts are not reported. Specimen set prices include specimen sets of all levels, all editions, all parts—but not all forms—unless otherwise indicated. Price information is believed to be correct as of 1970. Although every precaution has been taken to ensure accuracy, some prices may be in error and other prices may have changed. For complete and up-to-date price information, the latest catalog of a test publisher should be consulted.

l) SCORING AND REPORTING SERVICES. Scoring and reporting services provided by publishers are reported along with information on costs. Special computerized scoring and interpretation services are sometimes given in separate entries immediately following the test.

m) TIME. The number of minutes of actual working time allowed examinees and the approximate length of time needed for administering a test are reported whenever obtainable. The latter figure is always enclosed in parentheses. Thus, "50(60) minutes" indicates that the examinees are allowed 50 minutes of working time and that a total of 60 minutes is needed to administer the test. When the time necessary to administer a test is not reported or suggested in the test materials but has been obtained through correspondence with the test publisher or author, the time is enclosed in brackets.

n) AUTHOR. For most tests, all authors are reported. In the case of tests which appear in a new form each year, only authors of the most recent forms are listed. Names are reported exactly as printed on test booklets. Names of editors are generally not reported.

o) PUBLISHER. The name of the publisher or distributor is reported for each test; for their addresses, see the Publishers Directory and Index.

p) SUBENTRIES. Levels, editions, subtests, or parts of a test which are available in separate booklets are sometimes presented as subentries with titles set in small capitals. Sub-subentries are indented with titles set in italic type.

6) *Test References.* All known references—published articles and books and unpublished theses—on the construction, validity, use, and limitations of each test are reported immediately after the test entry. These references are arranged in chronological order by year of publication and alphabetically by authors within years. The test bibliographies are believed to be fairly complete through 1970; three references for 1971 are also included because they are cited in reviews. In order to assist students who wish to do selected reading on a particular test, references are given to abstracts in *Dissertation Abstracts International* and in *Psychological Abstracts.* For example, "(*DAI* 31:4160B)" refers to a thesis abstract beginning on page 4160 in volume 31, section B, of *Dissertation Abstracts International;* and "(*PA* 45:6636)" refers to abstract number 6636 in volume 45 of *Psychological Abstracts.* References are numbered consecutively for a given test through all MMY volumes. References which appeared in earlier volumes are referred to but are not repeated. For example, "1–7. See 6:86" means that the first seven references for the test will be found under entry 86 in *The Sixth Yearbook.* In cross references, "2:1243" refers to test 1243 in *The 1940 Yearbook,* and P:125 refers to test 125 in *Personality Tests and Reviews.*

7) *Original Test Reviews.* Original reviews of a particular test are arranged in alphabetical order by reviewers. Cited references which are also references for the test under review are indicated by the use of italic numbers in parentheses. Cited references which are not among the test references are indicated by the use of superscripts which refer to footnotes. At times, it will be necessary to consult an earlier MMY for the reference cited. Within test reviews only full titles of published tests are italicized; short titles and titles of unpublished tests are set in Roman type.

8) *Excerpted Test Reviews.* Excerpts from test reviews first published in journals follow immediately after the original test reviews in alphabetical order by journal.

9) *Cross References to Other Reviews.* Cross references to reviews in earlier year-books of the same test or earlier editions and cross references to related reviews in this year-book are presented following the last review or review excerpt.

10) *Classified Index of Books.* A roughly classified index presented at the beginning of the section Books and Reviews will assist the reader to locate books on a particular subject. In addition to using this index, readers are urged to skim over titles and excerpts in search for books of interest.

11) *Book Entries.* The books listed in the section Books and Reviews are arranged alphabetically by authors with anonymous books arranged alphabetically by title preceding the others. Rather complete bibliographic information is given for each book. Foreign publishers are not reported for books originating in the United States. Foreign publishers are, however, given for all books originating abroad even though the books are also published in the United States.

12) *Book Reviews.* Excerpts from book reviews first published elsewhere are arranged under each book in alphabetical order by journals.

13) *Catchwords.* The running heads include catchwords to assist readers in the location of particular materials. These catchwords are presented on right-hand pages. For the section Tests and Reviews, catchwords consist of the first test classification represented on the facing pages; for the section Books and Reviews catchwords consist of the first author represented on the facing pages.

14) *Indexes.* This yearbook contains six indexes: the previously mentioned Classified Index of Tests, in which all tests in a given area are grouped for quick reference; the Periodical Directory and Index, the major purpose of which is to serve as a key to the abbreviations used for journal titles from which excerpts have been taken; the Publishers Directory and Index, which furnishes the addresses of test and book publishers; the Index of Book Titles; the Index of Test Titles, which also serves as a keyword-in-title subject index; and the Index of Names, which lists the names of all reviewers, authors, editors, and others mentioned in test entries, book entries, excerpts, references, cross references, and footnotes. Detailed information on the use of each index is contained in the italic matter preceding the index.

Tests and Reviews

ACHIEVEMENT BATTERIES

REVIEWS BY *Georgia S. Adams, Dorothy C. Adkins, J. Stanley Ahmann, L. B. Birch, Frederick G. Brown, Miriam M. Bryan, Leonard S. Cahen, Courtney B. Cazden, Paul L. Dressel, Norman Frederiksen, Joseph L. French, Elizabeth Hagen, G. C. Helmstadter, A. N. Hieronymus. C. M. Lindvall, William A. Mehrens, Jack C. Merwin, James V. Mitchell, Jr., G. A. V. Morgan, Robert D. North, A. E. G. Pilliner, H. Bradley Sagen, Fred M. Smith, Robert L. Thorndike, Frank B. Womer, and Robert L. Wright.*

---

[1]

★**Academic Proficiency Battery.** College entrants; 1969; APB; 5 scores: social sciences, commercial sciences, natural sciences, mathematical sciences, languages (either English or Afrikaans); 1 form (50 pages, English and Afrikaans); preliminary manual (21 pages, English and Afrikaans); no data on validity; separate answer sheets (IBM 1230) must be used; R5 per 10 tests; R6 per 100 answer sheets; 70c per scoring stencil; R1.20 per manual; postpaid within South Africa; specimen set not available; 85(110) minutes; F. A. Fouché, N. F. Alberts, and C. L. J. Minnaar (test); Human Sciences Research Council. *

[2]

★**Adult Basic Education Student Survey.** Poorly educated adults in basic education classes; 1966–67; ABESS; 4 scores: reading comprehension, word recognition, arithmetic computation, arithmetic problems; Forms A ('66), B ('67), 29 pages in 2 booklets; manual ('67, 16 pages); profile ('66, 1 page); separate answer sheets must be used; $9.90 per 100 answer sheets; $1.50 per set of scoring stencils; $3 per 20 profiles; $1.50 per manual; postage extra; specimen set not available; (240–300) minutes in 2–4 sessions; Elvin Rasof and Monroe C. Neff; Educational Opportunities Division, Follett Educational Corporation. *
a) PARTS 1 AND 2. 2 scores: reading comprehension, word recognition; $6.60 per 20 tests.
b) PARTS 3 AND 4. 2 scores: arithmetic computation, arithmetic problems; $6.60 per 20 tests.

DOROTHY C. ADKINS, *Professor and Researcher, College of Education, University of Hawaii, Honolulu, Hawaii.*

This test, available in two forms, consists of two arithmetic subtests (computation and problems) and two verbal subtests (reading comprehension and word recognition). It is intended primarily to assist in class placement of adult basic education students. The 1966 manual for Form A states that norms were obtained by giving the tests to over a thousand adult basic education students from a large, multi-ethnic population (in Detroit, Michigan) and that the test and norms were then "used" on over four thousand students in and around Raleigh, North Carolina. It is not clear how the use of the original norms on a new sample justifies the conclusion in the 1967 manual that "the combined factors of North and South, urban and nonurban, and Negro and Caucasian resulted in a culturally unbiased instrument." The 1967 manual for Forms A and B states that "test results from both areas correlated with each other remarkably well" (whatever that means), and that the adults involved in the standardization of Forms A and B were located in 10 states. The norms in the later manual are identical with those in the earlier. It is said that "performance on both forms compares favorably," so that the same norms as those originally established for Form A on a sample of "over five thousand" will suffice for both forms. Whether the norms can be regarded as based on about 1,000 persons in the Detroit area, about 5,000 in the Detroit and Raleigh areas combined, or on some undefined larger number spread over 10 states is unclear. The manual should be more explicit.

The tests themselves, consisting of four-alternative multiple choice items, leave much to be desired from the standpoint of niceties of test construction. The directions for the arithmetic subtests are ineptly phrased (e.g., "Add these problems," "Subtract (take away) the following," "Divide these problems," "Do the problem the way the sign tells you"). Items in the reading comprehension subtest illustrate violations of well-known principles of test construction (e.g., alternatives that are non sequitur, either ideologically or grammatically; alternatives not parallel in structure; failure to ask a question or pose a clear problem; various types of specific determiners such as "a....eclipse," "circular is the shape of a....circle").

Although these are power tests, the scoring involves the familiar correction for guessing. The response tendency related to gambling probably could be better controlled by instructing subjects to respond to every question.

With respect to reliability, it is stated that 10 percent of the sample (which sample?) was retested with an alternate form at intervals of from one day to two months, the correlations ranging from .96 to .73. This information is followed by: "Note that the latter figure has not been corrected for the higher scores normally resulting from up to two months' study in adult basic education classes." If one were to apply a uniform correction for a particular time interval—and there would be no basis for any other—there would be no effect on the correlation. One factor that does have a tremendous impact on the reliability coefficients, however, is the range of talent, running from the grade equivalent of about 1 through 8. A second consideration is the skewness of the distributions. On the arithmetic problems subtest, for example, 27 percent of the norm sample obtained a score of zero. This will pronouncedly inflate the correlation between comparable forms. Aside from the skewness, the coefficients based on a wide range of talent are, of course, appro-

priate for the range but are liable to misinterpretation by the uninitiated.

The reported validity coefficients for predicting successful completion of skills training from bands of scores on the reading comprehension subtests range from .63 to .94. Thus for general machine operator, the coefficient for a band extending from grade equivalent 2.5 upward is reported to have a "predictive validity correlation" of .89. The manual states that "the validity correlations are based on reports from work-training counselors on the usefulness of Forms A and B in accurately predicting....the successful completion of skills training." A footnote indicates an N of 1,000, probably referring to the total group of 18 classes rather than to each class. It seems doubtful that the students were randomly assigned to training programs irrespective of ability. In fact, in the discussion of the validity correlations the manual states: "Readers unfamiliar with skills training for adult education students should be aware that these students normally do not select their training areas. Instead, they are counseled to register for classes in which it is felt they will succeed." Just how the "predictive validity correlations" were determined is still a complete mystery to this reader. The authors say that "these correlation figures, ranging from .63 to .94, are extremely respectable," but exhort the user to be cautious and review the section on "a tool for predicting success in skills training," where he finds that "the reader is warned against accepting statistics in lieu of his own professional experience." Several perusals of this section failed to enlighten this reviewer.

A. N. HIERONYMUS, *Professor of Education and Psychology, The University of Iowa, Iowa City, Iowa.*

Purposes are listed as: (*a*) "the gross sorting of ABE students," (*b*) "the measurement of their growth," (*c*) "the preparation....for the type of tests they would meet in life situations," and (*d*) success in skills training. A single battery is used for the entire range of adult literacy, although it is noted that the tests were "designed for the adult illiterate whose communication skills....[are] below the fourth-grade level."

There is no description of a prepublication item tryout; apparently there was none. There is no rationale for item selection, nor are content specifications provided. The items appear to be quite variable in quality. The reading tests consist of short passages, some of which appear to be interesting and appropriate for the adults in basic education. However, most of the items consist of short responses of the word-matching type, which measure only recognition of trivial factual detail with almost no emphasis on inferences and ideas.

The word recognition test, consisting of incomplete sentences with four alternatives each, appears to be competently constructed. While it is claimed that the items in each test are arranged in order of difficulty, the reading load and item difficulty throughout the test appear to be remarkably uniform. For example, the fourth item in Form A is, "To go on someone's property without any right is to *trespass*," whereas the next to the last item is, "Around means *about*."

The arithmetic computation test consists of 15 items each on the four fundamental processes with whole numbers, and an additional 15 items on fractions, decimals, and denominate numbers. The "Other" (open-ended) response is used with approximately one-third of the items, with little apparent reason for deletion in items in which there are many possible responses that cannot be accounted for with numerical distractors. For example, for $20 + 40$ the responses are 70, 60, 20, and Other; for $82916 + 43621$ the responses are 136535, 126537, 39395, and 145535.

The arithmetic problems test consists of few genuine problems. A majority are either straight computation (e.g., "$3 \times 23 = ?$") or numerical concept (e.g., "Which is the smallest number?").

It is implied that the test was constructed to avoid cultural bias. The authors state that traditional tests "inadvertently included a certain amount of cultural bias, having been standardized on middle-class samples rather than on the disadvantaged," as though standardization on disadvantaged groups would remove such bias. Later, as "evidence," they state, "Test results from both areas" (Detroit and Raleigh, North Carolina) "correlated with each other remarkably well, and thus the combined factors of North and South, urban and nonurban, and Negro and Caucasian resulted in a culturally unbiased instrument." This appears to imply that similar distributions of scores from diverse disadvantaged populations is evidence of lack of bias.

Normative scores provided are percentile ranks and T scores based on a disadvantaged population, and grade equivalents. The standardization population is vaguely described. In one place in the manual it is stated that the norms for Form A were established on 1,100 adults in basic education classes (in or around Detroit?). Further on in the manual, it is implied that norms for Form B (published a year later) were established on a diverse population in 10 states. Yet, the raw score conversion tables are identical for Forms A and B, and the norms published for the two forms are identical to those previously published for Form A. It is inconceivable to this reviewer that two forms constructed at different times, without item tryout, could yield identical raw score distributions for all four tests. This certainly casts doubt on the validity of the authors' recommendation that the two different forms be used for measuring growth. There is no information about how the grade-equivalent scores were derived.

Reliability data are scanty. Correlations "that ranged from .96 (when retesting occurred after one day) to .73 (when retesting occurred after two months)" were based on retesting "10 per cent of the sample population" with an alternate form. There is no indication whether these data were for individual subtests or some sort of total score.

Predictive validity data (for the reading test only) are similarly difficult to evaluate. A chart is presented which is purported to show the range of reading level (GE's) required for successful completion of training in each of 18 occupations. It is not clear what was used to determine where the bands begin and end. It is stated that the chart and accompanying validity correlations were "based on reports from work-training counselors on the usefulness of Forms A and B in accurately predicting....the successful completion of skills training."

This battery might be useful in administering and conducting adult basic education programs, but it meets few of even the minimum standards for test publication.

[3]

★**Adult Basic Learning Examination.** Adults with achievement levels grades 1–4, 5–8, 9–12; 1967–71; ABLE; 6 scores: vocabulary, reading, spelling, arithmetic (computation, problem solving, total); 3 levels; supplementary norms for Levels 1 and 2 available on request; publisher recommends use of local norms; $2.50 per specimen set of any one level, postage extra;

Bjorn Karlsen, Richard Madden, and Eric F. Gardner; Harcourt Brace Jovanovich, Inc. *

a) LEVEL 1. Adults with achievement levels grades 1–4; 1967; Forms A, B, (19 pages); 2 editions: hand scorable, MRC (spelling and arithmetic computation subtests must be hand scored); manual (40 pages); $17 per 35 hand scorable tests; 55¢ per MRC test booklet; MRC scoring service, 52¢ and over per test; (145) minutes.

b) LEVEL 2. Adults with achievement levels grades 5–8; 1967; Forms A, B, (23 pages); 2 editions: hand scorable, MRC (spelling and arithmetic computation subtests must be hand scored); manual (36 pages); $17 per 35 hand scorable tests; 55¢ per MRC test booklet; MRC scoring service, 55¢ and over per test; (145) minutes.

c) LEVEL 3. Adults with achievement levels grades 9–12; 1970–71; Forms A ('71, 30 pages), B ('70, 30 pages); manual ('71, 48 pages); separate answer sheets (IBM 1230, MRC) must be used; $17.50 per 35 tests; $2.80 per 35 IBM answer sheets; $10 per 100 MRC answer sheets; 80¢ per set of IBM scoring stencils; MRC scoring service, 45¢ and over per test; 207(250) minutes.

A. N. HIERONYMUS, *Professor of Education and Psychology, The University of Iowa, Iowa City, Iowa.* [Review of Levels 1 and 2.]

This battery is a highly professional publication. The tests, manuals, and accessory materials are attractive in format, and the manuals are well organized, and complete. The major purposes are to determine general educational level of adults who have not completed formal eighth grade education and to evaluate programs designed to raise their educational level. Other purposes are diagnosis of individual strengths and weaknesses, educational planning, and measurement of progress.

The vocabulary, spelling, and arithmetic problems (Level 1 only) tests are administered as listening tests to avoid contamination by reading. No separate answer sheets are used; rather the student marks directly in the test booklet (either hand-scorable or MRC machine-scorable).

Level 1 is intended to discriminate most reliably in the grade level range 1–4; Level 2 in the 5–8 range. Several of the tests appear to be overly difficult for optimum reliability in these ranges. For example, for Level 1, Form A, the arithmetic problem solving test consists of 20 items. A raw score of 10 converts to a GE of 4.6, which means that raw scores 1–10 separate grade levels 1.4 through 4.6. The raw score range 11–20 separates grade levels 5.1 to 6.0+; raw scores above 12 convert to an indeterminate 6.0+. On the Level 2 spelling test, raw scores above 29 (out of 40) convert to an indeterminate GE of 9.0+. This general criticism

applies to a somewhat lesser degree to all of the tests in the battery, with the possible exception of reading.

It was intended that the test material "be adult in content and orientation." An attempt was made to emphasize the vocabulary, reading, spelling, and arithmetic in the everyday life of adults. The authors appear to have succeeded very well in this attempt. Most of the items appear to be appropriate for the target group, and there is little or no obvious "cultural bias."

The items appear to be technically well constructed. The vocabulary test is intended to indicate "how well the student will be able to grasp verbal, school-type material in general." A possible criticism is that nouns appear to be overemphasized, especially in Level 1 in which 32 of the 50 vocabulary words (Form A) are nouns. Spelling ability is measured by a dictation-type test in which words are presented in context. The arithmetic computation tests are rather short, and a little too difficult for maximum efficiency, but reflect systematic sampling of skills. Only skills involving the fundamental processes applied to whole numbers are sampled in Level 1. In Level 2 there are five items in each form on fractions. The arithmetic problems tests appear to be suitable in content and technically well constructed.

The reading tests consist of short passages, in which the last word in most sentences is missing and must be selected from three alternatives. For this reviewer, this type of reading test has some serious shortcomings. Most of the passages consist of two or three sentences interrupted by missing words. The examinee must use the context of the remainder of each sentence to select the word which best fits the context. This type of item does not recognize the multi-faceted nature of reading comprehension. No emphasis is given to such skills as generalization, discerning the main idea, evaluating the purposes, attitudes, or intentions of the writer, etc. When one reads, he reads to get ideas, and it is difficult if not impossible to build items in which ideas with any degree of complexity can be represented by a one-word response.

The authors state, "The reading test establishes the general level at which a person can read sentences and paragraphs. It is a test of reading comprehension which, of course, is the primary objective of reading instruction. The test, then, is an overall evaluation of the reading act."

It is the last sentence which the reviewer questions. To be sure, reading comprehension is required in order to perform well on the test, and previous research has indicated that this type of sentence comprehension test correlates highly with tests intended to measure the whole range of comprehension objectives. But the test does not represent the kind of reading adults do, and selecting a word to fit a given context is not one of the *purposes* for which they read.

In reviewing a battery intended to assess basic education, one wonders why so little attention is paid to writing skills. The only test provided of writing is in spelling; nothing is provided for assessing capitalization, punctuation, and usage skills.

The only norms provided with the battery are grade-equivalent scores. These were established by equating ABLE to the *Stanford Achievement Test* in a large variable sample of school children. These are probably adequate for most purposes, because they indicate level of development in meaningful terms and provide a basis for evaluating growth. Because adult groups differ widely in characteristics, the authors recommend the use of locally developed percentile ranks and stanines to supplement GE scores.

Split-half reliabilities are reported for three groups: the school group used to obtain grade equivalents, Job Corps groups of approximately 500 and 300 each for Levels 1 and 2, respectively, and a group of approximately 450 adults enrolled in basic education classes. The reliabilities are quite satisfactory for all tests. The reliabilities of the tests in the basic education group are exceptionally high. The appropriateness of split-half reliabilities with this type of subject is open to question. If day-to-day fluctuations in attitude, attention, and motivation are as much of a problem as they are reputed to be, this source of error should have been included in reliability assessment.

The sections in the handbook for interpretation and use of test results are practical and point out the limitations as well as the positive values of the tests.

This is a well-conceived, well-constructed battery which should serve very well the purposes for which it was intended. Because it was developed specifically for use with adult groups, because of supporting data presented in a professional manner, and because of its generally high quality, the ABLE is recommended for use over the *Adult Basic Education Student Survey* or the *Tests of Adult Basic Education*.

J Counsel Psychol 16(3):278–80 My '69. Edward B. Fry. It is nice that the test makers have applied some of their skills to the socially desirable area of adult basic education. But the curriculum content of adult basic education is not very different from children's basic education or achievement batteries, as they are usually called. * The format for the test is pleasing * The chief empirical foundation for any formal test, the standardization group, was very hard to define. These test authors state that their test is for adults who have not completed eight grades of education, but what, pray tell, is normal achievement for an adult who has not completed eight grades of education? Theoretically, one could say, "we could draw a random sample of adults with under eighth-grade education and come up with a fine set of percentiles and stanines," but what would this really mean? The makers of this test have, I believe, correctly decided to give grade level norms based on administering the test to 1,000 pupils, Grades 2–7. * The authors....did not quite achieve the goal of having Level I of the ABLE suitable for Grades 1–4, and Level II for Grades 5–8. * In Form A, one of the major subtests, reading, has 16 of its 50 items which give grade-level designations 1.0–1.9. This same test has only four items to cover grade-level designations 4.0–4.8. When one jumps to the next higher form which is supposed to be Grades 5–8, it is seen that the reading subtest has nine items which cover grade-level designations 3.0–3.9. However, at the fifth-grade level where it is supposed to begin testing, there are only four items which cover the grade range 5.0–5.8, while three items cover the eighth grade. Hence, I believe the man who wrote the front page and probably the advertising copy for this test should state that Level I is most suitable for testing groups with first- and second-grade ability and Level II is suitable for students with third–eighth grade ability with much greater discrimination at the lower end. In fact, Level II would probably be considerably stronger if they attempted to cover only Grades 3, 4, and 5. * For accuracy in achievement, the user would be much better off simply using the regular Stanford Achievement Test or any other major achievement battery. This is particularly true if the user wishes to measure growth of an individual student. I believe I can drive this point home by stating that Test 4—Arithmetic Problem Solving for Level II of the ABLE has a total of 12 items which give a grade level range of 3–9. This means that the student can gain or lose ½ year by simply getting one more item right or wrong. The authors are to be commended for encouraging the user to develop local norms * The other statistical accouterments tend to be satisfactory. Split-half reliability coefficients tend to be in the 80s and 90s for each subtest and correlations between the ABLE and the Stanford Achievement subtest tend to be in the 70s which are about as good as achievement tests between different authors rate. Although inflation is rampant in the world, it came as a bit of shock to see that a package of 35 ABLE booklets costs $14.50 (versus $7.50 for the Stanford Achievement Primary Level or $7.35 for the California Achievement Elementary Level). This seems to be a rather high price to pay for a test which has a few items that appeal to adolescent or adult students and purports with somewhat erroneous aims to measure achievement either for Grades 1–4 or 5–7. Even though this purchase price will often be paid by some special federal government funds, I am afraid that as a taxpayer and a professional educator, I would recommend that both the teacher and the psychometrist would be better off using an achievement battery designed for the public schools. However, the ABLE could be used under the following conditions: (a) *when, for political or some other face validity situation, it is important to have a test that says it is aimed at adults;* (b) *when price is not an important consideration;* (c) *when grosser screening is the important testing objective, and not the finer measure of achievement as might be required in the measurement of growth of an individual due to training; and* (d) *when Level I is used with a group whose achievement hovers around Grades 1 and 2, and Level II is used when the group's achievement is around Grades 3 and 4.* Test publishers and authors are to be commended for putting some of their interest and effort into this important and socially significant area of adult basic skills. One approach that they might consider in the future is simply to make their main achievement batteries a little less child-oriented and hence a little less objectionable to adults. The

adult educators could then, with even greater impunity, use the much more powerful major achievement batteries.

J Ed Meas 5:271–4 f '68. James W. Hall. * In general, instructions for administration and scoring are clear, and inexperienced examiners should have little difficulty with them. The ABLE is intended to be "in all respects a power test," and no time limits are imposed. The greatest threat to this objective probably occurs with the Vocabulary and Spelling Tests, and for Level 2, the Arithmetic Problem Solving Test, since the items of these are read to examinees by the examiner. However, the authors' pacing instructions are quite clear and appropriate. Although the examiner is told that guessing is to be encouraged and no "correction formula" is to be used, the instructions to examinees are not sufficiently explicit on this point. Examiners are given the option of administering all tests in one session or distributing them over two or more sessions. Despite the appeal of such flexibility, certain questions are thereby raised with which the authors should have dealt. Which of the above administration procedures (massed or distributed) was used in obtaining their reliability and validity data? Can we safely assume equivalence of results across these conditions? Shouldn't each examiner adopt one of these alternatives and stick to it to obtain maximally useful norms? * Instructions for hand scoring are clear and the process is simple, except perhaps in the cases of Spelling and Arithmetic Computation where answers are constructed (rather than selected) by the examinee. The publishers offer a service whereby the test booklets are machine scored. If this service is desired, the Machine-Scorable Edition, rather than the Hand-Scorable Edition, must be ordered. However, machine scoring requires that the correctness of the constructed answers first be determined by the examiner. In other words, the Spelling and Arithmetic Computation sections must be hand scored before they can be machine scored, hardly an efficient procedure. In view of these complications the publishers probably are correct in anticipating relatively little demand for their scoring service. * All the reliability, validity, and normative data provided are based on administration of three preliminary forms of the ABLE at each level. On the basis of these data, one form at each level was eliminated. Items from the discarded forms "were used to replace poorly functioning items in the two final forms." Strictly speaking, then, no empirical data regarding the published forms of the ABLE are provided. Until this deficit is corrected, one must be guided solely by the preliminary data that we shall consider shortly. * The elementary school sample was described as having been selected to "provide a wide range of ability, but with a preponderance of pupils below average in academic achievement." The reasoning behind this selection is not discussed. Descriptions of the adult groups are fairly complete. * In terms of reliability, the weakest tests are Vocabulary and Arithmetic Problem Solving. Without additional data it is impossible to know whether or not changes from the preliminary forms to the final forms have strengthened these tests (as seems likely). Also needed are reliability data for the two forms (A and B) separately. The preliminary data suggest that reliability of the ABLE probably will be found to be satisfactory. Standard errors of measurement in raw score units are reported for the adult groups only. Unfortunately, there is no discussion of the relevance of these data so that they would be of value only to the more informed user. The authors state that "the Job Corps group is somewhat more variable (in terms of test standard deviations) than the school group....," but neglect to provide specific data or comments regarding consequences, without which such a statement carries little meaning. Concurrent validity data are reported with subtests of the Stanford Achievement Test as the criterion variables. The procedures used in deriving the reported correlation coefficients are clearly described, and the coefficients themselves are fairly impressive. * Tables are provided by which ABLE raw scores easily can be converted into grade equivalents based on the performance of the elementary school sample. The procedure used in deriving these norms, though reasonable enough, is described so briefly that relatively few consumers are likely to fully understand it. More important is the question of the relevance of norms such as these. The authors and this reviewer agree that "the use with adults of grade norms based on children's performance does present some unique problems." Some of these problems are discussed briefly by the authors, but of course they are not resolved. The authors wisely urge that local norms be developed by ABLE users. * At no point do the authors present any data regarding possible sex differences in performance. *Summary Evalua-*tion. The ABLE appears promising for the purposes for which it was developed. At present, however, its full capabilities cannot be assessed or realized because of inadequate empirical evidence. The most appropriate use at present may be in research regarding the effectiveness of various adult-education programs.

[4]

★Bristol Achievement Tests. Ages 8-0 to 9-11, 9-0 to 10-11, 10-0 to 11-11, 11-0 to 12-11, 12-0 to 13-11; 1969; BAT; 3 tests; Forms A, B, ['69, 7–8 pages]; 5 levels; administrative manual ['69, 8 pages] for each level; interpretive manual (78 pages); profile ['69, 2 pages] for each form; £1.90 per 25 tests; £1 per 25 profiles; 60p per teacher's set (without interpretive manual) of any one level of one test (must be purchased to obtain administrative manual and keys); 75p per interpretive manual; postage extra; Thomas Nelson & Sons Ltd. *

a) ENGLISH LANGUAGE. 6 scores: word meaning, paragraph meaning, sentence organisation, organisation of ideas, spelling and punctuation, total; 50(55) minutes for levels 1–3, 40(45) minutes for levels 4–5; Alan Brimer and Herbert Gross.

b) MATHEMATICS. 6 scores: number, reasoning, space, measurement, arithmetic laws and processes, total; 55(60) minutes; Alan Brimer.

c) STUDY SKILLS. 6 scores: properties, structures, processes, explanations, interpretations, total; 50(55) minutes; Alan Brimer, Margaret Fidler, Wynne Harlen, and John Taylor.

G. A. V. MORGAN, *Staff Inspector, Primary and Special Education, Education Office for Wales, Cardiff, Wales.*

These tests break new ground in both content and form. One innovation is the use of five levels, each covering a two-year stage and appropriate to an educational year, ranging from second year junior, which corresponds to ages 8–10, to the second year of secondary school, 12–14 years. This arrangement takes account of the pupil's length of schooling, rather than age alone. Construction of the tests allows for overlap of items with the levels above and below.

Another interesting feature of these tests is their novelty of content. It is implied that these tests represent the functional objectives of the modern primary school curriculum in Britain. The content has been based on sampling the current literature (psychological and educational); the tests represent general skills, strategies, and concepts rather than the content of a particular curriculum, which would obviously vary among schools.

The discussion of curriculum in the manual is, however, rather naive; it is denied that these tests represent specified objectives in a curriculum, but there would seem to be little purpose or relevance in tests unless they are appropriate evaluations and so are related closely to defined aims and objectives in the curriculum. The discussion of curriculum sampling fails to distinguish between the different levels of objective (from the general aims to the proximate objectives or the teaching programme in each classroom) between different aspects (content as compared with learning experiences) or levels of response (in terms of Bloom's taxonomy). As usually occurs when tests are devised for this wide purpose, they assess what is likely to be a reasonable common core or average set of concepts and skills, selected by the empirical trial of test content; consequently, these tests are directed, not to the specifics of skills and information based on particular teaching programmes, but to the higher level skills and concepts; to this degree, they are tests of general competencies and achievements, not tests of mastery of particular programmes.

The novelty of the test material varies. The content of the mathematics test successfully avoids the old depressing mixture of mechanical skills in computation and verbal problems in arithmetic; it brings in imaginative new content, set in challenging and interesting forms, based on essential experiences in primary school mathematics: classification, order, number sense, sets, use of tabular material, and the language of graphs. The study skills tests are the most novel aspect of this battery. They assess cultural and scientific knowledge of the environment. The tests of English language, however, despite their claims, rely on standard content in the form of vocabulary, reading, and mastery of mechanical skills, though there is an emphasis on the need for comprehension and creative response. This kind of content is almost unavoidable if the general skills of language are tested.

The tests are standardised on a satisfactory sample; between 1,200 and 1,500 children for each level took part in the first trial of test items. Age and sex were well distributed. Some 100 to 125 children at each level took part in the second trial and 1,072 to 1,265 children at each of the five levels took part in the final standardisation—and these again were well distributed by age and sex, except for a serious imbalance between boys and girls at level 3. No data are given on the number and distribution of schools or the kind of sampling undertaken; the manual states that they represented a nationally representative sample in England and Wales according to type, size, and urban-rural distribution of schools. The wide experience of the senior author in test construction and sampling should guarantee representative sampling.

Item discriminations and satisfactory standard deviation of trial tests confirm the appropriate choice of items, except possibly for some of the study skills tests.

The reliability of each main test at each level (English, mathematics, study skills) was calculated by correlating Form A and Form B on the same group over a fortnight interval. Form B was constructed and standardised to take into account that it would always be taken second. The reliabilities and standard errors are as expected for tests of this length (about 100 items) and are satisfactory for the classification of individual pupils. It is a pity, however, that no evidence is given on the internal consistency of the tests, on the grounds that this produces a spurious standard error. It is claimed in the manual that test-retest correlation is the more searching assessment of reliability, but close examination of the content of the tests suggests that the two parallel forms have been so devised that there is a rather high occurrence of very similar items and in some instances of practically identical items, particularly in the mathematics and study skills tests. In some instances, the parallel test forms contain questions which are practically identical, except for the reversal of wording or reorientation of a diagram.

Reliabilities are also given for part scores based on the five subtests in each main scale at each age level. These are good in relation to the very brief length of the test (from 10–31 items) but are not particularly satisfactory for the classification and guidance of individual pupils. When these reliabilities, as in some instances, reach values of .71 to .57, the standard error will clearly be large. As pointed out in the manual, fine discrimination between part scores is not justified, but the warning should be emphasised even more, possibly in capitals or italics, since elsewhere in the manual the use of subtest scores for differential diagnosis or checking on bias in the curriculum is recommended. It is doubtful, in view of the general and arbitrary definition of curriculum in the test content, whether the authors are justified in suggesting that their tests are a criterion of the effective balance of a particular school or class curriculum; only within the very wide score limits indicated in the test profile can individual differences in test scores be used for anything like a diagnostic purpose. In addition, it is clear from the tables given that there is a high degree of intercorrelation between the subtests within each main scale, such as English or mathematics; these correlations would need to be compared with the reliabilities of the subtests in order to establish significant difference scores between tests; this is not discussed in the manual. The main test scales vary in reliability. English and mathematics are, as would be expected from tried material, of satisfactorily high reliability (.92 to .96). The study skills tests, however, particularly at levels 4 and 5, fall below an acceptable level of reliability to .88 and .83, respectively. This may reflect the heterogeneous nature of the test content and processes and the dependence of these tests on an unknown mixture of environmental and cultural learning and school instruction.

The statistical validity of the tests is guaranteed by the item analysis, but there is no evidence on external validity in classifying pupils or predicting actual performance in school. Reference is made to the importance of construct or rational validity; it is claimed that rational validity can be satisfactorily defined by the appropriate definition and sampling of curriculum; but it has already been pointed out that these tests are based on an empirical choice of generalised skills and concepts, in turn based on logical, psychological, and other assumptions about what are the important content and processes in learning. In this sense, these test items have a face validity. There is no means, however, of determining whether the test material in fact measures directly the processes of the curriculum defined as suitable objectives. The rational validity referred to here is in fact a face validity, with all the traps that this can lead to. Direct comparison of performance on parts of the English tests with performance in English in school might well show that plausible content, such as scrambled sentences and sentence order tests in Section 4, though logically derived from a rather formal analysis of language skills, would prove to have a rather disappointing relationship with language work (either reading or writing) in school. Evidence on the external validity of tests in relation to the actual curriculum and achievement in school is to be added to the manual as this becomes available.

It has been noted that each main test at each age level is divided into five subtests, with separate timing, norms, and reliabilities. It is difficult to see, apart from symmetry, why the authors require five subtests at each level. For many purposes, it would be better to have fewer but longer subtests. It is implied in the manual that the content of each subtest differs significantly from that of others within the same main scale. The distinction in content or process between each subtest is not so clearly marked in English, for example, as it is in math. Despite claims made for the study skills test, that each subtest assesses a different aspect of cultural and scientific knowledge, items measuring ability to classify and infer and use symbols—in fact, items of similar appearance—occur in each subject (e.g., general information on the environment, interpretation of pictorial or diagrammatic presentations) and the correlations between each section suggest that they have a great deal in common. There is no clear evidence, therefore, apart from the authors' a priori classification, for the claimed differences between style and content of subtests in each main scale. There seems, rather, to be a gradation of content and a considerable overlap between subtests. The high degree of intercorrelation, not only between subtests within the main scales but indeed among the main scales, would suggest that these have a very considerable general factor of educational achievement. This casts further doubt on the recommendations in the manual (interesting though these are) for the use of comparisons between different achievement tests to group children into different levels of ability for teaching purposes.

Though subtests are separately timed, they are often so printed that one subtest overlaps onto a following page. This could lead pupils (especially the brighter and swifter ones) to begin working on the following test before time. This may be particularly true on retest with parallel forms when the pupil is familiar with the tests.

Norms are based on standard scores, worked out by modern standardisation methods; with a mean of 100 and a standard deviation of 15, they incorporate an age-allowance. Percentile equivalents are given for standardised scores for main test scales, to permit performance to be usefully compared between children. Deciles are given for part (subtest) scores because these do not discriminate so well; these use a median age for comparison and do not incorporate an age adjustment. The individual score and report sheet gives guidance on finding and recording standard scores and percentile and decile scores, together with the standard error limits for each total test and subtest. The graphic profile on the rear of the sheet reminds the teacher that the individual pupil does not have a fixed score on a test but could range within defined limits well above and below this score.

A very useful addition is the use of a predicted score (expected on the basis of reading skill, which is tested by the first subtest of the English test). There is, indeed, a considerable reading load throughout the tests in reading the instructions for test items. The predicted achievement score should be valuable in diagnostic work, suggesting how far backwardness in reading or reading failure has affected other forms of achievement.

Although the items in each subtest are claimed by definition to measure the same thing at each age level, there is no evidence that the concepts, skills, or processes remain the same. For example, tests of sentence sense, sentence order, etc. are unlikely to have the same validity at differing age levels, and an increase of difficulty is no guarantee that the test content assesses the same functions or is equally valid at different ages. Similarly, it is not clear how far the balance and weighting of subtests at each age level gives an optimal prediction of the total achievement defined and desired. It is clear, for example, that the content of the mathematics tests varies much more appropriately to suit different age levels than does the content of the English and study skills tests.

MATHEMATICS TESTS. The mathematics tests represent an ambitious and successful attempt to break out from the conventional approach involving a sequence of arithmetical skills into the areas covered by the newer approaches to primary and secondary school mathematics: to pattern, order, number base, sets, Venn diagrams, inductive thinking, probability, and graphic representation.

Part 1 assesses the conservation of number, ordinal aspects, use of number bases, understanding of magnitude, place and direction. Imaginative use is made of a domino pattern, up to Level 4, and items are based on an interesting "game" approach, which also helps the pupil without previous formal instruction in a particular aspect of arithmetic. As far as possible, an attempt is made to avoid verbal presentations.

Part 2 involves operation with sets and logical operations underlying algebra.

Part 3 emphasises Piagetian types of item and leans heavily on spatial representation and the ideas of proportion. It is clear that the spatial aspect is important, since boys do better on this than girls.

Part 4 introduces questions about directed space (angles, compass directions), the use of scale and, at Levels 1 to 3, a direct assessment of knowledge and skill in practical measurement. At Level 3, graphical representation is introduced, and elementary probability in a "game" setting. At Level 4, measurement of area enters. It is interesting that Part 4 is the least reliable subtest, possibly because it introduces materials which are taught in different ways in different schools.

Part 5 is, at all levels, devoted to the knowledge and use of arithmetical processes, but even here items are presented in such a form that they require the pupil to recognise patterns and apply relevant knowledge, not simply recall or carry out routine computation.

STUDY SKILLS TESTS. Study skills is the most novel and ambitious of the three areas of achievement. It is also the least reliable, especially at Levels 4 and 5. Study Skills is rather curiously named, since study skills in the sense of use of references, dictionary, indexing, etc. (as in the Iowa tests) are not assessed. These tests are rather an assessment of cultural knowledge and generalised concepts and skills related to the surrounding environment. It is significant, particularly with reference to the author's claims to have sampled the curriculum, that teachers feel that these tests are relevant to their pupils despite the absence of any similar content in their actual teaching. There appears to be a very strong influence of Piaget on much of the content.

Part 1 claims to deal with knowledge of materials and situations. There is much direct assessment of biological and physical information, e.g., about simple magnetism and evaporation, but there are also interesting items based on interpretations of diagrams or maps. Other items deal with simple physical properties, such as mirror reflection. The strength of this test is its emphasis on inference and general knowledge, not recall of specific information; it is, however, the second least reliable subtest in this area, with an average over all age levels of .71.

Part 2 is said to deal with structures in space involving size and movement; many of the items are essentially Piaget's conservation of substance, weight, etc. It also tests what used to be called mechanical and spatial knowledge, e.g., of balances and cog-wheels, as well as inferences from maps and graphs.

Part 3 is represented to measure sequences and "projection or interpolation in processes." It has a considerable overlap with Part 2 and similarly a considerable loading with mechanical knowledge.

Part 4 is said to be concerned with "explanation" of experiences. The actual content emphasises Piagetian conservation, classification of biological or physical objects, and scientific reasoning. It is the least reliable of all the study skills subtests, with an average correlation of .68 over all levels, sinking as low as .57 at Level 5.

Part 5 is the most distinct and directly valuable subtest, since it deals with knowledge of graphic and pictorial symbols, e.g., weather charts, graphs, isotypes, maps, and diagrams. In many respects it overlaps part of the mathematics tests.

Despite the claim for the distinctness of these tests, the intercorrelations suggest they have a very considerable amount of common content.

Some of the difficulties or weaknesses of these tests stem from the fact that since this material is so novel, sampling of content must to some degree be quite arbitrary; it is difficult, particularly at the later age levels, to ensure whether common concepts have been acquired from the environment or have been specifically taught in one school but not another.

One common feature, in the reviewer's opinion a disadvantage, of both the mathematics and study skills tests is their tendency to depend on blocks of items based on a common core, such as a diagram, table, or problem. In addition to reducing the variety of sampling and the flexibility of items, this dependence could lead to a spuriously increased reliability on retest.

ENGLISH TESTS. The English tests are most disappointing because of their essentially conventional nature and the failure to include well developed aspects of language work such as reference skills, long ago included in such tests as the Iowa battery. These tests assess very generalised aspects of language, such as vocabulary and reading, and reading is mainly at the level of primary and intermediate skills. A considerable advantage of the tests, to the teacher of English, is the requirement that children produce many of their own answers, not choose from alternatives; this means that scoring is more complicated, possibly subjective, and not reducible to machine scoring, but there is a considerable advantage in terms of getting real written response, rather than recall, from children.

Part 1 is a vocabulary test. It requires the pupil to read two sentences; the correct answer is a word in the second sentence that means the same as one in the first. The pupil must take account of the context and grammatical structure, as well as word meaning. The test discriminates well.

Part 2 is a reading test based on a series of continuous passages with gaps in them. The child is required to produce or complete written answers, governed by the sense of the paragraph rather than by difficulty of vocabulary. It is difficult to see why the author chose to impose on himself the handicap of using single continuous pieces of prose, rather than choosing more and shorter passages selected for varied content, difficulty, and level of answer. Apart from varying in difficulty, the pieces of prose do not seem to correspond to the very differing requirements of reading skills in the first years in primary and first years in secondary school. In Part 2, Levels 1 and 2 are very similar, on face value, and in fact correlate very highly.

Part 3 is an interesting and novel attempt to give the child an opportunity to write, for each item, a sentence with the same meaning as a key sentence but with controls allowing objective marking. This kind of valuable item type was developed some 15 years ago in Great Britain. This subtest is supposed to measure not only vocabulary and meaning but grasp of linguistic structure. A crude factor analysis of the intercorrelations between the English subtests suggests that Part 3 is the most representative of the verbal skills tested and is very closely related to vocabulary and reading.

Part 4, consisting mainly of jumbled words to be reassembled in a sentence and of sentences to be put in correct order, has the lowest reliability of all subtests in the entire battery. It also has lower correlation with the other subtests, i.e., is more specific. The reviewer knows of no evidence of good validity for this kind of test, despite its face validity. It assumes that this kind of anagram ability is related to real everyday writing ability, but this, in the reviewer's view, is unlikely to be so even in a very formal and structured approach to English teaching. On the other hand, the other item type in this subtest, the ability to produce three or five variants on a basic sentence, would appear to require considerable flexibility and knowledge of grammatical structure and creativity on the part of the child and is a very interesting item.

Part 5 is a conventional test of spelling (recognition of misspelling), capitalization, and punctuation, much too short to sample adequately at any specific age level. The punctuation skills would, in fact, appear to belong more to the preceding sentence sense items. This subtest is the least satisfactory in content and has a relatively low reliability because it is so short.

It is interesting that subtests 1, 2, 3, and 5 correlate quite highly, as would be expected in view of the fact that English skills have much in common and tend to be so taught that they become associated in the general and complex skills of reading and writing. The high intercorrelations of these tests suggest that there is a major verbal factor running through them and remarkably little which is specific. Because the tests are so short and so highly intercorrelated, it is doubtful whether they can usefully serve any differential diagnostic purpose.

ACCESSORIES. There is an excellent interpretive manual, well and lucidly written, containing full information on all aspects of development and standardisation of the tests' reliabilities, intercorrelations of main and subtest scores, item analyses, etc. There is a well-written popular account of the principles of testing and the use of simple statistics; it is to be hoped that teachers making use of these tests will study this manual, as it would considerably add to their understanding of the basic educational and statistical issues involved in the use of group tests. In making general and evaluative comments—e.g., on the respective merits of kinds of standard error—the manual might well give the appropriate reference in a bibliography, for the more sophisticated user.

The individual test report and profile sheet is concise, but one wonders whether it is too full of tabulated data and too compressed for easy use. Instructions for transferring raw scores to standard scores to deciles and for use of coding tables, could well be programmed more simply and explicitly step by step.

SUMMARY. Despite criticisms, these tests represent a great deal of very careful work in development and standardisation of novel forms of achievement testing. They are an imaginative and successful attempt to construct achievement measures which break away from the old conventional kind, and it is heartening to see the emphasis placed on the general concepts, skills, and applications of learning required in the modern primary school curriculum. Children are likely to enjoy the challenge and novelty of these tests. They are a valuable addition to the achievement measures available to users in school and classroom, and for general survey work.

A. E. G. PILLINER, *Director, Godfrey Thomson Unit for Academic Assessment, University of Edinburgh, Edinburgh, Scotland.*

This achievement test battery consists of tests of English Language, Study Skills, and Mathematics, each at five levels with two forms at each level—30 tests in all. There are 15 administrative manuals, one for each pair of forms. In addition, there is an unusually comprehensive interpretive manual which incorporates not only information already presented in the separate administrative manuals, but also the following: principles underlying selection of material; details of standardisation procedures; statistical information on reliability, intercorrelations among total and subtest scores, standard errors of measurement and prediction, sex differences, and the like; a general statement of the principles of mental measurement; and detailed recommendations for interpreting and utilising test results, in particular the use of profiles which are also a feature of this comprehensive and ambitious enterprise.

Part 1 of each of the English tests is concerned with reading for meaning; Part 2 with comprehension of continuous prose; and Parts 3, 4, and 5, respectively, with language expression, the production and organisation of ideas, and punctuation and spelling. The principles guiding content are stated at considerable length in the interpretive manual and rule out the use of standard multiple choice techniques. It is further prescribed that "reading at this level and for the purpose of these tests should be regarded as a skill instrumental in learning and therefore the tenor of the continuous passages would tend towards the didactic."

It is difficult to understand the reason for this prescription. It would seem to preclude, for example, reading for the sheer fun of it. However that may be, if the continuous passages are to have a didactic as well as a testing function, it is unfortunate that the passage on "Clouds" in a level 1 test should serve to perpetuate two common scientific errors. An unwarrantable distinction is made between steam and water vapour; and clouds, which consist of water droplets, are wrongly described as vapour. If the tests must also teach, it is as well that they should do so accurately.

Exception must also be taken to the method used in testing reading for meaning (Part 1). The rubric invites the child to "underline the one word in the second sentence that means the same as the word underlined in the first sentence." Now, for a word in one sentence to mean the same as another word in a different sentence, the two words must be interchangeable. In far too many of the items this is not so. Examples are: "He cut the _fat_ from the meat. The flat tin contained grease for the car" (answer: grease). Or: "The cat crept stealthily along and _pounced_ on the bird. He pounded down the path, sprang across the stream and landed lightly on his feet" (answer: sprang). Or again: "She _proved_ that she could cook. He was proud and he showed it" (answer: showed). This insensitivity to appropriateness in the use of language singularly fails to measure up to the criterion implied in the authors' insistence on the need to examine reading in context. The best that can be said about the words alleged to "mean the same" in many of these items is that they are vaguely in the same semantic area. In one item, incidentally, snakes are described as "slimy"; they are not.

Part 1 has been dealt with at some length because of the central role the authors assign to performance on it as an indicator of expected performance in other subsections of this test and of the tests of study skills and mathematics. The rest of the English test can be dealt with more briefly.

Part 2 consists of passages of continuous prose with gaps in which the testee must write words so as to maintain the sense throughout. There is much to be said for tests of this sort if they are well constructed, as most of these

are. Nevertheless, they present the marker with problems which the instructions provided do not entirely solve.

Some of the items in Part 3 again display the insensitivity in the use of language previously noted. It is a dubious proposition, for example, that the active and passive forms of a sentence mean "exactly the same," as the rubric claims. In Part 4 a number of headings are presented in scrambled order and must be "put into order for a story"—an excellent idea, but the marking scheme laid down is not easy to understand, still less to operate. The purpose of the spelling and punctuation of Part 5, we are told, is "to achieve an indication of whether a frame of reference exists within which the freedom to vary is an advantage." Why the inclusion of these basics should require such consequential justification is not clear.

The tests of study skills, we are told, "represent the most ambitious of the three areas of achievement measurement attempted." These tests are concerned with those parts of the curriculum relating to environmental studies and natural science. The emphasis throughout is on conceptualising, classifying, reasoning and abstraction, and away from factual information.

The work of the authors on this broad canvas displays considerable skill and imagination. Most of the items are well presented and many are ingenious. It is all the more unfortunate that the few blemishes observable cannot be dismissed as minor. Some of the science items are glaringly inaccurate. For instance, the preamble to one item asserts that "the same ball was bounced twice in exactly the same way each time, but it bounced higher the second time than the first time"—a nonsense statement. Worse still, to score a mark a child must attribute this difference in behaviour to chance. This is just plain wrong. In another item (of which the authors think so well that they include it in both forms of the test), the child is invited to predict the behaviour on release of a hoop with a weight, heavier than the hoop, attached to its periphery, the whole being placed on an inclined plane. The allegedly correct response is that the hoop will roll up the slope. The truly correct answer—that in the absence of more specific information about angles, relative weights, etc. whether it will roll up or down or stay put is anybody's guess—is not among the alternatives provided. In a test purporting to probe a child's ability to reason scientifically, there is no place for ill-conceived items such as these.

After these regrettable lapses, it is a relief to turn to the tests of mathematics. The statement in the interpretive manual of the principles on which they are based is surer in touch and more down-to-earth. The tests themselves reflect these principles faithfully. As examples of the (so-called) "new" mathematics in action they are very good, and it is hard to fault the component items. One nevertheless wonders what a nine-year-old will make of: "How many *more* letters are only in the second list than there are letters that are also in the first list?" One would surmise that the problem of understanding the question itself is more difficult than the task of sorting and counting which the question is about.

The material in the manuals accompanying the tests is comprehensive, clear and helpful. Profile sheets are provided on which a child's part-scores and total scores can be recorded together with their standard errors. As an impetus to record keeping, and as an aid to doing so, these should be useful. The interpretive manual, a *tour de force* of some 78 pages, serves to amplify the information in the test manuals and to provide a theoretical background against which to interpret test results. Despite the slightly pretentious tone of some of the writing ("The measurement of things and the measurement of man"), and the author's use of "data" as a singular noun, this manual is well worth reading. One slightly disturbing feature is the recorded difference (Table F) in mean raw score difficulty between Forms A and B for several of the tests—nearly 10 points in English Level 3. Another is that the tables of norms show some of the tests to be over-difficult. Thus for Mathematics Form A Level 5 (maximum possible score 100), the median raw score at median age is 19. Moreover, it is a little odd to find an age allowance incorporated in the norms for English Form A Level 5 and no age allowance in the norms for its partner Form B, while the corresponding regression coefficients of raw score on age are respectively .02 and .04.

In summary, this comprehensive battery is a more than usually ambitious enterprise which does not quite succeed. There is a great deal that is very good indeed, particularly in the mathematics tests, but also much to criticise in the English language tests on the ground that they do not foster enough feeling for language,

and in the study skills tests in which some of the science items are disastrously unscientific. One hopes that in subsequent editions these deficiencies will be put right. In the meantime, some tests are to be recommended individually, but the package as a whole is not.

For reviews of subtests, see 185 (1 review), 453 (1 review), and 776 (1 review).

[5]

*California Achievement Tests, 1970 Edition. Grades 1.5–2, 2–4, 4–6, 6–9, 9–12; 1934–70; CAT; previous edition (see 6:3) still available; 11 or 12 scores: reading (vocabulary, comprehension, total), mathematics (computation, concepts and problems, total), language (auding [level 1 only], mechanics, usage and structure, total, spelling), total; 1 form; 5 levels; subtests in reading, mathematics, and language available as separates; preliminary coordinator's handbook ('70, 49 pages); technical bulletin ('70, 35 pages); profile ('70, 1 page); $3 per 100 profiles; separate answer sheets (CompuScan [NCS], Digitek, IBM 1230) may be used in grades 4–12; $2.50 per coordinator's handbook; $2.50 per technical bulletin; postage extra; original edition by Ernest W. Tiegs and Willis W. Clark; CTB/McGraw-Hill. *
a) LEVEL 1. Grades 1.5–2; 2 editions; manual ('70, 87 pages); $2.45 per specimen set, postpaid; 114(171) minutes in 3 sessions.
  1) *Hand Scorable Booklet.* Form A ('70, 23 pages); $9 per 35 tests.
  2) *CompuScan Machine Scorable Booklet.* Form A ('70, 24 pages) in 2 booklets (reading, mathematics and language); $14.85 per 35 tests; scoring service, 40¢ and over per test.
b) LEVEL 2. Grades 2–4; 2 editions; manual ('70, 82 pages); prices same as for level 1; 123(177) minutes in 3 sessions.
  1) *Hand Scorable Booklet.* Form A ('70, 23 pages).
  2) *CompuScan Machine Scorable Booklet.* Form A ('70, 24 pages) in 2 booklets (reading, mathematics and language).
c) LEVEL 3. Grades 4–6; Form A ('70, 44 pages); manual ('70, 75 pages); $10 per 35 tests; $5 per 50 CompuScan answer sheets; $7.50 per 50 sets of Digitek answer sheets; $8 per 50 sets of IBM answer sheets; $4 per set of IBM hand scoring stencils; $2 per specimen set, postpaid; CompuScan scoring service, 32¢ and over per test; 152(212) minutes in 3 sessions.
d) LEVEL 4. Grades 6–9; Form A ('70, 43 pages); manual ('70, 77 pages); prices same as for level 3; 144(198) minutes in 3 sessions.
e) LEVEL 5. Grades 9–12; Form A ('70, 44 pages); manual ('70, 77 pages); prices same as for level 3; 153(207) minutes in 3 sessions.

REFERENCES

1. See 2:1193.
2–4. See 3:15.
5–12. See 4:2.
13–22. See 5:2.
23–41. See 6:3.
42. EBERT, ELIZABETH, AND SIMMONS, KATHERINE. *The Brush Foundation Study of Child Growth and Development: I, Psychometric Tests.* Monographs of the Society for Research in Child Development, Vol. 8, No. 2, Serial No. 35. Washington, D.C.: the Society, National Research Council, 1943. Pp. xiv, 113. * (*PA* 18:3322)
43. WILLIS, ROBERT N. "A Report of an Item Analysis Study." *Fla J Ed Res* 1:55–62 Ja '59. *
44. FRENCH, JOSEPH L. "A Predictive Test Battery." *Nursing Res* 10:104–5 sp '61. *

45. HOPKINS, KENNETH DEAN. *Validity Concomitants of Various Scoring Procedures Which Attenuate the Effects of Response Sets and Chance.* Doctor's thesis, University of Southern California (Los Angeles, Calif.), 1961. (*DA* 22:155)

46. RICHARDS, BERNA FLANDERS. *A Predictive Longitudinal Study of Intellective and Non-Intellective Factors Affecting School Achievement of Gifted Children.* Doctor's thesis, Ohio State University (Columbus, Ohio), 1961. (*DA* 22:3526)

47. SMITH, JOAN GEITGEY. *The Correlation Between California Achievement Test Scores and the Subjective Judgments of Elementary School Teachers.* Master's thesis, Stetson University (DeLand, Fla.), 1961.

48. IHINGER, ROBERT F. "Some Relationships Among Laterality Groups at Three Grade Levels in Performances on the California Achievement Tests," pp. 70–5. (*PA* 38:6656) In *Towards a Professional Identity in School Psychology.* California Association of School Psychologists and Psychometrists, Fourteenth Annual Conference, March 28–30, 1963. [Los Angeles, Calif.: the Association, 1963.] Pp. v, 97. *

49. IVERSON, ETHEL W. *Validity Comparison of Stanford Achievement Test and California Achievement Test.* Master's thesis, San Diego State College (San Diego, Calif.), 1963.

50. MICKLER, JACOB ERNEST, JR. *A Predictive Index of Academic Success for Alabama High School Graduates Entering the State Colleges and Universities.* Doctor's thesis, University of Alabama (University, Ala.), 1963. (*DA* 24:4086)

51. AMUNDSON, GORDON J. *A Study of the Correlation Between the California Achievement Test and the SRA Primary Mental Abilities Test.* Master's thesis, Northern Illinois University (DeKalb, Ill.), 1964.

52. DIZNEY, HENRY. "The Performance in Specific Skill Areas of Gifted, Elementary Underachievers." *Psychol Sch* 1:178–81 Ap '64. *

53. DIZNEY, HENRY, AND FLEMING, ELYSE. "Sex and I.Q. Differences in Discrepancies Between Predicted and Obtained Achievement." *J Sch Psychol* 3:26–31 au '64. * (*PA* 39:13032)

54. HOPKINS, KENNETH D. "Extrinsic Reliability: Estimating and Attenuating Variance From Response Styles, Chance, and Other Irrelevant Sources." *Ed & Psychol Meas* 24:271–81 su '64. * (*PA* 39:3152)

55. LETON, DONALD A., AND ANDERSON, HARRY E., JR. "Discriminant Analysis of Achievement Characteristics for Multi-Grade Grouping of Students." *J Exp Ed* 32:293–7 sp '64. * (*PA* 39:5994)

56. MILLMAN, JASON, AND LINDLOF, JOHN. "The Comparability of Fifth-Grade Norms of the California, Iowa, and Metropolitan Achievement Tests." *J Ed Meas* 1:135–7 D '64. * (*PA* 39:10143)

57. PARSLEY, KENNETH M., JR.; POWELL, MARVIN; AND O'CONNOR, HENRY A. "Further Investigation of Sex Differences in Achievement of Under-, Average-, and Over-Achieving Students Within Five IQ Groups in Grades Four Through Eight." *J Ed Res* 57:268–70 Ja '64. * (*PA* 39:5875)

58. WALDRON, CORMAC. *Differential Prediction of Achievement in Broad Curricular Areas in an Academic High School.* Doctor's thesis, Fordham University (New York, N.Y.), 1964. (*DA* 25:1764)

59. BOYCE, RICHARD W., AND PAXSON, R. C. "The Predictive Validity of Eleven Tests at One State College." *Ed & Psychol Meas* 25:1143–7 w '65. * (*PA* 40:3563)

60. HOPKINS, KENNETH D., AND WILKERSON, CAROLYN J. "Differential Content Validity: The California Spelling Test, an Illustrative Example." *Ed & Psychol Meas* 25:413–9 su '65. * (*PA* 39:15192)

61. LETON, DONALD A., AND HOLZ, MARGARET. "Discriminant Analysis of Achievement Profiles of Socially Maladjusted Pupils." *Psychol Sch* 2:228–33 Jl '65. *

62. BRISTOL, JOHN L. "Validity of the California Achievement and Mental Maturity Tests in Predicting Success in Five Different First Year High School Foreign Languages." *J Exp Ed* 34:57–61 sp '66. *

63. OLSON, ARTHUR V. "Relation of Achievement Test Scores and Specific Reading Abilities to the Frostig Developmental Test of Visual Perception." *Percept & Motor Skills* 22:179–84 F '66. * (*PA* 40:4750)

64. OLSON, ARTHUR V. "Relation of Achievement Test Scores and Specific Reading Abilities to the Frostig Test of Visual Perception." *Optom Weekly* 57:31–4 Jl 14 '66. *

65. TAGATZ, GLENN E.; LEMKE, ELMER A.; AND MEINKE, DEAN L. "Alpha Factor Analyses of Learning Concepts and Student Achievement Test Scores." *Teach Col J* 39:99–103 D '67. *

66. BUSZEK, BEATRICE R. "Differential Treatment of Test Scores." *Col & Univ* 43:294–307 sp '68. *

67. MEYERS, C. EDWARD; ATTWELL, ARTHUR A.; ORPET, RUSSELL E. "Prediction of Fifth Grade Achievement From Kindergarten Test and Rating Data." *Ed & Psychol Meas* 28:457–63 su '68. * (*PA* 42:19423)

68. THOMAS, HOWARD. *An Analysis of the California Test of Mental Maturity and the California Achievement Test for Discriminative Use at High Levels of Intelligence.* Master's thesis, Sacramento State College (Sacramento, Calif.), 1968.

69. WOLF, WILLAVENE; KING, MARTHA L.; AND HUCK, CHARLOTTE S. "Teaching Critical Reading to Elementary School Children." *Read Res Q* 3:435–98 su '68. * (*PA* 44:20663)

70. KENNEDY, WALLACE A. "A Follow-Up Normative Study of Negro Intelligence and Achievement." *Monogr Soc Res Child Develop* 34(2):1–40 '69. * (*PA* 45:1350)

71. MACARTHUR, RUSSELL S. "Some Cognitive Abilities of Eskimo, White, and Indian-Métis Pupils Aged 9 to 12 Years." *Can J Behav Sci* 1(1):50–9 Ja '69. * (*PA* 44:12319)

72. MORGAN, GORDON D. "Performance of East African Students on an Experimental Test Battery." *J Negro Ed* 38(4):378–83 f '69. *

73. WASHINGTON, ERNEST D., AND TESKA, JAMES A. "Relations Between the Wide Range Achievement Test, the California Achievement Tests, the Stanford-Binet, and the Illinois Test of Psycholinguistic Abilities." *Psychol Rep* 26(1):291–4 F '70. * (*PA* 45:4931)

For reviews by Jack C. Merwin and Robert D. North of the 1957 edition, see 6:3; for a review by Charles O. Neidt, see 5:2; for reviews by Warren G. Findley, Alvin W. Schindler, and J. Harlan Shores of the 1950 edition, see 4:2; for a review by Paul A. Witty of the 1943 edition, see 3:15; for reviews by C. W. Odell and Hugh B. Wood of an earlier edition, see 2:1193; for a review by D. Welty Lefever, see 1:876 (1 excerpt). For reviews of earlier editions of the subtests, see 6:251 (1 review), 5:177 (2 reviews), 5:468 (1 review), 4:151 (2 reviews), 4:411 (1 review), 4:530 (2 reviews, 1 excerpt), 2:1292 (2 reviews), 2:1459 (2 reviews), 2:1563 (1 review), 1:893 (1 review), and 1:1110 (2 reviews).

[6]

*Canadian Tests of Basic Skills. Grades 3–8; 1955–70; CTBS; Canadian adaptation of *Iowa Tests of Basic Skills;* 15 scores: vocabulary, reading comprehension, language (spelling, capitalization, punctuation, usage, total), work-study skills (maps, graphs and tables, reference materials, total), mathematics skills (concepts, problem solving, total), total; Forms 1 ('67, 97 pages), 2 ('68, 97 pages); 6 overlapping levels (grades 3, 4, 5, 6, 7, 8) in a single booklet; teacher's manual ('68, 99 pages); manual for administrators, supervisors, and counselors ('68, 77 pages); special percentile norms booklet for IQ levels ('70, 13 pages); profile ('67, 1 page); pupil report folder ('67, 4 pages); separate answer sheets (IBM 1230, MRC) must be used; Can $1.10 per test; $7.25 per 100 sets of IBM answer sheets; $4 per 35 MRC answer sheets; $1.50 per set of IBM response indicators; 90¢ per set of MRC scoring stencils; $1.24 per 35 report folders; $1.24 per 35 profiles; $1.20 per norms booklet for IQ levels; $1.65 per teacher's manual; $2.90 per administrator's manual; $3.25 per specimen set; postage extra; MRC scoring service, 32¢ and over per test; 279(315) minutes in 4 sessions; original test by E. F. Lindquist, A. N. Hieronymus, and others; adaptation by Ethel M. King; Thomas Nelson & Sons (Canada) Ltd. *

L. B. BIRCH, *Macdonald Professor of Education and Director of Graduate Studies, Faculty of Education, McGill University, Montreal, Quebec, Canada.*

The confidence with which test users make decisions upon the results of testing depends in considerable measure upon their confidence in the integrity and technical competence of the test makers. Unless a user is able to select an appropriate sample of subjects, carry out his own item analyses and reliability and validity studies, he must accept, on the reputation of the test designer, many of the bases upon which his conclusions are made. It is thus reassuring to be able to use a test like the *Canadian Test of Basic Skills* for it has such a long line of respected antecedents that its status need never be in doubt. It is, in fact, simply a Canadian version of the well-known *Iowa Test of Basic Skills*. The Iowa test is extensively reviewed in the *Fifth Mental Measurements Yearbook* so that, since the Canadian test is virtually identical in its form and layout, though the material is new, it would not be justifiable to review it at length.

The battery takes about five hours to administer, of which some four and a half hours are actual working time. It is recommended that testing be spread over four days; alternatively it may be given on four consecutive half days. However, this reviewer found that some experienced testers in Quebec Province have found it advantageous in many ways to reduce the length of the individual testing sessions with younger children.

The same level of technical sophistication that gave the Iowa test its fine qualities is evident in the design of the CTBS and the production of norms. Standardisation was on a group of over 30,000 children drawn from a stratified random sample of some 225 schools from the English speaking sector in all provinces of Canada. The sample took account of such school variables as location, size, type and confessionality and excluded from the sample children whose mother tongue was not English. It is claimed, with apparent justification, that the norms are truly representative of Canadian, English speaking pupils of grades 3 to 8, inclusive, as they were in the autumn of 1966.

In addition to the Canadian national norms it is possible to obtain local norms from the publisher. These should prove of considerable value and interest in a country as large and diverse as Canada. As in the U.S. version, all norms are expressed as grade equivalents. There are separate norms for each of the 11 subtests and these can be combined to give mean grade equivalents for each of the major areas or to provide one overall score for the whole battery. There are conversion tables in the manual for converting a pupil's grade equivalent score into a grade per-centile score. These are available for the start, the middle and the end of the school year. The use of grade-equivalent, instead of age-norms, has evoked some criticism among testers in Canada. At present they are probably as appropriate as they were in the United States when the Iowa test was made, but many areas in Canada are now experimenting with different forms of school organization which may make the grade equivalent score less meaningful in the future. It would not, of course, be difficult for large school boards or combinations of them to establish their own local norms.

The battery aims at the evaluation of generalised educational skills and abilities not content achievement. This is a concept which has been criticised from time to time and it may be that it needs to be reconsidered in the light of changes in the school curriculum. The vocabulary and arithmetic tests appear to be quite ordinary attainment tests and though the arithmetic test is now called a mathematics test it makes very few concessions to the newer mathematical syllabuses which are increasingly used in Canada. Similarly, the tests of capitalization and punctuation may soon be out of date as different emphases develop. The section on study skills still seems a most valuable one with its maps, graphs and reference materials. There would seem to be a need as the nature of curricula expand, to extend these skills to include, for example, the reading of a blueprint and the interpreting of a gear train.

However, for the present this is probably as useful an instrument as exists and so long as teachers do not fall into the error of teaching their classes along the lines of the tests, a practice not unknown, it is feared, it should prove valuable for the next few years at least.

[7]

★**Classification and Placement Examination.** Grade 8 and high school entrants; 1967–68; CAPE; 8 scores: aptitude (verbal, quantitative, total), achievement (reading, mathematics, English, total), total; Form A ('67, 16 pages); directions for administering ('67, 4 pages); guide for interpreting ('68, 8 pages); separate answer sheets (MRC) must be used; tests rented only; rental fee, $1 per student ($100 minimum); fee includes scoring service; $1.25 per specimen set; postage extra; 140(150) minutes in 1 or 2 sessions; Richard Madden and Eric F. Gardner; Harcourt Brace Jovanovich, Inc. *

Leonard S. Cahen, *Research Psychologist, Educational Testing Service, Princeton, New Jersey.*

According to the authors, the "three primary

purposes" of this battery of aptitude and achievement examinations "are to enable school personnel, through the use of a *secure* instrument, to select, classify, and place students as they move from one educational level to another." It is stated that "those aspects of student performance evaluated by CAPE subtests are not substantially different from those evaluated by widely-used, group-administered measures of mental ability and school achievement, such as the *Otis-Lennon Mental Ability Test* and the *Stanford Achievement Test.*" In the opinion of the publishers, "CAPE differs from these latter measures primarily because it is a secure test, i.e., its distribution is rigidly controlled by the publisher." The content of CAPE does, indeed, appear to be tapping many of the areas covered by such tests as the Otis-Lennon and Stanford.

The basic scoring services provided to the customer for each student include raw scores, local percentiles, and stanines for verbal, quantitative, and total aptitude, plus an IQ estimate for total aptitude; and raw scores, local percentiles, and stanines for the achievement sections dealing with reading, mathematics (concepts, computation, and problem solving), and English (usage, mechanics, and sentence structure), and total achievement. Grade equivalents for the achievement sections are also provided. Triplicate report listings, distributions and norms reports, permanent record labels, and individual profile reports, with local stanines plotted, are also provided in the basic scoring service package. The publishers caution the consumers that local CAPE norms will not be valid unless there are at least 100 students in the testing program. No evidence or elaboration is provided as to why the number of students must be equal to or greater than 100.

The publishers have gone to great lengths to preserve the "security" of the testing materials. The test booklets are made available on a rental only basis. Booklets are numbered, and booklet loss is controlled by checking all the booklet code numbers against a master list when the booklets are returned to the publisher.

The directions for administering are clearly written. Attention has been given to the potential danger of having a student spend too much time on one part of a multi-part testing section. The test administrator is told to announce, after a specific time allotment, that the students should move on to the next part.

The guide for interpreting CAPE contains information about test content and purpose, the utilization of scores, tables for converting raw scores to Stanford and Otis-Lennon equivalents, and technical characteristics. The early sections are written at a very elementary level; the later sections require some knowledge of elementary statistics. A weakness of the guide is that it provides too little guidance on how CAPE scores should and can be used by school districts for the three purposes stated by the publishers, i.e., the selection, classification, and placement of students as they move from one educational level to another.

Data presented in the guide indicate that Forms A and B are nominally parallel. Reliability and standard error of measurement data are reported with a warning that it is not recommended that all subtest scores be interpreted for individual students. While this warning seems reasonable and justifiable, it does reduce the usefulness of the subtest scores for the purposes of the battery as stated by the publishers.

All statistics reported in the guide are based on scores derived from the final edition of the test. It is hoped that the test publishers in the future will provide cross-validation information about the technical characteristics of CAPE.

The technical characteristics were determined by testing approximately 800 students in four diocesan school systems which participated in the developmental program. The locations of the school systems are identified but little additional information is provided to help answer the question of the representativeness of the students.

No information is provided about the amount of error involved in estimating Otis-Lennon IQ's and Stanford scores from CAPE scores.

A question can be raised about the last three items in the quantitative aptitude section. These items require the student to work in bases 2, 3, and 4 rather than base 10. These items would be more appropriate in the arithmetic computation achievement section than in the aptitude section, since they depend upon the mathematics curriculum of the student. The tests were standardized with students participating in "modern" mathematics curricula.

One aspect of the English mechanics part in Form A was disturbing to this reviewer. The potential problem involves the correctness of spelling a certain proper noun that appears seven times in the paragraph presented. The correct spelling of the proper noun was checked in an encyclopedia of American history, and it was learned that the proper noun can be spelled two different ways, one of which was used consistently in the paragraph. It is believed that this section could lead to correlated errors for students who had seen the optional spelling of this proper noun. The scoring key was not provided in the kit of reviewing materials so it was impossible for the reviewer to see how the selection of the optional spelling as an error would affect the score in this section.

This reviewer is not convinced that CAPE provides the potential consumer with anything better than presently exists in many other aptitude and achievement batteries. Success in breaking apart aptitude from achievement variance is not demonstrated from an examination of part-score correlations appearing in the guide.

As pointed out earlier, the publishers seemed to rest their case on the fact that CAPE, as compared to other available tests, is a *secure* test. The major users of this type of test are the schools which select a subset of students from a larger set of applicants for admission. This is rarely the case facing public school systems. Since most educational situations require schools to accept all students, emphasis should be placed on the utilization of test scores for the purpose of engineering the curriculum and instruction so that each student can succeed.

As in the selection of all test batteries, the potential consumer should carefully examine the content of the items, the nature and background of his testing population, and the ultimate purposes for which the test scores will be used.

[8]

★College-Level Examination Program General Examinations. 1–2 years of college or equivalent; 1964–70; for accreditation of nontraditional study, advanced placement, or assessment of educational attainment; tests administered monthly at regional centers throughout the United States; tests also available for institutional testing at any time; 13 scores: English composition, natural sciences (biological, physical, total), mathematics (basic skills, advanced topics, total), humanities (fine arts, literature, total), social sciences—history (social sciences, history, total); 2 editions; descriptive booklet ('68, 40 pages); for additional accessories, see 664; postpaid; 360(380) minutes in 2 sessions; program administered for the College Entrance Examination Board by Educational Testing Service. *
a) COMPLETE BATTERY. 5 tests in 2 booklets; Forms NCT2 ('65, 60 pages), OCT1, OCT2, ('66, 66 pages), PCT1, PCT2, ('67, 62 pages), RCT1 ('69, 65 pages), RCT2 ('69, 82 pages); separate answer sheets

(SCRIBE) must be used; rental and scoring fee, $5 per student.
1) *Book 1.* 3 tests: English composition, natural sciences, mathematics; 210(220) minutes.
2) *Book 2.* 2 tests: humanities, social sciences and history; 150(160) minutes.
b) SEPARATE TESTS. 5 tests; Forms MCT2 ('64, 12–16 pages), NCT1 ('65, 10–18 pages), NCT2 ('65, 12–16 pages), OCT1 ('66, 12–16 pages), OCT2 ('66, 13–17 pages), PCT1 ('67, 12–15 pages), PCT2 ('67, 12–17 pages) in each booklet; separate answer sheets (Digitek-IBM 805, IBM 1230, SCRIBE) must be used; rental and scoring fee, $1 per test; rental fee (local scoring), 75¢ per test.
1) *English Composition.* 60(70) minutes.
2) *Humanities.* 3 scores: fine arts, literature, total; 75(85) minutes.
3) *Mathematics.* 3 scores: basic skills, advanced topics, total; 75(85) minutes.
4) *Natural Sciences.* 3 scores: biological, physical, total; 75(85) minutes.
5) *Social Sciences and History.* 3 scores: social sciences, history, total; 75(85) minutes.

For reviews of the testing program, see 664 (3 reviews).

[9]

★Comprehensive Tests of Basic Skills. Grades 2.5–4, 4–6, 6–8, 8–12; 1968–70; CTBS; subtests in reading, arithmetic, language, and study skills available as separates; 13–15 scores: reading (vocabulary, comprehension, total), language (mechanics, expression, spelling, total), arithmetic (computation, concepts, applications, total), total, study skills (reference materials [except level 1], graphic materials [except level 1], total); 2 forms; 4 levels; profile for levels 1, 2–4, ('68, 2 pages); coordinator's handbook ('69, 62 pages); technical report ('70, 85 pages); supplementary Form Q norms for large city ['69, 35 pages] and Catholic ('68, 35 pages) schools; $2 per 100 profiles; separate answer sheets (CompuScan [NCS], Digitek, IBM 1230, Scoreze) may be used for levels 2–4; $2.50 per handbook; $2.50 per technical report; $2.50 per norms supplement; $8 per specimen set of all levels; postage extra; $1.75 per specimen set of any one level, postpaid; CTB/McGraw-Hill. *
a) LEVEL 1. Grades 2.5–4; 2 editions; Form Q manual ('68, 75 pages), Form R manual ('69, 74 pages); 184(252) minutes in 4 sessions.
1) *Hand Scorable Booklet.* Forms Q ('68, 25 pages), R ('69, 25 pages); $10.40 per 35 tests.
2) *CompuScan Machine Scorable Booklet.* Forms Q ('68, 24 pages), R ('69, 24 pages) in 2 booklets (reading and language, arithmetic and study skills); practice exercises ('69, 4 pages); $15.20 per 35 tests; $5 per 100 practice exercises; scoring service, 40¢ and over per test.
b) LEVEL 2. Grades 4–6; Forms Q ('68, 40 pages), R ('69, 40 pages); Form Q manual ('68, 67 pages), Form R manual ('69, 67 pages); practice exercises for CompuScan answer sheets ('69, 2 pages), for IBM 1230 answer sheets ('64, 1 page); directions: CompuScan, Digitek, IBM 1230, ('68, 3–4 pages); $12 per 35 tests; $5 per 50 CompuScan answer sheets; $5 per 50 sets of Digitek answer sheets; $10 per 50 sets of IBM answer sheets; $11 per 25 sets of Scoreze answer sheets; $8 per set of IBM hand scoring stencils for both forms; Digitek scoring stencils not available; $3 per 100 CompuScan practice exercises; $3 per 100 IBM practice exercises; 15¢ per directions; CompuScan scoring service, 32¢ and over per test; 195(257) minutes in 4 sessions.

c) LEVEL 3. Grades 6–8; Forms Q ('68, 43 pages), R ('69, 43 pages); Form Q manual ('68, 67 pages), Form R manual ('69, 67 pages); prices same as for level 2; 182(238) minutes in 4 sessions.
d) LEVEL 4. Grades 8–12; Forms Q ('68, 43 pages), R ('69, 43 pages); Form Q manual ('68, 65 pages), Form R manual ('69, 65 pages); Form Q supplementary norms for grades 11 and 12 ['69, 14 pages]; prices same as for level 2; 170(226) minutes in 4 sessions.

J. STANLEY AHMANN, *Professor of Psychology, Colorado State University, Fort Collins, Colorado.*

The *Comprehensive Tests of Basic Skills* are exactly what the title indicates, namely, measures of basic skills designed for and standardized on a wide variety of students. The basic skills are classified in four major tests (reading, language, arithmetic, and study skills), each of which is subdivided into two or three subtests. Two comparable forms of these tests have been developed for students in grade levels 2.5 through 10, with additional norms for grades 11 and 12. Moreover, norms are provided for three testing periods per year, that is, the beginning, middle, and end of the academic year.

In an attractive, well written manner, details about each test are provided in one of three coordinated publications. These are the Examiner's Manuals, the Test Coordinator's Handbook, and the Technical Report. A separate Examiner's Manual is available for each of the four levels of both forms of the CTBS, whereas the Test Coordinator's Handbook and the Technical Report include information about all levels of both forms.

NATURE OF THE TESTS. Great care was taken in the printing of the tests. The instructions to the students are clear and easy to read. The format is uncrowded and appealing to the eye. Also, the artwork associated with test items, particularly in the study skills tests, is well done and convenient to interpret.

Throughout all of the tests at all levels, objective test items of the multiple choice type are used. The student is to select the correct (or "best") answer from four or five options. These are typically arranged vertically to simplify examination by the student.

The reading tests have two subparts, namely, vocabulary and comprehension. In the former, the student identifies synonyms. In the latter, he reads a poem, story, or article and answers questions about it. The material to be read is often four or five paragraphs or stanzas long. It should be noted that there is no measure of reading speed. This is consistent with the emphasis in CTBS on the measurement of skills rather than speed.

Three subtests (mechanics, expression, and spelling) constitute the language section of CTBS. The mechanics section measures the student's ability to punctuate and use capital letters in stories and letters. In the expression section, the student must add the correct words and phrases to incomplete sentences, replace underlined parts of sentences in a story or poem, or recognize errors in usage. The measurement of spelling is limited to the recognition of incorrectly spelled words.

There are also three arithmetic tests—computation, concepts, and applications. In the first subtest, the student solves addition, subtraction, multiplication, and division problems involving various types of numbers. The concepts and applications subtests are composed of verbal problems. In the case of the former, the student is to recognize or use an appropriate numerical or geometric concept or technique in each test item. In the latter test, the tasks required of the student involve the ability to comprehend an arithmetic problem, to select the appropriate method for solving it, and to solve for the correct answer.

Two study skills tests are included in Levels 2, 3, and 4 of the CTBS, one measuring the student's ability to use reference materials and the other his ability to use graphic materials. Reference materials include books, dictionaries, and library materials such as catalog cards. In the graphic materials section, test items are based on maps, graphs, histograms, and tables.

NORMS. A total of 13 or 15 scores can be obtained from the CTBS. For Levels 2, 3, and 4, 10 of these are scores for each of the subtests, four are total scores for each of the major basic skill areas, and one is a total score for a combination of the reading, language, and arithmetic areas. Level 1 yields only 13 scores, since the study skills area is represented by only one test.

To obtain norms for these scores, a serious effort was made to draw a representative national sample of students in the public and, separately, Catholic schools. To obtain the public school sample, a two-stage sampling procedure was followed. First, a random sample of school districts was drawn. This was stratified according to enrollment, geographic region, and "educational-economic index." Second, a sample of schools was drawn from those districts selected in the first stage. Over 88 percent of all public school districts and 82 percent of all public schools chosen participated in the standardization testing.

A wide variety of norms are reported: percentiles, stanines, grade equivalents, and "expanded" standard scores. In view of the well-known weaknesses of grade equivalents, it is difficult to understand why they are included. Furthermore, at the same time that the authors recognize that the basic skills usually are not a part of the formal curriculum beyond junior high school, they extrapolate the grade equivalents upward to 12.9 for Level 3 tests. This, plus a willingness to provide grade equivalents for grades 11 and 12, needlessly weakens an otherwise strong effort to develop solid norms.

The "expanded" standard scores "are standard scores from a single, equal interval scale across all grades for use with all levels and both forms of CTBS." They have "a mean of 600 and a standard deviation of 100 at grade 10.1." These scores should "have unique advantages for measuring growth in achievement in basic skills, for research across all grades and schools in a district, for reporting performance of students at the high school level, and for measuring growth in basic skills for students in ungraded programs." On the other hand, it is regrettable that the authors found it necessary to introduce still another standard score to the already too-large group available!

In addition to the national public school norms, percentiles and stanines are published for all 13 or 15 scores for large city school districts (95,000 enrollment and over) and for Catholic schools. Comparison of the three sets of norms shows decided differences among them. For a given raw score, the student's relative performance will be reported consistently higher when the large city norms are used rather than the national norms. It will be the lowest of all when he is compared to Catholic school students.

VALIDITY AND RELIABILITY. The validity and reliability determinations follow closely the 1966 APA recommendations for psychological tests. Understandably, very close attention is given to the question of content validity. The Bloom taxonomy for the cognitive domain provided a basis for the classification of the objectives, each of which is stated in terms of student behavioral patterns.

A complete classification of the objectives for each test is shown in the Test Coordinator's Handbook, which includes two-dimensional tables of specifications for both forms of each test at each of the four levels. These tables of specifications are as complete as any published for tests of basic skills. One dimension, processes, is coded so that a direct relationship with an objective is established. The other, content, is sufficiently descriptive to identify without trouble the materials used in the test items. Most important of all, each test item is classified according to the particular process or content involved in it. Since it is identified by its number, any reviewer can examine the item and verify its classification if he wishes.

An almost hidden strength supporting the degree of content validity of the CTBS is that classroom teachers, supported by curriculum specialists, were used to write the original test items. These efforts, plus the assistance of testing specialists before and after extensive pretesting, provided a solid base for building a quality test.

The pretesting also established the desired gradients in the levels of difficulty of test items. This is revealed nicely by study of the norms for three grade levels using the same level of tests. For example, in Level 2, a given raw score in reading comprehension for a fourth grade student will yield a much higher percentile than the same score for a fifth grade student. Similarly, a pronounced drop occurs between fifth and sixth grade students who have the same raw score. When one considers the formal instruction which takes place in these years, the consistent downward shift in relative performance associated with a given raw score is reasonable and adds to our confidence in the test.

The prodigious effort to build the CTBS raises the question as to why the same publisher should continue to distribute the *California Achievement Tests*. One study of the degree of relationship between similar tests (reading, language, and arithmetic—a total of 9 scores) yielded correlations as high as .93. Most correlations were between .70 and .85. If equally large correlations between comparable tests are found repeatedly, use of both test batteries would be a wasteful mistake.

Numerous reliability determinations led to a common conclusion: Typical of basic skills tests, a high degree of reliability exists for subtest scores as well as for total scores. K-R 20 reliability coefficients were usually in the .85 to .95 region, although a few drifted downward as low as .75.

SCORING AND REPORTING. Although the many scoring and reporting services provided by the publisher are too numerous to mention, one should note several of their outstanding features. First, four different answer sheets can be used, namely, CompuScan, IBM 1230, Digitek, and Scoreze. Each has certain advantages and limitations, depending on the information desired. The CompuScan scoring service is quite useful for those who have in mind multiple uses of the test data—for example, item analysis to improve learning and instruction for both the individual student and the entire class.

Secondly, regression equations have been developed for the various tests of the CTBS and the *California Short-Form Test of Mental Maturity*. Oddly, all seven tests of the CTMM-SF are used for predicting achievement for each test of the CTBS. In view of what is known about the CTMM subtests, why not use only two or three scores for prediction—for instance, the language and nonlanguage IQ's? In any event, by means of a computer, anticipated achievement grade equivalents and standard scores are determined, thereby permitting comparison with a pupil's actual performance on the CTBS tests. Correlation coefficients between the scores of the CTBS tests and those of the CTMM-SF are unusually high, generally falling between .60 and .80. By the way, for those who wish to compare actual with anticipated achievement in the manner described, a combination CTBS/CTMM-SF answer sheet is available.

SUMMARY. Beyond a doubt, the CTBS is a well developed test which is packaged in a professional manner. It should be attractive to both student and teacher, since it has at least two advantages over currently available tests. In the first place, it has a very high ceiling in that it reaches well into the high school. In fact, separate eleventh and twelfth grade norms for Level 4, which are provided, should be helpful in remedial work. However, it should be noted that the authors made no specific effort to focus the tests in terms of their educational problems. Moreover, its recent development and use of teacher involvement has anchored it firmly in today's classroom. As successful and worthy as

other basic skills tests like the *Iowa Tests of Basic Skills* have been, it is unlikely that they can fully match the CTBS because of these two points.

The final verdict will, of course, come from the classroom after the tests have been used a number of years. Obviously, such evidence is not available now and may be negative, at least in part. At this point in time, such findings in any large measure seem unlikely.

FREDERICK G. BROWN, *Professor of Psychology, Iowa State University, Ames, Iowa.*

Any achievement battery purporting to provide "comprehensive" coverage of "basic skills" will have difficulty attaining its advertised coverage. The *Comprehensive Tests of Basic Skills* is no exception. Although the areas tested —reading, language, arithmetic, and study skills—are those skills most stressed in the elementary grades and consequently might lay some claim to the label of "basic skills," the battery is clearly not comprehensive at the upper elementary, junior high, and high school levels. But the overzealous claim should not overly detract from the battery.

PURPOSE. The CTBS is designed to "measure the extent to which students have acquired skills that are required for effective use of language and number in everyday living and for further academic study." Although the CTBS follows the traditional survey model, both hand and machine scoring procedures facilitate reporting performance on clusters of related items, thus enabling teachers to assess students' attainment of various instructional objectives. These procedures, and the discussions within the accompanying manuals, encourage the use of CTBS scores in planning and evaluating instruction rather than solely as tools for identifying individual differences in achievement among students.

ITEM SELECTION AND CONTENT. The authors attempted to write items which measured "broad concepts and abstractions" rather than specific knowledge which might be dependent upon particular classroom experiences. Although one can argue whether individual items measure factual knowledge or are tied to particular experiences, the CTBS probably contains no greater proportion of such items than do competing batteries. In terms of Bloom's *Taxonomy*, the skills of comprehension and application (e.g., recognition, analysis, translation, and interpretation) are stressed, rather than higher-order intellectual skills. The content of the various tests is quite traditional.

Item writing and pretesting were carefully done and resulted in items that are concise and unambiguous. All items are in multiple choice format, the only variation being the inclusion of some cluster multiple choice items.

DIFFICULTY. The data suggest that several subtests are relatively easy, particularly for the upper grade within each level (and presumably also for brighter students). The reviewer administered the CTBS to a 5th and an 8th grade student to determine their reactions. Both reported the tests to be easy and on several subtests obtained maximum scores while using only about half the allotted time.

Total scores tend to have a negatively skewed distribution with a noticeable ceiling effect. For example, at grade level 8.6 the mean of Form Q, Level 3, is 187 (out of a possible 268), the standard deviation is 48, and the median is 197. Although the publishers state that Level 4 (grades 8–10) can be used in grades 11 and 12, no data are provided to show that the test is appropriate at these grade levels.

ADMINISTRATION AND SCORING. The test administration should present few problems, even to the classroom teacher. The test taker's task is straightforward and procedures for administering the test are clearly detailed in the manuals. The only exception is on Level 1 (grades 2.5–4), where some items are overly crowded and thus may be confusing to a young child.

NORMS. The basic norm group is a national sample of 212,000 students in grades 2–10. Schools were randomly selected from districts chosen by stratifying all U.S. school districts by size, socioeconomic level, and geographic region. A high rate of cooperation (88 percent) was obtained, with replacements made by random sampling. The primary standardization was on Form Q; norms for Form R were derived by equating scores to Form Q, using an equi-percentile method, on samples of approximately 1,000 students per grade. No norms were developed for disadvantaged or minority groups, as the publishers felt such groups would be proportionately represented in the basic normative sample.

The use of local norms is stressed in the manuals. Procedures for constructing local norms are described and local normative data

are provided to schools using the publisher's scoring services.

SCORES. Scores can be reported as percentile ranks (within grades), as grade equivalents (except on Level 4), as stanines, and on a "Scale Score" system. The complexity of the Scale Score system makes these scores difficult to interpret for anyone other than a psychometrician. (The reviewer had difficulty comprehending their meaning and derivation.) The shortcomings of grade equivalent scores, though mentioned, are not adequately stressed. Thus the test user would be well advised to use percentile ranks when interpreting CTBS performance.

The user who administers the *California Test of Mental Maturity* with the CTBS can obtain Anticipated Achievement Scores (on the CTBS) if he uses the publisher's scoring service. Although these scores are derived by a procedure superior to the usual method, the limitations and potential misuse of such indices is not adequately stressed in the manuals.

CONSISTENCY. Internal consistency indices (K-R 20) show the subtests and tests to be quite homogeneous. In fact, the high degree of homogeneity of the total score (K-R 20's of .98–.99) might lead one to conclude that the CTBS measures a general "academic achievement" factor rather than the diversity of skills implied by the separate subtests.

Coefficients of equivalence for total and test scores cluster in the .80's and .90's. However, the low coefficients for a few subtests (in the .60's) indicate that the equating of forms was not completely successful.

Three other types of consistency data are also reported. One is a measure of Interlevel Articulation (the correlation between scores on adjacent levels of the test). These show acceptable consistency at the upper levels but lower correspondence at the lower levels (e.g., $r = .81$ for the total score between Levels 1 and 2). Second, Interlevel/Interform correlations are presented, but only for a small sample. Although more extensive data on these two types would be desirable, particularly if the user wants to measure growth from year to year, the publishers are to be commended for providing any data of this sort. Third, the standard error of measurement is reported with all reliability data. In addition, tables of empirically derived standard errors are presented; these, however, could be improved by grouping the data to increase N's, thus providing more stable data.

VALIDITY. The most obvious weakness of the CTBS is the lack of validity data. With the exception of data relating CTBS scores to *California Achievement Test* scores, no empirical relationships with external measures (e.g., grades, teachers' ratings, other achievement tests) are reported. On the other hand, one can argue that content validity is the sine qua non for an achievement measure. The conscientious construction procedures and certain internal measures (e.g., percent passing items at each grade) can be used to support the content validity of the CTBS. The question of whether the test reflects the particular objectives of a specific test user must be answered by the user himself. The manuals emphasize the need for this type of validation and provide suggestions to the user on how to determine the test's validity in his setting. Nevertheless, more validity data are essential.

SUMMARY. The CTBS is a carefully constructed and standardized achievement battery which covers the important skills, particularly at the elementary school level. The tests are easy to administer and will cause few problems for the test taker. While more reliability data are needed, the preliminary data suggest satisfactory consistency, though perhaps little differentiation between subtests. The lack of validity data is a glaring weakness.

The strongest point of the battery is the emphasis placed on using the tests to plan, evaluate, and improve instruction, and to help individual students learn, rather than just to rank students. For example, schools using the publisher's scoring services can obtain score distributions, printouts showing how each student responded to each item and cluster of items, and item analysis data. (The same data can be computed by the teacher willing to take the necessary time.) Use of tests in this manner can be of great value in improving instruction.

A school system selecting a basic achievement battery should consider the CTBS before making its choice.

J Ed Meas 6(2):117–9 su '69. Peter A. Taylor. * There is a question of the appropriateness of level 1 of the battery for pupils in Grade 2, the manual recommending it be used only with the more able students. There is, therefore, some subjectivity inherent in the de-

cision to administer the test at that level, but it should present no major problem. Unfortunately, the norms do not make it clear as to what were the precise characteristics of the Grade 2 children that constituted the standardization sample. * The examiner is provided with a list of suggestions for maximally effective testing that include the option of spreading the test administration over several days. No information is provided as to whether the technical data pertaining to the tests was obtained on massed or distributed administration or whether this option has been demonstrated to have no effect on the generation of validity and reliability data. It is a question as to whether one can assume equivalence of results under both conditions of administration. Surely it would be desirable to adopt one or the other strategy for optimal usage of norms? No explicit instructions are provided the examinee about guessing. There is a weak implication that the examinee should make as insightful a guess as he can, but more specific suggestions should help. * the examinee is required to blacken a circle of 1/16 inch radius * When the examinee is admonished not to "let your marks go out of the circle" one wonders the effect on a seven- or eight-year-old. Perhaps the younger child would appreciate a device requiring less precise muscular coordination. In general, the tests appear to be easy to hand score, and this should increase their applicability as well as contribute to the reliability of the scores. * the sampling for generation of the norms has been carefully and conscientiously done. Without implying any malpractice, the descriptions in the Technical Report (pp. 12–13) concerning the articulation of the normative data for adjacent test levels are comparatively vague. In a technical summary one could assume sufficiency of sophistication in the reader to justify more precise explication. The internal consistency of the battery is high. Kuder-Richardson 20 coefficients are all .98 and .99. * The number of students on which these data are based is not impressive and it will be interesting to observe how stable the initial data are as the sample sizes are increased. * it is clearly incumbent upon the publishers to establish the reliability satisfactorily under the more rigorous standards than internal consistency. As Form R is developed, one can hopefully look forward to parallel-form and test-retest data. Equally, validity data is, at this stage, barely existent. A serious attempt has been made to ensure content validity within the usual criteria framework. The data that are provided are encouraging, but it is the lack of criterion oriented validity information that is unfortunate. If the CTBS is to have any respected place in the library of tests, there is an urgent need for more data pertaining to both validity and reliability. It would have been desirable for these data to have been provided in a tentative sense even with this preliminary form. Tables are appended to each level's manual to enable raw scores to be converted to grade equivalents, scale scores, percentile ranks and stanines. These tables are easy to read and should be most helpful when based upon greater volume of data, the stability of which is established.

SUMMARY. The CTBS has every appearance of promise for the purpose for which it was developed. At the moment, some very fine and very careful work in the description of administrative routine is offset by some rather glaring lacks in empirical data. Since the publishers promise a steady effort to rectify these lacks, the user should be particularly alert to equip himself with the most recent technical data before committing himself to the use of the test.

J Ed Meas 7(1):60–2 sp '70. Verna White. "A Rejoinder From the Publisher to the Review by Peter A. Taylor." This rejoinder was written to answer some of the criticisms raised by the CTBS reviewer and to report that fortunately we are now able to meet many of the most cogent criticisms with the additional data collected for the second *Bulletin of Technical Data* now available. * [See rejoinder for statements about information not yet published at the time the review by Peter A. Taylor was prepared.]

Sch Counselor 18(3):220–1 Ja '71. Brooke B. Collison. * In general, the CTBS deserves consideration in the plans for a school testing program. Persons who read test manuals will be impressed with the care and comprehensiveness of statistical information, statistical description of item selection characteristics, etc. Curriculum directors will probably be pleased to see the Bloom Taxonomy concepts, and teachers who administer tests will be pleased with the clarity of directions and the attractiveness of test-book format. One could be overwhelmed with the reporting service, but this serves only as an advantage in being able to select what is needed. *

For reviews of subtests, see 514 (2 reviews), 685 (1 review), and 778 (1 review).

[10]

★**Cooperative Primary Tests.** Grades 1.5–2.5, 2.5–3; 1965–67; CPT; 2 levels labeled Forms 12, 23; both levels contain a common part, Word Analysis, referred to as Form 13; subtests also available as separates; pilot test ('65, 4 pages, a practice test which should precede administration of *a* below); manual ('67, 104 pages); $5 per 20 combined booklets; $3.25 per 20 separate booklets; $2 per 20 pilot tests; $3 per manual; $3 per specimen set; cash orders postpaid; (10–15) minutes for pilot test; Cooperative Tests and Services. *

a) FORMS 12A AND 12B. Grades 1.5–2.5; 4 scores: listening, word analysis, mathematics, reading; Forms 12A, 12B, ('65, 32 pages); (200) minutes in several sessions.

b) FORMS 23A AND 23B. Grades 2.5–3; 7 scores: listening, word analysis, mathematics, reading, writing skills (spelling, capitalization-punctuation-usage, total); Forms 23A, 23B, ('65, 36 pages); (250) minutes in several sessions.

REFERENCE

1. PICKERING, CHARLES THOMAS. *A Study of Intellectual Abilities of Culturally Disadvantaged Children as Predictors of Achievement in Reading, Mathematics, and Listening in Grade One.* Doctor's thesis, Ohio University (Athens, Ohio), 1969. (DAI 31:1085A)

Am Ed Res J 6(2):306–9 Mr '69. Esin Kaya. In reviewing tests published by the Educational Testing Service one need not be concerned with whether or not the tests are reliable, the norms are based on representative samples, or the forms are adequately equated. Indeed, ETS can hardly be surpassed in efficiency and thoroughness in obtaining and reporting test data. The....[test] under review....[reflects] this typical efficiency and thoroughness. * Even though there is an inconsistency in the report as to whether this is an achievement or ability test battery, the emphasis is on diagnosing pupils "in skills and concepts basic to future development" in the content areas. * The statistical data are a good example of the ETS efficiency and thoroughness mentioned earlier. * It is easy, especially for a non-technical school practitioner, to get the impression that statistical validity indices have contextual meaning of their own independent of the universe represented by the particular test content. Hence it is refreshing to see the new direction taken by ETS: its concern with content validity and with the logical and educational bases for the *Primary Tests.* Admittedly, there may be problems in leaving the content validation of tests to the local schools that will use them. Yet this move represents an attempt to face the problem of logical validity realistically, perhaps for the first time in the history of ETS. At least an attempt has been made to destroy the fictitious existence of a standard curriculum whose attainment and acquisition are tested by a standard test. Instead, it seems to be recognized that the validating criterion in our educational system changes from community to community and therefore must be established locally. If this is the beginning of a new direction for test development at ETS, it certainly deserves all the professional support it can get. Another important new step in testing at ETS is represented by the *Cooperative Primary Tests'* use of children's errors for diagnostic purposes. The notion that children's abilities need diagnosis and the emphasis on diagnosing individual children rather than predicting success for large groups are novel for ETS. It is heartening to see that the *Primary Tests* represent not only a philosophy of testing but also a philosophy of education. The educational implications of the new direction represented by the *Cooperative Primary Tests* are clear. What is not clear is whether educators are ready to accept and carry out the responsibilities placed on them as a result of this new direction. For example, will the local schools in fact establish their own criteria for content validation systematically and operationally? Will the suggested diagnosis of individual children's level of attainment be conducted and utilized adequately for instructional purposes? Since the new direction represents a philosophy of education, perhaps cooperation between the test developer and the test user may be initiated starting with this common denominator. Now that the test developers have taken a step toward bridging the gap between education and evaluation one can hope that other necessary steps will follow.

J Ed Meas 6(1):38–40 sp '69. Gerald S. Hanna. * Mid-percentile ranks are provided in convenient tables for fall of Grade 1 and fall and spring of Grades 2 and 3. This departure from the publisher's use of percentile bands may simplify the use of the test results and simultaneously increase potential overinterpretation in spite of warnings about imperfect reliability. The avoidance of the popular grade-equivalent scores will be appreciated by those concerned about their typical misuse and misinterpretation. Some kind of standard score, e.g., *T* scores or stanines, would have provided a desirable alternative to the percentile ranks. The grouping of the scaled scores, from which the percentile ranks are secured, into intervals

of two contributes to an unnecessary grouping error with a consequent reduction of derived-score reliability from the raw-score reliability findings reported. At its worst, this results in the following spring of Grade 1 conversions for Reading, Form 12A (Handbook, p. 36).

Raw Score	Scaled Score	Mid-percentile Rank
25–28	138–139	68
20–24	136–137	44
17–19	134–135	25

A raw score of 20 receives the same percentile rank as a raw score of 24 even though the scores differ by 1.2 standard error of measurement units. Raw scores of 24 and 25 convert to respective percentile ranks of 44 and 68; the raw scores differ by only .3 standard error units while their percentile ranks differ by 24. Agreeing that the Cooperative Primary Tests should "probe basic understandings of our verbal and quantitative world, rather than simple memorization of its arbitrary rules and so-called 'facts,'" (Handbook, p. 5) the reviewer rates the content validity of these tests outstanding. Some prospective users, however, may feel that the content sometimes departs so far from specific school learning that some of the items are more similar to intelligence test items than to achievement measures. Since social studies and science are not measured, schools using this battery will need to consider supplementary assessment of these fundamental areas. * The reliability section of the Handbook has at least three deficiencies. First, no data on reliability over periods exceeding two weeks are reported. Second, reliability data are not reported for separate schools but only for pooled samples of several schools. Third, reliability coefficients and standard errors of measurement are not reported for various levels of performance on the respective tests. Chance scores on most forms and levels yield very modest percentile ranks, the median being only 3. Deviating from this desirable tendency are both forms of the lower-level Reading test in which chance scores yield percentile ranks of 16 for fall of Grade 2 and 25 for spring of Grade 1. The only developmental item analysis program tried out no more items than were ultimately needed in the final tests. Consequently, inadequately functioning items were replaced in the final forms by untested items. The quality of the final items in spite of this serious developmental limitation is a tribute to the expertise of the authorial and editorial team; however, it is highly probable that a two-stage developmental item analysis program using more items would have resulted in more reliable tests. Public school districts enrolling over three hundred students were selected for invitation to participate in the standardization programs by means of a probability sampling procedure that rendered the chances of a pupil's inclusion in the sample independent of the size of the school district he attended. Unfortunately, this probability weighting by size of sampling unit was not applied to schools or classes; schools were randomly chosen within selected districts, and ten pupils per grade were randomly selected from each school. No stratification procedures were employed to *assure* representation proportional to the population on such features as socio-economic status of community, geographical region, or size of school district. The need seems especially evident for a stratified sampling design with replacement provision within strata in view of the fact that only 38 percent of the districts invited to participate in the standardizations elected to do so. The separate fall and spring standardization samples differed in representation of some regions of the country. The fall sample under-represented the southern region while the spring sample slightly over-represented that section; yet, the spring sample of Grade 1 pupils performed better on all tests than the spring-tested, Grade 1 pupils in schools that participated in the fall standardization. This surprising superiority of the sample with substantially greater southern representation may reflect the sampling design's neglect of one or more critical achievement-related, demographic variables. Community socio-economic level is probably the most important such variable. The laudable departure from the practice of obtaining multiple norms per year by means of linear interpolation from a single standardization is, ironically, the feature that revealed the inadequacies of the sampling design. Had only the usual single sample been used, the inadequacies in the sampling design would have, as usual, gone largely unnoticed. Commendable restraint was exhibited in not making adjustments that would have obscured the differences in performance of the two norm groups. The test user is candidly warned that the fall and spring norms are not strictly comparable. Another standardization limitation is that 1850 or fewer students comprised each set of norms. However, since the battery requires

hand scoring, since at least 170 schools comprised each set of norms, and since the publisher surpassed contemporary practices by providing separate fall and spring standardizations, the reasons for the small samples are apparent and are, perhaps, justified. The well-written items, clarity of directions, attractive, well-organized format, and highly competent measurement of understanding that characterize the Cooperative Primary Tests merit their serious consideration by schools wishing standardized assessment of primary achievement. Although several features that may detract from the usefulness of the battery have been pointed out, it is meritorious that the Handbook reports in so professional a fashion the information from which the tests may be evaluated.

[11]

★DIGEST: Diagnostic Inventory Group Evaluation Survey Tests. Grades 4-6, 7-9; 1967; for group measurement (names of examinees are not recorded), especially for evaluating projects designed for the culturally disadvantaged child; 3 tests; manual (24 pages); no data on reliability; no norms; separate answer sheets (DocuTran) must be used; the fee of $1.10 per student includes all test materials (Form A for pretesting and Form B for posttesting), scoring, and reporting of group test results (item and total scores for *a–b* and for 2 optional 20-item locally constructed tests, summary of responses for *c* by classroom, grade, and system; $1.35 per specimen set; postage extra; (90) minutes; Science Research Associates, Inc. * [Test withdrawn in 1971.]
a) COMPUTATIONAL SKILLS. Forms A, B, (4 pages); 2 levels.
b) READING SKILLS. Forms A, B, (4 pages); 2 levels.
c) ATTITUDE INVENTORY. Separate inventories for students (2 pages) and teachers (1 page).

REFERENCE
1. HOLLOWAY, REGINA HEMPLER. *The Effect of Special In-Service Training for Teachers of the Educationally Disadvantaged on Pupil Attitudes and Achievement.* Doctor's thesis, University of Tulsa (Tulsa, Okla.), 1969. (*DAI* 30: 1335A)

DOROTHY C. ADKINS, *Professor and Researcher, College of Education, University of Hawaii, Honolulu, Hawaii.*

These survey tests cover arithmetic and reading skills at two levels, grades 4–6 and grades 7–9. There are two forms for each level and an attitude inventory to be completed by both students and teachers. The tests, intended solely for group comparisons, are administered with anonymity of the subjects preserved. The original intent was to develop tools useful in evaluating special projects for the culturally disadvantaged. The authors also note that the surveys can serve as diagnostic tools.

It is argued that because the resulting scores are group measures, "a number of areas can be tested with very few items with no loss of reliability." Of course there is a loss. Perhaps the intent was to say that lower reliability is tolerable when a measure is intended for group rather than individual comparisons. Nevertheless, one would like at least a hint as to what reliability estimates have been obtained or are to be expected. No such data appear in the manual.

The items seem on an inspectional basis to meet the generally accepted rules for test construction; care appears to have been taken to insure comparability of the alternate forms. The general format is attractive. A little data surely would not have been amiss, however. For the research purposes for which the survey is intended, the content validation approach that was used is acceptable, but one can but wonder at the lack of any data at all on how any subjects at all have responded to the instruments.

NORMAN FREDERIKSEN, *Director, Division of Psychological Studies, Educational Testing Service, Princeton, New Jersey.*

DIGEST consists of a 30-item test of computational skills, a 20-item test of reading skills, and 30 attitude items (e.g., "I work hard in class, The teachers in this school don't like people like me, My friends tease me when I do well in class"). All answers are recorded by blackening circles on a DocuTran answer sheet. This sheet also provides answer spaces for two more 20-item tests that may be supplied by the school, for 10 more attitude items, and for recording other information about the examinee—sex, age, grade, group membership, and scores on two quantitative variables such as IQ. About 90 minutes are required for administration of the battery, not including any tests and attitude items that might be supplied by the school. There are two levels, one for grades 4–6 and one for grades 7–9, and there are two "parallel" forms for each level. (The attitude items are the same for all forms and levels.) Finally, there is another DocuTran answer sheet that gives the teacher an opportunity to rate the class as a whole on a parallel set of attitude items and to record other items of information about the class.

The computational skills test covers addition, subtraction, multiplication, and division of whole numbers; fractions; decimals; and percentages. The difference in content between tests at the two levels involves only addition and subtraction of whole numbers (included only at the lower level) and percentages (included only at the higher level). The manual presents a classification of the items into finer categories, such as "Find the lowest common denominator of two mixed numbers, subtract, and reduce to lowest terms." The items are of the multiple choice variety with four options, one of which is "answer not given." The *not given* answer is correct for three of the 30 items, and they occur early in the test, so that the examinee has an opportunity to learn soon that the correct answer is not always included among the options. The same scoring key fits all four versions of the computational skills test.

The reading skills test includes 5 items on understanding phrases (which ask the examinee to choose the phrase that might answer the question), 5 items on understanding sentences (choose the sentence that means the same as another sentence), 4 items on using contextual clues (choose the word that fits the sentence best), and 6 items on paragraph comprehension (read the paragraph, then answer the questions). Again, the same scoring key fits all four versions of the test.

The two forms of each test at each level are alleged to be parallel forms, and the SRA catalog recommends using Form A for pretesting and Form B for posttesting. In what sense can Forms A and B be said to be parallel? It will be useless to look in the manual for evidence of equal means, variances, reliabilities, and validities, because they are not there. In fact, no statistical information of any kind is presented, and there is no statement in the manual that implies that even an item analysis was ever performed.

The basis for the claim that tests are parallel is that pairs of items are matched with respect to type of operation; e.g., "$26\overline{)2158}$" in Form A is paired with "$34\overline{)3162}$" in Form B; and "Donna let the phone ring and ring before she (A. dialed B. heard C. answered D. called) it" in Form A is paired with "He got wet in the rain because he (A. cleaned B. wore C. forgot D. buttoned) his coat" in Form B. The matching is not always precise, however; in the long division items above, for example, only the first example requires borrowing. Equivalent operations do not necessarily mean that items are equally difficult or equally valid.

A scoring service comes with the tests. It

provides, for each grade, class, or other group designated, the number and percentage of students in each group that passed each item; and the N, mean, standard deviation, sum of scores, and sum of squared scores for each group on each test. Also, frequency distributions of scores, with percentile ranks, are supplied. For the attitude items, the frequency and percentage of the group choosing each response—Yes, ?, or No—is given for the group and for boys and girls separately. If the recommended procedure of giving Form A as a pretest and Form B as a posttest is followed, two such sets of reports are available for comparison. No norms exist; all reports are based only on raw scores for the local groups tested.

The battery was initially produced to aid in the evaluation of educational projects aimed at helping culturally disadvantaged children. The manual describes in very general terms a number of possible applications of DIGEST. Some of these uses imply comparison of pre- and posttest mean performance of the same group, others comparison of means of different groups, and still others merely inspection and evaluation of the records of performance of one group on items and categories of items. The manual states that "statistical analysis of group difference often is warranted after visual inspection," and a small-sample formula is offered for computing a t ratio—one which would, however, be appropriate for independent samples only, not for pretest-posttest comparisons of the same group, since no correlation term is included. The implication is that a do-it-yourself approach to evaluation is acceptable; but little hint of possible statistical complications is given beyond a statement that most introductory statistics texts tell how to interpret t. The possible need of a control group for evaluating educational treatments is scarcely hinted at.

DIGEST is referred to as a "group assessment battery" and is intended to provide information only about group performance. In fact, it is not possible to do more than get group statistics, since students are not identified on the answer sheets. The purpose of omitting names is presumably to encourage frankness in replying to the attitude items, but there may be effects on motivation also. We can be sure of one consequence: no correlational or regression analysis involving scores of individual students is possible, and the value of the data

for any serious educational research is thus diminished appreciably.

The absence of names introduces other problems concerned with data gathering. It is true that all the data on one answer sheet need not apply to the same student, if only group statistics are to be obtained, and therefore any answer sheet from the group could be returned to any student at a second testing session, for example. But absenteeism or dropout can cause difficulties. If the posttest group is smaller than the pretest group, how do we know which pretest answer sheets to discard in order to have the same students represented in both groups? Perhaps we are not supposed to worry about such trivialities.

DIGEST fails to meet almost all of the major recommendations in the *Standards for Educational and Psychological Tests and Manuals* that fall under the headings Validity, Reliability, and Scales and Norms. There is no discussion of validity in the manual except for one statement that might be construed as pertaining to content validity. The discussion of reliability comprises two sentences that contain the erroneous assertion that since DIGEST is a group measure, "areas can be tested with very few items with no loss of reliability." The discussion of norms is limited to such statements as "to assess group changes in skill mastery, raw scores provide all the information needed" and "[raw-score reports] meet the federal and state requirement that project reports be submitted in raw-score form." DIGEST appears to be the result of an attempt to take advantage of a market produced by requirements that evaluations be performed for Title I projects; it is not recommended to any user unless he decides solely on the basis of inspection of the test items that it provides just the information he needs for a particular purpose.

[12]
★**General Tests of Language and Arithmetic.**
Standards 5–7; 1964–67; GTLA; 3 scores: first language, arithmetic, second language; Forms EA, EB, ['67, 27 pages]; preliminary manual ('67, 20 pages); distribution of Form EB restricted to Psychological Services of the Department of Education; separate answer sheets (IBM 1230) must be used; R2 per 10 tests; R4 per 100 answer sheets; 30c per scoring stencil; 60c per manual; postpaid within South Africa; specimen set not available; Afrikaans edition available; 120(140) minutes; Human Sciences Research Council. *

[13]
★**Ligondé Equivalence Test.** Adults who left elementary or secondary school 15 to 20 years ago;

1967; LET; also called *School Equivalence Test;* Form GE (4 pages); manual (11 pages); norms are grade equivalencies; Can $2 per 25 tests; $3.50 per specimen set (must be purchased to obtain manual); postage extra; French edition (Forms EF, FF) available; 15(20) minutes; Paultre Ligondé; Institute of Psychological Research, Inc. *

[14]

Metropolitan Achievement Tests. Grades kgn–1.4, 1.5–2.4, 2.5–3.4, 3.5–4.9, 5.0–6.9, 7.0–9.5; 1931–71; MAT; 6 levels; subtests in reading (grades 2.5–9.5) and in mathematics (grades 3.5–9.5) available as separates; partial batteries without science and social studies tests are available at intermediate and advanced levels; teachers handbook ('71, 14–17 pages) for each level; 50¢ per handbook; $2 per specimen set of any one level; postage extra; Walter N. Durost, Harold H. Bixler, J. Wayne Wrightstone, George A. Prescott, and Irving H. Balow; Harcourt Brace Jovanovich, Inc. *

a) PRIMER. Grades kgn–1.4; 1971; 3 scores: listening for sounds, reading, numbers; Form F (12 pages); 2 editions; hand scorable, MRC scorable; directions (22 pages); $9.50 per 35 hand scorable tests; $14 per 35 MRC scorable tests; $1.30 per set of hand scoring stencils; MRC scoring service, 42¢ and over per test; (120) minutes in 8 sessions.

b) PRIMARY 1. Grades 1.5–2.4; 1931–71; 5 scores: reading (word knowledge, reading, total), word analysis, mathematics; Forms F ('70, 16 pages), G ('71, 16 pages); 2 editions: hand scorable, MRC scorable; directions ('70, 21 pages); $9.50 per 35 hand scorable tests; $14 per 35 MRC scorable tests; $1.50 per set of hand scoring stencils; MRC scoring service, 50¢ and over per test; (115–125) minutes in 3 or 4 sessions.

c) PRIMARY 2. Grades 2.5–3.4; 1932–71; 9 scores: reading (word knowledge, reading, total), word analysis, spelling, mathematics (computation, concepts, problem solving, total); Forms F ('70, 20 pages), G ('71, 20 pages); 2 editions: hand scorable, MRC scorable; directions ('70, 21 pages); $11 per 35 hand scorable tests; $15.50 per 35 MRC scorable tests; $1.70 per set of hand scoring stencils; MRC scoring service, 54¢ and over per test; (160–170) minutes in 5 sessions.

d) ELEMENTARY. Grades 3.5–4.9; 1932–71; 9 scores: reading (word knowledge, reading, total), language, spelling, mathematics (computation, concepts, problem solving, total); Forms F ('70, 20 pages), G ('71, 20 pages); 2 editions: hand scorable or reusable, MRC scorable; directions ('70, 13 pages); $11 per 35 hand scorable or reusable tests; separate answer folders (MRC) may be used; $15.50 per 35 MRC scorable tests; $17 per 100 answer folders; $1.70 per set of hand scoring stencils; $1.50 per set of MRC hand scoring stencils; MRC scoring service: 43¢ and over per answer folder, 54¢ and over per test booklet; (225–235) minutes in 7 sessions.

e) INTERMEDIATE. Grades 5.0–6.9; 1932–71; 11 scores: reading (word knowledge, reading, total), language, spelling, mathematics (computation, concepts, problem solving, total), science, social studies; Forms F ('70, 32 pages), G ('71, 32 pages); directions ('70, 19 pages); $14 per 35 tests; separate answer sheets (Digitek, IBM 805, IBM 1230, MRC, NCS) may be used; $8.40 per 35 sets of Digitek or IBM 1230 answer sheets; $6.90 per 35 sets of IBM 805 answer sheets; $10 per 100 MRC answer sheets; $32.50 per 250 NCS answer sheets; $2 per set of hand scoring stencils; $4 per set of Digitek scoring stencils; $4.80 per set of IBM scoring stencils; $1.20 per set of MRC hand scoring stencils; MRC scoring service, 35¢ and over

per test; IBM scoring service, $1.20 and over per test; 270(310–320) minutes in 6 sessions.

f) ADVANCED. Grades 7.0–9.5; 1932–71; 11 scores same as for intermediate level; Forms F ('70, 32 pages), G ('71, 32 pages); directions ('70, 19 pages); $15 per 35 tests; answer sheet, scoring stencil, and scoring service information same as for intermediate level; 265(305–315) minutes in 6 sessions.

REFERENCES

1–3. See 2:1189.
4–10. See 3:13.
11–20. See 4:18.
21–36. See 6:15.
37. REGER, ROGER. "Brief Tests of Intelligence and Academic Achievement." *Psychol Rep* 11:82 Ag '62. * (*PA* 37:5654)
38. MILLMAN, JASON, AND LINDLOF, JOHN. "The Comparability of Fifth-Grade Norms of the California, Iowa, and Metropolitan Achievement Tests." *J Ed Meas* 1:135–7 D '64. * (*PA* 39:10143)
39. PRENTICE, NORMAN M. "Individual Achievement Testing of Children With Learning Problems: A Clinical Guide." *J Proj Tech & Pers Assess* 28:448–64 D '64. * (*PA* 39:8660)
40. SARASON, SEYMOUR B.; HILL, KENNEDY T.; AND ZIMBARDO, PHILIP G. "A Longitudinal Study of the Relation of Test Anxiety to Performance on Intelligence and Achievement Tests." *Monogr Soc Res Child Develop* 29(7):1–51 '64. * (*PA* 39:15263)
41. ACKERMAN, THOMAS J. *Language Laboratory Instruction and the Achievement of First-Year Students of Spanish in Florida.* Doctor's thesis, Florida State University (Tallahassee, Fla.), 1965. (*DA* 27:134A)
42. BREEN, JOSEPH MICHAEL. *Differential Prediction of Intermediate Grade Skills Achievement From Primary Grade Aptitude and Achievement Measures.* Doctor's thesis, University of Connecticut (Storrs, Conn.), 1965. (*DA* 26:5260)
43. CARRINO, CAESAR AUGUSTUS. *Identifying Potential Dropouts in the Elementary Grades.* Doctor's thesis, Western Reserve University (Cleveland, Ohio), 1965. (*DA* 27:343A)
44. MULLIS, JESSE CARL. *The Prediction of Fifth Grade Achievement as Measured by Teacher Grades and Achievement Test Scores Using First-Grade Indices of Prediction.* Doctor's thesis, University of Georgia (Athens, Ga.), 1965. (*DA* 26:6515)
45. RAY, JOHN RICHARD. *The Predictive Value of Selected Factors for Achievement of Seventh Grade Pupils.* Doctor's thesis, University of Tennessee (Knoxville, Tenn.), 1965. (*DA* 26:4396)
46. GAY, CLEVELAND JOHNSON. *Academic Achievement and Intelligence Among Negro Eighth Grade Students as a Function of the Self Concept.* Doctor's thesis, North Texas State University (Denton, Tex.), 1966. (*DA* 27:112A)
47. SCHAIE, K. WARNER. *A Study of the Achievement Test Used in the Health Examination Surveys of Persons Aged 6–17 Years.* Public Health Service Publication 1000, Series 2, No. 24. Washington, D.C.: United States Government Printing Office, June 1967. Pp. viii, 60. *
48. BARZ, ANITA I. *Prediction of Secondary School Achievement From Primary Grade Aptitude and Achievement Measures.* Doctor's thesis, St. John's University (Jamaica, N.Y.), 1969. (*DAI* 30:3271A)
49. DE BOTTARI, LINDA. "Primary School Correlates of Secondary School Achievement." *Personnel & Guid J* 47(7):675–8 Mr '69. * (*PA* 43:13362)
50. EAGLE, NORMAN, AND HARRIS, ANNA S. "Interaction of Race and Test on Reading Performance Scores." *J Ed Meas* 6(3):131–5 f '69. * (*PA* 44:15298)
51. FOLLMAN, JOHN; HERNANDEZ, DAVID; AND MILLER, WILLIAM. "Canonical Correlation of Scholastic Aptitude and Critical Thinking." *Psychol* 6(3):3–6 Ag '69. * (*PA* 44:2853)
52. FOLLMAN, JOHN; MILLER, WILLIAM; AND HERNANDEZ, DAVID. "Factor Analysis of Achievement, Scholastic Aptitude, and Critical Thinking Subtests." *J Exp Ed* 38(1):48–53 f '69. * (*PA* 45:10901)
53. FOSTER, GARRETT R. "An Analysis of Teacher Assigned Grades at Nova and Three Control Schools." *Fla J Ed Res* 11(1):1–24 Ja '69. *
54. GOOLSBY, THOMAS M., JR.; FRARY, ROBERT B.; AND LASCO, RICHARD A. "Selecting and Supplementing an Appropriate Achievement Battery for an Experimental School—A Factor Analytic Approach." *Ed & Psychol Meas* 29(2):403–8 su '69. * (*PA* 44:17319)
55. MCELROY, ARTHUR ANDREW. *Comparison of Grade Equivalent Scores Among Batteries on Two Subtests of the Metropolitan Achievement Tests With Educable Mentally Retarded Children.* Doctor's thesis, University of Oregon (Eugene, Ore.), 1969. (*DAI* 30:4688A)
56. STROWIG, R. WRAY, AND ALEXAKOS, C. E. "Overlap Between Achievement and Aptitude Scores." *Meas & Eval Guid* 2(3):157–67 f '69. * (*PA* 44:11609)
57. ANNESLEY, FRED; ODHNER, FRED; MADOFF, ELLEN; AND CHANSKY, NORMAN. "Identifying the First Grade Underachiever." *J Ed Res* 63(10):459–62 Jl–Ag '70. *

58. BROWN, RALPH LOFTON. *The Utilization of Techniques for More Individualized Instruction for the Educable Mentally Retarded Student in the Junior High School.* Doctor's thesis, East Texas State University (Commerce, Tex.), 1970. *(DAI 31:4327B)*

59. CASSEL, RUSSELL N., AND KNOX, PATRICIA. "Improving High School Learning Predictions With Multiple Junior High Test Scores." *Calif J Ed Res* 21(1):14–20 Ja '70. *

60. HURT, MAURE, JR., AND MISHRA, SHITALA P. "Reliability and Validity of the Metropolitan Achievement Tests for Mexican-American Children." *Ed & Psychol Meas* 30(4):989–92 w '70. *

61. ROSEN, MARVIN; KIVITZ, MARVIN S.; CLARK, GERALD R.; AND FLOOR, LUCRETIA. "Prediction of Postinstitutional Adjustment of Mentally Retarded Adults." *Am J Mental Def* 74(6):726–34 My '70. * *(PA 44:17195)*

For reviews by Henry S. Dyer and Warren G. Findley of an earlier edition, see 6:15; for a review by Warren G. Findley, see 4:18; for reviews by E. V. Pullias and Hugh B. Wood, see 2:1189; for reviews by Jack W. Dunlap, Charles W. Odell, and Richard Ledgerwood, see 1:874. For reviews of earlier editions of subtests, see 6:627 (2 reviews), 6:797 (1 review), 6:877 (2 reviews), 6:970 (2 reviews), 4:416 (1 review), 4:543 (2 reviews), 2:1458.1 (2 reviews), 2:1551 (1 review), 1:892 (2 reviews), and 1:1105 (2 reviews).

[15]

*Metropolitan Achievement Tests: High School Battery. Grades 9–13; 1962–64; 11 scores: language arts (reading, spelling, language, study skills), social studies (study skills, vocabulary, information), mathematics (computation and concepts, analysis and problem solving), science (concepts and understandings, information); subtests in language arts, social studies, mathematics, and science available as separates; Forms Am ('62, 32 pages), Bm ('63, 32 pages); directions for administering ('62, 15 pages); revised interpretive manual ('64, 16 pages); revised norms booklet ('64, 12 pages); supplementary norms for grade 13 available on request; spelling and language worksheet ('62, 1 page); profile and report to parents ('63, 2 pages); score conversion tables (no date, 2 pages); Digitek directions ('65, 2 pages); IBM 1230 directions ('64, c1962, 1 page); separate answer sheets (Digitek, IBM 805, IBM 1230, MRC) must be used; $13.90 per 35 tests; $7.50 per 35 sets of IBM 805 answer sheets; $8.40 per 35 sets of IBM 1230 answer sheets; $8.40 per 35 Digitek answer sheets; $12 per 100 MRC answer sheets; $3 per 35 profiles; $2 per set of MRC hand scoring stencils; $3.60 per set of Digitek or IBM scoring stencils; $2 per specimen set (with interpretive manual); postage extra; MRC scoring service, 39¢ and over per test; IBM scoring service, 90¢ and over per test; 282(316) minutes in 7 sessions; Walter N. Durost, William H. Evans, James D. Leake, Howard A. Bowman, Clarke Cosgrove, and John G. Read; Harcourt Brace Jovanovich, Inc. *

ELIZABETH HAGEN, *Professor of Psychology and Education, Teachers College, Columbia University, New York, New York.*

Although the authors provide no information on the dates of the materials that were examined to prepare the specifications for the *Metropolitan Achievement Tests: High School Battery,* the data for item analysis on the experimental forms of the test were collected in November–December 1961. The instructional materials and sources used to develop the specifications for the tests could not have had a publication date later than 1960, and it is more likely that many had dates in the 1950's. In 1970, the content of the test appears to be out-dated; and the publishers have indicated in a personal communication to the reviewer that there are no plans to revise the test.

ITEMS. Since previous reviews of the test in *The Sixth Mental Measurements Yearbook* covered most of the points that need to be mentioned in relation to the test items, only a few additional comments about the items will be made here. This reviewer was bothered somewhat by the number of items in each subtest with stems that presented no well-defined problem to the examinee but was bothered much more by the "editorializing" in the stems of some items, for example, Social Studies Information, Form Bm, item 6, "A distinguished intellectual who opposed Eisenhower in the Elections of 1952 and 1956"; and the lack of precision in other items, for example, Science Information, Form Am, item 29, "Occurrence of an albino organism is called a (a) hybridization, (b) propagation, (c) recession, (d) mutation." In the Social Studies Vocabulary subtest, Form Bm, secondary school students in the 1970's might have difficulty in deciding whether the term, political issue, should be classified under (a) American Elections or (b) Military Action.

TECHNICAL CONSIDERATIONS. Most of the technical data for the tests are presented in the Guide for Interpreting. It appears as though data for item analysis and for standardization were collected on experimental forms of the test. The sample used for item analysis came from ten school systems in seven states. Normalized standard scores for each subtest were developed using a subsample of this group. Since the item analysis data were gathered in November–December 1961 and the standardization program was conducted in January–February 1962, there could not have been time to print new forms of the test containing only the items selected for the test. Apparently the authors of the test have assumed that the characteristics of the items were not affected by the items eliminated from the test. Such a procedure would affect the K-R 20 reliability estimates presented in Table 1 and Table 2. The estimates in these tables are probably high. It is difficult, though, to estimate how these have been affected since the other data on reliability presented in Table 8 are based on grades 10 and 11 combined.

The alternate forms reliability data are also based on grades 10 and 11 combined. The guide does not state the length of the time interval between the administration of the two forms. The reliabilities of the Reading test and the Language Study Skills test are in the low .70's; the rest tend to be in the low .80's. In general, the reliabilities are not impressive.

The authors give only very general information on the materials and methods used to develop specifications for the test. The item content outlines that are provided as a supplement to the Guide for Interpreting might help the potential user to determine the content and emphasis on each subtest, but they are too broad and general to be of much help. Supplementary Report No. 45 presents data on the correlations between scores on the battery and grade point averages for 357 freshmen entering a coeducational two-year college in Pennsylvania. These correlations range from a low of .15 for the Science Information subtest to a high of .38 for the Spelling and Language subtests. The Guide for Interpreting refers to item discrimination data as item validity data, which is undesirable.

In the Guide for Interpreting the authors state that "the Reading and Social Studies Information tests required separate treatment" from the other tests in establishing the normalized standard scores because of a timing factor. They state that the "raw scores on the final forms of these tests were corrected to allow for the influence of the speed factor," but nowhere do they explain how this correction was made.

The significance of Table 4, presenting correlations between final and experimental form raw scores, escapes this reviewer. The correlations are based on grades 9 through 12 combined and two-thirds of the items are common in the experimental and final forms. The correlations are high; so what?

NORMS. The normative sample is inadequately described, only the number of schools systems and the states from which they come being given. The authors make quite a point of norms based on students who are at-grade-for-age. However, this reviewer questions the usefulness of such norms since, in most schools, one never

finds only students who are at-grade-for-age. Norms for college preparatory students are also given, but these differ very little from the general norms.

INTERPRETATION. The uses suggested for the test results are very general and one cannot object to them. However, the authors appear to suggest a rather simplistic one-to-one comparison between performance on an intelligence test and on the achievement test. The statement in relation to stanines, "Therefore, a student's achievement in various areas as expressed in stanine terms is an accurate portrayal of relative strengths and weaknesses," may mislead the naive user and lead to overinterpretation of nonsignificant differences.

SUMMARY. Since the *Metropolitan Achievement Tests: High School Battery* are based on curriculum materials that are at least 10 years old and more probably 15 years old in 1970, there seems to be little reason for a secondary school to consider it for use.

FRANK B. WOMER, *Professor of Education, The University of Michigan, Ann Arbor, Michigan.*

The Sixth MMY contains three detailed reviews of the *Metropolitan Achievement Tests.* The High School Battery (HSB) has not been revised since then and there are no current plans (1971) for revision. Therefore, this review will summarize briefly the previous HSB reviews, will make some additional comments about points not previously covered, and then will summarize its strengths and weaknesses.

Of major concern when reviewing an achievement battery is the content validity of the subtests, as represented by the exercises that they contain. One of the previous reviewers praised the up-to-date coverage and the relationship of the exercises to current objectives (the HSB is copyrighted 1962 and 1963). A second reviewer considered the series "conservative," representing what curriculum is (in the early 1960's). The third reviewer criticized various "content" aspects, pointed out the similarity of the HSB to the *Essential High School Content Battery* of the early 1950's, and concluded that other achievement batteries are better for instructional purposes than the HSB. A range from praise to faint praise on the question of content validity in the early 1960's suggests that a new look is called for in 1971.

Two of the reviewers mentioned an emphasis

on skills and factual knowledge (rote memory) versus critical thinking or problem solving. Two of them praised the manuals as being very complete and containing valuable suggestions for users. Each reviewer raised a series of specific points, some favorable, some not.

Perhaps the major strength of the HSB is the care with which traditional test development techniques have been adhered to, and the candor of the manuals in describing that development. Test items were related to "analyses of current textbooks, courses of study, and expert formulations of the goals of instruction." Items were tried out to check discrimination, both within grade level and across grade levels. Reliability estimates were developed both from the item analysis sample and from an independent sample. The standardization process followed accepted procedures among test publishers. Two types of norms were developed: age-controlled and college preparatory. The *Otis Quick Scoring Mental Ability Test* was administered to the norm sample also, and Otis and HSB norms are related. No one could fault the general methods used, although specific aspects of the process are open to question.

The variety of norms that are available is an asset: age-controlled, college preparatory, and Otis-related. Also the suggestion for the development of local norms is good. The presentation of stanines and percentiles rather than grade equivalents certainly is to be commended.

Supplementary materials are well developed. It is possible to do a thorough review of the HSB from the manuals. More detailed information is available from the publisher if desired.

Several of the item formats are worthy departures from traditional techniques. Examples are the use of a rather long reading passage followed by questions that must be answered without referring back to the selection, and the requirement that incorrectly spelled words be written correctly.

Some aspects of the HSB are neither clearly advantages nor disadvantages, in this reviewer's opinion. The use of age-controlled norms, for example, is presented as a distinctive feature of the HSB (along with other Harcourt Brace Jovanovich tests). Clearly the authors and publisher feel that age-controlled norms are superior to traditional grade norms. Clearly the authors and publishers of other standardized achievement test batteries do not. This reviewer holds neither strong partiality for nor strong aversion to age-controlled norms, since either one can be understood by a potential user who is willing to give minimal thought to the question. Of greater importance is the availability of multiple norms, so that an individual student can be compared easily with a variety of peer groups.

Another aspect of the HSB that has potential utility in the hands of a skilled and trained user of test results, but also has potential for considerable misuse, is the Item Content Outline. The authors are cautious in their claims for the utility of content analysis, but perhaps not cautious enough. It seems to this reviewer that items chosen for a standardized test because they discriminate between high and low scoring examinees and because their difficulty level is in the midrange of item difficulty are not the best types of items to use to analyze students' knowledges and skills. Items built to be criterion-referenced rather than norm-referenced and with a greater range of item difficulties would be much more useful for content analysis. Certainly class statistics on the test items could be useful as supplementary information for a teacher knowing how to use such data, but should not form the basis of a teacher's analysis of his class's performance.

The HSB is available with four types of answer sheets. This certainly is an advantage. It would be well to know whether the norms have been checked against each format, but for a high school battery this probably is not as important as for an elementary battery.

The use of the Otis Gamma with the standardization population is stressed as a great asset, since one can relate the Metropolitan stanines or percentiles to Otis IQ's. It is not clear to this reviewer what a teacher really gains from this, except to see how two generalized measures of achievement relate to each other. It is interesting to note in Table 11 of the Guide for Interpreting that the median correlation between the Otis IQ and 10 of the HSB subtests (excluding Language Study Skills) is .68. From Table 10 one can determine that the median correlation between the Language Study Skills subtest and the other 10 subtests is .63. From this one could argue that the HSB could, through one of its subtests, serve as its own reference point rather than administer another test (the Otis).

Another point relating to the use of the Otis Gamma with the HSB is that the newer *Otis-*

Lennon Mental Ability Test is now available, but there are no norms relating it to the HSB.

The simultaneous administration of an achievement battery and intelligence test is quite common among test publishers. Whether it serves any major purpose other than to promote test sales is a moot question.

There are several points about the HSB that give this reviewer serious concern. Perhaps the most important one is its age. The series was copyrighted in 1962 and 1963, meaning that items were generated several years prior to that. No matter how well items were related to objectives and content in 1960, it is questionable whether they all have equal content validity in 1971. Relevance is an overused term these days, but it does apply to this situation.

It also bothers this reviewer that the standardization group was defined as "public school systems selected randomly from communities with populations between 10,000 and 99,999." Why big cities and rural areas were excluded is not explained. Certainly this would suggest that two sources of low achieving students were eliminated from the norm group, with subsequent potential bias.

Another similar point was the use of only ten schools in the item analyses, with seven of the ten schools from New England, four from New Hampshire. While New Hampshire is undoubtedly a fine state, it is questionable whether it is really representative of the entire country.

The use of identical norms for both forms is questionable, with alternate-form reliabilities ranging from .72 to .90 (median .84).

It is easy for a reviewer to establish some utopian standard for a test which he is reviewing, and then determine that nothing really measures up to his expectation. From a more practical viewpoint it is wiser to compare a given series with the available alternatives. In such a comparison this high school battery stands up rather well, for those schools that desire a traditional achievement battery at the high school level, and for those schools that feel the test content matches their own objectives and courses of study.

SUMMARY. The HSB has not changed its content in the last ten years, but curricula have changed—in many schools at least. Any secondary school considering the adoption of a new achievement series in the 1970's should examine the content of the HSB very carefully. Despite its careful attention to the details of test con-struction, the HSB is showing its age. The publisher's statement that no revision is contemplated now makes it even more "iffy" for any new adoptions. This generalization does not apply to schools already using the HSB, although it could well suggest to them that a new look at the battery's content and their own curricula is warranted.

For a review by Paul L. Dressel, see 6:15; for reviews by Henry S. Dyer and Warren G. Findley of both the elementary school and high school batteries, see 6:15. For reviews of subtests, see 200 (2 reviews), 479 (2 reviews), 792 (2 reviews), and 888 (2 reviews).

[16]

*National Educational Development Tests. Grades 7–8, 9–10; 1959–71; NEDT; tests administered annually in spring and fall by individual schools; 2 levels; separate answer sheets (DocuTran) must be used; tests rented only; postpaid; Science Research Associates, Inc. *

a) LEVEL 1. Grades 7–8; 1963–69; 6 scores: English usage, mathematics usage, social studies reading, natural sciences reading, word usage, total; supervisor's manual ('67, 15 pages); interpretive manual ('69, 23 pages); student interpretive booklet ('69, 15 pages); student information bulletin ('67, 14 pages); rental and scoring of tests, $1.10 per student; 180(220) minutes.
  1) [*Fall 1970 Program.*] Form A ('66, 32 pages).
  2) [*Spring 1971 Program.*] Form D ('67, 32 pages).
b) LEVEL 2. Grades 9–10; 1959–71; 7 scores: same as for *a* plus learning ability; test booklet includes the optional *Counselor's Program Questionnaire* (CPQ, '63, 5 pages, also called *Educational Planning Questionnaire*) by Samuel A. Stouffer; supervisor's manual ('70, 15 pages); interpretive manual ('70, 41 pages); student interpretive booklet ('70, 18 pages); student information bulletin ('70, 13 pages); rental and scoring of tests: $1.25 per student, $1.75 per student if optional CPQ is scored; 175(220) minutes, (30) minutes additional for optional CPQ; Test of Learning Ability by Thelma Gwinn Thurstone.
  1) [*Fall 1970 Program.*] Form 21A ('70, 36 pages).
  2) [*Spring 1971 Program.*] Form 22A ('71, 36 pages).

REFERENCES

1. KUSHINKA, MICHAEL. *The Predictive Components of Pupil Performance in Senior High School.* Doctor's thesis, Yeshiva University (New York, N.Y.), 1967. (*DA* 28:434A)
2. TOLOR, ALEXANDER. "Incidence of Underachievement at the High School Level." *J Ed Res* 63(2):63–5 O '69. *

For reviews by Willis W. Clark, Arthur E. Traxler, and Alexander G. Wesman of an earlier edition of Level 2, see 6:17.

[17]

★*Peabody Individual Achievement Test. Grades kgn–12; 1970; PIAT; 6 scores: mathematics, reading recognition, reading comprehension, spelling, general information, total; individual; 1 form; test plates: volumes 1 (mathematics, reading comprehension, 232 pages), 2 (reading comprehension, spelling, general information, 282 pages); manual (105 pages); $24 per set of test materials and 25 record booklets; $3 per 25 record booklets; postage extra; (30–40) minutes;

Lloyd M. Dunn and Frederick C. Markwardt, Jr.; American Guidance Service, Inc. *

JOSEPH L. FRENCH, *Professor of Special Education and Educational Psychology and Head of the Department of Special Education, The Pennsylvania State University, University Park, Pennsylvania.*

"The purpose of the PIAT is to provide a wide-range, screening measure of achievement in the areas of mathematics, reading, spelling, and general information." The five subscores and the total score may be converted into a variety of norms: grade scores, percentile ranks within grades, age scores, percentile ranks within ages, and normalized standard scores. Procedures for establishing basals and ceilings are effective for limiting administration to from 30 to 40 minutes. The PIAT test materials include two volumes of test plates on rings. The covers, which have been cleverly designed, can be assembled to form a display stand.

In a rather complete manual, the authors specify numerous limitations relative to the administration and interpretation of their test. No formal training is required to administer the PIAT. Para-professionals might be taught to use it; however, they should be carefully selected, trained and supervised; each must practice giving the instrument prior to its use in real life, if the norms are to be appropriate. Although the illustrations and format were designed to capture the interest of most subjects and to be appreciated by most examiners, the profile sets the stage for improper use by individuals who are not psychometrically oriented and do not take the time to read the cautions and limitations specified by the authors. Such phraseology as "basic percentile rank norms were computer-derived" may also suggest to the unwary that the numbers are more significant because they are "computer" rather than calculator derived.

The authors indicate that total test scores are a "reflection of overall school achievement only when this is defined as mathematics, reading, spelling and general information." In developing the test, extensive reviews were made of curriculum materials used at each grade level; the basic item pool evolved from this information. However, items were retained because of their statistical discrimination rather than their ability to test a critical content area. The authors do not represent the test as appropriately

sampling any curriculum. When a specific level of achievement needs to be obtained, the PIAT is recommended for locating the general level to be more thoroughly evaluated with a longer, more comprehensive achievement test.

The standardization sample was drawn from nine regions of the United States. Students tested were attending regular classrooms of public day schools. The authors believe that such standardization allows users of the test to make comparisons with "typical" persons of a given age. Such a population was easy to enumerate accurately and was most accessible for testing and gathering background data.

Test-retest reliabilities, based on a one-month interval, are presented for the total test (.82 to .92, median .89) and each of the subtests: mathematics (.52 to .84, median .74), reading recognition (.81 to .94, median .88), reading comprehension (.61 to .78, median .64), spelling (.42 to .78, median .65), and general information (.70 to .88, median .76). The reading recognition subtest has very nearly as much reliability as the total test.

Mean raw score differences between grade levels beyond grade 4 seem too small for more than rough screening. Although the authors have included many items in an attempt to get an adequate ceiling and a large range in scores, the mean scores within grades increase very slowly between grades 4 and 12. More confidence can be placed in the total score than in the subtest scores.

The authors report that correlations between PIAT total scores and PPVT IQ's range from .53 to .79 with median .68.

In summary the PIAT is a power test which can be administered by a well trained para-professional. The test will undoubtedly be well received as a screening device to help educational diagnosticians obtain a quick, rough estimate of educational levels. Often it will be used to suggest the point at which a more comprehensive test may be employed, should a more reliable and thorough estimate be desirable. The authors are to be commended for developing a test with five subtests covering such a broad age span and for providing such a comprehensive manual with cautionary notes for each of the scores used in interpretation. Perhaps the next yearbook will present a review of a revised PIAT with greater raw score mean differences between grade levels and more reliable subtests.

J Ed Meas 8(2):137–8 su '71. Howard B. Lyman. * easily the most attractively packaged test the reviewer has ever seen. The contents, though not attaining the clear superiority of the package, are good. The item content seems appropriate for each of the five tests; much of it seems interesting. The Directions seem clear, and there is little reason to believe that the test could not be administered meaningfully by anyone who has read and understood the directions. * The sampling procedure was slightly unorthodox, but it seems reasonably adequate and was efficient in terms of costs and examiner time. * The first subtest to be administered is Mathematics, "because it requires no reading, writing or oral response, and is interesting for most subjects, thus making it a good rapport establisher." (I'd like to see evidence in support of this statement from page 3 of the Manual.) * The general format of test, manual, and record booklet are superior. The procedures (determination of starting point, basal, ceiling, raw score, etc.) are identical for each subtest. An impressive amount of work has gone into the development of PIAT. There are a few less favorable features. Although there are advantages to having an *individual* achievement test, this one suffers in comparison to its *group* competitors. It has less demonstrated validity, lower test-retest reliability coefficients at most levels (though Mathematics and General Information seem reasonably high at most age levels), smaller standardization samples (inevitable, of course, with an individual test), and fewer subtests. Much more research is needed before the PIAT can be fully accepted as a valid test. The Record Booklet provides little room for writing even the minimal + or − information generally needed. Reading Recognition is the one test most obviously suited to individual administration. This subtest requires the greatest skill on the part of the examiner, because each item is scored as correct only when the examinee gives the exact correct pronunciation. Criteria are provided in a pronunciation guide in the manual or on a special extra-cost training tape. PIAT users need to recognize the importance of studying the correct pronunciation of words on both Spelling and Reading Comprehension (which together account for 40% of the Total score). It seems possible that some examiners may have difficulty in attaining proficiency in administering and scoring these two tests. The potential user should consider

whether the subtests are adequate for his needs. There are no subtests for science, social studies, or study skills. If such subtests are needed, the tester will need to look beyond the PIAT. All things considered, I like the PIAT. It does have some shortcomings, but I think that it can be very helpful in evaluating the achievement level of transfer students and other pupils who may be in need of special study. In short, the PIAT promises to be interesting.

[18]

*SRA Achievement Series. Grades 1–2, 2–4, 3–4, 4–9; 1954–69; 3 editions; technical report ('68, 38 pages); interpretive guide ('68, 30 pages); testing program handbook ('68, 14 pages); growth scale manual ('67, 65 pages); $3.15 per set of interpretive materials (technical report, interpretive guide, testing program handbook, and growth scale manual); postage extra; Louis P. Thorpe, D. Welty Lefever, and Robert A. Naslund; Science Research Associates, Inc. *
a) HAND SCORED EDITION. Grades 1–2, 2–4; 1955–68; subtests in arithmetic, reading, and language arts (grades 2–4 only) available as separates; 2 levels; pupil progress and profile chart ('64, 4 pages); $4.95 per 100 pupil progress and profile charts; $2.65 per specimen set of both levels.
  1) *Grades 1–2*. 1958–68; 10 scores: reading (verbal-pictorial association, language perception, comprehension, vocabulary, total), arithmetic (concepts, reasoning, computation, total), total; Forms C, D, ('63, 36 pages) for reading; Forms C, D, ('63, 21 pages) for arithmetic; examiner's manuals: Forms C ('64, 45 pages), D ('65, 42 pages); $5.85 per 25 reading tests; $4.35 per 25 arithmetic tests; 225(340) minutes in 7 sessions.
  2) *Grades 2–4*. 1955–68; 12 scores: language arts (capitalization and punctuation, grammatical usage, spelling, total), arithmetic (concepts, reasoning, computation, total), reading (comprehension, vocabulary, total), total; Forms C, D, ('63, 59 pages); examiner's manual ('64, 43 pages) for each form; $8.85 per 25 tests; 260(365) minutes in 7 sessions.
b) MACHINE SCORABLE EDITION. Grades 1–2, 3–4; 1955–68; 2 levels; $2.65 per specimen set of both levels; tests rented only; rental and scoring service, 90¢ and over per student.
  1) *Grades 1–2*. Scores same as for *a1*; uses same content as hand scored edition but with some differences in timing, sequence of items, and number and structure of items; Forms C ('68, c1958–63, 16 pages in 2 booklets), D ('68, c1963, 16 pages in 2 booklets) for reading; Forms C ('68, c1958–63, 8 pages), D ('68, c1963, 8 pages) for arithmetic; examiner's manual ('68, 41 pages); 210(325) minutes in 7 sessions.
  2) *Grades 3–4*. Scores same as for *a2*; based upon material from the hand scored edition; Forms C ('68, c1955–63, 8 pages), D ('68, c1957–63, 8 pages) for reading and arithmetic; Forms C ('68, c1954–63, 8 pages), D ('68, c1956–63, 8 pages) for language arts; examiner's manual ('68, 24 pages); 230(320) minutes in 4 sessions.
c) MULTILEVEL EDITION. Grades 4–9; 1955–69; 14 or 17 scores: social studies, science, language arts (capitalization and punctuation, grammatical usage, spelling, total), arithmetic (reasoning, concepts, computation, total), reading (comprehension, vocabulary, total), total, plus optional work-study skills (references, charts, total); subtests in arithmetic, language arts, reading,

science, and social studies available as separates; Forms C, D, ('63, 94 pages); 3 levels: blue (grades 4.5–6.5), green (grades 6.5–8.5), and red (grades 8.5–9) in a single booklet; work-study skills supplement: Forms C, D, ('63, 32 pages); $2.65 per specimen set; 310(363) minutes in 3 sessions for battery, 70(80) minutes for work-study skills supplement:

1) *SRA Scored.* Examiner's manual ('68, 27 pages); guide to individual item reports ('68, 88 pages); separate answer sheets (DocuTran) must be used.

(*a*) Complete Rental Plan. Rental and scoring service, 80¢ and over per student ($1 and over when work-study skills test is included).

(*b*) Scoring Only Plan. $26.25 per 25 tests; $10.35 per 25 work-study skills supplements; scoring service, 55¢ and over per student (65¢ and over when work-study skills test is included).

2) *School Scored.* Examiner's manuals: Digitek and IBM ('69, 38 pages), DocuTran ('68, 27 pages); conversion tables booklet ('64, 38 pages) for each level; pupil progress and profile charts ('64, 4 pages); separate answer sheets (Digitek, DocuTran, IBM 805, IBM 1230) must be used; $26.25 per 25 tests; $10.35 per 25 work-study skills supplements; $16.35 per 100 sets of Digitek or IBM 1230 answer sheets and conversion tables booklet for any one level; $9.30 per 100 DocuTran answer sheets and conversion tables booklet for any one level; $21 per 100 sets of IBM 805 answer sheets and conversion tables booklet for any one level; $4.95 per 100 pupil progress and profile charts; $2.10 per set of IBM 1230 hand scoring stencils for any one level; $2.10 per DocuTran hand scoring stencil for any one level; $3.75 per set of IBM 805 scoring stencils for any one level; Digitek scoring stencils not available.

REFERENCES

1–3. See 6:21.
4. HOPKINS, KENNETH DEAN. *Validity Concomitants of Various Scoring Procedures Which Attenuate the Effects of Response Sets and Chance.* Doctor's thesis, University of Southern California (Los Angeles, Calif.), 1961. (*DA* 22:155)
5. HOPKINS, KENNETH D. "Extrinsic Reliability: Estimating and Attenuating Variance From Response Styles, Chance, and Other Irrelevant Sources." *Ed & Psychol Meas* 24:271–81 su '64. * (*PA* 39:3152)
6. TAYLOR, ALTON L. "The Prediction of Success Using Programmed Science Materials." *J Res Sci Ed* 2(1):58–9 '64. *
7. HICKEY, DONALD E. *A Prediction of Success in Social Studies Based Upon Reading Scores From the SRA Achievement Series for Grades 6–9.* Master's thesis, Northern Illinois University (DeKalb, Ill.), 1965.
8. TAGATZ, GLENN E.; LEMKE, ELMER A.; AND MEINKE, DEAN L. "Alpha Factor Analyses of Learning Concepts and Student Achievement Test Scores." *Teach Col J* 39:99–103 D '67. *
9. CAWLEY, JOHN F., AND GOODMAN, JOHN O. "Interrelationships Among Mental Abilities, Reading, Language Arts, and Arithmetic With the Mentally Handicapped." *Arith Teach* 15:631–6 N '68. *
10. BARZ, ANITA I. *Prediction of Secondary School Achievement From Primary Grade Aptitude and Achievement Measures.* Doctor's thesis, St. John's University (Jamaica, N.Y.), 1969. (*DAI* 30:3271A)
11. HAYES, EDWARD MAJELLA. *The Relationship of Race and Sex to Academic Achievement in Selected Rural Elementary and High Schools Before and After Desegregation.* Doctor's thesis, University of Virginia (Charlottesville, Va.), 1969. (*DAI* 31:149A)
12. NEALE, DANIEL C.; GILL, NOEL; AND TISMER, WERNER. "Relationship Between Attitudes Toward School Subjects and School Achievement." *J Ed Res* 63(5):232–7 Ja '70. *

MIRIAM M. BRYAN, *Consultant, Cooperative Tests and Services, Elementary and Secondary School Programs, General Programs, Educational Testing Service, Princeton, New Jersey.*

Forms A and B, now out of print, were competently and thoroughly reviewed in the last two *Mental Measurements Yearbooks,* in which both the test batteries and each of the subtests making up the batteries were described by reviewers as being of generally high quality. Forms C and D can be similarly described. Indeed, insofar as the critical comments and suggestions for improvement made by the reviewers of the earlier forms have been heeded and other refinements have been introduced, and there has been much of this, Forms C and D are better than their predecessors.

THE COMPLETE BATTERIES. The content of the tests at all levels has been carefully planned, and the test questions have been written with obvious expertise. The tests give slower students in the lower grades for which they are intended some opportunity for success and at the same time they challenge faster learners in the higher grades. Some overlapping of questions from level to level gives continuity to the series and offers special advantages in comparing results when different levels are administered in the same classroom. Comparability of the two forms, both in content and in difficulty, has been achieved to a greater than usual degree. There is no indication that the tests are unusually speeded.

THE SEPARATE TESTS. *Reading.* At all levels the reading tests yield comprehension and vocabulary scores, plus a total score. The battery for grades 1 and 2 gives two additional subtest scores: verbal-pictorial association and language perception. These two subtests are highly commendable features of this particular battery.

The reading selections are drawn largely from fiction, biography, science, and social studies; in each of the tests at the highest level in the multilevel edition, there is an excellent selection from American poetry. At all levels the selections are interesting and lively, and appear to be of appropriate difficulty in sentence length, sentence complexity, and concept load.

While the reviewer is impressed with the intent and content of the reading tests, she is compelled to offer several critical comments—many of which have been offered by reviewers of earlier forms. First of all, except in the tests at the lower levels, the reading selections are all of considerable length. Shorter selections would offer the opportunity for a much wider variety of content without restricting the diversity of questions or the number of questions which might be based on them. Secondly, in the tests for the first four grades, from one-third to one-half of the questions offer "Yes," "No," and "We can't tell" as responses. These are high proportions for a question type that is known to present considerable difficulty for younger students in distinguishing between the two negative responses—difficulty which may be further aggravated by the statement of the third choice in the plural, implying common agreement. Thirdly, the use of vocabulary words exclusively from the selections, while it presents words in context, restricts the choice of words. Finally, the tests make no effort to measure speed of reading comprehension or flexibility in adjusting speed to suit different types of reading done for different purposes. Admittedly, test publishers generally have had little success in devising measures for these important reading skills for older students; these skills ought not, however, to be left unattended.

Arithmetic. The arithmetic tests give subscores in reasoning, concepts, and computation, plus a total score. The reasoning questions, built around situations presented in story form, require students to identify the facts relevant to a solution, select the arithmetical process to be used, and do the computation necessary to arrive at the solution. The questions on concepts canvass the student's ability to recognize number symbols, understand the cardinal and ordinal use of numbers, and handle time, money, and measures. The coverage in the concepts subtests is wide and comprehensive; the language of traditional mathematics is used. The situational approach in the reasoning subtests, while it no doubt adds an element of interest, does result in some interlocking of questions. An erroneous answer to a question having to do with the selection of the arithmetical process, for example, may result in an erroneous answer to a later question requiring computation. In the multilevel edition, the use of "None of these" as the fifth choice for all questions involving computation is to be commended.

Except for the computation subtests for the lowest level in the multilevel edition, for which chance scores give grade equivalent scores well into the lowest grade, the difficulty ranges of the various levels appear to be appropriate. The large number of questions contributing to each subscore cover quite adequately the traditional mathematics program.

Language Arts. At all levels, the punctuation, capitalization, and usage questions are presented in a series of stories and personal letters natural to the life of students at those levels. The coverage is quite complete. The questions range from the very obvious to the more exacting points in capitalization, from very simple to rather subtle points in punctuation, and from a choice between illiterate and literate English to some niceties of language usage to challenge the high scorers. On the whole the language arts tests, of all the tests in the basic skills areas, seem to have been most improved as a result of the comments of reviewers of Forms A and B.

Science. These tests are designed to measure "knowledge and understanding of certain representative facts and principles of science." To a reviewer without an extensive background in science, the tests seem to fulfill the stated purpose, with the areas of general science, biology, astronomy, geology, physics, and chemistry all represented, and important facts and principles taught in grades 4 through 9 in these areas covered. The questions are, however, primarily factual. It is regrettable that, with interpretation, application, and discovery being stressed in the newer science curricula, so few diagrams have been included and no attempt has been made to test ability to interpret reading selections, charts, and graphs, or to apply the principles of science to both familiar and unfamiliar situations.

The science tests contain the largest number of negatively stated questions encountered in the series. In both forms, 14 of 90 questions are of the NOT, LEAST, or EXCEPT types, a larger number than this reviewer would consider desirable. About the same number of questions, and many of them the same ones, are of the "Which of the following" type, which tend to result in the presentation of a series of true-false statements that frequently do not present very challenging alternatives. With these exceptions, the questions have been meticulously written and edited.

Social Studies. These tests are designed to measure "understanding and application of representative principles drawn from geography, history, government, and economics." The questions primarily measure recall of factual information rather than understanding and application of principles. The questions are, however, extremely well written and edited. There are few of the negatively expressed questions and the true-false sets objected to in the science tests. Again, it is to be regretted that there are no questions based on the interpretation of social studies materials and the application of social studies skills. Schools using the optional tests in work-study skills will, however, find that several of the skills applicable to the social studies are covered in those tests. The range of difficulty of the questions seems to be adequate.

Work-Study Skills. The tests in work-study skills are presented in attractive booklets; the items are well written; the charts, maps, and graphs clearly drawn; and the tables well assembled.

The tests may fulfill fairly well the purposes for which they were designed. The reviewer is, however, critical of the same characteristics of the tests that were criticized by reviewers of the earlier forms and wonders, with them, whether tests of just this type are really necessary.

The information sought in many of the questions on tables of contents could ordinarily be more easily and quickly located in indexes. Among the questions on the indexes are some that ask what can or cannot be found on certain pages; one does not usually approach an index from page number to topic. In the subtest on charts, some of the graphs and tables have been "milked" beyond the bone in an attempt to provide more questions than are really needed to measure the student's ability to locate the information desired and to interpret it. On the mythical maps, the cities are sometimes difficult to locate amid all the topographical features shown, and for one question (item 54 in Form C), the keyed response on the direction of flight from one city to another is imprecise.

There is no doubt that more work should be done in grades 4 through 9 with the development of work-study skills. There is a question, however, as to whether these skills, many of which are closely associated with work in specific subject areas, might not better be measured in tests designed for those areas. All but the questions concerned with the location of information in general references could be better incorporated in the arithmetic, science, and social studies tests, and a more comprehensive test of the location of information and the use of general references substituted for the tests of work-study skills.

INTERPRETIVE MATERIALS. The interpretive materials represent close to the epitome of what the knowledgeable test user expects the reputable test publisher to provide him with today.

Among these are the usual student records forms and progress and profile charts, and five booklets, variously described as guides, handbooks, manuals, and reports, several of which are commented upon below. In addition, various reports and analyses are available through SRA's centralized electronic scoring and reporting service.

The Guide to Individual Item Reports, an ingeniously contrived device for interpreting item scores, is made up of 78 overlays—one for each subtest of each form at each level in the multilevel edition. By aligning computer-printed class lists of individual items with the appropriate page in the guide, the teacher can read a description of the concept or fact tested in each item or group of items and see quickly and easily how each student and the entire class responded.

SRA Growth Scales have been developed for each of the subject matter areas shared by the *SRA Achievement Series* and the *Iowa Tests of Educational Development* to provide a way of expressing test results in the same units from the first through the twelfth grade. Although labeled "preliminary," the scales as presented can be used with considerable confidence in studying and predicting student growth.

The Technical Report gives clear and concise accounts of the development of the series and its standardization, and reports impressive test characteristics which show the tests to be generally of appropriate difficulty and length and the two forms of each test to be highly comparable. The reviewer would quarrel only with the emphasis put on grade-equivalent scores; such scores, showing regular and gradual increase in achievement from month to month, are "manufactured" scores that do not reflect the kind of irregular progress that is typical of the average classroom and are, therefore, subject to frequent and serious misinterpretation by teachers and parents. The estimates of reliability, while generally high, are K-R 20 estimates of internal consistency rather than parallel form estimates; no information is given regarding the discriminatory power of either individual items or tests; and no mention is made of concurrent or predictive validity—this in spite of the number of years the *SRA Achievement Series* had been available at the time the report was published.

Although distributions of school averages were not computed for the standardization sample, such distributions, based on results in schools using the SRA scoring service over a particular period of time, have more recently been made available for four different regions and, separately, for high-scoring user schools. Unfortunately, as a result of the method of selection, the schools represented are overwhelmingly parochial—over 80 percent for some of the distributions—and include a large number of very small schools. Test users interested in distributions of school scores need to be aware of these limitations.

SUMMARY. The *SRA Achievement Series* offers a program for testing basic skills and related areas from grades 1 through 9. In the basic areas, the emphasis is on the development of understanding and the application of learning rather than on the acquisition of factual knowledge only; to a somewhat lesser degree, this is true of the tests in the related areas.

On the credit side: The series has been carefully planned; the test content is appealing and appropriate; the test items are interesting and well written; the format of the test booklets and of the materials that accompany them is practical and attractive; the directions for administering are clear and adequate; the interpretive materials are many in number and generally comprehensive in coverage; the technical standards set for the series and met by it are quite acceptable.

On the debit side: A few of the item types and a small number of the items themselves are in need of review and improvement; the intent and content of the tests in related areas ought to be reexamined; less emphasis should be placed on grade-equivalent scores and more on kinds of scores that can be more easily explained and better justified; data should be provided concerning the statistical validity of the test questions; more substantial information should be given about the validity of the tests for the purposes for which they are recommended.

The commendable features of the *SRA Achievement Series* are many; the less than commendable, few. The series compares favorably with other series of its type currently available. For the school system whose purposes it can serve, it should not be overlooked when selection of a useful achievement battery is being made.

FRED M. SMITH, *Professor of Education and Director, Bureau of Educational Research,*

Louisiana State University, Baton Rouge, Louisiana.

Forms C and D represent extensive revisions of the earlier editions (Forms A and B) of this series. Although the basic content outline of Forms A and B was retained, items were revised to reflect newer educational objectives, and new tests in science and social studies were added. The emphasis on understandings and skills instead of memorized content was retained. The multilevel edition (grades 4–9) permits testing heterogeneous groups of students at the same time using the same booklets. This should also be economical, since theoretically fewer booklets should have to be purchased by the school system than would be the case with separate booklets for each level. At first it might seem that different levels within the booklet would be confusing for the student. Confusion has been minimized, however, by color coding and by the numbering arrangements on answer sheets.

VALIDITY. The validity of an achievement test is judged by the extent to which it reflects what is taught. To this end, as stated in the technical manual, the content of the battery was based on studies of elementary school curricula. An examination of the content outlines and test booklets indicates that the *SRA Achievement Series* reflects the content and objectives of elementary schools as well as most achievement batteries and better than some. For example, the inclusion of a science, a social studies, and a work-studies skills test makes this series more valid than the *California Achievement Tests*. Furthermore, it is one of the few achievement batteries which include tests of beginning reading skills at the primary level. The verbal-pictorial association and language perception tests should be much more useful in working with slow beginning readers at the second and third grade level than the usual reading comprehension tests of other batteries. For those schools which stress "modern" math, the *SRA Modern Math Understanding Test* may be substituted for the arithmetic test.

In attempting to match the curricula of all schools, however, a test may not match the curriculum of any one school very well. Teachers should examine the test booklets and manuals to determine the extent to which the battery possesses content validity for the local school. An excellent aid to such an examination, although it was not published for this particular purpose, is the Guide to Individual Item Reports. In this booklet, every item of every test in the series is classified according to content and objective measured. Content summary tables are also presented in the Interpretive Guide. The items of the social studies test should be closely reviewed, since they seem to depart from the emphasis on basic skills which is found in the other tests. At all levels, the social studies test seems to place primary emphasis on recall of information.

RELIABILITY. Reliability, in terms of K-R 20 coefficients and standard errors of measurement, is adequately described in the technical report. The authors are to be commended for adequate verbal descriptions of concepts and tables without long, theoretical, irrelevant discussions which only confuse the average reader and bore the specialist. They are also to be commended for reporting data for each grade level and on each score that is used, a practice that has not always been followed in other technical reports.

An examination of the reliability tables reveals, as one would expect, that part scores are not as reliable as composite scores. However, most subtest scores appear to have adequate, if not high, reliability for use with individuals as well as groups. Exceptions would be Form C of the reasoning and vocabulary subtests, and Form D of the vocabulary test, both at grade 1; Form D of the grammatical usage test at grade 3; both forms of the grammatical usage and reading comprehension subtests at grade 4; and both forms of the arithmetic concepts and arithmetic computation tests and Form D of the social studies test at grade 5. In each of the cases mentioned the coefficients were below .80.

Standard errors of measurement in terms of grade equivalents exceed .5 in a majority of the scores and exceed 1.0 in more than 50 of the 170 scores in grades 6–9. The increase of the standard error in the higher grades is explained in the manual as reflecting the increased range of grade equivalents at these levels. Regardless of the reason, such a large amount of error in a test score makes it highly susceptible to misuse by the average teacher.

Two studies of the comparability of Forms C and D are reported. In each study, the two forms were administered one year apart to a group of students. Correlation coefficients between corresponding tests and subtests of the two forms ranged from .62 to .93, indicating considerable similarity.

NORMS. The norms, as well as a complete description of their development, are contained in the Technical Report. A stratified sample of approximately 70,000 elementary school students based on geographic region and rural-urban community constitutes the norms groups. The authors are to be commended for presenting the number of students comprising the actual group used for each form and level of the test.

In addition to individual norms, regional frequency distributions of school averages are available. These "school norms" allow comparisons of an entire school's average with that of other schools in the region.

SCORES AND SCORING. Four types of derived scores are available with the battery: percentiles, stanines, grade equivalents, and SRA Growth Scale Values. The characteristics of each type of score and the relationships among the scores are clearly described in the Interpretive Guide. The authors should be commended for explaining the problems connected with using grade equivalents. However, as was stated earlier in this review, the large standard errors in terms of these scores make them susceptible to misuse by teachers, especially when individual diagnosis is attempted. SRA Growth Scale Values provide an opportunity for plotting growth curves in each content area and comparing scores at different levels of the test. Scores on the publisher's secondary school achievement battery, the *Iowa Tests of Educational Development*, have also been converted into Growth Scale Values so that a comparable curve from grades 2–12 may be plotted. The booklet which describes the growth scales and presents conversion tables is well written and complete, but the average teacher or principal would probably not be able to use it effectively without the aid of a specialist in measurement.

The usual extensive reporting services which large publishers currently offer are available. These include list report of scores, ranked lists, school and grade averages, local percentile norms, profile charts, and item analyses for groups or individuals.

Semi-transparent scoring keys to be used when hand scoring DocuTran answer sheets are color coded according to the different test levels; this provision should prevent a mix-up of levels, but not of forms. Editions at grades

1–2 and 3–4 are designed so that the student may place his answers in machine scorable booklets, an aid to both students and teachers. However, in many cases the teacher will still have to code each student's name in the numeric grid.

SUMMARY. The *SRA Achievement Series* is one of the better achievement batteries available today. It is about as reliable as other achievement batteries, and the length of the subtests makes them more reliable than those of some of the other achievement batteries on the market. Because of its greater content coverage and its emphasis on mental skills in line with current educational objectives, its potential for validity is greater than that of several other achievement batteries. The manuals and guides are complete and are clearly and concisely written. Used properly, it can be a useful tool for both diagnosis and survey testing.

For a review by Jacob S. Orleans of earlier forms, see 6:21; for reviews by Warren G. Findley and Worth R. Jones, see 5:21. For reviews of subtests, see 526 (1 review), 706 (1 review), 797 (1 review), 891 (1 review), 6:632 (1 review), 6:808 (1 review), 5:200 (2 reviews), 5:483 (2 reviews), 5:649 (2 reviews), and 5:696 (2 reviews).

[19]

*SRA High School Placement Test. Entering ninth grade students; 1957–70; HSPT; 7 or 8 scores: educational ability, reading achievement, language arts achievement, arithmetic or modern mathematics, total, social studies, science methodology, Catholic religion (optional); Series 72K ('70, 47 pages); new form published annually; optional religion test ('67, 7 pages); examiner's manual ('68, 37 pages); manual for religion test ('68, 12 pages); interpretive manual ('68, 30 pages); profile leaflet ('68, 4 pages); reliability data for earlier forms only; separate answer sheets (DocuTran) must be used; tests rented only; examination fee (with or without religion test), $1.25 per student, postage extra; fee includes scoring service and reporting of normed scores and local norms; 165(210) minutes, 30(35) minutes for religion test; Science Research Associates, Inc. *

REFERENCES

1–3. See 6:22.
4. BLUMENFELD, WARREN S. "Differentiating Between Low-Achievers With a Non-Verbal Pictorial Reasoning Measure: An 18-Month Follow-Up." *Psychol Rep* 15:985–6 D '64. * (*PA* 39:8681)
5. GILES, GEORGE C., JR. "Predictive Validity of Progressive Matrices and Two Other Nonlanguage Tests of Mental Ability." *J Ed Meas* 1:65–7 Je '64. * (*PA* 39:7757)
6. IMPELLITTERI, JOSEPH THOMAS. *A Study of the Prediction of Final Grades for a Sample of Ninth Grade Males Undertaking an Academic Program in Ten High Schools of the Diocese of Philadelphia.* Doctor's thesis, Fordham University (New York, N.Y.), 1964. (*DA* 26:868)
7. SIMMER, L., AND WICKISER, R. "SRA High School Placement Test Study of the Class of 1967." *Ill Sch Res* 1:28–9 N '64. *
8. WALDRON, CORMAC. *Differential Prediction of Achievement in Broad Curricular Areas in an Academic High School.* Doctor's thesis, Fordham University (New York, N.Y.), 1964. (*DA* 25:1764)
9. WITTMER, RUSSELL E. *A Study of the Science Research Associates High School Placement Test as a Predictor of Academic Achievement of Low Ability Students at Richwoods Community High School, Peoria Heights, Illinois.* Master's thesis, Northern Illinois University (DeKalb, Ill.), 1965.
10. MARINI, JOSEPH L. *A Study of the Use of the Science Research Associates High School Placement Test in the Early Identification of Potential Dropouts at LaSalle-Peru High School.* Master's thesis, Northern Illinois University (DeKalb, Ill.), 1966.
11. IMPELLITTERI, JOSEPH T. "Predicting Academic Achievement With the High School Placement Test." *Personnel & Guid J* 46:140–3 O '67. *

For reviews by Walter N. Durost and Charles O. Neidt of earlier forms, see 6:22; for reviews by Cyril J. Hoyt (with W. Wesley Tennyson) and William W. Turnbull, see 5:22.

[20]

★SRA Reading and Arithmetic Indexes. Job applicants with poor educational backgrounds; 1968; RAI; 2 tests; self-scoring test booklets; preliminary manual (12 pages); $5.95 per 25 tests; 40¢ per manual; $1.25 per specimen set; postage extra; (50–60) minutes; Science Research Associates, Inc. *
a) SRA ARITHMETIC INDEX. 1 form (7 pages).
b) SRA READING INDEX. 1 form (8 pages).

DOROTHY C. ADKINS, *Professor and Researcher, College of Education, University of Hawaii, Honolulu, Hawaii.*

These tests were designed to assess reading and computational abilities of persons over 14 years of age who are applying for entry-level jobs or special training programs, but whose basic skills are often too low to be evaluated by previously available tests. The authors urge specific job analyses to assure a realistic picture of job requirements and then the use of these (or similar) tests to avoid rejection of qualified applicants.

The *SRA Reading Index* is based on five rationally conceived proficiency levels: picture-word association, word decoding, comprehension of phrases, comprehension of sentences, comprehension of paragraphs. Likewise, the *SRA Arithmetic Index* comprises four levels: addition and subtraction of whole numbers, multiplication and division of whole numbers, basic operations involving fractions, and basic operations involving decimals and percentages. One can conceive of items at one of these levels that would be easier than the items in one or more of the levels below it. Nevertheless, the items selected for the different levels apparently do progress in mean difficulty. For each level, a critical score corresponding to 80 percent correct (or at least 50 percent of the items above what might be expected to be correct by chance) was set a priori. Both instruments are power tests, and the score is the highest developmental level passed. The method of establishing passing scores seems arbitrary at best. In addition, in its application, the authors appear not to have taken into account that the expected chance score for the five-choice arithmetic level scores is 20 percent instead of the 25 percent applicable to the reading level scores. Indeed, the critical scores given for the arithmetic test are more consistent with chance scores of 25 percent than with chance scores of 20 percent.

From larger pools of items, those for each level of each test were selected so as to maximize internal consistency within skill levels and minimize overlap between levels. The items in the Reading Index were subjected to the additional requirement that their correlation with the SRA Pictorial Reasoning Test not exceed .40. The total score on both the Reading Index for a sample of 81 and on the Arithmetic Index for a sample of 52 correlated .23 with the Pictorial Reasoning Test, which the authors refer to as a measure of "general ability." For a national sample of 12th grade vocational students, the Arithmetic Index correlated .16 with this test. One might like more evidence than is available to the reviewer that the Pictorial Reasoning Test is an adequate measure of general ability.

The K-R 20 reliability estimate, presumably for total raw score, was .87 for the Reading Index (N = 87) and .91 and .95 for the Arithmetic Index for two samples of 57 and 419 students, respectively. The items seem to have been adequately edited, pretested, and analyzed with respect to internal criteria and difficulty.

The reading measure, judged by the distribution of total scores for the Chicago final normative sample of 87, seems definitely too easy for the intended purpose, at least for the Chicago sample.

From plots of the reading and of the arithmetic levels against quarters of the distribution of scores on the Pictorial Reasoning Test (not quartiles, as the diagrams are erroneously labeled), the authors argue that 26 percent in reading and 42 percent in arithmetic have acquired basic skills below their potential as measured by the Pictorial Reasoning Test. But what of the large percentages who, by the same line of argumentation, have somehow managed to acquire skills above their ability levels? Is it possibly out of order to use a test that correlates only in the neighborhood of .15 to .25 with measures of skill as a criterion for determining

whether students are below, at, or above their potentials?

The burden of proof of validity of these tests in actual use rests squarely on the user, at least as of the time of publication of the Preliminary Manual. This is not to say that the tests may not prove useful in situations for which they appear to be appropriate.

[21]

*STS Closed High School Placement Test. Grade 9 entrants; 1955–69; HSPT; new series issued annually; 7 scores: ability (verbal, quantitative, total), skills (reading, modern mathematics or arithmetic, language), composite; series k ('69, 23 pages); a traditional arithmetic subtest ('69, 6 pages) may be substituted for the modern mathematics; general manual ('68, 38 pages, all statistical data based upon 1966 and earlier tests); directions manual ('69, 14 pages); profile ['69, 4 pages]; schools may choose at no extra cost 1 of the following 4 STS Placement Tests: Mechanical Aptitude ('66, 7 pages), Modern Mathematics ('66, 4 pages), Science ('66, 4 pages), Catholic Religion ('66, 4 pages); separate answer sheets (Digitek) must be used; rentai and scoring fee, $1.25 and over per student; an earlier edition (Series H, '66) is available for purchase and local scoring by schools: $24.50 per 35 tests, $6 per 50 answer sheets; postage extra; 135(160) minutes; Scholastic Testing Service, Inc. *

REFERENCES
1. DODSON, ROBERT GEORGE. A Factor Analytical Study of High School Placement Test, Battery for Entering Freshmen (Form A). Doctor's thesis, University of Oklahoma (Norman, Okla.), 1964. (DA 26:2049)
2. WESTPHAL, JOHN H. The Scholastic Testing Service, High School Placement Test, as a Predictor of Success for Ninth Grade Students in the Albert City-Truesdale Community School. Master's thesis, Drake University (Des Moines, Iowa), 1964.

For reviews by Marion F. Shaycoft and James R. Hayden of an earlier series, see 6:6; for reviews by William C. Cottle and Robert A. Jones of the 1955 "open" test, see 5:15.

[22]

★STS Educational Development Series: Scholastic Tests. Grades 2–3, 4–6, 6–9, 9–12; 1963–71; EDS; a battery of ability and achievement tests and questions on interests and plans; 14 reports and scores for grades 4–12: 3 interest areas (school plans, career plans, school interests), 3 ability scores (verbal, nonverbal, total), 7 achievement scores (reading, English, mathematics, basic skills total, science, social studies, everyday problems), composite of ability and achievement scores; 9 reports and scores for grades 2–3: omitting school plans, career plans, science, social studies, and everyday problems; 4 levels; manual ('66, 33 pages) for grades 4–12; content outline ['70, 2–3 pages] for each level; interpretive brochure ('70, 16 pages); student profiles: grades 2–3 ('68, 4 pages), grades 4–12 ('65, 6 pages); separate answer sheets (NCS) must be used; 15¢ per answer sheet; 5¢ per growth profile; 4¢ per student profile; 30¢ per content outline; 25¢ per interpretive brochure; $1 per specimen set of any one level; postage extra; scoring must be done by publisher; a basic skills battery (reading, English, and mathematics), a core achievement battery (reading, English, mathematics, science, and social studies), and an ability/skills battery (verbal, nonverbal, reading, English, and mathematics) are also available as separates (except for primary level for which only basic skills battery is available separately); Scholastic Testing Service. *

a) PRIMARY LEVEL. Grades 2–3; 1968–71; Form A ('68, 30 pages); directions for administering ['70, 16 pages]; technical report ('71, 15 pages); $16 per 20 tests; $2 per technical report; scoring service, 50¢ and over per test; rental and scoring of tests, 95¢ and over per student; 150(195) minutes in 3–5 sessions.

b) ELEMENTARY LEVEL. Grades 4–6; 1963–71; Form A ('63, 57 pages); directions for administering ['70, 20 pages]; technical report ('71, 46 pages); $20 per 20 tests; $2 per technical report; scoring service, 75¢ and over per test; rental and scoring of tests, $1.25 and over per student; 245(335) minutes in 4 sessions.

c) ADVANCED LEVEL. Grades 6–9; 1963–70; Forms A, B, ('63, 65 pages); directions for administering ['70, 24 pages]; technical report ('69, 57 pages); $22 per 20 tests; $2 per technical report; scoring service, 80¢ and over per test; rental and scoring of tests, $1.45 and over per student; 235(335) minutes in 2 sessions.

d) SENIOR LEVEL. Grades 9–12; 1965–70; Forms A ('65, 65 pages), B ('68, 65 pages); directions for administering ['70, 23 pages]; technical report ('67, 45 pages); prices and time same as for Advanced Level.

ROBERT D. NORTH, *Associate Director, Professional Examinations Division, The Psychological Corporation, New York, New York.*

The broad coverage of this relatively new series is unique. The inclusion of ability tests, achievement tests, and questions about plans and interests in a single booklet is designed to provide a battery that is useful for a wide range of evaluative, diagnostic, and guidance purposes.

For a series with a short history, the number of accessories available is impressive. Among these are separate manuals for administering each battery, pupil profile forms with score explanations, a booklet giving school administrators information about the report forms and the meaning of the results, and a content outline of the achievement and skills tests of each level of Form A. The editorial and printing quality is quite consistently high, especially with respect to readability and appearance.

At each of the four levels, pupils are asked to indicate on a nine-point scale their degree of liking for each of eight "school subjects"— music, art, mathematics, science, social studies, English, foreign languages, and vocations. While the goal of coordinating the batteries from one level to another as closely as possible is commendable, the wisdom of asking pupils in the second or third grade about their interests in foreign languages and vocations (explained as wood-work, metal-work, cooking, and sewing) is questionable. Similarly, the use of the word "chemistry" to help define science for

children in the primary grades seems inappropriate.

The parts dealing with school and career plans are identical in content from one battery to another in the grade range of 4–12. These parts are simply checklists, naming 16 career fields and 6 levels of educational goals. Although these checklists are likely to be useful in grades near or at the junior and senior high school levels, their utility may be limited for elementary grade pupils who are not able to make a decision on a matter such as whether they would like to "finish high school, and to finish four years of college, and then still go on for additional college training." On the other hand, perhaps a case might be made for using such an item to encourage some fourth grade youngsters to start thinking along these lines.

The items in the nonverbal reasoning part are comprised of sets of four or five drawings of objects or geometrical forms, with the student being required to identify the one that "doesn't belong with the others." The drawings are clear, and the set relationships seem to test logical reasoning adeptly over a wide range of ability. In this part, as well as in other parts, some items are unjustifiably repeated in identical form from one battery level to another, however. For example, items 16, 19 and 22 in the elementary level, Form A, appear in the advanced and senior levels with the same item numbers. Item 62 of the elementary level becomes item 64 of the senior level. Evidently the items are not consistently arranged in the order of their difficulty levels.

The verbal reasoning part, designed to test vocabulary and reasoning involving word relationships, consists of synonym items at the primary level, set items at the elementary level, and both of these types of items at the other two levels. As is the case for many verbal reasoning tests, knowledge in some specialized areas is required, in addition to reasoning ability, for successful performance. Areas sampled are music (composer's names), geography (coastal cities), geometry (plane figures), and military services (personnel ranks).

The reading, English, and mathematics achievement parts of all four levels and the science and USA in the World parts of the three upper levels provide a broad coverage of the typical, general curriculum in grades 2–12, with a relatively high ceiling of difficulty. Study skills items—tapping abilities such as using indices and reference books, chart and graph reading, and map reading—appear in most of these parts. In the main, the quality of the item writing is good.

In judging the appropriateness of the subject-matter content coverage for a given school or school system, some of the limitations of this series that should be considered are: the mathematics is mainly traditional, rather than "modern," with very sparse sampling in the areas of geometry, trigonometry, and algebra; the science material is geared to general courses; social studies coverage is restricted almost entirely to geography, history, government, and current events pertaining to the United States.

The Everyday Problems part of the three upper levels consists of items relating to school and careers, sources of personal assistance, and students' typical personal and social quandaries. A student's answers to these questions probably provide fruitful leads for guidance discussions. Oddly, however, the score on this part contributes to the battery composite score, along with the scores on the ability and achievement parts.

The national norms for the elementary, advanced, and senior levels are based on the scores of approximately 2,000 to 6,000 students in 6 to 62 schools per grade. Specific information about the types and locations of the schools comprising the norm groups is not given.

The STS processing service reports results in terms of raw scores, local stanines, and either national grade scores or national percentiles. The grade score system is a normalized standard score system, with the 50th percentile set equal to the grade placement of the students at the time of testing (apparently the fifth month of the school year). A normalized grade score unit of 1.0 is equal to one year on the grade scale, so that the 16th and 84th percentiles correspond respectively to points one year below and above the norm median. Only at the mid-grade point do these grade scores have the same meaning as the grade equivalent scores traditionally associated with achievement tests.

Advantages claimed for the STS grade score system over the traditional grade equivalent scale are described in the technical manuals for the senior and advanced levels. In this reviewer's opinion, an overriding disadvantage is that anyone who has only a passing familiarity with achievement tests in general and this series in particular is likely to interpret the grade

scores as though they were grade equivalent scores.

The within-grade K-R 20 reliabilities fall between .79 and .94 for the ability, achievement, and Everyday Problems parts, and .97 to .98 for the composite score. These coefficients compare favorably with those of well-established tests of similar types and lengths.

In summary, the *STS Educational Development Series* may be attractive to schools interested in a battery that offers broad coverage for evaluation and guidance purposes. If achievement measurement in terms of grade equivalent scores based on large-scale national norms is desired, attention might well be directed toward series such as the *Iowa Tests of Basic Skills, Metropolitan Achievement Test,* and *Stanford Achievement Tests.*

[23]

★**Scholastic Proficiency Battery.** Standards 8–10; 1969; SPB; 5 scores: social sciences, commercial sciences, natural sciences, arithmetic, languages (either English or Afrikaans); 1 form (48 pages, English and Afrikaans); preliminary manual (21 pages, English and Afrikaans); no data on validity; norms for standard 10 only; separate answer sheets (IBM 1230) must be used; R5 per 10 tests; R6 per 100 answer sheets; 70c per scoring stencil; R1.20 per preliminary manual; postpaid within South Africa; specimen set not available; 85(110) minutes; F. A. Fouché, N. F. Alberts, and V. H. Paul (test); Human Sciences Research Council. *

[24]

*Secondary School Admission Test: General School Ability and Reading.** Students in grades 6–10 who are applying for admission to independent secondary schools; 1957–70; SSAT; tests administered 4 times annually (January, April, May, December) at centers established by the publisher; 4 scores: reading comprehension, ability (verbal, quantitative, total); Form RST16 ('69, 31 pages); supervisor's manual ('70, 27 pages); bulletin of information for candidates ('70, 43 pages); descriptive booklet ('70, 11 pages); admission guide to independent schools ('66, 15 pages); counselor's score guide ('70, 11 pages); candidate's score guide ('70, 12 pages); separate answer sheets (SCRIBE) must be used; examination fee, $8 per student; fee includes reporting of scores to candidates, parents, and 6 schools designated at the time of testing; postpaid; 120(165) minutes; program administered for the Secondary School Admission Test Board, Inc. by Educational Testing Service. *

REFERENCES

1. See 6:24.
2. SCHUERGER, JAMES M., AND DIZNEY, HENRY F. "The Validity for Ninth Grade Achievement of the SSAT and Other Admission Criteria at a Private Secondary School." *Ed & Psychol Meas* 27:433–8 su '67. * (PA 41:12838)

For reviews by Charles O. Neidt and David V. Tiedeman of earlier forms, see 6:24.

[25]

*Stanford Achievement Test.** Grades 1.5–2.4, 2.5–3.9, 4.0–5.4, 5.5–6.9, 7.0–9.9; 1923–68; SAT; subtests in (grades 1.5–9.9) reading, (grades 4.0–9.9) spelling and language, arithmetic, and (grades 5.5–9.9) science and social studies available as separates; partial batteries without science and social studies are available at Intermediate 1 and higher levels; 5 levels; technical supplement ('66, 55 pages); expected grade score tables ('68, 10 pages) based on *Otis-Lennon Mental Ability Test* available on request; teachers guide ('65, 8 pages) for each level; separate answer sheets (Digitek, IBM 805, IBM 1230, MRC) may be used for grades 4.0–9.9; $2 per technical supplement; 50¢ per teachers guide; postage extra; Braille and large type editions of *b–e* available from American Printing House for the Blind; Truman L. Kelley, Richard Madden, Eric F. Gardner, and Herbert C. Rudman; Harcourt Brace Jovanovich, Inc. *

a) PRIMARY 1 BATTERY. Grades 1.5–2.4; 6 scores: word reading, paragraph meaning, vocabulary, spelling, word study skills, arithmetic; 3 editions; $1.75 per specimen set of hand or machine scorable edition; 127(160) minutes in 5 sessions.

1) *Hand Scorable Edition.* Forms W, X, ('64, 12 pages), Y ('65, 12 pages); manual ('64, 32 pages); $8 per 35 tests; $1 per key; scoring service, $2 per test.

2) *MRC Machine Scorable Edition.* Forms W, X, ('65, 12 pages); manual ('66, 32 pages); $12 per 35 tests; scoring service, 50¢ and over per test.

3) *i/t/a Edition.* Form W ('65, 12 pages); manual same as for *a*1; supplementary directions ['65, 1 page]; no norms; $8.80 per 35 tests; specimen set not available.

b) PRIMARY 2 BATTERY. Grades 2.5–3.9; 8 scores: word meaning, paragraph meaning, science and social studies concepts, spelling, word study skills, language, arithmetic computation, arithmetic concepts; 2 editions; $1.75 per specimen set; 200(235) minutes in 7 sessions.

1) *Hand Scorable Edition.* Forms W ('64, 16 pages), X ('64, c1963–64, 16 pages), Y ('65, 16 pages); manual ('64, 32 pages); $8.30 per 35 tests; $1.30 per key; scoring service, $2.25 per test.

2) *MRC Machine Scorable Edition.* Forms W, X, Y, ('65, 16 pages); manual ('65, 32 pages); $12.50 per 35 tests; scoring service, 51¢ and over per test.

c) INTERMEDIATE 1 BATTERY. Grades 4.0–5.4; 10 scores: word meaning, paragraph meaning, spelling, word study skills, language, arithmetic computation, arithmetic concepts, arithmetic applications, social studies, science; Forms W ('64, 31 pages), X ('64, c1963–64, 31 pages), Y ('65, 31 pages); manual ('64, 24 pages); supplementary directions ['64–66, 1–2 pages] for use with each type of answer sheet; Form X conversion table ('64, 1 page); $13.20 per 35 tests; $1.40 per key; $8.40 per 35 sets of Digitek or IBM 1230 answer sheets; $6.90 per 35 sets of IBM 805 answer sheets; $10 per 100 MRC answer sheets; $3.50 per set of Digitek or IBM scoring stencils; $1.20 per set of MRC hand scoring stencils; $2.25 per specimen set; IBM scoring service, $1.10 and over per test; MRC scoring service, 30¢ and over per test; 269(300) minutes in 7 sessions.

d) INTERMEDIATE 2 BATTERY. Grades 5.5–6.9; 9 scores: same as for Intermediate 1 Battery except for omission of word study skills; Forms W ('64, 31 pages), X ('64, c1963–64, 31 pages), Y ('65, 31 pages); manual ('64, 26 pages); supplementary directions ['64–66, 1–2 pages] for use with each type of answer sheet; Form X conversion table ('64, 1 page); $13.20 per 35 tests; $1.40 per key; $8.40 per 35 sets of Digitek or IBM 1230 answer sheets; $6.90 per 35 sets of IBM 805 answer sheets; $10 per 100 MRC answer sheets; $3.50 per set of Digitek or IBM 1230 scoring stencils; $4.20 per set of IBM 805 scoring stencils; $1.20 per set of MRC hand scoring stencils; $2.25 per specimen set;

scoring services same as for Intermediate 1; 267(303) minutes in 7 sessions.

e) ADVANCED BATTERY. Grades 7.0–9.9; 8 scores: same as for Intermediate 1 Battery except for omission of word meaning and word study skills; Forms W ('64, 32 pages), X ('64, c1963–64, 32 pages), Y ('65, 32 pages); manual ('64, 27 pages); supplementary directions ['64–66, 1–2 pages] for use with each type of answer sheet; Form X conversion table ('64, 1 page); $13.20 per 35 tests; $1.40 per key; $5.60 per 35 sets of Digitek answer sheets; $6.90 per 35 sets of IBM 805 answer sheets; $8.40 per 35 sets of IBM 1230 answer sheets; $10 per 100 MRC answer sheets; $2.80 per set of Digitek scoring stencils; $4.20 per set of IBM scoring stencils; $1.20 per set of MRC hand scoring stencils; $2.25 per specimen set; scoring services same as for Intermediate 1; 255(287) minutes in 6 sessions.

REFERENCES

1–34. See 3:18.
35–54. See 4:25.
55–73. See 5:25.
74–86. See 6:26.
87. McNEIL, OWEN R. *A Study of the Achievement of Three Grades at Peabody, Kansas According to Stanford Achievement Tests.* Master's thesis, Kansas State Teachers College (Emporia, Kan.), 1956.
88. SCHOLL, GERALDINE TERESA. *The Reading and Spelling Achievement of a Group of English Children as Judged by the Standards on an American Achievement Test.* Doctor's thesis, University of Michigan (Ann Arbor, Mich.), 1960. (DA 21:315)
89. HAAG, CARL HERBERT. *An Exploratory Study to Determine the Significance of Early Longitudinal Records of Ability and Achievement as Predictors of Academic Achievement in College.* Doctor's thesis, University of Michigan (Ann Arbor, Mich.), 1961. (DA 21:3702)
90. HARMS, CALLIS R. *The Relationship Between Intelligence, Physical Growth, Socio-Economic Status, Social Acceptance and Academic Achievement in the Elementary School.* Doctor's thesis, Arizona State University (Tempe, Ariz.), 1961. (DA 22:2631)
91. MORRISON, HUGH E., AND COLLISTER, E. GORDON. "The Use of Difference Scores in the Interpretation of Test Results in Elementary Schools." *Univ Kan B Ed* 16:19–25 N '61. *
92. IVERSON, ETHEL W. *Validity Comparison of Stanford Achievement Test and California Achievement Test.* Master's thesis, San Diego State College (San Diego, Calif.), 1963.
93. WEINER, LAWRENCE H. "The Performance of Good and Poor Braille Readers on Certain Tests Involving Tactual Perception." *Int J Ed Blind* 12:72–7 Mr '63. *
94. BERNARD, JACK. "A Common Fallacy in Achievement Test Norms." *Psychol Sch* 1:428–31 O '64. *
95. CARY, LEE ALLAN. *A Comparative Analysis of the Sub-Test Scores of Two Groups of Deaf Children for the Chicago Non-Verbal Examination and the Reading and Arithmetic Reasoning Sections of the Stanford Achievement Test.* Doctor's thesis, University of Denver (Denver, Colo.), 1964. (DA 25:7023)
96. HAAK, LOUIS ANDREW. *An Investigation of the Validation Characteristics of Four Statistical Techniques in the Prediction of Certain Educational Achievement Variables.* Doctor's thesis, University of Minnesota (Minneapolis, Minn.), 1964. (DA 26:867)
97. MOORE, EARL JAMES. *A Study of the Relationship Between High School and College Scholarship and Selected Test Results for Grades K–12.* Doctor's thesis, University of South Dakota (Vermillion, S.D.), 1964. (DA 27:679A)
98. NORTH, ROBERT D. "The 1964 Edition of the Stanford Achievement Test: Description and Initial Appraisal of Independent School Program Results." *Ed Rec B* 86:57–66 Jl '64. *
99. SPRINGER, OWEN LAVERLE. *A Study of the Relationships Between the Educational Characteristics Criterion, (ECC), the Stanford Achievement Test, and Selected Cost Factors.* Doctor's thesis, Michigan State University (East Lansing, Mich.), 1964. (DA 26:2027)
100. WOZENCRAFT, MARIAN. "Word Meaning Difficulties." *El Engl* 41:44–6 Ja '64. *
101. BERNARD, JACK. "Achievement Test Norms and Time of Year Testing." *Psychol Sch* 3:273–5 Jl '66. * (PA 41:1938)
102. CUNNINGHAM, WILLIAM. *A Thirteen-Year Retrospective Study of Standardized Test Data.* Doctor's thesis, Western Reserve University (Cleveland, Ohio), 1966. (DA 27:3305A)
103. EDUCATIONAL RECORDS BUREAU. "A Note on the Independent-School Norms for the 1964 Revision of the Stanford Achievement Test." *Ed Rec B* 89:51–2 F '66. *
104. HARTE, MARY LABOURE. *Anxiety and Defensiveness as Related to Measurable Intelligence and Scholastic Achievement*

of Selected Institutionalized Children. Doctor's thesis, Fordham University (New York, N.Y.), 1966. (*DA* 27:2884A)

105. OHNMACHT, FRED W. "Achievement, Anxiety and Creative Thinking." *Am Ed Res J* 3:131–8 Mr '66. *

106. RICH, ALAN E. *Determination of the Degree to Which Eighth Grade Stanford Achievement Test Results Can Be Used to Predict Four Year High School Academic Achievement at Haverhill Academy, Haverhill, New Hampshire.* Master's thesis, Plymouth State College (Plymouth, N.H.), 1966.

107. HAMMERMEISTER, FRIEDA KATHERINE. *The Stability of Reading Achievement in Deaf Adults.* Doctor's thesis, University of Pittsburgh (Pittsburgh, Pa.), 1967. (*DA* 28:4375A)

108. PUTTHOFF, RONALD. *Local Norms for the Stanford Achievement Test for the Roman Catholic Government Schools of British Honduras.* Master's thesis, University of Kansas (Lawrence, Kan.), 1967.

109. SCHAIE, K. WARNER. *A Study of the Achievement Test Used in the Health Examination Surveys of Persons Aged 6–17 Years.* Public Health Service Publication 1000, Series 2, No. 24. Washington, D.C.: United States Government Printing Office, June 1967. Pp. viii, 60. *

110. SINQUEFIELD, LARALEI. *A Study of the Relationship of Selected Personality Variables to Performance on the Stanford Achievement Test for Students at the Sixth Grade Level.* Master's thesis, Tennessee Technological University (Cookeville, Tenn.), 1967.

111. TAGATZ, GLENN E.; LEMKE, ELMER A.; AND MEINKE, DEAN L. "Alpha Factor Analyses of Learning Concepts and Student Achievement Test Scores." *Teach Col J* 39:99–103 D '67. *

112. TRIEGLAFF, ANNETTE L. *The Relationship Between the Wechsler Intelligence Scale for Children and Reading Scores for the Stanford Achievement Test.* Master's thesis, Sacramento State College (Sacramento, Calif.), 1967.

113. YATES, LOUISE GRAHAM. *Comparative Intelligence of Negro and White Children From a Rural-Southern Culture.* Doctor's thesis, University of North Carolina (Chapel Hill, N.C.), 1967. (*DA* 28:4768B)

114. BAUGHMAN, E. EARL, AND DAHLSTROM, W. GRANT. *Negro and White Children: A Psychological Study in the Rural South,* pp. 63–82, passim. New York: Academic Press Inc., 1968. Pp. xx, 572. *

115. BUSZEK, BEATRICE R. "Differential Treatment of Test Scores." *Col & Univ* 43:294–307 sp '68. *

116. CANNON, JOHN P. *An Investigation of Science Scores Received on the Stanford Achievement Test Compared to Teachers' Grades.* Master's thesis, Jersey City State College (Jersey City, N.J.), 1968.

117. CLAWAR, HARRY J. "Some Examples of Best-Weighted Combinations of Junior Scholastic Aptitude Test Verbal and Numerical Scores When Predicting Standardized Achievement Test Performance." *Ed Rec B* 93:34–40 F '68. *

118. EISENMAN, RUSSELL; PLATT, JEROME J.; AND DARBES, ALEX. "Creativity, Intelligence and Achievement." *Psychol Rep* 22:749–54 Je '68. * (*PA* 42:13739)

119. LEDERMAN, EDWARD. "Group Characteristics as a Factor in the Interpretation of Student Profile Scores on the Stanford Achievement Test." *Ed Rec B* 94:39–41 Jl '68. * (*PA* 44:21526)

120. OHNMACHT, FRED W. "Dimensionality of Change in Achievement, Anxiety, and Divergent Thinking." *Meas & Eval Guid* 1:163–7 f '68. * (*PA* 44:11228)

121. WEISS, RAYMOND ALLEN. *The Reliability of Change Scores in Scholastic Achievement.* Doctor's thesis, Columbia University (New York, N.Y.), 1968. (*DA* 29:4341A)

122. CARBUHN, WAYNE McKINZIE. *Job Corpsmen Selection and Prediction of Successful Completion of the General Education Development (GED) Program at Clearfield Urban Job Corps Center.* Doctor's thesis, University of Utah (Salt Lake City, Utah), 1969. (*DAI* 30:3774A)

123. MEHRENS, WILLIAM A., AND LEHMANN, IRVIN J. *Standardized Tests in Education,* pp. 170–86. New York: Holt, Rinehart & Winston, Inc., 1969. Pp. xi, 323. *

124. NAGEL, THOMAS SCOTT. *A Descriptive Study of Cognitive and Affective Variables Associated With Achievement in a Computer-Assisted Instruction Learning Situation.* Doctor's thesis, Michigan State University (East Lansing, Mich.), 1969. (*DAI* 30:5295A)

125. WEIDMAN, ABRAM H., JR. *A Comparison of the Composite and Sub-Test Scores of the Stanford Achievement Test With Relation to Seventh Grade Sectioning.* Master's thesis, Millersville State College (Millersville, Pa.), 1969.

126. COTTEN, JERRY DALE. *A Comparison of the Metropolitan Readiness Tests to the Stanford Achievement Test.* Master's thesis, California State College (Long Beach, Calif.), 1970.

127. JOHNSON, GERALD, AND BRADLEY, WILLIAM. "Some Correlational Aspects of Performance on the Art Scale of the WFPT Among Certain Variables in a Deaf Population." *J Exp Ed* 39(1):59–62 f '70. *

128. MAYCOCK, GEORGE ALBERT. *Emotional, Social, and Academic Adjustment of the Mentally Retarded as Related to Socio-Economic Level.* Doctor's thesis, Texas Technological University (Lubbock, Tex.), 1970. (*DAI* 31:3375A)

129. SKUBIC, VERA, AND ANDERSON, MARIAN. "The Interrelationship of Perceptual-Motor Achievement, Academic Achievement and Intelligence of Fourth Grade Children." *J Learn Dis* 3(8):413–20 Ag '70. *

130. UHL, NORMAN P., AND NURSS, JOANNE R. "Socio-Economic Level Styles in Solving Reading-Related Tasks." *Read Res Q* 5(3):452–85 sp '70. *

J Ed Meas 2:247–51 D '65. Peter F. Merenda. The Stanford Achievement Tests....are certainly the patriarch of the standardized achievement test batteries, and perhaps have been the most widely used tests of their kind over the longest period of time. The first edition appeared in 1923. * The format of the individual tests in the battery is excellent. They are attractive and appealing to the eye, and the test administration is facilitated by the color coding of the test booklets and answer sheets at each level. The two-color system, used in the Manual as well as the test booklets, is particularly helpful to the teacher who must distinguish between the directions she must read to the class and those which concern her privately regarding the technique of test administration. That the colorful attractive format contributes to the convenience of administration and scoring of the test is unquestionable. The authors should have been proud of themselves and content to leave it at that. However, in the Manual they go on to claim that the colorful format contributes to pupil motivation. This claim is without foundation, and should have either been omitted completely or qualified as reflecting the authors' opinion. * for the sake of the user who is ordinarily a school teacher unaware of the relative effectiveness and efficiency of the MRC machine over the IBM 805 machine in producing accurate results, the authors should have pointed this out in the Manual. The present reviewer has had considerable extensive and frustrating experience in maintaining even a tolerable level of inaccuracy of scores obtained from IBM answer sheets influenced by stray marks, incomplete erasures, pencils with insufficient graphite content, and relatively high water content of the answer sheets caused simply by increased humidity in the atmosphere. These conditions do not affect the scoring of answer sheets when using equipment such as MRC. * In general, the format appears to be very efficient. However, there are several ways in which it could be improved. For example, in the Arithmetic Computations Test in Intermediate I level, the size of type used for numerals is excellent. It corresponds with the type size in arithmetic textbooks for the fourth and fifth grades. But, in the Concepts and Applications Test, the type used for numerals is smaller and less bold. Similarly, the type size for the reading sections in both these tests appears to be too small and inconsistent with the type size in the usual textbooks for children at these grade levels. This situation can be generalized for other tests in the lower levels of the battery. * Local (city-wide) and regional norms are omitted in the Manual. This is a serious omission. Such data are certainly available and could prove to be very helpful and meaningful to the users of the tests. * there are some single tests for which....[a reliability coefficient] is reported in the low .70's or even in the .60's. The authors are somewhat remiss in not pointing out the inadvisability of employing tests with such reliability as individual tests, inasmuch as separate tests in an achievement battery are often used by teachers. To the authors' credit is the fact that the standard scores (in terms of grade scores) are given for each test, along with the split-half and the Kuder-Richardson reliability estimates. However, they fail to inform the user that for certain tests in the battery the standard errors may be so great that the scores must be interpreted with great caution, or they may not be useful at all. This reviewer is of the opinion that the authors failed to assume a great responsibility in this case. To expect the ordinary test user to figure this out for himself is simply too much to ask of him. Consequently, for the benefit of the user the 95% confidence limits for the least reliable test(s) at each level [have ranges, the upper limit minus the lower limit, varying from 1.0 to 5.2 grade levels] * While the reliability data seem to be generally adequate (with the exception possibly of those single tests noted above) and compare quite favorably with those for similar and commercially competitive batteries, the user is not given any direct empirical evidence of the stability of the individual tests in the battery nor of the battery as a whole. Since the SATs have been developed in four forms, it would seem reasonable to expect the authors to have conducted and reported some comparable forms of reliability studies, if not test-retest studies. Not that the internal consistency methods used are considered to be inappropriate here, but it would seem that in the 40 years that the tests have been available, the authors would have undertaken by now to conduct such studies. Furthermore, and what is more important here, is the

lack of reliability data on the entire battery. Achievement batteries such as the SAT are most generally used as batteries, either partial or complete. When single tests are administered as such, they most often are used in isolated instances for specific reasons. In former revisions of the SAT, it is quite understandable why such extensive reliability studies were not attempted. But in the present day and age, extremely large scale digital computers are readily accessible, and such applicable statistical procedures as Hotelling's canonical correlation methods and Tucker's interbattery factor analysis systems are generally known. Hence, it is difficult for this reviewer to understand why the authors have gone to such elaborate pains in revising the SAT in so many other respects, yet have failed to provide the user with important reliability data that would have been relatively easy to obtain. Empirical validity data are completely lacking. Suggestion of content or curricular validity is made through the statement that the authors "sought to insure content validity by examining appropriate courses of study and textbooks as a basis for determining the skills, knowledges, understandings, etc., to be measured." No interbattery correlation matrix is given. These r's would be important to know, since they would give some suggestion of overlap among the tests. For some tests, it would be expected that the degree of overlap is considerable. Such information would be useful to teachers and others who might find it expedient to reduce the battery. On this point, the authors apparently are content to ignore the criticisms of previous reviewers. While the tests are most widely used for evaluation purposes, there are many occasions in which the SAT battery is used for prediction purposes. For example, achievement test scores are often used as substitutes for teachers' ratings, course grades, etc., in selecting students for special classes and programs. No empirical validities such as those based on correlations between the SATs and these criterion measures, either predictive or concurrent, are reported. Neither are there any concurrent validities given showing what the correlations are between the SATs and the comparable tests on competitive batteries, e.g., Metropolitan, Iowa, SCAT, and the like. Perhaps the authors of the SAT have good cause to believe that in studies of this kind their tests should be used as the criteria for establishing the concurrent validity of the others.

However, it would have been helpful to the user to have this kind of information available to him. Better still, the canonical correlation data between different test batteries, taken as a whole, would be useful. An important kind of evidence of validity woefully lacking for the Advanced Battery in particular is that which guidance counselors might find valuable. Because of the lack of such data in the Manual, the SAT has not been shown to have validity for curriculum guidance. Yet guidance counselors constantly use standardized achievement test scores among other predictors in counseling students concerning the selection of courses and major programs of study. The same comments made earlier with reference to reliability are appropriate here regarding the failure of the authors to take advantage of the current availability of computers and of multivariate analysis statistical techniques. It is realized that the authors probably could not have done all the studies implied in this critique, nor would they necessarily be expected to have done so. However, in view of the length of time the SAT battery has been so widely used and the high status it has enjoyed as an achievement battery, it is reasonable to expect the authors to have encouraged these studies among their users and have reported these results in the Manual as have the authors of the DAT. In summary, this reviewer finds that the SAT battery remains at the forefront of such batteries available to school personnel below the senior high school level and recommends their continued adoption and use. It is unfortunate, however, that the authors who are capable of doing so have failed in this rather elaborate revision to have made it unique among its competitors.

For a review by Miriam M. Bryan, see 6:26 (1 excerpt); for a review by N. L. Gage of an earlier edition, see 5:25; for reviews by Paul R. Hanna (with Claude E. Norcross) and Virgil E. Herrick, see 4:25; for reviews by Walter W. Cook and Ralph C. Preston, see 3:18. For reviews of subtests, see 209 (2 reviews), 527 (1 review), 708 (1 review), 802 (1 review), 895 (1 review), 5:656 (2 reviews), 5:698 (2 reviews), 5:799 (1 review), 4:419 (1 review), 4:555 (1 review), 4:593 (2 reviews), 3:503 (1 review), and 3:595 (1 review).

[26]

★Stanford Achievement Test: High School Arts and Humanities Test. Grades 9–12; 1965–66; cata-log uses the title *Stanford High School Arts and Humanities Test;* Forms W, X, ('65, 5 pages); no specific manual; battery manual ('65, 48 pages); supplementary directions ('66, 4 pages) for each type of answer sheet; separate answer sheets (IBM 805, IBM 1230) must be used; $8.20 per 35 tests; $2.30 per 35 IBM 805 answer sheets; $2.80 per 35 IBM 1230 answer sheets; 70¢ per scoring stencil; $1.20 per battery manual; $2 per specimen set; postage extra; scoring service, 19¢ and over per test; 40(45) minutes; Eric F. Gardner, Jack C. Merwin, Robert Callis, and Richard Madden; Harcourt Brace Jovanovich, Inc. *

ROBERT L. WRIGHT, *Professor of American Thought and Language and Comparative Literature, Michigan State University, East Lansing, Michigan.*

Described in the publisher's catalogue as "a test of knowledge and understanding in the areas of classical and contemporary literature, music, art, dramatics, and philosophy," the Arts and Humanities Test requires 40 minutes working time and consists, in both Forms W and X, of 65 items.

Items are all multiple choice, with four foils, the correct response involving the completion of a sentence begun in the stem. Differences in color and type faces are used unobtrusively to make reading the items easy. Directions for administering the test appear conventional; stencil keys for scoring are provided.

Various kinds of within-grade reliability coefficients are reported, ranging from .84 to .93 with median .90. The items appear to represent reasonable and progressive levels of difficulty; unfortunately, no information is available concerning the discrimination of individual items. Some slight question of equivalency of forms might be raised since Form X contains a brief reading passage, followed by four items of which two seem to be substantially dependent upon reading ability.

According to the content description of Form W, 22 items are devoted to literature, 14 to music, 13 to art and architecture, 7 to performing arts, 6 to philosophy and religion, and 3 to "miscellaneous" (apparently other general areas or cross-disciplinary material). Form X contains, in literature, 24 items; music, 14 items; art and architecture, 16 items; performing arts, 7 items; philosophy and religion, 4 items; miscellaneous, no items.

Subject classifications of this nature are, of course, imprecise and inherently arbitrary. For example, the reviewer through inspection determined that Form W was in no way inferior to Form X in number of items in literature, and, indeed, gave a balanced distribution of items in English, American, and world literature (Form X seemed to bulge toward American literature).

The test authors have used detractors to give the impression of wider coverage than is actually the case (i.e., mention of a black author, a Scandinavian play, a writer representative of a particular movement). Stems occasionally provide too many clues. The writers and works may very well represent many high school curricula; that is, there is a substantial mixture of major and minor writers and little attention is paid to genuinely contemporary literary developments.

These criticisms are minor ones, however; a major reservation about the Arts and Humanities Test must be that most items ask only for ability to connect a writer with a book, an artist with a painting, a composer with an opus. Perhaps so doing is inevitable for an examination faced with so herculean a task as is this one. Perhaps the correlation between possession of such information and actual understanding is more than minimal, although one must surely give priority to understanding.

No test reviewer has a right to reject some items that deal simply and absolutely with quite clear matters of identification, but he does have a right to expect more. It is no easy matter to answer the music or literature teacher who says, "I really don't understand about statistics, but I know the things I hope my students learn are not, on the whole, the things tested here."

To close on a positive note, this reviewer had no real objection to any of the answers listed as correct, found not one item which he would describe as outrageous. He would recommend eliminating those areas for which only a few items appear (performing arts, for instance, in which items may seem often to deal with the ephemeral and which may quickly be outdated), reconsideration of objectives (now somewhat vague), inclusion of more cross-disciplinary items, and greater emphasis on items which test understanding of significant material. Such a test could fill a very real void.

[27]

★Stanford Achievement Test: High School Basic Battery. Grades 9–12; 1965–66; 9 scores: English, numerical competence, mathematics (Part A, total), reading, science (Part A, total), social studies, spelling; subtests (English and spelling combined) available as separates; referred to as the High School Battery when 3 supplementary tests (arts and humanities,

business and economics, and technical comprehension) are included; Forms W, X, ('65, 36 pages); Form S, a secure form, is also available; manual ('65, 48 pages); supplementary directions ('66, 7–11 pages) for each type of answer sheet; profile ('66, 2 pages); separate answer sheets (Digitek, IBM 805, IBM 1230, MRC) must be used; Digitek or MRC answer sheets must be used with supplementary tests; $16.50 per 35 tests; $4.60 per 35 sets of IBM 805 answer sheets; $5.60 per 35 sets of Digitek or IBM 1230 answer sheets; $10 per 100 MRC answer sheets; 10¢ per profile; $1 per set of MRC hand scoring stencils; $2.80 per set of Digitek or IBM 1230 scoring stencils; $3.50 per set of IBM 805 scoring stencils; $1.20 per manual; $3 per specimen set; postage extra; MRC scoring service, 36¢ and over per test; IBM scoring service, $1.10 and over per test; 320(350) minutes in 6 sessions; Eric F. Gardner, Jack C. Merwin, Robert Callis, and Richard Madden; Harcourt Brace Jovanovich, Inc. *

GEORGIA S. ADAMS, *Professor of Education, California State College, Los Angeles, California.*

Although the *Stanford Achievement Tests* have been published in successive editions since 1922, it was not until 1965 that this first High School Battery was published.

The authors have succeeded in preparing test items which, although they cannot be tailor-made to suit any specific new curriculum, go well beyond strictly factual questions to require the student to show comprehension of concepts and principles. Moreover, during the process of test development, item analyses were conducted for students in new, as well as traditional, curricula.

Items appear to be consistently well designed. Easy items are rarely easy because of clues; difficult items are rarely difficult because of triviality or irrelevant sources of difficulty. Time limits have been set so as to make the test primarily a power test.

Although textbooks and courses of study were surveyed and teachers and subject matter specialists consulted, no evidence is presented concerning the extent of their agreement on such important decisions as having about 45 percent more items in physical science than in biological science. It is obvious that it would be a herculean task to write the content specifications in only one subject area, e.g., for an 86-item, 60-minute test to sample the total high school science curriculum. One would like to be assured, however, that a number of well-informed judges participated in making the decisions concerning the proportion of items for each of the major content categories; and it would be desirable to know the extent of agreement among judges.

A detailed content description is given for each form of each test except for the Spelling Test. Moreover, local data on percentage of success on each item can be compared with item difficulty values based on the total tryout population.

For a number of reasons, however, the item difficulty values are not as helpful in curriculum evaluation as one might assume. Item difficulties are based on the *total* tryout samples for each grade, but the numbers tested would seem to justify separate item norms for college preparatory students. For example, of what value are *item* norms on the advanced, or B, sections of Mathematics and Science when approximately half of the mathematics items and one-third of the science items are answered at the chance level of success by the students in the total tryout samples? A large percentage of these students would not have had any elective courses in those areas.

The tryout sample for each grade should have been described in terms of the percentage of students at each grade level who had taken advanced mathematics and science courses. As it is, if a high school scores above average on item norms in these areas, one cannot infer that the school is doing a superior job of instruction; it may just have a higher-than-average percentage of students enrolled in these elective subjects.

Another problem in the use of these potentially valuable item norms is that they were *not* obtained on the standardization sample, tested in February and March, but on the national tryout sample, tested in October. No data are given concerning the comparability of the national tryout and standardization samples. Although both groups are of impressive size, no claim is made concerning representativeness of the tryout sample. Even if it were representative, item difficulty values obtained in October would undoubtedly be different from those obtained in March.

Data on grade-to-grade increases in means are reported and presented graphically. The small increases in means from grade to grade, as well as the large amount of overlapping of grade level distributions, show that, despite the use of many approved psychometric techniques, it has been impossible to develop 40-minute tests which are sensitive indicators of growth in achievement from one grade level to another. When results are summarized in mathematics

and science for "special semester" groups, which include only students who have had continuous instruction in a subject since the ninth grade, grade-level differentiation is appreciably better.

Four estimates are given of the reliability of each test at each grade level; however, all estimates are obtained by internal consistency methods (split-halves and Kuder-Richardson). It is highly desirable that reliability coefficients be obtained which estimate reliability across forms and across testing occasions.

Of the 108 reliability coefficients shown for grades 10 through 12 for subtests of the Basic Battery, only one coefficient is below .85; and 75 coefficients are .90 or above. Coefficients for grade 9 tend to be slightly lower. In general, a difference of more than one stanine between scores on different tests would be considered statistically significant.

Since the users of achievement tests wish to compare individuals *within* a single school or school system, it is recommended practice to present reliability coefficients for a number of different schools or school systems separately. Reliability coefficients, means, and standard deviations are not shown for individual school systems; however, median values are shown for reliability coefficients computed within each of seven school systems. The reviewer would prefer to see at least the range of coefficients, in addition to the median.

The norming sample was large (22,699 students in 58 schools) and selected so as to be representative of nine geographic regions; "regional representation was further checked against two socioeconomic indices which have been demonstrated to be positively related to educational achievement."

No data are given concerning community size; apparently, no cities of over 100,000 population were included. A table in the manual indicates that the norming samples were somewhat above average in academic aptitude and consequently in achievement. The mean IQ's for the ninth and tenth grade norming samples are 105 and 107, respectively, while those for the eleventh and twelfth graders, where there would be more dropouts, are 109 and 111, respectively.

Separate norms have been prepared at each grade level for students taking college preparatory subjects; these students tend to average seven points higher in IQ than the total group.

The mean IQ's for "special semester" norm samples (i.e., for students having had continuous instruction in a subject since grade 9) increase from 111 in tenth grade to 120 in twelfth grade, for science, the corresponding means are 108 and 117. These differences in average IQ for norming samples must be taken into account in interpreting the norms for achievement.

The development of separate norms for total, college preparatory, and "special semester" groups is highly commendable. To be commended also is the use of a common standard score scale for all students in grades 9 to 12. Conversion may be made into percentile ranks and stanines. One advantage of using stanines is that the standard error of difference for each pair of tests approximates one stanine; because of the loss of information involved in the use of stanines, however, and of the greater reliability of differences for groups, standard scores or percentile ranks should certainly be used in interpreting results for schools or school systems.

The manual presents a special set of norm tables indicating whether a student is achieving in the first, second, third, or fourth quarter in comparison with those who have the same stanine score on the Otis (Gamma). These supplementary tables can be very helpful in counseling students who are planning to attend selective colleges. It is when one examines norms for this highest stanine group that one appreciates the high ceiling on these tests. For no total test is there a score difference of less than three points between the median and the third quartile for students scoring in the top four percent on mental ability.

The manual acknowledges the difficulties involved in helping the individual student interpret his gains in subtest scores from year to year. The authors call the user's attention to the fact that data are not available on the retesting of the same students. Since scores in successive years would be highly intercorrelated, regression effects would have to be taken into consideration in interpreting gains.

SUMMARY. This test represents a high level of skill in item writing and makes use of adequate samples in item analysis and standardization. The tests have a high ceiling and may prove most useful to high schools in which many students are aiming for entrance into the more selective colleges. The tests do not appear adequate for (a) use in curriculum evaluation (except as item norms are used), (b) measurement of intra-individual differences (except for upper-grade students in major fields), or (c) study of individual student gains from year to year. Inclusion of more items of moderate difficulty for ninth and tenth graders would improve the battery's usefulness for the first two purposes, while compilation of data on individual student gains would be helpful for the third.

The authors have aspired to serve many different purposes; in terms of the time limits associated with marketability, they have done a craftsmanlike job. Before the next edition is prepared, decisions should be made on which purposes are the primary ones, or, if the multipurpose feature is retained, the tests should be lengthened.

Additional data on reliability (across forms and testing occasions) should be provided. More information on the decision making processes used in content selection should be provided, as well as correlations with other widely used achievement batteries.

G. C. HELMSTADTER, *Director, University Testing Services, Arizona State University, Tempe, Arizona.*

CONTENT SAMPLING. The most crucial judgment in determining the adequacy of an achievement test for use in a particular situation relates to the content which the test samples. While no educator can expect any nationally published test to reflect precisely that subject matter covered in his own "tailor-made" classroom, he should expect a sufficiently accurate description of the content sampled so that he can tell where the test fits and where it doesn't. In this respect, the user will not be disappointed in the *Stanford Achievement Test: High School Basic Battery,* since the publishers have taken a great deal of time to carefully classify each of the items according to specific content. If only these items had been classified by the type of behavior required as well as the content, the description would be as complete as any expert would demand. In addition to the item description, the presentation of rotated factor loadings for each test for each of the four grade levels is also helpful. However, the table in which the loadings are presented would be a little more meaningful if some attempt had been made to verbally label the three factors found.

TECHNICAL QUALITY. The excellence which is found in the content sampling of this test battery is generally maintained with respect to other technical characteristics of the instrument. This reviewer was particularly impressed with the care taken in the development and tryout of the items and in the detailed procedures followed to insure adequate norms for a general high school population. The development of special norms for college preparatory students, as well as the presentation of information by sex and grade level, is to be commended.

The reliabilities reported are certainly adequate for this type of test, and the information about the relationship between scores on the *Otis Quick Scoring Mental Ability Test* and performance on the *Stanford Achievement Test* could be helpful to conscientious teachers. Unfortunately, much of the potential usefulness of this latter information has been lost because of the way it is presented. Data cast in the form of expectancy tables showing what performance on the Stanford battery may be anticipated from students having various Otis IQ's would indeed have provided some highly useful information not generally available for most current achievement test batteries.

The major disappointment to this reviewer with the technical quality of the instrument concerns the lack of validity data which are specifically relevant to important school decisions that might be improved if they were made in the light of the Stanford scores. While gathering validity data for some of the uses recommended in the manual may be difficult, this is the very direction test publishers must take if such instruments are to be continued as useful tools in modern education. Although it might be argued that such validity studies should be carried out at the local level, an example or two reported in the test manual would go a long way toward promoting the effective use of test scores to improve the quality of education for our children.

USABILITY. Perhaps the greatest deficiency of the battery is the way in which some of the information is presented in the manual. Because of this, some users will be faced with several slight inconveniences when using this document. The first of the difficulties results from the presentation of information for the three separate-booklet tests in the same section of the manual as the information for the basic battery tests which are published in a single booklet edition. This arrangement may cause some confusion among teachers and school administrators who are not completely familiar with the *Stanford Achievement Tests* and who therefore are not fully aware of which tests comprise the basic battery and which tests are complementary to it. The second minor inconvenience is more likely to be annoying to the more sophisticated users. This results from the presentation of means for various norm groups in one table on one page of the manual and presentation of the associated standard deviations in another table on a different page. Finally, the reviewer fails to see what is gained by requiring the user to go first from raw scores to standard scores and then, in a different table, to convert standard scores to stanines and percentile ranks, when a direct translation of the raw score to the derived score would be possible.

SUMMARY. The *Stanford Achievement Test: High School Basic Battery* seems to provide an excellent sample of school achievement items taken from a clearly defined content universe. In addition, the technical quality of the instrument is high and the general usability is above average. The potential user who finds that the test's content sample reflects those subject matter areas he is interested in will, in this reviewer's opinion, be hard pressed to find another achievement battery which would serve his purposes more effectively.

For reviews of subtests, see 26 (1 review), 208 (2 reviews), 488 (2 reviews), 489 (2 reviews), 633 (1 review), 707 (2 reviews), and 801 (2 reviews).

[28]

★Stanford Early School Achievement Test. Grades kgn–1, 1.0–1.5; 1969–70; SESAT; 5 or 7 scores: environment, mathematics, letters and sounds, aural comprehension, word reading (level 2 only), sentence reading (level 2 only), total; 2 levels; postage extra; Richard Madden and Eric F. Gardner; Harcourt Brace Jovanovich, Inc. *
a) LEVEL I. Kgn–1; 1969; 1 form (12 pages); manual (23 pages); practice sheet for demonstration; $9 per 35 tests; $1.10 per scoring key and practice sheet; $1.50 per specimen set; scoring service, $1.50 and over per test; (90) minutes in 5 sessions.
b) LEVEL 2. Grades 1.0–1.5; 1970; 1 form (23 pages); manual (30 pages); $12.25 per 35 tests; $1.25 per scoring key; $1.75 per specimen set; scoring service, $2.25 and over per test; (140) minutes in 7 sessions.

ELIZABETH HAGEN, *Professor of Psychology and Education, Teachers College, Columbia University, New York, New York.* [Review of Level 1.]

This test has been designed to appraise "the child's cognitive abilities....upon entrance into kindergarten, at the end of kindergarten, or upon entrance to the first grade." The test consists of four parts: Environment, Mathematics, Letters and Sounds, and Aural Comprehension. It yields five scores, one for each subtest plus a total score.

ITEMS. The Environment subtest is a general information test with items about equally distributed between the social and natural sciences. The items on the mathematics test stress quantitative concepts. The first 14 items of the Letters and Sounds test require the recognition of upper and lower case letters and the last 14 test "the auditory perception of beginning sounds." In the Aural Comprehension test, short narrative paragraphs are read to the examinees, who are required to answer questions that largely require inference or following a sequence. All of the items are pictorial. In general, the items are well constructed and the pictures are clear and mostly free of fussy detail. A few, but very few, of the items could be criticized for having a middle class bias; for example, item 1, Environment, which asks the examinee the better way to care for your shoes. One of the pictures shows shoes in a neat row, the other shows the shoes in a disorderly pile. In all of the subtests, the first response position tends to be underused; correct answers tend to appear equally in the middle or last response position. Underuse of the first response position for correct answers might have been intentional since the authors caution teachers to watch for students who are marking all the first options for an entire subtest.

ADMINISTRATION. Directions for administration are clear. A section in the manual gives specific instruction for overcoming common difficulties in testing beginning kindergarten children. The first page of the test, 14 items, is devoted to practice, and the manual is quite specific as to what the examiner should observe while the students are doing the practice page. The practice page contains all the sample items; none is given before each subtest. Since the authors recommend giving the test in five settings, one or two practice items should probably be added in each of the last three tests. The additional sample items would probably be particularly helpful if the parts of the test were given on different days.

VALIDITY. The validity of SESAT is difficult to assess. The authors give no specific information about procedures used to determine the content of the test. The second paragraph under the rationale for the test implies that the content of kindergarten programs has influenced the content of the test, but no specific information is given about the sources used to make these decisions. In the third paragraph of the same section of the manual, there is an implication that the test is designed to assess the general experience background of the child when he enters kindergarten, but again no evidence is presented for this purpose. One might point out that authors of tests designed for this type of assessment rarely, if ever, give evidence on the validity of the test, so the authors of SESAT should not be too harshly criticized for following the cultural pattern.

RELIABILITY. Split-half reliability coefficients and intercorrelations of the five scores are given for the beginning of kindergarten and the beginning of first grade. No data are presented for the end of kindergarten. At the beginning of kindergarten the reliabilities range from .76 for scores on Aural Comprehension to .85 for scores on Environment. The other two subtests have reliabilities of .79. At the beginning of grade 1, the reliabilities are .77 for Aural Comprehension, .82 for Environment and for Mathematics, and .89 for Letters and Sounds. Each of the subtests appears to be a little too easy for beginning grade 1 students and a little too hard for beginning kindergarten students. Table 11, page 21 of the manual, gives proportions of correct responses, not percents.

That the intercorrelations among the part scores tend to be high makes one question the extent to which the different subtests are appraising different abilities. Except for the Letters and Sounds subtest, which has the lowest correlations with the other tests at both levels, the reliabilities of the differences between scores on the other subtests at the beginning of kindergarten are between .30 and .40 and at the beginning of the first grade they are between .20 and .30. Any user of the test should be extremely cautious in interpreting differences among scores on three of the four subtests. The authors do caution the user about over-interpretation of profile differences but the cautions are probably not strong enough. At the beginning of the first grade, three of the subtests—Environment, Mathematics, and Aural Comprehension—as well as the total score have substantial correlations (.65, .71, .65, respectively) with the total score on the *Otis-Lennon Mental Ability Test*.

NORMS. Stanine and percentile norms are given for beginning kindergarten and beginning first grade. The authors state that "beginning of the year norms are based on tests administered in the fall of 1968, and the end of kindergarten norms are based on tests administered in the spring of 1969." However, no end-of-kindergarten norms or any other data for this level are presented in the manual. The normative sample is described adequately and the standardization program appears to have been done carefully.

INTERPRETATIONS. The authors appear to have intended the test results to be used to plan instruction for individual students or groups of students. The manual includes a section advising a cautious interpretation of an individual's score. It also includes interpretations of four sample profiles. Some of the statements in these interpretations do not seem to be justified on the basis of the information supplied by the test. In the interpretation of the profile of Harold J, who had a stanine score of 7 on Environment, 2 on Mathematics, 3 on Letters and Sounds, 5 on Aural Comprehension, and 4 on Total score, the statement is made that "he is a very capable child." It is difficult to see how this inference was arrived at on the basis of the profile. On the other hand, Susan R, grade 1.1, who had stanine scores of 4 on Environment, 6 on Mathematics, 8 on Letters and Sounds, 4 on Aural Comprehension and 5 on Total, is described as "an average child who is being 'pushed' in Mathematics and in Letters and Sounds." Again, it is difficult to determine how these inferences were made from the profile, particularly since scores on the Mathematics test correlate .71 with total score on the *Otis-Lennon Mental Ability Test*. For Jeffrey B, who had a stanine score of 3 on the Aural Comprehension Test, the question is raised as to whether his hearing is good. Since the student received stanines of 7, 6, and 5 on other tests, all of which are presented orally, the question does not seem to be very pertinent. This section is the weakest section in the manual. Only the interpretation for Linda V appears to be relevant to the profile and to avoid encouraging unjustified inference.

The section on Analysis of the Class demonstrates how a teacher can organize the test data so that he can see more clearly the strengths and weaknesses of the class and the individuals who are potential candidates for subgroups for instructional purposes. This section is very well done.

Suggestions for instruction are given in each of the areas covered. Although most of the suggestions are rather general, no one is likely to take exception to them. In the section on suggestions to improve Aural Comprehension, the authors state, "It is quite conceivable that the test will predict third- or fourth-grade achievement better than kindergarten or first-grade achievement in reading or other subjects." The authors should present some evidence to support the statement.

SUMMARY. The SESAT is a well constructed test with moderate reliability; it can be used by schools to assess their kindergarten program if the objectives and content of their program are similar to those appraised by the test. The authors specifically state that SESAT is not a "readiness test"; however, if a first-grade program is based on the assumption that students have mastered the skills appraised by SESAT, then the results of the test might be useful in determining whether children should be placed in the first-grade program.

WILLIAM A. MEHRENS, *Professor of Education, Michigan State University, East Lansing, Michigan.* [Review of Level 1.]

SESAT is "designed to provide a measure of the child's cognitive abilities" but "does not assume a prescribed kindergarten program." The authors state that the results of this test will help establish a baseline so that teachers will know at what level to begin their instructional experiences.

GENERAL DESCRIPTION. The four subtests consist of 42, 28, 28, and 28 items, respectively. Each item shows a series of from two to five pictures (or numbers, letters, or designs) enclosed in a box. Under each picture is a circle and the student is to mark the circle under the picture that answers a question read aloud by the examiner. The Environment questions are taken from both the "social and natural environments." The Mathematics items measure such concepts as the following: "conservation of number, space and volume; counting; measurement; numeration, classification, simple operations;" and a few basic algorithms. The Letters and Sounds items measure two types of skills: (*a*) "the ability to recognize upper and lower case letters" (e.g., "mark under the letter y"), and (*b*) "the auditory perception of beginning sounds" (e.g., "mark under the [picture] that starts with the same sound as gate"). The Aural Comprehension items also are composed of two conceptually different types of tasks. For half of them a short story is read, a question is asked and then the story is repeated. For the other 14 items, the story is read only once and thus more memory on the part of the examinee is required. Both of these latter two tests should have been subdivided to provide part scores.

FORMAT AND ADMINISTRATION. The format of the test booklets is very good. The directions to the children are clear and few pupils, if any, should have trouble understanding the tasks. Two minor problems, however, do exist with respect to administering the test. It is to be given in three to five different sittings (normally five), but nowhere does the manual suggest a length of time between sittings. Is a 15-minute break enough, or should there be only one sitting a day? A second potential problem, and one common to many tests at this level, is in the teacher's reading of the test. We are all aware that teachers might give cues to the correct answer by some conscious or unconscious voice inflection. But in addition to the problem of cues, there is simply the problem of lack of standardization in diction. If a teacher has trouble differentiating the pronunciation of *b*, *p*, and *d*, for example, her students are handicapped on the Letters and Sounds subtest. One wonders why more standardized tests do not follow the lead of National Assessment and tape their directions. The expense of cutting tapes would be more than offset by the increased standardization.

ITEM QUALITY. No real data are provided regarding the original item analysis program used to select the items. We are told that two forms of an early edition were given and "the best items were then selected from those forms." More information regarding what qualities were assessed in choosing the "best" items and how good those best items were with respect to those qualities seems warranted. On the plus side, item difficulties are included in the manual. In general the questions seem to be well written. They appear to have both face and content validity.

NORMS. The manual itself presents only beginning-of-kindergarten norms (based on 8,310 pupils) and beginning of grade 1 norms (based on 11,106 pupils). End-of-kindergarten norms are available in multilith form. Both stanines and percentiles are provided. The norm tables suggest a few problems, but none serious, with respect to ceiling and floor effects. For example, a chance score on the Letters and Sounds subtest would place a kindergarten child at the 30th percentile. A perfect score would place a first grader at the 92nd percentile. There are no separate norms by sex. Separate norms for the two subtests within Parts 3 and 4 might have provided some useful information (this is related to my comment that separate subscores on these parts would have been useful).

RELIABILITY AND VALIDITY. Split-half reliabilities range from .76 to .85. The intercorrelations among part and total scores range from .53 to .90. For grade 1, correlations between the part and total scores and the *Otis-Lennon Mental Ability Test* are provided. The total score correlates .74 with the Otis-Lennon. The Mathematics subtest gives the next highest correlation with the Otis-Lennon (.71). Appropriate cautions about the "variability in measurement" are provided in the manual.

INTERPRETATION. Four different individual profile charts are illustrated in the manual and are accompanied by brief analyses of the performance. I felt these guides for interpretation left much to be desired. They somehow create the impression that the authors are interpreting the Environment section as measuring aptitude and the Mathematics and Letters & Sounds sections as measuring achievement. Harold, who receives a stanine of 7 on Environment, a 2 on Mathematics, and a 3 on Letters & Sounds is described as "a very capable child." Susan, who receives a stanine of 4 in Environment, a 6 in Mathematics, and an 8 in Letters & Sounds is described as "an average child who is being 'pushed' in Mathematics and in Letters and Sounds." These interpretations, in my mind, are unjustified—especially when one recalls that the Mathematics subtest correlates higher than the Environment subtest with the Otis-Lennon.

SUMMARY. The SESAT is a needed type of instrument. Data from such an instrument should be potentially useful in instructing students. The format, directions, and items themselves are generally good. Norm data are minimal but sufficient. Reliability data are average.

The biggest weakness, which this test shares with many others, is that teachers will not understand how to interpret and use the data. In this era of the "doubting Thomas" teacher regarding the usefulness of test data, authors need to give greater attention in their manuals to just how the data can be used.

[29]

★Survey of College Achievement. Grades 13–14; 1966–69; SCA; for institutional research use only; 5 scores: English composition, mathematics, social sciences and history, humanities, natural sciences; Forms ORP1, ORP2, ('66, 20 pages); supervisor's manual ('69, 21 pages); preliminary technical manual ('69, 35 pages); prospectus ('68, 12 pages); institutional norms based upon earlier edition; separate answer sheets (SCRIBE) must be used; examination fee (includes scoring service), $1.10 per student ($50 minimum); postage extra; 75(85) minutes; Educational Testing Service. *

PAUL L. DRESSEL, *Assistant Provost and Director, Institutional Research, Michigan State University, East Lansing, Michigan.*

This test is intended to be a measure of group achievement covering the first two years of college. It is provided in alternate forms, each one of which is divided into the following sections: English composition, 20 items; humanities, 19 items; mathematics, 15 items; natural sciences, 20 items; social sciences-history, 20 items. Each part is allowed 15 minutes for a total of 75 minutes of testing. The objectives to which the items are oriented are stated as: (*a*) knowledge of facts and concepts; (*b*) ability to perceive relationships; and (*c*) understanding of basic principles, all in the liberal arts. The instrument is designed for research. It should not, according to the technical manual, "be used in admissions, placement, selection of transfer students, or in any other individual evaluation." Summary statistics are reported for the total group and for non-overlapping subgroups. The items have been carefully chosen on the basis of statistical considerations, and they appear to be sampling the usual type of material, knowledges, and skills that are involved in such general or liberal education survey testing instruments. As is usual with the nature of these tests and the selection procedures involved, the SCA places a great deal of emphasis on knowledge of facts and concepts, but there definitely are items that involve something beyond this in the way of perception, relationships, and understanding.

TECHNICAL CONSIDERATIONS. The scores on the two forms are equated, with a mean of 50

and a standard deviation of 10. None of the raw score means on any of the subtests is as high as the middle difficulty value, and hence the tests may be thought of as somewhat difficult. The reported K-R reliabilities vary from .67 to .77 on Form 1, with humanities the lowest and English composition the highest, and from .57 to .73 on Form 2, with humanities again being the lowest and with social sciences-history being the highest. The correlations between forms vary from .53 to .67, figures which approximate the reliability figures indicating that the two forms are fairly well matched. For Form 1, the intercorrelations among the test scores range from .43 (mathematics and humanities) to .62 (natural sciences and social sciences-history and also natural sciences and mathematics). The intercorrelation of .62 between the natural sciences subtest and the social sciences-history subtest is a somewhat interesting phenomenon considering that the correlations between the same subtest scores in the two forms are of about that same order. The standard error of measurement of the mean of subtest scores is reported as only about one scale point even when the mean was based on as few as 25 students.

The norms are based upon 2,600 second semester sophomores and about the same number of second semester freshmen. The colleges and universities were selected with the probability of inclusion proportional to size within the various geographical areas of the country. With this approach, it gives each student rather than each institution an equal chance of being chosen. These norms are organized in such a way that an institution can obtain norms for men or women on each of the scores, and also summary statistics on institutional means, standard deviations, and the like. Profile charts also provide an illuminating way of exhibiting the data.

Recalling that the SCA is prepared for a group rather than individual utilization, the data provided suggest that it is adequate to the purpose.

RESEARCH APPLICATIONS. The manual suggests a number of studies which may be made using the SCA. Such matters as the achievement of the freshman class in comparison with normative subgroups or the comparison of subgroups within the freshman class, the growth or change in achievement of a student group with various subgroups by sex, major field, aptitude, grade-point averages, comparison with other factors, such as attitudes, are perhaps the more standard types of projects that institutions might think about. In addition to this, the manual indicates that the test might be used in delineating needs for curricular reform by considering the need for remedial programs, the elimination of certain courses, or the advanced placement of students. It is also suggested that the instrument might be used in comparing student achievement by major fields or in evaluating new programs. The test is also intended for use as a control variable in connection with a variety of studies, such as evaluation of teaching or in connection with the use of other instruments in the Institutional Research Program.

Because this instrument is a confidential one, the scoring and reporting are done by ETS. Individual scores and college summary information, including means and standard deviations, are provided by groups and for the total. In view of the fact that it is repeatedly emphasized that this test should be used only for group survey purposes, one may wonder whether it is wise to report the individual scores.

SUMMARY. A brief test of the type of the SCA is a very useful instrument in studies where an estimate of *group* achievement is needed to fulfill the research design. The SCA, both statistically and content-wise, is admirably suited to this usage.

H. Bradley Sagen, *Associate Professor of Education, The University of Iowa, Iowa City, Iowa.*

Despite the many exhortations about self-study and institutional evaluation there exist few standardized instruments which are brief enough to be included in a broad evaluation battery, which are convenient to administer, and which provide both comparative and diagnostic data for institutions engaged in self-study. To meet this need the Educational Testing Service has developed the Institutional Research Program for Higher Education. The four instruments comprising the program at present assess student attitudes (CSQ), the psychological environment of the campus (CUES), perceptions of institutional programs and policies (IFI), and group academic achievement.

The achievement measure, the *Survey of College Achievement,* is a relatively short research instrument which consists of five, 15-minute tests covering mathematics, English composi-

tion, humanities, natural sciences, and social sciences and history. According to the prospectus, the subject matter is similar to courses in the first two years of college and includes "knowledge of facts and concepts," "ability to perceive relationships" and "understanding of basic principles in the liberal arts." The test is published in two forms.

The tests are short forms of quite traditional achievement measures. English composition assesses grammatical usage and style. Mathematics, although the most difficult of the tests, contains only content taught in most secondary schools (general mathematics to analytic geometry).

Although each user must judge the appropriateness of the test items, some observations can be made regarding the subtests Social Sciences and History, Natural Sciences, and Humanities: (a) The items generally focus upon specific disciplines instead of tapping broader interdisciplinary perspectives. (b) About one-half of the items in each test require only the recall of facts and concepts. Those items which demand higher cognitive skills tend also to require specific information to reach the correct answer. (c) Although the tests emphasize those disciplines typically comprising general education programs, the balance among disciplines is sometimes uneven; e.g., one form of Humanities contains twice as many items from sculpture as from music; Social Sciences and History is heavily oriented toward history and government, but contains no items from sociology. While these properties are acceptable in an initial probe of institutional strengths and weaknesses, the test characteristics do not support generally the ETS suggestion that the test can be used to assess the impact of specific curricula.

The content of the several tests appears difficult for the student population now enrolled in less selective institutions. For example, the average mathematics raw score was less than one-half of the items and included negative scores for some students. (A correction for guessing formula is employed.)

With samples of over 100, the modified K-R 20 reliabilities ranging from .57 to .77 and the parallel form coefficients ranging from .53 to .67 should be adequate for assessment of group performance. Unless unusually large samples are available, however, such reliabilities are inadequate to assess changes in student achievement over time.

The norms, which consist of a distribution of institutional means obtained from a national sample, are appropriate for gross comparisons of student performance, although as the publisher notes, care should be taken not to interpret the relative standing on freshman and sophomore norms as an indication of institutional change.

The research services are well designed for general programs of self-study and evaluation. The SCA format and output are compatible with the other instruments in the ETS Institutional Research Program. Data are provided in both printout and punch-card form and provision is made for subgroups.

To summarize, as a short, broadly conceived measure of group academic achievement, the SCA fills a void in the institutional evaluation field. The major uses of the SCA appear to be as a quality control measure and as an initial diagnostic tool for evaluating institutional strengths and weaknesses. This reviewer is skeptical, however, of the SCA's potential to evaluate the impact of specific curricula or to ascertain changes in student performance over time.

[30]

★Test of Reading and Number: Inter-American Series. Grade 4 entrants; 1969; TRN; experimental form; 3 scores: reading, number, total; parallel editions in English and Spanish; English Form DE (13 pages); Spanish Form DEs (13 pages); English, Spanish, directions ['69, 4 pages]; no data on reliability and validity; no norms, publisher recommends use of local norms; separate answer sheets (IBM 805, IBM 1230) must be used; 10 or more tests, 16¢ each; $4 per 100 answer sheets; 10¢ per scoring stencil; 50¢ per specimen set; postage extra; 34(44) minutes; Herschel T. Manuel; Guidance Testing Associates. *

[31]

★Tests of Academic Progress. Grades 9-12; 1964-66; TAP; 7 scores: social studies, composition, science, reading, mathematics, literature, total; Forms 1, 2, ('64, 94 pages); 4 levels (grades 9, 10, 11, 12) in a single booklet; subtests available as separates; teacher's manual ('64, 62 pages); manual for administrators, supervisors, and counselors ('65, 45 pages); norms booklet for IQ levels ('66, 26 pages); student report folder ('64, 4 pages); profile ('64, 1 page); separate answer sheets (Digitek, IBM 805, IBM 1230, MRC) must be used; $1.14 per test; $42 per 250 sets of 2 Digitek answer sheets; $14.40 per 100 sets of 3 IBM 805 answer sheets; $17.10 per 100 sets of 3 IBM 1230 answer sheets; preceding answer sheets cover all levels; $8.55 per 100 MRC answer sheets for a given grade level; $3.60 per set of IBM scoring stencils; $2.40 per set of MRC hand scoring stencils; Digitek keys not available; $1.50 per 35 student report folders; $1.50 per 35 profiles; $1.20 per teacher's manual; 96¢ per manual for administrators, supervisors, and coun-

selors; 60¢ per norms booklet for IQ levels; $3 per specimen set; postage extra; MRC scoring service, 36¢ and over per test; 330(370) minutes in 3 sessions; Dale P. Scannell, Oscar M. Haugh (composition and literature), Alvin H. Schild (social studies), William B. Reiner (science), Henry P. Smith (reading), and Gilbert Ulmer (mathematics); Houghton Mifflin Co. *

C. M. LINDVALL, *Professor of Education, Learning Research and Development Center, University of Pittsburgh, Pittsburgh, Pennsylvania.*

The *Tests of Academic Progress,* an achievement battery for use in grades 9-12, includes subtests in social studies, composition, science, reading, mathematics, and literature. All subtests are contained in a single 94-page test booklet. Within each test there is an overlapping of test items between successive grades so that, for example, grade 9 students will use items 1 to 65, grade 10 will use 21 to 85, grade 11, 46 to 110, and grade 12, 66 to 130. Persons familiar with the *Iowa Tests of Basic Skills* will see this, and many other aspects of the format of the TAP, as being essentially identical with those of the ITBS. This is hardly surprising, since both are produced by the same publisher and have certain other things in common, including a joint standardization program and the availability of MRC scoring service.

The TAP uses the multiple choice item form throughout the test and format appears to be quite good for high school students. The authors seem to have been successful in developing items that test a variety of cognitive abilities. An examination of items, using the categories of the Bloom taxonomy, indicates that all subtests except social studies have substantial numbers of items measuring such higher order abilities as interpretation, comprehension, evaluation, and the application of principles and procedures. The social studies test probably has too large a proportion of items measuring knowledge only.

The teacher's manual for the tests is quite clear and complete and an experienced teacher should have no difficulty in administering the tests. Although most schools will likely use the publisher's scoring service, detailed instructions are given for hand scoring. Norms provided for the tests are limited to standard scores and percentile ranks. Percentile ranks are provided for each grade for fall, midyear, and spring testing. In addition, norms for school averages are available.

Anyone attempting to produce an achievement test battery for the secondary school is faced with the problem of how to produce one set of tests that is valid and useful for students taking a great variety of specialized programs. For example, a mathematics test must have validity for use with students whose high school math consists of only a general mathematics course taken in the ninth grade and also with those taking four years of math, including calculus and other advanced topics. The authors of the TAP have elected to address their testing to six "basic skill" content areas. In each area they appear to have attempted to base items largely on the abilities that would be developed in relatively basic courses and to do little with the content of advanced courses. However, it is no doubt true that a pupil's command of basic abilities in a given skill area is increased by further work in advanced areas. For this reason, persons using the TAP will find it important to temper their appraisal of a pupil's performance on a given subtest by considering the courses he has taken in this area. The authors and publishers would undoubtedly endorse this common sense injunction. However, it may be useful for producers of tests such as this to place a special emphasis on this type of warning. Pupils, and their parents, who have had experience with elementary school test batteries on which the basic skills tested are those for which all pupils have had equivalent course preparation, are likely to interpret results from these high school tests the same as results from the earlier tests. This is a danger to be avoided. However, it should be noted that a battery such as the TAP, in which each subtest is associated with a specific content area, lends itself much better to a diagnosis of the extent to which pupil performance is in keeping with amount of course work taken than does a test of "general development." This feature of this type of test also should mean that it has more direct implications for decisions as to where additional courses should be taken.

VALIDITY. As with any achievement test, the task of determining the validity of the *Tests of Academic Progress* is one that must be assumed by the test user in terms of his particular plans for using results and in terms of the specific abilities he wishes to measure. The manuals for this test provide little information on validity. However, for each subtest, the teacher's manual provides a rather extensive breakdown of the content covered by the items. This includes a

logically organized subject outline and an associated key for relating each test item to some specific element in the outline.

It is unfortunate that all of the subtests have not been analyzed in terms of both content and type of skill measured, as have the science and reading tests. The analyses of the other four tests, even in those cases where two types of outlines are provided, are, in the reviewer's judgment, restricted to an identification of the content covered. Of course, this type of outline cannot be the teacher's sole resource in determining whether or not a test measures what he wishes to have measured. Only an analysis of the items can do this. However, the outlines may be useful as a supplementary source of guidance in the necessary item-by-item skill and content analysis.

RELIABILITY. Split-test reliability coefficients and the standard error of measurement for each subtest at each grade level are provided. The reported coefficients are reasonably good, most being in the high .80's or low .90's. However, it should be noted that these data are only for Form 1 of the tests. The manual does include the warning that if an equivalent forms procedure with a time interval between testings had been used, the reliability coefficients probably would have been somewhat lower. It is hoped that in the near future the manual will provide the user with reliability data obtained through this equivalent forms procedure so that stability estimates will be available.

STANDARDIZATION. Normative data for the TAP were obtained from a coordinated standardization program which also involved the *Iowa Tests of Basic Skills* and the *Lorge-Thorndike Intelligence Tests*. Careful procedures were followed to see that the sample used in establishing norms was indeed representative of public and parochial school pupils in the nation. All of the standardization procedures followed appear to be equal to those used by other major test publishers in their larger test batteries.

SUGGESTED USES. The suggestions for using results from the TAP are rather typical of those found with most widely-used achievement batteries. It is likely that the conscientious teacher could find the tests quite valuable for certain types of student counseling and for the evaluation of curricula and instruction. The detailed suggestions provided for each subtest, if used with care and judgment, could make these tests an excellent aid in curriculum analysis and evaluation. This reviewer, however, notes with less enthusiasm that the manual includes the somewhat typical suggestion that the test data can be used "to individualize instruction." Obviously, a case can be made for this being a possibility. However, if published tests are ever going to serve this purpose for any significant number of teachers, important changes in test organization and in scoring procedures must be introduced. Tests will have to be made to yield scores that have clear-cut implications for instructional placement and treatment. Until achievement tests are built to yield criterion-referenced scores (instead of, or as a supplement to, currently used norm-referenced scores) and are specifically related to instructional sequences and suggested treatments, there is little likelihood that many teachers will be able to use them for individualizing instruction. It is to be hoped that a next step for producers of tests such as the TAP will be to provide teachers with such instruments.

SUMMARY. The *Tests of Academic Progress* represent a fine example of most of the best features of the current "state of the art" in achievement test batteries. Few better tests will be found in terms of general format, scoring procedures, adequacy of normative data, reliability, and accompanying instructions for administration and use. If used with care and judgment, these instruments could prove quite valuable in counseling and as an aid in assessing the academic program of a secondary school.

For reviews of subtests, see 210 (2 reviews), 225 (3 reviews), 491 (2 reviews), 710 (1 review), 805 (1 review), and 896 (1 review).

[32]

*Tests of Adult Basic Education. Adults at reading levels of children in grades 2-4, 4-6, 7-9; 1967, c1957-67; TABE; except for very minor changes, the tests are identical with the 1957 *California Achievement Tests* for grades 2-4, 4-6, and 7-9; 3 levels plus locator test; profile ('67, 2 pages); no data on reliability; no norms for adults (the grade norms presented are identical to the 1963 school-based norms for the *California Achievement Tests*); $1 per 25 profiles, postage extra; $3.60 per specimen set (including *d* below), postpaid; CTB/McGraw-Hill. *
a) LEVEL E. Adults at reading levels of children in grades 2-4; except for very minor changes, the tests are identical with the 1957 *California Achievement Tests* for grades 2-4; 6 scores: reading (vocabulary, comprehension, total), arithmetic (reasoning, fundamentals, total); Forms 1, 2, ('67, 22 pages); preliminary manual ('67, 19 pages); $6 per 25 tests; scoring service, 70¢ and over per test; 94(120) minutes in 2 sessions.

b) LEVEL M. Adults at reading levels of children in grades 4-6; except for very minor changes, the tests are identical with the 1957 *California Achievement Tests* for grades 4-6; 10 scores: same as for Level E plus language (mechanics, spelling, total), total; Forms 1 ('67, 30 pages), 2 ('67, 31 pages); preliminary manual ('67, 44 pages); $7.40 per 25 tests; 90¢ per set of keys; separate answer sheets (IBM 1230, Scoreze) must be used; $1.25 per 25 IBM answer sheets; $2.50 per 25 Scoreze answer sheets; $2.25 per set of IBM hand scoring stencils; IBM scoring service, 32¢ and over per test; 158(180) minutes in 3 sessions.
c) LEVEL D. Adults at reading levels of children in grades 7-9; except for very minor changes, the tests are identical with the 1957 *California Achievement Tests* for grades 7-9; 10 scores: same as for Level M; Forms 1, 2, ('67, 35 pages); preliminary manual ('67, 44 pages); answer sheets and prices same as for Level M; 176(200) minutes in 3 sessions.
d) PRACTICE EXERCISES AND LOCATOR TEST. 1967; for determining level of test to be administered; 1 form (6 pages); preliminary manual (10 pages); separate answer sheets (IBM 1230) may be used; $2.50 per 25 tests; 10¢ per key; $1.25 per 25 answer sheets; 75¢ per hand scoring stencil; (30) minutes.

A. N. HIERONYMUS, *Professor of Education and Psychology, The University of Iowa, Iowa City, Iowa.*

In each of the manuals for this test, it is stated, *"The Tests of Adult Basic Education* were developed to meet a growing need for instruments especially designed to measure adult achievement." Yet except for a very few relatively minor changes in some of the tests, this is not a specially designed instrument, but rather a repackaging of the 1957 edition of the *California Achievement Tests* with new covers and a new name. It is a battery which was originally designed for a population of elementary school children "to measure many of the most universal subject-matter objectives of the curriculum." It is now being marketed for use with adults in various educational and training programs with stated purposes of: (*a*) "obtaining pre-instructional information about an adult's status in the three basic skills areas of reading, arithmetic, and language"; (*b*) "identifying areas of weakness"; (*c*) "measuring an adult's growth"; (*d*) "involving the individual in the analysis and appraisal of his learning difficulties"; and (*e*) "assisting the teacher in preparing a remedial program for each individual, adapted to his special needs."

The two alternate forms should be regarded as paraphrased forms rather than equivalent forms. For most tests each item on Form 1 has a very similar item counterpart on Form 2, and frequently the items are identical. The rationale for this method of constructing alternate forms was discussed in the CAT Technical Manual but is not in the TABE manuals. Not only are the same keys used for both forms, but also the same tables for converting raw scores into grade scores are used. It was claimed that alternate forms of the *California Achievement Tests* were built of items "sensitively equated, resulting in the need for only one set of normative data at any one level." It seems to be tacitly assumed that the original equating still applies many years later with a different population and tests which have been at least minimally revised.

There is a very ingeniously designed three-sheet folder which contains 17 practice exercises to acquaint students with test-taking procedures and the use of a separate answer sheet, and a locator test of 50 vocabulary items (opposites) which is used to assist in the assignment of pupils to one of the three test levels. Considerable reading skill seems to be required in both the practice exercises and the locator test. No research or rationale is reported for the table which is used to "convert" raw scores to recommended levels.

The reading test consists of three sections: following written directions, finding information, and understanding what is read. The first has an academic flavor, is somewhat abstract, and probably would not appeal to adults as testing something important. The second has short sections on use of table of contents, use of index, interpreting a graph, map reading, and alphabetization. For the most part the items appear to measure rather simple objectives and require a minimum of understanding or application. This also appears to be true of the last section, which involves the interpretation of connected discourse.

The arithmetic test has three sections. The first is a concepts test of limited scope. The second is a test of word problems. The last is a computation test which appears to be very competently assembled.

The language test consists of sections on capitalization, punctuation, usage, and spelling. The other widely used adult batteries do not include tests of language mechanics.

There is a minimum of information to help the user interpret scores. There are no norms other than grade-equivalent scores which are based on the 1963 standardization of the 1957 *California Achievement Tests*. There are no reliability data, and, other than a brief presenta-

tion of the rationale for the battery, there is no discussion of validity.

On the Scoreze answer sheets and on the reverse side of the Profile Sheet is an "Analysis of Learning Difficulties," in which the user is encouraged to interpret raw scores derived from small groups of items—scores that are not reliable or unique enough to merit providing norms or reliability data. For example, for Level M, reference skills, four such scores are determined as follows: parts of a book (4 items), reading graphs (5), alphabetizing and use of index (5), and reading maps (6). Such scores are completely meaningless to this reviewer. Even for those who are seeking methods of developing content-referenced norms, the reference behavior for these raw scores is extremely vague. The authors discuss the reliability issue in a footnote in the CAT manual but give neither discussion nor caution in the TABE manuals. By contrast the authors of ABLE warn against the use of any such part scores derived from their battery for individual diagnosis.

The advantage of this battery over its competitors is the inclusion of a language mechanics test. The subject-matter content of the tests does not appear to be any more or less appropriate for adults than that of most other batteries developed for use in elementary schools. Whereas a tremendous quantity of data for the parent test was assembled on elementary school pupils, no research or experience is reported on the use of this adaptation with adult groups. Until such data are provided, the usefulness of the tests in adult programs must be determined through experience at the local level.

J Counsel Psychol 16(3):281-2 My '69. S. Alan Cohen. With all its inadequacies this battery may prove to be a useful tool for psychometricians and educators faced with populations of adult semiliterates, especially in a test market that has little else to offer for this population. * Tests of Adult Basic Education are a series of adult achievement tests in reading, arithmetic, and language on three levels, Level D (difficult), Level M (medium), Level E (easy). Each level has two alternate forms. In addition, a Locator test, that can be administered to 30 *S*s and scored in less than an hour, provides a short vocabulary test to determine the appropriate TABE level for each individual. The Locator test is also meant to provide test-taking training in using IBM answer sheets—a most useful provision that *might* reduce the effects of diverse cultural background and increase test reliability. However, since the battery was developed and published without reliability coefficients, the California Test Bureau (CTB) cannot report to what extent this "test preparation" technique works. * TABE is a collection of test items found in the California Achievement Tests (CAT) battery from primary through high school—adult. The items have been slightly revised to eliminate childish references, and a new adult format has been designed. Those familiar with the CAT instructions will probably agree that group administered California tests have about the easiest administration instructions of all standardized tests of this kind. * TABE's validity is said to be "inherited" from the CAT, since TABE is merely a collection of selected items slightly revised from the entire CAT battery. CAT was designed to measure school-learned academic behaviors. As such, the TABE Level D (difficult) items might be appropriate for adults moving into traditional community college curriculums. But Level D's validity can still be questioned on other grounds. The TABE has drawn its test items from at least three and possibly four different levels of the original CAT, has put this conglomeration into a new format and, furthermore, has rewritten these items in adult language. Can the validity, therefore, really be "inherited" from the previous CAT test battery? For Levels M, and especially E, content validity is highly questionable. What kinds of behavior should a test of literacy for disadvantaged, semiliterate, and illiterate adults tap? Should it assess the same things as are measured in middle-class elementary school children? It is doubtful. If a literacy test were to be designed for this population, one would want to perform behavioral analyses of the real life literacy demands of the job world or the adult education projects for this *level S*s. It certainly should not be assumed that such items as: "The index of a book is found in the ...." or that paragraphs about goats, farms, and birds in the park are real life literacy demands for this population. There is no reliability evidence to report. Given the change of format from the CAT, the rewriting of CAT items, the use of a practice test not present in the CAT, the usual low reliability coefficients for standardized tests when they are administered to disadvantaged populations, the use of an "inherited" reliability construct is impossible to accept in this case. CTB recognizes this and reports that reliability studies are under way. To publish a test without reliability coefficients, and, without compunction, announce that reliability testing is to come *after the fact* is totally indefensible. Is it so naive to assume that test reliability is relevant to sound standardized test construction? Can it be assumed that CTB will pull TABE off the market if the reliability coefficients are too low? * Why are the norms reported in grade levels? Because, says the manual, instructional materials are classified by grade level, and one major purpose of TABE is to identify the instructional level of the examinee. However, another reason grade levels are used is because of inherited norms. The grade levels appear to represent the levels of the test items in the original CAT, not the sampling of the population for whom the TABE battery was designed. If this logic were to be followed, a reading grade level score of 1.7 for a 32-year-old illiterate would place him in the Dick, Sally, and Spot primer. Would one care to try that prescription on a 32-year-old in Harlem? Conclusion. For those items appropriate to the real-world literacy demands upon adults for whom this battery was devised, the TABE helps teachers analyze specific behavioral deficiencies. California tests have always been designed to supply users with easy item analyses for diagnostic teaching. For this practice, the professions are indebted to CTB above all other test publishers. But the publishing of a test *before* the reliability coefficients are available opens up all sorts of questions about professional standards. To use a construct of item and validity inheritance from other tests designed for other uses with other populations is indefensible. To provide grade level norms based on other populations is absurd, especially when Grade Level 2 for a 7-year-old and Grade Level 2 for a 40-year-old mean very different things in terms of need, pedagogy, and appropriate material. Are the TABEs useless? In all likelihood, no. Many of the items, perhaps most of them, could be useful clinically, if not statistically. They may help pinpoint specific difficulties on which to build prescriptive educational programs. The battery could be used as a pre-post measurement for groups, but not for individuals. However, it is long past the time that publishers should refrain from publishing tests that have questionable validity and reliability and inappropriate norms.

For reference to reviews of the California Achievement Tests, *see 5.*

[33]

★**Tests of Basic Experiences.** Prekgn–kgn, kgn–grade 1; 1970–71; TOBE; test of experiences and concepts involving no reading; battery of 4 tests (language, mathematics, science, social studies) and a composite test (*General Concepts Test*) used for screening or as a post-test; 2 levels; proctor's instructions ('70, 2 pages); technical bulletin ('71, 18 pages); no information is presented on the age range or other characteristics of the "prekindergarten" children for whom the norms are applicable; $32.50 per 30 sets of the battery; $9 per 30 copies of any one test in the battery; $9.25 per 30 general concepts tests; postage extra; $3 per specimen set, postpaid; scoring service, $2.25 per battery of 4 tests; Spanish edition available; (100) minutes for the battery, (25) minutes for General Concepts; Margaret H. Moss; CTB/McGraw-Hill. *
a) LEVEL K. Prekgn–kgn; 1 form ('70, 34 pages) of each test; preliminary manual ('70, 52 pages).
b) LEVEL L. Kgn–grade 1; 1 form ('70, 18 pages) of each test; preliminary manual ('70, 52 pages).

COURTNEY B. CAZDEN, *Associate Professor of Education, Harvard University, Cambridge, Massachusetts.*

The TOBE is a set of group tests of the "richness of conceptual background" of children in preschool, kindergarten, or first grade. Each of the two levels has four separate tests—mathematics, language, science and social studies—and one composite test of general concepts which includes items from the other four. Each test contains 28 items, and requires approximately 25 minutes to administer. Test items seem to have been selected on a combination of norm-referenced and criterion-referenced criteria: "Items were selected to achieve a balance which avoided very easy and very difficult items" (norm-referenced) but "some items which appeared to be relatively easy or relatively difficult were retained due to the desirability of a measure of the concept inherent in the items" (criterion-referenced). In each item, the examiner gives a verbal direction and the child marks one out of four pictures in his test booklet.

Scoring can be done either by hand with the help of a well-designed Class Evaluation Record (CER), or by sending the tests back to the publisher. Scoring tables convert raw scores to standard scores, percentile ranks, or stanines. The CER for each test gives the proportion of children in the "national reference group" who gave the correct response. That standard-

ization group consisted of 10,300 children from all types of public and private schools from prekindergarten through second grade from all sections of the country.

In selecting the items, "every attempt was made to minimize the number of items based strictly on a knowledge of factual information and to maximize the number of items based on a child's understanding of educationally relevant concepts." This is an important aim, but some of the test items do not seem to meet this criteria.

In the mathematics test, there is a subtle difference between items which test basic concepts, items which depend on the use of those concepts in specific contexts, and items which demand knowledge based on custom. Examples, respectively, are "Mark the longest line"; "Mark the one where both hands are up" (among four clocks); "Mark the baby's cake" (with only one candle). A child could understand *up* and yet not have heard the preposition applied to clock or watch hands. He might understand about the relative age of babies and yet not be familiar with the custom of matching candles to age. Compared with the concept of *longest,* the latter two items seem much less educationally relevant. In the science test, there is a difference between knowledge about aspects of the natural world common to all children and more esoteric information. Examples, respectively, are "Mark the one with roots" (a tree) versus "Mark the one that lives in a cave" (a bear). One wonders if the more esoteric items were included to provide the desired range of scores. The social studies test combines knowledge about the social world with moralistic rules of behavior. For example, "Mark the one the fireman does not use" (a motorcycle), versus "Mark the one who is doing what she should not" (one girl pulling another girl's hair).

All the examples are from the K level, but comparable items are present at L level also. In each case, the first kind of item seems the most valid; and the test would be improved by elimination of items based on non-universal customs, esoteric information, and moralizing. But since tests for this age range are so rare, and because other aspects of the TOBE discussed below are very good, it will undoubtedly become widely used. In that case teachers should consider the above distinctions in interpreting scores.

A test for young children places heavy reliance on the intelligibility of the pictures. In general, TOBE pictures are good. Occasionally one is unclear; a picture of what presumably is a mayonnaise jar in answer to the question "What goes on a sandwich?" And some knowledge of pictorial conventions are probably falsely assumed; finger on chin to indicate "The one who does not understand the question" and a cherub blowing to represent "What moves the clouds."

Inevitably, tests require knowledge or skills outside of the intended focus. An important part of test design, especially for young children, is eliminating variance in scores from this source. As the manual makes commendably clear, concepts like "mark the" and "turn the page" must be understood. The manual suggests that the directions "may be supplemented with additional explanation, assistance and encouragement." With such young children, I would go further and urge teachers to teach these behaviors in separate sessions and make sure every child knows them before testing begins. Also commendable is the allowance for any "mark," not just the requested vertical line.

Group tests place particular demands on young children because they must keep up with a group pace, waiting when necessary without making extra marks, and attending to the right place on demand. For these reasons, many educators would not want to use any group test with prekindergarten children. For a group test, the TOBE procedures are very good. Proctors are required to assist the examiner—one for each 4–6 children at K level or 6–10 children at L level. Each proctor is assigned to particular children with whom they maintain contact for procedural assistance throughout the test. The test booklets are also designed to minimize inattention: there is only one item per page at K level and two items at L level; the left-hand page is always empty.

Problems in creating a group test of basic concepts for young children of widely different cultural backgrounds may be intrinsically insoluble. Questions are raised about the content of some test items, but otherwise the design of the test and conditions of its administration are probably as good as can be obtained.

[34]

*Tests of General Educational Development.
Candidates for high school equivalency certificates; 1944–70; TGED, also GED; 5 tests: correctness and effectiveness of expression, interpretation of reading materials in the social studies, interpretation of reading materials in the natural sciences, interpretation of literary materials, general mathematical ability; revised manual ('64, 15 pages); separate answer sheets (IBM 805) must be used; (120) minutes per test; General Educational Development Testing Service of the American Council on Education.

a) CIVILIAN RESTRICTED FORMS. Civilian adults including veterans; tests administered throughout the year only at Official GED Centers; Forms H ('61), J ('62), K ('65), L ('65), CC ('68), EE ('70), FF ('70); new form issued each September; revised official report form ('70, 1 page); tests rented only; annual rental fee: $6 per battery, $2 per set of scoring stencils; $1.25 per 25 answer sheets; 75¢ per 50 official report forms; postage extra; special editions available for blind and partially sighted.

b) MILITARY RESTRICTED FORMS. Military personnel on active duty; tests administered only at USAFI Testing Sections.

REFERENCES

1–11. See 3:20.
12–38. See 4:26.
39–77. See 5:27.
78. TURNER, CORNELIUS P. "Accreditation by Means of Tests," pp. 380–90. In Trends in Student Personnel Work. Edited by E. G. Williamson. Minneapolis, Minn.: University of Minnesota Press, 1949. Pp. x, 417. *
79. ASLIN, NEIL CLAY. The Development and Utilization of the High School Equivalency Certificate in Missouri. Doctor's thesis, University of Missouri (Columbia, Mo.), 1952. (DA 12:502)
80. BLEDSOE, JOSEPH C. "An Analytical Study of the Academic Performance of a Group of Students Accelerated on the Basis of College Level G.E.D. Test Scores." Col & Univ 29: 430–8 Ap '54. *
81. CAUFFMAN, PAUL F. A Study of the Validity of United States Armed Forces Institute Tests of General Educational Development (High School Level) for Determining Success in Maryland Colleges as Measured by Grades Received. Doctor's thesis, Temple University (Philadelphia, Pa.), 1954.
82. LETON, DONALD A. "Analysis of High School General Educational Development Test Scores." Calif J Ed Res 8:214–8 N '57. * (PA 33:6921)
83. KELLER, LOWELL J. A Comparative Investigation of the College Achievement of Selected GED Students and High School Graduates. Master's thesis, East Tennessee State University (Johnson City, Tenn.), 1958.
84. LAPINE, HARRY JOHN. A Study of the Validity of the United States Armed Forces Institute Tests of General Educational Development (High School Level). Doctor's thesis, University of Chicago (Chicago, Ill.), 1958.
85. BAIRD, THOMAS B. A Study of the College Achievement of GED Students in Relation to Seven Variables. Master's thesis, East Tennessee State University (Johnson City, Tenn.), 1960.
86. DENOYELLES, LESTER CHARLES. Administrative Policies and Practices for Granting the High School Diploma in the Evening High Schools in California. Doctor's thesis, University of Southern California (Los Angeles, Calif.), 1960. (DA 21:104)
87. PIPHO, CHRISTIAN CARLYLE. The General Educational Development (GED) High School Equivalency Certificate Program in Colorado. Doctor's research study No. 1, Colorado State College (Greeley, Colo.), 1965. (DA 26:5199)
88. FARLEY, EUGENE J.; WEINHOLD, CLYDE E.; AND CRABTREE, ARTHUR P. High School Certification Through the G.E.D. Tests. New York: Holt, Rinehart & Winston, Inc., 1967. Pp. v, 250. *
89. "General Educational Development Program (GED) Testing Program," pp. 387–90. In A Guide to the Evaluation of Educational Experiences in the Armed Services, 1968 Edition. Edited by Cornelius P. Turner. Washington, D.C.: American Council on Education, 1968. Pp. xxi, 530. *
90. BRENNA, DAVID W. "Use of the GATB in Predicting Success on the Tests of General Educational Development." J Employ Counsel 6(4):181–5 D '69. *
91. CARBUHN, WAYNE MCKINZIE. Job Corpsmen Selection and Prediction of Successful Completion of the General Education Development (GED) Program at Clearfield Urban Job Corps Center. Doctor's thesis, University of Utah (Salt Lake City, Utah), 1969. (DAI 30:3774A)
92. KLEIN, FREDA. Use of the General Aptitude Test Battery "G" Score for Predicting Achievement on the General Educational Development Test. Master's thesis, University of Nevada (Las Vegas, Nev.), 1969.
93. RUSSO, JOSEPH FRANK. Predicting Academic Achievement of Students in Arizona Junior Colleges. Doctor's thesis,

Arizona State University (Tempe, Ariz.), 1969. (*DAI* 30: 2309A)

94. SCHLICK, EARL FRANK. *Academic Success of Junior College Students Admitted on Basis of High School Equivalency Certificates.* Doctor's thesis, Arizona State University (Tempe, Ariz.), 1969. (*DA* 29:2077A)

95. CARBUHN, WAYNE M. "Predicting General Education Development (GED) Test Performance of Urban Job Corpsmen." *Ed & Psychol Meas* 30(4):993–8 w '70. *

96. KLEIN, FREDA, AND TRIONE, VERDUN. "Use of the GATB 'G' Score for Predicting Achievement on the GED." *J Employ Counsel* 7(3):93–7 Ag '70. *

97. KLEIN, MATTHEW AARON. *An Evaluation of the T.V. High School Project of the Detroit Urban Adult Education Institute and Michigan Blueshield.* Doctor's thesis, Michigan State University (East Lansing, Mich.), 1970. (*DAI* 31: 2091A)

98. SODERBERG, PATRICIA B. *Goal Achievement Following Successful Completion of the General Educational Development Test.* Master's thesis, Wisconsin State University (River Falls, Wis.), 1970.

For a review by Robert J. Solomon of earlier forms, see 5:27; for a review by Gustav J. Froehlich, see 4:26; for reviews by Herbert S. Conrad and Warren G. Findley, see 3:20. For reviews of individual tests, see 3:122 (1 review) and 3:528 (2 reviews).

[35]

*The Undergraduate Record Examinations: Area Tests. College; 1954–70; 3 tests (social sciences, humanities, natural science) in 1 booklet; Forms RUR1 ['68, 43 pages], RUR2 ['68, 42 pages]; tests available as separates for local scoring: Forms SUR1, SUR2, ('65, 12–17 pages) for each test; descriptive booklet ('70, 19 pages); score interpretation leaflet for freshmen and sophomores ('69, 4 pages); manual for local scoring ('70, 31 pages including insert); norms for seniors based on a 1954 reference group and a 70 minute time limit; norms for freshmen and sophomores estimated from 1963–64 administration of CLEP General Examinations; no norms for juniors; for more complete information, see 671; 60(70) minutes per test; Educational Testing Service. *

REFERENCES

1–9. See 6:9.

10. ELTON, CHARLES F. "The Use and Abuse of the Graduate Record Examination Area Tests." *Psychol Sch* 2:245–9 Jl '65. *

11. ASTIN, ALEXANDER W. "Undergraduate Achievement and Institutional 'Excellence.'" *Sci* 161:661–8 Ag 16 '68. *

12. ASTIN, ALEXANDER W., AND PANOS, ROBERT J. *The Educational and Vocational Development of College Students.* Washington, D.C.: American Council on Education, 1969. Pp. xii, 211. *

13. ROSCOE, JOHN T., AND HOUSTON, SAMUEL R. "The Predictive Validity of GRE Scores for a Doctoral Program in Education." *Ed & Psychol Meas* 29(2):507–9 su '69. * (*PA* 44:17512)

For reviews by Paul L. Dressel and Everett B. Sackett of earlier forms, see 6:9; for reviews by Benjamin S. Bloom and Frederick B. Davis, see 5:10. For reviews of the testing program, see 671 (2 reviews); for a review of an earlier testing program, see 5:601.

[36]

*Wide Range Achievement Test, Revised Edition. Ages 5-0 to 11-11, 12-0 and over; 1940–65; WRAT; 3 scores: spelling, arithmetic, reading; individual; 1 form ('65, 4 pages); 2 levels; manual ('65, 63 pages); $3.75 per 50 tests; $2.60 per manual; $2.75 per specimen set; postpaid; (20–30) minutes; J. F. Jastak, S. R. Jastak, and S. W. Bijou (test); Guidance Associates. *

REFERENCES

1–15. See 6:27.

16. REGER, ROGER. "Brief Tests of Intelligence and Academic Achievement." *Psychol Rep* 11:82 Ag '62. * (*PA* 37:5654)

17. BRICKER, AMY L.; SCHUELL, HILDRED; AND JENKINS, JAMES J. "Effect of Word Frequency and Word Length on Aphasic Spelling Errors." *J Speech & Hearing Res* 7:183–91 Je '64. * (*PA* 39:5601)

18. MATTHEWS, CHARLES G., AND FOLK, EARL D. "Finger Localization, Intelligence, and Arithmetic in Mentally Retarded Subjects." *Am J Mental Def* 69:107–13 Jl '64. * (*PA* 39: 2525)

19. OLDRIDGE, O. A. "A Congruent Validity Study of the Wide Range Achievement Test at Grade Seven." *Ed & Psychol Meas* 24:415–7 su '64. * (*PA* 39:5084)

20. SEYBOLD, FRED R., AND PEDRINI, DUILIO T. "The Relation Between Wechsler-Bellevue Subtests and Academic Achievement Using Institutionalized Retardates." *Psychiatric Q* 38:635–49 O '64. * (*PA* 39:12755)

21. STONE, F. BETH, AND ROWLEY, VINTON N. "Educational Disability in Emotionally Disturbed Children." *Excep Children* 30:423–6 My '64. * (*PA* 39:5920)

22. DALY, WILLIAM C. "The Relationship Between Reading and Anxiety in a Group of Mental Retardates." *Training Sch B* 62:113–8 N '65. * (*PA* 40:3299)

23. GARLOCK, JERRY; DOLLARHIDE, ROBERT S.; AND HOPKINS, KENNETH D. "Comparability of Scores on the Wide Range and the Gilmore Oral Reading Tests." *Calif J Ed Res* 16:54–7 Mr '65. * (*PA* 39:10108)

24. BERRY, ROSE AUERSPERG. *An Analysis of the Relationship Between Certain Variables of Students With Behavioral Disorders and Successful Completion of Vocational Training.* Doctor's thesis, University of Arkansas (Fayetteville, Ark.), 1966. (*DA* 27:1194A)

25. DAVIS, LEO J., JR.; HAMLETT, IONA C.; AND REITAN, RALPH M. "Relationship of Conceptual Ability and Academic Achievement to Problem-Solving and Experiential Backgrounds of Retardates." *Percept & Motor Skills* 22:499–505 Ap '66. * (*PA* 40:9152)

26. REGER, ROGER. "WISC, WRAT, and CMAS Scores in Retarded Children." *Am J Mental Def* 70:717–21 Mr '66. * (*PA* 40:6987)

27. SELLS, S. B. *Evaluation of Psychological Measures Used in the Health Examination Survey of Children Ages 6–11,* pp. 23–33. Public Health Service Publication No. 1000, Series 2, No. 15. Washington, D.C.: United States Government Printing Office, March 1966. Pp. viii, 67. * (*PA* 40:7217)

28. ANDERSON, HARRY E., JR.; KERN, FRANK E.; AND COOK, CHARLOTTE. "Correlational and Normative Data for the Progressive Matrices With Retarded Populations." *J Psychol* 67:221–5 N '67. * (*PA* 42:1396)

29. KAUFMAN, HARVEY ISIDORE. *Cognitive and Noncognitive Indices of Employability in a Sampling of 17 to 21 Year Old Mentally Retarded Individuals.* Doctor's thesis, Marquette University (Milwaukee, Wis.), 1967. (*DA* 28:3027A)

30. SCHAIE, K. WARNER. *A Study of the Achievement Test Used in the Health Examination Surveys of Persons Aged 6–17 Years.* Public Health Service Publication 1000, Series 2, No. 24. Washington, D.C.: United States Government Printing Office, June 1967. Pp. viii, 60. *

31. ANDERSON, HARRY E., JR.; KERN, FRANK E.; AND COOK, CHARLOTTE. "Sex, Brain Damage, and Race Effects in the Progressive Matrices With Retarded Populations." *J Social Psychol* 76:207–11 D '68. * (*PA* 43:4329)

32. BAE, AGNES Y. "Factors Influencing Vocational Efficiency of Institutionalized Retardates in Different Training Programs." *Am J Mental Def* 72:871–4 My '68. * (*PA* 42: 14397)

33. BURCH, CHARLES WILLIAM. *Assessment Variables Relevant to the Referral and Placement of Pupils in Educationally Handicapped Classes.* Doctor's thesis, University of Southern California (Los Angeles, Calif.), 1968. (*DA* 29:2995A)

34. MATTHEWS, CHARLES G.; CHUN, RAYMOND W. M.; GRABOW, JACK D.; AND THOMPSON, WAYNE H. "Psychological Sequelae in Children Following California Arboviros Encephalitis." *Neurology* 18:1023–30 O '68. * (*PA* 43:5771)

35. PINNEY, EDWARD L. "Reading and Arithmetic Scores and EEG Alpha Blocking in Disadvantaged Children." *Dis Nerv System* 29:388–90 Je '68. * (*PA* 42:15077)

36. RANKIN, RICHARD J. "Impact of Anxiety Produced by Delayed Auditory Feedback on Verbal Intelligence." *Percept & Motor Skills* 26:139–42 F '68. * (*PA* 42:10575)

37. SABATINO, DAVID A.; ASSISTED BY R. L. JONES, CURTISS BROWN, AND W. M. GIBSON. "The Relationship Between Twenty-Three Learning Disability Behavioral Variables," pp. 149–61. In *CEC Selected Convention Papers.* 46th Annual International Convention, 1968. Washington, D.C.: Council for Exceptional Children, [1968]. Pp. xii, 346. *

38. SABATINO, DAVID A.; WICKHAM, WILLIAM, JR.; AND BURNETT, CALVIN W. "The Psychoeducational Assessment of Learning Disabilities." *Cath Ed R* 66:327–41 My '68. *

39. VACC, NICHOLAS A. "A Study of Emotionally Disturbed Children in Regular and Special Classes." *Excep Children* 35:197–204 N '68. * (*PA* 43:13334)

40. WIENER, G.; RIDER, R. V.; OPPEL, W. C.; AND

HARPER, P. A. "Correlates of Low Birth Weight: Psychological Status at Eight to Ten Years of Age." *Pediatric Res* 2:110-8 Mr '68. * (*PA* 42:15299)

41. ATTWELL, ARTHUR A.; JAMISON, COLLEEN B.; AND FILS, DAVID H. "Relationship Between the WRAT, a Behavior Guide, and Achievement With Retarded Adolescents." *Am J Mental Def* 73(6):879-82 My '69. * (*PA* 43:13234)

42. AYRES, A. JEAN. "Deficits in Sensory Integration in Educationally Handicapped Children." *J Learn Dis* 2(3):160-8 Mr '69. * (*PA* 45:6978)

43. COCHRAN, MALCOLM L., AND PEDRINI, DUILIO T. "The Concurrent Validity of the 1965 WRAT With Adult Retardates." *Am J Mental Def* 73(4):654-6 Ja '69. * (*PA* 43:8574)

44. ELLIOTT, RAYMOND N., JR. "Comparative Study of the Pictorial Test of Intelligence and the Peabody Picture Vocabulary Test." *Psychol Rep* 25(2):528-30 O '69. * (*PA* 44:5541)

45. HOLLENDER, JOHN W., AND BROMAN, HARVEY J. "Intellectual Assessment in a Disadvantaged Population." *Meas & Eval Guid* 2(1):19-24 sp '69. *

46. LANGE, UNA ANN. *Differential Performances of Minimally Brain-Damaged Boys and of Non-Brain-Damaged Boys on Selected Tests.* Doctor's thesis, University of Nebraska (Lincoln, Neb.), 1969. (*DAI* 30:2852A)

47. OWENS, RICHARD THOMAS. *A Study of the Performance of Minimally Brain-Damaged and Emotionally Disturbed Boys on Six Selected Psychological Tests.* Doctor's thesis, University of Nebraska (Lincoln, Neb.), 1969. (*DAI* 31:383B)

48. REED, JAMES C., AND REITAN, RALPH M. "Verbal and Performance Differences Among Brain-Injured Children With Lateralized Motor Deficits." *Percept & Motor Skills* 29(3):747-52 D '69. * (*PA* 45:6334)

49. RICE, JAMES A. "Confusion in Laterality: A Validity Study With Bright and Dull Children." *J Learn Dis* 2(7):368-73 Jl '69. * (*PA* 45:6889)

50. SABATINO, DAVID A., AND CRAMBLETT, HENRY. "A Longitudinal Study of Children With Learning Disabilities Subsequent to Hospitalization for Viral Encephalitis Part 1." *J Learn Dis* 2(2):65-75 F '69. * (*PA* 45:6854)

51. SCHWARZ, ROBERT H. "Mental Age as It Relates to School Achievement Among Educable Mentally Retarded Adolescents." *Ed & Train Mental Retard* 4(2):53-6 Ap '69. *

52. SHEPHERD, CLYDE W., JR. "Childhood Chronic Illness and Visual Motor Perceptual Development." *Excep Children* 36(1):39-42 S '69. * (*PA* 44:21470)

53. CLARK, ALICE, AND FOSTER, JAMES. "Objective Measures and Occupational Success." *Mental Retard* 8(4):41-4 Ag '70. *

54. FERINDEN, WILLIAM E., JR., AND JACOBSON, SHERMAN. "Early Identification of Learning Disabilities." *J Learn Dis* 3(11):589-93 N '70. *

55. HARTLAGE, LAWRENCE C. "Differential Diagnosis of Dyslexia, Minimal Brain Damage and Emotional Disturbances in Children." *Psychol Sch* 7(4):403-6 O '70. * (*PA* 46:1422)

56. HIMES, JACK EDWARD. *An Investigation of the Haptic Abilities of Minimally Brain Injured and Normal Children.* Doctor's thesis, University of Texas (Austin, Tex.), 1970. (*DAI* 31:3374A)

57. HOFMEISTER, ALAN, AND ESPESETH, V. KNUTE. "Predicting Academic Achievement With TMR Adults and Teenagers." *Am J Mental Def* 75(1):105-7 Jl '70. *

58. KAUFMAN, HARVEY I. "Diagnostic Indices of Employment With the Mentally Retarded." *Am J Mental Def* 74(6):777-9 My '70. * (*PA* 44:17178)

59. LEWANDOWSKA, M. EDWARDINE. *A Comparative Study of Results Obtained on the Spelling Sections of the 1965 and 1966 Editions of the Wide Range Achievement Test.* Master's thesis, Cardinal Stritch College (Milwaukee, Wis.), 1970.

60. SABATINO, DAVID A., AND HAYDEN, DAVID L. "Information Processing Behaviors Related to Learning Disabilities and Educable Mental Retardation." *Excep Children* 37(1):21-9 S '70. * (*PA* 46:5527)

61. SABATINO, DAVID A., AND HAYDEN, DAVID L. "Psycho-Educational Study of Selected Behavioral Variables With Children Failing the Elementary Grades." *J Exp Ed* 38(4):40-57 su '70. * (*PA* 46:5680-1)

62. SABATINO, DAVID A., AND HAYDEN, DAVID L. "Variation in Information Processing Behaviors: As Related to Chronological Age Differences for Children Failing in the Elementary Grades." *J Learn Dis* 3(8):404-12 Ag '70. *

63. SIMPSON, ROBERT L. "Reading Tests Versus Intelligence Tests as Predictors of High School Graduation." *Psychol Sch* 7(4):363-5 O '70. * (*PA* 46:1870)

64. WASHINGTON, ERNEST D., AND TESKA, JAMES A. "Relations Between the Wide Range Achievement Test, the California Achievement Tests, the Stanford-Binet, and the Illinois Test of Psycholinguistic Abilities." *Psychol Rep* 26(1):291-4 F '70. * (*PA* 45:4931)

JACK C. MERWIN, *Professor of Educational Psychology and Dean, College of Education, University of Minnesota, Minneapolis, Minnesota.*

In a review of this test the persisting problem of differentiation between "intelligence" and "achievement" is boldly brought to the fore. This issue, confusing as it is for many, is further complicated in regard to this particular test. The author reports a "general" factor from "a clinical factor analysis" which accounts for 28 percent of the variance of each of the three scores (reading, spelling and arithmetic) and five group factors which the authors say "may be conceived of as true *personality* [reviewer's emphasis] variables." For example, the Group Factor I, labeled the "Verbal," said to be a personality variable unrelated to intelligence, is reported to carry 30 percent of the variance of the reading score and 24 percent of the variance of the spelling score. Careful examination of the materials leads one to seriously question why these authors chose to label this an "achievement" test.

The latest edition, like earlier editions, provides scores in: reading, "recognizing and naming letters and pronouncing words"; spelling, "copying marks resembling letters, writing the name, and writing single words to dictation"; and, arithmetic, "counting, reading number symbols, solving oral problems, and performing written computations." The individual user must determine the extent to which these activities reflect "achievement" in his own situation.

The authors make little effort to describe how this revised edition differs from earlier versions or the reason for the 1965 revision. They do note that the 1965 edition, unlike the earlier editions, is divided into two levels: Level 1 for ages 5-11 and Level 2 for ages 12 and over. In personal correspondence the author reports that, "the new form differs in content only in minor ways."

Administration interestingly involves sequential procedures. For example, parts one and two of the spelling subtest are not given to a person over 7 years 11 months if he has six or more successes in the dictation portion of the third part of that test. Similarly complex, if not confusing procedures of administration are followed in the other parts of the test. It is basically an individually administered test with provision for group administration of some parts under specified conditions.

The authors report that no attempt was made to obtain a representative national sampling for norming purposes. They note the seven states used in the administration for norming to arrive at sets of norms for six-month age groups from age five through adults for Level 1 and for age 9 through college student for Level 2. Sample size for the various sets of grade equivalents, standard scores, and percentile norms ranges from 86 to 691, half being based on 310 or fewer cases. In addition to number of cases, the only descriptive information regarding the norm group is a brief verbal description (no data provided) that an attempt was made to use IQ's available from a variety of tests to develop norms, "that would correspond to the achievement of mentally average groups with representative dispersions of scores above and below the mean." Thus a user can make comparisons with the norms provided, but with questionable meaning since the identity and nature of the groups serving as the basis for score interpretation is far from clear.

The authors report questionably high reliability coefficients by one-year age groupings. It is not possible to determine the extent to which the reported split-half coefficients based on "odd-even" scores are affected by the sequential administration and scoring procedures used for the test from the information provided. However, the procedures and the reported magnitude (e.g., low of .981 out of 14 coefficients on the reading test) make them suspect, at best.

There are several problems involved in assessing the value of the validity information provided in the manual. One of these relates to the above concern of what the potential user might consider achievement and the content validity of the items of this test for that individual user. While the authors provide several pages of "validity" data and discussion, it is not always clear when the data reported is based on results from the 1965 two-level edition.

The authors report that this test was designed as "an adjunct to tests of intelligence and behavior adjustment." They cite five ends which the method used in the test was devised to accomplish. The extent to which they have succeeded in attaining these ends is far from clear, as are some statements of the ends themselves, e.g., "to permit validity analyses by the method of internal consistency." The authors cite 11 ways in which the test reportedly "has been found of value" though no statistical evidence or research studies to support the statement are reported.

In summary, this "achievement" test is a unique, individually administered test. While possibly a potentially useful clinical tool for the psychologist working with specialized cases, for general school use it is impractical.

ROBERT L. THORNDIKE, *Professor of Psychology and Education, Teachers College, Columbia University, New York, New York.*

This is a brief test, in part individually administered, that provides a rough indication of three limited components of educational achievement. The components are spelling, decoding isolated printed words and pronouncing them correctly, and carrying out computational exercises in arithmetic and algebra. The adequacy with which these tasks represent the goals of education in today's schools is never questioned, and the content validity of the test is not considered by the authors at any point. This reviewer does not believe that it would be judged to be high.

The items in each part are stated to be arranged in order of difficulty. In order to spread out those young or mentally retarded individuals for whom even the easier items of the regular test would be too difficult, an oral section is provided for each, to be used below a specified age or for examinees who do poorly on the regular test. Though these vestibule tests have a certain plausibility, no evidence is offered that they are really measuring the same attribute that is dealt with by the main body of the test. Thus, the continuity between a task of copying geometric forms rapidly and accurately and spelling from dictation would seem at least open to question.

All parts of the test are timed, if not speeded, and in the word pronouncing test the task is stopped after a specified number of failures. Both of these features tend to inflate split-half reliabilities, and cause one to discount the rather startling values that the authors report. The correlations between Level 1 and Level 2, two separate forms differing in difficulty but printed in the same 4-page booklet, provide a more conservative estimate of reliability. The typical values for samples allegedly chosen to have a mean and standard deviation corresponding to the population of persons at that age, run about .90 for the spelling and word reading and about .85 for arithmetic. No data are provided on truly parallel forms, with any time interval between testing, or where forms were given by different examiners. Since strictness in timing and in scoring could vary appreciably from examiner to examiner, such factors could attenuate appreciably the precision of scores.

However, it is in the domain of validity that the most serious questions about this test would seem to arise. Here, the authors appear to have some bizarre conceptions, and to engage in somewhat exotic procedures. They state, for example, "Validity can be determined only by the comparison of one test score with those which measure entirely different abilities." Again, "It is acceptable practice to use criteria of internal consistency in the validation of tests. Criteria of internal consistency, if properly interpreted, are usually more meaningful and more valid than are external criteria of comparison." One finds it hard to reconcile these statements with each other or with the usual concepts of test validation.

The authors report, with considerable verbal elaboration but with no presentation of any of the data on which the interpretations are presumably based, a "clinical factor analysis" of the WRAT together with the WISC and the WAIS. Clinical factor analysis is described only as "successive regressions and score transformations in such a way as to obtain individual scores for each factor as it is extracted from the test comparisons." The exact nature of the procedure is apparently known only to the authors and God, and He may have some uncertainty.

The uses that the authors propose for the test are many, but few of them seem justified. For example, hopefully one would hesitate to count on it for "the accurate diagnosis of reading, spelling, and arithmetic disabilities" or to use it for "the selection of students for specialized technical and professional schools." Over-claiming seems fairly general in the test manual. This test may have some value in a clinical or a research setting in which one is testing individually persons of such diverse ability or background that one cannot tell in advance what level of test would be appropriate, and needs to get a quick estimate of each person's general level of ability and educational background. One would hesitate to recommend it for other purposes.

For reviews by Paul Douglas Courtney, Verner M. Sims, and Louis P. Thorpe of the 1946 edition, see 3:21.

CHARACTER AND PERSONALITY

REVIEWS BY *C. J. Adcock, Henry A. Alker, Anne Anastasi, Leonard L. Baird, Allan G. Barclay, Peter M. Bentler, Arthur L. Benton, Bruce Bloxom, Harold Borko, Thomas J. Bouchard, Jr., John R. Braun, Alvin G. Burstein, Maurice Chazan, D. F. Clark, Victor B. Cline, Richard W. Coan, Jacob Cohen, Andrew L. Comrey, John O. Crites, Richard H. Dana, R. G. Demaree, George Domino, Paul L. Dressel, James A. Dunn, William J. Eichman, Leonard D. Eron, H. J. Eysenck, Robert Fitzpatrick, Raymond D. Fowler, Jr., Sol L. Garfield, Gene V Glass, Goldine C. Gleser, Lewis R. Goldberg, Leonard D. Goodstein, Leonard V. Gordon, Harrison G. Gough, Malcolm D. Gynther, Dale B. Harris, Alfred B. Heilbrun, Jr., G. C. Helmstadter, Robert Hogan, Douglas N. Jackson, Carl F. Jesness, Joseph A. Johnston, David Jones, E. Lowell Kelly, James E. Kennedy, Philip M. Kitay, Benjamin Kleinmuntz, Paul Kline, Robert R. Knapp, John F. Knutson, Richard I. Lanyon, Julian J. Lasky, Wilbur L. Layton, S. G. Lee, Eugene E. Levitt, Lester M. Libo, William M. Littell, Paul R. Lohnes, Maurice Lorr, Robert W. Lundin, Clifford E. Lunneborg, David T. Lykken, Charles C. McArthur, Michael G. McKee, Douglas M. McNair, Paul McReynolds, Edwin I. Megargee, Manfred J. Meier, Joan J. Michael, Lovick C. Miller, James V. Mitchell, Jr., G. A. V. Morgan, Bernard I. Murstein, Warren T. Norman, David B. Orr, Stuart Oskamp, Jerome D. Pauker, R. W. Payne, Joan Preston, M. L. Kellmer Pringle, M. Y. Quereshi, Albert I. Rabin, James C. Reed, Willard E. Reitz, Marvin Reznikoff, James M. Richards, Jr., David A. Rodgers, Leonard G. Rorer, John W. M. Rothney, S. B. Sells, Melvyn I. Semmel, Rodney W. Skager, Hans H. Strupp, Richard M. Suinn, Norman D. Sundberg, Forrest L. Vance, Philip E. Vernon, James A. Walsh, Sheldon A. Weintraub, Joseph M. Wepman, Jerry S. Wiggins, Robert D. Wirt, Aubrey J. Yates, and Wayne S. Zimmerman.*

NONPROJECTIVE

[37]

★**Adaptive Behavior Scales.** Mentally retarded and emotionally maladjusted ages 3–12, 13 and over; 1969; ABS; ratings in 24 areas: Part 1 (independent functioning, physical development, economic activity, language development, number and time concept, occupation—domestic, occupation—general, self-direction, responsibilities, socialization), Part 2 (violent and destructive behavior, antisocial, rebellious behavior, untrustworthy behavior, withdrawal, stereotyped behavior and odd mannerisms, inappropriate interpersonal manners, inappropriate vocal habits, unacceptable or eccentric habits, self-abusive behavior, hyperactive tendencies, sexually aberrant behavior, psychological disturbances, use of medications) ; 2 levels: children, adults, (16 pages) ; manual (34 pages) ; "answer sheets" booklet (9 pages) for each level; "hand scoring sheet" ['69, 4 pages] for each level; no data on reliability, only inter-rater reliability reported (for adult level only) ; norms (consisting of means by age groups) based on institutionalized retardates; $5 per 10 tests; $5 per 25 "answer sheets"; $2.50 per 25 "hand scoring sheets"; $2.75 per manual; $7.50 per specimen set; postage extra; [20–25] minutes for children, [25–30] minutes for adults; Kazuo Nihira, Ray Foster, Max Shellhaas, and Henry Leland; American Association on Mental Deficiency. *

REFERENCES

1. LELAND, HENRY; SHELLHAAS, MAX; NIHIRA, KAZUO; AND FOSTER, RAY. "Adaptive Behavior: A New Dimension in the Classification of the Mentally Retarded." *Mental Retard Abstr* 4:359–87 N '67. * (*PA* 42:15922)
2. NIHIRA, KAZUO; FOSTER, RAY; AND SPENCER, LINDA. "Measurement of Adaptive Behavior: A Descriptive System for Mental Retardates." *Am J Orthopsychiatry* 38:622–34 Jl '68. * (*PA* 43:16602)
3. FOSTER, RAY, AND NIHIRA, KAZUO. "Adaptive Behavior as a Measure of Psychiatric Impairment." *Am J Mental Def* 74(3):401–4 N '69. * (*PA* 44:5544)
4. FRANK, HARRY, AND FIEDLER, EDNA R. "A Multifactor Behavioral Approach to the Genetic-Etiological Diagnosis of Mental Retardation." *Multiv Behav Res* 4(2):131–45 Ap '69. * (*PA* 43:16258)
5. NIHIRA, KAZUO. "Factorial Dimensions of Adaptive Behavior in Adult Retardates." *Am J Mental Def* 73(6):868–78 My '69. * (*PA* 43:13247)
6. NIHIRA, KAZUO. "Factorial Dimensions of Adaptive Behavior in Mentally Retarded Children and Adolescents." *Am J Mental Def* 74(1):130–41 Jl '69. * (*PA* 43:17820)
7. NIHIRA, KAZUO. "Three Factors of Adaptive Behavior in Mentally Retarded Children, Adolescents, and Adults." Abstract. *Proc 77th Ann Conv Am Psychol Assn* 4(2):777–8 '69. * (*PA* 44:1132)
8. NIHIRA, KAZUO. "Person Clusters on Two Dimensions of Adaptive Behavior." Abstract. *Proc 78th Ann Conv Am Psychol Assn* 5(2):715–6 '70. * (*PA* 44:19212)
9. NIHIRA, KAZUO, AND SHELLHAAS, MAX. "Study of Adaptive Behavior: Its Rationale, Method and Implication in Rehabilitation Programs." *Mental Retard* 8(5):11–6 O '70. *

LOVICK C. MILLER, *Director of Research, Child Psychiatry Research Center, Louisville, Kentucky.*

The ABS is a set of 111 items covering 24 areas of social and personal behavior for use in evaluating effectiveness in coping with environmental demands. The scales were designed to facilitate the classification of mentally retarded and emotionally disturbed persons based on the way in which the individual maintains personal independence and meets social expectations. The ABS is applicable to males and females and can be applied to all levels of mental retardation and to all ages beginning with age 3. The items are written clearly, organized logically, and presented in a well-constructed instruction booklet. Raters' recording booklets are separate. The authors state that any reasonably intelligent person can use the ABS providing he knows the child well. This reviewer lacks firsthand experience with the scales, but he believes that evidence will bear out the authors' assertions. Two forms have been prepared, one for children 12 and under, and an adult form for persons 13 and older.

Scale construction blended an extensive knowledge of the behavior of the mentally retarded with a proficiency in psychometrics. Inter-rater reliability, unfortunately only reported for the adult form, ranges from .40 to .86 on the 24 scales. No internal consistency measures are provided. Scoring instructions are somewhat awkward, but with several readings, clarity emerges. Mean scores by sex and by levels of intelligence are provided for ages 3 to 60+ for the 10 skill and habit domains and for ages 3 to 41 for 12 of the maladaptive scales. While these means are helpful, this reviewer believes that standard scores based on a population with a specified intelligence range would be more useful for comparisons across installations. Finally, the authors include for protocol scoring and key-punching a computer program which should be helpful where large numbers of subjects are involved.

The authors' goal was to construct an instrument that would describe the critical behavior upon which crucial decisions about the mentally retarded may be made. Face validity of the instrument suggests that this goal was achieved, and the authors cite four studies as evidence of empirical validity. While validity and utility evidence is minimal, I suspect that future studies will continue to validate the scales, for the authors have achieved a scholarly, practical, and down-to-earth instrument which should have wide applicability and great utility for persons charged with making decisions for the mentally retarded. Designed primarily for residential use, these scales are not limited to such applications, for they would be equally helpful in planning out-patient services under parent management.

Finally, the scales should facilitate much-needed research in social learning and social management and should throw more light on the relationship between intelligence and social skill. For example, correlations between the scale scores and IQ are not provided, but examination of the means suggests that the scales are most useful for children under 12 and for those at the extreme lower levels of intelligence. After 12, except for those of the lowest level of intelligence, the scales seem to provide essentially the same information as the IQ.

In summary, the *Adaptive Behavior Scales* is a welcome addition to the resources of the mental retardation field. The scales are well constructed, are easy to administer, and provide the essential information for making decisions about the mentally retarded. The scales should be useful for clinicians, administrators, and researchers.

MELVYN I. SEMMEL, *Professor of Special Education, Indiana University, Bloomington, Indiana.*

The ABS is designed to assess adaptive behavior of "mentally retarded" and "emotionally maladjusted" individuals. The authors follow the definition of adaptive behavior as introduced by the American Association of Mental Deficiency: "the effectiveness of an individual in coping with the natural and social demands of his environment." Each level consists of two parts. Part 1, containing 10 behavior domains, purports "to assess the individual's skills and habits in ten major areas considered important to the maintenance of personal independence in daily living." Part 2, consisting of 14 behavior domains, "is designed to provide measures of maladaptive behavior related to personality and behavioral disorders."

The ABS can be administered by informants who are well acquainted with the daily behavior of the individuals to be rated. Although the scale was originally developed for use in institutions, suggestions for use with other groups are presented. The scale appears to be relatively simple to administer. Subjectivity in interpreting some items appears to be a potential problem. A more detailed analysis of the behavior required in some form of a working definition would be helpful. In addition, some of the items appear to be inappropriate for children reared in institutionalized settings, e.g., items pertaining to money handling, budgeting, and shopping skills. The hand scoring system is relatively complex and requires careful reading of the manual's directions. Instructions for computer scoring are provided which would simplify and reduce scoring time of individual protocols. The scoring system provides raw scores in 24 areas ("behavior domains"). A detailed description of the derivation of the scoring key might have facilitated interpretation.

The scale was standardized on a sample consisting of approximately 2,800 patients from 63 residential institutions for the mentally retarded throughout the United States. The standardization sample was stratified by sex, intelligence, and age. The sample included relatively few cases at the younger age levels and upper levels of intelligence, hence, limiting the representativeness of norms. Revision of the norms on the basis of a more representative sample would be desirable. Inclusion in the norms of samples from various socioeconomic levels, minority groups, as well as non-institutionalized subjects would prove valuable. In order to determine more accurately a subject's position relative to the norms, derived scores for each domain should be included with the raw scores. This procedure would also facilitate intra-individual comparisons across behavior domains. Standard deviations of norms should be included to allow for more direct comparisons of domain scores at the various age levels. Although norms are presented, users may find local norms more suitable for their own purposes. In fact, the authors indicate that users may wish to develop their own local norms if they find certain behavior areas unnecessary for their purposes.

The reliability of the scale cannot be determined objectively since no reliability coefficients are provided. Test-retest reliability has yet to be determined. Inter-rater reliabilities are rather low—ranging from .43 to .86 with median .76 for the 10 ratings in Part 1 and .40 to .84 with median .55 for the 14 ratings in Part 2. These inter-rater correlations are for the adult level. No correlations are reported for the lower level.

Only scattered studies of validity are available. The authors report that factor analysis of the domain scores has delineated three major dimensions: "Personal Independence," "Social Maladaptation" and "Personal Maladaptation." Empirical estimates of concurrent and predictive validity are not provided, although there is evidence from a few studies indicating that the scale may possess satisfactory concurrent validity. However, as stated by the test authors, "The concurrent validity of the scale must rest upon what further research reveals regarding its concurrent and prognostic behavioral correlates, and its relationship to other psychological variables." Comparisons of the ABS with the *Vineland Social Maturity Scale,* the *Cain-Levine Social Competency Scale,* and the Stanford-Binet or WISC would be particularly meaningful. Continuing research on predictive validity with suitable and meaningful criterion measures is definitely required. The authors caution potential users "to evaluate the scale's practical validity, using different criteria for the retardate's adaptive behavior and varying environmental situations, and to avoid oversimplification of the concept of adaptive behavior."

In summary, at the present time, the *Adaptive Behavior Scales* appears to have considerable promise as a test of adaptive behavior of "mentally retarded" individuals. Potentially, the scale should prove valuable as a diagnostic tool within the area of mental retardation and in reaching decisions regarding possible institutionalization. Furthermore, accurate assessment of deficiencies in adaptive behavior may lead to the development of effective training programs and remediation adapted to the needs of the individual. However, the available norms should be regarded as tentative and require extension and revision on a more representative sample. The authors indicate that efforts are currently geared toward the assessment of non-institutionalized retardates as well as emotionally disturbed individuals. In addition, further revisions and refinements are planned. Continuing research on empirical reliability and validity with different samples and criteria is necessary. Effort should also be devoted toward improving interscore reliability of the various adaptive behavior domains for the adult form. The authors indicate that current studies are being carried out "to determine test-retest reliability and longitudinal behavior change under treatment, to compare ratings by different raters under different situations, to carry out typological analysis of the individual's score patterns and further factor analysis of the scale at the item level." In conclusion, it is the reviewer's opinion that the scale should be considered an experimental instrument with limited utility for non-institutionalized populations pending further standardization work.

[38]

★**The Adjective Check List.** Grades 9–16 and adults; 1952–65; ACL; 24 scores: number of adjectives checked, defensiveness, favorable adjectives checked, unfavorable adjectives checked, self-confidence, self-control, lability, personal adjustment, achievement, dominance, endurance, order, intraception, nurturance, affiliation, heterosexuality, exhibition, autonomy, aggression, change, succorance, abasement, deference, counseling readiness; 1 form ('52) ; 4 formats; manual ('65, 34 pages) ; $2.50 per manual; $2.50 per specimen set; postage extra; (15–20) min-

utes; Harrison G. Gough and Alfred B. Heilbrun, Jr. (manual) ; Consulting Psychologists Press, Inc. *

a) BOOKLET FORMAT. Test booklet (3 pages) ; profile ('65, 1 page) ; $2.75 per 25 tests; $1.25 per 25 profiles; hand scoring stencils must be prepared by test user.

b) IBM FORMAT. IBM 1230 test-answer sheet (2 pages) labeled Parker Answer Sheet; $5 per 50 IBM 1230 test-answer sheets.

c) NCS FORMAT. NCS test-answer sheet (2 pages) ; $4.75 per 50 tests; NCS scoring service and duplicate profiles; $1.25 to 90¢ per test (daily service), 80¢ to 50¢ per test ($20 minimum; weekly service).

d) DELA DATA FORMAT. Mark sense test-answer cards (6 pages) ; $5 per 50 tests; Dela Data scoring service and duplicate profiles, 75¢ to 50¢ per test.

REFERENCES

1–102. See P:4, also includes a cumulative name index to the first 102 references for this test.
103. SMITH, ALEXANDER FROTHINGHAM. *Some Characteristics of High Level Talent as Found in Selected Connecticut High Schools.* Doctor's thesis, University of Connecticut (Storrs, Conn.), 1953. (*DA* 13:1094)
104. GRIGG, AUSTIN EARNEST. *Speech Characteristics and Content of Client Statements as Cues for Clinical Judgment.* Doctor's thesis, State University of Iowa (Iowa City, Iowa), 1957. (*DA* 17:3091)
105. HEILBRUN, ALFRED B., JR. "Relationships Between the Adjective Check-List, Personal Preference Schedule and Desirability Factors Under Varying Defensiveness Conditions." *J Clin Psychol* 14:283–7 Jl '58. * (*PA* 33:8351)
106. CONNOR, RALPH GORDON. *The Self-Concepts of Alcoholics.* Doctor's thesis, University of Washington (Seattle, Wash.), 1961. (*DA* 21:3871)
107. GRIERSON, KENNETH MILLER. *A Study of the Self Concepts of a Group of Adolescent Students and the Relationship Between These Self Concepts and Behavioral Ratings.* Doctor's thesis, University of Oregon (Eugene, Ore.), 1961. (*DA* 21:2588)
108. BROXTON, JUNE A. *Interpersonal Attraction Factors Involved in Roommate Satisfaction Among College Freshmen.* Doctor's thesis, University of Kentucky (Lexington, Ky.), 1962. (*DAI* 31:2252B)
109. HEILBRUN, ALFRED B., JR. "A Comparison of Empirical Derivation and Rational Derivation of an Affiliation Scale." *J Clin Psychol* 18:101–2 Ja '62. * (*PA* 38:6906)
110. ROBINSON, MARCELLE. *A Study of Recall Set Utilizing Early Childhood Recollections and Recent Recollections.* Doctor's thesis, University of Southern California (Los Angeles, Calif.), 1962. (*DA* 23:302)
111. SMITH, DONALD C. *Personal and Social Adjustment of Gifted Adolescents.* CEC Research Monograph, Series A, No. 4. Washington, D.C.: Council for Exceptional Children, National Education Association, 1962. Pp. iv, 65. *
112. VON DER LIPPE, ROBERT PAUL. *Socialization of the Physician: A Study in the Sociology of the Professions.* Doctor's thesis, Stanford University (Stanford, Calif.), 1962. (*DA* 23:348)
113. GOLDBERG, LEWIS R. *Test-Retest and Other Item Statistics for an Adjective Check List.* ORI Research Monograph, Vol. 3, No. 5. Eugene, Ore.: Oregon Research Institute, November 1963. Pp. iii, 93. *
114. LAMBERT, PHILIP. "The 'Successful' Child: Some Implications of Teacher Stereotyping." *J Ed Res* 56:551–3 Jl–Ag '63. *
115. PALMER, ROBERT D. "Hand Differentiation and Psychological Functioning." *J Personality* 31:445–61 D '63. * (*PA* 38:8373)
116. PARKER, GEORGE VICTOR COMBS. *Some Concomitants of Dominance in the Psychotherapy Interview.* Doctor's thesis, State University of Iowa (Iowa City, Iowa), 1963. (*DA* 24: 4803)
117. SCHENDEL, JACK S. *The Differences Between the Psychological Characteristics of Ninth Grade, Twelfth Grade, and College Athletes and Non-Participants in Athletics.* Doctor's thesis, University of Oregon (Eugene, Ore.), 1963.
118. GOEN, JEAN NELLITA. *Explorations of Crites' Vocational Diagnostic System.* Doctor's thesis, State University of Iowa (Iowa City, Iowa), 1964. (*DA* 25:5111)
119. MITTMAN, HOWARD. *The Adjustment of Twins: An Evaluation of the Relationship Between Twinship, Patterns of Identification, and Adjustment.* Doctor's thesis, Yeshiva University (New York, N.Y.), 1964. (*DA* 25:3678)
120. SILLER, JEROME. "Personality Determinants of Reaction to the Physically Disabled." *Am Found Blind Res B* 7:37–52 D '64. * (*PA* 39:9978)
121. CASHDAN, SHELDON. *Personality and Creativity: A Study of Talented High School Students.* Doctor's thesis, University of North Carolina (Chapel Hill, N.C.), 1965. (*DA* 27:290B)

122. SCHEIBE, KARL E. "College Students Spend Eight Weeks in Mental Hospital: A Case Report." *Psychother Theory Res & Prac* 2:117–20 O '65. * (*PA* 40:3081)

123. FITZGERALD, EDWARD THOMAS. *The Measurement of Openness to Experience: A Study of Regression in the Service of the Ego.* Doctor's thesis, University of California (Berkeley, Calif.), 1966. (*DA* 27:955B)

124. GORDON, GALE LYNN. *Divergent and Spontaneous Art Strategy Comparison Profile for Art and Non-Art Female College Students.* Doctor's thesis, Pennsylvania State University (University Park, Pa.), 1966. (*DA* 27:3615A)

125. HANDY, DEIRDRE CATHLEEN PATRICK. *The Relationship of Hierarchical Need Level to Success of Peace Corps Trainees.* Doctor's thesis, University of Texas (Austin, Tex.), 1966. (*DA* 27:2882A)

126. HELSON, RAVENNA. "Personality of Women With Imaginative and Artistic Interests: The Role of Masculinity, Originality, and Other Characteristics in Their Creativity." *J Personality* 34:1–25 Mr '66. * (*PA* 40:8830)

127. NEWMAN, PHYLLIS MACY. *The Effects of Making Social Desirability Judgments on Personality Inventory Scores of Schizophrenics.* Doctor's thesis, University of Southern California (Los Angeles, Calif.), 1966. (*DA* 27:3293B)

128. QUENK, NAOMI LITT. *Fantasy and Personal Outlook: A Study of Daydreaming as a Function of Optimism, Pessimism, Realism, and Anxiety.* Doctor's thesis, University of California (Berkeley, Calif.), 1966. (*DA* 27:970B)

129. SCHWAB, LOIS OPPER. *Self-Perceptions of Physically Disabled Homemakers.* Doctor's thesis, University of Nebraska (Lincoln, Neb.), 1966. (*DA* 27:1270A)

130. SINGER, SUSAN KLUGMAN. *Factors Related to Participants' Memory for a Conversation.* Doctor's thesis, University of California (Berkeley, Calif.), 1966. (*DA* 27:1295B)

131. BARTLETT, WILLIS EDWARD. *Psychological Needs and Vocational Maturity of Manpower Trainees.* Doctor's thesis, Ohio State University (Columbus, Ohio), 1967. (*DA* 28:3456A)

132. CAVA, ESTHER LADEN. *Differences Between Interactions of Mothers With Their More Troublesome Children and Their Less Troublesome Children.* Doctor's thesis, Ohio State University (Columbus, Ohio), 1967. (*DA* 28:2619B)

133. CHAFFEE, GLENN ALBERT. *A Study of the Self Concepts, Occupational Personas, and Occupational Stereotypes of Engineering Students.* Doctor's thesis, Michigan State University (East Lansing, Mich.), 1967. (*DA* 28:3968A)

134. ISSEL, RICHARD PHILLIP. *Exploratory Research in Need for Approval, Approval Conditions, and Defensiveness in a Psychiatric Setting.* Doctor's thesis, Purdue University (Lafayette, Ind.), 1967. (*DA* 28:2625B)

135. JOHNSON, EDWARD G., JR. *A Comparison of Academically Successful and Unsuccessful College of Education Freshmen on Two Measures of "Self."* Doctor's thesis, University of Toledo (Toledo, Ohio), 1967. (*DA* 28:1298A)

136. PARKER, GEORGE V. C. "Some Concomitants of Therapist Dominance in the Psychotherapy Interview." *J Consult Psychol* 31:313–8 Je '67. * (*PA* 41:10543)

137. PARSONS, LOWELL BURT. *"Psychotherapists'" Behavior as a Function of Their Experience and Dominance and of Client Type.* Doctor's thesis, University of Texas (Austin, Tex.), 1967. (*DA* 28:214-B)

138. PEDERSON, M. GORDON. *Accelerating Client Therapeutic Growth Via Videotape.* Doctor's thesis, Marquette University (Milwaukee, Wis.), 1967. (*DA* 29:2969A)

139. ROWELL, WILLIAM JOSEPH. *Some Relationships Among Fathers' Perception of Sons' Problem-Solving Ability; Fathers' Teaching Methods; and Fathers' Descriptions of Self and Son.* Doctor's thesis, University of North Carolina (Chapel Hill, N.C.), 1967. (*DA* 28:4763B)

140. STRINGER, PETER. "A Comparison of the Self-Images of Art and Architectural Students." *Studies Art Ed* 9:33–49 au '67. *

141. TORTORELLA, WILLIAM MICHAEL. *The Effects of a Stressful Situation on a Creative Task.* Doctor's thesis, Fordham University (New York, N.Y.), 1967. (*DA* 28:1214B)

142. WOOD, WILLIAM DRANE. *Dominance as a Measure of Interaction in Married and Ad Hoc Dyads Under Different Task Conditions.* Doctor's thesis, University of North Carolina (Chapel Hill, N.C.), 1967. (*DA* 28:4768B)

143. ADAIR, FRED LAWRENCE. *The Development of a Scale to Measure the Service Orientation of Librarians: Preliminary Investigations.* Doctor's thesis, University of North Carolina (Chapel Hill, N.C.), 1968. (*DA* 29:2088A)

144. ALLAN, THOMAS KENNETH, AND HODGSON, EDWARD W. "The Use of Personality Measurements as a Determinant of Patient Cooperation in an Orthodontic Practice." *Am J Orthodontics* 54:433–40 Je '68. *

145. ALLEN, L. R., AND DOOTJES, I. "Some Personality Considerations of an Alcoholic Population." *Percept & Motor Skills* 27:707–12 D '68. * (*PA* 43:8469)

146. BODDEN, JOHN L., AND WALSH, W. BRUCE. "Increasing the Effectiveness of the Selection of Residence Counselors." *J Col Stud Personnel* 9:193–4 My '68. *

147. BOUCHARD, THOMAS J., JR. "Convergent and Discriminant Validity of the Adjective Check List and Edwards Personal Preference Schedule." *Ed & Psychol Meas* 28:1165–71 w '68. * (*PA* 44:6777)

148. CLIFF, NORMAN. "Adjective Check List Responses and Individual Differences in Perceived Meaning." *Ed & Psychol Meas* 28:1063–77 w '68. * (*PA* 44:6787)

149. DAVIS, ANNE JOE. *Self Concept, Occupational Role Expectations, and Occupational Choice in Nursing and Social Work.* Doctor's thesis, University of California (Berkeley, Calif.), 1968. (*DA* 29:3414A)

150. DAVIS, CLIFFORD E., AND WAGNER, PAULA D. *Evaluating and Counseling Prospective Church Workers: Supplement 1, Strong Vocational Interest Blank.* New York: Board of Christian Education, 1968. Pp. 19. *

151. DOMINO, GEORGE. "A Non-Verbal Measure of Intelligence for Totally Blind Adults." *New Outl Blind* 62:247–52 O '68. *

152. FOLKINS, CARLYLE H.; LAWSON, KAREN D.; OPTON, EDWARD M., JR.; AND LAZARUS, RICHARD S. "Desensitization and the Experimental Reduction of Threat." *J Abn Psychol* 73:100–13 Ap '68. * (*PA* 42:8261)

153. GOOD, RONALD GLENN. *An Analysis of the Self-Perceptions and Other Selected Characteristics of Effective and Ineffective Teachers: A Study Based on the Educational Philosophy of the Fifth-Year Program in Teacher Education at the University of North Carolina.* Doctor's thesis, University of North Carolina (Chapel Hill, N.C.), 1968. (*DA* 29:4373A)

154. GRAVES, WILLIAM HUGHES. *Some Differences in the Personality Characteristics of Premature Terminators in Two Types of Counseling Relationships.* Doctor's thesis, University of Florida (Gainesville, Fla.), 1968. (*DAI* 30:131A)

155. HAGEBAK, ROBERT WALDO. *An Experimental Study of Client Resistance as a Function of Client Dominance, Therapist Directiveness, and Type of Client Problem.* Doctor's thesis, University of Texas (Austin, Tex.), 1968. (*DA* 29:1841B)

156. HOLLANDER, MELVYN ARNOLD. *The Relationships Among Occupational Stereotypes, Certain Personality Dimensions, and Vocational Preferences of Adolescents.* Doctor's thesis, University of Oklahoma (Norman, Okla.), 1968. (*DA* 29:1754A)

157. KAPLAN, MARTIN F. "Elicitation of Information and Response Biases of Repressors, Sensitizers, and Neutrals in Behavior Prediction." *J Personality* 36:84–91 Mr '68. * (*PA* 42:15448)

158. LOVETT, SARAH LEE. *Personality Characteristics and Antecedents of Vocational Choice of Graduate Women Students in Science Research.* Doctor's thesis, University of California (Berkeley, Calif.), 1968. (*DA* 29:4287A)

159. MASON, EVELYN P.; ADAMS, HENRY L.; AND BLOOD, DON F. "Further Study of Personality Characteristics of Bright College Freshmen." *Psychol Rep* 23:395–400 O '68. * (*PA* 43:9714)

160. MERCER, CAROLYN MALINA. *Reading and Its Relationship With Parental Identification and Personality in a College Population.* Doctor's thesis, University of Houston (Houston, Tex.), 1968. (*DA* 29:2621B)

161. NEITHERCUTT, MARCUS G. *Predicting Outcomes of Federal Parolees.* Doctor's thesis, University of California (Berkeley, Calif.), 1968. (*DA* 29:3512B)

162. THORESEN, PAUL WALTER. *The Use of Self-Description in Identifying and Predicting Students Who Seek Help With Their Emotional Problems.* Doctor's thesis, Marquette University (Milwaukee, Wis.), 1968. (*DAI* 31:1552B)

163. BELL, DURWARD LYNN. *Background and Personality Variables as Correlates of Attitudes Toward and Information About Mental Health and Mental Illness.* Doctor's thesis, University of Texas (Austin, Tex.), 1969. (*DAI* 30:3379B)

164. BRUNNER, BURTON C. "Personality and Motivating Factors Influencing Adult Participation in Vigorous Physical Activity." *Res Q* 40(3):464–9 O '69. *

165. CAIN, ENOCH THOMAS, II. *Factors Operative in Curricular and/or Occupational Choice: A Study of Super's Theory.* Doctor's thesis, University of Idaho (Moscow, Idaho), 1969. (*DAI* 31:949A)

166. DAVIS, ANNE J. "Self-Concept, Occupational Role Expectations, and Occupational Choice in Nursing and Social Work." *Nursing Res* 18(1):55–9 Ja–F '69. * (*PA* 44:21061)

167. FISH, KATHLEEN D. *Paternal Availability, Family Role Structure, Maternal Employment, and Personality Development in Late Adolescent Females.* Doctor's thesis, University of Massachusetts (Amherst, Mass.), 1969. (*DAI* 30:4369B)

168. GOLDMAN, RUTH K., AND MENDELSOHN, GERALD A. "Psychotherapeutic Change and Social Adjustment: A Report of a National Survey of Psychotherapists." *J Abn Psychol* 74(2):164–72 Ap '69. * (*PA* 43:9900)

169. GRAHAM, WILLIAM K., AND CALENDO, JAMES T. "Personality Correlates of Supervisory Ratings." *Personnel Psychol* 22(4):483–7 w '69. * (*PA* 44:13524)

170. HAGEBAK, ROBERT W., AND PARKER, GEORGE V. C. "Therapist Directiveness, Client Dominance, and Therapy Resistance." *J Consult & Clin Psychol* 33(5):536–40 O '69. * (*PA* 44:2454)

171. HALL, WALLACE B., AND MACKINNON, DONALD W. "Personality Inventory Correlates of Creativity Among Architects." *J Appl Psychol* 53(4):322–6 Ag '69. * (*PA* 43:15815)

172. HEILBRUN, ALFRED B., JR. "Parental Identification and the Patterning of Vocational Interests in College Males and Females." *J Counsel Psychol* 16(4):342–7 Jl '69. * (*PA* 43:14837)

173. HERSCH, PAUL D.; KULIK, JAMES A.; AND SCHEIBE, KARL E. "Personal Characteristics of College Volunteers in Mental Hospitals." *J Consult & Clin Psychol* 33(1):30–4 F '69. * (*PA* 43:11408)

174. HOFFMAN, HARVEY E. "Scanning and the Counseling Readiness Scale." *Percept & Motor Skills* 29(2):645–6 O '69. * (*PA* 44:3800)

175. HOLLANDER, MELVYN A., AND PARKER, HARRY J. "Occupational Stereotypes and Needs: Their Relationship to Vocational Choice." *Voc Guid Q* 18(2):01–8 D '69. *

176. ISABELLE, LAURENT A., AND DICK, WILLIAM. "Clarity of Self-Concepts in the Vocational Development of Male Liberal Arts Students (An Abstract)." *Can Psychologist* 10(1):20–31 Ja–F '69. * (*PA* 43:16396)

177. JOESTING, JOAN, AND JOESTING, ROBERT. "Differences Among Self-Descriptions of Gifted Black College Students and Their Less Intelligent Counterparts." *Gifted Child Q* 13(3):175–80 sp '69. * (*PA* 44:13270)

178. KAYTON, ROBERT. *Sex-Role Identity, Parent Perception, and Psychopathology in Adult Males.* Doctor's thesis, University of Massachusetts (Amherst, Mass.), 1969. (*DAI* 30:4374B)

179. KULIK, JAMES A.; MARTIN, ROBERT A.; AND SCHEIBE, KARL E. "Effects of Mental Hospital Volunteer Work on Students' Conceptions of Mental Illness." *J Clin Psychol* 25(3):326–9 Jl '69. * (*PA* 44:3531)

180. LARSEN, MARY SUSAN FAABORG. *Female Achievement Conflict Related to Parental Sex-Typing and Identification.* Doctor's thesis, Michigan State University (East Lansing, Mich.), 1969. (*DAI* 30:4794B)

181. LOWRY, THOMAS WELLS. *The Effect of Training and Selected Cognitive and Personality Variables on Accuracy of Interpersonal Judgment.* Doctor's thesis, University of Texas (Austin, Tex.), 1969. (*DAI* 30:5692B)

182. PARKER, GEORGE V. C. "Sex Differences in Self-Description on the Adjective Check List." *Ed & Psychol Meas* 29(1):99–113 sp '69. * (*PA* 44:16715)

183. PARKER, GEORGE V. C., AND VELDMAN, DONALD J. "Item Structure of the Adjective Check List." *Ed & Psychol Meas* 29(3):605–13 au '69. * (*PA* 44:18733)

184. PEDERSEN, DARHL M. "Evaluation of Self and Others and Some Personality Correlates." *J Psychol* 71(2):225–44 Mr '69. * (*PA* 43:8342)

185. POE, CHARLES A. "Convergent and Discriminant Validation of Measures of Personal Needs." *J Ed Meas* 6(2):103–7 su '69. * (*PA* 44:12613)

186. REINEHR, ROBERT C. "Therapist and Patient Perceptions of Hospitalized Alcoholics." *J Clin Psychol* 25(4):443–5 O '69. * (*PA* 44:10768)

187. REUTER, MARK WILLIAM. *The Father-Son Relationship and the Personality Adjustment of the Late Adolescent Male.* Doctor's thesis, University of Massachusetts (Amherst, Mass.), 1969. (*DAI* 30:4379B)

188. RICHARDSON, BILLY K. *Prediction of Rehabilitation Counselor Effectiveness: The Relationship of Counselor Characteristics to Supervisors' Ratings.* Doctor's thesis, University of Iowa (Iowa City, Iowa), 1969. (*DAI* 30:3738A)

189. ST. DENIS, GERALD CHARLES. *Interracial Adoptions in Minnesota Self-Concept and Child Rearing Attitudes of Caucasian Parents Who Have Adopted Negro Children.* Doctor's thesis, University of Minnesota (Minneapolis, Minn.), 1969. (*DAI* 30:2633A)

190. SCARR, SANDRA. "Social Introversion-Extraversion as a Heritable Response." *Child Develop* 40(3):823–32 S '69. * (*PA* 44:2201)

191. SCHAEFER, CHARLES E. "The Prediction of Creative Achievement From a Biographical Inventory." *Ed & Psychol Meas* 29(2):431–7 su '69. * (*PA* 44:17333)

192. SCHAEFER, CHARLES E. "The Self-Concept of Creative Adolescents." *J Psychol* 72(2):233–42 Jl '69. * (*PA* 44:658)

193. VANDERPOOL, JAMES A. "Alcoholism and the Self-Concept." *Q J Studies Alcohol* 30(1A):59–77 Mr '69. * (*PA* 43:11588)

194. WADSWORTH, ALLEN PRATT, JR. *Social and Personality Factors Associated With Drop-Out From the Pastorate.* Doctor's thesis, University of North Carolina (Chapel Hill, N.C.), 1969. (*DAI* 30:3290A)

195. WELSH, GEORGE S. *Gifted Adolescents: A Handbook of Test Results.* Greensboro, N.C.: Prediction Press; June 1969. Pp. viii, 89. *

196. WHITTAKER, DAVID. "Masculinity-Femininity and Nonconformist Youth." Abstract. *Proc 77th Ann Conv Am Psychol Assn* 4(1):297–8 '69. * (*PA* 43:17481)

197. ZIEGLER, DANIEL JAMES. *The Relationship of Self-Concept and Vocational Interest to Vocational Preference in Male College Students.* Doctor's thesis, Temple University (Philadelphia, Pa.), 1969. (*DAI* 30:1911B)

198. ADAMS, HENRY L.; MASON, EVELYN P.; AND BLOOD, DON F. "Personality Characteristics of American and English, Bright and Average College Freshmen." *Psychol Rep* 26(3):831–4 Je '70. * (*PA* 45:1256)

199. ANDREW, JASON DANA. *The Relationship of Selected Counselor Characteristics to Counselor Satisfaction With and Participation in a Program of Continuing Education.* Doctor's thesis, University of Iowa (Iowa City, Iowa), 1970. (*DAI* 31:2676A)

200. BARRON, FRANK, AND ROSENBERG, MARVIN. "King Lear and His Fool: A Study of the Conception and Enactment of Dramatic Role in Relation to Self-Conception." *Ed Theatre J* 22(3):276–83 O '70. *

201. BARTLETT, WILLIS E. "Psychological Need Profiles of Manpower Trainees." *Voc Guid Q* 19(1):5–10 S '70. *

202. BATES, HENRY D. "Prediction of Self-Descriptions and Overt Behavior From a Scale of Assertiveness." *Newsl Res Psychol* 12(1):13–4 F '70. *

203. BOXER, LOUIS. "Mate Selection and Emotional Disorder." *Family Coordinator* 19(2):173–9 Ap '70. * (*PA* 44:16662)

204. CHINSKY, JACK M., AND RAPPAPORT, JULIAN. "Attitude Change in College Students and Chronic Patients: A Dual Perspective." *J Consult & Clin Psychol* 35(3):388–94 D '70. * (*PA* 45:4464)

205. CHISHOLM, MARGERY (MENGES). *A Study to Determine the Influence of Actual Self Observation on Selected Aspects of the Self Awareness of Participants in T-Groups.* Doctor's thesis, Boston University (Boston, Mass.), 1970. (*DAI* 31:2171A)

206. DOMINO, GEORGE. "Identification of Potentially Creative Persons From the Adjective Check List." *J Consult & Clin Psychol* 35(1):48–51 Ag '70. * (*PA* 44:20998)

207. EISENBERG, MYRON GAIL. *An Examination of a Procedure for Determining Personality Correlates to Independence of Judgment in Male University Students.* Doctor's thesis, Northwestern University (Evanston, Ill.), 1970. (*DAI* 31:4309B)

208. ERICKSON, CLARA; GANTZ, BENJAMIN S.; AND STEPHENSON, ROBERT W. "Logical and Construct Validation of a Short-Form Biographical Inventory Predictor of Scientific Creativity." Abstract. *Proc 78th Ann Conv Am Psychol Assn* 5(1):151–2 '70. * (*PA* 44:18715)

209. FRUIN, DAVID JOHN. *Response Styles and Creativity.* Doctor's thesis, Johns Hopkins University (Baltimore, Md.), 1970. (*DAI* 31:4361B)

210. GILBART, THOMAS EDGAR. *Self-Regard, Maladjustment, and Creative Potential Among College Counselees, Creatives, and Normals.* Doctor's thesis, St. John's University (Jamaica, N.Y.), 1970. (*DAI* 31:2177A)

211. HEILBRUN, ALFRED B., JR. "Adjective Check List Correlates of Social Conflict Problems in College Students." *Meas & Eval Guid* 3(3):158–63 f '70. * (*PA* 45:10634)

212. HEILBRUN, ALFRED B., JR. "Toward Resolution of the Dependency-Premature Termination Paradox for Females in Psychotherapy." *J Consult & Clin Psychol* 34(3):382–6 Je '70. * (*PA* 44:14749)

213. HELSON, RAVENNA, AND CRUTCHFIELD, RICHARD S. "Creative Types in Mathematics." *J Personality* 38(2):177–97 Je '70. * (*PA* 44:18669)

214. HELSON, RAVENNA, AND CRUTCHFIELD, RICHARD S. "Mathematicians: The Creative Researcher and the Average PhD." *J Consult & Clin Psychol* 34(2):250–7 Ap '70. * (*PA* 44:10374)

215. HENRY, GORDON HOWARD. *Open and Closed Mindedness, Values, and Other Personality Characteristics of Male College Students Who Served on or Appeared Before Judiciary Boards.* Doctor's thesis, University of North Dakota (Grand Forks, N.D.), 1970. (*DAI* 31:2106A)

216. HESS, ANNE L., AND BRADSHAW, H. L. "Positiveness of Self-Concept and Ideal Self as a Function of Age." *J Genetic Psychol* 117(1):57–67 S '70. * (*PA* 45:2111)

217. HOLLENDER, JOHN W., AND SCHALON, CHARLES L. "Personality Test Differences Between Vocational-Educational and Personal Adjustment Counseling Clients." *Meas & Eval Guid* 2(4):199–204 w '70. *

218. IVANOFF, JOHN M.; LAYMAN, JANE A.; AND VON SINGER, RONALD. "Changes in ACL Scales Corresponding to Changes in Educational Levels." *Psychol Rep* 27(2):359–63 O '70. * (*PA* 45:7042)

219. JOHNSON, RAY W. "Parental Identification and Vocational Interests of College Women." *Meas & Eval Guid* 3(3):147–51 f '70. * (*PA* 45:4977)

220. KELLY, MARYNELL ATWATER. *Active vs Passive Leadership Techniques With Development Groups.* Doctor's thesis, University of Arizona (Tucson, Ariz.), 1970. (*DAI* 31:2990B)

221. MENDELSOHN, GERALD A., AND GALL, MEREDITH D. "Personality Variables and the Effectiveness of Techniques to Facilitate Creative Problem Solving." *J Pers & Social Psychol* 16(2):346–51 O '70. * (*PA* 45:2395)

222. ROBERTS, MARJORIE KLAWITTER. *Change in Self-Concept of Leg Amputees After Prosthetic Replacement.* Doctor's thesis, Catholic University of America (Washington, D.C.), 1970. (*DAI* 31:3713B)

223. SCHAEFER, CHARLES E. "A Psychological Study of 10 Exceptionally Creative Adolescent Girls." *Excep Children* 36(6):431–41 F '70. * (*PA* 44:20978)

224. SHERMAN, RICHARD C., AND POE, CHARLES A. "Factor-Analytic Scales of a Normative Form of the EPPS." *Meas & Eval Guid* 2(4):243–8 w '70. *

225. SILVERMAN, IRWIN; SHULMAN, ARTHUR D.; AND WIESENTHAL, DAVID L. "Effects of Deceiving and Debriefing Psychological Subjects on Performance in Later Experiments." *J Pers & Social Psychol* 14(3):203–12 Mr '70. * (*PA* 44:7637)

226. VELDMAN, DONALD J., AND PARKER, GEORGE V. C. "Adjective Rating Scales for Self Description." *Multiv Behav Res* 5(3):295–302 Jl '70. * (*PA* 45:710)

227. VON SINGER, RON, AND PEDERSON, M. GORDON. "Behavioral Correlates of the ACL Heterosexual Scale." *Psychol Rep* 26(3):719–22 Je '70. * (*PA* 45:693)

228. WAGNER, M. K., AND BRAGG, R. A. "Comparing Behavior Modification Approaches to Habit Decrement—Smoking." *J Consult & Clin Psychol* 34(2):258–63 Ap '70. * (*PA* 44:10364)

229. WEISSMAN, HERBERT N. "Disposition Toward Intellectuality: Its Composition and Its Assessment." *J General Psychol* 82(1):99–107 Ja '70. * (*PA* 44:10452)

230. WEISSMAN, HERBERT N., AND RITTER, KENNETH. "Openness to Experience, Ego Strength and Self-Description as a Function of Repression and Sensitization." *Psychol Rep* 26(3):859–64 Je '70. * (*PA* 45:685)

231. WHITE, MARY ROBERT. *A Follow-Up Study of Candidates in a Religious Community of Women.* Doctor's thesis, Fordham University (New York, N.Y.), 1970. (*DAI* 31:3359A)

232. WOHL, JULIAN, AND PALMER, ALBERT B. "Correlations Between Adjective Check List and Edwards Personal Preference Schedule Measures of Murray's Needs." *Psychol Rep* 27(2):525–6 O '70. * (*PA* 45:6360)

233. ZIEGLER, DANIEL J. "Self-Concept, Occupational Member Concept, and Occupational Interest Area Relationships in Male College Students." *J Counsel Psychol* 17(2):133–6 Mr '70. * (*PA* 44:9412)

LEONARD G. RORER, *Research Associate, Oregon Research Institute, Eugene, Oregon.*

Since anyone who can read a dictionary can construct an adjective check list, one must wonder what Gough and Heilbrun did to entitle them to claim copyright protection for *The Adjective Check List.* Did they select the adjectives in such a way that they are, if not exhaustive, at least representative of some specifiable domain? Did they collect subsequent data to show that their list is sufficiently precise, exhaustive, or unique so that it can be recommended on one of those grounds? Do they present normative data for their adjectives and for the scales formed from them? Have they constructed scales for which validity or utility have been shown? Have they carried out studies to determine the structure or dimensionality of their list? The reader who wishes to be spared the details need read no further: the answer to all of these questions is no.

SELECTION AND CHARACTERISTICS OF THE ADJECTIVES. With regard to the construction of the initial list of 279 words, the manual states that, "The 171 words from Cattell's study were canvassed, and words thought to be more or less essential for describing personality from different theoretical vantage points were added." Cattell's 171 "words" are of the following form: [1]

ascetic ——————————— sensuous	
Abstinent, abstemious, Calvinistic.	Pleasure-seeking, self-indulgent, epicurean.

Just what use was made of them, beyond canvassing, is never stated. Inspection shows that

in some cases several words have been taken from a cluster, whereas in other cases, as in the example, none was used.

Since Cattell intended that his list should be exhaustive, and since he carried out a number of studies in which he identified clusters of items that he claimed would effectively span the domain of personality trait descriptors, and since Tupes and Christal [2] and Norman [3] have subsequently provided constructive replications, one would expect that Gough and Heilbrun would have availed themselves of this information and indicated those adjectives which had been included in the present list to mark the factors (clusters) identified in these studies. Such is not the case. No reference to these studies is made.

Not only is no claim made for the comprehensiveness of the original list, but the reader is told that when the list was first introduced in 1950, "It soon became apparent that a number of important words had been omitted." While it is possible to figure out that the number of "important" words was five, it is not possible to identify those words, or to determine the basis on which it became apparent that they were "important." The manual states that this increase to 284 words took place in 1961, whereas the present list of 300 was prepared in 1952. Whether this is an error or an intriguing fact requiring further explanation, it is representative of the care with which the manual was prepared.

With the exception of a mean (.54) and range (.01 to .86) of the mean test-retest reliability coefficients for the words in the list for one sample of 100 men, no itemmetric data (including normative data of any kind) are presented.

SCALES. The manual provides keys for 24 scales, but no easy self-scoring system is available. One scale is the total number of adjectives checked; two more give the number checked from the 75 adjectives selected as most and least desirable by 87 undergraduate psychology students. Six of the scales were empirically constructed—five to discriminate individuals rated high and low with respect to self-confidence, self-control, lability, personal adjust-

1 CATTELL, RAYMOND B. *Description and Measurement of Personality.* Yonkers, N.Y.: World Book Co., 1946. Pp. xx, 602. *

2 TUPES, ERNEST C., AND CHRISTAL, RAYMOND E. "Recurrent Personality Factors Based on Trait Ratings." *USAF ASD Tech Rep* 61–97:1–40 My '61. *

3 NORMAN, WARREN T. "Toward an Adequate Taxonomy of Personality Attributes: Replicated Factor Structure in Peer Nomination Personality Ratings." *J Abn & Social Psychol* 66:574–83 Je '63. *

ment, and counseling readiness; and one to discriminate maladjusted college students whose protocols "coincided" with their level of adjustment from similar students whose protocols did not. Scales to measure 15 of the Murray needs were rationally constructed by 19 graduate students who were given the descriptions contained in the manual for the *Edwards Personal Preference Schedule* and "asked to judge which adjectives, if endorsed, would indicate the presence of each need in the endorsers." It is interesting to note that adjectives such as orderly, nurturent, affiliative, autonomous, exhibitionistic, succorant, and deferent do not appear in the ACL. If these traits were sufficiently important that scales should be built to measure the need for them, why were they not sufficiently important to have been included in the list?

How are these diverse scales to be interpreted? The following paragraph is representative of those provided for each of the scales in the manual:

> The high-scoring subject on *Ach* is usually seen as intelligent and hard-working, but also as *involved* in his intellectual and other endeavors. He is determined to do well and usually succeeds. His motives are internal and goal-centered rather than competitive, and in his dealings with others he may actually be unduly trusting and optimistic. The low-scoring subject on *Ach* is more skeptical, more dubious about the rewards which might come from effort and involvement, and uncertain about risking his labors. He tends also to be somewhat withdrawn and dissatisfied with his current status.

Careful reading of this (and similar) paragraphs reveals a number of interesting facts. First, only one of the adjectives (intelligent) in this descriptive paragraph is both included in the ACL and scored on the Ach scale. (Does lack of intelligence preclude a need for achievement?) Four of the adjectives (trusting, optimistic, withdrawn, and dissatisfied) are included in the ACL, but not keyed on the scale. Now, no good empiricist would be surprised by the finding that the descriptors applied to someone are not necessarily those which he ascribes to himself. But the finding does raise some interesting questions: Is the person with a high need for achievement really the individual who checks the adjectives on the scale, or is he the individual who would be described by the adjectives on the scale? What are the adjectives that would be checked by the person who would be described by the adjectives in the present scale? And finally, what would be the appropriate desig-

nation be for an individual who checked those adjectives which are used to describe the individual who checks the adjectives on the scale?

The most intriguing thing about the description is that most of it is neither contained in the ACL nor easily expressible in terms of the adjectives contained therein. Since the adjectives hard-working, skeptical, dubious, and uncertain, for example, do not occur in the ACL, one wonders how Gough and Heilbrun learned that they were applicable to individuals scoring high on this scale. Did they collect their data on another check list? If these adjectives are really more salient than any of the adjectives in the ACL for describing high scorers on Ach, then why were these adjectives not included in the list?

More fundamentally, how did Gough and Heilbrun learn (of the high scorer on Ach) that "His motives are internal and goal-centered rather than competitive...."? Certainly not from *The Adjective Check List*. In opting to use any adjective check list, it must be recognized that many concepts such as this—or the concept of a "need," which 15 of the scales are supposed to measure—are difficult, if not impossible, to express in adjectival form. For one may have a need for achievement, or dominance, or heterosexuality, but not be achieving, dominating, or whatever, because, for example, achieving and heterosexing may be incompatible.

In short, it is one thing to maintain that those characteristics on which individuals differ in important ways will be encoded in the natural language, something further to maintain that they will be encoded in adjectival form, and something else again to claim that a particular set of adjectives exhaustively maps the domain of meaningful personality dimensions. As the above examples make clear, no such claim should be made for the ACL.

VALIDITY. The section on validity contains a wealth of information, but little evidence for validity. Not only does the manual contain citations which do not appear in the bibliography, but other data are reported without any citation whatsoever (e.g., pp. 18–19) and, therefore, cannot be evaluated. Tables are presented giving correlations (*a*) among the ACL scales, (*b*) between the ACL scales and the standard scales on the CPI and MMPI, and (*c*) between the ACL and the comparable EPPS scales. What these tables make abundantly clear is that, in general, the ACL scales correlate more highly with each other than with anything else. For illustrative purposes, consider Ach again. Its correlation with EPPS Ach is .01. "Ach has its highest correlation with CPI Do (dominance); however, a more interesting finding is that it correlates positively with CPI Ac (achievement via conformance) but negatively with Ai (achievement via independence)." Just why the latter finding is more interesting than the first is not clear, unless it is because the relationship is the reverse of that which would have been predicted. In any event, reference to the tables at the end of the manual reveals that the magnitude of the positive and negative coefficients in question is .30 and −.01, respectively. By way of contrast, correlations with other ACL scales for males, females, and combined samples, respectively, include Df (.41, .63, .51), Dom (.59, .80, .68), End (.55, .76, .64), Ord (.45, .70, .55), Suc (−.22, −.50, −.34), and Crs (−.42, .14, −.17). That's validity?

SCORING. Some of the validity problems may stem from a scoring system designed to control for "total checked" on the grounds that it is a "response set artifact." Even if one were to grant the premise on which the system is based, the system would still be far from optimal. Individuals are assigned to one of eight groups on the basis of their sex and the total number of adjectives they have checked. A separate table for converting raw scores to standard scores is provided for each group. Under this system, two individuals who checked the same number of adjectives on a scale will get different standard scores on that scale if they checked a different number of adjectives on other scales. For example, two males each of whom checked 15 Ach items will get standard scores of 73 and 61 if their total item counts are 75 and 76, respectively. Obviously, a continuous regression function would have been a more satisfactory way in which to make this correction. It should be recognized that, in either case, individual A may have a higher score than B, even though he checked fewer adjectives on the scale than B did. It must be left to the user to decide if, under these circumstances, it is appropriate to conclude that A has a higher need for achievement than B.

No normative data on raw scores are presented.

CHECK LIST RATIONALE: THE BASIC DILEMMA. An adjective check list can be used in two ways: either as the rating instrument itself, or as a device for obtaining samples or reports of behavior from which ratings are subsequently derived. Gough and Heilbrun suggest both uses for the ACL. Unfortunately, the criteria according to which the instrument should be evaluated vary as a function of the rationale for its use, and an instrument that is optimum from one point of view may not be optimum from the other. In the first case one looks for evidence that the instrument can provide ratings which are precise, exhaustive, and well structured, whereas in the second case he looks for evidence that the instrument elicits an optimum distribution of behaviors on the basis of which subsequent ratings may be made. In other words, the first conceptualization implies an orientation toward precision, whereas the latter implies a view of the instrument as a sort of projective device.

The case for a precise, exhaustive, and well-structured taxonomy of trait descriptors has been succinctly put by Norman.[4, 5] The ACL is clearly not it: the list is neither exhaustive nor representative of any specifiable domain; no attempt has been made to exhibit its structure; and the single words are less precise than the clusters (including opposites) that have been used by others. Even if the ACL did provide such a taxonomy, the problem of specifying those procedures by which the applicability of an adjective to a person is to be determined would remain. In the ascription of any adjective, one must have at least an implicit reference class (Is a 6′ 2″ basketball player "tall"?) and rules for ascribing the adjectives relative to that reference class (90th percentile? upper half?). The ACL has neither. Nor does it have a provision for indicating those adjectives which do not apply. In short, Gough and Heilbrun have chosen stimuli and instructions which are designed to increase the "projective" element in an individual's responses. (Small wonder that they think they have a problem with "checking tendency." If you do not tell people what you want them to do, it should not be surprising that they do different things.) The

4 NORMAN, op. cit.
5 NORMAN, WARREN T. 2800 Personality Trait Descriptors: Normative Operating Characteristics for a University Population. National Institute of Mental Health Grant No. MH 07195. Ann Arbor, Mich.: Department of Psychology, University of Michigan, 1967. Pp. 283. *

ACL is clearly inadequate as a rating instrument.

If one adopts the other point of view, namely, that the ascription of an adjective is to be viewed, not as a (self) rating but rather, in the empiricist tradition, as a response, the nontest correlates of which must be determined, then the utility of the instrument rests on the determination of those correlates. The meager validity data provided in the manual would not warrant the recommendation of the instrument on these grounds. Further, if one does not view the responses to the adjectives as the ratings themselves, then there is no longer an a priori case for the use of adjectives as the stimuli on the basis of which to elicit responses. A different rationale for their use must be developed, and data to support that rationale must be presented. In the case of the ACL, neither is forthcoming.

SUMMARY. If you want to use an adjective check list with moderate, noncontroversial terms appropriate for reasonably intelligent, well-educated subjects, you could use the ACL. But you could just as well make up a list of your own. You could even copyright it—call it *The Improved Adjective Check List*. I am saving *The Definitive Adjective Checklist* for my own use.

FORREST L. VANCE, *Professor of Psychology and Director of Counseling and Special Services, University of Rochester, Rochester, New York.*

The *Adjective Check List,* available since 1952, is an alphabetic list of adjectives from "absent-minded" to "zany," to which a subject responds by marking those that are self-descriptive.

"Subject" is the appropriate word because the ACL has been primarily a research instrument rather than a diagnostic or selection device. The instrument can be scored for 24 variables which include 15 needs, measures of personal adjustment, and counseling readiness plus some response-style variables and scales for self-confidence, self-control, and lability. The ACL represents the ultimate in item simplicity, and clearly demonstrates that simplicity at the beginning may devolve into complexity very quickly among test developers. A 24-scale profile is not easy to comprehend or interpret.

One of the most important uses of this instrument has been research work done by Gough and others at the Institute of Personality Assessment and Research (IPAR), at the University of California, Berkeley. His collection of ACL data on large numbers of subjects permits its use to give psychological meaning to dimensions or differences observed by other methods. Gough has, for example, been able to take a prediction equation, apply it to persons in the IPAR data bank, then look at the banked ACL results for high and low scorers on the equation in order to understand the psychological "meaning" of the equation. This is elegant and exciting theoretical work, and underscores the research value of the instrument, independent of the scales that are available for general use.

As might be expected, the scale development work for the ACL is sophisticated and sound. Scoring is complicated because different norm tables are required depending on the number of adjectives checked. However, the instrument is becoming more popular, and computer scoring service is available commercially. Practical considerations aside, there is some room for question concerning the organization of this instrument around the framework of need theory.

It is this reviewer's bias that few situations are illuminated by characterizing persons in terms of the need structure originally developed by Murray in the 1930's. The *Thematic Apperception Test* was, of course, originally devised by Murray to assess the inner needs (and outer presses) of his system. The TAT has remained a popular clinical instrument in spite of the fact that no one (I would wager) scores it routinely for Murray's needs. In part, this is because need-scoring the TAT is difficult, but it also reflects the fact that there are lots of other (more) interesting things to be found in a TAT protocol.

I would like to make something like the same claim for the ACL. It has more to offer than just being another device for assessing manifest needs. We still have the *Edwards Personal Preference Schedule* with us, and we have a newer and more elaborate need-measurer in Jackson's *Personality Research Form*. The EPPS is locked into the Murray need system, and the PRF is heavily invested in the same domain although it is very cleverly put together and could move in other directions. The ACL, as I read its history, got into the needs business fortuitously. The latter looked like a good thing and the ACL could do it economically and well.

Its beauty is that it can also be used to develop and understand other kinds of dimensions.

The most interesting aspects of the ACL to this reviewer are its utility for research, its economical assessment of general adjustment, and its potential for development in line with any user's special needs or theoretical preferences. It is a short, interesting task using machine-readable responses. It would be a mistake for the potential user or the publisher to view it as solely an inventory built around need theory.

[39]

*Babcock Test of Mental Efficiency. Ages 7 and over; 1930–65; BTME; formerly called *Babcock Test of Mental Deterioration;* individual; 10 scores: easy tests, repetition, initial learning, recall and recognition, motor A, motor B, perception time, easy continuous work, total efficiency (based on 8 previous scores), efficiency deviation; 1 form ('40); manual ('65, 70 pages including record booklet); record booklet ('64, 8 pages); reliability data the same as reported in 1940; $16.50 per set of testing materials, 25 record booklets, and manual; $7.50 per 25 record booklets; $5.50 per set of testing materials; $5.50 per manual; postpaid; (70) minutes; Harriet Babcock and Lydia Levy (test); Western Psychological Services. *

REFERENCES

1–14. See 2:1248.
15–35. See 3:71.
36–45. See 4:31.
46–51. See 6:64.
52–57. See P:13, also includes a cumulative name index to the first 57 references for this test.
58. JAMBOR, K. L. "Cognitive Functioning in Multiple Sclerosis." *Brit J Psychiatry* 115(524):765–75 Jl '69. * (*PA* 44: 7136)

AUBREY J. YATES, *Professor of Psychology, University of Western Australia, Nedlands, Australia.*

A distinction needs to be drawn between the theoretical contribution made by Babcock and the worth of the test battery she devised within this theoretical framework. The notion of impairment in efficiency of mental functioning embodied the important distinctions drawn by Thorndike between level (or power), speed, and persistence in performance as measured by intelligence tests (a distinction still largely neglected in the area of intelligence testing). The distinction between power and speed has remained a viable one and has mediated a good deal of recent experimental work, particularly in relation to the hypothesis that chronic schizophrenics are handicapped by being unable to process incoming information fast enough. In spite of the often muddled and strange notions to be found in Babcock's theoretical writings, credit should not be denied her for having seized upon an important distinction in relation to abnormal functioning.

The Babcock test itself, however, is an unbelievably clumsy, complex, and time-consuming device for measuring efficiency, the objections to which have been stated in previous reviews and need not be repeated here. If it is desired to assess whether a discrepancy between power and speed exists, then a test like the *Nufferno Tests of Speed and Level* would seem to be shorter, simpler, and more valid, especially as the Level version of that test is constructed in cyclic form, with the entire difficulty range sampled in each cycle; while the Speed versions successfully eliminate the confounding effects of difficulty. The Babcock test belongs to a past era when the massive "battery" approach was popular in clinical psychology. The time would appear to have arrived when the test should be decently interred and taken off the market. Little research has been published over the past ten years on this test, much of its content and norms are hopelessly dated; and it would not seem to be worth the effort of a rescue operation.

For reviews by D. Russell Davis and Seymour G. Klebanoff, see 4:31.

[40]

★Baker-Schulberg Community Mental Health Ideology Scale. Mental health professionals; 1967; CMHI; primarily intended for measuring groups; 1 form (4 pages); preliminary manual (12 pages, reprint of *1* below); norms consist of mean scores for various professional groups; $5.45 per 25 tests; 95¢ per set of scoring stencils; $1.75 per preliminary manual; $2.95 per specimen set; cash orders postpaid; [10–20] minutes; Frank Baker and Herbert C. Schulberg; Behavioral Publications, Inc. *

REFERENCES

1. See P:14.
2. BAKER, FRANK, AND SCHULBERG, HERBERT C. "Community Mental Health Ideology, Dogmatism, and Political-Economic Conservatism." *Commun Mental Health J* 5(6):433–6 D '69. * (*PA* 44:14694)
3. WALKER, LINDA J. *Differences and Similarities in the Degree to Which Clinicians and Members of the Community Endorsed a Community Mental Health Ideology.* Master's thesis, Smith College (Northampton, Mass.), 1970.

ROBERT FITZPATRICK, *Principal Research Scientist, American Institutes for Research, Pittsburgh, Pennsylvania.*

The authors originally viewed the community mental health ideology as having five major aspects: (1) focus on a population in a community rather than merely on those identified as sick at one time; (2) emphasis on prevention of mental illness through environmental intervention; (3) use of social adjustment as the goal of treatment; (4) recognition of need for comprehensive continuity of care, and (5) emphasis on desirability of total community involvement in mental health endeavors. A pool of 88 assertions representing these aspects of the ideology was drafted by the authors and pruned to 64 after review by a number of prominent exponents of the ideology. The 64 items were arranged in Likert style (strongly agree, moderately agree, slightly agree, slightly disagree, etc.) and administered to several groups thought to vary in the degree to which they embraced the ideology. Some of the groups are described by the authors, and by the publisher in promotional material, as random samples of the members of national professional groups. However, this is correct only in the limited sense that the authors apparently *requested* responses from random samples; since the best rate of response was 81 percent, the respondent groups were far from random.

On the basis of factor analysis and internal-consistency item analysis, a final set of 38 items was chosen to make the scale as homogeneous as possible. It is not quite accurate to say that the "cohesiveness of this ideology was demonstrated" (*2*) by the fact that the items of the final scale are fairly highly intercorrelated since they were designed, rather than discovered to be so.

The scale, furthermore, does not measure the ideology as originally defined. In the final scale, aspects (3) and (4) of the ideology are represented by so few items that they may be said to be effectively omitted. In other words, what was demonstrated was that belief in the social adjustment criterion for treatment and in the need for continuity of care are not part of the relatively homogeneous belief system represented by the other three aspects.

As is usual with the assertions which constitute the items in scales of this type, there are a number of ambiguities and other difficulties of interpretation. For example, consider item 10: "The mental health specialist should seek to extend his effectiveness by working through other people." Imagine the differing images evoked by this item in the psychoanalyst, the psychologist, the social worker, and the occupational therapist! Several of the items assume the concept of the psychiatrist as the chief treatment officer and may therefore arouse the ire of anti-medical-model psychologists and others. Item 34 contains a misprint which might be puzzling to some: "counsel" where "council" is intended.

Even the most conservative of the groups for which data on the scale are available (members of the American Psychoanalytic Association) responded on the average at about "slightly agree" with the ideology. It may be that those who responded were more favorable to the ideology than would be a truly random group of psychoanalysts. Nevertheless, it seems likely that most groups will be on the favorable side. This should not represent a major problem if the scale is used for comparing groups, as is the general intention.

The scale should be restricted in application to mental health professionals and others familiar with the methods and jargon in the mental health area. Reliability is adequate and a reasonable degree of content and construct validity has been demonstrated. (However, it is a highly questionable practice to state in a promotional brochure that: "Validity using nine criterion groups shows significance beyond the .001 level.")

For comparing groups of mental health professionals in their degrees of adherence to the modified community mental health ideology, the Baker-Schulberg scale appears to be adequate and is essentially without competition.

LESTER M. LIBO, *Professor of Psychiatry (Psychology), University of New Mexico School of Medicine, Albuquerque, New Mexico.*

One's adherence to the new ideology of community mental health can now be measured by a reliable and valid scale. The CMHI is a neat little instrument of only 38 items that is designed for use with mental health professionals, allied groups, citizen boards, and similar populations with some knowledge about the issues in mental health programs. The community mental health ideology consists of five major categories: "a population focus, primary prevention, social treatment goals, comprehensive continuity of care, and total community involvement." The scale first consisted of an 88-item preliminary questionnaire, which was submitted to a nationwide panel of 16 prominent leaders in mental health representing the various disciplines. Content validity was ascertained on the basis of these judges' ratings of the extent to which an "agree" or "disagree" response to each item would signify an endorsement of the community mental health philosophy. Inter-judge agreement and distribution of item "extremity" (for a "full gamut of opinion") were used to select the most promising items, and some items were rewritten at the judges' suggestion. The 64 items resulting, with a six-point Likert-type rating form, became the second version of the CMHI.

This second version of the CMHI was then given to 484 people from nine professional organizations, representing various orientations in mental health—from Harvard School of Public Health graduates at one extreme (community mental health model) to American Psychoanalytic Association members at the other (individual psychotherapeutic model). Items were then selected on the basis of item-total correlations (.44 or higher) and factor analysis (which supported the item-total correlations).

The result—the published final version—has 38 items, 19 positively and 19 negatively oriented. Three conceptual categories—population focus, primary prevention, and total community involvement—are proportionally more heavily represented in the final scale. These three categories, it seems, are what make the new ideology of community mental health distinctive.

The CMHI is clearly a unifactorial measure. The same 38 items derived from the item-total analysis received a factor loading of .44 or above on the first factor of the principal-components analysis. Reliabilities range from .92 to .95. Validity was assessed by means of several analyses: (a) Comparison of the nine criterion groups (with one understandable exception, the mean scores were distributed in the order predicted, with overall differences between groups highly significant, as were predicted differences on an inter-pair basis). (b) Comparison of the nine criterion group CMHI scores with their self-ratings of four orientations: somatic (organic), psychotherapeutic, sociotherapeutic (milieu), and community mental health (significant positive correlations of CMHI with community mental health orientation and with sociotherapeutic orientation, and low but significant negative correlations with somatic and with psychotherapeutic). (c) Comparison of high scorers and low scorers with regard to keeping up with new developments (more of the former followed community mental health, culture and personality, social psychiatry, epidemiology, group psychotherapy, and milieu therapy; more of the latter followed individual psychotherapy, biochemistry, genetics, neurology, and neuropharmacology). (d) Comparison of high scorers and low scorers

with regard to preferences in symposium topics (more of the former preferred community mental health and milieu therapy; more of the latter made psychotherapy their first choice). (e) Comparison of high scorers and low scorers on a 19-scale semantic differential (high scorers defined community mental health as good, effective, relevant, timely, new, progressive, wise, complex, right, sophisticated, broad, considered, realistic, needed, important, strong, productive, cooperative, and active; low scorers were less positive about community mental health, rating it less active and less potent).

The CMHI was also given to 140 members of citizen mental health boards in Massachusetts in a study of its (predicted negative) relationship to dogmatism (Rokeach D Scale) and conservatism (Political-Economic Conservatism Scale, 5 items). CMHI scores yielded significant negative correlations with dogmatism and conservatism.

Finally, an unpublished study cited in the manual indicates that the CMHI is sensitive to varying ideology patterns in a mental hospital undergoing change, sufficiently so as to discriminate among work groups and professional departments. Since the original nine-group sample of 484 professionals consisted only of psychiatrists, psychologists, and occupational therapists, it is important to study the CMHI with social workers, nurses, and other mental health groups, as well.

It would also be necessary to assess the validity of the CMHI on a new sample, different from the one on which the scale was developed and refined.

A small criticism: Three of the 38 items seem ambiguous: (a) "A significant part of the psychiatrist's job consists of finding out who the mentally disordered are and where they are located in the community" ("Consists" or "should consist"?); (b) "A mental health professional assumes responsibility....etc." ("Assumes" or "should assume"?); and (c) "It is a poor treatment policy to allow non-psychiatrists to perform traditional psychiatric functions" ("All" or "some"? "Traditional" includes prescribing medication.).

The CMHI has a preliminary manual, consisting largely of a reprint of a clearly-written, well-detailed descriptive article published in 1967. A companion test manual is promised. The test booklets are well printed, with clear instructions, and the four scoring templates are simple to use. The authors have done a most creditable job in constructing and assessing a relevant and useful scale; their studies are soundly conceived and executed, and their reports are clearly written. The CMHI is a valuable contribution to the advancement of research in community mental health.

[41]

*Barron-Welsh Art Scale: A Portion of the Welsh Figure Preference Test. Ages 6 and over; 1959–63, c1949–63; BWAS; a separate booklet printing of the art scale and revised art scale items from *Welsh Figure Preference Test, Research Edition;* 1 form ('49, 12 pages, published as a separate '63); no specific manual; instructions for administration, scoring, and interpretation contained in mimeographed preliminary manual ('59, 35 pages) for the parent test; manual supplement (no date, 1 page); reliability data, based on an earlier form, for revised art scale only; norms below adult level for ages 6–8 only; separate answer sheets (same as those used with parent test) must be used; $10.50 per 25 tests; $2.50 per 50 answer sheets; scoring stencils must be constructed locally; $1 per manual; $1.50 per specimen set; postage extra; (15–20) minutes; George S. Welsh and Frank Barron (test); Consulting Psychologists Press, Inc. *

REFERENCES

1–20. See P:15.
21. MACKINNON, D. W. "Fostering Creativity in Students of Engineering." *J Eng Ed* 52:129–42 D '61. * (*PA* 36: 4HD29M)
22. ROY, JAMES PETER. *The Relationship of Certain Religious Attitudes to Artistic Behavior.* Doctor's thesis, Pennsylvania State University (University Park, Pa.), 1961. (*DA* 22:184)
23. BARRON, FRANK. *Creativity and Psychological Health: Origins of Personal Vitality and Creative Freedom.* Princeton, N.J.: D. Van Nostrand Co., Inc., 1963. Pp. xi, 292. *
24. IRVINE, DAVID JAMES. *An Empirical Study of the Relationship Between Certain Pupil Characteristics and Selected Measures of Creativity.* Doctor's thesis, University of North Carolina (Chapel Hill, N.C.), 1963. (*DA* 25:4543)
25. WHITTEMORE, ROBERT GEORGE, JR. *Modification of Originality Responses in Academically Talented, Male University Freshmen.* Doctor's thesis, Arizona State University (Tempe, Ariz.), 1963. (*DA* 25:6403)
26. GETZELS, JACOB W., AND CSIKSZENTMIHALYI, MIHALY. *Creative Thinking in Art Students: An Exploratory Study.* An unpublished report to the U.S. Office of Education, Cooperative Research Project No. E-008, University of Chicago, 1964. Pp. vii, 202. * (ERIC ED 003 377)
27. BARRON, FRANK. Chap. 1, "The Psychology of Creativity," pp. 1–134. In *New Directions in Psychology II.* By Frank Barron and others. New York: Holt, Rinehart & Winston, Inc., 1965. Pp. x, 422. *
28. MORANO, NICHOLAS THOMAS. *Complexity-Simplicity: An Investigation of Cognitive, Motivational and Personality Correlates.* Doctor's thesis, Fordham University (New York, N.Y.), 1965. (*DA* 26:4079)
29. HELSON, RAVENNA. "Personality of Women With Imaginative and Artistic Interests: The Role of Masculinity, Originality, and Other Characteristics in Their Creativity." *J Personality* 34:1–25 Mr '66. * (*PA* 40:8830)
30. AIKEN, LEWIS R., JR. *A Review of Research on the Welsh Figure Preference Test.* Greensboro, N.C.: Creativity Research Institute of the Richardson Foundation, Inc., June 1967. Pp. i, 31. *
31. FORD, ELEANOR DIANE. *The Relationship of Certain Socio-Cultural Factors Among Junior High School Students to Creativity in Art.* Doctor's thesis, North Texas State University (Denton, Tex.), 1967. (*DA* 28:3502A)
32. MAGOWAN, ROBERT EVAN. *A Comparison of Pragmatical and Hypothetical Problems for Developing Creativity in Design.* Doctor's thesis, Texas A & M University (College Station, Tex.), 1967. (*DA* 28:1992A)
33. PLOGMAN, BERNARD EDWARD. *The Creative Relationship Between Art Teachers and Their Ninth Grade Art Students in Art Room Practices, Personality and Pencil Drawing in Catholic Schools.* Doctor's thesis, University of Cincinnati (Cincinnati, Ohio), 1967. (*DA* 28:3534A)
34. SKAGER, R. W.; KLEIN, S. P.; AND SCHULTZ, C. B. "The Prediction of Academic and Artistic Achievement at a School of Design." *J Ed Meas* 4:105–17 su '67. *

35. MCWHINNIE, HAROLD JAMES. "The Effects of a Learning Experience Upon the Preference for Complexity and Asymmetry in Fifth Grade Children." *Calif J Ed Res* 19:183–9 S '68. * (*PA* 43:5171)
36. PASNAK, MARY FRANCES DRAKE. *Fashion Innovators Compared With Non-Innovators on Clothing Attitudes, Self-Actualization, and Tolerance of Ambiguity.* Doctor's thesis, Pennsylvania State University (University Park, Pa.), 1968. (*DA* 29:1864B)
37. SHRY, STEPHEN ALLEN, JR. *The Relation of Creativity in College Students to Attention Cues.* Doctor's thesis, Oklahoma State University (Stillwater, Okla.), 1968. (*DAI* 30: 1368B)
38. BRAUN, JOHN R. "Search for Correlates of Self-Actualization." *Percept & Motor Skills* 28(2):557–8 Ap '69. * (*PA* 43:15764)
39. EISENMAN, RUSSELL. "Creativity, Awareness, and Liking." *J Consult & Clin Psychol* 33(2):157–60 Ap '69. * (*PA* 43:9747)
40. GARFIELD, S. JEFFREY; COHEN, HELEN A.; AND ROTH, ROBERT M. "Creativity and Mental Health." *J Ed Res* 63(4): 147–9 D '69. * (*PA* 46:4988)
41. MCWHINNIE, HAROLD J. "Some Relationships Between Creativity and Perception in Fourth Grade Children." *Acta Psychologica* 31(2):169–75 Ag '69. * (*PA* 44:14345)
42. PASNAK, MARY FRANCES DRAKE, AND AYRES, RUTH W. "Clothing Attitudes and Personality Characteristics of Fashion Innovators." *J Home Econ* 61(9):689–702 N '69. *
43. SCHAEFER, CHARLES E. "The Prediction of Creative Achievement From a Biographical Inventory." *Ed & Psychol Meas* 29(2):431–7 su '69. * (*PA* 44:17333)
44. ZIMMERMAN, SAUNDRA F.; PEDERSEN, DARHL M.; AND SMITH, KAY H. "The Factorial Determination of Types of Conforming Individuals." *J Psychol* 72(1):101–7 My '69. * (*PA* 43:15688)
45. BAKER, MARJORIE A. SWEENEY. *The Relationship of Creativity to Several Selected Personality Variables.* Doctor's thesis, Washington University (St. Louis, Mo.), 1970. (*DAI* 31:4324B)
46. EYSENCK, H. J., AND CASTLE, M. "A Factor-Analytic Study of the Barron-Welsh Art Scale." *Psychol Rec* 20(4): 523–6 f '70. * (*PA* 46:1193)
47. FRUIN, DAVID JOHN. *Response Styles and Creativity.* Doctor's thesis, Johns Hopkins University (Baltimore, Md.), 1970. (*DAI* 31:4361B)
48. GILBART, THOMAS EDGAR. *Self-Regard, Maladjustment, and Creative Potential Among College Counselees, Creatives, and Normals.* Doctor's thesis, St. John's University (Jamaica, N.Y.), 1970. (*DAI* 31:2177A)
49. HELSON, RAVENNA, AND CRUTCHFIELD, RICHARD S. "Mathematicians: The Creative Researcher and the Average PhD." *J Consult & Clin Psychol* 34(2):250–7 Ap '70. * (*PA* 44:10374)
50. HURLEY, JOHN DONALD. *The Relationship of Dogmatism With Two Measures of Originality.* Doctor's thesis, Boston University (Boston, Mass.), 1970. (*DAI* 31:2183A)
51. KEENAN, JUNE F. *The Relationship of Certain Socio-Cultural and Community Factors Among Sixth Grade Students to Creativity in Art.* Doctor's thesis, North Texas State University (Denton, Tex.), 1970. (*DAI* 31:3782A)
52. KROGER, ROLF O., AND TURNBULL, WILLIAM. "Effects of Role Demands and Test-Cue Properties on Personality Test Performance: Replication and Extension." *J Consult & Clin Psychol* 35(3):381–7 D '70. * (*PA* 45:6353)
53. KROP, HARRY. "Perceptual Preferences of the Mentally Retarded." *Training Sch B* 66(4):188–90 F '70. * (*PA* 44: 13178)
54. MCWHINNIE, HAROLD J. "A Third Study of the Effects of a Learning Experience Upon Preference for Complexity-Asymmetry in Fourth, Fifth, and Sixth Grade Children." *Calif J Ed Res* 21(5):216–25 N '70. * (*PA* 46:2721)
55. MCWHINNIE, HAROLD JAMES. "A Factor Analytic Study of Perceptual Behavior in 4th and 5th Grade Children." *Acta Psychologica* 34(1):89–97 S '70. * (*PA* 45:2179)
56. PARAMESH, C. R. "Value Orientations of Creative Persons." *Psychol Studies* 15(2):108–12 Jl '70. *
57. RENNER, VIVIAN. "Effects of Modification of Cognitive Style on Creative Behavior." *J Pers & Social Psychol* 14(3): 257–62 Mr '70. * (*PA* 44:8435)
58. SMITH, KAY H. "Conformity as Related to Masculinity, Self, and Other Descriptions, Suspicion, and Artistic Preference by Sex Groups." *J Social Psychol* 80(1):79–88 F '70. * (*PA* 44:12572)
59. WEISSMAN, HERBERT N. "Disposition Toward Intellectuality: Its Composition and Its Assessment." *J General Psychol* 82(1):99–107 Ja '70. * (*PA* 44:10452)
60. ZIMMERMAN, SAUNDRA F.; SMITH, KAY H.; AND PEDERSEN, DARHL M. "The Effect of Anticonformity Appeals on Conformity Behavior." *J Social Psychol* 81(1):93–103 Je '70. * (*PA* 44:18593)

LEONARD L. BAIRD, *Research Psychologist, Educational Testing Service, Princeton, New Jersey.*

The *Barron-Welsh Art Scale* has been used in a variety of studies of creativity and artistic preference. It consists of 62 black and white figures that elicited different reactions from a group of artists and art students than from a group of "people-in-general." Barron has interpreted the test as a nonverbal measure of complexity-simplicity related to artistic taste and talent. Barron (*23*) has described the correlates of the tests: "A liking for the complex figures is related negatively to rigidity, constriction, social conformity, subservience to authority, politico-economic conservatism, and ethnocentrism; it is related positively, however, to originality, verbal fluency, expression as opposed to repression of impulse, and to cathection of intellectual activity."

For each of the figures the subject is asked to indicate whether he likes or does not like it. The drawings are presented in a booklet containing 86 such figures, ranging from simple geometric forms to complex and diverse patterns and designs. Many are quite abstract.

A revised form of the scale, the Revised Art Scale (RA), was developed because a high score could be obtained on the original scale just by disliking many of the figures. For example, a score close to the mean for artists could be obtained just by disliking all the figures. The RA scale has a zero correlation with the total number of figures disliked, but a correlation of .85 with the BWAS scale.

Barron (*27*) reports an odd-even reliability of .96 and a test-retest reliabilitiy of .91 after six months. The manual reports test-retest reliabilities of .94 and .90 over one week for the RA.

Scoring is simply by agreement with the key. No interpretation is provided for scores; rather, some of the research studies using the test are summarized. It is not clear from these studies just what a high or low score means. (The "manual" is actually about three and one-half pages in the manual for the *Welsh Figure Preference Test*.)

It is difficult to assess the validity of the BWAS or RA scales without a clearer statement of what the test is designed to measure. The bulk of the studies using the test can be loosely grouped around the idea of creativity, so the test will be reviewed as an assessment of creative potential.

DIFFERENCES BETWEEN GROUPS. The BWAS has differentiated "creative" from "noncreative"

professional artists (*2*), writers, and architects and research scientists.[1] Other group studies are reported by Barron (*23*). This power to discriminate between creative and noncreative groups *within* professions that already involve some creativity is impressive. However, the differences *between* fields indicate that the BWAS should be interpreted carefully. Thus, the mean for the *most* creative male mathematicians is about the same as the mean for the *least* creative architects. The mean of the research scientists is three points less than the less creative women mathematicians. It is certainly debatable whether any of these fields involve substantially more creativity than the others. Also, intriguing as these studies are, they are generally based on small samples and have not been cross-validated. Again it is not entirely clear what these differences are due to.

RELATIONS TO CRITERIA OF CREATIVITY. In student samples, the results for the BWAS are mixed. Rosen (*2*) found a correlation of .40 between the BWAS and ratings of art students' originality and a correlation of .34 with course grades. But in a thorough study by Getzels and Csikszentmihalyi (*26*) the BWAS did not correlate with ratings of art students' creativity, nor to art grades in an art school. (Other measures produced significant correlations.) Helson (*17, 29*) found that the BWAS did not discriminate between students nominated as creative by faculty in a 1966 study, but did find it to discriminate in a 1968 study. (It did not work as well as other measures.) Schaefer (*20, 43*) found that it discriminated between "creative" and "noncreative" boys in art but did not discriminate in other creative areas for boys and did not discriminate for any girls' group. (Again it did not do as well as other measures among the boys in art.) Skager, Klein, and Schultz (*34*) found that a shortened version of the BWAS did not predict either academic or artistic achievement in a school of design.

CORRELATIONS WITH OTHER TESTS USED TO MEASURE CREATIVITY. The scale has been significantly correlated with fluency and originality scales from the Guilford battery (*39*). However, in a sample of art students Getzels and Csikszentmihalyi found no significant correlations between the BWAS and the Guilford

1 MACKINNON, DONALD W. Chap. 5, "Creativity in Architects," pp. 5-1 to 5-24. "The Creative Person": Proceedings of a Conference Presented at the Tahoe Alumni Center, October 13–17, 1961. An unpublished mimeographed report. Berkeley, Calif.: Institute of Personality Assessment and Research, University of California, 1961. Pp. 155. *

tests, the 16 PF, the *Study of Values,* word-association tests, or hidden figures tests, all of which have proved useful in other studies of creativity.

STUDIES OF OTHER CORRELATES AND THE MEANING OF THE PREFERENCES. Barron (*27*) has summarized the personality correlates of the BWAS as follows: "(1) Artistic preference is related positively to rapid personal tempo, verbal fluency, impulsiveness, and expansiveness. (2) It is related negatively to rigidity, control of impulse by repression, social conformity, ethnocentrism, and political-economic conservatism. (3) It is related positively to independence of judgment, originality, and breadth of interest." While all of these relations were found in various studies conducted at the University of California, Berkeley, only a few of them have been supported by other research. For example, Smith (*58*) found no relation between the BWAS and measures of conformity. However, the various research studies do suggest that the BWAS is consistently related to such traits as criticalness, touchiness, liberal attitudes, and independence.

The results from several studies have suggested that the BWAS scores are higher for people of higher social class. Preference for asymmetrical designs may be mediated by education and social class, possibly by opportunities to develop aesthetic sensitivity.[2] The research by Eisenman suggests that scores on the BWAS may be due to preferred styles of perception.

SUMMARY. While the BWAS discriminated between "creatives" and "noncreatives" in several professional groups, it did not do as well in a number of studies of art students and others. In these settings it seemed to be less useful than other measures, including biographical information, which, as Taylor and Holland[3] have pointed out, is the most consistent predictor of creative performance. The personality studies are fascinating, but except for a rather vague dimension of "complexity as a person" it is not clear what is the central underlying connection between BWAS scores and personality. The test seems to have restricted practical value, since it has not been shown to be a consistent predictor or correlate of creative or artistic performance. In addition, the meaning and interpretation of

the scores are difficult to assess. In sum, we can agree with the conclusions of an earlier review of research on the BWAS: "the correlations have not been large, the samples have generally been small, and the results have seldom been cross-validated....while the results are interesting and provocative, it is still not clear exactly what aspect or correlate of creativity is being measured" (*30*). More research about the meaning and uses of the BWAS seems to be needed.

G. C. HELMSTADTER, *Director, University Testing Services, Arizona State University, Tempe, Arizona.*

One of the difficulties faced by the person who chooses to buy the *Barron-Welsh Art Scale* will be that of discovering exactly what it is that the scale measures. Indeed, when he receives his materials, the purchaser may not even be sure the correct package has reached him. For, as it turns out, the answer sheet is labeled "Welsh Figure Preference Test or the Barron-Welsh Art Scale"; the test booklet is entitled "Barron-Welsh Art Scale" and "A Portion of the Welsh Figure Preference Test"; and the accompanying Preliminary Manual for the *Welsh Figure Preference Test* refers to a series of empirical scales, one of which seems to be labeled the *Barron-Welsh Art Scale* and another the Revised Art Scale.

Eventually, the user will discover that there is a single set of 86 black and white drawings which vary in line quality and which include a number of basic shapes. He will also note that while the examinee is expected to indicate whether he likes or does not like each of the drawings, not all items are included in the key for the *Barron-Welsh Art Scale.* The only insight that the user is likely to get as to the meaning of the resulting scores comes from inferences he is willing to make from the evidence that the scale does distinguish between artists and people-in-general and does differentiate between those persons who possess a cluster of personality characteristics which are sometimes associated with the artistic temperament and those persons who do not possess these traits.

TECHNICAL QUALITY. Since the items which comprise the BWAS were selected empirically from the larger pool of 400 items in the *Welsh Figure Preference Test* (which, in turn, was originally developed for use with clinical patients who didn't speak English) on the basis of whether or not they distinguish between

---

[2] CHILD, IRVIN L. "Personal Preferences as an Expression of Aesthetic Sensitivity." *J Personality* 30:496–512 S '62. *
[3] TAYLOR, CALVIN W., AND HOLLAND, JOHN L. "Development and Application of Tests of Creativity." *R Ed Res* 32:91–102 F '62. *

people-in-general and artists and art students, there is at least some evidence of validity. Even though the number of cases in the study was small, the resulting scale did in fact hold up when applied to a second sample of individuals. Additional evidence that the scale may be valuable in guidance work or as a selection device is presented in the form of a reported correlation of .40 between scores obtained on this scale by art students and ratings of the originality of art products which the students created.

Unfortunately, the original Barron-Welsh scale contains 24 items which are keyed "like" and 38 which are keyed "don't like." Thus, this scale is subject to the possibility of being affected by a response set to select only a few items as being liked. Apparently ignoring the possibility that this response set may contain some valid variance, the authors set about developing a revised scale, which would contain an equal number of "like" and "don't like" items. To accomplish this, 12 people who scored high and 12 who scored low (from a total pool of 250 persons) on the original scale were selected and their responses re-examined. Thus, the revised scale contains 60 items to which the 12 high-scoring and the 12 low-scoring persons on the original scale responded differently. No further crossvalidation of the revised scale to determine whether it did or did not distinguish between artist and non-artist is reported. However, a correlation of .85 between the revised scale scores and the scores on the original BWAS was obtained in a study of 100 psychiatric patients.

No reliability coefficients for the *Barron-Welsh Art Scale* per se are reported in the manual. However, one of the studies cited does refer to an odd-even correlation of .96, and the manual does report that one-week retestings of groups of 35 and 29 subjects resulted in test-retest reliabilities of .94 and .90, respectively.

Except for one table showing the means and standard deviations of scores obtained on 27 scales from the WFPT obtained by four groups (75 men, 75 women, 100 male VA neuropsychiatric patients, and 82 boys and girls), no normative data are provided. The only other information about typical levels of performance comes from the results of several studies cited in the manual which suggest that unselected adults will receive scores which average just under 20 while the mean scores for art students and artists will be around 40.

USABILITY. It is suggested that the WFPT can be used with children as young as six years old and even younger. Although it would seem that children at this age level can make judgments as to what they like and don't like, the directions given, as well as the answer sheet provided for the BWAS, may be confusing to children this young. Some confusion might be avoided if the directions omitted reference to other types of answer sheets than the one provided and if the item numbers on the answer sheet which is provided followed the items in the test booklet by going down columns rather than across rows. Also, the answer sheet might cause less consternation on the part of users if enough spaces were allowed between the edge of the paper and the lines on which personal data are to be recorded so that the respondent could print his name in other than miniature letters.

While the quality of printing in the test booklet and the answer sheet is good, the mimeographed preliminary manual is another matter. Also, the purchaser will find that he will have to construct his own scoring stencil from the list of items provided.

SUMMARY. The *Barron-Welsh Art Scale* consists of 86 line drawings taken from the *Welsh Figure Preference Test* which was originally developed for use with non-English-speaking neuropsychiatric patients. While there is some evidence that the BWAS does have validity for distinguishing between people-in-general and persons working in the field of art, similar data are not yet available for the Revised Art Scale, which makes use of the same test booklet but which is scored with a different key. Lack of more extensive validity studies, of evidence of score consistency over long periods of time, of normative data, and of a finished manual leads this reviewer to consider the BWAS more as a promising set of stimuli which can be used in a variety of research situations involving artists and art students than as a highly refined instrument. Any purchaser should be cautious about using this scale in investigations in which the validity of the instrument is assumed without question and about interpreting the results of this scale in guidance or selection situations where important decisions involving one's career might be made.

For a review by Harold Borko of the Welsh Figure Preference Test, *see 6:197 (1 excerpt).*

[42]

★**Behavior Status Inventory.** Psychiatric inpatients; 1969; BSI; ratings in 7 areas (personal appearance, manifest behavior, attitude, verbal behavior, social behavior, work or school behavior, cognitive behavior) and total patient asset score; 1 form (4 pages); instruction card (2 pages); profile (1 page); no data on reliability; $6.50 per 25 forms; $2.70 per 25 profiles; $1.50 per specimen set; cash orders postpaid; (5-10) minutes; William T. Martin; Psychologists and Educators Press. *

[43]

Biographical Inventory for Students. Grades 12–13; 1955–62; BIS; for research use only; 10 scores: action, social activities, heterosexual activities, religious activities, literature-music-art, political activities, socioeconomic status, economic independence, dependence on home, social conformity; Form KDRD1 ('58, c1955–58, 14 pages); mimeographed manual ('62, c1955–58, 38 pages); separate answer sheets (IBM 805) must be used; 25¢ per test; 5¢ per answer sheet; scoring stencils must be prepared locally; $1.50 per manual; cash orders postpaid; (55–60) minutes; Laurence Siegel; distributed by Educational Testing Service. *

REFERENCES

1–6. See 6:67.

JAMES M. RICHARDS, JR., *Professor of Psychology, University of Missouri, Kansas City, Missouri.*

The *Biographical Inventory for Students* is a 93-item research instrument designed to be appropriate for high school seniors and college freshmen. The manual presents information about the procedures for developing the 10 subscales and data for scale reliabilities, validities, and norms. Although these data are limited, they seem appropriate for a research instrument.

The BIS is now about 15 years old; consequently, some of the items are obsolete. For example, the student is asked the types of radio programs he listens to regularly but not the types of TV programs he watches. Similarly, there are few if any items relevant to many of the most pressing concerns of the current generation of students. Finally, there are only a few items tapping the kinds of information found most useful in other biographical inventory studies of adults and college students.[1] Therefore, a researcher wishing to use a biographical inventory to study students would almost cer-

1 HOLLAND, JOHN L. "The Prediction of Academic and Non-academic Accomplishment," pp. 44–51. In *Proceedings of the 1966 Invitational Conference on Testing Problems.* Princeton, N.J.: Educational Testing Service, 1966. Pp. ix, 123. *
OWENS, WILLIAM A., AND HENRY, EDWIN A. *Biographical Data in Industrial Psychology: A Review and Evaluation.* Greensboro, N.C.: Creativity Research Institute of The Richardson Foundation, Inc., 1966. Pp. i, 20. *

tainly be better advised to develop his own inventory emphasizing items relevant to his particular concerns.

[44]

★**Brook Reaction Test.** Ages 13 and over; 1969; BRT; experimental form; may be administered by examiner but tape recording is recommended; 27 scores: 22 interest scores (aesthetic, business, clothing, dances-social functions, entertainment, food and drink, agricultural, humanitarian, intellectual interests, practical, literary, law, military, outdoor activities, people, political, religion, biological sciences, physical sciences, secretarial, sport, travel) and 5 temperament indices (omissions, unclassifiable, questionable responses, sexual responses, multiple themes); 1 form; stimulus test words tape (3¾ ips tape, 5 inch reel); response sheet [no date, 4 pages]; manual in 3 parts: 1 (32 pages), 2 (46 pages), 3 [no date, 1053 pages, by sets of 13 pages]; score sheet (2 pages); reliability data for college students only; £15 per set of test materials and 25 response and score sheets; 65p per 25 response sheets; 50p per 25 score sheets; £2.37 per tape; £1.25 per part 1 or part 2 of manual, £9.50 per part 3 of manual; postage extra; 25(35) minutes; A. W. Heim, K. P. Watts, and V. Simmonds; NFER Publishing Co. Ltd. *

REFERENCES

1. BROOK, D. F., AND HEIM, A. W. "A Preliminary Note on the Brook Reaction Test." *Brit J Psychol* 51:347–56 N '60. * (PA 35:2813)
2. HARGREAVES, D. H.; HEIM, A. W.; AND WATTS, K. P. "An Experiment on the Effects of Mental Set in the Brook Reaction Test." *Brit J Ed Psychol* 33:236–9 N '63. * (PA 38:8418)
3. HEIM, A. W., AND WATTS, K. P. "The Brook Reaction Test of Interests." *Brit J Psychol* 57:171–85 My '66. * (PA 40:10624)
4. HEIM, A. W.; WATTS, K. P.; AND SIMMONDS, V. "The Brook Reaction as a Test of Temperament." *Brit J Social & Clin Psychol* 6:304–12 D '67. * (PA 42:7347)
5. HEIM, A. W. "The Brook Reaction as a Test of Interests and Temperament." *Occup Psychol* 42:105–10 Ap-Jl '68. *
6. KLINE, PAUL. "The Reliability of the Brook Reaction Test." *Brit J Social & Clin Psychol* 8(1):83–4 F '69. * (PA 43:7558)
7. KLINE, PAUL. "The Validity of the Brook Reaction Test." *Brit J Social & Clin Psychol* 9(1):42–5 F '70. * (PA 44:12609)

[45]

★**Burks' Behavior Rating Scale for Organic Brain Dysfunction.** Grades kgn-6; 1968; BBRS; ratings by teachers; 4 scores: vegetative-autonomic, perceptual-discriminative, social-emotional, total; 1 form (1 page); manual (114 pages); $2.50 per 25 scales; $4.50 per manual; $5.50 per set of manual and 10 tests; 10% extra for postage and handling; (5) minutes; Harold F. Burks; Arden Press. *

[46]

★**Burks' Behavior Rating Scales.** Preschool and kgn, grades 1–8; 1968–69; BBRS; experimental; ratings of problem children by teachers or parents in 18 or 20 areas: self blame, anxiety, withdrawal, dependency, ego strength, physical strength, coordination, intellectuality, academics (upper level), attention, impulse control, reality contact, sense of identity, suffering, anger control, sense of persecution, sexuality (upper level), aggressiveness, resistance, social conformity; 2 levels; $3.85 per 25 sets of scale and profile; $5 per manual and 10 sets of scale and profile; 10% extra for postage and handling; [10] minutes; Harold F. Burks; Arden Press. *
a) PRESCHOOL AND KINDERGARTEN. 1969; 1 form (4 pages); no manual (upper level manual needed for scoring directions); profile (1 page); no data on reliability; no norms.

b) [ELEMENTARY AND SECONDARY.] Grades 1–8; 1968–69; 1 form ('68, 4 pages); manual ('69, 91 pages); profile ('68, 1 page); $3.50 per manual.

REFERENCES

1. BEGLEY, JON C. "Overt Behavior Variables in Educationally Handicapped Children, by Higher IQ and Lower IQ." *J Learn Dis* 3(8):400–3 Ag '70. *

2. SABATINO, DAVID A., AND HAYDEN, DAVID L. "Variation in Information Processing Behaviors: As Related to Chronological Age Differences for Children Failing in the Elementary Grades." *J Learn Dis* 3(8):404–12 Ag '70. *

[47]

★**The California Life Goals Evaluation Schedules.** Ages 15 and over; 1966–69; CLGES; 10 scores: esteem, profit, fame, power, leadership, security, social service, interesting experiences, self-expression, independence; 2 editions; manual ('69, 32 pages plus tests and profile); profile ('66, 2 pages); tentative norms; $11.50 per examiner's kit of 25 tests, 25 profiles, and manual; $6.50 per 25 tests; $8.50 per 100 profiles; $5 per manual; postpaid; (30–45) minutes; Milton E. Hahn; Western Psychological Services. *
a) [CONSUMABLE BOOKLET.] Form D-S ('66, 6 pages).
b) REUSABLE BOOKLET. Form D-M ('66, 4 pages); separate answer sheets must be used; $8.50 per 100 answer sheets; $4.50 per set of scoring stencils.

REFERENCES

1. SINHA, SACHCHIDA NAND. *A Psychometric Study of Selected Dimensions of Vocational Maturational Motivation: Life Goals.* Doctor's thesis, University of California (Los Angeles, Calif.), 1964. (*DA* 25:5378)

2. KOHLER, ADAM THOMAS. *Some Possible Effects of Leader-Member, Similarity-Dissimilarity in the Counseling Technique of Group Psychoevaluation.* Doctor's thesis, University of California (Los Angeles, Calif.), 1969. (*DAI* 30:5240B)

3. SPIEGEL, DON, AND KEITH-SPIEGEL, PATRICIA. "Factor Analysis of 78 Variables From Nine Personality Tests and Scales." *J Proj Tech & Pers Assess* 33(2):160–7 Ap '69. * (*PA* 43:11352)

ROBERT W. LUNDIN, *Professor of Psychology and Chairman of the Department, The University of the South, Sewanee, Tennessee.*

CLGES is intended to elicit responses to determine "desired future conditions based on economic, social and political attitudes." The evaluation of future goals is intended as giving directions of motivation. Consequently, the general theoretical position, as stated in the manual, is that *"life goals,* in terms of the nomenclature used, *are future-oriented motivating attitudes."*

"The CLGES began with the adaptation of Centers' ten Life Goal classifications." The ten goals on which one is scored are esteem, profit, fame, power, leadership, security, social service, interesting experience, self-expression, and independence.

The subject is given a list of 150 debatable statements which he is asked to respond to on a five-point scale which varies from "strongly disagree" through "?" (neutral) to "strongly agree." After all questions are answered and scored, a profile is drawn up on the basis of the 10 life goals. The author indicates that the norms are still tentative. Different norms are used for males and females. Standardization samples were taken from university students, their parents and grandparents (when available). Mean scores on each of the life goals are presented for the mothers and fathers in terms of occupation. These are all tentative, based on relatively small samples (N's of 309 and 363).

Validities are also tentative. Regarding content validity, the author acknowledges that "whether or not the 15 items in each schedule comprise an adequate sampling of the concept involved must be determined by further use and research." The CLGES was developed to measure dimensions not duplicated by instruments such as the KPR-V, SV, and SVIB. Although relationships with interests and other personality variables appear, the evidence for concurrent validity, then, is not clear. "At present," the author states, "only clues to predictive validity are available." The manual cites a study with VA hospitals using small samples of male patients. It found that "patients who score high on Esteem, Profit, Fame and Power return to the community more quickly and remain out of the hospital longer than do those who score low on these Schedules."

Meager data on reliability are presented. One study of test-retest reliability using 41 upper division and graduate students with a 90-day interval between testing produced "reliabilities ranging from .71 for Social Service to .86 for Independence." Reliabilities for the other scales are not given, but one is led to assume that the reliabilities for the other eight scales range somewhere between these two figures.

Considerable space is given to interpretation, most of which does not tell us much but gives guidelines for future research of the scale. One point is that the CLGES should normally be given along with other tests and interviews. Low scores are represented to be as significant as high scores. One study found that the combination of high scores on Interesting Experiences, Self-Expression, and Independence *"occurs at all ages with individuals in the creative arts."* Generally speaking, however, the present data are too limited, according to the author, in occupational groupings to make strong generalizations.

In conclusion, then, the test is still in its experimental phase, and norms, reliabilities, and validities are tentative. However, opportunities for research are open using various socioeconomic, ethnic, and religious groups, as well as people with different political leanings and occupations.

[48]

★California Preschool Social Competency Scale.
Ages 2.5-5.5; 1969; CPSCS; ratings by teachers;
1 form (4 pages); manual (16 pages); $4 per 25
tests; $1.25 per manual; $1.50 per specimen set; postage extra; Samuel Levine, Freeman F. Elzey, and
Mary Lewis; Consulting Psychologists Press, Inc. *

[49]

*California Psychological Inventory. Ages 13 and
over; 1956-69; CPI; 18 scores: dominance (Do),
capacity for status (Cs), sociability (Sy), social presence (Sp), self-acceptance (Sa), sense of well-being
(Wb), responsibility (Re), socialization (So), self-control (Sc), tolerance (To), good impression (Gi),
communality (Cm), achievement via conformance
(Ac), achievement via independence (Ai), intellectual
efficiency (Ie), psychological-mindedness (Py), flexibility (Fx), femininity (Fe); 1 form ('56, 12 pages);
revised manual ('69, c1957, 40 pages); profile ('57,
2 pages); separate answer sheets (hand scored, Dela
Data, NCS) must be used; $6.25 per 25 tests; $3.75
per 50 sets of hand scored answer sheet and profile;
$4 per set of hand scoring stencils; $3.50 per 50 Dela
Data answer cards; $3.50 per 50 NCS answer sheets;
$3 per manual; $1 per specimen set; postage extra;
Dela Data scoring service, 45¢ and over per test;
NCS scoring service: $1 to 70¢ per test (daily service), 65¢ to 40¢ per test ($16.25 minimum; weekly
service); Dutch, French, German, Italian, and Spanish editions available; (45-60) minutes; Harrison G.
Gough; Consulting Psychologists Press, Inc. *

REFERENCES

1-33. See 5:37.
34-144. See 6:71.
145-393. See P:27, also includes a cumulative name index
to the first 393 references for this test.
394. GOUGH, HARRISON G.; McCLOSKY, HERBERT; AND
MEEHL, PAUL E. "A Personality Scale for Dominance." *J Abn
& Social Psychol* 46:360-6 Jl '51. * (*PA* 26:2181)
395. LINDZEY, GARDNER, AND URDAN, JAMES A. "Personality
and Social Choice." *Sociometry* 17:47-63 F '54. * (*PA* 29:731)
396. BELL, MARY MONROE. *Measurement of Selected Outcomes of Participation in Girls' High School Interscholastic
Basketball.* Doctor's thesis, State University of Iowa (Iowa
City, Iowa), 1955. (*DA* 15:1544)
397. ROKEACH, MILTON; McGOVNEY, WARREN C.; AND
DENNY, M. RAY. "A Distinction Between Dogmatic and Rigid
Thinking." *J Abn & Social Psychol* 51:87-93 Jl '55. * (*PA*
30:4166)
398. SARBIN, THEODORE R., AND HARDYCK, CURTIS D. "Conformance in Role Perception as a Personality Variable." *J Consult Psychol* 19:109-11 Ap '55. * (*PA* 30:624)
399. SCHAIE, K. WARNER. "A Test of Behavioral Rigidity."
J Abn & Social Psychol 51:604-10 N '55. * (*PA* 31:3074)
400. LANSKY, LEONARD MARVIN. *Patterns of Defense Against
Conflict.* Doctor's thesis, University of Michigan (Ann Arbor,
Mich.), 1956. (*DA* 16:2539)
401. PAYNE, DONALD E., AND MUSSEN, PAUL H. "Parent-
Child Relations and Father Identification Among Adolescent
Boys." *J Abn & Social Psychol* 52:358-62 My '56. * (*PA*
31:4438)
402. RECKLESS, WALTER C.; DINITZ, SIMON; AND MURRAY,
ELLEN. "Self Concept as an Insulator Against Delinquency."
Am Sociol R 21:744-6 D '56. * (*PA* 31:8432)
403. SUNDBERG, NORMAN D., AND BACHELIS, WARREN D.
"The Fakability of Two Measures of Prejudice: The California
F Scale and Gough's *Pr* Scale." *J Abn & Social Psychol* 52:
140-2 Ja '56. * (*PA* 31:2757)
404. WEITZENHOFFER, ANDRÉ MULLER. *Hypnotic Susceptibility as Related to Masculinity-Femininity.* Doctor's thesis, University of Michigan (Ann Arbor, Mich.), 1956. (*DA* 17:1397)
405. COHEN, HOWARD MARTIN. *The Relationship of the
Prison Program to Changes in Attitudes and Self Concepts of
Inmates: An Evaluation of Self-Concept, Acceptance of Self,
Ideal Self, and Predisposition Toward Crime and Delinquency
in Prison Inmates.* Doctor's thesis, New York University (New
York, N.Y.), 1957. (*DA* 18:653)
406. RECKLESS, WALTER C.; DINITZ, SIMON; AND KAY,
BARBARA. "The Self Component in Potential Delinquency and

Potential Non-Delinquency." *Am Sociol R* 22:566-70 O '57. *
(*PA* 33:1782)
407. REED, CHARLES F., AND CUADRA, CARLOS A. "The Role-
Taking Hypothesis in Delinquency." *J Consult Psychol* 21:386-
90 O '57. * (*PA* 33:1784)
408. RODEN, AUBREY HENRY. *The Effects of Residual, Background, and Stimulus on Contributing Behavior.* Doctor's thesis,
University of Texas (Austin, Tex.), 1957. (*DA* 18:503)
409. TRUUMAA, AARE. *The Effect of Masculinity on Projection as Elicited by Male and Female Figures and Situations.*
Doctor's thesis, Purdue University (Lafayette, Ind.), 1957.
(*DA* 17:1601)
410. TUMA, ABDUL H., AND GUSTAD, JOHN W. "The Effects
of Client and Counselor Personality Characteristics on Client
Learning in Counseling." *J Counsel Psychol* 4:136-43 su '57. *
(*PA* 32:5454)
411. DINITZ, SIMON; KAY, BARBARA ANN; AND RECKLESS,
WALTER C. "Group Gradients in Delinquency Potential and
Achievement Scores of Sixth Graders." *Am J Orthopsychiatry*
28:598-605 Jl '58. * (*PA* 33:10645)
412. JENTSCH, RICHARD C. *The Influence of Psychological-
Mindedness and Information on Accuracy of Prediction.* Doctor's thesis, State University of Iowa (Iowa City, Iowa), 1958.
(*DA* 19:570)
413. TEBOR, IRVING BENJAMIN. *Selected Attributes, Interpersonal Relationships, and Aspects of Psychosexual Behavior
of One Hundred Freshman Virgin Men.* Doctor's thesis, Oregon
State College (Corvallis, Ore.), 1958. (*DA* 19:900)
414. ALTROCCHI, JOHN. "Dominance as a Factor in Interpersonal Choice and Perception." *J Abn & Social Psychol* 59:
303-8 N '59. * (*PA* 34:5595)
415. COX, RICHARD HENRY. *A Comparison of Male Freshmen at Northwestern University From Public and Private
Secondary Schools Relative to Adjustmental, Personal'ty, Academic, and Socio-Economic Factors.* Doctor's thesis, Northwestern University (Evanston, Ill.), 1950. (*DA* 20:2141)
416. KEOGH, JOHN FRANCIS. *The Relationship of Motor
Ability and Athletic Participation in Certain Standardized
Personality Measures.* Doctor's thesis, University of California
(Los Angeles, Calif.), 1959.
417. MEADOW, ARNOLD, AND PARNES, SIDNEY J. "Evaluation
of Training in Creative Problem-Solving." *J Appl Psychol* 43:
189-94 Je '59. * (*PA* 34:5568)
418. PETERSON, DONALD R.; QUAY, HERBERT C.; AND ANDERSON, ARTHUR C. "Extending the Construct Validity of a
Socialization Scale." Abstract. *J Consult Psychol* 23:182 Ap
'59. *
419. SCHAIE, K. WARNER. "The Effect of Age on a Scale
of Social Responsibility." *J Social Psychol* 50:221-4 N '59. *
(*PA* 35:4895)
420. ZEDEK, MEIRA ELLEN. *The Conditioning of Verbal Behavior With Negative Cultural Connotations.* Doctor's thesis,
Boston University (Boston, Mass.), 1959. (*DA* 20:1873)
421. ASHMORE, D. L. *Predicting Delinquency With the
California Psychological Inventory and Social Data: A Comparison of Recidivists and Non-Recidivists.* Master's thesis,
University of Oregon (Eugene, Ore.), 1960.
422. BRENGELMAN, J. C. "Extreme Response Set, Drive
Level and Abnormality in Questionnaire Rigidity." *J Mental
Sci* 106:171-86 Ja '60. * (*PA* 35:6427)
423. GOUGH, HARRISON G., AND WOODWORTH, DONALD G.
"Stylistic Variations Among Professional Research Scientists."
J Psychol 49:87-98 Ja '60. * (*PA* 34:8513)
424. HICKS, R. A. *Factor Analytic Studies of the California Psychological Inventory.* Master's thesis, San Jose State
College (San Jose, Calif.), 1960.
425. LANSKY, LEONARD M. Chap. 12, "Mechanisms of Defense: 5, Sex Identity and Defenses Against Aggression," pp.
272-88. In *Inner Conflict and Defense.* By Daniel R. Miller
and others. New York: Henry Holt & Co., Inc., 1960. Pp. x,
452. *
426. MAHONEY, T. A.; JERDEE, T. H.; AND NASH, A. N.
"Predicting Managerial Effectiveness." *Personnel Psychol* 13:
147-63 su '60. * (*PA* 36:2LI47M)
427. NICHOLS, ROBERT C., AND BECK, KARL W. "Factors in
Psychotherapy Change." *J Consult Psychol* 24:388-99 O '60. *
(*PA* 35:5073)
428. O'DONNELL, JOHN A. *A Measure of Retreatism: An
Empirical Contribution to the Theory of Anomie.* Doctor's
thesis, University of Kentucky (Lexington, Ky.), 1960. (*DA*
26:4867)
429. OUELLETTE, EUGENE GEORGE. *A Study of Selected Variables and Their Relationship to Delayed Sidetone Response.*
Doctor's thesis, University of Washington (Seattle, Wash.),
1960. (*DA* 21:2406)
430. PIERCE-JONES, JOHN; MITCHELL, JAMES V., JR.; AND
KING, F. J. "Factor Structure and Factorial Invariance in the
California Psychological Inventory." Abstract. *Am Psychologist* 15:431 Jl '60. *
431. SCARPITTI, FRANK R.; MURRAY, ELLEN; DINITZ,
SIMON; AND RECKLESS, WALTER C. "The 'Good' Boy in a
High Delinquency Area: Four Years Later." *Am Sociol R*
25:555-8 Ag '60. * (*PA* 35:2020)
432. WINBORN, BOB BURTON. *The Effectiveness of Short-
Term Group Counseling Upon the Academic Achievement of*

Potentially Superior but Underachieving College Freshmen. Doctor's thesis, Indiana University (Bloomington, Ind.), 1960. (*DA* 21:550)

433. CARNEY, RICHARD E. "Some Correlates of Religiosity." *J Sci Study Relig* 1:143–4 O '61. *

434. CARNEY, RICHARD EDWARD. *An Analysis of University Student Behaviors With Measures of Ability, Attitude, Performance and Personality.* Doctor's thesis, University of Michigan (Ann Arbor, Mich.), 1961. (*DA* 22:2073)

435. DUNKLEBERGER, CLARENCE J., AND TYLER, LEONA E. "Interest Stability and Personality Traits." *J Counsel Psychol* 8:70–4 sp '61. * (*PA* 36:3FF70D)

436. GARWOOD, DOROTHY SEMENOW. *Some Personality Factors Related to Creativity in Young Scientists.* Doctor's thesis, Claremont Graduate School (Claremont, Calif.), 1961. (*DA* 22:3273)

437. HERZ, AUGUST J. *The Possible Use of the California Psychological Inventory in a Screening Program for Religious Candidates.* Master's thesis, University of Detroit (Detroit, Mich.), 1961.

438. LEVIN, JACOB LOUIS. *An Analysis of Certain Characteristics of Youthful Offenders in the Cook County Jail (Chicago, Illinois).* Doctor's thesis, Northwestern University (Evanston, Ill.), 1961. (*DA* 22:2692)

439. MacKINNON, D. W. "Fostering Creativity in Students of Engineering." *J Eng Ed* 52:129–42 D '61. * (*PA* 36:4HD29M)

440. MITCHELL, JAMES V., JR. "Statistical Relationships Between the Score Categories of the 16 PF and CPI Inventories." Abstract. *Am Psychologist* 16:386 Jl '61. *

441. ROSENBERG, LEON A.; McHENRY, THOMAS B.; ROSENBERG, ANNA MARIA; AND NICHOLS, ROBERT C. "The California Psychological Inventory as a Potential Screening Device in an Academic Setting." Abstract. *Am Psychologist* 16:371 Jl '61. *

442. SEARS, R. R. "Relation of Early Socialization Experiences to Aggression in Middle Childhood." *J Abn & Social Psychol* 63:466–92 N '61. * (*PA* 37:896)

443. SMELSER, WILLIAM T. "Dominance as a Factor in Achievement and Perception in Cooperative Problem-Solving Interactions." *J Abn & Social Psychol* 62:535–42 My '61. * (*PA* 36:4CN35S)

444. WEBB, ALLEN PAUL. *Sex-Role Preferences of Early Adolescents in Relation to Adjustment.* Doctor's thesis, University of Southern California (Los Angeles, Calif.), 1961. (*DA* 21:3859)

445. ALLER, FLORENCE DOROTHY. *The Role of the Self Concept in Student Marital Adjustment.* Doctor's thesis, University of Idaho (Moscow, Idaho), 1962. (*DA* 23:1598)

446. BECK, KARL WILHELM. *The Effects of Psychotherapy on Test Responses.* Doctor's thesis, Purdue University (Lafayette, Ind.), 1962. (*DAI* 30:5683B)

447. CHIGA, DOROTHY E. *Differences Identified in a Group of Psychiatric Nurses Through Use of the California Psychological Inventory.* Master's thesis, University of Utah (Salt Lake City, Utah), 1962.

448. FARROW, BOBBY J., AND SANTOS, JOHN F. "On Conditionability, Personality, and Perception." *Percept & Motor Skills* 15:578 D '62. * (*PA* 38:2620)

449. GILL, LOIS J., AND SPILKA, BERNARD. "Some Nonintellectual Correlates of Academic Achievement Among Mexican-American Secondary School Students." *J Ed Psychol* 53:144–9 Je '62. * (*PA* 37:2009)

450. HAVIGHURST, ROBERT J.; BOWMAN, PAUL HOOVER; LIDDLE, GORDON P.; MATTHEWS, CHARLES V.; AND PIERCE, JAMES V. *Growing Up in River City.* New York: John Wiley & Sons, Inc., 1962. Pp. xiii, 189. *

451. ISMIR, AWAD A., AND KLEBAN, MORTON H. "The Applicability of the Crown-Marlowe Social Desirability Scale to a Psychiatric Hospital Population." *J Clin Psychol* 18:144–6 Ap '62. * (*PA* 38:8494)

452. KLIEWER, VERNON DEAN. *Multiple Stylistic Effects and Self-Report Personality Assessment.* Doctor's thesis, University of Oregon (Eugene, Ore.), 1962. (*DA* 23:3966)

453. McCAUSLIN, JACK ALFRED. *Differences Between College Students Motivated to Seek Help With Their Problems and Those Who Are Not and Changes in the Attitudes of the Latter Following a Counseling Interview.* Doctor's thesis, University of Maryland (College Park, Md.), 1962. (*DA* 23:1583)

454. McCLAIN, EDWIN WAYNE. *The Relationship Between Student Teachers' Self-Reported Perceptions and Pupil Evaluations.* Doctor's thesis, University of Texas (Austin, Tex.), 1962. (*DA* 23:154)

455. MUSSEN, PAUL H. "Long-Term Consequences of Masculinity of Interests in Adolescence." *J Consult Psychol* 26:435–40 O '62. * (*PA* 39:1380)

456. NELSON, J. W. *Correlation Profile Analysis of the California Psychological Inventory and the Study of Values.* Master's thesis, San Jose State College (San Jose, Calif.), 1962.

457. ROSENBERG, LEON A.; McHENRY, THOMAS B.; AND ROSENBERG, ANNA MARIA. "Sociometric Ratings as Predictors of Academic Performance." *J Appl Psychol* 46:265–8 Ag '62. * (*PA* 37:3887)

458. SLOTE, GERALDINE MAE. *Feminine Character and Patterns of Interpersonal Perception.* Doctor's thesis, New York University (New York, N.Y.), 1962. (*DA* 23:1081)

459. SMYKAL, ANTHONY, JR. *A Comparative Investigation*

of Home Environmental Variables Related to the Achieving and Underachieving Behavior of Academically Able High School Students. Doctor's thesis, University of the Pacific (Stockton, Calif.), 1962. (*DA* 23:315)

460. BARRON, FRANK. *Creativity and Psychological Health: Origins of Personal Vitality and Creative Freedom.* Princeton, N.J.: D. Van Nostrand Co., Inc., 1963. Pp. xi, 292. *

461. CARNEY, RICHARD E. "Achievement Motivation, Anxiety, and Perceptual Control." *Percept & Motor Skills* 17:287–92 Ag '63. * (*PA* 38:7231)

462. CHILES, G. *Some California Psychological Inventory Scales as Indicators of Personal Adjustment and Academic Efficiency.* Master's thesis, Marshall University (Huntington, W.Va.), 1963.

463. FERGUSON, BETH ALLEN. *Personality Differences Between Adolescent Girls of High and Low Motor Performance.* Master's thesis, University of Colorado (Boulder, Colo.), 1963.

464. GAWRONSKI, DANIEL ANTHONY. *A Comparative Study of Differences Existing Among Overachieving, Normal Achieving and Underachieving High School Seniors.* Doctor's thesis, Northwestern University (Evanston, Ill.), 1963. (*DA* 25:292)

465. GOLDBERG, LEWIS R., AND RORER, LEONARD G. *Test-Retest Item Statistics Comparing Four Administrations of Items Differentiating "Yielders" From "Independents."* ORI Research Monograph, Vol. 3, No. 2. Eugene, Ore.: Oregon Research Institute, August 1963. Pp. iii, 56. *

466. GOTTFREDSON, DON M., AND BALLARD, KELLEY B., JR. *Interpersonal Maturity Measurement by the California Psychological Inventory.* Public Health Service Research Grant OM 823–2. Vacaville, Calif.: Institute for the Study of Crime and Delinquency, 1963. Pp. vii, 46. *

467. JAFFE, LESTER D. "Delinquency Proneness and Family Anomie." *J Crim Law & Criminol* 54:146–54 Je '63. * (*PA* 38:9006)

468. THORNE, GAYLORD L. "Discriminations Within the Delinquency Continuum Using Gough's Socialization Scale." Abstract. *J Consult Psychol* 27:183 Ap '63. *

469. WHITTEMORE, ROBERT GEORGE, JR. *Modification of Originality Responses in Academically Talented, Male University Freshmen.* Doctor's thesis, Arizona State University (Tempe, Ariz.), 1963. (*DA* 25:6403)

470. WILSON, JACK FRANCIS. *The Factor Structure and Some Correlates of Parental Identification.* Doctor's thesis, Pennsylvania State University (University Park, Pa.), 1963. (*DA* 24:3418)

471. ASTIN, ALEXANDER W. "Personal and Environmental Factors Associated With College Dropouts Among High Aptitude Students." *J Ed Psychol* 55:219–27 Ag '64. * (*PA* 39:5899)

472. BOHN, MARTIN J., JR. *Relationships of Counselor Dominance and Experience to Counseling Behavior.* Doctor's thesis, State University of Iowa (Iowa City, Iowa), 1964. (*DA* 25:5380)

473. BOSTROM, ROBERT N. "Dogmatism, Rigidity, and Rating Behavior." *Speech Teach* 13:283–7 N '64. *

474. CORTNER, FREDERICK DALE. *Personality Characteristics in Adolescents as Related to Length of Residence in a New School System.* Doctor's thesis, University of North Carolina (Chapel Hill, N.C.), 1964. (*DA* 26:3149)

475. EGAN, GERARD VINCENT. *Antecedents and Consequents of Cross-Identification in Adolescent Females.* Doctor's thesis, St. Louis University (St. Louis, Mo.), 1964. (*DA* 25:4814)

476. GARWOOD, DOROTHY SEMENOW. "Personality Factors Related to Creativity in Young Scientists." *J Abn & Social Psychol* 68:413–9 Ap '64. * (*PA* 39:1729)

477. GELLERMANN, WILLIAM PRESCOTT. *A Field Study of Process Variables in Interpersonal Relations.* Doctor's thesis, University of California (Los Angeles, Calif.), 1964. (*DA* 25:5422)

478. GOUGH, HARRISON G., AND FINK, MARTIN B. "Scholastic Achievement Among Students of Average Ability, as Predicted From the California Psychological Inventory." *Psychol Sch* 1:375–80 O '64. *

479. HAAN, NORMA. "The Relationship of Ego Functioning and Intelligence to Social Status and Social Mobility." *J Abn & Social Psychol* 69:594–605 D '64. * (*PA* 39:7560)

480. HETHERINGTON, E. MAVIS, AND FELDMAN, SOLOMON E. "College Cheating as a Function of Subject and Situational Variables." *J Ed Psychol* 55:212–8 Ag '64. * (*PA* 39:4799)

481. JONES, RICHARD R., AND GOLDBERG, LEWIS R. *An Alphabetical List of CPI Items With Corresponding MMPI Numbers.* ORI Technical Report, Vol. 4, No. 1. Eugene, Ore.: Oregon Research Institute, January 1964. Pp. 40. *

482. McCAULLEY, MARY H. *Dimensions of Masculinity-Femininity in Relation to Field Dependence, Dogmatism, and Other Estimates of Perceptual-Cognitive Differentiation.* Doctor's thesis, Temple University (Philadelphia, Pa.), 1964. (*DA* 25:4259)

483. McGURK, ETHEL LA NOUE. *Determinants of Differential Susceptibility to Visual Illusions.* Doctor's thesis, University of California (Berkeley, Calif.), 1964. (*DA* 25:7382)

484. MEGARGEE, EDWIN INGLEE. *Undercontrol and Overcontrol in Assaultive and Homicidal Adolescents.* Doctor's thesis, University of California (Berkeley, Calif.), 1964. (*DA* 25:2614)

485. MITTMAN, HOWARD. *The Adjustment of Twins: An*

Evaluation of the Relationship Between Twinship, Patterns of Identification, and Adjustment. Doctor's thesis, Yeshiva University (New York, N.Y.), 1964. (*DA* 25:3678)

486. SNIDER, JAMES GRANT. *Some Correlates of All-Inclusive Conceptualization in High School Pupils.* Doctor's thesis, Stanford University (Stanford, Calif.), 1964. (*DA* 25:4005)

487. STRICKER, LAWRENCE J., AND ROSS, JOHN. "Some Correlates of a Jungian Personality Inventory." *Psychol Rep* 14: 623–43 Ap '64. * (*PA* 39:1848)

488. TYLER, LEONA E. "The Antecedents of Two Varieties of Vocational Interests." *Genetic Psychol Monogr* 70:177–227 N '64. * (*PA* 39:10878)

489. WORDEN, ORIAN. *The Educational Significance of Styles of Categorization.* Doctor's thesis, Wayne State University (Detroit, Mich.), 1964. (*DA* 28:4500A)

490. BIRD, ANNE MARIE. *A Comparative Study of Certain Personality Characteristics of College Women Participating in Basketball and Modern Dance.* Master's thesis, University of Maryland (College Park, Md.), 1965.

491. BOHN, MARTIN J., JR. "Counselor Behavior as a Function of Counselor Dominance, Counselor Experience and Client Type." *J Counsel Psychol* 12:346–52 w '65. * (*PA* 40:3023)

492. CORDREY, LEROY JAY. *Characteristics of Curricularly Committed and Uncommitted Students.* Doctor's thesis, University of California (Berkeley, Calif.), 1965. (*DA* 26:7153)

493. FREEDMAN, MERVIN B. "The Role of the Educated Woman: An Empirical Study of the Attitudes of a Group of College Women." *J Col Stud Personnel* 6:145–55 Mr '65. *

494. GOUGH, HARRISON G. "Conceptual Analysis of Psychological Test Scores and Other Diagnostic Variables." *J Abn Psychol* 70:294–302 Ag '65. * (*PA* 39:15234)

495. JOHNSGARD, KEITH W., AND MUENCH, GEORGE A. "Group Therapy With Normal College Students." *Psychother Theory Res & Prac* 2:114–6 O '65. * (*PA* 40:3038)

496. LEARY, TIMOTHY; METZNER, RALPH; PRESNELL, MADISON; WEIL, GUNTHER; SCHWITZGEBEL, RALPH; AND KINNE, SARA. "A New Behavior Program Using Psilocybin." *Psychother Theory Res & Prac* 2:61–72 Jl '65. * (*PA* 40:3053)

497. LIPINSKI, BEATRICE GRACE. *Sex-Role Conflict and Achievement Motivation in College Women.* Doctor's thesis, University of Cincinnati (Cincinnati, Ohio), 1965. (*DA* 26: 4077)

498. McFADDEN, JACK DONALD. *The Relationship of Values, Attitude and Personality Characteristics of Student Teachers to Ratings by Their Supervisors.* Doctor's thesis, Northwestern University (Evanston, Ill.), 1965. (*DA* 26:7169)

499. MITCHELL, LESLIE HOWARD. *Dominance and Femininity as Factors in the Sex Role Adjustment of Parents and Children.* Doctor's thesis, University of California (Berkeley, Calif.), 1965. (*DA* 26:7440)

500. MORANO, NICHOLAS THOMAS. *Complexity-Simplicity: An Investigation of Cognitive, Motivational and Personality Correlates.* Doctor's thesis, Fordham University (New York, N.Y.), 1965. (*DA* 26:4079)

501. PARLOFF, MORRIS B., AND DATTA, LOIS-ELLIN. "Personality Characteristics of the Potentially Creative Scientist," pp. 91–106. In *Communications and Community.* Science and Psychoanalysis, Vol. 8. Edited by Jules H. Masserman. New York: Grune & Stratton, 1965. Pp. x, 309. *

502. ROSENBERG, JACK L. "Attitude Changes in Dental and Medical Students During Professional Education." *J Dental Ed* 29:399–408 D '65. *

503. SCHEIBE, KARL E. "College Students Spend Eight Weeks in Mental Hospital: A Case Report." *Psychother Theory Res & Prac* 2:117–20 O '65. * (*PA* 40:3081)

504. TOLLEFSON, NONA FALMLEN. *Relationship of Counselor Need Orientation to Counselor Effectiveness and Counselor Personality.* Doctor's thesis, Purdue University (Lafayette, Ind.), 1965. (*DA* 27:122A)

505. TORNOW, EUGENE WILLIAM. *A Study of the Relationship of Teachers' Perceptions of Decision Points and the Interactions of the Superintendent of Schools, the Director of Instruction and the High School Principal.* Doctor's thesis. University of Wisconsin (Madison, Wis.), 1965. (*DA* 27:643A)

506. VITZ, PAUL C., AND JOHNSTON, DONALD. "Masculinity of Smokers and the Masculinity of Cigarette Images." *J Appl Psychol* 49:155–9 Je '65. * (*PA* 39:13157)

507. WILDER, ALMARON MARSHALL. *The Development of a Group Movement Scale Which Will Reflect the Socialization Factor of a Group.* Doctor's thesis, Ohio State University (Columbus, Ohio), 1965. (*DA* 26:4113)

508. BOUCHARD, THOMAS JOSEPH, JR. *Personality, Problem Solving Procedure, and Performance in Small Groups.* Doctor's thesis, University of California (Berkeley, Calif.), 1966. (*DA* 27:3685B)

509. BROEKHOFF, JAN. *Relationships Between Physical, Socio-Psychological, and Mental Characteristics of Thirteen-Year-Old Boys.* Doctor's thesis, University of Oregon (Eugene, Ore.), 1966.

510. COLSON, DONALD BERNARD. *The Interaction of Sex-Role Conflict With the Experimental Manipulation of Masculinity-Femininity Test Scores of College Students.* Doctor's thesis, University of Cincinnati (Cincinnati, Ohio), 1966. (*DA* 27: 2131B)

511. DLABAL, JOHN JEROME, JR. *A Study to Identify Distinguishing Characteristics of Teachers Who Work Successfully With Culturally Deprived Children.* Doctor's thesis, University of Kansas (Lawrence, Kan.), 1966. (*DA* 27:1539A)

512. ENGRAM, WILLIAM CARL. *One Aspect of the Social Psychology of Experimentation: The E Effect and Related Personality Characteristics in the Experimenter.* Doctor's thesis, Cornell University (Ithaca, N.Y.), 1966. (*DA* 28:3260A)

513. GOLDEN, MARY CONSTANCE. *An Investigation of the Teaching Interests of Sisters, Their Personality Characteristics, and the Ratings of Their Supervisors.* Doctor's thesis, Fordham University (New York, N.Y.), 1966. (*DA* 27:2879A)

514. GUILLIAMS, CLARK IRVIN. *Predicting Creative Productivity in College Classes Where Creative Thinking Is Emphasized.* Doctor's thesis, University of Arkansas (Fayetteville, Ark.), 1966. (*DA* 27:675A)

515. HARDYCK, CURTIS D. "Personality Characteristics and Motor Activity: Some Empirical Evidence." *J Pers & Social Psychol* 4:181–8 Ag '66. * (*PA* 40:11183)

516. HARVEY, EDWARD. "Psychological Rigidity and Muscle Tension." *Psychophysiol* 3:224–6 O '66. * (*PA* 41:1253)

517. HELSON, RAVENNA. "Personality of Women With Imaginative and Artistic Interests: The Role of Masculinity, Originality, and Other Characteristics in Their Creativity." *J Personality* 34:1–25 Mr '66. * (*PA* 40:8830)

518. HILL, ARTHUR H. "A Longitudinal Study of Attrition Among High Aptitude College Students." *J Ed Res* 60:166–73 D '66. *

519. KEARNEY, DOROTHY LUCILLE. *Selected Non-Intellectual Factors as Predictors of Academic Success in Junior College Intellectually Capable Students.* Doctor's thesis, University of Southern California (Los Angeles, Calif.), 1966. (*DA* 27:395A)

520. LACROSSE, EDWIN ROBERT, JR. *The Relationship of Biological Sex, Psychological Sex, Intelligence, and Perceptual Rigidity to Visual Exploratory Behavior in Second and Sixth Grade, White, Southern Rural Children.* Doctor's thesis, University of North Carolina (Chapel Hill, N.C.), 1966. (*DA* 27: 2860B)

521. MADSON, DENNIS LEROY. *Factors Associated With Effectiveness as a Male Undergraduate Residence Hall Counselor.* Doctor's thesis, Ohio University (Athens, Ohio), 1966. (*DA* 27:3670A)

522. MARTIN, CLYDE V., AND ALVORD, JACK R. "Long-Term Effects of Intensive Short-Term Treatment of the Character and Personality Disorder." *Correct Psychiatry & J Social Ther* 12:433–42 N '66. * (*PA* 41:10584)

523. MEGARGEE, EDWIN I. "Undercontrolled and Overcontrolled Personality Types in Extreme Antisocial Aggression." *Psychol Monogr* 80(3):1–29 '66. *

524. MILLER, DON EDWARD. *Individual Differences in the Communication of Emotions.* Doctor's thesis, University of Utah (Salt Lake City, Utah), 1966. (*DA* 27:2141B)

525. MOSES, ELIZABETH. *Master's Students in Nursing Education.* Doctor's thesis, University of California (Berkeley, Calif.), 1966. (*DA* 27:1525B)

526. OLDS, CLAIRE MARIE. *Some Immediate Effects of Two Methods of Presenting Information About the Multiple Roles of Women to Selected College Sophomore Women.* Doctor's thesis, University of Denver (Denver, Colo.), 1966. (*DA* 27: 4102A)

527. PAPPAS, JOHN G. *The Effects of Three Approaches to College Orientation on Two Groups of Entering Freshmen Students at Kent State University.* Doctor's thesis, Kent State University (Kent, Ohio), 1966. (*DA* 28:401A)

528. RIDLEY, DAVID WENDELL. *Patterns of Dating Behavior Associated With Differences in Interpersonal Competence—A Twelfth Grade Sample.* Doctor's thesis, University of Oregon (Eugene, Ore.), 1966. (*DA* 27:2637A)

529. ROESSLER, ROBERT; BURCH, NEIL R.; AND CHILDERS, HAROLD E. "Personality and Arousal Correlates of Specific Galvanic Skin Responses." *Psychophysiol* 3:115–30 O '66. * (*PA* 41:1255)

530. SANDHU, HARJIT S. "Group Sessions in a Reformatory School in the Punjab (India)." *Correct Psychiatry & J Social Ther* 12:393–403 S '66. * (*PA* 41:3094)

531. SCHAAR, WILLIAM GEORGE, JR. *Changes in Academic Success and Self-Concept of Low Achieving Community College Freshmen.* Doctor's thesis, Michigan State University (East Lansing, Mich.), 1966. (*DA* 27:2750A)

532. SINGER, SUSAN KLUGMAN. *Factors Related to Participants' Memory for a Conversation.* Doctor's thesis, University of California (Berkeley, Calif.), 1966. (*DA* 27:1295B)

533. STEWART, LOUIS, AND LIVSON, NORMAN. "Smoking and Rebelliousness: A Longitudinal Study From Childhood to Maturity." *J Consult Psychol* 30:225–9 Je '66. * (*PA* 40:8868)

534. WEISS, ROBERT L. " 'Acquiescence' Response Set and Birth Order." Abstract. *J Consult Psychol* 30:365 Ag '66. *

535. ZIEGLER, FREDERICK J.; RODGERS, DAVID A.; AND KRIEGSMAN, SALI ANN. "Effect of Vasectomy on Psychological Functioning." *Psychosom Med* 28:50–63 Ja–F '66. * (*PA* 40:5830)

536. ALLAN, THOMAS KENNETH. "A Rationale for Organizing Studies Involving Personality Measures as Screening Instruments for Teacher Training." *SPATE* 6:13–20 f '67. *

537. BORG, WALTER R. "Teacher Effectiveness in Team Teaching." *J Exp Ed* 35:65–70 sp '67. *

538. BRUHN, JOHN G.; ADSETT, C. ALEX; AND BIRD, HENRY B. "Social Profiles and Academic Standing: A Study

of First Year Medical Students." *J Okla State Med Assn* 60: 538–44 O '67. *

539. CLAPP, RUFUS CARVEL. *The Relationship of Teacher Sex to Fifth Grade Boys' Achievement Gains and Attitudes Toward School.* Doctor's thesis, Stanford University (Stanford, Calif.), 1967. (*DA* 28:2433A)

540. COLLINS, DONALD J. "Psychological Selection of Drill Sergeants: An Exploratory Attempt in a New Program." *Mil Med* 132:713–5 S '67. * (*PA* 42:3024)

541. FINNEY, JOSEPH C. "Methodological Problems in Programmed Composition of Psychological Tests." *Behav Sci* 12: 142–52 Mr '67. * (*PA* 41:6439)

542. LIPSITT, PAUL D., AND STRODTBECK, FRED L. "Defensiveness in Decision Making as a Function of Sex-Role Identification." *J Pers & Social Psychol* 6:10–5 My '67. * (*PA* 41: 8396)

543. LYNCH, DENIS JOSEPH. *Future Time Perspective and Impulsivity in Old Age.* Doctor's thesis, Case Western Reserve University (Cleveland, Ohio), 1967. (*DA* 28:4296B)

544. MARTINO, THOMAS PATRICK. *Some Relationships Between a Measure of Self-Acceptance and Specific Criteria of College Adjustment.* Doctor's thesis, Catholic University of America (Washington, D.C.), 1967. (*DA* 28:2517A)

545. MATSCH, PHYLLIS L. *The Effects of Various Motivational Situations and Personality Factors Upon the Work Performance of College Women.* Master's thesis, University of Toledo (Toledo, Ohio), 1967.

546. MILLER, JEFFREY O. *Longitudinal Analysis of the Relationship Between Measures of Self-Differentiation and Social Interaction and Selected Physical Variables in Boys Twelve to Seventeen Years of Age.* Doctor's thesis, University of Oregon (Eugene, Ore.), 1967.

547. MOSHER, DONALD L.; OLIVER, WAYNE A.; AND DOLGAN, JEFFERY. "Body Image in Tattooed Prisoners." *J Clin Psychol* 23:31–2 Ja '67. * (*PA* 41:5685)

548. MOSKOVIS, LEFTERIE MICHAEL. *An Identification of Certain Similarities and Differences Between Successful and Unsuccessful College Level Beginning Shorthand Students and Transcription Students.* Doctor's thesis, Michigan State University (East Lansing, Mich.), 1967. (*DA* 28:4826A)

549. PANDYA, DASHARATHRAI NAVNITRAI. *Personality Characteristics and Level of Performance of Male County Extension Agents in Wisconsin.* Doctor's thesis, University of Wisconsin (Madison, Wis.), 1967. (*DA* 28:3115B)

550. PETERSON, RONALD SKEEN. *A Longitudinal Study of Nonintellective Characteristics of College Dropouts.* Doctor's thesis, University of Oregon (Eugene, Ore.), 1967. (*DA* 28: 2076A)

551. ROSENFELD, HERBERT MICHAEL. *Delinquent Acting-Out in Adolescent Males and Its Relationship to the Task of Sexual Identification.* Doctor's thesis, Smith College (Northampton, Mass.), 1967. (*DA* 28:4301B)

552. SUTTER, EMILY MAY GEESEMAN. *Individual Differences and Social Conditions as They Affect Learning by Computer-Assisted Instruction.* Doctor's thesis, University of Texas (Austin, Tex.), 1967. (*DA* 28:4012A)

553. TAFT, RONALD. "The Role of Personality Traits in the Social Assimilation of Immigrants." *Austral & N Zeal J Sociol* 3:19–31 Ap '67. * (*PA* 42:10447)

554. WHITE, HAZEL WILMA. *A Descriptive Analysis of a Group of AFDC (Aid to Families With Dependent Children) Recipients.* Doctor's thesis, University of New Mexico (Albuquerque, N.M.), 1967. (*DA* 28:3472A)

555. ABBOTT, KENNETH A. "The Use of the California Psychological Inventory in Intensive Study of Family Systems." *Psychol & Ed (Taipei)* 2:49–59 D '68. *

556. ADAIR, FRED LAWRENCE. *The Development of a Scale to Measure the Service Orientation of Librarians: Preliminary Investigations.* Doctor's thesis, University of North Carolina (Chapel Hill, N.C.), 1968. (*DA* 29:2088A)

557. ARONSON, ELLIOT, AND METTEE, DAVID R. "Dishonest Behavior as a Function of Differential Levels of Induced Self-Esteem." *J Pers & Social Psychol* 9:121–7 Je '68. * (*PA* 42: 12072)

558. ALLAN, THOMAS KENNETH. "The Relationship Between Supervisory Ratings and the Personality of Female Student Teachers." *SPATE* 6:84–90 sp '68. *

559. BARSCH, RAY H. "The California Psychological Inventory," pp. 323–8. In his *The Parent of the Handicapped Child: The Study of Child-rearing Practices.* Springfield, Ill.: Charles C Thomas, Publisher, 1968. Pp. xiii, 435. *

560. BASKETT, GLEN DALE. *Interpersonal Attraction as a Function of Attitude Similarity-Dissimilarity and Cognitive Complexity.* Doctor's thesis, University of Texas (Austin, Tex.), 1968. (*DA* 29:3931B)

561. BAYLEY, NANCY. Chap. 9, "Cognition and Aging," pp. 97–119. In *Theory and Methods of Research on Aging.* Edited by K. Warner Schaie. Morgantown, W.Va.: West Virginia University, 1968. Pp. iv, 197. *

562. BECKER, GILBERT. "Sex-Role Identification and the Needs for Self and Social Approval." *J Psychol* 69:11–5 My '68. * (*PA* 42:11989)

563. CLAYTON, HOWARD. *An Investigation of Personality Characteristics Among Library Students at One Midwestern University.* An unpublished report to the U.S. Office of Education, Project No. 7-8373, State University of New York at Brockport, 1968. Pp. vii, 127. * (ERIC ED 024 422)

564. COTTLE, THOMAS J. "Family Perceptions, Sex Role Identity and the Prediction of School Performance." *Ed & Psychol Meas* 28:861–6 au '68. * (*PA* 43:4515)

565. CROSS, JOHN A. *Relationships Between Selected Physical Characteristics of Boys at Twelve and Fifteen Years of Age and Their Personality Characteristics at Eighteen Years of Age.* Doctor's thesis, University of Oregon (Eugene, Ore.), 1968.

566. DORESS, IRVIN. *A Study of a Sampling of Boston University Student Activists.* Doctor's thesis, Boston University (Boston, Mass.), 1968. (*DA* 29:4563A)

567. EDWARDS, CARL N. "Cultural Dissonance and Dissimulation: A Study in Role Conflict." *J Consult & Clin Psychol* 32:607–10 O '68. * (*PA* 43:880)

568. ELDER, GLEN H., JR. "Occupational Level, Achievement Motivation, and Social Mobility: A Longitudinal Analysis." *J Counsel Psychol* 15:1–7 Ja '68. * (*PA* 42:6186)

569. FRANKE, BONNY. *A Study of Personality Differences Among College Freshmen as Measured by the California Psychological Inventory: The Survey of Study Habits and Attitudes, and the College Characteristics Index.* Master's thesis, Austin College (Sherman, Tex.), 1968.

570. GARMS, JOE D., AND RAY, J. B. "Authoritarian Attitudes and Scholastic Achievement." *Psychol* 5:47–51 N '68. * (*PA* 43:5964)

571. HAERTZEN, C. A., AND HOOKS, N. T., JR. "Effects of Adaptation Level, Context and Face Validity on Responses to Self-Report Psychological Inventories." *Psychol Rec* 18:339–49 Jl '68. * (*PA* 42:16412)

572. HELMICK, KENNETH DALE. *A Comparative Study of Personality Characteristics of Elementary and Secondary Education Majors: Using the California Psychological Inventory and the Strong Vocational Interest Blank.* Doctor's thesis, Oklahoma State University (Stillwater, Okla.), 1968. (*DAI* 30: 1048A)

573. HELSON, RAVENNA. "Effects of Sibling Characteristics and Parental Values on a Creative Interest and Achievement." *J Personality* 36:589–607 D '68. * (*PA* 43:6923)

574. HIPWOOD, STANLEY JAMES. *Pupil Growth as a Function of Teacher Flexibility, Student Independence, and Student Conformance.* Doctor's thesis, University of New Mexico (Albuquerque, N.M.), 1968. (*DAI* 30:169A)

575. KASL, STANISLAV V.; COBB, SIDNEY; AND BROOKS, GEORGE W. "Changes in Serum Uric Acid and Cholesterol Levels in Men Undergoing Job Loss." *J Am Med Assn* 206: 1500–7 N 11 '68. *

576. KASSERA, WAYNE JOSEPH. *Changes in Certain Selected Counselor Attitudinal Characteristics as a Concomitant of Counselor Education.* Doctor's thesis, University of Colorado (Boulder, Colo.), 1968. (*DA* 29:2962A)

577. KILCAWLEY, MARGARET PATRICIA. *Variables Associated With Academic Persistence Among Male Freshmen Students Enrolled in a College of Arts and Sciences.* Doctor's thesis, University of Maryland (College Park, Md.), 1968. (*DA* 29:1755A)

578. KINGSBURY, WARREN T. *A Study of Characteristics, Motivations, and Personality Patterns of National Foundation Chapter Volunteer Leaders.* Doctor's thesis, New York University (New York, N.Y.), 1968. (*DA* 29:4188A)

579. KORN, HAROLD A. Chap. 4, "Differences in Student Response to the Curriculum," pp. 18–206. In *No Time for Youth: Growth and Constraint in College Students.* Edited by Joseph Katz. San Francisco, Calif.: Jossey-Bass Inc., Publishers, 1968. Pp. xxii, 463. *

580. MCCLAINE, RICHARD EARL. *Factors in Executive Promotion and Demotion: An Empirical Study.* Doctor's thesis, Ohio State University (Columbus, Ohio), 1968. (*DA* 29: 1326A)

581. MCCONNEL, HELEN F. *The Relationship Between California Psychological Inventory Scores and Physical Fitness Test Scores for Selected Secondary School Girls.* Master's thesis, Chico State College (Chico, Calif.), 1968.

582. MCGUIRE, EDWARD C. *Psycho-Social Characteristics of Students Who Voluntarily Withdraw From Rutgers, The State University, Newark, New Jersey.* Doctor's thesis, Wayne State University (Detroit, Mich.), 1968. (*DAI* 30:552A)

583. MASON, EVELYN P. "Sex Difference in Personality Characteristics of Deprived Adolescents." *Percept & Motor Skills* 27:934 D '68. * (*PA* 43:8365)

584. MAY, MARIANNE BOWER. *Personality Characteristics of Secondary Home Economics Teachers of Homemaking and of Occupational Training.* Doctor's thesis, Oklahoma State University (Stillwater, Okla.), 1968. (*DAI* 30:1228B)

585. MICHIE, JACK. *Dominant Factors Influencing the Employment Success of a Selected Group of Disadvantaged Youth.* Doctor's thesis, University of California (Los Angeles, Calif.), 1968. (*DA* 28:4825A)

586. MITCHELL, JAMES V. "The Identification of Student Personality Characteristics Related to Perceptions of the School Environment." *Sch R* 76:50–9 Mr '68. * (*PA* 43:3006)

587. NEITHERCUTT, MARCUS G. *Predicting Outcomes of Federal Parolees.* Doctor's thesis, University of California (Berkeley, Calif.), 1968. (*DA* 29:3512B)

588. NEUFELD, JACOB A. *Factors Related to Choice of Transfer and Terminal Status in Junior College.* Doctor's thesis, University of North Dakota (Grand Forks, N.D.), 1968. *(DA 29:3045A)*

589. NUGENT, FRANK A. "Relationship of Kuder Preference Record Verification Scores to Adjustment: Implications for Vocational Development Theory." *J Appl Psychol* 52:429–31 D '68. * *(PA 42:3082)*

590. O'KANE, JAMES MICHAEL. *Upward Mobility Potential, Political Attitudes and Catholic Working-Class Adolescents.* Doctor's thesis, New York University (New York, N.Y.), 1968. *(DAI 30:833A)*

591. PAPPAS, JOHN G. "The Counseling Relationship: A Function of the Counselor's Personality." *Élan* 2:29–32 f '68. *

592. PARLOFF, MORRIS B.; DATTA, LOIS-ELLIN; KLEMAN, MARIANNE; AND HANDLON, JOSEPH H. "Personality Characteristics Which Differentiate Creative Male Adolescents and Adults." *J Personality* 36:528–52 D '68. * *(PA 43:6925)*

593. PESKIN, HARVEY. "The Duration of Normal Menses as a Psychosomatic Phenomenon." *Psychosom Med* 30:378–89 Jl–Ag '68. * *(PA 43:2882)*

594. RAWLS, DONNA J., AND RAWLS, JAMES R. "Personality Characteristics and Personal History Data of Successful and Less Successful Executives." *Psychol Rep* 23:1032–4 D '68. * *(PA 43:8822)*

595. ROGERS, MARTIN IRVING. *Self-Actualization as Process.* Doctor's thesis, Case Western Reserve University (Cleveland, Ohio), 1968. *(DAI 30:4380B)*

596. ROSENBERG, B. G., AND SUTTON-SMITH, B. "Family Interaction Effects on Masculinity-Femininity." *J Pers & Social Psychol* 8:117–20 F '68. * *(PA 42:5468)*

597. SAFFER, JERRY BENJAMIN. *Coping Mechanisms of Obese Men: A Psychometric and Behavioral Study.* Doctor's thesis, Illinois Institute of Technology (Chicago, Ill.), 1968. *(DA 29:1511B)*

598. SANFORD, NEVITT, AND SINGER, SUSAN. Chap. 9, "Drinking and Personality," pp. 348–75. In *No Time for Youth: Growth and Constraint in College Students.* Edited by Joseph Katz. San Francisco, Calif.: Jossey-Bass Inc., Publishers, 1968. Pp. xxii, 463. *

599. SAUNDERS, WALTER LANE. *Verbal-Numerical Achievement in a Required College Physical Science Course and Some Personality Correlates.* Doctor's thesis, Oregon State University (Corvallis, Ore.), 1968. *(DA 29:1053A)*

600. SEGNER, VENICE CHANDLER. *Effects of Early Experience on Later Interview Assessments of Social and Personal Adjustments.* Doctor's thesis, University of Georgia (Athens, Ga.), 1968. *(DA 29:4853B)*

601. SIMPKINS, RUTH E. *Verbal Performance Effected by Social Maturity and Social and Material Incentives.* Doctor's thesis, Temple University (Philadelphia, Pa.), 1968. *(DAI 30:1387B)*

602. SLAUGHTER, MARY HOKE. *An Analysis of the Relationship Between Somatotype and Personality Profiles of College Women.* Doctor's thesis, University of Illinois (Urbana, Ill.), 1968. *(DA 29:2554A)*

603. STANDRIDGE, CHARLES GARY. *The Predictive Value of Nonintellectual Factors and Their Influence on Academic Achievement.* Doctor's thesis, University of Arkansas (Fayetteville, Ark.), 1968. *(DA 29:1458A)*

604. STOCK, WILLIAM H., JR. *Some Psychological and Physiological Factors Affecting Excellence in Acting.* Doctor's thesis, Michigan State University (East Lansing, Mich.), 1968. *(DA 29:3716A)*

605. THOMPSON, SHEILAH DOREEN. *Some Personality Characteristics of Student Teachers of Guidance.* Doctor's thesis, University of British Columbia (Vancouver, B.C., Canada), 1968. *(DAI 30:556A)*

606. VARGAS, ROBERT. *A Study of Certain Personality Characteristics of Male College Students Who Report Frequent Positive Experiencing and Behaving.* Doctor's thesis, University of Florida (Gainesville, Fla.), 1968. *(DAI 30:142A)*

607. WALTON, FRANCIS XAVIER. *An Investigation of Differences Between More Effective and Less Effective Counselors With Regard to Selected Variables.* Doctor's thesis, University of South Carolina (Columbia, S.C.), 1968. *(DA 29:3844A)*

608. WATLEY, DONIVAN J. "Career Progress of Merit Scholars." *NMSC Res Rep* 4(1):1–23 '68. *

609. WILSON, DONNA JEAN. *The Use of the BIB in the Selection of College Seniors With Managerial Potential.* Doctor's thesis, Louisiana State University (Baton Rouge, La.), 1968. *(DA 29:801B)*

610. ZIEGLER, FREDERICK J.; RODGERS, DAVID A.; KRIEGSMAN, SALI ANN; AND MARTIN, PURVIS L. "Ovulation Suppressors, Psychological Functioning, and Marital Adjustment." *J Am Med Assn* 204:849–53 Je 3 '68. *

611. ALLEN, L. R. "Self-Esteem of Male Alcoholics." *Psychol Rec* 19(3):381–9 Jl '69. * *(PA 43:16025)*

612. ANDERSON, CARL EDWIN. *A Study of Selected Psycho-Social Correlates of College Student Protesters and Non-Protesters.* Doctor's thesis, University of Maryland (College Park, Md.), 1969. *(DAI 31:606A)*

613. BALDWIN, JEAN MARGARET. *An Analysis of the Relationship Between Self-Esteem, Academic Achievement, and Academic Level of Aspiration for a Group of College Students.* Doctor's thesis, University of Maryland (College Park, Md.), 1969. *(DAI 31:209A)*

614. BALL, MARY KAY. *Identification With Parents and Others as Predictors of Mental Health.* Doctor's thesis, Ohio University (Athens, Ohio), 1969. *(DAI 30:2901B)*

615. BARRILLEAUX, STEPHEN. *A Comparative Investigation of the Correlations Among the Variables of the California Psychological Inventory and the Strong Vocational Interest Blank on Two Eleventh Grade Female Populations.* Master's thesis, Catholic University of America (Washington, D.C.), 1969.

616. BECKER, GILBERT. "Ego-Defence Pattern, Extraversion-Introversion, and Sex-Role Adjustment." *Brit J Social & Clin Psychol* 8(3):275–86 S '69. * *(PA 44:3598)*

617. BEHAR, LENORE, AND SPENCER, ROGER F. "Relationship Between Psychosocial Adjustment and Perception of Maternal Attitudes." *J Abn Psychol* 74(4):471–3 Ag '69. * *(PA 43:15717)*

618. BENJAMIN, JEANETTE ANN. *A Study of the Social Psychological Factors Related to the Academic Success of Negro High School Students.* Doctor's thesis, Northwestern University (Evanston, Ill.), 1969. *(DAI 30:3543A)*

619. BENNETT, CHARLOTTE STUMPH. *Relationship Between Selected Personality Variables and Improvement in Academic Achievement for Underachieving Eighth Grade Boys in a Residential School.* Doctor's thesis, University of North Carolina (Chapel Hill, N.C.), 1969. *(DAI 30:3272A)*

620. BERGER, RICHARD A., AND LITTLEFIELD, DONALD H. "Comparison Between Football Athletes and Nonathletes on Personality." *Res Q* 40(4):663–5 D '69. *

621. BILLER, HENRY B., AND POEY, KENT. "An Exploratory Comparison of Sex Role-Related Behaviors in Schizophrenics and Nonschizophrenics." Abstract. *Develop Psychol* 1(5):629 S '69. * *(PA 43:17670)*

622. BOONE, LOUIS EUGENE. *The Diffusion of an Innovation: A Socio-Economic and Personality Trait Analysis of Adopters of Community Antenna Television Service.* Doctor's thesis, University of Arkansas (Fayetteville, Ark.), 1969. *(DAI 30: 465A)*

623. BOUCHARD, THOMAS J., JR. "Personality, Problem-Solving Procedure, and Performance in Small Groups." *J Appl Psychol Monogr* 53(1, pt 2):1–29 F '69. * *(PA 43:6351)*

624. BROWN, REX BENNETT. *Personality Characteristics Related to Injuries in Football.* Doctor's thesis, University of Arkansas (Fayetteville, Ark.), 1969. *(DAI 30:3758A)*

625. BUCK, CHARLES WARREN. *Crystallization of Vocational Interests as a Function of Exploratory Experience During the College Years.* Doctor's thesis, Columbia University (New York, N.Y.), 1969. *(DAI 30:4823A)*

626. CLINE, ELLIS WALLACE. *Confirming Behavior of School Executives.* Doctor's thesis, University of Florida (Gainesville, Fla.), 1969. *(DAI 31:1067A)*

627. COMPTON, NORMA H. "Characteristics of Clothing and Textile Students Compared With Those of Women in Fashion Careers." *J Home Econ* 61(3):183–8 Mr '69. *

628. CRISWELL, CYRUS ELLSWORTH. *A Study of the Relationship Between Delinquency Proneness and Social Maturity Among Junior High School Boys.* Doctor's thesis, Ohio University (Athens, Ohio), 1969. *(DAI 31:2100A)*

629. CROWNE, DOUGLAS P.; CONN, LANE K.; MARLOWE, DAVID; AND EDWARDS, CARL N. "Some Developmental Antecedents of Level of Aspiration." *J Personality* 37(1):73–92 Mr '69. * *(PA 43:12978)*

630. CURTIS, EUGENE LESTER. *A Study of the Differences Between a Group of Community College Students in an Adjustment Skills Course and a Control Group on Selected Personality and Non-Academic Characteristics.* Doctor's thesis, University of North Dakota (Grand Forks, N.D.), 1969. *(DAI 30:3720A)*

631. DAVIES, JOHN FRANKLIN. *Differential Perceptions of Delinquent Behavior.* Doctor's thesis, Ohio State University (Columbus, Ohio), 1969. *(DAI 31:841A)*

632. DOHERTY, ANNE. *The Relationship of Dependency and Perception of Parents to the Development of Feminine Sex Role and Conscience.* Doctor's thesis, Catholic University of America (Washington, D.C.), 1969. *(DAI 30:2415B)*

633. DOMINO, GEORGE. "Maternal Personality Correlates of Sons' Creativity." *J Consult & Clin Psychol* 33(2):180–3 Ap '69. * *(PA 43:9746)*

634. DREYER, DOROTHY E. *Listening Performance Related to Selected Academic and Psychological Measures.* Doctor's thesis, Michigan State University (East Lansing, Mich.), 1969. *(DAI 30:5735B)*

635. EISENTHAL, SHERMAN, AND SHERMAN, LEWIS J. "Psychological Characteristics of Neighborhood Youth Corps Enrollees." *J Consult & Clin Psychol* 33(4):420–4 Ag '69. * *(PA 43:15777)*

636. EVANS, JAMES D. "The Relationships of Three Personality Scales to Grade Point Average and Verbal Ability in College Freshmen." *J Ed Res* 63(3):121–5 N '69. *

637. FINNEY, BEN C., AND VAN DALSEM, ELIZABETH. "Group Counseling for Gifted Underachieving High School Students." *J Counsel Psychol* 16(1):87–94 Ja '69. * *(PA 43: 5923)*

638. FISH, KATHLEEN D. *Paternal Availability, Family Role*

Structure, Maternal Employment, and Personality Development in Late Adolescent Females. Doctor's thesis, University of Massachusetts (Amherst, Mass.), 1969. (*DAI* 30:4369B)

639. FONG, STANLEY L. M., AND PESKIN, HARVEY. "Sex-Role Strain and Personality Adjustment of China-Born Students in America: A Pilot Study." *J Abn Psychol* 74(5):563–7 O '69. * (*PA* 44:532)

640. FRANKEL, PHYLIS SCHWARTZ. *The Relationship of Self-Concept, Sex Role Attitudes, and the Development of Achievement Need in Women.* Doctor's thesis, Northwestern University (Evanston, Ill.), 1969. (*DAI* 30:3371B)

641. FULLERTON, JOHN REYNOLDS. *A Factor Analytic Study of Rehabilitation Role Perceptions Reported by Undergraduate Rehabilitation Students.* Doctor's thesis, Pennsylvania State University (University Park, Pa.), 1969. (*DAI* 31:607A)

642. GAINES, MICHAEL RIDGE. *An Empirical Study of the Relationships of Selected Personality Variables to Accounting Performance.* Doctor's thesis, University of Washington (Seattle, Wash.), 1969. (*DAI* 31:869A)

643. GALL, MEREDITH D.; HOBBY, AMOS K.; AND CRAIK, KENNETH H. "Non-Linguistic Factors in Oral Language Productivity." *Percept & Motor Skills* 29(3):871–4 D '69. *

644. GILBERT, CHARLES DAVID. *Interrelationships Among Interstaff Rankings of Elementary School Teachers in Respect to Classroom Management, Social Living Effectiveness, and Other Selected Factors.* Doctor's thesis, Ball State University (Muncie, Ind.), 1969. (*DAI* 30:489A)

645. GILMORE, SUSAN K. "Personality Differences Between High and Low Dogmatism Groups of Pentecostal Believers." *J Sci Study Relig* 8(1):161–4 sp '69. *

646. GOUGH, HARRISON G. "A Leadership Index on the California Psychological Inventory." *J Counsel Psychol* 16(4): 283–9 Jl '69. * (*PA* 43:14339)

647. GUADAGNOLO, FRANK BERNARD. *An Analysis of Personality Inventories as Identifiers of Leadership Ability Among California Youth Authority Wards.* Master's thesis, Sacramento State College (Sacramento, Calif.), 1969.

648. HALL, WALLACE B., AND MACKINNON, DONALD W. "Personality Inventory Correlates of Creativity Among Architects." *J Appl Psychol* 53(4):322–6 Ag '69. * (*PA* 43:15815)

649. HERSCH, PAUL D.; KULIK, JAMES A.; AND SCHEIBE, KARL E. "Personal Characteristics of College Volunteers in Mental Hospitals." *J Consult & Clin Psychol* 33(1):30–4 F '69. * (*PA* 43:11408)

650. HIGHRITER, MARION E. "Nurse Characteristics and Patient Progress." *Nursing Res* 18(6):484–501 N–D '69. *

651. HJELLE, LARRY A. "Personality Characteristics Associated With Interpersonal Perception Accuracy." *J Counsel Psychol* 16(6):579–81 N '69. * (*PA* 44:3605)

652. HOGAN, ROBERT. "Development of an Empathy Scale." *J Consult & Clin Psychol* 33(3):307–16 Je '69. * (*PA* 43: 12966)

653. HORNUNG, PHILIP E. *The Association Among the Variables of the California Psychological Inventory and the Strong Vocational Interest Blank on an Eleventh Grade Female Population.* Master's thesis, Catholic University of America (Washington, D.C.), 1969.

654. IBRAHIM, H. "Recreational Preference and Personality." *Res Q* 40(1):76–82 Mr '69. *

655. JANSSEN, JAN W. *The Relative Effectiveness of Students at Several College Levels to Lead Small Groups of Low-Achieving Freshmen in Academic Adjustment Counseling.* Doctor's thesis, West Virginia University (Morgantown, W.Va.), 1969. (*DAI* 31:1012A)

656. JENKINS, C. DAVID; HAMES, CURTIS G.; ZYZANSKI, STEPHEN J.; ROSENMAN, RAY H.; AND FRIEDMAN, MEYER. "Psychological Traits and Serum Lipids: 1, Findings From the California Psychological Inventory." *Psychosom Med* 31(2):115–28 Mr–Ap '69. * (*PA* 44:3322)

657. JEROME, WENDY C. F. *A Study of the Personality Characteristics of Female Athletes and Nonparticipants.* Master's thesis, University of Oregon (Eugene, Ore.), 1969.

658. JONES, IVAN ARMSTRONG, JR. *The CPI as a Moderator Variable in the Prediction of Grade Point Average From ACT Scores.* Doctor's thesis, Baylor University (Waco, Tex.), 1969. (*DAI* 30:2404B)

659. JUDD, LARRY R., AND SMITH, CAROLYN. "Predicting Success in the Basic College Speech Course." *Speech Teach* 18(1):13–7 Ja '69. *

660. KAYTON, ROBERT. *Sex-Role Identity, Parent Perception, and Psychopathology in Adult Males.* Doctor's thesis, University of Massachusetts (Amherst, Mass.), 1969. (*DAI* 30: 4374B)

661. KELLEY, SHARON L. *Personality Characteristics of Female High School Athletes and Nonparticipants in Athletics.* Master's thesis, University of Iowa (Iowa City, Iowa), 1969.

662. KOHFELD, DAVID L., AND WEITZEL, WILLIAM. "Some Relations Between Personality Factors and Social Facilitation." *J Exp Res Personality* 3(4):287–92 Ap '69. * (*PA* 43:14304)

663. LIPPMANN, GLENDA KATHRYN. *Personality Correlates of Differential Performance and Satisfaction in Self-Directed vs Teacher-Directed Instructional Strategies.* Doctor's thesis, University of Texas (Austin, Tex.), 1969. (*DAI* 31:1119A)

664. LOY, DONALD L. "Personality Correlates of Acceptance-Rejection of Behavior Modification Techniques." *Nursing Res* 18(2):154–6 Mr–Ap '69. * (*PA* 44:21073)

665. MCCLUNG, THOMAS E., AND WALSH, W. BRUCE. "Differences on Some Personality Variables Between Deans of Men and Women." *J Col Stud Personnel* 10(1):32–5 Ja '69. *

666. MCCONNEL, HELEN F. *The Relationship Between California Psychological Inventory Scores and Physical Fitness Test Scores for Selected Secondary School Girls.* Master's thesis, Chico State College (Chico, Calif.), 1969.

667. MARUYAMA, YOSHIO. *The Sense of Competence in Middle Adolescent Boys.* Doctor's thesis, Boston University (Boston, Mass.), 1969. (*DAI* 30:2405B)

668. MASON, EVELYN P. "Cross-Validation Study of Personality Characteristics of Junior High Students From American Indian, Mexican, and Caucasian Ethnic Backgrounds." *J Social Psychol* 77(1):15–24 F '69. * (*PA* 43:6793)

669. MAZER, MILTON, AND AHERN, JOHN. "Personality and Social Class Position in Migration From an Island: The Implications for Psychiatric Illness." *Int J Social Psychiatry* 15(3):203–8 su '69. * (*PA* 44:18460)

670. MEGARGEE, EDWIN I. "Influence of Sex Roles on the Manifestation of Leadership." *J Appl Psychol* 53(5):377–82 O '69. * (*PA* 44:1399)

671. MERIGOLD, FRANK A. "A Scale to Identify Male Dropouts at Liberal Arts Colleges." *Col Stud Survey* 3(1):19–22 sp '69. * (*PA* 43:14795)

672. MILLER, RICHARD E. *Impulsivity and Locus of Control Among Juvenile Delinquents.* Doctor's thesis, University of Pittsburgh (Pittsburgh, Pa.), 1969. (*DAI* 30:2340A)

673. MUELLER, DANIEL JOHN. *Differences in Social Responsibility Among Various Groups of College Students.* Doctor's thesis, University of Illinois (Urbana, Ill.), 1969. (*DAI* 31:646A)

674. MUTHARD, JOHN E., AND SALOMONE, PAUL R. "The Roles and Functions of Rehabilitation Counselors." *Rehabil Counsel B* 13(1-SP):81–165 O '69. *

675. PARKEY, WILLIAM W. "Project Self Discovery: Its Effect on Bright but Underachieving High School Students." *Gifted Child Q* 13(4):242–6 w '69. *

676. PENNELL, LILLIAN ADOLPHENA. *The Relationship of Certain Experiences to Psychological Adjustment in Persons With Spinal Cord Injury.* Doctor's thesis, University of Florida (Gainesville, Fla.), 1969. (*DAI* 31:232A)

677. PETERSEN, DWIGHT J. *CPI Achievement Motivation Scales in Differential Prediction of Academic Achievement.* Master's thesis, Utah State University (Logan, Utah), 1969.

678. PODSHADLEY, DALE W.; CHEN, MARTIN K.; AND SHROCK, JOHN G. "A Factor Analytic Approach to the Prediction of Student Performance." *J Dental Ed* 33(1, pt 2): 105–11 Mr '69. *

679. REUTER, MARK WILLIAM. *The Father-Son Relationship and the Personality Adjustment of the Late Adolescent Male.* Doctor's thesis, University of Massachusetts (Amherst, Mass.), 1969. (*DAI* 30:4379B)

680. REYNOLDS, CHRISTOPHER MACDONALD. *Personality Traits of Approving and Disapproving Responders to Controversial Theatre Material.* Doctor's thesis, University of Michigan (Ann Arbor, Mich.), 1969. (*DAI* 31:853A)

681. ROBERTSON, THOMAS R., AND MYERS, JAMES H. "Personality Correlates of Opinion Leadership and Innovative Buying Behavior." *J Marketing Res* 6(2):164–8 My '69. * (*PA* 44:5787)

682. ROHILA, PRITAM KUMAR. *Multivariate Relationships Between Personality and Vocational Interests.* Doctor's thesis, University of Oregon (Eugene, Ore.), 1969. (*DAI* 31:1022A)

683. RUDOFF, ALVIN, AND PILIAVIN, IRVING. "An Aid to Needy Children Program: A Study of Types and Responses to Casework Services." *Commun Mental Health J* 5(1):20–8 F '69. * (*PA* 44:3933)

684. SCHARF, MARY CHRISTINE. *Study of Differences in Selected Personality and Academic Characteristics of Low Achieving College Males.* Doctor's thesis, University of North Dakota (Grand Forks, N.D.), 1969. (*DAI* 30:1405A)

685. SCHNITZER, LEAH PALTIEL, AND STEWART, ROBERT A. C. "Originality and Personality Variables in High School Art Students." *Psychol* 6(1):36–9 F '69. * (*PA* 43:11334)

686. SCHREIBER, ELLIOTT H. "Personality Characteristics and Dental Disorders in Adolescents." *Psychol Rep* 24(2):626 Ap '69. * (*PA* 43:16056)

687. SCHULMAN, WILLIAM JOSEPH. *Personality and Behavior Characteristics of Assaultive Psychiatric Patients.* Doctor's thesis, University of Texas (Austin, Tex.), 1969. (*DAI* 30: 5698B)

688. SCHWARTZ, MELVIN L.; DENNERLL, RAYMOND D.; AND LIN, YI-GUANG. "Similarity of Personality Trait Interrelationships in Persons With and Without Epileptogenic Cerebral Dysfunction." *J Abn Psychol* 74(2):205–8 Ap '69. * (*PA* 43: 10204)

689. SMITH, JAMES M., AND SCHAEFER, CHARLES E. "Development of a Creativity Scale for the Adjective Check List." *Psychol Rep* 25(1):87–92 Ag '69. * (*PA* 44:3641)

690. SPEER, VINCENT JOSEPH. *Relationship of Masculinity-Femininity to Self-Concept, Adjustment, Body-Cathexis and Achievement in Vocational High School Students.* Doctor's thesis, St. John's University (Jamaica, N.Y.), 1969. (*DAI* 30: 1889B)

691. SPIEGEL, DON, AND KEITH-SPIEGEL, PATRICIA. "Factor Analysis of 78 Variables From Nine Personality Tests and

Scales." *J Proj Tech & Pers Assess* 33(2):160–7 Ap '69. * (*PA* 43:11352)

692. STEELE, CAROLYN IRENE. *Institutional Placement During Adolescence and Its Relationship to the Girl's Task of Sexual Identification.* Doctor's thesis, Smith College (Northampton, Mass.), 1969. (*DAI* 31:474A)

693. STROUP, ATLEE L., AND EFT, JOHN H. "The CPI as a Predictor of College Academic Success." *Alberta J Ed Res* 15(4):191–4 D '69. * (*PA* 46:1872)

694. TAYLOR, AZELLA L. *Teacher Dogmatism as Related to Classroom Questions and Pupil-Teacher Verbal Interaction.* Doctor's thesis, University of Washington (Seattle, Wash.), 1969. (*DAI* 30:4882A)

695. THELEN, MARK H. "Repression-Sensitization: Its Relation to Adjustment and Seeking Psychotherapy Among College Students." *J Consult & Clin Psychol* 33(2):161–5 Ap '69. * (*PA* 43:10377)

696. THOMSON, WILLIAM D. *Predicting Practical Nursing Course Grades From the California Psychological Inventory and the Differential Aptitude Test.* Master's thesis, Brigham Young University (Provo, Utah), 1969.

697. TRIMBLE, JOSEPH EVERETT. *Psychological Characteristics of Employed and Unemployed Western Oklahoma Male American Indians.* Doctor's thesis, University of Oklahoma (Norman, Okla.), 1969. (*DAI* 30:2156A)

698. WALDEN, RONALD LEE. *Flexible Scheduling: Factors Related to Change in Academic Achievement.* Doctor's thesis, Northwestern University (Evanston, Ill.), 1969. (*DAI* 30:2786A)

699. WATLEY, DONIVAN J. "Career Progress: A Longitudinal Study of Gifted Students." *J Counsel Psychol* 16(2):100–8 Mr '69. * (*PA* 43:10379)

700. WEINSTEIN, MALCOLM S. "Achievement Motivation and Risk Preference." *J Pers & Social Psychol* 13(2):153–72 O '69. * (*PA* 44:654)

701. WELKER, JAMES DOYT. *Selected Factors and Achievement in an Audio-Tutorial Introductory College Biology Course.* Doctor's thesis, Indiana University (Bloomington, Ind.), 1969. (*DAI* 31:249A)

702. WOLITZER, MORTON. *An Investigation of the Relationship Between Selected Personality Variables and the Involvement of Students in Social Protest Movements.* Doctor's thesis, New York University (New York, N.Y.), 1969. (*DAI* 30:4553A)

703. WORK, GERALD G. "CPI Patterns of College Male Disciplinary Cases and a Comparison Group." *J Col Stud Personnel* 10(4):223–6 Jl '69. *

704. ZIEGLER, FREDRICK J.; RODGERS, DAVID A.; AND PRENTISS, ROBERT J. "Psychosocial Response to Vasectomy." *Arch Gen Psychiatry* 21(1):46–54 Jl '69. * (*PA* 44:2257)

705. BARRON, FRANK, AND ROSENBERG, MARVIN. "King Lear and His Fool: A Study of the Conception and Enactment of Dramatic Role in Relation to Self-Conception." *Ed Theatre J* 22(3):276–83 O '70. *

706. BEECH, LAWRENCE A. "The California Psychological Inventory as a Measurement of Permissiveness-Restrictiveness and Love-Hostility." *Psychol Rep* 27(2):381–2 O '70. * (*PA* 45:6128)

707. BLANE, HOWARD T., AND YAMAMOTO, KAZUO. "Sexual Role Identity Among Japanese and Japanese-American High School Students." *J Cross-Cultural Psychol* 1(4):345–54 D '70. * (*PA* 45:9789)

708. BUTT, DORCAS SUSAN. "Socialization Dimensions and Their Correlates." Abstract. *Proc 78th Ann Conv Am Psychol Assn* 5(1):475–6 '70. * (*PA* 44:18653)

709. CANTY, JAMES JOSEPH, JR. *Personality and Behavior Correlates of Extreme Positive Self-Regard.* Doctor's thesis, Fordham University (New York, N.Y.), 1970. (*DAI* 31:3978B)

710. CLARK, WILLIAM HARRINGTON, III. *The Relationships of Personality and Performance to Motivator and Hygiene Orientations.* Doctor's thesis, Case Western Reserve University (Cleveland, Ohio), 1970. (*DAI* 31:3743B)

711. CLAYTON, HOWARD. "Femininity and Job Satisfaction Among Male Library Students at One Midwestern University." *Col & Res Libraries* 31(6):388–98 N '70. * (*PA* 45:7124)

712. CONNELL, DAVID M., AND JOHNSON, JAMES E. "Relationship Between Sex-Role Identification and Self-Esteem in Early Adolescents." Abstract. *Develop Psychol* 3(2):268 S '70. * (*PA* 44:20685)

713. COOK, PATRICK E., AND JOSEPHS, PAULA O. "The Community Adaptation Schedule and the California Psychological Inventory: A Validational Study With College Students." *Commun Mental Health J* 6(5):366–73 O '70. * (*PA* 45:6347)

714. COTTLE, THOMAS J.; EDWARDS, CARL N.; AND PLECK, JOSEPH. "The Relationship of Sex Role Identity and Social and Political Attitudes." *J Personality* 38(3):435–52 S '70. * (*PA* 45:4071)

715. DOHERTY, ANNE. "Influence of Parental Control on the Development of Feminine Sex Role and Conscience." Abstract. *Develop Psychol* 2(1):157–8 Ja '70. * (*PA* 44:4853)

716. DOMINO, GEORGE. "Interactive Effects of Achievement Orientation and Teaching Style on Academic Achievement." *ACT Res Rep* 39:1–9 D '70. *

717. DUNN, REGINA B. *Comparison of Personality Characteristics With Religious Ideals of High School Students.* Doc-

tor's thesis, Fordham University (New York, N.Y.), 1970. (*DAI* 31:4308B)

718. EISENBERG, MYRON GAIL. *An Examination of a Procedure for Determining Personality Correlates to Independence of Judgment in Male University Students.* Doctor's thesis, Northwestern University (Evanston, Ill.), 1970. (*DAI* 31:4309B)

719. FRANK, AUSTIN C., AND KIRK, BARBARA A. "Characteristics of Dental Hygiene Students." *Voc Guid Q* 18(3):207–11 Mr '70. *

720. GLASSMAN, BARRY M., AND SIEGEL, ALLEN. "Personality Correlates of Survival in a Long-Term Hemodialysis Program." *Arch Gen Psychiatry* 22(6):566–74 Je '70. * (*PA* 44:17240)

721. GOUGH, HARRISON G., AND KIRK, BARBARA A. "Achievement in Dental School as Related to Personality and Aptitude Variables." *Meas & Eval Guid* 2(4):225–33 w '70. *

722. HANSON, PHILIP G.; ROTHAUSE, PAUL; O'CONNELL, WALTER E.; AND WIGGINS, GEORGE E. "Diagnosis as a Predictor of Social Behavior in Human Relations Training." *Newsl Res Psychol* 12(3):29–33 Ag '70. *

723. HELSON, RAVENNA, AND CRUTCHFIELD, RICHARD S. "Creative Types in Mathematics." *J Personality* 38(2):177–97 Je '70. * (*PA* 44:18669)

724. HELSON, RAVENNA, AND CRUTCHFIELD, RICHARD S. "Mathematicians: The Creative Researcher and the Average PhD." *J Consult & Clin Psychol* 34(2):250–7 Ap '70. * (*PA* 44:10374)

725. HENSRUD, NEIL BARRY. *The Relation of Scores on the MTAI to Selected Non-Intellective and Demographic Variables.* Doctor's thesis, University of North Dakota (Grand Forks, N.D.), 1970. (*DAI* 31:2229A)

726. HICKSON, R. H., AND DRISKILL, J. C. "Needs for Achievement: Differences Between Honors and Non-Honors Students." *J Exp Ed* 38(3):37–8 sp '70. *

727. HOGAN, ROBERT. "A Dimension of Moral Judgement." *J Consult & Clin Psychol* 35(2):205–12 O '70. * (*PA* 45:4239)

728. HOGAN, ROBERT; MANKIN, DONALD; CONWAY, JOHN; AND FOX, SHERMAN. "Personality Correlates of Undergraduate Marijuana Use." *J Consult & Clin Psychol* 35(1):58–63 Ag '70. * (*PA* 44:20909)

729. IHLANFELDT, WILLIAM IVAN. *Personal Characteristics of Satisfied and Non-Satisfied Northwestern University Students.* Doctor's thesis, Northwestern University (Evanston, Ill.), 1970. (*DAI* 31:3293A)

730. KASL, STANISLAV V., AND COBB, SIDNEY. "Blood Pressure Changes in Men Undergoing Job Loss: A Preliminary Report." *Psychosom Med* 32(1):19–38 Ja–F '70. * (*PA* 44:14980)

731. KASSERA, WAYNE J., AND SEASE, WILLIAM A. "Personal Change as a Concomitant of Counselor Education." *Counselor Ed & Sup* 9(3):208–11 sp '70. * (*PA* 46:5561)

732. KILBURN, KENT L.; MCDOLE, GARY; AND SMITH, RUTH E. "The Strong Vocational Interest Blank as a Measure of Success in the Training of Psychiatric Technicians." *Psychol Rep* 26(3):883–6 Je '70. * (*PA* 45:764)

733. KISH, GEORGE B. "CPI Correlates of Stimulus-Seeking in Male Alcoholics." *Newsl Res Psychol* 12(2):15–6 My '70. *

734. KISH, GEORGE B. "Correlates of Active-Passive Food Preferences: Failure to Confirm a Relationship With Alcoholism." *Percept & Motor Skills* 31(3):839–47 D '70. * (*PA* 45:10246)

735. KISH, GEORGE B., AND TIMMONS, FRANK. "CPI Descriptions of Alcoholics Differing in Alienation." *Newsl Res Psychol* 12(4):7–9 N '70. *

736. KISH, GEORGE B., AND TIMMONS, FRANK. "CPI Descriptions of Alcoholics Differing in Locus of Control." *Newsl Res Psychol* 12(4):6–7 N '70. *

737. KRAUS, WILLIAM ARNOLD. *Laboratory Groups: Effect on the Tolerance Scale of the California Psychological Inventory.* Doctor's thesis, Ohio University (Athens, Ohio), 1970. (*DAI* 31:2686A)

738. KUNERT, KENNETH M. "Use of Profile Analysis in Predicting Academic Achievement." Abstract. *Proc 78th Ann Conv Am Psychol Assn* 5(2):661–2 '70. * (*PA* 44:19537)

739. LANDERS, DANIEL M. "Psychological Femininity and the Prospective Female Physical Educator." *Res Q* 41(2):164–70 My '70. *

740. LANYON, RICHARD I. "Development and Validation of a Psychological Screening Inventory." *J Consult & Clin Psychol Monogr* 35(1, pt 2):1–24 Ag '70. * (*PA* 44:18915)

741. LEVIN, JOSEPH, AND KARNI, ELIEZUR S. "Demonstration of Cross-Cultural Invariance of the California Psychological Inventory in America and Israel by the Guttman-Lingoes Smallest Space Analysis." *J Cross-Cultural Psychol* 1(3):253–60 S '70. * (*PA* 45:4050)

742. LUNNEBORG, PATRICIA W., AND LUNNEBORG, CLIFFORD E. "Factor Structure of MF Scales and Items." *J Clin Psychol* 26(3):360–6 Jl '70. * (*PA* 45:707)

743. MCCARTHY, DOROTHEA; ANTHONY, ROBERT J.; AND DOMINO, GEORGE. "A Comparison of the CPI, Franck, MMPI, and WAIS Masculinity-Femininity Indexes." *J Consult & Clin Psychol* 35(3):414–6 D '70. * (*PA* 45:4284)

744. MALLEY, PATRICK BRENDAN. *The Relationship of Selected Personality Variables to Employment as a School Counselor and Persistence in Graduate Education.* Doctor's thesis,

University of Pittsburgh (Pittsburgh, Pa.), 1970. (*DAI* 30: 4779A)

745. MEHRENS, WILLIAM A., AND ROGERS, BRUCE G. "Relations Between Grade Point Averages and Collegiate Course Grade Distributions." *J Ed Res* 64(4):169–71 D '70. *

746. MILLER, MARY BALL. "Meaningful Interpersonal Relationships and Mental Health Correlates." Abstract. *Proc 78th Ann Conv Am Psychol Assn* 5(1):347–8 '70. * (*PA* 44:18694)

747. MOSKOVIS, L. MICHAEL. "Similarities and Differences of College-Level Successful and Unsuccessful Shorthand Students." *Delta Pi Epsilon J* 12(2):12–6 F '70. *

748. OLCH, DORIS, AND SNOW, DAVID L. "Personality Characteristics of Sensitivity Group Volunteers." *Personnel & Guid J* 48(10):848–50 Je '70. *

749. QUINN, ALVIN WILLIAM. *An Assessment of Selected Personality Characteristics in Able Adolescent Science Students.* Doctor's thesis, University of Colorado (Boulder, Colo.), 1970. (*DAI* 31:2195A)

750. REESE, HAYNE W., AND PARNES, SIDNEY J. "Programming Creative Behavior." *Child Develop* 41(2):413–23 Je '70. * (*PA* 44:15509)

751. RUBINROIT, CARL IAN. *Leadership in Dyadic Groups as a Function of Dominance and Ethnic Composition.* Doctor's thesis, University of Texas (Austin, Tex.), 1970. (*DAI* 31: 2265B)

752. SCHLUDERMANN, SHIRIN, AND SCHLUDERMANN, EDUARD. "Generalizability of California Personality Inventory Factors." *J Psychol* 74(1):43–50 Ja '70. * (*PA* 44:10451)

753. SCHLUDERMANN, SHIRIN, AND SCHLUDERMANN, EDUARD. "Personality Correlations of Adolescent Self-Concepts and Security-Insecurity." *J Psychol* 74(1):85–90 Ja '70. * (*PA* 44: 10162)

754. SEARS, ROBERT R. "Relation of Early Socialization Experiences to Self-Concepts and Gender Role in Middle Childhood." *Child Develop* 41(2):266–89 Je '70. * (*PA* 44:14368)

755. SLAUGHTER, MARY. "An Analysis of the Relationship Between Somatotype and Personality Traits of College Women." *Res Q* 41(4):569–75 D '70. * (*PA* 46:4441)

756. SMITH, JoAnn HORN. *A Study of the Relationship Between Dogmatic and Rigid Attitudes in the Mother and Early Developmental Progress in the Infant.* Doctor's thesis, New York University (New York, N.Y.), 1970. (*DAI* 31:4160B)

757. SQUATRIGLIA, ROBERT WILLIAM. *The Impact of Short-Term Group Counseling on Student Values.* Doctor's thesis, University of South Carolina (Columbia, S.C.), 1970. (*DAI* 31:3280A)

758. STEIN, KENNETH B.; VADUM, ARLENE C.; AND SARBIN, THEODORE R. "Socialization and Delinquency: A Study of False Negatives and False Positives in Prediction." *Psychol Rec* 20(3):353–64 su '70. * (*PA* 45:8555)

759. STEWART, DENTON J., AND RESNICK, JEROME H. "Verbal Conditioning and Dependency Behavior in Delinquents." *J Abn Psychol* 76(3):375–7 D '70. * (*PA* 45:6636)

760. STROM, ROBERT D., AND LARIMORE, DAVID. "Predicting Teacher Success: The Inner City." *J Exp Ed* 38(4):69–77 su '70. *

761. STROUP, ATLEE L. "The Prediction of Academic Performance From Personality and Aptitude Variables." *J Exp Ed* 38(3):83–6 sp '70. *

762. TEPPER, BRENDA SCHLOSSBERG. *Contrast and Assimilation Effects in Dyadic Interaction.* Doctor's thesis, City University of New York (New York, N.Y.), 1970. (*DAI* 31:3718B)

763. THELEN, MARK H., AND VARBLE, DUANE L. "Comparison of College Students Seeking Psychotherapy With Nontherapy Students on Coping and Defense Scales." *J Clin Psychol* 26(1):123–4 Ja '70. * (*PA* 44:10572)

764. VANDERPOOL, JOHN P., AND BARRATT, ERNEST S. "Empathy: Towards a Psychophysiological Definition." *Dis Nerv System* 31(7):464–7 Jl '70. * (*PA* 45:2023)

LEWIS R. GOLDBERG, *Professor of Psychology, University of Oregon; and Research Associate, Oregon Research Institute; Eugene, Oregon.*

Taken together, the three previous MMY reviews of the CPI constitute a hung jury. E. Lowell Kelly evaluated the inventory highly: "All in all, however, the CPI in this reviewer's opinion is one of the best, if not the best, available instrument of its kind" (6:71). Lee J. Cronbach refused to return a verdict: "Gough is to be commended for pursuing his own contrary view skillfully, but the usefulness of his instrument is still in question" (5:37). And Robert L. Thorndike evaluated the inventory

negatively: "It is conceivable that there may be a role for a personality inventory developed by the procedures and following the rationale of the CPI. However, this reviewer feels that the role will not be that of providing a clear, efficient, and simple personality description" (5:37). What manner of beast serves to elicit such widely disparate appraisals?

The CPI consists of 480 items (e.g., "I enjoy social gatherings just to be with people."), 12 of which are duplicates; 178 of these items were taken directly from the MMPI item pool, and 35 more MMPI items were revised slightly for inclusion in the CPI (*188, 189, 481*). All items are presented with a true-false format. Of the 18 original CPI scales, three (Gi, Wb, and Cm) were developed mainly as potential indicators of response validity. The remaining 15 traits which the CPI purports to measure include a set of "folk concepts," defined as follows:

variables used for the description and analysis of personality in everyday life and in social interaction. It is theorized that such folk concepts, viewed as emergents from interpersonal behavior, have a kind of immediate meaningfulness and universal relevance which enhance their attractiveness as diagnostic concepts. Hopefully, diagnoses and forecasts of social behavior, if mediated by such concepts, will be more accurate and dependable than forecasts arrived at by way of other formulations (*494*).

The goal of the *California Psychological Inventory* is to measure those traits of character which arise directly and necessarily from interpersonal life, and which should therefore be relevant to the understanding and prediction of social behavior in any and all situations and in any culture. Specifically, the inventory seeks to assess "folk concepts" which are culturally universal (*194*).

That is, Gough equates the relative importance of a trait with its probability of occurrence in the natural language. The more important a trait is, the more people will notice it, wish to talk of it, and eventually invent a word for it. Moreover, Gough defines "folk concepts" by reference to the set of *all* natural languages: the more languages which have one or more terms for a particular kind of trait, the more universal—and hence more important—that trait is. While Gough did not utilize any cross-cultural linguistic studies in order to select the traits he included in the CPI, this would certainly have been a logical starting place for the development of such an inventory. On the other hand, of all inventory constructors, Gough has been among the most active in carrying out cross-cultural studies of his inventory scales *after* their construction (*192, 194, 232, 282, 283, 365, 366*).

Eleven of the CPI scales were constructed at least partially via an external strategy of scale construction (e.g., contrasted groups), and four (Sp, Sa, Sc, and Fx) via an internal strategy (e.g., item homogeneity). Like the other two popular externally constructed inventories, the MMPI and SVIB, the CPI was originally intended as an "open-ended" instrument, for which new scales could be constructed as the need arose. However, while new MMPI and SVIB scales have been proliferating on a yearly basis, Gough has not elected to expand the original CPI scale set, and only a few other investigators have constructed new scales from the CPI item pool (*132, 136, 234, 291, 331, 373, 652*). Instead, he has developed a series of regression equations, based on the original 18 CPI scales, to predict such criteria as leadership (*646*), social maturity vs. delinquency (*282, 366*), parole outcome (*233*), effectiveness in student teaching (*367*), college attendance among high aptitude students (*364*), graduation from high school (*284*), achievement in high school (*190, 478*), achievement in college courses in introductory psychology (*191*), achievement in dental school (*721*), and achievement in medical school (*193*). That is, Gough (like Cattell) has opted to utilize linear combinations of existing scales for applied prediction purposes, instead of developing new scales based upon the linear combination of items.

Both the assets and liabilities of the CPI closely parallel those of the MMPI and SVIB. Since a number of scales in all three inventories intercorrelate highly, critics tend to deplore the "redundancy" and "lack of parsimony" of the existing scale sets. Moreover, since factor analysts generally extract a number of factors equal to one-quarter the number of scales, it should come as no great surprise that the numerous factor analyses of the 18 CPI scales have generally tended to extract four factors (*66, 70, 100, 109, 135, 136, 138, 214, 218, 253, 310, 320*), while the MMPI's 12 scales have typically been reduced to three. Interestingly, however, inventories constructed by radically different strategies also produce a similar number of factors; as just one example, the 16PF, constructed by factor analytic tactics, has four "second-order" factors.

Nevertheless, it is certainly true that the three external inventories include scales with significantly higher intercorrelations than can be found in most inventories constructed by other strategies—in part because the same items are scored on more than one scale. For example, the SVIB Chemist and Physicist scales intercorrelate above .90, the MMPI Hypochondriasis and Hysteria scales intercorrelate about .75, and the CPI Dominance and Sociability scales intercorrelate about .65. Though some of these correlations are close to the maximum possible, given the reliabilities of the scales, only the first approaches that pinnacle reached by two of the four original Bernreuter scales, which correlated .96 with each other.

While it has been proposed that the CPI scale intercorrelations are the direct result of massive response sets or styles (*62*), this intriguing hypothesis has become increasingly less plausible as the research evidence has accumulated. More likely, a sizable proportion of CPI scale covariance stems from the actual covariation among the "folk concepts" targeted by the scales. As just one example, it would be quite strange if mean peer ratings of "dominance" and "sociability" were not at least moderately correlated in any heterogeneous sample of individuals; and were this correlation to reach .60, few psychologists would be surprised. Why, then, should one deplore *scale* intercorrelations of the same magnitude?

Given the rationale and purpose of the CPI, scale "redundancy" may be a pseudo-liability. However, three weaknesses of the inventory and its manual come easily to mind. First, the CPI (and other inventories as well) should include a few more duplicated items, and response consistency to these identical pairs should be scored as a gross measure of response validity; moreover, the inventory might well include a set of directly reversed items, again to provide another index for the same purpose. Second, the manual does not provide a detailed description of Gough's scale construction procedures; it should. And third, the manual devotes five and a half pages to a discussion of "interaction among scales" and "profile interpretation," and Gough explicitly encourages test users to intuit personality traits "clinically" from various profile configurations—in spite of (*a*) the paucity of research on CPI profiles (*95, 181*), (*b*) the failure of configural prediction schemes more generally,[1]

---

1 GOLDBERG, LEWIS R. "The Search for Configural Relationships in Personality Assessment: The Diagnosis of Psychosis vs. Neurosis From the MMPI." *Multiv Behav Res* 4(4):523–36 O '69. *

and (c) the model provided by Gough's own research, which has relied almost exclusively on linear regression equations.

On the other hand, the CPI shares with the MMPI and SVIB one overriding virtue: they are among the very small set of personality inventories for which enough empirical research has accumulated to allow the user to evaluate the probable utility of his predictions in industrial, clinical, and educational settings. Eventually, as research accumulates on the newer—psychometrically more polished—instruments, the CPI may become obsolete. But, at least for the next five years, the knowledgeable practitioner should be able to provide more valid nontest predictions from the CPI than from most other comparable instruments on the market today.

JAMES A. WALSH, *Professor of Psychology and Statistics, Iowa State University, Ames, Iowa.*

The CPI continues to be widely used in a variety of research settings, and for this reason but few others it merits review. It is no accident that most of the studies in which the CPI figures have highly applied and empirically oriented goals, such as personnel selection, for the CPI is an almost comically typical product of criterion-oriented test construction.

The 468 items of the CPI were formed into 18 redundant, highly intercorrelated scales almost wholly on the basis of their ability to discriminate between members of extreme groups on criteria such as rated popularity or rated citizenship. The criterion-oriented approach has liabilities enough of its own in that it usually results in scales without general or basic psychological meaning. When this approach is coupled with the practice of distinguishing between extreme groups, the psychological significance of the scales is likely to be no more than that of a classification schema for varieties of extreme behavior.

It might be argued that the repeated cross validation to which CPI scales have been subjected and their oft-praised capacity to provide intuitively meaningful descriptions of normal people in terms of socially useful personality characteristics are evidence that this charge is invalid. Research involving the CPI does not support this counterclaim, for most such studies appear to follow a highly predictable and quite circular sequence. Typically, the CPI is administered to some group about which little is known but which it would be convenient to be able to tag with some identifying "personality" characteristic: e.g., professional athletes are "dominant." Scores on all scales are obtained for the members of the group and means and standard deviations are computed. The sample mean is found to differ significantly from the mean of one or another norm group with respect to some scale such as Sociability, which was originally derived by selecting items which distinguished between extreme groups with respect to rated popularity and social participation. It is viewed as most reasonable that the group in question should be higher than the norm group on the Sociability scale, since it is, in retrospect, well known that members of this group are very sociable. This finding may be cross validated, but most likely it is not. Nevertheless, the group is now accepted as more sociable than the norm group—not more like one extreme group than another with respect to rated popularity, but sociable. Finally, the fact that the group being studied is sociable is taken as evidence for the validity of the Sociability scale. Validity claims based on reasoning of this sort are very dubious indeed.

The usefulness of the CPI scales is not improved by the all-hit-no-miss technique of interpretation described in the manual: "When the behaviors suggested by two or more extreme scores seem to be similar, they may well reinforce each other; if they seem opposing or contradictory, they may serve to counteract or ameliorate each other." Such interpretation amounts to no more than post hoc rationalization and should not be condoned. The CPP catalog is likewise guilty of a misdemeanor in citing the usefulness of the inventory in settings where "one is interested in identifying and maximizing the positive and favorable personality assets of individuals." The implication that the CPI can be directly useful in maximizing personality characteristics is misleading at best.

The strongest point of the CPI is undoubtedly the very sizable (more than 6,000 men and more than 7,000 women) and widely varied norm groups available. The male groups range from machine operators to military officers and the female groups from prison inmates to medical school students.

These large norm groups appear less useful in light of the moderate reliabilities of the scales. For non-incarcerated groups, the retest correlations are generally between .55 and .75 over a one year period. Given the fact that only four of the scales are in any sense homogeneous, these values should not be thought of as lower-bound estimates of reliability.

The correlations of the CPI scales with scales from other inventories are frequently quite substantial. There is a great deal of overlap, for example, between the *Guilford-Zimmerman Temperament Survey* and the CPI. Moreover, the sizable correlations between about one-third of the CPI scales and MMPI scales known to be saturated with social desirability raise the possibility of some response set contamination. It is possible that this danger is not serious, for Gough has been both imaginative and thorough in attempting to guard against, and also to assay the extent of, response set influence. Three scales are provided for these purposes.

Minor points deserving mention include the relative flimsiness of the test booklets. They fray and tear easily.

Overall, the reviewer cannot recommend the CPI, except possibly for the most purely empirical purposes. Its criterion-oriented mode of construction severely limits its generality and psychological meaningfulness. Much of its case for validity is based upon a circular mode of reasoning which is self-defeating. The CPI norm groups are large and varied, but reliabilities are quite modest. There is a possibility of response set contamination for several of the scales, and there is also a great deal of overlap with other inventories. Either the 16PF or the EPPS would probably serve as well as the CPI in most prediction situations, and, in addition, the scales of the former inventories possess the advantages of greater generality and clearer psychological meaning.

J Counsel Psychol 11:197–202, 299–306 su, f '64. John O. Crites. * As a measure of the normal personality, the CPI has considerable promise, but it also has some shortcomings, as Cronbach, Thorndike and others have pointed out (Buros, 1959). Not the least of these shortcomings has been the excessive number of scales in the CPI, which has made it difficult to interpret conceptually and cumbersome to use in counseling. The factor analyses which have been conducted on the CPI have reduced it to a more economic set of scales, however, and have increased its value for research, theory construction and practical application alike.

Further studies of the CPI might well investigate the behavioral correlates of the factorially-defined personality constructs in an essentially normal population and thereby determine the extent to which each of the sources of common variance in the scales is related to non-test criteria of academic and vocational performance, effectiveness in interpersonal relationships, adjustment to periods of stress and strain, etc. New departures in conceptualizing the normal personality might take Heath's model of ego functioning as a starting point and derive hypotheses which might then be tested with the CPI, such as "The *Reasonable Adventurer* comes from a familial interpersonal atmosphere in which the parents have encouraged self expression and independent action through attitudes of acceptance and understanding but have also fostered self-discipline and goal direction through the imposition of reasonable limits upon impulse gratification." And, uses of the CPI in counseling might be explored further by considering the implications for counseling goals and plans of the ways in which clients with different problems deviate from the various normal personality types identified in the factor analyses. The next review of the CPI will deal with this problem and suggest some answers to such questions as: What are the personalities of personal adjustment and vocational-educational clients? Why do they come for counseling? And, what is the relationship of their personalities to their problems? * [See original review for additional critical comments not excerpted.]

For a review by E. Lowell Kelly, see 6:71; for reviews by Lee J. Cronbach and Robert L. Thorndike, see 5:37 (1 excerpt).

[50]

★[Re California Psychological Inventory.] OP-TIMUM Psychodiagnostic Consultation Service. A computerized scoring and interpreting service for qualified users of the CPI or the MMPI; 1969; various types of interpretive reports are available: types 1 (for industrial psychologists and personnel counselors), 2 (for counselors and caseworkers), 3 (for correctional counselors), 4 (self-report to be given to patient by counselor or therapist), 5 (for physicians), 6 (standard report for psychiatrists and psychologists), 6C (standard report on delinquent patients), 7 (detailed report for use before psychoanalysis or intensive psychotherapy), 7C (detailed report on delinquent patients); each type of report (except type 4) available in full or brief form; although the reports may be based on either the CPI or the MMPI, publisher recommends that the CPI be used with types 1–3 reports and the MMPI with types 5–7 reports;

the interpretive report (except type 4) is a computer printout presenting a 1–6 page narrative report and 4–5 pages of scores on 18 CPI scales, 13 MMPI scales, 135 special research scales, 5 orthogonal factors, 16 Taulbee-Sisson scales, various other research indices, and a graph (types 6 and 7 only) of 12 MMPI scales; all of the scales are considered in the computerized narrative report; type 4 is a 1–2 page computer printout of narrative statements only; manual (12 pages) for psychiatrists and psychologists; special Digitek answer sheets must be used; scoring and computerized report fees: $15 per test for types 1–3, $20 for types 5, 6, or 6C, $30 for types 7 or 7C, (plus $5 additional for type 4 report on same client); psychiatrists and psychologists may request, in addition to their own report, type 2 ($5 additional) or type 5 ($10 additional) report for referring caseworker or physician; brief reports are $2–5.50 less than regular reports; reports are mailed within 2 days after receipt of answer sheets; postpaid; Joseph C. Finney, Charles Dwight Auvenshine, David Fulton Smith, and Donald E. Skeeters; Behavioral Sciences, Inc. * (For a review and references on the OPTIMUM Psychodiagnostic Consultation Service, see 107.)

[51]

★Chapin Social Insight Test. Ages 13 and over; 1967–68; CSIT; 1 form ('67, 4 pages); manual ('68, 15 pages); response booklet ('67, 4 pages); no norms; $3.75 per 25 tests; $6 per 50 response booklets; $3 per manual; $3.25 per specimen set; postage extra; (20–30) minutes; F. Stuart Chapin (test) and Harrison G. Gough (manual); Consulting Psychologists Press, Inc. *

REFERENCES

1–3. See P:34.

RICHARD I. LANYON, *Associate Professor of Psychology, Northeastern University, Boston, Massachusetts.*

This test was originally developed in 1942 to assess "the capacity to see into a social situation, to appreciate the implications of things said and to interpret effectively the attitudes expressed so as to appreciate the significance of past behavior, or to estimate the trend of future behavior" (*1*). The definition stresses the *diagnostic capacity* of the individual and not his own tendencies to behave in a more or less adaptive manner. The work of Chapin, an eminent sociologist, was largely ignored by psychologists until recently, when its potential was recognized by Harrison Gough, who conducted further validation research into the test and prepared the current manual.

The Chapin test consists of 25 short paragraphs describing situations in which a problem in interpersonal relations or personality dynamics is posed. The respondent is asked to choose, from among four multiple choice options, the one which offers the most insightful commentary or the wisest course of action. Chapin developed the test by assembling 45 such items and selecting the 25 which best differentiated between

persons rated high and those rated low on social insight according to the above definition. Development is adequately described in the manual and also in Gough's paper (*2*). The test takes 20–30 minutes to administer, and items are scored 1, 2, or 3 according to their differentiating power. Internal consistency reliabilities are in the range of .68–.78, which is adequate for the continuing use of the test in its present research status.

Reading the manual proved to be a pleasant experience for this reviewer. In the description of the development of the test, and particularly in the presentation of the relatively small amount of available validity evidence, great care has been taken to convey its exact developmental status. Reservations are stated freely, so that prospective users can feel comfortable in accepting the evaluations and recommendations which the manual offers.

Various kinds of validity data are presented. Direct validation is approached by attempting to delineate the personal characteristics of higher and lower Chapin test scorers, using (*a*) ratings made by psychologists after a five-day intensive study of their subjects, (*b*) correlations with eight standard tests of ability and aptitude, (*c*) the relative standing of various occupational and other groups, and (*d*) relationships with mean Q-sort descriptions from a panel of three psychologists, made after interviewing their subjects and observing them in various activities. In general, these validity data tend to be consistent with the intended meaning of the test. Thus, there are modest correlations with qualities such as good judgment and ability to communicate. Correlations with ability and aptitude tests, ranging from .24 to .40, are also approximately what would be expected; the lowest of these relationships is with mechanical comprehension, and the highest is with supervisory ability. However, no statement is made about the degree of homogeneity in ability level within each group studied. The Q-sort data are perhaps the most persuasive; the items which are the most highly related to Chapin scores stress ability for getting the cooperation of others and for being both a good leader and a good listener, and responsiveness to the subtleties of other people's behavior. The most negatively related items emphasize inflexibility, need for routine, and lack of interpersonal understanding. It should be noted that the possible role of general intelligence in mediating these relationships between Chapin scores and social insight is not dealt with directly in the manual.

Indirect validity evidence is provided by correlations of the Chapin scale with other tests. Correlations with the scales of the CPI, the MMPI, and the SV are low, with very few correlations reaching .30. Thus, the CSIT appears to be assessing a relatively specific personality or social attribute, and a careful reading of the manual conveys a satisfactory, though necessarily tentative, description of this attribute.

Several minor points should be raised about the test. For some of the questions, the correct response options seem somewhat arbitrary. This is a common complaint with multiple choice tests; however, since differential weighting of responses is used, Chapin might perhaps have improved his validity by keying more than one option as "correct," with different weights. Also, the wording of some of the questions and response options is somewhat outdated, though not irritatingly so. Third and more important, the manual contains means and standard deviations from a number of subject groups, but no norms in either percentile or standard score form. Such an inclusion would have been desirable, even at the test's present preliminary stage of development.

EVALUATION. Several other tests have been developed to assess constructs similar to this one. None of them is well known, and by the usual psychometric standards, none appears to be ready for serious consideration. Thus Chapin's test is, in this reviewer's opinion, the most promising available instrument for assessing social insight. Validity data are as yet sparse, but the candor displayed in the manual in identifying omissions and weaknesses makes the potential user's job of evaluating the test an easy one. If the suggested cautions are borne in mind, Chapin's test is recommended for continuing experimental use.

DAVID B. ORR, *President, Scientific Educational Systems, Inc., Washington, D.C.*

This test represents an interesting attempt to develop an instrument in the difficult area of assessing the sensitivity of individuals to the bases for interpersonal actions and feelings. The manual states the purpose as follows:

The purpose of the *Social Insight Test* is to assess the perceptiveness and accuracy with which an individual can appraise others and forecast what they might say and do. * The ability to evaluate an interpersonal situation also implies the ability to perceive what might be needed to bring about certain changes in any given situation, to improve it, perhaps, or to rectify disturbing tensions or conflicts.

Chapin drew upon case histories, literary descriptions, published analyses of conferences and discussions, and prior social scales to develop 45 paragraphs describing interpersonal situations. He constructed four options for each of these situational items, focused on the reasons for the situation, the implications of the situation, or next actions in the situation. One of the options was intended to be the "most accurate, or would represent the wisest thing to do in each situation."

These items were originally scored one point each, but in a subsequent study 200 subjects (not further defined), 100 high and 100 low on "social participation" (not defined) were used as an item analysis sample, and 25 of the 45 items were found to discriminate "adequately" (not defined). Based on these data (not given in the manual), differential scoring weights of 3, 2, and 1 were assigned to the items. For this shortened, 25-item scale, differentially weighted, the correlation with ratings of social insight improved from .21 for the original 45-item scale to .36 (biserial correlations) for two groups of "staff members," rated as 65 above average cases as opposed to 110 not-above-average cases.

To support this development of the test, several other studies are mentioned but not described by the manual. It is concluded that the high scorers on the test tended to come from samples tested in political, professional, social, and civic groups, whereas the low scorers came from testing done in youth organizations and business and religious groups; also, scores rose significantly over a school term for a small group of graduate students. The highest correlation obtained was .43 between social participation (in clubs and the like) and test score (N = 156).

The paragraphs are presented in a separate, reusable "Situations Booklet," with instructions and a sample situation given on the front of the booklet. The options are presented in the separate "Response Booklet." The subject can take as long as he likes, but is instructed that most people finish in 30 minutes or less, and to use that as a guideline. The administrative directions contain the rather unusual statement that the instructions to the student "may be modified as convenient," or that the test may be used as fully self-administering. This direction has serious implications for the "standardized" qualities of the test; however, it cannot interfere with the use of the norms—there are none!

Scoring is done entirely by hand, using a separate list of the correct options. There is no stencil form of the key, and the items are not printed in the Response Booklet in such a way as to facilitate the scoring operation. From the point of view of format, the test could profit from printing the situations together with the options in the same booklet, perhaps with one of the carbon-backed scoring sheet arrangements bound in. This arrangement would eliminate the constant looking back and forth between the two booklets and the possibility of scoring errors in applying and recording the item weights.

The evidence on the reliability of the test which is presented in the manual is sketchy. A corrected odd-even coefficient for a sample (undefined) of 100 males was .78. Other reliability estimates based on item-test correlations, projected by the Guilford method, for samples of 494 males and 215 females, produced values of .71 and .68. It is clear that the reliability of the instrument is hardly high enough to support the kind of use for which its nature would make it most valuable—individual diagnosis.

The evidence for the validity of the test is also rather sketchy, and is pieced together from a variety of small studies. For a sample of 100 military officers, the test correlated with ratings on "ability to communicate, ability to evaluate ideas, good judgment, and leadership" .31, .29, .27, and .26, respectively. Correlations with eight other tests, mostly cognitive, ranged from .24 to .40, with a median of .34. Although the highest correlation here was with *How Supervise?*, it should be noted that these correlations with cognitive tests were as high or higher than those between the *Social Insight Test* and the more relevant ratings given above. This suggests that the test has at least as much of a cognitive component as it does of social insight. Examination of the situations booklet suggests clearly that the test is heavily loaded with reading comprehension.

Nevertheless, the data taken together do suggest that something is being measured other than just reading comprehension. Mean scores of a variety of occupational groups show order-

ings which would be reasonable in terms of the social insight which might be expected to be required, and correlations for a sample of 66 students with a 50-item Q-sort rating by a panel of three psychologists seem favorable. This reviewer wishes that more of the data on this latter study had been included in the manual. The range for the 50 correlations was −.45 to .43, and the several descriptions having the highest correlations and the several having the lowest correlations did appear to describe the poles of a scale relevant to interpersonal perceptiveness and social acuity, which might be called social insight.

One of the more distinctive things which can be noticed about the data presented in the manual is that the validity coefficients are invariably low. A clue to the reason for this may be found in the item-test correlations, which were not reported individually, but which had *medians* of .30 for men and .28 for women. These data suggest, as we might expect, that we are not dealing with a unitary dimension, but rather with a multi-faceted, quite heterogeneous concept. This conclusion is further supported by examination of the situations themselves, which require everything from mind-reading to Freudian analysis to come up with the keyed answer. One is aided in this effort, however, by the weakness of some of the misleads, which lack parallelism and some of which would rarely be chosen by the intelligent respondent trying to select the right answer.

In summary, several points can be made. In spite of a certain diffuseness of concept, the test represents an interesting and useful attempt to measure potential interpersonal behavior, as it might occur in real-life situations. The validity data suggest that a multi-faceted concept which might be termed social insight is being measured, though barely beyond the level of reading comprehension required to take the test. The reliability is too low for individual work, but acceptable for group work. The test could be improved by reprinting in a single booklet with either stencil scoring or carbon-impression scoring. Some effort to reduce the reading load and to make the situations more homogeneous in construct would probably raise the level of the validity coefficients. The data reported in the manual should be made much more complete. Finally, interpretative aids such as norms are completely missing. The manual sums it up: "All of the above findings, it should be said again, are highly tentative and provisional. The relationships in all cases are moderate and do not justify strong claims or assertions."

[52]
The Child Behavior Rating Scale. Grades kgn–3; 1960–62; CBRS; ratings by teachers or parents; 6 adjustment scores: self, home, social, school, physical, total; 1 form ('62, 4 pages); manual ('62, 8 pages plus test); no data on reliability of subscores; $7.50 per 25 tests and manual; $6.50 per 25 tests; $2 per manual; postpaid; [5–10] minutes; Russell N. Cassel; Western Psychological Services. *

REFERENCE

1. See P:35.

JAMES A. DUNN, *Director, Developmental Systems Division, American Institutes for Research, Palo Alto, California.*

The CBRS is a 78-item rating scale described in the manual as offering an "objective assessment of personality adjustments" in the areas of: home adjustment, social adjustment, self adjustment, school adjustment, and physical adjustment. It is attractively packaged and the adjustment areas with which the instrument deals are of special importance to those working with children. The strategy of attempting to limit the scale to explicit, observable behaviors, and to the systematic identification of those behaviors from an empirical study of a large number of real life cases, is evidence of the soundness of the author's basic judgment. There are a number of technical and methodological questions, however, that raise serious concerns regarding use of the instrument.

The CBRS is intended for use with preschool children, primary grade children, and "children unable to read or handicapped in completing the conventional paper-and-pencil personality tests used in school testing programs." The manual does not state, however, what restrictions should be placed on the use of the instrument with this latter type of child; no data are given for the nonreading or "handicapped" child.

Some of the "purposes of the CBRS" cited in the manual are: (*a*) "To compare ratings of a specific child with the normative data of both typical children and emotionally handicapped children." (*b*) "To provide a single meaningful score to indicate total adjustment." (*c*) "To gain an understanding of the interpersonal relationships between raters and the child." (The manual does not give instructions how to do this, however.) (*d*) "To understand the dynamics of the home." (The manual does not give instructions as to how to do this either.)

The manual suggests the CBRS will provide "basic observations and evaluations dealing with the overt behavior, psychodynamics, and motivations of the child"; its use by teachers, counselors, and school personnel will help them better understand the "forces and circumstances operating in the life of the child"; that "if parents rate their children upon school entry and during the primary school years" (and make these data available to teachers and counselors) the data will enable them to "prevent the development of problems or to reduce existing unhealthy situations."

On scanning the CBRS, the reader is first struck by the fact that, in spite of the instrument's title, a high percentage of the items do not actually deal with child *behavior* per se. Many deal with rater inferences concerning the preferences, attitudes, and affect states of the child; degree of acceptance by peers; the child's physical health; the child-rearing practices of his parents; family religious commitments; living accommodations; and the like. Examples of items reflecting some of these are "Often prefers to be alone," "Parents often use corporal punishment," "Family lives in multiple family dwelling," and "Parents have little or no religious affiliations."

The second characteristic that strikes the reader inspecting the CBRS is the seeming inappropriateness of the rating scales for the wording of many of the items. All ratings are on a 6-point scale with the extremes labeled "yes" and "no." A number of the items, however, are worded in such a way that only a *binary* "yes-no" response would be appropriate. In these instances the existence of a 6-point rating scale is irrelevant. An example of an item of this type is the item "Immediate family is broken (death, divorce, etc.)." On the other hand, many other items are predicated on observer judgments of the *degree* to which a particular phrase is descriptive of the child; thus the "yes-no" cues on the rating scale seem particularly distracting.

The third problem apparent from simple inspection of the form is multiple referent items. For example, "Has uncorrected poor vision or poor hearing." Does a "no" answer mean his poor vision or poor hearing has been corrected? Or does it mean the child does not have poor vision; or vision which is only partially corrected? Or does it mean the rater is uncertain?

Fourth, no apparent attempt has been made to deal with response set, social desirability, response bias, or the like.

Finally, on inspecting the CBRS, one becomes very concerned regarding opposite items scored in an identical way. For example, "Often tends to be on the go and can't relax" is an indicator of poor adjustment, whereas the opposite, "Often doesn't have much energy or pep" is *also* an indicator of poor adjustment.

The items in the CBRS were obtained by screening "over 1,000" case studies of elementary school pupils referred for psychological or psychiatric services. The source of the referrals and the agencies to which referrals were made were not identified. "Items appearing most frequently in the records and considered critical for understanding children and their problems were selected for the CBRS." The manual gives no indication of the criteria by which items were judged to be "critical."

The 78 resultant items were then organized into five adjustment scales: (*a*) self adjustment; (*b*) home adjustment; (*c*) social adjustment; (*d*) school adjustment; and (*e*) physical adjustment. The assignments were made on the basis of a majority vote of "6 psychologists." There is no indication of how or why the five scales were identified or the basis for assigning items to the scales. There is no report in the manual of any empirical validation of the judgments of the six psychologists; nor was there any indication of the professional qualifications of the six judges.

No item intercorrelations, no form of empirical scale determination such as factor analysis, cluster analysis, or the like, is reported. There is no evidence that the scale was subject to field tryout, item analysis, or item revision. In short, very serious questions are raised regarding the process of scale construction. From the manual, the scale appears to have been developed in connection with a fairly short term and relatively small scale school-based research study.

Construct validity is implicitly defined in the manual as face validity plus predictive validity. The scale is "presumed to have high face validity," because "all the CBRS items were obtained directly from summary case reports made by highly trained persons in the different disciplines dealing with child behavior," (psychologists, psychiatrists, social workers, and pediatricians). Correlation coefficients between these weighted CBRS scale scores (the Personality Total Adjustment Score) and age, IQ, and academic achievement scores are offered as "construct validity indices."

As might be expected, teacher ratings of a child's emotional adjustment correlate more highly with IQ and achievement than do parent ratings. These "more valid" teacher ratings account for 2 percent of the arithmetic achievement variance, 13 percent of IQ variance, and 24 percent of language achievement variance. No rationale is given for why age and IQ are criterion variables for personality adjustment.

Still, under the heading of construct validity, the manual reports that since the correlations between mothers' and fathers' ratings are so "high" (.66), "it is not necessary to have ratings of both mother and father: either parent's ratings will do."

The author refers to concurrent validity as status validity and includes an elaborate set of data (from an uncited study) showing that, through the use of discriminate function analysis, three scales of the CBRS statistically differentiate between 200 "typical children, selected at random" and 200 "maladjusted" children. On this basis the major use of the CBRS discussed in the manual is the comparison of a student's adjustment profile with profiles of normal and emotionally handicapped children. There is almost no discussion of the nature of the sample of maladjusted children against which the CBRS was normed except that we are given statistics of their age and sex. Of particular importance, if one can rely on a parenthetical statement in the manual, is the fact that many of the 200 "maladjusted" children in his standardization sample *may not have been emotionally handicapped at all* inasmuch as the norming sample was drawn from a population of children *referred* for psychological services. They were *not* drawn from a population that had been *diagnosed* as emotionally handicapped. Further, the "typical" children and the children referred for psychological services were matched on sex only. The manual does not indicate any attempt to match them on age, IQ, academic achievement, or any other such variables.

A serious question may also be raised with regard to the use of discriminate function procedures to show the concurrent validity of an instrument which will be used, presumably, to make individual decisions. See, for example, J. D. Black's reviews of the *Test of Social Insight* and the *Leadership Ability Evaluation,* tests 190 and 133 respectively, in the *Sixth Mental Measurements Yearbook,* for an excellent discussion of this viewpoint.

With regard to reliability, Spearman-Brown odd-even reliabilities ranged from .59 for the "maladjusted" group to .87 for the normal group. In another study with 50 teachers as raters, reliability was reported as .74. The manual did not indicate the type of reliability however; i.e., test-retest, split-half, inter-rater. Still a third unspecified reliability check, involving 50 parents, gave a reliability of .91.

Regarding norms, the manual presents T scores for each of the five adjustment scales plus a Personality Total Adjustment Score (which excludes social and physical adjustment). These T scores apparently are based on the pooling of data on 2,000 subjects across grade levels. There is no description of this norming sample other than that it is a group of "2,000 typical primary grade pupils." Presumably, because the author makes a distinction between preschool and primary grade pupils, one must assume that the normative data pertain only to grades 1, 2, and 3. If this should be the case, then, it is difficult to see how the instrument can be used with preschool children as the author claims in the first sentence of the test manual. Even eliminating preschool children (preschool seems to be synonymous with kindergarten in the manual) given what is so well known about the socio-emotional growth and development of children in the early school years, it is hard to justify the use of norms that are not age differentiated. Younger children who are, by definition, less mature are going to be inappropriately diagnosed as poorly adjusted by the CBRS.

Considerable attention is devoted in the manual to the construction of adjustment profiles and then the comparison of these profiles to the norms for normal and maladjusted children. In addition to the questions regarding the representativeness of the norm group and the appropriateness of norms that are not age differentiated, we may raise the further question of the appropriateness of engaging in profile analyses using scores on subscales for which not a single bit of reliability or validity data is offered. Indeed, it is known from the discriminate function analyses, that two of the scales

in no way help to discriminate normal from "maladjusted" children.

In summary, apparent lack of attention to basic scaling questions, the lack of systematic empirical development, the problems cited in regard to standardization and to test interpretation, and apparent casualness in the preparation of the test manual, all suggest that the CBRS cannot be recommended for use where decisions regarding children are to be made. Because of the clearcut need for reliable and valid instruments in this area, however, it is hoped that the CBRS will be issued soon in a new, more rigorously developed, version.

[53]

Children's Embedded Figures Test. Ages 5–12; 1963; CEFT; revision of the Goodenough-Eagle modification (see *2* below) of the *Embedded Figures Test;* for research use only; 1 form (25 cards plus demonstration and practice materials); manual (15 pages); $6 per set of test materials, postage extra; [10–20] minutes plus practice session; Stephen A. Karp and Norma L. Konstadt; distributed by Consulting Psychologists Press, Inc. *

REFERENCES

1–2. See 6:74b.
3–9. See P:36.
10. ELKIND, SUE NATHANSON. *The Relationship of Orientation Toward Achievement to Convergent and Divergent Problem-Solving.* Doctor's thesis, University of California (Berkeley, Calif.), 1968. (*DAI* 30:1356B)
11. SCALLON, RICHARD J. *Field Articulation: A Study of the Perceptual Style of Enuretic Boys.* Doctor's thesis, St. John's University (Jamaica, N.Y.), 1968. (*DA* 29:4369B)
12. BLOOM, MARTIN; BLENKNER, MARGARET; AND MARKUS, ELLIOT. "Exploring Predictors of the Differential Impact of Relocation on the Infirm Aged." Abstract. *Proc 77th Ann Conv Am Psychol Assn* 4(2):731–2 '69. * (*PA* 44:1196)
13. BRUININKS, ROBERT H. "Auditory and Visual Perceptual Skills Related to the Reading Performance of Disadvantaged Boys." *Percept & Motor Skills* 29(1):179–86 Ag '69. * (*PA* 44:2835)
14. CARTER, HEATHER LILIAN. *A Study of the Ability of Primary School Children to Generalize Behavioral Competencies Acquired in Science to Other Content Settings.* Doctor's thesis, University of Maryland (College Park, Md.), 1969. (*DAI* 31:1067A)
15. DREYER, ALBERT S.; NEBELKOPF, EDWIN; AND DREYER, CECILY A. "Note Concerning Stability of Cognitive Style Measures in Young Children." *Percept & Motor Skills* 28(3):933–4 Je '69. * (*PA* 43:17146)
16. NASH, MARY SAUNDERS. *The Development of Depth Perception in Intermediate Age Children.* Doctor's thesis, University of Kentucky (Lexington, Ky.), 1969. (*DAI* 30:3894B)
17. SCALLON, RICHARD J., AND HERRON, WILLIAM G. "Field Articulation of Enuretic Boys and Their Mothers." *Percept & Motor Skills* 28(2):407–13 Ap '69. * (*PA* 43:15604)
18. WATSON, BILLY LESLIE. *Field Dependence and Early Reading Achievement.* Doctor's thesis, University of California (Los Angeles, Calif.), 1969. (*DAI* 31:656A)
19. CLACK, GERALD STERLING. *Effects of Social Class, Age, and Sex on Tests of Perception, Affect Discrimination, and Deferred Gratification in Children.* Doctor's thesis, Washington University (St. Louis, Mo.), 1970. (*DAI* 31:2275B)
20. GROSSMAN, MARVIN. "Perceptual Style, Creativity, and Various Drawing Abilities." *Studies Art Ed* 11(2):51–4 w '70. *
21. IRVING, DOUGLAS DORSET. *The Field-Dependence Hypothesis in Cross-Cultural Perspective.* Doctor's thesis, Rice University (Houston, Tex.), 1970. (*DAI* 31:3691B)
22. LOVANO, JESSIE J. "The Relation of Conceptual Styles and Mode of Perception to Graphic Expression." *Studies Art Ed* 11(3):39–51 sp '70. *
23. MUMBAUER, CORINNE C., AND MILLER, J. O. "Socioeconomic Background and Cognitive Functioning in Preschool Children." *Child Develop* 41(2):471–80 Je '70. * (*PA* 44:14201)
24. NEBELKOPF, EDWIN B., AND DREYER, ALBERT S. "Perceptual Structuring: Cognitive Style Differences in the Perception of Ambiguous Stimuli." *Percept & Motor Skills* 30(2):635–9 Ap '70. * (*PA* 46:6549)

SHELDON A. WEINTRAUB, *Assistant Professor of Psychology, State University of New York at Stony Brook, Stony Brook, New York.*

The *Children's Embedded Figures Test* (CEFT) is designed to measure an individual difference dimension initially labeled by Witkin as field dependence-independence and more recently as psychological differentiation.[1] This cognitive and perceptual style is viewed as an underlying process of development toward greater psychological complexity. Psychological differentiation is manifested in cognition by global versus articulated or delineated cognitive structuring, and in perception by field dependence-independence.

The dimension of field dependence is seen as the extent to which perception of part of a stimulus field is influenced by the entire field, or the ability to overcome embedded contexts in perception. It is measured by the Tilting Room-Tilting Chair, Rotating Room, and the Rod & Frame Test, where the subject is asked to discriminate the verticality of an object when cues from the surrounding field are misleading, and the less elaborate *Embedded Figures Test* (EFT), in which he must locate a simple figure embedded in a complex one.

The EFT has been the most widely used measure of field dependence in adults, but is much too difficult for young children. An easier version (CHEF) suitable for use with children between the ages of five and nine was constructed by Goodenough and Eagle (*2*), but it proved too unwieldy and complex to administer, necessitating the current revision (CEFT).

As in the adult form, the CEFT is composed of a series of items which require the subject to find a simple form in a complex one, but meaningful complex figures are used in order to make the task more attractive and to insure that the complex figure is perceived as a whole. The standard procedure involves the administration of an 11-item "tent" series in which a tent-like simple figure is to be found embedded in the stimulus figure, and a 14-item "house" series in which a house-like simple figure is to be found embedded in the stimulus figure. The subject's score is the total number of items correct on both series.

The test materials should prove attractive to children, and the task interesting and challenging. While the manual provides verbatim instructions for the administration of the CEFT, it stresses that these should serve merely as a guide. The examiner is urged to attune himself to the child's understanding of the task requirements and his readiness to perform, and modify his administration accordingly, varying amounts of "warm-up" and pretest training. This is good advice; rigid adherence to a verbatim set of instructions with young children and with a task of this sort often results in meaningless findings. The manual does fail to specify, however, a systematic way of handling the subject's requests for information about his performance, resulting in the possibly confounding effect of differential responsiveness to success and failure information. Procedures for scoring are clear and well-defined, credit being given only when the response meets a specific criterion.

Test development relied on item analysis procedures only, selecting those items that discriminated between the highest and lowest scorers on a large pool of potential items. Reliability and validity estimates were obtained from the standardization procedures conducted with boys and girls ranging in age from 5 to 12. No test-retest procedures were conducted by the test authors, but internal consistency reliability estimates were obtained for subjects aged 7 to 12. The five to six year olds were excluded from this analysis because they tended not to be given all items. (Testing is stopped if the subject fails a specified number of items.) Internal reliability estimates range from .83 to .90, and compare favorably with those obtained for EFT. A study (*15*) published subsequent to that of the manual demonstrates satisfactory test-retest stability of CEFT performance of five to six year olds over a six month period. The test-retest Pearson correlation between scores on CEFT in kindergarten and first grade was .87.

The only validity data reported are concurrent validity estimates using the EFT as the criterion measure, and conducted only with subjects aged 9 to 12. Using the EFT precluded concurrent validation with the younger children because of its difficulty, but the CHEF could not be used because many of its items are common to the CEFT. Correlations between CEFT and EFT for the 11 and 12 year old subjects are sizeable (.83 to .86) but somewhat lower for the 9 and 10 year old subjects (.70 to .73). The test authors note that this drop

1 WITKIN, H. A.; DYK, R. B.; FATERSON, H. F.; GOODENOUGH, D. R.; AND KARP, S. A. *Psychological Differentiation: Studies of Development.* New York: John Wiley & Sons, Inc., 1962. Pp. xii, 418. *

may be the result of lowered reliability of the EFT at age 9 (.75 as compared with .90 at age 11). When the nine year validity coefficients are corrected for attenuation of the EFT, they reach .80. Thus most all of the reliable variance of the CEFT may be accounted for by common variance with the EFT. Additionally, CEFT performance was noted to improve with increasing age but was unrelated to sex, both findings consistent with those obtained with the CHEF.

The authors note the need for additional data on concurrent validity as well as research on construct validity with measures which have been shown to reflect abilities similar to those tapped by EFT.

In summary, the CEFT serves as a satisfactory downward extension of the EFT, and should prove valuable in research on the development of the very interesting individual difference dimension of psychological differentiation. The utility and value of this dimension, however, is a separate issue from that of the research instrument CEFT, and can only be determined by further research and construct validation.

[54]

★Clinical Analysis Questionnaire, Research Edition. Ages 18 and over; 1970–71; CAQ; 37 scores (listed below): 28 primary factor scores and 9 second-order factor scores; 1 form ('70, 16 pages); 2 parts; manual ('71, 17 pages); no norms for second-order factor scores; separate answer sheets (Digitek) must be used; $17.50 per 25 tests; $5 per 50 answer sheets; scoring stencil not available; $1.25 per manual; $2 per specimen set; postage extra; scoring and interpreting service, $2 and over per test; (120) minutes for both parts; Karl H. Delhees and Raymond B. Cattell; Institute for Personality and Ability Testing. *

a) PART 1 [THE CLINICAL 16PF]. Shortened version of the *Sixteen Personality Factor Questionnaire;* the regular version of the 16PF may be substituted; 16 primary factor scores: reserved vs. outgoing (A), less intelligent vs. more intelligent (B), affected by feelings vs. emotionally stable (C), humble vs. assertive (E), sober vs. happy-go-lucky (F), expedient vs. conscientious (G), shy vs. venturesome (H), toughminded vs. tender-minded (I), trusting vs. suspicious (L), practical vs. imaginative (M), forthright vs. shrewd (N), self-assured vs. apprehensive (O), conservative vs. experimenting (Q_1), group-dependent vs. self-sufficient (Q_2), undisciplined self-conflict vs. controlled (Q_3), relaxed vs. tense (Q_4), plus 2 second-order factor scores: introversion vs. extraversion (I), low anxiety vs. high anxiety (II), tenderminded emotionality vs. tough poise (III), subduedness vs. independence (IV), broad superego vs. lack of self-sentiment (VIII); (45) minutes.

b) PART 2 [THE PATHOLOGY SUPPLEMENT]. 12 primary factor scores: low hypochondriasis vs. high hypochondriasis (D_1), zestfulness vs. suicidal disgust (D_2), low brooding discontent vs. high brooding discontent (D_3), low anxious depression vs. high anxious depression

(D_4), high energy euphoria vs. low energy depression (D_5), low guilt vs. high guilt (D_6), low bored depression vs. high bored depression (D_7), low paranoia vs. high paranoia (Pa), low psychopathic deviation vs. high psychopathic deviation (Pp), low schizophrenia vs. high schizophrenia (Sc), low psychasthenia vs. high psychasthenia (As), low general psychosis vs. high general psychosis (Ps), plus 4 second-order factor scores: general frustration depression (IX), restless depression (X), suicidal depression (XI), general maladjustment depression (XII); (60) minutes.

REFERENCE

1. CATTELL, RAYMOND B. "The Diagnosis of Schizophrenia by Questionnaires and Objective Personality Tests," pp. 104–24. In *Schizophrenia: Current Concepts and Research.* Edited by D. V. Siva Sankar. Hicksville, N.Y.: PJD Publications Ltd., 1969. Pp. vi, 944. *

[55]

★Clyde Mood Scale. Normals and schizophrenics; 1963; CMS; to measure changes produced by drugs by self ratings or ratings by others; 6 scores: friendly, aggressive, clear thinking, sleepy, unhappy, dizzy; 1 form; 2 formats: deck of 52 IBM cards, printed check list (1 page); manual (15 pages); [5–15] minutes; Dean J. Clyde; Biometrics Laboratory, University of Miami. * (*Out of print.*)

REFERENCES

1–12. See P:41.
13. ROESSLER, ROBERT; BURCH, NEIL R.; AND CHILDERS, HAROLD E. "Personality and Arousal Correlates of Specific Galvanic Skin Responses." *Psychophysiol* 3:115–30 O '66. * (*PA* 41:1255)
14. WINEMAN, EUGENIA WOLSK. *Some Psychophysiological Correlates of the Human Menstrual Cycle.* Doctor's thesis, University of California (Los Angeles, Calif.), 1967. (*DA* 28: 3084B)
15. DiTULLIO, WILLIAM M. *Mood Discrepancies in College Students as Indicated on the Clyde Mood Scale.* Master's thesis, Springfield College (Springfield, Mass.), 1968.
16. MAYFIELD, DEMMIE G. "Psychopharmacology of Alcohol: 1, Affective Change With Intoxication, Drinking Behavior and Affective State." *J Nerv & Mental Dis* 146:314–21 Ap '68. * (*PA* 42:14099)
17. MAYFIELD, DEMMIE G. "Psychopharmacology of Alcohol: 2, Affective Tolerance in Alcohol Intoxication." *J Nerv & Mental Dis* 146:322–7 Ap '68. * (*PA* 42:14100)
18. MORDKOFF, ARNOLD M., AND RAND, MELVIN A. "Personality and Adaptation to Coronary Artery Disease." *J Consult & Clin Psychol* 32:648–53 D '68. * (*PA* 43:4378)
19. BARRATT, ERNEST S., AND WHITE, ROBERT. "Impulsiveness and Anxiety Related to Medical Students' Performance and Attitudes." *J Med Ed* 44(7):604–7 Jl '69. * (*PA* 45:4877)
20. FISHER, MAURICE D.; HADDOX, VICTOR G.; AND JACOBSON, MILTON D. "Multitrait-Multimethod Analysis of the Validity of the Clyde Mood Scale." Abstract. *Proc 77th Ann Conv Am Psychol Assn* 4(1):129–30 '69. * (*PA* 43:17515)
21. KELLY, DESMOND; BROWN, CLINTON; AND SHAFFER, JOHN W. "A Controlled Physiological, Clinical and Psychological Evaluation of Chlordiazepoxide." *Brit J Psychiatry* 115(529):1387–92 D '69. * (*PA* 44:14811)
22. TRICE, HARRISON M.; ROMAN, PAUL M.; AND BELASCO, JAMES A. "Selection for Treatment: A Predictive Evaluation of an Alcoholism Treatment Regimen." *Int J Addic* 4(3):303–17 S '69. *
23. WHYBROW, P. C.; PRANGE, A. J., JR.; AND TREADWAY, C. R. "Mental Changes Accompanying Thyroid Gland Dysfunction: A Reappraisal Using Objective Psychological Measurement." *Arch Gen Psychiatry* 20(1):48–63 Ja '69. * (*PA* 43:11631)
24. MEYER, ROGER E.; DiMASCIO, ALBERTO; AND STIFLER, LAWRENCE. "Personality Differences in the Response to Stimulant Drugs Administered During a Sleep-Deprived State." *J Nerv & Mental Dis* 150(2):91–101 F '70. * (*PA* 44:12032)
25. SIMOPOULOS, A. M.; PINTO, ALCIDES; BABIKOW, PAUL W.; KURLAND, A.; AND SAVAGE, CHARLES. "Psychotomimetic Properties and Therapeutic Potentials of Dexoxadrol on Convalescing Alcoholics." *Dis Nerv System* 31(3):203–7 Mr '70. * (*PA* 44:12790)

DAVID T. LYKKEN, *Professor of Psychiatry and Psychology, University of Minnesota, Minneapolis, Minnesota.*

This sophisticated adjective checklist consists of 48 adjectives (such as efficient, impulsive, downhearted) which are to be rated on a four-point scale as to how well they describe the individual in question. Ratings may be done by doctors, nurses, relatives, or by the patient himself. Using data from 500 subjects, both patients and normals, each of whom rated both himself and some other person, groups of items were intercorrelated and were rotated to a varimax simple structure.

As presently used, the scale is computer scored by the publisher to provide six factor scores, labeled Friendly, Aggressive, Clear-thinking, Sleepy, Unhappy, and Dizzy. Hand-scoring is difficult because of the complex weighting system employed. Intraclass correlations between pairs of raters, as reported in the manual, range from .32 to .91 for the individual scale scores.

The CMS was originally designed for use as a dependent variable in controlled studies of psychoactive drugs and seems to have been useful in this application. No claim is made that the six factors represent basic dimensions of personality; rather they appear to be a convenient means of quantifying the results of adjective ratings, as compared, for instance, to merely listing the high-rated adjectives.

It is not clear that the complex scoring system adds significantly to the utility of the scale; research with other instruments has tended to show that validities obtained with item weights of 1 or 0 are seldom improved upon by more elaborate methods. There seems to be little information on the relative merits of self- versus other-ratings with this scale, nor do we yet know how it compares with other factored instruments for symptom or behavior ratings of patients.

The adjective checklist format is appealing mainly because of quickness and ease of administration. One suspects that this format is especially susceptible to the effects of test-taking attitudes and loaded on the ubiquitous Neuroticism factor. Because of the purpose for which it was designed, the *Clyde Mood Scale* factors, as well as the items themselves, seem most appropriate for use in drug studies. The investigator who wishes to employ an adjective checklist for other purposes would do well to consult the more general *Adjective Check List* formulated by Harrison Gough.

[56]

*College and University Environment Scales, Second Edition. College; 1962–69; CUES; an adaptation of the *College Characteristics Index;* students' conceptions of "the prevailing atmosphere or climate of the campus"; 7 scores: practicality, community, awareness, propriety, scholarship, campus morale, quality of teaching and faculty-student relationships; Form X-2 ('69, 7 pages); directions for administration ['69, 4 pages]; technical manual, second edition ('69, 55 pages); prospectus ('69, 8 pages); separate answer sheets (SCRIBE) must be used; 35¢ per test; 5¢ per answer sheet; $2.50 per technical manual; $3 per specimen set; postage extra; scoring and reporting service, 80¢ and over per answer sheet ($50 minimum); reporting service includes a 16 page printout with number and percentage responding in the keyed direction to each of the 160 items, 10 local option questions, and 4 information questions along with scores on the 5 basic scales and 2 subscales for 4 mutually exclusive subgroups and the total group; no normative data on printouts; reports are mailed approximately 4 weeks after receipt of answer sheets; (30) minutes; C. Robert Pace; Educational Testing Service. *

REFERENCES

1–40. See P:42, also includes a cumulative name index to the first 40 references for this test.
41. CENTRA, JOHN A. *Student Perceptions of Total University and Major Field Environments.* Doctor's thesis, Michigan State University (East Lansing, Mich.), 1965. (*DA* 27:664A)
42. DULING, JOHN ANDERSON. *College Environment as Perceived by Selected Student Subgroups.* Doctor's research study No. 1, Colorado State College (Greeley, Colo.), 1966. (*DA* 27:2006A)
43. GRIFFITHS, ANITA NETHKEN. *The Institutional Climate at Selected Universities and Junior Colleges in Florida.* Doctor's thesis, University of Florida (Gainesville, Fla.), 1966. (*DA* 27:3223A)
44. HAGSTROM, DAVID ALAN. *College Image and Organizational Character: Differentiated Perceptions of Various Groups in a Junior College.* Doctor's thesis, University of Illinois (Urbana, Ill.), 1966. (*DA* 27:2026A)
45. HENRY, JOAN LOUISE. *Student Characteristics and Perceptions of Indiana University.* Doctor's thesis, Indiana University (Bloomington, Ind.), 1966. (*DA* 27:1544A)
46. HOPPER, GORDON CLYDE. *Faculty, Freshman, and Upperclass Perceptions of the Environment at Northern Illinois University, DeKalb, 1965–66.* Doctor's thesis, Northern Illinois University (DeKalb, Ill.), 1966. (*DA* 27:2359A)
47. MEANS, HESTER RICE. *An Analysis of the First Freshman Class of the DeKalb Junior College.* Doctor's thesis, University of Georgia (Athens, Ga.), 1966. (*DA* 27:1552A)
48. MINISTER, EDWARD BOYD. *A Correlation Analysis of a Measure of Institutional Subgroups and a Measure of Attitude Toward Ethnic Groups.* Doctor's thesis, Columbia University (New York, N.Y.), 1966. (*DA* 28:3077A)
49. RUCH, CHARLES PIERCE. *Factors Associated With the Stability of College Choice.* Doctor's thesis, Northwestern University (Evanston, Ill.), 1966. (*DA* 27:2075A)
50. SHEMKY, ROBERT WILLIAM. *A Study of the Environment at Saint Joseph's College as Perceived by Administration, Faculty, and Students and as Anticipated by Entering Freshmen.* Doctor's thesis, Indiana University (Bloomington, Ind.), 1966. (*DA* 27:2016A)
51. STALLINGS, WILLIAM MARION. *A Study of Non-Intellective Factors in the Prediction of Academic Success for Master's Degree Level Students in the School of Education, Indiana University.* Doctor's thesis, Indiana University (Bloomington, Ind.), 1966. (*DA* 27:3324A)
52. CARBONE, GILBERT JOSEPH. *Characteristics of Entering Transfer Students' Perceptions of a Collegiate Institutional Environment.* Doctor's thesis, University of Washington (Seattle, Wash.), 1967. (*DA* 28:3406A)
53. DORWORTH, THOMAS R. "The Relationship Between the College and University Environment Scales (CUES) and Social Class." *Proc W Va Acad Sci* 39:71–4 '67. *
54. FERGUSON, DON WAYNE. *A Study of the Administration of Student Activities in Selected California Public Junior Colleges.* Doctor's thesis, University of California (Los Angeles, Calif.), 1967. (*DA* 28:1650A)
55. KAELKE, MICHAEL EDWIN. *A Study of the Influence of Selected Orientation Programs on the Environmental Perceptions of Community College Transfer Students Attending Michigan State University.* Doctor's thesis, Michigan State University (East Lansing, Mich.), 1967. (*DA* 28:3974A)
56. PAULUS, GEORGE STEPHEN. *A Multivariate Analysis Study of Student Activist Leaders, Student Government Lead-*

ers, and Non-Activists. Doctor's thesis, Michigan State University (East Lansing, Mich.), 1967. *(DA* 28:1902A)

57. SCHUCHMAN, BETTY JANE ENGLEMAN. *Real and Ideal College Environments Perceived by Freshmen.* Doctor's thesis, Indiana University (Bloomington, Ind.), 1967. *(DA* 28:2046A)

58. BROOKS, BONNIE SUE. *A Longitudinal Study of Perceptual Change Among Students.* Doctor's thesis, Indiana University (Bloomington, Ind.), 1968. *(DA* 29:3410A)

59. BUTLER, ROBERT DALE. *An Investigation of the Perceived Environment Between and Among the Existing Subcultures on a University Campus.* Doctor's thesis, East Texas State University (Commerce, Tex.), 1968. *(DA* 29:3412A)

60. DE MARS, MARY RITA. *How Students See Their Colleges: A Descriptive Analysis of Selected Institutional Climates Through Student Perceptions.* Doctor's thesis, University of Notre Dame (Notre Dame, Ind.), 1968. *(DA* 29:3828A)

61. FOXLEY, CECELIA H. *An Experimental Study and Evaluation of the 1967 University of Utah Freshman Orientation Program.* Doctor's thesis, University of Utah (Salt Lake City, Utah), 1968. *(DA* 29:2562A)

62. LANNON, JOHN ROBERT. *Personality Characteristics and Environmental Perceptions of Political and Social Activists and Nonactivists at a Large Urban Liberal Arts College.* Doctor's thesis, New York University (New York, N.Y.), 1968. *(DAI* 30:587A)

63. LEWIS, ALBA MYERS. *Comparisons of Student-Faculty Perceptions of Real and Ideal Environments at Five Negro Colleges, 1967–68.* Doctor's thesis, University of North Carolina (Chapel Hill, N.C.), 1968. *(DAI* 30:522A)

64. MASTERSON, RUSSELL WILLIAM. *An Elapsed Time Study of Changes in Perception of a College Environment as Measured by the "College and University Environmental Scales" at a Small, Liberal Arts, Church-Affiliated College.* Doctor's thesis, Boston College (Chestnut Hill, Mass.), 1968. *(DA* 29:4289A)

65. PATE, ROBERT HEWITT, JR. *A Study of Entering University Students: Environment Expected and Later Perceived.* Doctor's thesis, University of North Carolina (Chapel Hill, N.C.), 1968. *(DA* 29:4292A)

66. REEVES, TEDDY GLEN. *The Relationship Between Accuracy of Perception of Environment and Achievement Attrition, Satisfaction With the Environment, and Sex of First-Semester Freshmen.* Doctor's thesis, East Texas State University (Commerce, Tex.), 1968. *(DA* 29:3425A)

67. ROGERS, MARY ELEANOR PIPER. *Perception of the College Environment as a Factor in Attitude Change During the Freshman Year.* Doctor's thesis, Indiana University (Bloomington, Ind.), 1968. *(DA* 29:3472A)

68. SASAJIMA, MASU; DAVIS, JUNIUS A.; AND PETERSON, RICHARD E. "Organized Student Protest and Institutional Climate." *Am Ed Res J* 5:291–304 My '68. *

69. SIDLES, CRAIG WILLIAM. *The Relationship of Changes in Freshman Perceptions of Campus Environments to College Achievements and Attrition.* Doctor's thesis, University of Iowa (Iowa City, Iowa), 1968. *(DA* 29:3844A)

70. SPEERSTRA, BARBARA TUTTLE. *A CUES Environmental Study at a Small, Catholic, Liberal Arts College for Women.* Doctor's thesis, Indiana University (Bloomington, Ind.), 1968. *(DA* 29:4205A)

71. STILLION, GLENN WAYNE. *Values, Perceptions, and Characteristics of Student Leaders Compared With the General Student Population at Florida State University.* Doctor's thesis, Florida State University (Tallahassee, Fla.), 1968. *(DA* 29:1429A)

72. WIESE, HUGO. *The Relationship Between the Institutional Perceptions of Community College Freshmen and the Importance Ascribed to Certain Collegiate Experiences.* Doctor's thesis, University of Washington (Seattle, Wash.), 1968. *(DAI* 30:559A)

73. ADAMS, RAMONA SHEPHERD. *Evaluation of a Clustering Experience of College Freshmen.* Doctor's thesis, University of Utah (Salt Lake City, Utah), 1969. *(DAI* 30:4168A)

74. BROWN, WARREN SHELBURNE. *A Study of Campus Environment: A Comparative Study of the Perception of the Campus Environment by the Several Groups Affecting a Religiously Oriented Liberal Arts College.* Doctor's thesis, University of Southern California (Los Angeles, Calif.) 1969. *(DAI* 30:2741A)

75. BURNS, JOHN LUTHER. *The Relationship of Attitudinal Similarity to Collegiate Satisfaction and Degree of Role Orientation Identification.* Doctor's thesis, University of Texas (Austin, Tex.), 1969. *(DAI* 30:2844A)

76. CHICKERING, ARTHUR W. *Education and Identity,* pp. 165–84, 309–10, passim. San Francisco, Calif.: Jossey-Bass Inc., Publishers, 1969. Pp. xv, 367. *

77. CHICKERING, ARTHUR W.; McDOWELL, JAMES; AND CAMPAGNA, DENNIS. "Institutional Differences and Student Development." *J Ed Psychol* 60(4):315–26 Ag '69. * *(PA* 43:16308)

78. DANIELS, JACK L. "Differential Perceptions of College Environment: Faculty and Students." *South J Ed Res* 3(4): 268–72 O '69. *

79. DULING, JOHN A. "Differences in Perception of Environmental Press by Selected Student Subgroups." *J Nat Assn Women Deans & Counselors* 32(3):130–2 sp '69. *

80. FARREN, PHILLIP JOSEPH, JR. *Comparisons of Environ-*

mental Perceptions of Students, Faculty, and Administrators at a Military Oriented Junior College. Doctor's thesis, Colorado State College (Greeley, Colo.), 1969. *(DAI* 30:4140A)

81. FELDMAN, KENNETH A., AND NEWCOMB, THEODORE M. *The Impact of Colleges on Students: Vol. 1, An Analysis of Four Decades of Research,* pp. 355–8, passim. San Francisco, Calif.: Jossey-Bass Inc., Publishers, 1969. Pp. xiii, 474. *

82. FOXLEY, CECELIA H. "Orientation or Dis-Orientation?" *Personnel & Guid J* 48(3):218–21 N '69. *

83. GEHLHAUSEN, PAUL EDWARD. *An Exploration of Selected Factors Associated With Success of Beginning Engineering Students at Tri-State College.* Doctor's thesis, Purdue University (Lafayette, Ind.), 1969. *(DAI* 30:3724A)

84. GRANDE, PETER P., AND LOVELESS, EUGENE J. "Variability in the Measurement of Campus Climate." *Col & Univ* 44(3):244–9 sp '69. *

85. HANNAH, WILLIAM. *Dropout-Stayin Personality Differentials and College Environments.* Doctor's thesis, University of Southern California (Los Angeles, Calif.), 1969. *(DAI* 31:584A)

86. HEDEGARD, JAMES M., AND BROWN, DONALD R. "Encounters of Some Negro and White Freshmen With a Public Multiversity." *J Social Issues* 25(3):131–44 su '69. *

87. HERSEMANN, DARYLL DWAYNE. *A College Environment as Perceived by Campus Subcultures and the Student Personnel Staff.* Doctor's thesis, Northwestern University (Evanston, Ill.), 1969. *(DAI* 30:5237A)

88. HESKETT, SHARON L., AND WALSH, W. BRUCE. "Differential Perceptions of College Environment." *J Col Stud Personnel* 10(3):182–4 My '69. *

89. KENNEDY, MARY FRANCESCA. *Relationships Between College Policy Changes and Changes in Student Characteristics and Their Implications for Administrators.* Doctor's thesis, Columbia University (New York, N.Y.), 1969. *(DAI* 30:3686A)

90. KIDD, KEVIN A. J. *A Study of Student Perceptions and Student Attitudes in a Small Church-Affiliated Liberal Arts College and a Small Non-Denominational Liberal Arts College.* Doctor's thesis, Boston College (Chestnut Hill, Mass.), 1969. *(DAI* 31:228A)

91. LEMBKE, ROBERT THOMAS. *A Comparison of Perception of a Two-Year College Environment Between Native Students and Students Who Had Previously Attended Four-Year Institutions.* Doctor's thesis, University of South Dakota (Vermillion, S.D.), 1969. *(DAI* 30:3731A)

92. LINDEMUTH, MARVIN HERALD. *An Analysis of the Leader Behavior of Academic Deans as Related to the Campus Climate in Selected Colleges.* Doctor's thesis, University of Michigan (Ann Arbor, Mich.), 1969. *(DAI* 30:2765A)

93. McGAVIN, ROBERT JAMES. *An Analysis of Relationships Between High School Students' Perception of the University of Washington's College Environment and Academic Achievement.* Doctor's thesis, University of Washington (Seattle, Wash.). 1969. *(DAI* 30:1835A)

94. MAGRAB, PHYLLIS R. *Expectation-Press Congruence as a Psychological Variable in the Prediction of College Adaptation.* Doctor's thesis, University of Maryland (College Park, Md.), 1969. *(DAI* 30:5290A)

95. MARSHALL, JOHN FRANCIS, JR. *Manifestations of Dissonance in "Press" Expectations Versus "Press" Perceptions of College Freshmen.* Doctor's thesis, Pennsylvania State University (University Park, Pa.), 1969. *(DAI* 30:2806A)

96. MURLEY, ROBERT VINCENT. *An Analysis of the Relationship Between the Perception of the Illinois State University Campus Environment and Student Activity Patterns.* Doctor's thesis, Indiana University (Bloomington, Ind.), 1969. *(DAI* 30:989A)

97. OLSON, MARIAN LAHMAN. *A Comparison of Two Measures of College Environment.* Doctor's thesis, University of Tulsa (Tulsa, Okla.), 1969. *(DAI* 30:2351A)

98. PESQUEIRA, RICHARD ERNEST. *Comparisons of Perceptions of the College Environment Among Students, Faculty, Administration and Staff at the University of California, Riverside.* Doctor's thesis, University of California (Los Angeles, Calif., 1969. *(DAI* 30:4782A)

99. PITTS, ROBERT DUANE. *A Comparative Environmental Study of Four Denominational Colleges.* Doctor's thesis, Indiana University (Bloomington, Ind.), 1969. *(DAI* 30:4740A)

100. REINER, JOHN R., AND ROBINSON, DONALD W. "An Approach to Goal-Statement Evaluation." *N Central Assn Q* 44(2):241–5 f '69. *

101. REINER, JOHN ROBERT. *An Empirical Approach to the Evaluation of College Goal Statements Using Responses of Various Institutional Participant Groups on Locally-Derived Sub-Scales Based on College and University Environment Scales Items.* Doctor's thesis, Southern Illinois University (Carbondale, Ill.), 1969. *(DAI* 30:3254A)

102. RHODES, HENRY KENNETH. *A Study of Student Evaluation of Student Personnel Services and Campus Environment in Selected Junior Colleges.* Doctor's thesis, Texas Technological University (Lubbock, Tex.), 1969. *(DAI* 31:161A)

103. ROBINSON, LORA, AND SELIGMAN, RICHARD. "A Scale for Measuring Campus Morale." *J Ed Meas* 6(2):109–10 su '69. * *(PA* 44:13298)

104. ROMINE, BENJAMIN HOUSTON, JR. *The Effects of the Interaction Between a Personality Characteristic and an En-*

vironmental Characteristic on the Achievement of Female College Freshmen When Ability Is Controlled. Doctor's thesis, Duke University (Durham, N.C.), 1969. (*DAI* 30:5301A)

105. SHEARER, ROBERT ARTHUR. *Perceptions of the Environment at Florence State University as Perceived by Upperclass and Beginning Students.* Doctor's thesis, East Texas State University (Commerce, Tex.), 1969. (*DAI* 30:5247A)

106. SKELTON, DAVID RAY. *A Study of Relationships of Student and Institutional Attributes to Educational Objectives of Entering Freshmen.* Doctor's thesis, Indiana University (Bloomington, Ind.), 1969. (*DAI* 31:180A)

107. TAYLOR, DAVID STANTON. *A Study of Institutional Climate at Western Illinois University as Perceived by Selected Junior Class Students.* Doctor's thesis, Michigan State University (East Lansing, Mich.), 1969. (*DAI* 31:1044A)

108. TRIMBLE, MAXINE GENEVIEVE. *Measurement of Perceived Campus Press on Three Student Groups at the Kansas State Teachers College of Emporia.* Doctor's thesis, University of Arkansas (Fayetteville, Ark.), 1969. (*DAI* 30:505A)

109. VANDERHOOF, THOMAS JAY. *The Effects of Group Counseling on Low Achieving Students' Perception of Their College Environment.* Doctor's thesis, Colorado State College (Greeley, Colo.), 1969. (*DAI* 30:4237A)

110. VANDER WILT, ROBERT BOND. *Differences in Perception Among Students and Residence Hall Employees at Mankato State College.* Doctor's thesis, Iowa State University (Ames, Iowa), 1969. (*DAI* 30:2315A)

111. WALSH, W. BRUCE, AND McKINNON, RICHARD D. "Impact of Experimental Program on Student Environmental Perceptions." *J Col Stud Personnel* 10(4):310-6 S '69. *

112. CENTRA, JOHN A., AND LINN, ROBERT L. "On Interpreting Students' Perceptions of Their College Environments." *Meas & Eval Guid* 3(2):102-9 su '70. * (*PA* 45:1275)

113. CENTRA, JOHN A.; HARTNETT, RODNEY T.; AND PETERSON, RICHARD E. "Faculty Views of Institutional Functioning: A New Measure of College Environments." *Ed & Psychol Meas* 30(2):405-16 su '70. * (*PA* 45:2914)

114. DUGMORE, W. OWEN, AND GRANT, CLAUDE W. "Experiment in Cluster Registration of College Freshmen: Effects Upon Achievement, Anxiety and Perception of the College Environment." *J Ed Res* 63(5):216-8 Ja '70. * (*PA* 46:5422)

115. GARES, CHARLES WAYNE. *Comparisons of Existing and Idealized Perceptions of Afro-American, Spanish-American, Indian, and Caucasian Students Attending Eastern New Mexico University.* Doctor's thesis, University of Northern Colorado (Greeley, Colo.), 1970. (*DAI* 31:2703A)

116. GRANDE, PETER P. "How Objective Are Measures of Campus Climate," pp. 41–7. In *The Challenge and Response of Institutional Research.* Proceedings of the Ninth Annual Forum on Institutional Research. Athens, Ga.: Association for Institutional Research (c/o Cameron Fincher, University of Georgia), 1970. Pp. vii, 182. *

117. HANSEN, JOSEPH WILLIAM. *A Community College: Its Environmental Image as Perceived by Students, Faculty, and Administration.* Doctor's thesis, United States International University (San Diego, Calif.), 1970. (*DAI* 31:2005A)

118. HENDRICKS, JOHN T. *A Study of Administrative, Faculty, and Student Perceptions of the Campus Environment at the University of Tennessee.* Doctor's thesis, University of Tennessee (Knoxville, Tenn.), 1970. (*DAI* 31:3213A)

119. HOLLOWAY, ERNEST LEON. *Environmental Perceptions of Unsuccessful Students on Selected College Campuses.* Doctor's thesis, University of Oklahoma (Norman, Okla.), 1970. (*DAI* 31:2705A)

120. LEE, JAMES L., AND DORAN, WILLIAM J. "Vocational Persistence Among Seminarians." *Nat Cath Guid Conf J* 15(1):55-62 f '70. *

121. MAAS, McCLEDA GURLEY. *Differential Perceptions of Junior College Environment: Students, Staff, and Community.* Doctor's thesis, University of Nebraska (Lincoln, Neb.), 1970. (*DAI* 31:1546A)

122. McCLUSKEY, JIMMY DOW. *An Environmental Study of Arkansas State University as Perceived by Students and Faculty.* Doctor's thesis, University of Mississippi (University, Miss.), 1970. (*DAI* 31:2688A)

123. MOON, BRYDEN EARL. *Using College and University Environment Scales to Explore the Relationship of Selected Demographic Factors to Arkansas High School Seniors' Perceptions of the University of Arkansas.* Doctor's thesis, University of Arkansas (Fayetteville, Ark.), 1970. (*DAI* 31:1017A)

124. PACE, THERON. "Roommate Dissatisfaction in Residence Halls." *J Col Stud Personnel* 11(2):144-7 Mr '70. *

125. PATE, ROBERT H., JR. "Student Expectations and Later Expectations of a University Enrollment." *J Col Stud Personnel* 11(6):458-62 N '70. * (*PA* 45:8902)

126. PETERSON, ARLIN VERDAYNE. *A Comparison of Community College Transfer Students and Native University Students on Nonacademic Factors.* Doctor's thesis, Washington State University (Pullman, Wash.), 1970. (*DAI* 31:2709A)

127. POWELL, JOANN. *An Analysis of Factors Relating to Decisions to Transfer From Northwestern University by Freshman Women.* Doctor's thesis, Northwestern University (Evanston, Ill.), 1970. (*DAI* 31:3277A)

128. QUAY, ALAN TOWNSEND. *CUES: Before and After One Semester at Montgomery County Community College.* Doctor's thesis, University of Pennsylvania (Philadelphia, Pa.), 1970. (*DAI* 31:2710A)

129. REINER, JOHN R. "Students' Academic Ability and Perceptions of College Environment." *J Exp Ed* 38(3):69-71 sp '70. *

130. REINER, JOHN R., AND ROBINSON, DONALD W. "Perceptions of College Environment and Contiguity With College Environment." *J Higher Ed* 41(2):130-9 F '70. *

131. RICHARDS, JAMES M., JR.; SELIGMAN, RICHARD; AND JONES, PAUL K. "Faculty and Curriculum as Measures of College Environment." *J Ed Psychol* 61(4):324-32 Ag '70. * (*PA* 44:21503)

132. RISCH, THOMAS J. "Expectations for the College Environment." *J Col Stud Personnel* 11(6):463-73 N '70. * (*PA* 45:8904)

133. ROMINE, BEN H.; DAVIS, JUNIUS A.; AND GEHMAN, W. SCOTT. "The Interaction of Learning, Personality Traits, Ability, and Environment: A Preliminary Study." *Ed & Psychol Meas* 30(2):337-47 su '70. * (*PA* 45:5059)

134. ROWE, FREDERICK B. "How Ten Years of Change Affected One College Environment." *Col Board R* 76:28-9 su '70. *

135. SALZMAN, MURRAY. *Perceptions of the College Environment and Need Dispositions as Related to Expressed Satisfaction.* Doctor's thesis, University of Notre Dame (Notre Dame, Ind.), 1970. (*DAI* 31:1023A)

136. SPRADLING, JAMES W. *An Analysis of Personality and Environmental Press in Two Church Related Colleges and a State University.* Doctor's thesis, University of South Dakota (Vermillion, S.D.), 1970. (*DAI* 31:3356A)

137. STANFIEL, JAMES D., AND WATTS, FREDERICK P. "Freshman Expectations and Perceptions of the Howard University Environment." *J Negro Ed* 39(2):132-8 sp '70. *

138. STOVER, RAYMOND MUGGE. *An Exploration of Associations Among Selected Characteristics of Residence Halls and Residents' Perceptions of Their Environments.* Doctor's thesis, Columbia University (New York, N.Y.), 1970. (*DAI* 31:3242A)

139. WILSON, RONALD S., AND DOLLAR, ROBERT J. "Student, Teacher, and Administrator Perceptions of the Junior College Environment." *J Col Stud Personnel* 11(3):213-6 My '70. * (*PA* 45:4909)

PAUL L. DRESSEL, *Assistant Provost and Director, Institutional Research, Michigan State University, East Lansing, Michigan.*

The purpose of CUES is to help institutions define the cultural, social, and intellectual climate of the campus. The instrument is composed of 160 items (of which 60, at this time, are experimental and not included in the scales), requiring approximately 30 minutes for the student to complete. It may be administered either to groups or to individuals. The items are grouped into seven scales. The original five scales are: (*a*) Practicality (20 items). Environment emphasizes "enterprise, organization, material benefits, and social activities." (*b*) Community (20 items). Environment "friendly, cohesive, group-oriented." (*c*) Awareness (20 items). Environment emphasizes concern about "personal, poetic, and political" meanings. "Encouragement of questioning and dissent....tolerance of nonconformity and personal expressiveness." (*d*) Propriety (20 items). An environment that is polite, considerate, and decorous. (*e*) Scholarship (20 items). Environment emphasizes academic achievement and scholarship.

Two additional scales have been included in this edition: (*a*) Campus morale (22 items). Environment emphasizes "acceptance of social norms, group cohesiveness....commitment to in-

tellectual pursuits and freedom of expression."
(*b*) Quality of teaching and faculty-student
relationships (11 items). Environment is one
"in which professors are perceived to be scholarly, to set high standards, to be clear, adaptive,
and flexible."

The brief descriptions here provided are
inadequate summaries of the more elaborate
descriptions provided in the technical manual.
Ultimately, as in any instrument of this kind,
the definition of scales is best understood by
perusal of the items included in each scale.
Despite the very extensive statistical work
involving factor analysis and item discrimination data in defining the scales, there is some
overlapping and the critical user may find that
too-ready acceptance of the one-word characterization of the scales may be misleading.
Some indication of this problem is provided by
data given in the technical manual, where the
following correlations are reported: Awareness
with Practicality, $-.34$; Scholarship with Practicality, $-.50$; Awareness with Scholarship, .56.

This instrument provides only group scores.
Individual scores are not appropriate, and there
is no provision for computing them. Group
scores are obtained by (*a*) adding the number
of items answered by 66 percent or more of the
students in the keyed direction; (*b*) subtracting
the number of items answered by 33 percent or
fewer of the students in the keyed direction;
(*c*) adding 20 points to eliminate any possibility
of negative scores. Thus the instrument is a
kind of polling device which summarizes students' opinion with regard to the existence or
nonexistence of certain characteristics on the
campus. This poses two closely interrelated
issues. One is the sampling of the student body,
and the other is the existence of evidence that a
reasonable consensus exists. The manual recommends that freshmen not be given the instrument unless there is a definite intent to find out
something about freshmen expectations of environment. The reported experience is that
freshmen expectations are unrealistically high.
The manual recommends that the sample be
made up of students in the latter part of their
sophomore year and/or juniors and seniors.
Differences among the scores obtained from
these groups are reported as negligible. "In 35
such comparisons, 94 percent differed by 3
points or less, 88 percent of these by 2 points or
less." It is recommended that a minimum of 50
students be used for a sample, and a recom-

mended schedule from 50 to 350 is provided for
institutions of varying sizes of enrollment. This
involves a percentage sampling ranging downward from 5 per cent to 2 percent or less for
large institutions. There has been careful attention to developing norms based upon a national
reference group which is, in turn, divided into
eight subgroups. Data are available in a form
which permits an institution to compare itself
with what it deems to be an appropriate subgroup.

The question of reliability for an instrument
of this kind is distinctly different from that for
a test used for individual scoring. The problem
is to estimate the stability of the consensus
score for a single institution. The stability is a
function of the size of the sample and also of
the number of items falling close to the borderline of being counted or not counted in the
score. The manual reports that test-retest comparisons made from comparable samples of reporters over a one- or two-year period or comparisons of scores from different groups judged
to be qualified reporters have been summarized
for 25 different colleges and universities. The
finding is that of different groups within a
single institution 80 percent differed by 3 points
or less and 90 percent differed by 4 points or
less.

The problem of validity is rather more complicated even than that of reliability. The
manual provides an extensive set of tables showing intercorrelations between CUES scale
scores, college aptitude measured by mean SAT
scores of entering freshmen, and a wide variety
of other factors. Although these various relationships are reasonably congruent with expectations, one may certainly wonder just what
this fact has to say about the validity of the
instrument. The fact that student characteristics
and campus characteristics, attitudes and behavior of students, the atmosphere of the campus, and the dimensions of college environment
defined by various studies are generally similar
to those identified by CUES leaves unsettled
the question of just what the college environment is and what CUES is measuring. In fact,
most of the intercorrelations with the other
variables reported are not much higher than the
intercorrelations earlier reported among some
of the CUES scales themselves.

Kenneth A. Feldman [1] has commented exten-

1 FELDMAN, KENNETH A. "Research Strategies in Studying
College Impact." *ACT Res Rep* 34:1–23 My '70.

sively on these instruments. He points out the shortcomings of eliciting student perceptions of overall characteristics rather than seeking the student's personal feelings and observations. Fact and fiction are not separable. Feldman suggests further that widely shared views are not necessarily social norms which exert a press on behavior. The concept of environment is an ambiguous and elusive one, and there are many possible subenvironments. Even in a small college, residents in one hall may differ from those in others and majors in some fields may differ from those in others.

Two major approaches have been developed for the assessment of college environment. The CUES asks students to indicate whether certain statements characterize the environment as they perceive it. The Environmental Assessment Technique [2] avoids this perception approach with all of its subjectivity and uses eight objectively determined indices, including size and intellectual level of student body and percentage of student body awarded degrees in certain major areas.

There are indications in some studies that students' perceptions of their environment may be distorted by their own needs. This may confuse the interpretation of results, for personal views and environmental characteristics may be interdependent. Astin and Holland [2] suggest that "the attributes of the student body reflect a major portion of what has been called the college press or environment."

Another study (*116*), by Grande, raises some doubts about CUES as a reliable measure of campus climate. He reports data supporting Berdie's conclusion that the instrument may reveal something about parts of a university but is less useful in generalizing about the whole university (*16*). In fact, Grande found such differences between two groups of general psychology students at Notre Dame that he questions the objectivity of CUES even for description of subgroups.

We are left with the impression that CUES is most useful on the relatively small, uncomplicated campus. Even then, there is some uncertainty whether the instrument elicits the common orientations which are regarded as the important ones and ignores subgroup differences or whether it also is sensitive to distinctive sub-

cultures. Another issue is raised when a college is dissatisfied with its CUES profile and wishes to change. Would it be possible to change the environment, or would it be simpler to modify admissions criteria and seek a different student body? The answer is not evident.

JAMES V. MITCHELL, JR., *Associate Dean for Graduate Studies, College of Education, The University of Rochester, Rochester, New York.*

The *College and University Environment Scales* consist of 100 items taken from the earlier *College Characteristics Index* and arranged to yield the seven scores noted above, plus 60 "experimental" items which are not scored but which will be analyzed for possible incorporation in a later revision. According to the technical manual, this second edition of CUES was undertaken to improve and provide additional supportive evidence for the items and scales, to provide more representative norms, and to provide a basis for future attempts to update and improve the instrument. Scoring procedures are based upon an "opinion poll" rationale rather than the more traditional psychometric approach emphasizing individual differences and yielding indices of central tendency, dispersion, etc. Scale scores are obtained by adding the number of items answered by 66 percent or more of students in the keyed direction, subtracting the number answered by 33 percent or fewer in the keyed direction, and adding a constant of 20 to eliminate negative scores.

All items describe possible characteristics of a college environment (e.g., "Students set high standards of achievement for themselves"), and the respondent is instructed to answer True or False for each. The "opinion poll" approach, requiring consensus by at least 66 percent of the respondents before something may be judged characteristic or not characteristic of an environment, seems *prima facie* to make good sense. Pace's point is well taken that an item endorsed by one-half of the respondents, for example, can hardly be regarded as a dominant or outstanding characteristic of that environment. One is tempted to carry the opinion poll argument one step further: often the meanings of CUES scales seem overly broad and difficult to pinpoint and interpret, despite their supposed factorial unity; concentrating on the interpretation of *individual* items revealing high consensus may well provide a richer and more use-

2 ASTIN, ALEXANDER W., AND HOLLAND, JOHN L. "The Environmental Assessment Technique: A Way to Measure College Environments." *J Ed Psychol* 52:308–16 D '61. *

ful source of information about the college environment than the scale scores themselves.

The provision of relevant norms for an instrument like CUES raises some perplexing issues. Should the reference group be based upon the proportions of existing institutions of various kinds—or upon the proportions of students enrolled in these various kinds of institutions? Since there are many small liberal arts colleges enrolling relatively few students, and a relatively few large complex universities enrolling relatively many students, the issue has some far-reaching implications for norm development. In the new CUES edition, the issue is resolved by a compromise between these two approaches involving a straightforward averaging of the numbers or proportions determined by the two approaches for a sample of 100 institutions categorized in terms of region, level of program, form of control (public or private), and type of institution (liberal arts, teachers' college, etc.). The compromise effected may not be satisfactory to everyone; a more satisfactory resolution of these norm problems requires separate sets of norms for the different categories of institutions, some indication of their comparative standings, and a set of general norms as well. That the different types of institutions represent appreciable environmental differences is attested to by data provided in the manual; the average score for the teachers' colleges on the Scholarship scale, for example, represents a percentile equivalent 76 points lower than that for selective liberal arts colleges.

The revision of CUES was generally conducted in a professionally creditable manner. Defensible statistical criteria were established for identifying the best first-edition items for retention in the new edition. Not all of these criteria could be met consistently, especially those relating to the factor analytic composition of the scales. But the match of criteria with empirical results was generally satisfactory. The procedures resulted in a winnowing down to 20 items per scale in the new edition from the 30 per scale from the first edition, which was apparently accomplished with the retention of adequate (coefficient alpha) reliability. Intercorrelations among the five scales, although reduced from the first edition, still are appreciable for some variables (Community and Propriety, .53; Awareness and Scholarship, .56). A factor analysis of these scale intercor-

relations by the reviewer revealed a clear pattern of strong interrelationships that determined two distinct factors, the first defined by Community and Propriety and the second by Scholarship, Awareness, and (lack of) Practicality. This lack of statistical independence among score categories occasions some doubt about the defensibility of five separate scores.

The scales for Campus Morale and for Quality of Teaching and Faculty-Student Relationships are new to this edition. Composed of items overlapping those in the five major scales, they are of questionable usefulness at present. The manual contains no evidence of their validity.

Estimates of reliability for an instrument like CUES pose special problems. The reliability of CUES scores as measures of institutional differences was determined by means of Cronbach's coefficient alpha. These range from .89 to .94. But Pace points out that establishing the reliability of a CUES score for a single institution necessitates a departure from conventional psychometric procedure, since the CUES consensus or opinion poll scoring rationale yields only one score instead of the distribution of scores on which conventional estimates of reliability are based. Indeed, high conventional reliability based on high interindividual score variance would signify lack of consensus in this context, while strong consensus would mean low variance among individuals and a low reliability coefficient. "The problem for the single institution is to estimate the stability of its own consensus score," and Pace provides some guidelines for this purpose. One such guideline involves the determination of the likelihood that an item endorsed by a certain percentage of respondents in a given sample might or might not attain the 66–33 percent scoring criterion for another sample, and the relevant probability figures are presented. Stability in this context depends on the size of the sample and the proportion of "borderline" items in the original sample. Another guideline consists of empirical evidence of "test-retest comparisons made from comparable samples of reporters over a one- or two-year period, or comparisons of scores from different groups judged to be qualified reporters (such as sophomores, juniors, and seniors)." For 25 institutions and a total of 125 comparisons, it is reported, 80 percent of the scale scores differed by 3 points or less.

This last type of evidence is useful, but more such evidence needs to be presented, and in a more precise and systematic manner. Until it is, the reliability of CUES for the single institution must be regarded as a moot point. Affirmations about the typicality of intra-institutional consensus must also remain open to question, since such consensus was not always in evidence for the first edition (40). It would have been helpful if the test author had presented tables showing distribution characteristics of the intra-institutional standard deviations for his sample.

The CUES technical manual presents a variety of construct validity evidence. In addition to the factor analytic evidence noted earlier, evidence is offered on the "congruence" of campus atmosphere with student characteristics, attitudes, and behavior, and with academic programs offered; and on the similarity of dimensions of college environments identified by different studies and methods to those identified by CUES. The correlations reported reveal the expected relationships between the generally global variables of CUES and the often equally global reference variables; the real significance of that shared variance, however, is a matter of lingering doubt. Yet for instruments of this type such evidence as that provided may be all that can reasonably be expected.

Space is not available for a discussion of the general validity issue of whether measures of college environment involving student perceptions are adequate representations of the actual environment and of the additional question of whether those perceptions are related to and distorted by student personality characteristics. The CUES manual contains limited evidence pertaining to both. While that evidence may be reassuring to some, it should also be noted that research on CUES has revealed that there is greater likelihood of student consensus about a small campus than a large one and that student perceptions appear to be influenced by a frame of reference determined by the state of their knowledge concerning other institutions (112). These general issues are by no means resolved and will continue to plague all instruments of the CUES type.

In the practical setting, however, CUES should prove to be a useful resource for anyone looking for a systematic way of gathering data on student perceptions of the college environment and its impact on them. Provision for the reporting of responses for 10 local option ques-

tions developed by the user should enhance the value of the instrument, as should provision for the reporting of data for as many as four subgroups in addition to the total group. A most useful feature of the reporting service is the item analysis showing the number and percent responding in the keyed direction for each item. Appropriate norm tables are provided for evaluating these percentages. Consistent with earlier remarks is the reviewer's present impression that analysis and interpretation of item responses may well prove to be of greater benefit to the local user than reliance on the seven score categories. If one is taking an opinion poll, one couldn't wish for much more than the expression of opinion on 160 separate items!

[57]

★College Student Questionnaires. College entrants, students; 1965–69; CSQ; for research use only; institutional self-study of student populations; 2 editions; for optional test, see c below; supervisor's manual ['69, 19 pages]; technical manual, revised ('68, 64 pages); research prospectus ('68, 16 pages); publisher recommends use of local norms; separate answer sheets (SCRIBE) must be used; $2.50 per technical manual; $3 per specimen set; postage extra; scoring and reporting service, $1 and over per answer sheet ($50 minimum); reporting service includes a 39 page printout with item statements (including the number and percentage checking each item alternative), group statistics (mean, standard deviation, and frequency distribution) for each scale, and response frequency and percentage to 9 local option questions for 4 mutually exclusive subgroups and total; normative data included on printout; reports are mailed approximately 4 weeks after receipt of answer sheets; Richard E. Peterson (technical manual); Educational Testing Service. *
a) PART 1. College entrants; 7 scores: motivation for grades, family social status, family independence, peer independence, liberalism, social conscience, cultural sophistication; Form 200D ('65, 22 pages); 35¢ per test; 5¢ per answer sheet; (55–65) minutes.
b) PART 2. College students end of academic year; 11 scores: family independence, peer independence, liberalism, social conscience, cultural sophistication, satisfaction with faculty, satisfaction with administration, satisfaction with major, satisfaction with students, study habits, extracurricular involvement; Form 200D ('65, 22 pages); 35¢ per test; 5¢ per answer sheet; (55–65) minutes.
c) CONTROL TEST FOR ACADEMIC APTITUDE. CTAA; group measure of academic aptitude used in tandem with CSQ; test booklet title is *Control Test AA*; Form NQA ('65, 4 pages); responses made on answer sheets for Part 1 or Part 2; 15¢ per test; 12(20) minutes.

REFERENCES

1–2. See P:44.
3. MADSON, DENNIS LEROY. *Factors Associated With Effectiveness as a Male Undergraduate Residence Hall Counselor.* Doctor's thesis, Ohio University (Athens, Ohio), 1966. (DA 27:3670A)
4. WIDMAR, GARY E. *A Comparative Study of Fraternity and Sorority Membership Aspirations of Entering Freshmen at the Florida State University.* Doctor's thesis, Florida State University (Tallahassee, Fla.), 1966. (DA 27:2364A)
5. BORS, ADAM, JR. *A Study of Certain Biographical and Attitudinal Characteristics of Entering College Freshmen and*

the Grade Point Average Achieved During the First Semester of College. Doctor's thesis, Ohio University (Athens, Ohio), 1967. (DA 28:3063A)

6. PAULUS, GEORGE STEPHEN. A Multivariate Analysis Study of Student Activist Leaders, Student Government Leaders, and Non-Activists. Doctor's thesis, Michigan State University (East Lansing, Mich.), 1967. (DA 28:1902A)

7. WALKER, JIMMY REEVES. A Study of Selected Psycho-social Correlates of College Student Subcultures. Doctor's thesis, Oklahoma State University (Stillwater, Okla.), 1967. (DA 28:4883A)

8. WORK, GERALD GEORGE. Correlates of Academic Achievement for Female Sophomore Elementary Education Majors. Doctor's thesis, Ohio University (Athens, Ohio), 1967. (DA 28:2926A)

9. CALVERT, SAMUEL G. Comparison of Two Colleges, Attended Predominately by Negro Americans, as Measured by the College Student Questionnaire. Master's thesis, Fisk University (Nashville, Tenn.), 1968.

10. HARTNETT, RODNEY T., AND PETERSON, RICHARD E. "Religious Preference as a Factor in Attitudinal and Background Differences Among College Freshmen." Sociol Ed 41:227–37 sp '68. * (PA 42:18686)

11. PETERSON, RICHARD E. "The Student Left in American Higher Education." Daedalus 97:293–317 w '68. *

12. RICHARDSON, THOMAS EDWARD. The Relationship of Congruence Between Student Orientation Toward Higher Education and Campus Environment to Student Satisfaction on Selected Campuses. Doctor's thesis, Florida State University (Tallahassee, Fla.), 1968. (DA 29:2360A)

13. ROGERS, MARY ELEANOR PIPER. Perception of the College Environment as a Factor in Attitude Change During the Freshman Year. Doctor's thesis, Indiana University (Bloomington, Ind.), 1968. (DA 29:3472A)

14. APOSTAL, ROBERT A. "College Student Characteristics and Peer Independence Levels." Col Ed Rec 54(4):74–7 Ja '69. *

15. APOSTAL, ROBERT A. "College Subcultures and Peer Independence." Col Ed Rec 54(6):114–9 Mr '69. *

16. BUESCHER, RUTH MARIE. The Relationship Between Selected Noncognitive Variables and Academic Achievement of College Women in Various Fields of Study. Doctor's thesis, Fordham University (New York, N.Y.), 1969. (DAI 30:1858A)

17. BURNS, JOHN LUTHER. The Relationship of Attitudinal Similarity to Collegiate Satisfaction and Degree of Role Orientation Identification. Doctor's thesis, University of Texas (Austin, Tex.), 1969. (DAI 30:2844A)

18. FOLSOM, CLYDE H., JR. "An Investigation of Holland's Theory of Vocational Choice." J Counsel Psychol 16(3):260–6 My '69. * (PA 43:11955)

19. HARTNETT, RODNEY T., AND CENTRA, JOHN A. "Attitudes and Secondary School Backgrounds of Catholics Entering College." Sociol Ed 42(2):188–98 sp '69. *

20. HEDEGARD, JAMES M., AND BROWN, DONALD R. "Encounters of Some Negro and White Freshmen With a Public Multiversity." J Social Issues 25(3):131–44 su '69. *

21. KERPELMAN, LARRY C. "Concurrent Validity of a Brief Test of Academic Aptitude." Ed & Psychol Meas 29(4):891–4 w '69. * (PA 44:20988)

22. KIDD, KEVIN A. J. A Study of Student Perceptions and Student Attitudes in a Small Church-Affiliated Liberal Arts College and a Small Non-Denominational Liberal Arts College. Doctor's thesis, Boston College (Chestnut Hill, Mass.), 1969. (DAI 31:228A)

23. LaBACH, PATRICIA AVERY. Self-Actualization in College Students: Interrelationships of Self-Actualization, Personal Characteristics, and Attitudes in Subcultures of Liberal Arts Freshmen and Seniors. Doctor's thesis, Kent State University (Kent, Ohio), 1969. (DAI 31:1013A)

24. LINDSAY, CARL A., AND ALTHOUSE, RICHARD. "Comparative Validities of the Strong Vocational Interest Blank Academic Achievement Scale and the College Student Questionnaire Motivation for Grades Scale." Ed & Psychol Meas 29(2):489–93 su '69. * (PA 44:17506)

25. MAGRAB, PHYLLIS R. Expectation-Press Congruence as a Psychological Variable in the Prediction of College Adaptation. Doctor's thesis, University of Maryland (College Park, Md.), 1969. (DAI 30:5290A)

26. ROMINE, BENJAMIN HOUSTON, JR. The Effects of the Interaction Between a Personality Characteristic and an Environmental Characteristic on the Achievement of Female College Freshmen When Ability Is Controlled. Doctor's thesis, Duke University (Durham, N.C.), 1969. (DAI 30:5301A)

27. SANDEEN, ARTHUR. "Residence Groups and Program Planning." Col Stud Survey 3(3):55–6 w '69. * (PA 44:11196)

28. SKELTON, DAVID RAY. A Study of Relationships of Student and Institutional Attributes to Educational Objectives of Entering Freshmen. Doctor's thesis, Indiana University (Bloomington, Ind.), 1969. (DAI 31:180A)

29. SOCKLOFF, ALAN LEONARD. The Analysis of Student Characteristics Associated With Grades for Varying Levels of College Freshman Grade Complexity. Doctor's thesis, Emory University (Atlanta, Ga.), 1969. (DAI 31:903B)

30. STEWART, MARJORIE ANN. A Comparison of Commuting

and Resident Students on an Urban Campus. Doctor's thesis, Ohio State University (Columbus, Ohio), 1969. (DAI 30:2812A)

31. ZIMMERMAN, JOHN JAMES. Relationships Among Scholastic Aptitude, Attitudes Toward Various Facets of College Life, and Academic Performance of Students at Lycoming College. Doctor's thesis, Pennsylvania State University (University Park, Pa.), 1969. (DAI 30:4792A)

32. APOSTAL, ROBERT A. "Peer Independence and Personality." J Col Stud Personnel 11(2):107–10 Mr '70. *

33. APOSTAL, ROBERT A. "Personality Type and Preferred College Subculture." J Col Stud Personnel 11(3):206–9 My '70. * (PA 45:4876)

34. DEIULIO, ROBERT SALVATORE. An Analysis of College Freshmen Perceptions of Staff Members Who Functioned as Counselors Compared to Those Who Functioned as Teachers and Counselors. Doctor's thesis, Boston University (Boston, Mass.), 1970. (DAI 31:2101A)

35. DYER, PETER TURNER. Social Influence, Conformity, and Estimation Within a College Population. Doctor's thesis, State University of New York (Albany, N.Y.), 1970. (DAI 31:2734A)

36. FLORES, PEDRO V. A Comparative Study of Selected Filipino and American College Students' Satisfaction With the Administration, Faculty, and Student Body. Doctor's thesis, Pennsylvania State University (University Park, Pa.), 1970. (DAI 31:2703A)

37. FOLSOM, CLYDE H., JR., AND LUCY, WILLIAM. "Comparison of Education and Arts and Sciences Students on Family Background and Perceptions of Secondary School Experiences." J Col Stud Personnel 11(2):120–5 Mr '70. *

38. HARTNETT, RODNEY T. "Differences in Selected Attitudes and College Orientations Between Black Students Attending Traditionally Negro and Traditionally White Institutions." Abstract. Proc 78th Ann Conv Am Psychol Assn 5(2):609–10 '70. * (PA 44:19340)

39. HUMMERS, JO ANN. A Comparison of Selected Attitudes, Philosophies of Higher Education, and Characteristics of Students Known and Unknown to Student Personnel Staff of a Public Four Year College. Doctor's thesis, New York University (New York, N.Y.), 1970. (DAI 31:3292A)

40. IHLANFELDT, WILLIAM IVAN. Personal Characteristics of Satisfied and Non-Satisfied Northwestern University Students. Doctor's thesis, Northwestern University (Evanston, Ill.), 1970. (DAI 31:3293A)

41. JOHNSON, EDWARD. "Sophomore Fraternity Members Compared With Independents on the Biographical Scales of CSQ." J Col Stud Personnel 11(4):284–5 Jl '70. *

42. KRAMER, HOWARD C. "Interpretation of CSQ Scales." J Col Stud Personnel 11(1):28–32 Ja '70. *

43. KUDER, JAMES MICHAEL. A Comparative Study of Selected Characteristics of Junior and Senior Male University Students Residing in Fraternities and Residence Halls at Oregon State University. Doctor's thesis, Oregon State University (Corvallis, Ore.), 1970. (DAI 30:4244A)

44. MAJER, KENNETH. "Differential Relationships Between Personality and Performance Under Dissimilar Modes of Instruction." AV Commun R 18(2):169–79 su '70. * (PA 44:19555)

45. MORRISEY, ROBERT J. A Comparison of the Nonintellective Characteristics, as Determined by the College Student Questionnaire, of Freshman Probationary Student Dropouts and Persisters in an Urban University. Doctor's thesis, University of Missouri (Kansas City, Mo.), 1970. (DAI 31:1018A)

46. PETERSON, ARLIN VERDAYNE. A Comparison of Community College Transfer Students and Native University Students on Nonacademic Factors. Doctor's thesis, Washington State University (Pullman, Wash.), 1970. (DAI 31:2709A)

47. POWELL, JOANN. An Analysis of Factors Relating to Decisions to Transfer From Northwestern University by Freshman Women. Doctor's thesis, Northwestern University (Evanston, Ill.), 1970. (DAI 31:3277A)

48. RICHARDSON, THOMAS E. "Satisfaction With College: Its Relationship to Student-College Fit." Col Stud Survey 4(1):19–23 sp '70. * (PA 44:17307)

49. RIGGS, ROBERT OWEN. A Study of Non-Intellective Characteristics Associated With Differential Levels of Academic Over- and Underachievement. Doctor's thesis, Memphis State University (Memphis, Tenn.), 1970. (DAI 31:2745A)

50. ROMINE, BEN H.; DAVIS, JUNIUS A.; AND GEHMAN, W. SCOTT. "The Interaction of Learning, Personality Traits, Ability, and Environment: A Preliminary Study." Ed & Psychol Meas 30(2):337–47 su '70. * (PA 45:5059)

51. WATERMAN, ALAN S., AND WATERMAN, CAROLINE K. "Cross-Institutional Study of Personality Variables Relating to Satisfaction With College." Abstract. Proc 78th Ann Conv Am Psychol Assn 5(1):451–2 '70. * (PA 44:19352)

52. WATERMAN, ALAN S., AND WATERMAN, CAROLINE K. "The Relationship Between Ego Identity Status and Satisfaction With College." J Ed Res 64(4):165–8 D '70. *

53. WHITE, RUTH ANN MOORE. Student Subcultures on a University Campus. Doctor's thesis, East Texas State University (Commerce, Tex.), 1970. (DAI 31:2121A)

PAUL L. DRESSEL, *Assistant Provost and Director, Institutional Research, Michigan State University, East Lansing, Michigan.*

The *College Student Questionnaires* were developed to collect "biographical and attitudinal information about college student bodies." There are two questionnaires: Part 1, covering background, attitudes, and plans, is to be used for entering students. Part 2, to be used at the end of one or more years in college, includes sections on educational and vocational plans, college activities, and attitudes. Each questionnaire includes 200 multiple choice questions.

The range of information included should make them useful in institutional self-studies directed at understanding the student body and in making plans for changes in aspects of institutional operations as they affect students, although the responses to many questions may be of interest only to social scientists rather than to the faculty at large.

The technical manual emphasizes that these questionnaires are to be used to provide group summaries and not individual analyses. These cautions also extend to the 13 brief scales, ten items each, which are woven into the forms of the CSQ. Part 1 includes scales on family social status, motivation for grades, family independence, peer independence, liberalism, social conscience, and cultural sophistication. The last five scales are also included in Part 2, which in addition includes scales on satisfaction with faculty, satisfaction with the administration, satisfaction with the major, satisfaction with students, study habits, and extracurricular involvement. Comparative data are provided both on the scales and on the separate items of the questionnaires. Group average scores on the scales may be of interest, both in studying differences within groups on campus and in making comparisons from one institution to another to the extent that the norms make this possible, but most institutions and researchers will probably find that analysis of the individual item response frequencies will be the most significant part of their study.

One other feature of the CSQ should be noted. There are a number of optional research strategies and scoring arrangements. In addition, there are a number of optional items which an institution may fill in with questions of particular local interest. The institution can also designate up to four subgroups which can be treated separately in the analysis. While this does provide admirable flexibility in the instrument, there are also some complexities introduced which would seem to make it necessary for persons administering the questionnaires to be very careful in their instructions.

CONTROL TEST. For those institutions which may wish a statistical control for aptitude in studying the relationship of CSQ variables, or who desire a measure of aptitude in differentiating various groups of students, a brief *Control Test for Academic Aptitude* is provided. This test is composed of 30 items, 18 verbal and 12 mathematical, and requires 12 minutes. It is definitely a speeded test. The manual emphasizes that "it is entirely too brief to provide reliable measurement of the ability of individual students" and emphasizes that it has been provided only "to be used in tandem with the CSQ for research purposes." The reported reliability of .79 is quite adequate for a group measure. The evidence for validity is limited, largely based on the fact that some data which have accrued from its use are in accord with expectations.

RESEARCH APPLICATIONS. The technical manual provides numerous suggestions about the use of the CSQ in study and research. These suggestions include the possibility of using the questionnaire to provide a profile of entering freshmen, analysis of vocational and educational plans, studies of students in various major fields, studies of dropout and retention, student faculty relations, student satisfactions and dissatisfactions, descriptions of subgroups, and several others. It certainly should be suggested that any institution undertaking the use of these questionnaires should ascertain in advance just why. The questionnaires make available a very large mass of data, and it is commonplace for institutions to use such a questionnaire but then find that once the data are available, there is really no person, no group, no market for the information which results. Unless an institution has some particular problems or concerns, the sheer bulk of the information available is too likely to result in a voluminous report which does not bring any one issue into sufficient focus to attract any great attention or to bring about any action.

SUMMARY. The questionnaires are well conceived and carefully constructed. Institutions desirous of making surveys of their students will find them superior to anything that they can construct for themselves. However, only by careful review of the contents and by planning its use in advance is it likely that the cost and the effort will be rewarded.

HARRISON G. GOUGH, *Professor of Psychology, University of California, Berkeley, California.*

"Self-study" is an idea that holds great appeal for college administrators, as well it might. Few organizations are as loosely managed as the ordinary college, and few know as little about the raw material they receive and the products into which this material is somehow fashioned. It is not surprising that the last 10 to 15 years have seen the appearance of various psychometric tools and assessment devices that can assist the beleaguered academic official in learning more about the students for whose educational welfare he must be in part responsible.

The *College Student Questionnaires* are the answers given to the worried administrators by the Institutional Research Program for Higher Education of the Educational Testing Service. They include two 200-item inquiries: Part 1 for use with entering freshmen and transfer students, and Part 2 for use with enrolled undergraduates who have completed a year or more of study at the institution. The purpose of the pair of questionnaires is to provide evidence pertinent to overall trends and variations within large subgroups (e.g., majors in science vs. majors in the humanities, males vs. females), and not to permit diagnosis or evaluation of the individual case. The questionnaires are also not intended for use in admissions, although they might well be applied to bring to light the mischief that a planned admissions policy may have brought about.

Part 1, for entering students, includes questions in four domains: educational and vocational plans and expectations; activities and achievements in secondary school; family background; and personal attitudes. The items are in multiple choice format, and a very useful handbook of comparative data gives nationwide norms on each item for males, females, and total. For example, it is reported that 84 percent of entering males and 87 percent of entering females indicate that they have already reached a decision concerning the major field of study, and that the most popular choice is the social sciences (14.1% for all students), followed by education (12.5%), and the arts and humanities (11.6%). Summing the percentages for those

indicating a preference for biological science, physical science, and mathematics gives a figure of 16.6%.

The item pool in Part 1 may also be scored for seven scales: motivation for grades, family social status, family independence, peer independence, liberalism, social conscience, and cultural sophistication. Scale development was by a priori logic, and all items are completely transparent, as the following examples indicate: "In terms of your own personal satisfaction, how much importance do you attach to getting good grades?" "What is your best estimate of the total income last year of your parental family (not your own family if you are married)?" "How dependent on or independent of your parents do you consider yourself to be at the present time?" "Do you generally like to do things in your own way and without regard for what other students around you may think?" "Would you agree or disagree that conscientious objectors should be excused from military service during wartime?" "Are you concerned that persons who are not white-Anglo-Saxon-Protestant seem to have somewhat less opportunity in America?" and "How many of the following have you read: James Joyce, Leo Tolstoy, Thomas Mann?"

Part 2 repeats the questions asked in Part 1 about educational and vocational plans and personal attitudes. In place of Sections 2 and 3 of the first part, Part 2 includes 100 items asking about school activities, housing arrangements, reactions to faculty and students, scholastic performance, study techniques, and other issues. A useful handbook of comparative data is also furnished for Part 2, giving item statistics for a nationwide sample. In this handbook one can discover, for example, that 64 percent of students believed that grades during the past year under-represented their true ability and that 48 percent believed the college to have too much authority over student life.

Part 2 can be scored for 11 scales: satisfaction with faculty, satisfaction with administration, satisfaction with major, satisfaction with students, study habits, extracurricular involvement; and then a repetition of five scales included in Part 1: family independence, peer independence, liberalism, social conscience, and cultural sophistication.

Reliabilities for the 11 scales available in Part 2 are modest, ranging from .57 to .84, but sufficient for the purposes mentioned in the manual and illustrative literature sent to prospective users. Reliability of the individual items can be assumed to be on the order of .90 or above on the basis of prior work with biographical and attitudinal data of this kind.

Validity of the scales is documented in two ways: through correlations of the scales with individual items in the questionnaires (using only those items not scored on any scale), and through citation of group means. The liberalism scale, for example, gives rise to the following point biserial correlations with religious preferences: no formal religion, .44; Jewish, .28; Protestant, −.13; and Catholic, −.15. On the scale, Cultural Sophistication, the ranking of majors is as follows: humanities and fine arts, social science, natural science, education, engineering, and business.

Information gathered from the two questionnaires may be supplemented, if desired, by scores on a 12-minute, 30-item *Control Test for Academic Aptitude.* This measure produced median correlations of .60 and .62 with SAT-V and SAT-M, respectively, in three colleges, and a median coefficient of .40 with freshmen grades. It is included as a sort of addendum to the *College Student Questionnaires* for use where other aptitude data are not available and where the investigator wishes to have at least an approximate index of this factor. The user is firmly cautioned against using scores on the CTAA for individual evaluations.

These materials constitute an attractive and useful package for the college administrator interested in student personnel problems. The manual is informative and clearly written, and the supporting materials are excellent. Furthermore, a convenient scoring service is available and reporting conventions have been established that stress the research and survey implications of the questionnaires. Nonetheless, there are several deficiencies that future work on the questionnaires should seek to rectify. One of these concerns the choice of variables for scaling. Factor analysis already suggests considerable redundancy among the present scales, particularly those referring to satisfaction with various aspects of the educational institution. These scales could be consolidated into a briefer set, or possibly a single scale with two components. Other measures offering the kind of information administrators need and want should definitely be added, including scales for creative potential, professional aspirations (to

identify the proportion of students likely to go on to graduate or professional schools), personal stability, and some measure of the humanities-science continuum.[1]

The total length of the two booklets should also be reduced, to permit testing within a single class hour. Finally, there is a great need for correlational data relating the scales in Parts 1 and 2 to other measures often administered to incoming college classes—for example the *College and University Environment Scales,* the *College Characteristics Index,* and at least three or four of the personality inventories widely used in the testing of college students.

[58]

★Community Adaptation Schedule. Normals and psychiatric patients; 1965–68; CAS; for research use only; self-report measure of subject's relationship to the world outside of himself; primarily intended for measuring groups; 45 scores: work (employment, housework, family care, work potential, unemployment, volunteer, wage history, total), family (general living, spouse, children, parents, other relatives, total), social (general social, friends, dating, peers at work, neighbors, total), larger community (recreation, religion, organizations, communications, education, moving, civic, total), commercial (finances, shopping, transportation, modern technology, housing, total), professional (social services, other services, individual professionals, schools, total), affect, behavior, cognition, common question total, total, consistency; reliability data for an earlier form; norms consist of mean scores on earlier forms for 3 groups: normals, outpatients, patients; Form 5A ('68, 23 pages); preliminary manual ('68, 24 pages); separate answer sheets must be used; $11.95 per 25 tests; $4.95 per 50 answer sheets; $1.95 per set of scoring stencils; $2.95 per manual; $5.95 per specimen set; cash orders postpaid; (30–50) minutes; Sheldon R. Roen and Alan J. Burnes; Behavioral Publications, Inc. *

REFERENCES

1–2. See P:45.
3. GRIFFIN, CAROL LEE. *Dominance in Marriage and the Post-Hospital Adjustment of Male Psychiatric Patients.* Doctor's thesis, Boston University (Boston, Mass.), 1967. (*DA* 28:2136B)
4. HAMMARBACK, MARVIN DWAYNE. *An Investigation of the Community Adaptation Schedule With Educable Mentally Retarded Adolescents and Young Adults.* Doctor's thesis, University of Oregon (Eugene, Ore.), 1969. (*DAI* 30:4773A)
5. McDOWELL, RICHARD LANE. *An Evaluation of a Residential Treatment Program for Adolescents as Measured by Post-Hospital Adjustment: A Follow Up Study.* Doctor's thesis, University of Kansas (Lawrence, Kan.), 1969. (*DAI* 30:2855A)
6. COOK, PATRICK E., AND JOSEPHS, PAULA O. "The Community Adaptation Schedule and the California Psychological Inventory: A Validational Study With College Students." *Commun Mental Health J* 6(5):366–73 O '70. * (*PA* 45:6347)

JULIAN J. LASKY, *Clinical Research Branch, National Institute of Mental Health, Chevy Chase, Maryland.*

The *Community Adaptation Schedule* purports to measure an individual's relationship to six major aspects of his community. There is

1 GOLDSCHMID, MARCEL L. "Prediction of College Majors by Personality Tests." *J Counsel Psychol* 14:302–8 Jl '67. *

great need for such a device, especially in community mental health practice and for assessing patient post-hospital adjustment. The CAS appears to have the distinction of being the first of its kind based solely on the patient's self report.

The authors began by extrapolating 70 items from the interviewer-rated Barrabee-Finesinger Social Adjustment Scale and other similar inventories but then decided to add new concepts, items, and a self-report format.

The current schedule (Form 5A) contains 217 items grouped into six chapters and 33 subsections. Underneath each item in the booklet appears a 6-point scale, each point being defined by a descriptive word or phrase relevant to the question asked. All subjects respond to 114 questions. Each subsection has a heading which tells the subject whether or not he or she is to respond to the items in that subsection.

Scoring is accomplished by means of four templates (internal consistency, affect, behavior, and cognition) and by summing 41 scores (total score for subject, total score for common items, six chapter scores and 33 subsection scores) yielding 45 scores in all. Since the authors wished to reduce position set, they reversed the usual direction of response in 76 randomly selected items in the booklet. Before scoring begins, a reflection template is used to re-orient all items in one direction. Another desirable feature is the internal consistency score. Ten CAS items have been paired with 10 non-scored items to gauge consistency of subject performance. The 10 non-scored items are stated either in identical form to a paired item or in negative form. This score attempts to deal with a source of error which is frequently overlooked in patient self-reports when inadequate performance due to the patient's illness is often a problem. The social desirability value of the items, which is not considered, remains a problem.

The first 12 pages of the 20-page manual repeat most of the text and tables to be found in two previous publications by the authors (*1, 2*). The next section summarizes results of three unpublished studies in which the CAS was used. Directions for administration and scoring occupy the last two pages of the manual.

It would appear that most of the 217 items were constructed on an a priori basis. Reference is made to item analysis, but there is no published report in this regard. It is not clear why there are so many subsections; 16 of the 33

subsections contain five or fewer items. The origin and documentation for the three modal scales (affect, behavior and cognition) are not given.

The manual has several flaws. Whereas Form 5A of the CAS is offered to users, the data reported in the manual were collected using Forms 2A and 4A. Examination of the three forms reveals that this situation is not as serious as it might seem; Form 5A and Form 4A are virtually identical except for the numbering of the items. It would be reassuring to the user to have this fact pointed out in the next manual.

Table 1 presents 38 means and standard deviations representing CAS chapters and subsections (Form 2A) from a sample of 256 normals and 66 post-hospital psychiatric patients attending an aftercare clinic. The text reads, "Each of the other community chapters, except for Family Community, was responded to in a significantly less adaptive manner by aftercare patients than by normals." From this statement it would appear that significant differences were found for five of the six chapter mean scores. However, the *t* values in Table 1 do not support this statement; only three of the six chapter mean scores are significant.

None of the samples in the manual or supporting papers are described in terms of demographic characteristics, diagnoses, etc. They should be.

Table 2 presents another group differences study. Forty-five mental health professionals from nearby agencies, 58 outpatients from the same agencies, and 79 state psychiatric hospital patients are compared: *F* but not *t* values are presented; *t* values would be useful. Significant *F* values were found for each of the six chapters and for 15 of the 33 subsections, for each of the modal scales (affect, behavior, cognition) and for the two total scores. It is doubtful that the CAS is intended to measure the adjustment of mental health professionals to their community. Nor is it altogether clear that the *Community Adaptation Schedule* is appropriate for use with hospitalized inpatients. In any event, comparing the CAS performance of mental health professionals with that of state hospital inpatients does not constitute much of a challenge to the discriminating power of the CAS.

Test-retest correlations (one month interval) both for the professionals and for the inpatients are highly significant for very nearly all scores. This is encouraging, although it will be recalled that there is no alternate form of the CAS. Also, some CAS items represent enduring characterological traits, while other items reflect behavior and performance during the year prior to completion of the CAS. While this combination of items plus the memory of responses to the initial CAS would help produce the high test-retest correlations obtained, it would seem to adversely affect the sensitivity of the CAS to change in adaptation if the CAS were to be used as a change measure. Internal consistency reliability data are not presented.

Table 3 represents a further attempt to determine the validity of the CAS. The authors devised an a priori Social Activity Inventory (SAI) by writing 37 items, each of which is intended to represent a CAS chapter or subsection. The authors state, "The intent was to develop brief, parallel scales for purposes of cross validation." Twenty-two professionals completed the CAS and the SAI. Means, standard deviations and correlation coefficients are presented as an example of CAS "construct validity." Rather than a construct validity study, the left half of the table appears to be a study of alternate forms; that is, the same subjects during one session completed the full length CAS and a brief CAS, which the authors labelled SAI.

The other half of the table presents a more conventional validity study. Thirty outpatients completed the CAS. The SAI for these patients was completed by the professional worker who was most informed regarding the patient's functioning. Table 3 reveals that two (family, larger community) of the six chapter correlations are significant and that one (work) is not, but the correlations for the remaining three chapters are not presented. It is not clear why 19 of 37 correlation coefficients are not presented, especially when some nonsignificant correlations as low as .00 and .13 are presented. In any event, the results of this validity study are not convincing.

The final table presents a discriminant analysis classification study using the three samples (professional, outpatient, inpatient) referred to in Table 2. Previous comments apply: not a rigorous classification exercise.

In summary, there is great need for adequate measures of the adaptation of psychiatric outpatients to their community. Whether the CAS will answer this need remains to be seen; certainly more developmental work is indicated.

The authors clearly state that the manual is in preliminary form and that the CAS is still in its developmental stages and should be used for research purposes only. This caution is well advised.

LESTER M. LIBO, *Professor of Psychiatry (Psychology), University of New Mexico School of Medicine, Albuquerque, New Mexico.*

The *Community Adaptation Schedule* is designed to assess an individual's relationship to his environment—his life style, activities, interests, and satisfactions in a wide variety of self-environment transactions. The 217 questions in the CAS are divided into six "chapters" (work, family, social, larger, commercial, and professional communities), each of which has 4 to 7 subsections, for a total of 33 subsections, which include such areas as employment, marital relations, social life, neighbors, recreation, religious activity, financial management, housing, social service agencies, and schools. Each question is to be answered by use of a 6-point Likert-type scale.

The CAS is for research use only and the manual is labelled "Preliminary." The goal is to answer the need for an objective, standardized instrument in "psychological ecology" and community mental health. Such an environmentally-related instrument is needed to evaluate intervention programs, such as prevention and crisis consultation, in community mental health, as well as to represent a unit of analysis that is beyond the intrapsychic.

The authors state that "the questions define operationally what is meant by the concept of community adaptation. The schedule attempts to measure a person's perception of the community, affects toward it, and behaviors in it." When one looks at the questions, "community adaptation" becomes a bewildering mixture of frequency and intensity of involvement, interest, and satisfaction. The more one believes in and practices such upper middle class values as the pursuit of affluence, achievement, possession of material goods, interest in technology, having many friends, and trust in professionals and in community agencies, the higher one's adaptation score is. The following answers, for example, contribute to high community adaptation: *Annual income over $10,000;* feel *very close* to parents (including spending *very much* time with, *never* have serious arguments with, *completely* agree with); go out *very often* to movies, theater, or sporting events; go to religious services *more than once a week;* pay *over $150 each month* for housing; and like the police *very much.*

Is this community adaptation? Will these answers tell us that we have succeeded with our intervention programs?

The authors should call their instrument a community activity and interest schedule, or a social commitment schedule; but the items are too varied for any single title to be right. As it is, "adaptation" is quite value-laden (often substituting for health, in fact) and hence misleading and even dangerous in this application.

The test can be used to assess which social and community sectors an individual is involved in, how involved he is, and how he feels about these involvements, but the present additive scoring will becloud the important detail within. I believe the instrument, being too ambitiously broad-gauged, results in meaningless total scores.

The standardization sample on which the CAS was first developed consisted of 256 "normals" (presumed socially adapted) and 66 psychiatric patients in aftercare (presumed socially disrupted). Judging from the fact that middle class, conventional community groups were used for recruiting the "socially adapted" sample, and that only status as a psychiatric patient was used as the criterion for being "socially disrupted," one would wonder about the influence of socioeconomic status on CAS scores. However, neither sex nor socioeconomic status was found to be related significantly to CAS scores. This is surprising—until one remembers the restricted range in social status of the population used. The basic study of the present revised version of the CAS compared CAS scores of three groups: mental health professionals, outpatients at mental health agencies, and psychiatric hospital patients. In this study no analysis of the relationship of CAS scores to either sex or socioeconomic status is reported. This is unfortunate. The "normal" group, mental health professionals, is clearly of different social-educational status than the patients. The relationship of socioeconomic, educational, and sex differences to CAS scores needs to be studied further.

The preliminary manual is not clearly written. Sentences are lengthy, complex, and awkward, and there are numerous technical terms that can confuse and discourage the reader. The test booklet, however, is well-prepared, as are the answer sheet and scoring templates. The language in the test booklet instructions and questions is simple and clear. There are no double-barreled questions. Nevertheless, taking the schedule would seem a lengthy and difficult procedure for many respondents, particularly those of lower socioeconomic status, and many of the items are of a customarily private nature.

Laudably, there is an internal consistency scale and a means of checking response set. There are also three "mode of response" scores: affect, behavior, and cognition—an interesting and valuable byproduct—but these are not used to modify the subsection or total scores, leaving the latter a puzzling mixture of behavior, wish, satisfaction, etc.

Reliability (one-month retest) and validity studies have yielded varying, sometimes surprising, but generally promising results. Three studies using the CAS are briefly described. The authors recognize that much work remains to be done and they invite interested researchers to use the test and communicate with them. A great deal of effort has gone into developing and assessing the CAS. Statistical analyses are presented in detailed tables and text in the manual.

The general idea is good, the need is obvious, the quantitative work seems sound; but there are too many weaknesses in the conceptual and developmental foundation: the usual problems of a questionnaire format, the mixture of dimensions even within subsections, a marked social class and values bias in item selection and scoring, and the lack of a broadly representative standardization population.

In short, before more effort is expended on the statistical elements of test refinement, the conceptual basis should be reworked. The CAS (or its successor) might then become a useful instrument in community mental health research.

[59]

★**Comrey Personality Scales.** Ages 16 and over; 1970; CPS; 10 scores: trust vs. defensiveness (T), orderliness vs. lack of compulsion (O), social conformity vs. rebelliousness (C), activity vs. lack of energy (A), emotional stability vs. neuroticism (S), extraversion vs. introversion (E), masculinity vs. femininity (M), empathy vs. egocentrism (P), validity check (V), response bias (R); Form A (6 pages); manual (40 pages); profile (2 pages); only norms based upon college students and friends; separate answer sheets (Digitek, hand scored) must be used; $9.50 per 25 tests; $4.75 per 50 Digitek answer sheets; $3.75 per 50 hand scored answer sheets; $3.75 per 50 profiles; $2.50 per manual; $3 per specimen set; post-age extra; Digitek scoring service, 90¢ or less per test; administration time not reported; Andrew L. Comrey; Educational and Industrial Testing Service. *

REFERENCES

1. COMREY, ANDREW L. "Factored Homogeneous Item Dimensions in Personality Research." *Ed & Psychol Meas* 21:417–31 su '61. * (*PA* 36:2HF17C)
2. COMREY, ANDREW L. "A Study of Thirty-Five Personality Dimensions." *Ed & Psychol Meas* 22:543–52 au '62. * (*PA* 37:5004)
3. EDWARDS, ALLAN E., AND WINE, DAVID B. "Personality Changes With Age: Their Dependency on Concomitant Intellectual Decline." *J Gerontol* 18:182–4 Ap '63. * (*PA* 38:4099)
4. COMREY, ANDREW L. "Personality Factors Compulsion, Dependence, Hostility, and Neuroticism." *Ed & Psychol Meas* 24:75–84 sp '64. * (*PA* 39:1802)
5. WINE, DAVID B., AND EDWARDS, ALLAN E. "Intemperance: Psychological and Sociological Concomitants." *Q J Studies Alcohol* 25:77–84 Mr '64. *
6. COMREY, ANDREW L. "Scales for Measuring Compulsion, Hostility, Neuroticism, and Shyness." *Psychol Rep* 16:697–700 Je '65. * (*PA* 39:15184)
7. COMREY, ANDREW L. "Comparison of Personality and Attitude Variables." *Ed & Psychol Meas* 26:853–60 w '66. * (*PA* 41:4591)
8. COMREY, ANDREW L., AND JAMISON, KAY. "Verification of Six Personality Factors." *Ed & Psychol Meas* 26:945–53 w '66. * (*PA* 41:3707)
9. ROSENBERG, BETH; EDWARDS, ALLAN E.; AND HILL, RICHARD A. "Relationship Between Peripheral Vascular State, Personality, and Adaptive Response Under the Effects of Alcohol." Abstract. *Proc 74th Ann Conv Am Psychol Assn* 1:207–8 '66. * (*PA* 41:5635)
10. COMREY, ANDREW L., AND DUFFY, KIRT E. "Cattell and Eysenck Factor Scores Related to Comrey Personality Factors." *Multiv Behav Res* 3:379–92 O '68. * (*PA* 43:8363)
11. COMREY, ANDREW L.; JAMISON, KAY; AND KING, NATHAN. "Integration of Two Personality Factor Systems." *Multiv Behav Res* 3:147–59 Ap '68. * (*PA* 42:14724)
12. JAMISON, KAY, AND COMREY, ANDREW L. "Cross-Cultural Study of British and American Personality Factors." Abstract. *Proc 76th Ann Conv Am Psychol Assn* 3:167–8 '68. *
13. JAMISON, KAY, AND COMREY, ANDREW L. "Further Study of Dependence as a Personality Factor." *Psychol Rep* 22:239–42 F '68. * (*PA* 42:10607)
14. COMREY, ANDREW L. "Personality Factors, General Activity, Socialization, Compulsion, and Dependence." Abstract. *Proc 77th Ann Conv Am Psychol Assn* 4(1):151–2 '69. * (*PA* 43:17441)
15. DUFFY, KIRT E.; JAMISON, KAY; AND COMREY, ANDREW L. "Assessment of a Proposed Expansion of the Comrey Personality Factor System." *Multiv Behav Res* 4(3):295–307 Jl '69. * (*PA* 44:660)
16. EDWARDS, ALLAN E.; BLOOM, MARSHALL H.; AND COHEN, SIDNEY. "The Psychedelics: Love or Hostility Potion?" *Psychol Rep* 24(3):843–6 Je '69. * (*PA* 44:627)
17. FABIAN, JUDITH JANARO. *Comparison of Theoretical Viewpoints and Empirical Measures of Neuroticism.* Doctor's thesis, University of California (Los Angeles, Calif.), 1969. (*DAI* 30:4369B)
18. JAMISON, KAY, AND COMREY, ANDREW L. "A Comparison of Personality Factor Structure in British and American University Students." *J Psychol* 71(1):45–57 Ja '69. * (*PA* 43:5221)
19. COMREY, ANDREW L., AND BACKER, THOMAS E. "Construct Validation of the Comrey Personality Scales." *Multiv Behav Res* 5(4):469–77 O '70. * (*PA* 45:8241)
20. KUMAR, SANTOSH. *Personality Variables and Intellectual Abilities as Determinants of Concept Learning.* Doctor's thesis, University of Southern California (Los Angeles, Calif.), 1970. (*DAI* 31:1521B)

R. G. DEMAREE, *Professor of Psychology and Research Scientist, Institute of Behavioral Research, Texas Christian University, Fort Worth, Texas.*

The *Comrey Personality Scales* has much to commend it and can reasonably be expected to become a leading contender among self-report personality questionnaire instruments. Many investigators will agree with Comrey that his eight scales represent the major areas of the adult personality domain. The procedures which were followed in the development of the scales and the empirical findings associated with them are impressive. Comrey has reckoned well with past research concerning self-report instruments, and has come forth with an instrument which should not be regarded as just another self-report questionnaire. The seven-point rating scales for responses to each item and the sampling represented by the 20 items for each of the 8 scales (plus 8 items for a Validity scale and 12 items for a Response Bias scale) appear to give this instrument a decided edge over others in terms of scale homogeneities. Whether this edge will be upheld with different populations and testing situations than are represented in the data reported in the manual remains to be seen.

ITEM FORMAT AND SCORING. An important feature of the CPS is the use of seven-point scales for item responses. Following each item number in the booklet is either an X or Y, indicating whether Scale X (7, always; 6, very frequently; 5, frequently; 4, occasionally; 3, rarely; 2, very rarely; and, 1, never) or Scale Y (7, definitely; 6, very probably; 5, probably; 4, possibly; 3, probably not; 2, very probably not; and, 1, definitely not) is to be used.

The parallel structure of the response scales is worthy of note since it may minimize the burden on the respondent of frequently switching from one scale to the other. Indeed, it is suggested in the booklet for the CPS that "If the other answer scale seems more appropriate for you than the one indicated for the given statement, you may use it instead." Nevertheless, it is to be expected that the time required for completion of the 180 items of the CPS will be greater than for the same number of items in a two-choice format. Unfortunately, no information is given in the manual as to the time required for administration of the inventory.

The booklet for the CPS informs the respondent that if it is "impossible to select an answer that is even approximately correct for you, leave the answer space blank for the statement." Items for which no response is given are then scored as a "4." Hand scoring of the answer sheets is facilitated by the ordering of items in the booklet, whereby the items for each scale appear in two rows of the answer sheet. With provisions for reverse scoring of the negatively worded items, the raw score on each scale is a simple sum of the item scores.

USES. The focus of the CPS is on normal personality description. Studies to date with either forerunners or the present version of the CPS have been based predominately on college students who were furnished confidential profiles of scores in return for voluntary participation in the studies. Quite appropriately, the manual suggests that different conditions of administration may affect the measurement properties of the CPS. Upon this cautious note, the manual proceeds to suggest that the CPS may find many uses in research, school, college, and business settings.

DEVELOPMENT OF THE INSTRUMENT. The initial publication of the CPS represents the culmination of research spanning a period of over 15 years by Comrey and his associates. The analytic techniques employed in this research appeared to have served their purposes well. In general, the strategy of the research leading to the CPS was to seek parcels of items, called FHID's for "factored homogeneous item dimension," and to then enter scores on these into correlational analyses.

SAMPLING OF CONTENT. Each of the eight personality scales is based on five parcels of four items each. Each parcel is accorded a short label. With respect to the label, half of the items are positively worded and half are negatively worded. The simplicity and numerical symmetry thus afforded is beguiling and may have an appeal to users of the CPS, but is open to question on empirical grounds. To have the same number of items for every parcel and every scale is not the way to obtain evenness of measurement. It should also be noted that even though the parcels or FHID's were useful in the analyses leading to the eight scales, the five parcels associated with each scale are then merged, since the scale scores are formed by simply summing the 20 item scores.

In general, the correlations among the items in each FHID are impressive, but they do differ markedly in magnitude. For example, the absolute values of the intercorrelations for the four items of "No Stage Fright" ranged from .55 to .75, as compared to corresponding intercorrelations ranging from .20 to .30 for "Lack of Paranoia," and from .21 to .36 for "Trust in Human Nature." In the interest of evenness of measurement there would have been some justification for increasing the number of items for the less homogeneous parcels.

As might be expected, examination of individual items is less appealing than the short labels accorded to the FHID's. For example, two of the items in the FHID labeled "Order" are "My room is a mess," and "I am disorderly." While these two items were intercorrelated .66 in the normative sample, composed primarily of college students, one can only wonder about the applicability of these items to other populations of respondents. A particular problem is foreseen with certain of the items entering into the Validity and Response Bias scales. Surely more subtlety could have been mustered than is represented by the item on the Validity scale of "When I wake up in the morning, my heart is beating." Although it is probable that some respondents would be amused by such a "catch" item, other respondents might be led to question the seriousness or credibility of the instrument.

NORMATIVE DATA. According to the manual, the normative data are based "on 365 male and 362 female university students, their friends and family members, and some other university-connected individuals" who "volunteered to take the inventory in order to receive a confidential report on their own test results." Giving or taking a handful of individuals, this appeared to be the same sample as was used for the reliability studies and factor analyses.

RELIABILITIES. Excellent homogeneity coefficients are reported for the eight personality scales. Split-half reliabilities ranged from .87 for Masculinity vs. Femininity to .95 for Emotional Stability vs. Neuroticism and .96 for Extraversion vs. Introversion. Reliability estimates over occasions or situations remain to be made.

FACTOR RESULTS. Based on the correlations among the 40 FHID's, plus the Validity and Response Bias scales, age, and sex, a factor analysis was performed which led to an exceptionally clear, simple structure for eight uncorrelated factors. An oblique solution was also obtained in which the correlations among the factors closely resembled the correlations among the scales. Not unexpected was the finding that Masculinity vs. Femininity was the least well defined of the factors. Associated with this factor was the only FHID which had a higher loading on a factor other than hypothesized. This FHID, Tolerance for Vulgarity, had a loading of .34 on the Masculinity vs. Femininity factor, which was less than its loading of −.44 on Social Conformity vs. Rebelliousness. This result stemmed, at least in part, from the correlation of −.43 between Tolerance for Vulgarity and the Response Bias scale, which loaded .31 on the Social Conformity vs. Rebelliousness factor.

VALIDITY DATA. Reported in the manual are selected correlations between early or shortened forms of the CPS and scales from other self-report personality instruments. These results generally appeared to provide support for the labels placed on the CPS scales. Of greater interest, however, were the correlations, reported in the manual and in a recent article (*19*), between the CPS scales and self-report biographical items in a sample of 209 volunteer students. The Masculinity vs. Femininity scale, which was least well-defined from a psychometric point of view, was correlated .59 with sex (males scored 1 and females, 0). A correlation of −.36 was found between the number of mental problems listed and the Emotional Stability vs. Neuroticism scale. The strongest construct validity was shown, however, by the Social Conformity vs. Rebelliousness scale. The latter correlated −.54 with amount of marijuana used, −.39 with degree of participation in campus demonstrations, .39 with having some religious preference vs. having none, −.36 with amount of addictive drugs used, and −.27 with extent of premarital sexual activity. Other correlations with the CPS scales were generally quite low, although many of them, such as the correlation of .25 between the Empathy vs. Egocentrism scale and amount of interest in joining the Peace Corps, were in the expected directions.

SUMMARY. Based on data obtained primarily from volunteer college students, the CPS appears to be unusually promising in terms of the homogeneities of the eight scales, the distinctiveness of the scales, and correlations associated with biographical items. Data based on additional populations of respondents and conditions of administration are needed to confirm the reliability and validity of this instrument.

M. Y. QUERESHI, *Professor of Psychology, Marquette University, Milwaukee, Wisconsin.*

The CPS was designed to yield a "comprehensive, multi-dimensional" description of the major non-intellective aspects of the normal human personality. The inventory claims to accomplish this task by means of 160 mostly first-person pronoun statements, comprising 40 homogeneous item subscales (4 items per subscale and 5 subscales per factor) measuring eight personality dimensions labeled Trust, Orderliness, Social Conformity, Activity, Emotional Stability, Extraversion, Masculinity, and Empathy. Half of the items are positively and half negatively worded, and the examinee responds to each statement by using one of the two 7-choice rating scales. Another 20 items are included for providing a validity scale (8 items) and a response bias scale (12 items), bringing the total number of statements to 180.

An outstanding feature of the CPS, compared with other personality inventories, is the development of homogeneous item clusters, labeled as factored homogeneous item dimensions (FHID), to constitute various factors. The FHID's serve the same function as a subtest in a multiple aptitude battery having two or more subtests to measure each factor. The factor loadings thus obtained are much more reliable than those based on individual items. In addition, even individual items in the CPS provide a decided edge over a number of other inventories (e.g., 16 PF, MMPI, EPI, and CPI) because of the wider spread of item response choices (a seven-point scale instead of the ususal two- or three-choice items). The selection of items for each FHID, as well as the selection of FHID's for various factors, was made on the basis of both logical (i.e., whether the item was originally conceived to belong in a particular group) and empirical criteria (e.g., intercorrelations and factor loadings of items and FHID's). The items are generally clearly stated, with the exception of those designed to be ambiguous (i.e., the items for validity check). The inventory is self-administering and can be easily scored by hand or machine.

The manual is completely silent on how much time it usually takes to complete the CPS. Such information should be made available despite the fact that speed, as such, is irrelevant on self-report personality inventories. This reviewer went through the ritual of taking the inventory and completed the task in 50 minutes. However, during the course of this exercise, it became abundantly clear that the use of two 7-point scales could be noticeably annoying to the respondent. The mechanics of taking this inventory could be improved if the two response scales could be combined into one by the appropriate conjunction of response categories (e.g., 7 may stand for "always or definitely" and 1 for "never or definitely not").

It is easy for any college student or adult with high school education to see through the items. However, the emphasis in the CPS is on securing the subject's cooperation by means of appealing to his curiosity to gain knowledge about himself rather than relying on individual or institutional pressure techniques. This approach is apropos of the zeitgeist and obviates the objections emanating from the possibility of infringement upon individual rights and sensibilities. However, unlike the *Edwards Personality Inventory,* there are a number of items which a person may regard as too personal and, therefore, may not respond to them individually or, if given the choice, may not return his protocol for subsequent scoring and evaluation.

To obtain a personality profile the raw scores are converted into McCall's T scores for the two sexes separately. However, no information is provided about the shape of the raw score distributions themselves. Conversion into T scores is no guarantee of normalizing a distribution which suffers from extreme skewness or kurtosis. There is, however, ample justification for presenting separate norms for males and females since the differences between their mean performances are significant on 9 of the 10 scales. The norms are "based on 365 male and 362 female university students, their friends and family members, and some other university-connected individuals." No further information is provided about the normative subjects, although one would wish to know the number of students and nonstudents, their respective age and socioeconomic status and, especially for nonstudents, their educational and occupational levels. The norms, hence, must be considered tentative and of little use outside the population of college students who readily volunteer for their professors' research studies. The manual recognizes the limitations of the normative data, but expresses the hope that those who wish to use it with other groups will develop suitable norms.

Reliability indices presented in the manual are split-half estimates corrected for double length for each of the 10 scales. Excluding the validity and response set scales—for which internal consistency indices are unimportant—the estimates are impressive, ranging between .87 and .96. However, these estimates were obtained by correlating scores on 10 positively-worded statements with those on 10 negatively-worded statements for each of the scales and, therefore, probably indicate the upperbounds of internal consistency for the various scales. A more realistic estimate of internal consistency would be obtained if correlations were computed—and, of course, corrected for double-length—for each factor between two sets of 10 items constituted as follows: any randomly selected five positively-worded statements plus their negatively-worded counterparts versus the remaining items. In addition, no information is available about the stability (test-retest) reliability of factor scores. Such information is necessary despite the usual arguments advanced against test-retest estimates, since individuals as well as institutions are more often concerned with temporally generalized characteristics than with transitory phenomena. The manual should also report the standard error of measurement for each of the scales as well as the percent of variance attributable to each factor.

Personality inventories may be divided into three classes on the basis of the emphases and procedures their authors employ in determining the goodness of the scales: (*a*) those which are oriented toward construct development and validation, (*b*) those which are concerned with predicting practical criteria, and (*c*) those which have mainly used logical or linguistic analysis to sample a particular content domain. The CPS would seem to belong in category (*a*). Since very few claims are made about the predictive usefulness of the CPS—and there is very little evidence to justify any such claims—the goodness of this inventory must be judged mainly in the context of the construct validation data, especially of the factor analytic type. The evidence presented seems to indicate satisfactory factorial validity for five (Emotional Stability, Extraversion, Empathy, Trust, and Orderliness) of the eight factors, although it would be more informative to report such indices as Tucker's [1] coefficients of congruence, based on individual item loadings, in addition to factor loadings of various FHID's obtained in several studies. The correlations with a number of biographical indices presented in the manual are helpful, but cannot provide definitive evidence

1 TUCKER, LEDYARD R. *A Method for Synthesis of Factor Analysis Studies.* Personnel Research Section Report, No. 984. Washington, D.C.: Department of the Army, 1951. Pp. 120.

regarding construct validity of the scales unless the relationships are explicitly hypothesized and empirically verified. In this regard, the CPS, as well as other instruments intended for commercial distribution and sale, must provide adequate convergent and discriminant validity data a la Campbell and Fiske.[2] Furthermore, a number of statements regarding the uses of the CPS (e.g., "an extremely high score or an extremely low score on any scale almost inevitably is accompanied by aberrations in the subject's life style") are not supported by any empirical evidence.

In view of the empirical data available so far, the following statements regarding the possible uses of the CPS seem justified: (a) As a research tool measuring some important personality constructs, it is an important paper and pencil device and may be employed with as much confidence as any other instrument of its type. (b) As a means of self-understanding and self-guidance, it may be applied to volunteer college students and adults similar in their background to the standardization group. (c) As an instrument for diagnosis or prognosis, for any group whatsoever, its application is not justified at all. Only future research with the CPS can indicate whether it should be employed as a means of self-understanding and guidance with all sorts of normal groups between 16 and 60 and whether patterns of scores on this inventory can serve as a reasonable basis of psychological diagnosis and prognosis.

[60]

★The Conservatism Scale. Ages 12 and over; 1970; "general factor underlying social attitudes" variously labeled authoritarianism, fascism, dogmatism, rigidity, perseveration, and anti-scientific attitude; 1 form (1 page); manual (16 pages); 60p per 25 tests; 50p per manual; 60p per specimen set; postage extra; [10] minutes; Glenn D. Wilson and John R. Patterson; NFER Publishing Co. Ltd. *

REFERENCES

1. WILSON, GLENN D., AND PATTERSON, JOHN R. "A New Measure of Conservatism." Brit J Social & Clin Psychol 7: 264-9 D '68. * (PA 43:15017)
2. BOSHIER, ROGER. "A Study of the Relationship Between Self-Concept and Conservatism." J Social Psychol 77(1):139-40 F '69. * (PA 43:6892)
3. PATTERSON, JOHN R., AND WILSON, GLENN D. "Anonymity, Occupation, and Conservatism." J Social Psychol 78(2): 263-6 Ag '69. * (PA 44:6-55)
4. WILSON, GLENN D., AND PATTERSON, JOHN R. "Conservatism as a Predictor of Humor Preferences." J Consult & Clin Psychol 33(3):271-4 Je '69. * (PA 43:12974)
5. BAGLEY, CHRISTOPHER; WILSON, GLENN D.; AND BOSHIER, ROGER. "The Conservatism Scale: A Factor-Structure Comparison of English, Dutch, and New Zealand Samples." J Social Psychol 81(2):267-8 Ag '70. * (PA 44:20756)
6. KISH, GEORGE B. "Familial Resemblance in Conservatism." Newsl Res Psychol 12(4):9-10 N '70. *

2 CAMPBELL, DONALD T., AND FISKE, DONALD W. "Convergent and Discriminant Validation by the Multitrait—Multimethod Matrix." Psychol B 56:81-105 Mr '59. *

7. KISH, GEORGE B.; NETTERBERG, EDWARD E.; AND LEAHY, LOUIS. "Stimulus-Seeking and Conservatism." Newsl Res Psychol 12(1):19-22 F '70. *
8. STEWART, ROBERT A. C., AND WEBSTER, ALAN C. "Scale for Theological Conservatism, and Its Personality Correlates." Percept & Motor Skills 30(3):867-70 Je '70. * (PA 44:16675)
9. WILSON, GLENN D. "Is There a General Factor in Social Attitudes? Evidence From a Factor Analysis of the Conservatism Scale." Brit J Social & Clin Psychol 9(2):101-7 Je '70. * (PA 44:16708)

[61]

Cornell Medical Index—Health Questionnaire. Ages 14 and over; 1949-56; CMI; a questionnaire for use by physicians in collecting medical and psychiatric information from patients; separate forms ('49, 4 pages) for men and women; revised manual ('56, c1949, 15 pages including sample questionnaire and diagnostic sheet); diagnostic sheet ['53, 1 page]; no data on reliability; $3 per 50 questionnaires; $1.50 per 50 diagnostic sheets; postpaid; specimen set free; French Canadian and Spanish editions available; (10-30) minutes; Keeve Brodman, Albert J. Erdmann, Jr., and Harold G. Wolff; Cornell University Medical College. *

REFERENCES

1-77. See P:49, also includes a cumulative name index to the first 77 references for this test.
78. BRODMAN, KEEVE; ERDMANN, ALBERT J., JR.; LORGE, IRVING; AND WOLFF, HAROLD G.; WITH THE TECHNICAL ASSISTANCE OF TODD H. BROADBENT. "The Cornell Medical Index: An Adjunct to Medical Interview." J Am Med Assn 140:530-4 Je 11 '49. *
79. BRODMAN, KEEVE; ERDMANN, ALBERT J., JR.; LORGE, IRVING; AND WOLFF, HAROLD G.; WITH THE TECHNICAL ASSISTANCE OF TODD H. BROADBENT. "The Cornell Medical Index-Health Questionnaire: 2, As a Diagnostic Instrument." J Am Med Assn 145:152-7 Ja 20 '51. *
80. CULPAN, R. H.; DAVIES, B. M.; AND OPPENHEIM, A. N. "Incidence of Psychiatric Illness Among Hospital Outpatients: An Application of the Cornell Medical Index." Brit Med J 5176:855-7 Mr 19 '60. *
81. BOOKBINDER, LAWRENCE J. "Follow-Up Versus Discharge Status of Psychiatric Inpatients." J Clin Psychol 18:501-3 O '62. * (PA 39:5550)
82. KOLE, DELBERT MERRILL. A Study of Intellectual and Personality Characteristics of Medical Students. Master's thesis, University of Oregon Medical School (Portland, Ore.), 1962.
83. BRUHN, JOHN G.; CHANDLER, BETTY; LYNN, THOMAS N.; AND WOLF, STEWART. "Social Characteristics of Patients With Coronary Heart Disease." Am J Med Sci 251:629-37 Je '66. *
84. KADRI, Z. N. "Personality Appraisal of Southeast Asian University Students." J Am Col Health Assn 15:131-5 D '66. *
85. ROTH, HERBERT SAMUEL. Personal and Demographic Characteristics Associated With L-I-D Response Bias of Domiciled Veterans on an Institutional Interest Inventory. Doctor's thesis, University of Kansas (Lawrence, Kan.), 1966. (DA 28:1209B)
86. VERGHESE, ABRAHAM. Some Aspects of Chest Pains After Myocardial Infarction. Doctor's thesis, University of Melbourne (Parkville, Vic., Australia), 1966.
87. RHUDICK, P. J., AND GORDON, C. "Test-Retest IQ Changes in Bright Aging Individuals." Abstract. Gerontologist 7(3, pt 2):34 S '67. * (PA 41:16550)
88. RYLE, ANTHONY. Neurosis in the Ordinary Family: A Psychiatric Survey. London: Tavistock Publications Ltd., 1967. Pp. 156. *
89. VERGHESE, ABRAHAM. "Personality Traits and Coronary Heart Disease." Editorial. Austral & N Zeal J Psychiatry 1:62-3 Je '67. *
90. KENYON, F. E. "Physique and Physical Health of Female Homosexuals." J Neurol Neurosurg & Psychiatry 31: 487-9 O '68. * (PA 44:3835)
91. KENYON, F. E. "Studies in Female Homosexuality: 6, The Exclusively Homosexual Group." Acta Psychiatrica Scandinavica 44(3):224-3" '68. * (PA 43:17634)
92. BECK, JAMES DOUGLAS. Social Role Inconsistency and General Health Symptoms. Doctor's thesis, University of North Carolina (Chapel Hill, N.C.), 1969. (DAI 31:782B)
93. BOLENDER, CHARLES L.; SWOOPE, CHARLES C.; AND SMITH, DALE E. "The Cornell Medical Index as a Prognostic Aid for Complete Denture Patients." J Prosth Dent 22(1):20-9 Jl '69. *
94. GUNDERSON, E. K. ERIC, AND ARTHUR, RANSOM J. "A Brief Mental Health Index." J Abn Psychol 74(1):100-4 F '69. * (PA 43:8451)
95. MARTIN, IRENE; MARKS, I. M.; AND GELDER, M. "Conditioned Eyelid Responses in Phobic Patients." Behav Res & Ther 7(1):115-24 F '69. * (PA 43:10066)
96. MEADOW, ARNOLD, AND BRONSON, LOUISE. "Religious Affiliation and Psychopathology in a Mexican-American Popu-

lation." *J Abn Psychol* 74(2):177–80 Ap '69. * (*PA* 43:9838)

97. MUTHARD, JOHN E., AND SALOMONE, PAUL R. "The Roles and Functions of Rehabilitation Counselors." *Rehabil Counsel B* 13(1-SP):81–165 O '69. *

98. PILOWSKY, I., AND BOND, M. R. "Pain and Its Management in Malignant Disease: Elucidation of Staff-Patient Transactions." *Psychosom Med* 31(5):400–4 S–O '69. * (*PA* 44:12806)

99. PRUESKE, ELEONOR CHARLOTTE. *Relationship Between Hostility and Health Problems in College Students.* Doctor's thesis, University of Illinois (Urbana, Ill.), 1969. (*DAI* 31:769B)

100. SHELDON, ALAN, AND HOOPER, DOUGLAS. "An Enquiry Into Health and Ill-Health and Adjustment in Early Marriage." *J Psychosom Res* 13(1):95–101 Mr '69. * (*PA* 44:3521)

101. STOUT, CLARKE; WRIGHT, MARY ANN; AND BRUHN, JOHN G. "The Cornell Medical Index in Disability Evaluation." *Brit J Prev & Social Med* 23(4):251–4 N '69. *

102. WEISS, STEPHEN M. "Psychosomatic Aspects of Symptom Patterns Among Major Surgery Patients." *J Psychosom Res* 13(1):109–12 Mr '69. * (*PA* 44:3898)

103. AGULNIK, PETER L. "The Spouse of the Phobic Patient." *Brit J Psychiatry* 117(536):59–67 Jl '70. * (*PA* 45:2697)

104. CLUM, GEORGE A.; KOLE, DELBERT M.; PLAG, JOHN A.; AND HOIBERG, ANNE. "The Stability of Cornell Medical Index Scores and Symptoms in a Military Population." *J Clin Psychol* 26(2):188–91 Ap '70. * (*PA* 44:14624)

105. GROUNDS, DAVID; DAVIES, BRIAN; AND MOWBRAY, ROBERT. "The Contraceptive Pill, Side Effects and Personality: Report of a Controlled Double Blind Trial." *Brit J Psychiatry* 116(531):169–72 F '70. * (*PA* 44:18111)

106. KALIMO, ESKO; BICE, THOMAS W.; AND HOVOSEL, MARIJA. "Cross-Cultural Analysis of Selected Emotional Questions From the Cornell Medical Index." *Brit J Prev & Social Med* 24(4):229–40 N '70. *

107. KREITMAN, NORMAN; COLLINS, JOYCE; NELSON, BARBARA; AND TROOP, JANE. "Neurosis and Marital Interaction: 1, Personality and Symptoms." *Brit J Psychiatry* 117(536):33–46 Jl '70. * (*PA* 45:2702)

108. NELSON, BARBARA; COLLINS, JOYCE; KREITMAN, NORMAN; AND TROOP, JANE. "Neurosis and Marital Interaction: 2, Time Sharing and Social Activity." *Brit J Psychiatry* 117(536):47–58 Jl '70. * (*PA* 45:2705)

109. VERGHESE, ABRAHAM. "Relationships Between the Eysenck Personality Inventory N Score, the Cornell Medical Index M–R Score, and the Psychogalvanic Reflex." *Brit J Psychiatry* 116(530):27–31 Ja '70. * (*PA* 44:21183)

EUGENE E. LEVITT, *Professor of Clinical Psychology and Director, Section of Psychology, Indiana University School of Medicine, Indianapolis, Indiana.*

The CMI is designed to be a checklist adjunct to the standard medical examination or a substitute for it. It minimizes the time spent by the physician in obtaining a medical history, and helps to avoid inadvertently overlooking significant questions. The questionnaire is obviously based on the traditional, medical review of systems with a heavy emphasis on the psychiatric. Fifty-seven of the 195 questions are devoted to moods, feelings, and habits.

The CMI was intended to be used clinically, like its psychological counterpart, the *Mooney Problem Check List.* Its developers had no direct intention to determine a total score by the usual method of assigning unit value to each item and then counting the number of "yes" responses. It would be quite enough to identify the patient whose ankles were often badly swollen, or who suffered from frequent loose bowel movements. Thus the initial validity data (*78, 79*) was concerned with demonstrating that

more symptoms could be identified by using the CMI than by the conventional medical history interview.

Nevertheless, there was always an indication that the instrument's developers gave *some* consideration to the significance of a quantitative score based on unit value per question. The 1949 manual noted that if the identified symptoms were "scattered throughout the four pages of the CMI the medical problem is likely to be diffused, usually involving an emotional disturbance." This concept was extended in two further investigations (*1, 2*) which demonstrated that psychiatric patients obtained higher scores on the CMI than medical patients, who in turn obtained higher scores than non-patients. A similar finding for naval personnel was reported more recently by Arthur, et al. (*53*).

The fact that the total CMI score can be used as an index of emotional adjustment is not at all surprising. Psychiatric patients as a group are characterized by a high incidence of physical symptomatology. The clusters of physical and psychological symptoms on the CMI itself correlate about .60 (*101, 102*), approximately the same correlation as reported between the total CMI score and Taylor's Manifest Anxiety Scale (*102*).

The use of the CMI as a general psychiatric evaluation instrument is highly questionable. When only a total score is desired, there are any number of measures available which are more easily and quickly administered. In fact, a study by Gunderson and Arthur (*94*) strongly suggests that a short form of the CMI containing either 14 or 15 items will do as well in distinguishing psychiatric inpatients as the whole index.

The CMI is face valid as a symptom checklist. It is probably useful as a conserver of physician hours, but it is administratively unfeasible as a quantitative measure of psychological adjustment.

DAVID T. LYKKEN, *Professor of Psychiatry and Psychology, University of Minnesota, Minneapolis, Minnesota.*

This questionnaire, now more than 20 years old, was designed to be given by physicians in general practice to new patients and to provide a convenient starting point for getting a standardized medical history. It consists of 195 "yes-no" questions; e.g., "Are your joints often painfully swollen?" "Have you ever had anything seriously wrong with your genitals (privates)?" "Do you feel alone and sad at a party?" About one-third of the items are intended to tap psychiatric problems while the others are concerned with the conventional categories of medical complaint (ENT, cardiovascular, gastrointestinal, etc.). The number of "yes" answers in each category is supposed to be the physician's clue to potential problem areas.

As a psychometric instrument, the CMI is old-fashioned and naive in the extreme and the literature indicates that it has not been taken very seriously for this purpose. It no doubt could be shown to be highly loaded on "neuroticism" or "ego resiliency" or whatever one chooses to call the first factor of the MMPI and one could certainly expect to be able to derive a hypochondriasis scale from it as well. But there are obviously better alternatives available for serious psychiatric screening and one cannot imagine a reason for choosing the CMI for research or clinical psychological purposes. For the purpose for which it was intended, to be given by a GP's nurse to a new patient to facilitate the doctor's taking a medical history, it may be quite useful.

[62]

★Current and Past Psychopathology Scales. Psychiatric patients and nonpatients; 1966–68; CAPPS; the *Psychiatric Evaluation Form—Diagnostic Version* and the *Psychiatric History Schedule* have been stapled together and given a new title (the 2 component parts are no longer available as separates); rating scale and optional interview guide for use in diagnosing mental illness if any; judgments based upon various sources of information (subject, informant, case records, nurse's reports, etc.); the PEF-D section deals with the patient's current functioning over the past month, the PHS with his past functioning from age 12 up to the past month; computerized psychiatric diagnosis (DIAGNO II) produces for each subject 1 of 46 possible diagnoses, using the official nomenclature of the American Psychiatric Association for 44 of the diagnoses; Form C50 ('68, 11 pages, scales only); Form C51 ('68, 25 pages, scales and interview schedule); no manual; typewritten data sheets; for validity data, see *1* below; separate answer sheets must be used; 25¢ per test; 10¢ per answer sheet; postage extra; specimen set free; fee for editing, coding, key punching, and verifying protocol, 25¢ per subject; computerized psychiatric diagnosis (see *1* below) is available; (15–30) minutes for scales only, (60–120) minutes for scales with interview guide; Robert L. Spitzer and Jean Endicott; Biometrics Research, New York State Psychiatric Institute. *

REFERENCES

1. See P:53A.
2. MORROW, GEORGE M., JR. "Discussion: An Internist Assesses Future Computer Use." *Am J Psychiatry* 125(7, sup): 34–6 Ja '69. * (*PA* 43:9840)
3. MELROSE, J. PETER; STROEBEL, CHARLES F.; AND GLUECK, BERNARD C. "Diagnosis of Psychopathology Using Stepwise

Multiple Discriminant Analysis, 1." *Comprehen Psychiatry* 11(1):43–50 Ja '70. * (*PA* 45:4544)
4. SCHACHTER, JOSEPH. "Development of a Screening Questionnaire for Schizophrenia: A Pilot Study." *Arch Gen Psychiatry* 23(1):30–4 Jl '70. * (*PA* 44:18919)

WILLIAM J. EICHMAN, *Associate Professor of Psychology, The University of North Carolina; and Director of Psychology Service, John Umstead Hospital; Chapel Hill, North Carolina.*

The nature and use of the *Current and Past Psychopathology Scales* is very complex. Description itself has to be lengthy in order to communicate adequately. Consequently an overview will be presented first with description and documentation to follow.

Spitzer and Endicott's purpose in this endeavor is to provide a totally reliable procedure for establishing psychiatric diagnosis. Given a particular input (ratings on the CAPPS), the computer will always arrive at the same diagnosis. The purpose is highly laudable. Psychiatry's status has been much impaired over the years by the fact that so much subjectivity was present in the diagnostic process and so little reliability could be demonstrated. This fact alone impeded the development of adequate research and eventually led to a devaluation of the utility of diagnosis. Psychologists, in particular, have been highly critical of diagnostic criteria and have largely discarded these in favor of more behaviorally definable measures. Thus, it is interesting that a computer program could be derived which appears to function with approximately the same effectiveness as the individual psychiatrist who is making subjective decisions and weighting different variables in a manner that he could not always make explicit even to his own colleagues. As an exercise in learning the diagnostic process, every psychiatric resident could study this with profit.

At this point in our history, the disease/medical models of disturbed behavior are under severe attack. We find that even the defenders of the status quo devote less time to a rigorous diagnostic process and, instead, devote more time to treatment. We might wonder if Spitzer and Endicott's technique did not arrive 20 years too late. Had such a methodology been available earlier, it could have made psychiatric diagnosis more "respectable." Research with diagnostic groups could have been sharpened to the extent that our knowledge would be greater at the present time. Personally, I see considerable utility for the approach among those researchers who intend using psychiatric diagnosis as a defining characteristic for an experimental group. In the first place, they will be able to describe the sample much more completely than is typical, i.e., mean scores on the individual scales and mean scores on the summary scales (described below). The discerning reader and future research worker will be able to say, "Their schizophrenics are the same as (or different from) my schizophrenics." The more casual reader will also find comfort in the fact that the diagnoses in this instance have greater consensual validity than is typical.

It should be noted early that this is a time-consuming, laborious task for the clinical investigator. The time necessary for making the 171 judgments is somewhat imposing but it is dwarfed when one considers the depth of information needed about the patient. Although no esoteric information is needed, although all this information is a logical part of a "complete" psychiatric work-up, it seems doubtful that many psychiatrists or researchers are this rigorous at present. To those who are, I recommend the technique.

Attention should be paid to the *Current and Past Psychopathology Scales* itself. The authors have done a consummately fine piece of work here and I feel that this achievement deserves to be considered equally important as their goal of using these ratings as input for a diagnostic statement. First is the creative use of past history data as a basis for making ratings. This has a tremendous advantage over other psychiatric rating scales which use immediate behavior alone. Second, it is possible to use data supplied by sources other than the patient himself. Reported reliabilities for individual scales have a median of .90 (intraclass correlation). Given a particular set of data regarding a particular patient, it seems apparent that raters are in high agreement with each other. The ratings have been factored and the printout for each case contains summary scores for 8 "current" scales and 16 "past" scales. These scores might have greater utility for fine grain psychiatric research than diagnosis alone. Also they could be used as input for developing programs aimed at purposes other than diagnosis.

I personally rated three of my long-term psychotherapy cases and submitted them for the program. In each instance, the predicted diagnosis was identical with or similar to my own judgment and to those of hospital psychia-

trists. The process of rating was an enjoyable one. The scales are written well and do justice to the complexity of abnormal behavior over a long span of time. There is little redundancy and little omission of data that would be critical over a broad spectrum of cases. As stated above, it is a fine job. For those who are gathering information from the patient for the specific purpose of making the ratings, an excellent interview guide is presented.

In the area of psychiatric diagnosis, reliability and validity indices completely merge. There is no criterion for DIAGNO II except the diagnosis of one or more live psychiatrists. In the fact that DIAGNO II agrees with psychiatric diagnosis as well as psychiatrists making independent judgments, the instrument has achieved its purpose. It should be noted, however, that DIAGNO II has had limited field trial; the only reported study being conducted in a variety of New York settings among psychiatrists of similar theoretical training. The authors report in an informal communication that other investigators are obtaining similar results.

The methodology of DIAGNO II is quite complicated. Input consists of age and sex plus judgments from 94 scales in a "logical decision tree model similar to the differential diagnostic process used in internal medicine." Output is one of the 44 official diagnoses from the 1952 American Psychiatric Association nomenclature. In addition, two unofficial diagnoses are included: "nonspecific illness with mild symptomatology" and "not ill." An explanation of the "decision tree model" seems appropriate; the following is extracted from the authors' paper (*1*):

A flow chart which schematizes the basic logic implicit in the APA nomenclature and used in DIAGNO II is shown in figure 1. Thus the first question (shown by a circle with a 1 in it) is whether or not there are signs suggestive of an organic brain disorder. If not, the next question (shown by a circle with a 12 in it) is whether there are signs suggestive of a psychotic disorder. Then the transient situational disorders, the sociopathic disorders, the remaining personality disorders, the neuroses, the psychophysiologic reactions, mental retardation, and the diagnosis of *nonspecific illness* are considered. If all of these are eliminated, the patient is diagnosed as not ill.

Each question asked by the computer program is defined in terms of scale score cutoff levels and logical operators. Some decisions are simple. For example, question 1 (organicity?) is merely: "Is Disorientation-Memory (current state) less than 4?" If true, go to question 12. If false, go to question 2. Other decisions are very complex. For example, question 12 (psychosis?) considers evidence of current delusions, hallucinations, inappropriateness, speech disorganization, agitation-excitement, elation, grandiosity, retardation-lack of emotion, impairment in daily routine, evidence of past delusions, hallucinations, and speech disorganization, and an index determined by summing the scores across nine scales describing psychopathology characteristic of patients with chronic schizophrenia.

The flow chart provided by the authors makes this more clear but the precise nature and application of the program is very difficult to follow because of its complexity. For any wide scale application, the use of the computer is entirely necessary. The authors are to be commended for their painstaking care in the construction of this program. It amply documents the complexity of the oft criticized but little understood process of psychiatric diagnosis. Psychologists who are often appalled by the unspecified nature of the input in the conventional diagnostic process can profitably study this with care.

The authors' study provides considerable additional but complex data. An example lies in the critical area of agreement among diagnoses; obviously some nonidentical diagnoses are logically closer than others. Thus, a "weighted kappa" is used as an index of agreement but this takes some understanding in itself. The authors report a tendency for DIAGNO II to diagnose "not ill" more frequently than the psychiatrists. Agreement with psychiatrists is highest for the "nonspecific illness" and "not ill" group while lowest for the personality trait or pattern disturbances. Data from unpublished studies also indicate considerable discriminant power for the summary scores among major diagnostic groups.

It seems that this instrument is an excellent addition to the tools available for psychiatric and psychological research. Most needed at the present time are additional studies, conducted in a variety of settings and by investigators not connected with the Spitzer group. Because of its time-consuming nature, the instrument is not viewed as especially helpful in the daily diagnostic activities of most psychiatrists. It does appear to have considerable training potential, however, for psychiatric residency programs which are dedicated to the principle of accurate diagnosis.

RAYMOND D. FOWLER, JR., *Professor of Psychology and Chairman of the Department, University of Alabama, University, Alabama.*

CAPPS is a standardized interview form, on the basis of which the authors can provide a computerized output consisting of a psychiatric diagnosis and/or a rating on a variety of "scales" which represent dimensions of disturbance in psychological functioning.

The interview form itself consists of 171 items which are rated on a six-point scale. The questions represent a rather thorough coverage of most of the areas usually covered in a psychiatric evaluation. The form consists of one set of items which explores the present status of the subject and another set which examines the subject's history (prior to one month before the rating). The scales can be completed retrospectively on the basis of previous interviews, case records, and/or other information, or immediately on the basis of a single interview. The interview may be conducted by someone other than a psychiatrist, presumably even by a well instructed technician. An interview guide is provided, which gives carefully considered lead questions to assure thorough coverage of all areas of concern. The interview guide is optional, but the rater attempting to complete the CAPPS on the basis of a single interview would probably conserve time by following the guide faithfully. Otherwise, he would risk having to return and request further elaboration on an item for which he had not acquired sufficient information to rate.

No do-it-yourself scoring system is provided with CAPPS. The user has no alternative to sending the protocol to the authors for processing. The time factor could be critical if CAPPS were to be used to obtain information for immediate clinical decisions, but it is unlikely to receive extensive use in this way in its present form. All he loses, however, is time: it is doubtful that he could process it "in-house" for less than he would pay for the processing service, even if he had the necessary computer programs.

The two types of output require separate consideration. As indicated, the CAPPS may be scored to yield a psychiatric diagnosis and numerical scores on 106 scales which cover current and past functioning.

The most interesting aspect of the output is the psychiatric diagnosis. Although the hazards inherent in predicting a criterion so unreliable as psychiatric diagnosis are well known, the development of an automated method for assigning diagnoses is far from a trivial accomplishment. Whether or not one feels that the classification of patients into unstable and unreliable categories is a productive activity, the fact is that many thousands of professional man-hours are spent doing just that, and the possibility of having this activity, even if it is a ritualistic one, palmed off on a digital computer has a certain attraction.

More importantly, the system represents an excellent example of the simulation of clinical judgment. The computer program utilizes 94 of the scale-items and, by a method of successive examination of the items known to be related to various diagnostic categories, selects the most probable diagnosis from a total of 46 alternatives (44 standard APA classifications, one "not-ill" and one "non-specific illness"). The system, known as DIAGNO II, produces diagnoses which agree with a clinician's diagnoses as well as the agreement between two clinicians. The mean level of agreement, which is expressed in terms of kappa (proportion of agreement corrected for expected chance agreement), is .45 for DIAGNO II with psychiatrist, and also .45 for psychiatrist with psychiatrist. The ability of DIAGNO II to perform the diagnostic task as well as a skilled psychiatrist should give clinicians even more reason to question seriously the expenditure of interview and case conference time in formulating a differential diagnosis.

The second type of output, the print-out of scale scores, represents a more doubtful contribution. The Current and History sections of the CAPPS consist of 41 and 130 items respectively, each of which is rated on the six-point scale from "not present" to "extreme." On the basis of factor analysis, these have been reduced to 28 and 78 "scales." Some of these scales have as few as 2 items and none more than 11. Inasmuch as the items are based on quite subjective judgments, the brevity of the scales does not lead to much confidence in their stability. Nor do the scales represent any major transformation of the primary ratings on the constituent scales. In a short scale, the chances are that more information would be lost than gained by grouping. Nevertheless, it is reasonable to assume that using the questions and the interview guide would lead to a more thorough coverage of topics and a more objective method of recording observations than the usual unstructured psychiatric interview. As a means of providing new information to the clinician, these scales have relatively little to offer, but they could, to the extent that they are reliable, provide an excellent basis for comparing and

grouping patients. The preliminary reliability data, although sketchy and incomplete, suggest that the ratings, at least when done by two raters on the same interview, are quite reliable.

The utility of CAPPS must be considered in the light of the modest claims of its developers. They suggest that the CAPPS might be useful in the selection or description of subjects for research, in treatment evaluation, and in the comparison of different procedures for arriving at a computer diagnosis. While reserving judgment about the ultimate usefulness of CAPPS as a practical clinical tool, it would be difficult to dispute its success in meeting the authors' claims.

[63]

★Defense Mechanism Inventory. Ages 16 and over; 1968–69; DMI; for research use only; 5 scores: turning against object, projection, principalization, turning against self, reversal; separate forms for males, females, ('68, 11 pages); manual ('69, reprint of 3 below); profile ['69, 1 page] for each form; separate answer sheets must be used; $2 per 10 tests; $2 per 50 answer sheets; $2 per 50 profiles; 50¢ per Xerox copy of manual; $1.50 per specimen set (without manual); postpaid; (30–40) minutes; David Ihilevich and Goldine C. Gleser; Goldine C. Gleser. *

REFERENCES
1. COHEN, DAVID BENJAMIN. Frequency of Dream Recall Estimated by Three Methods and Related to Defense Preference and Anxiety Level. Doctor's thesis, University of Michigan (Ann Arbor, Mich.), 1968. (DA 29:3083B)
2. IHILEVICH, DAVID. The Relationship of Defense Mechanisms to Field Dependence-Independence. Doctor's thesis, University of Cincinnati (Cincinnati, Ohio), 1968. (DA 29:1843B)
3. GLESER, GOLDINE C., AND IHILEVICH, DAVID. "An Objective Instrument for Measuring Defense Mechanisms." J Consult & Clin Psychol 33(1):51–60 F '69. * (PA 43:11347)
4. BOGO, NORMAN; WINGET, CAROLYN; AND GLESER, GOLDINE C. "Ego Defenses and Perceptual Styles." Percept & Motor Skills 30(2):599–605 Ap '70. * (PA 46:6842)

JAMES A. WALSH, Professor of Psychology and Statistics, Iowa State University, Ames, Iowa.

Construction of the DMI was based upon the assumption that the major purpose of ego-defense mechanisms is resolution of conflicts between the perceptions and the values of an individual. A set of five "clusters" of defenses was hypothesized to be both comprehensive enough to account for the processes by which conflict is resolved and parsimonious enough to yield relatively independent measures.

The mechanisms of Turning against Object (TAO), Projection (PRO), Principalization (PRN), Turning against Self (TAS), and Reversal (REV) are measured by means of 12 stories, 2 for each of the conflict areas of authority, independence, masculinity (male form only), femininity (female form only), competition, and situational. Each individual taking this paper-and-pencil inventory reads the ten stories appropriate to his sex and responds to 4 questions following each story. Each question probes one of the four areas of : proposed actual behavior, impulsive behavior in fantasy, thoughts, and feelings. It must be answered by selecting both the alternative (from among five) which is most representative of the individual's behavior and the alternative which is least representative. The five responses of course represent the five defense mechanism clusters. Responses are differentially weighted and summed across questions and stories to obtain five scores, one for each cluster. The scores are ipsative since only one alternative can be chosen as most representative and one as least representative for each question. The clustering of stories into conflict areas was supported by high interrater agreement among a small group of expert judges, but the matching of responses to defense mechanisms was less than completely satisfactory for TAO and PRO.

In their journal article which serves as the manual for this test, the authors present convincing evidence that the ipsative scoring procedure affects primarily the elevation of the profile of scale scores and not the relationships among them. It does not appear to restrict variability enough to lower internal-consistency-based estimates of reliability below those found in most personality scales of similar length, i.e., an average of about .75. Stability coefficients for the scales range from .69 to .93, but are questionable because they are based upon small, atypically highly educated samples over a period of only one week.

Norms are presented in the form of means and standard deviations computed for males and females separately from three groups: college sophomores (N = 406) ; a "general adult" group (N = 114) ; and psychiatric outpatients (N = 234). The general adult sample was "unsystematically selected" and appears to have been strongly biased toward the upper end of the socioeconomic scale. As the authors noted, because TAO, PRN, and REV were correlated with age, and because the norm groups differed appreciably in age, observed differences between groups on these scales are probably largely a function simply of age.

A conflicting and, at best, partially confirmatory potpourri of studies was cited by the authors in support of the construct validity of their scales. For example, the correlations

among the scales portray a remarkably stable patterning across the three norm groups, but the several correlations are only loosely in line with predictions based on various theories of ego psychology. The unsystematic correlations of the DMI scales with MMPI scales do not strengthen the case for the validity of the DMI, but they do bolster the authors' claim to have minimized the effects of social desirability as defined by Edwards. However, the correlations of the TAO, PRO, and REV scales with the MMPI Lie Scale raise the possibility of a fairly pervasive approval-seeking set of the Crowne-Marlowe variety. In a more positive vein, predictions from theory about use of defense mechanisms by alcoholics coincided nicely with empirical findings, as did predictions of the relationships of TAS, REV, TAO, and PRO to measures of field dependency. Studies of defense mechanisms in relation to dream recall and time in psychotherapy generated very reasonable, but largely *post hoc,* interpretations.

In summary, the DMI has a number of problems. It rests on a less than rock-ribbed theoretical foundation. Keying is not unequivocally satisfactory for two of the five scales. The reliabilities are only moderately good. The norms are scanty and perhaps somewhat misleading. Response set contamination appears to be a possibility. The validity data are promising but not thoroughly supportive of the authors' contentions. Compared to other tests of defense mechanisms, however, the DMI rates well. It is sounder than any instrument of similar breadth, such as Haan's MMPI-based scales.[1] It cannot compare with the Byrne's Repression-Sensitization Scale [2] in terms of predictive validity, but it covers a broader set of mechanisms and is much less suspect because of social desirability considerations. All in all, use of the DMI for routine clinical assessment is obviously not justified at the present time, but it has equally obvious promise as a research instrument.

[64]

★The Demos D Scale: An Attitude Scale for the Identification of Dropouts. Grades 7–12; 1965–70; DDS; also called *Demos Dropout Scale;* 5 attitude scores : teachers, education, peers and parents, school behavior, total; 1 form ('65, 4 pages) ; manual ('70, 7 pages plus test) ; no data on reliability ; $7.50 per 25 tests and manual ; $6.50 per 25 tests ; $1.50 per manual ;

1 HAAN, NORMA. "Coping and Defense Mechanisms Related to Personality Inventories." *J Consult Psychol* 29:373–8 Ag '65. *
2 BYRNE, DONN; BARRY, JAMES; AND NELSON, DON. "Relation of the Revised Repression-Sensitization Scale to Measures of Self-Description." *Psychol Rep* 13:323–34 O '63. *

postpaid; (15–40) minutes; George D. Demos; Western Psychological Services. *

JOHN R. BRAUN, *Professor of Psychology and Chairman of the Department, University of Bridgeport, Bridgeport, Connecticut.*

The *Demos D Scale* consists of 29 statements with which the student indicates his degree of agreement by choosing one of five response categories: nearly always, most of the time, sometimes, very few times, nearly never; thereby earning from one to five points. The basis for keying of the items is logical rather than empirical, and is such as to make high scores supposedly associated with high dropout potential. For example, five points are earned by responding "nearly never" to the item "Teachers care about their students."

The publisher's 1970–1971 catalog describes the DDS as "widely used." The reviewer has mixed feelings about this claim. If not factually based, it represents deplorable misrepresentation. However, if the DDS is in fact widely used, we have pathetic naiveté on the part of numerous test purchasers.

To document the above, be advised that here is a device for which the manual presents absolutely no empirical data on reliability. We are told that Riker's researches in 1944 and 1945 "indicate that a logical approach to the development of attitudinal scales, such as the DDS, had retest reliability coefficients of correlation ranging from +.50 to +.86." Unfortunately, this statement still leaves us without data on the reliability of the device in hand.

In a similar way, not a single validity coefficient is presented. No norms are provided, although there are tables giving means for both the responses to the 29 individual items and to the total inventory. These tables represent performance of one nondropout group (N = 105 boys and girls; sex ratio not given), one group of 30 boys in a juvenile hall, and one group of dropouts (N = 30 boys and 12 girls). The manual states that there are "large mean significant differences between the dropout and non-drop groups." Specific *p* values are not given for these comparisons, and the amount of overlap between the distributions for the contrasted groups is not mentioned.

Additional tables provide a means of translating DDS scores into the clinical probability of the student dropping out of school. For total score this is done for five different score ranges, and involves probabilities of either 5, 25, 50, 70, or 90 chances in 100. The manual warns that DDS scores should not be used by themselves for definitive diagnostic purposes. This caution is eminently appropriate, since not a shred of empirical data is advanced to illustrate any basis for the probability tables. Likewise, the possibility that responses to the DDS might be faked is never considered.

In brief, the fundamental psychometric data needed in any test manual to enable one to evaluate the extent to which a device achieves what is claimed for it, are simply not presented for the DDS. There is, therefore, no justification for anyone making operational use of this device. As a matter of fact, there was no justification for the test author and test publisher to release the device commercially. Hopefully, both will take to heart the *Standards for Educational and Psychological Tests and Manuals* prior to any revision.

LEONARD V. GORDON, *Professor of Educational Psychology and Statistics, State University of New York at Albany, Albany, New York.*

The DDS consists of 29 school-related statements to each of which the student specifies his level of agreement on a five-point scale. Four area scores, as well as a total score based on their sum, are obtained. In the preparation of the DDS only those statements that had the unanimous agreement of seven judges regarding their degree of favorableness or unfavorableness were used. The 29 statements were categorized into the four areas by an undescribed method of analysis. Item analysis data from a very small sample of Mexican-American and Anglo-American students were then employed for the preparation of the final form.

The following summarizes the author's position regarding validity and reliability: "The primary purpose of the DDS is to determine verbalized opinions which reflect attitudes presumably related to dropping out of school. When such opinions are obtained, the DDS has accomplished its purpose, and can be said to possess validity" and "in the DDS validity and reliability are synonymous, and can be considered to be *high*, since DDS attitude responses are readily obtained."

The DDS *is* capable of obtaining "verbalized opinions" in the form of responses on the test booklet and some of these responses may be related to dropping out of school, although this relationship has not been adequately demonstrated by the author. However, since the DDS is scored, and the author provides procedures for using these scores, it is necessary to go beyond the fact that students *do* respond to the items in assessing the reliability and validity of the instrument. Traditionally, this type of appraisal is statistical. The author, while seemingly aware of this, provides no data on which such an appraisal can be made. For example, he cites reliability coefficients for *other* attitude scales as evidence for the presumed reliability of the DDS. He presents total score means for small samples of students and dropouts, referring to the differences as "significant," yet includes neither standard deviations nor a test of significance. Considering, among other things, the limited sample employed for the original item analysis, the statistical adequacy of the DDS for more generalized application can hardly be accepted on faith.

The section describing the interpretation and uses of the DDS is somewhat strange. Two methods of score interpretation are mentioned. In the first, the student's score is to be compared with those of the standardization groups —yet no information regarding the score distributions of the latter exists in the manual. In the second, the examiner may interpret a score in terms of the probability of the student dropping out of school. Tables developed on the basis of "clinical experiences with the DDS" are provided for this purpose. The meaningfulness of these tables is open to serious question. For example, for the total score, which is called "the most important DDS datum," a score in the range of 0 to 20 represents 5 chances in 100 of dropping out of school. The lowest possible total score on the DDS is 29.

The DDS has nothing to recommend its use for any professional purpose. Not only is its supporting material technically deficient, but little care appears to have gone into its preparation.

[65]

★Depression Adjective Check Lists. Grades 9–16 and adults; 1967; DACL; Forms A, B, C, D, E, F, G, (1 page); manual (16 pages); $3.50 per 25 tests; 75¢ per scoring stencil; $2.25 per specimen set; postage extra; (3–5) minutes; Bernard Lubin; Educational and Industrial Testing Service. *

REFERENCES

1–4. See P:57.
5. FOGEL, MAX L.; CURTIS, GEORGE C.; KORDASZ, FLORENCE; AND SMITH, WILLIAM G. "Judges' Ratings, Self-Ratings and Checklist Report of Affects." *Psychol Rep* 19:299–307 Ag '66. * (PA 40:12450)
6. LUBIN, BERNARD. "Fourteen Brief Depression Adjective Checklists." *Arch Gen Psychiatry* 15:205–8 Ag '66. * (PA 40:11201)
7. LEWINSOHN, PETER M., AND ATWOOD, GEORGE E. "Depression: A Clinical-Research Approach: The Case of Mrs. G." *Psychother Theory Res & Prac* 6(3):166–71 su '69. * (PA 44:3745)

LEONARD D. GOODSTEIN, *Professor of Psychology and Director of Professional Training in Psychology, University of Cincinnati, Cincinnati, Ohio.*

Since depression is probably the most common of the psychopathological conditions, for the past four decades there have been a number of attempts to develop a psychometric instrument for estimating depression.[1] The *Depression Adjective Check Lists* are clearly the most psychometrically sophisticated and potentially useful instruments of this type currently available.

There are seven different forms of the DACL, identified as Forms A through G. Each of the first four forms consist of 32 self-descriptive adjectives, while the last three forms each include 34 such adjectives. The form contains spaces for the respondent to give his name, age, sex, the date, and the highest grade he completed in school in addition to a box which is to be checked for each adjective which the respondent regards as descriptive of "how you feel now—Today." The form, which can be self-administering, can be completed by most persons within three to five minutes. Scoring for all seven forms is accomplished by use of a single cardboard overlay stencil and the score for each list consists of the total number of "plus" or depressive adjectives checked (such as "wilted," "miserable," or "gloomy") added to the total number of "minus" or positive adjectives *not* checked (such as "safe," "gay," or "lighthearted"). There is some possibility for confusion about the scoring of "minus" adjectives by clerical personnel which can be counteracted by careful training of scorers.

Norms are provided, in the form of means and standard deviations, for samples of 856 students (high school, college, and graduate), 61 senior citizens, 78 adolescent delinquents, and several groups of psychiatric patients (N's ranging from 15 to 100). Standard score equivalents for DACL raw scores, separately by sex, are also provided but these are based upon the student sample only which reduces their usefulness. The author reports in a personal com-

1 JASPER, HERBERT H. "The Measurement of Depression-Elation and Its Relation to a Measure of Introversion-Extroversion." *J Abn & Social Psychol* 25:307–18 O–D '30. *

munication that norms based on a national probability sample collected by the National Opinion Research Council are being prepared. The availability of these norms will greatly enhance the clinical usefulness of the DACL.

The DACL were empirically derived from a pool of 171 adjectives using the initial responses of 95 neuropsychiatric patients who had been rated as either "marked" or "severely" depressed in a psychiatric interview and the responses of a normal control group of 279 which had been matched on the basis of age and education. Lists A through D were developed using female subjects, 48 patients and 179 controls, while lists E through G were based on the data obtained from the male subjects, 47 patients and 100 normals. Those adjectives which statistically significantly ($p < .01$ for the males and $p < .001$ for the females) discriminated the patient responses from those of the normals were included in the final lists. The seven published lists were balanced so that lists A through D each consist of 22 "plus" adjectives and 10 "minus" adjectives while lists E through G have 22 "plus" adjectives and 12 "minus" to make the differentiating power of the lists similar. It should be noted that, as a result of this procedure, lists A through D have no overlapping items and lists E through G have none either, but there are overlapping items between these two sets of lists.

The intercorrelations among the lists were obtained by administering all seven lists, in scrambled order, to a new group of normal subjects. The obtained inter-list correlations ranged from .80 to .93, indicating that the lists are essentially comparable. Further, the intercorrelations among those lists with overlapping items were not different from those that are independent in content.

The manual presents an impressive amount of cross-validation data. Patients diagnosed as depressed obtain significantly higher scores on the DACL than do patients with other psychiatric disorders. Those patients with other psychiatric diagnoses, in turn, obtain higher DACL scores than do normal control subjects. The normal males, however, were significantly lower than the non-depressed male patients only on lists E through G, the lists originally developed with male subjects. Also there is clear evidence that females, in all three groups, obtain higher DACL scores than do the equivalent male groups, suggesting that lists A through D

might be more discriminating with females and lists E through G might be more effective with males, a caution not directly suggested by the author.

Fogel (5), in a study cited in the manual, reported a correlation of .79 between the ratings of an experienced psychiatrist and DACL scores, a correlation of .59 between the pooled ratings of two psychiatric residents and DACL scores, and a correlation of .95 between patient's self ratings of depression and DACL scores. The manual further reports that depressed patients score significantly higher on the DACL than do psychiatric patients diagnosed as having a personality disorder, psychoneurosis, or schizophrenia. Further, the manual reports consistently sensible correlations between DACL scores and those obtained from a number of other paper-and-pencil psychological inventories. For example, as one should expect, the highest correlation with the several clinical scales of the MMPI was the .57 obtained between the Depression scale and the DACL.

The internal consistency of the DACL ranges from .79 to .90, depending upon which form is used and the sex of the subjects. The split-half reliabilities range from .82 to .93 for normals and .86 and .93 for patients, again depending upon the form used and the sex of the respondents. The data presented suggest that, despite the brevity of each of the several forms, adequate reliability has been established.

From the foregoing it should be clear that the DACL has been successful in meeting the author's intention of providing a brief, reliable, and valid self-report measure of depression. It appears to this reviewer that the DACL is the most psychometrically sound of the several brief, self-report measures of depression now available and that the development of additional normative data will even further enhance this usefulness.

Douglas M. McNair, *Professor of Psychiatry, Boston University School of Medicine, Boston, Massachusetts.*

The DACL consists of two sets of parallel forms of adjective checklist measures of depressed affect. Set 1 includes four forms (A, B, C, D) each of which is 32 items in length. Set 2 includes three forms (E, F, G) each of which is 34 items in length. There is no item overlap between forms within the same set, but item overlap between forms in different sets ranges from 12 to 31 percent. Adjectives were selected for the Set 1 forms because they discriminated between normal women and female psychiatric patients rated as "markedly" or "severely" depressed. The items for the Set 2 forms were selected because they discriminated between similar groups of males. Crossvalidation studies have shown depressed patients of both sexes to differ significantly from normals on all seven checklists. However, the normal and patient groups employed in both the test development and the crossvalidation differed markedly in age and education as well as in degree of depressed affect.

Split-half and parallel form reliabilities appear quite satisfactory. The manual provides separate norms (T scores) for male and female normals. It is doubtful that these norms will prove of much value to most users because the normative groups are described only as a collection of high school, college and graduate students. Means and sigmas are presented for various patient samples and these should be helpful in interpreting checklist scores.

A major criticism of the DACL is that the author has completely ignored the factor analytic studies of mood and affective states. Other investigators [1] have found many of the adjectives included in the DACL to measure affective states other than depression. Other DACL items have been found by others to be factorially complex. No evidence is presented to indicate that the DACL is differentially sensitive to a depressed affective state as opposed to other affective states of the individual. The reviewer would interpret DACL scores as reflecting a complex and unknown combination of unpleasant affects, including depression, fatigue, lack of vigor, bewilderment and unfriendliness.

Various forms of the DACL correlate significantly with other measures of depression such as the MMPI D-scale, the Beck Inventory of Depression, Zung's *Self-Rating Depression Scale,* global ratings by clinicians and self-ratings. Typically, however, the DACL shares only from 10 to 30 percent of the variance with these other measures, which is about what most existing measures of depression seem to have in common. Clearly we need better definitions

1 BORGATTA, EDGAR F. "Mood, Personality, and Interaction." *J General Psychol* 64:105–37 Ja '61. *
McNAIR, DOUGLAS M., AND LORR, MAURICE. "An Analysis of Mood in Neurotics." *J Abn & Social Psychol* 69:620–7 D '64. *
NOWLIS, VINCENT, AND NOWLIS, HELEN H. "The Description and Analysis of Mood." *Ann N Y Acad Sci* 65:345–55 N 2 '56. *

of the domains of depressed affect and symptomatology and better separation of these domains from other types of affects and symptoms.

The manual suggests many uses for the DACL. Most of these are repeated measures applications, such as the measurement of psychiatric treatment effects. Only two repeated measures applications, however, are cited in the validity data, and in only one of these was the DACL shown to be sensitive to change. Considering all these limitations the DACL should be restricted to research uses, a restriction not suggested in the manual.

[66]

★**Devereux Adolescent Behavior Rating Scale.** Normal and emotionally disturbed children ages 13–18; 1967; DABRS; problem behaviors; 12 factor scores (unethical behavior, defiant-resistive, domineering-sadistic, heterosexual interest, hyperactive expansive, poor emotional control, need approval and dependency, emotional distance, physical inferiority-timidity, schizoid withdrawal, bizarre speech and cognition, bizarre action), 3 cluster scores (inability to delay, paranoid thought, anxious self-blame), 11 item scores (persecution, plotting, bodily concern, external influences, compulsive acts, avoids competition, withdrawn, socialization, peer dominance, physical coordination, distraction); 1 form (7 pages); manual (55 pages); $3.75 per 25 scales; $1 per manual; $4.50 per 25 scales and manual; sample copy of scale free; postpaid; (15) minutes; George Spivack, Jules Spotts, and Peter E. Haimes; Devereux Foundation Press. *

REFERENCE

1. See P:60.

CARL F. JESNESS, *Senior Behavioral Research Analyst, California Youth Authority, Sacramento, California.*

In the authors' words, the *Devereux Adolescent Behavior Rating Scale* was designed as a means for "describing and communicating the overt behavior symptoms which help define the total clinical picture of disturbed adolescents." The scale is not intended to provide a measure of personality traits, but to profile 15 problem behavior dimensions characteristic of youngsters aged 13 to 18.

In selecting items for inclusion, an attempt was made to cover the broad spectrum of problem behaviors that may be found among typical adolescents, and to define these items in terms that refer to immediately observable behavioral events. The items came from a perusal of relevant literature, from interviews with clinicians experienced in working with problem adolescents, and from a survey of the clinical records of institutionalized youngsters. Several factor analyses provided the primary rationale for item grouping. The standardization samples consisted of 548 adolescents from several different institutions. These were primarily seriously disturbed youngsters diagnosed as psychotic, mentally defective or brain damaged. Ratings on a group of 305 normal children were also obtained for comparative purposes.

The scale was designed to be usable by nonprofessionals. The authors claim that a rating can be completed in 15 minutes. Trial runs suggest that the time estimate is realistic, but that nonprofessionals may have difficulty with several of the items that are stated in psychiatric jargon ("preoccupied," "obsessed," "echolalia").

The manual reports a median correlation of .42 between ratings of independent raters, about that generally obtained with this type of rating scale. A median correlation of .82 is reported between average ratings made by the same group of raters on two separate occasions 7 to 10 days apart. These reliability data, although based on an unusually heterogeneous sample, seem adequate. The authors' attempt to suggest that the reliability is really higher than it appears, by using a generally unfamiliar statistic called a "coefficient of agreement," seems unnecessary. Some increase in reliability appears to have been achieved by including redundant items that may have increased scale reliability at the price of reducing validity. The authors fail to suggest that with reliability at this level it is highly advisable to use more than one rater and to combine scores for accuracy.

A great need exists for adequate rating scales usable with children and adolescents. The Devereux scale appears to be a helpful addition, but may be limited in its application. The primary limiting factor appears to be in the restriction of the difficulty level of the items, with most items referring to infrequently occurring abnormal symptomatic behaviors. Thus, it is highly doubtful that the scale will discriminate adequately between groups of normal, neurotic, or delinquent adolescents. On several scales only a very few points separate the vast bulk of scores obtained by subjects in these groups. Additionally, subtypes within these categories are not very likely to be sharply discriminated. For example, item content on the scale labeled "Physical Inferiority-Timidity" relates to fear of getting hurt in physical activities, lack of muscle tone, proneness to tire quickly, and shyness and timidity. The physically adequate but anxious adolescent would not achieve a remarkable score on this scale. Such a youngster would also not be identified by the scale labeled "Anxious Self-Blame," where three of the four items refer to extreme behaviors (obsessions, delusional beliefs, and blame or self-condemnation). Consequently, the scale seems most suited for very disturbed adolescents. Furthermore, although the authors suggest that the scale is behaviorally oriented, several of the items are poorly defined and require the rater to make inferences about intent, such as the following: "Intentionally tells lies," "wants to be a nonconformist." In addition, some of the terminology, "boy crazy" and "sneaky," for example, seems to need clarification, while other items introduce value judgments that detract from the objectivity of the scale.

The profile is conveniently constructed; it has the useful feature of indicating not only the distribution of scores of the normative sample (mostly institutionalized adolescents) but also the middle range of a "normal" group not included in the standardization sample.

The Devereux Adolescent Behavior Rating Scale should fill a useful function in clinical situations as well as in research studies. Because of the nature of the items, it does not appear that the scale will prove useful for making fine discriminations among normal children. However, as the scale's authors suggest, the instrument can be recommended for use with diagnosed groups of disturbed children, and as a help in identifying disturbed children.

[67]

★Devereux Child Behavior Rating Scale. Emotionally disturbed and mentally retarded children ages 8-12; 1966; DCBRS; ratings by clinicians, child care workers, parents, house parents, or others who have had "intimate living arrangement with the child over a period of time"; 17 scores: distractibility, poor self care, pathological use of senses, emotional detachment, social isolation, poor coordination and body tonus, incontinence, messiness-sloppiness, inadequate need for independence, unresponsiveness to stimulation, proneness to emotional upset, need for adult contact, anxious-fearful ideation, "impulse" ideation, inability to delay, social aggression, unethical behavior; 1 form (8 pages); manual (34 pages); $3.75 per 25 scales; $1 per manual; $4.50 per 25 scales and manual; sample copy of scale free; postpaid; (10-20) minutes; George Spivack and Jules Spotts; Devereux Foundation Press. *

REFERENCES

1-3. See P:61.

ALLAN G. BARCLAY, *Professor of Psychology, Saint Louis University, Saint Louis, Missouri.*

The *Devereux Child Behavior Rating Scale* was developed as an instrument for the assessment of atypical children from 8 through 12 years of age. Its use with younger, or older, children has apparently not been studied. The DCB was designed for use by raters knowledgeable about a given child's behavior. Scale items are of the form "Compared to normal children, *how often* does the child." The items themselves were derived from factor analytic studies based upon three groups: (*a*) 252 atypical children in four residential treatment centers, with a diversity of diagnoses and intellectual levels; (*b*) 100 retarded children from a state facility for the mentally retarded; and (*c*) 348 public school children. These factor analyses yielded the 17 factors listed in the entry preceding this review.

Although the manual is rather unsatisfactory in its reporting of the obtained factors, the research upon which it is based seems generally adequate.

Reliability data reported suggest reasonable scorer reliability, with a median correlation between two raters of .83, and although one would like somewhat more substantial evidence, it seems probable that adequate scorer reliability is obtainable on the DCB. Test-retest reliability, over a one-week period, was also reported at .83, while factor score reliability, using the same data, was reported to be .91. Since no validity data are reported, the relation of the obtained factors to external criteria remains an open question, and no additional data seem to be presently available to answer this question.

Since the DCB purports to be a descriptive system having no necessary theoretical rationale for its construction, the factors isolated are essentially empirical and would seem to be relatively similar to the general domain of behaviors noted by other investigators studying the child who manifests developmental disturbances based upon either an emotional or organic basis. As a classification instrument used for assigning children to groups (either diagnostic or treatment) or for assessing behavioral changes, the DCB offers a moderately useful technique. However, it does little to advance our understanding of the provenance of such factors, nor does it appear to provide much in the way of an heuristic impetus for further research. Further, the lack of additional research on the validity of the DCB continues to hamper its utility.

[68]

★**Devereux Elementary School Behavior Rating Scale.** Grades kgn–6; 1966–67; DESBRS; problem behaviors; 11 factor scores (classroom disturbance, impatience, disrespect-defiance, external blame, achievement anxiety, external reliance, comprehension, inattentive-withdrawn, irrelevant-responsiveness, creative initiative, need for closeness to the teacher), 3 item scores (unable to change, quits easily, slow work); 1 form ('67, 5 pages); manual ('67, 36 pages); $3.75 per 25 scales; $1 per manual; $4.50 per 25 scales and manual; sample copy of scale free; postpaid; (10) minutes; George Spivack and Marshall Swift; Devereux Foundation Press. *

REFERENCES

1–2. See P:62.
3. SWIFT, MARSHALL S., AND SPIVACK, GEORGE. "Clarifying the Relationship Between Academic Success and Overt Classroom Behavior." *Excep Children* 36(2):99–104 O '69. * (*PA* 44:21626)

WILLIAM M. LITTELL, *Professor of Psychology, San Francisco State College, San Francisco, California.*

The DESB is intended for use by elementary school teachers who wish to "better understand, describe and communicate the behavior problems of the children in their classes," and is oriented toward those overt behaviors which "interfere with the successful academic performance of the child." The scale should be administered only by someone who has direct contact with the child in the classroom, and who has had at least one month's experience with the child before making the rating.

The child is rated on 47 different items in terms of the relative frequency with which the described behavior occurs. These individual ratings are grouped into 11 different factors containing three, four or five items each, and three additional separate items. No item occurs in more than one factor, suggesting that the DESB should actually be looked upon as a collection of 14 separate rating scales. The factors are named from an examination of the items included. For example, Classroom Disturbance derives its score from the degree to which the child is rated to need control (item 11), tease (item 12), interfere with the work of others (item 13), and how quickly he is drawn into the talking or noisemaking of others (item 30). The DESB form includes a profile which allows the user to compare the child's scores with available norms. A large part of the manual is devoted to a discussion of the interpretation of the factors, and a number of possible uses are suggested ranging from "a means of identifying and measuring those classroom behaviors that may be interfering with achievement," to "an aid in group placement of children in classes."

A major strength of the DESB is the care

with which the items were selected and grouped into the rating scale. The DESB was developed as part of a program to identify and study achievement related classroom behaviors in children. Teachers of both normal and exceptional children were brought together to discuss and describe behaviors of the children in their classrooms that they saw as either disruptive of learning or as positively related to achievement. From these discussions a pool of items was made up from which the DESB was ultimately selected. This item pool was used to rate both normal and exceptional children, the data were factor analyzed, and the items best describing the factors which were common to both normal and exceptional children were retained in the final form. This instrument was then used in a number of studies in which DESB scores were related to various measures including academic achievement and effort. These data are referred to in the discussion of the interpretation and use of the scale.

Compared with the care given to the development of the scale, the manual shows a surprising lack of attention to the scale's reliability and validity. The short term (one week) stability of the ratings of individual teachers is reported (a median reliability of .87), but the more important matter of inter-rater reliability is not mentioned, and apparently was not investigated.

The validity of the ratings is dealt with only by implication in the discussion of the use of the scale, where statistically significant but characteristically low correlations with measures of achievement and effort are reported. There are two levels on which the validity of the scale should have been investigated and discussed. First, some of the behaviors rated appear to be sufficiently complex to warrant an examination of the degree to which the ratings by the teacher actually do measure the behavior described (e.g., disrespect). Further, there is little doubt that users will tend to interpret the ratings as measures of enduring characteristics (probably motivational) of the child. While the authors caution against making this interpretation of the factors, they themselves appear to do so as they discuss the meaning of some of the factors. For instance, Factor 2, Impatience, is stated to be "concerned with an inappropriate drive to enter into and to complete the work assigned." While the content validity of the items is compelling, the lack of an explicit

and careful treatment of validity is a major flaw in the scale.

The items included in the scale also must be seen to represent a common but somewhat restricted concept of teaching and of the relationship between teacher and student. A problem behavior is defined as "one which indicates that the child is not meeting the demands of the school as these are defined by the school structure and teacher." It is possible that the scale would not be especially useful in a classroom in which the problems of concern to the teacher are not the inability of the children to meet her demands. A teacher may also be surprised to find "treat teacher as an equal" given as an example of disrespect.

The DESB is a sophisticated and carefully developed rating scale. The behaviors to be rated are clearly described and instructions for rating are carefully given. The authors have been careful to caution that the scale "is not intended to provide a measure of 'personality' or character 'traits,'" but that it "provides a profile of 11 dimensions of overt problem behavior that experienced teachers have judged as being related to classroom achievement, and for which there is research evidence to this effect." If the users of the scale can confine themselves to this very conservative interpretation of the scale it will serve as a convenient tool in research and as an aid in communication about the behavior through which a child meets or fails to meet the demands of the teacher.

[69]

★The Differential Value Profile. College; 1963–69; DVP; 6 scores: aesthetic, humanitarian, intellectual, material, power, religious; Form A ('63, 4 pages); manual ('69, 46 pages); profile ['63, 1 page]; separate answer sheets must be used; 15¢ per test; 5¢ per answer sheet; 5¢ per profile; $1 per set of scoring stencils; $4 per manual; $5 per specimen set; postage extra; (30–45) minutes; Walter L. Thomas; Combined Motivation Education Systems, Inc. *

REFERENCES

1–2. See P:63.
3. KILLIAN, DAVID LAWRENCE. The General Social Values of Elementary School Teachers and Principals and the Acceptance of the Elementary Principal as Leader. Doctor's thesis, University of Michigan (Ann Arbor, Mich.), 1968. (DAI 30:93A)
4. SMALL, ROBERT MARTIN, JR. Value Characteristics and Academic Success of Marginal and Non-Marginal Freshmen at a State University. Doctor's thesis, Ball State University (Muncie, Ind.), 1969. (DAI 30:4159A)
5. THOMAS, WALTER LEE. The Initial Development of the Differential Value Profile. Doctor's thesis, University of Tulsa (Tulsa, Okla.), 1970. (DAI 31:2119A)

ROBERT HOGAN, Assistant Professor of Psychology, The Johns Hopkins University, Baltimore, Maryland.

The Differential Value Profile, designed for

use primarily with college students, measures six value clusters defined "by factor analyses." The scales are intended to provide information useful in a variety of areas of educational research (e.g., school-related personality changes, prediction of academic achievement, counselling).

The reusable test booklet contains 134 items; subjects check one of four response options (strongly agree, agree, disagree, strongly disagree). The items are conventional attitude statements with a naive and hysterical tone that some students will find offensive. Thus it is no surprise to find the following observation in the test manual: "The testee will often react strongly against the test after he has taken it," therefore, "The DVP must be taken in one sitting," or the testee may refuse to finish it.

The number of items on each scale varies between 35 and 40, guaranteeing considerable item overlap among the scales. Because of the item overlap and because the manual contains no information concerning correlations among the scales, one is prompted to speculate that the scales lack independence.

Both internal consistency and test-retest reliability estimates are presented in the manual. K-R 20 coefficients range from .76 to .88 and test-retest correlations across a 10-day interval varied between .83 and .94. These figures seem reasonable and appropriate in view of the well-known stability of interest scores in general.

The manual contains two kinds of validational evidence. First, 10 judges were asked to sort the 134 items into the six scales originally defined by factor analyses; they were able to do this with fair to good agreement. Thus the scales of the DVP have reasonable face validity. The second validational study compared 740 freshmen from "church-related" colleges with 740 freshmen from "public" colleges. Men were also compared with women. Eleven of the 12 resulting F tests were significant, enabling the author to conclude that "the Differential Value Profile is a valid instrument for discriminating among male and female, as well as church-related and public college freshmen." Magnitudes of relationships are not presented, however, and the existence of group differences *per se* is not theoretically enlightening. Concerning additional validational information, the manual contains only the following puzzling observation: "Although there is reason to believe from the author's studies in higher education that the DVP can efficiently *predict* college grades and college drop-outs, this manual is being written before such data is in reportable form."

The test manual itself is rather unsatisfactory. In addition to grammatical and spelling errors, the manual contains long and pointless statistical digressions and a number of seemingly irrelevant tables. Missing from the manual, on the other hand, are intra-scale correlations, information concerning the factor loadings which originally defined the scales, and the normally expectable correlations with standard intelligence measures and related inventories such as the *Study of Values,* FIRO-B, and the *Myers-Briggs Type Indicator.*

In a somewhat abbreviated theoretical section the author sketches "a basic conceptual statement for the value concept." The author has a good grasp of the inferential nature of values and their fundamental importance in the analysis of social conduct. On the other hand the particular set of values he proposes are suspiciously familiar. In particular the description of the DVP Aesthetic scale sounds very much like the Aesthetic scale of the *Study of Values.* The Humanitarian scale closely resembles the SV Social scale, while the Intellectual, Material, Power, and Religious scales parallel almost exactly the SV scales for Theoretical, Economic, Political, and Religious interests.

In summary, the *Differential Value Profile* provides stable, internally consistent, face valid measures of six well-known value clusters. However the items are somewhat offensive to the test-wise students of today, and the practical utility of this inventory for research in education and guidance remains to be demonstrated.

[70]

*Dynamic Personality Inventory. Ages 15 or 17 and over with IQ's of 80 and over; 1956–70; DPI; for research and experimental use only (not so labeled in distributor's catalog); 33 scores: hypocrisy, passivity, seclusion-introspection, orality, oral aggression, oral dependence, emotional independence, verbal aggression, impulsiveness, unconventionality, hoarding behavior, attention to details, conservatism, submissiveness, anal sadism, insularity, phallic symbol interest, narcissism, exhibitionism, active Icarus complex, passive Icarus complex, sensuality, Icarian exploits, sexuality, tactile impression enjoyment, creative interests, masculine sexual identification, feminine sexual identification, social role seeking, social activity interest, need to give affection, ego defense persistence, initiative; 1 form ('56, 7 pages); also available, in abbreviated form and without scores for orality, phallic symbol interest, and sexuality, under the title Likes and Interests Test ('56, 6 pages) for use with apprentices and employee applicants ages 15 and over; mimeographed temporary manual with supplements ('70, 108 pages); DPI score-norms sheets ('56, 6 sheets, separate sheets for male students, female students, general population males, general population females, male neurotics, female neurotics); LIT score-norms sheets ('56, 2 sheets, separate sheets for male apprentices, female technical college students); separate answer sheets must be used; 75p per 25 DPI tests; 40p per 25 DPI answer sheets; £7.70 per set of DPI scoring keys; 37p per 25 DPI score-norm sheets for any one population; £1.87 per DPI specimen set; £1.20 per 25 LIT tests; 65p per 100 LIT answer sheets; £1.25 per 100 LIT male apprentice score-norms sheets; £1.50 per 100 LIT female technical college student score-norms sheets; £2.05 per set of LIT scoring keys; £1.77 per LIT specimen set; £1.50 per manual; postage extra; (40) minutes; T. G. Grygier; distributed by NFER Publishing Co. Ltd. *

REFERENCES

1–7. See 6:86.
8–13. See P:65.
14. BISHOP, FRANCES V. *Anality, Privation, and Dissonance.* Doctor's thesis, New York University (New York, N.Y.), 1965. (*DA* 27:596B)
15. GORDON, CAROL M. "Some Effects of Clinician and Patient Personality on Decision Making in a Clinical Setting." *J Consult Psychol* 31:477–80 O '67. * (*PA* 41:16808)
16. STRINGER, PETER. "A Comparison of the Self-Images of Art and Architectural Students." *Studies Art Ed* 9:33–49 au '67. *
17. GLASBERG, H. MARK; BROMBERG, PHILIP M.; STEIN, MARVIN; AND LUPARELLO, THOMAS J. "A Personality Study of Asthmatic Patients." *J Psychosom Res* 13(2):197–204 Je '69. * (*PA* 44:12978)
18. LISH, JOAN ADLER. *The Influence of Oral Dependency, Failure, and Social Exposure Upon Self-Esteem and Depression.* Doctor's thesis, New York University (New York, N.Y.), 1969. (*DAI* 30:5692B)
19. GRYGIER, TADEUSZ. "Recent Studies With the Dynamic Personality Inventory." *Int Congr Rorsch & Other Proj Tech* 7:668–81 '70. *
20. HAMILTON, VERNON. "Non-Cognitive Factors in University Students' Examination Performance." *Brit J Psychol* 61(2):229–41 My '70. * (*PA* 44:15302)
21. KLINE, PAUL. "A Projective and Psychometric Study of the Oral Character." *Int Congr Rorsch & Other Proj Tech* 7:506–12 '70. *
22. STRINGER, PETER. "A Note on the Factorial Structure of the Dynamic Personality Inventory." *Brit J Med Psychol* 43(1):95 Mr '70. *

For a review by S. B. Sells, see 6:86.

[71]

★Early School Personality Questionnaire. Ages 6–8; 1966–70, c1963–70; ESPQ; 13 first order factor scores (reserved vs. outgoing, less intelligent vs. more intelligent, affected by feelings vs. emotionally stable, phlegmatic vs. excitable, obedient vs. assertive, sober vs. happy-go-lucky, expedient vs. conscientious, shy vs. venturesome, self-reliant vs. dependent, vigorous vs. doubting, forthright vs. shrewd, placid vs. apprehensive, relaxed vs. tense), 2 second order factor scores (extraversion, anxiety); orally administered; Form A, Parts A1 and A2 ('66, 4 pages, text for questions orally presented); answer booklets for either part ('66, 4 pages); profile ('66, 1 page); guidebook ('66, 19 pages); supplement ('70, 4 pages); no instructions for computing second order factor scores; 50¢ per test; $3 per 25 sets of answer booklets; $2.50 per set of keys; $2.50 per 50 profiles; 90¢ per guidebook; tape available for administration; $3.70 per specimen set; postage extra; (60–100) minutes in 2 sessions; Richard W. Coan and Raymond B. Cattell; Institute for Personality and Ability Testing. *

REFERENCES

1–7. See P:66.
8. NEWBERT, NANCY. *A Study of Certain Personality Correlates of the Middle Child in a Three-Child Family.* Doctor's thesis, Boston University (Boston, Mass.), 1967. (*DA* 29:4333A)
9. BAKER, RODNEY ROBERT. *Sex Differences in the Structure of Childhood Personality.* Doctor's thesis, University of Arizona (Tucson, Ariz.), 1968. (*DA* 29:1502B)
10. LAL, J. N. "Development of Hindi Form of Elementary School Personality Questionnaire." *Indian Psychol R* 5:76–80 Jl '68. *
11. ROSENBLATT, JOAN B. *Measures of Impulse Control as Related to First Grade Children's Socio-Economic Class and Ethnic Group Background.* Doctor's thesis, University of Arizona (Tucson, Ariz.), 1968. (*DA* 29:1510B)
12. BOSS, MARVIN WALTER. *An Experimental Investigation of the Acquisition of Positive and Negative Racial Attitudes.* Doctor's thesis, University of Maryland (College Park, Md.), 1969. (*DAI* 31:843A)
13. LAL, J. N. "Sex Differences in Children's Personality." *Indian Psychol R* 5(2):113–6 Ja '69. *
14. LAL, J. N. "A Study of the Development of Certain Personality Factors Among the Elementary School-Going Children." Doctoral thesis abstract. *Indian Psychol R* 5(2):207–9 Ja '69. *
15. AHAMMER, INGE M., AND SCHAIE, K. WARNER. "Age Differences in the Relationship Between Personality Factors and School Achievement." *J Ed Psychol* 61(3):193–7 Je '70. * (*PA* 44:13364)

LOVICK C. MILLER, *Director of Research, Child Psychiatry Research Center, Louisville, Kentucky.*

The *Early School Personality Questionnaire* is the third downward extension of Cattell's 16PF. The test is a verbal instrument for group administration to children 6 to 8 years of age. The ESPQ consists of 13 scales derived by factor analysis, purporting to describe personality dimensions which extend into adult life. Each scale has a technical and popular label identical with other IPAT instruments. The questionnaire is beautifully prepared, contains 80 items, presented in two parts. Each part takes 30 to 50 minutes to administer, and the authors suggest administration on two different days. Administration procedures and instructions are clear and make significant contribution to the techniques for testing young children. Scoring is simplified by a well-conceived test booklet with easy to score stencil keys. Raw scores are converted to standard sten scores and separate norms are provided for boys and girls at each of the ages 6, 7, and 8. No reliability or validity studies are reported.

The test is aimed at teachers and is accompanied by a test profile sheet with each dimension clearly labeled and described. In a matter of a few hours, then, a teacher can obtain through the ESPQ an image of what her students think about themselves.

What can one say about this test? It is beautifully packaged; it meets a major need, namely an objective personality instrument for young children, which has continuity through the life span; it seems to make a real contribution in the assessment of young children, both in the content of the verbal stimuli and in the ways they are presented; and finally, the test has behind it the experience and brilliance of the Cattell group. However, the failure to provide reliability and validity studies means that one can say nothing meaningful about the test. The authors do not even provide basic demographic and intelligence information on the population on which the sten scores were constructed. At this stage, the test is still experimental and should be used only by persons interested in personality research.

This reviewer is concerned with the ethics of publishing this test at this time, particularly when the test is designed primarily for the classroom teacher. Most teachers lack the training in theory, test construction, and personality assessment necessary for interpreting any test at this stage of development. Indeed, without reliability and validity studies, and without demographic data on the standardization sample, the test cannot be interpreted by anyone, regardless of the interpreter's background and training. The authors apparently recognize this fact, because they warn the user in the manual to be careful of over-generalizations. Further, on this reviewer's copy of the manual, the words "Research Edition" are hand-stamped. One wonders why this warning was not printed on the cover. There is a danger that the professional format, erudite language, impeccable logic, and the claims for a valid theoretical base will obscure the possibility that information obtained from the questionnaire may be meaningless, misleading, and possibly damaging to the child.

In brief, the ESPQ is a group personality test for young children, which partially extends Cattell's 16PF through the life span. To date, test development efforts have consisted of item selection, establishment of administration procedures, and packaging a pleasing and efficient test and scoring format. No effort has gone into studies of reliability; longitudinal effects of maturation; relationship of test scores to teacher, peer, parent or clinical observations or to other self-reporting instruments; or to the effects of situational and demographic variables. Such studies are possible and should be undertaken by competent research personnel. It is premature to use the test as a general assessment instrument.

Since this review was written, a guidebook supplement providing reliability and validity estimates of the test has been submitted.

Equivalence coefficients for the scale range from .28 to .84, with median .48 and homogeneity ranges from .31 to .83, with median .50. Scale intercorrelations demonstrate independence among the scales except for a few high correlations, which the authors attribute to "second-stratum factors." Factor validity ranges from .32 to .84, with median .62, while predictive validity with a behavior problem checklist ranges from −.29 to +.25.

These estimates partially mitigate the original criticisms. However, the reviewer has included the original review since the additional information does not alter the central critique, namely, that the test is published prematurely and that results may be misleading. For example, what do reliability estimates of .50 mean, other than that the scales do not meet usual standards of stability? Since there is little in the way of other child personality instruments to compare against, these results may be as good as can be expected. However, internal stability (homogeneity) or equivalence criteria of .50 appear low to this reviewer. The authors attempted to maximize factor reliability at the expense of stability, which is a legitimate strategy, but many test users will want high stability in order to know that change is a function of an independent variable and not of test unreliability.

The question of validity is even more complex. The authors demonstrate adequate factor validity (reconfirmation of the original factor structure) of children's verbal self reports. These self report scores, however, seem to have very little relationship to other behavioral measures, the highest correlation accounting for only nine percent of the variance when compared with a checklist. Clearly, what the child reports about himself on this test and what others report about him are not equivalent. This does not necessarily invalidate the test, but the user should recognize that self reports and behavioral observations have correlations approaching zero. This fact underscores the assertion that this test should be considered a research instrument until empirical investigation can relate its results to a larger body of theoretical knowledge.

[72]

Edwards Personal Preference Schedule. College and adults; 1953–59; EPPS; 15 scores: achievement, deference, order, exhibition, autonomy, affiliation, intraception, succorance, dominance, abasement, nurturance, change, endurance, heterosexuality, aggression; 1 form ('54, 8 pages); revised manual ('59, 25 pages); separate answer sheets (Digitek, hand scoring, IBM 805, IBM 1230, NCS) must be used; no instructions on the use of specific answer sheets; $4 per 25 tests; $3.20 per 50 Digitek or IBM 1230 answer sheets; $3 per 50 hand scoring or IBM 805 answer sheets; $3.50 per 50 NCS answer sheets; set of manual and stencils: 60¢ with hand scoring stencil, $3 with set of IBM 805 hand scoring stencils, $4.75 with set of IBM 805 machine scoring stencils; Digitek and IBM 1230 scoring stencils not available; 75¢ per specimen set; postage extra; NCS scoring service: $1.25 to 90¢ per test (daily service), 80¢ to 50¢ per test ($20 minimum; weekly service); (40–55) minutes; Allen L. Edwards; Psychological Corporation. *

REFERENCES

1–50. See 5:47.
51–326. See 6:87.
327–689. See P:67, also includes a cumulative name index to the first 689 references for this test.
690. DAY, BARBARA RUTH. *The Relationship of Need Patterns to Selection in the Formation of Courtship Couples and Same-Sex Friendships.* Doctor's thesis, University of Washington (Seattle, Wash.), 1956. (*DA* 16:2550)
691. LEWIS, WILLIAM ANDREW. *The Relationship Between Emotional Adjustment, the Amount of Need Satisfaction Achieved and the Ability to Differentiate Ways of Obtaining Need Satisfaction.* Doctor's thesis, University of Illinois (Urbana, Ill.), 1957. (*DA* 18:497)
692. STRAUSS, MARVIN E. *Need-Achievement and Instructions in Relation to Learning and Reminiscence.* Doctor's thesis, University of Pittsburgh (Pittsburgh, Pa.), 1957. (*DA* 17:1136)
693. THORPE, J. A. L. *A Study of Personality Variables Among Successful Women Professional Students and Teachers of Physical Education.* Master's thesis, Woman's College of the University of North Carolina (Greensboro, N.C.), 1957.
694. WALSH, RICHARD PATRICK. *Personality Factors in the Selection of Job Duties.* Doctor's thesis, University of Maryland (College Park, Md.), 1957. (*DA* 18:648)
695. BENDIG, A. W. "Predictive and Postdictive Validity of Need Achievement Measures." *J Ed Res* 52:119–20 N '58. * (*PA* 33:11016)
696. STONE, J. BLAIR. *Personal Factors Related to the College Performance of Physically Disabled Male College Students.* Master's thesis, University of Utah (Salt Lake City, Utah), 1958.
697. DOUGHERTY, M. FRANCES. *A Study of the Influence of a Creative Arts Laboratory on Selected Personality Characteristics of College Students.* Doctor's thesis, New York University (New York, N.Y.), 1959. (*DA* 20:3183)
698. EVANS, FRANKLIN B. "Psychological and Objective Factors in the Prediction of Brand Choice: Ford Versus Chevrolet." *J Bus* 22:340–69 O '59. *
699. KRAMER, KENNETH CALVERT. *A Comparison of Various Statistical Procedures and Methodological Techniques in the Selection of Life Insurance Agents.* Doctor's thesis, University of Houston (Houston, Tex.), 1959. (*DA* 20:3379)
700. LEVIN, BARRY LIVINGSTON. *The Use of Role Playing as a Method for Producing Self-Perceived Personality Change.* Doctor's thesis, Columbia University (New York, N.Y.), 1959. (*DA* 20:779)
701. MARSH, FRANK EUGENE, JR. *An Analysis of Failure Among University Freshmen.* Doctor's thesis, Boston University (Boston, Mass.), 1959. (*DA* 20:2101)
702. ROGERS, K. E. *A Comparison of Personality Variables of College Women Physical Education Majors Who Were Successful in Student Teaching With Those Who Were Less Successful.* Master's thesis, Woman's College of the University of North Carolina (Greensboro, N.C.), 1959.
703. LEIGHTON, ANN M. *A Study to Determine the Relation Between Body Build and Selected Personality Traits of Springfield College Women.* Master's thesis, Springfield College (Springfield, Mass.), 1960.
704. WEINICK, GEORGE DAVID. *The Comparative Effectiveness of Two Teaching Methods in Attaining Specific Course Objectives: An Evaluation of Two Different Methods of Teaching a Course in Psychology With Respect to the Students' Acquisition of Course Content and Changes in Personal Adjustment.* Doctor's thesis, New York University (New York, N.Y.), 1960. (*DA* 21:2996)
705. HELLER, KENNETH, AND GOLDSTEIN, ARNOLD P. "Client Dependency and Therapist Expectancy as Relationship Maintaining Variables in Psychotherapy." *J Consult Psychol* 25: 371–5 O '61. * (*PA* 37:336⁻)
706. HOLLYER, STEWART GORDON. *Social Status Factors and Achievement Needs as Related to Entry Into a Professional Field.* Doctor's thesis, University of Nebraska (Lincoln, Neb.), 1961. (*DA* 21:3844)

707. KJELDSEN, ERICK K. M. *A Study to Determine the Relationships Between the Edwards Personal Preference Schedule and Participation in Gymnastics.* Master's thesis, Springfield College (Springfield, Mass.), 1961.
708. LITCHARD, ROBERT M. *A Comparison of Scores on the Edwards Personal Preference Schedule of College Varsity Athletes Who Were Letter Winners, Non-Letter Winners and College Non-Athletes.* Master's thesis, Springfield College (Springfield, Mass.), 1961.
709. ROBINSON, DONALD W.; D'AMICO, LOUIS; AND MANOS, NICHOLAS E. "Edwards Personal Preference Schedule Scores for Students at Varying Levels of Ability and Achievement." *J Col Stud Personnel* 3:81–4 D '61. *
710. SCHUMER, HARRY. *Cohesion and Leadership in Small Groups as Related to Group Productivity.* Doctor's thesis, Ohio State University (Columbus, Ohio), 1961. (*DA* 22: 3735)
711. SNELBECKER, GLENN EUGENE. *Factors Influencing College Students' Person-Perceptions of Psychotherapists in a Laboratory Analog.* Doctor's thesis, Cornell University (Ithaca, N.Y.), 1961. (*DA* 22:3928)
712. TUKEY, RUTH SCHWEIGERT. *A Study of Differences Found Between Intellectually-Oriented and Socially-Oriented Superior Girls.* Doctor's thesis, Michigan State University (East Lansing, Mich.), 1961. (*DA* 22:4278)
713. BALLANTYNE, ROBERT HUBBARD. *An Analysis of Criteria for Selecting Freshmen Students for an Honors Program at Washington State University.* Doctor's thesis, Washington State University (Pullman, Wash.), 1962. (*DA* 23:2439)
714. COOPER, EUGENE BRUCE. *Patient-Therapist Relationships and Concomitant Factors in Stuttering Therapy.* Doctor's thesis, Pennsylvania State University (University Park, Pa.), 1962. (*DA* 23:4014)
715. HUTCHISON, RUSSELL STIRLING. *A Study of the Christian Education of Adults in Relation to the Needs and Values of Adults in Selected Protestant Churches in Muskingum County, Ohio.* Doctor's thesis, University of Pittsburgh (Pittsburgh, Pa.), 1962. (*DA* 23:2020)
716. KLIEWER, VERNON DEAN. *Multiple Stylistic Effects and Self-Report Personality Assessment.* Doctor's thesis, University of Oregon (Eugene, Ore.), 1962. (*DA* 23:3966)
717. KOLE, DELBERT MERRILL. *A Study of Intellectual and Personality Characteristics of Medical Students.* Master's thesis, University of Oregon Medical School (Portland, Ore.), 1962.
718. LUBIN, BERNARD; BRADY, JOHN PAUL; AND LEVITT, EUGENE E. "A Comparison of Personality Characteristics of Volunteers and Nonvolunteers for Hypnosis Experiments." *J Clin Psychol* 18:341–3 Jl '62. * (*PA* 39:1811)
719. MARLER, ROSE MARIE. *Personality Variables of Extramural Participant and Non-Participant Women Physical Education Majors.* Master's thesis, Illinois State University (Normal, Ill.), 1962.
720. RIBAL, JOSEPH EDWARD. *The Selfish Self: A Social Psychological Study of Social Character.* Doctor's thesis, University of Southern California (Los Angeles, Calif.), 1962. (*DA* 23:2615)
721. ROSENBERG, JUDAH JACOB. *Persuasibility in Personality and Culture.* Doctor's thesis, Columbia University (New York, N.Y.), 1962. (*DA* 26:2905)
722. SMITH, PATRICIA ANN. *Ego Strength in Males as a Motivational Variable in Mate Selection—A College Sample.* Doctor's thesis, University of Oregon (Eugene, Ore.), 1962. (*DA* 23:1612)
723. BECHTEL, LELAND PETERMAN. *Comparative Effects of Differentiated Teaching Methods on Certain Personality Characteristics of College Students: The Effect of the Traditional Approach to Teaching Psychology as Compared to an Interpersonal Approach to Teaching Psychology Upon Beliefs, Attitudes, Values and Adjustment of College Students in a Course in General Psychology.* Doctor's thesis, New York University (New York, N.Y.), 1963. (*DA* 24:3199)
724. DAUGHERTY, ROBERT ALTON. *Perceiving One's Own Performance Level as a Function of Cognitive Control and Motivation.* Doctor's thesis, Wayne State University (Detroit, Mich.), 1963. (*DA* 29:405B)
725. EVANS, FRANKLIN B., AND ROBERTS, HARRY V. "Fords, Chevrolets, and the Problem of Discrimination." *J Bus* 36: 242–9 Ap '63. *
726. HUGHES, THOMAS. *A Study of Personality Characteristics of a Selected Group of Springfield College Freshmen.* Master's thesis, Springfield College (Springfield, Mass.), 1963.
727. JOHNSON, KENNETH EDWIN. *Personal Religious Growth Through Small Group Participation: A Psychological Study of Personality Changes and Shifts in Religious Attitudes Which Result From Participation in a Spiritual Growth Group.* Doctor's thesis, Pacific School of Religion (Berkeley, Calif.), 1963. (*DA* 25:628)
728. KUEHN, ALFRED A. "Demonstration of a Relationship Between Psychological Factors and Brand Choice." *J Bus* 36:237–41 Ap '63. *
729. LACZEK, WILLIAM J. *Aggressive Motivation and Recognition Latencies to Aggressive Words.* Master's thesis, Springfield College (Springfield, Mass.), 1963.
730. NEAL, PATSY E. *Personality Traits of United States Women Athletes Who Participated in the 1959 Pan-American*

Games, as Measured by the Edwards Personal Preference Schedule. Master's thesis, University of Utah (Salt Lake City, Utah), 1963.

731. RAMSEY, LORENE MARIA. *A Comparison of the Personality Variables and Attitudes Toward Physical Education Between Highly Skilled Girls Participating in Varsity Programs and Girls' Athletic Association Programs.* Master's thesis, University of North Carolina (Greensboro, N.C.), 1963.

732. SCHNEIDER, WILBUR FRANK. *The Comparative Achievement of the Graduates of Public and Catholic High Schools in Their Freshman College Year.* Doctor's thesis, University of Colorado (Boulder, Colo.), 1963. *(DA 25:203)*

733. ADRIAN, MARLENE J. *Selected Motor and Psychological Changes in College Women.* Doctor's thesis, Springfield College (Springfield, Mass.), 1964.

734. DAVIDS, ANTHONY, AND ANDREWS, JEAN M. "Changes in Academic Attainment and Personality Characteristics Following a Special Educational Program for Underachieving Secondary School Boys." *Psychol Sch* 1:388–91 O '64. *

735. FAIRFIELD, PHILIP DEXTER. *A Study of Students Who Changed Programs of Studies at Springfield College.* Master's thesis, Springfield College (Springfield, Mass.), 1964.

736. FISHER, SEYMOUR. "Power Orientation and Concept of Self Height in Men: Preliminary Note." *Percept & Motor Skills* 18:732 Je '64. * *(PA 39:4781)*

737. HARRISON, LAWRENCE BRIGHT. *The Relationship Between Ordinal Position and Dependency, Dominance, Affiliation, Affection, and Task-Orientation.* Doctor's thesis, University of Oklahoma (Norman, Okla.), 1964. *(DA 25:3688)*

738. HETHERINGTON, E. MAVIS, AND FELDMAN, SOLOMON E. "College Cheating as a Function of Subject and Situational Variables." *J Ed Psychol* 55:212–8 Ag '64. * *(PA 39:4799)*

739. LEDERMAN, SELWYN. *A Study of the Relationship Between Parents' Self-Described Dependency Attitudes, Expectation for Achievement in Their Children and Observed Dependency Behavior in Their Children.* Doctor's thesis, Yeshiva University (New York, N.Y.), 1964. *(DA 25:36·6)*

740. LUBLIN, SHIRLEY CURRAN. *The Effects of Three Types of Reinforcement, Scholastic Aptitude, and Autonomy Need Upon Achievement in a Course in Programmed Instruction.* Doctor's thesis, Pennsylvania State University (University Park, Pa.), 1964. *(DA 26:1187)*

741. MAISEL, RICHARD N. *Psychological Concomitants of Chronic Disease: A Study of Hansen's Disease and Pulmonary Tuberculosis Patients Who Are Fast and Slow Recoverers.* Doctor's thesis, University of Miami (Coral Gables, Fla.), 1964. *(DA 25:5385)*

742. MILLS, DAVID HARLOW. *Liking as a Therapist Variable in the Psychotherapeutic Interaction.* Doctor's thesis, Michigan State University (East Lansing, Mich.), 1964. *(DA 25:6764)*

743. NELSON, ARTHUR H. *A Comparative Study of Personality Traits in Selected High School Students.* Master's thesis, Springfield College (Springfield, Mass.), 1964.

744. ROWLAND, MARTHA M. *An Investigation of the Predictive Value of the Edwards Personal Preference Schedule in Determining Grade Point Index and Reading Score.* Master's thesis, Boston University (Boston, Mass.), 1964.

745. SCHRADER, DONALD RALPH. *A Study of the Relations Among Sex, Social Position, Ethnic Group, Manifest Needs, and Academic Achievement in High School.* Doctor's thesis, Purdue University (Lafayette, Ind.), 1964. *(DA 25:2859)*

746. TONGAS, PHOEBUS N. *The Effects of Dependency Motivation on Persuasibility.* Doctor's thesis, State University of New York (Buffalo, N.Y.), 1964. *(DA 25:5391)*

747. VAN VURST, RAYNER. *An Investigation Into the Relationship Between Selected Personality Traits and Reactions to Frustration Among Religious Seminarians and Lay Students.* Master's thesis, University of Detroit (Detroit, Mich.), 1964.

748. FERRARI, LOUIS M. "Some Personality Characteristics of Male Psychiatric Nursing Assistants in One Facility." *Persp Psychiatric Care* 3(5):39–41 '65. *

749. FOLDS, JONELL HEMPHILL. *A Comparison of the Recall of Test Scores and Change in Self-Concept of College Students Following Three Methods of Test Interpretation.* Doctor's thesis, University of Georgia (Athens, Ga.), 1965. *(DA 26:2073)*

750. GAY, JAMES DONALD. *Personality Changes Associated With Workshop Participation.* Doctor's thesis, University of Kentucky (Lexington, Ky.), 1965. *(DAI 30:2436B)*

751. GLAD, JOAN ROGERS BOURNE. *Evaluation of the Remedial Reading Program in Utah Public Schools.* Doctor's thesis, University of Utah (Salt Lake City, Utah), 1965. *(DA 26:5864)*

752. KWELLER, IRVING IRA. *Impression Formation and Occupation.* Doctor's thesis, New York University (New York, N.Y.), 1965. *(DA 27:294B)*

753. McCRACKEN, OLIVER, JR. *Changes in the Personality, Attitudes, and Classroom Behavior of Beginning Elementary Teachers in Niles Township, Niles, Illinois.* Doctor's thesis, University of Missouri (Columbia, Mo.), 1965. *(DA 27:1663A)*

754. MILLS, DAVID H., AND ABELES, NORMAN. "Counselor Needs for Affiliation and Nurturance as Related to Liking for Clients and Counseling Process." *J Counsel Psychol* 12:353–8 w '65. * *(PA 40:3031)*

755. MINGE, MARVIN RONALD. *Counseling Readiness.* Doctor's thesis, Washington State University (Pullman, Wash.), 1965. *(DA 26:3487)*

756. OGDEN, WILLIAM EUGENE. *Field Dependency in a Sample of University Counseling Center Clients.* Doctor's thesis, University of Kansas (Lawrence, Kan.), 1965. *(DA 27:679A)*

757. PATERSON, JOHN GILBERT A. *Personality Characteristics of Undergraduate Education Students Associated With Differential Performance in Factual and Applied Educational Psychology Test Items.* Doctor's thesis, University of Washington (Seattle, Wash.), 1965. *(DA 27:119A)*

758. RENFRO, VIRGIL RALPH. *A Study of the Relationship Between Selected Influences and Changes of Attitude Toward Pupils That Occur During an Eighteen-Week Student-Teaching Experience.* Doctor's thesis, Oklahoma State University (Stillwater, Okla.), 1965. *(DA 27:407A)*

759. REZLER, AGNES G. "The Influence of Needs Upon the Student's Perception of His Instructor." *J Ed Res* 58:282–6 F '65. * *(PA 39:12984)*

760. RYCHLAK, JOSEPH F. "The Similarity, Compatibility, or Incompatibility of Needs in Interpersonal Selection." *J Pers & Social Psychol* 2:334–40 S '65. *

761. SCHLACHET, PETER J. "The Effect of Dissonance Arousal on the Recall of Failure Stimuli." *J Personality* 33:443–61 S '65. * *(PA 40:2277)*

762. SHEARER, ROBERTA. *A Comparative Study of American Graduate Student Friends of Foreign Students.* Doctor's thesis, Indiana University (Bloomington, Ind.), 1965. *(DA 26:5250)*

763. SISTRUNK, FRANCIS, AND McDAVID, JOHN W. "Achievement Motivation, Affiliation Motivation, and Task Difficulty as Determinants of Social Conformity." *J Social Psychol* 66:41–50 Je '65. * *(PA 39:15064)*

764. STROBLE, SHARON ELIZABETH. *The Relationship Among Selected Measures of Physical Fitness, Body-Image, Self-Concept, Movement-Concept, and Selected Personality Traits of College Physical Education Majors With Low Physical Fitness Indices.* Master's thesis, University of North Carolina (Greensboro, N.C.), 1965.

765. SULLIVAN, LINDA. *Relationships Between Self and Measured Perceptions of Physical and Personality Characteristics.* Master's thesis, Springfield College (Springfield, Mass.), 1965.

766. TEAL, CHARLES EDWARD. *A Study of the Relationship Between Selected Variables and the Time Devoted to Supervision of Instruction by Elementary School Principals.* Doctor's research study No. 1, Colorado State College (Greeley, Colo.), 1965. *(DA 26:5186)*

767. TOLLEFSON, NONA FALMLEN. *Relationship of Counselor Need Orientation to Counselor Effectiveness and Counselor Personality.* Doctor's thesis, Purdue University (Lafayette, Ind.), 1965. *(DA 27:122A)*

768. WIERSON, PHILLIP WAYNE. *An Evaluation of Short-Term Counseling.* Doctor's thesis, University of Missouri (Columbia, Mo.), 1965. *(DA 26:5256)*

769. WILSON, NORMAN EDWARD. *Personality Correlates of Person Perception Patterns Among School Counselors in Two Advanced Programs of Counselor Education.* Doctor's thesis, University of Texas (Austin, Tex.), 1965. *(DA 27:123A)*

770. ZYBON, GRETA. *Role Consensus, Need Complementarity and Continuance of Marriage.* Doctor's thesis, Western Reserve University (Cleveland, Ohio), 1965. *(DA 27:826A)*

771. ANDERSON, DONALD DUNWOODY. *A Comparison of Edwards Personal Preference Schedule Patterns of Elementary School Teachers in Open and Closed Organizational Climates.* Doctor's thesis, Auburn University (Auburn, Ala.), 1966. *(DA 27:1569A)*

772. ARKOFF, ABE, AND LETON, DONALD A. "Ethnic and Personality Patterns in College Entrance." *J Exp Ed* 35:79–83 f '66. *

773. BAKER, ELLIOT. *Psychological Factors Related to Competitive Performance in Middle and Long Distance Running.* Master's thesis, Temple University (Philadelphia, Pa.), 1966.

774. BERGER, EDWARD H. *The Relationships Among Personality, Perception, and Job Preference.* Doctor's thesis, Boston University (Boston, Mass.), 1966. *(DA 27:1614B)*

775. BERRIEN, F. KENNETH. "Japanese and American Values." *Int J Psychol* 1(2):129–41 '66. * *(PA 41:486)*

776. BOLLINGER, LAURENCE J. *An Investigation of the Psychological Characteristics of the Handicapped Employees in Industry.* Doctor's thesis, Wayne State University (Detroit, Mich.), 1966. *(DAI 30:375B)*

777. BRIGGS, MEROLD S. *A Comparative Study of the Characteristics of Personality Among Selected Groups of Freshmen in the Work-Study Program at Colorado State College.* Doctor's research study No. 1, Colorado State College (Greeley, Colo.), 1966. *(DA 27:2268A)*

778. BUCK, LUCIEN A., AND SCAMMON, MICHAEL W. "Perception of Incidental Success and Failure Stimuli by High and Low N Achievement Groups." *Percept & Motor Skills* 22:582 Ap '66. * *(PA 40:8318)*

779. BURKEEN, EMMETT D. *A Study of the Relationship of Certain Personal Characteristics to Acceptance-Rejection Attitudes Toward Professional Education Courses Among Teacher Education Graduates.* Doctor's thesis, University of Kentucky (Lexington, Ky.), 1966. *(DAI 30:2369A)*

780. BUXBAUM, JOAN. *Nurturance as a Factor in Wives' Appraisals of Their Aphasic Husbands.* Doctor's thesis, Columbia University (New York, N.Y.), 1966. (*DA* 27:955B)

781. CHARLES, LOUIS. *A Multiple Discriminant Analysis of the Effects of Personality Variables on Academic Achievement in a Dental Education Setting.* Doctor's thesis, University of Pittsburgh (Pittsburgh, Pa.), 1966. (*DA* 27:3303A)

782. COOPER, CECILIA ROSE. *A Comparison of Work Perceptions and Derived Satisfactions of Hospital Volunteers and Paid Employees.* Doctor's thesis, Boston University (Boston, Mass.), 1966. (*DA* 27:1618B)

783. DAYTON, LAURENCE LOUIS. *Instructions and Affiliation as Factors in the Categorizations of Love and Anger.* Doctor's thesis, University of Massachusetts (Amherst, Mass.), 1966. (*DA* 27:2868B)

784. DEAK, MARILYN RADINSKY. *The Effect of Motivation Arousal Conditions on Creativity Test Performance.* Doctor's thesis, State University of New York (Buffalo, N.Y.), 1966. (*DA* 27:1605B)

785. DIENER, RUSSELL EDWARD. *A Comparative Study of Selected Needs, Values, and Attitudes of Negro and White Elementary Education Students.* Doctor's thesis, University of Michigan (Ann Arbor, Mich.), 1966. (*DA* 27:2825A)

786. DINEEN, TIMOTHY PATRICK. *Verbal Learning, Dominance, and Tension.* Doctor's thesis, Columbia University (New York, N.Y.), 1966. (*DA* 27:962B)

787. FOWLER, THOMAS JACKSON. *Counselor Effectiveness in Relation to Role Concept and Psychological Needs.* Doctor's thesis, University of Alabama (University, Ala.), 1966. (*DA* 27:2826A)

788. GHEI, S. N. "A Cross-Cultural Study of Need Profiles." *J Pers & Social Psychol* 3:580–5 My '66. * (*PA* 40: 7594)

789. GOLDMAN, HARVEY. *A Study of the Teacher-Administrator Relationship and the Influence of Need Patterns.* Doctor's thesis, Michigan State University (East Lansing, Mich.), 1966. (*DA* 27:2778A)

790. GRAY, CLIFFORD FREDERICK. *A Comparison of Performance and Selected Personality Traits of Participants in a Total Enterprise Business Game.* Doctor's thesis, University of Oregon (Eugene, Ore.), 1966. (*DA* 27:1983A)

791. HALL, DAVID STANLEY. *Socio-Cultural and Personal Correlates of Differential Orientations of Dental Students to Dentistry.* Doctor's thesis, University of Kentucky (Lexington, Ky.), 1966. (*DAI* 30:2166A)

792. HOFMANN, LOUIS JOHN. *An Application of the Multitrait-Multimethod Matrix to the Study of the n-Achievement Construct.* Doctor's thesis, Michigan State University (East Lansing, Mich.), 1966. (*DA* 27:1262A)

793. LYON, JOHN THOMAS, JR. *An Experimental Investigation of the Relation Between Personality and Vocal Characteristics of Selected Beginning Adult Singers.* Doctor's thesis, Indiana University (Bloomington, Ind.), 1966. (*DA* 27:4285A)

794. MARCANTONIO, CHARLES. *Performance Expectancy as a Determinant of Actual Performance: With Particular Reference to Individual Difference Variables.* Doctor's thesis, State University of New York (Buffalo, N.Y.), 1966. (*DA* 28: 785A)

795. MAURATH, JEROME DONALD. *Selective Reinforcement vs Cognitive Structuring: Effects on "Motivational" Behavior.* Doctor's thesis, University of Illinois (Urbana, Ill.), 1966. (*DA* 27:4129B)

796. MILLER, AARON JULIUS. *A Study of Engineering and Technical Institute Freshman Enrollees and Dropouts in Terms of Selected Intellective and Non-Intellective Factors.* Doctor's thesis, Oklahoma State University (Stillwater, Okla.), 1966. (*DA* 27:4050A)

797. MINGE, M. RONALD. "Counseling Readiness as Readiness for Change." *J Col Stud Personnel* 7:197–202 Jl '66. *

798. MULLIKEN, RUTH KINNEY. *A Study of Parental Attitudes: Self Concepts and Personality Characteristics of Deviant Achievers of Average Ability.* Doctor's thesis, University of Utah (Salt Lake City, Utah), 1966. (*DA* 27:961A)

799. NELSON, DONALD THEODORE. *The Impact of Foreign Undergraduate Students Upon American Undergraduate Students.* Doctor's thesis, Indiana University (Bloomington, Ind.), 1966. (*DA* 27:2010A)

800. PARKER, ADAH DONOHUE. *Projections for the Selection, Training and Retention of Sub-Professional Recreation Leaders Based on an Analysis of Personality, Interest, Aptitude, and Preference Data.* Doctor's thesis, University of Illinois (Urbana, Ill.), 1966. (*DA* 27:2059A)

801. RIESS, DORIS GAIL FLOWERMAN. *The Effects of Compatibility and Accuracy of Interpersonal Information on Impression Formation.* Doctor's thesis, George Washington University (Washington, D.C.), 1966. (*DA* 28:788A)

802. SHERIN, CAROLYN RICHARDS. *Some Relationships Among Popularity, Friendship Choice, and Personality Variables.* Doctor's thesis, University of Miami (Coral Gables, Fla.), 1966. (*DA* 27:1931A)

803. STALLINGS, WILLIAM MARION. *A Study of Non-Intellective Factors in the Prediction of Academic Success for Master's Degree Level Students in the School of Education, Indiana University.* Doctor's thesis, Indiana University (Bloomington, Ind.), 1966. (*DA* 27:3324A)

804. TARWATER, JESSE W. "Chinese and American Stu-

dents' Interpersonal Values: A Cross-Cultural Comparison." *J Col Stud Personnel* 7:351–4 N '66. *

805. THIESSEN, IRMGARD. "Values and Personality Characteristics of Mennonites in Manitoba." *Mennonite Q R* 40:48–61 Ja '66. *

806. WILLIAMS, PAUL LEON. *A Study of Variables Related to Students' Perception of Classroom Tests.* Doctor's thesis, Illinois Institute of Technology (Chicago, Ill.), 1966. (*DA* 28:4288B)

807. ANDERSON, ROBERT E. "Seminar Experiences for Changing Attitudes of Graduating Seniors in Education." *J Exp Ed* 36:87–92 f '67. *

808. BORG, WALTER R. "Teacher Effectiveness in Team Teaching." *J Exp Ed* 35:65–70 sp '67. *

809. BREIMEIER, KENNETH H. *Relationship Between Various Psychological Measures in Use at Theological Seminaries.* Comments by James E. Dittes. Occasional Papers No. 1. Washington, D.C.: Ministry Studies Board, 1967. Pp. iii, 59. *

810. BROWN, OWEN BRUCE. *A Comparative Analysis of Certain Perceptual Effects Resulting From Two Methods of Initiating Counselor-Student Contact: Self-Initiated vs. Required.* Doctor's thesis, Boston University (Boston, Mass.), 1967. (*DA* 29:4274A)

811. CHAFFEE, GLENN ALBERT. *A Study of the Self Concepts, Occupational Personas, and Occupational Stereotypes of Engineering Students.* Doctor's thesis, Michigan State University (East Lansing, Mich.), 1967. (*DA* 28:3968A)

812. FOGG, CHARLES P., AND CALLA, VINCENT F. "The Comparative Influence of Two Testing Techniques on Achievement in Science and Critical Thinking Ability." *J Exp Ed* 35:1–14 sp '67. *

813. GOLDMAN, HARVEY, AND HEALD, JAMES E. "Teachers' Need Patterns and the Administrator." *Nat Assn Sec Sch Prin B* 51:93–104 D '67. *

814. HARTZELL, JOHN PAUL. *A Preliminary Study of Nurturant and/or Aggressive Therapists' Responsiveness to Expressions of Dependency and Hostility in the Initial Phase of Psychotherapy.* Doctor's thesis, Michigan State University (East Lansing, Mich.), 1967. (*DA* 28:1195B)

815. HILL, FREDERICK E. *The Attraction of Upper-Class and Under-Class Vocationally Undecided Male Students Towards a Counseling Relationship.* Doctor's thesis, Michigan State University (East Lansing, Mich.), 1967. (*DA* 29:122A)

816. KARR, BENJAMIN. *A Proposed Method for Test Interpretation.* Doctor's thesis, University of Cincinnati (Cincinnati, Ohio), 1967. (*DA* 28:3473B)

817. LAMB, ROBERT BRUCE. *Expectation and Achievement Motivation as Determinants of Performance.* Doctor's thesis, Washington University (St. Louis, Mo.), 1967. (*DA* 28: 4319B)

818. LECKWART, JOHN FRED. *Social Distance as an Interpersonal Dimension in Vertical Relationships.* Doctor's thesis, Western Reserve University (Cleveland, Ohio), 1967. (*DA* 28:1901A)

819. LIPSMAN, CLAIRE K. *The Relation of Socio-Economic Level and Occupational Choice to Needs and Vocational Behavior.* Doctor's thesis, Catholic University of America (Washington, D.C.), 1967. (*DA* 28:2073A)

820. NASH, DAVID C. *A Study Concerning the Relationship of Summer School Attendance and the Edwards Personal Preference Schedule With Academic Achievement of Pre-Admission Counselees at North Carolina State University, School of Engineering.* Master's thesis, North Carolina State University (Raleigh, N.C.), 1967.

821. PIETROFESA, JOHN JOSEPH. *A Comparison of the Need Structure of College Students Enrolled in Different Academic Majors.* Doctor's thesis, University of Miami (Coral Gables, Fla.), 1967. (*DA* 28:2520A)

822. PORTER, JANET B. "The Vocational Choice of Freshmen College Women as Influenced by Psychological Needs and Parent-Child Relationships," pp. 49–61. In *Parent-Child Relations: Research Status, Measurement, and Predictive Value.* By Harry J. Parker and others. Studies in the Assessment of Parent-Child Relationship, Monograph Series No. 1. Oklahoma City, Okla.: University of Oklahoma Medical Center Library, 1967. Pp. v, 61. *

823. SAMPSON, EDWARD E., AND HANCOCK, FRANCENA T. "An Examination of the Relationship Between Ordinal Position, Personality, and Conformity: An Extension, Replication, and Partial Verification." *J Pers & Social Psychol* 5:398–407 Ap '67. * (*PA* 41:7234)

824. SCHUTTE, EILEEN PAULINE. *Personality Characteristics of Typewriting and Shorthand Teachers.* Doctor's thesis, Northern Illinois University (DeKalb, Ill.), 1967. (*DA* 29: 1811A)

825. SHEYA, JUDY ANN. *The Relationship of Personality Variables to Choice of Physical Education Activity.* Master's thesis, Smith College (Northampton, Mass.), 1967.

826. SMITH, GENE M. "Personality Correlates of Cigarette Smoking in Students of College Age." *Ann N Y Acad Sci* 142:308–21 Mr 15 '67. * (*PA* 42:6913)

827. VESPRANI, GEORGE JOSEPH. *Accurate Empathy in a College Companion Program.* Doctor's thesis, University of Cincinnati (Cincinnati, Ohio), 1967. (*DA* 28:3483B)

828. VOGEL, ROBERTA BURRAGE. *A Projective Study of Dynamic Factors in Attempted Suicide.* Doctor's thesis, Michi-

gan State University (East Lansing, Mich.), 1967. (*DA* 28: 4303B)

829. WHITE, HAZEL WILMA. *A Descriptive Analysis of a Group of AFDC (Aid to Families With Dependent Children) Recipients.* Doctor's thesis, University of New Mexico (Albuquerque, N.M.), 1967. (*DA* 28:3472A)

830. WORKMAN, ARTHUR DAVID. *The Relationship Among Counselor N Achievement, Trait Attribution, and Verbal Reinforcement Behavior.* Doctor's thesis, University of California (Berkeley, Calif.), 1967. (*DA* 28:2526A)

831. ALLUMBAUGH, JAMES. *The Relationship of Structured and Non-Structured Stimuli for Art Production to Selected Personality Factors.* Doctor's thesis, North Texas State University (Denton, Tex.), 1968. (*DA* 29:1665A)

832. ASHMORE, BETTIE JANE. *An Investigation of Changes in Attitudes and Personality Characteristics Among Counselors in Three Types of Counselor Education Programs.* Doctor's thesis, University of Alabama (University, Ala.), 1968. (*DA* 29:1416A)

833. AUTEN, RICHARD T. *The Self Estimates of Need Strengths of High School Seniors and Their Scores on the Edwards Personality Preference Schedule.* Master's thesis, University of Tennessee (Knoxville, Tenn.), 1968.

834. BAYES, ANDREW HARTIN. *An Application of Hotelling's Canonical Correlation to Academic Prediction.* Doctor's thesis, University of Miami (Coral Gables, Fla.), 1968. (*DA* 29:2512A)

835. BLACKWELL, ROBERT BRENNAN. *A Study of Effective and Ineffective Teachers of the Trainable Mentally Retarded.* Doctor's thesis, Colorado State College (Greeley, Colo.), 1968. (*DA* 29:1147A)

836. BOUCHARD, THOMAS J., JR. "Convergent and Discriminant Validity of the Adjective Check List and Edwards Personal Preference Schedule." *Ed & Psychol Meas* 28:1165–71 w '68. * (*PA* 44:6777)

837. BRADSHAW, OTTIE LEON. *The Relationship of Selected Measures of Aptitude, Interest, and Personality to Academic Achievement in Engineering and Engineering Technology.* Doctor's thesis, Oklahoma State University (Stillwater, Okla.), 1968. (*DAI* 30:979A)

838. BRODY, ROBERT P., AND CUNNINGHAM, SCOTT M. "Personality Variables and the Consumer Decision Process." *J Marketing Res* 5:50–7 F '68. *

839. CLARY, ELDON GANDY, JR. *Predicting Student Teaching Behavior From Needs Profiles by Comparison With Sociometrically Defined Groups.* Doctor's thesis, North Texas State University (Denton, Tex.), 1968. (*DA* 29:3488A)

840. COHEN, EDMUND DAVID. *Some Related Variables in the Interpersonal Risk (IR) Theory.* Doctor's thesis, Case Western Reserve University (Cleveland, Ohio), 1968. (*DAI* 30:4787B)

841. CONLEY, JAMES LEROY. *A Study of Selected Biographical Data, Personality Characteristics and Attitudes of Elementary Intern Program Students at Michigan State University.* Doctor's thesis, Michigan State University (East Lansing, Mich.), 1968. (*DA* 29:3490A)

842. CURB, LAURA SOMERVILL. *Personality Traits of Elementary School Teachers Who Voted for or Against Sanctions.* Doctor's thesis, University of Oklahoma (Norman, Okla.), 1968. (*DA* 29:2559A)

843. CZAJKOWSKI, THEODORE JOSEPH, JR. *The Relationship of Confidence for Teaching to Selected Personal Characteristics and Performance of Student Teachers.* Doctor's thesis, Michigan State University (East Lansing, Mich.), 1968. (*DAI* 30:185A)

844. EDWARDS, CARL N. "Characteristics of Volunteers and Nonvolunteers for a Sleep and Hypnotic Experiment." *Am J Clin Hyp* 11:16–9 Jl '68. * (*PA* 43:912)

845. EMMER, ROBERT S. *A Comparison of Chronic Alcoholics and Psychiatric Patients on Three Scales of the Edwards Personal Preference Schedule.* Master's thesis, Springfield College (Springfield, Mass.), 1968.

846. FAULKNER, AUDREY OLSEN. *Myth and Circumstance: A Study of Priority Decision Making in the Pennsylvania Citizens Council.* Doctor's thesis, University of Pittsburgh (Pittsburgh, Pa.), 1968. (*DA* 29:965A)

847. GARMS, JOE D., AND RAY, J. B. "Authoritarian Attitudes and Scholastic Achievement." *Psychol* 5:47–51 N '68. * (*PA* 43:5964)

848. GARZETTA, LOUIS PETER. *Bias in Clinical Test Interpretation.* Doctor's thesis, Yeshiva University (New York, N.Y.), 1968. (*DA* 29:2191B)

849. GATES, CARL JAY. *A Study of Attitude, Need, and Personality Trait Correlates of Effective Teaching in Three Selected School Systems.* Doctor's thesis, University of Southern Mississippi (Hattiesburg, Miss.), 1968. (*DA* 29:3021A)

850. GHANNAD, REZA H. *The Effects of Planned Interaction of Adult Males With Institutionalized Mentally Retarded Boys Upon Their Sex-Role Identification and Self-Concept.* Doctor's thesis, Brigham Young University (Provo, Utah), 1968. (*DA* 29:3001A)

851. GILBERTS, RICHARD ALLAN. *A Comparison of Statistical Models for Predicting Counselor Responses From Personality Measures.* Doctor's thesis, University of Washington (Seattle, Wash.), 1968. (*DA* 29:2091A)

852. GRIMM, RONALD L. *Personality Traits of Women Athletes at the University of Montana as Measured by the Ed-*

wards Personal Preference Schedule. Master's thesis, University of Montana (Missoula, Mont.), 1968.

853. HAMNER, PATRICIA FULL. *Personality Characteristics of Home Economics Freshmen as Measured by the Edwards Personal Preference Schedule.* Master's thesis, Cornell University (Ithaca, N.Y.), 1968.

854. HENDERSON, DONALD RAY. *A Study to Determine the Personality Characteristics of Innovative Educational Administrators and Educational Administrators in Illinois and Indiana.* Doctor's thesis, Indiana University (Bloomington, Ind.), 1968. (*DA* 29:3375A)

855. HOOPER, DONALD BRUCE. *Differential Utility of Leadership Opinions in Classical and Moderator Models for the Prediction of Leadership Effectiveness.* Doctor's thesis, Ohio State University (Columbus, Ohio), 1968. (*DAI* 30:13A)

856. JORDAN, DAVID LEE. *A Comparison of the Effects of Didactic and Experiential Training on Accurate Empathy, Nonpossessive Warmth, and Genuineness.* Doctor's thesis, University of Colorado (Boulder, Colo.), 1968. (*DA* 29:3487B)

857. JOURARD, SIDNEY M., AND KORMANN, LEO A. "Getting to Know the Experimenter, and Its Effect on Psychological Test Performance." *J Humanistic Psychol* 8:155–9 f '68. * (*PA* 43:9637)

858. JOY, CAROL M. *A Study of the Relationship of Certain Personality Variables to Participation in Physical Education.* Master's thesis, Smith College (Northampton, Mass.), 1968.

859. KENWORTHY, JOY ANNE. *Personality Characteristics Associated With Effectiveness in Psychotherapy.* Doctor's thesis, Iowa State University (Ames, Iowa), 1968. (*DA* 29:3488B)

860. KETTERLING, MARVIN E., AND STOCKEY, MERREL R. "Personality Change During Nursing Education." *Meas & Eval Guid* 1:175–81 f '68. *

861. McINTIRE, WALTER GORDON. *A Comparative Study of Selected Personality Characteristics of Students Who Cheat and Do Not Cheat in an Academic Situation.* Doctor's thesis, University of North Dakota (Grand Forks, N.D.), 1968. (*DA* 29:3079B)

862. MAKOVIC, MARY VERNICE. *The Relationships Between Nun-Teachers' Manifest Psychogenic Needs and Attitudes Toward Students and Student Behavior.* Doctor's thesis, Case Western Reserve University (Cleveland, Ohio), 1968. (*DAI* 30:170A)

863. MALONEY, MICHAEL P. "The Question of Achievement in the Japanese American: A Comment on Cross-Cultural Research." *Psychologia* 11:143–58 D '68. * (*PA* 44:7267)

864. MARCUS, NATHANIEL SAMUEL. *Dropouts in Psychotherapy.* Doctor's thesis, University of California (Los Angeles, Calif.), 1968. (*DA* 29:1508B)

865. MASER, ARTHUR LYLE. *The Effect of Client Response and Counselor Personality on Counselor Response; and the Effect of Counselor Response on Client Response.* Doctor's thesis, University of Washington (Seattle, Wash.), 1968. (*DA* 29:2096A)

866. MEREDITH, GERALD M. "Personality Correlates to Religious Belief Systems." *Psychol Rep* 23:1039–42 D '68. * (*PA* 43:8236)

867. MILES, WILFORD GLENN, Jr. *An Investigation Into the Relationship Between Certain Personality Traits and Management Success.* Doctor's thesis, University of Arkansas (Fayetteville, Ark.), 1968. (*DA* 29:1341A)

868. MORRISON, HUGH E. *The Relationship of Expressed Psychological Needs of Teachers of Mentally Retarded Children to Occupational Success.* Doctor's thesis, University of Kansas (Lawrence, Kan.), 1968. (*DA* 29:1789A)

869. MOSLEY, LARRY A. *Effect of Skill and Personality on Activity Choice.* Master's thesis, Wisconsin State University (La Crosse, Wis.), 1968.

870. OURY, THOMAS HARRISON. *An Investigation of Sensitivity as a Predictor in Counselor-Trainee Selection Procedures.* Doctor's thesis, University of Southern California (Los Angeles, Calif.), 1968. (*DA* 29:2967A)

871. OWENS, WAYNE STANFORD. *An Analysis of the Characteristics of Selected Educational Administrators in Illinois and Indiana.* Doctor's thesis, Indiana University (Bloomington, Ind.), 1968. (*DA* 29:1728A)

872. PAPALIA, ANTHONY SEBASTIAN. *The Characteristics of Selected Low-Achieving, High-Potential Male College Freshmen Subjected to a Specialized Reading and Study Skills Program.* Doctor's thesis, State University of New York (Albany, N.Y.), 1968. (*DA* 29:3878A)

873. POWELL, GERTRUDE. *An Examination of Seminary Students' Scores on the Edwards Personal Preference Schedule.* Master's thesis, University of Maryland (College Park, Md.), 1968.

874. PSATHAS, GEORGE, AND PLAPP, JON. "Assessing the Effects of a Nursing Program: A Problem in Design." *Nursing Res* 17:336–42 Jl–Ag '68. * (*PA* 42:19503)

875. RADER, BLAINE BURDETTE. *Identification of Selected Personality Characteristics Which Make for Effectiveness in Pastoral Care.* Doctor's thesis, Drew University (Madison, N.J.), 1968. (*DA* 29:1849B)

876. RAWLS, DONNA J., AND RAWLS, JAMES R. "Personality Characteristics and Personal History Data of Successful and Less Successful Executives." *Psychol Rep* 23:1032–4 D '68. * (*PA* 43:8822)

877. RUSSELL, WILLIAM JOY CROSBY. *A Study of Changes*

in Measures of Inner-Direction, Open-Mindedness, and Intraception During Laboratory Training Designs of the Methodist Church. Doctor's thesis, Syracuse University (Syracuse, N.Y.), 1968. (*DA* 29:3887A)

878. SEAMAN, CAROLYN MUSSINA. *The Prediction of Length of Hospitalization From Personality Test Scores, Demographic and Social Variables According to the Process-Reactive Continuum.* Doctor's thesis, Ohio University (Athens, Ohio), 1968. (*DA* 29:1513A)

879. SEDLACEK, CAROLINE GLADYS. *Selected Factors Affecting Certainty and Persistence of Vocational Choice for College Women.* Doctor's thesis, University of North Dakota (Grand Forks, N.D.), 1968. (*DA* 29:3843A)

880. SEGNER, VENICE CHANDLER. *Effects of Early Experience on Later Interview Assessments of Social and Personal Adjustments.* Doctor's thesis, University of Georgia (Athens, Ga.), 1968. (*DA* 29:4853B)

881. SHACK, JOHN RICHARD. *Development of an Objective Factorial Learning Motivation Orientation Inventory.* Doctor's thesis, Case Western Reserve University (Cleveland, Ohio), 1968. (*DAI* 30:4383B)

882. SHAFFER, ROBERT H., AND DOWLING, LEO R. "Foreign Students and Their American Student Friends." *Sch & Soc* 96:245–9 Ap '68. *

883. SINDT, DORIS M. *An Investigation of the Relationship Between the Intolerance of Ambiguity Dimension of the Counselor's Personality and Counseling Behaviors and Certain Other Personality Dimensions.* Doctor's thesis, University of Kansas (Lawrence, Kan.), 1968. (*DA* 29:1759A)

884. SMITH, RICHARD MORTIMER. *A Study of the Relationship Between Personality Profiles and Vocational Preferences.* Doctor's thesis, St. Louis University (St. Louis, Mo.), 1968. (*DA* 30:1406A)

885. SWINDELL, DOROTHY H., AND LIEBERMAN, LEWIS R. "Effect of Sex on the Correlation Between the Dogmatism Scale and the Edwards Personal Preference Schedule." *Psychol Rep* 23:893–4 D '68. * (*PA* 43:9779)

886. TAFT, EDWARD JERRY. *The Role of a New Kind of Empathy in Understanding Marital Happiness.* Doctor's thesis, University of Arizona (Tucson, Ariz.), 1968. (*DA* 29:3223A)

887. TAYLOR, ELIZABETH ELLEN. *The Measurement of Need and Conflict in the Normal Person.* Doctor's thesis, Washington University (St. Louis, Mo.), 1968. (*DA* 29:4855B)

888. URBAN, THEODORE STANLEY. *Wives' Needs as Related to Perceptions of Their Husbands' Post-Mental Hospital Behavior.* Doctor's thesis, Pennsylvania State University (University Park, Pa.), 1968. (*DA* 29:3954B)

889. VAN ATTA, RALPH E. "Relationship of Personality Characteristics to Persistence in Psychotherapy." *J Consult & Clin Psychol* 32:731–3 D '68. *

890. WALBERG, HERBERT J., AND WELCH, WAYNE W. "Dimensions of Personality in Selected Physics Teachers." *J Res Sci Teach* 5(4):357–61 '67–68. *

891. WALLACE, FLORA TEAGUE. *A Measurement and Comparison of the Need Dispositions and Values Orientations of Secondary School Counselors and Teachers.* Doctor's thesis, University of New Mexico (Albuquerque, N.M.), 1968. (*DA* 29:4358A)

892. WEIGEL, RICHARD G., AND FRAZIER, JAMES E. "The Effects of 'Feeling' and 'Behavior' Instructions on Responses to the Edwards Personal Preference Schedule." *J Ed Meas* 5:337–8 w '68. * (*PA* 44:10442)

893. WENDT, MIRIAM JANE. *The Conditioning of Defensive Verbal Constructs in Schizophrenic Patients.* Doctor's thesis, Case Western Reserve University (Cleveland, Ohio), 1968. (*DA* 29:4857B)

894. WRIGHT, PAUL H. "Need Similarity, Need Complementarity and the Place of Personality in Interpersonal Attraction." *J Exp Res Personality* 3:126–35 D '68. *

895. YOUNG, JEAN ANN. *Implicit-Explicit Attitudes of Secondary Student Teachers.* Doctor's thesis, University of California (Berkeley, Calif.), 1968. (*DA* 29:4360A)

896. ADAMS, WESLEY JAMES. *Sex Composition in Group Discussion as Related to Acquisition of Knowledge and Attitudinal Change Among Women in a Family Life Course.* Doctor's thesis, Oregon State University (Corvallis, Ore.), 1969. (*DAI* 30:3093A)

897. ALDAG, JEAN C. KERZ. *Male Nurse Interest and Personality Characteristics.* Doctor's thesis, Washington University (St. Louis, Mo.), 1969. (*DAI* 30:5672B)

898. ANDERSON, DONALD D. "Personality Attributes of Teachers in Organizational Climates." *J Ed Res* 62(10):441–3 Jl–Ag '69. * (*PA* 46:5602)

899. ANDRISEK, JOHN RICHARD. *The Relationship of Formal Upward Communication to the Personality of the Principal and to Teacher Negotiations.* Doctor's thesis, Case Western Reserve University (Cleveland, Ohio), 1969. (*DAI* 30:3660A)

900. ARMLIN, NELSON JOSEPH. *Four Aspects of Counselor Behavior and Measured Personality Traits Related to the Open-Closed Cognitive Continuum of the Rokeach Dogmatism Scale.* Doctor's thesis, Florida State University (Tallahassee, Fla.), 1969. (*DAI* 30:4213A)

901. BAEHR, MELANY E.; FURCON, JOHN E.; AND FROEMEL, ERNEST C. *Psychological Assessment of Patrolman Qualifications in Relation to Field Performance.* Washington, D.C.: United States Government Printing Office, 1969. Pp. vii, 246. *

902. BAILEY, JUNE T., AND CLAUS, KAREN E. "Comparative Analysis of the Personality Structure of Nursing Students." *Nursing Res* 18(4):320–6 Jl–Ag '69. *

903. BARNA, JAMES DANIEL. *Development of a Scale of Causal Constructs and Its Relationship to Selected Personality Tests.* Doctor's thesis, St. Louis University (St. Louis, Mo.), 1969. (*DAI* 30:3861B)

904. BEHLING, MARY ALICE. *The Development of a Screening Program for the Selection and Retention of Women Physical Education Major Students.* Doctor's thesis, Florida State University (Tallahassee, Fla.), 1969. (*DAI* 30:4258A)

905. BELT, GORDON ANTHONY. *A Study of the Changes in Personality Variables and Attitudes of Students in an Education Class.* Doctor's thesis, Wayne State University (Detroit, Mich.), 1969. (*DAI* 31:1654A)

906. BERGIN, ALLEN E., AND JASPER, LAWRENCE G. "Correlates of Empathy in Psychotherapy: A Replication." *J Abn Psychol* 74(4):477–81 Ag '69. * (*PA* 43:15891)

907. BERKOWITZ, WILLIAM R. "Perceived Height, Personality, and Friendship Choice." *Psychol Rep* 24(2):373–4 Ap '69. * (*PA* 43:15719)

908. BERRIEN, F. KENNETH. "Familiarity, Mirror Imaging and Social Desirability in Stereotypes: Japanese *vs* Americans." *Int J Psychol* 4(3):207–15 '69. * (*PA* 45:6130)

909. BHATNAGAR, R. P. "A Study of Some EPPS Variables as Factors of Academic Achievement." *J Appl Psychol* 53(2): 107–11 Ap '69. * (*PA* 43:8752)

910. BROWN, EDWARD ALBERT. *A Comparative Study of Personality Traits of Varsity Skiers, Varsity Wrestlers, Varsity Swimmers, and Collegiate Non-Athletes at Selected Institutions of Higher Learning in the Intermountain Area.* Doctor's thesis, University of Utah (Salt Lake City, Utah), 1969. (*DAI* 30: 2826A)

911. CALLAHAN, LUKE J., AND WAUCK, LEROY A. "Characteristics of a Minor Seminary Population on the Edwards Personal Preference Schedule." *Nat Cath Guid Conf J* 13(3): 30–7 sp '69. * (*PA* 44:6579)

912. CHRISMAN, JAMES WELDON. *Some Factors Related to the Degree of Autonomy Exercised by Secondary School Principals in Missouri.* Doctor's thesis, University of Missouri (Columbia, Mo.), 1969. (*DAI* 30:1356A)

913. CLARK, AGNES LORRAINE HOWARD. *The Relationship of Selected Physiological Factors to Interpersonal Encounters.* Doctor's thesis, East Texas State University (Commerce, Tex.), 1969. (*DAI* 30:5228A)

914. COATES, THOMAS, AND MAZUR, STANLEY. "Personality Characteristics and Interpersonal Attraction." *Psychol* 6(1):2–9 F '69. * (*PA* 43:11298)

915. DANIELSON, HARRY A. "Personality of Prospective Elementary School Counselors: Implications for Preparation." *Counselor Ed & Sup* 8(2):99–103 w '69. *

916. DEED, MARTHA LOUISE. *Major Patterns of Religious Commitment Among Members of the Religious Society of Friends.* Doctor's thesis, Boston University (Boston, Mass.), 1969. (*DAI* 30:2396B)

917. DeWITT, CHARLES JAY. *A Study of Selected Variables in Discriminating Between Contrasting Levels of Student Teaching Performance.* Doctor's thesis, University of Virginia (Charlottesville, Va.), 1969. (*DAI* 31:260A)

918. DiGIORGIO, ANTHONY JOSEPH. *Discriminant Function Analysis of Measured Characteristics Among Committed Career Groups With Requisite Graduate Training.* Doctor's thesis, Purdue University (Lafayette, Ind.), 1969. (*DAI* 30:4769A)

919. DOHERTY, ANNE. *The Relationship of Dependency and Perception of Parents to the Development of Feminine Sex Role and Conscience.* Doctor's thesis, Catholic University of America (Washington, D.C.), 1969. (*DAI* 30:2415B)

920. DREWERY, J., AND RAE, J. B. "A Group Comparison of Alcoholic and Non-Alcoholic Marriages Using the Interpersonal Perception Technique." *Brit J Psychiatry* 115(520):287–300 Mr '69. * (*PA* 43:13083)

921. DREWERY, JAMES. "An Interpersonal Perception Technique." *Brit J Med Psychol* 42(2):171–81 Je '69. * (*PA* 44: 601)

922. DUNNING, DONALD. *Personality Differences Between Cigarette Smokers and Nonsmokers.* Master's thesis, Springfield College (Springfield, Mass.), 1969.

923. EBERLEIN, E. LARRY. "The Relationship Between School Climate and Edwards' Manifest Needs of the Elementary School Teacher." *Psychol Sch* 6(1):80–3 Ja '69. * (*PA* 43: 8729)

924. EIDE, LYLE JACOB. *Test Self-Estimates as Related to Needs, Vocational Interests, Ability, Achievement and Persistence of University Freshman Males.* Doctor's thesis, University of North Dakota (Grand Forks, N.D.), 1969. (*DAI* 30: 1818A)

925. FELDMAN, KENNETH A., AND NEWCOMB, THEODORE M. *The Impact of College on Students: Vol. 2, Summary Tables.* San Francisco, Calif.: Jossey-Bass Inc., Publishers, 1969. Pp. iv, 171. *

926. FINCH, KAYE. *Personality Variables and Sexual Status in Observer Performance.* Master's thesis, University of Alabama (University, Ala.), 1969.

927. FISHER, GARY. "Psychological Needs of Heterosexual Pedophiliacs." *Dis Nerv System* 30(6):419–21 Je '69. * (*PA* 44:7005)

928. Fiske, Donald W. "Subject Reactions to Inventory Format and Content." Abstract. *Proc 77th Ann Conv Am Psychol Assn* 4(1):137–8 '69. * (*PA* 43:17516)

929. Fitzgerald, Owen Ray. *Psychodynamics of Volunteers Serving Overseas: Religious Vocation Workers and Peace Corps Volunteers in a North African Country.* Doctor's thesis, Boston University (Boston, Mass.), 1969. (*DAI* 30:2126A)

930. Fitzpatrick, John Charles. *The Relationships Between the Relative Effectiveness of Two Teaching Methods and Selected Non-Cognitive Variables of College Students.* Doctor's thesis, Fordham University (New York, N.Y.), 1969. (*DAI* 30:5284A)

931. Foreman, Milton E., and James, Leonard E. "Vocational Relevance and Estimated and Measured Test Scores." *J Counsel Psychol* 16(6):547–50 N '69. * (*PA* 44:4197)

932. Frankel, Phylis Schwartz. *The Relationship of Self-Concept, Sex Role Attitudes, and the Development of Achievement Need in Women.* Doctor's thesis, Northwestern University (Evanston, Ill.), 1969. (*DAI* 30:3371B)

933. Fry, G. E., and Reinhardt, R. F. "Personality Characteristics of Jet Pilots as Measured by the Edwards Personal Preference Schedule." *Aerospace Med* 40(5):484–6 My '69. *

934. Gahlhoff, Peter Eric. *An Investigation of the Personal and Situational Factors Influencing School Counselors' Career Patterns.* Doctor's thesis, Purdue University (Lafayette, Ind.), 1969. (*DAI* 30:4771A)

935. Gayton, William, and Bernstein, Stephen. "Incompatible Need Strength and the Repression-Sensitization Dimension." *J Clin Psychol* 25(2):192–4 Ap '69. * (*PA* 43:14286)

936. Ghei, S. N. "Social Desirability Ratings and the Probability of Endorsement of Personality Statements in Two Cultures." Abstract. *Proc 77th Ann Conv Am Psychol Assn* 4(1): 421–2 '69. * (*PA* 43:17281)

937. Goldman, Harvey. "Differential Need Patterns: Implications for Principals." *Sch R* 77(3–4):266–75 S–D '69. *

938. Gordon, Leonard V., and Sait, Edward M. "Q-Typing in the Domain of Manifest Needs." *Ed & Psychol Meas* 29(1): 87–98 sp '69. * (*PA* 44:16711)

939. Goss, Allen. "Abasement Scores and Adjustment of Neuropsychiatric Patients." *J Psychol* 71(1):17–9 Ja '69. *

940. Goss, Allen. "Predicting Vocational Success for Neuropsychiatric Patients With the Edwards Personal Preference Schedule." *J Appl Psychol* 53(3):250–2 Je '69. * (*PA* 43: 11561)

941. Grant, Alfred Dixon. *A Study of the Personality Characteristics of the Acceptor and the Rejector of the Newer Educational Media Among Secondary Teachers of Wisconsin.* Doctor's thesis, University of Wisconsin (Madison, Wis.), 1969. (*DAI* 31:676A)

942. Greenspan, Carrie F., and Pollock, Kenneth C. "Response Variability and Personality Factors in Automated Audiometry." *J Auditory Res* 9(4):386–90 O '69. *

943. Gunderson, Maxine Murphy. "Relationships Between Expressed Personality Needs and Social Background and Military Status Variables." *J Psychol* 71(2):217–24 Mr '69. * (*PA* 43:8340)

944. Hansen, Andrew H. *The Relationship of Personality Factors to Academic Achievement in College.* Doctor's thesis, Brigham Young University (Provo, Utah), 1969. (*DAI* 30: 3277A)

945. Harmon, James Stephen. *Effects of a Multi-Media Environment in College Level Electronics.* Doctor's thesis, Colorado State College (Greeley, Colo.), 1969. (*DAI* 30:2250A)

946. Harper, John Hudson. *The Relative Effectiveness of Group Counseling Versus Individual Counseling as Indicated by Change in Grade-Point Average and Client Insight.* Doctor's thesis, Auburn University (Auburn, Ala.), 1969. (*DAI* 30: 1821A)

947. Hayward, Margaret Louise. *Correlates of Approval and Disapproval Received by Students at Selected Schools of Nursing.* Doctor's thesis, University of Pittsburgh (Pittsburgh, Pa.), 1969. (*DAI* 30:1865A)

948. Hedenberg, John Wesley, Jr. *Personality Types Via an Objective Multivariate Search Technique.* Doctor's thesis, University of California (Los Angeles, Calif.), 1969. (*DAI* 30:3868B)

949. Holley, Jeanne Lowry. *An Analysis of Personality Needs and Certain Background Factors Which May Influence Career Choice of Women Business Education Majors.* Doctor's thesis, University of Mississippi (University, Miss.), 1969. (*DAI* 31:223A)

950. Holt, Fred D., and Carr, James G. "Manifest Needs of CAUSE Selectees and NDEA." *J Employ Counsel* 6(3): 110–6 S '69. *

951. Huckabee, Malcom W. "Consistency in the Use of the Judgment of Equality and Its Relation to Personality Variables." *South J Ed Res* 3(4):262–7 O '69. *

952. Huckabee, Malcom W. "Personality and Academic Aptitude Correlates of Cognitive Control Principles." *South J Ed Res* 3(1):1–9 Ja '69. *

953. Jenkins, Norman Lee. *An Analysis of the Relationship Between Academic Achievement and Selected Criteria for Junior College Freshmen in Terminal and Transfer Curricula.* Doctor's thesis, Purdue University (Lafayette, Ind.), 1969. (*DAI* 30:3728A)

954. Johnson, S. W., and Stiggins, R. J. "A Cross-Cultural Study of Values and Needs." *Acta Psychologica* 31(3):277–84 O '69. * (*PA* 44:14442)

955. Krop, Harry. "Effects of Extrinsic Motivation, Intrinsic Motivation, and Intelligence on Creativity: A Factorial Approach." *J General Psychol* 80(2):259–66 Ap '69. * (*PA* 43:11332)

956. Larsen, Mary Susan Faaborg. *Female Achievement Conflict Related to Parental Sex-Typing and Identification.* Doctor's thesis, Michigan State University (East Lansing, Mich.), 1969. (*DAI* 30:4794B)

957. Lawson, David Herbert Otis. *An Investigation of the Inter-Relationship of Personality, Relevance and Conformity to Self-Assessment in Small Group Functioning.* Doctor's thesis, George Washington University (Washington, D.C.), 1969. (*DAI* 31:915B)

958. LeMay, Morris L., and Damm, Vernon J. "Relationship of the Personal Orientation Inventory to the Edwards Personal Preference Schedule." *Psychol Rep* 24(3):834 Je '69. * (*PA* 44:664)

959. Lord, Raymond Morrieson. *Profile Patterns of Selected Business Majors as a Basis for Intra-Occupational Differentiation.* Doctor's thesis, Indiana University (Bloomington, Ind.), 1969. (*DAI* 30:551A)

960. McClelland, Mary Elizabeth. *An Investigation of Selected Non-Intellectual Variables and Their Relationship to College Academic Achievement.* Doctor's thesis, Michigan State University (East Lansing, Mich.), 1969. (*DAI* 30:2339A)

961. McKee, Marjorie Ann Brand. *The Components of Academic Success Studied in Seventy-Five (75) Educable Retarded Children: A Descriptive Study of Selected Factors.* Doctor's thesis, Wayne State University (Detroit, Mich.), 1969. (*DAI* 30:3859A)

962. Mader, Charles Eugene. *Analysis of the Relationship Between the Involvement of the Supervisor in the Structure of School Organization and Measures of His Personality Characteristics.* Doctor's thesis, University of Illinois (Urbana, Ill.), 1969. (*DAI* 30:1368A)

963. Magnussen, Max G., and Kemler, William M. "Infant Feeding Preference as Related to Personality Test Scores." *J Clin Psychol* 25(3):258–60 Jl '69. * (*PA* 44:3609)

964. May, A. E. "A Cautionary Approach to Questionnaire Response." Letter. *Brit J Psychiatry* 115(526):1102–3 S '69. *

965. Moomaw, Robert C., and Hayden, Charles E. "Personality Differences Among Community College Students." *J Col Stud Personnel* 10(5):306–9 S '69. *

966. Moore, Shirley June Bohs. *Personality Characteristics and Preparation of Financial Aid Administrators.* Doctor's thesis, Colorado State College (Greeley, Colo.), 1969. (*DAI* 30:1784A)

967. Morton, Joyce. *Stability of High School Kuder Vocational Interests as Related to Edwards Personality Needs.* Master's thesis, East Tennessee State University (Johnson City, Tenn.), 1969.

968. O'Neill, Marion, and Kempler, Bernhard. "Approach and Avoidance Responses of the Hysterical Personality to Sexual Stimuli." *J Abn Psychol* 74(3):300–5 Je '69. * (*PA* 43:12986)

969. Ostrow, Andrew C. *The Aggressive Tendencies of Male Intercollegiate Tennis Team Players.* Master's thesis, University of Maryland (College Park, Md.), 1969.

970. Parrish, Mary Charles. "Parents of Autistic Children: Their Common Needs and Attitudes." *Correct Psychiatry & J Social Ther* 15(4):14–9 w '69. * (*PA* 46:7208)

971. Patros, Philip George. *An Investigation of the Relationship Between Certain Non-Intellective Factors and Academic Performance of Academically Bright Junior High School Girls.* Doctor's thesis, Boston College (Chestnut Hill, Mass.), 1969. (*DAI* 30:3734A)

972. Phillips, Jerry Louis, and Todd, Donald Franklin. *The Relationship of Principals' Leadership Training and Personality to the Organizational Climates of Schools.* Doctor's thesis, University of Southern California (Los Angeles, Calif.), 1969. (*DAI* 31:120A)

973. Poe, Charles A. "Convergent and Discriminant Validation of Measures of Personal Needs." *J Ed Meas* 6(2): 103–7 su '69. * (*PA* 44:12613)

974. Potter, Neil Reed. *The Relationships of Selected Student Characteristics to Teacher Ratings.* Doctor's thesis, Colorado State College (Greeley, Colo.), 1969. (*DAI* 30:1404A)

975. Reed, Robert Lynn. *An Application of the Joint Multiple Regression Model to the Prediction of Academic Success From Personality Variables.* Doctor's thesis, University of Kansas (Lawrence, Kan.), 1969. (*DAI* 30:5300A)

976. Reeling, Patricia Ann. *Undergraduate Female Students as Potential Recruits to the Library Profession.* Doctor's thesis, Columbia University (New York, N.Y.), 1969. (*DAI* 30:4470A)

977. Richardson, Frank C. "Effects of 'Feeling' and 'Behavior' Instructions on Responses to the EPPS: A Replication." *J Ed Res* 62(9):399 My–Je '69. *

978. Robertson, James Rice. *Teaching Styles, Teacher Attitudes and the New Social Studies.* Doctor's thesis, Utah State University (Logan, Utah), 1969. (*DAI* 30:3354A)

979. Rothman, Arthur I. "Teacher Characteristics and Student Learning." *J Res Sci Teach* 6(4):340–8 '69. *

980. Rothman, Arthur I.; Welch, Wayne W.; and

WALBERG, HERBERT J. "Physics Teacher Characteristics and Student Learnings." *J Res Sci Teach* 6(1):59–63 '69. *

981. SAWIN, MARGARET MAY. *A Study of Sunday Church School Teachers' Personality Characteristics and Attitudes Toward Children.* Doctor's thesis, University of Maryland (College Park, Md.), 1969. (*DAI* 31:245A)

982. SCHUSLER, RICHARD ALLEN. *Nonverbal Communication in Elementary School Classrooms.* Doctor's thesis, University of Missouri (Kansas City, Mo.), 1969. (*DAI* 30:3863A)

983. SCHWARTZ, MELVIN L.; DENNERLL, RAYMOND D.; AND LIN, YI-GUANG. "Similarity of Personality Trait Interrelationships in Persons With and Without Epileptogenic Cerebral Dysfunction." *J Abn Psychol* 74(2):205–8 Ap '69. * (*PA* 43:10204)

984. SINGER, ROBERT N. "Personality Differences Between and Within Baseball and Tennis Players." *Res Q* 40(3):582–8 O '69. *

985. STEIN, RITA F. "The Student Nurse: A Study of Needs, Roles, and Conflicts, Part 1." *Nursing Res* 18(4):308–15 Jl–Ag '69. *

986. STEIN, RITA F. "The Student Nurse: A Study of Needs, Roles, and Conflicts, Part 2." *Nursing Res* 18(5):433–40 S–O '69. *

987. SUINN, RICHARD M. "Limited Sensory and Social Deprivation and Operant Control of Affiliation and Deference Responses." *J Proj Tech & Pers Assess* 33(6):535–8 D '69. * (*PA* 44:6784)

988. SUNDBERG, NORMAN; SHARMA, VIJAY; WODTLI, TERRY; AND ROHILA, PRITAM. "Family Cohesiveness and Autonomy of Adolescents in India and the United States." *J Marriage & Family* 31(2):403–7 My '69. *

989. TANNER, C. E.; PASEWARK, R. A.; AND FITZGERALD, B. J. "Use of the Edwards Personal Preference Schedule With Paranoid Schizophrenics." *Psychol Rep* 24(3):988 Je '69. * (*PA* 44:964)

990. TAYLOR, DALMAS A.; ALTMAN, IRWIN; WHEELER, LADD; AND KUSHNER, ESTELLE N. "Personality Factors Related to Response to Social Isolation and Confinement." *J Consult & Clin Psychol* 33(4):411–9 Ag '69. * (*PA* 43:15789)

991. THIESSEN, IRMGARD; WRIGHT, MORGAN W.; AND SISLER, GEORGE C. "A Comparison of Personality Characteristics of Mennonites With Non-Mennonites." *Can Psychologist* 10(2):129–37 Ap '69. * (*PA* 43:15654)

992. VESPRANI, GEORGE J. "Personality Correlates of Accurate Empathy in a College Companion Program." *J Consult & Clin Psychol* 33(6):722–7 D '69. * (*PA* 44:3612)

993. WADE, MELVA JEAN. *Alienation, Manifest Needs, and Academic Achievement in College Students With Marginal Entrance Qualifications.* Doctor's thesis, New York University (New York, N.Y.), 1969. (*DAI* 30:2864A)

994. WALBERG, HERBERT J. "Predicting Class Learning: An Approach to the Class as a Social System." *Am Ed Res J* 6(4):529–42 N '69. * (*PA* 45:7078)

995. WALBERG, HERBERT J.; WELCH, WAYNE W.; AND ROTHMAN, ARTHUR I. "Teacher Heterosexuality and Student Learning." *Psychol Sch* 6(3):258–66 Jl '69. * (*PA* 44:4223)

996. WALSH, RICHARD P. "Test-Taking Anxiety and Psychological Needs." *Psychol Rep* 25(1):83–6 Ag '69. * (*PA* 44:4152)

997. WATERS, CARRIE WHERRY, AND WATERS, L. K. "Relationships Between a Measure of 'Sensation-Seeking' and Personal Preference Schedule Need Scales." *Ed & Psychol Meas* 29(4):983–5 w '69. * (*PA* 44:20996)

998. WATERS, L. K., AND KIRK, WILLIAM E. "Characteristics of Volunteers and Nonvolunteers for Psychological Experiments." *J Psychol* 73(1):133–6 S '69. * (*PA* 44:5149)

999. WEINSTEIN, MALCOLM S. "Achievement Motivation and Risk Preference." *J Pers & Social Psychol* 13(2):153–72 O '69. * (*PA* 44:654)

1000. WHEELER, D. K. "Edwards Personal Preference Schedule and National Characteristics." *Austral & N Zeal J Sociol* 5(1):40–7 Ap '69. *

1001. WOODSON, M. I. CHARLES E. "PL/I Program to Score the Edwards Personal Preference Schedule (EPPS)." *Ed & Psychol Meas* 29(1):203 sp '69. * (*PA* 44:15712)

1002. YUFIT, ROBERT I.; POLLOCK, GEORGE H.; AND WASSERMAN, EDWARD. "Medical Specialty Choice and Personality: 1, Initial Results and Predictions." *Arch Gen Psychiatry* 20(1):89–99 Ja '69. * (*PA* 21:11220)

1003. ADAMS, JERRY, AND KLEIN, LILYAN R. "Students in Nursing School: Considerations in Assessing Personality Characteristics." *Nursing Res* 19(4):362–6 Jl–Ag '70. *

1004. APOSTAL, ROBERT A., AND MURO, JAMES J. "Effects of Group Counseling on Self-Reports and on Self-Recognition Abilities of Counselors in Training." *Counselor Ed & Sup* 10(1):56–63 f '70. *

1005. BAILEY, ROGER LAWRENCE. *A Canonical Correlation Analysis of the Basic Interest Scales and the Edwards Personal Preference Schedule: A Test of Holland's Theory.* Doctor's thesis, University of Kansas (Lawrence, Kan.), 1970. (*DAI* 31:3259A)

1006. BARTOL, GEOFFREY H., AND DUERFELDT, PRYSE H. "Self-Reinforcing Behavior: The Effects of Base Rate and Dependency." *J General Psychol* 83(2):151–61 O '70. *

1007. BERNHARDSON, CLEMENS S., AND FISHER, RONALD J. "Personality Correlates of Dogmatism: Methodological Prob-

lems." Abstract. *J Consult & Clin Psychol* 34(3):449 Je '70. * (*PA* 44:14577)

1008. BIERSNER, ROBERT J., AND CAMERON, BERNARD J. "Betting Preferences and Personality Characteristics of Navy Divers." *Aerospace Med* 41(11):1289–91 N '70. *

1009. BROLLIER, CHESTINA. "Personality Characteristics of Three Allied Health Professional Groups." *Am J Occup Ther* 24(7):500–5 O '70. *

1010. CARLSON, STANLEY LLOYD. *Differences in Aptitude, Previous Achievement, and Nonintellectual Traits (Personality, Values, Interest, and Attitude Toward Mathematics) of Freshmen Mathematics Majors and Transfers From the Mathematics Major at the University of Northern Colorado.* Doctor's thesis, University of Northern Colorado (Greeley, Colo.), 1970. (*DAI* 31:3768A)

1011. CATALANO, JOHN F., AND BERGER, DAVID F. "The Effect of Need for Achievement and Normative Information on Rotary Pursuit Performance." *Psychon Sci* 18(2):69–71 Ja 25 '70. * (*PA* 44:6750)

1012. CUMMINGS, MARTHA ELIZABETH. *The Development and Evaluation of a Multi-Dimensional Scale for Predicting the Participation of High School Girls in Physical Activity.* Doctor's thesis, Boston University (Boston, Mass.), 1970. (*DAI* 31:2154A)

1013. CURTIN, MARY E.; GROSS, WILLIAM F.; AND CALVIN, JAMES S. "Factor Study of Alcoholics' EPPS Needs." *Newsl Res Psychol* 12(2):39–44 My '70. *

1014. DEIULIO, ROBERT SALVATORE. *An Analysis of College Freshmen Perceptions of Staff Members Who Functioned as Counselors Compared to Those Who Functioned as Teachers and Counselors.* Doctor's thesis, Boston University (Boston, Mass.), 1970. (*DAI* 31:2101A)

1015. DE MARTINO, HUGO A. *The Relations Between Certain Motivational Variables and Attitudes About Mental Illness in Student Psychiatric Nurses.* Doctor's thesis, St. John's University (Jamaica, N.Y.), 1970. (*DAI* 31:3036A)

1016. DEWALD, ANNA LUCILLE KENT. *A Study to Determine Factors Influencing Attitude Change of Student Teachers in the Elementary School.* Doctor's thesis, University of Houston (Houston, Tex.), 1970. (*DAI* 31:2769A)

1017. DIELMAN, T. E., AND WILSON, WARNER R. "Convergent and Discriminant Validity of Three Measures of Ability, Aspiration-Level, Achievement, Adjustment and Dominance." *J Ed Meas* 7(3):185–90 f '70. * (*PA* 45:4915)

1018. DISTEFANO, M. K., JR., AND PRYER, MARGARET W. "Predicting Vocational Outcome of Psychiatric Patients With the Edwards Personal Preference Schedule." *J Appl Psychol* 54(6):552–4 D '70. * (*PA* 45:4684)

1019. DIXON, PAUL W.; FUKUDA, NOBUKO K.; AND BERENS, ANNE E. "Cognitive and Personalogical Factor Patterns for Japanese-American High School Students in Hawaii." *Psychologia* 13(1):35–41 Mr '70. * (*PA* 45:8036)

1020. EBERLEIN, E. LARRY. "The EPPS Need Structure of In-Service Elementary School Teachers." *J Ed Res* 64(3):112–4 N '70. *

1021. EDWARDS, ALLEN L. *The Measurement of Personality Traits by Scales and Inventories.* New York: Holt, Reinhart & Winston, Inc., 1970. Pp. xiii, 306. *

1022. ERRINGTON, GARTH EDWARD. *An Analysis of Certain Factors Leading to the Predictability of Success and Failure in Elementary Student Teachers.* Doctor's thesis, Michigan State University (East Lansing, Mich.), 1970. (*DAI* 31:2228A)

1023. FENNELL, NANCY WILMINK, AND KENTON, ROBERT WILLIAM. *Some Effects on Personality of a Basic Encounter Group in a Community College Class.* Doctor's thesis, United States International University (San Diego, Calif.), 1970. (*DAI* 31:2493A)

1024. FINCH, KAYE; RICKARD, HENRY C.; AND WILSON, WARNER. "Personality Variables and Sexual Status in Observer Performance." *Psychol Rep* 26(2):676–8 Ap '70. * (*PA* 44:20819)

1025. FORMICOLA, ALLAN J.; WITTE, E. THOMPSON; AND CURRAN, PATRICK M. "A Study of Personality Traits and Acute Necrotizing Ulcerative Gingivitis." *J Peridont* 41(1):36–8 Ja '70. *

1026. FRANK, AUSTIN C., AND KIRK, BARBARA A. "Forestry Students Today." *Voc Guid Q* 19(2):119–26 D '70. *

1027. GALLESSICH, JUNE. "An Investigation of Correlates of Academic Success of Freshmen Engineering Students." *J Counsel Psychol* 17(2):173–6 Mr '70. * (*PA* 44:9340)

1028. HAMILTON, VERNON. "Non-Cognitive Factors in University Students' Examination Performance." *Brit J Psychol* 61(2):229–41 My '70. * (*PA* 44:15302)

1029. HAND, ROBERT; GADE, ELDON; AND APOSTAL, ROBERT. "A Comparison of the Manifest Psychological Needs of Employment Service Counseling and Office Managers." *J Employ Counsel* 7(3):89–92 Ag '70. *

1030. HARTNETT, JOHN J.; BAILEY, KENT G.; AND GIBSON, FRANK W., JR. "Personal Space as Influenced by Sex and Type of Movement." *J Psychol* 76(2):139–44 N '70. * (*PA* 45:4163)

1031. HICKSON, R. H., AND DRISKILL, J. C. "Needs for Achievement: Differences Between Honors and Non-Honors Students." *J Exp Ed* 38(3):37–8 sp '70. *

1032. HJELLE, LARRY A., AND ABOUD, JOHN, JR. "Some

Personality Differences Between Seminarians and Nonseminarians." *J Social Psychol* 82(2):279–80 D '70. * (*PA* 45:6287)

1033. HORNADAY, JOHN A., AND BUNKER, CHARLES S. "The Nature of the Entrepreneur." *Personnel Psychol* 23(1):47–54 sp '70. * (*PA* 44:17555)

1034. JORDAN, BRIAN T., AND KEMPLER, BERNHARD. "Hysterical Personality: An Experimental Investigation of Sex-Role Conflict." *J Abn Psychol* 75(2):172–6 Ap '70. * (*PA* 44:10820)

1035. KINNICK, BERNARD C., AND NELSON, THEODORE M. "The EPPS Norms: Reevaluation a Necessity." *J Exp Ed* 38(4):37–9 su '70. * (*PA* 46:5562)

1036. LIND, AMY I. "An Exploratory Study of Predictive Factors for Success in the Clinical Affiliation Experience." *Am J Occup Ther* 24(3):222–6 Ap '70. *

1037. LUNNEBORG, PATRICIA W. "EPPS Patterns and Academic Achievement in Counseling Clients." *Ed & Psychol Meas* 30(2):393–8 su '70. * (*PA* 45:3064)

1038. McCLAIN, EDWIN W. "Personality Correlates of Church Attendance." *J Col Stud Personnel* 11(5):360–5 S '70. * (*PA* 45:4043)

1039. McFALL, RICHARD M., AND SCHENKEIN, DIANE. "Experimenter Expectancy Effects, Need for Achievement, and Field Dependence." *J Exp Res Personality* 4(2):122–8 F '70. * (*PA* 44:10384)

1040. MALLEY, PATRICK BRENDAN. *The Relationship of Selected Personality Variables to Employment as a School Counselor and Persistence in Graduate Education.* Doctor's thesis, University of Pittsburgh (Pittsburgh, Pa.), 1970. (*DAI* 30:4779A)

1041. MARTIN, WILLIAM CHARLES. *A Study of the Relationship Between Specified Personality Dimensions and the Quality of Interpersonal Relations of Teachers and Semiprofessionals in Dyadic Work-Groups.* Doctor's thesis, Syracuse University (Syracuse, N.Y.), 1970. (*DAI* 31:3040A)

1042. MELCHISKEY, STEPHEN, AND WITTMER, JOE. "Some Personality Characteristics of Counselor Candidates Accepting and Rejecting Sensitivity Training." *Counselor Ed & Sup* 9(2):132–4 w '70. *

1043. MORRIL, RICHARD ALLEN. *Harmony of Self-Concept as a Factor Influencing the Vocational Development of Upper-Class and Graduate Male College Students.* Doctor's thesis, Michigan State University (East Lansing, Mich.), 1970. (*DAI* 31:3880A)

1044. O'CONNELL, WALTER E.; PATE, KENTON D.; AND HANSON, PHILIP G. "Verbal Participation and Group Behavior." *Newsl Res Psychol* 12(2):36–9 My '70. *

1045. O'SHEA, ARTHUR J. "Low-Achievement Syndrome Among Bright Junior High School Boys." *J Ed Res* 63(6):257–62 F '70. *

1046. OZEHOSKY, JOHN R.; McCARTHY, JAMES B.; AND CLARK, EDWARD T. "Manifest Needs Among ROTC and Non-ROTC Undergraduates." *Psychol Rep* 26(1):299–301 F '70. * (*PA* 45:4228)

1047. PAYNE, I. REED; RASMUSSEN, DELLA MAE; AND SHINEDLING, MARTIN. "Characteristics of Obese University Females Who Lose Weight." *Psychol Rep* 27(2):567–70 O '70. * (*PA* 45:6488)

1048. PELLEGRIN, VICTOR BRUCE HOLKER. *A Descriptive Study of a Midwestern Sample of Episcopal Clergy and Seminarians Categorized According to Various Criteria.* Doctor's thesis, University of Kansas (Lawrence, Kan.), 1970. (*DAI* 31:2690A)

1049. PESCI, MICHAEL LINDEN. *Psychological Differences Between Research, Development and Product Engineers and Their Implications for Placement Decisions.* Doctor's thesis, University of Minnesota (Minneapolis, Minn.), 1970. (*DAI* 31:3048B)

1050. PIETROFESA, JOHN J. "A Comparison of the Personality Need Structure of College Students Enrolled in Different Academic Majors." *Nat Cath Guid Conf J* 14(4):218–28 su '70. * (*PA* 45:2923)

1051. POSTHUMA, ALLAN B., AND NAVRAN, LESLIE. "Relation of Congruence in Student-Faculty Interests to Achievement in College." *J Counsel Psychol* 17(4):352–6 Jl '70. (*PA* 44:21606)

1052. PRYER, MARGARET W., AND DISTEFANO, M. K., JR. "Further Evaluation of the EPPS With Hospitalized Alcoholics." *J Clin Psychol* 26(2):205 Ap '70. * (*PA* 44:14885)

1053. RAINA, T. N. "Comparison of Personality Attributes of High and Low Authoritarian Student Teachers." *J Psychol Res* 14(2):43–9 My '70. *

1054. REITER, HENRY H. "Note on Some Personality Differences Between Heavy and Light Drinkers." *Percept & Motor Skills* 30(3):762 Je '70. * (*PA* 44:16671)

1055. REITER, HENRY H. "Similarities and Differences in Scores on Certain Personality Scales Among Engaged Couples." *Psychol Rep* 26(2):465–6 Ap '70. * (*PA* 44:20957)

1056. REITER, HENRY H. "Some EPPS Differences Between Smokers and Non-Smokers." *Percept & Motor Skills* 30(1):253–4 F '70. *

1057. ROBERTSON, CHARLES VERNON. *Personal Characteristics of Effective Teachers in Inner-City Secondary Schools.* Doctor's thesis, University of Oklahoma (Norman, Okla.), 1970. (*DAI* 31:3233A)

1058. ROBERTSON, JAMES R., AND HAAS, JOHN D. "Teacher

Personality and the New Social Studies." *J Ed Res* 64(3):133–8 N '70. * (*PA* 46:5634)

1059. ROTHFARB, HERBERT I. *A Study of the Psychological Needs and Self-Esteem of College Men Who Exercise Regularly.* Doctor's thesis, Boston College (Chestnut Hill, Mass.), 1970. (*DAI* 31:2727A)

1060. SALZMAN, MURRAY. *Perceptions of the College Environment and Need Dispositions as Related to Expressed Satisfaction.* Doctor's thesis, University of Notre Dame (Notre Dame, Ind.), 1970. (*DAI* 31:1023A)

1061. SANDERS, ROBERT GENE. *The Relationship of Achievement and Personality Variables for Graduating Seniors Between Test Performances on the American College Test and the Edwards Personality Preference Schedule.* Doctor's thesis, University of Oklahoma (Norman, Okla.), 1970. (*DAI* 31:648A)

1062. SAXTON, DOLORES FRANCES. *The Use of the Edwards Personal Preference Schedule to Identify Differences in Students Entering and Completing Associate Degree Nursing Programs.* Doctor's thesis, Columbia University (New York, N.Y.), 1970. (*DAI* 31:4159B)

1063. SHERMAN, RICHARD C., AND POE, CHARLES A. "Factor-Analytic Scales of a Normative Form of the EPPS." *Meas & Eval Guid* 2(4):243–8 w '70. *

1064. SHIPMAN, WILLIAM G.; HEATH, HELEN A.; AND OKEN, DONALD. "Response Specificity Among Muscular and Autonomic Variables." *Arch Gen Psychiatry* 23(4):369–74 O '70. * (*PA* 45:2693)

1065. SHIPMAN, WILLIAM G.; OKEN, DONALD; AND HEATH, HELEN A. "Muscle Tension and Effort at Self-Control During Anxiety." *Arch Gen Psychiatry* 23(4):359–68 O '70. * (*PA* 45:2694)

1066. SIMMONS, DALE D. "Development of an Objective Measure of Identity Achievement Status." *J Proj Tech & Pers Assess* 34(3):241–4 Je '70. * (*PA* 44:18735)

1067. SNIBBE, JOHN ROBINSON. *The Effects of Various Therapeutic Episodes on Dependency Feelings in Alcoholics as Measured by Four Tests.* Doctor's thesis, University of Utah (Salt Lake City, Utah), 1970. (*DAI* 31:4345B)

1068. STEWART, ROBERT A. C., AND WEBSTER, ALAN C. "Scale for Theological Conservatism, and Its Personality Correlates." *Percept & Motor Skills* 30(3):867–70 Je '70. * (*PA* 44:16675)

1069. STROM, ROBERT D., AND LARIMORE, DAVID. "Predicting Teacher Success: The Inner City." *J Exp Ed* 38(4):69–77 su '70. *

1070. TANCK, ROLAND H., AND ROBBINS, PAUL R. "Pupillary Reactions to Sexual, Aggressive, and Other Stimuli as a Function of Personality." *J Proj Tech & Pers Assess* 34(4):277–82 Ag '70. * (*PA* 44:20995)

1071. THOMAS, RUSSELL EARLE. *Discriminant Function Analysis of Probationary and Non-Probationary Students' Measured Values, Personality Needs, and Socio-Economic Background Factors.* Doctor's thesis, Purdue University (Lafayette, Ind.), 1970. (*DAI* 31:1589A)

1072. TSENG, M. S. "Locus of Control as a Determinant of Job Proficiency, Employability, and Training Satisfaction of Vocational Rehabilitation Clients." *J Counsel Psychol* 17(6):487–91 N '70. * (*PA* 45:2799)

1073. WALBERG, HERBERT J., AND AHLGREN, ANDREW. "Predictors of the Social Environment of Learning." *Am Ed Res J* 7(2):153–67 Mr '70. *

1074. WALSH, W. BRUCE, AND PALMER, DAVID A. "Some Personality Differences Between Law- and Non-Law-Oriented Students." *Voc Guid Q* 19(1):11–5 S '70. *

1075. WARDESKA, BRENDA C. *Psychological Needs as Measured by the Edwards Personal Preference Schedule of High Scorers Versus Low Scorers on the Remote Associates Test (A Test of Creativity).* Master's thesis, East Tennessee State University (Johnson City, Tenn.), 1970.

1076. WATSON, RILEY L.; PASEWARK, RICHARD A.; AND FITZGERALD, BERNARD J. "Use of the Edwards Personal Preference Schedule With Delinquents." *Psychol Rep* 26(3):963–5 Je '70. * (*PA* 45:966)

1077. WILLIAMS, JEAN M.; HOEPNER, BARBARA J.; MOODY, DOROTHY L.; AND OGILVIE, BRUCE C. "Personality Traits of Champion Level Female Fencers." *Res Q* 41(3):446–53 O '70. * (*PA* 46:1182)

1078. WINK, RICHARD L. "The Relationship of Self-Concept and Selected Personality Variables to Achievement in Music Student Teaching." *J Res Music Ed* 18(3):234–41 f '70. * (*PA* 45:8972)

1079. WOHL, JULIAN, AND PALMER, ALBERT B. "Correlations Between Adjective Check List and Edwards Personal Preference Schedule Measures of Murray's Needs." *Psychol Rep* 27(2):525–6 O '70. * (*PA* 45:6360)

1080. ZACCARIA, LUCY, AND CREASER, JAMES. "Personality Differences Between Counseled and Uncounseled Students: A Need for Replication Studies." *Meas & Eval Guid* 3(3):133–7 f '70. * (*PA* 45:4986)

ALFRED B. HEILBRUN, JR., *Professor of Psychology and Director of Clinical Training, Emory University, Atlanta, Georgia.*

Sixteen years and three *Mental Measurements Yearbooks* later, a reviewer is left with much the same critique of the EPPS as before. Edwards' publication of this instrument in 1954 came more as an exercise in test construction than as a serious entry into the market of validated tests. The EPPS served as a useful catalyst for research and psychometric debate over the role of social desirability response set and the effect of ipsative scaling, but when the dust began to settle over these controversies, the question of whether the EPPS measures the Murray needs which are nominally represented in its scales remained unresolved. Reviewers in the *Sixth Yearbook* consensually took the EPPS to task for the paucity of validity evidence. Since that time no new manual has appeared to collate validity evidence which would contradict these lingering concerns, if such evidence exists. A personal survey of the published research involving the EPPS since the last MMY fails to uncover a basis for altering these reservations about test validity.

Paradoxically, the EPPS has proven to be a most attractive research instrument gauging by the long bibliography of studies in which it is employed. Unfortunately, many of these studies are "empirical" in nature, usually meaning that the investigator is not able to predict what the results of the investigation should be. Thus, validity of the assessing instrument often seems to be presumed as personalogical "discoveries" emerge. The dangers in drawing inferences from such studies should be emphasized in light of the modest evidence for EPPS validity.

Lest this review present an overly critical impression of the EPPS, it should be said that this inventory possesses many positive technical features. The content of the EPPS, as evidenced by the scale names, represents an important cross-section of normal interpersonal dynamics. Scale reliabilities are satisfactory, norms are based on stable samples, and inter-scale correlations are reasonably low. The ipsative character of the raw scores does not appear to introduce any problems despite the conversion into normative standardized scores. In fact, the ipsative nature of the test allows for some interesting possibilities in individual profile coding which remain largely unexplored.

It is difficult to develop a summary recommendation regarding the use of the EPPS without fence-sitting. While the scanty evidence of validity lends considerable scepticism to any recommendation of its use, neither is there hard evidence that it does not have some predictive validity. It boils down to the amount of prudence which the user feels impelled to exercise with the test results.

MICHAEL G. McKEE, *Psychologist, Department of Psychiatry, Cleveland Clinic, Cleveland, Ohio.*

The EPPS was developed as a means of assessing the strength of 15 needs selected from Murray's list of manifest needs. The manual states that the EPPS "was designed primarily as an instrument for research and counseling purposes, to provide quick and convenient measures of a number of relatively independent normal personality variables." The emphasis in the section of the manual headed "Suggested uses for the EPPS" is on "stimulating discussions" in counseling sessions with normal persons. Such discussions can be useful in helping a student examine himself within the framework of Murray's need system, which has proved to be one of the most powerful conceptualizations of motivation within normal people, and also in helping a client look at what needs are most helpful in what vocational settings. The manual states that "If these [latter] discussions are openly recognized as being speculative and the counselee is encouraged to evaluate the judgments made and the questions raised in the light of his knowledge of past reactions, the discussions are frequently very fruitful." The manual is commendably cautious here as it is in discussing possible use of the EPPS in selection, where the statement is made that "research has not yet demonstrated the possible value of the EPPS in selection problems." But despite the cautious tone of the preceding statements from the manual, many test users are likely to assume that quick and convenient measures are also valid. In fact, validity is essential, for if quick and convenient measures were all that were needed in order to stimulate discussion, the counselee could simply rate himself on the needs, rendering the scales superfluous.

What then of validity for the EPPS? First, it is necessary to look at how the test was constructed. A major intent in developing the EPPS was to control for social desirability of the items, previous work of Edwards having demonstrated that there was a high positive correlation between students' endorsement of typical personality inventory items and the rated social desirability of the items. In an attempt to control this influence, the EPPS asks the respondent to choose in each case between two statements with equal social desirability scale value. However, context turns out to have a significant effect on social desirability. If two items that have the same social desirability are paired, that pairing may shift the balance, as may the environment of surrounding items, so that one of the pair is then seen as relatively more desirable than the other. Furthermore, it has been shown that equating items for social desirability as judged by groups may fail to equate them for individuals. Ratings of social desirability are also likely to vary from population to population, a point which is acknowledged in the manual. Practically, it has been demonstrated that response to the EPPS can be consciously faked in order to create a particular impression. The EPPS provides an inadvertent demonstration of the relative nature of absolute judgments.

Despite the psychometric skill applied in developing the instrument and the care used in demonstrating that social desirability values hold up over time, the EPPS has not fully achieved the attempted control and one can still question whether the EPPS effectively controls for social desirability. Whether it is necessary and desirable to do so is another question; effective control of social desirability would still leave open the question of validity.

The EPPS suffers a handicap from its inception since validity was not emphasized in scale development. To start with, there is not enough evidence to suggest that items within a scale are equivalent in the extent to which they measure a given need. One scale might be represented by items that are high measures of that need, another by items that are relatively low measures. Furthermore, the paired choice format that was used in an attempt to control for social desirability introduces significant problems. It is important to note that the paired choice format of the EPPS yields ipsative scores, a point which the manual should discuss but does not. The strength of each need is in terms of its relation to other needs of the individual instead of being an absolute measure. Just as absolute measures of social desirability don't hold up in context on a relative basis, relative measures of need may not hold up on an absolute basis. The T scores enable comparison of relative need strength in one person with relative need strength in another, but one person's 80 might reflect an intense need among a complex of strong ones, while another person's might reflect a weak need overriding a complex of feeble ones. The richness and intensity of personality is diminished by this measuring system which implies that one strong need must be offset by others being diluted. Also, the scales are not independent since there is intra- and inter-scale item overlap and each choice affects scores on two scales. Identical statements appear three or four times in different comparative pairs. This serves to inflate the reported internal-consistency reliability coefficients, leaving reliability uncertain since the other reliability data reported in the manual are based on test-retest data with only a week between test sessions. The ipsative measurement also confounds interpretation of correlation matrices and factor analyses using EPPS scores.

Although the manual is generally conservative in tenor, it fails by omission to point to the ipsative nature of the EPPS scores and the need for caution in using T scores based on such ipsative scores. Using such scores in a profile can be misleading for many test users who are likely to interpret them in an absolute sense. The manual gives a good presentation of the detailed procedures to be followed in administering and scoring the EPPS. It is faulty in not covering available research pertaining to validity of EPPS scales. The research that has been accomplished is often difficult to interpret because the ipsative nature of the scores was infrequently taken into account. On an overall basis, the research data provide insufficient justification for saying that the scales of the EPPS measure the constructs they intend to or that the scales are useful in the prediction of external, socially important criteria. At best, it can be said that some scales (particularly the Achievement scale) still have promise. While the face validity is adequate, with the disadvantage that the scales are relatively transparent, empirical validity is insufficient. Study of the test's origin, even when that origin is characterized (as with the EPPS) by psychometric elegance in attempted control of response style, inspection of the items in the scale, study of the theory to which the scales are related, even when (as with the EPPS) the scales are related to a powerful theoretical formulation, are insufficient steps for answering questions about what the scales measure and how well they do it. Here, further empirical research is necessary.

SUMMARY. The EPPS is an instrument that intends to measure a theoretically potent set of variables. Its paired comparison format and ipsative scoring confound interpretation of T score profiles and of much of the research data available on the EPPS. Attempted, but incomplete, control of social desirability seems to have been achieved at too high a cost, with the body of research on the EPPS failing to demonstrate many significant links between test scores and external behaviors or between test scores and underlying constructs. This reviewer would find instruments which have been developed with an emphasis on validity, such as the CPI, more useful in measuring personality characteristics of normally functioning individuals.

For reviews by John A. Radcliffe and Lawrence J. Stricker, see 6:87 (1 excerpt); for reviews by Frank Barron, Åke Bjerstedt, and Donald W. Fiske, see 5:47 (2 excerpts).

[73]

★Edwards Personality Inventory. Grades 11–16 and adults; 1966–67; EPI; 53 scores listed below; 5 booklets ('66, 13 pages); manual ('67, 54 pages); separate answer sheets (IBM 805, self scoring) must be used; $4.25 per 5 tests; $8.40 per 100 IBM 805 answer sheets for any one booklet; $4.25 per 25 self scoring answer sheets for any one booklet; $1.75 per manual; $5 per specimen set; postage extra; (40–50) minutes per booklet; Allen L. Edwards; Science Research Associates, Inc. *

a) BOOKLETS 1A AND 1B. 14 scores: plans and organizes things, intellectually oriented, persistent, self-confident, has cultural interests, enjoys being the center of attention, carefree, conforms, is a leader, kind to others, worries about making a good impression on others, seeks new experiences, likes to be alone, interested in the behavior of others.

b) BOOKLET 2. 11 scores: anxious about his performance, avoids facing problems, is a perfectionist, absent-minded, sensitive to criticism, likes a set routine, wants sympathy, avoids arguments, conceals his feelings, easily influenced, feels misunderstood.

c) BOOKLET 3. 15 scores: motivated to succeed, impressed by status, desires recognition, plans work efficiently, cooperative, competitive, articulate, feels superior, logical, assumes responsibility, self-centered, makes friends easily, independent in his opinions, is a hard worker, neat in dress.

d) BOOKLET 4. 13 scores: self-critical, critical of others, active, talks about himself, becomes angry, helps others, careful about his possessions, understands himself, considerate, dependent, shy, informed about current affairs, virtuous.

REFERENCES
1–2. See P:68.
3. FOWLER, ROY STANLEY, JR. *The Performance of Psychiatric Patients on a Set of Experimental Personality Scales.* Doctor's thesis, University of Washington (Seattle, Wash.), 1966. (DA 27:598B)
4. EDWARDS, ALLEN L. "Correlations Between Scores on Personality Scales When Items Are Stated in the First and Third Person Form." *Ed & Psychol Meas* 29(3):561–3 au '69. * (PA 44:18741)
5. OAKLAND, JAMES A. "Measurement of Personality Correlates of Academic Achievement in High School Students." *J Counsel Psychol* 16(5):452–7 S '69. * (PA 43:17997)
6. OAKLAND, JAMES A. "Personality Structures of Adolescents as Measured by the Edwards Personality Inventory." *Psychol Rep* 24(1):215–23 F '69. * (PA 43:14342)
7. BRAUN, JOHN R. "Edwards Personality Inventory, Booklet IV: Faking and Faking Detection." *Meas & Eval Guid* 3(2):86–7 su '70. * (PA 45:713)
8. LUNNEBORG, PATRICIA W. "Stereotypic Aspect in Masculinity-Femininity Measurement." *J Consult & Clin Psychol* 34(1):113–8 F '70. * (PA 44:6781)
9. OAKLAND, JAMES A. "Test-Retest Reliability and the Significance of Doubtful Responses in the Edwards Personality Inventory. *Psychol Rep* 26(2):659 64 Ap '70. * (PA 44:21002)
10. PEARSON, PAMELA H. "Relationships Between Global and Specified Measures of Novelty Seeking." *J Consult & Clin Psychol* 34(2):199–204 Ap '70. * (PA 44:10438)
11. PFISTER, GORDON C. *An Investigation of the Effectiveness of Laboratory Training in Increasing Interpersonal Communication Skills With Police Officers.* Doctor's thesis, University of Washington (Seattle, Wash.), 1970. (DAI 31: 3348A)

LEWIS R. GOLDBERG, *Professor of Psychology, University of Oregon; and Research Associate, Oregon Research Institute; Eugene, Oregon.*

Edwards has concluded that responses to, and scores from, most contemporary personality inventories are massively contaminated by what he calls a "social desirability response set," and he has set out to construct inventories with radically different properties. His first effort, the *Edwards Personal Preference Schedule,* employed a forced-choice item format to measure 15 manifest needs based upon the classification system devised by Henry Murray. In the new *Edwards Personality Inventory—* which unfortunately has the same initials as the *Eysenck Personality Inventory—*Edwards has eschewed both the forced-choice item format and the Murray needs. To eliminate "social desirability response set," Edwards has (a) focused primarily on items of relatively neutral desirability, and (b) changed the traditional self-report instructions to maximum-performance ones ("Your task....is to predict how people who know you well would mark each statement if they were asked to describe you"), though still within a true-false response format.

Few psychometricians will quarrel with Edwards' decision to exclude potentially "offensive" items in favor of items of relatively neutral desirability, if only because the elimination of items of extreme desirability will also tend to eliminate those of low inter-individual variance. However, contrary to the standard scientific practice of demonstrating the superiority of a technique before using it, Edwards introduced his new instructions in the EPI *prior* to any empirical comparison. In fact, research published two years after the publication of the EPI manual showed that there was essentially no difference between EPI scores based upon the traditional vs. the novel instructions (4).

Edwards' goal in developing the EPI was to construct a set of uncorrelated scales, each possessing both high internal consistency and a low correlation with his social desirability scale; hopefully, some small subset of these new scales would predict all other existing personality scales within the limits imposed by their reliabilities. During a sabbatical year in England, Edwards informally asked each of his acquaintances to describe some individual, and then after the conversation he jotted down the phrases they had used in their descriptions. Hundreds of such nonsystematic conversations produced some 5,000 descriptive statements, which—upon the elimination of all duplicate phrases and the addition of some new ones— constituted the initial 2,824-item pool used for the development of the EPI scales. These 2,824 phrases were grouped by intuitive procedures and later by cluster and factor analyses (based upon the responses of 221 college students) to develop 52 of the 53 scales included in the EPI.

The resulting inventory consists of 1,500 items (e.g., "He plans his work carefully") divided into five booklets of 300 items each. The first two booklets provide parallel forms of the same 14 scales. The rationale for including particular scales in each of the remaining three booklets is not discussed in the EPI manual. While 16 of the 1,500 items are not used to score any of the 53 EPI scales, they were retained to keep 300 items in each booklet. As a consequence of this unfortunate decision, the test administrator has no way to tell which booklet an individual filled out if he inadvertently responded on the wrong answer sheet.

The EPI scales vary in length from 10 items (four scales) to 58 items (one scale); most scales include from 15–30 items, and the typical scale includes around 20 items. No item is scored on more than one scale. Though once a prominent advocate of the importance of response sets and styles, Edwards appears to have capitulated completely on the issue of response "acquiescence." The topic is not even mentioned in the EPI manual, and 15 of the EPI scales have *all* of their items keyed true, with another 15 having only one or two false-keyed items.

For an inventory commercially published in the late 1960's, the EPI manual must be viewed as bizarre: (a) The size and composition of the standardization sample is clearly inadequate. Percentile norms are presented for 111 male and 163 female high school students and for 203 male and 329 female college students. (b) There is no section on validity whatsoever, and the only external (non-test) data presented are all focused upon the differences between the mean scores of university (N = 203) and junior college (N = 98) samples. (c) No test-retest reliability values are presented. (d) No correlations are given with the scales from any other inventory.

In the continuing controversy over the relative importance of *internal* (i.e., reliability) vs. *external* (i.e., validity) features of a test, Edwards appears to have taken a most extreme position. In fact, since the manual presents no evidence of any external correlates of the EPI scales, all that can be evaluated are internal data. K-R 20 reliability (homogeneity) coefficients for the 53 scales vary from a low of around .65 for "Logical" to a high of around .95 for "Sensitive to Criticism." Approximately 30 percent of the scales have reliability coefficients below .80, 40 percent have reliabilities in the .80's, and another 30 percent have reliabilities of .90 or more. Scale intercorrelations range up to the low .80's ("Is a Leader" and "Assumes Responsibility"). Though most of the intercorrelations are considerably lower, a number are in the .60's and .70's (e.g., "Persistent" and "Is a Hard Worker"); a factor analysis of the 53 EPI scales yielded 14 factors. Correlations between the EPI scales and Edwards' social desirability scale range up to the low .70's ("Self-Critical"), while nine others are above .40 (e.g., "Feels Misunderstood," "Shy," "Articulate," "Carefree," "Anxious About His Performance").

Nonetheless, *most* of the EPI scales are quite homogeneous, and most are virtually independent of each other and of the social desirability scale. If Edwards had elected to retain only 33, or even 43, of these 53 scales, the resulting product would have satisfied his own internal criteria. Instead, he elected to publish all 53 because he believed that some of the psychometrically inferior scales might prove to be the most useful in forecasting non-test behaviors. Ah, but there's the rub. Those internal properties, which Edwards elected to focus upon exclusively, do not insure that the scales possess the external properties necessary for the user. A scale with an internal consistency coefficient of .95 and a zero correlation with Edwards' social desirability scale might have near zero correlations with all other non-test behaviors the tester seeks to predict. For example, Oakland [1] correlated 21 EPI scores for 16 members of a college varsity basketball team with the mean ratings of the players on the same traits by the coach and assistant coach; only one of the 21 scales provided highly valid predictions ("Talks About Himself"), and eight of the scales (e.g., "Is a Hard Worker") were *negatively* correlated with the mean ratings. In addition, Oakland reported quite low correlations (ranging from −.27 to .43) between 11 EPI scores and mean peer ratings on the same traits for a sample of 32 college students.

Now Edwards is certainly aware of this problem: "It is anticipated that the EPI will in time prove to be of value for counseling, prediction, and research purposes. Before the EPI can properly be used as part of a placement or job-selection program or for other decision-making purposes, evidence must be obtained that the EPI scores are significantly related to appropriate criteria" (EPI manual, p. 1). The implication of this statement is, of course, that EPI scores can be used *only* for research, and solely for that sort of research aimed at discovering what the scales measure. Then why were the scales published commercially at this point? Ostensibly because Edwards, wishing other investigators to join him in EPI validity studies, reasoned that psychologists were more likely to be lured into this endeavor if the scales were commercially available. This argument would be more compelling if (*a*) neither Edwards nor his publisher stood to profit from the premature use of the inventory, and (*b*) if the EPI were appropriately labeled "FOR RESEARCH USE ONLY." Unfortunately, no such cautionary statement appears on either the test booklets or on the manual, which is labeled simply "Introductory Edition." As yet, the EPI is *considerably* less than that.

1 OAKLAND, J. A. Validity Studies of the *Edwards Personality Inventory* as Determined by the Agreement Between the Perceived Self, the Perceived Social Self, and the Expressed Opinion of Others. Paper presented at the meeting of the Western Psychological Association, Los Angeles, Calif., April 1970.

WARREN T. NORMAN, *Professor of Psychology, The University of Michigan, Ann Arbor, Michigan.*

The *Edwards Personality Inventory* is intended to provide scores on 53 personality variables on which normal individuals may be expected to differ from one another. An original pool of 2,824 items was developed by the author from interviews of persons who were asked to describe someone well known to them, from published biographies and autobiographies, and, in some cases, by an effort to tap a specific personality trait. By a combination of judgmental and empirical criteria including examination of item content, endorsement rates, desirability ratings, internal consistencies, and factor loadings, a final set of 52 scales, each semantically and statistically homogeneous, was derived from the pool. The items from 14 of these scales were divided into a pair of matched subsets to create equivalent forms (Booklets 1A and 1B) for these variables. The remaining 38 scales plus one additional scale of 33 items written a priori to assess a self-perceived reputation for "Virtuousness" were grouped into three additional booklets (2, 3, and 4).

As a multi-scale, personality inventory, the EPI is unusual—if not unique—in several particulars. First, the item content has been carefully edited to eliminate references to certain sensitive matters such as religious and political beliefs, family relations, health, and bodily functions. Second, the jargon of trait psychology and of psychopathology has been almost entirely avoided, not just in the item content, but in the labeling of the scales as well. Third, spurious contributions to interscale correlations owing to multiple keying of individual items have been avoided. Finally, and perhaps of greatest interest, the instructions to the respondent are such that the EPI is technically not a "self-report" inventory at all, at least not in the ordinary, direct sense of that concept. That is, the examinee is asked to respond to the items not in terms of whether he personally believes them to be true or false of himself but rather as "he believes those individuals who know him best would answer.... if *they* were asked to describe him."

The only norms currently available are percentile distributions for samples of 203 male and 329 female students from the University of Washington (all booklets) and a second set based on 111 male and 163 female high school juniors from two Seattle schools. The author recommends development of local norms and acknowledges the potential value of those based on broader reference groups, but as yet such general norms are not available.

In the manual the author states: "Although there are reliable individual differences in the self-descriptions obtained with the inventory, *there is no evidence at this time to indicate that these differences between individuals are related to success or failure in any occupation or course of study* [italics supplied]." The user is cautioned that the EPI should not be used for decision making for selection or placement until significant relationships between successful performance and scores on the inventory's scales have been established.

Finally, the manual states: "the EPI provides a comprehensive and systematic survey of the individual's perception of the self he displays to significant persons in his environment, and thus can be expected to be a useful tool for the clinician in his attempt to gain a better understanding of the individual." It is this feature of attempting explicitly to elicit the respondent's perceptions of others' impressions of himself, rather than direct self-descriptions, that most uniquely distinguishes the EPI from other available, multi-scale devices. In the manual, the author offers several justifications for this approach, including the possibility of obtaining greater objectivity on the part of the respondents, greater consistency in response, and direct information related to personal problems stemming from beliefs concerning others' perceptions of self. That any substantial increase in "objectivity" will result from this simple modification in the typical administrative format for self-report inventories seems to this reviewer unlikely. And any increases in response consistency achieved may well be a mixed blessing if they are attributable merely to the use of a more superficial and impoverished base of relevant information than the respondents actually have available and might otherwise be induced to employ.

One further comment concerning the use of this administrative procedure is noteworthy, although not explicitly mentioned in the manual. Current concerns about invasion of privacy stemming from the use of self-report personality tests hinge, within the law, upon protections against self-incrimination. The avoidance of "sensitive" content in the items of the EPI

has already been mentioned and is one step explicitly taken by the author in recognition of this problem. The use of an instructional set that calls for perceived impressions of others instead of direct self-reports provides an additional protection of a technical sort at least for both the respondent and the psychologist interested in the assessment of personality traits by such means.

Some empirical evidence exists[1] that perceived peer-perceptions and self-perceptions as recorded on a set of personality trait rating scales similar in their content to those of the EPI yield correlation structures and scale variances that are highly comparable in the two classes of data but means that are slightly more toward the desirable end of each scale under the direct self-report condition. Edwards (4) has reported additional data which bear even more directly on this matter as it pertains to the EPI. In this study items in Booklet 1B were rewritten in the first person and given, together with Booklets 1A and 1B, to a single sample of respondents. Not only were the correlations between first- and third-person versions of each scale of Booklet 1B similar to the corresponding correlations between Booklets 1A and 1B, but the variances and means were also highly similar to those obtained using either of the standard forms. The author cautions that these results might not extend to the variables contained in the other booklets in the set, but, if not, such anomalies would be of considerable interest from both a substantive and a methodological point of view.

In summary, the EPI is an instrument worthy of serious consideration by those interested in the assessment of a broad range of personality characteristics in "normal" adolescents and adults. I believe its usefulness will continue to grow as time passes and research evidence accumulates on the relationships of inventory scores and score profiles to relevant behavioral criteria of diverse sorts. At the moment, the absence of any appreciable information of this kind is the greatest deficiency this instrument possesses. Whether it will prove ultimately to be a defect as well remains to be seen.

Clin Psychologist 22(4):206–25 su '69. Thomas J. Bouchard, Jr. * The EPI utilizes

1 NORMAN, WARREN T., AND GOLDBERG, LEWIS R. "Raters, Ratees, and Randomness in Personality Structure." *J Pers & Social Psychol* 4:681–91 D '66. *

a standard true-false format, but introduces a new variation. The subject is instructed to answer all items the way those persons who know him best would describe him. These answers are considered the correct or right answers. All items are worded accordingly (e.g., He is never on time.). Edwards has attempted to eliminate all items that might in one way or another be considered offensive by examinees and almost all items with extreme social desirability ratings. Not coincidentally, none of the scales are designed to assess personal adjustment or psychiatric syndromes. The inventory is explicitly designed to assess dimensions on which normal individuals vary. * The final scales are the result of an extensive and sophisticated construction procedure. * retest reliabilities are not presented and would be highly desirable. Correlations between the comparable forms of 14 of the scales are reported for three samples. In most cases, they are almost identical to the K-R 20 coefficients, indicating excellent comparability. The inventory is easy to complete (each booklet takes about 40 minutes) in the sense that it is not difficult to decide how someone who knows you well would answer most of the items. Whether this test-taking set will yield greater consistency of self description as Edwards hopes, remains to be seen. It certainly would have been (and still will be) easy to answer this question simply by rewording the items in the more traditional "I" form and comparing their reliability with the current version. One of the consequences of requiring item homogeneity is short scales. Twenty-four of the 53 scales have 20 or fewer items. The result is that very large shifts in percentiles occur if a subject forgets an item or two or changes his mind on a retest. For example, Edwards suggests that the range of percentile scores can be divided into five levels, very high—94–99, high—70–93, average—32–69, low—8–31, very low—1–7. A change in scoring direction of only a few items can move a subject from very high or very low to average on many of the scales. Like all factor tests where item homogeneity is a goal, the items are repetitious and one gets the impression that a simple self rating schedule would serve the purpose just as well. * The self-scoring answer sheet contains complete instructions for scoring and profiling. It is quick and easy to use and will be greatly appreciated by users who handle a small number of protocols. The author pre-sents two factor analyses of the 53 scales, one each for the male and female university student samples. Each yields 14 factors that match up quite well (though some of the loadings on comparable factors have their signs reversed). Nevertheless, the author refuses to interpret the factors on the grounds that the procedure is subjective and intuitive. This argument is difficult to understand in view of the author's recommendation that the 53 scales be interpreted on the basis of content. The question also arises why only 14 factors of the 53 original scales were developed by factor analysis. The answer is that the analysis of items and scales took place at different conceptual levels, and there is no reason why they should yield the same results.[1] On the other hand, had Edwards used a different mix of items while developing his scales or used a different program capable of dealing with all of his items at one time,[1,2] it is likely that he would have generated a different structure. The points to be made here are that in spite of the technical sophistication used to develop the scales; a) there is nothing intrinsically special or scientific about them. The results are a function of the procedures and groupings of items used. Other procedures and groupings may have yielded different scales; b) Edwards presents no evidence that these particular scales have any generality outside of the university sample used to generate them. It is unlikely that they will have such generality.[3] Along these same lines, it is worth pointing out that Edwards presents no significant arguments as to why these scales may be of value apart from considerations based on the analysis of internal structure. The evidence indicates that scales constructed in this way are probably as good, but not better than scales constructed by other means.[4] All this leads us to ask why there is not more information about the meaning and functioning of the scales. It is no longer adequate to produce a technically good inventory, and the EPI is technically very good, and expect praise and acceptance. There are more personality inventories around than any other type

1 STEIN, KENNETH B. Chap. 5, "The TSC Scales: The Outcome of a Cluster Analysis of the 550 MMPI Items," pp. 80–104. In *Advances in Psychological Assessment, Volume One.* Edited by Paul McReynolds. Palo Alto, Calif.: Science Behavior Books, 1968. Pp. xiii, 336. *

2 TRYON, ROBERT C., AND BAILEY, DANIEL E. "The BC TRY System of Cluster and Factor Analysis." *Multiv Behav Res* 1:95–111 Ja '66. *

3 PETERSON, DONALD R. "Scope and Generality of Verbally Defined Personality Factors." *Psychol R* 72:48–59 Ja '65. *

4 HASE, H. D., AND GOLDBERG, L. R. "Comparative Validity of Different Strategies of Constructing Personality Inventory Scales." *Psychol B* 67:231–48 Ap '67. *

and a responsible test constructor should not introduce a new test unless he can show it is functionally superior to others now in existence or it serves some other meaningful purpose. For example, two inventories currently used in counseling, an area in which the use of the EPI has been recommended and will most likely generate the greatest demand, are the Omnibus Personality Inventory (OPI) and the California Psychological Inventory (CPI). There is much data relevant to the functioning of the scales on both of these tests. A potential user of the EPI should know where it stands with respect to these instruments. Do the scales overlap? Does the EPI make a unique contribution or tap an area that those instruments miss? At the very least, the manual should locate this instrument and its scales within the matrix of psychological tests with a similar function. Edwards claims most scales are free of S.D. and presents the evidence for us to judge. He also claims he attempted to avoid assessing adjustment and neuroticism. Where is the evidence? It would have been easy to collect pertinent data. Any new test should be correlated with an intelligence test of the same type (e.g., group or individual). There should be evidence that the test generates validity correlations higher than those for self-ratings on the same dimensions. There is evidence that this is often not the case.[4, 5] There should be data revealing the effects of dissimulation. There should be *some* evidence that the scales measure what they purport to measure. The answers to these and many other questions should have been generated and included in the manual. The failure to provide this information is a disservice to the potential user. How should we evaluate these scales? If we use Gough's [6] model for conceptual analysis, there are three important stages of evaluation. The first stage is primary evaluation. At this stage we ask; "how well [the scale] predicts what it seeks to predict, measures what it purports to measure, or defines what it is intended to define." The EPI manual presents only internal validity data on this point. The available data does not allow us to answer the questions meaningfully. Stage two is secondary evaluation. This stage "seeks to discover the psycho-

logical basis of measurement, to specify and clarify the meaning of that which is measured." The EPI manual presents almost no data relevant to this problem. Stage three is tertiary evaluation, and seeks to explicate the meaning "in use" of a scale or pattern of scales and their special consequences which may go beyond their originally intended purpose. Most test manuals never achieve this level of evaluation, therefore the EPI probably should not be faulted for failing to achieve it. In conclusion, the EPI is a carefully constructed and potentially very valuable inventory. Nevertheless, the manual is grossly inadequate for anything but research use. It should not be put to operational use until at least some evidence relevant to the ability of the scales to forecast or accurately index the behaviors they purport to assess has been developed. When this information has been developed, a new manual should be issued. Until then, the current manual should be stamped *"research use only."*

J Ed Meas 7(2):131–3 su '70. Benjamin Kleinmuntz. * The EPI differs from other personality inventories in a number of ways. * the items probe as little as possible into the privacy of each individual * Another way in which the EPI differs....is that the respondent is asked to assume the third person in his self-report. The respondent is asked to judge whether he believes if individuals who know him best would answer the item True or False. Professor Edwards hopes that this manner of responding may help the examinee to be more consistent in his self-description than if the first person is used. Whether or not this hope is fulfilled, at least in so far as evidence is brought to bear on this matter in the manual, is a moot point. * The test manual instructions, as well as the directions in front of each of the test booklets, are clear and unambiguous for both the test's administration and scoring. Taking this test, however, as a respondent may be an entirely different matter. This reviewer went through the motions of self-administering and self-scoring this test. No difficulty was experienced in scoring, but considerable difficulty was encountered in staying awake while attempting to respond to each of the items. Each and every item begins with the third person pronoun "He," and this can wear you out by the time you reach the 50th item. This format probably can be changed somewhat without violating the third person aspect of it. The test's development

5 CAMPBELL, DONALD T., AND FISKE, DONALD M. "Convergent and Discriminant Validation by the Multitrait-multi-method Matrix." *Psychol B* 56:81–105 Mr '59. *

6 GOUGH, HARRISON G. "Conceptual Analysis of Psychological Test Scores and Other Diagnostic Variables." *J Abn Psychol* 70:294–302 Ag '65. *

is in the best tradition of psychometric technology. * The reliability data....is impressive * It would have....been informative to obtain reliability coefficients on the test-retest stability of the various scales. The usual arguments about the meaninglessness of test-retest scores on personality scales should not be valid here because most of the scales developed by Edwards tend not to be mood scales in the same sense as the MMPI *D* or *M* scales. The main evidence presented in support of the validity of these scales is meager to say the least, but it must be remembered that at the time of the publication of the test manual no claims for the test's meaningfulness were made by its author. In fact, at the outset the author states: "Before the EPI can properly be used as part of a placement or job selection program or for other decision-making purposes, evidence must be obtained that the EPI scores are significantly related to appropriate criteria." * All in all then, the EPI has numerous innovative features, some of which reflect the latest thinking in personality test construction. Its reliability is adequate, although more data reflecting the test's stability over time should be accumulated. Evidence for EPI's validity is meager. It is an empirical question whether or not this test will have the impact, either in terms of the amount of research it inspires or in the extent of its usage, as the California Psychological Inventory (CPI) has had over the years. This reviewer feels that the CPI will be equally as difficult to displace as a forerunner among tests used with normals as the MMPI has proved to be in its own category.

[74]

★The Ego-Ideal and Conscience Development Test. Ages 12–18; 1969; EICDT; 9 scores: home and family, inner development, community relations, rules and law, school and education, romance and psychosexual, economic sufficiency, self-actualization, total; Forms A, B, (10 pages); manual (15 pages); profile (2 pages); separate answer sheets must be used; $15 per 25 tests; $1.25 per 25 answer sheets; $2.50 per 25 profiles; $2 per scoring stencil; $2 per manual; $5 per specimen set; postpaid; (50–60) minutes; R. N. Cassel; Monitor. *

REFERENCES

1. CASSEL, R. N., AND BLUM, L. P. "Computer Assist Counseling (COASCON) for the Prevention of Delinquent Behavior Among Teenagers and Youth." *Sociol & Social Res* 54(1):72–9 O '69. * (*PA* 45:8547)
2. CASSEL, RUSSEL N. "Computer Assisted Counseling (COASCON): A Basic Essential in Youth Correction Programs." *J Correct Ed* 21(2):21–3 sp '69. *
3. CHIU, ADA. *A Preliminary Evaluation of a Computer Assisted Counseling Program for Delinquent Youth.* Master's thesis, University of Wisconsin (Milwaukee, Wis.), 1969.
4. REISE, MELVIN W. *A Comparison Between Delinquent Youth and Typical Individuals on the Ego-Ideal and Con-*

science Development Test. Master's thesis, University of Wisconsin (Milwaukee, Wis.), 1969.
5. CASSEL, RUSSEL N. "Basic Fundamentals of an Effective Program for the Correctional Education of Delinquent Youth." *J Correct Ed* 22(2):4–8 sp '70. *

[75]

★Elizur Test of Psycho-Organicity: Children and Adults. Ages 6 and over, 10 and over; 1959–69; ETPO; brain injury; 3 scores: drawings, digits, blocks; individual; 1 form; 2 levels: children, adults; administration booklet ('69, 19 cards); manual ('69, 55 pages, see 4 below); record booklet ('69, 4 pages); no data on reliability; $19.50 per examiner's kit of testing materials, 25 record booklets, and manual; $9.50 per set of testing materials; $6.50 per 25 record booklets; $6.50 per manual; postpaid; (10–15) minutes; Abraham Elizur; Western Psychological Services. *

REFERENCES

1. ELIZUR, A. "A Combined Test Used for the Diagnosis of Organic Brain Condition." *A.M.A. Arch Neurol & Psychiatry* 81:776–84 Je '59. * (*PA* 34:5122)
2. ELIZUR, ABRAHAM. "The Psychological Evaluation of the Organic Child." *J Proj Tech & Pers Assess* 29:292–9 S '65. * (*PA* 39:15188)
3. ELIZUR, ABRAHAM. *Psycho-Organic Brain Disorders: Psychopathology and Psychotherapy.* Tel Aviv, Israel: Mental Hygiene Centre, 1965. Pp. xii, 276. *
4. ELIZUR, ABRAHAM. *The Psycho-Organic Syndrome: Its Assessment and Treatment: Including a Manual for the Elizur Test of Psycho-Organicity: Children and Adults.* Los Angeles, Calif.: Western Psychological Services, 1969. Pp. v, 54. *
5. KRAUS, J. "A Combined Test Used for the Diagnosis of Organic Brain Condition: Predictive Validity Based on Radiographic and Electroencephalographic Criteria." *J Abn Psychol* 75(2):187–8 Ap '70. * (*PA* 44:11034)

JOSEPH M. WEPMAN, *Professor of Psychology, Surgery and Education, The University of Chicago, Chicago, Illinois.*

To use this test it is necessary to accept the author's concept of brain function. In the test manual he neatly describes his tripartite thesis of brain organization and the relation of one part to the other. Thus, he postulates a neuro-organic and a psycho-organic basis for behavior with some area of overlap between the two. These are seen in juxtaposition to what he calls the "testing-organic," which partially overlaps both of the others. While his tests are designed to explore psycho-organicity, they cannot by his own schema differentiate people whose problems place them in the overlapped portion. Thus, emotional disturbances, neurological impairment, or so-called perceptual problems are not readily differentiated. While his theory holds for the separate testing-organic category, this seems to be an area where the results permit neither a neurological nor a psychogenic interpretation and therefore are relegated to an area demonstrated only by test behavior.

The test itself is made up of three parts, all three being common areas of investigation in other tests or test batteries. A drawing subtest is not unlike the items in the *Benton Visual Retention Test.* The digit recall subtest, like all such tests, is based on auditory retention and reproduction. The block design items are similar to items of the Kohs' *Block-Design Test*.

In the first and third instance the original tests from which these subtests were developed have a better chance to picture the abilities being tested than does the present test, if for no other reason than that they are longer. The drawing and blocks subtests of the ETPO have only four items each, which is good for reducing the time of testing but naturally reduces the sample of experience gained. Whether the testing of digit series by continuous repetition of 20 four- or five-digit units results in a more useful description of auditory recall, attention, and concentration is not demonstrated, but it is an interesting variation on digit series recall.

Nowhere in the material provided does the author indicate why visual motor memory, auditory recall, or block design construction are the areas of choice in determining organicity. The total lack of any test of verbal behavior, plus the questionable use of digit series as a test of auditory function, leaves one with considerable doubt as to the value of generalized observation from the test.

Aubrey J. Yates, *Professor of Psychology, University of Western Australia, Nedlands, Australia.*

The comprehensive manual issued as part of this test describes the author's views on what he calls "psycho-organicity"; the techniques he employs in treating the syndrome; and instructions for giving, scoring, and interpreting results on the test.

It is argued that much behavior disorder is the result of organic processes which are not detectable by standard tests of brain damage nor by standard neurological examination. It is, of course, true that massive brain damage may result in little or no detectable behavioral impairment; and conversely, that what has been termed "minimal brain damage" may lead to severe and ultimately detectable behavior disorder. However, as the author expatiates on his concept of psycho-organicity, it becomes clear that almost any form of behavior disorder may be attributed to the effects of psycho-organicity (P-O). Thus, the P-O syndrome may lead to *mental disturbances* (as indexed by narrowness of the field of consciousness, difficulties in concentration, perceptual difficulties, mild disorientation, defects in recent memory, concrete-

ness and lack of mental flexibility, and scholastic difficulties); *emotional disturbances* (as indexed by emotional instability, and fears and anxieties); *motor disturbances* (as indexed by psychomotor restlessness, tics, difficulty in learning motor skills, speech difficulties, and enuresis); *behavior disturbances* (as indexed by impulsiveness, asocial behavior, restricted behavior, suggestibility, and dependency); and *general disturbances* (as indexed by slowness, instability, use of substitutive aids to alleviate deficiencies, and oversensitivity to light and noise). Hysteria is considered to be a classic instance of the P-O syndrome; and the syndrome may manifest itself in otherwise normal persons as a result of physical or emotional stress as well as during critical life periods (early childhood, adolescence, pregnancy, the involutional period, and old age).

The test itself, which is thus diagnostic of almost any abnormalities of behavior, is claimed by the author to be a "new test for the specific purpose of diagnosing brain conditions" and is considered by him to be superior to current tests of organicity which he severely criticizes as being unidimensional, too time-consuming, originally designed for other purposes, dominated by "g" conceptions, and too subjective in their scoring. On examination, however, this test turns out to consist of three subtests (copying designs, copying blocks, and repeating digits), which are among those most commonly used as measures of organicity. For each of the subtests, a quantitative scoring key is given with sample reproductions for the user to practise on. For the blocks test, both time and error scores are recorded; for the other two only error scores are used. Separate material for use with children is provided. Three validation studies are reported, quantitative and qualitative analysis is discussed in some detail, and applications of the test battery are briefly mentioned. The validation studies reported do not in any way serve their purpose. The test was designed to identify patients manifesting the psycho-organic syndrome, but the two main validation studies compared the performance of known organics with non-organics. Not unexpectedly, the tests discriminated well between these two groups, but the results throw no light on the claimed ability of the test to identify psycho-organics. Indeed, logically, it is difficult to see how the test *could* be validated since, by definition, it is supposed to identify persons not detectable by standard psychological or neurological tests. Hence no independent criterion can be used. Even the little used but highly desirable criterion of predictive validity (identifying those patients who are not currently, but will subsequently be, detectable by neurological evidence) cannot be invoked here.[1]

In summary, the definition of psycho-organicity covers such a wide range of behavior disorders (one is tempted to conclude that Elizur would argue, if pressed, that *all* behavior is psycho-organically determined) that validation in the usual sense is ruled out. These short tests are almost certainly quite sensitive to impairment of functioning from some previously higher level. That impaired performance implies some subtle form of organic impairment which cannot be measured, is not only an unjustified (and unjustifiable) hypothesis but one which, if it were true, would be trivial, since such a diagnosis has no special implications for treatment over and above those which follow from consideration of the impaired performance itself without invoking a concept such as "psycho-organicity."

J Proj Tech & Pers Assess 34(1):76–7 F '70. Muriel D. Lezak. This test represents an ambitious undertaking. Dr. Elizur offers a set of tasks to "differentiate organics from non-organics" quickly, conveniently and objectively. * Scoring instructions range from precise through vague to obscure. No rationale or data are offered in explanation of either the kinds of errors selected for scoring, or the differences in point value given to errors. * There are no reliability studies; no studies correlating these data with other neuropsychological test results or with intelligence test data; no revalidation studies on other populations; no test of screening efficiency on other kinds of populations; no accounting for effects of institutionalization, education, socio-economic status; etc., etc. Three major purposes may be served by neuropsychological evaluation: differential diagnosis where neurological findings are limited, equivocal, or absent and organic pathology may be manifested behaviorally; discovery of the nature, extent, and ramifications of behavioral concommitants of brain damage for treatment and rehabilitation planning; and enhancement of

1 A recent study by Kraus (5) shows that this test has good predictive validity, but only against neurological criteria which are themselves of doubtful validity.

understanding of the relationship between neural substrate and behavior. This test fails each of these purposes. (1) While Dr. Elizur claims it can identify over 80% of a group of institutionalized diagnosed neurological cases, so can many other instruments and combinations thereof; what he has not shown is whether his test can reliably pick out patients with organic lesions who have passed through the standard neurological fine-comb. (2) This tripartite, essentially nonverbal test falls far short of Dr. Elizur's stated goal of creating a flexible, multidimensional instrument; its diagnostic potential is greatly restricted and it is essentially useless for treatment and rehabilitation planning. (3) As for its research possibilities, validity or reliability have yet to be demonstrated; it is limited both in range and in depth; and discrete functions are so confounded in complex tasks as to reduce its applicability in any sophisticated effort at relating brain and behavior. On the other hand, one or more of the subtests may prove to be a useful addition to the enterprising clinician's test battery if someone is willing to go through the trouble of standardizing and validating them. * While Dr. Elizur may be praised for his ambitiousness, exuberance, and creative imagination, this treatise lacks those qualities of sound scholarship required for serious scientific or professional consideration. Unfortunately, a number of useful clinical insights and suggestions are offered which, buried under conceptual looseness and methodological shoddiness, may never become generally available.

[76]

Eysenck Personality Inventory. Grades 9–16 and adults; 1963–69; EPI; revision of *Maudsley Personality Inventory;* 2 editions (identical except for 3 words and directions); 3 scores: extraversion, neuroticism, lie; no reliability data for the lie score; authors recommend use of both forms to obtain adequate reliability for individual measurement; postage extra; [10–15] minutes; H. J. Eysenck and Sybil B. G. Eysenck. * *a)* AMERICAN EDITION. Grades 9–16 and adults; 1963–69; Forms A, B, ('63, 2 pages); manual ('68, 27 pages); supplementary norms: college ['66, 2 pages], adult industrial ['69, 1 page]; the only norms for total scores on both forms are tentative college norms; no description of normative populations; $3.50 per 25 test-answer sheets; $1.50 per set of scoring stencils; $1.25 per manual; $2.25 per specimen set; scoring service, 45¢ or less per test; a printing with title *Eysenck Personal Inventory* is available for industrial use; Educational and Industrial Testing Service.
b) BRITISH EDITION. Adults; 1963–64; Forms A, B, ('64, 4 pages); manual ('64, 24 pages); norms consist of means and standard deviations for various groups; 32½p per 20 tests; 15p per scoring stencil;

22½p per manual; 42½p per specimen set; University of London Press Ltd.

REFERENCES

1. See 6:93.

2–53. See P:77, also includes a cumulative name index to the first 53 references for this test.

54. GREEN, LEONARD ROY. *Effects of Alcohol on "Introverted" and "Extraverted" Alcoholics.* Doctor's thesis, Boston University (Boston, Mass.), 1966. (*DA* 27:1448A)

55. RAMSAY, R. W. "Personality and Speech." *J Pers & Social Psychol* 4:116–8 Jl '66. * (*PA* 40:10092)

56. VERGHESE, ABRAHAM. *Some Aspects of Chest Pains After Myocardial Infarction.* Doctor's thesis, University of Melbourne (Parkville, Vic., Australia), 1966.

57. FREEDMAN, MARK J. *Homosexuality Among Women and Psychological Adjustment.* Doctor's thesis, Case Western Reserve University (Cleveland, Ohio), 1967. (*DA* 28:4294B)

58. VERGHESE, ABRAHAM. "Personality Traits and Coronary Heart Disease." Editorial. *Austral & N Zeal J Psychiatry* 1: 62–3 Je '67. *

59. BRIDGES, P. K., AND JONES, M. T. "Relationship of Personality and Physique to Plasma Cortisol Levels in Response to Anxiety." *J Neurol Neurosurg & Psychiatry* 31:57–60 F '68. * (*PA* 43:7142)

60. COMREY, ANDREW L., AND DUFFY, KIRT E. "Cattell and Eysenck Factor Scores Related to Comrey Personality Factors." *Multiv Behav Res* 3:379–92 O '68. * (*PA* 43:8363)

61. CONKLIN, R. C., AND OGSTON, D. G. "Prediction of Academic Success for Freshman at the University of Calgary." *Alberta J Ed Res* 14:185–92 S '68. * (*PA* 44:4244)

62. CRASKE, S. "A Study of the Relation Between Personality and Accident History." *Brit J Med Psychol* 41:399–404 D '68. * (*PA* 43:7142)

63. EYSENCK, S. B. G., AND EYSENCK, H. J. "The Measurement of Psychotism: A Study of Factor Stability and Reliability." *Brit J Social & Clin Psychol* 7:286–94 D '68. * (*PA* 43:15820)

64. FRITH, C. D. "Personality, Nicotine and the Salivary Response." *Life Sci* 7:1151–6 N 15 '68. *

65. GIBBINS, K. "Response Sets and the Semantic Differential." *Brit J Social & Clin Psychol* 7:253–63 D '68. * (*PA* 43:15821)

66. HESLET, FREDERICK ELLIS. *An Investigation Into the Experimental Balancing of Verbal Frequency in Small Problem Solving Groups.* Doctor's thesis, Ball State University (Muncie, Ind.), 1968. (*DA* 29:4283A)

67. HOWARTH, E., AND EYSENCK, H. J. "Extraversion, Arousal, and Paired-Associate Recall." *J Exp Res Personality* 3:114–6 D '68. *

68. KANEKAR, SURESH, AND DESHMUKH, MEENAXI. "A Study of Extraversion, Neuroticism, Authoritarianism and Misogyny Among Women." *Indian Psychol R* 5:21–7 Jl '68. *

69. KEUTZER, CAROLIN S. "Sex Differences in a Smoking Treatment Program." *Dis Nerv System* 29:529–33 Ag '68. * (*PA* 43:5324)

70. McCABE, OLIVER LEROY. *An Empirical Investigation of the Effects of Chemically (LSD-25)-Induced "Psychedelic Experiences" on Selected Measures of Personality, and Their Implications for Therapeutic Counseling Theory and Practice.* Doctor's thesis, Catholic University of America (Washington, D.C.), 1968. (*DA* 29:4849B)

71. McKERRACHER, D. W., AND WATSON, R. A. "The Eysenck Personality Inventory in Male and Female Subnormal Psychopaths in a Special Security Hospital." *Brit J Social & Clin Psychol* 7:295–302 D '68. * (*PA* 43:16011)

72. MORGAN, WILLIAM P. "Personality Characteristics of Wrestlers Participating in the World Championships." *J Sports Med* 8:212–6 D '68. *

73. MORGENSON, D. F., AND MARTIN, IRENE. "Personality, Awareness and Autonomic Conditioning." *Psychophysiol* 5:536–47 N '68. *

74. MUTHAYYA, B. C., AND RAJESWARI, S. "A Study of Personality and Achievement Motive of Backward and Normal Children." *J Psychol Res* 12:139–42 S '68. *

75. SMITH, STUART L. "Extraversion and Sensory Threshold." *Psychophysiol* 5:293–9 N '68. *

76. SMITHERS, A. G. "Some Characteristics of Business Students in a Technological University: 1, Personality Patterns." *Occup Psychol* 42:161–5 Ap–Jl '68. *

77. SMITHERS, ALAN. "Some Characteristics of Business Students in a Technology University: 2, Occupational Values." *Occup Psychol* 42:231–8 O '68. *

78. VINGOE, FRANK J. "Note on the Validity of the California Psychological Inventory." *J Consult & Clin Psychol* 32: 725–7 D '68. * (*PA* 43:4045)

79. WEINSTEIN, FRANCINE TODER. *The Effect of Personality Type on Systematic Desensitization and Structured Group Interaction in Reducing Examination Anxiety.* Doctor's thesis, Michigan State University (East Lansing, Mich.), 1968. (*DA* 29:3431A)

80. WILSON, JOHN D. "Predicting Student Performance in First Year Arts and Science." *Scottish Ed Studies* 1:68–74 My '68. *

81. AITKEN, R. C. B.; ZEALLEY, A. K.; AND ROSENTHAL, S. V. "Psychological and Physiological Measures of Emotion in Chronic Asthmatic Patients." *J Psychosom Res* 13(3):289–97 S '69. * (*PA* 44:12622)

82. ANDREWS, ROBERT THOMPSON, JR. *Oral Communications Practices of Extraverts and Introverts Regarding Selected Encoding Variables.* Doctor's thesis, Michigan State University (East Lansing, Mich.), 1969. (*DAI* 30:2649A)

83. BAILEY, JOHN E., AND METCALFE, MARYSE. "The MPI and the EPI: A Comparative Study on Depressive Patients." *Brit J Social & Clin Psychol* 8(1):50–4 F '69. * (*PA* 43: 8483)

84. BARTON, MICHAEL LON. *Differences in Critical Flicker Frequency as a Function of Extraversion, Reactive Inhibition, and Ego Motivation.* Doctor's thesis, Washington University (St. Louis, Mo.), 1969. (*DAI* 30:3378B)

85. BLOCK, SIDNEY, AND DAVIES, BRIAN. "Forearm Blood Flow in Anxious and Non-Anxious Patients." *Austral & N Zeal J Psychiatry* 3(2):86–8 Je '69. *

86. BOND, M. R., AND PEARSON, I. B. "Psychological Aspects of Pain in Women With Advanced Cancer of the Cervix." *J Psychosom Res* 13(1):13–9 Mr '69. * (*PA* 44:4072)

87. BROOKS, JOHN. "The Insecure Personality: A Factor Analytic Study." *Brit J Med Psychol* 42(4):395–403 D '69. * (*PA* 44:10714)

88. BUCKLEY, RICHARD EDWIN. *The Effect of Extraversion, Neuroticism, S-V Interval, and Time of Day on the Estimation of Unfilled Temporal Intervals.* Doctor's thesis, University of Southern Mississippi (Hattiesburg, Miss.), 1969. (*DAI* 30: 2921B)

89. CARR, GORDON DEMAREST. *Introversion-Extraversion and Vigilance Performance.* Doctor's thesis, Tufts University (Medford, Mass.), 1969. (*DAI* 31:2299B)

90. CHILD, DENNIS. "A Comparative Study of Personality, Intelligence and Social Class in a Technological University." *Brit J Ed Psychol* 39(1):40–6 F '69. * (*PA* 43:17888)

91. COLSTON, MALCOLM A. "The E and N Scales of the EPI —Some Further Australian Data." *Austral Psychologist* 4(1): 59–61 Jl '69. * (*PA* 45:8249)

92. DE, BIMALESHWAR, AND KHAN, AFTAB AHMAD. "Achievement Motivation and Two Personality Dimensions." *Psychol Studies* 14(2):137–9 Jl '69. *

93. DOTSON, ELSIE, AND TEMPLER, DONALD I. "Grades, Attendance, and Extraversion." *Psychol Rep* 25(2):369–70 O '69. * (*PA* 44:5702)

94. DRAKEFORD, G. C. "The EPI and Scales of Rigidity and Dogmatism." *Brit J Social & Clin Psychol* 8(1):9–12 F '69. * (*PA* 43:8364)

95. EYSENCK, H. J.; HENDRICKSON, A.; AND EYSENCK, S. B. G. Chap. 14, "The Orthogonality of Personality Structure," pp. 155–70. In *Personality Structure and Measurement,* see 96. *

96. EYSENCK, HANS J., AND EYSENCK, SYBIL B. G. *Personality Structure and Measurement.* San Diego, Calif.: Robert R. Knapp, Publisher, 1969. Pp. xiii, 365. *

97. FABIAN, JUDITH JANARO. *Comparison of Theoretical Viewpoints and Empirical Measures of Neuroticism.* Doctor's thesis, University of California (Los Angeles, Calif.), 1969. (*DAI* 30:4369B)

98. FARLEY, FRANK H., AND KUMAR, KRISHNA V. "Personality and Audiometric Response Consistency." *J Auditory Res* 9(2):108–11 Ap '69. * (*PA* 44:15831)

99. FRANCIS, R. D. "Neuroticism and Optical Pupil Changes in Response to Auditory Stimuli." *Brit J Social & Clin Psychol* 8(4):344–9 D '69. * (*PA* 44:6751)

100. GALE, ANTHONY; COLES, MICHAEL; AND BLAYDON, JENNIFER. "Extraversion-Introversion and the EEG." *Brit J Psychol* 60(2):209–24 My '69. * (*PA* 43:12980)

101. HALMIOVA, OLGA, AND UHERIK, ANTON. "Eysenck's Personality Dimensions and Properties of the Nervous System." *Studia Psychologica* 11(2):116–24 '69. * (*PA* 44:20442)

102. HARRISON, NOBLE W., AND McLAUGHLIN, ROBERT J. "Self-Rating Validation of the Eysenck Personality Inventory." *Brit J Social & Clin Psychol* 8(1):55–8 F '69. * (*PA* 43:8371)

103. HIRSCHMAN, WILLIAM. "Stability of Eysenck Personality Inventory Scores." *Newsl Res Psychol* 11(3):48 Ag '69. *

104. HOWARTH, E. "Expectations Concerning Occupations in Relation to Extraversion-Introversion." *Psychol Rep* 24(2): 415–8 Ap '69. * (*PA* 43:15780)

105. HOWARTH, E. "Personality Differences in Serial Learning Under Distraction." *Percept & Motor Skills* 28(2):379–82 Ap '69. * (*PA* 43:15781)

106. HOWARTH, EDGAR. "Extraversion and Increased Interference in Paired-Associate Learning." *Percept & Motor Skills* 29(2):403–6 O '69. * (*PA* 44:3128)

107. HUNTLEY, JACKSON RICHARD. *An Investigation of the Relationships Between Personality and Types of Instructor Criticism in the Beginning Speech-Communication Course.* Doctor's thesis, Michigan State University (East Lansing, Mich.), 1969. (*DAI* 30:5095A)

108. JALOTA, RAVI SHANKAR. "Personality Attitude Scores in the Context of General Ability and Social Desirability." *Indian Psychol R* 5(2):103–5 Ja '69. *

109. KELLY, M. R. "The Shor Personal Experiences Questionnaire: Some Personality Variables and College Achieve-

ment." *Austral J Psychol* 21(1):85–9 Ap '69. * (*PA* 43:13538)

110. KOLLER, K. M., AND CASTANOS, J. "The Eysenck Personality Inventory: Australian Experience With Normal and Abnormal Groups." *Austral Psychologist* 4(1):48–53 Jl '69. * (*PA* 45:8250)

111. KRAMER, ERNEST. "The Eysenck Personality Inventory and Self-Ratings of Extraversion." *J Proj Tech & Pers Assess* 33(1):59–62 F '69. * (*PA* 43:9774)

112. LUNGHI, M., AND RYLE, A. "The Stability of Scores of the Eysenck Personality Inventory in a University Population." *Brit J Psychiatry* 115(527):1201–2 O '69. * (*PA* 44:12643)

113. LYNN, R. "Personality Characteristics of a Group of Entrepreneurs." *Occup Psychol* 43(2):151–2 '69. * (*PA* 44:17595)

114. LYNN, RICHARD. "An Achievement Motivation Questionnaire." *Brit J Psychol* 60(4):529–34 N '69. * (*PA* 44:5167)

115. MANGAN, GORDON L., AND O'GORMAN, JOHN G. "Initial Amplitude and Rate of Habituation of Orienting Reaction in Relation to Extraversion and Neuroticism." *J Exp Res Personality* 3(4):275–82 Ap '69. * (*PA* 43:13947)

116. MARTIN, IRENE; MARKS, I. M.; AND GELDER, M. "Conditioned Eyelid Responses in Phobic Patients." *Behav Res & Ther* 7(1):115–24 F '69. * (*PA* 43:10066)

117. MASCIA, GEORGE VINCENT. *A Study of the Prediction of Alcoholics' Responsiveness to Treatment.* Doctor's thesis, University of Kansas (Lawrence, Kan.), 1969. (*DAI* 30:2912B)

118. MEHRABIAN, ALBERT. "Measures of Achieving Tendency." *Ed & Psychol Meas* 29(2):445–51 su '69. * (*PA* 44:17478)

119. ORWIN, WILLIAM. "Escape and Avoidance Learning in Extremely Neurotic and Extremely Stable Subjects." *Brit J Social & Clin Psychol* 8(4):362–74 D '69. * (*PA* 44:6754)

120. RAMSAY, R. W. "Salivary Response and Introversion-Extraversion." *Acta Psychologica* 29(2):181–7 Mr '69. * (*PA* 44:2337)

121. ROSENBERG, C. M. "Determinants of Psychiatric Illness in Young People." *Brit J Psychiatry* 115(525):907–15 Ag '69. * (*PA* 44:10505)

122. ROSENBERG, C. M. "Young Alcoholics." *Brit J Psychiatry* 115(519):181–8 F '69. * (*PA* 43:13086)

123. ROSENBERG, CHAIM M. "Young Drug Addicts: Background and Personality." *J Nerv & Mental Dis* 148(1):65–73 Ja '69. * (*PA* 43:14491)

124. SADLER, TIMOTHY GOODWIN. *The Role of Extraversion and Neuroticism in Human Operant Conditioning.* Doctor's thesis, University of Houston (Houston, Tex.), 1969. (*DAI* 30:5723B)

125. SHAW, G. K., AND HARE, E. H. "Eysenck Personality Inventory Scores of Patients With Depressive Illness. Letter. Reply by R. E. Kendell and W. J. DiScipio." *Brit J Psychiatry* 115(519):253–5 F '69. *

126. SIDDLE, DAVID A. T.; MORRISH, ROBERT B.; WHITE, KENNETH D.; AND MANGAN, GORDON L. "Relation of Visual Sensitivity to Extraversion." *J Exp Res Personality* 3(4):264–7 Ap '69. * (*PA* 43:14294)

127. SINGER, BARTON ALLEN. *Personality Variables and Conditioning in Alcoholics.* Doctor's thesis, Temple University (Philadelphia, Pa.), 1969. (*DAI* 30:1932B)

128. SOUEIF, M. I.; EYSENCK, H. J.; AND WHITE, P. O. Chap. 15, "A Joint Factorial Study of the Guilford, Cattell and Eysenck Scales," pp. 171–93. In *Personality Structure and Measurement,* see 96. *

129. STANLEY, GORDON. "Laymen's Identification of Item Content on the Eysenck Personality Inventory." *J Psychol* 72(1):99–100 My '69. * (*PA* 43:15837)

130. UHERIK, A. "Personality Traits and Bioelectrical Skin Reactivity (BSR) Under Conditions of a Load Situation." *Studia Psychologica* 11(4):307–17 '69. * (*PA* 44:20268)

131. VANDO, ALAN. *A Personality Dimension Related to Pain Tolerance.* Doctor's thesis, Columbia University (New York, N.Y.), 1969. (*DAI* 31:2292B)

132. WELLS, B. W. P. "Personality Characteristics of V.D. Patients." *Brit J Social & Clin Psychol* 8(3):246–52 S '69. * (*PA* 44:4087)

133. WHITE, KENNETH D.; MANGAN, GORDON L.; MORRISH, ROBERT B.; AND SIDDLE, DAVID A. "The Relation of Visual After-Images to Extraversion and Neuroticism." *J Exp Res Personality* 3(4):268–74 Ap '69. * (*PA* 43:14299)

134. WHITE, P. O.; EYSENCK, H. J.; AND SOUEIF, M. I. Chap. 19, "Combined Analysis of Cattell, Eysenck and Guilford Factors," pp. 239–50. In *Personality Structure and Measurement,* see 96. *

135. WHITE, P. O.; SOUEIF, M. I.; AND EYSENCK, H. J. Chap. 16, "Factors in the Eysenck Personality Inventory," pp. 194–217. In *Personality Structure and Measurement,* see 96. *

136. WILLIAMS, CLIVE. "Meaningfulness of the Eysenck Personality Inventory Lie Scale." *Austral Psychologist* 4(1):54–8 Jl '69. * (*PA* 45:8252)

137. BARTON, MICHAEL L. "Extroversion, Inhibition, and Adaptation Level Theory: An Unexpected Finding." Abstract. *Proc 78th Ann Conv Am Psychol Assn* 5(1):477–8 '70. * (*PA* 44:18684)

138. BATES, HENRY D. "Reinforcement Value, Sex, and Neuroticism." *Newsl Res Psychol* 12(1):16–7 F '70. *

139. BHUSHAN, L. I. "An Investigation Into Certain Personality Correlates of Leadership Preference." *Psychol Studies* 15(1):40–5 Ja '70. *

140. CROOKES, T. G., AND PEARSON, P. R. "The Relationship Between EPI Scores and 16 PF Second-Order Factors in a Clinical Group." *Brit J Social & Clin Psychol* 9(2):189–90 Je '70. * (*PA* 44:16699)

141. DANIEL, JOZEF, AND ŠKODACKOVA, JELA. "Correlations Among Various Forms of Secondary Load and Personality." *Studia Psychologica* 12(3):244–5 '70. * (*PA* 45:6308)

142. DAVIES, MARTIN. "Blood Pressure and Personality." *J Psychosom Res* 14(1):89–104 Mr '70. * (*PA* 44:16163)

143. DEB, MAYA. "Achievement in Engineering College and Neuroticism." *J Ed & Psychol* 27(4):378–9+ Ja '70. *

144. ENTWISTLE, N. J., AND ENTWISTLE, DOROTHY. "The Relationships Between Personality, Study Methods and Academic Performance." *Brit J Ed Psychol* 40(2):132–43 Je '70. * (*PA* 44:20948)

145. ENTWISTLE, N. J., AND WILSON, J. D. "Personality, Study Methods and Academic Performance." *Univ Q* 24(2):147–56 sp '70. *

146. FARLEY, FRANK H. "Comparability of the MPI and EPI on Normal Subjects." *Brit J Social & Clin Psychol* 9(1):74–6 F '70. * (*PA* 44:12616)

147. FARLEY, FRANK H. "Further Investigation of the Two Personae of Extraversion." *Brit J Social & Clin Psychol* 9(4):377–9 D '70. * (*PA* 45:8202)

148. FARLEY, FRANK H. "Generality of Faking Effects in the Dimensional Measurement of Personality." *Austral J Psychol* 22(3):265–8 D '70. * (*PA* 46:1206)

149. FARLEY, FRANK H., AND FARLEY, SONJA V. "Impulsiveness, Sociability, and the Preference for Varied Experience." *Percept & Motor Skills* 31(1):47–50 Ag '70. * (*PA* 45:4237)

150. GROUNDS, DAVID; DAVIES, BRIAN; AND MOWBRAY, ROBERT. "The Contraceptive Pill, Side Effects and Personality: Report of a Controlled Double Blind Trial." *Brit J Psychiatry* 116(531):169–72 F '70. * (*PA* 44:18111)

151. HORNE, DAVID J. DE L. "Minor Accidents and EPI Scores." Letter. *Brit J Med Psychol* 43(3):297–8 S '70. *

152. KANEKAR, SURESH, AND DOLKE, ASHOK M. "Smoking, Extraversion, and Neuroticism." *Psychol Rep* 26(2):384 Ap '70. * (*PA* 44:20911)

153. KEEHN, J. D. "Neuroticism and Extraversion: Chronic Alcoholics' Reports on Effects of Drinking." *Psychol Rep* 27(3):767–70 D '70. * (*PA* 45:10244)

154. KRAMER, ERNEST, AND ARONOVITCH, CHARLES D. "Voice Expression and Rated Extraversion." *J Proj Tech & Pers Assess* 34(5):426–7 O '70. * (*PA* 45:6363)

155. LEITH, G. O. M., AND WISDOM, BEATRICE. "An Investigation of the Effects of Error Making and Personality on Learning." *Program Learn & Ed Technol* 7(2):120–6 Ap '70. *

156. McKERRACHER, D. W.; ZWIRNER, W.; AND HARSHMAN, R. C. "Personality and Attainment: A Pilot Study." *West Psychologist* 1(2):62–70 Ja '70. *

157. McNEELY, JAMES BRICE. *Discriminant Function Analysis of Measured Characteristics of Male Undergraduates in Short Term, Educational-Vocational Counseling.* Doctor's thesis, Purdue University (Lafayette, Ind.), 1970. (*DAI* 31:1577A)

158. MEHRYAR, A. H. "An Attempt to Cross-Validate Eysenck's Hypothesis Regarding the Relationship Between Extraversion and Tough-Mindedness." *J Social Psychol* 80(1):109–10 F '70. * (*PA* 44:12390)

159. MEHRYAR, A. H. "Authoritarianism, Rigidity, and Eysenck's E and N Dimensions in an Authoritarian Culture." *Psychol Rep* 27(1):326 Ag '70. * (*PA* 45:6293)

160. MEHRYAR, A. H. "Some Data on the Persian Translation of the EPI." *Brit J Social & Clin Psychol* 9(3):257–63 S '70. * (*PA* 45:2414)

161. PAYNE, ROY. "Factor Analysis of a Maslow-Type Need Satisfaction Questionnaire." *Personnel Psychol* 23(2):251–68 su '70. * (*PA* 45:7134)

162. PLATMAN, S. R., AND PLUTCHIK, R. "Eysenck Personality Inventory as a Mood Test With Manic-Depressive Patients." *Psychol Rep* 27(3):947–52 D '70. * (*PA* 45:10341)

163. POWER, R. P., AND THOMPSON, W. T. "Simulation of Introversion and Extraversion on the Lemon Test." *Brit J Psychol* 61(1):91–3 F '70. * (*PA* 44:8468)

164. PRABHU, G. G. "Clinical Utility of Eysenck's Personality Inventory." *Indian J Appl Psychol* 7(1):21–3 Ja '70. *

165. ROBINSON, LISA. *Marihuana Use in High School Girls: A Psycho-Social Case Study.* Doctor's thesis, University of Maryland (College Park, Md.), 1970. (*DAI* 31:2196A)

166. SEGRAVES, ROBERT TAYLOR. "Personality, Body Build and Adrenocortical Activity." *Brit J Psychiatry* 117(539):405–12 O '70. * (*PA* 45:9557)

167. SKINNER, N. F.; HOWARTH, E.; AND BROWNE, J. A. "Note on the Role of Neuroticism and Extraversion in the 'Nice Personality' Stereotype." *Psychol Rep* 26(2):445–6 Ap '70. * (*PA* 44:21004)

168. SMITHERS, A. G., AND BATCOCK, ANGELA. "Success

and Failure Among Social Scientists and Health Scientists at a Technological University." *Brit J Ed Psychol* 40(2):144–53 Je '70. * (*PA* 44:20961)

169. SMITHERS, ALAN. "Personality Patterns and Levels of Dogmatism." *Brit J Social & Clin Psychol* 9(2):183–4 Je '70. * (*PA* 44:16654)

170. SOUEIF, M. I., AND EL-SAYED, A. M. "Curvilinear Relationships Between Creative Thinking Abilities and Personality Trait Variables." *Acta Psychologica* 34(1):1–21 S '70. * (*PA* 45:2374)

171. TROWN, E. ANNE. "Some Evidence on the Interaction Between Teaching Strategy and Personality." *Brit J Ed Psychol* 40(2):209–11 Je '70. * (*PA* 44:21644)

172. VERGHESE, ABRAHAM. "Relationships Between the Eysenck Personality Inventory N Score, the Cornell Medical Index M-R Score, and the Psychogalvanic Reflex." *Brit J Psychiatry* 116(530):27–31 Ja '70. * (*PA* 44:21183)

173. WARR, PETER B., AND COFFMAN, THOMAS L. "Personality, Involvement and Extremity of Judgement." *Brit J Social & Clin Psychol* 9(2):108–21 Je '70. * (*PA* 44:16679)

174. WHITEHILL, RICHARD P., AND JIPSON, JANICE A. "Differential Reading Program Performance of Extraverts and Introverts." *J Exp Ed* 38(3):93–6 sp '70. *

VICTOR B. CLINE, *Professor of Psychology, The University of Utah, Salt Lake City, Utah.*

The *Eysenck Personality Inventory,* as its authors state, "is, essentially, an improved version of the *Maudsley Personality Inventory.*" In the reviewer's opinion there is probably little justification in the change of name for this test or in the continued publication of the older MPI which is redundant and dated. The different titles of the two tests can be confusing and misleading to potential test purchasers, some of whom may incorrectly think that they are different or measure different personality traits. In the newer EPI some items of the older MPI have been rewritten in order to clarify and simplify their meaning. In addition, a Lie Scale (developed and adapted from the MMPI with some modifications) has been added. This test remains unchanged, except for an updated manual, from that reviewed by Lingoes in the Sixth MMY. Two equivalent forms have been developed for the EPI where only one is available for the older MPI. Item selection on the EPI's two primary scales E (extraversion-introversion) and N (neuroticism-stability) has been improved to reduce and eliminate the modest correlations which were present on the older MPI between these scales. The correlations between the E scale of the MPI and the EPI (and the N scale on both instruments) are as high as the reliabilities of either. With the various advantages of the EPI there appears to be little reason for any test user purchasing and using the older MPI unless possibly because he might have an accumulative bank of normative data which might be useful in certain business and industrial selection programs. Also, the MPI possibly might be considered as a third alternate form of the EPI which could in certain research settings have some use.

The manual (the American version) gives percentile norms using as a standardization group American college students. Test-retest reliabilities range between .80 and .97 and correlations between the two forms run from .75 to .91. Eysenck recommends combining Forms A and B where decisions are to be made about individuals. This would not be necessary in most research settings. Something in excess of 30,000 subjects were involved in the repeated factor analyses and research on the various sets of items which ultimately led to the E and N dimensions. The discussions of factorial, construct, and concurrent validity vary in quality and completeness. Correlations are presented between the E and N scales and MMPI and CPI involving small samples (40 and 66) without accompanying tables showing means and standard deviations. While N and E means and standard deviations are presented for a number of selected English reference samples such as salesmen, housewives, etc., nothing like this is given for American sample groups. Data are reported on the correlates of E, N, and the Lie Scale with judges' ratings and nominations of individuals and their behavior in real life.

According to a rather impressive array of data mustered by Eysenck, he and his coworkers have found two pervasive independent dimensions of personality, extraversion-introversion and neuroticism-stability which account for most of the variance in the personality domain. Eysenck refers to these two dimensions as "super factors." The theoretical background and the experimental validation of the concepts of extraversion and neuroticism are presented in a recent book (*96*) by the authors of the EPI. Eysenck's E factor, or dimension, resembles but is not identical with that discussed by Karl Jung. The high end is regarded as extroversion and applies to individuals tending to be outgoing, impulsive, and uninhibited, having many social contacts and frequently taking part in group activities. The introverted end is seen in a quite retiring sort of person, introspective, fond of books rather than people, one who has reserve and is distant except to intimate friends. He tends to plan ahead, looks before he leaps, and distrusts the impulse of the moment; he does not like excitement, he takes matters of everyday life with proper seriousness and likes a well-ordered mode of life. The high end of the neuroticism dimension is indicative of emotional instability and over-reactivity.

High scoring individuals tend to be emotionally over responsive and have difficulties in returning to a normal state after emotional experiences, such individuals frequently complain of vague somatic upsets of minor kinds such as headaches, digestive troubles, insomnia, backaches, etc. Such individuals are also predisposed to neurotic disorders under stress. Those with low scores on neuroticism tend in general to be better adjusted and more emotionally stable. The N and E dimensions are essentially uncorrelated.

Some diagnosticians may fault this test as being undynamic or limited and narrow in scope having only two dimensions versus the many that are avaliable on such tests as the MMPI, CPI, and other broad-range personality tests. Another concern some have with the EPI is that it is not very useful in assessing or differentiating between any standard psychiatric categories. Probably all it can do is grossly screen the psychiatrically sick and well, as well as measure the presence of pervasive anxiety.

In summary, for those who wish to measure the dimensions of neuroticism-stability and/or extroversion-introversion, the EPI is probably the best instrument now available and certainly is backed by superior research. It is, however, lacking in sufficient normative data and reference information which could make it more useful to the American population of subjects.

RICHARD I. LANYON, *Associate Professor of Psychology, Northeastern University, Boston, Massachusetts.*

The two personality factors of anxiety and extraversion, by these or similar names, have now reached central status in the literature on personality structure, as evidenced by their identification[1] in the 1968 *Annual Review of Psychology* as "the big two." The *Eysenck Personality Inventory*, which has evolved from the older *Maudsley Personality Inventory*, reflects Eysenck's many and prolific years of work in developing a theory of personality about these two concepts, and an evaluation of the test must necessarily involve reference to this broader work. The EPI can perhaps be best characterized as the basic assessment tool in research on Eysenck's formulation of personality structure.

The Eysenck test is a yes-no inventory with two parallel forms, each consisting of a 24-item

1 WIGGINS, JERRY S. "Personality Structure." *Ann R Psychol* 19:293–350 '68. *

extraversion (E) scale, a 24-item neuroticism (N) scale, and, as an addition beyond the MPI, a 9-item lie scale similar in format to the lie scale of the MMPI. The industrial form of the test (*Eysenck Personal Inventory*) is identical except for the title and the spaces for providing personal identifying data. Listed in the manual are other advantages claimed for the EPI over the MPI in addition to the two parallel forms and the lie scale: rewording of items to make them understandable at lower education and intelligence levels, re-selection of items to eliminate the small negative correlation existing between the MPI E and N scales, and higher reliabilities. The reader is referred to previous writings of Eysenck for an account of the enormous quantity of factor analytic work which went into the development of the E and N scales. The manual contains a large amount of detailed information on the characteristics and correlations of the EPI E and N scales, and it can be considered an excellent introduction to the use of the test for research related to Eysenck's theory of personality.

Do the EPI scales adequately reflect Eysenck's concepts of extraversion and neuroticism? For neuroticism, yes; for extraversion, yes with one reservation. Several critics have pointed out that in his theorizing Eysenck has favored the "European" definition of extraversion, which tends to identify the concept with relation to impulsiveness and weak superego controls, as opposed to the "American" usage, in which extraversion is more closely related to sociability. The item content of the E scale, however, identifies it with the American usage of extraversion to a greater extent than would be expected.

In the manual, the EPI is regarded as interchangeable with (though superior to) the MPI, and it is therefore reasoned that validity research for the MPI may also be used in support of the EPI. Unfortunately, correlations between the two tests are not presented, which is difficult to understand because the EPI was developed as long ago as 1963. These correlations are now available in the literature (e.g., *83, 146*) and they are generally in the .70's, indicating that the two tests may indeed be seen as comparable for many purposes. These intercorrelations approach the average test-retest reliabilities of the MPI scales (around .80), though reliabilities of the EPI scales are reported to be somewhat higher (around .85), and even higher reliabilities are obtainable (around .90) by using Forms A and B combined. Eysenck's attempt to remove, in the EPI scales, the small negative correlations which existed between the MPI E and N scales, appears to have been successful for Form A but less so for Form B (e.g., *47, 146*).

The manual is deficient in reporting norms, a shortcoming which the authors themselves acknowledge. A great deal of data on English populations are given in summary form, and some normative data on American college students are presented in percentiles. Since it is acknowledged that women tend to score higher than men on N and lower on E, the failure to state the proportion of men and women in the American norms is a serious omission.

One other deficiency with the test should be mentioned. The lie scale is not adequately researched and should be used with extreme caution. No reliability data are reported; this should be mandatory for a scale consisting of only nine items. Also, later studies (*50, 83*) show that the suggested cutting scores of 4 or 5 for the lie scale are probably too low, despite the norms given in the manual. It should be further noted that these percentile norms for the lie scale may be misleading, since it appears that "upper limits" to each score interval have been reported rather than the more usual "midpoints."

There are many interesting correlates of extraversion and neuroticism in educational, industrial, and clinical fields, and the reported research in these areas continues to indicate general though not unequivocal support for Eysenck's theory of personality. Critics and reviewers of Eysenck's work have never been comfortable with his declaration that the EPI may be used as a *clinical* instrument, and the relevant data presented in the manual do not give any new indications of clinical usefulness, except perhaps as a very general screening device for some purposes.

EVALUATION. The EPI has been developed as the basic assessment tool for research on Eysenck's personality theory, and its validity for this use is unquestioned. The manual presents an extremely wide variety of data and provides numerous references to the prolific literature dealing with Eysenck's work. There are some deficiencies with the American norms, and the lie scale should be used only with cau-

tion. As measures of the two major factors of personality, the EPI scales are as good as any.

Brit J Psychol 56:329–30 Ag '65. A. W. Heim. The Eysenck Personality Inventory (E.P.I.) is described as "a development of the Maudsley Personality Inventory (M.P.I.)." Like its predecessor, it claims to measure extraversion and neuroticism but the E.P.I. comprises two parallel forms, A and B, and it includes also a "lie scale" which may be used to eliminate subjects showing "desirability response set." We are, however, not told what to do with the "eliminated subjects." As Prof. Eysenck comments in a different publication, "when people are motivated to try and give as good an account of themselves as possible, questionnaires are almost entirely useless." Since psychological tests are used largely for purposes of selection and guidance, one might suppose that subjects do tend to be so motivated. But the corollary is not drawn in the E.P.I. manual—which reads, in fact, rather like an advertising brochure. Thus in the section on applications of the E.P.I. we find: "Wherever large bodies of data are being gathered the inclusion of the E.P.I. seems indicated" and, again, "For purposes of diagnosis and treatment, the E.P.I. should be administered routinely." In the short manual, room has even been found to denigrate other techniques: "This whole area has been very much neglected in motivation research, where unreliable and invalid 'projective techniques' have found favour." Yet "an enormous amount of applied work has been done in the area of market research with the M.P.I. and the E.P.I. in an attempt to discover personality correlates of consumption of different articles and brands of articles, of readership of different papers and journals, of participation in T.V., cinema going, and many other activities. The general finding has been that in almost every case where they have been looked for, these postulated personality differences have in fact been found." There is a tendency to assume the magic of numbers, e.g. "The total numbers involved in all this work are in excess of 30,000"; there is also a tendency, unsuited to a test manual, to blind with science, e.g. "T.V. viewing shows a strong, monotonic relationship with *N*, and a curvilinear one with *E*." (According to the statisticians, these relationships are by no means mutually exclusive.) Two main points strike the reviewer. The first is the smoothness with which the Eysencks glide from "personality tests" to personality differences, from E and N to extraversion and neurosis (as opposed to neuroticism). They attempt to draw this sting by invoking "phenotypic and genotypic aspects" and by actually stating that their near-zero correlations between E and N "should not be interpreted as *proving* the independence of E and N. This would imply a reification of these two conceptual entities which would be entirely inappropriate." Appropriate or inappropriate, however, such reification is repeatedly perpetuated in other sections of the manual. The second point is the paucity of validation data. The section called "Validity of the the scales" consists of two short paragraphs only. In the first of these it is held that since the E.P.I. scales closely resemble the M.P.I., and that validation "exists in profusion in relation to the M.P.I. (Knapp, 1962)," therefore "it seems reasonable to argue that this proof would also apply to the new scales. Independent proof would, of course, be required in due course, but is not yet available." The second paragraph contains the familiar "heads I win, tails you lose" element. Here a non-psychometric criterion was chosen, independent judges being "asked to nominate extraverted and introverted, or stable and unstable subjects." No figures are given but the subjects are said to "answer the E.P.I. in a corresponding manner. There is some evidence that where there is lack of agreement, it is the judges who are at fault, rather than the inventory answers"! Figures are given later, in two tables listing the mean scores of various normal and abnormal groups on the E.P.I. scales. Some of these figures confirm the doubts about validity already raised by the text. For example, the mean E scores of (normal) apprentices and G.P.O. telephonists are, respectively, 29.288 and 24.783, whilst those of depressives and schizophrenics are, respectively, 23.317 and 21.865. Again on the N, score, the mean of the (341) Army subjects, $m = 20.812$, is virtually the same as the mean of the (89) schizophrenics, $m = 20.843$. Apart from these and other curiosities, the manual seems to have been got out in a hurry. A test-retest correlation is given as 1/736 and the heading for the last column in Tables 4 and 5 is omitted. As to the questionnaire itself, this is open to the usual psychological objections of insisting on forced choice and of telling an intelligent subject that "there are no right or wrong answers," when the test includes such questions as "Have you ever been late for an appointment or work?"

Prof Psychol 1(4):413–5 su '70. James Linden. * Reliability indexes of acceptable magnitude are reported in the *Manual,* however, the associated Ns are small. Few validity data are reported for the EPI. However, the test's authors and others have conducted several experimental studies using the EPI's predecessor, the MPI, in which the MPI scales were shown to predict circumscribed real life behavioral criteria. EPI-MPI correlations are sufficiently high to support assertions that the experimental findings reported for the MPI also may apply to the EPI. * All norms provided for the EPI should be used with caution. Although the authors wisely suggest that it may be desirable for test users to develop their own local norms, they retain the responsibility of providing more relevant and representative reference data than they have to date. Certainly, interpretations of the EPI should mirror these considerations and be limited to persons with professional training and supervised experience in objective personality assessment. The presence of two parallel forms permits more rigorous estimations of the reliability of the EPI to be made and allows for more sophisticated experimental designs than usually is possible with other measures frequently used in objective personality assessment research. The factor analytic work leading to the development of the MPI and the refinements which resulted in the production of the EPI technically were sound. The use of only two factor scales provides perhaps a somewhat simplified but at the same time realistic and practical picture of the actual psychometric dimensions measured by most commonly used paper-and-pencil personality inventories. By definition, Scales E and N constitute two bipolar axes in a bivariate factor space. This permits a two dimensional graphic representation to be made of an individual's set of EPI scores or the depiction of the central tendency and variability among the scores of a given group of subjects. Such representations should facilitate the interpretation of the instrument and enhance efforts to formulate hypotheses for investigation. Although secondary in importance to the two major factor scales, the use of a Lie Scale does make possible a direct estimation of the impact of this response bias upon the performance of a given examinee. The *Manual* is informative and well referenced. Unfortunately, many references pertain to unpublished work. Reliability and validity data specific to American samples should be obtained prior to any extensive use of this instrument in the United States. Even though the two personality dimensions measured by this instrument have been found useful in psychological research and suggest promise for clinical use, the adequacy of this instrument for other than research purposes has yet to be verified.

For a review by James C. Lingoes, see 6:93.

[77]

★The Eysenck-Withers Personality Inventory (For I.Q. 50–80 Range). Institutionalized subnormal adults; 1965–66; EWPI; more than two thirds of the items are from the *Junior Eysenck Personality Inventory;* 3 scores: extraversion, neuroticism, lie; individual; 1 form ('65, 4 pages); manual ['65, 7 pages]; 32½p per 20 tests; 12½p per manual; 15p per scoring stencil; 30p per specimen set; postage extra; [20–30] minutes; Sybil B. G. Eysenck; University of London Press Ltd. *

REFERENCES

1. See P:78.
2. EYSENCK, HANS J., AND EYSENCK, SYBIL B. G. *Personality Structure and Measurement.* San Diego, Calif.: Robert R. Knapp, Publisher, 1969. Pp. xiii, 365. *
3. EYSENCK, S. B. G. Chap. 22, "Personality in Subnormal Subjects," pp. 317–22. In *Personality Structure and Measurement,* see 2. *

PAUL KLINE, *Lecturer in Psychology, University of Exeter, Exeter, Devon, England.*

The *Eysenck-Withers Personality Inventory* was administered to 426 patients with IQ's between 50 and 80 and the resulting inter-item correlations were subjected to factor analysis. Three clear factors emerged identified as Extraversion (E), Neuroticism (N), and Lie (L). After a few items were found too difficult and were rewritten, the test was given again to 330 of the former sample. The resulting factors were little different and the best items went into the final scale—20 N, 20 E and 12 L items.

Although the two factor analyses are not shown in the manual, Eysenck and Eysenck do report the loadings elsewhere (*2*). There can be little doubt that, in terms of face validity, personality factors very similar to those found by Eysenck with children and adults have been discovered in this subnormal population. The sample size is satisfactory for a restricted population of this type although it is unclear to what extent it is truly representative since its only description is "hospitalized in various institutions for the mentally subnormal." Ideally, we should like to know exactly how this sample was constituted.

One further point remains about this aspect of the test construction. It is clear that the testing was, in part at least, carried out by students at two British universities. To what extent their limited experience of testing affected the results is of course not clear but the use of any but the most skilled testers for an individual test is not entirely satisfactory.

RELIABILITY. The split-half reliabilities (E, .70; N, .88; L, .70) are satisfactory for a test of this type, just about sufficient for use with individuals. However, there is no indication of the sample size from which these figures were derived so that they can be regarded with no great confidence. The test-retest reliability (in fact the correlation between the two versions) calculated on 78 subjects was similar to that quoted above. We may conclude that the test is probably reliable although the data in the manual need supplementing.

NORMS. These are the most disappointing features of the test. Data from the standardisation sample (229 men, 197 women) showed no sex difference for E but a significantly higher score for N among the women. Thus we find in the manual "the sexes must clearly be kept apart in experimental and statistical analyses." Consequently, it is surprising to find the scores for E, N and L for groups of different intelligence are not presented separately for the sexes. The three IQ groups used where the N was around 100 in each are clearly too small for normative purposes.

No other norms are presented. Thus all we have are the scores from this one sample (whose constitution is unknown) in total and broken down into three IQ groups. Although there was no correlation with age in this sample, it would appear desirable to have norms for different age groups and for different disabilities perhaps even for different social classes. Until this is done practical application in the clinic must be severely limited.

VALIDITY. No evidence for the validity of these scales is offered other than the factor analysis described above. The emergence of factors defined by similar items to those defining E, N and L in other tests (which have some validation) is sound a priori evidence for validity. Nevertheless, some external evidence for validity, even if only correlations with ratings by nurses, would seem desirable for we cannot be certain to what extent these subnormal subjects understand and attribute the same meaning as do normals to these items. Further evidence of validity is needed.

ADMINISTRATION. The test items have to be read to the subject and in cases of difficulty, rephrasing is allowed. Thus there is a subjective element in the administration, although of a simple kind which experienced clinicians should be able to handle easily.

CONCLUSIONS. The construction of the *Eysenck-Withers Personality Inventory* and the similarity of the factor analyses of its items to the other Eysenck scales make it plausible that it is a valid measure of E and N in a subnormal population. Nevertheless, it must be realised that its validity has not been demonstrated. Similarly, it appears to be reliable though more work is needed on it with larger and more disparate samples. However the lack of norms means that its use in clinical *practice* as distinct from *research* must be cautious and limited until such norms are produced.

As an instrument of research into the personality of subnormal groups it does appear to be a useful and usable test at least as well supported as its counterpart from Illinois, the E level of the 16 PF. Which of these is to be preferred must depend upon the purpose of the research and the theoretical orientation of the researcher.

ROBERT D. WIRT, *Professor of Psychology, Child Development and Psychiatry and Director, Graduate Education in Clinical Psychology, University of Minnesota, Minneapolis, Minnesota.*

The EWPI, designed for use with adults having subnormal intelligence (IQ range 50–80), was developed by refinement of the items of the *Eysenck Personality Inventory*. All of the subjects tested thus far were hospitalized, mentally retarded adults. It is not yet known how persons of similar intelligence living in the community might score on the scales of this test.

From an original pool of 124 questions, 20 Extroversion (E), 20 Neuroticism (N), and 12 Lie (L) items were retained following a factor analysis using 426 subjects. The items must be read to each subject individually and his answer recorded by the examiner. During the standardization of the test, it was found necessary to refine the wording of some items even further. A retest of a sample of the original subjects showed the three factors to

have suitable stability, although the reliability of E is rather low ($r = .71$).

N scores are much higher in women than men and L scores somewhat higher in men than women. L clearly is correlated with mental age as research with both the EWPI and the JEPI show.

This test is still in a developmental stage. The research thus far gives some evidence that items can be found which show a personality structure in mentally defective persons which is similar to that of normal adults and children. However, the standardization sample was not large, was wholly institutionalized, and had to be tested individually (which may account for the high L scores). Further research is needed to show what, if any, relationship scores on these scales have to vocational and personal adjustment. There are no data yet available from non-English subjects.

[78]

*The FIRO Scales. Grades 9–16 and adults; 1957–67; 6 tests, of which all but FIRO-B are experimental tests; manual ('67, 19 pages); $3 per manual; $3.75 per set of tests and manual without keys; $5 per set of keys; postage extra; William C. Schutz; Consulting Psychologists Press, Inc. *

a) FIRO-B [FUNDAMENTAL INTERPERSONAL RELATIONS ORIENTATION—BEHAVIOR]. 1957–67; 6 scores of behavior toward others: inclusion (expressed, wanted), control (expressed, wanted), affection (expressed, wanted); 1 form ('67, 3 pages, identical with test copyrighted in 1957 except for directions and format); no high school norms; $3 per 25 tests; 50¢ per set of keys; $3.50 per specimen set; [8–15] minutes.

b) FIRO-F [FUNDAMENTAL INTERPERSONAL RELATIONS ORIENTATION—FEELINGS]. 1957–67; 6 scores of feelings toward others: inclusion (expressed, wanted), control (expressed, wanted), affection (expressed, wanted); 1 form ('67, c1957, 3 pages); no data on reliability; $3 per 25 tests; $1.75 per set of scoring stencils; $4.50 per specimen set; [8–15] minutes.

c) LIPHE [LIFE INTERPERSONAL HISTORY ENQUIRY]. 1962–67; retrospective childhood relationships with parents; 12 scores (6 scores for each parent): inclusion (behavior, feelings), control (behavior, feelings), affection behavior-feeling, perceived parental approval; 1 form ('62, 3 pages); no data on reliability; no norms; $3.25 per 25 tests; $1.50 per set of keys; $4.25 per specimen set; [20] minutes.

d) COPE [COPING OPERATIONS PREFERENCE ENQUIRY]. 1962–67; 5 scores: denial, isolation, projection, regression-dependency, turning-against-self; 1 form ('62, 4 pages); no data on reliability and validity; $3.25 per 25 tests; $3.25 per specimen set; [20] minutes.

e) MATE [MARITAL ATTITUDES EVALUATION]. 1967; 5 scores: inclusion (behavior, feelings), control (behavior, feelings), affection; separate forms for husbands and wives (3 pages); no data on reliability and validity; no norms; $4.25 per 25 tests; keys and specimen set not available; [8–15] minutes.

f) VAL-ED [EDUCATIONAL VALUES]. 1967; 14 scores: importance, mind, school-child control, teacher-child (control, affection), teacher-community (inclusion, control, affection), administrator-teacher (inclusion, control, affection), administrator-community (inclusion, control, affection) ; 1 form (4 pages) ; no data on reliability ; no norms ; $3.25 per 25 tests ; $1.75 per set of keys ; $4.50 per specimen set ; [15] minutes.

REFERENCES

1-15. See 6:94.
16-45. See P:79, also includes a cumulative name index to the first 45 references for this test.
46. EISENTHAL, SHERMAN. *The Dependence of Visibility of Values Upon Group Compatibility and Level of Need for Affection.* Doctor's thesis, University of Kansas (Lawrence, Kan.), 1961. (*DA* 22:2485)
47. COOPER, EUGENE BRUCE. *Patient-Therapist Relationships and Concomitant Factors in Stuttering Therapy.* Doctor's thesis, Pennsylvania State University (University Park, Pa.), 1962. (*DA* 23:4014)
48. FRANKS, THOMAS DANIEL. *A Study of Teacher Morale as Related to Selected Personal and Professional Factors.* Doctor's thesis, Indiana University (Bloomington, Ind.), 1963. (*DA* 24:3147)
49. ROSENBERG, JERRY MARTIN. *Perception of Automation Issues, Worker Background, and Interpersonal Behavior: An Analysis of Worker Attitudes Toward Automation and the Personality Needs and Personal History Factors That Relate to These Perceptions.* Doctor's thesis, New York University (New York, N.Y.), 1963. (*DA* 25:2644)
50. GARD, JOHN G. "Interpersonal Orientations in Clinical Groups." *J Abn & Social Psychol* 69:516-21 N '64. * (*PA* 39:7938)
51. GELLERMANN, WILLIAM PRESCOTT. *A Field Study of Process Variables in Interpersonal Relations.* Doctor's thesis, University of California (Los Angeles, Calif.), 1964. (*DA* 25:5422)
52. HARRISON, LAWRENCE BRIGHT. *The Relationship Between Ordinal Position and Dependency, Dominance, Affiliation, Affection, and Task-Orientation.* Doctor's thesis, University of Oklahoma (Norman, Okla.), 1964. (*DA* 25:3688)
53. KNAPP, DEANNE ERMA. *Interrelationships Among Measures of Affiliation Motivation.* Doctor's thesis, Purdue University (Lafayette, Ind.), 1964. (*DA* 25:6053)
54. ADLER, JACK. *Transfer of Interpersonal Behavior Among Emotionally Disturbed Adolescent Boys in Residential Treatment.* Doctor's thesis, Columbia University (New York, N.Y.), 1965. (*DA* 26:4433)
55. BECHTOLD, LAWRENCE A. *Administrative Typologies and Their Relationship to Interpersonal Needs of Teachers.* Doctor's thesis, University of Oklahoma (Norman, Okla.), 1965. (*DA* 27:2020A)
56. POWERS, JAMES RICHARD. *Trainer Orientation and Group Composition in Laboratory Training.* Doctor's thesis, Case Institute of Technology (Cleveland, Ohio), 1965. (*DA* 26:4065)
57. BORELLO, JOSEPH ANTHONY. *Psycho-Social Factors Related to Reported Marital Adjustment and Task-Efficiency.* Doctor's thesis, Yeshiva University (New York, N.Y.), 1966. (*DA* 27:1925A)
58. COHEN, JOEL BENJAMIN. *Interpersonal Response Traits and Consumer Behavior.* Doctor's thesis, University of California (Los Angeles, Calif.), 1966. (*DA* 27:1476A)
59. McDONOUGH, JOHN PAUL. *Hierarchically Grouped Social and Need Factors as a Means of Determining Dyadic Compatibility.* Doctor's thesis, Purdue University (Lafayette, Ind.), 1966. (*DA* 27:4130B)
60. PARAVONIAN, SAMUEL D. *The Effects of Counselor-Client Compatibility on the Client's Evaluation of the Effectiveness of the Counseling Relationship.* Doctor's thesis, Purdue University (Lafayette, Ind.), 1966. (*DA* 27:2051A)
61. PLUMMER, NOEL ARTHUR. *Patient-Therapist Need Compatibility and Expectation of Psychotherapeutic Outcome.* Doctor's thesis, University of Florida (Gainesville, Fla.), 1966. (*DA* 27:1628B)
62. ROARK, BILL. *The Effect of Training on Perceptions and Expectations of the Educational Administrative Role.* Doctor's thesis, Arizona State University (Tempe, Ariz.), 1967. (*DA* 28:1250A)
63. SHALINSKY, WILLIAM IRWIN. *The Effect of Group Composition on Aspects of Group Functioning.* Doctor's thesis, Western Reserve University (Cleveland, Ohio), 1967. (*DA* 28:793A)
64. SNYDER, LESTER MOSES, JR. *Some Effects of a Learning Systems Design in Counselor Education.* Doctor's thesis, University of Michigan (Ann Arbor, Mich.), 1967. (*DA* 28:2077A)
65. WALLACE, DONNEL GENE. *Group Loyalty, Communication, and Trust in a Mixed-Motive Game.* Doctor's thesis, University of Houston (Houston, Tex.), 1967. (*DA* 27:4569B)
66. YUKL, GARY ALLAN. *Leader Personality and Situational Variables as Co-Determinants of Leader Behavior.* Doctor's thesis, University of California (Berkeley, Calif.), 1967. (*DA* 29:406B)
67. DiTOSTO, EVELYN. *The Factors of Interpersonal Relations in Compatibility to Productivity of Student Teacher-Supervisor Dyads.* Doctor's thesis, West Virginia University (Morgantown, W.Va.), 1968. (*DAI* 30:1464A)
68. EDWARDS, WARREN P. *Interpersonal Relations Orientation*

Compatibility as Related to Outcome Variables in Group Psychotherapy. Doctor's thesis, Ohio University (Athens, Ohio), 1968. (*DA* 29:3909B)
69. JOHNSON, MONT LEATHAM. *Dissent and Agreement Regarding the High School Counselor's Role.* Doctor's thesis, University of Southern California (Los Angeles, Calif.), 1968. (*DA* 29:1424A)
70. KING, STANLEY H. "Characteristics of Students Seeking Psychiatric Help During College." *J Am Col Health Assn* 17:150-6 D '68. *
71. LAND, ARTHUR JULIAN. *Subordinates' Perceptions of Leadership Effectiveness Within the Idiographic Dimension and Their Relationship to the Interpersonal Needs of Status Leaders in Selected Florida Public Community Junior Colleges.* Doctor's thesis, University of Florida (Gainesville, Fla.), 1968. (*DAI* 30:96A)
72. LICHTENBERGER, EDGAR WILLIAM. *The Relationship of the Compatibility of Teachers and Their Principals in the Interpersonal Need Areas of Inclusion, Control, and Affection to the Continuation of Probationary Teachers in a Large Urban Public School System.* Doctor's thesis, Arizona State University (Tempe, Ariz.), 1968. (*DA* 29:2485A)
73. RIM, Y., AND COHEN, N. "Personality Variables in Making a Choice." *Psychologia* 11:191-7 D '68. *
74. RYAN, PETER LEIGHTON. *A Comparison of Three Theories of Group Behavior and Their Relationship to Behavioral Variables.* Doctor's thesis, University of California (Berkeley, Calif.), 1968. (*DAI* 30:1367B)
75. AELLEN, CAROL, AND LAMBERT, WALLACE E. "Ethnic Identification and Personality Adjustments of Canadian Adolescents of Mixed English-French Parentage." *Can J Behav Sci* 1(2):69-86 Ap '69. * (*PA* 44:12395)
76. ARNDT, GERALD MILTON. *An Investigation of the Influence of Interpersonal Compatibility on Counselor and Counselee Perceptions of the Initial Interviews.* Doctor's thesis, University of Rochester (Rochester, N.Y.), 1969. (*DAI* 30:977A)
77. BOUCHARD, THOMAS J., JR. "Personality, Problem-Solving Procedure, and Performance in Small Groups." *J Appl Psychol Monogr* 53(1, pt 2):1-29 F '69. * (*PA* 43:6351)
78. BRABBLE, ELIZABETH WILLIAMS. *Student Teacher-Supervising Teacher Compatibility and Its Relation to Success in Student Teaching.* Doctor's thesis, Pennsylvania State University (University Park, Pa.), 1969. (*DAI* 31:660A)
79. BRAMSON, ROBERT MARK. *Changes in Social Sensitivity in Group Training.* Doctor's thesis, University of California (Berkeley, Calif.), 1969. (*DAI* 31:823A)
80. BROWN, JEROME BANKS. *Some Factors in Response to Criticism in Group Therapy.* Doctor's thesis, University of Houston (Houston, Tex.), 1969. (*DAI* 30:376B)
81. DOLL, RICHARD E.; GUNDERSON, E. K. ERIC; AND RYMAN, DAVID H. "Relative Predictability of Occupational Groups and Performance Criteria in an Extreme Environment." *J Clin Psychol* 25(4):399-402 O '69. * (*PA* 44:11512)
82. ELBERT, WELDON EUGENE. *Changes in Self-Concept, Self-Actualization, and Interpersonal Relations as a Result of Video Feedback in Sensitivity Training.* Doctor's thesis, East Texas State University (Commerce, Tex.), 1969. (*DAI* 30:5233A)
83. FRIEDMAN, STEPHEN MARTIN. *Relationship Between Cognitive Complexity, Interpersonal Dimensions, and Spatial Preferences and Propensities.* Doctor's thesis, University of California (Berkeley, Calif.), 1969. (*DAI* 30:4776B)
84. GRADY, WILLIAM ELLIS. *Selected Variables Related to Academic Achievement of American and Canadian Male Freshmen at the University of North Dakota.* Doctor's thesis, University of North Dakota (Grand Forks, N.D.), 1969. (*DAI* 30:3725A)
85. HAGANS, REX WALTER. *School Climate and the Interpersonal Orientations of Elementary School Principals.* Doctor's thesis, University of Iowa (Iowa City, Iowa), 1969. (*DAI* 30:4184A)
86. HALL, WALLACE B., AND MacKINNON, DONALD W. "Personality Inventory Correlates of Creativity Among Architects." *J Appl Psychol* 53(4):322-6 Ag '69. * (*PA* 43:15815)
87. HETRICK, SUZANNE H. *An Analysis of "Client"-"Therapist" Compatibility and Its Effect on Transmissive and Receptive Communication in a Psychotherapy Analogue.* Doctor's thesis, Kent State University (Kent, Ohio), 1969. (*DAI* 31:1538B)
88. HIGHTOWER, EDWARD GLENN. *The Relationship of Perceived Effectiveness of Secondary School Principals and FIRO-B Data.* Doctor's thesis, University of Iowa (Iowa City, Iowa), 1969. (*DAI* 31:102A)
89. LUTJEMEIER, JOHN ARTHUR. *Organizational Climate, Teachers' Interpersonal Needs, and Pupil-Pupil Relations in Elementary Schools.* Doctor's thesis, University of Houston (Houston, Tex.), 1969. (*DAI* 30:2295A)
90. MEGATHLIN, WILLIAM LATIMER. *The Effects of Facilitation Training Provided Correctional Officers Stationed at the Atlanta Federal Penitentiary.* Doctor's thesis, University of Georgia (Athens, Ga.), 1969. (*DAI* 30:3282A)
91. MENDELSOHN, GERALD A., AND RANKIN, NEIL O. "Client-Counselor Compatibility and the Outcome of Counseling." *J Abn Psychol* 74(2):157-63 Ap '69. * (*PA* 43:10154)
92. RYAN, BRUCE ALLEN. *A Validation Study of the FIRO-*

B. Master's thesis, University of Alberta (Edmonton, Alta., Canada), 1969.

93. SCHULTZ, EDWARD WILLIAM. *A Study Concerning the Influence of Two Facilitative Conditions and Interpersonal Compatibility on Selected Educational Outcomes in a Tutorial Program.* Doctor's thesis, Syracuse University (Syracuse, N.Y.), 1969. (*DAI* 31:309A)

94. SHALINSKY, WILLIAM. "Group Composition as a Factor in Assembly Effects." *Hum Relations* 22(5):457–64 O '69. *

95. SNYDER, HENRY ALLEN. *The Relationship of Selected Interpersonal and Professional Characteristics of Administrative Interns and Their Supervisors to the Satisfaction of the Internship Experience.* Doctor's thesis, University of Minnesota (Minneapolis, Minn.), 1969. (*DAI* 30:4204A)

96. STEDTFELD, RICHARD WARREN. *Performance Level Effectiveness of Training Prospective Teachers in Interpersonal Skills.* Doctor's thesis, University of Minnesota (Minneapolis, Minn.), 1969. (*DAI* 30:5329A)

97. VRAA, CALVIN WOODROW. *The Relation of Selected Academic, Biographical and Personality Factors to the Achievement of Canadian College Freshmen.* Doctor's thesis, University of North Dakota (Grand Forks, N.D.), 1969. (*DAI* 31:168A)

98. ADINOLFI, ALLEN ANDREW. *The Characteristics of Highly Accepted, Highly Rejected and Relatively Unknown University Freshmen.* Doctor's thesis, University of Rochester (Rochester, N.Y.), 1970. (*DAI* 31:2271B)

99. BUCKEY, HAROLD M.; MUENCH, GEORGE A.; AND SJOBERG, BERNARD M. "Effects of a College Student Visitation Program on a Group of Chronic Schizophrenics." *J Abn Psychol* 75(3):242–4 Je '70. * (*PA* 44:11460)

100. COLLINS, MARGARET ANN. *An Investigation of the Influence of Interpersonal Compatibility on Pupil Achievement and Teacher and Pupil Perceptions of the Relationship.* Doctor's thesis, University of Rochester (Rochester, N.Y.), 1970. (*DAI* 31:1614A)

101. ERICKSON, CLARA; GANTZ, BENJAMIN S.; AND STEPHENSON, ROBERT W. "Logical and Construct Validation of a Short-Form Biographical Inventory Predictor of Scientific Creativity." Abstract. *Proc 78th Ann Conv Am Psychol Assn* 5(1):151–2 '70. * (*PA* 44:18715)

102. FROEHLE, THOMAS C. "Construct Validity of the FIRO-B Questionnaire: A Failure to Replicate?" *J Proj Tech & Pers Assess* 34(2):146–8 Ap '70. * (*PA* 44:15720)

103. GASSNER, SUZANNE MARIE. "Relationship Between Patient-Therapist Compatibility and Treatment Effectiveness." *J Consult & Clin Psychol* 34(3):408–14 Je '70. * (*PA* 44:14745)

104. LEVEEN, LOUIS. *On Becoming a Parent: Attitude and Feeling Changes.* Doctor's thesis, University of Southern California (Los Angeles, Calif.), 1970. (*DAI* 31:3067A)

105. McADAMS, CHARLES DEAN, JR. *A Comparison of Behavior Patterns of Music Teachers in Selected Universities Utilizing Interaction Analysis and the Fundamental Interpersonal Relations Orientation—Behavior Scale.* Doctor's thesis, East Texas State University (Commerce, Tex.), 1970. (*DAI* 31:2130A)

106. NEIDICH, JEROME FRED. *The Effect of Attention-Set on the Interpersonal Perceptual Accuracy of Open- and Closed-Minded Supervising Teachers.* Doctor's thesis, New York University (New York, N.Y.), 1970. (*DAI* 31:3395A)

107. NELSON, JOHN A., JR., AND HUTCHERSON, DONALD E. "A Pilot Study of the Relationships of Student-Teaching Grades to FIRO Compatibility Among the Student Teacher, Supervising Teacher, and University Supervisor." *J Teach Ed* 21(1):44–6 sp '70. *

108. PANEPINTO, JOSEPH VINCENT. *The Interpersonal Style of Parents and Their Children.* Doctor's thesis, West Virginia University (Morgantown, W.Va.), 1970. (*DAI* 31:3001B)

109. PARKS, DAVID JOHN. *A Study of Relationships Between Interpersonal Relations Orientations and Leader Behaviors of Elementary Principals.* Doctor's thesis, Syracuse University (Syracuse, N.Y.), 1970. (*DAI* 31:2657A)

110. PATTERSON, TOM W.; MARRON, JOHN P.; AND PATTERSON, NAOMI B. "Behavioral Patterns of Occupational Therapy Students on the FIRO-B." *Am J Occup Ther* 24(4):269–71 My–Je '70. * (*PA* 44:21560)

111. PFLAUMER, ELIZABETH MAE. *Personality Correlates of Effective Listening.* Doctor's thesis, Ohio State University (Columbus, Ohio), 1970. (*DAI* 31:3686A)

112. RILEY, RICHARD. *An Investigation of the Influence of Group Compatibility of Group Cohesiveness and Change in Self-Concept in a T-Group Setting.* Doctor's thesis, University of Rochester (Rochester, N.Y.), 1970. (*DAI* 31:3277A)

113. RYAN, BRUCE A.; MAGUIRE, THOMAS O.; AND RYAN, TONI M. "An Examination of the Construct Validity of the FIRO-B." *J Proj Tech & Pers Assess* 34(5):419–25 O '70. * (*PA* 46:1202)

114. STROM, ROBERT D., AND LARIMORE, DAVID. "Predicting Teacher Success: The Inner City." *J Exp Ed* 38(4):69–77 su '70. *

115. VERETT, GARY DWAYNE. *The Effect of a Summer Group Counseling Institute on Selected Attitudes and Personality Characteristics of Junior College Counselors.* Doctor's thesis, North Texas State University (Denton, Tex.), 1970. (*DAI* 31:3283A)

BRUCE BLOXOM, *Assistant Professor of Psychology, Vanderbilt University, Nashville, Tennessee.*

The FIRO scales are self-report questionnaires designed to assess a person's need for inclusion, control, and affection in various aspects of interpersonal situations. These aspects are: behavior which he directs towards others and which he desires others to direct towards himself (FIRO-B); feelings which he holds towards others and which he desires others to hold towards him (FIRO-F); feelings and behavior he remembers having desired of his mother and father plus feelings he remembers his mother and father having held towards him (LIPHE); feelings and behavior he desires of his spouse (MATE); and feelings and behavior he desires that teachers and school administrators should direct towards each other, towards children, and towards the community (VAL-ED). A questionnaire is included to assess a person's preferences among five defense mechanisms (denial, isolation, projection, regression, and turning-against-self) for resolving anxiety when his needs for inclusion, control, and affection are not met (COPE).

In each of the questionnaires, except for COPE, separate subscales are constructed to assess each of the three needs (inclusion, control, and affection). In the FIRO-B and FIRO-F questionnaires, subscales assess each need separately for each of two modes of expression: what is done or felt towards others and what is wanted of others. In the LIPHE and MATE questionnaires, subscales assess each need separately in the area of feelings and in the area of behavior. In the LIPHE and VAL-ED questionnaires, subscales also assess each need separately for persons in different roles, such as mother, father, and teacher.

In all questionnaires, except for COPE, the subscales contain nine single-statement items, each of which is to be answered on a 6-point scale. Each item is keyed dichotomously in such a way as to maximize the Guttman scale property of the subscale to which it belongs. This results in a high internal consistency of the keyed responses to the items in each subscale. However, this internal consistency is obtained at the expense of a loss of information deriving from many discriminations subjects make among the alternatives on the 6-point response scales. This loss of information may reduce the eventual utility of the scales for clinical diagnostic work. It should not, however, limit the usefulness of the scales for research in which only very broad measurement categories are used, e.g., the upper third of the distribution.

In the COPE questionnaire each item describes an interpersonal problem situation. Five defense mechanisms, described in nontechnical language, are given to be ranked in order by the subjects for the likelihood of being used in dealing with the problem. Since the same five types of defenses are ranked in each item, the total scores (the sum of the ranks for each defense) are interdependent, or ipsative. This results in low or negative correlations among the scores. This also means that the general level of the scales cannot be interpreted as indicating a person's general level of defensiveness.

Of the six FIRO questionnaires, only FIRO-B has been studied enough to be recommended for use in systematic research on the subject of interpersonal needs. The manual points out correctly that the other five questionnaires should be regarded as experimental. The manual contains some normative data for one of these five other scales, COPE, but no reliability data and scant validity data accompany those norms.

The manual presents rather complete psychometric data for the FIRO-B questionnaire. Internal consistency (the reproducibility index) is high for all subscales. All test-retest correlations are adequate (over .70). Subscale means and standard deviations are presented for a variety of student and occupational groups. The manual suggests interpretations can also be made of certain combinations of subscale scores, such as the difference between affection expressed towards others and affection wanted of others. Norm group means are given for these combination scores, but the absence of standard deviations for them makes the interpretation of them very tenuous.

The correlations among the FIRO-B subscales range from .06 to .49 with enough significant correlations to suggest the scales are not independent. These results should not necessarily be taken as indicators of poor test construction as suggested by the manual. Rather, they may indicate that there are substantive relationships among the variables being measured. The correlations suggest: expressed inclusion and wanted inclusion tend to reflect the same need, i.e., the need for inclusion; expressed affection and wanted affection

tend to reflect the same need, i.e., the need for affection; and that the need for inclusion is slightly and positively related to the need for affection.

Validity studies on the FIRO-B questionnaire suggest that its subscales are related to nontest interpersonal behavior as well as to other personality measures. Scale scores have been found to be correlated with: rated effectiveness of supervisors, production of good ideas in brain-storming groups, rated creativity, freshmen grades, and the diagnosis of schizophrenia. The number and strength of these relationships are not great enough to validate the use of FIRO-B for counseling and guidance, but they indicate it is definitely a worthwhile instrument for research.

The extensive use of FIRO-B subscales to study interpersonal compatibility has produced a mixture of positive and negative results. A typical study of this kind uses a comparison of the subscale scores of pairs of persons to create compatible or incompatible dyads, or, alternatively, uses the absolute difference of persons' scale scores as a measure of compatibility. Some of these studies show compatible dyads work better than incompatible dyads. Others of these studies show no results. Besides yielding these mixed empirical results, the potential of these studies is limited by the information lost when subscale scores are combined into a single measure of compatibility. A better design for this research would be to examine the main effects and interactions of needs of members of the dyad. This would enable the investigator to state his results most explicitly. For example, he could make a statement such as "A high need for inclusion therapist with a high need for inclusion patient produced the most positive feelings toward therapy."

In summary, the FIRO-B questionnaire is the only one of the six FIRO questionnaires well enough developed to be used for other than exploratory studies. Its subscales show a sufficient degree of relationship to interpersonal behavior and to personality measures to merit its use in research. However, the validity of the scales is not well enough documented to merit their use in guidance and counseling. The scales may be used to advantage to investigate dyadic need-compatibility provided that scores are not combined across persons to form a single indicator of compatibility.

[79]

*Family Relations Test. Ages 3–7, 7–15, adults; 1957–65; individual; 1 form ['57]; 3 levels; postage extra; (20–25) minutes; distributed by NFER Publishing Co. Ltd. *

a) FAMILY RELATIONS TEST: AN OBJECTIVE TECHNIQUE FOR EXPLORING EMOTIONAL ATTITUDES IN CHILDREN. Ages 3–7, 7–15; 1957; 2 levels; manual (59 pages); £6.75 per set of test materials; £1 per specimen set; Eva Bene and James Anthony.

   1) *Younger Children.* Ages 3–7; 40 item cards; 62p per 25 record booklets.

   2) *Older Children.* Ages 7–15; 86 item cards; 62p per 25 record booklets; 62p per 25 scoring blanks.

b) ADULT VERSION OF THE FAMILY RELATIONS TEST: AN OBJECTIVE TECHNIQUE FOR EXPLORING RECOLLECTED CHILDHOOD FEELINGS. Adults; 1965; 96 item cards; manual (30 pages); £5.37 per set of test materials; 62p per 25 record booklets; 62p per 25 scoring blanks; £1 per specimen set; Eva Bene.

REFERENCES

1. See 5:132.
2–13. See P:81.
14. FRANCIS WILLIAMS, JESSIE. Chap. 9, "A Serial Study of an Institutionalised Child Showing the Comparative Contribution to Rorschach Findings of Two Other Projective Techniques—the Children's Apperception Test and the Family Relations Test," pp. 110–23. In her *Rorschach With Children.* London: Pergamon Press Ltd., 1968. Pp. xi, 168. *
15. FROST, B. P. "Family Relations Test: A Normative Study." *J Proj Tech & Pers Assess* 33(5):409–13 O '69. * (PA 44:3632)
16. KAUFFMAN, JAMES MILTON. *Perception of Family and School Related Variables by School Adjusted, School Disordered, and Institutionalized Emotionally Disturbed Preadolescent Boys.* Doctor's thesis, University of Kansas (Lawrence, Kan.), 1969. (DAI 31:562A)
17. SMART, DAVID WAYNE. *Recalled Family Relations and Vocational Choice: A Test of Roe's Theory.* Doctor's thesis, University of Utah (Salt Lake City, Utah), 1969. (DAI 30:3741A)
18. SWANSON, BERNICE MARIAN. *Parent-Child Relations: A Child's Acceptance by Others, of Others, and of Self.* Doctor's thesis, University of Oklahoma (Norman, Okla.), 1969. (DAI 30:1890B)
19. KAUFFMAN, JAMES M. "Validity of the Family Relations Test: A Review of Research." *J Proj Tech & Pers Assess* 34(3):186–9 Je '70. * (PA 44:18748)
20. ROCHE, DERMOT D. J. "The Bene-Anthony Family Relations Test—Variations and Reliability of Administrative Procedure." *Papers Psychol* 4(1–2):12–5 Ap–O '70. *

Rorsch Newsl 12:38–9 Je '67. B. Semeonoff. * Although classified in the *Mental Measurement Yearbooks* under the heading "Character and Personality—Projective," the Family Relations Test has few, if any, strictly projective features. Methodologically, its closest affinities are perhaps with the card form of the MMPI; it is in fact really an inventory technique in disguise, since the questions asked are explicitly stated, and no interpretation is required of the tester. Like all forced-choice techniques it has its shortcomings, although provision is made to cover the most obvious contingency—i.e. the case where a statement can apply to more than one person. A further criticism might be that the tacit assumption of the distinction between "mild" and "strong" items is made irrespective of culture pattern. Thus, for example, "incoming positive strong" items are nearly all related to hugging, cuddling, etc., modes of behaviour very foreign to certain undemonstrative yet closely-knit families, as for example in the Scottish tradition. Conversely, "This person really understood me" rates as "mild." Difficulties may also arise resulting from the point in one's childhood at which one elects to think of oneself. The subject is allowed to answer different questions as at different ages, but it would seem that this might make for unreliability. One's evaluation of the technique must of course rest on experience in applying it; at a first examination it would appear to have distinct possibilities, if only as an aid to establishing contact with an inarticulate or inhibited subject. Trying it out informally on a few people has suggested that it "works," in the sense that the subject recognizes the inferences as valid. And while the basic device is obviously more suited to children than to adults, the fact that one is, in a sense, being deliberately invited to regress makes the introduction of a "play" element not inappropriate.

For reviews by John E. Bell, Dale B. Harris, and Arthur R. Jensen of children's levels, see 5:132.

[80]

★Fear Survey Schedule. College and adults; 1964–69; FSS; self-ratings on 108 fears; 1 form ('69, 3 pages); preliminary manual ('69, 7 pages); no data on reliability; norms (means and standard deviations only) based on 1964 edition consisting of first 73 items; $5 per 25 tests, postage extra; specimen set not available; (15) minutes; Joseph Wolpe and Peter J. Lang; Educational and Industrial Testing Service. *

REFERENCES

1. WOLPE, JOSEPH, AND LANG, PETER J. "A Fear Survey Schedule for Use in Behaviour Therapy." *Behav Res & Ther* 2:27–30 My '64. *
2. GROSSBERG, JOHN M., AND WILSON, HELEN K. "A Correlational Comparison of the Wolpe-Lang Fear Survey Schedule and Taylor Manifest Anxiety Scale." *Behav Res & Ther* 3:125–8 S '65. * (PA 40:2134)
3. HANNAH, F.; STORM, THOMAS; AND CAIRD, W. K. "Sex Differences and Relationships Among Neuroticism, Extraversion, and Expressed Fears." *Percept & Motor Skills* 20:1214–6 Je '65. * (PA 39:15353)
4. MANOSEVITZ, MARTIN, AND LANYON, RICHARD I. "Fear Survey Schedule: A Normative Study." *Psychol Rep* 17:699–703 D '65. * (PA 40:4235)
5. SUINN, RICHARD M. "The Desensitization of Test-Anxiety by Group and Individual Treatment." *Behav Res & Ther* 6:385–7 Ag '68. * (PA 43:3021)
6. CRIGHTON, J., AND JEHU, D. "Treatment of Examination Anxiety by Systematic Desensitization or Psychotherapy in Groups." *Behav Res & Ther* 7(3):245–8 S '69. * (PA 44:16783)
7. FAZIO, ANTHONY F. "Verbal and Overt-Behavioral Assessment of a Specific Fear." *J Consult & Clin Psychol* 33(6):705–9 D '69. * (PA 44:3630)
8. PAUL, GORDON L. "Inhibition of Physiological Response to Stressful Imagery by Relaxation Training and Hypnotically Suggested Relaxation." *Behav Res & Ther* 7(3):249–56 S '69. * (PA 44:16831)
9. SUINN, RICHARD M. "Changes in Non-Treated Subjects Over Time: Data on a Fear Survey Schedule and the Test Anxiety Scale." *Behav Res & Ther* 7(2):205–6 My '69. *
10. SUINN, RICHARD M. "The Relationship Between Fears and Anxiety: A Further Study." *Behav Res & Ther* 7(3):317–8 S '69. * (PA 44:16706)

11. WOLPE, JOSEPH. *The Practice of Behavior Therapy.* New York: Pergamon Press, Inc., 1969. Pp. x, 314. *
12. BATES, HENRY D. "Factorial Structure of Fears in a Clinical Population." *Newsl Res Psychol* 12(2):7–9 My '70. *
13. GIBBONS, DON; KILBORNE, LESLIE; SAUNDERS, ALAN; AND CASTLES, CHERYL. "The Cognitive Control of Behavior: A Comparison of Systemic Desensitization and Hypnotically-Induced 'Directed Experience' Techniques." *Am J Clin Hyp* 12(3):141–5 Ja '70. * (PA 44:14746)
14. KAMIL, LEONARD J. "Psychodynamic Changes Through Systematic Desensitization." *J Abn Psychol* 76(2):199–205 O '70. * (PA 45:4419)
15. LANG, PETER J.; MELAMED, BARBARA G.; AND HART, JAMES. "A Psychophysiological Analysis of Fear Modification Using an Automated Desensitization Procedure." *J Abn Psychol* 76(2):220–34 O '70. * (PA 45:2531)
16. ROTHSTEIN, WILLIAM, AND BOBLITT, WILLIAM EDGAR. "Expressed Fears of Psychiatric Inpatients." *J Clin Psychol* 26(3):277–9 Jl '70. * (PA 45:1022)
17. SPEIGLER, MICHAEL D., AND LIEBERT, ROBERT M. "Some Correlates of Self-Reported Fear." *Psychol Rep* 26(3): 691–5 Je '70. * (PA 45:683)

R. G. DEMAREE, *Professor of Psychology and Research Scientist, Institute of Behavioral Research, Texas Christian University, Fort Worth, Texas.*

According to the manual for the *Fear Survey Schedule* "its greatest value is in relation to *desensitization* techniques that deal with phobias and phobia-like reactions." Knowledge of an individual's responses to the 108 items of the FSS may indeed be useful to a therapist. As stated in the manual, the FSS "can frequently save a great deal of effort, revealing reactions to many stimulus classes, in a short time."

Within the context just described, fewer demands are placed on the FSS than if it were used as a psychometric instrument. Data to support its use as the latter is not presently available. From a psychometric point of view, therefore, the FSS should be considered only as a research instrument.

In an earlier, 73-item version of the FSS, the items were classified as follows: 9, animal; 16, social or interpersonal; 18, tissue damage, illness, death, or associated stimuli; 4, noises; 17, other classical phobias; and, 9, miscellaneous. This count of the items, however, overlooks the separate responses elicited for human and animal blood, and journeys by car, bus, and train. When these are counted as five items rather than two items, there are 76 items rather than 73 items in the earlier version of the FSS.

The latter constitutes the first 76 items (not the first 73 items, as stated in the manual) of the present 108-item schedule. Inspection of the additional 32 items did not reveal any particular theme, although seven of the items were sexual in nature.

In the booklet for the FSS, the respondent is informed that the items in the questionnaire "refer to things and experiences that may cause fear or other, related unpleasant feelings." Instructions are given to "Read each item and decide how much you are disturbed by it." Choices are marked in the booklet on a 5-point scale of 1, not at all; 2, a little; 3, a fair amount; 4, much; and, 5, very much.

Data have been reported on the earlier 73-item FSS for several samples of college students. Grossberg and Wilson (*2*) administered the FSS to 203 male and 302 female college students under conditions of anonymity. Summing the item scores led to scores for each of the six previously mentioned classes of items, as well as a total score over the 73 items. Means, standard deviations, and intercorrelations of these scores were reported separately for men and women. The results pointed to mean scores for women which were higher than for men on all classes of stimuli except noise. The correlations among the six subscores for the total sample ranged from .31 to .76, with a median of .55. The magnitude of these correlations suggests that the total score would be relatively reliable from an internal-consistency or generalizability point of view. The Taylor Manifest Anxiety Scale, which also was administered in this study, had a correlation of .46 with the total scores on the FSS.

Hannah, Storm, and Caird (*3*) administered the FSS and the *Maudsley Personality Inventory* to 1,154 male and 804 female college students. As in the study by Grossberg and Wilson, women received higher FSS scores on the average than did men. Total scores on the FSS correlated .41 with the neuroticism scores and −.14 with the extraversion scores of the *Maudsley Personality Inventory.*

In the two studies just cited, items most frequently responded to as "very much" disturbing were listed separately for men and women. Considerable agreement among men and women existed in both of these studies for social-interpersonal stimuli to be responded to most frequently as "very much" disturbing. "Failure" led the list with a response of "very much" by 25.1% of the men and 34.4% of the women in the Grossberg and Wilson study, and 21.7% of the men and 26.5% of the women in the Hannah, Storm, and Caird study. Apart from social-interpersonal stimuli, items to which phobic responses were given relatively often by both men and women were "dead people" and "prospects of a surgical operation." Results from a small sample of college students were reported by Manosevitz and Lanyon (4) which generally agree with the preceding.

Other findings of interest have been reported for fear survey schedules whose items contain many items which are similar or identical to those in the 108-item schedule. The 51-item schedule developed by Geer [1] and factor analyzed by Rubin et al.[2] is a good example. While the findings based on this instrument are not in disagreement with those cited for the 73-item FSS, the differences between these instruments in the instructions to respondents, response scales, and items can easily lead to differences in the psychometric properties of these instruments. This is particularly apt to be the case with factor analytic outcomes, based on different respondent populations and analytic techniques, as well as different instruments. The factor analyses of fear survey schedules reveal a plethora of interpretative distinctions. One can only guess as to the form the latter will take for data based on other populations than are represented by college students and under other conditions of administration.

In the judgment of the reviewer, the factor analytic findings and correlations with other measures which have been reported for fear survey schedules will be helpful mainly in the design of instruments and studies whereby sources of variance in responses to fear-evoking stimuli are systematically examined. Until studies of this nature have been accomplished, it is believed that fear survey schedules, such as the present 108-item schedule, should be restricted to use in research or as informal aids in behavior therapy.

[81]

The Forty-Eight Item Counseling Evaluation Test. Adolescents and adults; ICET; 1963; 7 problem area scores: anxiety-tension-stress, compulsive-obsessive-rigid behavior, depressive-defeatist thoughts and feelings, friendship-socialization, religious-philosophical goals, inadequacy feelings and behavior, total; 1 form (4 pages); manual (15 pages plus test); no data on reliability of subscores; $7.50 per examiner's kit of 25 tests, key, and manual; $6.50 per 25 tests; $1 per key; $1.50 per manual; postpaid; (10–20) minutes; Frank B. McMahon; Western Psychological Services. *

REFERENCE

1. McMAHON, FRANK B., JR. "Psychological Testing—A Smoke Screen Against Logic." *Psychol Today* 2(8):54–9 Ja '69. *

1 GEER, JAMES H. "The Development of a Scale to Measure Fear." *Behav Res & Ther* 3:45–53 Ag '65. *
2 RUBIN, BARRY M.; KATKIN, EDWARD S.; WEISS, BARRY W.; AND EFRAN, JAY S. "Factor Analysis of a Fear Survey Schedule." *Behav Res & Ther* 6:65–75 F '68. *

JOHN O. CRITES, *Professor of Psychology, University of Maryland, College Park, Maryland.*

One of the most critical functions which a counselor performs is to diagnose client problems and to assess general adjustment status. The purpose of such diagnosis and evaluation is usually twofold: to determine whether to accept a client for counseling, rather than referring him elsewhere, and to choose the most appropriate treatment for him. To aid the counselor in this decision-making process, the *Forty-Eight Item Counseling Evaluation Test* (ICET) was designed "to increase the accuracy in the identification of personal and emotional problems of adolescents and adults." As the title of this brief personality screening device indicates, it consists of 48 items which cover a wide range of self-descriptive behavioral content. (The first item is a sample, so that scores are actually based upon only 47 items.) The items are unique, in that they comprise two statements, the second of which is contingent on the first. For example, the sample item is as follows:

1. a. I like Mechanics magazines. T F
   b. IF FALSE: I prefer to read story-type magazines. T F

In other words, the examinee answers the second statement only if he has endorsed the first as indicated. The rationale for this item format is to identify a specific behavior or aspect of personality in the first statement which is of concern to the client and then to give him the opportunity to amplify it in the second statement.

Only the second statement in the diads is keyed in scoring the ICET, since it is answered only if the first statement has been endorsed in a predetermined diagnostically significant way. In other words, the scoring key is rationally derived to measure areas and symptoms of major maladjustments. In addition to a total score, which is the unweighted sum of the keyed responses to the second or contingency questions, six problem area scores are also calculated. These include the following, with the number of items for each in parentheses: Anxiety-Tension-Stress (11), Compulsive-Obsessive-Rigid Behavior (8), Depressive-Defeatist Thoughts and Feelings (5), Friendship-Socialization (7), Goals: Religious-Philosophical (7), and Inadequacy: Feelings and Behavior (9). How these subscales were constituted is not made clear in the manual. Item development is described sketchily as follows: "The selected 50 items [from a pool of 500] were tested on 260 subjects; on the basis of this study, the number of items was reduced to the present 48 items. Techniques used in the final selection included item analyses [sic] studies, discussions with professional Counselors who had used the experimental forms of the test, and suggestions made by counselees who had been tested." None of the item analysis data from this study or others are reported. A caveat to the user of the ICET is made, however, concerning score interpretation: "The validity of the Total Score is very high; the subscales (A-C-D-F-G-I) contain items for assisting in organizing responses into the general categories. The subscale validities are not equal to that of the Total Score." In fact, no validity data on the subscales are reported, and consequently considerable caution should be exercised in interpreting them, if they are used at all.

There are validity data on the total score, but they are less definitive than they are suggestive, and would not be generally interpreted as "very high." In three studies, the ICET was correlated (biserial r's) with subjects classified in response (Yes or No) to the question: "Do you feel the need for psychological assistance with your personal problems?" With N's of 59 junior college students, 100 sophomores, and 23 adult evening school students, the coefficients were .73, .71, and .73, respectively. These were considerably higher than the biserial r's of .56, .53, and .67 computed for a "partial" MMPI (not otherwise described) for the same groups. To assess the efficiency of a cutting score of 4 on the ICET, two other studies were conducted, in which a tetrachoric correlation of .92 (N = 25 vocational clients) was obtained for counselors' diagnoses of maladjustment and a mean total score of 12 (N = 16 psychiatric referrals) for admission to a hospital outpatient service. Similarly, one study of 64 vocational clients yielded a tetrachoric r of .81 between the same cutting score and case history, incomplete sentence, and personnel data criteria of maladjustment. Finally, two additional studies have investigated the relationship of the ICET to the *Minnesota Multiphasic Personality Inventory* and *Guilford-Zimmerman Temperament Survey*. For 21 subjects (not otherwise described), the tetrachoric r's were .95 (MM-

PI) and .87 (GZTS); for 49 clients, they were .89 (MMPI) and .76 (GZTS). These coefficients seem to be extraordinarily high, considering that the test-retest reliability of the ICET is reported as .80 for 42 college juniors over a three-week interval, which means that the upper limit for the correlation of the total score with other tests would be .80 even if the latter were perfectly reliable (.80 × 1.00).

The problem would appear to be that the N's in these studies are very small, with the exception of the one with 100 college sophomores. As a consequence, not only are the biserial and tetrachoric r's likely to be spuriously high but they are also probably unstable, i.e., not reproducible in larger, more heterogeneous samples. It is difficult to evaluate validity data based upon such meager N's, particularly when the studies are not fully reported in the manual. They are listed in outline form, which is easy to read but hard to appraise, and they raise more questions than they answer. For example: What was the "partial" MMPI which was used? What scores from it were correlated with the ICET? What were the base rates for the "cutting score" studies? How many false negatives and positives were there? Before the ICET can be used with confidence by counselors, these and similar questions concerning its empirical validity and usefulness must be answered in further research. There is a definite need for a test like the ICET, with its intriguing item format, and it warrants future systematic study, but at present it promises too much too soon. Claims in the manual that the total score has "very high" validity must be tempered with the quality and quantity of research data available to support them. Until more extensive empirical evidence is forthcoming, counselors might best use the ICET more as a "structured interview" technique than as a standardized and valid test.

[82]

★**The Gibson Spiral Maze.** Ages 8.5 and over; 1961–65; GSM; psychomotor performance associated with maladjustment, delinquency, mental illness, and accident proneness; 2 scores: time, error; individual; 1 form ('61, 1 page); manual ('65, 12 pages); no data on reliability and validity; only norms are for boys age 8.5–10; 50p per test; 20p per manual; 22½p per specimen set; postage extra; (2) minutes; H. B. Gibson; University of London Press Ltd. *

REFERENCES

1–2. See P:90.
3. GIBSON, H. B. "The Gibson Spiral Maze Test: Retest Data in Relation to Behavioral Disturbance, Personality and Physical Measures." *Brit J Psychol* 60(4):523–8 N '69. * (*PA* 44:4948)

4. MARTIN, D. N., AND CLARKE, R. V. G. "The Personality of Approved School Boy Absconders." Brit J Criminol 9(4): 366–75 O '69. * (PA 44:8825)

5. WHITING, H. T. A.; JOHNSON, G. F.; AND PAGE, M. "The Gibson Spiral Maze as a Possible Screening Device for Minimal Brain Damage." Brit J Social & Clin Psychol 8(2): 164–8 Je '69. * (PA 43:16244)

6. TUTOO, D. N. "The Performance of Socially Adjusted and Socially Maladjusted Subjects on the Gibson Maze Test." Indian J Psychol 45(2):165–74 Je '70. * (PA 46:1438)

D. F. CLARK, *Consultant Clinical Psychologist, North-East Regional Hospital Board, Ladysbridge Hospital, Banff, Scotland.*

This test of psychomotor speed and accuracy is a simple pencil and paper test designed for use primarily as a research tool to explore the association between a standardized psychomotor performance and certain limited personality characteristics, delinquency in particular. The author points out that the test may also be employed in conjunction with other techniques to investigate a variety of problems in experimental, clinical, educational, and personnel psychology.

The test consists of a card on which is printed a bold spiral of 9 inches diameter presenting a track rather than a maze (since there is only one way out without alternatives) on which are placed printed "O's" about half the width of the track to form obstructions.

The instructions are concise and simple and seem to give little room for misapprehension even on the part of dull subjects, although there may be some bias toward urging the candidate to work rapidly rather than to be accurate; twice he is asked to go as quickly as he can, but is asked only once to avoid touching the obstacles and the lines at the side of the track.

Only limited norms are available. Percentile norms are given for 392 primary school boys aged 8.5 to 10. Quartiles are also reported for 9 other groups (N's ranging from 22 to 97, median 40) including office girls, factory girls, approved school girls, maladjusted school boys, and depressive patients. Researchers using this test, however, should be prepared to establish their own norms and to consider carefully the effects of age and sex on their data.

It is when one comes to assess the validity of the test that one's misgivings are greatest. Gibson (1) originally validated scores against the degree of "naughtiness in school" as rated by class teachers. He divided test scores by median cuts as commented above and divided the boys into the categories of "good," "average," "naughty" on the basis of teachers' behaviour ratings. In discussing the contingency table

based on this classification, Gibson states that "'good' boys clearly predominate in the quick-and-accurate zone, 'naughty' boys predominate in both the quick-and-careless and slow-and-careless zones." This predominance is not clear to the reviewer and indeed no tests of significance appear to have been applied to this table. One would like to see the trend unequivocally assessed when the important hypothesis that the test is a good predictor of delinquency is implied by so much of what the author has written. It is important too to demonstrate that the naughty boys in class are in fact delinquent boys in the more general sense and if they are, would not the teacher's assessment which is the criterion simply be the best way of selecting them rather than by using the GSM? Just as there is no evidence of predictive validity, the evidence for concurrent validity is scanty. The best that can be achieved is a partial correlation of .33 between Porteus quantitative scores and GSM error scores with time scores held constant.

The manual does not present any information on the reliability of the two GSM scores. This is surprising.

In short, the GSM appears to have inadequate norms, to be of unknown reliability, and to have rather scanty evidence of validity. Perhaps it should be seen as a technique requiring development and standardization rather than a test at this stage. While the test offers scope for further investigation without expensive apparatus of the relationship of psychomotor skill to other variables, it clearly requires further development, especially in terms of reliability and validity. Even if users stick very closely to working with populations for which Gibson has supplied normative data, they will certainly wish to demonstrate that the test is reliable and valid for their purposes. The validity of the GSM cannot be assumed as it stands. Researchers interested in determining the test's validity in specific situations are likely to be the users of the *Gibson Spiral Maze;* others will be less interested.

Brit J Psychol 57:471 N '66. J. C. Raven. Maze tests have not always received the attention they merit. This is seen from Gibson's work with a simple spiral maze which takes about 2 minutes to administer. He uses a pencil and paper test, boldly printed on a 10 in. × 12 in. card. A person is asked to start at the centre and to get out as quickly as possible without touching the side lines or any of fifty-six obstacles placed in his path. There are no wrong turnings. The time taken to get out is recorded. Fifteen seconds after he starts a person is urged to go quickly. This is repeatedly used to create emotional stress. The number of times a person touches or penetrates a side line or obstacle is used to calculate his error score. The pencil and paper form of this test has the advantage over an electrically recorded form that a complete record is retained for comparative study. It has the limitation that what the psychologist says or does is the only emotional stress which can be applied. Gibson shows that, for normal children, T (the time taken to get out) decreases up to the age of 10 at least, but the E (errors) "do not appear to alter significantly with age in normal populations." He therefore calculates "adjusted E scores" in which T is partialled out to his own satisfaction. In some interesting tables and graphs Gibson shows for particular groups of children the time to get out, as well as the number of errors made, but it is not easy to evaluate group behaviour in terms of whether it is quick or slow as well as accurate or careless, as these two variables themselves correlate "around −0.5." From these tables and graphs, partialling out the time variable does not appear to be the solution. To compare errors of behaviour under stress, time could be kept constant by using a track which became visible and moved towards a person at regular speeds. Unfortunately this requires suitable apparatus. The merit of Gibson's test is its simplicity. For social studies this is important. In clinical work it is less essential.

Percept & Motor Skills 23:1339 D '66. C. H. Ammons. * Limited information on the test's validity is provided. While clinical use might be cautiously undertaken, as a task for experimental research the spiral seems highly appropriate.

[83]

★**Gottschalk-Gleser Content Analysis Scales.**
Ages 14 and over; 1969; GGCAS; content analysis by 2 or more scorers of 5 minute verbal samples tape recorded and then typed; 13 scores: anxiety (death, mutilation, separation, guilt, shame, diffuse, total), hostility directed outward (overt, covert, total), hostility directed inward, ambivalent hostility, social alienation-personal disorganization (schizophrenic); individual; manual (see *8* below); interpretive manual (see *6* below); $12.50 per interpretive manual; $6 per manual; postpaid; (10) minutes for verbal sample; Louis A. Gottschalk, Goldine C. Gleser, and Carolyn N. Winget (manual); University of California Press. *

REFERENCES

1. GOTTSCHALK, LOUIS A.; GLESER, GOLDINE C.; DANIELS, ROBERT S.; AND BLOCK, STANLEY. "The Speech Patterns of Schizophrenic Patients: A Method of Assessing Relative Degree of Personal Disorganization and Social Alienation." *J Nerv & Mental Dis* 127:153–66 Ag '58. * (PA 33:10726)
2. GOTTSCHALK, LOUIS A.; GLESER, GOLDINE C.; AND SPRINGER, KAYLA J. "Three Hostility Scales Applicable to Verbal Samples." *Arch Gen Psychiatry* 9:254–79 S '63. * (PA 38:4301)
3. MILLER, CLARENCE K. "The Psychological Impact of Coronary Artery Disease." *Newsl Res Psychol* 7:21–2 Ag '65. *
4. GOTTSCHALK, LOUIS A., AND FRANK, EDWARD C. "Estimating the Magnitude of Anxiety From Speech." *Behav Sci* 12:289–95 Jl '67. * (PA 41:13745)
5. IVEY, MELVILLE E., AND BARDWICK, JUDITH M. "Patterns of Affective Fluctuation in the Menstrual Cycle." *Psychosom Med* 30:336–45 My–Je '68. * (PA 42:18492)
6. GOTTSCHALK, LOUIS A., AND GLESER, GOLDINE C. *The Measurement of Psychological States Through the Content Analysis of Verbal Behavior.* Berkeley, Calif.: University of California Press, 1969. Pp. xxi, 317. *
7. GOTTSCHALK, LOUIS A.; KUNKEL, ROBERT; WOHL, THEODORE H.; SAENGER, EUGENE L.; AND WINGET, CAROLYN N. "Total and Half Body Irradiation: Effect on Cognitive and Emotional Processes." *Arch Gen Psychiatry* 21(5):574–80 N '69. * (PA 44:9141)
8. GOTTSCHALK, LOUIS A.; WINGET, CAROLYN N.; AND GLESER, GOLDINE C. *Manual of Instructions for Using the Gottschalk-Gleser Content Analysis Scales: Anxiety, Hostility, and Social Alienation-Personal Disorganization.* Berkeley, Calif.: University of California Press, 1969. Pp. vi, 176. *
9. WINGET, CAROLYN N.; GLESER, GOLDINE C.; AND CLEMENTS, WILLIAM H. "A Method for Quantifying Human Relations, Hostility, and Anxiety Applied to TAT Productions." *J Proj Tech & Pers Assess* 33(5):433–7 O '69. * (PA 44:3659)
10. GOTTSCHALK, LOUIS A.; GLESER, GOLDINE C.; CLEGHORN, JOHN M.; STONE, WALTER N.; AND WINGET, CAROLYN N. "Prediction of Changes in Severity of the Schizophrenic Syndrome With Discontinuation and Administration of Phenothiazines in Chronic Schizophrenic Patients: Language as a Predictor and Measure of Change in Schizophrenia." *Comprehen Psychiatry* 11(2):123–40 Mr '70. * (PA 45:6735)

S. B. SELLS, *Research Professor of Psychology and Director, Institute of Behavioral Research, Texas Christian University, Fort Worth, Texas.*

These scales are concerned with the measurement of transitory feeling states, or *affects,* that occur irregularly and with relatively small fluctuations of feeling. Affects are defined by the authors as a class of feeling states that have the attributes of quality and quantity, with subjective, purely psychological components, as well as physiological, biochemical, and behavioral concomitants. Affects thus defined are distinguished from two other types of feeling states: *mood,* which involves continuous mixtures of feelings of relatively long duration, and *emotions,* feeling states of relatively high intensity and variability. The focus of the anxiety scales is free anxiety, which is contrasted with bound anxiety; the principal aspect of the hostility scales included is anger; the schizophrenia scale emphasizes disturbances in the coherence and logicality of thinking as well as disturbances in human relations, particularly withdrawal, avoidance, and antagonism. The scales are designed so that nonprofessional persons can be trained as scorers; however, the reliability data presented do not reflect use by scorers trained outside the authors' organization.

Reliability estimates are presented for the anxiety and hostility scales, based on data for a single scorer and for the average of any two scorers. For anxiety total score, reliabilities reported for one scorer were .80, .73, and .86 in three different samples of 50 psychiatric outpatients, 65 mixed psychiatric inpatients, and 82 medical patients. The corresponding coefficients for any two scorers were .89, .84, and .93. Ranges of reliabilities for the six anxiety subscales were from .50 to .87, .62 to .88, and .60 to .82 in the three samples, but not in a constant rank order. In three similar samples of 50, 65, and 43 patients, respectively, reliabilities for the hostility scales, for one scorer, ranged as follows: hostility outward-overt, from .65 to .66, covert, from .82 to .96, total, .78 to .87; ambivalent hostility, from .76 to .92; hostility inward, from .78 to .89, also not in a constant rank order. The reliabilities for any two scorers are again higher, ranging from .76 to .98 across all measures. The correlation between two coders, on a sample of 35 male and 39 female chronic hospitalized schizophrenic patients, was reported as .90. On the whole, the reliabilities reported for the studies undertaken are impressive. In this reviewer's opinion, comparable reliabilities could be obtained by newly trained scoring technicians, but the training and quality controls required are rigorous and highly demanding and may be difficult to obtain in a clinical situation. The scoring procedures are, of course, crucial to the use of these scales, and special training and control procedures would be best justified in situations in which the level of use is high.

Data were also presented on generalizability of scores, indicating the extent to which these *state* scores, based on a single occasion, are indicative of comparability over occasions, indicating more enduring tendencies, or *traits*. For anxiety, it was concluded that no simple statement was possible, as estimates depend on subjects, intervals between tests, and types of situation. The data on hostility suggested that dependable, typical levels of inward or ambivalent hostility could be obtained from three to five verbal samples spaced over a limited interval of time; for outward hostility, a larger number of samples appears needed, especially for males. Generalizability was highest for the social alienation-personal disorganization

(schizophrenia) scale, as might be expected; the coefficient of generalizability of a set of scores on one occasion to a universe of possible scores during the week as scored by a single coder was .77 for males and .71 for females.

Normative data, in terms of percentile scores, were presented for anxiety total scales, for samples of 282 nonpsychiatric employees, 107 psychiatric inpatients, and 107 psychiatric outpatients. Percentile scores for hostility were presented for a sample of 322 nonpsychiatric subjects. For the schizophrenic scale, norms were reported by diagnostic groups (chronic schizophrenic, acute schizophrenic, brain syndrome, psychiatric nonschizophrenic, general medical, and "normal" employed), in terms of cumulative frequencies by score interval.

Validation studies were carried out by a variety of approaches and reflect the authors' commitment that psychological states have biological roots. The overall impression obtained from the data presented is favorable. Anxiety scale scores showed significant agreement with a variety of inventories and clinical ratings and differentiated well beyond chance in a number of psychophysiological, psychopharmacological, and psychobiochemical studies. Results with subscales varied considerably across these studies. The section on anxiety includes negative results, but in sum the results indicate that the scale would be useful in clinical settings as a basis for evaluating anxiety in patients in varying situations and over time during and after treatment. One advantage of this procedure is that it can be repeated without many of the problems encountered in testing.

Validation research with the hostility scales confirmed the need to consider inward, outward, and ambivalent hostility separately. Hostility inward correlates most highly with measures of depression and fatigue. There are significant sex differences in both inward and outward expression of verbal hostility and in their relations with other measures. The diverse approaches taken reflect the clinical and quantitative expertise of the authors and indicate valuable properties of the hostility scales which support their use in clinical situations as well as for research.

Correlations with clinical ratings and with several established measures were used to validate the schizophrenia scale. With the exception of samples in which the patient refused to communicate, the scale appears to have potential value in assessing the degree of schizophrenic disturbance.

The manual covers procedural considerations, such as the conditions for administering and recording the verbal protocols, procedures and training for coding and scoring, general procedures for content analysis, and specific procedures for each scale. Numerous examples of protocols are presented. Examples are provided for the subscales within each of the major scales.

In summary, the Gottschalk-Gleser scales appear to be reasonably valid and reliable measures of the manifest psychological states evidenced in verbal protocols. They thus provide a powerful psychometric tool in the diagnosis of psychological states of interest to clinical researchers and practitioners.

Cont Psychol 15(10):610–2 O '70. Kurt Salzinger. * The books [6, 8] under review provide an explicit method for the quantification of some of the ambiguous and elusive concepts of the theory of psychoanalysis. Although validation of psychoanalytic concepts was not the intention of the authors, such concepts did, in fact, serve as the basis for the constitution of the categories of their content analysis. The contribution of these books is primarily methodological, i.e., they provide operational definitions of the concepts supplemented by frequent examples. * Despite the (in this reviewer's opinion) shaky foundation of psychoanalysis, these books present important material: extensive discussion of methodology, including the way in which the behavior of interest is evoked from the subject, how the experimenter acts during the course of data collection, the methods by which the raw data are transformed into material amenable to precise descriptive analysis ready for hypothesis testing, and, finally, more insight into the process by which these investigators arrived at the concepts and tools in their work. The aim of these volumes is certainly unassailable, for it consists of making explicit a method of analysis to be applied to the most important kind of behavior in which human beings engage, namely verbal behavior. * the authors present a method for the content analysis of brief speech samples (typically five-minutes long) collected under standard instructions with minimal interference from the experimenter, who requires no special training beyond that of strictly following the

investigator's instructions. The work of the coder requires only a minimum amount of interpretation. * The Gottschalk-Gleser approach not only makes the system reliable but also translatable to investigators who have not themselves undergone analytic training. * Unlike the classical content analysis, which limits the analyst to presence-absence judgments, the Gottschalk-Gleser scales are also assigned weights with respect to degree or magnitude. * Although all the arithmetic operations can somehow be justified to arrive at a simple index rather than a measure of the category in question, the formula and its complexities result in a number, the origin of which cannot be substantively explained. It serves to hide the relationship of the raw data to the resultant number which is supposed to characterize those data. Furthermore, it does not state the relationship among the variables (the subcategories) which constitute the equation. In fact the Gottschalk-Gleser formula yields no verbal statement worthwhile making. And I think the authors would be among the first to admit that the formula in question has only the purpose of conveniently summarizing some data and does not state how the various kinds of anxiety (to take but one example) interact to yield the resultant overall anxiety. That is the greatest shame of all, and it applies not just to these authors and this study. Those of us working in psychopathology spend too much time worrying about the elegance of our summarizing measures and not enough time on their substantive meaning. In general, the estimates of reliability for the various categories are respectable, and the methods of arriving at these estimates are sophisticated, from a statistical standpoint. The validity studies include the usual ones, namely the relationship to results obtained through interviews, global ratings, subjective estimates, and personality tests, but there are also additional studies relating the indices to changes in physiological functioning, biochemical states, and drug effects. The sophistication of this content analysis is greater than is usually found in psychopathology. * On the other hand, the investigators have not wholly avoided the pitfall of the naming fallacy. Even if a particular category differentiates two populations, it does not necessarily follow that the name given it identifies the variable that differentiates them. * Establishment of a real difference among subjects or situations, or in response to different drugs, is a result only of an extensive investigation of the variables responsible for having produced the initial difference. Rather than reflecting a difference in the state of the organism, it may reflect the conditioning history of the subjects, the way people talk when given no feedback, or the discussion the subject had with others before entering the experimental situation. Finally, two specific problems in the content analysis should be noted: determination of the unit and determination of its size. It is incumbent upon content analysts to demonstrate the reliability of unitization, especially in the case of schizophrenic speech, which contains a large number of irrelevant words, making the boundaries of units rather uncertain. * In summary, although this reviewer disagrees with the writers in their choice of the basis for their categories and in some of their methodological decisions, he finds the explicitness of their approach, their attention to methodological detail, and their appreciation of the problem of validating their measures refreshing. Surely no investigator in the area of content analysis ought to construct a new system without at least seeing how Gottschalk, Winget, and Gleser handled it in these books.

[84]

★Grid Test of Schizophrenic Thought Disorder. Adults; 1967; GTSTD; 2 scores: intensity, consistency; individual; set of 8 photographs; manual (21 pages); no data on reliability; 8s. per set of photographs; 12s. per 25 record sheets; 12s. per 25 analysis sheets; 15s. per manual; postage extra; (15–25) minutes; D. Bannister and Fay Fransella; Psychological Test Publications. *

REFERENCES

1–8. See P:96.
9. FRANSELLA, FAY, AND ADAMS, B. "An Illustration of the Use of Repertory Grid Technique in a Clinical Setting." *Brit J Social & Clin Psychol* 5:51–62 F '66. * (*PA* 40:6806)
10. FOULDS, G. A.; HOPE, K.; McPHERSON, F. M.; AND MAYO, P. R. "Cognitive Disorder Among the Schizophrenias: 1, The Validity of Some Tests of Thought-Process Disorder." *Brit J Psychiatry* 113:1361–8 D '67. * (*PA* 42:9239)
11. FOULDS, G. A.; HOPE, K.; McPHERSON, F. M.; AND MAYO, P. R. "Cognitive Disorder Among the Schizophrenias: 3, Retardation." *Brit J Psychiatry* 115(519):177–80 F '69. * (*PA* 43:13128)
12. PRESLY, A. S. "'Slowness' and Performance on the Grid Test for Thought Disorder." *Brit J Social & Clin Psychol* 8(1):79–80 F '69. * (*PA* 43:8514)
13. ROMENY, DAVID. "Psychometrically Assessed Thought Disorder in Schizophrenic and Control Patients and in Their Parents and Siblings: Part I, Patients; Part II, Relatives." *Brit J Psychiatry* 115(526):999–1002 S '69. * (*PA* 44:10875)
14. GATHERCOLE, C. E.; BROMLEY, E.; AND ASHCROFT, J. B. "The Reliability of Repertory Grids." *J Clin Psychol* 26(4):513–6 O '70. * (*PA* 45:4530)
15. McPHERSON, F. M., AND BUCKLEY, FELICITY. "Thought-Process Disorder and Personal Construct Subsystems." *Brit J Social & Clin Psychol* 9(4):380–1 D '70. * (*PA* 45:8636)

DAVID JONES, *Lecturer in Psychology, Birkbeck College, University of London, London, England.*

The theoretical basis of the GTSTD is the personal construct theory of G. A. Kelly. Repertory grid tests involve sorting procedures on the part of the subject. As used by Kelly, the repertory grid method is not a standard test, but a flexible procedure in which the subject supplies names to fit various role titles provided by the examiner and also the constructs on which the named individuals will be judged. Bannister and Fransella have departed from this principle in their grid test to the extent that the subject is required to perform sortings of standard passport-type photographs on constructs named by the examiner. Bannister's theory is that thought disordered schizophrenics have an extremely loose construct system and that in consequence they show low intercorrelations between their constructs as measured by repertory grid tests; i.e., they have a low Intensity score. He also considers that thought disordered schizophrenics are unable to maintain the pattern of intercorrelations from one grid to the next and hence they have a low Consistency score.

The administration of the test is relatively easy. The eight photographs, four of men and four of women, are set out in front of the subject, who is required to rank them on six constructs presented in the order: kind, stupid, selfish, sincere, mean, and honest. The whole procedure is then repeated to obtain a second set of results. Administration of the test takes around 20 minutes and occasional subjects seem to find the procedure monotonous.

In contrast to the ease of administration, scoring the test is extremely tedious if carried out by hand. In the calculation of the Intensity score the original rankings are transferred to form two rank order tables, and 15 relationship scores based on Spearman's rank order correlations must be calculated for each grid. All 30 relationship scores contribute to the Intensity score. The Consistency score involves calculating the Spearman rank correlation of the two sets of relationship scores. Most users of this grid test employ computer scoring.

There are six different groups in the standardisation sample, including a group of thought disordered schizophrenics. As the number in each group is 30 or less, it is a little artificial to have the distribution of scores for the thought disordered schizophrenics shown as a table of percentages, although it is obviously more convenient to discuss cutoff points in terms of percentages. The selection of cutoff points for overlapping distributions is always a difficult problem, the decision being dependent upon the validity of the measures and the possible consequences of misdiagnosis. One must accept the argument of the test authors that in this case it is advisable to "minimise false positives." A recommended cutoff of below 1,000 on Intensity and below .49 on Consistency identifies 80 percent of the thought disordered schizophrenics but fails to distinguish them from 6.4 percent of non-thought disordered schizophrenics, neurotics, depressives, and normals. The group of patients with organic brain injury raises a special problem and are not easily distinguished from the thought disordered schizophrenics by the Grid Test. In particular, patients with diffuse organic damage seem to have low scores on Intensity and Consistency. The grid scores do not correlate with intelligence, but it has been found that this form of the test is not suitable for use with subnormals.

There is no published data on the reliability of the Grid Test.

In a prepublication copy of a paper by Bannister et al.[1] it is pointed out that there is a considerable increase in the Intensity score from the first to the second grid for all categories of subjects. However, non-thought disordered subjects show greater percentage Intensity gains than do thought disordered subjects.

The validity of the GTSTD is based on its ability to discriminate between thought-disordered schizophrenics and other subjects, the criterion of thought disorder being determined in the clinical interview situation. In the standardisation group, thought disorder was judged as present to the joint satisfaction of two psychiatrists and a psychologist, and in the forthcoming paper cited above, the judgments in the patients' clinical case notes have been accepted. No attempt seems to have been made to compare results on the Grid Test with other psychological tests which are claimed to measure thought disorder. It is emphasized in the manual that the Grid Test is a measure of schizophrenic thought disorder and not a diagnostic test of schizophrenia as such.

In summary, the Grid Test is able to identify patients who are assessed as showing thought disorder in the clinical interview situation. Since

1 BANNISTER, D.; FRANSELLA, FAY; AND AGNEW, JOYCE. "Characteristics and Validity of the Grid Test of Thought Disorder." *Brit J Social & Clin Psychol,* in press.

there are no correlations available for this test and other measures of thought disorder, one must judge the validity of the method in the wider context of the validity of personal construct theory. The standardisation group is relatively small, but further data are being assembled. The test is easy to administer, although use with large numbers of subjects is impractical without automated scoring facilities.

[85]

Guilford-Holley L Inventory. College and adults; 1953–63; GHLI; leadership behavior; 5 scores: benevolence, ambition, meticulousness, discipline, aggressiveness; 1 form ('53, 4 pages); manual ('63, 6 pages); separate answer sheets (IBM 805) must be used; $3.75 per 25 tests; 5¢ per answer sheet; $1.25 per scoring stencil; 5¢ per profile; 35¢ per manual; 55¢ per specimen set (complete test not included); postage extra; (25) minutes; J. P. Guilford and J. W. Holley; Sheridan Psychological Services, Inc. *

REFERENCE

1. HOLLEY, JASPER W. *The Isolation of Personality Traits in the Domain of Military Leadership.* Doctor's thesis, University of Southern California (Los Angeles, Calif.), 1951.

HARRISON G. GOUGH, *Professor of Psychology, University of California, Berkeley, California.*

This 150-item inventory is a derivative of a doctoral thesis in 1951 by Holley (*1*), on the identification of traits entering into military leadership. The "L" in the title reflects this starting point.

Factor analysis of the item sets used in the original study led to the specification of five relatively independent dimensions. These factors are listed below, along with descriptions from the manual, and representative items used in their measurement:

B—Benevolence, including an admiration for virtue, sympathy, helpfulness, concern for the feelings of others, and a need for approval. Sample items: "It is difficult for a dishonest person to be happy." "You go out of your way to give the other person a 'square deal.' "

Am—Ambition, including a desire for wealth, fame, success, and high position, impatience, and dislike of low position. "It is boresome for you to wait for a slow person to finish what he is saying or doing." "You would like to hold an important office in government."

Me—Meticulousness, including neatness, orderliness, cleanliness, liking for planning, compulsiveness, and liking for system and detail. "A person can judge a workman's character by the neatness of his workplace." "You like to keep your fingernails well manicured at all times."

Di—Discipline, including a belief in law enforcement, preference for strict rules at work and in the family, and a liking for decisiveness on the part of leaders and others. "In times of national peril, a citizen is either loyal to his country or he is a traitor." "The best training a boy can get is that of a military academy."

Agg—Aggression, including enjoyment of vicarious combat, readiness to attack, belief in revenge, the need to coerce others, and approval of aggression. "You prefer chewy kinds of candy such as taffy and caramel to other types." "You enjoy watching 'bonecrushing' wrestling matches."

Although the inventory originated in research on leadership and carries the designation "L" for leadership, the manual warns "it is not recommended that the scores be used in the selection of potentially successful leaders." It is stated, however, that the test can be informative as to the style of leadership an individual may manifest; for example, will he be democratic or authoritarian, coercive or cooperative, indulgent or strict? It is also mentioned that the test can be useful for measurement in areas other than management and leadership, e.g., in social welfare, but no research evidence is offered in support of these recommendations. Given the authors' own admission that no empirical findings are available to relate scores on the inventory to either quality or style of leadership, one must question the propriety of labeling the test "L" for leadership, or of suggesting that it can contribute to an understanding of other equally complex domains of human behavior.

The manual also asserts that the test is intended to provide "assessment of some traits not fully covered by other known instruments." One would expect to find this claim documented by correlational data comparing the "L" inventory to other tests, for example, the 16PF, EPPS, SIV, and others which contain scales for factors such as benevolence, aggression, cynicism, and surgency, which seem conceptually similar to those included in the Guilford-Holley. In fact, considering the ease with which inventory data may be gathered, it is a serious deficiency of this manual that its claim to uniqueness is not backed up by empirical evidence showing minimal relationships with competing devices such as those enumerated.

The manual does not carry a section on validity, and it appears from the discussion and from the list of 11 references in its bibliography

that no validation studies have been carried out. Inasmuch as the thesis itself was completed in 1951, it seems that at least a few validational studies could have been completed prior to the publication of the manual in 1963.

There is a certain degree of face validity in the items, although the dangers in trusting face validity are too well known to permit one to proceed very far on this basis. Furthermore, the greater the face validity of a set of items, the more vulnerable is that set to faking. The manual for the inventory says nothing whatsoever about faking, response distortions, and similar matters. Perusal of the scoring keys suggests that all five factors would be completely fakable.

For scales developed by factorial methods the strongest claim that can ordinarily be made is for reliability. Four estimates of the internal-consistency reliabilities for each variable are offered in the manual, giving the following median coefficients: benevolence, .70; ambition, .52; meticulousness, .84; discipline, .76; and aggression, .74. These are rather modest values, more representative of findings for empirically developed tests seeking to maximize external validity than of findings for factorial measures whose principal function is to specify dimensions of response to test items.

The norms for the instrument are extremely sketchy and have little to do with leadership or other suggested areas of application. Descriptive statistics are reported for 178 firemen from "a small industrial city in California," 100 students from New Mexico, 121 students from Cincinnati, and 213 "women." An additional 122 males are included in the total sample of 521 males on which C score, centile, and T score conversions are based, but their origin is unmentioned.

Handscoring is efficiently accomplished by means of a special answer sheet and a punched template. Seventeen of the items are scored for the "no" response, and the remainder for the "yes." A "?" response is allowed, and the manual states that this reply is "given the same weight as the 'Yes' or 'No' answer with the smaller frequency of occurrence for the particular item." However, no item frequencies are provided in the manual and the scoring stencil is not punched for any "?" responses. The user of the test must decide for himself how to solve this perplexing dilemma.

The manual recommends that this device be

used for research purposes only. This is good advice, and one can only add that the authors would do well to observe their own admonition. The next edition of the manual for the GHLI should carry extensive information on empirical validity, correlations with other well-known personality inventories, studies of faking and deliberate distortion of responses, and clinical evaluations of individual cases. It should also carry much more representative and extensive norms, and it should clear up present ambiguities and contradictions in the scoring instructions. Until the test's authors can fulfill these obligations, it is unlikely that psychologists should or will want to make very much use of the instrument.

WARREN T. NORMAN, *Professor of Psychology, The University of Michigan, Ann Arbor, Michigan.*

This instrument consists of 150 items written in the form of short declarative sentences, to each of which the respondent indicates his agreement, doubt, or disagreement. Thirty items are assigned to each of the five variables (Benevolence, Ambition, Meticulousness, Discipline, and Aggressiveness), every fifth item being scored on a given key. The predominantly keyed response is "Yes" for all five variables; only 1, 5, 6, 2, and 3 "No" responses are keyed on the five scales, respectively, and no "?" response is scored on any scale. Raw scores are obtained by a simple summation of keyed responses.

The manual states that the five variables scored on this inventory were "an outgrowth of an investigation of factors....believed to have relevance [to]....leadership behavior." Items were selected to represent one or another of the factors in this analysis if they correlated above .31 with their respective factorial criterion and less than this with all other criteria in the set. Subsets of items having similar content within each scale are listed and briefly described in manual as an aid to the interpretation of the scale. For example, the Benevolence scale contains 10 items that presumably reflect "admiration of common virtues," 7 items that imply "sympathy for others," 5 items for "helping others," 5 items expressing "concern for feeling of others," and 3 items indicating a "need to be approved and liked." No evidence of statistical homogeneity for these subsets of items nor of discriminability among subsets is presented.

Internal consistency (odd-even) estimates of reliability based on four samples range from the high .60's to the middle .80's on all scales except Ambition, where the four estimates are .56, .37, .48, and .57, and except for one estimate of .54 for the Benevolence scale. Ambition is conceded to be a trait probably "not as coherent as others." Benevolence is described as having a highly negatively skewed distribution, while Aggressiveness is skewed in the opposite direction. The practice, suggested in the manual, of interpreting subcategory scores where the full scale has low internal-consistency is recommended wholly without any supporting data but is probably a mistake, considering that the largest subcategory contains only 10 items.

Intercorrelations among the five scales based on two samples were generally low save that between Discipline and Meticulousness (moderately positive in both samples) and those relating Ambition to Meticulousness in both samples and to Aggressiveness in one sample and to Discipline in the same sample. On the basis of these limited data, a reasonable degree of independence seems to characterize these five variables.

Norms (C scores, centiles, and T scores) based on combined clump samples of 521 male and 213 female adults are presented in the manual, but these can hardly be considered representative of any population of broad general interest. Minor age, sex, and/or occupational differences detected in these samples are briefly commented on by the authors. However, given the adventitious character of the sampling frame from which these "norms" derive, any inferences based upon them may well be merely idiosyncratic and should tentatively be so-considered.

Regarding use of the L inventory, the authors explicitly state that it "is offered primarily as a research instrument." It is further and explicitly "not recommended that the scores be used in the selection of potentially successful leaders"—in spite of the instrument's title. What, then, can it be used for and what does it measure? The authors contend that "the scores should be informative as to the type of leader the individual would make; his style of managing others."

If any substantial evidence exists for this statement, it is entirely omitted from the manual. The assertion seems to rest wholly on a semantic evaluation of item content ("face validity"), coupled with a simplistic view of the relation between endorsement responses to such items and interpersonal behaviors more broadly considered. The inventory contains no built-in controls such as a forced-choice item format or balanced response option scoring keys to cope with stylistic response tendencies such as social desirability or acquiescence, nor are there even ancillary keys for assessing such potentially relevant attributes of respondents.

But by far the most critical defect is the *complete lack of any data in the manual on the relationships of various scale scores or profile types of actual leadership or managerial behaviors* (or to any other class of behaviors for that matter) from any sample of respondents. Until substantial amounts of such information are collected and reported, the offer of this device, even as a research instrument, carries with it an onerous and, in my view, excessive demand for local validation.

In summary, the five factors assessed by this instrument appear to be relatively independent and, in four of the five cases, to have moderately adequate internal consistencies. Against these modest virtues are arrayed a host of defects and deficiencies, including an easily misleading interpretation of the title in the introduction of the manual; unsubstantiated advice to the user regarding subcategory score interpretation; absence of any provision for the control or detection of faking, dissimulation, or other relevant test-taking attitudes; highly inadequate norms; and, of the gravest consequence, a presumption of validity and interpretability of scores and profiles based *exclusively* on the semantic content of the items. In the absence of any external evidence bearing on the validity and interpretability of this instrument, its release for publication was premature and can scarcely be viewed as a constructive contribution or service to the discipline.

[86]

★**Hostility and Direction of Hostility Questionnaire: Personality and Personal Illness Questionnaires.** Mental patients and normals; 1967; HDHQ; test booklet title is *Personality Questionnaire;* all items from *Minnesota Multiphasic Personality Inventory;* 7 scores: intropunitive (self criticism, guilt), extrapunitive (urge to act out hostility, criticism of others, projected delusional hostility), total hostility, direction of hostility; 1 form (4 pages); manual (20 pages); clinical diagram sheets for neurotics (1 page), psychotics (1 page); norms consist of means and standard deviations; 72½p per 20 tests; 20p per scoring stencil; 47½p per 20 clinical diagrams; 22½p per manual; 50p per specimen set; postage extra; [15–20] minutes; T. M. Caine, G. A. Foulds, and

K. Hope (diagrams and manual); University of London Press Ltd. *

REFERENCES

1. ADAMS, ANNE, AND FOULDS, G. A. "Depression and Personality." *J Mental Sci* 108:474–86 Jl '62. * (*PA* 37:3720)
2. ADAMS, ANNE, AND FOULDS, G. A. "Personality and the Paranoid Depressive Psychoses." *Brit J Psychiatry* 109:273–8 Mr '63. * (*PA* 38:3034)
3. FOULDS, G. A., AND OWEN, ANNA. "Are Paranoids Schizophrenics?" *Brit J Psychiatry* 109:674–9 S '63. * (*PA* 38:6487)
4. HESELTINE, G. F. "The Site of Onset of Eczema and Personality Trait Differences: An Exploratory Study." *J Psychosom Res* 7:241–6 D '63. * (*PA* 38:8360)
5. HOPE, KEITH. *The Structure of Hostility Among Normal and Neurotic Persons.* Doctor's thesis, University College, University of London (London, England), 1963.
6. CAINE, T. M. Chap. 13, "Changes in Symptom, Attitude, and Trait Measures Among Chronic Neurotics in a Therapeutic Community," pp. 262–91. In *Personality and Personal Illness,* see 9. *
7. FOULDS, G. A., AND ADAMS, ANNE. Chap. 10, "The Melancholic-Depressive Continuum," pp. 210–28 and Chap. 11, "The Paranoid-Melancholic Continuum," pp. 229–40. In *Personality and Personal Illness,* see 9. *
8. FOULDS, G. A., AND OWEN, ANNA. Chap. 12, "Analysis of Results in Terms of the Clinical Diagnosis," pp. 241–61. In *Personality and Personal Illness,* see 9. *
9. FOULDS, G. A.; IN COLLABORATION WITH T. M. CAINE AND WITH THE ASSISTANCE OF ANNE ADAMS AND ANNA OWEN. *Personality and Personal Illness.* London: Tavistock Publications Ltd., 1965. Pp. xii, 344. *
10. CAINE, T. M. "Response Consistency and Testing Levels." *Brit J Social & Clin Psychol* 6:38–42 F '67. * (*PA* 41:7319)
11. MAYO, P. R. "Some Psychological Changes Associated With Improvement in Depression." *Brit J Social & Clin Psychol* 6:63–8 F '67. * (*PA* 41:7562)
12. BLACKBURN, R. "Emotionality, Extraversion and Aggression in Paranoid and Nonparanoid Schizophrenic Offenders." *Brit J Psychiatry* 114:1301–2 O '68. * (*PA* 43:4254)
13. COOPER, ALAN J. "Hostility and Male Potency Disorders." *Comprehen Psychiatry* 9:621–6 N '68. * (*PA* 44:10471)
14. FOULDS, G. A. "Neurosis and Character Disorder in Hospital and in Prison." *Brit J Criminol* 8:46–9 Ja '68. * (*PA* 42:10847)
15. PHILIP, ALISTAIR E. "The Constancy of Structure of a Hostility Questionnaire." *Brit J Social & Clin Psychol* 7:16–8 F '68. * (*PA* 42:8267)
16. AITKEN, R. C. B.; ZEALLEY, A. K.; AND ROSENTHAL, S. V. "Psychological and Physiological Measures of Emotion in Chronic Asthmatic Patients." *J Psychosom Res* 13(3):289–97 S '69. * (*PA* 44:12622)
17. CAINE, T. M., AND SMAIL, D. J. Chap. 6, "The Effectiveness of the Treatment of Chronic, Hospitalized Neurotics by the Therapeutic Community Technique," pp. 102–32. In their *The Treatment of Mental Illness: Science, Faith and the Therapeutic Community.* New York: International Universities Press, Inc., 1969. Pp. 192. *
18. COCKETT, R., AND MARKS, V. "Amphetamine Taking Among Young Offenders." Abstract. *Brit J Psychiatry* 115(527):1203–4 O '69. * (*PA* 44:12889)
19. COOPER, ALAN J. "Some Personality Factors in Frigidity." *J Psychosom Res* 13(2):149–56 Je '69. * (*PA* 44:12563)
20. DALY, R. J. "Hostility and Chronic Intermittent Haemodialysis." *J Psychosom Res* 13(3):265–73 S '69. * (*PA* 44:12975)
21. FOULDS, G. A., AND HASSALL, CHRISTINE. "The Significance of Age of Onset of Excessive Drinking in Male Alcoholics." *Brit J Psychiatry* 115(526):1027–32 S '69. * (*PA* 44:10759)
22. HALL-SMITH, PATRICK, AND RYLE, ANTHONY. "Marital Patterns, Hostility and Personal Illness." *Brit J Psychiatry* 115(527):1197–8 O '69. * (*PA* 44:13196)
23. HOPE, K. "The Study of Hostility in the Temperaments of Spouses: Definitions and Methods." *Brit J Math & Stat Psychol* 22(1):67–95 My '69. * (*PA* 44:4336)
24. MAYO, P. R. "Women With Neurotic Symptoms Who Do Not Seek Treatment." *Brit J Med Psychol* 42(2):165–9 Je '69. * (*PA* 44:918)
25. MURTHY, VINODA NARAYANA. "Personality and the Nature of Suicidal Attempts." *Brit J Psychiatry* 115(524):791–5 Jl '69. * (*PA* 44:6985)
26. PHILIP, ALISTAIR E. "The Development and Use of the Hostility and Direction of Hostility Questionnaire." *J Psychosom Res* 13(3):283–7 S '69. * (*PA* 44:12611)
27. BLUM, DONNA M., AND VINCENT, M. O. "Personality Test Characteristics of Staff Physicians and Physicians as Psychiatric Patients." *J Clin Psychol* 26(3):389–90 Jl '70. * (*PA* 45:750)
28. CAINE, T. M. Chap. 27, "Personality and Illness," pp. 781–817. In *The Psychological Assessment of Mental and*

Physical Handicaps. Edited by Peter Mittler. London: Methuen & Co. Ltd., 1970. Pp. xxviii, 857. *
29. CLARK, I. S. "A Comparison of Two Hostility Inventories Using an Abnormal Population." *Brit J Psychiatry* 116(531):225 F '70. * (*PA* 44:18902)
30. HALEY, G. A. "Item-Analysis Procedures for Enhancing Validity of Existing Personality Scales." *Psychol Rep* 27(3): 847–53 D '70. * (*PA* 45:9984)
31. PHILIP, ALISTAIR E. "Traits, Attitudes and Symptoms in a Group of Attempted Suicides." *Brit J Psychiatry* 116(534):475–82 My '70. * (*PA* 45:984)
32. WALTON, H. J.; FOULDS, G. A.; LITTMANN, S. K.; AND PRESLY, A. S. "Abnormal Personality." *Brit J Psychiatry* 116(534):497–510 My '70. * (*PA* 45:965)

H. J. EYSENCK, *Professor of Psychology and Director of the Department, Institute of Psychiatry, University of London, London, England.*

This scale consists of 51 items from the MMPI, grouped in five sets which are supposed to measure: (*a*) urge to act out hostility, (*b*) criticism of others, (*c*) projected delusional (i.e., paranoid) hostility, (*d*) self criticism, (*e*) guilt. Correlations between these five sets of scores, and factor analysis of the intercorrelations, indicate the existence of two main factors, considered to represent amount of hostility (sum of the five sets) and direction of hostility (the first three vs. the last two). This is in line with intention: "the first three tests were designed to measure extrapunitive manifestations of hostility and the last two tests were designed to measure intropunitive manifestations of hostility." There are no direct attempts at assessing validity, but several indirect attempts are reported. "The validation of the first component depends on the assumption that psychotics have more aggression than neurotics, who in turn have more aggression than normals." No attempt is made to support this assumption, but the data reported do tend to show some such decline in total score from psychotic through neurotic to normal. As regards the direction of hostility, it was assumed that paranoid patients would be extrapunitive as compared with neurotics; this was found to be so. Normals, contrary to expectation, were even more extrapunitive than paranoids.

The authors claim that "the only approach to an estimate of reliability which is feasible in the case of the Hostility Battery is the calculation of test-retest correlations"; these are rather poor (.75 and .51 for the two components respectively). It is not clear why some form of K-R 20 coefficient could not have been calculated; the writers do not explain their reluctance to do so. Nor is the number of subjects on whom the test-retest reliability was established impressive; there were 15 men and 15 women,

tested and retested after one year. Means and standard deviations are provided for various (usually very small) neurotic and psychotic groups, and also normals. While well set out, the smallness of the groups makes it hazardous to use the information given.

The hostility scale correlates highly (−.58 and −.65) with the K scale of the MMPI; the authors regard this as an artifact "in so far as the K scale and the HDHQ contain the same seven items scored in opposite directions." They do not comment on the difficulties this correlation produces in the interpretation of scores. It has also been found that extraversion as measured by the MPI correlates highly with the hostility scale; this does not worry them either. It seems to the reviewer that the authors of this test have taken too many easy outs to make their inventory as useful, and their arguments as impressive, as they might have been. Starting with their 51 items, they should have intercorrelated these and factor-analyzed the resulting matrix; this would have established whether in fact the five sets into which they group the items have any separate existence. Factor scores should have been correlated with extraversion and neuroticism scores in order to see to what extent the hostility and direction of hostility factors (assuming them to emerge) measure anything beyond these well-established dimensions of personality. If results up to this stage were found to be positive, then factor scores for paranoid, neurotic and normal subjects could have been plotted and the various scores and other figures given in the manual derived. As things are, it is very difficult to interpret the scores or to know just how much reliability to attribute to them.

The reader is not helped by the fact that the manual is very badly constructed. He is given "the intercorrelations of the five tests of the HDHQ" on page 5, but is not told about these five tests until he reaches page 13; this does not make for good comprehension. The whole development is not set out in any logical fashion but jumps from one thing to another rather haphazardly. The reader is given some psychoanalytic propaganda in the first paragraph, but no evidence that any of the statements and assumptions there made have any basis in fact. This failure to put the manual together properly disguises the fact that such statistical work as has been done, has been done well; it is a pity that what was done did not include the steps outlined above. But above all, one would like to see some validation against an acceptable criterion; the criteria offered depend too much on unverified theory.

MAURICE LORR, *Professor of Psychology, Catholic University of America, Washington, D.C.*

The HDHQ "is designed to sample a wide, though not exhaustive, range of possible manifestations of aggression, hostility or punitiveness." It consists of 51 statements drawn from the MMPI. Responses yield scores for five subtests. The normal sample is limited to 47 hospital employees and surgical ward patients. Normative data derive from two neurotic samples representing consecutive admissions to two hospitals.

The authors postulate two dimensions: a hostility component and a bipolar extrapunitiveness vs. intropunitiveness. In the absence of criterion measures, the correlations among the five subtests within two neurotic samples and one normal sample were each subjected to a principal component analysis. In each case, two components proved to be sufficient to account for the correlations. The first component was interpreted as degree of hostility and the second as the bipolar dimension hypothesized. However, a simple transformation (as is usually applied) would have yielded simply an extrapunitive and an intropunitive dimension. On the basis of these analyses, Hostility is measured by the sum of the five subtest scores, and direction of hostility is computed as the difference between the weighted sum of scores on intro- and extrapunitive subtests. In effect, these scores represent overall level and profile difference scores. It is doubtful that there is any gain in this as opposed to a more conventional approach of measuring extrapunitiveness and intropunitiveness separately.

Measures of internal consistency are not offered. Instead, test-retest correlations for normals and neurotics for varying retest intervals are presented. Test-retest correlations for normals for a one-year period range from .23 to .70 for the subtests, and .75 and .51 for H and DH. Test-retest correlations for a neurotic sample split into failures and successes are higher for the failures (.85 and .68) than for the successes (.33 and .43) over a six-week period.

For purposes of validation, normals, neurotics, melancholics, paranoids and nonparanoid schizophrenics were contrasted with respect to their HDHQ scores. All diagnostic groups ranked in mean score as predicted on the direction of hostility. However, normals scored more extrapunitive than anticipated. To assess concurrent validity, the HDHQ scores in two samples were correlated with the K scale of the MMPI, the MPI, and the HOQ. The only significant relationships obtaining were with the K scale and they were attributed to item overlap. A discriminant function analysis of combined neurotic samples versus normals showed that the Direction score contributed 50 percent of the predictive power. However, the authors observe that six diagnostic subgroups included are too close together to warrant use of HDHQ as a diagnostic device. Instead, they recommend its use with the *Symptom-Sign Inventory*.

Most modern questionnaires include measures of response set and/or defensiveness, such as the K scale, a lie scale, or a measure of social desirability. The HDHQ lacks all of these. It is also surprising that the authors should use MMPI items and yet fail to relate their two measures to a few of the numerous MMPI scales. It should also be obvious that the personality dimensions assessed occur in a multivariate context and cannot be evaluated as to discriminant or convergent validity in a vacuum.

The manual is in need of simplification as far as the typical clinician is concerned. There is no explicit statement concerning intended uses of HDHQ. The numerous principal component tables might be relegated to an appendix for the ordinary reader. It should not require hunting to page 13 to discover the names of the subtests. The test form and the plastic scoring stencil are inconvenient to store because of their length. Figures 2 and 3 are more confusing than helpful.

SUMMARY. While the HDHQ has an interesting theoretical basis, there is as yet insufficient evidence for its discriminant and convergent validity. Safeguards against the influence of test-taking attitudes are needed. Thus it represents a worthwhile research tool that should be considered in experimental or clinical research on hostility. There seems to be no basis for choosing it over, say, the Gottschalk-Gleser hostility scales, the Buss-Durkee inventory, or the MMPI scales based on the Tryon analysis.

[87]

★The Hysteroid-Obsessoid Questionnaire: Personality and Personal Illness Questionnaires. Mental patients and normals; 1967; HOQ; test booklet title is *Self-Description Questionnaire;* 1 form (2 pages); manual (10 pages); norms consist of means and standard deviations; 32½p per 20 tests; 15p per scoring stencil; 15p per manual; 32½p per specimen set; postage extra; [10–15] minutes; T. M. Caine and K. Hope (manual); University of London Press Ltd. *

REFERENCES

1. ADAMS, ANNE, AND FOULDS, G. A. "Depression and Personality." *J Mental Sci* 108:474–86 Jl '62. * (*PA* 37:3720)
2. ADAMS, ANNE, AND FOULDS, G. A. "Personality and the Paranoid Depressive Psychoses." *Brit J Psychiatry* 109:273–8 Mr '63. * (*PA* 38:3034)
3. CAINE, T. M., AND HAWKINS, L. G. "Questionnaire Measure of the Hysteroid/Obsessoid Component of Personality: The HOQ." *J Consult Psychol* 27:206–9 Je '63. * (*PA* 38:977)
4. FOULDS, G. A., AND OWEN, ANNA. "Are Paranoids Schizophrenics?" *Brit J Psychiatry* 109:674–9 S '63. * (*PA* 38:6487)
5. FOULDS, G. A. "Personal Continuity and Psychopathological Disruption." *Brit J Psychol* 55:269–76 Ag '64. * (*PA* 39:5226)
6. FOULDS, G. A., AND OWEN, ANNA. "Speed and Accuracy on Mazes in Relation to Diagnosis and Personality." *Brit J Social & Clin Psychol* 3:34–5 F '64. * (*PA* 38:88-0)
7. CAINE, T. M. Chap. 3, "Obsessoid and Hysteroid Components of Personality," pp. 30–55. In *Personality and Personal Illness,* see 11. *
8. CAINE, T. M. Chap. 13, "Changes in Symptom, Attitude, and Trait Measures Among Chronic Neurotics in a Therapeutic Community," pp. 262–91. In *Personality and Personal Illness,* see 11. *
9. FOULDS, G. A., AND ADAMS, ANNE. Chap. 10, "The Melancholic-Depressive Continuum," pp. 210–28 and Chap. 11, "The Paranoid-Melancholic Continuum," pp. 229–40. In *Personality and Personal Illness,* see 11. *
10. FOULDS, G. A., AND OWEN, ANNA. Chap. 12, "Analysis of Results in Terms of the Clinical Diagnosis," pp. 241–61. In *Personality and Personal Illness,* see 11. *
11. FOULDS, G. A.; IN COLLABORATION WITH T. M. CAINE AND WITH THE ASSISTANCE OF ANNE ADAMS AND ANNA OWEN. *Personality and Personal Illness.* London: Tavistock Publications Ltd., 1965. Pp. xii, 344. *
12. BARRETT, WILLIAM; CALDBECK-MEENAN, JOHN; AND WHITE, JOHN GRAHAM. "Questionnaire Measures and Psychiatrists' Ratings of a Personality Dimension: A Note on the Congruent Validity of Caine's Self Description Questionnaire." *Brit J Psychiatry* 112:413–5 Ap '66. * (*PA* 40:10231)
13. CAINE, T. M., AND SMAIL, D. J. "Personal Relevance and the Choice of Constructs for the Repertory Grid Technique." *Brit J Psychiatry* 113:517–20 My '67. * (*PA* 41:12107)
14. HOPE, K.; PHILIP, A. E.; AND LOUGHRAN, J. M. "Psychological Characteristics Associated With XYY Sex-Chromosome Complement in a State Mental Hospital." *Brit J Psychiatry* 113:495–8 My '67. * (*PA* 41:12187)
15. MAYO, P. R. "Some Psychological Changes Associated With Improvement in Depression." *Brit J Social & Clin Psychol* 6:63–8 F '67. * (*PA* 41:7562)
16. HOPE, K., AND CAINE, T. M. "The Hysteroid Obsessoid Questionnaire: A New Validation." *Brit J Social & Clin Psychol* 7:210–5 S '68. * (*PA* 43:132)
17. MAYO, P. R. "Self-Disclosure and Neurosis." *Brit J Social & Clin Psychol* 7:140–8 Je '68. * (*PA* 42:17389)
18. BROOKS, JOHN. "The Insecure Personality: A Factor Analytic Study." *Brit J Med Psychol* 42(4):395–403 D '69. * (*PA* 44:10714)
19. CAINE, T. M., AND SMAIL, D. J. Chap. 6, "The Effectiveness of the Treatment of Chronic, Hospitalized Neurotics by the Therapeutic Community Technique," pp. 102–32. In their *The Treatment of Mental Illness: Science, Faith and the Therapeutic Community.* New York: International Universities Press, Inc., 1969. Pp. 192. *
20. CAINE, T. M., AND SMAIL, D. J. "The Effects of Personality and Training on Attitudes to Treatment: Preliminary Investigations." *Brit J Med Psychol* 42(3):277–82 Ag '69. * (*PA* 44:6850)
21. CAINE, T. M., AND SMAIL, D. J. "A Study of the Reliability and Validity of the Repertory Grid Technique as a Measure of the Hysteroid/Obsessoid Component of Personality." *Brit J Psychiatry* 115(528):1305–8 N '69. * (*PA* 44:14858)
22. MAYO, P. R. "Women With Neurotic Symptoms Who Do Not Seek Treatment." *Brit J Med Psychol* 42(2):165–9 Je '69. * (*PA* 44:918)
23. MURTHY, VINODA NARAYANA. "Personality and the Nature of Suicidal Attempts." *Brit J Psychiatry* 115(524):791–5 Jl '69. * (*PA* 44:6685)
24. AGULNIK, PETER L. "The Spouse of the Phobic Patient." *Brit J Psychiatry* 117(536):59–67 Jl '70. * (*PA* 45:2697)
25. CAINE, T. M. Chap. 27, "Personality and Illness," pp. 781–817. In *The Psychological Assessment of Mental and Physical Handicaps.* Edited by Peter Mittler. London: Methuen & Co. Ltd., 1970. Pp. xxviii, 857. *
26. PHILIP, ALISTAIR E. "Traits, Attitudes and Symptoms in a Group of Attempted Suicides." *Brit J Psychiatry* 116(534):475–82 My '70. * (*PA* 45:984)

H. J. EYSENCK, *Professor of Psychology and Director of the Department, Institute of Psychiatry, University of London, London, England.*

Each of the 48 items of this questionnaire is stated to belong to one of 11 traits listed in the manual as characterising hysteroids and obsessoids; scoring is always in the hysteroid direction. No data are given on the intercorrelations between these traits or the intercorrelations between items; the whole notion of the existence of traits, and even of a hysteroid-obsessoid dimension, rests on an insecure foundation, being supported entirely by reference to Janet's original hypotheses regarding these two "diseases" within the neurotic complex of disorders.

Test-retest reliabilities on small samples of normal and neurotic subjects, taken over a period of one year, are satisfactory (.74 to .85), but no K-R 20 reliabilities are reported. For validity the authors rely on the correlation between the scale and averaged ratings made by psychiatrists; average inter-rater reliability in a similar study was .70. Validity established in this way is approximately .68; this figure would be much lower if correlations were run with individual raters, rather than with groups of raters. Mean scores are reported for various normal, neurotic and psychotic samples; the only outstanding feature of the resulting table is that normals are more hysteroid than patients.

The manual reports high correlations (equalling the reliabilities of both questionnaires) between the HOQ and the E (extraversion) scale of the *Maudsley Personality Inventory* ($r = .81$ for a small normal sample). The authors give detailed E scores for six different diagnostic categories within their neurotic sample; one might have expected them, in a manual of the HOQ, rather to have given scores on their own questionnaire. They conclude that "it is clear that HOQ and E are, to a considerable extent, measuring the same dimension, and that part of the dimension which they measure is an aspect of personality which is slightly, but only slightly, correlated with diagnosis." Such a conclusion is only possible if the reliability of psychiatric diagnosis is reasonable; nothing is said about this point, and published figures regarding diagnostic reliability within a neurotic group of patients does not inspire confidence in its adequacy.

The authors argue that "although HOQ and E are measuring virtually the same dimension of personality, the authors do not claim that HOQ is a measure of extraversion-introversion"; their reason seems to be that it is not clear that the content of these inventories is in line with Jung's conception of extraversion-introversion. As the HOQ is clearly unable to distinguish psychiatrically diagnosed "hysterics" and "obsessionals," the terms "hysteroid" and "obsessoid" seem even less applicable. In any case, Jung's mythological ideas are hardly relevant to modern practice, and the term "extraversion" is nowadays used in a sense which has little in common with his "dynamic" notions. One might also object to the excessive ugliness of the terms used by Caine and Hope; Cattell's neologisms may be equally insubstantial, but at least they have a certain linguistic attractiveness which is entirely missing in "hysteroids" and "obsessoids."

This inventory, then, emerges as another extraversion questionnaire, similar in construction, and even in item content, to the *Maudsley Personality Inventory;* lacking the inter-item correlations and the factor analytic procedures which have been used to ensure the factorial purity of the latter, and also lacking the presence of items measuring N (Neuroticism), without which interpretation and prediction are seriously handicapped. The manual does in fact quote a correlation of −.40 between the HOQ and the N scale of the *Eysenck Personality Inventory;* this emphasizes the need for the inclusion of some form of N scale, and in particular some form of item analysis to exclude the intrusion of N-related variance. At the moment it looks as if the "obsessoid" score lies in the same quadrant as the Taylor MAS score, i.e., in the high N-introvert quadrant; the MAS correlates somewhat higher with N, the HOQ somewhat higher with introversion. No score is very meaningful which does not take the existence of two major dimensions into account. It is for this reason too, that attention has been drawn to the lack of correlational studies of the items used; it seems not unlikely that the scale in fact contains two dimensions, rather than one.

MAURICE LORR, *Professor of Psychology, Catholic University of America, Washington, D.C.*

The HOQ was constructed to measure a bipolar continuum observed by Janet in neurotics. It consists of 48 items devised to measure 11 traits. The total score is simply the sum of the weighted item responses. Measures of internal consistency either for traits or total score are conspicuously missing. However, test-retest correlations for normals, neurotics, and psychotics, re-examined after intervals of either six weeks or a year, ranged from .74 to .85. Thus internal consistency is probably adequate.

Total HOQ score was validated against the mean ratings received by two samples of neurotics observed by the professional staff in a hospital setting. However, for one sample, only 6 of the 11 traits correlated significantly with total HOQ rating. In the other sample, the correlation between averaged ratings and HOQ total score was .68. Thus there appears to be sufficient evidence of positive observer vs. HOQ self-description relationship.

The HOQ score was evaluated against the *Maudsley Personality Inventory* E scale (Extraversion-Intraversion) in two samples to yield correlations of .70 and .81. In a third sample of neurotics HOQ correlated .69 with the newer *Eysenck Personality Inventory* E scale. Assuming that the reliabilities of E and HOQ are .80 and that the typical validity coefficient is .75, the coefficient of attenuation is .94. Thus it seems clear, as the authors admit, that HOQ and E are measuring the same dimension.

The manual fails to describe the intended or possible uses of the HOQ. It is not at all obvious why a clinician might want to apply the HOQ nor how it might help in treatment selection, in prognosis, or in predicting behavior. Also lacking are auxiliary scales to assess defensiveness (lying), social desirability, or similar response sets. Because the plastic stencil and the form are 14 inches in length, they will be difficult to store in American filing cabinets. In general, the manual is prepared in the style of a research report and thus would benefit from a revision.

In conclusion, it can be said that the HOQ represents a promising measure of a broad dimension also available in the MPI and the EPI E scales. The latter devices are to be preferred presently because they offer a far broader range of norms, considerably more data on construct validity, and an associated scale of neuroticism.

[88]

*Inpatient Multidimensional Psychiatric Scale, 1966 Revision. Hospitalized mental patients; 1953–67; IMPS; 10 scores based on ratings following an interview: excitement, hostile belligerence, paranoid projection, grandiose expansiveness, perceptual distortions, anxious intropunitiveness, retardation and apathy, disorientation, motor disturbances, conceptual disorganization; question booklet ('66, 8 pages); answer-profile sheet ('66, 2 pages); manual ('67, c1966, 19 pages); scoring booklet ('66, 4 pages); separate answer-profile sheets must be used; $5 per 25 question booklets; $3.50 per 25 sets of scoring booklets and answer sheets; $1.75 per manual; $2 per specimen set; postage extra; (10–15) minutes following a 35–45 minute interview; original materials by Maurice Lorr, C. James Klett, Douglas M. McNair (scale), and Julian J. Lasky (scale); Consulting Psychologists Press, Inc. *

REFERENCES

1–26. See 6:126.
27–87. See P:124, also includes a cumulative name index to the first 87 references for this test.
88. ABRAMS, JULIAN. *Chlorpromazine in the Treatment of Chronic Schizophrenia: A Comparative Investigation of the Therapeutic Value of Chlorpromazine in Effecting Certain Psychological and Behavioral Changes in Chronic Schizophrenic Patients.* Doctor's thesis, New York University (New York, N.Y.), 1957. (DA 17:1589)
89. NORTON, JAMES BRADLEY. *Psychologists' Evaluations of Patients in Psychotherapy: Clinical and Projective.* Doctor's thesis, Columbia University (New York, N.Y.), 1962. (DA 23:1785)
90. HANLON, THOMAS E.; NUSSBAUM, KURT; WITTIG, BARBARA; HANLON, DOLORES D.; AND KURLAND, ALBERT A. "The Comparative Effectiveness of Amitriptyline, Perphenazine, and Their Combination in the Treatment of Chronic Psychotic Female Patients." *J New Drugs* 4:52–60 Ja–F '64. *
91. CENTOR, ARTHUR. *A Comparison of Prognosis and Improvement Rate of Two Differentiated Groups of Schizophrenics.* Doctor's thesis, New York University (New York, N.Y.), 1965. (DA 26:4071)
92. ROSENBERG, SIDNEY. *Cognitive Styles and Overt Symptomatology in Schizophrenia.* Doctor's thesis, Columbia University (New York, N.Y.), 1966. (DA 27:614B)
93. KELLAM, SHEPPARD G.; GOLDBERG, SOLOMON C.; SCHOOLER, NINA R.; BERMAN, AUDREY; AND SHMELZER, JUNE L. "Ward Atmosphere and Outcome of Treatment of Acute Schizophrenia." *J Psychiatric Res* 5:145–63 Je '67. * (PA 42:9243)
94. MILLER, ANTHONY GEORGE. *Nocturnal Body Motility Among Hospitalized Mental Patients.* Doctor's thesis, Washington State University (Pullman, Wash.), 1967. (DA 28:3498B)
95. STIER, SERENA AUSTER. *Developmental Attainment, Outcome and Symbolic Performance in Schizophrenia.* Doctor's thesis, University of California (Los Angeles, Calif.), 1967. (DA 28:4766B)
96. WILSON, IAN C.; RABON, ARCHIE M.; AND BUFFALOE, WILLIAM J. "Imipramine Therapy in Depressive Syndromes: Prediction of Therapeutic Outcome." *Psychosomatics* 8:203–7 Jl–Ag '67. * (PA 42:884)
97. DEROGATIS, LEONARD R.; BONATO, ROLAND R.; AND YANG, KENNETH C. "The Power of IMPS in Psychiatric Drug Research: As a Function of Sample Size, Number of Raters, and Choice of Treatment Comparison." *Arch Gen Psychiatry* 19:689–99 D '68. * (PA 43:7550)
98. GOLDBERG, SOLOMON C., AND MATTSSON, NILS B. "Schizophrenic Subtypes Defined by Response to Drugs and Placebo." *Dis Nerv System* 29(5, sup):153–8 My '68. * (PA 42:15603)
99. KLEIN, DONALD F.; HONIGFELD, GILBERT; AND FELDMAN, SYDNEY. "Prediction of Drug Effect by Diagnostic Decision Tree." *Dis Nerv System* 29(5, sup):159–87 My '68. * (PA 42:15608)
100. KURLAND, ALBERT A.; DESTOUNIS, NICHOLAS; SHAFFER, JOHN W.; AND PINTO, ALCIDES. "A Critical Study of Isocarboxazid (Marplan) in the Treatment of Depressed Patients." *Proc 4th World Congr Psychiatry* 1966(pt 3):1962–6 '68. *
101. LORR, MAURICE. "A Behavioral Perspective of Schizophrenia." *Dis Nerv System* 29(5, sup):45–52 My '68. * (PA 42:15790)
102. LORR, MAURICE, AND KLETT, C. JAMES. "Major Psy-

chotic Disorders: A Cross-Cultural Study." *Arch Gen Psychiatry* 19:652–8 D '68. * (PA 43:8455)
103. MARJERRISON, G.; JEDLICKI, S. M.; KEOGH, R. P.; HRYCHUK, W.; AND POULAKAKIS, G. M. "Carbamazepine: Behavioral, Anticonvulsant and EEG Effects in Chronically-Hospitalized Epileptics." *Dis Nerv System* 29:133–6 F '68. * (PA 42:13993)
104. SIMPSON, GEORGE M.; ANGUS, J. W. S.; SUGERMAN, A. ARTHUR; AND STOLBERG, HUBERT. "Two Pilot Studies of BC-347 in Chronic Schizophrenic Patients." *J Clin Pharmacol & J New Drugs* 8:196–9 My–Je '68. * (PA 42:12297)
105. WILSON, IAN C., AND RABON, ARCHIE M. "Differential Therapeutic Efficacy of Imipramine in Various Depressive Syndromes." *Proc 4th World Congr Psychiatry* 1966(pt 4): 1932–5 '68. *
106. GOLDSTEIN, B. J.; BRAUZER, B.; CLYDE, D. J.; AND CALDWELL, J. M. "The Differential Prediction of Response to Two Anti-Psychotic Drugs." *Psychosomatics* 10(3):193–7 My–Je '69. *
107. HAMLIN, ROY M., AND LORR, MAURICE. "Relative Effectiveness of Objective Tests and Symptom Ratings in Differentiating Psychiatric Disorders." Abstract. *Proc 77th Ann Conv Am Psychol Assn* 4(2):511–2 '69. * (PA 44:859)
108. KATZ, MARTIN M.; COLE, JONATHAN O.; AND LOWERY, HENRI A. "Studies of the Diagnostic Process: The Influence of Symptom Perception, Past Experience, and Ethnic Background on Diagnostic Decisions." *Am J Psychiatry* 125(7): 937–47 Ja '69. * (PA 43:7072)
109. KATZ, MARTIN M.; GUDEMAN, HOWARD; AND SANBORN, KENNETH. Chap. 9, "Characterizing Differences in Psychopathology Among Ethnic Groups: A Preliminary Report on Hawaii-Japanese and Mainland-American Schizophrenics," pp. 148–63. In *Mental Health Research in Asia and the Pacific.* Edited by William Caudill and Tsung-yi Lin. Honolulu, Hawaii: East-West Center Press, 1969. Pp. xv, 487. *
110. KATZ, MARTIN M.; SANBORN, KENNETH O.; AND GUDEMAN, HOWARD. "Characterizing Differences in Psychopathology Among Ethnic Groups in Hawaii." *Res Publ Assn Res Nerv & Mental Dis* 47:139–53 '69. *
111. LORR, MAURICE, AND KLETT, C. JAMES. "Cross-Cultural Comparison of Psychotic Syndromes." *J Abn Psychol* 74(4): 531–43 Ag '69. * (PA 43:15658)
112. LORR, MAURICE, AND KLETT, C. JAMES. "Psychotic Behavioral Types: A Cross-Cultural Comparison." *Arch Gen Psychiatry* 20(5):592–7 My '69. * (PA 43:16061)
113. SCHOOLER, CARMI, AND SILVERMAN, JULIAN. "Perceptual Styles and Their Correlates Among Schizophrenic Patients." *J Abn Psychol* 74(4):459–70 Ag '69. * (PA 43: 16089)
114. LORR, MAURICE, AND HAMLIN, ROY M. "Estimation of the Major Psychotic Disorders by Objective Test Scores." *J Nerv & Mental Dis* 151(3):219–24 S '70. * (PA 45:10216)

JEROME D. PAUKER, *Associate Professor of Psychiatry (Medical Psychology) and Psychology, University of Missouri, Columbia, Missouri.*

The *Inpatient Multidimensional Psychiatric Scale* provides a systematic means (or "schedule" as the authors refer to it) for rating the interview behavior of severely disturbed, psychiatric patients. Qualified users, according to the manual, are "trained interviewers and observers reasonably experienced in interviewing psychiatric patients and familiar with their symptomatology." Appropriate patients are functional psychotics or severe psychoneurotics who are communicative and who (if the norms are to apply) are not receiving active drug treatment.

There are 75 "standard" and 14 "experimental" items in the IMPS. Fifty-one of them are "intensity" items (e.g., "Compared to the normal person to what degree does he manifest speech that is slowed, deliberate, or labored?"). These items are scored on a nine-point scale which runs from "not at all" to "extremely," with adjectives used to designate each of the other seven points inbetween. Another 21 items are "frequency" items (e.g., "How often during the interview did he grimace peculiarly or otherwise exhibit unusual or bizarre frowns or other facial expressions?"). These are rated on a five-point scale ("not at all" to "very often"). The final 17 items are "dichotomous" items, with the rater responding "yes" or "no" to such questions as: "Does he believe that certain people are trying to or now do control his actions or thinking?"

Percentile norms for the ten psychotic syndromes (listed above) are presented in the manual for acute male (N = 1,605) and female (N = 681) samples and for a chronic male sample (N = 969). A separate scoring booklet provides a table for conversion of raw scores into T scores, again with separate scores for men and women (but with only one set here for the men and no indication of whether this represents a combination of the acute and chronic male samples). In addition, scores can be obtained for five second order factors (disorganized hyperactivity, schizophrenic disorganization, paranoid process, anxious depression, and hostile paranoia) and three tentatively defined "experimental" syndromes (depressive mood, impaired functioning, and obsessive-compulsive).

Factor analysis was used in the construction of the syndromes and the second order factors. Though this statistical tactic may not be everyone's cup of *t* in the definition of behavioral dimensions, it appears that it was carefully considered and carefully applied. At any rate, the crucial questions for such an instrument are ones concerning inter-rater reliability and validity.

Rater reliability is good, both for syndrome scores and for individual items. Correlations among the ten syndromes are remarkably low, a finding that indicates appropriate economy for a set of scores which, while conceived of by the authors as being an intercorrelated set of variables, is also described as constituting a set of syndromes each of which "is regarded as a unitary dimension of response."

The validity section of the manual summarizes four major kinds of evidence: (*a*) Factorial validity—analyses of IMPS data from several different patient samples reveal the same ten syndromes in each instance. (*b*) Variability in syndrome scores concomitant with various situational and diagnostic classifications of patients (e.g., open or closed ward; duration of hospitalization; psychiatric diagnosis). (*c*) Variability in scores concomitant with variations in psychiatric drug use, and the reverse. (*d*) Regularities in behavioral and social characteristics of patients who fit certain subclassifications according to the profile of IMPS syndrome scores (referred to by the authors as "psychotic types").

[This reviewer was impressed with the amount, quality, and control of work which has gone into the development and research of the IMPS. There are several admirable aspects of this instrument. The authors stress in their manual the importance of rating solely on the basis of behavior which is observed during the course of the interview, and not on other reports or on inference. In order to increase objectivity, they recommend the use of two raters, although this is not a necessity. They provide a concise rating guide at the back of the manual.]

The IMPS can be used as a part of the standard intake procedure, and could easily find additional use as a training method or reminder in interviewing psychiatric patients. Anyone using the IMPS would do well to read the article by Katz et al. (*47*) which documents differences which may occur among raters as a function of differences among them in their perception of pathology. [One would like to see additional data relating to probability levels in making predictions for individual patients, but the research thus far justifies the use of the IMPS as a criterion measure in psychiatric research, and certainly justifies further investigations of its applications in clinical use.]

[89]

★Institutional Functioning Inventory. College faculty and administrators; 1968–70; IFI; a measure of perceived institutional vitality; the first half of the inventory may be used with students; for research use only; 11 scores: intellectual-aesthetic extracurriculum, freedom, human diversity, concern for improvement of society, concern for undergraduate learning, democratic governance, meeting local needs, self-study and planning, concern for advancing knowledge, concern for innovation, institutional esprit; 1 form ('68, 8 pages); prospectus ('70, 18 pages); preliminary technical manual ('70, 70 pages); separate answer sheets (SCRIBE) must be used; 35¢ per test; 5¢ per answer sheet; $2.50 per technical manual; $3 per specimen set; postage extra; scoring and reporting service, $1 and over per answer sheet ($50 minimum); (20–30) minutes; Richard E. Peterson, John A. Centra, Rodney T. Hartnett, and Robert L. Linn; Educational Testing Service. *

REFERENCES

1. CENTRA, JOHN A. "Validation by Multigroup-Multiscale Matrix: An Adaptation of Campbell and Fiske's Convergent and Discriminant Validational Procedure." Abstract. *Proc 78th Ann Conv Am Psychol Assn* 5(1):135-6 '70. * (*PA* 44:17782)
2. CENTRA, JOHN A.; HARTNETT, RODNEY T.; AND PETERSON, RICHARD E. "Faculty Views of Institutional Functioning: A New Measure of College Environments." *Ed & Psychol Meas* 30(2):405-16 su '70. * (*PA* 45:2914)
3. OGDEN, GEORGE BARTON. *An Organizational Innovation in Residential Undergraduate Education and Its Effects on Student Behavior.* Doctor's thesis, University of Massachusetts (Amherst, Mass.), 1970. (*DAI* 31:2131A)

PAUL L. DRESSEL, *Assistant Provost and Director, Institutional Research, Michigan State University, East Lansing, Michigan.*

The *Institutional Functioning Inventory* was developed by ETS in cooperation with the Institute for Higher Education, of Teachers College, Columbia University. Originally, it represented an attempt to develop a measure of institutional vitality. The instrument includes 132 items, 48 of which are regarded as factual and answered "yes," "no," or "don't know," and the remainder regarded as opinions responded to by "strongly agree," "agree," "disagree," or "strongly disagree." Eleven scales of 12 items each define the variables listed in the entry preceding this review.

The instructions suggest use with faculty members, students, administrators, governing board members, and others. Students are told to respond only to the first 72 items. Materials provided indicate adequate reliability reflected by coefficient alpha reliabilities of from .81 to .97, based on 67 college means. The validity of such an instrument is not easily determined, although the manual does provide correlates of the various scales with various other types of evidence. Commendable effort was expended in tryouts and statistical analysis of the items and scales, and this is reflected in the clarity of the items.

The results from the inventory should provide evidence against which an institution can reflect its presumed purposes to determine whether its scholarly stance, service orientation, and capacity for self-renewal are actually reflected in the views of those responding to the inventory. Some institutions may find comparisons with the norms of interest.

Several issues may be raised with regard to the inventory. In this day of increasing student involvement, may it not be that students could respond to all items as effectively as faculty, administrators, or board members? Surely some students in some institutions have as much sense of the institution's willingness to innovate, of the effectiveness of leadership of administrators, and of communication as have some faculty. The items suggested are only a sample of those indicated as "off limits" for students. An institution using the instrument might well find its greatest significance in comparing the responses to *all* items and *all* scales for students, faculty, board members, alumni, and the general public.

A second issue arises in regard to the extent to which a complex institution can be characterized by the inventory. Innovation, the use of senior professors in freshman courses, and chamber music concerts may be found in some departments or colleges of a university, but essentially nonexistent or unknown in others.

A third and perhaps less significant issue is involved in the distinction between "factual" and "non-factual" items. For example, the following items are regarded as "factual":

6. There are established procedures by which students may propose new courses.

11. This institution deliberately seeks to admit a student body in which a variety of attitudes and values will be present.

84. The institution has a long-range plan based on a reasonably clear statement of goals.

Anyone who has spent much time on a campus in recent years surely must recognize that these are statements about which marked differences of opinion exist. "Established," "deliberately," and "reasonably" are surely judgmental rather than factual. These are no more factual than, for example: "The institution is currently doing a successful job in achieving its goals."

There is also some doubt as to just what an institution accomplishes by the use of this inventory. Will the profile and the analysis of the item responses and comparison with norms evoke change? Likely not, for an institution displaying a profile lacking dynamism or vitality will either ignore the results or condemn the inventory. The really vital institution will be too busy to bother with the instrument. However, evidence of profound differences in views among the several components of the institutional personnel might force a facing up to reality.

CLIFFORD E. LUNNEBORG, *Associate Professor of Psychology and Director, Bureau of Testing, University of Washington, Seattle, Washington.*

The IFI is a recent addition to the educational researcher's armamentarium of instruments designed to describe the perceived climate of institutions of higher education. Primarily developed to permit a survey of faculty members' judgments about their institutions, the inventory may be used, according to the authors, to contrast such results with the responses of administrators and, for certain scales, students well acquainted with the school. In its present form, distributed for research purposes only, the inventory consists of 132 yes-no-don't know or agree-disagree items divided for scoring into 11 scales of 12 items each. The preliminary technical manual is somewhat vague about a theoretical basis for this particular set of scales. The potential user must accept at face value that the following represent institutional characteristics worthy of assessment: Intellectual-Aesthetic Extracurriculum (IAE—availability of intellectual and aesthetic activities outside the curriculum); Freedom (F—academic freedom and freedom of personal conduct of faculty and students); Human Diversity (HD—heterogeneity of backgrounds and attitudes of students and faculty); Concern for Improving Society (IS—institution applies its skills and knowledge to improving social conditions); Concern for Undergraduate Learning (UL—emphasis placed on undergraduate teaching and learning); Democratic Governance (DG—involvement of students and faculty in institutional decision making); Meeting Local Needs (MLN —educational and cultural opportunities provided for the community); Self-Study and Planning (SP—importance of continuous long-range planning); Concern for Advancing Knowledge (AK—priority given faculty research and scholarship); Concern for Innovation (CI—commitment to educational experimentation); and Institutional Esprit (IE—faculty loyalty to the institution).

Scales were constructed from somewhat larger item pools. Twenty items were initially written for each of 12 scales (the present SP scale coalesced from two groups of items tentatively identified as Concern for Continuous Evaluation and Concern for Continuous Planning) and this set was administered to faculty samples at 67 colleges and universities. Classical item selection criteria (item-total and item-cross scale correlations, proportion endorsing, and proportion omitting item) were then used to reduce the number of items to 12 for each scale. Despite the paring, approximately 15 percent of the item-scale correlations show an accepted item to correlate higher with some other scale

in the inventory than with the one to which it was assigned. Notable in this regard, 3 of the 12 items making up the HD scale correlated more highly with IS, a fourth with F, and a fifth with both IS and F. Within-scale correlations, however, were high enough that coefficient alpha reliabilities average .92, ranging from .86 for SP to .96 for DG and AK.

Interscale correlations reported in the technical manual included some relatively high values; eight of the 55 were .60 or higher and an additional seven were in the .50's, and an interscale factoring of faculty means for 37 institutions suggested only four common factors. These were identified by the authors as Liberal (F, HD, IS, and CI), Community (SP, CI, IE, and DG), Intellectual (AK and IAE), and Ivory Tower (UL and the obverse of MLN). Scales cited are those which correlated in excess of .50 with the varimax factors. Despite the apparent overlap of measurement, the authors suggest that the preliminary nature of the IFI and the conceptual distinctness of the 11 scales argue in favor of retention of the multi-scale format. This reviewer is less sanguine in view of the absence of any compelling basis for the initial scale definitions.

Validity data reported in the technical manual are limited to a comparison of IFI scores with other information (published institutional data, CUES profiles, and data from a study of factors of student protest) already available for certain subgroups of the 67 schools participating in the preliminary testing and to comparisons of responses by administrators, faculty, and students. Because these measures represent what was available, they fall short of providing any definitive validation of the IFI. Many of the correlations are consistent with the scale definitions (research money and library size are highly correlated with AK), while others pose interesting questions (library size is also highly correlated with IS and the more selective a school in its admissions policy, the higher it is likely to score on DG).

Such validational data suggest one of the real problems with the use of such an instrument. It attempts measurement over a badly defined ground between demonstrable characteristics of a school and opinions about it, and the search for any satisfactory anchoring is certainly not easily defined, if, indeed, it is possible. Limited normative data based on faculty means for 37 schools are reported in the technical manual.

The 37 were selected, presumably, to be representative of the population of four-year U.S. colleges relative to location, type of control, and level of offering. Though that sounds appropriate, or would if the sample were somewhat larger, such information falls short of what would be most useful. It is more likely, for instance, that a privately controlled, nonsectarian liberal arts college would find a comparison of its faculty's perceptions with those of faculty at similar schools more illuminating than any comparison with all institutions offering the baccalaureate.

The inventory is still experimental. Additional normative and validity data will surely be forthcoming. As yet, however, it is not established that the IFI provides institutions with data about their functioning or perceived functioning that can lead to changes in that functioning.

[90]

★The Institutional Self-Study Service Survey, College Student Form. College students; 1960–71; ISS; also called *The ISS Survey Questionnaire, College Student Form;* designed to provide a college with student opinion concerning "its policies, practices, faculty, service, and programs" and to appraise student development; each "research report" consists of means, percentages, or correlations by sexes and total for 3 groups in the following 6 areas: *student goals and aspirations:* educational majors, vocational choices, vocational role preferences, educational aspirations, importance of college goals (academic, vocational, social, nonconventional) ; *student development:* intellectual pursuits outside of class (science-mathematics, humanities, social science), nonacademic achievements in college (leadership, social participation, art, social service, humanistic-cultural, religious, music, writing, dramatic arts, total), student ratings of progress in achieving selected college goals; *student evaluations of their collegiate experience:* instructors, college services, selected policies, practices, and facilities; *correlations between college grade point average and:* other measures of college progress, teacher characteristics, college services, policies, practices, and facilities; *cross tabulations between ACT scores and:* majors, intellectual pursuits outside of class, nonacademic achievements; *cross tabulations between college admission data and current status on:* major, vocational choice, aspirations, nonacademic achievements; 1 form ('70, 12 pages) ; modified forms for use with faculty and other nonstudent groups must be prepared locally; manuals ('70) : part 1, research planning (86 pages), part 2, using the research reports (122 pages) ; graphic interpretive materials ['71, 15 pages] ; separate answer sheets must be used ; scoring service, $1 per answer sheet (50¢ for any over 1000, $300 minimum) including test materials; postpaid; specimen set free; score reports include 2 copies each of a regular report (based on all persons studied) and up to 3 supplemental reports (based on subgroups) ; since each report gives statistics for 3 separate groups, analyses may be obtained for up to 12 groups (selected by the college) ; separate statistics given for men, women, and total for each group; (30–50) minutes; initial experimental form (*Survey of Educational Status and Progress*) by Donald P. Hoyt; Oscar T. Lenning; American College Testing Program. *

JAMES V. MITCHELL, JR., *Associate Dean for Graduate Studies, College of Education, University of Rochester, Rochester, New York.*

The American College Testing Program's Institutional Self-Study Service is one of several resources presently available to assist the administrator or institutional researcher who seeks greater knowledge of the characteristics of the college or university environment. The principal vehicle offered by ACT to effect this knowledge is the *Institutional Self-Study Service Survey,* a 247-item questionnaire covering student goals and aspirations, student development, and student evaluations of their college experiences. The total service package is both comprehensive and elaborate, with such features as : an ISS report of institutional results for 39 separate data categories, many of which involve individual item statistics ; the presentation of results separately for males and females ; numerous cross-tabulation and correlational tables ; the provision for three supplemental reports as well as the regular report, which permits the analysis of 12 different subgroups ; the opportunity to use and secure results for locally developed items and special ACT item sets ; the availability of data on punched cards and magnetic tape (at cost) for use in future research ; and the provision for parallel opinion surveys for nonstudent groups.

Anyone intending to make use of the Institutional Self-Study Service should be prepared to devote the considerable time and effort that will be necessary to use it effectively. The ACT claim that the ISS research service is comprehensive and flexible seems justified, but these very characteristics necessitate a great deal more than the usual amount of attention to planning and research design. Thorough familiarity with the ISS manual before participation is a sine qua non, particularly the chapter 2 material concerned with "Planning for Participation in the Self-Study Service." The opening paragraph of that chapter suggests that the ISS design and output are simple enough not to require an educational research specialist for implementation and interpretation, but adds nevertheless that "coordination by an able and experienced institutional researcher should prove to be a decided advantage in making optimum use of the service." This reviewer couldn't agree more. Without such an institutional researcher, or reasonable substitute thereof, the potential user had better make certain of the easy availability of consultative services from one of the regional ACT offices.

Despite this complexity and the associated caveat, there is the distinct possibility that the kind of in-depth planning required by the ISS service could serve as a stimulus for a thorough-going self-evaluation that could extend beyond the ISS survey itself. The suggestions for planning contained in chapter 2 of the manual are worthwhile in any context, and certainly more likely to be productive of useful results than any offhand attempt to secure instant knowledge by administering any environmental assessment instrument that happened to strike one's fancy —an increasing practice these days.

Item characteristics and report format also deserve thorough study before electing to participate in the ISS service. Since much of the interpretation of ISS questionnaire results focuses on the individual item, the face validity of the items for a particular campus assumes practical importance. Compared with the comprehensiveness and flexibility claimed for the total research service, item content may seem relatively restricted and sometimes lacking in potential for productive results. Questions about college goals and outcomes, and evaluations by students of college instruction, policies, practices, facilities, and services may constitute useful data to many. More questionable, perhaps, are the 100 items concerned with outside-of-class accomplishments. The manual indicates that the distributions of scores based on these items are extremely skewed, which presents not only statistical problems but also suggests a relatively low informational yield. This low yield is readily confirmed by consulting normative data. It is only the potential user, operating in a particular context, who can decide whether, on balance, an inventory with a particular set of items has a total yield to justify the effort involved.

There is also some question about the utility of some of the correlational and cross-tabulation data. Tables are presented showing median correlations of zero or near-zero for the normative sample for such variables as GPA and ratings of teachers. It is suggested that a departure from such nonsignificant correlations for the local institution should occasion analysis of the reasons for the discrepancy. Such analyses, on those few occasions when they are thought to be needed, may prove to be will-o'-the-wisp ventures, fraught as they are with problems related to possible capitalization on chance factors, determination of what constitutes a statistically significant departure, and the assessment of the practical significance of discrepancies. Similarly, some of the cross tabulations relating ability level to outside-of-class activities may be unfruitful.

The ISS manual obviously represents a strong effort on the part of the authors to provide effective guidance to those using the service. It is generally quite helpful, and probably more so than the typical manual in this area. The two parts of the manual ("Research Planning" and "Using the Research Reports") are very detailed, perhaps too much so in some cases, and sometimes uneven in their treatment of the various topics or in terms of the background expected of the user. The section on sampling procedures, for example, is much more elaborate than is typically found and probably requires some minimal level of statistical competence. Yet at another point in the manual the authors feel obliged to give a very global and freshman-level definition of the correlation coefficient!

This unevenness of treatment becomes particularly evident when comparisons are made with manuals for other environmental measures. The orientation in the ISS manual is toward the ISS as a *service, not* an *instrument,* and the manual places a much greater than usual emphasis on planning, procedures, research design, sampling, and interpretation of results; and a much less than usual emphasis on the psychometric properties of the ISS as a measuring instrument. Its major strength is its very evident focus on the practical concerns of the user; its related weakness is that in doing so it seems to direct comparatively little effort toward the vehicle itself. At its worst this combination could result in an unsettling perception by the user that he is being overwhelmed—by useless data.

The chapter in the manual on the technical aspects of the ISS instrument will seem lacking to many. It is indicated that items selected for inclusion in the instrument were sometimes taken from previous ACT research, sometimes from research conducted by others, and sometimes based on "expert opinion" and the literature in the area. Thus with few exceptions item selection has been governed by evidence acquired piecemeal from other sources and not from research directed toward the instrument itself. Claims for validity are based primarily on the same data; the manual states that "for most of the items the validity rests primarily on relevant research and consultation with experts in the field." An appeal is made for the content validity of the items. Emphasis is also placed upon studies purporting to show a lack of distortion in self-reports and others supporting their predictive validity. This generally casual approach to validity is in contrast to that for the *College and University Environment Scales* and the *Inventory of College Activities* and reflects the differences in orientation mentioned above.

Reliability estimates are a problem for the ISS instrument, not only because of the usual problems attending the reliability of group measures, but also because some of the data are presented as endorsement percentages for individual items. Reliability coefficients are provided, however, for the scales of Out-of-Class Activities, Nonacademic Achievement, and College Goals. These coefficients are lower than one might hope for but may still be adequate if the results for a given institution are based on a relatively large sample of students.

Normative data for the ISS inventory are disappointing. National norms are based on only 41 institutions, presumably representative of the larger population, and some tables involve even fewer than 41. The discussion of norm development is sketchy at best, but what does exist stimulates some doubt about the adequacy of the final result. Norm tables are both plentiful and specific, however, and include some useful institutional comparison tables that help to define one's institutional standing with respect to the entire distribution. It is hoped that subsequent editions of the ISS will see the development of a normative data base that will provide more justification for the existence of these numerous and elaborate tables.

The ISS, in short, is a mixed bag. Evaluated as a measuring instrument, as it must of necessity be evaluated in the present volume, it has its shortcomings. But considered in the context of a total institutional service, it has something more to offer. As a service it does have the comprehensiveness and flexibility claimed for it, and doubtlessly more of it than its nearest competitors. This comprehensiveness and flexi-

bility, however, are primarily functions of the structure for administering and interpreting the instrument and not the instrument itself. An exaggerated simile would be that of a vessel with a magnificent superstructure and an old, leaky hull. But because the service itself and the processes required for making use of it are themselves beneficial in an evaluative setting, the contribution of the total program package cannot be ignored. A potential user might best consider, in order: (1) the items and scales themselves and the utility of the data obtained from them; (2) the increase in utility from locally developed items or special sets of items; (3) the further increase in utility from the design features of the service itself. The judgmental process might terminate after step 1, but it might also continue through steps 2 and 3 and lead to the conclusion that the results obtained would justify the considerable effort involved.

[91]

★**Inter-Person Perception Test.** Ages 6–13, 14 and over; 1969; IPPT; no reading by examinees; Forms AC (11 pages, faces of children), AA (11 pages, faces of adults); mimeographed manual (6 pages); no data on validity; no norms; separate answer sheets must be used; $20 per 25 tests; $1.20 per 25 answer sheets; $2 per scoring stencil; $1.75 per manual; $4.75 per specimen set; postpaid; 15(25) minutes; F. K. Heussenstamm and R. Hoepfner; Monitor. *

[92]

★**Interpersonal Perception Method.** Married couples and other 2-person or 2-group situations; 1966; IPM; 6 scores: interdependence and autonomy, warm concern and support, disparagement-disappointment, contentions, contradiction and confusion, extreme denial of autonomy; 5 booklets (63 pages): he-she, she-he, he-he, she-she, we-they; manual (179 pages, see *1* below); score chart (2 pages, available in U.S. only); £2.62 per 12 tests; £1.75 per manual; postage extra; specimen set not available; (60–80) minutes; R. D. Laing, H. Phillipson, and A. R. Lee; distributed by NFER Publishing Co. Ltd. * (United States prices and distributor: $10 per 20 tests; $2.50 per 10 charts; $5.50 per manual; postpaid; $6.50 per specimen set including manual, postage extra; Springer Publishing Co., Inc.)

REFERENCES

1. See P:128.
2. KOTKAS, L. J. "Informal Use of the 'Interpersonal Perception Method' in Marital Therapy." *Can Psychiatric Assn J* 14(1):11–4 F '69. * (*PA* 43:16166)

BERNARD I. MURSTEIN, *Professor of Psychology, Connecticut College, New London, Connecticut.*

The *Interpersonal Perception Method* involves answering 60 dyadic issues on a four-point scale from very true to very untrue. Each issue is covered by 12 questions making a total of 720 questions to be answered. Average time required to complete these questions is 70 minutes.

The 60 issues themselves may be divided into six categories which are (a) "Interdependence and autonomy," (b) "Warm concern and support," (c) "Disparagement and disappointment," (d) "Contentions: fight/flight," (e) "Contradiction and confusion," and (f) "Extreme denial of autonomy."

This test focuses on the perception of the self and the other in a dyad when two individuals are engaged in a meaningful encounter or relationship. Five booklets are provided for different kinds of dyadic relationships: he-she, he-he, she-she, she-he, and we-they. The first word tells from whose point of view the test is being taken. In the marriage relationship (he-she, or she-he), four relationships are taken as objects of observation: the husband's relationship to himself (IIII), the wife's relationship to herself (WW), how he feels about her (HW), and how she feels about him (WH).

When an individual judges a relationship, for example, the wife judges her husband's relationship to himself, we have direct perspective, $W \rightarrow (HH)$. When the wife estimates her husband's judgment about his relationship to himself, we have a metaperspective, $W \rightarrow H \rightarrow (HH)$, and when the husband estimates the wife's estimate of his judgment of his relationship to himself, we have a meta-metaperspective, $H \rightarrow W \rightarrow H \rightarrow (HH)$.

Comparison of direct perspectives yields *agreement* or *disagreement*. Comparison of one individual's perspective with another's metaperspective yields *understanding* or *misunderstanding*. An individual's perspective compared with his own meta-metaperspective gives the feeling of *being understood* or *misunderstood*. Comparison of an individual's meta-metaperspective and another's metaperspective yields *realization* or *failure of realization*.

One strength of the IPM, therefore, would appear to be its measurement of a broad array of perceptions. In the case of marital discord, it might be possible to pinpoint the exact problem in terms of faulty perceptions. Does the problem lie in different perspectives or does he see her differently than the way she thinks he sees her? With the use of meta-metaperspectives, the complexity of perceptual comparisons exceeds that used heretofore in any other test.

Unfortunately, the limitations of this test are formidable. Very little information is given about the 60 issues used in the test except that the test was reduced gradually by item analysis from an original group of 2,000 items. On what grounds? No information is given in this regard. There are six categories under which the phrases are grouped. No information is given on how these were chosen.

The statements themselves seem rather vague and general, as the following examples show: "She believes in me," "I like her," "He blames me," "She is at one with me."

The authors do not take account of the fact that behavior is often role-determined rather than general. Perhaps "She believes in me" when I am alone with her but not when I say I'm only going to the Elks' convention to further business interests. "I like her" when she is being kind to me but not when she becomes a virago when preparing for a cocktail party.

Also, somewhat surprisingly, despite the complexity of the perceptions, the test provides no data on such crucial considerations as the expectation level against which to measure the various perceptions. Neither does it ask the testee to evaluate the importance of the items for him. The sentence "He makes me the center of the world" may mean little to an individual who thinks he *is* the center of the world. Yet, another individual might tolerate a lack of agreement and understanding on 59 items if on the 60th he might say "She makes me the center of her world."

Despite the assurance in the foreword that "those who are aware of their own experiences in relations with others will learn [the method] easily," the scoring and interpretation are respectively laborious and conceptually demanding. The test-retest reliability based on a small sample of 14 disturbed and 12 nondisturbed marriages tested for a second time after a lapse of four to six weeks is quite adequate for the nondisturbed group and adequate for the disturbed one.

The validation group consists of 12 disturbed and 10 nondisturbed couples. The various concepts mentioned earlier, as well as some additional ones, were all found to significantly differentiate these two groups, although (the authors do not make this point) these concepts are not all independent of each other. This finding validates the claim that in disturbed marriages the participants are more likely to "see things differently" than is the case in nondisturbed marriages. What is more debatable is whether this fact could have been ascertained without this laborious time-consuming task, and whether this test really pinpoints the specific areas of difficulty.

In sum, the IPM is probably the most complex person perception method yet devised. Although based on a very small sample, it appears to be adequately reliable and at least minimally valid. Limiting factors are the time required for administration and scoring, conceptual turbidity for interpretation, and a poor selection of items. Release of the test at this time seems to have been premature.

NORMAN D. SUNDBERG, *Dean, The Wallace School of Community Service and Public Affairs, University of Oregon, Eugene, Oregon.*

At the front of the book describing the theory and method of the *Interpersonal Perception Method* is a "Peanuts" cartoon. Charlie Brown and Lucy are each trying to figure out what the other is thinking as she holds a football for him to kick. In the end she pulls the football away as he runs up to kick, and he falls flat on the ground. She says, "I figured you knew that I knew you knew I knew that you knew I knew you knew, so I had to jerk it away!" This convoluted kind of thinking is what this questionnaire is all about.

After studying the IPM and trying it out, I feel about as confused and frustrated as Charlie Brown must have felt. The technique is an imaginative one in which respondents, such as a husband and a wife, are asked to answer questions directly about themselves, then to indicate how they think their partner answered the questions, and how the partner thinks the respondent answered the question. There are 60 issues, or topics, and 12 questions are asked about each one. For instance, item 26 on the HE-SHE form is as follows:

A. How true do you think the following are?
 1. She gets on my nerves.
 2. I get on her nerves.
 3. She gets on her own nerves.
 4. I get on my own nerves.
B. How would SHE answer the following?
 1. "I get on his nerves."
 2. "He gets on my nerves."
 3. "I get on my own nerves."
 4. "He gets on his own nerves."
C. How would SHE think you have answered the following?
 1. She gets on my nerves.
 2. I get on her nerves.
 3. She gets on her own nerves.
 4. I get on my own nerves.

One wonders how many people can answer 720 items on such a questionnaire without having it get on their nerves! Test-taking attitudes and understanding of the directions are serious problems for such a procedure. The authors state that the average time taken to answer the questionnaire is 70 minutes.

Even more irritating is the attempt to get the results translated into usable scores and summary data. I spent hours puzzling over the manual trying to figure out exactly how answers are to be recorded on a record sheet and then how they are to be coded. The authors should carefully show step-by-step how the results are to be transferred and organized. One finds by accident, for instance, that the intensity of positive and negative responses is ignored. Comparing the various answers of the two subjects gives scores on agreement and disagreement, understanding and misunderstanding (by comparing wife's answers with what husband thinks wife said) and realization or failure to realize that one is understood (by comparison of one's meta-meta perspective with the other's meta response). All these scores can be obtained on the 60 issues grouped into six subject matter areas such as "interdependence and autonomy" and "warm concern and support." Once responses are recorded and coded, the variety of possibilities is so staggering that the neophyte cannot make much meaning of them, although the authors say that one can detect "with a little practice, at one glance....the pattern of inter-experience and interaction as a whole."

It would seem that considerable training for use of the test would be needed.

Beyond these problems lie the usual questions about norms, reliability and validity. The manual's answers to such questions are very far from adequate. Although the word "norms" is used, there is nothing reported except some tables showing responses of 10 nondisturbed couples and 12 couples who sought marital counseling. The authors describe almost nothing about the background of these 22 dyads, such as the ages and problems of the couples. They do report some retest data in terms of percentages of agreement. There is high stability for the nondisturbed couples; over half the items showed 90 percent agreement between first and second administration. Disturbed subjects showed less consistency, but almost all of the items showed over 75 percent agreement.

The authors give little attention to validity

and do not list it in the content index of the manual. The manual does indicate that the method differentiates between disturbed and nondisturbed marital couples, although statistical tests are not used. There is less disjunction and more agreement and understanding among nondisturbed couples. The book demonstrates the clinical usage of the IPM by going into detail, often repetitively, concerning the responses of one couple. I find the presentation of that case unconvincing of the value of using the technique.

In sum, the IPM is time-consuming to administer and score, it is likely to be confusing to many subjects, the rationale for its six groups of issues is unclear, it possesses no adequate norms and has received little attention regarding reliability and validity. What good is it, then? There must be some good in everything!

As a psychometric or even clinical device, the IPM is not impressive yet. What is interesting is the potentiality of the theory and the method. The authors of the IPM are trying to confront what very few have dared to—namely, the complex perspectives and metaperspectives which people have of each other. The interplay of views of the other person and what he is thinking are undoubtedly involved in social and clinical behavior. What I think your intentions are and what I think you know about me do have an influence on my behavior. The authors point out that views of nations toward each other also have this character and recommend that surveys not only ask what people think directly, but what they think the average person's opinion is. An improved and simplified IPM may be very useful for research and practice in clinical and social psychology, but the instrument has a long way to go.

Brit J Psychiatric Social Work 9(1):39–40 '67. Inge Bergmann. "Human beings are constantly thinking about others, and about what others are thinking about them, and what others think they are thinking about others and so on." You may well think that this is a double think, but in fact it is the essence of the Interpersonal Perception Theory, which concerns itself with the study of the dyad, two people in a meaningful encounter. The three authors of Interpersonal Perception claim to shed a new light on the study of the interaction of two or more people. In traditional psychotherapy the patient uses his relationship with his therapist in order to explore his own personality structure. But in this book, the authors urge us to abandon the fruitless journey into the unconscious, forget the past, ignore the superego and the id, and only to concern ourselves with the here and now. We are asked to look at the patient in his setting, that is his family and the world he lives in. This has philosophical as well as psychological and therapeutic implications. Laing is concerned with the meaning of the self in relation to the universe. Here he expresses his existentialist views on the importance of the present, and he echoes many of Jaspers' ideas. The emphasis is on the understanding of the experience of life rather than the reason for living. To Social Workers the therapeutic implications of this theory are obvious, and not at all new. The authors show how their method can be used in marital therapy. * Translating their ideas into a complicated theory, the authors have devised the Interpersonal Perception Questionnaire, which is given to the dyad seeking therapy. The object of this is to ascertain the individuals position on the Interpersonal Perception Spiral. In this test, 60 issues between two people are constructed, and on each issue, twelve questions require to be answered. One such issue for example is, "Can I face up to my conflicts," with twelve variations on the theme. This makes a giddymaking total of 720 questions to be answered. On first sight, this theory provides a convenient solution to all one's problems. On second thoughts, alas, one is left with so many reservations, both theoretical and practical. The book claims to encompass "the full complexity of human experience" through a semantic interpretation of human behaviour. To scorn the past implies that one believes that learning has no part to play in human relationships, and that past attitudes are of no significance. Also what people say at any given point, is only part of the story. Often they feel things they can't express. The theory also assumes fixed attitudes, but we all feel different at various times. The aim of therapy surely must be to learn to live with oneself, which in itself affects one's relationship with others. Is it really so important to know what others think one thinks? I think not, but on the other hand you may think that I think wrongly, and unless we both take the test we shall never know.

Brit J Psychol 58:191 My '67. Michael Argyle. One or two psychoanalysts continue to produce ideas, based on their clinical material, which are valuable because they come from a more intensive analysis of individuals than is common in more rigorous research. In this case the work of the authors in family therapy has led them to an intensive study of the relationships between pairs of people, analysed in terms of mutual perceptions. The basic method is to ask each member of the pair 720 questions, e.g., "How would she think you have answered the following: 'She hates me'?" The questions refer to six areas of interpersonal behaviour, and are asked at three levels—how A sees B, how A thinks B sees A (meta-perspective), and how A thinks B thinks A sees B (meta-meta-perspective). By combining the scores of A and B at different levels it is possible to arrive at indices of agreement, understanding, feeling understood, together with more complex notions such as feeling misunderstood incorrectly, etc. This is not so much a test, as a method for studying in depth the mutual perceptions of two people. A small piece of validating data about the test is presented: 12 disturbed and 10 non-disturbed marriages are compared: there was significantly more misunderstanding for the disturbed partners. It would be interesting to know whether the meta-meta-perspective is of much importance; indeed it is doubtful how many people could understand this notion and answer meaningfully. Some case-studies are reported, one at length, of the complex ways in which two people can become confused about one another, and the impossible predicaments that can be generated. Some interesting, highly speculative, but possibly testable, ideas are put forward about how "spirals" of misunderstanding may develop: the general idea is that distrust generates further degrees of the same, e.g. "Jack may reason: 'Look at all the things that Jill is doing to try to prove to me that she loves me. If she really loved me she would not have to be so obvious about it and try so hard. The fact that she is trying so hard proves she is pretending. She must be trying to cover up her feelings—she must be trying to cover up her true feelings. She probably loves Tom.'" This monograph makes an interesting contribution to a hitherto neglected topic—the analysis of established relationships between people. It proposes a research technique and some novel hypotheses. It is, however, curiously out of touch with other work on person perception and social interaction, and the authors would be understood more accurately if they presented their material in a more readable way.

Brit J Social & Clin Psychol 8(1):89–90 F '69. Fay Fransella. * The language and symbols used make reading and understanding a rather laborious task. However, the effort required to overcome the complexity of the language is well worth while. * [The IPM] is concerned with measuring the degree of understanding and agreement between two individuals. Both members of the dyad answer from varying standpoints the IPM questionnaire, consisting of sixty "issues," each embodied in twelve questions. The 720 questions are detailed in the book. A dyadic relationship is measured at three levels of perspective: (i) A's view of X (direct perspective), (ii) A's view of B's view of X (metaperspective), (iii) A's view of B's view of A's view of X (metametaperspective). From the answers A and B give, measures of degree of agreement, understanding and "realization or failure of realization" are obtained at all three levels of perspective. Reliability and some normative data are included as well as a detailed analysis of one dyad. The book appears incomplete in that the authors rightly comment on the potential of the measure (e.g. as a measure of dyadic perception in international relations or between cultural groups), but all examples and normative data are restricted to married couples. The authors claim that the IPM can be used nomothetically and offer norms, but the basis for their claim that it is also an idiographic procedure is unclear since all the test items given are standard. There seems, however, to be no good reason why the "issues" should not be tailored to the language and outlook of individual couples. If this were done intra- and inter-dyad agreement could still be assessed even where questionnaire content differed. Perhaps the more important aspect of this book is that it reflects a welcome movement in psychology away from the rather artificial study of the "isolated" individual towards the study of the interpersonal process.

Cont Psychol 13:78+ F '68. N. L. Gage. * On the face of it, the authors seem to have developed an ingenious and sensible way of measuring psychological relationships between two persons. But they have ignored the work on interpersonal perception by their many predecessors in this field—Cronbach; Tagiuri; Bronfenbrenner, Harding, and Gallwey; and Hastorf, to name only a few. So they have proceeded in innocence of various substantive and methodological issues, such as the effects of consistent individual differences in tendency to respond in a socially desirable way, and the need for testing the efficacy of monadic variables before resorting to explanations involving dyadic variables. Their detailed 38-page analysis of the responses of one married couple proceeds without reference to the dangers of bogging down in a morass of artifactually interlocked variables. In short, the sophistication laboriously developed by previous workers is disregarded in the present enterprise. But the main problem is whether these so-called perceptions, meta-perceptions, and meta-metaperceptions, although they can easily be defined logically and operationally, actually exist psychologically, or phenomenologically. Do these variables actually make a difference in non-test, or real-life, behavior? It may be that we are incapable of handling more than one pair of reflections in these facing mirrors. That is, the infinitely regressing images of our images may be functionally nonexistent after one or two spirals of this kind. If so, the authors are playing with mere logical possibilities rather than significant psychological events. The authors' general approach has some promise. There may indeed be something useful to be learned from detailed analysis of two persons' responses to questions of this kind. But those potentialities will be realized only by taking into account the contributions of previous workers and by careful application of established techniques for the validation of psychometric and clinical instruments.

[93]

★The Inventory of College Activities. College; 1962–70; ICA; measure of characteristics of the college environment likely to have some influence upon student development; 33 scores: *peer environment* (competitiveness vs. cooperativeness, organized dating, independence, cohesiveness, informal dating, femininity, drinking vs. religiousness, musical and artistic activity, leisure time, career indecision, regularity of sleeping habits, use of the library, conflict with regulations, student employment, use of automobiles), *classroom environment* (involvement in the class, verbal aggressiveness, extraversion of the instructor, familiarity with the instructor, organization in the classroom, severity of grading), *administrative environment* (severity of administrative policy against drinking, against aggression, against heterosexual activity, against cheating), *college image* (academic competitiveness, concern for the individual student, school spirit, permissiveness, snobbishness, emphasis on athletics, flexibility of the curriculum, emphasis on social life); NCS test-answer booklet ('70, 4 pages); manual ('70, 78 pages, Xerox copy of manuscript); scoring

services to be provided by National Computer Systems; prices not yet determined; (20–25) minutes; Alexander W. Astin; American Council on Education. *

REFERENCES

1. Astin, Alexander W., and Panos, Robert. "Implications for Learning Climate and Student Personnel Administration of the American Council on Education Long-Range Student Development Studies." *NASPA* 5:203–9 O '67. *
2. Astin, Alexander W. *The College Environment.* Washington, D.C.: American Council on Education, 1968. Pp. xi, 187. *
3. Astin, Alexander W. "Personal and Environmental Determinants of Student Activism." *Meas & Eval Guid* 1:149–62 f '68. * (*PA* 44:11183)
4. Astin, Alexander W. "Undergraduate Achievement and Institutional 'Excellence.' " *Sci* 161:661–8 Ag 16 '68. *
5. Astin, Alexander W., and Panos, Robert J. *The Educational and Vocational Development of College Students.* Washington, D.C.: American Council on Education, 1969. Pp. xii, 211. *
6. Friis, Robert Harold. *Achievement Need-Press Discrepancy, Anomie and Unrest Among College Students.* Doctor's thesis, Columbia University (New York, N.Y.), 1969. (*DAI* 30:2148A)
7. Tupes, Ernest C., and Madden, Howard L. "Relationships Between College Characteristics and Later Performance of College Graduates." *Ed & Psychol Meas* 30(2):273–82 su '70. * (*PA* 45:3168)

James V. Mitchell, Jr., *Associate Dean for Graduate Studies, College of Education, The University of Rochester, Rochester, New York.*

The Inventory of College Activities is one of the more recent additions to a growing armamentarium of instruments designed to assist those who wish to study the college environment. It is seen by its author as an "objective means of describing and measuring some of the important differences among the environments of undergraduate institutions." The emphasis here on *objective* means is a critical aspect of the ICA rationale; it is regarded as objective because, unlike presently existing instruments, it employs a "stimulus" approach to environmental assessment. A "stimulus" is defined as: "Any behavior, event, or other observable characteristic of the institution capable of changing the student's sensory input, the existence or occurrence of which can be confirmed by independent observation." This "stimulus" approach is contrasted with the "image" approach of the *College Characteristics Index* (CCI) or the *College and University Environment Scales* (CUES), which are based on student perceptions of the total institutional climate, or with the Environmental Assessment Technique (EAT), which stresses the personal characteristics and orientations of the students themselves.

The ICA contains 275 items representing environmental stimuli from four broad categories: the peer environment (e.g., "Arranged a date for another student"); the classroom environment (e.g., "The class was taught by a graduate student") ; the administrative environment (e.g., severity of punishment expected for misdemeanors like "Cheating on examinations") ; and the physical environment (e.g., "Travel time to library"). How "observable" all of these "stimuli" really are is still open to conjecture ; knowing that your class is taught by a graduate student is more readily established in an objective sense, and less subject to perceptual distortion, than ascertaining that your instructor is "engaged in research of some kind." But generally the 275 items reflecting stimuli do seem to permit a more objective assessment than the image-type items. The image approach is not rejected altogether, however, for in addition to the 275 stimulus items the ICA contains 77 image-type items, many of which are similar to those found in CCI and CUES.

In order to identify general patterns of environmental stimuli and develop empirically based scoring categories, separate factor analyses were conducted on these five item groupings. This ultimately resulted in the factorial definition of 33 ICA dimensions representing peer, classroom, and administrative environment and the college image. Physical environment factors were omitted because of difficulties in obtaining adequate data and the generally unproductive results of the factor analysis. The 33 factor score dimensions are listed above with other descriptive data on the ICA.

Potential users of the ICA would do well to examine carefully the utility of the factor scores for their particular purposes. There is always the danger that a "stimulus" approach will in some instances reveal little more than what we already know or can observe—by definition. Perhaps the confirmation of that knowledge and the relating of it to normative data may in those instances be sufficient gain. Another danger is the overinterpretation or misinterpretation of factor scores derived from factor analyses in which the institution is used as the unit of sampling. The loadings for these factors are often a heterogeneous lot with a vaguely defined commonality of meaning. When in this situation every conceivable correlate is milked to ascribe meaning to a factor, the practical test user, discovering that his institution ranks high on a factor, may well assign a connotational aura to that score that bears little relationship to the situation existing on his campus. It is easy to overlook the fact that these factors define nothing more than collections of stimuli that seem to go together empirically in some degree in the sample of institutions selected for study. The two dangers described above may seem to be opposites ; that they can exist within the same instrument is evident from a score like "Use of the Library" on the one hand and "Cohesiveness" on the other.

ICA factor scores are typically estimated from the three variables with the highest regression weights for the factor. Some are estimated from the weights for only one or two variables. Intercorrelations among these factor scores seem low enough to justify their separate use, even when they are derived from separate analyses. Interestingly, although there are enough substantial correlations between the "stimulus" and "image" factors to provide some construct validity evidence for both, the two sets of variables appear sufficiently independent to suggest that they are measuring different aspects of institutional differences. The implications of this for the future measurement of institutional differences are pointed out by the test author in a recent monograph (2).

Reliability data for the ICA are inadequate and should be improved in subsequent editions of the manual. Environmental measures like ICA pose special reliability problems, since high inter-individual agreement within institutions, obviously a desideratum for instruments of this type, results in decreased variance and lower reliability coefficients as conventionally computed. Further complications arise for the ICA because the inclusion of only 1–3 items per scale precludes the use of split-half or other internal consistency methods. The test author confronts these problems by providing us with reliability coefficients based on the computation within each institution of factor scores for "odd" and "even" subjects (determined by student identification number) and the correlation of these across the entire sample of 246 institutions. These coefficients are generally satisfactory. It is probable that they are inflated, however, due to the author's original intent to select a sample of institutions that would "maximize heterogeneity." Additional evidence is needed. What is needed most particularly is evidence on the within-institution stability of factor scores over time, and the effects of any shifts in these on institutional standing with respect to norms. With so few items contributing to each factor score, the burden of proof of ICA reliability still remains with the author. Perhaps the "stimulus" approach requires fewer items to establish adequate reliability; the proof of this must come from more empirical evidence.

The validity of environmental measures is again a specialized kind of problem for which conventional approaches based on individual assessment are not always appropriate. The factor analysis of the ICA provided some evidence of construct validity. Other evidence of construct validity is derived from correlations between ICA factor scores and EAT scores, CUES scores, and the typological characteristics of institutions; and from studies on the effects of ICA factors on student development. In general the correlations are consistent with the meanings of the ICA factors. For some relationships this evidence is important and relatively convincing; for others, especially those for which the relationship is on a priori grounds seen as tangential, the evidence is less compelling. Some interesting findings concern the nature and degree of ICA-CUES overlap in variance and the effects of variables like Cohesiveness and Concern for the Individual Student on dropout rate and campus unrest. Assessing construct validity is a never-ending task; what is presented is useful, but additional evidence would strengthen the case.

The ICA is designed to be self-administered, but local scoring would involve the use of regression weights and conversion tables, probably prohibitive in terms of time, effort, and expense. The National Computer Systems will undertake the task and provide such useful extras as the total group profile and up to nine subgroup profiles and a tabulation of all item responses, by subgroup and total, including local (self-developed) items. Scores are reported as normalized standard scores with a mean of 500 and a standard deviation of 100, and mean ICA profiles are presented for two-year colleges, four-year colleges, and universities. The same data should also have been presented in more exact tabular form. Normative data, based on 246 institutions and 34,693 subjects, were systematically corrected for questionnaire return bias and institutional sampling bias. Rigorous procedures seem to have been followed, but there is only limited description of norm development procedures in a section in the appendix. It would be better if an expanded description were included in a technical manual or in a

section of the present manual devoted to technical procedures.

In the reviewer's judgment the ICA is still in an experimental phase of its development. Many of the "stimulus" factor scores have an artifactual quality about them that suggests lack of unity, psychological meaning, or utility. The items and scores could communicate useful information to the user, depending on his purposes. But any potential user should study carefully the actual item content for each score category (along with associated technical data, if possible) to determine whether those items and scores will in fact provide him with the kind of information he would judge to be useful in the understanding of his institutional environment.

For excerpts from related book reviews, see B50 (2 excerpts).

[94]

★**The Jesness Inventory.** Disturbed children and adolescents ages 8–18; 1966, c1962–66; JI; 11 scores: social maladjustment, value orientation, immaturity, autism, alienation, manifest aggression, withdrawal, social anxiety, repression, denial, asocial index; 1 form ('62, 4 pages); manual ('66, 32 pages); profile ('62, 2 pages); no data on the reliability of the asocial index, the score used for predicting delinquency; no data on predictive validity; administration tapes mentioned in the manual are not available; separate answer sheets (Dela Data) must be used; $4 per 25 tests; $4 per 50 sets of answer sheet and profile; $1.75 per set of scoring stencils; $2 per manual; $2 per specimen set; postage extra; scoring service, $1 or less per test; (20–30) minutes; Carl F. Jesness; Consulting Psychologists Press, Inc. *

REFERENCES

1–3. See P:133.
4. BUTLER, EDGAR W. "Personality Dimensions of Delinquent Girls." *Criminologica* 3:7–10 My '65. *
5. ROCHLIN, MARTIN. *Behavioral Seriousness and Impulse-Control Balance in Delinquency.* Doctor's thesis, University of Southern California (Los Angeles, Calif.), 1966. (*DA* 27:3680B)
6. COWDEN, JAMES E.; PETERSON, WILLIAM M.; AND PACHT, ASHER R. "The MCI vs. the Jesness Inventory as a Screening and Classification Instrument at a Juvenile Correctional Institution." *J Clin Psychol* 25(1):57–60 Ja '69. * (*PA* 43:9996)
7. KELLY, FRANCIS J., AND BAER, DANIEL J. "Jesness Inventory and Self-Concept Measures for Delinquents Before and After Participation in Outward Bound." *Psychol Rep* 25(3):719–24 D '69. * (*PA* 44:18960)
8. MARTIN, D. N., AND CLARKE, R. V. G. "The Personality of Approved School Boy Absconders." *Brit J Criminol* 9(4):366–75 O '69. * (*PA* 44:8825)
9. MOTT, JOY. *The Jesness Inventory: Application to Approved School Boys.* Studies in the Causes of Delinquency and the Treatment of Offenders 13. London: Her Majesty's Stationery Office, 1969. Pp. iv, 26. *
10. ROTHENBERG, EUGENIA. *The Effect of Self-Disclosure and Pseudo-Self-Disclosure on Social Adjustment of Institutionalized Delinquent Girls.* Doctor's thesis, University of New Mexico (Albuquerque, N.M.), 1969. (*DAI* 30:5246A)
11. BAKER, JOHN W., II, AND SPEILBERG, MIMI J. "A Descriptive Personality Study of Delinquency-Prone Adolescents." *J Res Crime & Del* 7(1):11–23 Ja '70. *
12. JOSEPH, JACOB JOSEPH. *An Analysis of the Post-Release Adjustment of Rehabilitated Delinquent Girls.* Doctor's thesis, United States International University (San Diego, Calif.), 1970. (*DAI* 31:2519A)
13. WOYCHICK, JAMES T. "Asociability Index Scores' Relationship to Adjustment of Youthful Offenders." *J Correct Ed* 22(2):12–3+ sp '70. *

SHELDON A. WEINTRAUB, *Assistant Professor of Psychology, State University of New York at Stony Brook, Stony Brook, New York.*

The *Jesness Inventory,* a self-report inventory for "disturbed children and adolescents," was developed as part of a five-year research program on delinquency. It was designed to (*a*) distinguish delinquents from nondelinquents; (*b*) provide a basis for the personality description and classification of both delinquents and nondelinquents; and (*c*) provide a measure sufficiently sensitive to change to enable its use as a valid measure of change in research and clinical studies. The instrument consists of 155 true-false items stated in fairly simple language designed to be comprehended by children as young as 8 years.

The inventory scales are as follows: Social Maladjustment; Value Orientation; Immaturity; Autism; Alienation; Manifest Aggression; Withdrawal; Social Anxiety; Repression; Denial; Asocialization Index. The first three scales were derived empirically from an item analysis using criterion groups; the remaining scales were derived statistically by cluster analysis; the final scale includes data from all scales and is based on a regression equation which combines attitude syndromes and personality traits into an index to predict delinquency.

Directions for administration are straightforward and scoring is simple; no special training is required to administer the test.

The normative samples consisted of 970 delinquent and 1,075 nondelinquent males, and 450 delinquent and 811 nondelinquent females. Subjects ranged in age from 8 to 19; the age distribution is similar in the delinquent and nondelinquent groups except for the lack of younger female delinquents. Both the item analysis and cluster analysis were based on the male sample only since males are much more frequently adjudged delinquent than females. Indeed, the cluster analyses were based only on delinquent boys aged 13 to 17.

Reliability has been only partially investigated. The manual reports split-half reliabilities, collected on a sample of 1,862 delinquent and nondelinquent boys ages 10 to 18, for the ten scales (excluding the Asocialization Index) ranging from .62 to .88 with median .71. Test-retest reliabilities over an eight-month period with a sample of 131 delinquent boys, ages 14 to 21, range from .40 to .79 with median .70. No information is given on the reliability of the Asocialization Index, the score used for predicting delinquency.

The validation data presented consist of correlations with the *California Psychological Inventory,* based on 324 male and female delinquents, ages 10–20, and relationships with behavior and test data in a sample of 210 delinquents, ages 10–14. The correlations, of course, describe concurrent validity and are straightforward. The criterion behavior and test data, unfortunately, are not described adequately to permit meaningful conclusions about empirical validation. For example, the manual states that high scores on one scale are associated with poor social relationship with peers and aggressive behavior, on another scale nonconforming, rule-violating behavior, lack of responsibility, and alienation in the relations between youngsters and adults are found. How these behaviors were measured is never described.

In a description of each of the scales, the manual indicates how an individual scoring high on the scale would appear. Usually this is accomplished by listing the behaviors and attitudes the individual attributes to himself. But occasionally the description seems to go far beyond the items. For instance: "His sensitivity to criticism suggests lack of ego strength, while other items imply failure in masculine identification," or "The picture is that of a most inappropriate facade of self-adequacy covering a very insecure person." These kinds of descriptions imply some greater knowledge than what the items themselves indicate.

There is no evidence presented of the utility of the *Jesness Inventory* in the description and classification of personality, the second objective of the test. The only validity data available are for distinguishing individuals who are currently delinquent from nondelinquents. Using a base rate for male delinquency of .20 and a cutoff score of 22, 74 percent of male delinquents may be correctly identified with a probability of .65 for a true positive and .35 for a false positive. The utility of the inventory with female subjects is greatly reduced, given the much lower base rate for female delinquency. Unfortunately, the data from which the cutoff scores are derived appear to be based on the normative data collected in the development of the test. No cross validation studies are reported for these classification norms. Even if these results held up on cross validation, however, this would demonstrate only that the inventory is useful in the *identification* of delinquency, not necessarily in the *prediction* of delinquency. Predictive validity is only provided by studies which follow up nondelinquents identified by the test to see which of them do indeed become delinquent.

In summary, the *Jesness Inventory* appears to be of limited usefulness. There is no evidence for its utility as a general personality test, or in predicting delinquency.

[95]

★**Job Analysis and Interest Measurement.** Adults; 1957–64; JAIM; for research use only; personal qualities influencing job success or failure; 37 scores: optimism, self confidence, moral absolutes, persistence, academic data, problem analysis, social interaction, mechanical interests, planning and organizing, activity-frequent change, group identification, authority identification, persuasive leadership, self assertiveness, move toward, move away, move against, rewards, punishment, knowledge of results, accept commands, accept routines, internal standards, independence, question authority, directive leadership, participative leadership, delegative leadership, empirical-intuitive, systematical-methodical, formal status, social service, approval from others, resourceful accomplishment, maintain standards, role conformity, self directive; Form 864 ('64, 18 pages); mimeographed manual ('64, 54 pages) contains statistical data for earlier forms only; separate answer sheets must be used; $2.50 per specimen set, cash orders postpaid; test materials may be reproduced locally; scoring keys not available; information on machine scoring service available from author (Center for Behavioral Sciences, George Washington University, Washington, D.C. 20006); (40–60) minutes; Regis Walther; distributed by Educational Testing Service. *

REFERENCES

1. WALTHER, REGIS H. "Self-Description as a Predictor of Success or Failure in Foreign Service Clerical Jobs." *J Appl Psychol* 45:16–21 F '61. * (*PA* 36:2LD16W)
2. WALTHER, REGIS H. "Self-Description as a Predictor of Rate of Promotion of Junior Foreign Service Officers." *J Appl Psychol* 46:314–6 O '62. *
3. WALTHER, REGIS H. "Job Analysis and Interest Measurement." *Ed* 83:279–82 Ja '63. *
4. WALTHER, REGIS HILLS. *The Prediction of Occupational Adjustment Through Measured Behavioral Styles.* Doctor's thesis, George Washington University (Washington, D.C.), 1963.
5. WALTHER, REGIS H. *The Psychological Dimensions of Work: An Experimental Taxonomy of Occupations.* An unpublished report to the U.S. Office of Education, Cooperative Research Project No. S-037, George Washington University, 1964. Pp. vi, 119. * (ERIC ED 003 075)
6. WALTHER, REGIS. *Orientations and Behavioral Styles of Foreign Service Officers.* Foreign Affairs Personnel Study No. 5. New York: Carnegie Foundation for International Peace, 1969. Pp. xv, 52. *
7. WALTHER, REGIS H., AND McCUNE, SHIRLEY D. "Juvenile Court Judges in the United States: Part 2, Working Styles and Characteristics." *Crime & Del* 11:384–93 O '65. *
8. WALTHER, REGIS H., AND McCUNE, SHIRLEY D. *Socialization Principles and Work Styles of the Juvenile Court: Goals for In-Service Training.* Washington, D.C.: Center for Behavioral Sciences, George Washington University, August 1965. Pp. xiii, 105. *
9. McCUNE, SHIRLEY DICKINSON. *An Exploratory Study of the Measured Behavioral Styles of Students in Five Schools of Social Work.* Doctor's thesis, Catholic University of America (Washington, D.C.), 1966. (*DA* 27:3123A)
10. LIPPITT, GORDON L., AND PETERSEN, PETER B. "Development of a Behavioral Style in Leadership Training: Combat Leadership Developed at Army Officer Candidate School." *Training & Develop* J 21:9–17 Jl '67. *
11. McCUNE, SHIRLEY D., AND MILLS, EDGAR W. *Continu-*

ing Education for Ministers: A Pilot Evaluation of Three Programs. Washington, D.C.: Ministry Studies Board, 1968. Pp. vi, 82. *
12. PETERSEN, PETER B., AND LIPPITT, GORDON L. "Comparison of Behavioral Styles Between Entering and Graduating Students in Officer Candidate School." *J Appl Psychol* 52:66–70 F '68. * (*PA* 42:6204)
13. TROJANOWICZ, ROBERT CHESTER. *A Comparison of the Behavioral Styles of Policemen and Social Workers.* Doctor's thesis, Michigan State University (East Lansing, Mich.), 1969. (*DAI* 30:2644A)
14. REEVES, EDGAR ALLEN, JR. *A Comparative Study of Behavioral Style as Measured by the Job Analysis Interest Measurement (JAIM) of Retired Adult Participation and Non-Participation in the Institute of Lifetime Learning, Washington, D.C.* Doctor's thesis, George Washington University (Washington, D.C.), 1970. (*DAI* 31:2093A)

[96]

★**Junior Eysenck Personality Inventory.** Ages 7–15; 1963–70; JEPI; downward extension of *Eysenck Personality Inventory;* 3 scores: extraversion, neuroticism, lie; 2 editions (identical except for 2 words and directions); postage extra; [15–20] minutes; Sybil B. G. Eysenck. *

a) AMERICAN EDITION. 1963–70; 1 form ('65, 3 pages); preliminary manual ('63, 11 pages); preliminary norms ['69–70, 2 sheets]; $4 per 25 tests; $1.50 per set of scoring stencils; $2.25 per specimen set; scoring service, 45¢ or less per test; Spanish edition available; Educational and Industrial Testing Service.

b) BRITISH EDITION. 1965; 1 form (4 pages); manual ['65, 16 pages]; 32½p per 20 tests; 15p per key; 15p per manual; 32½p per specimen set; University of London Press Ltd.

REFERENCES

1–7. See P:135.
8. LAUNGANI, D. "Personality and Verbal Conditioning." *Psychol Rep* 23:1134 D '68. * (*PA* 43:7720)
9. WATERS, THOMAS J. "The Validity of the Junior Eysenck Personality Inventory Lie Scale." *Ed & Psychol Meas* 28:1197–206 w '68. * (*PA* 44:6789)
10. ENTWISTLE, N. J., AND WELSH, JENNIFER. "Correlates of School Attainment at Different Ability Levels." *Brit J Ed Psychol* 39(1):57–63 F '69. * (*PA* 43:17988)
11. EYSENCK, H. J., AND COOKSON, D. "Personality in Primary School Children: 1, Ability and Achievement." *Brit J Ed Psychol* 39(2):109–22 Je '69. * (*PA* 44:6524)
12. EYSENCK, H. J., AND COOKSON, D. "Personality in Primary School Children: 2, Teachers' Ratings." *Brit J Ed Psychol* 39(2):123–30 Je '69. * (*PA* 44:6525)
13. EYSENCK, HANS J., AND EYSENCK, SYBIL B. G. *Personality Structure and Measurement.* San Diego, Calif.: Robert R. Knapp, Publisher, 1969. Pp. xiii, 365. *
14. EYSENCK, S. B. G. Chap. 21, "Personality Dimensions in Children," pp. 265–316. In *Personality Structure and Measurement,* see 13. *
15. FROST, BARRY P. "Extraversion and Educational Achievement." *West Psychologist* 1(1):5–18 S '69. * (*PA* 45:8976)
16. HALL, ERIC. "The Validity of the JEPI for ESN Children." *Brit J Social & Clin Psychol* 8(1):81–2 F '69. * (*PA* 43:8584)
17. SHEPHERD, JACQUELINE E. D. "Conformity and Personality: An Investigation Into the Relationship Between Conformity and Extraversion, Neuroticism, Attitude Toward Others, and Attitude Toward Self." *Papers Psychol* 3(1):36–8 Ap '69. *
18. COOKSON, D. "A Study of Difficulties in Reading and Understanding the Junior Eysenck Personality Inventory." *Brit J Ed Psychol* 40(1):8–14 F '70. * (*PA* 44:10446)
19. EYSENCK, H. J., AND COOKSON, D. "Personality in Primary School Children: 3, Family Background." *Brit J Ed Psychol* 40(2):117–31 Je '70. * (*PA* 44:20674)
20. EYSENCK, SYBIL B. G.; RUSSELL, T.; AND EYSENCK, H. J. "Extraversion, Intelligence, and Ability to Draw a Person." *Percept & Motor Skills* 30(3):925–6 Je '70. * (*PA* 44:16371)
21. FINLAYSON, D. S. "A Follow-Up Study of School Achievement in Relation to Personality." *Brit J Ed Psychol* 40(3):344–8 N '70. * (*PA* 45:706)
22. FROST, BARRY P. "A Note on Extraversion and Aggression." *West Psychologist* 1(3):111–2 My '70. * (*PA* 45:6313)
23. HARBISON, J. J. M. "The Relationship Between Two Children's Measures of Personality." *Brit J Social & Clin Psychol* 9(2):187–8 Je '70. * (*PA* 44:16712)
24. HOGHUGHI, M. S., AND FORREST, A. R. "Eysenck's Theory of Criminality: An Examination With Approved School Boys." *Brit J Criminol* 10(3):240–54 Jl '70. * (*PA* 46:1465)
25. STEWART, R. R.; WALKER, W.; AND SAVAGE, R. D. "A Developmental Study of Cognitive and Personality Character-

istics Associated With Haemolytic Disease of the Newborn."
Develop Med & Child Neurol 12(1):16–26 F '70. * (PA 44:
17249)
26. WILLIAMS, J. G. "Personality Factors and the Acquisi-
tioning of Swimming Skill." *Papers Psychol* 4(1–2):10–1 Ap–O
'70. *

MAURICE CHAZAN, *Senior Lecturer, Department of Education, University College of
Swansea, Swansea, Wales.*

The JEPI has the limited aim of measuring
two major personality dimensions in children,
extraversion/introversion and neuroticism/sta-
bility. Although the inventory does not claim
to probe deeply into a child's personality structure, it has already proved very useful to researchers and has been applied widely during
the last five years.

Split-half as well as test-retest reliability
coefficients are given in the manual, the test-
retest reliabilities (median .72) being somewhat
lower than the split-half coefficients. Reliability
tends to increase with age for extraversion,
somewhat less so for neuroticism. No claims
are made about the validity of the JEPI, though
the author hopes that further evidence will be
forthcoming on this following experimentation
with the scales.

The JEPI, in that it is the only British questionnaire personality test for children to have
undergone such rigorous standardisation, certainly merits experimental use on a wide scale,
even if estimates of a child's personality characteristics made on the basis of self-ratings must
be viewed with caution. The language employed
is clear and simple, though many of the questions are difficult to answer with a straightforward yes or no. In particular, the words
"often" and "sometimes" (frequently appearing in the questions) are likely to be interpreted
very differently by different respondents.
Younger children have special difficulties in
rating their own behaviour, in addition to which
Cookson (*18*) has shown, in an investigation
involving fourth-year junior school children,
that some of them cannot read or understand
a number of the items. He concludes that a
reading age of about 8 to 8½ years is probably
necessary for reading the inventory, and that
the understanding of the items is affected by
level of intelligence. He points out several items
which are particularly liable to misunderstanding. It is important, therefore, that reports of
studies using JEPI scores should give as much
detail as possible of the nature of the samples
used.

ROBERT D. WIRT, *Professor of Psychology,
Child Development and Psychiatry and Director, Graduate Education in Clinical Psychology,
University of Minnesota, Minneapolis, Minnesota.*

The *Junior Eysenck Personality Inventory* is
based on the extensive work of Hans Eysenck
and his colleagues. Eysenck's factor analytic
approach to the study of the adult personality
has led him to conclude that two essentially uncorrelated, higher order factors can account for
all of the clusters of human behavioral traits:
these are Extraversion (E) and Neuroticism
(N). Some have speculated that there may be
a smaller third factor of Psychoticism. Eysenck
has developed two widely used inventories to
assess these factors in adults, the *Maudsley Personality Inventory* and the *Eysenck Personality
Inventory*. A Lie (L) scale has been added to
each of these to determine the extent of faking.

The JEPI was designed to extend downward
Eysenck's method of personality measurement.
This was done by selecting items from the EPI,
rewriting some, and adding others. The 108
items, plus 16 Lie items, were administered to
two large samples of English children between
7 and 16 years old, and the results factor
analyzed. Only the first two factors, called E
and N, were considered further. Twenty-four
N, 24 E, and 12 L items were retained for the
final form of the JEPI.

The standardization procedures are well described in the manual, but a far more extensive
discussion is provided elsewhere (*14*). The
American edition contains data from one study
of 199 unselected public school children which
gives mean L scores well below those published
for English children and mean N scores well
above scores from both boys and girls studied
in England.

Several studies, using substantial samples,
have been conducted in England. These show
the test to have sufficient stability for use with
children above the age of 10. The data for 16-
year-olds are based on samples less representative of the general population than those from
younger age groups. If the JEPI does, in fact,
measure the same dimensions as the EPI, as it
appears to, the factors of E and N can be said
to be stable dimensions of personality from at
least age 10 into adulthood.

There is a fairly sizeable negative correlation
between N and L across ages, suggesting that
children with high L scores are attempting to

fake socially desirable scores. As has been found in studies of adults, E scores are higher for boys than girls, while N increases with age in girls and is generally higher than mean scores of boys. L decreases markedly with age.

The *New Junior Maudsley Inventory* and the *Junior Eysenck Personality Inventory* are very similar in item content, factor structure, and purposes for which they were designed. There seems little economic sense or scientific purpose in the development of two such similar instruments. The more extensive research and the more carefully designed standardization procedures suggest that the JEPI should be recommended for research use over the NJMI. Neither test has been given sufficient study using American children to recommend it for clinical use in the United States. The little research that has been reported here suggests that differences in scale score distributions will be found between normal groups in the two societies. If this is the case, then considerably more research will be required in both these and other countries using a variety of samples from different social groups.

In summary, the JEPI appears to have merit as an instrument for measuring E and N in children above the age of 10, but, as the author states, should be restricted to research use at this time.

Brit J Psychol 57:452–3 N '68. B. Semeonoff. * The published norms show, for E, a slight trend up and then down through the age range for both boys and girls; for N, an upward trend for girls and a downward trend for boys, with the boys' norms considerably lower than the girls', except at age 8. For the Lie scale there is a very marked downward trend for both sexes; at age 7 the mean L scores are as high as 9 for girls and 8 for boys. The status of the L scale seems in general to be rather dubious, since it shows substantial negative correlations (averaging over −0.3) with N. The implication that stable children tend to tell more lies is perhaps surprising: on the other hand, endorsement of the relevant items may indicate not lies but actual lower incidence of the behaviour in question among stable children. The interpretation would then be that stable children are slightly better behaved (or more priggish, if preferred) than those who score high in N. (A similar point is in fact made by the author in relation to observed negative correlations, at some ages, between L and E.) Split-half and test-retest reliabilities are quoted for all three scales, with a modal value of a little over 0.7. The position is least satisfactory for the E scale in the lower age ranges. This seems to confirm Mrs. Eysenck's suggestion, *à propos* of the factorial data, that the extraversion scale is of questionable applicability before the age of 9 or 10—the evidence indeed points to a still higher age. Face validity is nevertheless high; on empirical or predictive validity there are as yet no data. The Inventory is meantime offered "as an instrument for experimentation." It will no doubt prove valuable for large-scale research requiring groups of children graded on the relevant dimensions. Its potential usefulness in relation to the individual case is another matter; in particular, guidance on the handling of the Lie scale would have been welcome. The author concludes: "There is little need here to indicate the many ways in which a valid test of personality could help the educational psychologist as well as the clinical psychologist, both in his practical work and in the conduct of experiments; there are few areas of performance or behaviour where personality is not likely to be an important variable." This seems to imply a very narrow conception of variation in personality, one which goes little beyond a scaling of behaviour which would be very apparent to a psychologist who had in fact seen the child he was studying.

Occup Psychol 42:207 Ap–Jl '68. Gertrude H. Keir. * So far as validity is concerned, she [the author] is rightly cautious in discussing the use of the scale, other than as an instrument for experimentation. * Hence, at present it is clear that what is needed is intensive work with the inventory, and we must hope that further publications will yield information about the test as used not only with groups but with individual children presenting problems both in schools and clinics.

[97]

Jr.–Sr. High School Personality Questionnaire. Ages 12–18; 1953–69; HSPQ; 14 scores: reserved vs. warmhearted (A), dull vs. bright (B), affected by feelings vs. emotionally stable (C), undemonstrative vs. excitable (D), obedient vs. assertive (E), sober vs. enthusiastic (F), disregards rules vs. conscientious (G), shy vs. adventurous (H), tough-minded vs. tender-minded (I), zestful vs. circumspect individualism (J), self-assured vs. apprehensive (O), sociably group-dependent vs. self-sufficient (Q_2), uncontrolled vs. controlled (Q_3), relaxed vs. tense (Q_4); 2 editions; (40–50) minutes per form.

a) IPAT EDITION. 1953–69; Forms A, B, C, D, ('68, 8 pages, authors recommend administration of 2 or more forms) ; manual ('68, 16 pages) ; handbook ('69, 90 pages) ; profile ('68, 1 page) ; tentative norms ('68–'69, 6 pages) ; separate answer sheets (hand scored, Digitek) must be used ; $5.10 per 25 tests ; $3 per 50 hand scored answer sheets ; $3.50 per 50 hand scored answer-profile sheets ; $4 per 50 Digitek answer sheets ; $2.50 per 50 profiles ; $2.10 per scoring stencil ; 50¢ per tentative norms ; 60¢ per manual ; $5 per handbook ($7.50 hardbound) ; $4 per specimen set (without handbook) ; postage extra ; Digitek scoring service, 80¢ or less per test ($20 minimum) ; computer interpretation service, $4 or less per subject ($20 minimum) ; Raymond B. Cattell and Mary D. L. Cattell ; Institute for Personality and Ability Testing. *
b) BOBBS-MERRILL EDITION. 1958–60 ; Forms A, B, ('60, 8 pages, identical with out of print 1958 IPAT edition except for format, title, and directions) ; manual ('60, 24 pages) ; norms supplement ('60, 4 pages, identical with 1958 IPAT edition except for format and title) ; profile ('60, 1 page) ; separate answer sheets must be used ; $6.40 per 35 tests ; $2.80 per 35 answer-profile sheets ; 70¢ per scoring stencil ; $1.25 per manual and norms supplement ; $1.50 per specimen set ; Raymond B. Cattell, Richard W. Coan, and Halla Beloff ; Bobbs-Merrill Co., Inc. *

REFERENCES

1–4. See 5:72.
5–21. See 6:131.
22–51. See P:136, also includes a cumulative name index to the first 51 references for this test.
52. GALLIANI, CONO A. *Personality Factors Associated With Age-Mate Role and Status Designation.* Doctor's thesis, University of Texas (Austin, Tex.), 1960. (*DA* 21:124)
53. PITMAN, ARCHIE LEE. *Deception on Self-Scored Tests as a Function of Immediate, Background, and Residual Stimulus Factors.* Doctor's thesis, University of Texas (Austin, Tex.), 1960. (*DA* 20:4589)
54. D'ANGELO, RITA YVONNE. *An Evaluation of Group Psychotherapy With Institutionalized Delinquent Girls.* Doctor's thesis, Fordham University (New York, N.Y.), 1961. (*DA* 23:306)
55. McGUIRE, CARSON ; HINDSMAN, EDWIN ; KING, F. J. ; AND JENNINGS, EARL. "Dimensions of Talented Behavior." *Ed & Psychol Meas* 21:3–38 sp '61. * (*PA* 36:1KH03M)
56. TUKEY, RUTH SCHWEIGERT. *A Study of Differences Found Between Intellectually-Oriented and Socially-Oriented Superior Girls.* Doctor's thesis, Michigan State University (East Lansing, Mich.), 1961. (*DA* 22:4278)
57. CATTELL, R. B. ; YOUNG, H. BOUTOURLINE ; AND HUNDLEBY, J. D. "Blood Groups and Personality Traits." *Am J Hum Genetics* 16:397–402 D '64. * (*PA* 39:8006) [Correction of 25]
58. MITTMAN, HOWARD. *The Adjustment of Twins: An Evaluation of the Relationship Between Twinship, Patterns of Identification, and Adjustment.* Doctor's thesis, Yeshiva University (New York, N.Y.), 1964. (*DA* 25:3678)
59. BELLENGER, MARY ELLEN. *A Study of Prediction of Delinquent Behavior.* Doctor's thesis, University of Washington (Seattle, Wash.), 1965. (*DA* 27:105A)
60. DEZELLE, WALTER, JR. *A Comparative Study of the Changes in Personality in Academically Able Seventh-Grade Children Assigned or Not Assigned to an Accelerated Class in Mathematics Upon Entering Junior High School.* Doctor's thesis, University of Houston (Houston, Tex.), 1965. (*DA* 26:4438)
61. MILLER, DORIS KOTEEN. *A Study of Differences Between Auditory and Visual Learners in Respect to Extraversion-Introversion.* Doctor's thesis, New York University (New York, N.Y.), 1965. (*DA* 26:4078)
62. CATTELL, R. B. ; SEALY, A. P. ; AND SWENEY, A. B. "What Can Personality and Motivation Source Trait Measurements Add to the Prediction of School Achievement?" *Brit J Ed Psychol* 36:280–95 N '66. * (*PA* 41:804)
63. FLAX, MORTON LEWIS. *The Stability of Relationships Between Creativity and Personality Variables.* Doctor's research study No. 1, Colorado State College (Greeley, Colo.), 1966. (*DA* 27:2857B)
64. O'BRIEN, CAROL KATHLEEN. *The Relationship Between Personality and Attitude Toward Physical Activity.* Master's thesis, University of Wisconsin (Madison, Wis.), 1966.
65. REID, WALTER BROOK. *Some Aspects of Personality in Persistent Enuresis as Determined by Responses to Psychological Tests and to Drug Therapy.* Doctor's thesis, University of Houston (Houston, Tex.), 1966. (*DA* 27:1629B)

66. BOYLES, GARY EUGENE. *Psycho-Social Variables Related to Four Categories of School Persistence in a Rural County: Graduates and Potential Graduates, and Dropouts and Potential Dropouts.* Doctor's thesis, University of North Dakota (Grand Forks, N.D.), 1967. (*DA* 28:1673A)
67. CARDON, BARTELL W., AND ZURICH, GEORGE T. "Personality Characteristics of High School Dropouts of High Ability," pp. 4–10. In *Selected Convention Papers: 45th International CEC Convention, St. Louis, Missouri, 1967.* Washington, D.C.: Council for Exceptional Children, National Education Association, [1967]. Pp. ix, 285. *
68. CARLSON, LESTER ALVIN. *The Relationship of Delinquent Types of an Industrial School Setting to Personality-Motivation Profiles.* Doctor's thesis, Utah State University (Logan, Utah), 1967. (*DA* 29:1446A)
69. MEHROTRA, K. K. "Item-Analysis of the Hindi Version of Jr.–Sr. High School Personality Questionnaire." *Manas* 14(1):37–41 '67. * (*PA* 42:6386)
70. STAVELEY, BRYAN. *The Abilities and Interests of Craft and Technician Students of Mechanical Engineering.* Master's thesis, University of Manchester (Manchester, England), 1967. (Abstract: *Brit J Ed Psychol* 38:324)
71. CATTELL, RAYMOND B., AND BUTCHER, H. J. *The Prediction of Achievement and Creativity,* pp. 181–200, passim. Indianapolis, Ind.: Bobbs-Merrill Co., Inc., 1968. Pp. xiv, 386. *
72. CREW, JOHN LOWERY, SR. *An Investigation of Personality Profile Congruence Between Pupil and Teacher as a Predictor of Course Achievement.* Doctor's thesis, University of Maryland (College Park, Md.), 1968. (*DA* 29:1447A)
73. EDWARDS, ARTHUR B. *An Analysis of the Creative Ability Levels of the Potential Dropout in the Average Mental Ability Range.* Doctor's thesis, University of Tennessee (Knoxville, Tenn.), 1968. (*DA* 29:3828A)
74. HICKS, JOHN SHAVOR. *Introversion and Extraversion and Their Ralationship to Academic Achievement Among Emotionally Disturbed Children.* Doctor's thesis, Columbia University (New York, N.Y.), 1968. (*DA* 29:3462A)
75. PEARCE, CLIFFORD. "Creativity in Young Science Students." *Excep Children* 35:121–6 O '68. * (*PA* 44:9353)
76. REPLOGLE, JAMES ROBERT. *The Relation of Teacher-Pupil Profile Pattern Similarities on Measures of Interest and Personality to Grades and Perceived Compatibility.* Doctor's thesis, Lehigh University (Bethlehem, Pa.), 1968. (*DA* 29:1426A)
77. WICHIARAJOTE, NUANPEN KOSOLSRETH. *A Cross-Cultural Study of Societal Values and Personality of Thai and American Adolescents.* Doctor's thesis, University of Illinois (Urbana, Ill.), 1968. (*DAI* 30:179A)
78. BELL, DAVID BRUCE. *The Motivational and Personality Factors in Reading Retardation Among Two Racial Groups of Adolescent Males.* Doctor's thesis, Texas Technological University (Lubbock, Tex.), 1969. (*DAI* 31:909B)
79. BUTCHER, H. J. "The Structure of Abilities, Interests and Personality in 1,000 Scottish School Children." *Brit J Ed Psychol* 39(2):154–65 Je '69. * (*PA* 44:7217)
80. BUTCHER, H. J., AND PONT, H. B. "Predicting Arts and Science Specialisation in a Group of Scottish Secondary School Children: Some Preliminary Results." *Scottish Ed Studies* 1(3):3–10 Je '69. *
81. HAMILTON, DOROTHY DEE HOWE. *A Comparison of School Achievement, Teachers' Ratings, Self-Ratings, and a Personality Score as Predictors of Creative Thinking Potential.* Doctor's thesis, University of Nebraska (Lincoln, Neb.), 1969. (*DAI* 30:2905A)
82. JACOBS, JAMES ROGER. *Characteristics of Students Who Seek Counseling.* Doctor's thesis, University of Wisconsin (Madison, Wis.), 1969. (*DAI* 30:5238A)
83. KOENIG, FRANCES BECKER. *Comparative Analysis of Selected Personal and Social Background Characteristics of High School Girls at Three Levels of Participation in Basketball.* Doctor's thesis, Michigan State University (East Lansing, Mich.), 1969. (*DAI* 30:2361A)
84. LESSING, ELISE E., AND ZAGORIN, SUSAN W. "Some Demographic, Value, and Personality Correlates of Endorsement of Negro Militancy by Negro and White Youth." Abstract. *Proc 77th Ann Conv Am Psychol Assn* 4(1):295–6 '69. * (*PA* 43:17267)
85. MARTIN, D. N., AND CLARKE, R. V. G. "The Personality of Approved School Boy Absconders." *Brit J Criminol* 9(4):366–75 O '69. * (*PA* 44:8825)
86. PURCELL, K. ; MUSER, J. ; MIKLICH, D. ; AND DIETIKER, K. E. "A Comparison of Psychologic Findings in Variously Defined Asthmatic Subgroups." *J Psychosom Res* 13(1):67–75 Mr '69. * (*PA* 44:3896)
87. RICHARD, WAYNE C. ; MATES, CATHERINE G. ; AND WHITTEN, LAURA. "Personality Traits and Attitudes of Adolescent Girls With Behavior Disorders." *Correct Psychiatry & J Social Ther* 15(2):34–44 su '69. *
88. STERN, HERBERT, AND GROSZ, HANUS J. "H.S.P.Q. Personality Measurements of Institutionalized Delinquent Girls and Their Temporal Stability." *J Clin Psychol* 25(3):289–92 Jl '69. * (*PA* 44:3832)
89. SWAFFORD, JANE OLIVER. *A Study of the Relationship Between Personality and Achievement in Mathematics.* Doctor's thesis, University of Georgia (Athens, Ga.), 1969. (*DAI* 30:5353A)
90. VERBERNE, T. J. P. "The Personality Traits of Tattooed

Adolescent Offenders." *Brit J Criminol* 9(2):172–5 Ap '69. *
(*PA* 44:872)

91. WERNER, EMMY E., AND BACHTOLD, LOUISE M. "Personality Factors of Gifted Boys and Girls in Middle Childhood and Adolescence." *Psychol Sch* 6(2):177–82 Ap '69. * (*PA* 43:14130)

92. WOLDT, ANSEL LUVERNE. *Selected Characteristics of Senior High School Students Having Differential Counseling Referral Status.* Doctor's thesis, University of North Dakota (Grand Forks, N.D.), 1969. (*DAI* 30:1408A)

93. AHAMMER, INGE M., AND SCHAIE, K. WARNER. "Age Differences in the Relationship Between Personality Questionnaire Factors and School Achievement." *J Ed Psychol* 61(3): 193–7 Je '70. * (*PA* 44:13364)

94. CATTELL, RAYMOND B.; WAGNER, ANKA; AND CATTELL, MARY D. "Adolescent Personality Structure, in Q-Data, Checked in the High School Personality Questionnaire." *Brit J Psychol* 61(1):39–54 F '70. * (*PA* 44:8229)

95. DUNN, JOHN PATTERSON. *The Relationship Between Strength and Selected Social and Personality Factors.* Doctor's thesis, Texas A & M University (College Station, Tex.), 1970. (*DAI* 31:3318A)

96. McQUAID, JOHN. "A Personality Profile of Delinquent Boys in Scottish Approved Schools." *Brit J Criminol* 10(2): 147–57 Ap '70. * (*PA* 44:16951)

97. MAYCOCK, GEORGE ALBERT. *Emotional, Social, and Academic Adjustment of the Mentally Retarded as Related to Socio-Economic Level.* Doctor's thesis, Texas Technological University (Lubbock, Tex.), 1970. (*DAI* 31:3375A)

98. MOORE, JEAN TILMAN. *Personality Variables Between Selected Female High School Interscholastic Sports Participants.* Master's thesis, Springfield College (Springfield, Mass.), 1970.

99. MUSHIER, CAROLE LUCILLE. *A Cross-Sectional Study of the Personality Factors of Girls and Women in Competitive Lacrosse.* Doctor's thesis, University of Southern California (Los Angeles, Calif.), 1970. (*DAI* 31:635A)

100. PIERSON, GEORGE RAYMOND. *The High School Personality Questionnaire as a Delinquency Proneness Assessment Instrument.* Doctor's thesis, University of Oregon (Eugene, Ore.), 1970. (*DAI* 31:2964B)

101. ROBINSON, LISA. *Marihuana Use in High School Girls: A Psycho-Social Case Study.* Doctor's thesis, University of Maryland (College Park, Md.), 1970. (*DAI* 31:2196A)

102. RUSSO, WILLIAM J. *Relationship Between Dogmatism and Academic Achievement Among Male Academic High School Students.* Doctor's thesis, St. John's University (Jamaica, N.Y.), 1970. (*DAI* 31:2966B)

103. SHETTERLY, HENRY TITUS. *Self and Social Perceptions and Personal Characteristics of a Group of Suburban High School Marijuana Users.* Doctor's thesis, University of Denver (Denver, Colo.), 1970. (*DAI* 31:3279A)

104. WHITE, WILLIAM F., AND PORTER, THOMAS L. "Multivariate Analysis of Attitudes and Personality Characteristics Among 60 Youthful Offenders." *Psychol Rep* 26(2):487–91 Ap '70. * (*PA* 44:21224)

ROBERT HOGAN, *Assistant Professor of Psychology, The Johns Hopkins University, Baltimore, Maryland.* [Review of the IPAT Edition.]

The HSPQ was developed to assess "all of the more adequately research-demonstrated dimensions of personality" in the 12 to 18 age range. This 1969 version is the third edition of the test—the first appeared in 1953 and the second in 1963. The new form contains three modifications (in addition to new statndardization norms). First, item responses are now trichotomous (e.g.: a. yes; b. perhaps; c. no) rather than dichotomous, a change which should reduce subject resistance. Second, some items have been revised toward briefer statements phrased in more contemporary language. Third, the test is now available in four forms rather than two, a feature which researchers will find attractive. The answer sheet is neatly constructed so that all 14 scales may be scored with two keys in 2 or 3 minutes. Scoring services are

also available, as well as machine-produced profile interpretations and scores for several regression equations previously developed by the test's author.

The HSPQ was designed to measure 12 of the 16 factors appearing on Cattell's *Sixteen Personality Factor Questionnaire*. However, in in the sample used to develop the original form of the HSPQ, only 7 of 12 factors could be "unambiguously" matched with variables on the 16PF, and the average correlation for these 7 factors was .48. In a more recent comparison of the two tests, Goodwin, et al (*32*) observe, "There does not appear to be a consistent comparability between the scales common to the HSPQ and the 16PF. The correlations....range from .03 to .71 with most of the values hovering around .3 and .4, quite low considering the rationale for developing the articulated inventories."

Cattell maintains that the dimensions of the HSPQ have been replicated or confirmed by other psychologists. Anastasi,[1] on the other hand, remarks that, "Despite the extensive research conducted by Cattell and his associates over more than twenty years, the traits proposed by Cattell must be regarded as tentative." Both Cattell and Anastasi may be overstating the case. While all 14 dimensions have not been repeatedly confirmed, five of the HSPQ scales (E, A, G, C, and B—dominance, agreeableness, dependability, emotional stability, and intelligence) are certainly well accepted. (The other, perhaps less universal, dimensions are: excitability, D; surgency, F; shyness, H; toughmindedness, I; individualism, J; self-confidence, O; self-sufficiency, Q2; self-control, Q3; and tenseness, Q4.) Cattell also states that the dimensions of the HSPQ have *functional unity*. This assertion is puzzling in view of the fact that interscale correlations range from −.78 to +.69 for boys, and −.79 to +.79 for girls. Comparable figures for the *California Psychological Inventory*, a test constructed with little concern for scale independence, are −.30 and +.72 for boys, −.26 and +.78 for girls.

Because each scale contains only ten items, reliability is a problem. Over a one-year interval, the average test-retest reliability for 14 scales of one form of the test was .49. Using two forms of the test over the same interval, the average reliability was .63, prompting Cat-

[1] ANASTASI, ANNE. *Psychological Testing, Third Edition,* p. 451. New York: Macmillan Co., 1968. Pp. xiii, 665. *

tell to recommend that one form be used only under "dire necessity."

Cattell distinguishes between *relevance,* the correlation between a scale and "important, practical, concrete criteria," and *concept validity,* a scale's correlation with the pure factor it is supposed to measure. While recognizing the importance of non-test correlates, Cattell maintains nonetheless that the "scales stand or fall by their concept validity." Thus the HSPQ manual offers few correlations between the scales and external criteria.

The manual presents a wealth of material of varying degrees of importance. Test interpreters will find the extensive section on the psychological meaning of the scales quite helpful. Ample information is provided concerning sex differences and age changes. There is also a section describing the use of the HSPQ to predict complex behavioral patterns such as academic achievement, delinquency, neuroticism, creativity, popularity, and leadership. Unfortunately, with the exception of school achievement, no correlations are provided to indicate the size of the relationships mentioned in this section. Nor does there seem to be much value in Cattell's discussion of such topics as the "computer synthesis" procedure for variance re-allocation to enhance the validity of particular scales on the HSPQ. The manual contains no information about the relationships between the HSPQ and other personality and interest measures. Finally, and more curiously, 100 of the 212 references cited in the manual are either unpublished or available only through Cattell himself.

In summary the HSPQ provides a convenient and easy-to-use measure of 14 aspects of personality. The convenience, however, is not without its costs. Information derived from the test seems to represent only overt self-description; the reliability of the scales is modest, and their validity is indeterminate. Thus, while personality researchers in the factor analytic tradition may find the test useful, teachers and guidance counselors unschooled in Cattell's conceptual frame of reference may not.

Douglas N. Jackson, *Senior Professor of Psychology, The University of Western Ontario, London, Ontario, Canada.* [Review of the IPAT Edition.]

The HSPQ is a modification of most of the variables of personality contained in the adult 16PF to a form appropriate for adolescents. Two of the variables, D (Phlegmatic temperament vs. Excitability) and J ("Zeppia" vs. "Coasthenia"), do not appear in the 16PF, while four additional variables have been included in the 16PF but not in the HSPQ: L (Suspiciousness, Paranoia), M (Bohemianism, Hysterical Unconcern), N (Shrewdness), and Q1 (Radicalism vs. Conservatism). There are four forms available, each comprised of 142 items (ten items for each of the 14 scales, plus two filler items). The 1969 edition is similar to the earlier editions in terms of the number of forms available (four), the number of scales (14), the number of items per form (142), and the number of items per scale (10); the major differences are the scale revisions and the new norms.

In spite of the fact that this is not a new test, and that previous reviewers have called attention to serious inadequacies in the presentation of data, particularly validity data, reported for the earlier edition, one cannot help but be disappointed in this case by the negligible effect these reviews appear to have had upon the author in preparing a revision. This is especially true because the author is hardly ignorant of the issues involved.

The primary positive features of the test include Cattell's well-known supporting program of factor analytic work; an easy-to-read test booklet, with clear, concise directions regarding administration; and an easy-to-use scoring template.

The less than adequate features of the test include many omissions, ambiguities, and potentially misleading practices in the reporting of pertinent data in the HSPQ handbook. Its advertising brochure states it is "considerably more than the usual handbook accompanying a test; it is a description and compilation of the practical applications of basic research on personality at the junior-senior high school age-levels (12 to 18). Studded with 51 easy-to-read tables and 18 diagrams, all pertinent and useful in working with teen-agers, the HSPQ handbook will be of particular interest to counselors and guidance workers, teachers, principals, school and clinical psychologists, etc., both for guidance and research." But the average teacher or guidance counselor is ill-prepared to wade through a handbook which asks him to distinguish between "factor validity" and "factor trueness," of comprehending computer synthesis of weights derived from factor analysis, or of properly evaluating the authors' idiosyncratic and deceptive use of the term "validity." Clearly, this is not a test for the nonspecialist to apply in practical settings. The nature of its subject matter (personality), the technical inadequacies and omissions in the handbook, and the relative sophistication required properly to evaluate the authors' unsupported and often unsupportable assertions regarding the test, suggest that it should be used if at all only by test specialists, and only for research purposes.

A comprehensive discussion of all the frequently moot points raised by the authors in the handbook would require a very long review indeed, but some highlights are warranted. The authors assert that one of the prerequisites for a good test (which by implication apply to the HSPQ) is that it covers "*all* the major dimensions factor-analytically demonstrable in any attempt to describe individual differences comprehensively." Even a casual review of the literature reveals that there are a great number of demonstrable factors not incorporated into the HSPQ. It is by no means clear how one could establish such exhaustiveness, except, as the authors have done, by fiat. Presumably, traits not included in the HSPQ are not major dimensions.

One must also accept on faith most of the authors' assertions regarding the manner in which the test was constructed. A number of principles purportedly followed in construction of the HSPQ are outlined. These highlight care in item selection as exemplified by choosing only items loaded on a given factor, in counterbalancing irrelevant factor variance, or seeking subtlety in item content, in seeking external validity for scales, or avoiding response biases, or distributing valid items among all four forms, and in seeking the highest possible reliability consistent with short scales. No data are reported on the number of items analyzed by factor analysis or otherwise, and how many, if any, were rejected, whether by statistical or impressionistic criteria, or otherwise. In spite of the implication that the test was developed by factor analysis of items, no publication explicitly reporting data on a factor analysis of item relationships of HSPQ items has appeared, nor does the handbook state unequivocally that this has ever been done. The fact that each edition of the test has involved substantial changes of individual items suggests that item selection has been continuing, but no report

explicitly outlining the process is available. Indeed, on more than one occasion, Cattell has written rather contemptuously of item analysis. The notion that unwanted variance can be suppressed by counterbalancing items with certain irrelevant loadings with others having negative loadings with the irrelevant factors is an interesting theoretical proposal, but one which would be difficult to put into practice. No data are reported showing to what extent this was accomplished. Because items substantially loading a single factor will tend to correlate in the same direction with other factors, the possibility of demonstrating such effects is greatly increased with items having small relevant factor saturations. One would either have to begin with a prodigious number of items or be content with very poor ones. One can only guess at which, if either, of these alternatives was followed. To the extent that subtlety is achieved in a personality test, the price paid is ordinarily in terms of reliability and content saturation. If scales are to be short, as they are on the HSPQ, it is likely that homogeneity will be low, a fact borne out in the HSPQ homogeneity data. To achieve personality scales substantially free from the correlated irrelevancies of response biases is a laudable aim. This is best accomplished at the level of item analysis and scale construction. An obvious proposal within the factor analytic tradition is to identify factors for desirability responding, acquiescence, defensiveness, and extremity bias, and to seek to suppress these in scale construction. Instead, the only control for biases is the reported counterbalancing of "yes" and "no" alternatives in the *final* scales. It is not clear whether or not this counterbalancing was incorporated in any previous item analysis work. As for desirability, the authors argue that it is complex, and it "would be a mistake deliberately to eliminate desirability or acquiescence dimensions as such, completely, by statistical or test design allowances." But to the extent that these influences are test specific and invalid, they spuriously contribute to factor scores and to reliability, they serve as a source of error in the interpretation of individual scores, and because they cause test scores to intercorrelate for reasons other than those due to trait covariation, they detract from convergent and discriminant validity. Notwithstanding arguments regarding the possible empirical validity of certain response biases, their presence detracts from construct validity. As for faking, or what the authors term "Role Distortion," it is recommended that the nine scales on which shifts have occurred at one time or another between anonymous and "fake good" instructions be used to form a "Role Distortion Scale," although no norms for this purpose are provided in the handbook and the practitioner would be hard-pressed to follow the authors' recommendation of "taking the regression of the RD scale on the....factors which shift from distortion, and calculating from the given individual's RD score how much he is likely to have shifted on them." Putting such a practice into effect would not be consistent with the authors' view that a portion of this variance is valid. The authors are in error both in equating at one point faking and desirability, as these have repeatedly been shown to define different, although correlated, factors, and, on the basis of the faking data, to conclude that social desirability effects are not very dependable. The recommended check on random responding, of seeking evidence for an attenuation of homogeneity is not feasible with a single form, because the split-half reliabilities, ranging from .20 to .43, are already so low that a great many "false-positive" random responders would be uncovered by such a practice, as indeed, they have been demonstrated to be with the 16PF.

This very modest homogeneity of single scales, and the modest equivalent form correlations (range .27 to .50 for Forms A and B) are among the most serious technical inadequacies of the test. The authors argue that the homogeneities are *optimum,* implying that if they were higher, the scales might lack generalizability. This is specious reasoning; such concern is misplaced in this case. Like the attenuation paradox, serious lack of generalizability occurs at the upper ranges of homogeneity, ranges not even approached by single HSPQ scales. The simple fact is that a person taking Form A might get a very different score on the same factor than he would had he taken Form B. For individual assessment, there can be no justification for administering a single form of a test whose median "equivalent" form reliability is below .50. If predictions are made, or inferences drawn regarding his location on an underlying factor, an intolerable degree of error is present for most types of decisions. The user is cautioned in the handbook about this problem. He should reduce his test to a

single form "only under the most dire necessity," that normally, he should use two forms, preferably four. But even with two forms, the estimates of (corrected) parallel form equivalence are low, ranging from .43 to .67. One cannot estimate internal consistency reliability or stability with four forms, as no such data are given regarding Forms C and D. These data (as well as a variety of other data) are promised in future editions of the manual. The practice of publishing a test form prior to making data available about it is, to say the least, not a desirable test practice. Incidentally, it is not entirely clear how much of the reported data bear upon the present Forms A and B, or upon earlier editions. Neither is it clear how present forms differ from earlier ones. The published studies in the handbook reference list bearing on the HSPQ go back several years. A number of references are listed as "in preparation," which are, of course, not references at all.

Perhaps the most serious shortcoming in the handbook is the authors' deceptive misuse of the concept of validity in reporting test data. Modern treatments of validity, such as that of Campbell and Fiske, emphasize *heteromethod* validity, and place little stock in correlations between equivalent forms or similar methods of measurement as bearing critically on validity. The only correlational values listed in the handbook purporting to reflect validity are contaminated with common method variance, and are so inflated by the application of inappropriate statistical procedures as to make a mockery of the concept of validity as it has evolved in the twentieth century. In Table 6 Cattell and Cattell report on the multiple correlations between items in each scale and factors defined by the total scores of the scales for two forms and for one form. Values reported will appear high as "validity" estimates to the casual observer. But these values are inflated by virtue of: (a) the fact that they are part-whole correlations, reflecting linear dependence and correlated error, as well as variance due to common traits; (b) the property of the unreplicated multiple correlation to capitalize on chance; and (c) spurious inflation due to method variance. Similarly in Table 7, the authors take the square root of the equivalent form and split-half homogeneity coefficients as an estimate of "direct" validity. The square root of the value for the reliability is used in formulas in which correlations are corrected for attenuation, or, equivalently, for the denominator in the formula for estimating the correlation of the true score on a test with a criterion. These are *theoretical* values, reflecting the validity a test would have if all measurement errors were eliminated. Even as theoretical estimates, they have no place in a test manual as reflections of "validity," particularly when they merely reflect an inflated function of the reliability. The citation of Cureton as an authority in the use of the square root of the reliability as an estimate for validity is in error. He was dealing with stepped-up estimates of reliability, for longer tests. The authors also report a "computer synthesis" in which all scores on the HSPQ are used to estimate each factor by multiple correlational procedures. These values again are presented as validities, and invite the same criticisms as those directed at Table 7. In addition, the use of the multiple correlation will have the effect of increasing the correlations among the obtained scale scores, and thus will have a lowered level of convergent and discriminant validity for predicting factor-relevant criteria. The use of the "computer synthesis" procedures as described is improperly termed validity.

The authors present a number of what are purported to be factor loadings for each of the scales, but one cannot determine if these are obtained empirically from the studies, estimated on theoretical grounds, or some combination of the two. Citations to factor analytic studies are to studies done with young children and adults, and not with adolescents. Without pertinent data on current forms of the HSPQ, these factors can at best only be considered suggestive. Correlations between test scores (Table 28b) for all four forms vary over a wide range, but many are too high to justify considering the scales as independent factors. Considering only the highest absolute correlation for each scale with a second scale, these values range for males from .22 to .78, with a median of .58, hardly a sufficient degree of factorial purity to warrant the use of the term, "factor."

In summary, the HSPQ is perhaps characteristic of personality tests as they existed three decades ago. In spite of the solid contributions of the senior author to many areas of psychology, the HSPQ is, by contemporary standards, poorly crafted: its development, in spite of a lengthy handbook, is inadequately reported, with poor levels of homogeneity and scale equiv-

alence; evidence of validity is inadequate and misleading; and unwarranted claims are made for its utility. Other than for purely research applications, its use cannot be justified on the basis of data presented in the handbook or manual.

For reviews by C. J. Adcock and Philip E. Vernon of the 1958 IPAT and the 1960 Bobbs-Merrill Editions, see 6:131.

[98]

★**The Lüscher Color Test.** Adults; 1947–69; LCT; an 8-color patch version (also called *Short Lüscher Test*) of the 73-color patch *Full Lüscher Test* available in German edition only; a personality test sold through bookstores for self-administration or administration to others; individual; 1 form (no date, 8 color cards); manual ('69, 187 pages); no data on reliability and validity; $6.95 per manual, postage extra; (5–8) minutes; translated and edited by Ian A. Scott; Max Lüscher; Random House, Inc. *

S. G. LEE, *Professor of Psychology and Head of the Department, The University of Leicester, Leicester, England.*

Your reviewer's initial introduction to this test was in the pages of a newspaper color supplement—a most appropriate context.

Briefly, the subject is asked, twice, to place in order of preference, eight colors. This simple act will reveal to the trained user the subject's conscious and unconscious motives, glandular state, and subjective life situation. This, essentially, is the claim of the author. It is, I think, completely unjustified by fact. The "theory" underlying the test is credulous, simplistic, and anecdotal in the extreme: "Hundreds of thousands of snails gave their lives so that a Roman emperor could wear his robe of Tyrian purple while his subjects had to be content with unbleached cotton or linen, hides or wool," and "The sugar manufacturer knows, for example, that he must not try to sell his product in a green package, while beauty preparations in a brown jar will remain on the shelf long after others have gone."

"Experiments" purporting to show relationships between color and personality are cited, giving very odd results, but no adequate references are given in the text to enable the truth of these assertions to be checked. The manual is full of spurious "psychophysiology": "In this case, a preference for one color and a dislike for another means something definite and reflects an existing state of mind, of glandular balance, or of both." Or, "The heartbeat, for example, normally occurs at a rate kept within certain bounds by the balance struck between these two branches of the autonomic nervous systetm; but under the influence of physical (e.g., exertion, effort) or emotional (e.g., fear, anger, excitement) effects, the sympathetic system will override the parasympathetic and the heartbeat will speed up."

There is, too, some very questionable developmental psychology—for example, "A newly born child developing the ability to 'see' begins by being able to distinguish contrast, that is: 'brightness' and 'darkness'; next comes the ability to distinguish movement, and after that shape and form. The recognition of color is the last development of all." Or, again: "Color vision is similarly related to both educated and primitive brain, as was shown by Becker in 1953, when he proved that a network of nerve fibers led directly from a nucleus in the retina to the midbrain (mesencephalon) and to the pituitary system."

It is claimed by the author that defective color vision or even actual color blindness does not affect the validity of the *Lüscher Color Test* "since the acceptability of a particular color is somatically (from Greek 'soma,' body; somatic therefore means 'having to do with the body') related to the degree to which anabolism or catabolism is needed by the organism. If it is psychically or physically in need of emotional peace, physical regeneration and release from tension or stress, then the instinctive response will be to choose the darker colors. If the organism needs to dissipate energy by outgoing activity or in mental creativeness, then the instinctive response will be for the brighter colors." No adequate proof of any kind is offered for these wild and woolly beliefs, indeed most of the references to the past successes of the test have a *demi-mondaine* air of pseudo-psychology.

The claims made for the test are sweeping and grandiose. The test protocol, resulting from putting in order of preference a series of colours, "affords a wealth of information concerning the conscious and unconscious psychological structure of the individual, areas of psychic stress, the state of glandular balance or imbalance, and much physiological information of great value either to the physician or to the psychotherapist."

Another example of an unsupported claim is: "Physicians in Europe use this....test as a useful aid to diagnosis, since it has been found that such stresses show up in the Lüscher Test often long before their physiological results make themselves evident; in this, the test provides them with an incomparable 'early warning system' of stress ailments in their early stages—ailments such as cardiac malfunction, cerebral attack or disorders of the gastro-intestinal tract."

Because, in the nature of things, any rank order has certain mathematical properties, the test lends itself to quite complex jiggery-pokery in its "scoring." Despite intriguing headings such as "The Significance of the Eight Positions," your reviewer does not find the essentially fortune-telling approach convincing nor does he find impressive the "cook-book" list of color meanings. We learn, for example, that "Blue-green *represents* Elasticity of Will," *is* "Concentric, Passive, Defensive, Autonomous, Retentive, Possessive, Immutable, and that its affective aspects are Persistence, Self-assertion, Obstinacy, Self-esteem."

Interpretations are, throughout, psychomantic in type, on such bases as "Yellow corresponds symbolically to the welcoming warmth of sunlight, to the aspirational halo round the Holy Grail, to the Cheerful spirit and to happiness. Its sensory perception is piquancy, its emotional content is hopeful volatility, and its organs are the sympathetic and parasympathetic nervous systems," and are couched in typically fortune-telling terms—*vide* these, taken at random: "Inclined to luxuriate in things which give gratification to the senses, but rejects anything tasteless, vulgar or coarse." "Feels neglected, desiring greater security, warm affection and fewer problems." "Needs greater security and a more affectionate environment." "Hopes to obtain an improved position and greater prestige."

This reviewer has tried, by the use of quotations, to let the test "speak for itself" and any reputable psychologists are bound to share his doubts as to whether such an invaluable reference work as the MMY should have to concern itself with such disingenuous balderdash. On balance it is probably a good thing that humane and scientific psychology should have the opportunity of inspecting such an insult to the human psyche, pondering, and then utterly rejecting it.

Cont Psychol 15(10):648–9 O '70. Bernard I. Murstein. * The test is taken by shuffling eight color cards and then establishing an order of preference for the cards, followed a few minutes later by another choosing. * The test's rationale is very briefly described in a few pages, the bulk of the text containing information on how to score and interpret the varying resulting patterns. A bibliography regarding the test is given, but most of the references are in German and French. The English ones come mainly from *Medico,* a journal probably unknown to most psychologists. It will not be easy, therefore, to obtain further reading on the test in English. Despite the "deep" interpretations offered in the book, no empirical data are given. This absence, the nature of the language used in the text, and the tone of the book suggest that it is intended for nonprofessionals. In such hands, however, this is a potentially dangerous book. This conclusion is based on the fact that certain color patterns are interpreted as indicating severe maladjustment and others are said to suggest physical difficulties, such as cardiac trouble. The reviewer, unaware of any research with this test, does not state that the interpretations are invalid. However, anyone who has worked extensively in the area of personality assessment research will probably be very leery of the claims advanced in lieu of evidence. The fact that the back of the dust jacket makes a point of emphasizing that this "is NOT a parlor game" will only encourage the use of possibly invalid interpretations by untrained persons. The publisher and authors have failed to meet their responsibility either to restrict such a book to professionals or to provide sufficient data to back the extravagant claims made for the test. *

New Republic 162(5):26+ Ja 31 '70. David Sanford. Unlike most psychological tests there is less abuse potential than simple nonsense in the Lüscher Color Test, a new book purporting to reveal the psychological significance of color preferences, shamelessly published by Random House. * The test, which is in alleged wide use by *European* psychologists, grew out of certain notions Lüscher has about the significance of colors. Green, for example, represents "elastic tension," red connotes desire and therefore represents all forms of appetite and craving. Black says "no" to life. Once he had established the *meaning* of colors it was simple for Lüscher to devise a test in which the subject, by arranging eight color chips in the order of his liking, reveals his personality. The color cards that come with the test are numbered and every

conceivable combination of colors has an interpretation in the tables that bulk up the book. The tables are as explicit and applicable to life situations as a Jeane Dixon horoscope. I have administered Lüscher's little test to four or five friends, each of whom thought the resultant personality descriptions just right. It should be admitted however that the results are elastic, stretching to fit all sizes of psyche. One of my subjects played his cards in the order blue, green, yellow, brown, grey, black, lavender, and red. The arrangement yielded a number sequence which showed him to need a peaceful environment, wanting release from stress and freedom from conflicts or disagreement. He takes pains to control situations and problems by proceeding cautiously. He has "sensitivity of feeling" and "a fine eye for detail." My friend thought all this accurate and agreeable enough to believe that there might be something to the test. I also gave the test to Salvador Dali (not personally), whose penchant for blue and yellow reveals a need for affection and good fellowship, a readiness to be of help to others in exchange for warmth and understanding. That described Dali perfectly, not to mention everyone else on the planet, and precisely this generality of application is the key to Dr. Lüscher's success, not to mention phrenology and fortune cookies. The Lüscher test might have been great fun had there been anything amusing about the interpretations of color responses, but aside from brown, which has something to do with ability to enjoy sex, the answers are a bore. The publisher in its promotion of the book takes it all very seriously: "The Lüscher Color Test, despite the ease and speed with which it can be administered, is a 'deep' psychological test, developed for the use of psychiatrists, psychologists, physicians, and those who are professionally involved with the conscious and unconscious characteristics and motivations of others. It is NOT a parlor game and most emphatically it is not a weapon to be used in a general contest of one-upmanship." Now it would be interesting to know who the psychologist was who consulted with Random House in the wording of that statement, which rings true only when completely turned around. The book is not a text but a trade book, selling very well at bookstores everywhere, for frivolous if any use at all. I suppose Random House would say it is not a gyp.

*Percept & Motor Skills 31(1):339 Ag '70.
C. H. Ammons and R. B. Ammons.* * There is
no information given about standardization or
use in the field, except for a single table which
is too briefly presented to be useful. Despite
other extant literature and about 144 references,
no systematic provision in interpretation is made
for known effects of sex and age, for example.
Printing of the color cards is not impressive.
The publisher says the test is "a major diagnostic aid," but this is hardly convincing in view
of the book's content.

[99]

★**The Manchester Scales of Social Adaptation.**
Ages 6–15; '66; MSSA; adaptation of *Vineland Social
Maturity Scale;* 13 scores: social perspective (general,
sport, current affairs, aesthetic, scientific, total), self-
direction (socialisation of play, freedom of movement,
self-help, handling of money, responsibility in home,
total), total; individual; no reading by examinees; 1
form; manual (54 pages); scoring form (4 pages);
62p per 25 scoring forms; £1.50 per manual; £1.70 per
specimen set; postage extra; (30–40) minutes; E. A.
Lunzer; NFER Publishing Co. Ltd. *

REFERENCE

1. BRENNAN, W. K. *The Relation of Social Adaptation,
Emotional Adjustment and Moral Judgment to Intelligence in
Primary School Children.* Master's thesis, University of Man-
chester (Manchester, England), 1961.

G. A. V. MORGAN, *Staff Inspector, Primary
and Special Education, Education Office for
Wales, Cardiff, Wales.*

These scales were developed from the *Vineland Social Maturity Scale* to take account of
the cultural differences in experience between
the U.S. and Britain. Items appropriate for
only one sex, or biased in terms of experience
(e.g., use of telephone) by different age or
social groups are omitted. The standardisation
concentrates on the age range 6–15; 88 items
have been designed for more adequate discrimination; a new system of scoring allows for
different levels of response to the same item.

The scales are now defined as an assessment
of social adaptation (not "social maturity")
governed by the child's environment as well as
his innate assets or deficits. There are two main
scales: social perspective and self direction,
with separate norms. The social perspective
scale measures information on social situations,
sport, current affairs, and science. The self
direction scale measures practical acquaintance
with the environment, such as self-help items,
responsibility in the home, and competence
in play and leisure. These developments are
valuable.

Scoring is of specific observable responses

such as using a knife and fork, checked by
the examiner without reference to parents or
others. But items also measure generalized
aspects of social competence, e.g., interests and
knowledge of current affairs; alternative scorings give better discrimination over different
age levels, but introduce subjectivity.

To avoid the disadvantages of quotients,
scores are reported as percentile ranks for age
groups. Norms are given for total scale, social
perspective and self direction, and for subscales.
There is considerable overlap between the two
main scales judging by their intercorrelations.
One study suggests that social perspective is
more related to intelligence level, and self direction more to age and experience, for normal
subjects. Because of the low reliability of the
subscales at certain ages, however, they are not
useful as differential measures.

Unfortunately, the standardisation of a potentially useful scale is faulty. It was based on
approximately 20 children in each age group,
from 6–16 years on two samples, in 1958 and
1959. Changes were made in one scale between
the 2 years. The sample of children is small
but, more important, the standardisation was
based on a very small number of schools; the
author appears to have overlooked the known
need to ensure a representative random sample
of schools (number, size and type). Further,
there is no evidence that the sample reflects the
distribution of social class in the Manchester-
Cheshire area, let alone Great Britain. This is
only a provisional standardisation, already out
of date.

The reliabilities of the total scale and the
two main scales, based on item-scale correlations
of over .90 appear to be satisfactory for classification and prediction of individual status. The
reliabilities for the subscales fall below an
acceptable level. More relevant is the test-retest
reliability of examiners; 40 children aged 8–9,
and 43 children aged 13, were assessed by
random pairs of testers, experienced teachers
completing a university diploma course, but not
highly experienced in testing. Test-retest reliability for total score and for social perspective
are just acceptable; the reliability for self
direction is not acceptable. These examiners
improved with practice; the scales should prove
more reliable in the hands of experienced interviewers, but there is no evidence on probable
range of error.

There is little evidence on validity. In one investigation the scales discriminated between well-adjusted children and those who were not, but this was confused by differences in ability: these findings are not relevant to assessing social adaptation in normal or subnormal pupils. In another investigation, the scales had low correlations with IQ, particularly self direction, a valuable outcome.

Since the most useful application of the scale could be in assessing the social adaptation of children of different environments, educational and mental level, it is strange that statistical evidence is based on "normal" groups. The scale's value would have been enhanced by evidence on the responses of children who are educationally or mentally subnormal; such groups could appropriately have been included in the standardisation. No attempt has been made to undertake a direct comparison of Vineland and Manchester scales.

The manual frankly admits weaknesses in the scales. The user is rightly warned to use scores with due regard to the limits of standard error given for main scales and subscales. Full data are given on all items as percentage pass in age groups, 6–9, 9–12 and 12–15 years; item-scale correlation; and age at which 25, 50, and 75 percent success are gained. Correlations are given between subscales; mean scores are given for boys and girls. An analysis of variance indicates significant variation between the standardisations of 1958 and 1959. Sex differences are in the expected direction, e.g., higher scores by boys on sport and scientific knowledge, higher scores by girls on responsibility in the home, but only the difference in social perspective score is significantly in favour of boys. Separate sex norms would be useful if a new standardisation is undertaken.

The manual gives scrupulous but misapplied statistical detail on too restricted and unstable original data. The scoring form is simple and legible, but discussions of administration and scoring are complex and verbose. Much information on development is useful, but "academic." Their weaknesses will limit the value and wider use of the scales, which appear to have been based on academic research and are not adequately developed. They do not provide adequate measures of social competence in an acceptable sample of British children, suitable for routine diagnosis and guidance.

M. L. KELLMER PRINGLE, *Director, National Children's Bureau, London, England.*

The usefulness of the *Vineland Social Maturity Scale* as a diagnostic tool for the assessment of subnormal, delinquent, handicapped or otherwise deviant children has been demonstrated both in the United States and in the United Kingdom. The publication of the VSMS in 1936 was a useful first attack in a field where concepts were misty and ill-defined. Subsequent use has pointed up three needs: to expand the scale by increasing the number of items in each year group beyond the preschool stage; to produce a manual which gives more detailed descriptions of the behaviour required for the successful completion of each item; and to adapt and standardise the test for British children.

In devising the Manchester scales, Lunzer has addressed himself to meeting these needs and has done so with a considerable measure of success.

The age range covered is narrower than that of the Vineland, e.g., from 6 to 15 years. On the other hand, within this more restricted age band, there are many more items. Very few items of the Vineland scale have been retained. Moreover, the scales are quite differently designed and so is the system of scoring. Hence it is virtually a new test rather than an adaptation. There are two separate parts: a scale of Social Perspective and a scale of Self Direction. "The first bears more particularly on the *cognitive* aspects of social competence, or what might be called social '*know-that*'; the second deals with more *practical* aspects, or social '*know-how.*'" Each of the subscales is again subdivided into five areas of enquiry and the descriptive names of these 10 subsections are listed in the entry above. Since separate sets of norms are provided for each of the 10 subsections, a graphic profile may be constructed for a subject. Efforts have been made to include only such items as have very general relevance in Britain. Care has been taken to make directions for scoring unambiguous and to define criteria for success as precisely as possible. Scores are not transformed into social ages or quotients.

The area covered by the standardisation was confined to Manchester, Cheshire, and East Lancashire; altogether some 418 children, approximately 20 boys and 20 girls at each age, were interviewed by experienced teachers who had just completed a course in educational psychology. Mentally or educationally subnormal children were not included. The method of sampling was stratified for schools and random within schools.

The manual reports a correlation of .87 between different testers on two occasions for 400 8-year-olds; this indicates satisfactory reliability. Since the scales are relatively new, validation is "conspicuous by its almost total absence" (to quote the author).

Since attempts to measure the social aspects of human growth are as yet only in the beginning stages and our knowledge of norms of social development is still inadequate, an additional research and diagnostic tool is to be welcomed. It must also be welcomed as a much needed expansion of, and indeed improvement upon, the Vineland scale. To have a "home grown" clinical tool is still sufficiently rare in Britain to cause rejoicing. It might well be worthwhile to adapt the scales for use with American children.

The test manual and scoring form are simple and clear in design and presentation. However, the manual could be improved by adding a table of contents, by providing a sturdier cover, and by more careful proofreading (there are several misprints). The claim that the scoring form provides "ample space....for comments and details of information" is hardly justified even for those whose writing is minute. This too needs improving in future editions.

The scales necessitate interviewing the child himself whereas on the Vineland scale someone very familiar with him may act as informant. However, this point is not made explicit in the manual. Indeed, the explanatory comment for item 81 implies that the child does not always act as the informant.

The ten subscales cover a wide and diverse range of topics, so that the test can justly be said to tap many areas of social adaptation. However, the author has been less successful in choosing items in such a way as to appeal equally to both sexes. In the subscale Social Perspective (Sport), he has almost completely failed to do so: of the 10 questions, only 3 can, at best, be said to be fair to girls. Additionally, "boys are significantly more knowledgeable about current affairs and about science," and they also "apparently enjoy a greater freedom of movement at all ages" than is granted to girls. Therefore, it is regrettable that "con-

siderations of size of sample have led to the rejection of separate norms for boys and girls on the basis of existing standardisation." It must also be doubted whether the claim that "few adults would find difficulty in coping with more than one or two questions" is justified. A second criticism relates to the restricted geographical area from which the standardisation sample was drawn. Recent findings from a national study indicate marked regional differences in the behaviour, adjustment and achievement of children as young as 7 years; it is, therefore, likely that similar differences exist in social adaptation. Future revisions of the scales ought to take this into account.

In summary, then, this is a useful instrument which already looks very promising in its present provisional form. Therefore, its use as a clinical and research tool can be recommended.

Brit J Ed Psychol 37:269–70 Je '67. Maurice Chazan. * Apart from some misprints, the manual is a good one, being clear and informative. * The Standardisation procedures are quite fully described, and there is an interesting discussion of the concepts of social maturity and social competence. Dr. Lunzer's new scales are very welcome and he is to be congratulated on the progress he has made in a very difficult field. Most of the test items are easy to administer and in a form likely to produce a response from all but the most inhibited subjects. The availability of norms for each sub-scale and for each of the two parts is extremely valuable in that a profile of the child's social abilities is provided. While detailed comments should be withheld until the scales have been tried out over a wider area, some criticisms may be tentatively proffered at this stage. The standardisation sample (of twenty boys and twenty girls for each year) is hardly adequate. The scoring, while aiming at objectivity combined with some flexibility, is still somewhat subjective and complicated in places; and success in many of the Social Direction tests is dependent on what the child says he can do rather than on evidence of actual performance of social skills. The criteria for the cessation of testing in several sub-scales seem unduly harsh, seeing that a wide range of interests is covered and that the questions are not always in strict order of difficulty. Some of the items, too, in the Social Perspective section appear to test specialized interests, and their place in a general scale of social adaptation may be questioned. However, Dr. Lunzer makes it clear that he regards his present scales as provisional and that he intends to revise them after continued work. They should prove a valuable diagnostic instrument, and....we look forward to further reports on their use.

[100]

★**Martin S-D Inventory.** Clients and patients; 1970; MSDI; 1 form (2 pages); combined manual (12 pages) titled *Symptomatology and Evaluation of Depressed and Suicidal Patients* for this and test 133; preliminary norms consist of means and standard deviations for groups with 7 to 24 subjects; $3.75 per 25 forms; $1 per scoring stencil; $2.50 per specimen set (must be purchased to obtain manual); cash orders postpaid; (15) minutes; William T. Martin; Psychologists and Educators Press. *

[101]

Memory-For-Designs Test. Ages 8.5 and over; 1946–60; MFD; brain damage; individual; 1 form ('60, 15 cards, identical with cards distributed by the authors in 1946); revised manual ('60, 43 pages, reprinted from *12* below); norms-scoring examples booklet ('60, 12 pages, reprinted from manual); $8.50 per set of test materials including manual; $2.50 per manual; cash orders postpaid; (5–10) minutes; Frances K. Graham and Barbara S. Kendall; Psychological Test Specialists. *

REFERENCES

1–5. See 4:69.
6–23. See 6:140.
24–38. See P:163, also includes a cumulative name index to the first 38 references for this test.
30. JURKO, M. F., AND ANDY, O. J. "Psychological Aspects of Diencephalotomy." *J Neurol Neurosurg & Psychiatry* 27: 516–21 D '64. * (PA 39:9508)
40. HERON, ALASTAIR, AND CHOWN, SHEILA. *Age and Function.* London: J. & A. Churchill Ltd., 1967. Pp. x, 182. *
41. MICHAELSON, S.; ROSE, J. T.; AND MAY, A. E. "Controlling for 'Experimenter Effect' in the Psychometric Assessment of Brain Damage." *Brit J Med Psychol* 40:371–4 D '67. * (PA 42:12617)
42. CRONHOLM, BÖRJE, AND SCHALLING, DAISY. "Cognitive Test Performances in Cerebrally Palsied Adults Without Mental Retardation." *Acta Psychiatrica Scandinavica* 44(1): 37–50 '68. * (PA 43:2937)
43. SCOTT, JULESTER S. *The Relationship of Performance on the Memory-for-Designs Test to Reading Ability, Sex, and Socio-Economic Class.* Master's thesis, University of Wyoming (Laramie, Wyo.), 1968.
44. AFTANAS, M. S., AND ROYCE, J. R. "A Factor Analysis of Brain Damage Tests Administered to Normal Subjects With Factor Score Comparisons Across Ages." *Multiv Behav Res* 4(4):459–81 O '69. * (PA 44:11030)
45. BANNATYNE, ALEX D. "A Comparison of Visuo-Spatial and Visuo-Motor Memory for Designs and Their Relationship to Other Sensori-Motor and Psycholinguistic Variables." *J Learn Dis* 2(9):451–66 S '69. * (PA 45:6004)
46. BANNATYNE, ALEX D., AND WICHIARAJOTE, PENNY. "Hemispheric Dominance, Handedness, Mirror Imaging, and Auditory Sequencing." *Excep Children* 36(1):27–36 S '69. * (PA 44:20147)
47. BRUININKS, ROBERT H. "Auditory and Visual Perceptual Skills Related to the Reading Performance of Disadvantaged Boys." *Percept & Motor Skills* 29(1):179–86 Ag '69. * (PA 44:2835)
48. LANGE, UNA ANN. *Differential Performances of Minimally Brain-Damaged Boys and of Non-Brain-Damaged Boys on Selected Tests.* Doctor's thesis, University of Nebraska (Lincoln, Neb.), 1969. (DAI 30:2852A)
49. LILLISTON, LAWRENCE GRANT. *Dimensions of Schizophrenia as a Function of Performance on Tests of Cerebral Damage.* Doctor's thesis, Temple University (Philadelphia, Pa.), 1969. (DAI 30:1900B)
50. LYLE, J. G. "Reading Retardation and Reversal Tendency: A Factorial Study." *Child Develop* 40(3):833–43 S '69. * (PA 44:2706)
51. MURRAY, LOIS MIRIAM NELSON. *The Relationship Between Conceptual, Perceptual, and Electroencephalographic*

Factors in Process and Reactive Schizophrenics. Doctor's thesis, University of Arizona (Tucson, Ariz.), 1969. (DAI 30: 3872B)
52. OWENS, RICHARD THOMAS. *A Study of the Performance of Minimally Brain-Damaged and Emotionally Disturbed Boys on Six Selected Psychological Tests.* Doctor's thesis, University of Nebraska (Lincoln, Neb.), 1969. (DAI 31:383B)
53. QUATTLEBAUM, LAWRENCE F., AND WHITE, WILLIAM F. "Relationships Among the Quick Test, Two Measures of Psychomotor Functioning, and Age." *Percept & Motor Skills* 29(3):824–6 D '69. * (PA 46:5150)
54. TURLAND, D. N., AND STEINHARD, MARGARET. "The Efficiency of the Memory-For-Designs Test." *Brit J Social & Clin Psychol* 8(1):44–9 F '69. * (PA 43:8463)
55. VITALE, JOHN H.; STEINHELBER, JOHN C.; DRAKE, WILLIAM E., JR.; AND DAHLGREN, HELEN. "Psychological Dimensions of Cerebrovascular Insufficiency." *Percept & Motor Skills* 29(2):555–63 O '69. * (PA 44:3996)
56. WOHLFORD, PAUL, AND FLICK, GRAD L. "Sex-of-Rater Bias in Clinical Diagnosis of Organic Brain Damage Using the Bender-Gestalt and Memory-for-Designs Tests." *Percept & Motor Skills* 29(1):107–14 Ag '69. * (PA 44:2538)
57. ALEXANDER, DAVID A. "The Application of the Graham-Kendall Memory-for-Designs Test to Elderly Normal and Psychiatric Groups." *Brit J Social & Clin Psychol* 9(1):85–6 F '70. *
58. BURGESS, MICHAEL M.; KODANAZ, ALTAN; AND ZIEGLER, DEWEY K. "Prediction of Brain Damage in a Neurological Population With Cerebrovascular Accidents." *Percept & Motor Skills* 31(2):595–601 O '70. * (PA 45:6841)
59. BURGESS, MICHAEL M.; KODANAZ, ALTAN; ZIEGLER, DEWEY; AND GREENBURG, HOWARD. "Prediction of Brain Damage in Two Clinical Populations." *Percept & Motor Skills* 30(2):523–32 Ap '70. * (PA 46:7299)
60. GRUNDVIG, J. L.; NEEDHAM, W. E.; AND AJAX, E. T. "Comparison of Different Scoring and Administration Procedures for the Memory-for-Designs Test." *J Clin Psychol* 26(3): 353–7 Jl '70. * (PA 45:934)
61. GRUNDVIG, JOHN L.; NEEDHAM, WALTER E.; AJAX, ERNEST T.; AND BECK, EDWARD C. "The Use of the Sensory-Perceptual Examination in Diagnosis of Degree of Impairment of Higher Cerebral Functions." *J Nerv & Mental Dis* 151(2):114–9 Ag '70. * (PA 45:10499)
62. LEVITA, ERIC, AND RIKLAN, MANUEL. "Integrative Functions in Parkinsonism." *Percept & Motor Skills* 31(2): 379–85 O '70. * (PA 45:6405)
63. LILLISTON, LAWRENCE. "Tests of Cerebral Damage and the Process-Reactive Dimension." *J Clin Psychol* 26(2):180–1 Ap '70. * (PA 44:15126)
64. MAY, A. E.; URQUHART, A.; AND WATTS, R. E. "Memory-for-Designs Test: A Follow-up Study." *Percept & Motor Skills* 30(3):753–4 Je '70. * (PA 44:16746)

R. W. PAYNE, *Professor of Psychology and Chairman, Department of Behavioral Science, Temple University School of Medicine, Philadelphia, Pennsylvania.*

Since its original publication in 1946, the *Memory-for-Designs Test* has become one of the most popular tests for the assessment of brain damage in both children and adults. The test material consists of 15 simple straight line designs which the subject is shown one at a time for 5 seconds each. He is then required to reproduce each design from memory. An objective scoring system has been developed, which allows the accumulation of normative data.

The clinical usefulness of the test depends first of all upon its reliability and upon the adequacy of its standardization for different age groups, and for different non-brain-damaged. psychiatric populations. The reliability of the scoring procedure itself appears to be entirely satisfactory according to data presented in the test manual, and the test-retest reliabilities also appear to be comparable with many standard tests of intelligence (.72 to .90). New studies of the reliability since the test was reviewed in the 6th MMY have reported similar results; e.g., Richie and Butler (28) found a test-retest reliability of .77 in a mentally defective population and Heron and Chown (40) report a split-half reliability of .73. "Qualitative" scores are also possible, notably a measure of the tendency to "rotate" or misorient the designs. "Orientation error" can be measured reliably (32), test-retest indices ranging from .85 to .93. Standardization data for this score are available.

Since the test was last reviewed, additional normative data have become available. Davies (33) reports the norms for an English sample of 240, broken down by sex, and by each age decade from 20–29 to 70–79. These data suggest that the normal age decline may be greater than originally suggested. Thus, if the original norms are used, a number of "false positive" diagnoses of brain damage may result for older subjects. This finding is confirmed by Quattlebaum and White (53).

Although the age standardization for normal adults is probably adequate (it can hardly be claimed, however, that representative samples of any particular normal population have been obtained), the same cannot be said for the normative data available for different functional psychiatric groups. It is clear that some functional psychiatric disorders produce lower scores on this test. Unfortunately all the studies carried out lump the different functional psychiatric categories together, and none provides age norms for representative populations of functional psychiatric disorders. Thus it would be difficult from the presently available norms, to exclude the presence of a particular functional psychiatric disorder as an alternative explanation of a poor score, unless this alternative could be excluded on other grounds.

Much more important than the questions of reliability and standardization, however, is the question of validity. What are the possible practical uses of this test, or for that matter, of any test of "brain damage"? The studies summarized in the earlier review by Spreen suggest clearly that this test consistently differentiates between groups of patients clearly known to be brain damaged, and matched groups of normal people and psychiatric patients thought not to be brain damaged. Some subsequent studies confirm these earlier findings

(29, 33, 42, 54). However the practical implications of such findings are far from clear. In the first place all these studies beg the question of the definition of "brain damage." If brain damage refers to any amount of cell death in the cerebral cortex, regardless of cause, then it is likely that everyone over 30 is brain damaged, by virtue of age, if for no other reason. Common forms of birth trauma, anoxia and childhood injuries undoubtedly result in cell death in a large number of normal children. However for most of us, this "normal" brain damage is of no importance because we are not unduly functionally impaired. It is extremely difficult to accept that anybody could guarantee that the "non-brain damaged" groups for which there are data are really free of all cortical damage. All that is really implied by these group labels is that, as far as is known, the "non-brain damaged" samples exhibited no gross neurological signs, and no obvious functional impairment of the sort known to accompany certain types of brain damage, whereas the "brain damaged" groups showed both these features. The practical question which should be asked is not "Is this man of 45 brain damaged?" because the answer must surely be "yes," but "What are the practical consequences of a very abnormal MFD score in this man of 45?" It is possible to conceive of a number of such practical consequences. An abnormal score might imply damage in a particular cortical area, which might imply some other, previously unsuspected specific dysfunctions. It might imply the presence of some specific brain pathology, and hence some specific prognosis, such as a shortened life expectancy, and so on. However unless the score has been shown to have some such practical implication, it is difficult to know how to use it. Almost no such practical implications have ever been demonstrated for the MFD.

Although patients who are demonstrably and unambiguously brain damaged on this test clearly have abnormal scores, two studies suggest that there is a very low, usually insignificant correlation between MFD score, and a rating of the *severity* of brain damage as assessed by other medical (neurological) criteria such as EEG ratings (28, 56). Another study (54) suggests that when the test is given to a psychiatric group in which the presence or absence of brain damage is doubtful, the range of MFD scores produced is so wide that nothing can be said about the characteristic performance of such a group. If such a group had been followed up for a period of time, it might have been possible to determine whether the scores could have predicted the subsequent development of a clear cut neurological syndrome. However no such follow-up studies appear to have been carried out. Unfortunately, this test is most likely to be used clinically with just such doubtful cases.

One practical consequence of an abnormal MFD score which *has* been demonstrated is that the patient is likely also to have abnormal scores on several other tests of brain damage such as the *Bender Gestalt Test,* and the *Benton Visual Retention Test (36, 55)*. Aftanas and Royce (*44*) published the correlations between the MFD test and 34 other measures of brain damage for a normal sample of 100 people. Thus an abnormal MFD score might enable the clinical psychologist to uncover a previously unsuspected pattern of associated psychological abnormalities which, on a common sense level at least, might have implications for the adjustment of the patient.

One other potentially useful implication of an abnormal MFD score among children, is that one might anticipate difficulties in learning to read, as suggested by several studies (*14, 35, 47*).

For a review by Otfried Spreen, see 6:140.

[102]

★Mental Status Schedule. Psychiatric patients and nonpatients; 1964–66; MSS; standardized interview schedule and matching inventory of present-absent items descriptive of pathological behavior; 3 macro scores (feelings-concern, confusion-retardation, delusions-hallucinations), 13 factor scores (inappropriate-bizarre, belligerence-negativism, agitation-excitement, retardation-withdrawal, speech disorganization, suspicion-persecution-hallucinations, grandiosity, depression-anxiety, suicide-self mutilation, somatic concerns, social isolation, disorientation-memory, denial of illness), and 22 supplemental scores (anxiety, auditory hallucinations, conversion reaction, depression-suicide, dissociation, elated mood, grandiosity non-delusional, grandiose psychoticism, guilt non-delusional, inappropriate-bizarre, incoherence, schizophrenic, non-specific complaints, obsessions-compulsions, persecutory delusions, phobia, silliness, sociopath, somatic preoccupation, somatic delusions, somatic hallucinations, visual hallucinations); Form A ('64, 10 pages); manual ('66, 9 pages); inventory record sheet ('64, 2 pages); 50¢ per examiner's booklet; 5¢ per score sheet; 10¢ per inventory record sheet; 50¢ per manual; $3 per set of keys and teaching tape; postage extra; specimen set free; fee for editing, coding, key punching, and verifying score sheets, 25¢ per subject; scoring service with profile printout is available; (20–50) minutes; Robert L. Spitzer, Eugene I. Burdock (test), Anne S.

Hardesty (test), Jean Endicott (manual), and George M. Cohen (manual); Biometrics Research, New York State Psychiatric Institute. *

REFERENCES

1–8. See P:164.
9. BURDOCK, EUGENE I.; FLEISS, JOSEPH; AND HARDESTY, ANNE S. "A New View of Inter-Observer Agreement." *Personnel Psychol* 16:373–84 w '63. * (*PA* 38:6902)
10. PATTISON, E. MANSELL; HEADLEY, E. B.; GLESER, G. C.; AND GOTTSCHALK, L. A. "Abstinence and Normal Drinking: An Assessment of Changes in Drinking Patterns in Alcoholics After Treatment." *Q J Studies Alcohol* 29:610–33 S '68. *
11. ZUBIN, JOSEPH. Chap. 4, "Clinical, Phenomenological, and Biometric Assessment of Psychopathology With Special Reference to Diagnosis," pp. 68–98. In *The Definition and Measurement of Mental Health.* Edited by S. B. Sells. Public Health Service Publication No. 1873. Washington, D.C.: United States Government Printing Office, 1968. Pp. xii, 280. *
12. FAHY, T. J.; BRANDON, S.; AND GARSIDE, R. F. "Clinical Syndromes in a Sample of Depressed Patients: A General Practice Material." *Proc Royal Soc Med* 62(4):331–5 Ap '69. *
13. KATZ, MARTIN M.; COLE, JONATHAN O.; AND LOWERY, HENRI A. "Studies of the Diagnostic Process: The Influence of Symptom Perception, Past Experience, and Ethnic Background on Diagnostic Decisions." *Am J Psychiatry* 125(7): 937–47 Ja '69. * (*PA* 43:7072)
14. KATZ, MARTIN M.; GUDEMAN, HOWARD; AND SANBORN, KENNETH. Chap. 9, "Characterizing Differences in Psychopathology Among Ethnic Groups: A Preliminary Report on Hawaii-Japanese and Mainland-American Schizophrenics," pp. 148–63. In *Mental Health Research in Asia and the Pacific.* Edited by William Caudill and Tsung-yi Lin. Honolulu, Hawaii: East-West Center Press, 1969. Pp. xv, 487. *
15. WEINSTOCK, COMILDA SUNDEEN. *The Relations Between Social Isolation, Social Cognition and Related Cognitive Skills in the Aged.* Doctor's thesis, Columbia University (New York, N.Y.), 1969. (*DAI* 30:3376B)
16. GOTTSCHALK, LOUIS A.; GLESER, GOLDINE C.; CLEGHORN, JOHN M.; STONE, WALTER N.; AND WINGET, CAROLYN N. "Prediction of Changes in Severity of the Schizophrenic Syndrome With Discontinuation and Administration of Phenothiazines in Chronic Schizophrenic Patients: Language as a Predictor and Measure of Change in Schizophrenia." *Comprehen Psychiatry* 11(2):123–40 Mr '70. * (*PA* 45:6735)
17. HOLLAND, JIMMIE; MASLING, JOSEPH; AND COPLEY, DONALD. "Mental Illness in Lower Class Normal, Obese and Hyperobese Women." *Psychosom Med* 32(4):351–7 Jl–Ag '70. * (*PA* 46:1488)

SOL L. GARFIELD, *Professor of Psychology and Director, Clinical Psychology Program, Washington University, St. Louis, Missouri.*

The MSS is a standardized clinical interview for recording and appraising what has been called in psychiatry, the mental status of the patient: the patient's complaints, feelings, thoughts, perceptions and symptoms. The schedule consists of 82 questions with 51 supplementary questions which may be used to probe or clarify the responses secured from the patient. The interviewer, in turn, on the basis of the patient's overt behavior and the style and content of his oral communication, records the patient's responses as true or false on a 248-item inventory. Thus, the schedule focuses on observable and self-report behavior, and purposely leaves out speculation, interpretation and dynamics. The material describing the schedule states that the standard interview procedure is easily learned and this would appear to be true, particularly for someone who has worked with psychiatric patients and has some knowledge of psychopathology. However, specific training is required.

Originally, a total score was secured from this schedule which was interpreted as an index of psychopathology. Since then a number of clinical scales as well as factor-analytically derived scales have been derived. Anywhere from 6 to 20 clinical scales have been identified at various times, but probably most investigators who have need for such scores would tend to use the scores derived via factor analysis.

In terms of reliability, four small studies were reported early based on two to three psychiatrists who examined 15 to 21 patients. The intra-class correlations ranged from .92 to .97 for the total score, but those for six clinical subscales were lower, ranging from .48 to .99. The data on the factor-analyzed scores are more extensive and are based on 2,000 subjects in a majority of instances. The study (8) reporting this information would also appear to be the most important one for individuals who may want to use the schedule. Furthermore, since the factor analytically derived scores will most likely be used more frequently than the clinical scales, it may be worth saying a bit more about them.

The K-R 20 reliabilities of the three macroscales range from .86 to .92. The range for the 12 factor scales or subscales is from .51 to .91. Some data, based on a series of six studies with two or three judges and 13 to 63 patients, is provided on interjudge reliability. These on the whole are quite comparable to the values already reported for internal consistency. On the whole, one may state that the reliabilities for the total score and the macro scales are reasonably high whereas those for some of the separate factor scales are rather low.

Several kinds of validity studies are also reported which can be summarized very briefly. One type compares different diagnostic groups and populations. In general, inpatients, outpatients, Bowery residents, and community leaders tended to exhibit different patterns which can be interpreted meaningfully. Community leaders tend to have low scores on most of the scales, outpatients were highest on depression-anxiety, and inpatients were highest on confusion-retardation and delusions-hallucinations. Bowery men, incidentally, were highest in social isolation and in inappropriate or bizarre appearance. A similar comparison of psychotic depressive disorders, chronic brain syndromes, schizophrenic reactions, and neurotic reactions revealed that the three macro scales and 11 of

the 13 subscales did discriminate among these groups although some similarity in pattern between the neurotic and psychotic depressive groups was noted by this reviewer.

The MSS has also been compared to several other instruments such as the CMI, IMPS, KAS, and MMPI. These data are difficult to interpret in a brief manner since the various instruments vary considerably among themselves and in several instances were constructed to serve different purposes. However, in general the available information would appear to lend support to the claims of the authors of the MSS, particularly in terms of concurrent validity. The correlations with the IMPS, which is probably the most comparable instrument, are all positive and generally of moderate strength. Surprisingly, perhaps, the correlations with the MMPI are only slightly lower in terms of the comparisons which were made with scales judged to be measuring somewhat comparable attributes or syndromes. The Depression Scale on the MMPI, for example, correlated .68 with the factor scale, Depression-Anxiety, and .70 with the macro scale, Feelings-Concerns.

Thus, there are some data in support of the authors' claims concerning the reliability and validity of the MSS, and the authors have carried out studies pertaining to the relationship of the MSS to other instruments for appraising psychopathology and to the possible uses and limitations of this technique. At this point, some additional comments concerning the uses for such an instrument are in order. In terms of purpose and format, the MSS covers the ground of a mental status examination traditionally performed by the psychiatrist. As such, it tends to be concerned with the traditional and more severe aspects of psychopathology. For those who are interested in such an examination, and this would appear to the present reviewer to be primarily psychiatrists in mental hospitals, the MSS could be used as one means of securing such information in a fairly uniform and systematic way. Clinics which handle a fair number of severely disturbed individuals and make frequent referrals for hospitalization might also find some use for this instrument. In-patient settings in which drug studies and other types of related research are going on, also might want to examine the MSS for possible use. However, outpatient clinics and other settings which emphasize psychotherapy and relatively less disturbed populations, may not find it to their liking or suitable to their needs. As indicated, the MSS is derived from the traditional mental status examination, has a psychiatric orientation and is concerned with psychopathology, particularly the signs and symptoms associated with neurotic, psychotic, and organic brain disorders. As the authors point out, alcoholism, drug addiction, sociopathic behavior and normal personality traits are not covered. The MSS has also been adapted for computer use.

JULIAN J. LASKY, *Clinical Research Branch, National Institute of Mental Health, Chevy Chase, Maryland.*

The *Mental Status Schedule* has many of the desirable properties of a psychological test: a trained interviewer administers a mental status examination guided by a standard interview schedule and scores the responses objectively at intervals during the session. Several scoring systems have been published, some more adequate than others. Considerable reliability and validity data are available in published form.

The MSS is presented in a practical step-down booklet which is reusable with a separate scoring sheet for each subject. The manual is clearly written and readily understandable. The training procedures available to the user are excellent and include audio-tapes and prescored interview protocols along with the suggestion to conduct an interjudge reliability check before beginning a research study.

The MSS lacks an alternate form but the authors contend (with little evidence) that this does not constitute a problem.

When the MSS was first published in 1964, reliability and validity data were based primarily on total score, total score being the sum of items marked "True." Interjudge reliabilities for the total score were found to be over .90, the mean reliability being .94 based on four studies. MSS total score discriminated between psychiatric patients and nonpatients, and between outpatients and inpatients. MSS total scores were found to correlate .82 (Spearman rank order correlation) with independent psychiatrist ratings of severity of illness.

In 1967, the authors wisely recommended that total score no longer be used as a measure of severity of illness because more adequate scores were available (*8*). Two scoring systems were offered; one based on factor analytic studies and the other, intended as a supplementary system, based on rational diagnostic considerations. Two factor analytic studies, based on 1,000 MSS protocols each, yielded 3 "macro" and 13 factor-related scales.

The K-R 20 reliabilities for the macro scales ranged from .86 to .92. Ten of the 13 factor-related scales had internal consistency reliabilities below .80.

The median interjudge reliabilities for the macro scales ranged from .74 for Confusion-Retardation to .91 for Delusions-Hallucinations and .96 for Feelings-Concerns. Median interjudge reliabilities for the factor-related scales ranged from .58 (Speech Disorganization) to .97 (Depression-Anxiety); 4 of the factor-related scales (Inappropriate or Bizarre Appearance or Behavior, Agitation-Excitement, Speech Disorganization, and Grandiosity) occasionally had interjudge reliabilities below .50.

Interjudge reliability coefficients for the MSS compared favorably with those of a leading competitive scale, the *Inpatient Multidimensional Psychiatric Scale.*

In a validity study of 1,022 patients distributed over four broad diagnostic groups: psychotic depressed disorders, chronic brain syndromes, schizophrenic reactions, and neurotic reactions, each of the 3 macro scales and 11 of the 13 factor-related scales—but not Agitation-Excitement (8 items) nor Suicide-Self Mutilation (5 items)—discriminated among the four diagnostic groups. In another study, the MSS was completed for 704 schizophrenics diagnosed as paranoid, catatonic, hebephrenic, and acute or chronic undifferentiated. In general, the macro scales, but not the factor-related scales, discriminated between the four schizophrenia subtypes. Perhaps one of the major difficulties with the factor-related scales is that 6 of the 13 scales contain only five to ten items per scale.

As a measure of change the MSS, although adequate, does not appear particularly impressive in this regard.

The MSS user may also compute standard scores for his data by referring to means and standard deviations based on a sample of 1,413 newly admitted psychiatric patients. Although the demographic characteristics of this standardization sample have been published (*8*), the means and standard deviations of MSS raw scores for macro and factor-related scales have not been published but are available from the authors.

With reliability, validity and scoring accounted for, it might be interesting to look at the MSS in perspective. The item pool from which the MSS was developed was obtained by surveying standard psychiatric textbooks and by interviewing several hundred patients with preliminary forms of the MSS (*1*). As such, the item pool was derived from an empirical-descriptive set of observations made on hospital and clinic patients. The item pool and subsequent MSS may be faulted for lacking a broad theoretical base which might have profitably guided subsequent development. During usage, for example, it soon became apparent to the authors that the MSS does not sample certain deviant behaviors which are observed more frequently in the community than in the hospital, e.g., alcohol and drug addiction and various sociopathic behaviors. The MSS also does not assess the more positive and useful aspects of behavior such as social role functioning or constructive use of time. To remedy this situation, the principal author and his colleagues developed and published their *Psychiatric Status Schedule* which, in its first edition, interspersed the 248 MSS items among the 492 items which comprise the PSS. The second edition of the PSS contains 321 items; the reduction in length due to scale refinement procedures. Thus, it would appear that the PSS does everything the MSS does, only more and better. In addition to the PSS advantages referred to above, the user can send PSS scoring sheets to the authors who will furnish computerized psychiatric diagnoses using standard American Psychiatric Association nomenclature, batch scoring, and statistical services.

In summary, if one wishes to assess by means of interview the mental status (affect, thought, and behavior) of moderately to severely ill neurotic or psychotic patients as these patients are evaluated in the mode of descriptive psychiatry, and to conduct this assessment efficiently, systematically and reliably, the MSS is the best instrument available for this task. The domain of the scale may be too limited to adequately assess individuals with emotional problems in the community. However, the authors have developed an instrument similar to the MSS but broader in scope, the *Psychiatric Status Schedule,* for this latter purpose. In tracing the development of the MSS, it is gratifying to note the extensive developmental work and the steady evolution of improved scales, scoring systems, objective diagnostic

methods, and research support services provided by these authors.

[103]

★**Middlesex Hospital Questionnaire.** Ages 18 and over; 1970; MHQ; 7 scores: free-floating anxiety, phobic anxiety, obsessionality, somatic anxiety, depression, hysteria, total (neuroticism); 1 form (2 pages); manual (19 pages); no data on reliability of total score; norms consist of mean scores only; 15s. per 25 tests; 20s. per manual; postage extra; [25] minutes; A. H. Crisp and Sidney Crown; Psychological Test Publications. *

REFERENCES

1. CROWN, SIDNEY, AND CRISP, A. H. "A Short Clinical Diagnostic Self-Rating Scale for Psychoneurotic Patients: The Middlesex Hospital Questionnaire (M.H.Q.)." *Brit J Psychiatry* 112:917–23 S '66. * (PA 41:667)
2. McKERRACHER, D. W.; LOUGHNANE, T.; AND WATSON, R. A. "Self-Mutilation in Female Psychopaths." *Brit J Psychiatry* 114:829–32 Jl '68. * (PA 43:2787)
3. COCKETT, R. "A Short Diagnostic Self-Rating Scale in the Pre-Adult Remand Setting." *Brit J Psychiatry* 115(527): 1141–50 O '69. * (PA 44:12823)
4. CRISP, A. H., AND STONEHILL, E. "Aspects of the Psychological Status of Patients Treated With Cardiac Pacemakers." *Postgrad Med J* 45(525):423–7 Jl '69. *
5. CROWN, SIDNEY; DUNCAN, K. P.; AND HOWELL, R. W. "Further Evaluation of the Middlesex Hospital Questionnaire (M.H.Q.)." *Brit J Psychiatry* 116(530):33–7 Ja '70. * (PA 44:21165)

D. F. CLARK, *Consultant Clinical Psychologist, North-East Regional Hospital Board, Ladysbridge Hospital, Banff, Scotland.*

The authors of this test aver that "the need frequently arises both in research and in clinical practice for a means of rapid quantification of common symptoms and traits relevant to the conventional categories of psychoneurotic illness and personality disorder." The objective of the MHQ "is to obtain in five or ten minutes an approximation to the diagnostic information that would be gained from a formal clinical psychiatric examination."

There are 48 items, all of which are simply expressed and are answered by yes, no, sometimes, never, very, and a little. The response to each item is scored either 2, 1, or 0.

Since the test was designed to provide "clinical categorisations" similar to those used by psychiatrists, the authors have been careful to define these so-called dimensions in verbal terms. The dimensions are not, however, well defined factorially or psychometrically; there is a strikingly ad hoc quality about the way in which eight items have been used to assess each of the subscales. The authors used a simple form of item analysis to eliminate items which did not differentiate between psychoneurotics and normals.

Two methods of establishing validity were used. First, whether each subtest differentiated normal subjects from patients and second, whether the subtests correlated with clinical ratings by psychiatrists. On the first count significant differences were found for all subtests, but there was initially an unsatisfactory relationship of the score on the phobia subtest to clinical ratings. This is perhaps not altogether unexpected because of the limited sampling of specific phobias in only eight items. In another study comparing psychiatric outpatients with normal nurses and medical students, the obsessionality subtest scores did not correlate significantly with clinical ratings, but the other subscores were considered to be adequately validated. The phobia and obsessionality scores, therefore, need careful scrutiny.

The manual reports test-retest reliabilities based on testing 129 men over a one-year period for the subtests as ranging from .68 to .77 with median .72. Split-half reliabilities for five of the six subtests range from .48 to .85 with median .65. No reliability estimates are reported for the total score. These reliabilities appear to be adequate, especially when one allows for the fundamental paradox in attempting to devise a test which will tend to be highly stable and consistent from test to retest and yet at the same time take account of intra-individual differences over time.

In general, the manual is up-to-date and includes recent studies by the authors and others. The manual reports that age, social class, and IQ appear to have no important effect on MHQ scores. In one paper (5) the authors report that five of the six subtests show statistically significant differences between males and females; they urge further research to explain this. They then go on to say that "the 'hysteria' scale raises a number of important conceptual problems in psychiatric and personality research." It could be added that it is not the only scale which raises such problems. Since the authors have chosen to devise a test and have gone to some pains to make it psychometrically adequate in measuring these so-called variables, they are a bit late in the day in writing a sentence like this. To do them justice, however, the authors point out that the validity of individual subtests and the relationships between them need further research; they have been careful to point out the limitations and describe the development of the test in a way which is honest and comprehensive.

Some trouble has been taken to make the MHQ a worthwhile instrument within its terms of reference. It is its reference which one is inclined to question; it appears that the MHQ will be valuable mainly to psychiatrists who screen large populations, preferably of males over 18 years of age, and where the resulting data have to be given meaning only in the context of conventional psychiatric categories.

[104]

Minnesota Multiphasic Personality Inventory. Ages 16 and over; 1942–67; MMPI; 14 scores: hypochondriasis (Hs, '43), depression (D, '43), hysteria (Hy, '43), psychopathic deviate (Pd, '43), masculinity and femininity (Mf, '43), paranoia (Pa, '43), psychasthenia (Pt, '43), schizophrenia (Sc, '43), hypomania (Ma, '43), social (Si, '51), question (?), lie (L), validity (F, '43), test taking attitude (K, '46); 3 editions differing in format: individual, original group, rearranged group; revised manual ('67, 36 pages); *An MMPI Handbook* ('60, 579 pages, see 969 below) by W. Grant Dahlstrom and George Schlager Welsh, an essential supplement to manual; sections on scale descriptions and interpretation of scores omitted from 1967 manual; normative and reliability data unchanged since 1951; $1.50 per manual; $11.70 per MMPI Handbook; $23 per set of tapes for nonreading administration; postage extra; for computerized scoring and interpreting services see *105–9;* Spanish edition available; Starke R. Hathaway and J. Charnley McKinley; Psychological Corporation. *

a) INDIVIDUAL FORM ("THE CARD SET"). 1942–67; 550 cards plus sorting guides ('43); record blank ('48, 2 pages); $32 per set of testing materials including 50 record blanks; $4.20 per 50 record blanks; (30–90) minutes.

b) OLD GROUP FORM ("THE BOOKLET FORM"). 1943–67; items same as in individual form; test ('43, 15 pages); profile ('48, 2 pages); separate answer sheets (Hankes, IBM 805, IBM 1230, NCS) must be used; $6.50 per 25 tests; $4.50 per 50 sets of IBM 805 answer sheets and profiles; $4.60 per 50 sets of IBM 1230 answer sheets and profiles; $3.60 per 50 Hankes or NCS answer sheets; $6 ($7.50) per set of manual and IBM 805 hand scoring (machine scoring) stencils; $2 per specimen set; Hankes scoring service, $1.60 to $1.36 per test; NCS scoring service: 85¢ to 50¢ per test (daily service), 45¢ to 33¢ per test ($11.25 minimum; weekly service); (30–90) minutes.

c) NEW GROUP FORM (FORM R). 1965–67; c1943–67; new sequence of items with the 399 items used to obtain the 14 scores appearing first and the 167 research items last; shortened versions consist of the first 399 items or if K and Si scales are not wanted, 366 items; hard-cover booklet ('66, 23 stepdown pages) doubles as lapboard; separate answer sheets (NCS) must be used; $2 to $1.50 per test; $4.80 per 50 answer sheets; $4.50 per set of manual and hand scoring stencils; $3 per specimen set; NCS scoring service same as for old group form; (40–90) minutes for complete form, (40–75) minutes for shortened version.

REFERENCES

1–72. See 3:60.
73–283. See 4:71.
284–779. See 5:86.
780–1394. See 6:143.
1395–2460. See P:166, also includes a cumulative name index to the first 2460 references for this test.
2461. GLASER, ROBERT. "Predicting Achievement in Medical School." *J Appl Psychol* 35:272–4 Ag '51. *
2462. GOUGH, HARRISON G.; McCLOSKY, HERBERT; AND MEEHL, PAUL E. "A Personality Scale for Dominance." *J Abn & Social Psychol* 46:360–6 Jl '51. * (PA 26:2181)
2463. PHELAN, JOSEPH GERARD. *A Study of Psychological Diagnostic Skill as Employed in the Clinical Investigation of*

Personality. Doctor's thesis, Princeton University (Princeton, N.J.), 1951. (*DA* 13:599)

2464. BOLAND, JOHN LOUIS, JR. *A Comparison of Stutterers and Non-Stutterers on Several Measures of Anxiety.* Doctor's thesis, University of Michigan (Ann Arbor, Mich.), 1952. (*DA* 12:227)

2465. LAPLACE, JOHN PETER. *An Exploratory Study of Personality and Its Relationship to Success in Professional Baseball.* Doctor's thesis, Columbia University (New York, N.Y.), 1952. (*DA* 12:592)

2466. LEVINSON, HARRY. *The Relation of After-Image Duration to Certain Aspects of Personality.* Doctor's thesis, University of Kansas (Lawrence, Kan.), 1952. (*DA* 13:261)

2467. RENZAGLIA, GUY ANTHONY. *Some Correlates of the Self-Structures as Measured by an Index of Adjustments and Values.* Doctor's thesis, University of Minnesota (Minneapolis, Minn.), 1952. (*DA* 12:784)

2468. UECKER, ALBERT E. *A Comparative Study of the Vocational Interests, Aspirations, and Achievements of Selected Groups of Veteran Psychiatric Patients.* Doctor's thesis, University of Minnesota (Minneapolis, Minn.), 1952. (*DA* 12:392)

2469. WEBER, ROBERT JOHN. *A Study of the Relationship of Physical Fitness to Success in School and to Personality.* Doctor's thesis, State University of Iowa (Iowa City, Iowa), 1952. (*DA* 12:716)

2470. CRAWFORD, RONALD EUGENE. *Teacher-Pupil Personality Relationships.* Doctor's thesis, New York University (New York, N.Y.), 1953. (*DA* 13:589)

2471. CUADRA, CARLOS ALBERT. *A Psychometric Investigation of Control Factors in Psychological Adjustment.* Doctor's thesis, University of California (Berkeley, Calif.), 1953.

2472. MILL, CYRIL RALPH. *Personality Patterns of Socially Selected and Socially Rejected Male College Students.* Doctor's thesis, Michigan State College (East Lansing, Mich.), 1953. (*DA* 13:866)

2473. MOLDAWSKY, PATRICIA CORCORAN. *A Study of Personality Variables in Patients With Skin Disorders.* Doctor's thesis, State University of Iowa (Iowa City, Iowa), 1953. (*DA* 13:1260)

2474. RUDERMAN, VICTOR. *A Study of the Relationship Between Attitude Change and Post-Release Adjustment.* Doctor's thesis, New York University (New York, N.Y.), 1953. (*DA* 14:2396)

2475. SCODEL, ALVIN. "Passivity in a Class of Peptic Ulcer Patients." *Psychol Monogr* 67(10):1–15 '53. * (*PA* 28:4724)

2476. VITALE, JOHN HENRY. *An Investigation of Some Personality Correlates During the Clinical Course of Tuberculosis.* Doctor's thesis, Stanford University (Stanford, Calif.), 1953. (*DA* 14:401)

2477. WOLFF, WIRT MCCOY. *An Investigation of the Concept of Certainty in Human Behavior.* Doctor's thesis, Stanford University (Stanford, Calif.), 1953. (*DA* 13:893)

2478. ZUMWINKLE, ROBERT GORDON. *Factors Associated With the Compatibility of Roommates: A Test of the Birds-of-a-Feather Hypothesis.* Doctor's thesis, University of Minnesota (Minneapolis, Minn.), 1953. (*DA* 14:563)

2479. BERLIN, ASA JAIRUS. *An Exploratory Attempt to Isolate Types of Stuttering.* Doctor's thesis, Northwestern University (Evanston, Ill.), 1954. (*DA* 14:2433)

2480. BLUMBERG, EUGENE M. Chap. 3, "Results of Psychological Testing of Cancer Patients," pp. 30–71; discussion by Bruno Klopfer and J. F. T. Bugental. In *The Psychological Variables in Human Cancer.* Edited by Joseph A. Gengerelli and Frank J. Kirkner. Berkeley, Calif.: University of California Press, 1954. Pp. vi, 135. * (*PA* 29:4506)

2481. FEINER, ARTHUR H. *A Study of Certain Aspects of the Perception of Parental Figures and Sexual Identifications of an Obese Adolescent Female Group.* Doctor's thesis, New York University (New York, N.Y.), 1954. (*DA* 14:868)

2482. HILL, JULIUS MATHEW. *The Effects of Artificially Measured Low Aptitude Test Scores on Change in Vocational Interest.* Doctor's thesis, University of Michigan (Ann Arbor, Mich.), 1954. (*DA* 14:781)

2483. LABUE, ANTHONY CHARLES. *An Analysis of Some Factors Associated With Persistence of Interest in Teaching as a Vocational Choice.* Doctor's thesis, Syracuse University (Syracuse, N.Y.), 1954. (*DA* 14:2001)

2484. LEVY, SOL, AND FREEMAN, R. A. "Use of the Minnesota Multiphasic Personality Inventory in Measuring Adjustment of Prisoners." *J Social Ther* 1:33–9 O '54. * (*PA* 29:8777)

2485. SHUTTLEWORTH, MARGARET. *An Investigation of the Relationship Between Certain Psychological Factors and Childbirth.* Doctor's thesis, State University of Iowa (Iowa City, Iowa), 1954. (*DA* 14:716)

2486. TANNER, WILLIAM C., JR. "Personality Bases in Teacher Selection." *Phi Delta Kappan* 35:271–4+ Ap '54. *

2487. BLACK, JOHN D. "The Use of the MMPI With Normal Persons," pp. 33–48. In *New Perspectives in Counseling.* Edited by Vivian H. Hewer. Minneapolis, Minn.: University of Minnesota Press, 1955. Pp. v, 60. * (*PA* 29:7943)

2488. REED, MAX RODNEY. *A Study of the Masculinity-Femininity Dimension of Personality in "Normal" and "Pathological" Groups: An Investigation of Differences in MF Test Productions of Hospitalized and Non-Hospitalized Women.*

Doctor's thesis, Washington University (St. Louis, Mo.), 1955. (*DA* 15:1442)

2489. SARBIN, THEODORE R., AND HARDYCK, CURTIS D. "Conformance in Role Perception as a Personality Variable." *J Consult Psychol* 19:109–11 Ap '55. * (*PA* 30:624)

2490. SMUTZ, HAROLD TURK. *Investigation of a Reading Improvement Program in an Industrial Setting, Analyzing and Comparing the Reading Behavior With Measured Attitudes, Personality Attributes and Work Performance.* Doctor's thesis, Washington University (St. Louis, Mo.), 1955. (*DA* 15:1360)

2491. BARRON, F. Chap. 64, "Ego-Strength and the Management of Aggression," pp. 579–85. In *Basic Readings on the MMPI in Psychology and Medicine.* Edited by George Schlager Welsh and W. Grant Dahlstrom. Minneapolis, Minn.: University of Minnesota Press, 1956. Pp. xvii, 656. *

2492. BLACK, J. D. Chap. 17, "Adjectives Associated With Various MMPI Codes," pp. 151–72. In *Basic Readings on the MMPI in Psychology and Medicine.* Edited by George Schlager Welsh and W. Grant Dahlstrom. Minneapolis, Minn.: University of Minnesota Press, 1956. Pp. xvii, 656. *

2493. BLACK, J. D. Chap. 62, "MMPI Results for Fifteen Groups of Female College Students," pp. 562–73. In *Basic Readings on the MMPI in Psychology and Medicine.* Edited by George Schlager Welsh and W. Grant Dahlstrom. Minneapolis, Minn.: University of Minnesota Press, 1956. Pp. xvii, 656. *

2494. CUADRA, C. A. Chap. 27, "A Scale for Control in Psychological Adjustment (Cn)," pp. 235–54. In *Basic Readings on the MMPI in Psychology and Medicine.* Edited by George Schlager Welsh and W. Grant Dahlstrom. Minneapolis, Minn.: University of Minnesota Press, 1956. Pp. xvii, 656. *

2495. DRAKE, L. E. Chap. 19, "Scale 0 (Social Introversion)," pp. 181–3. In *Basic Readings on the MMPI in Psychology and Medicine.* Edited by George Schlager Welsh and W. Grant Dahlstrom. Minneapolis, Minn.: University of Minnesota Press, 1956. Pp. xvii, 656. *

2496. ENGEL, MARY. *The Stability of the Self-Concept in Adolescence.* Doctor's thesis, George Peabody College for Teachers (Nashville, Tenn.), 1956. (*DA* 17:1810)

2497. GOLDBERG, HYMAN; AMBINDER, WALTER J.; COOPER, LAWRENCE; AND ABRAMS, A. LEONARD. "Emotional Status of Patients With Acute Gingivitis." *N Y State Dental J* 22:308–20 Ag–S '56. *

2498. HATHAWAY, S. R. Chap. 10, "Scales 5 (Masculinity-Femininity), 6 (Paranoia), and 8 (Schizophrenia)," pp. 104–11. In *Basic Readings on the MMPI in Psychology and Medicine.* Edited by George Schlager Welsh and W. Grant Dahlstrom. Minneapolis, Minn.: University of Minnesota Press, 1956. Pp. xvii, 656. *

2499. HELLER, DORIS G. *The Relationship Between Sex-Appropriate Behavior in Young Children and the Clarity of the Sex-Role of the Like-Sexed Parents as Measured by Tests.* Doctor's thesis, New York University (New York, N.Y.), 1956. (*DA* 19:3365)

2500. HOLDER, WAYNE BUTLER. *The Relationship of Conformity and Consistency of Value Attitudes to Personal and Social Adjustment.* Doctor's thesis, University of Missouri (Columbia, Mo.), 1956. (*DA* 16:1277)

2501. LENFESTEY, FREDERICK THOMAS. *The Degree of Participation in Student Activities in Relation to the Presence of Certain Personality Characteristics.* Doctor's thesis, University of Florida (Gainesville, Fla.), 1956. (*DA* 16:2515)

2502. MEEHL, PAUL E. "Wanted—A Good Cookbook." *Am Psychologist* 11:263–72 Je '56. * (*PA* 31:6029)

2503. PILE, EVERETT NEWMAN. *Correlates of Retest Response Reversals on Selected Minnesota Multiphasic Personality Inventory Items.* Master's thesis, San Diego State College (San Diego, Calif.), 1956.

2504. PRELL, ARTHUR ELY. *The Effectiveness of a Penal Treatment Program and Its Relation to Parole Behavior.* Doctor's thesis, University of Minnesota (Minneapolis, Minn.), 1956. (*DA* 16:2549)

2505. P'SIMER, CHRISTINE. *An Experimental Study of the Effects of Counseling in Freshmen Halls.* Doctor's thesis, Florida State University (Tallahassee, Fla.), 1956. (*DA* 17:317)

2506. VAN DALSEM, ELIZABETH LOU. *Factors Related to Low Achievement in High School English.* Doctor's thesis, Stanford University (Stanford, Calif.), 1956. (*DA* 16:1233)

2507. WELSH, G. S. Chap. 29, "Factor Dimensions A and R," pp. 264–81. In *Basic Readings on the MMPI in Psychology and Medicine.* Edited by George Schlager Welsh and W. Grant Dahlstrom. Minneapolis, Minn.: University of Minnesota Press, 1956. Pp. xvii, 656. *

2508. ASCH, MORTON JAY. *Negative Response Bias and Personality Adjustment.* Doctor's thesis, Syracuse University (Syracuse, N.Y.), 1957. (*DA* 17:1704)

2509. CLANCY, DAVID DANA. *The Relationship of Positive Response Bias or Acquiescence to Psychopathology.* Doctor's thesis, Syracuse University (Syracuse, N.Y.), 1957. (*DA* 17:2054)

2510. DOUGLASS, ROBERT RAYMOND. *Personality of the Librarian.* Doctor's thesis, University of Chicago (Chicago, Ill.), 1957.

2511. GOOD, PATRICIA EILEEN KING-ELLISON. *A Psychological Study of the Effects of Regressive Electroshock Therapy.*

Doctor's thesis, University of Minnesota (Minneapolis, Minn.), 1957. (*DA* 17:2064)

2512. LEWIS, WILLIAM ANDREW. *The Relationship Between Emotional Adjustment, the Amount of Need Satisfaction Achieved and the Ability to Differentiate Ways of Obtaining Need Satisfaction.* Doctor's thesis, University of Illinois (Urbana, Ill.), 1957. (*DA* 18:497)

2513. LIPMAN, RONALD STEWART. *Some Relationships Between Anxiety, "Defensiveness" and Future Time Perspective.* Doctor's thesis, University of Connecticut (Storrs, Conn.), 1957. (*DA* 18:1518)

2514. SIMONS, WESLEY STANLEY. *The Personality Characteristics of the Residence Hall Assistant as Related to Job Performance.* Doctor's thesis, Michigan State University (East Lansing, Mich.), 1957. (*DA* 18:135)

2515. SINES, LLOYD K. *An Experimental Investigation of the Relative Contribution to Clinical Diagnosis and Personality Description of Various Kinds of Pertinent Data.* Doctor's thesis, University of Minnesota (Minneapolis, Minn.), 1957. (*DA* 17:2067)

2516. STERNITZKE, VINCENT L. *An Evaluation of the Reading and Study Methods Program of the University of Kansas for the Years 1953 to 1956.* Doctor's thesis, University of Kansas (Lawrence, Kan.), 1957. (*DA* 19:2856)

2517. ASPREY, GENE MAURICE. *The Effectiveness of Two Methods of Exercise Used in the Treatment of Back Pain.* Doctor's thesis, State University of Iowa (Iowa City, Iowa), 1958. (*DA* 19:1640)

2518. CALDWELL, ALEXANDER BRYAN. *Personality Impressions and Response Prediction.* Doctor's thesis, University of Minnesota (Minneapolis, Minn.), 1958. (*DA* 19:3019)

2519. CAMPBELL, EVERETT IHSEN. *A Study of Religious Conflict in Hospitalized Psychotics and Hospitalized Normals.* Doctor's thesis, University of Pittsburgh (Pittsburgh, Pa.), 1958. (*DA* 18:2236)

2520. FULKERSON, SAMUEL C.; FREUD, SHELDON L.; AND RAYNOR, GORDON H. "The Use of the MMPI in the Psychological Evaluation of Pilots." *J Aviat Med* 29:122–9 F '58. *

2521. HALBERSTAM, JACOB LEO. *Some Personality Correlates of Conditioning, Generalization, and Extinction of Experimental Anxiety.* Doctor's thesis, Columbia University (New York, N.Y.), 1958. (*DA* 19:360)

2522. MULLEN, ESTHER. *An Investigation of Some Aspects of Depression and Its Effect on the Perception of the Self and Others in a Non-Psychiatric Population.* Doctor's thesis, New York University (New York, N.Y.), 1958. (*DA* 19:2390)

2523. SWENSON, WENDELL MONSON. *A Study of Death Attitudes in the Gerontic Population and Their Relationship to Certain Measurable Physical and Social Characteristics.* Doctor's thesis, University of Minnesota (Minneapolis, Minn.), 1958. (*DA* 19:177)

2524. ADAMS, ADRAN DETAR. *Effects of Physical Conditioning Upon Physiological Stress Response and Psychological Adjustment.* Master's thesis, University of California (Los Angeles, Calif.), 1959.

2525. GARDNER, PAUL LEON. *Academic Failure, Reinstatement, and Follow-Up.* Doctor's thesis, Ohio State University (Columbus, Ohio), 1959. (*DA* 20:3627)

2526. DUBNO, PETER. *Group Effectiveness in Relation to the Interaction Between Decision Time Characteristics of Leaders and Task Conditions.* Doctor's thesis, New York University (New York, N.Y.), 1960. (*DA* 21:2390)

2527. GILLER, DONALD WAYNE. *Some Psychological Correlates of Recovery From Surgery.* Doctor's thesis, University of Texas (Austin, Tex.), 1960. (*DA* 21:2001)

2528. LAMBERT, PHILIP. "Mathematical Ability and Masculinity." *Arith Teach* 7:19–21 Ja '60. *

2529. MORGAN, PATRICIA KAYE. *Attitudes, Attitude Change and Group Conformity in the Psychopathic Personality.* Doctor's thesis, Louisiana State University (Baton Rouge, La.), 1960. (*DA* 21:2367)

2530. O'DONNELL, WILLIAM FRANCIS, JR. *The Effects of Individual Differences and Hostility Arousal on the Expression of Hostility in a Verbal Conditioning Situation.* Doctor's thesis, University of Washington (Seattle, Wash.), 1960. (*DA* 20:4723)

2531. VELDMAN, DONALD JOHN. *Hostility and Self-Evaluation.* Doctor's thesis, University of Texas (Austin, Tex.), 1960. (*DA* 21:2789)

2532. WALKER, GILWEE. *Social Pressure, Repression, and Cognitive Transformation.* Doctor's thesis, University of Washington (Seattle, Wash.), 1960. (*DA* 20:4726)

2533. WILSON, J. W.; DALTON, AND DYKMAN, ROSCOE A. "Background Autonomic Activity in Medical Students." *J Comp & Physiol Psychol* 53:405–11 Ag '60. * (*PA* 36:1DJ05W)

2534. YAMAMOTO, JOE, AND SEEMAN, WILLIAM. "Psychological Study of Castrated Males." *Psychiatric Res Rep Am Psychiatric Assn* 12:97–103 Ja '60. * (*PA* 35:6527)

2535. BOONE, JERRY NEAL. *A Study of the Effects of Anxiety on Auditory Perceptual Response to Threat.* Doctor's thesis, Vanderbilt University (Nashville, Tenn.), 1961. (*DA* 22:2062)

2536. DACHOWSKI, MARJORIE McCORMICK. *Inconsistency as Measured by Direct, Indirect and Projective Tests and Its*

Relationship to General Neuroticism. Doctor's thesis, University of Illinois (Urbana, Ill.), 1961. (*DA* 22:3740)

2537. DICKSON, STANLEY. *Differences Between Children Who Spontaneously Outgrew and Children Who Retained Functional Articulation Errors.* Doctor's thesis, University of Buffalo (Buffalo, N.Y.), 1961. (*DA* 22:151)

2538. DILLINGHAM, FRANCIS I., AND YOSHIMURA, SHIZUKO. *A Study of the Relationship of Selected Items on the Minnesota Multiphasic Personality Inventory to Clinical Practice Behaviors and Personality of Student Nurses in Selected Schools of Nursing.* Master's thesis, San Francisco State College (San Francisco, Calif.), 1961.

2539. KROEGER, VIRGIL JOHN. *A Study in the Classification of Delinquent Behavior.* Doctor's thesis, University of Minnesota (Minneapolis, Minn.), 1961. (*DA* 22:2097)

2540. LOWE, CARRINGTON MARSHALL. *A Study of the Nature of Guilt in Psychopathology.* Doctor's thesis, Ohio State University (Columbus, Ohio), 1961. (*DA* 22:909)

2541. McCLENAHAN, MARY LOUISE PHELPS. *The Relationship of Test-Defined Needs to Illuminance Matches of Need-Related Pictures.* Doctor's thesis, State University of Iowa (Iowa City, Iowa), 1961. (*DA* 21:3862)

2542. MOORE, ROSEMARIE KLEIN. *Susceptibility to Hypnosis and Susceptibility to Social Influence.* Doctor's thesis, Stanford University (Stanford, Calif.), 1961. (*DA* 22:1735)

2543. PARKES, EDWARD HARVEY. *The Effect of Situational Stress, Set-Strength, and Trait Anxiety on Problem-Solving Rigidity.* Doctor's thesis, University of Maryland (College Park, Md.), 1961. (*DA* 24:385)

2544. WINER, FRANK. *The Relationship of Certain Attitudes Toward the Mother to Sex-Role Identity.* Doctor's thesis, New York University (New York, N.Y.), 1961. (*DA* 22:4416)

2545. ASHBROOK, JAMES BARBOUR. *Evaluating Seminary Students as Potential Ministers.* Master's thesis, Ohio State University (Columbus, Ohio), 1962.

2546. BEAMISH, JEROME J., AND MALFETTI, JAMES L. "A Psychological Comparison of Violator and Non-Violator Automobile Drivers in the 16 to 19 Year Age Group." *Traffic Safety Res R* 6:12–5 Mr '62. *

2547. BLAUFARB, MYRNA TICKTIN. *Set and Bias in Clinical Judgment.* Doctor's thesis, University of Illinois (Urbana, Ill.), 1962. (*DA* 23:698)

2548. CUNNINGHAM, ANNE PATRICIA. *Cognitive Controls and Measures of Personality.* Doctor's thesis, University of Kentucky (Lexington, Ky.), 1962. (*DAI* 30:2432B)

2549. DVORAK, EDWARD JOHN. *Characteristics of University Students With Regard to Acceptance and Rejection of Polio Vaccination.* Doctor's thesis, University of Minnesota (Minneapolis, Minn.), 1962. (*DA* 23:3326)

2550. GUERRANT, JOHN; ANDERSON, WILLIAM W.; FISCHER, AMES; WEINSTEIN, MORTON R.; JAROS, R. MARY; AND DESKINS, ANDREW. Chap. 5, "Psychological Considerations," pp. 66–92. In their *Personality in Epilepsy.* Springfield, Ill.: Charles C Thomas, Publisher, 1962. Pp. xii, 112. *

2551. HOWARD, STEPHEN JAMES. *Determinants of Sex-Role Identifications of Homosexual Female Delinquents.* Doctor's thesis, University of Southern California (Los Angeles, Calif.), 1962. (*DA* 23:2588)

2552. ISMIR, AWAD A., AND KLEBAN, MORTON H. "The Applicability of the Crown-Marlowe Social Desirability Scale to a Psychiatric Hospital Population." *J Clin Psychol* 18:144–6 Ap '62. * (*PA* 38:8494)

2553. JOHNSON, LYNN ERIC. *Personality Changes in Emotionally Disturbed Students During Counseling.* Doctor's thesis, University of Utah (Salt Lake City, Utah), 1962. (*DA* 24:2985)

2554. KLIEWER, VERNON DEAN. *Multiple Stylistic Effects and Self-Report Personality Assessment.* Doctor's thesis, University of Oregon (Eugene, Ore.), 1962. (*DA* 23:3966)

2555. LIVINGSTON, MARTIN SANDELMAN. *The Repression Response to Induced Failure in Relation to Neurosis and Introversion-Extroversion.* Doctor's thesis, Columbia University (New York, N.Y.), 1962. (*DA* 23:3478)

2556. McCARTHY, M. KIERAN. *Masculinity Faking in a Validity Study of the Minnesota Multiphasic Personality Inventory (MMPI) and the FM Scale of the Strong Vocational Interest Blank for Women (SVIBW).* Master's thesis, Marquette University (Milwaukee, Wis.), 1962.

2557. MARSH, STEWART H. "Validating the Selection of Deputy Sheriffs." *Pub Personnel R* 23:41–4 Jl '62. * (*PA* 37:2051)

2558. SILVERMAN, SAUL A. *Exploration and Evaluation of Various Aspects of Personality and Self Concept Change in Functional Marriage Education With Special Regard to Those of Low Marriage Potential.* Doctor's thesis, Florida State University (Tallahassee, Fla.), 1962. (*DA* 23:1826)

2559. TAGGART, MORRIS. *A Study of Attitude Change in a Group of Theological Students.* Doctor's thesis, Northwestern University (Evanston, Ill.), 1962. (*DA* 23:2236)

2560. WILLIS, ROBERT NEAL. *The Use of the Galvanic Skin Reflex to Demonstrate Construct Validity of Personality Questionnaires.* Doctor's thesis, Florida State University (Tallahassee, Fla.), 1962. (*DA* 23:727)

2561. WILSON, WILLIAM EDWIN. *The Construct Validity of Several Perceived-Ideal Self Concept Discrepancy Measures.*

Doctor's thesis, Pennsylvania State University (University Park, Pa.), 1962. (*DA* 23:2600)

2562. ACHESON, SHIRLEY ANN. *Filicide: An MMPI Study of Mothers Who Murdered Their Children.* Master's thesis, San Diego State College (San Diego, Calif.), 1963.

2563. BARRON, FRANK. *Creativity and Psychological Health: Origins of Personal Vitality and Creative Freedom.* Princeton, N.J.: D. Van Nostrand Co., Inc., 1963. Pp. xi, 292. *

2564. BATES, CHARLES O. *A Study of Creative Potential as Found in Elementary Student Teachers.* Doctor's thesis, Ball State Teachers College (Muncie, Ind.), 1963. (*DA* 24:4561)

2565. CARR, GENEVIEVE DELTA. *A Psychosociological Study of Fertile and Infertile Marriages.* Doctor's thesis, University of Southern California (Los Angeles, Calif.), 1963. (*DA* 24: 5598)

2566. CHURCH, J. C. *Relationship Between Premorbid History and MMPI Profiles of Schizophrenics.* Master's thesis, University of North Carolina (Chapel Hill, N.C.), 1963.

2567. COELHO, VICTOR ANTHONY. *A Personality Scale for Candidates to the Priesthood.* Master's thesis, University of Detroit (Detroit, Mich.), 1963.

2568. EDWARDS, ALLEN L. "A Factor Analysis of Experimental Social Desirability and Response Set Scales." *J Appl Psychol* 47:308–16 O '63. * (*PA* 38:4230)

2569. GIBBENS, T. C. N.; WITH THE ASSISTANCE OF A. MARRIAGE AND A. WALKER. *Psychiatric Studies of Borstal Lads,* pp. 143–84. London: Oxford University Press, 1963. Pp. vi, 230. *

2570. GOLDBERG, LEWIS R., AND RORER, LEONARD G. *Test-Retest Item Statistics Comparing Four Administrations of Items Differentiating "Yielders" From "Independents."* ORI Research Monograph, Vol. 3, No. 2. Eugene, Ore.: Oregon Research Institute, August 1963. Pp. iii, 56. *

2571. HALL, CHARLES LAMONT, JR. *Patterns of Parental Identification as Related to Schizoid Behaviors in Grossly Normal Males.* Doctor's thesis, State University of Iowa (Iowa City, Iowa), 1963. (*DA* 26:7447)

2572. HALL, EVERETTE EARL, JR. *Psychological Correlates or Ordinal Position in the Two-Child Family.* Doctor's thesis, University of Florida (Gainesville, Fla.), 1963. (*DA* 24:2116)

2573. INGRAM, O. KELLY. "Student Recruitment." *Duke Divinity Sch B* 28:188–98 N '63. *

2574. JOHNSON, KENNETH EDWIN. *Personal Religious Growth Through Small Group Participation: A Psychological Study of Personality Changes and Shifts in Religious Attitudes Which Result From Participation in a Spiritual Growth Group.* Doctor's thesis, Pacific School of Religion (Berkeley, Calif.), 1963. (*DA* 25:628)

2575. KAKKAR, S. B. "A Diagnosis of Abnormal Personality Patterns." *Manas* 10(2):57–63 '63. * (*PA* 38:10195)

2576. LAND, MELVIN. "Psychological Tests as Predictors for Scholastic Achievement of Dental Students." *J Dental Ed* 27: 25–30 Mr '63. *

2577. MENA, ABELARDO. *Evaluation of Regressive Electroshock Treatments in Chronic Paranoid Schizophrenics.* Doctor's thesis, University of Minnesota (Minneapolis, Minn.), 1963. (*DA* 25:6763)

2578. PALMER, ROBERT D. "Hand Differentiation and Psychological Functioning." *J Personality* 31:445–61 D '63. * (*PA* 38:8373)

2579. QUINN, LEE WALTER, JR. *Factors Associated With Failure in Physical Education Due to Unsatisfactory Attendance.* Master's thesis, University of Florida (Gainesville, Fla.), 1963.

2580. SHAFFER, JOHN W. Chap. 24, "Masculinity-Femininity and Other Personality Traits in Gonadal Aplasia (Turner's Syndrome)," pp. 219–32. In *Advances in Sex Research: A Publication of the Society for the Scientific Study of Sex.* Edited by Hugo G. Beigel. New York: Hoeber Medical Division, Harper & Row, Publishers, Inc., 1963. Pp. xiv, 261. * (*PA* 39:8303)

2581. SMITH, TIMOTHY ANDRE. *A Study of the Temperament Factors of Tempo, Fluency, and Carefulness.* Doctor's thesis, University of North Carolina (Chapel Hill, N.C.), 1963. (*DA* 26:484)

2582. WHITTEMORE, ROBERT GEORGE, JR. *Modification of Originality Responses in Academically Talented, Male University Freshmen.* Doctor's thesis, Arizona State University (Tempe, Ariz.), 1963. (*DA* 25:6403)

2583. ALEAMONI, LAWRENCE MASSUD. *Analysis of Personality Measures and Measures Used to Predict Success in Science.* Master's thesis, University of Utah (Salt Lake City, Utah), 1964.

2584. BANAS, PAUL ANTHONY. *An Investigation of Trans-situational Moderators.* Doctor's thesis, University of Minnesota (Minneapolis, Minn.), 1964. (*DA* 26:1158)

2585. BEATTY, BILLIE CAMP. *Counselee-Counselor Identifications.* Doctor's thesis, University of California (Berkeley, Calif.), 1964. (*DA* 25:4255)

2586. BRODSKY, STANLEY LEON. *Language Patterns of Repressors and Sensitizers in Personal and Impersonal Descriptions.* Doctor's thesis, University of Florida (Gainesville, Fla.), 1964. (*DA* 25:4256)

2587. CHIA, FU-MING. *Effects of College Student Moodiness on Activities and Interpersonal Adjustment.* Doctor's thesis,

University of California (Los Angeles, Calif.), 1964. (*DA* 25:6385)

2588. CODKIND, DOROTHY. *Attitudes Toward the Imaginary: Their Relationship to Level of Personality Integration.* Doctor's thesis, University of Kansas (Lawrence, Kan.), 1964. (*DA* 27:1616B)

2589. CORDER, B. F.; HENDRICKS, A.; AND CORDER, R. F. "An MMPI Study of a Group of Wives of Alcoholics." *Q J Studies Alcohol* 25:551–4 S '64. *

2590. CROWNE, DOUGLAS P., AND MARLOWE, DAVID. *The Approval Motive: Studies in Evaluative Dependence.* New York: John Wiley & Sons, Inc., 1964. Pp. xiii, 233. *

2591. EDENS, LESTER WILLIAM. *An Analysis of Certain Socio-Psychological Characteristics of Unwed Mothers Referred to Private Agencies in Washington and Idaho.* Doctor's thesis, University of Idaho (Moscow, Idaho), 1964. (*DA* 25:5730)

2592. FISKE, DONALD W.; CARTWRIGHT, DESMOND S.; AND KIRTNER, WILLIAM L. "Are Psychotherapeutic Changes Predictable?" *J Abn & Social Psychol* 69:418–26 O '64. * (*PA* 39:8058)

2593. GILBREATH, STUART HENRY. *The Effects of Structured and Unstructured Group Counseling on Certain Personality Dimensions of Male College Students Who Underachieve.* Doctor's thesis, Michigan State University (East Lansing, Mich.), 1964. (*DA* 26:199)

2594. HETHERINGTON, E. MAVIS, AND FELDMAN, SOLOMON E. "College Cheating as a Function of Subject and Situational Variables." *J Ed Psychol* 55:212–8 Ag '64. * (*PA* 39:4799)

2595. JONES, RICHARD R., AND GOLDBERG, LEWIS R. *An Alphabetical List of CPI Items With Corresponding MMPI Numbers.* ORI Technical Report, Vol. 4, No. 1. Eugene, Ore.: Oregon Research Institute, January 1964. Pp. 40. *

2596. JORGENSEN, RONALD LELAND. *Perceptual Selectivity Effects and Personality Variables of Hospitalized Subjects.* Doctor's thesis, Purdue University (Lafayette, Ind.), 1964. (*DA* 26:1171)

2597. KELLY, EMMET EUGENE. *Group Counseling Interaction and Member Personality.* Doctor's thesis, University of Texas (Austin, Tex.), 1964. (*DA* 25:5117)

2598. KYRIAZIS, PETER WILLIAM. *The Relation Between Measured Hypochondriasis and Semantic Differential Profiles (Among College Students).* Doctor's thesis, George Washington University (Washington, D.C.), 1964.

2599. LEVINSON, ALMA. *A Comparison of Concepts of Self and Parental Figures in Selected Groups of Under-, Average and High Achieving High School Boys: A Comparison of a Group of Underachievers With Groups of Average and Above Average Achievers Selected for Intelligence, Age and Grade.* Doctor's thesis, New York University (New York, N.Y.), 1964. (*DA* 25:1320)

2600. MACANDREW, CRAIG, AND GEERTSMA, ROBERT H. "A Critique of Alcoholism Scales Derived From the MMPI." *Q J Studies Alcohol* 25:68–76 Mr '64. *

2601. NEVILLE, HELEN ANN. *A Diagnostic Evaluation of the PGS II as Compared to the MMPI.* Master's thesis, University of Detroit (Detroit, Mich.), 1964.

2602. SILLER, JEROME. "Personality Determinants of Reaction to the Physically Disabled." *Am Found Blind Res B* 7:37–52 D '64. * (*PA* 39:9978)

2603. SPACE, MARGARET NIVEN. *A Study of Individual Predictability Based on Intra-Individual Variability on Certain Achievement Measures.* Doctor's thesis, University of Minnesota (Minneapolis, Minn.), 1964. (*DA* 26:879)

2604. STRICKER, LAWRENCE J., AND ROSS, JOHN. "Some Correlates of a Jungian Personality Inventory." *Psychol Rep* 14: 623–43 Ap '64. * (*PA* 39:1848)

2605. VEAL, LELAND RAMON. *A Comparison of the Professional Growth of Student Teachers Under Two Different Time-Arrangements for Student Teaching at the Secondary Level.* Doctor's thesis, University of South Carolina (Columbia, S.C.), 1964. (*DA* 25:7104)

2606. ABOU-ALLAM, RAGAA MAHMOUD. *Personality Correlates of the Movement of Concepts in the Semantic Space: An Investigation of the Effect of Some Personality Variables on the Magnitude of Association Between Initially Meaningless Assigns and Previously Meaningful Signs.* Doctor's thesis, New York University (New York, N.Y.), 1965. (*DA* 27:382A)

2607. BORRELLI, NICHOLAS JOSEPH. *The Client's Perception of Therapist Potency and Changes in Psychotherapy.* Doctor's thesis, Michigan State University (East Lansing, Mich.), 1965. (*DA* 27:960B)

2608. BOURESTOM, NORMAN C., AND HOWARD, MARY T. "Personality Characteristics of Three Disability Groups." *Arch Phys Med & Rehabil* 46:626–32 S '65. *

2609. BRYSON, JEWELL GILBERT. *The Effectiveness of an Individualized Mechanical Pacing Device, the Strong-Pacer, in College Typewriting.* Doctor's thesis, University of Tennessee (Knoxville, Tenn.), 1965. (*DA* 26:4491)

2610. CHURCH, JANE CAROLYN. *A Short-Term Longitudinal Study of Factors Related to IQ Change in White Southern Rural Adolescents.* Doctor's thesis, University of North Carolina (Chapel Hill, N.C.), 1965. (*DA* 27:299B)

2611. FREEDMAN, MERVIN B. "The Role of the Educated Woman: An Empirical Study of the Attitudes of a Group of College Women." *J Col Stud Personnel* 6:145–55 Mr '65. *

2612. FRIEDMAN, ALICE LISA. *The Effect of Personality and*

Interest Variables on Learning by Linear and Scrambled Methods of Programmed Instruction. Doctor's thesis, New York University (New York, N.Y.), 1965. (*DA* 27:390A)

2613. GAY, JAMES DONALD. *Personality Changes Associated With Workshop Participation.* Doctor's thesis, University of Kentucky (Lexington, Ky.), 1965. (*DAI* 30:2436B)

2614. HEWITT, JACK LEE. *A Communications Approach to the Prediction and Alteration of Hypnotic Susceptibility.* Doctor's thesis, University of Kansas (Lawrence, Kan.), 1965. (*DA* 26:4075)

2615. IRVING, STEPHEN GARY. *Parental Empathy and Adolescent Adjustment.* Doctor's thesis, University of Florida (Gainesville, Fla.), 1965. (*DA* 27:967B)

2616. LEARY, TIMOTHY; METZNER, RALPH; PRESNELL, MADISON; WEIL, GUNTHER; SCHWITZGEBEL, RALPH; AND KINNE, SARA. "A New Behavior Program Using Psilocybin." *Psychother Theory Res & Prac* 2:61–72 Jl '65. * (*PA* 40:3053)

2617. LUTHER, BALDEV RAJ. *A Comparative Study of Some Arousal-Related Measures in Psychiatric Patients and Surgical Patients.* Doctor's thesis, University of Minnesota (Minneapolis, Minn.), 1965. (*DA* 27:2140B)

2618. MCBRIDE, DON W.; HAMMILL, DONALD D.; AND GILMORE, DOUGLAS. "Personality Factors in the Success of Classroom Teachers of the Handicapped." *Cereb Palsy J* 26:3–5 My–Je '65. * (*PA* 40:775)

2619. MANN, NANCY AMALIA. *Free Association and Preferred Defenses.* Doctor's thesis, University of Michigan (Ann Arbor, Mich.), 1965. (*DA* 27:611B)

2620. NAHUM, L. H. "The Computer and Personality Inventory." *Conn Med* 29:764+ N '65. *

2621. PATTERSON, G. R. "Parents as Dispensers of Aversive Stimuli." *J Pers & Social Psychol* 2:844–51 D '65. * (*PA* 40:2703)

2622. ROA, CLAYTON DURWARD. *An Investigation of Factors Leading to the Withdrawal of Waldorf Junior College Freshmen.* Doctor's thesis, Michigan State University (East Lansing, Mich.), 1965. (*DA* 27:681A)

2623. ROBERTS, F. J. "Some Psychological Factors in Religious Conversion." *Brit J Social & Clin Psychol* 4:185–7 S '65. * (*PA* 40:1488)

2624. SCHEIBE, KARL E. "College Students Spend Eight Weeks in Mental Hospital: A Case Report." *Psychother Theory Res & Prac* 2:117–20 O '65. * (*PA* 40:3081)

2625. SEGAL, BERNARD E., AND WEISS, ROBERT J. "Emotional Adjustment, Social Organization and Psychiatric Treatment Rates." *Am Sociol R* 30:548–56 Ag '65. *

2626. SLAWSON, PAUL FREDERIC. "Psychodrama as a Treatment for Hospitalized Patients: A Controlled Study." *Am J Psychiatry* 122:530–3 N '65. * (*PA* 40:3085)

2627. SWARR, RALPH ROHRER. *An Exploratory Study of Masculinity and the Attribution of Dominance and Love to Parents.* Doctor's thesis, Michigan State University (East Lansing, Mich.), 1965. (*DA* 26:4818)

2628. TOLLEFSON, NONA FALMLEN. *Relationship of Counselor Need Orientation to Counselor Effectiveness and Counselor Personality.* Doctor's thesis, Purdue University (Lafayette, Ind.), 1965. (*DA* 27:122A)

2629. VAN DER VEEN, FERDINAND, AND STOLER, NORTON. "Therapist Judgments, Interview Behavior and Case Outcome." *Psychother Theory Res & Prac* 2:158–63 D '65. * (*PA* 40:4327)

2630. WALKER, RONALD E., AND FIRETTO, ANTHONY. "The Clergyman as a Variable in Psychological Testing." *J Sci Study Relig* 4:234–6 Ap '65. *

2631. WHARTON, WILLIAM LOUIS. *Factors Associated With Success of Returning College Dropouts.* Doctor's thesis, University of Florida (Gainesville, Fla.), 1965. (*DA* 27:645A)

2632. WINKLER, LAWRENCE. *A Study of Minnesota Multiphasic Personality Inventories of Bright Achievers, Bright Underachievers, and Students With Designated Learning Difficulties.* Doctor's thesis, George Washington University (Washington, D.C.), 1965.

2633. ARNETTE, JOHNNY LESTER. *The Effect of Short-Term Group Counseling on Anxiety and Hostility of Newly Incarcerated Prison Inmates.* Doctor's thesis, University of Florida (Gainesville, Fla.), 1966. (*DA* 27:3299A)

2634. BALLAS, ARTHUR CHRISTY. *Counseling Process and Outcome Related to Client's Perception of Self and Counselor.* Doctor's thesis, Michigan State University (East Lansing, Mich.), 1966. (*DA* 28:117A)

2635. BINDMAN, STEPHEN STEWART. *Personality Characteristics of the Parents of Children Diagnosed as Schizophrenic.* Doctor's thesis, University of California (Los Angeles, Calif.), 1966. (*DA* 27:298B)

2636. BOLLINGER, LAURENCE J. *An Investigation of the Psychological Characteristics of the Handicapped Employees in Industry.* Doctor's thesis, Wayne State University (Detroit, Mich.), 1966. (*DA* 30:375B)

2637. CALLEJA, DORIS FLOR. *The Effect of Relaxation Training on Cognitive Functioning Under Psychological Stress.* Doctor's thesis, University of California (Berkeley, Calif.), 1966. (*DA* 27:3666B)

2638. CASHMAN, JEROME PATRICK. *A Study of the Relationship Between Organic Factors, Certain Selected Variables and Progress in a Reading Improvement Program.* Doctor's

thesis, Fordham University (New York, N.Y.), 1966. (*DA* 27:1648A)

2639. CASTO, GLENDON WEST. *Relationship Methods With Probationary Students.* Doctor's thesis, University of Utah (Salt Lake City, Utah), 1966. (*DA* 27:1649A)

2640. DOHERTY, MARY AUSTIN, AND WALKER, RONALD E. "The Relationship of Personality Characteristics, Awareness, and Attitude in a Verbal Conditioning Situation." *J Personality* 34:504–16 D '66. *

2641. DUNLOP, EDWIN, Editor. *Essentials of the Automated MMPI: A Compendium of Clinical Information.* Glendale, Calif.: Institute of Clinical Analysis, 1966. Pp. iii, 62. *

2642. EISENMAN, RUSSELL. "Psychopathology and Sociometric Choice." *J Abn Psychol* 71:256–9 Ag '66. * (*PA* 40:11330)

2643. FITZGERALD, EDWARD THOMAS. *The Measurement of Openness to Experience: A Study of Regression in the Service of the Ego.* Doctor's thesis, University of California (Berkeley, Calif.), 1966. (*DA* 27:955B)

2644. GREENBLATT, DAVID ROBERT. *Semantic Differential Analysis of the "Triangular System" Hypothesis in "Adjusted" Overt Male Homosexuals.* Doctor's thesis, University of California (Los Angeles, Calif.), 1966. (*DA* 27:4123B)

2645. GUILLIAMS, CLARK IRVIN. *Predicting Creative Productivity in College Classes Where Creative Thinking Is Emphasized.* Doctor's thesis, University of Arkansas (Fayetteville, Ark.), 1966. (*DA* 27:675A)

2646. HAKENWERTH, QUENTIN W. *The Effect of Religious Life on the MMPI Scores of Religious Brothers: A Longitudinal Study.* Master's thesis, Loyola University (Chicago, Ill.), 1966.

2647. HARDYCK, CURTIS D., AND MOOS, RUDOLF H. "Sampling Problems in Studies of Psychosomatic Disorders: Difficulties in Determining Personality Correlates." *J Psychosom Res* 10:171–82 S '66. * (*PA* 41:716)

2648. HAVENS, ROBERT INNIS. *An Exploratory Search for Characteristic Patterns of High Performance Rated and Low Performance Rated Counselor-Candidates in a Counseling Practicum.* Doctor's thesis, University of Michigan (Ann Arbor, Mich.), 1966. (*DA* 28:104A)

2649. HELLER, KENNETH; DAVIS, JOHN D.; AND MYERS, ROGER A. "The Effects of Interviewer Style in a Standardized Interview." *J Consult Psychol* 30:501–8 D '66. * (*PA* 41:2975)

2650. HELSON, RAVENNA. "Personality of Women With Imaginative and Artistic Interests: The Role of Masculinity, Originality, and Other Characteristics in Their Creativity." *J Personality* 34:1–25 Mr '66. * (*PA* 40:8830)

2651. HESTON, L. L.; DENNEY, D. D.; AND PAULY, I. B. "The Adult Adjustment of Persons Institutionalized as Children." *Brit J Psychiatry* 112:1103–10 N '66. * (*PA* 41:4721)

2652. HINTON, BERNARD LLOYD. *A Model of Creative Problem Solving Performance and the Effects of Frustration.* Doctor's thesis, Stanford University (Stanford, Calif.), 1966. (*DA* 27:2508B)

2653. HOGAN, ROBERT A. "Implosive Therapy in the Short Term Treatment of Psychotics." *Psychother Theory Res & Prac* 3:25–32 F '66. * (*PA* 40:6744)

2654. KLETT, WILLIAM G. "The Effect of Historically Based Inferences on the Behavior of Withdrawn Psychiatric Patients." *J Clin Psychol* 22:427–9 O '66. * (*PA* 41:2987)

2655. LAZARUS, RICHARD S.; TOMITA, MASATOSHI; OPTON, EDWARD, JR.; AND KODAMA, MASAHISA. "A Cross-Cultural Study of Stress-Reaction Patterns in Japan." *J Pers & Social Psychol* 4:622–33 D '66. * (*PA* 41:2760)

2656. MUIZZUDDIN, SHEIKH. *A Comparative Study of Personality Characteristics of Teachers in Training in Culturally Different Areas of West Pakistan.* Doctor's thesis, Indiana University (Bloomington, Ind.), 1966. (*DA* 27:2073A)

2657. NASH, CARROLL B. "Relation Between ESP Scoring Level and the Minnesota Multiphasic Personality Inventory." *J Am Soc Psychical Res* 60:56–62 Ja '66. * (*PA* 40:7155)

2658. NEWMAN, PHYLLIS MACY. *The Effects of Making Social Desirability Judgments on Personality Inventory Scores of Schizophrenics.* Doctor's thesis, University of Southern California (Los Angeles, Calif.), 1966. (*DA* 27:3293B)

2659. NOWICKI, STEPHEN, JR. "A Study of Personality Characteristics of Successful Policemen." *Police* 10:39–40 Ja–F '66. *

2660. PERSONS, ROY W. "Psychological and Behavioral Change in Delinquents Following Psychotherapy." *J Clin Psychol* 22:337–40 Jl '66. * (*PA* 41:1315)

2661. QUENK, NAOMI LITT. *Fantasy and Personal Outlook: A Study of Daydreaming as a Function of Optimism, Pessimism, Realism, and Anxiety.* Doctor's thesis, University of California (Berkeley, Calif.), 1966. (*DA* 27:970B)

2662. RAVSTEN, LYNN ALLEN. *Mood-Judgment From Vocal Cues and Its Relationship to Personality Variables and Group Psychotherapy.* Doctor's thesis, University of Utah (Salt Lake City, Utah), 1966. (*DA* 27:2876B)

2663. REITER, MICHAEL. *Variables Associated With the Degree of Preferred Directiveness in Therapy.* Doctor's thesis, University of Texas (Austin, Tex.), 1966. (*DA* 27:3679B)

2664. REYNOLDS, PHYLLIS CANTRELL. *The Relationship of Knowledge About Incarcerated Delinquent Boys to Training and Experience in Working With Them.* Doctor's thesis, University of Minnesota (Minneapolis, Minn.), 1966. (*DA* 27: 2877B)

2665. ROESSLER, ROBERT; BURCH, NEIL R.; AND CHILDERS, HAROLD E. "Personality and Arousal Correlates of Specific Galvanic Skin Responses." *Psychophysiol* 3:115–30 O '66. * (*PA* 41:1255)

2666. ROSENTHAL, TED LEE. "Anxiety-Proneness and Susceptibility to Social Influence." *Archiv für die Gesamte Psychologie* 118:18–33 Jl '66. * (*PA* 40:13195)

2667. ROSMARIN, MARTIN SUMNER. *Reaction to Stress and Anxiety in Chronically Underachieving High Ability Students.* Doctor's thesis, University of Florida (Gainesville, Fla.), 1966. (*DA* 27:1630B)

2668. ROSSILLON, JOSEPH P. *The Construction and Validation of a Forced-Choice Scale to Measure Students' Self-Concepts of Their Effectiveness as Speakers.* Doctor's thesis, Southern Illinois University (Carbondale, Ill.), 1966. (*DA* 27:3162A)

2669. ROTH, HERBERT SAMUEL. *Personal and Demographic Characteristics Associated With L-I-D Response Bias of Domiciled Veterans on an Institutional Interest Inventory.* Doctor's thesis, University of Kansas (Lawrence, Kan.), 1966. (*DA* 28:1209B)

2670. RUHLING, ROBERT O. *A Comparative Study of Introversion-Extroversion in Selected Varsity and Intramural Athletes Using the Composite MMPI Introversion-Extroversion Scale.* Master's thesis, University of Maryland (College Park, Md.), 1966.

2671. RUNDQUIST, EDWARD A. "Item and Response Characteristics in Attitude and Personality Measurement: A Reaction to L. G. Rorer's 'The Great Response-Style Myth.'" *Psychol B* 66:166–77 S '66. * (*PA* 40:12335)

2672. SCHMALE, ARTHUR H., JR., AND IKER, HOWARD P. "The Affect of Hopelessness and the Development of Cancer: 1, Identification of Uterine Cervical Cancer in Women With Atypical Cytology." *Psychosom Med* 28:714–21 S–O '66. * (*PA* 41:4832)

2673. SEGAL, BERNARD E.; WALSH, T. MYRICK; AND WEISS, ROBERT J. "Emotional Maladjustment in an Undergraduate Population: An Analytical Assessment of Six-Year Trends." *J Am Col Health Assn* 14:190–6 F '66. *

2674. SHOR, RONALD E.; ORNE, MARTIN T.; AND O'CONNELL, DONALD N. "Psychological Correlates of Plateau Hypnotizability in a Special Volunteer Sample." *J Pers & Social Psychol* 3:80–95 Ja '66. * (*PA* 40:2262)

2675. SINGER, SUSAN KLUGMAN. *Factors Related to Participants' Memory for a Conversation.* Doctor's thesis, University of California (Berkeley, Calif.), 1966. (*DA* 27:1295B)

2676. STEFFENHAGEN, RONALD ALBERT. *Socio-Psychological Factors in Rheumatoid Arthritis.* Doctor's thesis, State University of New York (Buffalo, N.Y.), 1966. (*DA* 27:833A)

2677. STIX, DANIEL LOUIS. *Overachievement in College as a Function of Anxiety, Repression and Attitudes.* Doctor's thesis, Temple University (Philadelphia, Pa.), 1966. (*DA* 27:969A)

2678. STOLER, NORTON. *The Relationship of Patient Likability and the A-B Psychiatric Resident Types.* Doctor's thesis, University of Wisconsin (Madison, Wis.), 1966. (*DA* 28:1213B)

2679. TWOMEY, JOHN F. *Personality Patterns of Coronary Heart Patients.* Doctor's thesis, Boston University (Boston, Mass.), 1966. (*DA* 27:2866B)

2680. WALSTER, ELAINE; ARONSON, VERA; ABRAHAMS, DARCY; AND ROTTMAN, LEON. "Importance of Physical Attractiveness in Dating Behavior." *J Pers & Social Psychol* 4:508–16 N '66. * (*PA* 41:536)

2681. WATMAN, WALTER A. "The Relationship Between Acting Out Behavior and Some Psychological Test Indices in a Prison Population." *J Clin Psychol* 22:279–80 Jl '66. * (*PA* 40:11312)

2682. WEHMER, GERALD MARVIN. *The Effect of a Stressful Movie on Ratings of Momentary Mood, Experienced Anxiety, and Plasma 17-Hydroxy-Corticosteroid Level in Three Psychiatric Groups.* Doctor's thesis, Vanderbilt University (Nashville, Tenn.), 1966. (*DA* 27:1632B)

2683. WESSMAN, ALDEN E., AND RICKS, DAVID F. *Mood and Personality.* New York: Holt, Rinehart & Winston, Inc., 1966. Pp. xiii, 317. *

2684. ZIEGLER, FREDERICK J.; RODGERS, DAVID A.; AND KRIEGSMAN, SALI ANN. "Effect of Vasectomy on Psychological Functioning." *Psychosom Med* 28:50–63 Ja–F '66. * (*PA* 40:5830)

2685. ZYLSTRA, JAMES LEROY. *Assessing Delinquent Juveniles From Their Responses to Verbal Conditioning.* Doctor's thesis, University of Washington (Seattle, Wash.), 1966. (*DA* 27:3301B)

2686. ACORD, LOREN DALE. *Psychopathy and Conditioning.* Doctor's thesis, Case Western Reserve University (Cleveland, Ohio), 1967. (*DA* 28:4289B)

2687. ANGERMEIER, ADOLF. *Perception of Verticality as an Information Processing Dimension of Personality.* Doctor's thesis, University of Delaware (Newark, Del.), 1967. (*DA* 29:1183B)

2688. BREIMEIER, KENNETH H. *Relationship Between Various Psychological Measures in Use at Theological Seminaries.*

Comments by James E. Dittes. Occasional Papers No. 1. Washington, D.C.: Ministry Studies Board, 1967. Pp. iii, 59. *

2689. CARDWELL, SUE WEBB. "The MMPI as a Predictor of Success Among Seminary Students." Comments by Charles A. Weisgerber and James E. Dittes. *Ministry Studies* 1:3–28 Ag '67. * (*PA* 42:1108)

2690. CARROLL, DAVID W. *Initial Psychological Prediction as Related to Subsequent Seminary Performance.* Doctor's thesis, Fordham University (New York, N.Y.), 1967. (*DA* 28:4292B)

2691. CAVIOR, NORMAN; KURTZBERG, RICHARD L.; AND LIPTON, DOUGLAS S. "The Development and Validation of a Heroin Addiction Scale With the MMPI." *Int J Addic* 2:129–37 sp '67. *

2692. CHRISTIANSEN, KENT M. "Student Adjustment and Use of an Automobile." *J Col Stud Personnel* 8:369–72 N '67. *

2693. DAVIS, CLIFFORD E., AND WAGNER, PAULA D. *Evaluating and Counseling Prospective Church Workers: Supplement 2, Minnesota Multiphasic Personality Inventory.* New York: Board of Christian Education, 1967. Pp. 23. *

2694. DEAN, ROBERT BRUCE. *Some MMPI and Biographical Questionnaire Correlates of Non-Institutionalized Male Homosexuals.* Master's thesis, San Jose State College (San Jose, Calif.), 1967. (*Masters Abstracts* 6:156)

2695. DUNTEMAN, GEORGE H. "A Discriminant Analysis of the MMPI for Female College Students in Health and Education." *J Exp Ed* 35:85–90 sp '67. *

2696. DVORAK, EDWARD J. "Educational and Personality Characteristics of Smokers and Nonsmokers Among University Freshmen." *J Am Col Health Assn* 16:80–4 O '67. *

2697. FINNEY, JOSEPH C. "Methodological Problems in Programmed Composition of Psychological Tests." *Behav Sci* 12:142–52 Mr '67. * (*PA* 41:6439)

2698. FORSYTH, DOUGLAS R. "MMPI and College Populations." *J Col Stud Personnel* 8:90–6 Mr '67. *

2699. GILBERT, ALBIN R. "Latency-Weighted Testing of Mental Patients." *Proc W Va Acad Sci* 39:62–6 '67. *

2700. GRANT, JOHN GERALD. *A Study of Deliberate Faking in the MMPI With Seminarians.* Doctor's thesis, Loyola University (Chicago, Ill.), 1967.

2701. GREEN, MARVIN. *An Examination of the Trait of Dishonesty in the Parents of Children Applying for Service in a Child Guidance Center.* Doctor's thesis, New York University (New York, N.Y.), 1967. (*DA* 28:1161B)

2702. JOHNSON, THOMAS HATCHER. *A Comparison of Male Maximum Participants and Male Non-Participants in a College Intramural Program.* Doctor's thesis, University of North Carolina (Chapel Hill, N.C.), 1967. (*DA* 28:3488A)

2703. KANIA, WALTER. "Healthy Defensiveness in Theological Students." Comment by John J. Rooney. *Ministry Studies* 1:1–24 D '67. * (*PA* 42:18809)

2704. LEMAY, MORRIS, AND MURPHY, THOMAS A. "MMPI Patterns of College Male Disciplinary Referrals." *J Col Stud Personnel* 8:85–9 Mr '67. *

2705. LIPSIG, FLORENCE S. *A Study of the Resolution of the "Identity Crisis" in Male Adolescents and Its Relationship to Adjustment.* Doctor's thesis, New York University (New York, N.Y.), 1967. (*DA* 28:4003A)

2706. LISTON, WALTER. *Differences in Perception of the College Advisory Program in Schools of Education From the Perspective of Students With Different Personality Patterns and From the Perspective of Faculty Advisors.* Doctor's thesis, North Texas State University (Denton, Tex.), 1967. (*DA* 28:126A)

2707. MCGRATH, JOHN H., III. *A Comparative Study of Adolescent Drug Users, Assaulters, and Auto Thieves.* Doctor's thesis, Rutgers—The State University (New Brunswick, N.J.), 1967. (*DA* 28:4290A)

2708. MACK, JAMES LEWIS. *An Objective Comparison of Parole Successes and Failures in Terms of Their History and Personality Adjustment.* Doctor's thesis, University of Minnesota (Minneapolis, Minn.), 1967. (*DA* 28:3475B)

2709. MAHONEY, M. FRANCES. *An Investigation Into Temperament and Teacher Potentiality in Selected Groups of College Women Students.* Doctor's thesis, St. John's University (Jamaica, N.Y.), 1967. (*DA* 28:4284B)

2710. MURSTEIN, BERNARD I. "The Relationship of Mental Health to Marital Choice and Courtship Progress." *J Marriage & Family* 29:447–51 Ag '67. * (*PA* 41:15153)

2711. NICHOLS, EDWIN J., AND SPIELBERGER, CHARLES D. "Effects of Medical Education on Anxiety in Students." *Mental Hyg* 51:74–9 Ja '67. *

2712. PETERSON, RONALD SKEEN. *A Longitudinal Study of Nonintellective Characteristics of College Dropouts.* Doctor's thesis, University of Oregon (Eugene, Ore.), 1967. (*DA* 28:2076A)

2713. PHILLIPS, CLINTON E. "Measuring Power of Spouse." *Sociol & Social Res* 52:35–49 O '67. * (*PA* 42:1009)

2714. PIOTROWSKI, ZYGMUNT A. "Psychological Testing of Intelligence and Personality," pp. 509–30. In *Comprehensive Textbook of Psychiatry.* Edited by Alfred M. Freedman and Harold I. Kaplan. Baltimore, Md.: Williams & Wilkins Co., 1967. Pp. xxv, 1666. *

2715. RAFTERY, FRANCIS MARITA. *An Investigation of the Influence of Religious Life on the Personality Adjustment of*

Sisters in the Formation Program of a Religious Congrega-tion of Women as Measured by the MMPI. Master's thesis, Catholic University of America (Washington, D.C.), 1967.

2716. RESCHKE, STEPHEN EMIL. *Mental Health Factors in College Students: A Test of the Motivation-Hygiene Theory.* Doctor's thesis, Western Reserve University (Cleveland, Ohio), 1967. (*DA* 28:1251B)

2717. SCHUTTE, EILEEN PAULINE. *Personality Characteristics of Typewriting and Shorthand Teachers.* Doctor's thesis, Northern Illinois University (DeKalb, Ill.), 1967. (*DA* 29:1811A)

2718. SEIBEL, DEAN W. "Predicting the Classroom Behavior of Teachers." *J Exp Ed* 36:26–32 f '67. *

2719. SMITH, J. REX. "Suggested Scales for Prediction of Client Movement and the Duration of Marriage Counseling." *Sociol & Social Res* 52:63–71 O '67. * (*PA* 42:1010)

2720. STEIBER, JUDITH KOHAN. *Counselor Anxiety and In-terview Behavior.* Doctor's thesis, Columbia University (New York, N.Y.), 1967. (*DA* 28:1699B)

2721. STIER, SERENA AUSTER. *Developmental Attainment, Outcome and Symbolic Performance in Schizophrenia.* Doc-tor's thesis, University of California (Los Angeles, Calif.), 1967. (*DA* 28:4766B)

2722. TAYLOR, GEORGE P., JR. *Predicted Versus Actual Re-sponse to Spinal Cord Injury: A Psychological Study.* Doc-tor's thesis, University of Minnesota (Minneapolis, Minn.), 1967. (*DA* 28:1214B)

2723. TEMPLER, DONALD IRVIN. *The Construction and Vali-dation of a Death Anxiety Scale.* Doctor's thesis, University of Kentucky (Lexington, Ky.), 1967. (*DAI* 30:2410B)

2724. VESPRANI, GEORGE JOSEPH. *Accurate Empathy in a College Companion Program.* Doctor's thesis, University of Cincinnati (Cincinnati, Ohio), 1967. (*DA* 28:3483B)

2725. VOGEL, ROBERTA BURRAGE. *A Projective Study of Dynamic Factors in Attempted Suicide.* Doctor's thesis, Michi-gan State University (East Lansing, Mich.), 1967. (*DA* 28:4303B)

2726. WALDO, GORDON P., AND DINITZ, SIMON. "Personality Attributes of the Criminal: An Analysis of Research Studies, 1950–65." *J Res Crime & Del* 4:185–202 Jl '67. *

2727. WILSON, IAN C.; RABON, ARCHIE M.; AND BUFFALOE, WILLIAM J. "Imipramine Therapy in Depressive Syndromes: Predicton of Therapeutic Outcome." *Psychosomatics* 8:203–7 Jl–Ag '67. * (*PA* 42:884)

2728. WILSON, M. ROBERT, JR.; SODERQUIST, RONALD; ZEMKE, ROBERT L.; AND SWENSON, WENDELL M. "Under-achievement in College Men: Evaluation of the Psychody-namics." *Psychiatry* 30:180–6 My '67. * (*PA* 41:15790)

2729. WILSON, WARNER, AND KAWAMURA, WALLACE. "Rigid-ity, Adjustment, and Social Responsibility as Possible Corre-lates of Religiousness: A Test of Three Points of View." *J Sci Study Relig* 6:279–80 f '67. * (*PA* 42:8804)

2730. WOOD, WILLIAM DRANE. *Dominance as a Measure of Interaction in Married and Ad Hoc Dyads Under Different Task Conditions.* Doctor's thesis, University of North Carolina (Chapel Hill, N.C.), 1967. (*DA* 28:4768B)

2731. ZALEN, GERALD W. *MMPI Profile Comparisons of the Michigan State Police Compared for Length of Time Spent at Command Posts.* Master's thesis, Central Michigan University (Mt. Pleasant, Mich.), 1967.

2732. ANASTASI, ANNE. *Psychological Testing, Third Edi-tion,* pp. 441–7. New York: Macmillan Co., 1968. Pp. xiii, 665. *

2733. ANDERSON, WAYNE. "Predicting Graduation From a School of Nursing." *Voc Guid Q* 16:295–300 Je '68. *

2734. ASHMORE, BETTIE JANE. *An Investigation of Changes in Attitudes and Personality Characteristics Among Counselors in Three Types of Counselor Education Programs.* Doctor's thesis, University of Alabama (University, Ala.), 1968. (*DA* 29:1416A)

2735. BAASEL, PATRICIA BRADFIELD. *Word Associations Given by College Students Having Normal and High SC-Scale MMPI Profiles.* Doctor's thesis, Ohio University (Athens, Ohio), 1968. (*DA* 29:1501B)

2736. BADEN, SAM ELLIOTT. *An Exploratory Attempt to "Purify" the Psychasthenia and Depression Scales of the Minnesota Multiphasic Personality Inventory.* Doctor's thesis, University of Minnesota (Minneapolis, Minn.), 1968. (*DA* 29:2625B)

2737. BANNER, RONALD HARLAN. *Anxiety, Personality and Birth Delivery.* Doctor's thesis, Colorado State University (Ft. Collins, Colo.), 1968. (*DA* 29:3906B)

2738. BAUERMEISTER, PAUL JOHN. *A Descriptive Study of Pastoral Counseling Subjects.* Doctor's thesis, University of Minnesota (Minneapolis, Minn.), 1968. (*DA* 29:3906B)

2739. BAUGHMAN, E. EARL, AND DAHLSTROM, W. GRANT. Chap. 11, "Eighth-Grade Children as Assessed by the Minne-sota Multiphasic Personality Inventory," pp. 232–59. In their *Negro and White Children: A Psychological Study in the Rural South.* New York: Academic Press Inc., 1968. Pp. xx, 572. *

2740. BENNETT, LAWRENCE A. *Sociopathy and Stress.* Doc-tor's thesis, Claremont Graduate School (Claremont, Calif.), 1968. (*DA* 29:2627B)

2741. BLOOM, STEPHEN LAWRENCE. *The Development of a Measure of State Anxiety.* Doctor's thesis, Pennsylvania State University (University Park, Pa.), 1968. (*DA* 29:3933B)

2742. BORGHI, JOHN H. "Premature Termination of Psycho-therapy and Patient-Therapist Expectations." *Am J Psychother* 22:460–73 Jl '68. * (*PA* 42:18915)

2743. BRANDT, JAMES E., AND HOOD, ALBERT B. "Effect of Personality Adjustment on the Predictive Validity of the Strong Vocational Interest Blank." *J Counsel Psychol* 15:547–51 N '68. * (*PA* 43:126)

2744. BRODSKY, STANLEY L. "Excessive Dispensary Users in the Military Prison." *Mil Med* 133:368–71 My '68. * (*PA* 42:14113)

2745. BROWN, ELEANOR JESSEN. *Some Psychological Differ-ences Between Neglected and Delinquent Adolescent Girls.* Doctor's thesis, University of Oklahoma (Norman, Okla.), 1968. (*DA* 29:1503B)

2746. CARROLL, LAWRENCE THOMAS. *An Investigation of the Internal-External Control Construct in a Population of Patients Addicted to Narcotic Drugs.* Doctor's thesis, Univer-sity of Kentucky (Lexington, Ky.), 1968. (*DAI* 30:1893B)

2747. CHABOT, DAVID RUSSELL. *An Investigation of the Effects of an Increased Emotional State on the Reliability of the MMPI in an Adolescent Population.* Doctor's thesis, Uni-versity of Minnesota (Minneapolis, Minn.), 1968. (*DA* 29:2629B)

2748. CHALKE, F. C. R., AND VANESS, N. L. "Personality and Peptic Ulcer." *Proc 4th World Congr Psychiatry* 1966(pt 4):2759–62 '68. *

2749. CLEARE, JULIE ANNE. *Personal and Semantic Meaning Among Students With Normal and Deviant MMPI Profiles.* Doctor's thesis, Fordham University (New York, N.Y.), 1968. (*DA* 29:3082B)

2750. CLUM, GEORGE ARTHUR. *The Relationships Between Measures of Classical and Operant Conditioning, Psychiatric Diagnoses and Statistically Derived Classificatory Groups.* Doc-tor's thesis, St. John's University (Jamaica, N.Y.), 1968. (*DA* 29:3899B)

2751. COHN, WERNER. "Personality, Pentecostalism, and Glossolalia: A Research Note on Some Unsuccessful Research." *Can R Sociol & Anthrop* 5:36–40 F '68. *

2752. CONGER, ANTHONY JOSEPH. *Dimensional Analysis of Binary Data: An Appraisal of the MMPI.* Doctor's thesis, University of Illinois (Urbana, Ill.), 1968. (*DAI* 30:367B)

2753. CURLEE, JOAN E. *A Comparison of Male and Female Patients at an Alcoholism Treatment Center.* Doctor's thesis, University of Minnesota (Minneapolis, Minn.), 1968. (*DAI* 30:843B)

2754. DAHLSTROM, W. GRANT. "The Minnesota Multiphasic Personality Inventory." *Inter Encycl Social Sci* 12:43–8 '68. *

2755. DAVIS, CLIFFORD E., AND WAGNER, PAULA D. *Evalu-ating and Counseling Prospective Church Workers: Supple-ment 1, Strong Vocational Interest Blank.* New York: Board of Christian Education, 1968. Pp. 19. *

2756. DICKSON, ROSE MARIE. *A Descriptive Study of the Relationship Between Specific Personality Factors and Or-dinal Position in the Family.* Doctor's thesis, Boston College (Chestnut Hill, Mass.), 1968. (*DA* 29:4278A)

2757. EARLEY, SHARON RUTH. *A Comparison of the Dif-ferential Efficiency of Least Squares and Simulation Tech-niques in Predicting Responses to MMPI Items.* Master's the-sis, Iowa State University (Ames, Iowa), 1968.

2758. EDMAN, MYRA. *Personality Profiles of a Group of Adult Public Aid Recipients Measured by the Minnesota Multi-phasic Personality Inventory.* Master's thesis, Eastern Illinois University (Charleston, Ill.), 1968.

2759. ELLIOTT, JERRY GORDON. *Factors Related to Inmate Participation in an Institutional Religious Program.* Doctor's thesis, School of Theology (Claremont, Calif.), 1968. (*DAI* 31:3016A)

2760. ERICKSON, MARILYN T. "MMPI Comparisons Be-tween Parents of Young Emotionally Disturbed and Organi-cally Retarded Children." *J Consult & Clin Psychol* 32:701–6 D '68. * (*PA* 43:4040)

2761. FALTZ, CHARLES ALBERT. *Prediction of Hospital Re-admission and Work Adjustment Among Released Psychiatric Patients.* Doctor's thesis, Purdue University (Lafayette, Ind.), 1968. (*DA* 29:3084B)

2762. FEINBERG, LAWRENCE HERBERT. *Relationships Be-tween College Students' Behavior and Attitudes Toward Stu-dent-Faculty Contact and the Students' Responses on the Social Introversion Scale of the Minnesota Multiphasic Personality Inventory.* Doctor's thesis, University of Wisconsin (Madison, Wis.), 1968. (*DA* 29:4281A)

2763. FINE, BERNARD J. "Personality Traits as Related to Symptomatology and Running Performance at Altitude Under Normal and Drug (Acetazoleamide) Conditions." *Percept & Motor Skills* 27:975–90 D '68. * (*PA* 43:8837)

2764. FORSYTH, DOUGLAS ROBERT. *The Effects of Pretesting, Test Batteries and Test Reactivity on the Behavior of Control Subjects.* Doctor's thesis, Colorado State University (Ft. Col-lins, Colo.), 1968. (*DA* 29:1187B)

2765. FOWLER, RAYMOND D., JR., AND MARLOWE, GUY H., JR. "A Computer Program for Personality Analysis." *Behav Sci* 13:413–6 S '68. * (*PA* 42:18075)

2766. FULLERTON, DONALD T.; WENZEL, FREDERICK J.; LOHRENZ, FRANCIS N.; AND FAHS, HAROLD. "Circadian Rhythm of Adrenal Cortical Activity in Depression: 1, A Comparison of Depressed Patients With Normal Subjects." *Arch Gen Psychiatry* 19:674–81 D '68. * (*PA* 43:8489)

2767. FULLERTON, DONALD T.; WENZEL, FREDERICK J.; LOHRENZ, FRANCIS N.; AND FAHS, HAROLD. "Circadian Rhythm of Adrenal Cortical Activity in Depression: 2, A Comparison of Types in Depression." *Arch Gen Psychiatry* 19:682–8 D '68. * (*PA* 43:8490)

2768. GASSNER, SUZANNE MARIE. *The Relationship Between Patient-Therapist Compatibility and Treatment Effectiveness.* Doctor's thesis, Syracuse University (Syracuse, N.Y.), 1968. (*DA* 29:4845B)

2769. GHANNAD, REZA H. *The Effects of Planned Interaction of Adult Males With Institutionalized Mentally Retarded Boys Upon Their Sex-Role Identification and Self-Concept.* Doctor's thesis, Brigham Young University (Provo, Utah), 1968. (*DA* 29:3001A)

2770. GILBERTS, RICHARD ALLAN. *A Comparison of Statistical Models for Predicting Counselor Responses From Personality Measures.* Doctor's thesis, University of Washington (Seattle, Wash.), 1968. (*DA* 29:2091A)

2771. GOLDBERG, LEWIS R. "Simple Models or Simple Processes?: Some Research on Clinical Judgments." *Am Psychologist* 23:483–96 Jl '68. * (*PA* 42:18999)

2772. GOOD, RONALD GLENN. *An Analysis of the Self-Perceptions and Other Selected Characteristics of Effective and Ineffective Teachers: A Study Based on the Educational Philosophy of the Fifth-Year Program in Teacher Education at the University of North Carolina.* Doctor's thesis, University of North Carolina (Chapel Hill, N.C.), 1968. (*DA* 29:4373A)

2773. GOTTESMAN, IRVING I. "The Maudsley-Bethlem Schizophrenic Twin Study." *Proc 4th World Congr Psychiatry* 1966(pt 4):1097–102 '68. *

2774. GRAVITZ, MELVIN A. "Masculinity-Femininity Orientation on the MMPI and Marital Status." *Psychol Rep* 23:1330 D '68. * (*PA* 43:8370)

2775. GREENBERG, GLORIA ULERT. *A Refinement of the Tennessee Self Concept Scale to Clarify Interpretation of Extremely Favorable Self Reports.* Doctor's thesis, University of Miami (Coral Gables, Fla.), 1968. (*DA* 29:770B)

2776. GUPTA, G. C. "Distribution of M.M.P.I. Scores in Two Samples of the Delhi University Students." *J Psychol Res* 12:153–5 S '68. *

2777. GYNTHER, MALCOLM D., AND BRILLIANT, PATRICIA J. "The Diagnostic Utility of Welsh's A-R Categories." *J Proj Tech & Pers Assess* 32:572–4 D '68. * (*PA* 43:10004)

2778. HAASE, RICHARD FRANK. *Non-Intellective Correlates of Value Congruence and Value Change in Counseling.* Doctor's thesis, Colorado State University (Ft. Collins, Colo.), 1968. (*DA* 29:2201B)

2779. HAERTZEN, C. A., AND HOOKS, N. T., JR. "Effects of Adaptation Level, Context and Face Validity on Responses to Self-Report Psychological Inventories." *Psychol Rec* 18:339–49 Jl '68. * (*PA* 42:16412)

2780. HARRISON, ROBERT H. "An Empirical Test of the Configural Scoring Hypothesis." *Ed & Psychol Meas* 28:395–402 su '68. * (*PA* 42:18093)

2781. HARRISON, ROBERT H., AND KASS, EDWARD H. "MMPI Correlates of Negro Acculturation in a Northern City." *J Pers & Social Psychol* 10:262–70 N '68. * (*PA* 43:3853)

2782. HEDLEY, CAROLYN NEAL. "Learning Relationship Differences and Curriculum Choice." *Improv Col & Univ Teach* 16:268–72 au '68. *

2783. HEDLEY, CAROLYN NEAL. "The Relationship of Personality Factors to Scientific and Mathematical Ability Factors." *Sch Sci & Math* 68:265–71 Ap '68. *

2784. HEIBERG, DAVID ALLISON. *Psychometric Correlates Within a Youthful Offender Population.* Doctor's thesis, University of Minnesota (Minneapolis, Minn.), 1968. (*DAI* 30:382B)

2785. HILL, HARRIS E.; HAERTZEN, CHARLES A.; AND YAMAHIRO, ROY A. "Addict Physician: A Minnesota Multiphasic Personality Inventory Study of the Interaction of Personality Characteristics and Availability of Narcotics." *Res Publ Assn Res Nerv & Mental Dis* 46:321–32 '68. *

2786. HIRT, MICHAEL; GOLDBERG, RICHARD; AND BERNSTEIN, I. LEONARD. "Interaction of Personality Variables and Allergic Predisposition in Asthma." *Psychosomatics* 9:340–3 N–D '68. * (*PA* 43:11678)

2787. JONES, RONALD BENNETT. *Suicidal Out-Patients: The MMPI and Case File Data.* Doctor's thesis, University of Oregon (Eugene, Ore.), 1968. (*DA* 29:2635B)

2788. KASTL, ALBERT J.; DAROFF, ROBERT B.; AND BLOCKER, W. WEBSTER. "Psychological Testing of Cerebral Malaria Patients." *J Nerv & Mental Dis* 147:553–61 D '68. * (*PA* 43:14654)

2789. KOGEN, JONATHAN BERNARD. *A Study of the Utility of Actuarial, Clinical, and Stereotypic Personality Descriptions.* Doctor's thesis, Southern Illinois University (Carbondale, Ill.), 1968. (*DA* 29:3913B)

2790. KURLAND, ALBERT A.; DESTOUNIS, NICHOLAS; SHAFFER, JOHN W.; AND PINTO, ALCIDES. "A Critical Study of Isocarboxazid (Marplan) in the Treatment of Depressed Patients." *Proc 4th World Congr Psychiatry* 1966(pt 3):1962–6 '68. *

2791. LANYON, RICHARD I. *A Handbook of MMPI Group Profiles.* Minneapolis, Minn.: University of Minnesota Press, 1968. Pp. xiii, 78. * (*PA* 43:7073).

2792. LANYON, RICHARD I., AND DROTAR, DENNIS. "Response Sets as Personality Concepts." *Psychol Rep* 23:751–6 D '68. * (*PA* 43:9726)

2793. LATTA, WILLIAM STEPHEN. *Projected Set and MMPI Scale Changes.* Doctor's thesis, University of Cincinnati (Cincinnati, Ohio), 1968. (*DA* 29:3914B)

2794. LAUDEMAN, KENT ALLEN. *Personality and Drinking Behavior of Alcohol and Non-Alcohol Offenders.* Master's thesis, Western Michigan University (Kalamazoo, Mich.), 1968. (*Masters Abstracts* 7:61)

2795. LEWIS, LAURA H. "Acquiescence Response Set: Construct or Artifact?" *J Proj Tech & Pers Assess* 32:578–84 D '68. * (*PA* 43:9763)

2796. LIN, PI-FONG, AND YEN, FANG. "A Study of Psychological After-Effect of the Contraceptive Operation of Tubal Ligation." *Acta Psychologica Taiwanica* 10:90–104 Mr '68. * (*PA* 45:4326)

2797. LONG, NICHOLAS KINSEY. *An Investigation of the Item Structure of Seven Marks-Seeman MMPI Code Types.* Doctor's thesis, University of Minnesota (Minneapolis, Minn.), 1968. (*DA* 29:3088B)

2798. LOPER, RODNEY G.; ROBERTSON, JAMES M.; AND SWANSON, EDWARD O. "College Freshman MMPI Norms Over a 14-Year Period." *J Col Stud Personnel* 9:404–7 N '68. *

2799. McCABE, OLIVER LEROY. *An Empirical Investigation of the Effects of Chemically (LSD-25)-Induced "Psychedelic Experiences" on Selected Measures of Personality, and Their Implications for Therapeutic Counseling Theory and Practice.* Doctor's thesis, Catholic University of America (Washington, D.C.), 1968. (*DA* 29:4849B)

2800. MARTIN, CLYDE V.; ALVORD, JACK R.; AND HORNER, GARY C. "The Prediction of Suicide Gestures." *Correct Psychiatry & J Social Ther* 14:153–65 f '68. *

2801. MASER, ARTHUR LYLE. *The Effect of Client Response and Counselor Personality on Counselor Response; and the Effect of Counselor Response on Client Response.* Doctor's thesis, University of Washington (Seattle, Wash.), 1968. (*DA* 29:2096A)

2802. MATIS, EDWARD EUGENE. *An Analysis of Differences in Interests, Personality Needs, and Personality Structures Between College Women Majoring in Speech Pathology and College Women Majoring in Other Professional Areas.* Doctor's thesis, University of Alabama (University, Ala.), 1968. (*DA* 29:4290A)

2803. MEDLER, BYRON WAYNE. *A Comparative Study of Selected Variables Between Students Completing the Elementary Education Curriculum and Those Students Who Left the Elementary Education Curriculum Due to Academic Disqualification or Change of Major.* Doctor's thesis, Ball State University (Muncie, Ind.), 1968. (*DA* 29:3503A)

2804. MENDOZA, BUENA FLOR H. *Predicting Counselor Effectiveness: A Multiple Regression Approach.* Doctor's thesis, Western Michigan University (Kalamazoo, Mich.), 1968. (*DAI* 30:552A)

2805. MILES, WILFORD GLENN, JR. *An Investigation Into the Relationship Between Certain Personality Traits and Management Success.* Doctor's thesis, University of Arkansas (Fayetteville, Ark.), 1968. (*DA* 29:1341A)

2806. MOORE, ROBERT A., AND WARD, GEORGE, II. "A Revised MMPI Scale for Measuring Psychopathy Among Prison Inmates." *Proc W Va Acad Sci* 40:212–4 '68. *

2807. MOOS, RUDOLF H. "Behavioral Effects of Being Observed: Reactions to a Wireless Radio Transmitter." *J Consult & Clin Psychol* 32:383–8 Ag '68. * (*PA* 42:17269)

2808. MORDKOFF, ARNOLD M., AND RAND, MELVIN A. "Personality and Adaptation to Coronary Artery Disease." *J Consult & Clin Psychol* 32:648–53 D '68. * (*PA* 43:4378)

2809. MORGAN, WILLIAM P. "Selected Physiological and Psychomotor Correlates of Depression in Psychiatric Patients." *Res Q* 39:1037–43 D '68. *

2810. MUMA, JOHN R.; LAEDER, RONALD L.; AND WEBB, CLARENCE E. "Adolescent Voice Quality Aberrations: Personality and Social Status." *J Speech & Hearing Res* 11:576–82 S '68. * (*PA* 45:4731)

2811. MURSTEIN, BERNARD I., AND GLAUDIN, VINCENT. "The Use of MMPI in the Determination of Marital Maladjustment." *J Marriage & Family* 30:651–5 N '68. * (*PA* 44:19078)

2812. ORME, J. E. "Are Obsessionals Neurotic or Are Neurotics Obsessional?" *Brit J Med Psychol* 41:415–6 D '68. *

2813. PAYNE, FRANK. *Substantive Homogeneity of MMPI Profile Types.* Master's thesis, University of Illinois (Urbana, Ill.), 1968.

2814. PAYNE, FRANK D., AND WIGGINS, JERRY S. "Effects of Rule Relaxation and System Combination on Classification Rates in Two MMPI 'Cookbook' Systems." *J Consult & Clin Psychol* 32:734–6 D '68. * (*PA* 43:4043)

2815. PENDERGAST, MARY CARITA. *Assessment of a Psychological Screening Program for Candidates to a Religious Congregation of Women.* Doctor's thesis, Fordham University (New York, N.Y.), 1968. (*DA* 29:2572A)

2816. PERLMAN, LEONARD G. *A Predictive Model for the Identification of Potential Dropouts From Vocational Training in a Comprehensive Rehabilitation Center.* Doctor's thesis, Pennsylvania State University (University Park, Pa.), 1968. (*DA* 29:3424A)

2817. ROHLF, RICHARD JOHN. *A Higher-Order Alpha Factor Analysis of Interest, Personality, and Ability Variables, Including an Evaluation of the Effect of Scale Interdependency.* Doctor's thesis, University of Kansas (Lawrence, Kan.), 1968. (*DA* 29:1758A)

2818. SANDMAN, CURT A.; CAUTHEN, NELSON R.; KILPATRICK, DEAN G.; AND DEABLER, HERDIS L. "Size of Figure Drawing in Relation to Depression." *Percept & Motor Skills* 27:945–6 D '68. * (*PA* 43:8447)

2819. SCHMAUK, FRANK J. *A Study of the Relationship Between Kinds of Punishment, Autonomic Arousal, Subjective Anxiety, and Avoidance Learning in the Primary Sociopath.* Doctor's thesis, Temple University (Philadelphia, Pa.), 1968. (*DAI* 30:1367B)

2820. SCOTT, SHEILA MANN. *Effects of Positive and Negative Verbal Reinforcement and Task Difficulty on the Verbal Discrimination Learning of Psychopathic and Non-Psychopathic Criminals.* Doctor's thesis, Temple University (Philadelphia, Pa.), 1968. (*DAI* 30:1368B)

2821. SEAMAN, CAROLYN MUSSINA. *The Prediction of Length of Hospitalization From Personality Test Scores, Demographic and Social Variables According to the Process-Reactive Continuum.* Doctor's thesis, Ohio University (Athens, Ohio), 1968. (*DA* 29:1513B)

2822. SHEPHERD, DAVID C., AND GOLDSTEIN, ROBERT. "Intrasubject Variability in Amplitude of Bekesy Tracings and Its Relation to Measures of Personality." *J Speech & Hearing Res* 11:523–35 S '68. * (*PA* 45:3372)

2823. SHEPPARD, CHARLES; FIORENTINO, DIANE; COLLINS, LOIS; AND MERLIS, SIDNEY. "Performance Errors on Ravens Progressive Matrices (1938) by Sociopathic and Schizotypic Personality Types." *Psychol Rep* 23:1043–6 D '68. * (*PA* 43:8462)

2824. SIMONO, RONALD B. "Anxiety and Involvement in Counseling." *J Counsel Psychol* 15:497–9 N '68. * (*PA* 43:1346)

2825. SIMONO, RONALD B. "Personality Characteristics of Athletes." *J Col Stud Personnel* 9:109–11 Mr '68. *

2826. SOLKOFF, NORMAN. "The Use of Personality and Attitude Tests in Predicting the Academic Success of Medical and Law Students." *J Med Ed* 43:1250–3 D '68. * (*PA* 44:7336)

2827. SPARE, GERALDINE HALLAM. *A Study of the Law of Enantiadromia, as It Relates to the Attitudes of Introversion-Extraversion.* Doctor's thesis, Washington State University (Pullman, Wash.), 1968. (*DA* 29:1850B)

2828. SPERO, JEANNETTE R. *A Study of the Relationship Between Selected Functional Menstrual Disorders and Interpersonal Conflict.* Doctor's thesis, New York University (New York, N.Y.), 1968. (*DA* 29:2905A)

2829. STAVRAKEY, KATHLEEN M. "Psychological Factors in the Outcome of Human Cancer." *J Psychosom Res* 12:251–9 D '68. * (*PA* 43:11783)

2830. SUSLAK, KENNETH V. *Diagnostic Insight: The Relationship Between Patient Self-Ratings on Major Psychiatric Dimensions, Ratings Based on Observation, and Ratings Based on the MMPI.* Doctor's thesis, University of Minnesota (Minneapolis, Minn.), 1968. (*DA* 29:3095B)

2831. THUMIN, FRED J. "Consumer Behavior as Related to Personality, Intelligence, Age and Education." *Psychol Rep* 23:1185–6 D '68. *

2832. TOWNSEND, JEANNETTE KATHRYN. *Reports of Parent Behavior (RPBI) Related to Current Behavior and MMPI Scores in Female Psychiatric Inpatients.* Doctor's thesis, University of North Carolina (Chapel Hill, N.C.), 1968. (*DA* 29:2642B)

2833. UECKER, ALBERT E.; KISH, GEORGE B.; AND BALL, MARGARET E. "Differentiation of Alcoholism From General Psychopathology by Means of Two MMPI Scales." *Newsl Res Psychol* 10:9–11 N '68. *

2834. VAN DE CASTLE, R. L. "Differences in Dream Content Among Psychiatric Inpatients." Abstract. *Psychophysiol* 4:374 Ja '68. * (*PA* 42:15697)

2835. VONDRACEK, FRED WILHELM. *The Manipulation of Self-Disclosure in an Experimental Interview Situation.* Doctor's thesis, Pennsylvania State University (University Park, Pa.), 1968. (*DAI* 30:1350D)

2836. WALES, MARY ELIZABETH. *An Investigation of MMPI Zero Items in a Patient Population With Varying Response Sets.* Doctor's thesis, University of Cincinnati (Cincinnati, Ohio), 1968. (*DA* 29:1851B)

2837. WALKER, RONALD E.; DAVIS, WILLIAM E.; AND FIRETTO, ANTHONY. "An Experimenter Variable: The Psychologist-Clergyman." *Psychol Rep* 22:709–14 Je '68. * (*PA* 42:13780)

2838. WARD, DOROTHY BALL. *Extraversion-Introversion and Neuroticism-Stability in Relation to Person Perception.* Doctor's thesis, University of Florida (Gainesville, Fla.), 1968. (*DAI* 30:394B)

2839. WEINBAUM, LOUIS. *A Study of Cumming's Extension of the Disengagement Theory Using Block's Rationale on the MMPI With Predictions on a Measure of Field-Dependence for Two Disengaged Samples.* Doctor's thesis, University of Kansas (Lawrence, Kan.), 1968. (*DAI* 30:1033A)

2840. WEINSTEIN, JOSHUA; AVERILL, JAMES R.; OPTON, ED-

WARD M., JR.; AND LAZARUS, RICHARD S. "Defensive Style and Discrepancy Between Self-Report and Physiological Indexes of Stress." *J Pers & Social Psychol* 10:406–13 D '68. * (*PA* 43:6909)

2841. WENDLAND, MARILYN MARIE. *Self-Concept in Southern Negro and White Adolescents as Related to Rural-Urban Residence.* Doctor's thesis, University of North Carolina (Chapel Hill, N.C.), 1968. (*DA* 29:2642B)

2842. WILSON, DONNA JEAN. *The Use of the BIB in the Selection of College Seniors With Managerial Potential.* Doctor's thesis, Louisiana State University (Baton Rouge, La.), 1968. (*DA* 29:801B)

2843. WILSON, IAN C., AND RABON, ARCHIE M. "Differential Therapeutic Efficacy of Imipramine in Various Depressive Syndromes." *Proc 4th World Congr Psychiatry* 1966(pt 4):1932–5 '68. *

2844. WINTERS, STEPHEN. *Response Style Correlates of Personality Traits: The Development of a Forced-Choice Instrument to Measure Independently Social Desirability and Acquiescence.* Doctor's thesis, University of Maryland (College Park, Md.), 1968. (*DA* 29:3904B)

2845. YOUSSEF, ZAKHOUR I. "The Role of Race, Sex, Hostility, and Verbal Stimulus in Inflicting Punishment." *Psychon Sci* 12:285–6 O 5 '68. * (*PA* 43:1870)

2846. ZIEGLER, FREDERICK J.; RODGERS, DAVID A.; KRIEGSMAN, SALI ANN; AND MARTIN, PURVIS L. "Ovulation Suppressors, Psychological Functioning, and Marital Adjustment." *J Am Med Assn* 204:849–53 Je 3 '68. *

2847. AGLE, DAVID P.; RATNOFF, OSCAR D.; AND WASMAN, MARVIN. "Conversion Reactions in Autoerythrocyte Sensitization: Their Relationship to the Production of Ecchymoses." *Arch Gen Psychiatry* 20(4):438–47 Ap '69. * (*PA* 43:16121)

2848. AIKEN, WILBUR JOHN. *The Use of the MMPI in the Prediction of the Rehabilitation Outcome of Male Inpatient Alcoholics.* Doctor's thesis, University of Missouri (Columbia, Mo.), 1969. (*DAI* 30:3712A)

2849. ALEXANDER, JAMES F., AND ABELES, NORMAN. "Psychotherapy Process: Sex Differences and Dependency." *J Counsel Psychol* 16(3):191–6 My '69. * (*PA* 43:11418)

2850. ANDERSON, BRUCE NILS. *The Utility of the Minnesota Multiphasic Personality Inventory in a Private Psychiatric Hospital Setting.* Master's thesis, Ohio State University (Columbus, Ohio), 1969.

2851. ANDERSON, LORNA M. "Personality Characteristics of Parents of Neurotic, Aggressive, and Normal Preadolescent Boys." *J Consult & Clin Psychol* 33(5):575–81 O '69. * (*PA* 44:2572)

2852. AUMACK, LEWIS. "MMPI Rational Subscales: A Question of Clinical Utility." *J Clin Psychol* 25(4):414–20 O '69. * (*PA* 44:10713)

2853. BACKUS, DONALD WILLIAM. *The Seven Deadly Sins: Their Meaning and Measurement.* Doctor's thesis, University of Minnesota (Minneapolis, Minn.), 1969. (*DAI* 30:2900B)

2854. BAILEY, JOHN P., JR.; JANTZEN, ALICE C.; AND DUNTEMAN, GEORGE H. "Relative Effectiveness of Personality, Achievement and Interest Measures in the Prediction of a Performance Criterion." *Am J Occup Ther* 23(1):27–9 Ja–F '69. * (*PA* 44:731)

2855. BARNA, JAMES DANIEL. *Development of a Scale of Causal Constructs and Its Relationship to Selected Personality Tests.* Doctor's thesis, St. Louis University (St. Louis, Mo.), 1969. (*DAI* 30:3861B)

2856. BERGIN, ALLEN E., AND JASPER, LAWRENCE G. "Correlates of Empathy in Psychotherapy: A Replication." *J Abn Psychol* 74(4):477–81 Ag '69. * (*PA* 43:15891)

2857. BLACKBURN, R. "Sensation Seeking, Impulsivity, and Psychopathic Personality." *J Consult & Clin Psychol* 33(5):571–4 O '69. * (*PA* 44:2520)

2858. BLUM, DONNA M. "Occupational Differences of Male Psychiatric Patients on the MMPI." *Psychol Rep* 25(1):117–8 Ag '69. * (*PA* 44:3670)

2859. BOCK, R. DARRELL; DICKEN, CHARLES; AND VAN PELT, JOHN. "Methodological Implications of Content-Acquiescence Correlation in the MMPI." *Psychol B* 71(2):127–39 F '69. * (*PA* 43:8377)

2860. BOGDAN, DONALD F.; BALENTINE, ROBERT W.; TARTAGLIA, CHARLES R.; AND KELIHER, THOMAS F. "A Psychological Study of Patients Referred to a Medical Diagnostic Clinic." *South Med J* 62(2):145–51 F '69. *

2861. BOTTRILL, JOHN H. "Personality Change in LSD Users." *J General Psychol* 80(2):157–61 Ap '69. * (*PA* 43:11280)

2862. BRADLEY, ROSALEE. *Measuring Loneliness.* Doctor's thesis, Washington State University (Pullman, Wash.), 1969. (*DAI* 30:3382B)

2863. BRITTON, PETER G., AND SAVAGE, R. DOUGLASS. "The Factorial Structure of the Minnesota Multiphasic Personality Inventory From an Aged Sample." *J Genetic Psychol* 114(1):13–7 Mr '69. * (*PA* 43:9577)

2864. BRUHN, JOHN G.; CHANDLER, BETTY; AND WOLF, STEWART. "A Psychological Study of Survivors and Nonsurvivors of Myocardial Infarction." *Psychosom Med* 31(1):8–19 Ja–F '69. * (*PA* 44:4073)

2865. BURGESS, MICHAEL M., AND DUFFEY, MARGERY. "The Prediction of Success in a Collegiate Program of Nursing." *Nursing Res* 18(1):68–72 Ja–F '69. *

2866. BUTCHER, JAMES NEAL. Appendix D, "Classification of MMPI Literature From 1959–1967," pp. 335–84. In his *MMPI: Research Developments and Clinical Applications,* see 2867. *

2867. BUTCHER, JAMES NEAL, EDITOR. *MMPI: Research Developments and Clinical Applications.* New York: McGraw-Hill Book Co., 1969. Pp. xiv, 402. *

2868. BUTLER, JOEL R., AND DAWSON, JOSEPH G. "Objective Measurement of an Hypnotically Induced Simulation of Psychopathology." *J Clin Psychol* 25(2):160–2 Ap '69. * (PA 43:14462)

2869. BUTTIGLIERI, MATTHEW W.; WOODSON, M. I. CHARLES E.; GUENETTE, MARIE; AND THOMSON, MAE. "Driver Accidents and the Neuropsychiatric Patient." Abstract. *J Consult & Clin Psychol* 33(3):381 Je '69. * (PA 43:13466)

2870. CARRINGTON, PATRICIA. *Dream Reports of Schizophrenic and Nonschizophrenic Women.* Doctor's thesis, Columbia University (New York, N.Y.), 1969. (DAI 30:4134A)

2871. CARSON, ROBERT C. Appendix A, "Interpretative Manual to the MMPI," pp. 279–96. In *MMPI: Research Developments and Clinical Applications,* see 2867. *

28-2. CARSON, ROBERT C. Chap. 2, "Issues in the Teaching of Clinical MMPI Interpretation," pp. 41–53. In *MMPI: Research Developments and Clinical Applications,* see 2867. *

2873. CATTELL, RAYMOND B., AND BOLTON, LAURA SPECHT. "What Pathological Dimensions Lie Beyond the Normal Dimensions of the 16 PF?: A Comparison of MMPI and 16 PF Factor Domains." *J Consult & Clin Psychol* 33(1):18–29 F '69. * (PA 43:11336)

2874. CAUTHEN, NELSON R.; SANDMAN, CURT A.; KILPATRICK, DEAN G.; AND DEABLER, HERDIS L. "DAP Correlates of Sc Scores on the MMPI." *J Proj Tech & Pers Assess* 33(3): 262–4 Je '69. * (PA 43:14346)

2875. CHRISTENSON, JEFFRY MILTON. *A Study of the Differences Between Seekers and Non-Seekers at a College Counseling Center.* Doctor's thesis, University of South Dakota (Vermillion, S.D.), 1969. (DAI 30:2326A)

2876. CLIPPINGER, JOHN; MARTIN, CLYDE; MICHAEL, VERNON; AND INGLE, JOANN. "Personality Characteristics of a Liberal Arts College Population." *Correct Psychiatry & J Social Ther* 15(4):27–37 w '69. * (PA 46:7390)

2877. CLUM, GEORGE A. "A Correlational Analysis of the Relationships Between Personality and Perceptual Variables and Discriminant GSR Conditioning." *J Clin Psychol* 25(1): 33–5 Ja '69. * (PA 43:9826)

28:8. COFFMAN, ROUTH NASH. *Role-Taking Defects as Correlates of Criminality and Mental Illness in Offender Populations.* Doctor's thesis, George Washington University (Washington, D.C.), 1969. (DAI 31:910B)

2879. CONGER, ANTHONY J. "A Dimensional Analysis of MMPI Items." *Multiv Behav Res* 4(3):309–27 Jl '69. * (PA 44:671)

2880. COOKE, GERALD. "The Court Study Unit: Patient Characteristics and Differences Between Patients Judged Competent and Incompetent." *J Clin Psychol* 25(2):140–3 Ap '69. * (PA 43:14463)

2881. CUMMINGS, S. THOMAS; GODFREY, ANNE E.; AND BURROWS, BENJAMIN. "Personality and Social Class Factors Associated With Occupational Disability in Patients With Chronic Obstructive Lung Disease: An Exploratory Study." *Am R Resp Dis* 99(6):872–8 Je '69. *

2882. DAHLSTROM, W. GRANT. Chap. 1, "Recurrent Issues in the Development of the MMPI," pp. 1–40. In *MMPI: Research Developments and Clinical Applications,* see 2867. *

2883. DAHLSTROM, W. GRANT. Chap. 13, "Invasion of Privacy: How Legitimate Is the Current Concern Over This Issue?", pp. 263–72. In *MMPI: Research Developments and Clinical Applications,* see 2867. *

2884. DARLEY, SUSAN A. *Cognitive and Personality Factors in Emotional Expression Under Conditions of False Heart-Rate Feedback.* Doctor's thesis, New York University (New York, N.Y.), 1969. (DAI 31:1370A)

2885. DAVIS, WILLIAM E., AND GILLETTE, ANTHONY P. "Relationship Between Patients' Responses to Objective Tests and Examiners' Characteristics." *Psychol Rep* 25(2):487–91 O '69. * (PA 44:5315)

2886. DICKEN, CHARLES. "Predicting the Success of Peace Corps Community Development Workers." *J Consult & Clin Psychol* 33(5):597–606 O '69. * (PA 44:2919)

2887. DIES, ROBERT; REZNIKOFF, MARVIN; HONEYMAN, MERTON; AND WHITE, COLIN. "Personality and Smoking Patterns in a Twin Population." *J Proj Tech & Pers Assess* 33(5):457–63 O '69. * (PA 44:3591)

2888. DIGIORGIO, ANTHONY JOSEPH. *Discriminant Function Analysis of Measured Characteristics Among Committed Career Groups With Requisite Graduate Training.* Doctor's thesis, Purdue University (Lafayette, Ind.), 1969. (DAI 30:4769A)

2889. DOORACK, RALPH. *The Predictive Value of Scholastic Averages and MMPI Scores of Candidates to the Religious Life.* Master's thesis, Marquette University (Milwaukee, Wis.), 1969.

2890. DUVALL, NANCY SHERMAN. *Field Articulation and the Repression-Sensitization Dimension in Perception and Memory.* Doctor's thesis, University of North Carolina (Chapel Hill, N.C.), 1969. (DAI 30:3864B)

2891. EASTMAN, WILLIAM F.; FROMHART, MICHAEL V.; AND FULGHUM, MARY SUSAN K. "Sexual Problems and Personality Adjustment of College Women." *J Am Col Health Assn* 18(2):144–7 D '69. *

2892. EDWARDS, ALLEN L., AND ABBOTT, ROBERT D. "Further Evidence Regarding the R Scale of the MMPI as a Measure of Acquiescence." *Psychol Rep* 24(3):903–6 Je '69. * (PA 44:673)

2893. ENDICOTT, NOBLE A.; JORTNER, SIDNEY; AND ABRAMOFF, EILEEN. "Objective Measures of Suspiciousness." *J Abn Psychol* 74(1):26–32 F '69. * (PA 43:8449)

2894. ERDBERG, STEPHEN PHILIP. *MMPI Differences Associated With Sex, Race, and Residence in a Southern Sample.* Doctor's thesis, University of Alabama (University, Ala.), 1969. (DAI 30:5236B)

2895. ERICKSON, MARILYN T. "MMPI Profiles of Parents of Young Retarded Children." *Am J Mental Def* 73(5):728–32 Mr '69. * (PA 43:10223)

2896. FALK, HILDA B. *Developmental Crisis, Perceived Family Relations and College Achievement.* Doctor's thesis, Yeshiva University (New York, N.Y.), 1969. (DAI 30:2906B)

2897. FELLER, RICHARD JOSEPH. *Changes in the MMPI Scores of a Group of Diocesan Seminarians First Year College Through Third Year Graduate Theology: A Longitudinal Study.* Master's thesis, Loyola University (Chicago, Ill.), 1969.

2898. FINCH, KAYE. *Personality Variables and Sexual Status in Observer Performance.* Master's thesis, University of Alabama (University, Ala.), 1969.

2899. FINE, BERNARD J., AND KOBRICK, JOHN L. "Note on Headache, Personality Traits and Visual Performance at Altitude." *Percept & Motor Skills* 29(2):521–2 O '69. * (PA 44:3078)

2900. FISHER, GARY. "The Repression-Sensitization Scale: Effects of Several Variables and Two Methods of Obtaining Scores." *J General Psychol* 80(2):183–7 Ap '69. * (PA 43:11601)

2901. FISKE, DONALD W. "Subject Reactions to Inventory Format and Content." Abstract. *Proc 77th Ann Conv Am Psychol Assn* 4(1):137–8 '69. * (PA 43:17516)

2902. FITZPATRICK, JOHN CHARLES. *The Relationships Between the Relative Effectiveness of Two Teaching Methods and Selected Non-Cognitive Variables of College Students.* Doctor's thesis, Fordham University (New York, N.Y.), 1969. (DAI 30:5284A)

2903. FLANAGAN, JOHN, AND LEWIS, GEORGE. "Comparison of Negro and White Lower Class Men on the General Aptitude Test Battery and the Minnesota Multiphasic Personality Inventory." *J Social Psychol* 78(2):289–91 Ag '69. * (PA 44:6578)

2904. FONTANA, ALAN F., AND GESSNER, THEODORE. Patients' Goals and the Manifestation of Psychopathology." *J Consult & Clin Psychol* 33(2):247–53 Ap '69. * (PA 43:9829)

2905. FORD, CHARLES V.; GLOBER, GARY A.; AND CASTELNUOVO-TEDESCO, PIETRO. "A Psychiatric Study of Patients With Regional Enteritis." *J Am Med Assn* 208(2):311–5 Ap 14 '69. * (PA 44:21467)

2906. FOWLER, RAYMOND D., JR. Chap. 6, "Automated Interpretation of Personality Test Data," pp. 105–26. In *MMPI: Research Developments and Clinical Applications,* see 2867. *

2907. FOWLER, RAYMOND D., JR. "The Current Status of Computer Interpretation of Psychological Tests." *Am J Psychiatry* 125(7, sup):21–7 Ja '69. * (PA 43:10000)

2908. FOWLER, RAYMOND D., JR., AND COYLE, F. A., JR. "Collegiate Normative Data on MMPI Content Scales." *J Clin Psychol* 25(1):62–3 Ja '69. * (PA 43:9772)

2909. FOWLER, RAYMOND D., JR., AND COYLE, F. A., JR. "MMPI Characteristics of Freshmen Entering College." *Psychol Rec* 19(2):263–71 Ap '69. * (PA 43:14338)

2910. FOWLER, RAYMOND D., JR., AND MILLER, MARVIN L. "Computer Interpretation of the MMPI: Its Use in Clinical Practice." *Arch Gen Psychiatry* 21(4):502–8 O '69. * (PA 44:8741)

2911. FRACCHIA, JOHN F.; FIORENTINO, DIANE; SHEPPARD, CHARLES; AND MERLIS, SIDNEY. "A Comparison of Techniques for the Scoring of Avoidable Errors on the Raven Progressive Matrices." *J Psychol* 72(1):93–8 My '69. * (PA 43:15804)

2912. FRANK, AUSTIN C., AND KIRK, BARBARA A. "Characteristics and Attributes of Prospective City and Regional Planners." *J Col Stud Personnel* 10(4):317–23 S '69. *

2913. GAINES, LAWRENCE S., AND FRETZ, BRUCE R. "Reliability of the Barron Ego Strength Scale in an Individual Form." *Psychol Rep* 25(2):513–4 O '69. * (PA 44:5173)

2914. GANNON, D. R., AND TYLER, D. W. "Effects of Paraphrasing of Interview Items on Structured Answers." *Newsl Res Psychol* 11(3):37 Ag '69. *

2915. GEIST, HAROLD. "Psychological Aspects of Rheumatoid Arthritis." Abstract. *Proc 77th Ann Conv Am Psychol Assn* 4(2):769–70 '69. * (PA 44:1156)

2916. GIEBINK, JOHN W., AND STOVER, DONALD O. "Adjustment, Mental Health Opinions, and Proficiency of Child Care Personnel." *J Consult & Clin Psychol* 33(5):532–5 O '69. * (PA 44:2403)

2917. GILBERSTADT, HAROLD. Chap. 3, "Construction and Application of MMPI Codebooks," pp. 55–70. In *MMPI: Research Developments and Clinical Applications,* see 2867. *

2918. GLATT, KENNETH M. "An Evaluation of the French, Spanish and German Translations of the MMPI." *Acta Psychologica* 29(1):65–84 F '69. * (PA 43:17524)

2919. GLESER, GOLDINE C., AND IHILEVICH, DAVID. "An Objective Instrument for Measuring Defense Mechanisms." *J Consult & Clin Psychol* 33(1):51-60 F '69. * *(PA 43: 11347)*

2920. GLUECK, BERNARD C., JR., AND STROEBEL, CHARLES F. "The Computer and the Clinical Decision Process: II." *Am J Psychiatry* 125(7, sup):2-7 Ja '69. * *(PA 43:10002)*

2921. GOLDBERG, LEWIS R. "The Search for Configural Relationships in Personality Assessment: The Diagnosis of Psychosis vs. Neurosis From the MMPI." *Multiv Behav Res* 4(4):523-36 O '69. * *(PA 44:10719)*

2922. GOLDSTEIN, STEVEN G., AND LINDEN, JAMES D. "Multivariate Classification of Alcoholics by Means of the MMPI." *J Abn Psychol* 74(6):661-9 D '69. * *(PA 44:3819)*

2923. GOLISCH, JOHN EDWARD WILLIAM. *Psychological Variables on Missouri Synod Lutheran Clergy.* Doctor's thesis, University of Minnesota (Minneapolis, Minn.), 1969. *(DAI 30:1396A)*

2924. GOSS, ALLEN, AND MOROSKO, THOMAS E. "Alcoholism and Clinical Symptoms." *J Abn Psychol* 74(6):682-4 D '69. * *(PA 44:3820)*

2925. GRAVITZ, MELVIN A. "Adult Norms at Several Age Levels for Hovey's MMPI Scale of CNS Disorder." *J Clin Psychol* 25(4):427-8 O '69. * *(PA 44:11009)*

2926. GRAVITZ, MELVIN A. "Direction of Psychosexual Interest and Figure Drawing Choice." *J Clin Psychol* 25(3):311 Jl '69. * *(PA 44:3655)*

2927. GRAVITZ, MELVIN A. "Figure Drawing Size as an Index of Depression and MMPI Depression Scores in Normal Adults." *J Clin Psychol* 25(1):77-9 Ja '69. * *(PA 43:10003)*

2928. GRAVITZ, MELVIN A. "Hypnotic-Like Experiences in a Large General Population Related to Personality Inventory Responses." *Am J Clin Hyp* 11(3):171-4 Ja '69. * *(PA 43: 14340)*

2929. GRESSETT, JOHN D. "Prediction of Job Success Following Heart Attack." *Rehabil Counsel B* 13(1):10-4 S '69. *

2930. HAERTZEN, CHARLES A. "Implications of Eysenck's Criterion Analysis for Test Construction: Is the MMPI Schizophrenia Scale a Criterion for Schizophrenia?" Abstract. *Psychol Rep* 24(3):894 Je '69. * *(PA 44:858)*

2931. HAERTZEN, CHARLES A., AND HOOKS, NALL T., JR. "Changes in Personality and Subjective Experience Associated With the Chronic Administration and Withdrawal of Opiates." *J Nerv & Mental Dis* 148(6):606-14 Je '69. * *(PA 44:875)*

2932. HAFNER, A. JACK; BUTCHER, JAMES NEAL; HALL, MARIAN D.; AND QUAST, WENTWORTH. Chap. 8, "Parent Personality and Childhood Disorders: A Review of MMPI Findings," pp. 181-9. In *MMPI: Research Developments and Clinical Applications*, see *2867*. *

2933. HAFNER, A. JACK; HALL, MARIAN D.; BUTCHER, JAMES NEAL; AND QUAST, WENTWORTH. Appendix B, "Comparison of MMPI Studies of Parents," pp. 297-321. In *MMPI: Research Developments and Clinical Applications*, see *2867*. *

2934. HALL, WALLACE B., AND MACKINNON, DONALD W. "Personality Inventory Correlates of Creativity Among Architects." *J Appl Psychol* 53(4):322-6 Ag '69. * *(PA 43:15815)*

2935. HARRELL, THOMAS W. "The Personality of High Earning MBA's in Big Business." *Personnel Psychol* 22(4): 457-63 w '69. * *(PA 44:13525)*

2936. HATHAWAY, STARKE R.; REYNOLDS, PHYLLIS C.; AND MONACHESI, ELIO D. "Follow-Up of the Later Careers and Lives of 1,000 Boys Who Dropped Out of High School." *J Consult & Clin Psychol* 33(3):370-80 Je '69. * *(PA 43: 13285)*

2937. HEDENBERG, JOHN WESLEY, JR. *Personality Types via an Objective Multivariate Search Technique.* Doctor's thesis, University of California (Los Angeles, Calif.), 1969. *(DAI 30:3868B)*

2938. HENRICHS, THEODORE F., AND KAUSCH, DONALD F. "The Edwards SD Scale: Further Evaluation and Comment." *J Clin Psychol* 25(3):300-3 Jl '69. * *(PA 44:3677)*

2939. HENRICHS, THEODORE F.; MACKENZIE, JAMES W.; AND ALMOND, CARL H. "Psychological Adjustment and Acute Response to Open Heart Surgery." *J Nerv & Mental Dis* 148(2): 158-64 F '69. * *(PA 43:14752)*

2940. HINER, DARLENE L.; OGREN, DAVID J.; AND BAXTER, JAMES C. "Ideal-Self Responding on the MMPI." *J Proj Tech & Pers Assess* 33(4):389-96 Ag '69. * *(PA 44:2358)*

2941. HIRT, MICHAEL, AND KURTZ, RICHARD. "A Reexamination of the Relationship Between Body Boundary and Site of Disease." *J Abn Psychol* 74(1):67-70 F '69. * *(PA 43:8626)*

2942. HOGAN, ROBERT. "Development of an Empathy Scale." *J Consult & Clin Psychol* 33(3):307-16 Je '69. * *(PA 43: 12966)*

2943. HOLMES, DOUGLAS S. "Sensing Humor: Latency and Amplitude of Response Related to MMPI Profiles." *J Consult & Clin Psychol* 33(3):296-301 Je '69. * *(PA 43:12967)*

2944. JACKSON, DOUGLAS N., AND MESSICK, SAMUEL. "A Distinction Between Judgments of Frequency and of Desirability as Determinants of Response." *Ed & Psychol Meas* 29(2):273-93 su '69. * *(PA 44:16713)*

2945. JACOBSON, JAMES L., AND WIRT, ROBERT D. Appendix C, "Comparisons of MMPI Results for Acceptable and Unacceptable Psychotherapy Groups and Normal Subjects," pp. 323-33. In *MMPI: Research Developments and Clinical Applications*, see *2867*. *

2946. JACOBSON, JAMES L., AND WIRT, ROBERT D. Chap. 9, "MMPI Profiles Associated With Outcomes of Group Psychotherapy With Prisoners," pp. 191-205. In *MMPI: Research Developments and Clinical Applications*, see *2867*. *

2947. JAKOBSON, THEODOR; BLUMENTHAL, MAX; HAGMAN, HARRIET; AND HEIKKINEN, ELSA. "The Diurnal Variation of Urinary and Plasma 17-Hydroxy-Corticosteroid (17-OHCS) Levels and the Plasma 17-OHCS Response to Lysine-8-Vasopressin in Depressive Patients." *J Psychosom Res* 13(4): 363-75 D '69. * *(PA 44:12907)*

2948. JARRAHI-ZADEH, ALI; KANE, F. J., JR.; VAN DE CASTLE, R. L.; LACHENBRUCH, P. A.; AND EWING, J. A. "Emotional and Cognitive Changes in Pregnancy and Early Puerperium." *Brit J Psychiatry* 115(524):797-805 Jl '69. * *(PA 44:6605)*

2949. JOHNSON, DALE T. "Introversion, Extraversion, and Social Intelligence: A Replication." *J Clin Psychol* 25(2): 181-3 Ap '69. * *(PA 43:14469)*

2950. JOHNSON, DUANE MONROE. *Educational and Personality Characteristics of Two Groups of College Disciplinary Offenders.* Doctor's thesis, University of Minnesota (Minneapolis, Minn.), 1969. *(DAI 30:1867A)*

2951. JOSHI, MOHAN C., AND SINGH, BEER. "Predictive Validity of Some MMPI Scales (I)." *Indian Psychol R* 5(2): 161-5 Ja '69. *

2952. KAHLER, RICHARD ALLEN. *Anxiety and Choice Behavior in Psychopathic and Nonpsychopathic Criminals.* Doctor's thesis, Indiana University (Bloomington, Ind.), 1969. *(DAI 30:3387B)*

2953. KATKIN, STEVEN. *The Relationship Between Professed Values and Emotional Adjustment of College Students.* Doctor's thesis, University of Georgia (Athens, Ga.), 1969. *(DAI 30:5690B)*

2954. KAUPPI, DWIGHT R., AND WEISS, DAVID J. "Efficiency of Commonly Used Measures in Predicting Inventory Validity." Abstract. *Proc 77th Ann Conv Am Psychol Assn* 4(2):691-2 '69. * *(PA 44:675)*

2955. KIRTLEY, DONALD, AND HARKLESS, RICHARD. "Some Personality and Attitudinal Correlates of Dogmatism." *Psychol Rep* 24(3):851-4 Je '69. * *(PA 44:642)*

2956. KISH, GEORGE B. "Explorations of the Relationships Between Food Preferences and Age, Sex, Education, and Some Personality Variables." *Newsl Res Psychol* 11(3):29-31 Ag '69. *

2957. KISH, GEORGE B. "Failure to Confirm a Relationship Between Alcoholism and Food Preferences." *Newsl Res Psychol* 11(3):31-4 Ag '69. *

2958. KISH, GEORGE B. "The Obscure Figures Test (OFT): 3, Relationships With Personality Variables (MMPI)." *Newsl Res Psychol* 11(2):16-7 My '69. *

2959. KISH, GEORGE B., AND BUSSE, WILLIAM. "MMPI Correlates of Sensation-Seeking in Male Alcoholics: A Test of Quay's Hypothesis Applied to Alcoholism." *J Clin Psychol* 25(1):60-2 Ja '69. * *(PA 43:10038)*

2960. KLEINMUNTZ, BENJAMIN. Chap. 5, "Personality Test Interpretation by Computer and Clinician," pp. 97-104. In *MMPI: Research Developments and Clinical Applications*, see *2867*. *

2961. KNEFF, DENNIS; BODENSTEINER, ROBERT T.; VODDE, THOMAS W.; AND GYNTHER, MALCOLM D. "The Clinical Utility of Block's Ego-Resiliency and Ego-Control Scales." *J Psychol* 72(2):165-8 Jl '69. * *(PA 44:862)*

2962. KNILL, FRANKLIN PETER, JR. *The Manipulation of Teacher Expectancies: Its Effect on Intellectual Performance, Self-Concept, Interpersonal Relationships, and the Institutional Behavior of Students.* Doctor's thesis, University of Cincinnati (Cincinnati, Ohio), 1969. *(DAI 30:5239B)*

2963. KOKOSH, JOHN. "MMPI Personality Characteristics of Physical and Social Science Students." *Psychol Rep* 24(3): 883-93 Je '69. * *(PA 44:634)*

2964. KOLLAR, EDWARD J.; PASNAU, ROBERT O.; RUBIN, ROBERT T.; NAITOH, PAUL; SLATER, GRANT G.; AND KALES, ANTHONY. "Psychological, Psychophysiological, and Biochemical Correlates of Prolonged Sleep Deprivation." *Am J Psychiatry* 126(4):488-97 O '69. * *(PA 44:9960)*

2965. KRAHENBUHL, GARY STUART. *The Relationship of Personality Traits and Catecholamine Excretion in Athletic Competition.* Doctor's thesis, Colorado State College (Greeley, Colo.), 1969. *(DAI 30:4144A)*

2966. KUNCE, JOSEPH T., AND CALLIS, ROBERT. "Vocational Interest and Personality." *Voc Guid Q* 18(1):34-40 S '69. *

2967. LAMPHEAR, STEVEN CLARK. *Personality and Recreation: A Study of Participant Behavior in Selected Outdoor Recreation Activities.* Doctor's thesis, University of Georgia (Athens, Ga.), 1969. *(DAI 30:5314B)*

2968. LEE, W. H., JR.; MILLER, W., JR.; ROWE, J.; JAIRSTON, P.; AND BRADY, M. P. "Effects of Extracorporeal Circulation on Personality and Cerebration." *Ann Thorac Surg* 7(6):562-70 Je '69. *

2969. LEVITT, HERBERT, AND BAKER, RALPH. "Relative Psychopathology of Marital Partners." *Family Process* 8(1):33-42 Mr '69. * *(PA 41:1032)*

2970. LEWINSOHN, PETER M., AND ATWOOD, GEORGE E. "Depression: A Clinical-Research Approach: The Case of Mrs.

G." *Psychother Theory Res & Prac* 6(3):166–71 su '69. * (*PA* 44:3745)

2971. LEZAK, MURIEL D., AND GLAUDIN, VINCENT. "Differential Effects of Physical Illness on MMPI Profiles." *Newsl Res Psychol* 11(2):27–8 My '69. *

2972. LIEBERMAN, LEWIS R. "Willingness to Accept Limitations and Personal Adjustment." *Percept & Motor Skills* 29(2):425–6 O '69. * (*PA* 44:3646)

2973. LOMONT, JAMES F.; GILNER, FRANK H.; SPECTOR, NORMAN J.; AND SKINNER, KATHRYN K. "Group Assertion Training and Group Insight Therapies." *Psychol Rep* 25(2):463–70 O '69. * (*PA* 44:5255)

2974. LOVE, HENRY G. I., AND ASHCROFT, LINDSAY M. "Errors in the A.C.E.R. Scoring Stencils for the M.M.P.I. Group Form." *Austral Psychologist* 4(2–3):193–5 N '69. * (*PA* 46:3088)

2975. McAREE, C. P.; STEFFENHAGEN, R. A.; AND ZHEUTLIN, L. S. "Personality Factors in College Drug Users." *Int J Social Psychiatry* 15(2):102–6 sp '69. * (*PA* 44:6730)

2976. McCLELLAND, JAMES N., AND RHODES, FEN. "Prediction of Job Success for Hospital Aides and Orderlies From MMPI Scores and Personal History Data." *J Appl Psychol* 53(1):49–54 F '69. * (*PA* 43:6974)

2977. McCULLOUGH, J. J., AND GILBERSTON, V. A. "Motivation Factors in Persons Seeking Early Diagnosis of Cancer." *Geriatrics* 24(5):117–25 My '69. *

2978. McGRAW, JAMES PAUL. *A Comparison of MMPI Scores and Other Variables With Subsequent Ratings of Nazarene Ministers by Their District Superintendents.* Doctor's thesis, University of Kansas (Lawrence, Kan.), 1969. (*DAI* 31:157A)

2979. MACK, JAMES L. "The MMPI and Recidivism." *J Abn Psychol* 74(5):612–4 O '69. * (*PA* 44:893)

2980. McLAUGHLIN, EDWARD J., AND WAUCK, LEROY A. "Quantitative Scoring of a Sentence Completion Test." *Nat Cath Guid Conf J* 13(2):121–7 w '69. * (*PA* 44:8473)

2981. MARKEL, NORMAN N. "Relationship Between Voice-Quality Profiles and MMPI Profiles in Psychiatric Patients." *J Abn Psychol* 74(1):61–6 F '69. * (*PA* 43:8456)

2982. MARKOWSKI, EDWARD. *The Effect of the Test Administrator and Testing Situation on the Land Anxiety Scales of the MMPI.* Master's thesis, East Tennessee State University (Johnson City, Tenn.), 1969.

2983. MARKS, PHILIP A., AND SINES, JACOB O. Chap. 4, "Methodological Problems of Cookbook Construction," pp. 71–95. In *MMPI: Research Developments and Clinical Applications,* see 2867. *

2984. MASCIA, GEORGE VINCENT. *A Study of the Prediction of Alcoholics' Responsiveness to Treatment.* Doctor's thesis, University of Kansas (Lawrence, Kan.), 1969. (*DAI* 30:2912B)

2985. MAYO, CLYDE C.; PURYEAR, HERBERT B.; AND RICHEK, HERBERT G. "MMPI Correlates of Religiousness in Late Adolescent College Students." *J Nerv & Mental Dis* 149(5):381–5 N '69. * (*PA* 44:8448)

2986. MEEHL, PAUL E. "Comments on the Invasion of Privacy Issue," pp. 273–8. In *MMPI: Research Developments and Clinical Applications,* see 2867. *

2987. MEGARGEE, EDWIN I. "Conscientious Objectors' Scores on the MMPI *O-H* (Overcontrolled Hostility) Scale." Abstract. *Proc 77th Ann Conv Am Psychol Assn* 4(2):507–8 '69. * (*PA* 44:677)

2988. MEIER, MANFRED J. Chap. 12, "The Regional Localization Hypothesis and Personality Changes Associated With Focal Cerebral Lesions and Ablations," pp. 243–61. In *MMPI: Research Developments and Clinical Applications,* see 2867. *

2989. MITSUKUNI, ABE. "The Japanese MMPI and Its Delinquency Scale." *Tohoku Psychologia Folia* 28(1–2):54–68 '69. * (*PA* 44:18897)

2990. MOHRBACHER, JOHN W. "MMPI and Rosen Scale Profiles in Relation to Type of Admission and Type of VA Hospital." *Newsl Res Psychol* 11(3):15–7 Ag '69. *

2991. MONACHESI, ELIO D., AND HATHAWAY, STARKE R. Chap. 10, "The Personality of Delinquents," pp. 207–19. In *MMPI: Research Developments and Clinical Applications,* see 2867. *

2992. MORROW, GEORGE M., JR. "Discussion: An Internist Assesses Future Computer Use." *Am J Psychiatry* 125(7, sup):34–6 Ja '69. * (*PA* 43:9840)

2993. MULLEN, JOHN ANDREW. *An Investigation of the Variable of Liking in Therapy: Its Relation to the Variables of Outcome, Empathy, and Therapist Experience.* Doctor's thesis, Michigan State University (East Lansing, Mich.), 1969. (*DAI* 31:1546B)

2994. MURRAY, LOIS MIRIAM NELSON. *The Relationship Between Conceptual, Perceptual, and Electroencephalographic Factors in Process and Reactive Schizophrenics.* Doctor's thesis, University of Arizona (Tucson, Ariz.), 1969. (*DAI* 30:3872B)

2995. NALVEN, FREDRIC B. "Ego Control Patterns and Hostility Expression: Correlation or Tautology?" *Psychol Rep* 24(1):16 F '69. * (*PA* 43:14291)

2996. NELSEN, EDWARD A. "Social Reinforcement for Expression vs. Suppression of Aggression." *Merrill-Palmer Q* 15(3):259–78 Jl '69. * (*PA* 44:8828)

2997. NEWTON, MARIANA. *A Study of the Effects of Diaze-pam on Stuttering.* Doctor's thesis, Northwestern University (Evanston, Ill.), 1969. (*DAI* 30:4833B)

2998. NORMAN, RUSSELL P. "Extreme Response Tendency as a Function of Emotional Adjustment and Stimulus Ambiguity." *J Consult & Clin Psychol* 33(4):406–10 Ag '69. * (*PA* 43:15785)

2999. O'DELL, JERRY W., AND KARSON, SAMUEL. "Some Relationships Between the MMPI and 16 PF." *J Clin Psychol* 25(3):279–83 Jl '69. * (*PA* 44:3638)

3000. O'DONOVAN, DENNIS. "An Historical Review of the Lie Scale—With Particular Reference to the Maudsley Personality Inventory." *Papers Psychol* 3(1):13–9 Ap '69. *

3001. OSBORNE, DAVID. *MMPI Validity: A Moderator Variable Approach.* Doctor's thesis, University of Minnesota (Minneapolis, Minn.), 1969. (*DAI* 30:1904B)

3002. PAIGE, PAUL E., AND ZAPPELLA, DAVID G. "The Incidence of MMPI Code High Combinations and Extreme Scores of a Select Group of Male Alcoholic Patients." *Psychol* 6(4):13–21 N '69. *

3003. PERLMAN, LEONARD G., AND HYLBERT, KENNETH W. "Identifying Potential Dropouts at a Rehabilitation Center." *Rehabil Counsel B* 13(2):217–25 D '69. *

3004. PERSONS, ROY W., AND MARKS, PHILIP A. "Self-Disclosure With Recidivists: A Study of Interviewer-Interviewee Matching." Abstract. *Proc 77th Ann Conv Am Psychol Assn* 4(2):531–2 '69. * (*PA* 44:895)

3005. PERSONS, ROY WOODVALL, JR. *Interpersonal Intimacy With Recidivists.* Doctor's thesis, Ohio State University (Columbus, Ohio), 1969. (*DAI* 30:1905B)

3006. PETERSON, HOWARD CHESTER. *A Comparison of Personality Characteristics of Persisters and Non-Persisters in an Undergraduate Engineering Program on the Minnesota Multiphasic Personality Inventory.* Doctor's thesis, University of South Dakota (Vermillion, S.D.), 1969. (*DAI* 30:3798A)

3007. PETZEL, THOMAS P., AND GYNTHER, MALCOLM D. "A Comparison of Psychiatric Diagnosis and Behavioral Classification as Criteria for Differentiating Psychiatric Patients." *J General Psychol* 80(2):219–27 Ap '69. * (*PA* 43:11571)

3008. PINO, CHRISTOPHER JOSEPH. *Illinois Institute of Technology Interaction in Sensitivity Training Groups.* Doctor's thesis, Illinois Institute of Technology (Chicago, Ill.), 1969. (*DAI* 30:2915B)

3009. PLUMMER, JACK MOORE, JR. *A Comparison of Successful and Unsuccessful Vocational Rehabilitation Clients From a Reformatory Population.* Doctor's thesis, Texas Technological University (Lubbock, Tex.), 1969. (*DAI* 31:2964B)

3010. POWELL, JUDITH ANN JOURDAN, AND BENSON, GERALD B. "Relationship Between Students' Personalities and Their Attitudes Toward Young Children." *J Home Econ* 61(9):687–92 N '69. *

3011. PRYOR, FELICIA A., AND BUTLER, JOEL R. "Test of the Unimportance of Particular Item Content Using the HTP and the MMPI." *Psychol Rep* 24(3):989–90 Je '69. * (*PA* 44:667)

3012. RAVENSBORG, MILTON R., AND FOSS, ADELINE. "Suicide and Natural Death in a State Hospital Population: A Comparison of Admission Complaints, MMPI Profiles, and Social Competence Factors." *J Consult & Clin Psychol* 33(4):466–71 Ag '69. * (*PA* 43:16032)

3013. REED, ROBERT LYNN. *An Application of the Joint Multiple Regression Model to the Prediction of Academic Success From Personality Variables.* Doctor's thesis, University of Kansas (Lawrence, Kan.), 1969. (*DAI* 30:5300A)

3014. RHODES, ROBERT J. "The MacAndrew Alcoholism Scale: A Replication." *J Clin Psychol* 25(2):189–91 Ap '69. * (*PA* 43:14477)

3015. RICE, DAVID G.; STERNBACH, RICHARD A.; AND PENN, NOLAN E. "Comparative Diagnostic Judgments From the Rorschach and the MMPI." *J Proj Tech & Pers Assess* 33(3):274–8 Je '69. * (*PA* 43:14334)

3016. RICH, CHARLES C., AND DAVIS, HARRY G. "Concurrent Validity of MMPI Alcoholism Scales." *J Clin Psychol* 25(4):425–6 O '69. * (*PA* 44:10735)

3017. ROHAN, WILLIAM P.; TATRO, R. L.; AND ROTMAN, S. R. "MMPI Changes in Alcoholics During Hospitalization." *Q J Studies Alcohol* 30(2A):389–400 Je '69. * (*PA* 44:886)

3018. ROHILA, PRITAM KUMAR. *Multivariate Relationships Between Personality and Vocational Interests.* Doctor's thesis, University of Oregon (Eugene, Ore.), 1969. (*DAI* 31:1022A)

3019. ROSECRANS, C. J., AND SUTTERER, J. R. "Perceptual, Concept Shift, and Personality Test Performance of Matched Psychiatric Outpatient Groups." *J Nerv & Mental Dis* 149(3):254–60 S '69. * (*PA* 44:6879)

3020. SAN DIEGO, ELLINOR AQUIO. *A Comparison of M-F Scores of American and Philippine Ss on the WAIS and the MMPI.* Master's thesis, Loyola University (Chicago, Ill.), 1969.

3021. SCHLUCK, CAROLYN GITZEN. *Predicting Teaching Style Using the MMPI.* Doctor's thesis, University of Minnesota (Minneapolis, Minn.), 1969. (*DAI* 31:1080A)

3022. SCHULMAN, WILLIAM JOSEPH. *Personality and Behavior Characteristics of Assaultive Psychiatric Patients.* Doctor's thesis, University of Texas (Austin, Tex.), 1969. (*DAI* 30:5698B)

3023. SCHWAB, FRANCIS JOSEPH. *A Comparison of Personality Profiles of Over- and Under-Achieving Students at South*

Dakota State University. Doctor's thesis, University of South Dakota (Vermillion, S.D.), 1969. *(DAI* 30:2343A)

3024. SCHWARTZ, MARK S. "'Organicity' and the MMPI 1-3-9 and 2-9 Codes." Abstract. *Proc 77th Ann Conv Am Psychol Assn* 4(2):519-20 '69. * *(PA* 44:1098)

3025. SEITZ, FRANK C. "A Behavior Modification Approach to Depression: A Case Study." *Newsl Res Psychol* 11(1): 10-2 F '69. *

3026. SEITZ, FRANK CHRYST. *A Psychotherapeutic Approach to Depression: The Immediate Impact of Videotape Confrontation and/or Psychotherapeutic Discussion on the Self-Concept and Behavior of Neurotically Depressed Patients.* Doctor's thesis, University of Colorado (Boulder, Colo.), 1969. *(DAI* 30:4797B)

3027. SELESNICK, SHELDON T.; MALMSTROM, EDWARD J.; YOUNGER, JESSE; AND LEDERMAN, ARTHUR R. "Induced Somatic Reactions in Asthmatic Adults (Their Reduction by Use of Psychotropic Drugs)." *Dis Nerv System* 30(6):385-91 Je '69. * *(PA* 44:7053)

3028. SHEPPARD, CHARLES; FIORENTINO, DIANE; COLLINS, LOIS; AND MERLIS, SIDNEY. "Comparison of Emotion Profiles as Defined by Two Additional MMPI Profile Types in Male Narcotic Addicts." *J Clin Psychol* 25(2):186-8 Ap '69. * *(PA* 43:14479)

3029. SMART, REGINALD G., AND FEJER, DIANNE. "Illicit LSD Users: Their Social Backgrounds, Drug Use and Psychopathology." *J Health & Social Behav* 10(4):297-308 D '69. * *(PA* 44:8423)

3030. SMITH, DAVID P.; PILLING, LORAN F.; PEARSON, JOHN S.; RUSHTON, JOSEPH G.; GOLDSTEIN, NORMAN P.; AND GIBILISCO, JOSEPH A. "A Psychiatric Study of Atypical Facial Pain." *Can Med Assn J* 100(26):286-91 F 8 '69. * *(PA* 44:17248)

3031. SMITH, WILLIAM H., AND COYLE, F. A., JR. "MMPI and Rorschach Form Level Scores in a Student Population." *J Psychol* 73(1):3-7 S '69. * *(PA* 44:5170)

3032. SPIEGEL, DON. "SPI and MMPI Predictors of Psychopathology." *J Proj Tech & Pers Assess* 33(3):265-73 Je '69. * *(PA* 43:14343)

3033. SPIEGEL, DON. "SPI Discriminators Among Four Psychological Health-Sickness Levels." *J Consult & Clin Psychol* 33(6):750-6 D '69. * *(PA* 44:3804)

3034. SPIEGEL, JOSEPH A. *Test Score Performance on Irish and Italian College Freshmen.* Doctor's thesis, Rutgers—The State University (New Brunswick, N.J.), 1969. *(DAI* 30: 3802A)

3035. STEELE, JAMES. "The Hysteria and Psychasthenia Constructs as an Alternative to Manifest Anxiety and Conflict-Free Ego Functions." *J Abn Psychol* 74(1):79-85 F '69. * *(PA* 44:8494)

3036. STEERE, JAMES LINDLEY. *The Relationship of a Measure of Personality Factors to a Measure of Motivation for Ministerial Work and Success in a Selected B. D. Program.* Doctor's thesis, Ball State University (Muncie, Ind.), 1969. *(DAI* 30:4235A)

3037. STEWART, ROBERT A. C. "Intolerance of Ambiguity, Ego Strength and Dominance." *Indian Psychol R* 5(2):97-9 Ja '69. *

3038. STOFFER, SHELDON S.; SAPIRA, JOSEPH D.; AND MEKETON, BETTY F. "Behavior in Ex-Addict Female Prisoners Participating in a Research Study." *Comprehen Psychiatry* 10(3):224-32 My '69. * *(PA* 44:14898)

3039. STRAUGHAN, JAMES H., AND DUFORT, W. HENRY. "Task Difficulty, Relaxation, and Anxiety Level During Verbal Learning and Recall." *J Abn Psychol* 74(5):621-4 O '69. * *(PA* 44:186)

3040. STRENGER, STUART BARRY. *Counterconditioning and Cognitive-Strategies in Systematic Desensitization.* Doctor's thesis, Vanderbilt University (Nashville, Tenn.), 1969. *(DAI* 30:4799B)

3041. STRICKER, GEORGE, AND MERBAUM, MICHAEL. "Social Desirability and the Marks and Seeman Atlas." Abstract. *Proc 77th Ann Conv Am Psychol Assn* 4(2):513-4 '69. * *(PA* 44:679)

3042. SULLIVAN, PATRICK F., AND ROBERTS, LYNN K. "Relationship of Manifest Anxiety to Repression-Sensitization on the MMPI." *J Consult & Clin Psychol* 33(6):763-4 D '69. * *(PA* 44:3648)

3043. SWOPE, ALAN JOSEPH. *Cognitive Controls and the Content of Reported Emotional Experience.* Doctor's thesis, Columbia University (New York, N.Y.), 1969. *(DAI* 30: 2918B)

3044. TALLENT, NORMAN, AND ROTMAN, SAUL R. "MMPI Profiles of Hospitalized Psychiatric Patients Placed on Suicidal Precautions." *Newsl Res Psychol* 11(3):2-4 Ag '69. *

3045. TAMKIN, ARTHUR S., AND SONKIN, NATHAN. "Use of Psychological Tests in Differential Diagnosis." *Psychol Rep* 24(2):590 Ap '69. * *(PA* 43:16017)

3046. TAYLOR, DALMAS A.; ALTMAN, IRWIN; WHEELER, LADD; AND KUSHNER, ESTELLE N. "Personality Factors Related to Response to Social Isolation and Confinement." *J Consult & Clin Psychol* 33(4):411-9 Ag '69. * *(PA* 43:15789)

3047. TELLEGEN, AUKE; GERRARD, NATHAN L.; GERRARD, LOUISE B.; AND BUTCHER, JAMES NEAL. Chap. 11, "Personality Characteristics of Members of a Serpent-Handling Religious Cult," pp. 221-42. In *MMPI: Research Developments and Clinical Applications*, see 2867. *

3048. TEMPLER, DONALD I. "Death Anxiety Scale." Abstract. *Proc 77th Ann Conv Am Psychol Assn* 4(2):737-8 '69. * *(PA* 44:647)

3049. THUMIN, FRED J. "A Correlational Study of the MMPI." *Meas & Eval Guid* 2(1):41-6 sp '69. * *(PA* 44: 12618)

3050. THUMIN, FRED J. "MMPI Scores as Related to Age, Education, and Intelligence Among Male Job Applicants." *J Appl Psychol* 53(5):404-7 O '69. * *(PA* 44:680)

3051. TRICE, HARRISON M.; ROMAN, PAUL M.; AND BELASCO, JAMES A. "Selection for Treatment: A Predictive Evaluation of an Alcoholism Treatment Regimen." *Int J Addic* 4(3):303-17 S '69. *

3052. TRUAX, CHARLES B., AND WARGO, DONALD G. "Effects of Vicarious Therapy Pretraining and Alternate Sessions on Outcome in Group Psychotherapy With Outpatients." *J Consult & Clin Psychol* 33(4):440-7 Ag '69. * *(PA* 43:15953)

3053. TSUBOUCHI, KOSUKE, AND JENKINS, RICHARD L. "Three Types of Delinquents: Their Performance on MMPI and PCR." *J Clin Psychol* 25(4):353-8 O '69. * *(PA* 44: 10803)

3054. TWOMEY, JOHN F., AND HENDRY, CHARLES H. "MMPI Characteristics of Difficult-to-Manage Federal Penitentiary Offenders." *Psychol Rep* 24(2):546 Ap '69. * *(PA* 43:16038)

3055. UECKER, ALBERT E. "Comparability of Two Methods of Administering the MMPI to Brain-Damaged Geriatric Patients." *J Clin Psychol* 25(2):196-8 Ap '69. * *(PA* 43:14484)

3056. UECKER, ALBERT E. "The Comparative Utility of Two Actuarial Systems of MMPI Interpretation in Classifying the Profiles of Male Alcoholic Inpatients." *Newsl Res Psychol* 11(3):41-3 Ag '69. *

3057. UECKER, ALBERT E. "The Validity of the MacAndrew Scale for Differentiating Male Alcoholic Inpatients From Nonalcoholic Psychiatric Inpatients." *Newsl Res Psychol* 11(2): 32-3 My '69. *

3058. UECKER, ALBERT E.; KISH, GEORGE B.; AND BALL, MARGARET E. "Differentiation of Alcoholism From General Psychopathology by Means of Two MMPI Scales." *J Clin Psychol* 25(3):287-9 Jl '69. * *(PA* 44:3809)

3059. VANDO, ALAN. *A Personality Dimension Related to Pain Tolerance.* Doctor's thesis, Columbia University (New York, N.Y.), 1969. *(DAI* 31:2292B)

3060. VESPRANI, GEORGE J. "Personality Correlates of Accurate Empathy in a College Companion Program." *J Consult & Clin Psychol* 33(6):722-7 D '69. * *(PA* 44:3612)

3061. VESTRE, NORRIS D., AND KLETT, WILLIAM G. "Admissions to a Neuropsychiatric Hospital With 'Normal' MMPI Profiles." Abstract. *Proc 77th Ann Conv Am Psychol Assn* 4(2):515-6 '69. * *(PA* 44:869)

3062. VESTRE, NORRIS D., AND KLETT, WILLIAM G. "Classification of MMPI Profiles Using the Gilberstadt-Duker Rules." *J Clin Psychol* 25(3):284-6 Jl '69. * *(PA* 44:3810)

3063. VESTRE, NORRIS D., AND KLETT, WILLIAM G. "Classification of MMPI Profiles Using the Gilberstadt-Duker Rules." *Newsl Res Psychol* 11(3):1 Ag '69. *

3064. VOORS, A. W.; RYTEL, M. W.; JENKINS, C. D.; PIERCE, W. E.; AND STEWART, G. T. "Prediction of Sickness in Naval Recruits by Minnesota Multiphasic Personality Inventory Scores." *Am R Resp Dis* 99(3):420-5 Mr '69. *

3065. WALES, BETH, AND SEEMAN, WILLIAM. "What Do MMPI Zero Items Really Measure: An Experimental Investigation." *J Clin Psychol* 25(4):420-4 O '69. * *(PA* 44:10746)

3066. WALKER, C. EUGENE, AND WARD, JAMES. "Identification and Elimination of Offensive Items From the MMPI." *J Proj Tech & Pers Assess* 33(4):385-8 Ag '69. * *(PA* 44:2536)

3067. WALKER, RONALD E.; NICOLAY, ROBERT C.; KLUCZNY, RITA; AND RIEDEL, ROBERT G. "Psychological Correlates of Smoking." *J Clin Psychol* 25(1):42-4 Ja '69. * *(PA* 43: 9698)

3068. WALSH, JAMES A.; PENBERTHY, DORIS K.; AND EARLEY, SHARON R. "Relationship Between Estimated Occurrence and Social Desirability Scale Value of Objective Personality Items." *Psychol Rep* 24(2):621-2 Ap '69. * *(PA* 43:15832)

3069. WARREN, LYNDA W., AND WEISS, DAVID J. "Relationship Between Disability Type and Measured Personality Characteristics." Abstract. *Proc 77th Ann Conv Am Psychol Assn* 4(2):773-4 '69. * *(PA* 44:1182)

3070. WATSON, CHARLES G. "An Attempt to Develop a Useful Process-Reactive Scale for the MMPI." *J Clin Psychol* 25(2):194-6 Ap '69. * *(PA* 43:14488)

3071. WEBB, JAMES T.; MILLER, MARVIN L.; AND FOWLER, RAYMOND D., JR. "Validation of a Computerized MMPI Interpretation System." Abstract. *Proc 77th Ann Conv Am Psychol Assn* 4(2):523-4 '69. * *(PA* 44:68)

3072. WEISGERBER, CHARLES A. *Psychological Assessment of Candidates for a Religious Order.* pp. 52-87, 154-6, 172-81. Chicago, Ill.: Loyola University Press, 1969. Pp. viii, 191. *

3073. WELSH, GEORGE S. *Gifted Adolescents: A Handbook of Test Results.* Greensboro, N.C.: Prediction Press, June 1969. Pp. viii, 809. *

3074. WHYBROW, P. C.; PRANGE, A. J., JR.; AND TREADWAY, C. R. "Mental Changes Accompanying Thyroid Gland

Dysfunction: A Reappraisal Using Objective Psychological Measurement." *Arch Gen Psychiatry* 20(1):48–63 Ja '69. * (*PA* 43:11631)

3075. WIEMER, MARLIN JAMES. *Dogmatism and Future Time Perspective in Seminary Students.* Doctor's thesis, University of Minnesota (Minneapolis, Minn.), 1969. (*DAI* 30:1910B)

3076. WIGGINS, JERRY S. Chap. 7, "Content Dimensions in the MMPI," pp. 127–80. In *MMPI: Research Developments and Clinical Applications,* see 2867. *

3077. WILLIAMS, CHRISTENE BLANTON, AND NICKELS, JAMES B. "Internal-External Control Dimension as Related to Accident and Suicide Proneness." *J Consult & Clin Psychol* 33(4): 485–94 Ag '69. * (*PA* 43:16034)

3078. WOLMAN, RICHARD, AND KEPECS, JOSEPH. "Ego Measurements of Patients and Staff on a Medical Ward." *Comprehen Psychiatry* 10(4):334–40 Jl '69. * (*PA* 44:14852)

3079. YOUNG, RHODES C., AND ADAMS, GORDON. "A Flexible Program for Keying and Standardizing Scales Developed From the Item Pool of the MMPI." *Ed & Psychol Meas* 29(3):713–4 au '69. * (*PA* 44:18744)

3080. ZIEGLER, FREDRICK J.; RODGERS, DAVID A.; AND PRENTISS, ROBERT J. "Psychosocial Response to Vasectomy." *Arch Gen Psychiatry* 21(1):46–54 Jl '69. * (*PA* 44:2257)

3081. APOSTAL, ROBERT A., AND HALCROW, JOHN H. "Personality Characteristics of Mental Health Center Patients Classified by Referral Source." *Mental Hyg* 54(2):295–7 Ap '70. * (*PA* 44:17253)

3082. ARMENTROUT, JAMES A. "Correspondence of the MMPI and Mini-Mult in a College Population." *J Clin Psychol* 26(4): 493–5 O '70. * (*PA* 45:4292)

3083. ARMENTROUT, JAMES A., AND ROUZER, DAVID L. "Utility of the Mini-Mult With Delinquents." Abstract. *J Consult & Clin Psychol* 34(3):450 Je '70. * (*PA* 44:14899)

3084. BATES, HENRY D. "Factorial Structure of Fears in a Clinical Population." *Newsl Res Psychol* 12(2):7–9 My '70. *

3085. BATES, HENRY D. "An MMPI Fear Scale." *Newsl Res Psychol* 12(2):1–3 My '70. *

3086. BATES, HENRY D. "MMPI Fear Scores in Normal, Neurotic, and Psychotic Samples." *Newsl Res Psychol* 12(2): 3–6 My '70. *

3087. BATES, HENRY D. "Predictions Based on Measures of 'Fearfulness' and Factor Scores." *Newsl Res Psychol* 12(2): 9–12 My '70. *

3088. BECKER, BRUCE. "The Projective Approach to the Study of Multiple Personality—A Case Study." *Int Congr Rorsch & Other Proj Tech* 7:423–38 '70. *

3089. BECKER, GILBERT, AND BAKAL, DONALD A. "Subject Anonymity and Motivational Distortion in Self-Report Data." *J Clin Psychol* 26(2):207–9 Ap '70. * (*PA* 44:14622)

3090. BEDNAR, RICHARD L., AND WEINBERG, STEVE L. "Clinical Judgments of Client Pathology and Subsequent Client Improvement." *J Clin Psychol* 26(4):443–6 O '70. * (*PA* 45: 4518)

3091. BERDIE, RALPH F.; PILAPIL, BONIFACIO; AND IM, IN JAE. "Entrance Correlates of University Satisfaction." *Am Ed Res J* 7(2):251–66 Mr '70. *

3092. BERNHARDSON, CLEMENS S. "Social Desirability as a Confounding Variable in the Reversed Item Approach to Studying Acquiescence in the MMPI." *Can J Behav Sci* 2(2):148–56 Ap '70. * (*PA* 44:14642)

3093. BIERSNER, ROBERT J., AND CAMERON, BERNARD J. "Betting Preferences and Personality Characteristics of Navy Divers." *Aerospace Med* 41(11):1289–91 N '70. *

3094. BLUM, DONNA M. "MMPI Characteristics of Males in a Private Hospital Population." *Psychol Rep* 26(1):234 F '70. * (*PA* 45:4522)

3095. BLUM, DONNA M., AND VINCENT, M. O. "Personality Test Characteristics of Staff Physicians and Physicians as Psychiatric Patients." *J Clin Psychol* 26(3):389–90 Jl '70. * (*PA* 45:750)

3096. BORSTEIN, IRVING JACOB. *Perceived Maternal Childbearing Patterns and Schizoid Behavior in "Normal" Males.* Doctor's thesis, Illinois Institute of Technology (Chicago, Ill.), 1970. (*DAI* 31:2273B)

3097. BOTTGER, JOAN E. *A Study of the Relationship Between the Percentage of Buccal Cell Nuclei Containing Barr Bodies and the Psychological Masculinity-Femininity Indices of 100 Freshman and Sophomore College Women.* Doctor's thesis, Texas Woman's University (Denton, Tex.), 1970.

3098. BRAATZ, GORDON A. "Preference Intransitivity as an Indicator of Cognitive Slippage in Schizophrenia." *J Abn Psychol* 75(1):1–6 F '70. * (*PA* 44:7048)

3099. BRODSKY ANNETTE MAE. *The Effect of Environmental Stimulation on Sensation Seeking Behavior of Criminals and Noncriminals.* Doctor's thesis, University of Florida (Gainesville, Fla.), 1970. (*DAI* 31:4327B)

3100. BROWN, WALTER A., AND MUELLER, PETER S. "Psychological Function in Individuals With Amyotrophic Lateral Sclerosis (ALS)." *Psychosom Med* 32(2):141–52 Mr–Ap '70. * (*PA* 44:17117)

3101. CANTY, JAMES JOSEPH, JR. *Personality and Behavior Correlates of Extreme Positive Self-Regard.* Doctor's thesis, Fordham University (New York, N.Y.), 1970. (*DAI* 31: 3978B)

3102. CARR, JOHN E. "Differentiation Similarity of Patient

and Therapist and the Outcome of Psychotherapy." *J Abn Psychol* 76(3):361–9 D '70. * (*PA* 45:6473)

3103. CASTELNUOVO-TEDESCO, PIETRO, AND KROUT, BOYD M. "Psychosomatic Aspects of Chronic Pelvic Pain." *Psychiatry Med* 1(2):109–26 Ap '70. *

3104. CASTON, JOSEPH; COOPER, LOWELL; AND PALEY, H. W. "Psychological Comparison of Patients With Cardiac Neurotic Chest Pain and Angina Pectoris." *Psychosomatics* 11(6):543–50 N–D '70. * (*PA* 45:8660)

3105. CHANDLER, MICHAEL J. "Self-Awareness and Its Relation to Other Parameters of the Clinical Inference Process." *J Consult & Clin Psychol* 35(2):258–64 O '70. * (*PA* 45: 2618)

3106. CLEELAND, CHARLES S.; MATTHEWS, CHARLES G.; AND HOPPER, CORNELIUS L. "MMPI Profiles in Exacerbation and Remission of Multiple Sclerosis." *Psychol Rep* 27(2):373–4 O '70. * (*PA* 45:6842)

3107. COLACICCO, MARY GRACE. *A Comparison of Item Responses on the MMPI by Selected American and Foreign Students.* Doctor's thesis, Purdue University (Lafayette, Ind.), 1970. (*DAI* 31:1572A)

3108. COWDEN, JAMES E., AND MORSE, EDWIN L. "The Relationship of Defensiveness to Responses on the Sex Inventory." *J Clin Psychol* 26(4):505–9 O '70. * (*PA* 45:4607)

3109. CRONBACH, LEE J. *Essentials of Psychological Testing, Third Edition,* pp. 527–47. New York: Harper & Row, Publishers, Inc., 1970. Pp. xxxix, 752. *

3110. CUMMING, GORDON HUGH. *A Study of Adjustment to a Family Crisis in the Form of a Disability to the Male Wage Earner.* Doctor's thesis, University of Southern California (Los Angeles, Calif.), 1970. (*DAI* 31:3667A)

3111. CURLEE, JOAN. "A Comparison of Male and Female Patients at an Alcoholism Treatment Center." *J Psychol* 74(2):239–47 Mr '70. * (*PA* 44:12859)

3112. DAMARIN, FRED. "A Latent-Structure Model for Answering Personal Questions." *Psychol B* 73(1):23–40 Ja '70. * (*PA* 44:3644)

3113. DAVIDS, ANTHONY. "Personality and Attitudes of Child Care Workers, Psychotherapists, and Parents of Children in Residential Treatment." *Child Psychiatry & Hum Develop* 1(1):41–9 f '70. *

3114. DAVIS, WILLIAM E.; GUSTAFSON, ROBERT C.; AND SCANLAN, JOHN W. "A Comparison of Currently Admitted Vietnam Era Psychiatric Patients With Currently Admitted World War II and Korean Era Psychiatric Patients." *Newsl Res Psychol* 12(4):12–3 N '70. *

3115. DAYRIES, JOHN L., AND GRIMM, RONALD L. "Personality Traits of Women Athletes as Measured by the Edwards Personal Preference Schedule." *Percept & Motor Skills* 30(1): 229–30 F '70. *

3116. DELHEES, KARL H., AND CATTELL, RAYMOND B. "Obtaining 16 PF Scores From the MMPI, and MMPI Scores for the 16 PF." *J Proj Tech & Pers Assess* 34(3):251–5 Je '70. * (*PA* 44:18740)

3117. DIAMANT, LOUIS. "Premarital Sexual Behavior, Attitudes, and Emotional Adjustment." *J Social Psychol* 82(1): 75–80 O '70. * (*PA* 45:4098)

3118. DITMAN, KEITH S.; MOSS, THELMA; FORGY, EDWARD; ZUNIN, LEONARD; FUNK, WAYNE; AND LYNCH, ROBERT. "Characteristics of Alcoholics Volunteering for Lysergide Treatment." *Q J Studies Alcohol* 31(2):414–22 Je '70. *

3119. DOBBS, NORMAN JAMES. *Predicting Length of Psychiatric Hospitalization Using Demographic and Psychological Test Data.* Doctor's thesis, Purdue University (Lafayette, Ind.), 1970. (*DAI* 31:2276B)

3120. EDWARDS, ALLEN L. *The Measurement of Personality Traits by Scales and Inventories.* New York: Holt, Rinehart & Winston, Inc., 1970. Pp. xiii, 306. *

3121. EDWARDS, ALLEN L.; ABBOTT, ROBERT D.; AND KLOCKARS, ALAN J. "Social Desirability and the TSC Scales: A Replication and Reply to Stein." *Multiv Behav Res* 5(3): 325–7 Jl '70. * (*PA* 45:714)

3122. EDWARDS, ALLEN L.; KLOCKARS, ALAN J.; AND ABBOTT, ROBERT D. "Social Desirability and the TSC MMPI Scales." *Multiv Behav Res* 5(2):153–6 Ap '70. * (*PA* 44: 16709)

3123. EDWARDS, KENNETH R., AND JONES, MARSHALL R. "Personality Changes Related to Pregnancy and Obstetric Complications." Abstract. *Proc 78th Ann Conv Am Psychol Assn* 5(1):341–2 '70. * (*PA* 44:19026)

3124. EISENBERG, MYRON GAIL. *An Examination of a Procedure for Determining Personality Correlates to Independence of Judgment in Male University Students.* Doctor's thesis, Northwestern University (Evanston, Ill.), 1970. (*DAI* 31: 4309B)

3125. EPSTEIN, PHILIP B. *Personality Characteristics of Skid Row Negro and White Chronic Alcoholics as Identified by the MMPI.* Master's thesis, George Washington University (Washington, D.C.), 1970.

3126. FINCH, KAYE; RICKARD, HENRY C.; AND WILSON, WARNER. "Personality Variables and Sexual Status in Observer Performance." *Psychol Rep* 26(2):676–8 Ap '70. * (*PA* 44:20819)

3127. FIORENTINO, DIANE; SHEPPARD, CHARLES; AND MERLIS, SIDNEY. "Emotions Profile Index (EPI) Pattern for Paranoid Personality Types: Cross-Validation and Extension." *Psychol Rep* 26(1):303–8 F '70. * (*PA* 45:4529)

3128. FRAAS, LOUIS A. "Sex of Figure Drawing in Identifying Practicing Male Homosexuals." *Psychol Rep* 27(1):172–4 Ag '70. * (*PA* 45:6638)

3129. FRACCHIA, JOHN; FIORENTINO, DIANE; SHEPPARD, CHARLES; AND MERLIS, SIDNEY. "Raven Progressive Matrices Avoidable Errors as a Measure of Psychopathological Ideational Influences Upon Reasoning Ability." *Psychol Rep* 26(2):359–62 Ap '70. * (*PA* 44:21168)

3130. FRACCHIA, JOHN; SHEPPARD, CHARLES; MERLIS, MICHAEL; AND MERLIS, SIDNEY. "Atypical Reasoning Errors in Sociopathic, Paranoid, and Schizophrenic Personality Types." *J Psychol* 76(1):91–5 S '70. * (*PA* 45:4560)

3131. FRITCHEY, KATHLEEN HARRIS. *The Effects of Anxiety and Threat on Self-Disclosure.* Doctor's thesis, University of Southern California (Los Angeles, Calif.), 1970. (*DAI* 31:4336B)

3132. GANNON, D. R., AND TYLER, D. W. "Effects of Paraphrasing Clinical Interview Items on Structured Responses." *Psychol Rep* 26(2):631–4 Ap '70. * (*PA* 44:21169)

3133. GASSNER, SUZANNE MARIE. "Relationship Between Patient-Therapist Compatibility and Treatment Effectiveness." *J Consult & Clin Psychol* 34(3):408–14 Je '70. * (*PA* 44:14745)

3134. GENDREAU, PAUL, AND GENDREAU, L. P. "The 'Addiction-Prone' Personality: A Study of Canadian Heroin Addicts." *Can J Behav Sci* 2(1):18–25 Ja '70. * (*PA* 44:12853)

3135. GIBBY, ROBERT G., AND LEE, WILLIAM M. "The Relationship of Rate of Change of Heart Rate to MMPI Variables." *J Clin Psychol* 26(4):491–3 O '70. * (*PA* 45:4534)

3136. GILBART, THOMAS EDGAR. *Self-Regard, Maladjustment, and Creative Potential Among College Counselees, Creatives, and Normals.* Doctor's thesis, St. John's University (Jamaica, N.Y.), 1970. (*DAI* 31:2177A)

3137. GILBERSTADT, HAROLD. *Comprehensive MMPI Code Book for Males.* Washington, D.C.: Veterans Administration Central Office, Psychology Division (116C), 1970. Pp. vi, 52. *

3138. GOLDBERG, LEWIS R. "Man Versus Model of Man: A Rationale, Plus Some Evidence, for a Method of Improving on Clinical Inferences." *Psychol B* 73(6):422–32 Je '70. * (*PA* 44:12828)

3139. GOORNEY, A. B. "MPI and MMPI Scores, Correlations and Analysis for a Military Aircrew Population." *Brit J Social & Clin Psychol* 9(2):164–70 Je '70. * (*PA* 44:16710)

3140. GOORNEY, A. B. "Psychological Measures in Air Crew." *Aerospace Med* 41(1):87–91 Ja '70. *

3141. GOORNEY, A. B. "Treatment of Aviation Phobias by Behaviour Therapy." *Brit J Psychiatry* 117(540):535–44 N '70. * (*PA* 45:10107)

3142. GORDON, ALAN STUART. *A Comparison of Homogeneous Versus Heterogeneous Grouping Using Client-Centered Therapy With Neurotics and Schizophrenics.* Doctor's thesis, University of Tulsa (Tulsa, Okla.), 1970. (*DAI* 31:3705B)

3143. GOSS, ALLEN, AND MOROSKO, THOMAS E. "Relation Between a Dimension on Internal-External Control and the MMPI With an Alcoholic Population." *J Consult & Clin Psychol* 34(2):189–92 Ap '70. * (*PA* 44:10761)

3144. GRAVITZ, MELVIN A. "Large Scale Normal Adult Base-Rates for MMPI 'Privacy' Items: 1, Sexual Attitudes and Experiences." *J General Psychol* 82(2):153–6 Ap '70. * (*PA* 44:14629)

3145. GRAVITZ, MELVIN A. "Validity Implications of Normal Adult MMPI 'L' Scale Endorsement." *J Clin Psychol* 26(4):497–9 O '70. * (*PA* 45:4297)

3146. GRAY, BERNADETTE G., AND GYNTHER, MALCOLM D. "Favorability Ratings of MMPI Sex Items: Stimulus Pull or Social Interaction Effects?" *J Proj Tech & Pers Assess* 34(3):245–50 Je '70. * (*PA* 44:18742)

3147. GYNTHER, MALCOLM D.; GRAY, BERNADETTE G.; AND STRAUSS, MILTON E. "Effects of Religious Affiliation, Religious Involvement, and Sex on the Social Desirability Ratings of MMPI Religion Items." *J Consult & Clin Psychol* 34(3):338–42 Je '70. * (*PA* 44:14644)

3148. HAIN, JACK D.; LINTON, PATRICK H.; EBER, HERBERT W.; AND CHAPMAN, MELINDA MUSGROVE. "Menstrual Irregularity, Symptoms and Personality." *J Psychosom Res* 14(1):81–8 Mr '70. * (*PA* 44:16666)

3149. HANSON, PHILIP G.; ROTHAUSE, PAUL; O'CONNELL, WALTER E.; AND WIGGINS, GEORGE E. "Diagnosis as a Predictor of Social Behavior in Human Relations Training." *Newsl Res Psychol* 12(3):29–33 Ag '70. *

3150. HARRELL, THOMAS W. "The Personality of High Earning MBA's in Small Business." *Personnel Psychol* 23(3):369–75 au '70. * (*PA* 45:9041)

3151. HARRIS, RICHARD J.; WITTNER, WILLIAM; KOPPELL, BERT; AND HILF, FRANKLIN D. "MMPI Scales vs Interviewer Ratings of Paranoia." *Psychol Rep* 27(2):447–50 O '70. * (*PA* 45:6583)

3152. HEACOCK, DELBERT DAVIS. *Relationships of the Minnesota Multiphasic Personality Inventory and the Word Preference Personality Inventory to Each Other and to Alcoholism.* Doctor's thesis, University of Utah (Salt Lake City, Utah), 1970. (*DAI* 31:3706B)

3153. HELSON, RAVENNA, AND CRUTCHFIELD, RICHARD S. "Creative Types in Mathematics." *J Personality* 38(2):177–97 Je '70. * (*PA* 44:18669)

3154. HELSON, RAVENNA, AND CRUTCHFIELD, RICHARD S. "Mathematicians: The Creative Researcher and the Average PhD." *J Consult & Clin Psychol* 34(2):250–7 Ap '70. * (*PA* 44:10374)

3155. HENNESSY, ROSALIE MYLIN. *Treatment Outcome of Process and Reactive Schizophrenics.* Doctor's thesis, Case Western Reserve University (Cleveland, Ohio), 1970. (*DAI* 31:4338B)

3156. HERR, VINCENT V. *The Personality of Seminarians: A Study Guide and Reference Work,* pp. 65–85. Staten Island, N.Y.: Alba House, 1970. Pp. xvii, 157. *

3157. HINTON, BERNARD L. "Personality Variables and Creative Potential." *J Creative Behav* 4(3):210–7 su '70. *

3158. HOFFMANN, HELMUT. "Depression and Defensiveness in Self-Descriptive Moods of Alcoholics." *Psychol Rep* 26(1):23–6 F '70. * (*PA* 45:4567)

3159. HOLLENDER, JOHN W., AND SCHALON, CHARLES L. "Personality Test Differences Between Vocational-Educational and Personal Adjustment Counseling Clients." *Meas & Eval Guid* 2(4):199–204 w '70. *

3160. HORTON, MARGARET, AND KRIAUCIUNAS, ROMUALDAS. "Minnesota Multiphasic Personality Inventory Differences Between Terminators and Continuers in Youth Counseling." *J Counsel Psychol* 17(2):98–101 Mr '70. * (*PA* 44:8995)

3161. HOUNTRAS, PETER T., AND FORREST, GARY G. "Personality Characteristics and Self-Disclosure in a Psychiatric Out-Patient Population." *Col Ed Rec* 55(9):206–13 Je '70. *

3162. HOUTS, DONALD CHARLES. *The Use of Ego Identity Measures in Evaluating a Seminary Curriculum.* Doctor's thesis, Northwestern University (Evanston, Ill.), 1970. (*DAI* 31:3362A)

3163. HUFF, FREDERICK W. "The Desensitization of a Homosexual." *Behav Res & Ther* 8(1):99–102 F '70. *

3164. HUGO, JOHN ADAM, II. *A Comparison of Responses of Negro and White Outpatient Alcoholics on the Minnesota Multiphasic Personality Inventory.* Master's thesis, University of Alabama (University, Ala.), 1970.

3165. HULSE, JAMES. *The Effect of Visual and Auditory Stimulation on Personality Traits as Measured by the Minnesota Multiphasic Personality Inventory.* Master's thesis, East Tennessee State University (Johnson City, Tenn.), 1970.

3166. JANSEN, DAVID G., AND ROBB, GEORGE P. "Differences Between Counseled and Non-Counseled Students on the MMPI." *J Clin Psychol* 26(3):391–3 Jl '70. * (*PA* 45:1318)

3167. JOHANSSON, CHARLES B. "Strong Vocational Interest Blank Introversion-Extraversion and Occupational Membership." *J Counsel Psychol* 17(5):451–5 S '70. * (*PA* 45:3003)

3168. JOHNSON, GFORGE R.; MARTIN, PATRICK L.; AND VOGLER, ROGER E. "Prediction of Rehospitalization of Family-Care Patients Using the MMPI." *Psychol Rep* 26(1):273–4 F '70. * (*PA* 45:2728)

3169. JOHNSON, RAY W. "A Configural Scoring of the MMPI and Diagnosis in Counseling." *J Clin Psychol* 26(1):84–6 Ja '70. * (*PA* 44:10447)

3170. JOHNSON, RAY W. "MMPI Characteristics of Successful and Unsuccessful Counseling Cases of Two Types." *J Col Stud Personnel* 11(2):111–4 Mr '70. *

3171. KATKOVSKY, WALTER. "Dental Reactions and Maladjustment." Abstract. *Proc 78th Ann Conv Am Psychol Assn* 5(1):345–6 '70. * (*PA* 44:18671)

3172. KIRTLEY, DONALD, AND HARKLESS, RICHARD. "Student Political Activity in Relation to Personal and Social Adjustment." *J Psychol* 75(2):253–6 Jl '70. * (*PA* 44:20780)

3173. KISH, GEORGE B. "Cognitive Innovation and Stimulus-Seeking: A Study of the Correlates of the Obscure Figures Test." *Percept & Motor Skills* 30(1):95–101 F '70. *

3174. KISH, GEORGE B. "Correlates of Active-Passive Food Preferences: Failure to Confirm a Relationship With Alcoholism." *Percept & Motor Skills* 31(3):839–47 D '70. * (*PA* 45:10246)

3175. KOELEGA, HENRY S. "Extraversion, Sex, Arousal and Olfactory Sensitivity." *Acta Psychologica* 34(1):51–66 S '70. * (*PA* 45:2022)

3176. KOLLAR, FRANCIS J. *An Investigation of the Existence of Pathological Personality Factors Among Athletes as Measured by the Minnesota Multiphasic Personality Inventory.* Master's thesis, Millersville State College (Millersville, Pa.), 1970.

3177. KRAMER, HOWARD C. "Interpretation of CSQ Scales." *J Col Stud Personnel* 11(1):28–32 Ja '70. *

3178. KUNCE, JOSEPH, AND ANDERSON, WAYNE. "Counselor-Client Similarity and Referral Bias." *J Counsel Psychol* 17(2):102–6 Mr '70. * (*PA* 44:8558)

3179. KUNCE, JOSEPH T., AND WORLEY, BERT. "Simplified Prediction of Occupational Adjustment of Distressed Clients." *J Counsel Psychol* 17(4):326–30 Jl '70. * (*PA* 44:21338)

3180. KUNCE, JOSEPH T.; MASUDA, MINORU; AND CARTER, TERRANCE E. "MMPI Scores, Psychiatric Disturbance and Catecholamine Metabolites." *J Clin Psychol* 26(3):291–5 Jl '70. * (*PA* 45:941)

3181. LACKS, PATRICIA B., AND POWELL, BARBARA J. "The Mini-Mult as a Personnel Screening Technique: A Prelimi-

nary Report." *Psychol Rep* 27(3):909–10 D '70. * (PA 45:
11068)

3182. LACKS, PATRICIA BRILLIANT. "Further Investigation
of the Mini-Mult." *J Consult & Clin Psychol* 35(1):126–7
Ag '70. * (PA 44:21177)

3183. LACKS, PATRICIA BRILLIANT, AND KEEFE, KATHRYN.
"Relationships Among Education, the MMPI, and WAIS
Measures of Psychopathology." *J Clin Psychol* 26(4):468–70
O '70. * (PA 45:4542)

3184. LACKS, PATRICIA BRILLIANT; ROTHENBERG, PETER J.;
AND UNGER, BETTY L. "MMPI Scores and Marital Status in
Male Schizophrenics." *J Clin Psychol* 26(2):221–2 Ap '70. *
(PA 44:14950)

3185. LANDERS, DANIEL M. "Psychological Femininity and
the Prospective Female Physical Educator." *Res Q* 41(2):
164–70 My '70. *

3186. LANGSTON, ROBERT D. "The MMPI and Perseverance
in the Convent." *Psychol Rep* 27(3):811–4 D '70. * (PA 45:
9944)

3187. LANYON, RICHARD I. "Development and Validation of
a Psychological Screening Inventory." *J Consult & Clin Psychol Monogr* 35(1, pt 2):1–24 Ag '70. * (PA 44:18915)

3188. LEBOVITS, BINYAMIN Z., AND OSTFELD, ADRIAN M.
"Personality, Defensiveness and Educational Achievement:
2, The Cattell 16PF Questionnaire." *J Clin Psychol* 26(2):
183–8 Ap '70. * (PA 44:14634)

3189. LESTER, DAVID. "Attempts to Predict Suicidal Risk
Using Psychological Tests." *Psychol B* 74(1):1–17 Jl '70. *
(PA 44:16905)

3190. LIEBERMAN, LEWIS R. "Attitudes Toward the Mentally Ill, Knowledge of Mental Illness, and Personal Adjustment." *Psychol Rep* 26(1):47–52 F '70. * (PA 45:4077)

3191. LINDNER, LEWIS A.; GOLDMAN, HAROLD; DINITZ,
SIMON; AND ALLEN, HARRY E. "Antisocial Personality Type
With Cardiac Lability." *Arch Gen Psychiatry* 23(3):260–7 S
'70. * (PA 45:4590)

3192. LUNNEBORG, PATRICIA W., AND LUNNEBORG, CLIFFORD
E. "Factor Structure of MF Scales and Items." *J Clin Psychol* 26(3):360–6 Jl '70. * (PA 45:707)

3193. LUSTIG, FELICIA M. *A Study of the Effect of a Pulmonary Rehabilitation Program on Anxiety, Medical Orientation, Social Introversion, Attitude Toward Work, and Engagement in Vocational Activities in Patients With Chronic Obstructive Pulmonary Emphysema (COPD).* Doctor's thesis, New
York University (New York, N.Y.), 1970. (DAI 31:3344A)

3194. McCARTHY, DOROTHEA; ANTHONY, ROBERT J.; AND
DOMINO, GEORGE. "A Comparison of the CPI, Franck, MMPI,
and WAIS Masculinity-Femininity Indexes." *J Consult & Clin
Psychol* 35(3):414–6 D '70. * (PA 45:4284)

3195. MALEY, ROBERT F. "The Relationship of Premorbid
Social Activity Level of Psychiatric Patients to Test Performance on the WAIS and the MMPI." *J Clin Psychol* 26(1):
75–6 Ja '70. * (PA 44:10494)

3196. MANDEL, KAY. *The Predictive Validity of On-the-Job
Performance of Policemen From Recruitment Selection Infor-
mation.* Doctor's thesis, University of Utah (Salt Lake City,
Utah), 1970. (DAI 31:2996B)

3197. MANOSEVITZ, MARTIN. "Early Sexual Behavior in Adult
Homosexual and Heterosexual Males." *J Abn Psychol* 76(3):
396–402 D '70. * (PA 45:6640)

3198. MANOSEVITZ, MARTIN. "Item Analyses of the MMPI
Mf Scale Using Homosexual and Heterosexual Males." *J Consult & Clin Psychol* 35(3):395–9 D '70. * (PA 45:6364)

3199. MATTHEWS, CHARLES G.; CLEELAND, CHARLES S.; AND
HOPPER, CORNELIUS L. "Neuropsychological Patterns in Multiple Sclerosis." *Dis Nerv System* 31(3):161–70 Mr '70. * (PA
44:13128)

3200. MAXSON, LINDA S., AND NEURINGER, CHARLES. "Evaluating Legal Competency." *J Genetic Psychol* 117(2):267–73
D '70. * (PA 45:6589)

3201. MEIKLE, STEWART, AND GERRITSE, RICHARD. "MMPI
'Cookbook' Pattern Frequencies in a Psychiatric Unit." *J Clin
Psychol* 26(1):82–4 Ja '70. * (PA 44:10449)

3202. MELNICK, BARRY. *Patient Therapist Identification in
Relation to Both Patient and Therapist Variables and Therapy
Outcome.* Doctor's thesis, Michigan State University (East
Lansing, Mich.), 1970. (DAI 31:4341B)

3203. MENDELSOHN, GERALD A., AND GALL, MEREDITH D.
"Personality Variables and the Effectiveness of Techniques to
Facilitate Creative Problem Solving." *J Pers & Social Psychol*
16(2):346–51 O '70. * (PA 45:2395)

3204. MOGAR, ROBERT E.; WILSON, WAYNE M.; AND HELM,
STANLEY T. "Personality Subtypes of Male and Female Alcoholic Patients." *Int J Addic* 5(1):99–113 Mr '70. *

3205. MOXLEY, ANN, AND SATZ, PAUL. "Effects of Statistical
Information on Clinical Judgment." Abstract. *Proc 78th Ann
Conv Am Psychol Assn* 5(2):545–6 '70. * (PA 44:18804)

3206. MURDOCH, PETER, AND PAULUS, PAUL. "Category Width
and Acquiescence." *Acta Psychologica* 32(2):162–78 Ap '70. *
(PA 44:16669)

3207. O'CONNELL, WALTER E., AND COWGILL, SALLIE. "Wit,
Humor, and Defensiveness." *Newsl Res Psychol* 12(1):32–3
F '70. *

3208. O'KEEFE, BETH E. "Accuracy of Patients' Predictions
of Their Mean State of Health on Release From Hospital."
Newsl Res Psychol 12(3):18–20 Ag '70. *

3209. OSBORNE, DAVID. "A Moderator Variable Approach to
MMPI Validity." *J Clin Psychol* 26(4):486–90 O '70. * (PA
45:4545)

3210. OWEN, DAVID R. "Classification of MMPI Profiles
From Non-Psychiatric Populations Using Two Cookbook Systems." *J Clin Psychol* 26(1):79–82 Ja '70. * (PA 44:10450)

3211. PALMER, ROBERT D. "Psychopathology and Seasonal
Preferences: An Aspect of Temporal Experience." *J Proj Tech
& Pers Assess* 34(6):513–8 D '70. * (PA 45:8251)

3212. PALMER, ROBERT D. "Psychopathology and Seasonal
Preferences: An Aspect of Temporal Experience." *Newsl Res
Psychol* 12(2):22–6 My '70. *

3213. PALMER, WARREN HALL. *Actuarial MMPI Interpretation: A Replication and Extension.* Doctor's thesis, University
of Alabama (University, Ala.), 1970. (DAI 31:6265B)

3214. PATRICK, JERRY H.; CONNOLLY, ARCH; AND OVERALL,
JOHN E. "Personality Correlates of Alcohol Abuse Among New
Admissions to a State Hospital." Abstract. *Proc 78th Ann Conv
Am Psychol Assn* 5(1):321–2 '70. * (PA 44:18938)

3215. PELLEGRIN, VICTOR BRUCE HOLKER. *A Descriptive
Study of a Midwestern Sample of Episcopal Clergy and Seminarians Categorized According to Various Criteria.* Doctor's
thesis, University of Kansas (Lawrence, Kan.), 1970. (DAI
31:2690A)

3216. PERSONS, ROY W., AND MARKS, PHILIP A. "Self-
Disclosure With Recidivists: Optimum Interviewer-Interviewee
Matching." *J Abn Psychol* 76(3):387–91 D '70. * (PA 45:
6631)

3217. PHILLIPS, CLINTON E. "A Study of Marriage Counselor's MMPI Profiles." *J Marriage & Family* 32(1):119–30 F
'70. * (PA 46:1259)

3218. PIERCE, RICHARD M., AND SCHAUBLE, PAUL G. "A
Note on the Role of Facilitative Responsibility in the Thera-
peutic Relationship." *J Clin Psychol* 26(2):250–2 Ap '70. *
(PA 44:14753)

3219. PLATMAN, S. R., AND WEINSTEIN, BETTE. "The Diagnosis Game." *Dis Nerv System* 31(8):561–6 Ag '70. * (PA
45:4547)

3220. PLATT, JEROME J.; POMERANZ, DAVID; EISENMAN, RUS-
SELL; AND DELISSER, OSWALD. "Importance of Considering Sex
Differences in Relationships Between Locus of Control and
Other Personality Variables." Abstract. *Proc 78th Ann Conv
Am Psychol Assn* 5(1):463–4 '70. * (PA 44:18699)

3221. POE, RICHARD; ROSE, ROBERT M.; AND MASON, JOHN W.
"Multiple Determinants of 17-Hydroxycorticosteroid Excretion
in Recruits During Basic Training." *Psychosom Med* 32(4):
369–78 Jl–Ag '70. * (PA 46:554)

3222. POLLEY, HOWARD F.; SWENSON, WENDELL M.; AND
STEINHILBER, RICHARD M. "Personality Characteristics of Pa-
tients With Rheumatoid Arthritis." *Psychosomatics* 11(1):45–9
Ja–F '70. * (PA 44:19252)

3223. RAYGOR, BETTY RUTH. "Mental Ability, School Achievement, and Language Arts Achievement in the Prediction of
Delinquency." *J Ed Res* 64(2):68–72 O '70. *

3224. REILLEY, ROBERT R., AND KNIGHT, GLENN E. "MMPI
Scores of Mexican-American College Students." *J Col Stud
Personnel* 11(6):419–22 N '70. * (PA 45:8903)

3225. REITAN, RALPH M. "Sensorimotor Functions, Intelligence and Cognition, and Emotional Status in Subjects With
Cerebral Lesions." *Percept & Motor Skills* 31(1):275–84 Ag
'70. * (PA 45:4773)

3226. RESH, MARY G. "Asthma of Unknown Origin as a
Psychological Group." Abstract. *J Consult & Clin Psychol*
35(3):429 D '70. * (PA 45:4666)

3227. RESH, MARY G. "Asthma of Unknown Origin as a
Psychological Group." *Newsl Res Psychol* 12(1):37–8 F '70. *

3228. RESH, MARY G., AND ANDERSON, DENNIS O. "Psychological Correlates of Hearing Aid Rejection." *Newsl Res Psychol* 12(1):38–9 F '70. *

3229. RICE, DAVID G., AND KEPECS, JOSEPH G. "Patient Sex
Differences and MMPI Changes—1958 to 1969." *Arch Gen
Psychiatry* 23(2):185–92 Ag '70. * (PA 45:952)

3230. RICHEK, HERBERT G.; MAYO, CLYDE D.; AND PURYEAR,
HERBERT B. "Dogmatism, Religiosity and Mental Health in
College Students." *Mental Hyg* 54(4):572–6 O '70. * (PA 45:
10428)

3231. RITTENHOUSE, JOAN DUNNE. "Endurance of Effect:
Family Unit Treatment Compared to Identified Patient Treatment." Abstract. *Proc 78th Ann Conv Am Psychol Assn* 5(2):
535–6 '70. * (PA 44:18805)

3232. ROSENMAN, MARTIN F., AND LUCIK, THOMAS W. "A
Failure to Replicate an Epilepsy Scale of the MMPI." *J Clin
Psychol* 26(3):372 Jl '70. * (PA 45:955)

3233. ROUZER, DAVID LEE. *Construct Validation of the Min-
nesota-Briggs History Questionnaire: Age and Personality Correlates.* Doctor's thesis, University of Minnesota (Minneapolis,
Minn.), 1970. (DAI 31:3006B)

3234. SAUNDERS, BRUCE T., AND PAPPANIKOU, A. J. "Minnesota Multiphasic Personality Inventory Sub-Scale Indices of
Effective Child-Care Personnel." *Devereux Sch Forum* 6(1):
19–25 f '70. *

3235. SCHWARTZ, MELVIN L., AND CAHILL, ROBERT. "Personality Assessment in Myasthenia Gravis With the MMPI."
Percept & Motor Skills 31(3):766 D '70. * (PA 45:10225)

3236. SEITZ, FRANK C. "Five Psychological Measures of

Neurotic Depression: A Correlation Study." *J Clin Psychol* 26(4):504–5 O '70. * (*PA* 45:4631)

3237. SHEKELLE, RICHARD B.; OSTFELD, ADRIAN M.; LEBOVITS, BINYAMIN Z.; AND OGLESBY, PAUL. "Personality Traits and Coronary Heart Disease: A Re-examination of Ibrahim's Hypothesis Using Longitudinal Data." *J Chronic Dis* 23(1): 33–8 Je '70. *

3238. SHEPPARD, CHARLES; O'NEIL, CAROLYN; FRACCHIA, JOHN; AND MERLIS, SIDNEY. "Levels of Personal Conflict Derived From Response to the Emotion Profile Index." *J Psychol* 74(2):143–8 Mr '70. * (*PA* 44:12658)

3239. SHIPMAN, WILLIAM G.; HEATH, HELEN A.; AND OKEN, DONALD. "Response Specificity Among Muscular and Autonomic Variables." *Arch Gen Psychiatry* 23(4):369–74 O '70. * (*PA* 45:2693)

3240. SHIPMAN, WILLIAM G.; OKEN, DONALD; AND HEATH, HELEN A. "Muscle Tension and Effort at Self-Control During Anxiety." *Arch Gen Psychiatry* 23(4):359–68 O '70. * (*PA* 45:2694)

3241. SHRAUGER, J. SIDNEY, AND KATKIN, EDWARD S. "The Use of Nonspecific Underlying Motivational Factors in the Systematic Desensitization of Specific Marital and Interpersonal Fears: A Case Study." *J Abn Psychol* 75(2):221–6 Ap '70. *

3242. SIMOPOULOS, A. M.; PINTO, ALCIDES; BABIKOW, PAUL W.; KURLAND, A.; AND SAVAGE, CHARLES. "Psychotomimetic Properties and Therapeutic Potentials of Dexoxadrol on Convalescing Alcoholics." *Dis Nerv System* 31(3):203–7 Mr '70. * (*PA* 44:12790)

3243. SINES, JACOB O. "Actuarial Versus Clinical Prediction in Psychopathology." *Brit J Psychiatry* 116(531):129–44 F '70. * (*PA* 44:18920)

3244. SINGER, MICHAEL I. "Comparison of Indicators of Homosexuality on the MMPI." *J Consult & Clin Psychol* 34(1):15–8 F '70. * (*PA* 44:7006)

3245. SMART, REGINALD G., AND JONES, DIANNE. "Illicit LSD Users: Their Personality Characteristics and Psychopathology." *J Abn Psychol* 75(3):286–92 Je '70. * (*PA* 44:14878)

3246. SMITH, ROBERT M., AND HAIN, JACK D. "Relationship Between Somatization and Effects of Stress on Electrogastric Waveforms in Humans." *Psychol Rep* 27(3):755–65 D '70. * (*PA* 45:0550)

3247. SMITH, WARREN C., AND FIGETAKIS, NICK. "Some Effects of Isometric Exercise on Muscular Strength, Body-Image Perception, and Psychiatric Symptomatology in Chronic Schizophrenics." *Am Correct Ther J* 24(4):100–4 Jl–Ag '70. *

3248. SNIBBE, JOHN ROBINSON. *The Effects of Various Therapeutic Episodes on Dependency Feelings in Alcoholics as Measured by Four Tests.* Doctor's thesis, University of Utah (Salt Lake City, Utah), 1970. (*DAI* 31:4345B)

3249. SNORTUM, JOHN R.; HANNUM, THOMAS E.; AND MILLS, DAVID H. "The Relationship of Self-Concept and Parent Image to Rule Violations in a Women's Prison." *J Clin Psychol* 26(3): 284–7 Jl '70. * (*PA* 45:991)

3250. SOLTZ, WILLIAM HOWARD. *Comparative Study of Negro-White Differences on the MMPI and PAS.* Doctor's thesis, University of Missouri (Columbia, Mo.), 1970. (*DAI* 31:3009B)

3251. SOSKIN, ROBERT A. "Personality and Attitude Change After Two Alcoholism Treatment Programs: Comparative Contributions of Lysergide and Human Relations Training." *Q J Studies Alcohol* 31(4):920–31 D '70. *

3252. SOUEIF, M. I., AND EL-SAYED, A. M. "Curvilinear Relationships Between Creative Thinking Abilities and Personality Trait Variables." *Acta Psychologica* 34(1):1–21 S '70. * (*PA* 45:2374)

3253. SPIEGEL, DON; HADLEY, PATRICIA A.; AND HADLEY, ROBERT G. "Personality Test Patterns of Rehabilitation Center Alcoholics, Psychiatric Inpatients and Normals." *J Clin Psychol* 26(3):366–71 Jl '70. * (*PA* 45:961)

3254. STEHBENS, JAMES A. "Comparison of MMPI Scores of Mothers of Enuretic and Control Children." *J Clin Psychol* 26(4):496 O '70. * (*PA* 45:4299)

3255. STEIN, EUGENE JONATHAN. *Ego-Resiliency, Ego-Control, and Risk Taking in Psychiatric Patients.* Doctor's thesis, University of Minnesota (Minneapolis, Minn.), 1970. (*DAI* 31: 3010B)

3256. STEIN, KENNETH B. "The TSC Scales: Social Undesirability or Personal Maladjustment? A Reply to Edwards, Klockars, and Abbott." *Multiv Behav Res* 5(2):157–8 Ap '70. * (*PA* 44:16717)

3257. STEIN, KENNETH B.; VADUM, ARLENE C.; AND SARBIN, THEODORE R. "Socialization and Delinquency: A Study of False Negatives and False Positives in Prediction." *Psychol Rec* 20(3):353–64 su '70. * (*PA* 45:8555)

3258. STEINER, J.; JARVIS, M.; AND PARRISH, J. "Risk-Taking and Arousal Regulation." *Brit J Med Psychol* 43(4):333–48 D '70. * (*PA* 45:8588)

3259. STEPHENS, JOSEPH H., AND SHAFFER, JOHN W. "A Controlled Study of the Effects of Diphenylhydantoin on Anxiety, Irritability, and Anger in Neurotic Outpatients." *Psychopharmacologia* 17(2):169–81 '70. * (*PA* 45:880)

3260. STEPHENSON, NORMAN LESLIE. *Some Empirical Relationships of an Actuarial Pattern Analysis of Basic Scales of the Strong Vocational Interest Blank.* Doctor's thesis, University of Minnesota (Minneapolis, Minn.), 1970. (*DAI* 31:3011B)

3261. STEWART, DENTON J., AND RESNICK, JEROME H. "Ver-

bal Conditioning of Psychopaths as a Function of Experimenter-Subject Sex Differences." *J Abn Psychol* 75(1):90–2 F '70. * (*PA* 44:7029)

3262. STONE, GAYLE VAUGHN. *The Relationship Between Personality and Work Need-Reinforcer Correspondence.* Doctor's thesis, University of Minnesota (Minneapolis, Minn.), 1970. (*DAI* 31:4346B)

3263. STRICKER, LAWRENCE J.; JACOBS, PAUL I.; AND KOGAN, NATHAN. "Veridicality of Implicit Personality Theories." Abstract. *Proc 78th Ann Conv Am Psychol Assn* 5(1):157–8 '70. * (*PA* 44:18743)

3264. SUTKER, PATRICIA B. "Vicarious Conditioning and Sociopathy." *J Abn Psychol* 76(3):380–6 D '70. * (*PA* 45:8589)

3265. TARTER, RALPH E. "Acquiescence in Chronic Alcoholics." *J Clin Psychol* 26(3):301–2 Jl '70. * (*PA* 45:2634)

3266. TAYLOR, GEORGE P., JR. "Moderator-Variable Effect on Personality-Test-Item Endorsements of Physically Disabled Patients." *J Consult & Clin Psychol* 35(2):183–8 O '70. * (*PA* 45:4700)

3267. TEMPLER, DONALD I. "The Construction and Validation of a Death Anxiety Scale." *J General Psychol* 82(2):165–77 Ap '70. * (*PA* 44:13636)

3268. THATCHER, KAREN; KAPPELER, THOMAS; WISECUP, PHILIP; AND FISCHER, ROLAND. "Personality Trait Dependent Performance Under Psilocybin, Part II." *Dis Nerv System* 31(3):181–92 Mr '70. * (*PA* 44:12034)

3269. THELEN, MARK H., AND VARBLE, DUANE L. "Comparison of College Students Seeking Psychotherapy With Nontherapy Students on Coping and Defense Scales." *J Clin Psychol* 26(1):123–4 Ja '70. * (*PA* 44:10572)

32-0. TRUAX, CHARLES B., AND LISTER, JAMES L. "Effects of Therapist Persuasive Potency in Group Psychotherapy." *J Clin Psychol* 26(3):396–7 Jl '70. * (*PA* 45:836)

3271. TRYON, ROBERT C., AND BAILEY, DANIEL E. *Cluster Analysis.* New York: McGraw-Hill Book Co., Inc., 1970. Pp. xix, 347. *

3272. TUFT, LAWRENCE H., AND BERMAN, MERRILL I. "Men of the Sea: A Description of a Psychiatric Population of Merchant Seamen Using the M.M.P.I." *Mental Hyg* 54(3):440–3 Jl '70. *

3273. TUFT, LAWRENCE H., AND BERMAN, MERRILL I. "Some Preliminary Observations on a Psychiatric Inpatient Merchant Seamen Population Using the MMPI." *South Med J* 63(1): 72–6 Ja '70. *

3274. UECKER, ALBERT E. "Differentiating Male Alcoholics From Other Psychiatric Inpatients." *Q J Studies Alcohol* 31(2):379–83 Je '70. *

3275. VAUGHAN, RICHARD P. "Seminary Training and Personality Change." *Relig Ed* 65(1):56–9 Ja–F '70. * (*PA* 44: 18679)

3276. WAINWRIGHT, BRUCE B. *Quantitative Scales for Scoring Human Figure Drawings.* Doctor's thesis, University of California (Los Angeles, Calif.), 1970. (*DAI* 31:1637A)

3277. WATSON, CHARLES G.; KLETT, WILLIAM G.; AND LOREI, THEODORE W. "Toward an Operational Definition of Anhedonia." *Psychol Rep* 26(2):371–6 Ap '70. * (*PA* 44:21292)

3278. WEBB, J. T. "Validity and Utility of Computer-Produced MMPI Reports With VA Psychiatric Populations." *Newsl Res Psychol* 12(2):117–21 My '70. *

3279. WEBB, JAMES T. "Validity and Utility of Computer-Produced MMPI Reports With Veterans Administration Psychiatric Populations." Abstract. *Proc 78th Ann Conv Am Psychol Assn* 5(2):541–2 '70. * (*PA* 44:18924)

3280. WEBB, JAMES T.; MILLER, MARVIN L.; AND FOWLER, RAYMOND D., JR. "Extending Professional Time: A Computerized MMPI Interpretation Service." *J Clin Psychol* 26(2): 210–4 Ap '70. * (*PA* 44:14645)

3281. WEST, KATHRYN L. "MMPI Correlates of Ulcerative Colitis." *J Clin Psychol* 26(2):214–9 Ap '70. * (*PA* 44:14982)

3282. WHITE, MARY ROBERT. *A Follow-Up Study of Candidates in a Religious Community of Women.* Doctor's thesis, Fordham University (New York, N.Y.), 1970. (*DAI* 31: 3359A)

3283. WILLIAMSON, RONALD W.; HECKEL, ROBERT V.; AND BOBLITT, WILLIAM EDGAR. "Reported Frequency of Dream Recall as Related to Repression-Sensitization and Intelligence." *J Clin Psychol* 26(3):300–1 Jl '70. * (*PA* 45:6:6)

3284. WOGAN, MICHAEL. "Effect of Therapist-Patient Personality Variables on Therapeutic Outcome." *J Consult & Clin Psychol* 35(3):356–61 D '70. * (*PA* 45:4396)

3285. WOLF, SIDNEY. *An Investigation of Counselor Type, Client Type, Level of Facilitative Conditions and Client Outcome.* Doctor's thesis, Catholic University of America (Washington, D.C.), 1970. (*DAI* 31:3013B)

3286. WOO-SAM, JAMES M.; ROGAL, RICHARD A.; AND ZIMMERMAN, IRLA LEE. "Influence of MMPI and Rorschach Indices of Hypochondriasis on the Rehabilitation of Brain-Injured Adults." Abstract. *Proc 78th Ann Conv Am Psychol Assn* 5(2):721–2 '70. * (*PA* 44:19166)

3287. WRIGHT, EDWIN T.; KYLE, N. L.; AND GUNTER, RALPH. "Personality Test Configurations in Acne Vulgaris." *Percept & Motor Skills* 30(1):191–201 F '70. *

3288. WRIGHT, EDWIN T.; MARTIN, ROSE; FLYNN, CATHERINE; AND GUNTER, RALPH. "Some Psychological Effects of Cosmetics." *Percept & Motor Skills* 30(1):12–4 F '70. *

3289. WRIGHT, FRED H., AND L'ABATE, LUCIANO. "On the

Meaning of the MMPI Mf and SVIB MF Scales." *Brit J Social & Clin Psychol* 9(2):171–4 Je '70. * (*PA* 44:16718)

3290. ZASTROW, CHARLES H. "Cheating Among College Graduate Students." *J Ed Res* 64(4):157–60 D '70. *

3291. HUGO, JOHN ADAM, II. *Abbreviation of the Minnesota Multiphasic Personality Inventory Through Multiple Regression.* Doctor's thesis, University of Alabama (University, Ala.), 1971. (*DAI* 32:1213B)

MALCOLM D. GYNTHER, *Professor of Psychology, St. Louis University, St. Louis, Missouri.*

The MMPI has survived two serious attacks by its detractors in the past decade, but may not continue much longer in its present form due to efforts of its proponents. The first onslaught was mounted primarily by Edwards (*1189, 1609*) and Messick and Jackson (*1128, 1223*) who said, in effect, the MMPI is not measuring what everyone had thought it was measuring, namely psychopathology, but rather responses to MMPI items are a function of the social desirability value of the item or the subject's tendency to go along with the statement, i.e., acquiescence, or both. After numerous authors published articles opposed to or in defense of one or the other of these positions, Block (*1750*) demonstrated forcefully that content is a more important determiner of item endorsement than any response set factor. MMPI interpreters continued to make their usual judgments about MMPI profiles throughout the 1960's, but no doubt felt less defensive about their activities since Block's masterful exposition. It might be noted that Edwards (*2173*) and Jackson (*2219*) have since modified their earlier more extreme positions. The second attempt to do away with the MMPI was principally championed by journalists in the muckraking tradition and wooly-minded editorial writers who said that the MMPI was a dastardly invasion of privacy which was being foisted on an innocent public by voyeuristic psychologists. (Civil libertarians also expressed concern, but were less melodramatic and hence received less publicity.) These critics asserted that the inventory was filled with questions concerning sex, religion and even such insidious, perhaps Communist-inspired inquiries as those which asked the subject if he thought his mother was a good woman. Congress gave psychologists some anxious moments in defense of this instrument [1] and its defenders hinted that book-burning akin to Nazi Germany (or at least test-burning) might take place in this country. Stripped of the emotional aspects

[1] "Special Issue: Testing and Public Policy." *Am Psychologist* 20:857–993 N '65. *

of the argument, the anti-test forces made a valid point but for the wrong reason. They said the test should not be used as a condition of employment, but the immorality of this enterprise, which they underlined, is almost completely irrelevant compared to the real issue which is that the test wasn't devised for this purpose and isn't effective for predicting who will be a good employee. It is a curious fact that no research was published concerning which items, if any, were objectionable until *after* the furore had subsided. Also, it is worth noting that few, if any, nonpsychologist writers on this subject mentioned the simple point that the subjects could and did omit items if they didn't feel like answering them.

The facts thus far acquired do not substantiate the hue and cry raised about the "indignities" suffered by subjects forced to respond to questions which concern intimate details of their lives. In the first place, extreme positive skews are found in distributions of MMPI item rejection. Rankin (*2421*), for example, found a modal rejection rate of 0 for males and 1 for females. Butcher and Tellegen (*1969*) found the median number of objections was 10, under standard instructions. A few people object to many of the items, but most people find very few items to be offensive. Secondly, the item content most often objected to has to do with elimination processes. Typically, sex and religion items are also found to be offensive. Yet rejection rates even for these sensitive categories do not exceed 15 percent. Thirdly, there is some evidence that females find more items objectionable than males, that more items are judged objectionable if the subject is told the test will be used for personnel selection, that fewer items are objected to on retesting than on initial testing, and that fewer objections are raised if the benefit of the inquiry to the subject is rated as high. No research has been published at the time of this writing relating number of items objected to to any kind of personality variable. In other words, we still do not know what kind of person finds being tested repugnant, what kind of person is indifferent, or what kind of person relishes the opportunity to reveal himself.

The MMPI has always been a cumbersome instrument. At 566 items, it is perhaps the longest inventory on the market. Yet more than 20 years passed before a true abbreviated form of the inventory was published. Others had used a so-called short form, but for all practical purposes this version merely amounted to eliminating the unscored items leaving the validity and clinical scales intact. In 1968, Kincannon, however, published a 71-item test called the Mini-Mult (*2386*) which may mean the end of the MMPI as we know it. Here is a test which takes 10–15 minutes to administer, can easily be given orally to disturbed patients, and has satisfactory scale score correspondence with the full form. Lacks (*3182*) has confirmed Kincannon's findings using psychiatric patients, but Armentrout and Rouzer (*3083*) using institutionalized juvenile delinquents were unable to predict the characteristics of full scale MMPI's very accurately from Mini-Mult data in individual cases. Many psychologists are trying this instrument out and it is possible that its popularity may rise to the point that Edwards and other critics will see the demise of the old MMPI. Those who work with college students may be interested to know that Hugo (*3291*) has developed a 174-item version of the MMPI for use with that population. Hugo's test includes Mf and Si which are conspicuous by their absence from Kincannon's version.

A powerful new force, however, is built on the full 566 items and may inadvertently prevent the development suggested above. Computer interpretation, which was virtually unknown in 1963–1964, has flourished in the latter half of the 1960's and clearly will expand even more in the 1970's. Since computer reports can with ease refer not only to the regular clinical and validity scales, but to dozens of other scales, and even to individual items, it seems clear that an abbreviation of the MMPI will not be welcomed by those who have devised these automated systems. A great deal of time and effort has been expended by Fowler (*2184*), Finney (*2697*), and others in the development of their interpretive programs; obviously, a change in test format would necessitate new programs which might require years to perfect. As separate reviews of these systems are available in the MMY, no specific evaluative comments will be made by this writer. However, it is clear that these systems can be no more accurate than the rules which govern them.

Efforts to determine the relative superiority of mechanically applied decision rules versus human judgments have continued. Also analyses of the relative merit of complex, configurational rules versus simple, linear rules have been conducted. With regard to the former issue, nearly all relevant studies have shown that the actuarial approach is equal or superior to the more time consuming, expensive clinical approach [2] (*3243*). Concerning the second issue, evidence by Goldberg (*1788*) favors the simple, linear rules. Goldberg (*3138*) has also shown that linear regression models of clinical judges can be more accurate diagnostic predictors than are the humans who are modeled. Unfortunately, the clinician still must make clinical judgments in the majority of cases due to the limited applicability of the rules so far derived. To illustrate, both of Goldberg's papers cited above are based on Meehl and Dahlstrom's (*1017*) sample of white males. Gynther (*1318*) has shown that if one attempts to apply the Meehl-Dahlstrom rules for discriminating psychotic from neurotic profiles to the incoming patients at a typical urban mental health center, only about 10–15 percent are even potentially suitable for analysis and only about half of that percentage are actually available (i.e., had taken the MMPI in addition to meeting the other criteria). The explanation of this apparent anomaly is that the rules are not applicable to the vast majority of patients—females, Negroes, those diagnosed organic or behavior disorder, or those with $L \geqq 70$, $F \geqq 80$, or $? \geqq 60$. Furthermore, the rules classify another fraction of patients' MMPI's as "indeterminate," which does not help the clinician searching for a specific label. Henrichs (*1646*) has attempted to rectify this situation by developing a character disorder classification, to be added to the Meehl-Dahlstrom classifications, which enables the rules to account for more MMPI's given by male patients. The same author (*2017*) also obtained approximately equivalent results with a female sample by changing cutting scores and modifying the rules slightly. Even with these extensions, however, the clinician will still find the rules inapplicable to many referrals or MMPI's.

A related important development in MMPI usage has been the construction of cookbooks, or as they are now more usually labeled, codebooks. This need was stressed by Meehl in his paper entitled "Wanted—A Good Cookbook" (*2502*), but nearly ten years passed until the publication of Marks and Seeman's (*1346*)

2 SAWYER, JACK. "Measurement *and* Prediction, Clinical *and* Statistical." *Psychol B* 66:178–200 S '66. * (*PA* 40:11647)

and Gilberstadt and Duker's (*1785*) codebooks. For the user of the MMPI, these publications were an innovation which promised much. In contrast with earlier research, which had produced information about psychiatric patients-in-general or prisoners-in-general or homosexuals-in-general (*2791*), this approach had relevant things to say about the *individual* profile. Knowledge of the average alcoholic or average paranoid schizophrenic profile did not give one much to write about when confronted by a profile from a given patient, but if a profile fit the rules governing the 16 profile types offered by Marks and Seeman or the 19 offered by Gilberstadt and Duker, immediately there were descriptive phrases, diagnostic statements, and symptoms that were applicable. For a while it appeared that the millennium had arrived, though some warned that unsophisticated users would be apt to mechanically reproduce statements from the books without much concern for their relevance in the individual case. Other problems soon appeared, however, especially the observation that the profile types which had accounted for so many patients in the derivation samples accounted for far fewer in other clinical installations. Where Marks and Seeman had found nearly 80 percent of all their profiles classifiable, others (*2076*) found only about 20 percent with the remainder needing to be approached by the old-time clinical methods. Even more serious are recent analyses which suggest that actuarial findings which are valid in one hospital setting may or may not be valid in another setting (*2373, 3213*). This approach loses much of its appeal if each clinic or hospital has to develop its own profile types. A more rigorous approach developed by Sines (*2100*) may lead to more generalizable findings. Basically, this procedure depends on a D^2 analysis which mathematically identifies profiles which cluster around the central prototype. At this time only one profile type and its correlates have been specified.

Another important series of findings for MMPI users took place in the 1960's. The effects of demographic factors on MMPI profiles were explored much more thoroughly than previously. Although most MMPI interpreters are aware, for example, that amount of education and field of interest must be taken into account to interpret Mf scores properly, little information concerning the effects of social status, age, intelligence, and especially race has

been available. It is now clear that MMPI's cannot be evaluated satisfactorily without this information (*1984, 2010, 2030*). The grossest case of neglect involved knowledge of Negro performance on the MMPI. By 1960, approximately 1,000 articles had been published concerning the MMPI of which 4 used Negro subjects; these were comprised entirely of prisoners or psychiatric patients. The first satisfactory studies of normal Negroes appeared in the mid-1960's (*1343, 1581*). McDonald and Gynther (*1343*) demonstrated that profiles given by Negroes tend to be higher than those given by whites, a result which was later confirmed by Baughman and Dahlstrom (*2739*). The unwary interpreter thus is apt to label Negroes as sicker than they actually are. More dramatic differences were disclosed by later studies (*2207, 2408*) which focused on patterns of item endorsement, as opposed to the traditional scale score analysis. Harrison and Kass (*2207*), for example, found that Negroes and whites differed significantly in their response to 213 out of the 566 items. These authors' factor analysis of the race-sensitive items revealed that estrangement, cynicism and religiosity are among the major underlying dimensions. Some new evidence [3] indicates that the inapplicability of white norms is so great, especially if limited education and rural residence are added to the race factor, that MMPI's should not be used with Negroes. Restandardization which includes an appropriate percentage of Negroes might be considered a solution, but the outcome of this procedure would be only slight shifts in scale means and standard deviations. The writer would recommend the classical approach: compare MMPI's of Negro adults-in-general with those given by salient categories of Negro psychiatric patients and construct new scales based on the configurations of items differentially endorsed by the clinical groups. Reconstruction would be expensive, but worthwhile in that diagnostic and/or clinically descriptive statements could then be made with confidence about the Negro segment of the psychiatric population.

To summarize, the current MMPI interpreter needs to be quite sophisticated. He must be aware that the actuarial approach will eventually replace him because machines possess near-

3 GYNTHER, MALCOLM D.; FOWLER, RAYMOND D.; AND ERDBERG, PHILIP. "False Positives Galore: The Application of Standard MMPI Criteria to a Rural, Isolated, Negro Sample." *J Clin Psychol* 27(2):234-7 Ap '71. *

perfect reliability. Yet he must recognize that that time has not yet arrived, since the rules and codebooks currently available are not comprehensive enough to handle even a majority of his cases. Furthermore, the task of cross validation of profile types already at hand has barely begun; what little evidence is available suggests that local rules based on local data may be essential to achieve predictive accuracy in a given setting. Hopefully, more rigorous actuarial procedures will obviate this impractical solution and yield generalizable profile types. Until these are available, however, the clinician will be largely dependent on his own skill. How he acquires these skills is a moot point, as the disappointing results of attempting to teach MMPI interpretive accuracy have shown.[4] In any case, he must be careful to avoid blind analysis and, indeed, should be extremely cautious in interpretations with only sex, age, and education available to him. Without information concerning race, social background, type of referral and other relevant factors, gross errors in interpretation may be made. The clinician should also be cognizant of new developments of the test itself: shortened versions which give greater flexibility for research or clinical practice are finally available and a whole new set of content scales has been developed by Wiggins (2119). These scales supplement the information obtained from the standard scales and may allow the test user to view a given clinical scale profile from a different perspective. Those psychologists who feel that the MMPI can serve a useful purpose in their installation but lack the time or skill to interpret the profiles may wish to investigate the computer interpretation services. Some process MMPI's quite inexpensively and rapidly. Checks on the validity of interpretations for one's own setting should, of course, be made. Another possibility for those who wish to play a more active role in MMPI interpretation, but distrust their own judgment, is offered by Hovey and Lewis' comprehensive statement library (2218). This format not only provides a substantial memory aid, but also allows the interpreter to avoid recording statements not compatible with each other or inconsistent with his personal impressions or the case history.

4 GOLDBERG, L. R., AND RORER, L. G. "Learning Clinical Inference: The Results of Intensive Training on Clinicians' Ability to Diagnose Psychosis vs Neurosis From the MMPI." Unpublished paper presented at Western Psychological Association annual meeting, Honolulu, Hawaii, 1965.

In conclusion, the MMPI is still the foremost instrument in the field of objective clinical assessment. No serious competitor has yet been devised. As a clinical tool, it leaves much to be desired, but as a source of research inspiration, it is without peer as the formidable listing of references in this volume attests.

DAVID A. RODGERS, *Head, Section of Psychology and Research, Department of Psychiatry, Cleveland Clinic, Cleveland, Ohio.*

At the time of this writing, the MMPI is almost certainly the psychological instrument of choice for the routine assessment of nature and degree of emotional upset in adult patients or other adult clients seeking help from the psychological, medical, or related professions for problems that do have or may have an emotional origin. One possible exception would be a patient population consisting of predominantly psychotic reactions, such as in a state hospital, where other instruments such as the *Rorschach* and *Thematic Apperception Test* may at least be competitive with the MMPI for routine utility, this being a population for which differential information obtained from the MMPI can be both limited and unreliable. Although most useful with an adult population, the MMPI has only slightly diminished utility with an adolescent population, down to the age of 13 or even 12. The primary hazard in using the test with adolescents is that a significant proportion of them show considerable discrepancy between verbal self-descriptions and life-situation behavior, such that they can, and often do in typical assessment settings, produce test results that either grossly overstate or understate the emotional pathology or upset that is clinically observable.

The MMPI is probably also the instrument of choice for screening or assessing emotional upset in a research population. It has some but much more limited utility in assessing emotional upset in an evaluation situation such as an employee screening program, in which the client's best interests are served by concealing emotional upset rather than, as in a patient-doctor context, by openly revealing it. The test is dependent for its power on verbal self-description. It was empirically developed from patient populations that were reasonably cooperative and reasonably motivated to reveal upset. In a differently motivated population, the test and its standard norms are not valid and can be grossly misleading.

The MMPI manual is inadequate as a guide to the use and background of the test. There is, though, a large literature on the test; and an adequate minimal library for the initial user is the Welsh and Dahlstrom's *Basic Readings on the MMPI in Psychology and Medicine* (669), Dahlstrom and Welsh's *An MMPI Handbook* (969), and Hathaway and Meehl's *An Atlas for the Clinical Use of the MMPI* (263).

A well-publicized strength of the MMPI is its empirical derivation and norming. This empiricism tempts the uninformed professional to assume that sophistication and interpretive skills are less important for this test than for other commonly used tests. Such unfortunately is not the case. The MMPI is a very complex psychometric instrument, as will be discussed, and can be a greater hazard in the hands of a naive interpreter than are tests which make no claim to prima facie validity and are not so seductively normed by quantified scores in a T score distribution. The test is valid and safe only in the hands of an MMPI expert and in my estimation is not, contrary to what has been suggested often enough in the literature, useful for the physician or psychiatrist who is psychometrically naive or the psychologist or psychiatrist who wants to use the test for only an infrequent assessment and who has not taken the time and effort both to become thoroughly familiar with the literature on the test and to become clinically experienced in its actual use. Paradoxically, considerable clinical sophistication in the use of the MMPI is necessary before its actuarial power can be appropriately utilized. It is this paradox that led to some justifiably negative early reviews of the test (e.g., Arthur L. Benton's reviews in the third and fourth *Mental Measurements Yearbooks*), even though this test has subsequently become perhaps the most frequently used of all psychological diagnostic instruments.

The test has many practical strengths that commend its use. In the hands of an expert, it can provide considerable valid and clinically useful information about the emotional status of a cooperative subject. This information goes well beyond simple diagnostic classification, a task for which the test was originally designed and one which in fact it does not always accomplish very well (although it may compare favor-

ably in this latter respect with clinical interview, which itself has limitations for making valid diagnostic classifications). The test is useful, for example, for assessing degree of depression or anxiety or suicidal risk or ego strength or potential for impulsive acting out, to mention a few variables that are somewhat independent of specific diagnostic classification. It is most useful to supplement rather than to replace information obtained by interview or clinical observation. Its use thus is not contraindicated simply because interview assessment is also obtained. Conversely, interview follow-up is seldom contraindicated simply because positive test results have already been obtained, although in many situations the test can appropriately be used to screen for desirability of psychological or psychiatric interview follow-up. More explicitly, the test's greatest utility is as an aid to patient assessment, and in this role it is one of the more powerful aids available. It has some but only limited use as an independent and purely actuarial patient assessment device, the clinical-versus-actuarial controversy to the contrary notwithstanding.

In addition to its assessment utility, which is its primary practical strength, the test is also economical of professional, if not assessee, time. It may take an hour or two of assessee time and 20 minutes of clerical time to score and profile. Actual professional evaluation of the profile itself by an experienced person normally requires less than five minutes, not counting time to become familiar with the referral problem and other relevant information, or time to write down the evaluation, which are additional important steps that may bring total professional assessment time closer to half an hour or an hour. This contrasts very favorably with the *Rorschach, Thematic Apperception Test,* or *Wechsler Adult Intelligence Scale* or other assessment devices that require much professional time just to obtain the initial data. For a cooperative subject population (but not, e.g., where a lawsuit is involved), the test can be done without supervision, with minimal initial instruction.

COMPUTERIZED INTERPRETATIONS. In suitable situations, scoring can be done by optical scanning and computer counting and profiling. Computer interpretations are also possible, by several private and commercially available programs. While the evaluation of these interpretive programs is beyond the scope of this review, it is this reviewer's opinion that some of them are first rate in abstracting the actuarial regularities within the test itself and in a "clinical-versus-statistical" contest would probably beat clinician interpretations. Nevertheless I regard them as basically dangerous except in the hands of a person who is sufficiently expert with the MMPI that he probably will not utilize the computer print-out or bother with the time delay inevitably involved in the commercial services. One exception may be psychiatrists and psychologists who are clinically sophisticated and comfortable ignoring, when indicated, the formally printed actuarial evaluations, and who gain sufficient experience with a particular interpretive service to learn the extent and limits of its utility in their own practice. This does *not* include the non-psychiatric physician or the occasional user obtaining assessment of the unusual case such that he cannot to a significant degree independently evaluate the validity of the computer print-out.

The basic problem with the computer interpretations, as with the straight actuarial use of the test for diagnostic classifications, is that they encourage the inexperienced user to draw nontentative conclusions, to neglect significant error probabilities, and often to act on information that lies outside his area of expertise. Actuarial tables and computers have little personal involvement in the consequences of their decisions; whereas a professional has much personal involvement, and, if competent, will minimize in his own setting the negative aspects of such consequences regardless of whether they might derive from correct or erroneous interpretations.

Of numerous examples, two may suffice to illustrate the hazards of misused computer information. A patient and her parents were directly and insensitively told by a non-psychiatrically-oriented general practitioner that the patient was a schizophrenic, and that the MMPI proved it. The experience was emotionally very destructive, regardless of whether or not the diagnosis was correct, and was made especially so by the weight of "psychometric certainty" of the computer print-out that was convincing to both physician and patient but that provided no professional resource either for evaluating the competency of the physician to utilize such information or for coping with the subsequent implications of the test results. If the test evaluation had been mediated through the typical psychologist or psychiatrist, this not-uncommon experience with computer data would probably have been either completely avoided or much detoxified.

In a second situation, an adolescent known to have committed both rape and murder in a very wanton fashion produced a within-normal-range MMPI profile that was devoid of any indication of anxiety, depression, remorse, or significant emotional pathology. If it had not been double checked with a professional who pointed out the serious implications of complete absence of evidence of personal upset under such circumstances, the very reassuring computer print-out could have become the basis for rather extreme therapeutic and legal neglect of an in fact severely emotionally disturbed boy. In this situation, the computer programs simply are not open to input of the unusual single-case information that in some cases can be diagnostically crucial and that is nearly always available to the on-the-scene professional. Thus, without seriously questioning the basic quality of some of the computer interpretive programs, I would suggest that essentially the same caution apply in their use as in the use of the MMPI itself, that they be used only by a professional familiar both with the MMPI and the computer program and with the professional implications of his diagnostic or interpretive decisions in his own setting.

The foregoing comments, which may apply in general to the use of all psychological test results, are especially relevant for the MMPI, because procedures of actual use and advertising have not only violated these cautions but have also strongly encouraged their neglect and violation.

PSYCHOMETRIC CONSIDERATIONS. If the MMPI did not work so well in a practical sense, it could be regarded as a psychometric monstrosity. The user should be aware of some of its metric limitations.

The test is called a "personality inventory" and indeed is often used to make judgments about personality, but its primary development and standardization had almost nothing to do with personality traits per se. Both conceptually and metrically, it was developed and validated as a psychiatric nosologic categorizing device. Schizophrenia, psychasthenia, hypochondriasis, and mania, to name a few of the scales, are not usually thought of as personality traits and do not in fact measure relevant "personality" dimensions. Indeed, the scale development was not metrically "dimensional" in nature, but instead was focused on dichotomous discrimination of a pathology group from a normal group.

The only metric justification for casting the scales into a T score format would be to determine a satisfactory "deviation from normal" cutting score to differentiate the target group from the normal population. Anyone scoring more than two standard deviations (above T score 70) from the normal mean could, with the usual 2½ percent one-tale probability, be excluded from the null hypothesis of normality and could be categorized as a schizophrenic, a hypomanic, a homoerotic invert, an hysteric, or what have you. It is the cutting score that is important for this discrimination, though, and not the scaled distribution.

Two essentially fallacious bases would argue for presenting the scores in scalar form, as has been done on the test. First, it might be argued that locating a person on a continuum allows a more precise judgment about whether or not to reject the null-hypothesis. Four standard deviations from the norm is of course a "safer" level of significance than is two standard deviations from the norm. This approach still assumes that the primary goal is dichotomous differentiation of a pathology group from the normal group, for purposes of nosologic classification. The problem with this approach is that the actuarial hazards of substituting "clinical" judgment of an acceptable level of significance for actuarial criteria are well known. If simple classification is the goal, then a simple classifying decision rule or cutting score (or perhaps even a "liberal" and "conservative" cutting score) would more accurately reflect the ostensible goals and metric development of the scales. T score scaling, varying from three standard deviations below the normal mean to seven standard deviations above, is metrically a grossly inappropriate format for such dichotomous classification, that strongly invites abuse in the form of treating the scales as dimensional rather than as classificatory.

The other fallacious basis for the present form of T score scaling might be that the scales were intended to measure dimensions rather than to discriminate into categories. That is, perhaps there was a desire to measure degree of hypochondriasis and not simply presence of hypochondriasis, or degree of depression and not simply presence of depression. This argument works reasonably well for some but certainly not all of the scales. For example, schizophrenia, paranoia, hypomania, and perhaps hysteria, psychopathic deviancy, homoerotic inversion, and psychasthenia are often thought of as being either present or absent in a given person, such that not every individual can be quantified on "dimensions" of schizophrenia, paranoia, etc. Even assuming, though, that these were to be regarded as dimensional characteristics, then the scale presentation as used is a metric anomaly. The variance unit (unit of standard deviation) is that of the normal population and not that of the population containing the "variable" to be scaled. Supposedly the particular "variable" being measured was more or less excluded from the normal population on which the scale was normed, such that the scales as published would seem to locate a person on a continuum of the normal population along a dimension that does not apply to the normal population.

Even if it could be argued that there is a dimensional quality to the MMPI scales and that standard deviations computed on a normal population are not inappropriate, the way in which the scales were developed still argues against a T score scaling. As has been well publicized, the test scales were empirically rather than rationally derived. On the positive side, this has meant that quite unexpected item combinations were identified that carried measurement precision substantially beyond the psychologic and psychiatric sophistication existing at the time the scales were developed. As a consequence of the empirical approach, most scales are multi-dimensional for the normal population, reflecting the unique multi-dimensional combination of traits that characterized each given pathology group and differentiated it from the normal. For example, Scale 3 ("hysteria") contains a set of complaint items (e.g., "Much of the time my head seems to hurt all over") and another set of items that essentially deny hostile feelings directed towards others (e.g., "At times I feel like swearing"—false—and "I think most people would lie to get ahead"—false). An hysteric with symptomatology characteristically scores high on both sets of items, which in the normal population are negatively correlated (756). Harris and Lingoes have detailed the item content for logical subdimensions of many of the MMPI scales (969). Such multidimensionality can add to the power of dichotomous discriminations, much in the fashion of a multidiscriminant analysis. Such multidimensionality *cannot* be linearly scaled, however, in any meaningful fashion, when the scaling pertains to the group in which nonhomogeneity along the target variables exists. For example, an elevation to T score 60 on Scale 3 can be obtained either because a person is complaining about many items or because a person is denying any feelings of resentment toward others or because of the particular combination of these two traits that characterize the hysteric which the scale was derived to identify. Thus, one is forced conceptually back to the only metrically justifiable use of the MMPI scales as being for dichotomous discrimination, i.e., for placing a particular subject either into or out of a particular nosologic category. For this task, T score scaling along a ten standard deviation scale is cumbersome and metrically undesirable.

The awkward scaling of the MMPI could be forgiven, and in fact probably would have been changed, if the test did what it was designed to do, i.e., reliably and validly categorize people into appropriate nosologic groups. At least in terms of the metric considerations that applied to its development, the test does not in fact do this. Each scale was initially validated as an independent measure, standing alone. Scale 3 was standardized to identify hysterics, Scale 8 was standardized to identify schizophrenics, etc. The nosologic categories are assumed to be essentially mutually exclusive. That is, one is not expected to be simultaneously a schizophrenic, an hysteric, and a psychopathic deviate. Patients nevertheless commonly obtain "significant" elevations on several of the MMPI scales simultaneously, such as the three scales just named. The simple decision rules that could apply to each scale taken separately are obviously invalidated in the face of such multiple classification, which occurs sufficiently frequently to make the test totally worthless if this were the only basis for interpretation. Hence, nosologic classification by the simple set of decision rules (more than statistically significant deviation from normal range on any given scale) that guided the development of the test becomes a nonworkable basis for using the test.

The test in fact is used as a personality assessment device, a use that runs contrary to the whole conceptual program of the test development, and it is this fact which, in my esti-

mation, requires a high degree of expertise if the test is to be used professionally. What seems to happen is a double order abstraction, whether done by a clinician or by a computer program. The first abstraction was of course the empirical identification of items that were associated with particular nosologic groups. The second abstraction is the inference that persons in particular nosologic groups, or at least persons scoring high on the scales that were derived to identify such groups, have certain personality characteristics. This second abstraction is partially in terms of identifiable logical subdimensions of the various scales and partially in terms of empirical regularities, regularities that may have been objectively or "intuitively" identified, on the basis of more or less valid and more or less insightfully abstracted clinical experience. The logical abstractions are perhaps the most easily detailed. For example, the complaint items that constitute a significant part of Scale 3, already mentioned, constitute the primary dimension in Scale 1 (20 of the 33 Scale 1 items appear also on Scale 3), whereas the denial-of-hostile-feelings dimension of Scale 3 constitutes a significant part of the K Scale (10 of the 30 K Scale items appear on Scale 3). Hence, the primary source of elevation of Scale 3 can be determined by observing the relative elevations on Scales K and 1, in conjunction with the Scale 3 elevation. Similarly, elevations on many of the other MMPI scales can also be "factorially clarified" by knowing in detail the dimensions that contribute to the elevations of various other scales, and then by making appropriate contingency allowances for what particular dimensions have to be represented by the items in order to produce the particular profile elevations obtained. Some clinicians may even sidestep this subjective "multiple correlation analysis" and formally score various subscales for various of the clinical scales to obtain more pure unidimensionality. Such purified dimensions often lend themselves to personality interpretations and to scaling throughout the normal range. Whether or not they improve nosologic classification remains somewhat controversial. There is no question, however, that such use of the test is *not* validated by the original developmental construction of the test.

Dimensions are also abstracted because they are either empirically shown, or are conceptually thought, to apply to particular nosologic groups or to particular scales. For example, a Scale 3 elevation may be translated into a measure of "repressiveness," because repression is a primary dimension in hysteria. Similarly, Scale 8 elevations may be translated in a dimension loosely characterized as "what-happens-to-me-is-not-under-my-own-control," which can vary from one end of the continuum indicating much feeling of personal control to another end of the continuum indicating very little personal control. In effect, then, the scales are often given personality-dimension meanings, the meaning for a given scale perhaps varying considerably depending on other scale elevations, on the particular level of elevation of that particular scale, and on the particular interpreter or interpretive program. Used in this fashion, the MMPI can approach the Rorschach and TAT as a projective device that allows remarkably wide latitude for professional interpretation and that is lacking to a surprisingly large degree in the safeguards of actuarial tables and clearly established validity that the empirical tradition of the test would suggest exists.

In addition to the aforementioned major metric considerations with which the user of the MMPI should be familiar, there are also a number of more minor ones. The test was originally standardized on a card-sort form in which each statement is on a card that is to be sorted into a "True," "False," or "Cannot Say" category and item order is randomly shuffled between each use. While this card-sort form is still used, it is much less common than the booklet form, in which item order follows a standardized sequence and in which the subject is expected to read an item in a booklet and mark either "True" or "False" on a separate answer sheet. There is no "Cannot Say" option in the booklet form and patients are encouraged not to omit answers. The booklet format is less expensive, much more portable, and more convenient for reasonably verbal and intellectually intact subjects. From a practical point of view, therefore, this transformation has been useful. The test has not been renormed for this format, however. From a metric point of view, major questions can and should be raised about the uncritical use of norms obtained with one format for profiles obtained with the other format. Of special relevance is the essential elimination of the "Cannot Say" category. The original standardization group on the average classified 30 items as "Cannot Say," and as many as 100

items could be so classified without exceeding normal range performance. It is rare in my experience for more than 4 or 5 items to be classified "Cannot Say" (i.e., omitted) with the booklet form. Since "Cannot Say" items are not scored as significant, the booklet form clearly draws far more significant—i.e., more pathology-indicating—answers than does the card-sort form. This should mean that the booklet form would result in somewhat higher elevations on the pathology scales than would the card-sort form. From a practical standpoint, this may be of relatively little importance, since the use of the test is usually to identify the presence of upset; in our present rather imprecise state of the art, erring in the direction of indicating slightly too much upset, as the booklet form may do, can be regarded as a conservative direction of error in most situations. This is especially true when the test is used as a dimensional measure (e.g., to measure "anxiety" rather than to identify presence or absence of psychasthenia), an application to which the original norms are not directly relevant in any case. While, therefore, there is no metric justification for the procedure (or lack of it) followed in shifting to another test format without renorming the test, in this situation, as in many others in the development of the MMPI, the pragmatic utility of the test is sufficiently great that the lack of metric precision is surprisingly unimportant. This is almost certainly an indication of the pragmatic orientation and clinical sophistication of the test developers rather than a merely chance phenomenon.

The empirical derivation of the test, on a geographically limited and rather atypical population (predominantly rural Minnesota adults with less than high-school education), could be expected to introduce many non-generalizable anomalies into the scale contents. This in fact has happened. For example, it seems reasonable that a person regularly reading a small town newspaper in Minnesota might claim unusual virtue by answering "False" to the item "I do not always read all the editorials in the newspaper every day," whereas this same claim would be ludicrous for a person who routinely subscribed to the *New York Times* and the *Wall Street Journal* in addition to his own metropolitan area newspaper. Perhaps because of similar considerations, the L Scale, on which this item appears, is poorly normed for metropolitan and cosmopolitan populations. Other specific examples can be given in which particular scale items are somewhat uniquely relevant to the Minnesota group. For example, the items, "I go to church almost every week" and "I believe in the second coming of Christ" indicate depression if answered in the negative, according to the Scale 2 norms. Failure to attend church or believe in the second coming of Christ may indeed have been associated with depression in rural Minnesota a few decades ago, but is not likely to be differentially associated with depression in, for example, a Los Angeles suburb or a college community at the present time.

Again, in spite of such items that inevitably add noise to scales actuarily derived on limited populations, the MMPI is remarkably robust and remarkably applicable in a wide range of cultures. Indeed, the test has worked with considerable adequacy when translated into other languages (there have been at least 39 translations so far) and when used in other countries with the same norms derived from the Minnesota population. There is, of course, no metric justification for failure to renorm the test according to different cultures, except possibly the pragmatic one that the Minnesota population norms seem to give clinically meaningful results.

Perhaps classifiable as a metric consideration is the inclusion in the standard test of 167 items that do not appear on any of the standard clinical scales. The test is already rather long, and the inclusion of these extra items adds considerably to patient resistance and testing time. The items are retained because some of them appear on some research scales and because there was the hope, well-realized in subsequent experience, that additional scales would be developed from this item pool. By 1960, 213 scales were available for publication in the Dahlstrom and Welsh handbook, and additional scales have been developed since. The expectation was that, with this item pool, the MMPI could "provide, in a single test, scores on all the more important phases of personality." This rather grandiose hope has not been realized, especially with respect to nonpathological dimensions of personality. The item pool was originally developed to measure pathology, and approximately half of its items are explicit symptoms (e.g., "I have a good appetite," "I have diarrhea once a month or more," "I have nightmares every few nights," etc.) that may

not figure prominently in personality characterization. With some notable exceptions such as Barron's Ego Strength Scale, non-pathology-oriented personality scales have tended to require an expanded item pool. A case in point is the *California Psychological Inventory,* a multiphasic test made up primarily of personality—as opposed to pathology—scales. The original development of the CPI scales was begun with the MMPI item pool, but most scales required additional items to achieve final adequate stability and validity.

This is perhaps a relevant place to point out that the rather inaccurate use of the concept of "Personality Inventory" for the MMPI highlights by omission almost more than by inclusion the desirability of looking at personality variables to understand pathology. I for one routinely use a combination of the MMPI and the CPI in clinical practice (the standard scales of both tests can be scored from a 700-item pool), because the MMPI alone provides inadequate information about interpersonal skills and personality variables that are critically important for many clinical decisions.

FUTURE IMPLICATION. The foregoing comments on the metric complexity of the MMPI and on its general use as being markedly deviant from the metric conceptions underlying its development should not be taken as belittling the accomplishment represented by the development of this test. It still remains, as indicated, the most useful single psychological test available in most clinical settings. What these comments should emphasize, however, is that the MMPI is simply a way-station in psychological test development. The MMPI's empirical approach has identified many unexpected dimensions in some of our standard pathological conditions. The clinical experience gained with the test has helped to clarify which of these dimensions are clinically important and which ones are accidental distractors. With such background and such experience, it should now be possible to go well beyond the MMPI to a better instrument, one that should have fewer metric problems but that could not have been written had the MMPI not provided a needed stepping stone. Until such a test is developed, the MMPI will well justify the professional investment required to become proficient in its use.

SUMMARY. The MMPI is one of the major psychological tests of the present time and is useful primarily for assessing degree and nature of intrapsychic pathology in an essentially cooperative patient population. Although it was empirically derived, with heavy emphasis placed on its actuarial development, the test is basically a psychometric nightmare that requires considerable sophistication and experience to use professionally. There is perhaps no better tribute to its value than the fact that it is well worth the investment of the professional psychologist to become proficient in its use in spite of, rather than because of, its metric characteristics.

For reviews by C. J. Adcock and James C. Lingoes, see 6:143; for reviews by Albert Ellis and Warren T. Norman, see 5:86; for a review by Arthur L. Benton, see 4:71; for reviews by Arthur L. Benton, H. J. Eysenck, L. S. Penrose, and Julian B. Rotter, see 3:60 (1 excerpt).

[105]

★[Re Minnesota Multiphasic Personality Inventory.] Computerized Scoring and Interpreting Services. For additional information and reviews, see the separate entries.
a) MMPI-ICA COMPUTER REPORT. See 106.
b) OPTIMUM PSYCHODIAGNOSTIC CONSULTATION SERVICE. See 107.
c) THE PSYCHOLOGICAL CORPORATION MMPI REPORTING SERVICE. See 108.
d) ROCHE MMPI COMPUTERIZED INTERPRETATION SERVICE. See 109.

WILLIAM J. EICHMAN, *Associate Professor of Psychology, The University of North Carolina; and Director of Psychology Service, John Umstead Hospital; Chapel Hill, North Carolina.*

The day of the automated/computerized MMPI is upon us. Meehl's 1956 call [1] for a "cookbook" of personality interpretations has been answered, at least in part. This narrative serves as a prologue to reviews of four interpretive services which are currently available to selected professionals on a commercial basis. In each instance, the service provides the professional with a kit of materials along with guidelines for the use of the service. Answer sheets are mailed to the service where they are scored and interpreted by computer. Narrative reports are then returned to the referring professional. These vary considerably, particularly in regard to complexity of the narrative and, indeed, one service offers several "levels" or types of reports, some of which are geared for

consumers who are not psychologists or psychiatrists.

The fact that computerized interpretation has emerged on a "commercial" basis seems to indicate a felt social need for the type of information provided. Arguments in favor of a more automated, actuarial, or cook-book approach are numerous. Exhaustive, individual assessment has proved to be prohibitive in cost for many clinical installations. Concurrently many psychologists have become disenchanted with (*a*) the social purposes to which assessment is put (e.g., psychiatric diagnosis), (*b*) current personality theory and/or models of psychopathology, and (*c*) the validity of the techniques themselves. The generally wide use of the MMPI is in part a reflection of these professional currents. As conventionally administered, the MMPI remains a low cost assessment procedure relative to the projective tests. There is probably a saving in interpretive time as well but this is not so apparent. A narrative report on any global personality test poses difficult problems, conceptually and semantically, that are not entirely solved by an empirical base or an instrument with psychometric properties. It is in this respect that the automated narrative report offers considerable saving of professional time.

A second argument has to do with validity or accuracy of the interpretations. Although, or perhaps because, the MMPI has such a vast research literature, no individual clinician is likely to be totally adequate to the task of interpretation. The automated interpretation, on the other hand, has few inadequacies. To the degree that the literature is adequate, the computer program can reflect the total knowledge of many clinicians. It can be completely reliable, following the same sequential model in each case and giving the same weight to each variable.

If one accepts the MMPI as a useful personality test or psychodiagnostic instrument, it is difficult to resist the appeal of reduced cost and greater validity. The automated personality assessment is here to stay. As one indication of this apparent fact, the American Psychological Association Council of Representatives adopted the following standards [2] in 1966:

The advent of sophisticated computer technology and recent psychological research has made it feasible and

---

1 MEEHL, PAUL E. "Wanted—A Good Cookbook." *Am Psychologist* 11:263–72 Je '56. *

2 FOWLER, RAYMOND D., JR. Chap. 6, "Automated Interpretation of Personality Test Data," pp. 105–26. In *MMPI: Research Developments and Clinical Applications.* Edited by James Neal Butcher. New York: McGraw-Hill Book Co., 1969. Pp. xiv, 402. *

desirable for consulting and service organizations to offer computer-based interpretation services for diverse clinical psychological measurement instruments. Since these services will be rendered to clients with varying degrees of training in psychological measurement and since improper use of such interpretations could be detrimental to the well-being of individuals, it is considered proper for the American Psychological Association to establish various conditions which must be met before such services should be offered to clients. (1) Any organization offering the services described above must have on its staff or as an active consultant a member of the American Psychological Association who is a Diplomate of the American Board of Examiners in Professional Psychology or who has essentially equivalent qualification. (2) Such services will be offered only to individuals or organizations for use under the active supervision of qualified professional personnel with appropriate training. The qualified person must be either a staff member or a responsible, active consultant to the individual or organization receiving such services. (3) Organizations offering scoring services must maintain an active quality control program to assure the accuracy and correctness of all reported scores. (4) Organizations offering interpretation services must be able to demonstrate that the computer programs or algorithms on which the interpretations rest are based on appropriate research to establish the validity of the programs and procedures used in arriving at interpretations. (5) The public offering of an automated test interpretation service will be considered as a professional-to-professional consultation. In this the formal responsibility of the consultant is to the consultee but his ultimate and overriding responsibility is to the client. (6) The organization offering service is responsible that their reports adequately interpret the test materials. They should not misinterpret nor over-interpret the data nor omit important interpretations that the consultee would reasonably expect to be included. (7) The organization offering services is responsible that their report be interpretable by the consultee. The technical level of the report should be understandable and not misleading to the consultee. The professional consultee is responsible for integrating the report into his client relationship. Where technical interpretations could be misleading, the organization offering service would be responsible either not to accept the referral, to modify the form of their report, or to avoid otherwise its misinterpretation.

For the most part, these are sensible and practical guidelines which are easy to follow. This is not the case for item 4, "must be able to demonstrate that the computer programs or algorithms on which the interpretations rest are based on appropriate research to establish the validity of the programs and procedures." Nor is standard 6 easily evaluated, "responsible that their reports adequately interpret the test materials. They should not misinterpret nor over-interpret the data nor omit important interpretations." Although the literature is replete with statistically significant relationships between MMPI scores and various criteria, many conservative statisticians and academic psychologists have long felt that these were not sufficiently strong for "individual" interpretation. Consequently there is likely to be wide diver-

gence of opinion regarding what constitutes "appropriate research" and what an "adequate" interpretation might be.

Validity has always been held to be the most important aspect of a test review yet, in this case, it is a most difficult matter to evaluate. We might well decide that the MMPI as an instrument is valid for many interpretations and purposes but at varying levels of effectiveness. This would be my position, in general. Yet it would also be possible to doubt the validity or "adequacy" of a global personality description based on the MMPI alone. Relatively few studies have made concerted attacks on the problem of global validity.[3] These were encumbered by methodological problems, but, regardless of this, results were quite disappointing. Using the devices of Q sorts and true-false rating scales, test judges agreed with therapists and/or interview judges with no greater correlation than .40. Yet, it is with the aspect of "global" validity that we are most concerned. It is a complex question. Suppose a given report makes 30 interpretive statements. We might expect, under the best of circumstances, that 15 were quite accurate, 10 were partially accurate, and 5 were inaccurate. What then is the composite validity? A simple average will not do since statements will vary along a dimension of clinical importance. Statements involving psychiatric diagnosis, prognosis, sexual deviance, etc. are likely to have greater impact on decision making than others. An additional complexity is the fact that many statements, describing etiology, deep dynamics, prognosis, etc., are not validatable on any practical level. In the meantime, the unvalidated or unvalidatable statement can assume the status of a self-fulfilling prophecy, i.e., the phrase, "poor risk for psychotherapy" will militate against such individuals being given the same attention as other clients.

In the typical clinical situation, the psychologist who interprets the MMPI has other information available to him. MMPI interpretations are modified accordingly. If a frankly psychotic patient produces an essentially nonpsychotic test result, the combination of the two pieces of information is likely to be of greater

3 GRAHAM, JOHN R. "A Q-Sort of the Accuracy of Clinical Descriptions Based on the MMPI." J Psychiatric Res 5:297–305 D '67. *
LITTLE, KENNETH B., AND SHNEIDMAN, EDWIN S. "Congruencies Among Interpretations of Psychological Test and Anamnestic Data." Psychol Monogr 73(6):1–42 '59. *
SINES, LLOYD K. "The Relative Contribution of Four Kinds of Data to Accuracy in Personality Assessment." J Consult Psychol 23:483–92 D '59. *

use than the "blind" interpretation of the MMPI alone. Ostensibly, the clinician who receives the automated report has other information about his patient and can formulate the patient's problem using multiple sources of data. The services providing automated interpretation generally advise use of the reports in a fashion similar to a clinical laboratory report. This is not an inappropriate analogy but neither is it exact. The physician is supplied with the chemical composition of the blood or urine. He then interprets the data with some knowledge of the variety of circumstances producing a particular result and with some knowledge of the reliability and validity of the technique itself. Although an MMPI profile in quantified form is provided to the user of the automated MMPI, we cannot presume equivalent knowledge on his part. In fact, we can be quite certain that many psychiatrists and some psychologists will be quite naive.

This, then, is a "blind" interpretation with all its attendant hazards. The use of this approach has been growing in recent years even without automation. Many larger clinical facilities are using technicians to administer a simple battery of tests, often including the MMPI, which are then interpreted without the professional ever seeing the patient. Economy, yes. Humanistic concern for the patient and optimal "validity," not necessarily.

Fowler [4] makes the following, very powerful statement:

In the final analysis, computerized MMPI reporting systems have deeper significance than the practical considerations of speed, economy, and wide availability. They offer an alternative to the endless cycle of training new personnel, generation after generation, to do approximately the same thing with test data as their predecessors did. The prediction of human behavior and the description of personality are far too complex to be subject to half-remembered norms and subjective extrapolation. Even a simple actuarial formula can usually exceed clinicians' accuracy in the prediction of phenotypic and genotypic descriptors. The economics involved in training clinical psychology students to accomplish what computers can already do is questionable; to train them to do what computers can potentially do is impossible. The computer can be a powerful tool to free the psychologist from tasks that he does not do well, while releasing him for responsibilities for which he is uniquely qualified.

While this argument has great merit and appeal, it avoids the paradoxical elements in the situation. As long as any doubt remains regarding the validity of the MMPI, perhaps we need the "endless cycle of training new personnel,"

4 FOWLER, op. cit.

at least in regard to knowing the basic construction of the test and its limitations. Personality assessment remains in a primitive state of development. Granted that the clinical psychologist is limited in knowledge and is inefficient. Nevertheless, if he abrogates his professional responsibility to a distant computer, he is running great professional risk. At least, he is a part of the situation in which his test results are to be used. He can modify his reports to fit local preferences and prejudices. Most importantly, he can choose to ignore the MMPI results, in whole or in part, if they do not "fit" other data. Thus, I am most comfortable in the situation where a mature professional is using this type of service. There can be a great increase of efficiency with little loss of the often intangible but important aspects of his professional role.

One further aspect of validity needs to be explored. We are, all of us, used to completely open documentation of our clinical instruments in journals, books, symposia, etc. This is not the case with three of the systems reviewed below. The Mayo-Psychological Corporation system is the exception. Their system is the simplest and is completely explicated in several publications. With the others, we have little or no precise information regarding the "computer programs or algorithms on which the interpretations rest." Apparently, it is not possible to copyright a computer program. Since each program represents an enormous investment of time, energy, and money, it is understandable that the developers want to realize some material gain. A second argument is on an ethical basis. If the programs were made public, certain unethical practices might well develop. I recognize the dilemma. Nevertheless, it seems to me that these services are in partial violation of the APA's principles in regard to establishing the validity of their procedures.

A reasonable compromise might be reached by research that proceeded from the narrative report itself. Independent judgment of patient behavior might be obtained in the usual fashion and then matched with selected statements from the automated report. However, this has not yet been accomplished. (Fowler reports such a study in progress.) In the meantime, a communications gap is evident. This reviewer is left in the awkward position of rendering judgment on the basis of face validity of the interpretations and on the basis of testimonials, i.e., that various users have found the reports helpful. Each of these services provided sample reports for this review. In addition, the reviewer had available to him a single case submitted to all three services (made available by W. Grant Dahlstrom and fully discussed in the Dahlstroms' forthcoming revision of the *MMPI Handbook*). In general, all of these reports appear to be "reasonable." By this, I mean that, if I were confronted with the same profile, I would arrive at a similar narrative. Often this was not the case with secondary interpretations, e.g., of a vocational or educational nature. Here it was impossible to tell whether the interpretation was a distant extrapolation of research known to me or was based on unfamiliar research or was based on the "hunch" of some expert. The point is that these reports are certain to generate some discomfort in the more rigorous scientist-professional until more data is made available.

To use or not to use? That is the question. The answer seems to reside in the degree of control one can exercise over the clinical and social uses of the narrative report once received. If the final recipient of the report is sophisticated in the use of psychological data or if he is generally competent and conservative in his use of information, the services can be of considerable use. I have absolutely no ethical concern regarding the use of such a report by any of the professionals who have had a rigorous course involving personality assessment from inventory measures. Although each of the services has developed safeguards in this respect, the most rigorous only demands professional status as a psychologist or psychiatrist. Consequently, I am as certain that the automated personality report will be misused as I am that it will be used. Furthermore, I am concerned with the timing. These techniques are emerging at a time when concern is at a maximum regarding the welfare of individuals and invasions of privacy. Any marginally unethical or controversial use of these procedures is likely to damage the status of all mental health professionals.

[106]

★[Re Minnesota Multiphasic Personality Inventory.] MMPI-ICA Computer Report. A computerized scoring and interpreting service for physicians, psychiatrists, and psychologists; 1963–67; the interpretive report is a 4 or 5 page computer printout presenting an emotional disturbance score (called *Multiphasic Index,* MI), probabilities of disturbances, descriptive and interpretative statements (regarding ability to cope, suggestions for improving coping, special coping problems, most frequent diagnosis, critical items, salient clinical features), scores on 4 validity scales, 10 clinical scales, and 17 special research scales [anxiety index (AI), internalization ratio (IR), anxiety factor (A), repression factor (R), ego strength (Es), contradictory response (Tr), dissimulation index (F–K), dissimulation (Ds), positive malingering (Mp), control (Cn), ego defensiveness (Ed), severity of illness (FNF), manifest anxiety (At), low back (Lb), rigidity defense (Rg), dependency (Dy), social dominance (Do)], and a profile of the validity and clinical scores; manual ('66, see *3* below, free on request); reference guide ['66, 12 pages]; reference guide abstract ['67, 15 pages]; special IBM 1230 answer sheets must be used; scoring and computerized report, $7.50 per test, postpaid; reports are mailed within 2 days after receipt of answer sheets; Edwin Dunlop (manual); Institute of Clinical Analysis. *

REFERENCES

1–2. P:167.
3. DUNLOP, EDWIN, EDITOR. *Essentials of the Automated MMPI: A Compendium of Clinical Information.* Glendale, Calif.: Institute of Clinical Analysis, 1966. Pp. iii, 62. *
4. SPIEGEL, DON. "SPI and MMPI Predictors of Psychopathology." *J Proj Tech & Pers Assess* 33(3):265–73 Je '69. * (PA 43:14343)
5. SPIEGEL, DON. "SPI Discriminators Among Four Psychological Health-Sickness Levels." *J Consult & Clin Psychol* 33(6):750–6 D '69. * (PA 44:3804)

WILLIAM J. EICHMAN, *Associate Professor of Psychology, The University of North Carolina; and Director of Psychology Service, John Umstead Hospital; Chapel Hill, North Carolina.*

Although the ICA interpretive service is offered to psychiatrists, psychologists, and physicians, the total effort appears to be primarily geared to the general practitioner. This orientation is indicated by language in ICA's brochures and interpretive manuals where considerable emphasis is placed on "holistic medicine" and the role of the general practitioner in treating psychiatric disturbance. Further impetus in this direction is provided by the extreme prominence of two measures of general disturbance in the reports with a consequent de-emphasis of typical configural interpretation of the MMPI. Third, there is a "symptom review" at the conclusion of the report; this makes considerable use of the critical items but also presents single items and clusters related to somatic symptoms, hyperactivity, dreams, sexual disturbance, anxiety, etc. The sum total appears to be a very readable report but one which is slanted to both the adequacies and inadequacies of the relatively untrained physician.

With the apparent intent of this service, focusing primarily on relatively untrained recipients, the need for appropriate manuals and literature is greater than with competing services. This need has been partially met by a 59-page manual which describes the MMPI as a test instrument along with specific description of each of the clinical and validity scales. The need is further met by a Reference Guide: Scale Interpretation of the MMPI-ICA Computer Print-Out which describes the special scales and indices reported. Relatively speaking, these documents are better than those provided to users of the competing services. One wonders, however, to what extent the physician reads this fine print (literally) and to what extent he is influenced by the narrative content of the report itself. Also, while the manuals contain appropriate precautionary statements for the most part, there is some "over-selling" of the validity of the interpretations. This is especially the case in regard to the Multiphasic Index where the following statements occur: "a computerized global rating that represents a breakthrough in behavioral science. Its mathematical model 'tells at a glance' whether the subject is normal or disturbed. * The M.I. is a new calculus of tensors. Purges semantic indigestion. Because it functions like a clinical thermometer, it has been referred to as an 'emotional temperature.' " This reviewer finds such promotional literature misleading and objectionable. It is hardly conducive to the conservative use of the MMPI report recommended elsewhere in their own literature.

A sequential review of the ICA report seems indicated. These generalizations are drawn from ten sample reports and from literature provided by the service. As mentioned above, the Multiphasic Index is presented first. This is reported in raw score form, with a range from 65 to 150 and is divided into five bands, ranging from "Normal" to "Markedly Elevated." The band is indicated next to the score. This is followed by a "Probability of Significant Disturbance" in a percentage value. Then, the following statement is printed, "Two separate and distinct methods of appraising emotional conflict are shown on scores above. Either score may suggest a disorder but clinical significance is greater when both scores are elevated." Next is a narrative statement regarding the Multiphasic Index. Samples in the "Normal" range contained this printout, "Reflects a mild degree of emotional conflict. Mild psychogenic symptoms are likely to develop under heavy stress." A "Markedly Elevated" M.I. received this printout, "reflects an emotional disorder of marked severity. Responses are inappropriate, unrealistic, and self-defeating."

Thus far, no mention has been made of the derivation of the M.I. On the basis of two unpublished reports, by Waltmann and Dunlop (1968) and Dishman, Birds, and Dunlop (undated), it appears to be little more than an estimate of the familiar first factor which has emerged in most factor analytic studies. The authors administered a variety of tests to normals and hospitalized patients, did a factor analysis, conducted discriminant function analysis, etc. From the MMPI scales and indices used in the analysis, a global index was developed which best separated the groups. In the smaller study (1968) with an N of 40, complete separation of patients from normals was found. In the larger study (undated) with an N of 232, 12 percent of normals and 28 percent of patients were misclassified. The smaller study appears to be a crossvalidation of the index but the patients seem to be more severely ill; it is not clear. At any rate, the Multiphasic Index appears to be a completely legitimate and potentially useful tool for screening of normal from abnormal groups. The extent to which it is more useful than simpler measures derived from the MMPI remains to be demonstrated among diverse samples and with independent investigation.

The next section of the report is labeled "Summary." It contains a restatement of the degree of disturbance, a diagnostic statement in some instances, a prognostic statement in some instances, an estimate of coping ability and some personality descriptors. Despite the variety of information presented here, these are very brief, well-written paragraphs. Quite likely they are in the statement library as intact paragraphs and are derived from a combination of the two-point code and the Multiphasic Index.

The next section is a brief interpretation of the validity scales followed by one or more of the following sections: (a) Personality description, (b) Positive traits, (c) Suggestions to improve coping, (d) Special coping problems and/or (e) Diagnostic impression. The number and pattern presented appears to be dependent upon the relative elevation of clinical scales. With "normal" profiles, only the "positive traits" section appears on two of the samples. With elevated profiles, most sections are present. The "Positive traits" are a list of adjectives but the other sections are in paragraph forms, once again brief (2–12 lines) and well written.

In general, the interpretation of the MMPI provided by ICA appears to be well grounded in the MMPI literature. It is, however, impossible for this reviewer to visualize the interpretive program, i.e., what statement comes from what score or combination of scores. In a letter to subscribers (undated) ICA states, "The MMPI-ICA is, today, probably the largest and most sophisticated program in medicine with almost a million positions of core storage." Later in the letter, they say, "Reliability of the ICA is further supported by years of actual use by hundreds of clinicians, universities, hospitals, and clinics for which over 50,000 reports have been processed." Yet there is a dearth of published literature and the material provided by ICA yields minimal information.

The final section of the report is a "Symptom Review." As stated above, this includes the critical items but also appears to rely on other single items or small clusters. Areas covered include anxiety, intropunitive, hyperactivity, sexual disturbance, unusual thoughts and experiences, dreams, somatic expression, hostility, family or marital problems, phobias and obsessions, depression, and, perhaps, more that do not appear on my sample reports. When a critical item appears, it is printed in its entirety and asterisked but the majority of entries are descriptive phrases, e.g., hostility, somewhat irritable or tense; hyperactivity, considerably agitated or restless; and dysphoric episodes.

Following the narrative report, there is a sheet of Technical Data, including T scores and relative elevation on the standardized MMPI scales, raw scores on 17 additional scales and indices with normal ranges, and scores on the obvious-subtle scales. The final page of the report is the familiar MMPI profile. This has an unusual shaded area surrounding a T score of 50, presumably indicating the error of measurement for each of the scales.

The total ICA report reflects the careful workmanship that certainly went into its development. Nevertheless, certain severe problems appear to be present. First, there is considerable overselling of the product both in the promotional literature and in the report itself which has none of the modest disclaimers appearing in competing reports. Since ICA's market appears to be largely composed of general practitioners, this is likely to be a particular disadvantage. The G.P. armed with such a report is likely to feel that he knows much more than is actually the case and proceed with radical treatment procedures. One aspect of this problem relates to diagnosis. This is stated in a very positive manner in some printouts. An example is with a markedly elevated 6248 profile where the following summary appears:

> This patient shows a marked degree of emotional disorder. Psychotic dynamics are fairly well indicated. These may be latent, incipient, or pre-psychotic. The patient is markedly calling attention to psychologic problems. Defenses are down and coping ability is very inadequate.

Later in this same report, the patient is referred to as "schizoid" and "paranoid" and the phrase "serious danger of destructive behavior" is used. While this description of the profile generally conforms to standard interpretive practice, there are none of the usual checks and balances which are present in most clinical situations. To what extent can we count on the physician to conduct independent, skilled interviewing, to collect other behavioral data, etc.? How many physicians are using the ICA report as a substitute for clinical judgment rather than as a supplement to it?

Consequently, the ICA report is seen as a two-edged sword. It can be extremely useful to the clinician who has skill in the use of psychometric-personality data; it can be misused badly by the naive recipient, especially if he does not have an optimum set of values regarding emotional problems.

A similar type of brashness in the ICA report is found in the handling of the symptom review. Absolutely no cautionary statement is presented regarding the unreliability of single items, the influence of response sets, etc. It is as though the developers of the program were regarding item endorsement as equivalent to a psychiatric interview, in the same naive manner as the original developers of personality inventories more than 50 years ago. Similarly, a highly elevated F score results in no statement of doubtful validity (or at least of exaggerated statements) as it does in other programs. The total ICA program has much of merit but could benefit greatly from critical review of promotional practices and of MMPI validity in general. Although the MMPI is an excellent instrument, it is not that good. Similarly, the developers of this system need to establish themselves in the general literature by conducting careful and conservative research.

[107]

★[Re Minnesota Multiphasic Personality Inventory.] OPTIMUM Psychodiagnostic Consultation Service. A computerized scoring and interpreting service for qualified users of the MMPI or the *California Psychological Inventory;* 1969; various types of interpretive reports are available: types 1 (for industrial psychologists and personnel counselors), 2 (for counselors and caseworkers), 3 (for correctional counselors), 4 (self-report to be given to patient by counselor or therapist), 5 (for physicians), 6 (standard report for psychiatrists and psychologists), 6C (standard report on delinquent patients), 7 (detailed report for use before psychoanalysis or intensive psychotherapy), 7C (detailed report on delinquent patients); each type of report (except type 4) available in full or brief form; although the reports may be based on either the CPI or the MMPI, publisher recommends that the CPI be used for types 1–3 reports and the MMPI for types 5–7 reports; the interpretive report (except type 4) is a computer printout presenting a 1–6 page narrative report and 4–5 pages of scores on 3 validity scales (excludes ? scale), 10 clinical scales, 18 CPI scales, 135 special research scales, 5 orthogonal factors, 16 Taulbee-Sisson scales, various other research indices, and a graph (types 6 and 7 only) of 12 validity and clinical scales (excludes ? and Si scales); all of the scales are considered in the computerized narrative report; type 4 is a 1–2 page computer printout of narrative statements only; manual (12 pages) for psychiatrists and psychologists; special Digitek answer sheets must be used; scoring and computerized report fees: $15 per test for types 1–3, $20 for types 5, 6, or 6C, $30 for type 7 or 7C, (plus $5 additional for type 4 report on same client); psychiatrists and psychologists may request, in addition to their own report, type 2 ($5 additional) or type 5 ($10 additional) report for referring caseworker or physician; brief reports are $2–$5.50 less than regular reports; reports are mailed within 2 days after receipt of answer sheets; postpaid; Joseph C. Finney, Charles Dwight Auvenshine, David Fulton Smith, and Donald E. Skeeters; Behavioral Sciences, Inc. *

REFERENCES

1. FINNEY, JOSEPH C. "The MMPI as a Measure of Character Structure as Revealed by Factor Analysis." *J Consult Psychol* 25:327–36 Ag '61. * (*PA* 37:1254)
2. FINNEY, JOSEPH C. "Development of a New Set of MMPI Scales." *Psychol Rep* 17:707–13 D '65. * (*PA* 40:4248)
3. FINNEY, JOSEPH C. "Effects of Response Sets on New and Old MMPI Scales." *Psychol Rep* 17:907–15 D '65. * (*PA* 40:4249)
4. FINNEY, JOSEPH C. "Factor Structure With the New Set of MMPI Scales and the Formula Correction." *J Clin Psychol* 22:443–9 O '66. * (*PA* 41:2896)
5. FINNEY, JOSEPH C. "Programmed Interpretation of MMPI and CPI." *Arch Gen Psychiatry* 15:75–81 Jl '66. * (*PA* 40:11167)
6. FINNEY, JOSEPH C. "Relations and Meaning of the New MMPI Scales." *Psychol Rep* 18:459–70 Ap '66. * (*PA* 40:8254)
7. FINNEY, JOSEPH C. "Methodological Problems in Programmed Composition of Psychological Test Reports." *Behav Sci* 12:142–52 Mr '67. * (*PA* 41:6439)
8. FINNEY, JOSEPH C. "Normative Data on Some MMPI Scales." *Psychol Rep* 23:219–29 Ag '68. * (*PA* 43:6943)
9. FINNEY, JOSEPH C.; AUVENSHINE, CHARLES DWIGHT; SMITH, DAVID FULTON; AND SKEETERS, DONALD E. "The OPTIMUM Program: Interpreting Psychological Tests for Schools." *J Ed Data Processing* 7(5):269–76 '70. *

WILLIAM J. EICHMAN, *Associate Professor of Psychology, The University of North Carolina; and Director of Psychology Service, John Umstead Hospital; Chapel Hill, North Carolina.*

The OPTIMUM consultation service offers a variety of different reports (see entry above) ranging from a brief screening type to a lengthy, complex "psychodynamic" report. The terminology, complexity, and length of the report is varied according to the qualifications and interests of the recipient. As might be expected, there is much overlapping of content and some overlapping of specific language among the different reports available. In general, the well-trained professional could infer most of the detail of the longer and the more complex forms from the language of the brief and the more simple forms.

The developers of this system have departed considerably from the trend of close adherence to the standard MMPI literature. First, Finney (*1*) did basic factor analytic work with the standard MMPI scales along with a number of additional, experimental scales. He states, "Our interpretations are based on eight factor scores (calculated from all scales for each case) as well as complex configurational analysis using all scales." Second, Finney has collected his own normative sample from which he develops normalized T scores (in contrast to the skewed T scores of the Minnesota norms). A third innovation is a correction for response set. In Finney's factor analytic study he found the usual first two factors, corresponding to Welsh's A and R, not important when rotating to oblique simple structure. In regard to interpretation, this implies under-interpreting a given score with a generally elevated profile and over-interpreting with a low profile. Although other interpreters of the MMPI have not generally used correction scores of this type, the principle is accepted by them and is probably used in a subjective manner. The fourth major innovation is the use of such a very large number of "additional" scales in the interpretive program itself and in addition to whatever contribution they make to the calculation of the factor scores.

The developers of this system deserve credit for their basic research with the MMPI. Each of the innovations described above represents a legitimate scientific attempt to improve understanding of the MMPI as a test instrument. When this knowledge is built into an interpretive program, however, a problem emerges. This system is somewhat more vulnerable than others in regard to establishing validity since it ultimately depends on the labors of only a few individuals. Competing systems, adhering closely to the MMPI literature, can more easily lay claim to "validity" in the sense that their reports resemble closely those written by individual psychologists. Finney states, "The principles used in my program, however, are well published. A psychologist familiar with the MMPI can look over a number of my reports, compare the statements with the scores, and tell for the most part how the statements are selected." This is not nearly so true as it is for the other systems described in this section. In this respect, part of the problem appears to be the greater complexity of this interpretive system. Another large part is the unusual nature of the scores reported. I could not generate the usual MMPI profile from the data reported nor do I have sufficient familiarity with the corrections used in this system even to speculate regarding the nature of the usual profile. This dilemma can, perhaps, be easily resolved by scoring an answer sheet in the usual manner before mailing it or the printout could be modified to present the usual profile along with the corrected profile. At present, however, the reviewer cannot make a definitive or subjective statement regarding "face validity."

The problems encountered in this review have no bearing on the validity of the Finney-Auvenshine interpretive system. This has not been investigated in any definitive manner. It is an empirical matter and deserves the early attention of the developers, perhaps to a greater extent than with the other systems which rest on somewhat more traditional foundations.

Sample reports seen by the reviewer are printed on standard computer printout sheets. While this may be impressive to some users of the service, the sheets must be folded to fit standard file folders and cannot be fastened in the manner used in most office files. The first three sheets contain a listing of scores on 165 scales. This is followed by another sheet of technical data. This is followed by the profile itself and by the narrative report.

A typical report cannot be described because of the great variety offered by this service. Finney (4) describes the order as:

a modified psychoanalytic developmental sequence: (1) evidences of validity and attitudes toward the tests; (2) psychosis or mental illness; (3) narcissism, guilt, and basic trust; (4) problems of dependency; (5) demandingness or oral aggression; (6) dependent masochism and bitterness; (7) anger or hostility and how the individual handles it; (8) response to authorities; (9) compulsive personality features; (10) hysterical personality features, including repression, conversion, unconscious acting-out, and some aspects of sexuality; and (11) the way the individual meets his responsibilities as an adult.

In general, the reports are more psychoanalytic in flavor than those of competing services. Conversely, they seem to be less "symptomatic." There is a decided attempt to extrapolate from the clinical setting into real life situations, especially work situations. To the extent that validity can be demonstrated, this is a decided virtue; too long have assessment reports only been concerned with clinical behaviors.

One must view the style and language of the report as a matter of personal preference. In general, this reviewer found them a bit too wordy and often redundant. In addition, the program prints out a "lead" sentence for each section of the report: e.g., "Now what about demandingness or oral aggression?" and "Next let's examine her anger or hostility and how she copes with it." These rhetorical questions or statements appear to be trite after reading several of the reports. Finney, in a number of his publications, alludes to the difficulties of transforming elements from the statement library into meaningful, comprehensible, and non-contradictory paragraphs. Indeed, it is a very demanding task. One sub-program (1965) for the use of the conjunctions "and," "but," and "though" had to be written. Contrary to the other automated programs which report individual statements (Mayo) or whole paragraphs (Fowler, ICA), this program is tremendously more daring and elaborate.

The reports designed for physicians, psychiatrists, and clinical psychologists conclude with a most likely diagnostic label and a list of other possible diagnoses. This section is prologued with the following statement.

Categorizing a patient with a diagnostic judgment must never be done from the results of psychological tests alone, nor from the reports of other laboratory tests alone. In making your diagnostic assessment of this patient, you will rely on the careful history that you have taken and on the shrewd observations that you have made of the patient's behavior in the interview.

Finney, Smith, Skeeters, and Auvenshine (undated report) conducted a validation study of the diagnostic part of the report at a state hospital (N = 40). This yielded statistically significant results but far from optimum prediction, i.e., 50 percent hit rate for the psychotic category and 86 percent hit rate for non-psychotics.

In short, Finney and his colleagues have taken a daringly innovative approach to the development of this MMPI interpretation system. This renders them more vulnerable to all the problems raised in the general commentary that precedes these reviews. As a consequence, the developers of the program should actively pursue further validity studies, especially by independent investigators. It also seems desirable to investigate the social impact and uses of these reports among the non-mental health personnel for whom some types of the report were developed. As with the other systems reviewed, this one can be highly useful to the recipient of the reports. Used responsibly and ethically, it can be helpful to the "patient" population served but the problem of social misuse continues to be an important issue.

[108]

★[Re Minnesota Multiphasic Personality Inventory.] The Psychological Corporation MMPI Reporting Service. A computerized scoring and interpreting service for qualified users of the MMPI; 1967; the interpretive report is a 1 page computer printout presenting 6 to 15 interpretive statements (selected from a population of 73 statements), scores on 4 validity scales, 10 clinical scales, and 13 special scales [first factor (A), second factor (R), ego strength (Es), low back pain (Lb), caudality (Ca), dependency (Dy), dominance (Do), social responsibility (Re), prejudice (Pr), status (St), control (Cn), tired housewife (Th), and worried breadwinner (Wb)], and a profile of the validity and clinical scores; none of the special scales are utilized in the computerized interpretive statements; manual ('67, 42 pages, entitled *A User's Guide to the Mayo Clinic Automated MMPI Program*); NCS answer sheets must be used; $3.60 per 50 answer sheets (Old Group Form); $4.80 per 50 answer sheets (Form R); $1.50 per manual; postage extra; scoring and computer interpretation service, $3 per single report; $2 each for 2–4; $1.50 each for 5–99 (by using prepaid report certificates, quantity prices apply even though for single reports); answer sheets must be sent to National Computer Systems; reports are mailed within 1 day after receipt of answer sheets; program and manual by John S. Pearson and Wendell M. Swenson; Psychological Corporation. *

REFERENCES

1–8. See P:168.
9. NAHUM, L. H. "The Computer and Personality Inventory." *Conn Med* 29:764+ N '65. *

WILLIAM J. EICHMAN, *Associate Professor of Psychology, The University of North Carolina; and Director of Psychology Service, John Umstead Hospital; Chapel Hill, North Carolina.*

The Mayo Clinic automated MMPI program received clinical trial with approximately 150,000 medical patients of great diversity. Consequently, it is a better established approach than others reviewed in this section. Much important actuarial data has accumulated in addition to experience in providing such a service to medical specialists. Contrary to the other automated programs, it has been fully

described in several publications (*1–9*). As a result, the system of interpretation can be applied by any person with access to the test materials and to the professional literature. Thus, the product offered by the Psychological Corporation and the developers of the program is basically one of clerical convenience, i.e., answer sheets are scored, profiles are developed, narrative statements are printed out.

As a clinical psychologist and as a teacher of assessment to graduate students, I am quite pleased with this program. I have been using it in my classes for some years as a first step toward the quite complex process of interpreting the MMPI. One of its virtues is simplicity. Basically, each of the 13 MMPI scales is categorized into five levels of elevation from "low" to "marked." A narrative statement is attached to each, printed in a sequence that generally conforms to relative elevation. From this modest schema, an astonishing number of different narrative reports can be generated. Further diversity is introduced by 11 "configural" rules, combinations of scores that occur frequently in particular clinical syndromes, e.g., "involutional pattern," "anxious psychopath," etc. When one of the configural rules apply, the usual narrative statement is suppressed and the configural statement is substituted for it.

In general terms, this program is a deliberate underinterpretation of the psychological test data. It was developed for use by "physicians in general." The authors hoped to stimulate the physician toward gaining greater knowledge of the instrument by reading appropriate literature and through cumulative clinical experience. Pearson and Swenson state:

At this stage of development, one should not expect the computer to do all his thinking for him relative to a complex instrument like the MMPI or the complexities of human emotions. However, by using the present modest but rigorous program for automated MMPI interpretation, professional people with little or no previous experience or knowledge of personality testing may stimulate and focus their thinking.

As illustration of the conservative nature of the narrative statements, consider the statement which is printed for the highest elevation on the Schizophrenia scale, "Probable feelings of unreality, bizarre or confused thinking and conduct. May have strange attitudes and false beliefs. Consider psychiatric evaluation." Similarly, marked elevation on the Paranoia scale is, "Resentful and suspicious of others, perhaps to point of fixed false beliefs."

The content of this statement library is almost completely descriptive or symptomatic. None of the statements involves diagnosis, etiology, prognosis, or recommendations for specific treatment. Only a few have direct implications regarding dynamics or underlying dispositions.

Twelve additional scales are scored and converted to T scores but, at present, are not interpreted in a narrative fashion. These are Welsh's first and second factor scales (A and R), Barron's ego strength scale, Hanvik's low back pain scale, Williams' caudality scale, Navran's dependency scale, Gough's dominance scale, the social responsibility scale, Gough's prejudice scale, Gough's status scale, Cuadra's control scale, and the "tired housewife" and "worried bread-winner" scales developed by Pearson et al. Presumably, this information is provided for the benefit of those with more specialized knowledge of the MMPI and more specialized interests.

The professional user of this service is provided a concise but informative User's Guide which describes the development of the MMPI, the development of scales and T scores, coding, content of each of the scales, a copy of the complete program, practical use of the program, suggested readings, etc.

This program and service can be highly recommended to the general physician for whom it was developed and to many psychiatrists and psychologists who consult with physicians. Similarly but with greater precautions, these reports could be useful to social agencies without full-time psychiatric or psychological staff. The understatement of results can always be supplemented by individual consultation and should be whenever a report does not appear to "fit" other data. Similarly, individual consultation is indicated when a particularly troubled or troublesome patient is involved. The "understatement" also renders the service *relatively* safe from misuse. The User's Guide recommends against allowing patients to read their own reports but cites experience where this has happened. They point out the fact that the MMPI is a self-report inventory and that negative interpretations are usually anticipated by the client who has endorsed negative statements about himself. Consequently, he is not surprised or overly chagrined. Relative to some other services, however, the Mayo system is far less inclined to make second-order inferences.

The client or patient endorses or rejects endorsement of 550 statements. His printout, then, essentially summarizes what he has said about himself. The highly sophisticated user of an MMPI service might well find this to be a disadvantage. If so, he should consider an alternative service.

In summary, the reviewer finds this service to be precisely what the authors claim, i.e., "a modest but rigorous program for automated MMPI interpretation." The cost is modest and is probably less than that involved in using local clerical workers.

[109]

★[Re Minnesota Multiphasic Personality Inventory.] Roche MMPI Computerized Interpretation Service. A computerized scoring and interpreting service for qualified users of the MMPI (clinical psychologists and psychiatrists for use in clinical practice and research); 1966-70; the interpretive report is a 3 page computer printout presenting a narrative report, scores on 4 validity scales, 10 clinical scales, and 14 special scales [first factor (A), second factor (R), ego strength (Es), low back pain (Lb), caudality (Ca), dependency (Dy), dominance (Do), responsibility (Re), prejudice (Pr), social status (St), control (Cn), manifest anxiety (At), social desirability (So-R), maladjustment (Mt)], reproduction of critical items with responses, and a profile of the validity and clinical scores; only 3 (A, Pr, Es) of the 14 special scales are utilized in the computerized narrative report; new subscriber kits consist of test booklet, 20 answer sheets with preprinted identification numbers, *The MMPI Notebook* ('66, 49 pages, including 1968 and 1970 additions), instructions for administration ['67, 6 pages], instructions for patient ['68, 1 page], record of patient numbers ['67, 1 page], 2 preaddressed envelopes, and 2 control cards; refill kits consist of test booklet and 20 answer sheets; $2.50 per new subscriber test kit (includes free reports on 2 patients); $1 per refill kit; scoring and computerized report, $2.50 per test; identification of subjects known only to test administrator; reports are mailed within 1 day after receipt of answer sheets; postpaid; program and manual by Raymond D. Fowler, Jr.; Roche Psychiatric Service Institute. *

REFERENCES

1-9. See P:169.
10. FOWLER, RAYMOND D., JR. Chap. 6, "Automated Interpretation of Personality Test Data," pp. 105-26. In *MMPI: Research Developments and Clinical Applications.* Edited by James Neal Butcher. New York: McGraw-Hill Book Co., 1969. Pp. xiv, 402. *
11. FOWLER, RAYMOND D., JR. "The Current Status of Computer Interpretation of Psychological Tests." *Am J Psychiatry* 125(7, sup):21-7 Ja '69. * (*PA* 43:10000)
12. FOWLER, RAYMOND D., JR., AND MILLER, MARVIN L. "Computer Interpretation of the MMPI: Its Use in Clinical Practice." *Arch Gen Psychiatry* 21(4):502-8 O '69. * (*PA* 44:8741)
13. WEBB, JAMES T.; MILLER, MARVIN L.; AND FOWLER, RAYMOND D., JR. "Validation of a Computerized MMPI Interpretation System." Abstract. *Proc 77th Ann Conv Am Psychol Assn* 4(2):523-4 '69. * (*PA* 44:68)
14. WEBB, JAMES T. "Validity and Utility of Computer-Produced MMPI Reports With Veterans Administration Psychiatric Populations." Abstract. *Proc 78th Ann Conv Am Psychol Assn* 5(2):541-2 '70. * (*PA* 44:18924)
15. WEBB, JAMES T.; MILLER, MARVIN L.; AND FOWLER, RAYMOND D., JR. "Extending Professional Time: A Computerized MMPI Interpretation Service." *J Clin Psychol* 26(2):210-4 Ap '70. * (*PA* 44:14645)

WILLIAM J. EICHMAN, *Associate Professor of Psychology, The University of North Carolina; and Director of Psychology Service, John Umstead Hospital; Chapel Hill, North Carolina.*

The Roche Laboratories have established a nonprofit interpretive service for the MMPI, using a program developed by Raymond Fowler. Altogether, it is a very impressive package that they offer at a very modest price. The service is primarily offered to clinical psychologists and psychiatrists in private practice. It is being extended to selected physicians in general practice and to psychiatric institutions. Highly desirable features of the service include: (*a*) maximum protection of the patient by the use of code numbers rather than names and (*b*) a continuing, intensive research effort in regard to the adequacy of the system.

In contrast to the Mayo system which might be termed a "screening" type of report, the Roche report is more "consultative" and more closely resembles a typical psychological report. It is in paragraph form and departs from a purely descriptive level to varying degrees, depending on the nature of the particular profile. Similarly the vocabulary level is more suitable to recipients who have had psychiatric/psychological training. Statements like the following are found: (*a*) "the pattern is a persistent one," (*b*) "assisting her to a better adjustment will probably require a combination of firm limits, warm support, and environmental modification," (*c*) "the long term prognosis is poor," (*d*) "she appears to be a person who utilizes repression as a defense." Each of these statements was drawn from a single report of a female patient with elevations above a T score of 80 on the Depression (D), Psychopathic Deviate (Pd), Psychasthenia (Pt), and Schizophrenic (Sc) scales, in that order. It can be quickly observed that inferences are made regarding temporal stability of a syndrome, the preferred treatment approach, prognosis, and ego-defensive mechanisms. Since neither the complete statement library (Fowler reports a statement library of 482 paragraphs and 2,100 sentences) nor the frequency of use of each statement were made available to the reviewer, it is impossible to determine relative occurrence of different types of statement. Certainly, it would seem that descriptive and/or symptomatic statements are most common but others, on a higher level of inference, occur quite frequently. Depending on one's point of view, this is a tremendous asset in the service or an example of clinical arrogance. The average clinician, psychiatric or psychological, expects more than a descriptive report when he seeks psychological assessment; he is likely to be somewhat more satisfied with this type of report than with a screening type. Similarly, he is likely to be sufficiently well trained to utilize it optimally. The more "scientifically" inclined, on the other hand, are likely to be disturbed at such important inferences being derived from a paper-pencil inventory.

The user of the Roche service receives a kit with MMPI booklets, answer sheets which are coded, instructions for administering the test, and instructions for use of the service. He is also provided with the *MMPI Notebook: A Guide to the Clinical Use of the Automated MMPI,* a 49-page manual in loose-leaf format which contains very general information regarding the MMPI and its interpretation along with somewhat more specific information regarding administration of the test and use of the service. In the introduction, it is stated, "The looseleaf format was selected to make it possible to augment the notebook with additional chapters and bulletins, which will be prepared and distributed periodically."

The following generalizations are based upon ten sample reports provided to the reviewer by the service. The report is a 3–4 page printout. The first page (or two) contains the narrative report along with the identifying code number and the age and sex of the client. The first paragraph relates to the elevations of the validity scales and their configuration. When none of these is unusually elevated, the following statement is printed:

> The test results of this patient appear to be valid. He (she) seems to have made an effort to answer the items truthfully and to follow the instructions accurately. To some extent this may be regarded as a favorable prognostic sign since it indicates that he (she) is capable of following instructions and able to respond relevantly and truthfully to personal inquiry.

The next paragraph is generated from the two-point code, i.e., the two highest scale scores, omitting consideration of the validity scales and, probably, the Masculinity-Femininity scale. Fowler states, "For each possible two-point code, there are a number of alternative statements depending upon the elevation of the highest two scales, the presence of other scale elevations, and such factors as sex, age, and marital status."

Succeeding paragraphs (numbering from 1–

6 in sample reports) interpret other scales of sufficient elevation in rank order of their T score. These paragraphs tend to be shorter than those based upon the high points, usually 2–4 sentences. They also appear to be somewhat more conservative in interpretation, e.g., a high Schizophrenia score not occurring as one of the two high points would result in this statement, "There are unusual qualities in this patient's thinking which may represent an original or eccentric orientation or perhaps some schizoid tendencies. Further information is required to make this determination." Generally, an Sc score of the same magnitude would receive stronger interpretation if it were one of the two high points. Generally, this trend is in keeping with the MMPI literature which has largely focussed on the two high points.

A last paragraph or two is sometimes included. These refer to: the presence of "emotional disorder" and/or the presence of "neurotic defenses." These statements also appear to be conservative in nature. One of the sample cases, coded 12″47′, resulted in the following two paragraphs:

This patient has a test pattern which suggests the possibility of severe emotional problems. Professional care is indicated.
This patient's condition appears to fall within the neurotic range. He is using neurotic defenses in an effort to control his anxiety.

Another patient with an 8*94″7′ profile received the following paragraph:

The test results are strongly suggestive of a major emotional disorder. The test pattern resembles those of psychiatric outpatients who later require inpatient care. Appropriate professional evaluation and care and continued observation are suggested.

It should be noted that the word "psychosis" is not used even in those cases where the individual clinician might be inclined to classify the profile as a "psychotic type."

A final "Note" is included in each narrative printout. This is:

Although not a substitute for the clinician's professional judgment and skill, the MMPI can be a useful adjunct in the evaluation and management of emotional disorders. The report is for professional use only and should not be shown or released to the patient.

The next page contains a listing of raw scores, K corrections, and T scores for the four validity scales and ten clinical scales of the MMPI. Raw scores and T scores based on the Minnesota norm group are also provided for 14 additional MMPI scales. This is followed by the Welsh code for the case and a listing of critical items which were answered in the deviant direction. The following admonition precedes the listing of the critical items:

These MMPI test items which were answered by the patient in the direction indicated, may require further investigation by the clinician. The clinician is cautioned, however, against over-interpretation of these isolated responses.

The caution is well-merited and, in fact, may not be sufficiently strong. A naive recipient of such a report might well forget the earlier narrative and focus unduly on one or more critical item responses which suggest psychosis, sexual deviance, or the like. Unless one has had long, painful experience with inventories, he is not likely to be completely aware that many subjects make unusual interpretations of individual test items, that they make clerical errors, that they have response sets, etc. Thus, inclusion of individual item content, particularly of the most bizarre items, is somewhat controversial.

So much for a description of the service and the type of reports developed. On the evaluative side, this appears to be an essentially conservative replica of the type report one would expect from an individual psychologist doing a blind interpretation of an MMPI. There are no "far out" interpretations. Aside from the two-point code paragraph, further configural interpretation did not seem to be present in the sample reports. Neither was there evidence of interpretation of the additional scales.

Validation studies of the interpretive system have been reported (13, 14). The samples involved were psychiatric outpatients and Veterans Administration inpatients. Clinicians working with these cases generally found the reports to be "valid descriptions" and to compare favorably with individually written reports. Bachrach (pre-publication report) found comparable results with a University Hospital population, using psychiatric residents as judges. He concludes, "The regard that the present group of psychiatrists has for the Roche MMPI report suggests that it is seen as a useful clinical tool that provides much information at a minimum cost of time and money."

It should be noted that these three "validity" studies rely upon rather global evaluatory statements from the recipients of the reports and, in no way, confront the more knotty issue of individual statements vis-à-vis independent observations of the patients. Fowler reports in personal communication that the problem is being met with a checklist of items, largely drawn from the library of statements, which will be rated by clinicians independently of MMPI results.

Finally, two unpublished papers by Webb illustrate the scientifically valuable information which is accruing as a consequence of the service. One report analyzes regional and sex differences with a sample of 2,010 patient records submitted by 1,267 professionals. This revealed many significant sex differences in the highest scale score of the profile but no regional differences. Another larger sample (12,174 cases) was used for more complex analysis of two-point codes according to age, sex, and educational level. All three of these demographic variables appear to be important sources of variance; they should receive considerable attention in future interpretive hypotheses and research. Webb reports that fully one third of the nation's psychiatrists in private practice are utilizing the service along with several hundred psychologists. Since all available outpatient data were used for these analyses, it seems quite likely that the sample is a close approximation to the total population of psychiatric outpatients seen in private practice.

In short, the Roche-Fowler computerized report has much to offer the professional psychiatrist or psychologist. All appropriate precautions appear to have been taken. If the professional user of the service follows instructions adequately, the patient is protected and the professional has an independent source of information for use in his care of the patient.

BENJAMIN KLEINMUNTZ, *Professor of Psychology, Carnegie-Mellon University, Pittsburgh, Pennsylvania.*

There are approximately eight automated personality test scoring and interpretation systems in commercial use at the present time, and of these, at least four are specially designed to interpret the MMPI. The Roche Psychiatric Service Institute's (RPSI) computerized service is in the latter category, and it is intended for "clinical psychologists and psychiatrists for use in clinical practice and research." The manual which accompanies the MMPI Kit further stipulates that the "system of interpretation was developed for patients who are in difficulty or distress because of disturbances in their behavior or emotional state. The Institute restricts its service to this area. *It is not suitable, therefore, for routine screening of presumably normal-range individuals who are largely symptom-free.* It should not be used for employee screening or any other nonclinical purpose." The author of this automated system, Raymond D. Fowler, Jr., further informed me in our correspondence that because "it is not designed for screening groups of presumably normal-range subjects or for college counseling, requests to use it this way have been refused." And then capturing the commendable spirit of the entire enterprise, Fowler goes on to say, "I have developed an alternative version of the program for college students, but I haven't yet felt entirely comfortable in making it available."

The system is designed to score and interpret the four validity scales (?, L, F, K) and ten clinical scales (Hs, D, Hy, Pd, Mf, Pa, Pt, Sc, Ma, Si) of the MMPI. The scores of 14 additional scales are printed out, but of these only three are used in the interpretation program: A (Welsh, 1956), Pr (Gough, 1951), and Es (Barron, 1953).

The MMPI user is provided with a three-page printout. The first page is the narrative report which is a compilation of paragraphs which the computer has selected according to specific instructions. The second page is a technical sheet, the top half of which includes the raw scores and the T scores of the 4 validity scales, 10 clinical scales and 14 special scales. The bottom half of the second page is a printout of certain "critical items," based on a selection of 38 MMPI items which, when answered in the scored direction, have implications for the presence of serious symptoms, impulses or experiences. The third page of the printout consists of the MMPI profile which contains the plotted graph of the four validity and ten clinical scales of the MMPI. Since the first of these three printout pages contains the most unique contribution of RPSI's service, most of this review will focus on it.

On the first page there are three types of information: basic identifying data (the coded case number which corresponds to the user's code; the RPSI code number, which probably serves a potential research purpose; the age and sex of the MMPI respondent; and the date on which the MMPI was administered); sets of interpretive statements corresponding to configurations found on the validity (or credibility) scales of the MMPI; and interpretive statements concerning the patterns found among the clinical scales. In addition, there is a note of caution appended at the end of the first page indicating that the interpretations are "not a substitute for the clinician's professional judgment and skill."

An obvious omission on the first page of the printout is some statement furnished by the user regarding the "reason for testing." That the author had intentions of including such information is evident from the fact that his published examples of the computer printout contain this item (*10*). At the present time the MMPI user is provided no opportunity to include this information when he submits his patient's answer sheet. Thus if he has a special question he would like to have answered (i.e., "is this patient psychotic or neurotic?"), he cannot pose it. Instead he may receive a set of interpretive comments that are not germane to his needs. Moreover, the omission of the "reason for testing" information can result in a loss of data which is of potential research usefulness both to the user and the RPSI.

The interpretive statements are the core of RPSI's offering to the MMPI user. These interpretations were accomplished by instructing the computer to inspect the various patterns of scale elevations on the MMPI. Depending on the patterns identified, the machine selects an appropriate description from any of several paragraphs stored in its statement library. These descriptive sentences or paragraphs are of two types, one type bears upon the question of whether or not an examinee's responses are credible; and the other is based on interpretations of the clinical scales. The statements are gleaned from reported research findings which have appeared in the MMPI literature over the years. Much of this information appears in Dahlstrom and Welsh's *MMPI Handbook* (1960), which is currently undergoing revision. Several descriptive sentences that are printed out by the RPSI system and which refer to the credibility of particular MMPIs are reproduced here:

THE TEST RESULTS OF THIS PATIENT APPEAR TO BE VALID. SHE SEEMS TO HAVE MADE AN EFFORT TO ANSWER THE ITEMS TRUTHFULLY AND TO FOLLOW THE INSTRUCTIONS ACCURATELY. TO SOME EXTENT THIS MAY BE REGARDED AS A FAVORABLE PROGNOSTIC SIGN SINCE IT INDICATES THAT SHE IS CAPABLE OF FOLLOWING INSTRUCTIONS AND ABLE TO RESPOND RELEVANTLY AND TRUTHFULLY TO PERSONAL INQUIRY.

IT APPEARS THAT THE PATIENT, IN HER RESPONSES TO THE TEST ITEMS, MAY HAVE BEEN OVERLY SELF-CRITICAL. THE VALIDITY OF THE TEST MAY HAVE BEEN SOMEWHAT AFFECTED BY HER TENDENCY TO ADMIT TO SYMPTOMS EVEN WHEN THEY ARE MINIMAL. THIS MAY SUGGEST THAT CURRENTLY SHE FEELS VULNERABLE AND DEFENSELESS, AND THAT SHE IS MAKING AN EFFORT TO CALL ATTENTION TO HER DIFFICULTIES IN ORDER TO ASSURE OBTAINING PROFESSIONAL HELP.

THE VALIDITY OF THIS PATIENT'S TEST RESULTS MAY HAVE BEEN ADVERSELY AFFECTED BY HER MARKED TENDENCY TO PRESENT HERSELF IN A FAVORABLE LIGHT. SHE APPEARS TO BE A SOMEWHAT UNCONVENTIONAL PERSON WHO STRONGLY RESISTS SELF-DISCLOSURE. THIS PATTERN IS LESS DEVIANT WHEN IT OCCURS IN EDUCATED AND RELATIVELY SUCCESSFUL INDIVIDUALS WHO ARE ACCUSTOMED TO MAINTAINING A GOOD SOCIAL APPEARANCE, ALTHOUGH IT DOES SUGGEST RIGIDITY AND OVER-COMPENSATION FOR FEELINGS OF INADEQUACY. IN AN INDIVIDUAL OF LOWER SOCIAL ATTAINMENT, IT MAY REFLECT AN EXTREME RIGIDITY AND DEFENSIVENESS. IN EITHER CASE THE DENIAL OF EMOTIONAL PROBLEMS COULD PORTEND DIFFICULTIES IN ESTABLISHING AND MAINTAINING A PSYCHOTHERAPY RELATIONSHIP.

SHE SEEMS TO BE ATTEMPTING TO MINIMIZE OR DENY FAULTS IN HERSELF. SHE IS HESITANT TO ADMIT PSYCHOLOGICAL PROBLEMS, PERHAPS BECAUSE SHE PERCEIVES THEM AS WEAKNESSES. IN SOME NORMAL FUNCTIONING INDIVIDUALS THIS APPARENT DEFENSIVENESS MAY REPRESENT SELF-ASSURANCE AND A GOOD SELF-CONCEPT. IN AN INDIVIDUAL WITH CURRENT DIFFICULTIES, HOWEVER, IT IS MORE LIKELY TO REPRESENT RESISTANCE AND RELUCTANCE TO ENTER TREATMENT.

Any MMPI interpreter who has performed the task of configural analysis of the four validity scales (?, L, F, K) will readily understand that formalization of a set of rules such as has been accomplished by the RPSI is indeed a contribution to the field. No matter how skilled the human interpreter may be, and regardless of how extensive is his information about interpretive heuristics and rules-of-thumb, he is essentially competing in an area in which he is uniquely unequipped. Not only does the automated system have a relatively greater storage capacity than the human, but once it is furnished with a set of rules (hopefully an optimal set), it can be expected to apply these rules uniformly, consistently, and cheerfully.

For the interpretation of the clinical scale elevations, the computer store is equipped with a statement library consisting of a collection of sentences also gleaned from the MMPI research literature. Several typical paragraphs are reproduced here:

THIS PATIENT SEEMS TO BE A PERSON WHO HAS DIFFICULTY MAINTAINING CONTROLS OVER IMPULSES. SHE BEHAVES IN A SOCIALLY UNACCEPTABLE MANNER, SHE IS LIKELY TO EXPERIENCE GUILT AND DISTRESS, ALTHOUGH HER CONCERN MAY REFLECT SITUATIONAL DIFFICULTIES RATHER THAN AN EXPRESSION OF INTERNAL CONFLICTS.

THIS PATIENT'S POORLY CONTROLLED ANGER MAY BE EXPRESSED IN TEMPER OUTBURSTS, OFTEN AS A RESPONSE TO THE FRUSTRATION OF CHILDISH DEMANDS FOR ATTENTION AND APPROVAL. SHE IS HIGHLY SENSITIVE TO REJECTION, AND HER ANGER IS ESPECIALLY LIKELY TO

BE DIRECTED TOWARDS FAMILY MEMBERS. WHEN HER ANGER IS SUPPRESSED AND INTERNALIZED SUICIDE ATTEMPTS ARE A POSSIBILITY. MOODINESS, DEPRESSION AND HEAVY DRINKING ARE FREQUENTLY FOUND IN SUCH INDIVIDUALS.

HE APPEARS TO BE AN IDEALISTIC INNER-DIRECTED PERSON WHO MAY BE SEEN AS QUITE SOCIALLY PERCEPTIVE AND SENSITIVE TO INTERPERSONAL INTERACTIONS. HIS INTEREST PATTERNS ARE QUITE DIFFERENT FROM THOSE OF THE AVERAGE MALE. IN A PERSON WITH A BROAD EDUCATIONAL AND CULTURAL BACKGROUND THIS IS TO BE EXPECTED AND MAY REFLECT SUCH CHARACTERISTICS AS SELF-AWARENESS, CONCERN WITH SOCIAL ISSUES AND AN ABILITY TO COMMUNICATE IDEAS CLEARLY AND EFFECTIVELY. IN SOME MEN, HOWEVER, THE SAME INTEREST PATTERN MAY REFLECT A REJECTION OF MASCULINITY ACCOMPANIED BY A RELATIVELY PASSIVE EFFEMINATE NON-COMPETITIVE PERSONALITY.

Again, comments similar to those made above regarding the interpretation of the validity scale configurations are in order here, except that the problem confronting the clinician is considerably more difficult because the number of scales is increased from 4 to 10. The formalization or freezing of available decision rules for this portion of MMPI interpretation, therefore, is a service of even greater importance for the MMPI user.

To gain some appreciation of how the author went about collecting data for the clinical scale statement library, several quotes from his recent work (*10*) are in order:

The computer is programmed to identify the two-point code and to locate the appropriate paragraph in the library. * First, a basic interpretative paragraph was prepared for each two-point code. Second, since the interpretation of the two-point code is influenced by the elevation of the two scales, variations were prepared to reflect various levels of elevation. Third, since the meaning of the two-point code is influenced by other profile characteristics, additional paragraphs were written to take other scale elevations and configurations into account. Fourth, such factors as sex, age, and marital status were considered, and alternative paragraphs were prepared. The result of this procedure was an elaborate set of interpretative rules and a number of alternative paragraphs for each two-point code.

Then, the author goes on to say, that several "decision rules" based on research were included in the program. These decision rules are those of Taulbee and Sisson,[1] Peterson,[2] Meehl and Dahlstrom,[3] and Kleinmuntz.[4] Only the first two of these are used in the interpretation system at the present time.

1 TAULBEE, EARL S., AND SISSON, BOYD D. "Configurational Analysis of MMPI Profiles of Psychiatric Groups." *J Consult Psychol* 21:413–7 O '57. *
2 PETERSON, DONALD R. "Predicting Hospitalization of Psychiatric Outpatients." *J Abn & Social Psychol* 49:260–5 Ap '54. *
3 MEEHL, PAUL E., AND DAHLSTROM, W. GRANT. "Objective Configural Rules for Discriminating Psychotic From Neurotic MMPI Profiles." *J Consult Psychol* 24:375–87 O '60. *
4 KLEINMUNTZ, BENJAMIN. "MMPI Decision Rules for the Identification of College Maladjustment: A Digital Computer Approach." *Psychol Monogr* 77(14):1–22 '63. *

Further information regarding the construction of the interpretive rules for clinical scale elevations has been furnished me by the author in personal correspondence:

Before preparing each of the paragraphs I collected all of the information that I could find on each two-point code, high-point code and various other configurations. The paragraph represents a boiling down into narrative prose of the essential interpretive information for each configuration. Often, for a single two-point code several statements were required. Sometimes alternative paragraphs are necessary depending on whether or not some other scale is elevated. For example, Scale 2 influences several two-point codes in that it modifies the statement one would make on the basis of the two-point code alone. Since each of these variables can require the preparation of two or more interpretive paragraphs, it is possible to have as many as eight alternatives for some configurations while others may have as few as two. The same goes for validity statements. In some cases, the paragraph is based on the three-point code, although the literature is fairly sparse on the three-point codes except in the Marks and Seeman, and Gilberstadt and Duker books.

It is appropriate now to ask ourselves whether or not the automated MMPI service offered by RPSI is a useful one. A partial answer to this question can be obtained by comparing it with standard procedures used by clinicians in eyeball scanning MMPI profile configurations in a clinical setting. In principle, such a comparison, as we emphasized above, favors the RPSI system because for this clinical decision-making task the human is no match for the computer. However, this is true only in fact *if, and only if,* the machine is furnished with a set of optimal decision rules. Therefore, in the present case, if in the process of profile interpretation, the human invokes and then applies the accumulated wisdom of MMPI folklore, then compared to the computer, he is at a considerable disadvantage. On the other hand, if the human has devised a sample-specific set of rules, or has discovered a particularly useful rule for performing an interpretive task, *and if he applies that rule consistently and invariably,* then the machine is no match for him.

In this regard, I have in mind Goldberg's rule [5] for discriminating psychotics vs neurotics, which is a simple linear function, and which is easily applied by the human in performing an MMPI analysis. The research evidence indicates that it is not only superior to the clinician, but that it attains a higher discrimination rate

5 GOLDBERG, LEWIS R. "Diagnosticians vs. Diagnostic Signs: The Diagnosis of Psychosis vs. Neurosis From the MMPI." *Psychol Monogr* 79(9):1–28 '65. *
GOLDBERG, LEWIS R. "The Search for Configural Relationships in Personality Assessment: The Diagnosis of Psychosis vs. Neurosis From the MMPI." *Multiv Behav Res* 4(4):523–36 O '69. *

than both the Taulbee-Sisson signs and the Peterson rules. It will be recalled that the RPSI system utilizes the latter two. It was disconcerting to learn from the author's personal correspondence that he has not modified the computer system to include Goldberg's rules. He states, "regarding the actuarial rules, I used the Taulbee-Sisson scale pairs and Peterson's rules; the former to make a psychotic-neurotic discrimination (it seems to be as good as any of the other systems except possibly Goldberg's which wasn't around when I wrote the program)." Considering the fact that Goldberg's rule was published in 1965 and again in 1969, the author's parenthetic remark is puzzling and hopefully not characteristic of RPSI's resistance to change. In any event, by not modifying the RPSI system we can conclude that there is at least one decision situation where the human being excels this computer program.

Another question that could be asked about the usefulness of RPSI's service is how it compares with the systems of its competitors. Such a comparative study, if properly designed to permit each automated service an equal opportunity to display its major strengths, should yield some interesting findings. Perhaps a study of this sort can be conducted by an investigator who is not involved in the commercial aspect of this competitive enterprise. Roche, for its part, judging from my experience with them, will be cooperative and helpful in supplying as much information as necessary to permit the launching of such an investigation. Moreover, RPSI caters to a large portion of the user market and it therefore can contribute a sizable sample to such a study.

At the present time there are two studies purporting to establish the validity and utility of RPSI's computer-produced reports. The more ambitious of these (*14*) is partially reported here. The author enlisted the cooperation of 16 VA stations (including 6 psychiatric hospitals, 6 general medical hospitals with psychiatric wards, 2 psychiatric out-patient clinics, and 2 centers), and collected data from each of these stations. Ten psychiatric patients from each station, who were judged to be representative of that station's patient population and who were well-known to the staff, served as the research sample. MMPIs were administered to these patients by the local staffs, these MMPIs were computer processed by RPSI, and reports were returned to the station. Upon receipt of these reports the interpretation was rated by the professional staff member most familiar with that patient. Of the total population, 158 ratings were returned (99% of the sample). Ninety-six percent of the raters indicated they knew their patients "very well," "well," or "moderately." Some of the findings are as follows: Eighty percent of the reports were rated as "well organized and clear" and 13% of the reports were rated as "not well organized and clear." Seventy-three percent of the reports were rated as "valid overall description of this patient" and 22% did not find these reports valid. Seventy-nine percent of the reports were rated as "accurate" and 17% were rated as not accurate. Moreover, in 84% of the reports patients' behaviors seemed to have been accurately predicted, and mood and feelings were correctly predicted in 83% of the reports. Interpersonal relationships were rated as having been accurately represented in 77% of the cases and predictions of response to therapy were deemed to be correct in 72% of the reports.

As impressive as this study seems to be at first blush, it does not provide convincing validating evidence. The fallacy of personal validation is well documented, and this study is merely a slight variation on the type of study where persons are favorably impressed by personality descriptions of themselves. Perhaps a future study might include "dummy" reports, or a matching procedure where clinicians select from among several reports the "most descriptive" one for a particular patient.

There are a number of other aspects of the RPSI system that deserve comment. As mentioned earlier, this reviewer found the author and RPSI most cooperative in furnishing information about their service and found them to be prompt (24 hours) in processing a set of 10 MMPI answer sheets submitted to them for scoring and interpreting.

The MMPI Kit itself is a convenient package, and the booklet which comes with the Kit, entitled Administering the MMPI, is attractively prepared and informative. This manual highlights the features of the system (simplicity of operation, speed with which MMPI answer sheets are processed, protection offered to the patient by assuring his anonymity, etc.) and interestingly offers to make "funds available for continuing research to increase further the sensitivity and usefulness of the MMPI."

The other impressive aspect of the MMPI

Kit, and a much more ambitious undertaking, is the *MMPI Notebook: A Guide to the Clinical Use of the Automated MMPI,* which was designed to serve as an introduction to both the MMPI and to the clinical use of the automated service. This notebook contains seven chapters including a general orientation to the MMPI as well as a guide to its administration. It has a loose-leaf format which was selected to make it possible to append materials as they become available in the area of interpreting MMPI profiles. To the extent that the *MMPI Notebook* reflects the types and numbers of revisions that the computer programs have undergone, it is somewhat disappointing. For example, although two of the appendices carry 1968 and 1970 copyrights, there is very little in them that is post-1965. Otherwise, however, it is a useful compendium of MMPI lore and wisdom, and it serves as a valuable aide to the understanding of the RPSI system.

In summary, then, it may be concluded that the RPSI offers a worthwhile service. Compared to the average clinician, it is probably a superior interpretive device—or if not superior, certainly an easier one on which to tally a hit and miss percent "boxscore." Potentially it is more flexible than any single clinician since its parameters (i.e., norms, cutoff points) are more easily regulated than those of clinicians. So far no comparisons have been made with other MMPI interpreting services, and there would seem to be no immediate need to conduct such comparative studies. There is a need, however, in the near future to furnish more convincing evidence that the RPSI system generates meaningful and valid test interpretations.

[110]

*Motivation Analysis Test. Ages 17 and over; 1959–70; MAT; 45 scores: 4 motivation scores (integrated, unintegrated, total, conflict) for each of 5 drives (mating, assertiveness, fear, narcism-comfort, pugnacity-sadism) and each of 5 sentiment structures (superego, self-sentiment, career, home-parental, sweetheart-spouse), plus 5 optional scores (total integration, total personal interest, total conflict, autism-optimism, information-intelligence); Form A ('64, 17 pages); manual, second printing ('64, 53 pages, with 1969 supplementation); preliminary manual for individual assessment ('69, 33 pages, with 1970 supplementation); profile ('64, 1 page); reliability data for total motivation scores only; separate answer sheets (Digitek, hand scored) must be used; $16 per 25 tests; $6 per 50 hand scored answer sheets; $5 per 50 Digitek answer sheets; $3.60 per set of hand scoring stencils; $4 per pad of 50 profiles; $2 per preliminary manual for individual assessment; $2.90 per manual; $5 per specimen set; postage extra; Digitek scoring service, $1.90 or less per test; computer interpretation service, $4 or less per subject; (55–65) minutes; Raymond B. Cattell, John L. Horn, and Arthur B. Sweney, with the assistance of John A. Radcliffe; Institute for Personality and Ability Testing. *

REFERENCES

1–6. See P:175.
7. TOLLEFSON, DONALD LLOYD. *Differential Responses to Humor and Their Relation to Personality and Motivation Measures.* Doctor's thesis, University of Illinois (Urbana, Ill.), 1961. (*DA* 22:1712)
8. MAY, MARVIN JEROLD. *The Effects of Electroshock Therapy on Repression and Other Phenomena Related to Personality, Motivation, and Education.* Doctor's thesis, Texas Technological College (Lubbock, Tex.), 1964. (*DA* 26:2322)
9. CARLSON, LESTER ALVIN. *The Relationship of Delinquent Types of an Industrial School Setting to Personality-Motivation Profiles.* Doctor's thesis, Utah State University (Logan, Utah), 1967. (*DA* 29:1446A)
10. HARRIS, GEORGE ALEXANDER. *Interpersonal Sensitivity in the Counselor-Client Relationship.* Doctor's thesis, University of Southern Mississippi (Hattiesburg, Miss.), 1967. (*DA* 28:3462A)
11. DONAHUE, MARY MARANS. *Personality Differences Between Volunteers and Professionals.* Doctor's thesis, St. John's University (Jamaica, N.Y.), 1968. (*DAI* 30:1863A)
12. LAWLIS, GARLAND FRANK. *Motivational Aspects of the Chronically Unemployed.* Doctor's thesis, Texas Technological College (Lubbock, Tex.), 1968. (*DA* 29:3915B)
13. BECHTOLD, DONALD WILLIAM. *Dynamic Structures of Occupational Choice of High School Seniors.* Doctor's thesis, Catholic University of America (Washington, D.C.), 1969. (*DAI* 30:2322A)
14. BEHRING, DANIEL WILLIAM. *Adaptive Functioning: A Rationale for the Prediction of Achievement in Nursing Education.* Doctor's thesis, Ohio University (Athens, Ohio), 1969. (*DAI* 31:1065A)
15. DAVIES, EVAN, AND BINKS, NOEL. "Some Motivational Characteristics of Senior Managers." *Austral Psychologist* 4(2–3):167–70 N '69. * (*PA* 46:3947)
16. DAVIES, EVAN; WYNDHAM, JOHN; AND BINKS, NOEL. "Psychological Changes in Sensitivity Training." *Austral Psychologist* 3(3):171–6 Mr '69. * (*PA* 45:7142)
17. SHONTZ, FRANKLIN C. *Perceptual and Cognitive Aspects of Body Experience,* pp. 190–202. New York: Academic Press Inc., 1969. Pp. xi, 250. *
18. STOCK, MARY JULE SCHRAUFNAGEL. *Separation Anxiety in College Women.* Doctor's thesis, St. Louis University (St. Louis, Mo.), 1969. (*DAI* 30:3879B)
19. VOLKSDORF, NORMAN RICHARD. *The Relationship of Ego-Strength to Ordinal Position and Sex.* Doctor's thesis, Texas Technological University (Lubbock, Tex.), 1969. (*DAI* 31:403B)
20. WILLIAMS, CARL D.; STEELE, MATTHEW W.; AND TEDESCHI, JAMES T. "Motivational Correlates of Strategy Choices in the Prisoner's Dilemma Game." *J Social Psychol* 79(2):211–7 D '69. * (*PA* 44:10332)
21. APOSTAL, ROBERT A., AND MURO, JAMES J. "Effects of Group Counseling on Self-Reports and on Self-Recognition Abilities of Counselors in Training." *Counselor Ed & Sup* 10(1):56–63 f '70. *
22. AXMAKER, LARRY WILLIAM. *The Effect of Group Counseling on the Self-Concept, on the Motivation to Achieve and on the Proportion of Dropouts Among Unselected Community College Students at Southwestern Oregon Community College.* Doctor's thesis, Oregon State University (Corvallis, Ore.), 1970. (*DAI* 30:4214A)
23. LITTLE, NEAL DEAN. *The Rehabilitation Center Dropout: A Demographic and Motivational Assessment.* Doctor's thesis, University of Arkansas (Fayetteville, Ark.), 1970. (*DAI* 31:2687A)
24. MAXON, LLOYD MELVIN. *The Relationship of Certain Mental Factors, Reading Factors, Aptitudes, and Situational Factors to Achievement in Selected Air Force Technical Courses.* Doctor's thesis, North Texas State University (Denton, Tex.), 1970. (*DAI* 31:3437A)

HENRY A. ALKER, *Assistant Professor of Psychology and Sociology, Cornell University, Ithaca, New York.*

This multimethod assessment inventory for five innate sources of reactive energy directed towards a goal ("ergs") and five acquired attitude aggregates ("sentiments") is primarily a research instrument. Cattell's theory of the "dynamic calculus" of motivation receives operationalization herewith. Each dynamic unit variable, be it an erg or sentiment (those measured are listed above), is assessed by two methods in both an "unintegrated" and an "integrated" form. The integrated (realistically expressed) form of a motivational unit is assessed by means of a forced, two choice word association test and an information test. Persons expressing motives can be expected to associate thematically relevant words and to be particularly well informed of particular information relevant to gratifying the sentiment or drive in question. Unintegrated (unexpressed, tension producing) motivational units are assessed by means of a forced choice "ends for means" test in which respondents indicate for which of two goals they would use a given resource and an estimation test presumed to measure autistic distortions in a dynamically gratifying direction.

Validities for these tests are generally only factorial. The experimental arousal of motives is neglected as a validational procedure. On the other hand, some data is available concerning the discriminant validity and incremental prediction utility of the inventory. This data, of course, is obtained within the framework of Cattell's other instruments and constructs. Persons seeking clarification of the relation of Cattell's constructs to Murray's needs, for example, will be disappointed.

A heteromethod heterotrait correlation matrix is neither contained in the manual nor referred to in any supplementary source. Method variance is discussed but mainly from the standpoint of ipsative measurement's capability of avoiding artifactual problems peculiar to normative measurement. Tables allowing a full, rather than a partial, ipsative scoring are promised for future publications. Partialling out confounding variables, such as intelligence (a serious problem on the information test), receives serious discussion. Normative data allowing the partialling out of (crystallized) intelligence is, unfortunately, not yet available. No discussion of social desirability problems (except as a problem plaguing other motive assessment devices) is given in the handbook. Sweney's valuable manual for individual assessment does mention that this problem is present in this inventory. Mention is made of the fact that careless, hurried or thoughtless responding can be detected on this test. It is to be detected, however, by comparing this inventory's estimate of intelligence with that obtained from another intelligence test (that presumably has been more carefully administered).

The median five week test-retest reliability for the 10 variables measured is .50; median alpha is .45. Parallel form reliability correctly regarded as crucial awaits a promised Form B. The authors assert that the "well informed psychometrist should recognize that homogeneity should not be too high in tests of this type." Descriptions of ambiguities in the interpretation of high and low scores provided in the descriptive manual call this claim into question. Possibly the low reliability and heterogeneity of the items account for the absence of convincing validation of the grand discrepancy score contrasting integrated with unintegrated motivation summed over each sentiment and erg. Intriguing sex differences on particular discrepancy scores are presented in the handbook. These findings and interesting speculations made in the descriptive manual concerning discrepancy scores for particular ergs and sentiments invite further serious research attention.

In summary, this inventory has some promise for intriguing future research on motivation. Recommended use in practical decisions must await validity, reliability, base rate and further normative data. Only true believing Platonists still staring at shadows in the cave will be impressed by the fact that all ten factors measured in this inventory have multiple correlations in the .90's between the subtests for each variable and the true factor.

ANDREW L. COMREY, *Professor of Psychology, University of California, Los Angeles, California.*

The MAT is a test designed to measure 10 factor analytically derived motivational traits: Career Sentiment, Home-Parental Sentiment, Fear Erg, Narcism-Comfort Erg, Superego Sentiment, Self-Sentiment, Mating Erg, Pugnacity-Sadism Erg, Assertiveness Erg, and Sweetheart-Spouse Sentiment. The 208 items are divided into four basic types: (*a*) forced choice "Uses" items, asking the respondent how he might prefer to spend his time and resources; (*b*) multiple choice "Estimates" items, asking the respondent to judge the correctness of certain alternatives of a factual kind; (*c*) "Paired Word" items, offering the respondent a word association test with two alternatives from which to choose; and (*d*) multiple choice "Information" items, dealing with a wide range of factual content. Using the same items, various scores other than the 10 trait scores are computed, including one to assess intelligence. A supplementary manual of interpretations is provided in addition to the regular test manual.

SUPPORTIVE DATA. Various types of reliability coefficients are reported for the 10 factor scales, well over half of them below .60. The "validity" coefficients reported are estimated correlations between the 10 factor scales and the factors they represent rather than correlations between the factor scales and external criteria. For evidence of the factor analytic basis for the traits, the reader is referred to published journal articles. No item statistics are given. The manual itself, therefore, does not contain data that would enable the reader to judge for himself whether the traits represent satisfactory factors of motivation and/or whether the scales are measuring what their names would suggest that they are measuring.

One school of test development holds that the apparent content of a test item means nothing, but rather it is what the item predicts that is the sole criterion of whether it is a good item or not. Although normally eschewed by factor analytically oriented test developers such as Cattell, this philosophy could be claimed as a basis for the MAT if adequate item and scale validity data were reported in the manual. In the absence of such information, it is necessary to fall back on an examination of item content, test structure, scoring, and other characteristics, in order to evaluate the test. The comments that follow concern what appear to the reviewer to be technical flaws in the test which have not been offset by convincing evidence that the test really does what it is supposed to do.

SCORING. Scoring the test by hand is rather laborious. More serious, however, is the fact that almost half of the items are scored on two of the trait scales. This practice seems inappropriate since the authors state that these traits are supposed to be relatively independent of one another. Such procedures introduce partial linear dependencies between scale scores.

SELF-SENTIMENT SCALE. Of the 10 scales, the Self-Sentiment scale will be singled out for special attention because it appears to be the most difficult to understand, despite the fact that it has twice as many items as the others. Examination of the items scored on this scale reveals a tremendous variety of content with no easily discernible common thread. The follow-

ing four items were chosen, one from each item type, to illustrate this problem (the number of points given for each response is presented in brackets) : "Marriage counseling should help you toward: (a) Providing for your spouse a home to be proud of [1], (b) Recognizing spiritual as well as physical aspects." "Research on the causes of dueling reports that ?% of the duels fought were over matters of self-regard: (a) 10%, (b) 20% [1], (c) 50% [2], (d) 70% [3]." "KNOW: (a) Self, (b) Facts [1]." "Which of the following is a drug used to limit interest in the opposite sex? (a) Saltpeter [1], (b) Sandlewood [sic] Oil, (c) Mercaptin, (d) Benzoin."

RELATION OF ITEMS TO CONSTRUCTS. Even with the more intuitively meaningful scales, there are still numerous items for which it is difficult to see a connection with the constructs they are supposed to be measuring. Several examples: "Which of the following materials characteristically holds a press, but may shrink when dry cleaned? (a) Wool (b) Nylon (c) Cotton (d) Dacron." If you choose c, you get a point on Assertiveness. "What is the process for freeing a person illegally held in jail? (a) Subpoena (b) Habeas Corpus (c) Tort de defense (d) Injunction." If you choose b, you get a point on Assertiveness. "Which one of the following was famous for the way he (or she) rode a horse? (a) Godiva (b) Paul Revere (c) Joan of Arc (d) Napoleon." If you choose a, you get a point on Narcism-Comfort. "When did the Bataan death march occur? (a) 1944 (b) 1943 (c) 1942 (d) 1941." Choice of c brings a point on the Fear Erg scale. "Which of the following organizations specializes in helping problem drinkers? (a) C.P.A. (b) T.W.A. (c) B.A.A.S. (d) A.A." If you choose d, you get a point on Narcism-Comfort. "Generally, which of the following jobs earns the most money? (a) Professors (b) Attorneys (c) Psychiatrists (d) Surgeons." If you choose d, you get a point on Pugnacity-Sadism. "Which of the following bombs is intended to kill *people* by fire? (a) Incendiary (b) Napalm (c) Pyro-bomb (d) Aerosol." If you choose b, you get a point on Pugnacity-Sadism.

At the basis of many information items seems to be the assumption that if you know something about that subject, it indicates a greater need investment. Thus, if you know about napalm, you must have some aggressive need. It seems to the reviewer, however, that individuals with an abhorrence for aggressive acts might be just as likely to know about napalm. The heavy dependence of the test on information and judgment items also tends to cause intelligent, well-informed people to have spuriously similar motivation profiles.

ITEM SUITABILITY FOR INTENDED USERS. The test is supposed to be appropriate for adults in general, but a number of items seem not to be suitable for some respondents. For example: "An extra hour added to each day could: (a) Allow more time for necessary duties, (b) Permit one more time with a sweetheart." This item does not seem suitable for married people. "If someone left me a lot of money, I might first spend some of it: (a) Helping my parents for their retirement, (b) Giving my sweetheart the finer things he (she) deserves." A respondent with no parents or sweetheart would have difficulty choosing an appropriate response.

SOCIAL DESIRABILITY. Quite a few items have alternatives that would be highly subject to social desirability response bias: "If I joined in a panel discussion, I would like the subject to be: (a) Gangsters in combat, (b) Jobs needing trust and dependability." "Being an army general could give a man: (a) A chance to 'knock hell' out of his country's enemies, (b) A sense of authority."

ITEM CLASSIFICATION. In a number of instances, an item seems to the reviewer to be as appropriate or more appropriate for some other scale than the one on which it is scored. For example, choosing "Home" over "Sex" as the preferred response to the stimulus word "LOVE" produces a point on the Home-Parental Sentiment scale, which seems reasonable, but choosing "Home" over "Virtue" as the preferred response to the stimulus word "IMPORTANT" produces a point on the Career Sentiment scale. A choice of "Lips" over "Cross" as a response to the stimulus word "RED" gives a point on the Mating Erg scale, which seems reasonable, but a response of "Kiss" chosen over "Parents" to the stimulus word "WONDERFUL" gives a point on the Self-Sentiment scale.

SUMMARY. The reviewer would be more favorably impressed with the MAT if the manual presented data which show that: (a) these factors constitute the important unitary dimensions of motivation; (b) the items are suitable measures of the factors on which they are scored; and (c) the trait scales are substantially correlated with external criteria in a way that would be predictable from a knowledge of the scale names.

J Ed Meas 2:245–6 D '65. Gilbert E. Mazer. * The MAT is by no means new in concept since it measures the same motivational structures as its companion the School Motivation Analysis Test. * The section of the manual dealing with technical data [and] the theoretical rationale for the test will present difficult reading for those unfamiliar with Cattell's personality theory and factor analysis. However, the remaining content is otherwise readily understood. The MAT has not fared well with regard to meeting the usual psychometric criteria of an acceptable test. Reliabilities are low and the traits measured seem particularly labile. While this lack of stability should not be overlooked, it may also mean that the test is very sensitive to momentary changes in temperament, as it should be. As an experimental device the MAT offers much promise. The ten scales are empirically derived and appear to have real structural existence. Furthermore the psychological content of most items is not easily discernible, eliminating the chief weakness of many such tests—transparency.

[111]

★**The Multidimensional Maturity Scale.** Grades kgn-12; 1968; MMS; ratings (based upon records, interviews, observations, and tests) in 6 areas: physiological, emotional, psychosexual, mental, educational, social; 1 form (3 pages); manual (8 pages); no data on reliability and validity; no norms; $6.30 per 35 scales; $1.50 per specimen set; postage extra; Barnard J. Hartman; Priority Innovations, Inc. *

[112]

★**Multiple Affect Adjective Check List.** Grades 8-16 and adults; 1960–67; MAACL; an extension of the *Affect Adjective Check List;* 3 scores: anxiety, depression, hostility; 2 formats: hand scoring ('65, 2 pages, Today Form for today's feelings and In General Form for general feelings with same items), IBM 1230 ('65, 1 page); manual ('65, 24 pages); mimeographed addendum ('66, 27 pages); norms-record sheet ('67, 2 pages) for Today's Form; $12.50 per 100 hand scoring test-answer sheets; $1.50 per set of hand scoring stencils; $12.75 per 100 IBM 1230 test-answer sheets; $2 per 25 norms-record sheets; $1.25 per manual; $2.25 per specimen set; postage extra; IBM 1230 scoring service, 45¢ or less per test; (5–10) minutes; Marvin Zuckerman and Bernard Lubin; Educational and Industrial Testing Service. *

REFERENCES

1–28. See P:176, also includes a cumulative name index to the first 28 references for this test.
29. FISCHER, HERBERT LEON. *Personal Versus Impersonal Test Administration as a Function of Various Subject Characteristics.* Doctor's thesis, Purdue University (Lafayette, Ind.), 1963. (*DA* 24:5543)
30. GIDDON, DONALD B. "Individual Differences in Average Affect Adjective Check List (AACL) Scores: Their Relation

to Psychological and Physiological Variables." *Psychol Rep* 14:541–2 Ap '64. * (*PA* 39:1730)

31. KEMP, C. GRATTON. "Self-Perception in Relation to Open-Closed Belief Systems." *J General Psychol* 70:341–4 Ap '64. * (*PA* 39:4812)

32. IRVING, STEPHEN GARY. *Parental Empathy and Adolescent Adjustment.* Doctor's thesis, University of Florida (Gainesville, Fla.), 1965. (*DA* 27:96-B)

33. LUBIN, BERNARD. "A Modified Version of the Self-Disclosure Inventory." *Psychol Rep* 17:498 O '65. * (*PA* 40:895)

34. WEAVER, THOMAS TODD, JR. *Effects of Positive and Negative Personality Evaluations on the Self-Concepts of High School Seniors.* Doctor's thesis, University of Florida (Gainesville, Fla.), 1965. (*DA* 26:1785)

35. BOURNE, PETER G.; COLI, WILLIAM M.; AND DATEL, WILLIAM E. "Anxiety Levels of Six Helicopter Ambulance Medics in a Combat Zone." *Psychol Rep* 19:821–2 D '66. * (*PA* 41:5159)

36. HODGES, W. F., AND SPIELBERGER, C. D. "The Effects of Threat of Shock on Heart Rate for Subjects Who Differ in Manifest Anxiety and Fear of Shock." *Psychophysiol* 2:287–94 Ap '66. * (*PA* 41:5675)

37. JOHNSON, DALE THEODORE. *The Effects of Stress, Relaxation Training, and the Passage of Time on Measures of Trait and State Anxiety.* Doctor's thesis, Vanderbilt University (Nashville, Tenn.), 1966. (*DA* 27:1623B)

38. MITCHELL, JOHN JACOB. *Anxiety as an Underlying Mechanism in Sensory Deprivation and Sensory Bombardment Affecting Performance on Complex Cognitive Tasks.* Doctor's thesis, Catholic University of America (Washington, D.C.), 1966. (*DA* 27:3315B)

39. ROSMARIN, MARTIN SUMNER. *Reaction to Stress and Anxiety in Chronically Underachieving High Ability Students.* Doctor's thesis, University of Florida (Gainesville, Fla.), 1966. (*DA* 27:1630B)

40. ZUCKERMAN, MARVIN, AND HOPKINS, T. ROBERT. "Hallucinations or Dreams? A Study of Arousal Levels and Reported Visual Sensations During Sensory Deprivation." *Percept & Motor Skills* 22:447–59 Ap '66. * (*PA* 40:8364)

41. CHAMBERS, ALMA CLYDE. *Anxiety, Physiologically and Psychologically Measured, and Its Consequences on Mental Test Performance.* Doctor's thesis, University of Southern California (Los Angeles, Calif.), 1967. (*DA* 28:4475A)

42. COLBERT, JOHN, AND HARROW, MARTIN. "Psychomotor Retardation in Depressive Syndromes." *J Nerv & Mental Dis* 145:405–19 N '67. * (*PA* 42:9228)

43. GEER, JAMES H., AND TURTELTAUB, ALAN. "Fear Reduction Following Observation of a Model." *J Pers & Social Psychol* 6:327–31 Jl '67. * (*PA* 41:11846)

44. MARKOWITZ, ARNOLD, AND FORD, LeROY H., JR. "Defensive Denial and Selection of a Target for Projection." *J Exp Res Personality* 2:272–7 D '67. * (*PA* 42:8927)

45. NICHOLS, EDWIN J., AND SPIELBERGER, CHARLES D. "Effects of Medical Education on Anxiety in Students." *Mental Hyg* 51:74–9 Ja '67. *

46. FOLKINS, CARLYLE H.; LAWSON, KAREN D.; OPTON, EDWARD M., JR.; AND LAZARUS, RICHARD S. "Desensitization and the Experimental Reduction of Threat." *J Abn Psychol* 73:100–13 Ap '68. * (*PA* 42:8261)

47. HODGES, WILLIAM F. "Effects of Ego Threat and Threat of Pain on State Anxiety." *J Pers & Social Psychol* 8:364–72 Ap '68. * (*PA* 42:8262)

48. JACOBSON, GARY. "The Briefest Psychiatric Encounter: Acute Effects of Evaluation." *Arch Gen Psychiatry* 18:718–24 Je '68. * (*PA* 42:17386)

49. JOHNSON, DALE T. "Effects of Interview Stress on Measures of State and Trait Anxiety." *J Abn Psychol* 73: 245–51 Je '68. * (*PA* 42:12163)

50. JOHNSON, DALE T. "Trait Anxiety, State Anxiety, and the Estimation of Elapsed Time." *J Consult & Clin Psychol* 32:654–8 D '68. * (*PA* 43:4056)

51. JOHNSON, DALE T., AND SPIELBERGER, CHARLES D. "The Effects of Relaxation Training and the Passage of Time on Measures of State- and Trait-Anxiety." *J Clin Psychol* 24: 20–3 Ja '68. * (*PA* 42:8924)

52. SMOUSE, ALBERT D., AND MUNZ, DAVID C. "The Effects of Anxiety and Item Difficulty Sequence on Achievement Testing Scores." *J Psychol* 68:181–4 Mr '68. * (*PA* 42:9430)

53. ZUCKERMAN, MARVIN. "Field Dependency as a Predictor of Responses to Sensory and Social Isolation." *Percept & Motor Skills* 27:757–8 D '68. * (*PA* 43:7658)

54. ZUCKERMAN, MARVIN, AND LINK, KATHRYN E. "Expectancy and Birth Order as Determinants of Affective Responses to Isolation." *Percept & Motor Skills* 27:279–86 Ag '68. * (*PA* 43:2528)

55. ZUCKERMAN, MARVIN; PERSKY, HAROLD; LINK, KATHRYN E.; AND BASU, GOPAL K. "Responses to Confinement: An Investigation of Sensory Deprivation, Social Isolation, Restriction of Movement and Set Factors." *Percept & Motor Skills* 27:319–34 Ag '68. * (*PA* 43:2529)

56. BIASE, D. VINCENT, AND DeLEON, GEORGE. "The Encounter Group—Measurement of Some Affect Changes." Abstract. *Proc 77th Ann Conv Am Psychol Assn* 4(2):497–8 '69. * (*PA* 44:784)

57. BIASE, D. VINCENT, AND MITCHELL, JOHN. "Anticipated Responses to Short-Term Sensory Deprivation." *Psychol Rep* 24(2):351–4 Ap '69. * (*PA* 43:15130)

58. BLANEY, JAMES G. *The Relation Between Environmental Stress, Psychoendocrine Responses, and Competitive Gymnastic Performance.* Master's thesis, Wisconsin State University (La Crosse, Wis.), 1969.

59. BLUMBERG, RICHARD W. *Client Dogmatism, Therapist Leadership and the Psychotherapeutic Relationship.* Doctor's thesis, University of Florida (Gainesville, Fla.), 1969. (*DAI* 31:389B)

60. BRINGMANN, WOLFGANG G.; BALANCE, WILLIAM D. G.; AND KRICHEV, ALAN. "Experimental Investigation of McLuhan's Ideas Concerning Effects of 'Hot' and 'Cool' Communications Media." *Psychol Rep* 25(2):447–51 O '69. * (*PA* 44:5113)

61. CRIGHTON, J., AND JEHU, D. "Treatment of Examination Anxiety by Systematic Desensitization or Psychotherapy in Groups." *Behav Res & Ther* 7(3):245–8 S '69. * (*PA* 44:16783)

62. DATEL, WILLIAM E., AND LIFRAK, STEPHEN T. "Expectations, Affect Change, and Military Performance in the Army Recruit." *Psychol Rep* 24(3):855–79 Je '69. * (*PA* 44:1412)

63. FISCHER, DONALD G.; KELM, HAROLD; AND ROSE, ANN. "Knives as Aggression-Eliciting Stimuli." *Psychol Rep* 24(3): 755–60 Je '69. * (*PA* 44:649)

64. FRANCIS, BARRY SHERWOOD. *The Psychological Measurement of Affect: A Comparison of Two Measurement Models.* Doctor's thesis, University of Arizona (Tucson, Ariz.), 1969. (*DAI* 30:4370B)

65. HANDAL, PAUL J. "The Relationship Between Subjective Life Expectancy, Death Anxiety and General Anxiety." *J Clin Psychol* 25(1):39–42 Ja '69. * (*PA* 43:9705)

66. HERRON, E. WAYNE. "The Multiple Affect Adjective Check List: A Critical Analysis." *J Clin Psychol* 25(1):46–53 Ja '69. * (*PA* 43:9762)

67. HODGES, WILLIAM F., AND SPIELBERGER, CHARLES D. "Digit Span: An Indicant of Trait or State Anxiety?" *J Consult & Clin Psychol* 33(4):430–4 Ag '69. * (*PA* 43: 15857)

68. LISH, JOAN ADLER. *The Influence of Oral Dependency, Failure, and Social Exposure Upon Self-Esteem and Depression.* Doctor's thesis, New York University (New York, N.Y.), 1969. (*DAI* 30:5692B)

69. LUBIN, BERNARD, AND ZUCKERMAN, MARVIN. "Level of Emotional Arousal in Laboratory Training." *J Appl Behav Sci* 5(4):483–90 O–D '69. * (*PA* 44:11467)

70. PLUTCHIK, R.; PLATMAN, S. R.; AND FIEVE, R. R. "Evaluation of Manic-Depressive States With an Affect Adjective Checklist." Abstract. *Proc 77th Ann Conv Am Psychol Assn* 4(2):521–2 '69. * (*PA* 44:925)

71. ZUCKERMAN, MARVIN. "Response Set in a Check List Test: A Sometimes Thing." *Psychol Rep* 25(3):773–4 D '69. * (*PA* 44:18737)

72. ZUCKERMAN, MARVIN; PERSKY, HAROLD; MILLER, LYNNE; AND LEVINE, BERNARD. "Contrasting Effects of Understimulation (Sensory Deprivation) and Overstimulation (High Stimulus Variety)." Abstract. *Proc 77th Ann Conv Am Psychol Assn* 4(1):319–20 '69. * (*PA* 44:16751)

73. BATES, HENRY D. "Locus of Control, Covert Hostility and Non-Assertive Behavior." *Newsl Res Psychol* 12(1):15–6 F '70. *

74. BATES, HENRY D. "Prediction of Self-Descriptions and Overt Behavior From a Scale of Assertiveness." *Newsl Res Psychol* 12(1):13–4 F '70. *

75. BATES, HENRY D. "Social Desirability Response Set and the Endorsement of Affect Adjectives." *Newsl Res Psychol* 12(1):2–3 F '70. *

76. BROWN, WALTER A., AND MUELLER, PETER S. "Psychological Function in Individuals With Amyotrophic Lateral Sclerosis (ALS)." *Psychosom Med* 32(2):141–52 Mr–Ap '70. * (*PA* 44:17117)

77. COHEN, ROBERTA. "The Effect of Specific Emotional Support on Anxiety Levels Prior to Electroconvulsive Therapy." *Nursing Res* 19(2):163–4 Mr–Ap '70. *

78. CROSS, HERBERT J., AND ALLEN, JON G. "Ego Identity Status, Adjustment, and Academic Achievement." Abstract. *J Consult & Clin Psychol* 34(2):288 Ap '70. * (*PA* 44:11185)

79. FREMONT, THEODORE; MEANS, GLADYS H.; AND MEANS, ROBERT S. "Anxiety as a Function of Task Performance Feedback and Extraversion-Introversion." *Psychol Rep* 27(2): 455–8 O '70. * (*PA* 45:6312)

80. JOHNSON, DALE T. "Response Set and an Adjective Check List: A Second Look." *J Clin Psychol* 26(1):88–90 Ja '70. * (*PA* 44:10488)

81. KAISER, CHARLES, AND ROESSLER, ROBERT. "Galvanic Skin Responses to Motion Pictures." *Percept & Motor Skills* 30(2):371–4 Ap '70. * (*PA* 46:6352)

82. PIPER, WILLIAM E., AND WOGAN, MICHAEL. "Placebo Effect in Psychotherapy: An Extension of Earlier Findings." Abstract. *J Consult & Clin Psychol* 34(3):447 Je '70. * (*PA* 44:14735)

83. PLATMAN, S. R., AND WEINSTEIN, BETTE. "The Diagnosis Game." *Dis Nerv System* 31(8):561–6 Ag '70. * (*PA* 45:4547)

84. ROESSLER, ROBERT, AND COLLINS, FOREST. "Personality Correlates of Physiological Responses to Motion Pictures." *Psychophysiol* 6(6):732–9 My '70. * (*PA* 45:5862)

85. STERN, RONALD. *The Effect of Anxiety on Verbal Learning as the Function of Total Time.* Master's thesis, Springfield College (Springfield, Mass.), 1970.

86. UNGER, BETTY LUE. *The Repression-Sensitization Scale as a Measure of Repression.* Doctor's thesis, Washington University (St. Louis, Mo.), 1970. (*DAI* 31:4348B)

87. ZUCKERMAN, MARVIN, AND LUBIN, BERNARD. *Bibliography for the Multiple Affect Adjective Check List.* San Diego, Calif.: Educational and Industrial Testing Service, 1970. Pp. 8. *

88. ZUCKERMAN, MARVIN; PERSKY, HAROLD; MILLER, LYNNE; AND LEVINE, BERNARD. "Sensory Deprivation Versus Sensory Variation." *J Abn Psychol* 76(1):76–82 Ag '70. * (*PA* 44:19926)

E. LOWELL KELLY, *Professor of Psychology, The University of Michigan, Ann Arbor, Michigan.*

The MAACL contains 132 adjectives, alphabetically arranged in three columns on one side of a single sheet. The other side of the sheet contains spaces for the subject's name, age, sex, highest grade completed and date. There are two forms of the checklist, printed in slightly different colors: the "In General" form and the "Today" form. These two forms differ only in the instructions to the subject: mark an *x* beside the words which describe "how *you generally feel*" or "how *you feel now—today*."

According to the authors, the MAACL "was designed to fill the need for a self-administered test which would provide valid measures of three of the clinically relevant negative affects: anxiety, depression, and hostility." Affect is "defined as the psychological aspects of emotion, or the emotional response which is assessed by means of verbal reports." From the instructions given to subjects, it is obvious that affect is also defined as "subjective feelings."

The General and Today forms of the test were devised to provide for the assessment of these three affects both as relatively stable traits and as states subject to change from day to day as a function of drugs, stress, or other external conditions. Just as a fever thermometer permits monitoring variations of a patient's body temperature, the Today form of the MAACL was designed to assess changes in the amount of these negative affects verbalizable by subjects from day to day.

The MAACL is an extension of the *Affect Adjective Check List* originally described by the senior author in 1960 (*1*). The AACL consisted of 61 adjectives; 21 of these were used to assess anxiety, the other 40 were buffer items. In 1965, 40 additional items were added to assess Depression: 20 plus (e.g., blue, sad, and unhappy) and 20 minus (e.g., fine, gay, and merry). At the same time, 28 items were added to assess Hostility: 16 plus (e.g., angry, disagreeable, and mad) and 12 minus (e.g., agreeable, kindly, and tender). Thus the MAACL includes 132 adjectives, 43 of which are not scored on any of the three scales.

Odd-even and plus-minus reliabilities for both the General and Today forms range from .17 to .92 (median .72) for different groups of subjects. Retest reliabilities (7–8 days) tend to be moderate (.54 to .70) for the General form and relatively low (.00 to .40) for the Today form. There is, however, one important exception to this general pattern of reliability coefficients; for psychiatric patients, retest reliabilities (one week) for all scales of the Today form are higher than the internal consistency estimates (.77, .79, and .84 compared to .73, .65, and .24); this suggests that patients (*a*) do not fluctuate as much from day to day or (*b*) are less able than normals to differentiate between the instructional sets of the two forms. Anxiety scores on the General and Today forms were found to correlate .43 for a college sample and .52 for a psychiatric sample.

In spite of the fact that no item is scored on more than one scale, the intercorrelations among the three scales with different names are very high—in fact, as high as their reliabilities.

Like all self-report instruments, the MAACL is subject to response sets. Siller and Chipman (*3*) report correlations of .05 to .48 between MAACL anxiety scores (General form) and various measures of acquiescence and *r*'s of −.33 and −.67 between the same anxiety score and Edwards Social Desirability. Anxiety scores (General form) tend to correlate significantly with MMPI F and K scales (.37 and .50, respectively) and all 3 of the Today scales show small negative *r*'s with the K scale. Apparently, subjects are more willing to admit socially undesirable feelings as a transient state than as a stable characteristic.

A potentially more serious type of response set is that associated with the actual number of adjectives checked. While instructions are to *"check all the words* that *describe* your feelings," subjects vary greatly in number of words actually checked. Herron (*66*) first called attention to this source of unwanted variance in checklist scores. Apparently, the correlation between number of items checked and affect scores is sometimes positive, sometimes negative and sometimes near zero. Furthermore, it may differ depending on whether the General or Today form of the MAACL is used. Even more disturbing are the findings reported by Zuckerman (*71*) showing marked regional differences in these correlations for large samples of college students. For example, the correlation between number of items checked and Anxiety scores ranged from +.04 to −.42, −.08 to −.72 with Depression scores and from +.07 to −.74 with Hostility scores. Such findings suggest the possible desirability of instructing subjects to check some specific number (e.g., 60) of words—those most descriptive of their feelings. In the absence of any correction for this particular kind of response set, Zuckerman recommends that users "examine the response set influence in their own data and.... remove it, if necessary, with covariance or partial correlation techniques."

A fair amount of normative data is presented in the manual and its mimeographed addendum; the score distributions vary considerably from one type of subject to another and according to whether the General or Today form was used. For this and other reasons, the authors wisely recommend using the inventory primarily as a research tool rather than for routine diagnostic applications.

As a research tool, the MAACL has been employed by dozens of investigators concerned with evaluating the effects of such varied stresses as sensory deprivation, examinations, frustration, failure, basic military training, confinement, and the threat of pain. It has also been used to evaluate the effectiveness of several possible agents or methods of stress reduction, e.g., alcohol, drugs, and different types of therapy. In spite of the very high interscale correlations noted above, the three scales of the MAACL appear to have sufficient differential validity to reflect meaningful changes in affect for *groups* of S's subjected to different types of stresses and stress-reducing manipulations. For example, among nurses in training, anxiety scores increase most on examination days or when threatened with an unannounced exam; among a group of soldiers in basic training, hostility scores increased most during days of KP duty and all affect scores dropped on weekends. Hypnotic induction of any of the three affects is reported to increase scores on all three scales, but the increase is consistently greatest on the relevant scale.

In summary, the MAACL, like other adjective checklists, is a relatively crude psychometric instrument. Reliabilities of the scores are generally high but the scores are clearly susceptible to response sets. The unique characteristic of the MAACL is that the Today form permits assessing transient levels of negative affect, at least for normal subjects. The three affect scores are very highly intercorrelated; whether this results from a lack of discriminant validity of the instrument or reflects the true intercorrelations among anxiety, depression, and hostility is not known. Whether the scores on this relatively brief checklist are more useful for research than are subjects' ratings of their feelings is an unanswered empirical question.

EDWIN I. MEGARGEE, *Professor of Psychology, Florida State University, Tallahassee, Florida.*

The *Multiple Affect Adjective Check List* was devised to provide brief state and trait measures of three negative affects: anxiety, depression, and hostility. The scores obtained when S's check how they *generally* feel are used as a trait measure; when S's are told to respond in terms of how they feel *today,* the results are regarded as a state measure. Some researchers maintain that a better state measure can be obtained if S's are told to respond as they feel *at this moment* rather than as they feel today.

DEVELOPMENT. The Anxiety and Depression scales were empirically derived by contrasting criterion samples of anxious and depressed psychiatric patients with normals. The operational definitions for these two scales would appear to involve traits more than states. The Hostility scale was derived by selecting those adjectives endorsed significantly more often by 10 women placed in a hypnotically induced state of hostility than by women not in a hostile state. This procedure would appear more likely to yield a state than a trait measure. No adjectives are included that require more than 8th grade reading ability and no item is included on more than one scale.

NORMS. Norms are available on various samples of normals and neuropsychiatric patients. The sample sizes tend to be small, typically ranging from about 20 to 50 S's and rarely involving more than 100 S's. The research emphasis has clearly been on establishing the construct validity of the instrument rather than on obtaining a broad stratified standardization sample.

RELIABILITY. The split-half reliability of both forms of the three MAACL scales is high when the items are divided by the traditional odd-even method. Studies using other, less appropriate splits, such as correlating the "plus" and "minus" scores, have yielded poorer results.

Unfortunately, there has not been sufficient research on the stability of the General form. Although a trait measure should show high test-retest reliability, the manual reports a retest reliability coefficient of only .68 for the Anxiety scale after a seven-day interval and contains no data on the other two scales. The addendum to the manual reports coefficients of .70, .65, and .54 for the Anxiety, Depression, and Hostility scales, respectively, but fails to specify the time interval.

Much more attention has been devoted to the temporal stability of the Today form, which is supposed to show day-to-day fluctuations and therefore have low test-retest coefficients. As expected, low coefficients of stability are typically found in normals but not in psychiatric patients.

VALIDITY. A number of good studies have been performed to test the validity of the MAACL, many of which are reviewed in the manual and the addendum. This review of the validational literature is the most comprehensive and nearly objective presentation of both negative and positive findings that this reviewer has encountered in a test manual; the authors' scholarship is to be commended.

In any measure that purports to assess both states and traits, a fundamental question is whether the state scores change over time and whether the nature of these changes is consistent with clinical expectations or observations. Much of the validity research on the MAACL has consisted of administering the Today form under conditions likely to elicit the relevant affective states and comparing the scores with those obtained under normal conditions. Investigators have tested students before and after examinations, military personnel during basic training, and actors before they go on stage. Hypnotically induced mood states, sensitivity training, stress interviews, tranquilizing medication, and induced relaxation have been used to alter mood states and the concomitant changes in the MAACL scores have been noted. By and large, the results of these studies have been positive. Stress typically raises the scores on the Anxiety scale signifi-cantly. The results with the Depression scale have been less satisfactory. Less work has been done on the Hostility scale than on the other two, but studies showing that hostility scores increase following frustration are consistent with the notion that state hostility (anger) is being assessed. Unfortunately, many of these studies suffer from a lack of control groups or from failure to give the General as well as the Today form of the test so that differences between state and trait scores could be observed.

Another approach to validity is to administer the instrument in conjunction with other measures of these affects and determine if they correlate as expected. Studies have been performed to relate the MAACL scales to clinical observations, to other psychological tests, and to autonomic measures. The results of these investigations indicate that the Anxiety and Depression scales do correlate, by and large, with clinical ratings of these dimensions but that the convergent validity of the Hostility scale is less adequate. A similar pattern can be observed in the correlations between the three scales and other personality test measures. As might be expected, the MAACL scales correlate better with other paper-and-pencil measures than they do with projective tests. The relationships to autonomic measures are inconsistent and unreliable. As is often the case, the picture is confused by the fact that a variety of autonomic measures and investigative procedures have been employed.

The manual reports correlations ranging from $-.33$ to $-.67$ between Anxiety and Edwards' SD scale and r's from .05 to .48 with measures of Acquiescence response set. No data are presented on the relation of the Depression and Hostility scales to these response sets. More alarming than these modest correlations is Herron's (66) recent report that a set to respond with many or few adjectives contributes a significant proportion of the variance on the MAACL.

SUMMARY. The data suggest that the MAACL Anxiety scale provides a brief, reasonably valid self-report state-trait measure of a negative affective condition. The Depression scale provides a somewhat less valid measure of this affect. The best name for this affective condition is probably "anxiety." The Hostility scale, which was derived from much smaller criterion groups, has had less research performed on it. The research that has been performed suggests that researchers should be cautious about relying on it as a state-trait measure of hostility or anger.

[113]

★The New Junior Maudsley Inventory. Ages 9–16; 1961–67; NJMI; 3 scores: neuroticism, extraversion, lie; 2 editions; (10–15) minutes; W. D. Furneaux and H. B. Gibson. *

a) [BRITISH EDITION.] 1961–66; items are identical to those in the *Junior Maudsley Inventory* ('61, JMI) except for sequence and the addition of items for the lie scale; norms for neuroticism and extraversion were derived from the JMI; 1 form ('66, 4 pages); manual ('66, 16 pages); 37½p per 20 tests; 62½p per set of keys; 25p per manual; 90p per specimen set; postage extra; University of London Press Ltd.

b) [AMERICAN EDITION.] 1966–67; for research use only; 1 form ('67, 4 pages, items identical with British edition except for 2 wording changes); manual ('66, 16 pages, identical with British edition except for imprint and introductory paragraph); all statistical data and norms based on British populations; $4 per 25 tests; $1.50 per set of scoring stencils; $2.25 per specimen set; postage extra; Educational and Industrial Testing Service.

REFERENCES

1–17. See P:179.
18. YATES, AUBREY J. "Level, Speed and Personality Factors in the Intellectual Performance of Young Children." *Brit J Ed Psychol* 36:312–6 N '66. * (*PA* 41:463)
19. LYTTON, H. "Some Psychological and Sociological Characteristics of 'Good' and 'Poor Achievers' (Boys) in Remedial Reading Groups." *Hum Develop* 11(4):260–76 '68. *
20. GIBSON, H. B. "The Gibson Spiral Maze Test: Retest Data in Relation to Behavioral Disturbance, Personality and Physical Measures." *Brit J Psychol* 60(4):523–8 N '69. * (*PA* 44:4948)
21. GIBSON, H. B. "The Significance of 'Lie Responses' in the Prediction of Early Delinquency." *Brit J Ed Psychol* 39(3):284–90 N '69. * (*PA* 44:8818)
22. McALLISTER, J., AND MARSHALL, T. F. "The New Junior Maudsley Inventory: Norms for Secondary Schoolchildren, Aged 11 to 14 Years." *Brit J Social & Clin Psychol* 8(2):160–3 Je '69. * (*PA* 43:15602)
23. MARTIN, D. N., AND CLARKE, R. V. G. "The Personality of Approved School Boy Absconders." *Brit J Criminol* 9(4):366–75 O '69. * (*PA* 44:8825)
24. HARBISON, J. J. M. "The Relationship Between Two Children's Measures of Personality." *Brit J Social & Clin Psychol* 9(2):187–8 Je '70. * (*PA* 44:16712)
25. HOGHUGHI, M. S., AND FORREST, A. R. "Eysenck's Theory of Criminality: An Examination With Approved School Boys." *Brit J Criminol* 10(3):240–54 Jl '70. * (*PA* 46:1465)
26. MEHRYAR, A. H., AND SHAPURIAN, R. "Some Normative Data on a Persian Form of the New Junior Maudsley Inventory." *Psychol Rep* 26(3):743–6 Je '70. * (*PA* 45:716)

PHILIP E. VERNON, *Professor of Educational Psychology, The University of Calgary, Calgary, Alberta, Canada.*

Eysenck's inclination for reducing personality differences as far as possible to two major dimensions, Neuroticism-Stability and Extraversion-Introversion, is well known. He is backed up by Cattell's discovery of two obviously similar second order factors underlying his 16 PF and HSPQ. While many American inventories nowadays are multidimensional, there is much to be said for a relatively short test which yields sufficiently reliable measures of only two major traits in a brief time. These do not, of course, correlate perfectly with other

instruments; in fact, a coefficient of only .47 was obtained between the JMPI N scale and Sarason's General Anxiety Scale. But this is not an atypical figure for personality tests aimed at the same trait; thus, the correlations between Eysenck's own adult and junior tests in a 14–15 year group reached only .51 to .60. On the other hand, Eysenck has managed to maintain low correlations between scales aimed at different traits. Correlations between Neuroticism and Extraversion in the NJMI are quoted as ranging from −.07 to −.21.

The original JMI was developed largely from Pintner's *Aspects of Personality*. The new inventory differs only in the addition of a Lie scale to the Neuroticism and Extraversion scales, and in some slight changes of item order. The test now contains 18, 22, and 22 items for these three scales, mixed together, and 2 sample items—a total of 64. The response to every item must be "same" or "different"; omissions are not allowed, and this should be checked by the tester before he accepts answer sheets. It is recommended that testing be done in groups by a psychologist or other trained person, but younger disturbed children can be tested individually, even orally. No precise information is available on the effects of this alteration.

The printing of test and instructions is clear, but the manual is unattractive and could be more lucidly organized. Card stencils are provided for scoring the three scales. Although some 6,000 British children have been tested, the bases of the various norms are rather obscure; indeed the Lie scale seems to have been normed on only 90 boys and 71 girls. Obviously none of these norms should be regarded as applicable in the United States without further standardization. The short-term retest reliability for the E scale is around .90 but is lower for the N scale, and the split-half figures are less satisfactory, dropping to .65 for the Lie scale. Since the standard deviations of the scales average about 3.5, the range and discriminating power of the scores are rather low. Thus in the middle of the range, 1 point of raw score corresponds to approximately 10 percentile points.

No further comment on the E and N scales is required, since the items are so similar to those found in other personality inventories. The usefulness of the Lie scale is not made very clear. At some points the manual seems to suggest that it is measuring another trait, namely the desire to make a good, or bad, impression. It correlates −.28 with N in boys, −.54 in girls, and negligibly with E. No reason for this sex difference is offered. Elsewhere, though, a high L score is taken to imply that N or E results should be accepted with reserve. It is also stated, though without evidence, that the L scores are "particularly susceptible to situational effects."

The reviewer is probably prejudiced against personality inventories, especially with children. However, the Eysenck scales for adults have proved themselves remarkably useful in a wide variety of contexts, and it is not unreasonable to hope that the Junior scales will show similar construct validity. The test is probably as good as most others that are being used to measure maladjustment or anxiety and extraversion. It looks less disturbing than many, and less liable to arouse teacher or parent resentment; and it is mercifully shorter.

ROBERT D. WIRT, *Professor of Psychology, Child Development and Psychiatry and Director, Graduate Education in Clinical Psychology, University of Minnesota, Minneapolis, Minnesota.*

The manual gives useful instructions, in simple language, for test administrators who may be relatively unqualified in psychology. The concept of traits as continua rather than types is well presented. Thus the authors prefer the concept of degrees of extroversion to the notion that people can be sorted into intraverts and extroverts. The idea of independent factors is also well explained.

The interpretation of the L scale is less satisfactorily explained than that for N and E because the relation of L to age is unknown, although there is some suggestion that L scale scores may decrease with age in boys and girls. Several studies of L show scores to be sensitive to the setting in which the children are tested. It cannot be determined from the test results whether low scores on L indicate boasting of naughty behavior, or high scores indicate defensiveness, or if either high or low scores may be related to a child's actual behavior or to an inaccurate perception of himself.

It is important that users of the NJMI be thoroughly familiar with the concepts of the N and E factors as developed by Eysenck and his colleagues. Jung would not have described a

highly extroverted person as unreliable, nor did Freud think people with little neuroticism to be phlegmatic.

There are slight differences in the test format between the British and American versions of the test. The American form will be more convenient for American users because of the standard size of the test form. The British form uses underlining on such words as *never* and *always* in L items while the American form does not. There are a few necessary spelling and word changes, as well, such as *colour-color* and *shopkeeper-grocer.*

The publisher warns that the data on which the test was constructed were obtained from English children and that American norms have not been developed.

Overall, the NJMI should prove to be a useful downward extension of Eysenck's method. Further normative studies are needed on a variety of populations before it can be said to be a useful clinical instrument in the United States; however, the British studies indicate such research would be worthwhile. The research completed thus far with the *Junior Eysenck Personality Inventory* is more extensive and more carefully designed. For these reasons, the JEPI is to be preferred for use over the NJMI.

[114]

★Nurses' Observation Scale for Inpatient Evaluation. Mental patients; 1965–66; NOSIE; manual title is *NOSIE-30: A Treatment-Sensitive Ward Behavior Scale;* 30 items yield 7 scores: social competence, social interest, personal neatness, irritability, manifest psychosis, retardation, total; 1 form ('66, 1 page); manual ('66, 13 pages); profile ('66, 1 page); no data on reliability of scores; norms based on adult male schizophrenics; 5¢ per test; 5¢ per profile; 5¢ per scoring key; postpaid; manual free on request; [3–5] minutes; Gilbert Honigfeld, Roderic D. Gillis, and C. James Klett (manual); Behavior Arts Center. *

REFERENCES

1. HONIGFELD, GILBERT, AND KLETT, C. JAMES. "The Nurses' Observation Scale for Inpatient Evaluation (NOSIE): A New Scale for Measuring Improvement in Chronic Schizophrenia." *Newsl Res Psychol* 6:22–3 My '64. *
2. HONIGFELD, GILBERT, AND KLETT, C. JAMES. "The Nurses' Observation Scale for Inpatient Evaluation: A New Scale for Measuring Improvement in Chronic Schizophrenia." *J Clin Psychol* 21:65–71 Ja '65. * (PA 39:12262)
3. HONIGFELD, GILBERT H.; ROSENBLUM, MARCUS P.; BLUMENTHAL, IRVING J.; LAMBERT, HENRY L.; AND ROBERTS, ARTHUR J. "Behavioral Improvement in the Older Schizophrenic Patient: Drug and Social Therapies." *J Am Geriatrics Soc* 13:57–72 Ja '65. *
4. KEITH-LEE, PATRICIA, AND SPIEGEL, DONALD E. "An Experimental Short Form of the Nurses' Observation Scale for Inpatient Evaluation." *Newsl Res Psychol* 7:43–5 N '65. *
5. HONIGFELD, GILBERT; GILLIS, RODERIC D.; AND KLETT, C. JAMES. "NOSIE-30: A Treatment-Sensitive Ward Behavior Scale." *Psychol Rep* 19:180–2 Ag '66. * (PA 40:12422)
6. SPIEGEL, DONALD E.; KEITH-SPIEGEL, PATRICIA; AND GRAYSON, HARRY M. "The Typical Mental Patient as Perceived by Hospital Personnel Groups." *Newsl Res Psychol* 8:54–7 N '66 .*

7. HONIGFELD, GILBERT, AND GILLIS, RODERIC. "The Role of Institutionalization in the Natural History of Schizophrenia." *Dis Nerv System* 28:660–3 O '67. * (*PA* 42:957)

8. MILLER, ANTHONY GEORGE. *Nocturnal Body Motility Among Hospitalized Mental Patients.* Doctor's thesis, Washington State University (Pullman, Wash.), 1967. (*DA* 28:3498B)

9. SPIEGEL, DONALD E.; KEITH-SPIEGEL, PATRICIA; AND GRAYSON, HARRY M. "Behavior of the Typical Mental Patient as Seen by Eight Groups of Hospital Personnel." *J Psychiatric Res* 5:317–25 D '67. * (*PA* 42:12180)

10. STIER, SERENA AUSTER. *Developmental Attainment, Outcome and Symbolic Performance in Schizophrenia.* Doctor's thesis, University of California (Los Angeles, Calif.), 1967. (*DA* 28:4766B)

11. FABREGA, HORACIO, JR.; SWARTZ, JON D.; AND WALLACE, CAROLE ANN. "Ethnic Differences in Psychopathology: 1, Clinical Correlates Under Varying Conditions." *Arch Gen Psychiatry* 19:218–26 Ag '68. * (*PA* 43:4230)

12. FABREGA, HORACIO, JR.; SWARTZ, JON D.; AND WALLACE, CAROLE ANN. "Ethnic Differences in Psychopathology: 2, Specific Differences With Emphasis on a Mexican American Group." *J Psychiatric Res* 6:221–35 D '68. * (*PA* 44:5399)

13. FRANCIS, RAYMOND WALTER. *A Study of the Relationships Among Acceptance of Psychological Disability, Self Concept and Body Image.* Doctor's thesis, State University of New York (Buffalo, N.Y.), 1968. (*DA* 29:770B)

14. KISH, GEORGE B. "Ward Behavior Ratings of Chronic Schizophrenics Who Differ in Level of Sensation-Seeking." *Newsl Res Psychol* 10:22–3 Ag '68. *

15. PRIEN, ROBERT F., AND COLE, JONATHAN O. "High Dose Chlorpromazine Therapy in Chronic Schizophrenia: Report of National Institute of Mental Health—Psychopharmacology Research Branch Collaborative Study Group." *Arch Gen Psychiatry* 18:482–95 Ap '68. * (*PA* 42:12292)

16. SIMPSON, GEORGE M.; ANGUS, J. W. S.; SUGERMAN, A. ARTHUR; AND STOLBERG, HUBERT. "Two Pilot Studies of BC-347 in Chronic Schizophrenic Patients." *J Clin Pharmacol & J New Drugs* 8:196–9 My–Je '68. * (*PA* 42:12297)

17. WENDT, MIRIAM JANE. *The Conditioning of Defensive Verbal Constructs in Schizophrenic Patients.* Doctor's thesis, Case Western Reserve University (Cleveland, Ohio), 1968. (*DA* 29:4857B)

18. FREEMAN, HARRY, AND FREDERICK, AMBELLUR N. D. "Comparison of Trifluoperazine and Molindone in Chronic Schizophrenic Patients." *Curr Ther Res* 11:670–6 N '69. *

19. KOLLAR, EDWARD J.; PASNAU, ROBERT O.; RUBIN, ROBERT T.; NAITOH, PAUL; SLATER, GRANT G.; AND KALES, ANTHONY. "Psychological, Psychophysiological, and Biochemical Correlates of Prolonged Sleep Deprivation." *Am J Psychiatry* 126(4):488–97 O '69. * (*PA* 44:9960)

20. RAVENSBORG, MILTON R. "Effects of Ward Change on Patient Behavior." *J Clin Psychol* 25(3):325–6 Jl '69. * (*PA* 44:3791)

21. RAVENSBORG, MILTON R., AND WILLENSON, DAVID. "Use of the NOSIE-30 Behavioral Rating Scale in Hospitals for the Mentally Ill and Retarded." *J Clin Psychol* 25(4):453–4 O '69. * (*PA* 44:10733)

22. KISH, GEORGE B. "Reduced Cognitive Innovation and Stimulus-Seeking in Chronic Schizophrenia." *J Clin Psychol* 26(2):170–4 Ap '70. * (*PA* 44:14866)

23. STERLIN, C.; BAN, T. A.; LEHMANN, H. E.; AND SAXENA, B. M. "Psychometric and Psychophysiological Test in the Prediction of Therapeutic Responsiveness in the Schizophrenias." *Int J Psychobiology* 1(1):85–91 F '70. *

24. WATSON, CHARLES G.; KLETT, WILLIAM G.; AND LOREI, THEODORE W. "Toward an Operational Definition of Anhedonia." *Psychol Rep* 26(2):371–6 Ap '70. * (*PA* 44:21292)

[115]

*Objective-Analytic (O-A) Anxiety Battery. Ages 14 and over; 1955–67; OAAB; revision of anxiety-to-achieve battery (U.I. 24) of *Objective-Analytic Personality Test Batteries* (see 5:90); individual in part (tests 246-I and 2410-I); 1 form ('60); 10 tests from which user may select those appropriate to his needs: 241-G (susceptibility to annoyance, 4 pages), 242-G (honesty in admitting common frailties, 2 pages), 243-G (modesty in assuming skill in untried performance, 7 pages), 244-G (critical severity vs. indulgent standards, 3 pages), 245-G (number of friends recalled, 2 pages), 246-I (increase or recovery of pulse rate), 247-G (emotionality of comment, 4 pages), 248-G (acceptance of good aphorisms, 1 page), 249-G (susceptibility to embarrassment, 5 pages), 2410-I (systolic blood pressure); manual ('60, 15 pages); second norm supplement ('67, 4 pages); no data on reliability of 246-I and 2410-I; no norms for 246-I and 2410-I; prices per 25 tests: $4 for 241-G

and 247-G, $2.40 for 242-G and 245-G, $5.60 for 243-G, $3.30 for 244-G, $1.25 for 248-G, $4.60 for 249-G; separate answer sheets may be used (except for 243-G, 245-G, 246-I, 2410-I); $3.50 per pad of 50 answer sheets; $2.70 per set of scoring stencils; $1.50 per manual; $8 per specimen set; postage extra; additional apparatus necessary for tests 246-I and 2410-I; (25–50) minutes for the complete battery; Raymond B. Cattell and Ivan H. Scheier; Institute for Personality and Ability Testing. *

REFERENCES

1–5. See 6:149.
6–11. See P:182.
12. RILEY, GLYNDON DAUGHTRY. *An Analysis of the Differences Between the Levels of Anxiety and Comention of Hyperconfident, Hypoconfident, and Normal Speakers.* Doctor's thesis, Florida State University (Tallahassee, Fla.), 1963. (*DA* 24:4871)
13. FABIAN, JUDITH JANARO. *Comparison of Theoretical Viewpoints and Empirical Measures of Neuroticism.* Doctor's thesis, University of California (Los Angeles, Calif.), 1969. (*DAI* 30:4369B)

ANDREW L. COMREY, *Professor of Psychology, University of California, Los Angeles, California.*

This battery consists of ten tests, all of which are intended to be measures of the anxiety factor. The tests were developed from earlier measures of this factor in Cattell's more comprehensive *Objective-Analytic Personality Test Batteries,* which assesses other dimensions as well as anxiety. Cattell also has a general purpose battery based on questionnaire measures and a specialized questionnaire anxiety scale, but the Objective-Analytic tests are supposed to be less subject to faking and less dependent on self-report than the questionnaire measures. Anxiety is described by the authors as being a factor which parallels the clinical concept of "free anxiety." The following characteristics are said to be descriptive of high anxiety: tension and emotionality, guilt and self-deprecation, irritability, susceptibility to embarrassment, loneliness and "separation," high expressed sex drive, and some suspicion and hostility. The authors go on to state that "anxiety is part, but not all, of what has been lumped together uncritically and intuitively as 'neurosis.' "

The manual contains the actual tests making up the battery which the buyer is permitted to reproduce for his own use, although tests 6 and 10 are only described. A 1967 supplement to the original manual gives norms for all the tests except 6 and 10. Average reliability estimates ranging from .56 to .90 are given for the same eight tests. The only other data given in the manual are average factor loadings for the tests on the anxiety factor. No descriptions are given of the investigations that produced these factor loadings, although references are cited. Average factor loadings, usually over several studies, for the separate tests ranged from .17 to .65. It is not clear whether the tests included in the manual are the earlier or the later versions. The value of .65 for the pulse rate test was based on only one study.

The pulse rate test merits special attention, not only because it had the highest factor loading, but also because it represents several tests in one. In one form of the test, increase in pulse rate after immersion of the arm in ice water is taken as a measure of anxiety. In another form of the test, length of time for the pulse to return to normal after removal of the arm from ice water is determined. A *faster* recovery means more anxiety. These two measures of anxiety are considered by the authors to be interchangeable, although no correlation between them is reported. Substituting an unexpected gunshot noise stimulus for immersing the arm in ice water is also considered to give equivalent results; hence only one factor loading is reported to represent these four distinct forms of the test. More data would be particularly valuable here since rapidity of normal pulse recovery as a measure of anxiety seems counter-intuitive to the reviewer.

The manual is not clear about the empirical basis of the claim that the test is measuring what clinicians in general call "free anxiety." Psychiatric evaluations of "free anxiety" are said to have loaded more highly on the anxiety factor than on any other factor, although it is not stated how high this loading was. The authors also state that "U.I. 24 [Anxiety] was the only one of 15 personality dimensions on which both of two independently-working psychiatrists agreed in having their anxiety evaluations load." Again, the size of the loadings is not given. Validity for the battery is also claimed on the basis of the presumed relationship between this Objective-Analytic measure of anxiety and the questionnaire measure of anxiety, although no correlation between the two is given. The authors state that "where comparative data are available, objective test measurement of Anxiety has proved to have essentially the same criterion relations as does questionnaire-measured Anxiety. * Therefore, known questionnaire associations of Anxiety can be used inferentially in the interpretation of Anxiety level as objectively measured in this battery."

The physical makeup of the manual itself leaves room for improvement. For example, many pages are printed on the wrong side of the paper. Some parts of the manual have not been revised to be consistent with changes made in the tests and the norm supplement.

In summary, the reviewer's main criticisms of the *Objective-Analytic Anxiety Battery* are (*a*) some of the tests are not intuitively convincing as measures of what clinicians in general call "free anxiety"; (*b*) correlations between the tests and independent criterion measures of free anxiety are inadequate; (*c*) the factor loadings for many of the tests with respect to the anxiety factor are low; and (*d*) the manual fails to present sufficient data about the tests and test items to allow the user to decide for himself whether the battery is measuring what it is supposed to measure.

For a review by Harold Borko, see 6:149 (1 excerpt).

[116]

*Omnibus Personality Inventory. College; 1968, c1959–68; OPI; 15 scores: thinking introversion (TI), theoretical orientation (TO), estheticism (Es), complexity (Co), autonomy (Au), religious orientation (RO), social extroversion (SE), impulse expression (IE), personal integration (PI), anxiety level (AL), altruism (Am), practical outlook (PO), masculinity-femininity (MF), response bias (RB), intellectual disposition category (IDC) based on the first 6 scores; Form F ('68, 11 pages); manual ('68, 71 pages); directions sheet ('68, 2 pages, reprinted from manual); norms for college freshmen only; separate answer sheets (MRC, NCS) must be used; $4.75 per 25 tests; $3.50 per 50 answer sheets; $8 per set of NCS scoring stencils and manual; directions sheets free on request; $2.50 per manual; $3 per specimen set; postage extra; MRC scoring service, 45¢ or less per test; NCS scoring service: 85¢ to 50¢ per test (daily service), 45¢ to 33¢ per test ($11.25 minimum; weekly service); (45–60) minutes; Paul Heist, George Yonge, T. R. McConnell (test), and Harold Webster (test); Psychological Corporation. *

REFERENCES

1–11. See 6:150.
12–70. See P:184, also includes a cumulative name index to the first 70 references for this test.
71. GORTNER, SUSAN REICHERT. *Nursing Majors in Twelve Western Universities: A Comparison of Registered-Nurse Students and Basic Senior Students.* Doctor's thesis, University of California (Berkeley, Calif.), 1964. (*DA* 25:3971)
72. McCAULLEY, MARY H. *Dimensions of Masculinity-Femininity in Relation to Field Dependence, Dogmatism, and Other Estimates of Perceptual-Cognitive Differentiation.* Doctor's thesis, Temple University (Philadelphia, Pa.), 1964. (*DA* 25:4259)
73. ROSE, HARRIETT ABRAHAM. *Prediction and Prevention of Freshman Attrition.* Doctor's thesis, University of Kentucky (Lexington, Ky.), 1964. (*DAI* 31:2264B)
74. TRENT, JAMES WILLIAM. *The Development of Intellectual Disposition Within Catholic Colleges.* Doctor's thesis, University of California (Berkeley, Calif.), 1964. (*DA* 25:6802)
75. THOMPSON, ALVIN HINTON. *The Secondary Teacher Experimental Program, University of California, Berkeley, 1963–1964.* Doctor's thesis, University of California (Berkeley, Calif.), 1965. (*DA* 26:7171)
76. ALBERTSON, ROBERT GRANT. *Values and the Curriculum.*

Doctor's thesis, Claremont Graduate School (Claremont, Calif.), 1966. (*DA* 28:4698A)

77. BROWN, ROBERT DONALD. *Manipulation of the Environmental Press in a College Residence Hall.* Doctor's thesis, University of Iowa (Iowa City, Iowa), 1966. (*DA* 27:1196A)

78. EVANS, LLOYD R.; INGERSOLL, RALPH W.; AND SMITH, EDWIN JAY. "The Reliability, Validity, and Taxonomic Structure of the Oral Examination." *J Med Ed* 41:651–7 Jl '66. *

79. TREZISE, ROBERT LEWIS. *A Descriptive Study of the Life Styles of a Group of Creative Adolescents.* Doctor's thesis, Michigan State University (East Lansing, Mich.), 1966. (*DA* 27:2754A)

80. BEACH, LESLIE R. "Study of Personality in the Church-Related Liberal Arts College." *J Col Stud Personnel* 8:105–8 Mr '67. *

81. ELTON, CHARLES F., AND ROSE, HARRIETT A. "Personality Characteristics of Male Scholarship Recipients." *J Col Stud Personnel* 8:260–4 Jl '67. *

82. ZAHN, JANE C. "Some Characteristics of Successful and Less Successful Overseas Community Development Advisers." *Adult Ed* 18:15–23 f '67. *

83. CALLAWAY, WEBSTER R. *A Study of the Relationship of a Holistic Conception of Creativity to Intelligence.* Doctor's thesis, Michigan State University (East Lansing, Mich.), 1968. (*DA* 29:475A)

84. DAVIES, BRIAN N., AND MOWBRAY, R. M. "Medical Students: Personality and Academic Achievement." *Brit J Med Ed* 2:195–9 S '68. *

85. ELTON, CHARLES F., AND ROSE, HARRIETT A. "Personality Characteristics of Students Who Write Letters to the Editor." *J Col Stud Personnel* 9:253–5 Jl '68. *

86. GREENLAND, THOMAS CHARLES. *Some Differential Relationships of Academic Ability and Personality Factors to Academic Status as Suggested by Inter-Institutional and Intra-Institutional Analyses of the Freshman Class at Four Campuses.* Doctor's thesis, University of Kentucky (Lexington, Ky.), 1968. (*DAI* 30:1921B)

87. HEIST, PAUL. Chap. 3, "Creative Students: College Transients," pp. 35–55. In his *The Creative College Student: An Unmet Challenge.* San Francisco, Calif.: Jossey-Bass Inc., Publishers, 1968. Pp. xviii, 253. *

88. HEIST, PAUL. *The Creative College Student: An Unmet Challenge,* pp. 218–22. San Francisco, Calif.: Jossey-Bass Inc., Publishers, 1968. Pp. xviii, 253. *

89. JOHNSON, BERKELEY, JR. *The Development of a Test of Commitment to Community College Values.* Doctor's thesis, University of California (Berkeley, Calif.), 1968. (*DA* 29: 4187A)

90. KING, SHIRLEY PATRICIA. *The Association of Selected Personality Characteristics With College Achievement.* Doctor's thesis, University of California (Berkeley, Calif.), 1968. (*DA* 29:3003A)

91. KORN, HAROLD A. Chap. 3, "Personality Scale Changes From the Freshman Year to the Senior Year," pp. 162–84. In *No Time for Youth: Growth and Constraint in College Students.* Edited by Joseph Katz. San Francisco, Calif.: Jossey-Bass Inc., Publishers, 1968. Pp. xxii, 463. *

92. KORN, HAROLD A. Chap. 4, "Differences in Student Response to the Curriculum," pp. 187–206. In *No Time for Youth: Growth and Constraint in College Students.* Edited by Joseph Katz. San Francisco, Calif.: Jossey-Bass Inc., Publishers, 1968. Pp. xxii, 463. *

93. PAYNE, JOHN WILEY. *Value Patterns of Seniors in Teacher Education as Revealed by Personality Factor Changes.* Doctor's thesis, University of Kentucky (Lexington, Ky.), 1968. (*DAI* 30:1928B)

94. ROBERTS, BRUCE BEN. *The Leader, Group, and Task Variables of Leader Selection in College.* Doctor's thesis, Claremont Graduate School (Claremont, Calif.), 1968. (*DA* 29:2360A)

95. ROSE, HARRIETT A., AND ELTON, CHARLES F. "Accepters and Rejecters of Counseling." *J Counsel Psychol* 15:578–80 N '68. * (*PA* 43:1404)

96. SANFORD, NEVITT, AND SINGER, SUSAN. Chap. 9, "Drinking and Personality," pp. 348–75. In *No Time for Youth: Growth and Constraint in College Students.* Edited by Joseph Katz. San Francisco, Calif.: Jossey-Bass Inc., Publishers, 1968. Pp. xxii, 463. *

97. SNYDER, BENSON R. Chap. 4, "The Education of Creative Science Students," pp. 56–70. In *The Creative College Student: An Unmet Challenge.* Edited by Paul Heist. San Francisco, Calif.: Jossey-Bass Inc., Publishers, 1968. Pp. xviii, 253. *

98. STANDING, GEORGE ROBERT. *A Typological Approach to the Study of Men's Residence Groups.* Doctor's thesis, Michigan State University (East Lansing, Mich.), 1968. (*DAI* 30: 816A)

99. STRINGHAM, MARION CAROL. *Factors Pertaining to the Utilization or Non-Utilization of Psychological Counseling Services in a Liberal Arts College.* Doctor's thesis, University of Michigan (Ann Arbor, Mich.), 1968. (*DAI* 30:556A)

100. TRENT, JAMES W., AND MEDSKER, LELAND L. *Beyond High School: A Psychosociological Study of 10,000 High School Graduates.* San Francisco, Calif.: Jossey-Bass Inc., Publishers, 1968. Pp. xxv, 333. *

101. WATTS, WILLIAM A., AND WHITTAKER, DAVID. "Pro-file of a Nonconformist Youth Culture: A Study of Berkeley Non-Students." *Sociol Ed* 41:178–200 sp '68. * (*PA* 42: 19260)

102. ADAMS, RAMONA SHEPHERD. *Evaluation of a Clustering Experience of College Freshmen.* Doctor's thesis, University of Utah (Salt Lake City, Utah), 1969. (*DAI* 30:4168A)

103. CALLAWAY, WEBSTER R. "A Holistic Conception of Creativity and Its Relationship to Intelligence." *Gifted Child Q* 13(4):237–41 w '69. * (*PA* 44:15338)

104. CHICKERING, ARTHUR W. *Education and Identity,* pp. 177–84, 310–9, passim. San Francisco, Calif.: Jossey-Bass Inc., Publishers, 1969. Pp. xv, 367. *

105. CHICKERING, ARTHUR W.; McDOWELL, JAMES; AND CAMPAGNA, DENNIS. "Institutional Differences and Student Development." *J Ed Psychol* 60(4):315–26 Ag '69. * (*PA* 43: 16308)

106. DUBLIN, JAMES E.; ELTON, CHARLES F.; AND BERZINS, JURIS I. "Some Personality and Aptitudinal Correlates of the 'A–B' Therapist Scale." *J Consult & Clin Psychol* 33(6):739–45 D '69. * (*PA* 44:3595)

107. DUGGER, JUNE ARMISTEAD. *A Study of Measurable Personal Factors of Leaders and Non-Leaders Among University Freshmen Women.* Doctor's thesis, Florida State University (Tallahassee, Fla.), 1969. (*DAI* 30:1817A)

108. ELTON, CHARLES F. "Patterns of Change in Personality Test Scores." *J Counsel Psychol* 16(2):95–9 Mr '69. * (*PA* 43:10296)

109. ELTON, CHARLES F. "Prediction of Educational Outcomes Among Junior College Students." *J Col Stud Personnel* 10(1):44–6 Ja '69. *

110. ELTON, CHARLES F., AND ROSE, HARRIETT A. "Differential Change in Male Personality Test Scores." *J Col Stud Personnel* 10(4):373–7 N '69. *

111. ELTON, CHARLES F., AND ROSE, HARRIETT A. "Personality Assessments Compared With Personality Inferred From Occupational Choices." *J Counsel Psychol* 16(4):329–34 Jl '69. * (*PA* 43:14327)

112. ELTON, CHARLES F., AND TERRY, T. RANKIN. "Factor Stability of the Omnibus Personality Inventory." *J Counsel Psychol* 16(4):373–4 Jl '69. * (*PA* 43:14337)

113. FELDMAN, KENNETH A., AND NEWCOMB, THEODORE M. *The Impact of College on Students: Vol. 2, Summary Tables.* San Francisco, Calif.: Jossey-Bass Inc., Publishers, 1969. Pp. iv, 171. *

114. FRANK, AUSTIN C., AND KIRK, BARBARA A. "Characteristics and Attributes of Prospective City and Regional Planners." *J Col Stud Personnel* 10(4):317–23 S '69. *

115. GALL, MEREDITH D. "The Relationship Between Masculinity-Femininity and Manifest Anxiety." *J Clin Psychol* 25(3):294–5 Jl '69. * (*PA* 44:3604)

116. GRUBERG, RONALD. "A Significant Counselor Personality Characteristic: Tolerance of Ambiguity." *Counselor Ed & Sup* 8(2):119–24 w '69. *

117. HANNAH, WILLIAM. *Dropout-Stayin Personality Differentials and College Environments.* Doctor's thesis, University of Southern California (Los Angeles, Calif.), 1969. (*DAI* 31:584A)

118. HEDEGARD, JAMES M., AND BROWN, DONALD R. "Encounters of Some Negro and White Freshmen With a Public Multiversity." *J Social Issues* 25(3):131–44 su '69. *

119. HOCHBERG, ARTHUR CHARLES. *A Study of the Outcomes of Same High School as Compared to Different High School Clustering of College Freshmen.* Doctor's thesis, University of Utah (Salt Lake City, Utah), 1969. (*DAI* 30: 1866A)

120. HOWDEN, J. ROBERT. *Predicting Teacher Competence: Using the OPI and the ETAS.* Doctor's thesis, University of California (Berkeley, Calif.), 1969. (*DAI* 31:1665A)

121. JOHNSON, PATRICIA CARROLLENE SMITH. *Institutional Change, Attitudes and Personality Characteristics of Medical Students.* Doctor's thesis, University of Southern California (Los Angeles, Calif.), 1969. (*DAI* 30:585A)

122. KIRK, BARBARA A., AND SEREDA, LYNN. "Accuracy of Self-Reported College Grade Averages and Characteristics of Non and Discrepant Reporters." *Ed & Psychol Meas* 29(1): 147–55 sp '69. * (*PA* 44:17475)

123. LONSWAY, FRANCIS A. "Personality Characteristics of Seminarians." *Voc Guid Q* 18(2):133–7 D '69. *

124. LONSWAY, FRANCIS A. "Some Notes on a Seminarian's Personality, Background and Goals." *Relig Ed* 64(3):212–7 My–Je '69. * (*PA* 43:14195)

125. MacMILLAN, THOMAS FERGUSON. *Establishing a Predictive Model for Early Recognition of Potential Community College Student Attrition.* Doctor's thesis, University of California (Berkeley, Calif.), 1969. (*DAI* 30:4226A)

126. MURPHY, PATRICIA DUREY. "Simplicity-Complexity in Thinking as Related to Preference for Dependence-Independence in Students." *J Ed Res* 62(5):206–10 Ja '69. *

127. NIKKARI, JOHN GARTON. *Freshman-to-Senior Personality Changes in Basic Collegiate Student Nurses as Compared to Changes in Females in a Liberal Arts College in a Large Midwestern State University.* Doctor's thesis, University of Michigan (Ann Arbor, Mich.), 1969. (*DAI* 31:774B)

128. ROSS, WESLEY F. *The Relation of Psycho-Social Variables to Mental Health Needs of a Freshman Class.* Doctor's

thesis, University of Kentucky (Lexington, Ky.), 1969. (*DAI* 30:3334A)

129. TREANOR, CAROL CAIRNS. *Using Multivariate Statistical Techniques to Assess Change in College Students.* Doctor's thesis, University of California (Berkeley, Calif.), 1969. (*DAI* 31:241A)

130. WALTON, H. F. "Personality Correlates of a Career Interest in Psychiatry." *Brit J Psychiatry* 115(519):211–9 F '69. * (*PA* 43:13021)

131. WHITTAKER, DAVID. "Masculinity-Femininity and Nonconformist Youth." Abstract. *Proc 77th Ann Conv Am Psychol Assn* 4(1):297–8 '69. * (*PA* 43:17481)

132. WHITTAKER, DAVID, AND WATTS, WILLIAM A. "Personality Characteristics of a Nonconformist Youth Subculture: A Study of the Berkeley Non-Student." *J Social Issues* 25(2):65–89 Ap '69. *

133. BRETON, GABRIEL RENÉ. *The Influence of Interaction Between Personality and Environment on Educational Outcomes.* Doctor's thesis, University of Michigan (Ann Arbor, Mich.), 1970. (*DAI* 31:2953B)

134. BROWN, ROBERT D. "Curricular Changers and Persisters: How Do They Differ?" *J Col Stud Personnel* 11(5):366–72 S '70. *

135. ELTON, CHARLES F. "Personality of Low Income Males: College Versus Noncollege." *J Col Stud Personnel* 11(3):210–2 My '70. * (*PA* 45:4881)

136. ELTON, CHARLES F., AND ROSE, HARRIETT A. "Male Occupational Constancy and Change: Its Prediction According to Holland's Theory." *J Counsel Psychol Monogr* 17(6):1–19 N '70. * (*PA* 45:5123)

137. HIGGINS, JERRY. "Personality Correlates of the Goodman Socio-Sexual Adjustment Scale." *J Abn Psychol* 75(3):276–7 Je '70. * (*PA* 44:14584)

138. KUUSINEN, SHARON. "Evidence for a Curvilinear Relationship Between Complexity and Originality." *J Personality* 38(3):329–43 S '70. * (*PA* 45:4565)

139. MAJER, KENNETH. "Differential Relationships Between Personality and Performance Under Dissimilar Modes of Instruction." *AV Commun R* 18(2):169–79 su '70. * (*PA* 44:19555)

140. MORGAN, MARGARET KNOX. *The OPI, the ACT and University Attrition: A Discriminant Analysis.* Doctor's thesis, University of Kentucky (Lexington, Ky.), 1970. (*DAI* 31:3906A)

141. OGDEN, GEORGE BARTON. *An Organizational Innovation in Residential Undergraduate Education and Its Effects on Student Behavior.* Doctor's thesis, University of Massachusetts (Amherst, Mass.), 1970. (*DAI* 31:2131A)

142. PEARSON, LOIS WILMA. *Personality Factors Implications for Independent Study in Teacher Education.* Doctor's thesis, University of Rochester (Rochester, N.Y.), 1970. (*DAI* 31:3397A)

143. PITTMAN, ROSEMARY, AND KERCHNER, LELA. "A Study of the Relationship Between Staff Attitudes and Dimensions of Supervisory Self-Actualization in Public Health Nursing." *Nursing Res* 19(3):231–8 My–Je '70. *

144. ROSE, HARRIETT A., AND ELTON, CHARLES F. "Personality Characteristics of Transfer Students." *J Col Stud Personnel* 11(4):266–70 Jl '70. * (*PA* 45:4901)

145. ROSSMANN, JACK E., AND KIRK, BARBARA A. "Comparison of Counseling Seekers and Nonseekers." *J Counsel Psychol* 17(2):184–8 Mr '70. * (*PA* 44:9247)

146. ROSSMANN, JACK E., AND KIRK, BARBARA A. "Factors Related to Persistence and Withdrawal Among University Students." *J Counsel Psychol* 17(1):56–62 Ja '70. * (*PA* 44:5658)

147. SHEPLER, MONTE PURVIS. *Changes in Attitudes and Values and Selected Factors in the Collegiate Environment Related to Change Among Freshmen Students.* Doctor's thesis, Columbia University (New York, N.Y.), 1970. (*DAI* 31:3303A)

148. SIMMONS, DALE D. "Development of an Objective Measure of Identity Achievement Status." *J Proj Tech & Pers Assess* 34(3):241–4 Je '70. * (*PA* 44:18735)

149. SMART, JOHN C.; ELTON, CHARLES F.; AND BURNETT, COLLINS W. "Underachievers and Overachievers in Intermediate French." *Mod Lang J* 54(6):415–20 O '70. *

150. SMITH, CHARLES P., AND WINTERBOTTOM, MIRIAM T. "Personality Characteristics of College Students on Academic Probation." *J Personality* 38(3):379–91 S '70. * (*PA* 45:5063)

151. VIA, MURRAY EUGENE. *Changes in Personality Characteristics and Attitudes of Male College Freshmen.* Doctor's thesis, Claremont Graduate School (Claremont, Calif.), 1970. (*DAI* 31:1636A)

152. WEISSMAN, HERBERT N. "Disposition Toward Intellectuality: Its Composition and Its Assessment." *J General Psychol* 82(1):99–107 Ja '70. * (*PA* 44:10452)

RICHARD W. COAN, *Professor of Psychology, The University of Arizona, Tucson, Arizona.*

The *Omnibus Personality Inventory* is a set of questionnaire scales that has evolved in a semi-orderly fashion over a period of several years. Its prime virtues and its major shortcomings can probably be traced to many of the same accidents in its history. The procedures by which the scales were constructed and developed are not adequately described in the test manual, and the reader might readily surmise that each scale was devised on a strictly rational basis to fit an a priori concept. There is no discussion of criterion correlation or other forms of analysis that evidently played some part in the development of the scales. Both theory and empirical findings regarding relationships among variables apparently influenced the ultimate choice of scales to be combined in the OPI.

This test is not the product of an organized systematic personality theory. Instead, it represents the interaction of a number of psychologists concerned with individual differences and personality development in college populations and it reflects bits of theorizing that have come from several sources. As a consequence, it taps a mixture of variables that are quite valuable for understanding college students and for helping them understand themselves better. In view of the overall content of the OPI and its demonstrated ability to make some appropriate discriminations, we may view it as an effective instrument for assessing the intellectual orientation and adjustment of college students. On the whole, it is probably as good as any alternative instrument that might be used for such a purpose.

From the standpoint of a subject, an obvious shortcoming of the test is its length. On the whole, the items are well formulated and concise, but their very number makes the chore of taking the test a bit tedious. Furthermore, the OPI does not yield as much information as one might hope to derive from 385 items, because there is a fair amount of redundancy among the scales. The redundancy is evident in some sizable intercorrelations among the scales and in factor analyses of such intercorrelations. The factor analyses reported in the manual were carried out only to the point of quartimax solutions, but it is evident from inspection of these that thorough rotation to optimal oblique solutions would leave the reported factor patterns essentially intact. The largest common factor loads the Practical Outlook scale in one direction and the scales for Autonomy, Complexity, Thinking Introversion, Religious Orientation, and Theoretical Orientation in the opposite direction. To be sure, each of these six scales yields some information that the other five do not, but obviously much of the information they yield as a group could be provided more economically by a single scale.

To capture some of the variance held in common by a number of scales, the authors propose the use of a graded series of Intellectual Disposition Categories. A subject is assigned to one of 8 categories in accordance with his standing on six scales. The six scales include all but one of the scales (Practical Outlook) loaded highly by the major common factor and include in addition Estheticism, which is loaded slightly by that factor. The Intellectual Disposition Categories thus constitute a rather crude and imprecise measure of the major common factor. No doubt these categories do provide some meaningful differentiation of subjects, but it would probably prove more fruitful to employ more efficient weighting schemes that would yield scores for three or four of the common dimensions that have actually been revealed by factor analysis.

A number of questions might be raised regarding the composition and interpretation of specific scales in this test. Two scales labeled Thinking Introversion and Social Extraversion have little correlation with each other, and it is not clear from available evidence how either is related to the various components of this domain that have been isolated in research with other questionnaires. As in a number of other inventories, a single Masculinity-Femininity scale is used to represent a host of loosely related attitude, interest, and disposition variables that distinguish the sexes. An adequate analysis of this realm remains a task for future research and test development.

Several scales are interpreted in terms of authoritarianism and nonauthoritarianism. The Autonomy and Religious Orientation scales in particular are singled out for such interpretation, although they can hardly represent this entire ill-charted territory very adequately. A dogmatic adherence to conventional religious beliefs and practices would undoubtedly correlate substantially with many other measures of conservatism and authoritarianism, but we can most safely interpret scores on Religious Orientation simply in terms of attitudes in the area of religion. To be sure, religious outlook is an area of some interest in its own right.

In brief, the OPI was developed for use in the assessment and guidance of normal college students. In comparison with other inventories that might be used for this purpose, it has particular strengths in the realm of intellectual orientation, but it does not provide an optimal measure of all the variables that it purports to tap. Judicious consideration of the results of multivariate analyses might point to many ways in which the OPI could be improved both with respect to the composition of individual scales and with respect to the total selection of scale variables included in the test.

PAUL McREYNOLDS, *Professor of Psychology, University of Nevada, Reno, Nevada.*

The OPI was designed primarily for use in research on college students, although it may also be, in certain instances, appropriately employed in student counseling. Utilizing a standard true-false format, the present—and presumably final—form, Form F, includes 385 items and yields 15 scores. The OPI is based on a long process of test development, which goes back to 1957 and includes a wide variety of research with and on earlier forms. It is, therefore, an instrument of considerable technical refinement, and one which, despite its recent date (1968), is to a large degree an older, established inventory.

Unlike many inventories, the OPI was not constructed in accord with an overall personality theory. Rather, the instrument, developed at the Center for the Study of Higher Education at the University of California at Berkeley, was devised to fill specific measurement needs in the research programs of that agency. Now, the absence of an underlying personality orientation in the construction of a personality inventory can be, and often is, overly restricting; this, however, does not appear to have been the case in the present instance. This is true, first, because the authors did have a consistent systematic position with respect to the kinds of variables they were trying to measure; and second, because while the test *is* somewhat restricted in its coverage, this fact, rather than being a disadvantage, can be a positive feature if one needs to assess in the area encompassed by the instrument. Thus, it can be argued that a test which focuses on a given domain for a given population can do this more adequately than an instrument which attempts to assay the entire personality for a wide range of adults. In the case of the OPI, the target population is college students, and the relevant domain is certain attitudes, values, and interests relevant to academic activity and the functioning of late adolescents in an educational context. Thus, in developing the instrument, emphasis was placed on the assessment of "intellectual vs. non-intellectual values and interests; liberal vs. conservative attitudes; and social-emotional adjustment characteristics." A particularly strong feature of the OPI's rationale is its focus on intrinsic, as differentiated from extrinsic, factors in learning. In accord with the generally pragmatic nature of the test's developmental history, most of the items (88 percent) were taken from some 13 other tests, including the MMPI and CPI.

The OPI includes 14 scales, with the number of items in each ranging from 20 (Anxiety Level) to 59 (Impulse Expression). For most scales there is some overlap of items with other scales, but this is generally minimal. One of the scales, Response Bias (RB), measures the degree to which the student is motivated to make a good impression, and can be used in identifying subjects who may not be presenting themselves on the test in a valid manner (it correlates .55 with Edwards' SD scale; correlations with other SD scales, such as that of Marlowe and Crowne, are not reported). The 13 substantive scales fall naturally into several groupings. The first group, known as the "primary intellectual scales," includes Thinking Introversion (TI), Theoretical Orientation (TO), Estheticism (Es), and Complexity (Co). A second major group, including Social Extroversion (SE), Impulse Expression (IE), Personal Integration (PI), and Anxiety Level (AL), focuses on "social-emotional adjustment." Two scales, Autonomy (Au) and Religious Orientation (RO), represent the authoritarian-nonauthoritarian orientation. The other scales, Altruism (Am), Practical Outlook (PO), and Masculinity-Femininity (MF), are not members of groups. In addition to these scales, a fifteenth score, termed Intellectual Disposition Category (IDC), can be obtained from a weighted combination of TI, TO, Es, Co, Au, and RO. All of the scales are of obvious relevance to the problems of adaptation at the college level, and, in principle, should add a great deal to the information furnished by the usual achievement-oriented tests. Of the various scales, those concerned with intellectual variables represent the most nearly unique contri-

bution of the OPI, as compared with other instruments.

The test appears to have adequate reliability. The K-R 21 and split-half estimates of internal consistency reported range from .73 to .91 for the substantive scales, and test-retest coefficients vary from .79 to .94. The problem of validity has been approached primarily through correlations with other inventories, and a large number of these, involving the CPI, EPPS, MBTI, MMPI, OAIS, SV, SVIB, and several other tests, are reported in the manual. In general, the obtained coefficients are in line with expectations. Nevertheless, this approach to validity can be considered as only extremely provisional, since the main thing it tells us is the extent to which the measures of one test can be translated into the measures of another. Such inter-inventory correlations mask major problems due to common response sets, verbal skills, test-taking anxieties, and the like. This is especially true when the items of a test are taken largely from other similar tests, as with the OPI. This general problem evidently is recognized by the authors and they do provide a few more direct assays of validity. Thus, students who frequently attend religious services score differently on the RO scale from students who attend infrequently; and the Co score correlates significantly with objective measures of preference for complex figures.

The manual, generally speaking, is excellent. It includes a lucid discussion of the scales, and helpful suggestions for their interpretations, including detailed presentation of several cases. T score norms based on 7,283 students are included. A serious limitation in the norms is that they are for college freshmen only.

The OPI, like all inventories, is marked by certain strong points and certain weak points. In this instance the former greatly outweigh the latter, provided the instrument is used for the purpose for which it was constructed. This purpose is research on problems of adaptation of young people to the college environment. The OPI seems to be especially useful with respect to the important intellectual attitudes and values, and probably handles this area better than any other current inventory; in particular, it is to be commended for its attention to intrinsic motivational factors in learning. Though there is considerable reason to believe that the OPI may also be useful in student counseling, its value in this respect has not as yet been clearly demonstrated.

For reviews by Paul M. Kjeldergaard and Norman E. Wallen of earlier forms, see 6:150 (1 excerpt).

[117]

Organic Integrity Test. Ages 5 and over; 1960–67; OIT; form perception as an indication of brain deficit unrelated to intelligence; individual; 1 form ('60, 20 cards) ; manual ['67, c1965, 36 pages, includes reprints of *2, 3, 4,* and *7* below] ; diagnostic chart ('60, 1 page) ; $25 per set of cards and manual, postpaid; (4–5) minutes; H. C. Tien; Psychodiagnostic Test Co. *

REFERENCES

1. See 6:152.
2–13. See P:186.
14. Aftanas, M. S., and Royce, J. R. "A Factor Analysis of Brain Damage Tests Administered to Normal Subjects With Factor Score Comparisons Across Ages." *Multiv Behav Res* 4(4):459–81 O '69. * (PA 44:11030)
15. Jacobs, Eleanor A.; Winter, Peter M.; Alvis, Harry J.; and Small, S. Mouchly. "Hyperoxygenation Effect on Cognitive Functioning in the Aged." Abstract. *Proc 77th Ann Conv Am Psychol Assn* 4(2):721–2 '69. * (PA 44:505)
16. Jacobs, Eleanor A.; Winter, Peter M.; Alvis, Harry J.; and Small, S. Mouchly. "Hyperoxygenation Effect on Cognitive Functioning in the Aged." *New Engl J Med* 281(14):753–7 O 2 '69. * (PA 44:7205)
17. Tien, H. C. "The Routine Use of Organic Integrity Test (OIT) in an EEG Laboratory." Abstract. *Electroencephalography & Clin Neurophysiol* 26(1):115–6 Ja '69. *
18. Tien, H. C. "The Theory of Pattern Recognition by Identity: Some Mathematical Origins of Psychosynthesis." *World J Psychosynthesis* 1(3):45–55 N '69. *
19. Engelsmann, Frank, and Drdkova, S. "Organic Integrity Test." *World J Psychosynthesis* 2(3):42–9 Mr '70. *
20. Tien, H. C. "Organic Integrity Test (OIT) in Monitoring Drug Effects." *Psychosomatics* 11(5):445–55 S–O '70. * (PA 45:6695)
21. Watts, Clark C., and Haerer, Armin F. "The Organic Integrity Test Evaluated." *J Clin Psychol* 26(1):77 Ja '70. * (PA 44:11464)

Ralph M. Reitan, *Professor of Neurological Surgery and Psychology, University of Washington, Seattle, Washington.*

Tien's OIT consists of 10 sets of three pictures each. All of the pictures, while recognizable as to type of object shown, are fragmentary, making identification of the objects more difficult. The test has no time limits and usually takes about five minutes to administer and score. One set at a time is offered to the subject and he is asked, "Which two *pictures* are alike?" The subject is then to match the free single card with one of the other two cards. The raw score is the number of form (as opposed to color) responses the subject makes. A numerical value, based on the frequency of correct responses to each set by normal subjects, is assigned to each of the 10 sets of cards, and the OIT value for any individual subject (sum of score on the 10 sets) is then used to determine diagnoses according to available tables and charts.

The manual states, "The O.I.T. (Organic Integrity Test) is a psychological test designed to detect the ability of the central nervous system in any subject to perceive gestalt, or form, or its inability to do so in one who has cortical damage due to any brain disease." Tien indicates that the test is modeled after a similar but unpublished version developed by Casagrandie. The test is based on the postulate that gestalt, or form perception, is a function of the intact central nervous system. From this postulate the author "deduced that subjects with an organic brain syndrome tend to lose their ability to perceive gestalt." Tien further states, "The OIT elicits form responses from the subjects only, and any color response is regarded as a decrease of the gestalt perceptual ability or the degree of brain damage. This decrease serves as a measure of loss of organic integrity."

The manual presents normative and validity information concerning children and adults. While the test is designed primarily to identify presence or absence of brain dysfunction, only one study presents data on subjects in whom brain damage is even reasonably certain. Two other studies using a total of 83 "organic" patients are referred to but no information about more specific neurological categories or diagnostic findings is reported. In Tien's own study (N = 52) the brain-damaged patients were all psychiatric in-patients. Diagnoses for these patients were made from review of hospital charts reporting neurological examinations of varying completeness. Subjects in the other group (psychotic, neurotic, normal) were not examined neurologically.

Normative data derived from the above studies and from one utilizing job applicants (N = 342) are also provided. While the manual states that 98 percent of persons without "organicity" or psychosis score above 51, the only available article not written by Tien does not confirm this. Watts and Haerer (*21*) found that 25.9 percent of armed forces inductees scored 50 or less and that these results were unrelated to age or intelligence test score. Tien also indicates that the OIT is not correlated with age or intelligence in adults.

A study of 1,300 children aged 5–17 did produce an age-related normative table. In another study, using groups of good readers, poor readers, and nonreaders, the test differentiated children who could read (mean IQ = 115) from those who could not (mean IQ = 71). Good readers (mean IQ = 115), however, were not differentiated from poor readers (mean IQ = 91). No neurological diagnostic information on any of these children was reported by the author. Nevertheless he concluded from these two studies that the test is applicable for use with children to screen for organicity and potential reading problems. Unless all reading problems are equated with low IQ, these conclusions are not supported by any data so far available.

The author claims that in addition to detecting brain damage, his test not only is useful in diagnosing psychoses but also yields data showing that paranoid schizophrenia may be a manifestation of an "organic brain syndrome." While this idea is hardly new, the data available on this test in no way affirm or deny his conclusions.

The test is based on the postulate that *any* form of brain dysfunction will result in the same behavioral manifestation, i.e., loss of ability to perceive form and a resultant tendency to respond to colors in matching stimulus figures. That all brain disorders have a single manifestation is hardly supported by the wealth of available information.[1]

The test also assumes that only persons with brain damage (or other conditions in which brain damage may be present, such as mental retardation and psychosis) will respond to color rather than form. The article by Watts and Haerer (*21*) indicates that many bright inductees recognized the need to choose on some basis and chose color over form apparently as a personal preference. The fact that other criteria of choice may be used, such as content or function, is ignored by Tien.

Data are presented in chart form, which gives the appearance of quantification as the basis for diagnoses. Actually, however, the method of inference utilized by this test is dependent upon the occurrence of specific pathological signs. The author states that occurrence of errors can be interpreted much as is the occurrence of a Babinski sign. However, because cerebral pathology has not been shown to be the sole cause of low OIT scores, their significance in any individual instance is difficult to interpret.

The test, in a general sense, appears to be sensitive to severe impairment in overall ability (*13*). Subjects who are severely brain-damaged, mentally retarded, or psychotic can be expected,

in the main, to do quite poorly. However, almost any psychological test can separate such groups from normals and the independent contribution of this test is unclear. The uncritical and sometimes irrelevant speculation into which the author is willing to venture makes it difficult to accept his claims without well-documented evidence. In no instance are the claims for this test supported by such evidence.

In summary, the lack of adequate neurological criterion information in the studies utilizing subjects with supposed brain damage and the naively simple model of brain functions represented by the behavior this test attempts to measure would appear to pose serious limitations for its value as a measure of the integrity of brain functions. While use of this test as part of a battery of tests is mentioned by the author, it was clearly developed and is currently used by him as a single diagnostic tool. Its possible contribution in conjunction with other tests is unexplored.

JOSEPH M. WEPMAN, *Professor of Psychology, Surgery, and Education, The University of Chicago, Chicago, Illinois.*

This test is based on a single premise; to wit, the effect of brain injury upon cognitive functioning is to reduce the individual to a primitive level of thought. This effect, the author believes, can be demonstrated by providing the subject with a binary choice (color or form) in categorization. If he sorts by primitive means, he will do so by accepting a color likeness. If he is capable, however, of more sophisticated judgment he will select a form relationship. Color sorting is then equated with the more likely choice of the brain injured; form comparison is less likely to be the choice of the brain injured, according to the author.

The test explores Goldstein's concrete-abstract dichotomy, which was tested by the *Weigl-Goldstein-Scheerer Color-Form Sorting Test.* The latter test in many ways seems superior to the present test simply because its material, as well as the task, seems less ambiguous. Unlike the CFST, the OIT forces a single decision between a readily discernible, unambiguous color comparison and a substantive but ambiguous form.

The author's results are relatively well stated, but of little assistance in making a distinction between schizophrenia and brain injury—both such patients sort their task on a primitive basis

1 YATES, AUBREY J. "Psychological Deficit." *Ann R Psychol* 17:111–44 '66. *

with no statistically significant difference between the two. The mentally retarded further confuse the statistics by also sorting in a primitive manner, so that the examiner is left with a dilemma—a given negative score may be interpreted as due to mental retardation, schizophrenia, or brain injury. Each of these indicates a degree of loss of integrity.

The test's merit lies in its ease and speed of administration, its ease of scoring and of interpretation. Research on patient populations reportedly finds the test useful in making the basic distinction between the impaired and unimpaired. The test is recommended by its author as useful in a battery of other procedures commonly used for neurological evaluation.

[118]

★PHSF Relations Questionnaire. Standards 6–10 and college and adults; 1969–70; PHSF; 12 scores: personal (self-confidence, self-esteem, self-control, nervousness, health), home (family influences, personal freedom), social (sociability—group, sociability —specific person, moral sense), formal relations, validity scale; 1 form ('69, 11 pages, English and Afrikaans); preliminary manual ('70, 32 pages, English and Afrikaans); norms for standard 10 only; separate answer sheets (IBM 1230) must be used; R2 per 10 tests; R6 per 100 answer sheets; R1.40 per set of scoring stencils; R1.20 per manual; postpaid within South Africa; specimen set not available; (30) minutes; F. A. Fouché and P. E. Grobbelaar; Human Sciences Research Council. *

[119]

★Parent-Adolescent Communication Inventory. High school and adults; 1968–69; PACI; Form A ('68, 4 pages) for adolescents, Form P ('69, 4 pages) for parents; manual ('69, 4 pages); no data on reliability and validity for Form P; tentative norms ['69, 1 page] for Form A; no norms for Form P; $2.50 per 25 tests; 35¢ per specimen set; postage extra; (20) minutes; Millard J. Bienvenu, Sr.; Family Life Publications, Inc. *

REFERENCES

1. BIENVENU, MILLARD J., SR. "Measurement of Parent-Adolescent Communication." *Family Coordinator* 18(2):117–21 Ap '69. *
2. TAYLOR, DONNA HODGKINS. *Parent-Adolescent Communication Patterns.* Master's thesis, Virginia Polytechnic Institute (Blacksburg, Va.), 1969.
3. LOVE, NASH W., JR. *Parent-Adolescent Communication as Related to Family Social Variables.* Doctor's thesis, Florida State University (Tallahassee, Fla.), 1970. (*DAI* 31:5629B)

DAVID B. ORR, *President, Scientific Educational Systems, Inc., Washington, D.C.*

The manual states that the inventory "was designed to help counselors, educators, and researchers assess parent-teen relations for purposes of individual counseling and for a better understanding of today's youth." It mentions the use of the inventory for clinical diagnosis, counseling aid, teaching and family life education purposes, and research.

The PACI is published in two forms, A for use by the adolescent age 13 and up, and P for use by the parent of an adolescent. Form A consists of 40 questions which may be answered Yes, No, or Sometimes, along with a few general, short-answer questions pertaining to the facts of the family situation (number of children, sibling position, parents' occupations and income, life goals, and perceptions of the parents). Form P is almost directly analogous, paraphrasing the questions from the parent's point of view. Typical Form A questions are "Do you feel that your father lectures and preaches to you too much?" and "Do you feel that your mother trusts you?"

The original version of the PACI consisted of 36 items developed by Bienvenu from reviews of the literature, from his clinical experience, and from the examination of other measures of family interaction. These items were submitted to a review panel consisting of a psychiatrist, a psychologist, and a psychiatric social worker, who agreed that the items were relevant to intrafamily communication. Scores of 376 high school students were then arrayed and a chi-square test was run for each item between score responses and being in the upper or the lower quarters on total score.

Based upon the above study and on a t-test comparison of regular session and summer school make-up students, a revision of the Inventory yielded 40 items. With this version, 358 high schoolers were studied, and all 40 items met the chi-square test of discrimination at the .01 level. Two additional studies revealed significant mean differences between 59 delinquents and 59 nondelinquents, and between 25 honors students and 20 remedial students; both showed results in the expected direction.

The reliability data given show an odd-even, corrected reliability of .86, based on 74 teen-age subjects. Percentile norms for Form A are based on 774 males and 782 females at the high school level. No grade or sex differences were found significant.

No further validity or developmental data are presented in the manual. However, some additional item analysis data are contained in an article (*1*) by the author. A doctoral study (*3*) reported confirmation of the relationship of all 40 items to a generalized factor called parent-adolescent communication and verified the high level of test-retest reliability. A master's thesis (*2*) reported no relationships between the inventory scores and sex, age, grade level, ordinal position in the family, rural-urban community, or source of family income. Significant relationships existed with socioeconomic status, level of father's education, and the respondent's choice of confidant (parent or other).

It should be noted that all of the data and results reported by the manual pertain to Form A, for adolescents. The assumption (perhaps a dubious one) seems to be that these statistics will apply equally well to Form P, for parents.

The PACI may best be thought of as a structured interview. There has apparently been no effort to define a psychometrically unitary dimension or to scale the questions in the usual sense. The scoring scheme is, as far as can be determined, entirely arbitrary. The fakability of the instrument is exceptionally high, but no consideration seems to have been given to this possibility. Rather, the responses are taken entirely at face value. On the other hand, the simple question format, ease of reading, and ease of application of the strip key should make the PACI easy, quick, and convenient to use. It might be more so if the troublesome differential scoring could be eliminated.

In general, the reliability seems good; the validity studies, while still sparse, appear to lend credibility to the inventory. This reviewer is not particularly impressed with those studies which merely indicate significantly different means, however, and further work might be directed to documenting the strength of such discriminations. It is further noted that the discrimination indices reported by the manual are based exclusively upon upper and lower quarters of the score distribution. Something is needed about the usefulness of the inventory for the middle half of the distribution.

In the opinion of this reviewer, the usefulness of Form P needs study just as much as that of Form A. It does not appear warranted to generalize the results of studying Form A to Form P.

In summary, then, the PACI appears to have promise as a device for organizing information about the familial communication situation and should be useful to the clinician and the counselor. It is still very much an experimental instrument and appears highly fakable. Many cautions and caveats are very much applicable to its use.

[120]

★The Perceptual Maze Test. Children, adults; 1955–69; PMT; brain damage; 2 levels; no data on reliability; no norms; £8.50 per 100 tests; [20] minutes for individual administration, (12–20) minutes for group administration; Alick Elithorn, Janice Smith (manual), and David Jones (manual); Medical Research Council. *
a) [CHILDREN'S EDITION.] Ages 6–16; 1969; test consists of 19 sheets; administration instructions (1 page); no data on validity.
b) [ADULT EDITION.] Adults; 1955–68; Forms VC 1 and VC 2 (referred to as Forms VO 1 and VO 2 when the solution numbers have been cut off), VCM 1 (a mirror image version of VC 1); test consists of 21 sheets stapled together; individual and group versions identical except for instructions; manual, called interim report ('67, 22 pages); no data on validity except in the journal literature.
c) RECTANGULAR VERSION. Adults; 1955–67; "while this version....has some advantages it has in general been superseded by the triangular version" (b above); test consists of 21 sheets stapled together; no data on validity except in the journal literature.

REFERENCES

1–23. See P:190A.
24. GROSS, MYRT L. The EEG and Performance on the Elithorn Mazes and a Hidden Figures Test. Master's thesis, Queens College (Flushing, N.Y.), 1968.
25. ELITHORN, ALICK, AND TELFORD, ALEX. "Computer Analysis of Intellectual Skills." Int J Man-Machine Studies 1(2):189–209 Ap '69. *
26. JAHODA, GUSTAV. "Cross-Cultural Use of the Perceptual Maze Test." Brit J Ed Psychol 39(1):82–6 F '69. * (PA 43:17908)

MANFRED J. MEIER, Professor of Psychology and Director, Neuropsychology Laboratory, University of Minnesota Medical School, Minneapolis, Minnesota.

The current version of the Perceptual Maze Test consists of a series of triangular lattices with dots superimposed at randomly selected junctions. The subject's task is to trace a course which passes through the maximal number of dots. The course is initiated at the vertex, which is oriented toward the subject, and follows from junction to junction. Since the subject has only two choices at each choice point (half left or half right, no regress to a previously passed choice point being allowed), the problems are binary mazes. It is this binary structure which allows precise mathematical definition of the properties of the maze. In the standard version, the number of dots along the maximal, or correct, course is located in the lower right corner of the test item sheet. Alternate forms of approximately equivalent difficulty range are available and can be administered without the solution number cue.

Conventional scoring simply involves notation of the number of mazes traced correctly; i.e., the number of times (in 18 problem attempts) the subject finds a path which passes through the maximum possible number of dots. Since the conventional scoring does not incorporate all of the data provided by the subject's performances, more refined graded scoring techniques (*11*) have been developed. These include quantitative credits based on difficulty level and incomplete solutions. The resulting scores increase the correlation between the PMT and *Progressive Matrices* significantly and may be more reliable.

The rationale for the construction of the PMT constitutes a significant departure from previous efforts to devise maze tracing tests of problem solving ability. Perhaps its closest predecessor is the *Porteus Maze Test,* an age scale in which variation in difficulty level is defined empirically. By contrast, the PMT difficulty range is defined rationally insofar as the specific dot distributions or arrays are generated by a computer program which sets their locations on the various lattices systematically. This systematization is achieved by varying the lattice size, the number of dots (saturation) and dot distribution (patterning). The difficulty level of each maze can be defined and analyzed by the use of matrix theory and subsequently correlated with the subjective or empirical difficulty of the test items. Although the correspondence between theoretical and empirical difficulty level is high, a rather sharp increase in the frequency of solution failures has been reported where the linearly accelerated theoretical difficulty approaches the upper levels in the order of presentation. A later version could include a problem sequence which conforms more to empirical difficulty if subsequent normative studies confirm such inequalities along the scale. An unlimited range of additional problems can readily be devised by means of an assortment of pattern generation programs available from the test author. Additional refinements in scoring can be achieved with programmed analysis of the frequency of point selection, pathway usage, and definable strategy selections of large subject pools. Even process control programs for on-line oscilloscopic presentation of the mazes, with response options such as back-tracking, can be introduced. Only the most elaborate behavioral laboratories would have the necessary hardware.

The applied literature for this instrument is just beginning to take shape. The PMT should be regarded as a research instrument, both as an approach to the development of systematically structured tests of problem solving ability and as a measure of organic cerebral dysfunction. Although the normative and validation data are as yet insufficient to permit routine use in the clinical or educational setting, the emerging literature favors significant future applicability of the PMT. Most of the work to date has been done with neurological samples and rather narrowly defined normal groups such as college students and RAF officers. One study (*10*) provides normative data for 540 members of the Medical Research Merseyside Volunteer Panel, subdivided into age decades and sex. This normative information would be expected to be listed in greater detail in the manual. Elithorn's manual, however, is introduced as an "interim report which is for private circulation only" and is not directed at the test consumer. The test, therefore, is deliberately presented as a research tool. The manual provides a description of the test, a relatively detailed account of its rationale and structure, a rather complete review of the supporting literature, and a summary of current research involving computer simulation and man-machine adaptations of PMT performances.

Despite the incompleteness of the available supporting information for purposes of clinical application, the emerging literature provides some noteworthy relevant findings. Test-retest reliabilities (.89) and alternate forms reliability (.81) are relatively high, although these values may be somewhat inflated by a learning factor. Clearly, more reliability data are needed. In the Davies normative study, a progressive decline in mean number of correct solutions is observed across decades from 20 to 80. Furthermore, there is a remarkable sex difference, in favor of men, in the number of correct solutions. This difference converges with increased age and almost disappears by the seventh decade.

It is well known that such age changes and sex differences are characteristic of visuospatial and complex perceptual tests. Whether these variables are more clearly expressed in PMT as compared with *Porteus Maze Test* performances, for example, remains an open question. Intercorrelations of the PMT with other cognitive measures such as the *Progressive Matrices* (.62 for men; .54 for women), *Mill Hill Vocabulary Scale* (.23 for men; .42 for women), and Wechsler-Bellevue Vocabulary (.46) and Block Design (.74) subtests are remarkably similar to corresponding relationships between such measures and the *Porteus Maze*

Test quotient. Similarly, factor analyses have yielded significant PMT loadings with a visuospatial component of intelligence, a bipolar educational/noneducational factor, and a specific spatial ability—"perceptual span."

PMT performances are expected to correlate highly with the Porteus. This expectation is based more on the intercorrelational similarities noted above than on the apparent overlap of content. Although serial maze tracing is involved in both tasks, a critical difference may well favor the Porteus as a measurement approach to problem-solving ability. This difference involves the availability of definitive confirmatory information which the subject may use at the choice points of the Porteus. Although the subject may not use the information correctly, he can determine whether or not his course is correct up to that point without scanning the entire maze. On the PMT, such confirmatory feedback must be sought by scanning the entire maze, repeatedly on the more difficult problems. This format probably accounts for the specific "perceptual span" factor loading of the PMT and may confound short-term (visuospatial) memory with problem-solving ability to some extent. The latter conceivably could reduce the validity of the PMT as a measure of problem-solving ability. The PMT was designed to minimize the participation of memory processes in finding solutions but may not have fully achieved this goal. To be sure, Porteus Maze performances can be affected by memory functioning but, a priori, do not seem as likely to involve such cognitive processes, at least not in a major contributing sense.

Despite these considerations, the emerging course of PMT validation research seems to bear a striking similarity to the history of the *Porteus Maze Test*. The selection of external criteria and the corresponding results have favored the sensitivity of both tests to CNS dysfunction, particularly in the frontal lobes. Among a sizable group of neuropsychological tests, the PMT ranked fifth in discriminating "brain damaged" from normal controls. As with the Porteus, impaired performances on the PMT are more frequently reported in patients with lesions of the right or nondominant cerebral hemisphere. This deficit selectivity in relation to right hemisphere involvement, in the context of an extensive literature implicating the right hemisphere in the mediation of visuospatial abilities, provides the major empirical finding bearing on the construct validity of the PMT. Claims for the PMT's sensitivity to frontal and temporal lobe lesions will necessarily await larger samples and more precise descriptions of the clinical criteria to determine the location of the focal cerebral lesions. However, these shortcomings apply to much of the Porteus Maze literature as well.

In summary, the PMT appears to hold considerable promise as a test of visuospatial functioning with potential applicability in the assessment of cerebral dysfunction, particularly in relation to lesions of the right cerebral hemisphere. The systematically derived item structure constitutes a significant innovation in the construction and analysis of visuospatial and maze-tracing functions. Although there are critical differences in test content, the construct validation of the PMT will likely interface considerably with that of the *Porteus Maze Test*. Whether the *Perceptual Maze Test,* or its automated offspring, will provide an improvement over the Porteus as a clinical assessment technique remains to be determined.

Aubrey J. Yates, *Professor of Psychology, University of Western Australia, Nedlands, Australia.*

Each item of this test consists of a pattern made up of a lattice background of diagonally intersecting dotted lines. A variable number of heavy black dots are placed at a proportion of the intersections. The task involves finding a path through the lattice which connects the largest number of dots, with the restrictions that the subject must keep to the dotted lines and may not double back. For each item, only one solution is correct. The number of dots which must be connected is printed on the form in one version of the test but not in the other. In the former case, the subject will know whether his solution is the correct one or not. The earliest version of the test used a square or rectangular background; later versions use a binary or V-shaped background. The unique characteristics of the PMT have resulted in a number of investigations into its formal analytical properties (*4, 5, 7, 8, 11, 12, 17, 21*). Factorial analysis of the test (*2, 9*) indicates that the ability producing individual differences in performance cannot be reduced to verbal reasoning, fluency, or spatial ability, although it does appear to involve auditory verbal activity to some degree. Elithorn (*2, 8*) has suggested that the test involves a perceptual scanning mechanism, individual performance differences being a function of the size of unit the subject can handle and of his rate of scanning. Scanning is distinguished from more rigid sequential search, the latter becoming more important as an alternative strategy to scanning as the latter becomes less efficient with increase in item difficulty.

The test has increasingly been regarded as a possibly useful instrument for the measurement of localized brain damage. Early suggestions (1) that the test would discriminate anterior from posterior (post-Rolandic) lesions have not been supported by subsequent results, although the possibility that discrimination may be positive when item difficulty is taken into account cannot yet be ruled out (7). However, there is now very strong evidence that the test discriminates significantly between left-sided and right-sided lesions, the latter performing at a higher level on the test than the former (3, 7, 16, 18, 19, 22). The discrimination holds up even when dysphasic patients are excluded from the left-sided group.

The test has not been "officially" issued for use and the material provided with the test is inadequate.[1] Instructions for administration are included with the forms, but no details are provided covering the genesis and nature of the test, standardization data are not provided, and it is presumably assumed that the user is fully familiar with the literature on the test, a good deal of which is in relatively inaccessible journals. A good deal of data relating to the performance of brain-damaged patients with left- and right-sided lesions are available in the literature (3, 7, 16, 18, 19, 22). However, the only large-scale standardization study so far published suggests extreme caution in the use of the test for diagnostic purposes. Davies (10), using the Triangular version (three sizes of maze and three values of saturation, factorially combined), provided data on a sample of 540 normal subjects (50 men and 40 women in each of the age decades from 20–29 up to 70–79). The mean number of items attempted showed no relation to age or sex. However, the mean correct score showed a significant negative correlation with age for men (−.545) and women (−.281), while males were significantly

superior to females at all age levels except the two oldest. The negative correlation with age has been confirmed in other studies (1, 3, 20), as has the sex difference, both at older (20) and at younger age levels (9). A test-retest (14-day interval) study showed a very significant practice effect. Thus, any attempt to use the test as a diagnostic test of brain-damage (3) or to discriminate left- from right-sided lesions (3, 7, 16, 18, 19, 22) must take account of age and sex differences. Standardization data for brain-damaged subjects with focal lesions, by age and sex, are essential if the test is to be used for diagnostic purposes. Cross-validation studies have not been carried out, nor is it known to what extent the test will correctly identify brain-damaged subjects who are not readily identifiable by standard neurological tests.

In summary, this is a unique kind of test with special properties; it has shown signs of developing into a useful diagnostic instrument for the identification of unilateral lesions. It appears to be at least as promising as many of the other tests currently in use (3). However, further validation studies and a properly constructed manual are essential before the *Perceptual Maze Test* can be considered as other than a research instrument.[2]

[121]

★**Personal Orientation Inventory.** Grades 9–16 and adults; 1962–68; POI; 12 scores: time competent, inner directed, self-actualizing value, existentiality, feeling reactivity, spontaneity, self regard, self acceptance, nature of man, synergy, acceptance of aggression, capacity for intimate contact; 1 form ('63, 8 pages); manual with 1968 supplementation ('66, 39 pages); profile ('65, 2 pages); separate answer sheets (Digitek, hand scoring, IBM 1230) must be used; $9.50 per 25 tests; $3.75 per 50 hand scoring answer sheets; $4.50 per 50 Digitek or IBM answer sheets; $7 per set of hand or IBM scoring stencils; $3.75 per 50 profiles; $1.75 per manual; $2.25 per specimen set; postage extra; Digitek scoring service, 85¢ or less per test; (30–40) minutes; Everett L. Shostrom; Educational and Industrial Testing Service. *

REFERENCES

1–26. See P:193, also includes a cumulative name index to the first 26 references for this test.
27. GERBER, BARBARA WITTER. *A Study of Relationships Between Psychological Health and Creativity.* Doctor's thesis, Syracuse University (Syracuse, N.Y.), 1964. (*DA* 25:5733)
28. FORD, RICHARD WILLIAM. *The Relationship of Psychological Health of Elementary School Principals to the Organizational Climate of Schools.* Doctor's thesis, Syracuse University (Syracuse, N.Y.), 1966. (*DA* 28:900A)
29. GIBB, LEONARD LOUIS. *A Study of Differences in Sex, Home Background, Educational Background, Work Experience, Extra-Curricular Participation, and Self-Actualization Attainment in College Juniors.* Doctor's thesis, Northern Illinois University (DeKalb, Ill.), 1966. (*DA* 27:2358A)

1 An "interim report, which is for private circulation" only, is available and is currently being updated; it will probably be issued as a formal manual (personal communication from the author).

2 Recent published and unpublished studies indicate that administration of the test may be computerized, thus enabling on-line investigation of intellectual performance, both in normal and abnormal subjects (see, for example, 25).

30. GREEN, RUDOLPH VALENTINO. *Self-Actualizing Values and Occupational Aspirations of Culturally Different Youth.* Doctor's thesis, University of Kentucky (Lexington, Ky.), 1966. (*DAI* 30:2848A)

31. GROSSACK, M. M.; ARMSTRONG, T.; AND LUSSIEV, G. "Correlates of Self-Actualization." *J Humanistic Psychol* 6:87–91 sp '66. *

32. HOOVER, HELENE MAE PERRY. *Concept Development of College Students Exposed to Systematic, Organized Learning Experiences in Family Relationships.* Doctor's thesis, Oklahoma State University (Stillwater, Okla.), 1966. (*DA* 27:4465B)

33. PEARSON, OZIAS. *Effects of Group Guidance Upon College Adjustment.* Doctor's thesis, University of Kentucky (Lexington, Ky.), 1966. (*DAI* 30:4738A)

34. SWIFT, MARSHALL S. *Parent Child-Rearing Attitudes and Psychological Health of the Parent.* Doctor's thesis, Syracuse University (Syracuse, N.Y.), 1966. (*DA* 27:1274A)

35. ACKER, MARY BRYANT. *The Relation of Achievement Need, Time Perspective, and Field Articulation to Academic Performance.* Doctor's thesis, University of California (Berkeley, Calif.), 1967. (*DA* 29:1492B)

36. BERTOCH, MICHAEL R. *A Study of the Relationship of Counseling Theory Concepts to the Self-Concepts and Values of Counselors in Training.* Doctor's thesis, Boston University (Boston, Mass.), 1967. (*DA* 29:4272A)

37. FREEDMAN, MARK J. *Homosexuality Among Women and Psychological Adjustment.* Doctor's thesis, Case Western Reserve University (Cleveland, Ohio), 1967. (*DA* 28:4294B)

38. JOHNSON, EDWARD G., JR. *A Comparison of Academically Successful and Unsuccessful College of Education Freshmen on Two Measures of "Self."* Doctor's thesis, University of Toledo (Toledo, Ohio), 1967. (*DA* 28:1298A)

39. RESCHKE, STEPHEN EMIL. *Mental Health Factors in College Students: A Test of the Motivation-Hygiene Theory.* Doctor's thesis, Western Reserve University (Cleveland, Ohio), 1967. (*DA* 28:1251B)

40. WHITSETT, DAVID ANDERSON. *Self-Actualization and the Modern Formal Organization.* Doctor's thesis, Western Reserve University (Cleveland, Ohio), 1967. (*DA* 28:2616B)

41. BRAUN, JOHN R., AND ASTA, PATRICIA. "Intercorrelations Between Personal Orientation Inventory and Gordon Personal Inventory Scores." *Psychol Rep* 23:1197–8 D '68. * (*PA* 43:8368)

42. COHEN, EDMUND DAVID. *Some Related Variables in the Interpersonal Risk (IR) Theory.* Doctor's thesis, Case Western Reserve University (Cleveland, Ohio), 1968. (*DAI* 30:4787B)

43. DALE, VERDA M. *An Exploration of the Relationship of Home Managers' Self-Actualization to Participation by Family Members in Home Activities.* Doctor's thesis, Michigan State University (East Lansing, Mich.), 1968. (*DAI* 30:728B)

44. DORESS, IRVIN. *A Study of a Sampling of Boston University Student Activists.* Doctor's thesis, Boston University (Boston, Mass.), 1968. (*DA* 29:4563A)

45. EIBEN, RAY EUGENE. *Counselor-Counselee Personal Orientation and Post-Interview Affect.* Doctor's thesis, Ohio State University (Columbus, Ohio), 1968. (*DA* 29:796A)

46. GIBB, LEONARD L. "Home Background and Self-Actualization Attainment." *J Col Stud Personnel* 9:49–53 Ja '68. *

47. HOOD, WESLEY DELL. *Counselor-Client Similarity of Self-Actualization Level and Its Effect on Counseling Outcome.* Doctor's thesis, Ball State University (Muncie, Ind.), 1968. (*DA* 29:3831A)

48. JORGENSON, RONALD DUANE. *Relationship of Teacher Perception to Student and Teacher Self-Actualization.* Doctor's thesis, Ball State University (Muncie, Ind.), 1968. (*DAI* 30:134A)

49. LAMB, DONALD WAYNE. *Demonstrated Internal-External Reward Expectancies as a Variable in Group Counseling.* Doctor's thesis, North Texas State University (Denton, Tex.), 1968. (*DA* 29:2568A)

50. LAMOTT, JAMES ROBERT. *A Study of Personal Value Orientations Associated With Anticipated Career Specialty Choices of a Population of Medical Students.* Doctor's thesis, University of Washington (Seattle, Wash.), 1968. (*DA* 29:2122A)

51. LEWIS, SINCLAIR O. *A Test of Small-Group Procedures in College Adjustment.* Doctor's thesis, University of Kentucky (Lexington, Ky.), 1968. (*DAI* 30:2337A)

52. McCABE, OLIVER LEROY. *An Empirical Investigation of the Effects of Chemically (LSD-25)-Induced "Psychedelic Experiences" on Selected Measures of Personality, and Their Implications for Therapeutic Counseling Theory and Practice.* Doctor's thesis, Catholic University of America (Washington, D.C.), 1968. (*DA* 29:4849B)

53. MURRAY, MURIEL ELOISE. *Self-Actualization and Social Values of Teachers as Related to Students' Perception of Teachers.* Doctor's thesis, Pennsylvania State University (University Park, Pa.), 1968. (*DAI* 30:1026A)

54. PASNAK, MARY FRANCES DRAKE. *Fashion Innovators Compared With Non-Innovators on Clothing Attitudes, Self-Actualization, and Tolerance of Ambiguity.* Doctor's thesis, Pennsylvania State University (University Park, Pa.), 1968. (*DA* 29:1864B)

55. PELLEGRENO, DOMINICK DANIEL, JR. *The Personal Constructs of Counselor Enrollees.* Doctor's thesis, University of Toledo (Toledo, Ohio), 1968. (*DA* 29:1107A)

56. REYNOLDS, EDWARD NEAL. *Interpersonal Risk and Self-Actualization in Four Religious Groups.* Doctor's thesis, Case Western Reserve University (Cleveland, Ohio), 1968. (*DAI* 30:4019A)

57. RIDGE, RICHARD ALLEN. *Self-Actualization, Achievement and Other Factors as a Function of College Students in Selected Housing Settings.* Doctor's thesis, University of Florida (Gainesville, Fla.), 1968. (*DAI* 30:139A)

58. ROGERS, MARTIN IRVING. *Self-Actualization as Process.* Doctor's thesis, Case Western Reserve University (Cleveland, Ohio), 1968. (*DAI* 30:4380B)

59. RUSSELL, WILLIAM JOY CROSBY. *A Study of Changes in Measures of Inner-Direction, Open-Mindedness, and Intraception During Laboratory Training Designs of the Methodist Church.* Doctor's thesis, Syracuse University (Syracuse, N.Y.), 1968. (*DA* 29:3887A)

60. SALVA, DAVID MATTHEW. *Self-Actualization and Its Relationship to Intensity of Vocational Interests of Male College Freshmen.* Doctor's thesis, University of Kansas (Lawrence, Kan.), 1968. (*DAI* 30:837B)

61. SILVERSTEIN, A. B., AND FISHER, GARY. "Is Item Overlap Responsible for a 'Built-In' Factor Structure?" *Psychol Rep* 23:935–8 D '68. * (*PA* 43:9778)

62. SMITH, MIRIAM LOUISE HOGUE. *The Facilitation of Student Self-Directed Learning as Perceived by Teachers With High and Low Levels of Self Actualization and Dogmatism.* Doctor's thesis, Pennsylvania State University (University Park, Pa.), 1968. (*DA* 29:1467A)

63. STEIN, FRANKLIN. *Consistency of Cognitive, Interest, and Personality Variables With Academic Mastery: A Study of Field-Dependence-Independence, Verbal Comprehension, Self-Perception, and Vocational Interest in Relation to Academic Performance Among Male Juniors Attending an Urban University.* Doctor's thesis, New York University (New York, N.Y.), 1968. (*DA* 29:1429A)

64. THOMPSON, SEABORN ADAMS. *A Study of the Relationship Between Personality Factors of Counselors and Counselee Perceptions of These Counselors.* Doctor's thesis, Auburn University (Auburn, Ala.), 1968. (*DA* 29:3427A)

65. THOMPSON, SHEILAH DOREEN. *Some Personality Characteristics of Student Teachers of Guidance.* Doctor's thesis, University of British Columbia (Vancouver, B.C., Canada), 1968. (*DAI* 30:556A)

66. WALKER, NORMA PEDEN. *Clothing Expenditures as Related to Selected Values, Self-Actualization, and Buying Practices: An Exploratory Study.* Doctor's thesis, Pennsylvania State University (University Park, Pa.), 1968. (*DA* 29:4836B)

67. BRAUN, JOHN R. "Search for Correlates of Self-Actualization." *Percept & Motor Skills* 28(2):557–8 Ap '69. * (*PA* 43:15764)

68. BRAUN, JOHN R., AND ASTA, PATRICIA. "A Comparison of 'Real' *VS.* 'Ideal' Self With Self-Actualization Inventory." *J Psychol* 72(2):159–64 Jl '69. * (*PA* 44:670)

69. BRAUN, JOHN R., AND LA FARO, DOLORES. "A Further Study of the Fakability of the Personal Orientation Inventory." *J Clin Psychol* 25(3):296–9 Jl '69. * (*PA* 44:3643)

70. DAMM, VERNON J. "Overall Measures of Self-Actualization Derived From the Personal Orientation Inventory." *Ed & Psychol Meas* 29(4):977–81 w '69. * (*PA* 44:20997)

71. DAWSON, FORD. *An Analytical Study of the Effects of Maternal Employment, of Same-Sex Chum Denial in Preadolescence, and of Residential Mobility on Self-Actualization Achievement in a Sample of Adolescents.* Doctor's thesis, American University (Washington, D.C.), 1969. (*DAI* 31:925A)

72. ELBERT, WELDON EUGENE. *Changes in Self-Concept, Self-Actualization, and Interpersonal Relations as a Result of Video Feedback in Sensitivity Training.* Doctor's thesis, East Texas State University (Commerce, Tex.), 1969. (*DAI* 30:5233A)

73. FISHER, GARY, AND SILVERSTEIN, A. B. "Self-Actualization Values of Felons." *J Humanistic Psychol* 9(1):66–70 sp '69. * (*PA* 44:6987)

74. FISHER, GARY, AND SILVERSTEIN, A. B. "Simulation of Poor Adjustment on a Measure of Self-Actualization." *J Clin Psychol* 25(2):198–9 Ap '69. * (*PA* 43:14507)

75. FISHER, THOMAS LEE. *A Prediction of Counselor Facilitation From Communication and Discrimination Indexes and a Personality Measure.* Doctor's thesis, University of Georgia (Athens, Ga.), 1969. (*DAI* 31:147A)

76. FOULDS, MELVIN L. "Positive Mental Health and Facilitative Genuineness During Counseling." *Personnel & Guid J* 47(8):762–6 Ap '69. *

77. FOULDS, MELVIN L. "Self-Actualization and Level of Counselor Interpersonal Functioning." *J Humanistic Psychol* 9(1):87–92 sp '69. * (*PA* 44:7107)

78. FOULDS, MELVIN L. "Self-Actualization and the Communication of Facilitative Conditions During Counseling." *J Counsel Psychol* 16(2):132–6 Mr '69. * (*PA* 43:9852)

79. GATTSHALL, GERALD WALTER. *Imprisonment's Affects Upon the Self Concept and the Actualizing Process.* Doctor's thesis, Ball State University (Muncie, Ind.), 1969. (*DAI* 30:5235A)

80. GROENEVELD, LEROY CHARLES. *The Positive Experience Group Encounter and Its Effect Upon Self-Actualization.* Doc-

tor's thesis, Ball State University (Muncie, Ind.), 1969. (*DAI* 30:3726A)

81. GUNTER, LAURIE M. "The Developing Nursing Student: Part 1, A Study of Self-Actualizing Values." *Nursing Res* 18(1):60–4 Ja–F '69. * (*PA* 44:21066)

82. JEPSON, PETER. *Some Effects of Self-Actualizing Growth Psychology on Teenagers.* Doctor's thesis, United States International University (San Diego, Calif.), 1969. (*DAI* 31:224A)

83. KAMMEIER, MARY LEO. *Biographic, Cognitive, Demographic and Personality Differences Between Adolescents From Families With Identifiable Alcohol Problems and From Families Without Identifiable Alcohol Problems.* Doctor's thesis, University of North Dakota (Grand Forks, N.D.), 1969. (*DAI* 30:1398A)

84. LABACH, PATRICIA AVERY. *Self-Actualization in College Students: Interrelationships of Self-Actualization, Personal Characteristics, and Attitudes in Subcultures of Liberal Arts Freshmen and Seniors.* Doctor's thesis, Kent State University (Kent, Ohio), 1969. (*DAI* 31:1013A)

85. LEMAY, MORRIS L. "Self-Actualization and College Achievement at Three Ability Levels." *J Counsel Psychol* 16(6):582–3 N '69. * (*PA* 44:4231)

86. LEMAY, MORRIS L., AND DAMM, VERNON J. "Relationship of the Personal Orientation Inventory to the Edwards Personal Preference Schedule." *Psychol Rep* 24(3):834 Je '69. * (*PA* 44:664)

87. LIBENSON, MICHAEL A. *Relationship of Academic Performance to Perceptual Congruence Between Selected College Freshmen and Their Parents.* Doctor's thesis, Boston University (Boston, Mass.), 1969. (*DAI* 31:156A)

88. LOW, GARY ROY. *A Study of Counselor Trainee Changes in Two Types of Practicum.* Doctor's thesis, East Texas State University (Commerce, Tex.), 1969. (*DAI* 30:5240A)

89. MARGULIES, NEWTON. "Organizational Culture and Psychological Growth." *J Appl Behav Sci* 5(4):491–508 O–D '69. * (*PA* 44:10309)

90. MAZER, GILBERT E. "Attitude and Personality Change in Student Teachers of Disadvantaged Youth." *J Ed Res* 63(3):116–20 N '69. * (*PA* 46:5629)

91. MORITZ, FLOYD C. *A Human Relations Laboratory as an Inservice Education Program.* Doctor's thesis, Arizona State University (Tempe, Ariz.), 1969. (*DAI* 30:3694A)

92. PASNAK, MARY FRANCES DRAKE, AND AYRES, RUTH W. "Clothing Attitudes and Personality Characteristics of Fashion Innovators." *J Home Econ* 61(9):689–702 N '69. *

93. POST, HARRY H., JR. *Self-Actualization and the Interpersonal Relationship Environment.* Doctor's thesis, Boston University (Boston, Mass.), 1969. (*DAI* 31:383B)

94. SCHENK, KATHERINE NIXON. *Factors Associated With Planned Change in Baccalaureate Nursing Programs.* Doctor's thesis, University of Florida (Gainesville, Fla.), 1969. (*DAI* 31:268B)

95. SHERMAN, LILLIAN LASKAW. *Movers and Perseverers in Education: An Investigation of Interests, Values, Personality Factors, Self-Actualization, Need Satisfaction and Job Satisfaction Among Movers Into Counseling and Into Administration and Among Perseverers in Teaching.* Doctor's thesis, New York University (New York, N.Y.), 1969. (*DAI* 31:1023A)

96. STOCKTON, REX ARTHUR. *An Investigation of the Effect of Sensitivity Training on the Attitudes of Teacher Education Students.* Doctor's thesis, Ball State University (Muncie, Ind.), 1969. (*DAI* 30:2156A)

97. WEIR, WILLIAM, AND GADE, ELDON. "An Approach to Counseling Alcoholics." *Rehabil Counsel B* 12(4):227–30 Je '69. *

98. YEAGER, JOSEPH CORNELIUS. *The Effectiveness of a Training Program in Human Relations.* Doctor's thesis, University of Pittsburgh (Pittsburgh, Pa.), 1969. (*DAI* 31:2344B)

99. ZIMMERMAN, SAUNDRA F.; PEDERSEN, DARHL M.; AND SMITH, KAY H. "The Factorial Determination of Types of Conforming Individuals." *J Psychol* 72(1):101–7 My '69. * (*PA* 43:15688)

100. BURDG, MARVIN LEWIS. *Relationship of Student Attrition Rates and Self-Actualization of Community College Teachers.* Doctor's thesis, United States International University (San Diego, Calif.), 1970. (*DAI* 31:2169A)

101. CARPENTER, JAMES CLINTON. *Patterns of Self-Disclosure and Confirmation in Mother-Daughter Communication.* Doctor's thesis, Ohio State University (Columbus, Ohio), 1970. (*DAI* 31:4331B)

102. DAMM, VERNON J. "Creativity and Intelligence: Research Implications for Equal Emphasis in High School." *Excep Children* 36(8):565–9 Ap '70. * (*PA* 46:1754)

103. DEIULIO, ROBERT SALVATORE. *An Analysis of College Freshmen Perceptions of Staff Members Who Functioned as Counselors Compared to Those Who Functioned as Teachers and Counselors.* Doctor's thesis, Boston University (Boston, Mass.), 1970. (*DAI* 31:2101A)

104. EMRICK, CHAD D. "Abstinence and Time Perception of Alcoholics." *Q J Studies Alcohol* 31(2):384–93 Je '70. *

105. FISHER, IJOURIE STOCKS. *The Relationship Between Selected Personality Characteristics and the Effects of Training to Develop Small Group Productivity Skills and Interpersonal Competence.* Doctor's thesis, University of Miami (Coral Gables, Fla.), 1970. (*DAI* 31:1617A)

106. FOULDS, MELVIN L. "Effects of a Personal Growth

Group on a Measure of Self-Actualization." *J Humanistic Psychol* 10(1):33–8 sp '70. * (*PA* 46:6737)

107. GRAFF, ROBERT W., AND BRADSHAW, HARLEY E. "Relationship of a Measure of Self-Actualization to Dormitory Assistant Effectiveness." *J Counsel Psychol* 17(6):502–5 N '70. * (*PA* 45:2917)

108. GRAFF, ROBERT W.; BRADSHAW, HARLEY E.; DANISH, STEVEN J.; AUSTIN, BRIAN A.; AND ALTEKRUSE, MICHAEL. "The POI: A Validity Check." *Ed & Psychol Meas* 30(2):429–32 su '70. * (*PA* 45:2408)

109. GUINAN, JAMES F., AND FOULDS, MELVIN L. "Marathon Group: Facilitator of Personal Growth?" *J Counsel Psychol* 17(2):145–9 Mr '70. * (*PA* 44:8431)

110. KELLY, MARYNELL ATWATER. *Active vs Passive Leadership Techniques With Development Groups.* Doctor's thesis, University of Arizona (Tucson, Ariz.), 1970. (*DAI* 31:2990B)

111. LUZZI, MATTHEW HENRY. *A Study of the Relationship of Self-Acceptance and Social Values to Effectiveness of Male Rehabilitation Counselor Trainees.* Doctor's thesis, Boston University (Boston, Mass.), 1970. (*DAI* 31:2111A)

112. MCCLAIN, EDWIN W. "Further Validation of the Personal Orientation Inventory: Assessment of Self-Actualization of School Counselors." *J Consult & Clin Psychol* 35(1):21–2 Ag '70. * (*PA* 44:21001)

113. PELLEGRIN, VICTOR BRUCE HOLKER. *A Descriptive Study of a Midwestern Sample of Episcopal Clergy and Seminarians Categorized According to Various Criteria.* Doctor's thesis, University of Kansas (Lawrence, Kan.), 1970. (*DAI* 31:2690A)

114. PHELAN, JOSEPH G.; BROOKS, RICHARD; AND BRASHEARS, GLADYS C. "Relationship of Kinesthetic Figural Aftereffect to Masculinity-Femininity and Expectation for Internal Versus External Control of Reinforcement." *Percept & Motor Skills* 31(3):863–6 D '70. * (*PA* 45:9967)

115. ROMANO, ROBERT JOHN. *Counseling Outcomes Related to Family Background of Delinquent Male Adolescents.* Doctor's thesis, Boston University (Boston, Mass.), 1970. (*DAI* 31:3004B)

116. SANDS, BILLIE LOUISE. *An Exploratory Study of Self-Actualization and Self-Perception of Competency Among Michigan Family Life Teachers.* Doctor's thesis, Michigan State University (East Lansing, Mich.), 1970. (*DAI* 31:3425A)

117. SHERIDAN, KATHLEEN, AND SHACK, JOHN R. "Personality Correlates of the Undergraduate Volunteer Subject." *J Psychol* 76(1):23–6 S '70. * (*PA* 45:2397)

118. SMITH, OSLER PAUL, JR. *Changes in Self-Actualization and Self-Concept as a Result of the Use of Visual Feedback in Marathon Sensitivity Training.* Doctor's thesis, East Texas State University (Commerce, Tex.), 1970. (*DAI* 31:3280A)

119. SQUATRIGLIA, ROBERT WILLIAM. *The Impact of Short-Term Group Counseling on Student Values.* Doctor's thesis, University of South Carolina (Columbia, S.C.), 1970. (*DAI* 31:3280A)

120. STEWART, ROBERT A. C., AND WEBSTER, ALAN C. "Scale for Theological Conservatism, and Its Personality Correlates." *Percept & Motor Skills* 30(3):867–70 Je '70. * (*PA* 44:16675)

121. WALL, JOAN B. "Relationship of Locus of Control to Self-Actualization." *Psychol Rep* 27(1):282 Ag '70. * (*PA* 45:6305)

122. YOUNG, EDWARD R., AND JACOBSON, LEONARD I. "Effects of Time-Extended Marathon Group Experiences on Personality Characteristics." *J Counsel Psychol* 17(3):247–51 My '70. * (*PA* 44:12729)

123. ZIMMERMAN, SAUNDRA F.; SMITH, KAY H.; AND PEDERSEN, DARHL M. "The Effect of Anticonformity Appeals on Conformity Behavior." *J Social Psychol* 81(1):93–103 Je '70. * (*PA* 44:18593)

BRUCE BLOXOM, *Assistant Professor of Psychology, Vanderbilt University, Nashville, Tennessee.*

The *Personal Orientation Inventory* is a self-report instrument designed to assess values, attitudes, and behavior relevant to Maslow's concept of the self-actualizing person. Specific variables assessed are (*a*) inner support (I), which is the tendency of a person to quite generally act on and be guided by his own principles and motives in contrast to responding to a wide variety of external pressures, and (*b*) time competence (Tc), which is the tendency of the person to live primarily in the present free of hangups over past events and future uncertainties. The inner-support variable is broken down into five facets of self-actualization in the interpersonal sphere. Each facet consists of a pair of closely related, but contrasting, variables. The first pair deals with the facet of interpersonal values: self-actualizing values (SAV), which is the valuing of acting on one's own principles, and existentiality (Ex), which is the valuing of flexibility in applying these principles. The second pair deals with admitted responsivity to one's feelings: feeling reactivity (Fr), which is sensitivity to one's own feelings, and spontaneity (S), which is free expression of these feelings. The third pair deals with attitudes toward the self: self-regard (Sr), which is the liking of one's self as a person, and self-acceptance (Sa), which is the attitude of acceptance of one's own weaknesses. The fourth pair is very broadly described as "awareness": nature of man (Nc), which is the attitude that man is basically good, and synergy (Sy), which is the perception of opposites in life (e.g., lust and love) as really having something in common. The fifth facet deals with sensitivity to important aspects of interpersonal relations: acceptance of aggression (A), which is the acceptance of one's own hostile feelings, and a capacity for intimate contact (C), which is the desire to respond to expectations and obligations without becoming a slave to them and without using them to exploit people. For each of these five facets a person is said to be self-actualizing if and only if both aspects of the facet are characteristic of him.

The POI contains a scale for each of the variables just described. The Tc and I scales have 23 and 127 items, respectively. The remaining scales are subscales, containing from 9 to 32 items taken mostly from the I scale. As noted in the test manual, these subscales have a number of items overlapping and are, therefore, not statistically independent. The most extreme instance of this is the Sy scale which has seven of its nine items in common with the SAV scale. Each of the subscales has at least five items in common with some other subscale, making it very difficult to make substantive interpretations of the subscale intercorrelations reported in the manual.

In part, the item overlap may be due to a lack of parsimony in the conceptual schema used to define the facets of self-actualization. The lack of parsimony is most obvious when one critically compares the definitions of the variables. For example, feeling reactivity and acceptance of aggression both imply an awareness and acceptance of hostile feelings. Therefore, it is not surprising that the scales for these two variables should have a number of items in common. Perhaps the creation of fewer and different facets in the self-actualization schema could have prevented this problem.

In general, the content validity of the scales of the POI is good. The variables being assessed by the items are broadly defined. The content of the items in each scale is appropriately quite varied. Since the use of a broad range of content can lower the indices of internal consistency (e.g., the K-R 20 coefficient) such indices should be reported in the manual, which they are not.

The major psychometric data reported in the manual are test-retest reliability correlations and normative data. The reliability coefficients range from a moderate .55 to a good .85. Only three subscales have coefficients that might be regarded as substandard (say, less than .70): A (.55), Nc (.66), and Fr (.69). The A and Fr scales measure variables that are affect-related and, as such, may be measuring fluctuation in mood states from test to retest. It is not clear why No has a relatively low reliability.

The normative data in the manual are biased towards the college student population. The standard score profile sheet is based on norms of 2,607 entering college freshmen. Three out of nine group profiles presented are for college groups. Other groups for which profiles are given are business supervisors, Peace Corps volunteers, high school students, hospitalized psychiatric patients, delinquent sailors, and male alcoholics. Unfortunately, no norms or profiles are provided for psychiatric outpatients. The manual stresses that a good use of the inventory is in therapy and counseling, in which case it might be helpful to have outpatient norms.

Even with this bias in the normative data, the test user should base his interpretations on the standard score profiles only and not on the time-ratio and support-ratio scores which are suggested by the manual as providing information above and beyond the profiles. The ratio scores are completely determined by and positively related to the Tc and I scale scores. Furthermore, no data are presented to back up some of the manual's exaggerated claims to validity of the ratio scores (e.g., "with a [time] ratio of $1:3$ he is time incompetent about $\frac{1}{4}$ of the time").

The validity of the POI can be well documented by summarizing the results of studies of the I scale. Studies of the subscales are not reviewed here since most of them fail to take the statistical interdependence of those scales into account.

The I scale appears to show a considerable degree of validity as a measure of feelings, values, and attitudes appropriate to self-actualization. In five of six therapy studies using that scale, the scores of patients increased from pretherapy to posttherapy more than was the case for nonpatient controls. In studies using person-rating methods, I scores were found to be positively related to clinical ratings of self-actualization, to ratings of empathy and facilitative genuineness in practicum students, and to ratings of teachers' concern for their students. In studies using other measures of individual differences as criteria, I scores were negatively correlated with neuroticism, dogmatism, and the D, Pt, and Si scales of the MMPI. I scale scores were positively correlated with extraversion, college grades, and creativity measures.

In contrast to these, some studies indicate that the I scale lacks some of the properties desirable in a complete measure of self-actualization. In one study, a negative correlation was found between I scores of student teachers and supervisors' ratings of their performance. In another study, college counselors with low I scores effected more changes in their clients than did counselors with high I scores. In a study of middle aptitude college students, over-achievement was found to correlate negatively with I scores. These studies suggest that although persons with high I scores are acting, thinking, and feeling like self-actualizers, they are not necessarily utilizing all of their capabilities (which is an integral part of complete self-actualization).

In summary, the POI lacks some desirable properties as an inventory because of the rather pervasive item overlap in its subscales. However, its two major scales, time competence and inner support, are free of this problem if used by themselves. A number of studies indicate that the inner support scale measures feelings, values, and attitudes appropriate to Maslow's concept of self-actualization, but that persons scoring high on these attitudes and values are not necessarily utilizing all of their capabilities in a way consistent with complete self-actualiza-

tion. Researchers and practitioners who keep these features of the POI in mind should find it a useful instrument.

RICHARD W. COAN, *Professor of Psychology, The University of Arizona, Tucson, Arizona.*

The *Personal Orientation Inventory* represents an effort to assess a number of variables involved in sound personal functioning, or "self-actualization." In the past, both theory and measurement in the personality realm have centered too much around concepts of psychopathology. Theorists have increasingly recognized the importance of focusing directly on sound functioning, and there is now an obvious need for instruments that can tap components of sound functioning, rather than just the presence or absence of pathology. In taking a bold psychometric leap into the land of self-actualization, Shostrom is attempting to perform a much-needed service. When one leaps into darkness, however, one runs the risk of unforeseen hazards, and we may ask whether Shostrom's jumping style is the one best suited to the circumstances.

The nature of the optimal personality, whether we speak of it in terms of self-actualization, personality integration, positive mental health, or some other common phrase, has been the object of much speculation in recent years. The little systematic research that has been addressed to this topic suggests that theorists have grossly oversimplified the problem. We need to deal with a variety of independent components, and we have much to learn about the nature of these. Shostrom uses extant theory as his springboard, particularly the thinking of Maslow, Riesman (whose name is consistently misspelled in the test manual), May, and Perls. Apparently the scale variables were all selected on theoretical grounds, and the items were constructed and assembled by essentially rational procedures.

The actual choice of variables necessarily reflects the biases of the author. There is a rather strong emphasis on individual autonomy. Most of the items are scorable in terms of a contrast between other-support and inner-support, and a greater than average emphasis on the latter is viewed as one of the basic characteristics of the self-actualizer. It is recognized that inner-directedness can be carried too far, and an optimal balance—or optimal range of balances—is specified. We may hope that future theoretical and empirical analyses will enable us to specify and assess more clearly the particular forms in which other-support and inner-support are desirable.

A second major contrast concerns the use and experience of time. All items not scorable for the above dichotomy are scored for this. Each item involves a choice between a "time competent" and a "time incompetent" alternative. Time competence, which is obviously to be preferred, is conceptualized in terms of living "more fully in the here-and-now" and experiencing present events in a meaningful continuity with both the past and the future. Actually, a mere emphasis in test responses on present experience would seem to favor a "time-competent" score balance. It is obvious that an individual who is overly preoccupied with either the past or the future must lead a life of limited zest and spontaneity, but on logical grounds we may question whether the score ratio that Shostrom considers desirable necessarily represents an optimal condition.

Examination of the remaining more specific scales, and of the items in the test as a whole, suggests an additional bias in favor of extraversion. There is considerable emphasis on overt expression, but not an inner experience. This impression of the POI is supported by its correlations with the various scales of the MMPI, the *Eysenck Personality Inventory,* and the *Study of Values.*

Other features of item formulation must be noted. In each item, the subject is asked to choose between two opposing statements, instead of just marking a single statement true or false. The use of double-statement items makes the test seem a little monotonous, but it often provides the subject with a more clearly delineated choice than he would otherwise have. Its advantages seem to outweigh its shortcomings. It is a bit more disturbing, however, to find that so many statements are expressed in an absolute, or categorical, form. The testee is frequently confronted with a demand to choose between two extremes, neither of which comes close to describing his attitudes or life situation. Since the items tend to be very general or abstract in content, we might expect intellectual sophistication in the psychological realm to play a large role in the choice that is made. In a few items where only one of the alternatives is expressed in absolute form, the choice

may be governed by a set to accept or reject statements in this form.

A still more serious problem is that a large number of items appear to reflect a naive conception of the relationship between test taking behavior and measured psychological variables. What is it that leads a subject to endorse or reject any of the following statements?

> I am afraid to be myself.
> I accept my weaknesses.
> For me, past, present and future is in meaningful continuity.
> I can accept my mistakes.
> I live in terms of my wants, likes, dislikes and values.

The scoring system evidently assumes that any statement endorsed by a subject is literally true or, at least, that it tends to be. The assumption is clearly not credible for items of this general character. To assert that one is not afraid to be himself or that one can accept his weaknesses may well betoken a defensiveness that is not reckoned in the scoring or interpretation of this test.

In the face of these difficulties, it is reassuring to find some supportive validity data for the test. Scores tend to be higher for subjects designated by clinical psychologists as relatively self-actualized, and they tend to rise as a consequence of psychotherapy. In view of the item characteristics of the test, however, we must wonder to what extent such observed differences can be explained in terms of relatively superficial differences or changes in sophistication with respect to current thought regarding psychological growth and soundness. There appear to be no construct validity data bearing on the individual scales of the test. The positive intercorrelations among the scales are in accord with theoretical expectations, but the magnitude of these correlations underscores the need for further clarification of the overall structure of the region assessed by the test.

Since there have been relatively few attempts to measure components of self-actualization, the POI may be welcomed as an effort to fill a large and regrettable void. Unfortunately, it represents an arbitrary and theoretically biased selection of variables, and it suffers from a lack of sophistication in questionnaire item formulation. In view of the need that it is intended to meet, the test deserves exploratory research use at present. It must be recognized, however, that the whole realm of variables encompassed by concepts of optimal personal functioning is in need of greater clarification through systematic multivariate research, and we may hope that much more adequate instruments will appear in the not-too-distant future.

[122]

★Personal Values Inventory. Grades 12–13; 1941–69; PVI; for predicting academic achievement; 12 scores: high school self report, need for achievement, direction of aspirations, socioeconomic status, peer influence, home influence, planning, persistence, self control, total of persistence and self control, faking, self insight; separate editions for men and women; Student Form ('64, 7 pages); mimeographed preliminary manual, revised ('69, 72 pages, identical with manual published in 1967 except for 4 page appendix); the test may currently be used only by colleges interested in carrying out validation research; separate answer cards must be used; $3 per manual, postpaid; specimen set not available; examination fee, 20¢ per student; fee includes test booklet, answer card, scoring service, and research report on the validity of the test for predicting grades in the participating college; (50) minutes; George E. Schlesser, John A. Finger, and Thomas Lynch (manual only); Colgate University Testing Service. *

REFERENCES

1–15. See P:195.
16. GRANDE, PETER P. "Persistence and Change of Educational Objectives of Engineering Freshmen." J Col Stud Personnel 6:98–101 D '64. *
17. RIVERA, EMILIO, JR. The Contribution of Non-Intellectual Variables to the Prediction of Academic Performance of Junior High School Pupils. Doctor's thesis, New York University (New York, N.Y.), 1967. (DA 28:4058A)

HENRY A. ALKER, Assistant Professor of Psychology and Sociology, Cornell University, Ithaca, New York.

This inventory represents 30 years of continuing effort at developing measures for predicting and explaining college academic achievement. The focus has been consistently on achieving incremental validity in prediction beyond that obtainable with SAT predictors. In a period when the SAT exams are under attack for their questionable validities, especially with culturally disadvantaged groups, such a goal is particularly timely. Unfortunately, validity data concerning various aspects of this problem are, as yet, incomplete.

Data in the manual fail to make it clear, for example, how much incremental validity is achieved by the PVI when SAT predictors and high school rank in class, presumably standardized, are included. This problem arises because validity studies from 25 colleges reported in the manual never include the students' actual high school rank in class in correlation with the PVI scales. Instead, the authors use a self-reported grade point average. Schlesser reports (personal communication) that in two

available samples self-reported high school record and actual numerical high school average correlated only .64 and .80. Within these constraints, using only self-reported high school record and the two best PVI scales (Direction of Aspirations and Persistence), predictions of about .50 for freshman GPA have been achieved. The median (apparently not cross validated) multiple regression prediction, including both SAT-V and SAT-M, was .60. A focus on incremental prediction from the standpoint of the college admissions office requires this missing information. Other dependent variables such as graduation, four-year GPA, transfer, and graduate admission have received little attention. One study of dropouts reported that negligible though statistically significant prediction was possible.

As the reader may suppose, the extensive focus in predicting college achievement has resulted in a rather narrow selection of "personal values." Why persistence, home influence, and peer influence are called "personal values" at all is not made clear. There is little informed discussion in the manual or elsewhere about the causal priority of the "values" or the behavior those values presumably control.

Good scale reliabilities, promising faking scales, adequate norms, and some validity data on the nonintellective scales, together with an excellent discussion of several case studies, suggest that this inventory has some value as an aid in counseling college students. Whether it would surpass or even reach the utility of the California Psychological Inventory as a counseling aid is open to question. The practical incremental predictive utility of this inventory, moreover, is rather modest. Further research, particularly with disadvantaged groups, may, however, prove rewarding.

ROBERT R. KNAPP, Director, Educational and Industrial Testing Service, San Diego, California.

The Personal Values Inventory is a group administered, self-report inventory, empirically developed to measure noncognitive variables for use in predicting academic achievement at the college level.

At present the PVI is intended primarily for use as a research instrument although case studies and other material for use in individual interpretation are presented in the 1969 revision of the handbook, and its use in selection and counseling is suggested. Further, the research restriction is not clearly noted in the handbook.

The development of the PVI is reported in the manual as dating back to preliminary work initiated in 1941, although only a very few published articles have appeared. No theoretical framework of personality was followed in construction of the inventory and the research results reported seem to provide few new insights into the personality determinants of college success. Item development was initiated with an item pool based on personality traits, study habits lists, principles of learning, and interest items. Items vary in format from brief descriptions of student life styles, answered by the degree to which they describe the examinee, to questions such as "Do you avoid wild parties?" The original item pool was administered to a beginning college sample and first semester marks used as a criterion in preliminary item selection. Cluster analysis was used to group items. Analyses based on two independent samples yielded three corresponding clusters identified as "steady, persistent effort," "moral self-control," and "dislike of rashness (particularly needless physical risks)."

From the clues provided in this preliminary work, additional items were developed and empirically tested through the years. Scales tapping other dimensions, including the Autobiographical Inventory and Socioeconomic scale, were added, with only items significantly related to scholastic performance being retained. Although many items were subsequently tested and scales added, the authors report that few correlated as well with grade point average as the scale measuring persistence.

Reported reliability of the scales appears satisfactory, with median coefficients ranging from .75 to .91. All but one scale, Independence in Planning, yielded reliabilities of .80 or above. The authors do not state the method used in determining reliability, and the concept (attributed to Guilford) that for maximum reliability, indicating homogeneity of the scale, items of equal difficulty are required, while for validity items of differing difficulty are required is, of course, true for estimates of *internal consistency* reliability and not *test-retest* estimates.

Validity data are presented in the form of multiple correlation coefficients showing the relative importance of combinations of PVI scales and the SAT in predicting GPA. The average multiple correlation obtained with these variables is reported as approximately .60, ranging in various samples from .42 to .79. The authors report that in every college, nonintellective variables contributed at least as much to the prediction of GPA as did the intellective variables, with the PVI scales of Persistence, Direction of Aspiration, and the self-reported high school record accounting for the greatest amount of the noncognitive variance.

Validity data are considered in the handbook for each of the nine noncognitive PVI scales. Correlations between the scales and GPA presented in the handbook are based on samples of 2,493 from 11 men's colleges and 1,261 from 9 women's colleges. Median correlations of nine PVI scales against GPA range from $-.08$ (Socioeconomic) to .41 (Persistence) for men and from $-.13$ (Socioeconomic) to .45 (Direction of Aspirations) for women. Patterns of intercorrelations of the scales against self-reported high school record are similar to those against the GPA criteria. Scales interpreted as measuring Direction of Aspirations and Persistence, and to a lesser degree Need for Achievement and Self-Control, clearly account for the greatest portion of variance in relating PVI scales to GPA and to the high school record scale.

As suggested from the above, the two most promising PVI scales are the Direction of Aspiration and Persistence scales. Although absence of scale scoring instructions makes outside critical examination of scale content and interpretation impossible, some evidence is presented in the handbook. The Direction of Aspiration scale is interpreted by the authors as reflecting orientation toward academic excellence rather than other pursuits. Median correlations of this scale with GPA are reported as .40. Median correlations with scholastic aptitude, as measured by the SAT, range from .02 to .25.

The Persistence scale is interpreted as reflecting a student's perceived self-reputation with regard to persistence and effort. The median correlation in all samples between the Persistence scale and GPA is reported as .42. Median correlations of .07 and .08 against SAT Verbal and Mathematical, respectively, are reported. The goal of obtaining a scale significantly correlated with GPA but independent of intellectual factors is best represented in the PVI by the Persistence scale.

As is the case generally with empirically

developed instruments, the PVI might be expected to find its greatest usefulness when applied for the specific purpose for which items were selected; i.e., to predict first semester college grade point average. In this reviewer's estimation, the attempt to identify diagnostically useful scales yet retain significant item-criterion (GPA) correlations has not been overly successful. Several PVI scales do not meet the criteria of significant correlation with GPA, yet the scope of the inventory doesn't adequately cover any single domain. Examples of scales not meeting the criteria of significant correlation with GPA are the Socioeconomic scale and the Self-Insight scale. The Socioeconomic scale correlates only −.08 and −.13 for men and women, respectively, against GPA and the Self-Insight scale yielded correlations of −.03 and −.02 against the criterion.

Counselors wishing to consider the PVI results will find the illustrative case studies to be helpful in understanding and interpreting results. However, they will find the PVI wanting in the coverage of meaningful traits and behavior. Missing are diagnostically useful indices of study habits and the broader range of attitudes and values useful in the counseling situation. Indications are not provided for those areas of interest beyond academic success. The authors might follow a course of action designed to provide a single scale for the prediction of GPA with associated diagnostic scales developed independent of the GPA criterion for use in counseling.

Of particular interest would be correlations with other personality trait measures and correlations with scales from similarly developed instruments such as the Achiever Personality scale of the OAIS. Correlations with established trait measures might be expected to provide greater insight into the personality characteristics associated with academic achievement, an area about which considerably more knowledge should be gained.

Those considering research use of the PVI will, of course, critically review the evidence for the possible usefulness of the inventory as an adjunctive instrument only to their entrance examination battery. Lacking the availability of further data, the contribution of the PVI would seem to be limited to an increment in prediction of the college GPA criteria, a contribution which may be useful for certain purposes.

[123]

★**Personality Research Form.** College; 1965–68; PRF; 2 forms; 2 editions; manual ('67, 31 pages); $8.75 per 25 tests; $1.90 per 25 answer sheets; $2.10 per 25 profiles; $2.25 per hand scoring stencil; $4 per manual; $1.50 per specimen set, excluding manual and stencils; cash orders postpaid; Douglas N. Jackson; Research Psychologists Press, Inc. *

a) STANDARD EDITION. 1965–68; 15 scores: achievement, affiliation, aggression, autonomy, dominance, endurance, exhibition, harm avoidance, impulsivity, nurturance, order, play, social recognition, understanding, infrequency; Forms A ('68, 6 pages, identical with test copyrighted in 1965), B ('65, 6 pages); profile ('67, 2 pages); separate answer sheets (Digitek, hand scored) must be used; Digitek scoring stencils not available; (30–45) minutes.

b) LONG EDITION. 1965–67; 22 scores: same as for Standard Edition plus abasement, change, cognitive structure, defendence, sentience, succorance, desirability; contains the 300 items of the Standard Edition plus 140 additional items intermixed; Forms AA, BB, ('65, 8 pages); profile ('67, 2 pages); separate answer sheets (hand scored) must be used; (40–70) minutes.

REFERENCES

1–13. See P:201.
14. OSBORNE, WILBUR JOSEPH. *An Investigation of Interpersonal Persuasiveness as a Factor of Personality.* Doctor's thesis, Pennsylvania State University (University Park, Pa.), 1966. (*DA* 28:1148A)
15. HOFFMANN, HELMUT. "Performance on the Personality Research Form Under Desirable and Undesirable Instructions: Personality Disorders." *Psychol Rep* 23:507–10 O '68. * (*PA* 43:9773)
16. JOHNSON, GERALD W. *A Validation Study of the Personality Research Form.* Master's thesis, Chico State College (Chico, Calif.), 1968.
17. BENTLER, P. M., AND PRINCE, CHARLES. "Personality Characteristics of Male Transvestites: III." *J Abn Psychol* 74(2):140–3 Ap '69. * (*PA* 43:10049)
18. BITHER, STEWART WALLACE. *A Study of the Relationship Among Personalities in Groups and Group Task Performance.* Doctor's thesis, University of Washington (Seattle, Wash.), 1969. (*DAI* 30:2196A)
19. BRAUN, JOHN R., AND ASTA, PATRICIA. "Changes in Personality Research Form Scores (PRF, Form A) Produced by Faking Instructions." *J Clin Psychol* 25(4):429–30 O '69. * (*PA* 44:10428)
20. BUTT, DORCAS SUSAN, AND FISKE, DONALD W. "Differential Correlates of Dominance Scales." *J Personality* 37(3): 415–28 S '69. * (*PA* 44:6748)
21. FISKE, DONALD W. "Subject Reactions to Inventory Format and Content." Abstract. *Proc 77th Ann Conv Am Psychol Assn* 4(1):137–8 '69. * (*PA* 43:17516)
22. HOLTZMAN, WAYNE H. "Precursors of Later Personality Traits in Children." Abstract. *Proc 77th Ann Conv Am Psychol Assn* 4(1):289–90 '69. * (*PA* 43:17227)
23. JACKSON, DOUGLAS N. "Multimethod Factor Analysis in the Evaluation of Convergent and Discriminant Validity." *Psychol B* 72(1):30–49 Jl '69. * (*PA* 43:12045)
24. JACKSON, DOUGLAS N.; NEILL, JOHN A.; AND BEVAN, ANN R. "Interpersonal Judgmental Accuracy and Bias as a Function of Degree of Acquaintance." Abstract. *Proc 77th Ann Conv Am Psychol Assn* 4(1):135–6 '69. * (*PA* 43:17394)
25. LAY, CLARRY H., AND JACKSON, DOUGLAS N. "Analysis of the Generality of Trait-Inferential Relationships." *J Pers & Social Psychol* 12(1):12–21 My '69. * (*PA* 43:11309)
26. MERRENS, MATTHEW ROY. *An Examination of Extreme Response Style.* Doctor's thesis, University of Montana (Missoula, Mont.), 1969. (*DAI* 30:4396B)
27. ADINOLFI, ALLEN A. "Characteristics of Highly Accepted, Highly Rejected, and Relatively Unknown University Freshmen." *J Counsel Psychol* 17(5):456–64 S '70. * (*PA* 45:2994)
28. ADINOLFI, ALLEN ANDREW. *The Characteristics of Highly Accepted, Highly Rejected and Relatively Unknown University Freshmen.* Doctor's thesis, University of Rochester (Rochester, N.Y.), 1970. (*DAI* 31:2271B)
29. BRAUN, JOHN R., AND COSTANTINI, ARTHUR. "Faking and Faking Detection on the Personality Research Form, AA." *J Clin Psychol* 26(4):516–8 O '70. * (*PA* 45:4273)
30. HOFFMANN, HELMUT. "Note on the Personality Traits of Student Nurses." *Psychol Rep* 27(3):1004 D '70. * (*PA* 45:9986)
31. HOFFMANN, HELMUT. "Personality Characteristics of Alcoholics in Relation to Age." *Psychol Rep* 27(1):167–71 Ag '70. * (*PA* 45:6613)

32. HOFFMANN, HELMUT. "Personality Pattern of Depression and Its Relation to Acquiescence." *Psychol Rep* 26(2):459–64 Ap '70. * (*PA* 44:21171)

33. KUSYSZYN, IGOR, AND GREENWOOD, DON E. "Marlowe-Crowne Defensiveness and Personality Scale Faking." Abstract. *Proc 78th Ann Conv Am Psychol Assn* 5(1):343–4 '70. * (*PA* 44:18728)

34. MARKS, EDMOND. "Individual Differences in Perceptions of the College Environment." *J Ed Psychol* 61(4):270–9 Ag '70. * (*PA* 44:21521)

35. MERRENS, MATTHEW R., AND RICHARDS, WILLIAM S. "Acceptance of Generalized Versus 'Bona Fide' Personality Interpretation." *Psychol Rep* 27(3):691–4 D '70. * (*PA* 45: 9965)

36. NEILL, JOHN A., AND JACKSON, DOUGLAS N. "An Evaluation of Item Selection Strategies in Personality Scale Construction." *Ed & Psychol Meas* 30(3):647–61 au '70. * (*PA* 45:4285)

37. PEARSON, PAMELA H. "Relationships Between Global and Specified Measures of Novelty Seeking." *J Consult & Clin Psychol* 34(2):199–204 Ap '70. * (*PA* 44:10438)

38. PIERCE, ROBERT A. "Roommate Satisfaction as a Function of Need Similarity." *J Col Stud Personnel* 11(5):355–9 S '70. *

39. ROTHMAN, ARTHUR I., AND FLOWERS, JOHN F. "Personality Correlates of First-Year Medical School Achievement." *J Med Ed* 45(11, pt 1):901–5 N '70. *

40. SIESS, THOMAS F., AND JACKSON, DOUGLAS N. "Vocational Interests and Personality: An Empirical Integration." *J Counsel Psychol* 17(1):27–35 Ja '70. * (*PA* 44:5695)

ANNE ANASTASI, *Professor of Psychology and Chairman of the Department, Fordham University, New York, New York.*

Designed as a self-report personality inventory for use within the normal range, the *Personality Research Form* is available in two parallel short forms (A and B) yielding 14 trait scores and two parallel longer forms (AA and BB) yielding the same 14 scores plus 6 additional trait scores. The trait scales have also been grouped into a few broader units suggested partly by theoretical considerations and partly by the results of several factor-analytic studies. For instance, Measures of Impulse Expression and Control include five scales: Impulsivity and Change at one pole and Harmavoidance, Order, and Cognitive Structure at the other.

There are also two "validity scales" (in the sense of test-taking attitudes): an Infrequency scale in the short form and an additional Desirability scale in the long form. Based on the number of highly unlikely responses chosen by the respondent, the Infrequency scale provides an index of carelessness, failure to understand directions, and other nonpurposeful responding. A Desirability scale is included in the long forms, although desirability bias was substantially reduced in advance by the procedures employed in item development and selection. The manual correctly points out that high or low scores on the Desirability scale may indicate not only atypical test-taking attitudes (e.g., deliberate attempt to create a favorable impression vs. malingering) but also important personality characteristics in their own right (e.g.,

high self-regard or high degree of conventional socialization vs. low self-regard).

Unusual care was exercised in the original formulation of items so as to conform to the theoretically-based trait definitions and to ensure distinctness among traits and reduction of irrelevant variance. Taking Henry Murray's personality framework as a starting point, the author reformulated the trait definitions in the light of subsequent research and theoretical developments. All scales are bipolar, half of the items being expressed in terms of one pole and half in terms of the other. This procedure also provides an effective control of acquiescence response bias. From an initial pool of nearly 3,000 items, provisional scales were prepared and administered to samples of college students totalling over 1,000 cases. Items were selected on the basis of high biserial correlation with total score on their own scales and low correlation with total scores on other trait scales and on the Desirability scale. Items yielding extreme endorsement proportions were also eliminated at this stage. Through a specially developed computer program, the selected items were assigned to the two parallel forms in terms of endorsement frequencies and biserial correlations with total scale score.

The inventory is self-administering, although the manual recommends that it be given under supervision to ensure standard conditions. Reusable answer sheets are hand scored with a template, the items in each scale having been arranged in a simple pattern to facilitate scoring. If the two halves of the template were differently colored, scoring would be further facilitated by permitting ready identification of the pair of columns whose responses are combined in finding each scale score.

Separate profile sheets based on male and on female norms are available for the short and long forms. When raw scores on each scale are transferred to these profile sheets, they are automatically expressed as T scores derived from samples of over 1,000 male and over 1,000 female students from more than 30 North American colleges and universities. Parenthetically, these T scores are truly normalized standard scores, unlike the misnamed T scores of certain other personality inventories. Tables are also given in the manual for the numerical conversion of raw scores to both T scores and percentiles.

Reliability was checked in several ways and

compares favorably with that of other personality scales of equal length. Odd-even reliability coefficients for the individual 20-item trait scales range from .48 to .90; K-R coefficients range from .54 to .86. The manual suggests the combined use of the parallel forms if time permits, in order to increase score reliability. Odd-even reliabilities of Forms A and B, administered over a two-week interval and combined to yield a single score for each scale, range from .72 to .92. Retest reliability of Form AA administered to 135 college students during a class period and a week later at home ranged from .69 to .90. It should also be noted that the 14 trait scales of the short forms tend to be more reliable than the six scales added in the long forms. For the former, reliability coefficients—by whatever method obtained—clustered close to .80 and none fell below .60.

Special investigations of response bias in the final scales suggested that both acquiescence and desirability bias have been satisfactorily controlled.

Both convergent and discriminant validity of the trait scales have been investigated. The manual cites three studies of college students in which PRF scores were correlated with pooled peer ratings as well as self-ratings. In one study, combined scores on the two parallel forms yielded a median r of .52 with peer ratings and a median r of .56 with self-ratings. In the other studies, correlations were somewhat lower because a single form was used and the criterion ratings were less reliable. The data from 202 college students were subjected to a multimethod factor analysis, using a 60 × 60 matrix with 20 traits and 3 methods (PRF, peer rating, self-rating). The trait factors that emerged across different methods corresponded so closely with the original trait scales as to provide good evidence of both convergent and discriminant validity.

Because of the rapid proliferation of personality inventories, any new inventory needs to be carefully scrutinized to decide whether such an addition is justified. In the case of the PRF, sufficient progress in test construction procedures is indicated to provide this justification. In part, the level of technical sophistication represented by the PRF reflects its author's extensive prior research on response styles, the factorial composition of personality inventories, and other related problems. Some of the procedures followed in item selection, moreover,

would have been well-nigh impossible before computers had reached their present state of development. At the same time, it is noteworthy that sound judgment and knowledge of psychological theory were employed throughout the development of the PRF as a corrective to purely statistical procedures. In accordance with proper test construction practice, reliability and validity were built into the test in the initial stages of item construction and selection. The manual is written with commendable restraint. The user is cautioned, for instance, to reassess the degree of desirability bias in the scores if the PRF is given in situations where motivation to dissemble is high and to recheck the norms if the test is used with groups that are very different from college populations. Technically the PRF appears to be exemplary; the extent to which it may prove useful in a variety of practical situations, such as selection and counseling, remains to be seen. As a research instrument, it has high promise.

E. LOWELL KELLY, *Professor of Psychology, The University of Michigan, Ann Arbor, Michigan.*

The PRF constitutes a welcome addition to the list of available inventories to provide for the multidimensional assessment of normal persons in a wide variety of settings. Its publication in 1967 occurred only after several years of systematic effort on the part of the author to develop an instrument which would make possible the measurement of personality traits with levels of precision and validity formerly associated only with intellectual abilities and scholastic achievement. On the basis of the evidence thus far available, it would appear that he has achieved this goal to a degree not heretofore considered possible.

In developing the PRF, the author sought to measure those personality variables broadly relevant to the functioning of normal individuals. In this respect, the PRF is much more similar to the CPI than to the MMPI. As a basis for selecting the most relevant and comprehensive set of personality traits, the author began with the set of variables of personality originally defined by Murray and his colleagues in 1938. Although conceptual modifications of these traits were made in the course of the development of this inventory, the names given to the personality traits assessed by it are very similar to those used to designate Murray's basic needs. However, there is a very important conceptual difference between Murray's original needs and those measured by the PRF. While needs were considered by Murray to represent a continuum ranging from low to high, PRF variables are all conceived as truly bipolar dimensions, in fact half of the items for each scale are written in terms of the opposite poles of each of the named variables.

More specifically, the PRF provides measures of 20 personality traits and two validity scales. Parallel Forms A and B each include 300 self-descriptive items, 20 items for each of 15 scales. The parallel Forms AA and BB include the 300 items of Forms A and B and an additional 140 items to provide measures of six additional personality variables and one additional validity scale.

The manual provides a description of high scoring individuals on each of the 22 traits. For the 20 personality variables, the manual also lists a series of defining trait adjectives; for example, the individual scoring high on "Cognitive Structure" is described as follows: Does not like ambiguity or uncertainty in information; wants all questions answered completely; desires to make decisions based on definite knowledge, rather than upon guesses or probabilities. For this same trait the defining adjectives are: precise, exacting, definite, seeks certainty, meticulous, perfectionistic, clarifying, explicit, accurate, rigorous, literal, avoids ambiguity, defining, rigid, needs structure.

To facilitate the interpretation of the resulting raw scores for individuals, the author has provided separate profile sheets for the shorter and longer forms. By merely encircling the raw score for each of the traits in the several columns, the user obtains a profile of the individual automatically converted to normalized T scores. Because of sex differences in both the mean and distribution of scores for most of the variables, separate profile sheets based on male and female norms are provided on the two sides of a single page. These norms are based on separate samples of over a thousand college students of each sex, selected from a larger group approximately twice as large in order to be representative of colleges varying widely in size, geographical setting, public or private support, and nature of the student body. Although in no sense strict probability samples, the author reports that the stability of normative statistics from one college and region to another

proved to be encouragingly high. Appropriately, the manual warns persons using the PRF with other than college samples against applying the college norms without first evaluating possible group differences.

In order to facilitate the detection of invalid records, each of the four forms of the inventory includes 20 items yielding scores on an "Infrequency Scale." The infrequency scale is composed of items which would almost never be answered true by anyone. Examples are: "I was born over ninety years ago" and "I have never seen an apple." Obviously, a high score on this scale indicates that the subject has either purposely distorted his responses, failed to use the proper spaces for a number of the items or in some other way responded in a careless fashion.

The longer Forms AA and BB each include 20 items scored for social desirability. These two scales, although heterogeneous in content and composed of items selected to avoid psychopathological content, have a K-R 20 reliability of about .83 suggesting considerable consistency in response to this group of highly diverse items. The author suggests that high scores on the social desirability scale may indicate "either conscious distortion or impression management, on the one hand, or the more subtle influences of atypically high self regard or of a high degree of conventional socialization." Conversely, he suggests that the very low scores may indicate, "possible tendencies toward malingering or, more likely, atypically low self regard."

The manual provides extensive information concerning two aspects of the reliability of the PRF scores: homogeneity (internal consistency) and stability over time. Even though each of the 22 scores is based on only 20 items, the author has succeeded in developing scales with encouragingly high reliabilities for a personality inventory. The manual reports a median K-R 20 coefficient of .76 for the 20 personality variables included in Forms AA and BB and of .78 for the 14 variables assessed by Forms A and B. The comparable odd-even median reliabilities are .78 and .81. If more reliable scores are needed, the user may administer both forms of the inventory; the median odd-even reliabilities for the resulting 40-item scales are .86 for the 20 scales and .88 for the 14 personality scales included in Forms A and B.

In addition to these encouragingly high indices of the internal consistency, initial evidence indicates considerable stability of PRF scores over time. PRF Form AA was administered on two occasions separated by an interval of one week, the first administration was conducted in class; on the second occasion subjects responded to the items at home. In spite of the fact that testing conditions on these two occasions were not identical, the median test-retest correlation was .81. In general, reliabilities, both of homogeneity and stability, are somewhat higher for the 14 content scales included in Forms A and B than for the six additional ones in Forms AA and BB.

These encouragingly high reliabilities are even more impressive because of the author's systematic and largely successful efforts to eliminate response biases in PRF scores. Acquiescence was suppressed by employing equal numbers of true and false keyed items in each of the scales. A systematic study by Jackson and Lay, using four different types of scales —positively worded original, positively worded reversal of the original content, negations of positively worded originals and negation of the positively worded reversals—indicated that the content scales are substantially free of acquiescence bias.

The author went to considerable effort to suppress or at least to minimize the second major response bias, social desirability. Starting with many more items than eventually used, he computed biserial correlations between each item response and (a) the total provisional scale of which it was a member, (b) related scales and (c) for a large set of heterogeneous items previously scaled for desirability. Items were retained for further analysis only if they showed higher correlations with the scale to which they belonged than to any irrelevant scale including desirability. In a further effort to minimize social desirability response bias, each item was evaluated on the basis of a Differential Reliability Index, which is presented as reflecting that portion of the variance of an item associated with the total scale score for the trait it was designed to measure *less* the variance shared by the item and a social desirability scale.

The author's efforts to minimize the response bias associated with social desirability was reasonably successful. Only 3 of the 20 content scales correlate as high as .40 with the social desirability scale and the median correlation (irrespective of sign) is in the low .20's for both sexes.

The manual presents intercorrelation matrices of the 22 PRF variables for each sex separately. Analysis of these tables reflects clearly the author's success in developing relatively independent scales for each of the variables. The median of the absolute values of the resulting 231 correlations is .17 for males and .16 for females; none of the scales correlate nearly as high with any other scale as their reliabilities would permit. In fact only 7 (for females) or 8 (for males) of the 231 intercorrelations have absolute values of .50 or higher, indicating not only the absence of any general factors of response bias but also suggest that each of the scales provides relatively unique information.

With respect to validity of the PRF scales, the manual summarizes the results of several studies using behavior ratings, trait ratings and self ratings as external criteria. For each of the 20 scales, the resulting validity coefficients are not only significant but most of the correlations with these independent criteria are substantial. For example, in a study using 51 California college students, the median correlation of the trait scores and behavior ratings by peers was .52; for this same sample, the median correlation with trait ratings was .56. Other studies of the relationship between PRF variables and personality ratings yield validities of similar magnitude in spite of what must have been criterion judgments with only modest reliabilities.

On the whole, the evidence concerning the construct of validity for the PRF scales is extremely encouraging. There is as yet but meager evidence regarding the empirical validity of the PRF scales in predicting life criteria. The manual does include tables showing the intercorrelations of the PRF scales with SVIB and CPI scores, both of which were developed on the basis of external criteria.

Regrettably the manual does not include matrices showing the intercorrelations of PRF scores and scores on other multidimensional inventories designed to sample broadly the entire personality domain; e.g., the Cattell 16 PF and the Guilford-Martin or Guilford-Zimmerman inventories. Such obviously useful information will certainly be provided soon by someone, and hopefully will be incorporated in the next edition of the manual. In the meantime,

Jackson does suggest that the 22 PRF scores may usefully be organized into 7 superordinate categories based "in part on the basis of theoretical considerations and in part on the results of a number of factor analytic studies." Quite properly, however, the author emphasizes that each of the 22 scales has enough unique true variance to justify its use as a separate scale and to be potentially useful in predicting relevant external criteria.

In summary, the PRF represents a welcome contribution to the field of personality assessment. By spending years in its development and using appropriate statistical techniques for item analysis and scale development, the author has produced an extremely promising assessment device; it provides reliable and valid measures on a score of relatively independent personality traits and the yield of information is certainly great in proportion to the time required for administration and scoring. The test booklets are attractively printed and the answer sheets, scoring stencils and profile sheets are easy to use. Finally, the author had the modesty to publish his test—not as an all purpose device for personality assessment, but to title it simply: *Personality Research Form.*

JERRY S. WIGGINS, *Professor of Psychology, University of Illinois, Champaign, Illinois.*

There is more to the PRF than meets the eye of the reader of its manual. The publication of a personality inventory based on the need constructs of Murray is hardly a singular event. But the theoretical and psychometric principles which guided the detailed procedures for item selection and scale construction represent a significant departure from the established traditions of previous rational, empirical, and factor analytic inventories. Jackson's touchstone for rigorous personality measurement is to be found in Loevinger's [1] elaboration of the notion of construct validity in psychological tests. The principal considerations here are those relating to the content, structure, and external validity of personality scales. The content of test items and the structural (statistical) relations that exist among test items are matters of great concern to investigators whose work is guided by explicit theoretical considerations regarding the nature of personality. The external validity of personality scales, or at least that aspect of

validity that relates to the prediction of socially-relevant criteria, is the predominant concern of the test consumer in educational, clinical, and industrial settings. It is Jackson's contention that personality scales which meet the substantive and structural standards of the researcher will best serve the needs of the test consumer as well.

On the basis of empirical and theoretical considerations (that are not shared with the reader of the PRF manual), 20 personality variables were selected from Murray's taxonomy and redefined as a guide for item writing. The reader of the manual is informed that an attempt was made to specify both the characteristics implied by each trait definition and those that would be excluded by the definition. A team of item writers generated over 100 items for each trait. Critical review by two or more editors reduced these to a preliminary pool of 2,554 items. This preliminary item pool was administered to samples of college students for purposes of item analysis.

Forty items were selected for each of 20 traits on the basis of (*a*) high correlations with a provisional content scale, (*b*) low correlations with irrelevant scales, (*c*) nonextreme endorsement frequencies (5–95%), and (*d*) high item "content saturation" as determined by a comparison of variance shared with a provisional content scale and variance shared with a specially derived social desirability scale. During the item writing phase, an attempt was made to construe each trait dimension in a "bipolar" fashion. Thus, the trait of Social Recognition is represented by endorsement of positive statements ("I consider it important to be held in high esteem by those I know") and by rejection of negative statements ("I don't try to 'keep up with the Joneses'"). Although such a procedure did not guarantee that the functional opposite of the positive pole of each trait was measured, it did permit the selection of 20 positive and 20 negative statements relative to each trait. This balanced representation of each content dimension minimizes the possible contribution of acquiescence to total scale scores.

These item analytic procedures were designed to produce scales that were internally consistent, relatively independent of each other, comprised of items of moderate endorsement frequencies, and relatively free of the possibly distorting influences of social desirability and acquies-

1 LOEVINGER, JANE. "Objective Tests as Instruments of Psychological Theory." *Psychol Rep* 3:635–94 D '57. *

cence. Parallel forms of each scale were constructed by an iterative procedure that exchanged items between two 20-item sets until the sets were nearly identical in terms of scale means and scale internal consistencies. The Standard Edition of the inventory appears in parallel forms (A and B), each of which permits the scoring of 14 content scales, plus an Infrequency scale to detect random responding. The latter validity scale is similar in conception to the MMPI F scale, but less confounded with psychopathology; it is composed of items which have extreme endorsement frequencies (e.g., "I am able to read English"). The Long Edition is available in parallel forms (AA and BB), each of which includes all the scales of the Standard Edition, plus six additional content scales and a Desirability scale. The Desirability scale was developed in such a way as to provide a reliable measure of desirability responding that is relatively free of both psychopathology and specific content saturation.

The PRF appears to have been developed primarily for purposes of personality research and secondarily for appraisal in "schools and colleges, clinics and guidance centers, and in business and industry." Consequently, the present edition of the PRF manual does not reflect much concern for the problems of the test consumer in applied settings. Although large samples of college students were employed in the development of the test, no breakdown is provided on the manner in which different samples were utilized for item selection, construction of parallel forms, assessment of internal consistency, or the computation of normative data. The author's decision to spare the reader such details is at variance with the generally accepted purpose of a test manual. Test consumers who wish to apply the normalized PRF standard scores and percentiles to other than college populations are warned to "exercise caution." Since virtually no demographic correlates of the PRF scales are reported, test consumers in applied settings are very much on their own.

Evidence for the construct validity and potential usefulness of the PRF is presented in sections dealing with (a) "structural properties" (reliability), (b) "freedom from response biases," and (c) "convergent and discriminant validities of the PRF scales." Complete reliability data (test-retest, odd-even, K-R 20) are presented only for the longer Form AA. The internal consistency and temporal stability

of what would presumably be the most widely used versions (Form A and Form B) are not evaluated. Despite this serious oversight, there is little doubt that the majority of PRF scales represent both homogeneous and stable dimensions of self-report. As would be expected from the attention devoted to the elimination of response biases in the construction of the PRF, the final scales are relatively free of the possibly distorting influences of social desirability and acquiescence, as these variables are defined by Jackson.

Evidence for the convergent validities of PRF scales is presented from three studies in which PRF scale scores were correlated with independently obtained peer ratings and with self-ratings on an adjective rating form and nine-place rating scales. The author's conclusion that "these values....exceed those typically reported for personality inventories by a comfortable margin" appears justified by the data reported. Correlations are presented between the PRF scales and scales from the SVIB and CPI. Correlations with the SVIB scales are generally slight, although sensible where they do occur. Correlations with the CPI scales are more substantial and more relevant to convergent validity, such as the correlation of .78 between the dominance scales of the two inventories. Surprisingly, the PRF was not compared with the EPPS, which contains 12 of the same need scales. This is unfortunate, since the EPPS is the most obvious competitor of the PRF. Similarly, it would have been helpful to have compared the PRF with the recent *Adjective Check List* need scales (nine of which overlap with the PRF) or with the *Stern Activities Index,* which shares 15 need scales in common with the PRF.

Jackson places heavy emphasis on the evaluation of both the convergent and discriminant validities of PRF scales within the framework of the multitrait-multimethod distinctions proposed by Campbell and Fiske.[2] At least one set of data, involving peer ratings, self-ratings, and PRF scale scores was available for such an analysis. But the data were not analyzed by the conventional Campbell-Fiske method, nor were the necessary intercorrelations provided for the reader who might wish to draw his own conclusions. Notable omissions from the manual

2 CAMPBELL, DONALD T., AND FISKE, DONALD W. "Convergent and Discriminant Validation by the Multitrait-Multimethod Matrix." *Psychol B* 56:81–105 Mr '59. *

include the intercorrelations among traits measured by different methods and the correlations between simple self ratings and peer ratings, which, when compared with the correlations between PRF scales and peer ratings, would permit an evaluation of the incremental validity of the PRF scales. Instead, only the partial results of a "multimethod factor analysis" (*23*) are presented. This method of analysis was designed to ignore the contribution of method variance peculiar to a single method of measurement. Although the results presented in the manual appear striking in terms of both convergent and discriminant validity, it should be noted that there may be serious shortcomings to this method of analysis [3] and that the data are considerably less striking when viewed in terms of Campbell and Fiske's original distinctions.

The limitations of the present test manual should not detract from the fact that the PRF is among the most methodologically sophisticated personality inventories presently available. Careful attention to issues of substantive, structural, and external validity during the scale construction phase has resulted in an inventory of commendable psychometric properties. Whether these scale construction efforts, and particularly the attention paid to substantive considerations, will guarantee significant incremental validities in applied settings is another question. But it is probably the most important question facing personality assessment today. At this writing, the PRF should, as its title indicates, be considered as primarily a *research* instrument. As research workers gain a fuller appreciation of the theoretical and empirical issues underlying the development of the test,[4] it is likely that the PRF will become a major focus of investigation during the next decade.

Am Ed Res J 6(2):302–6 Mr '69. Ruth Wessler and Jane Loevinger. * an objective, omnibus personality inventory that aims to achieve bias-free measures of theoretically defined personality traits * The traits defining the several scales are derived from Murray's taxonomy of personality variables, which was also the source for Edwards' Personal Preference Schedule. Oddly, there is no comparison of the

PRF with the EPPS. The forced-choice format of the EPPS results in ipsative rather than normative scales, and the PRF (wisely, we think) avoided this whole bag of troubles by using single stimulus items. Jackson uses another route to meet the perennial problem of response bias. The items chosen for each scale showed maximum correlation with a content measure for the variable and minimum correlation with a measure of desirability, i.e., tendency to favorable self-description. Murray's list of personality variables has been modified, Jackson claims, on the basis of recent research evidence, but he does not intimate what that evidence might be. Murray's distinction between needs and behaviors is omitted; hence there is no recognition of latent needs. There is no inkling of distinction between levels of personality. The topic or topics referred to by terms such as conscience, guilt, and superego seem to be unrepresented in the PRF, although present in Murray's list and the subject of much recent work elsewhere. Perhaps Jackson's expressed intention to study only normal functioning is his reason for this deliberately superficial view of personality, but it does not suffice. Normal people have latent needs and conscience. There is another difficulty with regard to trait definition. In some places Jackson stresses that the traits are bipolar and that items were constructed for both poles. The descriptions given, however, correspond only to the high pole. Moreover, in validational studies using rating scales corresponding to each scale, the judges were asked to rate the degree to which each trait was present or absent. This appears to be an inconsistency. Certainly no evidence is brought to bear on the question of bipolarity. To compound the matter, the traits are also organized into "superordinate categories," with different scales apparently defining opposite poles of the supertraits, again without supporting evidence beyond vague mention of factor analysis. An example of a superordinate category is "Measures of Impulse Expression and Control." At one pole are the traits Impulsivity and Change, at the other, Harmavoidance (which seems to be the closest he comes to including a measure of anxiety), Order, and Cognitive Structure (which might better have been called rigidity or intolerance of ambiguity). Although Jackson invokes Loevinger's notion of the structural aspect of construct validity, he has not adopted its central tenet. (The

3 CONGER, ANTHONY J. "An Evaluation of Multimethod Factor Analysis." *Psychol B* 75(6):416–20 Je '71. *
4 JACKSON, DOUGLAS N. "The Dynamics of Structured Personality Tests: 1971." *Psychol R* 78(3):229–48 My '71. *
JACKSON, DOUGLAS N. "A Sequential System for Personality Scale Development," pp. 61–96. In *Current Topics in Clinical and Community Psychology, Vol. 2.* Edited by Charles D. Spielberger. New York: Academic Press, Inc., 1970. Pp. 217.

problem of trait bipolarity can also appropriately be called an aspect of structure.) Loevinger's suggestion was that the scoring keys of a test should reflect the empirical clustering of items. Jackson, instead, continues the use of the earlier method of internal consistency. That is, he constructed items to fit traits defined *a priori,* then selected those items showing the highest correlation with the original total pool for the trait (and meeting his other criteria). The acid test of a personality inventory, as Jackson says, lies in the Campbell-Fiske notion of convergent and discriminant validity, and it is to these ideas that he has done most violence. He does indeed show good correlations between behavior ratings and self ratings of traits corresponding to the PRF scales. Nowhere, however, does he show the intercorrelation of the behavior ratings among themselves nor of the self-ratings among themselves, data that are necessary for the Campbell-Fiske evaluation. Intercorrelations of the PRF scales with each other are presented, but not in a way that facilitates their comparison with the correlations with the ratings. As evidence for discriminant validity, Jackson cites results obtained by a method of factor analysis specially worked out so that "method variance common only to a single method of measurement cannot intrude to determine common factors (p. 25)." The major purpose of the Campbell-Fiske matrix, to determine the relative weight of trait variance and method variance, is thus circumvented. If we put together data from Table 15, showing the intercorrelation of PRF scales, and data from Table 9, showing heteromethod validity coefficients, we find that the highest correlations between PRF scales are of about the same order of magnitude as the corresponding validities, higher in some cases, lower in others. As Campbell and Fiske point out, this is par for the course. Some curious small lapses occur. Table 3 seems to refer to a study not reported in the text of the manual. In another case, for a sample described only as containing 192 cases, Forms AA and BB were administered two weeks apart. Although he describes this as a study of stability, Jackson reports only the odd-even reliabilities for the forms separately and combined. To the extent that the odd-even coefficients were influenced by instability over time or non-parallel content of the forms, they would in fact be raised. Failure to report the correlations between first testing and second or

between Form AA and Form BB (these were not identical because half were given each form first) was no doubt due to carelessness, but it does not engender confidence. Perhaps the most serious criticism of the PRF scoring manual is that nowhere is there a straightforward presentation of all the samples used, together with a statement of the exact form given to them and the uses of the data, whether for item selection, norm construction, or reliability or validity studies. Table 6, for example, reports KR-20 coefficients for each scale for the original pool and for the best 40 items. Apparently both male and female subjects are included in the sample; for personality tests data for men and women should in general be treated separately. Moreover, computation of the coefficients on the best 40 items is misleading, since no form of the test uses more than 20 items for a scale. Further, since these were the data used to pick the best items, the coefficients should have been reported for a new set of data. These errors operate to inflate the reported coefficients. * We are told about the normative samples only that there were over 1000 each of males and females, all were college students and probably all volunteers, and the groups were from over 30 North American colleges and universities, though we are not told whether Harvard or Grambling was among them. The following questions are not answered: Do these 2000 cases include the several samples cited elsewhere in the manual for other studies, or are they an additional sample? Were the norms computed from cases given the forms as they are published, or are the norms synthesized from data obtained with the original pool of items? Were the cases used to select items also used for the norms? As a general rule, if two forms are made equivalent using one set of data, they will be somewhat different using a new set of data; Jackson forecloses the possibility by presenting just one set of norms for the two forms. Comparing the manual for the PRF test with the manual for Thorndike's Dimensions of Temperament (TDOT) test, Thorndike comes out ahead. He reports many more studies, and they are reported in a clearer, more straightforward fashion. For example, the samples used in standardization are listed giving the number of cases, grade level, community, and school. Data are also given on the relation of the scales to certain demographic variables, as should be done in every test manual. Jackson's manual bears the marks of haste and insufficient thought. Publication should have been delayed. Jackson claims to have spent a great deal of time composing items, and he has indeed assembled an appealing and lively collection of items. If we compare the tasks presented to the subject on the PRF, the TDOT, and the EPPS, probably the PRF is the pleasantest to take. Thorndike, Edwards, and Jackson have chosen different approaches to what has become the central problem of measuring personality, namely, controlling response bias. Thorndike asks the subject to pick the three most characteristic and three least characteristic for himself from each block of 10 statements. Edwards requires picking one of each pair. Both Thorndike and Edwards choose each of the alternatives in an item from a different scale; so both have evolved ipsative measures. (One consequence is that the sum total of scores on all scales is the same for every subject; there is no score indicating a general level.) Jackson has the subject accept or reject each statement, and counts on item selection to reduce response bias, probably not altogether successfully, to the extent one can judge from his fragmentary data. There is an obvious way of getting out of the response bias bag without climbing into the ipsative bag, but it does not appear to have been used on any omnibus scale as yet. This method is forced choice between two more or less opposed statements on a single topic, scored with respect to only one scale. Rotter, Tomkins, and Loevinger have used this method in tests of limited scope. The crucial test will be to see whether it reduces the method variance in an omnibus personality test.

J Counsel Psychol 16(2):181–4 Mr '69. John O. Crites. * probability sampling procedures were not used. Furthermore, the author of the PRF points out that: "While experience has indicated that noncollege samples conform reasonably well in terms of summary statistics, investigators using the PRF with groups which are very different from college students should exercise caution in applying standard PRF norms without first evaluating differences [Manual, p. 8]." No discussion is provided in the Manual concerning profile interpretation, nor are the scales even grouped on the profile according to the factorial-theoretical clusters mentioned above. * the use of the Infrequency and Desirability scales to detect careless and/or biased endorsement of items is dealt with at length. Of the two, the Infrequency scale would appear to be the more useful, in order to identify nonpurposeful responding and scoring errors, since the Desirability scale correlated negligibly with most of the need scales (Achievement and Aggression are notable exceptions), indicating that this source of response bias is not a particularly important one in the PRF. As compared with most new measures of personality, the reliability and validity data on the PRF are both more complete and more promising. * Validity data on the PRF are only slightly less encouraging than those on its reliability. There are some instances of inconsistencies in the relationships of the PRF to other variables, such as the −.41 *r* between Social Recognition and the Good Impression scale of the CPI, but in general the findings are as would be expected. * *Conclusions.* The PRF is a well-conceived and well-developed personality inventory, whose psychometric characteristics are more than adequate. It is relatively free from response bias; it measures largely independent variables; it is reliable, both structurally and temporally; and, it correlates with variables it should correlate with and not with those it should not correlate with. The norms for the PRF are restricted in scope, which limits its applicability at present, but future research should produce the needed data. If the PRF has a shortcoming, it may be the lack of appeal that Murray's need constructs may have among counselors and personnel workers, who tend to be oriented more toward behavioral, psychoanalytic, self, and trait-and-factor theories of personality.

Prof Psychol 1(1):82–3 N '69. Lonnie D. Valentine, Jr. * reliabilities are higher than those generally obtained for personality scales * scales of the PRF appear to be well defined and soundly constructed. They evidence high internal consistency and test-retest reliability, and there is evidence that they measure those characteristics they were intended to measure. Of the two "validity" scales, Infrequency is probably the more useful, since Desirability was controlled in scale construction (those few scales which show some modest correlation with Desirability probably *should* be correlated with it). The instrument should prove to be highly useful in a considerable variety of psychological research problems.

[124]

★The Piers-Harris Children's Self Concept Scale (The Way I Feel About Myself). Grades 3–12; 1969; CSCS; 1 form (6 pages); manual (29 pages); 1–99 tests, 20¢ each; 50¢ per key; $1 per manual; $1.25 per specimen set; postage extra; (15–20) minutes; Ellen V. Piers and Dale B. Harris (test); Counselor Recordings and Tests. *

REFERENCES

1. MAYER, C. LAMAR. A Study of the Relationship of Early Special Class Placement and the Self Concepts of Mentally Handicapped Children. Doctor's thesis, Syracuse University (Syracuse, N.Y.), 1965. (DA 27:143A)
2. COX, SAMUEL HARRY. Family Background Effects on Personality Development and Social Acceptance. Doctor's thesis, Texas Christian University (Ft. Worth, Tex.), 1966.
3. MILLEN, L. The Relationship Between Self-Concept, Social Desirability and Anxiety in Children. Master's thesis, Pennsylvania State University (University Park, Pa.), 1966.
4. WING, SARAH WILLIAMSON. A Study of Children Whose Reported Self-Concept Differs From Classmates' Evaluation of Them. Doctor's thesis, University of Oregon (Eugene, Ore.), 1966. (DA 27:959B)
5. FARLS, ROBERT JAMES. High and Low Achievement of Intellectually-Average Intermediate Grade Students Related to the Self-Concept and Social Approval. Doctor's thesis, University of Pittsburgh (Pittsburgh, Pa.), 1967. (DA 28:1205A)
6. ASHBY, MARY LAVERNE. The Effect of Self Concept on Children's Learning in Religious Education. Doctor's thesis, George Peabody College for Teachers (Nashville, Tenn.), 1968. (DAI 30:1035A)
7. HUGO, MIRIAM JEANNE. The Effects of Group Counseling on Self-Concepts and Behavior of Elementary School Children. Doctor's thesis, Ohio University (Athens, Ohio), 1969. (DAI 30:3728A)
8. SISENWEIN, MARTIN. A Comparison of the Self Concepts of Negro and White Children in an Integrated School. Doctor's thesis, Columbia University (New York, N.Y.), 1970. (DAI 31:1633A)

PETER M. BENTLER, Associate Professor of Psychology, University of California, Los Angeles, California.

The CSCS consists of 80 first-person declarative statements of the type "I am a happy person"; the child responds "yes" or "no." The items are declarative sentences, half of them worded to indicate a positive self concept and slightly more than half to indicate a negative self concept. Negative terms such as "don't" are avoided because they can be confusing to young children. When the items are read by the examiner, children below the third grade level can take the test.

The scale was standardized on 1,183 children in grades 4–12 of one Pennsylvania school district. There appear to be no consistent sex or grade differences in means. The internal consistency of the scale ranges from .78 to .93 and retest reliability from .71 to .77. Correlates with similar instruments are in the mid-sixties, and the scale possesses teacher and peer validity coefficients on the order of .40. Care was taken that the scale not correlate unduly with social desirability, and reasonable success was achieved; however, quite high correlations, −.54 to −.69, exist with a measure of anxiety. The authors believe this correlation represents a true trait correlation rather than one of response style. Thus, the scale possesses sufficient reliability and validity to be used in research, as recommended by the authors.

The authors not only have produced a psychometrically adequate scale, but have written about it in a direct and honest manner. The research use of the scale is emphasized, in contrast to applications for which the scale is not yet validated. It is recommended for studies of change in self concept; the appropriate recommendation to use a control group is urged, because scores on the scale tend to increase slightly with retesting. In applied use of the scale with individual cases, the authors point out that it is primarily the low scorer who might be viewed with concern. Regarding changes in score for an individual, the manual carefully points out that the magnitude of the standard error of measurement requires at least a 10-point score difference before a change can be considered statistically reliable.

Although the CSCS was designed to be unidimensional, a principal components factor analysis indicated that at least six factors might be present. It is worthwhile to look at this result in greater depth than has been done in the manual, since if the scale is indeed six-dimensional, the single total score for the scale must lose a lot of useful information. This reviewer, however, suspects that the scale is rather more unidimensional than the manual indicates. Unfortunately, crucial information regarding the size of the latent root associated with the first unrotated principal component is not presented at all. Only certain aspects of the final rotated solution are available. It seems likely, however, that the first unrotated dimension accounts for by far the largest portion of the total variance of the items. Analyses of item pools in this content area generally lead to such a result. In addition, there is the characteristic finding that a principal components analysis of binary items such as those used in the scale tends to result in too many, and some spurious, factors as compared to a more appropriate procedure such as that of monotonicity analysis.[1] Internal evidence of the loading patterns indicates that all but two of the factors have a sufficiently large imbalance of positive and negative items with high loadings to lead one to suspect that response style has interacted

1 BENTLER, PETER M. "A Comparison of Monotonicity Analysis With Factor Analysis." Ed & Psychol Meas 30(2):241–50 su '70. *

sufficiently with the content to distort the desired content factors. The worst example is found in factor three, physical appearance and attributes, which has 11 out of 12 items keyed in the positive direction. Thus it is quite likely that fewer content factors than six actually exist on this instrument, lending support to the total score that is described psychometrically and for which normative data are available.

Some of the more admirable features of the manual are its accuracy and its caution. For example, the principal components analysis described above yielded suggested combinations of items that can be scored to yield "cluster" scores, a correct designation, in contrast to the more usual but inaccurate label "factor" scores. In addition, the manual indicates that the cluster scores are at the moment sufficiently tentative that their main application should be in research.

Future editions of the manual should concentrate on correcting the existing minor technical problems that can be found in it. For example, internal consistency coefficients are not presented for the final scale. Instead, coefficients are presented for an earlier version with a larger number of items. While this increase in items would tend to make the internal consistency appear higher than warranted, another technical error mitigates this effect; the use of K-R 21 as a measure of consistency tends to depress the appropriate value. Consequently, it is difficult to get an accurate picture of the internal consistency of the final scale. The test-retest coefficient of .77 technically should be an upper limit for internal consistency. Yet this reviewer suspects that the consistency may be higher, on the order of about .85, since a rather lengthy, "two and four month," test-retest interval was used to estimate reliability. Further data gathering and analysis can clear up these problems.

A few sections of the manual require simple re-editing and rewriting. As they stand, they can be misleading. For example, a test development sample that took a 140-item version of the scale is referred to in a section called "Standardization." As far as this reviewer can determine, standardization was conducted separately using over 1,000 subjects with the appropriate final 80-item version of the scale. In addition, it appears as if the norms, which are presented in percentile and stanine fashion, are not the "true" norms for the scale. Apparently the negative skewness of scores was taken into account, and the scores were normalized through area equivalents prior to the computation of percentile data. While such a practice is followed frequently in the test construction literature, this reviewer does not recommend it. At the very least, it would seem that discrepancies between the presented norms and the uncorrected raw score norms ought to be discussed.

[125]

*Progress Assessment Chart of Social Development.** Mentally handicapped children, mentally handicapped adults; 1962–69; behavior checklist for assessing progress in 4 areas: self-help, communication, socialisation, occupation; 3 levels; manual ('69, 94 pages); descriptive folder ('68, 4 pages); no data on reliability; £1 per 25 charts; £1.62½ per 5 norms and record folders; £1.12½ per manual; 50p per specimen set (without manual); postpaid; French, Norwegian, Portuguese, Spanish, and Swedish editions available; H. C. Gunzburg; SEFA (Publications) Ltd. *
a) PRIMARY PROGRESS ASSESSMENT CHART, FIFTH EDITION. Profoundly handicapped children and adults; 1966–69; PPAC; 1 form ('66, 4 pages); norms and record folder ('69, 4 pages, entitled *Primary Progress Evaluation Index*).
b) PROGRESS ASSESSMENT CHART I, NINTH EDITION. Children unsuitable for education at school; 1962–69; PAC 1; 1 form ('65, 4 pages); norms and record folder, third edition ('67, 4 pages, entitled *Progress Evaluation Index 1*).
c) PROGRESS ASSESSMENT CHART 2, SEVENTH EDITION. Older mentally handicapped trainees; 1963–69; PAC 2; 1 form ('69, 4 pages); norms and record folder ('69, 4 pages, entitled *Progress Evaluation Index 2*).

REFERENCES

1–5. See P:216.
6. MARSHALL, ANNE. *The Abilities and Attainments of Children Leaving Junior Training Centres.* London: National Association for Mental Health, 1967. Pp. i, 62. *

[126]

★Psychiatric Evaluation Form.** Psychiatric patients and nonpatients; 1967–68; PEF; an interview guide and rating scale for recording scaled judgments (based upon various sources of information: subject, informant, case records, nurses' notes, etc.) of a person's functioning over a one week period in 19 psychopathological dimensions and role impairment in 3 occupational roles and 2 social roles; Form R2 ('68, 20 pages); manual ('68, 20 pages); no norms; $1 per booklet; 10¢ per score sheet; 50¢ per manual; postage extra; specimen set free; fee for editing, coding, key punching, and verifying score sheets, 10¢ per subject; (2–4) minutes; Robert L. Spitzer, Jean Endicott, Alvin Mesnikoff, and George Cohen; Biometrics Research, New York State Psychiatric Institute. * [The Diagnostic Version, PEF-D ('68, 13 sheets, same as regular edition except for the addition of 12 scales and the coverage of a person's functioning over the past month) is available only as a part of *Current and Past Psychopathology Scales*.]

REFERENCE

1. SPITZER, ROBERT L.; ENDICOTT, JEAN; AND FLEISS, JOSEPH L. "Instruments and Recording Forms for Evaluating Psychiatric Status and History: Rationale, Method of Development, and Description." *Comprehen Psychiatry* 8:321–43 O '67. * (*PA* 42:7466)

GOLDINE C. GLESER, *Professor of Psychology and Director, Psychology Division, University of Cincinnati College of Medicine, Cincinnati, Ohio.*

The *Psychiatric Evaluation Form* consists of an optical scanning form for computer recording of ratings on 19 dimensions of psychopathology, an overall evaluation, and five areas of possible role impairment, in addition to other data such as identification, date, age, sex, diagnosis, duration of illness, and the like, needed for both clinical and research files. Severity ratings are made on six-point scales ranging from "none" to "extreme." There is also a space for indicating that a particular scale is inapplicable or unratable.

The PEF is normally used in conjunction with an interview guide conveniently arranged so that the scale definitions and appropriate questions are opposite the scale being rated. The time period on which the judgments are based is the week up to and including the day of evaluation. Both "intensity and duration" of symptoms are considered in making judgments but inferences are avoided. Questions may be added or omitted to obtain the desired information from the interview and supplementary records may be consulted.

A salient aspect of the manual is the emphasis placed by the authors on the importance of training in obtaining reliable and valid judgments. Two case histories are presented and rated to indicate what evidence is used for each scale and how it is interpreted quantitatively. In addition, a tape is available with two interviews that can be rated and compared to the key. It would be desirable if even more practice material were made available, particularly in the form of examples of responses classified as mild, moderate, severe, etc., on each of the scales. Unless such objectification can be accomplished, ratings are not likely to be highly comparable from one center to another.

The current version of the manual has no psychometric data on these scales for various clinical populations. However, additional information was provided by the authors. Two reliability studies have been undertaken. In the first study, 64 newly-admitted psychiatric inpatients were interviewed by two first-year medical students who had had three weeks of intensive training in the use of the PEF. It was not indicated whether both were present at each interview or whether tape recordings were employed. The intraclass correlations ranged from .51 to .95, with a median of .74. Another study of 31 inpatients in which four raters were paired in various combinations yielded intraclass correlation coefficients ranging from .69 to 1.00, with a median of .90. Minimal agreements were obtained in both studies for ratings of "inappropriate affect" and "anxiety." The lower coefficients obtained by the medical students would certainly indicate the advisability of obtaining raters with adequate psychiatric training and experience. One wonders, however, whether the design of the second study might not have tended to result in inflated coefficients, since variance attributable to difference in interviewers was confounded with subject effects. The inadequate attention paid to rater main effects is a weakness of these and other such rating scales.

Intercorrelations among the 19 rating scales are available on 433 patients. These have been factored to yield six clusters or syndromes, namely: disorganization, grandiosity-externalization, withdrawal, antisocial, depression, anxiety. Some evidence is available that the rating scales can differentiate inpatient, outpatient, and nonpatient samples, and among various diagnostic groups.

The PEF form and interview guide is much easier to handle and administer than the *Mental Status Schedule* by the same authors. It remains to be seen, however, which type of scaling will yield the more meaningful results. Certainly the rating form will appeal more to psychiatrists and is potentially useful for a broader range of patients.

JEROME D. PAUKER, *Associate Professor of Psychiatry (Medical Psychology) and Psychology, University of Missouri, Columbia, Missouri.*

The PEF is one of several related rating instruments to come out of Biometrics Research of the New York State Department of Mental Hygiene. It is a means for evaluating the functioning of a subject over a short period of time; the authors recommend one week as the target period but also allow for studies involving special time periods. Seven days is seen by them as being long enough to cover a reasonable sampling of the person's behavior and short enough to be handled in a manageable rating scale. The information on which the ratings are based can come from a variety of sources, including interviews with the patient, interviews with other informants, hospital records, and other documents. Judgments are made about 19 dimensions of psychopathology called the Comprehensive Psychopathology Scales, plus an additional scale called Overall Severity of Illness. The other scales carry such titles as Agitation-Excitement, Hallucinations, Belligerence-Negativism, and Daily Routine-Leisure Time. Each dimension is given a definition which the rater must follow. If the subject meets specified criteria for the roles of wage earner, housekeeper, student or trainee, mate, or parent, his degree of role impairment is also rated.

Ratings are made on a six-point scale ranging from "none" to "extreme." The score sheet upon which the ratings are marked consists of an original and two self-marking duplicates. Another clever device is a reusable scoring booklet into which the score sheet is placed. The booklet is set up in such a way that the definition of a dimension is next to the place where it is to be marked, with the opposite page providing a guide to aid in eliciting information appropriate to that dimension when an interview is used.

A second part of the PEF is used if the subject is a new admission to a psychiatric facility. This part deals with the duration of the most recent illness or episode, the stress of precipitating events, and the primary reason for admission.

Unfortunately, there is relatively little information to which a potential user can refer if he wishes to evaluate the PEF. It appears that the content of the PEF dimensions is derived for the most part from factored and other scales which are a part of other psychiatric rating methods developed by these authors or their associates, but there is little to show how well the scales fare in the transformation. There is a manual of instructions, which describes the PEF and provides some material for practice, but there is no manual which presents data about scale construction, reliability, or validity, nor are there as yet any other publications in which such material is presented. A section in an unpublished progress report provided by the authors presents some of the results of interrater reliability studies (demonstrating reasonable reliability), intercorrelations among scales, factor analyses among the psychopathology scales (resulting in six summary scales), data

concerning differentiation among psychiatric populations, and expected changes in psychopathology as a function of time. The information is sketchy, however, with respect to such crucial information as population characteristics, research design, and significance levels.

Personal communication with one of the authors reveals that further information will be published, and that the results of additional factor analyses and reliability and validity studies are in preparation. This is fortunate, because it is apparent that a good deal of effort has gone into the development of the PEF. Until such time as much more background and pertinent research results are available, however, the PEF will have to be rated as a potentially useful instrument which is worthy of further investigation. At the present time, if you are looking for a rating scale which has considerable overlap with the PEF dimensions, you might consider the *Inpatient Multidimensional Psychiatric Scale,* which uses ratings based on an interview.

[127]

★The Psychiatric Status Schedules: Subject Form, Second Edition. Psychiatric patients and nonpatients; 1966–68; PSS; a standardized interview schedule for gathering information from a subject needed to fill out a matching inventory designed to evaluate social and role functioning as well as mental status; most of the sections dealing with signs and symptoms of psychiatric disorder are from the *Mental Status Schedule;* 18 symptom scores (inappropriate affect-appearance-behavior, interview belligerence—negativism, agitation-excitement, retardation—lack of emotion, speech disorganization, grandiosity, suspicion-persecution-hallucinations, reported overt anger, depression-anxiety, suicide—self-mutilation, somatic concerns, social isolation, daily routine—leisure time impairment, antisocial impulses or acts, alcoholic abuse, drug abuse, disorientation memory, denial of illness), 5 role functioning scores (wage earner, housekeeper, student or trainee, mate, parent), 5 summary symptom and role scales (subjective distress, behavioral disturbance, impulse control disturbance, reality testing disturbance, summary role), and 20 supplemental scores (anxiety, auditory hallucinations, catatonic behavior, conversion reaction, delusions-hallucinations, depression-suicide, disassociation, elated mood, guilt, lack of emotion, obsessions-compulsions, persecutory delusions, phobia, psychomotor retardation, sex deviation, silliness, somatic delusions or hallucinations, visual hallucinations, miscellaneous, validity check); Subject Form ('68, 15 pages); manual ('68, 15 pages); for reliability and validity data, see 5 below; norms based upon newly admitted psychiatric patients; $3 per booklet; 10¢ per score sheet; 50¢ per manual; $4 per set of keys and teaching tape; postage extra; specimen set free; fee for editing, coding, key punching, and verifying score sheet, 50¢ per subject; scoring service with either profile printout or a computerized psychiatric diagnosis (DIAGNO I) using standard American Psychiatric Association nomenclature is available; (25–50) minutes; Robert L. Spitzer, Jean

Endicott, and George Cohen; Biometrics Research, New York State Psychiatric Institute. *

REFERENCES

1. SPITZER, ROBERT L.; ENDICOTT, JEAN; AND FLEISS, JOSEPH L. "Instruments and Recording Forms for Evaluating Psychiatric Status and History: Rationale, Method of Development, and Description." *Comprehen Psychiatry* 8:321–43 O '67. * (*PA* 42:7466)
2. COOPER, JOHN E.; KENDELL, ROBERT E.; GURLAND, BARRY J.; SARTORIUS, NORMAN; AND FARKAS, TIBOR. "Cross National Study of Diagnosis of the Mental Disorders: Some Results From the First Comparative Investigation." *Am J Psychiatry* 125(10, sup):21–9 Ap '69. * (*PA* 43:11554)
3. SPITZER, ROBERT L.; COHEN, GEORGE; MILLER, J. DAVID; AND ENDICOTT, JEAN. "The Psychiatric Status of 100 Men on Skid Row." *Int J Social Psychiatry* 15(3):230–4 su '69. * (*PA* 44:18922)
4. PLATMAN, S. R., AND WEINSTEIN, BETTE. "The Diagnosis Game." *Dis Nerv System* 31(8):561–6 Ag '70. * (*PA* 45:4547)
5. SPITZER, ROBERT L.; ENDICOTT, JEAN; FLEISS, JOSEPH L.; AND COHEN, JACOB. "The Psychiatric Status Schedule: A Technique for Evaluating Psychopathology and Impairment in Role Functioning." *Arch Gen Psychiatry* 23(1):41–55 Jl '70. * (*PA* 44:18923)

HANS H. STRUPP, *Professor of Psychology, Vanderbilt University, Nashville, Tennessee.*

HISTORY AND USE. The PSS is one of an integrated group of instruments. Its specific role is "to improve the research value of clinical judgments of psychopathology and role functioning based on data collected during a psychiatric interview." Although the procedure can be used for the clinical evaluation or description of an individual subject, its major use is in the research comparison of groups of patients or nonpatients. The schedule is appropriate for a single evaluation but can also be administered repeatedly to evaluate change. Investigators have used the PSS in such areas as rehabilitation of mental patients, psychiatric evaluation, cross-cultural and cross-group comparisons, community assessment of care facilities, subject selection, instructional aid, psychiatric research, and epidemiological studies. The authors have utilized these research findings to improve the existing schedule and to construct related instruments and services.

CONTENT AND FORMAT. Information of demonstrated relevance was culled from the professional literature, textbooks, available scales, and hospital records before preliminary forms were constructed and submitted to experienced clinicians and researchers for their critical opinion. The items, calling for dichotomous (true/false) judgments, "are brief, non-technical descriptions of small units of observed or reported overt behavior." Each item to be judged contains only words or phrases explicitly defined within the context of the measure. All judgments are made and recorded during the interview. This task is facilitated by the convenient step-down format and other helpful features in the design of the interview schedule and answer sheet.

ADMINISTRATION. The interviewer need not be an experienced clinician, but he must be trained to use the PSS. The interview schedule format is best suited for situations where the assessor has no clinical responsibility for the subject. The manual provides explicit and complete directions covering all aspects of the interview interaction and judgment-making processes. Training tapes provide essential practice and demonstrate proper techniques. Accompanying keys present a supporting discussion for the "correct" scoring, based on the judgments of experienced observers.

SCORING. The basic scoring system yields scales at either of two levels of summarization. Level one provides the 23 symptom and role functioning scales. The scales are based on a range of 6 to 38 items, and most are derived from factor analytic studies performed on data from 2,000 subjects. Level two provides the summary role scale, scored "by averaging the standard scores of those occupational role scales which are applicable for the subject," and the four summary symptom scales, scored by summing the raw scores of their constituent scales. The latter were achieved through applying a principal component-varimax factor analysis to the correlations among the symptom scales, based on data from 1,760 subjects from 11 studies. The user can select the level of summarization most appropriate for his purposes; however, the use of the summary scales is recommended when more detail is not needed. The supplementary scoring procedure yields 19 additional scales which are used in presenting a detailed clinical portrait of psychopathology along traditional diagnostic lines and in providing input for the computer program, DIAGNO I.

All PSS raw scores are converted to standard scores to facilitate comparisons across different scales. No item is included in more than one scale, and some items are weighted to increase their fidelity to clinical judgments of severity. The item ratings are conservative, so errors fall in the direction of greater health rather than in assigning a symptom on little or infrequent evidence.

COMPUTER PROGRAMS. Available subroutines are RECORD, providing the "subject's standard scale scores, the items judged true with their weights, and....a computer diagnosis";

PROFILE, which "displays the subject's scale scores graphically"; and GRAPH, which visually shows group comparisons on scales.

DIAGNO I is a branch analysis program which utilizes data from the PSS to approximate the diagnoses arrived at by psychiatrists in the usual clinical procedure. A later version, DIAGNO II, considers data based on any source of information, using as input age, sex, and 94 scales derived from the six-point scales of the *Current and Past Psychopathology Scale* (CAPPS) covering current state over a one-month period and past history after age 12. The agreement with hypothetical cases is .60 for DIAGNO I and .61 for DIAGNO II. The mean agreement with clinicians on real cases is .28 for DIAGNO I and .45 for DIAGNO II. The greater validity of DIAGNO II is probably attributable to the addition of historical information. DIAGNO II is able to boast an "agreement between computer diagnoses and clinical diagnoses equal to the diagnostic agreement between clinicians given the same information" and has "been shown to have substantial agreement with diagnoses made by psychiatrists functioning in a setting where they knew the subject well."

PSYCHOMETRIC PROPERTIES. *Internal Consistency.* The K-R 20 reliabilities range from .80 to .89 for the four summary symptom scales; .43 to .93 (median .74) for the 17 symptom scales; and .65 to .80 for the six role scales.

Interjudge Reliability. Intraclass correlation coefficients for a single rater, for 46 newly admitted patients, ranged from .90 to .98 for the four summary symptom scales; .57 to .99 (median .89) for the symptom scales; .94 for the summary role scale; and .66 to .98 for the role scales. In a separate study, the average coefficient was .86.

Test-Retest Reliability. Different interviewers assessed 25 newly-admitted psychiatric patients twice within a week's time. Scale score coefficients ranged from .30 to .85 (median .57). "Generally the scales based on verbal content [were] more stable than the scales based on overt physical behavior."

Intercorrelations Among the Scales. For the standardization sample, the correlations among the symptom scales within each summary scale tended to be higher than the correlations among symptom scales included in different summary scales. Subjective Distress, Behavioral Disturbance, and Impulse Control were virtually independent of each other; while Reality Testing Disturbance was correlated with both Subjective Distress and Behavioral Disturbance; and Summary Role was correlated with Subjective Distress and Impulse Control Disturbance.

Concurrent Validity Studies. A series of concurrent validity studies have demonstrated the PSS to be an effective instrument in differentiating contrasting populations of inpatients, outpatients, and nonpatient community residents; differentiating contrasting diagnostic groups of organic brain syndrome, schizophrenia, and neurosis, drug addiction and alcoholism, and the four common schizophrenic subtypes; and the measurement of change in 40 newly admitted psychiatric patients, interviewed on admission and again four weeks later, who showed the expected improvements on all but two scales, and 12 manic-depressive patients who, when interviewed during the three phases of their illness, showed specific changes in scale scores.

STRENGTHS. Some advantages of the PSS are (*a*) an interview format which eliminates error variance due to response sets, failure to understand questions, or inability to perform the task; provides information on personal appearance, speech, delusions, etc.; allows probes into areas of uncertainty; and maintains sufficient flexibility for establishing rapport; (*b*) a standardized procedure; (*c*) judgments based on specific, defined, small units of behavior; and (*d*) a wide range of coverage.

LIMITATIONS. The role scales appear to be of limited value in assessing role impairment in highly disorganized patients, as they show almost no correlation with Behavioral Disturbance and Reality Testing. Their greatest value is for patients primarily disturbed in the area of subjective distress.

RECOMMENDATION. To increase the value of the PSS for the researcher, it would be desirable to compile in a single manual a unitary and concise presentation of all the background and supporting information which now appears in diverse places.

CONCLUSION. The PSS provides researchers with an interview schedule which does a fine job of combining clinical flexibility with systematic, comprehensive, and standardized assessment. Its psychometric properties are sound, with reliability and validity well documented. Users of the PSS will find the investment of time and training necessary for optimum use of the schedule to be amply rewarded if their research needs are consonant with the purposes for which the instrument was designed. The scale construction is a model of excellence in both conception and execution. A close study of the PSS should aid anyone engaged in psychiatric interviewing, whether or not he elects to use the instrument for research purposes.

[128]

*Psychotic Inpatient Profile. Mental patients; 1961-68; PIP; ratings by nurses and psychiatric aides; revision of still-in-print *Psychotic Reaction Profile;* 12 scores: excitement, hostile belligerence, paranoid projection, anxious depression, retardation, seclusiveness, care needed, psychotic disorganization, grandiosity, perceptual disorganization, depressive mood, disorientation; 10 of the scores are "essentially equivalent" to the 10 scores obtained on the *Inpatient Multidimensional Psychiatric Scale,* the 2 new scores are seclusiveness and care needed; 1 form ('68, 6 pages); manual ('68, 15 pages plus test); $8.50 per 25 tests and manual; $7.50 per 25 tests; $2.50 per manual; postpaid; [10] minutes; Maurice Lorr and Norris D. Vestre; Western Psychological Services. *

REFERENCES

1. HALL, WILSON B.; VESTRE, NORRIS D.; SCHIELE, BURTRUM C.; AND ZIMMERMANN, ROBERT A. "A Controlled Comparison of Haloperidol and Fluphenazine in Chronic Treatment-Resistant Schizophrenics." *Dis Nerv System* 29:405-8 Je '68. * (PA 42:15606)
2. LORR, MAURICE, AND VESTRE, NORRIS D. "The Psychotic Inpatient Profile: A Nurse's Observation Scale." *J Clin Psychol* 25(2):137-40 Ap '69. * (PA 43:14474)
3. VESTRE, NORRIS D., AND ZIMMERMANN, ROBERT. "Validation Study of the Psychotic Inpatient Profile." *Psychol Rep* 27(1):3-7 Ag '70. * (PA 45:6597)
4. WATSON, CHARLES G.; KLETT, WILLIAM G.; AND LOREI, THEODORE W. "Toward an Operational Definition of Anhedonia." *Psychol Rep* 26(2):371-6 Ap '70. * (PA 44:21292)

GOLDINE C. GLESER, *Professor of Psychology and Director, Psychology Division, University of Cincinnati College of Medicine, Cincinnati, Ohio.*

PIP is an inventory designed to summarize currently observable behavior of a patient over a three-day period on a psychiatric inpatient ward. It consists of 74 statements to be scored on a 4-point scale based upon the frequency with which the specified behavior is observed, and 22 statements to be scored true or false on the basis of talking to the patient. Item scores are summed to provide measures of 12 dimensions of psychotic behavior. Ratings are made by nurses or psychiatric aides having adequate opportunity to observe and interact with the patients.

Ten of the dimensions measured by this inventory consist of behavior observations of syndromes corresponding to those elicited by a psychiatric interview schedule, the *Inpatient Multidimensional Psychiatric Scale.* The two additional dimensions of PIP are seclusiveness and need for care. These oblique factors were obtained by analysis and modification of the *Psychotic Reaction Profile,* on the apparent assumption that it should be possible to describe psychotic behavior along the same dimensions as had been obtained from interview data.

Normative data were obtained from 12 state and university hospitals. Both centile ranks and T scores are given for 135 males and 277 females diagnosed as functional psychotic and observed prior to any drug treatment. Separate norms are also given for 236 men and 368 women who were on "mild or moderate dosages of tranquilizers." It is interesting to note that substantially more patients were found who were already taking drugs when admitted than who were drug-free. Also, despite the fact that such drugs tend to obscure or suppress symptoms, the mean scores on all dimensions except anxious depression, retardation, and depressive mood are considerably higher for the drug-treated samples than for those not on drugs. This may imply that the most severely disturbed patients were almost invariably given drugs, so that patients not on drugs may actually have represented a restricted or truncated sample of the range of psychotic behavior. If this is so, the use of separate norms could give misleading results.

Disappointingly little information is available on the contribution of raters and items to the variance of scores. Intraclass correlations between raters in a sample of 57 cases from one hospital are presented in the manual. These range from .74 for perceptual distortion to .99 for grandiosity, with a median coefficient of .88. It would be helpful for the design of drug and other treatment research to know something about the extent to which mean scores of raters in the same and in different institutions vary on these measures. It would also be desirable to know something about the internal consistency of the behaviors scored on each dimension in order to be able to better judge the usefulness of obtaining 12 separate scores.

In summary, PIP is an instrument for rating the ward behavior of psychotic patients during a three-day period. It takes into account both the nature and relative frequency of various actions to obtain the 12 scores. The instrument is sophisticated in design and based on considerable knowledge of relevant behavior and of psychometric techniques. It is disappointing, however, that so little of the analysis of the data is shared with the readers of the manual.

For a review by Wilson H. Guertin of the first edition, see 6:167.

[129]

★**Pupil Behavior Inventory.** Grades 7–12; 1966; PBI; a rating scale; 5 scores: classroom conduct, academic motivation, socio-emotional, teacher dependence, personal behavior; 1 form (1 page); manual (70 pages plus set of scoring stencils); $2.50 per 100 forms; $2.15 per manual; postage extra; specimen set not available; (5–10) minutes; Robert D. Vinter, Rosemary C. Sarri, Darrel J. Vorwaller, and Walter E. Schafer; Campus Publishers. *

JOHN W. M. ROTHNEY, *Professor of Counseling and Guidance, University of Wisconsin, Madison, Wisconsin.*

This instrument is a by-product of a demonstration research project designed "to evaluate group work service as an approach in resolving problems of....misconduct and underachievement among pupils in elementary and secondary schools." The authors report that it was used as "an expedient device for collecting standardized information from several teachers with a minimum of time and effort."

The inventory consists of 34 items. Teachers rate each pupil on each item by indicating whether the behaviors have been observed very frequently, frequently, sometimes, infrequently or very infrequently. Since there are no guides for frequency counts, one teacher's "sometimes" may be another's "infrequently." The ratings presumably provide scores in the five areas noted above. In the teacher dependence area, for example, a student is rated on two items, "Seeks constant assurance," and "Possessive of teacher." If his behavior rating was "very infrequently" on those two items, he would have a score which is said to indicate that he is highly independent of his teachers. Similar procedures are used for the 12 items on classroom conduct, 9 on academic motivation and performance, 5 on socio-emotional state, and 6 on personal behavior.

Reliability is inferred from what is called high consistency in item factor loadings on ratings done at eight-month intervals, and a difference-of-means test between two "normal" and two "malperforming" groups. The efforts indicate that there is little difference in group means but there is no evidence about an individual's consistency.

Evidence of validity was obtained by comparing scores of a random sampling of youth "which we shall classify as normal" with those of students "designated as malperformers." The latter included both "underachieving and misbehaving pupils." The differences between the two groups "were significant at the .01 level of confidence on all items, permitting the inference that this result would be obtained 99 percent of the time when comparing normal and malperforming *individuals or groups* in the participating schools [italics added]." This inference about validity is not justified by the data.

Selective examples of findings resulting from use of the scale are that ratings made in the spring are consistently lower than those made in the fall; that English, language, and social science teachers tend to rate pupils highest, music and art teachers lowest, with others between these extremes; changes in ratings reflected differences resulting from the treatment offered during the major experiment conducted by the authors.

There seems to be no good reason for purchasing this inventory. The items are similar to those one finds on many pupil rating and report card forms. The too elaborate scoring, clerical, and statistical treatments will not be welcomed by, or helpful to, teachers. The scale seems to have been useful in the experiment conducted by the authors, but there is little in the manual which suggests that it could be employed with profit in ordinary school circumstances.

[130]

★**The Purpose in Life Test.** Adults; 1962–69; PIL; 1 form ('69, 4 pages); manual ('69, 4 pages); $2 per 25 tests; $1 per specimen set; cash orders postpaid; (10–15) minutes; James C. Crumbaugh and Leonard T. Maholick; Psychometric Affiliates. *

REFERENCES

1. CRUMBAUGH, JAMES C., AND MAHOLICK, LEONARD T. "An Experimental Study in Existentialism: The Psychometric Approach to Frankl's Concept of *Noogenic* Neurosis." *J Clin Psychol* 20:200–7 Ap '64. * (PA 39:8454)
2. BALLARD, REX EUGENE. *An Empirical Investigation of Viktor Frankl's Concept of the Search for Meaning: A Pilot Study With a Sample of Tuberculosis Patients.* Doctor's thesis, Michigan State University (East Lansing, Mich.), 1965. (DA 26:1165)
3. STROM, KENNETH R., AND TRANEL, NED N. "An Experimental Study of Alcoholism." *J Relig & Health* 6:242–9 Jl '67. *
4. BUTLER, ALAN C., AND CARR, LESTER. "Purpose in Life Through Social Action." *J Social Psychol* 74:243–50 Ap '68. * (PA 42:10435)
5. CRUMBAUGH, JAMES C. "Cross-Validation of Purpose-in-Life Test Based on Frankl's Concepts." *J Indiv Psychol* 24:74–81 My '68. * (PA 42:11401)
6. RICHMOND, BERT O.; MASON, ROBERT L.; AND SMITH, VIRGINIA. "Existential Frustration and Anomie." *J Nat Assn Women Deans & Counselors* 32(3):136–8 sp '69. *
7. CRUMBAUGH, JAMES C.; RAPHAEL, MARY; AND SHRADER, RAYMOND R. "Frankl's Will to Meaning in a Religious Order." *J Clin Psychol* 26(2):206–7 Ap '70. * (PA 44:14434)

JOHN R. BRAUN, *Professor of Psychology and Chairman of the Department, University of Bridgeport, Bridgeport, Connecticut.*

The *Purpose in Life Test* is a logically-keyed attitude scale intended as a measure of Viktor E. Frankl's concept of "existential vacuum": a failure to find a meaning and purpose in life— a "state of emptiness, manifested chiefly by boredom." The PIL has three parts. Part A consists of 20 items to be rated on a seven-point scale. In each case, position 4 is defined as neutral, and different descriptive terms are presented as anchors for points 1 and 7. For example, the item "My life is" has "empty, filled only with despair" as anchor for point 1, and "running over with exciting good things" as point 7 anchor. Total score involves the adding across all items of the scale points selected by the subject with higher scores indicating higher degrees of meaning and purpose in life. Part B involves 13 sentence completion items, and Part C requires the writing of a paragraph on personal aims, ambitions, and goals. Part A is the only one which is routinely treated quantitatively, and has been the subject of most research efforts to date. It will therefore be the focus of this review.

Split-half reliabilities have been demonstrated to be adequate in two separate studies (.90 and .92). Consistency over time has apparently not been investigated.

For a group of 50 outpatient neurotics, a correlation of .38 was found between PIL scores and therapist ratings of degree of purpose and meaning exhibited by the patient. Likewise, with a group of 120 Protestant parishioners, a correlation of .47 was found with ministers' ratings.

The test authors also cite as evidence of construct validity the correct predicting of the order of PIL means of four normal populations: successful business and professional personnel, active and leading Protestant parishioners, college undergraduates, and indigent nonpsychiatric hospital patients. The reviewer finds this evidence unconvincing, since the theoretical basis for predicting this order is not clear. Also, the difference between the means of the undergraduates and the indigent patients is surprisingly small (108.45 vs. 106.40).

The manual presents intercorrelations between the PIL and about 13 other personality measures including the MMPI, 16PF, etc. Among these measures was Frankl's Question-naire, an informal series of questions used by Frankl to estimate the presence of existential vacuum. A correlation of .68 was obtained with this measure in a group of 136 patients and nonpatients, thus providing evidence on convergent validity. However, in view of the high correlations found with some other measures (e.g., −.65 with D scale of MMPI, .63 with CPI achievement via conformance scale, .57 with Marlowe-Crowne social desirability, −.51 with Elmore General Anomie factor, etc.) discriminant validity has not been established. It would be highly useful to have a systematic investigation of both the convergent and discriminant validity of the PIL using the Campbell and Fiske multitrait-multimethod matrix. Multiple measures of existential vacuum might well include the Frankl Questionnaire and scores derived from Parts A, B, and C of the PIL, while measures of anomie, depression, and social desirability would also appear desirable for the matrix.

The PIL manual indicates that it may be useful for individual counseling purposes when used with the cautions necessary for any self-report device. In addition, it is recommended for group administration for research purposes. Examples of the latter are recent studies using the PIL to evaluate the effects of counseling, as well as attempts to relate it to degree of participation in social action, and to employment status in middle-aged women. Since the PIL manual has only four pages, a more informative revision should be published.

Although still requiring additional basic research dealing with reliability and validity, the PIL nevertheless stands as an interesting and promising tool.

GEORGE DOMINO, *Associate Professor of Psychology and Director, Counseling Center, Fordham University, New York, New York.*

The *Purpose-in-Life Test* is a brief nontimed attitude scale consisting of three sections: Part A contains 20 sentence stems each with seven response alternatives, with extreme and neutral points defined, Part B consists of 13 sentence completion stems, and Part C directs the respondent to write a paragraph describing in detail aims, ambitions, goals in life, and progress being made in achieving these. Parts B and C are not scored and little consideration is given them in either the manual or published research reports; consequently, the following discussion pertains only to Part A.

The PIL reflects the existential viewpoint of Viktor E. Frankl and is intended as a measure of Frankl's concept of "existential vacuum," a state of emptiness experienced by one who fails to find meaning and purpose in life. The PIL is thus an attempt to quantify a concept drawn from an important philosophical-therapeutic orientation which has been often criticized for its inherent vagueness and lack of empirical underpinnings; as such, the PIL is a commendable effort.

The test protocol leaves something to be desired. The printing is large, of the type found in children's beginning readers. There is at least one typing error (heridity), and the prominent title reinforces the transparency of the items. The manual is brief (four pages), contains some minor errors (e.g., Frankle) and appears highly condensed. Much of the validity data, for example, might be better presented in tables than in the text. The articles by Crumbaugh and Maholick (1) and by Crumbaugh (5) contain most of the information available in the manual, but in a much clearer format.

The 20 items can be completed in less than ten minutes, are quite obvious, and rather loaded in social desirability (a correlation coefficient of .57 is reported with the Marlowe-Crowne social desirability scale for a group of 40 college undergraduates). A respondent's score is the sum of the numerical values circled and can theoretically range from 20 to 140.

There is little indication of the manner in which the items were selected. Crumbaugh and Maholick (1) indicate that the items were selected from an examination of the literature on existentialism, and more specifically, on logotherapy. A pilot study of 25 items resulted in half of them being discarded and new items substituted; 22 items stood up in a subsequent item analysis. No specific information is presented in the manual as to what criteria were used for dropping or retaining items, nor what specific analyses were performed. Assuming the authors proceeded in a standard manner and began with the best items they could develop, one wonders about such a high mortality rate, as well as the source of the new items. Crumbaugh and Maholick (1) do indicate that 20 of the items correlate above .40 with the total score, with coefficients ranging from −.06 to .82. Crumbaugh (5) indicates that two items

requiring negative scoring were omitted for simplicity, leaving a 20-item test. Thus, one major area of information required by the serious user is not presented: that of individual item behavior. Without this information, one may well wonder whether a single item such as "How meaningful is your life?" might not be as valid as the entire scale.

Reliability appears satisfactory with reported odd-even reliabilities in the low .90's. No other type of reliability is reported. The manual presents extensive validity data in the form of both means for various patient and normal groups, and correlations with a wide variety of other scales, including MMPI and CPI scales. In general, most of the validity data presented are positive and support both the theortical underpinnings of the PIL and its empirical functioning.

The PIL significantly distinguishes patient from nonpatient samples and reflects a progressive decrease in means consonant with logotherapeutic theory.

The PIL correlates substantially with both the Srole Anomie Scale and the MMPI Depression scale, showing considerable overlap, yet sufficient variance to allow the PIL to stand on its own.

The PIL appears to be a worthwhile instrument to consider, with much additional work needed, however, before it can be incorporated (no pun intended) into the main stream of psychological research.

[131]

★The Q-Tags Test of Personality. Ages 6 and over, ages 12 and over; 1967–69; QTTP; individual; 2 forms; mimeographed manual ['69, 27 pages]; directions sheet ('69, 1 page); record form ('69, 1 page); norms consist of means and standard deviations; Can $4 per set of testing materials and 25 record forms; $1.50 per 25 record forms; postage extra; (60–80) minutes in 2 sessions; Arthur G. Storey and Louis I. Masson (manual); Institute of Psychological Research, Inc. *

a) [BIOGRAPHICAL FORM.] Ages 6 and over; 13 scores: 6 factor scores (affective, assertive, effective, hostility, reverie, social) in each of 2 areas (he or she is, he or she should be), correlation of self and idealself; 2 parts labeled Forms h, s, ('67, 54 cards plus paradigm); norms for ages 6–12 only.

b) [AUTOBIOGRAPHICAL FORM.] Ages 12 and over; 13 scores: 6 factor scores (same as a above) in each of 2 areas (I am, I wish I were), correlation of self and idealself; 2 parts labeled Forms i, w, ('67, 54 cards plus paradigm).

REFERENCES

1–5. See P:225.
6. STOREY, ARTHUR G., AND SAINTY, J. E. "Personality Characteristics of Prisoners Compared With Non-Prisoners." Can J Correct 9:306–12 O '67. *
7. STOREY, ARTHUR G. "Of Personality and Q-Technology." Can Psychologist 10(4):447–55 O '69. * (PA 44:6783)

JOAN PRESTON, *Assistant Professor of Education, The Ontario Institute for Studies in Education, Toronto, Ontario, Canada.*

This test consists of 54 statement cards, nine statements for each of the six factors. The items were selected by item and factor analysis from a larger pool of 77 items coming primarily from the MMPI. The cards are first sorted into two piles: statements descriptive of the individual and those not descriptive of him. The cards are then sorted into 11 columns, representing categories ranging from "most unlike me" to "describes me best." The score for an item corresponds to the number of the column in which it was placed. Scores for the nine items of each factor are then summed to give the six factor scores. This procedure is used to administer both the self and ideal-self paradigms, and the correlation between the self and ideal self is calculated from the item scores of the two paradigms. If the individual is doing the sorting for himself the autobiographical form is used, while the biographical form is employed when a person who knows the individual well is doing the sorting.

The test-retest reliabilities of Form i, based on 180 grade 7 and 8 students, with a time interval of 5 days, are reported as affective, .65; assertive, .73; effective, .61; hostility, .69; reverie, .50; and social, .60.

The evidence for validity presented in the manual is very weak. Concurrent validity was obtained using 100 grade 8 students who completed Form i, with their teachers completing Form h. Low but statistically significant correlations were obtained for four of the factors: assertive (.26), effective (.36), hostility (.21), and reverie (.22). More promising validity evidence is presented in other published papers. Storey (*1*) found that school decelerates differed significantly from both accelerates and potential accelerates on all factors except social. Masson and Gough (*3*) obtained different patterns among factor correlations for the four groups of regular high school boys and girls and vocational program boys and girls.

The test authors state that the scales measure whatever is implied by the items making up the scale, although many of the items probably have a high social desirability component. The test seems to be interesting to the examinee, but its usefulness is limited by the unimpressive reliability and validity data currently available.

[132]

★**Reid Report.** Job applicants; 1969; RR; for predicting the likelihood of employee theft; 1 form (24 pages); no manual; only data on reliability and validity and norms in *1* below; examination fee, $11 per applicant; fee includes scoring service; postpaid; specimen set free; [45–75] minutes; John E. Reid and Associates. *

REFERENCE

1. ASH, PHILIP. "Validation of an Instrument to Predict the Likelihood of Employee Theft." Abstract. *Proc 78th Ann Conv Am Psychol Assn* 5(2):579–80 '70. * (PA 44:19568)

[133]

★**S-D Proneness Checklist.** Clients and patients; 1970; SDPC; 3 ratings: suicidal, depressive, total; 1 form (2 pages); combined manual (12 pages) titled *Symptomology and Evaluation of Depressed and Suicidal Patients* for this and test 100; no data on reliability and validity; basis for score interpretations not presented; $3.75 per 25 forms; $1.50 per specimen set (must be purchased to obtain manual); cash orders postpaid; (5–10) minutes; William T. Martin; Psychologists and Educators Press. *

[134]

★**School Interest Inventory.** Grades 7–12; 1966, c1959–66; SII; revision of *Life Adjustment Scale, Number 1* ('58); for identifying potential dropouts who "should receive counseling"; 1 form (4 pages); manual (19 pages); no norms, publisher recommends use of local norms; $12 per 100 MRC test-answer booklets; $1.05 per set of hand scoring stencils; 48¢ per manual; 90¢ per specimen set; postage extra; scoring service, 33¢ per test; (20–30) minutes; William C. Cottle; Houghton Mifflin Co. *

REFERENCES

1–9. See P:236.
10. NEWBURY, DAVID NORMAN. *An Evaluation of a Dropout Prevention Project in Hazel Park, Michigan.* Doctor's thesis, Wayne State University (Detroit, Mich.), 1967. (DA 28:2907A)
11. RENFROW, OMER WILLIAM. *Dropout Prone and Non-Dropout Prone High School Boys: A Study of Differences.* Doctor's thesis, University of Illinois (Urbana, Ill.), 1968. (DA 29:449A)
12. DAVENPORT, CHRISTOPHER M. *A Study of the Feasibility of Developing a Delinquent Girl Scale for the School Interest Inventory.* Doctor's thesis, Boston College (Chestnut Hill, Mass.), 1969. (DAI 31:215A)
13. GAETANO, CARL ROGER. *A Comparative and Experimental Study of Selected Characteristics of Disadvantaged and Non-Disadvantaged Rural Youth.* Doctor's thesis, Ohio University (Athens, Ohio), 1969. (DAI 30:2331A)
14. PATROS, PHILIP GEORGE. *An Investigation of the Relationship Between Certain Non-Intellective Factors and Academic Performance of Academically Bright Junior High School Girls.* Doctor's thesis, Boston College (Chestnut Hill, Mass.), 1969. (DAI 30:3734A)
15. UBER, THOMAS BARCLAY. *Delinquency Prediction With the School Interest Inventory.* Doctor's thesis, Boston College (Chestnut Hill, Mass.), 1969. (DAI 30:3-42A)
16. O'SHEA, ARTHUR J. "Low-Achievement Syndrome Among Bright Junior High School Boys." *J Ed Res* 63(6):257–62 F '70. *

GENE V GLASS, *Professor of Education and Co-director, Laboratory of Educational Research, University of Colorado, Boulder, Colorado.*

This instrument was constructed by selecting self-report questionnaire items which discriminated between dropouts and "stay-ins," i.e., persisters. The final form consists of 150 items in the form of declarative statements which the pupil reports as being either true or false for him. The resulting instrument is actuarial, being based on no psychological theory or reasoning about persistence in school. The items reflect the strictly empirical character of the inventory: "We rent our home"; "I like to skip school"; "School is fun." Items were selected from an earlier edition by determining which of the original items correlated significantly with membership in either a group of 150 dropouts or 150 matched (on grade, sex, age, school, and course of study) stay-ins. The two groups were selected from a population of 25,000 pupils in grades 7–9, containing about 800 dropouts. Such empirical keying of subsets of larger pools of items capitalizes on chance variation; the 150 most discriminating items could be expected to be less discriminating in any cross validation of the item validity coefficients.

Separate scoring keys for boys (90 items) and for girls (86 items) are provided. Many items could elicit ambiguous responses: 15 items ask for data on the pupil's father, while no provisions are made for pupils without fathers; statements about brothers or sisters are not infrequent; etc. (One wonders about the meaning of the responses of a fatherless only child.)

Unweighted and weighted scoring keys are provided. An unweighted total score for a pupil is derived by counting the number of times he marked items with the response (T or F) typical of dropouts. Though it is nearly certain on a priori psychometric grounds that differential weighting of nearly 100 items will not improve reliability or validity appreciably, the author of the inventory has been misled into thinking that his weighted scoring key is to be preferred: "The improvement in differentiation by use of the weighted scores can be seen by examining the figure and tables." The figure and tables referred to show only that weighted scores have a larger variance, which is to be expected. Cottle reported that weighted and unweighted scores correlated above .96—as was to be expected—but apparently he failed to realize that there could not be any practical difference between the validity or reliability of such highly correlated weighted and unweighted scores. The user of the inventory should not spend 33 cents per test for scoring services to obtain weighted scores.

The stability reliability of the inventory is high. Test-retest correlations with one to two weeks between administrations ranged from .78 to .92 on eight groups, with an average of 90 pupils per group. The stability of scores over a longer period of time was not reported in the manual; memory could have permitted consistency of responses across only one to two weeks. Test-retest reliability across a school year is more important but is not reported.

Validity data on the inventory are fragmentary; fortunately, they were gathered on an independent crossvalidation group. Mean differences between dropouts and persisters are reported for 215 boys and 236 girls of each type selected in an unspecified manner from more than 20 schools. Mean differences on total inventory scores for the two groups are statistically reliable. Goodwin (review excerpted below) found evidence of moderate predictive validity for the SII over a period of one year. However, teacher estimates of future dropouts were more valid than the inventory predictions.

No normative data are presented. The manual recommends that scores be interpreted on an intra-institutional basis, which has the alleged advantage of yielding recommendations based on a given school rather than on schools in general. The point may be well taken, but it will be unconvincing to the majority of schools lacking resources for local norm construction. With so much data presumably available on the inventory, one wonders why more are not reported in the manual.

The validity of the *School Interest Inventory* is not extensively investigated in the manual. Stability reliability for decision-making about pupils was established only for a short time period. The user should not bother with the recommended weighted scoring system. No norms are presented. However, the genuine utility of the inventory rests on a question of "incremental validity," viz., can it predict school dropouts better than a five-item, half-page questionnaire measuring a pupil's race, family income per family member, welfare status, father's occupation, and personal educational aspirations? It is doubtful.

Leonard V. Gordon, *Professor of Educational Psychology and Statistics, State University of New York at Albany, Albany, New York.*

Designed primarily to identify students who are likely to drop out of high school and who accordingly may be referred to the school counseling service, the inventory consists of 150 items, 90 for boys and 86 for girls. Seventy-two items are common to both scales and 46 are experimental and unscored. Two scoring methods are available. The one using unit weights is recommended for hand scoring, and the other, using differential weights of 1 to 9, is employed by the publisher's scoring service, which also provides, for each pupil, the number of items answered in the dropout direction in each weight category. The value of the latter information is not clear. The two scoring methods correlate .97, suggesting that on the whole the gain achieved with the more complex system is likely to be small. The test-retest reliabilities, mostly "in the .80's," seem acceptable for screening purposes. No norms are provided, the student's relative standing within his own school being the recommended method of interpretation.

A weakness in the instrument is the non-applicability of a number of items to some students. Such items may refer to nonexistent siblings, or deceased, unknown, or absent parents. Further, it is left to the individual student to call the irrelevance of these items to the examiner's attention, a very questionable testing procedure.

The validity information is poorly presented; it suffers from incomplete reporting, an overworking of data from small samples, and analyses that overstate the test's effectiveness. For example, the manual states that "examination of individual school results....is more appropriate than a study of results obtained by combining schools," but then includes validity data for *one* school, followed by summary data for combinations of 4 schools and then 17 schools. It surely would have been more meaningful to have presented the total array of validity coefficients by individual school, with some indication of each school's socioeconomic and ethnic makeup.

The effectiveness of the test is over-represented in that many of the comparisons are based on equal-sized matched samples of stay-ins and dropouts, the actual dropout rate being about 5 percent. Consequently, the reported point-biserial validities are spuriously high. A two-page graphic display based on these matched samples is deceiving in that the discriminating power of the test appears much greater than would be the case in practice. In this same display, the use of the same scale units for the weighted and unweighted scores visually exaggerates the relatively small differences in validity between them. The use of comparable units, such as standard scores, would

have been proper. The same flavor of overstatement occurs in the text. For example, slippage in predictive power is rationalized in terms of family and social pressures that may cause "false positives" to remain in school, and intentional falsification that may result in low scores for the "false negatives."

While it is reported that about 22 percent of the dropout students in the massive two-year follow-up study turned in void papers and accordingly were not included in the analyses, this problem is not further discussed. It would be important to know the percentage of stay-in students whose papers were void, as well as the validity associated with proper versus improper completion of the inventory. As it stands, the counselor has neither guidance nor an empirical basis for deciding what rank in the counseling order to assign to students who turn in void papers, and in some schools the proportion is likely to be fairly large. Of equal relevance is the extent to which invalidity was associated with such things as grade level and the socio-economic status of the schools sampled, and intellective, subcultural and socioeconomic characteristics of the students. This would be important information for the counselor who is to decide on the appropriateness of the inventory for his intended application. Finally, the extent to which the omission of potentially non-applicable items contributed to test invalidity is not specified. If at all significant, an immediate revision of the inventory, with such items deleted, would be indicated.

The manual states that "scores obtained should be used in close conjunction with other available information for determining which students should receive counseling. School records of academic achievement, attendance, teachers' opinions, and age relative to school grade are some of the factors to be considered; the inventory serves as a supplement to these sources of information." Since the inventory includes a substantial number of heavily weighted items relating to school grades and attendance, it would be most important to know the correlation between inventory scores and the latter variables, as well as the incremental validity, if any, of the inventory in predicting school dropout. No such data are provided.

The manual on the whole is characterized by a conceptual barrenness. No mention is made of the test content nor of its relationship to other important reference variables. This is particularly regrettable in view of the extensive research on which the inventory was based. One is left with the feeling that significant information regarding school dropout proneness may lie buried in the instrument, unrevealed by the total score.

The inventory is described as providing a "valuable supplement to information about individual pupils in grades seven through twelve so that a more effective placement of the student may be achieved either in the school system or in the work setting outside of school." Considering the meager information presented in the manual, the instrument is unlikely to be of value to the counselor for either purpose. For the simple identification of "potential drop-outs" for counseling purposes, the use of available data, such as school grades and attendance records, not only may be as effective as the inventory but would avoid problems of test invalidity associated with the latter.

J Ed Meas 6(3):200–1 f '69. *William L. Goodwin.* * Of the items, 75 are scored for both males and females, 15 for just males, and 11 for just females. Curiously, 49 of the items have no function in determining inventory scores. They are included because other scales are under development; it is unclear that the author's welcome for "inquiries or reports of scores using this inventory" is any justification for subjecting students to the nonfunctional items in the interim period. * A question not considered, yet an important one, is the predictive strength of the instrument compared with other available measures, such as attendance, previous grades, or counselor and teacher opinion. It is strange that these other readily accessible measures were not examined during test development. Examining those items receiving the greatest weights, the direct relation of most of them to these other measures is obvious * no mention is made of any factor analyses conducted regarding items in the inventory. In an effort to understand the instrument better, it was administered....to all the seventh-, eighth-, ninth-, and tenth-graders ($N = 736$) in a central Pennsylvania school district * Additionally, teachers in the district were asked to indicate in writing those pupils that they considered potential dropouts. * In the year following administration of the test, 20 students dropped out. Of the 20, 19 had been identified as likely dropouts by at least one

teacher and, on the average, by four teachers. Six of the 20 did not score over 30 on the School Interest Inventory (the initial cutoff score suggested in the manual) * Thus, the predictive validity of the instrument was substantiated at a tolerable level. At the same time, teachers in this small secondary school situation were even more impressive in identifying possible dropouts correctly. It would seem that the Inventory has merit, but also that its value can be increased substantially if other factors, such as teacher judgment, are given careful scrutiny. Additionally, its greatest value might be realized in large urban schools where evidence of student anonymity is marked.

[135]
★**School Motivation Analysis Test, Research Edition.** Ages 12–17; 1961–70; SMAT; downward extension of *Motivation Analysis Test;* 40 scores: 4 motivation scores (unintegrated, integrated, total, difference [conflict]) for each of 6 drives (assertiveness, mating, fear, narcism, pugnacity-sadism, protectiveness) and each of 4 sentiments (self-sentiment, superego, school, home); Form A ('70, 20 pages); preliminary manual ('70, 18 pages); no data on reliability; separate answer sheets (Digitek) must be used; $15 per 25 tests; $4 per 50 answer sheets; scoring stencils not available; $1 per manual; $1.50 per specimen set; postage extra; scoring service, 75¢ and over per test; (50–60) minutes; Arthur B. Sweney, Raymond B. Cattell, and Samuel E. Krug; Institute for Personality and Ability Testing. *

REFERENCES

1. CATTELL, RAYMOND B.; SWENEY, ARTHUR B.; AND RADCLIFFE, JOHN A. "The Objective Measurement of Motivation Structure in Children." *J Clin Psychol* 16:227–32 Jl '60. * (PA 36:2FF27C)
2. CATTELL, R. B.; RADCLIFFE, J. A.; AND SWENEY, A. B. "The Nature and Measurement of Components of Motivation." *Genetic Psychol Monogr* 68:49–211 Ag '63. * (PA 39:10186)
3. CATTELL, RAYMOND B.; RADCLIFFE, JOHN A.; AND SWENEY, ARTHUR B. "Components in Motivation Strength in Children Compared With Those in Adults." *J General Psychol* 70:95–112 Ja '64. *
4. JOHNSON, HENRY SIOUX. *Ethnic Group Differences in Certain Personal, Intellectual, Achievement, and Motivational Characteristics.* Doctor's thesis, University of Southern California (Los Angeles, Calif.), 1964. (DA 25:3396)
5. PIERSON, GEORGE R. "A Refinement in the Use of School Motivation Analysis Test (SMAT) as a Predictor of School Achievement of Delinquent Boys." *Ed & Psychol Meas* 24:929–34 w '64. * (PA 39:8709)
6. PIERSON, GEORGE R.; BARTON, VIRGINIA; AND HEY, GORDON. "SMAT Motivation Factors as Predictors of Academic Achievement of Delinquent Boys." *J Psychol* 57:243–9 Ja '64. * (PA 39:2617)
7. CATTELL, R. B.; SEALY, A. P.; AND SWENEY, A. B. "What Can Personality and Motivation Source Trait Measurements Add to the Prediction of School Achievement?" *Brit J Ed Psychol* 36:280–95 N '66. * (PA 41:804)
8. ROACH, ARTHUR JAMES, JR. *Some Characteristics Differentiating Adolescent Religious Candidates Perceived as Superior From Those Perceived as Inferior: A Cross-Sectional, Exploratory Investigation Into Various Psychosocial Characteristics of Christian Brothers Candidates.* Doctor's thesis, University of Notre Dame (Notre Dame, Ind.), 1966. (DA 27:3732A)
9. HUNDLEBY, JOHN D., AND CATTELL, RAYMOND B. *Personality Structure in Middle Childhood and the Prediction of School Achievement and Adjustment.* Monographs of the Society for Research in Child Development, Serial No. 121; Vol. 33, No. 5. Chicago, Ill.: University of Chicago Press, 1968. Pp. iv, 61. *
10. BELL, DAVID BRUCE. *The Motivational and Personality Factors in Reading Retardation Among Two Racial Groups of Adolescent Males.* Doctor's thesis, Texas Technological University (Lubbock, Tex.), 1969. (DAI 31:909B)

[136]

★Self Perception Inventory. Ages 12 and over; 1967–69; SPI; 12 scores: general adjustment (consistency, self-actualization, supervision, total), general maladjustment (uncommon response, rigidity-dogmatism, authoritarianism, anxiety, depression, paranoia, total), time; 1 form ('69, 8 pages); manual ('69, 16 pages); profile ('69, 1 page); separate answer sheets must be used; $13.50 per examiner's kit including 10 tests, 25 answer and profile sheets, keys, and manual; $3.50 per specimen set; cash orders postpaid; (20–35) minutes; William T. Martin; Psychologists and Educators Press. *

REFERENCES

1. MARTIN, WILLIAM T. "Self Perception Inventory: A New Test of Personality." *Psychol Rep* 23:961–2 D '68. * (*PA* 43: 9775)
2. BRAUN, JOHN R., AND TINLEY, JOHN J. "Faking Study of Scores on the Self-Perception Inventory." *Psychol Rep* 26(1): 118 F '70. * (*PA* 45:4294)
3. MARTIN, WILLIAM T. "Transparency of Pseudo-Transparency on the Subscales of the Self-Perception Inventory." *Psychol Rep* 26(2):401–2 Ap '70. * (*PA* 44:21000)

[137]

★Self-Rating Depression Scale. Adults; 1965–67; SDS; intensity of depression regardless of diagnosis; booklet entitled *The Measurement of Depression* ('67, 18 pages) presents directions, key, norms, and 12 copies of scale; no charge for test materials; a 22 minute 16 mm. sound and color film on the scale's use is available on loan without charge; Chinese, Czech, Dutch, French, German, Italian, Japanese, Slovak, Spanish, Swedish, and Thai editions of the scale available; (5) minutes; William W. K. Zung; the Author. *

REFERENCES

1–8. See P:242.
9. JACOBS, THEODORE J.; FOGELSON, SUSAN; AND CHARLES, EDWARD. "Depression Ratings in Hypochondria." *N Y State J Med* 68:3119–22 D 15 '68. * (*PA* 44:7015)
10. JACOBSON, GARY. "The Briefest Psychiatric Encounter: Acute Effects of Evaluation." *Arch Gen Psychiatry* 18:718–24 Je '68. * (*PA* 42:17386)
11. MORGAN, WILLIAM P. "Selected Physiological and Psychomotor Correlates of Depression in Psychiatric Patients." *Res Q* 39:1037–43 D '68. *
12. CROSBY, ALLAN R. "The Use of the Self-Rating Depression Scale After Traumatic Injuries." *J Am Osteopath Assn* 69(3):269–70 N '69. * (*PA* 45:8735)
13. KELLY, DESMOND; BROWN, CLINTON; AND SHAFFER, JOHN W. "A Controlled Physiological, Clinical and Psychological Evaluation of Chlordiazepoxide." *Brit J Psychiatry* 115(529):1387–92 D '69. * (*PA* 44:14811)
14. LAMONT, JOHN NORMAN. *Resistance to Influence in Depressives.* Doctor's thesis, University of Washington (Seattle, Wash.), 1969. (*DAI* 30:5240B)
15. MIKESELL, R. H., AND CALHOUN, L. G. "Faking on the Zung Self-Rating Depression Scale." *Psychol Rep* 25(1):173–4 Ag '69. * (*PA* 44:3636)
16. ROCKLIFF, BURTON W. "A Brief Self-Rating Questionnaire for Depression (SRQ-D)." *Psychosomatics* 10(4):236 Jl-Ag '69. * (*PA* 44:16913)
17. SMITH, GERALD HERSCHEL. *A Differentiation Between Suicidal and Non-Suicidal Schizophrenic Patients.* Master's thesis, Western Michigan University (Kalamazoo, Mich.), 1969. (*Masters Abstracts* 7:196)
18. ZUNG, WILLIAM W. K. "A Cross-Cultural Survey of Symptoms in Depression." *Am J Psychiatry* 126(1):116–21 Jl '69. * (*PA* 44:921)
19. DESILVERIO, ROBERT V.; RICKELS, KARL; WEISE, CHARLES C.; CLARK, EDWARD L.; AND HUTCHINSON, JAMES. "Perphenazine-Amitriptyline in Neurotic Depressed Outpatients: A Collaborative Study." *Am J Psychiatry* 127(3):322–9 S '70. * (*PA* 45:8421)
20. MIKESELL, RICHARD H., AND CALHOUN, LAWRENCE G. "Response Set on the Zung Self-Rating Depression Scale." *Percept & Motor Skills* 30(1):22 F '70. *
21. MORGAN, WILLIAM P. "Physical Working Capacity in Depressed and Non-Depressed Psychiatric Females: A Preliminary Study." *Am Correct Ther J* 24(1):14–6 Ja-F '70. *
22. RICKELS, KARL; HESBACHER, PETER; AND DOWNING, ROBERT W. "Differential Drug Effects in Neurotic Depression." *Dis Nerv System* 31(7):468–75 Jl '70. * (*PA* 45:2566)
23. SEITZ, FRANK C. "Five Psychological Measures of Neurotic Depression: A Correlation Study." *J Clin Psychol* 26(4): 504–5 O '70. * (*PA* 45:4631)
24. ZUNG, WILLIAM W. K., AND WONNACOTT, THOMAS H. "Treatment Prediction in Depression Using a Self-Rating Scale." *Biol Psychiatry* 2(4):321–9 O '70. *

LEONARD D. GOODSTEIN, *Professor of Psychology and Director of Professional Training in Psychology, University of Cincinnati, Cincinnati, Ohio.*

Depression is perhaps the most common of all psychopathological states and psychologists have been attempting to develop a useful scale for tapping this area of disturbance since Jasper's work [1] in 1930. The *Self-Rating Depression Scale* is one recent attempt to provide a relatively simple and direct procedure for evaluating the severity of clinical depression. The scale itself consists of 20 self-report items which the respondent answers as true of himself "None or a little of the time," "Some of the time," "Good part of the time," or "Most or all of the time." These qualitative responses are given arbitrary numerical values of 1 to 4 in scoring the scale.

In selecting the 20 items for inclusion in the scale the author attempted to include those behaviors or symptoms which were cited in the literature as most characteristic of depressive disorders, regardless of the etiology of the depression. Using previously reported factor analytic studies of depression as the basis, the author used his judgment to select those items which he regarded as adequately tapping three important areas of disturbance which characterize depression: affective (two items), biological (eight items), and psychological (ten items) disturbance. The basis for deciding upon the number of items to tap each of these areas is not made clear by the author. In order to avoid the problems involved in establishing a positive response set, half of the items were worded so that a negative response would be the scored one.

The scale itself is printed on 5½ by 8½" sheets bound into a convenient booklet which includes 12 copies of the scale and an overlay scoring stencil. Unfortunately, the scale form does not provide any space for either the respondent's name or the date, which information would seem necessary for any record keeping or filing. Further, there are no standardized instructions to the respondent printed on the form. The directions for administration

1 JASPER, HERBERT H. "The Measurement of Depression-Elation and Its Relation to a Measure of Introversion-Extroversion." *J Abn & Social Psychol* 25:307–18 O-D '30. *

which are included as part of the general directions for the professional user and which are printed on the booklet covers are quite nonspecific. Considering the confusion which is so typical of depression, the failure to include carefully worked out and pretested instructions is somewhat surprising.

Each respondent's raw score is then transformed into an SDS Index which is nothing more than the actual percentage obtained of the 80 possible scale points. In this age of more sophisticated scaling techniques, this procedure both seems inadequate and might delude naive users into considering such scores with more seriousness than they deserve. Crude norms are provided in the booklet, giving the mean and range of SDS Index scores for a group of normal controls and five groups of psychiatric patients. While the number of cases on which these norms are based is not explicated in the booklet, the research referenced by the author (1, 2) suggests that there were 100 subjects in the normal control group and approximately 200 subjects in the five other groups.

It is important to note that there is no evidence on the reliability of SDS scores reported, either in the booklet or in the other relevant research published by the test author or others. While the problem of reliability of such a mood or symptom scale is a complex one, the potential user would be in a better position to decide upon this issue if there were some data available on the scale.

While SDS scores have been shown to be independent of marital status, sex difference, intelligence, and family income, there was a significant relationship reported between SDS scores and total years of education ($r = -.28$), suggesting that more highly educated patients are less likely to admit to depressive symptoms (6). Whether this obtained difference reflects a true difference in the distribution of depression or is a consequence of greater defensiveness as a function of education is not possible to determine from the available evidence.

Of more concern, however, are the findings of Mikesell and Calhoun (15), who not only report that the SDS is easily "faked," especially in the direction of greater admission of symptomatology, but that presumably normal adolescents with no history of psychiatric disturbance give SDS scores in the clinical range when asked to respond to the SDS truthfully. While it is difficult to determine the reasons for this

finding, it would appear that age is an important consideration in determining SDS scores, a finding supported by a report by Zung (5) himself with "normal" geriatric persons who gave elevated SDS scale scores. Thus, the need for carefully derived normative data, including separate age norms, would seem apparent.

On the other hand, there is fair evidence available on the concurrent validity of the SDS scores. Scores on the SDS do differentiate depressive patients from those with other psychiatric disorders (1, 2), are significantly correlated (.43 to .65) with global ratings of depression made by psychiatrists in the United States and six other countries (18), and are significantly correlated (.59 to .75) with scores on the MMPI Depression scale (2). Further, changes in SDS scores were shown to be significantly related to clinical changes following treatment for depression (1, 2).

On the basis of the currently available data, the SDS would appear to be only marginally successful in meeting the author's intention of providing a brief, simple, self-administering, and quantified scale for measuring clinical depression. While the SDS clearly is brief, simple, and self-administering, there are serious questions about the quantified data this procedure provides. The failure to provide any estimates of the reliability of the instrument and to provide adequate scaling must be seen as seriously limiting the usefulness of the SDS, especially as a clinical tool. It is unfortunate that these limitations have not been more adequately handled, in view of the promising early validity data now available. Those persons in need of a brief measure of depression would be better advised to use the *Depression Adjective Check Lists,* despite their greater cost.

[138]

Shipley-Institute of Living Scale for Measuring Intellectual Impairment. Adults; 1939-46; SILS; 4 scores: vocabulary, abstractions, total, conceptual quotient; 1 form ('39, 2 pages); manual ('46, 4 pages, identical with manual copyrighted in 1940 except for title); $6.50 per 50 tests, postpaid; specimen set not available; 20(25) minutes; Walter C. Shipley; distributed by Mrs. John H. Boyle. *

REFERENCES
1-25. See 3:95.
26-48. See 5:111.
49-61. See 6:173.
62-99. See P:244, also includes a cumulative name index to the first 99 references for this test.
100. PHELPS, HENRY BEVERIDGE. *Conceptual Ability and the Perception of Interaction in Movement by Elderly Persons.* Doctor's thesis, Columbia University (New York, N.Y.), 1960. (*DA* 21:2007)
101. ROBLES, ALBERT G. *The Shipley-Hartford Scale as a Measure of Intellectual Efficiency and as a Predictor of Aca-*

demic Success. Master's thesis, Fresno State College (Fresno, Calif.), 1960.

102. BOOKBINDER, LAWRENCE J. "Follow-Up Versus Discharge Status of Psychiatric Inpatients." *J Clin Psychol* 18:501–3 O '62. * (*PA* 39:5550)

103. JUDGE, CAROLE HESSE. *Thought Disorder in Parents of Schizophrenics.* Doctor's thesis, University of Minnesota (Minneapolis, Minn.), 1967. (*DA* 28:3473B)

104. GILBERSTADT, HAROLD. "Relationships Among Scores of Tests Suitable for the Assessment of Adjustment and Intellectual Functioning." *J Gerontol* 23:483–7 O '68. *

105. MALERSTEIN, A. J., AND BELDEN, E. "WAIS, SILS, and PPVT in Korsakoff's Syndrome." *Arch Gen Psychiatry* 19:743–50 D '68. * (*PA* 43:8472)

106. BELL, HOWARD A.; WEINGOLD, HAROLD P.; AND LACHIN, JOHN M. "Measuring Adjustment in Patients Disabled With Alcoholism." *Q J Studies Alcohol* 30(3A):634–9 S '69. * (*PA* 44:6972)

107. DAY, H. I., AND LANGEVIN, R. "Curiosity and Intelligence: Two Necessary Conditions for a High Level of Creativity." *J Spec Ed* 3(3):263–8 f '69. * (*PA* 44:14614)

108. HARTLAGE, LAWRENCE C. "Nonvisual Test of Spatial Ability." Abstract. *Proc 77th Ann Conv Am Psychol Assn* 4(1):163–4 '69. * (*PA* 33:16635)

109. KISH, GEORGE B. "GATB and Shipley Profiles of 71 Male Alcoholics." *Newsl Res Psychol* 11(4):16–7 N '69. *

110. KISH, GEORGE B. "Relationships Between the Shipley and the GATB in a Group of Male Alcoholics." *Newsl Res Psychol* 11(4):18–9 N '69. *

111. KISH, GEORGE B., AND BALL, MARGARET E. "Low Education Level as One Factor Producing a Verbal-Abstract Disparity on the Shipley-Institute of Living Scale." *J Clin Psychol* 25(2):183–4 Ap '69. * (*PA* 43:14471)

112. BARTZ, WAYNE R., AND LOY, DONALD L. "The Shipley-Hartford as a Brief I.Q. Screening Device." *J Clin Psychol* 26(1):74–5 Ja '70. * (*PA* 44:10407)

113. BLUM, DONNA M., AND VINCENT, M. O. "Personality Test Characteristics of Staff Physicians and Physicians as Psychiatric Patients." *J Clin Psychol* 26(3):389–90 Jl '70. * (*PA* 45:750)

114. KISH, GEORGE B. "Alcoholics' GATB and Shipley Profiles and Their Interrelationships." *J Clin Psychol* 26(4):482–4 O '70. * (*PA* 45:4569)

115. LEMMON, DONNA BERNHARDT. *The Performance of Women on the Shipley-Institute of Living Scale.* Master's thesis, California State College (Long Beach, Calif.), 1970.

116. MACK, JAMES L. "A Comparative Study of Group Test Estimates of WAIS Verbal, Performance, and Full Scale IQs." *J Clin Psychol* 26(2):177–9 Ap '70. * (*PA* 44:14870)

117. MARCIA, JAMES E., AND FRIEDMAN, MEREDITH L. "Ego Identity Status in College Women." *J Personality* 38(2):249–63 Je '70. * (*PA* 44:18674)

118. MURRAY, MICHAEL D.; PAGE, JAMES; STOTLAND, EZRA; AND DIETZE, DORIS. "Success on Varied Tasks as an Influence on Sense of Competence." *J Clin Psychol* 26(3):296–8 Jl '70. * (*PA* 45:1020)

119. PAULSON, MORRIS J., AND LIN, TIEN-TEH. "Predicting WAIS IQ From Shipley-Hartford Scores." *J Clin Psychol* 26(4):453–61 O '70. * (*PA* 45:4546)

120. WILKINSON, A. EARL. "Relationship Between Measures of Intellectual Functioning and Extreme Response Style." *J Social Psychol* 81(2):271–2 Ag '70. * (*PA* 44:21200)

AUBREY J. YATES, *Professor of Psychology, University of Western Australia, Nedlands, Australia.*

This test is based on the doubtful assumption that in mental disorder vocabulary remains resistant to decline, whereas performance on conceptual tasks (abstraction) suffers. Hence, vocabulary may be used as a measure of pre-breakdown level of functioning and the conceptual quotient (the discrepancy between vocabulary level and abstract reasoning level) as a measure of the amount of decline which has occurred as a result of behavioral disturbance.

In spite of the doubtful validity of the basic assumptions, and in spite of the failure to control, in the standardization data, for confounding variables such as age, sex, educational

level, and the effects of slowness of responding, the test has remained a popular clinical instrument, largely because of its brevity. As a result, a good deal of effort has been expended over the past ten years in attempts to improve the usefulness of the test. Thus, studies carried out have related to the effects of age, sex, and educational level on normative data (*65, 68, 69, 79, 83, 93*); psychiatric group normative data (*74, 76, 94*); the test's reliability (*75, 82, 90, 97*) and validity (*78, 81, 85, 98*); and its prognostic value (*70, 87, 88, 91*). The results have not been particularly encouraging or consistent. For example, Corotto (*79*) gave the test to 110 males and 114 females, stratified by age, and found no sex differences, whereas age differences appeared to be a confounding factor. In Corotto's study, age correlated with abstraction −.14, whereas Palmer (*69*), using adolescents aged 12–18, found that age and abstraction correlated +.47. On the other hand, Lewinsohn (*67*) measured the Shipley performance of 45 patients tested before and after treatment and found that whereas there was no change in vocabulary score, there was significant improvement in abstraction score.

The test, used with due caution because of possible confounding factors listed above, remains a useful screening device or indicator of change where more intensive or direct experimental investigation is not possible.

For reviews by E. J. G. Bradford, William A. Hunt, and Margaret Ives, see 3:95.

[139]

*Sixteen Personality Factor Questionnaire.** Ages 16 and over; 1949–70; 16PF; 22 scores: 16 primary factor scores: reserved vs. outgoing (A), less intelligent vs. more intelligent (B), affected by feelings vs. emotionally stable (C), humble vs. assertive (E), sober vs. happy-go-lucky (F), expedient vs. conscientious (G), shy vs. venturesome (H), tough-minded vs. tender-minded (I), trusting vs. suspicious (L), practical vs. imaginative (M), forthright vs. shrewd (N), self-assured vs. apprehensive (O), conservative vs. experimenting (Q_1), group-dependent vs. self-sufficient (Q_2), undisciplined self-conflict vs. controlled (Q_3), relaxed vs. tense (Q_4), plus 6 second-order factor scores: introversion vs. extraversion (I), low anxiety vs. high anxiety (II), tenderminded emotionality vs. tough poise (III), subduedness vs. independence (IV), naturalness vs. discreetness (V), cool realism vs. prodigal subjectivity (VI); 3 levels; handbook, 1970 edition ('70, 395 pages); $9.95 per handbook ($14.50 hardbound); postage extra; computer scoring services below not available for Form E; Digitek scoring service, 80¢ to 45¢ per test ($20 minimum); computer interpretation service, $4 to $1.50 per subject ($20 minimum); NCS scoring service: $1.20 to 70¢ per test ($2.50 minimum; daily service),

65¢ to 40¢ ($16.25 minimum; weekly service); Raymond B. Cattell, Herbert W. Eber, and Maurice M. Tatsuoka (handbook); Institute for Personality and Ability Testing. *

a) FORMS A AND B. 1949–70; authors recommend that both forms (374 items) be used; 2 editions; manual ('62, 22 pages); profile ('67, 1 page); separate answer sheets (Digitek, hand scored, NCS) must be used; $12.50 per 25 tests; $4.50 per 50 hand scored answer sheets; $4 per 50 Digitek or NCS answer sheets; $5.50 per 50 combined hand scored answer sheet-profiles; $4 per 50 profiles; $2.25 per set of scoring stencils; 80¢ per manual; $5 per specimen set; (50–60) minutes.

　1) *1961–62 Edition.* 1949–70; Forms A ('62, 10 pages), B ('61, 10 pages); norms supplement ('62, 23 pages); $1.25 per norms supplement; experimental German and Spanish editions available.

　2) *1967–68 Edition.* 1956–70; Forms A, B, ('67, 10 pages); norms supplement ('70, 42 pages); $2 per norms supplement.

b) FORMS C AND D. Reading levels grades 6 and over; 1954–70; short forms (105 items) using less difficult vocabulary; 2 editions (Form C); 1957 handbook supplement for Form C, second edition ('62, 25 pages); profile ('67, 1 page); separate answer sheets (Digitek, hand scored, NCS) must be used; $12.50 per 25 tests; answer sheet and profile prices same as for Forms A and B; $2 per scoring stencil; $1.50 per handbook supplement; $4.30 per specimen set; industrial edition published under title *Employee Attitude Series: 16P.F.*, by Industrial Psychology, Inc.; (30–40) minutes.

　1) *[1956 Edition.]* Form C ('56, 7 pages); authors recommend that all three forms (A, B, and C) making a total of 479 items) be used for important research.

　2) *1969 Edition.* Forms C, D, ('69, 7 pages, authors recommend administration of both forms); administration of all four forms (A, B, C, and D making a total of 584 items) is recommended for important research; tentative norms ('70, 9 mimeographed pages); $1.50 per tentative norms.

c) FORM E. Reading levels grades 3–5; 1965–70; experimental edition; Form E ('67, 10 pages); mimeographed interim manual ['67, 8 pages, with 1968 norms]; profile ('67, 1 page); no data on reliability; no data on validity for subjects at reading levels grades 3–5; tape recording is available for oral administration to persons reading below the grade 3 level; separate answer sheets must be used; $12.50 per 25 tests; $4.50 per 50 answer sheets; $4 per 50 profiles; $1.80 per scoring stencil; $25 per tape; 50¢ per manual; $2.80 per specimen set; [20–30] minutes.

REFERENCES

1–8. See 4:87.
9–29. See 5:112.
30–108. See 6:174.
109–357. See P:245, also includes a cumulative name index to the first 357 references for this test.
358. MILES, HENRY W.; WALDFOGEL, SAMUEL; BARRABEE, EDNA L.; AND COBB, STANLEY. "Psychosomatic Study of 46 Young Men With Coronary Artery Disease." *Psychosom Med* 16:455–77 N–D '54. *
359. HERMAN, DAVID OVENDEN. *A Factorial Study of Research Potential in Chemistry.* Doctor's thesis, Ohio State University (Columbus, Ohio), 1959. (*DA* 20:4164)
360. MARSHALL, JAMES W., AND WAXMAN, BRUCE D. "An Empirical Study of the Relationship Between Certain Personality Dimensions and the Incidence of Accidental Injuries." *Conn Health B* 73:337–52 N '59. *
361. TUMA, JAMES WOOD. *UDT Candidate Attrition, U.S. Navy: The Influence of Exercise and Diet Supplement (Wheat Germ Oil) on Fitness Changes During Training.* Doctor's thesis, University of Illinois (Urbana, Ill.), 1959. (*DA* 20:3189)
362. BECKER, WESLEY C. "The Matching of Behavior Rating and Questionnaire Personality Factors." *Psychol B* 57:201–12 My '60. * (*PA* 35:6414)
363. BOONE, JERRY NEAL. *A Study of the Effects of Anxiety on Auditory Perceptual Response to Threat.* Doctor's thesis, Vanderbilt University (Nashville, Tenn.), 1961. (*DA* 22:2062)
364. MITCHELL, JAMES V., JR. "Statistical Relationships Between the Score Categories of the 16 PF and CPI Inventories." Abstract. *Am Psychologist* 16:386 Jl '61. *
365. REISER, MARTIN. *The Effects of Group Counseling on Interpersonal Relationships, Anxiety Level, Intellectual Functioning, and Certain Personality Characteristics in a Planned Workshop Experience.* Doctor's thesis, Temple University (Philadelphia, Pa.), 1961. (*DA* 22:325)
366. TOLLEFSON, DONALD LLOYD. *Differential Responses to Humor and Their Relation to Personality and Motivation Measures.* Doctor's thesis, University of Illinois (Urbana, Ill.), 1961. (*DA* 22:1712)
367. HENDRIX, VERNON LEE. *A Critical Analysis of the Relationships Between Administrative Policies and Procedures and Certain Faculty Characteristics.* Doctor's thesis, University of Texas (Austin, Tex.), 1962. (*DA* 23:3721)
368. ARNHOFF, FRANKLYN N., AND LEON, HENRY V. "Personality Factors Related to Success and Failure in Sensory Deprivation Subjects." *Percept & Motor Skills* 16:46 F '63. * (*PA* 38:912)
369. PARSONS, DAVID ROY. *Personality Traits of National Representative Swimmers—Canada 1962.* Master's thesis, University of British Columbia (Vancouver, B.C., Canada), 1963.
370. FOGARTY, BRYCE MARTIN. *Characteristics of Superintendents of Schools and Centralization-Decentralization of Decision-Making.* Doctor's thesis, University of Wisconsin (Madison, Wis.), 1964. (*DA* 25:3928)
371. GETZELS, JACOB W., AND CSIKSZENTMIHALYI, MIHALY. *Creative Thinking in Art Students: An Exploratory Study.* An unpublished report to the U.S. Office of Education, Cooperative Research Project No. E-008, University of Chicago, 1964. Pp. vii, 202. * (ERIC ED 003 377)
372. GOTTESMAN, DONALD T. *Relationships Between Cattell's Sixteen Personality Factor Questionnaire and Physique, Strength, and Motor Traits of College Men.* Doctor's thesis, University of Oregon (Eugene, Ore.), 1964.
373. HILL, EVELYN FOSTER. *Affect Aroused by Color, a Function of Stimulus Strength.* Doctor's thesis, Catholic University of America (Washington, D.C.), 1964. (*DA* 25:2611)
374. HOSINSKI, MARION. *Self, Ideal Self, and Occupational Role: Perceptual Congruence in Vocationally Committed College Women: A Cross Sectional Study of Self Perception, Self Aspiration, and Occupational Perception Among University Nursing Students.* Doctor's thesis, University of Notre Dame (Notre Dame, Ind.), 1964. (*DA* 28:4481A)
375. MAY, MARVIN JEROLD. *The Effects of Electroshock Therapy on Repression and Other Phenomena Related to Personality, Motivation, and Education.* Doctor's thesis, Texas Technological College (Lubbock, Tex.), 1964. (*DA* 26:2322)
376. ABOU-ALLAM, RAGAA MAHMOUD. *Personality Correlates of the Movement of Concepts in the Semantic Space: An Investigation of the Effect of Some Personality Variables on the Magnitude of Association Between Initially Meaningless Assigns and Previously Meaningful Signs.* Doctor's thesis, New York University (New York, N.Y.), 1965. (*DA* 27:382A)
377. ANDERSON, DUANE L. *A Comparative Descriptive Analysis of First-Year Agriculture Short Course and Degree Students at Michigan State University.* Doctor's thesis, Michigan State University (East Lansing, Mich.), 1965. (*DA* 26:4320)
378. CHANCE, WILLIAM GEORGE. *A Study of Selected Factors as They Relate to the Establishment of Interpersonal Relations by Student Teachers.* Doctor's thesis, Oklahoma State University (Stillwater, Okla.), 1965. (*DA* 27:47A)
379. FLINT, FRIEDA SNYDOVER. *A Validation and Developmental Study of Some Interpretations of the Bender Gestalt Test.* Doctor's thesis, New York University (New York, N.Y.), 1965. (*DA* 27:608B)
380. GRANDE, PETER P. *Rapport in the School Counseling Interview in Relation to Selected Personality Characteristics of Religious and Layman (Nonreligious) Counselors: An Exploration.* Doctor's thesis, University of Notre Dame (Notre Dame, Ind.), 1965. (*DA* 27:391A)
381. HUNDLEBY, JOHN D.; PAWLIK, KURT; AND CATTELL, RAYMOND B. *Personality Factors in Objective Test Devices: A Critical Integration of a Quarter of a Century's Research.* San Diego, Calif.: Robert R. Knapp, Publisher, 1965. Pp. iii, 542. *
382. JONES, WYATT CLAIBORNE. *Correlates of Social Deviance: A Study of Unmarried Mothers.* Doctor's thesis, New York University (New York, N.Y.), 1965. (*DA* 27:3958A)
383. JOSHI, MEERA M. "A Study of Source Trait B in Cattell's 16 P.F. Test." *J Gujarat Res Soc* 27:103–5 Ap '65. *
384. KIRCHMAN, MARGARET M. "The Personality of the Rheumatoid Arthritis Patient." *Am J Occup Ther* 19:160–4 My–Je '65. * (*PA* 39:15978)
385. McCORD, HALLOCK. "Use of a Psychological Pencil-and-Paper Test to Predict Hypnotizability." *J Am Soc Psychosom Dent & Med* 12:45–6 Ap '65. * (*PA* 39:15734)
386. MEISGEIER, CHARLES. "The Identification of Successful Teachers of Mentally or Physically Handicapped Children." *Excep Children* 32:229–35 D '65. * (*PA* 40:3409)
387. ROTHBERG, JUNE SIMMONDS. *Dependence and Anxiety*

in Male Patients Following Surgery: An Investigation of the Relationship Between Dependence, Anxiety, and Physical Manifestations of Recovery Following Surgery in Male Patients. Doctor's thesis, New York University (New York, N.Y.), 1965. (DA 27:525B)

388. SCHEIER, IVAN H. "Creative Personality and the Nature of the Creative Process." High Sch J 48:474–9 My '65. *

389. WAGGONER, BERNICE E. A Comparison of the Profiles of Temperament Traits of Women Undergraduate Students and Full-Time Teachers in Physical Education Departments in Selected Colleges and Universities in the United States, With Implications for the Guidance of Young Women Seeking Careers in This Field. Doctor's thesis, Texas Woman's University (Denton, Tex.), 1965.

390. WILLIAMS, HOWARD YOLEN. College Students' Perceptions of the Personal Traits and Instructional Procedures of Good and Poor Teachers. Doctor's thesis, University of Minnesota (Minneapolis, Minn.), 1965. (DA 27:3644A)

391. BANKS, ROBERT RICHARD. Selected Social and Psychological Variables Related to Role Satisfaction Among Graduate Ministerial Students in a Seventh-Day Adventist Seminary. Doctor's thesis, University of Notre Dame (Notre Dame, Ind.), 1966. (DA 27:2384A)

392. BOHLEBER, MICHAEL EDGAR. Conditions Influencing the Relationships Between Leadership Style and Group Structural and Population Characteristics. Doctor's thesis, University of Wisconsin (Madison, Wis.), 1966. (DA 28:776A)

393. CAFFREY, CLETUS BERNARD. Behavior Patterns and Personality Characteristics as Related to Prevalence Rates of Coronary Heart Disease in Trappist and Benedictine Monks. Doctor's thesis, Catholic University of America (Washington, D.C.), 1966. (DA 28:2619B)

394. CATTELL, RAYMOND B., AND SCHEIER, IVAN H. "Personality Measurement in Applied Psychology as Illustrated by the 16 Personality Factor Test." Revista de Psicologia Normal e Patológica 11:42–58 Ja–S '66. * (PA 41:588)

395. DAVIS, HARRY GRAYSON. Variables Associated With Recovery in Male and Female Alcoholics Following Hospitalization. Doctor's thesis, Texas Technological College (Lubbock, Tex.), 1966. (DA 27:3669B)

396. DOHERTY, MARY AUSTIN, AND WALKER, RONALD E. "The Relationship of Personality Characteristics, Awareness, and Attitude in a Verbal Conditioning Situation." J Personality 34:504–16 D '66. *

397. EDWARDS, RAYMOND LEWIS, JR. Familial Characteristics and Personality Profiles of Graduate Social Work Students. Doctor's thesis, Florida State University (Tallahassee, Fla.), 1966. (DA 28:307A)

398. KAPOOR, S. D. "A Study of 'Lie' Variable in 'The 16 P.F. Test (VKSJ)' I." Manas 13(2):53–61 '66. *

399. MADDI, SALVATORE R., AND ANDREWS, SUSAN L. "The Need for Variety in Fantasy and Self-Description." J Personality 34:610–25 D '66. *

400. MASUDA, MINORU, AND BAKKER, CORNELIS B. "Personality, Cathecholamine Metabolites, and Psychophysiological Response to Diazepam." J Psychiatric Res 4:221–34 D '66. * (PA 41:10044)

401. MURPHY, JOSEPH ALLISON, JR. An Investigation Into Certain Personality Factors of Elementary School Teachers and Principals With Reference to the Organizational Climate of the School. Doctor's thesis, University of Georgia (Athens, Ga.), 1966. (DA 27:3670A)

402. RYAN, ROBERT PATRICK. The Role of the Experiencing Variable in the Psychotherapeutic Process. Doctor's thesis, University of Illinois (Urbana, Ill.), 1966. (DA 27:971B)

403. SARGENT, JAMES CURRIER. An Analysis of Principal and Staff Perceptions of High School Organizational Climate. Doctor's thesis, University of Minnesota (Minneapolis, Minn.), 1966. (DA 27:2344A)

404. SIMONS, JOSEPH BERNARD. Congruence Between Self and Religious Role Percepts: A Descriptive Study of Satisfaction With the Religious Life Among Seminarians in Differential Stages of Preparation for the Priesthood. Doctor's thesis, University of Notre Dame (Notre Dame, Ind.), 1966. (DA 29:4295A)

405. WESSMAN, ALDEN E., AND RICKS, DAVID F. Mood and Personality. New York: Holt, Rinehart & Winston, Inc., 1966. Pp. xiii, 317. *

406. ADCOCK, C. J. Humour Preferences and Personality. Victoria University of Wellington Publications in Psychology No. 21. Wellington, New Zealand: Department of Psychology, the University, 1967. Pp. iii, 15. *

407. ALLEN, JOHN ELLIS. The Adoption of Innovations and the Personality of the Superintendent of Schools. Doctor's thesis, Ohio State University (Columbus, Ohio), 1967. (DA 28:2005A)

408. BAKKER, CORNELIS B. "Psychological Factors in Angina Pectoris." Psychosomatics 8:43–9 Ja–F '67. * (PA 42:1062)

409. BELL, THOMAS O. A Study of Personality Characteristics of School Superintendents in Relation to Administrative Behavior. Doctor's thesis, Utah State University (Logan, Utah), 1967. (DA 29:2049A)

410. BORG, WALTER R. "Teacher Effectiveness in Team Teaching." J Exp Ed 35:65–70 sp '67. *

411. BOYLES, GARY EUGENE. Psycho-Social Variables Related to Four Categories of School Persistence in a Rural County: Graduates and Potential Graduates, and Dropouts and Potential Dropouts. Doctor's thesis, University of North Dakota (Grand Forks, N.D.), 1967. (DA 28:1673A)

412. CARTER, ROBERT EARLE. A Personality Study of Elementary School Teachers of Mentally Retarded Children in Selected Michigan Public School Systems. Doctor's thesis, Wayne State University (Detroit, Mich.), 1967. (DA 29:1148A)

413. DELL, HELEN LUCILE DAVIS. The Evaluation of Teaching Procedures Designed to Increase Empathic Ability. Doctor's thesis, Ball State University (Muncie, Ind.), 1967. (DA 29:1447A)

414. GIVENS, PAUL R.; PINKARD, CAROLYN A.; AND RICH, THOMAS A. "Relationship of Personality Factors, Creativity and Academic Achievement Among High School Seniors." Fla J Ed Res 9:45–56 Ja '67. *

415. GOLDSTEIN, MARGARET W. Mental Health, Social Status, and Maslow's Need System. Doctor's thesis, Yeshiva University (New York, N.Y.), 1967. (DA 28:2123B)

416. GRANT, CARMEN RITA HILL. Age Differences in Self Concept From Early Adulthood Through Old Age. Doctor's thesis, University of Nebraska (Lincoln, Neb.), 1967. (DA 28:1160B)

417. HINMAN, EDNA FULLMER. Personality Characteristics of Clark County School District Principals Related to the Degree of Their Implementation of Innovation. Doctor's thesis, Utah State University (Logan, Utah), 1967. (DAI 30:3234A)

418. KOSIER, KENNETH P., AND DeVAULT, M. VERE. "Differential Effects of Three College Instructional Approaches on Personality Traits of Beginning Elementary Teachers." J Exp Ed 35:19–27 su '67. *

419. LEITHWOOD, KENNETH A. The Personality Characteristics of Three Groups of Weight Trainers. Master's thesis, University of British Columbia (Vancouver, B.C., Canada), 1967.

420. McPHERSON, B. D.; PAIVO, A.; YUHASZ, M. S.; RECHNITZER, P. A.; PICKARD, H. A.; AND LEFCOE, N. M. "Psychological Effects of an Exercise Program for Post-Infarct and Normal Adult Men." J Sports Med 7:95–102 Je '67. *

421. MASON, EDWARD A. Identifying Creativity in Art Students With the Sixteen Personality Factor Questionnaire. Master's thesis, Brigham Young University (Provo, Utah), 1967.

422. MEYER, ROBERT GEORGE. The Relationship of Blood Pressure Levels to the Chronic Inhibition of Aggression. Doctor's thesis, Michigan State University (East Lansing, Mich.), 1967. (DA 28:2099A)

423. MORRISON, W. LEE, AND ROMOSER, R. C. "Personality Structure and Dimensions of Teacher Attitudes." J Exp Ed 36:55–8 w '67. *

424. MULLENS, BARBARA NELSON. A Perceptual and Cognitive Taxonomy of Character Disorders. Doctor's thesis, George Washington University (Washington, D.C.), 1967. (DA 28:2145B)

425. STEVENS, THOMAS GRANVILLE. Congruency Between Diagnostic Dimensions of Personality Theories and Personality Tests. Master's thesis, California State College (Fullerton, Calif.), 1967. (Masters Abstracts 6:21)

426. TUMAMPOS, RUSTICA S. An Analysis of the Personality Profiles of B.S.E.Ed. Women Students of Divine Word College, Tagbilapan City, Philippines as Revealed on the IPAT 16 Personality Factor Questionnaire. Master's thesis, Fresno State College (Fresno, Calif.), 1967.

427. ALLMAN, THOMAS S., AND WHITE, WILLIAM F. "Birth Order Categories as Predictors of Select Personality Characteristics." Abstract. AERA Paper Abstr 1968:178–9 '68. *

428. AX, ALBERT F., AND BAMFORD, JACQUELINE L. "Validation of a Psychophysiological Test of Aptitude for Learning Social Motives." Psychophysiol 5:316–32 S '68. * (PA 43:3943)

429. BAKKER, CORNELIS B. "The Influence of Personality Patterns on Response to Psychotropic Drugs." Proc 4th World Congr Psychiatry 1966(pt 3):2142–4 '66. *

430. BUTLER, JOHN HARRISON. Personality Factors as Correlates of Receptivity to Electronic Music. Doctor's thesis, University of Georgia (Athens, Ga.), 1968. (DA 29:4514A)

431. CARY, THORNLEY C. Effects of Human Resources Development Institutes Upon Employment Service Employees as Measured by the Sixteen Personality Factor Questionnaire. Master's thesis, University of South Carolina (Columbia, S.C.), 1968.

432. CATTELL, RAYMOND B., AND BUTCHER, H. J. The Prediction of Achievement and Creativity. Indianapolis, Ind.: Bobbs-Merrill Co., Inc., 1968. Pp. xiv, 386. *

433. CLEMENTS, WILLIAM HENRY. Marital Adjustment and Marital Interaction. Doctor's thesis, University of Cincinnati (Cincinnati, Ohio), 1968. (DA 29:1839B)

434. COMREY, ANDREW L., AND DUFFY, KIRT E. "Cattell and Eysenck Factor Scores Related to Comrey Personality Factors." Multiv Behav Res 3:379–92 O '68. * (PA 43:8363)

435. CORDINER, CONSTANCE M. "Personality Testing of Aberdeen Student Nurses." Nursing Times 64:178–80 F 9 '68. *

436. CREW, JOHN LOWERY, SR. *An Investigation of Personality Profile Congruence Between Pupil and Teacher as a Predictor of Course Achievement.* Doctor's thesis, University of Maryland (College Park, Md.), 1968. (*DA* 29:1447A)

437. CROUCH, JOYCE G. *The Role of Sex, Anxiety and Independence as Moderator Variables in Achievement of College Freshmen.* Doctor's thesis, University of Tennessee (Knoxville, Tenn.), 1968. (*DA* 29:3827A)

438. DAUW, DEAN C. "Creativity Research on Actuaries." *J Creative Behav* 2:274–80 f '68. * (*PA* 43:14316)

439. DEBLASSIE, RICHARD R. "Diagnostic Usefulness of the 16PF in Counseling." *J Col Stud Personnel* 9:378–81 N '68. *

440. EDGECOMBE, WILLIAM DAVID. *The Interrelationships Between Certain Personality Factors of the Elementary School Principal, His Interpersonal Perception, and the Morale of His Faculty.* Doctor's thesis, Case Western Reserve University (Cleveland, Ohio), 1968. (*DAI* 30:3673A)

441. FINE, BERNARD J. "Personality Traits as Related to Symptomatology and Running Performance at Altitude Under Normal and Drug (Acetazoleamide) Conditions." *Percept & Motor Skills* 27:975–90 D '68. * (*PA* 43:8837)

442. GATES, CARL JAY. *A Study of Attitude, Need, and Personality Trait Correlates of Effective Teaching in Three Selected School Systems.* Doctor's thesis, University of Southern Mississippi (Hattiesburg, Miss.), 1968. (*DA* 29:3021A)

443. GETZELS, J. W., AND CSIKSZENTMIHALYI, M. "The Value-Orientations of Art Students as Determinants of Artistic Specialization and Creative Performance." *Studies Art Ed* 10:5–16 f '68. *

444. HEILMAN, HENRIETTA. *A Study of the Relationships Between Certain Factors Associated With Employability and the Rehabilitation Status of Selected Psychiatric Clients in a Vocational Rehabilitation Program.* Doctor's thesis, New York University (New York, N.Y.), 1968. (*DA* 29:2564A)

445. HENDERSON, DONALD RAY. *A Study to Determine the Personality Characteristics of Innovative Educational Administrators and Educational Administrators in Illinois and Indiana.* Doctor's thesis, Indiana University (Bloomington, Ind.), 1968. (*DA* 29:3375A)

446. HENDRY, L. B. "Assessments of Personality Traits in the Coach-Swimmer Relationship, and a Preliminary Examination of the Father-Figure Stereotype." *Res Q* 39:543–51 O '68. *

447. JOHNSON, DALE ARDEN. *A Study of Relationships Between Participation in Decision Making, Job Satisfaction, and Selected Personality Variables of Secondary School Principals.* Doctor's thesis, University of Minnesota (Minneapolis, Minn.), 1968. (*DA* 29:3377A)

448. JONES, RICHARD GARNER. *A Factored Measure of Ellis' Irrational Belief System, With Personality and Maladjustment Correlates.* Doctor's thesis, Texas Technological College (Lubbock, Tex.), 1968. (*DA* 29:4379B)

449. KAPOOR, S. D. "Differential Sensitivity of 'Lie-Scale' to Sex and Socio-Economic Variables in Personality Questionnaires." *Manas* 15(1):43–9 '68. * (*PA* 43:11338)

450. KLECKNER, JAMES HERBERT. *An Investigation Into the Personal Characteristics and Family Backgrounds of Psychedelic Drug Users.* Doctor's thesis, Columbia University (New York, N.Y.), 1968. (*DA* 29:4380B)

451. LAWLIS, GARLAND FRANK. *Motivational Aspects of the Chronically Unemployed.* Doctor's thesis, Texas Technological College (Lubbock, Tex.), 1968. (*DA* 29:3915B)

452. LAWRENCE, CLIFFORD JEX. *Personality Characteristics of School Superintendents Who Implement Innovation in the Public Schools.* Doctor's thesis, Utah State University (Logan, Utah), 1968. (*DA* 29:1397A)

453. LEFF, J. P. "Perceptual Phenomena and Personality in Sensory Deprivation." *Brit J Psychiatry* 114:1499–508 D '68. * (*PA* 43:9727)

454. LEVAKE, KEITH ROBERT. *The Relationship of Personality Characteristics to Acceptance and Rejection of Reported Achievement Test Scores.* Doctor's thesis, University of Missouri (Columbia, Mo.), 1968. (*DA* 29:2529A)

455. LEWIS, LAURA H. "Acquiescence Response Set: Construct or Artifact?" *J Proj Tech & Pers Assess* 32:578–84 D '68. * (*PA* 43:9763)

456. LYNN, R. "Anxiety and Economic Growth." Letter. *Nature* 219:765–6 Ag '68. * (*PA* 44:14444)

457. McCLAIN, EDWIN W. "Is the Counselor a Woman?" *Personnel & Guid J* 46:444–8 Ja '68. * (*PA* 42:9568)

458. McCLAIN, EDWIN W. "Sixteen Personality Factor Questionnaire Scores and Success in Counseling." *J Counsel Psychol* 15:492–6 N '68. * (*PA* 43:1417)

459. MALUMPHY, THERESA M. "Personality of Women Athletes in Intercollegiate Competition." *Res Q* 39:610–20 O '68. *

460. MARSHALL, JOSEPH JEMERSON. *Non-Cognitive Variables as a Predictor of Academic Achievement Among Freshmen, Sophomores, and Juniors at Abilene Christian College.* Doctor's thesis, Baylor University (Waco, Tex.), 1968. (*DA* 29:3833A)

461. MEREDITH, GERALD M. "Personality Correlates to Religious Belief Systems." *Psychol Rep* 23:1039–42 D '68. * (*PA* 43:8236)

462. MEREDITH, GERALD M. "Stereotypic Desirability Profiles for the 16 P.F. Questionnaire." *Psychol Rep* 23:1173–4 D '68. * (*PA* 43:8373)

463. MOSEY, ANNE CRONIN. *Dependency and Integrative Skill as They Relate to Affinity for and Acceptance by an Assigned Group.* Doctor's thesis, New York University (New York, N.Y.), 1968. (*DA* 29:483A)

464. OGILVIE, BRUCE C. "Psychological Consistencies Within the Personality of High-Level Competitors." *J Am Med Assn* 205:780–6 S 9 '68. * (*PA* 43:4006)

465. OWENBY, DAVID JACK. *Perceptions of Organizational Climate and Leader Behavior in Southern Independent Schools.* Doctor's thesis, University of Tennessee (Knoxville, Tenn.), 1968. (*DA* 29:3810A)

466. OWENS, NORMA F. *A Study of Personality Changes in Males With Severe Facial Deformity During the First Six Months of Adjustment After Radical Surgery for Cancer.* Doctor's thesis, New York University (New York, N.Y.), 1968. (*DAI* 30:722B)

467. OWENS, WAYNE STANFORD. *An Analysis of the Characteristics of Selected Educational Administrators in Illinois and Indiana.* Doctor's thesis, Indiana University (Bloomington, Ind.), 1968. (*DA* 29:1728A)

468. PAM, ELEANOR. *Ego Strength, Consistency in Problem Perception and Expectation of Counseling Assistance: A Study in Counselor Role Expectancy.* Doctor's thesis, New York University (New York, N.Y.), 1968. (*DA* 29:462A)

469. PEARCE, CLIFFORD. "Creativity in Young Science Students." *Excep Children* 35:121–6 O '68. * (*PA* 44:9353)

470. PERROW, MAXWELL VERMILYEA. *A Description of Similarity of Personality Between Selected Groups of Television Viewers and Certain Television Roles Regularly Viewed by Them.* Doctor's thesis, University of Southern California (Los Angeles, Calif.), 1968. (*DA* 29:1956A)

471. PHILLIPS, JAY D., AND DELHEES, KARL H. *A Personality Analysis of Drug Addicts by the 16 Personality Factor and Evaluation of the Influence of Rehabilitation.* [Riverside, Calif.: Jay D. Phillips], 1968. Pp. 18. *

472. PILOWSKY, I., AND WALKER, WENDY L. "The Measurement of Change During Psychotherapy." *Austral & N Zeal J Psychiatry* 2:209–14 O '68. *

473. PUGH, RICHARD C. "Evidence for the Validity of the Behavioral Dimensions of Teaching—Characteristics Schedule Scales." *Ed & Psychol Meas* 28:1173–9 w '68. * (*PA* 44:5884)

474. PYECHA, JOHN NICHOLAS. *An Experimental Investigation of the Comparative Effects of Judo and Selected Physical Education Activities on Personality Traits of Male University Freshmen.* Doctor's thesis, University of North Carolina (Chapel Hill, N.C.), 1968. (*DA* 29:2551A)

475. REDDING, ARTHUR JOEL. *The Relationship Between Training in Verbal Interaction Analysis and Selected Counseling Process Variables.* Doctor's thesis, University of North Dakota (Grand Forks, N.D.), 1968. (*DA* 29:3840A)

476. REPLOGLE, JAMES ROBERT. *The Relation of Teacher-Pupil Profile Pattern Similarities on Measures of Interest and Personality to Grades and Perceived Compatibility.* Doctor's thesis, Lehigh University (Bethlehem, Pa.), 1968. (*DA* 29:1426A)

477. SEGNER, VENICE CHANDLER. *Effects of Early Experience on Later Interview Assessments of Social and Personal Adjustments.* Doctor's thesis, University of Georgia (Athens, Ga.), 1968. (*DA* 29:4853B)

478. SHATIN, LEO; KOTTER, WALLACE; AND DOUGLAS-LONGMORE, GLADYS. "Personality Profile of Successful Music Therapists." *J Music Ther* 5:111–3 D '68. * (*PA* 43:15829)

479. SHATIN, LEO; KOTTER, WALLACE; AND LONGMORE, GLADYS. "Personality Traits of Music Therapists." *Psychol Rep* 23:573–4 O '68. * (*PA* 43:9719)

480. SLAUGHTER, MARY HOKE. *An Analysis of the Relationship Between Somatotype and Personality Profiles of College Women.* Doctor's thesis, University of Illinois (Urbana, Ill.), 1968. (*DA* 29:2554A)

481. THOMPSON, SEABORN ADAMS. *A Study of the Relationship Between Personality Factors of Counselors and Counselee Perceptions of These Counselors.* Doctor's thesis, Auburn University (Auburn, Ala.), 1968. (*DA* 29:3427A)

482. TRENT, SHIRLEY JEAN. *A Study of the Relationship of Personality Factors to Academic Achievement.* Doctor's thesis, University of Tennessee (Knoxville, Tenn.), 1968. (*DA* 29:2129A)

483. TURNER, MARY MALISSA. *Personality Factors for Major Students in Health, Physical Education, and Recreation.* Doctor's thesis, University of Alabama (University, Ala.), 1968. (*DA* 29:3861A)

484. WALTER, JAMES IRBY. *A Comparative-Descriptive Study of Sixty Incarcerated Criminals Utilizing the Variables of Personality as Measured by the Sixteen Personality Factor Questionnaire, Reading Scores, Age, Time in Prison and Disciplinary Actions.* Doctor's thesis, Auburn University (Auburn, Ala.), 1968. (*DA* 29:1114A)

485. WILLIAMS, RICHARD C. "Teacher Personality Factors as Related to Membership in Teacher Organizations." *H Sch J* 51:165–72 Ja '68. *

486. ABERMAN, HUGH M. *An Investigation Into the Relationship Between Individual Personality Characteristics and Perceived Behavior in Small Groups.* Doctor's thesis, Temple University (Philadelphia, Pa.), 1969. (*DAI* 31:1062A)

487. ADAMS, WALTER DALE. *Survival Training: Its Effect on the Self Concept and Selected Personality Factors of Emotionally Disturbed Adolescents.* Doctor's thesis, Utah State University (Logan, Utah), 1969. (*DAI* 31:388B)

488. ALUMBAUGH, RICHARD V.; DAVIS, HARRY G.; AND SWENEY, ARTHUR B. "A Comparison of Methods for Constructing Predictive Instruments." *Ed & Psychol Meas* 29(3): 639–51 au '69. * (*PA* 44:18722)

489. ANDERSON, EDGAR JAMES. *A Correlational Study: Personality Characteristics and Changes in Semantic-Differential Meaning as Exhibited by Teachers Who Have Experienced Title I Inservice Training.* Doctor's thesis, Arizona State University (Tempe, Ariz.), 1969. (*DAI* 30:574A)

490. ANDERSON, GILBERT WERNER. *The Characteristics of Voluntary and Involuntary Counselees at Thorton Junior College.* Doctor's thesis, University of Arizona (Tucson, Ariz.), 1969. (*DAI* 30:3713A)

491. AYERS, JERRY B.; BASHAW, W. L.; AND WASH, JAMES A. "A Study of the Validity of the Sixteen Personality Factor Questionnaire in Predicting High School Academic Achievement." *Ed & Psychol Meas* 29(2):479–84 su '69. * (*PA* 44: 17499)

492. BERENDS, EUGENE HOWARD. *Perceptions of the Principal's Personality: A Study of the Relationships to Organizational Climate.* Doctor's thesis, Michigan State University (East Lansing, Mich.), 1969. (*DAI* 30:3210A)

493. BOTTRILL, JOHN H. "Personality Change in LSD Users." *J General Psychol* 80(2):157–61 Ap '69. * (*PA* 43: 11280)

494. BOYKIN, JOHN HENRY. *A Comparative Study of Students in Different Fields of Study.* Doctor's thesis, University of Tennessee (Knoxville, Tenn.), 1969. (*DAI* 30:3273A)

495. BRAUN, JOHN R., AND LaFARO, DOLORES. "Faking and Faking Detection on the 16 PF-Form A." *J Psychol* 71(2): 155–8 Mr '69. * (*PA* 43:8362)

496. BROOKS, JOHN. "The Insecure Personality: A Factor Analytic Study." *Brit J Med Psychol* 42(4):395–403 D '69. * (*PA* 44:10714)

497. BRUCE, LARRY RHEA. *A Determination of the Relationships Among SCIS Teachers' Personality Traits, Attitude Toward Teacher-Pupil Relationship, Understanding of Science Process Skills and Question Types.* Doctor's thesis, Michigan State University (East Lansing, Mich.), 1969. (*DAI* 30: 4850A)

498. BUTT, DORCAS SUSAN, AND FISKE, DONALD W. "Differential Correlates of Dominance Scales." *J Personality* 37(3):415–28 S '69. * (*PA* 44:6748)

499. BYRAM, NANCY KLAHN. *The Influence of Selected Transitory States on Personality Traits.* Doctor's thesis, Northwestern University (Evanston, Ill.), 1969. (*DAI* 30:4786B)

500. CAFFREY, BERNARD. "Behavior Patterns and Personality Characteristics Related to Prevalence Rates of Coronary Heart Disease in American Monks." *J Chronic Dis* 22(2):93–103 Jl '69. *

501. CAINE, T. M., AND SMAIL, D. J. Chap. 5, "The Personalities of Psychiatrists," pp. 87–101. In their *The Treatment of Mental Illness: Science, Faith and the Therapeutic Community.* New York: International Universities Press, Inc., 1969. Pp. 192. *

502. CAINE, T. M., AND SMAIL, D. J. "The Effects of Personality and Training on Attitudes to Treatment: Preliminary Investigations." *Brit J Med Psychol* 42(3):277–82 Ag '69. * (*PA* 44:6850)

503. CATTELL, RAYMOND B. "Is Field Independence an Expression of the General Personality Source Trait of Independence, U. I. 19?" *Percept & Motor Skills* 28(3):865–6 Je '69. * (*PA* 43:17514)

504. CATTELL, RAYMOND B., AND BOLTON, LAURA SPECHT. "What Pathological Dimensions Lie Beyond the Normal Dimensions of the 16 PF?: A Comparison of MMPI and 16 PF Factor Domains." *J Consult & Clin Psychol* 33(1):18–29 F '69. * (*PA* 43:11336)

505. CHALMERS, ELDEN MOSES. *The Relationship Between Personality Characteristics and Performance in the Seventh-Day Adventist Ministry.* Doctor's thesis, University of Tennessee (Knoxville, Tenn.), 1969. (*DAI* 31:3043B)

506. CHERRY, ADA LOU. *A Comparison of Selected Characteristics of Graduated Students and Academically Disqualified Students Who Were Admitted With Warning to Ball State University Autumns, 1963 and 1964.* Doctor's thesis, Ball State University (Muncie, Ind.), 1969. (*DAI* 30:4217A)

507. COCKETT, R., AND MARKS, V. "Amphetamine Taking Among Young Offenders." Abstract. *Brit J Psychiatry* 115 (527):1203–4 O '69. * (*PA* 44:12889)

508. CORNWELL, HENRY G. "Figure Preference and Personality." *Percept & Motor Skills* 29(3):812–4 D '69. *

509. DALY, R. J. "Hostility and Chronic Intermittent Haemodialysis." *J Psychosom Res* 13(3):265–73 S '69. * (*PA* 44: 12975)

510. DAVIS, T. N., AND SATTERLY, D. J. "Personality Profiles of Student Teachers." *Brit J Ed Psychol* 39(2):183–7 Je '69. * (*PA* 44:7309)

511. DE ANDRADE, E. M.; ALVES, D. DE GODOY; AND FORD, JOHN J. "A Comparison of North-American and Brazilian College Students' Personality Profiles in the 16 PF Questionnaire." *Int J Psychol* 4(1):55–8 '69. * (*PA* 44:6590)

512. DONNAN, HUGH H.; HARLAN, GRADY E.; AND THOMPSON, SEABORN A. "Counselor Personality and Level of Functioning as Perceived by Counselees." *J Counsel Psychol* 16(6): 482–5 N '69. * (*PA* 44:4196)

513. DUNN, DENNIS JAMES. *Adjustment to Spinal Cord Injury in the Rehabilitation Hospital Setting.* Doctor's thesis, University of Maryland (College Park, Md.), 1969. (*DAI* 31: 911B)

514. EMBREE, JAMES EDWARD. *The Relationship of Life Experience Patterns and Personality Factors Indicating Innovative Potential.* Doctor's thesis, Utah State University (Logan, Utah), 1969. (*DAI* 30:3223A)

515. EMMERICH, WALTER. "The Parental Role: A Functional-Cognitive Approach." *Monogr Soc Res Child Develop* 34(8): 1–71 '69. *

516. ERICKSON, WILLIAM IVAN. *Personality Characteristics of the 1967–68 NASSP Administrative Interns as Measured by the Cattell Questionnaire.* Doctor's thesis, University of Southern California (Los Angeles, Calif.), 1969. (*DAI* 30:515A)

517. EYSENCK, H. J.; WHITE, P. O.; AND SOUEIF, M. I. Chap. 17, "Factors in the Cattell Personality Inventory," pp. 218–28. In *Personality Structure and Measurement,* see 518. *

518. EYSENCK, HANS J., AND EYSENCK, SYBIL B. G. *Personality Structure and Measurement.* San Diego, Calif.: Robert R. Knapp, Publisher, 1969. Pp. xiii, 365. *

519. FELDMAN, KENNETH A., AND NEWCOMB, THEODORE M. *The Impact of College on Students: Vol. 2, Summary Tables.* San Francisco, Calif.: Jossey-Bass Inc., Publishers, 1969. Pp. iv, 171. *

520. FINE, BERNARD J., AND KOBRICK, JOHN L. "Note on Headache, Personality Traits and Visual Performance at Altitude." *Percept & Motor Skills* 29(2):521–2 O '69. * (*PA* 44: 3078)

521. FORBES, A. R. "The Validity of the 16 PF in the Discrimination of the Hysteroid and Obsessoid Personality." *Brit J Social & Clin Psychol* 8(2):152–9 Je '69. * (*PA* 43: 16003)

522. FRANCIS, R. D. "Introversion and Isolation Tolerance." *Percept & Motor Skills* 28(2):534 Ap '69. * (*PA* 43:15792)

523. FRIEDMAN, VICKI SHARON. *The Effects of Sensitivity Training on Students at a Major Metropolitan University.* Doctor's thesis, St. Louis University (St. Louis, Mo.), 1969. (*DAI* 31:2102A)

524. GEORGE, JULIUS R. *Organizational Structure, Teacher Personality Characteristics and Their Relationship to Organizational Climate.* Doctor's thesis, Claremont Graduate School (Claremont, Calif.), 1969. (*DAI* 31:581A)

525. GIVONE, ROBERT. *The Personality of Basketball Players From Rural and Urban Areas as Measured by the Cattell Sixteen Personality Factor Questionnaire.* Master's thesis, University of Massachusetts (Amherst, Mass.), 1969.

526. GODSHALL, TRICIA A. *An Investigation of the Influence of Teacher Anxiety Upon the Anxiety Level of Students From the Lowest Socio-Economic Level.* Doctor's thesis, University of Miami (Coral Gables, Fla.), 1969. (*DAI* 30:3320A)

527. GOLIGHTLY, CAROLE, AND REINEHR, ROBERT C. "16 PF Profiles of Hospitalized Alcoholic Patients: Replication and Extension." *Psychol Rep* 24(2):543–5 Ap '69. * (*PA* 43:16027)

528. GOODWIN, KATHRYN S., AND SCHAIE, K. WARNER. "Age Differences in Personality Structure." Abstract. *Proc 77th Ann Conv Am Psychol Assn* 4(2):713–4 '69. * (*PA* 44:674)

529. HARVILLE, DENNIS L. "Early Identification of Potential Leaders." *J Col Stud Personnel* 10(4):333–5 S '69. *

530. HAYES, VIRGINIA. *A Study of Personality and Achievement Variables of Successful and Unsuccessful Shorthand Students at the University of Alabama.* Doctor's thesis, University of Alabama (University, Ala.), 1969. (*DAI* 31:66A)

531. HEDDENDORF, RUSSELL HOWARD. *The Student Teacher and Professional Values.* Doctor's thesis, University of Pittsburgh (Pittsburgh, Pa.), 1969. (*DAI* 30:4853A)

532. HENDRY, L. B. "A Personality Study of Highly Successful and 'Ideal' Swimming Coaches." *Res Q* 40(2):299–304 My '69. *

533. HENJUM, ARNOLD. "A Study of the Significance of Student Teachers' Personality Characteristics." *J Teach Ed* 20(2): 143–7 su '69. * (*PA* 44:2824)

534. HOPKINS, JUNE H. "The Lesbian Personality." *Brit J Psychiatry* 115(529):1433–6 D '69. * (*PA* 44:14911)

535. HORVAT, GEORGE LITTLE. *A Study of Relationships Between Counselor Supervisor Personality and Counselor Trainee Growth in Practicum.* Doctor's thesis, St. Louis University (St. Louis, Mo.), 1969. (*DAI* 30:3278A)

536. HOY, RICHARD M. "The Personality of Inpatient Alcoholics in Relation to Group Psychotherapy as Measured by the 16-P.F." *Q J Studies Alcohol* 30(2A):401–7 Je '69. * (*PA* 44:882)

537. JOHNSON, DALE T.; NEVILLE, CHARLES W., JR.; AND WORKMAN, SAMUEL N. "Field Independence and the Sixteen Personality Factor Questionnaire: A Further Note." *Percept & Motor Skills* 28(2):670 Ap '69. * (*PA* 43:16004)

538. JONES, JANIE LOUISE. *Personality in Vocational Occupations.* Doctor's thesis, Colorado State University (Ft. Collins, Colo.), 1969. (*DAI* 30:4223A)

539. KARSON, SAMUEL. "Some Relations Between Personality Factors and Job Performance in Radar Controllers." *Aerospace Med* 40(8):823–6 Ag '69. *

540. KULDAU, VON DEAN. *A Study of Selected Characteristics of Freshman Students Who Requested Counseling as Compared to Those Who Did Not Request Counseling.* Doctor's thesis, Ball State University (Muncie, Ind.), 1969. (*DAI* 30:1823A)

541. LARTER, S. J., AND TAYLOR, P. A. "A Study of Aspects of Critical Thinking." *Manitoba J Ed* 5(1):35–53 N '69. *

542. LEVONIAN, EDWARD. "Personality and Communication-Mediated Opinion Change: The Influence of Control." *J Commun* 19(3):217–26 S '69. *

543. LOY, JOHN W., JR. "Social Psychological Characteristics of Innovators." *Am Sociol R* 34(1):73–82 F '69. * (*PA* 44:8446)

544. LYNN, R., AND HAYES, B. "Some International Comparisons of Tobacco Consumption and Personality." *J Social Psychol* 79(1):13–7 O '69. * (*PA* 44:6595)

545. LYNN, RICHARD. "An Achievement Motivation Questionnaire." *Brit J Psychol* 60(4):529–34 N '69. * (*PA* 44:5167)

546. MCCLAIN, EDWIN W., AND ANDREWS, HENRY B. "Some Personality Correlates of Peak Experiences: A Study in Self-Actualization." *J Clin Psychol* 25(1):36–8 Ja '69. * (*PA* 43:9728)

547. MCCLENNEY, BYRON NELSON. *A Comparison of Personality Characteristics, Self-Concepts, and Academic Aptitude of Selected College Men Classified According to Performance on a Test of Physical Fitness.* Doctor's thesis, University of Texas (Austin, Tex.), 1969. (*DAI* 30:1423A)

548. MCCONAUGHY, JOHN B., AND PALMER, J. DAVID. "Personality and Performance of Federal Field Executives in South Carolina." *Pub Personnel R* 30(4):205–10 O '69. *

549. MATTSSON, KENNETH DALE. *Relationships Between Certain Personality Factors of Student Teachers, Success in Student Teaching and Certain Responses From Dropout-Prone Pupils.* Doctor's thesis, University of Minnesota (Minneapolis, Minn.), 1969. (*DAI* 30:1899A)

550. MEGATHLIN, WILLIAM LATIMER. *The Effects of Facilitation Training Provided Correctional Officers Stationed at the Atlanta Federal Penitentiary.* Doctor's thesis, University of Georgia (Athens, Ga.), 1969. (*DAI* 30:3282A)

551. MEHRABIAN, ALBERT. "Measures of Achieving Tendency." *Ed & Psychol Meas* 29(2):445–51 su '69. * (*PA* 44:17478)

552. MEREDITH, GERALD M., AND HARRIS, MARJORIE M. "Personality Traits of College Women in Beginning Swimming." *Percept & Motor Skills* 29(1):216–8 Ag '69. * (*PA* 44:2798)

553. MEREDITH, GERALD MARVIN. *Acculturation and Personality Among Japanese-American College Students in Hawaii.* Doctor's thesis, University of Hawaii (Honolulu, Hawaii), 1969. (*DAI* 30:5677B)

554. MINNICK, MICHAEL LINDEN. *An Analysis of the Interrelationship Between Selected Cornell Index Groups and Their Sixteen Personality Factor Questionnaire Scores.* Doctor's thesis, Ball State University (Muncie, Ind.), 1969. (*DAI* 30:3327A)

555. MUELLER, E. JANE, AND LYMAN, HOWARD B. "The Prediction of Scores on the State Board Test Pool Examination." *Nursing Res* 18(3):263–6 My–Je '69. *

556. MUTHARD, JOHN E., AND SALOMONE, PAUL R. "The Roles and Functions of Rehabilitation Counselors." *Rehabil Counsel B* 13(1-SP):81–165 O '69. *

557. NEUFELD, GERALD G. *How Personality, Foreign Language Aptitude, and Anomie Relate to Foreign Language Acquisition.* Doctor's thesis, University of California (Berkeley, Calif.), 1969. (*DAI* 31:1651A)

558. O'DELL, JERRY W., AND KARSON, SAMUEL. "Some Relationships Between the MMPI and 16 PF." *J Clin Psychol* 25(3):279–83 Jl '69. * (*PA* 44:3638)

559. OLSON, HARRY, JR. "Distributive Education Teacher-Coordinators: Relationship Between Personality and Job Satisfaction." *Delta Pi Epsilon J* 11(3):4–20 My '69. *

560. PALLONE, NATHANIEL J.; DRISCOLL, JOHN; AND DROBA, MARIAN. "Correlates of Vocational Satisfaction Among Nuns and Brothers." *Nat Cath Guid Conf J* 14(1):5–20 f '69. * (*PA* 44:8310)

561. PANDEY, JAGDISH. "Problems of Adjustment of Adolescents in Relation to Their Personality Variables." Doctoral thesis abstract. *Indian Psychol R* 5(2):212–4 Ja '69. *

562. PEACHEY, THOMAS J. *The Influence of Music Upon Performance on the 16 PF Among Male and Female College Students.* Master's thesis, East Tennessee State University (Johnson City, Tenn.), 1969.

563. PEARSON, ELIZABETH. *Personality Correlates of Course Critiques by College Students.* Doctor's thesis, St. Louis University (St. Louis, Mo.), 1969. (*DAI* 30:3331A)

564. POSTON, WILLIAM KENNETH, JR. *Educational Administrator Job Performance and Training Program Admission Criteria.* Doctor's thesis, Arizona State University (Tempe, Ariz.), 1969. (*DAI* 30:532A)

565. RASHEED, ROBERT NADEEM. *The Relationship Between Factors of Personality and Academic Achievement in a Programed Learning Situation Among College Students.* Doctor's thesis, Auburn University (Auburn, Ala.), 1969. (*DAI* 31:1646A)

566. RHOADES, CHRISTOPHER D., AND EDMONSTON, WILLIAM E., JR. "Personality Correlates of Hypnotizability: A Study Using the Harvard Group Scale of Hypnotic Susceptibility, the 16-PF and the IPAT." *Am J Clin Hyp* 11(4):228–33 Ap '69. * (*PA* 43:13654)

567. ROBERTS, POLLY CABE. *Personality Characteristics of Groups in Physical Education and Related Professional Areas.* Doctor's thesis, University of North Carolina (Chapel Hill, N.C.), 1969. (*DAI* 30:3768A)

568. ROHR, MICHAEL EUGENE. *An Exploratory Study of Two Measures and Two Correlates of Accurate Empathy.* Doctor's thesis, University of Tennessee (Knoxville, Tenn.), 1969. (*DAI* 30:4783A)

569. ROSENSTIEL, LUTZ V. "Capacity for Empathy: A Function of Anxiety in the Production of H-Responses." *J Proj Tech & Pers Assess* 33(4):336–42 Ag '69. * (*PA* 44:2376)

570. RUSHALL, BRENT SYDNEY. *The Demonstration and Evaluation of a Research Model for the Investigation of the Relationship Between Personality and Physical Performance Categories.* Doctor's thesis, Indiana University (Bloomington, Ind.), 1969. (*DAI* 30:2837A)

571. RUSSELL, JACK. *An Investigation of the Relationship Between College Freshman Withdrawal and Certain Critical Personality and Study Orientation Factors.* Doctor's thesis, University of Southern California (Los Angeles, Calif.), 1969. (*DAI* 30:1437A)

572. SCHUSTER, DONALD H., AND SCHUSTER, LOCKY. "Study of Stress and Sex Ratio in Humans." Abstract. *Proc 77th Ann Conv Am Psychol Assn* 4(1):335–6 '69. * (*PA* 43:17294)

573. SHERMAN, LILLIAN LASKAW. *Movers and Perseverers in Education: An Investigation of Interests, Values, Personality Factors, Self-Actualization, Need Satisfaction and Job Satisfaction Among Movers Into Counseling and Into Administration and Among Perseverers in Teaching.* Doctor's thesis, New York University (New York, N.Y.), 1969. (*DAI* 31:1023A)

574. SHONTZ, FRANKLIN C. *Perceptual and Cognitive Aspects of Body Experience,* pp. 188–202. New York: Academic Press Inc., 1969. Pp. xi, 250. *

575. SIEVERS, FARRELL PATRICK. *A Study of Variables Differentiating Counselors.* Doctor's thesis, University of South Dakota (Vermillion, S.D.), 1969. (*DAI* 30:3740A)

576. SMITH, ROBERT D. *An Analysis of the Relationship Between Personality Traits and Success in Swimming and Diving.* Master's thesis, Wisconsin State University (La Crosse, Wis.), 1969.

577. SNIPES, PAUL DAVID. *Communication Behavior and Personal Adjustment Among American and Foreign Students at Indiana University.* Doctor's thesis, Indiana University (Bloomington, Ind.), 1969. (*DAI* 30:1880A)

578. SOUEIF, M. I.; EYSENCK, H. J.; AND WHITE, P. O. Chap. 15, "A Joint Factorial Study of the Guilford, Cattell and Eysenck Scales," pp. 171–93. In *Personality Structure and Measurement,* see 518. *

579. SPRUELL, MICHAEL NORRIS. *The Development of Facilitative Training for a Group of Alcoholics.* Doctor's thesis, University of Georgia (Athens, Ga.), 1969. (*DAI* 30:5679B)

580. STOCK, MARY JULE SCHRAUFNAGEL. *Separation Anxiety in College Women.* Doctor's thesis, St. Louis University (St. Louis, Mo.), 1969. (*DAI* 30:3879B)

581. TAMKIN, ARTHUR S., AND SONKIN, NATHAN. "Use of Psychological Tests in Differential Diagnosis." *Psychol Rep* 24(2):590 Ap '69. * (*PA* 43:16017)

582. TAYLOR, A. J. W. "Ability, Stability and Social Adjustment Among Scott Base Personnel, Antarctica: A Preliminary Study." *Occup Psychol* 43(2):81–93 '69. * (*PA* 44:17609)

583. TITUS, H. EDWIN. "Prediction of Supervisory Success by Use of Standard Psychological Tests." *J Psychol* 72(1):35–40 My '69. * (*PA* 43:16503)

584. TITUS, H. EDWIN, AND GOSS, RICHARD G. "Psychometric Comparison of Old and Young Supervisors." *Psychol Rep* 24(3):727–33 Je '69. * (*PA* 44:1447)

585. TRICE, HARRISON M.; ROMAN, PAUL M.; AND BELASCO, JAMES A. "Selection for Treatment: A Predictive Evaluation of an Alcoholism Treatment Regimen." *Int J Addic* 4(3):303–17 S '69. *

586. VOLKSDORF, NORMAN RICHARD. *The Relationship of Ego-Strength to Ordinal Position and Sex.* Doctor's thesis, Texas Technological University (Lubbock, Tex.), 1969. (*DAI* 31:403B)

587. WEAVER, WENDELL W.; KINGSTON, ALBERT J.; BICKLEY, A. C.; AND WHITE, WILLIAM F. "Information-Flow Difficulty in Relation to Reading Comprehension." *J Read Behav* 1(3):41–9 su '69. * (*PA* 45:2355)

588. WHITE, P. O.; EYSENCK, H. J.; AND SOUEIF, M. I. Chap. 19, "Combined Analysis of Cattell, Eysenck and Guilford Factors," pp. 239–50. In *Personality Structure and Measurement,* see 518. *

589. WILSON, PHILIP K. "Relationship Between Motor Achievement and Selected Personality Factors of Junior and Senior High School Boys." *Res Q* 40(4):841–4 D '69. *

590. WORSHAM, JOHN WILLIAM, JR. *An Investigation of Effective Visual Speech Reception: Its Relationship to Personality Variables, Sex, Intelligence, and Conditionability.* Doctor's thesis, Texas Technological College (Lubbock, Tex.), 1969. (*DAI* 30:3858B)

591. ABERMAN, HUGH M., AND CHANSKY, NORMAN. "Factor Analysis of Two Personality Tests With Differing Conceptual Frameworks." *Psychol Rep* 27(2):475–80 O '70. * (*PA* 45:6344)

592. ADAMS, JERRY, AND KLEIN, LILYAN R. "Students in Nursing School: Considerations in Assessing Personality Characteristics." *Nursing Res* 19(4):362–6 Jl–Ag '70. *

593. ANDERSON, GLADYS MARY. *Personality Characteristics of Aspiring Teachers and Experienced Teachers: A Discriminant Analysis.* Doctor's thesis, Ohio State University (Columbus, Ohio), 1970. (*DAI* 31:4323B)

594. BACHTOLD, LOUISE M., AND WERNER, EMMY E. "Personality Profiles of Gifted Women: Psychologists." *Am Psychologist* 25(3):234–43 Mr '70. * (*PA* 44:15615)

595. BARLOW, DANIEL LENOX. *The Relationship Between the Counselors' Inferred Self Perceptions of Students and the Same Students' Scores on the Sixteen Personality Factor Questionnaire.* Doctor's thesis, Arizona State University (Tempe, Ariz.), 1970. (*DAI* 31:1570A)

596. BERNHARDSON, CLEMENS S., AND FISHER, RONALD J. "Personality Correlates of Dogmatism: Methodological Problems." Abstract. *J Consult & Clin Psychol* 34(3):449 Je '70. * (*PA* 44:14577)

597. CATTELL, RAYMOND B.; EBER, HERBERT W.; AND TATSUOKA, MAURICE M. *Handbook for the Sixteen Personality Factor Questionnaire (16 PF) in Clinical, Educational, Industrial and Research Psychology for Use With All Forms of the Test.* Champaign, Ill.: Institute for Personality and Ability Testing, 1970. Pp. xxv, 388. *

598. CHARLTON, LARRY HOGGE. *Teacher Personality and Acceptance of Team Teaching.* Doctor's thesis, Utah State University (Logan, Utah), 1970. (*DAI* 30:5280A)

599. CLAYTON, DIANE ELTHEA. *The Relationships Among Attitudes Toward Physical Activity, Personality, and Self-Concept.* Master's thesis, University of Washington (Seattle, Wash.), 1970.

600. COLEMAN, RAYMOND J., AND RILEY, M. J. "The Chief Executive: His Personality Characteristics and the Firm's Growth Rate." *Personnel J* 49(12):994–1001 D '70. *

601. CONNOR, GEORGE N., AND BOBLITT, WM. EDGAR. "Reported Frequency of Dream Recall as a Function of Intelligence and Various Personality Test Factors." *J Clin Psychol* 26(4):438–9 O '70. * (*PA* 45:4235)

602. COWDEN, JAMES E.; PACHT, ASHER R.; AND BODEMER, OTTMAR A. "The 16 PF vs. the MCI in a Group Testing Program of Reformatory Inmates." *J Clin Psychol* 26(4):510–3 O '70. * (*PA* 45:4586)

603. CROOKES, T. G., AND PEARSON, P. R. "The Relationship Between EPI Scores and 16 PF Second-Order Factors in a Clinical Group." *Brit J Social & Clin Psychol* 9(2):189–90 Je '70. * (*PA* 44:16699)

604. CROOKES, T. G., AND PEARSON, P. R. "WAIS IQ, Sixteen PF B Score and Education." *J Clin Psychol* 26(3):348–9 Jl '70. * (*PA* 45:672)

605. DELHEES, KARL H., AND CATTELL, RAYMOND B. "Obtaining 16 PF Scores From the MMPI, and MMPI Scores From the 16 PF." *J Proj Tech & Pers Assess* 34(3):251–5 Je '70. * (*PA* 44:18740)

606. EISENBERG, MYRON GAIL. *An Examination of a Procedure for Determining Personality Correlates to Independence of Judgment in Male University Students.* Doctor's thesis, Northwestern University (Evanston, Ill.), 1970. (*DAI* 31:4309B)

607. EVANS, RAY B. "Sixteen Personality Factor Questionnaire Scores of Homosexual Men." *J Consult & Clin Psychol* 34(2):212–5 Ap '70. * (*PA* 44:10804)

608. GALLOP, R. "A Study of the B.Ed. Student." Thesis Abstract. *Brit J Ed Psychol* 40(2):220 Je '70. *

609. GORMAN, BERNARD S. "16 PF Correlates of Sensation-Seeking." *Psychol Rep* 26(3):741–2 Je '70. * (*PA* 45:689)

610. GOTTSCHALK, LOUIS A.; GLESER, GOLDINE C.; CLEGHORN, JOHN M.; STONE, WALTER N.; AND WINGET, CAROLYN N. "Prediction of Changes in Severity of the Schizophrenic Syndrome With Discontinuation and Administration of Phenothiazines in Chronic Schizophrenic Patients: Language as a Predictor and Measure of Change in Schizophrenia." *Comprehen Psychiatry* 11(2):123–40 Mr '70. * (*PA* 45:6735)

611. GRIFFIN, JOHN J., JR. *An Investigation of the Work Satisfaction of Priests of the Archdiocese of Boston.* Doctor's thesis, Boston College (Chestnut Hill, Mass.), 1970. (*DAI* 31:3018A)

612. HAYNES, JACK R. "Factor-Analytic Study of Performance on the Bender-Gestalt." *J Consult & Clin Psychol* 34(3):345–7 Je '70. * (*PA* 44:13618)

613. HAYNES, JACK R., AND CARLEY, JOHN W. "Relation of Spatial Abilities and Selected Personality Traits." *Psychol Rep* 26(1):214 F '70. * (*PA* 45:4238)

614. HAYWARD, A. E. "The 16-PF and a General Psychiatric Factor." *Brit J Social & Clin Psychol* 9(4):382–3 D '70. * (*PA* 45:8498)

615. HUBELE, GLEN EDWARD. *An Investigation of Personality Characteristics of Counselors, Administrators, Teachers and "Non-Helping" Professionals.* Doctor's thesis, University of Illinois (Urbana, Ill.), 1970. (*DAI* 31:2108A)

616. IANNOTTI, MARY MARGARET. *The Relationship Between Certain Noncognitive Factors and the Academic Achievement of Junior College Women.* Doctor's thesis, Fordham University (New York, N.Y.), 1970. (*DAI* 31:3271A)

617. JENKINS, KENNETH DONALD. *The Relationship Among Selected Pupil Personality Characteristics, Relevant Pupil Perception, and Failure in a Nongraded Secondary School.* Doctor's thesis, University of Miami (Coral Gables, Fla.), 1970. (*DAI* 31:1512A)

618. JOHNSON, RICHARD J., AND LEONARD, LOUISE C. "Psychological Test Characteristics and Performance of Nursing Students." *Nursing Res* 19(2):147–50 Mr–Ap '70. *

619. KEAR-COLWELL, J. J. "The B Factor Scale of the 16 PF as a Measure of Intelligence in Psychiatric Patients." *J Clin Psychol* 26(4):477–9 O '70. * (*PA* 45:4540)

620. KLINE, PAUL. "The Validity of the Brook Reaction Test." *Brit J Social & Clin Psychol* 9(1):42–5 F '70. * (*PA* 44:12609)

621. LAHEY, HENRY CHARLES. *Personality Differentiation of Elevated Outdoor and Literary Kuder Preference Record Scales in an Urban Population.* Doctor's thesis, University of Connecticut (Storrs, Conn.), 1970. (*DAI* 31:1014A)

622. LEBOVITS, BINYAMIN Z., AND OSTFELD, ADRIAN M. "Personality, Defensiveness and Educational Achievement: 2, The Cattell 16PF Questionnaire." *J Clin Psychol* 26(2):183–8 Ap '70. * (*PA* 44:14634)

623. LEWIS, CHARLES E., AND EASTON, RICHARD. "Community Medicine: Personality Characteristics, Career Interests, Observed Health Behavior, and Teaching." *Arch Environ Health* 21(1):99–104 Jl '70. *

624. LEWIS, WAYNE M. *A Study of the Relationship Between Personality and Intelligence.* Master's thesis, Springfield College (Springfield, Mass.), 1970.

625. MCCLAIN, EDWIN W. "Personality Correlates of Church Attendance." *J Col Stud Personnel* 11(5):360–5 S '70. * (*PA* 45:4043)

626. MCCLAIN, EDWIN W., AND CHRISTIANSEN, MARK A. "Personality Characteristics of Students Preparing to Teach High School English." *Res Teach Engl* 4(2):149–56 f '70. *

627. MCGOWAN, BARBARA, AND LIU, PHYLLIS Y. H. "Creativity and Mental Health of Self-Renewing Women." *Meas & Eval Guid* 3(3):138–46 f '70. * (*PA* 45:4872)

628. MCKERRACHER, D. W.; ZWIRNER, W.; AND HARSHMAN, R. C. "Personality and Attainment: A Pilot Study." *West Psychologist* 1(2):62–70 Ja '70. *

629. MAI, F. M. M., AND PIKE, ANNE. "Correlation of Rhesus (Rh) and Personality Factors." *Brit J Social & Clin Psychol* 9(1):83–4 F '70. *

630. MATTIE, EDWARD C. *Personality Factors in the Discrimination of Medical, Surgical and Obstetrical Specialists.* Doctor's thesis, Catholic University of America (Washington, D.C.), 1970. (*DAI* 31:2189A)

631. MUSHIER, CAROLE LUCILLE. *A Cross-Sectional Study of the Personality Factors of Girls and Women in Competitive Lacrosse.* Doctor's thesis, University of Southern California (Los Angeles, Calif.), 1970. (*DAI* 31:635A)

632. NORSTED, LEROY VERNON. *Personality Factors of Teachers and the Acceptance of Audio-Visual Instructional Media Relative to Classroom Instruction.* Doctor's thesis, University of Minnesota (Minneapolis, Minn.), 1970. (*DAI* 31:2018A)

633. OLLEY, PETER C. "Age, Marriage, and Distress: A Study of Personality Factors in Women Referred for Therapeutic Abortion." *Seminar Psychiatry* 2(3):341–51 Ag '70. *

634. PALM, HAROLD JOHN. *The Differential Effects of Verbal Conditioning Upon Dominant and Submissive College Students in a Counseling Setting.* Doctor's thesis, Arizona State University (Tempe, Ariz.), 1970. (*DAI* 31:2114A)

635. PHILIP, ALISTAIR E. "Personality and Attempted Suicide: Traits Related to Having Prior History of Suicidal Attempts." *Appl Social Studies* 2(1):35–40 F '70. *

636. PHILIP, ALISTAIR E. "Traits, Attitudes and Symptoms in a Group of Attempted Suicides." *Brit J Psychiatry* 116(534):475–82 My '70. * (*PA* 45:984)

637. PORTER, RUTHERFORD B. "Test Results as an Aid in Personnel Selection." *J Employ Counsel* 7(1):36–9 Mr '70. *

638. PUGH, RICHARD C., AND CHASE, CLINTON I. "Test Content as a Determiner of Response Habits." *J Clin Psychol* 26(1):32–4 Ja '70. * (*PA* 44:10439)

639. PYECHA, JOHN. "Comparative Effects of Judo and Selected Physical Education Activities on Male University Freshman Personality Traits." *Res Q* 41(3):425–31 O '70. * (*PA* 46:1897)

640. ROSS, JANE E. "Simplification of Human Abilities With Age in Four Social Class Groups." Abstract. *Proc 78th Ann Conv Am Psychol Assn* 5(2):685–6 '70. * (*PA* 44:18417)

641. ROTHMAN, ARTHUR I., AND FLOWERS, JOHN F. "Personality Correlates of First-Year Medical School Achievement." *J Med Ed* 45(11, pt 1):901–5 N '70. *

642. SLAUGHTER, MARY. "An Analysis of the Relationship Between Somatotype and Personality Traits of College Women." *Res Q* 41(4):569–75 D '70. * (*PA* 46:4441)

643. SOSKIN, ROBERT A. "Personality and Attitude Change After Two Alcoholism Treatment Programs: Comparative Contributions of Lysergide and Human Relations Training." *Q J Studies Alcohol* 31(4):920–31 D '70. *

644. SPRADLING, JAMES W. *An Analysis of Personality and Environmental Press in Two Church Related Colleges and a*

State University. Doctor's thesis, University of South Dakota (Vermillion, S.D.), 1970. (*DAI* 31:3356A)

645. SWENSON, CHARLES DENNIS. *The Relationship Between Certain Personality Traits of Advanced Counselor Trainees and Their Ability to Express Congruence, Empathy and Positive Regard.* Doctor's thesis, Arizona State University (Tempe, Ariz.), 1970. (*DAI* 31:1027A)

646. TATSUOKA, M. M., AND CATTELL, R. B. "Linear Equations for Estimating a Person's Occupational Adjustment, Based on Information on Occupational Profiles." *Brit J Ed Psychol* 40(3):324–34 N '70. * (*PA* 45:7030)

647. TSENG, M. S. "Locus of Control as a Determinant of Job Proficiency, Employability, and Training Satisfaction of Vocational Rehabilitation Clients." *J Counsel Psychol* 17(6):487–91 N '70. * (*PA* 45:2799)

648. WALTON, H. J.; FOULDS, G. A.; LITTMANN, S. K.; AND PRESLY, A. S. "Abnormal Personality." *Brit J Psychiatry* 116-(534):497–510 My '70. * (*PA* 45:965)

649. WEIANT, ELIZABETH A. *An Experiment in Voluntary Group-Centered Counseling: Dedham House of Correction.* Doctor's thesis, Boston University (Boston, Mass.), 1970. (*DAI* 31:2120A)

650. WILLIAMS, JEAN M.; HOEPNER, BARBARA J.; MOODY, DOROTHY L.; AND OGILVIE, BRUCE C. "Personality Traits of Champion Level Female Fencers." *Res Q* 41(3):446–53 O '70. * (*PA* 46:1182)

651. WILSON, ALFRED P. *Personality Characteristics of Teachers in Relation to Performance in an Individually Prescribed Instruction Program.* Doctor's thesis, Utah State University (Logan, Utah), 1970. (*DAI* 30:5218A)

652. WITTMER, JOE. "Homogeneity of Personality Characteristics: A Comparison Between Old Order Amish and Non-Amish." *Am Anthrop* 72(5):1063–7 O '70. *

THOMAS J. BOUCHARD, JR., *Associate Professor of Psychology, University of Minnesota, Minneapolis, Minnesota.*

The 16PF purports to assess most of the important dimensions of personality with 12 factors derived from both the questionnaire and rating domains and 4 factors derived from the questionnaire domain alone. The authors claim that the test measures functional or "source traits," as opposed to the arbitrary or subjective surface traits measured by other tests.

The potential user of this test should not be unduly impressed by such claims. Almost all test constructors would claim a form of nonarbitrary uniqueness for their scales and this reviewer knows of no arbitrary scales. Some tests derive their dimensions from theories, e.g., Murray's need theory as expressed in Jackson's *Personality Research Form.* Some derive them from the domain to which they expect the test to apply, e.g., the world of work as expressed in the scales of the *Strong Vocational Interest Blank.* The 16PF began in the world of everyday description and has been refined by means of factor analysis to reflect the world of oblique (correlated) factors. Cattell's version of factor analysis (there are others) is simply one of many possible theoretical schemes through which a test user may filter the world. Each scheme generates a different set of abstractions. The average test user must decide for himself which test is most valid for his purposes.

With the important exceptions to be noted below, the 1970 handbook is an outstanding accomplishment and should serve as a model for other test authors. Although the discussions are not always supported by sufficient data, they are almost always lucid and informative. A large number of powerful statistical aids are clearly described and made accessible to the user. There are extensive discussions of the test's design and construction, the psychometric properties of the scales, the problems and complexities of standardization, the meaning of each of the primary and secondary source traits, and the criterion evidence. Chapters 9, 10, 12, and 13 closely approximate what this reviewer conceives of as an ideal treatment of construct validity. Chapters 9 and 10 *conceptualize* the variables and give them psychological meaning. Chapters 12 and 13 *evaluate* the evidence (albeit in an idiosyncratic fashion) and provide the empirical basis for *generalizing* this meaning. The rich store of "specification equations" (regression equations), normative data, and occupational profiles are a psychometrician's delight and provide the major justification for using this test. Full utilization of the available information will require computer analysis (to be discussed below).

The handbook has serious deficiencies. The manual of any test should supply the correlations between it and other tests of similar function in order to locate it in the matrix of available instruments. It is inexcusable not to be able to find correlations between the 16PF and at least four or five widely used similar instruments, such as the *Omnibus Personality Inventory,* the *Guilford-Zimmerman Temperament Survey,* the *California Psychological Inventory,* and the *Minnesota Multiphasic Personality Inventory.* One should also be able to find correlations between specific factors and other well established measures of the same trait. The 16PF's Factor B purports to measure a facet of intelligence, yet there are no correlations between it and similarly constructed (e.g., group) intelligence tests. The first 12 factors are said to correspond to similar factors in the realm of ratings, yet we find no matrix of correlations in the handbook. These data were requested in an earlier review (4:87) of the 16PF and many are considered VERY DESIRABLE by the *Standards for Educational and Psychological Tests and Manuals.* The authors are irresponsible in omitting them. It would also be of interest to see how the 16PF correlates with various interest, aptitude, creativity, and intelligence measures. In spite of the above omissions, we are given the regression weights for estimating the GZTS and the MMPI from the 16PF. The original correlations themselves would have been much more useful. The regression coefficients are likely to be population specific and of limited generality. A large number of regression equations for predicting adjustment, adaptation, effectiveness, etc. in various occupations are also given, but the validity coefficients are nowhere to be seen! It is therefore impossible to evaluate them without looking up each original study.

Before discussing the question of validity in general, I wish to emphasize that there are four regular forms of the 16PF (A, B, C, D) and the correlations between forms (even pairs of forms) are so low that data gathered with one form or pair of forms may simply not be generalizable to all forms. There are also old and new forms (revisions). The 1967–68 Form A and B revisions differ considerably from the 1961 Form B and 1962 Form A. For example, assuming that any change in wording (question or answer) is meaningful, an average of 43 percent of the items have been changed on the 16 scales (range 12–75 percent). These changes are so massive that they make most of the empirical or predictive validity data on the earlier forms obsolete. No arguments about purity of factor structure and increase in concept validity are relevant to this verdict. The applied user who will be making individual decisions with these new forms should assume he is using a semi-experimental instrument.

Forms C and D contain a motivational distortion scale made up of items that show maximum shift from an anonymous to a job-seeking situation. This should prove useful to applied users. Forms A and B do not contain any faking scales. This is a shame, in view of the ease with which brief scales can be built to detect random answering, faking good and faking bad. Mean scores for the latter two response sets are presented in the handbook, but they are pooled for both sexes in spite of the discussion in the text that indicates there are significant sex differences.

The first 12 factors purport to represent functional measurement in the sense that they represent natural personality concepts found in the worlds of both factor analysis and ratings. This claim is invalid. The authors consistently cite Schaie [1] on this point. Schaie's results were "equivocal" by his own report and dealt with only five factors. Work by Becker (362) and Peterson [2] demonstrate very little convergent or discriminant validity between the 16PF factors and ratings. If a test user wants ratable traits, he should look for another instrument.

Are the 16PF factors "source traits"? Source traits supposedly work together to determine a particular behavioral response. According to Cattell, they can be combined to predict particular behaviors more efficiently than surface traits or other types of scales. The handbook does not present any comparative data on this question but data that will throw light on the question are available. The handbook gives the regression equations used for predicting academic achievement (grades) in four different samples. It is not reported whether these equations were crossvalidated and might therefore shrink. Each equation makes use of all 16 factors. The multiple r's are .55, .63, .37, and .56. The CPI has also been used to predict grades. In one study,[3] a six-variable regression equation yielded a crossvalidated multiple r of .56 with grade point average. In a second study,[4] another six-variable equation yielded crossvalidated multiple r's of .46 for males and .43 for females. Anyone familiar with multiple regression will realize that inclusion of all 18 CPI scales would boost all of these multiple r's. I conclude from these and other data that factor derived scales or "source traits" have no inherent superiority over empirical scales when used in multiple regression equations.

Summarizing, the 16PF does not appear to measure dimensions that correspond to the rating domain. The various forms of the test are not as comparable as they should be. The dimensions measured do not appear to be special or fundamental in any "source trait" sense and the handbook, in spite of its size, still has significant deficiencies.

The publisher provides computer interpretation of the 16PF for the convenience of the test's users. Instead of using raw scores, the program computes new "true" sten scores using

1 SCHAIE, K. WARNER. "On the Equivalence of Questionnaire and Rating Data." Psychol Rep 10:521–2 Ap '62. *
2 PETERSON, DONALD R. "Scope and Generality of Verbally Defined Personality Factors." Psychol R 72:48–59 Ja '65. *
3 GOUGH, HARRISON G. "Academic Achievement in High School as Predicted From the California Psychological Inventory." J Ed Psychol 55:174–80 Je '64. *
4 GOUGH, HARRISON G., AND FINK, MARTIN B. "Scholastic Achievement Among Students of Average Ability as Predicted From the California Psychological Inventory." Psychol Sch 1:375–80 O '64. *

a computer synthesis method of consolidating variance from all scales for each scale score. This procedure is highly touted. One IPAT news release says "How much validity are you willing to pay for?" continues to be a more reasonable statement of the case than the answer to the question "What is the validity of the test?" This is sheer nonsense. It assumes that the factor model underlying the 16PF provides an ultimate criterion and can always meet the needs of the test user better than tests based on other models. This is simply not true. The validity of an instrument for most users rests in its capacity to relate to significant external criteria. Empirical or predictive validity coefficients continue to constitute the crucial test of any instrument designed for operational, rather than strictly "scientific," use. Research with the 16PF has generated an enormous number of empirical validity coefficients, both of the simple and multiple regression type, as well as a great deal of normative data for assessing profiles. It seems to this reviewer that the computer's time would be better spent calculating regression equations for predicting criteria and generating contrasts called for by the user rather than calculating more precise sten scores and making age corrections. For example, a long list of equations could be made available and the user could choose those he wanted. I mention this possibility in order to prod the potential user into making demands on the computer scoring service. The program is an open system, constantly changing and potentially responsive to the demands of users. Its ultimate effectiveness is therefore partially their responsibility.

Each interpretation begins with the client's profile plotted in much the same way as it appears on the conventional profile sheet. Since these scores are based on computer synthesis equations they may differ considerably from the raw input scores. The profile is followed by three statements that index "Broad Influence Patterns." They are (a) level of extraversion, (b) interpersonal style (e.g., focus on relationships vs. rational and objective considerations), and (c) life style (e.g., subdued and accepting vs. striving to achieve control of the environment). Each of the three statements is modified by adjectives indicating the appropriate level of intensity (e.g., very high, high average, equal emphasis on both tendencies, etc. for the low end). These three statements constitute the basic personological analysis. This section of

the report is extremely weak and could use considerable strengthening.

The next section is "Clinical Observations." Brief statements dealing with level of adjustment, level of anxiety, rigidity, and acting out behavior are modified in the same way as those in the first section. The third section is labeled "Treatment Considerations." The statements given on the printouts examined for this review were generally not very informative. Since the 16PF is relatively insensitive to pathology and was not designed for drawing clinical inferences, these two sections are extremely misleading and should be withdrawn from the program (they are optional and can be suppressed).

The program also has a related option which I consider highly undesirable. A user can, at his request, simply supply the computer with a statement he wants printed (e.g., slight possibility of brain damage). There is a strong tendency even among professionals to respond to what comes out of the computer as truth. Since all the other statements printed by the program are asserted to be empirically based, this option will simply mislead users, especially if they did not supply the input. One of the values of the computer printout is its lack of contamination by the clinician or counselor. It should remain in that pristine state. It is of course the professional user's responsibility to reject a printout if he feels it is inadequate, but he should not be allowed to make his own judgments look more objective than they are.

The last three sections that appear are "Vocational Observations," "Some Further Vocational Patterns," and "Occupational Fitness Projections." Although the statements that appear in these sections are based on empirical studies with the 16PF in the world of work, it seems to this reviewer that if a user were primarily interested in vocational counseling he should use a more appropriate instrument (e.g., the *Strong Vocational Interest Blank*). The statements do, however, provide a useful supplementary source of information.

The section on "Occupational Fitness Projections" indicates how similar the test taker is to 24 different occupational groups. They are divided into five sections: artistic professions (3), community and social service (2), scientific and technical personnel (10), clerical personnel (2), and academic professions (7). Similarity is based on the profile similarity coefficient which is described in the handbook. Unfortunately, the coefficient itself is not reported, but rather a fitness rating is given (7-point scale ranging from extremely high to extremely low). The user should be aware that the term *fitness* is being used in a special sense and that there are no data that demonstrate predictive validity for the approach. Nevertheless, the information provided is very informative.

I strongly recommend that each report be ended with some sort of statement of caution. For example, "This report is intended for professional use only. It should not be shown or released to the client. It should be considered only a partial report and a useful aid, but not a substitute for careful professional judgment."

It would also be very useful if the interpretation were accompanied by a brief manual, perhaps only two or three pages, documenting the original sources for the equations used in the program.

In summary, this program has a great deal of potential; it provides much useful information that is typically unavailable to a test interpreter; but it is weak in spots, and a number of sections are inappropriate and should be deleted.

LEONARD G. RORER, *Research Associate, Oregon Research Institute, Eugene, Oregon.*

For more than 30 years Cattell has pursued a program of research which, from the beginning, had as its goals the identification of the basic dimensions of personality and the development of a set of instruments to measure those dimensions across different data domains. The technique of choice in both cases has always been factor analysis. Cattell's single-minded pursuit of his goals has resulted both in a prodigious outpouring of books and articles dealing with the theoretical, methodological, and statistical problems of personality assessment and in the development and publication of an interrelated set of personality assessment instruments, of which the 16PF is probably the best known. Developed as an integral part of the research program, the assessment instruments serve to demonstrate and evaluate the theory and methodology which are the real focus of the program.

While the prominence of the 16PF is attributable primarily to its position as premier exemplar of the Cattellian research program, this review is concerned with the evaluation of the 16PF as an instrument to be used by the applied practitioner for prediction, evaluation, and general personality assessment, i.e., with the extent to which the 16PF conforms to the *Standards for Educational and Psychological Tests and Manuals.*

After 20 years during which the 16PF was accompanied by only an inadequate manual, both a 413-page handbook and a 40-page tabular supplement were published in the fall of 1970. The manual contains instructions for administration and scoring, and brief descriptions of the scales. The tabular supplement includes norm tables, age corrections, and item keys for the 1967–68 revision of Forms A and B of the 16PF, and will presumably become part of either the handbook or the manual. The handbook suggests textbooks of general personality theory as sources of information concerning the 16PF, but of those cited, none includes more than incidental or illustrative information concerning the design, construction, standardization, or interpretation of the test. With good reason, even the handbook does not recommend the journals. The 16PF user is left, then, with the handbook as a potential source of background and interpretive information.

The handbook often reflects the brilliance of its authors, but the overwhelming impression it leaves is one of disorganization, contradiction, and confusion. For example, it contains original theoretical material on profile similarity. While this material might make a significant journal article, it has nothing to do with the 16PF as such, and as a result, is simply distracting when included in the handbook. Or consider the cornerstone of the entire enterprise—the factor structure on which the ESPQ, CPQ, and HSPQ, in addition to the six forms of the 16PF, are all supposed to be based. The number of primary factors is variously estimated to be 16, 18, 19, 22, 23, and 28, at least. Since these primaries, however many there are, are not orthogonal, "second stratum" factors can be calculated. The number of these is variously reported to be 8, 9, 14, and 16. No effort is made to account for these seemingly inconsistent findings or to reconcile them with the repeated allusions to a stable pattern which has clearly and consistently emerged over the years. Nor are the data that would allow the reader to evaluate the results presented. Indeed, there is no indication of any awareness that there may be even an appearance of inconsistency, or that anything remains to be explained.

The handbook presents no information concerning the origins of the test. There is no indication as to where the items came from, or how they were selected; nor is there any indication of the way in which various editions of the 16PF differ, or the reasons for the revisions. There is nothing concerning the construction of the test, beyond the fact that it had something to do with factor analysis and simple structure; but the factor analytic model is never presented and simple structure is never discussed. Nor is the theoretical system on which the 16PF is based anywhere described. Some of the textbooks cited would be helpful in this regard, but the links between the theoretical system and the 16PF are missing.

The information that is in the handbook is primarily of three kinds: (*a*) There are imaginatively written but lightly documented descriptions that purportedly characterize high and low scorers on the primary and secondary scales. (*b*) There are average profiles for cultural, vocational, educational, and clinical groups of all kinds. These data are impressive, both for their sheer numerosity and the general plausibility of the descriptive text accompanying them. Unfortunately, it is one thing to present a lot of profiles, another to show that valid description (classification) on the basis of those profiles is possible. (*c*) There are what Cattell calls "specification equations" for predicting many diverse criteria. These should give some indication of the extent to which valid prediction on the basis of the profiles is possible. But while the weights to be used in these equations are given to two decimal places, the corresponding validity coefficients are rarely reported. Furthermore, the references for the descriptions, the profiles, and the specification equations, when references are given, cover the entire 30-year span of Cattell's research. Seldom is there any indication as to whether the study employed the current 1967–68 edition of the test, or the 1961–62 edition, or the 1956–57 edition, or the 1949 edition, or some still earlier preliminary editions. Considering the variable nature of regression weights from sample to sample, the prediction equations presented in the handbook would be of dubious validity in new samples, even if evidence of their original validity were presented. In view of the fact that they may have been derived on earlier editions of the

test, they may be said, in the Cattellian tradition of coining phrases, to possess face fatuity.

The handbook does present correlations between equivalent scales for Forms A and B and for Forms C and D of the 16PF. For Forms A and B one "equivalence coefficient" is in the .70's, two are in the .60's, five in the .50's, four in the .40's, three in the .30's, and one in the .20's. Furthermore, when the Spearman-Brown formula is applied to the coefficients for Forms A and B, in order to estimate the correlation between scales of combined length, and the resulting estimates are compared to the intercorrelations among scales, four of the 16 scales correlate more highly with some other scale than with themselves. Since there is no basis on which to believe that the correlations with presumably equivalent previous editions would be significantly "better" than these correlations between presumably equivalent forms of the present edition, it must be concluded that most of the material in the handbook is unusable, because its relevance to the present form of the test is indeterminate. The potential user of the 16PF should simply ignore both the handbook and the scale descriptors which are given both in the manual and on the answer sheet. For all practical purposes, the 16PF is composed of 16 scales of indeterminate origin and unknown significance, for which there are available test-retest and split-half reliabilities, intercorrelations, and norms, based on samples selected in an unknown way, for males and females in high school, college, and the general population. It is possible to know whether or not someone has responded deviantly, but not what the correlates of his responses may be.

In conception and design, the 16PF is unique, and a priori may well be the best personality inventory there is. Furthermore, after 20 years of research, much of the data, which would allow the instrument to be evaluated on its merits, must exist. It is tragic that these essential data have not been made available in coherent and usable form. Until they are, the 16PF should be used for the derivation of prediction and classification functions only in those situations in which scale or profile interpretation is not desired.

For a review by Maurice Lorr, see 6:174; for a review by C. J. Adcock, see 5:112; for reviews by Charles M. Harsh, Ardie Lubin, and J. Richard Wittenborn, see 4:87.

[140]

★**Slosson Drawing Coordination Test for Children and Adults, 1967 Edition.** Ages 1.5 and over; 1962–67; SDCT; brain dysfunction and perceptual disorders; 1 form ('67, 2 pages); manual ('67, 52 pages); 75¢ per 20 tests; $3.75 per 40 tests and manual; postpaid; (10–15) minutes; Richard L. Slosson; Slosson Educational Publications. *

ARTHUR L. BENTON, *Professor of Neurology and Psychology, The University of Iowa, Iowa City, Iowa.*

This 12-item figure drawing test was "designed to identify individuals with various forms of brain dysfunction or perceptual disorders where eye-hand coordination is involved." The 12 figures are arranged in order of increasing difficulty level and thus "make up a crude developmental scale." Detailed directions for scoring the drawings are given. The population samples from which the normative standards were derived are not described in sufficient detail to be informative nor are descriptive statistics on their performances presented. A test-retest study of 200 subjects ranging widely in age and IQ yielded a reliability coefficient of .96. The validity of the test as a method for disclosing brain damage is discussed but no supporting data, other than illustrative case reports, are provided. Some ancillary materials of questionable relevance (a diagram from Morgan's *Physiological Psychology,* some definitions from Birch's *Brain Damage in Children* and testimonials from school principals and social service workers concerning the value of the *Slosson Intelligence Test*) are included in the manual.

This is still another copying-of-designs test. The basis for its standardization is obscure and evidence bearing on its validity or distinctive merits in identifying cerebral dysfunction in children or adults is not offered. So far as can be seen, it offers nothing which is not provided by existing tests of this type and it compares unfavorably with them in respect to demonstrated clinical utility.

JAMES C. REED, *Associate Professor of Psychology, Tufts University School of Medicine, Boston, Massachusetts.*

The *Slosson Drawing Coordination Test* cannot be recommended to identify individuals with various forms of brain dysfunction where eye-hand coordination is involved because: the subsets of the population on which the norms are based are ill defined and probably subject to bias

of an unknown degree; the sample used for determining the reliability of the test overestimates the reliability for most situations in which the test would be used; the evidence for the validity of the test is inadequate.

The test, which can be group administered, consists of 12 geometric figures to be copied three times. The number of items to be attempted depends on the age of the subject. Each reproduction of each drawing is scored on a plus-minus basis. The directions for scoring are clear, and a sufficient number of examples of passes and failures are shown so that scoring difficulties are minimal. The accuracy score is the percentage of reproductions scored as pluses. An accuracy score below 85 percent places the subject in the brain damaged classification.

The author recommends that the test be used as a screening device and that individuals who earn accuracy scores below 85 percent be given a thorough neurological examination. The overall purpose of this assessment is to identify children with organically based learning difficulties so that they may be placed in appropriate school curricula. Likewise, according to the author, adults who have some form of brain damage may need vocational rehabilitation.

The standardization population came from New York State. It included samples of children from urban and rural populations; Negro, white and American Indian. Children were also selected from well-child conferences, nursery schools, public and parochial schools. The adults came from rural and urban settings and included Negroes and whites. Many were referrals from Division of Vocational Rehabilitation. For neither the children nor the adults was the size of the sample categories given nor were there any percentages which indicated the portion of the various subsets taken. It is impossible to tell from the manual what biases or degree of representativeness were present in the standardization samples.

The reliability coefficient of .96 was obtained by a test-retest procedure. One testing was done at the beginning of an interview and the other done at the end of the same interview. The coefficient was calculated from an N of 200, ages 4–52. The number included at each age was not given. Since reliability coefficients vary with range of ability, the reported coefficient overestimates the reliability that would be found in a more homogeneous group, a second grade class, say.

The validity of the test is unknown. Apparently two methods were used for validation. First, individuals who departed from the norm were checked with a neurological examination and with case history information to see if there was a relationship between the test classification and brain dysfunction. The magnitude of the relationship, if any, was not reported nor was any information given about correct hits or percentages of false positives and false negatives.

Second, individuals who were known to be brain damaged, epileptic, suffering from cerebral palsy, birth injuries or accidents were tested and their drawing observed. The majority of these individuals fell below the accuracy score of the 85 percent. The size of this conglomerate group was not given, nor were the number of individuals in each diagnostic classification listed. Most importantly, no mention was made as to how the author knew the individuals were indeed brain damaged; nothing was stated concerning the type of criterion information (clinical neurological examination, case history, contrast studies, EEG tracing) used to make the diagnosis of brain damage.

The foregoing weaknesses are sufficient to make the test questionable for use in identifying brain-damaged individuals. In addition, the use of a cut-off score, indeed, the concept of a screening test, is based on certain assumptions for which no evidence was given. Why does a teacher want to identify children who have brain damage? If the lesion is recent and progressive, far more sensitive tests are available. If the lesion is chronic and static in course, does the test provide useful information? No evidence was presented to support the notion that children with chronic cerebral dysfunction need or will benefit from pedagogical procedures which differ materially from those used in the regular classroom. Even more, no evidence was given to suggest that children who have difficulty copying geometric designs do, indeed, develop learning problems.

In summary the author has not furnished sufficient data to show that the SDCT is valid for the identification of brain damage. The author has failed to give a rationale for the assumption that children with either poor eye-hand coordination or chronic cerebral dysfunction develop learning disabilities which require special teaching procedures.

[141]

★**State-Trait Anxiety Inventory.** Grades 9–16 and adults; 1968–70; STAI; title on test is *Self-Evaluation Questionnaire;* 2 scores: state anxiety, trait anxiety; 1 form ('68, 2 pages); 2 parts labeled Forms X-1 (state), X-2 (trait); manual ('70, 25 pages); $2.25 per 25 tests; 50¢ per key; $2.50 per manual; $3 per specimen set; postage extra; (15–20) minutes; C. D. Spielberger, R. L. Gorsuch, and R. Lushene; Consulting Psychologists Press, Inc. *

REFERENCES

1. SPIELBERGER, CHARLES D. Chap. 1, "Theory and Research on Anxiety," pp. 3–20. In his *Anxiety and Behavior.* New York: Academic Press Inc., 1966. Pp. xv, 414. *
2. SPIELBERGER, CHARLES D., AND GORSUCH, RICHARD L. Chap. 4, "Anxiety and Verbal Conditioning and the Development of the State-Trait Anxiety Inventory," pp. 32–41; Appendix C, "The Development of the State-Trait Anxiety Inventory," pp. 45–72. In their *Mediating Processes in Verbal Conditioning.* An unpublished report to the National Institutes of Mental Health (MH 7229 and 7446) and the Child Health and Human Development, U.S. Public Health Service (HD 947), Vanderbilt University, 1966. Pp. i, 72. *
3. JOHNSON, DALE T. "Effects of Interview Stress on Measures of State and Trait Anxiety." *J Abn Psychol* 73:245 51 Je '68. * (*PA* 42:12163)
4. TAYLOR, DALMAS A.; WHEELER, LADD; AND ALTMAN, IRWIN. "Stress Reactions in Socially Isolated Groups." *J Pers & Social Psychol* 9:369–76 Ag '68. *
5. BARTON, KEITH. *Block Manipulation by Children as a Function of Social Reinforcement, Anxiety, Arousal, and Ability Pattern.* Doctor's thesis, George Peabody College for Teachers (Nashville, Tenn.), 1969. (*DAI* 30:5219B)
6. DIBLIN, JOAN EDNA. *Anxiety in Counselor Trainees.* Doctor's thesis, Arizona State University (Tempe, Ariz.), 1969. (*DAI* 30:3721A)
7. EIGENBROD, FREDERICK A., JR. *The Effects of Territory and Personality Compatibility on Identity and Security.* Doctor's thesis, Michigan State University (East Lansing, Mich.), 1969. (*DAI* 30:2329A)
8. KASS, EMIL LEOPOLD. *The Effect of Short-Term Group Desensitization on Test Anxiety.* Doctor's thesis, Arizona State University (Tempe, Ariz.), 1969. (*DAI* 30:3729A)
9. LAMB, DOUGLAS HART. *The Effects of Public Speaking of Self-Report Physiological, and Behavioral Measures of Anxiety.* Doctor's thesis, Florida State University (Tallahassee, Fla.), 1969. (*DAI* 31:2284B)
10. MONKE, ROBERT HERMAN. *The Effect of Systematic Desensitization on the Training of Counselors.* Doctor's thesis, Arizona State University (Tempe, Ariz.), 1969. (*DAI* 30:1401A)
11. NIXON, GEORGE FREDERICK, JR. *The Relationship Between Anxiety-Trait and Anxiety-State With the Approach of Final Examinations.* Doctor's thesis, East Texas State University (Commerce, Tex.), 1969. (*DAI* 30:5296A)
12. O'NEIL, HARRY F., JR.; SPIELBERGER, CHARLES D.; AND HANSEN, DUNCAN N. "Effects of State-Anxiety and Task Difficulty on Computer-Assisted Learning." *J Ed Psychol* 60(5): 343–50 O '69. * (*PA* 44:2872)
13. STOUDENMIRE, JOHN ALEXANDER, JR. *Methodological Variables in the Reduction of State and Trait Anxiety Using Relaxation Training.* Doctor's thesis, University of Southern Mississippi (Hattiesburg, Miss.), 1969. (*DAI* 30:5703B)
14. WORTH, JAMES WELDON. *Anxiety, Permissiveness, and Social Desirability in Teachers With High and Low Authoritarian Principals.* Doctor's thesis, Colorado State College (Greeley, Colo.), 1969. (*DAI* 30:2429B)
15. ALLEN, GEORGE J. "Effect of Three Conditions of Administration on 'Trait' and 'State' Measures of Anxiety." *J Consult & Clin Psychol* 34(3):355–9 Je '70. * (*PA* 44:14621)
16. EDELMAN, ROBERT I. "Effects of Progressive Relaxation on Autonomic Processes." *J Clin Psychol* 26(4):421–5 O '70. * (*PA* 45:4418)
17. HODGES, WILLIAM F., AND FELLING, JAMES P. "Types of Stressful Situations and Their Relation to Trait Anxiety and Sex." *J Consult & Clin Psychol* 34(3):333–7 Je '70. *
18. KAMEN, GARY BEST. *The Effects of a Stress Producing Film on the Test Performance of Adults.* Doctor's thesis, University of Missouri (Columbia, Mo.), 1970. (*DAI* 31:2989B)
19. KNOX, WILMA J., AND GRIPPALDI, RICARDO. "High Levels of State or Trait Anxiety and Performance on Selected Verbal WAIS Subtests." *Psychol Rep* 27(2):375–9 O '70. * (*PA* 45:6319)
20. RATZLAFF, CLIFFORD NELSON. *Effects of Relaxation of Self-Report Measures of a Basic-Encounter Group Experience.* Doctor's thesis, Arizona State University (Tempe, Ariz.), 1970. (*DAI* 31:2116A)

[142]

*Stern Activities Index. Grades 7–16 and adults; 1950–70; SAI; personal needs (see 143 for related tests of environmental press covering the same areas) ; 48 scores: 30 need scores (abasement-assurance, achievement, adaptability-defensiveness, affiliation, aggression-blame avoidance, change-sameness, conjunctivity-disjunctivity, counteraction, deference-restiveness, dominance-tolerance, ego achievement, emotionality-placidity, energy-passivity, exhibitionism-inferiority avoidance, fantasied achievement, harm avoidance-risk taking, humanities and social science, impulsiveness-deliberation, narcissism, nurturance, objectivity-projectivity, order-disorder, play-work, practicalness-impracticalness, reflectiveness, science, sensuality-puritanism, sexuality-prudishness, supplication-autonomy, understanding), 12 factor scores (self-assertion, audacity-timidity, intellectual interests, motivation, applied interests, orderliness, submissiveness, closeness, sensuousness, friendliness, expressiveness-constraint, egoism-diffidence), 4 second-order factor scores (achievement orientation, dependency needs, emotional expression, educability), 1 validity score, 1 academic aptitude score; also 5 composite culture factor scores (expressive, intellectual, protective, vocational, collegiate) based on combinations of needs scores with environmental press scores; 1 form ('58, 7 pages); research report entitled *People in Context* ('70, see *128* below) ; norms booklet ('58, 60 pages) for SAI and *College Characteristics Index;* NCS individual profile ('63, 1 page) for any norm group and for all scores; scale score profiles (1 page) : individual ('68), group ('66) ; factor score profiles (1 page): individual ('68), group ('63), blank ('66) ; diagnostic summary profile ('65, 1 page) ; college culture profiles (1 page) : individual ('68), group ('68), blank ('68), vectors ('68), circumplex ('66) based upon SAI and *College Characteristics Index;* separate answer sheets (Digitek, IBM 1230, NCS) must be used; 25¢ per test; $3.50 per 50 NCS answer sheets; 7¢ per Digitek answer sheet; 5¢ per IBM 1230 answer sheet; 5¢ per profile; $6 per set of NCS hand scoring stencils; $13.95 per research report; postage extra; norms booklet available free on request from Psychological Research Center; NCS scoring service, 80¢ to 50¢ per test; (20–90) minutes; George G. Stern; profiles (except NCS profile) and Digitek and IBM answer sheets available only from Psychological Research Center; research report available only from John Wiley & Sons, Inc.; other materials distributed by National Computer Systems. *

REFERENCES

1–27. See 6:180.
28–68. See P:255, also includes a cumulative name index to the first 68 references for this test.
69. HISCOX, ELIZABETH ANN WILSON. *An Investigation of the Relationship Between Certain Personality Characteristics and Achievement in Freshman English Courses at the Ohio State University.* Doctor's thesis, Ohio State University (Columbus, Ohio), 1958. (*DA* 19:2658)
70. CHILMAN, CATHERINE STREET. *A Comparative Study of Measured Personality Needs and Self-Perceived Problems of Ninth and Tenth Grade Students: Half of the Group Possessing Characteristics Associated With Early School Leaving and the Other Half Not Possessing Such Characteristics.* Doctor's thesis, Syracuse University (Syracuse, N.Y.), 1959. (*DA* 20:3190)
71. COLE, DOROTHY AGNES. *Some Emotional Factors in Couples Presenting a Pattern of Habitual Abortion.* Doctor's thesis, Syracuse University (Syracuse, N.Y.), 1959. (*DA* 20:749)
72. GARDNER, PAUL LEON. *Academic Failure, Reinstatement, and Follow-Up.* Doctor's thesis, Ohio State University (Columbus, Ohio), 1959. (*DA* 20:3627)
73. DUCANIS, ALEX J. *An Investigation of Institutional Environment and Student Satisfaction.* Doctor's thesis, University of Pittsburgh (Pittsburgh, Pa.), 1961. (*DA* 22:3935)
74. HERMAN, SIMON. *An Investigation of the Relationship Between Interpersonal Effectiveness, Orientation to Authority, and Social Perception.* Doctor's thesis, Wayne State University (Detroit, Mich.), 1962. (*DA* 28:4708A)
75. SOLDAHL, THOMAS ALAN. *Secondary School Counselors Concept of Role in Relation to Personal Data and Psychogenic Needs.* Doctor's thesis, University of Minnesota (Minneapolis, Minn.), 1962. (*DA* 24:4089)
76. DONOIAN, GEORGE. *A Study of Self-Perception: An Assessment of the Changes in the Modes of Thinking Among a Selected Group of Teachers Over a Period of Time.* Doctor's thesis, Wayne State University (Detroit, Mich.), 1963. (*DA* 25:6326)
77. VANBUSKIRK, CHARLES, AND YUFIT, ROBERT I. "A Comparison of Two Techniques for Personality Assessment." *J Proj Tech & Pers Assess* 27:98–110 Mr '63. * (*PA* 38:989)
78. GILBREATH, STUART HENRY. *The Effects of Structured and Unstructured Group Counseling on Certain Personality Dimensions of Male College Students Who Underachieve.* Doctor's thesis, Michigan State University (East Lansing, Mich.), 1964. (*DA* 26:199)
79. LUKENS, LOIS GRAHAM. "The Nurse Stereotype Must Go." *Voc Guid Q* 13:95–9 w '64–65. * (*PA* 39:7943)
80. NORRED, ROBERT GAINES. *The Effect of Certain Selected Variables on Performance in Football.* Doctor's thesis, University of Alabama (University, Ala.), 1964. (*DA* 25:7066)
81. STERN, GEORGE G. "B = f(P, E)." *J Proj Tech & Pers Assess* 28:161–8 Je '64. * (*PA* 39:5008)
82. HINER, EDWARD SHELLY. *Differential Need Patterns of Business, Service, and Science Majors in a Catholic Liberal Arts College.* Doctor's thesis, University of Kansas (Lawrence, Kan.), 1965. (*DA* 27:1657A)
83. CALLIHAN, DOROTHY JEANNE GLAZENER. *An Analysis of Differences in Experiential Background and Personality Variables Between Work-Study and Non-Work-Study Freshmen at the University of Alabama.* Doctor's thesis, University of Alabama (University, Ala.), 1966. (*DA* 27:2869A)
84. DAVIS, WILLIAM ROBERT. *An Analysis of Certain Relationships Between Student Needs, College Environment, and Academic Achievement.* Doctor's thesis, Washington State University (Pullman, Wash.), 1966. (*DA* 27:2722A)
85. KIRKLAND, MARJORIE CREWS. *An Investigation of the Characteristic Needs, Beta Presses, and Certain Resultant Behaviors of Selected Auburn University Freshmen.* Doctor's thesis, Auburn University (Auburn, Ala.), 1966. (*DA* 27:3272B)
86. MADDI, SALVATORE R., AND ANDREWS, SUSAN L. "The Need for Variety in Fantasy and Self-Description." *J Personality* 34:610–25 D '66. *
87. STEINHOFF, CARL ROBERT. *Organizational Climate in a Public School System.* Doctor's thesis, Syracuse University (Syracuse, N.Y.), 1966. (*DA* 27:4093A)
88. VOSS, DONALD HENRY. *The Relationship of Environmental Change to Student Performance and Attrition.* Doctor's thesis, Michigan State University (East Lansing, Mich.), 1966. (*DA* 28:790A)
89. COHEN, ROGER D. *Students and Colleges: Need-Press Dimensions for the Development of a Common Framework for Characterizing Students and Colleges.* Doctor's thesis, Syracuse University (Syracuse, N.Y.), 1967. (*DA* 28:1534A)
90. DWORKIN, SAMUEL F. "Personality Interactions With Dental Education: An Hypothesis and Exploratory Study." *J Dental Ed* 31:368–77 S '67. *
91. GODBOLD, DONALD HORACE. *A Comparison of Attitudes Towards School, Self-Perception, and Achievement of Eighth Grade Pupils Attending Junior High Schools in Communities of Different Levels of Economic Affluence.* Doctor's thesis, University of Michigan (Ann Arbor, Mich.), 1967. (*DA* 28:3460A)
92. NEWPORT, DONALD LEE. *An Ecological Analysis of Factors Related to the Habituation Process of Students Transferring to the University of Michigan.* Doctor's thesis, University of Michigan (Ann Arbor, Mich.), 1967. (*DA* 28:1996A)
93. OUZTS, DAMARIS HOLLAND. *Relationships Among Types and Levels of Teacher Training and the Acceptance and Knowledge of Exceptional Children.* Doctor's thesis, University of Georgia (Athens, Ga.), 1967. (*DA* 28:4388A)
94. WEBB, SAM C. *The Relations of College Grades and Personal Qualities Considered Within Two Frames of Reference.* Multivariate Behavioral Research Monographs, No. 67-2. Ft. Worth, Tex.: Texas Christian University Press, 1967. Pp. 53. * (*PA* 42:9511)
95. BENNETT, JAMES WELDON. *The Interrelationship of College Press, Student Needs, and Academic Aptitudes as Measured by Grade Point Average in a Southern Denominational College.* Doctor's thesis, North Texas State University (Denton, Tex.), 1968. (*DA* 29:474A)
96. CROWDER, TRUMAN HOMER, JR. *The Dental Student and Social Responsibility: A Study of the Personality Needs and Environmental Pressures Within a Dental School.* Doctor's thesis, University of Alabama (University, Ala.), 1968. (*DA* 29:1421A)
97. EUBANK, JOHN YOUNG, JR. *The Relationship Between Preconception and Conception of Environment and Academic Achievement of High Ability Male Students.* Doctor's thesis, University of Tennessee (Knoxville, Tenn.), 1968. (*DA* 29:3871A)
98. HAMM, BETTY HUGHIE. *A Study of Enrollee Characteristics in Schools of Nursing in Georgia.* Doctor's thesis, University of Georgia (Athens, Ga.), 1968. (*DA* 29:4324A)
99. HEDLEY, WILLIAM HENRY. *Freshman Survival and Attrition at a Small, Private, Liberal-Arts College: A Discriminant Analysis of Intellectual and Nonintellectual Vari-*

ables. Doctor's thesis, Washington State University (Pullman, Wash.), 1968. (*DA* 29:461A)

100. KING, STANLEY H. "Characteristics of Students Seeking Psychiatric Help During College." *J Am Col Health Assn* 17:150–6 D '68. *

101. KIRKPATRICK, PAUL RUCKER. *Staff Selection for Men's Residence Hall Programs From Undergraduate and First-Year Graduate Students.* Doctor's thesis, University of Arkansas (Fayetteville, Ark.), 1968. (*DA* 29:1366A)

102. MCKEEL, JAMES THOMAS, JR. *A Study of the Relationship of Personality Needs, Environmental Presses, and Need-Press Interaction to the Academic Performance of Engineering Students at the Pennsylvania State University.* Doctor's thesis, Pennsylvania State University (University Park, Pa.), 1968. (*DAI* 30:107-A)

103. MATIS, EDWARD EUGENE. *An Analysis of Differences in Interests, Personality Needs, and Personality Structures Between College Women Majoring in Speech Pathology and College Women Majoring in Other Professional Areas.* Doctor's thesis, University of Alabama (University, Ala.), 1968. (*DA* 29:4290A)

104. MITCHELL, JAMES V. "The Identification of Student Personality Characteristics Related to Perceptions of the School Environment." *Sch R* 76:50–9 Mr '68. * (*PA* 43:3006)

105. RIDDLE, LYNNE. *Relationships Between Physical Education Activity Preference, Socioeconomic Status, and Personality Needs of Freshman and Sophomore College Women.* Doctor's thesis, Syracuse University (Syracuse, N.Y.), 1968. (*DAI* 30:1005A)

106. SINCO, EDELMIRA D. *Student Needs and College Environments of Selected Universities in the Philippines.* Doctor's thesis, Michigan State University (East Lansing, Mich.), 1968. (*DAI* 30:141A)

107. TILLER, THOMAS COLUMBUS, JR. *A Study at Lynchburg College of the Relationship Between Congruence and Non-Congruence of Student Needs With College Environmental Press and Selected Attitudes and Behaviors.* Doctor's thesis, Florida State University (Tallahassee, Fla.), 1968. (*DA* 29:1378A)

108. WHISENTON, JOFFRE TRUMBULL. *A Comparison of the Values, Needs, and Aspirations of School Leavers With Those of Non-School Leavers.* Doctor's thesis, University of Alabama (University, Ala.), 1968. (*DA* 29:822A)

109. BAUER, GEORGE RAY. *A Study of the Environment of a High School, Using the Need-Press Construct of H. A. Murray and the Instrumentation of George Stern.* Doctor's thesis, University of Kansas (Lawrence, Kan.), 1969. (*DAI* 30:2367A)

110. BROWN, JOHN MUIR, JR. *Personality and Environmental Factors Related to Success in the College of Engineering at Cornell University.* Doctor's thesis, Cornell University (Ithaca, N.Y.), 1969. (*DAI* 30:979A)

111. EDENS, FRANK NEWTON. *A Study of Relationships of Personality Needs and Biographical Data to Work-Activity Choice in a Selected Group of Physicists.* Doctor's thesis, University of Texas (Austin, Tex.), 1969. (*DAI* 30:5116A)

112. FELDMAN, KENNETH A., AND NEWCOMB, THEODORE M. *The Impact of College on Students: Vol. 2, Summary Tables.* San Francisco, Calif.: Jossey-Bass Inc., Publishers, 1969. Pp. iv, 171. *

113. HUNT, WILLIAM ORLAND. *Academic and Co-Curricular Correlates of College Students' Need-Press Dissonance.* Doctor's thesis, Illinois Institute of Technology (Chicago, Ill.), 1969. (*DAI* 30:2419B)

114. KLEIN, JENNY W. *Maternal Attitude Changes in Nursery Schools for Mentally Retarded Children.* Doctor's thesis, University of Maryland (College Park, Md.), 1969. (*DAI* 30:1869A)

115. LACHICA, GENARO M. *The Relationship Between Factors of Personality and Academic Achievement of Selected Groups of Tenth Grade Students.* Doctor's thesis, Fordham University (New York, N.Y.), 1969. (*DAI* 30:1435A)

116. MARSHALL, JOHN FRANCIS, JR. *Manifestations of Dissonance in "Press" Expectations Versus "Press" Perceptions of College Freshmen.* Doctor's thesis, Pennsylvania State University (University Park, Pa.), 1969. (*DAI* 30:2806A)

117. RICHMAN, JOEL, AND CASSELL, WILFRED. "Needs, Expectations, and Ability in Groups Reporting Symptoms of Physical Illness." *J Col Stud Personnel* 10(4):258–63 Jl '69. *

118. SAUNDERS, D. R. "A Factor Analytic Study of the AI and the CCI." *Multiv Behav Res* 4(3):329–46 Jl '69. * (*PA* 44:1242)

119. TRIMBLE, MAXINE GENEVIEVE. *Measurement of Perceived Campus Press on Three Student Groups at the Kansas State Teachers College of Emporia.* Doctor's thesis, University of Arkansas (Fayetteville, Ark.), 1969. (*DAI* 30:505A)

120. WEISBERG, MICHAEL. *A Study of the Relationships Among High School Learning Environments, Student Needs and Academic Achievement.* Doctor's thesis, University of Rochester (Rochester, N.Y.), 1969. (*DAI* 31:650A)

121. YUFIT, ROBERT I. "Variations of Intimacy and Isolation." *J Proj Tech & Pers Assess* 33(1):49–58 F '69. * (*PA* 43:9700)

122. BUHL, ANTHONY JOSEPH. *The Compared Perceptions of a Senior High School by Teachers and Students as Measured by the Stern High School Characteristics Index.* Doctor's

thesis, Oregon State University (Corvallis, Ore.), 1970. (*DAI* 31:3331A)

123. CHAMBLISS, CHARLES ALVAH. *The Use of Personality Variables and Personal Data in Predicting Student Preference for a Proposed Set of Degree Requirements.* Doctor's thesis, University of Arkansas (Fayetteville, Ark.), 1970. (*DAI* 31:1031A)

124. HANSEN, JAMES C., AND WARNER, RICHARD W., JR. "Environmental Press, Student Needs, and Academic Adjustment." *J Ed Res* 63(9):404–6 My–Je '70. * (*PA* 46:5427)

125. LAWLOR, GEORGE F. "An Analysis of Institutional Press in a College of Business Administration." *J Exp Ed* 38(3): 48–53 sp '70. *

126. PEARSON, PAMELA H. "Relationships Between Global and Specified Measures of Novelty Seeking." *J Consult & Clin Psychol* 34(2):199–204 Ap '70. * (*PA* 44:10438)

127. SHOCKLEY, VERNON LEE. *An Analysis of Differences Between Baccalaureate and Associate Students in Terms of Academic Press Expectations, Personality Needs and Related Academic Achievement.* Doctor's thesis, Pennsylvania State University (University Park, Pa.), 1970. (*DAI* 31:2711A)

128. STERN, GEORGE G. *People in Context: Measuring Person-Environment Congruence in Education and Industry.* New York: John Wiley & Sons, Inc., 1970. Pp. xxvi, 402. *

129. WHISENTON, JOFFRE T., AND LOREE, M. RAY. "A Comparison of the Values, Needs, and Aspirations of School Leavers With Those of Non-School Leavers." *J Negro Ed* 39(4):325–32 f '70. * (*PA* 45:10943)

WILBUR L. LAYTON, *Vice President for Student Affairs and Professor of Psychology, Iowa State University, Ames, Iowa.*

The *Stern Activities Index,* purporting to measure 30 personal needs derived from the theorizing of Murray, was developed for use in research on person-environment interaction. Needs, according to Stern, are "taxonomic classification of the characteristic spontaneous behaviors manifested by individuals in their life transactions." Personality tests according to Stern are "indexes of cognitive organization, of anticipated responses in hypothetical environments." What do the preceding two sentences mean? To this reviewer there is a logical inconsistency between "spontaneous behaviors" and "cognitive organization of anticipated responses," but let us look at Stern's "personality test" purporting to measure needs to seek clarification of the meaning of the sentences.

The *Stern Activities Index* is a self-administered questionnaire consisting of 300 items distributed among 30 need scales of ten items each. The items describe activities or events. The examinee responds "L" if the item describes something he would like, enjoy, or find more pleasant than unpleasant, and "D" if the item describes something he would dislike, reject, or find more unpleasant than pleasant. "Being quite changeable in my likes and dislikes" is item 6 of the index!

The prototype of the Activities Index, the Interest Index, was developed from a pool of over 1,000 items describing activities and feelings which appeared to represent unambiguous manifestations of need processes as judged by eight psychologists. Two assumptions underlie this procedure according to Stern: characteristic classes of interactions as conceptualized by need constructs are reflected in specific activities; and the manifestation of interest in these activities is an index to actual participation in such interactions. The Interest Index was revised several times and renamed the Activities Index in 1953. The present version, Form 1158, derived from analyses of all the preceding forms in some unspecified manner.

Form 1158 was administered to students in over 100 institutions. A total of 1,076 student questionnaires were identified from 23 colleges in a haphazard sample. Men and women were about equally represented in the group. Nearly four-fifths of the group were seniors, and most of the rest were juniors, "except for a small number of sophomores who were also inadvertently included." Item analyses, estimation of reliability of the 30 scales, and a factor analysis executed by Saunders (*118*) were based on this group.

The norms for the 30 needs scales and the 12 first order and four second order factor scales were based on the group of 1,076 cases. The norms for individuals should be viewed as tentative because of the haphazard sampling. No norms are provided for institutions even though Stern makes institutional comparisons in his research.

Item discrimination indexes were computed for each item. The index was the proportion of persons answering an item in the scored direction in the upper and lower 27 percent of scores on a given scale. The score on the item itself was left in when determining the total score on the scale. Thus, the item indices are spuriously high. Remember, there are only ten items in a scale. Given ten uncorrelated items of equal difficulty, the spurious item criterion coefficient would be .32. The average coefficients for the 30 scales reported by Stern ranged from .27 to .81 with a grand mean of .57. Seemingly, no attempt was made to increase the rather low internal consistency of the 30 scales through selection on the basis of item analysis data and the tryout of new items. The item data presented add little to an understanding of the measurement characteristics of the 30 need scales.

The SAI is subject to response distortion. As reported by Stern, Schultz found that students were able to select responses reflecting a given personality type described to them in behavioral terms, but were not able to slant responses for occupational types.

The correlations between needs scores as freshmen and Social Acceptability (Desirability?) ratings of the needs scores obtained in the sophomore year from a group of 250 students were extremely high, averaging .82, and the correlation between means of scales scored for needs and also scored for Social Acceptability is .74. Given the reliabilities of the scales, one wonders if there is any variance not accounted for by Social Acceptability.

RELIABILITY. The K-R 20 reliabilities of the 30 need scales range from .40 to .88, with mean, median, and mode falling in the low .70's. Test-retest reliabilities are somewhat lower. The reliabilities for 14 of the scales fall below .70. Five of the scales have reported reliabilities of .80 or above. Some of the reliabilities reported are fairly good for ten-item scales, but the scales should be used only in differentiating groups and not for assessing individuals.

VALIDITY. Validity exists for the extent to which the test author is able to identify the sources of variance in test scores and hence give meaning to the scores. As indicated above, eight psychologists agreed that the 300 items included reflect the 30 needs supposedly measured by the SAI.

Stern discusses two kinds of validity. The first of these is validation by equivalence. Equivalent validity according to Stern is the agreement of a given appraisal with other appraisals, either objective or judgmental. The second kind of validity is validation by consequence. It is evident if some form of consequent behavior which was predicted to occur by the appraiser does occur. The evidence for validity offered by Stern is meager.

As evidence for equivalent validity, Stern reports Scanlon's study of a class of medical students and Mueller's study of counselors. In Scanlon's research the SAI profiles of 76 subjects "were classified by vector summaries into ten subgroups and compared with student ratings of personality characteristics of classmates assigned to each group." Differences between vector subgroup ratings were significant beyond the .001 level and significant positive correlations were obtained between rating and vector angle.

Mueller identified 11 subjects with maximally distinctive SAI summary vectors from a population of 50 certified secondary school counselors.

Judges' efforts to predict the counselors' SAI responses on the basis of tapes of their interviews with clients were successful, but were accounted for by only six scales. Furthermore, the judges varied considerably in their relative accuracy among each of these individual variables.

Stern summarizes a number of studies that have shown differences between several occupational and professional groups on various scales on the SAI. The fact that there are group differences on the SAI scales does not directly validate the scales in terms of the labels applied to them. The Activities Index may have some practical validity in the sense of being able to differentiate amongst various kinds of groups, but the *Strong Vocational Interest Blank* does a more impressive job!

It is unfortunate that there is no more evidence for construct validity for the SAI scales than is presented by Stern for, as it is, one is prone to attribute more psychological meaning to scale differences than is warranted by the evidence presented.

Saunders (*118*) factor analyzed the SAI and CCI (*College Characteristics Index*) scale scores of the sample of 1,076 men and women from 23 schools. Twelve SAI factors and 11 CCI factors were identified. The 12 SAI factors were refactored yielding four second order dimensions labelled Achievement Orientation, Dependency Needs, Emotional Expression and Educability. The Educability factor partially overlapped Achievement Orientation and Dependency Needs.

Stern has demonstrated that the Activities Index factor scales do differentiate the student bodies of various kinds of colleges classified by administrative types, for example, liberal arts colleges versus state universities and denominational colleges. Although this fact is interesting, it does not add much to the psychological meaning of the various scales.

This reviewer recommends that the *Stern Activities Index* not be used in an attempt to assess the needs or other personality characteristics of individuals. The low reliabilities of the scales, their susceptibility to response distortion, and the lack of evidence of substantial validity, indicate the need for psychometric refinement of the index. The use of the index in further research aimed at differentiating groups should await the development of a better instrument.

RODNEY W. SKAGER, *Associate Professor of Education, University of California, Los Angeles, California.*

The *Stern Activities Index* was constructed to provide a profile of the kinds of activities persons like to engage in as an expression of their individual personality needs. The instrument is meant to be used along with one of four other indices designed to reveal the extent to which a given institution (university, high school, evening or day school, or generalized organization) facilitates the behavioral expression of those needs. The SAI should not be evaluated solely on its merits as a personality inventory, but rather in terms of the information provided when used in conjunction with one of the other instruments.

The SAI contains 300 items describing behavioral manifestations of 30 personality needs. The items were selected from a large pool on the basis of the unanimous agreement by eight psychologists that each provided an unambiguous measure of a need process. A like-dislike response format is used without an indifferent category, a requirement which frequently forced this reviewer to make a difficult choice between two extreme categories, neither of which was applicable. The author's argument that the 2-choice format produces the same "results" does not compensate for the difficulty caused the examinee. Moreover, using the like-dislike response mode, rather than one in which the examinee indicates the relative frequency that a given behavior is manifested, can cause confusion. For example, on a number of items this reviewer was uncertain about giving a very hypothetical "like" response to an activity he seldom or never engages in, and vice versa.

Norms, reliability estimates, and profiles by which the scales are combined into first and second order factor composites are based on data from 1,076 cases from 23 colleges, all collected before 1961. This sample, in addition to being dated, is not representative of U.S. institutions of higher education either in terms of type or geographical distribution. For example, large private institutions are not represented and large state universities are vastly underrepresented. K-R 20 reliabilities of the 30 ten-item scales vary from .40 to .88 with a mean of .71. Since each scale has only 10 items these reliabilities are relatively high, although the suitability of many of the scales for individual diagnosis is certainly open to question.

At the time of this review a complete and up-to-date test manual was not available. A concise summary of descriptive, scoring, and technical information is badly needed. A vast amount of information on this extensively researched instrument is available, however, in the author's *People in Context* (*128*). Much of this information bears on the validity of the instrument as used in conjunction with the *College Characteristics Index* (CCI). This book also summarizes the factor analytic treatment of the data used to construct group and individual factor score profiles. The former can be used to contrast institutions or groups within institutions in terms of patterns of personality needs. The profiles group 12 first order factor scales under three second order factors. Interpretation of the resulting profiles is considerably complicated by the fact that four of the first order factor scales appear on two of the second order scales, *but with signs reversed*. For example, three of the seven scales on the second order Dependency factor are plotted in the opposite direction from the one in which they appear on the other two second order factors. What goes up in this case must go down, often producing spectacular peaks and valleys in the profile via what can only be characterized as a psychometric sleight of hand.

A variety of validity information is available on the SAI. Dealing first with factors which may produce response distortion, one study shows a correlation of .74 between mean SAI scale scores and mean social desirability ratings for 250 students. While this high a relationship might seem damning to some, one can always argue, as does Stern, that people merely see their own personal characteristics as desirable. With respect to faking, one study shows that students were unable to distort the profiles when instructed to take the test twice while role playing two different occupations. Profiles were markedly different, however, when a second group of students was instructed to contrast aggressive and withdrawn personality types.

A very large number of validity studies have revealed that the SAI does distinguish between the student bodies in different types of institutions (such as liberal arts vs. denominational), between the two sexes, between students with differing majors (across colleges), and the like. A less numerous group of validity studies provides some evidence of construct validity. These involved testing predictions that groups having

certain SAI profiles would behave in certain ways, based on assumptions about what the SAI measures. Another type of information, of a more qualitative type, is provided by SAI profiles of students in individual colleges or types of colleges, which, when interpreted, seem consistent with what one knows, or thinks one knows, about the institution or institutions in question. Finally, factor scores for institutions based on a joint analysis of SAI and CCI (environmental data) show patterns which one might predict based on general knowledge about the institutions involved. For example, institutions like Bennington and Bryn Mawr are high on an Intellectual Culture factor.

An assumption basic to the use of the SAI along with one of the related environment or press indices such as the CCI is that the environment presents "conditions that represent impediments to a need as well as those that are likely to facilitate its expression." This reviewer infers that a basic rationale underlying the construction of the SAI and its related instruments is the assumption that people will be more productive, more satisfied, or happier in environments whose press matches their personal pattern of needs. It would seem that an important consideration bearing on the joint validity of the instruments would be an empirical test of this assumption. This reviewer failed to locate such information. In fact, the relationship between needs and press, as measured by the two instruments, is very complex indeed. The author stresses that a one-to-one correspondence between need (SAI) and press (CCI) scales (the latter written to parallel need scales) does not exist. Moreover, for individual subjects correlations between need and press approximate zero, though there are positive correlations between the SAI and CCI for institutional means for student groups across and within colleges. Since the modern higher educational institution is composed of so many subcultures it would seem essential that the above assumption be tested. For one thing, a given individual could easily find a compatible student-faculty subculture facilitating the expression of his own needs, though the dominant institutional press is of a different nature. More fundamentally, the assumption that it is better if need and press as measured by the SAI and CCI are congruent for a given individual does need to be tested.

The SAI is a carefully researched instrument

in spite of the gaps noted above. Its main use appears to have been in institutional research, although one clinical investigation on a single individual is reported in Stern's book. Whether or not one should use this particular test and its associated environmental indices depends on what one wants to find out. If one is interested in describing students and their institution in terms of traditional personality variables like needs for achievement, aggression, reflectiveness, and the like, then the SAI is as good or better a choice than any other instrument measuring similar factors. But in an age when college students are so saliently characterized by ideological imperatives, alienation, activism and dropping out, the variables measured by the SAI seem to harken from a rather distant and far more comfortable past.

For additional reviews, see B594 (3 excerpts).

[143]

*Stern Environment Indexes. Grades 9–13, 13–16, adults, employees; 1957–70; SEI; environmental press (see 142 for a related test of personal needs covering the same areas); 30 press scores (abasement-assurance, achievement, adaptability-defensiveness, affiliation, aggression-blame avoidance, change-sameness, conjunctivity-disjunctivity, counteraction, deference-restiveness, dominance-tolerance, ego achievement, emotionality-placidity, energy-passivity, exhibitionism-inferiority avoidance, fantasied achievement, harm avoidance-risk taking, humanities and social science, impulsiveness-deliberation, narcissism, nurturance, objectivity-projectivity, order-disorder, play-work, practicalness-impracticalness, reflectiveness, science, sensuality-puritanism, sexuality-prudishness, supplication-autonomy, understanding) for each index plus press factor scores and composite culture factor scores based on combinations of environmental press scores with needs scores specific to each edition as listed below; 4 editions; *c* for research use only; research report entitled *People in Context* ('70, see *141* below); NCS profile ('63, 1 page) for any norm group; separate answer sheets (Digitek, IBM 1230, NCS) must be used; 25¢ per test; $3.50 per 50 NCS answer sheets; 7¢ per Digitek answer sheet; 5¢ per IBM 1230 answer sheet; 5¢ per profile sheet; $6 per set of NCS hand scoring stencils; postage extra; NCS scoring service, 50¢ to 80¢ per test; (20–90) minutes; profiles for *b* and Digitek and IBM answer sheets available only from Psychological Research Center; other materials distributed by National Computer Systems. *

a) HIGH SCHOOL CHARACTERISTICS INDEX. Grades 9–13; 1960–70; HSCI; Form 960 ('64, 7 pages, identical with form copyrighted in 1960 except for format and directions); 40 scores: 30 press scores listed above, 7 factor scores (intellectual climate, expressiveness, group life, personal dignity, achievement standards, orderliness, practicalness) based on combinations of the press scores, and 3 second-order factor scores (development press, orderliness, practicalness); George G. Stern.

b) COLLEGE CHARACTERISTICS INDEX. Grades 13–16; 1957–70; CCI; 1 form ('58, 7 pages); 49 scores: 30 press scores listed above, 11 factor scores (aspiration level, intellectual climate, student dignity, academic climate, academic achievement, self-expression, group life, academic organization, social form, play-work, vocational climate) based on combinations of the press scores, 3 second-order factor scores (intellectual climate, non-intellectual climate, impulse control), and 5 composite culture factor scores (expressive, intellectual, protective, vocational, collegiate) based on combinations of need scores with press scores; norms booklet ('58, 60 pages) for CCI and *Stern Activities Index;* scale score profiles (1 page): individual ('63), group ('66); factor score profiles (1 page): individual ('66), group ('63), blank ('66); culture factor profiles (1 page): individual ('68), group ('68), blank ('68), vectors ('68), circumplex ('66) based on CCI and *Stern Activities Index;* norms booklet free on request from Psychological Research Center; George G. Stern and C. Robert Pace.

c) EVENING COLLEGE CHARACTERISTICS INDEX. Adults; 1961–70; ECCI; Form 161 ('61, 7 pages); 30 press scores as listed above; George G. Stern, Clifford L. Winters, Jr., N. Sidney Archer, and Donald L. Meyer.

d) ORGANIZATIONAL CLIMATE INDEX. Employees; 1958–70; OCI; Form 1163 ('63, 7 pages); three norm groups; school districts: 47 scores: 30 press scores listed above, 6 factor scores (intellectual climate, achievement standards, practicalness, supportiveness, orderliness, impulse control) based on combinations of the press scores, 2 second-order factor scores (development press, control press), 6 composite culture factor scores (protective, achievement, development, emotional, friendliness, submissiveness) based on combinations of the need and press scores, 3 second-order composite culture factor scores (conventional, expressive, warmth); Peace Corps: 38 scores: 30 press scores listed above, 6 factor scores (group life vs. isolation, intellectual climate, personal dignity, achievement standards, orderliness, impulse control) based on combinations of the press scores, 2 second-order factor scores (development press, control press); Peace Corps factor score profile ('66, 1 page); industrial sites: 38 scores: 30 press scores listed above, 6 factor scores (intellectual climate, organizational effectiveness, personal dignity, orderliness, work, impulse control) based on combinations of the press scores, 2 second-order factor scores (development press, control press); industrial factor score profile ['66, 1 page]; George G. Stern and Carl R. Steinhoff.

REFERENCES

1–19. See 6:92.
20–84. See P:256, also includes a cumulative name index to the first 84 references for this test.
85. DUCANIS, ALEX J. *An Investigation of Institutional Environment and Student Satisfaction.* Doctor's thesis, University of Pittsburgh (Pittsburgh, Pa.), 1961. (*DA* 22:3935)
86. BREWER, JUNE HARDEN. *An Ecological Study of the Psychological Environment of a Negro College and the Personality Needs of Its Students.* Doctor's thesis, University of Texas (Austin, Tex.), 1963. (*DA* 24:2777)
87. RAINES, BILL. "An Approach to Practicum for the Elementary School Counselor." *Personnel & Guid J* 43:57–9 S '64. *
88. ROWE, FREDERICK B. "Stability of a College Environment." *J Col Stud Personnel* 5:242–9 Je '64. *
89. STANDING, G. ROBERT, AND PARKER, CLYDE A. "The College Characteristics Index as a Measure of Entering Student Preconceptions of College Life." *J Col Stud Personnel* 6:2–6 O '64. *
90. STERN, GEORGE G. "B = f(P, E)." *J Proj Tech & Pers Assess* 28:161–8 Je '64. * (*PA* 39:5008)
91. WEISS, ROBERT FRANCIS. *Student and Faculty Perceptions of Institutional Press at Saint Louis University.* Doctor's thesis, University of Minnesota (Minneapolis, Minn.), 1964. (*DA* 26:883)
92. HINER, EDWARD SHELLY. *Differential Need Patterns of Business, Service, and Science Majors in a Catholic Liberal Arts College.* Doctor's thesis, University of Kansas (Lawrence, Kan.), 1965. (*DA* 27:1657A)
93. PERRY, WILMA IRENE. *A Taxonomy of Nonintellective Factors Germane to the Drop-Out Problem: A Study of a Small, Church-Related Liberal Arts College and the Value Pat-*

terns of Its Faculty and Students. Doctor's thesis, University of Oregon (Eugene, Ore.), 1965. (DA 26:5877)

94. BAKER, S. R. "The Relationship Between Student Residence and Perception of Environmental Press." J Col Stud Personnel 7:222–4 Jl '66. *

95. CAUDILL, ANNE CONRAD. Student Perceptions of a Midwestern High School Environment. Doctor's thesis, Indiana University (Bloomington, Ind.), 1966. (DA 28:118A)

96. DAVIS, WILLIAM ROBERT. An Analysis of Certain Relationships Between Student Needs, College Environment, and Academic Achievement. Doctor's thesis, Washington State University (Pullman, Wash.), 1966. (DA 27:2722A)

97. HOOVER, BASIL. College Students Who Did Not Seek Counseling During a Period of Academic Difficulty. Doctor's thesis, University of Florida (Gainesville, Fla.), 1966. (DA 28:1298A)

98. KIRKLAND, MARJORIE CREWS. An Investigation of the Characteristic Needs, Beta Presses, and Certain Resultant Behaviors of Selected Auburn University Freshmen. Doctor's thesis, Auburn University (Auburn, Ala.), 1966. (DA 27: 3272B)

99. MARTIN, GEORGIA M. Differences in Evaluation of College Climate Between Freshman and Senior Women at the University of Georgia. Doctor's thesis, University of Georgia (Athens, Ga.), 1966. (DA 27:4135A)

100. STEINHOFF, CARL ROBERT. Organizational Climate in a Public School System. Doctor's thesis, Syracuse University (Syracuse, N.Y.), 1966. (DA 27:4093A)

101. VOSS, DONALD HENRY. The Relationship of Environmental Change to Student Performance and Attrition. Doctor's thesis, Michigan State University (East Lansing, Mich.), 1966. (DA 28:790A)

102. COHEN, ROGER D. Students and Colleges: Need-Press Dimensions for the Development of a Common Framework for Characterizing Students and Colleges. Doctor's thesis, Syracuse University (Syracuse, N.Y.), 1967. (DA 28:1534A)

103. GODBOLD, DONALD HORACE. A Comparison of Attitudes Towards School, Self-Perception, and Achievement of Eighth Grade Pupils Attending Junior High Schools in Communities of Different Levels of Economic Affluence. Doctor's thesis, University of Michigan (Ann Arbor, Mich.), 1967. (DA 28: 3460A)

104. HAMATY, GEORGE GREGORY. Some Behavioral Correlates of Organizational Climates and Cultures. Doctor's thesis, Syracuse University (Syracuse, N.Y.), 1967. (DA 28:4849A)

105. JOHNSON, RICHARD W., AND KURPIUS, DEWAYNE J. "A Cross-Sectional and Longitudinal Study of Students' Perceptions of Their College Environment." J Col Stud Personnel 8:199–203 My '67. *

106. NEWPORT, DONALD LEE. An Ecological Analysis of Factors Related to the Habituation Process of Students Transferring to the University of Michigan. Doctor's thesis, University of Michigan (Ann Arbor, Mich.), 1967. (DA 28: 1996A)

107. SKORPEN, HAROLD CONRAD. The Impact of Organizational Differences on the Educational Relevancy of University Residence Halls. Doctor's thesis, Purdue University (Lafayette, Ind.), 1967. (DA 28:2077A)

108. WHITE, ANDREW WILLIAM. An Analysis of Environmental Press Differences in Five Institutions Preparing Candidates for a Religious Teaching Order. Doctor's thesis, University of Minnesota (Minneapolis, Minn.), 1967. (DA 28: 3392A)

109. CROWDER, TRUMAN HOMER, JR. The Dental Student and Social Responsibility: A Study of the Personality Needs and Environmental Pressures Within a Dental School. Doctor's thesis, University of Alabama (University, Ala.), 1968. (DA 29:1421A)

110. EUBANK, JOHN YOUNG, JR. The Relationship Between Preconception and Conception of Environment and Academic Achievement of High Ability Male Students. Doctor's thesis, University of Tennessee (Knoxville, Tenn.), 1968. (DA 29: 3871A)

111. HEDLEY, WILLIAM HENRY. Freshman Survival and Attrition at a Small, Private, Liberal-Arts College: A Discriminant Analysis of Intellectual and Nonintellectual Variables. Doctor's thesis, Washington State University (Pullman, Wash.), 1968. (DA 29:461A)

112. KING, CHARLES WILLIAM. Relation of Personal and Environmental Factors to Faculty Service in Church Related Colleges. Doctor's thesis, University of Minnesota (Minneapolis, Minn.), 1968. (DAI 30:94A)

113. LEAFGREN, FREDERICK ALDEN. An Investigation of Images of the University and Student Role Expectations. Doctor's thesis, Michigan State University (East Lansing, Mich.), 1968. (DAI 30:134A)

114. MCKEEL, JAMES THOMAS, JR. A Study of the Relationship of Personality Needs, Environmental Presses, and Need-Press Interaction to the Academic Performance of Engineering Students at the Pennsylvania State University. Doctor's thesis, Pennsylvania State University (University Park, Pa.), 1968. (DAI 30:1077A)

115. MOORE, ALEXANDER M. A Survey of Student Perceptions of the Environment of an Inner-City Segregated High School. Doctor's thesis, Indiana University (Bloomington, Ind.), 1968. (DA 29:4291A)

116. SINCO, EDELMIRA D. Student Needs and College Environments of Selected Universities in the Philippines. Doctor's thesis, Michigan State University (East Lansing, Mich.), 1968. (DAI 30:141A)

117. TILLER, THOMAS COLUMBUS, JR. A Study at Lynchburg College of the Relationship Between Congruence and Non-Congruence of Student Needs With College Environmental Press and Selected Attitudes and Behaviors. Doctor's thesis, Florida State University (Tallahassee, Fla.), 1968. (DA 29:1378A)

118. BAUER, GEORGE RAY. A Study of the Environment of a High School, Using the Need-Press Construct of H. A. Murray and the Instrumentation of George Stern. Doctor's thesis, University of Kansas (Lawrence, Kan.), 1969. (DAI 30:2367A)

119. BROOKER, RICHARD A. Comparative Analysis of the Results of the College Characteristics Index Administered at a Single University. Doctor's thesis, University of Arkansas (Fayetteville, Ark.), 1969. (DAI 30:1354A)

120. BROWN, JOHN MUIR, JR. Personality and Environmental Factors Related to Success in the College of Engineering at Cornell University. Doctor's thesis, Cornell University (Ithaca, N.Y.), 1969. (DAI 30:979A)

121. BUCKLEY, HAROLD DONALD. The Relationship of Achievement and Satisfaction to Anticipated Environmental Press of Transfer Students in the State University of New York. Doctor's thesis, Syracuse University (Syracuse, N.Y.), 1969. (DAI 31:1369A)

122. FELDMAN, KENNETH A., AND NEWCOMB, THEODORE M. The Impact of College on Students: Vol. 1, An Analysis of Four Decades of Research, pp. 355–8, passim. San Francisco, Calif.: Jossey-Bass Inc., Publishers, 1969. Pp. xiii, 474. *

123. FELDMAN, KENNETH A., AND NEWCOMB, THEODORE M. The Impact of College on Students: Vol. 2, Summary Tables. San Francisco, Calif.: Jossey-Bass Inc., Publishers, 1969. Pp. iv, 171. *

124. GANTZ, BENJAMIN S.; STEPHENSON, ROBERT W.; AND ERICKSON, CLARA O. "Ideal Research and Development Climate as Seen by More Creative and by Less Creative Research Scientists." Abstract. Proc 77th Ann Conv Am Psychol Assn 4(2):605–6 '69. * (PA 44:1425)

125. GOTTHEIL, EDWARD; THORNTON, CHARLES C.; CONLY, SAMUEL S., JR.; AND CORNELISON, FLOYD S. "Stress, Satisfaction, and Performance: Transition From University to Medical College." J Med Ed 44(4):270–7 Ap '69. *

126. HUNT, WILLIAM ORLAND. Academic and Co-Curricular Correlates of College Students' Need-Press Dissonance. Doctor's thesis, Illinois Institute of Technology (Chicago, Ill.), 1969. (DAI 30:2419B)

127. KUNTZELMAN, WILLIAM P., AND CAMP, WILLIAM L. "Use of Stern's High School Characteristics Index Survey in Study of Student and Faculty Perceptions." Ill Sch Res 5(2):15–8 F '69. *

128. LABELLE, JOSEPH EMIL. Leadership Patterns of Chief Administrators in Six Christian Brothers' Colleges. Doctor's thesis, University of Minnesota (Minneapolis, Minn.), 1969. (DAI 31:1038A)

129. RICHMAN, JOEL, AND CASSELL, WILFRED. "Needs, Expectations, and Ability in Groups Reporting Symptoms of Physical Illness." J Col Stud Personnel 10(4):258–63 Jl '69. *

130. ROYSE, NYAL DAILEY. A Study of the Environment of Harding College as Perceived by Its Students and Faculty and as Anticipated by Entering Students. Doctor's thesis, Memphis State University (Memphis, Tenn.), 1969. (DAI 30:3799A)

131. SAUNDERS, D. R. "A Factor Analytic Study of the AI and the CCI." Multiv Behav Res 4(3):329–46 Jl '69. * (PA 44:1242)

132. SPEEGLE, JAMES REED. College Catalogs: An Investigation of the Congruence of Catalog Descriptions of College Environments With Student Perceptions of the Same Environments as Revealed by the College Characteristics Index. Doctor's thesis, Syracuse University (Syracuse, N.Y.), 1969. (DAI 31:1026A)

133. WEISBERG, MICHAEL. A Study of the Relationships Among High School Learning Environments, Student Needs and Academic Achievement. Doctor's thesis, University of Rochester (Rochester, N.Y.), 1969. (DAI 31:650A)

134. BRETON, GABRIEL RENÉ. The Influence of Interaction Between Personality and Environment on Educational Outcomes. Doctor's thesis, University of Michigan (Ann Arbor, Mich.), 1970. (DAI 31:2953B)

135. CAMPANILE, SALVATORE C. Prediction of Academic Success and Description of Students in a Comprehensive Community College. Doctor's thesis, Rutgers—The State University (New Brunswick, N.J.), 1970. (DAI 31:3331A)

136. DONATO, DONALD J., AND FOX, GARY C. "Admissions Officer, Faculty, and Student Perceptions of Their College Environment." J Col Stud Personnel 11(4):271–5 Jl '70. * (PA 45:4867)

137. HANSEN, JAMES C., AND WARNER, RICHARD W., JR. "Environmental Press, Student Needs, and Academic Adjustment." J Ed Res 63(9):404–6 My–Je '70. * (PA 46:5427)

138. IANNOTTI, MARY MARGARET. The Relationship Between Certain Noncognitive Factors and the Academic Achievement of Junior College Women. Doctor's thesis, Fordham University (New York, N.Y.), 1970. (DAI 31:3271A)

139. NASIADKA, MARY JAN. *The Relationship Between Perception of College Environment and Scholastic Achievement for Students Enrolled in a Community College.* Doctor's thesis, Fordham University (New York, N.Y.), 1970. (*DAI* 31: 3275A)

140. SHOCKLEY, VERNON LEE. *An Analysis of Differences Between Baccalaureate and Associate Students in Terms of Academic Press Expectations, Personality Needs and Related Academic Achievement.* Doctor's thesis, Pennsylvania State University (University Park, Pa.), 1970. (*DAI* 31:2711A)

141. STERN, GEORGE G. *People in Context: Measuring Person-Environment Congruence in Education and Industry.* New York: John Wiley & Sons, Inc., 1970. Pp. xxvi, 402. *

142. TARASUK, PAUL E. *A Study of the Perceptions of Frequently and Infrequently Counseled Senior Students in Five High Schools for Military Dependents.* Doctor's thesis, University of North Dakota (Grand Forks, N.D.), 1970. (*DAI* 31:2119A)

143. WRIGHT, WILLIAM RONALD. *Environmental Press as Perceived by High School Students and Its Relationship to Organizational Climate.* Doctor's thesis, Purdue University (Lafayette, Ind.), 1970. (*DAI* 31:1562A)

WILBUR L. LAYTON, *Vice President for Student Affairs and Professor of Psychology, Iowa State University, Ames, Iowa.*

It is unfortunate that so much effort and money has been expended on research using the *Stern Activities Index* and the *Stern Environment Indexes* because the psychometric inadequacies of the instruments preclude obtaining substantial research results. The SAI and the SEI were developed to allow research on person-environment interaction. The *Stern Activities Index,* designed to measure personal characteristics, is reviewed separately so no detailed discussion of it is needed in this review except to say it served as a model for the development of the environmental indexes.

The *College Characteristics Index,* the *Evening College Characteristics Index,* the *High School Characteristics Index,* and the *Organizational Climate Index* were developed to measure environmental characteristics, consensual beta press. The concept of consensual beta press derives from the theorizing of Murray (P:P606) and of Stern, Stein, and Bloom (P:P776). Beta press refers to the phenomenological world, the private interpretation each individual makes of the context in which he lives. Presumably, persons to some extent have certain common interpretations of their context. The mutually held interpretation is labeled consensual beta press.

According to Stern, "Press may be defined (like needs) as a taxonomic classification of characteristic behaviors manifested by aggregates of individuals in their mutual interpersonal transactions." Stern believes that press can be inferred from self-estimates of the resources, expectancies, and behaviors likely to be characteristic of others in a given situation and that the press distinctions of interest are sub-

cultural phenomenon, perceptions shared only by persons in the same subculture.

The first three environment indexes developed describe activities and events in different types of academic settings. The *Organizational Climate Index* is more general and presumably can be applied to any organization regardless of setting.

The environment indexes are self-administered questionnaires with the same basic format, each index consisting of 300 items distributed among 30 scales of ten items each. The environmental indexes' scales parallel those of the Activities Index and purport to reflect the environmental press conditions likely to facilitate or impede the expression of the behavioral manifestations of the various needs variables.

The subject responds "true" or "false" to the questionnaire statements. If he thinks a statement is generally true or characteristic of the academic setting, or of the organization, is something which occurs or might occur, is the way people tend to feel or act, he responds "true." If he thinks a statement is generally false or not characteristic of the academic setting, or of the organization, is something which is not likely to occur, is not the way people feel or act, he responds "false."

The *Stern Activities Index* was the model for the *College Characteristics Index,* the first of the environment indexes to be constructed. Each of the 30 needs scales items was reformulated in a parallel version reflecting a collegiate environment. This reformulation presents difficult theoretical considerations. Is there a press analogue of a need for succorance? May there not be several press counterparts for a given need? Stern has not adequately addressed himself to such theoretical questions and, unfortunately, the design of the environment indexes will not permit the collection of data to suggest answers to these questions.

This review will concentrate on the CCI because Stern has given more attention to its development than he has to the other indexes. The shortcomings of the CCI are also the shortcomings of the other instruments.

The present forms of the CCI and the SAI were administered to a haphazard sample of several thousand students in over 100 colleges. From the larger sample were drawn CCI and SAI questionnaires of 1,076 men and women who had completed both. They came from 23 colleges. Nine more schools at which the CCI alone had been given were added to bring the total of CCI cases to 1,993. The sample of 1,076 cases was used for a factor analysis of the SAI and CCI scales by Saunders (*131*). Studies of item and scale characteristics, and norms for the 30 scales and the factor scales for the CCI were based on the group of 1,993 persons.

At first glance, the Activities Index appears to have been intended to discriminate among persons on dimensions of personality and the environmental indexes appear to have been intended to discriminate among organizations, or institutions, or subcultures on dimensions of environment. However, Stern has attempted to use the indexes, personality and environment, to study individuals and groups. Obviously the dual purpose measuring instruments desired by Stern must be standardized with both purposes in mind. Item design and selection, reliability estimation, validation, and norming must all be accomplished in consideration of the two objectives. Stern attempted to standardize the Activities Index and the environment indexes using methods appropriate to differentiation among individuals and ignored the special conceptual and methodological considerations necessary for standardizing instruments useful in differentiating groups. The result is confusion. This confusion is sharply exemplified in Stern's discussion of reliability of the CCI.

Stern analyzed the items of the CCI and the HSCI only by determining item discrimination indexes which reflect the effectiveness of each item in discriminating between the extreme high and low scoring subjects on each scale. As Menne and Tolsma [1] correctly point out, an index reflecting the effectiveness of the item in discriminating among groups is an appropriate one to use in selecting items for instruments like the environment indexes. Menne and Tolsma recommended using as a selection criterion that 20 percent of the total sum of squares for an item be attributable to between groups with the remainder attributable to within groups. In a study of 16 high schools, Tolsma, Menne, and Hopper found that only 12 of the 300 HSCI items met the recommended criterion.[2]

Stern seems to have had some understanding

of the above rationale when he estimated the reliabilities of the scales of the CCI. He used an average of the within-schools item variance as an estimate in the Kuder-Richardson formulas 20 and 21. More appropriate estimates could be made using an analysis of variance method allowing the combination of variance components into the categories of "true" and "error" variance.

Norms for the CCI were based on the group of 1,993 students from 32 colleges. The sample has already been called haphazard, but it should be emphasized that in the case of the CCI the sampling of institutions, as well as persons within institutions, was haphazard. This is crucial for norms for the CCI should have been developed for *institutions* rather than *persons,* as was done. It is misleading to compare institutional averages to norms based on individuals.

The scores of individuals on the scales of the CCI, HSCI, and OCI have been factor analyzed. No factor analyses have been conducted on institutions. Person's scores do cluster and one would expect institutional averages to cluster, also. An item factor analysis based on individuals and on institutions would be highly important in the refinement of the environment indexes because Stern seemingly wants the same instruments to differentiate individuals and institutions.

This reviewer recommends that the environment indexes not be used, even for research. The experience Stern has gained to date might very well be used by him to develop instruments which will have measuring characteristics necessary to accomplish the research aims of Stern and his like-minded colleagues.

RODNEY W. SKAGER, *Associate Professor of Education, University of California, Los Angeles, California.*

COLLEGE CHARACTERISTICS INDEX. The CCI is designed to measure characteristics or "press" of higher educational institutions which facilitate (or, conversely, impede) the expression of each of 30 hypothesized personality needs. It is meant to be used along with the *Stern Activities Index,* a personality questionnaire providing information on the extent to which those same need processes are manifest in the behavior of individuals. Much of the research bearing on the CCI also involves the SAI, so the former is most appropriately evaluated as one of a pair of instruments.

1 MENNE, JOHN W., AND TOLSMA, ROBERT J. "A Discrimination Index for Items in Instruments Using Group Responses." *J Ed Meas* 5(1):5–7 sp '71. *
2 TOLSMA, ROBERT J.; MENNE, JOHN W.; AND HOPPER, GORDON C. "Measurement Characteristics of the HSCI." Unpublished paper presented at the American Educational Research Association meeting, Minneapolis, Minnesota, 1970.

The CCI contains 300 items, answered "true" if the institutional characteristic described in the item is "Generally true or characteristic of the college" and "false" if "Generally false or not characteristic of the college." Each item was written to parallel one of the categories of personal needs measured by the SAI. For example, CCI items written to measure environmental press relating to the need to achieve (SAI) describe tutorial and honors programs, etc. Preferences for an orderly environment (SAI) have their complement in CCI items describing highly structured institutional practices such as assigned seating or attendance taking in the classroom.

CCI norms and one set of reported reliability coefficients were based on a sample of 1,993 students in 32 colleges, all data having been collected before 1961. Although a variety of institutions are represented in the sample, the developer of the CCI does not claim that the sample is representative. Large private institutions are not in the sample and large state universities are very much under-represented. There is strong north and southeastern regional bias as well. Factor profiles which combine CCI scales into first and second order composites are based on a subsample of 1,076 students from 23 institutions on which both SAI and CCI data were available. K-R 20 reliabilities for the 30 CCI scales computed on the smaller sample range from .34 to .81, with a mean of .66. These values are certainly adequate for comparing groups of students, but are not always high enough for reliable use in counseling or diagnosing individual students, if such is indeed, one of the functions to which the CCI is addressed.

At the time of this review an up-to-date test manual was not available. Although a great deal of information on the CCI and the findings resulting from its use is provided in *People in Context* (*141*), a concise and organized manual summarizing descriptive, scoring, and technical information is badly needed. Much of the work reported in *People in Context* in one way or another bears on the validity of the CCI, especially as used with its companion instrument. Factor profiles available for the CCI group 11 first order factors under two second order factors, "Intellectual Climate" and "Non-Intellectual Climate." Interpretation of the profiles is complicated by the fact that two first order factor scales appear on both second order scales,

although with signs reversed, and one first order factor appears on both second order scales bearing the same sign. The resulting factor profiles are thus not independent. Particularly objectionable are the two cases of reversed scales, since this procedure forces the profile to go down on one second order factor where it went up on the other second order factor, often producing interesting but misleading profiles.

Because they are intended to be used jointly, the relationship between SAI and CCI scores is a matter of paramount concern with regard to the validity of both instruments. An initial question in this regard is whether or not individual subjects merely project their own personality needs (SAI) on to their perceptions of the college environment. One study shows that correlations computed across individual subjects at a single institution between needs as measured by the SAI and press on the CCI were generally around zero. A relatively small number of individual items descriptive of the college environment were found to be related to need measures, but these were primarily directed at aspects of the college with which students were likely to be unfamiliar. Similar results occurred for a second analysis of individual students across the 23 institutions of the norm sample. Likewise, the fact that relatively independent SAI and CCI factors resulted from a combined analysis of the two scales was also taken as counterindicative to the hypothesis that perceived institutional press is a simple projection of personal needs.

Another and more extensive type of validity information deals with the extent to which the CCI actually reflects forces operating in the college environment. Such a variety of this type of information is available that its nature can only be indicated by examples. In one study, three types of liberal arts colleges (independent, university affiliated, and denominational) show quite different profiles, with independent schools high on first order factors relating to emphasis on the academic, and low on vocational and social press factors. These results are interpreted to mean that the different types of schools represent an "ecological niche" for different types of students, though data is not presented relating to student satisfaction with the institution. Likewise, within one large university perceived press does differentiate between groups of students in different colleges and schools. Finally, independent measures of college characteristics such as number of Merit Scholars per 1,000 students or mean SAT Verbal score show rather high correlations (.59 and .83, respectively) with a composite CCI "Intellectual Climate" score. This type of information, as well as a variety of other validation findings do, by confirming our expectations, suggest that the instrument reflects differences in institutional climate as perceived by students. What they do not do is tell us anything that is really new, unless we are unfamiliar with the particular institution or student group in question.

The major problem in evaluating the CCI lies in the implicit assumption that a match between need (SAI) and press (CCI) must exist if students are to be happy, or productive, or whatever in the institution they are attending. That this assumption seems reasonable does not establish it as fact. Nor does the additional finding that institutional means on the CCI and SAI tend to be correlated, in contrast to the relative lack of correlation between corresponding scales of the two instruments when based on data from individual students. This does not tell us, for example, that a student with a need to express aggression is really better off in an institution he views as facilitating the expression of that aggression.

Nevertheless, the CCI is an extensively researched instrument and one that is well enough known among institutional researchers to insure some degree of common understanding as to what is being measured. The decision about using the instrument is really dependent on whether one wishes to describe an institution in terms of factors which may facilitate the expression of one system of personality needs, or whether one wishes to view the institution in terms of some other kind of conceptual structure. Certainly the CCI is based on psychologists' notions about how institutions are to be described. Sociologists, anthropologists, and members of other disciplines might tend to select a different framework. Perhaps the most critical issue transcends disciplinary points of view. The forces operating on and within the college in the 1970's are social and ideological in nature. The differences between, say, architects and medical students in terms of perceived press as measured by the CCI do not seem to be nearly so important as the differences between the committed and uncommitted, the alienated

and adapted, with regard to life style, participation in the governance of the institution, and relation to the society at large.

HIGH SCHOOL CHARACTERISTICS INDEX. The HSCI, developed from the parent *College Characteristics Index,* is designed to measure the environmental "presses" operating in a high school which would facilitate or inhibit the expression of 30 personality needs. Where necessary, items from the CCI were rewritten to be appropriate for the high school context, though the parallelism between CCI and HSCI items is ordinarily quite obvious. Respondents are asked to respond "true" if each statement is "generally TRUE or characteristic of your high school" and "false" if the reverse is true. There is no middle or uncertain category.

Data reported on the HSCI in *People in Context* were collected in the early 1960's on 947 students in 12 high schools. The sample was not designed to be representative of U.S. high schools, though the institutions do vary including both public and private (one of the latter a military school) and progressive and traditional. The sample is mainly drawn from the Northeast and includes both urban and suburban schools, probably with a strong middle-class bias.

Reliabilities (K-R 20) computed on the 30 scales over the entire sample varied considerably (.28 to .77), though the typical scale appears to be reliable enough for making contrasts between groups. Other analyses contrasted private schools (high intellectual orientation) with parochial schools (high pressure for dependency), and with public schools (high autonomy). Taken together, these studies do suggest that the HSCI differentiates successfully between differing types of high schools, and in a predictable fashion.

Each of the 30 scales differentiates at a statistically significant level between schools in the sample, though a more intensive study was conducted on four of the schools, contrasting two "creative" schools with two "traditional" institutions. The former, for example, were found to be higher on scales relating to intellectual emphasis, but lower on press to attain purely academic achievement.

Seven first order factors were extracted from an analysis of the scales, and these were further combined into three second order factors (Development Press, Orderliness, and Practicalness). In general, the factor results on the

HSCI are similar to those for the CCI, although the Practicalness factor did not emerge for the latter. Additional factor analyses have been conducted by other investigators with partly different results that might be attributed to different extraction procedures.

It is somewhat early to conclude whether or not to recommend the use of the HSCI in studying the American high school. It does have the advantage of comparability with the CCI, a much more extensively researched instrument. The real question is whether or not one wants to describe the high school in terms of presses favoring the expression of the particular set of personality variables chosen, or in terms of other types of variables. Comments made regarding the CCI are relevant to this point.

EVENING COLLEGE CHARACTERISTICS INDEX. The items on the ECCI were also derived from the *College Characteristics Index* (CCI). The ECCI is actually misnamed, since the content of the 30 scales is geared to any nonresident institution of higher education, including day schools and community colleges. Many items on the ECCI also appear on the CCI, with differences occurring where CCI items referred to practices or events which do not occur in nonresidential institutions.

Norms and reliabilities for the ECCI are not reported in *People in Context,* though there is every reason to believe that reliabilities of ECCI scales would be quite similar to those reported for the CCI. One study relating to the validity of the ECCI is reported showing differences in scale profiles between new and old undergraduate students in one evening college. Since much less is known about the ECCI than about the CCI, the review of the latter should be referred to when considering whether to use this instrument for institutional research or other purposes.

ORGANIZATIONAL CLIMATE INDEX. The OCI is the latest of the environmental indices derived from the CCI. In contrast to the HSCI and the ECCI, items on the OCI are directed at the generalized institutions by avoiding reference to students, educational policy, and the like. However, OCI items were written to be parallel to CCI items and generally so appear on inspection.

Initial work with the OCI involved administering the instrument to three separate groups: (a) all teaching and administrative staff of elementary and secondary schools in a single city school district, with 931 completed questionnaires returned from 43 schools, (b) all participants in some 65 Peace Corps training units at 48 host institutions, with 2,505 questionnaires returned from some 63 training programs, and (c) 223 cases from three widely scattered industrial sites. These data, of course, cannot be considered representative of any definable populations, but do make it possible to contrast three highly disparate groups.

Scale reliabilities (K-R 20) are comparable to those of other environment indices in this family of instruments, ranging, in the case of the school district sample, from .23 to .87, though reliabilities of factor scores combining scales are of course much higher. Separate factor analyses were conducted on each of the three groups, resulting in six factor solutions in each case. There appears to be a good deal of similarity between these three solutions and with earlier factor analyses of the parent CCI. Evidence for validity is similar to that provided for the other environmental indices. For example, two Peace Corps training units show dramatic contrasts in perceived press consistent with independent information on local administrative emphasis. Other kinds of differences were observed in the school sample between elementary and high school climates. Finally, school climates isolated through combined factor analyses of the OCI and the *Stern Activities Index* were found to differentiate between grade levels and to be related to other measures such as pupil achievement and teacher turnover.

The above validating information does suggest that the OCI is capable of distinguishing between institutional environments in ways that might be expected, given other information on the organizations studied. While not as extensively developed, the OCI does draw on a body of information collected about the other instruments in the series, especially the CCI. As in the case of the other instruments, the basic assumption that a match should exist between personality needs and institutional presses does not appear to have been tested in any way, though the assumption sounds reasonable enough. Whether or not one chooses to use the OCI is dependent on what it is one wants to measure. The institutional counterparts of human personality characteristics provide only one framework for describing institutions. The kind of organizational or structural variables which a sociologist might select would certainly pose one alternative.

For additional reviews, see B594 (3 excerpts).

[144]

★**Structured Clinical Interview.** Mental patients; 1963–69; SCI; 11 scores: anger-hostility, conceptual dysfunction, fear-worry, incongruous behavior, incongruous ideation, lethargy-dejection, perceptual dysfunction, physical complaints, self depreciation, sexual problems, total; individual; 1 form ('68, 4 pages); manual ('69, 60 pages plus test); scoring sheet-profile ('68, 2 pages); no reliability data for subtest scores; $7.50 per 25 tests; $3.50 per manual; cash orders postpaid; (20–30) minutes; Eugene I. Burdock and Anne S. Hardesty; Springer Publishing Co., Inc. *

REFERENCES

1. BURDOCK, EUGENE I., AND HARDESTY, ANNE S. "Contrasting Behavior of Normals and Mental Patients on a Screening Interview." Abstract. *Proc Ann Conv Am Psychol Assn* 73:347–8 '65. * (*PA* 39:15859)
2. BURDOCK, EUGENE I., AND HARDESTY, ANNE S. "Behavior Patterns of Chronic Schizophrenics." *Proc Am Psychopath Assn* 54:182–204 '66. *
3. BURDOCK, EUGENE I., AND HARDESTY, ANNE S. "Psychological Test for Psychopathology." *J Abn Psychol* 73:62–9 F '68. * (*PA* 42:7448)
4. ZUBIN, JOSEPH. Chap. 4, "Clinical, Phenomenological, and Biometric Assessment of Psychopathology With Special Reference to Diagnosis," pp. 68–98. In *The Definition and Measurement of Mental Health.* Edited by S. B. Sells. Public Health Service Publication No. 1873. Washington, D.C.: United States Government Printing Office, 1968. Pp. xii, 280. *
5. BURDOCK, EUGENE I., AND HARDESTY, ANNE S. "A Research Tactic for Evaluation of Drug Specificity in Schizophrenia," pp. 174–81. In *Schizophrenia: Current Concepts and Research.* Edited by D. V. Siva Sankar. Hicksville, N.Y.: PJD Publications Ltd., 1969. Pp. vi, 944. *
6. JOHNSON, GORDON. "Differential Response to Lithium Carbonate in Manic Depressive and Schizo-Affective Disorders." *Dis Nerv System* 31(9):613–5 S '70. * (*PA* 45:6533)
7. PLATMAN, S. R., AND WEINSTEIN, BETTE. "The Diagnosis Game." *Dis Nerv System* 31(8):561–6 Ag '70. * (*PA* 45:4547)

DOUGLAS M. McNAIR, *Professor of Psychiatry, Boston University School of Medicine, Boston, Massachusetts.*

The SCI is intended for the screening, evaluation, and measurement of change in psychopathology. It consists of both a standard interview protocol and an inventory of 179 dichotomous (Yes-No) behavioral items. The interview involves 45 specific stimulus questions for eliciting psychopathology, plus standard probes and qualifying phrases for special circumstances. The examiner records his judgments of the subject's behavior as the interview progresses. About two-thirds of the ratings concern verbal and behavioral responses to specific questions. The remaining third of the items require the recording of behaviors appearing at any point during the interview.

There is great merit in using a highly standardized interview for eliciting, measuring, and evaluating the signs and symptoms of psychopathology. By eliminating many sources of bias and error in observations, such a method should prove eventually to be a major step in assuring comparability of the results of mental status examinations from interviewer to interviewer, from rater to rater, and from setting to setting. The authors should be applauded for their efforts and their considerable progress to date. It is the reviewer's opinion, however, that the present form of the SCI should be considered as a preliminary and tentative instrument. Much more research is needed to produce a clinically useful product. Yet even in its present stage the SCI can be considered potentially useful for many kinds of research, such as evaluative studies of therapeutic methods.

Many flaws exist in the present execution of the SCI. A major reservation concerns whether the SCI measures 10 distinct and meaningful dimensions of psychopathology. The 10 subtests are basically clinically rather than empirically derived categories of behaviors. It is difficult to comprehend why many of the items were assigned to specific subtests or, indeed, why many of the items were retained in the rating form. Apparently the main criterion for assignment of items to subtests was the crude procedure of inspecting the correlations of each item with *only* its own subtest score and with the total SCI score. As more than 25 percent of the current SCI items have total score correlations that are equal or higher than their subtest correlations, it appears that clinical or other preconceptions often overrode even this objective criterion. An additional problem is that about one-third of the behaviors rated on the SCI were observed in less than two percent of a patient sample of 183 psychiatric inpatients. Nearly three-fourths of the items in one lengthy subtest (Incongruous Ideation) are of this variety. Almost 10 percent of the SCI items were observed with zero percent frequency! While such rarely observed behaviors can certainly constitute critical pathognomic signs, the authors report no objective basis for determining what if any dimension of behavior low frequency items measure. The above considerations and an inspection of the item-subtest correlations suggest that the internal consistency reliabilities of the SCI subtests (not given) may be unsatisfactory.

Interrater reliabilities of the subtests are given. These vary considerably, from .34 to .93 depending on the sample and the subtest. In general they appear rather low, but not definitely unsatisfactory, for subtests of such length.

Norms for the SCI present another problem. Standard scores and clinical profile charts for nine of the subtests are based on a group of 95 "normal" clients of a vocational counseling agency. No other information is given about the normative group. Standard scores for one subtest are based on the sample of 183 psychiatric inpatients. The unrepresentativeness and the meager size of the normative group are obvious. Perhaps, at this time, it would have been more useful to present tentative norms based on the inpatient sample.

Many mean profiles are presented for various groups of patients. These suggest the SCI has considerable promise as a method for objectively distinguishing various diagnostic groups and for evaluating treatment results. Usually the groups compared are rather small and no tests of the significance of profile differences are offered.

The authors recommend that the SCI be used by psychologists with supervised experience with the technique. No detailed recommendations are offered concerning the kind and amount of required training. There also is no obvious reason why interested psychiatrists should not also experiment with the SCI and, perhaps, further contribute to its much needed development as a clinical and research instrument.

S. B. Sells, *Research Professor of Psychology and Director, Institute of Behavioral Research, Texas Christian University, Fort Worth, Texas.*

The SCI was developed to supplement the *Ward Behavior Inventory,* an instrument that describes "pathological behavior observed naturalistically on the ward." The purpose of the SCI is to "test the readiness of a subject to disclose psychopathology through his discourse in the context of an interview." The authors emphasize that "the SCI is a psychological, not a psychiatric technique."

The test contains somewhat ambiguous open-ended questions that set a relatively mild tone of inquiry but that, nevertheless, provide the subject with an opportunity to express ideation and behavior from which the psychologist can judge the presence or absence of psychopathology. The SCI is intended for use both as a screening instrument (in the community as well as in admission services of hospitals and clinics) and as an assessment tool for determination of changes in psychopathology with the passage of time.

The SCI provides measures of level and pattern of psychopathology. It is comparatively brief and has a generally neutral impact on the subject. It is therefore most appropriately placed first in a battery of tests, followed by more probing instruments to explore the source and depth of the psychopathology uncovered. According to the authors, "the comparatively neutral stimuli used in the SCI are intended to minimize any tendency of the subject toward acquiescence or disavowal."

The SCI consists of an interview schedule together with an inventory of 179 observational and rating items to be marked yes or no by the examiner during the interview on the basis of the subject's answers.

The total score provides an overall measure of severity of symptoms. The items have been rationally clustered into 10 nonoverlapping subtests (listed above) which describe areas of potential psychopathology in psychological terms. Item assignments to subtests were based on clinical and theoretical criteria, and were verified by point biserial correlations which were cross-validated on a fresh sample. Interobserver reliability was based on comparison of the results by two or more simultaneous but independent observers. Intraclass correlations for total scores ranged from .64 to .92 (median .83) for patient groups varying in size from 10 to 83. Interobserver reliabilities for the subtests ranged from .34 to .93 with median .73. Correlations of .35 to .68 were found between the WBI and the SCI in samples of 73 and 16, respectively; "while for an unstructured psychiatric interview with 73 patients the correlation with the WBI was insignificant, only .22" (3).

Although based on relatively small samples, the manual and additional references listed above report an impressive amount and variety of research which demonstrates the usefulness of the SCI to predict improvement in the intensive treatment of schizophrenia, to differentiate the score profiles of clinical groups (manic versus depressed patients, depressives versus schizophrenics, schizoaffectives versus manics and schizophrenics), and to measure changes following treatment.

A strongly recommended use of the SCI is in the screening for psychopathology in the general population, as in epidemiological surveys. Two sets of norms, in terms of standard score equivalents for raw scores, are available for the ten subtests, one for adults and one for adolescents. The total standard score is the arithmetic mean of the subtest scores. The mean standard score is zero and positive scores represent deviation in units of standard deviation. Negative scores are not clinically significant.

In evaluating the validity of the SCI, it is noteworthy that the basic data are observations of behavior in more or less standardized situations rather than diagnostic categories based on psychiatric nosology, which are notoriously unreliable. The SCI appears to reflect scrupulously careful developmental research and is one of the best instruments of its genre to become available.

Brit J Psychiatry 117(537):233-4 Ag '70. J. R. M. Copeland. * The interview....consists of a set of standard, open-ended questions which serve as controlled stimuli to which the subject responds by expressing his ideas and behaviour. The interviewer then makes judgements on the presence or absence of symptoms. No other questions are allowed. * High scores on hospitalized schizophrenic patients are shown to be predictive of poor outcome of treatment. Although depressed patients and those with schizophrenia are clearly distinguished on symptom profiles, the profiles of schizophrenic and manic patients are very similar. Some of the differences which do exist between the profiles of these two conditions are partly due to the selection of patients, e.g. none of the 12 manic patients chosen by them had "perceptual distortion" (i.e. hallucinations etc.), and so, by contrast to the schizophrenic patients, they scored nothing on this subtest. For its purpose this is a well standardized tool, unique among psychology assessment techniques for the care which has been put into producing the present form. It is suitable for the research worker who is willing to undergo the course of training recommended and is interested in assessing quantitative alterations in a patient's or subject's behaviour, or in seeking to discriminate subjects showing abnormal behaviour from a normal population, provided he is content with symptoms spontaneously presented by the patient and is not relying on the interview for making a diagnosis.

J Proj Tech & Pers Assess 34(5):439-40 O '70. Richard H. Dana. * a landmark instrument that enables the functions of a test to be served within an interview format. Of course, this is exactly what we have always *said* we have done with projective techniques for assessment. However, heretofore, our own idiosyncratic clinical prerogatives when combined with an inferential model have obscured consensus and made repeated evaluations, or evaluations by independent clinicians, difficult to compare. Whatever else we do as assessors, we are certainly obligated to monitor those aversive behaviors that define patient status in order to minimize the time period any person spends under the label "patient." * The consequences of using the SCI are immediate. Diagnosis can be accomplished as a reliable practice based on a standardized interview procedure. Diagnosis would then be founded on frequency and kind of aversive behaviors. As a result, we would no longer have to use the Rorschach and TAT for diagnosis per se, but could restrict these projective techniques to purposes that demand an inferential model. I plan to begin this fall (1970) teaching the use of the SCI to second year clinical graduate students who have already become sophisticated in inferential assessment. It is essential that both descriptive and inferential models of assessment be incorporated into our assessment repertoire.

[145]

★**Student Attitude Inventory.** College; 1967; formerly called *Study of Professional Education Attitude Inventory;* for research purposes only; 7 scales: academic, intellectual, political-economic liberalism, social liberalism, pragmatism, dogmatism, cynicism; 1 form (4 pages); manual (36 pages); no data on reliability; no norms; Aus 50¢ per 10 tests; $1.50 per set of scoring stencils; $1 per manual; $2.60 per specimen set; postpaid within Australia; (10-20) minutes; D. S. Anderson and J. S. Western; Australian Council for Educational Research. *

REFERENCES

1. ANDERSON, D. S., AND WESTERN, J. S. "Attitudes of Students Entering Professional Faculties." *Austral J Psychol* 21(3): 291-9 D '69. * (PA 45:6162)
2. ANDERSON, D. S., AND WESTERN, J. S. "State Differences in Authoritarian Attitudes." *Austral J Psychol* 22(3):261-4 D '70. * (PA 46:1842)

[146]

*Study of Values: A Scale for Measuring the Dominant Interests in Personality, Third Edition.** Grades 10-16 and adults; 1931-70; SV, also AVL; for British adaptation, see P:259A; 6 scores: theoretical, economic, aesthetic, social, political, religious; 1 form (identical with test copyrighted in 1951); 2 editions; manual ('70, 29 pages); 96¢ per specimen set, postage extra; (20) minutes; Gordon W. Allport, Philip E. Vernon, and Gardner Lindzey; Houghton Mifflin Co. *

a) HAND SCORED EDITION. 1 form ('60, 12 pages) ;
$4.50 per 35 tests.
b) MACHINE SCORABLE EDITION. 1 form ('68, 8 pages) ;
$7.50 per 35 tests ; scoring service, 45¢ per test ($22.50
minimum).

REFERENCES

1–61. See 3:99.
62–86. See 4:92.
87–143. See 5:114.
144–280. See 6:182.
281–475. See P:259, also includes a cumulative name index
to the first 475 references for this test.
476. GRANT, DONALD LINDSAY. *An Exploratory Study of
Halo Effect in Rating.* Doctor's thesis, Ohio State University
(Columbus, Ohio), 1952. (*DA* 18:1096)
477. WATSON, DOROTHY JEANNE. *Some Social Psychological
Correlates of Personality: A Study of Usefulness of Psychoanalytic Theory in Predicting to Social Behavior.* Doctor's thesis, University of Michigan (Ann Arbor, Mich.), 1953. (*DA*
13:447)
478. LINDZEY, GARDNER, AND URDAN, JAMES A. "Personality
and Social Choice." *Sociometry* 17:47–63 F '54. * (*PA* 29:731)
479. TANNER, WILLIAM C., JR. "Personality Bases in
Teacher Selection." *Phi Delta Kappan* 35:271–4+ Ap '54. *
480. SMUTZ, HAROLD TURK. *Investigation of a Reading Improvement Program in an Industrial Setting, Analyzing and
Comparing the Reading Behavior With Measured Attitudes,
Personality Attributes and Work Performance.* Doctor's thesis,
Washington University (St. Louis, Mo.), 1955. (*DA* 15:1360)
481. KLEYENSTEUBER, CARL JOHN. *Attitudes and Behaviors
of Groups of School Administrators.* Doctor's thesis, University of Wisconsin (Madison, Wis.), 1956. (*DA* 17:797)
482. SHAFFER, CHARLES LOUIS. *Corporate Membership and
Individual Values.* Doctor's thesis, New York University (New
York, N.Y.), 1956. (*DA* 16:2230)
483. VEROFF, JOSEPH. *Development and Validation of a
Projective Measure of Power Motivation.* Doctor's thesis, University of Michigan (Ann Arbor, Mich.), 1956. (*DA* 16:2518)
484. COX, CHRISTINE. *A Study of the Religious Practices,
Values, and Attitudes in a Selected Group of Families.* Doctor's thesis, Cornell University (Ithaca, N.Y.), 1957. (*DA*
17:2703)
485. KEMP, CLARENCE GRATTON. *Changes in Patterns of Personal Values in Relation to Open-Closed Belief Systems.* Doctor's thesis, Michigan State University (East Lansing, Mich.),
1957. (*DA* 19:271)
486. SIMONS, WESLEY STANLEY. *The Personality Characteristics of the Residence Hall Assistant as Related to Job Performance.* Doctor's thesis, Michigan State University (East
Lansing, Mich.), 1957. (*DA* 18:135)
487. PROPHET, WALLACE W. *The Effect of Value on the
Perception of Distance.* Doctor's thesis, University of Florida
(Gainesville, Fla.), 1958. (*DA* 19:1127)
488. BECK, ISABEL HOLDERMAN HANDLEY. *A Study of Criteria of Social Perception and Some Related Variables.* Doctor's
thesis, University of Southern California (Los Angeles, Calif.),
1959. (*DA* 20:2372)
489. GORDON, BARBARA JANE ARTHUR. *The Determination
and Study of Academic Underachievement in the New York
State College of Home Economics at Cornell University With
Implications for Counseling and Admissions.* Doctor's thesis,
Cornell University (Ithaca, N.Y.), 1959. (*DA* 20:1675)
490. MILLER, JERRY LEE LAMASNEY. *Occupational Choice:
The Construction and Testing of a Paradigm of Occupational
Choice for the College Graduate.* Doctor's thesis, Florida State
University (Tallahassee, Fla.), 1959. (*DA* 20:3422)
491. O'HARA, ROBERT P., AND TIEDEMAN, DAVID V. "The
Vocational Self-Concept in Adolescence." *J Counsel Psychol*
6:292–301 w '59. * (*PA* 35:3279)
492. MURPHY, RAYMOND ORIN. *Non-Intellectual Factors in
Early Discontinuances of the 1959–1960 Freshman Class in
Engineering of the Pennsylvania State University.* Doctor's
thesis, Pennsylvania State University (University Park, Pa.),
1960. (*DA* 21:2536)
493. EISENTHAL, SHERMAN. *The Dependence of Visibility of
Values Upon Group Compatibility and Level of Need for
Affection.* Doctor's thesis, University of Kansas (Lawrence,
Kan.), 1961. (*DA* 22:2485)
494. FOWLER, WILLIAM H. *A Comparative Study of Evaluative Attitudes of Outstanding Varsity Athletes and Junior
Varsity Athletes.* Master's thesis, Springfield College (Springfield, Mass.), 1961.
495. PROCTOR, ROBERT ALLEN, JR. *A Study of Attitude
Changes in Theological Students During One Year of Seminary Training.* Doctor's thesis, Temple University (Philadelphia, Pa.), 1961. (*DA* 22:343)
496. DENNY, TERRY PATRICK JAMES. *The Academic Achievement of Roman Catholic Students in Public High Schools.*
Doctor's thesis, University of Illinois (Urbana, Ill.), 1962.
(*DA* 23:155)
497. HUTCHISON, RUSSELL STIRLING. *A Study of the Christian Education of Adults in Relation to the Needs and Values
of Adults in Selected Protestant Churches in Muskingum
County, Ohio.* Doctor's thesis, University of Pittsburgh (Pittsburgh, Pa.), 1962. (*DA* 23:2020)
498. LUBIN, BERNARD; BRADY, JOHN PAUL; AND LEVITT,
EUGENE E. "A Comparison of Personality Characteristics of
Volunteers and Nonvolunteers for Hypnosis Experiments." *J
Clin Psychol* 18:341–3 Jl '62. * (*PA* 39:1811)
499. BECHTEL, LELAND PETERMAN. *Comparative Effects of
Differentiated Teaching Methods on Certain Personality Characteristics of College Students: The Effect of the Traditional
Approach to Teaching Psychology as Compared to an Interpersonal Approach to Teaching Psychology Upon Beliefs, Atti-
tudes, Values and Adjustment of College Students in a Course
in General Psychology.* Doctor's thesis, New York University
(New York, N.Y.), 1963. (*DA* 24:3199)
500. CREEKMORE, ANNA MARY. *Clothing Behaviors and Their
Relation to General Values and to the Striving for Basic
Needs.* Doctor's thesis, Pennsylvania State University (University Park, Pa.), 1963. (*DA* 24:1599)
501. DUSTAN, LAURA CORBIN. *Characteristics of Students in
Three Types of Nursing Education Programs.* Doctor's thesis,
University of California (Berkeley, Calif.), 1963. (*DA* 24:
3697)
502. LYSAUGHT, JEROME P. "An Analysis of Factors Related
to Success in Constructing Programed Learning Sequences."
J Programed Instr 2:35–42 f '63. * (*PA* 38:10415)
503. RAULERSON, AL. "Values of Doctoral Students in Major
Subject Fields." *Fla J Ed Res* 5:37–40 Ja '63. *
504. SOSTEK, ALAN BERNARD. *The Relation of Identification
and Parent-Child Climate to Occupational Choice.* Doctor's
thesis, Boston University (Boston, Mass.), 1963. (*DA* 24:
1690)
505. WHITTEMORE, ROBERT GEORGE, JR. *Modification of Originality Responses in Academically Talented, Male University
Freshmen.* Doctor's thesis, Arizona State University (Tempe,
Ariz.), 1963. (*DA* 25:6403)
506. ADRIAN, MARLENE J. *Selected Motor and Psychological
Changes in College Women.* Doctor's thesis, Springfield College (Springfield, Mass.), 1964.
507. CLEMENTS, BARTON ELBERT. *The Effects of Group
Counseling With College-Bound High School Seniors on Their
Anxiety and Parent-Child Empathy.* Doctor's thesis, Arizona
State University (Tempe, Ariz.), 1964. (*DA* 25:3966)
508. GETZELS, JACOB W., AND CSIKSZENTMIHALYI, MIHALY.
Creative Thinking in Art Students: An Exploratory Study. An
unpublished report to the U.S. Office of Education, Cooperative
Research Project No. E-008, University of Chicago, 1964. Pp.
vii, 202. * (ERIC ED 003 377)
509. GORTNER, SUSAN REICHERT. *Nursing Majors in Twelve
Western Universities: A Comparison of Registered-Nurse Students and Basic Senior Students.* Doctor's thesis, University of
California (Berkeley, Calif.), 1964. (*DA* 25:3971)
510. REDMAN, BARBARA DARLIEN KLUG. *Clinical Nursing Instructors' Perceptions of Students' Attitudes Toward Selected
Interpersonal Relationships.* Doctor's thesis, University of Minnesota (Minneapolis, Minn.), 1964. (*DA* 26:2549)
511. SERVIS, MARGERY ANN. *Qualities Related to Success in
Women's Physical Education Professional Preparation Program.*
Doctor's thesis, Springfield College (Springfield, Mass.), 1964.
512. BITNER, GEORGE HULL. *Religious Attitudes and Values
and Religious Activities and Counseling Experiences of Upper-
class Students at a State and a Church College.* Doctor's thesis,
Pennsylvania State University (University Park, Pa.), 1965.
(*DA* 27:696A)
513. CASHDAN, SHELDON. *Personality and Creativity: A Study
of Talented High School Students.* Doctor's thesis, University
of North Carolina (Chapel Hill, N.C.), 1965. (*DA* 27:290B)
514. HAWKINS, NANCY E., AND MEYER, MERLE E. "Social
Values and Conformity." *Psychon Sci* 2:31–2 Ja 15 '65. *
(*PA* 39:7634)
515. HINER, EDWARD SHELLY. *Differential Need Patterns of
Business, Service, and Science Majors in a Catholic Liberal
Arts College.* Doctor's thesis, University of Kansas (Lawrence,
Kan.), 1965. (*DA* 27:1657A)
516. LIBERTY, PAUL G., JR.; DOUGHTIE, EUGENE B., JR.; AND
EMBREE, ROYAL B., JR. "Value and Trait Comparisons of
Clinical and Counseling Students: An Exploratory Study."
Psychol Rep 17:157–8 Ag '65. * (*PA* 40:846)
517. LUEBKEMANN, HEINZ HERMAN. *The Effects of Selected
Student Teaching Program Variables on Certain Values and
Certain Verbal Behaviors of Student Teachers.* Doctor's thesis,
Pennsylvania State University (University Park, Pa.), 1965.
(*DA* 27:689A)
518. MENDOZA, ANGELITA RODRIGUEZ. *Clothing Values and
Their Relation to General Values: A Cross-Cultural Study.*
Doctor's thesis, Pennsylvania State University (University
Park, Pa.), 1965. (*DA* 26:6688)
519. RAPP, MARJORIE LEE. *Factors Related to the Impressions
Made on One Another by Members of a Discussion Group.*
Doctor's thesis, University of California (Los Angeles, Calif.),
1965. (*DA* 25:7087)
520. ROCHESTER, DEAN EDWARD. *Attitude and Personality
Changes of Counselor Trainees in Eight Academic Year Long
NDEA Guidance and Counseling Institutes.* Doctor's thesis,
Florida State University (Tallahassee, Fla.), 1965. (*DA* 26:
4458)
521. SHEARER, ROBERTA. *A Comparative Study of American*

Graduate Student Friends of Foreign Students. Doctor's thesis, Indiana University (Bloomington, Ind.), 1965. (*DA* 26:5250)

522. SINGH, AMAR J. *Interests, Values and Personality Traits of Students Specialising in Different Fields of Study in University.* Master's thesis, University of London (London, England), 1965. [Abstract: *Brit J Ed Psychol* 39(1):90–1 (*PA* 43:17900)]

523. SMITH, ANTHONY J. "Developmental Changes in Cognitive Balance." *J Psychol* 60:39–50 My '65. * (*PA* 39:14613)

524. WILSON, NORMAN EDWARD. *Personality Correlates of Person Perception Patterns Among School Counselors in Two Advanced Programs of Counselor Education.* Doctor's thesis, University of Texas (Austin, Tex.), 1965. (*DA* 27:123A)

525. ZUSNE, LEONARD. "Metaphysical Parallels of the Study of Values." *Psychol Rec* 15:537–43 O '65. * (*PA* 40:1476)

526. ATTEA, WILLIAM JOHN. *A Study of the Relationships Between Specified Characteristics of Teacher Preparation, Experience, and Values and the Reading Achievement Attained by Pupils in First Grade.* Doctor's thesis, State University of New York (Buffalo, N.Y.), 1966. (*DA* 27:1571A)

527. BANKS, ROBERT RICHARD. *Selected Social and Psychological Variables Related to Role Satisfaction Among Graduate Ministerial Students in a Seventh-Day Adventist Seminary.* Doctor's thesis, University of Notre Dame (Notre Dame, Ind.), 1966. (*DA* 27:2384A)

528. BROWN, L. B. "The Structure of Religious Belief." *J Sci Study Relig* 5:259–72 sp '66. * (*PA* 41:1465)

529. BURNS, ROBERT JOHN. *A Study of the Relationships of Certain Values, Personal Preferences, and Activities of Pre-Retired and Retired Professional Engineers.* Doctor's thesis, University of Michigan (Ann Arbor, Mich.), 1966. (*DA* 27:3717A)

530. CUNNINGHAM, THOMAS SIDNEY. *A Study of Some Family Influences and Other Social Factors Affecting Participation in Religious Activities Among a Group of College Students Professing a Common Faith.* Doctor's thesis, Oklahoma State University (Stillwater, Okla.), 1966. (*DA* 27:4146A)

531. DECKARD, NOBLE SHERMAN. *An Investigation of the Interrelationship of an Individual's Interaction Patterns in Two Different Work Group Settings and His Task-Frame-of-Reference: An Empirical Case Study of Environmental Sanitarians.* Doctor's thesis, University of Washington (Seattle, Wash.), 1966. (*DA* 27:823A)

532. DIENER, RUSSELL EDWARD. *A Comparative Study of Selected Needs, Values, and Attitudes of Negro and White Elementary Education Students.* Doctor's thesis, University of Michigan (Ann Arbor, Mich.), 1966. (*DA* 27:2825A)

533. FALCK, FRANCES ELIZABETH. *An Analysis of Achievement and Attitudes of Freshman Participants in the Federal Work-Study Program at the University of Colorado.* Doctor's thesis, University of Colorado (Boulder, Colo.), 1966. (*DA* 28:1263A)

534. GOLD, JOEL ARTHUR. *The Attitude Toward Government and Values.* Doctor's thesis, Colorado State University (Ft. Collins, Colo.), 1966. (*DA* 27:4574B)

535. HALL, DAVID STANLEY. *Socio-Cultural and Personal Correlates of Differential Orientations of Dental Students to Dentistry.* Doctor's thesis, University of Kentucky (Lexington, Ky.), 1966. (*DAI* 30:2166A)

536. HAMPTON, CAROL DEAN. *An Analysis of Pupil Progress as Related to Selected Teacher Behaviors: A Study of the Senior High School Associate Teachers Enrolled in the Fifth-Year Program in Teacher Education at the University of North Carolina, 1964–1965.* Doctor's thesis, University of North Carolina (Chapel Hill, N.C.), 1966. (*DA* 27:3755A)

537. HARTLEY, EUGENE L., AND SCHWARTZ, SHIRLEY. "Self-Consistency, Value Strength and Aesthetic Judgments." *Psychol Rep* 19:367–70 O '66. * (*PA* 41:565)

538. JOHNSON, RUSSELL MARION. *A Comparison of Gifted Adolescents From High and Low Socioeconomic Backgrounds on School Achievement and Personality Traits.* Doctor's thesis, University of Denver (Denver, Colo.), 1966. (*DA* 27:3226A)

539. KINNICK, BERNARD CONRAD. *An Experimental Study and Analysis of Attitudinal Change Toward Negroes and School Desegregation Among Participants in a Summer Institute Sponsored Under the Civil Rights Act of 1964.* Doctor's thesis, Auburn University (Auburn, Ala.), 1966. (*DA* 27:3315A)

540. LARSON, RAYMOND O. *School Board Members' Values, Belief Systems, and Satisfaction With the School Board Role.* Doctor's thesis, University of Wisconsin (Madison, Wis.), 1966. (*DA* 28:906A)

541. McAULIFFE, MARY EILEEN. *Manifest Anxiety, Ascendance, and Values in Students Planning to Teach.* Doctor's thesis, Northwestern University (Evanston, Ill.), 1966. (*DA* 27:2403A)

542. MEYERING, CHESTER. *Values of Nazarene Seniors in Higher Educational Institutions.* Doctor's thesis, University of Denver (Denver, Colo.), 1966. (*DA* 27:2741A)

543. MILLER, AARON JULIUS. *A Study of Engineering and Technical Institute Freshman Enrollees and Dropouts in Terms of Selected Intellective and Non-Intellective Factors.* Doctor's thesis, Oklahoma State University (Stillwater, Okla.), 1966. (*DA* 27:4050A)

544. MOSES, ELIZABETH. *Master's Students in Nursing Education.* Doctor's thesis, University of California (Berkeley, Calif.), 1966. (*DA* 27:1525B)

545. NELSON, DONALD THEODORE. *The Impact of Foreign Undergraduate Students Upon American Undergraduate Students.* Doctor's thesis, Indiana University (Bloomington, Ind.), 1966. (*DA* 27:2010A)

546. OLDS, CLAIRE MARIE. *Some Immediate Effects of Two Methods of Presenting Information About the Multiple Roles of Women to Selected College Sophomore Women.* Doctor's thesis, University of Denver (Denver, Colo.), 1966. (*DA* 27:4102A)

547. SARGENT, JAMES CURRIER. *An Analysis of Principal and Staff Perceptions of High School Organizational Climate.* Doctor's thesis, University of Minnesota (Minneapolis, Minn.), 1966. (*DA* 27:2344A)

548. SIMONS, JOSEPH BERNARD. *Congruence Between Self and Religious Role Percepts: A Descriptive Study of Satisfaction With the Religious Life Among Seminarians in Differential Stages of Preparation for the Priesthood.* Doctor's thesis, University of Notre Dame (Notre Dame, Ind.), 1966. (*DA* 29:4295A)

549. STRØMNES, FRODE J. "Development and Differentiation of Acquaintance in Engaged and Married Couples." *Scandinavian J Psychol* 7(1):34–42 '66. * (*PA* 40:6581)

550. WHITE, JACK. *The Relationship Between Values and Success in Student Teaching.* Doctor's thesis, George Peabody College for Teachers (Nashville, Tenn.), 1966. (*DA* 27:1289A)

551. AUSTIN, CLYDE NEAL. *The Measurement and Modification of the Attitudes of College Students Toward Older Workers.* Doctor's thesis, University of Houston (Houston, Tex.), 1967. (*DA* 28:5225B)

552. BERTOCH, MICHAEL R. *A Study of the Relationship of Counseling Theory Concepts to the Self-Concepts and Values of Counselors in Training.* Doctor's thesis, Boston University (Boston, Mass.), 1967. (*DA* 29:4272A)

553. BRIDGMAN, JOHN NORTHAN, JR. *Selected Teacher Characteristics and Their Relationships With Certain Behavior Patterns and Teaching Effectiveness.* Doctor's thesis, University of North Carolina (Chapel Hill, N.C.), 1967. (*DA* 28:3524A)

554. CANNON, FRANCES CLAIRE. *Selected Personal Characteristics of Undergraduate Recreation Majors Who Are Successful in a Recreation Curriculum.* Doctor's thesis, Columbia University (New York, N.Y.), 1967. (*DA* 28:3985A)

555. DELL, HELEN LUCILE DAVIS. *The Evaluation of Teaching Procedures Designed to Increase Empathic Ability.* Doctor's thesis, Ball State University (Muncie, Ind.), 1967. (*DA* 29:1447A)

556. EVANS, K. M. "Teacher Training Courses and Students' Personal Qualities." *Ed Res* 10:72–7 N '67. * (*PA* 42:9394)

557. FERRY, ROBERT D. *The Relationship Between the Values of Counselees, Counselors, and Counselors in Role Playing Situations as Measured by the Allport-Vernon-Lindzey Scale of Values.* Master's thesis, Northern Illinois University (DeKalb, Ill.), 1967.

558. KESSEL, PAUL. *Control of Verbal Behavior as a Function of Social Reinforcement, the Subject's Conception of the Interviewer's Values Relative to His Own, and Need for Social Approval; A Psychotherapy Analogue Study.* Doctor's thesis, Temple University (Philadelphia, Pa.), 1967. (*DA* 28:1198B)

559. MAZAK, RUTH MARJORIE JOHNSON. *The Relationship of Selected Characteristics of Junior College Pre-Engineering Students to Their Success and Persistence in Upper-Division Professional Education for Engineering.* Doctor's thesis, University of California (Los Angeles, Calif.), 1967. (*DA* 28:470A)

560. RAMSLAND, DOROTHY ELIZABETH ANN. *Values Underlying Family Utilization of Home Furnishings.* Doctor's thesis, Michigan State University (East Lansing, Mich.), 1967. (*DA* 28:5100B)

561. SCHUBERT, JOE DAVID. *The Impact of Selected Colleges on Students' Values.* Doctor's thesis, University of Southern California (Los Angeles, Calif.), 1967. (*DA* 28:63A)

562. SCHUTTE, EILEEN PAULINE. *Personality Characteristics of Typewriting and Shorthand Teachers.* Doctor's thesis, Northern Illinois University (DeKalb, Ill.), 1967. (*DA* 29:1811A)

563. SEIFERT, KENNETH ROBERT. *Interaction of Political Subsystems: School Administrators and Community Influentials.* Doctor's thesis, Cornell University (Ithaca, N.Y.), 1967. (*DAI* 31:124A)

564. WALKER, JIMMY REEVES. *A Study of Selected Psychosocial Correlates of College Student Subcultures.* Doctor's thesis, Oklahoma State University (Stillwater, Okla.), 1967. (*DA* 28:4883A)

565. WALTNER, SUSAN KAY. *Attitudes Toward Modern Dance Among College Students as a Function of Social Values, Academic Major, and Sex.* Master's thesis, University of Wisconsin (Madison, Wis.), 1967.

566. APOSTAL, ROBERT A. "Student Subcultures and Personal Values." *J Col Stud Personnel* 9:34–9 Ja '68. *

567. BENTZ, V. JON. Chap. 3, "The Sears Experience in the Investigation, Description and Prediction of Executive Behavior," pp. 59–152. In *Predicting Managerial Success.* Edited by John A. Myers, Jr. Ann Arbor, Mich.: Foundation for Research on Human Behavior, April 1068. Pp. v, 173. *

568. BRINK, DEBORA CATHARINA. *The Characteristics of Personally Meaningful Intellectual Experience.* Doctor's thesis, Columbia University (New York, N.Y.), 1968. (*DA* 29:3465B)

569. CLARK, JAMES VAL. *Characteristics Related to Prefer-*

ences for Different Procedural Approaches to Counseling. Doctor's thesis, University of Texas (Austin, Tex.), 1968. (*DA* 29:476A)

570. CURB, LAURA SOMERVILL. *Personality Traits of Elementary School Teachers Who Voted for or Against Sanctions.* Doctor's thesis, University of Oklahoma (Norman, Okla.), 1968. (*DA* 29:2559A)

571. DONAHUE, MARY MARANS. *Personality Differences Between Volunteers and Professionals.* Doctor's thesis, St. John's University (Jamaica, N.Y.), 1968. (*DAI* 30:1863A)

572. EVANS, K. M. "Teachers and Some Others: A Comparative Study." *Ed Res* 11:153–6 F '68. *

573. GETZELS, J. W., AND CSIKSZENTMIHALYI, M. "The Value-Orientations of Art Students as Determinants of Artistic Specialization and Creative Performance." *Studies Art Ed* 10: 5–16 f '68. *

574. GILBERTS, RICHARD ALLAN. *A Comparison of Statistical Models for Predicting Counselor Responses From Personality Measures.* Doctor's thesis, University of Washington (Seattle, Wash.), 1968. (*DA* 29:2091A)

575. GOOD, RONALD GLENN. *An Analysis of the Self-Perceptions and Other Selected Characteristics of Effective and Ineffective Teachers: A Study Based on the Educational Philosophy of the Fifth-Year Program in Teacher Education at the University of North Carolina.* Doctor's thesis, University of North Carolina (Chapel Hill, N.C.), 1968. (*DA* 29:4373A)

576. HARVEY, THEODORE FERRILL, JR. *Relationships Between Body Expression, Graphic Expression, and Personality in Art: A Correlational Analysis.* Doctor's thesis, Illinois State University (Normal, Ill.), 1968. (*DA* 29:3929A)

577. HEIST, PAUL. Chap. 3, "Creative Students: College Transients," pp. 35–55. In his *The Creative College Student: An Unmet Challenge.* San Francisco, Calif.: Jossey-Bass Inc., Publishers, 1968. Pp. xviii, 253. *

578. HEIST, PAUL. *The Creative College Student: An Unmet Challenge,* pp. 214–8. San Francisco, Calif.: Jossey-Bass Inc., Publishers, 1968. Pp. xviii, 253. *

579. HICKNER, MARYBELLE R. *Authoritarianism in Personality Organization of Supervising Teachers as Related to Values and Accuracy of Judgment of Student Teachers.* Doctor's thesis, University of Minnesota (Minneapolis, Minn.), 1968. (*DA* 29:3896A)

580. JONES, MURIEL KATHLEEN. *Esteem Accorded to Clothed Figures as Related to Fashion and Perception.* Doctor's thesis, Ohio State University (Columbus, Ohio), 1968. (*DAI* 30:271B)

581. JONES, RONALD EVERETT. *Characteristics, Perceptions, and Values of Students Who Were Placed on Disciplinary Probation or Suspended at the University of Tennessee During the Academic Years 1964–65 and 1965–66.* Doctor's thesis, University of Tennessee (Knoxville, Tenn.), 1968. (*DA* 29:2481A)

582. KENWORTHY, JOY ANNE. *Personality Characteristics Associated With Effectiveness in Psychotherapy.* Doctor's thesis, Iowa State University (Ames, Iowa), 1968. (*DA* 29:3488B)

583. KING, SHIRLEY PATRICIA. *The Association of Selected Personality Characteristics With College Achievement.* Doctor's thesis, University of California (Berkeley, Calif.), 1968. (*DA* 29:3003A)

584. KINNICK, BERNARD C., AND PLATTOR, STANTON D. "Relationship of Authoritarian, Ethnocentric, and Segregationist Attitudes With Basic Values Among Public School Personnel." *SPATE* 7:22–32 f '68. *

585. LEWIS, KATHRYN LUCETTA. *Correlates of College Choice Satisfaction.* Doctor's thesis, University of Southern California (Los Angeles, Calif.), 1968. (*DA* 29:2095A)

586. LLOYD, THOMAS C. *The Relationship of Selected Characteristics of Teacher Education Students and Selected Measures of Achievement in Teacher Education.* Doctor's thesis, Texas Technological College (Lubbock, Tex.), 1968. (*DA* 29:3332A)

587. McCANDLESS, JANE BARDARAH. *Correlates of Prayer Behavior Among Students at Five Church-Related Colleges.* Doctor's thesis, University of Pittsburgh (Pittsburgh, Pa.), 1968. (*DAI* 30:798A)

588. McCLOUD, WILLIAM THURLOW. *Student Characteristics Associated With Use and Nonuse of Washington State University Student Counseling Services.* Doctor's thesis, Washington State University (Pullman, Wash.), 1968. (*DA* 29:2964A)

589. MARTIN, RAY IVAN. *Prayer Patterns of Ministerial Couples in Worcester County, Massachusetts.* Doctor's thesis, Boston University (Boston, Mass.), 1968. (*DA* 29:1947A)

590. MASER, ARTHUR LYLE. *The Effect of Client Response and Counselor Personality on Counselor Response; and the Effect of Counselor Response on Client Response.* Doctor's thesis, University of Washington (Seattle, Wash.), 1968. (*DA* 29:2096A)

591. MASON, EVELYN P.; ADAMS, HENRY L.; AND BLOOD, DON F. "Further Study of Personality Characteristics of Bright College Freshmen." *Psychol Rep* 23:395–400 O '68. * (*PA* 43:9714)

592. MEHROTRA, CHANDRA MOHAN NATH. *Behavioral Cognition as Related to Interpersonal Perception and Some Personality Traits of College Students.* Doctor's thesis, Ohio State University (Columbus, Ohio), 1968. (*DAI* 30:3~2B)

593. MURRAY, MURIEL ELOISE. *Self-Actualization and Social Values of Teachers as Related to Students' Perception of Teachers.* Doctor's thesis, Pennsylvania State University (University Park, Pa.), 1968. (*DAI* 30:1026A)

594. NEUFELD, JACOB A. *Factors Related to Choice of Transfer and Terminal Status in Junior College.* Doctor's thesis, University of North Dakota (Grand Forks, N.D.), 1968. (*DA* 29:3045A)

595. NORWALK-POLSKY, ZITA. *A Preliminary Study of the Belief Systems and Selected Values and Attitudes of Faculty and Students in a State College for Teachers.* Doctor's thesis, New York University (New York, N.Y.), 1968. (*DA* 29:1466A)

596. OWENBY, DAVID JACK. *Perceptions of Organizational Climate and Leader Behavior in Southern Independent Schools.* Doctor's thesis, University of Tennessee (Knoxville, Tenn.), 1968. (*DA* 29:3810A)

597. QASHU, MARIAN FAYE. *The Relation of Commitment, Creativity, and Openness to Successful Interaction With Children.* Doctor's thesis, University of Arizona (Tucson, Ariz.), 1968. (*DA* 29:487A)

598. RADER, BLAINE BURDETTE. *Identification of Selected Personality Characteristics Which Make for Effectiveness in Pastoral Care.* Doctor's thesis, Drew University (Madison, N.J.), 1968. (*DA* 29:1849B)

599. SHAFFER, ROBERT H., AND DOWLING, LEO R. "Foreign Students and Their American Student Friends." *Sch & Soc* 96:245–9 Ap '68. *

600. SINGH, A. "Interests, Values and Personality Traits of Students Specializing in Different Fields of Study in University." *Ed R* 21:41–55 N '68. *

601. SMITH, RICHARD MORTIMER. *A Study of the Relationship Between Personality Profiles and Vocational Preferences.* Doctor's thesis, St. Louis University (St. Louis, Mo.), 1968. (*DAI* 30:1406A)

602. STILLION, GLENN WAYNE. *Values, Perceptions, and Characteristics of Student Leaders Compared With the General Student Population at Florida State University.* Doctor's thesis, Florida State University (Tallahassee, Fla.), 1968. (*DA* 29:1429A)

603. TALLEY, WILLIAM MARTIN. *An Exploratory Study of the Dogmatism and Values of Persons Who Trace Their Ancestry.* Doctor's thesis, Ohio State University (Columbus, Ohio), 1968. (*DA* 29:3884A)

604. TANSEY, DAVID PHILLIPS. *Altruism and Teacher Behavior.* Doctor's thesis, University of California (Los Angeles, Calif.), 1968. (*DA* 29:1691A)

605. TAYLOR, LUCY C., AND COMPTON, NORMA H. "Personality Correlates of Dress Conformity." *J Home Econ* 60:653–6 O '68. *

606. WALBERG, HERBERT J., AND WELCH, WAYNE W. "Dimensions of Personality in Selected Physics Teachers." *J Res Sci Teach* 5(4):357–61 '6~–68. *

607. WALKER, NORMA PEDEN. *Clothing Expenditures as Related to Selected Values, Self-Actualization, and Buying Practices: An Exploratory Study.* Doctor's thesis, Pennsylvania State University (University Park, Pa.), 1968. (*DA* 29:4836B)

608. WHITE, THOMAS ROBERT. *A Study of the Values and Attitudes of Distributive Education Teacher-Coordinators as Compared to Two Groups of Potential Teacher-Coordinators.* Doctor's thesis, Ohio State University (Columbus, Ohio), 1968. (*DAI* 30:610A)

609. ARMLIN, NELSON JOSEPH. *Four Aspects of Counselor Behavior and Measured Personality Traits Related to the Open-Closed Cognitive Continuum of the Rokeach Dogmatism Scale.* Doctor's thesis, Florida State University (Tallahassee, Fla.), 1969. (*DAI* 30:4213A)

610. BAZIK, ANNA MARIE. *Characteristics of Junior College Male Students Who Seek Counseling Services.* Doctor's thesis, Northwestern University (Evanston, Ill.), 1969. (*DAI* 30:2793A)

611. BOYKIN, JOHN HENRY. *A Comparative Study of Students in Different Fields of Study.* Doctor's thesis, University of Tennessee (Knoxville, Tenn.), 1969. (*DAI* 30:3273A)

612. BRADY, CONSTANCE CLINE. *The Functions, Characteristics and Limitations of Psychological Openness.* Doctor's thesis, Ohio State University (Columbus, Ohio), 1969. (*DAI* 30:4216A)

613. CARLSON, RAE, AND PARKER, JANET. "Personality and Esthetic Sensitivity." *J Proj Tech & Pers Assess* 33(6):530–4 D '69. * (*PA* 44:6749)

614. CHURCHILL, WILLIAM DeLEE. *A Case Study Approach to the Investigation of Parental Influence on the Vocational Attitudes and Values of Adolescent Males.* Doctor's thesis, University of Rochester (Rochester, N.Y.), 1969. (*DAI* 30:3717A)

615. CORNWELL, HENRY G. "Figure Preference and Personality." *Percept & Motor Skills* 29(3):812–4 D '69. *

616. CURTIS, EUGENE LESTER. *A Study of the Differences Between a Group of Community College Students in an Adjustment Skills Course and a Control Group on Selected Personality and Non-Academic Characteristics.* Doctor's thesis, University of North Dakota (Grand Forks, N.D.), 1969. (*DAI* 30:3720A)

617. FELDMAN, KENNETH A., AND NEWCOMB, THEODORE M. *The Impact of College on Students: Vol. 2, Summary Tables.* San Francisco, Calif.: Jossey-Bass Inc., Publishers, 1969. Pp. iv, 171. *

618. FINCH, CURTIS R. "The Trade and Industrial Education Teacher's Background, Values, and Attitude Toward Teaching." *J Indus Teach Ed* 6(2):55–64 w '69. *

619. FITZGERALD, OWEN RAY. *Psychodynamics of Volunteers Serving Overseas: Religious Vocation Workers and Peace Corps Volunteers in a North African Country.* Doctor's thesis, Boston University (Boston, Mass.), 1969. (*DAI* 30:2126A)

620. GARDNER, R. C.; REYNOLDS, A. G.; AND BEINAROVICS, VENERANDA. "Personal Values and the Meaningfulness of Value-Related Words." *Psychol Rep* 24(3):939–42 Je '69. * (*PA* 44:568)

621. GEISS, DORIS THERESA. *Faculty and Administrator Perceptions of the Decision-Making Authority in Collegiate Nursing Programs.* Doctor's thesis, Columbia University (New York, N.Y.), 1969. (*DAI* 30:1359A)

622. GUYER, RICHARD WAYNE. *A Study of Selected Value Characteristics of Secondary Public School Principals in the Greater Indianapolis Area Related to Criteria Expressed by Educational Authorities.* Doctor's thesis, Ball State University (Muncie, Ind.), 1969. (*DAI* 30:4183A)

623. HALL, WALLACE B., AND MACKINNON, DONALD W. "Personality Inventory Correlates of Creativity Among Architects." *J Appl Psychol* 53(4):322–6 Ag '69. * (*PA* 43:15815)

624. HINRICHS, J. R. "Comparison of 'Real Life' Assessments of Management Potential With Situational Exercises, Paper-and-Pencil Ability Tests, and Personality Inventories." *J Appl Psychol* 53(5):425–32 O '69. * (*PA* 44:1442)

625. HOGAN, ROBERT. "Development of an Empathy Scale." *J Consult & Clin Psychol* 33(3):307–16 Je '69. * (*PA* 43:12966)

626. HUCKABEE, MALCOM W. "Personality and Academic Aptitude Correlates of Cognitive Control Principles." *South J Ed Res* 3(1):1–9 Ja '69. *

627. KRATOCHVIL, DANIEL W. "Changes in Values and in Interpersonal Functioning of Counselor Candidates." *Counselor Ed & Sup* 8(2):104–7 w '69. *

628. LARTER, S. J., AND TAYLOR, P. A. "A Study of Aspects of Critical Thinking." *Manitoba J Ed* 5(1):35–53 N '69. *

629. LATHROP, ROBERT CHARLES. *A Study of Various Characteristics of Vocational-Technical Students and Community College Students.* Doctor's thesis, Washington State University (Pullman, Wash.), 1969. (*DAI* 30:4225A)

630. LOWREY, GEORGE ANDREW, JR. *A Multivariate Analysis of the Relationship Between Selected Leisure Behavior Variables and Personal Values.* Doctor's thesis, University of Illinois (Urbana, Ill.), 1969. (*DAI* 30:2867A)

631. MCCLELLAND, MARY ELIZABETH. *An Investigation of Selected Non-Intellectual Variables and Their Relationship to College Academic Achievement.* Doctor's thesis, Michigan State University (East Lansing, Mich.), 1969. (*DAI* 30:2339A)

632. MAGNUSSEN, MAX G., AND KEMLER, WILLIAM M. "Infant Feeding Preference as Related to Personality Test Scores." *J Clin Psychol* 25(3):258–60 Jl '69. * (*PA* 44:3609)

633. MATELL, MICHAEL STEVEN. *The Psychometric Characteristics of Likert-Type Rating Scales Consisting of Two-Through Nineteen-Steps.* Doctor's thesis, Purdue University (Lafayette, Ind.), 1969. (*DAI* 30:4406B)

634. NICHOLS, CHARLIE DONALD. *A Study of Values Among Selected Secondary Teachers and Principals as Related to Success Criteria.* Doctor's thesis, North Texas State University (Denton, Tex.), 1969. (*DAI* 30:2382A)

635. PADOVER, ANN FEINGOLD. *Impact on Attitudes, Personality Factors, and Behavior of an N.D.E.A. Summer Institute for Teachers and Other Professional School Personnel of Disadvantaged Youth.* Doctor's thesis, University of Michigan (Ann Arbor, Mich.), 1969. (*DAI* 30:4780B)

636. REELING, PATRICIA ANN. *Undergraduate Female Students as Potential Recruits to the Library Profession.* Doctor's thesis, Columbia University (New York, N.Y.), 1969. (*DAI* 30:4470A)

637. RHOADES, WILLIAM JAY. *Comparison of Values of Selected Academic Groups of Doctoral Students at Florida State University as Measured by the Study of Values.* Doctor's thesis, Florida State University (Tallahassee, Fla.), 1969. (*DAI* 30:5245A)

638. RICHMOND, BERT O.; MASON, ROBERT L.; AND SMITH, VIRGINIA. "Existential Frustration and Anomie." *J Nat Assn Women Deans & Counselors* 32(3):136–8 sp '69. *

639. ROCHESTER, DEAN E., AND COTTINGHAM, HAROLD F. "A Comparison of NDEA Institute Enrollees With Personnel and Guidance Norms on the Allport-Vernon-Lindzey Study of Values." *Counselor Ed & Sup* 8(3):220–5 sp '69. *

640. ROTHMAN, ARTHUR I. "Teacher Characteristics and Student Learning." *J Res Sci Teach* 6(4):340–8 '69. *

641. ROTHMAN, ARTHUR I.; WELCH, WAYNE W.; AND WALBERG, HERBERT J. "Physics Teacher Characteristics and Student Learnings." *J Res Sci Teach* 6(1):59–63 '69. *

642. SHERMAN, LILLIAN LASKAW. *Movers and Perseverers in Education: An Investigation of Interests, Values, Personality Factors, Self-Actualization, Need Satisfaction and Job Satisfaction Among Movers Into Counseling and Into Administration and Among Perseverers in Teaching.* Doctor's thesis, New York University (New York, N.Y.), 1969. (*DAI* 31:1023A)

643. SPIEGEL, DON, AND KEITH-SPIEGEL, PATRICIA. "Factor Analysis of 78 Variables From Nine Personality Tests and

Scales." *J Proj Tech & Pers Assess* 33(2):160–7 Ap '69. * (*PA* 43:11352)

644. VAN HALL, RICHARD. *The Relationship Between Personality Factors and the Choice of Selected Major Fields in Education.* Doctor's thesis, North Texas State University (Denton, Tex.), 1969. (*DAI* 30:548A)

645. WALKER, RONALD E.; NICOLAY, ROBERT C.; KLUCZNY, RITA; AND RIEDEL, ROBERT G. "Psychological Correlates of Smoking." *J Clin Psychol* 25(1):42–4 Ja '69. * (*PA* 43:9698)

646. WEICK, RAY KAY. *A Study of Personal Values and Their Relationship to Perception of Organizational Elements.* Doctor's thesis, North Carolina State University (Raleigh, N.C.), 1969. (*DAI* 30:4761A)

647. WEISGERBER, CHARLES A. *Psychological Assessment of Candidates for a Religious Order,* pp. 133–9. Chicago, Ill.: Loyola University Press, 1969. Pp. viii, 191. *

648. WELCH, WAYNE W. "Some Characteristics of High School Physics Students: Circa 1968." *J Res Sci Teach* 6(3):242–7 '69. *

649. WHITTAKER, DAVID. "Masculinity-Femininity and Nonconformist Youth." Abstract. *Proc 77th Ann Conv Am Psychol Assn* 4(1):297–8 '69. * (*PA* 43:17481)

650. WITHYCOMBE-BROCATO, CAROL JEAN. *The Mature Graduate Woman Student: Who Is She?* Doctor's thesis, United States International University (San Diego, Calif.), 1969. (*DAI* 31:2973B)

651. ZOLLINGER, LELAND HALE. *A Comparison of Values Expressed by Students in a Seventh-Day Adventist College to Values Held by Students in Other Colleges and Universities.* Doctor's thesis, University of Tennessee (Knoxville, Tenn.), 1969. (*DAI* 30:4702A)

652. ABBOTT, ROBERT D. "Stylistic Response Variance and Trait Inference From the Study of Values." *Psychol Rep* 27(3):911–4 D '70. * (*PA* 45:9982)

653. ADAMS, HENRY L.; MASON, EVELYN P.; AND BLOOD, DON F. "Personality Characteristics of American and English, Bright and Average College Freshmen." *Psychol Rep* 26(3):831–4 Je '70. * (*PA* 45:1256)

654. ARSENIAN, SETH. "Change in Evaluative Attitudes During Twenty-Five Years." *J Appl Psychol* 54(4):302–4 Ag '70. * (*PA* 44:21514)

655. BLOIS, MARSDEN SCOTT, III. *Child-Rearing Attitudes of Hippie Adults.* Doctor's thesis, University of Washington (Seattle, Wash.), 1970. (*DAI* 31:3329A)

656. CARLSON, STANLEY LLOYD. *Differences in Aptitude, Previous Achievement, and Nonintellectual Traits (Personality, Values, Interest, and Attitude Toward Mathematics) of Freshmen Mathematics Majors and Transfers From the Mathematics Major at the University of Northern Colorado.* Doctor's thesis, University of Northern Colorado (Greeley, Colo.), 1970. (*DAI* 31:3768A)

657. DIXIT, RAMESH C., AND SHARMA, DEO DUTTA. "A Study of Student-Teacher Relationship in Terms of Value Incorporation." *J Psychol Res* 14(2):57–63 My '70. *

658. ELLENBERG, NORMAN LESLIE. *The Relationship of Personal Value Systems and Administrative Orientations of Selected Elementary School Principals.* Doctor's thesis, New York University (New York, N.Y.), 1970. (*DAI* 31:2044A)

659. FORTIN, CLIFFORD CHARLES. *The Relation of Certain Personal and Environmental Characteristics of School Librarians to Their Life Values and Work Satisfactions.* Doctor's thesis, University of Minnesota (Minneapolis, Minn.), 1970. (*DAI* 31:3573A)

660. GABLE, MYRON. *The Value Orientations and Actual and Perceived Level of Economic Understanding of New York Businessmen.* Doctor's thesis, New York University (New York, N.Y.), 1970. (*DAI* 31:3411A)

661. GALLOP, R. "A Study of the B.Ed. Student." Thesis Abstract. *Brit J Ed Psychol* 40(2):220 Je '70. *

662. HELSON, RAVENNA, AND CRUTCHFIELD, RICHARD S. "Creative Types in Mathematics." *J Personality* 38(2):177–97 Je '70. * (*PA* 44:18669)

663. HELSON, RAVENNA, AND CRUTCHFIELD, RICHARD S. "Mathematicians: The Creative Researcher and the Average PhD." *J Consult & Clin Psychol* 34(2):250–7 Ap '70. * (*PA* 44:10374)

664. HENRY, GORDON HOWARD. *Open and Closed Mindedness, Values, and Other Personality Characteristics of Male College Students Who Served on or Appeared Before Judiciary Boards.* Doctor's thesis, University of North Dakota (Grand Forks, N.D.), 1970. (*DAI* 31:2106A)

665. JUAN, ISABEL R., AND HALEY, HAROLD B. "High and Low Levels of Dogmatism in Relation to Personality, Intellectual, and Environmental Characteristics of Medical Students." *Psychol Rep* 26(2):535–44 Ap '70. * (*PA* 44:20939)

666. LIND, AMY I. "An Exploratory Study of Predictive Factors for Success in the Clinical Affiliation Experience." *Am J Occup Ther* 24(3):222–6 Ap '70. *

667. LOCKE, CHARLES KENNETH. *Small Group Counseling Compared With Freshman Orientation Classes in Reducing Attrition of Freshman Junior College Students.* Doctor's thesis, North Texas State University (Denton, Tex.), 1970. (*DAI* 31:1576A)

668. LUZZI, MATTHEW HENRY. *A Study of the Relationship of Self-Acceptance and Social Values to Effectiveness of*

Male Rehabilitation Counselor Trainees. Doctor's thesis, Boston University (Boston, Mass.), 1970. (*DAI* 31:2111A)

669. McGowan, Raymond Peter. *Line Managers and College Business Students: A Differential Analysis of Personality Variables and Value Concepts.* Doctor's thesis, St. John's University (Jamaica, N.Y.), 1970. (*DAI* 31:3745B)

670. McKerracher, D. W.; Zwirner, W.; and Harshman, R. C. "Personality and Attainment: A Pilot Study." *West Psychologist* 1(2):62–70 Ja '70. *

671. May, W. Theodore, and Ilardi, Robert L. "Change and Stability of Values in Collegiate Nursing Students." *Nursing Res* 19(4):359–62 Jl–Ag '70. *

672. Mehryar, A. H. "An Attempt to Cross-Validate Eysenck's Hypothesis Regarding the Relationship Between Extraversion and Tough-Mindedness." *J Social Psychol* 80(1): 109–10 F '70. * (*PA* 44:12390)

673. Mehryar, A. H. "A Cross-Cultural Investigation of Eysenck's Hypothesis Regarding the Relationship Between Personality and Attitudes." *Brit J Social & Clin Psychol* 9(3):216–21 S '70. * (*PA* 45:2237)

674. Merz, Walter Samuel. *A Study of Dogmatism, Values, and Demographic Variables as They Affect Attrition of Male Teachers in Lutheran Elementary and Secondary Schools.* Doctor's thesis, George Peabody College for Teachers (Nashville, Tenn.), 1970. (*DAI* 31:2776A)

675. Murphy, Glenn W. "Content Centered vs. Process Centered Biology Laboratories: Part 3, The Relationship of Student Values to Success." *Sci Ed* 54(1):37–40 Ja–Mr '70. *

676. Pace, Jesse Leonard, Jr. *Relationships of the Dominant Value Constructs to Achieved Grade Point Averages of High and Low Ability Transfer Students in Two Age Groups at Phillips County Community College.* Doctor's thesis, University of Mississippi (University, Miss.), 1970. (*DAI* 31:1039A)

677. Pesci, Michael Linden. *Psychological Differences Between Research, Development and Product Engineers and Their Implications for Placement Decisions.* Doctor's thesis, University of Minnesota (Minneapolis, Minn.), 1970. (*DAI* 31: 3048B)

678. Pierleoni, Robert G., and Lysaught, Jerome P. "A Decision Ladder for Predicting Programmer Success." *NSPI J* 9(5):6–7+ Je '70. *

679. Ranney, James Larry. *Dogmatism, Values, and Self-Concepts of College Freshmen With Either Public or Parochial Schooling.* Doctor's thesis, Southern Illinois University (Carbondale, Ill.), 1970. (*DAI* 31:3230A)

680. Rochester, Dean E. "Persistence of Attitudes and Values of NDEA Students—Two Year Post Institute." *Counselor Ed & Sup* 9(3):205–7 sp '70. * (*PA* 46:5579)

681. Sciortino, Rio. "Allport-Vernon-Lindzey Study of Values: 1, Factor Structure for a Combined Sample of Male and Female College Students." *Psychol Rep* 27(3):955–8 D '70. * (*PA* 45:9990)

682. Simon, William E. "Self-Concept and the Validity of the Allport-Vernon-Lindzey Study of Values." *Percept & Motor Skills* 31(1):263–6 Ag '70. * (*PA* 45:6240)

683. Sorhaindo, Alphonso Lorenzo. *The Relationship Between Value-Expectancy Discrepancy and Alienation in College Students.* Doctor's thesis, Ohio State University (Columbus, Ohio), 1970. (*DAI* 31:4345B)

684. Squatriglia, Robert William. *The Impact of Short-Term Group Counseling on Student Values.* Doctor's thesis, University of South Carolina (Columbia, S.C.), 1970. (*DAI* 31:3280A)

685. Thomas, Russell Earle. *Discriminant Function Analysis of Probationary and Non-Probationary Students' Measured Values, Personality Needs, and Socio-Economic Background Factors.* Doctor's thesis, Purdue University (Lafayette, Ind.), 1970. (*DAI* 31:1589A)

686. Vanderpool, John P., and Barratt, Ernest S. "Empathy: Towards a Psychophysiological Definition." *Dis Nerv System* 31(7):464–7 Jl '70. * (*PA* 45:2023)

687. White, Ruth Ann Moore. *Student Subcultures on a University Campus.* Doctor's thesis, East Texas State University (Commerce, Tex.), 1970. (*DAI* 31:2121A)

Robert Hogan, *Assistant Professor of Psychology, The Johns Hopkins University, Baltimore, Maryland.*

In the spring of 1968 the *Study of Values* was given to a national sample of high school students in grades 10, 11, and 12 (males, N = 5,320; females, N = 7,296). Norms from that testing are now included in a revised manual, which also contains directions for the use of an optional machine-scored edition of the test itself. Although the *Study of Values* was origi-

nally designed for use with persons with "some college," the high school and college norms are surprisingly similar. The major difference is found on the Aesthetic scale, due primarily to the low aesthetic interests of high school girls (mean 38.2) when compared with college women (mean 43.9).

The manual mentions using the test with undergraduates as an introduction to personality measurement. However, personal experience with this technique suggests that students may complain about the "transparency" of the *Study of Values;* they also seem annoyed occasionally by the content and format of the items. Such reactions may reflect increasing undergraduate ambivalence toward psychological testing in general, rather than a problem specific to the *Study of Values.*

In an earlier review, Gage (5:114) cited criticism that the test content confounds interests and values. In a different context, Mowrer [1] amplified this point by noting that the word "values" is "an essentially useless term, which has recently come into vogue....as a sort of lowest common denominator for all who recognize, however vaguely, the reality of some sort of axiological dimension in human existence * the term, unless extensively qualified, verges on meaninglessness, and certainly lacks power and precision." Thus there seems to be some question concerning what, exactly, the test measures.

Previous reviewers (4:92, 6:182) cautioned about the validity of the test when used with individual cases and observed that the scales of the 1951 revision require separate validation. Although the manual still lacks information concerning these points, there is little doubt that the test taps something significant. Two recent studies (*623, 663*) found the *Study of Values* significantly related to creative performance among adults in the "real world." Moreover, Feldman and Newcomb [2] remark that "this instrument provides the best single source of information about value changes during the college years."

The theoretical base of the *Study of Values* —i.e., Spranger's types—was questioned in all previous MMY reviews, reflecting a widespread aversion among psychologists to "non-

---

[1] Mowrer, O. Hobart, Editor. *Morality and Mental Health,* p. viii. Chicago, Ill.: Rand McNally & Co., 1967. Pp. xviii, 669. *

[2] Feldman, Kenneth A., and Newcomb, Theodore M. *The Impact of Colleges on Students: Vol. 1, An Analysis of Four Decades of Research,* pp. 18–9. San Francisco, Calif.: Jossey-Bass Inc., Publishers, 1969. Pp. xiii, 474. *

empirical" concepts. There are perhaps four reasons for this antipathy. First, traits (the traditional variables of choice) seem actually to reside in people, while types have a fictional flavor; traits appear veridical, while types seem only nominal. Second, while several psychologists have recently attempted to assess the universe of trait terms, few have studied seriously the taxonomy of personalities, for which type concepts would be essential. Third, the authors of the *Study of Values* were primarily concerned with the manner in which personality is expressed through values. Consequently, they made no attempt to explicate or defend the logic of ideal types. Finally, psychologists tend to associate type concepts exclusively with Dilthey, Spranger, and the fuzzy-minded psychology of *verstehen*.

Two points should be noted concerning ideal types. First, neither trait *nor* type concepts exist in reality; they are theoretical inferences of equally uncertain validity. Furthermore, there are no a priori grounds for concluding that one form of concept is, in principle, preferable to the other. Second, Dilthey and Spranger were by no means the only European social scientists to employ the methodology of ideal types. The sociologist-historian Max Weber provided one of the earliest and clearest statements of this analytical method, arguing that the choice is always between logically coherent and relatively well-defined concepts somewhat removed from empirical reality and concepts which are heavily qualified but close to the scientist's original observations. More recently, Kurt Lewin, in distinguishing between Aristotelian and Galilean modes of thought, argued for the necessity of abstract and formal concepts which transcend conclusions tied closely to empirical observations. Spranger's types, in Lewin's terms, are Galilean concepts.

Clearly, then, there is nothing in the nature of Spranger's types per se that makes them unacceptable as a theoretical basis for a test. There are, however, two other theoretical issues concerning the test which can be raised. The first concerns the degree to which value scores are related to nontest variables in a manner consistent with the type-theory. On this issue the evidence is clear; the scale scores predict a variety of criteria in the theoretically expected manner. For example, "gifted" students tend to score high on the Theoretical and Aesthetic scales (*124, 217*); "creatives" score high on

the theoretical and low on the Religious scales (*623, 663*); a high Theoretical-Economic-Political profile is "masculine," a high Aesthetic-Social-Religious profile is "feminine." The second question concerns the adequacy of Spranger's types as a taxonomy of personality. Here the types have two shortcomings. First, as a result of the manner in which the scales are defined conceptually, individual characterizations derived from the *Study of Values* are always honorific. There are no provisions within the system to classify blackguards, villains, or demonic men. Second, the types have a pervasive middle class flavor; the yeoman has no place in Spranger's scheme. In this regard, the six types defined by Holland's *Vocational Preference Inventory*, for example, although paralleling Spranger's in many ways, seem preferable because they are capable of classifying farmers and mechanics as well as college students.

In summary, in spite of several problematic features (i.e., ipsative scoring and the associated difficulties of interpreting correlations of subscales across persons, a restricted range of usage, the poorly defined nature of "values"), the *Study of Values* is a surprisingly viable test. When used with cooperative subjects, it provides dependable and pertinent information concerning individual cases. In addition, the steadily mounting bibliography of the *Study of Values* suggests the test will also have continuing usefulness as a research device.

For reviews by John D. Hundleby and John A. Radcliffe, see 6:182; for a review by N. L. Gage of the second edition, see 5:114; for reviews by Harrison G. Gough and William Stephenson, see 4:92 (1 excerpt); for a review by Paul E. Meehl of the original edition, see 3:99.

[147]

*Survey of Personal Attitude "SPA" (With Pictures): Individual Placement Series. Adults; 1960-66; SPA; 3 scores: social attitude, personal frankness, aggressiveness; Form A ('60, 14 pages); no specific manual; series manual ('66, 107 pages); separate answer sheets must be used; $30 per 20 tests; $4 per 100 answer sheets; $1 per scoring stencil; $2.50 per series manual; $5.15 per specimen set; cash orders postpaid; [20–30] minutes; J. H. Norman; Personnel Research Associates, Inc. *

HAROLD BORKO, *Professor of Psychology, School of Library Service, University of California, Los Angeles, California.*

The *Survey of Personal Attitude* is one of a series "of eight basic tests that have been developed for the specific purpose of objectively appraising abilities and potentials of adults" and is suggested "for screening applicants and appraising employees for transfer and promotion." The manual contains data on all eight tests, but this review is on the SPA only.

The SPA is a nonverbal test consisting of pairs of pictures; for each the subject is asked to select the picture that gives him the "more comfortable or pleasing feeling." He may also indicate that neither one gives him this feeling or that both are equally pleasant. The testing format is reasonably efficient. The test is not timed but is generally completed within 30 minutes. It is scored for three variables: Social Attitude, Personal Frankness, and Aggressiveness. The manual states that the interpretation of the results requires professionally trained personnel and should not be attempted by an unqualified person. Four examples of profile interpretation are included.

The report on the reliability and validity of the test leaves much to be desired. In the opening paragraph of the manual, it is stated that "Test scores on more than 30,000 individuals are included in normative data which represents a cross section of adults in industry in the United States." This reviewer has been unable to find any data in the manual based upon this large an N. The table of normative data does not indicate the size of the N. Some numbers are provided in the section on validity, and it is best to quote them directly, for they are hard to believe: "One study of a group of 21 junior engineers showed a positive but not significantly high correlation between scores obtained on the 'SPA' and job performance. Another study of 17 plant foremen revealed a positive relationship between the 'S' and 'P' factors and job success, but only a slightly positive correlation with the 'A' factor and the same criterion." The author then goes on to say, "Research with other tests and test factors has shown both positive and negative relationships." These statements speak for themselves. The test seems to be of unknown reliability and of low validity. The most charitable comment that can be made is that the test might be used for research purposes if anyone wished to spend his time collecting normative and validation data.

WAYNE S. ZIMMERMAN, *Test Officer and Professor of Counseling and Testing, California State College at Los Angeles, Los Angeles, California.*

This test consists of two parts, the first containing 84 paired drawings, and the second containing an additional 36 pairs, making 120 items in all. In Part 1 the examinee is asked to decide which one of two paired pictures gives him a more comfortable or pleasing feeling. He is also given the option of marking "neither" or "equally." For 22 of the items he is asked additionally to indicate whether he has participated in the life situation illustrated in either of the paired pictures.

Of the 120 paired line drawings, 110 illustrate common life situations. Ten additional drawings resembling inkblots are included. All 120 items are scored for one of the two categories of Social Attitude and Aggressiveness. In addition, the 22 items for which the examinee indicates personal participation are scored for Personal Frankness. For these items at least one of the paired pictures portrays an activity in which nearly everyone would be expected to have been a participant at one time or another.

Only 11 of the 107 pages in the manual for the eight-test battery are devoted to the SPA. The general format gives the impression that the manual has been professionally prepared. Cautionary statements in the use and interpretation of tests are made in appropriate sections.

Correlations between SPA scores and job performance are reported for 21 "junior engineers" and 17 "plant foremen." The correlations for the engineers are low and not statistically significant; .26, .19, and .08 for social attitudes, personal frankness, and aggressiveness, respectively. The corresponding correlations for the foremen are .61, .47, and .53. No further information is reported on the groups studied or the performance measure used. The manual also reports "low or negative correlations," based on 67 cases, with all 13 factors of the Guilford inventories GAMIN, GMPI, and STDCR.

Test-retest reliabilities, based on 46 cases not otherwise described, of ".833," ".814," and ".721" are claimed for aggressiveness, social attitudes, and personal frankness, respectively. The crucial time period between test administrations is not given. No other reliability data are furnished. Reporting reliabilities to three places based on such a small N suggests either extreme statistical naiveté or deliberate over-selling.

This is the extent of the statistical data presented on reliability and validity. Nevertheless, other sections of the manual contain such statements as: "Many years of research in industry preceded the development of the 'SPA.' * As employees with 'undesired' attitudes came up for promotion or participated in special studies, the items on the 'SPA' were evaluated for their ability to discriminate and to identify the deviate. * It was established in one study of 18 assembly inspectors that low average scores were obtained on the best performers and very high scores by the poor performers. * Follow-up studies have been of value in describing the three specific factors of the test." In no case, however, is there a reference to research reports, published or unpublished, anywhere in the manual.

The authors have applied an interesting technique in the assessment of personal attitudes. Asking an examinee to react to a pictured or graphically illustrated life situation in terms of whether he is more comfortable or has a pleasing feeling about it opens the way for an objectively scored projective type test unencumbered by a restrictive multiple choice format. The use of this technique, however, demands that a tremendous amount of research data be collected and analyzed before there can be hope of establishing satisfactory reliabilities and validities. The authors maintain that they have done this, but they present very little evidence to support their claim.

While some of the items present relatively unambiguous situations wherein it is relatively clear to the examinee what life situation is supposed to be portrayed, other items are quite ambiguous. The directions to the examinee do not specify that he should identify with any particular person. In some instances, the total life situation might be considered pleasing or comfortable for an examinee who would identify with one person, but would be considered unpleasing or uncomfortable if he were to identify with another person in the picture. Whereas it can be argued that stimulus ambiguity is a positive characteristic of a projective test, such an argument would overlook the fact that in writing items for objectively scored tests there are two kinds of ambiguity to consider. One provides an ambiguous stimulus to which one of several unambiguous responses may be expected in a reliable and consistent fashion. The other provides an ambiguous stimulus that evokes one response from an individual under a given set of circumstances but a different response by the same individual under the same set of circumstances at another time. The first situation can yield a reliable score, the second cannot. It would appear to this reviewer that many items in the SPA present the second kind of ambiguity and must therefore suffer from low item reliability.

It is difficult for this reviewer to decide whether he should or should not recommend the use of this test in industry as proposed by the authors. If he were to accept at face value the author's claims that many years of research preceded the development of the test, that several or many item analyses have been conducted, and that research with the test has revealed its usefulness time and time again, then it follows that the test can and should be recommended. On the other hand, the reviewer is confronted with the fact that no statistical summaries of item validity and of item consistency or homogeneity are presented, and that the very few statistics presented on reliability and validity are based on very small samples. The reviewer is forced to question why only these fragmentary results are presented rather than reports of the many studies that are so frequently referred to in the text.

In the absence of more convincing support from reports of further studies conducted in the ten years since the test was published, this reviewer feels that he must fall back on the tried and true psychologist's cop-out and recommend the test as a research instrument only and suggest that for any other application it should be employed only with extreme caution.

[148]

★Survey of Personal Values. Grades 11–16 and adults; 1964–67; SPV; 6 scores: practical mindedness, achievement, variety, decisiveness, orderliness, goal orientation; 1 form ('65, 3 pages); manual ('67, 16 pages); no adult norms; $4.50 per 25 tests; 85¢ per scoring stencil; 60¢ per manual; $2 per specimen set; postage extra; (15–20) minutes; Leonard V. Gordon; Science Research Associates, Inc. *

REFERENCES

1–3. See P:263.
4. SHERMAN, CHARLES EVANS. Differences in the Personal and Interpersonal Values of Negro and White College Freshmen. Doctor's thesis, Northern Illinois University (DeKalb, Ill.), 1969. (DAI 30:3800A)
5. STEIN, SANDRA LOU. The Interrelationships Among Self-Esteem, Personal Values, and Interpersonal Values. Doctor's thesis, Northern Illinois University (DeKalb, Ill.), 1969. (DAI 30:3803A)
6. BELLUCCI, JOSEPH T. The Contribution of Values in Predicting Success in Practical Nursing Training Programs. Doc-

tor's thesis, Lehigh University (Bethlehem, Pa.), 1970. (*DAI* 31:2731A)

7. KIRCHNER, ELIZABETH P. "Values and Value Changes During and After Graduate Study in Psychology." *J Clin Psychol* 26(2):252–6 Ap '70. * (*PA* 44:13586)

8. MURRAY, ROBERT. *Rating of Job Applicants by Principals as Related to Similarity-Dissimilarity in Value Orientation.* Doctor's thesis, State University of New York (Albany, N.Y.), 1970. (*DAI* 31:2652A)

9. THOMMES, MARTIN JOHN. *Changes in Values, Perceptions, and Academic Performance of College Freshmen Underachievers in a Remedial Program.* Doctor's thesis, United States International University (San Diego, Calif.), 1970. (*DAI* 31:2969B)

GENE V GLASS, *Professor of Education and Co-director, Laboratory of Educational Research, University of Colorado, Boulder, Colorado.*

If it is to become anything of significance, the *Survey of Personal Values* must compete with the older and established *Study of Values* by Allport, Vernon, and Lindzey. Both instruments are designed to probe the same broad domain of behavior, which happens *not* to be valuing. However, where the authors of the SV recognized this semantic lapse and corrected it immediately in the subtitle ("A Scale for Measuring the Dominant Interests in Personality"), the author of the SPV has been less emphatic in denying that values are measured by the survey. In asking the examinee what is "most important" to him, Gordon does come closer to eliciting genuine statements of value than do Allport, Vernon, and Lindzey when they ask for "likes" and "preferences." But suffice it to say that values, the standards and criteria with which we judge worth and goodness, are synonymous with neither "basic motivational patterns" nor with "dominant interests" as in the SV. Little harm results—except to language—if the user realizes that both the SPV and SV measure broad areas of interest and not values.

The SPV comprises 30 triadic forced-choice items. Each of six scales is represented once in about 15 triads. Commendably, the items of each triad are matched on ratings of social desirability. Within each triad, the examinee is directed to select what are for him the "most important" and "least important" statements. The score for an examinee on a scale is the number of times an item representing the scale is marked "most important" plus the number of times items not representing the scale in question in the same triads are marked "least important." The scales were developed by means of factor analyses of items apparently generated after an "extensive review of the literature relating to values." On this point, i.e., rationale

for the interest dimensions, the SPV comes off second best to the SV. Regardless of how highly one regards the use of Spranger's *Lebensformen* as a basis for the SV, it clearly led Allport, Vernon, and Lindzey to a richer, more encompassing measure of interests than did Gordon's literature review. Gordon's six scales for the SPV are as follows: Practical Mindedness (getting one's dollar's worth); Achievement (doing a hard job well); Variety (doing new things); Decisiveness (making up one's mind and sticking to it); Orderliness (being well-organized); Goal Orientation (having definite goals clearly in mind). The last scale was suggested by Guilford's convergent thinking factors; "Decisiveness," by Guilford's "dislike of ambiguity" factor; the other four scales appear to have been suggested by nothing in particular. These six scales are based on the small coin of human motivation; they hardly possess the romantic appeal and fundamental significance of Spranger's Theoretical-, Economic-, Political-, Religious-, Social- and Aesthetic-Men in the SV.

The test-retest reliabilities of the scales of the SPV are reported to range from .74 (for Decisiveness) to .92 (for Variety) over a period of seven to ten days (N of 97). The long-term reliability of the scales must currently be only presumed. However, there is little reason to suppose that the 30 triadic-item SPV is substantially less reliable than the 30 dyadic plus 15 triadic-item SV which has shown substantial stability across two months (no scale with reliability below .84) and remarkable validity over 20 years (no scale below .32). That the items of the SPV are less specific ("experience the unusual," "always get my money's worth") than the SV (Would you prefer to read *Scientific Age* or *Arts and Decorations?* Are you more interested in Florence Nightingale, Napoleon, Henry Ford or Galileo?) probably enhances their stability. The SPV might be said to have "face reliability" in lieu of the needed data.

No single, observable criterion exists against which any one of the SPV scales can be validated. Accordingly, Gordon attempted to determine what the scales were measuring by studying their intercorrelations, their correlations with other better established scales, and the pattern of mean differences for various groups of persons. To criticize or worry about the SPV because the scales have primarily negative intercorrelations is simply unjustified. It is a mathematical certainty that ipsatively scored scales will intercorrelate negatively on the average; to be exact, the average correlation will equal $-1/(k-1)$ for k scales with equal variances. (To the extent that life forces choices upon us, it too is "negatively intercorrelated"; lying on one's face on the beach correlates -1.00 with lying on one's back.) The choice to measure interests in a *forced-choice* rather than a *normative* format is always an open question in this domain of measurement. However, the empirical, psychometric research needed to resolve the question is not complete. Gordon chose a format for his inventory that has proved successful in the past.

Correlations of the scales of SPV with other instruments and mean differences between various demographic groups are presented as a construct validation of the inventory. In part, the data are relevant and illuminating. Five of the six scales have statistically significant correlations (between .25 and .41 in absolute value) with either the Economic or the Aesthetic scale of the SV, but with no other SV scales. The SPV scales are virtually unrelated to aptitude measures. However, the "construct validation" of the SPV runs aground of the lack of any compelling rationale for the selection of its scales. There is no nomological network of interests which permits predictions of patterns of correlations among SPV scales with other variables or which predicts mean differences among classes of persons. Does the lack of correlation of SPV scales with aptitude measures count in favor of the inventory because interests should be shaped by aptitudes? Does the fact that Peace Corps volunteers score lower than students-in-general on Practical-Mindedness count for more in favor of the inventory than the fact that the two groups do not differ on Variety counts against it? And what is the import of all of the data on mean differences on the scales for Japanese versus American males and females in high school and college, Japanese college students in education versus industrial arts, Asian Indians versus Americans, etc.? Do such data tell us something about the scales, something about the cultures, both or neither? Perhaps the relevance of such data for the construct validation of the instrument depends on knowledge from cultural anthropology and sociology from which predictions of group differences can be made. The requisite knowledge either does not exist or was simply not included. Without it, the evidence presented for the validity of the SPV is merely a collection of interesting facts, the raw material of a process of validation yet to be seriously undertaken.

The norms consist of percentiles corresponding to raw scores on each of the six scales for the four groups: college male (N = 984), college female (N = 1,080), high school male (N = 298) and high school female (N = 324). The college students came from 13 colleges "selected so as to represent all major regions of the country." However, since "sampling" may have been quite selective within colleges (on the average about 150 students were taken from each school), one wonders more about how representative the selected students are of students-in-that-college than how representative the 13 colleges are of colleges-in-general. The high school norms are based solely on data from students of the San Mateo (California) School District; as such, they are not very useful. The norms for the SPV are considerably less complete than those of the SV.

SUMMARY. The *Survey of Personal Values* is an interesting addition to that domain of personality assessment which has long been dominated by the Allport-Vernon-Lindzey *Study of Values*. Its reliability appears adequate, though more evidence is needed. The long, arduous process of learning what its scales measure has only begun. Its norms are skimpy. In its author's own words, "pending analysis and reporting of additional data, however, the SPV should be viewed as a research instrument." The potential user of the inventory would do well to weigh heavily this frank recommendation from the author against the publisher's enthusiasm for immediate dissemination and use.

[149]

★Symptom Sign Inventory: Personality and Personal Illness Questionnaires. Mental patients; 1968; orally administered; 2 editions; manual (35 pages); 40p per set of keys; 37½p per manual; 72½p per specimen set; postage extra; G. A. Foulds and K. Hope (manual); University of London Press Ltd. *
a) [REGULAR EDITION.] SSI; differential diagnosis among 8 categories (anxiety state, neurotic depression, hysteria, obsessional state, non-paranoid schizophrenia, paranoid schizophrenia, mania, psychotic depression) and 2 scales (personality disturbance, psychotic vs. neurotic); 1 form (4 pages); 62½p per 20 tests; [30–35] minutes.
b) SHORT VERSION. SSI/PD; consists of the 20 items of the personal disturbance scale of regular edition; may be used as a screening device; 1 form (1 page); 37½p per 20 tests; [10] minutes.

REFERENCES

1. ADAMS, ANNE, AND FOULDS, G. A. "Depression and Personality." *J Mental Sci* 108:474–86 Jl '62. * (*PA* 37:3720)
2. FOULDS, G. A. "A Quantification of Diagnostic Differentiae." *J Mental Sci* 108:389–405 Jl '62. * (*PA* 37:3215)
3. ADAMS, ANNE, AND FOULDS, G. A. "Personality and the Paranoid Depressive Psychoses." *Brit J Psychiatry* 109:273–8 Mr '63. * (*PA* 38:3034)
4. FOULDS, G. A., AND OWEN, ANNA. "Are Paranoids Schizophrenics?" *Brit J Psychiatry* 109:674–9 S '63. * (*PA* 38:6487)
5. FOULDS, G. A. "Personal Continuity and Psychopathological Disruption." *Brit J Psychol* 55:269–76 Ag '64. * (*PA* 39:5226)
6. FOULDS, G. A., AND OWEN, ANNA. "Speed and Accuracy on Mazes in Relation to Diagnosis and Personality." *Brit J Social & Clin Psychol* 3:34–5 F '64. * (*PA* 38:8870)
7. FOULDS, G. A. "The Significance of Intra-Individual Diagnostic Levels." *Brit J Psychiatry* 111:761–8 Ag '65. * (*PA* 40:1588)
8. FOULDS, G. A., AND ADAMS, ANNE. Chap. 10. "The Melancholic-Depressive Continuum," pp. 210–28 and Chap. 11, "The Paranoid-Melancholic Continuum," pp. 229–40. In *Personality and Personal Illness*, see 10. *
9. FOULDS, G. A., AND OWEN, ANNA. Chap. 12, "Analysis of Results in Terms of the Clinical Diagnosis," pp. 241–61. In *Personality and Personal Illness*, see 10. *
10. FOULDS, G. A.; IN COLLABORATION WITH T. M. CAINE AND WITH THE ASSISTANCE OF ANNE ADAMS AND OWEN. *Personality and Personal Illness*. London: Tavistock Publications Ltd., 1965. Pp. xii, 344. *
11. FOULDS, G. A. "Some Differences Between Neurotics and Character Disorders." *Brit J Social & Clin Psychol* 6:52–9 F '67. * (*PA* 41:7336)
12. FOULDS, G. A., AND MAYO, P. R. "'Neurotic' Symptoms, Intropunitiveness, and Psychiatric Referral." *Brit J Med Psychol* 40:151–2 Je '67. * (*PA* 42:12419)
13. MAYO, P. R. "Some Psychological Changes Associated With Improvement in Depression." *Brit J Social & Clin Psychol* 6:63–8 F '67. * (*PA* 41:7562)
14. PHILIP, A. E., AND McCULLOCH, J. W. "Social Pathology and Personality in Attempted Suicide." Abstract. *Brit J Psychiatry* 113:1405–6 D '67. * (*PA* 42:9200)
15. FOULDS, G. A. "Neurosis and Character Disorder in Hospital and in Prison." *Brit J Criminol* 8:46–9 Ja '68. * (*PA* 42:10847)
16. PHILIP, ALISTAIR E., AND McCULLOCH, J. W. "Some Psychological Features of Persons Who Have Attempted Suicide." Abstract. *Brit J Psychiatry* 114:1299–300 O '68. * (*PA* 43:4183)
17. CAINE, T. M., AND SMAIL, D. J. Chap. 6, "The Effectiveness of the Treatment of Chronic, Hospitalized Neurotics by the Therapeutic Community Technique," pp. 102–32. In their *The Treatment of Mental Illness: Science, Faith and the Therapeutic Community*. New York: International Universities Press, Inc., 1969. Pp. 192. *
18. FOULDS, G. A., AND HOPE, K. "A Delusional Scale." *Brit J Psychiatry* 115(520):335–7 Mr '69. * (*PA* 43:13077)
19. FOULDS, G. A.; HOPE, K.; McPHERSON, F. M.; AND MAYO, P. R. "Cognitive Disorder Among the Schizophrenias: 3, Retardation." *Brit J Psychiatry* 115(519):177–80 F '69. * (*PA* 43:13128)
20. HALL-SMITH, PATRICK, AND RYLE, ANTHONY. "Marital Patterns, Hostility and Personal Illness." *Brit J Psychiatry* 115(527):1197–8 O '69. * (*PA* 44:13196)
21. KEAR-COLWELL, J. J. "Neuroticism (Cattell) and Its Relationship to the Presence of Neurotic Symptomatology." *Multiv Behav Res* 4(2):223–33 Ap '69. * (*PA* 43:16005)
22. McPHERSON, F. M. "Thought-Process Disorder, Delusions of Persecution and 'Non-Integration' in Schizophrenia." *Brit J Med Psychol* 42(1):55–7 Mr '69. * (*PA* 43:11669)
23. MAYO, P. R. "Women With Neurotic Symptoms Who Do l t Seek Treatment." *Brit J Med Psychol* 42(2):165–9 Je '69. * (*PA* 44:918)
24. MURTHY, VINODA NARAYANA. "Personality and the Nature of Suicidal Attempts." *Brit J Psychiatry* 115(524):791–5 Jl '69. * (*PA* 44:6685)
25. CAINE, T. M. Chap. 27, "Personality and Illness," pp. 781–817. In *The Psychological Assessment of Mental and Physical Handicaps*. Edited by Peter Mittler. London: Methuen & Co. Ltd., 1970. Pp. xxviii, 857. *
26. GIEL, R. "Some Patterns of Thinking and Feeling in Fifty Neurotic Ethiopian Students." *Psychiatria, Neurologia, Neurochirurgia* 73(1):49–57 Ja–F '70. *
27. GORDON, ADRIEN V., AND GREGSON, R. A. M. "The Symptom-Sign Inventory as a Diagnostic Differentia for Paranoid and Non-Paranoid Schizophrenics." *Brit J Social & Clin Psychol* 9(4):347–56 D '70. * (*PA* 45:8496)
28. PHILIP, ALISTAIR E. "Traits, Attitudes and Symptoms in a Group of Attempted Suicides." *Brit J Psychiatry* 116(534):475–82 My '70. * (*PA* 45:984)
29. PHILIP, ALISTAIR E., AND McCULLOCH, J. W. "Test-Retest Characteristics of a Group of Attempted Suicide Patients." *J Consult & Clin Psychol* 34(2):144–7 Ap '70. * (*PA* 44:10778)
30. SMAIL, D. J. "Neurotic Symptoms, Personality and Personal Constructs." *Brit J Psychiatry* 117(541):645–8 D '70. *
31. WALTON, H. J.; FOULDS, G. A.; LITTMANN, S. K.; AND PRESLY, A. S. "Abnormal Personality." *Brit J Psychiatry* 116(534):497–510 My '70. * (*PA* 45:965)

H. J. EYSENCK, *Professor of Psychology and Director of the Department, Institute of Psychiatry, University of London, London, England.*

The SSI has been compiled as an aid to the differential diagnosis of the mentally ill. It contains 80 items, 10 for each of 8 diagnostic classes; 4 of these are neurotic and 4 psychotic. These classes, together with the number of male and female patients used to standardise the inventory, follow: anxiety state (48 males, 60 females), neurotic depression (34, 59), hysteria (18, 52), obsessional state (10, 13), non-paranoid schizophrenia (52, 30), paranoid schizophrenia (33, 37), mania (12, 8), psychotic depression (33, 63), and normals (0, 69).

The inventory must be administered by a qualified psychologist; it "is not intended to be a paper-and-pencil test, and attempts to use it as such have not been successful." Detailed instructions concerning administration and scoring are given. A scoring scheme was constructed on the basis of the protocols which were collected in various hospitals over a number of years. "So far as possible, patients were tested in the acute phase of their illness, and every effort was made to test them within a few days of admission"; we are not told how successful these efforts were. "The omission of patients with chronic illnesses renders the samples more homogeneous than they otherwise would have been"; it is suggested that for the purpose of classification it is probably necessary to treat chronic schizophrenics as quite separate from acute schizophrenics. Scores were derived from the protocols, and the power of these scores to discriminate the different types of patients is discussed in detail; Tables 6 and 7 give the correlation ratios for each discriminator in the pair of diagnostic groups from which it was derived, for men and women separately. (This includes the normal group of women; there were no normal men, and the male patients are compared with the normal women.) The writers are aware of the fact that they could have used some of the classical methods of multivariate analysis, such as canonical analysis of discriminance; their reasons for not doing so seem weak. Such an analysis might have thrown much light on the dimensionality of the universe spanned by the eight categories used; it does not seem likely that categorical allocation of cases is the most efficient way of dealing with the problem of diagnosis. The writers do not even consider alternative (dimensional) possibilities.

The SSI presents an interesting attempt to quantify the process of diagnosis and make it more objective; there are, however, a number of criticisms which must be discussed. In the first place, the number of cases in many of the categories is obviously too small to make scores based on them very useful; for example, there are only eight manic women! Even worse, there are no normal men. Before publishing such an inventory, and before carrying out the considerable statistical labour involved, it would surely have been useful to have collected a larger number of cases. In the second place, the scheme stands and falls with the reliability and validity of the psychiatric diagnoses; these, we are told, "were contributed by scores of psychiatrists in a dozen different hospitals," but no information is given of their reliability, and validity is not even mentioned. A multivariate analysis might have shown that the psychiatric model did not in fact agree with the actual data collected; perhaps it is for this reason that no such analysis was carried out. In the third place, one must wonder about the accuracy of a procedure which discriminates normals from neurotics and psychotics no better than one group of patients from another; only about one-third of the variance discriminating normals from male non-paranoid schizophrenics is contributed by the SSI. This is very poor indeed. In the fourth place, no evidence is given about the reliability of the scales when used on the same patients by different psychologists; such information is absolutely essential and should have been collected and published. Altogether, one has the impression that publication of the scales and the manual was somewhat premature; more data should have been collected, reliabilities established, and proper multivariate analyses carried out before confronting the outside world with the SSI.

Maurice Lorr, *Professor of Psychology, Catholic University of America, Washington, D.C.*

The SSI is an 80-item questionnaire designed "as an aid in the differential diagnosis" of four neurotic and four psychotic classes. Ten items of the SSI were written for each of the eight diagnostic classes. All questions are to be administered orally by a qualified psychologist. The normative samples of male and female psychotics and neurotics are fairly substantial but the normal controls consist of only 69 women.

While the items written for each diagnostic class tend to be more frequent in the class to which they belong, there are numerous exceptions. The discriminatory power of each item was determined "by taking each pair of diagnostic groups in turn and forming the 2×2 contingency table for each of the 80 items." Each discriminator of two groups was given a weight of $+1$ or -1. "The weight is positive if the first-named group gives a positive response more often than the second-named. In the opposite case the weight is negative." Efficiency is assessed in part by the percentage of persons classified by the discriminators in agreement with the diagnostician. Other evidence consists of correlation ratios for each discriminator in the pair of groups in which it was derived; these range from .53 to .93. Individual cases are allocated to one of the eight diagnostic classes through the application of cutting scores to any comparison between two groups. A patient's total score is the sum of his positive and negative scores. The diagnostic class with the highest score is the group to which a patient is assigned.

Tables are presented that show how well SSI diagnoses compare overall with the original psychiatric diagnoses. These indicate poor differentiation among the neurotic classes with the exception of obsessional states. The psychotic classes are much better differentiated, with the exception of nonparanoid schizophrenia among men. Since differential diagnosis is at issue, base rates are highly relevant in judging the success of the SSI for its stated purpose. However, base rates are not given or compared with the rate of correct diagnosis.

Also lacking are test-retest data on the stability of the eight scores over time, as well as evidence of the reliability of the original psychiatric diagnoses. The latter are important when one considers how uncertain such judgments usually are. No measures of test-taking attitudes seem to have been considered, although these are currently regarded as essential in questionnaire construction.

The manual is fairly complete but not easy to follow. The technical development might well be presented separately from the section describing uses, administration, and method of scoring for differential diagnosis. The test form and the keys are easy to apply but of an awkward length for storing or filing. The need for an oral interview conducted by scarce personnel is also likely to restrict the application of the SSI. Most hospitals and clinics in the U.S. would be reluctant to use such a device routinely.

In conclusion, it may be said that the SSI represents a carefully designed and ingeniously analyzed tool for differential diagnosis. However, since the SSI has never been applied to a set of diagnostic groups other than the original, its power for differential diagnosis cannot be assessed. Nor do the authors provide information on concurrent validity with comparable devices such as the MMPI. For these reasons, the SSI can only be recommended as a promising research questionnaire.

B Brit Psychol Soc 22(74):60–1 Ja '69. D. J. Smail. * The aim of the test is to differentiate patients who are acutely ill, purely at the symptom level. This avoids confusing symptoms with personality attributes—a confusion which most former diagnostic tests of the questionnaire type have failed to avoid. * The validity of the inventory is established by the extent of its agreement with psychiatric diagnosis. Depending on the kind of task required of it, the SSI varies between 50 and 100% concordance with psychiatric opinion and validities are particularly satisfactory where the decision is limited to a differential diagnosis between two possible categories. Stability is not taken into account, but is probably not a concept which could usefully be applied to scores from acutely ill patients in psychiatric hospitals. The statistical tables provided are helpful in allowing the clinician a certain amount of flexibility in determining the weight to attach to scores which may arise. The tables (12 and 13) referring to the "psychotic versus neurotic" scale in the manual and the corresponding items in the scoring key are, or so it seems after a perplexed search through the text, only poorly explained. Some of the statistical jargon in the manual may baffle the clinician (as it did the reviewer) who cannot lay claim to considerable mathematical sophistication. The items themselves are administered orally, with

some discretion being allowed the examiner to judge from a patient's answer whether or not an item should be scored. This makes a welcome change from the rigidly mechanistic administration so often insisted on by test constructors— it seems psychologically preferable for patients to understand what is required of them than to sacrifice their comprehension to some metaphysical notion concerning the virtues of objectivity. The scoring of the inventory is with practice mastered easily enough, and in most cases should not take more than a few minutes. Patients are assigned to one member of the various pairs of categories on the basis of a cutting score, though it should be noted that one of the more serious criticisms of the material is that this cutting score frequently coincides with or is included in the range of "doubtful scores" which, in the authors' words, means that a patient's "assignment to one or other of the two groups cannot be made with any confidence." This appears to constitute (at worst) a contradiction or (at best) a logical confusion which badly needs clarification. However, considered as a whole this material is a very useful addition to the clinical psychologist's test library in providing him with a "pure" symptom measure of the questionnaire type, standardized on British psychiatric patients, and in many ways an improvement on forerunners.

[150]

★Systematic Interview Guides. Mothers; 1967; SIG; for gathering information from mothers about the early development of their children; 2 guides; manual (11 pages); no data on reliability and validity; no norms; 17½p per manual; 52½p per specimen set; postage extra; interview time not reported; D. H. Stott; University of London Press Ltd. *
a) NO. 1—BIRTH TO 5 YEARS. 9 scores: physical abnormality, behavior disturbance, birth complication, condition at birth, epidemic illness, functional impairment, adverse health conditions, retardation in development, trauma; 1 form (8 pages); £1.87 per 20 guides; 12½p per key.
b) NO. 2—PRENATAL. 8 scores: adverse health conditions, mental stress, nervous condition, reproductive abnormality, smoking habits, trauma, unwanted pregnancy, working conditions; 1 form (4 pages); 92½p per 20 guides; 7½p per key.

Brit J Psychiatry 115:501–2 Ap '69. Michael Rutter. The aim of these Guides is ambitious: "to bring system into the information obtained from the mother about her child's early development." No. 1 covers the period birth to five years and No. 2 the prenatal period. They are intended for use in "child and family casework, professional training and research....in child care and welfare, child guidance, social work and probation....in paediatrics and general health nursing." It is doubtful whether the Guides meet any of these needs satisfactorily. The Guides consist for the most part of a series of statements which are to be underlined when they apply to the child in question. Thus, neurological defects noticed soon after birth are covered by: "Didn't move arms, legs properly (one, both sides)/twitching, tremor—due to low calcium/low blood sugar/put on sedative"; and affection one to five years by "loving/did not like cuddling or sitting on knee/only liked cuddling when ill/treated us impersonally (as if we were just objects around him)." It seems improbable that this kind of thing could avoid the need for freely written interview reports (as is claimed), as least as regards psychiatric assessment. Very little attention is paid to how this information should be obtained, and no data on the reliability or validity of the Guides are given. The section in the manual on retrospective recall gives a misleadingly rosy view of its accuracy. Apart from one of Stott's own papers, the only reference to the literature on the subject is that by Haggerty and his colleagues (and even that is given as Haggard *et al.*, in the text). A well designed interview guide would be useful for both clinical and research work, but this reviewer can see no place for this set of publications. It is a pity that they were put on the commercial market before carrying out even elementary tests of their reliability, validity or usefulness for any particular purpose.

[151]

★Tennessee Self Concept Scale. Ages 12 and over; 1964-65; TSCS; 2 scoring systems referred to as Counseling Form and Clinical and Research Form; 1 form ('64, 6 pages); manual ('65, 31 pages); separate answer sheets must be used; 26¢ per test, 1-99 copies; 16¢ per answer sheet (including score and profile sheets), 1-99 copies; 90¢ per set of scoring keys for both forms; 70¢ per manual; 90¢ per specimen set; postage extra; scoring service, 50¢ per test; (10-20) minutes; William H. Fitts; Counselor Recordings and Tests. *

a) COUNSELING FORM. 15 profiled scores: self criticism, 9 self esteem scores (identity, self satisfaction, behavior, physical self, moral-ethical self, personal self, family self, social self, total), 3 variability of response scores (variation across first 3 of the self esteem scores, variation across the last 5 self esteem scores, total), distribution score, time score.

b) CLINICAL AND RESEARCH FORM. 30 profiled scores: the 15 scores in a above and the following 15: response bias, net conflict, total conflict, 6 empirical scales (defensive positive, general maladjustment, psychosis, personality disorder, neurosis, personality integration),

deviant signs, 5 scores consisting of counts of each type of response made.

REFERENCES

1-30. See P:266, also includes a cumulative name index to the first 30 references for this test.
31. CONGDON, CLYDE S. *Self Theory and Chlorpromazine Treatment.* Doctor's thesis, Vanderbilt University (Nashville, Tenn.), 1958. (*DA* 19:2654)
32. DEITCHE, JOHN HOWARD. *The Performance of Delinquent and Non-Delinquent Boys on the Tennessee Department of Mental Health Self-Concept Scale.* Doctor's thesis, Indiana University (Bloomington, Ind.), 1959. (*DA* 20:1437)
33. HAVENER, PHILIP HENRY. *Distortions in the Perception of Self and Others by Persons Using Paranoid Defenses.* Doctor's thesis, Vanderbilt University (Nashville, Tenn.), 1961. (*DA* 22:322)
34. KICKLIGHTER,, RICHARD HAMPTON. *Reported Self-Concept and Immediate Recall.* Doctor's thesis, University of Florida (Gainesville, Fla.), 1962. (*DA* 23:2793)
35. PURINTON, DAWN E. *The Effect of Item Familiarity on Self-Concept Sorts.* Doctor's thesis, University of Nebraska (Lincoln, Neb.), 1965. (*DA* 26:2325)
36. BUTTERFIELD, MARY LANE. *The Effect of Certain Group Activities on the Self Report of Selected High School Students.* Doctor's thesis, University of Miami (Coral Gables, Fla.), 1966. (*DA* 28:488A)
37. GAY, CLEVELAND JOHNSON. *Academic Achievement and Intelligence Among Negro Eighth Grade Students as a Function of the Self Concept.* Doctor's thesis, North Texas State University (Denton, Tex.), 1966. (*DA* 27:112A)
38. SCHALON, CHARLES LAWRENCE. *Performance Following Failure Stress as a Function of Level of Self-Esteem.* Doctor's thesis, University of Iowa (Iowa City, Iowa), 1966. (*DA* 27:3296B)
39. SHERIN, CAROLYN RICHARDS. *Some Relationships Among Popularity, Friendship Choice, and Personality Variables.* Doctor's thesis, University of Miami (Coral Gables, Fla.), 1966. (*DA* 27:1931A)
40. TOEWS, WILMA F. *Self-Esteem, Perception of Parental Control and Hostility of Adolescents.* Doctor's thesis, Brigham Young University (Provo, Utah), 1966. (*DA* 27:1130A)
41. WRIGHTSMAN, LAWRENCE S.; RICHARD, WAYNE C.; AND NOBLE, FRANK C. "Attitude Changes of Guidance Institute Participants." *Counselor Ed & Sup* 5:212-20 su '66. * (*PA* 41:5051)
42. BRANN, RALPH AUSTIN. *A Study of the Effect of Teaching Self-Evaluation Procedures on the Self-Concept of Student Teachers.* Doctor's thesis, Oklahoma State University (Stillwater, Okla.), 1967. (*DA* 28:4843A)
43. FLEMISTER, IDA MORRIS. *The Effect on Self Concept of the Chattanooga Neighborhood Youth Corps and of Education, Vocational Aspiration, and Sex Role.* Doctor's thesis, University of Tennessee (Knoxville, Tenn.), 1967. (*DA* 28:2069A)
44. GRANT, CARMEN RITA HILL. *Age Differences in Self Concept From Early Adulthood Through Old Age.* Doctor's thesis, University of Nebraska (Lincoln, Neb.), 1967. (*DA* 28:1160B)
45. HUGHES, THOMAS MEARS. *A Study of the Relationship of Coping Strength to Self-Concept, School Achievement, and General Anxiety Level in Sixth Grade Pupils.* Doctor's thesis, University of Tennessee (Knoxville, Tenn.), 1967. (*DA* 28:4001A)
46. BROOK, ROBERT CHARLES. *Self Concept Changes as a Function of Participation in Sensitivity Training as Measured by the Tennessee Self Concept Scale.* Doctor's thesis, Michigan State University (East Lansing, Mich.), 1968. (*DA* 29:1700A)
47. CARROLL, JEROME F. X. *The Acceptance or Rejection of Differences Between Adoptive and Biological Parenthood by Adoptive Applicants as Related to Various Indices of Adjustment/Maladjustment.* Doctor's thesis, Temple University (Philadelphia, Pa.), 1968. (*DA* 29:1503B)
48. DALY, EDWARD JOSEPH. *Projected Sex-Blame and Religiosity in College Men.* Doctor's thesis, Michigan State University (East Lansing, Mich.), 1968. (*DA* 29:3480B)
49. FURR, HENRY BEDFORD. *Some Influences of a Course in Business Speaking on Certain Personality Traits of College Students.* Doctor's thesis, North Texas State University (Denton, Tex.), 1968. (*DA* 29:3460A)
50. GHANNAD, REZA H. *The Effects of Planned Interaction of Adult Males With Institutionalized Mentally Retarded Boys Upon Their Sex-Role Identification and Self-Concept.* Doctor's thesis, Brigham Young University (Provo, Utah), 1968. (*DA* 29:3001A)
51. GREENBERG, GLORIA ULERT. *A Refinement of the Tennessee Self Concept Scale to Clarify Interpretation of Extremely Favorable Self Reports.* Doctor's thesis, University of Miami (Coral Gables, Fla.), 1968. (*DA* 29:770B)
52. IGLINSKY, CLYDE LEE. *Intellectual and Non-Intellectual Factors Affecting Academic Success of College Freshmen.* Doctor's thesis, East Texas State University (Commerce, Tex.), 1968. (*DA* 29:1423A)
53. LAMB, DONALD WAYNE. *Demonstrated Internal-External Reward Expectancies as a Variable in Group Counseling.* Doc-

tor's thesis, North Texas State University (Denton, Tex.), 1968. (*DA* 29:2568A)

54. PADGETT, HARRY G., AND GAZDA, GEORGE M. "Effects of Group Guidance and Group Counseling on the Self Concept and Professional Attitude of Prospective Teachers." *SPATE* 6:42–9 w '68. *

55. PASSONS, WILLIAM RICHARD. *The Relationship of Counselor Characteristics and Empathic Sensitivity.* Doctor's thesis, Washington State University (Pullman, Wash.), 1968. (*DA* 29:2968A)

56. PETERS, DOROTHY MARIE. *The Self-Concept as a Factor in Over- and Under-Achievement.* Doctor's thesis, Indiana University (Bloomington, Ind.), 1968. (*DA* 29:1792A)

57. SCHWAB, JOHN J.; HARMELING, JAMES D.; AND MCGINNIS, NANCY H. "Anxiety, Self Concept, and Body Image: Psychosomatic Correlations: 1, A Preliminary Report." *Proc 4th World Congr Psychiatry* 1966(pt 4):2715–7 '68. *

58. SOFFEN, FAYE. *Teaching for Improvement of Self Concept.* Doctor's thesis, University of Pennsylvania (Philadelphia, Pa.), 1968. (*DA* 29:1468A)

59. VARGAS, ROBERT. *A Study of Certain Personality Characteristics of Male College Students Who Report Frequent Positive Experiencing and Behaving.* Doctor's thesis, University of Florida (Gainesville, Fla.), 1968. (*DAI* 30:142A)

60. WALKER, KENNETH DELEON. *Effects of Social and Cultural Isolation Upon the Self-Concepts of Negro Children.* Doctor's thesis, University of Miami (Coral Gables, Fla.), 1968. (*DAI* 30:596A)

61. ADAMS, WALTER DALE. *Survival Training: Its Effect on the Self Concept and Selected Personality Factors of Emotionally Disturbed Adolescents.* Doctor's thesis, Utah State University (Logan, Utah), 1969. (*DAI* 31:388B)

62. ALEXANDER, ALBERT ANDRIA. *The Effect of a Residential Camping Experience on the Self-Concept of Boys From Low Income Families.* Doctor's thesis, Boston University (Boston, Mass.), 1969. (*DAI* 31:629A)

63. BALL, MARY KAY. *Identification With Parents and Others as Predictors of Mental Health.* Doctor's thesis, Ohio University (Athens, Ohio), 1969. (*DAI* 30:2901B)

64. BERRYMAN, BERLE WAYNE. *The Effects of Group Counseling Upon Visual Perception and Its Relationship to Other Forms of Perception.* Doctor's thesis, North Texas State University (Denton, Tex.), 1969. (*DAI* 30:2793A)

65. CHRISTIAN, QUENTIN ADRIS. *Relationship Between Physical Fitness and Self Concept.* Doctor's thesis, East Texas State University (Commerce, Tex.), 1969. (*DAI* 30:2827A)

66. COOK, KEITH EMERY. *Differences Between Self-Concepts of Disadvantaged and Non-Disadvantaged High School Students Within Certain Types of Rural and Urban Communities.* Doctor's thesis, University of Maine (Orono, Me.), 1969. (*DAI* 31:1615A)

67. COTNAM, JOHN DALE. *Variance in Self-Report Measures of Disadvantaged Young Adults as a Function of Race and Stated Purpose of Testing.* Doctor's thesis, University of Rochester (Rochester, N.Y.), 1969. (*DAI* 30:3719A)

68. CULP, WILLIAM HARRISON. *Changes in Behavior and Attitude as a Result of Receiving Direct Feedback and Participating in Group Counseling.* Doctor's thesis, West Virginia University (Morgantown, W.Va.), 1969. (*DAI* 31:1007A)

69. DIBARTOLO, RUSSELL. *Self-Concept and the Attainment of Esophageal Speech.* Doctor's thesis, State University of New York (Buffalo, N.Y.), 1969. (*DAI* 30:2890B)

70. EIGENBROD, FREDERICK A., JR. *The Effects of Territory and Personality Compatibility on Identity and Security.* Doctor's thesis, Michigan State University (East Lansing, Mich.), 1969. (*DAI* 30:2329A)

71. ELBERT, WELDON EUGENE. *Changes in Self-Concept, Self-Actualization, and Interpersonal Relations as a Result of Video Feedback in Sensitivity Training.* Doctor's thesis, East Texas State University (Commerce, Tex.), 1969. (*DAI* 30:5233A)

72. FADALE, VINCENT EDWARD. *An Experimental Study of the Effects of Videotape Feedback in a Basic Encounter Group.* Doctor's thesis, East Texas State University (Commerce, Tex.), 1969. (*DAI* 30:5234A)

73. GARRIS, DONALD LEE. *Self-Reference Changes of Teacher Trainees Undergoing Differing Types of Human Relations Training.* Doctor's thesis, Ball State University (Muncie, Ind.), 1969. (*DAI* 30:3828A)

74. GATTSHALL, GERALD WALTER. *Imprisonment's Affects Upon the Self Concept and the Actualizing Process.* Doctor's thesis, Ball State University (Muncie, Ind.), 1969. (*DAI* 30:5235A)

75. GEORGE, FLAVIL HALL. *The Relationship of the Self Concept, Ideal Self Concept, Values, and Parental Self Concept to the Vocational Aspiration of Adolescent Negro Males.* Doctor's thesis, North Texas State University (Denton, Tex.), 1969. (*DAI* 30:4772A)

76. GRANT, CARMEN HILL. "Age Differences in Self-Concept From Early Adulthood Through Old Age." Abstract. *Proc 77th Ann Conv Am Psychol Assn* 4(2):717–8 '69. * (*PA* 44:639)

77. HEALEY, GARY WILLIAM. *Self Concept: A Comparison of Negro-, Anglo-, and Spanish-American Students Across Ethnic, Sex, and Socioeconomic Variables.* Doctor's thesis, New Mexico State University (University Park, N.M.), 1969. (*DAI* 30:2849A)

78. HERSKOVITZ, FRIEDA SCHREIBER. *The Effects of an Edu-cational-Vocational Rehabilitation Program Upon the Self-Concepts of Disadvantaged Youth.* Doctor's thesis, University of Pennsylvania (Philadelphia, Pa.), 1969. (*DAI* 30:2801A)

79. KELTON, DALE L. *The Self Concept of Juvenile Delinquents: A Study of Maladaptives, Losers and Integrators.* Doctor's thesis, University of Oklahoma (Norman, Okla.), 1969. (*DAI* 30:1899B)

80. KHAN, EHSAN ULLAH. *Susceptibility to the Mueller-Lyer Illusion as a Function of Conflicts in Self Concept and the Characteristics of the Stimulus.* Doctor's thesis, North Texas State University (Denton, Tex.), 1969. (*DAI* 30:836B)

81. LATHROP, ROBERT CHARLES. *A Study of Various Characteristics of Vocational-Technical Students and Community College Students.* Doctor's thesis, Washington State University (Pullman, Wash.), 1969. (*DAI* 30:4225A)

82. LETNER, RODNEY CHARLES. *The Effect of Group Counseling on the Self Concept as Measured by the Tennessee Self Concept Scale.* Doctor's thesis, Ball State University (Muncie, Ind.), 1969. (*DAI* 30:2803A)

83. LEVY, JUDITH MOSKOWITZ. *Phenomenological Aspects of Childbearing.* Doctor's thesis, University of Florida (Gainesville, Fla.), 1969. (*DAI* 31:2994B)

84. LOW, GARY ROY. *A Study of Counselor Trainee Changes in Two Types of Practicum.* Doctor's thesis, East Texas State University (Commerce, Tex.), 1969. (*DAI* 30:5240A)

85. MINTER, JOSEPH ROBERT. *The Effects of Sensitivity Training on Self Concept and Attitudes of Student Teachers.* Doctor's thesis, East Texas State University (Commerce, Tex.), 1969. (*DAI* 30:5323A)

86. PEKAREK, ROBERT CHARLES. *Differential Perceptions Held by Selected Publics of the Fraternity System at the Florida State University.* Doctor's thesis, Purdue University (Lafayette, Ind.), 1969. (*DAI* 30:3735A)

87. PUGH, DWIGHT ALLEN. *A Comparison of Changes Over a Period of Time in the Self-Concepts of Students Enrolled in Vocational and Non-Vocational Curricula.* Doctor's thesis, Ohio University (Athens, Ohio), 1969. (*DAI* 30:3737A)

88. QUEEN, RENEE. *A Study of the Relationship Between the Self Concepts and Ethnocentricism of Student Teachers and Their Teaching Behavior.* Doctor's thesis, New York University (New York, N.Y.), 1969. (*DAI* 30:3353A)

89. RICHARD, WAYNE C.; MATES, CATHERINE G.; AND WHITTEN, LAURA. "Personality Traits and Attitudes of Adolescent Girls With Behavior Disorders." *Correct Psychiatry & J Social Ther* 15(2):34–44 su '69. *

90. ROHR, MICHAEL EUGENE. *An Exploratory Study of Two Measures and Two Correlates of Accurate Empathy.* Doctor's thesis, University of Tennessee (Knoxville, Tenn.), 1969. (*DAI* 30:4783A)

91. SEIDMAN, SYLVIA K. *The Self-Concept of Elementary School Student-Teachers and Its Relationship to Classroom Verbal Interaction.* Doctor's thesis, New York University (New York, N.Y.), 1969. (*DAI* 30:3355A)

92. SMITH, CLYDE RAYMOND. *An Analysis of the Effectiveness of a College Preparatory Program for the Visually Impaired.* Doctor's thesis, University of Tennessee (Knoxville, Tenn.), 1969. (*DAI* 31:1653A)

93. SWIHART, P. J.; DELEON, P. H.; AND SWENSEN, C. H. "Life History and Personality Correlates of Dominant-Submissive Behavior." *Percept & Motor Skills* 28(2):491–8 Ap '69. * (*PA* 43:15800)

94. THOMAS, MURPHY MCNEEL. *Personality Integration and Cognitive Processes.* Doctor's thesis, George Peabody College for Teachers (Nashville, Tenn.), 1969. (*DAI* 31:402B)

95. VANDERPOOL, JAMES A. "Alcoholism and the Self-Concept." *Q J Studies Alcohol* 30(1A):59–77 Mr '69. * (*PA* 43:11588)

96. AXMAKER, LARRY WILLIAM. *The Effect of Group Counseling on the Self-Concept, on the Motivation to Achieve and on the Proportion of Dropouts Among Unselected Community College Students at Southwestern Oregon Community College.* Doctor's thesis, Oregon State University (Corvallis, Ore.), 1970. (*DAI* 30:4214A)

97. BUTLER, OSCAR PERRY, JR. *A Comparative Study of the Self-Concept of Black and White Freshman Students From the Midwest and South.* Doctor's thesis, Michigan State University (East Lansing, Mich.), 1970. (*DAI* 31:3331A)

98. COLLINS, HARDIN A., AND BURGER, GARY K. "The Self Concepts of Adolescent Retarded Students." *Ed & Train Mental Retard* 5(1):23–30 F '70. *

99. CORRIGAN, FRANCIS VINCENT, JR. *A Comparison of Self Concepts of American Indian Students From Public or Federal School Backgrounds.* Doctor's thesis, George Washington University (Washington, D.C.), 1970.

100. COUCH, JERRY DEE. *Prospective High School Teachers' Self Concepts as Reflected by the Tennessee Self Concept Scale at the University of Arkansas.* Doctor's thesis, University of Arkansas (Fayetteville, Ark.), 1970. (*DAI* 31:1113A)

101. CUMMINGS, MARTHA ELIZABETH. *The Development and Evaluation of a Multi-Dimensional Scale for Predicting the Participation of High School Girls in Physical Activity.* Doctor's thesis, Boston University (Boston, Mass.), 1970. (*DAI* 31:2154A)

102. FURR, H. BEDFORD. "Influences of a Course in Speech-Communication on Certain Aspects of the Self-Concept of College Freshmen." *Speech Teach* 19(1):26–31 Ja '70. *

103. GROSS, WILLIAM F., AND ALDER, LINDA O. "Aspects

of Alcoholics' Self-Concepts as Measured by the Tennessee Self-Concept Scale." *Psychol Rep* 27(2):431–4 O '70. * (*PA* 45: 6612)

104. HOBBS, GEORGE WILLIAM. *An Investigation of Certain Factors Related to Self-Concept, Sexual Knowledge, and Attitude Toward Sex Education of a Group of Elementary Teachers.* Doctor's thesis, North Texas State University (Denton, Tex.), 1970. (*DAI* 31:3388A)

105. LEITER, N. ZWI. *Some Personality Factors in Extreme Religiosity.* Doctor's thesis, Catholic University of America (Washington, D.C.), 1970. (*DAI* 31:2962B)

106. McCARY, PATRICK WELLINGTON. *The Effects of Small Self-Understanding Groups on the Self-Concept and Anxiety Level When Group Composition Has Been Varied.* Doctor's thesis, Michigan State University (East Lansing, Mich.), 1970. (*DAI* 31:2112A)

107. MEIGHAN, THOMAS. *An Investigation of the Self Concept of Blind and Partially Seeing Adolescents and of the Relation of Their Self Concepts to Academic Achievement in Language and Paragraph Reading.* Doctor's thesis, Catholic University of America (Washington, D.C.), 1970. (*DAI* 31:2191A)

108. MILLER, MARY BALL. "Meaningful Interpersonal Relationships and Mental Health Correlates." Abstract. *Proc 78th Ann Conv Am Psychol Assn* 5(1):347–8 '70. * (*PA* 44:18694)

109. MORRIL, RICHARD ALLEN. *Harmony of Self-Concept as a Factor Influencing the Vocational Development of Upper-Class and Graduate Male College Students.* Doctor's thesis, Michigan State University (East Lansing, Mich.), 1970. (*DAI* 31:3880A)

110. RESNICK, HARVEY; FAUBLE, MARIANNE LEESON; AND OSIPOW, SAMUEL H. "Vocational Crystallization and Self-Esteem in College Students." *J Counsel Psychol* 17(5):465–7 S '70. * (*PA* 45:3008)

111. ROTHFARB, HERBERT I. *A Study of the Psychological Needs and Self-Esteem of College Men Who Exercise Regularly.* Doctor's thesis, Boston College (Chestnut Hill, Mass.), 1970. (*DAI* 31:2727A)

112. SMITH, OSLER PAUL, JR. *Changes in Self-Actualization and Self-Concept as a Result of the Use of Visual Feedback in Marathon Sensitivity Training.* Doctor's thesis, East Texas State University (Commerce, Tex.), 1970. (*DAI* 31:3280A)

113. SWAN, ANDREW COBURN. *Personality Integration and Perceived Behavior in a Sensitivity Training Group.* Doctor's thesis, George Peabody College for Teachers (Nashville, Tenn.), 1970. (*DAI* 31:3717B)

114. TAYLOR, THEODORE DAVID. *Effects of Group Counseling on Self Concept and Academic Achievement of Selected High School Sophomore Health Classes.* Doctor's thesis, Oregon State University (Corvallis, Ore.), 1970. (*DAI* 31:1582A)

115. VERETT, GARY DWAYNE. *The Effect of a Summer Group Counseling Institute on Selected Attitudes and Personality Characteristics of Junior College Counselors.* Doctor's thesis, North Texas State University (Denton, Tex.), 1970. (*DAI* 31:3283A)

116. VIA, MURRAY EUGENE. *Changes in Personality Characteristics and Attitudes of Male College Freshmen.* Doctor's thesis, Claremont Graduate School (Claremont, Calif.), 1970. (*DAI* 31:1636A)

117. WILLIAMS, ROBERT L., AND BYARS, HARRY. "The Effect of Academic Integration on the Self-Esteem of Southern Negro Students." *J Social Psychol* 80(2):183–8 Ap '70. * (*PA* 44: 14461)

118. YOUNG, JAMES ROBERT. *The Effects of Laboratory Training on Self-Concept, Philosophies of Human Nature, and Perceptions of Group Behavior.* Doctor's thesis, George Peabody College for Teachers (Nashville, Tenn.), 1970. (*DAI* 31:3696B)

PETER M. BENTLER, *Associate Professor of Psychology, University of California, Los Angeles, California.*

The TSCS consists of 100 self-description items, of which 90 assess the self-concept and 10 assess self criticism (the self-criticism items are all MMPI Lie scale items). For each item, the respondent chooses one of five response options labeled from "completely false" to "completely true." Fourteen scores are derived from these items in the Counseling Form of the scale; this version is considered appropriate for feedback to an individual. The same items are also utilized in the Clinical and Research Form. This version is considered appropriate

for research and clinical assessment; 30 scores are derived and reported in the Profile Sheet.

Items for the scale were written according to a type of two dimensional facet design, involving the following aspects of the self: Identity, Self-Satisfaction, Behavior, Physical Self, Moral-Ethical Self, Personal Self, Family Self, and Social Self. Each of these aspects of the self receives a subscore based on relevant items. In addition, major additional scores are derived: Total Positive Score, reflecting the overall level of self-esteem; Variability Scores, reflecting the amount of consistency from one area of self-perception to another; and Distribution Score, a measure of extremity response style. In addition, the Clinical and Research Form yields scores for True-False Ratio, a measure of response style; Net Conflict Score, reflecting responses to positive vs. negative items; Empirical Scales for group discrimination of various sorts; and Number of Deviant Signs Score, a count of the number of deviant features on all other scores. The various content areas are well conceived, and the scale yields a vast amount of information from only 100 test items.

Several scores from the scale have remarkably high correlations with other measures of personality functioning. For example, the Taylor Anxiety Scale correlates −.70 with Total Positive. Correlations from .50 to .70 are common with the *Cornell Medical Index* and an unpublished Inventory of Feelings. Correlations with various MMPI scales are frequently in the .50's and .60's. Thus it seems safe to conclude that the scale overlaps sufficiently with well-known measures to consider it a possible alternative for these measures in various applied situations. The scale was normed on a sample of 626 persons of varying age, sex, race, and socioeconomic status. The sample does not reflect the distribution of these variables in the population, but it will suffice for many practical purposes. Retest reliability, while varying for different scores, is in the high .80's, sufficiently large to warrant confidence in individual difference measurement. Thus many psychometric qualities of the scale meet the usual test construction standards that should exist in an instrument that hopes to receive wide usage.

The manual, as well as the scale that is described, suffers from two major, possibly fatal, interrelated defects. The first defect reflects the virtually complete absence of information regarding the internal structure of the scale; the second, the high degree of over-interpretation, relative to the data base, that is made regarding various aspects of data involving the scale. These defects will be discussed in turn.

No information whatsoever is presented on the internal consistency of the scale, or on any of the scale subscores. This reviewer suspects that the internal consistency coefficients would doubtless be quite high, considering the large correlations obtained between scale scores and other measures such as MMPI scales. Another reason for such an expectation is found in the 29 variable intercorrelation matrix; the major subscores correlate highly, up to .91. While many of the scale scores are thus likely to be quite unidimensional, some of the scores might not be so. At any rate, there is no reason for the psychological or educational profession to accept a manual or a trait measure in the 1970's without this elementary information being available.

A more profound problem occurs whenever multiple scores are computed from an instrument. While it has been fashionable to continue multiplying scales, even in such well-known instruments as the MMPI, there are severe difficulties with such a procedure. Certainly such subscores are generally not uncorrelated and simply duplicate one another extensively. While there are over 200 MMPI scales, the MMPI certainly measures nowhere near that number of dimensions. The *Tennessee Self Concept Scale* provides scores for up to 29 variables. While the intercorrelations among these scores are presented, no principal components analysis or factor analysis is reported. It would be trivial to compute such an analysis of the internal structure of the scale; the analysis could easily be accomplished at the item level with today's computers (indeed, it should be carried out at this level because of the many artificial interdependencies among subscores). This reviewer would suspect that two or three dimensions at best exist in the scale; in view of the high correlation found with the Taylor Anxiety Scale, there might even be less. If there are only a few independent dimensions, multiplying scales in the fashion reported would serve mainly to confuse the user of the instrument and lead him to over-interpretations that are simply not warranted

on the basis of data. The issue is particularly acute in this case, since in the introductory paragraph of the manual the author implies that the scale fulfills the need for a measure that is "multi-dimensional in its description of the self concept." No evidence is presented that would verify this assertion. Lack of these data is hard to understand in this instance, since the scale has been in development for over a decade and since the publisher has been careful to include such data in other published tests.

While some old-style clinicians may appreciate the depth and care with which the author of the scale formulates hypotheses and proceeds to test them using data of the scale, this reviewer finds such a practice misleading and quite overinterpretive relative to the available data base. To illustrate, the manual cites an unpublished study in which the scale was used to predict changes through therapy. Although only six patients were used in the study, 88 predictions were made with respect to scale changes. In another study of 54 patients in two groups, 1,110 scale score changes were predicted. This is a remarkable amount of information to be assessed by 100 items; it becomes impossible to deal with statistically when the various scale scores are not independent. In future editions of the scale, the author would be well advised to consult with a psychometrician or a statistician in dealing with the above problems. Combining the author's clinical sensitivity with a more hard-nosed data analysis approach would no doubt yield a far more useful instrument.

Finally, the potential user should be aware that the scoring method is quite cumbersome. A rather extensive procedure must be followed; it is, however, very well organized in the accompanying answer sheet, score sheet, and profile sheet package. The drawbacks of scoring, however, compound the structural problems of the scale. One must remember to compare the possible benefits and drawbacks to be obtained from this scale with those obtained from competing measures such as the Taylor scale or the MMPI.

RICHARD M. SUINN, *Professor of Psychology and Associate Head of the Department, Colorado State University, Fort Collins, Colorado.*

The *Tennessee Self Concept Scale* is a self-administering instrument comprised of 100 self-descriptive statements. It is suitable for subjects age 12 or older and having at least a sixth grade reading level. The test may be given to normal or severely disturbed clients. The Counseling Form of the scale is used where self interpretation is desired or where the administrator is relatively unsophisticated in psychometrics. The Clinical and Research Form "is more complex in scoring, analysis, and interpretation" and requires a skilled examiner. Both forms use the same test items.

The TSCS is an extremely intriguing instrument that is the result of much painstaking work. The items in the original pool were derived from surveys of the literature on the self concept and from analyses of patient self-reports. The final items were selected by seven clinical psychologists who were asked to classify each item as to its fit with defined constructs. The final items included only those on which the judges showed perfect agreement. The determination of the various scores that reflect differing traits also demonstrates the work invested by the author in his scale. Some 27 different scores are reported; most of these scores appear to have been derived through a careful system of logical analyses and deductions. However, it is this very care and meticulousness which makes the manual so disappointing. The feeling that is conveyed is that an authority in assessment and test construction developed the scale and initiated the research, but that the reporting of the psychometric data in the manual was aimed toward an unsophisticated readership. Significantly absent are such crucial kinds of information as descriptive statistics on the normative sample, method for selection of samples cited, and the exact nature of results leading to the author's various conclusions. For example, the manual reports that "the norms are overrepresented in number of college students, white subjects, and persons in the 12 to 30 year age bracket"; nevertheless, the author concludes that "it has been apparent that samples from other populations do not differ appreciably from the norms, provided they are large enough samples." It would have been good practice for the author to cite the research leading to this conclusion, and to report the exact demographic data on the normative sample, perhaps in a single table. Since the test appears to be especially valuable in differentiating normals from psychiatric patients, again more information should have been presented to identify the nature of the patients

examined, the procedure for their selection, the criteria for exclusion of subjects, etc.

Some comments should be directed toward the scores of the TSCS. In some respects the TSCS shares something in common with the Stanford-Binet and with the MMPI. As with the Stanford-Binet, the meaning of the TSCS scores will in all likelihood be clarified through the gradual accumulation of research and clinical experience. In essence, although the scores seem to have certain content validity, there has been little work directed toward empirical validation of *individual* scores, e.g., what does the acquiescence conflict score relate to behaviorally—is this score a reflection of acquiescence response set, or of defensiveness? The value of the Stanford-Binet lies not only in the meaningfulness of the original concept of mental age, but also in the incredible amount of both concurrent and longitudinal types of data lending meaning to the scores. The TSCS is well along the road to stimulating enormous numbers of research studies. What is needed is for these to be summarized in a revised manual, with an emphasis upon works which may shed light upon the meaning, or the behavioral correlates, of the various scores.

The TSCS scores are similar to the MMPI scale in that they are recorded on a profile scoring sheet. In addition, the TSCS includes items from the Lie scale of the MMPI. Finally, the Empirical scales of the TSCS were derived by including items which empirically differentiated subjects of one group from another, a procedure identical to that used in the development of the MMPI scales. Again, there is some promise of better things to come, since the author holds out some hope that profile or pattern analysis may be eventually forthcoming. There is little doubt that the strongest aspect of the TSCS current scoring materials is the Empirical scales, items which were found on initial standardization to discriminate among the following groups: normals, psychotics, neurotics, personality disorders, defensive positive subjects, and personality integration subjects. Although the percentages of false positives and false negatives which occur vary with the particular scale under study (e.g., 20 percent of normals will be misidentified as deviant on the basis of the Number of Deviant Signs score; 38 percent of psychotics will be misidentified as nonpsychotic on the basis of the Psychosis Scale), nevertheless these Empirical scales provide a useful screening system. In addition, the test-retest reliabilities are quite substantial for these scales for a college student sample. Again, the manual fails to report on reliability data for other samples, such as patient samples (one coefficient is mentioned, but not for the Empirical scales scores).

The proper use of the nonempirical scales depends heavily upon the knowledge and intuitions of the examiner. Since the behavioral correlates of these scales are not yet fully available, the examiner must relate these scores to what he knows about psychopathology or personality development. For example, if Row 2 P score is reflective of self acceptance, then what is the interpretation of Row 1 P score (Identity) or Row 3 P score (Behavior)? It should be noted that although a majority of the important scale scores appear to have high reliability, a number of scores are unstable, e.g., some of the variability and conflict subscores. Finally, it must be acknowledged that the scoring procedures for both the Counseling Form and the Clinical and Research Form are tedious; the psychometrist must follow two and one-half pages of instructions for scoring.

Because of the two-fold nature of the TSCS, validation data must be examined (*a*) in terms of the test's usefulness in differentiating normals from non-normals, and (*b*) in terms of its capability of measuring self concept variables. Regarding the former, the manual cites cross-validation data which strongly suggest that the Empirical scales do a competent job of aiding in group discrimination. Regarding the latter, the problem is one which faces all research on self concept assessment, i.e., how does one select the criterion variable? For the TSCS, it was assumed that changes in self concept would occur from certain significant experiences (such as psychotherapy, sensitivity training, or hospitalization) or membership in certain groups (for example, minority groups or delinquency groups). In general, the results are supportive, although some unexpected findings have occurred. For example, psychotherapy, hospitalization, and group membership (delinquency) do seem to affect TSCS scores. On the other hand, sensitivity training did not lead to significant changes. In addition, scores for the normative sample led the author to conclude that race had negligible effects on scores; yet other studies have demonstrated that TSCS scores for southern Negro students appeared to be different from those of Caucasians. This adds construct validity to the scale, but raises questions about the representativeness of the normative sample.

One final set of data must be mentioned regarding validation studies. Although the TSCS is divided into several scales, each with presumed differing information, some factor analytic work has reported conflicting results. Rentz and White (*17*) identified three factors with primary loadings on one (called self-acceptance). Vacchiano and Strauss (*25*) found 20 factors but failed to find support for the three theorized measures of Identity, Self Satisfaction, and Behavior.

In summary, the TSCS ranks among the better measures combining group discrimination with self concept information. The Empirical scales are useful as a means of screening clients for pathology, while some of the other scales seem to add some intuitive data about self perceptions. A multitude of research has been stimulated by the instrument, and it is hoped that a future manual will summarize the more important results related to test interpretation and validation. The current manual leaves much to be desired in terms of providing pertinent details for fully evaluating the instrument. In addition, the scoring of the test remains a tedious process. In all, the TSCS offers great potential as a promising clinical instrument. Given the current information, it must be used as an aid to assessment subject to the cautions indicated in this review.

J Counsel Psychol 12:330–1 f '65. John O. Crites. * If any questions are raised about the Scale at this stage of its development, they most likely will pertain to its rationale instead of its construction. Thus, it can be asked: What are the particular advantages of this instrument over its long line of precursors, e.g., the Bills *Index of Adjustment and Values,* the various published Q-sorts, etc.? It is incumbent upon the author to demonstrate that his Scale is "simpler for the subject, more widely applicable, better standardized, etc." than other similar measuring devices. But, more importantly, it can be asked by died-in-the-wool "self concepters," such as Combs (1962), whether the Scale *is* a measure of the self concept. The Scale does not allow the examinee, for example, to use his *own words* to describe himself and consequently some would argue that it is not truly phenomenological. The author has not dealt with this issue in the Manual, but it would seem to be a critical one to resolve, if he wants to relate his Scale to self concept theory.

[152]

★Tests of Social Intelligence. High school and adults; 1965–66; TSI; 6 tests; 5 scores: implications (test *a*), classes (test *b*), systems (tests *c, d*), transformations (tests *e, f*), composite (tests *a, b, c, f*); manual ('66, 8 pages); norms for grade 10 only; separate answer sheets (IBM 805) must be used; 7¢ per answer sheet (space for all 6 tests); $2 per set of scoring stencils; 50¢ per manual; $2 per specimen set (complete test not included); postage extra; Maureen O'Sullivan, R. deMille (*c, d, e*), and J. P. Guilford; Sheridan Psychological Services, Inc. *

a) CARTOON PREDICTIONS. Form A ('65, 8 pages); $5 per 25 tests; 8(13) minutes.

b) EXPRESSION GROUPING. Form A ('65, 8 pages); $5 per 25 tests; 10(15) minutes.

c) MISSING CARTOONS. Form A ('65, 16 pages); $7 per 25 tests; 16(21) minutes.

d) MISSING PICTURES. Form A ('65, 12 pages); $7 per 25 tests; 12(17) minutes.

e) PICTURE EXCHANGE. Form A ('65, 12 pages); $7 per 25 tests; 12(17) minutes.

f) SOCIAL TRANSLATIONS. Form A ('65, 4 pages); $2.50 per 25 tests; 8(13) minutes.

REFERENCES

1. See P:272.
2. TENOPYR, MARY L. "Social Intelligence and Academic Success." *Ed & Psychol Meas* 27:961–5 w '67. * (*PA* 42:9509)
3. CLARK, LYNN FRED. *Repressor-Sensitizer Personality Styles and Associated Levels of Verbal Ability, Social Intelligence, Sex Knowledge, and Quantitative Ability (Neutral Content)*. Doctor's thesis, University of Kansas (Lawrence, Kan.), 1968. (*DAI* 30:842B)

DOUGLAS N. JACKSON, *Senior Professor of Psychology, The University of Western Ontario, London, Ontario, Canada.*

These tests are a continuation of the comprehensive treatment of intellectual abilities undertaken by Guilford and his collaborators within the context of the structure of intellect model. They represent an attempt to extend this work into the area of social interaction and cognition. Social cognition, according to these authors, "involves knowing or understanding the nature of the mental states of other persons, including what they are attending to, perceiving, thinking, feeling, or intending to do, by using visual cues from the expressive behavior of those others."

The emphasis is upon pictorial and graphical material both in material presented and in response format, rather than upon semantic materials, an emphasis which is quite understandable in the light of early research in this area. Factor analytic studies convincingly provided one of the earliest examples of a test being invalidated by too high a correlation with an irrelevant criterion. Tests purporting to measure social intelligence were insufficiently differentiated from general intelligence. Although the structure-of-intellect model hypothesizes 30 different facets of social intelligence, the study on which the present tests are based sought to identify 6 of these. These hypothesized factors were abilities to cognize or understand behavioral units, classes, relations, systems, transformations, and implications. The authors proffer the opinion that these abilities encompass what is commonly referred to as social sensitivity, empathy, and person perception. The authors administered 23 tests spanning this domain to 240 eleventh-grade middle-class students, and chose to publish six of the more successful of these tests, reflecting factors of the psychological products of classes, systems, transformations, and implications, with two tests showing some slight variance reflecting units and relations. For the population sampled, these tests proved to be substantially independent of tests of semantic content of the type commonly found on IQ tests.

Expression Groupings, a measure of the factor, cognition of behavioral classes, involves abstracting common attributes from a set of three line drawings showing various behavioral reactions and selecting one of four pictures best representing this common attribute. Missing Pictures and Missing Cartoons are essentially similar tests in which one of a set of four pictures or cartoons depicting two or more interacting persons is missing. The examinee chooses one from a set of three which would complete the story. The test loaded a factor identified as cognition of behavioral systems. Picture Exchange, involving a task in which one of three pictures is chosen as a substitute for one marked picture so that it will change the meaning of the story, is identified as a univocal measure of cognition of behavioral transformations. In Social Translations the examinee chooses between one of three given alternative pairs of people between whom a given verbal statement will have a changed behavioral meaning, different from what it would be if spoken between members of another given pair. This test is also primarily associated with the cognition of behavioral transformation factor, with a secondary loading on cognition of behavioral relations. Cartoon Predictions, in which the examinee chooses one of three alternative cartoons that shows what is most likely to result from a given cartoon situation, is a relatively easy test of the cognition of behavioral implications.

Reliability and normative data are presented based on a second sample administered slightly revised versions of the above tests. In general, reliabilities are in the moderate range, ranging from .32 for Picture Exchange to .85 for Social Translations. The authors state that "except in two instances [Social Translations and Missing Cartoons], the reliabilities would ordinarily be considered to be too low for measurement of individuals," but point out that all factor loadings were above .50 on hypothesized factors in the initial study. Data for three composite scores are also presented, the most promising of which appears to be the social cognition composite, with a reliability of .88. Since males and females did not differ on any of the tests significantly, norms are given for the two sexes combined. Norms are based on 266 tenth-grade students from a Fullerton, California, high school. Validity data are limited to reference to the initial factor analysis.

Clearly these are tests primarily suitable for research purposes. In their present form, too little is known about the presumed attributes being measured, their real-life social and behavioral consequences, and the validity of these particular measures, for recommending them in applied settings. Clearly, such research appears warranted based on the present preliminary factor analytic findings.

Further development and refinement of these tests might proceed in a number of ways. A careful examination of the items suggests that they are almost certainly not equally good or equally efficient, and would benefit from item analysis. In addition, although the authors have preferred orthogonal rotations, it is clear that their factors are correlated, resulting in undesirable complexity in their tests. (The intercorrelation matrix of these six tests is not reported in the manual.) Identifying items which are univocal or factorially pure, or, alternatively which suppress unwanted variance, would result in tests of higher technical quality.

Proponents of factor analytically derived tests have argued for the superiority of this method over others on methodological grounds. However, assessment specialists increasingly have come to appreciate the advantages of heteromethod identification of factors, particularly when the social or behavioral consequences of traits are at issue. For example, in the case of social intelligence, it has been demonstrated that reliable judgments by peers are possible and have resulted in a separation of social from "academic" intelligence. Experimental criterion tasks, such as the variant of the leaderless group discussion, would also be possible. Clearly, reliance on correlations between paper and pencil tests should be merely a starting point in test construction.

In an area like social cognition, cultural expectations and conventions play a dominant role. The degree to which tests of this type are affected by cultural and subcultural influences is not known. Pictorial material and cartoons of complex social interaction are perhaps more susceptible to this influence than are materials involving facial expression of emotions, but this is not certain. The degree to which materials like these, designed for high school and college students, are suitable for adults or for other subgroups needs further investigation, but certainly one should not assume equal applicability across subcultures.

In conclusion, *Tests of Social Intelligence* is a pioneering venture seeking to assess socially important but neglected factors of social cognition. It is the most promising set of materials available in an area where there is virtually no competition. Nevertheless, the absence of data relating to heteromethod validity, and the possible restrictiveness of the norms and of the appropriateness of materials to upper-level school age individuals, would suggest that these materials be employed at present in research contexts exclusively, where there is a possibility of appraising their relevance to criterion performance variables.

[153]

★**The Thomas Self-Concept Values Test.** Ages 3-9; 1967-69; TSCVT; experimental form; 19 scores: value scores (happiness, size, sociability, ability, sharing, male acceptance, fear of things, fear of people, strength, cleanliness, health, attractiveness, material independence), self concept scores (self as subject, mother, teacher, peer, total); no reading by examinees; revised manual ('69, 53 pages); answer-profile sheet ('67, 2 pages); 10¢ per answer-profile sheet; $24 per manual, postage extra; (10-20) minutes; Walter L. Thomas; Combined Motivation Education Systems, Inc. *

JOAN J. MICHAEL, *Associate Professor of Educational Psychology, California State College at Long Beach, Long Beach, California.*

The TSCVT is an individually administered scale designed to assess the self-concept of young children using the self-report format.

The child is asked to respond to the same series of 14 bipolar adjectival items four times: first from the standpoint of his own perceptions, then from the standpoint of his perceptions of others' perceptions of him, namely, his mother's, his teacher's, and his peers'. Thus, each test yields a total of 19 scores: 14 item scores (one for each item for all four scales combined), four scale scores comprised of 14 items each, and a total score for all scales combined.

The author has spent the first 16 pages of the manual reviewing past literature and research and evolving a model and rationale around which the instrument has been constructed, certainly a plus factor for a scale of this type.

Instructions to examiners appear to be complete—however, at times lacking in standardization. For example, it is suggested in light of limitations of attention span of the typical four-year-old, that the test be administered in various numbers of sittings, depending upon the child. While this reviewer agrees with the rationale here, it seems that different norms should be made available for different time schedules for administration.

The scale is inherently easy to score with its +1 and −1 format for each item. It is then recommended that in order to compare individuals, raw scores be converted to standard scores, and a T scale table is furnished for that purpose. However, it is unclear in the manual from what type and number of data these standard scores were derived. Did the data meet the criterion of being normally distributed? If not, these standard scores may be unreliable or misleading.

In the manual, extensive item analysis data are presented; however, the average user might find this information difficult to interpret and use. Few students with masters degrees in education—even in educational measurement—would be able to comprehend the technical aspects of this manual. The sample of Headstart children would suggest a restriction of range and hence an atypical item analysis. Moreover, these coefficients seem unusually high—a circumstance suggesting the possibility of an acquiescent response set, either positive or negative.

The reported reliability (test-retest) estimate for this scale was .78 for the total score with .82 for the self-referent scale, .68 for the teacher-referent scale, and .61 for the peer-referent scale. The reliability estimate for the mother referent scale was omitted. For the 14 self-value items the derived coefficients ranged between .34 (health) and .93 (sharing). The average (Fisher z-transformation) internal consistency measure of reliability was given as .73. Thus there appears to be further support for the conclusion that the four self-concept referent scales are substantially related to each other.

For construct validity, the author writes: "the particular item format, the logically selected item content, the independent scale scores are all cited as maximizing the possible construct validity of the Thomas Self-Concept Values Test." This reviewer believes that this statement is perhaps a necessary but not a sufficient condition of construct validity and that it holds true for almost any kind of validity. Is this not more akin to face validity than to construct validity? Then as evidence of concurrent validity, the author reports the results of an experimental investigation based upon his theory in which hypotheses were for the most part confirmed. Although the author has termed this evidence to be in support of concurrent validity, this reviewer believes that it is more closely related to construct validity in light of the prediction and confirmation of "typologies."

Finally the manual reports research with various demographic data, such as, number of siblings, amount of father's education, age of child, and child's IQ, all of which would be of interest to anyone considering using the instrument for a research investigation.

It is this reviewer's summative analysis that the TSCVT would be a useful tool in clinical assessment of the self concept of a young child. The items and format seem appropriate for the age level stipulated; however, the user would be wise to exercise great caution in attempting to use the scale for purposes of research. Finally, although it is recognized that extensive effort (certainly far more than one often finds for a scale of this type) has already been put forth in establishing norms, doing item analyses, and estimating reliability and validity, further work is certainly warranted.

RICHARD M. SUINN, *Professor of Psychology and Associate Head of the Department, Colorado State University, Fort Collins, Colorado.*

The *Thomas Self-Concept Values Test* is a very brief scale measuring self-evaluative responses. In the introductory section of the test manual, the author quite correctly points out the need for more appropriate scales of intellect, ability, and personality, for children of preschool and early elementary school ages. In addition, he recognizes the desirability of keeping the testing time to a minimum because of the short attention span of very young examinees. A unique aspect of the test is the reliance upon a Polaroid camera snapshot of the examinee to enable the child to focus his attention on a tangible topic when taking the test. The examiner photographs the child, props the portrait before the child, then asks the child several questions to elicit a self-description, with the photograph as a reminder to the child that he is to describe himself.

Although the TSCVT is purported to measure self-concept, the instrument in fact emphasizes questions involving self-evaluation and the scores are termed *value scores*. Several assumptions are made: (*a*) the self-concept involves self-evaluative descriptions; (*b*) the crucial dimensions for self-evaluation are those assumed to be highly valued by "cultural demands of middle-class" society; (*c*) the self-concept is shaped by significant others (namely mother, teacher, classmates), and therefore the scores include a total self-concept score which is the sum of the scores derived from answers to questions of how "mother, teacher, your classmates think of you"; (*d*) young children are able to assume the role of these significant others in replying to the questions; and (*e*) the 14 self-value factors represent the basic demands and cultural values which, if measured, will provide the needed information for assessment and prediction.

The TSCVT is characterized by simplicity in administration and in scoring. The child is asked to respond to forced-choice questions which are worded in simple language, e.g., "Does [your] mother think that [you] are happy or sad?" Scoring involves assigning a value of $+1$ or -1, summing these scores, then converting to standard scores from a table. The scoring sheet provides a means for drawing a profile for quick visual inspection.

Intriguing though the instrument may be, there are several major theoretical and statistical problems. The author admits that there are no factor analytic studies of values at early childhood ages from which to select the dimensions for assessment. Consequently, he pro-

ceeded to survey the literature and apparently extracted his 14 factors on the basis of at least two criteria: they seemingly represent culturally approved values, and they appear to be necessary for normal personality growth. Some of these factors are at least somewhat supported by rigorous research, but others (such as size) are justified on the basis of statements by a cultural anthropologist. The reviewer agrees with the author that the selections were "a result of speculative decision." Although the test is directed towards children ages 3–9, the scoring scheme fails to take into account possible change in values across age levels, such as occur in parental tolerance or valuation of dependency. The author does take minimal account of differences across sexes by reversing the scoring weights for some items; however, a critical deficiency exists in the absence of any norms by age level or by sex.

Test-retest reliability coefficients obtained over a two-week period show that 14 of the scores have reliabilities at or below .78. These figures raise some question regarding the stability of the scores and their use for individual diagnosis. In addition, they call into doubt the manual's instruction that parts of the test may be administered after a delay of as long as three weeks. As a differing way of expressing reliability, tetrachoric correlations are reported and again the majority of the correlations are less than satisfying, with a range from .10 to .93.

Two major types of validation data are provided. For construct validity, the author simply cites definitions of terms and concepts such as "value," "self-concept," "test item." This gives the reader some grasp of the point of view held by the author, but fails to supply any substantive validation of the particular instrument. As further validity information, the author cites the relationship between TSCVT scores and membership in various criterion groups, e.g., "highly privileged and underprivileged." Of 19 scores examined, 8 showed differences between the two groups where the differences were higher than one standard deviation. However, when the data are examined in detail, it is clear that the underprivileged subjects' scores were all within one standard deviation of the standard score mean, with nine scores being within 2 points of the standard score mean of 50.

In view of the lower reliability coefficients,

and the absence of normative data, and the scarcity of adequate validation materials, the TSCVT is best relied upon as an experimental instrument or an interview guide, rather than as a tool for individual diagnosis or prediction. The questions may be valuable for eliciting the child's perceptions of how he views himself on specific dimensions, how others view him, and the congruency between his self-perception and his perception of how others see him. Although the author emphasizes the issues of the disadvantaged child, early-start programs, and adjustment in his introductory remarks, the TSCVT has not reached the stage of psychometric development which would justify its current use as a means for making major decisions related to such matters.

[154]

★Thorndike Dimensions of Temperament. Grades 11–16 and adults; 1963–66; TDOT; 10 scores: sociable, ascendant, cheerful, placid, accepting, toughminded, reflective, impulsive, active, responsible; 1 form ('63, 7 pages); manual ('66, 35 pages); norms for grades 11–13 only; separate answer sheets (IBM 805) must be used; $3.80 per 25 tests; $3 per 50 answer sheets; $2 per set of hand scoring stencils and manual; $2.25 per set of machine scoring stencils and manual; $2.50 per specimen set; postage extra; (45–55) minutes; Robert L. Thorndike; Psychological Corporation. *

REFERENCES

1–2. See P:276.
3. COLQUHOUN, DOROTHY REBECCA. *The Relationship Between Ontario Nurse Registration Examinations and Certain Criterion Measures.* Doctor's thesis, Columbia University (New York, N.Y.), 1967. *(DA* 28:3459B)
4. BRAUN, JOHN R., AND TINLEY, JOHN. "Control for Social Desirability in the Thorndike Dimensions of Temperament." *Psychol Rep* 23:1150 D '68. * *(PA* 43:8369)
5. THORNDIKE, ROBERT L. "A Verification Key for the Thorndike Dimensions of Temperament." *J Ed Meas* 5:331–3 w '68. * *(PA* 44:10441)
6. SAPPENFIELD, BERT R. "Stereotypical Perception of a Personality Trait in Fraternity Members." *Percept & Motor Skills* 29(2):460–2 O '69. * *(PA* 44:3563)
7. SAPPENFIELD, BERT R. "Stereotypical Perception of a Personality Trait in Personal Acquaintances." Abstract. *Proc 77th Ann Conv Am Psychol Assn* 4(1):409–10 '69. * *(PA* 43:17406)
8. LEDERMAN, EDWARD. *An Evaluation of the Rationale for the Forced-Choice Structure of the Thorndike Dimensions of Temperament.* Doctor's thesis, Columbia University (New York, N.Y.), 1970. *(DAI* 31:2258B)

C. J. ADCOCK, *Retired Professor of Psychology, Victoria University of Wellington, Wellington, New Zealand.*

The title of this personality inventory suggests a query as to what the author had in mind. The term "temperament" has usually been used to refer to aspects of personality largely due to genetic factors, but it has also been somewhat loosely used to refer to any stable personality dimension. The nature of the instrument suggests that the term is used in the latter sense. If this is so, both the ambiguity and the lack of precision seem undesirable.

The choice of the dimensions to be measured is a vital problem in any personality test. Eysenck and Eysenck's recent text [1] highlights the need for a firmly based set of dimensions for personality measurement. Unless designed for a specific purpose, a general test of personality is most usefully based upon dimensions which are as far as possible factorially pure and which remain largely invariant from population to population. Both Guilford and Cattell have made major contributions in this respect and Eysenck's acceptance of primary factors underlying his own broad second-order factors has brought his system into accord with Cattell's general schema, although the specific primary factors differ very much.

The ten dimensions which the inventory aims to measure have been inspired largely, it would appear, by the *Guilford-Zimmerman Temperament Survey.* Five dimensions, as evidenced by correlational data provided, represent G-Z measures: Sociable (.48), Ascendant (.73), Active (.61), Tough-minded (masculine) (.71), Reflective (thoughtfulness) (.55). Impulsive and Responsible have correlations of −.50 and .44, respectively, with G-Z Restraint and are themselves negatively correlated to the extent of −.56, which makes one suspect that these two dimensions may be largely measuring the same thing but with reversed scales. The data regarding correlations with average peer ratings reinforce this suspicion. Again, the correlations of Impulsive with the peer rating of Impulsive is .37, while its correlation with the peer rating of Responsible is −.36.

Since the three remaining TDOT scales have overlapping relations with the G-Z scales but are themselves relatively independent (highest mean r is .38), it might be surmised that the TDOT provides the best structuring of this area.

In the light of recent research, as, for example, the extensive study by Eysenck and Eysenck, it would appear that the TDOT dimensions are in accord with the general trend of evidence. Comment on the individual dimensions may be useful:

Sociable. This is a widely-evidenced dimension but it is not always clear whether what is involved is a desire to participate in group

1 EYSENCK, HANS J., AND EYSENCK, SYBIL B. G. *Personality Structure and Measurement.* London: Routledge and Kegan Paul, 1969. Pp. xiii, 365. *

activities, to lead such activities, or simply to have some contact with other human beings and so avoid loneliness. The first and last of these are assumed by Thorndike. Two subfactors could be involved, but there is doubtless a common core.

Ascendant. This is a well-attested factor of social leadership, the tendency to dominate in a social situation regardless of group size. Vocational implications of this and the preceding dimension are obvious.

Active. This is a measure not represented in the 16PF system, but there is good evidence for it in other research and it appears to be of considerable vocational importance. Perhaps "energetic" might have been a better term for it.

Tough-minded. There is general agreement on this factor, which Cattell refers to as sensitivity and Guilford as masculinity, thereby emphasising the importance of sex differences.

Reflective. This appears in some form in the major systems but the measures are not necessarily equivalent. Here we have a stress on intellectual and aesthetic interests and one would expect an appreciable correlation with educational level.

Cheerful. This corresponds to the surgency of Cattell and rhathymia of Guilford. It involves not merely a high average cheerfulness but a quick recovery from setbacks and a general tendency to be free from undue worry.

Placid. This seems to correspond to the second-order factor of anxiety in the 16PF, the neuroticism of Eysenck and the earlier emotionality of Burt. Essentially, one might describe it as a low threshold for autonomic involvement. Some correlation with the previous factor could be expected, since worry and depression become accentuated by high emotional reaction.

Accepting. This spans the friendliness and personal relations scales of the G-Z but seems to have very much in common with the protension of the 16PF. The dimension seems to be one of trustfulness versus suspicion.

Impulsive. Many tests have found it almost impossible to distinguish between the effects of high ego-control and low emotionality on the stability of behaviour. The present scale seems to relate to the former. The items suggest planned action with careful thought to the consequences. There is little doubt about the existence and importance of such a factor and

it is rather a pity that it here seems to be confused with responsibility. However, study of the test items suggests that it is the latter dimension which is suspect, since so many of its items involve some degree of impulsivity or planning.

Responsible. Theoretically this is a very satisfactory dimension which would be well justified by research studies, but unfortunately it is here very much contaminated by the impulsivity factor. Inspection of the test items involved clearly indicates why. The majority of these items need complete rewriting.

A major aim in the preparation of the test has been to avoid contamination by social desirability effects. This has led to the adoption of a forced-choice approach. The procedure adopted is commendable in principle if one is prepared to accept ipsative scores. It involves grouping test items in groups of 10 to cover the 10 dimensions to be measured and asking testees to select the three items which are most like them and the three which are least like them, and to ignore the others, thereby scoring all on a 3-point scale. The presumption is that in trying to maximise social desirability the testee will be frustrated by the competing claims of different items. However, for this to work, all items must be scored in the same direction relative to social desirability. The aim of this procedure becomes completely nullified if half the items are in negative form since six items can be given maximum scores for social desirability and the four items least socially desirable can be left to the neutral category. Strangely this requirement has been completely overlooked in compiling the test and the number of negatives in each set ranges from two to eight. This range controls response bias but largely eliminates control of social desirability. Both aims could have been given maximum effect by keeping negative (re desirability) items within their own groups where testees would wish to score all items in the same direction.

Some people will question the effectiveness of forced choice methods in controlling social-desirability effects. Scott [2] has shown that individual differences with regard to the desirability of traits make it impossible to resort to any really effective system of automatically elimi-

2 Scott, William A. "Social Desirability and Individual Conceptions of the Desirable." *J Abn & Social Psychol* 67:574-85 D '63. *

nating this factor,[3] and Braun and LaFaro (*2*) report the ineffectiveness of the present approach. Thorndike compiled a verification key which he claims catches 83 percent of the "faked" scores at the expense of including only 6 percent of the "honest" scores. Under these circumstances it might be considered much better to drop the ipsative approach altogether, since ipsative scores have negative correlations built into them and this gravely distorts correlational studies.

Reliability of the scales ranges from .54 to .87 for high school students and seems to be satisfactory for a test of this kind. Validity cannot be easily assessed, since there are no standard criteria and no factorial studies are presented to indicate construct validity. Data with regard to correlation with other known tests would suggest to the reviewer that mean validity for the scales probably approaches .70 if one omits the Responsibility scale. This could make it a very useful test if it is used with discretion. With suitable revision it could be excellent for vocational guidance but its ipsative character would raise doubts as to its suitability for some forms of research. Percentile norms based on large samples give a good basis for comparison.

ALFRED B. HEILBRUN, JR., *Professor of Psychology and Director of Clinical Training, Emory University, Atlanta, Georgia.*

The *Thorndike Dimensions of Temperament* is a self-report personality questionnaire in which one is asked to describe himself on ten dimensions of "temperament." The person is presented with sets of ten statements, one representing each dimension, and he is asked to choose the three statements most like him and the three least like him. Presentation of 20 such sets allows for each trait to be compared with each of the other 9 traits 20 times. Scores may range from -20 to $+20$ on each dimension; in the former case, the person must have chosen the statement representing a given dimension as among the three most like him within every set, whereas in the latter case the person must have selected the given dimensional statement as among the three least like him on each occasion.

One need go little further than the name of this inventory to take issue with it. It is diffi-

cult to conceptualize what Thorndike considers to be the essence of temperament when the ten dimensions he has chosen for measurement are considered. Thomas, Chess, and Birch [1] in a recent book on temperament in children define their subject matter as "the characteristic tempo, rhythmicity, adaptability, energy expenditure, mood, and focus of attention of a child, independent of the content of any specific behavior." Yet the TDOT includes not only what appear to be acceptable dimensions of temperament (e.g., placid-irritable, impulsive-planful, active-lethargic) but also some variables which clearly reflect the content of social behavior (e.g., sociable-solitary, ascendant-withdrawing, accepting-critical). The manual fails to deal conceptually with the nature of temperament, except to mention the factor analytic origin of those variables included in the TDOT. Anyone considering the use of this inventory must proceed cautiously in inferring that any unitary umbrella covers the TDOT variables unless it is something as broad and nebulous as "personality."

The origins of the TDOT are rooted in the assumption that social desirability response set must be deterred as a pervasive determinant of item responses on personality inventories. While this particular issue has been the basis for long debate and no apparent resolution, the importance attributed to the structural attempts to deter social desirability as a source of variance requires at least one parting shot. Even the more elegant test development procedures which went into the *Edwards Personal Preference Schedule* were found ultimately not to be particularly effective in presenting the *individual* with options equal in social desirability. The TDOT, which utilized a cruder method of matching, should prove even less effective in this regard. But what is more important is that social desirability responding has been enormously oversold as a determinant of test behavior and does not merit the attention Thorndike has given it.

Consideration which will now be given to the major technical attributes of the TDOT as a psychological test will be based upon information provided in the manual. The first of these, reliability of the scales, is reported only in terms of an internal consistency coefficient. While the range of corrected split-half coefficients, .46 to

---

3 It should be noted that when vocational selection is involved the ideal profile which the testee may wish to project will vary according to the job involved and any general corrective factor could be quite misleading.

1 THOMAS, ALEXANDER; CHESS, STELLA; AND BIRCH, HERBERT G. *Temperament and Behavior Disorders in Children.* New York: New York University Press, 1968. Pp. vii, 309. *

.88, is rather wide, the fact that most are in the .70's and .80's attests to some degree of homogeneity of intra-scale item content. However, the statement in the manual to the effect that low internal consistency may be expected when "a trait represents a rather loosely organized constellation of behaviors" fails to add that the same result occurs given faulty item selection. It would also have been valuable to present us with test-retest reliability figures to see how well the TDOT holds up over time.

Since interscale correlations are consistently low, it is safe to assume that the TDOT is comprised of independent trait measures. The degree of relationships between the scales and various indices of intellectual ability are also low enough to allow our viewing this inventory as a nonintellective instrument.

The percentile norms presented in the manual appear at first glance to be quite satisfactory, including as they do separate norms by sex and by high school versus college attendance based upon sizeable N's. However, the norms are based on a very narrow age range, almost all of the roughly 5,500 high school juniors and seniors and college freshmen in the normative samples presumably falling in the 16–19 year range. It must be seriously questioned whether the sampling has been adequate to consider the present norms as representative even of "high school" and "college" populations.

Perhaps the most serious limitation of the TDOT, as far as one is able to discern from the manual, is the almost complete absence of evidence of its validity. While some correlations with previously published tests and with self and peer ratings are presented, no bibliography can be found to suggest a serious effort on the part of the test developer or anyone else to expose the inventory to a systematic critical analysis of its validity.

The summary impression which comes from these evaluative comments is that the TDOT was made commercially available before it should have been. Certainly, the lack of stability estimates, the restricted norms, and the paucity of evidence regarding scale validities could have been alleviated by a more thorough pre-publication effort. Compounding this uneasiness is the bald statement made early in the manual that "the inventory appears to be quite successful in providing a differentiated picture of the manifest personality," followed by suggestions for use in making counseling, career development, and personnel utilization decisions. *Caveat emptor!*

Since some of the criticisms leveled at the TDOT are concerned with errors of omission or correctable limitations such as the norms, the test could still turn out to be a useful one. However, it strikes me that the test developer (and the publisher) should assume the basic responsibility for demonstrating usefulness and not the consumer.

Am Ed Res J 5:281–4 Mr '68. Lawrence J. Stricker. * The traits measured....are based largely on....factors identified by Guilford and Zimmerman. Items were written that were believed to correspond to the factors, and item analysis was employed to select the items that correlated highly with the set of items for their own factor but did not correlate highly with the sets of items for the other factors. In this way, 20-item scales were obtained for each of ten traits * Roughly half the items in each scale are positively worded and half are negatively worded. These items are cast into a forced-choice format, based on sets of 10 items. Each of the 20 sets consists of one item from each scale, all the items in the set having similar endorsement frequencies. The examinee is instructed to pick the three items from each set that are most like him and the three from the set that are least like him. The score for each TDOT scale is the number of positive items endorsed and negative items rejected in the 20 sets. Two features of the test-construction procedures—matching items from different scales on some index of their favorability and then pitting the items against each other—are common to other forced-choice inventories and have serious limitations. One is that matching is fine in principle but difficult to achieve in practice. Even if it were possible to match items *exactly* on some favorability index, the index is likely to be multidimensional, and interaction or context effects may occur when items are contrasted with each other. These matching procedures can therefore provide no assurance that all the items in a set are equally favorable to a subject. Hence distortion may not be reduced substantially, if at all. It is paradoxical that the TDOT manual reports no data on the inventory's resistance to distortion since solving this problem was a major concern in the TDOT's design. Another limitation is that forcing a choice between items from different scales inevitably produces ipsative scores. These scores reflect intraindividual differences unlike normative scores, which reflect interindividual differences. Ipsativity complicates score interpretations and appraisals of the statistical relationships among the scores as well as between the scores and other variables. Factor analysis and other multivariate techniques are either precluded or must be drastically modified. It is likely, however, that the particular forced-choice format of the TDOT—six choices from each 10-item set—has made these ipsative effects somewhat less serious than they are on the *Edwards Personal Preference Schedule,* for example, which uses a paired-comparison format. What is the content of the scales? In view of their factor analytic origin, it would have been useful to factor analyze the scales before they were matched in order to determine if they tapped different factors, but no such study is reported. A cursory inspection of the items on each scale reveals both heterogeneity and a kind of pseudo-homogeneity. Several items have no apparent connection with the name of their scale or with the other items on it (e.g., "You find it hard to 'let yourself go' " is on the Ascendant scale; "You feel most foreign governments are not to be trusted" is on the Reflective scale). Perhaps more seriously, a number of items are simply rewordings of each other (e.g., "You rarely forget to do anything you are supposed to do" vs. "You are likely to forget things you are supposed to do"). The reliability of the scales is particularly distressing, judging from the data that are available. The medians of the split-half reliability coefficients in four student groups range from .68 to .74—and reliability coefficients as low as .46 are reported. In the absence of evidence that these internal-consistency reliability data are substantially lower than other kinds of reliability estimates—no parallel-form or retest reliability data are presented—there is serious doubt about the usefulness of interpreting individuals' scores on this inventory. In contrast to the sparse or nonexistent data on other important issues, extensive data are reported to demonstrate that the scales are relatively independent. Indeed, the intercorrelations are generally moderate, but, unfortunately, the interpretation of these correlations is difficult because of the ipsativity of the scales, which affects the pattern of correlations, and the low reliability of many of the scales, which atten-

uates their correlations. Validity data are scanty. They consist of the correlations of the TDOT with other tests and inventories, ratings on the traits measured by the TDOT, and demographic characteristics. No predictive validity data are provided. Most relevant are the TDOT's correlations with the *Guilford-Zimmerman Temperament Survey* and the ratings, which provide evidence of the inventory's convergent and discriminant validity. The correlations between similar scales on the two inventories are generally substantial and consistently higher than the correlations between dissimilar scales on the two devices. Especially persuasive are the correlations of the TDOT with self- and peer-ratings. The TDOT scales correlate higher with their corresponding ratings than they do with the other ratings, but the correlations are not always sizeable. Separate norms are furnished for male and female high school students and college freshmen. The norms are not based on representative samples, but the subjects are drawn from a variety of schools scattered across the country and the number of cases is large. In summary, the blueprint for the TDOT has some laudable features, but the actual product seems to have fallen short of the mark. The structural limitations of the TDOT, its marginal reliability, and its lack of adequate validity data provide no justification for its use in real-life situations. The inventory's use in research, though hampered by many of these same problems, may conceivably uncover fruitful applications for this instrument.

J Ed Meas 6(1):54–5 sp '69. Donald J. Veldman. * The author suggests the Dimensions of Temperament (DOT) for use as an adjunct to counseling, especially when psychopathology is not an issue. He also suggests its use in career development and personnel utilization problems in industry. No validity data are offered in the manual, however, to guide the user in such applications of the inventory. Research and classroom demonstrations are also mentioned as possible uses. Percentile norms are provided for male and female high school students (Grades 11 and 12) and college freshmen. The author claims that the inventory is suitable for adults of educational levels comparable to those included in the normative sample, but no norms are provided for older adults. Although the forced-choice structure of the inventory does control the influence of social desirability response set, it should be noted that this does not insure that the profiles of scores are free from the effects of conscious bias toward what the respondents may feel is wanted in a particular context, such as career development. Normative data collected under such conditions might differ significantly from those provided in the manual. The most interesting feature of the DOT inventory is the unique structure of the item set and the response format. In one sense, the instrument contains only 20 items. Each "item" consists of a set of ten statements, phrased with second-person pronouns. The respondent is asked to indicate the three statements in each set which are most like him, and the three that are most unlike him, leaving the other four unmarked. This partially forced-choice procedure is economical compared to all possible item-pairings or complete ranking, and has the definite advantage of decreasing subject resistance to the task. The resulting scale scores have a potential range of 41 points, with each item being essentially a three-point scale. Items within each set were selected for comparable endorsement value, in order to reduce the influence of social desirability response set. Sets are arranged in the booklet so that those with the lowest endorsement values are in the middle of the series. Reliability values given in the manual vary from .54 to .87. Although less reliable than the scales of the Guilford-Zimmerman instrument, the internal consistency of the DOT scales appears adequate. The intercorrelations of the ten scales of the DOT are considerably lower than those of the Guilford-Zimmerman variables. Thorndike attributes this logically to the forced-choice structure of his instrument, and claims greater differential precision for his measures on this basis. In this reviewer's opinion, the author has not adequately supported this contention. The relatively low scale intercorrelations may in fact reflect the reduced influence of social desirability response set. However, it does not follow automatically that precision of trait measurement has been increased at the same time. Forced-choice structuring tends to result in negative scale relationships, a kind of hydraulic effect. The low scale intercorrelations undoubtedly reflect this artifact to some extent. To state the point another way, it is not true that the high scale correlations obtained with the usual independent-item scales are necessarily spurious, nor is it true that the forced-choice format necessarily results in more precise measurement

of traits. The trade-off between influence of social desirability and the artificial constriction of responses imposed by the set structure may have resulted in no net gain in precision of measurement. What is badly needed here is a definitive comparison of the reliability and validity of scores from these two formats, applied to the same item statements. Thorndike includes in his manual a variety of validity data concerning relationships between the DOT scales and comparable ratings by self and peers. As might be expected, the self-ratings correlate with the DOT scales at a level somewhat lower than the DOT scale reliabilities, while the peer ratings correlate with the DOT at a much lower level. Also included are correlations between DOT scales and various ability/achievement test scores. A rather surprising finding was that the Impulsive scale correlated positively with these measures, while the Responsibility scale correlated negatively with them in a number of samples. In summary, the information provided in the manual supports the author's statement that the inventory "portrays the individual both as he sees himself and as others see him." The level of assessment is frankly superficial: "....it does not pretend to delve into deep layers of personality dynamics ...." The traits measured are very much like those assessed by the older Guilford-Zimmerman Temperament Survey. The unique feature of the instrument is its semi-forced-choice structure, which is probably more acceptable to most respondents than the usual independent-item format. Although social desirability set is almost certainly reduced by this device, the author's contention that precision of trait measurement is consequently increased remains open to question and deserves to be studied empirically.

Prof Psychol 1(4):416–7 su '70. Kenneth B. Stein. * The traits are based on the factors in the *Guilford-Zimmerman Temperament Survey.* The apparent purpose for the development of a new test to measure these similar traits is the utilization of a format that presumably controls for social desirability. * A salient question is whether the inventory actually controls for social desirability. Matching items for popularity scores based on proportion of endorsement does not guarantee that the instrument is free of social desirability distortion. The manual surprisingly contains no studies to indicate that the inventory is resistive to systematic error due to a faking set. However, a subsequent study by Braun and LaFaro (1967) demonstrated rather clearly that when subjects on a second administration of the TDOT were asked to answer the items with the set to make a good impression, significant shifts occurred in the scores on all 10 traits. This led Thorndike (1968) to develop a verification key based on the Braun and LaFaro (1967) sample. The best cut-off scores based on this sample of 86 subjects resulted in approximately 23–29% misses. The effects of the opposite set, namely, to make a bad impression, have not as yet been studied. The above studies place into question the advantage and justification of the TDOT format. If the format does not eliminate or sharply reduce response set distortion and if verification keys are required to locate invalid protocols, it would seem important to question whether other formats such as True-False, Likert-type rating scales or ranking procedures could do as well or better for the purpose of the measurement of these traits. In the development of the items an attempt was made to find those that were homogeneous within the trait but independent of other traits. This design ideally could be implemented by factorization procedures, but these were not employed. Using other statistical procedures, relatively independent scales were nevertheless achieved. The intercorrelations between traits are generally quite low and the author demonstrates that TDOT traits are more independent than the Guilford-Zimmerman measures. The TDOT correlations, however, are based on a format which yields ipsative scores and such scores tend to produce low coefficients. The apparent independence of the traits may be merely an artifact of an ipsative instrument. As to the homogeneity of the traits, the split-half reliability data shed some light on this problem. The reliabilities across four samples range from .54 to .87 with the median in the low .70s. These magnitudes incidentally are augmented by corrections for variance attenuation. It is apparent that the internal consistency is not as large as one would desire, particularly for a number of scales, in order to be useful for application to the individual case. It is noted in the manual that the intention was to obtain a broad range of content within the traits and to avoid mere repetition or rephrasing of the same content, and that such an effort does tend to lower the intra-item scale correlations. The burden then

becomes one of finding adequate validational criteria against which to analyze the items. It should be noted that other types of reliability have not as yet been studied, namely, test-retest and alternate forms. Norms in the form of percentile equivalents for raw scores are provided for college freshmen and combined eleventh and twelfth graders, but separately for males and females. Even though the number of participants is quite respectable, it is not clear how the 20 high schools and the 10 colleges supplying subjects were selected and whether they are representative of such institutions across the country. * The manual recommends the TDOT for use in personal counseling, personnel decisions, and research. Certainly such dimensions might be quite useful in understanding manifest aspects of personality and such knowledge might facilitate decision making of importance to the counselee as well as to management in personnel selection. The adequacy of the reliability and validity of an inventory is important to its usefulness. The TDOT inventory discloses magnitudes of reliability which leave something to be desired as far as application to the individual case is concerned. Although characteristics of each trait are described in the manual, very little is available on the interpretation of patterns or the interactional effects of two traits. Case examples of TDOT use in counseling and personnel decisions are not provided and this may introduce difficulties for counselors. It is suggested that at this stage the inventory might be utilized to provide initial hypotheses for free discussion between the counselor and counselee. Although the validity data thus far are promising, additional studies concerned with practical application are needed. If the inventory is presumably an attempt to build an improved measure of the Guilford-Zimmerman traits, future studies will have to determine whether the goal has been achieved. Its format certainly is intriguing, but whether such an ipsative measure proves to be more effective than a more conventional one remains to be seen by future research.

[155]

★Trait Evaluation Index. College and adults; 1967–68; TEI; 22 scores (social orientation, compliance, benevolence, elation, ambition, motivational drive, self confidence, dynamism, independence, personal adequacy, caution, self organization, responsibility, propriety, courtesy, verbal orientation, intellectual orientation, perception, self control, fairmindedness, adaptability, sincerity) plus 4 general supplementary scores (over-all adjustment, masculinity, femininity, consistency) and 3 supplementary scores for engineers (employment stability, productivity-creativity, job satisfaction); 1 form ('67, 4 pages); manual ('68, 38 pages); supplement ['68, 4 pages]; profile for college, adults, ('67, 2 pages); no norms for adult females; separate answer sheets (IBM 1230) must be used; $6 per 20 tests; $3.25 per 20 answer sheets; $6 per set of scoring stencils; $3.25 per 20 profiles; $2.75 per manual; $7.50 per specimen set; cash orders postpaid, 10% extra on charge orders; German edition available; (30–50) minutes; Alan R. Nelson; Martin M. Bruce, Ph.D., Publishers. *

REFERENCE

1. BRAUN, JOHN R., AND SEAMON, JOHN. "Control for Social Desirability in the Trait Evaluation Index." *J Proj Tech & Pers Assess* 33(3):279–80 Je '69. * (PA 43:14344)

HAROLD BORKO, *Professor of Psychology. School of Library Service, University of California, Los Angeles, California.*

The *Trait Evaluation Index* purports to measure 22 personality trait variables. The instrument consists of 125 triads of positive-sounding adjectives descriptive of personality. It is a self-rating test; that is, the subject—a normal adult—is asked to select the adjective within the group of three that is most descriptive of himself and the one that is least descriptive. The selections are recorded on a separate answer sheet and are manually scored by use of a template.

The test developer is well aware of the many difficulties involved in measuring personality and in using a self-rating procedure in particular. The adjectives used in the instrument were carefully selected and rated for social desirability before being included. Each triad grouping was selected so that the three adjectives would have approximately the same social desirability value, thus preventing an easy, nondiscriminating choice. Deliberate biasing was made more difficult by utilizing a forced-choice format. And finally, eight triad items were repeated to provide a measure of consistency in the self-ratings.

The validity of the instrument has been evaluated by two separate procedures. In one instance the TEI was administered to 87 college students who were later asked to rate themselves, using a five-point scale, on each of the 22 test variables. The correlations were reasonably high, ranging between .52 and .79, with one exception; adaptability scored .31. In the second procedure, 49 college students took both the TEI and the *Survey of Interpersonal Values*. The correlations between the 22 TEI and the six SIV scales are reported, and the significant correlations appear to be in the expected directions. Item validity was also calculated by measuring the relationship of each item to the scale in which it has been keyed. These scores are all significant at the .05 level or above.

Although the validating samples are small, the test has been planned and constructed with care. The claims made are refreshingly modest. To quote from the manual, "At its present stage of development this index is a research instrument of potential value in counseling."

JACOB COHEN, *Professor of Psychology and Chairman, Quantitative Psychology Area, New York University, New York, New York.*

This instrument yields measures on 22 a priori "normal" personality traits plus seven supplementary scores. Each of its 125 items is a triad of positive-sounding personality-descriptive adjectives selected to be equated for social desirability. Each item requires the choice of the most and the least descriptive adjective of the three. The manual argues that the use of this item format effectively rules out the operation of the response sets of social desirability and acquiescence and that its use of positively valued adjective traits minimizes defensiveness and task rejection. These claims are quite reasonable. The TEI is offered explicitly for use in counseling and research but is presumably suitable for any of the innumerable purposes for which one might use a general personality inventory.

Despite its attention to response set contamination, there is something quite old-fashioned about the TEI, specifically the basis for deciding which personality traits to measure, which adjectives to use for each, and the structural organization of the measurement scheme. About the selection of the traits to measure, the manual merely states, "Initially an extensive list of personality variables was compiled." One courts committing the nominal fallacy when one selects a list that "makes sense," without either on the one hand providing a coherent theory of personality which dictates the measurement of one trait rather than another (a la Murray) or, on the other, using some multivariate grouping procedure like factor analysis, to yield a battery of relatively nonredundant scales (a la Cattell or Guilford). Otherwise one does not know whether one's list is too long or too short, over-representing some regions of the personality sphere at the cost of others, or, in general, where one stands.

Some 283 adjectives were garnered from thesaurus sources and catalogued, a priori, under the initial set of traits. An unspecified number of traits were then eliminated because they had "insufficient" adjectives. Then the surviving adjectives were rated for social desirability and ambiguity and further reduced to 190 on arbitrary but reasonable criteria on these ratings, two more traits being lost in the process.

At this point there were 22 traits with varying numbers of adjectives subsumed under each. The manual at this point becomes vague and a bit confused, but the result was the formation of 125 triads of adjectives coming from different a priori scales, within each of which the social desirability ratings of the three adjectives were essentially constant.

Now this procedure produces two kinds of asymmetry, completely glossed over in the manual. First, each triad can be considered as representing three pair of traits, so that there is room for 3 times 125 (375) pairings. There are a total of 232 distinct trait-pairs (not 484, as the manual suggests). Not all pairs can occur equally, since 375 is not a multiple of 210. Moreover, the constraint of equal desirability within triads operates further to imbalance pairings. The second, and probably more serious, asymmetry lies in the inequality of numbers of adjectives per trait, which results, in those traits for which there is a paucity of adjectives, in the repeated use of the same adjective to represent the trait in many triads. For example, Benevolence is represented by 12 different adjectives in 19 triads, Compliance by only 5 adjectives in 16 triads (the adjective "willing" appearing 5 times), and Elation by 10 adjectives appearing in only 13 triads. These asymmetries create certain problems in reliability, scale intercorrelations, and, generally, the adequacy with which traits are measured.

RELIABILITY. "Split-half" and "odd-even" reliabilities (a difference is apparently intended but not made clear) are fairly high, ranging from .70 to .92. Unfortunately, these are spuriously high to varying degrees, since the repetition of adjectives within scales treats what should be adjective(item)-specific error variance as if it were true trait variance. The high test-retest coefficients support the idea that the trait *scores* are stable, but these scores contain varying amounts of item-specific variance.

SCALE INTERCORRELATIONS. These are offered as a basis for clustering the scales into five groups for some unspecified purposes of interpretation. The author expresses some awareness of the fact that the forced-choice structure minimizes positive scale intercorrelations but does not pursue the implications of this state of affairs. Every correlation coefficient between scales has a negative component relative to what its value would be in a free rating situation (indeed, the majority are negative). But because of the first asymmetry noted above, this negative component does not operate uniformly over the intercorrelations but depends on the unequal amounts of pairings between scales in triads. Thus, the correlations reflect "true" correlation between traits plus a *varying* and unknown amount of forced choice negative covariance.

SUPPLEMENTARY SCALES. An Over-All Adjustment score is found by summing four of the scales, the choice being a priori. One questions the utility of a composite based on four scales having a mean intercorrelation of −.01 in both of the two matrices provided. A Consistency score is obtained by the repetition of one triad eight times. Feminine and Masculine Orientation scales were obtained empirically. In a large-scale study of engineers, scales for Employment Stability, Productivity/Creativity, and Job Satisfaction were generated empirically by using standard test construction procedures on the adjective choices.

VALIDITY. Despite the stress on the ipsative nature of the index in the introduction, no evidence on the ipsative validity is offered. Correlations with self-ratings for college students are presented and are predominantly in the .60's. Comparable correlations for engineers under less well-controlled conditions are distinctly lower. Correlations with scales from the MMPI, EPPS, GZTS, and the total score on the *Association Adjustment Inventory* are generally trivial (the EPPS, similarly constructed, is a partial exception). The manual does not interpret them, but merely calls them "enlightening."

NORMS. Percentile norms are offered for males in Business and Industry (no N given, but may be 107), engineers (N = 1,081), college males (N = 120) and college females (N = 180), the latter two restricted to New York City. The only clearly adequate norming with regard to size and representativeness is that for engineers.

SUMMARY. The a priori nature of the traits selected for measurement and of the assignment of adjectives, taken together with the structural problems of an unbalanced forced-choice format with unequal numbers of adjectives per trait, makes this an unpromising candidate for use. This does not necessarily mean that some psychologists would not find the test useful in counseling, but evidence for validity, and particularly validity for its intended ipsative use, is lacking. Given a need for an instrument of this general type, a test user would be better advised to try the EPPS (on which the TEI is partially modeled), or the 16PF (with its impressive theoretical and empirical factor-analytic basis), or the CPI.

[156]

Triadal Equated Personality Inventory. Adult males; 1960–63; TEPI; 22 scores: dominance, self confidence, decisiveness, independence, toughness, suspiciousness, conscientiousness, introversion, restlessness, solemnity, foresight, industriousness, warmth, enthusiasm, conformity, inventiveness, persistence, sex drive, recognition drive, cooperativeness, humility-tolerance, self control; 1 form ('61, 4 pages); administration and technical manual ('63, 4 pages); norms manual ('61, 4 pages); profile ('61, 1 page); separate answer sheets must be used; $4 per 25 tests; $2 per 25 answer sheets; $2 per 25 profiles; $22 per specimen set (must be purchased to obtain manuals and scoring stencils); cash orders postpaid; scoring service, $1 per test; (60–80) minutes; Research Staff, United Consultants; Psychometric Affiliates. *

JACOB COHEN, *Professor of Psychology and Chairman, Quantitative Psychology Area, New York University, New York, New York.*

Composed of 211 triads of adjectival terms, the TEPI yields scores on 22 personality trait variables. The three terms in each triad, each from a different trait, are equated for social desirability and the respondent's task is to select the most and least self-descriptive terms in each triad. The manual states that the trait list was chosen so as to "represent" variables of both factorial and prefactorial historical origin, which "establish approximate synonym measures for practically all variables heretofore isolated in psychology's 45 years of personality research." Beyond this ringing claim, not a further word (to say nothing of data) is offered by way of its substantiation.

Very little information is given about the construction of the TEPI. All that is said in the manual about the formation of triads is "terms were recombined into various factorial combinations...." Now there are $(22)(21)(20)/(3)(2) = 1,540$ different triads of 22 variables, so not all the possible triads can appear in 211. At the level of pairs, each triad represents three pairs, making $3(211) = 633$ pairings possible. There are $(22)(21)/2 = 231$ distinct pairs, but 633 is not a multiple of 231 so that the possible pairs cannot be equally represented in the 211 triads. A further source of imbalance is due to the necessary inequality of terms (231) among the 22 traits, which leads to some inequality in repetition of terms. Thus there is some unknown amount of "lumpiness" in the structure. This has an important bearing on the scale intercorrelations. The forced-choice format builds in a negative component in each intercorrelation (in fact, 117 of the 232 scale intercorrelations are negative). Since the number of pairings within triads varies among scale pairings, the size of this negative component varies among the intercorrelations. Thus, a given correlation may overstate or understate the relationship between two variables depending upon whether they were paired less than or more than the average number of pairings. This obviously bears on the validity of the interpretation of the "type and/or syndrome patterns" and of individual profiles. The manual states that "Construct ('internal') validity data are richly interlaced" in these intercorrelations.

RELIABILITY. Split-half reliabilities on 263 cases (apparently "sales applicants") are predominantly in the .70's and .80's, ordinarily quite adequate. However, since each adjectival term is used an average of $633/231 = 2.74$ times, the same terms are appearing in both of the split halves, so that term-specific, hence measurement-error variance, is being treated as true variance, thus increasing the reliabilities. Moreover, this, too, is occurring to a varying and unknown degree from scale to scale.

VALIDITY. In addition to the "construct" validity claimed by the scale intercorrelations (see above), correlations are offered with length of stay in a rehabilitation program for 100 alcoholics. Two of the 22 scales yield small and barely significant correlations. Differences are exhibited among the mean profiles of these alcoholics, college men, and sales applicants. For one scale, Dominance, correlations of about .6 with group membership and self-ratings are offered. This "validity" information is at best inadequate, and at worst, irrelevant. It makes for an embarrassing contrast with the hyperbole in the manual's introduction.

NORMS. Separate percentile norms are offered for a national sample of 374 "Key Personnel" (of which 210 are sales applicants), 77 alcoholics in a Salvation Army rehabilitation program, and 417 college men not further described. The absence of adequate description leaves the question of representatives of these samples an open one, at best, and, similarly, the utility of these norms.

SUMMARY. The positive aspects of the TEPI (control of social desirability, intensiveness and breadth of coverage) are more than offset by its unbalanced construction and lack of adequate validity information and norms, a particularly noteworthy set of defects for a test which is nine years since publication.

[157]

*Vocational Preference Inventory, Sixth Revision. Grades 12–16 and adults; 1953–65; VPI; "a personality test employing occupational item content"; formerly called *Holland Vocational Preference Inventory*; 11 scores: realistic, intellectual, social, conventional, enterprising, artistic, self-control, masculinity, status, infrequency, acquiescence; 1 form ('65, 2 pages); manual ('65, 65 pages); profile (no date, 2 pages); separate answer sheets must be used; $1.25 per 25 sets of tests; $3.75 per 50 sets of answer sheets and profiles; $1 per scoring stencil; $3 per manual; $4.50 per specimen set; postage extra; (15–30) minutes; John L. Holland; Consulting Psychologists Press, Inc. *

REFERENCES

1–13. See 6:115.
14–44. See P:283, also includes a cumulative name index to the first 44 references for this test.
45. RAND, LEONARD PETER. *A Study of the Relationship Between the Matching of Student and Institutional Characteristics and College Choice Satisfaction.* Doctor's thesis, University of Iowa (Iowa City, Iowa), 1966. (*DA* 27:2832A)
46. MARIN, GENARO. *Some Interaction Correlates of Self-Estimation and Self-Acceptance on Performance Among the Culturally Deprived.* Doctor's thesis, Southern Illinois University (Carbondale, Ill.), 1967. (*DA* 28:4487A)
47. WALL, HARVEY W.; OSIPOW, SAMUEL H.; AND ASHBY, JEFFERSON D. "SVIB Scores, Occupational Choices, and Holland's Personality Types." *Voc Guid Q* 15:201–5 Mr '67. *
48. BANDUCCI, RAYMOND. *Accuracy of Stereotypic Perceptions of Types and Levels of Occupations in Relation to Selected Background and Personal Characteristics of High School Senior Boys.* Doctor's thesis, University of Iowa (Iowa City, Iowa), 1968. (*DA* 29:3825A)
49. CORLEY, DOLORES D. *The Social Scale of the Vocational Preference Inventory in Relation to Peer and Self-Ratings of Eleventh Grade Students.* Master's thesis, University of Nevada (Reno, Nev.), 1968.
50. KILCAWLEY, MARGARET PATRICIA. *Variables Associated With Academic Persistence Among Male Freshmen Students Enrolled in a College of Arts and Sciences.* Doctor's thesis, University of Maryland (College Park, Md.), 1968. (*DA* 29:1755A)
51. McDOWALL, WILLIAM H. *A Comparison of Faculty-Community and Student Orientation Patterns in a Junior College Setting.* Doctor's thesis, University of North Dakota (Grand Forks, N.D.), 1968. (*DA* 29:3878A)
52. NEAL, ROBERT GORDON. *A Comparison of Multivariate and Univariate Techniques for Classifying Engineering Students.* Doctor's thesis, University of Missouri (Columbia, Mo.), 1968. (*DA* 29:2967A)
53. ROORDA, TIMOTHY. *Characteristics of the Holland Vocational Preference Inventory and Other Selected Variables for a Group of School Psychologists.* Master's thesis, California State College (Hayward, Calif.), 1968.
54. SALOMONE, PAUL ROBERT. *Rehabilitation Counselor Job*

Behavior and Vocational Personality: Needs and Work Style. Doctor's thesis, University of Iowa (Iowa City, Iowa), 1968. (*DA* 29:1759A)
55. SCHMIDT, MARLIN RUTH. *Relationship Between Sorority Membership and Changes in Selected Personality Variables, Goals and Attitudes.* Doctor's thesis, University of Iowa (Iowa City, Iowa), 1968. (*DA* 29:3843A)
56. SCOTT, GARY JULIAN. *Vocational Behavior as a Function of Person-Environment Interactions: A Test of Holland's Theory.* Doctor's thesis, Pennsylvania State University (University Park, Pa.), 1968. (*DAI* 30:1082A)
57. BAIRD, LEONARD L. "Factors in the Continuance of Accomplishment From High School to College." *Meas & Eval Guid* 2(1):5–18 sp '69. * (*PA* 44:11406)
58. BAIRD, LEONARD L. "Relation of Vocational Interests to Life Goals, Self-Ratings, and Potentials for Achievement." Abstract. *Proc 77th Ann Conv Am Psychol Assn* 4(2):689–90 '69. * (*PA* 44:1289)
59. BATDORF, RICHARD LEWALLEN. *An Investigation of the Applicability of Holland's Theory to Adjudicated Female Adolescent Delinquents.* Doctor's thesis, Washington State University (Pullman, Wash.), 1969. (*DAI* 30:4214A)
60. BATES, GORDON L. *The Relationship of Personality and Work Adjustment of Vocational Rehabilitants: A Test of Holland's Theory.* Doctor's thesis, University of Oklahoma (Norman, Okla.), 1969. (*DAI* 30:126A)
61. BEHRING, DANIEL WILLIAM. *Adaptive Functioning: A Rationale for the Prediction of Achievement in Nursing Education.* Doctor's thesis, Ohio University (Athens, Ohio), 1969. (*DAI* 31:1065A)
62. DENISON, WALTER MARSHALL. *A Study of Three Interest Inventories Currently in Use at Central Virginia Community College.* Doctor's thesis, University of Virginia (Charlottesville, Va.), 1969. (*DAI* 31:996A)
63. HOLLAND, JOHN L.; WHITNEY, DOUGLAS R.; COLE, NANCY S.; AND RICHARDS, JAMES M., JR. "An Empirical Occupational Classification Derived From a Theory of Personality and Intended for Practice and Research." *ACT Res Rep* 29: 1–22 Ap '69. * (*PA* 45:3132)
64. HORVAT, GEORGE LITTLE. *A Study of Relationships Between Counselor Supervisor Personality and Counselor Trainee Growth in Practicum.* Doctor's thesis, St. Louis University (St. Louis, Mo.), 1969. (*DAI* 30:3278A)
65. INGRAM, RICHARD THOMAS. *Holland's Typology of Personality in the Prediction of Certain Counseling Outcomes.* Doctor's thesis, University of Maryland (College Park, Md.), 1969. (*DAI* 31:151A)
66. KRISTJANSON, RONALD W. *Personality Types and Their Hypothesized Attributes: An Application of Holland's Vocational Choice Theory.* Master's thesis, University of North Dakota (Grand Forks, N.D.), 1969.
67. MASTEN, ELLSWORTH EDWARD. *Modes of Dissonance Reduction in Relation to Cognitive Dissonance Concerning Vocational Choice.* Doctor's thesis, University of Iowa (Iowa City, Iowa), 1969. (*DAI* 30:5241B)
68. OSIPOW, SAMUEL H. "Cognitive Styles and Educational-Vocational Preferences and Selection." *J Counsel Psychol* 16(6):534–46 N '69. * (*PA* 44:4204)
69. RAVENSBORG, MILTON R. "Psychiatric Technicians' Ranking of Five Potential Employment Screening Tests." *Personnel J* 48(1):39–41 Ja '69. * (*PA* 44:2910)
70. VAN HALL, RICHARD. *The Relationship Between Personality Factors and the Choice of Selected Major Fields in Education.* Doctor's thesis, North Texas State University (Denton, Tex.), 1969. (*DAI* 30:548A)
71. WALL, ROBERT ERNEST. *Engineering Freshmen Responses to the Holland Vocational Preference Inventory and Persistence in the University of Maryland College of Engineering.* Doctor's thesis, University of Maryland (College Park, Md.), 1969. (*DAI* 31:614A)
72. WALSH, EDWARD PIERCE. *A Study of Graduate Student-Institutional Environment Interaction.* Doctor's thesis, State University of New York (Buffalo, N.Y.), 1969. (*DAI* 30:2347A)
73. WALSH, W. BRUCE, AND LACEY, DAVID W. "Perceived Change and Holland's Theory." *J Counsel Psychol* 16(4):348–52 Jl '69. *
74. WERNER, JEANNE ELDER. *A Study of Holland's Theory of Vocational Choice as It Applies to Selected Working Women.* Doctor's thesis, State University of New York (Buffalo, N.Y.), 1969. (*DAI* 30:1832A)
75. WERNER, WAYNE ELON. *A Study of Holland's Theory of Vocational Choice as It Applies to Vocational High School Students.* Doctor's thesis, State University of New York (Buffalo, N.Y.), 1969. (*DAI* 30:1832A)
76. BAIRD, LEONARD L. "The Relation of Vocational Interests to Life Goals, Self-Ratings of Ability and Personality Traits, and Potential for Achievement." *J Ed Meas* 7(4):233–9 w '70. * (*PA* 45:8910)
77. BATES, GORDON L.; PARKER, HARRY J.; AND McCOY, JOHN F. "Vocational Rehabilitants' Personality and Work Adjustment: A Test of Holland's Theory of Vocational Choice." *Psychol Rep* 26(2):511–6 Ap '70. * (*PA* 44:21319)
78. BODDEN, JACK L. "Cognitive Complexity as a Factor in Appropriate Vocational Choice." *J Counsel Psychol* 17(4):364–8 Jl '70. * (*PA* 44:21547)

79. Posthuma, Allan B., and Navran, Leslie. "Relation of Congruence in Student-Faculty Interests to Achievement in College." *J Counsel Psychol* 17(4):352–6 Jl '70. * (PA 44: 21606)

80. Rose, Harriett A., and Elton, Charles F. "Ask Him or Test Him?" *Voc Guid Q* 19(1):28–32 S '70. *

81. Schmidt, Marlin R. "Personality Change in College Women." *J Col Stud Personnel* 11(6):414–8 N '70. * (PA 45:8906)

82. Southworth, J. Alfred, and Morningstar, Mona E. "Persistence of Occupational Choice and Personality Congruence." *J Counsel Psychol* 17(5):409–12 S '70. * (PA 45: 3009)

83. Walsh, W. Bruce, and Lacey, David W. "Further Exploration of Perceived Change and Holland's Theory." *J Counsel Psychol* 17(2):189–90 Mr '70. * (PA 44:8439)

Joseph A. Johnston, *Associate Professor of Education, University of Missouri, Columbia, Missouri.*

The VPI is intended primarily as a personality inventory designed to "yield a broad range of information about the subject's interpersonal relations, interests, values, self-conception, coping behavior, and identifications." It consists of 160 occupational titles to which the subject indicates his likes or dislikes. Fifteen to 30 minutes of testing time yields 11 scores, the first 6 of which can be used as vocational interest type scales: realistic, intellectual, social, conventional, enterprising, and artistic. The remaining 5 are more clearly personality scales: self-control, masculinity, status, infrequency, and acquiescence.

The author stresses its *"most desirable* use is as a *brief, screening inventory* for high school and college students, and employed adults." According to the author, "It is unlikely that the VPI has more validity than comparable inventories; instead its chief value is its economical use of time and money." In the reviewer's opinion, the VPI can be helpful in identifying both the nature and the extent of the vocational exploration done by individuals. It can identify individuals in vocational conflict or other kinds of conflict, suggest types of counseling (vocational or personal) that would be most appropriate, and provide numerous cues to the nature of these difficulties. Researchable hypotheses in these areas are offered in Holland's book (*28*) and the interested reader should consult that reference for additional ideas.

The manual is clearly written and accurate but not as extensive as would be desirable. The rationale for the instrument is well described in the manual but supporting evidence is not well presented. This is a surprising flaw since there is considerable evidence available in the literature on the reliability, validity, and usefulness of the inventory. The 1970 manual, identical to the 1965 manual except for the enlarged bibliography, should have been updated. The manual should include more complete descriptions of populations used in various normings, a summary of the existing data supporting the rationale for the inventory, and elimination of some not particularly impressive studies lending only marginal support to inferences made considering the various ways to interpret VPI scores. The VPI is based on heuristic theory which needs continual reinterpretation; such is available in the literature but not in the manual. Anyone wishing to use the instrument should consult Holland's book (*28*) for a more thorough explanation of the rationale and possible uses. A report by Holland et al. (*63*) provides important data on recent revisions of the theory and a particularly good section on possible uses of both the theory and the instrument.

The VPI is an inexpensive, straightforward, easy to administer and score, non-threatening personality inventory of value to the counselor both in screening and in counseling. Holland stresses accurately that its neutral content reduces the need to "fake" since the occupational content does not seem related to personal adjustment; most subjects see the inventory as a "vocational test." In fact, the VPI probably has more validity and usefulness as a vocational inventory than as a personality measure. Most of the research supporting its usefulness has been in the vocational area.

The VPI features of nominal cost, hand scoring, and face validity offer some advantages over other inventories of similar nature. The personality indices provide added information about the nature of the client and his vocational experiences and ought to prove helpful in vocational counseling. The VPI categories promote the student's finding occupational information which is closely related to his measured interests. Perhaps most important, the inventory is tied to a theoretical framework that appears to be quite promising in explaining the vocational choice process for at least a significant portion of the adult population.

There are some limitations. Occupational titles included may cover too much of the total spectrum of jobs. The titles include college oriented occupations as well as many entry level job titles which require minimal education. The range of titles is between the ranges in the SVIB and the MVII. The validity of the VPI is dependent on the individual having had reasonable exposure to the occupational titles mentioned; this is not likely to be the case for many lower class college bound students. With these students the inventory can be used but with certain cautions and obviously different norms. The user should collect appropriate norms (a relatively easy task with this instrument). When this is not done, the user should keep in mind that the available middle-class norms are only helpful when one can make some interpolation based on social class differences in vocational exploration behavior. Further, more titles will be unfamiliar to this group and hence the instrument may lose some face validity although this does not become a serious limitation if one is prepared for it and instructs the individual accordingly. Taken into account in the administration and interpretation, these limitations are not serious, and, in fact, can add to one's understanding of the individual and his personality. Available norms are now at best minimal; particularly important will be more norms on populations actually employed at various jobs. A great deal of material on the validity and norms should be incorporated into a new manual along with information on the relationship of VPI scores with other established instruments.

The VPI is a promising inventory that is deserving of serious attention. Use by counselors will help them better understand firsthand what all is involved in vocational decision making or decision making in general. This seems a benefit not often derived from use of similar inventories. I can endorse its use as outlined by the author in the manual.

PAUL R. LOHNES, *Professor of Education, State University of New York at Buffalo, Buffalo, New York.*

The VPI asks the subject to decide whether he likes or dislikes each of 160 jobs. In his review of the third revision of the VPI in *The Third Yearbook,* French judged as "reasonable" the underlying assumption that job preferences reflect the operation of significant personality variables. He characterized the inventory as "an ingenious empirical approach to personality measurement" and gave it his warm endorsement as a research instrument, which was all that version claimed to be. Since then Holland has published a book (*28*) on the personality theory behind the VPI, several excellent research studies (*35, 42, 63*) and this sixth edition

of the VPI. Holland describes the VPI as a screening device applicable to high school and college students and employed adults to measure interests, to assess the six personality types in the Holland theory, and to stimulate occupational explorations.

This reviewer applauds Holland's perseverance in the program of research on the VPI, unequivocally endorses the proposed counseling applications, and suggests a widespread use of the instrument in career development research. The reviewer will argue that the VPI is the *best* choice of an interest inventory for either counseling or research in most situations and will support this contention with his own knowledge of what Project TALENT has revealed about interests in relation to career development.

This review has, however, one negative comment to discharge. The VPI's dark side is its report of four scales named Self-Control, Masculinity, Infrequency, and Acquiescence and a general slant of the manual toward a clinical psychology market, evident in the bizarre and often offensive clinical interpretations suggested for score profiles, especially in reference to these four scales. Possibly Holland is giving these customers what they expect and demand of a personality inventory, in which case this is more evidence for the dismal suspicions this educational psychologist harbors about assessment practices in clinical psychology. The reader should take the VPI himself (it's easy and fun) and apply the language of the manual to his own ego before he rejects this criticism as prejudiced. This reviewer considers the six vocational preference scales and the Status scale to be the bright side of the VPI, and suggests that ACT Research Reports 25 (*42*) and 29 (*63*) provide a better manual for career counseling and research applications than does the official manual.

Holland casts his theory in terms of six personality types corresponding to six scales on the VPI. A person's type is indicated by the scale for which he has the highest percentile score. Vocations are classified by highest mean on the six scales. So far the approach bears striking resemblance to that of the *Study of Values* and there are obvious similarities of scale constructs between the two inventories. Also like the *Study of Values,* the VPI concedes that a person is not properly conceived as purely of one type and directs attention to the profile of his scores on all scales. In irresolution reminiscent of the quantum versus wave dilemma, Holland vacillates between classification analysis and correlation analysis. In the manual he urges that the scales be viewed as traits, but in the research (*42, 63*) he concentrates on classes, greatly expanded in number by classifying according to the three or four highest scale scores *and their order*. The reviewer concludes that the taxonomic gambit is very useful for many practical purposes, such as organizing job titles and vocational information libraries, but that in theory the VPI constructs are continuous dimensions of preferences.

Most interest inventories report many more than six dimensions. The reviewer's[1] factor analyses of Project TALENT's 17 interest scales (based on likes and dislikes for 122 occupations and 83 activities) supported only four uncorrelated interest dimensions. The VPI scales—with their TALENT correspondents, if any, in parentheses—are Realistic (Outdoor and Shop), Intellectual (Science), Artistic, Social (Cultural), Enterprising, and Conventional (Business). Since the VPI scales are modestly intercorrelated, and Holland gives .68 as the intraclass correlation of Enterprising and Conventional (*63*), there is substantial agreement between Lohnes and Holland that only a small number of scales are needed to span the vocational interests measurement space. Indeed, Holland's ingenious hexagonal model for the six main types can be viewed as suggesting that most interest variance exists in one plane of the space. Rapoport,[2] defining parsimony, says, "To know more means, operationally speaking, *to be able to explain (or predict) more by assuming less.*" Although the VPI still needs a buildup of predictive validity studies, Holland and Whitney's (*42*) study of changes in vocational plans and the many predictive validities for the four TALENT interest factors established by Cooley and Lohnes[3] clearly suggest that the new look in interest assessment is to explain more career adjustments from fewer interest variables. Note that Cooley and Lohnes

agree with Holland and Lutz (*35*) that since stable career plans explain themselves, it is changes in plans for which inventoried interests must show predictive validities. Luckily, they do.

Anne Roe's[4] pioneering vocational taxonomy had one advantage which Cooley and Lohnes carried over into the TALENT Career Development Tree model and which is lacking in the Holland theory of six families of vocations, and that is the concept of *level* of aspiration and achievement. The TALENT work scaled an educational aspiration variable called scholasticism, which turned out to be as important in prediction studies as the four interest factors. This variable was constructed to be uncorrelated with the interests, although it was of course correlated with important ability factors. The VPI scale called Status is more of a socio-economic aspiration variable, and would presumably be a useful complement to scholasticism in prediction studies. Anyway, the reviewer now believes that Roe's people-thing interest dichotomy was overworked in the TALENT tree and that four to six categories of the VPI sort make better sense for the advanced stages of a career patterns tree structure. A new tree model incorporating Holland's theory is in order.

In summary, Holland's theory and the VPI instrument will continue to be significant in the research enterprise and appear to be ready for widespread deployment in the career guidance enterprise. The claims for clinical psychology applications boggle the reviewer's mind, but so does much of the clinical psychology enterprise.

For reviews by Robert L. French and H. Bradley Sagen of an earlier edition, see 6:115.

[158]

*WLW Personal Attitude Inventory. Business and industry; 1954–69; 6 scores: emotional stability, friendliness, aggressiveness, humility and insight, reliability, leadership; 2 editions: third edition ('55, 3 pages), fifth edition ('60, 4 pages); mimeographed manual ('69, 15 pages); profile ('56, 1 page); norms for men only; $17 per 100 tests, postpaid; [20] minutes; Robert W. Henderson; third edition by W. E. Brown, T. L. Chappell, L. D. Edmonson, W. H. E. Geiger, R. L. Kaiser, L. C. Steckle, and L. E. Saddler; William, Lynde & Williams. *

JAMES E. KENNEDY, *Professor of Psychology, The University of Wisconsin, Madison, Wisconsin.*

This is a self-report inventory which, accord-

1 LOHNES, PAUL R. *Measuring Adolescent Personality:* Project TALENT Five-Year Follow-Up Studies, and Interim Report 1. U.S. Office of Education, Project No. 3051, Contract No. OE-6-10-065. Pittsburgh, Pa.: American Institutes for Research, 1966. Pp. 226. *

2 RAPOPORT, ANATOL. *Operational Philosophy: Integrating Knowledge and Action.* New York: Harper & Brothers, Publishers, 1953. Pp. xi, 258. *

3 COOLEY, WILLIAM W., AND LOHNES, PAUL R. *Predicting Development of Young Adults:* Project TALENT Five-Year Follow-Up Studies, Interim Report 5. U.S. Office of Education, Project No. 3051, Contract No. OE-610-065. Palo Alto, Calif.: American Institutes for Research, 1968. Pp. ix, 224. *

4 ROE, ANNE. "A New Classification of Occupations." *J Counsel Psychol* 1:215–20 w '54. *

ing to its manual, "gives what a person thinks of himself or wants to have others think how he sees himself." It is available in two editions with slightly different formats. The Fifth Edition has 64 items and the respondent chooses the one phrase of three that best fits him. The Third Edition has half as many items and the respondent chooses two of six phrases. Examples of these phrases are: "Seldom budget my time," "Listen more than I talk," "Sometimes feel foolish." The Third and Fifth Editions yield scores on six scales: Emotional Stability, Friendliness, Aggressiveness, Humility and Insight, Reliability, and Considerate and Democratic Leadership. (A Sixth Edition differs in that the Considerate and Democratic Leadership Scale is replaced by an Initiating Structure and Task Orientation Scale. This edition is reserved for exclusive use of the publishers.)

This inventory was developed in an industrial setting. The publishers claim, "Extreme scores often highlight the most outstanding psychological characteristics of the individual. In the hiring situation, for example, it is often sufficient to determine if the individual seems to fall within normal limits. If he does not, the Inventory results can serve as a red flag that demands additional checks and precautions."

The test manual provides item-total scale correlations for most items in the Third Edition and norms based on 1,884 cases of predominately middle management males for the Fifth Edition. Split-half scale reliabilities ranging from .73 to .89 are reported but the manual does not say for which edition. There is no discussion of the original basis for choosing items. Those items appearing on the final forms were presumably selected from a larger pool of similar items on the basis of an internal consistency item analysis.

A section of the manual devoted to "Interpretation of Scales" consists of a casual discussion of what, in the opinions of the authors, scores on the various scales indicate. Nowhere in the 14-page manual is the issue of validity approached. Three rather pitiful "illustrative cases" are discussed. For example, one notes that "an industrial supervisor who has never done a fully effective job because of his tendency to fold under job pressure" had a very low emotional stability score.

In summary, the authors of this test offer no theoretical explanation as to why they believe these items arranged into these scales should provide a meaningful and useful self-description for any purpose. They offer no empirical evidence that the test is valid according to any definition of validity. Until such time as this information is available there seems to be nothing to recommend its use except for experimental purposes. For those believing it is appropriate to use self-description inventories for personnel selection and upgrading, a number of available instruments would seem to be preferable at this time. Considerable information is now available in the literature concerning the validity of, for example, *California Psychological Inventory, Edwards Personal Preference Schedule,* or *Gordon Personal Inventory.*

[159]
★Walker Problem Behavior Identification Checklist. Grades 4–6; 1970; WPBIC; ratings by teachers; 6 scores: acting-out, withdrawal, distractability, disturbed peer relations, immaturity, total; 1 form (2 pages); manual (9 pages plus checklist); $9.50 per 100 checklists and manual; $8.50 per 100 checklists; $2.50 per manual; postpaid; [2–5] minutes; Hill M. Walker; Western Psychological Services. *

REFERENCE
1. WALKER, HILL MONTAGUE. *Construction and Validation of a Behavior Checklist for the Identification of Children With Behavior Problems.* Doctor's thesis, University of Oregon (Eugene, Ore.), 1967. (DA 28:978A)

[160]
William, Lynde & Williams Analysis of Personal Values, Second Edition. Business and industry; 1958–62; APV; 6 scores: theoretical, practical, social, personal power, aesthetic, religious; 1 form ('60, 4 pages); mimeographed combined manual ('62, 8 pages) for this and test 1041; no data on reliability and validity; $12.50 per 100 tests, postpaid; [15] minutes; R. W. Henderson; William, Lynde & Williams. *

WAYNE S. ZIMMERMAN, *Test Officer and Professor of Counseling and Testing, California State College at Los Angeles, Los Angeles, California.*

This brief survey (40 short answer items) of values, like the *Study of Values,* is based essentially on the six types of men originally described by Spranger. The authors state, "Because the Study of Values is mainly academic in its content and intent, we have developed the WLW Analysis of Personal Values for business and industry." Two of the original Spranger types—economic and political—have been replaced by "practical" and "personal power" to obtain pairs which may be treated as opposites: theoretical and practical, social and personal power, and aesthetic and religious.

Each of the 40 ipsative items presents the examinee with a choice of responses representing one of three of the values. The 20 possible combinations of 6 values taken 3 at a time are presented twice for each combination; hence, the 40 items.

The authors describe briefly in two pages of the manual their concept of the six values by descriptive phrases such as, "He tends to be," "He strives to," and "He likes the,"—an approach which is convenient for putting together a summary description using selected phrases directly from the manual.

In the manual, the authors maintain that the instrument is designed "to help any person explore his value system as it relates to his business and personal life." They also declare that it and another of their tests "are satisfactory discussion evoking instruments." Thus, to the authors' credit, there is the implication that the instrument is not intended for use in selection and placement. An actual statement to this effect, however, is missing.

The APV must be criticized for familiar reasons. This test, first published in 1958 and revised in 1962, was listed in the 1965 MMY with the statement "no data on reliability and validity." There is still no documentary evidence of follow-up research beyond developmental work in constructing the inventory. No data are presented that would indicate that there has been any attempt to establish either reliability or validity. The 7-page, mimeographed manual provides only median scores for managers, salesmen, and technicians, based on N's of 212, 26, and 52, respectively. The test user is apparently free to draw his own conclusions regarding the significance of differences among these scores. The ipsative form of the score distributions complicates comparisons, but maximum differences of two raw score points between the medians of managers and the medians of either salesmen or technicians, and maximum differences of three between salesmen and technicians on the six scales, suggest that an acceptable statistical significance of difference would be difficult to establish.

Since the inventory continues to be published and sold, there must be data which could be analyzed with respect to both reliability and validity. The author and publisher must be criticized for not reporting research results based on data accumulated, or which should have been accumulated, during the 12 years since the first edition was published. They must be further criticized for not labeling the instrument as experimental.

In the absence of essential data pertaining to reliability and validity and in view of the limited normative data, the reviewer is unable to recommend use of the APV for other than research purposes. The application of the instrument in a business or industrial setting except perhaps for "evoking discussion" is open to serious question.

[Other Tests]

For other tests new or revised since *The Sixth Mental Measurements Yearbook,* see the following in *Personality Tests and Reviews:*

3. ★Addiction Research Center Inventory (15 references)
8. ★Anxiety Scale for the Blind (3 references)
20. *Bristol Social Adjustment Guides (6 references)
22. ★CYR Youth Survey (2 references)
30. ★Cardiac Adjustment Scale (1 reference)
38. *Children's Personality Questionnaire (14 references)
40. ★Clinical Behavior Check List and Rating Scale
52. *Courtship Analysis
71. *Embedded Figures Test (47 references)
89. ★Getting Along (2 references)
94. *Grassi Block Substitution Test (13 references)
99. ★Group Psychotherapy Suitability Evaluation Scale (1 reference)
106. ★Hartman Value Inventory (2 references)
108. ★Hellenic Affiliation Scale
109. ★Hill Interaction Matrix
110. *Hoffer-Osmond Diagnostic Test (22 references)
111. *Hooper Visual Organization Test (7 references)
119. *IPAT Humor Test of Personality (8 references)
122. ★Independent Activities Questionnaire (2 references)
125. *Institute of Child Study Security Test (4 references)
125A. ★Integration Level Test Series (12 references)
132. ★JIM Scale
138. ★Katz Adjustment Scales (10 references)
139. *Kuder Preference Record—Personal (9 references)
140. ★Kundu's Neurotic Personality Inventory (5 references)
144. ★Level of Aspiration Board (9 references)
146. ★M-Scale
148. *M-B History Record (3 references)
151. ★Mandel Social Adjustment Scale (2 references)
160. ★Maryland Parent Attitude Survey (6 references)
181. ★Object Sorting Scales
183. ★Ohio College Association Rating Scale
185. *Opinion, Attitude, and Interest Survey (19 references)
190. ★PRADI Autobiographical Form
202. ★Personnel Reaction Blank
205. ★Polarity Scale (1 reference)
212. ★Preschool Self-Concept Picture Test (1 reference)
213. *Press Test (1 reference)
218. ★Psychological Audit for Interpersonal Relations
228. ★Richardson Emergency Psychodiagnostic Summary
230. ★Russell Sage Social Relations Test (3 references)
232A. *STS Junior Inventory (4 references)
233. *STS Youth Inventory (2 references)
234. ★Scale of Socio-Egocentrism
235. *Scale to Measure Attitudes Toward Disabled Persons (14 references)
249. *Social Competence Inventories for Adults and for Older Persons

252. ★Stamp Behaviour Study Technique
254. *Stanford Profile Scales of Hypnotic Susceptibility (4 references)
257. ★Stockton Geriatric Rating Scale (2 references)
258. ★Student Description Form
259A. ★Study of Values: British Edition
268. *Test of Basic Assumptions
273. *Theological School Inventory (5 references)
275. ★Thorman Family Relations Conference Situation Questionnaire
281. *Vineland Social Maturity Scale (21 references)
285. ★Ward Behavior Inventory (14 references)

PROJECTIVE

[161]

*[Bender-Gestalt Test.] Ages 4 and over; 1938–69; individual; the original Bender-Gestalt is listed as *a* below; the modifications listed as *b-e* consist primarily of alterations in administration procedure, new scoring systems, or expanded interpretive procedures, rather than changes in the test materials; *b-e* use essentially the same administration procedure as the basic testing procedure; *c* and *d* provide, in addition, for use of the materials as projective stimuli for associations.

a) VISUAL MOTOR GESTALT TEST. Ages 4 and over; 1938–46; VMGT; 1 form ('46, 9 cards); pictures are also available as 35 mm. slides for group administration; manual ('38, 187 pages, see 5 below); directions for administering ('46, 8 pages); no data on reliability; $1.50 per set of cards and directions; $5.50 per manual; $10 per set of slides and directions; postpaid; [10] minutes; Lauretta Bender; American Orthopsychiatric Association, Inc. *

b) THE BENDER GESTALT TEST. Ages 4 and over; 1951; BGT; utilizes same test cards as *a*; scoring sheet ['51, 1 page]; manual (287 pages, see 41 below); $2.25 per pad of 50 scoring sheets; $10 per manual; postage extra; (10) minutes; Gerald R. Pascal and Barbara J. Suttell; Grune & Stratton, Inc. *

c) *THE HUTT ADAPTATION OF THE BENDER-GESTALT TEST. Ages 7 and over; 1944–69; HABGT; formerly called *Revised Bender-Gestalt Test;* 1 form ['60, 9 cards, same as cards of *a* except for modification in 1 design and in drawing method throughout]; manual, second edition ('69, 200 pages, see 429 below); revised record form ('68, 4 pages); no data on reliability of scored factors; $1.25 per set of cards; $5.25 per 25 record forms; $6.75 per manual; postage extra; [45–60] minutes; Max L. Hutt; Grune & Stratton, Inc. *

d) THE BENDER VISUAL MOTOR GESTALT TEST FOR CHILDREN. Ages 7–11; 1962; utilizes same test cards as *a*; manual (72 pages); record form (4 pages); no data on reliability and validity; $3 per set of cards; $6.50 per 25 record forms; $6.50 per manual; postpaid; (10) minutes without associations; Aileen Clawson; Western Psychological Services. *

e) THE BENDER GESTALT TEST FOR YOUNG CHILDREN. Ages 5–10; 1964; a developmental scoring system; utilizes same test cards as *a*; manual (206 pages, see 259 below); $8.50 per manual, postage extra; administration time not reported; Elizabeth Munsterberg Koppitz; Grune & Stratton, Inc. *

f) THE VISUAL MOTOR GESTALT TEST TWO-COPY DRAWING FORM. 1964; 1 form (1 page plus backing sheet); $6.50 per 25 forms, postpaid; Western Psychological Services. *

REFERENCES

1–8. See 3:108.
9–42. See 4:144.
43–160. See 5:172.
161–259. See 6:203.

260–429. See P:415, also includes a cumulative name index to the first 429 references for this test.

430. KRASNER, JACK DANIEL. *The Psychological Effects of Regressive Electroshock Therapy.* Doctor's thesis, New York University (New York, N.Y.), 1952. (DA 12:591)

431. HILER, EDWARD WESLEY. *An Investigation of Psychological Factors Associated With Premature Termination of Psychotherapy.* Doctor's thesis, University of Michigan (Ann Arbor, Mich.), 1954. (DA 14:712)

432. SEGAL, STANLEY JACOB. *The Role of Personality Factors in Vocational Choice: A Study of Accountants and Creative Writers.* Doctor's thesis, University of Michigan (Ann Arbor, Mich.), 1954. (DA 14:714)

433. WAXENBERG, SHELDON EDWARD. *Psychosomatic Patients and Other Physically Ill Persons: A Comparative Study.* Doctor's thesis, Columbia University (New York, N.Y.), 1954. (DA 14:1818)

434. VERNIER, CLAIRE M. Chap. 18, "Predictability in Treatment of Tuberculosis Patients," pp. 344–52. In *Personality, Stress, and Tuberculosis.* Edited by Phineas J. Sparer. New York: International Universities Press, Inc., 1956. Pp. xviii, 629. *

435. TRACHTMAN, GILBERT M. *Personality and Developmental Characteristics of Children Rated Most and Least Ready for First Grade by Their Kindergarten Teachers.* Doctor's thesis, New York University (New York, N.Y.), 1958. (DA 19:3028)

436. CRARY, WILLIAM GRAHAM. *An Investigation of Some Indications of Total, Covert and Overt Anxiety in the Bender Visual-Motor Gestalt Test.* Master's thesis, San Diego State College (San Diego, Calif.), 1959.

437. FAULS, JOHN THOMAS. *Superior Readers Versus Mediocre Readers: A Comparison of Ego Organizations.* Doctor's thesis, Florida State University (Tallahassee, Fla.), 1959. (DA 20:3376)

438. HABER, WILFRED. *The Contribution of Selected Variables to Success or Failure in a Vocational Rehabilitation Evaluation.* Doctor's thesis, New York University (New York, N.Y.), 1959. (DA 20:4171)

439. ROYO, D., AND MARTIN, F. "Standardized Psychometrical Tests Applied to the Analysis of the Effects of Anti-Convulsive Medication on the Intellectual Proficiency of Young Epileptics." *Epilepsia* 1:189–207 D '59. *

440. SHUBERT, SHELDON LAWRENCE. *The Relationship of the Bender-Gestalt Test to Juvenile Delinquency.* Master's thesis, Texas Christian University (Ft. Worth, Tex.), 1959.

441. HILER, E. WESLEY, AND NESVIG, DAVID. "Changes in Intellectual Functions of Children in a Psychiatric Hospital." *J Consult Psychol* 25:288–92 Ag '61. * (PA 37:1495)

442. KLAUSNER, MAX. *The Attitudes of Mothers Toward Institutionalized and Non-Institutionalized Retarded Children.* Doctor's thesis, New York University (New York, N.Y.), 1961. (DA 22:915)

443. PEOPLES, LANDON CROCKER. *A Study of Important Stimuli in the Lives of Men With Lung Cancer.* Doctor's thesis, University of Tennessee (Knoxville, Tenn.), 1961. (DA 22:2071)

444. YANAGI, GARRET HONORU. *An Appraisal of Psychologic Deficit in Children With Cerebral Palsy.* Doctor's thesis, University of Tennessee (Knoxville, Tenn.), 1961. (DA 22:4088)

445. GUERRANT, JOHN; ANDERSON, WILLIAM W.; FISCHER, AMES; WEINSTEIN, MORTON R.; JAROS, R. MARY; AND DESKINS, ANDREW. Chap. 5, "Psychological Considerations," pp. 66–92. In their *Personality in Epilepsy.* Springfield, Ill.: Charles C Thomas, Publisher, 1962. Pp. xii, 112. *

446. OVERDEER, ABNER RAY, JR. *Some Correlates of Premorbid Adjustment in Schizophrenia.* Doctor's thesis, Vanderbilt University (Nashville, Tenn.), 1962. (DA 23:708)

447. HUTT, MAX L. Chap. 15, "The Bender Gestalt Test," pp. 241–56. In *The Genain Quadruplets.* Edited by David Rosenthal. New York: Basic Books, Inc., Publishers, 1963. Pp. xv, 609. * (PA 38:9070)

448. O'CONNELL, APRIL WELSH. *Sensori-Perceptual Differences Between Academically and Non-Academically Retarded Children.* Doctor's thesis, Ohio State University (Columbus, Ohio), 1963. (DA 24:4782)

449. SKLAR, MAURICE. "Relation of Psychological and Language Test Scores and Autopsy Findings in Aphasia." *J Speech & Hearing Res* 6:84–90 Mr '63. * (PA 38:1201)

450. BUTLER, ALFRED J., AND CONRAD, W. GLENN. "Psychological Correlates of Abnormal Electroencephalographic Patterns in Familial Retardates." *J Clin Psychol* 20:338–43 Jl '64. * (PA 39:10572)

451. EDENS, LESTER WILLIAM. *An Analysis of Certain Socio-Psychological Characteristics of Unwed Mothers Referred to Private Agencies in Washington and Idaho.* Doctor's thesis, University of Idaho (Moscow, Idaho), 1964. (DA 25:5730)

452. ESLER, HAROLD DEAN. *An Investigation of the Causes of Suicide in Patients Diagnosed as Schizophrenic.* Doctor's thesis, Michigan State University (East Lansing, Mich.), 1964. (DA 26:1169)

453. JURKO, M. F., AND ANDY, O. J. "Psychological Aspects of Diencephalotomy." *J Neurol Neurosurg & Psychiatry* 27:516–21 D '64. * (PA 39:9508)

454. LANDMARK, MARGRETE, AND GRINDE, TURID. "Children's Bender Drawings From 1938 to 1962: A Study of the Litera-

ture." *Nordisk Psykologi* 16(2):65–104 '64. * (*PA* 39:7902)

455. REITMAN, E. EDWARD, AND CLEVELAND, SIDNEY E. "Changes in Body Image Following Sensory Deprivation in Schizophrenic and Control Groups." *J Abn & Social Psychol* 68:168–76 F '64. * (*PA* 38:5172)

456. THRONE, FRANCES M.; KASPAR, JOSEPH C.; AND SCHULMAN, JEROME L. "Performance Time and Brain Damage Ratings." *Am J Mental Def* 68:656–9 Mr '64. * (*PA* 39:2484)

457. SILBERBERG, NORMAN ESAU. *An Investigation to Identify Intellectual and Perceptual Correlates of Disability in Word Recognition.* Doctor's thesis, State University of Iowa (Iowa City, Iowa), 1965. (*DA* 26:878)

458. ADAMS, JERRY. *An Investigation of the Performance of School Children on Canter's Background Interference Procedure for the Bender-Gestalt Test.* Master's thesis, University of Iowa (Iowa City, Iowa), 1966.

459. CASHMAN, JEROME PATRICK. *A Study of the Relationship Between Organic Factors, Certain Selected Variables and Progress in a Reading Improvement Program.* Doctor's thesis, Fordham University (New York, N.Y.), 1966. (*DA* 27:1648A)

460. McELHANEY, MARK LUCAS. *A Comparison of Temporal Lobe With Non-Temporal Lobe Brain Damage as Shown by Various Psychological Tests.* Doctor's thesis, University of Houston (Houston, Tex.), 1966. (*DA* 27:1625B)

461. BRENNER, MAY WOOLF; GILLMAN, SELMA; ZANGWILL, O. L.; AND FARRELL, MARGARET. "Visuo-Motor Disability in School Children." *Brit Med J* 4:259–62 N 4 '67. *

462. COLBERT, JOHN, AND HARROW, MARTIN. "Psychomotor Retardation in Depressive Syndromes." *J Nerv & Mental Dis* 145:405–19 N '67. * (*PA* 42:9228)

463. FLEMING, JEAN McKEY. *Body Image and Learning of Deaf and Hearing Boys.* Doctor's thesis, University of Florida (Gainesville, Fla.), 1967. (*DA* 29:144A)

464. HEMPHILL, AUGUSTA S. *A Comparison of the Bender Visual Motor Gestalt Test and the Metropolitan Readiness Test, Form B, as Measures of First Grade Readiness.* Master's thesis, Southern Methodist University (Dallas, Tex.), 1967.

465. OBERLEDER, MURIEL. "Adapting Current Psychological Techniques for Use in Testing the Aging." *Gerontologist* 7(3, pt 1):188–91 S '67. * (*PA* 42:3801)

466. SIMPSON, SEYMOUR AARON. *Perceptual Functions in Cerebral-Palsied Children.* Doctor's thesis, Yeshiva University (New York, N.Y.), 1967. (*DA* 28:508A)

467. STEINMAN, WARREN M. "The Use of Ambiguous Stimuli to Predict General Competence." *J Sci Lab Denison Univ* 48:7–14 Je '67. * (*PA* 42:2590)

468. WALRAVEN, MAURICE PETER. *Perceptual Relationships: Personality-Reading.* Doctor's thesis, University of Oklahoma (Norman, Okla.), 1967. (*DA* 27:3742A)

469. ADAMS, JERRY RAYMOND. *An Application of the Canter Background Interference Procedure to the Prediction of Brain Damage in Mentally Retarded Children.* Doctor's thesis, University of Iowa (Iowa City, Iowa), 1968. (*DA* 29:2197B)

470. ANDREWS, JOSEPH KARL. *The Relationship of Body Image to Verbal Learning and Perceptual Motor Ability in Young Children.* Doctor's thesis, Syracuse University (Syracuse, N.Y.), 1968. (*DA* 29:4373B)

471. ANTHONY, GEORGE A. *Cerebral Dominance as an Etiological Factor in Dyslexia (Severe Reading Disability).* Doctor's thesis, New York University (New York, N.Y.), 1968. (*DAI* 30:1425A)

472. BIETZ, DONALD C. *The Test-Retest Reliability of the Bender-Gestalt Test With Children Certified as Educationally Handicapped Minors Using the Koppitz Developmental Scoring System.* Master's thesis, Sacramento State College (Sacramento, Calif.), 1968.

473. BOROSAGE, VERA. *A Study of the Effect of Nursery School Experience on Intellectual Performance at Two Socio-Economic Levels.* Doctor's thesis, Michigan State University (East Lansing, Mich.), 1968. (*DA* 29:2993A)

474. BRYNJOLFSSON, KENNETH LEE. *An Investigation of the Concurrent Validity of the Bender Gestalt Test.* Doctor's thesis, University of Illinois (Urbana, Ill.), 1968. (*DAI* 30:127A)

475. BURCH, CHARLES WILLIAM. *Assessment Variables Relevant to the Referral and Placement of Pupils in Educationally Handicapped Classes.* Doctor's thesis, University of Southern California (Los Angeles, Calif.), 1968. (*DA* 29:2995A)

476. CONNOR, MARJORIE WELLS. *Learning Characteristics of Able Nonachievers in Audiolingual Foreign Language Classes.* Doctor's thesis, University of Cincinnati (Cincinnati, Ohio), 1968. (*DA* 29:1446A)

477. FERRITTO, MARY CABRINI. *An Evaluation of the Bender-Gestalt Test as a Measure of Assessing Reading Readiness.* Master's thesis, St. John College (Cleveland, Ohio), 1968.

478. FREED, EARL X. "Type II Rotations on the Bender-Gestalt Test." *Newsl Res Psychol* 10:4–5 N '68. *

479. GATES, MAXINE FULLER. *A Comparison of the Learning Characteristics of Hyperactive and Hypoactive Children With Related Central Nervous System Dysfunctions.* Doctor's thesis, Ohio State University (Columbus, Ohio), 1968. (*DAI* 30:166A)

480. GILBERSTADT, HAROLD. "Relationships Among Scores of Tests Suitable for the Assessment of Adjustment and Intellectual Functioning." *J Gerontol* 23:483–7 O '68. *

481. GOFF, ANNE FUNKHOUSER. *An Empirical Study of Reliability and Concurrent Validity for the Koppitz Scoring System of the Bender Gestalt Test With Primary School Children.* Doctor's thesis, Southern Illinois University (Carbondale, Ill.), 1968. (*DA* 29:3417A)

482. KASTL, ALBERT J.; DAROFF, ROBERT B.; AND BLOCKER, W. WEBSTER. "Psychological Testing of Cerebral Malaria Patients." *J Nerv & Mental Dis* 147:553–61 D '68. * (*PA* 43:14654)

483. KEOGH, BARBARA K. "The Copying Ability of Young Children." *Ed Res* 11:43–7 N '68. * (*PA* 45:6067)

484. KEOGH, BARBARA K., AND KEOGH, JACK F. "Pattern Walking: A Dimension of Visuomotor Performance." *Excep Children* 34:617–8 Ap '68. * (*PA* 42:17546)

485. LUONG, CORINA K. MONGCAL. *An Analysis of Factors Related to Difficulties in Learning and Adjustment Among Minority Group Children.* Doctor's thesis, Bryn Mawr College (Bryn Mawr, Pa.), 1968. (*DAI* 30:4795B)

486. MILLICHAP, J. GORDON; AYMAT, FERNANDO; STURGIS, LORETTA H.; LARSEN, KATHERINE W.; AND EGAN, ROSEMARY A. "Hyperkinetic Behavior and Learning Disorders: 3, Battery of Neuropsychological Tests in Controlled Trial of Methylphenidate." *Am J Dis Children* 116:235–44 S '68. * (*PA* 43:4123)

487. RAINWATER, HAROLD G. "Reading Problem Indicators Among Children With Reading Problems." *Psychol* 5:81–3 N '68. *

488. SNYDER, ROBERT T., AND KALIL, JOHN. "Item Analysis, Inter-Examiner Reliability and Scoring Problems for Koppitz Scoring on the Bender Gestalt for Six-Year-Olds." *Percept & Motor Skills* 27:1351–8 D '68. * (*PA* 43:9808)

489. SPERGEL, PHILIP. *The Relationship Between Vocational Interest, Aptitude and Personality Integration With Disadvantaged Youth.* Doctor's thesis, Temple University (Philadelphia, Pa.), 1968. (*DA* 29:1760A)

490. THELEN, M. H.; VARBLE, D. L.; AND JOHNSON, JANE. "Attitudes of Academic Clinical Psychologists Toward Projective Techniques." *Am Psychologist* 23:517–21 Jl '68. * (*PA* 42:18843)

491. WIENER, G.; RIDER, R. V.; OPPEL, W. C.; AND HARPER, P. A. "Correlates of Low Birth Weight: Psychological Status at Eight to Ten Years of Age." *Pediatric Res* 2:110–8 Mr '68. * (*PA* 42:15299)

492. WISE, JAMES H. "Stick Copying of Designs by Preschool and Young School-Age Children." *Percept & Motor Skills* 27:1159–68 D '68. * (*PA* 43:9547)

493. YULIS, SERGIO. *Performance of Normal and Organic Brain Damaged Subjects on the Canter Background Interference Procedure Test as a Function of Drive.* Doctor's thesis, University of Iowa (Iowa City, Iowa), 1968. (*DA* 29:4390B)

494. ABRAM, HARRY S.; ALLAN, J. HAMILTON; HUGHES, DEANNA; SMITH, BURKE M.; HALL, WILLIAM E.; AND LEWIS, DAVID W. "A Multidisciplinary Computerized Approach to the Study of Adjustment to Lower Limb Amputation." *South Med J* 62(9):1072–6 S '69. *

495. ABRAMS, STANLEY. "The Upper Weight Level Premature Child." *Dis Nerv System* 30(6):414–7 Je '69. * (*PA* 44:6420)

496. ADAMS, JERRY. "On Reconciling the 'Multidimensional' and 'Unitary' Concepts of Brain Damage." *Percept & Motor Skills* 29(2):579–98 O '69. * (*PA* 44:3998)

497. ADAMS, JERRY, AND CANTER, ARTHUR. "Performance Characteristics of School Children on the BIP Bender Test." Abstract. *J Consult & Clin Psychol* 33(4):508 Ag '69. * (*PA* 43:15802)

498. ALLEN, ROBERT M. "The Developmental Test of Visual Perception and the Bender Gestalt Test Achievement of Educable Mental Retardate." *Training Sch B* 66(2):80–5 Ag '69. * (*PA* 44:4029)

499. ALLEN, ROBERT M. "An Empirical Tautology." *Percept & Motor Skills* 29(1):50 Ag '69. * (*PA* 44:2709)

500. ALLEN, ROBERT M., AND ADAMO, CYNTHIA. "A Study of the Bender Gestalt Figure and Visual Perception." *Acta Psychologica* 31(4):394–6 D '69. * (*PA* 44:14603)

501. AMES, LOUISE BATES. "Children With Perceptual Problems May Also Lag Developmentally." *J Learn Dis* 2(4):205–8 Ap '69. * (*PA* 45:6985)

502. ARMSTRONG, RENATE G. "The Bender-Gestalt: A Replication of Comparisons of Recalled Reproductions and an Investigation of Effects of Varying Instructions." *Newsl Res Psychol* 11(3):39 Ag '69. *

503. BAUMANN, KAREN SUZANN. *The Effects of an Educational Program on the Test Performance of Children With Psychoneurological Learning Disabilities.* Doctor's thesis, Oklahoma State University (Stillwater, Okla.), 1969. (*DAI* 31:3865A)

504. BECKER, JOHN T. *The Effect of Group Administration of Selected Individual Tests of Language, Visual Perception, and Auditory Perception to Kindergarten, First-, Second- and Third-Grade Children.* Doctor's thesis, Catholic University of America (Washington, D.C.), 1969. (*DAI* 30:2367A)

505. BROADHURST, ANNE, AND PHILLIPS, C. J. "Reliability and Validity of the Bender-Gestalt Test in a Sample of British School Children." *Brit J Social & Clin Psychol* 8(3):253–62 S '69. * (*PA* 44:3009)

506. CANTER, ARTHUR, AND STRAUMANIS, JOHN J. "Performance of Senile and Healthy Aged Persons on the BIP

Bender Test." *Percept & Motor Skills* 28(3):695-8 Je '69. * (*PA* 43:17618)

507. CONNOR, JAMES P. "Bender Gestalt Test Performance as a Predictor of Differential Reading Performance." *J Sch Psychol* 7(4):41-4 '68-69 ['69]. * (*PA* 44:2852)

508. DIBNER, ANDREW S., AND KORN, ERIC J. "Group Administration of the Bender Gestalt Test to Predict Early School Performance." *J Clin Psychol* 25(3):263-8 Jl '69. * (*PA* 44:4245)

509. DIERKS, DARRELL, AND CUSHNA, BRUCE. "Sex Differences in the Bender Gestalt Performance of Children." *Percept & Motor Skills* 28(1):19-22 F '69. * (*PA* 43:11067)

510. DOUBROS, STEVE G., AND MASCARENHAS, JULIET. "Relations Among Wechsler Full-Scale Scores, Organicity-Sensitive Subtest Scores and Bender-Gestalt Errors Scores." *Percept & Motor Skills* 29(3):719-22 D '69. * (*PA* 46:4666)

511. EDMUNDS, ROBERT. *An Evaluation of Current Scoring Systems of the Bender-Gestalt Test for Children.* Doctor's thesis, University of Utah (Salt Lake City, Utah), 1969. (*DAI* 30:3778A)

512. ELTERICH, KENNETH W. *The Effectiveness of a Perceptual Program as Indicated by the Bender-Gestalt Test.* Master's thesis, Southern Connecticut State College (New Haven, Conn.), 1969.

513. FIEDLER, MIRIAM F., AND SCHMIDT, ELLEN P. "Sex Differences in Bender-Gestalt Drawings of Seven-Year-Old Children." *Percept & Motor Skills* 29(3):753-4 D '69. *

514. FREED, EARL X. "Actuarial Data on Bender-Gestalt Test Rotations by Psychiatric Patients." *J Clin Psychol* 25(3):252-5 Jl '69. * (*PA* 44:3799)

515. GOFF, ANNE F., AND PARKER, AILEEN W. "Reliability of the Koppitz Scoring System for the Bender Gestalt Test." *J Clin Psychol* 25(4):407-9 O '69. * (*PA* 44:10142)

516. GRAVITZ, HERBERT LEONARD. *Examiner Expectancy Effects in Psychological Assessment: The Bender Visual Motor Gestalt Test.* Doctor's thesis, University of Tennessee (Knoxville, Tenn.), 1969. (*DAI* 30:5238B)

517. HENDERSON, NORMAN B.; BUTLER, BRUCE V.; AND GOFFENEY, BARBARA. "Effectiveness of the WISC and Bender-Gestalt Test in Predicting Arithmetic and Reading Achievement for White and Nonwhite Children." *J Clin Psychol* 25(3):268-71 Jl '69. * (*PA* 44:4246)

518. HURLEY, MICHAEL EUGENE. *Group Administration of the Bender-Gestalt With Retarded Children.* Master's thesis, Chico State College (Chico, Calif.), 1969.

519. HUTT, MAX L. "Potentiality of a Measure of Perceptual Adience-Abience in Predicting Inner Psychological Adaptability." Abstract. *Proc 77th Ann Conv Am Psychol Assn* 4(2):509-10 '69. * (*PA* 44:941)

520. JACOBS, ELEANOR A.; WINTER, PETER M.; ALVIS, HARRY J.; AND SMALL, S. MOUCHLY. "Hyperoxygenation Effect on Cognitive Functioning in the Aged." Abstract. *Proc 77th Ann Conv Am Psychol Assn* 4(2):721-2 '69. *

521. JACOBS, ELEANOR A.; WINTER, PETER M.; ALVIS, HARRY J.; AND SMALL, S. MOUCHLY. "Hyperoxygenation Effect on Cognitive Functioning in the Aged." *New Engl J Med* 281(14):753-7 O 2 '69. * (*PA* 44:7205)

522. KALIL, ALBERT JOHN. *A Reliability Study of the Bender Visual Motor Gestalt Test When Administered and Scored Under Special Conditions.* Doctor's thesis, Catholic University of America (Washington, D.C.), 1969. (*DAI* 30:2378A)

523. KEIM, RICHARD PAUL. *Visual-Motor Training, Readiness, and Intelligence of Kindergarten Children.* Doctor's thesis, Temple University (Philadelphia, Pa.), 1969. (*DAI* 31:1076A)

524. KENNY, THOMAS JOSEPH. *The Utility of the Background Interference Procedure as an Assessment Instrument for Use by Guidance Counselors to Evaluate Special Learning Problems in Children.* Doctor's thesis, Catholic University of America (Washington, D.C.), 1969. (*DAI* 30:2335A)

525. KEOGH, BARBARA K. "The Bender Gestalt With Children: Research Applications." *J Spec Ed* 3(1):15-22 w-sp '69. * (*PA* 44:15304)

526. KROP, HARRY D., AND SMITH, CORINNE ROTH. "Effects of Special Education on Bender-Gestalt Performance of the Mentally Retarded." *Am J Mental Def* 73(5):693-9 Mr '69. * (*PA* 43:10347)

527. LILLISTON, LAWRENCE GRANT. *Dimensions of Schizophrenia as a Function of Performance on Tests of Cerebral Damage.* Doctor's thesis, Temple University (Philadelphia, Pa.), 1969. (*DAI* 30:1900B)

528. LINGREN, RONALD H. "Performance of Disabled and Normal Readers on the Bender-Gestalt, Auditory Discrimination Test, and Visual-Motor Matching." *Percept & Motor Skills* 29(1):152-4 Ag '69. * (*PA* 44:2803)

529. MCNAMARA, J. REGIS; PORTERFIELD, CHARLES L.; AND MILLER, LAWRENCE E. "The Relationship of the Wechsler Preschool and Primary Scale of Intelligence With the Coloured Progressive Matrices (1956) and the Bender Gestalt Test." *J Clin Psychol* 25(1):65-8 Ja '69. * (*PA* 43:9766)

530. MECKE, VIOLA. "Centration: A Perceptual Process Diacritic of Intellection and a Differential Diagnostic Criterion." *Percept & Motor Skills* 29(3):827-34 D '69. *

531. MORDOCK, JOHN B. "Effect of Stress on Perceptual-Motor Functioning of Adolescents With Learning Difficulties." *Percept & Motor Skills* 29(3):883-6 D '69. * (*PA* 46:5523)

532. MORDOCK, JOHN B. "A Procedural Critique of 'Bender Gestalts of Organic Children: Accuracy of Clinical Adjustment.'" *J Proj Tech & Pers Assess* 33(6):489-91 D '69. * (*PA* 44:6954)

533. MORDOCK, JOHN B.; TERRILL, PATRICIA ANN; AND NOVIK, ELLEN. "The Bender-Gestalt Test in Differential Diagnosis of Adolescents With Learning Difficulties." *J Sch Psychol* 7(4):11-4 '68-69 ['69]. * (*PA* 44:2682)

534. MOSELEY, DOLLY ANN. *The Performance of Deprived Children on the Bender Gestalt Test.* Doctor's thesis, University of Oklahoma (Norman, Okla.), 1969. (*DAI* 30:3329A)

535. NIELSEN, HELLE H., AND RINGE, KIRSTEN. "Visuo-Perceptive and Visuo-Motor Performance of Children With Reading Disabilities." *Scandinavian J Psychol* 10(4):225-31 '69. * (*PA* 44:9351)

536. NORFLEET, MARY ANN. *The Bender Gestalt as a Group Screening Instrument for Reading Readiness.* Doctor's thesis, University of Oregon (Eugene, Ore.), 1969. (*DAI* 31:1083A)

537. O'CONNOR, WILLIAM J. "The Relationship Between the Bender-Gestalt Test and the Marianne Frostig Developmental Test of Visual Perception." *Proc Ann Conv Int Read Assn* 13(3):72-81 '69. *

538. PORTERFIELD, CHARLES L. "Adaptive Mechanisms of Young Disadvantaged Stutterers and Nonstutterers." *J Proj Tech & Pers Assess* 33(4):371-5 Ag '69. * (*PA* 44:2144)

539. PRABHU, G. G. "The Clinical Utility of Bender-Gestalt and Minnesota Percepto Diagnostic Tests." *Indian J Appl Psychol* 6(2):69-73 Jl '69. *

540. QUATTLEBAUM, LAWRENCE F., AND WHITE, WILLIAM F. "Relationships Among the Quick Test, Two Measures of Psychomotor Functioning, and Age." *Percept & Motor Skills* 29(3):824-6 D '69. * (*PA* 46:5150)

541. ROSECRANS, C. J., AND SCHAFFER, HARRIET B. "Bender-Gestalt Time and Score Differences Between Matched Groups of Hospitalized Psychiatric and Brain-Damaged Patients." *J Clin Psychol* 25(4):409-10 O '69. * (*PA* 44:10737)

542. ROSECRANS, C. J., AND SUTTERER, J. R. "Perceptual, Concept Shift, and Personality Test Performance of Matched Psychiatric Outpatient Groups." *J Nerv & Mental Dis* 149(3):254-60 S '69. * (*PA* 44:6879)

543. ROSICKI, MARIA. *A Comparison of the Critical Flicker Frequency and Other Perceptual Tasks in Mental Defectives and Normals.* Doctor's thesis, Fordham University (New York, N.Y.), 1969. (*DAI* 30:5697B)

544. SABATINO, DAVID A. "Auditory and Visual Perceptual Behavioral Function of Neurologically Impaired Children." *Percept & Motor Skills* 29(1):35-40 Ag '69. * (*PA* 44:2686)

545. SABATINO, DAVID A. "The Construction and Assessment of an Experimental Test for Auditory Perception." *Excep Children* 35(9):729-37 My '69. * (*PA* 44:19177)

546. SABATINO, DAVID A. "Identifying Neurologically Impaired Children Through a Test of Auditory Perception." *J Consult & Clin Psychol* 33(2):184-8 Ap '69. * (*PA* 43:10203)

547. SABATINO, DAVID A., AND BECKER, JOHN T. "Relations Among Five Basic Tests of Behavior." *Percept & Motor Skills* 29(2):487-90 O '69. * (*PA* 44:3428)

548. SABATINO, DAVID A., AND CRAMBLETT, HENRY. "A Longitudinal Study of Children With Learning Disabilities Subsequent to Hospitalization for Viral Encephalitis—Part 1." *J Learn Dis* 2(2):65-75 F '69. * (*PA* 45:6854)

549. SABATINO, DAVID A., AND CRAMBLETT, HENRY G. "A Longitudinal Study of Children With Learning Disabilities Subsequent to Hospitalization for Viral Encephalitis—Part 2." *J Learn Dis* 2(3):124-35 Mr '69. * (*PA* 45:6855)

550. SCHWARTZ, MELVIN L., AND DENNERLL, RAYMOND D. "Immediate Visual Memory as a Function of Epileptic Seizure Type." *Cortex* 5(1):69-74 Mr '69. * (*PA* 44:1114)

551. SONG, A. Y., AND SONG, R. H. "The Bender-Gestalt Test With the Background Interference Procedure on Mental Retardates." *J Clin Psychol* 25(1):69-71 Ja '69. * (*PA* 43:10238)

552. SUINN, RICHARD M., AND OSKAMP, STUART. *The Predictive Validity of Projective Measures: A Fifteen-Year Evaluative Review of Research*, pp. 94-100, 130-2. Springfield, Ill.: Charles C Thomas, Publisher, 1969. Pp. xv, 161. *

553. VITALE, JOHN H.; STEINHELBER, JOHN C.; DRAKE, WILLIAM E., JR.; AND DAHLGREN, HELEN. "Psychological Dimensions of Cerebrovascular Insufficiency." *Percept & Motor Skills* 29(2):555-63 O '69. * (*PA* 44:3996)

554. WAGNER, EDWIN E. "A Reply to Mordock's 'Critique.'" *J Proj Tech & Pers Assess* 33(6):492 D '69. * (*PA* 44:6957)

555. WAGNER, EDWIN E., AND MURRAY, ALICE Y. "Bender-Gestalts of Organic Children: Accuracy of Clinical Judgment." *J Proj Tech & Pers Assess* 33(3):240-2 Je '69. * (*PA* 44:14487)

556. WARD, WILLIAM JOSEPH. *A Comparison of Distortion Scores on the Bender Visual Motor Gestalt Test Using Circular and Rectangular Protocol Sheets.* Doctor's thesis, University of Tulsa (Tulsa, Okla.), 1969. (*DAI* 30:1883A)

557. WEDELL, K., AND HORNE, I. EDNA. "Some Aspects of Perceptuo-Motor Disability in 5½-Year-Old Children." *Brit J Ed Psychol* 39(2):174-82 Je '69. * (*PA* 44:6514)

558. WEISS, A. A. "Bender-Gestalt Performance and Con-

cept Formation." *Israel Ann Psychiatry* 7(1):76–81 Ap '69. * (*PA* 45:6061)

559. WEISS, A. A. "Directionality in 4 Bender-Gestalt Figures." *Percept & Motor Skills* 29(1):59–62 Ag '69. * (*PA* 44:2347)

560. WOHLFORD, PAUL, AND FLICK, GRAD L. "Sex-of-Rater Bias in Clinical Diagnosis of Organic Brain Damage Using the Bender-Gestalt and Memory-for-Designs Tests." *Percept & Motor Skills* 29(1):107–14 Ag '69. * (*PA* 44:2538)

561. YULIS, SERGIO. "The Relationship Between the Canter Background Interference Procedure (BIP) and Intelligence." *J Clin Psychol* 25(4):405–6 O '69. * (*PA* 44:11041)

562. ZACH, LILLIAN, AND KAUFMAN, JUDITH. "The Effect of Verbal Labelling on Visual Motor Performance." *J Learn Dis* 2(4):218–22 Ap '69. *

563. ADAMS, JERRY. "Canter Background Interference Procedure Applied to the Diagnosis of Brain Damage in Mentally Retarded Children." *Am J Mental Def* 75(1):57–64 Jl '70. * (*PA* 45:2616)

564. BECKER, JOHN T. "Spatial Orientation and Visual Discrimination." *Percept & Motor Skills* 31(3):943–6 D '70. * (*PA* 46:894)

565. BENDER, LAURETTA. "The Use of the Visual Motor Gestalt Test in the Diagnosis of Learning Disabilities." *J Spec Ed* 4(1):29–39 w-sp '70. *

566. BENNETT, RONALD C. *The Teaching of Concrete Thinking Strategies to Five Year Old Children and Its Effect of Performance on the Bender Gestalt Test.* Master's thesis, Utah State University (Logan, Utah), 1970.

567. BEN-YISHAY, YEHUDA; GERSTMAN, LOUIS; DILLER, LEONARD; AND HAAS, ALBERT. "Prediction of Rehabilitation Outcomes From Psychometric Parameters in Left Hemiplegics." *J Consult & Clin Psychol* 34(3):436–41 Je '70. * (*PA* 44:15081)

568. BURGESS, MICHAEL M.; KODANAZ, ALTAN; AND ZIEGLER, DEWEY K. "Prediction of Brain Damage in a Neurological Population With Cerebrovascular Accidents." *Percept & Motor Skills* 31(2):595–601 O '70. * (*PA* 45:6841)

569. BURGESS, MICHAEL M.; KODANAZ, ALTAN; ZIEGLER, DEWEY; AND GREENBURG, HOWARD. "Prediction of Brain Damage in Two Clinical Populations." *Percept & Motor Skills* 30(2):523–32 Ap '70. * (*PA* 46:7299)

570. CHOYNOWSKI, MIECZYSLAW. "Curve-Fitting as a Method of Statistical Correction of Developmental Norms, Shown on the Example of the Bender-Koppitz Test." *J Clin Psychol* 26(2):135–41 Ap '70. * (*PA* 44:13625)

571. COHEN, I.; FLIEGELMAN, S.; GLUCK, Z.; AND KELMAN, D. "Study of Early Differentiation Between Schizophrenia and Psychotic Manifestations in Adolescence." *Israel Ann Psychiatry* 8(2):163–72 Jl '70. *

572. CULLEN, BETTE. *An Investigation of the Bender Visual Motor Gestalt Test Scored by Koppitz Developmental Scoring System and Specific Reading Skills of Second Graders.* Master's thesis, Wisconsin State University (River Falls, Wis.), 1970.

573. DE-LEVIE, ARI. "Bender-Gestalt Distortion on Recall Associated With Recent Physical Trauma." Abstract. *Proc 78th Ann Conv Am Psychol Assn* 5(2):711–2 '70. * (*PA* 44:18903)

574. EGELAND, BYRON; DI NELLO, MARIO; AND CARR, DONALD. "The Relationship of Intelligence, Visual-Motor, Psycholinguistic and Reading-Readiness Skills With Achievement." *Ed & Psychol Meas* 30(2):451–8 su '70. * (*PA* 45:3056)

575. FERINDEN, WILLIAM E., JR., AND JACOBSON, SHERMAN. "Early Identification of Learning Disabilities." *J Learn Dis* 3(11):589–93 N '70. *

576. FINE, E. W.; LEWIS, D.; VILLA-LANDA, I.; AND BLAKEMORE, C. B. "The Effect of Cyclandelate on Mental Function in Patients With Arteriosclerotic Brain Disease." *Brit J Psychiatry* 117(537):157–61 Ag '70. * (*PA* 45:4442)

577. FRETZ, BRUCE R. "Factor Structure of Intellectual, Visual Perception, and Visuomotor Performance of Poorly Coordinated Boys." *J Motor Behav* 2(2):69–78 Je '70. *

578. FURR, KARL D. "Standard Scores for the Koppitz Developmental Scoring System." *J Clin Psychol* 26(1):78–9 Ja '70. * (*PA* 44:10410)

579. GIEBINK, JOHN W., AND BIRCH, ROBERT. "The Bender Gestalt Test as an Ineffective Predictor of Reading Achievement." *J Clin Psychol* 26(4):484–5 O '70. * (*PA* 45:5055)

580. GILBERSTADT, HAROLD. "Detection of Organicity With a Bender Recall Sign." *Newsl Res Psychol* 12(2):58–61 My '70. *

581. HAFNER, LAWRENCE E.; WEAVER, WENDELL W.; AND POWELL, KATHRYN. "Psychological and Perceptual Correlates of Reading Achievement Among Fourth Graders." *J Read Behav* 2(4):281–90 f '70. * (*PA* 46:5663)

582. HARMAN, CHARLES E., AND RAYMOND, CHRISTOPHER S. "Computer Prediction of Chronic Psychiatric Patients." *J Nerv & Mental Dis* 150(6):490–503 Je '70. * (*PA* 45:8497)

583. HARTLAGE, LAWRENCE C. "Differential Diagnosis of Dyslexia, Minimal Brain Damage and Emotional Disturbances in Children." *Psychol Sch* 7(4):403–6 O '70. * (*PA* 46:1422)

584. HAYDEN, BENJAMIN S.; TALMADGE, MAX; HALL, MARJORY; AND SCHIFF, DONALD. "Diagnosing Minimal Brain Damage in Children: A Comparison of Two Bender Scoring Systems." *Merrill-Palmer Q* 16(3):278–85 Jl '70. *

585. HAYNES, JACK R. "Factor-Analytic Study of Performance on the Bender-Gestalt." *J Consult & Clin Psychol* 34(3):345–7 Je '70. * (*PA* 44:13618)

586. HIRSCH, ERNEST A. *The Troubled Adolescent: As He Emerges From Psychological Tests.* New York: International Universities Press, Inc., 1970. Pp. xv, 645. *

587. HIRSCHENFANG, SAMUEL; FABRIKANT, MURIEL B.; AND BENTON, JOSEPH G. "Perceptual Impairment in Patients With Multiple Sclerosis." *Am Arch Rehabil Ther* 18(4):90–4 D '70. *

588. HOWARD, JUDITH. "The Group Bender Gestalt Test as a Screening Procedure for the Identification of Children With Lags in Visual Perceptual Development." Abstract. *J Sch Psychol* 8(1):64–5 '70. * (*PA* 44:10138)

589. HUTT, MAX L., AND GIBBY, ROBERT GWYN. *An Atlas for the Hutt Adaptation of the Bender-Gestalt Test.* New York: Grune & Stratton, Inc., 1970. Pp. ix, 285. *

590. JORDAN, SIDNEY. "Projective Drawings in a Cerebellar Disorder Due to Chicken Pox Encephalitis." *J Proj Tech & Pers Assess* 34(3):256–8 Je '70. * (*PA* 44:18910)

591. KAPLAN, MARVIN L.; COLARELLI, NICK J.; GROSS, RUTH BRILL; LEVENTHAL, DAVID B.; AND SIEGAL, SAUL M. *The Structural Approach to Psychological Testing.* New York: Pergamon Press, Inc., 1970. Pp. xi, 195. *

592. KELLY, THOMPSON J., SR., AND AMBLE, BRUCE R. "IQ and Perceptual Motor Scores as Predictors of Achievement Among Retarded Children." *J Sch Psychol* 8(2):99–102 Ap–Je '70. * (*PA* 44:15325)

593. KEOGH, BARBARA K., AND SMITH, CAROL E. "Early Identification of Educationally High Potential and High Risk Children." *J Sch Psychol* 8(4):285–90 '70. * (*PA* 46:1866)

594. KEOGH, BARBARA K.; VERNON, MCCAY; AND SMITH, CAROL E. "Deafness and Visuo-Motor Functions." *J Spec Ed* 4(1):41–7 w-sp '70. *

595. KOPPITZ, ELIZABETH MUNSTERBERG. "Brain Damage, Reading Disability and the Bender Gestalt Test." *J Learn Dis* 3(9):429–33 S '70. *

596. LACKS, PATRICIA BRILLIANT; COLBERT, JOHN; HARROW, MARTIN; AND LEVINE, JACOB. "Further Evidence Concerning the Diagnostic Accuracy of the Halstead Organic Test Battery." *J Clin Psychol* 26(4):480–1 O '70. * (*PA* 45:4541)

597. LAMBERT, NADINE M. "An Evaluation of Scoring Categories Applicable to Children's Performance on the Bender Visual Motor Gestalt Test." *Psychol Sch* 7(3):275–87 Jl '70. * (*PA* 45:4922)

598. LEEK, WILLIAM R. *A Visual Perception Study of First Grade Compensatory Education Children Using the Bender Visual Motor Gestalt Test.* Master's thesis, Sacramento State College (Sacramento, Calif.), 1970.

599. LESSLER, KEN; SCHOENINGER, D. W.; AND BRIDGES, JUDITH S. "Prediction of First Grade Performance." *Percept & Motor Skills* 31(3):751–6 D '70. * (*PA* 45:10959)

600. LILLISTON, LAWRENCE. "Tests of Cerebral Damage and the Process-Reactive Dimension." *J Clin Psychol* 26(2):180–1 Ap '70. * (*PA* 44:15126)

601. MALONEY, MICHAEL P., AND WARD, MICHAEL P. "Bender-Gestalt Test Performance of 'Organic' and 'Functional' Mentally Retarded Subjects." *Percept & Motor Skills* 31(3):860 D '70. * (*PA* 45:10525)

602. MORRISON, MARY JANE, AND KAHN, HARRIS. "A Comparison of Visual and Motor Modalities in Bender-Gestalt Performance." *Am Correct Ther J* 24(1):3–5 Ja–F '70. *

603. MURSTEIN, BERNARD I., AND WOLF, STEVEN R. "An Empirical Test of the 'Levels' Hypothesis With Five Projective Techniques." *Int Congr Rorsch & Other Proj Tech* 7:558–72 '70. *

604. MURSTEIN, BERNARD I., AND WOLF, STEVEN R. "Empirical Test of the 'Levels' Hypothesis With Five Projective Techniques." *J Abn Psychol* 75(1):38–44 F '70. * (*PA* 44:6794)

605. NURSS, JOANNE R. "A Diagnostic Comparison of Two Third Grade Reading Classes," pp. 42–54. In *Reading Difficulties: Diagnosis, Correction, and Remediation.* Edited by William K. Durr. Newark, Del.: International Reading Association, 1970. Pp. vii, 276. *

606. ORME, J. E. "A Practical Guide to Estimating Intelligence, Attainments and Intellectual Deficit." *Acta Psychologica* 32(2):145–61 Ap '70. * (*PA* 44:16684)

607. POPE, PEGGY, AND SNYDER, ROBERT T. "Modification of Selected Bender Designs and Interpretation of the First Graders' Visual-Perceptual Maturation With Implications for Gestalt Theory." *Percept & Motor Skills* 30(1):263–7 F '70. *

608. SABATINO, DAVID A., AND HAYDEN, DAVID L. "Information Processing Behaviors Related to Learning Disabilities and Educable Mental Retardation." *Excep Children* 37(1):21–9 S '70. * (*PA* 46:5527)

609. SABATINO, DAVID A., AND HAYDEN, DAVID L. "Psycho-Educational Study of Selected Behavioral Variables With Children Failing the Elementary Grades." *J Exp Ed* 38(4):40–57 su '70. * (*PA* 46:5680–1)

610. SABATINO, DAVID A., AND HAYDEN, DAVID L. "Variation in Information Processing Behaviors: As Related to Chronological Age Differences for Children Failing in the Elementary Grades." *J Learn Dis* 3(8):404–12 Ag '70. *

611. SCHWARTZ, MELVIN L., AND DENNERLL, RAYMOND D. "Neuropsychological Assessment of Children With, Without, and With Questionable Epileptogenic Dysfunction." *Percept & Motor Skills* 30(1):111–21 F '70. *

612. STAVRIANOS, BERTHA K. "A Bit of Ammunition for Wagner and Some Answers to Mordock's Questions." *J Proj Tech & Pers Assess* 34(2):87 Ap '70. * (*PA* 44:16916)

613. STEWART, R. R.; WALKER, W.; AND SAVAGE, R. D. "A Developmental Study of Cognitive and Personality Characteristics Associated With Haemolytic Disease of the Newborn." *Develop Med & Child Neurol* 12(1):16–26 F '70. * (*PA* 44:17249)

614. VEGA, MANUEL, AND POWELL, ARNOLD. "The Effects of Practice on Bender Gestalt Performance of Culturally Disadvantaged Children." *Fla J Ed Res* 12(1):45–9 Ja '70. *

615. WAGNER, EDWIN E. "Results of Psychological Testing on a Child With Gilles De La Tourette's Disease." *J Clin Psychol* 26(1):52–7 Ja '70. * (*PA* 44:10955)

616. WATKINS, JULIA MARY HERNDON. *Comparison of a Normal and Emotionally Disturbed Sample of Children Using the Plenk Scoring System for the Bender Gestalt Test.* Doctor's thesis, University of Utah (Salt Lake City, Utah), 1970. (*DAI* 31:2750A)

617. WEISS, A. A. "Frequency of Distortions, Rotations, Perseverations, Simplifications, and Contaminations etc. on the Bender Visual-Motor Gestalt Test in a Non-Clinical Population." *Israel Ann Psychiatry* 8(1):75–80 Ap '70. *

618. WEISS, A. A. "Reproduction From Memory and Frequency of Recall of Bender-Gestalt Figures in Non-Clinical Subjects of Different Ages." *Israel Ann Psychiatry* 8(2):143–5 Jl '70. *

619. WEISS, SAMUEL A.; FISHMAN, SIDNEY; AND KRAUSE, FRED. "Symbolic Impulsivity, the Bender-Gestalt Test, and a Prosthetic Adjustment in Amputees." *Arch Phys Med & Rehabil* 51(3):152–8 Mr '70. *

620. WILLIS, DIANE JANICE. *Perceptual and Cognitive Performance of Children as Functions of Socio-Economic Class.* Doctor's thesis, University of Oklahoma (Norman, Okla.), 1970. (*DAI* 31:3045A)

621. YULIS, SERGIO. "Performance of Normal and Organic Brain-Damaged Subjects on the Canter Background Interference Procedure Test as a Function of Drive." *J Consult & Clin Psychol* 34(2):184–8 Ap '70. * (*PA* 44:11040)

PHILIP M. KITAY, *Professor of Psychology, Adelphi University, Garden City, New York.*

The *Bender-Gestalt Test* occupies a unique position among major clinical diagnostic instruments as a brief test that is both projective and nonprojective. Bender (*242*) changed Wertheimer's verbal perceptual technique into a nonverbal measurement of gestalt functioning in the perceptual-motoric sphere by substituting copying designs for describing them, only to have others, especially Hutt and Briskin (*192*), superimpose a projective function. This innovation has met loud protest from some clinicians, especially from Bender (*242*), though with some equivocation. Hutt and Briskin, by adding to the standard copying phase an elaboration, an association, and a testing-the-limits phase, have grafted onto the test a Rorschach-type procedure. It is not clear whether their intent is to duplicate Rorschach findings or to assess personality dimensions untapped by the Rorschach. It would seem to be more profitable to create a new projective technique capitalizing on insights from Bender-Gestalt findings than to demonstrate virtuosity in projective interpretation by extracting every last drop of projective material from a test not designed for that purpose.

The development of scoring systems to provide objectivity and quantification, e.g., the work of Pascal and Suttell (*41*), Koppitz (*259*), and most recently Hutt (*429*), has encouraged much research. Although the scores themselves have not been of much help to clinicians, the signs or items of the systems have provided useful frames of reference. Much of the research stimulated by this approach has dealt with concurrent validity of the scoring systems, whereas the urgent need is for research on construct validity, i.e., the meaning of what the test measures. Instead of being limited to the specifics of the Bender-Gestalt, research should be extended into the more general area of graphic and perceptual maturation and regression to provide a better conceptual framework for the test. Fabian's (*7*) developmental study of children's verticalization in copying horizontal lines and of attempts by six and seven year olds to achieve vertical orientation by head and arm twisting represents early work of this type but unfortunately has led to little further research. Hutt (*410*) has offered the provocative hypothesis that nonverbal measurements in the perceptual-motor sphere may tap very deep and early modes of personality functioning dating from pre-verbal stages of development.

Since the test has relatively low retest reliabilities and, as Bender has cautioned in her 1946 instructions booklet, is easily affected by fatigue, much more research is needed on the causes of fluctuation in performance, on the influence of modification of directions for administering the test, and of experimental manipulation of extra-individual and intra-individual variables upon test performance. Research has indicated that advance information as to the number of designs to be copied, position of stimulus cards relative to copy sheet, and shape and size of copy sheet affect performance. Bender's directions, "just copy them [the designs] the way you see them," and Hutt's (*429*) directions, "copy the drawing on the paper as well as you can," would seem to make a difference in test performance. Allowing or not allowing the examinee to move the stimulus card and the copy sheet from their original positions will affect performance. It is very important for the researcher and clinician to be aware of the effects of specific administration procedures employed.

Schulberg and Tolor's (*216*) survey conducted in 1960 revealed that four out of five psychologists sampled considered the Bender of some or great value in their work and that it was a popular device for differential diagnosis involving organicity, but not often used for other types of differential diagnosis. Forty-four percent of the clinicians responding reported little confidence in the Bender for evaluating personality dynamics. Currently, most clinicians probably include the Bender-Gestalt in their batteries primarily for detecting brain damage; some use it as a supplement in personality evaluation. Clinicians frequently use a combination of clinical intuition and an inspection system. Tolor and Schulberg (*242*) believe that the inferential analysis method of hypothesis testing proposed by Hutt and Briskin (*192*) offers a desirable combination of clinical intuitiveness with statistical refinement. This system, similar to sequence analysis on the Rorschach, seems to provide a legitimate and promising strategy.

The brevity of the *Bender-Gestalt Test,* its innocuousness and its usefulness as an opener or icebreaker appeal to clinicians but are unlikely to impress nonclinical researchers. The Hutt and Briskin elaboration, association, and testing-the-limits phases militate against these advantages without offering any compensatory values that could not be obtained from Rorschach, drawings, and TAT.

Some valuable contributions to differential diagnosis of organicity with the Bender have been made by Canter (*343*) and by Smith and Martin (*398*). Canter has found that organics have greater difficulty in copying the designs on a jigsaw-lined sheet of paper (background interference procedure) than on the usual blank sheet of paper. Nonorganics manifest this differential much less often. Smith and Martin found that the number of cues needed to perceive and correct rotations is greater in organics than in nonorganics, facilitating the detection of false positives.

Low predictive validities reported for the Bender are in the general range typical for projective techniques. As Rabin [1] has aptly indicated, specific predictions from projective techniques are disappointing since the clinician has to make inferences from test data that were not intended to be directly relevant to his specific predictions. Much criticism of the Bender as inadequate in differentiating patients in various

psychiatric diagnostic categories is unjustified since psychiatric syndromes are not clean-cut categories in which all patients become stereotyped likenesses regardless of pre-morbid personality. Furthermore, clinicians use test behavior, material from other tests, and case history in assigning weight to a given test response for a particular diagnosis, whereas the researcher working with a single instrument does not have this latitude.

Koppitz's (*259*) developmental Bender scoring system and scoring manual for emotional indicators for use on children ages five to ten provide very useful aids in the burgeoning applications of the Bender to the study of children's problems. Work in this area should be further encouraged.

In this reviewer's opinion, the major reliance for the projective evaluation of personality dynamics should continue to be on the Rorschach, drawing techniques, and the TAT. In differential diagnosis for organicity, Anglin, Pullen, and Games (*303*) found the *Memory-For-Designs Test,* consisting of 15 designs presented tachistoscopically for copying, to be equal to the Bender in validity and easier to score, especially for inexperienced examiners. However, the vast research literature on the Bender undoubtedly makes it the instrument of choice. The Bender-Gestalt should be included, if possible, in every diagnostic examination of adults and of children from age five because of its unique contributions to the evaluation of perceptual-motor functioning, neurological impairment, expressive styles, and maladjustment. Elaborate projective use of the instrument should be employed with caution. This instrument deserves its popularity among clinicians; indications are that this will grow and that the full potentialities of this test have not yet been realized.

For a review by C. B. Blakemore, see 6:203 (1 excerpt); for reviews by Arthur L. Benton and Howard R. White, see 4:144.

[162]

Buttons: A Projective Test for Pre-Adolescent and Adolescent Boys and Girls. Grades 7–9; maladjustment; 1963; 3 scores: initial, content, total; 1 form (7 pages); manual (36 pages plus test and scoring booklet); scoring booklet (4 pages); no data on reliability of scores; $8.50 per examiner's kit of 10 tests, 10 scoring booklets, and manual; $3.50 per manual; postpaid; (45) minutes; Esther P. Rothman and Pearl H. Berkowitz; Western Psychological Services. *

1 RABIN, A. I. Chap. 19, "Adapting and Devising Projective Methods for Special Purposes," pp. 611–26. In his *Projective Techniques in Personality Assessment: A Modern Introduction.* New York: Springer Publishing Co., Inc., 1968. Pp. x, 638. *

WILLARD E. REITZ, *Associate Professor of Psychology, The University of Western Ontario, London, Ontario, Canada.*

Buttons is a projective test in cartoon format which purports to measure maladjustment in adolescent and pre-adolescent boys and girls. In the manual, it is stated that "Buttons *differentiates well-adjusted* pupils from those pupils with *gross deviations in personality, attitudes and behaviour.*" When used in groups, "it provides....a rapid method for *identifying children with problems.*" It is also stated that "Buttons identifies children in need of guidance, counseling, or psychological-psychiatric services." The test is made up of 11 four-picture animal cartoon sequences (Buttons is a rabbit) each of which sets up a school situation or problem and requires resolution, and one blank item for which the pupil writes his own story.

Scoring is accomplished by coding a child's open-ended responses as acceptable or unacceptable. The scoring scheme assumes that "a well-adjusted pre-adolescent or adolescent behaves in a manner acceptable to society and satisfying to himself." The Initial score is determined by scoring each response as either acceptable or unacceptable. Examples of these categories are given in the manual for each of the sequences. The Content score is determined by evaluating responses in seven diagnostic areas (Anxiety, Aggression, Withdrawal, Self-Concept, Authority, Structuring, and Value Judgment). Again, each response is scored as either positive or negative, although a given response here may be scorable in more than one content area. The manual provides examples of positive and negative responses in each of the diagnostic domains. The Total score is simply the sum of the Initial and Content scores. Since the test is designed to measure maladjustment, only the minus (unacceptable) scores are considered in forming the Total score. The Total score is deemed to be most significant and is used to evaluate adjustment.

Only interscorer reliabilities (two scorers) are reported and only for the Total score. For ten selected groups (how or why they were selected is not specified) ranging in size from 35 to 91, the median interscorer reliability was .95 (range .90–.98). Nothing, however, is mentioned as to who the scorers were, their level of training, or what safeguards were set up to insure independence of scoring. For a test designed for clinical use, not only should such information be reported, but different pairs of scorers should have been used across different groups to produce confidence in the scoring procedure. If such confidence were present, the conclusion would be that individuals working independently can arrive at similar numerical values for the Total score. It does not follow, however, that a similar statement can be made for the component parts of the Total score. In addition, for the general trait-like construct of maladjustment, indexes of internal consistency and temporal stability are appropriate but are totally lacking.

Equally serious is the total lack of normative data regarding Initial, Content and Total scores, as well as the relationships among these. Norms are most appropriate for the Total scores, given the explicit claims made for the test, but are not provided. The importance of norms for a test designed to measure important clinical constructs like maladjustment can scarcely be overstressed. In the present case even general norms are not provided, much less age-graded norms.

Finally, even though the various Content scores are not explicitly claimed to measure constructs indicated by their label, an implicit assumption of a quantitative nature is made regarding them. That is, it is assumed that the more unacceptable aggression responses there are, for example, the more maladjusted a child is in the aggression domain. A score sheet is provided to tally such responses for visual comparisons. This whole process could well mislead an unsuspecting user to misuse the Content scores. It should be underscored that there are *no norms and no reliability or validity evidence for any of the Content scores.*

"Standardization studies" are reported in the manual on "approximately 700 children" in New York City schools (grades 7, 8 and 9). The tables presented, however, reveal analysis on a total of only 511 subjects (256 boys and 255 girls). Of these, 373 were from regular schools and 138 from Bellevue Psychiatric Hospital. These pupils were distributed, based upon their Total score, into three groups: Well Adjusted, Mild Maladjustment, and Disturbed. No rationale or analysis is given for the cutoff scores used. No rationale is given for the ten subgroups analysed. Some clearly differ on the variables of sex, grade, or hospitalization, but not all.

With regard to the identification of well-adjusted and disturbed pupils, the Total score was compared with "judgment of teachers" (particular judgment not specified), counselors, *Mooney Problem Check List,* and evaluations by psychologists using the Rorschach. Considering well-adjusted pupils, it is reported that percentage agreements with these criteria were 43, 45, 60, and 75, respectively. When disturbed pupils were considered, the percentage agreements were 21, 38, 42, and 89, respectively.

The "high agreement" between Total score and psychologists' ratings is taken as indicating "that *Buttons* findings correlate highly with the clinical judgments of professional Psychologists." Inspection of the appropriate table, however, reveals that the total sample of pupils on which Rorschach comparisons were made reached only 25 (16 well adjusted and 9 disturbed). Furthermore, the conditions under which the Rorschach was used are not specified. Were the conditions blind, for example, or could base rate information have done as well or better?

The major validity information is given in the form of comparisons of Total score with psychiatric diagnoses for 91 disturbed boys and 47 disturbed girls in Bellevue Hospital. Agreements reported are 90 and 83 percent, respectively. Again, however, nowhere is it indicated whether or not elementary safeguards were instituted in scoring *Buttons.* If the protocols were known, for example, to have come from a hospital population, experimenter bias could have operated in the direction of raising scores and artifactually inflating agreements. In addition, no rationale is given for scoring agreements between Total scores and psychiatric diagnoses. Do all diagnostic categories, for example, represent maladjustment?

In sum, as a psychometric instrument *Buttons* falls far short of acceptable evidence of reliability and validity criteria. What evidence is provided is very weak and not bolstered with appropriate controls and safeguards. The absence of age-grade norms is a serious shortcoming. No rationale or analysis is given for cutoff scores of the central construct being measured. Information is presented in a misleading way in the manual. The cartoon format, which can portray school situations at a moderate level of specificity, is an interesting and potentially useful feature but poorly developed in the present instance. Finally, the assumption that children will more readily identify with animals is questionable, especially for those in the recom-

mended age range. The test cannot be recommended for use. Any use should be reserved to research efforts aimed at remedying the instrument's substantial problems.

[163]

★**Color Pyramid Test.** Ages 6 and over; 1951–65 (English edition, 1964–65); CPT; nonverbal "technique for the study of the role of emotion and affect"; English revision of *Der Farbpyramiden-Test nach Max Pfister* (1951) by Robert Heiss and Hildegard Hiltmann; 1 form ('65); manual ('64, 295 pages, see *4* below); summary of administration and scoring instructions ('65, 6 pages); color code chart ('65, 1 card); record blank ('65, 1 page); separate profiles ('65, 1 page) for males, females; Fr. 20 per set of color chips; Fr. 8 per pad of 50 record blanks; Fr. 5 per 25 profile sheets for either sex; Fr. .80 per summary instructions; Fr. 1 per color code chart; Fr. 1.80 per set of 2 pyramid form cards; Fr. 40 ($11) per complete set of preceding test materials; Fr. 38 ($12) per manual; postage extra; (25–50) minutes; K. Warner Schaie and Robert Heiss; Hans Huber. * (United States distributor: Grune & Stratton, Inc.)

REFERENCES

1–9. See P:420.
10. SCHAIE, K. WARNER. "Mass Psychological Screening of Young Children With the Color Pyramid Test." *Int Congr Rorsch & Other Proj Tech* 7:292–9 '70. *

S. G. LEE, *Professor of Psychology and Head of the Department, The University of Leicester, Leicester, England.*

A test procedure can, ultimately, be no stronger than the rationale on which it is based, for upon this rationale the interpretation of individual differences in response will depend. It is always easy to set up stimuli which will evoke varied responses from human subjects— so complex are the minds of men—and it is a truism that behaviour so elicited is a reflection of the personality of each subject. It is in the *interpretation* of these acts that false conclusions can be drawn. In the past, most of the attacks on projective techniques as such might more profitably have been levelled first against the theoretical beliefs that caused the test stimuli to be constructed in any particular way, and then against the same theoretical biases that distorted the conclusions drawn.

In the present instance it is claimed by the authors that:

The CPT has all the attributes of a projective technique, although perhaps with better defined stimulus dimensions and scoring procedures than most others currently available. Test interpretation may therefore be approached with all the principles well-known and appropriate for techniques such as the Rorschach or TAT. On the other hand, the CPT also has the attributes of a truly objective test (CATTELL, 1959). The CPT is an objective test in that the S is not aware of the dimensions on which he is being examined while at the same time the S's response is rigorously and unambiguously defined. Since the number of scoring variables is large and the empirically observed relations among these variables are low, the CPT is thus eminently suitable also for actuarial methods of personality description.

These are large, if muddled, claims. Let us look at the reality. The subject is asked to make, consecutively and in two dimensions, three "pretty" pyramids, each of 15 squares, culled from a large assortment of colours and hues available to him. He then has to make three "ugly" pyramids, and it was only on page 136 of the manual that your reviewer became aware that the "pretties" are intended to reveal "manifest emotional structure," while the "uglies" will represent latent or unconscious modes of affective response. No reason is given as to why these relationships should exist.

At the base of all this lies a grossly simplified system of hypothesized relationships, Red: happy : excited : blood : : black : sad : depressed : earth, etc., etc. Shades of Empedocles! These are bolstered by a *mélange* of (*a*) "biological cue functions" (Goethe, Tinbergen, Lorenz, Hess), (*b*) "symbolic meanings" ("Thus red is known as the violent colour of revolution but at the same time represents the humanistic [*sic*] characteristics of the International Red Cross"), and (*c*) "laboratory studies of the meaning of colour" (mostly colour preferences or semantic associations with colour from a variety of criterion groups, including psychotics and children). The last of these supports for the reasoning behind the CPT is probably the strongest, in type, but the results cited are so varied and discrepant as to be almost worthless.

The "biological" functions are very sketchily covered, with almost incredible apparent naïvete. Either they are almost completely beside the point, or the implication rests that your reviewer, a human being, is affected by colour differences in much the same way as is a male stickleback or blue jay! The enormous cross-cultural variations in colour symbolism are hardly mentioned. For example, among the Zulu, a string of pink and white beads sent to her lover by a girl would read: "My heart is full of love (White) but you have no cattle to marry me with (Pink)."

But even if, for whatever reasons, such simple-minded relationships exist between the human psyche and colours, these do not imply veridical relationships between the hundreds of "scores" that can, by permutation and combination, be elicited from any collection of CPT protocols and the dozens of traits listed in the "prediction equations" of Appendix II. Here is a very short list, roughly sampled, from the norms given: "Considerate, cheerful, unquestioning, suspicious, conventional, egotistical, timid, 'quitting,' baffled, intelligent, brave." The inferential leaps to these, from a basis of mere colour choice and use, are too great to command the credulity of your reviewer.

The manual teems with statistics of many kinds, often with special pleading involved: "For the re-analysis it was decided to count as a prediction error only those ratings where the predicted rating disagreed with both criterion raters. The revised procedure leads to far more encouraging results." All validatory evidence is culled from the use of differing criterion groups (not usually selected on a hypothetico-deductive basis), and the group results cited may have some validity. A great deal of painstaking—if, in my opinion, misguided—work has been done using the test, much of it reminiscent of some of the earlier attempts to put graphology on a scientific basis. Indeed, over the years, with possible correlation with refined physiological measures, longitudinal studies on the same individual, etc. the test may acquire some validity for the diagnosis of individual personality characteristics. At present I do not see this as a practical possibility.

In view of the crudity of the rationale, I am puzzled whether colour-blind subjects should be just rather mixed-up kids or lacking whole ranges of emotional activity. But we are told "clinical experience with some color blind Ss suggests that these will respond with great similarity to the performance of normals." Why?

Probably, the statement that sticks most in my gullet is: "The content validity of the CPT is demonstrated simply by showing (as in Fig. 2) that an adequate sample of hues in the color spectrum has been included in the test material." Validity for what?

ALBERT I. RABIN, *Professor of Psychology, Michigan State University, East Lansing, Michigan.*

The subject is given more than 200 chips which represent the 24 hues. He is asked to make a total of three "pretty" and three "ugly" pyramids.

This nonverbal method works well, according to the authors, with anxious and resistant subjects. It may be given in the beginning of an entire test battery. The only qualifications and counterindications to the use of the test are defective color vision and an inability to make a choice between stimuli.

The CPT is not a psychometric instrument in the conventional sense of the word. Its authors consider it a projective technique primarily because of the greater freedom of response (wide choice of chips and patterns of their combination in the construction of the pyramids) and because respondents are not aware of the meaning that is attributed to their responses and performance. However, so many variables of this technique are so well-quantified, and so much normative information is reported that it compares favorably with the available information in manuals of the more standardized questionnaires and personality tests.

The first half of the manual describes the CPT and its basic theoretical principles. The remaining half of the book (about 150 pages) contains a series of appendices of tabular normative data obtained from children and adults.

In addition to an exposition of some historical and folklore-based associations between color and personality variables and of the symbolic meaning of some colors, experiments concerned with the meaning of color and the historical antecedents of the CPT are also discussed. It was Pfister who originally suggested the use of color pyramids as a technique for personality assessment. Others picked up the idea and elaborated upon it until the present form resulted.

Detailed instructions for test administration and a description of the test materials are also presented. Although the relationship between the "pretty" and "ugly" pyramids is not too clear, a variety of quantitative indices based on the six pyramids which result from the test performance are proposed.

Essentially, there are two types of scores: color scores and form scores. In the former category there is scoring of the choice of hues, color groups (red, green, etc.), sequence, "color syndromes" (e.g., normal, consisting of red, green, and blue; stimulation syndrome, consisting of red, orange, and yellow; and so on), and the color characteristics of the total record (rank order of colors, and the dominance of "warm" and "cold" colors).

The form scoring involves patterns of color domination, color separation, and organization (12 patterns).

Some experiments involving comparisons of different groups of adults and children on the CPT are reported. Form dominance tends to show "significant developmental increments" from kindergarten to age 13 for boys and to age 14 for girls (9). In addition to some data concerning significance of test-retest reliability, construct validity, concurrent validity, and predictive validity are summarized in the text. For example: "Lienert administered LSD to a group of 30 college students who were tested prior to the drug administration and four hours thereafter * differences in the expected direction were significant at the 5% level of confidence [sic] for purple, brown, and blue" and not for yellow, black, and orange, as predicted. Schizophrenics were differentiated from some other groups, but no clear differential diagnostic patterns appeared when epileptics and neurotics were compared. Some positive relationships between test predictions and teacher behavior ratings are reported in support of "predictive validity." At best, these are rather slim pickings. It may be wondered, of course, whether all this labor was worthwhile in order to differentiate, at a low level of probability, between some diagnostic groupings but not between others. Of course, the main problem is actually the articulation of the meaning of the variables (color and form) with personality variables that presumably constitute the relevant pathological syndromes. Burdick's (7) study with 50 normals shows very little relationship between the CPT and MMPI personality variables. The central claim for the meaning of the test is that it yields information "relevant to affect expression and impulse control." It basically deals with the "emotional tension system." However, this we have to accept on faith, since the several types of validity and the experiments do not point very clearly and specifically to this aspect of personality. Thus, for example, we are told that the bright-dark dichotomy refers to mood states, since bright is associated with daylight, etc. "This leads to a description of White as the representation of lightness, release, unboundedness, but also of emptyness and lack of identification. Black on the other hand comes to signify depression, constraint, taciturnity and inhibition."

Overall, despite a good many meticulously reported statistical tables and factor analyses of the numerous form and color variables resulting from the test, there seems to be little sound rationale for interpretation of this test. Personality is dealt with on a common-sense level. There is no information as to how the meanings of the various scores can be integrated into a sophisticated or dynamic description of personality. The available quantitative material does not really support the alleged meaning of the performance characteristics, which are semantically connected with folklore-based interpretation. It offers an illustration of a technically well performed empirical exercise without much theoretical basis or psychological rationale.

Brit J Psychiatry 111:1130–1 N '65. L. J. Clements. [Review of the manual (4).] * The Color Pyramid Test is a non-verbal technique for personality assessment which has received much attention in the German psychological literature in recent years. This volume is the first presentation available in English, and represents an extension of the original intuitive concepts by application of psychometric approaches and experimental procedures. * The use of paper pyramid forms and "an abundance" of one-inch square coloured gummed papers, however, has many disadvantages as test materials, and the alternative permanent pyramid and coloured chips is the only satisfactory form of the test materials. Ironically, the major criticism of the book is the lack of the use of colour in the figures, necessitating a constant referral back to the one coloured plate. Half the volume is taken up with two appendices containing tables of norms and trait prediction equations. The confused layout of the tables given in Appendix II makes interpretation and comparison of test results very tedious, and if, as the authors claim, the administration and scoring of the test is simple, this manner of presentation of data adds to the complexity of assessment. However, this approach to personality assessment is remarkably absent from studies in this country, and for those who are concerned in this aspect of investigation the book provides a well-prepared account of one method that might be used.

Brit J Social & Clin Psychol 7:69 F '68. Moyra Williams. [Review of the manual (4).] Although the Color Pyramid Test....has been in use on the continent for the past twelve years,

this is the first book about it which has been specifically written for English-speaking psychologists. * consists of a box of 1-inch squares of coloured paper or chips in twenty-four different hues (covering ten different colours in varying shades of brightness) and a 15-field pyramid form, onto which the subject is instructed to make (a) As pretty a pyramid as you can, (b) a second pretty pyramid, (c) as ugly a pyramid as possible * Interpretation of the test is based on the colours chosen, the sequence formula (e.g. the stability of choices in the two pretty pyramids), the difference between pretty and ugly pyramids, and the form of the patterns made (e.g. "carpets," "layers," "staircases," etc.). According to its authors, this test is designed to yield information on affective expression and impulse control. Intellectual ability and "instinctive drives" do not influence performance, although "A global view of the person may emerge by inferring behaviour characteristics which would be expected on the basis of observed emotional structure" (p. 112). A large part of this volume is taken up with tables giving normative data from which readers can form their own conclusions regarding the test's usefulness. Those who feel the need for a test of emotional expression which to some extent combines the advantage of projective techniques with those of standardized methods of scoring may find this the answer. It clearly has considerable potentiality in the fields of research and vocational guidance, but in the opinion of the present reviewer the number of occasions on which it could give enough information to be of value in the clinical field is very small.

Percept & Motor Skills 22:667 Ap '66. C. H. Ammons. [Review of the manual (4).] The Color Pyramid Test, an ipsative procedure, is described carefully so that one is made aware of the limitations and possible sources of bias in the individual studies performed in the course of developing the test. Details of administration, scoring, and interpretation are given in a single volume in English. This should stimulate greater use of this nonverbal, projective-like test which is scored objectively.

[164]

★The Columbus: Picture Analysis of Growth Towards Maturity. Ages 5–20; 1969; individual; 1 form (24 pictures); manual (76 pages); no data on reliability and validity; Fr. 59 per set of pictures and manual; Fr. 30 per specimen set; postage extra; [30–60] minutes; M. J. Langeveld; S. Karger AG. *

REFERENCE
1. LANGEVELD, M. J. "A Short Preliminary Note on Some Presuppositions of the Columbus-Test for Children." *Folia Psychiatrica Neurologica et Neurochirurgica Neerlandica* 61: 178–82 '58. *

J Proj Tech & Pers Assess 34(4):342 Ag '70. Steven G. Vandenberg. This is a projective test somewhat similar to the TAT, but designed for children and adolescents from 5 to 18 years of age. It was developed in Holland, so that some of the pictures show Dutch suburbs or farms, but these are similar enough to comparable items in other European countries. It is claimed that the pictures are appropriate for non-western countries. Card 6 shows an old fashioned room with a bed built into a closet, an oil lamp over the table and a large hearth with a kettle over an open fire, which may seem somewhat odd to testees in the USA. Card 18 shows soccer players, which is an unfamiliar sight in the USA. The other cards show either interiors that could be almost anywhere or outside settings that are not too foreign looking. The author is unduly sanguine about the cross-cultural suitability of his test. It may well be that the presence of only two "unusual" pictures out of a total of 24, of which 3 are in color, will not cause too much of a problem, but the extent of the influence should be determined empirically. The manual contains a number of suggestions regarding use of the test and its interpretations, but no general scheme for "scoring" is proposed. Some of the pictures seem very well chosen and it would appear that either the total set or some selection from them may be useful for research. No information on the reliability or validity of the test is furnished; in fact, the general tone of the discussion in the manual is such that one would expect the author to attribute little value to such data. In an indirect way, this test gives a good insight into the nature of clinical work with children in Holland. The pictures were apparently chosen so that they would tap important psychological problems: being ill, being excluded from a group, being out late at night, etc. *

Percept & Motor Skills 31(1):339 Ag '70. C. H. Ammons and R. B. Ammons. The construction of a projective test using a series of 21 black and white pictures and 3 in color to "facilitate projective examination of children from a very early age up to maturity" (5 yr. on) (p. 5) is described following apologies for attention to "projective" investigation. Pro-

cedures for age-sequences were derived from responses of 80 children in each of 4 age groups (8, 10, 14, 16 yr.) and from several other groups, overlapping in age. As is often the case with European test manuals, details are sparse, statistical analysis nonexistent, and procedures fragmentarily depicted. Despite these problems the work seems to have been orderly, even systematic, but this reporting of the work may discourage many researchers and clinicians from trying to use the materials.

[165]

The Draw-A-Person. Ages 5 and over; 1963; DAP; 1 form; manual (38 pages plus sample copies of record and interpretive booklets); record booklet (4 pages); interpretive booklet (4 pages); $6.50 per 25 record booklets; $6.50 per 25 interpretive booklets; $6 per manual; postpaid; [5–10] minutes; William H. Urban; Western Psychological Services. *

DALE B. HARRIS, *Professor of Psychology, The Pennsylvania State University, University Park, Pennsylvania.*

This catalog of categories and suggested interpretative hypotheses has been assembled from the works of Bender, Buck, Goodenough, Hammer, Jolles, Machover and other specialists, with the greatest debt to Jolles[1] and Machover.[2] The entries, alphabetically arranged, combine five distinct categories of concepts: qualities to be inferred or concluded (e.g., aggression, dependency, perseveration, etc.); drawing characteristics (e.g., dim lines, eyes, shoes, etc.); diagnostic categories (e.g., obsessive-compulsives, paranoids, schizophrenia); behavioral characteristics (e.g., reluctance to draw); and subject matter of drawings (e.g., nudes, stick figures, themes, etc.).

Generally, when listed, the indicators reference clinical interpretations; clinical conditions or states reference features of the drawing which are considered to be diagnostic. Inevitably there is overlapping and contradiction among signs and indicators. In some instances, the source of authority (Machover or Jolles) for the conclusion is indicated; in most instances, no source is given.

There is a 4-page protocol booklet which permits the clinician systematically to record, feature by feature, the clinical indicators, e.g., mood and appearance; placement on page; areas

1 JOLLES, ISAAC. *A Catalogue for the Qualitative Interpretation of the H-T-P.* Beverly Hills, Calif.: Western Psychological Services, 1952. Pp. 97. *
2 MACHOVER, KAREN. *Personality Projection in the Drawing of the Human Figure: A Method of Personality Investigation.* Springfield, Ill.: Charles C Thomas, Publisher, 1949. Pp. ix, 183. *

of disproportion, erasure, and shading; head, shoulder, arm, and hand features; sexually symbolic areas; and control features. Two checklists are provided: a 16-item Severe Mental/Emotional Disturbance checklist, and a 14-item Organic Brain Damage checklist. The four-page Interpretative Report permits a description of the subject's behavior while drawing, evaluated by a checklist of possible behaviors and their significance, the examiner's impressions of the DAP figures on 24 graphic rating scales, and a comparison of the M and F figures on 10 qualitative dimensions. The author's untimely death undoubtedly accounts for a lack of evaluative discussion of and evidence for these forms.

The drawing of the human figure is one of the most widely used projective tests in psychological clinics. Projective tests, by definition, consist of fairly unorganized amorphous stimuli, on which the subject imposes organization in order to achieve an interpretation. A difficulty is that the examiner can likewise "project" in his interpretations of the subject's constructions, unless well-developed criteria for classifying and interpreting the subject's responses exist. The DAP presumably reveals unconscious features of the personality—dispositional qualities as well as behavioral syndromes. Thus, a fundamental assumption for the use of this device is that the drawing of a person represents an unconscious projection of the self-image. Most of the literature on draw-a-person tests makes the further assumption that diagnosis may be made through a study of qualitative features of drawings. The commonest approach is to inspect certain features or body parts considered as "signs." How these are defined and treated is illustrated from Urban's manual. Aggression, for example, is shown by "talon fingers," "a figure with dark piercing eyes," "flattened nose," or "emphasized nostrils." Clinicians who have discussed DAP interpretations clearly make extensive use of analogy to widely accepted general concepts. The talon fingers, presumably indicating hostility and aggression toward the world, are a very obvious analogy to an image deeply embedded in folklore. The "emphasized nostrils," further interpreted in Urban's manual as indicating "unsophisticated primitive anger: literally 'snorting with anger,'" refer to another widespread stereotype. Urban says concerning "Belt (also see Waistline)": "Traditionally the belt, since it separates the upper and lower halves of the body, has been

a symbol of control. Physiologically the belt cuts off the upper or intellectually controlling part of the body from the lower or sexually expressing part of the body. The belt also provides a place for a purse, weapons, or other symbols of power and authority." Further isomorphy is seen in such items as the unusually small figure drawing, which presumably indicates the shrunken ego. While such assumptions are clearly made throughout the literature of the DAP, only Raven [3] has explicitly acknowledged the assumptions of analogy and isomorphy. From the outset of the projective use of drawings, these assumptions have been utilized without question concerning their validity.

Because most of these signs are based on dynamic theories of personality which often proceed by a species of dialectical logic, such lists of signs as the Urban manual or the earlier comprehensive catalog by Bell [4] contain many apparent contradictions. For example, in the Urban manual indicators of "inadequacy feelings" are found in "very small figures" and "very large, weak or grandiose figures." Similarly, a large head may indicate "strong intellectual strivings" or "feelings of intellectual inadequacy, with compensatory stress on intellectual achievement"; an unusually large human figure may indicate "overwhelming inadequacy with compensatory trying to prove self on paper," or it may show "excessively high self esteem." Such curvilinear rather than rectilinear relationships between characteristics of a drawing and psychological characteristics suggest that blind analysis is risky indeed; evaluation of drawings must be done in concert with a variety of other evidences concerning personality. Hence, the DAP may have more value as accessory evidence than as a primary diagnostic tool, though in practice it is often used for diagnosis.

In comprehensive surveys of the DAP Swensen,[5] Harris,[6] and Roback,[7] have concluded that very little research support exists for validity

3 RAVEN, J. C. Controlled Projection for Children, Second Edition. London: H. K. Lewis & Co., Ltd., 1951. Pp. 176. *
4 BELL, JOHN ELDERKIN. Projective Techniques: A Dynamic Approach to the Study of the Personality. New York: Longmans, Green & Co., Inc., 1948. Pp. xvi, 533. *
5 SWENSEN, CLIFFORD H. "Empirical Evaluations of Human Figure Drawings." Psychol B 54:431–66 N '57. *
  SWENSEN, CLIFFORD H. "Empirical Evaluations of Human Figure Drawings: 1957–66." Psychol B 70:20–44 Jl '68. *
6 HARRIS, DALE B. Children's Drawing as Measures of Intellectual Maturity: A Revision and Extension of the Goodenough Draw-A-Man Test. New York: Harcourt, Brace & World, Inc., 1963. Pp. xv, 367. *
7 ROBACK, HOWARD B. "Human Figure Drawings: Their Utility in the Clinical Psychologist's Armamentarium for Personality Assessment." Psychol B 70:1–19 Jl '68. *

of a sign approach to personality characteristics. One of the very few exceptions to this statement is found in the work of Koppitz.[8]

In addition to the basically questionable validity of signs or indicators, there is considerable evidence [9] that with children, at least, there is so much variability from drawing to drawing that particular features in any one drawing become too unreliable an index for prediction. There is also evidence that experts accustomed to using the test may show only a very modest agreement among themselves in interpretation. Cassel, Johnson, and Burns,[10] for example, found that experienced clinicians agreed on diagnoses only to the extent of a mean inter-correlation of .33; after considerable discussion and agreement on scoring standards, this value rose to .71. This low inter-scorer reliability even after training is not surprising, considering the unclear, amorphous character of the signs as they are stated in this manual and in the general DAP literature. There is also considerable evidence [11] that nonpsychologists, including secretaries and clerk typists, do quite as well as psychologists and psychiatrists in interpreting drawings on a global basis. A number of studies suggest that when an overall or qualitative approach to drawings is used rather than a sign approach, the general quality of goodness, or perhaps artistic ability of the subject becomes the quality judged.

In children's drawings it has been the contention of several investigators [12] that the cognitive component is so large as to rather overwhelm any noncognitive aspects which may be there. With adults, mental retardation can be diagnosed from figure drawings. These facts are further evidence of the dubious character of many "projective" claims for the DAP.

More promising than the sign approach may be the evaluation of drawings according to more comprehensive, abstract principles. For example, Mildred Martin [13] found ratings of such qualities as degree and kind of organization of the sketch, symbolism, and rigidity to separate clinically distinct groups. On the other hand, W. Martin,[14] using analogous complex abstract principles, failed to confirm Wolff's [15] dynamic hypotheses concerning children's figure drawings.

It is sometimes maintained that the sign approach, feature by feature, is an inadequate approach and that a more global, overall approach should be used. Here, there is more evidence that the DAP may differentiate between normals and particularly selected clinical groups, despite the tendency of clinicians to judge on a general dimension of "goodness" of drawing. Schaeffer [16] has shown, for example, that though samples of drawings on the whole are not diagnosed on a better than chance basis, certain drawings in the series are always correctly classified by all judges and certain other drawings are never correctly classified by any judge. Swensen [17] concludes that there is some evidence that a drawing as a whole may perhaps indicate severe psychopathology or organicity by the presence of bizarre features, disproportions, and the like. However, it is clear from his survey that this relationship is of such a low order that individual prediction is extremely hazardous (see also Stone [18] and Hammer and Kaplan,[19] two of the few studies to find any positive evidence favoring "signs").

In view of the overwhelmingly negative evidence, Watson [20] states that the profession is due for a reevaluation of the DAP, and Murstein [21] wonders why the DAP continues to be such a popular test but refuses to speculate

8 KOPPITZ, ELIZABETH MUNSTERBERG. *Psychological Evaluation of Children's Human Figure Drawings.* New York: Grune & Stratton, Inc., 1968. Pp. x, 341. *

9 HAMMER, MAX, AND KAPLAN, ARTHUR M. "The Reliability of Children's Human Figure Drawings." *J Clin Psychol* 22:316-9 Jl '66. *

10 CASSEL, ROBERT H.; JOHNSON, ANNA P.; AND BURNS, WILLIAM H. "Examiner, Ego Defense, and the H-T-P Test." *J Clin Psychol* 14:157-60 Ap '58. *

11 FISHER, SEYMOUR, AND FISHER, RHODA. "Test of Certain Assumptions Regarding Figure Drawing Analysis." *J Abn & Social Psychol* 45:727-32 O '50. *

PLAUT, ERIKA, AND CRANNELL, C. W. "The Ability of Clinical Psychologists to Discriminate Between Drawings by Deteriorated Schizophrenics and Drawings by Normal Subjects." *Psychol Rep* 1:153-8 S '55. *

12 BUCK, JOHN N. "The H-T-P Technique: A Qualitative and Quantitative Scoring Manual." *J Clin Psychol* 5:37-76 Ja '49. *

RUBIN, HAROLD. "A Quantitative Study of the HTP and Its Relationship to the Wechsler-Bellevue Scale." *J Clin Psychol* 10:35-8 Ja '54. *

13 MARTIN, MILDRED H. "Some Reactions of Pre-school Children to Discipline." *Nerv Child* 9:125-30 '51.

14 MARTIN, WILLIAM E. "Identifying the Insecure Child: 3, The Use of Children's Drawings." *J Genetic Psychol* 86:327-38 '55.

15 WOLFF, WERNER. *The Personality of the Preschool Child: The Child's Search for His Self.* New York: Grune & Stratton, Inc., 1946. Pp. xvi, 341. *

16 SCHAEFFER, ROBERT W. "Clinical Psychologists' Ability to Use the Draw-A-Person Test as an Indicator of Personality Adjustment." Abstract. *J Consult Psychol* 28:383 Ag '64. *

17 SWENSEN, op. cit.

18 STONE, PHILIP M. *A Study of Objectively Scored Drawings of Human Figures in Relation to the Emotional Adjustment of Sixth Grade Pupils.* Doctor's thesis, Yeshiva University (New York, N.Y.), 1952. (*DA* 13:1265)

19 HAMMER AND KAPLAN, op. cit.

20 WATSON, CHARLES G. "Interjudge Agreement of Draw-A-Person Diagnostic Impressions." *J Proj Tech & Pers Assess* 31:42-5 Je '67. *

21 MURSTEIN, BERNARD I., EDITOR. *Handbook of Projective Techniques,* p. 609. New York: Basic Books, Inc., Publishers, 1965. Pp. xxv, 934. *

concerning this matter. This reviewer believes that in the present state of the art, noting in the last two decades a considerable regression from psychometrics to the use of more "clinical" judgments in diagnosis, the assumption of isomorphy is all too easily made. There is a long history of such logic in human thought, going back to the "sympathetic magic" of primitive man. Perhaps a superstition dies hard!

As one who has worked a good many years with children's drawings, this reviewer must confess to his personal conviction that the individuality and uniqueness of drawings, the great variety of ways in which a subject can portray the human figure, plus the fact that many individuals adopt and follow an individual, recognizable style in their drawing, lead to the persisting belief that drawings must tell something about the person's interests, preoccupations and perhaps unconscious dynamics. Clearly, however, research must be initiated along different psychological dimensions of drawings than those used to date.

If this systematic catalog leads to much-needed research to *break away* from such lists, the author will have done no small service to clinical psychology. In view of the evidence, it would be regrettable if the catalog encourages further uncritical application of indicators to drawings in order to derive clinical diagnoses.

PHILIP M. KITAY, *Professor of Psychology, Adelphi University, Garden City, New York.*

The Draw-A-Person Catalogue for Interpretative Analysis is essentially an alphabetically arranged compilation of signs for DAP interpretation, suggested by Jolles catalogue[1] for the H-T-P. Most of the material was taken from Jolles and Machover; the rest was extracted from Bender, Buck, Goodenough, Hammer, and Levy with no bibliographic references for any of these except as indicated here. The manual is sophomoric, amateurish, and unprofessional. Level of scholarship is abysmally low. The major purpose of this catalogue, it would appear, is to enable the unqualified to make cookbook diagnoses from the DAP. Even though Jolles, a major source for Urban, revised his 1952 catalogue in 1964,

Urban's manual was reprinted in 1967 and 1968 without revision. It is not an up-to-date compilation. The naïveté and simplism of the manual are manifested in the gratuitous advice offered, such as thanking the examinee for his cooperation, recording the name, age, sex of subject and date of administration, and not forcing insights obtained from the test upon the examinee. Drawing with faint line is listed in the catalogue with the interpretation "spiritual" with no supporting bibliographic source. Slipshod treatment of drawing signs is seen in the failure to distinguish interpretation of dimly drawn face from that of omitted face. Urban fails to point out that some signs listed as pathognomic may also be found in normals; e.g., he does not note that omission of hands in drawings is a frequent finding and of equivocal significance.

Ogdon's *Psychodiagnostics and Personality Assessment: A Handbook*[2] is far superior to Urban's manual in level of scholarship, sophistication, accuracy, documentation, bibliographic references, and up-to-dateness. In addition to guides for the DAP, it provides guides for interpretation of the Wechsler, the Rorschach, the H-T-P, and the Bender-Gestalt.

Urban's Protocol Booklet provides for checking off drawings of male and female in regard to mood portrayed, placement, areas of disproportion, shading and erasures, and treatment of body zones. It is useful in summarizing the major features of the drawings and in comparing drawings of male and female figures. No instructions are offered. The booklet also contains two checklists, a 16-item checklist for severe emotional disturbance and a 14-item one for organic brain damage, scored by summation of checked items. Arbitrary cut-off scores for severity of diagnosis are presented with no data offered in support of them. In the emotional disturbance checklist, drawing of internal organs on a person, a highly pathognomic sign, is given the same weight as heavy shading of eyes and ears, a less significant sign.

The Interpretative Report booklet is of dubious and limited value. It provides rating scales for the examiner's use in rating the examinee's appearance and his reactions to the test and the examiner, and for summarizing the examiner's impressions of the drawings. A series of

1 JOLLES, ISAAC. *A Catalogue for the Qualitative Interpretation of the H-T-P.* Beverly Hills, Calif.: Western Psychological Services, 1952. Pp. 97. *
  JOLLES, ISAAC. *A Catalogue for the Qualitative Interpretation of the House-Tree-Person (H-T-P). Revised 1964.* Beverly Hills, Calif.: Western Psychological Services, 1964. Pp. ii, 64. *

2 OGDON, DONALD P. *Psychodiagnostics and Personality Assessment: A Handbook.* Beverly Hills, Calif.: Western Psychological Services, 1967. Pp. v, 96. *

questions is offered to assist the examiner in deciding whether identification was with male or female figure. No instructions are provided for use with this booklet. It is a waste to publish a 4-page booklet of such limited value.

The main usefulness of the Urban type of catalogue might be in the training of graduate students in the use of the DAP; however, the Urban catalogue is so watered down and lacking in documentation that the training obtained would be stultifying and inaccurate. In their present form, neither the catalogue nor the protocol and interpretative booklets are worthy of publication. Fortunately, Ogdon's handbook provides an interpretive aid that meets standards of scholarship.

[166]

*The Family Relations Indicator, Revised Edition. Emotionally disturbed children and their parents; 1962–67; FRI; intra-family relationships; 1 form ['67, 24 cards]; manual ('67, 31 pages); record sheet ['67, 1 page]; no data on reliability; £7.35 per set of cards, 20 record sheets, and manual; postage extra; (60) minutes in 2 sessions; John G. Howells and John R. Lickorish; Oliver & Boyd. *

REFERENCES

1. See 6:212.
2. See P:427.
3. HOWELLS, JOHN G., AND LICKORISH, JOHN R. "A Projective Technique for Assessing Family Relationships." *J Clin Psychol* 25(3):304–7 Jl '69. * (PA 44:3928)
4. HOWELLS, JOHN G., AND LICKORISH, JOHN R. "The Family Relations Indicator (FRI)." *Int Congr Rorsch & Other Proj Tech* 7:936–42 '70. *

PAUL KLINE, *Lecturer in Psychology, University of Exeter, Exeter, Devon, England.*

This projective technique involves the presentation of 24 cards to both parents and children in a family, and if the family has children of each sex 16 additional cards are administered to the parents. Among the advantages of this revised edition, according to its authors, are that the pictures have been redesigned to make them more "applicable in a wider range of cultural environments"; that the technique may be meaningfully divided into sessions, thus allowing a measure of reliability; and, finally, that the validation studies have been improved.

The importance of good rapport is, of course, stressed in the manual and the tester is left fairly free as to how he will encourage spontaneous responses. The danger of a Greenspoon effect is obvious. There are clearly difficulties in the physical recording of responses. Constant writing by the tester can destroy the rapport and tape recordings may be hard to decipher. Trivial points, maybe, but ones which make it essential to know the inter-tester reliability of the test.

The replies to each picture have to be analysed into units according to their grammatical and syntactical structure. This means that the data record must be extremely accurate, far more so than in many other projective techniques. The units are then classified into descriptions, verbal or physical interactions, personal features, and an "other" category. The categories are then set out visually on a grid so that the amounts and kinds of interactions in the family can be observed. In view of the problems of recording the data and the possible difficulties in correctly categorising, inter-scorer reliability must be known if the technique is to be used with any confidence.

No reliabilities are quoted. To this reviewer, this omission makes use of the test extremely dubious. The authors try to defend the absence of test-retest reliabilities on the grounds that environmental changes may affect an individual's perceptual world, and hence the scores on retest. However, if a variable fluctuates to such an extent over time, the value of measuring it at all may be questioned. Furthermore, a test-retest study on a clinical sample could hope to show that any changes in scores were indeed a reflection of environmental change if this were in fact the case. Another important point is the internal consistency of the test, in which the cards are arranged in four "parallel" series. To what extent are these parallel or equivalent? Urgently required are inter-scorer correlations, test-retest reliabilities, and evidence of internal consistency.

The one validity study quoted in the manual demands careful scrutiny. The FRI aims to measure a subject's perception of his family relationships (*not* the actual family situation as it is). The validity study examined the relationship between scores on the FRI and the perceptions of the family (as scored by a psychiatrist) of 24 subjects—children and parents in 14 families who were attending the Institute of Family Psychiatry. If there was agreement between the views of the subjects on the FRI and the psychiatric rating, an item was scored correct; if not, it was scored incorrect. The rationale was that if the FRI truly revealed the percepts of subjects, there would be significantly more correct than incorrect opinions. Use of the chi-square technique found this to be the case for mothers and children but not for fathers. However, it is to be noted that this is not a powerful test of validity. Thus, for example, in the case of the mothers there were 102 correct and 47 incorrect statements. Though this difference is significant, there are still 47 wrong responses and the clinician has no way of knowing which of these are incorrect from the test alone. Indeed, overall there were 251 correct responses and 130 incorrect—a significant difference in the right direction but hardly good evidence for the validity of the test. The test does better than chance; that is about all. In view of these figures it is difficult to accept the claim in the manual that the FRI is a valid technique.

I am not arguing that this test is bad: merely that there is a lack of evidence concerning both reliability and validity. Consequently, its use as a test in clinical practice cannot be recommended. On the other hand, to use it in research and to examine its reliability and validity do seem worthwhile. In summary, this test demands much further work before it can be fully assessed or used.

Appl Social Studies 1(2):132–3 Je '69. Alistair Munro. * Many psychologists are unconvinced of the value of projective techniques in general, since much depends on relatively subjective interpretations of psychological material. Validation always proves a difficult task and the authors report that, as regards the Family Rélations Indicator, their validation study has proved only "reasonably correct." This suggests that the prediction value of the data it produces is relatively limited, especially in the hands of non-experts. From the psychiatrist's point of view, it is often valuable to record data which are not strictly objective but which may facilitate assessment and management of the patient. It is largely this type of information the Family Relations Indicator aims to record and since it is slanted towards the family rather than the individual situation it may encourage the therapist to note valuable material which could otherwise be overlooked. Unfortunately the method is cumbersome and one could not, for example, recommend it to the social worker as a handy means of history-taking. * projective tests are now regarded as unreliable scientific tools and it seems unlikely that this particular one will prove any more satisfactory. At best, one could say that it may possibly be of use to those workers who deal

particularly with psychological problems in families and who wish to record their information more systematically. This reviewer is not impressed by its potential as a diagnostic aid.

Brit J Psychiatry 114:1190 S '68. R. F. Barbour. * [this test] consists of a red plastic folder containing 40 cards depicting family scenes, a Manual, and some simple score sheets referred to as *The Relationships Grid.* * This is a revised and enlarged edition; the pictures have been redrawn in a more stylized, that is a more ambiguous, form, in order to reduce specific cultural and social characteristics. The faces are often no more than a dot for an eye and a line for the mouth: profiles often contain no indication of eyes or ears. Extra pictures have been added so that only half the cards need to be shown at any one time and a re-test is therefore possible. Some of the cards have been markedly altered, for instance, the one with the boy/girl and the broken vase is now more uncertain of interpretation—the vase might just have been found broken—while in the first edition the boy, at any rate to this reviewer, appeared to be more clearly linked with the damage. One of the claims of the new edition is that the cards, being now printed on solid plastic sheets with "the ink bonded into the plastic" are extremely "durable and washable." The set of cards sent to me were badly smudged after being used by children some ten times (they were not asked to wash their hands), and when an attempt was made to clean the card with water even more of the card became smudged. Dr. Howells is well known as a keen exponent of family psychiatry, but whether it has made individual psychiatry "obsolete," as the Manual claims, is open to doubt. Naturally a projective test based on the concept of the family as a clinical entity is desirable, and this set of pictures has certain advantages over the *Jackson Family Attitudes Test,* as there are more pictures and a wider range of situations, and compared to *Pickford's Projective Pictures* the cards all illustrate possible real family scenes. * The designers of the test suggest that when it is given to adults their comments should be tape-recorded and then typed. Each comment is then divided into "Information Units" and these are categorized as simple descriptions, personal interactions, personal features indicating adult's feelings or traits, the fourth category being "odd words, exclamations, interjections." Each Information Unit is then entered on the *Relationships Grid* under the heading of the person to whom it relates. The Manual is discursive, lacks clarity, and also contains several errors, for instance, cards P.2 and P.4 do not illustrate "parents with children" as stated on the last line of page 6. The new validation study is based on work with families and not only on work with children, and is, according to the writers, a more rigorous statistical evaluation; even so, results are claimed as being only "reasonably correct." If the cards were re-issued with a more satisfactory form of printing they could be useful, but the full technique is elaborate, and probably few psychologists would find time to use it, though the cards might well be used to structure an interview and act as stimuli for discussion.

For reviews by C. B. Blakemore and Walter Katkovsky of the original edition, see 6:212.

[167]

The Group Personality Projective Test. Ages 11 and over; 1956–61; GPPT; formerly called *Kahn Stick Figure Personality Test;* 7 scores: tension reduction quotient, nurturance, withdrawal, neuroticism, affiliation, succorance, total; 1 form ('58, 17 pages); manual ('61, 20 pages, reprint of 4 below); directions for interpretation ('60, 2 pages); separate answer sheets (IBM 805) must be used; $13.50 per examiner's kit of 12 tests, 100 answer-profile sheets, set of scoring stencils, and manual; $2 per manual; cash orders postpaid; specimen set not available; (40–45) minutes; Russell N. Cassel and Theodore C. Kahn; Psychological Test Specialists. *

REFERENCES

1–7. See 6:214.
8–9. See P:434.
10. Moss, Allen Miller. *Differences in Academic Achievement, Motivation, and Personality Traits Between High School Dropouts and Persisters.* Doctor's thesis, University of Alabama (University, Ala.), 1968. (*DA* 29:4832B)
11. Buckham, H. F. "The Group Personality Projective Test: An Australian Application." *Austral Psychologist* 4(2–3): 153–4 N '69. * (*PA* 46:3309)
12. Ong, Jin. "Manifest and Projective Anxiety." *Psychol Rep* 24(3):707–8 Je '69. * (*PA* 44:666)
13. Abe, Clifford. *The Prediction of Academic Achievement of Mexican-American Students.* Doctor's thesis, University of Arizona (Tucson, Ariz.), 1970. (*DAI* 31:4535A)
14. Brozovich, Richard. "Fakability of Scores on the Group Personality Projective Test." *J Genetic Psychol* 117(2): 143–8 D '70. * (*PA* 45:6346)

Edwin I. Megargee, *Professor of Psychology, Florida State University, Tallahassee, Florida.*

The *Group Personality Projective Test* consists of 90 simple drawings, mostly of stick figures. The respondent must choose which of five alternative explanations best describes the scene portrayed. The assumption is that because the drawings provide minimal cues, the respondent will project his own needs.

Whether any instrument that restricts the number of response options can be really "projective" is debatable. On the GPPT the situation is compounded by the fact that on some items two or three response options can easily be eliminated as unreasonable. The question of whether or not the test is truly "projective" is of more than semantic interest, for the GPPT was developed by means of rational item selection and keying. Therefore, the validity of the test constructors' assumption that projection rather than cognition is the primary response determinant is important, since this assumption no doubt guided their item selection.

DEVELOPMENT. One of the major deficiencies of the GPPT is a lack of adequate information in the manual regarding the item selection procedures. All that is stated is that on the basis of a priori reasoning, 15 scales were constructed to measure personal needs (aggression, dominance, achievement, passivity, and withdrawal), social needs (affiliation, nurturance, psychosexual or romance, succorance, and distrust), and emotional needs (anger, happiness, conciliation, perplexity, and dejection). The number of items on each of these scales and the guidelines for their selection are not reported. When the 15 scales were intercorrelated and factor analyzed, they yielded five factors. The first factor was bipolar and one pole was used to comprise the Withdrawal scale, while the other served as the basis for the Affiliation scale. The second factor was also bipolar and was incorporated as the Tension Reduction Quotient, which consisted of the ratio of items reflecting Dejection relative to those reflecting either Happiness or Dejection. The remaining three unidimensional factors were used to make up the Neuroticism, Succorance, and Nurturance scales. Unfortunately, the manual does not provide data which would enable the user to evaluate the adequacy of this factor labeling.

In addition to these scales, there is also a total score, which consists of the weighted sum of the raw scores on the six subscales. The theoretical rationale of this total score is murky but the data show that of the GPPT scales it has the highest correlations with overt behavior.

NORMS. The authors have spent more time and care in collecting normative data than is typical with projective tests. Normative data are reported for high school boys and girls, unselected normal adults, Air Force cadets, adult neuropsychiatric patients, juvenile delinquents, and Spanish-American high school students. For many of these groups T score conversion tables are also provided so that the test data may be profiled with reference to the most appropriate set of norms.

RELIABILITY. The manual provides split-half reliabilities and coefficients of stability for all of the scales on large samples of normals and clinical groups. The split-half reliabilities range from .25 to .84, with median .50. The test-retest reliabilities range from .41 to .85, with median .60. Unfortunately, the test authors neglected to indicate the time interval between the test and retest.

FACE VALIDITY. In order to demonstrate the "face" validity of the GPPT, the test authors administered the test to various samples of students and military personnel and found that the vast majority recognized the GPPT as a psychological test and that 80 percent asked to obtain their scores. These data indicate that despite the fact that the test calls for a number of quite arbitrary judgments, it is accepted as a meaningful task by respondents.

CONVERGENT VALIDITY. In a factorially derived instrument such as the GPPT, the first question that must be answered is whether the factor structure is reproducible. Further research reported by the authors suggests that the same five factors could be obtained from a new batch of data. The rotated factor loadings for the GPPT scales were generally appropriate, with the exception of the Succorance scale. Although the Succorance scale was devised as a measure of Factor IV, it had its highest loading on Factor II.

Further evidence for the construct validity comes from correlations of the various scales with measures of social insight, leadership, scholastic achievement, and other variables. Given the large sample sizes employed, many of the correlation coefficients are statistically significant; however, few are high enough to engender much confidence in the usefulness of the scales in individual assessment. The largest coefficient reported is −.46 and the present reviewer's rough count shows no more than 19 percent of the reported coefficients with an absolute value greater than .25.

A serious deficiency in the construct validity of the GPPT is the relative dearth of good studies determining whether the individual scales assess the traits suggested by their names. Surveying the correlational data for the Neuroticism scale, for example, one learns that the scale has significant positive correlations with measures of leadership and class standing and significant negative correlation with the grade point average of high school students. While these data are interesting, they are not fitted into a nomological network of predictions that would make them adequate tests of the scale's construct validity. One could just as reasonably have predicted that a Neuroticism scale would relate negatively to leadership and positively to academic achievement.

DISCRIMINANT VALIDITY. A major problem of the GPPT, and one that is surprising on a factorially derived instrument, is the lack of discriminant validity. Although the authors do not supply the first order correlations among the scales, the pattern of factor loadings and correlations with other measures suggests to this reviewer that several of the scales covary with one another. A lack of discriminant validity is particularly evident with respect to low scores on the various scales. T scores below 40 on the Tension Reduction Quotient, the Withdrawal scale, the Neuroticism scale, and the Succorance scale are all interpreted as indicating "general emotional immaturity," and a T score below 40 on the Affiliation scale is interpreted as an indicator of "general psychosexual immaturity."

PRACTICAL VALIDITY. The GPPT's strongest suit is in the realm of practical validity. Beta weights are provided for the discrimination between normal adults and neuropsychiatric patients and for the discrimination between normal high school students and juvenile delinquents. A cutoff score of 60 on the weighted composite score would, for example, identify 94 percent of the sample of neuropsychiatric patients and 54 percent of a sample of prisoners, at the expense of misclassifying 11 percent of a normal population. The care of the test authors in providing comparative frequency distributions and computing hit rates of various cutoff scores is to be commended.

STUART OSKAMP, *Professor of Psychology, Claremont Graduate School, Claremont, California.*

The GPPT's development began with some clever ideas and added a promising start on statistical analysis, but inappropriate and insufficient procedures have left the test development incomplete and have vitiated any value which the test might have had.

The test consists of 90 multiple choice items, the stimulus for each item being a stick-figure drawing of one or more persons in some kind of action and the responses being five short interpretive statements such as "he is trying to hurt the other person" or "they are only playing a game of tag."

The idea of a group-administered, objectively-scored, easy-to-take projective test of personality needs might well sound attractive to many clinicians and educators, especially when presented in an interesting cartoon-like format. Also, the scoring of responses in terms of personality needs seems intuitively plausible. Unfortunately, these good ideas have been allowed to wither on the vine due to later errors of omission and commission.

The manual, though it made a good start at statistical analysis, was inadequate when published in 1961 and badly needs a complete restructuring. It is marred by errors, inconsistencies, ambiguity, and unsupported statements. The amount of information given is inadequate for determining the test's validity for various purposes and also for clarifying interpretation of test scores. In addition, it is oversimplified in approach; crucial distinctions are obscured and important questions left untouched. The theory behind the test, concerning layers of personality, is unclearly stated and operationally meaningless.

The test development information is completely inadequate. Only the words "a priori" on page 25 hint that item construction was rational rather than empirical. However, many alternative responses do not seem to correspond with their stated scale (e.g., 6c, 13c, 64b, 66a, 71e), an important weakness if the construction was rational. Similarly, items indicating succorance and items indicating distrust, though rationally opposite in meaning, are combined on one scale due to the factor-analytic results. The forced-choice format of the test may help to decrease its fakability, but it would have much more value if the alternative responses had been equated for social desirability.

The factor-analytic data are also inadequate and often involve improper procedures and incorrect statements. There is no information on how the items were scored in order to compute intercorrelations, a particular problem because each item is now scored on five scales, one for each alternative response, making the scale scores highly non-independent. The sample of cases for the factor analysis was a peculiar combination of normal and abnormal individuals, and the unlikely and unsupported claim is made that a second factor analysis found the same results as the first one. As a result of the factor analysis, 15 original scales were cut down to 7, but there is no mention of elimination of any items or responses nor of construction of any new ones, and, miraculously, all five responses to every item are still scored on one of the seven remaining scales. Another strange procedure was the retention of two scales (Withdrawal and Affiliation) which represent only one factor. The reliability of the total score is adequate (above .80 for high school students), but odd-even reliabilities for the Nurturance, Withdrawal, and Affiliation scales are as low as .25, .42, and .36, respectively, with some samples.

A vital question in using the test is how to interpret the scores. The claim is made, without any support, that "healthy" or "good" scores on each scale are in the middle, between T scores of 40 and 60. T scores below 40 are said to indicate "emotional immaturity," but this claim conflicts with the normative data for 558 "unselected normals," of whom 24 percent were below this level, indicating that it is not an appropriate cutoff point for interpreting pathology.

If "healthy" GPPT scores were in the middle of the scale, then these scales would be expected to have curvilinear relationships with other variables such as leadership or school achievement. However, no curvilinear correlation coefficients were computed. Similarly, fakability of scores would be decreased if "healthy" scores were midscale scores, but since this point is in dispute, the authors' conclusions of low fakability must also be questioned. The most reasonable interpretation of low scores seems to be that they show adequate satisfaction of the need. This interpretation, incidentally, reaffirms the value of the product-moment correlations presented.

Other problems in the manual abound. Correlations as low as −.13 and −.11 with other measures are interpreted as meaningful in spite of explaining negligible variance. Crossvalidation studies of predictive validity are mentioned, but no empirical data are cited. The basic T score norms show some fairly major errors (e.g., on the TRQ score) where unequal raw score intervals are given equal T score intervals. The recommendation not to use standard error estimates (which are provided) with the subscales is indefensible. Finally, the manual's conclusion of the GPPT's low fakability is not supported by the study cited. It showed that it was easy to "fake bad," and "faking good," though harder, was certainly not impossible. Braun's study (9) concludes that college students were able to "fake good" successfully.

In summary, the GPPT represents some appealing ideas gone astray. With a thorough reconstruction of items, a new statistical analysis, and restandardization, it might yet be rescued. But in its present state it cannot be recommended to any user who wants meaningful results.

MARVIN REZNIKOFF, *Professor of Psychology and Director of Clinical Training, Fordham University, New York, New York.*

This instrument, based on projective technique principles, can be administered individually or in groups to subjects, 11 years of age or older, having a reading knowledge of English. The test is described as being a rapid (45 minutes or less) and inexpensive yet effective way of screening large groups of children and adults for emotional maladjustment. It "is concerned with assessing the amount of anxiety-producing tension, and the degree of activeness of certain psychological needs" at the time of testing. It is also said to detect proneness to delinquency and to identify persons who lack leadership qualities.

The "underlying theory" of the test, discussed in an exceedingly sketchy fashion in the manual, is in terms of Murray's three layers of personality. Without offering a real rationale, the authors feel that the GPPT is geared to the middle layer, that is, "the mask one wears in relation to one's self" in contrast to an outer layer, which is the "mask which one wears in relation to others" and a deeper layer, consisting of "symbolic responses."

The test uses ambiguous stick drawings accompanied by five descriptions from which the examinee chooses one. Seven scale values are obtained. T score profiles are provided to facilitate comparisons of the individual's performance with group norms for unselected normal individuals, neuropsychiatric patients, delinquent or imprisoned individuals, and Spanish-Americans. Normative data for both sexes are combined.

Odd-even and test-retest reliabilities are given for the six scales (range .25 to .78, median .59) and the total (range .59 to .85, median .70) for five groups.

The authors report a variety of validity studies. A section on face validity, defined as "the degree to which a test resembles the psychological instrument that it purports to be," cites the results of several dubious studies and could easily be deleted from the manual with no great loss. A factor analytic validity study, on the other hand, is presented essentially in the abbreviated form of a table of factor loadings and could benefit greatly from some explanation and discussion of the tabular material. In addition, since this analysis has the stated purpose of "re-checking the factor structure found for the earlier experimental edition of the test," it would have been helpful to include data on the earlier factor analysis beyond the brief description of the five factors initially extracted.

Construct validity is dealt with by correlating GPPT scores with scores on a variety of social insight, leadership, and scholastic achievement measures. In no real sense, however, are these correlation data developed to the point of helping to explain the theoretical underpinnings of the GPPT. Furthermore, as candidly indicated by the test authors, one finding runs directly counter to expectation, namely, that for the unselected normal individual the greater the tension and the poorer the personality adjustment scores, the better the leadership value scores. Concurrent and predictive validity studies indicate that the GPPT does successfully differentiate between sundry groups, including psychiatric patients, normals, and delinquents. In this regard, beta weights are given for discriminating between neuropsychiatric patients and normals, but the tabular presentation and the related text seem contradictory or at best unclear as to whether the normals were an unselected group.

It is stated that the test is essentially "self-administering" and that it can be completed at home without supervision. Interpretation, however, according to the publisher, "demands specific training in the use of projective techniques." To aid in interpretation, a short paragraph is provided for each of the scales, describing what is being measured and what various T score ranges may indicate. In the case of "anxiety-producing tension" expressed in terms of a Tension Reduction Quotient, it is not a T score, but rather a percentage of the negative feelings the subject projects, that is meaningful in assessing emotional maturity and mental health. The total score is also employed as an index of mental health. Apart from a very short discussion of T score patterning when emotional disturbance occurs with emotional immaturity, there is no effort to deal with the scales configurationally.

At this writing, the GPPT suffers from a curious dearth of research studies. Virtually all of the published research this reviewer was able to locate appeared in the late 1950's or early 60's, with Cassel serving as senior author. Why the GPPT has failed to stimulate more current research and by investigators other than its authors, is unclear at this juncture. Unfortunately, in one of the few studies not done by Cassel and of more recent vintage, the claim that the GPPT cannot be faked is disputed. Braun (9) administered the GPPT to several groups of college students who were asked to give "good impressions" on a repeat administration. The results revealed that the students were successful in faking in a positive direction.

The test booklets are well designed and the individual items appear to have a good deal of intrinsic interest which should readily enlist the cooperation of the subject. The scoring and recording procedures are straightforward and easily followed. On the other hand, the manual could benefit substantially from a far more comprehensive and in-depth treatment of "interpretation." The training in the area of projective tests that is recommended as a requisite for interpreting the GPPT would seem to have minimal relevance to the kind of largely perfunctory and overly brief treatment of the meaning of the various scales presently included in the manual. It is to be recognized, of course, that while the GPPT uses partially structured, ambiguous stimulus material in common with other projective instruments, its multiple choice approach obviously curtails the potential range and richness of the subject's projections.

The format and objective scoring system of the GPPT would certainly enable the GPPT to compete with self-descriptive personality inventories as a convenient group screening instrument. And, it could have important advantages over the latter type of test in eliciting information from the very defensive subject who is vigorously guarding against self-disclosure. Such evaluations of the GPPT, however, will have to remain in the purely conjectural realm until further research data are available.

[168]

★HFD Test. Ages 5–12; 1968; HFDT; human figure drawing test, drawing of a whole person; level of mental ability score and 30 emotional indicator signs; manual (350 pages, see 7 below); no accessories; no norms for total number of emotional indicators; $10.75 per manual, postage extra; (10–30) minutes; Elizabeth Munsterberg Koppitz; Grune & Stratton, Inc. *

REFERENCES

1–8. See P:436.
9. KOPPITZ, ELIZABETH MUNSTERBERG. "Emotional Indicators on Human Figure Drawings of Shy and Aggressive Children." J Clin Psychol 22:466–9 O '66. * (PA 41:2915)
10. KOPPITZ, ELIZABETH MUNSTERBERG. "Emotional Indicators on Human Figure Drawings of Boys and Girls From Lower and Middle-Class Backgrounds." J Clin Psychol 25(4):432–4 O '69. * (PA 44:10143)
11. LANGE, UNA ANN. Differential Performances of Minimally Brain-Damaged Boys and of Non-Brain-Damaged Boys on Selected Tests. Doctor's thesis, University of Nebraska (Lincoln, Neb.), 1969. (DAI 30:2852A)
12. McNAMARA, J. REGIS, AND PORTERFIELD, CHARLES L. "Levels of Information About the Human Figure and Their Characteristic Relationship to Human Figure Drawings in Young Disadvantaged Children." Develop Psychol 1(6):669–72 N '69. * (PA 44:2141)
13. FULLER, GERALD B.; PREUSS, MICHELE; AND HAWKINS, WILLIAM F. "The Validity of the Human Figure Drawings With Disturbed and Normal Children." J Sch Psychol 8(1):54–6 '70. * (PA 44:9578)
14. HALL, LEON P., AND LADRIERE, M. LAVERNE. "A Comparative Study of Diagnostic Potential and Efficiency of Six Scoring Systems Applied to Children's Figure Drawings." Psychol Sch 7(3):244–6 Jl '70. * (PA 45:4921)
15. SNYDER, ROBERT T., AND GASTON, DIANE S. "The Figure Drawing of the First Grade Child—Item Analysis and Comparison With Koppitz Norms." J Clin Psychol 26(3):377–83 Jl '70. * (PA 45:523)

DALE B. HARRIS, Professor of Psychology, The Pennsylvania State University, University Park, Pennsylvania.

One of clinical psychology's most popular devices, the drawing of a person, has been systematized by Koppitz as the HFD Test. The author has derived two scales for the evaluations of children's drawings of a person (sex not specified). In common with many writers in this area, the author assumes that asking a child to "draw 'a whole person' seems to lead the child to look into himself and into his own feelings when trying to capture the essence of 'a person.'" Thus, the task becomes a kind of portrait of the child's inner self and of his attitudes. The interpretation of the test is best described as qualitative and clinical but is based on two lists of items, one of developmental items and the other of emotional indicators.

The chief advantages of both scales are brevity and ease of scoring. The items are simple, and "self evident," and thus quite objective. Inter-scorer reliability was determined by two psychologists who independently evaluated 25 drawings for 30 developmental items and 30 emotional indicators. Ninety-five percent of the total judgments made were checked by both psychologists. On 10 of the drawings there was perfect agreement on scoring. No evidence is given concerning test-retest reliability, but this is undoubtedly quite high, to judge from the extensive published literature on children's drawings.

To establish the developmental scale, 30 items were selected largely on the basis of the Goodenough and the Goodenough and Harris scales and on the author's own clinical experience. These items are scored on a present or absent basis but are not accumulated as point scores. Rather, the developmental progression of the items is determined across successive age samples of children from 5 through 12, and the percentages of inclusion separated into four frequency categories: expected items, common items, not unusual items, and exceptional items.

Thus, the "score" on the developmental scale is not a point score recording the total number of points attained. Rather, it is based on the table of items distributed across these four categories at each age level. For each expected item omitted one point is subtracted and for each exceptional item included one point is added. The items typically given by 16 to 85 percent of children in an age group, whether passed by a particular child or not, are ignored in such a score. In effect, the score depends on a few exceptional items included by children who deviate more than one standard deviation from the mean in each direction. The author's preference for this somewhat unconventional scoring method is in line with her desire to see the instrument used as a clinical tool and with her reluctance to depend on IQ techniques for drawing analysis. This method thus permits only a qualitative comparison with an IQ derived from a standard intelligence test.

The identification of emotional indicators was conducted in a somewhat different fashion. Three types of potential indicators were identified from the projective literature: quality signs, special features not usually found on human figure drawings, and omissions of body parts that are almost universally included in children's drawings. Thirty-eight potential items were subjected to the following criteria: Such items must differentiate between children with and without emotional problems; such items must occur in less than 16 percent of children at a given age level who are not psychiatric patients; and they must not be related to age and maturation. Thirty-two items survived the application of these criteria and were subjected to further study.

Seventy-six public school children from 5 to 12 years of age, of average or better intelligence, and stated to be outstanding all-around students with good social, emotional, and academic adjustment were paired in sex, age, and intelligence with a like number of children who were patients in a psychiatric clinic. While 58 of the 76 normal subjects included no emotional indicators in their drawing, only 7 of the 76 clinical cases failed to include at least one of the emotional indicators. The author argues that rare occurrence of an indicator in the general population may actually enhance the clinical validity of an item. However, the problem of base rate of occurrence of a phenomenon is a critical matter in determining the probability level at which statistical significance will be found. The value of the author's procedure, of course, lies in the confidence one has in subjective as opposed to objective criteria.

For the emotional indicators there are no published "norms" in the usual sense. A table is provided indicating which indicators appear significantly more often (p = .10) in one of eight different clinical groups and those which merely appear more often in the clinical group but fail to satisfy the 10 percent level of significance. There is a qualitative discussion, indicator by indicator, which combines evidence from the literature, from the author's general experience, and from occasionally cited case studies, bearing out the value and significance of each feature. The emotional indicators occur as significant most often in the group by which they were originally validated. On substudies with "shy," "aggressive," "psychosomatic," "stealing," "brain injury," "poor school achievement," and "special class" groups fewer items appear as significant; in measurement, this is generally the case with new, or cross-validating, samples.

While a score based on the number of Emotional Indicators would undoubtedly be more reliable and perhaps more definitive than any one item or combination of few items, the author is reluctant to use this method, as it would imply an "average" degree of disturbance, which to her is nonsensical. She has suggested a cutoff score of 2 or more Emotional Indicators as significant of disturbance.

The HFDT is not, then, a test but an evaluation of presumptive clinical evidence. It adds little that is objective or quantifiable to the subjective or "clinical" use of drawings which has been found quite undependable by an impressive array of evidence (see my review of test 165).

Unquestionably this volume contributes usefully to the literature of research on children's drawings. The drawing "test" itself should not be used as a diagnostic or even as a screening device for personality study, for it has not been constructed according to the accepted concepts and assumptions of measurement. Depending on the psychologist's use of and belief in qualitative and subjective evidence, the HFDT may be used along with other evidence, qualitative or quantitative, to illuminate and clarify the clinical picture of personality where disturbances are known or strongly suspected.

For additional reviews, see B364 (3 excerpts).

[169]

The Holtzman Inkblot Technique. Ages 5 and over; 1958–66; HIT; 22 scores: reaction time, rejections, location, space, form definiteness, form appropriateness, color, shading, movement, pathognomic verbalization, integration, content (human, animal, anatomy, sex, abstract), anxiety, hostility, barrier, penetration, balance, popular; 2 formats; manual ('61, 428 pages, see 7 below) not adapted for group administration; $8 per manual, postage extra; for computerized scoring and interpreting service, see P:440; (75) minutes; Wayne H. Holtzman, Joseph S. Thorpe (manual), Jon D. Swartz (manual), and E. Wayne Herron (manual); Psychological Corporation.

a) [INDIVIDUAL TEST.] 1958–61; Forms A, B, ('58, 47 cards); administration and scoring guide ('61, 171 pages, reprinted in part from manual); record form ('58, 8 pages) for each form; summary sheet ('58, 2 pages); $29 per set of cards for either form, 25 record forms, and administration and scoring guide; $52 per set of cards and accessories for both forms; $2.75 per 25 record forms and summary sheets; $3.25 per administration and scoring guide.

b) [GROUP TEST.] 1958–66; Form A ('58, set of 35 mm. Kodaslides); no specific manual; group record form ('66, 2 pages); $55 per set of Kodaslides; $2.40 per 50 group record forms; Donald R. Gorham (record form).

REFERENCES

1–22. See 6:217.
23–112. See P:439, also includes a cumulative name index to the first 112 references for this test.
113. PAREIS, EGBERT NELSON. *Inkblot Perception and Personality: An Experimental Departure From the Rorschach Test.* Doctor's thesis, University of Texas (Austin, Tex.), 1958. (DA 19:1118)
114. YOUNG, HARL H., JR. "A Test of Witkins Field-Dependence Hypothesis." *J Abn & Social Psychol* 59:188–92 S '59. * (PA 34:2798)
115. SWARTZ, JON DAVID. *The Holtzman Inkblot Technique: A Normative Study of Elementary School Children.* Master's thesis, University of Texas (Austin, Tex.), 1961.
116. LEVINE, MURRAY, AND SPIVACK, GEORGE. "Human Movement Responses and Verbal Expression in the Rorschach Test." *J Proj Tech* 26:299–304 S '62. * (PA 37:3197)
117. REITMAN, ELI EDWARD. *Changes in Body Image Following Sensory Deprivation in Schizophrenic and Control*

Groups. Doctor's thesis, University of Houston (Houston, Tex.), 1962. (DA 23:3481)
118. CODKIND, DOROTHY. *Attitudes Toward the Imaginary: Their Relationship to Level of Personality Integration.* Doctor's thesis, University of Kansas (Lawrence, Kan.), 1964. (DA 27:1616B)
119. GORDON, HELEN GAIL. *Developmental Changes in Responses on the Holtzman Inkblot Technique.* Master's thesis, University of Texas (Austin, Tex.), 1964.
120. HARDISON, JIMMIE LEE. *An Investigation of the Relationships Between Several Inkblot Variables and Impulse Control.* Doctor's thesis, University of Kentucky (Lexington, Ky.), 1964. (DAI 30:2439B)
121. HILL, EVELYN FOSTER. *Affect Aroused by Color, a Function of Stimulus Strength.* Doctor's thesis, Catholic University of America (Washington, D.C.), 1964. (DA 25:2611)
122. HOLTZMAN, WAYNE H. "Recurring Dilemmas in Personality Assessment." *J Proj Tech & Pers Assess* 28:144–50 Je '64. * (PA 39:5153)
123. HUDSPETH, MARY ALICE BARNES. *An Analysis of Pathognomic Verbalization in the Holtzman Inkblot Technique.* Master's thesis, University of Texas (Austin, Tex.), 1964.
124. MEGARGEE, EDWIN INGLEE. *Undercontrol and Overcontrol in Assaultive and Homicidal Adolescents.* Doctor's thesis, University of California (Berkeley, Calif.), 1964. (DA 25:2614)
125. MUELLER, WILLIAM J., AND ABELES, NORMAN. "The Components of Empathy and Their Relationship to the Projection of Human Movement Responses." *J Proj Tech & Pers Assess* 28:322–30 S '64. * (PA 39:7908)
126. REITMAN, E. EDWARD, AND CLEVELAND, SIDNEY E. "Changes in Body Image Following Sensory Deprivation in Schizophrenic and Control Groups." *J Abn & Social Psychol* 68:168–76 F '64. * (PA 38:5172)
127. BRASFIELD, CHARLES, AND PAPAGEORGIS, DEMETRIOS. "Manifest Anxiety and the Effect of a Dissonant Self-Relevant Communication on Self-Perception." Abstract. *Proc Ann Conv Am Psychol Assn* 73:193–4 '65. *
128. BRASFIELD, CHARLES RANDOLPH. *Manifest Anxiety and the Effect of a Discrepant Self-Relevant Communication on Self-Perception.* Master's thesis, University of Texas (Austin, Tex.), 1965.
129. COLEMAN, KATHERINE ANN. *The Significance of Eye Responses on the Holtzman Inkblot Technique as Measured by the Minnesota Counseling Inventory.* Master's thesis, Springfield College (Springfield, Mass.), 1965.
130. DE LEONARD, CARMEN COOK. "Problems in the Translation of Spanish (Mexican) Protocols Into English." *Proc Interam Congr Psychol* 9(1964):271–7 ['65]. *
131. EISMAN, HOWARD DAVID. *Inhibition and the Human Movement Response in Children.* Doctor's thesis, Boston University (Boston, Mass.), 1965. (DA 26:2865)
132. KRIPPNER, STANLEY. "The Relationship of Reading Improvement and Scores on the Holtzman Inkblot Technique." Abstract. *Am Psychologist* 20:484 Jl '65. *
133. MOSELEY, EDWARD C. "Some Results of Cross-Cultural Computer Scoring of Mexican, Panamanian, Chinese, and American Students." *Proc Interam Congr Psychol* 9(1964):277–81 ['65]. *
134. SCHIEBEL, DOUGLAS REMIGIUS. *Tactile Behavior in Psychopathology.* Doctor's thesis, University of Michigan (Ann Arbor, Mich.), 1965. (DA 27:616B)
135. BREESKIN, JOHN. *The Development of Time Estimation in Children.* Doctor's thesis, University of Texas (Austin, Tex.), 1966. (DA 27:3267B)
136. CLEVELAND, SIDNEY E., AND SIKES, MELVIN P. "Body Image in Chronic Alcoholics and Non-Alcoholic Psychiatric Patients." *J Proj Tech & Pers Assess* 30:265–9 Je '66. * (PA 40:10241)
137. HOLTZMAN, WAYNE H. "Intelligence, Cognitive Style, and Personality: A Developmental Approach," pp. 1–32. In *Intelligence: Perspectives 1965: The Terman-Otis Memorial Lectures.* By Orville G. Brim, Jr., Richard S. Crutchfield, and Wayne H. Holtzman. New York: Harcourt Brace & World, Inc., 1966. Pp. x, 101. *
138. LERNER, BARBARA. "Rorschach Movement and Dreams: A Validation Study Using Drug-Induced Dream Deprivation." *J Abn Psychol* 71:75–86 Ap '66. * (PA 40:6668)
139. MEGARGEE, EDWIN I. "Undercontrolled and Overcontrolled Personality Types in Extreme Antisocial Aggression." *Psychol Monogr* 80(3):1–29 '66. *
140. ROESSLER, ROBERT; BURCH, NEIL R.; AND CHILDERS, HAROLD E. "Personality and Arousal Correlates of Specific Galvanic Skin Responses." *Psychophysiol* 3:115–30 O '66. * (PA 41:1255)
141. SHULTZ, TIMOTHY DAVID. *A Comparison of the Reactions and Attitudes Toward Stress of Two Psychosomatic Symptom Groups.* Doctor's thesis, Washington University (St. Louis, Mo.), 1966. (DA 27:616B)
142. WOODS, MARCELLA DARLENE. *An Exploration of Developmental Relationships Between Children's Body Image Boundaries, Estimates of Dimensions of Body Space, and Performance of Selected Gross Motor Tasks.* Doctor's thesis, Ohio State University (Columbus, Ohio), 1966. (DA 27:4119A)
143. GORHAM, DONALD R. "Validity and Reliability of a

Computer Scoring System for Inkblot Responses." *Proc Interam Congr Psychol* 10(1966):276–90 '67. *

144. LAIRD, DON ROBERT. *Reading Achievement in Children: A Developmental Analysis by Means of the Holtzman Inkblot Technique.* Master's thesis, University of Texas (Austin, Tex.), 1967.

145. LARSEN, VIRGINIA L.; BRODSACK, JEANNE; HARMON, JUDITH E.; MARTIN, LORETTA; AND EVANS, THEODORA. "Prediction of Early Post Partum Adjustment." Abstract. *Am J Orthopsychiatry* 37:397–8 Mr '67. * (*PA* 41:8820)

146. MOSELEY, EDWARD C. "Multivariate Comparison of Seven Cultures: Argentina, Colombia (Bogota), Colombia (Cartagena), Mexico, Panama, United States and Venezuela." *Proc Interam Congr Psychol* 10(1966):291–304 '67. *

147. MOSHER, DONALD L.; OLIVER, WAYNE A.; AND DOLGAN, JEFFERY. "Body Image in Tattooed Prisoners." *J Clin Psychol* 23:31–2 Ja '67. * (*PA* 41:5685)

148. OBERLEDER, MURIEL. "Adapting Current Psychological Techniques for Use in Testing the Aging." *Gerontologist* 7(3, pt 1):188–91 S '67. * (*PA* 42:3801)

149. SWARTZ, JON D. "The Roles of Culture, Age, Sex, and Father's Occupational Level in Children's Responses to the Holtzman Inkblot Technique." *Proc Interam Congr Psychol* 10(1966):130–42 '67. *

150. SWARTZ, JON D.; TAPIA, LUIS LARA; AND THORPE, JOSEPH S. "Perceptual Development of Mexican School Children as Measured by Responses to the Holtzman Inkblot Technique." *Revista Interamericana de Psicología* 1:289–95 D '67. * (*PA* 42:9008)

151. FABREGA, HORACIO, JR.; SWARTZ, JON D.; AND WALLACE, CAROLE ANN. "Ethnic Differences in Psychopathology: 1, Clinical Correlates Under Varying Conditions." *Arch Gen Psychiatry* 19:218–26 Ag '68. * (*PA* 43:4230)

152. FABREGA, HORACIO, JR.; SWARTZ, JON D.; AND WALLACE, CAROLE ANN. "Ethnic Differences in Psychopathology: 2, Specific Differences With Emphasis on a Mexican American Group." *J Psychiatric Res* 6:221–35 D '68. * (*PA* 44:5399)

153. FOX, DONALD LEE. *Influence of Examiner Affect and Subject's Response Length on Holtzman Inkblot Scores.* Master's thesis, University of Texas (Austin, Tex.), 1968.

154. GARDNER, RILEY W., AND MORIARTY, ALICE. Chap. 7, "Individuality in the Holtzman Inkblot Test," pp. 119–28, passim. In their *Personality Development at Preadolescence: Explorations of Structure Formation,* see 155. *

155. GARDNER, RILEY W., AND MORIARTY, ALICE. *Personality Development at Preadolescence: Explorations of Structure Formation.* Seattle, Wash.: University of Washington Press, 1968. Pp. xi, 344. *

156. GOTTLIEB, SYBIL. *Modeling Effects on Fantasy.* Doctor's thesis, City University of New York (New York, N.Y.), 1968. (*DA* 29:1840B)

157. HIRT, MICHAEL; GOLDBERG, RICHARD; AND BERNSTEIN, I. LEONARD. "Interaction of Personality Variables and Allergic Predisposition in Asthma." *Psychosomatics* 9:340–3 N–D '68. * (*PA* 43:11678)

158. HOLTZMAN, WAYNE H. "Cross-Cultural Studies in Psychology." *Int J Psychol* 3(2):83–91 '68. * (*PA* 43:745)

159. KERNALEGUEN, ANNE PAULE. *Creativity Level, Perceptual Style and Peer Perception of Attitudes Towards Clothing.* Doctor's thesis, Utah State University (Logan, Utah), 1968. (*DA* 29:2960B)

160. KLIEGER, DOUGLAS MYLES. *An Investigation of the Influence of Response Sets on the Holtzman Projective Technique.* Doctor's thesis, Iowa State University (Ames, Iowa), 1968. (*DA* 29:4848B)

161. MAHER, JOHN JAMES. *Barrier Score-Body Image, or Behavior Tendency?* Doctor's thesis, University of Georgia (Athens, Ga.), 1968. (*DA* 29:2480B)

162. MORDKOFF, ARNOLD M., AND RAND, MELVIN A. "Personality and Adaptation to Coronary Artery Disease." *J Consult & Clin Psychol* 32:648–53 D '68. * (*PA* 43:4378)

163. SANDERS, JEFFREY L.; HOLTZMAN, WAYNE H.; AND SWARTZ, JON D. "Structural Changes of the Color Variable in the Holtzman Inkblot Technique." *J Proj Tech & Pers Assess* 32:556–61 D '68. * (*PA* 43:9801)

164. SANDERS, JEFFREY LANCE. *A Longitudinal Study of the Holtzman Inkblot Technique Variable of Color and Its Elements.* Master's thesis, University of Texas (Austin, Tex.), 1968.

165. WESTWOOD, DALE. *Repeat Holtzman Inkblots in Flared and Quiescent Arthritis.* Doctor's thesis, University of Utah (Salt Lake City, Utah), 1968. (*DA* 29:1514B)

166. BRANTON, JOAN. "The Holtzman Inkblot Technique: A Preliminary Study With a British Delinquent Sample." *Brit J Proj Psychol & Pers Study* 14(1):23–6 Je '69. * (*PA* 46:5188)

167. BRENER, ELLIOT MAYNARD. *Castration Anxiety, Sexual Fantasy, and Sexual Adjustment.* Doctor's thesis, Boston University (Boston, Mass.), 1969. (*DAI* 30:2412B)

168. CLELAND, CHARLES C., AND SWARTZ, JON D. "Work Deprivation as Motivation to Work." *Am J Mental Def* 73(5):703–12 Mr '69. * (*PA* 43:10262)

169. DAHLIN, GERALDINE. *The Relationship of Personality to Subcultural Membership in Middle Class Adults.* Doctor's thesis, Illinois Institute of Technology (Chicago, Ill.), 1969. (*DAI* 30:2414B)

170. DARBY, JOEL ALBERT. *Alteration of Some Body Image Indices in Schizophrenics via Induced Somatic Awareness.* Doctor's thesis, Michigan State University (East Lansing, Mich.), 1969. (*DAI* 30:2903B)

171. EDWARDS, KENNETH ROBERT, JR. *Psychological Changes Associated With Pregnancy and Obstetric Complications.* Doctor's thesis, University of Miami (Coral Gables, Fla.), 1969. (*DAI* 30:3864B)

172. ENDICOTT, NOBLE A.; JORTNER, SIDNEY; AND ABRAMOFF, EILEEN. "Objective Measures of Suspiciousness." *J Abn Psychol* 74(1):26–32 F '69. * (*PA* 43:8449)

173. GEIST, HAROLD. "Psychological Aspects of Rheumatoid Arthritis." Abstract. *Proc 77th Ann Conv Am Psychol Assn* 4(2):769–70 '69. * (*PA* 44:1156)

174. GRAY, JAMES J. "The Effect of Productivity on Primary Process and Creativity." *J Proj Tech & Pers Assess* 33(3):213–8 Je '69. * (*PA* 43:14302)

175. GRAY, JAMES J. "Effect of Productivity on Primary Process Thinking and Creativity." Abstract. *Proc 77th Ann Conv Am Psychol Assn* 4(1):157–8 '69. * (*PA* 43:17495)

176. HAHN, KENNETH V. *Repression-Sensitization and Its Relation to the Anxiety, Hostility and Barrier Measures of the Holtzman Inkblot Test.* Master's thesis, Pennsylvania State University (University Park, Pa.), 1969.

177. HERRON, E. WAYNE. "Value of Experimental Manipulation in Multivariate Studies of Personality." Abstract. *Proc 77th Ann Conv Am Psychol Assn* 4(1):131–2 '69. * (*PA* 43:17519)

178. HIRT, MICHAEL, AND KURTZ, RICHARD. "A Reexamination of the Relationship Between Body Boundary and Site of Disease." *J Abn Psychol* 74(1):67–70 F '69. * (*PA* 43:8626)

179. HOLTZMAN, WAYNE H. "Precursors of Later Personality Traits in Children." Abstract. *Proc 77th Ann Conv Am Psychol Assn* 4(1):289–90 '69. * (*PA* 43:17227)

180. HOLTZMAN, WAYNE H.; DIAZ-GUERRERO, ROGELIO; SWARTZ, JON D., AND TAPIA, LUIS LARA. "Cross-Cultural Longitudinal Research on Child Development: Studies of American and Mexican Schoolchildren." *Minn Symposia Child Psychol* 2:125–72 '69. *

181. KAMEN, GARY B. "Effects of a Stress-Producing Film on the Test Performance of Adults." *J Proj Tech & Pers Assess* 33(3):281–5 Je '69. * (*PA* 43:14224)

182. KOSKI, MAIJA-LIISA. "The Coping Process in Childhood Diabetes." *Acta Paediatrica Scandinavica Supplement* 198:1–56 '69. *

183. LEHRER, ARNOLD CURTIS. *The Personality Correlates of Creativity in Undergraduates.* Doctor's thesis, Colorado State College (Greeley, Colo.), 1969. (*DAI* 31:397B)

184. LEVITZ, LEONARD A., AND ULLMANN, LEONARD P. "Manipulation of Indications of Disturbed Thinking in Normal Subjects." *J Consult & Clin Psychol* 33(6):633–41 D '69. * (*PA* 44:3762)

185. NEWTON, PETER McDANIELS. *Recalled Dream Content and the Maintenance of Body Image.* Doctor's thesis, Columbia University (New York, N.Y.), 1969. (*DAI* 30:2424B)

186. PENK, WALTER. "Developmental Patterns in Children's Inkblot Responses." *Develop Psychol* 1(1):55–64 Ja '69. * (*PA* 43:6749)

187. PETERS, BILL BAILEY. *Experimental Stress and the Holtzman Anxiety Scale.* Master's thesis, University of Texas (Austin, Tex.), 1969.

188. ROSENSTIEL, LUTZ V. "Capacity for Empathy: A Function of Anxiety in the Production of H-Responses." *J Proj Tech & Pers Assess* 33(4):336–42 Ag '69. * (*PA* 44:2376)

189. STOUT, ROBERT JAMES. *The Effect of Test Anxiety Upon Perception in Projective Testing.* Doctor's thesis, Colorado State College (Greeley, Colo.), 1969. (*DAI* 30:4161A)

190. SWARTZ, JON DAVID. *Pathognomic Verbalizations in Normals, Psychotics, and Mental Retardates.* Doctor's thesis, University of Texas (Austin, Tex.), 1969. (*DAI* 30:5703B)

191. TAYLOR, DALMAS A.; ALTMAN, IRWIN; WHEELER, LADD; AND KUSHNER, ESTELLE N. "Personality Factors Related to Response to Social Isolation and Confinement." *J Consult & Clin Psychol* 33(4):411–9 Ag '69. * (*PA* 43:15789)

192. TORRETA, DELFINA MARQUEZ. *Somesthetic Perception of Clothing Fabrics in Relation to Body Image and Psychological Security.* Doctor's thesis, Utah State University (Logan, Utah), 1969. (*DAI* 30:3731B)

193. WEST, B. BRADLEY. *A Study of Computer Scored Group Holtzman Inkblot Variables as Related to Student Teaching Success, Major Teaching Fields, and Sex.* Doctor's thesis, Michigan State University (East Lansing, Mich.), 1969. (*DAI* 31:1128A)

194. BENTLER, P. M.; SHERMAN, RICHARD W.; AND PRINCE, CHARLES. "Personality Characteristics of Male Transvestites." *J Clin Psychol* 26(3):287–91 Jl '70. * (*PA* 45:1004)

195. BOWERS, KENNETH S., AND VAN DER MEULEN, SANDRA J. "Effect of Hypnotic Susceptibility on Creativity Test Performance." *J Pers & Social Psychol* 14(3):247–56 Mr '70. * (*PA* 44:8441)

196. BRANTON, JOAN. "A Short Form of the Holtzman Inkblot Technique." *Brit J Proj Psychol & Pers Study* 15(1):25 Je '70. *

197. BUCHANAN, EDITH BEAN. *The Relationship of Affec-*

tive Behavior to Movement Patterns, Body Image, and Visual Perception in Four- and Five-Year Old Children. Doctor's thesis, University of California (Los Angeles, Calif.), 1970. (*DAI* 31:3406A)

198. COOPER, LOWELL, AND CASTON, JOSEPH. "Physical Activity and Increases in M Response." *J Proj Tech & Pers Assess* 34(4):295–301 Ag '70. * (*PA* 44:21007)

199. CREMER, ALMA GRACE. *Relationships Between Body Size Estimates, Body Image Boundaries, and Health Practices in Preadolescents.* Doctor's thesis, Ohio State University (Columbus, Ohio), 1970. (*DAI* 31:4150B)

200. DARBY, JOEL A. "Alteration of Some Body Image Indexes in Schizophrenics." *J Consult & Clin Psychol* 35(1): 116–21 Ag '70. * (*PA* 44:21275)

201. DAVIS, RUTH MEREDITH. *The Relations Between Body Image Boundary and Physical Fitness in Children From a Trainable Program for Mental Retardates.* Doctor's thesis, Ohio State University (Columbus, Ohio), 1970. (*DAI* 31: 3316A)

202. EDWARDS, KENNETH R., AND JONES, MARSHALL R. "Personality Changes Related to Pregnancy and Obstetric Complications." Abstract. *Proc 78th Ann Conv Am Psychol Assn* 5(1):341–2 '70. * (*PA* 44:19026)

203. GORHAM, DONALD R. "Cross-Cultural Research Based on the Holtzman Inkblot Technique." *Int Congr Rorsch & Other Proj Tech* 7:158–64 '70. *

204. HARTUNG, JURGEN R.; MCKENNA, SHEILA A.; AND BAXTER, JAMES C. "Body Image and Defensiveness in an LSD-Taking Subculture." *J Proj Tech & Pers Assess* 34(4): 316–23 Ag '70. * (*PA* 44:20907)

205. HOLTZMAN, WAYNE H. "Cross-Cultural Studies of Inkblot Perception and Personality." *Int Congr Rorsch & Other Proj Tech* 7:252–62 '70. *

206. HOLTZMAN, WAYNE H.; SWARTZ, JON D.; AND SANDERS, JEFFREY L. "Effects of Stimulus Variation on Responses to the Group Version of the Holtzman Inkblot Technique." *J Consult & Clin Psychol* 34(1):64–6 F '70. * (*PA* 44:6790)

207. HOLZMAN, PHILIP S., AND ROUSEY, CLYDE. "Monitoring, Activation, and Disinhibition: Effects of White Noise Masking on Spoken Thought." *J Abn Psychol* 75(3):227–41 Je '70. * (*PA* 44:14564)

208. KAMEN, GARY BEST. *The Effects of a Stress Producing Film on the Test Performance of Adults.* Doctor's thesis, University of Missouri (Columbia, Mo.), 1970. (*DAI* 31:2989B)

209. LAKE, A. E., III, AND TEDFORD, W. H., JR. "Influence of Creativity on Formation of Subjective Units." *J General Psychol* 83(2):227–37 O '70. * (*PA* 45:2406)

210. MAUSNER, BERNARD, AND GRAHAM, JUDITH. "Field Dependence and Prior Reinforcement as Determinants of Social Interaction in Judgment." *J Pers & Social Psychol* 16(3): 486–93 N '70. * (*PA* 45:4127)

211. NEWTON, PETER M. "Recalled Dream Content and the Maintenance of Body Image." *J Abn Psychol* 76(1):134–9 Ag '70. * (*PA* 44:21350)

212. PENK, WALTER. "Developmental Patterns in Children's Inkblot Responses." *Int Congr Rorsch & Other Proj Tech* 7:266–77 '70. *

213. ROSENZWEIG, STANLEY P., AND HARFORD, THOMAS. "Correlates of the Psychotic Reaction Profile in an Outpatient Psychiatric Sample." *J Consult & Clin Psychol* 35(2):244–7 O '70. * (*PA* 45:4549)

214. ROUTH, DONALD K., AND SCHNEIDER, JOHN M. "Word Association and Ink Blot Responses as a Function of Instructional Sets and Psychopathology." *J Proj Tech & Pers Assess* 34(2):113–20 Ap '70. * (*PA* 44:16914)

215. SHALIT, BENJAMIN. "Environmental Hostility and Hostility in Fantasy." *J Pers & Social Psychol* 15(2):171–4 Je '70. * (*PA* 44:12571)

216. SHIPMAN, WILLIAM G.; HEATH, HELEN A.; AND OKEN, DONALD. "Response Specificity Among Muscular and Autonomic Variables." *Arch Gen Psychiatry* 23(4):369–74 O '70. * (*PA* 45:2693)

217. SHIPMAN, WILLIAM G.; OKEN, DONALD; AND HEATH, HELEN A. "Muscle Tension and Effort at Self-Control During Anxiety." *Arch Gen Psychiatry* 23(4):359–68 O '70. * (*PA* 45:2694)

218. SWARTZ, JON D.; WITZKE, DONALD B.; AND MEGARGEE, EDWIN I. "Normative Item Statistics for the Group Form of the Holtzman Inkblot Technique." *Percept & Motor Skills* 31(1):319–29 Ag '70. * (*PA* 45:6378)

Am J Psychol 77:687–8 D '64. Raymond J. McCall. [Review of the manual (7).] This is a serious and, on the whole, successful attempt to put the interpretation of standardized inkblots upon a sound psychometric foundation. After 40 years the Rorschach is still a vehicle for the intuitive operation of clinical impression and not an instrument of testable (let alone sig-

nificant) reliability or validity. Things, however, are looking up. The senior author, Wayne Holtzman of the University of Texas and the Hogg Foundation, exhibited no false modesty in naming the technique HIT, after himself, as he deserves credit for having fathered a clinical research program of considerable scope and for having, with the help of his collaborators, carried it through to an impressive conclusion. The crucial variable in inkblot interpretations, number of responses, has been controlled by using a greater number (two alternate forms of 45 blots each) of stimuli and permitting only one response per card. Thereupon, using only slight modifications of traditional scoring categories such as Location, Form Definiteness, Form Appropriateness, Color, the HIT has demonstrated satisfactory levels of inter-judge and odd-even reliability, and alternate form reliabilities which, though modest, are far better than anything hitherto achieved with the Rorschach. The HIT also seeks to capture formally certain aspects of verbal interpretation of inkblots that are not explicitly scored, though regularly noted by clinicians, in the Rorschach. Most important among these is the behavior which the authors designate "pathognomic verbalization" which includes fabulation, incoherence, contamination, and self-reference. Regarding this category the authors note that "more effort was expended in developing an explicit rationale and scoring system for Pathognomic Verbalization than for any other variable in the Holtzman Inkblot Technique." It is unfortunate that this effort did not include consulting a good dictionary, for there the authors would have found that what they are interested in is correctly designated *pathognomonic verbalization,* and that the word "pathognomic," though perfectly legitimate, has a meaning quite different from that which they give to it. The impression of semiliterateness that this kind of mistake, repeated dozens and dozens of times throughout the volume, leaves is not dissipated by a style that is singularly lacking in elegance or precision and that at times achieves an almost wooden incoherence. Consider: "Credit for Movement is given only when the subject voluntarily ascribes movement or potential for movement to the percept....Since movement is designed to reflect the degree of movement, tension, or dynamic energy projected into the percept by the subject, it is important that concepts clearly involving tension and dynamic energy not be excluded merely because they may not be perceived in actual motion." Does a subject ascribe movement *voluntarily* (as opposed to involuntarily), or do the authors perhaps mean *spontaneously?* And is such movement ascribed to the *percept,* or to the object *perceived?* Or is it ascribed to neither, since the authors speak of *concepts* that "may not be perceived in actual motion"? It is hard to say which is more confused here, the epistemology or the mode of expression. On the psychometric side, fortunately, the authors do far better than in the philosophical or stylistic. Fifteen different samples were employed in the standardization, embracing a wide developmental and diagnostic range, including pre-school and school children from the 5-year to the 11th grade level, middle class housewives and city firemen, college students, schizophrenics, depressives, and mentally retarded adults. A total of 1239 cases was employed in establishing percentile norms for the various scoring categories, providing a statistically reliable foundation for evaluating different kinds of inkblot interpretations. * Using a centroid factor analysis on the matrix of intercorrelated scores, the authors are able to extract three clear and two less clear factors. Factor I has significant loadings on the HIT equivalents of Z, M, H, P and FC/FY. Factor II is identified by the equivalents of CF and YF, and factor III chiefly by verbalizations that are "pathognomic," anxious, or hostile. These results point to an underlying similarity of the Holtzman and Rorschach techniques that should facilitate the gradual replacement of the latter by the metrically sounder HIT. The successful use of Fisher's discriminant function with HIT scores as a technique for differentiating between normals and paranoid schizophrenics also suggests fascinating possibilities for future exploration. After a lengthy and rather belaboredly obvious case analysis, the volume concludes with appendices on the scoring of location, popularity, and form appropriateness for the two versions of the HIT.

J Counsel Psychol 15:481–4 S '68. David G. Martin. * developed to overcome some of the psychometric shortcomings of the Rorschach, while "preserving (its) rich qualitative projective material." This attempt has been partially successful. A psychometrically "cleaner" instrument has been developed, but many of the difficulties inherent in the Rorschach method

have not been eliminated and some Rorschach users claim useful information is lost by the HIT. The HIT uses only the first response to each of 45 cards, controlling the total number of responses relatively well (rejections still occur) and avoiding disproportionate stimulus effects for any one blot. This innovation also eliminates the troublesome nonlinear relationship between total number of responses (R) and many Rorschach scores * More formal shortcomings of the HIT will be discussed below. Informally, some Rorschach users say that in clinical use, the price paid for psychometric improvement is the loss of a measure of productivity (R) and of sequence of response to a single blot; there is no opportunity to observe improvement or deterioration of later responses to a single blot. * it is unlikely that the suggested HIT procedures eliminate the examiner effect. In fact, one study of this problem....has shown an effect of examiner "coldness" on HIT protocols—a finding distressingly similar to many examiner-subject (E-S) interaction variables found with the Rorschach. One solution to the E-S problem for which the HIT is more appropriate than the Rorschach is group administration. The need for only one response per card makes written responses practicable. * Parenthetically, this reviewer and many other clinicians have found the HIT more cumbersome and time consuming to administer than the Rorschach. This may reflect only greater familiarity with the Rorschach, since Holtzman's group (not surprisingly) reports greater ease with the HIT. As Murstein....has pointed out, the most disappointing aspect of HIT administration is the retention of the Rorschach inquiry method of self-report of the determinants. Baughman....has shown that most Ss do not know the determinants of their responses. Perceptual discrimination (systematically varying blot characteristics during inquiry) appears to be a better method; a clever innovation is needed to make this process less cumbersome, but retaining the old method does not seem justified. * Scoring criteria appear in the manual and are quite adequate for the experienced tester. * Intrascorer and interscorer reliabilities reported for the HIT's major variables are adequate when scorers are well trained and experienced. Interscorer reliabilities for the 22 minor variables tend to be lower than is acceptable for individual evaluation but most are adequate for research applications. * No attempt is made to report normative profiles of scores; only separate scores are presented. * Some HIT scores have been given names such as "anxiety" or "hostility" and might tempt the less sophisticated test user to make unwarranted interpretations, believing that the presence of norms indicates the usefulness of the scores. * Supporters of the HIT now face the task of showing not that they have a well-constructed instrument but what it is that their instrument measures. This effort has just begun. The most promising results of validation attempts to date have been in identifying gross pathological groups. * Correlations with paper-and-pencil measures of personality have yielded relatively consistent negative results. Commenting on this fact Holtzman states that, "it is important to keep in mind that Anxiety and Hostility as scored in the HIT are strictly ratings at a fantasy level which are not necessarily related in any simple direct way to overt behavior that is judged to be anxious or hostile [p. 180]." Whether HIT scores do reflect fantasy, however, is itself a validity question. There is no evidence on which to accept or reject Holtzman's explanation. * For the counselor who has found the Rorschach useful, the HIT might offer some advantages, especially if administration could be automated or conducted in a group. The most justifiable clinical application of the HIT at present seems to be in diagnosing schizophrenia. This reviewer suspects that, in spite of its psychometric superiority, the HIT will not replace the Rorschach for a long time, if at all, in the clinic. Inertia among testers already familiar with the Rorschach will undoubtedly be a factor. But, in addition, superior validity and usefulness in the clinic setting have not been demonstrated for the HIT. In research applications where inkblots are the measure of choice, the HIT is clearly superior. However, the use of the HIT scores as criteria is not justified without more extensive validity data. We may face another generation of validity research with a new and better set of inkblots, or we may see an increasing movement toward other methodologies in personality research. This reviewer expects the latter.

For reviews by Richard W. Coan, H. J. Eysenck, Bertram R. Forer, and William N. Thetford, see 6:217.

[170]

The Howard Ink Blot Test. Adults; 1953–60; HIBT; individual; 1 form ('53, 12 cards); 1953 manual ('53, 47 pages, reprint of *1* below); 1960 manual ('60, 207 pages, see *4* below); no data on reliability; $12.50 per set of cards; $2 per 1953 manual; $5 per 1960 manual; cash orders postpaid; (90–105) minutes; James W. Howard; Clinical Psychology Publishing Co., Inc. *

REFERENCES

1–3. See 5:141.
4. See 6:219.
5. See P:442.

Brit J Social & Clin Psychol 7:76 F '68. John Graham White. * Howard originally developed his blots for group testing and designed them to stimulate quantity and range of response, an effect which the twelve blots selected for the individual test also seem capable of producing. The method of scoring, which follows Beck's, and of interpreting the scores is set out in great detail and with ample illustration. * Clearly, this technique is no less time-consuming, both in the initial training (fifty cases as a minimum for the novice) and in scoring and interpreting than the original Rorschach. The author does not wish his technique to be regarded as a standardized test in any psychometric sense and makes no claims for its reliability or validity; in fact, he specifically disclaims inter examiner reliability for the individual case on p. 2. Although he provides means and standard deviations for his scoring categories he warns against using these as any but a rough guide in interpreting results. The samples from which his score distributions were derived consisted of normal subjects (510), "pseudo-normals" (173 people with "problems" but not seeking psychiatric advice) and much smaller groups of psychiatric patients. The normal sample appears to have been "super normal" in that all subjects were "above high average in general intelligence" as measured by one or other of Wechsler's tests. This would appear, then, to exclude 66 per cent of the population not defined as either "borderline" or mentally defective. The clinical groups, on the other hand, though comparable in age, tended to be lower in educational and intellectual status. The many significant mean differences in score between the normal and the clinical groups may, therefore, reflect differences in intelligence as much as they do differences in the variables represented by the scores. These scores carry much the same implications for behaviour as those derived from the Rorschach. Thus, whole responses imply "planning ability," quality of form "control of personal inclinations," use of colour emotional responsiveness, movement responses independence or dependence, according to whether it is "expansile" or "contractile." The evidence for the assertion of such relationships between test response and actual performance is presumably largely clinical; but many of them are susceptible to empirical test, even when they are qualified by "other features of the record." Before embarking on the use of a very laborious clinical technique, one should, in this day and age, have some notion of the validity of the inferences one is going to make from verbalized perceptions to behaviour. Dr. Howard, however, has been content to leave matters as they have stood for many years with the Rorschach; wisely, no doubt, since most investigations into the validity of the latter technique have, as Payne (1955) pointed out ten years ago, failed to substantiate most of the inferences commonly made by Rorschach users. Those psychologists who still work with Rorschach-like procedures will certainly find the Howard Inkblot Test at least as useful as either the Rorschach itself or Holtzman's method.

For reviews by Jesse G. Harris, Jr. and Bernard I. Murstein, see 6:219 (1 excerpt); for a review by C. R. Strother, see 5:141 (1 excerpt).

[171]

★Ka-Ro Inkblot Test. Ages 3 and over; 1970; designed as "a Rorschach parallel series"; individual; 1 form (10 cards); manual (148 pages, see 1 below); record booklet (6 pages); no data on reliability; $15 per set of cards; $8 per 25 record booklets; $10 per manual; postage extra; administration time not reported; Yasufumi Kataguchi and the Ka-Ro Research Group (manual and record booklet); Kaneko Shobo Publisher. *

REFERENCE

1. KATAGUCHI, YASUFUMI. *Psychology: Manual for Ka-Ro Inkblot Test.* Tokyo, Japan: Kaneko Shobo Publisher, 1970. Pp. 157. *

[172]

Miner Sentence Completion Scale. Managers and management trainees; 1961–64; MSCS; motivation; item and rare scores in 7 areas (authority figures, competitive games, competitive situations, masculine role, imposing wishes, standing out from group, routine administrative functions), total, and popularity level; 1 form ('61, 4 pages); scoring guide ('64, 64 pages); scoring sheet ('61, 1 page); data on reliability and validity available only in 4 below; $8.50 per 50 sets of scale and scoring sheet; $2.75 per scoring guide; postpaid; specimen set not available; [30] minutes; John B. Miner; Springer Publishing Co., Inc. *

REFERENCES

1–2. See 6:230a.
3–5. See P:456.

6. MINER, JOHN B. "The Managerial Motivation of School Administrators." *Ed Adm Q* 4:55–71 w '68. *
7. MINER, JOHN B., AND SMITH, NORMAN R. "Managerial Talent Among Undergraduate and Graduate Business Students." *Personnel & Guid J* 47(10):995–1000 Je '69. *

C. J. ADCOCK, *Retired Professor of Psychology, Victoria University of Wellington, Wellington, New Zealand.*

The *Miner Sentence Completion Scale* is simple in form, consisting of 40 incomplete sentences, the completion of which provides scores on seven scales (five items per scale and five buffer items) with two additional scales based on the test as a whole.

The rationale of the test is that good managers will be highly motivated to manage and will manifest this drive in their reactions to typical situations. It is contended that they will manifest approving attitudes to authority figures, will enjoy competitive games and competitive situations, will appreciate masculine roles, will desire to impose wishes on others, and will enjoy standing out from the group. Keys based on a minimum of ten examples for each category (+, ?, −) for each sentence are provided for the scoring of responses in these six areas. Routine Administrative Functions is the seventh scale, and two general scales complete the test.

The six major scales seem reasonable in concept, and empirical evidence is presented which indicates their significant performance in a number of studies in which validity was assessed using various criteria of occupational success. "Masculine Roles" failed in the earlier studies but in later samples achieved significance. Item analysis data would be interesting. One may doubt the relevance of shooting a rifle in modern life (not to mention contamination effects from war service) and it may be doubted whether driving a car is necessarily masculine now. The seventh scale is retained, despite obvious limitations, on the grounds that it did produce consistent, useful results in a department store study and should not be prematurely abandoned. It seems likely that further evidence could lead to substantial improvement with regard to both choice of scales and items to be included in them. Nevertheless, it seems certain that this approach can produce significant measures. The crucial question is probably whether the test needs to be specifically tailored for the sample to which it is to be applied. Cultural factors are obviously important and caution is needed in using the MSCS on populations different from the ones on which it was developed. For example, "Getting my shoes shined" and "Country club dances" would be foreign to New Zealand experience.

The Supervisory Job scale is based on the ranking of the five items which contribute to each scale, in terms of the number of plus scores obtained in the normative group, which, it is recommended, should preferably be specific to the sample studied, although norms from a representative group of 160 managers are provided. The rank 1 score for the testee is the number of pluses obtained for the top ranking item of each of the seven scales, the rank 2 score similarly being based on the number of pluses for the seven rank 2 items. The same procedure is used independently for the minus scores so that one ends up with five pairs of scores, each with a limit of 7. Presumably this is a detailed measure of conformity to the group pattern, but why this should be a measure of supervisory ability is not very clear. One can only conclude that it is based on similarity to a group which represents superior ability in this direction, but if so, would it not be desirable to choose the normative group on the basis of suitably approved criteria and not include "all levels of management below the company officer level"? A rather surprising aspect of the rankings provided from the sample of 160 managers studied is the lack of agreement between the ranks obtained from the plus and minus scores. One would expect these to be complementary but a sampling check on the correlations gives values of $-.20$, $.00$ and $-.20$. This effect is due to the unequal use of the "?" category and may justify the separate handling of the two sets.

The Rare Score scale is specially favoured by the author but again it is difficult to fully appreciate the rationale. It is not the originality of response which is involved here but rather a rare pattern of response. For each of the seven sets of items all possible patterns of plus and minus scores are considered and those which occur in fewer than five percent of the cases are regarded as rare. The responses are considered singly, in pairs, in sets of three, four, or five— altogether, three patterns for each sign. Since the presence of a single rare response in any scale area is regarded as contributing a unit to the score, once a rare has been found, no further examination is needed and the next scale area can be examined.

It will be noted that the Supervisory Job score is essentially a popular response score and gives some approximation to a mean correlation coefficient. It lacks accuracy in that it does not take into account the extent of departure from the normal rank order and it can give the suggestion of appreciable agreement when the mean rank correlation is zero, and this apart from the complication that the suggested norms do not involve complementary positive and negative ranks. On the other hand, it is easily calculated and its separate positive and negative scores can be useful as mentioned above. The question arises, however, as to how one can reconcile a score based on *conformity* to popular responses with one based on *nonconformity,* which is assumed to have, and empirically is found to have, positive correlation with it (as much as .86) and with both scales predicting managerial capacity. Superficially at least, there appears to be a problem here.

The justification for the rare score approach may best be appreciated if it is compared to answering correctly very difficult problems in an intelligence test. One really difficult item may here be much more significant than many simple ones and a comparable situation may apply in the attitude area so far as individual items are concerned, but when we come to unusual *combinations* of items, the matter is complicated. If the combination includes a rare separate, it will qualify on this basis and one wonders why, in fact, such combinations are even referred to in the norms. If only the combination is unusual, it may be due to a lack of consistency in the responses, to the operation of contaminating factors, or to the unreliability which could be expected in projective test items. With such possibilities, one is rather more doubtful of the significance of such rare scores and would like to see a study analysing the specific relevance of different types of rare scores. One might even suggest that nonconformity is itself the mark of leadership but no claim is made for this and the scores may not indicate it at all.

Apart from the Supervisory Job scale and the Rare Score scale, an additional general score can be obtained by subtracting the total minus scores from the total plus scores. This gives the combined effect of all the specific scales and has the advantage of being based on a large number of items and so is relatively stable. However, the Rare Score scale has almost equal reliability on 10-week retest; a split-half reliability cannot be calculated in this case.

The success achieved by this test in research situations encourages the hope that it may provide a very promising, relatively objective type of "projective" test in an area where there is a dearth of useful measures. On the other hand, there are a number of improvements in form which could be undertaken and further light could be thrown on the rationale of the more obscure aspects. For do-it-yourself executives, a warning should be given that the test may be very sensitive to cultural differences and should not be given too much weight until suitable data indicate its validity for the population concerned. Moreover, despite the finding that the examinees seem to be unaware of what is being measured, specific evidence is required to indicate what is the likely effect of motivation to fake. There seems little doubt that this would appreciably distort the results in some way. The reviewer hopes that the test will be widely studied.

[173]

Pickford Projective Pictures. Ages 5–15; 1963; PPP; 1 form (120 cards); manual (130 pages, see 5 below); no data on reliability; £1.25 per set of cards; £1.50 per manual; postage extra; to be administered about 6 pictures at a time over about 20 therapy sessions; R. W. Pickford with the assistance of Ruth Bowyer and John Struthers; NFER Publishing Co. Ltd. *

REFERENCES

1–5. See 6:234.

Brit J Psychiatry 110:455–6 My '64. R. F. Barbour. * What is new in these pictures and technique is that Pickford is trying to provide psychologist, psychotherapist and school teacher with a therapeutic technique as well as a diagnostic tool. Many therapists are accustomed to providing play material or enquiring about dreams. This series will allow a new series of 6 pictures to be shown to a child each week for 20 weeks. If these are selected from the sets of cards indicating a special topic, for instance, "child alone or rejected," the child's stories may be expected to show changes as therapy proceeds. This combination of diagnosis and therapy, using the one set of material, is both the weakness and the strength of the technique as set out. The test can barely be said to be standardized as a diagnostic tool. It has not been given to normal children. * As a basis for therapy it is again rather difficult to evaluate the pictures. The author describes five cases

which he treated by means of the cards with satisfactory results. The material seems to be especially suitable for the pre-adolescent who sometimes finds play-room material too childish; the cards have the advantage of being light and not taking up too much room, though the reviewer doubts whether they will stand up to much use, as the present cards are thin. The reviewer found them especially useful in treating two in-patients on a paediatric ward where a very small office did not lend itself either to play material or free painting. A therapist visiting a school might find them similarly useful. * The Pickford Projective Pictures provide a field for research and for experimentation by any therapist to whom the showing of cards appeals as a basis for starting an interview. At present, owing to the relative absence of frequency tables and norms, a good deal has to be left to the therapist's own experience and awareness of his own unconscious fantasies.

J Proj Tech & Pers Assess 28:113–5 Mr '64. Albert I. Rabin. One must be brave and wise, these days, to add still another projective method to the existing array of techniques. That courage is needed there is no doubt, for projective techniques have been encountering an increasingly hostile and critical public. The need for wisdom, for learning from experience in the design of new techniques, is apparently not so widely recognized. The author of this book and inventor of this new method is, perhaps, brave, at any rate. Pickford's method consists of 120 "projective pictures," essentially line drawings, which represent a wide variety of situations encountered by children, mainly preadolescents, for whom the technique is primarily intended. A *post hoc* classification of 15 categories into which the pictures may be placed with respect to content is proposed by the author. * It is interesting to note....that anal issues are not directly highlighted. The number of pictures in the aforementioned categories range from 24 to *one*. Obviously, the classification was imposed upon the material after this large range of situations described by the drawings was decided upon. There was not, apparently, any other guiding principle to begin with. It is the author's recommendation that only six pictures at a time be administered. The child is asked "to invent a story about each of them." Moreover, "Emphasis should be placed upon the idea of inventing a story as long, complex or irrelevant as the child likes." * We shall....concern ourselves with the "evidence" concerning the usefulness of this method therapeutically and/or diagnostically. In a brief chapter (9 pages) L. R. Bowyer illustrates the Rogerian approach and the remedial education approach via the projective pictures. All we are given are quotations from stories, told to certain pictures, by several children. The comments relate to the parallelism between the story content and the problems of the children. However, we are not offered much about the *operations* of the therapist and how the improvement has come about. Nor, certainly, can we see the advantage of employing the pictures in the process. It is not at all clear why *these* particular drawings are to be preferred to some other projective device that may be used as a part of psychotherapeutic procedure. The author reports favorable data about workers' reactions to the diagnostic and therapeutic value of these pictures. Information is classified as "diagnostic value, therapeutic value, no value and value not stated." We do not know, however, what percentage of these evaluations is based on the author's information and what proportion on that of the reactions of other workers. Besides, these testimonials are singularly uninformative for they do not tell us *why* value was seen or not seen in the application of the method. We agree that "In order to estimate more exactly the success in using the pictures, a carefully planned research would be needed." Such information would be highly desirable *before* the publication of a technique rather than some time after it. With a nod in the diagnostic direction some normative data on the figures identified in the pictures, and of the major themes involved in the stories, are given at the end of the book. Two remarks are in order in this connection. First, although the data reported on the first 23 pictures are based on more than 100 stories, the number of stories decreases until it dwindles to *only five stories* for the last five pictures. There is hardly a sufficient N for normative information; for comparative purposes it is practically useless, especially since both sexes are represented in these small numbers. A second difficulty with the "norms" is that they are based on a rather selected sample—patients from the child guidance clinics in Glasgow. Data from such a source can hardly be used as a valid standard from which deviations in hero identification and theme content can be usefully interpreted. In conclusion, the basic question

must be asked—"Do we need this new projective method?" (Rabin 1963). In order to answer such a blunt query we must also ask whether this new technique contributes something novel and original to the theory of projective techniques, to personality theory or to procedure. With respect to the first two, projective and personality theory, the contribution is nil. With respect to procedure, the material presented in the book is unconvincing. Therapeutically, it may well be that this method, a sort of derivative of play technique at the preadolescent level, is effective. However, its contribution to the process is not clear. Moreover, we have no comparative information, beyond the testimonials contained in some of the tables, regarding the relative effectiveness of psychotherapy or counseling *with* or *without* these pictures. We do need new methods which will determine the parameters of personality to be dealt with at the start and deal explicitly with the interpretative process in relation to the determined stimulus value of the material presented (Forer *et al*, 1961). We can no longer be satisfied with global testimonials regarding the clinical effectiveness, whether diagnostic or therapeutic, of new arrivals in the camp of psychological armamentarium.

For a review by Stanley J. Segal, see 6:234 (3 excerpts).

[174]

*The Picture Impressions Test. Adolescents and adults; 1956–69; PIT; for investigating the patient-therapist relationship; individual; separate forms for men, women, ['56, 4 cards]; manual ('69, 17 pages); response sheet ['56, 1 page]; no data on reliability; $2.50 per set of 8 cards; $3.75 per 25 response sheets; $2.50 per manual; $4.50 per specimen set; postage extra; (20–30) minutes; Lester M. Libo; Consulting Psychologists Press, Inc. *

REFERENCES

1. See 5:152.
2. See P:464.
3. LIBO, LESTER M. *Measuring Group Cohesiveness.* University of Michigan, Institute for Social Research, Research Center for Group Dynamics, No. 3. Ann Arbor, Mich.: University of Michigan Press, 1953. Pp. ix, 111. * (*PA* 28:8654)
4. HELLER, KENNETH, AND GOLDSTEIN, ARNOLD P. "Client Dependency and Therapist Expectancy as Relationship Maintaining Variables in Psychotherapy." *J Consult Psychol* 25:371–5 O '61. * (*PA* 37:3367)

EUGENE E. LEVITT, *Professor of Clinical Psychology and Director, Section of Psychology, Indiana University School of Medicine, Indianapolis, Indiana.*

The PIT is a thematic picture technique which is employed in a semi-projective manner. It consists of four simple line drawings, each of which suggests a psychotherapeutic, or at least a healing, situation. The subject is required to respond in writing to four questions that seek to determine his impression of what is occurring in the picture, what the people involved are feeling, what has led up to the situation, and what is going to happen.

According to the manual, thema are scorable only if a doctor or therapist, a patient, and a diagnostic or therapeutic function are included, and if it is clear that the respondent's self rather than another is involved. The procedure given in the manual for analyzing and scoring responses seeks to determine the extent to which the patient or client is "attracted" or "not attracted" to the therapist and the therapeutic situation. Thema are scored plus or minus. Any total score for the four cards that is plus is interpreted to indicate that the patient is "attracted." Any total score of zero or lower is interpreted to mean that the patient is "not attracted." The manual also suggests that a subject giving two or more unscorable stories should be judged as "not attracted." No rationale for this interpretation is given in the manual.

Reliability of total scores in terms of interscorer agreement is generally high. In the handful of investigations utilizing the PIT, agreement between scorers on total scores ranged from 82 to 97 percent. Similarly, agreement on "number of stories receiving a score" is usually reported as above 95 percent.

The PIT was designed to investigate the psychotherapeutic process—specifically, to study the patient-therapist relationship, to estimate the degree of therapist resistance to change, to examine the effects of different therapeutic variables on the treatment dyad, and to predict whether or not a patient would return for the next scheduled interview. The latter factor is labeled in the manual "an operational criterion of attraction," and provided the initial validity data.

Libo (*1*) found that total scores on the PIT correctly predicted return or termination in 75 percent of a group of outpatients, largely Negro females. Mullen and Abeles (*2*) correctly predicted 90 percent of the cases when the subjects were college student counselees.

The PIT first appeared in 1956 and was copyrighted for commercial sale in 1969. In the intervening years, the instrument seems to have been seldom used experimentally. In view of the tremendous volume of psychotherapy research during those years, the neglect suggests

that psychotherapy investigators as a group have not been impressed by the PIT's potential as a research tool. There are several possible explanations. The theoretical utility of a projective test lies in its ability to evoke feelings and attitudes which are below the level of awareness, or which might be deliberately withheld or distorted by the respondent. Positive or negative valence of the therapy situation does not seem to be a phenomenon that requires tapping by a projective procedure. There is no reason to believe that reliable and valid responses to direct questions could not be obtained from patients and clients. The value of the PIT is thus doubtful.

Even if it is assumed that a projective measure is needed, the PIT, on examination, is unimpressive. The drawings are unimaginative; an investigator might reasonably predict that he would do as well merely by asking subjects to make up a story about a therapeutic situation. Indeed, the simple question is likely to be more productive than the PIT, since the latter does not always elicit therapy thema. There is another weakness of the instrument, one which is practically ignored by the manual. There is no indication of the anticipated percentage of unscorable thema, as well as no explanation of the interpretation that multiple unscorable thema represent negative attraction.

This weak face validity may be the reason that the PIT has rarely been employed to investigate aspects of the therapeutic situation other than the attraction-nonattraction variable. Also, the manual does not provide a guide to any other type of scoring of responses.

The PIT is easily administered and is amenable to reliable scoring but does not appear to be useful in psychotherapy research. Or, at least that is the consensus of psychotherapy researchers to date.

See 5:152 (1 excerpt).

[175]

*Rorschach. Ages 3 and over; 1921–66; variously referred to by such titles as Rorschach Method, Rorschach Test, Rorschach Ink Blot Test, Rorschach Psychodiagnostics; many variations and modifications are in use with no one method of scoring and interpreting generally accepted; unless otherwise indicated, the word Rorschach may be interpreted as referring to the use of the Psychodiagnostic Plates listed as *f* below. *a*) BEHN-RORSCHACH TEST. 1941–56; BRT; a parallel set of inkblots; also called *The Bero-Test;* 1 form ('41, 10 cards); manual ('56, 198 pages, see *2156* below, translation of the German edition published in 1941); record blank ('51, 1 page); Fr. 19 ($11) per set of cards; Fr. 9 ($3.50) per pad of 100 record blanks; Fr. 25 ($8) per manual; postage extra; Hans Zulliger; Hans Huber. (United States distributor: Grune & Stratton, Inc.) *

b) ★THE DAVIS RORSCHACH MINIATURE LOCATION CHARTS IN COLOR (BRUNO KLOPFER SCORING AREAS). 1966; 1 card; $4.50 per card, postpaid; Julian C. Davis; Western Psychological Services. *

c) HARROWER'S GROUP RORSCHACH. Ages 12 and over; 1941–45; HGR; set of original Rorschach inkblots on 35 mm. slides; group blank (no date, 24 pages); 1 set per set of slides; $7 per 25 group blanks; postage extra; (70–90) minutes; M. R. Harrower; distributed by Psychological Corporation. *

d) HARROWER'S MULTIPLE CHOICE TEST. Ages 12 and over; 1943–45; HMCT; for use with either cards or slides; 1 form ('43, 4 pages); $4.25 per 25 record blanks, postage extra; M. R. Harrower; distributed by Psychological Corporation. *

e) *HARROWER'S PSYCHODIAGNOSTIC INKBLOT TEST. Ages 16 and over; 1945–66; HPIT; a parallel set of inkblots; formerly called *Psychodiagnostic Inkblots;* 1 form ('66, 10 cards, identical with set copyrighted in 1945 except for finish); expendable set of inkblots also available; manual, third edition ('66, 85 pages plus record booklet); record booklet ('66, 4 pages); $26.50 per examiner's kit of set of cards, 5 sets of expendable inkblots, 25 record booklets, and manual; $12.50 per set of cards; $7.50 per 10 sets of expendable inkblots; $6.50 per 25 record booklets; $7.50 per manual; postpaid; Molly R. Harrower; Western Psychological Services. *

f) PSYCHODIAGNOSTIC PLATES, FIFTH EDITION. 1921–54; 1 form ('54, 10 cards, identical with original edition copyrighted in 1921); manual, fifth edition ('51, 263 pages, translation of the 1942 German edition with the addition of a bibliography; record blank ('47, 1 page); Fr. 27 ($12.50) per set of cards; Fr. 8.50 ($3.75) per pad of 100 record blanks; Fr. 23 ($7) per manual; postage extra; Hermann Rorschach; Hans Huber. (United States distributor: Grune & Stratton, Inc.) *

g) *THE REVISED RORSCHACH EVALOGRAPH. 1954–65; record booklet ('65, 16 pages); $8.50 per 25 booklets, postpaid; Morse P. Manson and George A. Ulett; Western Psychological Services. *

h) RORSCHACH COMBINED LOCATION AND RECORD FORM. 1957; 1 form (12 pages); $2.75 per 25 booklets; 30¢ per specimen set; postpaid; Nicholas De Palma; the Author. *

i) ★THE RORSCHACH CONCEPT EVALUATION TECHNIQUE. Adults; 1965; CET; 3 conceptual scores: precision (J), conformity (V), deviance (C); manual (18 pages plus record booklet); record booklet (4 pages); $6.50 per examiner's kit of 25 record booklets and manual; $5.50 per 25 record booklets; $2 per manual; postpaid; set of Rorschach inkblots necessary for administration; Paul McReynolds; Western Psychological Services. *

j) RORSCHACH LOCATION CHARTS (BECK'S SCORING AREAS). 1951–54; 1 form ('54, 12 cards, identical with set copyrighted in 1951); Fr. 9.50 ($3.25) per set of cards, postage extra; Julian C. Davis; Hans Huber. (United States distributor: Grune & Stratton, Inc.) *

k) RORSCHACH METHOD OF PERSONALITY DIAGNOSIS: INDIVIDUAL RECORD BLANK, REVISED EDITION. 1942–60; 1 form ('60, 4 pages); directions ('60, 4 pages); tabulation and scoring sheet ('60, 1 page); $4.20 per 35 blanks, postage extra; Bruno Klopfer and Helen H. Davidson; Harcourt Brace Jovanovich, Inc. *

l) *THE RORSCHACH MINIATURE INKBLOTS IN COLOR: A LOCATION AND RECORD FORM. 1955–64; $7.50 per pad of 100 sheets, postpaid; Morse P. Manson; Western Psychological Services. *

m) STRUCTURED-OBJECTIVE RORSCHACH TEST: PRELIMINARY EDITION. See P:477.

REFERENCES

1–147. See 2:1246.
148–598. See 3:73.
599–1219. See 4:117.
1220–2297. See 5:154.
2298–3030. See 6:237.
3031–3749. See P:470, also includes a cumulative name index to the first 3749 references for this test.

3750. HARROWER-ERICKSON, M. R. Chap. 20, "Psychological Studies of Patients With Epileptic Seizures," pp. 546–74. In *Epilepsy and Cerebral Localization.* By Wilder Penfield and Theodore C. Erickson. Springfield, Ill.: Charles C Thomas, Publisher, 1941. Pp. x, 623. * (*PA* 16:4045)

3751. HARROWER-ERICKSON, M. R. "Clinical Use of Psychological Tests." *McGill Med J* 11:105–9 D '41. *

3752. HARROWER-ERICKSON, M. R. "The Patient and His Personality: A Short Discussion of the Rorschach Method of Personality Assessment and Its Use in Clinical Medicine." *McGill Med J* 11:25–40 O '41. *

3753. HALLOWELL, A. "Some Psychological Characteristics of the Northeastern Indians," pp. 195–225. In *Man in Northeastern North America.* Edited by Frederick Johnson. Papers of the Robert S. Peabody Foundation for Archaeology, No. 3. Andover, Mass.: the Foundation, Phillips Academy, 1946. Pp. xi, 347. *

3754. ORR, DAVID HAMILTON. *A Field Study of a Psychiatric Aide Applicant Group at a State Mental Hospital.* Doctor's thesis, University of Kentucky (Lexington, Ky.), 1950. (*DA* 18:666)

3755. EYLEY, HERSHEL E. *A Rorschach Study of Psychological Changes in Alcoholics Following the Administration of Adrenal Cortex Extract.* Master's thesis, Texas Christian University (Ft. Worth, Tex.), 1951.

3756. PHELAN, JOSEPH GERARD. *A Study of Psychological Diagnostic Skill as Employed in the Clinical Investigation of Personality.* Doctor's thesis, Princeton University (Princeton, N.J.), 1951. (*DA* 13:599)

3757. ABRAMS, ARNOLD. *Effects of Group Therapy Upon Certain Personality Characteristics of a Selected Group of Institutionalized Male Sex Offenders.* Doctor's thesis, New York University (New York, N.Y.), 1952. (*DA* 13:114)

3758. BARRON, JULES. *A Personality Study of Individuals With Seen and Unseen Physical Handicaps.* Doctor's thesis, New York University (New York, N.Y.), 1952. (*DA* 13:114)

3759. BERGER, DAVID G. *The Emotional Reaction on Admission to a Tuberculosis Hospital.* Doctor's thesis, Michigan State College (East Lansing, Mich.), 1952. (*DA* 14:550)

3760. CALIMAN, ALVIS WAYMAN. *Personality Adjustment of Aging Women.* Doctor's thesis, Michigan State College (East Lansing, Mich.), 1952. (*DA* 13:862)

3761. COHEN, GEORGE. *Psychological Differences in Relapsing and Non-Relapsing Tuberculous Patients.* Doctor's thesis, New York University (New York, N.Y.), 1952. (*DA* 13:118)

3762. ELKIN, VICTOR B. *The Relationship Between Personality Characteristics and Efficiency in the Use of Aural Sensory Aids by a Group of Acoustically Handicapped Patients.* Doctor's thesis, New York University (New York, N.Y.), 1952. (*DA* 13:202)

3763. GABRIELE, ANTHONY BENEDICT. *The Relationship of Day Center Attendance to Several Psychological and Socio-Economic Characteristics in a Group of Older Persons in New York City: A Comparative Analysis and Evaluation of Rorschach Records, Adult Activity Inventory Scores, and Socio-Economic Characteristics of Three Groups of Individuals Over Sixty Years of Age Some of Which Attend Day Centers for Older Persons of the New York City Department of Welfare.* Doctor's thesis, New York University (New York, N.Y.), 1952. (*DA* 13:516)

3764. GORDON, MYRON H. *A Clinical Study of Personality Patterns in Children With Reading Disability.* Doctor's thesis, New York University (New York, N.Y.), 1952. (*DA* 13:68)

3765. GÜNZBURG, H. C. "Maladjustment as Expressed in Drawings by Subnormal Children." *Am J Mental Def* 57:9–23 Jl '52. * (*PA* 27:3628)

3766. KATZ, ARNOLD. *A Study of the Relationships Among Several Measures of Rigidity.* Doctor's thesis, State University of Iowa (Iowa City, Iowa), 1952. (*DA* 12:590)

3767. KRASNER, JACK DANIEL. *The Psychological Effects of Regressive Electroshock Therapy.* Doctor's thesis, New York University (New York, N.Y.), 1952. (*DA* 12:591)

3768. MENAKER, LEON. *A Study of the Personality of the Asthmatic Adult Male.* Doctor's thesis, New York University (New York, N.Y.), 1952. (*DA* 12:727)

3769. MICHAEL, JOHN FRANCIS. *An Attempt to Check and Extend the Ethnocentrism-Rigidity Hypothesis.* Doctor's thesis, Ohio State University (Columbus, Ohio), 1952. (*DA* 18:1100)

3770. NORGARB, BRIAN A. Chap. 8, "Rorschach Psychodiagnosis in Hypnotic Regression," pp. 178–214. In *Experimental Hypnosis: A Symposium of Articles on Research by Many of the World's Leading Authorities.* Edited by Leslie M.

LeCron. New York: Macmillan Co., 1952. Pp. xix, 483. * (*PA* 27:7619)

3771. PEARLMAN, SAMUEL. *An Investigation of the Problem of Academic Underachievement Among Intellectually Superior College Students.* Doctor's thesis, New York University (New York, N.Y.), 1952. (*DA* 12:599)

3772. RAIFMAN, IRVING. *An Investigation of the Personality Factors of Dependency and Overcompensatory Goal Striving Behavior Associated With the Development of Peptic Ulcer in a Group of Veteran Male Patients.* Doctor's thesis, New York University (New York, N.Y.), 1952. (*DA* 12:539)

3773. TINDALL, RALPH HAROLD. *Relationships Among Indices of Adjustment Status.* Doctor's thesis, Ohio State University (Columbus, Ohio), 1952. (*DA* 19:2155)

3774. BARD, MORTON. *The Relationship of the Personality Factor of Dependence to Psychological Invalidism in Women Following Radical Mastectomy.* Doctor's thesis, New York University (New York, N.Y.), 1953. (*DA* 13:716)

3775. KATZ, WILLIAM D. *A Study of the Changes in Personality Structure in Depression by Means of Psychological Tests.* Doctor's thesis, New York University (New York, N.Y.), 1953. (*DA* 13:592)

3776. KULICK, WILLIAM. *Personality Traits and Academic Standing of Probationary Engineering Students Before and After Counseling: An Evaluation of the Effectiveness of Non-Directive Counseling by Means of the Rorschach Test.* Doctor's thesis, New York University (New York, N.Y.), 1953. (*DA* 13:584)

3777. LOFCHIE, STANLEY H. *The Performance of Adults Under Distraction Stress: A Developmental Approach.* Doctor's thesis, Clark University (Worcester, Mass.), 1953. (*DA* 13:865)

3778. MILL, CYRIL RALPH. *Personality Patterns of Socially Selected and Socially Rejected Male College Students.* Doctor's thesis, Michigan State College (East Lansing, Mich.), 1953. (*DA* 13:866)

3779. MYERS, JULIAN S. *The Effect of Testosterone Upon Certain Aspects of Personality in Male Paraplegics.* Doctor's thesis, New York University (New York, N.Y.), 1953. (*DA* 14:397)

3780. SALTZMAN, SIDNEY S. *An Investigation of Certain Psychological Aspects of Personality in Three Allergic Groups.* Doctor's thesis, New York University (New York, N.Y.), 1953. (*DA* 13:1251)

3781. WEXLER, MURRAY. *The Relationship Between Personality Organization and Electroshock: A Comparative Study of the Personality Characteristics of Psychotic Patients Who Improve or Do Not Improve From Electroshock Therapy.* Doctor's thesis, New York University (New York, N.Y.), 1953. (*DA* 14:2281)

3782. ZEICHNER, ABRAHAM M. *Psychosexual Identification and Conception of Sexual Role in Paranoid Schizophrenia.* Doctor's thesis, New York University (New York, N.Y.), 1953. (*DA* 13:593)

3783. deVINCENTIS, G., AND FERRACUTI, F. "Preliminary Investigations by Means of the Rorschach Test and Other Projective Techniques in a Group of Sexual Offenders." *Schweizerischen Zeitschrift für Psychologie und Ihre Anwendungen* 25:151–5 '54. * (*PA* 30:3150)

3784. FABIAN, WALTER ALBERT, JR. *An Investigation of the Relationship Between Measures of Insight and Measures of Projection and Distortion in Ratings.* Doctor's thesis, University of Buffalo (Buffalo, N.Y.), 1954. (*DA* 14:711)

3785. HILER, EDWARD WESLEY. *An Investigation of Psychological Factors Associated With Premature Termination of Psychotherapy.* Doctor's thesis, University of Michigan (Ann Arbor, Mich.), 1954. (*DA* 14:712)

3786. KADINSKY, D. "On the Significance of Anatomy Responses in the Rorschach." *Schweizerischen Zeitschrift für Psychologie und Ihre Anwendungen* 25:85–102 '54. * (*PA* 30:2889)

3787. KAVKEWITZ, HENRY. *The Relationship Between Personality and Success in a Vocational Rehabilitation Program: A Comparative Study of the Success and Failure of Schizophrenic Veterans of World War II in a Veterans' Administration Vocational Rehabilitation Training Program.* Doctor's thesis, New York University (New York, N.Y.), 1954. (*DA* 14:870)

3788. RUSSELL, G. HUGH. *Experimental, Clinical and Behavioral Measures of Perceptual Distortion as Related to Form Preferences.* Doctor's thesis, Purdue University (Lafayette, Ind.), 1954. (*DA* 14:1822)

3789. SEGAL, STANLEY JACOB. *The Role of Personality Factors in Vocational Choice: A Study of Accountants and Creative Writers.* Doctor's thesis, University of Michigan (Ann Arbor, Mich.), 1954. (*DA* 14:714)

3790. SHARPE, SUSIE McMILLAN. *The Relation of Personality Factors to Intellectual Functioning and Achievement in Nine and Ten Year Old Children.* Doctor's thesis, New York University (New York, N.Y.), 1954. (*DA* 14:2278)

3791. SHIRE, ALBERT. *Personality Correlates of Preferences Among Psychoanalytic Defense Mechanisms.* Doctor's thesis, University of Michigan (Ann Arbor, Mich.), 1954. (*DA* 14:715)

3792. STEIN, HARRY. *An Investigation of Developmental Changes in Fantasy and Imagination in Three Groups of Children.* Doctor's thesis, New York University (New York, N.Y.), 1954. (*DA* 14:1815)

3793. VACCA, E., AND BREDA, R. "The Application of the Rorschach Test to an Ethnical Group (Sermoneta, Italy)." *Schweizerischen Zeitschrift für Psychologie und Ihre Anwendungen* 25:103–15 '54. * (*PA* 30:2793)

3794. WAXENBERG, SHELDON EDWARD. *Psychosomatic Patients and Other Physically Ill Persons: A Comparative Study.* Doctor's thesis, Columbia University (New York, N.Y.), 1954. (*DA* 14:1818)

3795. BERLINER, ANNA. "The Rorschach Determinant in Terms of Visual Psychology." *Optom Weekly* 46:13–7+ Ja 6 '55. * (*PA* 29:7257)

3796. LEVIT, HERBERT I. *A Study of the Effects of Electroconvulsive Therapy on Certain Psychological and Physiological Functions in Paranoid Schizophrenia.* Doctor's thesis, Temple University (Philadelphia, Pa.), 1955. (*DA* 15:1440)

3797. TONG, JOHN E. "Abstraction Ability and Impairment. The Barrow Hospital Sorting Test in Clinical Psychological Testing." *Brit J Med Psychol* 28:19–28 pt 1 '55. * (*PA* 30:1065)

3798. BROWN, DONALD VAUGHN. *An Investigation of the Influence of Prejudice, Race, and Sex Factors in a Testing Situation.* Doctor's thesis, Purdue University (Lafayette, Ind.), 1956. (*DA* 17:404)

3799. HELLER, DORIS G. *The Relationship Between Sex-Appropriate Behavior in Young Children and the Clarity of the Sex-Role of the Like-Sexed Parents as Measured by Tests.* Doctor's thesis, New York University (New York, N.Y.), 1956. (*DA* 19:3365)

3800. JACKSON, JOHN THOMAS, JR. *A Comparison of Poliomyelitis and Tuberculosis Patients on the Basis of the Rorschach Method of Personality Diagnosis.* Master's thesis, Texas Christian University (Ft. Worth, Tex.), 1956.

3801. RITCHIE, JAMES E. *Basic Personality in Rakau.* Victoria University of Wellington Publications in Psychology No. 8; Monographs on Maori Social Life and Personality No. 1. Wellington, New Zealand: Department of Psychology, the University, 1956. Pp. ix, 187. *

3802. SANUA, VICTOR D. *Differences in Personality Adjustment Among Different Generations of American Jews and Non-Jews.* Doctor's thesis, Michigan State University (East Lansing, Mich.), 1956. (*DA* 19:3358)

3803. SEYMOUR, JOHN H. *Some Changes in Psychometric, Perceptual and Motor Performance as a Function of Sleep Deprivation.* Doctor's thesis, New York University (New York, N.Y.), 1956. (*DA* 16:2216)

3804. VERNIER, CLAIRE M. Chap. 18, "Predictability in Treatment of Tuberculosis Patients," pp. 344–52. In *Personality, Stress, and Tuberculosis.* Edited by Phineas J. Sparer. New York: International Universities Press, Inc., 1956. Pp. xviii, 629. *

3805. WEISS, BERTRAM ARTHUR. *Relationships Between Developmental Experiences and Choice of Defensive Behavior: Study I, Males.* Doctor's thesis, University of Houston (Houston, Tex.), 1956. (*DA* 17:1392)

3806. ABRAMS, JULIAN. *Chlorpromazine in the Treatment of Chronic Schizophrenia: A Comparative Investigation of the Therapeutic Value of Chlorpromazine in Effecting Certain Psychological and Behavioral Changes in Chronic Schizophrenic Patients.* Doctor's thesis, New York University (New York, N.Y.), 1957. (*DA* 17:1589)

3807. ARNAUD, SARA HAYES. *Children of Multiple Sclerotics: Their Psychological Characteristics.* Doctor's thesis, Boston University (Boston, Mass.), 1957. (*DA* 17:1809)

3808. ASCH, MORTON JAY. *Negative Response Bias and Personality Adjustment.* Doctor's thesis, Syracuse University (Syracuse, N.Y.), 1957. (*DA* 17:1704)

3809. CLANCY, DAVID DANA. *The Relationship of Positive Response Bias or Acquiescence to Psychopathology.* Doctor's thesis, Syracuse University (Syracuse, N.Y.), 1957. (*DA* 17:2054)

3810. CLIGGETT, DONALD P. *An Investigation of Cognitive Style as a Function of the Perception of Human Movement in Ink Blots.* Doctor's thesis, New York University (New York, N.Y.), 1957. (*DA* 18:652)

3811. ESKENAZI, ALBERT. *Personality Development of Pre-Adolescent Boys as a Function of Mothers' Defenses and Parental Attitudes.* Doctor's thesis, University of Houston (Houston, Tex.), 1957. (*DA* 18:1862)

3812. JORDY, GERTRUDE BARNES. *The Rorschach as an Objective Measure of Adjustment and Its Relationship to Academic Achievement.* Master's thesis, San Diego State College (San Diego, Calif.), 1957.

3813. LOWENHEIM, HENRY. *The Relationship Between Personality Rigidity and Acceptance of Physical Disability: Perceptual and Attitudinal Correlates of Adjustment to Physical Disability.* Doctor's thesis, New York University (New York, N.Y.), 1957. (*DA* 18:1493)

3814. PODELL, JEROME EDWARD. *Personality and Stimulus Factors in Adult Cognition: A Developmental Analysis of Decontextualization.* Doctor's thesis, Clark University (Worcester, Mass.), 1957. (*DA* 18:311)

3815. ROTH, BERNARD. *A Study of Selective Memory Changes After Electroshock Treatments.* Doctor's thesis, New York University (New York, N.Y.), 1957. (*DA* 18:1502)

3816. ROTHSTEIN, CHARLES. *The Role of Hostility and Dependency Conflicts in Peptic Ulcer Etiology.* Doctor's thesis, University of Buffalo (Buffalo, N.Y.), 1957. (*DA* 17:174)

3817. SINES, LLOYD K. *An Experimental Investigation of the Relative Contribution to Clinical Diagnosis and Personality Description of Various Kinds of Pertinent Data.* Doctor's thesis, University of Minnesota (Minneapolis, Minn.), 1957. (*DA* 17:2067)

3818. STONE, THOMAS E. *The Effect of Anxiety on Fantasy.* Doctor's thesis, New York University (New York, N.Y.), 1957. (*DA* 21:963)

3819. TALKOFF, ALVIN ROY. *The Consistency of Control Function in Non-Patient and Patient Populations: An Evaluation of Intra-Individual Control in the Self, the Ego, and Behavior in Non-Hospitalized Persons and in Groups of Patients Diagnosed as Paranoid Schizophrenia.* Doctor's thesis, New York University (New York, N.Y.), 1957. (*DA* 18:670)

3820. WECHSLER, RUTH R. *An Investigation of Certain Psychodynamic Aspects of the Personality of Individuals Who Have Suffered Manic and Depressive Attacks.* Doctor's thesis, New York University (New York, N.Y.), 1957. (*DA* 18:672)

3821. WEINBERG, GEORGE HENRY. *Clinical Versus Statistical Prediction With a Method of Evaluating a Clinical Tool.* Doctor's thesis, Columbia University (New York, N.Y.), 1957. (*DA* 17:1602)

3822. DUBIN, WILLIAM. *Toward a Definition of Effective Functioning.* Doctor's thesis, Columbia University (New York, N.Y.), 1958. (*DA* 18:1858)

3823. KIMMEL, JAMES. *A Comparison of Children With Congenital and Acquired Orthopedic Handicaps on Certain Personality Characteristics: An Evaluation of Self-Concept, Anxiety, Defense Mechanisms, and Adjustment in Children With Orthopedic Handicaps.* Doctor's thesis, New York University (New York, N.Y.), 1958. (*DA* 19:3023)

3824. MULLEN, ESTHER. *An Investigation of Some Aspects of Depression and Its Effect on the Perception of the Self and Others in a Non-Psychiatric Population.* Doctor's thesis, New York University (New York, N.Y.), 1958. (*DA* 19:2390)

3825. RILL, HERBERT J. *Effects of Sparine and a Total-Push Program on the Psychopathological Functions of Paranoid Schizophrenics.* Doctor's thesis, Temple University (Philadelphia, Pa.), 1958. (*DA* 19:3371)

3826. SCHULMAN, DORIS. *A Study of the Relationships Between Mothers' Attitudes Toward Their Children, and the Personality Adjustment and School Behavior of These Children.* Doctor's thesis, New York University (New York, N.Y.), 1958. (*DA* 19:734)

3827. TRACHTMAN, GILBERT M. *Personality and Developmental Characteristics of Children Rated Most and Least Ready for First Grade by Their Kindergarten Teachers.* Doctor's thesis, New York University (New York, N.Y.), 1958. (*DA* 19:3028)

3828. WEINBERG, NORRIS H. *Cognitive Development, Self-Orientation, and Piaget's Notion of Ego-Centricity.* Doctor's thesis, University of Pennsylvania (Philadelphia, Pa.), 1958. (*DA* 18:2222)

3829. WESTON, DONALD LESLIE. *Motor Activity and Depression in Juvenile Delinquents.* Doctor's thesis, Boston University (Boston, Mass.), 1958. (*DA* 19:2391)

3830. WYLIE, ALEXANDER ARTHUR. *Concept Formation in Pre-School Children.* Doctor's thesis, University of Houston (Houston, Tex.), 1958. (*DA* 18:1874)

3831. ALLRED, DALE LEROY. *Consistency of Color Usage and Some Correlates.* Doctor's thesis, Purdue University (Lafayette, Ind.), 1959. (*DA* 20:1874)

3832. COLE, DOROTHY AGNES. *Some Emotional Factors in Couples Presenting a Pattern of Habitual Abortion.* Doctor's thesis, Syracuse University (Syracuse, N.Y.), 1959. (*DA* 20:749)

3833. FAULS, JOHN THOMAS. *Superior Readers Versus Mediocre Readers: A Comparison of Ego Organizations.* Doctor's thesis, Florida State University (Tallahassee, Fla.), 1959. (*DA* 20:3376)

3834. HOFFER, BARBARA DIANE. *Some Symbolic Associations to Three Rorschach Cards.* Master's thesis, San Diego State College (San Diego, Calif.), 1959.

3835. LINDZEY, GARDNER. "On the Classification of Projective Techniques." *Psychol B* 56:158–68 Mr '59. * (*PA* 34:1389)

3836. MARLENS, HANNA S. *A Study of the Effect of Hospitalization on Children in a Metropolitan Municipal Institution: A Comparative Study of Emotional Attitudes Toward Self and the Environment of Children Hospitalized and Those Non-Hospitalized With Similar Physical Complaints.* Doctor's thesis, New York University (New York, N.Y.), 1959. (*DA* 20:3385)

3837. ACKMAN, PHYLLIS. *The Effects of Induced Regression on Thinking Processes.* Doctor's thesis, University of Michigan (Ann Arbor, Mich.), 1960. (*DA* 21:365)

3838. CROOKES, T. G., AND KELLER, ANNA J. "Rorschach Card Rejection and IQ." *J Clin Psychol* 16:424–6 O '60. * (*PA* 37:3140) Duplication of 2615.

3839. LANDAU, MIRIAM FELDMAN. *Body Image in Paraplegia as a Variable in Adjustment to Physical Handicap.* Doctor's thesis, Columbia University (New York, N.Y.), 1960. (*DA* 21:960)

3840. LEDYARD, FRANCIS MONROE. *Developmental Differences Between Successful and Unsuccessful Intellectualizers.* Doctor's thesis, University of Houston (Houston, Tex.), 1960. (*DA* 20:4439)

3841. BERNSTEIN, LEWIS. "Psychological Testing: 2, The Rorschach Test." *J Child Asth Res Inst & Hosp* 1:313–24 S '61. *

3842. FINZI, HILDA. *Interchangeability of Perceptual and Motor Activity in the Release of Organismic Tension.* Doctor's thesis, New York University (New York, N.Y.), 1961. (*DA* 22:4078)

3843. KAHN, PAUL. *Time Orientation and Perceptual and Cognitive Organization With Special Reference to Reading Achievement.* Doctor's thesis, Yeshiva University (New York, N.Y.), 1961. (*DA* 26:6838)

3844. WILLIAMS, ROBERT LEE. *The Relationship of Body-Image to Some Physiological Reactivity Patterns in Peptic Ulcer and Rheumatoid Arthritic Patients.* Doctor's thesis, Washington University (St. Louis, Mo.), 1961. (*DA* 22:4415)

3845. BLAUFARB, MYRNA TICKTIN. *Set and Bias in Clinical Judgment.* Doctor's thesis, University of Illinois (Urbana, Ill.), 1962. (*DA* 23:698)

3846. CORNETT, STEPHEN J., JR. *An Analysis of Variables in an Experimental Measurement of Attitudes of Psychiatric Patients.* Doctor's thesis, University of Kentucky (Lexington, Ky.), 1962. (*DAI* 30:1816A)

3847. GOCHMAN, DAVID SAMUEL. *System Theory and Adaptability.* Doctor's thesis, University of Colorado (Boulder, Colo.), 1962. (*DA* 23:3965)

3848. GUERRANT, JOHN; ANDERSON, WILLIAM W.; FISCHER, AMES; WEINSTEIN, MORTON R.; JAROS, R. MARY; AND DESKINS, ANDREW. Chap. 5, "Psychological Considerations," pp. 66–92. In their *Personality in Epilepsy.* Springfield, Ill.: Charles C Thomas, Publisher, 1962. Pp. xii, 112. *

3849. HOWARD, STEPHEN JAMES. *Determinants of Sex-Role Identifications of Homosexual Female Delinquents.* Doctor's thesis, University of Southern California (Los Angeles, Calif.), 1962. (*DA* 23:2588)

3850. LUBIN, BERNARD; BRADY, JOHN PAUL; AND LEVITT, EUGENE E. "A Comparison of Personality Characteristics of Volunteers and Nonvolunteers for Hypnosis Experiments." *J Clin Psychol* 18:341–8 Jl '62. * (*PA* 39:1811)

3851. PRYOR, DAVID BRUCE. *Regression in the Service of the Ego: Psychosexual Development and Ego Functions.* Doctor's thesis, Michigan State University (East Lansing, Mich.), 1962. (*DA* 23:3982)

3852. REIFF, CAROLYN GRACE GIRARD. *An Investigation of Relationships Among Body Image and Some Ego Functions Involved in Formal Thought Processes.* Doctor's thesis, New York University (New York, N.Y.), 1962. (*DA* 23:2208)

3853. WITKIN, H. A.; DYKE, R. G.; FATERSON, H. F.; GOODENOUGH, D. R.; AND KARP, S. A. *Psychological Differentiation: Studies of Development.* New York: John Wiley & Sons, Inc., 1962. Pp. xii, 418. * (*PA* 37:819)

3854. BARRON, FRANK. *Creativity and Psychological Health: Origins of Personal Vitality and Creative Freedom.* Princeton, N.J.: D. Van Nostrand Co., Inc., 1963. Pp. xi, 292. *

3855. BLOCK, WILLIAM E. "Clinical Validation of Adaptation-Level Theory as a Framework for Projective Testing." *J Clin Psychol* 19:304–9 Jl '63. * (*PA* 39:7885)

3856. DERI, SUSAN K. "Genotropism in the Framework of a Unified Theory of Choice." *Schweizerischen Zeitschrift für Psychologie und Ihre Anwendungen* 47:39–74 '63. *

3857. KLEIN, HELEN THERESE. *Maternal Anxiety and Abnormalities of Birth: Relationship Between Anxiety Level During Pregnancy and Maternal-Fetal Complications.* Doctor's thesis, Yeshiva University (New York, N.Y.), 1963. (*DA* 25:2049)

3858. KLEIN, RALPH. *The Self Image of Adult Males in an Andean Culture. A Clinical Exploration of a Dynamic Personality Construct.* Doctor's thesis, New York University (New York, N.Y.), 1963. (*DA* 24:2986)

3859. PIOTROWSKI, ZYGMUNT A. Chap. 17, "Rorschach Diagnostic Evaluations," pp. 269–306. In *The Genain Quadruplets.* Edited by David Rosenthal. New York: Basic Books, Inc., Publishers, 1963. Pp. xv, 609. * (*PA* 38:9070)

3860. ROSENTHAL, DAVID, AND PIOTROWSKI, ZYGMUNT A. Chap. 18, "The Beck-Molish Rorschach Typology With Respect to the Genain Family," pp. 307–14. In *The Genain Quadruplets.* Edited by David Rosenthal. New York: Basic Books, Inc., Publishers, 1963. Pp. xv, 609. * (*PA* 38:9070)

3861. SIERACKI, EDWARD ROBERT. *Body-Image as a Variable in the Acceptance of Disability and Vocational Interests of the Physically Disabled.* Doctor's thesis, State University of New York (Buffalo, N.Y.), 1963. (*DA* 24:1249)

3862. SINGER, MARGARET THALER. Chap. 19, "A Rorschach View of the Family," pp. 315–25. In *The Genain Quadruplets.* Edited by David Rosenthal. New York: Basic Books, Inc., Publishers, 1963. Pp. xv, 609. * (*PA* 38:9070)

3863. SKLAR, MAURICE. "Relation of Psychological and Language Test Scores and Autopsy Findings in Aphasia." *J Speech & Hearing Res* 6:84–90 Mr '63. * (*PA* 38:1201)

3864. TUTKO, THOMAS ARTHUR. *Need for Social Approval and Its Effect on Responses to Projective Tests.* Doctor's thesis, Northwestern University (Evanston, Ill.), 1963. (*DA* 24:3429)

3865. ALSTON, LESTER THOMAS. *An Investigation of the*

Relationship Between Some Ego Factors and Memory Styles. Doctor's thesis, New York University (New York, N.Y.), 1964. (*DA* 27:4546B)

3866. CROWNE, DOUGLAS P., AND MARLOWE, DAVID. *The Approval Motive: Studies in Evaluative Dependence,* pp. 171–85. New York: John Wiley & Sons, Inc., 1964. Pp. xiii, 233. *

3867. FISKE, DONALD W.; CARTWRIGHT, DESMOND S.; AND KIRTNER, WILLIAM L. "Are Psychotherapeutic Changes Predictable?" *J Abn & Social Psychol* 69:418–26 O '64. * (*PA* 39:8058)

3868. GERDINE, PHILIP VAN HORN, JR. *Patterns of Ego Function in Psychophysiological Skin Disorders.* Doctor's thesis, Boston University (Boston, Mass.), 1964. (*DA* 25:3108)

3869. KETTELL, MARJORIE EDYTHE. *Integrity of Ego Processes in Aged Females.* Doctor's thesis, Boston University (Boston, Mass.), 1964. (*DA* 25:3111)

3870. LERNER, PAUL MARVIN. *Resolution of Intrafamilial Conflict in Families of Schizophrenic Patients.* Doctor's thesis, University of Illinois (Urbana, Ill.), 1964. (*DA* 25:6761)

3871. MAISEL, RICHARD N. *Psychological Concomitants of Chronic Disease: A Study of Hansen's Disease and Pulmonary Tuberculosis Patients Who Are Fast and Slow Recoverers.* Doctor's thesis, University of Miami (Coral Gables, Fla.), 1964. (*DA* 25:5385)

3872. THOMAS, CAROLINE BEDELL; ROSS, DONALD C.; AND FREED, ELLEN S. *An Index of Rorschach Responses: Studies on the Psychological Characteristics of Medical Students—I.* Baltimore, Md.: Johns Hopkins Press, 1964. Pp. xlv, 741. *

3873. ACKERMAN, BERNARD R. *The Relationship of Certain Personality Variables to the Executive Role in the Funeral Service Industry: An Evaluation of the Personality Variables of Rigidity, Lability, Self-Concept and Interests in Executive and Technical Personnel in the Funeral Service Industry.* Doctor's thesis, New York University (New York, N.Y.), 1965. (*DA* 27:606B)

3874. ARTHUR, BETTIE. Chap. 4, "The Forced Confabulation Technique: An Extension of the Rorschach Method for Use With Children," pp. 37–55. In *Psychological Test Modifications.* Edited by Milton Kornrich. Springfield, Ill.: Charles C Thomas, Publisher, 1965. Pp. xii, 265. *

3875. BACHELIS, LEONARD A. *Body-Field Perceptual Differentiation as a Variable in Creative Thinking.* Doctor's thesis, Yeshiva University (New York, N.Y.), 1965. (*DA* 26:3475)

3876. BOYER, L. BRYCE; KLOPFER, BRUNO; BOYER, RUTH M.; BRAWER, FLORENCE B.; AND KAWAI, HAYAO. "Effects of Acculturation on the Personality Traits of the Old People of the Mescalero and Chiricahua Apaches." *Int J Social Psychiatry* 11:264–71 au '65. * (*PA* 40:2752)

3877. CASSELL, WILFRED A. "Body Perception and Symptom Localization. *Psychosom Med* 27:171–6 Mr–Ap '65. * (*PA* 39:12906)

3878. FULGENZI, LAWRENCE BENJAMIN. *The Repression-Sensitization Personality Dimension and Aggressive Behavior.* Doctor's thesis, University of Oklahoma (Norman, Okla.), 1965. (*DA* 26:1774)

3879. FULKERSON, SAMUEL C. "Some Implications of the New Cognitive Theory for Projective Tests." *J Consult Psychol* 29:191–7 Ap '65. * (*PA* 39:12389)

3880. GIBEAU, PHILIP JOSEPH. *Field Dependency and the Process-Reactive Dimension in Schizophrenia.* Doctor's thesis, Purdue University (Lafayette, Ind.), 1965. (*DA* 26:1775)

3881. JOHNSTON, JAMES ORRIN. *Relationships Between Intelligence and Personality Variables.* Doctor's thesis, Oklahoma State University (Stillwater, Okla.), 1965. (*DA* 27:315B)

3882. KAPLAN, BERT, AND LAWLESS, RICHARD. "Cultural and Visual Imagery: A Comparison of Rorschach Responses in Eleven Societies," pp. 295–311. In *Context and Meaning in Cultural Anthropology.* Edited by Melford E. Spiro in honor of A. Irving Hallowell. New York: Free Press, 1965. Pp. xxii, 442. *

3883. KENT, ROSE. *Children of Mothers With Authoritarian Ideology.* Doctor's thesis, Yeshiva University (New York, N.Y.), 1965. (*DA* 26:2313)

3884. KORNRICH, MILTON. Chap. 16, "Eliciting 'New' Rorschach Responses," pp. 213–7. In his *Psychological Test Modifications.* Springfield, Ill.: Charles C Thomas, Publisher, 1965. Pp. xii, 265. *

3885. LANGS, ROBERT J. "First Memories and Characterologic Diagnosis." *J Nerv & Mental Dis* 141:318–20 S '65. * (*PA* 40:5532)

3886. LIPGAR, ROBERT MAURICE. *Subjective Probability Notions, Guessing Behavior and Their Personality Correlates.* Doctor's thesis, University of Chicago (Chicago, Ill.), 1965. (*DAI* 30:1348B)

3887. MANN, NANCY AMALIA. *Free Association and Preferred Defenses.* Doctor's thesis, University of Michigan (Ann Arbor, Mich.), 1965. (*DA* 27:611B)

3888. MUKHERJEE, KAMAL. "Personality of Criminals: A Rorschach Study." *B Council Social & Psychol Res* 5:15–8 Jl '65. * (*PA* 40:2960)

3889. ORBACH, CHARLES E., AND TALLENT, NORMAN. "Modification of Perceived Body and of Body Concepts: Following the Construction of a Colostomy." *Arch Gen Psychiatry* 12:126–35 F '65. * (*PA* 39:8295)

3890. PATERSON, JOHN GILBERT A. *Personality Characteristics of Undergraduate Education Students Associated With*

Differential Performance in Factual and Applied Educational Psychology Test Items. Doctor's thesis, University of Washington (Seattle, Wash.), 1965. (*DA* 27:119A)

3891. RAYCHAUDHURI, MANAS, AND MAITRA, AMAL KUMAR. "Developmental Parallels in the Rorschach Responses: An Approach to the Test Validation." *B Council Social & Psychol Res* 5:1–7 Jl '65. * (*PA* 40:2142)

3892. TOLLEFSEN, NONA FALMLEN. *Relationship of Counselor Need Orientation to Counselor Effectiveness and Counselor Personality.* Doctor's thesis, Purdue University (Lafayette, Ind.), 1965. (*DA* 27:122A)

3893. TSUJI, SHOZO. "Some Investigations of Parental Preference in Early Childhood." *Rorsch Newsl* 10:37–41 Je '65. * (*PA* 40:2706)

3894. WRIGHT, NANCY A., AND ABBEY, DAVID S. "Perceptual Deprivation Tolerance and Adequacy of Defense." *Percept & Motor Skills* 20:35–8 F '65. * (*PA* 39:9155)

3895. ZIMNY, GEORGE H. "Body Image and Physiological Responses." *J Psychosom Res* 9:185–8 O '65. * (*PA* 40:5503)

3896. ALLEN, ROBERT M. *Student's Rorschach Manual: An Introduction to Administering, Scoring and Interpreting Rorschach's Psychodiagnostic Inkblot Test.* New York: International Universities Press, Inc., 1966. Pp. xvii, 280. * (*PA* 41:5980)

3897. BACHELIS, FAITH G. *Regional Origin, Personality, and Mothers' Attitudes of Jewish Day School Students.* Doctor's thesis, Yeshiva University (New York, N.Y.), 1966. (*DA* 28:1154B)

3898. BENNETT, DEWEY EUGENE. *Myers-Briggs Validation of Rorschach Experience Balance.* Master's thesis, San Diego State College (San Diego, Calif.), 1966.

3899. BRIGGS, L. D. *The Impact of Failure on Elementary School Pupils.* Doctor's thesis, North Texas State University (Denton, Tex.), 1966. (*DA* 27:2719A)

3900. DOBBS, DARREL D. *The Blurred Rorschach: Effects of the Amorphous.* Doctor's thesis, University of Kentucky (Lexington, Ky.), 1966. (*DAI* 30:1817A)

3901. GOLDFRIED, MARVIN R. "A Suggested Approach to Evaluation of Projective Techniques." *Psychol Rep* 18:111–4 F '66. * (*PA* 40:6665)

3902. HAER, JOHN LESTER. *Aspects of Aggression in Psychotherapy Groups.* Doctor's thesis, Claremont Graduate School (Claremont, Calif.), 1966. (*DA* 28:2138B)

3903. HARDYCK, CURTIS D. "Personality Characteristics and Motor Activity: Some Empirical Evidence." *J Pers & Social Psychol* 4:181–8 Ag '66. * (*PA* 40:11183)

3904. HOWARD, GEORGE HERBERT. *The Relationship Between Two Patterns of Personality Factors and the Use of Kinesthetic Cues in the Solution of Visual Learning Problems.* Doctor's thesis, New York University (New York, N.Y.), 1966. (*DA* 27:2893B)

3905. KANTROWITZ, JUDY LEOPOLD. *The Effects of Crisis on Academic Achievement.* Doctor's thesis, Boston University (Boston, Mass.), 1966. (*DA* 27:1623B)

3906. KIMBRELL, DON L., AND LUCKEY, ROBERT E. "Remotivation of Institutionalized Epileptics." *Percept & Motor Skills* 23:770 D '66. * (*PA* 41:7722)

3907. LEVIN, RACHEL B. "An Empirical Test of the Female Castration Complex." *J Abn Psychol* 71:181–8 Je '66. * (*PA* 40:8985)

3908. McELHANEY, MARK LUCAS. *A Comparison of Temporal Lobe With Non-Temporal Lobe Brain Damage as Shown by Various Psychological Tests.* Doctor's thesis, University of Houston (Houston, Tex.), 1966. (*DA* 27:1625B)

3909. MADSEN, JOAN CAROLE. *The Expression of Aggression in Two Cultures.* Doctor's thesis, University of Oregon (Eugene, Ore.), 1966. (*DA* 27:2513B)

3910. MALEV, J. S. "Body Image, Body Symptoms and Body Reactivity in Children." *J Psychosom Res* 10:281–9 D '66. * (*PA* 41:5792)

3911. MOTANKY, GUY URBAN. *Behavioral Reactions Following Brain Damage to Cardiac Patients.* Doctor's thesis, Illinois Institute of Technology (Chicago, Ill.), 1966. (*DA* 28:4298B)

3912. PIOTROWSKI, ZYGMUNT. "Some Basic Psychologic Investigations Relevant to Schizophrenia." *Mental Hyg* 50:536–40 O '66." *

3913. REID, WALTER BROOK. *Some Aspects of Personality in Persistent Enuresis as Determined by Responses to Psychological Tests and to Drug Therapy.* Doctor's thesis, University of Houston (Houston, Tex.), 1966. (*DA* 27:1629B)

3914. RICKELS, KARL, AND DOWNING, ROBERT. "Compliance and Improvement in Drug-Treated and Placebo-Treated Neurotic Outpatients." *Arch Gen Psychiatry* 14:631–3 Je '66. * (*PA* 40:10202)

3915. ROGOLSKY, MARYROSE MARGARETTEN. *Artistic Creativity: Adaptive Regression and Independence of Judgment in Third Grade Children.* Doctor's thesis, Harvard University (Cambridge, Mass.), 1966. (*DA* 27:4556B)

3916. ROSANES, MARILYN BLITZER. *Psychological Correlates to Myopia Compared to Hyperopia and Emmetropia.* Doctor's thesis, Yeshiva University (New York, N.Y.), 1966. (*DA* 27:2125B)

3917. SARETSKY, THEODORE. "Effects of Chlorpromazine on Primary-Process Thought Manifestations." *J Abn Psychol* 71:247–52 Ag '66. * (*PA* 40:11345)

3918. SILVER, ALBERT W., AND DERR, JOHN. "A Comparison of Selected Personality Variables Between Parents of Delinquent and Non-Delinquent Adolescents." *J Clin Psychol* 22:49–50 Ja '66. * (*PA* 40:4414)

3919. SILVERMAN, LLOYD H., AND GOLDWEBER, ARTHUR M. "A Further Study of the Effects of Subliminal Aggressive Stimulation on Thinking." *J Nerv & Mental Dis* 143:463–72 D '66. * (*PA* 41:10488)

3920. TÄHKÄ, VEIKKO. Chap. 4, "Rorschach Findings," pp. 69–118. In his *The Alcoholic Personality: A Clinical Study.* Helsinki, Finland: Finnish Foundation for Alcohol Studies, 1966. Pp. 279. * (*PA* 41:3075)

3921. WATMAN, WALTER A. "The Relationship Between Acting Out Behavior and Some Psychological Test Indices in a Prison Population." *J Clin Psychol* 22:279–80 Jl '66. * (*PA* :11312)

3922. WATMAN, WALTER ALAN. *The Capacity to Delay Gratification and Its Relationship to Perceptual Developmental Level, Ego Strength and Anxiety Level: A Study of Prisoners.* Doctor's thesis, Michigan State University (East Lansing, Mich.), 1966. (*DA* 28:354B)

3923. WESSMAN, ALDEN E., AND RICKS, DAVID F. *Mood and Personality.* New York: Holt, Rinehart & Winston, Inc., 1966. Pp. xiii, 317. *

3924. ALLEN, THOMAS W. "Effectiveness of Counselor Trainees as a Function of Psychological Openness." *J Counsel Psychol* 14:35–40 Ja '67. * (*PA* 41:4840)

3925. ASSAEL, MARCEL; KOHEN-RAZ, REUVEN; AND ALPERN, SUZY. "Developmental Analysis of EEG Abnormalities in Juvenile Delinquents." *Dis Nerv System* 28:49–54 Ja '67. * (*PA* 41:7530)

3926. BRIGHAM, BRUCE W. *A Study of the Reading Achievement and Certain Characteristics of Adult Males Convicted of Felonies.* Doctor's thesis, Temple University (Philadelphia, Pa.), 1967. (*DA* 28:4279B)

3927. CARDONE, SAMUEL STEVE. *The Effect of Chlorpromazine on the Body Image of Chronic Schizophrenics.* Doctor's thesis, Illinois Institute of Technology (Chicago, Ill.), 1967. (*DA* 28:4291B)

3928. COMPTON, NORMA H. "Body Build, Clothing, and Delinquent Behavior." *J Home Econ* 59:655–9 O '67. *

3929. FEDER, JACK. *An Investigation Into the Relationship Between Vividness of Recall of Early Childhood Experiences, Proximal Sensory Modalities, and Proprioceptive Awareness.* Doctor's thesis, New York University (New York, N.Y.), 1967. (*DA* 28:1188B)

3930. FISH, CAROLINE CHANDLER. *Impulsivity in Culturally Deprived Children.* Doctor's thesis, Boston University (Boston, Mass.), 1967. (*DA* 29:4322A)

3931. GINSBERG, ANIELA MEYER; AZZI, ENZO; AND PIRES, NELSON CAMPOS. "Projective and Experimental Methods in Personality Assessment." *Bulletin de l'Association Internationale de Psychologie Appliquée* 16:52–61 sp '67. * (*PA* 42:752)

3932. GORDON, CAROL M. "Some Effects of Clinician and Patient Personality on Decision Making in a Clinical Setting." *J Consult Psychol* 31:477–80 O '67. * (*PA* 41:16808)

3933. GRAYSON, HENRY TATE, JR. *Psychosexual Conflict in Adolescent Girls Who Experienced Early Parental Loss by Death.* Doctor's thesis, Boston University (Boston, Mass.), 1967. (*DA* 28:2136B)

3934. GREENSPOON, CHARLES D., AND GERSTEN, JOEL. "A New Look at Psychological Testing: Psychological Testing From the Standpoint of a Behaviorist." *Am Psychologist* 22:848–53 O '67. *

3935. HAYASHI, SHUZO. "A Rorschach Study of Identical Twins Discordant for Schizophrenia." *B Osaka Med Sch Sup* 12:192–6 '67. *

3936. KIZU, MASAHARU. "The Personalities of Parents of Schizophrenics With Special Reference to the Rorschach Test." *B Osaka Med Sch Sup* 12:184–91 '67. *

3937. McBROOM, PATRICIA. "The Rorschach Tested." *Sci News* 92:182–3 Ag 12 '67. *

3938. MARTIN, ROBERT M. "Symposium: 'The Role of Experiential Data in Personality Assessment': Introduction." *J Proj Tech & Pers Assess* 31:3 Ag '67. *

3939. MATULEF, NORMAN JAY. *Future Time Perspective and Personality Characteristics of Male Adolescent Delinquents and Non-Delinquents.* Doctor's thesis, Washington University (St. Louis, Mo.), 1967. (*DA* 28:1204B)

3940. MIGDOLE, SAMUEL MARK. *An Investigation of Orality, Depression, and Denial in Obese and Non-Obese Adolescent Females.* Doctor's thesis, Boston University (Boston, Mass.), 1967. (*DA* 29:4850B)

3941. OBERLEDER, MURIEL. "Adapting Current Psychological Techniques for Use in Testing the Aging." *Gerontologist* 7(3, pt 1):188–91 S '67. * (*PA* 42:3801)

3942. OKI, TADAHIKO. "A Psychological Study of Early Childhood Neuroses." *B Osaka Med Sch Sup* 12:344–59 '67. *

3943. OTSUKA, FUMIO. "Rorschach Study of Schizophrenia, With Special Reference to the Problem of Heterogeneity." *B Osaka Med Sch Sup* 12:173–83 '67. *

3944. PEEBLES, RICHARD R. "Telophasic Theory and Depressive Conflict in Adolescent Girls." *Adolescence* 2:359–94 f '67. * (*PA* 42:7119)

3945. PIOTROWSKI, ZYGMUNT A. "Psychological Testing of Intelligence and Personality," pp. 509–30. In *Comprehensive*

Textbook of Psychiatry. Edited by Alfred M. Freedman and Harold I. Kaplan. Baltimore, Md.: Williams & Wilkins Co., 1967. Pp. xxv, 1666. *

3946. STEINMAN, WARREN M. "The Use of Ambiguous Stimuli to Predict General Competence." *J Sci Lab Denison Univ* 48:7–14 Je '67. * (*PA* 42:2590)

3947. STIER, SERENA AUSTER. *Developmental Attainment, Outcome and Symbolic Performance in Schizophrenia.* Doctor's thesis, University of California (Los Angeles, Calif.), 1967. (*DA* 28:4766B)

3948. STRAUSS, ELSA LOVITT. "The Rorschach as an Encounter." *Psychiatric Q Sup* 41:255–61 pt 2 '67. * (*PA* 44:8479)

3949. WATSON, LAWRENCE CRAIG. *The Effect of Urbanization on Socialization Practices and Personality Development in Guajiro Society.* Doctor's thesis, University of California (Los Angeles, Calif.), 1967. (*DA* 28:1327B)

3950. WINTER, GERALD DAVID. *Intelligence, Interest, and Personality Characteristics of a Selected Group of Students: A Description and Comparison of White and Negro Students in a Vocational Rehabilitation Administration Program in Bassick and Harding High Schools, Bridgeport, Connecticut.* Doctor's thesis, Columbia University (New York, N.Y.), 1967. (*DA* 28:4920A)

3951. ANASTASI, ANNE. *Psychological Testing, Third Edition,* pp. 495–9. New York: Macmillan Co., 1968. Pp. xiii, 665. *

3952. ANDERSON, CATHERINE J.; PORRATA, ELENA; LORE, JAMES; ALEXANDER, SHIRLEY; AND MERCER, MARGARET. "A Multidisciplinary Study of Psychogeriatric Patients." *Geriatrics* 23:105–13 F '68. * (*PA* 42:14051)

3953. ARMSTRONG, HUBERT E., JR. "Relationship Between a Dimension of Body Image and Two Measures of Conditioning." *J Consult & Clin Psychol* 32:696–700 D '68. * (*PA* 43:4010)

3954. BECK, SAMUEL J. "The Rorschach Test." *Inter Encycl Social Sci* 12:568–73 '68. *

3955. BOREHAM, JOHN. "An Atypical Depressive Record." *Brit J Proj Psychol & Pers Study* 13:3–6 D '68. *

3956. BRYAN, VINCENT. *The Experimental Induction of Stress in Relation to Field Articulation.* Doctor's thesis, Yeshiva University (New York, N.Y.), 1968. (*DAI* 30:1354B)

3957. CHAPMAN, MARY VERONICA. *Measuring Thought Process as an Ego Function in Schizophrenic, Mentally Retarded and Normal Adolescents by Means of the Rorschach.* Doctor's thesis, University of Southern California (Los Angeles, Calif.), 1968. (*DA* 29:1504B)

3958. CONNOLLY, CHRISTOPHER GEORGE. *The Psychosocial Adjustment of Children With Dyslexia.* Doctor's thesis, Northwestern University (Evanston, Ill.), 1968. (*DA* 29:3456A)

3959. COOPER, SHAWN. *An Exploration of Ego Defense Mechanisms and Related Processes in Clinic and Non-Clinic Families.* Doctor's thesis, University of Massachusetts (Amherst, Mass.), 1968. (*DA* 29:348-8B)

3960. DUDEK, S. Z. "Regression and Creativity: A Comparison of the Rorschach Records of Successful vs. Unsuccessful Painters and Writers." *J Nerv & Mental Dis* 147:535–46 D '68. * (*PA* 43:14264)

3961. DUDEK, S. Z., AND LESTER, E. P. "The Good Child Facade in Chronic Underachievers." *Am J Orthopsychiatry* 38:153–60 Ja '68. * (*PA* 42:17778)

3962. FINNIE, FRANCES RUTH. *The Relationship Between Perceptual Field Articulation and Intellectual Functioning in Paranoid Male Schizophrenics.* Doctor's thesis, George Washington University (Washington, D.C.), 1968.

3963. FRANCIS-WILLIAMS, JESSIE. *Rorschach With Children: A Comparative Study of the Contribution Made by the Rorschach and Other Projective Techniques to Clinical Diagnosis in Work With Children.* London: Pergamon Press Ltd., 1968. Pp. xi, 168. *

3964. FRÖBÄRJ, GÖSTA, AND HOLLEY, JASPER W. "A Q Factor Analysis of Some Rorschach Protocols of Epileptic and Normal Persons." *Psychol Res B* 8(6):1–19 '68. * (*PA* 42:15489)

3965. GADOL, IRWIN. *The Incremental and Predictive Validity of the Rorschach Test in Personality Assessments of Normal, Neurotic and Psychotic Subjects.* Doctor's thesis, Louisiana State University (Baton Rouge, La.), 1968. (*DA* 29:3482B)

3966. GARDNER, RILEY W., AND MORIARTY, ALICE. *Personality Development at Preadolescence: Explorations of Structure Formation.* Seattle, Wash.: University of Washington Press, 1968. Pp. xi, 344. *

3967. HALL, MARIE MABRY, AND HALL, GEORGE C. "Antithetical Ideational Modes of Left Versus Right Unilateral Hemispheric Lesions as Demonstrated in the Rorschach." Abstract. *Proc 76th Ann Conv Am Psychol Assn* 3:657–8 '68. *

3968. HALL, MARIE MABRY; HALL, GEORGE C.; AND LAVOIE, PAUL. "Ideation in Patients With Unilateral or Bilateral Midline Brain Lesions." *J Abn Psychol* 73:526–31 D '68. * (*PA* 43:3524)

3969. HARPER, RANDOLPH THOMAS. *The Influence of Selected Aspects of Cognitive and Affective Development Upon Preferences for Delayed Versus Immediate Gratification.* Doctor's thesis, Ohio State University (Columbus, Ohio), 1968. (*DAI* 30:381B)

3970. KASTL, ALBERT J.; DAROFF, ROBERT B.; AND BLOCKER, W. Webster. "Psychological Testing of Cerebral Malaria Patients." *J Nerv & Mental Dis* 147:553–61 D '68. * (*PA* 43: 14654)

3971. KISSIN, BENJAMIN; ROSENBLATT, SIDNEY M.; AND MACHOVER, SOLOMON. "Prognostic Factors in Alcoholism." *Psychiatric Res Rep Am Psychiatric Assn* 24:22–43 Mr '68. * (*PA* 43:1099)

3972. LARSEN, EILEEN A. *A Pre-Normative and Predictive Study of the College Student Rorschach.* Doctor's thesis, University of Colorado (Boulder, Colo.), 1968. (*DA* 29:2204B)

3973. LERNER, BARBARA. "A New Method of Summarizing Perceptual Accuracy on the Rorschach." *J Proj Tech & Pers Assess* 32:533–6 D '68. * (*PA* 43:9813)

3974. LEVY, MARTIN RAY. *Examiner Bias on the Rorschach Test as a Function of Patients' Socioeconomic Status.* Doctor's thesis, Ohio University (Athens, Ohio), 1968. (*DA* 29:3491B)

3975. LYTTON, H. "Some Psychological and Sociological Characteristics of 'Good' and 'Poor Achievers' (Boys) in Remedial Reading Groups." *Hum Develop* 11(4):260–76 '68. *

3976. MAJUMDAR, P. K., AND MUKERJI, K. "Examination of Certain Rorschach Ratios: A Factorial Study." *Manas* 15:71–8 D '68. * (*PA* 43:11359)

3977. MEAD, MARGARET. *The Mountain Arapesh: Vol. 1, The Record of Unabelin With Rorschach Analyses.* Garden City, N.Y.: Natural History Press, 1968. Pp. xv, 218. *

3978. MOSES, HELEN M. *The Relation of Degree of Autonomy to Degree of Cognitive Expansiveness in Adolescent Girls.* Doctor's thesis, City University of New York (New York, N.Y.), 1968. (*DA* 29:1846B)

3979. MUKERJI, K., AND MAJUMDAR, P. K. "A Comparison of Direct and Projective Method of Personality Assessment." *Manas* 15(1):19–24 '68. * (*PA* 43:11340)

3980. OBERHOLZER, EMIL, JR. "Rorschach—the Man and the Test." *J Proj Tech & Pers Assess* 32:502–8 D '68. * (*PA* 43:9814)

3981. OGDON, DONALD P.; BASS, CAROLYN LEBO; THOMAS, EDWIN R.; AND LORDI, WILLIAM. "Parents of Autistic Children." *Am J Orthopsychiatry* 38:653–8 Jl '68. * (*PA* 43: 17672)

3982. PAL, S. K. "Personality Structure of Engineering Students." *J Psychol Res* 12:136–8 S '68. *

3983. PETERSEN, PAUL A. *The Clinical Utility of Projective Techniques.* Doctor's thesis, Illinois Institute of Technology (Chicago, Ill.), 1968. (*DAI* 30:2913B)

3984. PHELAN, THOMAS W. *Effects of Guardedness and Openness on the Rorschach Performance of Psychiatric Patients.* Master's thesis, Loyola University (Chicago, Ill.), 1968.

3985. PHILLIPS, LESLIE. *Human Adaptation and Its Failures,* pp. 91–6, passim. New York: Academic Press Inc., 1968. Pp. xv, 271. *

3986. PIENAAR, WYNAND D. "Body Awareness in Certain Types of Speech Defective Individuals." *J Proj Tech & Pers Assess* 32:537–41 D '68. * (*PA* 43:10189)

3987. PIOTROWSKI, ZYGMUNT A. "Psychological Test Prediction of Suicide," pp. 198–208. (*PA* 43:7114) In *Suicidal Behaviors: Diagnosis and Management.* Edited by H. L. P. Resnik. Boston, Mass.: Little, Brown & Co., 1968. Pp. xxvii, 536. *

3988. SCHIMEK, J. G. "Cognitive Style and Defenses: A Longitudinal Study of Intellectualization and Field Independence." *J Abn Psychol* 73:575–80 D '68. * (*PA* 43:3996)

3989. SEMEONOFF, BORIS. "The Equivalence of Rorschach and Zulliger's Test in a Selection Context." *Brit J Proj Psychol & Pers Study* 13:11–2 D '68. * (*PA* 46:6949)

3990. SPARE, GERALDINE HALLAM. *A Study of the Law of Enantiadromia, as It Relates to the Attitudes of Introversion-Extraversion.* Doctor's thesis, Washington State University (Pullman, Wash.), 1968. (*DA* 29:1850B)

3991. STARK, STANLEY. "Drama, Inner Creation, and Role-Taking (Empathy): 2, Leadership, Historiography, and Winston Churchill." *Percept & Motor Skills* 27:1263–93 D '68. * (*PA* 43:9699)

3992. STARK, STANLEY. "Toward a Psychology of Knowledge: 6, The Sublime, the Mystical, and the Inner Creative." *Percept & Motor Skills* 27:767–86 D '68. * (*PA* 43:7491)

3993. TALBOT, AMY. *Differences Between Good and Poor Prognosis Schizophrenics in Defensive Behavior, Perceptual Organization, Concept Formation, and Developmental and Social Experiences.* Doctor's thesis, University of Houston (Houston, Tex.), 1968. (*DA* 29:4854B)

3994. TAMARIN, GEORGES R. "Notes on Some Specific Forms of Perseveration in the Rorschach Test." *Israel Ann Psychiatry* 6:143–8 D '68. *

3995. TAYLOR, ANN. "Institutionalized Infants' Concept Formation Test." *Am J Orthopsychiatry* 38:110–5 Ja '68. * (*PA* 42:17003)

3996. THELEN, M. H.; VARBLE, D. L.; AND JOHNSON, JANE. "Attitudes of Academic Clinical Psychologists Toward Projective Techniques." *Am Psychologist* 23:517–21 Jl '68. * (*PA* 42:18843)

3997. TOWNES, BRENDA, AND CHRIST, ADOLPHE E. "Psychological Testing: Its Usefulness in Teaching Psychotherapy and Psychodynamics to Medical Students." *Arch Gen Psychiatry* 19:487–90 O '68. * (*PA* 43:4068)

3998. TRACHTMAN, JOAN P. *Socio-Economic Class Bias in Rorschach Diagnosis: Contributing Psychosocial Attributes of the Clinician.* Doctor's thesis, New York University (New York, N.Y.), 1968. (*DAI* 30:392B)

3999. VAN DE MARK, STEVEN N. *Rorschach and Body Image: Induced Somatic Awareness and Perception of Ink Blots.* Doctor's thesis, University of Kansas (Lawrence, Kan.), 1968. (*DA* 29:2212B)

4000. WHIPPLE, CHARLES M., JR. *The Effect of Short Term Classroom Bibliotherapy on the Personality and Academic Achievement of Reformatory Inmate Students.* Doctor's thesis, University of Oklahoma (Norman, Okla.), 1968. (*DA* 29: 2214B)

4001. WOODRUFF, JAMES WILSON. *The Effect of Degree of Personality Integration as Influenced by Social and Racial Group Membership Upon Adolescent Educational Achievement and Vocational Exploratory Behavior.* Doctor's thesis, Wayne State University (Detroit, Mich.), 1968. (*DAI* 30:145A)

4002. WOODWARD, CHRISTEL ALMA GUNKEL. *Combining Methods of Description in Personality Assessment.* Doctor's thesis, Ohio State University (Columbus, Ohio), 1968. (*DA* 29:1851B)

4003. YARNELL, THOMAS DONALD. *Influence of Mother, Father, and Self Conceptualizations on Choice of Mother, Father, and Self Cards on the Rorschach Test.* Doctor's thesis, Louisiana State University (Baton Rouge, La.), 1968. (*DA* 29:382B)

4004. AGLE, DAVID P.; RATNOFF, OSCAR D.; AND WASMAN, MARVIN. "Conversion Reactions in Autoerythrocyte Sensitization: Their Relationship to the Production of Ecchymoses." *Arch Gen Psychiatry* 20(4):438–47 Ap '69. * (*PA* 43:16121)

4005. ALDRICH, C. KNIGHT. "Experimental Self-Regulated Readdiction to Morphine." *Int J Addic* 4(3):461–70 S '69. *

4006. ALKOFF, THOMAS DAVID. *An Investigation of the Affective Meanings of the Rorschach Inkblot Plates.* Doctor's thesis, Syracuse University (Syracuse, N.Y.), 1969. (*DAI* 30:5682B)

4007. ANDERSEN, DENNIS O., AND SEITZ, FRANK C. "Rorschach Diagnosis of Homosexuality: Schafer's Content Analysis." *J Proj Tech & Pers Assess* 33(5):406–8 O '69. * (*PA* 44:3661)

4008. AZCARATE, EDUARDO. "Body Boundary and Psychological Control in an Arthritic Population." *J Proj Tech & Pers Assess* 33(6):493–500 D '69. * (*PA* 44:7178)

4009. BECK, NORMA, AND HERRON, WILLIAM G. "The Meaning of the Rorschach Cards for Children." *J Proj Tech & Pers Assess* 33(2):150–3 Ap '69. * (*PA* 43:11353)

4010. BELMONT, IRA; BELMONT, LILLIAN; AND BIRCH, HERBERT G. "The Perceptual Organization of Complex Arrays by Educable Mentally Subnormal Children." *J Nerv & Mental Dis* 149(3):241–53 S '69. * (*PA* 44:7170)

4011. BERTRAND, SHARON, AND MASLING, JOSEPH. "Oral Imagery and Alcoholism." *J Abn Psychol* 74(1):50–3 F '69. * (*PA* 43:8470)

4012. BLATT, S. J.; ALLISON, JOEL; AND FEIRSTEIN, ALAN. "Capacity to Cope With Cognitive Complexity." *J Personality* 37(2):269–88 Je '69. *

4013. BOULAY, MAURICE A. "Verbal Reinforcement and Rorschach Productivity." *J Clin Psychol* 25(3):310 Jl '69. * (*PA* 44:3662)

4014. BRODSKY, MARVIN; BREWER, JOHN; VRANA, MARGARET; AND WERGIN, JOHN. "Rorschach Content and Arousal Level." Abstract. *Proc 77th Ann Conv Am Psychol Assn* 4(2):503–4 '69. * (*PA* 44:686)

4015. CAMPO, VERA, AND JUBERT, ELENA NOEMI. "Dissociation and M." *Brit J Proj Psychol & Pers Study* 14(2): 17–22 D '69. * (*PA* 46:5013)

4016. CARDONE, SAMUEL S., AND OLSON, RONALD E. "Chlorpromazine and Body Image: Effects on Chronic Schizophrenics." *Arch Gen Psychiatry* 20(5):576–82 My '69. * (*PA* 43:16118)

4017. CARLSON, RAE. "Rorschach Prediction of Success in Clinical Training: A Second Look." *J Consult & Clin Psychol* 33(6):699–704 D '69. * (*PA* 44:3697)

4018. CARTER, ROSS EDWARD. *Rorschach Signs, Thinking Disorganization, and Withdrawal in Process and Reactive Schizophrenics.* Doctor's thesis, Michigan State University (East Lansing, Mich.), 1969. (*DAI* 31:1531B)

4019. CHAPMAN, LOREN J., AND CHAPMAN, JEAN P. "Illusory Correlation as an Obstacle to the Use of Valid Psychodiagnostic Signs." *J Abn Psychol* 74(3):271–80 Je '69. * (*PA* 43:13004)

4020. COCKING, RODNEY R.; DANA, JEAN M.; AND DANA, RICHARD H. "Six Constructs to Define Rorschach M: A Response." *J Proj Tech & Pers Assess* 33(4):322–3 Ag '69. * (*PA* 44:2371)

4021. COLE, SPURGEON; WILLIAMS, ROBERT L.; AND MOORE, CHARLES H. "Parental Interpretation of Rorschach Cards IV and VII Among Adjusted and Maladjusted Subjects." *J General Psychol* 81(1):131–5 Jl '69. * (*PA* 44:5179)

4022. COOPER, LOWELL. "Motility and Fantasy in Hospitalized Patients." *Percept & Motor Skills* 28(2):525–6 Ap '69. * (*PA* 43:16058)

4023. CUCCIARE, SAMUEL. *The Human Movement Factor of the Rorschach Test as a Predictor of Intelligence.* Master's thesis, University of the Pacific (Stockton, Calif.), 1969.

4024. DAVIDS, ANTHONY; LAFFEY, JOHN J.; AND CARDIN, PAUL J. "Intellectual and Personality Factors in Effective Child Care Workers." *Am J Orthopsychiatry* 39(1):68–76 Ja '69. * (*PA* 45:757)

4025. DUDEK, S. Z. "Intelligence, Psychopathology and Primary Thinking Disorder in Early Schizophrenia." *J Nerv & Mental Dis* 148(5):515–27 My '69. * (*PA* 44:700)

4026. DUDEK, S. Z. "Interaction Testing as a Measure of Therapeutic Change in Groups." *J Proj Tech & Pers Assess* 33(2):127–37 Ap '69. * (*PA* 43:11471)

4027. EXNER, JOHN E., JR. "Rorschach Responses as an Index of Narcissism." *J Proj Tech & Pers Assess* 33(4):324–30 Ag '69. * (*PA* 44:2372)

4028. EXNER, JOHN E., JR. *The Rorschach Systems.* New York: Grune & Stratton, Inc., 1969. Pp. viii, 381. *

4029. FAST, IRENE. "Concrete and Abstract Thought: An Alternative Formulation." *J Proj Tech & Pers Assess* 33(4):331–5 Ag '69. * (*PA* 44:2373)

4030. FISHER, SEYMOUR, AND CLEVELAND, SIDNEY E. "Rejoinder to Hirt and Kurtz' 'A Reexamination of the Relationship Between Body Boundary and Site of Disease.'" *J Abn Psychol* 74(2):144–7 Ap '69. * (*PA* 43:10268)

4031. FISHER, SEYMOUR, AND CLEVELAND, SIDNEY E. "Rejoinder to Mitchell's 'The Body Image Boundary Construct: A Study of the Self-Steering Behavior Syndrome.'" *J Proj Tech & Pers Assess* 33(4):318–21 Ag '69. * (*PA* 44:2657)

4032. FOX, ELIZABETH, AND BLATT, SIDNEY J. "An Attempt to Test Assumptions About Some Indications of Negativism on Psychological Tests." *J Consult & Clin Psychol* 33(3):365–6 Je '69. * (*PA* 43:12965)

4033. GEIST, HAROLD. "Psychological Aspects of Rheumatoid Arthritis." Abstract. *Proc 77th Ann Conv Am Psychol Assn* 4(2):769–70 '69. * (*PA* 44:1156)

4034. GOODMAN, LISL MARBURG. *Perceptual Preferences in Relation to Aspects of Personality.* Doctor's thesis, New School for Social Research (New York, N.Y.), 1969. (*DAI* 31:380B)

4035. GREENBERG, NATHAN. "The Use of the Rorschach Prognostic Rating Scale With Foster-Home Children." *J Proj Tech & Pers Assess* 33(5):451–3 O '69. * (*PA* 44:3663)

4036. GREENBERG, NATHAN; RAMSAY, MARIA; RAKOFF, VIVIAN; AND WEISS, ABRAHAM. "Primary Process Thinking in Myxoedema Psychosis: A Case Study." *Can J Behav Sci* 1(1):60–7 Ja '69. * (*PA* 44:13015)

4037. HARTUNG, JURGEN R.; MCKENNA, SHEILA A.; AND BAXTER, JAMES C. "Test-Taking Attitudes and Rorschach Pathognomic Verbalization." *J Proj Tech & Pers Assess* 33(2):146–9 Ap '69. * (*PA* 43:11356)

4038. HODGE, JAMES R., AND WAGNER, EDWIN E. "The Effect of Trance Depth on Rorschach Responses." *Am J Clin Hyp* 11(4):234–8 Ap '69. * (*PA* 43:14350)

4039. HORN, JOHN L. "The Utility of Projective Techniques and the Function of the Clinical Psychologists." *Mental Hyg* 53(4):654–6 O '69. *

4040. IRIZARRY, RAYMOND. *Anxiety, Repression and Varieties of Anti-Social Behavior in Psychopaths.* Doctor's thesis, Columbia University (New York, N.Y.), 1969. (*DAI* 30:2420B)

4041. IWAWAKI, SABURO; ZAX, MELVIN; AND MITSUOKA, SUSUMU. "Extremity of Response Among Japanese and American Children." *J Social Psychol* 79(2):257–9 D '69. * (*PA* 44:10214)

4042. JAIN, K. S. PRABHACHANDRA. "Measurement of Congruence/Deviation Factor of Personality by Rorschach Content Analysis: A Contribution to Rorschach Methodology." *J General Psychol* 81(2):177–88 O '69. * (*PA* 44:6798)

4043. KAMIL, LEONARD JEFFREY. *Psychodynamic Changes Through Systematic Desensitization.* Doctor's thesis, University of Texas (Austin, Tex.), 1969. (*DAI* 30:5689B)

4044. KAYE, J. D. "Percept Organisation as a Basis for Rorschach Interpretation." *Brit J Proj Psychol & Pers Study* 14(1):7–14 Je '69. * (*PA* 46:5014)

4045. KESSEL, PAUL; HARRIS, JAY E.; AND SLAGLE, SARAH J. "An Associative Technique for Analyzing the Content of Rorschach Test Responses." *Percept & Motor Skills* 29(2):535–40 O '69. * (*PA* 44:3664)

4046. KLOPFER, WALTER G. "Consensus Rorschach in the Primary Classroom." *J Proj Tech & Pers Assess* 33(6):549–52 D '69. * (*PA* 44:6528)

4047. KRIAUCIUNAS, ROMUALDAS. "Rorschach Movement Before and After a Rest." *Percept & Motor Skills* 28(2):586 Ap '69. * (*PA* 43:15845)

4048. LEFCOURT, HERBERT M. "Need for Approval and Threatened Negative Evaluation as Determinants of Expressiveness in a Projective Test." *J Consult & Clin Psychol* 33(1):96–102 F '69. * (*PA* 43:11357)

4049. LEVY, MARTIN R., AND KAHN, MARVIN W. "Interpreter Bias on the Rorschach Test as a Function of Patients' Socioeconomic Status." Abstract. *Proc 77th Ann Conv Am Psychol Assn* 4(2):525–6 '69. * (*PA* 44:864)

4050. LEVY, NISSIM. "Affective Preference for Card IV or VII of the Rorschach as Related to Sex and Age." *Percept & Motor Skills* 28(3):741–2 Je '69. * (*PA* 43:17530)

4051. LICHTENSTEIN, KAREN R. "Anxiety, 'Color Shock,' and Order Effect on Reaction to Inkblots." *J Proj Tech & Pers Assess* 33(4):353–6 Ag '69. * (*PA* 44:2374)

4052. LONG, FRANCIS J., AND KARON, BERTRAM P. "Rorschach Validity as Measured by the Identification of Individual Patients." *J Proj Tech & Pers Assess* 33(1):20–4 F '69. * (*PA* 43:10011)

4053. MAJUMDAR, P. K., AND MUKERJI, K. "Examination of Certain Rorschach Ratios: A Factorial Study With Criminal Population." *Indian J Appl Psychol* 6(2):82–8 Jl '69. *

4054. MANDEL, HARVEY PHILIP. *Validation of Developmental Theory of Psychopathology: Diagnostic Categorization Versus Symptomatology.* Doctor's thesis, Illinois Institute of Technology (Chicago, Ill.), 1969. (*DAI* 30:2911B)

4055. MARCUS, SANDER IRA. *Diagnostic Classification of Alcoholics According to Developmental Theory.* Doctor's thesis, Illinois Institute of Technology (Chicago, Ill.), 1969. (*DAI* 30:2424B)

4056. MARTIN, MICHAEL. *Rorschach Evaluation of Students Having Highly Favorable and Highly Unfavorable Attitudes Toward a Student-Centered Class.* Doctor's thesis, Kansas State Teachers College (Emporia, Kan.), 1969.

4057. MARWIT, SAMUEL J. "Communication of Tester Bias by Means of Modeling." *J Proj Tech & Pers Assess* 33(4):345–52 Ag '69. * (*PA* 44:2375)

4058. MARWIT, SAMUEL JOEL. *An Investigation of the Communication of Tester-Bias by Means of Modeling.* Doctor's thesis, State University of New York (Buffalo, N.Y.), 1969. (*DAI* 30:3390B)

4059. MITCHELL, KENNETH R. "The Body Image Boundary Construct: A Reply to Fisher and Cleveland." *J Proj Tech & Pers Assess* 33(5):470–3 O '69. * (*PA* 44:3665)

4060. MITCHELL, KENNETH R. "The Body Image Boundary Construct: A Study of the Self-Steering Behaviour Syndrome." *J Proj Tech & Pers Assess* 33(4):311–7 Ag '69. * (*PA* 44:2659)

4061. MORRISON, DELMONT, AND CENTERS, LOUISE. "Investigation of the Convergent Validity of Different Measures of Cognitive Style." *J Proj Tech & Pers Assess* 33(2):168–72 Ap '69. * (*PA* 43:11569)

4062. MUKERJI, MAYA. "Rorschach Indices of Love, Aggression and Happiness." *J Proj Tech & Pers Assess* 33(6):526–9 D '69. * (*PA* 44:6800)

4063. MURPHY, RICHARD F., JR., AND DANA, RICHARD H. "Peebles' Rorschach Content Scoring System: Reliability, Normative Data, and Validity." *J Proj Tech & Pers Assess* 33(6):518–25 D '69. * (*PA* 44:6801)

4064. NAIMAN, DORIS WEINKLE. *The Relation of Verbal Language Ability to Psychological Differentiation in the Adult Deaf.* Doctor's thesis, New York University (New York, N.Y.), 1969. (*DAI* 31:2261B)

4065. NELSON, PETER. *Selected Rorschach Response Differences Between Urban and Rural Lower Socio-Economic Class Juvenile Delinquents.* Master's thesis, Central Michigan University (Mt. Pleasant, Mich.), 1969.

4066. NICKERSON, EILEEN T. "Some Correlates of *M.*" *J Proj Tech & Pers Assess* 33(3):203–12 Je '69. * (*PA* 43:14306)

4067. NORMAN, RUSSELL P. "Extreme Response Tendency as a Function of Emotional Adjustment and Stimulus Ambiguity." *J Consult & Clin Psychol* 33(4):406–10 Ag '69. * (*PA* 43:15785)

4068. PIOTROWSKI, ZYGMUNT A. "Long-Term Prognosis in Schizophrenia Based on Rorschach Findings: The LTPTI," pp. 84–103. In *Schizophrenia: Current Concepts and Research.* Edited by D. V. Siva Sankar. Hicksville, N.Y.: PJD Publications Ltd., 1969 Pp. vi, 944. *

4069. RICE, DAVID G.; STERNBACH, RICHARD A.; AND PENN, NOLAN E. "Comparative Diagnostic Judgments From the Rorschach and the MMPI." *J Proj Tech & Pers Assess* 33(3):274–8 Je '69. * (*PA* 43:14334)

4070. ROBERTS, ALAN H., AND ERIKSON, ROBERT V. "Measuring Impulse Control in Institutionalized Delinquents Using Rorschach Content and Thought Process Scales." *J Abn Psychol* 74(5):632–4 O '69. * (*PA* 44:688)

4071. ROSECRANS, C. J., AND SUTTERER, J. R. "Perceptual, Concept Shift, and Personality Test Performance of Matched Psychiatric Outpatient Groups." *J Nerv & Mental Dis* 149(3):254–60 S '69. * (*PA* 44:6879)

4072. RYCHLAK, JOSEPH F., AND BOLAND, GERTRUDE C. "Empirical Cross-Validation of Hermann Rorschach's Theory of Perception." *J Proj Tech & Pers Assess* 33(1):11–9 F '69. * (*PA* 43:9815)

4073. SCHOOLMAN, DAVID A. *Empirical Validity of the Thorne Sex Inventory and Sexual Perceptions on the Rorschach.* Master's thesis, Pennsylvania State University (University Park, Pa.), 1969.

4074. SCHUBERT, JOSEF. "Rorschach Protocols of Asthmatic Boys." *Brit J Proj Psychol & Pers Study* 14(1):16–22 Je '69. * (*PA* 46:5391)

4075. SCHWARTZ, MARK S., AND EWERT, JOSEPHINE C. "A Study of Weiner's Deviant Tempo Rorschach Signs for the Psychodiagnosis of Schizophrenia." *J Clin Psychol* 25(3):308–9 Jl '69. * (*PA* 44:3803)

4076. SHEVRIN, HOWARD; SMITH, WILLIAM H.; AND FRITZLER, DEAN E. "Repressiveness as a Factor in the Subliminal Activation of Brain and Verbal Responses." *J Nerv & Mental Dis* 149(3):261–9 S '69. * (*PA* 44:6310)

4077. SINGER, PAUL R. Chap. 9, "Psychological Testing: Thematic Apperception Test, Rorschach Test, and WAIS

Vocabulary Scale," pp. 110–43. In *The Psychological World of the Teen-Ager: A Study of Normal Adolescent Boys.* By Daniel Offer and others. New York: Basic Books, Inc., Publishers, 1969. Pp. xiv, 286. *

4078. SMITH, WILLIAM H., AND COYLE, F. A., JR. "MMPI and Rorschach Form Level Scores in a Student Population." *J Psychol* 73(1):3–7 S '69. * (*PA* 44:5170)

4079. SPIEGEL, DON, AND KEITH-SPIEGEL, PATRICIA. "Volunteering for a High-Demand, Low-Reward Project: Sex Differences." *J Proj Tech & Pers Assess* 33(6):513–7 D '69. * (*PA* 44:6759)

4080. SPITZER, STEPHEN P. "Test Equivalence of Unstructured Self-Evaluation Instruments." *Sociol Inquiry* 10(2):204–15 sp '69. *

4081. STARK, STANLEY. "Inner Creation in Knower and Known, Observer and Observed, Theorist and Theorized: 2, Illustrations of Anti-Equilibriumism or Dialecticalism in Psychology and Sociology." *Percept & Motor Skills* 28(3):939–56 Je '69. * (*PA* 43:16559)

4082. STARK, STANLEY. "Schachtel's *Metamorphosis*: 1, On the Confounding of Creativity Contexts." *Percept & Motor Skills* 28(2):367–77 Ap '69. * (*PA* 43:15816)

4083. STARK, STANLEY. "Suggestion Regarding *Gemeinschaft*, Inner Creation, and Role-Taking (Empathy): 2, David Bakan on 'Communion and Agency.'" *Psychol Rep* 24(2):611–9 Ap '69. * (*PA* 43:15636)

4084. STARK, STANLEY. "Toward a Psychology of Charisma: 2, The Pathology Viewpoint of James C. Davies." *Psychol Rep* 24(1):88–90 F '69. * (*PA* 43:14296)

4085. STAVRIANOS, BERTHA K., AND LANDSMAN, SYLVIA C. "Personality Patterns of Deficient Readers With Perceptual-Motor Problems." *Psychol Sch* 6(2):109–23 Ap '69. * (*PA* 43:14671)

4086. STEELE, NANCY M., AND KAHN, MARVIN W. "Kinesthesis and the Rorschach *M* Response." *J Proj Tech & Pers Assess* 33(1):5–10 F '69. * (*PA* 43:9816)

4087. SUINN, RICHARD M., AND OSKAMP, STUART. *The Predictive Validity of Projective Measures: A Fifteen-Year Evaluative Review of Research*, pp. 3–58, 117–25. Springfield, Ill.: Charles C Thomas, Publisher, 1969. Pp. xv, 161. *

4088. TALKINGTON, LARRY, AND REED, KATHY. "An Evaluation of Rorschach Indicators of Psychosis With Mentally Retarded." *J Proj Tech & Pers Assess* 33(5):474–5 O '69. * (*PA* 44:3808)

4089. TALKINGTON, LARRY, AND REED, KATHY. "Rorschach Response Patterns of Hearing-Impaired Retardates." *Percept & Motor Skills* 29(2):546 O '69. * (*PA* 44:4055)

4090. TAMKIN, ARTHUR S., AND SONKIN, NATHAN. "Use of Psychological Tests in Differential Diagnosis." *Psychol Rep* 24(2):590 Ap '69. * (*PA* 43:16017)

4091. VAN DE MARK, STEVEN N., AND NEURINGER, CHARLES. "Effect of Physical and Cognitive Somatic Arousal on Rorschach Responses: An Experimental Test of the Assumption That Body Image Influences the Perceptual Organization of Unstructured Stimuli." *J Consult & Clin Psychol* 33(4):458–65 Ag '69. * (*PA* 43:15846)

4092. WAGNER, EDWIN E., AND SLEMBOSKI, CLARENCE A. "Construct Validation of Piotrowski's Interpretation of the Rorschach Shading Response." *J Proj Tech & Pers Assess* 33(4):343–4 Ag '69. * (*PA* 44:2377)

4093. WEBB, PHILIP A. "Rorschach Assessment of Business Executives." *Austral Psychologist* 4(2–3):171–4 N '69. * (*PA* 46:3914)

4094. WILLI, JÜRG. "Joint Rorschach Testing of Partner Relationships." *Family Process* 8(1):64–78 Mr '69. * (*PA* 44:1036)

4095. WOLMAN, RICHARD, AND KEPECS, JOSEPH. "Ego Measurements of Patients and Staff on a Medical Ward." *Comprehen Psychiatry* 10(4):334–40 Jl '69. * (*PA* 44:14852)

4096. WRIGHT, NANCY A., AND ZUBEK, JOHN P. "Relationship Between Perceptual Deprivation Tolerance and Adequacy of Defenses as Measured by the Rorschach." *J Abn Psychol* 74(5):615–7 O '69. * (*PA* 44:689)

4097. ZECHOWY, ALLEN CHARLES. *The Influence of Social Class on the Psychodynamics of Obesity.* Doctor's thesis, State University of New York (Buffalo, N.Y.), 1969. (*DAI* 30:2920B)

4098. ALSTON, LESTER. "Ego Functioning and Memory Style." *J Consult & Clin Psychol* 34(3):348–54 Je '70. * (*PA* 44:13801)

4099. AMES, LOUISE BATES. "Projecting the Future of a Projective Technique." *J Proj Tech & Pers Assess* 34(5):359–65 O '70. * (*PA* 45:4308)

4100. BANIK, SAMBHU N. "Diagnosis of LSD-Induced Psychosis on Rorschach." *Int Congr Rorsch & Other Proj Tech* 7:601–5 '70. *

4101. BARKER, G. B. "Rorschach Study of Young Female Heroin-Dependent Patients." *Int Congr Rorsch & Other Proj Tech* 7:588–600 '70. *

4102. BASIT, A. "Personality Development in Identical and Fraternal Twins." *Int Congr Rorsch & Other Proj Tech* 7:278–85 '70. *

4103. BECK, NORMA. "The Meaning of the Rorschach Cards for Children." *Int Congr Rorsch & Other Proj Tech* 7:264–5 '70. *

4104. BECKER, BRUCE. "The Projective Approach to the

Study of Multiple Personality—A Case Study." *Int Congr Rorsch & Other Proj Tech* 7:423–38 '70. *

4105. BEIZMANN, CECILE. *Handbook for Scorings of Rorschach Responses: After H. Rorschach, S. J. Beck, C. Beizmann, and M. Loosli-Usteri.* Translated by Samuel J. Beck. New York: Grune & Stratton, Inc., 1970. Pp. vii, 244. *

4106. BERRY, JOYCE HAMILTON. *The Rorschach Inkblot Test as an Indication of Empathy.* Doctor's thesis, University of Kentucky (Lexington, Ky.), 1970. (*DAI* 31:4980B)

4107. BERSOFF, DONALD N. "Rorschach Correlates of Traumatic Neurosis of War." *J Proj Tech & Pers Assess* 34(3):194–200 Je '70. * (*PA* 44:18900)

4108. BHAN, RAJNATH. "Social Factors in Creative Potentiality." *Manas* 17(1):21–7 My '70. * (*PA* 46:9064)

4109. BLATT, SIDNEY J. "An Evaluation of Some Methodological Issues in Research With Projective Techniques." *Int Congr Rorsch & Other Proj Tech* 7:120–30 '70. *

4110. BLATT, SIDNEY J.; BAKER, BRUCE L.; AND WEISS, JAY. "Wechsler Object Assembly Subtest and Bodily Concern: A Review and Replication." *J Consult & Clin Psychol* 34(2):269–74 Ap '70. * (*PA* 44:10408)

4111. BOAS, CONRAD VAN EMDE; VAN STEENDEREN, ESTELLA; AND EYGENSTEIN, WILLEM F. "The Value of the Rorschach-Test to Assess Suitability for Therapeutic Abortion." *Int Congr Rorsch & Other Proj Tech* 7:901–6 '70. *

4112. BONDY, MILOS. "Two Cases of Psychiatric Symptoms Following Exposure to the Rorschach." *J Proj Tech & Pers Assess* 34(5):432–4 O '70. * (*PA* 45:4523)

4113. BRAR, HARCHAND S. "Rorschach Content Responses of East Indian Psychiatric Patients." *J Proj Tech & Pers Assess* 34(2): 88–94 Ap '70. * (*PA* 44:16896)

4114. BROEKMANN, NEIL C. "A Psychophysiological Investigation of the Rorschach Colour and Form Determinants." *J Proj Tech & Pers Assess* 34(2):98–103 Ap '70. * (*PA* 44:16722)

4115. CAMPO, VERA, AND RABINOVICH, DIANA. "Review of the Meaning of Shading Responses in the Rorschach." *Int Congr Rorsch & Other Proj Tech* 7:88–94 '70. *

4116. CAMPO, VERA; JACHEVASKY, LUCY; AND PAGOLA, MARTA. "Human Movement Responses and Behavior." *Int Congr Rorsch & Other Proj Tech* 7:711–6 '70. *

4117. CASTELNUOVO-TEDESCO, PIETRO, AND KROUT, BOYD M. "Psychomatic Aspects of Chronic Pelvic Pain." *Psychiatry Med* 1(2):109–26 Ap '70. *

4118. CASTROGIOVANNI, PAOLO; DEL CARLO-GIANNINI, GIULIA; MAFFEI, GIUSEPPE; PASQUINUCCI, PAOLO; LIJTMAER, NORMA; AND ZAMPOLLI, ANTONIO. "Linguistic Analysis of the Responses to the Rorschach Test by Schizophrenics and Neurotics Patients and Their Relatives." *Int Congr Rorsch & Other Proj Tech* 7:733–43 '70. *

4119. COHEN, I.; FLIEGELMAN, S.; GLUCK, Z.; AND KELMAN, D. "Study of Early Differentiation Between Schizophrenia and Psychotic Manifestations in Adolescence." *Israel Ann Psychiatry* 8(2):163–72 Jl '70. *

4120. COONS, W. H., AND PEACOCK, E. P. "Interpersonal Interaction and Personality Change in Group Psychotherapy." *Can Psychiatric Assn J* 15(4):347–55 Ag '70. * (*PA* 44:21108)

4121. CRONBACH, LEE J. *Essentials of Psychological Testing, Third Edition*, pp. 633–7. New York: Harper & Row, Publishers, Inc., 1970. Pp. xxxix, 752. *

4122. DANA, RICHARD H.; COCKING, RODNEY R.; AND DANA, JEAN M. "The Effects of Experience and Training on Accuracy and Configural Analysis." *J Clin Psychol* 26(1):28–32 Ja '70. * (*PA* 44:10456)

4123. DAVIS, ROBERT WM. "Comment on H. S. Brar: Rorschach Content Responses of East Indian Psychiatric Patients." *J Proj Tech & Pers Assess* 34(2):95–7 Ap '70. * (*PA* 44:16897)

4124. DE ANDRADE, L. D. "An Existential Approach to Rorschach—Anatomy Content Responses." *Int Congr Rorsch & Other Proj Tech* 7:976–80 '70. *

4125. DE SLULLITEL, SOFIA I., AND SORRIBAS, ELIZABETH. "The Rorschach Test in a Research on Artists." *Int Congr Rorsch & Other Proj Tech* 7:519–32 '70. *

4126. DOWNING, R. W., AND RICKELS, K. "Patient Personality and Demographic Factors as Predictors of Early Response to Psychotropic Drug Treatment." *Comprehen Psychiatry* 11(6):568–75 N '70. *

4127. DREY-FUCHS, CHRISTEL. "Projective Theory of Rorschach Technique as a Theory of Anxiety Structure." *Int Congr Rorsch & Other Proj Tech* 7:690–701 '70. * (*PA* 45:8260)

4128. DUDEK, S. Z. "The Artist as Person: Generalizations Based on Rorschach Records of Writers and Painters." *J Nerv & Mental Dis* 150(3):232–41 Mr '70. * (*PA* 45:8260)

4129. DUDEK, S. Z. "Effects of Different Types of Therapy on the Personality as a Whole." *J Nerv & Mental Dis* 150(5):329–45 My '70. * (*PA* 46:1275)

4130. EXNER, JOHN E. "Rorschach Manifestation of Narcissism." *Int Congr Rorsch & Other Proj Tech* 7:449–56 '70. *

4131. FARBEROW, NORMAN L.; DARBONNE, ALLEN R.; STEIN, KENNETH; AND HIRSCH, SOPHIE. "Self-Destructive Behavior of Uncooperative Diabetics." *Psychol Rep* 27(3):935–46 D '70. * (*PA* 45:10562)

4132. FAST, IRENE, AND PAWL, JEREE H. "The Sense of

Being Dead and of Dying: Some Perspectives." *J Proj Tech & Pers Assess* 34(3):190–3 Je '70. * (*PA* 44:19017)

4133. FELDMAN, JUDITH. "Selected Rorschach Inkblot Test Determinants in Leadership Studies." *Int Congr Rorsch & Other Proj Tech* 7:184–9 '70. *

4134. FRANCIS-WILLIAMS, JESSIE. "The Use of the Rorschach in the Study of the Personality Development of Cerebral Palsied Children." *Int Congr Rorsch & Other Proj Tech* 7:319–29 '70. *

4135. FROMM, ERIKA; OBERLANDER, MARK I.; AND GRUENEWALD, DORIS. "Perceptual and Cognitive Processes in Different States of Consciousness: The Waking State and Hypnosis." *J Proj Tech & Pers Assess* 34(5):375–87 O '70. * (*PA* 45:3386)

4136. GANZER, VICTOR J.; SARASON, IRWIN G.; GREEN, CAROL T.; AND RINKE, CAROLYN. "Effects of Model's and Observer's Hostility on Rorschach, Interview and Test Performance." *J Proj Tech & Pers Assess* 34(4):302–15 Ag '70. * (*PA* 44:21013)

4137. GINSBERG, ANIELA. "Problems of Validation of Some Projective Methods in Personality Assessment." *Int Congr Rorsch & Other Proj Tech* 7:614–21 '70. *

4138. GOLDFRIED, MARVIN R. "The Use of the Rorschach as a Diagnostic Instrument: Suicide Indicators." *Int Congr Rorsch & Other Proj Tech* 7:907–12 '70. *

4139. GRAUMANN, H. M. "The Rorschach Psychogram: Suggestions for Our Work With the Rorschach Test." *Int Congr Rorsch & Other Proj Tech* 7:702–10 '70. *

4140. GROSSMAN, EDITH KATE. *Effects of Anxiety on Task Performance.* Doctor's thesis, New York University (New York, N.Y.), 1970. (*DAI* 31:4337B)

4141. HALL, MARIE M., AND HALL, GEORGE C. "Antithetical Ideational Modes of Left Versus Right—Unilateral Hemispheric Lesions as Demonstrated in the Rorschach." *Int Congr Rorsch & Other Proj Tech* 7:880–4 '70. *

4142. HARRIS, SANDRA, AND MASLING, JOSEPH. "Examiner Sex, Subject Sex, and Rorschach Productivity." *J Consult & Clin Psychol* 34(1):60–3 F '70. * (*PA* 44:6797)

4143. HARROWER, MOLLY. "Mental Health Potential, as Measured by the Projectives, in Relation to Therapeutic Outcome." *Int Congr Rorsch & Other Proj Tech* 7:817–30 '70. *

4144. HAYS, JAMES RAY. *An Analysis of the Function of Color in the Rorschach.* Doctor's thesis, University of Georgia (Athens, Ga.), 1970. (*DAI* 31:4994B)

4145. HERDT, BERYL F. "The Human Movement Factor (M) in the Rorschach, Motor Activity, and Behavior." *J Motor Behav* 2(2):134–9 Je '70. *

4146. HERSEN, MICHEL. "Sexual Aspects of Rorschach Administration." *J Proj Tech & Pers Assess* 34(2):104–5 Ap '70. * (*PA* 44:16902)

4147. HERTZ, MARGUERITE R. *Frequency Tables for Scoring Rorschach Responses: Code Charts, Normal and Rare Details, F+ and F— Responses, and Popular Responses, Original Responses,* Fifth Edition. Cleveland, Ohio: The Press of Case Western Reserve University, 1970. Pp. ix, 274. *

4148. HIRSCH, ERNEST A. *The Troubled Adolescent: As He Emerges From Psychological Tests.* New York: International Universities Press, Inc., 1970. Pp. xv, 645. *

4149. HOLLEY, JASPER W. "The Methodology of Rorschach Validation." *Int Congr Rorsch & Other Proj Tech* 7:682–9 '70. *

4150. HUIZINGA, RALEIGH J. "The Individual Testing Situation as a Two-Person Group: The Role of Interactional Variables on Performance and Test Interpretation." *Int Congr Rorsch & Other Proj Tech* 7:150–5 '70. *

4151. ISRAEL, HOWARD MARK. *A Measurement of Affect Discrimination: A Validational Study.* Doctor's thesis, University of Montana (Missoula, Mont.), 1970. (*DAI* 31:2282B)

4152. JACKLI, ERNST. "Rocheck/Convert: A Program System for Quantitative Analysis and Documentation of Rorschach-Test Data." *Computer Progr Biomed* 1(1):23–35 Ja '70. *

4153. JONES, KENNETH J., AND JONES, PRISCILLA P. "Contribution of the Rorschach to Description of Personality Structure Defined by Several Objective Tests." *Psychol Rep* 26(1):35–45 F '70. * (*PA* 45:4281)

4154. JUBANY, HELENA. "Rorschach Study of a Colour Blindness Case." *Int Congr Rorsch & Other Proj Tech* 7:407–17 '70. *

4155. KALTER, NEIL, AND MARSDEN, GERALD. "Response Productivity in Rorschach Research: A Caution on Method." *J Proj Tech & Pers Assess* 34(1):10–5 F '70. * (*PA* 44:8477)

4156. KAMIL, LEONARD J. "Psychodynamic Changes Through Systematic Desensitization." *J Abn Psychol* 76(2):199–205 O '70. * (*PA* 45:4419)

4157. KAPLAN, MARVIN L.; COLARELLI, NICK J.; GROSS, RUTH BRILL; LEVENTHAL, DONALD B.; AND SIEGAL, SAUL M. *The Structural Approach to Psychological Testing.* New York: Pergamon Press, Inc., 1970. Pp. xi, 195. *

4158. KARON, BERTRAM P., AND O'GRADY, PAUL. "Quantified Judgments of Mental Health from the Rorschach, TAT, and Clinical Status Interview by Means of a Scaling Technique." *J Consult & Clin Psychol* 34(2):229–35 Ap '70. * (*PA* 44:10723)

4159. KATAGUCHI, YASUFUMI. Chap. 3, "The Comparison Between Rorschach Series and Ka-Ro Series," pp. 39–48,

passim. In *Psychology: Manual for Ka-Ro Inkblot Test.* Tokyo, Japan: Kaneko Shobo Publisher, 1970. Pp. 157. *

4160. KEMPLER, HYMAN L., AND SCOTT, VALORIE. "Can Systematically Scored Thematic Stories Reflect the Attributes of the Antisocial Child Syndrome?" *J Proj Tech & Pers Assess* 34(3):204–11 Je '70. * (*PA* 44:18911)

4161. KLATSKIN, ETHELYN H., AND ERON, LEONARD D. "Projective Test Content During Pregnancy and Postpartum Adjustment." *Psychosom Med* 32(5):487–94 S–O '70. *

4162. KUNKE, TH. "Rorschach Investigations in Cases of Change of Sex." *Int Congr Rorsch & Other Proj Tech* 7:798–806 '70. *

4163. LANDIS, BERNARD. "Ego Boundaries." *Psychol Issues* 6(4):1–178 '70. *

4164. LANDIS, BERNARD. "Rorschach Assessment of Ego Boundary Permeability-Impermeability." *Int Congr Rorsch & Other Proj Tech* 7:131–43 '70. *

4165. LESTER, DAVID. "Attempts to Predict Suicidal Risk Using Psychological Tests." *Psychol B* 74(1):1–17 Jl '70. * (*PA* 44:16905)

4166. LEVY, MARTIN R. "Issues in the Personality Assessment of Lower-Class Patients." *J Proj Tech & Pers Assess* 34(1):6–9 F '70. * (*PA* 44:8467)

4167. LEVY, MARTIN R., AND KAHN, MARVIN W. "Interpreter Bias on the Rorschach Test as a Function of Patients' Socioeconomic Status." *J Proj Tech & Pers Assess* 34(2):106–12 Ap '70. * (*PA* 44:16906)

4168. LEWINSOHN, PETER M.; FLIPPO, JOSEPH R.; AND BERGQUIST, WILLIAM H. "Leveling-Sharpening: Its Relation to Repression-Sensitization and Memory." *Psychol Rep* 27(1):211–4 Ag '70. * (*PA* 45:6290)

4169. LYONS, JOSEPH. "Existentialism and the Rorschach." *Int Congr Rorsch & Other Proj Tech* 7:981–4 '70. *

4170. MACCOBY, MICHAEL, AND FOSTER, GEORGE M. "Methods of Studying Mexican Peasant Personality: Rorschach, TAT, and Dreams." *Anthropol Q* 43(4):225–42 O '70. *

4171. McCULLY, ROBERT S. "Archetypal Qualities Underlying the Rorschach Experience." *Int Congr Rorsch & Other Proj Tech* 7:30–9 '70. *

4172. MARINKOV, MILICA; BERGER, JOSIP; AND STOJANOVIĆ, LJUBINKA. "The Validity of an Additional Testing Procedure With the Rorschach Technique." *Int Congr Rorsch & Other Proj Tech* 7:717–20 '70. *

4173. MARSDEN, GERALD. "Intelligence and the Rorschach Whole Response." *J Proj Tech & Pers Assess* 34(6):470–6 D '70. * (*PA* 45:7873)

4174. MITCHELL, KENNETH R. "The Body Image Barrier Variable and Level of Adjustment to Stress Induced by Severe Physical Disability." *J Clin Psychol* 26(1):49–52 Ja '70. * (*PA* 44:10980)

4175. MURAWSKI, BENJAMIN J., AND JONES, KENNETH J. "Correlation of Somatic, Biochemical, Perceptual, and Rorschach Data on 40 Healthy Male Subjects." *Psychophysiol* 6(6):61–72 My '70. * (*PA* 45:5584)

4176. MURSTEIN, BERNARD I., AND WOLF, STEVEN R. "An Empirical Test of the 'Levels' Hypothesis With Five Projective Techniques." *Int Congr Rorsch & Other Proj Tech* 7:558–72 '70. *

4177. MURSTEIN, BERNARD I., AND WOLF, STEVEN R. "Empirical Test of the 'Levels' Hypothesis With Five Projective Techniques." *J Abn Psychol* 75(1):38–44 F '70. * (*PA* 44:6794)

4178. OBERLANDER, MARK I.; GRUENEWALD, DORIS; AND FROMM, ERIKA. "Content and Structural Characteristics of Thought Processes During Hypnosis." Abstract. *Proc 78th Ann Conv Am Psychol Assn* 5(2):843–4 '70. * (*PA* 44:17853)

4179. ORNITZ, HILDA WANE. *A Developmental Study of Errors of Commission in Recall.* Doctor's thesis, City University of New York (New York, N.Y.), 1970. (*DAI* 31:3711B)

4180. PIOTROWSKI, ZYGMUNT A. "Mutual Dependency of Theory and Technique in Projective Personality Tests." *Int Congr Rorsch & Other Proj Tech* 7:25–9 '70. *

4181. POGGIALI, BRUNO, AND MARCHESCHI, MARA. "The Rorschach Test in the Psychotic Disorders of Mentally Retarded Children." *Int Congr Rorsch & Other Proj Tech* 7:343–8 '70. *

4182. PROLA, MAX. "A Re-evaluation of the Motor Inhibition: Fantasy Hypothesis." *J Proj Tech & Pers Assess* 34(6):477–83 D '70. * (*PA* 45:8257)

4183. REISMAN, JOHN M. "The Effect of a Direct Inquiry on Rorschach Scores." *J Proj Tech & Pers Assess* 34(5):388–90 O '70. * (*PA* 45:4309)

4184. SCHMEIDLER, GERTRUDE R., AND LeSHAN, LAWRENCE. "An Aspect of Body Image Related to ESP Scores." *J Am Soc Psychical Res* 64(2):211–8 Ap '70. * (*PA* 44:15604)

4185. SCHUBERT, JOSEF. "The Diagnostic Significance of Changes in Rorschach Scores After Testing the Limits." *Brit J Proj Psychol & Pers Study* 15(1):3–11 Je '70. *

4186. SCOTT, BEATRICE. "Intelligence and Rorschach Patterns of Response." *Int Congr Rorsch & Other Proj Tech* 7:105–19 '70. *

4187. SEIM, SOL. "The Teenagers Grow Up." *Int Congr Rorsch & Other Proj Tech* 7:387–98 '70. *

4188. SELVINI-PALAZZOLI, MARA. "Anorexia Nervosa—A New Rorschach Scoring Enhances the Understanding of the

Syndrome." *Int Congr Rorsch & Other Proj Tech* 7:894–900 '70. *

4189. SILVEIRA, ANÍBAL. "Impulsiveness and Ways of Mastering It: Rorschach Data With 100 Adults." *Int Congr Rorsch & Other Proj Tech* 7:479–93 '70. *

4190. SLOANE, PATRICIA. "Art and Art Token in Tests Involving Art Evaluation." *Psychol Rec* 20(2):191–6 sp '70. * (*PA* 45:2366)

4191. SLOANE, PATRICIA. "The Ink Blot Test, 'Psychodiagnostics' and Hermann Rorschach's Aesthetic Views." *J Aesthetics & Art Criticism* 29(1):105–19 f '70. * (*PA* 45:4310)

4192. STERNE, SPENCER B. "Some Indices of the Passive Aggressive Personality Constellation as Reflected in the Rorschach Protocols of One Hundred Male Juvenile Delinquents." *Int Congr Rorsch & Other Proj Tech* 7:494–501 '70. *

4193. STRAUSS, MILTON E., AND MARWIT, SAMUEL J. "Expectancy Effects in Rorschach Testing." Abstract. *J Consult & Clin Psychol* 34(3):448 Je '70. * (*PA* 44:14648)

4194. STRICKER, GEORGE. "The Rorschach as an Index of Organic Brain Damage." *Int Congr Rorsch & Other Proj Tech* 7:921–5 '70. *

4195. STUCKI, M. E. "Rorschach's Ambiequals and Abstractionists." *Int Congr Rorsch & Other Proj Tech* 7:514–8 '70. *

4196. TEDFORD, W. H., JR., AND LAKE, ALVIN E., III. "Influence of Stimulus Symmetry on the Movement Response." *J Proj Tech & Pers Assess* 34(1):16–8 F '70. * (*PA* 44:8474)

4197. TOLOR, ALEXANDER, AND JALOWIEC, JOHN E. "Body Boundary, Parental Attitudes and Internal-External Expectancy." *Int Congr Rorsch & Other Proj Tech* 7:144–9 '70. *

4198. WAGNER, EDWIN E. "Results of Psychological Testing on a Child With Gilles De La Tourette's Disease." *J Clin Psychol* 26(1):52–7 Ja '70. * (*PA* 44:10955)

4199. WAGNER, EDWIN E., AND HOOVER, THOMAS O. "Intra-Protocol Plate Failures: An Investigation of Rorschach Card Meaning." *J Proj Tech & Pers Assess* 34(6):484–6 D '70. * (*PA* 45:8512)

4200. WEINER, IRVING B. "Rorschach Diagnosis of Schizophrenia: Empirical Validation." *Int Congr Rorsch & Other Proj Tech* 7:913–20 '70. *

4201. WEISS, A. A. "Frequency of 'Primary Process' Responses on the Rorschach Test in Non-Clinical Subjects." *Israel Ann Psychiatry* 8(1):81–6 Ap '70. *

4202. WEISS, LILLIE, AND MASLING, JOSEPH. "Further Validation of a Rorschach Measure of Oral Imagery: A Study of Six Clinical Groups." *J Abn Psychol* 76(1):83–7 Ag '70. * (*PA* 44:21185)

4203. WOO-SAM, JAMES M.; ROGAL, RICHARD A.; AND ZIMMERMAN, IRLA LEE. "Influence of MMPI and Rorschach Indices of Hypochondriasis on the Rehabilitation of Brain-Injured Adults." Abstract. *Proc 78th Ann Conv Am Psychol Assn* 5(2):721–2 '70. * (*PA* 44:19166)

4204. YEN, YI-SHIU. "On the Modified Bias." *Acta Psychologica Taiwanica* 12:101–11 Mr '70. * (*PA* 45:8513)

ALVIN G. BURSTEIN, *Professor of Psychology and Chief of the Division, The University of Texas Medical School, San Antonio, Texas.*

There is a certain irony in the fact that two psychiatrists, Rorschach and Wolpe, have revolutionized—or at least radicalized—American clinical psychology, and in ways that are not only inconsistent with the basic theoretical orientation of the innovator but also diametrically opposed to each other. Hermann Rorschach's experiment, devised in a non-dynamic, structuralist tradition, was to become the darling of the Freudian set, while Wolpe, ultimately committed to molar psychological behavior as an epiphenomenon of biological events, popularized a purely psychological, though anti-dynamic, approach to behavior alteration.

Recent years have not been kind to Rorschach's test—in part for reasons that might be regarded as scientific and in part for reasons which are basically sociocultural. The test's initial popularity as a diagnostic device and the patterns of role collaborations among phy-

sicians and paramedical personnel led to the test's being highly identified with the practice of clinical psychology. As psychological practitioners began to invade the domains of psychotherapy and social planning, diagnostic testing in general, and its paradigm, Rorschach's test, began to generate feelings similar to those of a first generation offspring toward his immigrant parent, the reminder of an embarrassing past. And since, in our culture, fees and salary levels are so directly tied to fashion, financial differentials added fuel to this social evolution.

The urge to disaffiliate has gained further urgency from the scientific critics. As the canons of scientific research purified and laboratory procedures became more stringent, increasing doubt—particularly for the past 20 years—has been cast on almost all diagnostic procedures. Such doubt has more recently extended to traditional psychotherapeutic proceedings and soon, perhaps, will be extended to the social manipulations of the newest look in psychological practitioners.

It is an operational truism that no psychological test can be considered except as defined by the stimuli used, the procedures followed, and the scores developed. Nevertheless, much of what has been written about Rorschach's test overlooks this elementary point.

Polemic exchanges about the virtue of projective techniques are familiar to all psychologists. As suggested above, their tone suggests generational conflict or religious warfare rather than scientific difference; my opinion is that psychology's involvement with projective techniques and with the Rorschach will be a function of the extent to which the field comes to view itself as objective and behavior oriented or mind and experience oriented. If the quality and content of human experience and consciousness remain a legitimate concern of psychology, then projective techniques, including the Rorschach, will be elaborated as legitimate devices for scientific and therapeutic use.

While the bulk of the criticism directed at Rorschach's test is ideological, some has been methodological and concerned with making hopefully constructive alterations in the nature of the stimulus or in the procedures followed. Thus, a series of "neo-Rorschachs" has developed, including such examples as *Harrower's Multiple Choice Test,* the *Holtzman Inkblot Test,* the *Structured-Objective Rorschach Test,* the Concept Evaluation Technique, and the

Consensus Rorschach. While the neo-Rorschachs constitute an important and interesting field, the focus of this review will be on Rorschach's test, defined as the conventional series of cards to which the patient is asked to respond in an unstructured fashion and whose associations are later explored by means of an inquiry. Even this limiting convention leaves play in the definition of the test in that scoring procedures vary considerably. The most widely used of the conventional systems are those of Beck, Klopfer, and Schafer and Rapaport; basic familiarity with these conventional systems is assumed for the purpose of the review. Unfortunately, common practice in some settings is to substitute for formal scoring a system of impressionistic reaction. Therefore, I shall make another limiting convention, that the protocol is then systematically scored in the tradition of Beck et al.

A review of the basic scoring systems reveals multiple inconsistencies and confusions, defects which occur across systems and with which various writers have attempted to deal. The central purpose of this review will be to describe these defects and the proposed remedies.

As most readers will be aware, basic Rorschach scoring is done in three components: the location score, the determinant score, and the content score. Beyond these three components, note is sometimes made of qualitative aspects of the response, such as its degree of originality, confused quality, etc. These components are basically those suggested by Hermann Rorschach, and an important historical factor is that they were developed largely in isolation from dynamic, motivationally oriented personality theory. Perhaps the most serious scientific limitation of the Rorschach as a personality test is that it was not linked in its conception to a comprehensive theory of personality. The most notable attempt to remedy this defect is the work of Holt on the primary process rating scale. This scale, currently in experimental form, is viewed as a supplement to conventional scoring systems. It involves an attempt to rate the patient's responses in terms generated by psychoanalytic theory, namely the nature or level of the impulse, the intensity of "raw" drive involved (defense demand), and effectiveness of the defense deployed against drive (defense effectiveness). These ratings are based on qualitative aspects of the content of

patient's response, and more will be said about this system in the section on content scoring.

The initial component of conventional Rorschach scoring systems, the location score, serves two purposes. It identifies the locus of the response to facilitate further scoring—for example, of form level—that may be location specific, and it also is intended to reflect a specific psychological process. With respect to this second purpose, the location score is highly suspect in that it confounds two variables, the complexity of the stimulus used and the rarity with which the stimulus is used. While these are not entirely unrelated, they are logically (and interpretively) quite distinct. Assigning the conventional interpretive meaning of integrative ability and/or ambition to the very common instant whole responses is unwarranted, just as is overlooking the integrative effort involved in complex detail responses. Rapaport (3707) attempted to deal with this problem by developing a finer typology of W scorings; Mayman's (3600) form-level ratings represent a more recent attempt. Both appear to be excellent beginnings. For reasons mentioned, simple tabulations of W% or of ratio of whole to non-whole responses are not likely to have meaning. It is probably essential to retain the localizing potential of this score, but it would be very helpful to develop independent ways of noting the rarity of the stimulus utilized and its complexity. Beck makes an effort in this direction with his organization score but continues to rely on a highly confounded location variable.

An additional use of the location score is to note whether white space has been utilized in the response. The importance of noting the white space responses is a function of the presumptive relationship between reversal of figure-ground relationships and psychological traits of oppositionality, innovativeness, etc. Yet, scoring systems commonly fail to distinguish between the use of white space involving figure-ground reversal from the use of white space as an elaboration of a commonly perceived figure.

The incoherence which characterizes location scoring is also reflected in the determinant sector. The scoring of determinants is a highly complex issue which cannot be exhaustively discussed in this review, but a few illustrative difficulties can be presented. The presumed purpose of the determinant scoring is to note the ways in which the patient justifies his response and the appropriateness of his justification or of the content of his response. The first is reflected in the nature of the determinant (form, color, shading, etc.), the latter in the so-called form level. The form-level issue brings us to the first of difficulties we shall discuss. It is clearly questionable to restrict the judgment of appropriateness to form dominated percepts or—as in the case of the F+% or Lambda scores—to pure form percepts. Attempts to rectify these limitations are those of the extended F+% of Schafer and the B+% of Lerner (3496). These are but partial remedies; what is needed are separate systems of evaluating appropriateness of content and appropriateness of justification, given content.

A second difficulty related to form scores is that two distinct types of justification tend to be noted as F responses. The first category includes those responses in which the patient makes explicit reference to articulation, contour, or extension in space. The prototype of the second category is that response in which the patient says "it just looks like it." It is apparent that widely different psychosocial processes are reflected in the two categories and to score them additively is a major error.

A third issue in the determinant sector has to do with a blurring of the basis of determinant scoring, which sometimes reflects the aspects of the stimulus thought by the examiner to determine the response, sometimes the justification by the response adduced by the patient, and sometimes the patient's elaboration of the nature of the percept. Scoring determinants in the first way is probably simply an error. On the other hand, it is probably important to note systematically, in ways currently not provided for, the degree to which the patient tends to offer justifications (utilizing form, color, chiaroscuro), as opposed to elaborating and sharing his experience (utilizing perspective, movement, texture).

Many additional questions about determinant scoring could be explored, but limitations of space preclude doing more at this time than simply noting that fact.

Scoring of content, too, is highly problematic. A very complete review of this area is available by Draguns et al. (3572, 3584, 3673), and no attempt will be made here to duplicate or summarize their excellent and stimulating work. Rather, note will simply be taken that numerous attempts to develop quantitative estimates of various psychological processes have been undertaken. These efforts have moved well beyond the early content scoring, which involved little more than categorization by the examiner (for example H%, A%, etc.). Spivack and Levine's (3302) work on repressive activity is of interest, though it seems to reflect a highly simplified view of repression. It yields a simple score reflecting the patient's access to affectively saturated material, but not the flexibility of that access. Fisher and Cleveland (2409) have attempted to view the content of Rorschach responses from the point of view of body-image theory and have developed barrier and penetration scores, which may be related to cognitive styles. Singer (3520) has developed a system of scoring communication defects in schizophrenics which is of interest and may be generalizable. Most ambitious has been the attempt of Holt (2645, 3481) to develop his primary process scoring system. This would appear to be a system of great sensitivity and promise, but one which requires considerable effort to learn and use and which Holt regards as being still in the experimental phase.

Basically, content scoring seems to involve two issues: (a) identifying the type of object(s) toward which the patient orients himself in the environment and in terms of which he seeks gratification and (b) identifying the style in which the recognition procedure occurs, noting, for example, whether it is affectively rich, highly systematized, carefully checked, etc. Conceptually, many aspects of the recognition process would be captured in the determinant sector of the scoring, and an artificial barrier between this aspect of the two sectors is misleading.

Given the almost ramshackle status of Rorschach scoring and the lack of stability, coherence, and unanimity about personality theory, it is a tribute to the vigor of the core notion that the test has survived. The view that recognition, the act of construing an unfamiliar stimulus, taps central components of personality function is one that will remain crucial in any psychology committed to the understanding of human experience. Further use of the Rorschach, or of some derivative or related task, will await a worker with the ingenuity and patience to redo in a theoretically sophisticated and scientifically adequate fashion our system of noting the behavior.

JOHN F. KNUTSON, *Assistant Professor of Psychology, The University of Iowa, Iowa City, Iowa.*

A review of a test for *The Mental Measurements Yearbook* is somewhat unique since the review is typically preceded by several reviews in earlier Yearbooks. When preparing a review of a previously reviewed test, it is a reasonable strategy to attempt to complement the material made available in earlier reviews. Based upon such a premise, the present article is an attempt to offer the reader a brief examination of those data which reflect upon previous Rorschach reviews as well as to enumerate instances of innovative efforts with the instrument occurring since the last series of reviews.

An examination of past MMY Rorschach reviews yields an indication of a general trend within clinical psychology to consider the Rorschach in an increasingly negative fashion. In the Third MMY, both Rorschach reviewers noted inadequacies in Rorschach research and knowledge; yet in a vein of optimism, Wittenborn indicated that the Rorschach was the most promising method for evaluating personality, and Krugman concluded that the Rorschach was "the most important single psychological instrument for the measurement of personality." The Fourth MMY review presented a similar opinion. Sargent acknowledged the paucity of validity data but hoped improved research methodology and refined criteria measures would contribute support for the Rorschach technique. The Fifth MMY reviews presented far less unanimity than those of the preceding volumes and reflected the rather marked disagreement developing among psychologists with respect to the use of the Rorschach. Beck concerned himself with the differing systems of Rorschach analysis and McCall anticipated the possibility of a content analysis of the Rorschach based upon an integration of clinical methods and research. Eysenck, however, noted that the methodological improvements which characterized later Rorschach research were associated with increasingly negative results. Recognizing similar trends, Shaffer asked how long an instrument or a method can stay promising in the face of extensive negative evidence. In the last MMY, Dana suggested that the era of the Rorschach *as a test* was over. Eron asserted that the Rorschach, when considered as a structured interview, has considerable clinical value and that a rigorous

empirically-based content analysis would result in support for this widely used clinical instrument. In that same volume, Jensen seemed to voice the attitude of a growing number of psychologists when he concluded, "Meanwhile, the rate of scientific progress in clinical psychology might well be measured by the speed and thoroughness with which it gets over the Rorschach."

Six years have passed and psychology has not gotten over the Rorschach. Several of the recently published books on the Rorschach demonstrate the continued interest in and variety of approaches to this technique. A number of these books reflect a commitment to empirical considerations of the Rorschach.

Zubin, Eron, and Schumer (*3437*) offer a unique contribution to the analysis of the Rorschach. Their work presents an unusually rigorous and empirically-based approach emphasizing the scoring and interpretation of the content of the subjects' responses. Molish [1] indicated that this book might offer an optimistic position during an era of dwindling support for the Rorschach. Unfortunately, this book does not seem to have exerted any major influence upon the Rorschach research literature. It would be difficult to assess its influence upon the clinical uses of the Rorschach; however, the Zubin, Eron, and Schumer scales are unlikely to receive frequent use in clinical settings because of the complicated and lengthy scoring procedure. Levine and Spivack (*3030*) presented an empirically derived Rorschach scale. Their monograph deals with a Rorschach scale designed to assess proneness to repress and is worth examination by those interested in the projective assessment of repression. Thomas and others have authored two large volumes (*3425, 3872*) of Rorschach responses by medical students. Although these are interesting reference works, the restricted population included in these books may seriously limit their value.

These books may all be contrasted with several recently published works which lack this research emphasis. *Rorschach With Children* by Francis-Williams (*3963*) and a second edition by Beck and Molish (*3555*) are dominated by case studies and, with all the weaknesses inherent in single case descriptions, do little to clarify the generally poor picture

1 MOLISH, H. BARRY. "Doubtless There Are Other Paths." *J Proj Tech & Pers Assess* 31:3-6 D '67. *

of Rorschach validity research. Similarly, Schachtel's (3516) blending of phenomenology and psychoanalysis in an attempt to understand Rorschach's test not only lacks sufficient empirically established data but is unlikely to evolve in an empirical direction. Thus, all the Rorschach positions, from empirical researcher to advocates of subjective interpretation, have been represented by recent books.

Although the general picture of the Rorschach has not changed markedly during the past six years, some indication of differences in use can be found in the literature. Modifications in the use of the Rorschach as a psychological instrument may reflect changes in research on the instrument itself, changes in clinical psychology, or a subtle blending of both. Recent trends in clinical psychology would seem likely to result in a marked decrement in the use of the Rorschach. Breger [2] has suggested that psychological test results do not determine the treatment programs which might be used with a patient. He also indicated that the use of lengthy test batteries might actually be detrimental to therapeutic progress.

The Rorschach's primary clinical use has centered on diagnostic procedures. With a decreased emphasis on diagnosis and serious questions regarding testing in general, it is unlikely that the Rorschach will fare well in a general reduction in testing. The increasing use of therapy techniques based upon learning principles [3] may hasten the trend toward a decreasing use of the Rorschach, as well as of other tests. Treatment programs which incorporate testing but minimize the emphasis upon underlying dynamics and deeper personality characteristics are also likely to contribute to a decrease in Rorschach usage.

While these trends seem readily apparent, it is interesting to note a semblance of recent support for the use of the Rorschach (and projective techniques in general) from some unlikely quarters. Greenspoon and Gersten (3934), considering psychological testing from a behaviorist's position, hypothesized Rorschach variables which might predict responsivity to specific contingencies of reinforcement in an operant conditioning program. They suggested the form level of the Rorschach record might

discriminate those patients who would benefit from the self-control procedures discussed in the behavior modification literature. Although the role of reinforcement in the Rorschach test situation has been considered (2676), the possibility of the Rorschach's playing a role in operant behavior modification remains speculative.

Following the decision-theory model of Cronbach and Gleser,[4] Fulkerson (3879) discussed how projective techniques, and specifically the Rorschach, could be considered by means of the decision-theory parameters of value, uncertainty, and risk. The Fulkerson model is unique, since it attempts to account for both subject and examiner behavior with exactly the same theoretical parameters, a strategy rarely taken by the more popular Rorschach systems. Frequently, users of the Rorschach have criticized research on it on the grounds that the research has not accurately paralleled the true clinical use of the instrument. This decision-theory model of the Rorschach seems to offer a reasonable attempt to assess the actual behaviors of the subject in the Rorschach situation and of the clinician then and during subsequent interpretations. The Rorschach is not the only instrument which has been discussed from the decision-theory model. Arthur [5] has advocated supplanting the diagnostic model with a decision model of testing. If such an approach receives widespread support, then Fulkerson's approach may result in a new direction in Rorschach research.

In a sense, the variety of administrative and scoring systems precludes any possibility of discussing the Rorschach. Exner's book (4028) offers an explication of the five major Rorschach scoring systems, those of Beck, Klopfer, Piotrowski, Rapaport and Schafer, and Hertz. A book for acquainting students with the characteristics of the various systems, it could also serve as a reference book to reacquaint Rorschach users with the different ways a single response might be scored and interpreted. This systematic comparison underscores the degree of uncertainty in clinical Rorschach interpretation.

In spite of administrative, scoring, and interpretive differences, there has been some

2 BREGER, LOUIS. "Psychological Testing: Treatment and Research Implications." *J Consult & Clin Psychol* 32:176–81 Ap '68. *
3 LEVIS, DONALD J., EDITOR. *Learning Approaches to Therapeutic Behavior Change.* Chicago, Ill.: Aldine Publishing Co., 1970. Pp. 280.

4 CRONBACH, LEE J., AND GLESER, GOLDINE C. *Psychological Tests and Personnel Decisions.* Urbana, Ill.: University of Illinois Press, 1957. Pp. x, 165. *
5 ARTHUR, A. Z. "Diagnostic Testing and the New Alternatives." *Psychol B* 72(3):187–92 S '69. *

commonality among the various Rorschach systems. Within the past six years several research articles have raised questions regarding some of these widely practiced procedures and interpretations. Huberman (*3357*) reports three studies which led him to question whether testing the limits reflects an extension of the performance proper, and he speculated that behavior during testing the limits is more likely related to a willingness to accept suggestions from others, especially those in authority. Perceptual accuracy in most systems has been based upon the extent to which the form of the percept is the primary determinant of the response, but Lerner (*3973*) has presented support for the inclusion of all form determinants, including form even if it is not a primary determinant. Acceptance of this procedure would result in radical changes in all systems of Rorschach interpretations.

Many additional articles present data which question frequently practiced clinical procedures. Validity of card III as an index of sexual identification has been questioned (*3477*), as has the concept of the universal sex role of animal responses frequently included in psychoanalytic Rorschach interpretation (*3581*). References to the "mother card" (VII) and "father card" (IV) abound in the literature and clinical reports, but this too has been seriously questioned (*3608*). Research on color preferences should cause Rorschach users to reexamine the validity of interpretations based on the presence or absence of color determinants in the Rorschach record (*3499, 3566*). In short, within the past six years more questions have been raised regarding Rorschach interpretation.

Early research and clinical use in the area of the Rorschach were consistent with the original projective test hypothesis [6] that the response of the subject was primarily determined by his unique personality. Gradually, more importance has been accorded to the eliciting stimuli, and several studies have dealt with the manipulation or consideration of the stimulus value of the Rorschach and how this stimulus value determines the response (*2251*). Recent articles have continued to consider the role of the stimulus in determining the response, demonstrating the importance of the complexity of the Rorschach stimuli (*3552*) and how the stimulus may be modified (*3460, 3630*). A more important trend

6 FRANK, LAWRENCE K. "Projective Methods for the Study of Personality." *J Psychol* 8:389–413 O '39. *

in the literature is the large number of studies which have attempted to alter Rorschach responding by manipulating situation variables. Magnussen (*3607*) demonstrated that Rorschachs administered after the Draw-an-Animal Test (DAA) and the *Children's Apperception Test* (CAT) resulted in significantly more animal responses than Rorschachs administered prior to the DAA and the CAT. A comparable study completed with adults achieved similar results; Rorschach tests which followed a draw-a-person test and the *Thematic Apperception Test* resulted in a significantly greater number of human responses than Rorschachs which preceded the DAP and the TAT (*3310*). These data strongly suggest that the items included in a test battery and their order of presentation can exert a powerful influence on Rorschach performance.

That the examiner influences the responses of the subject in the Rorschach test situation has long been recognized in the literature, and the journals are replete with articles on the effect of examiner differences upon subjects' scores (e.g., *982, 1079, 1344, 1525*). This area of concern in Rorschach research has continued. In an interesting study, Masling (*3385*) trained graduate students in a quick course in the Rorschach and then indicated to half of the students that "experienced" Rorschach examiners obtain more human content than animal content. The other half of the group of students were told that "experienced" examiners get more animal content than human content. These students then administered Rorschachs to undergraduate volunteers and each group obtained a H:A relationship consistent with the indoctrination it had experienced. Careful analysis of the students' verbal behavior did not reveal the source of these differences and the author suggested that examiners influenced the subjects via postural, gestural, and facial cues. These data have serious implications when multiplicity of graduate student Rorschach indoctrination is considered. The specific training of Rorschach examiners could be contributing an inordinately large amount of variance to the test situation. The fact that systematic Rorschach scoring errors have been associated with examiner differences reflected in specific scale elevations on the *Edwards Personal Preference Scale* compounds this problem (*3539*).

Another article which poses a serious question with respect to the interpretative validity of the Rorschach demonstrated that a Rorschach record labeled as one produced by a subject from a low socioeconomic group received an interpretation of more pathology and poorer prognosis than the same record with a middle class label (*4167*). The fact that experienced Rorschachers also displayed the same interpretation bias, although less frequently than novices, should increase concern about the clinical utility of Rorschach-determined prognoses.

Strauss (*3735*) seemed distressed that Rorschach trainees ignored test data and wrote reports primarily on the basis of anamnestic pretest information. Results of other studies suggest that the trainees might have been on firm ground. A factor analytic Rorschach study resulted in a Rorschach scale factor which correlated significantly with outcome data on a large number of patients but was not as good a predictor as such demographic data as marital status, religion, length of time in the service, and length of previous hospitalizations (*3462*). If readily available demographic variables predict as well or better than the Rorschach indices, then these indices are superfluous.

As already noted, several previous reviews have suggested that the emphasis in Rorschach interpretation should be shifted from the formal determinants to the actual contents of the response. Indeed, Klopfer (*3689*) suggests that content scoring has predictive value far beyond the formal scoring procedures. The approach of Zubin, Eron, and Schumer (*3437*) places such an emphasis, but, as I have noted, the long-term impact of that work is yet unknown. The content literature has been reviewed extensively in three successive articles considering traditional, nontraditional, and theoretical formulations of Rorschach content (*3572, 3584, 3673*). These reviews covered the research rather thoroughly but they were too uncritical of many of the articles cited. In fact, an article which they singled out as "a model for the exploration of the interpretative significance attributed to specific contents" was the article which gave impetus to Lykken's examination [7] of methodological problems in psychology. Several other recent reviews within the Rorschach literature assume a rather benign position with respect to the reviewed research. Frequently, after noting a series of conflicting, non-replicated or methodologically inadequate experiments, a review author will conclude that, although it is not supported, there is no reason *not* to include the Rorschach in a test battery (e.g., *3390*). Taking such positions has probably been instrumental in maintaining the low quality of Rorschach research and probably has fostered many invalid clinical interpretations.

In 1964 Lebovits,[8] in support of projective techniques and in response to critics of them, said that the critics had based their positions upon studies which included (*a*) poorly worded hypotheses, (*b*) inadequate subject populations and clinicians without adequately described backgrounds, and (*c*) basic methodological weaknesses. It seems totally inappropriate to support the use of an instrument without adequate validity research because the negative results studies are poor. A series of recent articles which might be considered supportive of the use of the Rorschach display the same errors that Lebovits sees as characterizing the studies in the Rorschach detractor's bibliography.

Finn and Neuringer (*3677*) noted the equivocal nature of the research relating white space responding to oppositional characteristics. After demonstrating that left-handed subjects show more white space responses than right-handed subjects, the authors concluded that they had demonstrated that left-handed subjects were more oppositional! Equally unsupported conclusions were made in two attempts to relate Rorschach responses to creativity (*3625, 3708*) These articles identified Rorschach determinants associated with artists engaged in teaching. In addition to ignoring possible training contributions and background differences and using a rather pedestrian control procedure, the authors developed conclusions which are not consistent with their data. Showing that teaching artists give more whole (W) responses does not lend much support to the use of W in the prediction of creativity. Similarly, an article purporting to demonstrate the validity of the Rorschach Prognostic Rating Scale establishes only that it correlated significantly with ratings by psychiatrists and social workers (*3647*). No statements were made with respect to the later behavior of the patients, which would be a far more relevant criterion for prognostic scales. In comparing the diagnostic judgments based upon the MMPI and Rorschach, Rice, Sternbach, and Penr

7 LYKKEN, DAVID T. "Statistical Significance in Psychological Research." *Psychol B* 70:151-9 S '68. *

8 LEBOVITS, BINYAMIN Z. "On Empty Bathtubs: A Reply to Meehl." *J Proj Tech & Pers Assess* 28:307-13 S '64. *

(*4069*) noted how often there was concurrence between the two instruments, but when the tests differed, primacy was accorded the Rorschach. Using only three clinicians, these authors concluded that the results were representative because the clinicians had been trained in different geographical locations and were employed in different settings. Although this article is likely to be accorded a position supporting the Rorschach, it suffers from as major a sampling error as any anti-Rorschach article. All these articles, potentially considered as supporting the use of the Rorschach, display serious errors.

In an attempt to establish "clinical" validation of the Rorschach, Long and Karon (*4052*) demonstrated that a well-trained Rorschach trainee could correctly qualify 9 out of 13 male and 6 out of 16 female patients. Unfortunately, none of the salient features of the procedure are explicated. The probability of this study being replicated is severely diminished by such poor exposition.

Neuringer (*3390*) had suggested that in the interest of preventing suicide, a level of significance more liberal than .05 be used in assessing suicide signs on the Rorschach! This rather erroneous position has been aptly criticized by Lester (*4165*). Such research "liberalism" has a tendency to occur with considerable frequency in the Rorschach literature and has contributed considerably to the poor quality of Rorschach research.

Kalter and Marsden (*4155*) recently noted that corrections for response productivity have resulted in erroneous conclusions in many widely accepted journal articles supporting Rorschach use in specific interpretations. These authors concluded that Cronbach's 1949 statement suggesting that 90 percent of the Rorschach conclusions were unsubstantiated because of unsound analyses is equally appropriate today.

Psychologists who support the use of the Rorschach are regularly confronted with such negative data or demonstrations that results previously considered to be sound are no longer acceptable. Some proponents continue to assert that there is a strong need for this instrument in the assessment of personality (*3589, 3603, 3612, 3632*), while others seem to be looking for innovations which will serve to resurrect the technique. Molish [1] hoped for a "coalescence between the subjectivists and the so-called super-objectivists." The approach of Zubin,

Eron, and Schumer (*3437*) might be his answer. Other innovations have included attempts at computerized Rorschachs (*3287*) and the use of the contagious Poisson distribution to deal more effectively with Rorschach scores (*3605*). The consensus Rorschach is a recent attempt to salvage the Rorschach. This approach can involve a number of variations about the theme of administering the Rorschach to a group of subjects and getting consensus responses to each card (*3271, 3275, 3667, 4046*). The consensus Rorschach is a logical consequence, consistent with an increasing emphasis upon group processes and family therapy. Unfortunately, the literature has produced primarily position papers supplemented with a few case studies. These papers will not be sufficient to blunt the continuing attack by the Rorschach's critics, and unless empirical support of the consensus Rorschach is forthcoming, it will not improve the Rorschach's position.

There are two indices to the future of the Rorschach, current trends in its use, and provisions for training in the Rorschach technique. Through 1965, the use of the Rorschach as a research instrument had been declining in frequency at an irregular rate which was slightly faster than the decline in use of projective techniques in general.[9] There is no reason to believe that the rate of Rorschach use in research will not continue to decline. Clinically, however, the Rorschach has been and still is a widely used instrument. In American Psychological Association-approved internship facilities, the clinical directors saw the importance of the Rorschach second only to the Wechsler scales.[10] These directors noted, however, that the interns were displaying a waning interest in the Rorschach and displayed less preparation when they arrived for their internship than had the interns of previous years. A survey of Rorschach teaching (*3483*) noted the enormous variation in both course work and practica associated with the Rorschach at APA-approved graduate programs in clinical psychology. At training institutions, students are primarily exposed to literature, rather than to clinical use.

9 CRENSHAW, DAVID A.; BOHN, SUZANNE; HOFFMAN, MARLENE R.; MATHEUS, JOHN M.; AND OFFENBACH, STEFAN G. "The Use of Projective Methods in Research: 1947–1965." *J Proj Tech & Pers Assess* 32:3–9 F '68. *
MILLS, DAVID H. "The Research Use of Projective Techniques: A Seventeen Year Survey." *J Proj Tech & Pers Assess* 29:513–5 D '65. *
10 McCULLY, ROBERT S. "Current Attitudes About Projective Techniques in APA Approved Internship Training Centers." *J Proj Tech & Pers Assess* 29:271–80 S '65. *

Perhaps these students are becoming increasingly negative toward the Rorschach. A more recent study (3996) lends support to that position by demonstrating that academic clinicians show declining interest in the Rorschach and indicate that current research does not support its use. Interestingly, academic clinicians who have done research on the projectives do not support the Rorschach technique more than academic clinicians who have not done research in the area. The Thelen et al. study also noted that only 43 percent of the academic clinicians felt the Rorschach was important for the practicing clinician. Although 86 percent of the clinical directors in the McCully study supported its use, continued waning interest in the Rorschach among the new young clinicians is a reasonable prediction.

The Rorschach has continued to be characterized by numerous systems and an overwhelming amount of negative research. The current prediction is that Rorschach use will follow a gradual but accelerating decline in the next decade. Although six additional years of negative research have not cooled the ardor of the Rorschach supporter, decreasing emphasis in diagnostic testing in psychology and a lack of training in the area of the Rorschach among an increasing number of clinicians will cause this decline. The protest of the clinical user is to be expected, but surely if the Rorschach were instrumental clinically, some positive research analogues would have been produced by now.

CHARLES C. McARTHUR, *Psychologist to the University Health Services, Harvard University, Boston, Massachusetts.*

The Rorschach asks the most open-ended question devised by man: "What can you see in these inkblots even though both of us know there is nothing there?" Faced with so ill-defined a problem, the examinee can take any number of task sets. In the end he must do some intellectual work—to generate a series of images—but meanwhile he displays all sorts of social and autonomic self-expression. Everything he does and says is recorded.

Of each of the images he reports, there are four things we can always say: (a) The response uses all or some part of the blot; (b) it uses one or more properties of the blot, like form, color, or shading; (c) it uses some class of content, like human, animal, or thing; and (d) it is a picture seen by other people commonly or rarely. These four aspects of each substantive response must later be systematically labelled and so they are targets of an inquiry and then of some testing of the limits of the respondent's ability to use each of these kinds of evidence.

Interpretations of the Rorschach are simply observant descriptions of the patterns of perceptual, cognitive, emotional, and social strategies the subject used in coping with the situation and the task. Available constructs facilitate exegesis of the record, but in the end, analysis shows what forces elicit from him the styles of responses and hence implies the interactions in life that are likely to elicit similar patterns of response from him. Behavior predicts behavior.

NOT A "MEASURE." Rorschach began by talking about "this experiment." The Rorschach is not a "test," in the sense of "tests and measures." It is a behavior sample—a standardized sample, however. It was Rorschach's stroke of genius to perceive that inkblots could give us a standard task in which very, very many aspects of the person were engaged all at once, even in one response. Of all the instruments the psychologist uses to pick up signals from another man's personality, the Rorschach is the instrument that has the broadest band. It is the richest behavior sample we know how to collect. We never know in advance what we will find in it, but we always find a lot that is of value. In a technology full of tests "of" some one dimension, only the Rorschach allows us to watch another person in full flight.

It seems too bad that the systematic categorizing of the four inevitable aspects of each Rorschach response has come to be called "scoring." These labels are clinical shorthands, not names of test scores. These four kinds of categories are only part of the Rorschach. Both in the clinic and whenever research hypotheses are tested, the data include diction, gesture, changes of pace, or autonomic signs (2705). A Rorschach is a slice of total behavior.

Paradoxically, a literature has grown up around the "psychometrics" of this nontest. To review the pseudo-psychometric literature is justifiable only because, pained as we are at how badly current psychometric models fit what goes on during a Rorschach experiment, we yet dare to hope that one day we may be offered less shoddy models from the mathematicians' shelf.

FREQUENCY DISTRIBUTIONS. Rorschach "scores" persistently occur with frequencies that do not generate any of the psychometrically fashionable distributions. The normal curve is not the one they follow, nor can they be made to fit it by any of the usual arithmetic transformations.

The writer (*3605*) has recently shown that frequencies of Rorschach symbols may follow one of the many "contagious Poisson" distributions. (Simple Poisson formulae ordinarily do not give a good fit.) In terms of probability theory, the corresponding urn model would be one in which when a black ball is drawn, two are replaced. It is too soon to tell if this finding will stand up. If it does, it could imply auto-contagion, individual differences in proneness to each kind of response, or differing rates of emission from a potential store of such responses. If this should be the generating function of Rorschach frequencies, we are not justified in doing usual psychometrics, perhaps not even in using Pearson's *r*.

RELIABILITY. Many studies—see past reviews and, more recently, Schimek (*3714*) and Voigt (*3313*)—have shown that test-retest reliability varies widely from "score" to "score," often showing values of .80 or .90—higher than commonly found in objective tests—but sometimes showing values as low as .00. The low reliabilities are usually artifacts of the rare occurrence of the symbol in question (C, for example), but so can the high ones be! However, high reliabilities are also found for categories that occur often enough to give meaning to the index. The old (*795*) criticism that these reliabilities result from the partial correlation of each "score" with total response number does not apply: when we control for response number, the reliabilities go up.

Split-half reliability is not intended to exist in the Rorschach experiment, each blot being a distinctive stimulus. However, odd-even reliabilities can also be seen to be very high or very low.

It is difficult to know what reliability coefficients are supposed to mean, not just in view of the dubious applicability of correlation coefficients but because of the Rorschach rules of succession. An examinee who gave three W responses to a blot on first testing and three W followed by two D on retesting could be assigned a reliability coefficient of 1.00! This because on both occasions he was going down the track of the same regular succession. There was a reliable sequence in which his apples fell off the bough. In short, the problem of "reproducibility" of the Rorschach is not adequately handled by any "reliability coefficient." Perhaps Guttman scaling contains the seeds of an appropriate mathematical model—unless, of course, the order in which the respondent did things got reversed by satiation. Retesting after a short interval may evoke a test set of "To be creative, I'll have to think of something different." This phenomenon is known in the TAT.

Interscorer reliability is surely more apropos. When thoroughly trained, scorers consistently reach 95 percent agreement. Reliable scoring (or interpretation) can never be attained if the judges are not given sufficient information. That is why Rorschachers must conduct a clever and patient inquiry. The lack of proper inquiry is the source of unreliability that destroys all forms of group Rorschach tests.

A potentially more serious fault of the Rorschach is suggested by the very few articles that show low inter-interpreter reliability. Jensen (6:237) has a shrewd suggestion: "They do not seem to be shooting at the same targets." In so rich a behavior sample, different observers may well extract different parts of the data, blind-men-and-the-elephant fashion.

FACTOR STRUCTURE. Rorschach scores are cited by Guilford[1] as prize instances of "When Not to Factor Analyze." His moral is that psychologists should not "apply a gimcrack transformation and then go ahead and factor." Instead he recommends that they "do not factor at all," lest they add to "the number of misuses of factor analysis that are appearing from time to time in published articles." His reason is the inapplicability to Rorschach (and to the Strong, the Kuder, the MMPI, etc.) of Pearson's *r*.

But psychometrists go on factoring the Rorschach. They then conclude that the Rorschach is not "really" structured as its theory says (though inspection of their own data may give this conclusion the lie) and that the Rorschach is "merely" a test of response number. The latter result they attain by failing to heed Cronbach's (*795*) warning not to include *R* unwittingly in other percents and indices. A more reasoned position is taken by Wittenborn (*1058*) but he, too, fails to take the basic step

[1] GUILFORD, J. P. "When Not to Factor Analyze." *Psychol B* 49:26–37 Ja '52. *

of factoring within approach, within determinants, etc., which has never been done.

PROBLEMS OF VALIDATION. What the Rorschach offers is "a means not only for appraising capacity, both intellectual and emotional, but for analyzing the way in which capacity is used in problem-solving, in adaptation, and in control of thinking and impulse" (Sargent, 4:117).

Everything else is second-order inference—diagnostic labels, for example. They are administrative predictions and require a knowledge of the thinking process of the doctor who does the diagnosis. Psychiatric labels are notoriously unreliable. They are not given directly by the Rorschach experiment.

"Validation" studies have for the most part used just such predictions of administrative outcome as criteria. The results have been very mixed, with positive findings more often occurring when the experiment (a) entered the world of the examinee rather than trusting to a regression equation, (b) was done by Rorschachers who were old pros, (c) used the Rorschach as part of a battery, and (d) made more use of the determinants than of the contents. Negative findings more often arose when (a) simplistic categories and simplistic scores had been used, (b) the criterion to be predicted was administrative, (c) content was used exclusively or primarily, (d) the criterion was itself less reliable and valid than the Rorschach (outcome of therapy being a prize instance), and (e) the criterion was a wastebasket word: organicity, schizophrenia, homosexuality. Above all, negative findings have been caused by poor theoretical linking between the Rorschach and the criterion.

In an earlier review, Dana (6:237) pointed out that "our research subculture has stereotyped the kinds of questions which may be legitimately asked." The Rorschach experiment is not a simple-minded VAR(M-N) problem. Therefore, it has been often (Jensen, 6:237; Eysenck, 5:154; McCall, 5:154) drummed out of all science!

Which seems a shame in an era when we are beginning to be able to hope for mathematical models that do not contort our observations. No one has tried crude but contemporary models like information theory. The Rorschach is as "redundant" as a Mozart melody. Rorschach succession is more intricate than a Markov chain but it is not too complex an idea for mathematical psychology that the same act is not the same act when it is preceded by and followed by differing acts. Perhaps each examinee could be characterized by a transformation matrix—and this matrix would come nearer to speaking to the man's "conditions for behaving this way or that way" rules than has any statistic yet tried. Surely the respondent's choice of options for his next response can be modeled by some kind of decision theory. The difficulties that respondents have with Card IX look very like the kind of troubles information theory predicts with a "filtering" task. Is color shock measurable as filtering? Or maybe the Rorschach problem is yet more abstruse; the mathematics of an experiment that allows people to act like folks ought not to be simple.

RORSCHACH THEORY. The richness of the data available in even an ill-conducted inkblot experiment has encouraged non-Rorschach theorists to co-opt the Rorschach as their own. To its detriment. Thus, Rorschach theory is *not* psychoanalytical, and recent distortions by those who "interpret" only content show the vice of so narrow a theory. The Rorschach is *not* a projective test. The projective mechanism occurs in only one kind of response. Nor is Lindzey (*3835*) correct in calling it an associative procedure. Above all, it is not psychometric, nor even a *measure*. Recent American Zeitgeist has led to the usage of labeling the Rorschach as "The Rorschach Test" and has thus erected for the delight of the captious a straw man easy to knock down.

Past reviewers have complained that the Rorschach is based on its own special theory, which it is, and that that theory lies outside of general psychology, which it does not. A much-needed updating of good Rorschach theorizing has been provided by Schachtel (*3516*) in his *Experiential Foundations of Rorschach's Test*. Schachtel delineates the hundreds of ways that the Rorschach taps the perceiving of the examinee and so reveals in different people different relatedness to objects, which is to say, to their world. To describe how a man handles his worldful of experience is precisely the task of the inkblot experiment.

A thing never said—perhaps because both Rorschachers and psychometrists make the false assumption that the other man understands what is to them obvious—is that there is an irreconcilable difference between procedures which assume one or more dimensions to be known and procedures which seek to discover what dimensions exist. Psychometricians assume they know; clinicians assume they know not. This is the Ur-ground of their conflict and the issue that remains unexamined in a mountainous literature. The Rorschach and the TAT (except as bowdlerized by McClelland) are the only techniques in all of psychology (unless one includes Kelly's Rep Test) that take as their goal to discover what, in fact, the relevant dimensions for understanding John Jones may be, given the common sense assumption that John Jones does not obey the laws that govern Abel Harriman. The Rorschach is unique among psychological techniques in that it takes seriously the mission of entering John Jones's and Abel Harriman's worlds. Few psychologists and no psychometrists nowadays feel that this operation matters. But it is the only satisfaction in practising psychology.

CURRENT STATUS. Despite wistful pronunciamentos to the contrary (*3937*), the Rorschach was at last count [2] second only to the TAT as a research tool, with all other choices bad also-rans. The variety of its applications and misapplications is wondrous: since the last MMY, it has been applied to facial disfigurement, reading disability, gang rape, shamanism, children on a holiday, murderers, married couples, left-handers, and Athenians, to name a few. We may regret to see so much research on group differences and so little on deeper issues. There still is none of the personality psychology for which Beck used to plead, in which the unit counted is the person.

The Rorschach is also used daily in clinics— perhaps still, as an earlier reviewer (McCall, 5:154) estimated, a million times a year.

The mystery of why the Rorschach will not die has baffled psychometrically oriented reviewers for years. Is it because Rorschachers don't read the literature? (They do.) Is it an instance of the madness of crowds? (McCall, 5:154) (We hope not!) The best answer is to be found in having the Rorschach experience. You can't beat something with nothing. What "test" lets us get to know a man, live and functioning? To make his acquaintance? To see him operate? Well, to a lesser degree, the TAT. The Wechsler, to a small extent, and it is symptomatic of testers' hunger to sample full-blooded behavior that they stretch their

2 CRENSHAW, DAVID A.; BOHN, SUZANNE; HOFFMAN, MARLENE R.; MATHEUS, JOHN M.; AND OFFENBACH, STEFAN G. "The Use of Projective Methods in Research: 1947–1965." *J Proj Tech & Pers Assess* 32:3–9 F '68.*

Wechsler data far beyond its natural elasticity to try to make it yield inferences well beyond those its scores provide. By contrast, measurements "of" something limit our getting-acquainted process to an exchange of formalities. Our need to be able to observe a broad band of the person's behavior still leads us back to the Rorschach.

It is the only game in town.

SUMMARY. The rich sample of patterned interactions among a man's perceptual, cognitive, emotional, and social sides that appears in even one Rorschach response is neither matched nor approximated by any other psychological tool. The Rorschach is not really a measure; it is a behavior sample. Its psychometrics have not yet been properly examined; we may hope that contemporary mathematical psychology will provide better models than psychometrics have. Its validation has been against a wild variety of group differences, seldom against appropriate psychodynamic variables, never in studies in which the person was the unit. Results have been as various as the criteria employed. Yet the Rorschach continues to be one of the modal tools used both in the clinic and in research, probably for a simple reason: if the examiner wants a broadband spectrum of the examinee's response patterns, the Rorschach is the only tool now in existence that receives so many messages. It is not better than its competitors; no competitive tool has ever been invented.

ALBERT I. RABIN, *Professor of Psychology, Michigan State University, East Lansing, Michigan.*

There can be little doubt that research productivity with the Rorschach method has dropped off in recent years. An examination of the bibliographies in *Personality Tests and Reviews* and of the tables of contents of the more clinically oriented journals would support this impression.

The importance of the Rorschach as a discipline to be taught to clinicians is not uniformly high in the opinion of teachers of clinical psychology (*3996*). Although 43 percent think it is "very important" that students be taught the method, 43 percent feel that it is of "some" importance while 8 and 4 percent consider it of "little" and "no" importance, respectively.

However, when one looks at these attitudes in the broader context of valuation of different clinical activities, it appears that the relatively reduced esteem in which the Rorschach is held is part of the decline of diagnosis as an important clinical area. Psychodiagnosis rates fourth in importance (next to theory, research, and psychotherapy) as a field of training and activity among university-based clinicians.

Reasons for this reduced interest in diagnosis have been recently reviewed by Holt (3707) and need not be further documented in this context. Suffice it to say that, at least in part, the reduced activity in the Rorschach field is a function of the overall lesser concern of clinicians with diagnostic testing. They have been "investing their libido" in a variety of other activities such as individual and group psychotherapy, community mental health, and others.

Despite the foregoing, there is a good deal of evidence that the vitality of the Rorschach as a clinical and research instrument has not diminished tremendously. The numerous publications that cannot, of course, all be reviewed in our limited space attest to this fact. Although even workers in the field (3720) admit that the method is "old fashioned and unsophisticated either psychometrically or in relation to personality theory," it nevertheless continues to stimulate research, much of it on higher levels both psychometrically and theoretically. It must be admitted, however, that some of the reports continue to be pedestrian and unimaginative. The trend is away from the research use of the Rorschach as a diagnostic instrument of the "total personality" (wide band) to greater concentration upon the adoption of the method (3706) for purposes of "narrow band" investigation of limited numbers of variables.[1]

Some attempts to deal with the Rorschach as a "test," with its psychometric characteristics and with the validity of individual variables, continue to appear in the literature (3577). The "long-range stability of selected Rorschach scores," based on examinations of a group of subjects at ages 10, 14, 17, and 24 (3714), is reported. The results show "a significant and consistent stability of all of the main categories after age 14." This assessment is based on product-moment correlations. Ratings of intellectualization obtained from the Rorschach also

tend to remain stable from childhood to adulthood (3988).

Studies of individual Rorschach determinants have also produced some validating data. Thus, for example, when W is not just counted and is not related to general intelligence but is scored by means of Friedman's (946) qualitative scoring system, it shows that its level of complexity is related to problem-solving efficiency (3220, 3334). The movement response (M) continues to interest numerous researchers. According to Fisher's review (3577) in 1967, "over 15 studies have been undertaken to test the hypothesis that M is increased by conditions that intensify muscular inhibition. The majority have supported Rorschach's view" (p. 166). By now, the count has increased (3568, 3593). Support for additional hypotheses concerning the meaning of M has also been given in more recently published reports (3670, 3674). Moreover, a recent study (3219) even lends support to the relationship between experience balance (M:C ratio) and the introversion-extroversion dichotomy, as originally hypothesized by Rorschach.

Although the color variables (C, CF, FC) have fared less well at the hands of researchers, a reinterpretation (3577) of a previously published critical review (2961) of the color response yields the conclusion that "two out of three" studies tend to confirm the link between C and CF, and impulsivity. The "box score" may be enhanced by some additional findings (3659, 3749). The shading response has also received some recent attention (3345, 3660).

Thus, despite the advice of Eron (6:237) and others (3437) that the Rorschach not be considered as a perceptual method, workers in the field have not entirely abandoned the enterprise. The work with individual perceptual variables is apparently not altogether without dividends, as noted above.

Various sign approaches continue to be employed. Klopfer's Prognostic Rating Scale (based on M, FM, m, Shading, Color, and Form Level) continues to predict psychotherapeutic outcome successfully (2970, 3243). Similarly, an index "based on ego psychological conceptualization of an optimal personality picture" was employed with the Kelly and Fiske data obtained from trainees in clinical psychology (4017). This measure turned out to be more effective in predicting success in clinical training than the more successful pre-

---

[1] LEVINE, DAVID. Chap. 17, "Why and When to Test: The Social Context of Psychological Testing," pp. 553–80. In *Projective Techniques in Personality Assessment: A Modern Introduction.* Edited by A. I. Rabin. New York: Springer Publishing Co., Inc., 1968. Pp. x, 638. *

dictors reported in the original Kelly and Fiske study. A good deal of activity in the quest for empirical score combinations for the purpose of differential diagnosis may still be noted (*3572*). In this "pigeonholing" activity (*3707*) the Rorschach does not seem to be worse off than some of the more popular "objective" methods (*4090*). It is seriously questioned whether this classificatory preoccupation is the primary goal of the clinician and whether the aim is not really the production of a "verbal model of personality" (*3707*) which will ensue in the understanding of the individual. Thus, clinician *cum* technique, rather than the method alone, is intertwined in the diagnostic process (see Dana's review, 6:237).

Much of current Rorschach work is involved in testing specific hypotheses. An example of this trend is the series of studies concerned with oral imagery and its relationships to several disorders (*3611, 3698, 4011, 4202*). By using Rorschach content classified as representing dependency or sadistic trends, the investigators were able to confirm a number of psychodynamic hypotheses. Complete coverage of the efforts in this category is beyond the scope of this review.

Among the flourishing fields of research activity are the extensions of the use of the Rorschach beyond the diagnosis of the "total personality." The proliferation of studies of the Fisher and Cleveland "barrier" and "penetration" scores (*2409*) is one such example (*3577*). A convincing demonstration of the "effects of physical and cognitive somatic arousal on Rorschach responses" was recently reported by Van De Mark and Neuringer (*4091*).

Holt's method (*3481, 3707*) has stimulated numerous studies in which primary process thinking and defensiveness are reported with clinical groups and in different experimental settings. Recent examples are uses of his system in successfully predicting tolerance for perceptual deprivation (*3894, 4096*).

A most recent development is the study of group processes by means of the Consensus Rorschach (*3655, 3658, 3667, 3676, 3721, 3748*). Klopfer notes (*3691*) that this development represents a "resurrection" of the Rorschach as a clinical instrument "for purposes that fit the current mores of clinical psychology."

Some recent statistical developments in the treatment of Rorschach data may be noted in the work of several investigators (*3355, 3588, 3964*). Validation of the psychometric use of the method is demonstrated in some of these papers.

Before closing this brief review, a comment about the three reviews in the last MMY is in order. These reviews represent a wide spectrum of opinion and reflect different models of the human personality. On the one extreme, the "danger" of the continued clinical use of the Rorschach was stressed (Jensen), while on the other, a very tolerant attitude for its continued use as part of the clinician's evaluation procedures was advocated (Dana). In the middle was the conditional approach to "content only." These divergent approaches reflect different expectancies on the part of the reviewers who in many instances referred to the same studies and arrived at different conclusions. On the one hand, there is the strict psychometric approach to the Rorschach as a "test." Most will admit that it is not a test; it lacks the statistical prerequisites of a standardized test, although research attempts continue in this direction. On the other hand, when the Rorschach is viewed as a means for describing personalities in clinical contexts and in relation to other available material, it remains an important source of data for understanding individual differences and personality dynamics. One must agree with the reviewer who stresses the tendency on the part of clinicians to ignore the research literature. Familiarization with the increasingly sophisticated and theory-oriented research would certainly contribute greatly to the refinement of the psychodiagnostic process. However, it is very questionable whether great effort should be expended on the diagnostic actuarial classification enterprise. In view of the shakiness of the criterion in psychopathology and personology [2] (*3684*), clinicians will do best in describing personality and researchers in following the recently developed avenues outlined above.

In conclusion, and at the risk of repetition, it should be stated that the Rorschach is not a test. It is a clinical technique, or a pool of techniques, which some clinicians employ for their purposes with a good deal of success. It is also a field of study and research which permits workers to investigate such diverse concepts as body image, primary process think-

2 FRANK, GEORGE H. "Psychiatric Diagnosis: A Review of Research." *J General Psychol* 81(2):157–76 O '69. *

ing, hypnotizability, orality, and ego strength. Not unlike a good deal of the general psychological literature, many Rorschach studies deal with trivialities, are inconsistent, are not replicated, and are inconclusive. Yet "it is probably fair to say that the state of the Rorschach literature is neither more nor less confusing or disappointing than that which today typifies most areas of psychological research" (3577). Although research activity in the area has abated and concern with diagnosis among clinicians is lessened, Rorschach's ten inkblots persist in providing important stimulation to psychologists in producing increasingly challenging and useful research and applications (3656).

Marvin Reznikoff, *Professor of Psychology and Director of Clinical Training, Fordham University, New York, New York.*

Perhaps the most compelling question that can be asked about the Rorschach at this time is whether yet another review of this test is, in fact, necessary or even desirable. Writing in *The Sixth Mental Measurements Yearbook,* Jensen, for example, takes the rather extreme point of view that "the rate of scientific progress in clinical psychology might well be measured by the speed and thoroughness with which it gets over the Rorschach."

From a comparison of the percentages of references reported in *Personality Tests and Reviews* for the Rorschach and MMPI for the period from 1964 through 1968, it is obvious that the Rorschach has already lost its position of research preeminence among personality measures. In this period the Rorschach has averaged 10.1 percent of all references to personality tests in the literature, contrasted with a high of 39.3 percent in 1943, while the MMPI has maintained an average percentage of 16.7. In actual numbers, there were 900 MMPI references in these five years, contrasted with 533 Rorschach references.

The central issue, however, with respect to the somewhat diminished interest in the Rorschach, along with other projective instruments, is the current relatively low appeal of psychodiagnostic testing. Considering the reasons for this in a very thoughtful and perceptive analysis, Holt (3707) emphasizes, among other factors, that the clinician is now called upon to engage in a far broader range of professional activities than formerly. He is no longer con-

fined largely to the role of a "tester," with the frustrating restraints this role may impose on him in terms of meaningful and sustained interaction with his patients. Rather, he can, for instance, become a practicing psychotherapist or serve in a consultative capacity to a variety of burgeoning community mental health programs—both of which may be far more gratifying and challenging than assessment.

Holt also stresses the "oversell" of personality tests, with the Rorschach probably being the prime example of an instrument to which a near magical quality was initially ascribed. However, once research and clinical experience revealed the Rorschach to be considerably less potent diagnostically than was at first assumed, an overreactive and sweepingly indiscriminate negation of its usefulness ensued.

Despite some reduction in the popularity of the Rorschach and the grave questions repeatedly raised about its reliability and validity, it nevertheless remains a clinically vigorous technique and as such deserves attention. Furthermore, a perusal of the numerous critical reviews of the Rorschach literature hardly leaves one with a sense of confidence in dismissing the test as grossly inadequate and useless, for what is most conspicuous is the notable lack of consensus among the reviewers over its basic parameters. Although increasingly sophisticated methodology and statistical analyses are now employed more and more in Rorschach research, the regularity with which markedly contradictory findings occur does suggest that definitive studies are apparently yet to be done on a number of very fundamental issues.

The bulk of evidence, however, has shown the Rorschach to have serious limitations as a psychometric instrument based on a formal scoring system for the perceptual determinants of associations to the inkblots. Among many others, Anastasi (3951) and Zubin, Eron, and Schumer (3437) have written convincingly of the psychometric insufficiencies of traditional Rorschach scoring procedures and have indicated that the test may be more fruitfully regarded as a clinical interview with an emphasis on the content elicited. In light of such critical evaluations, this review will first consider the Rorschach as essentially akin to an interview situation in which the interviewee is exposed to a set of standardized stimuli under relatively standard conditions. Research stressing psychometric aspects of the instrument will then be covered briefly. The studies selected will be the most recent ones, the majority of them published in 1968 and 1969.

Very possibly the Consensus Rorschach represents the most innovative current application of the test (*3691*). As perceived by Wynne (*3748*), the Consensus Rorschach affords a standardized situation in which the interaction of two or more people can be studied directly as they endeavor to arrive at a mutually agreeable Rorschach percept. The struggles for dominance and the patterns of resistance that may take place in this group Rorschach situation, according to Blanchard (*3658*), parallel group behavior in life situations, affording the observer significant insights into the latter. Furthermore, Blanchard asserts that in contrast to the defensive withholding that may pervade an individually administered Rorschach, the Consensus Rorschach stimulates spontaneity and contributes to a greater variety of individual responses. Cutter (*3665*) addresses himself to issues of analyzing verbal transcriptions of Consensus Rorschach, determining the effects of different groups on Consensus records and assessing relationships between individual and group Rorschach protocols obtained separately. The Consensus Rorschach is used with couples and families (*3655, 3721*), as well as with groups in which the members are unrelated. It has been administered in serial form (*3667*) and repeated testing has been employed to tap changes occurring in therapy groups (*4026*).

In a very different vein, the Rorschach continues to be a valuable instrument for probing the dimensions of creativity. Rawls and Slack (*3708*) were able to differentiate between groups of artists and non-artists using quantitative and qualitative Rorschach variables. Dudek (*3960*) found that M, human movement percepts, is related to creativity but fails to reveal the degree of talent or motivation or the capacity to utilize a potential for creative productivity.

The M response category has in the past proven to be probably the most empirically viable of Rorschach determinants and is still being investigated, presently with somewhat equivocal findings. In a study of a group of paraplegics, Nickerson (*4066*) concluded that the Rorschach notions of M as a reflection of kinesthetic imagery and as a measure of ego delay function were supported by her data, although Cooper (*4022*) found that the amount

of ward activity of a group of borderline psychotics was inversely related to the number of M's they produced. On the other hand, Steele and Kahn (*4086*), using electromyographic recordings with a group of undergraduates, did not obtain increases in muscle potential with M, FM, or imagined movement. In another study (*4020*), a number of constructs potentially related to M were conceptualized and experimentally explored. Intelligence, time estimation, and fantasy correlated significantly with human movement.

An important line of Rorschach research encompasses studies of the influence of age changes on various aspects of test performance. Schimek (*3988*), in a longitudinal investigation of the stability of the defense of intellectualization as assessed by the Rorschach, indicated that Rorschach ratings of intellectualization remain stable from childhood to young adulthood. Comparing the content of Rorschach responses of groups of 10- and 13-year-old boys, Coleman (*3664*) determined that significant changes do occur between the two age levels, a finding which he felt is meaningful in terms of theories of child development. Several age groups were contrasted on a series of semantic differential ratings of both the Rorschach inkblots and the percepts given to the blots by Loiselle, Fisher, and Parrish (*3695*). Beck and Herron (*4009*) obtained normative data, with comparisons between sexes, for a group of elementary school children regarding their choice of mother, father, family, and me cards and which cards they like best and least. Examining the situation from the standpoint of parents, Ogdon, Bass, Thomas, and Lordi (*3981*) concluded that there was Rorschach evidence that parents' personalities influence the development of autism.

Noteworthy are several researches related to the work of Fisher and Cleveland (*2409*) on body image and their Rorschach Barrier and Penetration Index scores. Pienaar (*3986*) found significant differences in body interior and boundary awareness among groups of boys with stuttering problems and articulation deficits, and those having normal speech. Van De Mark and Neuringer (*4091*) demonstrated experimentally, using somatic arousal stimuli, that body image states influence the perceptual organization of the Rorschach inkblots.

Equally interesting are two studies utilizing the Rorschach as a measure of cognitive processes. Lerner (*3693*) ascertained that cognitive perceptual functioning, defined by a Rorschach genetic level score, was closely allied to level of social effectiveness evidenced on a social competence index. In another research, levels of cognition in terms of primary versus secondary thinking were found to relate to types of conscience development (*3657*).

There are still, of course, a number of more psychometrically oriented Rorschach investigations being published; these address themselves essentially to traditional diagnostic problems, validity issues, and formalistic scoring procedures. Representative of these types of studies, that of Long and Karon (*4052*) found that individual schizophrenic patients could be identified significantly beyond chance through blind analysis of their Rorschach protocols. Brevity of the record was the key factor that contributed to misidentification. The differential diagnostic ability of the Rorschach, along with several other measures, was reported by Tamkin and Sonkin (*4090*) to be markedly limited in a research they conducted on psychiatric patients. Talkington and Reed (*4088*) found that 2 of 13 Rorschach "indicators" significantly differentiated between psychotic and nonpsychotic retardates. In a study of Rorschach indicators of homosexuality, Chapman and Chapman (*4019*) noted that both practicing psychodiagnosticians and a large group of undergraduates consistently focused on a number of the Wheeler signs of homosexuality that research has established as invalid, while curiously ignoring several valid content signs. Andersen and Seitz (*4007*), however, were "highly successful" in differentiating heterosexuals, those with disturbances in sexual role, and homosexuals by applying Schafer's content signs. Overt homosexuals were compared with several other patient groups and a control group of college students in a Rorschach study by Exner (*4027*). The homosexuals produced more reflection responses and also more color percepts of a less form-bound character, both of which the author established in a second part of his study as clearly indicative of narcissism.

One well designed Rorschach prediction study deserves mention. Carlson (*4017*) developed a Rorschach index of the optimal personality picture of the successful VA trainee in clinical psychology. This carefully conceived index proved superior to the *Miller Analogies Test* and the *Strong Vocational Interest Blank* in predicting success and identifying failures for "personality reasons."

Among the studies investigating specific Rorschach scoring factors, Wagner and Slemboski (*4092*) found confirmation for Piotrowski's special interpretation of the Rorschach shading variable. The results of a study by Fox and Blatt (*4032*) indicated that the Rorschach measure of oppositionality reflected in white space percepts was significantly related to a WAIS indicator of negativism—namely number of digits remembered backward exceeding the number recalled in a forward order. Combining several scoring determinants, Lerner (*3973*) presents a method of summarizing perceptual accuracy on the Rorschach, while Rychlak and Boland (*4072*) endeavored to cross validate Hermann Rorschach's theory of perception.

In attempting to improve Rorschach content analysis, Kessel, Harris, and Slagle (*4045*) offer a technique which relies on the patient's own associations to his responses, paralleling an approach used in dream interpretation. Some research has set out to compare Rorschach and HIT scoring determinants. In one such study an overlapping longitudinal design employed the Holtzman technique with 6-, 9-, and 12-year-old children to examine the color variables.[1] The developmental trends for color elicited by the Holtzman procedure were found to be in agreement with prior longitudinal studies of color on the Rorschach.

Not to be overlooked in any consideration of Rorschach test performance is the "examiner effect." This has long been a subject of study, generally in terms of the examiner's personality and explicit test behavior. In a very recent investigation in this particular area, Harris and Masling (*4142*) found that even so fundamental a variable as the pairing of a male examiner and a female subject elicited more responses than any other sex pairing, which is consistent with Rosenthal's finding that this combination produces "unique results." Concentrating on other factors involved in Rorschach productivity, Hartung, McKenna, and Baxter (*4037*) noted that test-taking attitudes stemming from an "instructional set" given the subject could influence not only the production of Rorschach percepts indicative of inner disturbance but also the number of self-referential responses.

1 SANDERS, JEFFREY L.; HOLTZMAN, WAYNE H.; AND SWARTZ, JON D. "Structural Changes of the Color Variable in the Holtzman Inkblot Technique." *J Proj Tech & Pers Assess* 32:556–61 D '68. *

In sum, when the Rorschach is viewed from a strict psychometric framework and the emphasis is placed on its formalistic scoring determinants and tabulation procedures, its reliability and validity failings readily appear. Even within this context, however, there are some marked disagreements over basic aspects of the instrument and more potent evaluative studies are clearly still to be done.

A far more productive approach to the Rorschach is to regard it as essentially a standardized interview and to focus, therefore, primarily on content variables. With this orientation, the Rorschach emerges as an exceedingly flexible technique that can be utilized in some very diverse and innovative ways. Recently, the Rorschach has been employed in various group constellations to assess interpersonal behavior. It has been used to investigate aspects of creativity and cognition and to probe body image concepts. Work has been done with it in studying developmental changes and processes.

Thus, while the Rorschach may be psychometrically moribund, there is convincing evidence that it is gaining new vigor as a very novel interview situation that has meaningful applications in exploring a broad spectrum of personality dimensions.

For reviews by Richard H. Dana, Leonard D. Eron, and Arthur R. Jensen, see 6:237; for reviews by Samuel J. Beck, H. J. Eysenck, Raymond J. McCall, and Laurance F. Shaffer, see 5:154; for a review by Helen Sargent, see 4:117; for reviews by Morris Krugman and J. R. Wittenborn, see 3:73.

[176]

★**School Apperception Method.** Grades kgn–9; 1968; SAM; individual; 1 form (22 cards); pictures are also available as 35 mm. transparencies for group administration; manual (35 pages); no directions for use of transparencies; no data on reliability and validity; no norms; $10 per set of cards and manual; $12 per set of transparencies (without manual); postage extra; (30–45) minutes; Irving L. Solomon and Bernard D. Starr; Springer Publishing Co., Inc. *

REFERENCES

1–2. See P:473.
3. STARR, BERNARD D. "The School Apperception Method." *Int Congr Rorsch & Other Proj Tech* 7:376–80 '70. *

WILLARD E. REITZ, *Associate Professor of Psychology, The University of Western Ontario, London, Ontario, Canada.*

The *School Apperception Method* falls squarely within the projective tradition of personality assessment. The aim was to create a thematic projective device with situational specificity—that of a school situation—for use by school psychologists. Children portrayed in the SAM stimuli are of "median elementary school age."

Three explicit claims are made regarding the SAM. It is claimed, first, that "the stimuli are situationally relevant to the environment in which the school must understand the behavior of problem children." The pictures do portray a variety of school scenes at a moderate level of structuredness. One can, however, question the extent to which the stimuli sample typical school problems. In this regard, the authors say that picture content was determined by their "varied experience in school psychology." They apparently made no attempt to survey problems typically dealt with by other psychologists in different school settings.

The second claim is related to the first: that "the very content of the stimuli assures school-oriented associations." This claim is supported by the inclusion of 11 illustrative cases in the manual. Given school-oriented pictures and administration of the test by school psychologists in schools, it seems likely that school-associated responses would be elicited. Nonetheless, norms are not presented to document the claim. (A side issue here is that if a child's problems originate outside of or are extrinsic to school, *assurance* of school-related responses may be a serious shortcoming.) While the 11 cases are useful, they are insufficient to document the claim of school-related associations. Age-graded thematic norms would be required for each picture to effectively document this claim.

The existence of such age-graded norms is also essential to the third claim: that responses "provide data from which the school psychologist or other trained personnel can formulate hypotheses concerning strategies for classroom management and other school decisions. These hypotheses would not be as readily available through other techniques." As worded, this statement avoids any explicit quantitative claim. The authors point out that the SAM is intended to be used as a wide-band, low-fidelity, qualitative instrument and they deny any intention of the SAM's being used to obtain precise psychometric measures. To the extent that this intention is so and appropriately communicated, the SAM should not be assessed according to quantitative standards. The authors point out, however, that responses can be interpreted within diverse theoretical frameworks—for example, Murray's or Bellak's. Such systems, of course, utilize quantitative measures and thus would be required to hold to the usual rules of reliability and validity for supporting it. In the present instance, reliability and validity evidence is nil and claimed to be unnecessary.

The authors go on to suggest their own framework within which to evaluate SAM responses. They list nine areas around which to organize responses as an interpretational aid. While many of the categories involve qualitative considerations, there is also an implicit assumption that the more aggressive responses, say, the more aggression (or aggressive concern, or the like) the child has. The authors suggest, in this regard, that they have no new answers to these questions and wisely recommend the use of auxiliary information "abundantly available in the school setting" to supplement SAM findings. The total lack of norms and of reliability and validity data, however, is inconsistent with assumptions of a quantitative nature, even if the level of measurement assumed is weak. Categorizing a child as having certain kinds of attitudes or characteristics as opposed to others, of course, is a measurement operation at a nominal level.

The authors discuss other similar or related projective tests. They conclude that existing techniques "neglect or deal inadequately with the school setting."

In summary, the SAM is a new projective instrument designed to be situationally relevant to schools. There is, however, little evidence presented that its stimuli represent typical school problems broadly conceived. Norms and reliability and validity data are totally lacking. There has been no demonstration of its being more useful, reliable, or valid than existing procedures. It can thus be characterized as a new, untried set of projective stimuli which will require a great deal of research to document its characteristics and specify any potential usefulness. Outside of use by very experienced, competent professional psychologists, its application should be restricted to such research.

NORMAN D. SUNDBERG, *Dean, The Wallace School of Community Service and Public Affairs, University of Oregon, Eugene, Oregon.*

The *School Apperception Method* is another form of the TAT. The 22 drawings are of school children and school personnel in a variety of situations intended to encourage stories about relations with teachers, principals, and schoolmates; attitudes toward school work; anger, aggression, and other themes one might expect. In addition to the 12 basic pictures, there are 10 additional ones which can be substituted in or added to the original series. Five of the additional ones show both blacks and whites in school situations; others show special problems, such as two children playing with matches. Instructions for administration are very similar to those for the TAT and other thematic techniques. The manual by Solomon and Starr does not give any scoring procedure. The authors suggest that the interpreter notice the formal qualities and a variety of aspects of content and context in the stories, such as attitudes toward teachers and schoolmates, achievement orientation, situations that trigger anger or are frustrating, and relations between home and school. The manual gives a series of examples together with brief interpretations.

The authors suggest that the SAM would be primarily of use to school psychologists and mental health workers. It might also be of use for training and research with student teachers. The manual suggests using the method with parents and children in Head Start programs. No reports of norms, reliability, or validity are provided in the manual or the two earlier articles.

The authors justify their publication of the SAM at this early stage of development because of its "content validity" (referring to the school-related nature of the stimulus pictures) and because of its "apparent usefulness as an assessment technique with school children." They state that "criterion validation is quite inappropriate for an assessment technique in its early development." They imply that Cronbach advises that "assessment techniques" do not need the careful attention to reliability and validity that "psychometric tests" require. They point out that thousands of decisions are being made about children every day and that the SAM is advantageous because it introduces a systematic approach and utilizes a degree of objectivity.

The authors were probably referring to Cronbach's distinction between broad and narrow bandwidth devices, a point made in his latest book,[1] as well as to the earlier one to which

[1] CRONBACH, LEE J. *Essentials of Psychological Testing, Third Edition,* pp. 179–82, 679–80. New York: Harper & Row, Publishers, Inc., 1970. Pp. xxx, 752. *

they refer. Cronbach indicates that initial explorations of cases or research areas often require wide-ranging interviews or techniques. However, this need does not justify ignoring the usual concern for reliability and validity. When the authors claim that the SAM adds something to the psychological examination of a child, one wonders what evidence there is for that claim. Would the time taken to give the SAM have been better used in an interview or in observation of the child? As Cronbach points out, dynamic assessment in comparison with more direct methods adds stages of inference about personality constructs that make predictions (and decisions) much more prone to error. Some research studies have shown that predictions are better if based only on case history information without added information from projective techniques. Psychologists interpreting the Rorschach and the TAT tend, for instance, to exhibit strong biases towards pathology rather than health. It is possible, following this line of reasoning, that the psychologist might be doing a poorer job for school children by using the SAM, Rorschach, or other technique than he would by using ordinary interviewing, observing, and checking of records.

The authors' assertion that the thematic stimuli used with school children should be pertinent to the school situation seems eminently reasonable. In this regard, the *School Apperception Method* is likely to be better for school testing than the other thematic techniques. It is also true that storytelling is often an interesting and nonthreatening approach with children. Testers should recognize that the clever child would still be able to discern the intent of the SAM and to "throw" his responses toward what he conceives as proper answers, if he wished. The dilemma of projective techniques is whether to make the stimuli very ambiguous and run the danger of not eliciting relevant responses or to make them clear and run the danger of bias from deliberate attempts to deceive or avoid topics. The SAM has opted for considerable clarity. The procedure is therefore very dependent, as is the interview, on the personal skill of the psychologist and his relationship with the child. Until evidence is forthcoming that the SAM, or any similar procedure, is effective for producing relevant and important information for decision making,

there is no reason to prefer it over many other approaches to understanding children.

[177]

★**The Self Explorations Inventory.** College and adults; 1966; SEI; for research use only; no scores: 12 questions allowing for "projective-type" responses; 1 form (3 pages); mimeographed manual (13 pages); no data on reliability and validity; no norms; $4.50 per 20 tests; $1 per single copy; $1 per manual; postage extra; [15-25] minutes; Sheldon J. Lachman; Psychological Publications Press. *

[178]

★**Sentence Completion Blank.** College and adults; 1955-66; SCB; 2 forms; mimeographed manual ('65, 15 pages); no data on reliability; no norms; $1.25 per manual, postage extra; Sheldon J. Lachman; Psychological Publications Press. *
a) LONGER FORM. 1 form ('66, 4 pages); $5 per 20 tests; $1 per single copy; [45-60] minutes.
b) SHORTER FORM. 1 form ('66, 2 pages, consists of 50 of the 80 items on Longer Form); $3 per 20 tests; $1 per single copy; [25-35] minutes.

[179]

★**Seven Squares Technique.** Ages 5 and over; 1952-68; SST; also called *7-Squares Test;* no set scoring or interpretation procedures; individual; 1 form (no date, white board and 7 graduated black paper squares); English translation of manual ('68, 19 pages); no data on reliability and validity in manual; no norms; Sw. kr. 33 per test; Sw. kr. 17 per manual; postage extra; German and Swedish manuals available; [10] minutes; Heinz Hector; English translation of manual by Daniel James Bradley; Skandinaviska Testförlaget AB. *

REFERENCES

1. YSSEL, G. J. "The Reliability of Preferences of 7-Squares Test Patterns." *J Nat Inst Personnel Res* 7:137 Jl '58. * (*PA* 33:11116)
2. YSSEL, G. J. "The Reliability of Ratings of 7-Squares Test Patterns on a Scale: 'Rigid-Flexible-Labile.'" *J Nat Inst Personnel Res* 7:135-6 Jl '58. * (*PA* 33:11117)
3. FABIAN, H. "An Experiment With Two Forms of the 7-Squares Test." *J Nat Inst Personnel Res* 8:56-8 S '59. * (*PA* 34:5579)
4. HECTOR, H. "Relationship Between Paired Comparisons and Rankings of 7-Squares Test Patterns." *J Nat Inst Personnel Res* 8:65-6 S '59. * (*PA* 34:5582)
5. HECTOR, H., AND HUDSON, W. "Pattern Specificity in a Sample of Mozambique Tribesmen on the 7-Squares Test." *J Nat Inst Personnel Res* 7:156-61 Ap '59. *
6. ICHIMURA, K. "Results From the 7-Squares Test Applied in Japan." *J Nat Inst Personnel Res* 7:201-2 Ap '59. *
7. MORGAN, P. "Observations and Findings on the 7-Squares Test With Literate and Illiterate Black Groups in Southern Africa." *J Nat Inst Personnel Res* 8:44-7 S '59. * (*PA* 34:5588)
8. BRADLEY, D. J. "The Ability of Black Groups to Produce Recognisable Patterns on the 7-Squares Test." *J Nat Inst Personnel Res* 8:142-4 D '60. * (*PA* 35:5383)
9. HECTOR, H.; DLODLO, M. S.; AND DU PLESSIS, C. F. "An Experiment on Silhouette Recognition and Projection With Bantu Children of Different Ages." *J Nat Inst Personnel Res* 8:195-8 S '61. * (*PA* 36:4FF95H)
10. DANA, RICHARD H., AND VOIGT, WALTER H. "The Seven-Squares Test." *Percept & Motor Skills* 15:751-3 D '62. *
11. HECTOR, H. "Psychodiagnostic Theory of the Seven-Squares Test." *Percept & Motor Skills* 17:567-9 O '63. * (*PA* 38:6095)
12. BRADLEY, DANIEL J. "Problems of Recognition in Bantu Testing." *Percept & Motor Skills* 19:718 D '64. * (*PA* 39:6358)
13. HECTOR, H., AND SHMUKLER, D. "Observation on Schizophrenic Seven-Squares Test Patterns." *Percept & Motor Skills* 18:856 Je '64. * (*PA* 39:5022)
14. BRADLEY, DANIEL J. "The Null Hypothesis vs the Differential Hypothesis." *Percept & Motor Skills* 20:114 F '65. * (*PA* 39:10256)
15. DANA, RICHARD H. "The Seven Squares Test: Phenom-

enon Naming vs. Casual Naming." *Percept & Motor Skills* 20:69–70 F '65. * (*PA* 39:10258)
16. BRADLEY, DANIEL J. "A Psychophysical Approach to the Seven Squares Technique (SST)." *Percept & Motor Skills* 29(1):169–70 Ag '69. * (*PA* 44:2361)
17. BRADLEY, DANIEL J. "Seven Squares: Research Emphasis Past and Present." *Percept & Motor Skills* 30(3): 683–6 Je '70. * (*PA* 44:15775)
18. HECTOR, HEINZ. "Seven Squares: Bibliography of German References 1952–67." *Percept & Motor Skills* 30(2):502 Ap '70. * (*PA* 46:6899)

[180]

*A Test of Family Attitudes. Ages 6–12; 1952–66; individual; 1 form ('65, 8 pictures, identical with pictures published in 1952 except for format); manual ('66, 69 pages); recording sheet ('66, 1 page); no data on reliability; Fr. 250 per set of pictures; Fr. 100 per 100 recording sheets; Fr. 300 per manual; Fr. 305 per specimen set; postage extra; French edition available; (30–60) minutes; Lydia Jackson; Editest. *

REFERENCES

1–2. See 5:163.
3–4. See P:504.

For a review by John E. Bell, see 5:163.

[181]

Thematic Apperception Test. Ages 4 and over; 1935–43; TAT; individual; 1 form ('43, 20 cards); manual ('43, 20 pages); no data on reliability; $6 per set of testing materials; 50¢ per manual; cash orders postpaid; 100(120) minutes in 2 sessions 1 day apart; Henry A. Murray; Harvard University Press. *

REFERENCES

1–101. See 3:103.
102–299. See 4:136.
300–610. See 5:164.
611–897. See 6:245.
898–1236. See P:484, also includes a cumulative name index to the first 1236 references for this test.
1237. PHELAN, JOSEPH GERARD. *A Study of Psychological Diagnostic Skill as Employed in the Clinical Investigation of Personality.* Doctor's thesis, Princeton University (Princeton, N.J.), 1951. (*DA* 13:599)
1238. GORDON, MYRON H. *A Clinical Study of Personality Patterns in Children With Reading Disability.* Doctor's thesis, New York University (New York, N.Y.), 1952. (*DA* 13:68)
1239. LOWINGER, LOUIS. *The Psychodynamics of Stuttering: An Evaluation of the Factors of Aggression and Guilt Feelings in a Group of Institutionalized Children.* Doctor's thesis, New York University (New York, N.Y.), 1952. (*DA* 12:725)
1240. MENAKER, LEON. *A Study of the Personality of the Asthmatic Adult Male.* Doctor's thesis, New York University (New York, N.Y.), 1952. (*DA* 12:727)
1241. RAIFMAN, IRVING. *An Investigation of the Personality Factors of Dependency and Overcompensatory Goal Striving Behavior Associated With the Development of Peptic Ulcer in a Group of Veteran Male Patients.* Doctor's thesis, New York University (New York, N.Y.), 1952. (*DA* 12:539)
1242. BARD, MORTON. *The Relationship of the Personality Factor of Dependence to Psychological Invalidism in Women Following Radical Mastectomy.* Doctor's thesis, New York University (New York, N.Y.), 1953. (*DA* 13:716)
1243. BRENNER, ROSE. *A Study of Some of the Psychological Factors Contributing to the Stability or Instability of the Marriages of Neurotic Veterans.* Doctor's thesis, New York University (New York, N.Y.), 1953. (*DA* 14:630)
1244. MILL, CYRIL RALPH. *Personality Patterns of Socially Selected and Socially Rejected Male College Students.* Doctor's thesis, Michigan State College (East Lansing, Mich.), 1953. (*DA* 13:866)
1245. MYERS, JULIAN S. *The Effect of Testosterone Upon Certain Aspects of Personality in Male Paraplegics.* Doctor's thesis, New York University (New York, N.Y.), 1953. (*DA* 14:397)
1246. SALTZMAN, SIDNEY S. *An Investigation of Certain Psychological Aspects of Personality in Three Allergic Groups.* Doctor's thesis, New York University (New York, N.Y.), 1953. (*DA* 13:1251)
1247. ZEICHNER, ABRAHAM M. *Psychosexual Identification and Conception of Sexual Role in Paranoid Schizophrenia.* Doctor's thesis, New York University (New York, N.Y.), 1953. (*DA* 13:593)
1248. NEWMAN, CARL. *A Study of the Relationship Between Attitudes Toward Certain Authority Figures and Adjustment to the Military Service.* Doctor's thesis, New York University (New York, N.Y.), 1954. (*DA* 14:2402)

1249. OSEAS, LEONARD. *A Study of Some Language Correlates of Passivity in Personality.* Doctor's thesis, Northwestern University (Evanston, Ill.), 1954. (*DA* 14:1812)
1250. WAXENBERG, SHELDON EDWARD. *Psychosomatic Patients and Other Physically Ill Persons: A Comparative Study.* Doctor's thesis, Columbia University (New York, N.Y.), 1954. (*DA* 14:1818)
1251. WHEELER, HARRY EVERETT, JR. *Apperceptive Distortion in Clinical Judgments.* Doctor's thesis, Washington University (St. Louis, Mo.), 1954. (*DA* 14:1819)
1252. HARLOW, ROBERT GRANVILLE. *The Perception of Persons: An Exploratory Study of Some of the Determinants of Self Perception and Social Perception.* Doctor's thesis, Clark University (Worcester, Mass.), 1956. (*DA* 16:2220)
1253. RUSH, BERNARD HOLLANDER. *An Investigation of Parent-Child Relationships, in Broken Homes and Their Relationship to School Behavior.* Doctor's thesis, New York University (New York, N.Y.), 1956. (*DA* 16:1509)
1254. SEYMOUR, JOHN H. *Some Changes in Psychometric, Perceptual and Motor Performance as a Function of Sleep Deprivation.* Doctor's thesis, New York University (New York, N.Y.), 1956. (*DA* 16:2216)
1255. BERENBERG, ALBERT N. *A Study of the Relationship Between Skills in Certain Cognitive Areas and Certain Patterns Involving Attitudes, Interests and Identifications in Eighth Grade Students.* Doctor's thesis, New York University (New York, N.Y.), 1957. (*DA* 18:651)
1256. GLASS, HARVEY L. *The Effects on Fantasy of Achievement Motivation Based on "Fear of Failure" and "Hope of Success."* Doctor's thesis, University of Pennsylvania (Philadelphia, Pa.), 1957. (*DA* 18:645)
1257. HABER, RALPH NORMAN. *The Prediction of Achievement Behavior by an Interaction of Achievement Motivation and Achievement Stress.* Doctor's thesis, Stanford University (Stanford, Calif.), 1957. (*DA* 17:2686)
1258. WECHSLER, RUTH R. *An Investigation of Certain Psychodynamic Aspects of the Personality of Individuals Who Have Suffered Manic and Depressive Attacks.* Doctor's thesis, New York University (New York, N.Y.), 1957. (*DA* 18:672)
1259. COBURN, THURMAN EUGENE. *The Temporal Orientation of Emotionally Disturbed Boys.* Doctor's thesis, University of Oklahoma (Norman, Okla.), 1958. (*DA* 19:728)
1260. FARLEY, NANCY BESS. *The Temporal Orientation of the Female Juvenile Delinquent.* Doctor's thesis, University of Oklahoma (Norman, Okla.), 1958. (*DA* 19:1012)
1261. MOSS, HOWARD ALAN. *The Generality of Cautiousness as a Defense Behavior.* Doctor's thesis, Ohio State University (Columbus, Ohio), 1958. (*DA* 19:879)
1262. RIESSMAN, FRANK, AND MILLER, S. M. "Social Class and Projective Tests." *J Proj Tech* 22:432–9 D '58. * (*PA* 34:1268)
1263. SCHULMAN, DORIS. *A Study of the Relationships Between Mothers' Attitudes Toward Their Children, and the Personality Adjustment and School Behavior of These Children.* Doctor's thesis, New York University (New York, N.Y.), 1958. (*DA* 19:734)
1264. SMITH, AARON. *Discrepancy in the Meaning of Self in a Multilevel Personality System and Emotional Disturbance.* Doctor's thesis, University of Illinois (Urbana, Ill.), 1958. (*DA* 19:1120)
1265. WILSON, HELEN ELIZABETH. *Overt and Fantasied Hostility as a Function of Channels of Expression.* Doctor's thesis, University of Utah (Salt Lake City, Utah), 1958. (*DA* 19:1440)
1266. GIER, JAMES DALE. *The Relationship of Physical Ability to Certain Psychological Scores and Ratings Among Mentally Retarded Boys.* Master's thesis, University of Washington (Seattle, Wash.), 1959.
1267. KINGSMORE, JOHN M. *Relationship Between Physical Capacity Scores of College Male Freshmen and Aggressive and Sexual Tendencies as Measured by Certain Projective Tests.* Master's thesis, University of Maryland (College Park, Md.), 1959.
1268. LINDZEY, GARDNER. "On the Classification of Projective Techniques." *Psychol B* 56:158–68 Mr '59. * (*PA* 34: 1389)
1269. MARLENS, HANNA S. *A Study of the Effect of Hospitalization on Children in a Metropolitan Municipal Institution: A Comparative Study of Emotional Attitudes Toward Self and the Environment of Children Hospitalized and Those Non-Hospitalized With Similar Physical Complaints.* Doctor's thesis, New York University (New York, N.Y.), 1959. (*DA* 20:3385)
1270. MEADOW, ARNOLD, AND PARNES, SIDNEY J. "Evaluation of Training in Creative Problem-Solving." *J Appl Psychol* 43:189–94 Je '59. * (*PA* 34:5568)
1271. PILKEY, LORAINE. *Role Playing as a Technique for Increasing Empathic Ability of Mentally Subnormal Adolescents.* Doctor's thesis, University of Missouri (Kansas City, Mo.), 1959. (*DA* 28:504A)
1272. SILVERMAN, MORTON. *The Relation of Ego Control to Overt and Fantasy Aggression.* Doctor's thesis, Syracuse University (Syracuse, N.Y.), 1959. (*DA* 20:2908)
1273. YOUNG, MAXIM F. *An Investigation of Narcissism and Correlates of Narcissism in Schizophrenics, Neurotics, and*

Normals. Doctor's thesis, Temple University (Philadelphia, Pa.), 1959. (DA 20:3394)

1274. BARWICK, JANICE MARIE. A Study of the Relationship Between Parental Acceptance and the Academic Achievement of Adolescents. Doctor's thesis, Boston University (Boston, Mass.), 1960. (DA 21:3698)

1275. DEWOLFE, RUTHANNE KATHERINE SOBOTA. The Effect of Drive Level on the Language Behavior of Process and Reactive Schizophrenics. Doctor's thesis, Northwestern University (Evanston, Ill.), 1960. (DA 21:3162)

1276. HEDVIG, ELEANOR HERSON. A Study of the Effects of Immediately Preceding Experiences Upon Early Childhood Recollections. Doctor's thesis, Northwestern University (Evanston, Ill.), 1960. (DA 21:2784)

1277. POWELL, KATHRYN SUMMERS. Maternal Employment in Relation to Family Life. Doctor's thesis, Florida State University (Tallahassee, Fla.), 1960. (DA 21:2269)

1278. BOONE, JERRY NEAL. A Study of the Effects of Anxiety on Auditory Perceptual Response to Threat. Doctor's thesis, Vanderbilt University (Nashville, Tenn.), 1961. (DA 22:2062)

1279. BREGER, LOUIS. Conformity and the Expression of Hostility. Doctor's thesis, Ohio State University (Columbus, Ohio), 1961. (DA 22:3738)

1280. DACHOWSKI, MARJORIE McCORMICK. Inconsistency as Measured by Direct, Indirect and Projective Tests and Its Relationship to General Neuroticism. Doctor's thesis, University of Illinois (Urbana, Ill.), 1961. (DA 22:3740)

1281. GARWOOD, DOROTHY SEMENOW. Some Personality Factors Related to Creativity in Young Scientists. Doctor's thesis, Claremont Graduate School (Claremont, Calif.), 1961. (DA 22:3273)

1282. JOHNSON, NANCY MARIMON. The Relation of Training and Other Variables to the Content and Accuracy of Predictions Made From Thematic Test Materials. Doctor's thesis, University of North Carolina (Chapel Hill, N.C.), 1961. (DA 23:702)

1283. LASKY, DAVID ISAAC. The Relationship Between Spontaneous Fantasy, Induced Fantasy, and Behavioral Measures of Hostility. Doctor's thesis, Temple University (Philadelphia, Pa.), 1961. (DA 22:4408)

1284. REISER, MARTIN. The Effects of Group Counseling on Interpersonal Relationships, Anxiety Level, Intellectual Functioning, and Certain Personality Characteristics in a Planned Workshop Experience. Doctor's thesis, Temple University (Philadelphia, Pa.), 1961. (DA 22:325)

1285. HOWARD, STEPHEN JAMES. Determinants of Sex-Role Identifications of Homosexual Female Delinquents. Doctor's thesis, University of Southern California (Los Angeles, Calif.), 1962. (DA 23:2588)

1286. KAGAN, JEROME, AND MOSS, HOWARD A. Birth to Maturity: A Study in Psychological Development. New York: John Wiley & Sons, Inc., 1962. Pp. xiii, 381. *

1287. MADDI, SALVATORE R.; CHARLENS, ALAN M.; MADDI, DOROTHY-ANNE; AND SMITH, ADRIENNE J. "Effects of Monotony and Novelty on Imaginative Productions." J Personality 30:513–27 D '62. * (PA 39:1784)

1288. QUINN, THOMAS LEO. Differences in Motivational Patterns of College Student Brothers as Revealed in the TAT, the Ratings of Their Peers, and the Ratings of Their Superiors: A Validation Study. Doctor's thesis, Loyola University (Chicago, Ill.), 1962.

1289. RUBIN, SAMUEL SOLOMON. The Relation of Fantasy Productions to Test Intelligence. Doctor's thesis, Columbia University (New York, N.Y.), 1962. (DA 23:1080)

1290. SELKIN, JAMES. Vocational Adjustment and Personality: A Study of Some Mediating Variables. Doctor's thesis, University of Colorado (Boulder, Colo.), 1962. (DA 23:2200)

1291. WITKIN, H. A.; DYKE, R. G.; FATERSON, H. F.; GOODENOUGH, D. R.; AND KARP, S. A. Psychological Differentiation: Studies of Development. New York: John Wiley & Sons, Inc., 1962. Pp. xii, 418. * (PA 37:819)

1292. BARRON, FRANK. Creativity and Psychological Health: Origins of Personal Vitality and Creative Freedom. Princeton, N.J.: D. Van Nostrand Co., Inc., 1963. Pp. xi, 292. *

1293. NEUGARTEN, BERNICE L. Chap. 17, "Personality and the Aging Process," pp. 321–34. In Process of Aging: Social and Psychological Perspectives. Edited by Richard H. Williams and others. New York: Atherton Press, 1963. Pp. xix, 587. *

1294. SILVAROLI, NICHOLAS JOSEPH. Intellectual and Emotional Factors as Predictors of Children's Success in First Grade Reading. Doctor's thesis, Syracuse University (Syracuse, N.Y.), 1963. (DA 24:5008)

1295. TUTKO, THOMAS ARTHUR. Need for Social Approval and Its Effect on Responses to Projective Tests. Doctor's thesis, Northwestern University (Evanston, Ill.), 1963. (DA 24:3429)

1296. WONDERLING, LAWRENCE VERNON. The Effects of Stimulus Variations in the Thematic Apperception Test on the Response Process. Master's thesis, San Diego State College (San Diego, Calif.), 1963.

1297. BENTON, JOHN A., JR. Perceptual Characteristics of Episcopal Pastors. Doctor's thesis, University of Florida (Gainesville, Fla.), 1964. (DA 25:3963)

1298. BLUHM, PHILIP M. Discrimination Reaction Time as a Function of Incentive-Related DRQ Anxiety and Task Diffi-

culty. Doctor's thesis, Florida State University (Tallahassee, Fla.), 1964. (DA 25:2609)

1299. COHEN, ARLENE FREEMAN. Achievement Motivation and Rehabilitation of the Physically Disabled. Doctor's thesis, Boston University (Boston, Mass.), 1964. (DA 25:3105)

1300. CROWNE, DOUGLAS P., AND MARLOWE, DAVID. The Approval Motive: Studies in Evaluative Dependence, pp. 171–85. New York: John Wiley & Sons, Inc., 1964. Pp. xiii, 233. *

1301. ELLIS, NORMAN CALVIN. Zipf's Law, Schizophrenia, and Long-Term Institutionalization. Doctor's thesis, University of Kansas (Lawrence, Kan.), 1964. (DA 26:490)

1302. FISKE, DONALD W.; CARTWRIGHT, DESMOND S.; AND KIRTNER, WILLIAM L. "Are Psychotherapeutic Changes Predictable?" J Abn & Social Psychol 69:418–26 O '64. * (PA 39:8058)

1303. GARWOOD, DOROTHY SEMENOW. "Personality Factors Related to Creativity in Young Scientists." J Abn & Social Psychol 68:413–9 Ap '64. * (PA 39:1729)

1304. HAWARD, L. R. C. "Thematic Apperception Analysis as a Forensic Technique." J Forensic Sci Soc 4:209–16 O '64. *

1305. LEVINSON, ALMA. A Comparison of Concepts of Self and Parental Figures in Selected Groups of Under-, Average and High Achieving High School Boys: A Comparison of a Group of Underachievers With Groups of Average and Above Average Achievers Selected for Intelligence, Age and Grade. Doctor's thesis, New York University (New York, N.Y.), 1964. (DA 25:1320)

1306. MADDI, SALVATORE R., AND BERNE, NAOMI. "Novelty of Productions and Desire for Novelty as Active and Passive Forms of the Need for Variety." J Personality 32:270–7 Je '64. * (PA 39:7907)

1307. MALIVER, BRUCE L. Anti-Negro Bias Among Negro College Students. Doctor's thesis, Yeshiva University (New York, N.Y.), 1964. (DA 25:2660)

1308. MEGARGEE, EDWIN INGLEE. Undercontrol and Overcontrol in Assaultive and Homicidal Adolescents. Doctor's thesis, University of California (Berkeley, Calif.), 1964. (DA 25:2614)

1309. SHERMAN, VIVIAN MABEL STANLEY RUSHWORTH. Personality Correlates of Differential Performance on Intelligence and Creativity Tests. Doctor's thesis, Stanford University (Stanford, Calif.), 1964. (DA 25:4004)

1310. WOHLFORD, PAUL FREDERICK. Determinants of Extension of Personal Time. Doctor's thesis, Duke University (Durham, N.C.), 1964. (DA 25:4255)

1311. CERVANTES, LUCIUS F.; WITH THE ASSISTANCE OF GRACE PLATTS HUSTED. Chap. 5, "Psychological Tendencies of the Dropout," pp. 175–95. In their The Dropout: Causes and Cures. Ann Arbor, Mich.: University of Michigan Press, 1965. Pp. viii, 244. *

1312. DYK, RUTH B., AND WITKIN, HERMAN A. "Family Experiences Related to the Development of Differentiation in Children." Child Develop 36:21–55 Mr '65. * (PA 39:11936)

1313. EPSTEIN, MARVIN. An Investigation of Certain Aspects of Cognitive Controls and Reading Comprehension. Doctor's thesis, Temple University (Philadelphia, Pa.), 1965. (DA 26:1764)

1314. FRIEDMAN, ALICE LISA. The Effect of Personality and Interest Variables on Learning by Linear and Scrambled Methods of Programmed Instruction. Doctor's thesis, New York University (New York, N.Y.), 1965. (DA 27:390A)

1315. HARRIS, NORMAN. Controlling Maternal Attitudes: Clinical and Socio-Cultural Implications. Doctor's thesis, Yeshiva University (New York, N.Y.), 1965. (DA 26:6837)

1316. KEEFE, JEFFREY FRANCIS. A Study of Two Seminary and Two Non-Seminary High School Groups on Selected Aspects of Maturity. Doctor's thesis, Fordham University (New York, N.Y.), 1965. (DA 26:4076)

1317. KRASS, ALVIN. A Comparative Study of Attitude Towards Authority Among Parents of Institutionalized Antisocial Boys and Parents of Non-Antisocial Boys. Doctor's thesis, New York University (New York, N.Y.), 1965. (DA 27:396A)

1318. LIPGAR, ROBERT MAURICE. Subjective Probability Notions, Guessing Behavior and Their Personality Correlates. Doctor's thesis, University of Chicago (Chicago, Ill.), 1965. (DAI 30:1348B)

1319. LUBORSKY, LESTER. Chap. 18, "Clinical Manual for the Evaluation of Patients' Self-Interpretations of T.A.T. Stories," pp. 242–65. In Psychological Test Modifications. Edited by Milton Kornrich. Springfield, Ill.: Charles C Thomas, Publisher, 1965. Pp. xii, 265. *

1320. MADDI, SALVATORE R.; PROPST, BARBARA S.; AND FELDINGER, IRWIN. "Three Expressions of the Need for Variety." J Personality 33:82–98 Mr '65. * (PA 39:10204)

1321. MEEHL, PAUL E. "Seer Over Sign: The First Good Example." J Exp Res Personality 1:27–32 Mr '65. * (PA 39:10206)

1322. MITCHELL, KEVIN MICHAEL. An Elaboration of a Study of the Schizophrenogenic Mother Concept by Means of the Thematic Apperception Test. Doctor's thesis, Michigan State University (East Lansing, Mich.), 1965. (DA 27:960B)

1323. MORANO, NICHOLAS THOMAS. Complexity-Simplicity: An Investigation of Cognitive, Motivational and Personality

Correlates. Doctor's thesis, Fordham University (New York, N.Y.), 1965. (*DA* 26:4079)

1324. REISS, NORMAN BERTRAM. *A Study of the Relationship Between Tolerance for Unrealistic Experiences and Originality.* Doctor's thesis, New York University (New York, N.Y.), 1965. (*DA* 27:305B)

1325. SEWARD, GEORGENE H.; WAGNER, PHILIP S.; HEINRICH, JEROME F.; BLOCK, SAUL K.; AND MYERHOFF, H. LEE. "The Question of Psychophysiologic Infertility: Some Answers." *Psychosom Med* 27:533–45 N–D '65. * (*PA* 40:5774)

1326. TODD, BEVERLEY CATHCART. *A Comparative Study of Mother-Child Relationships With Disturbed Children and Their Siblings.* Doctor's thesis, Temple University (Philadelphia, Pa.), 1965. (*DA* 26:4819)

1327. TOLLEFSON, NONA FALMLEN. *Relationship of Counselor Need Orientation to Counselor Effectiveness and Counselor Personality.* Doctor's thesis, Purdue University (Lafayette, Ind.), 1965. (*DA* 27:122A)

1328. TSUJI, SHOZO. "Some Investigations of Parental Preference in Early Childhood." *Rorsch Newsl* 10:37–41 Je '65. * (*PA* 40:2706)

1329. TYAGI, A. K. "A Study of Personality Differences in University Students With the Help of the TAT." *Manas* 12(1):47–63 '65. * (*PA* 40:2965)

1330. ANDERSON, LYNN R. "Leader Behavior, Member Attitudes, and Task Performance of Intercultural Discussion Groups." *J Social Psychol* 69:305–19 Ag '66. * (*PA* 40:12282)

1331. BARSKY, MARILYN LEE. *The Relationship of Some Aggressive Characteristics to Reading Achievement in Fifth and Sixth Grade Males and Females.* Doctor's thesis, Rutgers —The State University (New Brunswick, N.J.), 1966. (*DA* 27:1257A)

1332. EPSTEIN, SEYMOUR. "Some Theoretical Considerations on the Nature of Ambiguity and the Use of Stimulus Dimensions in Projective Techniques." *J Consult Psychol* 30:183–92 Je '66. * (*PA* 40:8870)

1333. FROMME, DONALD KARL. *An Approach-Avoidance Analysis of Aggression and the Thematic Apperception Test.* Doctor's thesis, University of Iowa (Iowa City, Iowa), 1966. (*DA* 27:608B)

1334. GOLD, DOLORES. *Psychological Changes Associated With Acculturation.* Doctor's thesis, University of Saskatchewan (Saskatoon, Sask., Canada), 1966. (*DA* 27:3514A)

1335. HELSON, RAVENNA. "Personality of Women With Imaginative and Artistic Interests: The Role of Masculinity, Originality, and Other Characteristics in Their Creativity." *J Personality* 34:1–25 Mr '66. * (*PA* 40:8830)

1336. KANTROWITZ, JUDY LEOPOLD. *The Effects of Crisis on Academic Achievement.* Doctor's thesis, Boston University (Boston, Mass.), 1966. (*DA* 27:1623B)

1337. KATZ, EVELYN WALKER. "A Content-Analytic Method for Studying Themes of Interpersonal Behavior." *Psychol B* 66:419–22 N '66. * (*PA* 41:659)

1338. KNIGHT, MARCIA S.; REZNIKOFF, MARVIN; AND TOLOR, ALEXANDER. "The Assessment of Ambivalence in Schizophrenic Patients." *J Clin Psychol* 22:407–11 O '66. * (*PA* 41:3137)

1339. LOGAN, DANIEL LANIER. *An Empirical Investigation of the Cultural Determinants of Basic Motivational Patterns.* Doctor's thesis, University of Arizona (Tucson, Ariz.), 1966. (*DA* 27:2874B)

1340. MCCLELLAND, DAVID C. "Longitudinal Trends in the Relation of Thought to Action." *J Consult Psychol* 30:479–83 D '66. * (*PA* 41:2919)

1341. MARCH, JUDITH V. *A Study in Time Orientation: The Relationship Between Memory for Past Experience and Orientation to the Future.* Doctor's thesis, New York University (New York, N.Y.), 1966. (*DA* 27:2141B)

1342. MEGARGEE, EDWIN I. "Undercontrolled and Overcontrolled Personality Types in Extreme Antisocial Aggression." *Psychol Monogr* 80(3):1–29 '66. *

1343. MURICKAN, JOSE VARKEY. *Family Systems in India and the United States: A Cross-Cultural Comparison of Educational Adequacy.* Doctor's thesis, St. Louis University (St. Louis, Mo.), 1966. (*DA* 27:1128A)

1344. REID, WALTER BROOK. *Some Aspects of Personality in Persistent Enuresis as Determined by Responses to Psychological Tests and to Drug Therapy.* Doctor's thesis, University of Houston (Houston, Tex.), 1966. (*DA* 27:1629B)

1345. ROSENFELD, HOWARD M. "Relationships of Ordinal Position to Affiliation and Achievement Motives: Direction and Generality." *J Personality* 34:467–79 D '66. * (*PA* 41:10197)

1346. ROTH, HERBERT SAMUEL. *Personal and Demographic Characteristics Associated With L-I-D Response Bias of Domiciled Veterans on an Institutional Interest Inventory.* Doctor's thesis, University of Kansas (Lawrence, Kan.), 1966. (*DA* 28:1209B)

1347. RYAN, ROBERT PATRICK. *The Role of the Experiencing Variable in the Psychotherapeutic Process.* Doctor's thesis, University of Illinois (Urbana, Ill.), 1966. (*DA* 28:971B)

1348. SANDHU, HARJIT S. "Group Sessions in a Reformatory School in the Punjab (India)." *Correct Psychiatry & J Social Ther* 12:393–403 S '66. * (*PA* 41:3094)

1349. SHOR, RONALD E.; ORNE, MARTIN T.; AND O'CONNELL, DONALD N. "Psychological Correlates of Plateau Hypnotizability in a Special Volunteer Sample." *J Pers & Social Psychol* 3:80–95 Ja '66. * (*PA* 40:2262)

1350. TAYLOR, MARGARET FORD. *An Investigation of Physiological Measures in Relation to the Moment of Stuttering in a Group of Adult Males.* Doctor's thesis, University of Southern California (Los Angeles, Calif.), 1966. (*DA* 27:3532A)

1351. THIESSEN, IRMGARD. "Values and Personality Characteristics of Mennonites in Manitoba." *Mennonite Q R* 40:48–61 Ja '66. *

1352. TITUS, WALTER FRANKLIN. *Relationship of Need for Achievement, Dependency and Locus of Control in Boys of Middle and Low Socioeconomic Status.* Doctor's thesis, Indiana University (Bloomington, Ind.), 1966. (*DA* 27:1674A)

1353. TOOLEY, KAY MCDONALD. *Ego Adaptation in Late Adolescence.* Doctor's thesis, University of Michigan (Ann Arbor, Mich.), 1966. (*DA* 28:106A)

1354. TURBERG, JESSIE. *An Investigation of the Association of Maternal Attitudes and Childhood Obesity and the Self-Concept of the Obese Child.* Doctor's thesis, New York University (New York, N.Y.), 1966. (*DA* 28:243B)

1355. WEISBERGER, STANLEY EARL. *An Analysis of Stuttering as a Function of the Stutterer's Response to an Array of Standard Projective Stimuli Involving Themes of Sexuality, Aggression and Parental-Authority.* Doctor's thesis, New York University (New York, N.Y.), 1966. (*DA* 27:2654A)

1356. WESSMAN, ALDEN E., AND RICKS, DAVID F. *Mood and Personality.* New York: Holt, Rinehart & Winston, Inc., 1966. Pp. xiii, 317.*

1357. WOHLFORD, PAUL. "Extension of Personal Time, Affective States, and Expectation of Personal Death." *J Pers & Social Psychol* 3:559–66 My '66. * (*PA* 40:7300)

1358. ALPER, THELMA G., AND GREENBERGER, ELLEN. "Relationship of Picture Structure to Achievement Motivation in College Women." *J Pers & Social Psychol* 7:362–71 D '67. * (*PA* 42:3964)

1359. BARCLAY, ANDREW MICHAEL. *The Effect of Hostility on Physiological and Fantasy Responses.* Doctor's thesis, University of Minnesota (Minneapolis, Minn.), 1967. (*DA* 28: 3259A)

1360. BARRINGTON, BYRON L. Chap. 14, "The Differential Effectiveness of Therapy as Measured by the Thematic Apperception Test," pp. 337–52. In *The Therapeutic Relationship and Its Impact: A Study of Psychotherapy With Schizophrenics.* Edited by Carl R. Rogers. Madison, Wis.: University of Wisconsin Press, 1967. Pp. xix, 625. *

1361. DERELI, ATILA HASAN. *Parental and Authority Relationships of Turkish College Students: A Cross-Cultural TAT Study.* Doctor's thesis, University of Oregon (Eugene, Ore.), 1967. (*DA* 28:938A)

1362. FELZ, GERALD ANTHONY. *Group Process as an Enabling Activity in an Elementary Teacher Preparation Curriculum.* Doctor's thesis, Arizona State University (Tempe, Ariz.), 1967. (*DA* 27:2913A)

1363. FOGEL, MAX L. "Picture Description and Interpretation in Brain-Damaged Patients." *Cortex* 3:433–48 D '67. * (*PA* 42:10991)

1364. GOODMAN, ELLEN. *A Study of Certain Aspects of the Social-Emotional Adjustment of Nonpromoted Elementary School Children.* Doctor's thesis, Lehigh University (Bethlehem, Pa.), 1967. (*DA* 28:3997A)

1365. GRAYSON, HENRY TATE, JR. *Psychosexual Conflict in Adolescent Girls Who Experienced Early Parental Loss by Death.* Doctor's thesis, Boston University (Boston, Mass.), 1967. (*DA* 28:2136B)

1366. JAMES, PATRICIA B., AND MOSHER, DONALD L. "Thematic Aggression, Hostility-Guilt and Aggressive Behavior." *J Proj Tech & Pers Assess* 31:61–7 F '67. * (*PA* 41:13678)

1367. KLINGER, ERIC. "Modeling Effects on Achievement Imagery." *J Pers & Social Psychol* 7:49–62 S '67. * (*PA* 41:15309)

1368. KUKUK, WILLIAM DUANE. *Modern Art Preferences, Problem-Solving Ability, and Time Perspective of Open- and Closed-Minded Persons.* Doctor's thesis, Brigham Young University (Provo, Utah), 1967. (*DA* 28:3051B)

1369. MCKINNON, DAN WILLARD. *Some Effects of Concomitant Group Counseling Experience on Students in the Counseling Practicum.* Doctor's thesis, Arizona State University (Tempe, Ariz.), 1967. (*DA* 28:2561A)

1370. MONDY, LEWIS W. "A Failure to Obtain Defensive Projection." *Psychol Rep* 20:1009–10 Je '67. * (*PA* 41:12982)

1371. OBERLEDER, MURIEL. "Adapting Current Psychological Techniques for Use in Testing the Aging." *Gerontologist* 7(3, pt 1):188–91 S '67. * (*PA* 42:3801)

1372. PEEBLES, RICHARD R. "Telophasic Theory and Depressive Conflict in Adolescent Girls." *Adolescence* 2:359–94 f '67. * (*PA* 42:7119)

1373. PIOTROWSKI, ZYGMUNT A. "Psychological Testing of Intelligence and Personality," pp. 509–30. In *Comprehensive Textbook of Psychiatry.* Edited by Alfred M. Freedman and Harold I. Kaplan. Baltimore, Md.: Williams & Wilkins Co., 1967. Pp. xxv, 1666. *

1374. PYTKOWICZ, ANN ROTH; WAGNER, NATHANIEL N.; AND SARASON, IRWIN G. "An Experimental Study of the Reduction of Hostility Through Fantasy." *J Pers & Social Psychol* 5:295–303 Mr '67. * (*PA* 41:5424)

1375. SHELTON, PATRICIA BROOKS. *Achievement Motivation in Professional Women.* Doctor's thesis, University of California (Berkeley, Calif.), 1967. (*DA* 28:4274A)

1376. SHORE, MILTON F.; MASSIMO, JOSEPH L.; AND MORAN, JANET K. "Some Cognitive Dimensions of Interpersonal Behavior in Adolescent Delinquent Boys." *J Res Crime & Del* 4:243–7 Jl '67. *

1377. TSUSHIMA, WILLIAM TORAO. *A Comparative Study of the Attitudes of Irish and Italian Patients of Two Social Levels Under Pre-Operative Stress.* Doctor's thesis, Fordham University (New York, N.Y.), 1967. (*DA* 28:1216B)

1378. WATSON, LAWRENCE CRAIG. *The Effect of Urbanization on Socialization Practices and Personality Development in Guajiro Society.* Doctor's thesis, University of California (Los Angeles, Calif.), 1967. (*DA* 28:1327B)

1379. BETHE, DONALD RAY. *Success in Beginning Handball as a Function of the Theory of Achievement Motivation.* Doctor's thesis, Ohio State University (Columbus, Ohio), 1968. (*DA* 29:1769A)

1380. BRODSKY, STANLEY L., AND DIXON, JAMES C. "Impersonal and Personal Language Patterns of Repressors and Sensitizers." *J General Psychol* 78:27–33 Ja '68. * (*PA* 42: 7273)

1381. BROWN, WILLIAM THOMAS. *Consideration of the Interrelationship of Five Aptitude and Achievement Factors in Successful Male Undergraduate Students at the University of Montana.* Doctor's thesis, University of Montana (Missoula, Mont.), 1968. (*DA* 29:3411A)

1382. BURTON, LINDY. *Vulnerable Children: Three Studies of Children in Conflict: Accident Involved Children, Sexually Assaulted Children, and Children With Asthma.* New York: Schocken Books Inc., 1968. Pp. x, 277. *

1383. CANSEVER, GÖKÇE. "The Achievement Motive in Turkish Adolescents." *J Social Psychol* 76:269–70 D '68. * (*PA* 43:3857)

1384. CARROLL, JEROME F. X. *The Acceptance or Rejection of Differences Between Adoptive and Biological Parenthood by Adoptive Applicants as Related to Various Indices of Adjustment/Maladjustment.* Doctor's thesis, Temple University (Philadelphia, Pa.), 1968. (*DA* 29:1503B)

1385. CHAUBEY, N. P. "Frustration-Reactions of High and Low n-Achievement." *Indian Psychol R* 5:52–6 Jl '68. *

1386. CHU, CHENG-PING. "The Remodification of TAT Adapted to Chinese Primary School Children: 1, Remodification of the Pictures and Setting Up the Objective Scoring Methods." *Acta Psychologica Taiwanica* 10:59–73 Mr '68. * (*PA* 45:4301)

1387. CHU, CHENG-PING. "The Remodification of TAT Adapted to Chinese Primary School Children: 2, The Application and Evaluation of Pictures." *Acta Psychologica Taiwanica* 10:74–89 Mr '68. * (*PA* 45:4302)

1388. CLEMENTS, WILLIAM HENRY. *Marital Adjustment and Marital Interaction.* Doctor's thesis, University of Cincinnati (Cincinnati, Ohio), 1968. (*DA* 29:1839B)

1389. COLEMAN, JOHN C. "Independence in Adolescence." *Brit J Proj Psychol & Pers Study* 13:7–10 D '68. *

1390. DRESSLER, RICHARD M. *Relationships Among Needs, Interests, and Curricular Choice in a Sample of College Men.* Doctor's thesis, Temple University (Philadelphia, Pa.), 1968. (*DAI* 30:1356B)

1391. ELDER, GLEN H., JR. "Achievement Motivation and Intelligence in Occupational Mobility: A Longitudinal Analysis." *Sociometry* 31:327–54 D '68. * (*PA* 43:3861)

1392. GARDNER, RILEY W., AND MORIARTY, ALICE. *Personality Development at Preadolescence: Explorations of Structure Formation.* Seattle, Wash.: University of Washington Press, 1968. Pp. xi, 344. *

1393. GREENWALD, EDDE R. *Perceptual Style in Relation to Role Choices and Motivational Variables.* Doctor's thesis, Yeshiva University (New York, N.Y.), 1968. (*DA* 29:2192B)

1394. HALL, LINCOLN HERBERT. *Selective Variables in the Achievement or Nonachievement of Junior College Students From Different Socioeconomic Backgrounds.* Doctor's thesis, University of Southern California (Los Angeles, Calif.), 1968. (*DA* 29:1674A)

1395. HENDRICKS, RONALD WAYNE. *An Investigation of the Relationship Between Certain Perceptions of Self and Evidences of Congruence, Empathy, and Positive Regard in Counselor Trainees.* Doctor's thesis, Arizona State University (Tempe, Ariz.), 1968. (*DA* 29:1451A)

1396. HENRY, WILLIAM E. "The Thematic Apperception Test." *Inter Encycl Social Sci* 12:573–9 '68. *

1397. HOLMES, DAVID S., AND TYLER, JOHN D. "Direct Versus Projective Measurement of Achievement Motivation." *J Consult & Clin Psychol* 32:712–7 D '68. * (*PA* 43:4029)

1398. HUMES, CHARLES WARREN, JR. *Group Counseling with Educable Mentally Retarded Adolescents in a Public School Setting: A Description of the Process and a Quantitative Assessment of Its Effectiveness.* Doctor's thesis, University of Massachusetts (Amherst, Mass.), 1968. (*DA* 29:1105A)

1399. INGHAM, JOHN MICHAEL. *Culture and Personality in a Mexican Village.* Doctor's thesis, University of California (Berkeley, Calif.), 1968. (*DA* 29:4492B)

1400. JOSHI, PURUSHOTTAM. "Attitudes Study in Uttar-Pradesh: Northern India." *Psychologia* 11:81–5 Je '68. * (*PA* 44:6628)

1401. KIEFER, CHRISTIE WEBER. *Personality and Social Change in a Japanese Danchi.* Doctor's thesis, University of California (Berkeley, Calif.), 1968. (*DA* 29:1246B)

1402. KINGSMORE, JOHN MACK. *The Effect of a Professional Wrestling and Professional Basketball Contest Upon the Aggressive Tendencies of Male Spectators.* Doctor's thesis, University of Maryland (College Park, Md.), 1968. (*DA* 29:3859A)

1403. LARSEN, EILEEN A. *A Pre-Normative and Predictive Study of the College Student Rorschach.* Doctor's thesis, University of Colorado (Boulder, Colo.), 1968. (*DA* 29:2204B)

1404. LETT, WARREN ROBERT. *Some Postulated Correlates of Creativity and Need Achievement.* Doctor's thesis, University of California (Berkeley, Calif.), 1968. (*DA* 29:1106A)

1405. LEVINE, FREDERIC J. "Color-Word Test Performance and Drive Regulation in Three Vocational Groups." *J Consult & Clin Psychol* 32:642–7 D '68. * (*PA* 43:4002)

1406. MARTIN, JAMES G., AND STRANGE, WINIFRED. "Determinants of Hesitations in Spontaneous Speech." *J Exp Psychol* 76:474–9 Mr '68. * (*PA* 42:8897)

1407. MENDELL, DAVID; CLEVELAND, SIDNEY E.; AND FISHER, SEYMOUR. "A Five-Generation Family Theme." *Family Process* 7:126–32 Mr '68. * (*PA* 43:8379)

1408. MITCHELL, KEVIN M. "An Analysis of the Schizophrenogenic Mother Concept by Means of the Thematic Apperception Test." *J Abn Psychol* 73:571–4 D '68. * (*PA* 43:4048)

1409. MUTHAYYA, B. C. "Personality Variables and Their Relation to Achievement Motive." *Psychol Studies* 13:98–100 Jl '68. * (*PA* 43:5336)

1410. PETERSEN, PAUL A. *The Clinical Utility of Projective Techniques.* Doctor's thesis, Illinois Institute of Technology (Chicago, Ill.), 1968. (*DAI* 30:2913B)

1411. PIOTROWSKI, ZYGMUNT A. "Psychological Test Prediction of Suicide," pp. 198–208. (*PA* 43:7114) In *Suicidal Behaviors: Diagnosis and Management.* Edited by H. L. P. Resnik. Boston, Mass.: Little, Brown & Co., 1968. Pp. xxvii, 536. *

1412. SCHAW, LOUIS C. *The Bonds of Work: Work in Mind, Time, and Tradition.* San Francisco, Calif.: Jossey-Bass Inc., Publishers, 1968. Pp. xix, 300. *

1413. SHORE, MILTON F.; MASSIMO, JOSEPH L.; MACK, RONALD; AND MALASKY, CHARLOTTE. "Studies of Psychotherapeutic Change in Adolescent Delinquent Boys: The Role of Guilt." *Psychother Theory Res & Prac* 5:85–8 Je '68. * (*PA* 42:17308)

1414. SPERO, JEANNETTE R. *A Study of the Relationship Between Selected Functional Menstrual Disorders and Interpersonal Conflict.* Doctor's thesis, New York University (New York, N.Y.), 1968. (*DA* 29:2905A)

1415. TAMHANKAR, VASANT S. "Analysis of Protocols of Indian Subjects on TAT in Ach Test." *Jap Psychol Res* 10:63–9 Jl '68. * (*PA* 44:2369)

1416. TAYLOR, ELIZABETH ELLEN. *The Measurement of Need and Conflict in the Normal Person.* Doctor's thesis, Washington University (St. Louis, Mo.), 1968. (*DA* 29:4855B)

1417. THELEN, M. H.; VARBLE, D. L.; AND JOHNSON, JANE. "Attitudes of Academic Clinical Psychologists Toward Projective Techniques." *Am Psychologist* 23:517–21 Jl '68. * (*PA* 42:18843)

1418. TINIO, FILIPINAS SANTOS. *Two Indices of Aggression: Aggressive Fantasy and Change in Pupil Size.* Master's thesis, Western Michigan University (Kalamazoo, Mich.), 1968. (*Masters Abstracts* 6:126)

1419. TOWNES, BRENDA, AND CHRIST, ADOLPHE E. "Psychological Testing: Its Usefulness in Teaching Psychotherapy and Psychodynamics to Medical Students." *Arch Gen Psychiatry* 19:487–90 O '68. * (*PA* 43:4068)

1420. WENDT, MIRIAM JANE. *The Conditioning of Defensive Verbal Constructs in Schizophrenic Patients.* Doctor's thesis, Case Western Reserve University (Cleveland, Ohio), 1968. (*DA* 29:4857B)

1421. WHEATON, CHARLES HOWARD. *The Effect of Hostility-Guilt on Responses to TAT Stimuli.* Master's thesis, Ohio State University (Columbus, Ohio), 1968.

1422. WILLIS, JOE DON. *Achievement Motivation, Success, and Competitiveness in College Wrestling.* Doctor's thesis, Ohio State University (Columbus, Ohio), 1968. (*DA* 29: 1443A)

1423. ABRAM, HARRY S.; ALLAN, J. HAMILTON; HUGHES, DEANNA; SMITH, BURKE M.; HALL, WILLIAM E.; AND LEWIS, DAVID W. "A Multidisciplinary Computerized Approach to the Study of Adjustment to Lower Limb Amputation." *South Med J* 62(9):1072–6 S '69. *

1424. ALKER, HENRY A. "Rationality and Achievement: A Comparison of the Atkinson-McClelland and Kogan-Wallach Formulations." *J Personality* 37(2):207–24 Je '69. *

1425. BARCLAY, A., AND CERVANTES, L. F. "The Thematic Apperception Test as an Index of Personality Attributes Characterizing the Adolescent Academic Dropout." *Adolescence* 4(16):525–40 w '69. * (*PA* 44:15283)

1426. BARCLAY, ANDREW M. "The Effect of Hostility on Physiological and Fantasy Responses." *J Personality* 37(4): 651–67 D '69. * (*PA* 44:8024)

1427. BEHRING, DANIEL WILLIAM. *Adaptive Functioning: A Rationale for the Prediction of Achievement in Nursing Education.* Doctor's thesis, Ohio University (Athens, Ohio), 1969. (*DAI* 31:1065A)

1428. BRENER, ELLIOT MAYNARD. *Castration Anxiety, Sexual Fantasy, and Sexual Adjustment.* Doctor's thesis, Boston University (Boston, Mass.), 1969. (*DAI* 30:2412B)

1429. CLARK, EDWARD T., AND PROPPER, MARTIN M. "Inter-Scorer Reliability of Davids' Three Projective Measures of Alienation." *Psychol Rep* 25(1):123–6 Ag '69. * (*PA* 44:3653)

1430. CLELAND, CHARLES C., AND SWARTZ, JON D. "Work Deprivation as Motivation to Work." *Am J Mental Def* 73(5): 703–12 Mr '69. * (*PA* 43:10262)

1431. COHEN, HELEN A., AND LIEBOWITZ, BERNARD. "A Family With Twins Discordant for Schizophrenia: A Case Study." *J Proj Tech & Pers Assess* 33(6):542–8 D '69. * (*PA* 44:7060)

1432. COLEMAN, JOHN C. "Changes in TAT Responses as a Function of Age." *J Genetic Psychol* 114(2):171–8 Je '69. * (*PA* 43:17223)

1433. CUMMINGS, S. THOMAS; GODFREY, ANNE E.; AND BURROWS, BENJAMIN. "Personality and Social Class Factors Associated With Occupational Disability in Patients With Chronic Obstructive Lung Disease: An Exploratory Study." *Am R Resp Dis* 99(6):872–8 Je '69. *

1434. DAHLIN, GERALDINE. *The Relationship of Personality to Subcultural Membership in Middle Class Adults.* Doctor's thesis, Illinois Institute of Technology (Chicago, Ill.), 1969. (DAI 30:2414B)

1435. DANESINO, ANGELO, AND LAYMAN, WILLIAM A. "Contrasting Personality Patterns of High and Low Achievers Among College Students of Italian and Irish Descent." *J Psychol* 72(1):71–83 My '69. * (*PA* 43:157·6)

1436. DAVIDS, ANTHONY; LAFFEY, JOHN J.; AND CARDIN, PAUL J. "Intellectual and Personality Factors in Effective Child Care Workers." *Am J Orthopsychiatry* 39(1):68–76 Ja '69. * (*PA* 45:757)

1437. DESIDERATO, OTELLO, AND KOSKINEN, PATRICIA. "Anxiety, Study Habits, and Academic Achievement." *J Counsel Psychol* 16(2):162–5 Mr '69. * (*PA* 43:10360)

1438. DICKSTEIN, LOUIS S. "Prospective Span as a Cognitive Ability." *J Consult & Clin Psychol* 33(6):757–60 D '69. * (*PA* 44:3616)

1439. DONOFRIO, ILENE ANNA. *The Effect of Examiner Variables on Amount of Self-Disclosure in TAT Stories.* Doctor's thesis, State University of New York (Buffalo, N.Y.), 1969. (DAI 30:2904B)

1440. ELMAN, LUBA. *Interpersonal Influences on Academic Achievement and Non-Achievement Among Disadvantaged College Students.* Doctor's thesis, City University of New York (New York, N.Y.), 1969. (DAI 30:844B)

1441. HALL, LINCOLN H. "Selective Variables in the Academic Achievement of Junior College Students From Different Socioeconomic Backgrounds." *J Ed Res* 63(2):60–2 O '69. *

1442. HURST, JUSTIN FRED. *The Influence of Color and/or Movement Added to Thematic Apperception Test to Evoke Need Achievement.* Doctor's thesis, Utah State University (Logan, Utah), 1969. (DAI 30:3322A)

1443. IRIZARRY, RAYMOND. *Anxiety, Repression and Varieties of Anti-Social Behavior in Psychopaths.* Doctor's thesis, Columbia University (New York, N.Y.), 1969. (DAI 30: 2420B)

1444. KADUSHIN, PHINEAS; CUTLER, CAROLINE; WAXENBERG, SHELDON E.; AND SAGER, CLIFFORD J. "The Family Story Technique and Intrafamily Analysis." *J Proj Tech & Pers Assess* 33(5):438–50 O '69. * (*PA* 44:3656)

1445. KAPLAN, MARTIN F. "The Ambiguity of TAT Ambiguity." *J Proj Tech & Pers Assess* 33(1):25–9 F '69. * (*PA* 43:9790)

1446. KAPLAN, MARTIN F. "Expression of TAT Hostility as a Function of Self-Reported Hostility, Arousal and Cue Characteristics." *J Personality* 37(2):289–96 Je '69. *

1447. KAPLAN, MARTIN F. "Reply to Murstein's 'Comment on "The Ambiguity of TAT Ambiguity."'" *J Proj Tech & Pers Assess* 33(6):486–8 D '69. * (*PA* 44:6791)

1448. LESTER, DAVID, AND SCHUMACHER, JOAN. "Schizophrenia and Death Concern." *J Proj Tech & Pers Assess* 33(5):403–5 O '69. * (*PA* 44:3879)

1449. LEVINE, FREDFRIC J. "Thematic Drive Expression in Three Occupational Groups." *J Proj Tech & Pers Assess* 33(4):357–63 Ag '69. * (*PA* 44:2365)

1450. LIPGAR, ROBERT M. "Treatment of Time in the TAT." *J Proj Tech & Pers Assess* 33(3):219–29 Je '69. * (*PA* 43:14368)

1451. LOWENHERZ, LILA, AND FEFFER, MELVIN. "Cognitive Level as a Function of Defensive Isolation." *J Abn Psychol* 74(3):352–7 Je '69. * (*PA* 43:13002)

1452. MANDEL, HARVEY PHILIP. *Validation of Developmental Theory of Psychopathology: Diagnostic Categorization Versus Symptomatology.* Doctor's thesis, Illinois Institute of Technology (Chicago, Ill.), 1969. (DAI 30:2911B)

1453. MARCUS, SANDER IRA. *Diagnostic Classification of Alcoholics According to Developmental Theory.* Doctor's thesis, Illinois Institute of Technology (Chicago, Ill.), 1969. (DAI 30:2424B)

1454. MASLING, JOSEPH, AND HARRIS, SANDRA. "Sexual Aspects of TAT Administration." *J Consult & Clin Psychol* 33(2):166–9 Ap '69. * (*PA* 43:9855)

1455. MAY, ROBERT. "Deprivation-Enhancement Fantasy Patterns in Men and Women." *J Proj Tech & Pers Assess* 33(5): 464–9 O '69. * (*PA* 44:3657)

1456. MELNICK, BARRY, AND HURLEY, JOHN R. "Distinctive

1457. MITCHELL, KEVIN M. "Concept of 'Pathogenesis' in Parents of Schizophrenic and Normal Children." *J Abn Psychol* 74(4):423–4 Ag '69. * (*PA* 43:16083)

1458. MITCHELL, KEVIN M. "Social Class and the Schizophrenogenic Mother Concept." *Psychol Rep* 24(2):463–9 Ap '69. * (*PA* 43:16084)

1459. MORRISON, EVELYN. "Underachievement Among Preadolescent Boys Considered in Relationship to Passive Aggression." *J Ed Psychol* 60(3):168–73 Je '69. * (*PA* 43:13387)

1460. MUHLENKAMP, ANN F. "A Comparison of Reification Frequencies in Thematic Apperception Test Stories." *J Clin Psychol* 25(1):82–3 Ja '69. * (*PA* 43:9795)

1461. MURRAY, EDWARD J.; SEAGULL, ARTHUR; AND GEISINGER, DAVID. "Motivational Patterns in the Families of Adjusted and Maladjusted Boys." *J Consult & Clin Psychol* 33(3):337–42 Je '69. * (*PA* 43:12803)

1462. MURSTEIN, BERNARD I. "Comment on 'The Ambiguity of TAT Ambiguity.'" *J Proj Tech & Pers Assess* 33(6): 483–5 D '69. * (*PA* 44:6793)

1463. NESTER, EMERY WALTER, JR. *The Relationship Between Certain Student Personality Characteristics and Choice of College and Related Curricula.* Doctor's thesis, Arizona State University (Tempe, Ariz.), 1969. (DAI 30:934A)

1464. NORMAN, RUSSELL P. "Extreme Response Tendency as a Function of Emotional Adjustment and Stimulus Ambiguity." *J Consult & Clin Psychol* 33(4):406–10 Ag '69. * (*PA* 43:15758)

1465. ODELL, MARTHA QUERY. *Sex Differences in the Relationship Between Anxiety and Need for Achievement and in the Relationship Between Anxiety and Need for Affiliation.* Doctor's thesis, George Washington University (Washington, D.C.), 1969. (DAI 30:1904B)

1466. OLCZAK, PAUL V., AND KAPLAN, MARTIN F. "Originality and Rate of Response in Association as a Function of Associative Gradient." *Am J Psychol* 82(2):157–67 Je '69. * (*PA* 43:15754)

1467. OSTROW, ANDREW C. *The Aggressive Tendencies of Male Intercollegiate Tennis Team Players.* Master's thesis, University of Maryland (College Park, Md.), 1969.

1468. SHAPIRO, KENNETH J., AND ALEXANDER, IRVING E. "Extraversion-Introversion, Affiliation, and Anxiety." *J Personality* 37(3):387–406 S '69. * (*PA* 44:6758)

1469. SHARMA, G. C., AND SHARMA, G. C. "Personality of Artists." *Indian J Appl Psychol* 6(1):31–4 Ja '69. *

1470. SIMS, JOHN H. "The Federal Civil Service Executive: The Psychodynamics of a Social Role." Abstract. *Proc 77th Ann Conv Am Psychol Assn* 4(2):615–6 '69. * (*PA* 44:1445)

1471. SINGER, PAUL R. Chap. 9, "Psychological Testing: Thematic Apperception Test, Rorschach Test, and WAIS Vocabulary Scale," pp. 110–43. In *The Psychological World of the Teen-Ager: A Study of Normal Adolescent Boys.* By Daniel Offer and others. New York: Basic Books, Inc., Publishers, 1969. Pp. xiv, 286. *

1472. SMART, REGINALD G., AND FEJER, DIANNE. "Illicit LSD Users: Their Social Backgrounds, Drug Use and Psychopathology." *J Health & Social Behav* 10(4):297–308 D '69. * (*PA* 44:8423)

1473. SPITZER, STEPHEN P. "Test Equivalence of Unstructured Self-Evaluation Instruments." *Sociol Inquiry* 10(2): 204–15 sp '69. *

1474. SUINN, RICHARD M., AND OSKAMP, STUART. *The Predictive Validity of Projective Measures: A Fifteen-Year Evaluative Review of Research,* pp. 61–82, 125–8. Springfield, Ill.: Charles C Thomas, Publisher, 1969. Pp. xv, 161. *

1475. THIESSEN, IRMGARD; WRIGHT, MORGAN W.; AND SISLER, GEORGE C. "A Comparison of Personality Characteristics of Mennonites With Non-Mennonites." *Can Psychologist* 10(2):129–37 Ap '69. * (*PA* 43:15654)

1476. TINIO, FILLIPINAS, AND ROBERTSON, MALCOLM. "Examination of Two Indices of Hostility: Fantasy and Change in Pupil Size." Abstract. *Proc 77th Ann Conv Am Psychol Assn* 4(1):173–4 '69. * (*PA* 43:17032)

1477. TREPPA, JERRY ANTHONY. *An Investigation of Some of the Dynamics of the Interpersonal Relationship Between Pairs of Multiple Therapists.* Doctor's thesis, Michigan State University (East Lansing, Mich.), 1969. (DAI 30:1909B)

1478. WANG, MAY-JANE. "Report on the Revision of the Thematic Apperception Test." *Acta Psychologica Taiwanica* 11:24–41 Mr '69. * (*PA* 44:8475)

1479. WICKSTROM, MARGARET LEE. *The Relationship of Future Time Perspective to Rehabilitation Performance on a Leg Prosthesis.* Doctor's thesis, Columbia University (New York, N.Y.), 1969. (DAI 30:4802B)

1480. WINGET, CAROLYN N.; GLESER, GOLDINE C.; AND CLEMENTS, WILLIAM H. "A Method for Quantifying Human Relations, Hostility, and Anxiety Applied to TAT Productions." *J Proj Tech & Pers Assess* 33(5):433–7 O '69. * (*PA* 44:3659)

1481. WINTER, SARA K. "Characteristics of Fantasy While Nursing." *J Personality* 37(1):58–72 Mr '69. * (*PA* 43: 12863)

1482. WINTER, WILLIAM D., AND FERREIRA, ANTONIO J. "Talking Time as an Index of Intrafamilial Similarity in

Personality Attributes of Child-Abusing Mothers." *J Consult & Clin Psychol* 33(6):746–9 D '69. * (*PA* 44:3841)

Normal and Abnormal Families." *J Abn Psychol* 74(5):574–5 O '69. * *(PA* 44:1037)

1483. WOLOWITZ, HOWARD M., AND SHORKEY, CLAYTON. "Power Motivation in Male Paranoid Children." *Psychiatry* 32(4):459–66 N '69. * *(PA* 44:16761)

1484. YUFIT, ROBERT I. "Variations of Intimacy and Isolation." *J Proj Tech & Pers Assess* 33(1):49–58 F '69. * *(PA* 43:9700)

1485. BECKER, BRUCE. "The Projective Approach to the Study of Multiple Personality—A Case Study." *Int Congr Rorsch & Other Proj Tech* 7:423–38 '70. *

1486. BORSTEIN, IRVING JACOB. *Perceived Maternal Child-bearing Patterns and Schizoid Behavior in "Normal" Males.* Doctor's thesis, Illinois Institute of Technology (Chicago, Ill.), 1970. *(DAI* 31:2273B)

1487. BUIRSKI, PETER, AND KRAMER, ERNEST. "Literature as a Projection of the Author's Personality." *J Proj Tech & Pers Assess* 34(1):27–30 F '70. * *(PA* 44:8470)

1488. CASTELNUOVO-TEDESCO, PIETRO, AND KROUT, BOYD M. "Psychomatic Aspects of Chronic Pelvic Pain." *Psychiatry Med* 1(2):109–26 Ap '70. *

1489. COHEN, I.; FLIEGELMAN, S.; GLUCK, Z.; AND KELMAN, D. "Study of Early Differentiation Between Schizophrenia and Psychotic Manifestations in Adolescence." *Israel Ann Psychiatry* 8(2):163–72 Jl '70. *

1490. CRONBACH, LEE J. *Essentials of Psychological Testing, Third Edition,* pp. 651–8. New York: Harper & Row, Publishers, Inc., 1970. Pp. xxxix, 752. *

1491. EISENMAN, RUSSELL, AND FOULKS, EDWARD F. "Usefulness of Mussen's TAT Scoring System: 1, Differences Among Guatemalan Indians, Ladinos, and Mengalas on a Modified TAT; 2, Attitudes Toward the Physically Disabled as Related to Nurturance and Deference." *Psychol Rep* 27(1):179–85 Ag '70. * *(PA* 45:6372)

1492. EMRICK, CHAD D. "Abstinence and Time Perception of Alcoholics." *Q J Studies Alcohol* 31(2):384–93 Je '70. *

1493. GOLDSTEIN, MICHAEL J.; GOULD, EDWARD; ARMAND, ALKIRE; RODNICK, ELIOT H.; AND JUDD, LEWIS L. "Interpersonal Themes in the Thematic Apperception Test Stories of Families of Disturbed Adolescents." *J Nerv & Mental Dis* 150(5):354–65 My '70. * *(PA* 46:1231)

1494. GRISSO, J. THOMAS. "Verbal Behavior and the Action-Thought Dimension." *J Abn Psychol* 76(2):265–9 O '70. * *(PA* 45:4615)

1495. HANDEL, GERALD. "Projective Techniques and the Social Psychology of the Family." *Int Congr Rorsch & Other Proj Tech* 7:928–35 '70. *

1496. HARTMAN, A. ARTHUR. "A Basic TAT Set." *J Proj Tech & Pers Assess* 34(5):391–6 O '70. * *(PA* 45:4304)

1497. HERMANS, HUBERT J. M. "A Questionnaire Measure of Achievement Motivation." *J Appl Psychol* 54(4):353–63 Ag '70. * *(PA* 44:21518)

1498. HIRSCH, ERNEST A. *The Troubled Adolescent: As He Emerges From Psychological Tests.* New York: International Universities Press, Inc., 1970. Pp. xv, 645. *

1499. HOLZMAN, PHILIP S., AND ROUSEY, CLYDE. "Monitoring, Activation, and Disinhibition: Effects of White Noise Masking on Spoken Thought." *J Abn Psychol* 75(3):227–41 Je '70. * *(PA* 44:14564)

1500. KALTER, NEIL. "Self-Selection of TAT Cards: A Technique for Assessing Test-Restraint Children." *J Proj Tech & Pers Assess* 34(3):324–7 Ag '70. * *(PA* 44:211~4)

1501. KAMIL, LEONARD J. "Psychodynamic Changes Through Systematic Desensitization." *J Abn Psychol* 76(2):199–205 O '70. * *(PA* 45:4419)

1502. KAPLAN, MARTIN F. "A Note on the Stability of TAT Interjudge and Intrajudge Ambiguity Scores." *J Proj Tech & Pers Assess* 34(3):201–3 Je '70. * *(PA* 44:18747)

1503. KAPLAN, MARTIN F.; SIMON, SEYMOUR; AND DITRICHS, RAYMOND. "Observational Learning of TAT Theme Commonality." *J Exp Res Personality* 4(3):176–80 Je '70. * *(PA* 44:16648)

1504. KAPLAN, MARVIN L.; COLARELLI, NICK J.; GROSS, RUTH BRILL; LEVENTHAL, DONALD B.; AND SIEGAL, SAUL M. *The Structural Approach to Psychological Testing.* New York: Pergamon Press, Inc., 1970. Pp. xi, 195. *

1505. KARON, BERTRAM P., AND O'GRADY, PAUL. "Quantified Judgments of Mental Health From the Rorschach, TAT, and Clinical Status Interview by Means of a Scaling Technique." *J Consult & Clin Psychol* 34(2):229–35 Ap '70. * *(PA* 44:10723)

1506. KEILLOR, JAMES SHERWOOD. *The Effects of Experimentally Induced Consciousness Expansion and Consciousness Control Upon Creativity and Intellectual Functioning.* Doctor's thesis, Wayne State University (Detroit, Mich.), 1970. *(DAI* 31:4339B)

1507. KLATSKIN, ETHELYN H., AND ERON, LEONARD D. "Projective Test Content During Pregnancy and Postpartum Adjustment." *Psychosom Med* 32(5):487–94 S–O '70. *

1508. LESTER, DAVID. "Attempts to Predict Suicidal Risk Using Psychological Tests." *Psychol B* 74(1):1–17 Jl '70. * *(PA* 44:16905)

1509. LESTER, DAVID. "Factors Affecting Choice of Method of Suicide." *J Clin Psychol* 26(4):437 O '70. * *(PA* 45:4579)

1510. LEVY, MARTIN R. "Issues in the Personality Assessment of Lower-Class Patients." *J Proj Tech & Pers Assess* 34(1):6–9 F '70. * *(PA* 44:8467)

1511. MACCOBY, MICHAEL, AND FOSTER, GEORGE M. "Methods of Studying Mexican Peasant Personality: Rorschach, TAT, and Dreams." *Anthropol Q* 43(4):225–42 O '70. *

1512. MASLING, JOSEPH, AND HARRIS, SANDRA. "On Alternative Interpretations of Experimental Findings: A Reply to Wolf." *J Consult & Clin Psychol* 35(3):330–1 D '70. * *(PA* 45:6374)

1513. MURSTEIN, BERNARD I., AND WOLF, STEVEN R. "An Empirical Test of the 'Levels' Hypothesis With Five Projective Techniques." *Int Congr Rorsch & Other Proj Tech* 7:558–72 '70. *

1514. MURSTEIN, BERNARD I., AND WOLF, STEVEN R. "Empirical Test of the 'Levels' Hypothesis With Five Projective Techniques." *J Abn Psychol* 75(1):38–44 F '70. * *(PA* 44:6794)

1515. ORNITZ, HILDA WANE. *A Developmental Study of Errors of Commission in Recall.* Doctor's thesis, City University of New York (New York, N.Y.), 1970. *(DAI* 31:3~11B)

1516. PALMER, ROBERT D. "Visual Acuity and Stimulus-Seeking Behavior." *Psychosom Med* 32(3):277–84 My–Je '70. * *(PA* 44:18697)

1517. PASSINI, FRANK THOMAS, JR. *Peer Nomination Assessment of Resultant Motivation.* Doctor's thesis, University of Michigan (Ann Arbor, Mich.), 1970. *(DAI* 31:4369B)

1518. PROLA, MAX. "A Re-evaluation of the Motor Inhibition: Fantasy Hypothesis." *J Proj Tech & Pers Assess* 34(6):477–83 D '70. * *(PA* 45:8257)

1519. PROPPER, MARTIN M. "Direct and Projective Assessment of Alienation Among Affluent Adolescent Males." *J Proj Tech & Pers Assess* 34(1):41–4 F '70. * *(PA* 44:824~)

1520. REES, ANN H., AND PALMER, FRANCIS H. "Factors Related to Change in Mental Test Performance." *Develop Psychol Monogr* 3(2):1–57 S '70. * *(PA* 45:464)

1521. SANTOSTEFANO, SEBASTIANO. "Assessment of Motives in Children." *Psychol Rep* 26(2):639–49 Ap '70. * *(PA* 44:20681)

1522. SCHAEFER, CHARLES E. "A Psychological Study of 10 Exceptionally Creative Adolescent Girls." *Excep Children* 36(6):431–41 F '70. * *(PA* 44:20978)

1523. SHALIT, BENJAMIN. "Environmental Hostility and Hostility in Fantasy." *J Pers & Social Psychol* 15(2):171–4 Je '70. * *(PA* 44:12571)

1524. SMITH, J. M. "A Note on Achievement Motivation and Verbal Fluency." *J Proj Tech & Pers Assess* 34(2):121–4 Ap '70. * *(PA* 44:16655)

1525. STARKER, STEVEN, AND GOODENOUGH, DONALD R. "Effects of Sleep State and Method of Awakening Upon Thematic Apperception Test Productions at Arousal." *J Nerv & Mental Dis* 150(3):188–94 Mr '70. * *(PA* 45:8258)

1526. STRAUSS, F. H. "A Modification in TAT Technique." *Int Congr Rorsch & Other Proj Tech* 7:640–4 '70. *

1527. TSENG, M. S., AND CARTER, A. R. "Achievement Motivation and Fear of Failure as Determinants of Vocational Choice, Vocational Aspiration, and Perception of Vocational Prestige." *J Counsel Psychol* 17(2):150–6 Mr '70. * *(PA* 44:9309)

1528. VASSILIOU, VASSO; KATAKIS, HARRIS; AND VASSILIOU, GEORGE. "Milieu Related Variations of Motivational Patterns of Pre-Adolescents in Greece as Revealed by Story Sequence Analysis." *Int Congr Rorsch & Other Proj Tech* 7:349–56 '70. *

1529. WERNER, MARTHA; STABENAU, JAMES R.; AND POLLIN, WILLIAM. "Thematic Apperception Test Method for the Differentiation of Families of Schizophrenics, Delinquents, and 'Normals.'" *J Abn Psychol* 75(2):139–45 Ap '70. * *(PA* 44:10513)

1530. WOHLFORD, PAUL, AND HERRERA, JORGE A. "TAT Stimulus-Cues and Extension of Personal Time." *J Proj Tech & Pers Assess* 34(1):31–7 F '70. * *(PA* 44:8218)

1531. WOLF, MARTIN G. "An Alternative Interpretation of Masling and Harris' Study on the Sexual Aspects of TAT Administration." *J Consult & Clin Psychol* 35(3):328–9 D '70. * *(PA* 45:6379)

1532. ZIMRING, FRED M.; NAUMAN, COLSTON; AND BALCOMBE, JACK K. "Listening With the Second Ear: Selective Attention and Emotion." Abstract. *Proc 78th Ann Conv Am Psychol Assn* 5(1):471–2 '70. * *(PA* 44:18704)

1533. STOLOROW, ROBERT D. "Causality-Interpretation and Obsessive Versus Hysterical Functioning." *J Proj Tech & Pers Assess* 35(1):32–7 F '71. * *(PA* 46:6905)

RICHARD H. DANA, *Professor of Psychology, University of Arkansas, Fayetteville, Arkansas.*

This review covers over 100 studies that appeared in three dozen journals, with roughly one-third from the *Journal of Projective Techniques and Personality Assessment* and one-sixth from the *Journal of Consulting and*

Clinical Psychology. When these tallies are compared with journal sources for the previous review, it is apparent that publication outlets have become more restricted. These studies do not form a cohesive body of knowledge about the TAT or its application to personality evaluation. However, these studies do represent the current thinking about the TAT as a projective device for tapping fantasy in a manner that leads to conceptualizations of individual personality or group dynamics and to theories of personality.

All studies using non-TAT pictures as well as many reports of single need variables have been excluded. The need scores are not often used in clinical practice, although such applications are feasible (*1196*). Traditional clinical assessment has been global and related to dynamic personality theories. As Lazarus has indicated (*1113*), need scores emphasize instrumental activities, or secondary process content, while clinical interpretation has been focused on primary process content. For this reason, the need constructs have stronger validational evidence because of their more direct relationship to behavior, as well as their more systematic research development. The relevant consideration here is that the history of TAT validation has not made this distinction clearly. The assumption that TAT fantasy and overt behavior are related has often been made, but the conditions under which this relationship obtains have been infrequently stated. Fantasy, unless blocked, is probably directly related to behavior whenever one measures fantasy in terms of secondary process TAT content. However, as other writers have indicated, fantasy may also be a substitute for behavior, a perceptual style, or even a learned response tendency when measured from TAT content that reflects primary process activity. The relationship of fantasy to behavior is complex and idiographic.

Perspective on the TAT stimulus may be found in extensive reviews by Kenny (*774, 1006*) and discussions by Epstein (*1332*) and Murstein (*1063*). Kenny (*1006*) has presented three models for thematic test stimuli: the *pure relative frequency* of the standard TAT, containing many stimuli to assess many personality dimensions; the *specific relative frequency* of custom-built, single dimension measures; and the *cumulative homogeneity* of stimuli scaled to decrease ambiguity for single dimensions.

The studies reviewed here represent all models to the extent that standard cards were used.

Attempts to define the stimulus values for TAT cards have dealt both with physical picture cues and with the number of alternative decoding reactions. There is now consensus on this latter definition, either by semantic differential ratings (*999, 1050*), or Murstein's direct use of the number of alternative coding reactions as the measure of ambiguity (*1011*). Murstein has provided normative data for college students on all cards and reports few sex differences, except that women produce richer stories (*1121*). High ambiguity cards tend to decrease verbal fluency (*1131*), a finding anticipated by clinicians.

Epstein's hypothesis [1] that low stimulus-value cards are drive-relevant while high stimulus-value cards are conflict relevant, has been generally supported for hostile-aggressive thematic content, regardless of scoring system used or degree of psychological disturbance (*1032, 1165, 1218, 1445*), and for sexual thematic content.[2] However, when the overt behavior of adolescent boys is the criterion, the Epstein relationship apparently does not hold (*1151, 1172, 1366*), perhaps because the design format is reversed.

A potpourri of other stimulus studies, while interesting, cannot be related to context within this review. Megargee (*1171*) found differential responses by sex when he varied arousal instructions and card stimulus-values; sensitizing and repressing women expressed hostile content differentially. Murstein (*1064*) found that students can control hostile TAT content to accord with their perceived selves rather than with their overt behavior. And arousal by insult produces greater hostility to age-equivalent male TAT figures for both sexes.[3] When color is added to TAT pictures, it has a subtle and stimulating effect on fantasy productions (*1056, 1144*).

Some of the conditions of examiner-examinee interaction now have been delineated as they affect story content. Examiner bias, particularly in cross-sex administrations, is clearly opera-

[1] EPSTEIN, SEYMOUR. "The Measurement of Drive and Conflict in Humans: Theory and Experiment." *Neb Symposium Motiv* 10:127–206 '62. *

[2] EISLER, RICHARD M. "Thematic Expressions of Sexual Conflict Under Varying Stimulus Conditions." *J Consult & Clin Psychol* 32:216–20 Ap '68. *

[3] FESHBACH, SEYMOUR; SINGER, ROBERT D.; AND FESHBACH, NORMA. "Effects of Anger Arousal and Similarity Upon the Attribution of Hostility to Pictorial Stimuli." *J Consult Psychol* 27:248–52 Je '63. *

tive: male examiners apparently do not clearly separate their social and professional roles while female examiners are more task-oriented (*1454*). Examiners also differ in the type of TAT content elicited (*853*), and the administration conditions—indirect examiner effects—do make a difference (*988, 1126, 1162*).

Issues in the assessment of lower-class persons have finally been reviewed (*1510*). TAT pictures represent middle class persons (*1262*). Middle class examiners typically misinterpret subcultural referrents by focusing on nonshared behaviors and minimizing the relevance of shared behaviors (*1109*). Such distortions have been mediated by the outdated belief in personality as a fixed condition existing within the person. Part of this misinterpretation is also due to a confounding of perceptual bias and cultural distinctness (*1006*). Any study making cross-cultural or subcultural comparisons must first demonstrate an equivalence between groups in the functional stimulus meaning, i.e., the existence of similar decoding systems to identify and categorize thematic content. Finally, the survival qualities for the lower class environment are often judged by middle class standards; e.g., lower class persons have transitory interpersonal relations, an inadequate self concept, a predominantly physical mode of self-expression with primitive defenses, little delay, and much hostility and aggression.

It is mandatory to articulate our own class-typed and sex-typed examiner bias and to look at TAT content as a joint expression of goodness of fit between the examinee and his environmental status and between the examiner and examinee expectancies for interaction. A next logical step is the delineation of personality characteristics that are relevant for participation in our increasingly separate, different, and dissident subcultures.

One solution to the examiner bias inherent in the traditional focus on nonshared behaviors has appeared in the study of family interactions. Historically, separate testings of each family member were followed by a combined interpretation of all data (*584*). Then separate testings were followed by a joint testing during which mutually agreed-upon responses were required, or a single testing was used with the requirement of either agreed-upon stories or family-content stories [4] (*1091, 1103, 1142, 1444*). All

of these approaches use selected TAT cards and familiar content scores, e.g., Fine (*481*) or Hafner and Kaplan (*720*), in order to find consistent differences in TAT content as a function of family adjustment.

Although most of this research has been on the development of new techniques using familiar cards and scores, several studies suggest the future. A delineation of cognitive styles within a family permits blind matching of children and their parents (*1081*). Thus, it is not surprising that families are consistent in their theme usage across generations (*1407*). There are also characteristic differences in content between well-adjusted and poorly-adjusted couples, as determined by scores from new scales for Human Relations, Hostility Directed Outward, and Anxiety (*1480*). Similarly, mothers of maladjusted boys are more responsive to external cues than mothers of adjusted boys, using a TAT experience-balance score (*1461*).

The question of what the TAT taps, with whom and under what conditions, has received renewed attention in studies by direct and indirect assessment using self-report or projective techniques. The sophistication of the subject clearly affects content (*1060*), although social desirability influences have not been readily demonstrable (*1022*). "Willingness" vs. "ability" to be self-revealing may be contrasted by the motivation to create a favorable impression (*638*). In other words, the level of the assessment may determine the response (*1067, 1097, 1184, 1397*). Homogeneous subjects, however, may respond equivalently, regardless of level assessed (*1519*), and the nature or uniformity of the trait or state assessed may determine the characteristic level at which self-revelation takes place (*1130, 1172*). Such issues are not resolved by piecemeal, unsystematic research, but some of the relevant variables have been suggested.

There are a variety of studies on newly articulated personality dimensions. Time span, retrotensive and protensive, provides a matrix of empirical correlates [5] (*1236, 1357, 1530*), especially since it is apparently unrelated to verbal IQ (*1438*) and is part of the human subjective probability system (*1450*). Locus of control has been assessed as an independent variable (*1197*) and as a causality notion that is intimately tied in to the obsessive-hysteroid

4 WINTER, WILLIAM D., AND FERREIRA, ANTONIO J. "A Factor Analysis of Family Interaction Measures." *J Proj Tech & Pers Assess* 34(1):55–64 F '70. *

5 RICKS, DAVID; UMBARGER, CARTER; AND MACK, RONALD. "A Measure of Increased Temporal Perspective in Successfully Treated Adolescent Delinquent Boys." *J Abn & Social Psychol* 69:685–9 D '64. *

personality dimension (*1533*). Adolescent expressive style (*1183*), deprivation-enhancement fantasy [6] (*1455*), ego sufficiency (*758, 1068*), extremeness (*1205*), guilt (*1030, 1366*), human relations (*1480*), openness (*1163*), and rebelliousness (*1037, 1111*) are conspicuous. These dimensions may well be precursors of a descriptive rubric that fits modern man in an age of transition and crisis.

Personality theory per se is equally represented by activation and psychoanalysis. Scores for novelty (*1287*) and variety [7] (*1320*), are receiving the beginnings of systematic attention (*1096, 1287, 1306*). The psychoanalytic proponents have presented hypothesis-testing (*1024, 1099, 1141*), and one classic exposition of a global ego strength scale, including the TAT, that deserves wide readership.[8] Two studies suggest Piaget's influence (*1183, 1200*).

In order to document that the practice of labeling convenient if not homogeneous groups is still present, there are studies of the aged (*1371, 1432*), asthmatic and allergic children (*1145*), bilinguals (*996*), brain damaged (*1363*), delinquents (*1228*), executives (*1154*), foster home children (*1122*), mental retards (*1052*), nurses (*1045, 1460*), and obesity (*1170*). Case studies, however, have become infrequent, e.g., female temporomandibular joint dysfunction (*1117*), and phantom pain (*1073*).

In striking contrast to these studies are normative data for sex (*1121*), minority (*1057, 1118*), and IQ groups (*1025*), as well as expositions of consistency between drive expression and métier (*1107, 1449*). Similarly, the literature on "schizophrenia" as a distinct entity is disappearing and instead there are systematic inquiries into origin (*1174, 1408, 1457*), and various behavioral dimensions [9] (*997, 1143, 1212*).

Now that there appears to be tacit acceptance of Tomkins' dictum that the TAT is a methodology for personality study and not a test per se, the emphasis on validation research has diminished. Instead, there is a more flexible use of scoring variables and scoring systems, coupled with a sensitivity to changes in clinical practice with social class and family groups. Simultaneously, there is sustained relevance to an empirical base for personality theory, with minor reference to hypothesis testing derived from newer personality theories. A burgeoning of systematic research in which stimulus values, arousal conditions, subject characteristics, and examiner biases are studied concurrently provide this base. Increasingly, the clinical usage and the research scrutiny are separate events, with the clinical practice modeled on the TAT as a method of observation and the research predicated on an absence of blind necessity for immediate nourishment of clinical practice.

LEONARD D. ERON, *Professor of Psychology, University of Illinois at Chicago Circle, Chicago, Illinois.*

The TAT, introduced in 1935, is a procedure in which the subject makes up stories in response to a series of pictures. Inferences are made by the examiner about the motivations, attitudes, and habits of the subject on the basis of the characteristics of the stories he tells—the themes, affects, relationships among characters, outcomes, emotional tone of the stories, etc. How reliable and valid these inferences are or can be has been the subject of countless articles in the past 30 years. In my review of the TAT in *The Fifth Mental Measurements Yearbook,* it was pointed out that the TAT is probably not a very efficient clinical tool but it has many worthwhile functions and applications in personality research. Adcock, in *The Sixth Mental Measurements Yearbook,* took the position that "as an indicator of general interests, important current sources of motivation, areas of emotional disturbance, and clues for clinical discussion, the test has excellent possibilities but it is not suitable for providing a profile of personality traits or a reliable measurement of any one trait." He based his views on the accumulated evidence of reliability and validity, which he felt was adequate for group differentiation but not for trait identification in specific individuals.

Nothing has appeared in the literature in the last five years which would serve to refute these conclusions with any degree of conviction. Reasonable reliability is obtained when the measure is agreement between two judges in their ratings of responses on various scales of content and

6 MAY, ROBERT. "Fantasy Differences in Men and Women." *Psychology Today* 1:42–5+ Ap '68. *

7 MADDI, SALVATORE R., AND ANDREWS, SUSAN L. "The Need for Variety in Fantasy and Self-Description." *J Personality* 34:610–25 D '66. *

8 BELLAK, LEOPOLD; HURVICH, MARVIN; SILVAN, MARK; AND JACOBS, DAVID. "Toward an Ego Psychological Appraisal of Drug Effects." *Am J Psychiatry* 125:593–603 N '68. *

9 LEBOW, KENNETH E., AND EPSTEIN, SEYMOUR. "Thematic and Cognitive Responses of Good Premorbid Schizophrenics to Cues of Nurturance and Rejection." *J Consult Psychol* 27:24–33 F '63. *

form. However, it has been shown that the responses themselves are subject to conscious control by the subject [1] (*1163, 1397*) and that sophisticated subjects (clinical psychologists and advanced graduate students) are more apt to fake successfully than naive subjects (undergraduates) (*1060*). Retest reliability in terms of stability over 20 years has been demonstrated by Skolnick (*1134*), who analyzed the TAT protocols of 93 subjects obtained at ages 17 and 37. All stories were scored for four kinds of motivation: achievement, affiliation, power, and aggression. Agreement in scoring between judges ranged between .76 and .85. For male subjects, power and aggression showed moderate stability ($r = .34$ and $.27$, respectively); for females, all four showed positive trends but only achievement was significant ($r = .24$). These results are consistent with other findings about differences in stability of personality traits according to sex (*1286*).

Findings from Skolnick's longitudinal study were also brought to bear upon the central problem of validity, i.e., the relation between fantasy imagery as reflected in TAT stories and overt behavior in real life. This was possible since there were behavioral measures taken at the same time the TAT's were administered. "The results suggest that it is not possible to make a statement about the relation between TAT fantasy and behavior that will hold for all motives, ages, and both sexes, although the predominant effect seems to be direct rather than inverse" (*1133*). Essentially the same conclusion had been stated by the present reviewer in *The Fifth Mental Measurements Yearbook.*

One of the factors which has been shown to affect the relation between TAT fantasy and overt behavior of the story teller is the stimulus relevance of the picture to the trait in question. The general finding has been that the ambiguity of the picture is inversely related to the degree of relationship between story content and overt behavior (*1011, 1063, 1445*). This has been demonstrated particularly for aggression and/or hostility (*1032, 1151, 1165, 1218*), with no difference between men and women (*1121*), although for achievement motivation, pictures of medium ambiguity seem to be most valuable (*1121*). Stimulus ambiguity

has also been found to be associated with hesitant and disrupted speech on the part of the narrator (*1131*). There is some evidence that young children, in contrast to adults, respond more productively to ambiguous pictures,[2] however, than to appropriately structured ones.

All the TAT cards are black and white. It has been postulated that this at least partially accounts for the predominantly sombre emotional tone of the majority of TAT productions. A few studies have introduced color into the cards as an experimental variable (*1056, 1144*). Both of the studies cited found little difference in productivity and emotional tone between the color and noncolor series, although both sets of authors felt that color might have a subtle effect on the conceptual and aesthetic attributes of fantasy production. In further exploration of the stimulus value of the TAT pictures, semantic differential type scales have been administered in at least two studies (*999, 1050*). Results have been no different from previous studies with other kinds of scaling techniques: each picture has its own stimulus value, which must be taken into account before the significance of any single response to that picture can be validly determined.

Variations in scoring have been introduced in order to improve the validity of inferences made from TAT stories (*1068, 1179*), and the utility of computer scoring of content has been explored with encouraging results (*1208, 1230*). Interesting new scales have been developed to measure need for variety (*1320*) and perceived locus of control, i.e., whether internal or external (*1197*). For the scoring of achievement, affiliation, and power, it has been demonstrated that simply counting stories in which the given motive appears is superior to summing the number of motive cues across all stories for a given subject.[3] A manual for scoring communication deviances has been used to discriminate parents of young adult schizophrenics from parents of neurotic patients (*1132*).

Concurrent validity in terms of similarity of inferences from TAT scoring and assessments with other procedures has not been encouraging. For example, Murray need constructs were not equivalently tapped by the *Adjective Check*

1 GUTMAN, GLORIA M. "A Note on the MPI: Age and Sex Differences in Extraversion and Neuroticism in a Canadian Sample." *Brit J Social & Clin Psychol* 5:128–9 Je '66. *

2 BUDOFF, MILTON, AND VACCHIANO, RALPH B. "Developmental Study of Ambiguity Level in Picture-Story Stimuli." *J Proj Tech & Pers Assess* 29:465–72 D '65. *
3 TERHUNE, KENNETH W. "A Note on Thematic Apperception Scoring of Needs for Achievement, Affiliation and Power." *J Proj Tech & Pers Assess* 33(4):364–70 Ag '69. *

List, Edwards Personal Preference Schedule, and TAT (*1214*). Nor did aggressive content scales, based on the TAT and *Holtzman Inkblot Technique,* agree in relating to 11 different independent criteria of overt aggression (*1172*). In another study (*1148*), dreams and TAT responses of 13 subjects were scored according to the Murray need-press system. It was found that for some needs, e.g., dominance, there was a negative correlation between appearance in dreams and TAT responses. In all these concurrent validity studies in which TAT findings are compared with those of another assessment procedure it is moot which one, if either, is the "really" valid technique.

Concurrent validity, in terms of differential results with contrasted groups of subjects, remains satisfactory, indicating that there may indeed be some justification for including the TAT in a diagnostic work-up of patients. The most surprising finding is how well the TAT does in differentiating parents of schizophrenic children from parents of normal children (*1132, 1174, 1408, 1529*). However, there has been less striking success in the differentiation of parents of 20 boys described as maladjusted from the parents of a carefully matched control group of 20 adjusted boys (*1461*). The TAT has also been used successfully to differentiate patients with heart complaints from normals (*1088*), paranoid from nonparanoid psychiatric populations (*1143*), brain damaged patients from controls (*1363*), women who made good post-partum adjustments from women whose post-partum adjustment was poor (*1507*), and foster home children from children living with their natural parents (*1122*). However, it should be pointed out that none of these findings were cross validated on new contrasting groups of similar type subjects and thus it is uncertain how generalizable the findings are beyond the specific samples contrasted. Lindzey (*1061*) reported 95 percent accuracy in blind prediction by a clinician of which of a group of protocols belonged to homosexual college students and which to normal ones. He found also that by using an actuarial formula comprising 20 objective indices his success rate was almost as high. However, when the same actuarial method was applied to differentiating homosexual from normal prisoners, the actuarial formula was a complete failure, whereas two clinicians were successful in predicting the criterion.

Another demonstration of the use of the TAT with contrasted groups is its application in cross-cultural studies. Protocols of samples of subjects from Brazil,[4] and from Yucatan (*1105*), of Tibetan boys,[5] Arab university students (*1010*), and of subjects from West Africa [6] have been compared to protocols from American subjects. Within the United States there have been cross-cultural comparisons between Negro, Mexican-American, and Anglo psychiatric patients (*1057*) and lower class white and Negro juvenile delinquents (*1118*). The last cited author points up the danger of making inferences about basic racial personality structure on the basis of projective tests without careful matching on other variables, particularly IQ. Levy (*1510*) makes a similar point about comparing lower class patients with middle class norms.

As mentioned above, the use of the TAT in personality research, other than in diagnostic differentiation, has been extensive. The utility of TAT-type tasks in assessing and manipulating motivation and its consequents was originally proposed by David McClelland and his associates. Most of the subsequent work has been done with achievement motivation, although affiliation, aggression, approval, dominance, dependence, deference, and many other offshoots of the Murray need-press system have also been studied extensively. It is beyond the scope of this review to summarize and evaluate this vast body of literature. However, it is apparent that many research psychologists interested in personality consider the TAT and its many adaptations as an acceptable procedure for assessing motivation, attitude, and habit, especially when consideration is given to the stimulus value of the pictures and when the analyst takes into account both positive and negative indications of the variable in question. There is less agreement about the utility and efficiency of the TAT as a clinical diagnostic tool.

For a review by C. J. Adcock, see 6:245; for reviews by Leonard D. Eron and Arthur R. Jensen, see 5:164; for a review by Arthur L.

4 ANGELINI, ARRIGO L. "Measuring the Achievement Motive in Brazil." *J Social Psychol* 68:35–40 F '66. *
ROSEN, BERNARD C. "The Achievement Syndrome and Economic Growth in Brazil." *Social Forces* 42:341–54 Mr '64. *
5 MEHROTRA, K. K., AND MEHROTRA, V. K. "A TAT Study of Tibetan Boys." *Psychol Res* 2(1–2):37–42 '67.
6 BOCQUET, FANNY. "De l'application du T.A.T. à un groupe d'étudiants africains occidentalisés." *Archivio di Psicologia Neurologia e Psichiatria* 26:554–65 '65. *

Benton, see 4:136; for reviews by Arthur L. Benton, Julian B. Rotter, and J. R. Wittenborn, see 3:103 (1 excerpt).

[182]

★**Washington University Sentence Completion Test.** Ages 12 and over; 1962–70; WUSCT; various titles used by authors; ego development; Form 9-62 for women ('62, 2 pages); 6 additional forms ('62–68, 2–3 pages, including another for women, 3 for men, 1 for girls, and 1 for boys) are also presented in manual; manual ('70, 266 pages, see 4 below); scoring manual for women and girls ('70, 476 pages, see 5 below); reliability data and scoring directions only for Form 9-62 for women; scoring method is intended to be applicable to other stems as well; $25 per set of manuals, postage extra; tests must be reproduced locally; (20–30) minutes; Jane Loevinger, Ruth Wessler, and Carolyn Redmore (scoring manual); Jossey-Bass Inc., Publishers. *

REFERENCES

1. BEDNAR, MARY ANN. *Changes in Social Perception in Adolescents During Group Psychotherapy.* Doctor's thesis, Washington University (St. Louis, Mo.), 1964. (*DA* 26:1166)
2. HEZEL, JOHN DONALD. *Some Personality Correlates of Dimensions of Delinquency.* Doctor's thesis, St. Louis University (St. Louis, Mo.), 1968. (*DA* 29:3087B)
3. LOEVINGER, JANE. Chap. 8, "The Relation of Adjustment to Ego Development," pp. 162–80. In *The Definition and Measurement of Mental Health.* Edited by S. B. Sells. Public Health Service Publication No. 1873. Washington, D.C.: United States Government Printing Office, 1968. Pp. xii, 280. *
4. LOEVINGER, JANE, AND WESSLER, RUTH. *Measuring Ego Development: Vol. 1, Construction and Use of a Sentence Completion Test.* San Francisco, Calif.: Jossey-Bass, Inc., Publishers, 1970. Pp. xxi, 245. *
5. LOEVINGER, JANE; WESSLER, RUTH; AND REDMORE, CAROLYN. *Measuring Ego Development: Vol. 2, Scoring Manual for Women and Girls.* San Francisco, Calif.: Jossey-Bass, Inc., Publishers, 1970. Pp. xix, 457. *

For a review, see B395 (1 excerpt).

[183]

★**The Zulliger Individual and Group Test.** Ages 3 and over; 1948–69; ZT; formerly called *Z-Test;* 2 editions: individual ['54, 3 cards], group ['48, 3 slides]; manual ('69, 603 pages, see 11 below, combined English-language edition of two German volumes: group test manual, second edition, published in 1959 and individual test manual, second edition, published in 1962); scoring sheet ('53, 1 page); no data on reliability; Fr. 9 ($4) per set of cards; Fr. 32 ($10) per set of slides; Fr. 5 per 50 ($2.50 per 100) scoring sheets; $15 per manual; postage extra; (5–20) minutes for individual test, (15–20) for group test; Hans Zulliger; English manual edited by Fritz Salomon, translated by Dusya T. Dubrovsky; Hans Huber. (United States distributor: International Universities Press, Inc.) *

REFERENCES

1. KRAUS, ANTHONY R. "An Experiment With Blurred Exposures of Zulliger's Ink-Blot Slides." Abstract. *Am Psychologist* 11:401 Ag '56. *
2. GLADSTON, ELAINE R., AND AMADO-HAGUENAUER, GINETTE. "Fluidity in the Limits of the Self." *Int J Social Psychiatry* 6:260–8 au '60. *
3. GLADSTON, ELAINE R., AND AMADO-HAGUENAUER, GINETTE. "A Note on the Z-Test Results of 37 Schizophrenics." *Rorsch Newsl* 5:23–4 D '60. *
4. GLADSTON, ELAINE R., AND HAGUENAUER, GINETTE. "The Clinical Use of the Z-Test." *Rorsch Newsl* 5:8–16 Je '60. *
5. EBLE, SELMA J.; FERNALD, L. DODGE, JR.; AND GRAZIANO, ANTHONY M. "The Comparability of Quantitative Rorschach and Z-Test Data." *J Proj Tech & Pers Assess* 27:166–70 Je '63. * (*PA* 38:2692)
6. SEMEONOFF, BORIS. "The Z-Test as a Quick Substitute for Rorschach." *Rorsch Newsl* 8:15–21 Je '63. *
7. LEFKOWITZ, MONROE M. "Screening Juvenile Delinquents for Psychopathology by Use of the Z-Test." *J Proj Tech & Pers Assess* 32:475–8 O '68. * (*PA* 43:5574)
8. SCHMID, FRED W. "Projective Tests in Vocational Counseling." *J Proj Tech & Pers Assess* 32:10–5 F '68. * (*PA* 42:9004)
9. SEMEONOFF, BORIS. "The Equivalence of Rorschach and Zulliger's Test in a Selection Context." *Brit J Proj Psychol & Pers Study* 13:11–2 D '68. * (*PA* 46:6949)
10. SEMEONOFF, BORIS. "On the Equivalence of the Rorschach and Zulliger's." *Int Congr Rorsch & Proj Meth* 6(4): 733–7 '68. *
11. ZULLIGER, HANS; EDITED BY FRITZ SALOMON. *The Zulliger Individual and Group Test.* Translated by Dusya T. Dubrovsky. New York: International Universities Press, Inc., 1969. Pp. xi, 592. * [A translation, with duplications eliminated, of the author's *The Zulliger Group Test, Second Edition,* 1959 and *The Zulliger Individual Test, Second Edition,* 1962.]
12. BASH, K. W., AND BASH-LIECHTI, J. "Z Test Findings Among Iranian Peasants and Nomads." *Int Congr Rorsch & Other Proj Tech* 7:244–51 '70. *
13. SCHUT, DIEN; BESIJN, J. W.; BOEKE, P. E.; AND ULEMAN, A. L. "Psychological Examination Before and After Stereotactic Operations in Parkinson Patients." *Psychiatria, Neurologia, Neurochirurgia* 73(5):375–86 S-O '70. *

Cont Psychol 15(3):206+ Mr '70. Bernard I. Murstein. [Review of the manual.] The Zulliger Test is a three-card inkblot test devised by Hans Zulliger, a Swiss psychologist and a student and friend of Hermann Rorschach. In 1948 he published, in German, a book describing the group-form utilization of the test and in 1954 an individual-test adaptation. These two books have been, in essence, combined, edited, and translated into English in the present volume. This book's misfortune is that it appeared in 1969 instead of 1939. At that time justifying an analysis by saying "Rorschach said so," would have given a Swiss author osmotic status. Clinical psychologists might have cheered when Zulliger attacked those who relied on "coarse summaries" of an inkblot test instead of profound depth analysis by saying "This error is made by those who believe that the science of testing is nothing else but a purely mathematical and statistical task and....expect to be able to capture and delineate human souls with the aid of averages, curves, and other such mechanical contrivances [pp. 257–258]." We might even have swallowed the statement that *land map* responses in children "are indicative of the ambition to *excel* in school [p. 118]," and that "as a rule, subjects who produce responses that contain *many small animals*—insects, wood lice, spiders, etc.—do not have a good relationship with their siblings [p. 134]" and not have asked for substantiating data. Zulliger is of the "every response is psychologically meaningful" rather than "part wheat, part chaff" school. Differences in performance on test-retesting, in his opinion, thus, are never due to the unreliability of responses but to the instability of the subject. Accordingly, he reported that of 100 Swiss army subjects tested on two occasions, the *experience balance* (ratio of movement responses to the sum of weighted color perceptions) had changed so that 13–15 *extratensive* subjects (color greater than movement) became *introversive* (color less than movement) and 10–12 recruits who had been introversive subjects became extravertive. Of 100 recruits who were originally ambiequal (movement equals color) 66 became extratensive and the rest intratensive. One weakness of ratio scores is that the reliability of the ratio is not apparent in its numerical value; thus a ratio of 2:1 could come from two movement to one color response or ten movement to five color responses. If the number of color responses is unreliable (and with only three cards in the test this is practically a foregone conclusion), the ratio may change drastically on the basis of a single response and thus alter the psychological interpretation. An introversive person with a 2:1 ratio becomes ambiequal with the addition of only one color-form response. The nearest thing to a validation study in the book is the mention that test diagnoses and observations in military service agree 80–90%, with no explanation of how this statement was arrived at. A suggested "validation" study of the Zulliger, Rorschach and Behn-Rorschach tests in all possible combinations lists only five combinations instead of the actually possible six. In the absence of empirical data, or indeed of an index, there are a multitude of case studies and interpretations for those who like their interpretations excathedra. This book is outdated.

J Proj Tech & Pers Assess 34(2):150–1 Ap '70. Margaret Mercer. [Review of the manual.] * The book is a distillation of the long experience of a sensitive self-critical clinician. It has a nostalgic quality, belonging with the work of Rorschach and Behn. The test can be used easily by persons experienced in the Rorschach method. The book can be read with pleasure by anyone who values what Rapaport called the "cogwheeling of the perceptual and associational processes" as a means of understanding a patient's private world. However if the test is to contribute to the process of personality assessment as it is practiced at the present time, much work needs to be done to find out to what degree it can be depended upon when it is used by someone less clinically sophisticated and less familiar with it than Zulliger himself. As is frequently the case with projective techniques, it will be necessary to accumulate data from various carefully described populations in order to define the groups and conditions for which the test is valid and reliable.

For an additional review, see B664 (1 excerpt).

[Other Tests]

For other tests new or revised since *The Sixth Mental Measurements Yearbook,* see the following in *Personality Tests and Reviews:*

416. *Blacky Pictures (39 references)
417. ★Braverman-Chevigny Auditory Projective Test (2 references)
419. *Children's Apperception Test (18 references)
421. *Curtis Completion Form (3 references)
423. *Draw-A-Person Quality Scale (3 references)
433. ★Graphoscopic Scale (8 references)
437. *H-T-P: House-Tree-Person Projective Technique (24 references)
438. *Hand Test (12 references)
440. ★[Re Holtzman Inkblot Technique.] Computer Scoring Service for the Holtzman Inkblot Technique (5 references)
449. *Lowenfeld Kaleidoblocs
453. *Marriage Adjustment Sentence Completion Survey
454. ★Measurement of Self Concept in Kindergarten Children
457. *Minnesota Percepto-Diagnostic Test (19 references)
458. *Object Relations Technique (5 references)
459. ★PRADI Draw-A-Person Test
460. ★Percept and Concept Cognition Test
463. ★Picture Identification Test (17 references)
465. ★Picture Story Test Blank
466. *Picture World Test (1 reference)
473B. ★Social Relations Test (1 reference)
474. ★Sound-Apperception Test (3 references)
480. *Szondi Test (24 references)
481. ★Tasks of Emotional Development Test (1 reference)
483. ★Test of Subjective and Objective Factors in Relationship to Communication Skills

ENGLISH

REVIEWS BY *Nicholas Anastasiow, Fred H. Borgen, M. A. Brimer, Nancy W. Burton, John B. Carroll, William E. Coffman, Clarence Derrick, Paul B. Diederich, Vincent R. D'Oyley, Ralph D. Dutch, Leonard S. Feldt, Robert Fitzpatrick, R. Gulliford, David P. Harris, Thomas D. Horn, Joan J. Michael, Walter J. Moore, Stanley Nisbet, Ellis Batten Page, Osmond E. Palmer, William H. Perkins, Robert C. Pooley, Alan C. Purves, Carleton B. Shay, John C. Sherwood, David A. Walker, George P. Winship, Jr., Blaine R. Worthen, and Albert H. Yee.*

[184]

*Advanced Placement Examination in English. High school students desiring credit for college level courses or admission to advanced courses; 1954–70; Forms RBP ('69, 10 pages), SBP ('70, 14 pages) in 2 booklets (objective, essay); for more complete information, see 662; 180(200) minutes; program administered for the College Entrance Examination Board by Educational Testing Service. *

REFERENCE

1. SMITH, EUGENE H. "English Composition in the Advanced Placement Program." *Engl J* 54:495–501 S '65. *

For a review of the testing program, see 662.

[185]

★Bristol Achievement Tests: English Language. Ages 8-0 to 9-11, 9-0 to 10-11, 10-0 to 11-11, 11-0 to 12-11, 12-0 to 13-11; 1969; 6 scores; word meaning, paragraph meaning, sentence organisation, organisation of ideas, spelling and punctuation, total; Forms A, B, ['69, 7–8 pages]; 5 levels; administrative manual ['69, 8 pages] for each level; battery interpretive manual (78 pages); battery profile ['69, 2 pages] for each form; £1.90 per 25 tests; £1 per 25 profiles; 60p per teacher's set (without interpretive manual) of any one level (must be purchased to obtain administrative manual and keys); 75p per interpretive manual; postage extra; 50(55) minutes for levels 1–3, 40(45) minutes for levels 4–5; Alan Brimer and Herbert Gross; Thomas Nelson & Sons Ltd. *

RALPH D. DUTCH, *Principal Lecturer in Educational Psychology, Aberdeen College of Education, Aberdeen, Scotland.*

Many of the attainment tests commonly used by British teachers and educational researchers are pitifully inadequate, and at this time of major changes in curricula and methods, teachers especially are desperately in need of well standardised tests, tailored to modern behavioural objectives, to rescue them from a fog of uncertainty and anxiety as to what results all these changes are producing. Fortunately, most adult teachers have now outgrown the fashion of regarding any form of evaluation as a symbol of reaction and academic fettering, and the *Bristol Achievement Tests* are consequently coming on the market at an opportune time.

From the start, this reviewer wishes to emphasise that, whatever shortcomings in detail these tests have, it is his opinion that as a complete battery they represent, both in sophistication of design and comprehensiveness of range if not yet in subject matter, a considerable advance in testing practice in Britain. Although this review will be concerned with the English tests, the aim of the whole battery is to provide a profile of a child's cognitive skills in the basic areas of numeracy and literacy, together with the basic concepts and understandings underlying performance in the social and scientific areas. Sets of Mathematics and Study Skills tests are therefore provided, equivalent in range and standardisation to the English tests described below.

The English tests cover five overlapping age ranges, from second year junior to second year secondary, the norms for each test being designed to cover a whole school year group (called level). This means that each child will have his scores compared with children of the same age and amount of school experience rather than with age peers who may have had a very different time of exposure to teaching. There are parallel forms at each of the five levels so that progress during a school year can always be evaluated against performance on a fresh but equivalently difficult test.

The standardisation of the tests was carried out on large samples of children selected with the intention of forming a nationally representative sample, and the interpretive manual contains an unusually full and open account of how this was done. The interpretation of raw scores offers several novel features. First, the raw scores are converted to standardised scores, then each subtest score is changed to the decile or percentile equivalent for that level and age group. Then, for each of the other subtests, the score is found that might have been expected from the child's reading ability as shown on one subtest, and finally the error limits of each score are calculated and shown on a profile, along with the actual score and the expected score. Reliability coefficients are based, not on internal consistency measures, but on correlations between scores on Form A and Form B. Standard errors of measurement are given and form an important consideration in interpreting test scores. The authors hope to counteract the tendency of teachers to read too much meaning into a single score or difference between scores by using the standard errors of the subscores to show the range within which a true score is likely to be. Unfortunately, some of the reliability measures, especially on the Organisation of Ideas subtests, are low (down to .59), and the range of error is so wide that educational decisions would be very hard for teachers to make on the basis of such variability. The authors are aware of this danger and suggest using 95 percent confidence limits where decisions to the possible detriment of a child are concerned and 68 percent where positive remedial action might be taken. This seems an unrealistic distinction and one beyond the patience or expertise of most teachers. In fact, to get the most out of these tests demands a degree of statistical understanding sadly lacking in most of the teachers who might use them; the Profile Sheet instructions could usefully be expanded and simplified.

After all this sophistication, the actual test contents are somewhat disappointing. The authors realise the need to test underlying principles and strategies rather than specific attainments and they have largely just played their hunches as to what these principles and strategies are where skill at English is concerned. At each level there are five subtests, covering the same areas at each level, though the more advanced levels have more items on expressive skills and fewer on reading comprehension. In Part 1 (Word Meaning), the child has to underline the word in a sentence that corresponds to the word underlined for him in a preceding sentence. The second sentence contains ingenious decoy words. For Part 2 (Paragraph Meaning), the child completes gaps in a continuous narrative, the missing words being either simple or previously mentioned, so that vocabulary by itself matters little. Part 3 (Sentence Organisation) consists of items in which the child has to complete, modify, or unscram-

ble the words of a sentence. In Part 4 (Organisation of Ideas), the child has in one section to put a series of ideas in the best order to produce a story and in the other to rearrange a sentence to give as many different meanings as possible. Part 5 (Spelling and Punctuation) means what it says and the authors are unnecessarily apologetic about including these measures in their test.

Now, in the absence of any factorial analysis of the contents or any attempt at even a concurrent validity measure, it is impossible to say whether the authors have caught the important English skills or not. Nor is it possible to use some of these tests diagnostically in the sense that they clearly indicate a course of generalisable remedial action. In these respects the tests are promising but still at an early stage in their development.

In general, then, these tests represent an honest and thorough attempt at an updated coverage of English language skills; in some respects they need working up and supplementing, and evidence on validity is urgently required, but for teachers who are prepared to make the effort to get the maximum use from them, they form part of a battery with distinct advantages over similar British productions in this field. The excellent interpretive manual is a must.

For a review of the complete battery, see 4.

[186]

★**CLEP Subject Examination in English Composition.** 1 year or equivalent; 1965–70; for college accreditation of nontraditional study, advanced placement, or assessment of educational achievement; tests administered monthly at regional centers throughout the United States; tests also available for institutional testing at any time; Form NCT ('65, 20 pages); optional essay supplement: Form NCT-A ('65, 3 pages); for program accessories, see 664; rental and scoring fee, $5 per student; postpaid; essay supplement scored by the college; 90(95) minutes, same for essay supplement; program administered for the College Entrance Examination Board by Educational Testing Service. *

DAVID P. HARRIS, *Professor of Linguistics, and Director, The American Language Institute, Georgetown University, Washington, D.C.* [Review of Form NCT.]

This is a 90-minute objective test consisting of 120 five-choice items; it may be supplemented with a 90-minute optional essay section, which requires the student first to paraphrase a given passage and then to organize two sets of information into separate paragraphs, using specified methods of development. (No advice on scoring the essay section is provided.) The purpose of the test, in the words of the publisher, is "to measure....knowledge of the theoretical aspects of writing usually taught in a beginning two-semester college course in composition and....ability to put into practice the principles of good writing." Thus, the test aims at measuring not only writing skill as such but also "a knowledge of the fundamental principles of rhetoric and of such elements of language facts, grammar, and logic as may be useful for the improvement of writing skill." In the objective portion, on which this review will concentrate, three types of problems account for about three-fourths of the test content.

Error-recognition items are used to measure the student's ability to write sentences that are grammatically, stylistically, and mechanically acceptable. Each item consists of a sentence with four underlined segments, one of which may contain an "error" according to the "requirements of standard written English"; otherwise, the student selects the fifth—"no error"—option. Though some of the sentences contain blatant "errors," those that do are mixed in with others which, in the reviewer's opinion, test recognition of stylistic faults of too subtle a nature to be useful discriminators. Moreover, a couple of the "no-error" items are written so infelicitously that it seems criminal to allow them to pass as acceptable. (Three English professors, given this 21-item section by the reviewer, each made at least two "mistakes.")

Sentence-conversion items test the student's sentence-writing dexterity. Here, sentences are to be rewritten according to specific directions (e.g., "Change the first verb to a noun used as the subject of the sentence"). The student does the rephrasing in his head or in the margins of his test book, then selects the one option containing a word or phrase that occurs in his revised version. If none of the options fits his sentence, he is advised to "rephrase the sentence again so that it includes a word or phrase that is listed." The revised sentences are seldom superior to the originals; the purpose of these items is to have the student demonstrate his ability to construct various sentence types upon demand. For the most part, the terminology of the instructions is fairly basic, though there are instances where a reasonably competent writer might not understand the technical description of sentences he is quite capable of creating on

his own: e.g., "Substitute an infinitive for the first gerund." A rather elaborate set of directions is required for this kind of exercise, filling nearly a full page in the test book.

Paragraph-analysis items consist of sets of questions, each of which is based on a given paragraph, designed to test the student's understanding of the author's overall strategy, method of organization, use of stylistic devices, and the like. In some cases the student is asked to identify faults in the writing or to select the best rewriting of a specific sentence. The analytic questions set the widest possible range of tasks, from explaining an author's choice of punctuation to giving technical names for literary devices. There are six such paragraph-analysis sets, which, very wisely, are spaced throughout the test to avoid monotony.

The remaining quarter of the test items probe the student's knowledge of the history of the English language and of modern English grammar, his understanding of the principles of coherence and logic in writing, and his ability to use bibliographical tools and the conventions of the documented paper. Most of this miscellaneous matter seems appropriate in terms of the stated test objectives, though as always one might quarrel with isolated items. Should we expect our freshman composition students to know Greek prefixes on sight, to know the chief foreign source of the technical vocabulary of hairdressers, or to know the function of *Baird's Manual* (luckily, only a distractor)? Fortunately, relatively few such questionable items appear.

In the test as a whole, the quality of the item writing is high. The reviewer puzzled over only two or three problems and found only one item (item 47) where there are definitely multiple right answers, due to a careless wording of the question. Except for the necessarily lengthy explanation for the sentence-conversion items, the test directions are brief but unequivocal. Particularly welcome are the very explicit instructions about guessing.

Test results are reported as scaled scores ranging from 20 to 80 with a mean of 50 and a standard deviation of 10. Norms were obtained in May-June 1965 by administering the test to full-time undergraduate students near the end of freshman composition courses. The test analysis of September 1965 indicates that the norms group found the test rather difficult and slightly speeded. The K-R 20 reliability was .87. Two related criteria were used for one study of validation: course grades estimated by instructors before the final examination (r = .50) and final course grades (r = .57). The publisher's attractive Score Interpretation Guide also includes normative data in the form of percentile ranks and graphs comparing distributions of scores with grades received in appropriate courses.

The matter of test validity leads the reviewer to voice one cautionary note. As may be observed from the summary of test content, the test designers clearly had in mind a very traditional kind of composition course, one that gives almost equal attention to writing and *talk about* writing, with the discussion couched in fairly technical language. (A rough tally indicates that about one item in five requires an understanding of one or more specialized terms: "compound verb," "analysis by partition," "synecdoche," "epigrammatic," etc.) For institutions where composition is still taught in this manner, the test could be expected to prove reasonably valid and useful. Where composition classes are less terminology-oriented, the test might be considerably less appropriate. Thus, for some of the recommended academic uses, such as the evaluation of "nontraditional college-level education....[and] the placement, accreditation, and admission of transfer students," the test requires cautious use. For the same reason there is a danger that the test will be misapplied by the nonacademic types of users whom the publisher has (secondarily) in mind: "business and industrial educators, and individuals responsible for certification and licensing programs." It is hoped that they, and all other potential users, will read with care the publisher's admirably thorough descriptive material.

For reviews of the testing program, see 664 (3 reviews).

[187]

*California Achievement Tests: Language, 1970 Edition. Grades 1.5–2, 2–4, 4–6, 6–9, 9–12; 1933–70; previous edition (see 6:251) still available; 4 or 5 scores: auding (level 1 only), mechanics, usage and structure, total, spelling; 1 form; 5 levels; for battery manuals and accessories, see 5; separate answer sheets (CompuScan [NCS], Digitek, IBM 1230) may be used in grades 4–12; postage extra; original edition by Ernest W. Tiegs and Willis W. Clark; CTB/McGraw-Hill. *
a) LEVEL 1. Grades 1.5–2; Form A ('70, 6 pages); $5 per 35 tests; $2.45 per specimen set, postpaid; 37(65) minutes.

b) LEVEL 2. Grades 2–4; Form A ('70, 6 pages); prices same as for level 1; 35(60) minutes.
c) LEVEL 3. Grades 4–6; Form A ('70, 15 pages); $6 per 35 tests; $2.50 per 50 CompuScan or Digitek answer sheets; $3 per 50 IBM answer sheets; $1 per IBM hand scoring stencil; $2 per specimen set, postpaid; CompuScan scoring service, 22¢ and over per test; 43(70) minutes.
d) LEVEL 4. Grades 6–9; Form A ('70, 15 pages); prices same as for level 3; 43(70) minutes.
e) LEVEL 5. Grades 9–12; Form A ('70, 15 pages); prices same as for level 3; 47(75) minutes.

REFERENCES
1–3. See 5:177.
4. See 6:251.
5. TURNER, DANIEL. *A Study of Speech Effectiveness and Personal and Social Adjustment Among Ninth Grade Pupils.* Doctor's thesis, Boston University (Boston, Mass.), 1957. (*DA* 17:2902)
6. PALATE, E. L. "The Measurement of Sentence Structure of Deaf Children." *Alberta J Ed Res* 8:39–44 Mr '62. * (*PA* 37:3492)

For a review by Richard E. Schutz of an earlier edition, see 6:251; for reviews by Constance M. McCullough and Winifred L. Post, see 5:177; for reviews by Gerald V. Lannholm and Robert C. Pooley, see 4:151; for reviews by Harry A. Greene and J. Paul Leonard, see 2:1292. For reviews of earlier editions of the complete battery, see 6:3 (2 reviews), 5:2 (1 review), 4:2 (3 reviews), 3:15 (1 review), 2:1193 (2 reviews), and 1:876 (1 review, 1 excerpt).

[188]

*College Board Achievement Test in English Composition. Candidates for college entrance; 1943–71; test administered each January, March, May, July, and December at centers established by the publisher; for more complete information, see 663; 60(80) minutes; program administered for the College Entrance Examination Board by Educational Testing Service. *

REFERENCES
1–6. See 4:178.
7–20. See 5:204.
21–26. See 6:287.
27. CLARK, EUGENE WARREN. *An Evaluation of Predictive Criteria for a Group of High Ability College Freshmen.* Doctor's thesis, University of Denver (Denver, Colo.), 1963. (*DA* 25:957)
28. COLLEGE ENTRANCE EXAMINATION BOARD. *Manual of Freshman Class Profiles, 1964 Edition.* Princeton, N.J.: the Board, 1964. Pp. xiv, 584. * (Earlier editions published in 1961, 1962, and 1963.)
29. FRENCH, JOHN W. "New Tests for Predicting the Performance of College Students With High-Level Aptitude." *J Ed Psychol* 55:185–94 Ag '64. * (*PA* 39:5979)
30. IVANOFF, JOHN M.; MALLOY, JOHN P.; AND ROSE, JANET R. "Achievement, Aptitude, and Biographical Measures as Predictors of Success in Nursing Training." *Ed & Psychol Meas* 24:389–91 su '64. * (*PA* 39:5972)
31. SHOSTAK, JEROME. *How to Prepare for College Board Achievement Tests: English Composition and the Writing Sample.* Great Neck, N.Y.: Barron's Educational Series, Inc., 1964. Pp. vi, 116. *
32. BARTH, CARL A. "Kinds of Language Knowledge Required by College Entrance Examinations." *Engl J* 54:824–9 D '65. *
33. HALLADAY, ROY ELDON. *The Effect of Certain Subcultural Background Factors on the Prediction of Grades at the University of Michigan.* Doctor's thesis, Michigan State University (East Lansing, Mich.), 1966. (*DA* 27:2780A)
34. MARSHALL, JOSEPH JEMERSON. *Non-Cognitive Variables as a Predictor of Academic Achievement Among Freshmen, Sophomores, and Juniors at Abilene Christian College.* Doctor's thesis, Baylor University (Waco, Tex.), 1968. (*DA* 29:3833A)
35. ELLEDGE, SCOTT. "For the Board's English Tests: As

an Old Era Ends, What Lies Ahead?" *Col Board R* 71:22–7 sp '69. *

36. PUGH, RICHARD C.; MORGAN, JAMES M.; AND LUDLOW, H. GLENN. *Predicting Success for Indiana University Freshmen Using the CEEB Achievement Tests, the CEEB Scholastic Aptitude Test, and High School Rank.* Indiana Studies in Prediction, No. 13. Bloomington, Ind.: Bureau of Educational Studies and Testing, Indiana University, April 1970. Pp. xi, 39. *

For reviews by Charlotte Croon Davis, Robert C. Pooley, and Holland Roberts of earlier forms, see 6:287; for a review by Charlotte Croon Davis (with Frederick B. Davis), see 4:178. For reviews of the testing program, see 6:760 (2 reviews).

[189]

★**College English Placement Test.** College entrants; 1969; CEPT; 1 form (12 pages); Part 2 consists of 2 optional essay questions; manual (16 pages); no information on marking, reliability, or norms presented for Part 2; separate answer sheets (IBM 1230, MRC, self-marking) must be used; $7.50 per 50 tests; $5.70 per 100 IBM 1230 answer sheets; $4.95 per 50 self-marking answer sheets; $3 per 100 MRC answer cards; 60¢ per IBM 1230 scoring stencil; 45¢ per manual; 90¢ per specimen set; postage extra; MRC scoring service, 18¢ per test; 45(55) minutes for Part 1; Oscar M. Haugh and James I. Brown; Houghton Mifflin Co. *

CLARENCE DERRICK, *Professor of Humanities, University of Florida, Gainesville, Florida.*

The stated purpose of this test is to give "an objective guide for the placement of college freshmen in English composition classes." The basic assumption is that the "usual steps in writing a composition" can be analyzed and reformulated into groups of objective test items. Even if one accepts the principle that most measurement is indirect, not everyone will accept the assumption and the actualization of the assumption of this test. As one takes the test, one wonders if the test is *really* the kind of mental activity that is involved when one *really* writes a composition. In Part 1, the objective part of the test, there are 13 different sets of items to be answered in 45 minutes. An unstated skill being tested is the ability to change gears; there is plenty of opportunity for gear shifting in this test. It does not help when two of the three sample exercises presented to "familiarize yourself with the kinds of items in the test" are not in the test in that form.

Earlier tests of "mechanics of expression" and "usage" designed to be used in sectioning freshmen emphasized spelling, punctuation, capitalization, usage, etc. The CEPT gives little emphasis to these categories. The various sections of the test include judgments relating to the selection of a subject for a composition; identification of dominant, subordinate, and irrelevant topics from unorganized data; grouping related and unrelated topics; judging which transitional connectives are best; distinguishing which sentence in a group is most effectively expressed; verbal analogies; an artificial language exercise; and finally a set of 21 usage items.

The manual contains this statement: "The 106 items in Part One of CEPT are all objective and *thus only one answer is correct for each question* [italics added]." An objective test has been defined as a test which can be *scored* by someone who has no knowledge of the subject matter. There is subjectivity in objective tests and room for some variation of opinion. Not always is there only one correct answer. Item 73, for example, is in a group of items that requires a decision whether a given sentence creates an unfavorable impression or a favorable impression. Would everyone agree that *He's frugal* creates a favorable rather than an unfavorable impression? Would frugality be recognized as a cardinal virtue by all college freshmen, particularly when they write home for funds at the end of the month? Item 51 requires a student to select Sentence B as more effective than Sentence C.

> B. Some loose boards laid on the railroad ties provided a footing for the man and his executioners.
>
> C. Some loose boards laid on the ties supporting the rails provided a footing for the man and his executioners.

The only difference is between "railroad ties" and "ties supporting the rails." Conceivably there could be a context when "ties supporting the rails" fits the writer's intention.

Part 2 of CEPT is an optional essay section. Its inclusion is based on the theory that a combination of objective items with an essay is more valid than either type of item alone. In the first of two essays, within a 25-minute time limit the student writes on one of two propositions. In the second essay, with a time limit of 35 minutes, the student attacks or defends a single proposition. The essay topics are well chosen, and most college freshmen should be able to write on them. The evaluation of these essays has to be done locally without the kind of assistance the STEP Essay Tests provide with their samples of student essays.

The CEPT has been carefully constructed and standardized. The manual contains the right amount of information that can be understood by a teacher with some familiarity with norms, validity, reliability, and standard errors of measurement. One lack is any information about the speededness of the test. With so many different item types in one test, the student will use a certain amount of time figuring out just what he is expected to do. Most test constructors want a test to be relatively unspeeded and use as a criterion that at least 75 percent of the students finish the test within the time limits. The fact that the directions for the CEPT call for students to begin item 40 after 21 minutes is a hint that students may not have time to complete all parts of the test.

The manual states that additional validity studies are being planned but are not yet available. The most important correlation that should be sought is a correlation between CEPT and a measure of verbal aptitude. This reviewer suspects that what CEPT measures is verbal aptitude, which is, of course, reasonably well correlated with ability to write. However, if a good measure of verbal aptitude is already available for all freshmen, the usefulness of CEPT is reduced.

In summary, CEPT is a recent test that differs from most screening tests used to evaluate freshmen competence in writing. The test authors have a point of view and a plan which they have carried out at a high level of competence.

OSMOND E. PALMER, *Professor, Office of Evaluation Services, Michigan State University, East Lansing, Michigan.*

This is an original, exciting, and extremely well prepared test. The authors decided to examine systematically all the things involved in composition. They devote only 27 of 106 items to matters of grammar and mechanics. The rest of the test involves items on limiting a topic, organizing materials in narrative and expository paragraphs, securing continuity within paragraphs, and making logical connections between the various parts of a sentence. There is a vocabulary section involving both like and unlike words and there are items getting at the connotation rather than the denotation of words.

Probably one of the things which gives this test its unique quality is its flexibility. The authors are not committed to any one form of item or to any set number of foils. In multiple choice items they use five responses when the responses are short, but when responses are long, as in the items on effective sentence structure, they use four. Often they use key-list items, and the keys contain from two to five responses. For the section on connotation the key is simply favorable-unfavorable. For some organization items they do not go beyond the logical three-part choice: a main topic, a subtopic, irrelevant. The items on mechanics refer to underlined portions of an essay, and the student uses a five-point key to indicate what, if anything, is wrong: capitalization, form, punctuation, spelling, no error. The test on vocabulary increases its range and simplifies directions by using the proportion technique: "Conspicuous is to hidden as PROXIMITY is to" or "Genuine is to authentic as EXOTIC is to."

The format of the test is also good. The items on the page are well spaced and the pages are usually not crowded.

The most interesting innovation is the creation of a nonsense verb and its principal parts and the requirement that the student supply the proper part in a series of sentences. It seems to me this is an economical way to get at a student's understanding of the English verbal system.

I take exception to only four items in the test. Item 37 asks the student to pick out a sentence in which there is no transitional word. I think that all of the sentences contain a transitional word: the *first* in sentence 3 locates an event in time as well as the *after* in sentence 2. Item 40 is tricky. Foil B introduces a sentence pattern which occurs in handbooks as the proper way to handle the construction, but then by omitting the word *other,* it is made illogical. Several of my colleagues and I missed this omission. Item 94 is supposed to illustrate the use of the wrong form of a word; but the choice is between *in* and *into,* and I do not consider *into* a morphological change of *in.* The one really ambiguous item is item 76. The student has to decide "Which underlined word has the widest range of application?" and he has to choose among *lie, falsehood, untruth, fib, misrepresentation.* I think that this depends too much on the authors' interpretation of "widest." I chose *untruth.* The authors want *misrepresentation* as the right response; to me this word suggests a specific, though unnamed, object with which I can compare a given statement. But when we say *untrue* we are simply putting a thing in a class with all other false things.

I also quarrel with this test on the basis of an omission. The authors suggest the need to have an essay in addition to the objective test and they present two essay topics at the end of the test booklet which the colleges can use if they wish. But they do not suggest that the topics have been tried out to see if they work well, and they have no advice to give the reader about grading the essays. The authors missed a golden opportunity, as part of the standardization, to have essays written. If they had given them the multiple readings involved in a recent College Board study [1] and correlated the essay scores with the part and total scores of their objective test, they could have assured prospective users of their test that the objective test did, in fact, correlate highly with students' ability to write. For the first time on a national scale it could have been pointed out that well-prepared and well-balanced objective tests do measure something very close to students' ability to write. A more immediate and practical benefit could have followed. Annotated samples of inferior, average, and superior papers could have been printed in the manual to serve as a guide to those colleges using the essays as part of the test.

[190]

*College Placement Test in English Composition. Entering college freshmen; 1962–70, c1958–70; CPTEC; irregularly scheduled reprintings of inactive forms of *College Board Achievement Test in English Composition;* Forms RPL1, RPL2, ['69, reprint of 1966 tests] in a single booklet (25 pages); for more complete information, see 665; 60(70) minutes; program administered for the College Entrance Examination Board by Educational Testing Service. *

REFERENCES

1. JACOBS, PAUL I. "Effects of Coaching on the College Board English Composition Test." *Ed & Psychol Meas* 26:55–67 sp '66. * (*PA* 40:9225)
2. HILTON, THOMAS L., AND MYERS, ALBERT E. "Personal Background, Experience and School Achievement: An Investigation of the Contribution of Questionnaire Data to Academic Prediction." *J Ed Meas* 4:69–80 su '67. * (*PA* 42:4570)
3. BURGESS, THOMAS C. "Estimating Average Freshman Class Ability From Preliminary Information." *J Col Stud Personnel* 10(3):161–3 My '69. *

JOHN C. SHERWOOD, *Professor of English, University of Oregon, Eugene, Oregon.*

The College Placement Test Program, of which this test forms a part, is intended "to place students at the appropriate level of study in college" through "the sensitive matching of student and course"; the individual college is

1 GODSHALK, FRED I.; SWINEFORD, FRANCES; AND COFFMAN, WILLIAM. *The Measurement of Writing Ability.* New York: College Entrance Examination Board, 1966. Pp. viii, 84.

advised not to use any of the tests without a preliminary validity survey to determine local applicability and to establish local norms for actual placement—full instructions for both validation and placement are provided in the manual.

The composition test is specifically "designed to measure the ability to write clear, effective English." This statement can be accepted only with some qualification. In the first place, as everyone knows, such tests are not tests of writing but of certain critical skills thought to have some correlation with writing skill; as far as the exercise resembles any part of the creative process, it resembles the stage of revision and proofreading—except that it is not his own ideas which the student is revising. Second, whatever the test measures, it measures only in one-sentence units; there is no demand to criticize, much less produce, larger units of composition and more extended patterns of thought. Thirdly, "clear, effective" might be better translated as "following the traditional conventions of standard written English as expounded by conservative handbooks"; clarity is seldom an issue, since even the faulty examples are not really obscure, and if effectiveness means rising above mere mechanical correctness in the direction of eloquence, that issue arises in only one section and then in a limited form. (There may, of course, be an unexpressed assumption that correctness is ipso facto effective.) Finally, of the problems relevant to the issues of clarity and effectiveness, some are heavily emphasized and others slighted; punctuation is hardly covered at all.

The test booklet contains not one but two tests, exactly parallel in structure and with very similar items. In either case, the first section contains 35 one-sentence exercises, in each of which four words or phrases are underlined; one or none may be faulty, and the student must pick out (but not diagnose) the one error or pronounce the sentence faultless. The faulty items are chiefly offenses against balance, symmetry, and consistency; they are of the each-of-us-brought-their-book, to-run-sing-and-to-dance sort of thing, and liberals might doubt whether some of them are really errors. The items seem generally unambiguous if one accepts the conventions of the test-makers.

In the second section the student faces another 35 possibly faulty sentences; each must be either pronounced correct or identified as exhibiting one of four errors: faulty diction (words which are not exact, not idiomatic, or not acceptable in standard written English); wordiness; clichés and inappropriate metaphors; faulty grammar and sentence structure (a category which has roughly the same emphasis as Part A of the test). Again the items seem generally unambiguous (especially the wordiness and cliché items!), though there might be some hesitation in ruling whether certain structural flaws offend against idiom (hence diction) or against grammar; the distinction may often be more semantic than real. The wordiness and cliché categories do genuinely raise the issue of rhetorical effectiveness as distinguished from mechanical correctness; it might, however, be wondered whether these particular problems of effectiveness deserve to be stressed and so many others passed over. The last section is the most ingenious and creative; here the student must actually construct sentences, if only in his mind. What we have is a series of single-sentence items, not necessarily faulty; in each case a change in the structure of one part of the sentence is suggested, and the student must determine what effects the change will have on other parts of the sentence —a process which requires him to rephrase the whole sentence and thus to approximate the creative process. For instance, offered the sentence "Poetry, like all the other arts, is to a very large degree a mode of imitation," he could be asked to consider the effect of beginning with the words "Poetry and all the other arts" (the example comes from a descriptive booklet rather than the test itself and is more obvious and mechanical than most). Many of the items could be answered only by someone who has both a quick, sharp mind and a well-developed sense of English syntax.

What are we to conclude about the usefulness of the test—or, to put the matter in more practical terms, can we conclude that it is promising enough to justify the "validity test" which the publishers honestly suggest as preliminary to any local use? Probably yes, if a comparison with comparable tests seems to suggest that it best fits the local need or emphasis. On the one hand, its use does involve an act of faith: one must assume a correlation between the skills tested and such untested skills as organization and punctuation, and between critical ability and actual writing performance. On the other hand, the test is carefully done,

generally unambiguous, sometimes ingenious. Success on the test would certainly indicate a clarity of mind and feeling for style which ought to enable the possessor to produce good expository prose, though the contrary might not be true—failure to solve some of the test's puzzles need not indicate incompetence in simple expression. The test need be viewed with no more suspicion than is appropriate to any objective test of writing.

For reviews by Charlotte Croon Davis, Robert C. Pooley, and Holland Roberts of earlier forms, see 6:287; for a review by Charlotte Croon Davis (with Frederick B. Davis), see 4:178. For a review of the testing program, see 665.

[191]
★**Comprehensive Tests of Basic Skills: Language.** Grades 2.5–4, 4–6, 6–8, 8–12; 1968–70; 4 scores: mechanics, expression, spelling, total; 2 forms; 4 levels; for battery manuals and accessories, see 9; separate answer sheets (CompuScan [NCS], Digitek, IBM 1230, Scoreze) must be used for levels 2–4; postage extra; $1.75 per specimen set of any one level, postpaid; CTB/McGraw-Hill. *
a) LEVEL 1. Grades 2.5–4; Forms Q ('68, 8 pages), R ('69, 8 pages); $5.35 per 35 tests; 35(55) minutes.
b) LEVEL 2. Grades 4–6; Forms Q ('68, 10 pages), R ('69, 10 pages); $5.75 per 35 tests; $2.50 per 50 Digitek or IBM answer sheets; $3 per 50 CompuScan answer sheets; $2.75 per 25 Scoreze answer sheets; $1 per IBM hand scoring stencil; CompuScan scoring service, 17¢ and over per test; 38(58) minutes.
c) LEVEL 3. Grades 6–8; Forms Q ('68, 13 pages), R ('69, 13 pages); prices same as for level 2; 37(57) minutes.
d) LEVEL 4. Grades 8–12; Forms Q ('68, 13 pages), R ('69, 13 pages); prices same as for level 2; 35(55) minutes.

For reviews of the complete battery, see 9 (2 reviews, 3 excerpts).

[192]
*English Progress Tests.** Various ages 7-3 to 15-6; 1952–70; 17 levels; 5p per test; 7p per manual for any one level except *f* (no manuals for *g* and *l–q*, mimeographed directions free on request from NFER); postpaid within U.K.; published for the National Foundation for Educational Research in England and Wales; Ginn & Co. Ltd.*
a) ENGLISH PROGRESS TEST A. Ages 8-0 to 9-0; 1952–60; 1 form ['52, 6 pages]; manual ['60, 8 pages]; (40–45) minutes; A. F. Watts.
b) ENGLISH PROGRESS TEST B. Ages 9-0 to 10-6; 1956–62; 1 form ['56, 7 pages]; manual ['62, 7 pages]; norms for ages 8-6 to 10-0 only; (40–45) minutes; M. A. Brimer.
c) ENGLISH PROGRESS TEST C. Ages 10-0 to 11-0; 1952–60; formerly called *English Grading Test 3;* 1 form ['52, 8 pages]; revised manual ('60, 7 pages); (45–50) minutes; A. F. Watts.
d) ENGLISH PROGRESS TEST D. Ages 11-0 to 12-0; 1956; 1 form ['56, 7 pages]; manual ['56, 8 pages]; pro-

isional norms; (40–45) minutes; M. A. Brimer and
A. F. Watts.

) ENGLISH PROGRESS TEST E. Ages 12-0 to 13-0; 1956;
  form ['56, 8 pages]; manual ['56, 8 pages]; pro-
  isional norms; (40–45) minutes; M. A. Brimer and
  A. F. Watts.

) ENGLISH PROGRESS TEST F. Ages 13-0 to 14-0; 1953;
  form ['53, 8 pages]; manual ['53, 10 pages]; no
  ata on reliability; 8p per manual; (40–50) minutes;
  A. F. Watts.

) ENGLISH PROGRESS TEST G. Ages 13-0 to 15-6; 1962;
  form ['62, 8 pages]; mimeographed directions ['62,
  pages]; no data on reliability; no norms; (35–45)
  ninutes; S. M. Unwin.

) ENGLISH PROGRESS TEST A2. Ages 7-3 to 8-11;
  962–66; 1 form ['62, 8 pages]; manual ['66, 8 pages];
  40–50) minutes; Betsy Barnard.

) ENGLISH PROGRESS TEST B2. Ages 8-6 to 10-0; 1959–
  0; 1 form ['59, 7 pages]; manual ['60, 7 pages]; (40–
  5) minutes.

) ENGLISH PROGRESS TEST C2. Ages 9-6 to 11-0; 1961;
  form ['61, 8 pages]; manual ['61, 7 pages]; (40–
  5) minutes; Valerie Land.

) ENGLISH PROGRESS TEST D2. Ages 10-6 to 12-0; 1963–
  4; 1 form ['63, 8 pages]; manual ['64, 7 pages]; (40–
  5) minutes; Jennifer Henchman.

) ENGLISH PROGRESS TEST E2. Ages 11-0 to 12-6; 1962–
  3; 1 form ['62, 8 pages]; mimeographed directions
  '63, 6 pages]; no data on reliability; no norms;
  5(50) minutes; S. M. Unwin.

n) ENGLISH PROGRESS TEST F2. Ages 12-0 to 13-6; 1963;
  form ['63, 8 pages]; mimeographed directions ['63,
  5 pages]; no data on reliability; no norms; 45(50)
  ninutes; Jennifer Henchman and Elsa Hendry.

) ENGLISH PROGRESS TEST B3. Ages 8-0 to 9-6; 1970;
  form ['70, 8 pages]; mimeographed directions ['70,
  4 pages]; no data on reliability; no norms; (45–50)
  ninutes.

) ENGLISH PROGRESS TEST C3. Ages 9-0 to 10-6; 1970;
  form ['70, 6 pages]; mimeographed directions ['70,
  5 pages]; no data on reliability; no norms; (45–50)
  ninutes.

) ENGLISH PROGRESS TEST D3. Ages 10-0 to 11-6; 1970;
  form ['70, 6 pages]; mimeographed directions ['70,
  4 pages]; no data on reliability; no norms; (45–50)
  minutes.

) ENGLISH PROGRESS TEST F3. Ages 12-0 to 13-6;
  1969; 1 form ['69, 8 pages]; mimeographed directions
  ['69, 6 pages]; provisional norms ('69, 1 page); no
  ata on reliability; no norms for ages 12-0 to 12-8;
  norms free on request from NFER; (40–45) minutes.

*For reviews by Neil Gourlay and Stanley
Nisbet of Tests A–F, see 5:187.*

[193]

*English Tests (Adv.). Ages 12-0 to 13-11; 1954–
67; 4 tests; distribution restricted to directors of education; 7p per test; 8p per manual for any one test
except d; postpaid within U.K.; 50(55) minutes; published for the National Foundation for Educational
Research in England and Wales; Ginn & Co. Ltd. *
a) ENGLISH TEST (ADV.) 1. 1954–55; 1 form ['54, 11
pages]; manual ('55, 11 pages); G. A. V. Morgan.
b) ENGLISH TEST (ADV.) 3. 1958; 1 form ['58, 12
pages]; manual (9 pages).
c) ENGLISH TEST (ADV.) 4. 1960; 1 form ['60, 12
pages]; manual (10 pages).
d) ENGLISH TEST (ADV.) 5. 1962–67; 1 form ['62, 12
pages]; mimeographed directions for administration
['62, 10 pages]; provisional norms ['67, 1 page]; directions and norms free on request from NFER.

STANLEY NISBET, *Professor of Education, University of Glasgow, Glasgow, Scotland.*

This series for the 12–14 age group was
produced between 1954 and 1962. In general
design and standardization procedure it follows
the pattern of the well-known Moray House
tests (which also include a series for this age
range). The tests are almost wholly objective
in form, though each test includes a few open-
ended items which involve a slight degree of
subjectivity in scoring. The usual fields are covered—comprehension, vocabulary, usage, word
formation, sentence structure, spelling, and the
like. The tables of norms enable test scores to
be translated into standardized scores with a
mean of 100 and an SD of 15. No indication
is given as to the purposes for which the tests
should be used, but one may assume, from their
character and from certain comments in the
handbooks, that they were designed as instruments of selection.

The construction and standardization of the
tests would seem to be sound and the handbooks
are reasonably informative. A few features of
the norms, however, make one wonder if the
standardizing groups (usually containing between 1,500 and 2,000 boys and girls) were
truly representative. For instance, the conversion tables for Tests 1 and 3 show a steep
increase of score with age, that for Test 4
shows a very small increase, and that for Test
2,[1] where separate norms for boys and girls are
given, shows a steep increase for boys and
hardly any for girls. When we come to Test 5,
we are told that the age increment is so small
that age has been ignored in the table altogether.

Coming to the content of the tests, we find
that the items vary considerably in validity, or
at least in face validity. (a) Some items strike
one as being very good indicators of ability in
English, such as those which require the selection of the best word to fill the blank in a
sentence (e.g., items 68–74, Test 1) or the
creative completion of a sentence beginning
and/or ending with given words (e.g., 55–61,
Test 1; 41–5, Test 2). (b) Some items, good
enough in themselves as items, appear to be
testing general intelligence more than ability
in English, e.g., the reconstruction of a long
sentence by rearranging eight groups of words
(45–61, Test 5). Other examples are 14–20,
Test 1; 18–22 and 31–40, Test 2; 12–21, Test

1 Test 2, published in 1957, is out of print.

3; 54–61 and 68–73, Test 5. (*c*) Other items are just faulty items—awkward wording, puzzling instructions, omission of necessary punctuation, items penalizing children whose dialect deviates slightly from standard English pronunciation, and even an apparent misprint (94, Test 3) and a misspelling (99, Test 2). The reviewer has reason to find fault at least with the following: 31–2, 43–9, and 98, Test 1; 14, 46, 49, 52, 85, 87–90, and 92, Test 2; 24, 35, 50, 60, 67–8, and 75, Test 3; 36, 38, 50, 52, and 92, Test 4; and 8–9, 20, and 27, Test 5.

The most disquieting feature of these English tests, however, is nothing less than the uneven quality of the English which they themselves contain. One comes across poor English everywhere—in items, in instructions, in passages for comprehension. To take a single example, the bottom third of page 5 and most of page 6 in Test 2 are hardly likely to inspire confidence in the test as an instrument claiming to appraise mastery of written English.

The reviewer would therefore hesitate to recommend the tests as tests of English, though they would probably be effective as tests of verbal intelligence.

For a review by A. E. G. Pilliner of Tests 1–4, see 6:262.

[194]

*English Tests 13–20. Ages 10-0 to 11-11; 1951–70; 8 tests (12 pages for *a–d,* 8 pages for *e–h*); new test published annually except for 1970; distribution restricted to directors of education; 7p per test (*a–d*); 5p per test (*e–h*); 8p per manual; postpaid within U.K.; 50(55) minutes for *a–e,* 45(50) minutes for *f–h;* published for the National Foundation for Educational Research in England and Wales; Ginn & Co. Ltd. *
a) ENGLISH TEST 13. 1962–63; forms 13A, 13B, ['62]; manual ('63, 12 pages) for each form.
b) ENGLISH TEST 14. 1963–64; 1 form ['63]; manual ('64, 12 pages).
c) ENGLISH TEST 15. 1964–65; 1 form ['64]; manual ('65, 12 pages).
d) ENGLISH TEST 16. 1965–66; 1 form ['65]; manual ('66, 12 pages).
e) ENGLISH TEST 17. 1966–67; 1 form ['66]; manual ('67, 12 pages).
f) ENGLISH TEST 18. 1967–68; 1 form ['67]; manual ('68, 12 pages).
g) ENGLISH TEST 19. 1968–69; 1 form ['68]; manual ('69, 12 pages).
h) ENGLISH TEST 20. 1969–70; 1 form ['69]; manual ('70, 12 pages).

REFERENCE

1. See 6:264.

R. GULLIFORD, *Senior Lecturer in Education, The University of Birmingham, Birmingham, England.*

These well constructed tests were prepared for use in selection procedures for secondary education in England. Interest in this review centres on how the test constructors, with considerable experience behind them, have modified their procedures through the eight tests in response to recent developments in the teaching of English and to the increased influence of linguistics.

The test constructors' awareness of the need for change is obvious from the variety of items which have been tried and from statements in the test manuals such as, "new types of item have been introduced to test the appropriate use of words and the appreciation of well-written English" and "the [test] marks a further stage in the development of tests of the mainly creative response type in which the emphasis on formal grammar is kept to a minimum."

A comparison of the earlier and later tests in the series from 13 to 20 does not show as much change as one might hope for in the direction of more open-ended, truly creative responses. Nevertheless, the trend is in the right direction. Examination of the marking keys for the later tests shows a much greater range of acceptable alternative answers and greater discretion left to the marker.

There is a discernible change in the test content. Whereas Test 13, for example, includes many questions on word structure (making plural and tense changes, substituting pronouns for nouns), Test 19 places the emphasis on sentences (rewriting jumbled sentences, sequencing sentences, selecting or producing words or phrases indicated by the syntax and meaning of a continuous passage) and greater weight is given to the ability to read and comprehend a continuous passage. Reduction by half in the number of items in Test 17 onwards but with the same time allowed is further evidence of the greater degree of judgment and thought required instead of an immediate response.

Tests of the ability to manipulate sentence structures are attempted in several ways: sequencing phrases, rewriting jumbled sentences and rewriting sentences using the passive transformation. The latter prompts the question whether items involving other transformations could not have been devised and whether sentence completion from a supplied beginning would not have been feasible—presumably problems of ensuring optimum pupil response and of marking may have proved limiting factors.

In general, the more recent tests show a marked development towards testing language in more adequate contexts so that they leave one with less of the feeling of having skipped arbitrarily through innumerable situations and artificial sentences.

A technique which is included in two tests—identifying the meaning of a nonsense word from several sentence contents—is not used in the last two tests, though, strangely, an item based on homophones continues to be used. One wonders what the rationale of this is since it might prompt teachers to give attention to a rather insignificant aspect of teaching English.

While there are certain consistencies of content in these eight tests (all contain passages for comprehension, some punctuation tasks, and vocabulary items), there are also variations from test to test and one wonders what are the underlying assumptions about attainment in English. This is not adequately discussed in any of the manuals and since test content is likely to influence teaching, it might be useful to state explicitly the range of language skills which the testers are trying directly or indirectly to sample. Such a statement might help schools to avoid the danger of assuming that test techniques devised to probe certain kinds of linguistic skills are necessarily desirable and profitable as teaching procedures.

For reviews by Stanley Nisbet and H. J. Sants of earlier tests, see 6:264.

[195]

★**Grammar, Usage, and Structure Test and Vocabulary Test.** College entrants; 1963–68; 2 tests in one booklet; 1 form ('63, 9 pages); combined manual ('68, 43 pages) for this test and R:57; separate answer sheets must be used; $4 per 20 tests; $1 per manual; 50¢ per specimen set; postpaid; answer sheets must be obtained locally; 60(65) minutes for both tests; William A. McCartney; the Author. *

[196]

***Hoyum-Sanders English Tests.** I, 2 semesters in grades 2–4, 5–6, 7–8; 1962–64; first published 1962–63 in the Every Pupil Scholarship Test series; 3 tests; Forms A, B, ('64, 4 pages); 2 levels labeled Tests I, 2; manual ('64, 5 pages); $1.75 per 25 tests, postage extra; 75¢ per specimen set of any one test, postpaid; 40(45) minutes; Vera Davis Hoyum and M. W. Sanders; Data Processing and Educational Measurement Center. *

a) HOYUM-SANDERS ELEMENTARY ENGLISH TEST. I, 2 semesters in grades 2–4.
b) HOYUM-SANDERS INTERMEDIATE ENGLISH TEST. I, 2 semesters in grades 5–6.

c) HOYUM-SANDERS JUNIOR HIGH SCHOOL ENGLISH TEST. I, 2 semesters in grades 7–8.

PAUL B. DIEDERICH, *Senior Research Associate, Educational Testing Service, Princeton, New Jersey.*

Although this publisher is not noted for care or sophistication in test construction, these English tests for grades 2–8 seem to be good, useful measures of knowledge of rules governing correctness in writing and ability to apply the rules to the kinds of sentences that students write. The points covered are those that are stressed in composition textbooks for the grades for which these tests are intended, and they correspond pretty well to the types of errors in student writing. There are very few items about which even the most permissive of linguists would argue that the alternatives are equally acceptable, and there are almost none that concern fine points, disputed usages, or problems that do not arise in ordinary student writing. The sentences that present these problems deal with matters that students in these grades often write about themselves. They are easy to understand, and they do not sound like the artificial sentences that grammarians so often concoct. Grammatical terminology is avoided almost entirely up to the tests for grades 7–8, and then it is limited to terms needed to explain why the option chosen is correct. There is one final section in each test of 10 items on alphabetization, included for obvious reasons, but apart from that, everything included in these tests contributes to the impression that a student has or has not mastered the ordinary conventions of writing. If a teacher does not expect these tests to reveal anything more than this, he ought to find them quite useful as measures of status and growth and, to a limited extent, as pointers toward areas in which a class needs to improve.

For the last-mentioned purpose of class diagnosis, it is unfortunate that some sections of these tests have different numbers of items in Forms A and B. For example, it would be hard to tell whether a class had improved in usage when there are 50 items of this sort in Form A of the intermediate tests and 40 items in Form B. Teachers would have to change raw scores to percent correct, and many would forget or not take the trouble to do so. It is so easy to produce large numbers of items like these and to make sure that those selected for published forms are equal in difficulty that there is no apparent reason for inequality in numbers of items in sections of forms intended to be equivalent.

All 12 forms of these tests have six sections: Sentence Recognition, Capitalization, Punctuation, Contractions and Possessives, Usage, and Alphabetization. The manual gives the impression that the intermediate and junior high tests do not have the section Contractions and Possessives and substitute a section on "reference materials, such as guide words and index" for Alphabetization, but this is inaccurate; the same six sections appear throughout. The section "Contractions, Possessives" has "Plurals" included in some forms and "Spelling" in others, usually because one or two items (out of 10 or 15)—like "monkeys, monkies" or "sheep, sheeps"—might be classified either way. These items might better be eliminated, since the label should not give the impression that these tests include spelling.

The main objection I would have to these tests is that they must be highly speeded. With a uniform time limit of 40 minutes, there are 95 items in the elementary tests, either 115 or 120 in the intermediate tests, and 135 in the junior high tests. The test of this sort that I admire most, the *Writing Skills Test* (for grades 9–12) by Macklin Thomas, published by SRA, has 70 items with the same time limit, and I doubt that the operations involved (except in one final section of 10 items) take more time than those of the Hoyum-Sanders tests. The norms tables for the latter, however, seem to indicate that the norms population was almost incredibly fast. In Test 1, Form A, for example, the average student got 69 out of 95 items right in grade 4, 92 out of 120 right in grade 6, and 93 out of 135 right in grade 8. The 90th percentile student got about four-fifths right in these grades. If this is representative, the use of the split-half method is not seriously questionable in computing reliabilities, which range from .86 to .93.

The same manual of four pages is used for the tests at all three levels—elementary, intermediate, and junior high. As usual, it does not give enough information about the development, tryout, and validation of the tests to satisfy the sophisticated, but the one serious error occurs in a paragraph explaining the norms. There are four tables of raw scores corresponding to percentiles (at intervals of 5) for Tests 1-A, 1-B,

2-A, and 2-B, and each table has columns for grades 2 through 8. These tables would be easier to interpret if headings were added to indicate that the columns for grades 2, 3, and 4 are based on the elementary tests, columns for grades 5 and 6 on the intermediate tests, and columns for grades 7 and 8 on the junior high tests. In the catalogue it is stated that Test 1 at each level is for the first semester and Test 2 for the second; Forms A and B of each test are equivalent. In the manual, however, one is directed to use Form A norms for all scores made in the first half of the school year, Form B norms for the second—apparently for both Test 1 and Test 2. This must be wrong, since the Form B norms show no consistent advance over Form A norms; instead, they bear out the catalogue statement that these forms are equivalent. The Test 2 norms, however, are slightly but consistently higher than the Test 1 norms, bearing out the catalogue statement that Test 1 is for the first semester and Test 2 for the second. This paragraph in the manual concludes, "Be sure to use the correct Table with reference Mid-year and End of Year and test form." No spik English?

The manual also says that raw scores may be converted into grade equivalent scores by using these norms tables but fortunately does not tell how. Only a mathematician could do it, and if he had a conscience, he would refuse, since there are different numbers of items and differences in content at successive levels and no administrations to justify placing all three levels on the same scale.

[197]
Language Arts: Minnesota High School Achievement Examinations. Grades 7, 8, 9, 10, 11, 12; 1955–70; new form issued each May; Form GJ Rev. ('70, 6–7 pages); 6 levels; no specific manual; series manual ('70, 16 pages); no data on reliability; 12¢ per test, postage extra; $1.10 per specimen set, postpaid; 60(65) minutes; edited by V. L. Lohmann; American Guidance Service, Inc. *

For a review by Marvin D. Glock of earlier forms, see 6:268; for a review by Roger A. Richards, see 5:186.

[198]
★Language Arts Tests: Content Evaluation Series.* Grades 7–9; 1969; Form 1; 3 tests in 1 booklet (33 pages); manual (24 pages); series technical manual (21 pages); separate answer sheets (MRC) must be used; $15 per 35 tests; $4.20 per 35 answer sheets; $1.05 per set of hand scoring stencils; 60¢ per manual; 90¢ per technical manual; $1.35 per specimen set of series; postage extra; scoring service, 27¢ per test booklet; 40(50) minutes per test; Elsa Graser

(a), Leonard Freyman (b), Ruth Reeves (c);
Houghton Mifflin Co. *
a) LANGUAGE ABILITY TEST: CONTENT EVALUATION
SERIES.
b) COMPOSITION TEST: CONTENT EVALUATION SERIES.
c) LITERATURE TEST: CONTENT EVALUATION SERIES.

JOAN J. MICHAEL, *Associate Professor of Educational Psychology, California State College at Long Beach, Long Beach, California.*

The *Language Arts Tests* measure achievement in three general areas: language ability, composition, and literature. To the great credit of this set of tests, the authors have taken considerable pains in the construction of a detailed outline of the major and specific objectives for each of the three tests. To assist the reader in evaluating the content, the authors have prepared item classifications which indicate how each item is related to the particular outline. Thus, a prospective user is provided with an effective means of deciding upon content validity for any particular curriculum. Kudos, for this feature!

In the Language Ability Test the two major objectives stated are "to assess the student's understanding of the basic structure of the English language" and "to assess the student's ability to use sentence elements effectively in standard patterns." Of the 58 items comprising this test, only 14 are devoted to "basic structure," and the remaining 44 are devoted to the use of sentence elements. Appropriate selection of language usage problems from both the traditional and the newer patterns of English instruction have been included. Before using, however, a teacher has to decide whether the balance of items between traditional and new patterns is appropriate for a given curriculum. This reviewer raises some question about the variety of the format of items. In 40 minutes of testing time the examinee is required to read, understand, and implement eight different sets of instructions for answering the questions. Especially for lower ability students, this task in itself would appear to be formidable.

Of course, the continued challenge by teachers of English to the use of multiple choice items to evaluate students' composition skills remains. If the reader can accept the premise that this type of test offers a useful complement but not a substitute for actual samples of writing, then the Composition Test may be judged upon its merits as one form of assessment. The major objectives as set forth in the outline of the Composition Test are those of invention, arrangement, and style. Of the 60 items in this test, 31 were devoted to arrangement, 24 to style, and 5 to invention. As would be expected for this type of test, the choosing and restricting of the subject and stating of the purpose receive less emphasis than do the problems of organization and style. The content of this test appears to be based upon a rather thorough analysis of student errors; however, for the 7th, 8th, and 9th grade levels, this test seems to be a rather difficult undertaking. Moreover, in 40 minutes of testing time, the examinee is required to read and understand over 60 items, and to implement some 13 different sets of instructions.

The Literature Test is directed not toward factual content, but rather toward the significance and understanding of literary works. The teacher's manual outlines the three major objectives of this test as "overall comprehension," "response to techniques common to imaginative literature," and "literary interpretations." Of the 45 items, 16 are devoted to comprehension; 18 to techniques such as figurative language, contrast, emphasis, or implications; and 11 to literary interpretations of fiction, poetry, essay, and drama. The subject matter of the selections appears quite appropriate for the junior high level; however, the amount of reading required in a 40-minute time span to answer the 45 items is rather sizable. Students with poor reading skills might possibly be overwhelmed with the task involved.

The teacher's manual provides the user with administration and scoring directions, an explanation of the various types of scores suggested, conversion tables, bibliography, as well as the aforementioned outlines of the three tests. With respect to the various types of scores provided, the percentile ranks and stanines seem appropriate; however, the manner in which the standard scores were derived from a normalized curve seems so unusual as to lessen their usability. These standard scores were derived from the *total* weighted distribution of students in grades 7, 8, and 9. This weighted distribution interferes with ease of interpretation at any given grade level on a given test.

Split-half reliability estimates for the subtests range from .84 to .95. The high intercorrelations among the subtests (.69 to .75) are possibly a result of the sizable reading factor involved in the tests. No validity coefficients are shown; however, the outlines of specifications for the tests do serve this purpose. Finally, as an indication of criterion-related validity, an expectancy table pitting Language Ability Test scores against final English grades is shown.

In summary, the *Language Arts Tests* seem to this reviewer to be thoughtfully conceived and implemented but difficult and quite possibly inappropriate for lower ability students.

BLAINE R. WORTHEN, *Co-director, Laboratory of Educational Research, University of Colorado, Boulder, Colorado.*

Specific purposes of these three tests are to assess student progress in the three subject areas over the three junior-high years and to diagnose areas of strength and weakness for individual students.

TEST CONTENT. The teacher's manual contains a rationale and content outline for each of the tests and a classification of the items according to that outline. Each item number is listed with a numerical indicator of the point in the outline that the item is designed to measure. Attempting to use these two lists to determine how a content classification is represented by test items is laborious and the lists should be combined with items listed under each point in the outline.

The Language Ability Test is concentrated on areas which research seems to indicate are of greatest importance in language development— the structure of basic English and use of sentence elements in standard sentence patterns. Although the rationale states that no particular grammatical method is tested and no traditional grammatical terms are used, the student who has been exposed to structural grammar may have an advantage. The student must know what "sentence patterns" or "standard patterns of usage" are for 19 of the 58 items; 16 items use nonsense sentences that might be most readily deciphered by students familiar with structural grammar.

The Composition Test is designed to assess student ability to manipulate his language effectively; three principles of classical rhetoric— invention, organization, and style—are proposed as vehicles for this assessment. Inspection of the test shows that 21 of the 60 items cover choosing the main headings and subheadings of an outline. Twenty-three other items involve choosing among sentences embodying such considerations as "judicious infinitive splitting," "faulty reference," or "use of subordinate clauses." Two sets of items are interdependent;

one set includes 16 items which require arranging topics in an outline and another includes 6 items which require arranging sentences in a paragraph. Within each set, responding to one item influences the responses to the remaining items. This means that only 38 of the items on the test are independent. More seriously, a student could conceivably miss over one-third of the items by making only two wrong choices.

The Literature Test is intended to measure ability to identify important types of literature and "feeling for literature." Questions refer to five passages: one story, one essay, two poems, and one play. The questions stress analysis; 20 of the 45 items deal with "the central thought," "tone," or "implications." Although the level of reading difficulty appears to be appropriate for the other two tests, the required reading level in this test may be too high for a number of students in grades 7–9. Leaving the literary passages aside, some questions are unnecessarily complex and may penalize students who have considerable "feeling for literature" but have not been introduced to specific technical terms. Several questions require knowledge of terms such as "alliteration," "stanza," "simile," "metaphor," "rhyme scheme," and "unaccented syllables."

All three tests were difficult for seventh graders in the standardization group. The average seventh grade score for each was less than half the items. The median score for seventh graders on two of the tests—Composition and Literature—is not significantly different from chance; i.e., for half the seventh graders, one cannot be confident that the student did not achieve his score by random guessing.

TEST USE. The test format is excellent for all three tests. Directions for preparing for the test period and administering the test are quite explicit and will likely prove especially helpful to the beginner. Directions for scoring and reporting results are also clear and complete.

Scores for each test can be reported in four ways: raw scores, within-grade percentiles, within-grade stanines, and across-grade standard scores (normalized T scores). The latter "is provided so that scores from different subject areas and grade levels can be compared." One infers that such scores would be used to construct profiles, but no further discussion is given. Conversion tables are supplied in both the technical and teacher's manuals.

It is indicated in the manuals that the test

results might be used diagnostically with individual students. This seems unwarranted, since there are far too few items in most content areas to permit any reliable diagnoses. These tests should be viewed as group tests and appropriate for diagnostic use at that level only.

ITEM ANALYSIS. It is stated in the technical manual that item analyses were performed on preliminary forms of the test. The criteria were "a suitable range of difficulty" and "discrimination powers." Unfortunately, these criteria are not specified and item analysis data are not reported. It is also unfortunate that in the age of computers, discrimination indices were computed using the upper and lower 27 percent method rather than point-biserial coefficients or other indices of discrimination.

NORMS. Three factors were considered in drawing the sample for test standardization: community size, community location, and grade. Within these categories, the sampling plan used in the Project Talent survey was adopted and schools were selected randomly from the "community size by location" categories. Rates of noncooperation, mortality, and unusable results were not reported. "In all, 50,336 tests were administered in 27 schools from 21 districts representing 17 states." However, this selection of schools did not fully meet the specified sample requirements. There was marked overrepresentation of rural Northeast communities and underrepresentation of rural West and urban Southeast communities. Overall, rural communities were overrepresented and urban communities underrepresented. A weighting system was employed. "Actual returns were reported in 112 cells....these cells were then weighted to more closely meet the requirements of the sample." Unfortunately, the weighting system is inadequately described and test users are left to wonder how closely the weighted results meet the sample requirements. Given this ambiguity, one must also wonder how useful norms from this sample will be for interpreting test results in metropolitan schools. A further description of the sample (by sex, school and district size, race, socioeconomic status, etc.) would better enable users to determine the applicability of the norms to their schools.

RELIABILITY. Means, standard deviations, and standard errors of measurement for both raw and standard scores, and split-half correlations are reported for all three tests. These statistics were computed from "a systematic sample of 400 tests per grade per test." The system for selecting this sample is not reported.

Split-half reliabilities range from .84 to .95. These reliability coefficients are described as representing "the degree to which the performance of the student remains stable." However, the split-half method is a measure of internal consistency, not stability. Since the tests are to be used three times (at grades 7, 8, and 9) for assessing progress, the manual should give a reliability coefficient that does indicate stability over time. Particularly, one needs data on potential practice effects, since the same test, same form, could be used three times.

A more serious drawback of the split-half method, however, is the effect of speededness on the coefficient. Precisely 40 minutes are allotted for each test and instructions stress enforcing this time limit. There is no evidence that this period allows most students to finish the test. It may be that the high number of seventh grade scores which are not significantly different from chance reflects the effect of speed rather than test difficulty.

Although standard errors of measurement are listed for both raw and standard scores, useful information on the interpretation of these data are not included.

VALIDITY. Validity data on the *Language Arts Tests* are limited. Content validity is based on (*a*) an analysis of leading textbooks and courses of study for content and weighting of test specifications, and (*b*) examination of the specifications by curriculum experts to confirm appropriateness and coverage of content. However, no description of the specifications or experts' reactions to them are provided; agreement of experts with the final selection of items is implied, but no supporting data are offered.

Criterion-related validity is limited to a single study; the expectancy tables presented show positive relationships between scores on each of the tests and final eighth-grade English grades. Although correlation coefficients would have given more information about validity, the failure to use an independent criterion is a more serious deficiency. No mention is made of possible criterion contamination—any effect of the test scores on the final grades is ignored. In short, one can have confidence only in claims for content validity, and even there considerable appeal to faith is necessary.

SUMMARY. In spite of the criticisms noted above, the *Language Arts Tests* are appropriate for assessing end-of-year achievement in the three specified language areas, especially in grades 8 and 9. They are interesting tests with a blend of traditional and innovative content. Content validity for the tests appears acceptable, but an explicit description of content validation processes is needed before one can be confident about such validity. Inclusion of a stability reliability index is a must, especially in view of the use of the same tests across three grade levels. Users should be provided better descriptions of norm groups and criteria used in the item analyses. Item interdependencies should be reduced or eliminated in the Literature Test and item difficulties and time limits should be reconsidered on all three tests. If these inadequacies can be corrected, these tests should prove very useful in assessing proficiency in the three language areas. In the meantime, interpretation of test results will be most difficult and the tests should be used only by those who understand the limitations involved.

[199]

*Mechanics of Written English. High school; 1940–66; 6 scores: punctuation, recognition of non-standard usage, capitalization, vocabulary, spelling, total; 1 form ('66, 11 pages, identical with Form 59B published in 1959 except for title page); mimeographed scoring directions [no date, 3 pages, identical with directions for Form 59B except for omission of norms]; no data on reliability; no norms; $1 per 10 tests, postpaid; 25¢ per single copy, cash orders only; 50(55) minutes; R. S. Hunting; High School Testing Service, Purdue University. *

[200]

*Metropolitan Achievement Tests: High School Language Tests. Grades 9–13; 1962–64; catalog uses the title *Metropolitan High School Language Tests;* 4 scores: reading, spelling, language, language study skills; Forms Am ('62, 12 pages), Bm ('63, 12 pages); manual ('64, 28 pages); for battery accessories, see 15; separate answer sheets (Digitek, Harbor, IBM 805, IBM 1230) must be used; $8.50 per 35 tests; $2.80 per 35 Digitek answer sheets; $2.90 per 35 IBM 805 answer sheets; $3.30 per 35 IBM 1230 answer sheets; $6 per 100 sets of Harbor answer cards; 70¢ per Digitek scoring stencil; $1.40 per set of IBM scoring stencils; $1.50 per specimen set; postage extra; Harbor scoring service, 19¢ and over per test; IBM scoring service, 33¢ and over per test; 95(112) minutes; Walter N. Durost, William H. Evans, James D. Leake, Howard A. Bowman, Clarke Cosgrove, and John G. Read; Harcourt Brace Jovanovich, Inc. *

LEONARD S. FELDT, *Professor of Education, The University of Iowa, Iowa City, Iowa.*

The original edition of the *Metropolitan Achievement Tests* was published approximately 40 years ago. Its long history is rivaled by only one or two competing batteries, including the *Stanford Achievement Tests,* distributed by the same publisher. The high school battery is a relatively new addition to the testing scene, however, having first appeared in 1962. The forms under review bear copyright dates of 1962 and 1963. Thus, they appear to be the original extensions of the Metropolitan battery to grades 9–13.

The first three passages of the reading test follow the traditional pattern of such instruments. Each selection is approximately 400–500 words in length and is followed by a series of seven or eight questions. The final passage presents an innovation at the high school level. A fairly long selection (about 800 words) is presented to the examinee for 10 minutes of preliminary study. At the end of this period, he turns the page and must answer a series of questions without opportunity to reread the material. This is apparently an attempt to reflect in the test the kind of recall situation commonly encountered in school work. However, there is no evidence in the manual to indicate that this approach reveals a unique aspect of the reading process. If there is a new recall element introduced, do we want to see the student with a facile memory receive a higher reading score than a classmate not similarly blessed? This may be an academic question, since the variance associated with differences in memory may be insignificant. The recall period is, after all, very short.

The authors state that the questions bear on four aspects of the selections: main idea or purpose of the passage, inferences from the passage, perception of details, and deduction of the meanings of words from the context. The manual does not indicate the category to which each item belongs. This reviewer found few items which he would consider very penetrating or which require a high level of critical insight. Perhaps this follows from the fact that the passages themselves, while quite interesting, do not include any that seem very meaty or demanding. In their daily work, high school juniors and seniors are confronted with more sophisticated material than these tests offer. Competing reading tests, such as those found in the STEP and ITED batteries, pose more of a challenge, with questions that probe more deeply than do the materials represented here.

The spelling and language exercises include a response that may be unique to this battery.

t is "don't know." This option may provide relief from the frustration some examinees feel when forced to choose one answer from several equally attractive possibilities. But surely most students and practically all teachers will realize that no credit can be earned by selecting this response. If any students are tempted to mark it (there are no data in the manual on this point), the scores become unnecessarily and undesirably sensitive to the test-taking skills and naiveté of the examinee.

The spelling test, involving 55 items of the 'right-wrong-don't know" variety, and one of the language usage subtests introduce another novelty: a worksheet on which the examinee records the correct spelling or the correct grammatical form of words that are incorrect in the test exercises. The teacher uses these worksheets for diagnosis if he wishes, but they are ignored in the scoring of the tests. They would seem to open the way to some interesting research possibilities. They could be used, for example, to document the contention that those who recognize an error do know the correct language forms. No such studies are reported in the test manual.

The capitalization and punctuation subtest proved somewhat confusing to this reviewer when he used the IBM 1230 answer sheet. The item responses are printed on the sheet, and one must constantly bear in mind that the response space which applies to an option *follows* rather than *precedes* it. This can be forgotten. Also, the text material in this subtest includes obvious errors which the student must ignore. The directions might have noted this fact.

In general, the language tests represent a compromise between identifying errors and specifying the reasons why a usage is unacceptable. Some teachers may consider the reasons important and be happy that the test demands this knowledge. But others might have preferred some items devoted to effectiveness of phrasing, organization of ideas, and so on. The entire test deals exclusively with issues of right and wrong, rather than better or worse.

The test scores can be interpreted via norms based on "age-controlled" samples (pupils who have been regularly promoted) or the scores of students enrolled in college preparatory curriculums. The former have been used for many years in conjunction with the lower levels of this battery. As a previous reviewer has pointed out (6:15), the specifications for the national standardization may have been well formulated, but the execution of the plan probably fell short of the publisher's hopes. Fewer than 30 school systems are represented in the norms.

The manual describes the developmental program quite well, but validity rests solely on the efforts of the authors to build tests consistent with "expert pronouncements," "current research," "representative courses of study," and "widely used textbooks." How well they succeeded, each teacher must decide for himself. The reliability data must be considered with caution. K-R 20 coefficients were computed from the same data and samples used to make the final item selection—a procedure which leads to biased coefficients. Split-half estimates are based on two school systems and, more crucially, on scores from grades 10 and 11 combined. Such pooling of grade data is not a sound procedure. Why samples from the national standardization were not used for reliability estimation is not explained.

In summary, this reviewer finds both the reading and the language tests less penetrating and narrower in scope than multiple choice tests can be. Where the decision on their use is not tied to adoption of the battery as a whole, he would strongly suggest consideration of competing instruments.

DAVID P. HARRIS, *Professor of Linguistics and Director, The American Language Institute, Georgetown University, Washington, D.C.*

These tests are comprised of four separate measures which can be used independently. Test 1, Reading, consists of 40 four-choice items based on four selections. The first three passages in Form Am range roughly between 450 and 500 words in length; those in Form Bm are all slightly shorter. These passages are followed by seven or eight items each. The fourth selection is about twice as long as the others, and students are to answer the 17 questions without referring back to the passage. Test selections are interesting and varied in content, and the items are soundly written. Factual questions are interspersed with inferential problems and questions about the author's purpose, as well as with a few pure vocabulary items. The inclusion of one section testing recall is appropriate, though the choice of subject for the Am passage seems questionable: it is for the most part a conventional discussion of reading techniques, and the student who has been taught anything about intensive and extensive reading and skimming ought to be able to answer seven or eight items on the basis of prior knowledge alone.

Test 2, Spelling, presents the 55 test words in one-sentence contexts. The student marks each word R (right), W (wrong), or DK (don't know). Words he considers misspelled are then to be spelled correctly on a work sheet. These spellings are not counted in the scoring; they are intended to provide additional information for the teacher. Unfortunately, no advice is given the student as to whether it is better to guess or to mark the DK option (which is also used in Tests 3 and 4), and one supposes that the test-wise student will gain an advantage by limiting himself to R and W choices. Most of the test words are reasonably appropriate for high school students, though a handful of words in each form seem to have been chosen primarily for their spelling peculiarities, not for their probable utility value: *lacquer, silhouette, exhilaration,* etc.

Test 3, Language, is divided into three parts: punctuation and capitalization (25 items based on a passage in which most punctuation and capitalization have been omitted); correct usage (35 sentences with underlined words); and sentence style and structure (13 sentences which either are acceptable or contain one of several designated types of "errors"). Though this should be one of the strongest tests in the battery, it is, alas, the weakest. It is hard to believe that, after so many years of emphasis on descriptive grammar and levels of usage, we should still find tests demanding that the "rules" of formal written English be applied to highly colloquial contexts. Can we still reasonably insist that our students mark as incorrect "I wish today *was* Saturday"? Does anyone still find it appropriate to drill "This is *he* speaking"? This test puts far too much emphasis on the traditional shibboleths: e.g., *"these* kind of apples," "taller than *me,"* "it was *him,"* *"all the farther* I read." And surely if such matters of divided usage are worthy of any attention at all, it is only when they appear in formal or semiformal writing and spoil the general tone. To drill or test them in contexts that suggest conversation between friends is to set back our understanding of the language by several decades.

Of far greater potential value is the section on sentence style and structure, where faulty sentences of various kinds are presented to the student for analysis. But this part of the test has only 13 problems (compared with 25 for punctuation and capitalization), and the student has only to select an appropriate description of the sentence faults: "Modifier is misplaced," "Sentence is incomplete," etc. The reviewer would strongly urge, first, that this part of the test be considerably expanded and, second, that at least some items require the student to choose the best of alternative ways of expressing the same idea, so that his task would be more than simply attaching labels.

Test 4, Language Study Skills (only 32 items), is concerned with the student's ability to interpret dictionary entries and to utilize various reference sources (tables of contents, card catalogue, *Readers' Guide,* etc.). The test measures some useful learnings, though the 12 dictionary items, based on three highly simplified dictionary entries, seem repetitive and rather easy. High school students should certainly be able to handle the standard "college" dictionaries, and a more valid and challenging test could be constructed around a reproduced page from such a dictionary, as was done in the old *Cooperative Dictionary Test.*

The publisher provides a wide range of clear and helpful information on the tests. Results are expressed in terms of a normalized standard score scale having a mean of 50 and a standard deviation of 15. Tables are given for converting standard scores to percentile ranks and stanines, with separate norms for age-controlled and college-preparatory groups. Separate test data on both test forms are provided for the 9th through 12th grades. Reliability has been estimated by three methods: K-R 20, split-half, and alternate forms. K-R 20 coefficients for Form Bm of Test 1 and for both forms of Test 4 are below .85, suggesting cautious use of these tests as measures of individual performance. Unfortunately, no data are offered on combinations of the tests, nor is there any information on degree of speededness, which would be particularly helpful in the case of Test 1, Reading.

The manual proposes four specific uses for the tests: (*a*) appraisal of student progress, (*b*) educational and vocational guidance, (*c*) evaluation of instructional programs "as a basis for curriculum revision," and (*d*) evaluation of instructional material. Certain of the tests, and particularly Test 1, Reading, might be of some use as diagnostic or achievement instruments. On the other hand, the extremely old-fashioned character of Test 3, Language, renders it inappropriate for most diagnostic or achievement testing, and to use it as a basis for curriculum reform or as a measure of the adequacy of modern instructional materials could prove downright destructive.

For reviews of the complete battery, see 15 (2 reviews) and 6:15 (3 reviews).

[201]

★**Missouri College English Test.** Grades 12–13; 1964–65; MCET; Forms B, C, ('64, 8 pages); Form C is restricted to colleges; manual ('65, 16 pages); supplementary grade 12 norms available on request; separate answer sheets (Digitek, IBM 805, IBM 1230) must be used; $7 per 35 tests; $2.30 per 35 IBM 805 answer sheets; $2.80 per 35 Digitek or IBM 1230 answer sheets; 70¢ per scoring stencil; $1.50 per specimen set; postage extra; IBM scoring service, 19¢ and over per test; 40(50) minutes; Robert Callis and Willoughby Johnson; Harcourt Brace Jovanovich, Inc. * (Form A is out of print.)

REFERENCE

1. WILLIS, CARL G., AND NICHOLSON, JAMES. "Series II SCAT as a College Aptitude Measure." *Ed & Psychol Meas* 30(4):971–5 w '70. *

JOHN B. CARROLL, *Senior Research Psychologist, Educational Testing Service, Princeton, New Jersey.*

This is a competently constructed, well standardized test which is, as the manual puts it, "generally concerned with the mechanics and the effectiveness of written expression." One is impressed with the amount of effort that apparently went into the drawing up of specifications, the writing of items, the obtaining of comments and suggestions from subject-matter specialists, the updating of the test in 1962–63 after it was discovered that entering college freshmen were increasingly better prepared, and the final norming.

Each of the three equivalent forms has three parts. Part 1 requires the examinee to register whether each of 60 underlined segments in a group of themes contains an error in the mechanics of expression and, if so, whether the error is one of capitalization, "grammar," punctuation, or spelling. Most of the errors are of the rather elementary sort that continually plague teachers of English composition, and the segments that are keyed as having no error contain expressions that will often tempt the unsure student to believe there is an error. Throughout, the emphasis is on standards of formal correctness; occasionally the student is expected to recognize such a standard even though it may be somewhat unrealistic, as when

he must identify a "grammatical" error in the phrase "who we are sure we can trust," even though the phrase in question occurs in a quoted, informal conversation.

Part 2 has 10 items requiring the student to decide which one of four sentences best expresses an idea; the distractors are awkward, ungainly sentences that would never be approved by a good editor, yet item difficulty data included in the manual reveal that significant proportions of students do not recognize the keyed choices. Occasionally, however, even a good editor might disagree with the key (e.g., items 65 and 70 in Form A), and sometimes the keyed choices are of dubious excellence stylistically (e.g., item 69, Form A). The difficulty and discrimination indices tend to confirm these judgments.

Part 3 asks the student to indicate the order in which sentences should be arranged in four 5-sentence paragraphs, for a total of 20 items.

The user of this test should note that by far the largest portion of the test is concerned with elementary mechanics of expression. Apparently this is what English instructors are most worried about. (Incidentally, the test authors should attend to their own mechanics: in Table 10 of the manual, we find a mention of the "principle [sic] parts" of verbs.)

The authors claim this is a power test because "it was determined that a 90-item test could be completed in 40 minutes by the vast majority of college freshmen." Nevertheless, they make the common mistake of reporting split-half reliability coefficients without pointing out that they may be inflated because of possible speededness.

The norms for the test appear to be highly adequate, based on data obtained from freshmen enrolled at 81 two- and four-year public and private colleges. Supplementary data available from the publisher give norms for 968 students completing 12th grade English in five comprehensive high schools in New York State. It is somewhat saddening to note the relatively poor showing of all these students; the median score for all college freshmen is about 51 right out of 90, and the distribution extends down to the level of chance scores.

On the basis of the technical excellence of its standardization and the trouble the authors took to insure its content validity, this test can be recommended to high school and college English teachers who want a global measure of knowledge of the ordinary mechanics of English expression at the 12th grade or college freshman level. Its usefulness as a diagnostic test, however, would be limited both by the fact that relatively small numbers of items pertain to each category of error and by the fact that obtaining diagnostic information from the answer sheets would entail considerable effort. Its main use would be for placement in college freshman writing courses or for the identification of students needing remedial teaching.

CLARENCE DERRICK, *Professor of Humanities, University of Florida, Gainesville, Florida.*

The item types used to evaluate objectively what the test constructor hopes is related to writing proficiency are of two general types—"mechanics" items and "effectiveness" items. Since 60 of the 90 items in this test are "mechanics" items, the *Missouri College English Test* will serve best in those situations where punctuation, capitalization, spelling, and grammar are emphasized. (The writers of this test do not make the distinction between the terms *grammar* and *usage.*)

The mechanics items are presented in "selections....adapted from essays written by college students" with certain underlined parts to be examined for errors in capitalization, "grammar," punctuation, and spelling. The fifth possibility is that the underlined portion contains no error. Supposedly the use of student essays presents a natural situation. Although this item type has been used frequently in other tests, this reviewer has never liked it. The test taker is put in a proofreading situation, and how many of us are good proof readers? Too much depends on visual acuity. The person who would not misspell a particular word may fail to detect that a letter is missing. Another limitation is that the underlined portion may not present a situation where all the categories are live options. For example, an item in Form B: "Considering the *remarkable facility of the minature* camera as...." Is capitalization a possibility? Is punctuation? Is "grammar"? Essentially this item is a two-choice item—spelling or no error.

In Part 2, the examinee selects from four sentences the one that expresses the idea best. Of the three item types in the test, this item type seems to have the most "face validity" for evaluating proficiency in writing. To state that one item type is preferable to another type is

not to say that all items using that format are equally good. The trick in the item type in Part 2 is to have as the keyed answer a sentence that most people would regard as better expressing the idea in the sentence and still not have the choice too obvious—not an easy trick.

Part 3 uses another familiar item type. The examinee is presented with five sentences in scrambled order and then responds to a series of questions: "Which sentence should be placed *first?* Which *second?*" etc. This reviewer has never been sure exactly what is being measured by this item type, but he doubts that it has much to do with the ability to organize one's own sentences, which is presumably the rationale for it. Furthermore, the experienced test taker knows that his performance on this item type is facilitated if he writes a number by each sentence in what he considers the proper sequence and then answers the questions. However, the directions for the *Missouri College English Test* do not permit him to write in the test booklet.

The *Missouri College English Test* is a device to separate sheep from goats in the traditional freshman composition course and to urge students to follow the path of "correctness." Those who want a test that gives less emphasis to mechanics and more emphasis to stylistic matters and diction should examine such tests as the *Cooperative English Tests* and the *College English Placement Test.*

[202]

*Moray House English Tests. Ages 8.5–10.5, 10–12, 12–14; 1935–70; 3 levels; distribution restricted to education authorities; £1 per 20 tests; 5p per single copy; 12½p per manual for any one form of any one test; postage extra; 40(50) minutes; Godfrey Thomson Unit, University of Edinburgh; University of London Press Ltd. *

a) MORAY HOUSE JUNIOR ENGLISH TEST. Ages 8.5–10.5; 1952–70; 4 forms: *Junior English Test 1* ['52], *Junior English Test 3* ('64), 5 ('70), 6 ('70), (11–12 pages); manual [dates same as for tests, 12 pages] for each form.

b) MORAY HOUSE ENGLISH TEST. Ages 10–12; 1935–69; 1–2 new forms issued annually; 10 forms (12 pages) currently available: forms 33 ['61], 34 ['62], 35 ['63], 36 ('64), 37 ('65), 38 ('65), 39 ('66), 40 ('67), 41 ('68), 42 ('69); manual (dates same as for tests, 11–12 pages) for each form.

c) MORAY HOUSE ENGLISH TEST (ADV.). Ages 12–14; 1947–58; forms 1 ['56], 2 ['58], (12 pages); manual [dates same as for tests, 12 pages] for each form.

REFERENCES

1–7. See 6:271.
8. MACNAMARA, JOHN. "Zero Error and Practice Effects in Moray House English Quotients." *Brit J Ed Psychol* 34:315–20 N '64. * (*PA* 39:8704)

For a review by M. Alan Brimer, see 6:271.

[203]

*National Teacher Examinations: English Language and Literature. College seniors and teachers; 1940–70; Forms RNT1 ('69, 23 pages), RNT2 ('69, 21 pages), SNT ('70, 23 pages); descriptive booklet ('70, 8 pages); for more complete information, see 582; 120(165) minutes; Educational Testing Service. *

REFERENCE

1. MEDLIN, YANCEY LEONARD. *An Analysis of Some Aspects of the English Proficiency of White Secondary School Teacher Candidates in North Carolina, 1959–1961.* Doctor's thesis, University of North Carolina (Chapel Hill, N.C.), 1962. (*DA* 24: 1495)

For a review by Holland Roberts of an earlier form, see 6:259. For reviews of the testing program, see 582 (2 reviews), 6:700 (1 review), 5:538 (3 reviews), and 4:802 (1 review).

[204]

★Pacific Tests of English Attainment and Skills: Pacific Test Series. Job applicants in Papua and New Guinea; 1933–68; PTEAS; 3 tests; manual ('68, 31 pages); Aus $2.50 per manual; $3 per specimen set; postpaid within Australia; I. G. Ord; Australian Council for Educational Research. *
a) PACIFIC READING COMPREHENSION TEST. 1933–68; PRCT; adaptation of Part 3 of *A.C.E.R. Silent Reading Test,* Forms A and B (see 5:616); Forms A, B, ('68, 3 pages, each form consists of 12 items from Form L plus 4 more difficult items), L ('68, 4 pages); Aus 75¢ per 10 tests; 10(15) minutes for Forms A and B, 12(17) minutes for Form L.
b) PACIFIC WORD KNOWLEDGE TEST. 1933–68; PWKT; 1 form ('68, 2 pages); Aus 50¢ per 10 tests; 12(17) minutes.
c) PACIFIC WORD FORMATION TEST. 1968; PWFT; 1 form (4 pages); Aus $1 per 10 tests; 19(24) minutes.

[205]

★Picture Story Language Test. Ages 7–17; 1965; PSLT; a developmental scale for written language; 5 scores: productivity (total words, total sentences, words per sentence), syntax, abstract-concrete; record form (4 pages); test picture (1 card); manual ('65, 292 pages) title is *Development and Disorders of Written Language: Vol. 1, Picture Story Language Test;* $7.50 per 100 record forms; $4.75 per picture; $8.50 per manual; postage extra; (20–30) minutes; Helmer R. Myklebust; Grune & Stratton, Inc. *

REFERENCES

1. MYKLEBUST, HELMER R. *Development and Disorders of Written Language: Vol. 1, Picture Story Language Test.* New York: Grune & Stratton, Inc., 1965. Pp. xiii, 278. *
2. MASON, CHARLES WILBURN. *An Analysis of the Interrelationships of Variables in Selected Language Skills of Intermediate and Upper Elementary School Students.* Doctor's thesis, Southern Illinois University (Carbondale, Ill.), 1968. (*DA* 29:3043A)
3. MOORE, ANTHONY BRYAN. *Reasoning Ability and Verbal Proficiency in Deaf and Hearing Children.* Doctor's thesis, University of Massachusetts (Amherst, Mass.), 1968. (*DA* 29:4381B)
4. O'TOOLE, THOMAS JAMES. *The Effect of a Long-Term Functional Articulation Problem on the Language Skills of Seventh Grade Boys.* Doctor's thesis, University of Maryland (College Park, Md.), 1968. (*DAI* 30:3424B)
5. LEWIS, FRANKLIN D.; BELL, D. BRUCE; AND ANDERSON, ROBERT P. "Reading Retardation: A Bi-Racial Comparison." *J Read* 13(6):433–6, 474–8 Mr '70. *

NICHOLAS ANASTASIOW, *Director, Institute for Child Study, Indiana University, Bloomington, Indiana.*

This test is a relatively new diagnostic, clinical instrument for assessing the writing development of children. The test manual is a clothbound book in which the author discusses his rationale for how children's writing skills develop. He maintains that deficits in writing ability are related to abnormalities in the peripheral and central nervous system, caused by psychogenic disturbances and psycho-social deprivation. A major purpose of the test is to serve "as a diagnostic instrument for the study of children with language disorders and other types of learning disabilities." The child is presented with a picture about which he is asked to write a story. From these written stories, scales are developed to measure length (productivity), correctness of expression (syntax), and to attempt to measure content or meaning of the sentence (abstract-concrete). Thus, number of words, number of sentences, and words per sentence are counted; accuracy of word usage, of word endings, and of pronunciation is rated; and errors of additions, omissions, substitutions, and word order are counted.

The norming sample is described as consisting of three types of public school populations from one Midwestern state. A group of educators chose the schools as being representative but what they are representative of is not clear. Only odd years from ages 7 to 17 were sampled. The described norming procedures are very inadequate.

The means and standard deviations are presented by age and sex. Some growth curves are not linear. There is a large overlapping across ages in the range of scores for each scale but the author fails to comment upon these findings. For example, for total words a mean of 90.4 with a standard deviation of 51.5 was obtained at age 9 and a mean of 116.0 and standard deviation 56.0 at age 11. All scales were determined on the same sample; the description of how these data were obtained is inadequate. The author states that the instrument appears to be a valid test. However, validity is not adequately described. The author refers to studies with handicapped children, which are to be reported in a second volume. However, at this time, five years after the publication of the first volume, the second volume has not been published.

Reliability is based on test-retest and split-half data. The author reports that the test-retest correlations were statistically significant but does not present the data for the reader to determine what the statement means. This could be very misleading, as these correlations may be beyond chance, but as reported in his book the odd-even reliabilities range from .38 to .84 for words per sentence and from .52 to .92 on the syntax scale. Thus, most of the reliabilities are below adequate levels of test standards. Interrater reliabilities are below .90 on some of the scales. For the syntax scale, for example, the ranges are from .34 to .95 for individual ratings by three trained examiners.

In summary, the data as presented do not provide sufficient confidence that the test is either a reliable or valid measure of a child's writing skills. In addition, the author interpolates scores for ages not sampled. This is a dubious practice, considering the large standard deviation for the ages sampled. The *Picture Story Language Test* is a relatively untried projective technique with inadequate psychometric data presented to support the supposition the author maintains.

WILLIAM H. PERKINS, *Professor in Communicative Disorders, University of Southern California, Los Angeles, California.*

The *Picture Story Language Test* is intended as a diagnostic instrument for appraising normal and abnormal development of written language. This test evolved from several theoretical constructs: (*a*) that language is more than a signalling device; it is a system for attaching meaning to abstract symbols for expression of ideas; (*b*) that writing follows reading, which follows speech; (*c*) that whereas speech depends on integrity of the auditory system for learning, reading also depends on the visual system, and writing on coordination of these sensory processes with the motor system. Written language is therefore viewed as man's highest verbal achievement, and disorders of writing can reflect inability to learn auditorally, visually, tactually, or motorically.

The PSLT is a landmark test of written language. Not only is it based on a defensible theoretical foundation, but it has also been developed as a standardized test of facility with the written word and as an instrument for differential diagnosis of learning disabilities. The normal sample of 747 children from one Midwestern state was drawn from three school populations: metropolitan, rural, and suburban. Both sexes were represented about equally at

six age levels from 7 to 17, and a wide range of socioeconomic levels and cultural backgrounds was included. Although these norms probably apply to all children with average school experience, no evidence is yet available on geographic differences in written language development. The handicapped were studied separately and the data on those with learning disabilities, mental retardation, speech defects, social-emotional disturbance, and reading disabilities were to be reported separately in a second volume which, unfortunately, never was published.

Such evidence as is available indicates that the PSLT is a valid test of facility with the written word. Although the various tests have not been factor analyzed to determine the extent to which they test separate functions, they do have face validity. As normal children mature, their scores on the productivity, syntax, and abstract-concrete scales tend to improve. Too, handicapped children for whom language impairment would be expected reflect linguistic limitations in PSLT results. By comparison with such other tests as purport to measure the same functions, the PSLT appears to be a valid measure of written language.

For reliability, test-retest and odd-even methods have been used. The syntax and words-per-sentence scores meet acceptable standards of reliability, although reliability coefficients are lowest at age levels 11 and 13, suggesting greater performance variability at these ages. Using trained and untrained groups to determine interscorer reliability, the productivity and abstract-concrete scales emerge as scales that can be reliably administered irrespective of training. Training in use of the syntax scale, however, is critical for its use.

The PSLT is a valuable instrument for assessing facility with written language. Although it could also be used to evaluate spoken language, this is not a purpose for which it was designed, nor would it be particularly useful. The assumption underlying the test is that the spoken form is basic to the written form, an assumption supported by evidence that acquisition of reading and writing correlates highly with intelligence, whereas acquisition of speech requires only minimal intellectual capacity. For its purpose, this test stands apart as a valid reliable instrument for which normative data are available.

Cont Psychol 11:458 S '66. Joseph M. Wepman. * a manual for a new and relatively untried test for the development of written language in children. It has little theoretical substance and perhaps is better described as a statement of position rather than one of theory. Its greatest virtue lies in the care in which the author has elaborated the presentation and scoring principles for the new test. For the psychologist interested in a written projective test, the "picture story language test" might well provide the basis for a good psychological analysis. At the present time it is used as a study of the development of syntax more than anything else.

Percept & Motor Skills 22:667 Ap '66. C. H. Ammons. * The manual contains tables of normative data, illustrations of stories, and some specific information concerning reliability and validity. Several indices reflecting consistency suggest that reliability is reasonable. However, assessment of validity will require considerable ingenuity and further work. On this basis then, the interpretation of test protocols should be tentative at best.

[206]

*SRA Achievement Series: Language Arts. Grades 2–4, 4–9; 1954–69; 4 scores: capitalization and punctuation, grammatical usage, spelling, total; 2 forms; 4 levels in 2 booklets; no specific manuals; for series manuals and accessories, see 18; postage extra; Louis P. Thorpe, D. Welty Lefever, and Robert A. Naslund; Science Research Associates, Inc. *
a) HAND SCORED EDITION. Grades 2–4; 1955–68; test booklet title is *How Should We Say This?*; Forms C, D, ('63, 18 pages); $3.75 per 25 tests; 60(85) minutes in 2 sessions.
b) MULTILEVEL EDITION. Grades 4–9; 1963–69; Forms C, D, ('63, 27 pages); 3 levels: blue (grades 4.5–6.5), green (grades 6.5–8.5), and red (grades 8.5–9) in a single booklet; separate series answer sheets (Digitek, DocuTran, IBM 805, IBM 1230) must be used; $8.70 per 25 tests; $9.30 per 100 DocuTran answer sheets; 70(85) minutes.

REFERENCE

1. See 6:277.

For a review by Miriam M. Bryan of earlier forms, see 6:277; for reviews by Constance M. McCullough and Winifred L. Post, see 5:200. For reviews of the complete battery, see 18 (2 reviews), 6:21 (1 review), and 5:21 (2 reviews).

[207]

★Senior English Test. Technical college entrants; 1963–64; 1 form ['63, 8 pages]; mimeographed manual ('64, 8 pages); provisional norms ['63]; 5p per test, postpaid within U.K.; manual and norms free on request from NFER; 60(65) minutes; published for the National Foundation for Educational Research in England and Wales; Ginn & Co. Ltd. *

M. A. BRIMER, *Head of Research Unit, School of Education, University of Bristol, Bristol, England.*

The *Senior English Test* has been constructed with the cooperation of teachers to meet a particular need in England and Wales to measure general skills in the comprehension and use of English amongst entrants to technical college courses. Since the test is still in a developmental stage, despite its first introduction in 1963–64, the administrative manual (dated 1964) and a set of tentative norms are issued in duplicated form. No data on construction, reliability, or validity are reported.

Nineteen of the 56 items elicit a free response from the student and 13 require the construction of complete sentences. Vocabulary is tested through a "cross-word" item type, though independence of items is largely retained. Reading comprehension, sentence construction, the organisation of ideas in continuous prose, competence in syntactical usage, spelling, and insertion of periods are also represented, though with too few items to yield part scores.

Scoring is not entirely objective. Judgement of the quality of the response in relation to criteria given in the marking key is demanded in the case of 19 items. Moreover, in other items, where misspellings are not penalised, the marker must judge whether or not the subject's intention was to write the correct word, however it is spelled. Inevitably this must lead to increase in between-marker variation and to reduced reliability. Yet the loss in reliability may be compensated by improved construct validity.

Provisional t-score norms are offered for age groups 15–0 to 15–11 and 16–0 to 16–11, based, respectively, on 206 and 271 engineering student entrants to technical colleges. The absence of further data on the constitution of the sample, on construction, reliability, or validity precludes the possibility of a full assessment of the test. Only the reputation of the NFER would inspire confidence in an instrument which is so lacking in relevant data.

DAVID A. WALKER, *Formerly Director, The Scottish Council for Research in Education, Edinburgh, Scotland.*

This test was designed to assess the basic

knowledge of English possessed by entrants to courses in technical colleges. It contains 51 items, in 5 of which the candidate can earn two marks, the remainder carrying one mark each. The test begins with an easy crossword puzzle and continues with exercises in reading comprehension, word completion, punctuation, rearrangement of parts of a paragraph, completion of a paragraph using given phrases, and sentence construction. The manual gives clear instructions on the administration of the test and a marking key. Provisional conversion tables for 15-year-olds and 16-year-olds enable the test user to convert raw scores for these age-groups to T scores with mean at 50 and standard deviation of 10.

While the intention behind the test is praiseworthy, the execution unfortunately falls much below the standard expected from the National Foundation for Educational Research in England and Wales. The first reading comprehension passage, which is characterised by figurative language, is more appropriate to the material handled by able pupils following an academic course. The second passage contains vocabulary which is quite inappropriate for students of the type entering technical courses. The weight given to correctness of spelling seems unduly great; a candidate who knows that lines which meet at infinity are parallel, but misspells "parallel" scores zero. The test of punctuation is a satisfactory one, but the marking scheme makes nonsense of the section in that a candidate who supplies a sufficiently large number of strokes between words is certain to collect full marks but is not penalised for the surplus and incorrect strokes he has inserted. Nineteen of the responses are open-ended; although instructions for allocating marks are given in the manual, it is doubtful whether they are sufficiently precise to obviate differences between markers.

The provisional norms which are supplied are based on relatively small numbers of students. The manual, which was prepared in 1964, expresses the hope that standardisation data to be obtained for the period 1963–65 would enable more widely based conversion tables to be produced. An inquiry at the Foundation in August 1970 revealed that no further information had been made available and that there was none at that date on the reliability and validity of the test.

On the whole, it would appear to be wise to regard this test as an experiment in a difficult field.

[208]

★Stanford Achievement Test: High School English and Spelling Tests. Grades 9–12; 1965–66; catalog uses the title *Stanford High School English and Spelling Tests;* subtest of *Stanford Achievement Test: High School Basic Battery;* Forms W, X, ('65, 9 pages) ; no specific manual; battery manual ('65, 48 pages) ; supplementary directions ('66, 4 pages) for each type of answer sheet; separate answer sheets (IBM 805, IBM 1230) must be used; $8.20 per 35 tests; $2.30 per 35 IBM 805 answer sheets; $2.80 per 35 IBM 1230 answer sheets; $1.40 per set of scoring stencils; $1.20 per battery manual; $2 per specimen set; postage extra; scoring service, 19¢ and over per test; 60(65) minutes; Eric F. Gardner, Jack C. Merwin, Robert Callis, and Richard Madden; Harcourt Brace Jovanovich, Inc. *

VINCENT R. D'OYLEY, *Professor of Education, The Ontario Institute for Studies in Education, The University of Toronto, Toronto, Ontario, Canada.*[1]

These tests form part of a new comprehensive battery, designed as an extension of the *Stanford Achievement Test* series for grades 1–9. The English test consists of 85 items spread over three sections, mechanics, style, and paragraph organization; the spelling test has 60 items, each consisting of four unrelated words, one of which is misspelled.

There is much evidence of careful planning, imaginative writing, and thorough analysis in every phase of the development of these tests. The manual is clearly organized and comprehensive. It is readable, even by the unsophisticated teacher; its content is neatly outlined in such a way as to assist local administrators in test selection. The norming procedures are difficult to fault, and the norms themselves, presented in stanines and percentiles for each of grades 9–12, are easy to determine from the charts. The acceptable and unacceptable uses of the tests are spelled out in simple though very general terms. For the teacher, item statistics and charts denoting standard errors of differences for the whole battery are rendered more helpful by the use of illustrative examples of their use.

The directions for administering the test are clear and not too verbose; the illustrative examples appear suitable and adequate. On the basis of these factors, the high school test selector should be well pleased with this instrument.

1 The reviewer wishes to acknowledge with thanks the assistance of Dr. Warrick Elley in the preparation of this review.

Turning to the content of the tests themselves, however, he may wish to ponder some of the following points: The English test consists of 85 objective items designed to measure "as many of the important objectives of a modern comprehensive high school as possible." While it is recognized that essay writing cannot be sampled in an objective test, it is somewhat unfortunate that only 10 of the 85 items are devoted to writing style, an important objective. Items on paragraph arrangement have a superficial appeal in this respect, but the evidence concerning this type of item obtained in the ETS study on the measurement of writing ability [2] is scarcely promising enough to warrant 25 items. In this study, paragraph arrangement items proved the least valid of seven item types. One suspects that such questions simulate rather imperfectly the task faced by children in composing their own thoughts.

The heavy emphasis on mechanics (59 percent of the items) may reflect what is currently found in "appropriate courses of study and textbooks." Whether such emphases correspond to actual teaching time and whether these routine skills are predictive of success in writing ability, the "important objective," are debatable points, however. It is disappointing to see as many as 11 spelling items in the mechanics section, when it is realized that spelling is adequately tested elsewhere. And if the test is not to be used diagnostically, then the inclusion of 13 items on capitalization seems excessive. Some of this testing time could have been devoted to more basic writing skills, which are objectively assessable with reasonable validity through such items as the sentence completion, construction shift, and sentence combining. Then the "backwash" effects on instruction could well be healthier than that of a test which calls for superficial skills.

The test constructors have shown considerable ingenuity in placing their mechanics items within continuous, interesting paragraphs. The classification of errors according to type (capitalization, grammar, punctuation, spelling, and no error) is an interesting departure, presumably designed to pinpoint more precisely the student's ability to recognize the nature of the error involved. This approach runs into difficulty only when an item requires a change in

punctuation or capitalization, as in "So when the local newspaper announced her engagement, we were shocked, it was, to say the least, quite a surprise" and "He had been at all the famous battles, he had fought good." Many of these items are not really five-choice, since some of the underlined sections could not contain spelling or capitalization errors plausible enough to attract high school students. Since the reliability of the test is high, however, it is likely that this feature has been carefully watched in item selection. Nevertheless, the utility of some of these items should be studied carefully over the next few years.

The 10 items on style are well constructed and unambiguous, a feature not easy to ensure when the student's task is to choose amongst four expressions of the same ideas. One wonders only about the efficiency of such items in terms of time. Students must read 60 to 80 words, usually with some repetition, in order to score one point. It is likely that sentence completion and sentence correction items could achieve the same end in considerably less testing time.

The spelling test requires the student to identify 60 misspelt words from groups of four. Most of the 240 words included are definitely common errors or potential errors in students' writing. A few, however, seem implausibly misspelt (e.g., "costomers," "slepped") and such distractors as "favorable" and "oftener" are not wisely chosen. Some critics may question the use of isolated words as a valid test of spelling, but the authors do report that a correlation of .87 was found between this kind of spelling item and a dictated test at grade 8 level. One might have wished for further information on this point. The face validity of most of the words chosen and the reliability coefficients of .87 to .94 make for considerable confidence in the value of this test for those who like a comprehensive measure of spelling ability.

The authors went to considerable pains to describe the procedures adopted for establishing equivalence of forms, but they failed to report equivalent forms reliability, so that the high coefficients presented for single form administrations could well be misleading. The extent of speededness is not reported and with 85 items to complete in 40 minutes, time may well have been a problem. And since the internal reliability coefficients were calculated on the total

2 GODSHALK, FRED I.; SWINEFORD, FRANCES; AND COFFMAN, WILLIAM E. *The Measurement of Writing Ability*. New York: College Entrance Examination Board, 1966. Pp. viii, 84.

standardization sample, they would, then, be spuriously high. Some reassurance on these matters is surely to be expected.

It is unfortunate that no validity statistics are presented in this manual. True, the subtest intercorrelations are helpful, but the high correlations between English and Otis IQ's (around .80) raise some doubts which are not completely settled by an inspection for content validity. Some correlations with other measures of important objectives in English would have been an asset.

One further matter bothered this reviewer. The fact that the norms are midyear should have been reported either in the introduction or with the norms table. Teachers wishing to use the tests in the fall for placement and planning, or in the spring for end-of-year evaluation, will need to adjust the norms for their purposes, and guidance on this matter might have been helpful.

LEONARD S. FELDT, *Professor of Education, The University of Iowa, Iowa City, Iowa.*

In *The Sixth Mental Measurements Yearbook* the reviewer of a widely used English test offered this judgment: "The test undoubtedly serves some use in measuring a student's ability to criticize writing, but the only adequate test of effectiveness is to give the student a subject, a blank sheet of paper, and a pen, and ask him to write" (6:256). The very large number of English teachers who share this skepticism for multiple choice exercises are likely to find their views reinforced by the Stanford Achievement Test in English. Even those more favorably disposed may have several reservations about it.

To live within the restrictions of the multiple choice format, English test authors generally require the examinee to perform one or two editorial tasks: (*a*) indicate the errors they find in a composition, or (*b*) select the best of several suggested revisions which remedy possible defects in a composition. Neither of these, as the quoted reviewer so succinctly puts it, is equivalent to producing either the original version or its revision. But if a choice must be made between these approaches, most teachers would probably prefer the second—recognition of error coupled with awareness of a satisfactory revision. Part A of the Stanford test, which includes 50 of the 85 items, requires only the correct categorization of the error as one

of capitalization, grammar, punctuation, or spelling. Correction of the error—even by a recognition process—is not demanded.

The potential weakness of this approach may be illustrated by an item taken from a paragraph on the flags of the Confederacy. It begins as follows:

There <u>were three confederate flags.</u> The first of
41
these was called the <u>"Stars and bars."</u>
42

In exercise 41 there is obviously an error in capitalization, and it is so keyed. But the student is not asked about, or permitted to challenge, this uninspired opening sentence. Were various revisions presented for his consideration, he could be required both to diagnose the error in capitalization and to show sensitivity to this lackluster beginning. In exercise 42, the wayward student who feels the quotation marks should be omitted will incorrectly categorize the error as one of punctuation. But what of the student who feels no initial upper case letters are called for and hence classifies the error as one of capitalization? He would get the item correct—unfortunately.

It may be that the great majority of high school students who choose the proper error classification for any item do so for the right reasons. Perhaps appropriate categorization of an error can be taken as a trustworthy sign that the examinee could correct the error. However, the manual presents no evidence on these points.

It is worth noting with respect to this first portion of the language test that 9 or 10 items actually contain spelling errors. Moreover, the "error in spelling" option is available in every exercise, and hence it exerts additional influence as a distractor. Since the battery includes a 60-item spelling test bound in the same booklet as the English test, one wonders why spelling was given this additional emphasis.

Parts B and C of the test pose somewhat different tasks for the student. Each exercise of Part B presents four variations of a single sentence, and the examinee selects the best phrasing. Unlike items in Part A, these *do* require more than categorization of errors. There are only 10 such exercises, however.

In Part C, the student must indicate the optimal order of the five sentences of a paragraph. This is an attempt to measure sensitivity to logical sequence in the development of ideas. The item format is ingenious, but many students may respond on the basis of grammatical clues. For example, in a paragraph summarizing the stages of a man's career, one sentence begins: "The next period includes." Another starts: "Then, the years from about 60 or 65." The introductory phrases suggest immediately that these could not be the opening sentences of the paragraph. This reviewer found that he paid about as much attention to the construction of the sentences as to their content. In several of the paragraphs two or three different sequences could be justified if one considered only the ideas conveyed by the sentences. The presence of telltale words and phrases, rather than an inherent organizational logic, often seems to dictate which order conforms to the key.

The spelling exercises are of the "find-the misspelled-word" variety, with four words per item. All of the most prevalent types of error seem to be represented, but the authors appear to have given the social utility principle little weight on occasion. Such words as *pestiferous, mnemonic, impious, cuneiform,* and *archipelago* seem more appropriate for a spelling bee.

The manual for the Stanford battery is unusually complete and, in general, a model of good reporting practices. Though short on information relating the scores to data external to the tests, the manual does contain a wealth of information: the developmental steps leading to publication, raw and standard score means and standard deviations, the results of a factor analysis, correlations among subtests, individual item classifications, item difficulty values by grade. Normative data are reported for several different populations: total grade groups, college preparatory students of each grade, groups which have taken a continuous sequence of courses in such areas as mathematics or science, and groups at different levels of Otis intelligence. In view of the normative data provided, one regrettable omission is information on the reliability of the scores *within IQ levels.*

This reviewer would take issue with the authors' interpretations of the standard scores, which are based on the distributions of combined samples from grades 9 through 12. The usual claim is made that any standard score value, like 57, "has the same meaning for all forms and tests in the battery." Yet if one takes the authors' illustrative value and checks it through the various norms tables, the data tend to contradict this contention. In grade 9, for example, the percentile rank of standard score

57 varies between 82 and 92. In grade 12 it varies between 46 and 66. These inconsistencies, while not surprising, raise questions regarding the soundness of the suggested test-to-test comparisons of standard scores.

To sum up, this reviewer is very favorably impressed by the test manual but less so by the test itself. Because it is so complete, the manual could be used effectively to supplement the textbook in a course in educational measurement. But English teachers may find other instruments better designed to measure effectiveness of written expression.

For reviews of the complete battery, see 27 (2 reviews).

[209]

*Stanford Achievement Test: Spelling and Language Tests. Grades 4.0–5.4, 5.5–6.9, 7.0–9.9; 1940–68; catalog uses the title *Stanford Language Tests;* same as spelling and language subtests of *Stanford Achievement Test;* 2 scores: spelling, language; 2 forms; 3 levels; battery technical supplement ('66, 55 pages); expected grade score tables ('68, 10 pages) based on *Otis-Lennon Mental Ability Test* available on request; battery teachers guide ('65, 8 pages) for each level; supplementary directions ['64–66, 1–2 pages] for each type of answer sheet; $7.50 per 35 tests; 60¢ per key; separate answer sheets (Digitek, Harbor, IBM 805, IBM 1230) may be used; $2.30 per 35 IBM 805 answer sheets; $2.80 per 35 Digitek or IBM 1230 answer sheets; $6 per 100 sets of Harbor answer cards; $1.40 per set of Digitek or IBM scoring stencils; $2 per technical supplement; 50¢ per teachers guide; $1.75 per specimen set of any one level; postage extra; Harbor or IBM scoring service, 19¢ and over per spelling or language subtest; Braille and large type editions available from American Printing House for the Blind; Truman L. Kelley, Richard Madden, Eric F. Gardner, and Herbert C. Rudman; Harcourt Brace Jovanovich, Inc. *
*a) INTERMEDIATE 1. Grades 4.0–5.4; Forms W, X, ('64, 8 pages); manual ('64, 11 pages); 56(70) minutes in 2 sessions.
*b) INTERMEDIATE 2. Grades 5.5–6.9; Forms W, X, ('64, 9 pages); manual ('64, 12 pages); 63(75) minutes in 2 sessions.
*c) ADVANCED. Grades 7.0–9.9; Forms W, X, ('64, 9 pages); manual ('64, 12 pages); 61(75) minutes in 2 sessions.

WILLIAM E. COFFMAN, *E. F. Lindquist Professor of Educational Measurement, The University of Iowa, Iowa City, Iowa.*

The purposes of the authors of the *Stanford Achievement Test* are set forth in the manuals that accompany the three levels. The test battery was

developed to measure the important knowledges, skills, and understandings commonly accepted as desirable outcomes of the major branches of the elementary curriculum. The tests are intended to provide dependable measures of these outcomes, comparable from subject to subject and grade to grade, for use in connection with improvement of instruction, pupil guidance, and evaluation of progress. The tests have been planned with a view toward simplicity of administration, scoring, and interpretation, so that they may be used effectively by persons with little or no formal training in the use of standard tests.

With respect to validity, the manual states:

> The validity of *Stanford Achievement Test* is best thought of as the extent to which the content of the test constitutes a representative sample of the skills and knowledges which are the goals of instruction. This *content*, or *curricular*, validity must be assessed through a careful analysis of the actual content of each subtest in relation to the objectives of instruction in the various fields.

Since the authors rest their case for validity on the nature of the content, it seems appropriate to begin the evaluation of the tests by examining the content in some detail. Since they have aimed at simplicity of administration, scoring, and interpretation, it seems appropriate to ask how well they have achieved their purposes and at the same time to inquire concerning possible unintended effects.

Each level of the tests provides two scores, a score for spelling and a score for language. The language score is based on five separately timed sections containing questions in usage, punctuation, capitalization, dictionary skills, and sentence sense. No attempt is made to measure effectiveness of expression, in contrast to correctness of expression.

Although there are slight differences in format from level to level, the Intermediate 2 level illustrates the essential elements of the format and content. Each of the 56 items in this level of the spelling test consists of four words, one of which is spelled incorrectly.

The usage section of the language test consists of sentences, each with two alternate options for a word or phrase in the sentence. The examinee marks one of three responses: only option 1 makes the sentence correct, only option 2 makes the sentence correct, or neither option is correct. The punctuation and the capitalization sections consist of passages printed without either punctuation or capitalization. Certain words are underlined and numbered. In the punctuation section, two marks of punctuation are suggested to follow each numbered word, the student indicating which of the marks is correct or that neither is appropriate. Some of the words that should be followed by punctuation are not underlined. In the capitalization section, the examinee is to select one of two choices, C (capital letter) or s (small

letter), for each of the underlined words and mark the appropriate answer space. Some of the words that should be capitalized in a corrected passage are not underlined. The dictionary skills section consists of four-choice questions based on simulated dictionary entries. Some require that the examinee read a sentence and decide which of four definitions in a simulated dictionary entry corresponds to the use of the word in a sentence given in the item. Finally, the sentence sense subtest consists of word groupings to be placed in one of three categories: can be correctly punctuated as one sentence, could be punctuated as two sentences, or not a complete sentence. Altogether, eight different coding operations are involved in making responses when marking answers in the test booklet.

Only a single set of conversions from raw scores to grade scores is provided, but no evidence is cited to support the assumption that scores are equivalent regardless of whether answers are marked in the test booklet, on IBM 805, IBM 1230, Harbor, or Digitek answer sheets. The impression one gets in working through the test is that a considerable amount of clerical aptitude is involved. One might also wonder whether or not this form of testing is likely to encourage teachers to drill their pupils using exercises like those in the test in preference to giving them exercises providing practice in writing and editing connected discourse.

In general, sound test development procedures were followed in building the test package. The test items were written and coded according to a detailed content outline, test items were pretested on carefully chosen samples prior to the assembly of the final forms, national norms were established on the basis of sound sampling techniques, special norms by IQ level are reported, item difficulty values based on the norms sample are provided, and tables relating scores on these tests to scores on corresponding tests in earlier editions of both the *Stanford Achievement Test* and the *Metropolitan Achievement Test* are included in the technical supplement. There are, however, no regional norms for individuals and no norms for schools, even at the national level. The user is cautioned not to interpret subscores for individuals, but the normative data that are provided—the 25th, 50th, and 75th percentiles for individuals in the national sample—are hardly the proper norms for interpreting group performance.

Reliability coefficients and standard errors of measurement are reported for each test at half-grade intervals over the range of grades for which each form is intended. These data are sufficient for users trained in technical aspects of testing. However, "persons with little or no formal training in the use of standard tests" will need additional guidance if they are to avoid misinterpretation. Unfortunately, no further assistance is provided in the manual regarding interpretation of errors of measurement. Furthermore, grade scores clearly in the chance range are generated without any clear indication that they are suspect.

In summary, the spelling and language tests of the Stanford battery provide scores on certain aspects of correctness of expression in writing. The normative data, as far as they go, do permit comparisons of scores from subject to subject and grade to grade. It is doubtful, however, that teachers who lack training in technical aspects of measurement can develop sound interpretations without guidance beyond that provided in the manual. Finally, a detailed examination of the content of the test does not support the claim that it constitutes a representative sample of the skills and knowledges which are the goals of instruction in language and spelling. Rather, it constitutes a highly artificial and indirect approach to the measurement of certain of those knowledges and skills. Whenever such indirect measurement is proposed, it is necessary to show that the advantages of such an approach outweigh the disadvantages. Teachers who view the goal of language instruction as skill in communicating in correct and effective written discourse will have serious reservations about the appropriateness of the types of items included in these tests. They will seek other tests containing objective items that simulate more closely the activity of the pupil as he writes and edits his own manuscript.

Unfortunately, the greater the departure of the test item from the direct task it is attempting to simulate, the greater the temptation to drill pupils directly on items like those in the test—or even on the test items themselves. Good teachers have always resisted the temptation, knowing that the validity of indirect measurement depends on its remaining indirect. Recently, however, there has developed an interest in "accountability" and school systems in various parts of the country, according to newspaper accounts, have contracted with private corporations to bring the students' achievement scores up to or above national grade-level norms. It is to be devoutly hoped that the *Stanford Achievement Test: Spelling and Language Tests* will not become the criterion measures for any of these performance contracts. As models of what should be taught in the schools, they fall quite short.

As indirect measures of certain of the skills teachers attempt to develop in the elementary school years, and in the hands of teachers adequately trained in the interpretation of standardized tests, these particular tests may have value. The value will be greater if the tests are used as part of the Stanford battery so that scores in spelling and language may be related to scores in other areas, particularly reading and vocabulary. The value will be enhanced if the tests are being used in the context of a continuing testing program with local norms and longitudinal data. The value will be enhanced if scores on the test are related to measures of other aspects of language instruction, particularly "effectiveness of expression" in contrast to "correctness of expression." The value will be enhanced if teachers resist vigorously the temptation to teach for the test. For the school with a long history of use of these tests, their continued use may be justified. For schools looking for a separate test of spelling and language, competing tests should be examined carefully.

CARLETON B. SHAY, *Professor of Education and Associate Dean, School of Education, California State College, Los Angeles, California.*

The Spelling and Language Tests comprise two of the six to ten subtests (according to level) of the *Stanford Achievement Test* battery. Available in booklets separate from the battery at only the upper three levels, they share battery answer sheets, norms, teacher's guides for interpretation, and technical data. Color coding is used as a convenient means of distinguishing materials at each level. At successive levels, the 15-minute spelling test consists of 50, 56, and 58 items of the one-misspelled-of-four multiple choice variety. The language portion consists of five separately timed tests: usage, punctuation, capitalization, dictionary skills, and sentence sense, yielding a single overall score. With the exception of a portion of the dictionary skills items, the language test deals only with aspects of grammar.

The only information upon which to evaluate content validity consists of general descriptions of test content and, for language only, item content outlines. According to the authors, content validation "demands a systematic comparison of the test's contents with the curriculum used by the school." This is certainly true, and the authors are to be commended for insisting on this comparison and resisting any claim of satisfactory content validity. At the same time, more information could have been given to help in making this evaluation, such as clearer definitions of the content universe sampled and identification of textbook series, courses of study, word lists, and other material used. Correlations between the scores on the 1953 and 1964 editions (.79 to .87) are presented as additional evidence of validity. This is important information, but of dubious value in the context of validity, since an edition which is being replaced is considered an adequate criterion. Other validity-related data, of use primarily to the test specialist, are tables which show that "mean scores on the test increase for successively higher grades" and within-grades correlation coefficients between the Stanford and the *Otis Quick-Scoring Mental Ability Test,* which range from .55 to .65 for spelling and .70 to .75 for language.

Split-half reliability coefficients and K-R 20 reliability coefficients are given for each grade for each test. These coefficients are high, as might be expected: .91 to .94. The technical supplement discusses the effect of speededness on reliability (it spuriously inflates reliability coefficients), and concludes that for the Stanford, "speededness is a negligible factor." This conclusion is based on a study of the influence of speed on scores, which used the 1953 edition and was assumed valid for the 1964 edition. As a result of this study, ratios of items to time were reduced for five battery subtests; unfortunately, these subtests are not identified. Since the serial position of items is only roughly in order of increasing difficulty, and there are marked exceptions, particularly on the subtests of capitalization and dictionary skills, it is hoped that the language test was among those whose ratios of items to time were reduced. Comprehensive tables of other reliability data are given, including standard errors of measurement and language part-score reliability coefficients. No

equivalent-forms reliability coefficients are given, however—a serious omission which invalidates the contention that alternate forms of the test are interchangeable. In lieu of these vital data, only a general description of the equating program is given. There are no test-retest reliability data either, although we are assured that "as this type of reliability data becomes available, it will be duly reported."

The standardization group is not a representative sample of the country as a whole, and, technically, it is not claimed to be. Nevertheless, a technicality does not absolve the publisher from the responsibility of providing such a norm group, since users will treat the norms as representative whether they are or not. The consequences of decisions based on nonrepresentative norms can be extreme. Test users should also heed this advice: applicability of norms demands a systematic comparison of the standardization sample with the pupils tested by the school. If the groups are not alike, the results are not interpretable with respect to the norms. Corrections may be applied but should be avoided, as they imply a false accuracy easily overinterpreted. Selection of another test with suitable norms, or the establishment of local norms are desirable alternatives.

The standardization group warrants closer scrutiny. Otis IQ medians for grades 4 through 9 are 109, 109, 109, 108, 108, and 106. Not only are these IQ's high, but they decrease with grade level, contrary to the increase found in most studies. No children less than nine years of age at grade 4, ten years at grade 5, eleven years at grade 6, etc., were included in the standardization sample. At the same time, students up to two years and eleven months more than this minimum were included. It would appear, at first glance, that the standardization sample is simply overage and over-intelligent, but the bias is even more serious when it is realized that the IQ level is high despite the exclusion of the youngest, and generally brightest, students from the standardization group. We are informed that integrated, segregated, and private sectarian and nonsectarian schools were included and that median family income and number of years of schooling were in "essential agreement" with census figures. This is reassuring, but no data are given; the only other demographic data are a distribution of school systems by region and a list of standardization communities, which shows an underrepresentation of data from large city school systems. It is clear from the data, for example, that the Stanford is not appropriate for a large urban school system with a significant minority population. To reiterate: the norm group is *not* representative.

Norms include grade scores (grade equivalents without decimal points), percentile ranks, and stanines. Tables provided allow correction of grade scores as a function of Otis IQ stanines, or alternately, a comparison with grade scores corresponding to quartile points for Otis stanines. Directions for interpretation of scores with each type of norm are clear and fairly complete, though hazards of overinterpretation could be emphasized more in the technical supplement. The tests should be easy to give and score with all types of answer sheets; directions are clear and concise.

The teachers' guides are, in some respects, useful and innovative and, in other respects, disappointing. A review of test content is followed by a section on interpretation which includes samples of individual cases and an explanation of the use of class analysis chart. The basic thesis of "Diagnose, Evaluate, Plan" is well conceived, clearly explained, and, when used with the battery, realistically useful to teachers. Data are limited to stanines and are presented so as to provide a conscientious but unsophisticated teacher the minimum opportunity to overinterpret. Suggestions for interpretation are of less use to spelling and language test users than for users of the whole battery, since relative strengths and weaknesses are an important component of the diagnostic scheme. The suggestions given for remedial instruction are disappointing. Remediation must be based on careful diagnosis, and the tests are not intended to perform this function. Some suggestions imply that the teacher should construct his own diagnostic instruments based on skills presumably tested but not specifically related to test content, rather than using available tests designed for that purpose. Others describe general observations or methods which should already be in the teacher's repertoire.

In short, the content of the *Stanford Achievement Tests: Spelling and Language Tests* has been carefully prepared, and the tests should be easy to use. Technical information reported is accurate. The efforts thus far named are impressive, but the standardization group is not representative, some vital technical informa-

tion is not reported, and the attempts to educate those who would benefit most by such information are insufficient for the 1970's. In these days of guaranteed performance contracts, or the equivalent politically, tests must be better, users more enlightened, and data more complete. Specifically, the user must assure himself that the test content matches his curriculum and the norm group matches his pupils. The test should be renormed on a nationally representative sample if any inferences are to be made with regard to "national norms." The publisher should provide more technical and interpretive information, especially that dealing with the standardization group, retesting and alternate forms. And, finally, the number of items per grade level should be increased if grade norms continue to be used. If the test user is unwilling to apply the above comparisons and the publisher unable to supply the necessary data, use of the Stanford language and spelling tests is ill-advised.

For reviews of the complete battery, see 25 (1 excerpt), 6:26 (1 review, 1 excerpt), 5:25 (1 review), 4:25 (2 reviews), and 3:18 (2 reviews).

[210]

★**Tests of Academic Progress: Composition.** Grades 9–12; 1964–66; Form 1 ('64, 15 pages); 4 levels (grades 9, 10, 11, 12) in a single booklet; no specific manual; battery teacher's manual ('64, 62 pages); battery manual for administrators, supervisors, and counselors ('65, 45 pages); battery norms booklet for IQ levels ('66, 26 pages); separate answer cards (MRC) must be used; 30¢ per test; $3 per 100 MRC answer cards; $1.20 per battery teacher's manual; 96¢ per battery administrator's manual; 60¢ per battery norms booklet; $3 per specimen set of the complete battery; postage extra; scoring service, 27¢ per test; 60(70) minutes; Dale P. Scannell and Oscar M. Haugh; Houghton Mifflin Co. *

REFERENCE

1. GOOLSBY, THOMAS M., JR. "The Appropriateness of the Tests of Academic Progress for an Experimental School." *Ed & Psychol Meas* 30(4):967–70 w '70. *

ELLIS BATTEN PAGE, *Professor of Educational Psychology, University of Connecticut, Storrs, Connecticut.*

CONTENT. For each grade, the test content consists of some sample printed documents (letters or parts of essays such as a high school student might write) which contain unmarked errors. The lines of each document are numbered for reference; each document is followed by 10 to 13 questions. Each question contains some stem, such as "Which is the best way to write line 1?" or "How should lines 1, 2, and 3 be punctuated?" or "Which is the correct way to write the first three words in line 14?" or even "Which, if any, is the correct way to divide the last word that is hyphenated on line 16?" Then each stem is followed by four provided alternatives, only one of which is "correct."

Often these questions center on particular problems, such as how a verb should be formed or how a quotation should be punctuated. At other times, the question asks what kind of change, if any, might be necessary in a line. Some items are quite independent of the passage, such as identifying first-order spelling errors (misspellings in any context, like *thier*). Other items require study of the entire sample document: picking a paragraph's topic sentence from among all the sentences, or deciding how the document should be paragraphed.

This reviewer (a former teacher of English) took the test to study face validity and was not very satisfied. In some cases, the prose was so poorly constructed that the specific questions seemed a playing at the fringe. And since some fundamental errors are uncorrected, taking the test will not be wholly constructive as a learning experience. Also, at times there is an extrinsic logical tip-off (as in the common "all-of-the-above" construction). And some solutions themselves seem, at best, highly debatable (for example, sympathised, a commonplace British spelling, is keyed as flatly "wrong").

FORMAT. But the most serious criticism of the test's face validity concerns its format. The usual multiple choice item, in the usual test, calls upon the student to keep track of *two* sequences: the questions in the booklet, and the responses on the answer sheet. This composition test calls upon the student to keep track of at least *three* sequences, since it is necessary to consult the passage itself, as well as the question and the answer card. And for some items (for example, where one is asked to choose the "transitional word" from among four possible alternatives), the student has to keep track of six different locations! And all of these are indexed by different numbers, not letters. There may be four competing locations in four different line numbers (or even combinations of lines), and then there may be the inhibition created by the question number (in both booklet and card) and alternative choices (in both booklet and card). The student's final choice, then, may be doggedly encoded as "lines 22–23, which are alternative 3, for question 17." The

necessary intensive, clerical concentration must indicate something, but its relevance to composition is surely unproved. It is urged that test builders stay away from this format. To lessen confusion, alternatives and questions should all be incorporated with the test passage.

INSTRUCTION ABOUT GUESSING. One of the standing dilemmas in honest test administration is what to say about guessing (see Page, 6:14). The student instructions for the TAP battery include the admonition: "If you have *no* idea *whatsoever* about the answer, omit the exercise on the answer sheet." In other words, the student should leave it blank. Yet no penalty is levied for wrong answers, and the student who follows this instruction will lower his score compared with the next student who, wisely or cynically, disregards it. Furthermore, in applying the suggested rule, a student will often be too self-critical. He may not "think" he knows the answer, but he *might* be able to eliminate one or two competing alternatives, in which case his chance of raising his score would be even better than chance.

A study of the norms reveals just how much guessing can accomplish. Let us assume a student "knows" enough answers to reach the 48th percentile on the 9th grade norms and then "blindly" guesses the rest. He will, by disregarding the instruction and by guessing only with average luck, raise his performance to the 90th percentile—a gain of 42 percentile points! If the 11th grade student at the 46th percentile does the same, he will jump to the 88th. And if a student at the 75th percentile does it, he will jump to the 98th percentile—from above average, to very superior. By their instruction, then, the test publishers seem to be penalizing students for obedience. Instructions not to guess should be abolished, and all students should be encouraged to try all items, even where a "correction" is applied.

INFORMATION ABOUT THE TEST. The battery is accompanied by a fairly flossy package of manuals and auxiliary services. In the Manual for Administrators, Supervisors, and Counselors, a chapter on interpretation leaves much to be desired. The "standard score" (SS) is discussed as if it were a great improvement over the raw score in "meaning." But for most grades, since there is no easy significance of the SS *except in terms of the 11th grade norms*, the improvement is not clear. The grade-adjusted percentile rank (PR) is of course more meaningful, but to obtain it we must make a double transformation, first to the SS, *then* to the PR. Where such conversion is done by hand, new tables would have to be derived for efficiency, since they are not supplied by the publisher. When one *does* compare the raw score with the PR, one realizes just how fragile, or unstable, many PR differences will inevitably be.

This instability is not recognized clearly in the manual. Where profiles are discussed, only standard scores are compared, and not always wisely. A sample profile treats a student tested in his 10th and 11th grades. (As we have seen, if the same form were used, this would result in exactly the *same* items over about two-thirds of the test.) In discussing the profile, the manual states that, where gains of three or four SS points have been made (about the same number of raw score points), these are regarded as "normal" growth. Where one subtest has only *one* point change, this is regarded as "growth.... less than one would expect." And where six points of change occur, this is regarded as "progress....greater than average." The manual suggests that "Reasons for such growth should be sought." Given the stated levels of reliability, especially interform agreement, all such conjectures would be based upon trivial observed differences. Pursuing "the reasons" for such differences is probably a waste of time and should not be encouraged.

RELIABILITY. Such skepticism is supported by evidence from the same manual, where the standard errors of measurement for the Composition Test are shown to range *about 3.6 raw score points*. And these standard errors, as is customary for commercial tests, are based upon split-half reliabilities (averaging about .90), rather than the always lower coefficients which would be derived from test-retest experiments over time, or from inter-form agreement.

VALIDITY. A still more damaging consideration, however, concerns statistical validity. The user who searches for persuasive evidence of such validity will simply search in vain. In the manual, printed in 1965, it is stated that "At the time of this printing, the authors have not had an opportunity to collect comprehensive evidence of concurrent or predictive validity." This is puzzling, since some of the norm schools could easily have reported student grades. In any case, when the present reviewer contacted the test company five years later, he was not reassured. There are some unpublished tables

from a small local study in Billings, Montana. These show correlations for 380 students between the various subtests and *overall* grade-point average (*r*'s in the high .60's). There were other unpublished results from Billings for correlations of the subtests with Otis IQ (also in the high .60's). There was nothing more.

In other words, even after five years, there was *no statistical evidence for specific validity of any subtest*. Particularly for composition, this negligence seems inexcusable, since natural compositions are easy to obtain and can be reliably appraised by judge panels.

SUMMARY. The *Test of Academic Progress: Composition* seems questionable in some of its contents and unnecessarily confusing in student procedure. It lacks any evidence of statistical validity, even after five years of sale. There are some good aspects to the test but, on balance, these negative criticisms seem central and severe. They suggest that school testers search elsewhere before selecting this test.

OSMOND E. PALMER, *Professor, Office of Evaluation Services, Michigan State University, East Lansing, Michigan.*

This test, unlike most, consists of 142 items only some of which are answered at each grade level. Ninth graders start with item 1 and work through 70; tenth do items 23–92; eleventh, 47–117; and twelfth, 71–142. Thus there is a 40-odd item overlap between successive grades. Only the ninth and twelfth graders take totally different tests. The justification for this is that it permits testing more specifically for those things covered in a given year and that it provides a more accurate measure of progress.

In the case of English, there is probably less need to make a distinction among grades than elsewhere, because in English classes the same things are reviewed from year to year and it is not likely that the same things are covered in a given year in different school systems. For instance, this test measures the use of footnoting only at the twelfth-grade level; but footnoting is probably not taught in some schools at all—the National Council of Teachers of English recommends against it—and in some schools it is taught as early as the ninth grade.

It might be enlightening to know exactly how much improvement tenth graders show on the items taken by ninth graders, and so forth, but the data presented in the manuals do not tell us this. In the norms sample, eleventh graders scored somewhat better than ninth graders. But since the tables report in terms of standard scores, one does not know exactly what this means in terms of improvement in number of items right. One can tease something out from the last table given in the teacher's manual, which shows the raw score necessary to achieve a certain standard score. The ninth grade test is somewhat easier for ninth graders than the twelfth grade test is for twelfth graders. The tenth and eleventh grade results fall between these two. If it is true that the tests become increasingly difficult, then the mean raw scores might drop slightly. Is this the reason why raw scores were suppressed in the manuals? For the teacher, it is probably best to look at the tests themselves, to see what they cover and how well they cover it.

The test attempts to involve all aspects of the writing situation: mechanics, including spelling; sentence structure; word choice; and organization. The attempt to be so comprehensive involves rigorous decisions on inclusion and exclusion, but the test does not seem to show this, as my comments on several aspects of it will illustrate.

Only about a dozen items deal with verbs, verbals, or tense sequence. Two of these (7 and 39) deal with *should of* and *must of,* which have more to do with the transcription of the spoken language and careful proofreading than with showing (as the manual states) that the student is "having difficulty with his verbs." Three (52, 55, 56) have to do with the agreement of subject and verb, none at the twelfth grade level; and three (43, 67, 94) with tense sequence, one at the twelfth grade level. Beyond these, item 68 involves a dangling participle and item 133 a split infinitive, the latter having two acceptable answers in addition to the split itself, which is not a bad one. Only one item tests for the problem involved in verbs frequently confused (lie-lay) and one (item 39) suggests that *forgotten* may be the only past participle of *forget.* One obviously cannot do much curriculum revision or reteaching from this smattering of information about how the student handles verbs and tense sequences.

One can also quarrel with the items testing capitalization. There is no item which invites the student to capitalize a point of the compass or a season of the year; there is none on proper adjectives or geographical places; in titles, only the capitalization of short adjectives is involved.

And about half of these items are dubious. The girl who capitalizes Recipe Book (61) (probably a substitute title for her mother's) and Burnt Sugar Cake (63) should have the option of doing so. A student who looked up C(?)opperhead (a Southern sympathizer in the 1860's) in the current series of Merriam-Webster dictionaries would pick 2 (rather than 3) as the right answer for item 111.

In the light of the failure to measure certain things adequately, one is annoyed to find some things that *are* tested for. Item 64 insists that Sam must use an apostrophe in his store title, Sam's Superette, but Consumers Power (of Michigan) does not. One of the few items on agreement between subject and verb, item 52, involves the combination of *neither-nor* with a change of number—sufficiently rare to be passed over. With only six to nine spelling items in each grade level of the test, one wishes the authors had skipped words like "sympathise" and "karmelize." The applicant for a job as errand boy must write "advertisement" rather than "ad," according to item 72.

Several of the questions on matters of style are, it seems to me, matters of personal taste. The letter of application seemingly suffers from overuse of the word I, but since one of the revisions (78) eliminates two uses, I find no good answer for item 79. Similarly, item 104 calls for making a fourth paragraph in an essay of about 160 words; I look for a response which would reduce the paragraphing. The review of the movie *David Copperfield* uses (several times) "pals," which various dictionaries list as slang or colloquial. Item 50 asks how the student would write a particular expression in this essay in formal English; but to introduce the sentence keyed as right is to do violence to the tone of the essay. Response 2 would not be bad and response 1 is not taboo on the basis of the current Merriam-Webster dictionaries.

Item 121 in the second scrambled paragraph exercise demands a special comment. One has to decide which sentence should follow Sentence B and he is supposed to pick Sentence D. The sentences are these: "B. His books, *Alice In Wonderland* and *Through The Looking Glass,* are known the world over; and have been translated into many languages. D. These books also contained many humerous [*sic*] poems such as *Jabberwocky,* a poem containing words that had never been used before." To me, the *also* of Sentence D suggests that the previous sentence had been detailing the major content and that this sentence is going on to talk about content. But obviously Sentence B is not about content: it simply mentions the titles of Carroll's two children's books and talks about their popularity. Since the topic of this essay is to show that Lewis Carroll is famous for his children's books and not for his teaching or his books on logic and mathematics, one suspects that this sentence was intended to be irrelevant and marked for omission, like one in the previous exercise. But *humerous* (a spelling item) crept into it and since it contained the only occasion to test for the use of quotation marks for the title of a poem, somebody forgot the original intention. (One also wonders why the second capital T was left in *Through The,* since it is not tested for, and whether at one stage it was planned to have a question on the tense of *contained.*)

A lot of thought seems to have gone into the conception of this test, but the child which was produced was not nourished properly.

For a review of the complete battery, see 31.

[211]

★**Tests of Basic Experiences: Language.** Prekgn-kgn, kgn-grade 1; 1970–71; 1 form; Levels K ('70, 34 pages), L ('70, 18 pages); for battery manual and accessories, see 33; $9 per 30 tests, postage extra; scoring service, $1.20 per test; (25) minutes; Margaret H. Moss; CTB/McGraw-Hill. *

REFERENCE

1. Moss, MARGARET H. *Performance of Disadvantaged and Middle-Class Preschool Children on a Language Coding Test of Space and Location.* Doctor's thesis, George Washington University (Washington, D.C.), 1968.

For a review of the complete battery, see 33.

[212]

*****Walton-Sanders English Test.** 1, 2 semesters in grades 9–13; 1962–64; first published 1962–63 in the Every Pupil Scholarship Test series; Forms A, B, ('64, 8 pages); 2 levels labeled Tests 1, 2; manual ('64, 6 pages); no norms for college freshmen; $1.75 per 25 tests, postage extra; 75¢ per specimen set, postpaid; 50(55) minutes; Charles E. Walton and M. W. Sanders; Data Processing and Educational Measurement Center. *

[213]

★**Watson English Usage and Appreciation Test, Fourth Edition.** Grades 4–8; 1966; 1 form (8 pages); manual (8 pages); no data on reliability; Can $2.75 per 25 tests; 25¢ per manual; 40¢ per specimen set; postage extra; 30(40) minutes; G. Milton Watson; Book Society of Canada Ltd. *

VINCENT R. D'OYLEY, *Professor of Education, The Ontario Institute for Studies in Edu-*cation, *The University of Toronto, Toronto, Ontario, Canada.*[1]

This test sets out to measure a variety of English skills in order to assist teachers in grade placement and diagnosis. It is designed for pupils in grades 4 to 8, but it reports grade equivalent scores ranging from grades 1.1 to 12.0 and age equivalents from 6–11 to 17–1.

Apart from the laudable aims of the test constructor, it is difficult to make positive statements about the test. Clearly, it has been produced by a well-meaning educator but with little concern for the APA Standards. The manual contains no information on reliability coefficients or standard errors of measurement. There is only a hint of validity-consciousness in the statement that "there is a significantly positive correlation between scores on this test and the ability to write and speak correct, lucid English." No technical supplement has been planned, although at least four to five thousand students write the test annually in one Ontario city alone.

The norming sample is described most inadequately: "about 1,300 pupils from grades 4 to 8" representing "a wide cross-section of social background, and [ranging] in I.Q. from 70 to 140." The only graph presented refers to results from two schools only. The misconceptions evident in the section relating to interpretation of scores must be seen as unfortunate. The determination of achievement level as a function of the test is played down at the seventh and eighth grade levels because the scores in the standardization sample departed slightly from normality, the apparent ideal of the test constructor. The extraordinary generalization is made that pupils scoring 12 percent below their grade median should be retested or retaught. A cursory inspection of the chart from which this conclusion was drawn is sufficient to show that the raw scores which are 12 percent below the median lie between the 25th and 75th percentiles in grades 4–7 and below the 25th percentile in grade 8. The blindness to such other interpretative factors as the background of children and suitability of the test in relation to curricular objectives makes this generalization a dangerous one. For the percentage-oriented teacher, formulae are presented to convert raw score (out of 200) to a percentage appropriate

[1] The reviewer wishes to acknowledge with thanks the assistance of Dr. Warrick Elley in the preparation of this review.

for each grade level. The application of this formula results in more than one quarter of the grades 6–7 standardization sample receiving percentages above 100.

No information is given about the calculations or extrapolations required for the grade and age equivalents presented, in very awkward format, in the manual. We are told only that the extreme norms "have been established by exterpolation [*sic*] and comparison with standardized *reading* tests giving grade levels." The meaningfulness of a grade equivalent of 1.1 on a test designed primarily for children around grade 6 is puzzling. But how such refinement of scale could be attained from a sample of 1,300, providing equivalent norms for 12 grade levels, is positively perplexing. It is unlikely that 10 students scored below grade 2 level, yet grade equivalents are given for every month from 1.1 upwards. We sincerely hope that teachers do not use these test results for grade placement, as the manual recommends.

The test itself leaves much to be desired. There is no explanation of how the skills to be tested and the weightings for each topic were arrived at, but the lack of correspondence between subtest title and item content suggests that such a blueprint would not have contributed helpfully to content validity. For instance, the Organization subtest contains items requiring the selection of descriptive adjectives and verbs, the Word Meanings subtest calls for homonyms, and the Appreciation subtest for general knowledge about trees.

The instructions intended for pupils are inadequate in content and confused in style. They give no directions about guessing or changing answers, no practice exercises, and no statements about how to mark correct answers in multiple choice questions. The diversity of question types must present a bewildering task for the pupil: the first eight questions require him to answer in no less than six different ways.

Matching questions typically contain the same number of items in each list, and many of these lists are so heterogeneous that pupils can score highly with only limited knowledge. Many completion items are sufficiently ambiguous to cast doubt on the claimed objective nature of the items—e.g., "I tiptoed into the room as _____ as possible."

The Word Usage subtest contains some original items on the expression of mood, spoilt only by the ambiguity involved in deciding which subject or person is supposed to experience the mood—the author, or one or more of the persons or animals referred to in the sentences.

The heavy emphasis on grammar and its technical terms make this test unsuitable for teachers who stress a more functional approach to language; the educational value of many other items is difficult to defend. Of what predictive or diagnostic utility, to grade 6 pupils, is knowledge of the word "lye," or information about when "a knell [is] rung"?

The test has been carelessly proofread. For instance, two items on page 7 have omitted the underlinings mentioned in the instructions; *then* is used incorrectly as a conjunction in the instructions at the top of page 8. The manual refers to nonexistent charts "on pages 5 and 6," and later it reports that "the intervals....*does* not vary." Many possible alternative answers could have been included in the answer key, but it should be pointed out that any further additions to this cumbersome key would make it virtually unusable. Teachers will be unenthusiastic about this aspect of the test.

In short, there is little to recommend in the *Watson English Usage and Appreciation Test.* Even the title is unfortunate. One noun used adjectivally is permissible; three are too many. Mention of usage and appreciation seems arbitrary in this hotchpotch of topics ranging over paragraph organization, reading comprehension, vocabulary knowledge, idiomatic expressions, sentence classification, plurals and possessives, parts of speech, and sentence structure. Of the 165 items, only 10 measure appropriate English usage, and 10 measure appreciation. The title of the test is as likely to mislead the teacher as much as the results it produces.

[214]

★**Writing Test: McGraw-Hill Basic Skills System.** Grades 11–14; 1970; also called *MHBSS Writing Test;* although designed for use with the MHBSS instructional program, the test may be used independently; 4 scores: language mechanics, sentence patterns, paragraph patterns, total; Forms A, B, (14 pages); manual (34 pages); separate answer sheets (Digitek, IBM 1230, Scoreze) must be used; $6 per 25 tests; $2.50 per 50 IBM or Digitek answer sheets; $3 per 25 Scoreze answer sheets; $1 per IBM or Digitek scoring stencil; postage extra; $1.25 per specimen set, postpaid; IBM scoring service, 25¢ and over per test ($20 minimum) ; 45(55) minutes; Alton L. Raygor; McGraw-Hill Book Co., Inc. *

LEONARD S. FELDT, *Professor of Education, The University of Iowa, Iowa City, Iowa.*

In reviewing standardized achievement tests, one occasionally encounters a curious phenomenon. An instrument may strike the reviewer as quite unattractive in terms of item quality, content, or skill coverage, but the test may be accompanied by an excellent manual. Normative data may have been conscientiously gathered, the technical information competently analyzed, and the facts fully reported. The effort appears to be wasted, however, on essentially a poor test. In other instances one encounters the opposite situation. The test itself may offer many interesting exercises and represent a commendable effort at measuring important skills, but it may be poorly documented in a technical sense. The norms may be so biased as to be useless, the validity data very limited, and the facts on reliability suspect. This latter description seems to fit the MHBSS *Writing Test.*

This instrument was developed primarily for use in conjunction with the instructional materials that comprise the McGraw-Hill Basic Skills System: Writing. The test is sold separately, however, and teachers may wish to consider it solely on its own merits. Whether or not the instructional materials from which the test stems can be successfully used to improve the user's language skills (and to raise the test scores) cannot be considered here. Composition teachers should evaluate these materials quite apart from the test. But it is worth noting that the test was developed to accompany the instructional materials and hence is closely coordinated with them.

Some of the introductory statements in the manuals make a fairly strong pitch for the diagnostic potential of the test. Its two forms constitute the initial and final phases of an instructional system involving diagnosis, prescription, instruction, and evaluation. Later statements back off a bit from any promise of highly detailed, individual diagnosis, claiming that the *Writing Test* is designed "to be diagnostic only in a general way." Determination of student weaknesses is officially sanctioned only through consideration of the three part scores, but there are hints that more detailed analysis of item responses may pay dividends.

The distribution of exercises and the three part scores suggest the skills of concern to the authors. The first score is derived from 30 items concerned with mechanics: capitalization, punctuation, and grammar (tense, pronoun forms, subject-verb agreement, and so forth).

The second score is based on 26 items which require classification of sentence types (complex, compound, etc.), choice of pronouns (who, which, etc.), detection of nonparallel constructions, and feel for appropriate transitional words and phrases to introduce or connect sentences. The final part presents 15 exercises bearing on the construction of paragraphs: identification of appropriate topic sentences, development sentences, and concluding sentences; awareness of the proper sequence of sentences; and judgment of the most appropriate division of sentences into paragraphs. Those familiar with objective tests in this area will probably recognize the unique emphasis given to paragraph construction. In summary, about 40 items deal with matters of right and wrong, 20 items concern issues of effectiveness or appropriateness, and 10 items involve classification of sentence types, including sentence fragments.

A few supplementary observations about the types of exercises used in the test may head off possible disappointment. First, the mechanics items of Part 1 do not yield separate scores for punctuation, capitalization, and usage. Also, they require that the examinee merely classify an error, not select a correct version of the offending words or phrases. Error detection, but not correction, is also characteristic of the pronoun and parallelism exercises of Part 2. Second, very few of the exercises require the student to choose the most effective, appropriate, precise, or colorful word or phrase to express an idea, rather than to detect an outright error. Part 3 deals largely with the appropriateness of the content of entire sentences, not with the phrasing of ideas in small segments of a composition. Finally, in attempting to assess the several aspects of writing in 45 minutes, the authors were forced to limit the number of exercises that deal with each. Despite these limitations, many teachers may find the test more attractive than competing instruments, particularly because of its concern for paragraph construction.

Turning now to the technical characteristics of the test, we find a number of serious limitations. Apparently the publishers could not fully convince themselves of the need to invest the effort in norming and validation that are now accepted as part of test publication. Three sets of norms are provided, corresponding to the three populations for which the instruction system is intended: (*a*) college-bound students in grades 11 and 12, (b) two-year college students, and (c) freshmen in four-year colleges. The samples used to develop the norms were chosen by very casual procedures—so casual, in fact, that the manual frankly warns the user that no sample can be considered to represent the population implied by the norm-group designation. The extent of the differential biases in these samples may be suggested by the fact that the high school groups have a median of 48.5 and the four-year college freshmen a median of 43.5 on Form B. The user would be well advised to heed the publisher's advice about developing local norms.

Reliability and item data are based on all three samples combined, a procedure not considered appropriate even with the best of samples. Even within this artificially heterogeneous group, reliability of the part scores is relatively modest for individual diagnosis—below .70 for about half of the parts on the two forms. Though the test was developed for use before and after a specific course, no studies are available as to the impact of the course on the test scores. The publishers recommend this instrument for sectioning classes in English composition, a function it may be well designed to serve. But surprisingly, they disclaim responsibility for demonstrating its value for this purpose. Another fault is the absence of correlations among the part scores, data that are easily obtained and quite important for diagnostic tests. The manual is very frank in recognizing these shortcomings, but this sincerity—while refreshing—does not offset the handicaps that they impose on the user.

With reactions as mixed as these, one is hard pressed to arrive at a balanced summary statement. The test deserves consideration by those who agree with the authors' skill emphasis. But users should be prepared to develop their own norms and to invest more than the usual effort in the study of local reliability and validity.

LITERATURE

[215]

★CLEP Subject Examination in Analysis and Interpretation of Literature. 1 year or equivalent; 1964–70; for college accreditation of nontraditional study, advanced placement, or assessment of educational achievement; tests administered monthly at regional centers throughout the United States; tests also available for institutional testing at any time; Form MCT ('64, 16 pages); optional essay supplement: Form MCT-A ('64, 2 pages); for program accessories, see 664; rental and scoring fee, $5 per student; postpaid; essay supplement scored by the college; 90(95) minutes, same for essay supplement; program administered for the College Entrance Examination Board by Educational Testing Service. *

For reviews of the testing program, see 664 (3 reviews).

[216]

★CLEP Subject Examination in English Literature. 1 year or equivalent; 1970; for college accreditation of nontraditional study, advanced placement, or assessment of educational achievement; tests administered monthly at regional centers throughout the United States; tests also available for institutional testing at any time; Forms SCT1, SCT2, (17 pages); optional essay supplement: Form SCT1A (3 pages); for program accessories, see 664; rental and scoring fee, $5 per student; postpaid; essay supplement scored by the college; 90(95) minutes, same for essay supplement; program administered for the College Entrance Examination Board by Educational Testing Service. *

For reviews of the testing program, see 664 (3 reviews).

[217]

★College Board Achievement Test in Literature. Candidates for college entrance; 1968–71; test administered each January and May at centers established by the publisher; for more complete information, see 663; 60(80) minutes; program administered for the College Entrance Examination Board by Educational Testing Service. *

REFERENCES

1. PURVES, ALAN C. "Designing the Board's New Literature Achievement Test." *Col Board R* 67:16–20 sp '68. *
2. ELLEDGE, SCOTT. "For the Board's English Tests: As an Old Era Ends, What Lies Ahead?" *Col Board R* 71:22–7 sp '69. *

[218]

★College Placement Test in Literature. Entering college freshmen; 1968–70; CPTL; irregularly scheduled reprintings of inactive forms of *College Board Achievement Test in Literature;* Form SPL ['70, reprint of 1968 test, 12 pages]; for more complete information, see 665; 60(70) minutes; program administered for the College Entrance Examination Board by Educational Testing Service. *

For a review of the testing program, see 665.

[219]

*The Graduate Record Examinations Advanced Literature in English Test. Graduate school candidates; 1939–70; 4 current forms ('67–70, 32–40 pages); descriptive booklet ('70, 10 pages); for more complete information, see 667; 180(200) minutes; Educational Testing Service. *

REFERENCE

1. LANNHOLM, GERALD V.; MARCO, GARY L.; AND SCHRADER, WILLIAM B. *Cooperative Studies of Predicting Graduate School Success,* pp. 34–45. Graduate Record Examinations Special Report No. 68-3. Princeton, N.J.: Educational Testing Service, August 1968. Pp. 92. *

For a review by Robert C. Pooley of an earlier form, see 5:215. For reviews of the testing program, see 667 (1 review) and 5:601 (1 review).

[220]

*Hollingsworth-Sanders Junior High School Literature Test. 1, 2 semesters in grades 7–8; 1962–64; first published 1962–63 in the Every Pupil Scholarship Test series; Forms A, B, ('64, 4 pages); 2 levels labeled Tests 1, 2; manual ('64, 2 pages); $1.75 per 25 tests, postage extra; 75¢ per specimen set, postpaid; 40(50) minutes; Leon Hollingsworth and M. W. Sanders; Data Processing and Educational Measurement Center. *

PAUL B. DIEDERICH, *Senior Research Associate, Educational Testing Service, Princeton, New Jersey.*

These literature tests must have been based on a particular anthology, not named in the manual or catalogue, since they consist mainly of factual items on a large number of selections that can hardly be common to all anthologies used in grades 7–8. Test 1, Form A, for example, has 90 factual items based on 52 selections, 31 represented by one item apiece, 15 by two items, 4 by three items, and one each by four and five items, together with eight items unconnected with particular selections.

Most of the factual items would be easy if a student had read the selection and remembered anything at all about it. They are fairly represented by such stems as "Selection A is about" (in which the responses are the names of five sports) and "Selection B is a" (poem, short story, play, etc.). More difficult items ask which of five authors wrote the selection or which of five names was the name of a principal character. A small number of items test recall of details that hardly seem worth remembering. For example, one of the few selections that may be remembered by teachers who have not used this anthology is the story of "The Cat and the Pain Killer" from *The Adventures of Tom Sawyer.* One would expect an item on what was the point of this episode, or what Aunt Polly learned from it. Not so; the question asks for the name of the cat.

An item unconnected with a particular selection is, "One of Mark Twain's early jobs was" (soldier, cub pilot, minstrel singer, organ player, printer). The keyed answer is "cub pilot," but Mark Twain had been a printer for nine years (1847–56) before he took up piloting and became a soldier immediately afterwards (1861). This mistake is important mainly because it reveals the lack of an independent critical review and pretesting before publication.

"Factual" items on literary works need not be trivial. For example, in one tryout form of a test on *Huckleberry Finn,* one item asks, "In which direction do Huck and Jim travel on the Mississippi River?" (north, south, east, west). I included this item reluctantly, thinking that no one could possibly get it wrong, but in a large tryout population only 56 percent got it right; 34 percent thought the characters were going north! How one could float north on a raft on a river that runs south is beyond my power to imagine, and the mistake reveals serious confusion and unawareness of the setting. The factual items in the tests under review, however, are not of this order. Once you know what, in general, a selection is about, who wrote it, the names of the principal characters, and whether it is a short story, poem, play, etc., you are likely to get a high score. On the average over the four forms, there are also 14 quotations with a choice of five titles of selections from which they were taken, and 17 words (not necessarily literary terms) with a choice of five brief definitions. The objectives of the study of literature at this stage of development are hardly represented at all.

The only manual, called Manual of Directions, is printed on both sides of a small sheet. The stated objective is "to measure understanding and knowledge of literature," and the items are said to have undergone numerous revisions based on statistical studies of test results and the criticism of teachers and test construction specialists. There is a table of percentiles for grades 7 and 8, said to be based on January and April administrations in the Nation-Wide Every Pupil Scholarship Testing Programs of 1962 and 1963, and the number of cases ranges from 1,494 to 1,743. Split-half reliabilities of .88 to .93 are reported for each form in grades 7 and 8. Since the tests could hardly be used unless one happened to be using the anthology on which they are based and since they test only memory of salient points in or about these selections, there is no point in commenting on the weaknesses of the manual.

[221]

*Hoskins-Sanders Literature Test. 1, 2 semesters grades 9–13; 1962–64; first published 1962–63 in the Every Pupil Scholarship Test series; Forms A, B, ('64, 4 pages); 2 levels labeled Tests 1, 2; manual ('64, 3 pages); no norms for college freshmen; $1.75

per 25 tests, postage extra; 75¢ per specimen set, post-paid; 40(45) minutes; Thomas Hoskins and M. W. Sanders; Data Processing and Educational Measurement Center. *

ALAN C. PURVES, *Professor of English, University of Illinois, Urbana, Illinois.*

The *Hoskins-Sanders Literature Test* consists of four forms of 150 four-choice items each. Almost all of the items call for recall of authors, titles, characters, incidents, lines, or tropes from English and American literature (with a few questions on world literature). Each form has about four items dealing with literary terms, but most items are of the type, "He was a famous after-dinner speaker, conversationalist, and poet: 1. Thoreau 2. Emerson 3. Whittier 4. Holmes" or "This novel is really an allegorical presentation of man's struggle with nature and with evil: 1. Chance 2. The Man of Property 3. The Scarlet Letter 4. Moby Dick." Needless to say, many of the other items are as unanswerable as these two.

Accompanying the tests is a manual indicating that the items deal with "35 classical selections"; I count 35 in the first third of each form and wonder whether Saki's "The Interlopers" (as good a short short story as it may be) is even a neglected classic. There are several items on such untaught authors as Louis Bromfield, Albert Bigelow Paine, and Helen Hunt Jackson, and no items dealing with black literature. There are norms—purportedly national—of 1962–63, which are revealing. Even then, before the great curriculum reforms had fully taken hold, the 99th percentile at grade 12 averages 91 out of 150 and the 75th percentile averages 59. Evidently, few students even then read the handbooks of literature that Hoskins and Sanders are testing.

These tests are, then, picayune, invalid, and unrepresentative of the secondary school English curriculum. They are also poorly edited. Representing, as they do, all that education in literature and testing in literature have been moving away from in the past twenty years, they should be avoided by all.

[222]

★**A Look at Literature: The NCTE Cooperative Test of Critical Reading and Appreciation.** Grades 4–6; 1968–69; 3 scores: Parts 1 (selections read aloud by examiner while read silently by examinee), 2 (selections read silently by examinee), total; Forms A ('68, 16 pages), B ('68, 19 pages); manual ('69, 38 pages); use of the unnamed part scores not discussed; norms for highly selected fifth graders only; $7 per 20 tests; separate answer sheets (Digitek-IBM 805) may be used; $4 per 100 answer sheets; $2 per manual; $2.50 per specimen set; cash orders postpaid; (60–70) minutes; developed and sponsored jointly by Research Foundation of the National Council of Teachers of English and Educational Testing Service; Cooperative Tests and Services. *

NANCY W. BURTON, *Fellow, Laboratory of Educational Research, University of Colorado, Boulder, Colorado.*

A Look at Literature, developed jointly by an NCTE committee and ETS, reflects well on both—the literature selections and questions are good and the construction and statistical procedures were sound.

The authors clearly wish to encourage the inclusion of literature in the elementary curriculum. By constructing a test they seem to be using the old saw, tests limit curriculum, backhand. To further their commendable design, more than half of the three pages of suggestions for using the test covers ways to use the test to teach literature. The other uses discussed are research, evaluation, and instructional planning. General use is restricted because the test has not been standardized or normed. Furthermore, for an unnormed test, it is expensive.

Each form contains 14 short literary selections and 50 four-option multiple choice questions. The first half of the test is to be read aloud by the administrator, partially to decrease the effect of students' reading ability. This interesting notion enhances the instrument's research value and, in one sense, content validity, although the oral reading factor would restrict standardization procedures. The test booklets are attractive and well laid out.

The literary selections are of high quality—diverse, appealing, and generally up-to-date. Excerpting from longer selections was very well done. The vocabulary level is not high—most difficult words are to be read aloud. Many questions, however, call for sophistication of interpretation; the rationale underlying the keyed responses was not always obvious to the reviewer.

The test development was competently done and completely reported. A couple of aspects deserve special mention: (*a*) The selection of passages and editing of items appear to have been done entirely by the test developers. No outside experts, beyond the NCTE committee, or literature search are mentioned. (*b*) An apparently successful effort was made to statistically equate the two forms by using a common equating test. The equating procedure is, however, not described adequately for most test users.

The authors have been most conscientious in explaining methods and limitations. Means, standard deviations, standard errors of measurement, K-R 20 reliabilities, correlations with STEP Reading, and average biserial discriminations and average difficulties are reported.

No content validity is insured beyond that provided by the NCTE committee's expertise. As might be expected, correlations of .78 and .79 between total LAL scores and STEP Reading "suggest that whatever is being measured is not distinct from reading in general." The K-R 20 reliabilities are only moderately good, ranging from .68 to .76 for part scores and .83 for total scores.

The mean item difficulties for Forms A and B are reported as .53 and .56, respectively, somewhat lower than optimum .625. This would not in itself be serious, but the sample was a high-ability group of fifth graders whose mean STEP reading score was at the 89th percentile. One should therefore be very cautious in giving the test to average and low-ability students in fifth or sixth grade, or to *any* fourth graders.

SUMMARY. The advantage of *A Look at Literature* is its freshness. The test is the only one of its kind, the literary selections are not tired or shopworn, the idea of reading part of the test aloud is interesting, and the conscientious reporting in the manual is refreshing. Its disadvantages are in interpretation. Without norms or validity data, its use is pretty much limited to criterion referenced testing or to districts that wish to develop local norms.

WALTER J. MOORE, *Professor of Elementary Education, University of Illinois, Urbana, Illinois.*

This test is described in the manual as a research instrument, designed to measure "the ability to respond critically to specific literary selections." According to the authors, "Responding to *A Look at Literature* calls for such operations as interpreting, valuing, comparing, inferring, appreciating, restating, attending to, relating, identifying with, and understanding." Selections were chosen to represent as many as possible of the modes of literary expression found in imaginative prose and poetry deemed suitable for children. Thus, under the general heading of prose are found such categories as

description, fanciful dialogue, realistic dialogue, fable, myth, fanciful narrative, realistic narrative, and the tall tale. Under poetry are found humorous and lyric subdivisions.

Certain "response modes were defined prior to the development of the test and item writers tried to write questions that would fit into one of three categories": translation, extension, and awareness. Translation involves "low-level inferences, comprehension of meanings, definition, restatement, recognition of elements." Extension includes "interpretation, prediction, comparison, higher-level inferences, use of the givens to go beyond the givens." Awareness is said to be exhibited by "perception of styles and their relationships, recognition of points of view and of the author's craft and its effects." The categories are not mutually exclusive.

The manual frankly discusses the limitations of the test. The test contains a few questions and their associated selections that have succeeded in discriminating between those students who score high on each part of the test and those who score low. As one reviews the test, certain concerns are felt, and one of these is the statistical validity of the test. The manual confesses that "only face validity is considered" and that before statistical validity can be established, further research is required. A real limitation on the generalizability of the results of the use of the tests resides in an absence of "norms on which to base interpretations of the test scores. The students whose test results are reported....are a select, not a random, group. By and large, they are middle-class urban and suburban pupils of average or above-average general ability, and they are above-average readers."

"*A Look at Literature* will need to be supplemented by other tests and data-gathering procedures. * [Its sponsors hope that] it will give rise to the development of companion instruments aimed also at the measurement of response and sensitivity." They rightly recognize the necessity for the establishment of the statistical validity of the test. The NCTE committee of teachers, librarians, and specialists in literature for children had as their goal the development of a research instrument—this they now have and it is a good one. It is suggested in the manual that the test may be used "informally as an aid in instruction" and as "a useful resource in teacher education, both pre-service and in-service." This reviewer feels that these ends may well be served by the test in its present state and recommends its use in these areas.

[223]

Objective Tests in American Anthology. High school; 1959–64; 2 forms; no manual; no data on reliability; no norms; $3.45 per complete specimen set; postage extra; [60] minutes per test; Perfection Form Co. *

a) FIRST SERIES. 1959–61; 6 tests: 5 tests ('59, 4 pages) on specific periods and a final examination ('61, 6 pages); 10 or more tests same title, 15¢ each; $1.75 per specimen set; Carl H. Larson.

b) ALTERNATE SERIES. 1964; series title is *Alternate Objective Tests in American Anthology;* 7 tests: 6 tests (4 pages) on specific periods and a final examination (4 pages); separate answer sheets (IBM 805) must be used; 10 or more tests same title, with answer sheets, 15¢ each; 25 or more answer sheets, 3¢ each; $2.15 per specimen set; Dorothy A. Mason.

[224]

Objective Tests in English Anthology. High school; 1959–64; 2 forms; no manual; no data on reliability; no norms; $4.75 per complete specimen set; postage extra; [60] minutes per test; Perfection Form Co. *

a) FIRST SERIES. 1959; 8 tests: 7 tests (4 pages) on specific periods and a final examination (6 pages); 10 or more tests same title, 15¢ each; $2.45 per specimen set; Carl H. Larson.

b) ALTERNATE SERIES. 1964; series title is *Alternate Objective Tests in English Anthology;* 9 tests: 7 tests (4 pages) on specific periods, a final examination (5 pages), and a test entitled *The English Novel* (4 pages); separate answer sheets (IBM 805) must be used; 10 or more tests same title with answer sheets, 15¢ each; 25 or more answer sheets, 3¢ each; $2.75 per specimen set; Dorothy A. Mason.

[225]

★Tests of Academic Progress: Literature. Grades 9–12; 1964–66; Form 1 ('64, 15 pages); 4 levels (grades 9, 10, 11, 12) in a single booklet; no specific manual; battery teacher's manual ('64, 62 pages); battery manual for administrators, supervisors, and counselors ('65, 45 pages); battery norms booklet for IQ levels ('66, 26 pages); separate answer cards (MRC) must be used; 30¢ per test; $3 per 100 MRC answer cards; $1.20 per battery teacher's manual; 96¢ per battery administrator's manual; 60¢ per battery norms booklet; $3 per specimen set of the complete battery; postage extra; scoring service, 27¢ per test; 50(60) minutes; Dale P. Scannell and Oscar M. Haugh; Houghton Mifflin Co. *

REFERENCE

1. GOOLSBY, THOMAS M., JR. "The Appropriateness of the Tests of Academic Progress for an Experimental School." *Ed & Psychol Meas* 30(4):967–70 w '70. *

ROBERT C. POOLEY, *Professor Emeritus of English, University of Wisconsin, Madison, Wisconsin.*

Part of a battery entitled *Tests of Academic Progress,* this literature test undertakes to measure the success of students in grades 9 through 12 in reading and interpreting six types of literature: the short story, novel, essay, narrative poem, lyric poem, and drama. Responses are made by choosing one of four options in multiple choice questions. To keep the test within bounds of space and time (50 minutes) the selections are necessarily very brief; for example, the sample of the whole field of drama offered a ninth grade student is a quotation of 22 lines. The two longest selections consist of 47 lines each.

To cover the four years of high school in one test, the exercises are overlapping. Of the total of 126 test items, the first 60 are performed by ninth grade students; tenth grade students begin at item 21 and continue through item 82, and so on. The ninth grade performs 60 items, the tenth grade 62 items, the eleventh grade 64 items, and the twelfth grade 66 items. If the test were repeated annually, more than half of the items for grades 10 through 12 would be repeated by the same students.

The selections of literature are well chosen to provide unfamiliar but typical quotations from standard authors. In Form 1 the authors total 12 and include Harte, Frost, Crane, Hawthorne, Thoreau, Byron, Keats, and Shakespeare. Each grade level is tested by items including the six types of literature. The test items, which are questions or statements based on the reading of the sample quotations, are classified into four general categories: understanding meaning in context; understanding the content of a literary selection; understanding literary devices; and using literary background. The last category includes exercises in identifying literary types, identifying authors by textual evidence or simple elimination, and identifying characteristics and styles of writing. A table on page 40 of the teacher's manual classifies each item for Forms 1 and 2 (only Form 1 is available), providing not only an analysis of the content of the tests, but also the means to a diagnostic analysis of individual pupil performance as a method of determining areas of competence and insufficiency.

The test items are ingeniously devised. For example, the words picked out for identification of meaning in the ninth grade test can all be determined by the context, requiring no previous knowledge of the word but exercising the skill of recognizing meaning in context. I find no objection to the questions calling for recognition of figures of speech, nor for such literary devices as alliteration, assonance, simile, and onomatopoeia, which appear for the first time in the tenth grade portion of the test. In a test of this nature I seriously question the significance of identifying terms of prosody such as iambic pentameter, trochaic tetrameter, iambic tetrameter, and trochaic pentameter, or, more erudite, the identification of such stanza forms as Chaucerian, Spenserian, ottava rima, and terza rima. I doubt whether the majority of high school English teachers could make these identifications correctly. Too many of the items for grades 11 and 12 contain these gratuitous technicalities. On the other hand, a large portion of the items require inferences from the content and context; these are well done and are, in my opinion, the most valuable part of the test.

The manual for administrators presents within-grade reliability coefficients ranging from .85 to .90. These coefficients are high enough to warrant confidence in the measuring worth of the test in its own narrow sphere, but they point to caution in the interpretation of the score of any particular student, especially at the midpoint of the range.

The authors state in the same manual that the Literature test measures four general categories of literary knowledge (listed above) "which reflect the major goals of the teaching of literature." This is a considerable overstatement. Few teachers of English would agree that the four categories employed by the authors constitute "the major goals" of teaching literature. More accurate is this statement in the teacher's manual: "The purpose of *Test 6: Literature* is to determine how well a student can apply what he has learned in his English classes to the reading and interpretation of the following six types of literature: the short story, novel, essay, narrative poem, lyric poem, and drama." This is a true description which emphasizes that this is a reading test for a specific field; it measures with some degree of accuracy the success of students in reading pieces of literature for meaning, for the detection of literary devices, and for the application of past literary experience to a present reading. These skills are valuable in achieving the goals of literature in the curriculum, but they are not in themselves the major goals.

In a report which has influenced the teaching of English for over 50 years [1] these excerpts are among the listed goals for teaching literature in high schools: (*a*) "broaden, deepen, and

enrich the imaginative and emotional life of the student," (*b*) "arouse in the minds of pupils an admiration for great personalities," (*c*) "raise the plane of enjoyment in reading to progressively higher levels," (*d*) "give to the student....a sense of [the] abundance of interesting material, and a trained ability and desire to find for himself such intellectual and spiritual food as he may need," and (*e*) "feel more sensitively and deeply, and to imagine more vividly, but to think more accurately and intelligently."

If these are the fundamental goals for the teaching of literature in high schools, and I believe the majority of English teachers would accept them as such, then the materials measured in this test bear very slight relationship to these goals. The test is not at fault; it is the title that is wrong. The test in its present form measures specific skills; these skills undoubtedly assist in achieving the goals for teaching literature, but these skills are not the goals. It must be admitted that the accepted goals are very difficult, if not impossible, of quantitative measurement. This problem has plagued the makers of tests of literature since objective testing began. Practically all teachers of English recognize the present impossibility of testing for gains in achieving the true goals of literature instruction. The authors of this test are at fault only in labelling the test "Literature" without qualification and for the statement that the four categories of the test items "reflect the major goals of the teaching of literature."

The potential harm of this claim lies in the assumption that a teacher who teaches exclusively the skills measured in this test is a superior teacher of literature and that a teacher whose students do not do so well on this test is thereby an inferior teacher. School administrators and an uninformed public sometimes make such assumptions. The end result might be the neglect of the true goals of literature instruction in favor of skills which can be measured. The test itself is a satisfactory instrument for the measurement of specific contributory skills to the reading of literature, as an index of progress in these skills. It should be titled not "Literature," but "A Test of Basic Skills in the Reading of Literature."

ALAN C. PURVES, *Professor of English, University of Illinois, Urbana, Illinois.*

The literature test consists of 12 passages of

---

[1] HOSIC, JAMES FLEMING, COMPILER. *Reorganization of English in Secondary Schools,* pp. 63-4. Bulletin, 1917, No. 2, Bureau of Education. Washington, D.C.: United States Government Printing Office, 1917. Pp. 181. *

prose, verse, and drama, each with 9 to 12 four-choice items related to it. The test is so arranged that ninth grade students do passages 1–6; tenth grade students, 3–8; eleventh grade students, 5–10; and twelfth grade students, 7–12. The tests have a median reliability for the four levels of .88 and have norms based on good national samples. There is an item classification consisting of 13 subcategories grouped into four categories (understanding meanings in context, understanding content, understanding literary devices, and using literary background).

The test package has a statistical and marketing sheen that would lead the careless user to accept the test as a measure of literary understanding. Underneath this sheen, however, is a trivial test of reading comprehension (interestingly, the test has a .83 correlation with the reading test in the same series).

To take the items and the item classification first, one sees that the items measuring an understanding of literary devices simply ask the student to identify the devices. Calling something a simile is not understanding it. Of the items dealing with understanding main ideas, a good number ask the student to give a title to the work; others ask him to indicate the author's purpose, e.g., to narrate, describe, persuade, or explain. Neither of these kinds of items measures the understanding of main ideas save indirectly (and often ambiguously).

Beyond the problem of the classificatory terms is the balance of the test. Seventy-six of the items measure understanding meanings and understanding content, in other words, comprehension of the substance of the passages; of these, 21 are vocabulary items. There is nothing wrong with testing literal comprehension in a literature test, but the dominance of this kind of item leads a student to think that this is all there is to literary understanding. No items appear dealing with the relationships of part to part, part to whole, style to thought, or language to tone, dealing with the structure, the tone, or the attitude of the writer, or dealing with the justification of interpretation of the passage; surely these are major aspects of literary study. Further, the items connected with a passage seem to have no functional relationship to the passage; there seems to be no reason for asking those particular questions. As a whole, then, the test borders on the trivial.

So much of the test also seems to be measuring test wiseness. Specific determiners abound, as in these four options: expository, descriptive, narrative, narrative and descriptive. There are many "none of the above" and "all of the above" items, including one on a passage from Thoreau (in which there is reference to the author by name): "Who wrote this selection? (1) Thackeray (2) Tolstoy (3) There is no way of telling who wrote this selection (4) None of the above." Another item asks for the best title for a selection; a sharp student would see that the title is printed in the acknowledgments.

The selections chosen are generally adequate, but not "advanced and challenging" as the manual claims. One of the selections, from Hawthorne's *The Scarlet Letter* should have been avoided, since the work is so widespread in the curriculum and since two of the items test more the student's knowledge of the work than his ability to read the passage with literary acumen.

There are so many flaws in the content of this test that it is hard to summarize one's judgment of it, but one suspects that the definition of literary ability that produced the specifications and the items was reinterpreted by the psychometric editors and not carried through by those knowledgeable about literary study. It would seem, too, that all of the effort went into the norming process and not enough into the validation process. Validity in a literature test is based less on the pedigree of the passages chosen than on the behaviors measured by the items. By that definition of validity these tests are invalid and certainly inferior to the publisher's other literature test, that in the Content Evaluation series. Prospective users of the *Tests of Academic Progress: Literature* should be very careful not to use the literature portion of the tests to make judgments about a student's literary ability.

JOHN C. SHERWOOD, *Professor of English, University of Oregon, Eugene, Oregon.*

The battery of *Tests of Academic Progress* is intended "to provide an efficient and comprehensive appraisal of student progress toward the most widely accepted academic goals of secondary education"; the tests provide, in other words, a mechanism by which a local school or system can rate individuals or classes for purposes of placement, course planning, and the like. Each test consists of four different but overlapping grade level tests (e.g., grade 9 will answer exercises 1–60; grade 10, exercises 21–82), so that it can serve for all four grades. There is a considerable mass of statistical material, including not only norms for various levels and even times of the year but also "Special Percentile Norms for IQ Levels" directed to educators rash enough to attempt to identify over- and under-achievement (to be honest, the accompanying instructions clearly warn against any hasty judgments in such matters). The literature test is designed to find out how well the student "can interpret selections taken from many different kinds of literature" (actually "the short story, novel, essay, narrative poem, lyric poem, and drama") or, more specifically, to test "the ability to understand the meaning of words, phrases, and sentences in context; the ability to understand the content of literary selections; the ability to understand the use of literary devices." If such phrases as "ability to understand the content" seem on the vague side, an analysis of the test may help to define more sharply what is actually being tested: (a) Ordinary unspecialized reading comprehension, the ability to understand the text, sometimes taking the form of mere attentiveness (e.g., the ability to identify a selection as from "a play of more than one act" from the fact that it is plainly labeled "Act One"). (b) A type of reading comprehension more specifically literary, such as the ability to estimate a character from clues in the dialogue. (c) Knowledge of certain formal and technical matters, such as genre, meter, and figures of speech. (d) Finally, command of some odds and ends of literary history, as evidenced by the ability to identify authors and periods from clues in style and content.

In considering the usefulness of the test, we might first ask whether the inclusion of items from literary history is expedient in a test ostensibly intended to measure interpretation. It certainly muddles the issue, for although interpretation might be thought of as a kind of unity, history is a large and amorphous realm, which really ought to be tested in terms of identified areas such as English, continental, or classical. Of the authors actually quoted, all are English or American, mostly of the nineteenth century. An idea of the kind of traditional curriculum the editors had in mind is suggested by their defensive statement that the answer to one item would be obvious to "any-

one who knows that Frost was a poet, that Stevenson did not write of incidents concerning broncos and Mexican dialect, and that the language is unlike anything written by Joel Chandler Harris." Even assuming that it is important to know what Stevenson did *not* write, we are getting a rather provincial view of literary history; a student could be widely read in the masterpieces of Western culture and still come to grief with the items on this test. It would seem better to test literary history separately and more systematically, unless, to be sure, the group tested had exactly the background the editors had in mind, in which case the questions might seem rather easy.

Turning to the genuinely interpretive items, we note little of subtlety, little of that sense of the complexity and ambiguity of literature which the formalist school has taught us so much about. There is likewise no attempt to assess literary taste or value judgments; and perhaps for these reasons the questions tend to be unambiguous, with answers which the experienced reader can easily spot. Some seem to be little more than exercises in labeling. The student may be asked to determine whether a passage is "vivid," "wordy," "exact," or "colorful," to decide whether an author's purpose was "to tell a story," "to describe a scene," "to criticize a way of life," or "to entertain the reader with an amusing situation." Such categories are crude and vague and ambiguities are not lacking; pity the student who must choose between the labels "autobiographical" and "humorous" with reference to a passage which has elements of both categories. Much of the questioning involves matters of fact—what is going on? where is the scene? who are the persons involved?—or involves defining the obvious prose significance. Problems of tone and attitude, much less the more elusive shades of meaning, do not get much beyond asking whether the author "approved" or "disapproved" of the events or whether a passage shows a "humorous vein" or an "ironic sense."

We might conclude by asking what progress a student would have made if his performance on the test did in fact improve over the years. We should expect that he had extended somewhat his knowledge of literary history, especially of the nineteenth century; that he had extended his vocabulary; that he had acquired a good command of the formal mechanics of literature—meter, rhyme schemes, figures, and the like—though this command might not go beyond the ability to identify, and need not involve the ability to show how such devices function in context. He would have maintained or increased his ability to read a text closely and attentively with a strong sense of detail, especially factual detail, but not necessarily with a sense of literary meaning as that has been understood since the new critics burst on the scene; as for the recently revived concern with the social and political bearings of literature, this simply belongs to a different world from the one assumed by the editors. Admittedly the skills emphasized are important to literary study; probably a student who did well on this test would have no great trouble in adjusting to college literature courses. But the fact remains that for the twelfth grade at least the test operates at a more pedestrian level than is appropriate to much secondary study today.

For a review of the complete battery, see 31.

[226]
★**The Undergraduate Record Examinations: Literature Tests.** College; 1969–70; 2 tests: field, modular; descriptive booklet ('70, 12 pages); for more complete information, see 671; Educational Testing Service. *
a) LITERATURE TEST. Forms RUR ('69, 28 pages), SUR ('70, 27 pages); 120(140) minutes.
b) EUROPEAN AND AMERICAN LITERATURE TEST: A MODULAR TEST DESIGNED TO COMPLEMENT THE TWO-HOUR LITERATURE TEST. Form SUR ('70, 13 pages); 45(55) minutes.

For reviews of the testing program, see 671 (2 reviews).

SPELLING

[227]
*****Kansas Spelling Tests.** I, 2 semesters in grades 3, 4–6, 7–8; 1962–64; first published 1962–63 in the Every Pupil Scholarship Test series; 3 tests; Forms A, B, ('64, 4 pages); 2 levels labeled Tests I, 2; manual ('64, 5 pages); $1.75 per 25 tests, postage extra; 75¢ per specimen set of any one test, postpaid; 15(20) minutes; Connie Moritz, Alice Robinson, Mary T. Williams, and M. W. Sanders; Data Processing and Educational Measurement Center. *
a) KANSAS ELEMENTARY SPELLING TEST. I, 2 semesters in grade 3.
b) KANSAS INTERMEDIATE SPELLING TEST. I, 2 semesters in grades 4–6.
c) KANSAS JUNIOR HIGH SCHOOL SPELLING TEST. I, 2 semesters in grades 7–8.

[228]
★**N.B. Spelling Tests.** Standards 1–3, 3–5, 6–8, 8–10 for English pupils and 3–5, 6–8, 8–10 for Afrikaans pupils; [1964]; Forms A, B, (2 pages); 4 levels labeled Series 2, 3, 4, 5; Series 5 for English pupils only; preliminary manual (18 pages); 20c per 10 tests; 30c per scoring key; 40c per manual; postpaid within South Africa; specimen set not available; Afrikaans edition available; (45) minutes; Human Sciences Research Council. *

[229]
*****Sanders-Fletcher Spelling Test.** I, 2 semesters in grades 9–13; 1962–64; first published 1962–63 in the Every Pupil Scholarship Test series; Forms A, B, ('64, 4 pages); 2 levels labeled Tests I, 2; manual ('64, 4 pages); no norms for college freshmen; $1.75 per 25 tests, postage extra; 75¢ per specimen set, postpaid; 30(35) minutes; Gwen Fletcher and M. W. Sanders; Data Processing and Educational Measurement Center. *

THOMAS D. HORN, *Professor of Curriculum and Instruction and Chairman of the Department, The University of Texas, Austin, Texas.*

Four forms are available for grades 9–12 and college freshmen. 1A and 1B are described as equivalent for the first semester of instruction; 2A and 2B are equivalent for the second semester. However, the manual refers to 4 equivalent forms. Each contains 150 items requiring a total of 315 word judgments. Part 1 of each form requires the testee to mark correct spellings with a plus, misspellings with a minus; Part 2 of each form requires the selection of the correct word from a choice of two within sentences (some foils are misspelled; however, some are homonyms, e.g., *cereal, serial,* and some are correctly spelled but do not fit in the sentence, e.g., *desert, dessert,* which adds a vocabulary dimension to the test); Part 3 of each form requires the testee to select the misspelled word from five possibilities (no *none* response). No information is given concerning the number of words used more than once in the four tests.

Directions for giving the test are printed on the test blanks which require the testee to read the directions and answer the items as directed. The extent to which scores for pupils with reading difficulties would be affected by no assistance in test orientation is not known. This reviewer found the small print size used on the tests increased the likelihood of error.

Although the test manual states that the words were selected on the "basis of functional significance, frequency of usage, and incidence of misspellings" by using "the Buckingham Extension of the Ayres Spelling Scale, the New Standard High School Spelling Scale, the Thorndike word list, and a number of recognized spelling tests," no criteria for selection are identified. In checking the test words against

Ernest Horn's list of 10,000 words most commonly used in writing, the number of words found in Horn were: (*a*) Test 1A, 163 words of 315 judgments (some used more than once); (*b*) Test 1B, 117 of 315; (*c*) Test 2A, 175 of 315; and (*d*) Test 2B, 135 of 315. This appears to reflect an overabundance of spelling "demons" and/or infrequently written words in the tests. Geographic bias in the selection of words is represented in the use of *Wichita* and *Manhattan*. Words never seen or heard by a testee, e.g., *rhapsody, tiara,* represent special problems for disadvantaged populations. Words with more than one pronunciation, e.g., *variegate,* which may be pronounced with either three or four syllables, add to the spelling difficulty of a particular word. Nevertheless, these examples would provide "top" to a high school test.

Concurrent with the issue of word-selection validity is the use of words with more than one correct spelling, e.g., *acknowledgment* and *acknowledgement; saleable* and *salable; obligato* and *obbligato; eerie* and *eery; guerilla* and *guerrilla.* In some cases, the preferred spelling was not used, thus a student knowing a correct preferred spelling, but not alternative spellings, would receive no credit for what he did know. The trade name *Sanforized* appears, in form 2B, item 62, as *Sanforize* as a correct spelling, thereby requiring a wrong answer to receive credit. A key error occurs in Test 2B, item 80.

In addressing themselves to the issue of whether or not an objective spelling test is an adequate measure of spelling ability, the authors set up a pattern "so that each grade would have a fair distribution of easy, moderately difficult, and difficult words." The pattern is not described. As tentative lists were assembled, they were "administered to students both as objective tests and as pronounced lists and error studies made on each set." This procedure seems essential if incorrect spellings are to serve as challenging foils.

In some cases, an element of luck exists when the testee faces a relatively easy misspelling, e.g., *concurr,* followed by *chandelier, carrion, fabrikoid,* and *lustre* (for which the preferred spelling is *luster*) as foils. Also, the student's background and mental set on misspellings out of context may lead him to see *solder* as a misspelling of *soldier.*

Normative data "were computed from 20,423 high school student scores which were reported by cooperating schools in four nation-wide testing programs." However, this population is not described. It is obvious that linguistically different students in the inner city or in migrant populations would not have an easy time with words such as *iridescent, plagiarize* and *crystalline.* Percentile norms are provided for each of grades 9–12.

Test reliability was determined by the split-half method. Coefficients of reliability ranged from .79 to .90 among the various grade levels.

The authors suggest five ways the test results may be used:

a) "For determining student achievement": This is questionable since the measures on this test are norm-referenced. Information about general performance levels may be obtained, but the components of any given spelling program might differ widely from the measures used in the test. One can see that criterion-based measures, e.g., 100 percent mastery of a given corpus of words, would evoke different interpretations.

b) "For checking the efficiency of instruction": For much the same reasons as were indicated in *a*) above, using scores in this way has serious limitations. The greatest validity for instructional efficiency would hold for those teachers who "teach the test."

c) "For assigning school marks": In the light of current trends in high school English curricula, and because of the nature of norm-referenced measures, the authors' suggested practice of translating percentile scores into school marks seems rather dubious.

d) "For analyzing student and class weaknesses": The fact that this test is dealing with norm-referenced measures results in the weakness identified by Klein,[1] that of "failing to provide specific information about particular skill development and needs." Also, no means for the analysis of spelling difficulties is provided in the manual, other than admonishing the user that "after the specific weaknesses and handicaps are located, remedial measures may be applied intelligently." Problems of phonetic misspellings, homonyms, or misspellings due to mispronunciation are examples of problem clusters which could have been provided for teacher and student analysis. With individual and class error information for the foregoing problem areas, instructional prescriptions could then be intelligently made.

1 KLEIN, STEPHEN. "Evaluating Tests in Terms of the Information They Provide." *Eval Comment* 2(2):1–6 Je '70. *

e) "For motivating student effort" : While it is true that some students rise to the occasion when undertaking a test and some actually enjoy the competitiveness of test taking or regard the experience as something of a game, there are significant numbers of other students who face a testing session with fear, resentment, or a "couldn't care less" attitude. Here again, we are facing the issue of norm-referenced versus criterion-referenced measures in terms of relevant instructional objectives in spelling.

In summary, this reviewer has some doubts concerning the validity of word selection for this test. The lack of test orientation for testees and the overly small print size would appear to handicap unsophisticated test takers. Most importantly, the suggested uses of the test do not appear to be appropriate.

[230]

★Spelling Test: McGraw-Hill Basic Skills System. Grades 11–14; 1970; also called *MHBSS Spelling Test;* although designed for use with the MHBSS instructional program, the test may be used independently; Forms A, B, (7 pages) ; manual (31 pages) ; separate answer sheets (Digitek, IBM 1230, Scoreze) must be used; $4.90 per 25 tests ; $2.50 per 50 Digitek or IBM answer sheets; $3 per 25 Scoreze answer sheets ; $1 per Digitek or IBM scoring stencil ; postage extra ; $1.25 per specimen set, postpaid ; IBM scoring service, 25¢ and over per test ($20 minimum) ; 20(30) minutes; Alton L. Raygor; McGraw-Hill Book Co., Inc. *

THOMAS D. HORN, *Professor of Curriculum and Instruction and Chairman of the Department, The University of Texas, Austin, Texas.*

Each form of this test consists of 50 items ; Form A requires 215 word judgments and Form B requires 219 word judgments, the difference caused by the number of paired homonyms or easily confused words selected. Each test item appears as one or two sentences. The student determines "which one, if any, of the four underlined words in each item is misspelled ; a 'none wrong' response is provided for each item." Homonyms and easily confused words are forced into context by the sentence in which they appear. The manual states that no word or derivative of that word about which the testee must make a judgment appears more than once in the same form ; "it recurs neither as an answer choice in another item nor in the context of another sentence." However, five exceptions to this were found as shown below. The manual provides extremely useful tables of : (*a*) misspellings ; (*b*) the word list for each form in alphabetical order with the item num-

ber for each word ; and (*c*) words repeated, but not in the same form (i.e., ninth and ninety), are listed alphabetically with the form and item number indicated. Unfortunately, the confusing actual title of this last table, "Words Not Repeated in the Same Form," apparently confused the table compiler. A check of the tests reveals that five words are actually in the same form in both Form A and Form B, i.e., secretary, seized, subtle, superintendent and tremendous. Also, the word *attempting* indicated as being included in item 38, Form B, does not appear there ; *governors,* identified as being included in item 18, Form A, does not appear ; *ninety,* identified as item 56, Form B, should be item 46. Gremlins also got into the word list for Form B, with *benefit* and *obvious* being misspelled.

Complete and detailed directions for administering the test are provided in the manual. Testee directions are clear and each form provides a practice item.

The words selected for these tests were drawn from Pollack's study of misspellings and seven other lists of words commonly misspelled by high school and college students. The "spelling demons" of these lists were combined by computer in a collated list which included the frequency with which each word appeared on the eight lists. Again, the computer was used to select, "first the most frequently misspelled word on the Pollack list, and then, using a table of random numbers, it selected randomly three other words from the collated list. These four words together [plus a 'none' response], were used to create a test item. The second test item's words were selected in a similar manner. The second most frequently misspelled word on the Pollack list was grouped with three other randomly selected words" plus the "none" response. This was continued until enough items were secured for a try-out edition. Using the words and sentences, an "experimental version of the test was then tried out on other populations [not identified] for the purpose of gathering item analysis data. Items were selected from these try-outs on the basis of their difficulty and discrimination indices." This reviewer checked the words finally selected for the published tests against Horn's *Basic Writing Vocabulary.* Form A contains 170 words (79 percent) which are also in Horn ; Form B contains 172 words (79 percent). This appears to reflect significantly higher validity when compared with the

Sanders-Fletcher Spelling Test and probably also reflects the intended population for which the MHBSS test was designed, i.e., "high school juniors or seniors who are planning to attend college....two-year college students, and ....students in the early years of four-year colleges and universities." Students found to be poor spellers may be guided by test results "toward remedial or developmental instruction in spelling." In addition, the authors are careful to point out that criterion-related validity must be determined by test users in terms of instructional objectives.

K-R 20 reliabilities of .89 and .90 are reported for the two forms. No claim is made that any of the normative populations represent a random sample. Tables are provided to convert raw scores to percentile ranks, stanines, and standard scores. The section describing norming procedures is written in quite an informative and readable way, particularly for the nonspecialist administrator.

The section describing scoring, reporting, and interpreting test results is, likewise, informative and readable. Although the list of words used in developing this test was the same as that used in developing the McGraw-Hill Basic Skills System Instructional Materials in spelling, the manual manages to maintain low-key suggestions to use the latter materials. The desirability of building an atlas of norms, e.g., representing geographic and linguistic differences, is reflected by the author's comment concerning use of local norms. Use of the test scores for diagnostic interpretations is realistic in only a general way. The SCOREZE answer sheet does provide a useful, though limited, analysis of learning difficulties by identifying the items representing such errors as vowel substitution, double consonants, and homonyms. However, the incidence of items representing particular difficulties is not always proportional between forms, e.g., Form A has 8 double-consonant items, Form B contains 2; Form A contains 11 vowel-substitution items, Form B contains 15. The number of "none" responses is the same for both forms.

In short, this test is recommended for use, keeping in mind the issues involved in criterion-related validity. It is hoped that the discrepancies identified in the foregoing paragraphs may be eliminated in the next edition of the materials.

ALBERT H. YEE, *Professor of Curriculum and Instruction, University of Wisconsin, Madison, Wisconsin.*

The McGraw-Hill Basic Skills System (MHBSS) provides diagnosis and training for college-bound high school juniors and seniors and college freshmen and sophomores in six academic skill areas—reading, writing, spelling, vocabulary, study skills, and mathematics. Each area's materials contain a diagnostic test, a self-instructional, remedial program with workbook and audiotape, and a second test to evaluate the student's achievement after his training.

The MHBSS Spelling Test is not complex, and explicit directions in the manual make test administration quite clear and simple to follow. A raw score of total correct responses is easily converted to a standard T score, stanine, and percentile ranking. No subscales were developed for diagnosis of specific problems, because the test authors were not able to find reliable information on diagnostic schemes. Thus, the test authors suggest that on the basis of total score results, "A student's adviser must make a subjective judgment in selecting....an activity for the student."

Thus, such guidance leads to quite generalized interpretation of results. The high scorer is identified as being capable of spelling when he wants to do so and probably able to recognize situations when he needs aid. A low score indicates that a student does not recognize his spelling errors and may have a poor attitude toward improving his spelling proficiency. The test authors say those students scoring in the middle range are potentially the most willing and able to profit from remedial instruction, such as provided by the MHBSS worktext, *Basic Spelling Skills: A Program to Self-Instruction.*

The test items require the examinee to identify one or none of four underlined words in one or two sentences as being incorrectly spelled. The test words were selected from a frequency count of 4,482 different misspelled words and word-groups of students that Pollack[1] collected from 599 college English teachers in 1950. The passage of 20 years could make a difference in what words are misspelled and what problems students have. The English proficiency of high school graduates has steadily improved in the last two decades and has

[1] POLLACK, THOMAS CLARK. "Spelling Report." *Col Engl* 16:102–9 N '54. *

reached the level where many universities, such as the University of Wisconsin, have abolished the traditionally required year of English for most freshmen. However, the respectable work done to standardize the test appears to make it up-to-date and provides norms relevant to modern students. The standardization sample included freshmen from five 4-year colleges or universities, first year students from 14 junior colleges, and college preparatory juniors and seniors from 13 high schools distributed in the four main geographic regions of the USA.

The basis of the MHBSS Spelling Test, therefore, is simply students' accuracy in recognizing correctly spelled and misspelled words. The test authors claim that spelling recognition items produce test scores that correlate positively with proficiency in spelling dictated words. To support such a claim, they report a correlation of .85 between an experimental version of the test and the spelling section of the *Cooperative English Test,* Form OM ; but the manual does not report the sample size and is not completely clear concerning the details of the item analyses conducted with the responses of other samples. The discussion of test validity is brief and vague ; it does not appear that adequate crossvalidation was accomplished. Since the spelling section of the *Cooperative English Test,* Form OM, is also comprised of recognition-type items, the empirical question remains open of whether the test predicts the criterion. Even if spelling recognition scores correlate as well as .85, there remains about 28 percent of the variance that is still unexplained.

The criterion of spelling behavior in this test follows the traditional definition of spelling that one envisions in school spelling lists and spelling "bees." Ability to reproduce spellings upon demand is a significant aspect of spelling achievement but there is more to spelling than that. Personke and Yee [2] have developed a theoretical model of spelling behavior that incorporates all pertinent behaviors involved in spelling and systematically structures them into five distinct yet complementary channels of processing spelling behavior. Based in part on modern communications and systems theories, the model specifies what decisions and operations follow

2 PERSONKE, CARL R., AND YEE, ALBERT H. "A Model for the Analysis of Spelling Behavior." *El Engl* 43:278–84 Mr '66. *
PERSONKE, CARL R., AND YEE, ALBERT H. "The Situational Choice and the Spelling Program." *El Engl* 45:32–7+ Ja '68. *

different spelling contingencies and their relative efficiency in achieving the desired outcome.

Pure rote spelling without conscious effort to reproduce the words as one writes his thoughts, is efficient, mature spelling. However, there are different levels of spelling response, such as occasions when spelling may be consciously produced through phonetic rules or with the aid of one or several external sources and/or verified in various ways. Students need to learn rote spelling, rules, situational choices, etc., through practice and instruction to develop comprehensive spelling behavior. Schools need to systematize their instructional programs accordingly. The traditional spelling programs for elementary and middle school students provide skills and exercises that may be viewed as steps toward comprehensive, if not systematic, instruction ; but the criterion behavior all such programs focus upon is narrowly perceived, as can be found in the MHBSS Spelling Test. Thus, the test provides little diagnostic help beyond classifying scores as high, medium, and poor. Advisers are asked to make their own judgments of specific student needs and strengths. As with all other existing spelling tests, its construct validity leaves much to be desired.

From a technical point of view, the MHBSS Spelling Test appears to have been given adequate attention as to standardization, item discrimination, internal consistency, and intercorrelation with three of the other five MHBSS tests (with reading, .55 ; vocabulary, .47 ; and mathematics, .38). The test authors state that correlations with writing and study skills will be computed later when those tests are completed. Also, reliability will be estimated later with test-retest and Form A and B correlations to assess test stability and equivalence.

Although this reviewer finds serious fault with its construct validity and would like to see some crossvalidation done, the MHBSS Spelling Test compares well with other traditional spelling tests available.

VOCABULARY

[231]

*Bruce Vocabulary Inventory.** Business and industry ; 1959–67 ; 1 form ('59, 4 pages) ; manual ('59, 4 pages) ; supplementary norms ['63 and '67, 1 page] ; reliability data for raw scores only ; $6 per 20 tests ; 35¢ per key ; separate answer sheets (IBM 805) may be used; $3.25 per 20 answer sheets; $1 per set of scoring stencils; $1.50 per manual; $2.25 per specimen set with hand scoring key, $2.50 with scoring stencils; cash orders postpaid, 10% extra on charge orders; (15–25) minutes; Martin M. Bruce; Martin M. Bruce, Ph.D., Publishers. *

FRED H. BORGEN, *Research Psychologist, National Merit Scholarship Corporation, Evanston, Illinois.*

The *Bruce Vocabulary Inventory* is presented as an aid for personnel decisions in industry and business, presumably throughout the range of white collar employees. The manual does not specify just what uses might be most appropriate for the test, but it implies that it might be used as a brief measure of intelligence, as well as a measure of verbal comprehension and usage. The test consists of 100 four-alternative multiple choice items, each with the correct alternative meaning the same or most nearly the same as the key word. The 100 key words, which were randomly selected from the *Oxford Universal Dictionary,* are roughly arranged in terms of increasing difficulty. There is no time limit, and "a person with a high school education will generally complete the form in about 15–20 minutes."

Few vocabulary tests specify how words were selected, and the author of this test is to be commended for using a precise method of compiling the sample of words. The nature of the particular vocabulary domain, however, may not be appropriate for many business uses and the user may prefer a vocabulary test containing words with more functional and pragmatic usage.

The selection of items and the wise use of distractors make for a wide range of difficulty among the items; hence, the instrument can be expected to make reliable discriminations over a wide variety of applicant groups, particularly those of average or higher ability. The distractors have been carefully selected to foil the respondent with incomplete knowledge of a word, and correct guessing is therefore minimized. Unfortunately, some of the distractors are more difficult than the key word; distractors for moderately difficult words include such stumpers as, rani, adiposity, virgule, nipa, and intaglio.

The manual appropriately warns that "too heavy reliance on this test as a vocabulary measure and as an indicator of intellectual level is discouraged. The test user should view test results as suggestive rather than as definitely diagnostically significant."

The manual claims that a special value of this particular vocabulary test is the availability of norms for industrial and business groups. This claim places a major burden on the adequacy of the norms the author provides, yet in several respects the norms appear deficient. The manual lists the job titles in the various norm groups but gives no evidence that the groups are representative of any naturally occurring population. For example, the white collar group contains such diverse workers as statisticians and switchboard operators, but one suspects, in the absence of evidence to the contrary, that the composition of the white collar group is ad hoc, rather than representative of the general population of white collar workers. The norm group for the "total employed population" is a simple composite of most of the available groups and is rather heavily weighted, to some unspecified extent, with persons of well above average education.

Further, there is a disturbing lack of agreement between the norms in the manual (1959) and the supplemental norms issued in 1963 and 1967. Median score for the "total employed population" is listed as 77 in the manual, while the supplementary norms for "countrywide evaluatees" give a median of 65. Similarly, for "white collar" personnel there is a major discrepancy between the 1959 norms and the supplementary norms: medians of 77 versus 67, respectively. These are discrepancies of nearly a full standard deviation, raising a red flag cautioning the user about the meaningfulness of the norms for his setting. The performance levels for many of the norm groups seem to be exceptionally high, particularly for executives and middle management. A raw score of 75 correct for the 100 items falls at the 2nd percentile for executives, 15th percentile for middle management, 50th percentile for engineers, and *also* at the 50th percentile for the total employed population. Some of these group differences suggest that the test administration or sampling conditions may have been quite different for the various norm groups. Finally, one's confidence in the technical adequacy of the norms is further shaken by the fact that in four out of nine cases the median score listed in the manual for a specific norm group does not correspond with the score falling at the 50th percentile in the norms! In view of these reservations about the accuracy and generalizability of the norms, the usual recommendations about the development of local norms need even greater emphasis for this test.

The manual gives the pretense of offering validity data, but, in fact, criterion-related validity information showing the utility of the instrument as a selection device is critically lacking. One looks in vain for a correlation between scores on this test and job performance. The "validity" section of the manual merely presents correlations between this test and other tests of vocabulary knowledge and general ability. The correlations with general ability tests range from .53 to .67, and despite the manual's claim that "vocabulary development is consistently highly correlated with intelligence," these values are not high enough to support the use of this test as an adequate substitute for a longer measure of general ability, particularly if decisions about individuals are required.

The APA Task Force on Employment Testing of Minority Groups [1] warns against the possibility of unfair personnel practices resulting from the use of a job-irrelevant or unduly difficult aptitude test to screen applicants or candidates for promotion. The difficulty level and apparent irrelevance of many of the words to business usage raise questions about the fairness of the instrument with disadvantaged populations. It is conceivable that one may get a good measure of social background with this test but not a measure of adequacy of word usage in any practical setting. The method of selection of the words, by sampling from a dictionary, tends to make some of the key words archaic and infrequently used in everyday communications. Such an emphasis is laudable for a test designed to predict skill at solving crossword puzzles, but if the task is to identify people with an adequate vocabulary for a particular employment role, it is *logically* difficult to justify the use of this test. It may be *empirically* quite defensible, but we are given no information to decide this issue. In the absence of empirical evidence for the validity of this test with culturally different groups, extreme caution is urged in the use of this test for selection purposes in any setting where applicants come from diverse social backgrounds.

In summary, the vocabulary domain repre-

1 APA TASK FORCE ON EMPLOYMENT TESTING OF MINORITY GROUPS. "Job Testing and the Disadvantaged." *Am Psychol* 24(7):637–50 Jl '69. *

sented by this test has been carefully specified and the items are well constructed. Although the manual fails to emphasize the value of locally developed norms, this need is particularly intense in this case because of the apparent deficiencies in the published norms. Insufficient validity information is given to justify the use of this instrument as a selection device. Ideally, the user of this test should be able to conduct validity studies within his own organization with special attention, where appropriate to the validity of the test, to specific jobs and specific groups of applicants.

ROBERT FITZPATRICK, *Principal Research Scientist, American Institutes for Research, Pittsburgh, Pennsylvania.*

In the brief manual for this test, the author justifies the development of still another vocabulary test on the grounds that no other such test has been standardized on employed groups. But he could have developed norms using employed groups for any of several other vocabulary tests, to essentially the same effect. The normative data he has provided, though useful and reasonably well described, are not so extensive or unusual as to outweigh the disadvantages of proliferating tests.

The 100 stimulus words for the test, according to the manual, "were chosen at random from the even numbered pages of the Oxford Universal Dictionary." This can scarcely have been the whole method, since all the words are nouns, verbs, or adjectives. Whatever the exact method, it resulted in a rather odd set of words. The greatest oddity is that two of the words are *applaud* and *applause*.

The *Oxford Universal Dictionary* is an abridgement of the *Oxford English Dictionary,* a classic work which is both relatively old and British. Thus, item 83, *defedation,* does not appear in the *Random House Dictionary of the English Language* (1967, hereafter abbreviated as RH) and is listed as archaic in *Webster's Third New International Dictionary* (1966, hereafter WT). For the stimulus word *hoyden,* the keyed synonym *clown* does not appear in RH and appears in WT only as part of a definition labeled obsolete: "a rude clownish youth." Similarly, *overflow* for *redound* is not given by RH and is labeled archaic by WT.

Some other questionable pairings: the key for *theory* is *hypothesis;* for *commissary, commissioner;* for *espy, spy;* for *treadle, lever;* for *tangential, erratic* (the last scarcely justified by one definition in WT: "deviating widely and sometimes erratically"). As a synonym for *jovial, happy* is keyed in preference to another choice, *pleasant;* for *substantiate, prove* is preferred to *bolster;* and for *pointless, meaningless* to *rounded.* (Some of these pairings might be suitable for examinees who speak the British version of the language. However, the norms appear to be based wholly on Americans and the test is marketed in the United States.)

Such difficulties are usually thought likely to lead to considerable guessing by examinees, to reduced reliability, and to poor validity. Other vocabulary tests have achieved useful results without such ambiguities, archaisms, and odd definitions. Even if some gain in validity of one kind or another resulted from these means, it might not be worth it. A test serves many functions, intended or not. It is, for example, a learning experience for the examinee. The examinee also judges the whole testing movement on the basis of his perceptions of the fairness and relevance of the tests he takes. Surely it is important on a number of grounds to be as accurate, fair, and relevant as we can in our tests.

The idea of sampling words for a vocabulary test from a dictionary is a superficially attractive one. But a dictionary is a repository of (not entirely obsolete) words and does not distinguish, other than by the length of the listings, the relative importance of the words. How should the items in a vocabulary test be chosen? Many would agree that the stimulus words should represent a sample from some population of words. But what is the best population? In a spelling test developed for the *Clerical Skills Series,* Bruce chose the stimulus words on the basis of his observations of common errors in business contexts. For the applications to industry intended by Bruce, it might be appropriate to sample from the *Wall Street Journal* or *Business Week.* Then, one could assess the degree to which the examinee has a relevant vocabulary. The basic difficulty is not the choice of an old British dictionary to sample from, but the choice of any dictionary.

The directions give the examinee no hint of whether he should guess if uncertain of the answer. Since the score is the number correct, the examinee who guesses has an advantage.

Reliability and validity are discussed only very briefly in the manual. Reliability is on the low side but is adequate as reported. Validity data consist entirely of correlations with other tests. More data are available on the vocabulary test of the *Clerical Skills Series,* consisting of the odd-numbered items of this test. The latter data are generally favorable and suggest that, if data are collected for the full version, they may be better than inspection of the test suggests.

It is possible that the *Bruce Vocabulary Inventory* may have some value in rather specialized applications, but its use at present, especially for persons who learned English in America, is not recommended.

[232]

RBH Vocabulary Test. Applicants for clerical and stenographic positions; 1948–63; 1 form ('48, 2 pages); manual ['63, 8 pages]; directions (no date, 2 pages); no data on reliability; $3.50 per 25 tests; 50¢ per key; $1.50 per manual; $1.50 per specimen set; postage extra; 5(10) minutes; Richardson, Bellows, Henry & Co., Inc. *

FRED H. BORGEN, *Research Psychologist, National Merit Scholarship Corporation, Evanston, Illinois.*

The *RBH Vocabulary Test* is designed as a brief measure of verbal skills for use in the "screening and selection of applicants of both sexes for a variety of clerical and stenographic positions." Sixty-four pairs of words are presented on a single page and the examinee is given a total of five minutes to decide whether the words in each pair mean the same thing, are opposite in meaning, or are neither the same nor opposite. Inspection of the items substantiates the manual's claim that the items are appropriate for a wide range of clerical applicants, with item-difficulties apparently suitable for all but the marginally literate and the exceptionally able.

Two pairs of words, which are synonyms in this reviewer's dictionary, are incorrectly keyed. The words *effrontery-temerity* are incorrectly keyed as opposites and *limpid-lucid* are incorrectly keyed as being neither synonyms nor antonyms. Such carelessness is a matter of concern on a test as brief as this where reliability is likely to be marginal even when the test is correctly scored.

Wisely, the normative and other data have been presented separately for men and women; the normative data for women, representing both applicant and employee groups, are somewhat more precise. However, this apparent preciseness of the norms is seductive, since the composition of the norm groups is neither well specified nor representative of any significant population. Cross-checking of the tables in the manual reveals that a single oil company was the source for *all* of the women in the employees' norm group and 91 percent of the men in the male norm group. Thus, the norms are not representative of any widely relevant reference group and, at best, will have only suggestive value in most settings. Users should take seriously the authors' injunction that "norms developed on local populations are always of most value."

For some unexplained reason, the authors present no reliability data to demonstrate either internal consistency or temporal stability for scores on this test. If one were evaluating a test for personnel decisions and were forced to have either reliability *or* validity data, he no doubt would choose validity data. The fact that the present validity data show some non-zero relationship of *Vocabulary Test* scores with job performance does indicate minimal reliability for this 64-item test. Moreover, the correlations for this test with other tests do at least give some lower-bound estimates of the reliability of this instrument. For example, scores on this test are shown to correlate .77 with scores on the *RBH Test of Language Skills*. But why must we perform such mental gymnastics to divine the reliability of this test when the authors could easily have calculated reliability coefficients? Such information should be considered mandatory, particularly for an instrument which consists of only a five-minute sample of behavior.

It is refreshing to see validity data reported with such candor. The manual presents eight small-scale validity studies in samples of clerical workers, usually with annual performance ratings as the criterion. Regrettably, the authors do not make clear whether the coefficients reflect concurrent or predictive validity. Five of the eight validity coefficients fall between .15 and .21, and—here the candor enters—two of the coefficients are embarrassingly negative at −.08 and −.14. Because of the very small size of most of the validation samples, the correlations are statistically significant for only two studies; however, if one is willing to pool the results over the several studies, he should be able to conclude confidently that there is a generally significant relationship between test score

and clerical performance. For seven of the eight validity studies the manual explicitly reports that this vocabulary test was used, at least in part, for the selection of the employees in the validation samples. Consequently, there is some truncation of test score variance in these samples and the obtained correlations probably underestimate the actual validity of the test as a selection device. It seems fair to conclude that the test has a promising, though quite modest, capacity to predict performance in some clerical occupations.

The authors have made a good beginning in presenting validity data. Confidence in the instrument will be enhanced by continued development of more extensive and more precise validity information. Future studies should be based on larger samples, and some studies should include other predictive variables to indicate the incremental validity of this particular test. Such extended information should help the potential user identify the kinds of situations where this test is likely to be most appropriate as a selection device.

In summary, this is an attractively packaged test which *appears* to be a well-designed quick measure of the verbal skills of applicants for clerical and stenographic positions. The data presented in the manual partially confirm these expectations for the test, although the manual is distressingly brief and is particularly negligent in failing to report reliability data. No claims can be made for the generality of the norms; users will be better served by locally developed norms. Because of the sparseness of the information in the manual, the ideal user of this test should be qualified to judge the merit of this instrument for personnel decisions in his own setting. This effort would include: (*a*) modifying the present scoring key for the two items which are miskeyed; and (*b*) collecting local normative, reliability, and validity data. Potential users not prepared to undertake these steps should probably await appropriate revisions and clarification by the test publishers.

[233]

*Sanders-Fletcher Vocabulary Test. 1, 2 semesters in grades 9–13; 1938–64; first published 1938 in the Every Pupil Scholarship Test series; Forms A, B, ('64, 4 pages); 2 levels labeled Tests 1, 2; manual ('64, 3 pages); $1.75 per 25 tests, postage extra; 75¢ per specimen set, postpaid; 40(45) minutes; Gwen Fletcher and M. W. Sanders; Data Processing and Educational Measurement Center. *

[234]

*Survey Test of Vocabulary. Grades 3–12; 1931–65; Forms X₄ ('40, 4 pages, identical with Form X copyrighted 1931), Z₄ ('65, 4 pages); no manual; key-norms sheets (no dates); no data on reliability; $2.25 per 50 tests, postage extra; 25¢ per specimen set, post-paid; 20(25) minutes; L. J. O'Rourke; O'Rourke Publications. *

REFERENCES
1. See 3:167.
2–4. See 5:239.

For reviews by Verner M. Sims and Clifford Woody, see 3:167.

[235]

Vocabulary Test for High School Students and College Freshmen. Grades 9–13; 1964; Forms A, B, (2 pages); manual (9 pages); reliability data for longer experimental form only; provisional norms; $3.60 per 35 IBM 1230 test-answer sheets; $1 per set of scoring stencils; 60¢ per specimen set; postage extra; 15(20) minutes; Arthur E. Traxler; Bobbs-Merrill Co., Inc. *

REFERENCE
1. Traxler, Arthur E. "Some Aspects of the Vocabulary of Independent Secondary School Pupils." *Ed Rec B* 87:44–9 F '65. *

George P. Winship, Jr., *Professor of English and Chairman of the Department, King College, Bristol, Tennessee.*

Two neat little vocabulary tests, 50 words apiece, not in booklets but printed directly on IBM answer sheets, promise great usefulness. They are simple to administer, take only 15 minutes of working time, and cost about a dime a copy.

The tests were copyrighted in 1964, having been constructed and tried out in the early '60's. The words and definitions were chosen, however, not on the basis of what students were then reading and having trouble in understanding, but rather from the Thorndike-Lorge frequency list (published in 1944 but based upon much earlier books) and from the *Thorndike Century Senior Dictionary* of 1941. The impression given by the tests is strangely quaint, like that of a reprinted Montgomery Ward catalog or a McGuffey *Reader.*

The stem words are given in a sentence or brief context, but the compiler appears to have worked from his frequency list and his dictionary in isolation from the living language on which students are to be tested. An item reads, "Her dress has longitudinal stripes," although that adjective is generally employed for a horizontal dimension, and dresses are always described with the wearer standing. (Even the *Shorter Oxford Dictionary* marks the vertical use as obsolete.) *Combustible* is matched to *inflammable* in spite of the confusion recently

created by the revival of *flammable* in this sense. For "She has a *seductive* manner," the correct answer is *captivating,* in spite of what high school and college students have been reading the past few years. "He used the native *parlance*" is to be equated with *language,* as if *parlance* were normally used for Spanish, French, Swahili, or the like. Any of these items might have been produced with a dictionary by a foreigner knowing a little English, or by a computer. Few items do anything to teach or to test a really sensitive command of idiomatic English, and some of them actually penalize the well-read student who has met the words in a variety of literary contexts.

Mental measurements are not diagnostic tools in isolation from the whole process of education; they are an element in education. A vocabulary test may render a young person more or less aware of the meanings and use of words. The student is a living being, and the cells of his intellect ought not to be killed under the microscope.

J Ed Meas 3:71–2 sp '66. Joan Bollenbacher. * An unfortunate misprint in Table 4 should be noted * "*ACT* Total Score" is listed in error, instead of "*ACE* Total Score." While the ACE Total Score is discussed in the text, the casual reader who looks only at the statistical table could misinterpret this statistic as relating to the American College Test. * the manual....is clearly written and should be understood even by those who are scared of statistics * In the view of English curriculum consultants whom the writer consulted, the range of difficulty of the items is such that it should make the test a useful instrument to determine which pupils are weak in vocabulary, which are proficient. The instructions are clear and should cause no problem. The pale blue print of the IBM 1230 answer sheet, however, may be difficult for some pupils to read. Perhaps a darker ink compatible to the 1230 could be located for the next printing. The item choices are well done and contain no clues that would give the word away. In summary, the test is a good one to provide just what the author said—"a simple, easily and quickly administered test of general vocabulary for use with high school students and freshmen entering college."

[236]

★Vocabulary Test: McGraw-Hill Basic Skills System. Grades 11–14; 1970; also called *MHBSS*

Vocabulary Test; although designed for use with the MHBSS instructional program, the test may be used independently; Forms A, B, (7 pages); manual (31 pages); separate answer sheets (Digitek, IBM 1230, Scoreze) must be used; $4.90 per 25 tests; $2.50 per 50 Digitek or IBM answer sheets; $3 per 25 Scoreze answer sheets; $1 per Digitek or IBM scoring stencil; postage extra; $1.25 per specimen set, postpaid; IBM scoring service, 25¢ and over per test ($20 minimum); 12(22) minutes; Alton L. Raygor; McGraw-Hill Book Co., Inc. *

GEORGE P. WINSHIP, JR., *Professor of English and Chairman of the Department, King College, Bristol, Tennessee.*

These tests are part of the extensive battery of tests, tapes, books, and cards comprising the McGraw-Hill's Basic Skills System. Though only the vocabulary test is discussed here, it should be considered in relation to all these materials.

They have been produced, according to the publisher, largely for the sake of ill-prepared students who are attempting the college experience under open admissions policies. Specifically, the materials begin at a tenth-grade level of difficulty with content from college subjects. There are tests to diagnose deficiencies in several distinct elements of intellectual skill (listening, skimming, taking notes, and the like)— more than a dozen skills grouped in six tests, of which vocabulary, at 12 minutes, is the shortest. There are instructional and practice materials for each of the skills, and a parallel form of each test to confirm after the practice that the skill has indeed been learned.

The purpose is worthy, for the sake of the millions who have the maturity, ambition, and intelligence to profit from college but who lack the techniques of study. These are not only the "disadvantaged"; recommended youngsters from good schools need some of this help.

The vocabulary tests are in two parts. First are 30 words to be identified by meaning (6 minutes), then 25 problems in interpreting roots and affixes (the rest of the student's 12 minutes); for an average score he should finish about half the items correctly. The words are drawn from fields studied in college (examples are, *morphology, anode, antecedent, primogeniture*); the items are carefully ordered by difficulty. This part is directly diagnostic of the deficiencies in vocabulary which will give a student trouble. The second part tests ability to use etymology to master hard words. It contains artificial combinations for which he must select plausible meanings (*neophobia* he should iden-

tify as "fear of newness," *reduct,* as "to lead again").

The part with artificial words will seem to most teachers the more interesting, I believe, and to most students the more bewildering. A highly qualified student who has been taught to notice etymology will be put off by some insensitively constructed nonce words: the unlikely *nonvoluta* and *satisverus* may make him pause (and lose points). For *malvert* he is required to select "a bad turn," but he ought to boggle at it for a moment, searching in vain for the proper equivalent, "to turn badly" ("a bad turn" might be a *malversion*). So the best student will be penalized. But this ideal student was not intended to use the MHBSS in the first place.

Much more likely is that the *average* student on the first, or diagnostic, test will be so confused by this unfamiliar way of gauging his knowledge that he will score deceptively low. Such has been my experience when a class meets a problem that is novel or original; and I have tried this kind of etymological exercise. There are wide differences in the students' ability to cope with the unfamiliar. This ability, of course, is important to success in college, but it is not the same as knowing words. The present test is supposed to diagnose a particular weakness and to measure the success of particular MHBSS materials. But it is certainly possible that the second test, after the instruction, will come as a more familiar and much less formidable task; would the second scores not be higher, for many students, whether the instruction had been effective or not? (Only trials in which students take both tests without intervening lessons in etymology can resolve this possible ambiguity of the test scores.)

In view of our sense of urgency to meet the needs of the ill-prepared and of the advent of schemes that promise quick and measurable gains for problem students, we must take great care that our measures are valid as well as reliable.

[237]

Word Clue Tests. Grades 7–13 and adults; 1962–65; designed primarily for use with instructional booklets in the Word Clues series; 2 tests; manual ('65, 6 pages); no data on reliability; no norms; separate answer sheets must be used; 25¢ per test; $2 per 100 answer sheets; 20¢ per scoring stencil; 50¢ per manual (free with 25 or more tests); postage extra; (40–45) minutes; Stanford E. Taylor, Helen Frackenpohl, and Arthur S. McDonald; Educational Developmental Laboratories, Inc. *

a) WORD CLUE TEST. WCT; Forms A, B, ('62, 15 pages); 65¢ per specimen set.
b) WORD CLUE APPRAISAL. WCA; special edition available to nonprofessionals for self appraisal; Forms AA ('62, 15 pages), BB ('65, 15 pages).

[238]
★**Word Understanding.** Grades 6–12; 1969; WU; 1 form; 2 editions; manual ['69, 3 pages]; norms for

junior high school only; $3.75 per 25 tests; 50¢ per manual; $1 per specimen set of either edition; postpaid; 8(10) minutes; R. Hoepfner, M. Hendricks, and R. H. Silverman; Monitor. *
a) REUSABLE EDITION. 1 form (3 pages); separate answer sheets (IBM 805) must be used; $1 per 25 answer sheets; 50¢ per scoring stencil.
b) CONSUMABLE EDITION. Form C (3 pages); 50¢ per key.

FINE ARTS

REVIEWS BY *Richard Colwell, Edwin Gordon, Paul R. Lehman, Robert W. Lundin, John McLeish, and Roger P. Phelps.*

ART

[239]
★**Art Vocabulary.** Grades 6–12; 1969; AV; 1 form; 2 editions; manual ['69, 3 pages]; norms for grade 7 only; $7.50 per 25 tests; 50¢ per manual; $2 per specimen set of either edition; postpaid; 20(25) minutes; R. H. Silverman, R. Hoepfner, and M. Hendricks; Monitor. *
a) REUSABLE EDITION. 1 form (7 pages); separate answer sheets (IBM 805) must be used; $1 per 25 answer sheets; $1 per scoring stencil.
b) CONSUMABLE EDITION. Form C (7 pages); $1 per scoring key.

[240]
The Meier Art Tests. Grades 7–16 and adults, 9–16 and adults; 1929–63; 2 tests; postage extra; Norman Charles Meier; Bureau of Educational Research and Service. *
a) THE MEIER ART TESTS: 1, ART JUDGMENT. Grades 7–16 and adults; 1929–42; revision of *Meier-Seashore Art Judgment Test;* 1 form ('40, 101 pages); manual ('42, 24 pages); separate answer sheets (IBM 805) must be used; 5–24 tests, $1.50 each; 6¢ per answer sheet; 60¢ per set of machine scoring stencils; 6¢ per hand scoring record sheet; 20¢ per hand scoring key; 40¢ per manual; $1.75 per specimen set; (45–60) minutes.
b) THE MEIER ART TESTS: 2, AESTHETIC PERCEPTION. Grades 9–16 and adults; 1963; 1 form (53 pages); preliminary manual (4 pages); no data on reliability; tentative norms; separate record sheets must be used; 5–24 tests, $1.75 each; 6¢ per record sheet; 30¢ per hand scoring key; $1.85 per specimen set; administration time not reported.

REFERENCES
1–15. See 2:1326.
16–19. See 3:172.
20–28. See 4:224.
29–36. See 6:346.
37. MILLMAN, MARCIA, AND CHANG, TERESA. "Inter-Correlations Among Three Widely Used Art Tests." *Percept & Motor Skills* 23:1002 D '66. *
38. KEESEE, CURTIS GORDON, JR. *The Relationship of Performance on the Scholastic Aptitude Test, the Meier Art Judgment Test, and the Graves Design Judgment Test to Successful Completion of Freshmen Commercial Art Courses.* Doctor's thesis, University of Virginia (Charlottesville, Va.), 1967. (*DA* 28:2516A) (Abstract: *Ed R* 5:58–60)
39. QUEENEY, DONNA SUSAN SUTIN. *A Study of Aesthetic Value and Aesthetic Sensitivity as Related to the Home.* Doctor's thesis, Pennsylvania State University (University Park, Pa.), 1967. (*DA* 28:3771B)
40. ROGERS, DONALD WESLEY. *A Comparison of Selected Art Abilities of Elementary School Students From Varying Socioeconomic Levels.* Doctor's thesis, University of Connecticut (Storrs, Conn.), 1967. (*DA* 28:3381A)
41. SCHROTH, MARVIN L. "Spatial Aptitude and Its Relationship to Art Judgment." *Percept & Motor Skills* 24:746 Je '67. *
42. STALLINGS, WILLIAM M., AND ANDERSON, FRANCES E. "Some Characteristics and Correlates of the Meier Art Test of Aesthetic Perception Under Two Systems of Scoring." *J Ed Meas* 6(3):179–85 f '69. * (*PA* 44:14571)
43. SLOANE, PATRICIA. "Art and Art Token in Tests Involving Art Evaluation." *Psychol Rec* 20(2):191–6 sp '70. * (*PA* 45:2366)

J Counsel Psychol 11:98 sp '64. Laurence Siegel. [Review of test 2.] * the presently available preliminary manual is supposed to provide for the test's use until the revision is published. This manual does not provide even the minimum amount of statistical evidence ordinarily anticipated for operational instruments. Even the scoring key now distributed with the test is tentative. This key "....represents a combination of judgments of a limited number of artists and about 350 art students and teachers." The way in which these judgments were combined to produce a scoring key is not clarified. The earlier experimental form of the test, consisting of 70 items, was administered to a pilot group. Item analyses of the resultant data produced the present set of 50 items. The manual states that when these 50 items were tested, the results indicated that the new version was "....a far superior and sensitive instrument." Presumably, the comparison here implied was with the pre-item analysis version. The test as published has been administered to approximately 350 high school students taking art and to 350 college-adult subjects. The results of these administrations provide what norms are now available. Reliability data are not cited. Validity of a sort is inferred from a progression of mean test scores obtained for mature artists, younger artists, and high school students taking art. In view of the paucity of data now available for *Aesthetic Perception,* including the lack of reported correlations with other tests, the reviewer was surprised by the following rather strong statement in the manual: "Insofar as the test is not predicated upon learning, general intelligence, or general physiological maturation, it would seem very probable that the test is measuring something basic in the art-ability complex." Although the test may not be *predicated* upon learning, intelligence, or maturation, it may nevertheless be reflecting some or all of these conditions in spite of its face validity. *Summary. Aesthetic Perception* is an experimental test probably measuring something related to artistic ability. The nature and utility of the functions measured are not clarified by the data provided in the preliminary manual. The independence of these functions from those measured by the *Art Judgment Test* also remains to be demonstrated.

For a review by Harold A. Schultz of test 2, see 6:346; for a review by Harold A. Schultz of test 1, see 4:224; for a review by Edwin Ziegfeld, see 3:172; for reviews by Paul R. Farnsworth and Aulus Ward Saunders of the original edition of test 1, see 2:1326.

[241]
*National Teacher Examinations: Art Education. College seniors and teachers; 1961–70; Forms K-ONT ('69, 21 pages), RNT ('69, 23 pages), SNT1 ('70, 19 pages), SNT2 ('70, 20 pages); descriptive booklet ('70, 8 pages); for more complete information, see 582; 120(165) minutes; Educational Testing Service. *

For a review by Harold A. Schultz of earlier forms, see 6:345. For reviews of the testing program, see 582 (2 reviews), 6:700 (1 review), 5:538 (3 reviews), and 4:802 (1 review).

[242]
★The Undergraduate Record Examinations: Art History Test. College; 1970; Form SUR (33 pages); descriptive booklet (8 pages); for more complete information, see 671; 120(140) minutes; Educational Testing Service. *

For reviews of the testing program, see 671 (2 reviews).

MUSIC

[243]
*The Graduate Record Examinations Advanced Music Test. Graduate school candidates; 1951–70; 3 current forms ('66–70, 40–52 pages); descriptive booklet ('70, 8 pages); for more complete information, see 667; 180(200) minutes; Educational Testing Service. *

For a review by William S. Larson of an earlier form, see 5:247. For reviews of the testing program, see 667 (1 review) and 5:601 (1 review).

[244]
★The Gretsch-Tilson Musical Aptitude Test. Grades 4–12; 1938; 1 form (33⅓ rpm record); manual (4 pages); $4.25 per record; $2.20 per 100 answer sheets; 50¢ per scoring stencil; postage extra; (25) minutes; Lowell Mason Tilson; Fred Gretsch Co., Inc. *

REFERENCES
1. TILSON, LOWELL MASON. "A Study of the Prognostic Value of the Tilson-Gretsch Musical Aptitude Tests." *Teach Col J* 12:110–2 My '41. *
2. JUNG, JOSEPH WEILAND. *A Study of the Factors Associated With Music Participation by Secondary School Pupils in the Suburban Areas of Minneapolis and St. Paul.* Doctor's thesis, University of Minnesota (Minneapolis, Minn.), 1954. (*DA* 14:2007)

[245]
★Iowa Tests of Music Literacy. Grades 4–12, 7–12; 1970; ITML; 9 scores: tonal concepts (aural perception, reading recognition, notational understanding, total), rhythmic concepts (aural perception, reading recognition, notational understanding, total), total; 1 form (4 pages, MRC test-answer folder); Levels 1–3 for grades 4–12, Levels 4–6 for grades 7–12; tape recording (1½ mil) for each level; Xerox copy of manual manuscript (156 pages); $48 per set of tapes; 10¢ per test-answer folder; $1.50 per set of hand scoring stencils; $3.50 per manual; $4 per specimen set; postpaid; scoring service, 30¢ per student; 72(90) minutes in 2 sessions; Edwin Gordon; Bureau of Educational Research and Service. *

REFERENCES
1. HUYSER, BETTY H. *The Effects of Orff Rhythm Activities on Selected Scores of the Iowa Tests of Music Literacy.* Master's thesis, Drake University (Des Moines, Iowa), 1970.
2. SWINDELL, WARREN C. *An Investigation of the Adequacy of the Content and Difficulty Levels of the Iowa Tests of Music Literacy.* Doctor's thesis, University of Iowa (Iowa City, Iowa), 1970. (*DAI* 31:4827A)

[246]
*Knuth Achievement Tests in Music: Recognition of Rhythm and Melody. Grades 3–4, 5–6, 7–12; 1936–68; KATM; manual title is *Achievement Tests in Music;* reissue of the 1936 edition using filmstrips and prerecorded tapes; Forms A, B, ['68, filmstrip and 7½ ips tape, identical with tests copyrighted in 1936 except for format]; 3 levels; manual ('67, 10 pages, with 1936 reliability data and norms); $25 per set of filmstrips and tapes for all levels of one form, 100 answer sheets, scoring stencil and manual; $2 per manual; postage extra; [40–50] minutes; William E. Knuth; Creative Arts Research Associates, Inc. *
a) DIVISION 1. Grades 3–4.
b) DIVISION 2. Grades 5–6.
c) DIVISION 3. Grades 7–12.

REFERENCES

1. See 2:1332.
2. SLAGLE, HAROLD CLAYTON. *An Investigation of the Effect of Seven Methods of Instruction on the Musical Achievement of Elementary Education Majors.* Doctor's thesis, University of Illinois (Urbana, Ill.), 1967. (*DA* 28:5098A)

For a review by Carl E. Seashore, see 2:1332; for reviews by Jay W. Fay and James L. Mursell, see 1:1085.

[247]

★**Measures of Musical Abilities.** Ages 7–14; 1966; MMA; 1 form (33⅓ rpm record); manual (8 pages); £1.65 per set of record and manual; 37½p per 25 answer sheets; 12½p per manual; postage extra; 21 (30) minutes; Arnold Bentley; George G. Harrap & Co. Ltd. * (United States distributor: October House, Inc.)

REFERENCES

1. BENTLEY, ARNOLD. *A Study of Some Aspects of Musical Ability Amongst Young Children, Including Those Unable to Sing in Tune.* Doctor's thesis, University of Reading (Reading, England), 1963.
2. BENTLEY, ARNOLD. *Musical Ability in Children and Its Measurement.* London: George G. Harrap & Co. Ltd., 1966. Pp. 151. *
3. McLEISH, JOHN, AND HIGGS, GEOFFREY. *An Inquiry Into the Musical Capacities of Educationally Sub-Normal Children.* Occasional Research Papers No. 1. Cambridge, England: Cambridge Institute of Education, [1967]. Pp. ii, 12. *
4. BENTLEY, ARNOLD. "Monotones, Musical Abilities and the Larynx." *J Ed (Vancouver)* 14:44–55 Ap '68. *
5. BENTLEY, ARNOLD. "Musical Abilities of Children." *J Ed (Vancouver)* 14:36–43 Ap '68. *
6. McLEISH, JOHN. "The Validity and Reliability of Bentley's Measures of Musical Abilities." *Brit J Ed Psychol* 38:201 Je '68. * (*PA* 42:16419)
7. BENTLEY, ARNOLD. "Measurement and Development of Musical Abilities: Some Research Interests and Findings." *J Res Music Ed* 17(1):41–6 sp '69. *
8. BENTLEY, ARNOLD. "Some Research Interests and Findings." *J Res Music Ed* 17(1):41–6 sp '69. *
9. CLEAK, RONALD E. "Measurement and Development of Musical Abilities: Educational and Social Factors." *J Res Music Ed* 17(1):51–6 sp '69. *
10. ROWNTREE, JOHN P. "Measurement and Development of Musical Abilities: Evaluation of Bentley Measures." *J Res Music Ed* 17(1):88–9 sp '69. *
11. ROWNTREE, JOHN PICKERING. *A Critical Evaluation of the Bentley "Measures of Musical Ability" With Particular Reference to Practice Effect on Various of the Subtests.* Master's thesis, University of Newcastle Upon Tyne (Newcastle Upon Tyne, England), 1969.
12. BENTLEY, ARNOLD. "A Comparison of a Musician's Assessments With Data From the Bentley 'Measures of Musical Abilities.'" *Council Res Music Ed B* 22:17–24 f '70. *
13. ROWNTREE, JOHN P. "The Bentley 'Measures of Musical Abilities'—A Critical Evaluation." *Council Res Music Ed B* 22:25–32 f '70. *

RICHARD COLWELL, *Professor of Secondary and Continuing Education and Music, University of Illinois, Urbana, Illinois.*

The *Measures of Musical Abilities* was developed as a test of musical ability in young children, ages 7 to 12. Norms are also provided for ages 13 and 14. There are several advantages in this battery which have led to its acceptance. Primary among these are the clarity of the directions, the reasonableness of the testing time for younger students, and general acceptance by the music profession of the tasks required. Of the four subtests in the battery, pitch discrimination, tonal memory, and rhythmic memory are similar in nature to tasks in the Seashore and other older measures. The fourth section, chord analysis, resembles a subtest in the *Wing Standardised Tests of Musical Intelligence.*

Use of the sine wave oscillator and the pipe organ to produce the sounds, subjects the tests to the same criticisms of nonmusicality and artificiality that have long been voiced against the Seashore, Kwalwasser and other aptitude tests. However, restriction of the range of these sounds to those of the singing range of the small child, and the use of larger intervals, three cycles per second being the finest discrimination in the pitch section with a range to 26 cycles per second (a semitone), make the tests less difficult than the Seashore. The test is well paced with instructions given slowly and understandably. The timing between items is not rushed and the seven-year-old should not be confused. Several examples are given in an instructional manner for each subtest. For example, in the chord analysis section, a chord is defined, the notes are played arpeggiated, and a clear explanation is given of exactly what is expected of the student in distinguishing a two-, three-, or four-note chord. In the test, the chord is played in the normal fashion.

Both the seven-page manual which accompanies the test, and the text *Musical Ability in Children* (*2*) are deficient in giving the type of data recommended in *Standards for Educational and Psychological Tests and Manuals.* Some of these will be pointed out in the course of this review. Bentley argues that he is measuring basic ability because the gain of an entire class, on an immediate second testing, is only about three percent. Scores increase over a year's time span at the rate of six to seven percent. Second, he claims that because the range of scores is great at each grade level, this is a further indicator of aptitude. The scores of graduate music majors, of string teachers and of choral students, which are much higher than the general population, are cited as additional proof of criterion-related validity.

The gain scores are rather significant. Scores on the standardization sample increase from 20.4 at seven years of age to 42.0 at fourteen, a gain of almost 34 percent. The work of other researchers indicates an even greater gain; Rowntree (*13*) reports a 28 percent gain from grades 7 to 10. Bentley has probably isolated factors which are easily teachable with formal musical instruction but are not emphasized in the regular school program. This would account for the range of scores across age levels found in his heterogeneous population and for the high scores of the select groups.

The validity of the chord analysis section has been seriously challenged. The author believes that "it is necessary for the singer or monophonic instrumentalist to be aware of the different sounds of other singers or instrumentalists in performance and the greater his awareness, the more appropriate one's contribution to the ensemble is likely to be." His own work, however, found that children do not achieve more than a chance score in this subtest before the age of 11—yet the test is designed for children 7 to 14 (2). This age level criterion is crucial in appraising the test, as the test has little discrimination with older students. Music graduates obtain correct answers on more than 90 percent of the questions and even with unselected adults, over 86 percent of the tonal and rhythmic memory sections are marked correctly. Rowntree (11) has also challenged the nature of the children's responses to this section of the test. It appears that the section might well be dropped; however, this would materially affect the entire battery as the chord analysis subtest is a major part, weighting the test in difficulty and number of items.

Bentley fails to give adequate information on standardization procedures and sampling techniques. He worked carefully with several small groups on various problems and there is an indication that data exist for approximately 1,200 subjects, at least with respect to sex differences, but most data are based on samples of from 90 to 150. Reliability, using 90 boys and girls 9.1 to 11.9 years of age and a mean age of 10.9, is reported as .84 obtained by test-retest with a time interval of four months. Grouping by age levels, of course, leads to a spuriously high reliability. Rowntree's work with a block sample of 3,000 children between the ages of 7 and 11 indicates that the reliability for 10-year-old subjects is closer to .60. Similar discrepancies occur for reliabilities of the subtests.

Bentley does an excellent job in the seven-page manual of suggesting some cautions in interpreting data from the test. He elects to give norms by grade level only in the following manner: A for the top 10 percent, B for the next 20 percent, a grade of C for the middle 40 percent, and so on. He feels that more exact norms might be misleading. Further questions

about the reliability of the battery can be asked in view of this broad normative system. On a test-retest, with an interval of one year, 57 percent of his standardization sample would be in a different category (A, B, C, etc.), 30 percent moving up by *at least* one letter grade, 27 percent moving down. His norms have been challenged by at least two researchers; Rowntree suggests that the mean for seven-year-olds should be 14.2 rather than 20.4 and that for ten-year-olds, 31.0 rather than 28.6. The combined work of Bentley, Jack[1] and Rowntree would lower the mean score by four points for seven-year-olds and raise it nearly two points for the ten-year-olds. Use of a correction for guessing formula, seldom recommended by this reviewer, might be of real help in interpreting the norms for this test. The grade of E for the bottom 10 percent of the standardization sample is below chance score for grades 7 through 10. A score of as few as one or two points above chance would still be a low score, even for young children, in a test that accurately measures their musical potential.

With the exception of the chord analysis section, the test comprises the type of tasks one can reasonably expect of a young child. However, even though the tunes section is reasonable, it may not accurately reflect a student's native ability. Young students may become so busy counting the notes in order to answer in the required fashion that they find it difficult to listen with the proper degree of attention. Counting in the rhythm section does not present the same disadvantage, because the testee listens and counts with the beat. This, rather than note counting, is the normal task in music.

Part intercorrelations are rather high (.40 and higher for tonal memory, chord recognition, and pitch). One explanation is that much of this is a general musical factor, but this does require further investigation.

Bentley is obviously a careful, knowledgeable worker in test construction, and the instructions for the administration and interpretation of test results are good. The manual does not, however, provide item analysis data nor is an indication given that this has been done by grade level. Some indication of difficulty is given for the

[1] JACK, DAVID A. *Testing Musical Ability: An Investigation and Review of Dr. Arnold Bentley's Measures of Musical Abilities.* Unpublished paper, 1967, available from Music Department, Wellington Teachers College, Wellington, New Zealand.

pitch and chordal analysis subtest but only in the most general terms.

The test is an excellent research tool and very usable due to the data available from a variety of small studies and the time length of the test. However, these data must be interpreted in terms of research completed subsequent to the publication of the test. The *Musical Aptitude Profile* or the *Seashore Measures of Musical Talents,* less usable but more reliable instruments, should continue to be used where normative data are a critical factor.

JOHN McLEISH, *Professor of Educational Psychology, University of Alberta, Edmonton, Alberta, Canada.*

This test can be used with confidence for measuring musical ability of children 9 years of age and older. It is easy to use, interesting to both musical and nonmusical children, and is highly satisfactory from the standpoint of validity and reliability. Adapting it for individual testing (by re-recording the items on tape, and permitting frequent rest pauses) it has been used successfully with eight-year-old educationally subnormal children.

In comparison with Seashore's and Wing's tests it was found to be much more economical of time, generated much less test anxiety and was more convenient to use (being on two sides of one record). In testing fairly young children (ages 8–11), the reviewer found that the Wing and Seashore tests each demanded a whole morning whereas the Bentley could be administered easily within a 40-minute period. The Seashore and Wing tests both presented difficulties to these children: no similar problems were encountered in using Bentley's measures. The instructions are particularly clear, concise, and comprehensive and are included on the record; this noticeably improves *rapport*. The interval between test items is adequate for the population for which the test was designed. The factor loadings on musical ability were found by this reviewer to be higher, on the average, than in the Wing and Seashore tests: Seashore, .62; Wing, .47; Bentley, .65. After one year, the test-retest reliability was found to be .83 (N = 105).

Two criticisms may be voiced, both rather tentatively. Although the test is particularly useful with children of relatively low intelligence and low musical talent, it appears to be inadequate in "headroom." A marked bunching of scores at the upper end of the scale is obtained with children who are in no way exceptionally talented. The other criticism relates to the "chords" subtest. Although this has a factor loading of .53 with the musical ability factor, it remains unclear what aspect of musical ability this subtest is measuring. Indeed, the theoretical rationale of the measures as a whole has not been made out. This criticism does not detract from their usefulness in practice. Whatever the Seashore and Wing tests are measuring, the Bentley measures more economically, more conveniently, and over a broader range of intellectual and musical abilities.

Cont Psychol 12:69–70 F '67. Paul R. Farnsworth. [Review of *Musical Ability in Children and Its Measurement (2).*] * The music aptitude tests now on the market have been planned so as to give ample top to the older and more musical testees but yet to keep some of the items easy enough for use on fourth graders. Dr. Bentley, the author of the book under review, has adopted a rather different strategy. He has devised a music aptitude test with young children in mind, dipping down as low as age seven. He has taken his test ideas largely from Seashore and Wing and offers subtests covering pitch discrimination, tonal memory, rhythmic memory, and chord analysis. * With only 60 items in the entire battery it is obvious that the subtests can have little reliability. In fact, the battery as a whole was found to have a retest reliability of only .84 when given to 90 children ranging in age from 9 years 10 months to 11 years 9 months. This figure would, of course, be a bit smaller for a single year and far smaller for persons in the older years where the test has little top. This lack of top is most serious and Bentley admits that even at age eight there were children in his normative group who made perfect scores on the two memory tests. Professor Bentley's little book is essentially a description of the conception and development of his music test battery. He has made the sorts of analyses all good testers make on their tests * With a bibliography of only 30 items, the book is not intended as a scholarly work but rather as an aid to unstatistically minded educators, particularly those in Britain. Dr. Bentley obviously hopes that his battery's major appeal will come from its validity data. He has employed four criteria of validity: estimates of musical ability by music teachers, progress in music, scores of skilled musicians, and comparisons with other measures of music ability. To the reviewer these data are not overly impressive. Dr. Bentley would seem better advised to spend less time trying to impress the music educators and to devote more attention to the improvement of his test battery. He should enlarge his test to insure better reliability and include more difficult items to furnish top for his more musical subjects. But even with such improvements he may find that his test battery is not well adapted to the enormous age range with which he desires to deal.

J Res Music Ed 15:91–2 sp '67. Richard R. Bentley. [Review of *Musical Ability in Children and Its Measurement (2)*.] * essentially a manual for a new musical ability test * thorough coverage * I do not feel....that there is sufficient evidence presented to support the conclusion that musical ability is largely innate * a significant book for those....particularly interested in the measurement of musical ability * also a significant book for all who are interested in the musical learning and development of children *

[248]

★Music Achievement Tests. Grades 3–12; 1967–70; MAT; first edition called *Elementary Music Achievement Tests*; 4 tests; interpretative manual for Tests 1 and 2 ('69, 142 pages), for Tests 3 and 4 ('70, 253 pages); separate answer sheets (Digitek) must be used; $6 per record; $4.50 per interpretative manual; $1.50 per manual; $1.50 per sample set; postage extra; scoring service available only from H. Robert Andrews (Prairie State College); Richard Colwell; Follett Educational Corporation. *
a) TEST 1. Grades 3–12; 1967–69; 4 scores: pitch discrimination, interval discrimination, meter discrimination, total; 1 form ['68, 33⅓ rpm record]; manual ('68, 31 pages); $4.02 per 35 answer sheets and scoring stencil; scoring service, 4¢ and over per test; 18(25) minutes.
b) TEST 2. Grades 4–12; 1967–69; 6 scores: major-minor mode discrimination, feeling for tonal center, auditory-visual discrimination (pitch, rhythm, total), total; 1 form ['68, 33⅓ rpm record]; manual ('68, 35 pages); $5.01 per 35 answer sheets and scoring stencil; scoring service, 7¢ and over per test; 28(35) minutes.
c) TEST 3. Grades 4–12; 1970; 5 scores: tonal memory, melody recognition, pitch recognition, instrument recognition, total; 1 form ['70, 33⅓ rpm record]; manual (32 pages); $5.01 per 35 answer sheets and scoring stencil; scoring service, 7¢ and over per test; 32(39) minutes.
d) TEST 4. Grades 5–12; 1970; 7 scores: musical style (composers, texture, total), auditory-visual discrimination, chord recognition, cadence recognition, total; 1 form ['70, 33⅓ rpm record]; manual (32 pages); $5.01 per 35 answer sheets and scoring stencil; scoring service, 7¢ and over per test; 38(45) minutes.

REFERENCES
1. SWINCHOSKI, ALBERT A. "A Standardized Music Achievement Test Battery for the Intermediate Grades." *J Res Music Ed* 13:159–68 f '65. * (*PA* 40:46)
2. SLAGLE, HAROLD CLAYTON. *An Investigation of the Effect of Seven Methods of Instruction on the Musical Achievement of Elementary Education Majors.* Doctor's thesis, University of Illinois (Urbana, Ill.), 1967. (*DA* 28:5098A)
3. STANDIFER, JAMES ALLRED. *Effects of Aesthetic Sensitivity of Secondary General Music Courses Designed to Develop Perception of Elements of Musical Expressiveness.* Doctor's thesis, Case Western Reserve University (Cleveland, Ohio), 1968. (*DAI* 30:3978A)
4. HINTON, THOMAS EARL. *An Investigation of Instructional Provisions and Student Achievement in Music in Tennessee Elementary Schools.* Doctor's thesis, George Peabody College for Teachers (Nashville, Tenn.), 1969. (*DAI* 31:1310A)
5. COLWELL, RICHARD. "The Development of the Music Achievement Test Series." *Council Res Music Ed B* 22:57–73 f '70. *

PAUL R. LEHMAN, *Professor of Music Education, Eastman School of Music, The University of Rochester, Rochester, New York.*

The four tests of the *Music Achievement Tests* are designed to measure achievement in certain basic skills of aural perception generally regarded as important in the school music curriculum. They are intended for use by either the classroom teacher or the music specialist, and each test may be used independently. The test stimuli are recorded by piano, violin, viola, and cello, and each test is presented on a single 33⅓ rpm recording. Other instruments are included in the Instrument Recognition subtest.

The content of MAT is based on the objectives stated or implied by eight leading basic series of music textbooks. Content validity is claimed on this basis and on the basis of consultation with leading music educators and examination of existing and proposed curriculums. A correlation of .92 between scores and teachers' selections of their five best and five poorest students is reported as evidence of criterion-related validity for Tests 1 and 2. Further, according to the manual, students with instrumental training consistently score higher than those without. Predictive validity is suggested by a reported correlation of .65 between scores for 26 seventh graders beginning instrumental study in September and their teachers' ratings the following June.

Tests 1 and 2 are based on objectives for grades 3 through 5 and Tests 3 and 4 are based on objectives for grades 6 through 8. However, because of the diversity among school music programs, norms are provided through grade 12 as follows: Test 1, each grade from 3 through 8, grades 9–12 combined, and grades 4–12 combined; Test 2, each grade from 4 through 8, grades 9–12 combined, and grades 4–12 combined; Test 3, each grade from 4 through 12; and Test 4, each grade from 5 through 12.

In addition, for Tests 3 and 4 norms are provided for grades 4–6 combined, grades 7–9 combined, and grades 10–12 combined, as well as for students with and without piano experience and instrumental experience. Similar norms for each subtest are included.

K-R 21 reliabilities are given for each test, subtest, and sub-subtest for each grade from 4 through 12 except that for Tests 1 and 2 grades 9–12 have been combined and for Test 4 the data begin with grade 5. The median reliabilities for the four tests, respectively, are .87, .91, .85, and .85. The medians of the within-grade reliabilities on the four tests range from .80 in grade 4 to .88 in grades 9–12. The subtest reliabilities, of course, tend to be lower. The medians of the within-grade reliabilities for the subtests of Test 1 are .83, .67, and .66; of Test 2, .69, .59, and .91 (Part 3 total); of Test 3, .72, .53, .65, and .62; and of Test 4, .74 (Part 1 total), .70, .77, and .39.

The Interpretative Manual for Tests 1 and 2 describes the process by which the tests were standardized and provides means and standard deviations for the various grades according to whether music was taught by a music specialist or by a classroom teacher, sex, geographic section of the country, and size of the community. For Test 2 there is also a breakdown according to the type of musical experiences the students have had. The percentile rank and standard score corresponding to each raw score are shown by grade level and by subtest for each test.

The Interpretative Manual for Tests 3 and 4 includes means, along with their standard deviations and reliabilities, according to grade, sex, geographic section, size of the school system, years of piano experience, if any, and years of instrumental experience, if any. Difficulty and discrimination indexes for each item are included in both manuals, as well as intercorrelations between the parts of the tests. There is also an Administrative and Scoring Manual for each test.

Tests 1 and 2 were standardized on a population of more than 20,000 students, representing 158 school systems in 43 states. Tests 3 and 4 were standardized on approximately 9,000 students, representing some 71 school systems in 29 states. The norms are based on nonselective groups.

The tests have been carefully constructed. They include several item types not previously used on standardized tests in music. The manuals are complete, the explanatory materials adequate, and the claims made for the tests are realistic.

The *Music Achievement Tests* are useful in providing students and teachers with evidence of progress toward meeting the objectives of the curriculum and in providing information of use in student guidance and in program evaluation. They may also be useful in group diagnostic work and in identifying students who will benefit from instrumental instruction. The author suggests that they can be of help in sectioning prospective classroom teachers for fundamentals and methods courses and that they can be used for "selected purposes" with college music majors, although no supporting data are offered. Despite a reference to the existence of college norms, no such norms are included.

"The author....has attempted to construct a test so that the teacher can give one part at a time, or use only two or three parts, without materially affecting the reliability." He has been only partially successful in this endeavor, however, and the existence of 22 scores does not suggest that all are equally useful. Colwell tacitly endorses the view of Leonhard and House that .80 represents the minimum reliability useful in the measurement of individuals and .50 constitutes the minimum for groups. By this standard, the total scores on all four tests are useful for individual work except for Test 3 in grades 4, 5, and 6. However, of the 36 subtest reliabilities given for Test 3, only 1 is as high as .80, and of the 48 subtest reliabilities for Test 4, only 5 exceed .80. Clearly these subtests are of limited utility for work with individuals. Similarly, Parts 2 and 3 of Test 1 are not useful, and Parts 1 and 2 of Test 2 are useful only at the high school level.

For group work, on the other hand, most subtests are useful except for those of Test 3 at the lower grade levels. Part 4 of Test 4 is a notable exception in that the highest reliability obtained at any level was .46. Perhaps because they are newer, Tests 3 and 4 are not yet as highly refined as Tests 1 and 2. The author claims, however, to have information suggesting that K-R 21 provides a low estimate of the true reliability of MAT.

In a few instances, often coinciding with low reliabilities, the item discrimination indexes also tend to be low. In Part 4 of Test 4, for example, they range from − .034 to .378 for grades 7–9, with a median of .227. Others which tend to be low include Part 2 of each test for grades 4–6, as well as parts 3 and 4 of Test 3; Part 2 of Test 3 for grades 7–9; Part 4 of Test 4 for grades 10–12; and Part 1a of Test 4 for all levels.

Many teachers will probably welcome a standardized measure in which the student must identify instruments. This subtest, however, calls for some subtle discriminations as, for example, between flute and piccolo, violin and viola, and claves and wood block. These discriminations are not unreasonable, but, particularly since a "none" option is included, they require that the sound reproducing equipment used be of better quality than that available in some classrooms.

Despite its limitations in assessing individuals, MAT is the best, most comprehensive, and most widely useful standardized achievement test battery in music currently available. Ultimately its usefulness to the teacher will be determined by the degree of correspondence between the skills that he is attempting to teach and the skills measured by the tests. Although some important aspects of musicianship are missing from MAT, this correspondence will normally be high. MAT is an important and valuable general-purpose test for use in a wide variety of situations.

[249]

★**Musical Aptitude Profile.** Grades 4–12; 1965; MAP; 11 scores: tonal imagery (melody, harmony, total), rhythm imagery (tempo, meter, total), musical sensitivity (phrasing, balance, style, total), total; stimulus material presented on 3 7½ ips tapes; manual (127 pages); student report (4 pages); record folder (3 pages); separate answer sheets (IBM 1230, MRC) must be used; $27 per set of tapes; $5.70 per 100 IBM 1230 answer sheets; $8.55 per 100 MRC answer sheets; $1.20 per set of IBM scoring stencils; $1.05 per set of MRC hand scoring stencils; $3.15 per 100 student reports; $9.60 per 100 record folders; $3.60 per manual; 96¢ per specimen set (without tapes or manual); postage extra; MRC scoring service, 30¢ per test; 110(150) minutes in 3 sessions; Edwin Gordon; Houghton Mifflin Co. *

REFERENCES

1. Fosha, Revone Leon. *A Study of the Concurrent Validity of the Musical Aptitude Profile.* Doctor's thesis, State University of Iowa (Iowa City, Iowa), 1964. (*DA* 25:5319)
2. Tarrell, Vernon Virgil. *An Investigation of the Validity of the Gordon Musical Aptitude Profile.* Doctor's thesis, State University of Iowa (Iowa City, Iowa), 1964. (*DA* 25:5326)
3. Culver, Florence Reusch. *Study of the Musical Aptitude Profile.* Master's thesis, University of Iowa (Iowa City, Iowa), 1965.
4. Gordon, Edwin. "The Music Aptitude Profile: A New and Unique Musical Aptitude Test Battery." *Council Res Music Ed B* 6:12–6 f '65. * (*PA* 40:4606)
5. Raim, Roland L. *A Comparison of the Musical Aptitude Profile and the Seashore Measures of Musical Talent.* Master's thesis, University of Iowa (Iowa City, Iowa), 1965.
6. Tarrell, Vernon V. "An Investigation of the Validity of the Musical Aptitude Profile." *J Res Music Ed* 13:195–206 w '65. * (*PA* 40:3589)
7. Lee, Robert Edward. *An Investigation of the Use of the Musical Aptitude Profile With College and University Freshman Music Students.* Doctor's thesis, University of Iowa (Iowa City, Iowa), 1966. (*DA* 27:1301A)
8. Brown, Merrill Edwin. *An Investigation of the Optimum Length of Musical Aptitude Profile Subtests.* Doctor's thesis, University of Iowa (Iowa City, Iowa), 1967. (*DA* 28:2706A)
9. Gordon, Edwin. "A Comparison of the Performance of Culturally Disadvantaged Students With That of Culturally Heterogeneous Students on the Musical Aptitude Profile." *Psychol Sch* 4:260–2 Jl '67. * (*PA* 41:15117)
10. Gordon, Edwin. "Implications for the Use of the *Musical Aptitude Profile* With College and University Freshman Music Students." *J Res Music Ed* 15:32–40 sp '67. * (*PA* 41:12500)
11. Gordon, Edwin. "The Musical Aptitude Profile." *Music Ed J* 53:52–4 F '67. *
12. Gordon, Edwin. *A Three-Year Longitudinal Predictive Validity Study of the Musical Aptitude Profile.* University of Iowa Monograph, Studies in the Psychology of Music, Vol. 5. Iowa City, Iowa: University of Iowa Press, 1967. Pp. xi, 78. *
13. Harrington, Charles Jay. *An Investigation of the Experimental Version Primary Level Musical Aptitude Profile for Use With Second and Third Grade Students.* Doctor's thesis, University of Iowa (Iowa City, Iowa), 1967. (*DA* 28:2713A)
14. Hatfield, Warren Gates. *An Investigation of the Diagnostic Validity of the Musical Aptitude Profile With Respect to Instrumental Music Performance.* Doctor's thesis, University of Iowa (Iowa City, Iowa), 1967. (*DA* 28:3210A)
15. Lee, Robert E. "An Investigation of the Use of the Musical Aptitude Profile With College and University Freshman Music Students." *J Res Music Ed* 15:278–88 w '67. * (*PA* 42:9424)
16. Bixler, John. "Musical Aptitude in the Educable Mentally Retarded Child." *J Music Ther* 5:41–3 Je '68. * (*PA* 43:2976)
17. Dittemore, Edgar Erwin. *An Investigation of Some Musical Capabilities of Elementary School Students.* Doctor's thesis, University of Iowa (Iowa City, Iowa), 1968. (*DA* 29:4516A)
18. Froseth, James Owen. *An Investigation of the Use of Musical Aptitude Profile Scores in the Instruction of Beginning Students in Instrumental Music.* Doctor's thesis, University of Iowa (Iowa City, Iowa), 1968. (*DA* 29:1916A)
19. Gordon, Edwin. "The Contribution of Each Musical Aptitude Profile Subtest to the Overall Validity of the Battery: A Note From the Author." *Council Res Music Ed B* 12:32–6 w '68. * (*PA* 42:9719)
20. Gordon, Edwin. "A Study of the Efficacy of General Intelligence and Musical Aptitude Tests in Predicting Achievement in Music." *Council Res Music Ed B* 13:40–5 sp '68. *
21. Gordon, Edwin. "The Use of the Musical Aptitude Profile With Exceptional Children." *J Music Ther* 5:37–40 Je '68. * (*PA* 43:2619)
22. Hill, John D. "The Musical Achievement of Culturally Deprived and Advantaged Children: A Comparative Study at the Elementary Level." *J Music Ther* 5:77–84 S '68. * (*PA* 43:5161)
23. Hill, John D. *A Study of the Musical Achievement of Culturally Deprived Children and Culturally Advantaged Children at the Elementary School Level.* Doctor's thesis, University of Kansas (Lawrence, Kan.), 1968. (*DA* 29:2738A)
24. Standifer, James Allred. *Effects of Aesthetic Sensitivity of Secondary General Music Courses Designed to Develop Perception of Elements of Musical Expressiveness.* Doctor's thesis, Case Western Reserve University (Cleveland, Ohio), 1968. (*DAI* 30:3978A)
25. Brown, Merrill. "The Optimum Length of the Musical Aptitude Profile Subtests." *J Res Music Ed* 17(2):240–7 su '69. * (*PA* 44:1252)
26. Gordon, Edwin. "Intercorrelations Among Musical Aptitude Profile and Seashore Measures of Musical Talent Subtests." *J Res Music Ed* 17(3):263–71 f '69. * (*PA* 44:7263)
27. Harrington, Charles J. "An Investigation of the Primary Level Musical Aptitude Profile for Use With Second and Third Grade Students." *J Res Music Ed* 17(4):359–68 w '69. * (*PA* 44:11218)
28. McCarthy, Kevin Joseph. *Effects of Participation in School Music Performance Organizations on the Ability to Perceive Aesthetic Elements in Recorded Music.* Doctor's thesis, Case Western Reserve University (Cleveland, Ohio), 1969. (*DAI* 30:3974A)
29. Young, William Thomas. *An Investigation of the Relative and Combined Power of Musical Aptitude, General Intelligence, and Academic Achievement Tests to Predict Musical Attainment.* Doctor's thesis, University of Iowa (Iowa City, Iowa), 1969. (*DAI* 30:758A)
30. Gordon, Edwin. "First-Year Results of a Five-Year Longitudinal Study of the Musical Achievement of Culturally

Disadvantaged Students." *J Res Music Ed* 18(3):195–213 f '70. *

31. GORDON, EDWIN. "Taking Into Account Musical Aptitude Differences Among Beginning Instrumental Students." *Am Ed Res J* 7(1):41–53 Ja '70. *

32. McGLOTHLIN, DONALD ERNEST. *An Investigation of the Efficacy of Ability Grouping Prospective Teachers Enrolled in Elementary Music Methods and Materials Courses.* Doctor's thesis, University of Iowa (Iowa City, Iowa), 1970. (*DAI* 31:1312A)

33. RICE, JAMES A. "Abbreviated Gordon Musical Aptitude Profile With EMR Children." *Am J Mental Def* 75(1):107–8 Jl '70. *

ROBERT W. LUNDIN, *Professor of Psychology and Chairman of the Department, The University of the South, Sewanee, Tennessee.*

This test of musical aptitude, the most recent to appear on the market, is the result of more than six years of research. Like most other musical aptitude tests its rationale lies in the subject's ability to make fine musical discriminations. According to the author the tests provide diagnostic appraisal of specific aspects of tonal and rhythmic aptitudes and musical appreciation.

The first two parts of the test, Tonal and Rhythmic Imagery, are perfectly objective and in a rough way correspond to other tests where discriminations are called for which are either right or wrong. The third main part, Musical Sensitivity, consists of three subtests, phrasing, balance and style. These really are a matter of musical taste, since the examinee is asked to indicate a preference for one of two selections according to the stated criteria. This last test resembles to some degree the last four subtests of the *Wing Standardised Tests of Musical Intelligence,* except that the Wing test uses a piano.

Reliability coefficients vary considerably for the different subtests and populations. Generally speaking, they are lower for the lower grades. On the separate subtests, the reliabilities run from the .60's to .80's; for the main division composites, in the .80's and .90's; and in the .90's for the total battery.

Initial validation studies published in the manual involve primarily concurrent validity using teachers' ratings of talent as the criterion. Although the range is considerable the correlations run in the .60's and .70's for part scores, and .70's to .90's for the composite score. A study by Culver (*3*) correlated test scores and judges' ratings of taped performances of individual subjects. These tended to run considerably lower.

A three year follow-up predictive validity study by Gordon (*12*) using a variety of criteria compared favorably with other validation studies, particularly when the total composite score was used. Environmental factors were also estimated from a questionnaire. Test scores did not seem to be significantly correlated with practice, per se, but with the subjects' attitudes toward practice (motivation?).

The taped selections were performed by professional musicians using original musical phrases. The manual states that the quality of reproduction is high, but in this reviewer's opinion it is only fair. All instructions for taking the test are recorded on the tapes so the individual administrator is left with only minimal preliminary instructions which are also provided in the manual.

The reason for choosing violin and cello over other sources (such as piano) is not explained. The test is long and in this reviewer's opinion and in the opinion of a sample of music students to whom the test was given, listening to violins and cello played repeatedly, singly and together, for so long a period becomes extremely monotonous. Further, if one wishes to purchase all of the materials available, including tapes, answer sheets, scoring keys, manual and individual file folders, the total outlay can easily come to $60 or more. This is quite expensive compared to other tests which employ single discs or tapes such as the Drake, Seashore, and Wing tests.

However, the test would appear to be a valid instrument; although no information is available comparing it with other current tests in use. A great many years have been spent in its development. The manual contains a vast amount of statistical data for those who care to plow through it. The normative sample is very adequate.

JOHN McLEISH, *Professor of Educational Psychology, University of Alberta, Edmonton, Alberta, Canada.*

This is, without a doubt, the best test of its kind on the market. It conforms to all the criteria of excellence not only in test construction and validation, but in musicality. The task is clearly defined, instructions are concise, the test material is interesting and well presented, and the answer sheets are well designed and suitable for group use and machine scoring. The manual is well produced in durable materials; it presents the basic validation data and norms in as interesting a way as this kind of writing permits; the print is pleasing and legible. Although repetitive, the music content is pleasing and is played by violinist and cellist with both musical finesse and psychometric expertise.

The test is suitable for grades 4–12 but can also be used to test the highest levels of musical sophistication. If anything, the test seems to be more successful in measuring musical aptitude in the older group. Analysis by the reviewer reveals a general factor which accounts for approximately 58 percent of the test variance at grade 11, in comparison with 48 percent at grade 5. This is in favorable contrast to the Seashore and Wing tests in which the first factor accounts for approximately 30 and 45 percent of the test variance respectively. Gordon's test relies heavily on musical memory which, together with perception of tone, is, of course, the sine qua non of musical aptitude. His test succeeds in measuring the higher level functions of musical aptitude, and avoids the trap of measuring the effects of training. The simple nature of the task (discrimination between two pieces of music in terms of "same" or "different") and the nature of the stimuli, insure that differences in intelligence, previous training and musical interest have little effect on the score.

[250]

*National Teacher Examinations: Music Education. College seniors and teachers; 1957–70; Forms K-ONT ('69, 22 pages), RNT ('69, 25 pages), SNT1 ('70, 25 pages), SNT2 ('70, 20 pages); descriptive booklet ('70, 8 pages); for more complete information, see 582; 120(165) minutes; Educational Testing Service. *

PAUL R. LEHMAN, *Professor of Music Education, Eastman School of Music, The University of Rochester, Rochester, New York.* [Review of Forms SNT1 and SNT2.]

Like the other Teaching Area Examinations of the National Teacher Examinations program, the Music Education examination seeks to determine what the student knows about his field. It does not claim to measure performance skills, teaching aptitude, interests, attitudes, or personal or social characteristics. It does not claim to determine what kind of person the subject is or how effective he will be in the classroom, though the publisher acknowledges the importance of these considerations. For this reason, the examination is intended not for use by itself but rather as a supplement to college transcripts, interviews, auditions, and personal recommendations.

The questions cover a wide variety of topics.

The examination is based on the assumption that the music teacher is or should be qualified to teach the broad spectrum of vocal, instrumental (including strings and winds), and general music at the elementary, junior high, and senior high school levels, and that he is familiar with the techniques of supervision. For the majority of teachers, however, this assumption is no longer valid. Most now specialize in one field or another. It is true that the teacher should be familiar with the overall program, but the tendency to specialize has undoubtedly undermined the hypothesis upon which the examination is based. Today, particularly, music teachers' responsibilities vary so widely, sometimes even within the same school system, that it is questionable whether any single paper-and-pencil test can contribute effectively to identifying candidates with the prerequisite knowledge.

The test items which are factual in nature, such as those in music history and theory, are generally sound. Some of those which depart from strictly cognitive learning, such as those that deal with methodology, however, reveal possible weaknesses. The difficulty in preparing such an examination, of course, is that in certain types of items the distracters tend to be either so obviously incorrect as to be ineffectual or so close to being acceptable that experts might argue over them. As a result, the examination contains items which represent oversimplifications or overgeneralizations, which are based on questionable premises, or which may be slightly misleading. A few items are weakened by faulty wording even though the underlying ideas are sound, and occasionally even the best answer may not be entirely adequate. Further, numerous options include qualifications which could indicate to the knowledgeable test taker whether they are likely to be correct or incorrect.

The National Teacher Examinations are prepared by nationally recognized authorities in their respective fields. The Educational Testing Service relies on these test development procedures to ensure content validity. It would be helpful, however, if additional validating criteria could be identified and the resulting data made available.

The Kuder-Richardson reliability for the most recent form for which data are available is claimed to be .91.

The Music Education examination is useful

for making gross discriminations and for identifying obvious misfits. For other purposes, it provides one additional source of information for use in conjunction with other data, such as information on performing ability, conducting, sight-singing, and keyboard proficiency. For making fine discriminations, the examination is of limited usefulness. It does not quite meet the usual standards of the Educational Testing Service, but the task it sets out to accomplish is inordinately difficult because of the complex nature of the subject.

ROGER P. PHELPS, *Professor of Music Education, New York University, New York, New York.* [Review of Forms K-ONT and RNT.]

The purpose of the NTE area examinations is to assess those aspects of teacher education which may be measured by a paper-and-pencil test. No attempt is made to measure teaching aptitude, interests, attitudes, or personal-social characteristics. The area examinations basically determine what a prospective teacher knows about his field by measuring his ability to relate concepts and factual knowledge through simulation of hypothetical situations which he may encounter on the job.

NTE scores may be used for different specific purposes by local and state school systems and by colleges and universities. For example, a local school system might use NTE scores to select new teachers, whereas a state could use the scores as a basis for awarding teaching certificates. A college or university, on the other hand, might note weak areas which a student could strengthen through further study.

The comments which follow relate to comparisons of Forms K-ONT and RNT of the Music Education examination. The K-ONT form appeared in 1966, and again in 1969. The RNT form is a slightly different 1969 version.

Each form of the Music Education test has a time limit of two hours. The test subject is directed to select a correct response for each of 150 questions from the five choices given. The questions may be in the form of providing a response to an incomplete statement or determining an answer to a question. The last questions—11 of K-ONT and 13 of RNT—require in addition a choice based on the words *least* or *except*.

This reviewer categorized the questions on both forms into the following areas: music education philosophy and information, teaching concepts and techniques, music literature and history, and music theory. The designations are purely for the purpose of trying to evaluate content; no doubt some other reviewer might consider them differently, for several questions could be placed in more than one category. The comparative designations are represented as follows: teaching concepts and techniques—69 questions (46 percent) for both K-ONT and RNT; music theory—35 questions (23 percent) in K-ONT, 27 questions (18 percent) in RNT; music literature and history—25 questions (17 percent) in K-ONT, 31 questions (21 percent) in RNT; music education philosophy and information—21 questions (14 percent) in K-ONT, 23 questions (15 percent) in RNT.

According to the NTE Prospectus, the content validity is essentially based on a priori evidence related to the planning and construction of the tests, two aspects not very specific statistically. Concurrent validity is determined by the relationship between scores on the examinations and grade-point averages. Based on correlations between weighted common examinations total scores and cumulative grade-point averages for seniors at 11 teacher-training institutions, the average correlation is .57. These criteria for validity undoubtedly will not be completely satisfactory for all who use the tests, because it is unlikely that all users will agree on what prospective teachers need to know. Until such time as agreement on these criteria is reached, or until a test is designed for one specific group or purpose—for example, to measure minimum standards of knowledge in music for certification purposes—the establishment of statistically sound validity coefficients will be difficult.

The Music Education tests appear to be excellent instruments. They should be especially valuable for college and university music departments in determining whether or not their graduating seniors appear to have the requisite knowledge regarded as essential for a beginning teacher. By pinpointing areas of weakness, the tests make it possible for a student to be advised where to concentrate in his post-baccalaureate study. Although the tests consist entirely of objective questions, the prospective teacher, through analysis and deduction, can make application to a hypothetical situation of the concepts and factual information he has learned. Statistical data which have been provided are generally very impressive and help to reinforce the claims made for the tests by the publisher. However, more empirical data on validity would add strength to the utility of these tests. Statements to the effect that validity coefficients are difficult to compute statistically because of the diverse objectives of the tests are not very convincing.

For a review by William S. Larson of earlier forms, see 6:350. For reviews of the testing program, see 582 (2 reviews), 6:700 (1 review), 5:538 (3 reviews), and 4:802 (1 review).

[251]

★Snyder Knuth Music Achievement Test. Elementary education and music majors; 1968; SKMAT; Forms A, B, (2 filmstrips and 2 7½ ips tapes); manual (9 pages); tentative norms; separate answer sheets (IBM 805) must be used; $25 per set of testing materials, 100 answer sheets, and manual; $2 per manual; postage extra; (65) minutes; Alice Snyder Knuth; Creative Arts Research Associates, Inc. *

REFERENCES

1. SNYDER, ALICE M. *The Development, Construction and Standardization of a Test of Music Achievement.* Doctor's thesis, University of Oregon (Eugene, Ore.), 1958. (*DA* 19:738)
2. SLAGLE, HAROLD CLAYTON. *An Investigation of the Effect of Seven Methods of Instruction on the Musical Achievement of Elementary Education Majors.* Doctor's thesis, University of Illinois (Urbana, Ill.), 1967. (*DA* 28:5098A)
3. GARDER, BARBARA WORK. *A Comparison of the Teaching of Music Fundamentals by the Traditional Method With the Omnibus Approach.* Doctor's thesis, Oklahoma State University (Stillwater, Okla.), 1969.

RICHARD COLWELL, *Professor of Secondary and Continuing Education and Music, University of Illinois, Urbana, Illinois.*

The manual for this test is only seven pages in length, but a more complete report on the test is available in the author's dissertation (1) completed in 1958. Some information for this review has been taken from the dissertation. The author states that the test was designed to measure understanding of music notation. She states that the test may be used as a placement examination to determine the music background of college elementary education majors, and to measure the musical achievement of "music majors at both the secondary school and college levels" and of elementary school pupils.

The tapes and filmstrip are adequate in quality but extremely awkward to use. Proper use of the tape should ensure constant timing but no precautions are given about stopping the tape or about giving additional help.

The manual is inadequate, containing only minimal administrative instructions, some data on reliability, means, and standard deviations for elementary education majors and music

majors for both forms, and a single table of norms. The strength of the test lies in the interesting and varied tasks presented. There is, however, no apparent logic in the weighting of the test in terms of number of questions for each part.

Content validity is based upon the author's many years of experience with elementary education majors. Here the test is strong. Although the primary purpose of the test is predictive, unfortunately no evidence of predictive validity is given. A score of 80, or slightly above the mean, is arbitrarily cited as the cutoff score for determining whether a student should be placed in a basic or advanced music course. This is of special significance when one considers that the two forms are not equivalent, the mean score for Form A being 75.6 and for Form B, 81.5 for elementary education majors.

There is doubt whether the tasks in some of the subtests are typically encountered in regular music instruction, i.e., following a melody by the use of contour lines (6 questions), or measuring one's ability to perceive and understand music symbols (35 questions). The analogy section may provide an indication of intelligence, as well as of musical knowledge and understanding. The other tasks of recognizing major and minor, recognizing a melody from notation, placing the appropriate chord designations under a given melodic line, hearing whether a melody is moving scalewise or skipping, and selecting like phrases in a melody are common music tasks.

There is a wide variety of tasks in the test. In 46 of the 53 questions in Part 1, the student selects from four written alternatives the music he hears performed. In the other seven questions, he must select the proper chord sequence appropriate to harmonize a melody. Part 2 measures at least four different skills: six questions require the student to match a melody with a graph line indicating the "shape" of the melody; ten questions pertain to whether the melody moves scalewise; four questions test ability to select like phrases in a melody; and seven questions ask for recognition of whether the melody is in major or minor mode. Part 3 is the analogies test and Part 4 (a four-minute section) consists of 10 questions which require the student to match four bars of notation with the correct title of the melody selected from four choices. The variety of tasks within a subtest contributes to specious reliability. Pilot work on the sections and the test was accomplished with samples of about 30 students, too few upon which to accept or reject items. Trial work with the test resulted in the dropping of 18 items from the original 300. The author states that she had some difficulty in finding discriminating items for the analogies test, and consequently 13 items are repeated in both forms.

Reliability is given in terms of the correlation between forms for music and elementary education majors. The correlation given for elementary education majors is .993 and for music majors, .998! This is incorrect. The formula used to determine reliability, given on page 69 of the dissertation, is in error. This may be a misprint; however, the author also used the sums of the scores in the formula rather than individual scores to compute reliability. This procedure results in X equalling Y and a correlation of 1.0! The slightly lower figures obtained by the test author are due only to rounding errors. Consequently, no reliability estimate is currently available.

The norms provided in the manual are supposedly applicable to either form of the test. They were arrived at by combining the results of the two forms (which are nearly six raw points apart in mean scores) and then adjusting them to fit a normal probability curve. With a sample of only 311, all from one school, additional norming is necessary before confidence can be placed in the norms. Slagle (*2*) found the mean scores nine points below those reported by Knuth. Garder (*3*) reports mean scores of 13 to 16 points lower than those of Knuth. Slagle's posttest (after a one-semester course in music fundamentals) provided scores more nearly equal to the published norms. Norms are not given for music majors or for elementary school students. A simplified type of item analysis providing a rough difficulty index was used to eliminate a few items. Of concern is that the published test differs from that given in Appendix 7 of the dissertation by having five fewer items on each form, thus invalidating published norms which are identical with those in the dissertation. Another factor lessening the value of the norms is that nearly one-fourth of the standardization sample was absent from the administration of one form, thus providing a source of some bias.

The Snyder Knuth test remains an interesting research tool. With adequate development and research it could prove to be a useful test with elementary education majors. However, at the present time the *Music Achievement Tests* and the *National Teacher Examinations: Music Education* provide a more reliable source of data for use with this population.

EDWIN GORDON, *Professor of Music and Education, The University of Iowa, Iowa City, Iowa.*

The *Snyder Knuth Music Achievement Test* is primarily designed to evaluate the musical backgrounds of elementary education majors at the college and university level. The author suggests that test scores "may help the music education staff to determine whether or not these students need to take a basic music fundamentals course, prerequisite to an elementary music methods course."

There are two equivalent forms of the test, each containing 136 items, most of which are multiple choice. Each of the forms comprises four parts: (1) Listening and Seeing, (2) Listening, (3) Music Comprehension, and (4) Tonal Memory. The piano is the musical stimulus. The entire test, including directions and practice exercises, is tape recorded. A filmstrip is used in conjunction with the recording.

Although the titles are nondescript, the content of the test parts is not outlined in the brief test manual. Actually, Part 1 tests the ability to recognize in tonal and rhythm notation, and through chord symbols, what is heard on the recording; Part 2 tests the ability to perceive aurally keynotes, tonic chords, octaves, steps and skips in tonal intervals, like and different phrases, duple and triple meters, and major and minor tonalities. For Parts 3 and 4, no music is performed. The former deals with the intellectual understanding of musical signs and symbols, and the latter with the recognition of familiar melodies from musical notation.

Only equivalent forms reliability for the complete test (not for the separate parts) is reported in the manual. Albeit a total test score is expected to yield a higher reliability coefficient than a part score, equivalent forms reliability is generally found to be lower than split-half reliability for a given test. Nonetheless, the test author states in the manual that the equivalent forms reliability of the test is .993 for elementary education majors and .998 for advanced music majors. An error was obviously made in the computation of these figures. The reliability is unbelievably high when the following factors are taken into account: (*a*) Practice exercises are not always given for specific tasks required in different sections within parts of the test. (*b*) The majority of items in the test are performed only once. This is particularly a limitation in Part 1 where the subject must concurrently associate the correct tonal and rhythmic notation with what is heard on the recording. (*c*) It would seem difficult to determine which of four phrases are alike or different in Part 2 because the beginnings and endings of the phrases are not easily distinguishable. (*d*) Correct choices of chord symbols for some items in Part 1 could be a matter of preference. (*e*) The spoken directions on the tape recording are not always articulate. (*f*) The sound reproduction of the piano on the tape recording is not consistently desirable nor are the items always performed in a musical manner, especially when upbeats are encountered.

There is no experimental validity for the test reported in the manual. As the author states, "For the purpose of this test, content validity, which is the amount of agreement between the test item content and the content of music books currently in use, is the only concern." It is suggested that the test user examine for himself the validity of the test "by checking the test items against courses of study, textbooks, or curriculum guides prepared for teachers in the elementary school, and for teacher training in the colleges."

Percentile rank norms for the unweighted total test score are based on the test results of 311 elementary education majors. A further description of the students who participated in the standardization program is not given in the manual.

The author suggests that if a student earns a raw score less than 80 (the 55th percentile), it is likely that he should be enrolled in a basic music fundamentals course before he registers for an elementary music methods course. No explanation of how this point was determined is given in the manual. Nor is it explained that if, as suggested in the manual, Form A of the test is administered at the beginning of the year or semester and Form B at the end, the teacher will need somehow to determine for himself what constitutes typical and exceptional student growth.

Undoubtedly there is a need for a well de-

signed and standardized musical achievement test for elementary education majors. The *Snyder Knuth Music Achievement Test,* considering the wealth of tonal and rhythmic dimensions which it comprises, represents a contribution to this need.

[252]

★The Undergraduate Record Examinations: Music Tests. College; 1969–70; 2 tests: field, modular; descriptive booklet ('70, 12 pages) ; for more complete information, see 671 ; Educational Testing Service. *
a) MUSIC TEST. Form RUR ('69, 28 pages) ; 120(140) minutes.
b) AURAL MUSIC: A MODULAR TEST DESIGNED TO COMPLEMENT THE TWO-HOUR MUSIC TEST. Forms RUR ('69, 16 pages), SUR ('70, 16 pages) ; 12-inch record (33⅓ rpm) for each form; 45(55) minutes.

ROGER P. PHELPS, *Professor of Music Education, New York University, New York, New York.* [Review of Form RUR.]

THE MUSIC TEST. Objectives of the Music Test are to: (*a*) measure specific competencies and skills achieved by a college or university senior music major, (*b*) evaluate an undergraduate student's achievement to determine his competence for graduate music study, (*c*) obtain information useful in counseling the student, and (*d*) assist in institutional, curricular, and departmental self-evaluation.

The Music Test objectively evaluates the components of musical achievement that can be measured by means of a written test. Music theory and music history and literature, two areas that normally constitute at least one-half of the music courses of an undergraduate music major's program, are covered extensively and in considerable depth in this two-hour examination. For each of the 150 incomplete questions or statements, the test subject must select one correct response from the five suggested answers or completions.

Specific areas covered with the number of questions in each are: music fundamentals (27), harmony (19), counterpoint (10), instrumentation and orchestration (14), repertory (21), forms (23), stylistic elements (32), and sources of musical information (4). Because of these emphases the Music Test is eminently well suited for all music majors. The areas of concentration are those which provide a solid foundation for any subsequent advanced instruction.

The very useful Group Item Summary Worksheet provides normative data showing that all students reached item 97 ; 98 percent, item 138; and 58 percent, item 150, the last item. Time limits obviously are not a constraining factor in the Music Test. The UP interpretive manual presents data showing percentages of those who answered each question correctly, incorrectly, or omitted the question. Items of varying difficulty occur throughout various sections of the test.

The reliability of the test is .95, which makes it the most reliable of all the Field Tests.

Content validity has largely been based on the assumption that sampling procedures can be controlled by the inclusion of participants from different types of institutions in various parts of the country. Herein lies a weakness. The handbook states that participating faculty members who devised the test determined its utility according to whether or not the questions were relevant to the course content at their local institutions. In the absence of uniform curricular content such an explanation seems plausible, but it is not very convincing statistically. Predictive validity also is stated in rather vague terms.

The UP Music Test provides a generally thorough and objective measure of the areas of music theory and music literature and history, other than aural, for an undergraduate music major. The questions are varied enough to retain a test subject's interest for two hours and at the same time offer him a challenge. The Music Test also can be a useful instrument for college and university departments of music which are earnestly seeking to evaluate the effectiveness of their curricula. On the other hand this strong emphasis on music literature and history and music theory could be somewhat disconcerting to a student who attends an institution where these areas are not stressed. This test can indicate pointedly the necessity for more substantive programs in such institutions. Not unexpectedly there is a complete absence of questions relating to concepts and pedagogical trends with which a music education student is expected to be conversant. It would appear to this reviewer that the *National Teacher Examinations: Music Education,* which includes questions on basic musical background as well as those pertinent to teaching, would make a good supplement to the UP Music Test. This most reliable of all the UP Field Tests suffers somewhat in precision from the lack of objective statistical data on validity. It is to be hoped that more stress will be placed on statistical validation in subsequent revisions of the UP Music Test.

THE AURAL MUSIC TEST. This Modular Test may be used alone or as a complement to the Music Field Test. Included on this highly specialized 45-minute test are elements of ear training and sight reading that cannot be measured by a written test. The musical stimuli have been recorded on a single monaural record. There are 63 multiple choice questions, selection of the correct answer to be made from five choices in 44 questions and from three choices in 19 others.

Following are the nine aspects of aural recognition, with the number of items for each in parentheses: intervals (10), scales and modes (5), rhythmic patterns (10), cadences (4), four-part harmonic progressions (5), nonharmonic tones (4), modulations (5), figured bass (4), and recognition of musical forms, styles, and composers (16). The number of times each example is presented varies from one to two depending on the musical element measured. The 10-second interval following each item seems adequate for a student to determine and record his answer.

It would appear to this reviewer that the four-part harmonic progressions and the figured bass items should be played three times instead of two. These are the most difficult parts of the test and it may be that the intent of the author was to provide examples of this difficulty to offset some of the easier ones.

The rhythmic patterns section, conversely, seems to be one of the easiest parts of the test, therefore this reviewer questions whether or not the items should be presented twice. Other more difficult examples, notably modulations, are played only once; another playing no doubt would result in a higher percentage of correct scores.

Directions for each of the nine sections of the Aural Music Test are given not only on the record but also in the test booklet. The practical and realistic approach to the everyday musical sounds that a test subject encounters in the Aural Music Test is a refreshing contrast to the hypothetical and often uninteresting examples found in many music tests. This salient feature is evident in the variety of orchestral instruments used singly and in ensemble. A few choral and piano examples are included also. Noteworthy is the high proportion of excerpts which are taken directly from standard literature, an encouraging and gratifying trend that is evident in some other recently published music tests also.

A review of normative data for the spring of 1969 indicates that all subjects completed the 63 questions but this was due, no doubt, to the use of a record, which conditioned the test subjects to conform to a routine time schedule in answering questions. The item analysis of percentage of those answering questions correctly on the rhythmic patterns test ranges from a high of 97 to a low of 71. On the four-part harmonic progressions and figured bass tests the percentage of correct responses, with one exception, ranges from a high of 41 to a low of 23. As indicated earlier, both of these tests are difficult so perhaps another trial would have been beneficial in improving the percentage of correct responses. The lowest correct response figure is in the area of modulations, with only 12 percent getting one specific item correct. In these exercises, as indicated earlier, the test subject has one trial for each example to indicate the key to which the composition has modulated. In addition to insufficient trials it is possible that the low number of correct responses may be due to insufficient stress on this type of

material at many colleges and universities. Another possibility is that the test author intended to make a clear delineation between students with extremely sensitive and relatively insensitive ears.

Reliability of the Aural Music Test is .84. No validity coefficients are given; criteria for content and predictive validity have been given but without statistical verification. It is to be hoped that sufficient data will be obtained from subsequent testings to establish meaningful validity coefficients.

This UP Modular Test, with its emphasis on measuring a highly specialized type of musical behavior, makes an excellent complement to the UP Music Field Test. Its relatively short length (45 minutes), plus the fact that it is presented on a record with varying musical stimuli, can in itself be a strong motivating force. The reliability coefficient is excellent, but the validity coefficients remain largely conjectural statistically. This excellent test will become even more useful when validity coefficients based on more objective criteria than those presently used are provided.

For reviews of the testing program, see 671 (2 reviews).

FOREIGN LANGUAGES

Reviews by *John B. Carroll, Clinton I. Chase, John L. D. Clark, George Domino, Michio Peter Hagiwara, A. Ralph Hakstian, Walter V. Kaulfers, Robert Lado, Walter F. W. Lohnes, Joseph A. Murphy, T. F. Naumann, Josephine Bruno Pane, Gino Parisi, Glen W. Probst, Jean-Guy Savard, Jack M. Stein, and Paolo Valesio.*

[253]

*Common Concepts Foreign Language Test. Students in any grade who are at the Level 1 stage of achievement; 1962–66; CCFLT; 3 aural comprehension tests: French, German, Spanish; may be administered using live voice but tape recording (3¾ ips) is recommended; Forms 1, 2, ('62, 31 pages, the same booklet is used for both forms and all 3 languages); manual ('66, 41 pages); separate answer sheets (IBM 1230) must be used; $1.10 per test; $2.50 per 50 answer sheets; $5.95 per tape recording; 75¢ per scoring stencil for a given form and language; $1 per manual; postage extra; $2.25 per specimen set (without tape), postpaid; scoring service, 22¢ and over per test; (40–45) minutes; Bela H. Banathy, Miles V. Zintz, W. James Popham, Joseph M. Sadnavitch, Rena Krichbaum, Fred B. Gannon, Valdemar Hempel, and Klaus A. Mueller; CTB/McGraw-Hill. *

Walter V. Kaulfers, *Professor of Foreign Language Education, University of Illinois, Urbana, Illinois.*

Although the title page of the manual suggests that the battery includes English as a foreign language, the current edition is incomplete in this respect. "An English version had been contemplated at one time, but was subsequently dropped. Users in situations demanding an English edition are urged to utilize the appropriate language and simply reverse the process; that is, the preliminary instructions should be given in the native tongue (French, for example) and the stimulus sentences spoken in English." Since no supporting data are available to substantiate the validity and reliability of this procedure, it is doubtful if users of the test should place much confidence in scores for English obtained in this manner.

In fact, the title of this test does not indicate that it is exclusively a test of aural comprehension. The test requires no ability whatsoever to read, write, or speak the foreign language. With changes in the directions, it could be administered to illiterates in almost any language. It is therefore difficult to accept the authors' claim that a student's "basic language competence can be estimated more readily by testing aural comprehension or oral production than by using measurement techniques based on the secondary skills of reading and writing." This would seem true only if "basic language competence" is narrowly defined in esoteric terms to describe the most primitive of language skills. The claim that the examination "is designed primarily to measure and evaluate overall level of proficiency in another language" is therefore not warranted in this reviewer's judgment.

In structure the examination is exclusively a multiple choice test "presenting a stimulus sentence which is heard in the foreign language while the student looks at a panel of four small pictures. The student's task is to identify from the four frames [i.e., choices] the one picture which matches the spoken sentence. * Twenty-three clearly delineated, multi-colored pictures are used for the eighty test sentences that are incorporated in each form of the test. These are common scenes that are easily interpretable." The pictures, while small, are generally attractive, interesting, and readily intelligible.

Tapes in Spanish, French, and German (one for each of the two forms for each language, but none for English) are available for administering the test entirely by tape recorder. The directions (given in impeccable English by a separate administrator) are clear and so detailed as to occupy over a third of each recording. The test sentences are spoken by a male native. The same male voice is heard exclusively throughout both forms of the test for each language. The recordings are of high fidelity, the voices pleasing, and the diction that of educated natives. However, the use of only one native voice throughout (using only the Latin American pronunciation in the case of Span-

ish) seems an unfortunate limitation in a test measuring nothing but aural comprehension.

Use of the tapes should simplify administration of the test and is recommended to assure uniformity of administration when data are to be obtained for comparative purposes from students taught by different methods. Their use is also desirable if the scores are to provide a measure of how well the students can understand German, French, or Spanish when the language is spoken by someone other than their teacher.

Statistically, the *Common Concepts Foreign Language Test* compares favorably with the better foreign language achievement tests now on the market. The reliability of the two forms for French, German, and Spanish extends from .73 for elementary school pupils in French to .96 for junior high school students in Spanish. Most reliability coefficients in the three languages fall within the .88–.92 range. As measured by the correlation of raw scores with teachers' course marks, the validity of the test ranges from .40 in junior high school Spanish (71 cases only) to .72 in elementary school Spanish (172 cases).

Tables giving percentiles, standard scores, and stanine reference distributions for the elementary school, junior high school, and senior high school levels are included for each language and form in the manual. However, since the publishers do not indicate whether the data are based on tape recorded administrations of the test, derived from administration by the students' own teachers, or from scores obtained by a mixture of methods, these "reference distributions" have very limited application. Comparison of a particular student's score with scores other than the average for his own classmates is unwarranted because of (*a*) the lack of data concerning the norming population, (*b*) the impracticability of providing separate norms for highly selected vs. unselected groups, and (*c*) the impracticability of providing norms for specific grades—because of the wide variations in the number of contact hours in different schools.

The chief limitations of the *Common Concepts Foreign Language Test,* however, are qualitative rather than statistical. Five deserve attention:

a) The 80 items of each form of the test consist almost exclusively of simple declarative sentences. In all of Form 1 of the German test, for example, nine items are simple questions, but only two items are exclamatory. No items whatever are compound, complex, or complex-compound in structure and only one (one of the exclamations) is imperative. The French and Spanish forms have comparable shortcomings. A picture identification test apparently does not lend itself readily to other than simple declarative statements.

b) The tests are phrased almost exclusively in the present indicative. For example, Form 1 of the French examination contains not a single sentence in a past or present perfect tense and only one future tense. In the German and Spanish tests, the number of other than simple present indicative statements is much too limited for evaluative purposes.

c) Apparently none of the tests are scaled in difficulty from easiest item first to hardest item last. Translated into English, item 43 in Form 2 of the French test reads, "They walk, ride, and drive to school," while item 80 at the end of the test simply says, "The walls are green." A relatively hard item early in a test often disheartens an examinee unnecessarily.

d) No evidence is available showing to what extent the two forms for each language are statistically of equal difficulty. Thus, if a pupil scores 10 points higher on Form 2 at the end of the third semester than he scores on Form 1 at the end of the second, no one can be sure whether the gain is a measure of the student's progress, or a measure of the degree to which Form 2 is easier.

e) Correct answers can at times be selected without necessarily comprehending the statement as a whole. In translation, item 59 in Form 2 of the French test reads, "I see the number 50." Since only one picture in the booklet contains this number, a pupil would not necessarily have to understand the entire sentence to choose the right answer. Just recognizing the French word for "fifty" would suffice.

In summary, the *Common Concepts Foreign Language Test* can provide a rough measure of the extent to which a pupil understands spoken French, German, or Spanish when the speaker talks almost exclusively in the present tense and rarely in other than short, simple declarative sentences. In no circumstances should it be used as the sole means for measuring and evaluating "overall level of proficiency in another language."

[254]

*MLA Cooperative Foreign Language Tests. 1–2 years high school or 2 semesters college, 3–4 years high school or 4 semesters college; 1963–65; 2 levels; 5 tests; for additional information and reviews, see the separate test entries; Cooperative Tests and Services. *
a) FRENCH. See 277.
b) GERMAN. See 290.
c) ITALIAN. See 302.
d) RUSSIAN. See 312.
e) SPANISH. See 322.

J Ed Meas 2:234–44 D '65. John L. D. Clark. * Although a number of specific criticisms of these tests may be advanced, it should be borne in mind that the emphasis and scope of these tests is such as to secure for them a very important place in present day language teaching and evaluation endeavors. * Listening and Speaking norms for level L are given only for "audio-lingual" classes at the first and second year high school levels, since tests of these two skills were not considered appropriate for the "traditional" courses at these levels. Although it is certainly true that the development of listening and speaking skills usually receives greater stress in "audio-lingual" courses, even the more traditional courses do provide at least some opportunity for listening and speaking practice, if only through the occasional repetition of memorized material or the reading of blackboard sentences. Thus, it would appear suitable (and particularly helpful for comparative and other research purposes) to provide listening and speaking norms for "traditional" groups as well. * At the college level, general norms are provided for all four skills at each of two levels: first year (level L) and second year (level M). A worthwhile future undertaking might be to provide separate "audio-lingual" and "traditional" norms at the elementary *college* level; a candid view of beginning undergraduate courses will suggest considerable variations in course content and emphasis which would make the definition of different norming groups appropriate. For the most part, the normative data described above are uniformly available across languages; in a few instances, however, and particularly for certain Italian and Russian groups, the total number of cases tested was too small to permit even tentative norming; test users in these two languages particularly should make sure that norms are listed for the forms and levels to be used. * For the most part, considerable care seems to have been taken to assist the user in his interpretation of the norms tables and other statistical information presented. * Although claims made for the measurement applications of the tests are in general carefully delineated, a few rather serious overstatements seem to have been made concerning their potential usefulness for *diagnostic* purposes for pinpointing specific language areas in which individual students or test groups are experiencing difficulty. The Handbook states in this respect that the tests will be found useful for "discovering the kinds of errors that foreign language students make," and for "identifying idioms and structures in a foreign language that are troublesome for a class or for individual students." The reviewer seriously doubts that either the test developers or potential users would be able to identify in most of the items the unitary linguistic features which are both necessary and sufficient for success or failure on that item. The linguistic redundancies always present in meaningful continuous discourse, both spoken and written, make it extremely difficult to specify particular lexical or syntactical elements which the student must "know" to answer the item correctly. Put somewhat differently, there are usually a number of "linguistic roads" (or detours) that the student may follow in passing or failing an item; and from the item response alone, it is generally impossible to determine which particular route the student has taken. * A clear warning against the attempted use of the tests for diagnostic purposes is particularly in order in view of the recent establishment by ETS of a scoring-reporting service for the "A" forms of the Listening and Reading tests. This service provides the teacher with such item analysis data as the percentage of students passing each item, the group frequency of answer alternatives, and individual student response patterns including the designation of correctly and incorrectly answered items and indication of the particular answer options chosen. A leaflet describing the scoring service states among other things that the data provided will "facilitate the use of test results in improving instruction" and will permit the identification of "common difficulties revealed by the individual response patterns." It is somewhat ironic that this type of scoring is not available for the Speaking and Writing tests—the two tests which do in certain limited instances permit the identification of particular linguistic problems (the pronunciation of certain sounds and the knowledge of tense, gender,

and number markers, respectively). But to expect that similarly close identifications will be afforded by commercial or private analysis of responses to Listening and Reading test items (or by private analysis of most Speaking and Writing test items) is to court disillusionment. In keeping with the above discussion, it is suggested that the Cooperative tests will *not* be found appropriate in such content-oriented applications as the following: 1) determining student grades, insofar as such grades are expected to reflect the extent to which particular linguistic patterns, vocabularies, etc. have been learned; 2) evaluating the success of training programs in meeting goals cast in specific linguistic terms (for example, as given in course syllabi); 3) identifying particular linguistic problems for diagnostic and correctional purposes, either on an individual or group basis. On the other hand, as more general-purpose tests of the level of students' competence in different skill areas, the Cooperative tests could be expected to serve effectively in such measurement tasks as: 1) determining the standing of certain schools or school districts with respect to the overall outcomes of the language programs; 2) establishing the general level of competence of individual students for such purposes as initial class placement, assignment to teaching sections, and so forth; 3) determining, for counseling or other purposes, the relative standings of particular students with respect to "developed proficiency" in any or all of the four skill areas, by reference either to the performance of other students in a locally defined group or to the performance of a nationwide sample of students engaged in "similar" language programs. In these and comparable undertakings, the fact that the Cooperative tests are not bound to materials presented in a specific textbook or training sequence gives appreciable assurance that the tests will be "fair" to large numbers of students regardless of the particular classrooms or school systems in which they have studied. * the Cooperative series is made up of four entirely different tests, each with unique characteristics and logic of measurement corresponding to the particular skill involved * The order in which the tests are discussed below is established for convenience only; the suggested order of administration is not made clear in the test literature, although it may be an important variable in the light of possible "warm-up" or practice effects among the different tests. * *Reading.* In the Reading tests....the reading passages, questions, and answer alternatives are all in the foreign language. Although it would appear generally desirable to reduce the use of English as much as possible in foreign language tests, measurement validity may be adversely affected. Thus, in the Reading test, the student's inability to understand a particular printed question may prevent a proper response to that item, regardless of his overall comprehension of the passage itself. * In the absence of distracting factors of the type described above, it may fairly be said that the Cooperative Reading tests measure the student's ability to comprehend various written passages to the extent that he is able to answer certain questions based on the factual content and, for some of the upper level items, the "tone" of the material involved. * *Listening.* * When played on a high quality and properly adjusted reproducing system, the sound quality of both the Listening and Speaking tapes is unquestionably excellent. * the speech heard on these tapes may be considered somewhat "too good" in that it often exceeds in clarity and carefulness the speech which would usually be employed in the various real-life situations being modeled * It is not suggested that test constructors are ill-advised to seek high electronic and vocal quality in test tapes (on the contrary, there are cogent pedagogical and evaluative justifications for such an approach), but rather that students who respond successfully in the various situations presented on the Listening test tapes might not by this token be expected to perform with comparable facility in analogous real-life situations encountered, for example, during a trip abroad. A more serious problem with the Listening tests lies in the fact that these tests are to a certain extent tests of *reading* ability: the student must read and understand the answer alternatives in order to indicate his responses to the spoken stimuli. Here, as with the Reading tests, it is always possible that the student may understand the test passages themselves but experience confounding difficulties with the "answer" portions. In the Listening tests, however, the problem is compounded, since an entirely different linguistic modality is involved, a modality in which the student may well not be expected to have the requisite degree of facility. Indeed, for those language classes that postpone the introduction of printed material in favor of intensive pre-

liminary work on listening comprehension and speaking, the necessity for the student to *read* a number of printed answer alternatives may in some instances proscribe use of these tests as valid measures of aural comprehension. Teachers who wish to make use of the Listening tests in their own classes should determine through careful prior examination of the test booklets that their students would probably not have difficulty in understanding the printed alternatives. Another potential problem with the Listening tests is the occasional inclusion of spoken passages based on factual or historical material. In Spanish Listening MA, for example, a passage is read describing the history of bullfighting; in Spanish Listening MB, there is a description of the history and geography of Bolpebra, a rather well-known city near the borders of Bolivia, Peru, and Brazil. In these and similar cases, students who have had previous exposure to the factual material presented (not necessarily in a language learning situation) are in a more favorable position to answer the questions correctly than persons for whom the material is entirely novel. For that matter, students who are well acquainted with the probable content of a given passage may need to catch only a few random words to "understand" quite clearly what the passage is about. Fortunately, such factual passages are in the minority, and most of the conversations, dialogues, and other passages used appear to have been created expressly for the tests, a procedure that insures against prior familiarity with the content of the passages. *Writing.* * Although the Writing test is subjectively scored in the sense that trained human judgment is required, the inter-rater scoring reliability (independent scoring by two judges) seems to be quite high. * In general terms, the producers of the Writing tests appear to have struck a happy balance between, on the one hand, a structuring of student responses sufficient to allow for well-defined grading procedures, and on the other, provision for a certain amount of freedom in the actual writing process including the "creation" of an entire paragraph. Like the Listening tests, the Writing tests do not measure exclusively the language skill for which they are named. On the contrary, the student is required to read and understand a number of foreign words and sentences to fill in the required words or alter the sentences as requested. Not all tests of writing skill necessarily require some element of reading proficiency in the foreign language: for example, the simple direction "Write a story about...." would successfully bypass questions of reading ability altogether. However, in view of the fact that the Cooperative test constructors for a number of practical reasons have elected to construct the Writing test in a way which includes a reading ability factor, the test user should satisfy himself that his students are experiencing little difficulty with the reading of the sentences as such if he intends to consider the obtained results to be reflections of writing ability *per se*. Certain possibly minor problems in the mechanics of the Writing test may be suggested. For example, is the test so arranged as to place a premium on handwriting speed? In this connection, it is interesting to note that the scoring directions ask the rater to overlook "minor errors that might be due to hurried copying of words in the model sentence." Another question is raised by a sentence in the scoring directions which asks the rater to "overlook a student's failure to observe" an instruction printed in the test booklets (for some languages) that only a certain number of words (e.g. from 3 to 10) are to be used in composing certain responses. There seems to be in these instances no legitimate reason to misinform the student as to the nature of the task requested. Aside from such minor considerations, which are probably easily correctable, the Writing tests appear to provide a convenient and straightforward means for presenting the student an opportunity to produce words, phrases, and longer passages in the foreign language with attention to spelling, agreement of persons and gender, proper sequence of tenses, and so forth, all of which are certainly valid elements in the totality of performance known as "writing in the foreign language." *Speaking.* Among the tests in the four skill areas, the development of a valid and reliable test of speaking ability is at once of the most immediate importance to the teaching profession and of the greatest technical difficulty in terms of the measurement problems encountered. * the undertaking on the part of the MLA-ETS group to provide alternate forms of a speaking test for five different languages at each of two ability levels is of major significance. Although the tests so produced may be considered in many respects the least successful of the four Cooperative skill tests, the importance of the undertaking cannot be overempha-

sized: rather than curse the darkness which has surrounded the evaluation of foreign language speaking ability, the Cooperative test constructors have lit several candles for which the entire language profession may be grateful. Administration of the Speaking test requires the use of the test booklet, a test tape, and in addition, blank tapes (locally obtained) for recording the student responses. Administration is almost necessarily confined to the language laboratory, where the number of student recording positions available sets an upper limit on the number of students who may be tested at one time. * In the first part of the Speaking test, the student listens to short utterances that he repeats aloud, attempting to imitate the model voice as closely as possible. * The second section of the test asks the student to read a short printed passage aloud * In the third section, the student looks at simple line drawings (for example, a book lying on a table) and answers a spoken question about each drawing ("Where is the book?"). * In the fourth and final part of the test, the student looks at and "tells a story about" both a single picture (for example, a wife bringing her husband a cake from the kitchen) and a series of four pictures (for example, a family visiting the zoo). * A number of questions may immediately be raised concerning the first section of the test (sound imitation). First, there is some indication that trained judges may not be able to rate consistently the right-wrong quality of the imitated sounds. * In the same connection, it may be wondered whether sounds produced by native speakers themselves would be uniformly judged as "right," or whether certain features of the speakers' idiolects might be considered "wrong" by the judges. In the latter case, the validity of the right-wrong scoring method might be called into question. For the picture description sections, one could ask whether rather laconic native speakers might be assigned lower scores than more verbose speakers; presumably, such individual personality factors would be out of place in a test of basic speaking skill. In the absence of validity information obtained through the administration of the Speaking (and other skills) tests to representative groups of native speakers, these and similar questions which might be raised about test performance must go unanswered. It should be noted briefly that the reading section of the Speaking test again involves two different linguistic modalities, and that student scores on this part of the test might be expected to vary to some extent on the basis of their prior exposure to printed materials. A serious practical shortcoming in the use of the published Speaking test norms is that these norms have been based on the scoring performance of "largely native or very fluent" speakers of the test language who had also participated in a number of preliminary training sessions at ETS. Since an in-field test usage would involve a rather different group of scorers (presumably, high school and college teachers with varying degrees of linguistic proficiency and no preliminary practice in the judging procedure) the scores assigned by these raters might not be comparable to those which would have been assigned in the same cases by the norming judges. The in-field scoring problem is addressed, at least in a nominal way, by the provision at the end of each Speaking test tape of a special section containing responses of one student "judged by his teacher to have a high degree of competence for a student at this level." Suggested ratings for this model student on the various sections of the test are not provided, nor is there any discussion of the linguistic merits or shortcomings of the responses made. Further, in the absence of other recordings made by "poor" or "average" students, little idea of the range of possible responses can be obtained through listening to the single voice provided on the practice tape. It would not be technically difficult to produce and make available a detailed "scorer training tape" for each language that would contain a number of representative student performances together with a detailed discussion of the scores to be assigned in each case. The scoring directions for the Writing test do in fact present samples of student responses, giving both the particular scores assigned in each case and the rationale underlying their assignment; in the case of the Speaking test, an aural analog for this type of scoring aid would seem clearly in order. *Summary.* The MLA Cooperative Foreign Language Tests are considered to represent, for the most part, well based and carefully developed measures of overall linguistic achievement at the beginning and intermediate levels of proficiency. Their wide scope and general orientation make them especially suitable for use in larger-scale testing programs which cut across lines of particular course content. On the individual student level, the tests allow for broadly

defined statements of competence which should be of value in such areas as initial course placement and academic counseling. The MLA tests are not recommended for use in measuring the attainment of particular linguistic goals, such as the knowledge of specific lexicon, control of certain syntactical patterns, and so forth. Although individual linguistic elements may be isolated for some of the items, the tests as a whole do not lend themselves to such analysis. In certain tests or test sections, the confounding of linguistic modalities as a consequence of the format employed makes it advisable for the user to determine that students who are to take the tests would not reasonably experience difficulty as a result. Additional research on various other aspects of test performance may be suggested, including a detailed examination of the responses of native speakers to the linguistic tasks presented. The MLA Cooperative tests are to be praised for their extensiveness and for the emphasis which they bring to the testing of all four language skills. It can be hoped that the precedent so established will be followed by both the MLA-ETS group and others in continuing the work that has been so auspiciously begun.

For reviews of individual tests, see 277, 290, 302, 312, and 322.

[255]
★Modern Language Aptitude Test—Elementary. Grades 3–6; 1960–67; EMLAT; downward extension of the *Modern Language Aptitude Test;* 5 scores: hidden words, matching words, finding rhymes, number learning, total; Form EA ('65, 15 pages); manual ('67, 12 pages); 3¾ ips test tape, 5 inch reel; $4.50 per 25 tests; 60¢ per set of keys; $7.50 per test tape; 40¢ per manual; $1.20 per specimen set; postage extra; 61(75) minutes; John B. Carroll and Stanley M. Sapon; Psychological Corporation. *

A. RALPH HAKSTIAN, *Associate Professor of Educational Psychology, University of Alberta, Edmonton, Alberta, Canada.*

The EMLAT contains many of the features found in the older, well-conceived MLAT (for grades 9 and over). In Part 1, Hidden Words, the examinee must find a synonym or definition for a stimulus consisting of a group of letters which, when uttered, approximates an English word (e.g., "silns," for which the correct answer is "quiet"). Both vocabulary and sound-symbol association—verbal and auditory skills, respectively—are presumably measured. In Part 2, Matching Words, two sentences are presented together, the task being to find the word in the second sentence having the same syntactic function as a particular word in the first. "Sensitivity to grammatical structure" is said to be measured. In Part 3, Finding Rhymes, the examinee must identify, from a list, the word that rhymes with the stimulus word, so that, although both stimulus and response are written, something akin to sound discrimination—an auditory skill—is measured. In Part 4, Number Learning, the examinee learns the names of numbers in an artificial language and then must write them down when he hears them presented. Thus, memorizing ability is measured along with, perhaps, "auditory alertness." Parts 1, 2, and 4 are found in the MLAT; Part 3 is totally new.

ADMINISTRATION AND SCORING. Instructions are given almost entirely on a tape. The test stimuli for Parts 1, 2, and 3 are in an expendable test booklet; for Part 4, on the tape. All responses are recorded in the test booklet. Thus, test booklets and a single tape recording are needed for administration. The test booklets are hand scored using stencils which are provided. Overall, administration and scoring are clearly explained in the manual and require no special training other than in the operation of a tape recorder.

INTERPRETATION AND NORMS. Norms are based on a fairly small but adequately representative sample (18 elementary schools), and are given for both sexes in each of grades 3 to 6. Since normative data are provided only for total scores, the diagnostic purposes for which this test can be used are rather limited. The part scores and the constructs which they represent are not discussed or interpreted in the manual. Although in the higher-level MLAT norms are available only for total scores, some information is given in the manual on using part scores to diagnose learning difficulties (it might prove difficult, of course, to know what is really a "low" score without norms). It seems reasonable that if language aptitude can be conceived of as multi-factorial, the uses to which a test such as the EMLAT could be put might well have been extended beyond prediction to include diagnosis.

The very sensible feature, present also in the MLAT, of norms reported in terms of percentile bands is found in the manual. Unfortunately, however, and unlike the MLAT, no mention is made of developing local normative data. Some directions are given on using scores for placement and guidance. Overall, however, some important interpretive uses of the test have been overlooked.

RELIABILITY AND VALIDITY. The statistical data gathered on the EMLAT are particularly well presented. The inappropriateness for speeded tests of the usual split-half method of estimating reliability is acknowledged (three of the four parts may be considered speeded), and instead an alternative estimate is presented, based upon independently administered and timed half-tests, with the resulting correlations corrected with the Spearman-Brown formula. The obtained reliabilities, data on which were gathered from four schools, and which were estimated at each of the four grade levels for each sex, are extremely high, ranging from .93 to .96. Also included are standard errors of measurement and an excellent explanation of their uses.

Reliabilities (based on the same groups) of the part scores range between .70 and .95. Also presented are the intercorrelations among the parts for samples comprising each of the eight sex-by-grade-level combinations. Part 1, Hidden Words, and Part 3, Finding Rhymes, tend to correlate highly—from .55 to .81 over the samples. The other interpart correlations tend to be lower, but still substantial enough (approximately half of the 48 interpart correlations— six each for the eight samples—are above .50), when one considers the shortness and hence deflated reliabilities of the parts, to call into question the authors' contention that the interpart correlations are "only moderate" and represent evidence that the parts measure "distinct aspects of aptitude." It would appear that the separate component skills are quite substantially interrelated.

Evidence for criterion-related validity is presented in the form of correlations between total scores and course grades given two to three months later. The authors correctly acknowledge that such correlations can be more properly considered concurrent than predictive validity estimates. Forty samples were used in the validation study, with N's ranging between 26 and 89. Although each sample was homogeneous with regard to sex, grade, language (French or Spanish), and school (seven were used), the obtained validity estimates are impressively high, ranging between .23 and .84 over the 40 coefficients presented, with 37 at or above .40

and 10 above .60. The validities could perhaps have been even higher had the authors combined the students examined into larger subsets with consequently less restriction in the range of ability, but such estimates would not have been nearly as meaningful. Some demographic information on the schools in the study, however, might have helped the prospective user better estimate the test's validity for his school. In any case, the criterion-related validity appears more than adequate to make this test a useful predictor of success in foreign language learning. In short, reliability and validity are not only excellent, but also well documented.

SUMMARY. The EMLAT appears to be a carefully constructed and useful instrument for assessing language aptitude in grades 3–6. In spite of certain interpretative failings of the manual—such as no emphasis on establishing local norms and no way to interpret part scores —this test can be used to make reliable and valid assessment of language aptitude among young students. It is hoped that subsequent manuals will offer more direction on possible interpretive uses of the test.

[256]

★Pimsleur Language Aptitude Battery. Grades 6–10; 1966–67; 5 scores: grade-point average, interest, verbal, auditory, total; Form S ('66, 4 pages); manual ('66, 19 pages); student performance chart and report to parents ('67, 2 pages); separate answer sheets (Digitek, IBM 805, IBM 1230) must be used; $7 per 35 tests; $9.50 per 7½ ips test tape, 7 inch reel; $2.30 per 35 IBM 805 answer sheets; $2.80 per 35 Digitek or IBM 1230 answer sheets; $1.40 per set of scoring stencils; $2.70 per 35 student performance charts; $2.25 per specimen set; postage extra; IBM scoring service, 33¢ and over per test; (50–60) minutes; Paul Pimsleur; Harcourt Brace Jovanovich, Inc. *

REFERENCES

1. PIMSLEUR, PAUL; STOCKWELL, ROBERT P.; AND COMREY, ANDREW L. "Foreign Language Learning Ability." J Ed Psychol 53:15–26 F '62. * (PA 37:2003)
2. PIMSLEUR, PAUL. "Predicting Success in High School Foreign Language Course." Ed & Psychol Meas 23:349–57 su '63. * (PA 38:1387)
3. FAY, BETTE LANNERT. A Study of the Validity of the Pimsleur Language Aptitude Battery With Beginning French Students. Master's thesis, Ohio State University (Columbus, Ohio), 1965.
4. PIMSLEUR, PAUL, AND STRUTH, JOHANN F. "Knowing Your Students in Advance." Mod Lang J 53(2):85–7 F '69. *
5. THOMAS, JESSE C. A Study of the Correlation Between the Pimsleur Language Aptitude Battery and Foreign Language Grade Point Average Among Seventh Grade Students in the Anaheim Union High School District. Master's thesis, Chapman College (Orange, Calif.), 1969.

A. RALPH HAKSTIAN, Associate Professor of Educational Psychology, University of Alberta, Edmonton, Alberta, Canada.

The Pimsleur Language Aptitude Battery is composed of six parts: (1) Grade Point Average, (2) Interest, (3) Vocabulary, (4) Language Analysis (from a list of foreign expressions and their English equivalents, deducing how sentences may be formed in the foreign language), (5) Sound Discrimination (differentiating between pitch, orality, and nasality in spoken words), and (6) Sound-Symbol Association (associating sounds with their written symbols). The four factors seen by the author as underlying language aptitude, and on which part scores are used, are GPA, Interest, Verbal (Parts 3 and 4), and Auditory (Parts 5 and 6).

ADMINISTRATION AND SCORING. In Part 1, GPA, the examinee records from memory his last letter grade in English, social studies, mathematics, and science. From a predictive viewpoint, such an assessment appears weak, not only because considerable inaccuracy is probable, but also because the precise meaning of letter grades can vary over local settings; longer-term GPA's with greater predictive efficacy could be obtained from school records. Perhaps, however, the advantage of not having to search out these grades outweighs any small loss in predictive power. One wonders whether the equal weighting of grades in the four subjects, when summing to get the GPA score, could not effectively be replaced by some optimal unequal weighting system, since it is unlikely that grades in the four subjects predict foreign language aptitude equally well.

Part 2, Interest, is assessed via a single item with a 5-point scale running from "Rather uninterested" (in studying a modern foreign language) through "Strongly interested." Such an assessment seems very unreliable, since the measurement of such fluctuating, noncognitive constructs is somewhat unreliable at best. It seems strange that a longer interest test used experimentally by the author and referred to in the manual was abandoned.

Parts 3 through 6 are administered by using directions on tape; Parts 3 and 4 have the test stimuli in a booklet, whereas Parts 5 and 6 have the stimuli also on tape. Responses to all parts are recorded on machine scorable answer sheets. Thus, test booklets, answer sheets, and a single tape recording are needed. Overall, no special training is required of the teacher giving the test, and directions for administration and scoring are clear and complete.

INTERPRETATION AND NORMS. Norms, based on an admirably large and representative standardization sample, are provided in terms of both percentile ranks and stanines at four levels—the beginning of grades 7, 8, and 9, and the end of a first-level course—for total raw scores, verbal scores, and auditory scores. The manual unfortunately stresses the use of the stanine, the disadvantages of which seem to far outweigh the merits. Comparative judgments among students can more accurately be made with such other standard scores as the T score. Further, the size of stanines 1 and 9 is *not* equal to that of the others (although in the manual one is informed that all nine intervals are of equal size), and the reflection of truly exceptional scores—both low and high—is somewhat precluded. Percentile bands (used, for example, in the *Modern Language Aptitude Test*) would have constituted a preferable acknowledgment of the errors of measurement in mental testing.

Thorough interpretive information is presented. The user is advised to interpret scores cautiously and always with an eye to the most relevant norms group. Highly commendable are the rationale and directions provided for establishing local normative information using expectancy tables. Further, multiple regression analysis is suggested, and the publisher offers such a service. Advice is included on using the test for selection, classification, and diagnosis.

RELIABILITY AND VALIDITY. Corrected split-half reliability estimates, based on scores in the normative samples, are presented for Parts 3 through 6 separately and for the total of these parts, for four levels. Reliabilities appear adequate—running from .57 to .82 for the part scores and .85 to .89 for the composite scores—for tests of such length (Part 4, for example, has only 15 items), although it is not clear just how much elevating effect speededness may have had on these estimates. One can only guess, of course, at the reliability of the one-item interest test. Test-retest reliability estimates are promised in a future publication. It is most unfortunate that standard errors of measurement are not presented, as (a) they tend to be considerably more stable, over samples differing in homogeneity, than do the associated reliability coefficients, and (b) they can be used to set limits about obtained scores for more judicious interpretation. Their absence, then, must be considered a shortcoming.

The construct validation procedures are described, and tables of intercorrelations among the six part scores are presented at four levels. These correlations, varying between .14 and .50, are presented as evidence that the abilities measured are relatively distinct. Actually, however, the .14 and most of the correlations below .20 involve the interest test, which undoubtedly has low correlations with the other parts because of low reliability. In fact, of the remaining correlations presented, the majority are above .35, and many above .40. Given the short tests used to measure the six components, it would seem that the constructs represented are quite highly interrelated.

Concurrent validity data are the results of two studies. In one, correlations between total raw scores and (a) final grades in first-level courses in French and Spanish and (b) scores on experimental forms of the Pimsleur tests of Reading and Listening Comprehension ranged (over samples) between .44 and .79 for final grades, .25 and .72 for the Reading Comprehension Test, and .39 and .78 for the Listening Comprehension Test. Unfortunately, a different set of weights than that recommended in the manual was used with Parts 1 and 2 of the aptitude battery. In the other study, part scores, but not total scores, were correlated with the same criteria. Some predictive validity data are presented with the criterion being the *MLA—Cooperative Foreign Language Tests: French*, but again regression weights different from those recommended were used. Thus, no substantial predictive or concurrent validity data for the present test are presented. Had the test been published a year later, perhaps adequate validity data could have been included, rather than merely promised in a future publication.

SUMMARY. It may be true that data on the first two components of language aptitude— GPA and Interest—could be more effectively obtained by means other than the same test used to assess verbal and auditory ability. Overall, however, the *Pimsleur Language Aptitude Battery* appears to offer easy administration and scoring, adequate interpretive guidelines, but, as yet, incomplete reliability and validity data (although the reliability and validity may well be quite adequate). It is hoped that as these data are obtained they will be made available to users of the test.

J Counsel Psychol 15:299–300 My '68. Donald C. Ryberg. * The norms....summarize data for nearly 4,000 students beginning Grades 7, 8, and 9 in the fall of 1965–1966. Means and standard deviations are reported for each level by sex and with sexes combined for each of the parts and for the total scores. Intercorrelations are given. However, data are cross-sectional, and the population sample is not specified. * Correlations of Aptitude scores with final course grades and with raw scores for the Pimsleur Listening and Reading Comprehension Tests in French and Spanish are reported. Aptitude scores (total raw scores) yield coefficients ranging from .44 to .79, with final course grades ranging from .39 to .78 with Listening Test raw scores and from .31 to .72 with Reading Comprehension Test raw scores. While these data provide information on performance, the measures were obtained concurrently and cannot be considered evidence of predictive validity. * The LAB appears to be appropriate to the age levels for which it was intended and appears to measure relevant characteristics for foreign language learning. The battery is easily administered and scored. Given the scores, prediction and guidance, however, should proceed cautiously. The part scores seem particularly useful. For example, scores on Part 1 indicating general academic achievement could tell a great deal about perseverance and application in general, and scores on Part 2 indicating interest in studying a modern foreign language could be crucial when there is an unusually low score in either verbal or auditory ability. The interest score depends largely on a student's background of information and interests rather than on interest which may be developed through contact, study, and maturity. Total score on this type of test is of questionable value when one considers the various abilities or skills that make up the spectrum of language learning. Scores on the various parts of the battery will tell more about the facets of language learning that might pose problems for the student. The manual suggests that local norms collected over a period of years may be most helpful. The norms presented in the manual are useful references, but are not necessarily relevant to local groups of students and programs of instruction. On the other hand, once local norms are established, it may be valuable to compare them with those quoted in the manual as a basis for judgments about the program itself. Validity and reliability data in the manual are incomplete. The publisher is reporting results of investigations in progress as they are available. *

[257]

★**Pimsleur Modern Foreign Language Proficiency Tests.** First, second level courses in grades 7–12 or

first, second semesters college; 1967; 3 tests; for additional information and reviews, see the separate test entries; Harcourt Brace Jovanovich, Inc. *
a) PIMSLEUR FRENCH PROFICIENCY TESTS. See 279.
b) PIMSLEUR GERMAN PROFICIENCY TESTS. See 292.
c) PIMSLEUR SPANISH PROFICIENCY TESTS. See 325.

J Ed Meas 6(1):44–6 sp '69. A. Ralph Hakstian. * *Administration and Scoring.* Clear and detailed instructions for administration and scoring are provided in the manual. The fifteen minute listening comprehension test is administered via tape and answers are recorded on machine-scorable answer sheets. The thirty-five minute reading comprehension test utilizes test booklets and machine-scorable answer sheets. The speaking and writing proficiency tests, requiring sixteen and thirty-five minutes, respectively, represent necessarily more subjective scoring (spoken answers to the former are recorded on tape; written answers to the latter, in a booklet), but commendable attempts have been made to make the scoring as objective as possible. * *Interpretation and Norms.* Substantial interpretive materials are provided in the manual. Relevant information is given on the standardization sample. The sample seems admirably representative, geographically, and certainly large enough—8595 students in all, from 90 schools and 21 states. There is no information given on the degree of selectivity introduced as a function of the degree to which schools showed a willingness to participate. It is interesting to note that when teachers were asked to send back only every fifth *writing* test booklet in order to facilitate scoring in the standardization program, the listening and reading test scores of this "random" sample were slightly higher than those for the total normative group. * It is somewhat unfortunate that considerable stress is given to the stanine scale, since this scale does little more than add additional crudeness to already crude measures. The manual points out that a difference of two stanines or more between a person's scores on two of the subtests can be considered a reliable difference. Actually, however, the standard error of a difference for a difference between listening and reading comprehension scores on Form A of the French test, for example, is 1.28 stanines. Thus, the probability by chance alone, of a difference of two stanines on these two tests for an individual whose scores are at the top of the lower stanine and the bottom of the upper stanine could be as high as .28, clearly too high to consider such a difference reliable. A weakness in the interpretive tables lies in the fact that percentiles and stanines are based upon the total first- and second-level standardization groups. The first-level norming group contains students from grades 8 to 12; the second-level group, from grades 9 to 12. It might be more informative for teachers to be able to make comparisons with more finely delineated reference groups or at least have data showing the degree of similarity of performance between the various grades included in each level. With these few exceptions, however, the interpretive materials are informative and well presented. *Validity and Reliability.* Data on validity are well presented in the manual. A breakdown of items into well defined categories constitutes the content validity data, and the author wisely suggests that prospective users of the tests use this analysis in judging the appropriateness of the tests for their own language program. * Concurrent validity is presented in terms of correlations of the various tests (except for speaking proficiency) with final grades and teachers' ratings in a sample of students other than the standardization sample. Unfortunately, it is not clear from the manual whether or not teachers had knowledge of their students' scores on the tests prior to assignment of final grades and ratings. It is interesting to note that Form A of the French writing test, for example, correlates more highly with teachers' ratings of listening (.63) than does the listening test (.52). Similarly, the writing test correlates as highly with teachers' ratings of reading (.60) as does the reading test (.58). Also, the reading test appears to correlate more highly with the teachers' ratings of listening (.59) than does the listening test (.52). It is the reviewer's belief that these seeming incongruities are attributable to halo effect, in that teachers are more familiar with a student's reading and writing capabilities, perhaps, than his listening ability and knowledge of these more familiar skills transfers to assessment of listening ability. These results also bring up the issue of the relative purity of the four tests in all three languages, and the discriminant validity inherent in the tests. The listening test, and, to a lesser degree, the speaking test, are somewhat contaminated with a reading component. In the former, the student hears a sentence and chooses among four *written* alternatives the one he thinks he has heard. As Scherer and Wert-

heimer (1964) have suggested,[1] a better measure of listening as a separate skill would have been to have the alternatives also presented on tape. Moreover, the relatively high correlations among the listening, reading, and writing tests (.56 to .78) and between these three tests and teachers' ratings of speaking (.48 to .72) suggest, as Scherer and Wertheimer found, that, even had the tests been as free as possible of the overlapping of hypothesized skills, the existence of four language communication skills as meaningfully discriminable entities may be an unwarranted conception among teachers of foreign languages. * It is a mystery, though, why the Kuder-Richardson formula 21 was used in estimating reliabilities for the writing proficiency test, when it was freely admitted in the manual that assumptions implied in formula 21 were not met (the possible scores on some of the items of this test range from 0 to 3). * In general, however, validity and reliability data are clearly presented and complete. *Summary.* With the few exceptions noted, the Pimsleur Tests are well designed technically, and clearly and completely documented in the manual. The tests for each language will be discussed at greater length in the following sections.

For reviews of individual tests, see 279, 292, and 325.

ARABIC

[258]

★First-Year Arabic Qualifying Examination. 1 year college; 1964; 1 form (25 pages); manual (4 pages); no data on reliability; no norms, publisher recommends use of local norms; separate answer sheets (IBM 805) must be used; $3 per test and manual, postage extra; answer sheets free; (110–130) minutes; Sami A. Hanna; Middle East Center, University of Utah. *

CHINESE

[259]

★Harvard-MLA Tests of Chinese Language Proficiency. College and adults; 1959–65; 2 tests; manual ('65, 12 pages); no data on reliability; 35¢ per test; 5¢ per answer sheet; 35¢ per manual; cash orders postpaid; Modern Language Association of America and Educational Testing Service; program administered by Educational Testing Service. *
a) PICTORIAL AUDITORY COMPREHENSION TEST. 2 semesters; 1959–65; PACT; 1 form ('59, 21 pages);

7½ ips tape, 7 inch reel; separate answer sheets may be used; $5 per tape; (30–40) minutes; John B. Carroll and Wai-Ching Ho.

b) INTERMEDIATE READING COMPREHENSION TEST IN MODERN CHINESE. 4 semesters; 1964–65; 4 scores: vocabulary, structure, reading comprehension, total; 1 form ('64, 31 pages); separate answer sheets must be used; (120–130) minutes; K. P. Chou, John de Francis, Y. K. Kao, H. C. Mills, R. C. Pian, and J. Wrenn.

ENGLISH

[260]

★A Comprehensive English Language Test for Speakers of English as a Second Language. Nonnative speakers of English; 1970; CELT; 3 tests; preliminary manual (16 pages); tentative norms; publisher recommends use of local norms; separate answer sheets must be used; $4 per 100 answer sheets, postage extra; David P. Harris and Leslie A. Palmer; McGraw-Hill Book Co. *

a) LISTENING. Administered orally or by a recording; Form L-A (7 pages); examiner's book (13 pages); $8 per 20 tests; $20 per 20 tests, 100 answer sheets, examiner's book, and 3¾ ips tape recording ($15 with 33⅓ rpm record instead of tape); $3 per specimen set; (35–45) minutes.

b) STRUCTURE. Form S-A (10 pages); directions (1 page); $8 per 20 tests; $10.50 per 20 tests and 100 answer sheets; $2.50 per specimen set; 45(55) minutes.

c) VOCABULARY. Form V-A (10 pages); directions (1 page); $8 per 20 tests; $10.50 per 20 tests and 100 answer sheets; $2.50 per specimen set; 35(45) minutes.

JOHN B. CARROLL, *Senior Research Psychologist, Educational Testing Service, Princeton, New Jersey.*

To judge from the data arrayed in the preliminary manual, this battery would appear to be a promising instrument for gauging the English proficiency of persons (high school age and above) who are learning English as a second language. It is "comprehensive" in the sense that it provides information in three critical areas: listening comprehension, knowledge of "structure," and reading vocabulary. The intertest correlations are not so high as to suggest that the subscores are all measuring the same thing, yet they are not so low as to give the impression that they are measuring totally different domains. The materials evidently went through a considerable amount of pretesting, item analysis, and refinement. Sufficient normative data, although of a provisional character, are offered to enable the user to interpret scores with some confidence. The authors are to be commended for presenting data on the performance of native English speakers on the tests—data that show that American high school students of only moderate ability achieved "extremely high scores" on

them. Thus, one may infer that the tests measure fundamental rather than high-level skills in English.

It is unlikely that there will ever be a perfect all-purpose test of English as a second language; any battery of reasonable length must be designed with particular purposes in mind. This test is intended for persons who have had some formal instruction in English, usually abroad, and who come to the U.S. for further training or education. All parts of the test assume reading knowledge of English. Thus, the listening test is a test not only of aural comprehension but also of reading skill, even though the authors claim to have taken care "to keep the printed alternatives brief and lexically and grammatically simple so as to minimize the reading factor." Nevertheless, one can find items in which the total word count for the four alternatives (which must be inspected within the 15 seconds allowed for selecting the answer) is as high as 40. A learner of English with a native language background in a non-Roman alphabet or syllabary, or with just poor reading ability, might do poorly on the test despite good aural comprehension. Occasionally the items demand more than comprehension, that is to say, they demand the making of inferences about fairly complex situations. On the other hand, a few items seem too simple, depending almost exclusively on the recognition of introductory question words (*what, how,* etc.). But on the whole, given the assumptions on which it was based, this is a good test of global auditory comprehension of idiomatic American English spoken at a relatively rapid rate. Unless they object to the particular American dialect used in the recordings, users are strongly encouraged to employ the tape or phonograph recording that is available rather than to try to have the script read aloud locally —requiring the use of three speakers, two males and one female.

The structure test is introduced as a test of how well the learner knows the "grammar" of English. This is a correct claim only if one assumes that "knowing the grammar of English" corresponds to the ability to read and select constructions that are acceptable and idiomatic in choice of words or word order. These are constructions that tend to cause difficulty for foreign learners. Teachers of English as a second language justifiably place much emphasis on such constructions, hoping that the student who masters them will be more likely to speak and write acceptably. One could imagine, however, a student with a rather good technical knowledge of the theory of English grammar who might nevertheless fail to recognize, say, that "lunch room" is more idiomatic than "room for lunches," or to find a better word order than "hardly ever he leaves his house now." But this structure test will please most teachers of English as a second language, for the constructions tested are well selected and the items well written.

If any of the subtests can be rather seriously faulted, it would be the vocabulary test. According to the authors, the 280 words included in the test (counting words in both stems and alternatives) "were selected to represent the vocabulary which students might encounter in mature reading materials of the kinds assigned in general college courses." This reviewer was struck, however, with the rather high frequency of what he would call "everyday household words" like *shrink, rake, dyed,* and *strap* that would be more likely to occur in *Woman's Day* magazine than in mature college reading material; conversely, core concept words like *excel* and *reject* were poorly represented in the test. By selecting only words from the 4th to the 7th thousand in frequency-rank in the Thorndike-Lorge *Teacher's Word Book of 30,000 Words,* the authors missed the opportunity to test some of the less usual meanings of words occurring in the 1st to 3rd thousand of the frequency list. Incidentally, item 25 of the vocabulary test Form V-A is miskeyed in the scoring key that was supplied to the reviewer (the answer should be D, not B).

Since CELT comes in three separate modules, it will be convenient and economical to use only those parts that are appropriate for one's purpose. It is to be hoped that more forms will become available so that it may be used for varied purposes in placement and in the measurement of course achievement. As a practical and flexible test that can be easily procured by a teacher (in contrast to "secure" tests like the ETS *Test of English as a Foreign Language*), it will fill a need. The CELT total score is reported as having a correlation of .91 with the TOEFL scores in one group of 29 students.

[261]

★**English Knowledge and Comprehension Test.** High school; 1965; EKCT; Form 165 ['65, 13 pages]; mimeographed manual ['65, 14 pages]; authors recommend use of local norms; separate answer sheets must be used; Rs. 1.60 per test; Rs. 75 per 50 tests; Rs. 6 per 100 answer sheets; Rs. 3.50 per scoring stencil; Rs. 4 per manual; postage extra; 90(100) minutes; S. Chatterji and M. Mukerjee; S. Chatterji. *

[262]

*English Usage Test for Non-Native Speakers of English.** Non-native speakers of English; 1955–70; Forms U-A ('62, 8 pages), G, H, I, ('63, 8 pages), J ('67, 8 pages), K ('70, 8 pages); directions sheets: Form U-A ('62, 2 pages), Forms G-K ('67, 2 pages); combined manual ('67, 15 pages) for this and tests 263, 265, and 267; distribution of Forms G-K restricted to the Agency for International Development and the Bureau of Educational and Cultural Affairs of the U.S. Department of State; distribution of Form U-A restricted to the Department of State; separate answer sheets must be used; manual free on request; 60(65) minutes; David P. Harris and Leslie A. Palmer; American Language Institute. *

[263]

*Listening Test for Students of English as a Second Language.** Non-native speakers of English; 1961–67; administered orally or by tape recording; Forms A ('61, 7 pages), B ('62, 7 pages), C ('64, 7 pages); examiner's booklets: Forms A ('61, 10 pages), B ('62, 10 pages), C ('64, 10 pages); combined manual ('67, 15 pages) for this and tests 262, 265, and 267; distribution restricted to the Agency for International Development and the Bureau of Educational and Cultural Affairs of the U.S. Department of State; separate answer sheets must be used; manual free on request; (25) minutes; David P. Harris and Leslie A. Palmer; American Language Institute. *

[264]

*Michigan Test of English Language Proficiency.** Applicants from non-English language countries for admission to American colleges; 1961–65; MTELP; Forms A ('61, 15 pages), B, revised ('65, 16 pages); manual ('62, 15 pages); separate answer sheets must be used; $8 per 20 tests, 100 answer sheets, scoring stencil, and manual; $3 per 100 answer sheets; $2 per specimen set; postpaid; 75(90) minutes; test by John Upshur, Geraldine May, Leslie Palmer (A), John Harris (A), Miho Tanaka (B), and Rudolph Thrasher (B); manual by Division of Testing and Certification, English Language Institute, University of Michigan; distributed for the Institute by Follett's Michigan Book Store, Inc. *

REFERENCES

1. DIZNEY, HENRY. "Concurrent Validity of the Test of English as a Foreign Language for a Group of Foreign Students at an American University." *Ed & Psychol Meas* 25: 1129–31 w '65. * (*PA* 40:3566)
2. URSUA, AURORA RICARDO. *The Relationship Between Adeptness in the English Language and Social Adjustment of Foreign Graduate Students.* Doctor's thesis, Catholic University of America (Washington, D.C.), 1969. (*DAI* 30:2390A)

For a review by John B. Carroll of Form A, see 6:360.

[265]

*Oral Rating Form for Rating Language Proficiency in Speaking and Understanding English.** Non-native speakers of English; 1959–67; also called *AULC Interview Rating Form;* 6 ratings by interviewers: comprehension, pronunciation, grammar and word-order, vocabulary, general speed of speech and sentence length, total; individual; 1 form ('62, 2 pages, identical with form published in 1959 except for title); manual ('60, 11 pages); combined manual ('67, 15 pages) for this and tests 262-3 and 267; distribution restricted to the Agency for International Development and the Bureau of Educational and Cultural Affairs of the U.S. Department of State; manual free on request; (15-30) minutes; [David P. Harris]; American Language Institute. *

[266]

★Test of English as a Foreign Language. Applicants from non-English language countries for admission to American colleges; 1964-70; TOEFL; test administered 4 times annually (January, March, June, October) in approximately 100 countries; 6 scores: listening comprehension, English structure, vocabulary, reading comprehension, writing ability, total; 4 forms published annually; last 3 forms: Forms SEF2 ('70, 26 pages), SEF3 ('70, 25 pages), SEF4 ('70, 25 pages); bulletin of information ('70, 16 pages); handbook for candidates ('70, 19 pages); supervisor's manual ('70, 24 pages); revised interpretive manual ('70, 31 pages); listening comprehension subtest administered by record or tape; supervisor's script ['70, 7 pages]; separate answer sheets (SCRIBE) must be used; examination fee, $10 per student; fee includes reporting of scores to the examinee and to 3 colleges designated at time of application; 140(160) minutes; program sponsored jointly by the College Entrance Examination Board and Educational Testing Service; Educational Testing Service. *

REFERENCES

1. HARRIS, DAVID. "English as a Second Language: Testing." *Overseas* 3:22-5 Ja '64. *
2. LADO, ROBERT. "English and the Foreign Student." *Nat Cath Ed Assn B* 61:210-2 Ag '64. *
3. DIZNEY, HENRY. "Concurrent Validity of the Test of English as a Foreign Language for a Group of Foreign Students at an American University." *Ed & Psychol Meas* 25:1129-31 w '65. * (*PA* 40:3566)
4. PALMER, LESLIE A. "TOEFL: Testing of English as a Foreign Language." *Nat Cath Ed Assn B* 62:235-8 Ag '65. *
5. CHASE, CLINTON I., AND STALLINGS, WILLIAM M. *Tests of English Language as Predictors of Success for Foreign Students.* Indiana University, Monograph of the Bureau of Educational Studies and Testing, Indiana Studies in Prediction, No. 8. Bloomington, Ind.: the Bureau, 1966. Pp. 24. *
6. MAXWELL, ALICE. *A Comparison of TOEFL and the UCB/EFL Test.* Master's thesis, Sacramento State College (Sacramento, Calif.), 1966.
7. HWANG, KWO-YANN. *A Study of TOEFL Test Scores and Academic Success for Chinese Graduate Students at an American University.* Master's thesis, University of Oregon (Eugene, Ore.), 1969.
8. DARNELL, DONALD K. "Clozentropy: A Procedure for Testing English Language Proficiency of Foreign Students." *Speech Monogr* 37(1):36-46 Mr '70. *
9. HWANG, KWO-YANN, AND DIZNEY, HENRY F. "Predictive Validity of the Test of English as a Foreign Language for Chinese Graduate Students at an American University." *Ed & Psychol Meas* 30(2):475-7 su '70. *
10. VROMAN, CLYDE, AND WILCOX, LEE. "Research on A.I.D. Sponsored Foreign Students." *Col & Univ* 45(4):717-23 su '70. *

CLINTON I. CHASE, *Professor of Educational Psychology and Chairman of the Department; and Director, Bureau of Educational Studies and Testing; Indiana University, Bloomington, Indiana.*

This test is designed to assess the English language skills of persons whose native language is not English and who are applicants for admission to American colleges and universities. There are five subtests: Listening Comprehension, English Structure, Vocabulary, Reading Comprehension, and Writing. A total score is also reported.

The Listening Comprehension test has three parts: direct questions, conversation followed by questions, and a lecture followed by questions on its content. Tape recordings provide the stimuli in all parts of this subtest. The first two parts are general in content and only casually exploit the verbal skills that reflect one's ability for movement within the American culture. Also, the first part deals heavily with personal responses, using 16 American given names, such as Bob and Eloise, in 20 items. While the lecture provided in the third part of Listening Comprehension appears to simulate activity in which students will participate in college, one wonders what is being measured. Is it understanding of English, ability to take permitted notes, recall of details, general intelligence, or prior knowledge of the topic of the lecture? Certainly more than listening skill goes into this subscale.

The second section of TOEFL is English Structure. Each item provides a segment of a dialogue with a blank and four options from which the examinee selects the correct response with which to fill the blank. This subtest deals with tense, sequence of nouns and adjectives, etc., but no rationale is given for the selection of structure included. Although rules of grammar are important to communication, it is clear that much communication goes on amid obvious violations of these rules. The responses demanded by this subtest simulate little behavior that will be required of a foreign student in an American college.

Vocabulary, Part A, is basically like English Structure in that it uses a "fill in the blank" procedure with four options. Part B provides definitions or synonyms with four options, one of which corresponds to the stimulus. There are 15 items in Part A and 25 in Part B, a meager sample of total vocabulary. Another format, possibly selecting synonyms, would have allowed a much wider sampling of vocabulary in essentially the same amount of time, divorced from any burden of sentence reading. With an obvious overlap in format between the Vocabulary and the English Structure subtests, it is not surprising to see that the intercorrelation between them is substantial, .72. Further, there is no rationale presented for selecting the vocabulary in the test. With the number of word counts available, it seems reasonable to believe that a test based on graded difficulty and abstractness could be developed.

The fourth subtest is Reading Comprehension. A short text is provided and several questions asked about the content. Text and questions are on the same page and students may refer to the reading passage to look up the answers to the questions. A test-wise student would first scan the questions and skim the passage for the answers. This is an important skill for research work in college but is not what is typically defined as reading comprehension.

The last subtest is Writing Ability. Part A contains sentences with four words or phrases underlined in each sentence. The underlinings are labelled A, B, C, D. In each sentence one underlined word or phrase is incorrect. The letter of that word is to be marked on the answer sheet. Part B contains incomplete sentences with four options presented for completing each statement. This subtest, like English Structure, is essentially tied to basic grammar. The format of the test is so similar to other subtests that it is not surprising that it correlates in the .70's with several other subtests. Again, this test asks the student to do nothing that he will be asked to do later in his college career. Recognition of an inconsistency in grammatical form tells us very little about how the student would manage the form in his own writing. A writing sample like that used in the *Sequential Tests of Educational Progress,* although difficult to manage, would clearly be more intimately associated with writing tasks the student will be asked to perform in college than is the TOEFL writing ability exercise.

The TOEFL manual is clearly written and provides a considerable amount of useful data. The test results are reported in percentile ranks based on nearly 114,000 persons tested between 1964 and 1969.

Reliabilities, based on K-R 20, are relatively substantial, ranging from .84 for Reading Comprehension to .91 for Vocabulary. For the total test the reliability was .97. However, these reliabilities are none too high for tests designed for making decisions about individuals. The tests are timed, but the degree of their speededness is probably not a major factor in their reliability, since for the most part at least 90 percent of the examinees finish within the time limits.

The manual states that "the part scores are particularly relevant for diagnostic....interpretation." This statement is highly questionable. The intercorrelation between the subtest scores is substantial, ranging from .54 to .79 with a median of .68. The reliability of the difference score between the most reliable and least reliable subtests would be .60. A considerable score difference would have to appear between these two subtests before it could be considered more than a chance variation. The test reliabilities and intercorrelations suggest that this generalization would be true for all tests in the battery. Therefore, diagnostic application of the test is clearly limited.

The validity of the TOEFL is reflected in three types of studies: concurrent validity studies, predictive studies, and construct validity studies.

Studies of concurrent validity typically correlate TOEFL with either ratings of proficiency in English or with other test scores. Although ratings are typically less than satisfactory assessments, the TOEFL total score has been shown to correlate with them in the .70 and .80 range. TOEFL also has correlated with other tests of English well into the .80 range (.89 with the *Michigan Test of English Language Proficiency*). It should, however, be pointed out that test-taking behavior common to these tests may be increasing their intercorrelation. In any case, TOEFL is measuring about the same things as other tests of English, although it should be noted that most of the studies are based on rather small groups of students with little information on their mode of selection.

Studies showing the validity of TOEFL as a predictor of later criterion performance, typically grade point average, produce much lower correlations than do the concurrent validity studies. The correlations are, in fact, so low (e.g., .17 at the University of California, .26 at the University of Washington) as to suggest that the test may be of almost no value as a predictor of grade achievement.

Although all of the above data are relevant to construct validation of the test, the use of construct validity as described in the manual is scarcely permissible. There is little evidence of a nomological network out of which hypotheses may be constructed and tested. Hence, the nature of the construct is obscure.

In summary, the TOEFL subscales appear by title to be assessing important subskills in language behavior; however, there is obvious overlap in format from test to test, and many common behaviors are required by the various subtests in the battery. This contention is supported by the substantial intercorrelations between the subtests. Reliabilities are satisfactory, but the reliability of differences between two subtest scores is so low that making diagnostic decisions about individuals becomes perilous. The test has evidence of acceptable concurrent validity where other measures of English language ability are used as criteria. However, TOEFL is not a useful predictor of grade achievement. The manual suggests that TOEFL is best used for admission only in conjunction with corroborating data on the candidate. This appears to be excellent advice for the test user.

George Domino, *Associate Professor of Psychology and Director, Counseling Center, Fordham University, New York, New York.*

The TOEFL is designed to test competence in English of foreign students applying for admission to American colleges and universities. It is an objective test divided into five timed sections: Listening Comprehension, English Structure, Vocabulary, Reading Comprehension, and Writing Ability. Part scores, based on a mean of 50 and a standard deviation of 10, as well as a total score, are reported for each candidate, with the interpretive manual indicating that "the part scores are particularly relevant for diagnostic, as well as admissions, interpretation."

Normative data are given so that part scores can be translated into percentile ranks; these ranks were, however, computed on the basis of all candidates taking the TOEFL within a five year period, rather than a breakdown by sex, undergraduate versus graduate status, and intended field major. These breakdowns are available for total scores. Mean total scores for candidates classified by native language and by native country are also given, with an explicit cautionary note that mean differences may be the result of myriad factors rather than a reflection of native differences.

Kuder-Richardson reliability coefficients for the individual subparts range from .84 to .91 and appear satisfactory. Intercorrelations of the five subparts range from .54 to .79; although these values are high, the interpretive manual argues that each of the parts contributes something unique to the total since these values are all lower than the K-R reliability coefficients. Statistically, this may be a cogent argument; practically, one wonders whether for admission purposes, there is much redundancy. The sub-

parts may be differentially relevant to both diagnostic interpretations and admissions decisions, but there is little if any empirical evidence either to support or to dispute this.

Thirteen validation studies are reported in the interpretive manual, seven focusing on concurrent validity, five concerned with predictive validity, and one with construct validity. The seven concurrent validity studies report substantial correlations of TOEFL total scores with performance on other English proficiency tests, and in several instances, with faculty ratings. Most of the five studies focusing on predictive validity report low correlations between TOEFL scores and grade point average. As the manual points out, however, grades may not be a reasonable criterion of the validity of the TOEFL, since proficiency in English is a necessary but not sufficient prerequisite for academic achievement.

Finally, the manual contains a useful example for setting up institutional norms and expectancies tables, while repeatedly underscoring the fact that academic decisions should not be based solely on TOEFL scores and that there are no cut off scores of general applicability.

As with most ETS tests, the TOEFL appears to be a carefully constructed test. The manual and other interpretive aids are well written, and skillfully present a proper balance of technical details and interpretive comments. Although there are other English proficiency tests available of comparative validity, none approach the TOEFL in general availability both to the foreign applicant and to American institutions.

From the consumer's viewpoint, however, it has been this reviewer's experience that a number of foreign student advisors and admissions committees use (misuse?) the TOEFL either to assess in a global manner a candidate's English proficiency or to predict his potential for academic achievement. If, indeed, institutions are merely interested in knowing whether a candidate possesses a minimal knowledge of English, then a standard vocabulary test might be as satisfactory. If prediction of academic achievement is the major goal, then the effort is doomed at the beginning.

[267]

*A Vocabulary and Reading Test for Students of English as a Second Language, Revised Edition.** Non-native speakers of English; 1960-67; Forms A ('61, 11 pages), VR-B ('62, 11 pages); directions sheets: Form A ['60, 2 pages], Form VR-B ('62, 2 pages); combined manual ('67, 15 pages) for this and tests 262-3 and 265; distribution restricted to the Agency for International Development and the Bureau of Educational and Cultural Affairs of the U.S. Department of State; separate answer sheets must be used; manual free on request; 60(65) minutes; David P. Harris and Leslie A. Palmer (VR-B); American Language Institute. *

FRENCH

[268]

*Advanced Placement Examination in French. High school students desiring credit for college level courses or admission to advanced courses; 1954-70; Forms RBP ('69, 15 pages), SBP ('70, 17 pages) in 2 booklets (objective, essay); listening comprehension tapes: 7½ ips for Form RBP, 3¾ ips for Form SBP; tape script ['69-70, 5 pages] for each form; for more complete information, see 662; 180(200) minutes; program administered for the College Entrance Examination Board by Educational Testing Service. *

REFERENCES
1-3. See 6:368.
4. "CEEB Advanced Placement Examination in French." French R 39:439-49 D '65. *

For a review of the testing program, see 662.

[269]

*College Board Achievement Test in French. Candidates for college entrance with 2-4 years high school French; 1901-71; test administered each January at centers established by the publisher; for more complete information, see 663; 60(80) minutes; program administered for the College Entrance Examination Board by Educational Testing Service. *

REFERENCES
1-7. See 4:237.
8-9. See 5:263.
10-13. See 6:366.

For a review by Walter V. Kaulfers of earlier forms, see 4:237. For reviews of the testing program, see 6:760 (2 reviews).

[270]

*College Placement Test in French Listening Comprehension. Entering college freshmen; 1962-70, c1955-70; CPTFLC; irregularly scheduled reprintings of inactive forms of College Board Achievement Test in French Listening Comprehension; Forms NPL ['65, reprint of 1963 test], QPL ['68, reprint of 1967 test] in a single booklet (13 pages); test administered by 7½ ips tape recording; for more complete information, see 665; 30(40) minutes; program administered for the College Entrance Examination Board by Educational Testing Service. *

REFERENCE
1. ALEAMONI, LAWRENCE M., AND MATSUNAGA, ALLEN. A Study of Foreign Language at the University of Illinois Using the CEEB Foreign Language Placement Tests and End-of-Course Grades. Research Report No. 317. Champaign, Ill.: Measurement and Research Division, Office of Instructional Resources, University of Illinois, 1970. Pp. i, 42. *

For a review of the testing program, see 665.

[271]

*College Placement Test in French Reading. Entering college freshmen; 1962-70, c1955-70; CPTFR; irregularly scheduled reprintings of inactive forms of College Board Achievement Test in French; Forms SPL1 ('70, reprint of 1963 test), SPL2 ('70, reprint of 1964 test) in a single booklet (19 pages); for more complete information, see 665; 60(70) minutes; program administered for the College Entrance Examination Board by Educational Testing Service. *

REFERENCE
1. ALEAMONI, LAWRENCE M., AND MATSUNAGA, ALLEN. A Study of Foreign Language at the University of Illinois Using the CEEB Foreign Language Placement Tests and End-of-Course Grades. Research Report No. 317. Champaign, Ill.: Measurement and Research Division, Office of Instructional Resources, University of Illinois, 1970. Pp. i, 42. *

For a review by Walter V. Kaulfers of earlier forms, see 4:237. For a review of the testing program, see 665.

[272]

*Common Concepts Foreign Language Test: French. Students in any grade who are at the Level 1 stage of achievement; 1962-66; aural comprehension; same booklet also used to test German and Spanish; may be administered using live voice but tape recording (3¾ ips) is recommended; Forms 1, 2, ('62, 31 pages) in a single booklet; manual ('66, 41 pages); separate answer sheets (IBM 1230) must be used; $1.10 per test; $5.95 per tape recording; $2.50 per 50 answer sheets; 75¢ per scoring stencil for either form; $1 per manual; postage extra; $2.25 per specimen set (without tape), postpaid; scoring service, 22¢ and over per test; (40-45) minutes; Bela H. Banathy, Miles V. Zintz, W. James Popham, Joseph M. Sadnavitch, Rena Krichbaum, Fred B. Gannon, Valdemar Hempel, and Klaus A. Mueller; CTB/McGraw-Hill. *

For a review covering the three languages, see 253.

[273]

*First Year French Test, [Revised Edition]. High school and college; 1956-68; FYFT; Form A ('68, 2 pages); manual ('68, 2 pages); no data on reliability; $1.75 per 25 tests, postage extra; 75¢ per specimen set, postpaid; 50(55) minutes; Jean Leblon and Minnie M. Miller; Data Processing and Educational Measurement Center. *

For reviews by Nelson Brooks and Mary E. Turnbull of an earlier edition, see 5:266.

[274]

*The Graduate Record Examinations Advanced French Test. Graduate school candidates; 1939-70; 3 current forms ('64-69, 32-36 pages); descriptive booklet ('70, 8 pages); for more complete information, see 667; 180(200) minutes; Educational Testing Service. *

For a review by Nelson Brooks of an earlier form, see 6:376; for a review by Walter V. Kaulfers, see 5:270. For reviews of the testing program, see 667 (1 review) and 5:601 (1 review).

[275]

*Graduate School Foreign Language Test: French. Graduate level degree candidates required to demonstrate reading proficiency in French; 1963–71; GSFLTF; 3 current forms ('70–71, 31–32 pages); for more complete information, see 668; 100(120) minutes; Educational Testing Service. *

REFERENCES

1. BARTLETT, ALBERT ALLEN. "The Foreign Language Requirement for the Ph.D.: A New Approach." *Foreign Lang Ann* 2:174–84 D '68. *
2. CLARK, JOHN L. D. "The Graduate School Foreign Language Requirement: A Survey of Testing Practices and Related Topics." *Foreign Lang Ann* 2:150–64 D '68. *
3. HARVEY, PHILIP R. "Minimal Passing Scores on the Graduate School Foreign Language Tests." *Foreign Lang Ann* 2:165–73 D '68. *

For a review by Clarence E. Turner of an earlier edition, see 6:377.

[276]

*MLA Cooperative Foreign Language Proficiency Tests: French. French majors and advanced students in college; 1960–68; formerly called *MLA Foreign Language Proficiency Tests for Teachers and Advanced Students: French;* 7 tests in 3 booklets (formerly in 7 booklets); Forms HA ('61, identical except for format and directions with earlier tests variously designated Forms A, JML1, and K-JML1), HB ('66, identical except for format and directions with tests copyrighted in 1961 and variously designated Forms B, JML2, K-JML2, and OML1); temporary series directions for administering ('68, 12 pages); series norms ('66, 2 pages); mimeographed series score conversion directions ['68, 8 pages]; separate answer sheets (Digitek, SCRIBE) must be used except for speaking and writing tests; $4 per 100 answer sheets, cash orders postpaid; Digitek scoring stencils not available; SCRIBE scoring and statistical analysis service, 35¢ per student for all tests except speaking and writing; scoring by special arrangement with language specialists: $3 per speaking test tape, $1.50 per writing test; Modern Language Association of America and Educational Testing Service; Cooperative Tests and Services. *

a) BOOK 1: READING, LISTENING COMPREHENSION, SPEAKING. Forms HA (24 pages), HB (21 pages); $9 per 10 tests; 90¢ per single copy; $12 per 7½ ips listening/speaking test tape; blank tapes for student responses must be obtained locally; 40(50) minutes for reading, (20–30) minutes for listening comprehension, (15–30) minutes for speaking.

b) BOOK 2: WRITING. Forms HA (8 pages), HB (7 pages); $6 per 20 tests; 30¢ per single copy; 45(55) minutes.

c) BOOK 3: APPLIED LINGUISTICS, CIVILIZATION AND CULTURE, PROFESSIONAL PREPARATION. Forms HA, HB, (29 pages); professional preparation test is common to all languages in series; $9 per 10 tests; 90¢ per single copy; 40(50) minutes for linguistics, 30(40) minutes for civilization and culture, 45(55) minutes for professional preparation.

REFERENCES

1–3. See 6:379.
4. PAQUETTE, F. ANDRÉ; WALLMARK, MADELINE; SPENCER, RICHARD E.; AND CHURCHILL, FREDERICK J. *A Comparison of the MLA Foreign Language Proficiency Tests for Teachers and Advanced Students With the MLA Foreign Language Cooperative Tests.* An unpublished report to the U.S. Office of Education, Project No. BR-6-2619. Modern Language Association of America, 1966. Pp. 58. * (ERIC ED 019 017)
5. TOLLINGER, SUZANNE, AND PAQUETTE, F. ANDRÉ, EDITORS. *The MLA Foreign Language Proficiency Tests for Teachers and Advanced Students: A Professional Evaluation and Recommendations for Test Development,* pp. 1–23, 118–24, 144–7, 161–5, passim. Sections on this test by Dora S. Bashour, Michel Beaujour, Jacques Ehrmann, Alexander Hull, Tora T. Ladu, James C. McKinney, Douglas C. Sheppard, and Rebecca M. Valette. An unpublished report to the U.S. Office of Edu-

cation, Project No. BR-6-2619, Modern Language Association of America, June 1966. Pp. viii, 366. * (ERIC ED 019 016)
6. CARROLL, JOHN B. "Foreign Language Proficiency Levels Attained by Language Majors Near Graduation From College." *Foreign Lang Ann* 1:131–51 O '67. *
7. DIZNEY, HENRY F., AND GROMEN, LAUREN. "Predictive Validity and Differential Achievement on Three MLA-Cooperative Foreign Language Tests." *Ed & Psychol Meas* 27: 1127–30 w '67. * (PA 42:9417)
8. PAQUETTE, F. ANDRÉ; WITH THE COOPERATION OF MADELINE WALLMARK. *The MLA Foreign Language Proficiency Tests for Teachers and Advanced Students: Analysis of the Performance of Native Speakers and Comparison With That of NDEA Summer Institute Participants.* An unpublished report to the U.S. Office of Education, Project No. BR-6-2619, Modern Language Association of America, June 1968. Pp. ii, 42. * (ERIC ED 019 017)
9. PERKINS, JEAN A. "State Certification and Proficiency Tests: The Experience in Pennsylvania." *Foreign Lang Ann* 2:195–9 D '68. *
10. CARROLL, JOHN B. "What Does the Pennsylvania Foreign Language Project Tell Us?" *Foreign Lang Ann* 3(2): 214–36 D '69. *
11. OTTO, FRANK. "The Teacher in the Pennsylvania Project." *Mod Lang J* 53(6):411–20 O '69. * (PA 44:21642)
12. SMITH, PHILIP D., JR. "The Pennsylvania Foreign Language Research Project: Teacher Proficiency and Class Achievement in Two Modern Languages." *Foreign Lang Ann* 3(2):194–207 D '69. *

JOSEPH A. MURPHY, *Professor of French, Lycoming College, Williamsport, Pennsylvania.*

In evaluating the MLA Proficiency tests, one cannot avoid reference to the central issue in evaluating any teacher-education program: Are the in-put experiences on which the program (or test) rests predictive of the competencies required of the practitioner? In this age of deep educational malaise, the reviewer should look beyond a mere correlation between these variables to the values on which current educational practice stands. More specifically, is the discipline involved in a program or test battery attuned to the perceived needs of those served by it? Only after this nagging question has been confronted, however unsatisfactorily, can we meaningfully consider the problem of test efficiency.

Proficiency in something called the four skills has long been the central objective of foreign language programs. This logical categorization has led to very real kinds of separation in preparing curriculum objectives, activities, and tests. The MLA Proficiency tests represent the ultimate in compartmentalization of skills. Given the lack of demonstrated correlation between teacher proficiency and student achievement,[1] doubts must be raised about this separatist form of teaching and testing. This thought will reappear in the analysis of particular tests.

THE WRITING TEST. In the first of the two sections, the student completes sentences with structure words. In the second he corrects a

1 SMITH, PHILIP D., AND BARANY, HELMUT A. *A Comparison Study of the Effectiveness of the Traditional and Audiolingual Approaches to Foreign Language Instruction Utilizing Laboratory Equipment.* Unpublished report to the U.S. Office of Education, Project No. 7-0133, Pennsylvania State Department of Public Instruction, October 1968. (ERIC ED 030 013)

poorly written passage. The former stands as an effective procedure for testing key grammatical concepts. The items themselves span elementary to low-level advanced French grammar. However, there is something unnatural about a test in which a student revises incorrect French that is not his own. A more authentic question type would encourage students to produce synonyms or paraphrased equivalents for underlined words. This does not qualify as an authentic writing test if by writing one means the production of original language patterns. French grammar will continue to be treated as a static body of knowledge until national examinations provide model evaluations of comprehensive writing samples. Despite serious administrative and scoring difficulties, ways should be found to test writing as a total skill. Knowledge of structure cannot be *realistically* tested except in a situation where the student is given some freedom to decide content as well as form. Objectivity must be re-defined within a nonstatistical framework.

THE READING TEST. The first section of the reading test contains 15 multiple choice items about idioms. Other sections contain many vocabulary recognition and implication type questions. The last part presents five questions on analysis of poetry. In general, the questions appear carefully designed. There is a balance between the word-study inventory and the comprehension questions themselves. It is notable that there are no questions which stimulate analogous, logical (in the sense of cause-effect recognitions), or evaluative thinking. In this area too the test provides teacher education programs with powerful motivation for sustaining the inertia of present low thought levels. For example, five efficient questions requiring higher mental operations would be more revealing of reading aptitude than all the questions assigned to word study. As a reading test it succeeds only partially as a measure of the process of reading.

THE SPEAKING TEST. The first thing notable about this test is the angry voice of the announcer. Despite such a frightening beginning, the test does offer the means of evaluating oral production. It consists of a taped sampling of oral French cued in three ways. First one repeats 15 sentences, each of which contains two phonetic elements for scoring. In the next part the subject reads a passage "in a natural colloquial style, treating liaison in accord with

this style." The final section requires one to comment on pictures—in isolation, in a series, and with general directions in English.

These three question types afford the test a commendable pedagogical balance. The first and last parts especially seem to have been prepared with a keen critical sense. In Part A most of the phonetic units are quite appropriately vowel sounds. The few consonants chosen for testing are dentals and liquids. A minor recommendation might be to substitute initial plosives for the relatively simple and insignificant dentals. Degrees of acceptability might be more easily detected for plosives. In fact, none of the consonant mistakes are likely to interfere with comprehension of a message. Moreover, specific intonation features were not tested in this part but were relegated to the more subjective sections in which rating scales were used. Intonation should be tested more rigorously.

In Part C the pictures are simple and clear, but rich enough in detail to stimulate a series of coherent utterances. They command speech involving narration, description, and "formules de politesse," while allowing the imaginative student to go beyond the physical stimulus.

Part B might be questioned on the reasoning that few if any undergraduate courses stress the precise characteristics of colloquial versus formal French, especially as applied to optional liaisons. Basing an entire section on this precarious foundation undoubtedly introduces an emotional shock with a concomitant error factor, the extent of which would be difficult to ascertain. Clearer directions would require the subject to make obligatory liaisons and to refrain from forbidden ones.

THE LISTENING TEST. In the listening test 36 questions are cued in three ways. First, short snatches of conversation are followed by four possible written responses. Next a radio broadcast is followed by oral questions and four written answers. Finally a three-minute "dramatic" scene is followed by eight oral true-false questions. The style of the utterances progresses from carefully enunciated to rapid colloquial in the last section. The items in both forms have been meticulously constructed. Most are difficult for beginners but attainable by a person with average sound discrimination ability and moderate exposure to the foreign tongue. It is improbable that a subject without foreign experience could perform successfully in the last part. Moreover, there are some disturbing facts that warrant further study. Because the answers are read, the purity of the listening factor becomes tainted. In Form HA especially, there seem to be some items in which an unreasonably brief pause is given to peruse the printed answers and make a selection. This is not to argue against combining skills in a testing situation for that would only lead to further compartmentalization. What is needed is synchronization based on an average reading speed of representative test subjects. Without this kind of knowledge, a speed reading factor is introduced into a test where listening skill should dominate. Also, because the test is administered in a language laboratory, one can only wonder about the effect of moving the booklet around so that printed answers are always within normal seeing distance. There is definite distraction in manipulating the answer booklet in a crowded space. Despite these doubts, the listening test remains a fair and significant measure within realistic limits.

THE APPLIED LINGUISTICS TEST. The applied linguistics test includes 55 items covering pronunciation and phonetics, the writing system, morphology and syntax, general linguistics, and historical linguistics. The questions are pertinent, treating the kind of knowledge taught in the better applied linguistics courses. Moreover, it contains many application questions in which knowledge of principles must be accompanied by a more practical penetrating kind of intelligence. Such a test presents a problem for the many institutions lacking trained personnel to teach modern applied linguistics. However, this gives no legitimate basis for abandoning evaluation of this vital related discipline.

THE CIVILIZATION AND CULTURE TEST. To test culture and civilization, there are 60 objective questions about French history, politics, literature, geography, economics, religion, education, and sports. The range of questions is commendable. The underlying assumption can be identified with the validity of a "culture" in the broad French meaning. Regardless of the inherent value of such a "culture," problems arise in the course of achieving and evaluating it. Specific aspects of this assumption will have to receive honest investigation. Is the information embodied in the questions of greatest worth to the student of French life? Is the scope of the test realistic for a novice teacher? Does any part of the test reflect a compromise with the scientific view of culture as a social science?

Does the test provide an excuse for continuing the boring un-intellectual approaches to the teaching of culture and civilization? If the test contained the germs of positive response to these questions, it would be analyzed further at this point.

THE PROFESSIONAL PREPARATION TEST. The professional preparation test contains 65 multiple choice questions of pedagogical interest. As stated in the preceding section, the most crucial question about an "objective" question is "What information is most worth examining?" The 65 questions can be categorized as pertaining to either fact or theory. There is little justification in an "objective" test of "right" answers for the latter. In the absence of convincing research, it is intellectually dishonest to parade theories as facts. For example, there is no "right" answer as to whether choral or individual drills are more effective, whether dictation is inappropriate for the language laboratory, whether the mental discipline argument for learning a language is less defensible than the pragmatic one, whether literature is a better tool for learning culture than history, geography, or economics, or whether one method of dialogue presentation is superior to another. On the other hand, professional questions like that dealing with the values of linguistics for a language teacher, should be kept and increased. The test could be made considerably more objective by including application questions on topics like the use of the media, psychological foundations on which a consensus has been reached, unit planning, and evaluation procedures. The absence of such professional topics and the inclusion of so much partisan bias tarnish a potentially important test.

CONCLUSION. Results of external validation of the MLA Proficiency tests have not yet appeared in the professional literature, but such studies are not necessary to raise doubts about the importance to be granted this battery. Given the inherent limitations of the separate tests, no educator can securely interpret scores on this test as a predictor of teaching effectiveness. This is true mostly because the static parts separately united do not create a dynamic whole. The test does offer an uneven gauge of mastery of a few skills and a mass of factual information.

JEAN-GUY SAVARD, Research Officer, International Center for Research on Bilingualism;

and Assistant Professor of Linguistics, Université Laval, Quebec, Canada.

The *MLA Foreign Language Proficiency Tests: French* are worthy of top-rank listing among present-day foreign language testing materials for advanced students and foreign language teachers. This reviewer made it a point personally to answer each item contained in this test, so that an analysis of each of the subtests might bring forth a more accurate evaluation of the test as a whole.

READING. The 40 minutes allotted for the 50 items of the reading test seem more than adequate. I wonder, however, about the use of certain difficult and rarely used words and expressions, such as: "mettre le grappin dessus," "primesautier," and "lamente la faiblesse" in a test of reading comprehension. On the other hand, in one item the correct word, "cafard," might be selected by a greater number of testees simply because the other choices are so outstandingly irrelevant to the meaning of the sentence. To be fair with the examinees it would also seem advisable to mention the author of a literary quotation, and perhaps the year in which it was written. The interpretation of the meaning may depend on whether the passage was taken from works signed Corneille, Rousseau, Sartre, etc. This test definitely measures what it was meant to measure, the meanings of words and sentences, knowledge of grammatical categories (nouns, pronouns, adverbs, prepositions, verbs, etc.) and structures. In a sense, it could be said that the test measures more than what it is intended to measure. Some questions appear to measure a degree of intelligence as well as a degree of proficiency in literary analysis. Unfortunately, it does not seem possible to specify the equivalence of the two forms owing to the lack of statistical data.

LISTENING COMPREHENSION. In this test it would seem quite admissible to allow for an occasional and perhaps intentional flaw in articulation. In fact, such is the case in several items where the first three words are literally dropped. This minor detail is a bit more obvious with the hissing sounds in the first four spoken words of one item. The testmakers are to be complimented for the commendable feature of alternating masculine and feminine voices on the test tape. The only drawback here is that the feminine voice, in certain instances, tends to exaggerate the natural flow of enunciation. In general, the masculine and feminine voices in

Form HB have a twangy tone on the tape and slurring seems unnecessarily overdone. At this advanced level, however, this procedure could very well be admissible. Assuming that this procedure is part of the intentional difficulties included in the test, it would be advisable to present them in both forms. At present the difficulties differ from one form to the other. In Form HA, item 7, the intonation is a little misleading; it seems to lack the upward movement of the pitch needed to make it sound like a question. In item 11 the rolling of *rrr* as in "aller et retour" seems somewhat excessive at a normal speed of conversation. Item 13 is given rather rapidly on tape, and thereby seems to skip syllables. These are reasons for doubting the equivalence of the forms.

The spacing of questions given on tape deserves some attention. The following is the result of our trial in timing the tape. In the first part, a statement is given, and 10 seconds are allotted to choose the correct answer. It takes approximately 5 seconds to read the four choices and then another 3 to 4 seconds to select the answer. More time could be given: 2 additional seconds would suffice. In the third part, the description of a scene seems to be a bit long and drawn out. The dialogue must be retained and recalled. The student may easily forget what he has heard. In this case we tend to measure memorizing ability rather than listening comprehension.

SPEAKING. Both forms of the test are well balanced, well constructed, adequate, and comprehensive. Part A, Form HA, tends to measure the 16 phonemes most apt to create certain difficulties for English-speaking students learning French. Time allotment for reading of the text in Part B is quite sufficient. The reading calls for a natural colloquial style of speech. In Part C the examinee is asked to give an oral description of pictures and he may also give his version of what they suggest. This pictorial feature is well chosen and should give rise to favorable comments. Objective evaluation of this type of test would, however, bring about certain problems in scoring. The testmakers are to be commended on their effort to give clear and concise instructions in order to avoid a completely subjective scoring system. Nevertheless, Parts B and C most likely present certain scoring difficulties. I should imagine that even trained judges could interpret differently the meaning of "Performance like a native who reads well," "Easily intelligible," or "Frequent approximation of native features," etc. In all fairness we must admit that this particular problem of scoring method is not peculiar to the MLA tests. The authors of the MLA battery have devised a worthy measuring instrument. The five-point scale which they have devised will no doubt help to reduce the error factor.

WRITING. Part A (HA) of this test mostly measures the use of function words: relative pronouns, demonstrative pronouns, prepositions, articles, adverbs, and auxiliary verbs. The relative importance of each of these grammatical categories has been fairly well determined. Among 30 measured elements there are 11 prepositions. It is a well-known fact that prepositions do bring about numerous problems to students learning a foreign language. In Part B-1 (HA), the choice of words and structures to be measured is entirely relevant. However, in Part B-2 (HA), the word "matineux," which is so archaic that few native speakers could be expected to understand the subtleties of its usage, is a good example of French language subtleties which should be avoided in this type of test. It may be noted that poorly written passages which "present some incorrect forms for students to correct" are, according to item 58 of the Professional Preparation Test (HA), the LEAST desirable practice in constructing a foreign language test.

APPLIED LINGUISTICS. In this subtest, a good knowledge of French phonetics, morphology, and syntax is a requisite. If a diploma is to be of importance then it is high time to demand that foreign language teachers be proficient in the language they intend to teach. The authors have wisely de-emphasized the importance of a knowledge of historical linguistics. Items 23, 24, 27, and 50 in Form HA are long and complicated. They present such comprehension difficulties that I wonder if they truly measure the knowledge of the grammar rule involved. In Form HB the range and order of item difficulties are questionable. For a native speaker items 9 and 12 seem much easier to answer than item 1. Statistical data only could prove the validity of such an observation.

CIVILIZATION AND CULTURE. It is undoubtedly an excellent idea to include a sound knowledge of French culture and civilization among the requirements for advanced students and future teachers of French. Indeed, true bilingualism supposes a certain degree of biculturalism. The construction of this type of test, however, involves many difficulties. It should be pointed out to users of the test that the answers given in the Table of Correct Answers should be checked for possible modifications due to the passage of time. I would also be inclined to put considerably less emphasis on the history and economy of France. It would then be possible to include a few questions concerning ways and customs and institutions of contemporary French-speaking communities (la Francophonie) throughout the world with particular reference to North America. It would be a means of giving better balance to this subtest, thereby rendering it a bit more comprehensive.

PROFESSIONAL PREPARATION. This subtest is of utmost importance to those who have chosen language teaching as a profession. The purpose of this test is to measure knowledge of principles and techniques of language teaching at the primary and secondary levels. Granted that there is a world of difference between theory and practice, we must still take available means to ascertain the degree of professional competency of teachers of a foreign language. The content of the subtest seems to correspond to a curriculum based on the audio-lingual approach to foreign language teaching. The theories and practices which this test emphasizes are hardly questionable, and it takes much careful probing to single out questions which could be considered irrelevant. In this perspective, even the less satisfactory questions are still acceptable. In order to answer items 25 and 63 (HA) the testee would have to be familiar with the specific documents mentioned. This point in itself deprives the test of its universal character. The same remark applies to items 25 and 62, where reference is made to the abbreviation FLES. Current fashions should be banned by testmakers. The importance given to the audio-lingual approach in language teaching may lead one to wonder whether the pedagogical value of this test is not as important as its measuring value. As a means for measuring knowledge of audio-lingual methodology this test is undoubtedly adequate.

CONCLUSIONS. The one problem to which a definite answer had yet to be found when this test was designed was that of content: linguistic, cultural, or professional. This observation can be applied, in a very general manner, to all known language tests and professional preparation tests. *We do not know exactly what to test because we do not know exactly what to teach.* In practice, we do make a choice, but is it always the best one? In the light of what is currently known on the subject, the authors were wise in giving priority to their own most pressing needs. This, however, does not eliminate the need for a new approach to research in the field. It should be possible to establish a more or less precise operational definition of the subject matter to be taught at the different stages of language teaching. Only such an operational definition could constitute an adequate criterion for the validity of a test.

It appears that constructors of this MLA test have achieved the proposed objectives at a high level. The techniques and procedures are in conformity with the specifications supplied by responsible authorities. The committees designated to make up the test have without doubt succeeded in devising a measuring instrument which permits an evaluation of the candidates' (future teachers) degree of proficiency. Classification is then established as minimal, good, or superior.

Those who might find the testing time excessive should be reminded that the professional objectives pursued by this test fully justify the required four to five hours. Independently of correlations between subtests, it is quite evident that the seven lengthy subtests will enable administrators to establish a more reliable diagnosis of specific weaknesses and skills.

A complete and well organized manual giving the coefficients of reliability and validity, as well as a detailed item analysis for HA and HB forms, would be of great value. Data from the NDEA experimental testing of native speakers (*8*) and other programs and surveys should be available in one exhaustive report. The figures compiled up to now are encouraging; for example, the following reliability coefficients were reported: Listening (.91), Reading (.93), Writing (.94), Applied Linguistics (.87), Civilization and Culture (.86), and Professional Preparation (.87).

This MLA French test is, to my knowledge, the most adequate, comprehensive, and objective test of its kind. Notwithstanding all the aforementioned observations, I do not hesitate in recommending the *MLA Cooperative Foreign Language Proficiency Tests: French* to those who have the responsibility of selecting and appointing teachers of French as a foreign language.

For reviews by Paul Pimsleur and James H. Ricks, Jr., see 6:379.

[277]

*MLA-Cooperative Foreign Language Tests: French. 1–2 years high school or 2 semesters college, 3–4 years high school or 4 semesters college; 1963–65; 4 tests in a single booklet: listening, speaking, reading, writing; writing test available as separate; 2 forms; 2 levels; no specific manual; series directions for administering and scoring ('64, 40 pages); series handbook ('65, 24 pages); series booklet of norms ('65, 82 pages); student bulletin ('65, 2 pages) for each level; $7 per 10 tests; $5 per 20 writing tests only; separate answer sheets (Digitek, Digitek-IBM 805, IBM 1230, SCRIBE) may be used for listening and reading tests; $4 per 100 answer sheets; $1.25 per 10 IBM 805 or IBM 1230 scoring stencils (answer pattern must be punched out locally); Digitek scoring stencils not available; $8.50 per 3¾ ips tape, 5 inch reel, for listening test; $8.50 per 3¾ ips tape, 5 inch reel, for speaking test (blank tapes or discs for recording student responses must be obtained locally); $2 per series directions for administering and scoring; $2 per series handbook; $2 per series norms booklet; $3 per 100 student bulletins; $3 per specimen set; cash orders postpaid; SCRIBE scoring and statistical analysis service (listening and reading tests), 35¢ per student; no scoring service for speaking and writing tests, but arrangements for professional scoring can be made; 25(35) minutes for listening, 10(20) minutes for speaking, 35(40) minutes for reading, 35(40) minutes for writing; prepared in cooperation with the Modern Language Association of America; Cooperative Tests and Services. *
a) [LOWER LEVEL.] 1–2 years high school or 2 semesters college; Forms LA ('63, 23 pages), LB ('63, 24 pages); writing test: Forms LA, LB, ('63, 8 pages).
b) [HIGHER LEVEL.] 3–4 years high school or 4 semesters college; Forms MA, MB, ('63, 25 pages); writing test: Forms LA, LB, ('63, 9 pages).

REFERENCES

1. PAQUETTE, F. ANDRÉ; WALLMARK, MADELINE; SPENCER, RICHARD E.; AND CHURCHILL, FREDERICK J. *A Comparison of the MLA Foreign Language Proficiency Tests for Teachers and Advanced Students With the MLA Foreign Language Cooperative Tests.* An unpublished report to the U.S. Office of Education, Project No. BR-6-2619, Modern Language Association of America, 1966. Pp. 58. * (ERIC ED 019 017)
2. SPENCER, RICHARD E. "The Influence of Disc or Tape Language Laboratory Equipment on Foreign Language Speaking Test Scores." *Mod Lang J* 50:207–8 Ap '66. *
3. VOCOLO, JOSEPH M. "The Effect of Foreign Language Study in the Elementary School Upon Achievement in the Same Foreign Language in High School." *Mod Lang J* 51:463–9 D '67. *
4. MUELLER, THEODORE H. "Programmed Language Instruction—Help for the Linguistically 'Underprivileged.'" *Mod Lang J* 52:79–84 F '68. * (*PA* 44:20888)
5. ALEAMONI, LAWRENCE M., AND SPENCER, RICHARD E. "A Comparison of Biserial Discrimination, Point Biserial Discrimination, and Difficulty Indices in Item Analysis Data." *Ed & Psychol Meas* 29(2):353–8 su '69. * (*PA* 44:17314)

MICHIO PETER HAGIWARA, *Associate Professor of French, University of Michigan, Ann Arbor, Michigan.*

Foreign language methodology that has been dominant in the past two decades is the "audiolingual" approach. It aims to develop the four fundamental language skills of listening comprehension, speaking, reading, and writing in a systematic manner, with a stress on the first two, often called "primary communication skills," in the early stages of instruction. The advent of this teaching method made traditional reading-oriented proficiency tests all too inadequate. The *MLA-Cooperative Foreign Language Tests* were issued in 1963 in the light of the "new key" method. They measure the linguistic competence of a student in the four basic language skills at two different levels.

LISTENING COMPREHENSION. Forms LA and LB have 45 items (45 maximum points), and MA and MB, 40 items (4 maximum points), to be completed in 25 minutes. Pure auditory test items are found only in LA and LB, where the first four items require the student to choose the one of four simple line drawings that matches the statement he has heard. The remainder of the items are a conventional "hybrid" type combining listening and reading. They are also grouped according to general topics, so that the context of the sentences does not jump abruptly from one item to another. Forms LA and LB contain 13 and 12 items, respectively, after the pictorial-cue items, and each item is a single utterance for which the student chooses one out of four possible answers that are printed in the booklet. The next 13 or 14 items are "conversations" between two speakers, usually a male and a female. The student is to select a printed statement that best describes each conversation. In the next 10 items, the auditory stimuli are lengthened, up to four utterances per item; in each item, however, there are normally two cues embedded, so that missing one out of several sentences may not adversely affect the selection of the correct response. The pauses are also longer in order to accommodate the increased amount of reading. Items 41 through 43 concern a brief telephone conversation, and the student is to play the role of the second speaker in answering statements made by the first speaker which are heard on the tape. Finally, the last two items are preceded by a dialogue of 12 lines or more and two questions concerning its content. Forms MA and MB follow the same patterns as LA and LB, except that there are no picture-based items and the auditory stimuli are much longer and somewhat more complicated.

The heavy reliance on hybrid test items to evaluate listening comprehension is rather unfortunate. Although the 10–15 second pauses may enable most students to glance over the printed multiple choice answers quickly, the slow reader will more likely be penalized as the answers become progressively longer. Furthermore, there is a possibility that a wrong response may be due to a faulty reading of the answers or an unfamiliarity with their vocabulary, rather than to a misunderstanding of the auditory cues. As a result, the score on this test may reflect reading ability as much as listening comprehension. A more extensive use of pictorial multiple choice items would be preferable for both levels. As an additional means of increasing the difficulty level, the phonation rate of the aural stimuli might have been gradually increased, or some background noise or "white noise" might have been introduced in the last few items. The telephone conversation that occurs in all the tests could have utilized the actual pitch and timbre of voices on the telephone.

SPEAKING. This is probably the most original of the four tests. It aims to evaluate the student's oral production on the basis of pronunciation, grammar, vocabulary, and fluency, through 32 items with a maximum possible score of 82 points. The test, which lasts 10 minutes, requires the student to record his oral responses on a tape. The first 15 items measure his pronunciation in terms of mimicry. The student repeats 10 short utterances given by the master tape, each sentence within 3 or 4 seconds. The responses are checked according to specific sounds or successions of sounds and basic intonation patterns, each item to be scored as right or wrong. The next 10 items are embedded in a short passage containing a dialogue which the student reads aloud from his test booklet. Each item is scored right or wrong even though it contains several sounds. There is also a global rating scale (item 26) on which the student's general ability to pronounce accurately is judged on a five-point scale. The first part can be scored relatively objectively by a trained ear, but in the second part scorer subjectivity increases. Obviously, in speech production the correct pronunciation of a sequence of phonemes is more important than that of single phonemes. But since each item is made up of several sounds, an error in any one sound segment will mark the entire item wrong even if the remainder are pronounced acceptably. No intonation patterns are checked in the second part. In both parts, certain sound segments that are often mispronounced by students, such as /i/ and /a/, are not tested alone, but each is combined with at least one other sound. The rising intonation is not sufficiently covered in any of the four test forms. Perhaps the reading passage should be a dialogue without extraneous descriptive elements and should test intonation, linking of syllables, liaison, and a limited number of morphologically important segments, such as the /d/ of *vendent* as against *vend,* /n/ of *italienne* as against *italien,* /l/ of *journal* as against *journaux,* and so forth.

Part 3 consists of four questions concerning simple line drawings, thus combining auditory comprehension and speaking. Each response is globally rated on a 0–3 point scale, so that the total possible score is 12 points. Subjectivity increases in this part, since the definition of "major" versus "minor" errors is lacking, and relative weights of vocabulary, grammar, and pronunciation in scoring are not clearly established in the instructions. The last part consists of a single picture and a series of four sequential pictures telling a story, to be described in 60 and 120 seconds, respectively. The student responses are scored in terms of vocabulary, pronunciation, structure, and fluency, each factor on a 0–5 point scale. There is a brief description of these scoring categories to aid the teacher.

The testing method, patterned after similar items in the *MLA Cooperative Foreign Language Proficiency Tests,* is ingenious but it also has several drawbacks. Since the tests consist of a few pictures, the transmission of items from one student to another is almost inevitable unless it can be insured that all students take the test simultaneously. Secondly, speaking activity is seldom a monologue, and the one-sidedness of the responses may not accurately reflect the student's ability to communicate in the target language. True speaking fluency may be better measured by a panel of judges in interviews or role playing, even though such procedures are more time-consuming and have less scorer reliability. In any case, the evaluative criteria of these tests do not take into account the total length of the responses. The recorded sample student responses for the single-picture item were 53, 40, 25, and 20 seconds, respectively, for the four forms, and for the sequential picture item, 27, 67, 40, and 27 seconds. Obviously, as any experienced teacher can testify, the longer the response, the more errors it is likely to contain. Therefore, length should be considered in scoring speech production, perhaps along with a simple measure of the ability to phonate a certain number of syllables within so many seconds. Moreover, in view of the short sample responses, the maximum recording time for the last two items could be reduced by at least one-third, which would also facilitate scoring. The evaluation could be based on the first ten utterances, in terms of grammar and vocabulary, on a more simplified scoring scale, with a global rating of pronunciation and fluency for each picture description. It should be noted, in fact, that pronunciation seems to receive an inordinate emphasis in the speaking test, to the disadvantage of those students who have acquired a reasonable control of structure and vocabulary but who speak with an obvious "foreign" accent.

In order to guide the teacher in applying the rating scales, sample student responses are recorded on the test tape, without extraneous pauses, and separated from the test itself by a white leader tape. Each of the four male and female students is judged to have a "high degree of competence for a student" at the given level. Contrary to our expectation, there is no discussion whatsoever of the scoring procedures to be applied to these sample responses, and the excellent answers given by the students offer little clue as to how their responses were actually graded. It should also be mentioned that the student answering the single-picture item in Form LA tended to enumerate the objects in the picture despite the instructions to "describe what seems to be going on" rather than simply list all the objects. The directions to the student could be more specific; for example, the master tape could tell him to make up an imaginary dialogue or tell a story in the first person from the viewpoint of one of the persons depicted in the picture.

READING. This test is composed of two parts with a total of 50 items (50 maximum points), to be administered in 35 minutes. Part 1, consisting of 25 items in LA and LB and 20 in MA and MB, contains statements which must be completed with appropriate words or expressions supplied in multiple choice. There appears to be a rather heavy emphasis on vocabulary. In order to answer as many as two-thirds of LA or LB, the student needs to know especially the single key word in each statement as well as the fill-in items. According to the handbook these forms are "specifically aimed at the middle of the second year"; they will prove excessively difficult for students who have completed only one year of language instruction, particularly through the audio-lingual method, which intentionally limits the number of lexical items in the early stages in favor of a more firm mastery of structures. False cognates are not utilized to any appreciable extent.

As many as 8 out of 20 items in MA and MB are idiom-oriented. One might question on what basis certain idioms have been selected; for instance, *se faire prier* and *en savoir gré* instead of *s'agir de, au lieu de,* or *avoir beau.* Since there are numerous reading materials available today, the criteria used for the choice of lexical items and idiomatic expressions for the construction of the reading tests should be listed as a guide to the teacher who needs to determine the suitability of the test as a measuring instrument for his particular purpose. If the test writers do not wish to publish such lists, they should at least state whether or not the vocabulary is based on any known frequency list.

The second part consists of 8 to 10 journalistic and literary prose readings, including dramatic scenes, with multiple choice questions that must be answered. The reading passages are longer and more difficult in MA and MB, as they should be. There is again the question of the criteria for selecting the lexical items, idiomatic expressions, and structural points employed in this part. In order to respond correctly, the student must either find *corroborating* information in the passage or judge what is *implied* in it. The first type demands a good knowledge of vocabulary and structure, while the second requires a somewhat more sophisticated analysis of the text in order to draw the necessary inferences. Forms LA and LB appear to contain about an equal number of both types of items. On the other hand, in MA and MB, less than one-third of the items seem to be inference-oriented. This is somewhat surprising since at more advanced levels of language instruction there is an increased amount of reading, and the discussions of stories in terms of plot, characterization, apparent themes, underlying ideas, and the author's intentions are more frequent. Furthermore, students who have reached the fourth-year level are often introduced to the fundamental concepts of the *explication de texte,* an important part of French literary studies. There are, however, no items requiring elementary stylistic analysis, even though the majority of the passages are literary rather than journalistic prose.

WRITING. The writing test, to be completed in 35 minutes, consists of four parts which combine reading and writing. Part 1 is made up of 25 fill-in items in LA and LB, and 30 items in MA and MB. The student inserts one word in each of the sentences, none of which are related to the other. The context in these sentences requires a relative pronoun, question word, object pronoun, preposition, verb in the appropriate tense and form, and so on. Forms LA and LB concentrate on somewhat more elementary aspects of grammar, such as the use of articles, noun-markers, relative pronouns, and object pronouns. Forms MA and MB, in addition to the type of structural points found in the lower forms, contain items such as demonstrative pronouns, adjectives, and verbs requiring a preposition before a dependent infinitive, and verb tenses used in "contrary-to-fact" statements. One may question the validity of the selection criteria for certain items. While the coverage of the grammatical points in the four forms combined seems fairly comprehensive, some common constructions are missing: the passive voice, the comparison of adjectives and adverbs, and simple idioms with *avoir,* to name a few. On the other hand, somewhat idiomatic expressions such as *en vouloir à* and *s'en aller* are included in MA. Grading is simple and rapid, for each item receives one point or zero.

Part 2 of LA and LB consists of five sentences. The student must rewrite the verb in the embedded clause of each sentence to match its tense with the verb in the main clause which has been already rewritten so as to provide a cue. The verb tenses involved are the future and the *passé composé,* and there is no attempt made to check the correct use and form of the imperfect tense. Grading here is also one point or zero per item. Part 3 of LA and LB comprises 15 items requiring the student to rewrite sentences according to the changes indicated, usually a switch in the gender or number of the key nouns or pronouns. Most items do not check syntax but rather the adjective and verb morphology. Scoring is based on a 0–3 point scale, and there is a short description of each category to assist the scorer. The distinction of these categories depends mostly on the number of errors found in each sentence as well as on the nature of the errors (major or minor).

Scoring can thus be quite subjective, particularly because the number of changes to be effected by the student in each sentence is not kept uniform.

Part 2 of MA and MB consists of seven questions to be answered with the appropriate object pronouns, and Part 3 has eight pairs of sentences to be combined by embedding one sentence into the other. The grading procedure is the same as in the corresponding parts of LA and LB. We may question whether or not it is desirable to have seven or eight items on a single grammatical point, such as the object pronouns and the subjunctive, with a high maximum score for the part. Furthermore, the verb tenses in the pronoun substitution items are exclusively in the past tense, thus penalizing some students as many times as they have failed to make the agreement of the past participle with the preceding direct object pronoun. The change in the subject occurs twice, from *vous* to *je,* with a concomitant change in the auxiliary verb, adding still another operation to perform in these sentences. One of them even requires the addition of a negative element. Perhaps the majority of the sentences should have been in the present tense, with a mandatory change of subject from *je* to *vous* or vice versa. At least one item should have dealt with the affirmative imperative, in which the sequence of object pronouns differs from the normal pattern. The scoring could have been greatly simplified by using a uniform 0–1 point scale for the object pronouns, for the verb form (preferably a common irregular verb), and for the rest of the sentence.

In Part 4 of Forms LA and LB, the student must write a short dialogue based on a **given** topic, including in his sentences the words or expressions listed in the booklet. Scoring is in terms of the number of specified words covered in the response, their appropriate use, the accuracy of each sentence, the continuity of meaning, and a global rating, to each of which are assigned 0, 1, 3, or 5 points. In order to assist the scorer, sample responses are given, with an indication of the scores on each of the five factors. The scoring fails to distinguish between major and minor errors which affect differently the general intelligibility of the dialogue. In fact, a single minor error can result in a loss of two points rather than one, since the scoring system does not permit assigning four points. The total scores of students on this part

of the examination may thus show considerable variation without reflecting accurately the intelligibility or the originality of their compositions.

Part 4 of MA and MB consists of a very long connected passage, approximately half of which is "dehydrated." Students are to use all the given elements in completing sentences, while supplying grammar to them in view of the given context. It is an excellent way of testing writing, inasmuch as the passage as a whole has a good continuity of meaning and the responses are controlled just enough to facilitate evaluation. The scoring method, however, is similar to that for the lower forms and is subject to the same type of criticism. It is extremely time-consuming to have to count the words used by the student to determine how many of the specified elements (63 in MA, 78 in MB) have been included in the response. It would have been much simpler and far more efficient to divide the expected answers into segments, such as *le monde/attendait/avec impatience,* or *faire/une longue promenade/à bicyclette.* One point or zero can be assigned to each segment, with a global rating using a 0–5 point scale at the end.

CONCLUSION. The MLA-Cooperative tests were produced after rigorous item analyses and correlation studies. They should prove to be of use to many language teachers who are acquainted with statistical methods of interpreting test results. However, as has been mentioned earlier, they are not really designed to measure the four basic language skills separately. Listening, speaking, reading, and writing are interdependent activities in the language classroom. The extensive use of hybrid test items may be justifiable but it will give only broad indications of the relative strength or weakness of a student or group of students in regard to the different linguistic skills involved in language learning. According to the handbook, one of the purposes of the tests is the identification of the "idioms and structures in a foreign language that are troublesome for a class or for individual students." Yet the implied "sensitivity" of the test batteries may be questioned, particularly in view of the biases present in some of the tests, such as the vocabulary emphasis in reading and pronunciation emphasis in speaking, and the rarity of pure test items. There are, moreover, no lists indicating the sources of the vocabulary, idioms, and structures that are utilized in the tests. As pointed out earlier, such lists are essential to the users, especially because of the myriad of instructional materials available today and of the numerous psycholinguistic research projects that require the use of reliable standardized tests. The avoidance of English as test items is also regrettable. Translation is an important activity in our culture and is utilized by many language teachers, even though the early audio-lingual methodology proscribed it in language instruction. The avoidance of English has resulted in an outright exclusion from these tests of many problems of pattern conflicts and vocabulary distinctions which are found commonly in classroom quizzes and examinations. Finally, the reliability and the norms of the tests need to be re-examined in view of the developments in language methodology and instructional materials since 1963. The findings of contrastive linguistic analysis, along with the experience of many teachers with their locally-produced tests, should be considered in the revision of the tests.

It should be pointed out that the criticisms of the MLA-Cooperative tests by no means detract from their excellent overall quality and usefulness. They reflect both the traditional and "new key" teaching methods and constitute an admirable attempt to introduce innovation as well as renovation in the field of foreign language testing. The need for nationally standardized tests has been felt for a long time, and these tests have made significant contributions, particularly in the areas of evaluating speaking and writing skills.

For an excerpted review of the series, see 254.

[278]

★National Teacher Examinations: French. College seniors and teachers; 1970–71; modified version of secure form of *MLA Foreign Language Proficiency Tests for Teachers and Advanced Students: French;* Form TNT1 ('71, 22 pages); descriptive booklet ('70, 8 pages); listening comprehension section administered by 3¾ ips tape recording; for more complete information, see 582; 120(165) minutes; Educational Testing Service. *

For reviews of the testing program, see 582 (2 reviews), 6:700 (1 review), 5:538 (3 reviews), and 4:802 (1 review).

[279]

★Pimsleur French Proficiency Tests. First, second level courses in grades 7–12 or first, second semesters college; 1967; 4 scores: listening, speaking, reading, writing; 1 form; 2 levels labeled Forms A, C; manual (23 pages); no college norms; $1.75 per manual;

$1.75 per specimen set (without tapes or manual); postage extra; Paul Pimsleur; Harcourt Brace Jovanovich, Inc. *

a) TEST 1, LISTENING COMPREHENSION. Digitek, IBM 805, and IBM 1230 test-answer sheets (2 pages); 7½ ips test tape, 5 inch reel; $7.50 per test tape; $3.80 per 35 test-answer sheets; $1.40 per set of scoring stencils; IBM scoring service, 33¢ and over per test; 15(25) minutes.

b) TEST 2, SPEAKING PROFICIENCY. Test (4 pages); scoring sheet (2 pages); 7½ ips test tape, 5 inch reel; $7.50 per test tape; $4.50 per 35 tests; $2.70 per 35 scoring sheets; 16(26) minutes.

c) TEST 3, READING COMPREHENSION. Test (4 pages); separate answer sheets (Digitek-IBM 805, IBM 1230) must be used; $4.50 per 35 tests; $2.30 per 35 Digitek-IBM 805 answer sheets; $2.80 per 35 IBM 1230 answer sheets; 70¢ per scoring stencil; IBM scoring service, 19¢ and over per test; 35(45) minutes.

d) TEST 4, WRITING PROFICIENCY. Test (6 pages); answer key and scoring directions (4 pages); $7.40 per 35 tests; 35(45) minutes.

REFERENCE
1. PIMSLEUR, PAUL. "A French Speaking Proficiency Test." *French R* 34:470–9 Ap '61. *

JOHN L. D. CLARK, *Examiner in Foreign Languages, Test Development Division, Educational Testing Service, Princeton, New Jersey.*

The *Pimsleur French Proficiency Tests* consist of two batteries, each containing four separate skills tests: Listening Comprehension, Speaking Proficiency, Reading Comprehension, and Writing Proficiency. The two levels are labeled Form A and Form C. These are somewhat misleading designations, because the two batteries are not alternate forms but rather two different sets of instruments designed for students completing either a "first-level" course (Form A) or a "second-level" course (Form C). The absence of true alternate forms at each level renders problematical the use of the Pimsleur tests for pre- and post-testing of a single group of students or for other applications requiring the use of equivalent instruments. The test manual, advisedly, does not recommend such use but suggests that tests at either level be used on a year-to-year basis to compare the achievement of different class groups using a stable curriculum or to evaluate the results of modifications in the language teaching program (under the apparent assumption that inherent student ability remains constant over the time period in question).

Normative information consisting of raw score percentile ranks and stanine score equivalents is presented for the listening, reading, and writing tests at each level, but similar data are regrettably not available for the Speaking Proficiency test. According to the manual, the speaking test did not undergo a complete norming analysis but was subjected to a "smaller, separate study." Results of this study are shown only in the form of a simple table of suggested proficiency ratings of "good," "fair," and "poor" for each of three raw-score ranges; in addition, the user is cautioned that "because of the nature of this test and the limitations of the study on which the classifications are based," even these limited ratings should be considered only as estimated cutting points. Reliability coefficients, means, standard deviations, analysis group size, and related statistical data are completely lacking. The upshot is quite simply that the Pimsleur battery contains only three standardized tests: listening, reading, and writing. Evaluation of student competence in speaking must for all practical purposes be limited to comparisons based on local norms, and in view of the apparently unsatisfactory results of the test developers' own analysis of the speaking test data, it is difficult to be sanguine about the reliability and usefulness of similar analyses carried out at the local level.

Normative data for the listening, reading, and writing tests are based on the results of a standardization study involving 4,543 "first-level" students and 3,052 "second-level" students from junior and senior high schools in the U.S. "First" and "second" levels are not explicitly defined in either the test catalog or manual. Although most language teachers would be expected to have a general notion of the curricula and student attainment levels implied by these two designations, a closer definition in terms of various combinations of course length and grade level (e.g., two years of junior high school study, one year of high school study, one semester of college study, etc.) or the number of units covered in widely used language programs would allow the potential test user to determine more accurately the appropriateness of the tests for a particular group of students.

The composition of the two norming groups is not clearly indicated in the test literature. The manual mentions the use of 90 participating schools that are described as having been selected on the basis of responses to a school questionnaire covering such factors as amount of material covered in the French classes, the type of language program, and the size and geographical location of the school system. Unfortunately, only the geographical distribution of the schools is shown in the manual. More crucial breakdowns such as the type of schools represented (public, private, parochial) and, especially, their instructional orientation (e.g., "audio-lingual," "traditional," "eclectic") are not given. In the absence of specific information in these areas, the prospective user can only guess as to the particular "mix" of schools and instructional emphases represented by the standardization groups and the degree of correspondence of these groups to the local group whose performance he intends to evaluate. In this regard, one may wonder why only one general norms group was identified at each level rather than two or more separate groups, such as "audio-lingual" and "traditional." The information needed to make such categorizations would presumably have been available from the school questionnaires, and the total number of students tested would easily have permitted the establishment of two or more norming groups at each level.

Norming considerations notwithstanding, the Pimsleur test manual presents a considerable amount of useful information in other areas of test usage and interpretation. Administration instructions for each test are set forth clearly and completely, and the test user should have little difficulty in following them correctly. The very detailed instructions for administering the Speaking Proficiency test—including the procedures to be followed in labeling the student response tapes, setting the tape recorder controls, and even threading the tape ("thread to the take-up reels, and make a few turns")—should help to reassure the nontechnically oriented user and increase the chances of a smooth and valid administration.

It should be pointed out that the order of administration of the four skills tests is not specified but is left to the judgment of the test user. As discussed elsewhere (see 254) in my review of the *MLA Cooperative Foreign Language Tests,* different administration sequences may produce varying warm-up or practice effects for one or more tests in a skills battery. Thus, in the absence of a single prescribed administration sequence, the user would be well advised to adopt a specific administration order of his own and to follow this order in testing any and all groups whose performance he will later wish to compare.

The authors of the test manual are candid and helpful in their discussion of the proper interpretation of test results. A basic caveat not often emphasized in test literature is succinctly stated in the Pimsleur manual: "standardized tests can measure only a representative sample of those aspects of learning commonly accepted as being important and measurable"; for this reason, "the extent to which the content and objectives actually correspond to those of a local program must be determined by the prospective test user." To aid in this determination, test items from those sections of the speaking and writing tests that lend themselves to close content analysis are classified in the manual according to the pronunciation feature or grammatical element represented. Although these classifications should not be used as a substitute for careful examination of the tests themselves, they do provide a succinct content overview of the test sections involved and should also be of value in any post-test analysis of individual item results.

Separate descriptions and discussions of each test in the Pimsleur battery are given below. Unless otherwise indicated, all comments apply to both first-level and second-level tests.

READING COMPREHENSION. The content of this test is typical of several other published reading tests: the student reads French passages of varying lengths and degrees of difficulty and answers multiple choice questions, also in French, dealing with the literal meaning of the passage or with easily drawn inferences about it. At both levels, the passages chosen are well varied in style and content and include brief selections on general topics as well as the usual literary narratives and dramatic scenes. Several passages have been drawn, with considerable adaptation, from well-known authors, including Maupassant, Jean-Jacques Rousseau, Théophile Gautier, and Saint-Exupéry (*Le Petit Prince*). With the exception of *Le Petit Prince*—which may have been encountered by some students—prior acquaintance with the reading passages would not be expected; nonetheless, the careful test user may wish to verify this fact through prior examination.

Although each of the reading tests has only 36 items, odd-even split-half reliabilities are satisfactorily high (.85 and .88 for first and second levels, respectively). Mean raw scores of 15.5 and 19.5 for the first and second level norming samples indicate that the tests are reasonably well pitched in difficulty, at least for the "general" standardization group. However, in view of the wide difference in emphasis accorded the reading skill under "traditional"

and "audio-lingual" methods (especially at the first level), the presentation of separate "traditional" and "audio-lingual" norming data would have been quite welcome.

LISTENING COMPREHENSION. The format of the listening test differs in that there is no student test booklet. Instead, a special answer sheet is used on which the answer options for each question are printed immediately beside the corresponding answer spaces. This technique deserves some praise as it substantially reduces the amount of paper handling which the student must do in the course of the test.

The test has two parts. In the first part, the student listens to short tape-recorded sentences such as "Charles ne la voit guère" and chooses from among four printed sentences the one that was spoken: "Charles ne la voit guère/Charles la voit à la guerre/Charles a la voix gaie/ Charles voit la gare." The testing intent of this section, as stated in the manual, is to "measure the student's ability to listen attentively, to distinguish individual French sounds in the context of a complete sentence, and to associate these sounds with their written symbols." Although the first two goals would probably have the general approval of language teachers regardless of their instructional philosophy, there may well be some question about using at the elementary or intermediate level—and particularly with audio-lingually trained students—a testing procedure that requires the student to deal with a wide variety of sound-grapheme relationships. Although most students, even those in audio-lingual courses, would have had some exposure to elementary reading tasks by the time they were tested, it is questionable whether they would have mastered the sound-spelling correspondences involved in discriminating among such sentences as: "J'ai su sauter/Je sais sauter /J'ai sursauté/Je sais souder" or "Vous dites qu'il était déçu?/Vous dites qu'il était dessus?/ Vous dites qu'il était dessous?/Vous dites qu'il était dissous?" One should also note the uncommon vocabulary required in some cases to make meaningful parallel sentences.

The sound-grapheme discrimination problem is compounded by the short (8 seconds) pauses allowed for student responses. If it is assumed that two of the 8 seconds are used for mechanically marking the response and the remaining 6 seconds for reading the options, it may be calculated that an average reading speed of 187 words per minute would be required to answer each of the second-level questions in the time allotted and 195 words per minute to answer the first-level questions. Reading speed for individual questions ranges from a low of 110 words per minute (item 18, first level) to a high of 300 words per minute (item 12, first level).

The manual states candidly that "the four tests in the Pimsleur series do not measure the individual skills in isolation" and suggests that "the teacher must therefore be alert to the possibility of interactions among the skills in evaluating performance." This advice is especially applicable to the first part of Listening Comprehension, in which the reading load and the speed with which the student is required to respond may for some student groups largely invalidate this section of the test as a measure of aural comprehension.

The second part of the test makes use of "rejoinder" questions, in which the student hears a conversational statement or question in French and chooses from among four printed French choices the most appropriate reply. Although student reading ability is also at issue in this part of the test, the printed choices are generally shorter than in the first part and embody a much more common vocabulary.

In both parts of the test, the spoken material for each question consists of a short utterance by a single voice. The student hears no spoken dialogues, radio broadcasts, *récits,* or other longer passages typical of other published listening tests. Since the Pimsleur test tapes run only about 15 minutes and since the manual suggests that a full class period be set aside for each test, it may be wondered why a somewhat longer test was not specified, both to increase total test reliability beyond the rather low figure of .74 reported for both levels and to permit the inclusion of various other types of spoken material.

An interesting feature of the listening test tapes is that the speakers read their scripts throughout at a normal to slightly rapid speed and elide mute E's wherever phonetically possible. The prospective test user would be advised to listen in advance to the test tapes to determine whether the speed of delivery is generally in keeping with the type of listening practice that his students have had in the classroom. If classroom speech has for the most part been at a slower pace, it may be helpful for the teacher to devote one or more preliminary class periods to practice in listening at a somewhat faster speed.

WRITING PROFICIENCY. This test uses a free response format in which the student writes all of his answers in the test booklet; the tests must therefore be scored individually by the classroom teacher or some other person competent in French. In the first part of the test, the student reads a French paragraph in which certain words have been omitted and writes in the appropriate completions. The missing words include pronouns, demonstrative adjectives, prepositions, and other grammatical elements. For the most part, the sentence context is such that only one specific word can be considered correct. The scoring instructions state, however, that the teacher should give credit for the occasional use of some other correct word that is not shown on the scoring key. No partial credit is allowed, and the word must be spelled correctly, including any necessary accents.

The second part, which is also a fill-in exercise, tests the student's ability to write verb forms in various persons and tenses. The first-level test includes present, imperfect, past indefinite, and future tenses of regular and common irregular verbs; the second-level test adds the conditional and present subjunctive.

In the third part, the student writes complete sentences based on model sentences but requiring certain modifications, such as changing the number or gender of adjectives, converting nouns to direct and indirect object pronouns, and so forth. For example, "J'ai un beau manteau blanc (robe)" would be rewritten: "J'ai une belle robe blanche." Scoring is on a right-wrong basis for each critical element (in this example, the correct formation of the three feminine adjectives).

The fourth and final part consists of somewhat freer writing tasks based on pictorial stimuli. In the first-level test, the student writes descriptive sentences for each of several pictures; the time cue "maintenant" or "hier" written above each picture indicates whether present or past tense is to be used. In the second-level test, the student writes a single paragraph describing a series of chronologically related pictures. For both levels, scoring of the fourth part is carried out subjectively on the basis of guidelines provided in the scoring instructions leaflet.

The Writing Proficiency test appears to be a quite straightforward measure of such basic components of writing skill as verb formation, grammatical agreement, and pronoun selection and placement. Inter-scorer reliabilities for the entire test are .988 (first level) and .979 (second level), reported for the independent rating of a sample of 50 tests by two scorers. Within-scorer reliability is not indicated, except for the results of a limited study in which one rater rescored the fourth part of 82 second-level tests with a reliability of .961.

It should be noted in evaluating these statistics that scoring was carried out by raters who had undergone special preliminary training and had discussed the rating procedure in detail in group meetings. Although one would not expect in-field users to have difficulty in scoring the essentially right-wrong items in the first three parts of the test, there might be some question as to whether persons scoring the test locally and having recourse only to the printed scoring guides could reach reported reliability levels for the less structured exercises in the fourth part. A somewhat stronger case for the reliability of the writing test in general and of the fourth part in particular could have been made by asking teachers to administer and score the tests just as they would in the school situation. Reliabilities based on these more realistic conditions would be of both practical and research interest.

SPEAKING PROFICIENCY. The Pimsleur speaking test may be administered on a group basis in language laboratories equipped to record the responses of each student on an individual tape. Although not so indicated in the manual, the test may also be administered on an individual student basis through the use of two regular tape recorders, one to play the test tape and the other to record student responses. This technique would of course be feasible only for rather small groups of students.

Test instructions to the student are recorded on the master tape, and the tape also automatically times the approximately 16 minutes required for administration. A useful feature of the Pimsleur test is that the student is instructed to start and stop his own tape recorder so as to record only those portions of the test in which he is actually speaking. In this way, the overall length of each student-response tape is reduced to about six and one-half minutes, and the listening time of the person scoring the test is substantially reduced. By contrast, the student-response tapes for the MLA Cooperative speaking test run approximately 11 minutes, and

the person scoring these tapes must either listen to long periods of re-recorded instructions or laboriously shuttle the tape back and forth to locate the spots at which the student is speaking. In either case, the time and effort involved is substantially greater than for the Pimsleur tests.

In the first part of the speaking test (Vocabulary), the student looks at line drawings depicting common objects and is given four seconds per drawing to name the object aloud in French. Use of the definite article is not required. This use of pictures to test spoken vocabulary is a potentially rewarding technique in that a great number of scorable items can be introduced within a short time span. By the same token, it is possible to sample a number of different vocabulary domains (such as *vêtements, parties du corps, articles de cuisine,* etc.) within a relatively brief period. The technique is limited to those vocabulary items that can be easily and unambiguously pictured, but for beginning and intermediate language courses, which typically involve common noun vocabulary to a large extent, this restriction should not be critical. Scoring reliability of a pictured vocabulary section should be very high, since only one specific response would be considered correct in most cases. Novel correct responses might occasionally be made, but these could be easily resolved by the teacher-scorer.

In the second part of the test (Pronunciation), the student reads aloud a number of printed French sentences. For each sentence, the scorer judges as right or wrong the student's pronunciation of two "critical sounds." For example, the phrase "Buvez du café" is evaluated for the proper pronunciation of the two /e/ sounds. In "C'est une question de temps," the /k/ of *question* and the nasal vowel of *temps* are scored as right or wrong. It is the reviewer's opinion, based on close acquaintance with similar sound judging exercises in other testing situations, that satisfactory scoring reliability is difficult to attain even through the use of scorers who are both highly sophisticated in the phonetic considerations at issue and thoroughly practiced in the judging standards to be applied to a particular test form. Neither the Pimsleur nor the MLA test manual provides information on the scoring reliability that could be expected in regular in-field use of the test, and it may be seriously doubted that many teachers or other local persons would be able to score accurately the sound-judging section of either the Pimsleur or the MLA Cooperative test simply on the basis of their own phonetic backgrounds and the printed scoring instructions.

In the third and final part of the test (Fluency), the test booklet is not used. Instead, the student listens to simple questions such as "Quelle est la date d'aujourd'hui?" or "Où allez-vous après l'école?" and answers the questions using complete French sentences. Scoring is done on a four-point scale in accordance with reasonably specific verbal criteria. There is considerable face validity to this part of the test in that question-answer sequences are an important aspect of everyday conversation. It is also worth noting that no printed materials are required and that the procedure is thus entirely audio-lingual in nature. However, the question of scoring reliability may again be raised, and it is unfortunate that specific information on this matter is not available in the manual.

As previously discussed, the major shortcoming of the Speaking Proficiency test is the unavailability of normative and other statistical data that would allow it to be classified and used as a standardized test. This second-class status of the Speaking Proficiency test in comparison to the other three tests in the battery is unfortunate in that the absence of suitable interpretive information will in all probability reinforce the already apparent trend on the part of school systems and research groups to forego direct testing of student speaking ability as a regular part of their evaluation programs. When lack of standardization of the Pimsleur speaking test is added to the list of drawbacks already identified for speaking tests in general (complexity of administration, time and expense of scoring, problems of reliability), those in the language teaching and testing professions who continue to see important advantages to the formal evaluation of speaking skill will have an even more difficult battle.

MICHIO PETER HAGIWARA, *Associate Professor of French, University of Michigan, Ann Arbor, Michigan.*

Though it appears that the preliminary version of these tests had at least two equated sets, the present tests are available only in one form for each level, thereby lessening somewhat their usefulness in educational research where independent measures of language competence for groups of students are needed.

LISTENING COMPREHENSION. The listening test, consisting of two parts with 20 items each, has a maximum total score of 40 points and is administered in approximately 15 minutes. All aural stimuli are read at normal conversational speed by alternating male and female voices on the test tape. Part 1 presents basically sound-symbol association items. The student matches within an eight-second pause the sentence he has heard with one of the four similar-looking sentences printed on the answer sheet. Generally, the aural stimulus is a single utterance composed of four to seven words. Form C has a comparatively larger number of items based on verb morphology, since students completing two years of French will have learned many verb tenses and forms which often sound alike. The sound-symbol association takes up exactly 50 percent of the entire test, and we may question whether or not such inordinate emphasis is warranted. Furthermore, there is no attempt to graduate the difficulty level of the test items. As a result, the sentences at the beginning are just as long as those occurring toward the middle or the end of this part. Thus, the student who is a slow reader or who has a short auditory retention will undoubtedly be handicapped from the outset. It would have been more desirable to begin the test with single words or short phrases and gradually increase the length of utterances.

In Part 2, the student matches the aural cue, usually a question or a statement, with one of the four printed sentences that constitutes the most appropriate answer or rejoinder. As in the other Pimsleur tests, some of the test items in Form A are repeated in Form C, in order to elicit responses from underachievers and also to discriminate among the varying abilities of students. The aural cues are repeated twice in succession, unlike the practice of many other standardized listening comprehension tests, to insure that many students will attempt to answer most of the items. The test items do not appear to be graded according to their difficulty levels. From the beginning, there are fairly long spoken cues and equally long multiple choice answers, to the disadvantage of slow readers. The aural cues are almost invariably single utterances and do not become longer throughout the twenty items. Some items are based on auditory discrimination of two or three sound segments—rather than on vocabulary, structure, or context—and should have been incorporated in Part 1. Since there is no attempt to group the test items on the basis of common general topics, the context jumps from one item to another. In Form C, several items have a distinct vocabulary bias: the student cannot select the correct response unless he knows the key words or expressions—such as *avocat, veuve,* and *s'en aller*—used in the aural stimuli. Although the hybrid types are more economical to produce, it would have been preferable to include a few items in which simple line drawings replace printed sentences, as used, though insufficiently, in the MLA Cooperative tests. It also would have been desirable either to increase the length of the aural cues progressively or to include one or two short connected passages. Background noise or an increased rate of phonation might also have been used. Except for the addition of the sound-symbol association items—which are rather excessive in number—the Pimsleur listening comprehension test is less systematic and sophisticated than its counterparts in the MLA and the College Board tests.

SPEAKING. Speaking skill is measured by a three-part test of approximately 16 minutes with a maximum possible score of 91. Part 1, scored one point or zero per item, consists of 27 drawings designed to elicit vocabulary. Spontaneity, one of the aspects of speech fluency, is also tested inasmuch as the recording time for each item hardly exceeds three seconds. Pronunciation is not an important factor since the scoring instructions state that it "need not be perfect, but the word must be readily understandable," implying that all kinds of substitution of English phonemes are permissible as long as the substitution does not distort a given French word to the point of making it unintelligible. Although the use of pictorial cues is an excellent idea, one may wonder if a set of 27 lexical items is really sufficient to evaluate the student's active vocabulary. The vaguely stated criterion for the evaluation of pronunciation does not seem to qualify this part as a true speaking test. We note, in addition, that several illustrations are culturally unauthentic, such as the pictures of an American church, kitchen, breakfast, and bread. They may give an erroneous impression that the semantic range—connotational, denotational, and circumstantial

—of the 27 words is identical in English and French.

Part 2 is a combination of mimicry and reading pronunciation test in that first the 20 short utterances are heard first on the master tape and the student is allowed to follow them with the test booklet open. The pause allowed for the recording of each sentence is approximately three to four seconds. The model on the master tape may encourage some students to mark the difficult words as they follow the text while listening. The embedding of two test items in each short utterance, recorded in rapid succession, will make scoring extremely difficult without stopping the answer tapes frequently. Moreover, as many as 14 phonemes in Form A and 8 in Form C occur twice in the same sentence, potentially adding to the confusion of the inexperienced scorer and penalizing students twice for the same kind of error. At least 7 items in Form A and 11 in Form C border on sound-symbol association in that the sounds to be produced are represented by the *c* of *lac,* and *ch, s,* and *x,* while the absence of sounds as indicated by the verb ending *-ent* and the plural marker of nouns occur also as pronunciation items. The sound /œ̃/, virtually nonexistent in the standard Parisian French, is included although the more important /œ/ is not. Finally, there are no items designed to check the intonation patterns and syllabification. As a result, Part 2 measures pronunciation only imperfectly, despite the fact that it is assigned a maximum of 40 points in the entire speaking test.

Part 3 is made up of eight questions, all of which begin with question words. They center around a vaguely common topic so that the context does not jump abruptly from one question to another. In order to insure correct listening comprehension and to elicit appropriate responses, each question is repeated. Five items in Form A and seven in Form C require personalized answers, such as, "What time did you get up this morning?" and "Where do you go after school?" Students are told to respond in complete sentences, and each response is scored globally in terms of pronunciation, meaning, and grammar on a 0–3 point scale. Scorer subjectivity is inherent in this type of evaluation. There is no sample recording, but a brief description of the scoring categories is given. Unlike the MLA Cooperative tests, this test provides no items to check the continuous speech production of the student.

READING. Reading comprehension (35 minutes) is tested by 12 short paragraphs representing authentic as well as adapted journalistic and literary prose. Each passage is followed by three multiple choice completion items, with a maximum score of 36 points. The lexical items used in both the paragraphs and statements are quite simple, so that there is little vocabulary bias in the two tests, as contrasted with the MLA Cooperative and the College Board tests. Six items from Form A are repeated in Form C. The manual mentions that the "ability to locate and understand information set forth" in the passage and the ability to make inferences are more or less evenly tested, 18 to 18 items in Form A, and 17 to 19 in Form C. However, such a distinction is so subtle that another person analyzing the contents can easily come up with different results. This reviewer's classification shows that the ratio of the two types of test items is 21 to 9 in Form A, with 6 items bordering on both categories, and 19 to 12 in Form C, with 5 items having both characteristics. The only general agreement thus seems to be that Form C has a comparatively larger number of items requiring the ability to draw inferences from a given passage. These tests are adequate for Levels 1 and 2 of secondary-school French or the first and second semester of college French, even though the difficulty levels of the test items and the length of paragraphs are not graduated.

WRITING PROFICIENCY. Writing competence is evaluated in four parts, to be completed in 35 minutes. Part 1, scored one point or zero per item, consists of 19 fill-in items in Form A and 22 in Form C. The sentences, which require a preposition, noun marker, object pronoun, and so forth, constitute a connected passage.

On Part 2, scored the same as the preceding part and containing 9 items in Form A, the student is to supply the correct forms of the verbs whose infinitives are given in parentheses. The verb tenses involved are the present, future, imperfect, and the passé composé of regular and common irregular verbs. Each of the 10 items in Form C consists of a pair of sentences, a complete model and an incomplete transformation for which the correct verb form must be supplied. In addition to the tenses already mentioned, the conditional and the present subjunctive are included. As is the case with the MLA Cooperative tests, the number of verbs is extremely limited and the choice seems almost arbitrary.

Part 3 contains 10 sentences to be rewritten to incorporate the transformation required by a change in the noun, object pronoun, adjective, or verb in the original. The scoring shows an improvement over the similar test items in the MLA Cooperative tests in that *each* change receives one point or zero, thereby insuring a higher degree of scorer objectivity. The number of changes to be made varies from one sentence to another, so that the maximum score for each item ranges between one and four points. Form C duplicates three sentences (nine points) of Form A. Students who make mistakes in copying the unchanged portion of the sentences will be penalized, the degree of penalty depending on the type of errors involved.

Part 4 is the most original section of the writing test. In Form A, the student describes each of four unrelated pictures in a sentence and then writes three sentences concerning a scene that contains a good number of details. The scoring is global for each of the five sentences, based on a 0–3 point scale, and there is a description of each numerical category with sample responses. Although the scoring is simpler than for the comparable part of the MLA Cooperative tests, scorer subjectivity cannot be avoided. Furthermore, those students who have chosen more "original" expressions and sentence patterns have more chances of being penalized for the possible number of errors they may make, as compared to those who stay with the conventional subject-verb-object type of sentence structure. If the subject of each sentence were indicated in the test booklet, perhaps more varied constructions might be elicited.

Form C contains eight sequential drawings representing a simple story. There is no limit to the number of sentences the student can write to tell the story, again with the possibility that the longer the composition, the more errors it may contain. No credit is given for originality of expressions, and the student who writes a series of simple sentences will be better off than the one who attempts to produce complex and compound sentences. Scoring is global: the composition is evaluated from the viewpoint of grammar, verb formation and usage, and content (completeness, continuity, vocabulary, appropriate use of idioms, and the absence of extraneous sentences). Each of these factors is to be rated on a 0–4 point scale and the resultant score to be multiplied by two. The doubling of the score is necessary in order to weight this part of the test and give a sufficient range of scores. Nevertheless, it also increases the likelihood of magnifying scorer errors. In addition, the "content" factor could be divided into at least two separate categories, vocabulary and idioms on one hand, and completeness and continuity on the other.

A rather high interscorer agreement is claimed in the manual, the tables indicating the results of scoring Parts 1–3 and of Part 4 by two similarly trained scorers and that of one scorer evaluating the same compositions of Part 4 twice. The crucial point of the degree of unanimity among three or more scorers remains to be established. As with the MLA Cooperative tests, the Pimsleur tests preclude the use of English as test cues. As a result, many pattern conflicts and vocabulary distinction problems are not included, even though they constitute very common errors made by students in their writing assignments. Moreover, there are no items dealing with relative pronouns, interrogative pronouns and adverbs, and the various equivalents of the English *how* plus adjectives. The writing test is somewhat fragmentary in Parts 1–3, and the nature of Part 4, particularly in Form A, is such that it may not be comprehensive enough to yield a sufficient sampling of the student's writing ability.

CONCLUSION. The *Pimsleur French Proficiency Tests* serve basically the same objectives as the MLA Cooperative tests. They can assess the linguistic competence of a student or a group of students in terms of national or local norms. They are useful to some extent in evaluating the effectiveness of a local language curriculum and may also be used for guidance and counseling purposes. Both batteries of tests will reveal to a degree the relative strengths and weaknesses of students in the four fundamental language skills. The choice between the Pimsleur tests and the MLA Cooperative tests will depend on the purchasing and scoring cost factors. Generally speaking, the Pimsleur tests are shorter and much less complicated to administer and score, an important point to consider if a fairly large-scale local scoring is contemplated. The usefulness of the Pimsleur tests as a diagnostic instrument is somewhat superior, since they provide some information concerning the content and objectives of each test. Simplicity and economy seem to have been a key factor in the production of the Pimsleur tests. They are not necessarily an improvement over the MLA Cooperative tests, and in certain areas they tend to magnify the latter's defects. Form A of the Pimsleur tests provides a more appropriate instrument to evaluate the language proficiency of the first-year French students at the high school level, for whom the Forms LA and LB of the MLA Cooperative tests will prove to be rather difficult. On the other hand, for Level 2 and above, the MLA tests, despite their shortcomings, may be more effective because of their amplitude and systematic treatment of testing methods. Furthermore, the usefulness of the Pimsleur tests is severely limited because they lack alternate forms, college norms, and more advanced tests for third-year and fourth-year high school French students.

J Ed Meas 6(*1*):46–7 sp '69. C. Richards Pusey. The most serious weaknesses....are in the listening and speaking tests. Noticeable positive features of these tests include clear, authentic, French recordings, ample time to record responses, adequate increase in question difficulty from Form A to Form C, and answer choices all expressed in correct language. Negative features observed in the listening and speaking tests include questions requiring only vocabulary knowledge for a correct answer and some ambiguity in the choice of answers. These two tests appear to be strongly influenced by two common misconceptions held by teachers of foreign languages; first that French (or any other "foreign" language) has its real meaning in English, and second, that language and writing are the same thing. Evidence of these negative features is found in the translation used in the directions of the listening proficiency test and in the highly objectionable use of reading skills to measure listening comprehension. The listening comprehension test should be revised so as to measure aural and not visual discriminations. In the listening test directions, Part 2, contrary to what Mr. Pimsleur says on the tape, the French speaker did not say "I'm sick today"; she said "Je suis malade aujourd'hui." The author is wrongfully assuming that French has its real meaning in English. This, of course, is not so, nor should the author assume that it is so for students taking his test. In the speaking test the author might just as well cause direct translation by using written English words to evoke the pronunciation of French vocabulary items as to cause indirect translation by using American drawings of objects. It would, however, be much more appropriate to have the student use the picture-suggested noun in a complete sentence than to simply record the noun with neither a context nor an article indicating its gender. The second part of the test called pronunciation measures oral reading ability rather than speaking proficiency. It is unfortunate that the speaking test, along with its questions and answers, makes no use of the statement-comment, or rejoinder exercise, an extremely appropriate means of measuring student ability to interact in a language, for speaking proficiency is "interaction in the language" rather than vocabulary recall, pronunciation, or oral reading. The reading test presents varied and interesting passages and thought-provoking questions. For some reason, not immediately apparent to this reviewer, this test is much more advanced than either the listening test or the speaking test. This discrepancy in difficulty levels contradicts commonly accepted modern foreign language pedagogy which demands more listening and speaking than reading and writing experience in the first two years of language study. The reason for identical passages in Forms A and C is not apparent. There is an objectionable ambiguity of answer choice in at least four of the questions causing the student's point of view to determine his response rather than the information given him in the reading passage. It is commendable that in the writing test any right answer is to be considered correct even though not found on the correction sheet, and that no answer using English is to be accepted. This reviewer finds it difficult to see why the student is never required to write the future tense in the more advanced form of the test and only once in the first level form. The directions telling the student not to write everything he can about the rather detailed picture in his test booklet do not seem to be necessary. Why not simply give a less detailed picture? Suggestions for improvement would include the use of "action" pictures as opposed to "thing" pictures in both the listening and speaking tests. In conclusion, the Pimsleur French Proficiency Tests show a noble aim if not noteworthy marksmanship. The listening and speaking tests need serious revision; the reading and writing tests are well designed and for the most part valid.

[280]

*Second Year French Test, [Revised Edition]. High school and college; 1956–68; SYFT; Form A ('68, 2 pages); manual ('68, 2 pages); no data on reliability; $1.75 per 25 tests, postage extra; 75¢ per specimen set, postpaid; 50(55) minutes; Jean Leblon and Minnie M. Miller; Data Processing and Educational Measurement Center. *

JOHN L. D. CLARK, *Examiner in Foreign Languages, Test Development Division, Educational Testing Service, Princeton, New Jersey.*

The *Second Year French Test* is a paper-and-pencil test containing 100 items. The entire test is printed on the front and back of a single sheet of paper, on which the student makes all of his responses. Seven of the ten parts use a multiple choice format in which the student writes in the number (not letter) corresponding to the intended answer. (There are five true-false items in one part.) The remaining three parts use questions of the "completion" type, in which the student must fill in a word or words to complete a sentence.

Extremely sketchy information on test use and interpretation is given in a one-page Manual of Directions. Administration instructions are presented in only two sentences: "After the students have filled in the blanks on the first page, direct them to read the directions and answer the items of each part. Allow exactly 50 minutes of working time." The students are not told, for example, how they should indicate a changed answer or, for the multiple choice items, how they should handle questions about which they are not certain (since there is no correction for guessing, the appropriate instruction would be for the student to attempt to answer every question).

Normative information is restricted to a single percentile table based on the scores of 240 "students of second-year French classes." The number of classes represented, the type and location of the participating schools, and the course history of the students tested are not described. In the absence of more specific information about the norming group, the potential user is at a loss to evaluate the appropriateness of the norms for a local test group. Basic statistical data, such as whole-test reliability and standard deviation of the norming group scores, are also lacking.

The test places heavy weight on reading-related tasks and on grammatical exercises. Of the ten parts, three involve recognitional vocabulary and textual reading, and five are concerned with verb formation and usage, pronoun selection, contraction of articles, use of preposition, and other basic grammatical features.

In the reading area, there are two multiple choice parts in which the student finds synonyms and antonyms for various nouns, verbs, and idiomatic expressions. A third part presents a reading passage of about 240 words on which are based four 3-option multiple choice questions and five true-false questions. Rather than base the entire reading part on a single passage representing only one writing style and topical area, it would be preferable to use two or three shorter passages by different authors and on different topics. One may also wonder why 3-choice questions were used rather than the more reliable 4- or 5-choice questions.

The largest proportion of the test—five parts and 51 items—is devoted to questions testing grammatical points. The student is asked to identify appropriate verb forms, select correct pronouns or other forms for a given context, supply the correct person and tense of verbs given in the infinitive, convert a short paragraph written in the present tense into a past-tense narration by changing the verbs into the past indefinite or imperfect, and write in pronouns or prepositions drawn from a short list of designated forms.

In working through the test, the student may be hindered by the extremely cramped format used to print the entire test on a single sheet of paper; this is particularly likely for the fill-in questions.

A single part containing five multiple choice items is addressed to questions of pronunciation. The student sees a word (such as maison) and is asked to choose from among three other words (monsieur, pompe, donner) the one which has "the same sound" as the boldface letters in the stimulus word. Under the perhaps questionable assumption that there is a high correspondence between the ability to recognize similar-sounding elements in printed words and the ability accurately to produce the same sounds, this part of the test could be considered to deal with one aspect of pronunciation. However, since the part consists of only five items, the overall contribution of the "pronunciation" section to total test score is minimal.

The last part of the test consists of ten multiple choice questions on French civilization and culture. Teachers who attempt to give their students a broader picture of French history,

customs, and daily life than that represented by a simple collection of facts about dates, places, and famous personages will find this part of the test insufficient.

No provision is made to test listening comprehension, either directly or indirectly. For this reason, many teachers would probably wish to supplement the *Second Year French Test* with a tape-recorded listening test produced locally or obtained from some other source. Any intention to evaluate student speaking ability would also call for the administration of a supplementary test specifically aimed at this skill.

In summary, the *Second Year French Test* may be of general informational use to the teacher who has by the time of testing given his students suitable exposure to the various vocabulary-reading and grammatical tasks represented. In the absence of sufficient normative information, student performance on the test should not be evaluated in other than local terms; and for classes in which all four language skills receive emphasis, the use of additional tests of listening comprehension and speaking ability would be indicated.

For reviews by Geraldine Spaulding and Clarence E. Turner of an earlier edition, see 5:271.

[281]
★**The Undergraduate Record Examinations: French Test.** College; 1969–70; Form K-RUR ('69, 21 pages); descriptive booklet ('70, 8 pages); for more complete information, see 671; 120(140) minutes; Educational Testing Service. *

JOSEPH A. MURPHY, *Professor of French, Lycoming College, Williamsport, Pennsylvania.*

This new standardized test of achievement in French has the following stated purposes:

To measure the level of certain kinds of competence achieved by the college senior who has majored in French.
To provide information useful in assessing a student's achievement in undergraduate work and his competence for further study.
To serve as one useful source of information for student counseling.
To provide information that will prove useful in institutional self-evaluation, both curricular and departmental.

It is a two-hour test of reading comprehension, literature (including literary history, criticism and interpretation), and culture and civilization.

The test is reported to have a reliability coefficient of .93, one of the highest reported for a UP test. However, the content validity of the test is more difficult to ascertain. Following ETS guidelines for determining validity, one must decide (a) to what extent the test questions are representative of particular courses of study, and (b) the extent to which the questions are representative of the content to which the person has been exposed.

With the limited data published at this time, one can only make inferences about validity from an item analysis of the reference-group sample. In that analysis only 64 of the 110 items fell within the difficulty range of 40 to 75 percent. A significant number of questions (32) were missed by more than 60 percent of students while only 14 items were answered correctly by 60 percent or more of the student population. Although a good test should contain a wide range of item difficulty, such a sustained high level of difficulty creates doubt as to whether the test is a representative sampling of subject matter actually taught by the institutions serviced. A more detailed analysis will clarify the strengths and weaknesses of this test.

An analysis of the 49 items testing reading comprehension has revealed them to be fair and discriminating. The questions span many cognitive areas from vocabulary recognition, paraphrasing, implications, comparative thinking, and evaluation. This large subsection would certainly be useful to individuals and institutions wishing to evaluate reading competence.

Although there is no section numbering, it is possible to place the questions into ten sets. Five sets test exclusively reading comprehension, vocabulary and literary analysis. Two sets treat culture and civilization, with one set apiece for literary terms, literary characters, and literary criticism. In terms of item-weight per area of achievement, 61 items measure reading comprehension and literary analysis, while 18 items are assigned to literary criticism, 16 to culture and civilization, 8 to literary terms, and 7 to literary characters. It is thus clear that the instrument is above all a test of reading comprehension and literature. There are no questions pertaining to customs and values of everyday French life. Moreover, the small sampling of questions in the culture-civilization sets does not permit reliable generalizations about individual competence in those areas. This is perhaps the most serious deficiency in a test that purports to provide comprehensive individual and institutional self-evaluation. With rare exceptions the

questions are well written and challenging. There are perhaps two questionable items, items 48 and 83.

In testing factual information about culture and civilization, one should select material having the utmost significance and applicability. Most of the questions meet this criterion, but with only 13 questions asked about geography, history, and music, it does not seem balanced to select names like Jean Monnet and Leon Blum as bases for questions. In this section also, the questions are technically effective and demanding. It is the size of the sampling and the absence of culture with a small "c" that render this part useless for generalizations.

Only one of the eight questions on literary terminology was answered correctly by a majority of students in the reference group. While a few of the difficult items would seem appropriate for undergraduate testing ("pasticher," "hiatus," "romanesque," "le vers régulier"), others lend themselves to more sophisticated literary study at the graduate level (Voltaire's "pamphlets," "chevilles," "le drame selon Victor Hugo," "ouvrages inédits"). These kinds of questions would be more appropriate in a graduate examination. In general the literary questions should be reviewed item by item by a number of experienced undergraduate teachers. These are precisely the questions that seem to function the least efficiently.

As stated above, the test performs most adequately as a measure of the level of reading competence. It performs less effectively as a measure of literary knowledge and ability, and is of little use as a test of culture and civilization. If institutions are to evaluate comprehensively their undergraduate programs, they will need supplementary modular tests in culture and civilization, listening, speaking, and writing skills. In the interim, this test will provide useful feedback on reading skills.

For reviews of the testing program, see 671 (2 reviews).

GERMAN

[282]

*Advanced Placement Examination in German. High school students desiring credit for college level courses or admission to advanced courses; 1954–70; Forms RBP ('69, 17 pages), SBP ('70, 15 pages) in 2 booklets (objective, essay); listening comprehension tapes: 7½ ips for Form RBP, 3¾ ips for Form SBP;

tape script ['69–70, 6 pages] for each form; for more complete information, see 662; 180(200) minutes; program administered for the College Entrance Examination Board by Educational Testing Service. *

REFERENCES

1–5. See 6:385.
6. "The Advanced Placement German Examination of 1965." *German Q* 38:480–505 S '65. *
7. LEDERER, HERBERT. "Evaluating Advanced Placement Candidates: Notes From the Chief Reader's Desk." *German Q* 38:506–13 S '65. *
8. REICHARD, JOSEPH R. "The First Ten Years of German Advanced Placement: Theory and Practice." *German Q* 38:440–9 S '65. *
9. SCHEIDER, ROSE M. "The Role of Educational Testing Service in the German Advanced Placement Program." *German Q* 38:514–21 S '65. *

For a review by Herbert Schueler of an earlier form, see 5:273. For a review of the testing program, see 662.

[283]

*College Board Achievement Test in German. Candidates for college entrance with 2–4 years high school German; 1901–71; test administered each January at centers established by the publisher; for more complete information, see 663; 60(80) minutes; program administered for the College Entrance Examination Board by Educational Testing Service. *

REFERENCES

1–3. See 4:244.
4–6. See 5:272.

For a review by Gilbert C. Kettelkamp of earlier forms, see 6:383; for a review by Harold B. Dunkel, see 5:272; for a review by Herbert Schueler, see 4:244. For reviews of the testing program, see 6:760 (2 reviews).

[284]

*College Placement Test in German Listening Comprehension. Entering college freshmen; 1962–70, c1955–70; irregularly scheduled reprintings of inactive forms of *College Board Achievement Test in German Listening Comprehension;* Forms PPL1 ('67, reprint of 1966 test), PPL2 ('67) in a single booklet (12 pages); test administered by 7½ ips tape recording; for more complete information, see 665; 30(40) minutes; program administered for the College Entrance Examination Board by Educational Testing Service. *

REFERENCES

1. SPENCER, RICHARD E., AND SEGUIN, EDMOND L. "The Relative Effectiveness of Earphones and Loudspeakers as a Means of Presenting a Listening Test in a Foreign Language." *Mod Lang J* 48:346–9 O '64. *
2. ALEAMONI, LAWRENCE M., AND MATSUNAGA, ALLEN. *A Study of Foreign Language at the University of Illinois Using the CEEB Foreign Language Placement Tests and End-of-Course Grades.* Research Report No. 317. Champaign, Ill.: Measurement and Research Division, Office of Instructional Resources, University of Illinois, 1970. Pp. i, 42. *

For reviews by Harold B. Dunkel and Herbert Schueler of earlier forms, see 6:384. For a review of the testing program, see 665.

[285]

*College Placement Test in German Reading. Entering college freshmen; 1962–70, c1957–70; CPTGR; irregularly scheduled reprintings of inactive forms of *College Board Achievement Test in German;* Forms QPL1 ['68, reprint of 1965 test], QPL2 ['68, reprint

of 1966 test] in a single booklet (24 pages); for more complete information, see 665; 60(70) minutes; program administered for the College Entrance Examination Board by Educational Testing Service. *

REFERENCES

1. SPENCER, RICHARD E., AND SEGUIN, EDMOND L. "The Relative Effectiveness of Earphones and Loudspeakers as a Means of Presenting a Listening Test in a Foreign Language." *Mod Lang J* 48:346–9 O '64. *
2. ALEAMONI, LAWRENCE M., AND MATSUNAGA, ALLEN. *A Study of Foreign Language at the University of Illinois Using the CEEB Foreign Language Placement Tests and End-of-Course Grades.* Research Report No. 317. Champaign, Ill.: Measurement and Research Division, Office of Instructional Resources, University of Illinois, 1970. Pp. i, 42. *

For a review by Gilbert C. Kettelkamp of earlier forms, see 6:383; for a review by Harold B. Dunkel, see 5:272; for a review by Herbert Schueler, see 4:244. For a review of the testing program, see 665.

[286]

*Common Concepts Foreign Language Test: German. Students in any grade who are at the Level 1 stage of achievement; 1962–66; aural comprehension; same booklet also used to test French and Spanish; may be administered using live voice but tape recording (3¾ ips) is recommended; Forms 1, 2, ('62, 31 pages) in a single booklet; manual ('66, 41 pages); separate answer sheets (IBM 1230) must be used; $1.10 per test; $5.95 per tape recording; $2.50 per 50 answer sheets; 75¢ per scoring stencil for either form; $1 per manual; postage extra; $2.25 per specimen set (without tape), postpaid; scoring service, 22¢ and over per test; (40–45) minutes; Bela H. Banathy, Miles V. Zintz, W. James Popham, Joseph M. Sadnavitch, Rena Krichbaum, Fred B. Gannon, Valdemar Hempel, and Klaus A. Mueller; CTB/McGraw-Hill. *

WALTER F. W. LOHNES, *Professor of German, Stanford University, Stanford, California.*

This test, designed to measure proficiency in German after the first level of instruction, is an aural comprehension test based on visual cues. It was developed in the early 1960's, following the widespread introduction of the audio-lingual method. The assumption upon which the test is based is that listening and speaking are primary skills and more basic than the secondary skills of reading and writing. Hence, these primary skills should be tested without recourse to the printed or written word. To date, no satisfactory way has been found to test speaking on a large scale, but the authors claim that "aural comprehension is a better index of oral production than the ability to read or write the language." Thus, though measuring only listening comprehension, this test should also give an indication of the student's manifest or latent speaking ability.

The test is ingeniously devised. There are 80 items in all, each requiring the student to identify one of four pictures in a set. There are, however, only 23 multicolored pictures of familiar scenes. On the tape, each of these scenes is described in a few sentences, prior to the actual test, thus familiarizing the student with the content of the pictures. From picture 24 on, the first 23 reappear in various arrangements; subsequent questions deal with different aspects of the pictures, and as the aural stimuli increase in difficulty, the student becomes increasingly familiar with the pictures. The stimuli are all complete utterances rather than isolated words, so that each item creates a mini-situation connecting the spoken word with its visual representation. There are various types of sentences; some are descriptive, some narrative, others are statements that could be made by one of the people in the pictures.

The nature of the test also circumscribes its limitations. It cannot be used to test proficiency in all skills; however, if given in a strictly audio-lingual situation, where the mode of instruction is exclusively aural-oral, it is very well suited indeed. The content of both pictures and aural stimuli is such that use of the test beyond a certain age limit, say the second year in high school, would seem precarious.

There are two parallel forms of the test, both based on the same set of pictures, but with different stimuli. Aside from the fact that there are more statistical data available for Form 1 than for Form 2, the two are interchangeable.

The test can be administered by the teacher, but, in order to achieve uniform results, use of the tape is mandatory. The quality of the taped instructions, including the description of the pictures, is very good, but the German stimulus sentences are not as clearly spoken as they could be. The voice of the (male) speaker is somewhat distorted and muffled. (In one instance, it took three replays to determine whether the word spoken was *badet* or *wartet*.)

By and large, the German sentences are idiomatic and well suited for the age level and achievement level of the presumed test population. There are, however, a number of words one would not expect in the vocabulary of beginning German students, e.g., *Fächer* or *Karton*. In item 76 of Form 1, there is a sudden shift of gears that is apt to throw the student off. Some of the stimuli are somewhat far-fetched (Hier schläft wahrscheinlich ein Mann), a few others have lost their idiomatic genuineness in favor of simplification.

The manual contains a description of the test,

statistical data, directions for administration and scoring, and the stimulus sentences as well as their translations. The manual is not as logically and clearly arranged as it might be; it takes several readings before its scope is completely understood. For instance, the reader is informed that pauses will be indicated throughout the test script, but this is true only of the introductory section of the script where the pauses are not needed; in the test proper, these indications are missing, although it is here that the length of pauses is most crucial if the test is not administered by tape.

The tables of percentile, standard score, and stanine distributions are based on rather small populations: 55 cases for Form 2, Junior High, 1–3 semesters, to 866 cases for Form 1, Senior High, 1–3 semesters; the highest number of cases for over three semesters is 230 for Senior High. For this reason, and also "because of vast differences in foreign language instructional programs, especially at the elementary and junior high levels, the norms have been presented as illustrative 'reference distributions.' "

As an instrument for testing listening comprehension in the early stages of audio-lingual instruction, this test is excellent. It is hoped that the flaws pointed out above will be corrected in an early revision.

For a review covering the three languages, see 253.

[287]

*The Graduate Record Examinations Advanced German Test. Graduate school candidates; 1939–70; 2 current forms ('70, 32 pages); descriptive booklet ('70, 8 pages); for more complete information, see 667; 180(200) minutes; Educational Testing Service. *

For reviews of the testing program, see 667 (1 review) and 5:601 (1 review).

[288]

*Graduate School Foreign Language Test: German. Graduate level degree candidates required to demonstrate reading proficiency in German; 1963–71; GSFLTG; 3 current forms ('70–71, 31–33 pages); for more complete information, see 668; 100(120) minutes; Educational Testing Service. *

REFERENCES

1. BARTLETT, ALBERT ALLEN. "The Foreign Language Requirement for the Ph.D.: A New Approach." *Foreign Lang Ann* 2:174–84 D '68. *
2. CLARK, JOHN L. D. "The Graduate School Foreign Language Requirement: A Survey of Testing Practices and Related Topics." *Foreign Lang Ann* 2:150–64 D '68. *
3. HARVEY, PHILIP R. "Minimal Passing Scores on the Graduate School Foreign Language Tests." *Foreign Lang Ann* 2:165–73 D '68. *

For a review by Jack M. Stein of an earlier edition, see 6:391.

[289]

*MLA Cooperative Foreign Language Proficiency Tests: German.** German majors and advanced students in college; 1960–68; formerly called *MLA Foreign Language Proficiency Tests for Teachers and Advanced Students: German;* 7 tests in 3 booklets (formerly in 7 booklets); Forms HA ('61, identical except for format and directions with earlier tests variously designated Forms A, JML1, and K-JML1), HB ('66, identical except for format and directions with tests copyrighted in 1961 and variously designated Forms B, JML2, K-JML2, and OML1); temporary series directions for administering ('68, 12 pages); series norms ('66, 2 pages); mimeographed series score conversion directions ['68, 8 pages]; separate answer sheets (Digitek, SCRIBE) must be used except for speaking and writing tests; $4 per 100 answer sheets, cash orders postpaid; Digitek scoring stencils not available; SCRIBE scoring and statistical analysis service, 35¢ per student for all tests except speaking and writing; scoring by special arrangement with language specialists: $3 per speaking test tape, $1.50 per writing test; Modern Language Association of America and Educational Testing Service; Cooperative Tests and Services. *

a) BOOK 1: READING, LISTENING COMPREHENSION, SPEAKING. Forms HA (24 pages), HB (21 pages); $9 per 10 tests; 90¢ per single copy; $12 per 7½ ips listening/speaking test tape; blank tapes for student responses must be obtained locally; 40(50) minutes for reading, (20–30) minutes for listening comprehension, (15–30) minutes for speaking.

b) BOOK 2: WRITING. Forms HA (8 pages), HB (7 pages); $6 per 20 tests; 30¢ per single copy; 45(55) minutes.

c) BOOK 3: APPLIED LINGUISTICS, CIVILIZATION AND CULTURE, PROFESSIONAL PREPARATION. Forms HA, HB, (29 pages); professional preparation test is common to all languages in series; $9 per 10 tests; 90¢ per single copy: 40(50) minutes for linguistics, 30(40) minutes for civilization and culture, 45(55) minutes for professional preparation.

REFERENCES

1–3. See 6:393.
4. PAQUETTE, F. ANDRÉ; WALLMARK, MADELINE; SPENCER, RICHARD E.; AND CHURCHILL, FREDERICK J. *A Comparison of the MLA Foreign Language Proficiency Tests for Teachers and Advanced Students With the MLA Foreign Language Cooperative Tests.* An unpublished report to the U.S. Office of Education, Project No. BR-6-2619, Modern Language Association of America, 1966. Pp. 58. * (ERIC ED 019 017)
5. TOLLINGER, SUZANNE, AND PAQUETTE, F. ANDRÉ, EDITORS. *The MLA Foreign Language Proficiency Tests for Teachers and Advanced Students: A Professional Evaluation and Recommendations for Test Development,* pp. 24–41, 125–7, 148–50, 161–75, passim. Sections on this test by Frederick J. Churchill, Tora T. Ladu, James C. McKinney, James W. Marchand, Klaus A. Mueller, Helmut Rehder, Frank G. Ryder, and Douglas C. Sheppard. An unpublished report to the U.S. Office of Education, Project No. BR-6-2619, Modern Language Association of America, June 1966. Pp. viii, 366. * (ERIC ED 019 016)
6. CARROLL, JOHN B. "Foreign Language Proficiency Levels Attained by Language Majors Near Graduation From College." *Foreign Lang Ann* 1:131–51 O '67. *
7. DIZNEY, HENRY F., AND GROMEN, LAUREN. "Predictive Validity and Differential Achievement on Three MLA—Cooperative Foreign Language Tests." *Ed & Psychol Meas* 27: 1127–30 w '67. * (PA 42:9417)
8. PAQUETTE, F. ANDRÉ; WITH THE COOPERATION OF MADELINE WALLMARK. *The MLA Foreign Language Proficiency Tests for Teachers and Advanced Students: Analysis of the Performance of Native Speakers and Comparison With That of NDEA Summer Institute Participants.* An unpublished report to the U.S. Office of Education, Project No. BR-6-2619, Modern Language Association of America, June 1968. Pp. ii, 42. * (ERIC ED 019 017)
9. PERKINS, JEAN A. "State Certification and Proficiency Tests: The Experience in Pennsylvania." *Foreign Lang Ann* 2:195–9 D '68. *
10. CARROLL, JOHN B. "What Does the Pennsylvania For-
eign Language Project Tell Us?" *Foreign Lang Ann* 3(2): 214–36 D '69. *
11. SMITH, PHILIP D., JR. "The Pennsylvania Foreign Language Research Project: Teacher Proficiency and Class Achievement in Two Modern Languages." *Foreign Lang Ann* 3(2):194–207 D '69. *

For reviews by Harold B. Dunkel and Herbert Schueler, see 6:393.

[290]

*MLA-Cooperative Foreign Language Tests: German.** 1–2 years high school or 2 semesters college, 3–4 years high school or 4 semesters college; 1963–65; 4 tests in a single booklet: listening, speaking, reading, writing; writing test ('63, 8 pages) available as separate; 2 forms; 2 levels; no specific manual; series directions for administering and scoring ('64, 40 pages); series handbook ('65, 24 pages); series booklet of norms ('65, 82 pages); student bulletin ('65, 2 pages) for each level; $7 per 10 tests; $5 per 20 writing tests only; separate answer sheets (Digitek, Digitek-IBM 805, IBM 1230, SCRIBE) may be used for listening and reading tests; $4 per 100 answer sheets; $1.25 per 10 IBM 805 or IBM 1230 scoring stencils (answer pattern must be punched out locally); Digitek scoring stencils not available; $8.50 per 3¾ ips tape, 5 inch reel, for listening test; $8.50 per 3¾ ips tape, 5 inch reel, for speaking test (blank tapes or discs for recording student responses must be obtained locally); $2 per series directions for administering and scoring; $2 per series handbook; $2 per series norms booklet; $3 per 100 student bulletins; $3 per specimen set; cash orders postpaid; SCRIBE scoring and statistical analysis service (listening and reading tests), 35¢ per student; no scoring service for speaking and writing tests, but arrangements for professional scoring can be made; 25(35) minutes for listening, 10(20) minutes for speaking, 35(40) minutes for reading, 35(40) minutes for writing; prepared in cooperation with the Modern Language Association of America; Cooperative Tests and Services. *

a) [LOWER LEVEL.] 1–2 years high school or 2 semesters college; Forms LA ('63, 23 pages), LB ('63, 24 pages).

b) [HIGHER LEVEL.] 3–4 years high school or 4 semesters college; Forms MA, MB, ('63, 24 pages).

REFERENCES

1. PAQUETTE, F. ANDRÉ; WALLMARK, MADELINE; SPENCER, RICHARD E.; AND CHURCHILL, FREDERICK J. *A Comparison of the MLA Foreign Language Proficiency Tests for Teachers and Advanced Students With the MLA Foreign Language Cooperative Tests.* An unpublished report to the U.S. Office of Education, Project No. BR-6-2619, Modern Language Association of America, 1966. Pp. 58. * (ERIC ED 019 017)
2. ALEAMONI, LAWRENCE M., AND SPENCER, RICHARD E. "A Comparison of Biserial Discrimination, Point Biserial Discrimination, and Difficulty Indices in Item Analysis Data." *Ed & Psychol Meas* 29(2):353–8 su '69. * (PA 44:17314)

T. F. NAUMANN, *Professor of Psychology, Central Washington State College, Ellensburg, Washington.*

The stated purpose of the MLA-Cooperative tests is to measure the learner's knowledge of structures which are common in speech and writing, and to assess his knowledge of vocabulary and idiom in their receptive and productive aspects. By design the tests measure language skills in a functional context of the language for which skills are tested.

No specific study or discussion of validity

was found. It can be assumed fairly safely that adequate content validity has been obtained due to the outstanding technical know-how of ETS and the specialists selected by MLA.

The content of the Listening Test seems adequate, but some minor improvements are indicated. For example on Form LA item 39 should begin the response stems C and D with "Über's" or "Über das." Also, in the same test item 43 should have an idiomatically more adequate introduction on the tape containing "erzahlte mir meine Schwester" instead of "meine Schwester had mir erzahlt." Item 7, Form MB, should use the term "Butterbrote" (sandwiches) instead of "Brote" (breads) in the taped conversation. When listening to items 35 to 37 of the same form the question arises to what extent memory is tested rather than listening comprehension skill. It is suggested that the taped directives give more often the number of the page to be turned to. Scoring of the listening skill test is objective and simple.

In the Speaking Test, the learner interacts with a test tape, recording his own statements on a separate tape. Scoring is subjective with specific directions provided for the tester. The learner's responses are scored for proper reproduction of German sounds ("mimicry"), adequacy of expression within word groups, rhythm, intonation patterns, correctness, naturalness and meaningfulness of responses. For a number of responses a point system is applied. This is obviously the weakest section of the tests since it is open to rater bias and the scorer's own competency in German.

The Reading Test consists of 50 multiple choice items which range from selecting small parts of speech in a given sentence to completing a dialogue or a paragraph from multiple choices. Scoring is objective. This is the most comprehensive of the four subtests. With the native German speaker sample referred to above, reading had the highest correlation with other subtests, viz., .41 with listening and .42 with writing, the first a receptive communication skill, the other an expressive skill.

The types of responses in the 50-item Writing Test range from filling in small parts of speech to rewriting sentences and, finally, writing a dialogue or paragraph based on a specified situation or topic. Part of the scoring is subjective with items scored on a point system. Item 39 of Forms MA and MB should be changed to

avoid unnecessary ambiguity with respect to gender in the third person singular.

The MLA-Cooperative German tests are undoubtedly the best of this type available. Improvements of small details here and there could readily be made in a new edition. The potential user should realize that the tests are for students beyond beginner's level. Reports of validity studies should be made available as soon as possible, particularly with data on predictive validity. On the whole, these tests set standards which deserve emulation.

For an excerpted review of the series, see 254.

[291]
★National Teacher Examinations: German. College seniors and teachers; 1970–71; modified version of secure form of *MLA Foreign Language Proficiency Tests for Teachers and Advanced Students: German;* Form TNT1 ('71, 21 pages); descriptive booklet ('70, 11 pages); listening comprehension section administered by 3¾ ips tape recording; for more complete information, see 582; 120(165) minutes; Educational Testing Service. *

For reviews of the testing program, see 582 (2 reviews), 6:700 (1 review), 5:538 (3 reviews), and 4:802 (1 review).

[292]
★Pimsleur German Proficiency Tests. First, second level courses in grades 7–12 or first, second semesters college; 1967; 4 scores: listening, speaking, reading, writing; 1 form; 2 levels labeled Forms A, C; manual (23 pages); no college norms; $1.75 per manual; $1.75 per specimen set (without tapes or manual); postage extra; Paul Pimsleur; Harcourt Brace Jovanovich, Inc. *
a) TEST 1, LISTENING COMPREHENSION. Digitek, IBM 805, and IBM 1230 test-answer sheets (2 pages); 7½ ips test tape, 5 inch reel; $7.50 per test tape; $3.80 per 35 test-answer sheets; $1.40 per set of scoring stencils; IBM scoring service, 33¢ and over per test; 15(25) minutes.
b) TEST 2, SPEAKING PROFICIENCY. Test (4 pages); scoring sheet (2 pages); 7½ ips test tape, 5 inch reel; $7.50 per test tape; $4.50 per 35 tests; $2.70 per 35 scoring sheets; 16(26) minutes.
c) TEST 3, READING COMPREHENSION. Test (4 pages); separate answer sheets (Digitek-IBM 805, IBM 1230) must be used; $4.50 per 35 tests; $2.30 per 35 Digitek-IBM 805 answer sheets; $2.80 per 35 IBM 1230 answer sheets; 70¢ per scoring stencil; IBM scoring service, 19¢ and over per test; 35(45) minutes.
d) TEST 4, WRITING PROFICIENCY. Test (6 pages); answer key and scoring directions (4 pages); $7.40 per 35 tests; 35(45) minutes.

WALTER F. W. LOHNES, *Professor of German, Stanford University, Stanford, California.*

These tests examine proficiency in the four skills: listening, speaking, reading, and writing. Both forms, A and C, follow the same pattern, the sole difference being the degree of difficulty of the material tested. The primary usefulness of the tests is for high school testing and as an instrument for placing incoming freshmen into early college courses. The content of parts of the tests, notably the reading and writing tests, does not seem to be suitable for today's college students and may, in fact, soon outlive its appeal to high school students as well. The tests can be used for other purposes: evaluating individual and class achievement as well as evaluating local German programs.

The Pimsleur tests were developed during several years of thorough research and experimentation, starting in 1960. They follow the pattern set by the *MLA Foreign Language Proficiency Tests for Teachers and Advanced Students* and closely resemble the *MLA Cooperative Foreign Language Tests.* The manual reflects the thoroughness with which the tests were produced. It contains not only easy-to-follow directions for administering and scoring the tests, but also detailed statistical information on the interpretation of test results and on validity and reliability.

The tapes for the Listening and the Speaking Tests are excellent. The English instructions are clear and precise; the German voices, one male and one female, are very good; all texts are spoken at normal speed.

The Listening Test has two parts. Part 1 tests sound discrimination. For each of the 20 spoken sentences, the student has to identify the correct written equivalent from among four printed choices. Each item concentrates on one problem, such as *s* versus *z*. Each sentence is spoken only once. In Part 2, the student hears 20 statements or questions, each spoken twice, and has to select the most logical rejoinder from among four printed choices. There are a few unhappy choices of words; for example, the German equivalent of *athlete* is not *Athlet,* but *Sportler.* By and large, however, the items are very good, some with excellent distractors that play on possible misunderstandings of the stem. In Part 1 of Form C, a few items are quite artificial, doubtless due to the fact that it is very difficult in German to find minimal pairs (let alone minimal quadruplets) of phonemic distinction. There is some duplication of items in the two forms, presumably for equating purposes.

Part 1 of the Speaking Test tests vocabulary. The student has to identify 27 nouns (article not required) from simple line drawings in the test booklet. This part appears to test speaking proficiency only secondarily. Speed is of the essence here, and if the student cannot think of the correct word immediately, he will miss out, no matter how good his speaking ability. It can be argued, of course, that the ability to transfer instantaneously a visual image into sound is a major part of speaking proficiency. Part 2 tests pronunciation. Each item contains two critical sounds: vowels, consonants, diphthongs, or glottal stops. (A classification of these items is given in the manual.) All 20 phrases and sentences are read by the speaker; the student records them from his printed text only after he has heard all of them, thus being forced to rely on what he has learned and knows rather than on immediate imitation of the taped voice. In Part 3, the student hears eight questions, to which he must respond freely, though in complete sentences. This is apt to create artificial statements, since the normal way of responding to questions such as these is in incomplete sentences. In a revision of the test, it might be advisable to increase the number of questions and to encourage the student to reply as he would in a normal conversation.

Both forms of the Reading Test contain ten very short passages and a total of 36 multiple choice questions; thus, the same answer sheet can be used for both. Again, there is an overlap between the two forms: two passages appear in both, though the choices are scrambled differently. As far as language is concerned, this is the poorest of the four tests. The wording of some of the passages, especially in Form A, simply does not ring true. There are a number of ungrammatical forms in the choices as well. In a revision of the test, some of the texts should be improved or replaced by passages of more immediate concern to the student.

The format of the Writing Test is again the same for both forms. Strictly speaking, only Parts 1 and 4 test the student's writing ability. In Part 1, the student is given a passage with a number of function words left out; this type of exercise has proved to be an excellent indicator of writing ability. In Part 4, the student is asked to write freely, using pictures as cues. Parts 2 and 3 simply require the student to rewrite a number of sentences, either by changing tenses or by substituting other indicated elements, which necessitates some additional changes. These two parts demand nothing more than the kind of manipulation required in pattern drills. A classification of the items in Parts 1, 2, and 3 is provided in the manual. Like the Reading Test, the Writing Test could profit from some updating.

The interpretation of test results in the manual gives percentiles and stanines based on standardization samples of 2,390 students for Level 1 and 2,025 students for Level 2 in 21 states across the United States.

Two final points: In the next printing of the test booklets, the digraph ß should be used instead of *ss,* and on the cover of the test package, the picture of Hohenschwanstein, which is about as representative of Germany as Disneyland is of the United States, should be replaced by a more appropriate picture.

Despite my criticisms and suggestions for revision, I consider the Pimsleur Tests one of the best available test batteries. Its shortcomings are primarily of a linguistic nature and can be easily remedied in a future revision.

Jack M. Stein, *Professor of German, Harvard University, Cambridge, Massachusetts.*

The *Pimsleur German Proficiency Tests* are an excellent medium for evaluating achievement in the first and second levels of German study in grades 7–12. They are less useful for college placement purposes (more below). Separate tests in each of the four skills combine to make a larger unit, while each can be administered independently. The tests make use of established techniques; there are no innovations. A splendid 25-page printed manual gives accurate descriptions of the separate units, including excellent classification tables, item by item. The manual provides careful guidance in administering and scoring the tests, with copious tables. There are also lucid sections on interpreting and using the test results, including some cautious but sound advice on evaluating individual and class achievement, as well as on evaluating the local language program as a whole. The manual also contains six pages describing the validity and reliability of the tests. Reliability coefficients, item analysis summaries (difficulty, discrimination), and other detailed information are given in statistical tables.

The overwhelming majority of the items in all the tests are sound, natural, and functional. There are occasional slips, however, which, it seems, could easily have been eliminated. I noticed the following: in each listening comprehension test there was at least one sentence which was spoken on tape with an unnatural intonation. On the second level test, the sentences "Verzieh es nicht" and "Er wäscht nicht" are spoken. Both are artificial. In the vocabulary part of the speaking tests, where pictures are given to elicit nouns from the student, the pictures are occasionally ambiguous. Since the responses must be given with very little deliberation, this is all the more objectionable. For instance, a theater ticket looks a lot like a safety razor blade; a store front could be any number of things, etc. One picture in Form C shows an unmistakably American farmer (der Farmer? der Bauer?). Part 2 of the Form A speaking test, which tests pronunciation, contains a silly sentence: "Sie ist dünn und müde." In Part 3 of each speaking proficiency test occurs the most serious fault. This part tests fluency by requiring responses to basic questions. The directions insist that the student respond in "simple but complete German sentences." The reason for the directions is clear, but the technique is nonetheless artificial. The natural response would in most cases be an incomplete sentence. Occasionally a complete sentence would be downright unnatural, e.g., the response to "Wohin werden Sie heute nach der Schule gehen?" In the writing test there are a couple of bad sentences, e.g., "Die Jungen essen immer viele Brötchen und werden später krank," which is to be rewritten as "Robert isst immer viel Brot und wird später krank." One would think he (or they) would eventually learn not to.

These and a few additional examples notwithstanding, the Pimsleur tests are in general excellent and are certain to give reliable achievement scores when administered as advised in the excellent printed manual (the test packet includes in addition a 3-page brochure giving the information from the 25-page manual in summary form; if this offers any temptation not to read the full manual carefully, it should be eliminated). The tests can be administered at any time after a certain minimum amount of material has been covered, defined in the manual as "at least two-thirds of a first-level German course" for Form A and "at least two-thirds of a second-level German course" for Form C. Form A is too elementary for college placement; Form C could be used for college placement only if none of the entering students had had more than two years of secondary school German. It is simply not advanced enough to be reliable otherwise. For this reason it is not an acceptable alternative for college placement purposes to the Higher Level of the *MLA-Cooperative Foreign Language Tests: German.*

J Ed Meas 6(1):47–8 sp '69. Garold N. Davis. Although a nominal effort is made to test the four language skills independent of one another, this effort is never entirely successful. The listening test, for example, could not be taken by even a native speaker of German if he had not yet learned to read. The speaking test is also dependent in part on the ability to read. Since it is assumed that the students taking the tests will have been trained in the four skills, this relationship between the spoken and the written language is not necessarily a disadvantage as long as the tests are taken as a unit. Any attempt to use the individual parts to test one of the skills independently will be unsuccessful. The vocabulary and structure used for the Form A tests seem to be of adequate difficulty for students with one year of high school training in German. The language proficiency level tested with the Form C tests, however, does not seem to be much higher than that of the Form A tests. Of the 20 sentences presented in the Form C listening test, for example, 5 sentences are repetitions from Form A. Such repetitions are found throughout the Form C tests. There are a few unfortunate test items. On the Form C listening test students are asked to distinguish from a single hearing the difference between "machst du" and "magst du." Although a phonetic distinction does exist, I found that a Professor of German Linguistics whose native language is English, and a native speaker of German were both unable to identify the distinction as it was presented on the test tape without several hearings and a lengthy discussion. Also, the Form C reading test includes the strange construction: "Diese Reise wäre ein Grund, damit ich zeitlebens barfuss ginge," instead of the more normal: "Diese Reise wäre ein Grund für mich, dass ich...." Such items which will tend to confuse even the better students should be eliminated from the tests. Fortunately these confusing items are few in number. Perhaps there is no simple, efficient way to test reading comprehension. The "reading" test in both Form A and Form C

is actually an exercise in identifying the synonymous relationship between words or phrases used in a prose passage with the words or phrases used in the "questions." For example, a reading passage contains the sentence: Konrad hat ein Auto, aber er ist kaputt." In the "question" section the student sees the partial sentence: "Sie fahren mit dem Bus, denn Konrads Auto....," followed by four possible "completions." The correct completion in this case is "fährt nicht." Thus if the student knows that "kaputt" and "fährt nicht" are used synonymously he will mark the correct completion. It is possible that a student could read and understand the prose passage, however, and still not be able to identify the correct completion. Perhaps as long as it is understood that the "answers" as well as the reading passages constitute a part of the "reading" test, there is no problem. There will be no way to identify the source of the error, however, without further testing. The most outstanding part of the test in my estimation is the writing test, which makes use of drawings to stimulate written responses. This attenuates the possibility of interference from a written English model, and seems to be the most natural way to conduct a controlled writing test. The problem of this part of the test is in the scoring, but even here the author has done an admirable job of preparing an objective and uniform method of grading the written responses. Since testing is still one of the most neglected phases of language teaching, these tests will be a welcome addition to the materials available, and, taking into consideration the problems suggested in this review, they will be a useful tool to the teacher who wants to evaluate the relative progress of a group of students.

[293]
★**The Undergraduate Record Examinations: German Test.** College; 1969–70; Forms K-RUR ('69, 23 pages), SUR ('70, 23 pages); descriptive booklet ('70, 11 pages); for more complete information, see 671; 120(140) minutes; Educational Testing Service. *

For reviews of the testing program, see 671 (2 reviews).

GREEK

[294]
***College Board Achievement Test in Greek.** Candidates for college entrance with 2–3 years high school Greek; 1901–71; test administered at local sec-

ondary schools in February; candidates must also be registered to take Achievement Tests (see 663*b*) during a regular program administration; 3 parts (candidate takes only one): Attic prose, Homeric poetry, Attic prose and Homeric poetry; descriptive booklet ('70, 7 pages); supervisor's manual ('71, 14 pages); no data on reliability; no additional fee; 90(100) minutes; program administered for the College Entrance Examination Board by Educational Testing Service. *

For a review by Konrad Gries of an earlier form, see 5:277. For reviews of the testing program, see 6:760 (2 reviews).

[295]

*College Placement Test in Greek.** Entering college freshmen; 1962–70, c1957–70; CPTG; irregularly scheduled reprintings of inactive forms of *College Board Achievement Test in Greek;* Form K-KPLI ['62, reprint of 1957 test]; 2 tests (student takes only one): Attic prose (10 pages), Homer and Attic prose (11 pages); for more complete information, see 665; 60(70) minutes per test; program administered for the College Entrance Examination Board by Educational Testing Service. *

For a review by Konrad Gries (then Form FAC), see 5:277. For a review of the testing program, see 665.

HEBREW

[296]

*College Board Achievement Test in Hebrew.** Candidates for college entrance with 2–4 years high school Hebrew; 1961–71; test administered each January at centers established by the publisher; for more complete information, see 663; 60(80) minutes; program administered for the College Entrance Examination Board by Educational Testing Service. *

For reviews of the testing program, see 6:760 (2 reviews).

[297]

★College Placement Test in Hebrew Reading.** Entering college freshmen; 1962–70, c1961–70; CPTHR; irregularly scheduled reprintings of inactive forms of *College Board Achievement Test in Hebrew;* Form SPL ('70, reprint of 1964 test, 19 pages); for more complete information, see 665; 60(70) minutes; program administered for the College Entrance Examination Board by Educational Testing Service. *

For a review of the testing program, see 665.

[298]

★[NCRI Achievement Tests in Hebrew.]** Grades 5–7, 7–9; 1965–67; 2 levels; 2 forms; directions ['65, 1 page]; combined interpretation guide ('67, 14 pages) for this test and 6:397; no data on reliability; separate answer sheets (IBM 1230) must be used; 15¢ per test; 2¢ per answer sheet; scoring stencil not available; 5¢ per directions sheet; 75¢ per interpretation guide; 10% extra for postage, cash orders only; scoring service, 9¢ per test; [40–50] minutes; Simon Bugatch and

Judah Pilch (test); National Curriculum Research Institute, American Association for Jewish Education. *
a) ACHIEVEMENT TEST IN HEBREW. Grades 5–7; Forms 1, 2, ['65, 8 pages].
b) ACHIEVEMENT TESTS IN HEBREW. Grades 7–9; 2 forms labeled Tests 3, 4, ('65, 8 pages).

ITALIAN

[299]

*College Placement Test in Italian Listening Comprehension.** Entering college freshmen; 1962–70; irregularly scheduled reprintings of inactive forms of *College Board Achievement Test in Italian Listening Comprehension;* Form PPL ['67, reprint of 1966 test, 9 pages]; test administered by 7½ ips tape recording; for more complete information, see 665; 30(40) minutes; program administered for the College Entrance Examination Board by Educational Testing Service. *

PAOLO VALESIO, *Associate Professor of Romance Languages and Literatures, Harvard University, Cambridge, Massachusetts.*

In dialogue 9, the expression *Stasera danno l'Aida a Caracalla* is perhaps too concise and allusive. A version like *Stasera danno l'Aida al Teatro Comunale* (where the presence of the common noun *teatro* clarifies the context) would spare the listener some difficulty.

In the dialogue "La signorina Rossi e il direttore d'ufficio," there are some points which do not seem to me to be fully idiomatic: (*a*) *Capoufficio* (or *capo ufficio,* or *capufficio*) is more appropriate than *direttore d'ufficio.* (*b*) The phrase *scuola media,* with no further qualification, usually designates in Italian the period of schooling between 10 and 13 years; a 20-year-old Italian typist would probably name a *scuola commerciale* or *scuola professionale* as her recent scholastic background. (*c*) In Italy one speaks of *chilometri* (at least in a technical, nonliterary context such as this one) rather than *miglia.* (*d*) Unlike the English phrase *letters of recommendation,* the superficially equivalent Italian phrase *lettere di raccomandazione* implies a very informal kind of communication; a more appropriate equivalent here would be *lettere di presentazione.*

Perhaps an effort could be made to make these short dialogues slightly broader in scope and more lively. For instance, one or two of the shorter exchanges could have a polemical, or a humorous tone, and the longer dialogue could concern some historical or cultural problems relevant to Italy.

In general, this test seems to be adequate to

the task of evaluating the familiarity of the candidate with the everyday use of the language.

For a review of the testing program, see 665.

[300]

*College Placement Test in Italian Reading. Entering college freshmen; 1962–70, c1957–70; CPTIR; irregularly scheduled reprintings of inactive forms of *College Board Achievement Test in Italian Reading and Essay;* Form PPL ('67, reprint of 1966 test, 12 pages) ; for more complete information, see 664 ; 60(70) minutes ; program administered for the College Entrance Examination Board by Educational Testing Service. *

PAOLO VALESIO, *Associate Professor of Romance Languages and Literatures, Harvard University, Cambridge, Massachusetts.*

The criteria implicit in the lists of lexical items in sections 1, 2, and 3 seem to be different for each section : in 1 there are three items (A, B, D) which are clearly out of place in the proposed context, and two (C, E) of which only one is the normal answer but which are semantically and phonologically very close, although morphologically unrelated ; in 2 there are no special relationships (phonological, morphological, or semantic) among the five items ; in 3, three of the items (A, D, E) are morphologically related, insofar as they are all formed on the basis of the same suffix, and to that extent they are also semantically related (the relation between A and D is particularly close). It is not clear to me whether this different treatment was planned or not, i.e., whether or not there is a plan to put lexical choices within a specific phonological and/or morphological framework. Concerning section 3, the form *scarpellino* is less usual in Italian than *scalpellino.*

In 5, it seems confusing to present D and E as mutually exclusive choices, since the distinction between them is essentially graphemic ; the form in E is the most usual, but the form in D, although less common in modern Italian writing, is not incorrect.

In section 11, there is a sort of semantic hierarchy : although A is the normal solution, E is still possible as an answer here, while the other three items are clearly "out." It seems to me that such a hierarchy is missing in sections 9 and 10 ; in each of them there is only one likely answer, while the other answers are clearly not normal in the context. (Answer C in 10 could be an exception, if one considers *cucinare* as a metaphor for the making of the

movie ; but if so, this should have been made clearer.) This situation (hierarchy of acceptability in one section versus absence of such a hierarchy in the other two sections) could puzzle the reader.

In section 14, since the verb *sentire* in Italian may refer to either acoustic or tactile perceptions, it is not clear whether answer B is meant as an unacceptable answer or as a less acceptable but still possible answer with respect to the normal one, E.

The most interesting and delicate problem arises in connection with sentence 4, *Domani mattina voi....questo o niente!* This sentence is syntactically ambiguous, in the context of the available choices, because it can have two different interpretations, for both of which the sentence is grammatical : in one interpretation, it can be paraphrased in English as "Tomorrow you will eat this, otherwise you will not get anything," (from the answer presented as correct, A, it is obvious that the writers had this interpretation in mind) ; in the other interpretation, the sentence can be paraphrased in English as "Tomorrow you would be capable of refusing to eat, if you were not offered this," implying an (admirative or ironical) "this-is-the-kind-of-person-you-are" attitude. In other words, this sentence can be interpreted *either* as a descriptive statement (although, as things now stand, this is not completely true, as will be shown later) in which, given the choices available and the reference to the future expressed by the adverbial phrase (*Domani mattina*), the appropriate choice is the future tense form (A), *or* as an emphatic statement, for which the Italian "conditional mood" form, *mangereste* (C), would be the appropriate choice. The ambiguity could be solved (but not fully, even for a native speaker of Italian, because of intonation problems in reading an incomplete sentence) if the sentence were uttered, because the intonation symbolized by the exclamation point in connection with the first interpretation, although it could be generically described as "emphatic," is different from the intonation symbolized by the exclamation point in connection with the second interpretation. But since this is a printed sentence presented to a reader, the ambiguity remains. This ambiguity is all the more damaging because the two interpretations presuppose two opposite attitudes of the subject of the sentence toward the action described : in the first interpretation, the presupposition is that the subject (the group of persons designated by the pronoun *voi*) does not want to eat the thing referred to, while in the second interpretation, the presupposition is that the subject strongly wants to eat it.

Since it is almost impossible to find a sentence, in any language, whose surface syntactic structure does not possess some measure of ambiguity, inconveniences like these are probably unavoidable. But if this is true, it shows that clearcut evaluations of grammaticality such as the ones required in these tests have relatively little to do with the actual linguistic knowledge of the speaker. However, it is perhaps possible to clarify this sentence. In the first interpretation (the one desired by the test writers) the sentence remains grammatical even if a different, less emphatic intonation is adopted. In fact, in the framework of the first interpretation, the emphatic intonation symbolized by the exclamation point adds an imperative meaning to the sentence; a less emphatic intonation, symbolized by a period, would make of the sentence a descriptive statement (the indication of a choice), without a specific imperative implication. On the other hand, the second interpretation implies a structure which requires the kind of emphatic intonation represented by the exclamation point, in order for the sentence to be grammatical; the only other kind of intonation normally possible would be the "suspensive," usually one represented by a comma. Then, the conditional form would make of this structure merely a clause in a complex sentence, and thus the sentence as presented in the text would be ungrammatical (as required). One could, therefore, simply substitute a period for the exclamation point here; in this way, the solution desired for the test would really become the only one which is normally acceptable in the language.

In conclusion, provided that some adjustments are made, this test should prove useful.

For a review of the testing program, see 665.

[301]

*MLA Cooperative Foreign Language Proficiency Tests: Italian.** Italian majors and advanced students in college; 1961–68; formerly called *MLA Foreign Language Proficiency Tests for Teachers and Advanced Students: Italian;* 7 tests in 3 booklets (formerly in 7 booklets); Form HA ('61, identical except for format and directions with earlier tests variously designated Forms A, JML1, and K-JML1); temporary series directions for administering ('68, 12 pages); series norms ('66, 2 pages, Italian norms tentative);

mimeographed series score conversion directions ['68, 8 pages]; separate answer sheets (Digitek, SCRIBE) must be used except for speaking and writing tests; $4 per 100 answer sheets, cash orders postpaid; Digitek scoring stencils not available; SCRIBE scoring and statistical analysis service, 35¢ per student for all tests except speaking and writing; scoring by special arrangement with language specialists: $3 per speaking test tape, $1.50 per writing test; Modern Language Association of America and Educational Testing Service; Cooperative Tests and Services. *

a) BOOK 1: READING, LISTENING COMPREHENSION, SPEAKING. Form HA (24 pages); $9 per 10 tests; 90¢ per single copy; $12 per 7½ ips listening/speaking test tape; blank tapes for student responses must be obtained locally; 40(50) minutes for reading, (20–30) minutes for listening comprehension, (15–30) minutes for speaking.

b) BOOK 2: WRITING. Form HA (8 pages); $6 per 20 tests; 30¢ per single copy; 45(55) minutes.

c) BOOK 3: APPLIED LINGUISTICS, CIVILIZATION AND CULTURE, PROFESSIONAL PREPARATION. Form HA (29 pages); professional preparation test is common to all languages in series; $9 per 10 tests; 90¢ per single copy; 40(50) minutes for linguistics, 30(40) minutes for civilization and culture, 45(55) minutes for professional preparation.

REFERENCES

1–3. See 6:403.
4. TOLLINGER, SUZANNE, AND PAQUETTE, F. ANDRÉ, EDITORS. *The MLA Foreign Language Proficiency Tests for Teachers and Advanced Students: A Professional Evaluation and Recommendations for Test Development,* pp. 42–61, 128–9, 151–4, 161–75, passim. Sections on this test by Pierina B. Castiglione, Robert J. Di Pietro, Tora T. Ladu, Graziana Lazzarino, Archibald T. MacAllister, James C. McKinney, Paul R. Olson, and Douglas C. Sheppard. An unpublished report to the U.S. Office of Education, Project No. BR-6-2619, Modern Language Association of America, June 1966. Pp. viii, 366. * (ERIC ED 019 016)
5. PAQUETTE, F. ANDRÉ; WITH THE COOPERATION OF MADELINE WALLMARK. *The MLA Foreign Language Proficiency Tests for Teachers and Advanced Students: Analysis of the Performance of Native Speakers and Comparison With That of NDEA Summer Institute Participants.* An unpublished report to the U.S. Office of Education, Project No. BR-6-2619, Modern Language Association of America, June 1968. Pp. ii, 42. * (ERIC ED 019 017)

JOSEPHINE BRUNO PANE, *Associate Professor of Foreign Language Education, Rutgers, The State University, New Brunswick, New Jersey.*

These tests are based on the 1955 MLA "Qualifications for Secondary School Teachers of Modern Foreign Languages." The MLA statement establishes three levels of proficiency: Minimal, Good, Superior, for seven areas of competency: Listening Comprehension, Speaking, Reading, Writing, Applied Linguistics, Culture and Civilization, and Professional Preparation.

To review in 1970 tests which appeared in 1961 is difficult. At the time the MLA Proficiency Tests were written, the foreign language profession was in the midst of re-evaluating itself. In all of the areas, but especially in applied linguistics, culture and civilization, and professional preparation, it was treading on unfamiliar ground. Since there was uncertainty regarding content, it follows naturally that there had to be uncertainty in the matter of testing it. The MLA Proficiency Tests are a reflection of their time.

Since then, however, the foreign langúage profession has moved forward both in definition of content and in the science of testing. In view of these facts, this reviewer suggests that the MLA Proficiency Tests be revised to reflect these advances. In most urgent need of revision is Book 3 (Applied Linguistics, Culture and Civilization, and Professional Preparation) because these areas are constantly changing and must be kept contemporary, and also because their relationship to modern foreign language teaching is now better defined.

The science of linguistics, for example, is growing and changing rapidly. The Applied Linguistics Test reflects neither the growth nor the changes, the most obvious omission being any mention of transformational grammar. In addition, it is the application of linguistics to foreign language teaching that is being stressed today. Yet, this aspect is not emphasized in the test. Interestingly, whatever items there are on applied linguistics actually appear in the Professional Preparation Test. Perhaps the most important result of this test is that it has forced foreign language teachers to investigate the science of linguistics.

The Culture and Civilization Test is another which needs constant up-dating, because it must include items of contemporary culture along with those of basic, unchanging character. In addition, the foreign language teaching profession now has a clearer understanding of culture in the anthropological sense and of its relation to foreign language teaching. In the Italian Culture and Civilization Test little mention is made of language as culture or of contrasts in culture. Instead, the test stresses fine arts, history, music, architecture, and literary appreciation. The last of these, incidentally, might better be included in the Reading Test. As for the identification questions, luck might play a very important part in answering some of them. In the items connected with pictures, for example, the unlucky examinee might know all of the cathedrals in Italy except the one pictured in the test item whereas the lucky examinee might know no other cathedral but that one!

The Professional Preparation Test also needs constant up-dating. The original criticism of this test, that it is biased toward the audio-lingual approach, still holds true. In 1970, it shows, in addition, serious omissions in areas reflecting recent developments in research, media, curriculum, and the "New Key" itself.

In the Listening Comprehension Test the examinee hears spoken passages (questions, monologues, conversations) and chooses appropriate responses from those printed in his booklet. In general, the spoken passages are too long. This is unfortunate, because it limits the kinds of situations and themes that can be presented and therefore also the variety and levels of language usage. Also, if the examinee does not know the key words, he is at a loss on too large a number of items. In addition to being too long, the spoken passages are also overinvolved and contain too many people, with the result that it is difficult to remember who is who and who did what. All of this raises the important question of whether the test really measures comprehension, or, rather if it measures retention. As for the answers themselves, they often require knowledge of unimportant details rather than ideas. Much of the vocabulary is either uncommon or archaic and the structural forms are often so involved as to sound unnatural and contrived. The voices are native and represent several regions of Italy.

The Speaking Test includes mimicry, reading from a script, and describing a picture or a series of pictures. This reviewer seriously questions the mimicry section. Is it not more important to judge the examinee's own performance instead of his ability to mimic a model? Especially since in some cases the model's speech is open to question. Furthermore, even a native speaker of Italian from one region of Italy would have difficulty reproducing the pronunciation and intonation of a native from another region. In any case, the ability to imitate is not the same as the ability to speak. As for scoring, it is difficult to achieve reliability on speaking tests, because it cannot be done objectively, and so much depends upon the expectations and linguistic prejudices of the judges.

The Reading Test sets out to measure vocabulary and reading comprehension. The format is similar to previous reading tests. The questions emphasize vocabulary more than reading, however; in many cases the correct answer depends not on understanding an idea but rather on a specific word. To make matters worse, many of the words and idioms are unusual, and the passages are long and abstruse.

The Writing Test shares the format of the

writing tests in the other four languages. According to the MLA Statement of Qualifications, even the minimal level of proficiency in writing includes "the ability to write" in the foreign language. Yet, nowhere in the proficiency tests is the examinee asked to write. Instead, he fills blanks and corrects passages. Filling in the blanks limits the morphological items that can be tested. As for the correction of passages, one such exercise might be sufficient instead of three. The remainder of the test might be devoted to writing a passage, in the manner of the Speaking Test. This reviewer would recommend such a change, even with the attendant problems that it would create for scoring.

In 1966 the MLA conducted an evaluative study (4) of the existing forms of the MLA tests with teams of foreign language teachers as reviewers. This study points out many weaknesses in the tests. It also points out the strengths, the chief ones being that they evaluate teacher proficiency objectively, and perform well statistically. (In regard to the latter, data on the Italian tests should be considered as tentative because of the small numbers involved.)

To help in validating the tests the MLA sponsored another study (5) which analyzes the performance of native speakers and compares it with that of NDEA Institute participants. Listening Comprehension, Speaking, Reading, and Writing were given to native speakers in the corresponding country in the summer of 1964. Results show that the native speaker groups performed at a level considerably higher than that achieved by the NDEA Institute participants in the posttest, and suggest that because of some overlap in performance "the best among the NDEA participants approach the 'educated native speaker' in competence." The fact that native speakers sometimes received mediocre or even low scores in speaking points to the difficulty of scoring the speaking test. The fact that some native speakers scored lower in reading than non-native speakers suggests that they might have had difficulty with those parts of the test which require literary analysis.

The *MLA Cooperative Foreign Language Proficiency Tests* represent an important achievement in the foreign language profession. They still remain the only such tests available, serve an important need, and are being used extensively in research projects of all kinds. A number of states use the scores on these tests as a basis for certification of foreign language teachers. Both of the studies sponsored by the MLA point out the strengths and weaknesses of the tests and can be very helpful in the interpretation of test results. This reviewer recommends that users of the MLA tests read these studies.

[302]

*MLA-Cooperative Foreign Language Tests: Italian.** 1–2 years high school or 2 semesters college, 3–4 years high school or 4 semesters college; 1963–65; 4 tests in a single booklet: listening, speaking, reading, writing; writing test ('63, 8 pages) available as separate; 2 forms; 2 levels; no specific manual; series directions for administering and scoring ('64, 40 pages); series handbook ('65, 24 pages); series booklet of norms ('65, 82 pages); student bulletin ('65, 2 pages) for each level; $7 per 10 tests; $5 per 20 writing tests only; separate answer sheets (Digitek, Digitek-IBM 805, IBM 1230, SCRIBE) may be used for listening and reading tests; $4 per 100 answer sheets; $1.25 per 10 IBM 805 or IBM 1230 scoring stencils (answer pattern must be punched out locally); Digitek scoring stencils not available; $8.50 per 3¾ ips tape, 5 inch reel, for listening test; $8.50 per 3¾ ips tape, 5 inch reel, for speaking test (blank tapes or discs for recording student responses must be obtained locally); $2 per series directions for administering and scoring; $2 per series handbook; $2 per series norms booklet; $3 per 100 student bulletins; $3 per specimen set; cash orders postpaid; SCRIBE scoring and statistical analysis service (listening and reading tests), 35¢ per student; no scoring service for speaking and writing tests, but arrangements for professional scoring can be made; 25(35) minutes for listening, 10(20) minutes for speaking, 35(40) minutes for reading, 35(40) minutes for writing; prepared in cooperation with the Modern Language Association of America; Cooperative Tests and Services. *
a) [LOWER LEVEL.] 1–2 years high school or 2 semesters college; Forms LA, LB, ('63, 25 pages).
b) [HIGHER LEVEL.] 3–4 years high school or 4 semesters college; Forms MA, MB, ('63, 24 pages).

JOSEPHINE BRUNO PANE, *Associate Professor of Foreign Language Education, Rutgers, The State University, New Brunswick, New Jersey.*

The lower level Listening test has 45 items and the higher level, 40. Instructions, narrative passages, and questions are presented on tape and the student selects the appropriate answer from the multiple choices printed in the test booklet. The spoken passages are usually single utterances, conversations, or prose selections. To be sure, the listening tests are also partially reading tests, since they require a reading knowledge of Italian in order to answer the questions. To the credit of these examinations, the reading load is usually no greater than the difficulty presented in the spoken material. And further, the answers do give the student the opportunity to demonstrate understanding of ideas as well as words. The situations are varied, thereby giving opportunity for different levels of language, vocabulary and structure. The voices are native, the Italian is authentic, the speed of delivery is normal.

The Speaking test for both levels contains 38 items. Instructions and questions are spoken and students' responses are recorded on their own individual tapes. The test includes mimicry, reading from a script, answering questions about line drawings, and describing a picture or a series of pictures that tell a story (the drawings and pictures are in the test booklet). Speaking stimuli, both spoken and pictured, are very good. The drawings are clear, and present a variety of situations. The weakest part of this test is the mimicry section. Certainly the ability to imitate is not the same as the ability to speak; good imitators may not be able to speak the language while good speakers may not be able to imitate. Perhaps the greatest problem with any test of speaking is the scoring, since it is open to subjectivity on the part of the scorer.

The Reading test for both levels has 50 items. The format is not unlike some reading tests which preceded it, consisting, as it does, of reading selections followed by multiple choice items. Where it does differ from them is in the questions, which really test ideas rather than just vocabulary. The Italian is largely contemporary, and always appropriate contextually.

The Writing test for both levels has 50 items. It is intended as a test of structure, but like all writing tests necessarily implies reading comprehension and vocabulary. The first part calls for filling in blanks and includes such items as articles, prepositions, pronouns, and subjunctive. Another section calls for rewriting sentences requiring such changes as tense, person, number, mood. The last part requires writing a composition on a given subject. Too many testmakers shy away from actual writing items because of the difficulty of scoring them. The MLA is to be congratulated first for including the item and then for giving helpful suggestions for scoring.

One aspect of these tests which ought to be studied is the matter of lexicon in the first level. It is difficult to know what formula was used for determining the vocabulary found in all four skill tests. One even wonders if such a formula could be devised and herein lies the greatest difficulty in all first-level tests. In the first year of foreign language instruction, vo-

cabulary acquisition is based on the textbook used. Vocabulary selection in textbooks is anarchic, with the result that there is very little common vocabulary across the lower level materials. This is not so much a problem in upper level tests because students at this stage of the language sequence should be able to handle vocabulary across a wide range of frequency. This is not intended as a criticism of the tests, but rather as a comment on the vocabulary situation in the lower level in general.

The MLA-Cooperative test in Italian is not only the first and only one available for measuring the four skills, but it is also an excellent one. This reviewer recommends it highly to teachers of Italian at both the high school and college level.

For an excerpted review of the series, see 254.

LATIN

[303]

*Advanced Placement Examination in Latin. High school students desiring credit for college level courses or admission to advanced courses; 1954–70; 4 tests (candidate elects 1 or 2): Comedy, Lyric, Prose, Vergil; Forms RBP ('69, 10–11 pages), SBP ('70, 10–11 pages) in 2 booklets (objective, essay); for more complete information, see 662; 90(100) minutes; program administered for the College Entrance Examination Board by Educational Testing Service. *

For a review of the testing program, see 662.

[304]

*College Board Achievement Test in Latin. Candidates for college entrance with 2–4 years high school Latin; 1901–71; test administered each January and May at centers established by the publisher; for more complete information, see 663; 60(80) minutes; program administered for the College Entrance Examination Board by Educational Testing Service. *

REFERENCES

1–2. See 4:250.
3. See 5:280.

For a review by Konrad Gries of an earlier form, see 5:280; for a review by Harold B. Dunkel, see 4:250. For reviews of the testing program, see 6:760 (2 reviews).

[305]

*College Placement Test in Latin Reading. Entering college freshmen; 1962–70, c1955–70; CPTLR; irregularly scheduled reprintings of inactive forms of *College Board Achievement Test in Latin*; Forms PPL1 ['67, reprint of 1963 test], PPL2 ['67, reprint of 1964 test] in a single booklet (15 pages); for more complete information, see 665; 60(70) minutes; program administered for the College Entrance Examination Board by Educational Testing Service. *

For a review by Konrad Gries of an earlier form, see 5:280; for a review by Harold B. Dunkel, see 4:250. For a review of the testing program, see 665.

[306]

*Emporia First Year Latin Test. 1 year high school; 1962–64; first published 1962–63 in the Every Pupil Scholarship Test series; Forms A, B, ('64, 2 pages); 2 levels labeled Tests 1, 2; manual ('64, 3 pages); $1.75 per 25 tests, postage extra; 75¢ per specimen set, postpaid; 40(45) minutes; Bernadine Sitts, Minnie M. Miller, Lillian A. Wall, and M. W. Sanders; Data Processing and Educational Measurement Center. *

[307]

*Emporia Second Year Latin Test. 2 years high school; 1962–64; first published 1962–63 in the Every Pupil Scholarship Test series; Forms A, B, ('64, 2 pages); 2 levels labeled Tests 1, 2; manual ('64, 3 pages); $1.75 per 25 tests, postage extra; 75¢ per specimen set, postpaid; 40(45) minutes; Bernadine Sitts, Minnie M. Miller, Lillian A. Wall, and M. W. Sanders; Data Processing and Educational Measurement Center. *

RUSSIAN

[308]

*College Placement Test in Russian Listening Comprehension. Entering college freshmen; 1962–70; irregularly scheduled reprintings of inactive forms of *College Board Achievement Test in Russian Listening Comprehension;* Form SPL ['70, reprint of 1968 test, 13 pages]; test administered by 7½ ips tape recording; for more complete information, see 665; 30(40) minutes; program administered for the College Entrance Examination Board by Educational Testing Service. *

REFERENCE

1. ALEAMONI, LAWRENCE M., AND MATSUNAGA, ALLEN. *A Study of Foreign Language at the University of Illinois Using the CEEB Foreign Language Placement Tests and End-of-Course Grades.* Research Report No. 317. Champaign, Ill.: Measurement and Research Division, Office of Instructional Resources, University of Illinois, 1970. Pp. i, 42. *

For a review of the testing program, see 665.

[309]

★College Placement Test in Russian Reading. Entering college freshmen; 1962–70; CPTRR; irregularly scheduled reprintings of inactive forms of *College Board Achievement Test in Russian;* Forms PPL1 ['67, reprint of 1964 test], PPL2 ['67, reprint of 1965 test] in a single booklet (28 pages); for more complete information, see 665; 60(70) minutes; program administered for the College Entrance Examination Board by Educational Testing Service. *

For a review of the testing program, see 665.

[310]

*Graduate School Foreign Language Test: Russian. Graduate level degree candidates required to demonstrate reading proficiency in Russian; 1963–70; GSFLTR; 2 current forms ('68–69, 47–49 pages); for more complete information, see 668; 100(120) minutes; Educational Testing Service. *

REFERENCES

1. BARTLETT, ALBERT ALLEN. "The Foreign Language Requirement for the Ph.D.: A New Approach." *Foreign Lang Ann* 2:174–84 D '68. *
2. CLARK, JOHN L. D. "The Graduate School Foreign Language Requirement: A Survey of Testing Practices and Related Topics." *Foreign Lang Ann* 2:150–64 D '68. *
3. HARVEY, PHILIP R. "Minimal Passing Scores on the Graduate School Foreign Language Tests." *Foreign Lang Ann* 2:165–73 D '68. *
4. ALEAMONI, LAWRENCE M., AND MATSUNAGA, ALLEN. *A Study of Foreign Language at the University of Illinois Using the CEEB Foreign Language Placement Tests and End-of-Course Grades.* Research Report No. 317. Champaign, Ill.: Measurement and Research Division, Office of Instructional Resources, University of Illinois, 1970. Pp. i, 42. *

[311]

*MLA Cooperative Foreign Language Proficiency Tests: Russian. Russian majors and advanced students in college; 1960–68; formerly called *MLA Foreign Language Proficiency Tests for Teachers and Advanced Students: Russian;* 7 tests in 3 booklets (formerly in 7 booklets); Forms HA ('61, identical except for format and directions with earlier tests variously designated Forms A, JML1, and K-JML1), HB ('66, identical except for format and directions with tests copyrighted in 1961 and variously designated Forms B, JML2, K-JML2, and OML1); temporary series directions for administering ('68, 12 pages); series norms ('66, 2 pages); mimeographed series score conversion directions ['68, 8 pages]; separate answer sheets (Digitek, SCRIBE) must be used except for speaking and writing tests; $4 per 100 answer sheets, cash orders postpaid; Digitek scoring stencils not available; SCRIBE scoring and statistical analysis service, 35¢ per student for all tests except speaking and writing; scoring by special arrangement with language specialists: $3 per speaking test tape, $1.50 per writing test; Modern Language Association of America and Educational Testing Service; Cooperative Tests and Services. *

a) BOOK 1: READING, LISTENING COMPREHENSION, SPEAKING. Forms HA (24 pages), HB (21 pages); $9 per 10 tests; 90¢ per single copy; $12 per 7½ ips listening/speaking test tape; blank tapes for student responses must be obtained locally; 40(50) minutes for reading, (20–30) minutes for listening comprehension, (15–30) minutes for speaking.

b) BOOK 2: WRITING. Forms HA (8 pages), HB (7 pages); $6 per 20 tests; 30¢ per single copy; 45(55) minutes.

c) BOOK 3: APPLIED LINGUISTICS, CIVILIZATION AND CULTURE, PROFESSIONAL PREPARATION. Forms HA, HB, (29 pages); professional preparation test is common to all languages in series; $9 per 10 tests; 90¢ per single copy; 40(50) minutes for linguistics, 30(40) minutes for civilization and culture, 45(55) minutes for professional preparation.

REFERENCES

1–3. See 6:417.
4. TOLLINGER, SUZANNE, AND PAQUETTE, F. ANDRÉ, EDITORS. *The MLA Foreign Language Proficiency Tests for Teachers and Advanced Students: A Professional Evaluation and Recommendations for Test Development,* pp. 62–89, 131–5, 155–6, 161–75, passim. Sections on this test by Robert L. Baker, David Chandler, Edith Ignatieff, Tora T. Ladu, James C. McKinney, Charles A. Moser, Douglas C. Sheppard, and Leon I. Twarog. An unpublished report to the U.S. Office of Education, Project No. BR-6-2619, Modern Language Association of America, June 1966. Pp. viii, 366. * (ERIC ED 019 016)
5. CARROLL, JOHN B. "Foreign Language Proficiency Levels Attained by Language Majors Near Graduation From College." *Foreign Lang Ann* 1:131–51 O '67. *
6. PERKINS, JEAN A. "State Certification and Proficiency Tests: The Experience in Pennsylvania." *Foreign Lang Ann* 2:195–9 D '68. *

For a review by Wayne D. Fisher, see 6:417.

[312]

*MLA-Cooperative Foreign Language Tests: Russian. 1–2 years high school or 2 semesters college, 3–4 years high school or 4 semesters college; 1963–65; 4 tests in a single booklet: listening, speaking, reading, writing; writing test ('63, 8 pages) available as separate; 2 forms; 2 levels; no specific manual; series directions for administering and scoring ('64, 40 pages); series handbook ('65, 24 pages); series booklet of norms ('65, 82 pages); student bulletin ('65, 2 pages) for each level; $7 per 10 tests; $5 per 20 writing tests only; separate answer sheets (Digitek, Digitek-IBM 805, IBM 1230, SCRIBE) may be used for listening and reading tests; $4 per 100 answer sheets; $1.25 per 10 IBM 805 or IBM 1230 scoring stencils (answer pattern must be punched out locally); Digitek scoring stencils not available; $8.50 per 3¾ ips tape, 5 inch reel, for listening test; $8.50 per 3¾ ips tape, 5 inch reel, for speaking test (blank tapes or discs for recording student responses must be obtained locally); $2 per series directions for administering and scoring; $2 per series handbook; $2 per series norms booklet; $3 per 100 student bulletins; $3 per specimen set; cash orders postpaid; SCRIBE scoring and statistical analysis service (listening and reading tests), 35¢ per student; no scoring service for speaking and writing tests, but arrangements for professional scoring can be made; 25(35) minutes for listening, 10(20) minutes for speaking, 35(40) minutes for reading, 35(40) minutes for writing; prepared in cooperation with the Modern Language Association of America; Cooperative Tests and Services. *

a) [LOWER LEVEL.] 1–2 years high school or 2 semesters college; Forms LA, LB, ('63, 24 pages).

b) [HIGHER LEVEL.] 3–4 years high school or 4 semesters college; Forms MA, MB, ('63, 25 pages).

REFERENCES

1. BAIR, RAYMOND L. "The MLA Cooperative Foreign Language Tests in Russian." *Slavic & East Europ J* 9:308–14 f '65. *
2. ALEAMONI, LAWRENCE M., AND SPENCER, RICHARD E. "A Comparison of Biserial Discrimination, Point Biserial Discrimination, and Difficulty Indices in Item Analysis Data." *Ed & Psychol Meas* 29(2):353–8 su '69. * (PA 44:17314)

Slavic & East Europ J 9:308–14 f '65. Raymond L. Bair. * The first test in form LA, the Listening Test, is....to be given to the students on tape * these questions are excellent and the range of difficulty extremely wide * However, language, unlike Gaul, does not lend itself so neatly to division into four parts (listening, speaking, reading, and writing). Although this first test is labeled "Listening," it is not just that. This portion of the entire test requires the student not only to comprehend spoken Russian, but also to read Russian. In the test booklet, four answers are given for each question, and the student must read all four in order to select the correct one. This test might be more accurately labeled "Listening and Reading." This may sound like a picayune criticism, but having taken the MLA *Proficiency Tests for Teachers* at NDEA Institutes four times, I vividly recall having had much more difficulty with reading the phrases jammed with poly-syllabic words that I had never seen, than with comprehending what was being said by the voice on the tape. If listening is actually being tested, why not have the voice on the tape read the answer choices? * If two skills are to be combined in order to provide a testing situation, why not combine listening and writing? A short passage might be read in Russian, then a question asked in Russian to be answered by the examinee in Russian in his test booklet. This answer need be graded only for content, not for form. The present number of questions, forty or forty-five, could be reduced to thirty while retaining the same accuracy. The present questions, with four choices in each answer, mean that every fourth question might be guessed right. If the examinee wrote his answer in Russian, this possibility would be less likely. Listening and writing might make a more reliable appraisal of the student's progress in Russian than listening and reading. The second section of the MLA *Cooperative Russian Tests,* "Speaking," contains thirty-eight questions with a total of eighty-two points. This test is comprehensive and cleverly devised. Mimicry; reading aloud; questions about pictures, to be answered in Russian; descriptions, the first of a single picture and the second of a four-picture sequence, are the techniques employed to test speaking ability. * The method used for rating speaking performance is excellent and deserves the highest praise. * the vocabulary is carefully and fairly chosen * The "Reading" test has fifty questions of the multiple-choice type, each with four answers. * "Passages drawn from periodicals and appropriate literary sources are used to test word and phrase discrimination and ability to understand the main idea, find details, and draw conclusions." Once again the range of difficulty is wide, and the questions, for the most part, well chosen. My weakest student answered five correctly, the strongest—forty-five. Some of the first twenty-five questions are what would have been called a few years ago vocabulary questions, but here they are dressed up to suit the label "Reading." * The reading passages that follow are well chosen as to vocabulary and topics. * These passages are appropriate and seem to increase gradually in degree of difficulty. It is unfortunate that five of them can be answered without reference to the selection from which the information for the answer is supposed to come. This is true of questions 26, 29, 34, 37, and 42 * The final test in form

LA, the "Writing" test, sems to me the weakest of the four. This test contains one hundred units of credit. The range of questions is limited and several grammatical categories neglected. The consequence of this is to make it pedagogically unsound. It is obvious that teachers will use these tests as syllabi for their teaching of Russian. In the lower level form LA and in the higher level form MA there is no question to test aspect. These MLA *Cooperative Foreign Language Tests* are of such scope that in the future they will determine the mode of instruction of Russian. It is, therefore, vital that they contain a fair sampling of questions covering the entire grammar of Russian. Here is my count of the parts of speech covered in form LA: pronouns—3, adjectives—8, correlatives—2, numbers—1, nouns—29, adverbs—3, prepositions—5, verbs—19, demonstrative adjectives—3, possessive adjectives—7. Not questioned at all were: aspect, inflection of cardinal and ordinal numbers, reflexive verbs, future tense of perfective or imperfective verbs, verb prefixes, actual and potential verbs, imperatives, and the declension of *sebja, sam,* and *čej,* to mention a few. Although verbs are requested nineteen times, six of these are to be written in the past tense, for regular verbs a rather easy task in Russian. The features that make Russian verbs difficult—consonant mutation, changing stress, and aspect—go untested. Evidence that some of the question forms were written with a language other than Russian in mind can be found in the contradiction in the directions. For questions 31 to 36 they read: "Rewrite each of the following sentences so that the word or words printed on the line below it fit correctly into the new sentence. Make all changes necessary to produce a correct Russian sentence, but do not add any words and do not leave any out." Immediately below, a Russian sentence must be changed from the positive to the negative and a double negative used—ergo a word added. * Sentence 34 is to be rewritten in the past tense and the model is in the present. The verb is "to be," which is expressed in the past and not in the present and therefore must be added here to make a correct sentence, contrary to the directions! * In order to rewrite the next sentence correctly two words must be deleted and two added. * A tabulation of the parts of speech of the "Writing" test of the higher level form MA shows an increase in the percentage of nouns asked for. The declension of nouns is tested

thirty-one times; 38 percent of the words asked for are nouns. Fifteen verbs must be altered or supplied, and this number represents 19 percent of the words tested. In descending order then are adjectives, prepositions, pronouns, and adverbs. For the most part there is only *one* word each for the remaining speech categories. After four years of secondary school Russian, aspect, declension of cardinals, actual and potential verbs, and a few more categories go untested. For us secondary school teachers, it is comforting to know exactly what is to be taught during the first, second, third, and fourth years of Russian language study. These tests will serve as outlines for teachers, to guide them as to how to teach and what to teach. In the past we have often noticed a reluctance on the part of publishers and experienced teachers to state dogmatically just exactly what to teach, at what speed, and how. * The importance of the MLA *Cooperative Foreign Language Tests* hinges on the fact that these tests include listening and speaking sections. Students are reluctant to recognize the worth of listening and speaking, if these skills are not tested and credit given for them in a formal manner. This, then, is the real contribution of the MLA *Cooperative Foreign Language Tests.* Who can fool a student? He knows full well that when listening and speaking are not tested as part of the final examination they are not as important as reading and writing. *

For an excerpted review of the series, see 254.

SPANISH

[313]

*Advanced Placement Examination in Spanish. High school students desiring credit for college level courses or admission to advanced courses; 1954–70; Forms RBP ('69, 16 pages), SBP ('70, 17 pages) in 2 booklets (objective, essay); listening comprehension tapes: 7½ ips for Form RBP, 3¾ ips for Form SBP; tape script ['69–70, 5–6 pages] for each form; for more complete information, see 662; 180(200) minutes; program administered for the College Entrance Examination Board by Educational Testing Service. *

REFERENCES

1. See 6:421.
2. ENGLEKIRK, JOHN E. "The Evolution of the College Board Advanced Placement Program in Spanish: What Will the 1968 Program Be Like?" *Hispania* 50:558–68 S '67. *
3. TURNER, ALBERT R. "New Developments in the Spanish Advanced Placement Program of the College Entrance Examination Board." *Hispania* 50:348–53 My '67. *

For a review of the testing program, see 662.

[314]

*College Board Achievement Test in Spanish.
Candidates for college entrance with 2-4 years high
school Spanish; 1902-71; test administered each January at centers established by the publisher; for more
complete information, see 663; 60(80) minutes; program administered for the College Entrance Examination Board by Educational Testing Service. *

REFERENCES

1-3. See 4:259.
4. See 5:287.
5. See 6:419.

*For reviews of the testing program, see 6:760
(2 reviews).*

[315]

*College Placement Test in Spanish Listening
Comprehension. Entering college freshmen; 1962-
70, c1955-70; irregularly scheduled reprintings of inactive forms of *College Board Achievement Test in
Spanish Listening Comprehension;* Forms NPL ('65,
reprint of 1963 test), OPL ('66, reprint of 1964 test)
in a single booklet (18 pages); test administered by
7½ ips tape recording; for more complete information,
see 665; 30(40) minutes; program administered for
the College Entrance Examination Board by Educational Testing Service. *

REFERENCES

1. See 6:422.
2. ALEAMONI, LAWRENCE M., AND MATSUNAGA, ALLEN. *A
Study of Foreign Language at the University of Illinois Using
the CEEB Foreign Language Placement Tests and End-of-
Course Grades.* Research Report No. 317. Champaign, Ill.:
Measurement and Research Division, Office of Instructional
Resources, University of Illinois, 1970. Pp. i, 42. *

For a review of the testing program, see 665.

[316]

*College Placement Test in Spanish Reading.
Entering college freshmen; 1962-70, c1955-70;
CPTSR; irregularly scheduled reprintings of inactive
forms of *College Board Achievement Test in Spanish;*
Forms PPL1, PPL2, ['67, reprint of 1963 tests] in a
single booklet (20 pages); for more complete information, see 665; 60(70) minutes; program administered for the College Entrance Examination Board
by Educational Testing Service. *

REFERENCE

1. ALEAMONI, LAWRENCE M., AND MATSUNAGA, ALLEN. *A
Study of Foreign Language at the University of Illinois Using
the CEEB Foreign Language Placement Tests and End-of-
Course Grades.* Research Report No. 317. Champaign, Ill.:
Measurement and Research Division, Office of Instructional
Resources, University of Illinois, 1970. Pp. i, 42. *

For a review of the testing program, see 665.

[317]

*Common Concepts Foreign Language Test:
Spanish. Students in any grade who are at the Level
I stage of achievement; 1962-66; aural comprehension; same booklet also used to test French and German; may be administered using live voice but tape
recording (3¾ ips) is recommended; Forms 1, 2, ('62,
31 pages) in a single booklet; manual ('66, 41 pages);
separate answer sheets (IBM 1230) must be used;
$1.10 per test; $5.95 per tape recording; $2.50 per 50
answer sheets; 75¢ per scoring stencil for either form;
$1 per manual; postage extra; $2.25 per specimen set
(without tape), postpaid; scoring service, 22¢ and
over per test; (40-45) minutes; Bela H. Banathy,
Miles V. Zintz, W. James Popham, Joseph M. Sadna-

vitch, Rena Krichbaum, Fred B. Gannon, Valdemar
Hempel, and Klaus A. Mueller; CTB/McGraw-Hill. *

*For a review covering the three languages,
see 253.*

[318]

*First Year Spanish Test. High school and college;
1947-68; FYST; revision of *Kansas First Year Spanish Test;* Form A ('68, 2 pages); manual ('68, 2
pages); no data on reliability; $1.75 per 25 tests,
postage extra; 75¢ per specimen set, postpaid; 50(55)
minutes; Oscar F. Hernández and Minnie M. Miller;
Data Processing and Educational Measurement Center. *

[319]

*The Graduate Record Examinations Advanced
Spanish Test. Graduate school candidates; 1946-70;
3 current forms ('64-69, 24-28 pages); descriptive
booklet ('70, 9 pages); for more complete information,
see 667; 180(200) minutes; Educational Testing Service. *

GINO PARISI, *Assistant Professor of Spanish,
Georgetown University, Washington, D.C.*
[Review of Form RGR.]

There are different ways of grouping the 200
items that make up this test. Exact analysis is
difficult because some items test several factors
simultaneously. The breakdown used by the
publisher follows: (*a*) Literature, 50 items (33
Spanish, 17 Spanish-American); (*b*) Culture
and Civilization, 60 items (40 Spanish, 20
Spanish-American); (*c*) Structure and Linguistics, 40 items; (*d*) Reading Comprehension, 49 items.

The analysis shows the Literature section to
be the most difficult and the language sections
(*c* and *d*) the easiest. Reliability for the total
test is highest of all the GRE tests: within a
range of .83 to .96, the Spanish has a coefficient
of .96, shared only by the Music test. However,
the prime consideration in this case is not the
reliability, which may be expected in a test of
predominantly factual material, but the predictive validity of the scores, which must be determined by each graduate department as it
collects data over the years.

A three-way classification along different
lines shows the following proportions: (*a*)
Factual information, 4 parts; (*b*) Literary
appreciation, 2 parts; (*c*) Language proficiency, 1 part. The desirability of such a preponderance of factual material must be judged
by each graduate school according to its program. For those requiring a high level of proficiency, the important question is whether there
is a sufficient degree of language ability implicit
in the literature and culture sections of this test.

In view of the fact that acquisition of the language is often a goal in itself, there could be a better balance between what may be called simple language proficiency on the one hand and knowledge of literature, culture, and linguistics on the other. Furthermore, the scores in each area could be explicitly stated. Although the subscores are used in the publisher's analysis, apparently the usual practice is to report only the total score to the graduate school.

The items in different categories are grouped in short sections alternating throughout the test. A majority of the answers are five-choice; some are four-choice; and one section uses a format in which four questions are matched with five answers. This last device would seem to complicate the guessing factor as a student eliminates the possible answers.

Usage is tested in items that cover the fundamental areas of verbs, syntax, and vocabulary. Except for one item, apparently based on prescriptive rules, the knowledge required is appropriate for college level.

The section on linguistics contains only 10 items, mostly in the field of dialectology. For a school offering a program in linguistics this number is too small to be significant, and for a literature program the section is irrelevant. It is not clear why it has been included, except for the contemporary sound of the label "linguistics."

The prose and poetry selections require the student to understand both the literal and the implied meaning. He must be aware of the tone of the writer, the literary devices employed, and the period represented. There is one section in Old Spanish with the attendant problems of orthography and vocabulary.

In conclusion, this is a highly reliable test of the student's achievement in Spanish and Spanish-American literature and culture; language proficiency, primarily passive skills, is tested for the most part indirectly. Users should first satisfy themselves that the content is appropriate for their programs, then decide how much weight to give to the scores. For the future, a test with clearly labeled subtests and subscores in different areas—language, literature, culture, linguistics—might facilitate this task. It would also be advantageous for the student or school to be able to use only parts of the test. Finally, predictive validity studies must be carried out by the schools themselves. Judgment concerning the value of GRE scores must

therefore be deferred until more data are accumulated.

For reviews of the testing program, see 667 (1 review) and 5:601 (1 review).

[320]

★**Graduate School Foreign Language Test: Spanish.** Graduate level degree candidates required to demonstrate reading proficiency in Spanish; 1963-70; GSFLTS; 2 current forms ('69-70, 29-31 pages); for more complete information, see 668; 100(120) minutes; Educational Testing Service. *

REFERENCES

1. BARTLETT, ALBERT ALLEN. "The Foreign Language Requirement for the Ph.D.: A New Approach." *Foreign Lang Ann* 2:174-84 D '68. *
2. CLARK, JOHN L. D. "The Graduate School Foreign Language Requirement: A Survey of Testing Practices and Related Topics." *Foreign Lang Ann* 2:150-64 D '68. *
3. HARVEY, PHILIP R. "Minimal Passing Scores on the Graduate School Foreign Language Tests." *Foreign Lang Ann* 2:165-73 D '68. *

ROBERT LADO, *Dean, School of Languages and Linguistics, Georgetown University, Washington, D.C.*

The *Graduate School Foreign Language Test: Spanish* is designed to measure the ability to read and understand professional literature in Spanish. It was developed to test reading proficiency in fulfilling the foreign language requirement for advanced degrees. It may also be used to measure reading at the end of an undergraduate program of study or a graduate reading course, or to assess the reading proficiency of those who judge their preparation to be adequate without formal course work.

An initial version of the test was developed in 1967. The present version, Form RFG, is the result of a 1969 revision, which incorporated a specialized reading section with a choice of three fields: humanities, natural sciences, and social sciences, making the Spanish test parallel to the French, German, and Russian forms of the same program. The test is administered nationally by the Educational Testing Service, which provides scaled and percentile scores. The scaled scores range from 200 to 800, with a mean of 500. Since this is a new version, score interpretation charts are based on the scores of approximately 625 students who took the test in November 1969. The total test reliability estimates are .94 for humanities, .92 for natural sciences, and .93 for social sciences. These are in the same range as those for the French, German, and Russian tests.

Administration of the test, which consists of two sections, requires 100 minutes: 40 minutes for Section 1 and 60 minutes for Section 2.

Section 1 consists of 60 multiple choice items. Section 2 consists of passages in the humanities, the natural sciences, and the social sciences, drawn from professional literature in Spanish. All candidates take Section 1 and choose one of the options of Section 2 according to their field of professional interest. The passages vary in length from about 75 to 300 words, each passage being followed by a series of multiple choice questions in English that are to be answered through comprehension of the Spanish text.

This is a test developed in the pattern of the Educational Testing Service in which the ETS cooperates with qualified members of the profession in the preparation of items and the refinement and standardization of the test on the basis of statistical analysis of field performance. The present revision in format followed a survey of the language requirements and testing practices of 1,604 graduate school departments in the spring of 1967. The availability of this test service in Spanish represents a welcome advance in the assessment of the reading proficiency of graduate students in fulfilling their foreign language requirement. We now have the option of a professionally prepared objective instrument to substitute for the great variety of practices with subjective and often arbitrary procedures and standards which contribute to the fear and frustration on the part of graduate students and the waste of valuable hours of faculty time. Any reservations one might have about the validity of the test for a particular student or program or about the various parts and items of the test do not begin to compare with the weaknesses of the various practices which were the only fare before the appearance of this test.

The ability to read connected texts at an advanced level in a foreign language is in itself a complex skill. The reader must be able to extract the meanings of lexical items that are brought up by the context; to understand stylistic variations; and to handle longer sequences of material. Section 1 of the test is intended to measure the candidate's knowledge of specific structure elements, while Section 2 concentrates on the more complex task of overall comprehension and abstraction of meaning.

Section 1 consists of two parts, A and B, with 30 items each. The 30 items of Part A present Spanish sentences with a blank for certain words or phrases, followed by four suggested choices of possible fillers. The functional structure elements, such as verbs, sequence signals, and adverbs are emphasized. Vocabulary is not tested directly, although a good command of the lexical meanings of the sentences is required in order to establish the context. The validity of this section can be justified in terms of the specific elements being tested. However, the skill that is being measured seems to be productive knowledge of Spanish structure rather than interpretation of structural elements as an aid to comprehension. A candidate who has followed a reading course, or who intends to use his second language only for reading purposes, will probably have been trained in the recognition and interpretation of Spanish texts that are already stylistically and grammatically well formed. The task of choosing items to be used in active production is more demanding and may lead to some frustration, particularly at the beginning of the test, since many of the choices present stylistic or grammatical distractors rather than matters of interpretation of meaning. Thus, some of the choices offer answers with no semantic difference, although one of the two may be chosen as stylistically more appropriate or more 'correct' according to grammar norms. It is true that the students who are able to choose a stylistically or grammatically more appropriate form are likely to understand the meaning better, but the two abilities are not the same and therefore the substitution of one for the other introduces an unnecessary problem of validity.

The 30 items of Part B, Section 1, are more directly related to the task of determining whether the candidate understands specific Spanish items. Here the student is presented with complete Spanish sentences where certain words or phrases have been underlined. Following each sentence are four English words or phrases among which the candidate is to select the one that is the best translation of the underlined items in the stimulus sentence. A wider sample of language elements is evaluated in this section, including idioms, vocabulary, and the main grammatical categories. Most of the items offer good distractors, although a few include choices that may be decided on the basis of English criteria: that is, the student may decide on the correct item by judging which one of the choices will fit into the English version of the Spanish sentence. In some cases there may be a doubt as to whether to choose an item because it is the best translation of the Spanish—as specified in the directions—or because it represents better English.

The three specialized options of Section 2 measure the candidate's ability to extract meaning from longer texts in a broad area within which his own field of specialization falls. A frequent objection to this necessarily broad field in the selection of the reading passages is the fact that the student's research interests may be highly specialized by the time he reaches this advanced stage of his graduate studies. There is no question that the ability to read with understanding the professional literature in Spanish depends in part upon the student's knowledge of the concepts, methods, and terminology in his own special field. But these are most likely to be similar across languages and therefore most will be readily understandable to the student if he is able to read the foreign language in the general context of the humanities, natural sciences, or social sciences. Therefore, a well-developed objective test of reading in the broader field is likely to be more valid and reliable than an ad hoc translation or a reading chosen from material which is specifically within the student's field.

In the present test the natural sciences option seems to contain the largest number of questions that might be answered merely from knowledge of subject matter without reading the Spanish text, since the questions are based on natural facts and phenomena with which the student may be familiar. This may be inherent in any test of reading in the natural sciences that discusses realistic material.

In all sections most of the questions and choices seem to focus on the student's general reasoning ability and on his skill at making inferences from the authors' statements. Relatively few questions test his grasp of the specific language clues to a given meaning. Some of the selections, particularly in the humanities and social sciences, include paragraphs of unusual complexity. The English questions and choices themselves are also quite complex and will test the candidate's general reading ability and power of abstraction in his own language. Efficient readers of English may have more than the usual advantage in decoding the subtleties involved in the various choices.

The test is not intended as a speeded instrument and the standardization procedures report that enough students finished both parts to eliminate the factor of speed. This is presumably a desideratum in a reading test for students who will be doing untimed reading of some critical source material in their research. Actually, the ability to read at an efficient speed is also important. Future revisions might consider a speed section as well.

The need for a second language at the advanced level of graduate study, where the scholar needs to have access to professional literature written abroad, has always been great and will continue to be so in spite of the availability of translations of most major works. The increasing volume of periodical literature and professional journals will continue to require a knowledge of foreign languages in order to have up-to-date information on new developments reported in such publications. The task of measuring a graduate's proficiency in a second language can be greatly simplified by using tests such as GSFLT. Maximum simplification would have been achieved by adopting national norms and standards for passing scores with a range for superior to minimum performance. In the absence of such national norms, each school or department may establish its own standards. Suggestions for relating the scaled and percentile scores on the test to other scores and criteria for passing are presented in the Guide to the Interpretation of Scores.

This, then, is a professionally developed test of reading prepared according to correct professional standards and administered within the practices of the ETS. It can be used with confidence for its intended purpose.

[321]

*MLA Cooperative Foreign Language Proficiency Tests: Spanish. Spanish majors and advanced students in college; 1960–68; formerly called *MLA Foreign Language Proficiency Tests for Teachers and Advanced Students: Spanish;* 7 tests in 3 booklets (formerly in 7 booklets) ; Forms HA ('61, identical except for format and directions with earlier tests variously designated Forms A, JML1, and K-JML1), HB ('66, identical except for format and directions with tests copyrighted in 1961 and variously designated Forms B, JML2, K-JML2, and OML1) ; temporary series directions for administering ('68, 12 pages) ; series norms ('66, 2 pages) ; mimeographed series score conversion directions ['68, 8 pages] ; separate answer sheets (Digitek, SCRIBE) must be used except for speaking and writing tests; $4 per 100 answer sheets, cash orders postpaid; Digitek scoring stencils not available; SCRIBE scoring and statistical analysis service, 35¢ per student for all tests except speaking and writing; scoring by special arrangement with language specialists; $3 per speaking test tape, $1.50 per writing test; Modern Language Association of America and Educational Testing Service; Cooperative Tests and Services. *

a) BOOK I: READING, LISTENING COMPREHENSION, SPEAKING. Forms HA (24 pages), HB (21 pages); $9 per 10 tests; 90¢ per single copy; $12 per 7½ ips listening/speaking test tape; blank tapes for student responses must be obtained locally; 40(50) minutes for reading, (20–30) minutes for listening comprehension, (15–30) minutes for speaking.
b) BOOK 2: WRITING. Forms HA (8 pages), HB (7 pages); $6 per 20 tests; 30¢ per single copy; 45(55) minutes.
c) BOOK 3: APPLIED LINGUISTICS, CIVILIZATION AND CULTURE, PROFESSIONAL PREPARATION. Forms HA, HB, (29 pages); professional preparation test is common to all languages in series; $9 per 10 tests; 90¢ per single copy; 40(50) minutes for linguistics, 30(40) minutes for civilization and culture, 45(55) minutes for professional preparation.

REFERENCES

1–3. See 6:427.
4. PAQUETTE, F. ANDRÉ; WALLMARK, MADELINE; SPENCER, RICHARD E.; AND CHURCHILL, FREDERICK J. *A Comparison of the MLA Foreign Language Proficiency Tests for Teachers and Advanced Students With the MLA Foreign Language Cooperative Tests.* An unpublished report to the U.S. Office of Education, Project No. BR-6-2619, Modern Language Association of America, 1966. Pp. 58. * (ERIC ED 019 017)
5. TOLLINGER, SUZANNE, AND PAQUETTE, F. ANDRÉ, EDITORS. *The MLA Foreign Language Proficiency Tests for Teachers and Advanced Students: A Professional Evaluation and Recommendations for Test Development,* pp. 90–112, 136–9, 157–60, 161–75, passim. Sections on this test by Joan E. Ciruti, David Griffin, Tora T. Ladu, James C. McKinney, Robert G. Meade, Jr., Lucrecia Ruisanchez-Lopez, Douglas C. Sheppard, and George W. Wilkins, Jr. An unpublished report to the U.S. Office of Education, Project No. BR-6-2619, Modern Language Association of America, June 1966. Pp. viii, 366. * (ERIC ED 019 016)
6. CARROLL, JOHN B. "Foreign Language Proficiency Levels Attained by Language Majors Near Graduation From College." *Foreign Lang Ann* 1:131–51 O '67. *
7. DIZNEY, HENRY F., AND GROMEN, LAUREN. "Predictive Validity and Differential Achievement on Three MLA–Cooperative Foreign Language Tests." *Ed & Psychol Meas* 27:1127–30 W '67. * (*PA* 42:9417)
8. PAQUETTE, F. ANDRÉ; WITH THE COOPERATION OF MADELINE WALLMARK. *The MLA Foreign Language Proficiency Tests for Teachers and Advanced Students: Analysis of the Performance of Native Speakers and Comparison With That of NDEA Summer Institute Participants.* An unpublished report to the U.S. Office of Education, Project No. BR-6-2619, Modern Language Association of America, June 1968. Pp. ii, 42. * (ERIC ED 019 017)
9. PERKINS, JEAN A. "State Certification and Proficiency Tests: The Experience in Pennsylvania." *Foreign Lang Ann* 2:195–9 D '68. *

GLEN W. PROBST, *Professor of Spanish, Michigan State University, East Lansing, Michigan.*

Several years have passed since the publication of this test. And although much has been said and done in conjunction with it, there are still some questions which need to be answered, as well as some updating and revision that need to be accomplished.

The listening, reading, and writing parts of this test have acceptable reliability coefficients, but those for the other parts are questionable. An attempt at securing a validity index was carried out by administering the test to samples of native speakers in Latin America and Spain. The results were not conclusive enough to establish the test's validity for determining language proficiency in non-native speakers of Spanish. Therefore, its role in testing for certification purposes and institutional testing programs may be limited.

Listening comprehension skill is tested in combination with the testing of reading skill. The examinee must choose his response from the printed options. This hybrid-type test may deliver inaccurate results because the score achieved is dependent upon the examinee's ability to recognize the correct response from the written word. It does not test one's ability to listen to and understand spoken Spanish without reference to the written word. Although reality cannot be duplicated as long as the examinee knows he is being tested, an attempt must be made to represent it as closely as possible by not testing one skill based on ability in another skill.

Part A of the Speaking test aims at an evaluation of ability to pronounce with correct intonation while repeating model sentences spoken by a native speaker on the tape. Part B tests the ability to read aloud from the printed page. Both of these parts are weak in their attempt to deliver valid results concerning the examinee's ability to speak. Part C does a much better job by asking the examinee to respond extemporaneously to certain situations which are cued through the use of visuals. This part has three subparts, each one setting up a different situation. A negative aspect of the two latter parts is that the situations illustrated are too contrived and restrict the examinee to a narrow line of theme development. A lack of knowledge or lapse in recall of key words could inhibit the examinee's performance in general. Wider contextual situations are needed which will allow the examinee flexibility in topic choice and development.

The Reading test appears to be the least valid part of the examination. The primary disadvantage of the Reading test is that the vocabulary treats more the rare, exceptional, and obscure than the common, real life situations. Since extensive vocabulary acquisition is not a primary goal in audio-lingual teaching, it seems to be a paradox that many items are based upon a knowledge of very low frequency vocabulary, and not of structure and syntax. The structure and syntax need to be given more attention while a common, high frequency vocabulary inventory is used. The Reading test takes for granted a good basic proficiency in reading skill and aims at testing a proficiency based too much on a knowledge of obscure vocabulary in a literary context. This is a narrow dimension when compared with all the different kinds of content available in Spanish reading material. Perhaps the test is an accurate measure of one's ability to handle literary readings at the upper college level. If this is the case, it will serve to define the competence of a narrow segment of individuals in the profession. A check on the difficulty of the Reading test was made by this reviewer by applying the Spaulding Spanish Readability Formula [1] to seven passages in both test forms. Three of the passages were rated "exceptionally difficult," two were rated "difficult," and two were rated "moderately difficult."

The Writing test does not measure the examinee's ability to write. It measures his ability to understand grammar or appropriate word choice controlled by a contrived word environment. The test reveals no indication of the examinee's proficiency at writing out his thoughts in Spanish or at accurately recording on paper Spanish sounds which he has heard; nor does it give any indication as to the examinee's ability to extemporize in writing on a given subject. The Writing test requires more reading comprehension skill than writing skill. It reveals that the examinee has either not understood what he has read, if he is unable to fill in the blank correctly, or that he does not know a specific word or the grammar concept involved. Instead of measuring ability in writing skill, this examination tests the production of grammar.

In the Applied Linguistics test the questions posed in the negative would be clearer and more easily understood if stated in the affirmative. Question 24, Part B of Form HB is more of a pedagogical question than a linguistic question and should be deleted.

The Civilization and Culture test contains too much information concerning formal culture. About 20 percent of this section of the test on both forms deals with anthropological culture. In order to establish a more valid basis for testing, at least a balance, if not an overbalance in favor of anthropological culture, needs to be included in the questions of this part of the test. Some questions on formal culture have no apparent validity or relevance. For example, one question asks what country leads the Hispanic world in motion-picture production. Until more information concerning the social be-

havior patterns of the people is included in this test, it will remain a weak indicator of the examinee's knowledge of the target cultural patterns.

The Professional Preparation test impresses this reviewer as the most valid for its purpose of the seven tests in the battery. Several changes and modifications could be made in order to update and improve it. Question 8, Form HB is cloudy because the wording is misleading. Question 22 of the same form should be updated to include ACTFL as a possible answer. Question 36, Form HB should be placed in the Applied Linguistics section or deleted. Questions 43 and 52, Form HB are based too much on subjectivity which could result in more than one correct answer among the four possibilities. Question 5, Form HA also has as its correct answer a statement which has not yet been established as being more pedagogically sound than some of the alternate possibilities. Five of the questions on the two forms are asked in the negative. These would be better put in the affirmative.

This MLA battery may reveal some relative differences between those examinees who take it, but it could be missing the target completely in testing the four basic skills and knowledge of culture and civilization because of an apparent lack of content validity in these areas. An examinee's results in the four basic skills tests may not be a realistic representation of his true ability since the Spanish used is of a low frequency vocabulary, the skills are mixed in testing, and there is too much emphasis on the production of grammar. The Culture and Civilization test results might not be representative of the examinee's knowledge because it relies too heavily on formal culture content instead of anthropological culture content.

It is quite possible that many prospective teachers could fail this test battery and still become adequate teachers in the classroom at the beginning levels of instruction. Perhaps too many have already been screened out in such a manner. In light of the weaknesses discussed here, it is suggested that administrators judiciously use a candidate's results on this test, keeping in mind that the degree of proficiency should be commensurate with the requirements of the position—not way beyond them, nor in a semi-related content area.

In summary, these MLA tests in Spanish were designed to serve a definite need and give impetus to a field which was almost nonexistent

---

1 SPAULDING, SETH. "A Spanish Readability Formula." *Mod Lang J* 40:433–41 D '56. *

until their publication. However, no one should consider the tests valid enough to use them as the only criterion in selecting students for graduate study, for certification, or for hiring Spanish teachers. The administrator who is selecting students for graduate study may rely on the candidate's results in certain sections of the test, while the administrator who is seeking prospective teachers may rely more on the candidate's proficiency in other sections of the test, depending on the requirements for the position involved. In all cases it is strongly suggested that the results of this test be used in conjunction with other methods of measuring achievement, such as a personal interview in Spanish or recommendations from previous advisors to the candidate in question.

For a review by Walter V. Kaulfers, see 6:427.

[322]

*MLA-Cooperative Foreign Language Tests: Spanish. 1–2 years high school or 2 semesters college, 3–4 years high school or 4 semesters college; 1963–65; 4 tests in a single booklet: listening, speaking, reading, writing; writing test ('63, 8 pages) available as separate; 2 forms; 2 levels; no specific manual; series directions for administering and scoring ('64, 40 pages) ; series handbook ('65, 24 pages) ; series booklet of norms ('65, 82 pages) ; student bulletin ('65, 2 pages) for each level; $7 per 10 tests; $5 per 20 writing tests only; separate answer sheets (Digitek, Digitek-IBM 805, IBM 1230, SCRIBE) may be used for listening and reading tests; $4 per 100 answer sheets; $1.25 per 10 IBM 805 or IBM 1230 scoring stencils (answer pattern must be punched out locally) ; Digitek scoring stencils not available; $8.50 per 3¾ ips tape, 5 inch reel, for listening test; $8.50 per 3¾ ips tape, 5 inch reel, for speaking test (blank tapes or discs for recording student responses must be obtained locally) ; $2 per series directions for administering and scoring; $2 per series handbook; $2 per series norms booklet; $3 per 100 student bulletins ; $3 per specimen set; cash orders postpaid; SCRIBE scoring and statistical analysis service (listening and reading tests), 35¢ per student; no scoring service for speaking and writing tests, but arrangements for professional scoring can be made; 25(35) minutes for listening, 10(20) minutes for speaking, 35(40) minutes for reading, 35(40) minutes for writing; prepared in cooperation with the Modern Language Association of America; Cooperative Tests and Services. *
a) [LOWER LEVEL.] 1–2 years high school or 2 semesters college; Forms LA, LB, ('63, 24 pages).
b) [HIGHER LEVEL.] 3–4 years high school or 4 semesters college; Forms MA, MB, ('63, 24 pages).

REFERENCES

1. PAQUETTE, F. ANDRÉ; WALLMARK, MADELINE; SPENCER, RICHARD E.; AND CHURCHILL, FREDERICK J. *A Comparison of the MLA Foreign Language Proficiency Tests for Teachers and Advanced Students With the MLA Foreign Language Cooperative Tests.* An unpublished report to the U.S. Office of Education, Project No. BR-6-2619, Modern Language Association of America, 1966. Pp. 58. * (ERIC ED 019 017)
2. ALEAMONI, LAWRENCE M., AND SPENCER, RICHARD E. "A Comparison of Biserial Discrimination, Point Biserial Discrimination, and Difficulty Indices in Item Analysis Data." *Ed & Psychol Meas* 29(2):353–8 su '69. * (PA 44:17314)

ROBERT LADO, *Dean, School of Languages and Linguistics, Georgetown University, Washington, D.C.*

The MLA tests were developed specifically to measure language learning by the audiolingual approach. With major emphasis being given to audio-lingual skills in the teaching of languages after World War II and especially after the enactment of the National Defense Education Act in 1958, the need for tests that would measure these skills became imperative.

The tests are aimed at two levels: the L or low level for the second year of high school and second semester in college, and the M or middle level for the fourth year of high school and fourth semester in college.

These tests are designed to measure Spanish language skills functionally and are completely in Spanish except for directions on taking the test, which are given in English. Since they test the four skills separately and functionally, they can be used for traditional as well as progressive classes by simply omitting or including the audio-lingual tests.

Approximately 40,000 tests were administered to 10,000 students in the pretesting phase of the work. These tests plus the development of the *MLA Cooperative Foreign Language Proficiency Tests* constitute the largest undertaking in the history of the profession with regard to testing.

The preparation of the test followed the general procedures of the ETS, first bringing together the various tests committees to draw up test specifications and outlines, then writing test items for three experimental forms at each level, submitting them to extensive pretesting and detailed item analyses, and finally selecting items from every three pretested forms for the two final forms of each test. The pretesting phase was more elaborate than usual because of the new ways of testing language achievement being attempted.

The listening test gives the instructions and the utterances to be comprehended on a tape-recording. The utterances are single sentences, short conversations, paragraphs read by a speaker, telephone conversations, and dramatic scenes played by several speakers. The student responds by selecting one of four choices in his test booklet.

The speaking test gives instructions and questions on a tape and the student records his spoken responses on another tape. "He repeats ....short statements that he hears; he reads from a printed script; he answers spoken questions that refer to simple line drawings; and he describes, at some length, a picture or series of pictures that convey a message or story."

The reading test consists of 50 multiple choice items of two types. Approximately one-half of the items are incomplete sentences. These items seem to require only reading comprehension since the selection of the correct choice depends on the meaning of the context and the choices, and the distractors must be rejected on the basis of their meaning rather than grammatical incorrectness. The remaining items test comprehension of paragraphs selected from periodicals and appropriate literary sources. The paragraphs of the L forms are simple, straightforward factual prose free from archaisms. Those of the M forms are slightly longer and more literary but still clearly within the style limits that a student can be expected to understand if he has succeeded in learning.

The writing test breaks up the skill into five partial tasks that are involved in writing. They are (1) filling a blank with a word that fits the context lexically and grammatically. There are 24 items of these, requiring such words as *a, la, del, que, es, le,* etc. Only one of these seems dubious in each L form (LA item 3, LB item 3) because it requires a lexical item representing a cultural choice rather than a grammatical one. Forms MA and MB have twenty items each in this section. They all require grammatically and lexically determined words or in some cases words required as part of an idiom. (2) The second task is to supply the appropriate verb form in a sentence. The items cleverly obviate the need for using the technical names of the tenses by giving a base sentence with two verbs and providing a transformed sentence with the test verb left blank. The student knows what tense is required by analogy with the one supplied. The example makes this clear:

Primero como y luego trabajo
Primero comí y luego *trabajé*

In this fashion the test requires that the student use tenses that are difficult, e.g., the subjunctive, the imperfect indicative, etc. (3) In the third type of task the student has to rewrite a sentence changing the number, gender and/or

person to agree with one word that has been changed. Again no grammatical terminology is necessary: if the word is the 3rd person singular pronoun *él,* and the base sentence is in 1st person plural *nosotros* the response must change the sentence accordingly. Each form has eight items of this type.

The first three parts can be scored objectively since only one response per item is fully acceptable. The fourth and fifth tasks are obviously intended to approximate actual writing more closely, and they allow more than one acceptable answer. This is commendable in the crucial problem of developing a valid test, but it represents the loss of fully objective scoring. In task (4) several content words are given and the student has to write a complete sentence in Spanish using all of the words in the order given, changing their form if necessary and adding other necessary words. For example,

Libro/mesa/sala
Tus libros están en una mesa en la sala

This sample item could be answered correctly in many different ways, e.g., *Los libros de mi hermano habían quedado sobre la mesa monumental detrás de la Sala.* This response is within the 7 to 15 word limit of the instructions. It uses more complicated tenses and phrase structure. The problem is how do we score this if a mistake is made in an element that the simpler answer did not attempt? It may well be that if this student had attempted the simpler sentence he might have been successful.

The last task (5) is to write a six- or seven-line dialogue using a given expression in each line. The scoring on this part is done on a four-slot scale (5, 3, 1, 0) applied separately on five variables: coverage of elements, correct word, sentences and phrases meaningful in themselves, sentences and phrases contributing to paragraph meaning, and general quality. As the scale and variables clearly show, there is room for considerable subjectivity in scoring this part in spite of the controls imposed by the expressions and the particular speakers and situation given.

The test norms are given for first through fourth year high school and first through second year of college. The first and second year high school norms for reading and writing are given separately for traditional and audio-lingual classes. Audio-lingual norms for first and second year high school are given only for audio-lingual classes. Third and fourth year high school norms and those for first and second year college are for undifferentiated groups as to teaching method and are called "general." The number of cases in the norming samples seems small in several cases. It would seem that establishing national percentile norms on samples of less than 100 cases must be taken as very preliminary. Such is the case with the listening and speaking, L level, high school audio-lingual norms, first year (91 students), second year (95 students) ; listening and speaking, level M, high school general norms, third year (58 students), fourth year (79 students).

The norms show a steady progression from first through fourth year high school Spanish and from first through second year college. This progression must be assumed to include a factor of selection of students as they advance to the later years.

Reliability is high for all the tests. This is particularly noticeable for the speaking and the writing tests, which one would expect to have lower reliabilities due to the subjective scoring. The reliability of both these tests was computed on samples with greater spread of language study (college and high school samples were included), but even so, the highest reliability is that reported for LB Writing (.96) which did not include college grades.

SUMMARY. It is obvious that the MLA tests represent a major effort and accomplishment of the profession. They give fully equal status to the audio-lingual skills (listening and speaking) ; they do away with translation altogether; they introduce items that approximate actual functional use of the language; they are objective for the most part; and they are professionally developed and standardized.

With these credentials the tests can be recommended and used confidently. Naturally, they are not everything we might need, and their limitations must be pointed out. They are diagnostic as to the four skills—i.e., they show separate scores for them, but they are not diagnostic in detail (nor were they designed to be) within each skill. They are general level tests and may be used as achievement tests in general but not as the single achievement measure for a particular course. They are not speed tests, and they are not exhaustive power tests; they are based on samples on which typical performance may be measured.

The norms are internal and relative for the population of students intended. They do not tell us if a student will know enough to perform well in typical real life use of the language with native speakers. The cost of scoring the speaking and writing tests limits their use on a mass scale. Finally, the absence of new forms will eventually diminish their usefulness through possible compromise of the present forms.

For an excerpted review of the series, see 254.

[323]
National Spanish Examination. 1, 2, 3, 4, 5 years junior high school and high school; 1957–70; NSE; new form issued annually for administration in April at local secondary schools or centers established by local chapters of the AATSP; 4 scores: aural, usage, reading comprehension, total; 5 levels; Forms O1S, O2S, O3S, O4S, O5S, ('70, 4 pages) used in 1970 program; tape recording (7½ ips, 7 inch reel) for each level of aural subtest; directions for administering ['70, 3 pages, mimeographed]; no data on reliability; summary of results (based on locally scored papers returned to the test development committee) is published in *Hispania* in September following the testing program; 15¢ per test; separate answer sheets may be used; $5.50 per tape recording; postpaid; answer sheets must be obtained locally; copies of previous year's tests and tapes available at the same prices; 70(90) minutes; [Test Development Committee, American Association of Teachers of Spanish and Portuguese]; the Association (distributed by local chapter treasurers and the national chairman). *

REFERENCES

1–8. See 6:428.
9. CHARLY, HARRY T. "History of the AATSP National Spanish Examination Program." *Hispania* 50:857–9 D '67. *

WALTER V. KAULFERS, *Professor of Foreign Language Education, University of Illinois, Urbana, Illinois.* [Review of 1969 and 1970 forms.]

Since March 1957, some 25,000 *National Spanish Examinations* have been administered yearly as a basis for allocating the 300 awards sanctioned by the American Association of Teachers of Spanish and Portuguese. Because of the AATSP Test Development Committee's 14-year experience in the preparation of objective achievement tests, the examinations reveal a high level of expertise in test construction. The directions are clear, the Spanish is idiomatic, and the high-fidelity tape recordings are impeccable in diction and intonation.

Since new examinations have to be prepared each year, time limitations prevent standardization of the tests in such a way as to make them comparable in reliability, validity, and difficulty to those of previous years. That the examinations are not statistically comparable is revealed in the variations in medians and means since

1957. In 1957, for example, the mean for the 100-item Level 3 Examination (first or second semester of the third year) was 73.4 while in 1965 it was 57.57—a difference of nearly 16 points.

Inspection of the medians, means, and percentile distributions of scores for the 1969 tests (structured along lines similar to those of 1970) leads the reviewer to believe that the reliability of the examinations as a whole should be .85 or better. It is unfortunate that coefficients of reliability have not actually been reported for previous years, since the tests for the preceding term are commonly available for use either as achievement tests or as means for acquainting prospective contestants with the general nature and scope of the *National Spanish Examinations* for the current academic year. Where the previous year's examination is used as an achievement test, the median, mean, and percentile distribution of scores can serve as norms in evaluating individual achievement.

In any case, tryout of prospective contestants on one or more earlier examinations is strongly recommended for the following reasons:

a) The oral directions for some of the subtests of auditory discrimination and aural comprehension are given only once on tape and hence promote a feeling of insecurity because of their complexity. Note, for example, the following exclusively oral directions for Part 1 of the 1970 Auditory Discrimination Test:

For each item you will hear a series of three words. If all three words are identical in sound, mark *A* on your answer sheet or in your test booklet. If two of the words are identical and a third is different, indicate your choice of answer as *B*. If all three are different, mark answer *C*. Each set of words will be read once.

Note also the insecurity that the following directions for the true-false section are likely to produce when given only once orally, exclusively on tape, without printed confirmation of the directions on the students' answer sheets:

You will now hear a series of simple statements in Spanish. Select the letter *A* on your answer sheet or in your test booklet if the statement is generally true. Select the letter *B* if the statement is logically false. Select the letter *C* if the statement could be considered either true or false, or is only partially true.

The reviewer feels strongly that student response on these parts of the test may in many cases be as much a measure of ability to comprehend and remember the directions as of actual performance in Spanish. In fact, some of the items require a level of philosophical discrimination comparable to that needed to make a value judgment between tweedledee and tweedledum.

b) The voices on the tapes are those of adult males. Students who have been taught exclusively by women teachers, with little opportunity to hear other than feminine voices in Spanish, may find themselves disadvantaged without advance practice using the tests for a previous year.

c) The pronunciation on the tapes is exclusively Highland Latin American. Students who have been taught the pronunciation of Castile or have grown up in families of Castilian descent may find themselves somewhat disadvantaged if they have not had frequent exposure to pronunciation different from that of Old or New Castile. The difference in pronunciation and intonation is in some respects as great as the difference between Oxford English and Midwest American.

If the reviewer has any specific suggestion for the improvement of the examinations (beyond those implied in the preceding paragraphs), it is that the Auditory Discrimination subtest be eliminated. It is essentially a *diagnostic* test of aural acuity. As such it does not belong in a functional test of actual ability to use Spanish in connected discourse in everyday life. Diagnostic tests have their place in locating the *reasons* for inferior or superior performance, not in evaluating achievement or performance itself.

[324]

★**National Teacher Examinations: Spanish.** College seniors and teachers; 1970–71; modified version of secure form of *MLA Foreign Language Proficiency Tests for Teachers and Advanced Students: Spanish;* Form TNT1 ('71, 19 pages); descriptive booklet ('70, 8 pages); listening comprehension section administered by 3¾ ips tape recording; for more complete information, see 582; 120(165) minutes; Educational Testing Service. *

For reviews of the testing program, see 582 (2 reviews), 6:700 (1 review), 5:538 (3 reviews), and 4:802 (1 review).

[325]

★**Pimsleur Spanish Proficiency Tests.** First, second level courses in grades 7–12 or first, second semesters college; 1967; 4 scores: listening, speaking, reading, writing; 1 form; 2 levels labeled Forms A, C; manual (23 pages); no college norms; $1.75 per manual; $1.75 per specimen set (without tapes or manual); postage extra; Paul Pimsleur; Harcourt Brace Jovanovich, Inc. *
a) TEST I, LISTENING COMPREHENSION. Digitek, IBM 805, and IBM 1230 test-answer sheets (2 pages);

7½ ips test tape, 5 inch reel; $7.50 per test tape; $3.80 per 35 test-answer sheets; $1.40 per set of scoring stencils; IBM scoring service, 33¢ and over per test; 15(25) minutes.

b) TEST 2, SPEAKING PROFICIENCY. Test (4 pages); scoring sheet (2 pages); 7½ ips test tape, 5 inch reel; $7.50 per test tape; $4.50 per 35 tests; $2.70 per 35 scoring sheets; 16(26) minutes.

c) TEST 3, READING COMPREHENSION. Test (4 pages); separate answer sheets (Digitek-IBM 805, IBM 1230) must be used; $4.50 per 35 tests; $2.30 per 35 Digitek-IBM 805 answer sheets; $2.80 per 35 IBM 1230 answer sheets; 70¢ per scoring stencil; IBM scoring service, 19¢ and over per test; 35(45) minutes.

d) TEST 4, WRITING PROFICIENCY. Test (6 pages); answer key and scoring directions (4 pages); $7.40 per 35 tests; 35(45) minutes.

GINO PARISI, *Assistant Professor of Spanish, Georgetown University, Washington, D.C.*

The emphasis during the sixties on teaching the four skills, which brought about fundamental changes in textbooks and methodology, has obviously influenced the writers of these tests. It has become acceptable to discuss the four skills as independent areas. Yet the feasibility of such a separation is open to question. As pointed out in the manual, "The four tests.... do not measure the individual skills in isolation * The teacher must therefore be alert to the possibilities of interaction among the skills in evaluating performance."

Prospective users of these tests should become thoroughly acquainted with the manual beforehand. Its description of the tests and various tables give a clear idea of the abilities measured in the four tests, each of which will be taken up in turn below.

PASSIVE SKILLS: LISTENING COMPREHENSION. In the 20 items of the first part, or Side 1, the student hears a short sentence once and must match it with the correct written form by choosing among four possibilities. The tapes are clear, with male and female voices alternating; pronunciation is Spanish-American. The four choices are often subtle, differing only by a phoneme, a syllable, or an intonation pattern indicated by the punctuation. A considerable amount of rapid reading is required. Recognizing individual differences in mental processes, one might assume that some students would continue repeating silently what they heard as they scan the four options. In such a case, the written sentences might cause a student to forget or confuse what he heard. Furthermore, the slow or careless reader might be handicapped even if he understood the Spanish perfectly, especially when the correct choice was the fourth one listed.

Another factor relative to the validity of items of this type is the difficulty of perceiving minimal differences unaided by context. The formal test situation provides none of the code redundancy that characterizes natural conversation and facilitates comprehension.

The 20 items of Side 2 are based less on fine distinctions. They consist of oral sentences to be matched by suitable rejoinders, chosen from four printed possibilities. As in Side 1, the reading factor is important, but here the procedure seems more reasonable because the correct rejoinder is completely different from the incorrect ones and therefore easily distinguishable.

It is unfortunate that listening and reading are combined in this test. Understandably, the burden on one's memory would be excessive if the four choices were presented orally. On the other hand, if this test were presented entirely in written form, it would be false to attribute a student's mistakes to either a listening deficiency or a reading deficiency. He simply would not know the items, regardless of the skill involved.

An idea of the difficulty of the levels can be formed from a comparison of the verb tenses used in each test. The first level (Form A) uses mostly present tense in both parts, with an occasional preterite or imperfect form. In the second level (Form C), the first part consists of slightly more than half present tense and the remainder preterite, imperfect, and present perfect; in the second part, about three-fourths of the verbs are in the present and one-fourth are in the preterite. This information is not included in the manual for the Listening test.

PASSIVE SKILLS: READING COMPREHENSION. In this test the student reads short passages of one to nine sentences followed by three questions with four-choice answers. Form A uses simple narratives, dialogues, and letters. Vocabulary and verb forms seem appropriate. Form C also includes literary, historical, and cultural examples; the prose is more sophisticated.

Ability to draw inferences as well as to understand literal meaning is tested. The manual provides a table which classifies the questions according to these two factors. A reasonable knowledge of synonyms is required, but meanings are straightforward and the authors have avoided the type of item in which all interpretation hinges on an unusual idiom or a punch line.

This is a fairly traditional type of test and easily controlled. Based on samples of from 500 to 2,340 students per grade from grades 8 to 12, split-half reliability coefficients range from .83 to .88, a natural consequence of the complete objectivity of scoring. The lower figures of .72 to .83 for the Listening test, also objectively scored, may be attributable to the many skills tested simultaneously.

Table 10 of the manual gives the results of a comparison of the Listening and Reading tests. For Form A, based on over 5,000 subjects, the mean score for Listening is 19.8 (50% of possible score) and for Reading, 13.6 (38%); and the correlation between the two is .60. These figures should be interpreted carefully for many reasons. They imply that students perform better in listening than in reading, but such a conclusion would be a result of the assumption that the two tests are testing the same material in different form, an assumption not borne out by close examination. In length, variety, and complexity, the Reading test is more advanced than the Listening test. No significant conclusions can be drawn unless the two tests deal with the same level of material. Nor is it valid to argue that the reading skill requires a more developed vocabulary than the listening skill. Because of the elementary level of these tests, all its vocabulary could be called conversational. The major difference between these two tests is one of quantity. The student clearly has to know more Spanish for the Reading test.

ACTIVE SKILLS: WRITING PROFICIENCY. Part 1 consists of a dialogue, with missing items to be supplied from the context. Form A contains 19 items; Form C contains 26, with longer sentences and more advanced syntax. The words required are mostly prepositions, articles, and pronouns, plus a few verbs.

Here again the overlapping of the separate tests is apparent. The missing words are no more peculiar to writing than to speaking. Their inclusion in this section is obviously due to the practical consideration of control. A student might be able to produce these forms in writing without having the necessary fluency to speak them; on the other hand, if a student did not know these forms in writing it is safe to assume that he would not be able to use them in speaking either. Thus the relation between writing and speaking, if only measurable negatively through mistakes, is real and could be made explicit if the techniques were available.

This observation is equally applicable to Parts 2 and 3. Part 2 tests recognition (reading) and production (writing) of verb forms in 10 items. In Form A the student is expected to recognize the tense used in one part of the sentence and match it by conjugating the infinitive given in the other part. In Form C the student changes a verb from one tense to another on cue. One item which calls for a choice between preterite or imperfect seems ambiguous.

These devices to test control and usage of verb forms are an improvement over the once common practice of asking for a specific tense of a verb given in parentheses. Yet they require recognition before production and thus serve to underline the difficulty of separating active and passive skills.

Part 3 of both forms consists of nine items of the pattern drill type, involving cued changes in number and gender. The directions for correction specify that copying errors are not to be considered. Since such items could easily be tested orally, there seems to be no reason for calling this a test of writing rather than speaking proficiency.

At issue is not the relevance of a given ability to the skill being tested, but rather the implication that such an ability is more relevant to one skill than to another. Indeed, pattern drills are usually associated with oral practice and involve both active and passive skills.

Part 4, Form A, asks the student to write one sentence about each of four pictures and a three-sentence description of a larger picture. Form C is similar to Form A, except that eight pictures tell a story which must be written in the past tense. For scoring there is a factor guide which gives credit for content, verb formation and usage, and structure. Instructions for scoring are detailed, mentioning completeness of story, vocabulary, phrasing, smoothness, word order, spelling, tense usage, and many other aspects.

Obviously, the most important consideration in Part 4 is scorer reliability. The manual gives data based on two studies, one involving the same scorer and a set of 82 tests corrected at two different times, and another involving two scorers and a set of 50 tests. Correlations are high: .96 for the first study and .94 for the second. The conclusion arrived at in the manual is the following: "Although the extremely high correlation coefficients and the marked agreements in means and standard deviations may reflect to a certain extent the training and backgrounds of the scorers, classroom teachers should also be able to achieve high reliability in scoring *if they follow carefully and conscientiously the prescribed scoring system* [italics added]." This is far from convincing. First, as is frankly stated in the manual, the coefficients are based on figures treated as though the total of points arrived at by applying scoring standards (Part 4) is comparable to a number of separate items answered correctly (Parts 1, 2 and 3). Second, the classroom teacher may not be highly trained. And third, objectivity is difficult when a teacher knows the students whose work he is evaluating. The only valid conclusion is that there is a *possibility* of high scoring reliability, subject to the important variables of care, conscience, training, and background. These are precisely the qualities one expects in a standardized test. It does not seem fair to shift the responsibility to the teacher. It would be safer to use the scoring service provided by the publishers and trust that all the trained scorers are equally competent. For writing proficiency (and speaking proficiency) there continues to be a need for reliability studies involving significant numbers of scorers. Indeed, elimination of scorer subjectivity should be the goal. As long as the teacher is required to use his own judgment he might operate more effectively within the framework of classroom tests which he could control according to his particular needs.

ACTIVE SKILLS: SPEAKING PROFICIENCY. In Part 1 of both forms the student is asked to record without the article the names of 27 pictured items. Directions for correcting instruct the scorer that "pronunciation need not be perfect, but the word must be readily understandable." The format dictates that all the items be concrete nouns.

A voice on the master tape paces the student by reading numbers, so that a reasonable speed of response is maintained. Aside from this, what is tested is vocabulary, and the omission of the article does not seem well advised. A sure control of gender is certainly essential for speaking.

Part 2 tests pronunciation by having the student first listen to all of 20 sentences of two to seven words as he reads them in the test booklet. Then he records all the sentences as a voice reads the numbers, again controlling the speed. What is being tested, rather than simple pronunciation, is ability to read orally.

The scoring focuses on two sounds in each sentence, disregarding all other elements. Test results would be affected if a student trained to read had had any oral practice, since some of the mistakes anticipated involve pronouncing Spanish letters ("silent h") as in English. A suggested improvement would be to lengthen the test so that the student would have more than one sentence devoted to each sound. This repetition would allow discrimination between those who never mispronounce, those who sometimes mispronounce, and those who habitually mispronounce.

Part 3, Form A, includes eight taped questions to be answered orally by the student, preferably in complete sentences, and in the present tense. In Form C five answers are in the present and three in the past tense. Some of the questions are personal and would require answers of varying length from different individuals. Listening ability is a factor in this section.

The answer tape runs 6 to 7 minutes, including only the student's responses for Parts 1 and 2, and both questions and answers for Part 3.

As noted above, very little can be said about scorer reliability for this test. No norms are given, and no scoring service is available. When one considers that to correct 100 test tapes—a reasonable number for high school—the teacher would have to spend about 13 hours, there is little advantage in using this test. A good teacher could probably evaluate his students' pronunciation informally with as much accuracy. There is no need to consider the poor teacher; he would have difficulty correcting the tapes objectively in any event.

For the teacher the promise of a standardized test is uniformity and ease of correction. A test which shifts the burden of reliability back on the teacher does not answer any purpose. It has only the appearance of objectivity. The teacher's evaluation is at least frankly subjective and therefore more honest. The teacher should be aware of the problems connected with standardization of speaking (and writing) proficiency tests and not assume that they have been solved yet.

CONCLUSION. The eight tests of this series cover about one-half of a complete language course, judging by the fact that virtually no subjunctives have been included. They have been carefully developed, the Spanish is consistently appropriate, and many pertinent statistical tables are published in the manual. They can be said to represent the best of the past decade; but if we are to take seriously the publisher's promise—"A new decade, a new challenge. Old concepts must go and new ones take their place"—these tests must be judged unsatisfactory. Face validity is still the guiding factor in many cases: the student speaks for a speaking test; he writes for a writing test.

The chief shortcoming is the overlapping of the abilities in the separate tests. This stems from the framework which dictates that the four skills can or should be tested independently, creating a problem of validity for all tests and of reliability for Speaking and Writing. Perhaps a new approach will focus on the elements or abilities rather than the skills. In the search for new techniques, the following questions may be kept in mind: (a) What is the approximate range of the student's vocabulary? (b) Is there any difference between his oral and written command of this vocabulary? (c) How does his active vocabulary compare to his passive vocabulary? (d) At what speed of delivery is he competent in listening? (e) How much code noise can he tolerate? (f) Is he able to distinguish between Spanish and non-Spanish—e.g., how many of the following are not Spanish nouns: *masa, maso, casa, caso?* (g) Does he know the patterns of derivation as well as all the words to which they apply— e.g., is it *conocimento* or *conocimiento?* (h) How secure is his command of verbs, oral or written? (i) How correct is his pronunciation? (j) Does he command both formal and informal styles? The new tests may try to tell us first *what* the student knows, then *how* he is able to manifest that knowledge.

J Ed Meas 6(1):48–50 sp '69. E. E. Bilyeu. * basically well constructed and contain many excellent testing techniques. However, they do not completely avoid some of the pitfalls common to standardized testing. There is a lack of procedure from the simple to the complex in each part of the tests as well as from Form A to Form C. With few exceptions, the testing techniques of the two forms are identical, and

Level C is not always sufficiently more difficult than Level A. Indeed, many of the test items appear without change in both forms. For example, items 31 through 36 of the Reading Comprehension Test of Form A are repeated as items 1 through 6 of Form C. In the Listening and the Reading Comprehension Tests the questions are multiple choice. In enough test items to be of some concern, two of the four alternatives could be considered logical responses. To illustrate: in an item the student hears "¿Qué hay allí?" (What's over there?). Two of the four alternatives are easily eliminated, leaving "No tiene nada" and "No veo nada." A student might legitimately argue that "He has nothing" is as logical an answer as "I see nothing." Once an oral statement or a reading passage has been understood, it is desirable that the correct response be readily apparent and that the matter of student conjecture be eliminated. One minor problem pertains only to Part I of the Listening Comprehension Test. The student hears a statement and from four similar sentences printed on the answer sheet he must choose the one he heard. For example, he hears: "Caminó hacia la universidad." He reads: Caminó hasta la universidad, Caminó hacia la universidad, Camino hasta la universidad, Camino hacia la universidad. If it occurs to the student to read ahead in order to identify the areas of contrast and to listen attentively to *only* those areas, he will have a distinct advantage over the student who fails to make the analogy in time and who continues to treat all of the sounds of all four sentences as problems demanding his attention as he attempts to remember what he has heard. Thus, the possibility exists that the student's success may relate directly to his ability to discover a test-taking technique. The above item reveals another problem of greater concern—the interdependence of skills. Although, in the above example, the student must correctly perceive the oral stimulus, his success, nevertheless, depends upon his ability to relate what he has heard to the graphic representation. The emphasis upon visual perception is so great that the student who has been taught by an intensive audio-lingual approach, with little emphasis on reading and writing, will find himself at a distinct disadvantage. Of greater significance is the over emphasis throughout the tests on the student's knowledge of vocabulary. Reference is not made here to those areas of the test which are constructed to test vocabulary knowledge, but rather to certain parts of the tests which are designed to measure a compre-hensive skill, but in which the student's success is dependent upon his knowledge of a particular vocabulary item. The problem is particularly prevalent in the Listening and in the Reading Comprehension Tests. In many cases it is pos-sible that the student may have understood the oral statement or the reading passage, yet may answer the test item incorrectly because a par-ticular word among the alternatives is unfa-miliar to him. One example, chosen at random from many, will illustrate the point. One reading passage discusses the return of a student from Peru. To successfully complete one of the fol-lowing test items the student must know the idioms *acabar de* (to have just) and *hacer un viaje* (to take a trip), neither of which appears in the reading passage. Thus, the item does not actually measure the student's ability to read and understand the passage, but rather assesses his knowledge of vocabulary equivalency. In spite of the above problems, the Pimsleur tests are a good measure of the basic skills of listen-

ing, speaking, reading and writing. Representa-tive samples of most of the major structures of the language are included, and matters of sound, order, form, and choice are adequately tested. Particularly excellent are the Writing Proficiency Tests and the Fluency portions of the Speaking Tests. Much thought and con-siderable effort clearly have been employed in constructing all the tests. Certainly, they must be recognized as a worthwhile contribution to the profession.

[326]
*Second Year Spanish Test. High school and col-lege; 1953-68; SYST; revision of *Kansas Second Year Spanish Test;* Form A ('68, 4 pages); manual ('68, 2 pages); no data on reliability; $1.75 per 25 tests, postage extra; 75¢ per specimen set, postpaid; 50(55) minutes; Oscar F. Hernández and Minnie M. Miller; Data Processing and Educational Measure-ment Center. *

[327]
★The Undergraduate Record Examinations: Spanish Test. College; 1969-70; Form K-RUR ('69, 17 pages); descriptive booklet ('70, 8 pages); for more complete information, see 671; 120(140) minutes; Edu-cational Testing Service. *

For reviews of the testing program, see 671 (2 reviews).

INTELLIGENCE

REVIEWS BY *J. Stanley Ahmann, Anne Anastasi, J. Douglas Ayres, Leonard L. Baird, Robert H. Bauernfeind, George K. Bennett, Alvin G. Burstein, H. J. Butcher, Joel T. Campbell, John B. Carroll, Clinton I. Chase, Roberta R. Collard, Lee J. Cronbach, Richard F. Docter, Robert C. Droege, Philip H. DuBois, James A. Dunn, Dorothy H. Eichorn, John P. Foley, Jr., David Freides, Joseph L. French, Eric F. Gardner, Bert A. Goldman, Marcel L. Goldschmid, Russel F. Green, Albert J. Harris, Philip Himelstein, Marshall S. Hiskey, Raymond H. Holden, Marjorie P. Honzik, Kenneth D. Hopkins, John L. Horn, Jane V. Hunt, Arthur R. Jensen, Raymond A. Katzell, James E. Kennedy, Kenneth Lovell, Howard B. Lyman, Boyd R. McCandless, Arthur C. MacKinney, William B. Michael, John E. Milholland, Alice E. Moriarty, T. Ernest New-land, John Nisbet, Stanley Nisbet, Robert D. North, Jum C. Nunnally, R. T. Osborne, David A. Payne, John H. Rosenbach, Richard E. Schutz, Melvyn I. Semmel, A. B. Silverstein, Charles D. Smock, Erwin K. Taylor, Hugh Taylor, Robert L. Thorndike, Carol K. Tittle, Philip E. Vernon, David A. Walker, Wimburn L. Wallace, Henry Weitz, and Emmy E. Werner.*

GROUP

[328]
*A.C.E.R. Advanced Test B40. Ages 13 and over; 1940-66; formerly called *Adult Test (B40)*; I form ['65, 4 pages, identical with test copyrighted in 1940 except for 2 revised items]; mimeographed manual ('66, 9 pages, identical—including norms—with manual published in 1964 except for key to 2 items); Aus 50¢ per 10 tests; 40¢ per manual; 45¢ per specimen set;

postpaid within Australia; 55(65) minutes; Australian Council for Educational Research. *

REFERENCES
1-3. See 5:296.
4. ANDERSON, A. W. "Reading Ability and Intelligence of Students: A Study of New Admissions to the University of Western Australia in 1957." *Educand* 3:108-12 Mr '57. *
5. HOGBEN, D. "School of Entry and First Year Perform-ance of Medical Students in the University of Western Aus-tralia." *Austral J Higher Ed* 2:79-83 N '64. *
6. ANDERSON, A. W. "Intelligence and Reading Scores of Entrants to the University of Western Australia 1954-65." *Austral J Higher Ed* 2:177-82 N '65. *

7. HOGBEN, D. "The Prediction of Academic Success in Relation to Student Selection in Medicine at the University of Western Australia." *Austral J Higher Ed* 2:152–60 N '65. *

For a review by C. Sanders, see 5:296.

[329]

★A.C.E.R. Lower Grades General Ability Scale, Second Edition. Ages 6-6 to 9-1; 1962–66; 5 scores: picture vocabulary, picture arrangement, picture analogies, picture series, total; 1 form ['64, 16 pages in 2 booklets labeled Part A and Part B]; test identical with first edition copyrighted in 1962 except for minor revisions in format; manual ('66, 45 pages); no norms for part scores; Aus $1.50 per 10 tests; $1 per set of keys; $1.25 per manual; $2.45 per specimen set; postpaid within Australia; (110–120) minutes in 2 sessions; M. L. Clark (manual) and the Australian Council for Educational Research; the Council. *

[330]

*ACT Test Battery of the American College Testing Program. Candidates for college entrance; 1959–70; ACT; tests administered 5 times a year (October, December, February, April, July) at centers established by the publisher; 5 scores: English usage, mathematics usage, social studies reading, natural sciences reading, composite; test booklet also includes a biographical inventory (Student Profile Section) of nonacademic achievements, aspirations, special campus needs, and perceptions of college; 3 new forms published annually; supervisor's manual, 1970–71 edition ('70, c1968, 20 pages); counselor's handbook ('70, 39 pages); technical report ('65, 43 pages); student information booklet ['70, 24 pages]; interpretive booklet for students ('70, 32 pages); guide for use of ACT services on campus ('70, 35 pages); reprint of student profile section ('70, 8 pages); announcement of ACT research services ('70, 44 pages); separate answer sheets (MRC) must be used; examination fee, $6 per student; fee includes reporting of scores to the student, his high school, and 3 colleges designated at time of application; 195(240) minutes; American College Testing Program. *

REFERENCES

1–14. See 6:1.
15. RAY, PHILIP BOND. *A Descriptive Study of Certain Characteristics of "High Creative" Freshman Arts College Students as Compared With "High Academic Potential" Students.* Doctor's thesis, University of Minnesota (Minneapolis, Minn.), 1962. (*DA* 24:1924)
16. ADKINS, ARLIE ANDREW. *Prediction of College Success at Middle Tennessee State College.* Doctor's thesis, University of Florida (Gainesville, Fla.), 1963. (*DA* 25:211)
17. CHASE, CLINTON I.; LUDLOW, H. GLENN; POMEROY, MARTHA C.; AND BARRITT, L. SPENCER. *Predicting Individual Course Success for Entering Freshmen.* Indiana Studies in Prediction No. 2. Bloomington, Ind.: Bureau of Educational Studies and Testing, Indiana University, 1963. Pp. i, 41. *
18. CHASE, CLINTON I.; LUDLOW, H. GLENN; POMEROY, MARTHA C.; AND BARRITT, L. SPENCER. *Predicting Success for University Freshmen.* Indiana Studies in Prediction No. 1. Bloomington, Ind.: Bureau of Educational Studies and Testing, Indiana University, 1963. Pp. vi, 47. *
19. FRIESEN, WALTER S. *A Descriptive Study of Freshman Performance in English Composition I at Kansas State University, 1961, in Relation to Fifty-Two Variables.* Doctor's research study No. 1, Colorado State College (Greeley, Colo.), 1963. (*DA* 25:290)
20. HIGGINS, WILLIAM. *A Comparison of the ACT Program With Other Available Criteria for Predicting Success of Students at Bismarck Junior College.* Master's thesis, Northern State College (Aberdeen, S.D.), 1963.
21. LIBBY, DOUGLAS F., JR. *The American College Testing Program and High School Achievement as Contributing Predictors of Success for Technical Institute Students.* Doctor's thesis, Boston University (Boston, Mass.), 1963. (*DA* 25:1657)
22. MAY, LOMAX LOUIS. *A Study of the Relationships Between Achievement on a Complex Visual-Auditory Learning*

Task and Certain Selected Variables. Doctor's thesis, University of Alabama (University, Ala.), 1963. (*DA* 25:1750)
23. VAUGHAN, GEORGE ELLIS, JR. *Some Characteristics of College Freshmen According to Sex and Ethnic Group and the Relationship of These Characteristics to Academic Achievement.* Doctor's thesis, North Texas State University (Denton, Tex.), 1963. (*DA* 25:1017)
24. BLEDSOE, LUTHER, AND WARD, GEORGE. "An Analysis of the West Virginia State College Admissions Policy and Academic Performance at Marshall University." *Proc W Va Acad Sci* 36:184–7 S '64. *
25. BOYCE, RICHARD W. "The Prediction of Achievement in College Algebra." *Ed & Psychol Meas* 24:419–20 su '64. * (*PA* 39:5976)
26. BROWN, MARY MARGARET. *A Study of the Relationships of Selected Tests and Grade Point Averages for a Land Grant Institution.* Doctor's thesis, University of South Dakota (Vermillion, S.D.), 1964. (*DA* 27:664A)
27. DIZNEY, HENRY F., AND ROSKENS, RONALD W. "Comparing Aptitude and Achievement of American and Foreign Students in an American University." *J Col Stud Personnel* 5:146–51 Mr '64. *
28. FIRNBERG, JAMES W. *The Use of the American College Testing Program Test in the Prediction of Academic Achievement.* Master's thesis, Louisiana State University (Baton Rouge, La.), 1964.
29. FISHER, JAMES LEE. *Factors Affecting Academic Success.* Doctor's thesis, Northwestern University (Evanston, Ill.), 1964. (*DA* 25:3970)
30. KELLOGG, T. E.; TRUMP, PAUL L.; PEARSON, RICHARD; FOOSE, ROBERT L.; BENSON, LOREN; AND GROESBECK, BYRON L. "National Admissions Testing Programs—Their Value to Colleges—Their Impact on Secondary Schools." *Col & Univ* 39: 488–514 su '64. *
31. LINDQUIST, E. F. "Equating Scores on Non-Parallel Tests." *J Ed Meas* 1:5–9 Je '64. * (*PA* 39:7777)
32. NORRED, ROBERT GAINES. *The Effect of Certain Selected Variables on Performance in Football.* Doctor's thesis, University of Alabama (University, Ala.), 1964. (*DA* 25:7066)
33. PETERSEN, LORENZ J. *The Significance of Score Discrepancies on a Test Battery.* Master's thesis, Illinois State University (Normal, Ill.), 1964.
34. QUINLAN, CLAIRE A. *The Prediction of Freshman Academic Success at Colorado State College by Means of Selected Standardized Tests and Admission Data.* Doctor's research study No. 1, Colorado State College (Greeley, Colo.), 1964. (*DA* 25:5124)
35. RYAN, ROBERT DALE. *A Study of Student Performance in First Year Technical Drawing at St. Cloud State College as Related to Certain High School Courses and ACT Scores.* Doctor's research study No. 1, Colorado State College (Greeley, Colo.), 1964. (*DA* 25:5031)
36. WALKER, PETER. *Is Either the SAT or the ACT a Superior Instrument for Predicting Academic Success at National College of Education.* Master's thesis, National College of Education (Evanston, Ill.), 1964.
37. WEBER, LOUISE A. *The Predictive Validity of the SCAT and the ACT at a Liberal Arts College for Women.* Master's thesis, John Carroll University (Cleveland, Ohio), 1964.
38. BOSSEN, DORIS STEPHENS. *The Relation of Four Nonintellective Factors to the Matriculation of High School Senior Girls.* Master's thesis, Ohio State University (Columbus, Ohio), 1965.
39. BOYCE, RICHARD W., AND PAXSON, R. C. "The Predictive Validity of Eleven Tests at One State College." *Ed & Psychol Meas* 25:1143–7 w '65. * (*PA* 40:3563)
40. BOYD, JOSEPH D. "Vocational Interest Measurement in High School: What Do the Findings Mean?" *J Assn Col Adm Officers* 10:9–14 w '65. *
41. BROWN, FREDERICK G., AND WOLINS, LEROY. "An Empirical Evaluation of the American College Testing Program." *Personnel & Guid J* 43:451–6 Ja '65. * (*PA* 39:10813)
42. CHASE, CLINTON I. *The University Freshman Dropout.* Indiana University, Monograph of the Bureau of Educational Studies and Testing, Indiana Studies in Prediction, No. 6. Bloomington, Ind.: the Bureau, 1965. Pp. 36. *
43. CRAIG, MARY J. *A Study of the Effectiveness of the Interpretation of the ACT Program Scores Through Group Guidance With Freshman Women.* Master's thesis, Texas Woman's University (Denton, Tex.), 1965.
44. CRIBB, GEORGE ROBERT. *The Comparative Effectiveness of Conventional and Programed Instructional Procedures in Teaching Fundamentals of Music.* Doctor's thesis, North Texas State University (Denton, Tex.), 1965. (*DA* 25:7098)
45. DeSENA, PAUL A., AND WEBER, LOUISE ANN. "The Predictive Validity of the School College Ability Test (*SCAT*) and the American College Test (*ACT*) at a Liberal Arts College for Women." *Ed & Psychol Meas* 25:1149–51 w '65. * (*PA* 40:4603)
46. DIZNEY, HENRY F.; ELFNER, ELINOR A.; AND PAGE, HORACE A. "American College Test (ACT) Performance as a Function of Examinee Acceptance of Test." *Ed & Psychol Meas* 25:547–53 su '65. * (*PA* 39:15223)
47. DuBOIS, LLOYD VERRELL. *A Study of Factors Related to Persistence and Withdrawal Among Sophomore Students in the College of Education at Oklahoma State University.*

Doctor's thesis, Oklahoma State University (Stillwater, Okla.), 1965. (*DA* 27:50A)

48. ELLIOTT, EUGENE W. "An Evaluation of Some Tests for Placement in College Chemistry." *Mont Acad Sci* 25:106–9 '65. *

49. FOSTER, JAMES M., AND DANSKIN, DAVID G. "The American College Test (ACT) Tested Three Ways." *Personnel & Guid J* 43:904–9 My '65. * (*PA* 39:16438)

50. FUNCHES, DELARS. "A Correlation Between the ACT Scores and the Grade Point Averages of Freshmen at Jackson State College." *Col & Univ* 40:324–6 sp '65. *

51. GALLANT, THOMAS FRANCIS. *Academic Achievement of College Freshmen and Its Relationship to Selected Aspects of the Student's Background.* Doctor's thesis, Western Reserve University (Cleveland, Ohio), 1965. (*DA* 26:6468)

52. GARLAND, CALVIN BOOTH. *A Comparative Study of High School Grades, Class Rank, and ACT Test Scores as Predictors of College Success at East Tennessee State University, 1964–65.* Master's thesis, East Tennessee State University (Johnson City, Tenn.), 1965.

53. HOLLAND, JOHN L., AND RICHARDS, JAMES M., JR. "Academic and Non-Academic Accomplishment: Correlated or Uncorrelated?" *ACT Res Rep* 2:1–26 Ap '65. *

54. HOLLAND, JOHN L., AND RICHARDS, JAMES M., JR. "Academic and Nonacademic Accomplishment: Correlated or Uncorrelated?" *J Ed Psychol* 56:165–74 Ag '65. * (*PA* 39:15293)

55. JOHNSON, RICHARD W. "Are SVIB Interests Correlated With Differential Academic Achievement?" *J Appl Psychol* 49:302–9 Ag '65. * (*PA* 39:15357)

56. KEEFER, KARL ELTON. *Self-Prediction of Academic Achievement by College Students.* Doctor's thesis, University of Tennessee (Knoxville, Tenn.), 1965. (*DA* 26:4337)

57. McIFF, LYLE HATCH. *The Relationship of Certain Selected Factors to the Success or Failure of Second-Quarter Accounting Students at Utah State University.* Doctor's thesis, University of Southern California (Los Angeles, Calif.), 1965. (*DA* 26:5767)

58. MUNDAY, LEO. "Comparative Predictive Validities of the American College Tests and Two Other Scholastic Aptitude Tests." *ACT Res Rep* 6:2–14 Ag '65. *

59. MUNDAY, LEO. *An Investigation of the Relationships of Selected Factors to the Predictability of College Grades.* Doctor's thesis, State University of Iowa (Iowa City, Iowa), 1965. (*DA* 26:2591)

60. MUNDAY, LEO. "Predicting College Grades in Predominantly Negro Colleges." *J Ed Meas* 2:157–60 D '65. *

61. MUNDAY, LEO, AND HOYT, DONALD P. "Predicting Academic Success for Nursing Students." *Nursing Res* 14:341–4 f '65. *

62. PHAY, JOHN E., AND McDONALD, DOUGLAS. *Four Years of Academic Achievement and Disposition of the 1961–62 Entering Freshmen at the University of Mississippi Compared With American College Test Scores.* University, Miss.: Bureau of Institutional Research, University of Mississippi, 1965. Pp. xvi, 161. *

63. RICHARDS, JAMES M., JR., AND HOLLAND, JOHN L. "Academic and Nonacademic Accomplishment: Correlated or Uncorrelated?" Abstract. *Proc Ann Conv Am Psychol Assn* 73:309–10 '65. * (*PA* 39:15293)

64. ROA, CLAYTON DURWARD. *An Investigation of Factors Leading to the Withdrawal of Waldorf Junior College Freshmen.* Doctor's thesis, Michigan State University (East Lansing, Mich.), 1965. (*DA* 27:681A)

65. ROBINSON, FRANCES K. *An Investigation of the Value of the ACT Battery, the College Board Scholastic Aptitude Test, the Differential Aptitude Test Battery, and the University of Kansas Placement Battery as Predictors of University of Kansas Freshmen Grades.* Master's thesis, University of Kansas (Lawrence, Kan.), 1965.

66. SASSENRATH, JULIUS M., AND PUGH, RICHARD. "Relationships Among CEEB Scholastic Aptitude Test and American College Test Scores and Grade Point Average." *J Ed Meas* 2:199–205 D '65. *

67. STANSBERRY, CHARLES WAYNE. *A Comparative Study of First Year Academic Achievement as Related to Predicted Achievement of Freshmen Enrolled in Elementary Education at Frostburg State College.* Doctor's thesis, Pennsylvania State University (University Park, Pa.), 1965. (*DA* 26:2028)

68. STEINBRECHER, ANDREW W. *Characteristic Personality Factors of Students With Marked Interest Variability on the A.C.T.* Master's thesis, Illinois State University (Normal, Ill.), 1965.

69. ABE, CLIFFORD. "A Factor Analytic Study of Some Non-Intellectual Indices of Academic Achievement." *J Ed Meas* 3:39–44 sp '66. *

70. ANDERSON, ROGER CLARE. *A Study of Academic and Biographical Variables for Predicting Achievement in Technical Programs at the North Dakota State School of Science.* Doctor's thesis, University of North Dakota (Grand Forks, N.D.), 1966. (*DA* 27:2046A)

71. BAILEY, CLARENCE W. *Description of Patterns of the American College Testing Program Scores of Academically Dismissed Students at Plymouth State College, Plymouth, New Hampshire.* Master's thesis, Plymouth State College (Plymouth, N.H.), 1966.

72. BRADLEY, NOLEN EUGENE, JR. *The Negro Undergraduate Student: Factors Relative to Performance in Predominantly White State Colleges and Universities in Tennessee.* Doctor's thesis, University of Tennessee (Knoxville, Tenn.), 1966. (*DA* 27:1534A)

73. BRISTOW, RONALD MILTON. *English and Native Language Test Score Relationships to College Grade Point Average for Japanese Students.* Doctor's thesis, University of Southern California (Los Angeles, Calif.), 1966. (*DA* 27:2062A)

74. BROWN, FREDERICK G., AND SCOTT, DAVID A. "The Unpredictability of Predictability." *J Ed Meas* 3:297–301 w '66. *

75. CHANDLER, JOSEPH DOUGLAS. *An Analysis of Competence in the Social Sciences by Elementary Education Majors at the University of Tennessee.* Doctor's thesis, University of Tennessee (Knoxville, Tenn.), 1966. (*DA* 27:3246A)

76. CHASE, CLINTON I., AND BARRITT, L. SPENCER. "A Table of Concordance Between ACT and SAT." *J Col Stud Personnel* 7:105–8 Mr '66. * Comment by William H. Angoff and reply by the authors, 7:194–6 Jl '66. *

77. COLLINS, MILTON EUGENE. *A Predictive and Item Study of the Cognitive Structure of a College Aptitude Test.* Doctor's thesis, University of Michigan (Ann Arbor, Mich.), 1966. (*DA* 27:3287A)

78. COPPEDGE, FLOYD LEVON. *The Relationship of Selected Factors to Occupational and College Success.* Doctor's thesis, University of Oklahoma (Norman, Okla.), 1966. (*DA* 26:6441)

79. DEMOS, GEORGE D., AND WEIJOLA, MERRILL J. "Achievement-Personality Criteria as Selectors of Participants and Predictors of Success in Special Programs in Higher Education." *Calif J Ed Res* 17:186–92 S '66. * (*PA* 41:1923)

80. DOHNER, CHARLES WESLEY. *The Relation of Non-Intellective Factors to the Academic Achievement of College Freshmen at the Ohio State University.* Doctor's thesis, Ohio State University (Columbus, Ohio), 1966. (*DA* 27:2826A)

81. HALL, WESTON ADRIAN. *The Construction of Scales From Selected Variables for Predicting Academic Success in a Junior College.* Doctor's thesis, University of Houston (Houston, Tex.), 1966. (*DA* 27:3325B)

82. HANSON, ROBERT NELTON. *Visual Stimulus Versus Combined Audio-Visual Stimuli for Out-of-Class Practice in First-Semester College Gregg Shorthand.* Doctor's thesis, University of North Dakota (Grand Forks, N.D.), 1966. (*DA* 27:3224A)

83. HOLLAND, JOHN L. "The Research and Development Division in the American College Testing Program." *J Counsel Psychol* 13:117–9 sp '66. *

84. HOLLAND, JOHN L., AND RICHARDS, JAMES M., JR. "Academic and Non-Academic Accomplishment in a Representative Sample Taken From a Population of 612,000." *ACT Res Rep* 12:1–28 My '66. * (*PA* 40:10451)

85. HOOVER, HELENE MAE PERRY. *Concept Development of College Students Exposed to Systematic, Organized Learning Experiences in Family Relationships.* Doctor's thesis, Oklahoma State University (Stillwater, Okla.), 1966. (*DA* 27:4465B)

86. HOYT, DONALD P. "Predicting Grades in Two-Year Terminal Programs: An Experiment in Predicting the College Ability of 'Non-Academically Oriented' Students." *Jun Col J* 36:20–3 F '66. *

87. HOYT, DONALD P., AND MUNDAY, LEO. "Academic Description and Prediction in Junior Colleges." *ACT Res Rep* 10:1–22 F '66. * (*PA* 40:8035)

88. JEX, FRANK B. *Predicting Academic Success Beyond High School.* Salt Lake City, Utah: University of Utah Bookstore, 1966. Pp. vi, 41. *

89. JOHNSON, RICHARD W. "Interpretation of ACT Difference Scores." *J Col Stud Personnel* 7:109–12 Mr '66. *

90. KAHNK, DONALD LEE. *Differential Value of Selected Pre-Matriculation Data for Predicting Collegiate Persistence.* Doctor's thesis, University of Nebraska (Lincoln, Neb.), 1966. (*DA* 27:1263A)

91. LEWIS, LESLIE. *A Multivariate Analysis of Variables Associated With Academic Success Within a College Environment.* Doctor's thesis, Oklahoma State University (Stillwater, Okla.), 1966. (*DA* 27:4134A)

92. LINS, L. JOSEPH; ABELL, ALLAN P.; AND HUTCHINS, H. CLIFTON. "Relative Usefulness in Predicting Academic Success of the ACT, the SAT, and Some Other Variables." *J Exp Ed* 35:1–29 w '66. *

93. MILLER, AARON JULIUS. *A Study of Engineering and Technical Institute Freshman Enrollees and Dropouts in Terms of Selected Intellective and Non-Intellective Factors.* Doctor's thesis, Oklahoma State University (Stillwater, Okla.), 1966. (*DA* 27:4050A)

94. MOSLEMI, MARLENE H. *ACT English Scores and General Studies English Grade Point Average as Predictors of Academic Achievement on the Undergraduate Level at Southern Illinois University.* Master's thesis, Southern Illinois University (Carbondale, Ill.), 1966.

95. MUNDAY, LEO A.; HOYT, DONALD P.; AND LUTZ, SANDRA W. *College Student Profiles: Norms for the ACT Assessment, 1966–67 Edition.* Iowa City, Iowa: American College Testing Program, Inc., 1966. Pp. xii, 292. * (*PA* 41:10950)

96. PAPPAS, JOHN G. *The Effects of Three Approaches to College Orientation on Two Groups of Entering Freshmen*

Students at Kent State University. Doctor's thesis, Kent State University (Kent, Ohio), 1966. (*DA* 28:401A)

97. RAND, LEONARD PETER. *A Study of the Relationship Between the Matching of Student and Institutional Characteristics and College Choice Satisfaction.* Doctor's thesis, University of Iowa (Iowa City, Iowa), 1966. (*DA* 27:2832A)

98. RICHARDS, JAMES M., JR.; HOLLAND, JOHN L.; AND LUTZ, SANDRA W. "The Prediction of Student Accomplishment in College." *ACT Res Rep* 13:1–38 Je '66. * (*PA* 40: 11491)

99. RIVIERE, ANN L. *A Study of the Relationship Between American College Test Scores and College Grade Point Averages of Selected Tennessee Technological University Education Majors.* Master's thesis, Tennessee Technological University (Cookeville, Tenn.), 1966.

100. RUNDE, ROBERT M. "Freshman Placement Uses of a Nationwide Test." *Col & Univ* 41:190–8 w '66. *

101. SASSENRATH, JULIUS M., AND PUGH, RICHARD. "Note: Relationships Among CEEB Scholastic Aptitude Test and American College Test Scores and Grade Point Average: A Replication." *J Ed Meas* 3:37–8 sp '66. *

102. SEGRIST, ALLEN EDWARD. *Admission of Transfer Students.* Doctor's thesis, Ohio State University (Columbus, Ohio), 1966. (*DA* 27:2053A)

103. SHANA'A, JOYCE ADRIAN. *A Statistical Analysis of the Placement Program in Mathematics for Freshmen at the University of Oklahoma.* Doctor's thesis, University of Oklahoma (Norman, Okla.), 1966. (*DA* 27:1629A)

104. SHRADER, EDWARD FRANKLYN. *A Descriptive Study of Students in the Precollege Summer Session Program, the University of Maryland, 1964–1965.* Doctor's thesis, George Washington University (Washington, D.C.), 1966. (*DA* 27:4104A)

105. SIMONIAN, CHARLES. *A Descriptive Analysis of Selected Male Freshmen Majoring in Physical Education at the Ohio State University.* Doctor's thesis, Ohio State University (Columbus, Ohio), 1966. (*DA* 27:2858A)

106. SPARKS, THOMASINE P. *A Study of the Relationships Between ACT Scores and Grades of Female Elementary Education Students.* Master's thesis, Texas College of Arts and Industries (Kingsville, Tex.), 1966.

107. WALKUP, MARY JO COLEMAN. *The Predictability of Success in Bowling and Badminton.* Doctor's thesis, University of Iowa (Iowa City, Iowa), 1966. (*DA* 27:4119A)

108. WILLIAMS, JACK. *An Investigation of the Relationships Between Selected Factors Concerning Student Teachers and Their Success in Student Teaching.* Doctor's thesis, University of Houston (Houston, Tex.), 1966. (*DA* 27:2820A)

109. ANDERSON, JAMES, AND WHITTEMORE, ROBERT G. "Predictive Utility of Certain Criteria for Advanced Freshman Mathematics Courses." *Math Teach* 60:619–20 O '67. *

110. BAIRD, LEONARD L. "The Educational Goals of College-Bound Youth." *ACT Res Rep* 19:1–28 Ap '67. *

111. BAIRD, LEONARD L. "Family Income and the Characteristics of College-Bound Students." *ACT Res Rep* 17:1–26 F '67. *

112. BARNETT, THOMAS MARVIN. *The Predictive Validities, as Measured by Multiple Correlation, of Two Batteries Using Academic Achievement as Criterion.* Doctor's thesis, North Texas State University (Denton, Tex.), 1967. (*DA* 28:2006A)

113. BOWERS, JOHN E. "Prediction of Freshman Achievement With a Moderator Model." *Ed & Psychol Meas* 27: 427–8 su '67. * (*PA* 41:14213)

114. BOWERS, JOHN E. "A Test of Variation in Grading Standards." *Ed & Psychol Meas* 27:429–30 su '67. * (*PA* 41:12822)

115. BROWN, F. G., AND SCOTT, D. A. "Differential Predictability in College Admissions Testing." *J Ed Meas* 4:163–6 f '67. *

116. DAVIS, KENNETH MARTIN. *Predicting College Success for Five Area Schools.* Master's thesis, Eastern Illinois University (Charleston, Ill.), 1967.

117. ELTON, CHARLES F. "Male Career Role and Vocational Choice: Their Prediction With Personality and Aptitude Variables." *J Counsel Psychol* 14:99–105 Mr '67. * (*PA* 41:7879)

118. ELTON, CHARLES F., AND ROSE, HARRIETT A. "Traditional Sex Attitudes and Discrepant Ability Measures in College Women." *J Counsel Psychol* 14:538–43 N '67. * (*PA* 42:4471)

119. FUNCHES, DeLARS. "Correlation Between Secondary School Transcript Averages and Grade Point Averages and Between ACT Scores and Grade Point Averages of Freshmen at Jackson State College." *Col & Univ* 43:52–4 f '67. *

120. HENDERSON, HARVEY CRIMMINS. *The Relationship Between Scholastic Aptitude and Confirmed vs. Non-Confirmed Responses to a Linear Program in the Physics of Sound as It Relates to Phonation.* Doctor's thesis, Ohio University (Athens, Ohio), 1967. (*DA* 28:3797A)

121. HIMMEL, KEITH LaVERN. *The Number of Years of High School Science as a Predictor of First Year College Success Compared With Other Predictors.* Doctor's thesis, Montana State University (Missoula, Mont.), 1967. (*DA* 28:3364A)

122. HOLLAND, JOHN L., AND RICHARDS, JAMES M., JR. "Academic and Nonacademic Accomplishment in a Repre-

sentative Sample of Students Taking the American College Tests." *Col & Univ* 43:60–71 f '67. *

123. HOLT, JUDITH MARKHAM. *A Study of the Relationship Between American College Test Scores and Achievement of Indian Students at Brigham Young University.* Master's thesis, Brigham Young University (Provo, Utah), 1967.

124. HUSTON, BEATRICE MOORE. *A Normative Survey of the Personal and Academic Characteristics of the Freshmen Women Students Enrolled in Mary Hardin-Baylor College, 1966–1967.* Doctor's thesis, Baylor University (Waco, Tex.), 1967. (*DA* 28:1209A)

125. JOHNSON, RICHARD, AND WARD, GEORGE, II. "A Comparison of the Wherry-Doolittle and Multiple Cutting Score Methods in Predicting Academic Performance." *Proc W Va Acad Sci* 39:75–7 '67. *

126. LANE, JAMES ALBERT. *Assessment of Physically Handicapped Adult Students in College.* Doctor's thesis, Ohio State University (Columbus, Ohio), 1967. (*DA* 28:3511A)

127. McCARY, ARTHUR DALE. *Personality Variables Associated With Five Levels of Academic Achievement Within Five Levels of Ability.* Doctor's thesis, University of Mississippi (University, Miss.), 1967. (*DA* 28:56A)

128. MARZOLF, STANLEY S. "Individual Variability on the ACT Tests." *J Ed Res* 61:184–5 D '67. *

129. MORRISON, W. LEE, AND ROMOSER, R. C. "'Traditional' Classroom Attitudes, the A.C.T. and the 16 P.F." *J Ed Res* 60:326–9 Mr '67. *

130. MUNDAY, LEO. "Predicting College Grades Using ACT Data." *Ed & Psychol Meas* 27:401–6 su '67. * (*PA* 41:14221)

131. PASSONS, WILLIAM R. "Predictive Validities of the ACT, SAT and High School Grades for First Semester GPA and Freshman Courses." *Ed & Psychol Meas* 27:1143–4 w '67. * (*PA* 42:9427)

132. POWELL, HOBART L. *A Comparative Study of the Relationship Between ACT Composite Scores and G.P.A. of Washington County Students at ETSU, 1965–66.* Master's thesis, East Tennessee State University (Johnson City, Tenn.), 1967.

133. RANGE, LEO HARRY. *A Comparison of ACT and SAT Standard Scores.* Master's thesis, St. Louis University (St. Louis, Mo.), 1967.

134. RICHARDS, JAMES M., JR., AND LUTZ, SANDRA W. "Predicting Student Accomplishment in College From the ACT Assessment." *ACT Res Rep* 21:1–38 Ag '67. * (*PA* 41:15295)

135. RICHARDS, JAMES M., JR.; HOLLAND, JOHN L.; AND LUTZ, SANDRA W. "Prediction of Student Accomplishment in College." *J Ed Psychol* 58:343–55 D '67. * (*PA* 42:4582)

136. SASSENRATH, J. M. "Anxiety, Aptitude, Attitude, and Achievement." *Psychol Sch* 4:341–6 O '67. * (*PA* 42:2949)

137. SMITH, HAROLD T. *An Analysis of Intellectual Factors Bearing on Success in the College of Business, Brigham Young University, Provo, Utah.* Doctor's thesis, Brigham Young University (Provo, Utah), 1967. (*DA* 28:2048A)

138. STEINBERG, MARVIN; SEGEL, RUEBEN H.; AND LEVINE, HARRY D. "Psychological Determinants of Academic Success: A Pilot Study." *Ed & Psychol Meas* 27:413–22 su '67. * (*PA* 41:14226)

139. VAN ERDEWYK, ZENO MARTIN. *Academic and Non-Academic Variables Related to Persistence, Transfer, and Attrition of Engineering Students.* Doctor's thesis, University of North Dakota (Grand Forks, N.D.), 1967. (*DA* 28:4453A)

140. WALKER, JIMMY REEVES. *A Study of Selected Psychosocial Correlates of College Student Subcultures.* Doctor's thesis, Oklahoma State University (Stillwater, Okla.), 1967. (*DA* 28:4883A)

141. WALTERS, ALTON W. *An Analysis of Freshman Year Grade Point Average and Expected Grade Point Average Compared to ACT Research Predictions.* Master's thesis, East Tennessee State University (Johnson City, Tenn.), 1967.

142. WILLIAMS, JACK, AND FOX, A. M. "Prediction of Performance in Student Teaching." *Ed & Psychol Meas* 27: 1169–70 w '67. * (*PA* 42:9491)

143. WORK, GERALD GEORGE. *Correlates of Academic Achievement for Female Sophomore Elementary Education Majors.* Doctor's thesis, Ohio University (Athens, Ohio), 1967. (*DA* 28:2926A)

144. ZIMMERMAN, WAYNE S., AND MICHAEL, WILLIAM B. "A Comparison of the Criterion-Related Validities of Three College Entrance Examinations With Different Content Emphases." *Ed & Psychol Meas* 27:407–12 su '67. * (*PA* 41: 12845)

145. ABRAMS, AMANDA ULM. *Magic Thinking and Anxiety in Junior College Freshmen.* Doctor's thesis, University of Maryland (College Park, Md.), 1968. (*DA* 29:3450A)

146. BAIRD, LEONARD L. "The Achievements of Bright and Average Students." *Ed & Psychol Meas* 28:891–9 au '68. * (*PA* 43:4514)

147. BAIRD, LEONARD L., AND RICHARDS, JAMES M., JR. "The Effects of Selecting College Students by Various Kinds of High School Achievement." *ACT Res Rep* 23:1–30 F '68. *

148. BAKKEN, ORLIN D. *Does the American College Test Serve as a Valid Predictor for the Electronics Technology Curriculum at the North Dakota State School of Science.* Master's thesis, North Dakota State University (Fargo, N.D.), 1968.

149. BENNETT, JAMES WELDON. *The Interrelationship of College Press, Student Needs, and Academic Aptitudes as Measured by Grade Point Average in a Southern Denominational College.* Doctor's thesis, North Texas State University (Denton, Tex.), 1968. (*DA* 29:474A)

150. BRADSHAW, OTTIE LEON. *The Relationship of Selected Measures of Aptitude, Interest, and Personality to Academic Achievement in Engineering and Engineering Technology.* Doctor's thesis, Oklahoma State University (Stillwater, Okla.), 1968. (*DAI* 30:979A)

151. BROOKS, WINONA NOLAND. *Relationships of Variables Identified With Success in College Clothing Construction Courses: A View Toward Advanced Placement and Improved Learning.* Doctor's thesis, University of Southern California (Los Angeles, Calif.), 1968. (*DA* 29:1701A)

152. BROWN, THOMAS O. *The Urban University Student: Selected Factors Related to Continuation and Withdrawal.* Doctor's thesis, Kent State University (Kent, Ohio), 1968. (*DA* 29:4318A)

153. BROWN, WILLIAM THOMAS. *Consideration of the Interrelationship of Five Aptitude and Achievement Factors in Successful Male Undergraduate Students at the University of Montana.* Doctor's thesis, University of Montana (Missoula, Mont.), 1968. (*DA* 29:3411A)

154. CLEVENGER, WALTER SCHOBAL. *A Study to Determine the Relationship Between Certain Academic Factors and the Grade Earned in Business Education 347 at Northern Illinois University.* Master's thesis, Northern Illinois University (DeKalb, Ill.), 1968. (Abstract: *Nat Bus Ed Q* 38:9)

155. CORSINI, RAYMOND J., AND BORGATTA, EDGAR F. "The Quick Number Test (QNT)." *J Exp Ed* 36:7–10 su '68. *

156. DOBBINS, HOWARD JACK. *The Relationship of the Variability of the Subtest Scores on the American College Test and Prediction of Academic Achievement of College Freshmen.* Doctor's thesis, University of Tulsa (Tulsa, Okla.), 1968. (*DAI* 30:128A)

157. FISHER, RHEUA DALE SPICKELMIER. *A Study of Grades and Test Scores in a Selective Admissions Program for Teacher Education.* Doctor's thesis, Oklahoma State University (Stillwater, Okla.), 1968. (*DAI* 30:986A)

158. GRAY, STUART C. "A Study of the Relationships of Prospective Teachers' Choice of Subject Matter Field to Their Academic Aptitudes." Abstract. *J Teach Ed* 19:116–7 sp '68. *

159. GREEN, JOHNNIE HENDERSON. *An Analysis of Academic Proficiency of the 1965–66 Beginning Freshman Class, School of Business, Texas Southern University, Houston, Texas.* Doctor's thesis, University of Houston (Houston, Tex.), 1968. (*DA* 29:3323A)

160. HANSEN, EDA A. *The Relationship Between Grade Point Averages of the Henmon-Nelson Test of Mental Ability and the American College Test.* Master's thesis, Utah State University (Logan, Utah), 1968.

161. HOYT, DONALD P. "Description and Prediction of Diversity Among Four-Year Colleges." *Meas & Eval Guid* 1:16–26 sp '68. *

162. HOYT, DONALD P. "Description and Prediction of Diversity Among Junior Colleges." *Personnel & Guid J* 46:997–1004 Je '68. *

163. HOYT, DONALD P. "Forecasting Academic Success in Specific Colleges." *ACT Res Rep* 27:1–52 Ag '68. *

164. HOYT, DONALD P. "Generalized Academic Prediction in Four-Year Colleges." *Personnel & Guid J* 47:130–6 O '68. * (*PA* 43:11926)

165. HOYT, DONALD P., AND MUNDAY, LEO A. *Your College Freshmen: Interpretive Guide to ACT Research Services for Higher Education, 1968–69 Edition.* Iowa City, Iowa: American College Testing Program, Inc., 1968. Pp. vii, 249. *

166. HUMPHREYS, LLOYD G. "The Fleeting Nature of the Prediction of College Academic Success." *J Ed Psychol* 59:375–80 O '68. * (*PA* 42:19409)

167. JENNINGS, JO ANN. *Preadmission Information and First Quarter Persistence of Freshman Students Admitted on Probation at a Large Midwestern University.* Doctor's thesis, St. Louis University (St. Louis, Mo.), 1968. (*DA* 29:2481A)

168. KISH, GEORGE B., AND DONNENWERTH, GREGORY. "Sex Differences in the Relationship Between Sensation-Seeking and Scholastic Aptitude." *Newsl Res Psychol* 10:10–2 My '68. *

169. LEDBETTER, PEGGY JEAN. *An Analysis of the Performance of Graduates of a Selected Baccalaureate Program in Nursing With Regard to Selected Standardized Examinations.* Doctor's thesis, University of Alabama (University, Ala.), 1968. (*DA* 29:3381A)

170. LUTZ, SANDRA W. "Do They Do What They Say They Will Do?" *ACT Res Rep* 24:1–31 Mr '68. *

171. MARSHALL, JOSEPH JEMERSON. *Non-Cognitive Variables as a Predictor of Academic Achievement Among Freshmen, Sophomores, and Juniors at Abilene Christian College.* Doctor's thesis, Baylor University (Waco, Tex.), 1968. (*DA* 29:3833A)

172. MERCADO, AUREA ADRIAS. *American College Test Assessment of Educational Hierarchies and Scholastic Survival at the University of the Philippines.* Doctor's thesis, University of Maryland (College Park, Md.), 1968. (*DA* 29:3422A)

173. MILLER, RICHARD HADDEN. *A Descriptive Study of the Relationship Between Potential and Performance of Freshman Students at the University of South Dakota.* Doctor's thesis, University of South Dakota (Vermillion, S.D.), 1968. (*DA* 29:2612A)

174. MONTERO, PAUL. *The Predictive Validity of the National Merit Scholarship Qualifying Test, the American College Test, and Three Year High School Grade Point Average for Academic Success at Louisiana State University in New Orleans.* Master's thesis, University of Alabama (University, Ala.), 1968.

175. MUNDAY, LEO. "Correlations Between ACT and Other Predictors of Academic Success in College." *Col & Univ* 44:67–76 f '68. *

176. MUNDAY, LEO A. "A Comparison of Junior College Students in Transfer and Terminal Curricula." *J Col Stud Personnel* 9:325–9 S '68. *

177. PAVEK, FRANCIS LESLIE. *The Relationship of Non-Academic High School Variables to College Achievement and Participation in Selected Extra-Curricular Activities.* Doctor's thesis, University of North Dakota (Grand Forks, N.D.), 1968. (*DA* 29:2968A)

178. PETERS, BILL EUGENE. *Comparison of 1966 and 1967 Freshman Students at the Colorado State College Admitted Under Two Sets of Admission Standards.* Doctor's thesis, Colorado State College (Greeley, Colo.), 1968. (*DA* 29:2492A)

179. PLANISEK, R. J., AND MERRIFIELD, P. R. "Ability, Study Habits, and Academic Performance Correlates of the Theoretical-Practical Value Characteristics Inventory (TPCI)." Abstract. *Proc 76th Ann Conv Am Psychol Assn* 3:159–60 '68. *

180. PRATT, MICHAEL, AND ALEAMONI, LAWRENCE M. *Predicting the Academic Performance of the Fall, 1967 Freshmen Engineering Students.* Research Report No. 277. Champaign, Ill.: Measurement and Research Division, Office of Instructional Resources, University of Illinois, 1968. Pp. 6. *

181. PUGH, RICHARD C., AND SASSENRATH, JULIUS M. "Comparable Scores for the CEEB Scholastic Aptitude Test and the American College Test Program." *Meas & Eval Guid* 1:103–9 su '68. * (*PA* 44:9266)

182. READ, JOHN WILLIAM. *An Investigation of the Relationship of Selected Variables to Sight-Singing Ability.* Doctor's thesis, North Texas State University (Denton, Tex.), 1968. (*DAI* 30:358A)

183. REDFORD, JEANETTE. *A Comparison of Selected Factors in the Prediction of Academic Success at Southwest Mississippi Junior College.* Doctor's thesis, University of Southern Mississippi (Hattiesburg, Miss.), 1968. (*DA* 29:1109A)

184. RICHARDS, JAMES M., JR., AND LUTZ, SANDRA W. "Predicting Student Accomplishment in College From the ACT Assessment." *J Ed Meas* 5:17–29 sp '68. * (*PA* 42:14503)

185. SEVERINSEN, K. NORMAN. "A.C.T., W.A.I.S. Test Scores and College Grades." *J Ed Meas* 5:161–2 su '68. *

186. SPENCER, RICHARD E., AND STALLINGS, WILLIAM M. "The Student Profile Section of ACT Related to Academic Success." *J Col Stud Personnel* 9:177–9 My '68. *

187. SPURLIN, MELVIN DAVID. *A Study of the Relationship of Sex, Ability Level and Biology Preparation to Achievement in Freshman Biology at Metropolitan State College.* Doctor's thesis, University of Colorado (Boulder, Colo.), 1968. (*DA* 29:1173A)

188. TURNER, VERAS DEAN. *Prediction of Success as a Mathematics Major at the Minnesota State Colleges.* Doctor's thesis, University of Oklahoma (Norman, Okla.), 1968. (*DA* 29:2099A)

189. TURNIPSEED, JORJA POUND. *Academic Success of Junior College Transfer Students as Compared to Native Students at the University of Southern Mississippi.* Doctor's thesis, University of Southern Mississippi (Hattiesburg, Miss.), 1968. (*DA* 29:2908A)

190. YARINGTON, DAVID JON. *A Study of the Relationships Between the Reading Done by College Freshmen and Aptitude and Scholastic Achievement.* Doctor's thesis, University of Pennsylvania (Philadelphia, Pa.), 1968. (*DA* 29:1694A)

191. *The Two-Year College and Its Students: An Empirical Report.* Monograph Two. Iowa City, Iowa: American College Testing Program, 1969. Pp. vii, 157. *

192. BAIRD, LEONARD L. "Prediction of Academic and Nonacademic Achievement in Two-Year Colleges From the ACT Assessment." *Ed & Psychol Meas* 29(2):421–30 su '69. * (*PA* 44:17500)

193. BAIRD, LEONARD L. "The Prediction of Grades in Occupational and Academic Curricula in 2-Year Colleges." *J Ed Meas* 6(4):247–54 w '69. * (*PA* 44:17501)

194. BALDWIN, JEAN MARGARET. *An Analysis of the Relationship Between Self-Esteem, Academic Achievement, and Academic Level of Aspiration for a Group of College Students.* Doctor's thesis, University of Maryland (College Park, Md.), 1969. (*DAI* 31:209A)

195. BECHTOLD, DONALD WILLIAM. *Dynamic Structures of Occupational Choice of High School Seniors.* Doctor's thesis, Catholic University of America (Washington, D.C.), 1969. (*DAI* 30:2322A)

196. BOGUE, E. G., AND FOX, RAY P. "Feedback of College Grades to High Schools." *Personnel & Guid J* 48(3):210–7 N '69. *

197. CASSEL, RUSSELL N., AND EICHSTEADT, ARDEN C. "Factorial Structure of CQT, ACT, and SAT Test Scores for 50

Available College Freshmen." *J Psychol* 71(2):199–204 Mr '69. * (*PA* 43:8675)

198. CHRISTENSON, JEFFRY MILTON. *A Study of the Differences Between Seekers and Non-Seekers at a College Counseling Center.* Doctor's thesis, University of South Dakota (Vermillion, S.D.), 1969. (*DAI* 30:2326A)

199. COLE, NANCY S. "Differential Validity in Tests of Academic Ability." Abstract. *Proc 77th Ann Conv Am Psychol Assn* 4(1):175–6 '69. * (*PA* 43:17904)

200. COLE, NANCY S. "Differential Validity in the ACT Tests." *ACT Res Rep* 30:1–8 Ag '69. * (*PA* 45:2943)

201. DENISON, WALTER MARSHALL. *A Study of Three Interest Inventories Currently in Use at Central Virginia Community College.* Doctor's thesis, University of Virginia (Charlottesville, Va.), 1969. (*DAI* 31:996A)

202. DUBLIN, JAMES E.; ELTON, CHARLES F.; AND BERZINS, JURIS I. "Some Personality and Aptitudinal Correlates of the 'A-B' Therapist Scale." *J Consult & Clin Psychol* 33(6):739–45 D '69. * (*PA* 44:3595)

203. DYRHAUG, DONALD ROBERT. *Expectations Concerning the College Experience as They Relate to the Academic Achievement and Persistence of Freshmen.* Doctor's thesis, University of Minnesota (Minneapolis, Minn.), 1969. (*DAI* 30:2373A)

204. ELTON, CHARLES F. "Prediction of Educational Outcomes Among Junior College Students." *J Col Stud Personnel* 10(1):44–6 Ja '69. *

205. ELTON, CHARLES F., AND SHEVEL, LINDA R. "Who Is Talented? An Analysis of Achievement." *ACT Res Rep* 31:1–13 S '69. * (*PA* 45:3058)

206. FAIRCHILD, PATRICIA CARLETTE. *Grade Point Average and Variance as Criteria of College Academic Performance.* Doctor's thesis, University of Oklahoma (Norman, Okla.), 1969. (*DAI* 30:3318A)

207. FLAMINI, DOMINIC WILLIAM. *Competitive Strategies in Obtaining Grades.* Doctor's thesis, University of Oklahoma (Norman, Okla.), 1969. (*DAI* 30:580A)

208. GOLDBERG, LEONARD SEYMOUR. *Negroid-Caucasoid Differences Among College Freshmen.* Doctor's thesis, Ohio State University (Columbus, Ohio), 1969. (*DAI* 30:2724A)

209. GORDON, JAMES HALE. *A Comparison of Selected Characteristics of Students Entering Five Campuses of Ohio University.* Doctor's thesis, Ohio University (Athens, Ohio), 1969. (*DAI* 30:2332A)

210. GRADY, WILLIAM ELLIS. *Selected Variables Related to Academic Achievement of American and Canadian Male Freshmen at the University of North Dakota.* Doctor's thesis, University of North Dakota (Grand Forks, N.D.), 1969. (*DAI* 30:3725A)

211. GROENKE, GLENN RUSSELL. *The Relationship of the Entrance Examination Score to Grade Point Average of Junior College Freshmen When Classified by Age, Sex, and Curriculum.* Doctor's thesis, Arizona State University (Tempe, Ariz.), 1969. (*DAI* 30:3709A)

212. HARMAN, ROBERT LEE. *Predicting Persistence in College From Information in High School Cumulative Records.* Doctor's thesis, University of Nebraska (Lincoln, Neb.), 1969. (*DAI* 30:1397A)

213. HARRINGTON, CHARLES. "Forecasting College Performance From Biographical Data." *J Col Stud Personnel* 10(3):156–60 My '69. *

214. HAYES, VIRGINIA. *A Study of Personality and Achievement Variables of Successful and Unsuccessful Shorthand Students at the University of Alabama.* Doctor's thesis, University of Alabama (University, Ala.), 1969. (*DAI* 31:66A)

215. HOWLETT, JOHN L. "A Study of Placement Methods for Entering College Freshmen in the Proper Mathematics Sequence at Michigan Technological University." *Math Teach* 62(8):651–9 D '69. *

216. HUCKABEE, MALCOM W. "Personality and Academic Aptitude Correlates of Cognitive Control Principles." *South J Ed Res* 3(1):1–9 Ja '69. *

217. IRVIN, FLOYD S. "The Relationship Between Manifest Anxiety and Measures of Aptitude, Achievement, and Interest." *Ed & Psychol Meas* 29(4):957–61 w '69. * (*PA* 44:20950)

218. JONES, ANN O. *The Prediction of Physical Education Skill Grade Point Average Based Upon Motor Ability and ACT Scores.* Master's thesis, San Diego State College (San Diego, Calif.), 1969.

219. KEEFER, KARL E. "Self-Prediction of Academic Achievement by College Students." *J Ed Res* 63(2):53–6 O '69. *

220. LENNING, OSCAR THOMAS. *Student Factors Related to Educational Growth at a Church Related Liberal Arts College.* Doctor's thesis, University of Iowa (Iowa City, Iowa), 1969. (*DAI* 30:4225A)

221. LENNING, OSCAR T.; MUNDAY, LEO A.; AND MAXEY, E. JAMES. "Student Educational Growth During the First Two Years of College." *Col & Univ* 44(2):145–53 w '69. *

222. LONNING, PHILIP EUGENE. *Characteristics of Full-Time Students Enrolled in Area II and Area V Community Colleges.* Doctor's thesis, Iowa State University (Ames, Iowa), 1969. (*DAI* 30:4779A)

223. McCLENNEY, BYRON NELSON. *A Comparison of Personality Characteristics, Self-Concepts, and Academic Aptitude of Selected College Men Classified According to Performance*

on a Test of Physical Fitness. Doctor's thesis, University of Texas (Austin, Tex.), 1969. (*DAI* 30:1423A)

224. MAIN, NOBLE JAMES. *A Study of the Dropouts Among Music Majors in Four Church Related Liberal Arts Colleges.* Doctor's thesis, University of Oklahoma (Norman, Okla.), 1969. (*DAI* 30:3281A)

225. MOEGENBURG, LOUIS ARTHUR. *An Experimental Comparison of Programed Instruction Versus Video-Tape Television in Teaching Selected Orthographic Projection Concepts.* Doctor's thesis, Texas A & M University (College Station, Tex.), 1969. (*DAI* 30:4802A)

226. MOORE, JAMES C. "Using 'ACT' Battery to Recruit Honors Students." *Improving Col & Univ Teach* 17(3):215–6 su '69. *

227. MRIZEK, DAVID EMIL. *The Effects of Interest and Scholastic Ability Upon Listening Retention.* Master's thesis, Eastern Illinois University (Charleston, Ill.), 1969.

228. NIELSON, CHARLES L. *A Study of the Relation Between Selected Academic Factors and Performance on the I-E Scale.* Doctor's thesis, University of North Dakota (Grand Forks, N.D.), 1969. (*DAI* 30:1402A)

229. PARASKEVOPOULOS, JOHN, AND ROBINSON, L. F. "Comparison of College Performance of Cold War Veterans and Non-Veterans." *Col & Univ* 44(2):189–91 w '69. *

230. PARSONS, TERRY WAYNE. *A Descriptive Analysis of the Achievement Level Realized by Grant-in-Aid Athletes as Compared to Matched Non-Athletes at the Ohio State University.* Doctor's thesis, Ohio State University (Columbus, Ohio), 1969. (*DAI* 30:4263A)

231. PEERSON, RICHARD HAWES. *Analysis of Variables Predictive of Student Success in Community Colleges.* Doctor's thesis, United States International University (San Diego, Calif.), 1969. (*DAI* 30:2808A)

232. PROUSE, HOWARD, AND TURNER, V. DEAN. "Factors Contributing to Success in Calculus II." *J Ed Res* 62(10):439–40 Jl–Ag '69. *

233. RAMOS, ROBERT ANTHONY. *An Investigation of the Effect of Moderator Variables on the Regression and Factor Structure of Predictors and Criteria.* Doctor's thesis, University of Tennessee (Knoxville, Tenn.), 1969. (*DAI* 30:5275B)

234. REID, BARBARA ANN. *A Comparison Between Undergraduate Special Education Students Who Changed and Those Who Did Not Change Their Major.* Doctor's thesis, Colorado State College (Greeley, Colo.), 1969. (*DAI* 30:1757A)

235. RUSSO, JOSEPH FRANK. *Predicting Academic Achievement of Students in Arizona Junior Colleges.* Doctor's thesis, Arizona State University (Tempe, Ariz.), 1969. (*DAI* 30:2309A)

236. SCHLICK, EARL FRANK. *Academic Success of Junior College Students Admitted on Basis of High School Equivalency Certificates.* Doctor's thesis, Arizona State University (Tempe, Ariz.), 1969. (*DA* 29:2077A)

237. SIEVEKING, NICHOLAS A., AND SAVITSKY, JEFFREY C. "Evaluation of an Achievement Test, Prediction of Grades, and Composition of Discussion Groups in College Chemistry." *J Res Sci Teach* 6(4):374–6 '69. *

238. STALLINGS, WILLIAM M., AND ANDERSON, FRANCES E. "Some Characteristics and Correlates of the Meier Art Test of Aesthetic Perception Under Two Systems of Scoring." *J Ed Meas* 6(3):179–85 f '69. * (*PA* 44:14571)

239. STONE, THOMAS CARL. *A Case Study: Predictors of Success in Post-High School Vocational Trade, Industrial, and Technical Programs.* Doctor's thesis, Colorado State University (Ft. Collins, Colo.), 1969. (*DAI* 30:4348A)

240. TAYLOR, RONALD G., AND HANSON, GARY R. "Pre-College Math-Workshop and Freshman Achievement." *J Ed Res* 63(4):157–60 D '69. *

241. TOWNER, JOHN C. *The Relationship Between Area of Study and American College Testing Scores of Recent Degree Graduates at Wisconsin State University—River Falls.* Master's thesis, Wisconsin State University (River Falls, Wis.), 1969.

242. VRAA, CALVIN WOODROW. *The Relation of Selected Academic, Biographical and Personality Factors to the Achievement of Canadian College Freshmen.* Doctor's thesis, University of North Dakota (Grand Forks, N.D.), 1969. (*DAI* 31:168A)

243. WELKER, JAMES DOYT. *Selected Factors and Achievement in an Audio-Tutorial Introductory College Biology Course.* Doctor's thesis, Indiana University (Bloomington, Ind.), 1969. (*DAI* 31:249A)

244. WHEELER, JUDITH E. *Usefulness of the ACT Scores and High School Rank in Predicting Academic Success of Freshmen at Wisconsin State University—Platteville.* Master's thesis, Wisconsin State University (Platteville, Wis.), 1969.

245. WHIPKEY, KENNETH LEE. *A Study of the Interrelationship Between Mathematical Attitude and Mathematical Achievement.* Doctor's thesis, Case Western Reserve University (Cleveland, Ohio), 1969. (*DAI* 30:3808A)

246. WHORTON, JAMES EDWARD. *A Study of Academic Predictors for College Students Majoring in Special Education.* Doctor's thesis, Colorado State College (Greeley, Colo.), 1969. (*DAI* 30:1904A)

247. WORSLEY, ROGER LEWIS. *An Analysis of Selected Variables and the Prediction of the Educational Achievement of Junior College Freshmen.* Doctor's thesis, Arizona State University (Tempe, Ariz.), 1969. (*DAI* 30:3705A)

248. WORTHINGTON, LOIS ELAINE HUCKO. *A Study of Factors Related to First Quarter Academic Success at the University of Utah.* Doctor's thesis, University of Utah (Salt Lake City, Utah), 1969. (*DAI* 30:1884A)

249. ABE, CLIFFORD. *The Prediction of Academic Achievement of Mexican-American Students.* Doctor's thesis, University of Arizona (Tucson, Ariz.), 1970. (*DAI* 31:4535A)

250. ABELL, WILLIAM RUSSELL. *A Comparison of Selected Characteristics of Successful and Unsuccessful Students in a Junior College Remedial Program.* Doctor's thesis, Wayne State University (Detroit, Mich.), 1970. (*DAI* 31:3284A)

251. BERDIE, RALPH F.; PILAPIL, BONIFACIO; AND IM, IN JAE. "Entrance Correlates of University Satisfaction." *Am Ed Res J* 7(2):251–66 Mr '70. *

252. BIGGS, DONALD A., AND TINSLEY, DIANE J. "Student-Made Academic Predictions." *J Ed Res* 63(5):195–7 Ja '70. *

253. CARLSON, STANLEY LLOYD. *Differences in Aptitude, Previous Achievement, and Nonintellectual Traits (Personality, Values, Interest, and Attitude Toward Mathematics) of Freshmen Mathematics Majors and Transfers From the Mathematics Major at the University of Northern Colorado.* Doctor's thesis, University of Northern Colorado (Greeley, Colo.), 1970. (*DAI* 31:3768A)

254. CHAMBLISS, CHARLES ALVAH. *The Use of Personality Variables and Personal Data in Predicting Student Preference for a Proposed Set of Degree Requirements.* Doctor's thesis, University of Arkansas (Fayetteville, Ark.), 1970. (*DAI* 31:1031A)

255. DAVIS, SAMUEL C.; LOEB, JANE W.; AND ROBINSON, LEHYMANN F. "A Comparison of Characteristics of Negro and White College Freshman Classmates." *J Negro Ed* 39(4):359–66 f '70. *

256. ELTON, CHARLES F., AND ROSE, HARRIETT A. "Male Occupational Constancy and Change: Its Prediction According to Holland's Theory." *J Counsel Psychol Monogr* 17(6):1–19 N '70. * (*PA* 45:5123)

257. ERNEST, DAVID J. "The Predication of Academic Success of College Music Majors." *J Res Music Ed* 18(3):273–6 f '70. * (*PA* 45:8994)

258. GANSER, CARL J. "Understanding of Economic Concepts by Business Education and Social Studies Undergraduate Teaching Majors." *Delta Pi Epsilon J* 12(4):10–21 Ag '70. *

259. HANSON, GARY R., AND TAYLOR, RONALD G. "Interaction of Ability and Personality: Another Look at the Drop-Out Problem in an Institute of Technology." *J Counsel Psychol* 17(6):540–5 N '70. * (*PA* 45:3036)

260. HARRIS, GEORGE. *A Study Predicting Probable Success in College Among Freshmen at Tougaloo College Utilizing ACT Scores.* Master's thesis, Jackson State College (Jackson, Miss.), 1970.

261. HOFLAND, DEAN MYRON. *A Study of Selected Characteristics of Freshman Male Students Who Choose a Major and Those Who Do Not Choose a Major Upon Matriculation.* Doctor's thesis, University of South Dakota (Vermillion, S.D.), 1970. (*DAI* 31:3269A)

262. HOUNTRAS, PETER T., AND BRANDT, KENNETH R. "Relation of Student Residence to Academic Performance in College." *J Ed Res* 63(8):351–4 Ap '70. *

263. HOUNTRAS, PETER T.; GRADY, WILLIAM E.; AND VRAA, CALVIN W. "Manifest Anxiety and Academic Achievement of American and Canadian College Freshmen." *J Psychol* 76(1):3–8 S '70. * (*PA* 45:3037)

264. KIMBALL, JACK E., AND TOLMAN, HUBERT. "College ACT Data Information Storage and Retrieval." *J Ed Data Processing* 7(4):229–38 '70. *

265. LAUTZ, ROBERT; MACLEAN, G. DONALD; VAUGHAN, ANDREW T.; AND OLIVER, THOMAS C. "Characteristics of Successful Students Following Academic Suspension." *Col & Univ* 45(2):192–202 w '70. *

266. LOEB, JANE W., AND MUELLER, DANIEL J. "The Use of a Scale of High Schools in Predicting College Grades." *Ed & Psychol Meas* 30(2):381–6 su '70. * (*PA* 45:3063)

267. MILLSAPS, TEDDY W. *A Study Using the ACT and Four Year GPA to Establish the Predictive Validity for Academic Success at Middle Tennessee University for Graduates of Red Bank High School.* Master's thesis, University of Alabama (University, Ala.), 1970.

268. MORGAN, MARGARET KNOX. *The OPI, the ACT and University Attrition: A Discriminant Analysis.* Doctor's thesis, University of Kentucky (Lexington, Ky.), 1970. (*DAI* 31:3906A)

269. MUNDAY, LEO A. "Factors Influencing the Predictability of College Grades." *Am Ed Res J* 7(1):99–107 Ja '70. *

270. NASH, JOHN MORTON. *Prediction of Academic Achievement of Women at a Private Junior College Through Use of Certain Intellective and Family Relationships Measures.* Doctor's thesis, Boston University (Boston, Mass.), 1970. (*DAI* 31:2113A)

271. PARASKEVOPOULOS, JOHN, AND ROBINSON, L. F. "Comparison of Regression Equations Predicting College Performance From High School Record and Admissions Test Scores for Males and Females." *Col & Univ* 45(2):211–6 w '70. *

272. PARKS, KATHRYN J. *A Study to Determine the Relationship of Motor Educability and American College Test Scores to Skill Achievement.* Master's thesis, San Diego State College (San Diego, Calif.), 1970.

273. PEHRSON, PATRICIA J. *A Comparison of Student Achievement in Shorthand and Performance on the Turse Test and the ACT Test at Mankato State College.* Master's thesis, Mankato State College (Mankato, Minn.), 1970.

274. PITTMAN, FRANK MALLORY, JR. *An Investigation of the Predictive Value of Selected Factors on Achievement in Beginning Woodworking, Metalworking, and Electricity-Electronics Courses at the College Level.* Doctor's thesis, Texas A & M University (College Station, Tex.), 1970. (*DAI* 31:2149A)

275. SANDERS, ROBERT GENE. *The Relationship of Achievement and Personality Variables for Graduating Seniors Between Test Performances on the American College Test and the Edwards Personality Preference Schedule.* Doctor's thesis, University of Oklahoma (Norman, Okla.), 1970. (*DAI* 31:648A)

276. SMART, JOHN C.; ELTON, CHARLES F.; AND BURNETT, COLLINS W. "Underachievers and Overachievers in Intermediate French." *Mod Lang J* 54(6):415–20 O '70. *

277. SOLES, JAMES HENRY. *A Comparative Study of the Academic Performance of Three Selected Groups of Students Entering Troy State University.* Doctor's thesis, University of Alabama (University, Ala.), 1970. (*DAI* 31:1554A)

278. WILLIAMS, OSCAR C. *A Study of the Relationship Between High School Averages and College Success and Between ACT Composite Score and College Success.* Master's thesis, Jackson State College (Jackson, Miss.), 1970.

279. WYNNE, JOHN T., AND MURPHY, PATRICK S. "Using the Strong Vocational Interest Blank Diversity Scale Score as a Predictor of Freshman Academic Success." *Col Ed Rec* 55(9):203–6 Je '70. *

WIMBURN L. WALLACE, *Director, Professional Examinations Division, The Psychological Corporation, New York, New York.*

The American College Testing Program was initiated in 1959. Its adoption as a college admission examination has grown very rapidly since that time to the point where nearly a million students now take it annually throughout the country.

ACT's student assessment program comprises four tests of educational development and scholastic ability plus a questionnaire about high school grades, vocational and educational plans, family background, extracurricular activities, etc. The four tests are in English usage, mathematics usage, social studies reading, and natural sciences reading. They are direct descendants of the *Iowa Tests of Educational Development.*

Recent forms of the English usage test contain 75 items with a 40-minute time limit. Earlier forms contained 80 items with a time of 50 minutes. The test consists of four fairly lengthy, contiguous reading passages in which words or phrases are underlined and alternates of "no change" or different expressions are offered for the underlined sections. The task is to select the alternative "that best expresses the idea, makes the statement grammatically correct or [sic] more precise, or is worded most consistently with the style and tone of the passage as a whole." With these somewhat vague instructions, unequivocal right answers might occasionally be difficult to defend. Several ACT publications state that this test "measures the student's understanding and use of the basic elements in correct and effective writing—punctuation, capitalization, usage, phraseology, style, and organization." Although such may be the intent or goal, no evidence is presented that the test actually does measure these skills, especially the student's use of the basic elements listed.

The mathematics usage test consists of 40 items in arithmetic, algebra, and plane geometry with a 50-minute time limit. The emphasis on geometry varies among different forms of the test. The problems are of the traditional variety, reflecting little or no "modern mathematics." In an apparent attempt to give the test some flavor of practicality, there are many wordy problems; the stem for one item contains 69 words. This format would seem to vitiate the independence of this test from the three other parts of the ACT which are all essentially reading tests.

The social studies reading test contains 52 items. Although earlier forms with the same number of items had a time limit of 40 minutes, current forms allow only 35 minutes. Thirty-seven of the items are based on four reading passages, and the remaining 15 are miscellaneous information from the social studies area. Descriptions about the test state that it measures "the evaluative reasoning and problem-solving skills needed in the social studies." Evidence for this claim is lacking; indeed, it would be most difficult to substantiate any such statement.

Similarly, the natural sciences reading test is a 52-item, 35-minute (formerly 40-minute) section with 37 of the items based on four reading passages of scientific content and 15 items of general science knowledge. Content is not limited to "natural" science as differentiated from "physical science"; the section could more simply and accurately be labeled just "science." It is claimed that the test "measures the critical reasoning and problem-solving skills required in the natural sciences." This assertion generates an appreciable degree of skepticism.

All the items in the ACT are of the multiple choice type. Those in the mathematics section have five options, while the rest have four options. The reason for this discrepancy is not evident. The arrangement of the items in the test booklets is excellent with adequate spacing and easy readability. However, the quality of the construction of many of the items is poor. Stems often fail to define the question or problem at all, and nonparallel

options are not uncommon. Following are some examples of inadequate stems:

> The weight of an object
> The deadlock between Hindu and Moslem
> Speaker 4's argument is
> Joule's experiments were
> Which of the following is most likely true of the author?
> Why is $(7 - 5) - 3 \neq 7 - (5 - 3)$?
> Which of the following is a name for 1?

For this last item, one option is "$2[(\frac{1}{3})(\frac{3}{2})]$," and another is "none of these."

Among the social studies and natural science items there are a great many stems which begin, "Which of the following" usually requiring the student to read through all the options to find the accurate one. This type devolves into a series of four true-false statements rather than a central question or problem to be recognized and answered.

Although most ACT publications are revised and updated annually, the latest ACT Technical Report available for this review was the 1965 edition. The report describes the development and equating of new test forms, scales and norms, reliability estimates, and summaries of some validity studies.

Draft items for new forms of the ACT are tried out on Iowa high school students, and item analysis is performed with the ITED as the criterion measure. Final forms are equated by the equipercentile method to old forms, using principally students at regular ACT centers in Iowa. Since each of the ACT subtests is equated to the corresponding ITED subtest, the national norms for the latter can be used for interpreting ACT scores of high school students. Beyond that, ACT has developed many sets of norms for individual colleges, regions, type of school, etc. There is a great abundance of normative data on the ACT fully accompanied by helpful descriptive information.

The scale score system used for the ACT is the same as that for the ITED. Scale scores range from 1 to 36 with the standard deviation intentionally set at approximately 5 so that the probable error of measurement would conveniently be about one scale score unit if the reliability coefficient were .91. Unfortunately, reliabilities for the ACT tend to be lower than for ITED, so the rule of thumb about the probable error of measurement does not so readily apply. The mean scale score for unselected first semester high school seniors is approximately 16, while the mean for college bound seniors is about 20.

Although summaries or distributions of item analysis data are not published for the ACT, printouts of item difficulties and validities and of distributions of responses on the forms used in 1968–1969 were provided to this reviewer. In general these data are satisfactory despite the fact that the discrimination index for several items fell below .20 with one reaching into the negative area at −.09. Item difficulties have a wide range. The difficulty of the mathematics items is such that an average of about 45 percent of the students get each item correct, while an average of about 60 percent answer each item correctly in the English usage test. The mean difficulty of items in the other two tests falls between these extremes. Why such a discrepancy was created among the tests is not evident.

Reliabilities of successive forms of the ACT are estimated by the odd-even procedure. The Technical Report asserts that this method is recommended by Gulliksen in his *Theory of Mental Tests,* whereas actually Gulliksen (pp. 236–237) specifically warns against the use of this procedure with speeded tests. Since many students do not finish the parts of the ACT within the time limits, it may be concluded that the reliability coefficients reported are spuriously high. One inadequate study of parallel form reliability is reported in the Technical Report. It is based on 433 high school students who had been nominated for a competitive scholarship program in 1964. Interform correlations ranged from .69 in natural sciences to .86 on the Composite. Further studies of alternate form reliability are needed. Current evidence indicates that ACT reliabilities may be somewhat low for individual decisions.

Validation of the ACT has been very extensive with consistently good results. There is a vigorous and ongoing program of checking the validity of the ACT for predicting college grades. For every participating college that cooperates by providing the necessary criterion data, separate validity studies are performed. Furthermore, the predictive effectiveness of the ACT scores is analyzed by course or subject-matter groupings within schools as well as by programs such as business administration, engineering, education, and art. This wide variety of situations, of course, yields a broad range of validity coefficients, but it is estimated that the central tendency of the distribution of correlations between ACT Composite scores and overall grade point averages is about .50. In spite of the numerous criticisms of the ACT in this review, it must be emphasized that the most crucial characteristic of the examination, its predictive validity, proves to be as satisfactory as the state of the measurement art currently permits.

To enhance the accuracy of the prediction of college grades, ACT regularly incorporates self-reported high school grades with the test scores. The combined index provides a moderate gain in validity coefficients over either predictor alone, as might be expected.

In the Technical Report and other ACT literature there is an appeal to reviewers to consider the content validity of the ACT. It asks the reader "to try to determine the intellectual processes required to respond correctly to each item. In this way the reviewer can determine for himself to what degree the skills and understandings required by [sic] the examinee are similar to those required for the student in reading and study situations in college." This suggestion is patently inappropriate. In the case of the ACT, the topic of validity should be left well enough alone with the ample evidence of good predictive validity.

The few available reports of intercorrelations among the four ACT tests yield sets of data somewhat different from each other presumably because of sampling variations. In general these interrelationships are high, tending to confirm the observation that the ACT contains a redundancy of similar intellectual exercises all dependent to some degree on reading comprehension. A more telling indication of this condition is the fact that there is extremely little incremental validity gained by the addition of more of the parts of the ACT after the first test in a multiple correlation pattern. Indeed, all four parts optimally weighted appear to have practically no advantage over the one best predictor of the four.

There have been essentially no efforts made toward the development of new test types for the ACT. There is need for such work. A reasonable portion of the resources of ACT should be devoted to the exploration of improved testing techniques. Some varieties of assessments of intellectual skills are particularly called for in this battery which currently comprises such a concentration of reading comprehension. Although the ITED prototype has proved useful in the prediction of academic success, some improvements on that 30-year-old model should be attempted.

The ancillary services offered by ACT are extensive and splendid. The Student Profile Report contains a good deal more information beyond the ACT scores themselves. All the information gathered in the personal questionnaire section of the ACT is reflected in potentially useful categorized form on the report. High school grade averages in the areas corresponding to the parts of the ACT appear next to the test scores, and both local (for the college to which the scores are sent) and national percentile equivalents are provided for the ACT standard scores. Furthermore, for colleges participating in ACT's basic research service by providing grades, Student Profile Reports contain tables of grade predictions and probabilities of students' attaining C or higher in separate curricular areas and overall. Detailed, attractive, clear, helpful manuals accompany the reports containing useful guides to interpretation and suggestions for uses of the host of data provided.

Research services offered to participating colleges at no cost include distributions of ACT scores, high school grades, and college freshman grades; multiple regression analyses of ACT scores and high school grades as predictors of college grades; intercorrelations of all these variables; and comparative local and national norms. Subgrouping and local predictors are also included in analyses under certain conditions. A 250-page book entitled *Your College Freshmen* is provided with reports as an interpretive guide to the results of the research services. When unusual findings occur in the results of the research services for any college, individual communications are directed to that college concerning them.

ACT offers additional services associated directly in some instances and peripherally in others with the testing program itself. These include special punched card reports, magnetic tape reports, high school and college address files, financial aid information and reports, and a high school profile service. Most of these extra services are at additional cost.

Generally distributed periodic publications of ACT include *ACTivity,* a newsletter of the organization, and ACT Research Reports, which describe discrete studies in measurement or student personnel fields and are usually of general interest and high quality.

In summary, ACT is one of the two most widely used admission testing programs in the country. The other is the *College Board Scholastic Aptitude Test.* ACT contains four tests in English usage, mathematics usage, social studies reading, and natural sciences reading. A student profile questionnaire of background, high school grades, educational plans, and occupational goals is also an integral part of the program. Results are reported to the students and colleges in a very complete fashion with ample explanation accompanying them.

There is an overdependence on reading comprehension in the ACT. The four tests have high intercorrelations and the incremental validities of the addition of the second, third, and fourth tests in predicting collegiate success are minuscule. Reliabilities of the four tests are low for individual student assessment. Construction of the items in the ACT is of uneven quality; many of the items could benefit from more careful editing. There are extensive norms for the ACT, well developed and described and appropriately selected for the intended uses and interpretations of the test results. Despite some of the psychometric weaknesses of the ACT cited, the tests display highly satisfactory predictive validities against criteria of college grades, and this is in essence the most important property of all.

There has been a reprehensible neglect of new test development or experimentation associated with the ACT. Intensive attempts toward the evolvement of more varied yet pertinent measures of intellectual skills are long overdue.

The ancillary services of ACT in the forms of explanatory publications, extensive individual reports, local analyses of test and associated data, and research services for participating colleges are well executed, attractively presented, and potentially highly useful to those who will peruse them.

ACT suffers by comparison with the SAT in psychometric care and sophistication, is about equal in validity for predicting collegiate success, and excels somewhat in the variety and extent of ancillary services offered.

For reviews by Max D. Engelhart and Warren G. Findley of an earlier program, see 6:1 (1 excerpt).

[331]

*AH4, AH5, and AH6 Tests. Ages 10 and over, 13 and over, 16 and over; 1955–70; 2 levels: general intelligence, high-level intelligence; 4 tests; separate answer sheets must be used; 50p per 25 answer sheets; postage extra; A. W. Heim, K. P. Watts (AH6), and V. Simmonds (AH6); NFER Publishing Co. Ltd. *

a) AH4: GROUP TEST OF GENERAL INTELLIGENCE (1968 REVISION). Ages 10 and over; 1955–70; 1 form ('68, 14 pages); revised manual ('70, 18 pages); £2 per 25 tests; 10p per key; 50p per manual; £1 per specimen set; 20(30–45) minutes.

b) AH5: GROUP TEST OF HIGH-GRADE INTELLIGENCE. Ages 13 and over; 1956–68; 1 form ['56, 8 pages]; revised manual ('68, 25 pages); £1.15 per 25 tests; 15p per key; 50p per manual; £1 per specimen set; 40(60–70) minutes.

c) AH6: GROUP TESTS OF HIGH-LEVEL INTELLIGENCE. Ages 16 and over; 1970; 2 tests (12 pages): SEM for Scientists, Engineers and Mathematicians (potential or qualified), AG for Arts and General; manual (30 pages); £2.25 per 25 tests; 30p per set of keys; 70p per manual; £1.37 per specimen set; 40(60–75) minutes for SEM, 35(60–75) minutes for AG.

REFERENCES

1–11. See 5:390.
12. BEARD, R. M. "The Structure of Perception: A Factorial Study." *Brit J Ed Psychol* 35:210–22 Je '65. *
13. KELVIN, R. P.; LUCAS, C. J.; AND OJHA, A. B. "The Relation Between Personality, Mental Health and Academic Performance in University Students." *Brit J Social & Clin Psychol* 4:244–53 D '65. * (PA 40:4573)
14. TARPEY, M. SIMEON. "Personality Factors in Teacher Trainee Selection." *Brit J Ed Psychol* 35:140–9 Je '65. * (PA 39:16480)
15. LUCAS, C. J.; KELVIN, R. P.; AND OJHA, A. B. "Mental Health and Student Wastage." *Brit J Psychiatry* 112:277–84 Mr '66. * (PA 40:7958)
16. PILKINGTON, G. W., AND HARRISON, G. J. "The Relative Value of Two High Level Intelligence Tests, Advanced Level, and First Year University Examination Marks for Predicting Degree Classification." *Brit J Ed Psychol* 37:382–9 N '67. * (PA 42:6148)
17. CORTIS, G. A. "Predicting Student Performance in Colleges of Education." *Brit J Ed Psychol* 38:115–22 Je '68. * (PA 42:17717)
18. DACEY, J.; MADAUS, G.; AND ALLEN, A. "The Relationship of Creativity and Intelligence in Irish Adolescents." *Brit J Ed Psychol* 39(3):261–6 N '69. * (PA 44:8234)
19. BANKS, C.; KARDAK, V. S.; JONES, E. M.; AND LUCAS, C. J. "The Relation Between Mental Health, Academic Performance and Cognitive Test Scores Among Chemistry Students." *Brit J Ed Psychol* 40(1):74–9 F '70. * (PA 44:11366)
20. GALLOP, R. "A Study of the B.Ed. Student." Thesis abstract. *Brit J Ed Psychol* 40(2):220 Je '70. *
21. HAMILTON, VERNON. "Non-Cognitive Factors in University Students' Examination Performance." *Brit J Psychol* 61(2):229–41 My '70. * (PA 44:15302)
22. MEHRYAR, A. H., AND SHAPURIAN, R. "The Application of a High-Grade Intelligence Scale (AH5) in Iran." *Brit J Ed Psychol* 40(3):307–13 N '70. * (PA 45:6335)
23. POVEY, ROBERT M. "Arts/Science Differences: Their Relationship to Curriculum Specialization." *Brit J Psychol* 61(1):55–64 F '70. * (PA 44:9215)

JOHN NISBET, *Professor of Education, University of Aberdeen, Aberdeen, Scotland.*

AH4 and AH5 have proved popular as measures of general ability for research studies in Britain over the past 15 years. One reason is that they have an attractive face validity, for they include both verbal and nonverbal items in equal numbers, with at least four different types of problems in each part, all within a reasonable time limit. The researcher in a hurry, with a limited budget and an already crowded test battery, might find these all-purpose tests convenient.

A recent revision has improved the older tests in this series. The original versions were criticised for poor printing and amateurish drawings and lettering (6:506). These defects have been removed in the 1968 reprinting of AH4. (The marked improvement in layout may invalidate the old norms.) New manuals have been issued for AH4 and AH5, with more extensive norms and fuller details on validity and reliability. Norms, however, are still presented in the crude form of score distributions from a variety of samples, and provide only a broad five-point categorization from A (top 10 percent) to E (bottom 10 percent), varying for each reference group. The process of revision has been taken a step further by the publication in 1970 of AH6, designed to improve on AH5 by a more appropriate mixture of verbal (V), numerical (N) and diagrammatic (D) items, and by the provision of separate norms for the V, N and D categories. Two forms of AH6 have been issued: SEM for those specializing in science, engineering and mathematics, and AG for the somewhat vague group described as "Arts and General Subjects." SEM has equal numbers of V, N and D items, while AG has more V and fewer N and D, but the two forms have a substantial overlap of common items. SEM has norms for V, N and D separately, based on 1,189 university science students; AG has norms for V and (N + D) based on 1,710 school and college students.

The manuals give a clear statement of testing procedure and precise information on validity and reliability. Emphasis is laid on the proper presentation of the practice items which precede the tests. No less than 18 practice items are given for AH6, and, unlike some tests, these examples are of the same level of difficulty as the first items in the test proper. The claim is made (in the manuals for AH4 and AH5, but not for AH6) that these tests are less dependent on speed than most others of their kind, but this is open to question. For AH4 the time limit allows only nine seconds per item on average; but all the manuals prescribe that "nothing should be said....about speed of work." For AH4, test-retest reliability is .92; for AH5 and AH6 it is lower as the tests are designed for selected groups (AH6, AG total score, .83 on test-retest). For all tests a range of reliability coefficients is given, derived from different samples and by different methods. Validity is reported in the form of correlations with other comparable tests and with other criteria, mostly academic performance.

The tests are good examples of their kind, relying on the conventional types of problem, such as analogies, relations and series in verbal, numerical and diagrammatic forms. For AH6 the items have been devised imaginatively, especially the verbal problems which make use of words with more than one meaning. The timed group test, relying on a variety of items to secure wide coverage and sustain interest, will continue to be useful as a research instrument, but will not be used, one hopes, for individual assessment or as a basis for counseling. AH6, with its alternative bias, is likely to arouse most interest. The rationale of the design of the two forms of this test is argued in the manual. Giving weight to verbal items with the AG group is surely correct; for science-based courses also, verbal items give a fair prediction of achievement. The argument is less convincing for retaining diagrammatic items if the test is regarded as a measure of scholastic aptitude. The manual argues that "visuality" is important for the scientist, but it does not report any factor analysis of the test, and the correlations reported between D scores and scores on other similar tests are all below .50. (The manual is at least to be commended for reporting the correlations fully—even one on the wrong side of zero.) It is to be hoped that those who use the separate score categories will bear in mind the small number of items from which these subtest scores are derived. Comparison across SEM and AG will be based on the still smaller number of common items. Nevertheless, AH6 represents an interesting development of this series and provides a welcome addition to the measures available for assessing high-ability subjects. However, the established pattern of scholastic aptitude test, with its two categories, verbal and numerical, is not yet seriously challenged by this development.

For a review by John Liggett of AH5 and the original edition of AH4, see 6:506; for reviews by George A. Ferguson of AH4 and J. A. Keats of AH5, see 5:390.

[332]
*Academic Alertness "AA": Individual Placement Series.** Adults; 1957–66; 7 scores: general knowledge, arithmetic, vocabulary, reasoning ability, logical sequence, accuracy, total; Forms A, B, ('57,

6 pages); no specific manual; series manual ('66, 107 pages); no data on reliability of part scores; separate answer sheets must be used; $25 per 20 tests; $4 per 100 answer sheets; 50¢ per key; $2.50 per series manual; $4.45 per specimen set; cash orders postpaid; 20(25) minutes; J. H. Norman; Personnel Research Associates, Inc. *

JOEL T. CAMPBELL, *Senior Research Psychologist, Educational Testing Service, Princeton, New Jersey.*

This 100-item measure of general intelligence is arranged in spiral form, each spiral having groupings of five items for each subarea. An additional score, called accuracy, is calculated from the ratio of items correct to items completed.

The items are in a free response format; the scoring key lists several variations of acceptable responses (or a range of responses) but this still leaves the scorer with judgmental decisions.

The question wording has been kept short and simple, but at a cost of ambiguity in a number of instances. For example, in one question, "What is the largest city in the United States?" the term "largest" is used to mean population rather than area. However, in a similar question "smallest" is used to mean area. For a few questions, the keyed response will not be acceptable to specialists in the area, although no doubt most of the general population would consider the response correct.

Possibly the most serious challenge to question wording will come from the standpoint of minority groups who will have considerable justification in claiming that the test has irrelevant cultural detail. This test was developed about 1956, before employers' attention had been forcibly directed to the problem of minority employment and differences in cultural background. Some of the questions ask for fairly common knowledge or for common sense interpretations or for fairly simple arithmetic computation. Other questions call for more esoteric information and it would be difficult to justify the need for such information on most jobs.

No item analyses are given. Correlations of the area scores with the total score range from .72 to .78, while area score intercorrelations range from .36 to .53. These correlations are low enough to indicate that the areas measure somewhat different abilities.

Table 1 in the manual is supposed to show the equivalence of the two forms, but the reviewer is unable to understand it. Columns 2 and 3 of this table, for example, give "number of misses" for each area and the total, but "number of misses" is nowhere defined. Test-retest reliability is given as .92 for an undescribed group of 100.

Evidence of validity is presented in three ways. Correlations of the two forms of the test with the Wonderlic, Army Beta, and Army General Classification Tests range from .69 to .88. Median scores by job classifications (total scores and area scores) for 20 different jobs show reasonable progression by job level from laborer to engineer. A third way in which validity information is presented is by expectancy charts for four occupations, comparing test performance with rated job performance.

Here, however, there is confusion in the figures for at least one of the charts. The text says "The length of each bar on the charts reflects the percent of employees who were rated as above average employees who scored in a given interval. Chart 6, for example, indicates that 88 percent of the guards who scored between 54 and 100 had been rated as superior performers; whereas only 12 percent of those who scored between 0 and 43 were rated as superior performers." The middle category had 57 percent. Since chart 6 was based on an N of 12, it is not possible to come up with any grouping of numbers which will permit these percentages!

In fairness, it should be stated that the other three expectancy charts are based on more respectable N's. They report, however, lower validity coefficients: .32 for 45 assembly engineers, .45 for 72 machine parts inspectors, and .18 for 116 junior engineers.

Normative data are based on unusually large numbers of cases. The total industry norm is based on 31,143 cases. Norms are also reported for clerical workers, shop workers, engineers, and supervisors.

The reviewer does not feel that this test can be recommended over such alternate possibilities as the verbal and numerical tests of the *Fundamental Achievement Series,* for lower level jobs, and the *Personnel Tests for Industry* for somewhat higher level factory or office jobs, even though these alternatives do require more testing time than does the AA.

[333]

*Adaptability Test. Job applicants; 1942–67; Forms A, B, ('42, 3 pages); manual ('67, 12 pages); $5.30 per 25 tests; 40¢ per manual; $1.25 per specimen set;

postage extra; 15(20) minutes; Joseph Tiffin and C. H. Lawshe; Science Research Associates, Inc. *

REFERENCES

1–3. See 3:216.
4–16. See 5:305.
17. PAGE, HOWARD E. "A Note on Norms for the Purdue Industrial Mathematics Test and the Adaptability Test." *J Appl Psychol* 34:306–8 O '50. * (*PA* 26:559)
18. CHANDLER, ROBERT E. *Validation of Apprentice Screening Tests in an Oil Refinery.* Doctor's thesis, Purdue University (Lafayette, Ind.), 1956. (*DA* 27:325B)
19. KAZMIER, LEONARD J. "Normative Data Information Exchange, No. 12–22." *Personnel Psychol* 12:504 au '59. *
20. GRUENFELD, LEOPOLD WILHELM. *Selection of Executives for a Training Program.* Doctor's thesis, Purdue University (Lafayette, Ind.), 1960. (*DA* 21:1247)
21. BUEL, WILLIAM D., AND BAEHNER, VIRGINIA M. "The Assessment of Creativity in a Research Setting." *J Appl Psychol* 45:353–8 D '61. * (*PA* 37:1211)
22. GUION, ROBERT M. "Synthetic Validity in a Small Company: A Demonstration." *Personnel Psychol* 18:49–63 sp '65. * (*PA* 39:16490)

For a review by John M. Willits, see 5:305; for reviews by Anne Anastasi and Marion A. Bills, see 3:216.

[334]

★Analysis of Learning Potential. Grades 1, 2–3, 4–6, 7–9, 10–12; 1970; ALP; *complete test option:* 2 scores derived from the same total raw score: learning potential ("estimate of the pupil's general learning ability" compared to his age group), general composite ("estimate of the pupil's general learning ability" compared to his grade group); in grades 4–12 a reading-mathematics difference score (called "reading-mathematics composite prognostic differential") is also reported; *reading prognostic subtests option:* reading composite prognostic score ("an estimate of the pupil's capacity for school learning" in reading compared to his grade group); *mathematics prognostic subtests option:* mathematics composite prognostic score ("an estimate of the pupil's capacity for school learning" in mathematics compared to his grade group); the same test booklets but different answer sheets are used for the 3 options; 1 form; 5 levels; preliminary technical report (59 pages); no data on predictive validity; no norms for difference scores; use of local norms recommended; separate answer sheets (Digitek, IBM 805, IBM 1230, MRC) must be used for grades 4–12; $5.50 per 35 Digitek or IBM 1230 answer folders; $4.20 per 35 IBM 805 answer folders; $10 per 100 MRC answer sheets; $1.20 per set of MRC hand scoring keys; $2 per technical report; MRC scoring service: complete test (56¢ and over for grades 1–3, 43¢ and over for grades 4–12), either the reading prognostic subtests or the mathematics prognostic subtests (51¢ and over for grades 1–3, 38¢ and over for grades 4–12); postage extra; Walter N. Durost, Eric F. Gardner, Richard Madden, and George A. Prescott; Harcourt Brace Jovanovich, Inc. *
a) PRIMARY I BATTERY. Grade 1; Form A (12 pages); 2 editions: hand scored, MRC scored; manual (35 pages); norms (8 pages); $10.80 per 35 hand scored tests; $1 per key; $2 per specimen set; $13.80 per 35 MRC scored tests; (84) minutes in 3 sessions for complete test, (32) for reading, (27) for mathematics.
b) PRIMARY 2 BATTERY. Grades 2–3; Form A (12 pages); 2 editions: hand scored, MRC scored; manual (34 pages); norms (10 pages); $11 per 35 hand scored tests; $1 per key; $2 per specimen set; $14 per 35 MRC scored tests; (85) minutes in 3 sessions for complete test, (32) for reading, (31) for mathematics.
c) ELEMENTARY BATTERY. Grades 4–6; Form A (9 pages); manual (38 pages); norms (10 pages);

$11.50 per 35 tests; $2.10 per set of Digitek or IBM keys; $2.25 per specimen set; 50(75) minutes in 2 sittings for complete test, 19(28) for reading, 22(30) for mathematics.

d) ADVANCED 1 BATTERY. Grades 7–9; Form A (12 pages); manual (40 pages); norms (11 pages); $11.50 per 35 tests; $2.80 per set of Digitek or IBM 1230 keys; $2.10 per set of IBM 805 keys; $2.25 per specimen set; 68(93) minutes in 2 sittings for complete test, 23(31) for reading, 21(29) for mathematics.

e) ADVANCED 2 BATTERY. Grades 10–12; Form A (12 pages); manual (40 pages); norms (10 pages); prices same as for *d*; 68(93) minutes in 2 sittings for complete test, 31(40) for reading, 21(29) for mathematics.

LEE J. CRONBACH, *Vida Jacks Professor of Education, Stanford University, Stanford, California.*

ALP is made up of newly designed subtests which allegedly "have demonstrated their ability to predict specific criteria of scholastic success while....relatively free from....[content] specifically taught in school." The Index of Learning Potential is an indicator of "general capacity for school learning." A more accurate claim would be that the test measures the pupil's present level of general educational development; it requires reasoning, vocabulary, and computational skill.

Let us deal thoroughly with the Elementary battery, and examine its statistics at grade 5. Regarding batteries for earlier and later grades, it will then be necessary to note only a few variations from this basic pattern. The seven subtests at the Elementary level are for the most part variations on old themes. The variations are ingenious and avoid the "guess what I have in mind" character of items in many group mental tests. Verbal classification here takes the form

door   kitchen   painted   garage   basement   porch

Number series is turned into a sort of analogy item:

(4,2)   (5,3)   (7,—)   3 4 5 6 7

A numerical-reasoning task requires one to fill the blanks in

$$\frac{\square \quad 8}{5 \quad 6} \quad \square$$

with the same digit, so as to make a sound calculation. To do this, one must decide whether addition, subtraction, or multiplication fits the problem. These numerical items require school-learned content, but it is content all pupils taking this battery will have covered. Facility in using and adapting very basic skills is tested, and performance hence will not reflect local variations

in curricula. The items in all subtests are abstract and formal. There is no attempt to interest pupils by referring to real situations.

The total score is converted to ILP, a standard-score-within-age-group; 50 is the scale mean and 15 the standard deviation. The *Test Standards* urge publishers to employ a 50-10 scale unless there is a compelling reason for some alternative, since proliferation of scales confuses users. There is no warrant for this 50-15 scale. The authors recommend *stanines* (in an obscure paragraph certain to be overlooked by users) as "the most desirable method of interpreting scores on ALP." The manuals, however, at all points discuss the 50-15 standard scores, and the norm booklet makes an extra stage of conversion necessary to get stanines (or percentiles). Surely most users will mistakenly employ the over-refined standard-score scale.

Such labels as "learning potential" and "capacity" are even more objectionable than the term "intelligence," which the authors studiously avoid. The only sensible meaning that can be given to "learning potential" is "what the pupil could achieve if he were hereafter to be given the instruction optimal for him." There is of course no evidence to support such an interpretation here. ILP is a measure of what the pupil's past education, in school and out, has taught him. It indicates the rank in achievement to be anticipated for him if the school does nothing more effective in the future than it did in the past. To label the mediocre achiever as having mediocre "potential" is simply to reassure the school that it has done the best it could for him. The authors recommend that ILP be used together with other data in making educational plans for the pupil. Clearly, if ILP is less favorable than the other evidence, it has to be ignored, for how can a pupil achieve beyond his potential? If ILP is significantly higher than other indicators, the school should heed its signal. But in what fraction of cases will there be such a disparity? The manual gives no direct evidence, but it appears that ALP will agree so closely with concurrent achievement tests that disparity is likely to be noise, not signal.

The total score is also converted to GCSS (General Composite Standard Score), a number on a 50-15 scale that compares the pupil with the norm for his half-grade. ILP and GCSS will agree except for the child whose age is atypical for his grade. For raw score 70 in the first half of grade 5, the GCSS stanine is 5; and the ILP stanine is also 5 for pupils of normal age (10-3 to 11-5). For a 9-year-old the stanine is 7. The authors propose that GCSS, not ILP, be the basis for ability grouping, where ability grouping is practiced.

The statistics for the total score are what one would expect for a test requiring 75 minutes. Reliability (taking into account short-term pupil variability and form-to-form variability) is .90; the standard error is about six-tenths of the stanine unit. ILP correlates .83 with Lorge-Thorndike Verbal and Total IQ's, .70 with Non-Verbal. The concurrent correlation of GCSS with single subtests of the Metropolitan and Stanford Achievement batteries is generally in the .70's, and the (unreported) correlation with an achievement total is probably close to .90. The statistics support the view, then, that this is a transfer test of academic achievement over the verbal and numerical areas.

The composite score on an achievement battery is a good predictor of next year's success, and it is a reasonable guess that this measure will have predictive validity in the same range. There are, however, no predictive data of any sort on this test, a fact that is obscured by the authors' liberal use of the words "predictive" and "prognostic" in discussing data from concurrent testing. It is hard to believe that ALP will be a better predictor of achievement than the *Iowa Tests of Basic Skills* or some other fundamental-skills battery. Such a battery has immediate diagnostic relevance, and is not subject to intrusive misinterpretations invoked by words like "capacity." Hence it is hard to understand why ALP should be used in preference to an achievement battery, for start-of-year planning.

THE PROGNOSTIC COMPOSITES. The idea of predicting specific achievements, quoted in the first sentence of this review, is an echo of early plans that collapsed under the weight of evidence. An attempt was made to develop separate composites relevant to reading, mathematics, science, language arts, and social studies, using the subtests in different combinations. As the data came in the authors faced up to the fact that GCSS is at least as good a (concurrent) predictor of achievement in science as any set of subtests. Likewise for other categories of achievement. Hence GCSS is clearly the predictor to use and the manual says so.

It is possible for a school interested solely in reading to administer just the three subtests in the reading composite (RCPS). This short scale works reasonably well. Other three- or four-subtest combinations can be separately administered where information relevant specifically to mathematics (MCPS) or any other single subject is desired.

Hope dies hard. The authors have retreated step by painful step from their intent to offer a differential battery, and in the manuals, score reports, etc., the composites are not yet properly subordinated to GCSS. While the authors recommend that subscales not be interpreted, they suggest that the RCPS-MCPS difference be examined; a confidence-band technique is used to suppress small differences. Even though conclusions about the true difference reach the level of differential reliability customary in profile interpretation, its differential validity is in serious doubt. More significant is the fact that in any event teachers can make no practical decision on the basis of norm-referenced differences in these two variables. It appears to me that the score should not be calculated, and if reported should not be used.

Although the authors prize their "measurement technology," they are not up to date. They preserve the interpretation of confidence bands symmetric around the observed score, which Lord and Novick [1] have exposed as fallacious. The authors ignore recent work [2] on theory of difference scores; further limitations of classical work in this field are still emerging.[3]

OTHER LEVELS. The Advanced batteries require 93 minutes, and include a fairly difficult spatial subtest. The Syntactic Clues subtest is intriguing, with items like this: "Priffles and wurfles were umping piskly in the opple popple. Whangles are usually wurfy but not while _____." The correct answer choice is "umping" rather than "piskly" or another non-verb.

The GCSS reliability coefficient rises to about .93 in grade 6 and above. Concurrent correlations of GCSS with achievement battery sub-

[1] LORD, FREDERIC M., AND NOVICK, MELVIN R. *Statistical Theories of Mental Test Scores.* Reading, Mass.: Addison-Wesley Publishing Co., Inc., 1968. Pp. xvii, 568. *
[2] LORD, FREDERIC M. Chap. 2, "Elementary Models for Measuring Change," pp. 21–38. In *Problems in Measuring Change.* Edited by Chester W. Harris. Madison, Wis.: University of Wisconsin Press, 1963. Pp. x, 259. *
STANLEY, JULIAN C. "General and Special Formulas for Reliability of Differences." *J Ed Meas* 4:249–52 w '67. *
[3] CRONBACH, LEE J., AND FURBY, LITA. "How We Should Measure 'Change'—Or Should We?" *Psychol B* 74(1):68–80 Jl '70. *

tests spread over the range .70 to .85. The story on predictive composites is essentially the same as for the Elementary battery.

Primary 2, for grades 2 and 3, requires no reading. A dictated test asks the pupil to judge whether a word such as "suspect" does or does not apply to a picture (man behind bars). Other tasks have to do with computation, everyday information, figure series and vocabulary. A picture-story task displays two silhouette pictures that start a story, plus four additional pictures. The pupil is to mark 3 beneath the picture that fits as third in the sequence, and 4 beneath the correct fourth panel. This subtest falls below the usual excellence of execution: the task is complex, the drawings are tiny, and responses other than the keyed ones can be defended.

For Primary 2 the reliability of GCSS holds up, but concurrent correlations with achievement subtests drop to the .50's and .60's. At this level the attempt to interpret the RCPS-MCPS difference is abandoned, though the option of administering half the test to get either composite remains.

Primary 1 is similar. There are more pictorial tests, and numerical tasks are replaced with one on quantitative concepts. Primary 1 is more nearly a pictorial test of verbal and general abilities than are the achievement-related tests at later levels. It includes a maddening perceptual task calling for selection of similar *kanji*. In general, the demands upon visual acuity and attentiveness seem large for school beginners. A considerable concession to children's interests is made at this level, however. Reliability over a short interval falls off to .80. At this level in particular one wants the missing information on stability over several months, and on predictive validity.

EVALUATION. The manual and technical report are disappointing. The developers obviously made an effort to give honest advice, to qualify statements, and to present extensive evidence. Outright conflict with the *Test Standards* is rare. Yet the manual and technical report seem unlikely to give users a sound understanding of the test. The facts I have found salient in assessing the test are located in widely scattered places, sometimes deeply buried. Some of the needed statistics are not reported even though the data were in hand. There was massive data collection, yet no resources were allocated to one-year follow-up studies. Tabular data are amassed to the point of throwing dust in the reader's eyes. It is agreed, for example, that alternate-forms reliabilities are pertinent, and internal-consistency coefficients less suitable. Why precede the two tables of relevant alternate-forms coefficients with *three* tables of K-R 20 coefficients? (Worse, the K-R 20 values are computed by a lazy-man's formula that probably inflates the coefficients.)

In the discussion of norms the information overload is even greater. The three-stage sampling plan appears to have been very well designed. The technical report offers three tables by way of evidence on the adequacy of the norms. The first table defends the representativeness of the first-stage selection of 2,000 school districts, but leaves us with no direct report on the 69 systems actually used in the norms. The second table, presented without comment, is a regional breakdown of the actual sample. The careful reader discovers that pupils in the Southeast region are overrepresented by 50 percent, with corresponding deficits in Midwest and West. Since the Southeast usually has conspicuously different score distributions, this suggests that the norms are more in error than the developers intended. How much difference does this make? What went wrong in the sampling? Why is the unrepresentativeness not discussed? The third table displays, for each grade, the percentage of standardization cases from various sizes of school system, and shows that each of these distributions matches the distribution for the U.S. population for all grades pooled. But is the U.S. distribution uniform in all grades? One suspects not. In sum, despite a flood of technical information, our confidence in the norms has to rest on our confidence in the authors.

ALP is a carefully made test. Preparation of items is good on the whole. The technical characteristics are entirely adequate, despite the faults noted. Probably ALP will forecast end-of-year grades as well as other tests do, at least in grades beyond the second. Yet it is hard to see what niche it will fit into. It cannot supplant the achievement test a good testing program uses early in the school year. It will do less than a good test of nonverbal reasoning to shake up the school by detecting the many pupils who can reason well but who have not mastered basic educational skills. ALP is conservative in conception, identifying the child's achievement to date with his "potential" and emphasizing pre-

diction to the exclusion of diagnosis and prescription.

ARTHUR R. JENSEN, *Professor of Educational
Psychology; and Research Psychologist, Institute of Human Learning; University of California, Berkeley, California.*

The ALP is the result of a major effort to
produce a series of group mental tests for
school use which can fully compete with the
best and most widely used group intelligence
tests now available. To this reviewer, the effort
appears to have been successful.

The various subtests can be classified by inspection of their item contents as Word Relational Concepts, Number Concepts, and Figure
Concepts, although, as we shall see, the factorial
complexity of the tests is not as great as all the
diverse subtest labels might suggest.

The time required for administration is reasonable and comparable to other good tests. The
tests are given in two or three sittings.

The manual for administration is excellent
and contains all the information one could wish
to find in a test manual.

PUBLISHER'S CLAIMS VS. REALITY. In the present climate of popular criticism of intelligence
tests, which has culminated in their being
banned in some school systems, the publishers
of ALP seem to have gone all-out to make their
product appear to be something other than what
it actually is, namely, a good intelligence test.
The publisher's blurb, for example, claims the
"ALP is more than just a new measure of
scholastic aptitude—it is a totally new concept
for assessing school ability." The title of the
test itself is misleading. There is nothing "analytic" about the scores it yields; there are no
profiles or special diagnostic ratios. And the
concept of "potential" is quite meaningless with
respect to scores on any psychological tests.
Some readers are apt to construe the test's title
as suggesting a measure of innate ability—a
claim not made by the publishers and for which
no appropriate evidence is available. Moreover,
the test is not best regarded as a measure of
"learning" ability. If "learning ability" means
rate of acquisition of skills or knowledge, independent of initial status, then the ALP, to the
extent that it is like other intelligence tests, is
not a measure of "learning ability." The ALP
is very much like most other intelligence tests,
and ample research has shown that intelligence
test scores have relatively low correlations with

learning measures or "gain scores" which are
independent of initial status.

WHAT ALP MEASURES. Actually, the ALP
measures nothing new, nothing different from
what is measured by, say, the *Lorge-Thorndike
Intelligence Tests.* It is old wine in a new bottle.
But the old wine is excellent and the new bottle
is indeed attractive. As anyone who has had
much experience in factor analyzing a large
variety of mental ability tests can readily see
from casual inspection of the various ALP subtests, the old wine is nothing other than Spearman's g, the general intelligence factor. The
various subtests would be somewhat differentially loaded on what Cattell calls "fluid" and
"crystallized" g, and they can also be grouped
in a way that would correspond quite closely to
the verbal and nonverbal parts of the Lorge-
Thorndike. Through factor analytic experience
with many kinds of tests one comes readily to
recognize the types of items most heavily loaded
with g. It would be extremely difficult to make
up more different kinds of g-loaded items than
the authors have succeeded in composing—
g-loaded items appropriate in difficulty and
interest for every grade level from I to 12. This
heavy g characteristic of the ALP tests is most
interesting in view of its authors' emphasizing
in the manual for administration that the ALP
"was *not* developed within a specific theoretical
framework concerning the nature of mental
ability or intelligence. Thus, the tests were
designed to measure neither a single, general
ability factor nor to provide factorially 'pure'
measures of somewhat discrete mental functions. Tests appearing in each battery were selected solely from the standpoint of their contribution to the prediction of academic success."

FACTORIAL COMPOSITION. To determine the
factorial complexity of the ALP, this reviewer
performed a factor analysis separately on
Forms A and B of each of the five batteries,
using the matrix of subtest intercorrelations for
each battery provided by the publisher. (Specifically, a principal components analysis was
done, followed by a varimax rotation of the
components having Eigenvalues greater than
I.) Factorially, Forms A and B are very equivalent. A general factor accounts for between 42
and 59 percent of the total variance in each
battery. With few exceptions the various subtests are highly similar in the g loadings, which
are almost uniformly high (i.e., .70 to .80). In
two of the batteries (Primary I and Elemen-

tary) no second factor emerged. And in no battery did more than two factors emerge. Rotation of these factors simply divides the variance between verbal and nonverbal factors. In brief, the reviewer's analysis indicates that the variance in these tests is mainly attributable to a large general factor (g), accounting on the average for about 52 percent of the variance, and to two small group factors, verbal and nonverbal (or numerical-spatial), together accounting for about 10 to 13 percent of the variance. The remaining 30 to 35 percent of the variance is attributable to measurement error (less than 10 percent) and to factors specific to the various subtests (about 20 to 25 percent). We can estimate that the total score on the ALP correlates with g between .65 and .77 for the various batteries, with an average correlation of about .72. In this respect, then, the ALP closely resembles most other good tests of general intelligence, which means that it measures, more than anything else, the subject's ability to see complex or abstract relationships, or in Spearman's words, "the eduction of relations and correlates." Whether we like it or not, this is the ability which, more than any other, enters into scholastic achievement under the instructional conditions of present-day schools and as assessed by the traditional criteria of school grades and achievement test scores.

"CULTURE-FAIRNESS." In their manual the authors warn that "Pupils who are poorly motivated or who have not had the opportunity to learn the broad, general types of behaviors sampled by the tests should have these limiting factors taken into consideration by teachers and counselors in interpreting the test results. This is particularly true for pupils who have experienced severe cultural deprivation." Does this mean that the ALP has lower validity in predicting the scholastic performance of "culturally deprived" children? We do not know. But we can guess from experience with similar tests that it will predict scholastic achievement (under normal school conditions and assessed by standard tests) as well for the disadvantaged as the majority of children. If it is realized that the *causes* of any particular child's score are unknown (unless specifically investigated) and that the score is simply a statistical predictive device, there need be no concern about the test's "fairness" to all subpopulations of pupils. However, if one should imagine that he is getting at something more "profound" than this, he should

be made aware that the test is no more "culture-fair" than most other group tests now on the market. So far as we know, all tests with a high g saturation, whether or not they are called "culture-fair" or look "culture-fair," show very substantial social class differences in performance. The ALP will be no exception. We can expect lower socio-economic status children, on the average, to score about one standard deviation below middle-class children on the ALP.

This reviewer would regard tests like the ALP (and all other standard intelligence tests) as "unfair" only in the sense that they assess such a limited and homogeneous set of abilities. These abilities can be called "intelligence" or g, which is indeed highly correlated with scholastic performance. But g is not the whole spectrum of human ability, nor is it the only ability that can be marshaled for scholastic achievement. One would like to see a broader assessment of children's abilities, especially among groups who are relatively low in g, in hopes of finding other abilities and talents which can serve in the educational process of making schooling rewarding even for children with below average academic aptitude. Although tests like the ALP may give the impression, with all their diverse subtests, that they are getting at a broad assessment of many abilities, they are actually very unidimensional. Unless supplemented by other forms of assessment they tend to rank-order pupils along a single dimension of aptitude. Does the form of school instruction in turn attempt to maximize the correlation between "scholastic aptitude" (as represented by non-scholastic tests of g) and scholastic achievement? Highly homogeneous tests of ability, yielding a single score, may not be the most useful instruments in schools tending toward a diversity of curricula and instructional programs intended to make school beneficial to a wide range of individual differences. Only by inventing additional tests with low loadings on g will we be able to discover possible areas of educationally relevant strengths in those children who are below the average in g-type abilities. Unfortunately, there is no standard test battery one can recommend at present to fill this need.

NORMS. The ALP norms are based on a sample of 165,000 pupils in 75 school systems selected so as to be highly representative of the U.S. school population according to the latest census. Norms for different regions of the U.S.

or for different types of communities (e.g., rural-urban, lower–class—middle–class, etc.) are not provided. The authors suggest that school systems should develop their own local norms, presumably by accumulating large numbers of test results and converting the raw ALP scores to normalized standard scores. A further step would be to determine the regression equation for the school's particular achievement measures as "predicted" from the ALP. Local norms, if properly established and maintained up-to-date, make a good deal of sense, considering the fact that the average level of scholastic achievement in a school or a community is highly related to a host of community characteristics over which the schools themselves have little or no control, such as the educational level of the adult population, home ownership, cost of housing, proportion of native-born whites, rate of unemployment, proportion of professional workers, etc. Comparison of a particular school's or community's scores with overall national norms, though it may serve the purpose of describing one aspect of the school population, is of little or no value in dealing with an individual pupil. On the other hand, there may be some value in comparing an individual's score on an intelligence test with an assessment of his scholastic achievement. This is best done by putting the intelligence and achievement scores on the same scale (e.g., normalized standard scores with the same mean and standard deviation) normed on the same reference population. The authors of the ALP emphasize, correctly, I believe, that the subtests are designed, for the most part, to be "relatively free from specific school-learned skills. The tests ....do assess learned abilities gained from a number of somewhat diffuse sources whose exact nature cannot be clearly specified." The detection of large and reliable discrepancies between a measure of extra-scholastically acquired skills and measures of scholastic achievement can be of diagnostic value, both for individual children and for the means of classrooms and of whole schools. Detection of "underachievers" for special attention is a useful function of ability tests. The ALP can serve this purpose as well as any other intelligence tests on the market. The "cut-off" discrepancy between ALP and achievement scores that would pick out "underachievers" is not specified, but it is a largely arbitrary matter anyway. (It should probably be at least twice the test's standard error of estimate.) The fact

that there will be about as many "overachievers" as "underachievers" belies the test's label, "Analysis of Learning *Potential*," since theoretically no one should be able to exceed his "potential."

SCALES AND SCORES. The ALP provides five types of derived scores, all of which can be found in tables in the Norms-Conversion Booklet. The Index of Learning Potential (ILP) is a normalized standard score with a mean of 50 and a standard deviation of 15. The reference group is based on chronological age, within 2 or 3 month intervals. Although the term IQ is assiduously avoided by the authors, the ILP is essentially a deviation IQ, comparing the individual's standing among others of his age, and thus it has the same meaning that IQ has on the Lorge-Thorndike or any other up-to-date tests of intelligence which provide deviation IQ's. To put the ILP on the same scale as the IQ, one must simply add 50 to the ILP.

The General Composite Standard Score (GCSS) is normed on pupils making normal progress within grade levels limited to an 18-month age range within each grade level, a range that comprises the middle 80 to 90 percent of pupils in any one grade. The GCSS also has a mean of 50 and a SD of 15.

So, if you want to know where a pupil stands with respect to those of similar chronological age, regardless of their grade level, you use the ILP. If you want to see where a pupil stands in relation to others in his grade who are making normal progress (presumably the middle 80 to 90 percent of the age range of children in regular classes), you use the GCSS.

The Composite Prognostic Score (CPS), also with a mean of 50 and a SD of 15, is a score based on a weighted combination of several subtests that correlates maximally with either reading or mathematics achievement. The CPS provides hardly any appreciable gain over the total ILP or GCSS in terms of correlation specifically with achievement in verbal or quantitative curricula.

Finally, the ALP raw scores can be converted to percentile ranks and to stanines.

The most useful score, one might think, would be one which is on the same scale as the scholastic achievement test, so that direct comparison of "intelligence" (i.e., extra-scholastic achievement) and scholastic achievement would be possible. But most standard achievement tests provide normalized T scores with a mean of 50 and a standard deviation of 10. The ILP unfortunately combines the mean of achievement tests (i.e., 50) with the standard deviation of IQ tests (i.e., 15).

Scoring of the ALP by hand (made easy by simple templates) or by machine is possible. IBM, MRC, and Digitek answer sheets are available, and scoring can be done locally or by the publisher's scoring service.

RELIABILITY. The internal consistency reliability (Kuder-Richardson) is very high, ranging from .92 to .97 in different grades. The alternate-forms reliability is also quite satisfactory (.80 to .94).

VALIDITY. The ALP is expressly intended to predict scholastic achievement. Its validity was established by correlating the GCSS scores at each grade level. In the high school grades the validities are nearly as high as reliability will permit. If the authors' chief aim was to "predict" concurrent scholastic achievement with the ALP, it is hard to see how they could have been any more successful. The ILP score was not used in the validation evidence but would probably yield validity coefficients very similar to those for the GCSS.

The ALP correlates .83 with Lorge-Thorndike total IQ (at grade 5) and has correlations between .29 (Mechanical) and .86 (Verbal Reasoning + Numerical Ability) with various parts of the *Differential Aptitude Tests*.

TECHNICAL INFORMATION. In addition to the very complete printed manual that accompanies the test, the publishers have prepared a mimeographed Preliminary Technical Report which contains much more detailed information about the construction and validation of the ALP. It contains information which will be of primary interest to educational researchers and could also serve as a model in courses on the theory and practice of test construction. One of its most useful features is an appendix which gives normalized standard scores, with a mean of 500 and SD of 50, for the entire five batteries. This puts all the five tests, spanning grades 1 to 12, on the same scale, a feature which enhances the test's usefulness for longitudinal studies. The method of scaling the various tests is fully described in this report.

USEFULNESS. If one wants to use a test of "general intelligence," or "IQ," or "scholastic aptitude," the ALP is about as good as any of the current top competitors in the field. Since

it correlates almost as highly with tests of scholastic achievement as reliability permits, one might ask, Why use the ALP at all? Why not just measure achievement? Indeed, why not? Unless the school authorities have some special purpose intended which calls for a measure of ability which is not directly based on the subject matter of the curriculum, there would seem to be little justification for the time, bother, and expense involved in getting group-administered intelligence test scores on all pupils in a school. Achievement scores should suffice for most purposes. Other diagnostic measures (including nonscholastic measures of general intelligence) would be called for in those cases where a pupil's scholastic performance is markedly deviant. As previously suggested, an intelligence test used along with achievement tests can spot the underachievers who may then receive further diagnosis to determine the causes of the underachievement. Since the correlation is so high between ALP and achievement, those pupils who show a marked discrepancy between the two scores would warrant special attention, especially if achievement scores are markedly *below* the ALP scores. The ALP scores, reflecting more extra-school influences, could also be used in the same way for comparing the average achievement of whole classes, schools, or communities. The ALP can also serve as a control variable in educational experiments.

SUMMARY. From both technical and practical standpoints, the *Analysis of Learning Potential* (despite its title being a misnomer for "intelligence test") is an excellent battery of five group tests, covering grades 1 to 12, for measuring general intelligence or scholastic aptitude by means of test materials for the most part not specifically taught in school. Its correlations with tests of scholastic achievement are exceptionally high. The ALP appears to be fully competitive with the best group intelligence tests currently available.

[335]

★Boehm Test of Basic Concepts. Grades kgn–2; 1969–70, c1967–69; BTBC; Form A ('69, 16 pages in 2 booklets) ; manual ('70, 22 pages) ; $5.90 per 30 tests; 50¢ per manual; $1 per specimen set; postage extra; Spanish edition available; (30–40) minutes in 2 sessions; Ann E. Boehm; Psychological Corporation. *

REFERENCE

1. BOEHM, ANN ELIZABETH. *The Development of Comparative Concepts in Primary School Children*. Doctor's thesis, Columbia University (New York, N.Y.), 1966. (DA 27: 4109B)

BOYD R. MCCANDLESS, *Professor of Education and Psychology and Director, Educational Psychology, Emory University, Atlanta, Georgia.*

The purpose of the test, as stated by the author, is "to assess beginning school children's knowledge of frequently used basic concepts widely but sometimes mistakenly assumed to be familiar to children at their time of entry into kindergarten or first grade." The reviewer considers this statement accurate, modest, and realistic.

The test was inspired by the author's awareness that many children beginning school do not comprehend many of the printed or spoken instructions taken as "givens" by most teachers, and by her assumption (well supported by survey data) that deficits at the beginning of school are cumulative over time. She hopes to provide an instrument to pinpoint these deficits, lead the way to remedying them, and thus prevent irrelevant interference with school progress.

The initial item content was empirically and apparently somewhat subjectively determined by inspection of curriculum materials, together with checks to see what concepts were difficult or unfamiliar to substantial numbers of children.

The test was finally narrowed to 50 items placed in two test booklets to facilitate administration in two sessions to children in grades K, 1, 2, and 3. Items proved so easy for third graders that the final form of the test includes norms for only grades K through 2, but the test is too easy to be of great value for first graders from middle or higher socioeconomic levels or for second graders of any social class.

Two waves of preliminary testing were conducted before the final form of the test was set up. Item selection was made according to conservative and acceptable principles—e.g., sampling of a range of concepts, point biserial correlations exceeding .30, "even rises of percent-passing values across age levels," and "normal distribution of percent-passing values, centered around .50 for the kindergarten pupils."

Testing with two booklets, each including 25 questions to be answered by making X's on pictures, requires 15 to 20 minutes per booklet. Instructions to teachers state that groups of 8 to 12 may be tested. Although the reviewer has not tried the test with kindergartners, he is skeptical that it can be feasibly administered to groups of this size unless there is a generous supply of proctors.

The booklets are made up of black line drawings on white (Booklet 1) or buff (Booklet 2). For the most part, the drawings are clear, though a few seem ambiguous. The people in the illustrations are appropriately integrated racially. Scoring instructions are clear and the mechanics are about as simple as is possible when working with test protocols for children in kindergarten and grades 1 and 2.

The standardization sample came from five cities, one western, one south-midwestern, one southeastern, and two northeastern. School personnel in each city were asked to administer the test within one high, one middle, and one low socioeconomic school. A disproportionate number of the low socioeconomic class children come from the southeastern city school system. The test author makes no pretense to having a representative U.S. normative sample, but has sampled widely in reasonably representative school systems.

No validity evidence other than face validity is presented, although the face validity is convincing enough. As anyone familiar with kindergarten and first grade instruction will realize, the items tap concepts that children need to know. The author represents the BTBC modestly as a screening device and a guide for instruction. Used thoughtfully, it can be quite useful to teachers. A section in the manual devoted to interpretation and use of the results in instruction is very practical.

CHARLES D. SMOCK, *Professor of Psychology, The University of Georgia, Athens, Georgia.*

Children enter school with a variety of experiential backgrounds and variation in knowledge of the physical and social environments. Current interest in cognitive developmental theory and enrichment of the environments of "disadvantaged" children has increased concern for adequate assessment of their intellectual level upon entering school. Also, curriculum development specialists have found it necessary to modify the typical first grade curriculum in order to create effective learning conditions for these children. Of particular importance is the fact that both the available curriculum materials and "readiness" tests assume a set of fundamental concepts which many disadvantaged children do not yet understand; for example, the understanding necessary to follow directions in the procedures designed to determine "readiness" is often questionable. The primary reason for development of the *Boehm Test of Basic Concepts* was the recognition of this fact: the assumption that all children have mastered these fundamental concepts is fallacious.

The Boehm assessment procedure consists of 50 items concerning the child's understanding of space (location, direction, orientation, dimensions); time and quantity (number); plus a few miscellaneous concepts selected on the basis of their contribution to the internal consistency and validity of the test.

The criteria governing the initial item selection included both empirical and educational considerations. That is, the concepts selected were important for the understanding and following of directions and occurred frequently in curriculum materials but were not generally part of the usual instructional process. The final 50 items selected met the following criteria: correlation of each item with the total score on the 25-item booklet in which the item appeared; a fairly even increase in percent passing across the age levels; and a final set of items which would yield a normal distribution of percent passing with the kindergarten children achieving a 50 percent level. Tables of percent passing, based on subsequent data collections, for each item by grade and socioeconomic level at the beginning and middle of each year are presented. Reliability coefficients ranging from .68 to .90 are reported. "Content validity," the only validity reported, seems adequate since the items were selected on the basis of the relevance to currently used curriculum materials in kindergarten, first, and second grades.

The Boehm procedures should be valuable to teachers in the detection and remediation of deficiencies in verbal understanding. Appropriate qualifications and cautions are presented in the manual regarding interpretation of obtained scores; e.g., the scores do not reflect general intellectual level. The directions and test items (pictorial form) are clear and concise; the test could be administered by aides or paraprofessional personnel. The manual gives explicit instructions on procedures for administration and offers suggestions to the teacher on how to use the results to plan remedial instructional work for children who have not acquired specific concepts.

J Ed Meas 7(2):139-40 su '70. Victor H. Noll. * The manual presents various reasons for concept difficulty and suggests procedures for remedial instruction. It is emphasized that ideally instruction should result in mastery, though training on the test items is to be avoided "if post-training test results are to reflect more than rote memorization." This would seem to pose some difficulties if, as appears likely, synonyms for such concepts as top, bottom, whole, every, etc. are to be found and used without equating them directly with their counterparts in the test. * The norms tables reveal that the test is still too easy for second graders with mean scores of 43.5, 46.7, and 47.8 out of a possible 50 for the three socioeconomic levels. It appears that it also may be too easy for the upper levels of Grade 1. The mean score for the middle socioeconomic level of Grade 1 is 43.8 while that for the highest level of second graders is 47.8. It might therefore be concluded that the test is adequate in difficulty only for kindergarten and the lowest socioeconomic levels of first graders. For a test of 50 items at these grade levels, reliabilities are surprisingly good. * It is in this matter of validity that the Boehm Test is most seriously open to question. This weakness has two aspects. In the first place no information is given as to what materials the author examined and only vague statements descriptive of methods used to determine what concepts were to be retained as a basis for the test. The statement is made that they "occurred with considerable frequency." Further, we are told that they "were seldom if ever explicitly defined or were defined in their simple forms but subsequently used in complex forms without adequate transitions." Finally, that "they represented relatively abstract basic concepts or ideas." Such statements as "considerable frequency," "seldom if ever," "adequate transitions," and "relatively abstract" are too general and imprecise to convey any adequate understanding of the criteria. In the second place, the author supplies no information on the question of how necessary these concepts really are to "achievement in the first years of school." Is there any relation between mastery of them and quality of school achievement? If there is none or even very little, the whole *raison d'etre* for the test as a test would seem to disappear unless some evidence on this point can be determined. A teacher who gave the test, tabulated the results, and proceeded with careful remedial instruction would seem to be wasting time. In summary, the author of this test has gone through most of the accepted and established procedures for constructing and standardizing a test but has not provided adequate and essential information on how the concepts on which the test is based were determined and the evidence, if any is available, to show that these concepts are indeed "necessary for achievement in the first years of school." Perhaps someone might claim that it is self-evident that no child could do well in the first years of school without mastery of them. But the author presents no evidence in support of such a claim. Directions for administering are clear and complete. The publishers have done a fine job of production. The test may have considerable usefulness as a teaching device to help identify group and individual lack of understanding of the 50 concepts tested. However, for this purpose most of the statistical data provided are superfluous.

J Spec Ed 4 (2):249–51 sp–su '70. Barton B. Proger. * Interpretation of test results is clearly and carefully delineated in the manual. * This reviewer was pleased to see that the author provides guidelines for using the *BTBC* in pretest-posttest gain analyses to evaluate the effectiveness of remediation efforts. Teachers should be encouraged to engage in, at least, informal program evaluation; far too many shy away from it. * by and large, that the test items possess a high degree of internal consistency. The consistency of scores over time cannot be gauged from the manual, since test-retest co-efficients are not provided; such data are most desirable. It should also be noted that no internal consistency reliability measures are given for start-of-the-year scores, although such information would have been easy to provide. Boehm is to be commended for her discussion of confidence intervals and standard errors of measurement. * In the areas of conceptualization, standardization, interpretation, reliability, etc., the Boehm test is better than most new test instruments appearing on the market. However, this is not saying much! The *BTBC* must be severely criticized on the grounds of insufficient validity studies. The author begs the issue: "For the *Boehm Test of Basic Concepts,* like any other test of educational achievement or mastery, validity is primarily a matter of the relevance of the test content to the school curriculum. This type of validity is usually called *content validity*" (p. 17). Content validity is important, but predictive, construct, and concurrent validity are also important and have been neglected here. Indeed, only one research reference is provided in the whole manual: Boehm's dissertation (1966). Also, a test's technical manual should provide a representative (and perhaps comprehensive) review of the literature relevant to the issues underlying the test's development. The *Boehm* fails us here as well. Unfortunately, a dearth of documentation is by no means peculiar to the *BTBC*. In summary, the manual and test materials for the *Boehm Test of Basic Concepts* appear to be of high quality; its rationale has considerable appeal. It is an instrument that the teacher can administer, interpret, and utilize in remedial work. It has implications for both the disadvantaged and the handicapped. Limitations in standardization efforts, and lack of validation studies and of test-retest reliability should make the user cautious in its deployment.

Nat Cath Guid Conf J 14(3):200–1 sp '70. George Lawlor. * The items appear to be well selected from a survey of curriculum material in the areas of reading, arithmetic and science. * The standardization sample was adequate, however, no nursery school subjects were used. * it is strongly felt that a sample of pre-kindergarten subjects should have been included. Furthermore, the test Booklet 1 appears too easy for grade 2 since only two items reported less than 90% passing. Booklet 2 presents a slightly better use for grade 2. * More meaningful validity information should have accompanied the test rather than the generalized and well known cliché concerning this important aspect of the test. The classification of concepts with four content categories is well developed in the test form. However, there is a preponderance of items dealing with space, e.g., 56%, 36% pertains to quantity; 26% to time, and 10% to miscellaneous. There is overlapping in that 7% of the items test two concepts and 6% tap a triad in one item. The question arises when the teacher sets up remediation: which concept was known or unknown? Is further testing needed to determine whether one, two, or three basic concepts were unknown? Maybe the test would serve its purpose better if each item dealt with only *one* basic concept. The statistics are adequately presented. The Tables are easy to interpret. The table to determine per cents passing each item is very useful and can be used in any situation with forty or less subjects. However, this reviewer found no statement for the teacher regarding the cut-off level determining the difficulty of a given item for a grade level. Should this be 50, 75, or 90%? The directions are well stated. The booklets are easily handled by young children and the pictures are large enough to be readily identified. Non-white subjects are used in the test illustrations. In the local situation the teacher may find the Boehm Test useful in the identification of individual children with deficiencies in the area of certain basic concepts. The test may have further use in pointing out the individual concepts which may be unfamiliar to many students in a class.

Prof Psychol 1(5):490 f '70. Frank S. Freeman. * The usual standardization procedures were followed, but the areas from which the population was drawn, as the author of the test recognizes, are not representative of the nation as a whole. Still, the test items can be useful in any class if the teacher believes the concepts included should be empirically tested. Validation was by content, the items having been selected from "relevant curriculum materials." The data provided in the manual, unfortunately, are inadequate to permit judgment regarding comprehensiveness and representativeness of the selected items as to the curriculum materials. Justification of selected items is given entirely in general terms. Split-half reliability correlations are fairly good (.60–.90) * This type of instrument can be useful only in providing teachers with symptoms, or clues, as to children's concept mastery or ignorance. Granted that the selected concepts are valid as to curriculum content, they cannot represent the entire range of concepts that a child should know, ideally, or needs to know. * I am often surprised by statements that reveal deficient information in the subject under discussion. Dr. Boehm states, "It is only in the last few years that attention has been focused on these developmental differences (in cognitive development) with respect to their nature, their origins, modifiability, and implications for future achievement" [Test Manual, p. 3]. This astonishing statement ignores the very considerable research and the many publications on nature-nurture and individual differences, as well as on the differences in instructional materials and methods demanded by individual differences. Dr. Boehm's statement also ignores the fact

that children's differences in concept mastery have for many years been tested, in one way or another, by means of individual and group tests of intelligence, although these were not devised exclusively for that purpose, for example, Stanford-Binet, Wechsler scales, California Test of Mental Maturity, Lorge-Thorndike, Terman-McNemar, and among the very early scales, Dearborn Group Tests, Pintner-Cunningham Primary Test, the Non-Language Multi-Mental Test, and others. Dr. Boehm's unwarranted claim, however, does not reduce the value the test has for the purpose intended.

[336]

★**CGA Mental Ability Tests.** Grades 6–9, 9–12; 1957–68; items identical with *The Henmon-Nelson Tests of Mental Ability;* for use in Canada only; Forms A, B, ['62, 4 pages]; 2 levels; manuals: grades 6–9 ['68, 8 pages], grades 9–12 ['68, 10 pages]; Can $2.47 per 25 tests; 97¢ per scoring stencil; 30¢ per manual; $2.44 per specimen set of either level; 15% extra for postage and handling; 30(35) minutes; Canadian Guidance Associates; distributed by Guidance Centre. *

[337]

*California Short-Form Test of Mental Maturity, 1963 Revision.** Grades kgn–1.0, 1.5–3, 3–4, 4–6, 6–7, 7–8, 9–12, 12–16 and adults; 1938–65; CTMM-SF; all items drawn from the long form, *California Test of Mental Maturity;* 7 scores: logical reasoning, numerical reasoning, verbal concepts, memory, language total, nonlanguage total, total; 1 form; 8 levels; interpretation guide ('64, 38 pages) for long and short forms; technical report ('65, 25 pages) for long and short forms; supplementary norms ('65, 5–8 pages) for levels 1, 1H, 2, and 3; $3 per 100 profiles; $1 per interpretation guide; $1.50 per technical report; postage extra; $1.25 per specimen set of any one level, postpaid; Elizabeth T. Sullivan, Willis W. Clark, and Ernest W. Tiegs; CTB/McGraw-Hill. *
a) [HAND SCORED LEVELS.] Grades kgn–1.0, 1.5–3, 3–4; profile ('62, 1 page, also on back of test booklet) ; $5.75 per 35 tests; scoring service, 45¢ and over per test.
1) *Level 0.* Grades kgn–1.0; 1963 S-Form ('62, 11 pages) ; manual ('63, 49 pages) ; 34(39) minutes.
2) *Level 1.* Grades 1.5–3; 1963 S-Form ('62, 12 pages) ; manual ('63, 53 pages) with 1964 norms; 41(46) minutes.
3) *Level 1H.* Grades 3–4; 1963 S-Form ('62, 10 pages) ; manual ('64, 56 pages) with 1965 norms; 42(47) minutes.
b) [MACHINE SCORABLE LEVELS.] Grades 1.5–3, 3–4, 4–6, 6–7, 7–8, 9–12, 12–16 and adults; profile ('61, 1 page, also on back of test booklet and back of answer sheet) ; Digitek directions ('68, 4 pages) for levels 2–5; IBM 1230 directions ('65, 4 pages) for levels 2–5; separate answer sheets (CompuScan [NCS], Digitek, IBM 1230, Scoreze) may be used for levels 2–5; tape recorded directions (3¾ ips) for administration of levels 2–5 available at $5.95 each.
1) *Level 1.* Grades 1.5–3; 1963 S-Form ('62, 12 pages) ; manual ('63, 53 pages) with 1964 norms; $8 per 35 tests; $1 per scoring key; CompuScan scoring service, 27¢ and over per test; 41(46) minutes.
2) *Level 1H.* Grades 3–4; 1963 S-Form ('62, 10 pages) ; manual ('64, 56 pages) with 1965 norms;

prices same as for machine scorable level 1; 42(47) minutes.

3) *Level 2*. Grades 4–6; 1963 S-Form ('61, 11 pages); manual ('63, 59 pages); $6 per 35 tests; $2.50 per 50 CompuScan, Digitek, or IBM answer sheets; $2.50 per 25 Scoreze answer sheets; 5¢ per NCS answer sheet; 75¢ per Digitek or IBM hand scoring stencil; CompuScan scoring service, 22¢ and over per test; IBM scoring service, 25¢ and over per test; NCS scoring service, 14¢ and over per test; 43(48) minutes.

4) *Level 2H*. Grades 6–7; 1963 S-Form ('61, 11 pages); manual ('63, 60 pages); prices same as for level 2; 41(46) minutes.

5) *Level 3*. Grades 7–8; 1963 S-Form ('61, 11 pages); manual ('63, 57 pages); prices same as for level 2; 41(46) minutes.

6) *Level 4*. Grades 9–12; 1963 S-Form ('61, 11 pages); manual ('63, 53 pages); prices same as for level 2; 39(45) minutes.

7) *Level 5*. Grades 12–16 and adults; 1963 S-Form ('61, 11 pages); manual ('63, 47 pages); prices same as for level 2; 39(45) minutes.

REFERENCES

1–15. See 5:313.

16–26. See 6:443.

27. McHugh, Ann F. *An Investigation of the Reliability and Concurrent Validity of Two Levels of the California Test of Mental Maturity, Short Form.* Master's thesis, Fordham University (New York, N.Y.), 1957.

28. Rooks, Ila. *Teaching Satisfaction in Relation to Intelligence, Interests, and Grade-Point Average of Selected University of Georgia Graduates.* Doctor's thesis, University of Georgia (Athens, Ga.), 1957. (DA 17:1953)

29. Bashaw, Joan Ann. *The Effects of Three Methods of Group Test Interpretation on Self-Esteem.* Doctor's thesis, Florida State University (Tallahassee, Fla.), 1962. (DA 23:527)

30. Denum, Donald C. "The Use of the Stanford-Binet Intelligence Scale, Form L-M, 1960 Revision as a Criterion Instrument for Norming All Levels of the 1963 Revision of the California Test of Mental Maturity Series." *Yearb Nat Council Meas Ed* 20:50–3 '63. * (PA 38:8409)

31. Mattick, William E. "Predicting Success in the First Grade." *El Sch J* 63:273–6 F '63. *

32. Mickler, Jacob Ernest, Jr. *A Predictive Index of Academic Success for Alabama High School Graduates Entering the State Colleges and Universities.* Doctor's thesis, University of Alabama (University, Ala.), 1963. (DA 24:4086)

33. Altenhaus, Corrinne Batlin. *An Exploration of the Relationship of Intelligence to Creativity in School Children.* Doctor's thesis, Rutgers—The State University (New Brunswick, N.J.), 1964. (DA 25:2842)

34. Cauble, Ben Leroy. *Anxiety in Intermediate Grade Children and Its Relationship With Their Scores on Measures of Intelligence, Academic Achievement, and Several Personality Factors.* Doctor's thesis, Southern Illinois University (Carbondale, Ill.), 1964. (DA 25:5150)

35. Drew, Alfred S. "The Relationship of General Reading Ability and Other Factors to School and Job Performance of Machine Apprentices." *J Indus Teach Ed* 2:47–60 f '64. *

36. Shaffer, Raymond George. *A Study of Four Group Intelligence Tests to Identify Ambiguous Pictures as a Factor Which Causes Some Children to Select Incorrect Answers.* Doctor's research study No. 1, Colorado State College (Greeley, Colo.), 1964. (DA 25:1014)

37. West, L. W., and MacArthur, R. S. "An Evaluation of Selected Intelligence Tests for Two Samples of Metis and Indian Children." *Alberta J Ed Res* 10:17–27 Mr '64. * (PA 39:12328)

38. Frost, Barry P. "Intelligence, Manifest Anxiety and Scholastic Achievement." *Alberta J Ed Res* 11:167–75 S '65. * (PA 40:1948)

39. Johnson, Halvin Sherwood. *The Relationship of Scores on Aptitude and Achievement Tests Taken at Late Elementary and Junior High School Levels to Scholarship in Ninth Grade.* Doctor's thesis, University of South Dakota (Vermillion, S.D.), 1965. (DA 26:4449)

40. Rainey, Robert G. "A Study of Four School-Ability Tests." *J Exp Ed* 33:305–19 su '65. * (PA 39:12306)

41. Slayton, Wilfred George. *A Comparison of Successful and Unsuccessful Bible College Students With Respect to Selected Personality Factors.* Doctor's thesis, University of Arizona (Tucson, Ariz.), 1965. (DA 26:1487)

42. Swan, Robert J., and Hopkins, Kenneth D. "An Investigation of Theoretical and Empirical Chance 'Scores on

43. Allen, Joyce Carmen Yandell. *A Study of the Relationships Between Achievement and Intelligence Test Scores for Charleston High School Juniors and Sen ors.* Master's thesis, Eastern Illinois University (Charleston, Ill.), 1966.

Selected Standardized Group Tests." *Calif J Ed Res* 16:34–41 Ja '65. * (PA 39:10156)

44. Bristol, John L. "Validity of the California Achievement and Mental Maturity Tests in Predicting Success in Five Different First Year High School Foreign Languages." *J Exp Ed* 34:57–61 sp '66. *

45. Finley, Carmen J.; Thompson, Jack M.; and Cognata, Albert. "Stability of the California Short Form Test of Mental Ability: Grades 3, 5, and 7." *Calif J Ed Res* 17:157–68 S '66. * (PA 41:996)

46. Jenkins, Alice Crawford. *The Relationship of Certain Measurable Factors to Academic Success in Freshman Biology.* Doctor's thesis, New York University (New York, N.Y.), 1966. (DA 27:2279A)

47. Kopff, Richard Garms. *Manager Performance as Related to Goal Setting, Intelligence, and Selected Personality Characteristics.* Doctor's thesis, Columbia University (New York, N.Y.), 1966. (DA 27:677A)

48. Mayhon, Woodrow G. *The Relationship of Creativity to Achievement and Other Student Variables.* Doctor's thesis, University of New Mexico (Albuquerque, N.M.), 1966. (DA 27:1713A)

49. Olson, Arthur V. "Relation of Achievement Test Scores and Specific Reading Abilities to the Frostig Developmental Test of Visual Perception." *Percept & Motor Skills* 22:179–84 F '66. * (PA 40:4750)

50. Olson, Arthur V. "Relation of Achievement Test Scores and Specific Reading Abilities to the Frostig Test of Visual Perception." *Optom Weekly* 57:31–4 Jl 14 '66. *

51. Barnett, Thomas Marvin. *The Predictive Validities, as Measured by Multiple Correlation, of Two Batteries Using Academic Achievement as Criterion.* Doctor's thesis, North Texas State University (Denton, Tex.), 1967. (DA 28:2006A)

52. Hanna, Gerald S. "The Use of Students' Predictions of Success in Geometry and Year of High School to Augment Predictions Made From Test Scores and Past Grades." *J Ed Meas* 4:137–41 f '67. *

53. MacNeil, Ronald Lauchlin. *A Study of the Effectiveness of the SCAT and CTMM-SF to Predict First Semester Averages.* Master's thesis, St. Francis Xavier University (Antigonish, N.S., Canada), 1967.

54. Olson, Norinne Hilchey. *An Analysis of the Relationship Between Conventional Reading Readiness Measures and Intellectual Functioning.* Doctor's thesis, University of Georgia (Athens, Ga.), 1967. (DA 28:4490A)

55. Burke, Barbara Patricia. *An Exploratory Study of the Relationships Among Third Grade Negro Chidren's Self-Concept Creativity and Intelligence and Teachers' Perceptions of Those Relationships.* Doctor's thesis, Wayne State University (Detroit, Mich.), 1968. (DAI 30:1327A)

56. Carbonari, Joseph Phillip, Jr. *An Investigation of Residual Gain and Its Correlates.* Doctor's thesis, Northern Illinois University (DeKalb, Ill.), 1968. (DA 29:2559A)

57. MacArthur, R. S. "Assessing Intellectual Potential of Native Canadian Pupils: A Summary." *Alberta J Ed Res* 14:115–22 Je '68. * (PA 44:4170)

58. Ramirez, Walter Gene. *Measures of Three Types of Information Processing Related to Language and Non-Language Intelligence.* Doctor's thesis, University of Oregon (Eugene, Ore.), 1968. (DA 29:3470A)

59. Bushey, James Thomas. *The Relationships Between a Preschool Measure of Readiness and Subsequent Test Performances Among a Group of Private Elementary School Children.* Doctor's thesis, Wayne State University (Detroit, Mich.), 1969. (DAI 30:3816A)

60. Carron, Theodore J. "Validity of Tests for Chemical Plant Personnel." *Personnel Psychol* 22(3):307–12 au '69. * (PA 44:9414)

61. Cashen, Valjean M., and Ramseyer, Gary C. "The Use of Separate Answer Sheets by Primary Age Children." *J Ed Meas* 6(3):155–8 f '69. * (PA 44:15297)

62. Furr, Karl D., and Wilson, F. Robert. "The California Short-Form Test of Mental Ability 1963 Edition as a Screening Device for Educable Mentally Retarded Programs." *J Sch Psychol* 7(4):47–9 168–69 ['69]. * (PA 44:2793)

63. Hall, Lucien Talmage, Jr. *The Prediction of Success in Each of Six Four-Year Selections of Secondary Mathematics Courses.* Doctor's thesis, University of Virginia (Charlottesville, Va.), 1969. (DAI 30:4141A)

64. McCullough, James Leonard, Sr. *A Study of the Predictive Efficiency of the California Short-Form Test of Mental Maturity, Level 2, for Negro and White Subjects.* Doctor's thesis, Mississippi State University (State College, Miss.), 1969. (DAI 30:2260A)

65. Oas, Robert T. *A Study of the Relationships of Students' Aptitude, Academic Achievement and Attitude Toward School for Selected School Populations.* Doctor's thesis, University of South Dakota (Vermillion, S.D.), 1969. (DAI 30:3644A)

66. Mars, Paul Arne. *High School Geometry Achievement as Related to Reading Achievement, Arithmetic Achievement, and General Intelligence in the Public Schools of Lincoln Ne-*

braska. Doctor's thesis, University of Nebraska (Lincoln, Neb.), 1970. (*DAI* 31:1691A)

67. MILLER, BERNEICE BEADLES. *The Effects of Continuing or Changing Foreign Languages on Listening Comprehension and Selected Tests as Predictors of Success in S^anish or French at the Seventh-Grade Level.* Doctor's thesis, University of Oklahoma (Norman, Okla.), 1970. (*DAI* 31:2618A)

For a review by Julian C. Stanley, see 6:443; for a review by Cyril Burt of an earlier edition, see 5:313; see also 4:282 (1 excerpt). For reviews of the regular edition, see 338 (2 reviews), 5:314 (2 reviews), 4:282 (1 excerpt), 3:223 (1 review, 2 excerpts), 2:1384 (2 reviews, 1 excerpt), and 1:1042 (3 reviews, 1 excerpt).

[338]

*California Test of Mental Maturity, 1963 Revision. Grades kgn–1.0, 1.5–3, 4–6, 7–9, 9–12, 12–16 and adults; 1936–65; CTMM; for short form, see preceding entry; 8 scores: logical reasoning, spatial relationships, numerical reasoning, verbal concepts, memory, language total, non-language total, total; 1 form; 6 levels; interpretation guide ('64, 38 pages) for long and short forms; technical report ('65, 25 pages) for long and short forms; $2 per 100 profiles; $1 per interpretation guide; $1.50 per technical report; postage extra; $1.25 per specimen set of any one level, postpaid; Elizabeth T. Sullivan, Willis W. Clark, and Ernest W. Tiegs; CTB/McGraw-Hill. *

a) HAND SCORED LEVELS. Grades kgn–1.0, 1.5–3; profile ('62, 1 page, also on back of test booklet); $7.30 per 35 tests; scoring service, 70¢ and over per test.

1) *Level 0.* Grades kgn–1.0; 1 form ('62, 15 pages); manual ('64, 60 pages); 48(58) minutes.

2) *Level 1.* Grades 1.5–3; 1 form ('62, 16 pages); manual ('64, 68 pages); 63(73) minutes.

b) MACHINE SCORABLE LEVELS. Grades 4–6, 7–9, 9–12, 12–16 and adults; 1 form ('61, 19 pages); profile ('61, 1 page, also on back of test booklet and back of answer sheet); practice exercises ('64, 2 pages) for IBM answer sheets; IBM directions ('65, 4 pages); separate answer sheets (IBM 1230, Scoreze) may be used; $5 per 50 sets of IBM answer sheets; $5 per 25 sets of Scoreze answer sheets; $1.50 per set of IBM hand scoring stencils; $3 per 100 practice exercises; 15¢ per IBM directions; IBM scoring service, 25¢ and over per test.

1) *Level 2.* Grades 4–6; manual ('64, 66 pages); $8 per 35 tests; 83(93) minutes.

2) *Level 3.* Grades 7–9; manual ('64, 63 pages); $8 per 35 tests; 83(93) minutes.

3) *Level 4.* Grades 9–12; manual ('64, 61 pages); $8.80 per 35 tests; 81(91) minutes.

4) *Level 5.* Grades 12–16 and adults; manual ('64, 53 pages); $8.80 per 35 tests; 81(91) minutes.

REFERENCES

1–5. See 2:1384.
6–15. See 3:223.
16–39. See 4:282.
40–73. See 5:314.
74–103. See 6:444.
104. CLARK, JERRY H. "Interest Variability on the California Test of Mental Maturity in Relation to the Minnesota Multiphasic Personality Inventory." *J Consult Psychol* 14:32–4 F '50. * (*PA* 24:4112)
105. RAWLINGS, TRAVIS DEAN. *Mental Organization as a Function of Brightness.* Doctor's thesis, University of Kentucky (Lexington, Ky.), 1956. (*DA* 21:2778)
106. MOE, IVER L. *Auding as a Predictive Measure of Reading Performance in Primary Grades.* Doctor's thesis, University of Florida (Gainesville, Fla.), 1957. (*DA* 18:121)
107. GUNDERSEN, RICHARD OSCAR. *The Significance of Divergencies Between Verbal and Nonverbal Intelligence Scores.*

Doctor's thesis, State University of Iowa (Iowa City, Iowa), 1959. (*DA* 20:2142)
108. HAROOTUNIAN, BERJ AVEDIS. *The Relationships Among Tests of Intelligence, Learning, and Reasoning.* Doctor's thesis, University of Pennsylvania (Philadephia, Pa.), 1959. (*DA* 20:203)
109. CURRY, ROBERT LEE. *The Effect of Intelligence on the Scholastic Achievement of Sixth-Grade Children of Comparable Socio-Economic Status.* Doctor's thesis, University of Oklahoma (Norman, Okla.), 1960. (*DA* 20:3995)
110. HOFFMAN, CARL BENTLEY. *The Relationship of Immediate Recall, Delayed Recall, and Incidental Memory to Problem-Solving Ability.* Doctor's thesis, University of Pennsylvania (Philadelphia, Pa.), 1960. (*DA* 21:813)
111. JOHNSON, WYNNE ELTON. *Prediction of High School Achievement by the Use of an Attitude Scale and a Group Intelligence Test.* Doctor's thesis, Washington State University (Pullman, Wash.), 1960. (*DA* 21:2215)
112. VERTEIN, LESTER DALE. *A Study of the Personal-Social and Intellectual Characteristics of a Group of State College Students Preparing to Teach.* Doctor's thesis, University of Wisconsin (Madison, Wis.), 1960. (*DA* 21:1473)
113. McGUIRE, CARSON; HINDSMAN, EDWIN; KING, F. J.; AND JENNINGS, EARL. "Dimensions of Talented Behavior." *Ed & Psychol Meas* 21:3–38 sp '61. * (*PA* 36:1KH03M)
114. WELTER, M. BORROMEO. *A Comparison of the California Test of Mental Maturity and the Pikunas Graphoscopic Scale as Measures of Intelligence and Academic Achievement.* Master's thesis, University of Detroit (Detroit, Mich.), 1961.
115. OLSON, D. R., AND MACARTHUR, R. S. "The Effect of Foreign Language Background on Intelligence Test Performance." *Alberta J Ed Res* 8:157–66 S '62. * (*PA* 37:8270)
116. RUBIN, SAMUEL SOLOMON. *The Relation of Fantasy Productions to Test Intelligence.* Doctor's thesis, Columbia University (New York, N.Y.), 1962. (*DA* 23:1080)
117. *Basic Data for Factor Analytic Studies With the California Test of Mental Maturity, 1963 Revision.* Monterey, Calif.: California Test Bureau, 1963. Pp. 34. *
118. GARDNER, SHELDON FRANK. *Creativity in Children: A Study of the Relationship Between Temperament Factors and Aptitude Factors Involved in the Creative Ability of Seventh Grade Children With Suggestions for a Theory of Creativity.* Doctor's thesis, University of Southern California (Los Angeles, Calif.), 1963. (*DA* 24:822)
119. HOPKINS, KENNETH D., AND BIBELHEIMER, MILO H. "Two and Four Year Constancy of CTMM Language and Non-Language IQs," pp. 93–7. (*PA* 38:6058) In *Towards a Professional Identity in School Psychology.* California Association of School Psychologists and Psychometrists, Fourteenth Annual Conference, March 28–30, 1963. [Los Angeles, Calif.: the Association, 1963.] Pp. v, 97. * (*PA* 38:4904)
120. MUMAW, MYRON JAY. *Test Predictability for Culturally Deprived Students.* Master's thesis, Ohio State University (Columbus, Ohio), 1963.
121. PLESSAS, GUS P. "Auding and Intelligence." *Calif J Ed Res* 14:90–4 Mr '63. * (*PA* 38:1415)
122. WALSH, NANCY E. *The Relationship Between Performance on Certain Long Problems and Intelligence Factors.* Doctor's thesis, Rutgers—The State University (New Brunswick, N.J.), 1963. (*DA* 24:2–93)
123. ANDERSON, HARRY E., JR., AND LETON, DONALD A. "Factor Analyses of the California Test of Mental Maturity." *Ed & Psychol Meas* 24:513–23 f '64. * (*PA* 39:3176)
124. BISH, GERTRUDE GANTZ. *A Study of the Relationships of Intelligence, Achievement, Creativity, Anxiety, and Confidence Among Intermediate Grade Pupils in a Suburban Area Elementary School.* Doctor's thesis, George Washington University (Washington, D.C.), 1964.
125. BONEY, JEW DON. *A Study of the Use of Intelligence, Aptitude, and Mental Ability Measures in Predicting the Academic Achievement of Negro Students in Secondary School.* Doctor's thesis, University of Texas (Austin, Tex.), 1964. (*DA* 25:5726)
126. BRADSHAW, DONALD H. "Stability of California Test of Mental Maturity IQ's From the Second to the Fourth Grade." *Ed & Psychol Meas* 24:935–9 w '64. * (*PA* 39:7741)
127. BUCK, JAMES R., JR. *Some Identifiable Characteristics of Students Entering Negro Senior Colleges in Mississippi.* Doctor's thesis, George Peabody College for Teachers (Nashville, Tenn.), 1964. (*DA* 25:5039)
128. COBB, BART B. "Problems in Air Traffic Management: 5, Identification and Potential of Aptitude Test Measures for Selection of Tower Air Traffic Controller Trainees." *Aerospace Med* 35:1019–27 N '64. * (*PA* 39:16518)
129. DE BOER, DOROTHY LOUISE. *A Study of the Relationship of Creativity to Intelligence and Achievement.* Doctor's thesis, Northwestern University (Evanston, Ill.), 1964. (*DA* 25:3968)
130. DIZNEY, HENRY. "The Performance in Specific Skill Areas of Gifted, Elementary Underachievers." *Psychol Sch* 1:178–81 Ap '64. *
131. DIZNEY, HENRY, AND FLEMING, ELYSE. "Sex and I.Q. Differences in Discrepancies Between Predicted and Obtained Achievement." *J Sch Psychol* 3:26–31 au '64. * (*PA* 39:13032)

132. JONGEWARD, PAUL A. *The Relationship of Reading Ability to Performance on the California Test of Mental Maturity.* Master's thesis, Sacramento State College (Sacramento, Calif.), 1964.

133. SMITH, ROBERT HOUSTON. *A Study of Pre-Adolescent Boys Demonstrating Varying Levels of Creativity With Regard to Their Social Adjustment, Peer Acceptance and Academically Related Behavior.* Doctor's thesis, North Texas State University (Denton, Tex.), 1964. (DA 25:4553)

134. TRITES, DAVID K. "Problems in Air Traffic Management: 6, Interaction of Training-Entry Age With Intellectual and Personality Characteristics of Air Traffic Control Specialists." *Aerospace Med* 35:1184–94 D '64. * (PA 39:16533)

135. WALDRON, CORMAC. *Differential Prediction of Achievement in Broad Curricular Areas in an Academic High School.* Doctor's thesis, Fordham University (New York, N.Y.), 1964. (DA 25:1764)

136. BOYCE, RICHARD W., AND PAXSON, R. C. "The Predictive Validity of Eleven Tests at One State College." *Ed & Psychol Meas* 25:1143–7 w '65. * (PA 40:3563)

137. BRADY, WILLIAM JOSEPH. *Twenty Quantitative Predictors of Academic Success in College as Measured by Grade Point Averages.* Doctor's thesis, University of Connecticut (Storrs, Conn.), 1965. (DA 26:5121)

138. BREEN, JOSEPH MICHAEL. *Differential Prediction of Intermediate Grade Skills Achievement From Primary Grade Aptitude and Achievement Measures.* Doctor's thesis, University of Connecticut (Storrs, Conn.), 1965. (DA 26:5260)

139. GUILFORD, J. P.; HOEPFNER, RALPH; AND PETERSEN, HUGH. "Predicting Achievement in Ninth-Grade Mathematics From Measures of Intellectual-Aptitude Factors." *Ed & Psychol Meas* 25:659–82 au '65. * (PA 40:3376)

140. McCALL, ROZANNE A., AND McCALL, ROBERT B. "A Comparison of First Grade Reading Tests." *Ill Sch Res* 2:32–7 O '65. *

141. McCAULEY, JOHN HOWARD, JR. *Rorschach, WISC, and ITBS Patterns of Nine-Year-Old School Boys With Labile and Stabile IQ Scores.* Doctor's thesis, University of Maryland (College Park, Md.), 1965. (DA 27:1663A)

142. SPIERS, DUANE EDWIN. *A Study of the Predictive Validity of a Test Battery Administered to Theological Students.* Doctor's thesis, Purdue University (Lafayette, Ind.), 1965. (DA 26:1488)

143. BONEY, J. DON. "Predicting the Academic Achievement of Secondary School Negro Students." *Personnel & Guid J* 44:700–3 Mr '66. * (PA 40:8064)

144. COPPEDGE, FLOYD LEVON. *The Relationship of Selected Factors to Occupational and College Success.* Doctor's thesis, University of Oklahoma (Norman, Okla.), 1966. (DA 26:6441)

145. COPPEDGE, LLOYD LEON. *A Study of the Causes for Pupil Failure in High School.* Doctor's thesis, University of Oklahoma (Norman, Okla.), 1966. (DA 27:1579A)

146. CUNNINGHAM, WILLIAM. *A Thirteen-Year Retrospective Study of Standardized Test Data.* Doctor's thesis, Western Reserve University (Cleveland, Ohio), 1966. (DA 27:3305A)

147. DIRR, PIERRE MARIE. *Intellectual Variables in Achievement in Modern Algebra.* Doctor's thesis, Catholic University of America (Washington, D.C.), 1966. (DA 27:2873A)

148. FUQUA, NORMAN VINCE. *An Analysis of the Relationships and Differences Among Measures of Creative Thinking and Selected Other Factors in Educable and Less Educable Groups of Negro Children.* Doctor's thesis, Wayne State University (Detroit, Mich.), 1966. (DA 27:2314A)

149. GRIESS, JERALD ALFRED. *Selection of Trainees for a Twelve-Week Pre-Occupational Basic Education Program.* Doctor's thesis, Pennsylvania State University (University Park, Pa.), 1966. (DA 27:3704A)

150. GUILFORD, J. P., AND HOEPFNER, RALPH. "Creative Potential as Related to Measure of IQ and Verbal Comprehension." *Indian J Psychol* 41:7–16 Mr '66. * (PA 41:2877)

151. HAROOTUNIAN, BERJ. "Intellectual Abilities and Reading Achievement." *El Sch J* 66:386–95 Ap '66. *

152. HAROOTUNIAN, BERJ. "Intelligence and the Ability to Learn." *J Ed Res* 59:211–4 Ja '66. * (PA 40:6627)

153. KANDEL, ARTHUR. *Discrepancies Between the Stanford-Binet and Three Group Tests of Intelligence in the Identification of Low I.Q. Children.* Doctor's thesis, Catholic University of America (Washington, D.C.), 1966. (DA 27:1659A)

154. KEACH, CHARLES CAMPBELL. *Discrepancies Between the Stanford-Binet and Three Group Tests of Intelligence in the Identification of High I.Q. Children.* Doctor's thesis, Catholic University of America (Washington, D.C.), 1966. (DA 27:1660A)

155. PARISH, ROBERT L. *A Comparison of Scores Made on the Primary and Elementary Forms of the California Test of Mental Maturity and Their Relationship to Report Card Grades.* Master's thesis, San Jose State College (San Jose, Calif.), 1966.

156. PARKER, ADAH DONOHUE. *Projections for the Selection, Training and Retention of Sub-Professional Recreation Leaders Based on an Analysis of Personality, Interest, Aptitude, and Preference Data.* Doctor's thesis, University of Illinois (Urbana, Ill.), 1966. (DA 27:2059A)

157. BRENDEMUEHL, FRANK LOUIS. *The Influence of Reading Ability on the Validity of Group Non-Verbal Intelligence Tests.* Doctor's thesis, University of Minnesota (Minneapolis, Minn.), 1967. (DA 28:2088A)

158. CLEVELAND, GERALD ARTHUR, AND BOSWORTH, DOROTHY L. "A Study of Certain Psychological and Sociological Characteristics as Related to Arithmetic Achievement." *Arith Teach* 14:383–7 My '67. *

159. FULLER, GERALD B., AND ENDE, RUSSELL. "The Effectiveness of Visual Perception, Intelligence and Reading Understanding in Predicting Reading Achievement in Junior High School Children." *J Ed Res* 60:280–2 F '67. *

160. GILMAN, ROBERT H. *A Study of Intellectual Change of Deaf Students as Measured by Standard Tests of Intelligence.* Master's thesis, Springfield College (Springfield, Mass.), 1967.

161. LLOYD, BRUCE A., AND LLOYD, ROSALIE. "A Comparison of the Reading Readiness and Mental Maturity Scores of Selected First Grade Pupils in an American School and in a Belgian School: A Pilot Study." *J Read Specialist* 7:14–7 O '67. *

162. MANDEL, ROBERT. *A Study of the Performance of Disadvantaged Seventh Grade Males on the Colored Raven Progressive Matrices and the California Test of Mental Maturity.* Master's thesis, University of Tennessee (Knoxville, Tenn.), 1967.

163. TILKER, HARVEY A., AND SCHELL, ROBERT E. "Concurrent Validity of the Porteus Maze Test: A Comparative Study of Regular and Educationally Handicapped High School Students." *Ed & Psychol Meas* 27:447–55 su '67. * (PA 41:12840)

164. TRITES, DAVID K.; KUREK, ADOLPH; AND COBB, BART B. "Personality and Achievement of Air Traffic Controllers." *Aerospace Med* 38:1145–50 N '67. *

165. TULLY, G. EMERSON. "Test-Retest Reliability of the Raven Progressive Matrices Test (Form 1938) and the California Test of Mental Maturity, Level 4 (S-F 1963)." *Fla J Ed Res* 9:67–74 Ja '67. *

166. WAGNER, HILMAR ERNEST. *A Study of Physical, Mental and Musical Characteristics of Selected Band Members.* Doctor's thesis, North Texas State University (Denton, Tex.), 1967. (DA 28:2285A)

167. ARTH, ALFRED ARTHUR. *A Study of the Relationship Between Non-Completion and Intelligence Exhibited by Sixth Grade Elementary School Students.* Doctor's thesis, University of Oklahoma (Norman, Okla.), 1968. (DA 29:1666A)

168. COLGAN, RICHARD THOMAS. *A Longitudinal Study of the Relationship of Teacher Judgment Versus Objective Test Data With Respect to College Success.* Doctor's thesis, Southern Illinois University (Carbondale, Ill.), 1968. (DA 29:3413B)

169. COOKE, BRYAN EDWARD MARSHALL. *The Relationship Between Balance and Cognitive Abilities of Children Aged Eight to Thirteen Years.* Doctor's thesis, University of Illinois (Urbana, Ill.), 1968. (DAI 30:154A)

170. DEICH, RUTH F. "Correlations Between the PPVT and the CTMM." *Psychol Rep* 22:856 Je '68. * (PA 42:12982)

171. HATFIELD, ROBERT C. *A Study of the Relationships of Selected Components of Creativity, Cognitive Style, and Self-Concept Identified in a Random Sample of Twelfth Grade Students in One High School With Their Learning of Selected Information in the Social Studies.* Doctor's thesis, Wayne State University (Detroit, Mich.), 1968. (DAI 30:1334A)

172. LAUTEN, DORIS ANNE HIGGINS. *The Relationship Between Intelligence and Motor Proficiency in the Intellectually Gifted Child.* Doctor's thesis, University of North Carolina (Greensboro, N.C.), 1968. (DAI 31:1521B)

173. McLEOD, JACK DONALD. *Prediction of Independent Study Performance in Secondary School.* Doctor's thesis, Stanford University (Stanford, Calif.), 1968. (DA 29:3044A)

174. MARSHALL, JOSEPH JEMERSON. *Non-Cognitive Variables as a Predictor of Academic Achievement Among Freshmen, Sophomores, and Juniors at Abilene Christian College.* Doctor's thesis, Baylor University (Waco, Tex.), 1968. (DA 29:3833A)

175. RATTAN, M. S., AND MacARTHUR, R. S. "Longitudinal Prediction of School Achievement for Metis and Eskimo Pupils." *Alberta J Ed Res* 14:37–41 Mr '68. * (PA 44:4249)

176. RAY, MARTHA ROBERTS. *A Study of the Relationship Between Children's Test Scores on the Sensory Perception Block and the California Test of Mental Maturity.* Master's thesis, University of Tennessee (Knoxville, Tenn.), 1968.

177. THOMAS, HOWARD. *An Analysis of the California Test of Mental Maturity and the California Achievement Test for Discriminative Use at High Levels of Intelligence.* Master's thesis, Sacramento State College (Sacramento, Calif.), 1968.

178. ANDERSON, HARRY E., JR.; WHITE, WILLIAM F.; AND STEVENS, JOHN C. "Student Creativity, Intelligence, Achievement, and Teacher Classroom Behavior." *J Social Psychol* 78(1):99–107 Je '69. * (PA 43:16427)

179. BARZ, ANITA I. *Prediction of Secondary School Achievement From Primary Grade Aptitude and Achievement Measures.* Doctor's thesis, St. John's University (Jamaica, N.Y.), 1969. (DAI 30:3271A)

180. CALLAWAY, WEBSTER R. "A Holistic Conception of Creativity and Its Relationship to Intelligence." *Gifted Child Q* 13(4):237–41 w '69. * (PA 44:15338)

181. COPPEDGE, FLOYD L. "Relation of Selected Variables

From High School Records to Occupational and College Success." *J Ed Res* 63(2):71-3 O '69. *

182. Cox, Otis. *Creative Thinking in a High School Experimental Humanities Program.* Doctor's thesis, University of Alabama (University, Ala.), 1969. (*DAI* 31:214A)

183. Hieronymus, A. N., and Stroud, James B. "Comparability of IQ Scores on Five Widely Used Intelligence Tests." *Meas & Eval Guid* 2(3):135-40 f '69. * (*PA* 44:13285)

184. Hopkins, Kenneth D., and Sitkei, E. George. "Predicting Grade One Reading Performance: Intelligence vs. Reading Readiness Tests." *J Exp Ed* 37(3):31-3 sp '69. *

185. Krop, Harry. "Effects of Extrinsic Motivation, Intrinsic Motivation, and Intelligence on Creativity: A Factorial Approach." *J General Psychol* 80(2):259-66 Ap '69. * (*PA* 43:11332)

186. Lovett, Carl James. *An Analysis of the Relationship of Several Variables to Achievement in First Year Algebra.* Doctor's thesis, University of Texas (Austin, Tex.), 1969. (*DAI* 30:1470A)

187. Maples, Virginia S. *The Use of the California Mental Maturity Test in Predicting Differential Aptitude Scores.* Master's thesis, Texas Technological College (Lubbock, Tex.), 1969.

188. Shields, Ruth V., and Gordon, Mary Alice. "Schematic Concept Formation in Relationship to Mental Ability in Adolescents." *Psychon Sci* 17(6):361-2 D 25 '69. * (*PA* 44:6539)

189. Smith, Philip D., Jr. "The Pennsylvania Foreign Language Research Project: Teacher Proficiency and Class Achievement in Two Modern Languages." *Foreign Lang Ann* 3(2):194-207 D '69. *

190. Sutherland, Kelley. *The Predictive Value of School and College Ability Test, Sequential Test of Educational Progress, Differential Aptitude Test, Iowa Silent Reading Test, and California Test of Mental Maturity Scores at Clintwood High School, Clintwood, Virginia.* Master's thesis, East Tennessee State University (Johnson City, Tenn.), 1969.

191. Willmarth, John Gary. *Factors Affecting the Vocational Choice of Women of Different Ages Selecting Clerical and Secretarial Occupations.* Doctor's thesis, Washington State University (Pullman, Wash.), 1969. (*DAI* 30:991A)

192. Arena, Thomas. "Social Maturity in the Prediction of Academic Achievement." *J Ed Res* 64(1):21-2 S '70. *

193. Caldwell, James R.; Michael, William B.; Schrader, Donald R.; and Meyers, C. E. "Comparative Validities and Working Times for Composites of Structure-of-Intellect Tests and Algebra Grades and Composites of Traditional Test Measures and Algebra Grades in the Prediction of Success in Tenth-Grade Geometry." *Ed & Psychol Meas* 30(4):955-9 w '70. *

194. Canabal, Juana Villanueva. *Comparison of Deaf and Normally Hearing Children on Analogy Items Under Different Methods of Instruction at Different Age Levels.* Doctor's thesis, St. John's University (Jamaica, N.Y.), 1970. (*DAI* 31:3700B)

195. Carroll, Imogene Vass. *A Comparison of the Intelligence Quotients of Sixth-Grade Children of Negro and Caucasian Educators and Non-Educators.* Doctor's thesis, University of Alabama (University, Ala.), 1970. (*DAI* 31:3161A)

196. Corrigan, Francis Vincent, Jr. *A Comparison of Self Concepts of American Indian Students From Public or Federal School Backgrounds.* Doctor's thesis, George Washington University (Washington, D.C.), 1970.

197. Damm, Vernon J. "Creativity and Intelligence: Research Implications for Equal Emphasis in High School." *Excep Children* 36(8):565-9 Ap '70. * (*PA* 46:1754)

198. Gates, John Anthony. *Selective Factors in Predicting Success in Learning Basic Sight Words and First Grade Reading Achievement.* Doctor's thesis, West Virginia University (Morgantown, W.Va.), 1970. (*DAI* 31:3775A)

199. Johnson, Janice K. "Effects of the Process Approach Upon I.Q. Measures of Disadvantaged Children." *Sci Ed* 54(1):45-8 Ja-Mr '70. *

200. Jones, Kenneth J., and Jones, Priscilla P. "Contribution of the Rorschach to Description of Personality Structure Defined by Several Objective Tests." *Psychol Rep* 26(1):35-45 F '70. * (*PA* 45:4281)

201. McCracken, Robert A., and Mullen, Neill D. "The Validity of Certain Measures in an I.R.I.," pp. 104-10. In *Reading Difficulties: Diagnosis, Correction, and Remediation.* Edited by William K. Durr. Newark, Del.: International Reading Association, 1970. Pp. vii, 276. *

202. Moulin, Eugene K. "The Effects of Client-Centered Group Counseling Using Play Media on the Intelligence, Achievement, and Psycholinguistic Abilities of Underachieving Primary School Children." *El Sch Guid & Counsel* 5(2):85-98 D '70. *

203. Ringness, Thomas A. "Identifying Figures, Their Achievement Values, and Children's Values as Related to Actual and Predicted Achievement." *J Ed Psychol* 61(3):174-85 Je '70. * (*PA* 44:13397)

204. Skubic, Vera, and Anderson, Marian. "The Interrelationship of Perceptual-Motor Achievement, Academic Achievement and Intelligence of Fourth Grade Children." *J Learn Dis* 3(8):413-20 Ag '70. *

205. Younge, James W. "A Study of High School Preparation and Freshman Failures at North Carolina College at Durham." *J Negro Ed* 39(1):96-9 w '70. *

Bert A. Goldman, *Dean of Academic Advising, The University of North Carolina at Greensboro, Greensboro, North Carolina.*

The CTMM purports to measure functional capacities deemed basic to learning, problem-solving, and responding to new situations, by means of five factors for each of six school levels and for adults. Although the 1963 series retains the rationale and basic structure of earlier editions, the authors maintain that it has undergone extensive modification in test content and composition and that it has been rescaled at all levels. Some of the changes include: replacement of the ratio IQ with the deviation IQ to conform to the 1960 revision of the Stanford-Binet; introduction of new items; rearrangement of tests and factors; modification of time limits; revision of the directions for administration; redrawing of all artwork; adoption of a new format and color scheme for the test booklets, manuals, and accessories; and simplification of the process of calculating derived scores.

An earlier review criticized the test authors "for using the term 'factors' for scores derived from tests whose development was not based on factor analysis" (Milholland, 5:314). This complaint may no longer be registered because the authors say they have factor analyzed the test employing the Thurstone centroid method which produced five discrete factors. They say that as a result of this factor analysis the only major revision involved transferring the Inferences test from the Logical Reasoning factor to the Verbal Concepts factor. Surprisingly, no statistical information concerning the factor analysis is provided in the Technical Report. The reader is simply referred to "a more complete report" (*117*) prepared by the California Test Bureau in 1963 but not listed in their catalog. This information should have been included in the Technical Report.

The standardization population seems to be representative. However, no explanation is given for using 49 instead of all 50 states. The excluded state is not identified.

Overall, the reliability coefficients indicate adequate reliability. Levels 0 and 1 present the weakest coefficients and when coefficients for the five factors are compared across all levels, it is noted that Spatial Relationships has the poorest reliability. The K-R 21 reliabilities reported for each type of score follow: the five factor scores, .48 to .94, median .77; language total, .71 to .95, median .90; nonlanguage total, .79 to .93, median .86; and total, .86 to .96, median .93.

Considerable validity data for the Short Form of the CTMM are presented, but no data are provided for the Long Form. As an earlier reviewer pointed out, there is need for evidence of the Long Form's use for "educational selection, prediction, and guidance at each of the several age and grade levels" (Freeman, 5:314). Also lacking are validity and reliability data indicating use with the intellectual extremes (i.e., mentally deficient and superior).

No rationale is given for using eight school levels with the Short Form and only six school levels with the Long Form. Further, five factors are included in the Long Form and only four in the Short Form. No reason is given for eliminating the Spatial Relationships factor from the Short Form. However, earlier in this review it was pointed out that among the five factors this one provided the poorest reliability coefficients.

In sum, as far as group tests of intelligence are concerned, the CTMM appears to rate among the best. Its format is clear and easy to follow, its material appears durable, the norms appear representative, and its reliability while being weaker at the lower levels generally seems satisfactory. Data on validity are lacking, but if its shorter version is comparable, then considerable evidence suggests that the Long Form is valid. This leads to a question that has long stood in this reviewer's mind. Why both tests? Why not just the CTMM-SF? The Short Form takes less time to administer than the Long Form, research is available concerning its validity, and in terms of reliability it does not contain the Long Form's weakest factor (Spatial Relationships).

JOHN H. ROSENBACH, *Professor of Educational Psychology and Head of the Department, State University of New York at Albany, Albany, New York.*

In reading the publisher's literature on the CTMM series, one gets the definite impression of a test package designed to provide something for everyone: an omnibus IQ test to estimate Stanford-Binet (S-B) scores; language non-language, and total IQ's in the spirit of the

Wechsler scales; factor scores for those who lean toward differential aptitudes; mental ages for those who were brought up in the old S-B tradition; short forms and long forms; tests for kindergarteners to adults; color-coded booklets; and student profile charts on which the data-oriented teacher can record a multitude of numbers—IQ's, MA's, standard scores, stanines, and even I.S.I.'s and A.A.G.P.'s, which translate to Intellectual Status Index and Anticipated Achievement Grade Placements.

Certainly the CTMM is presented to us in an attractive fashion. But what does it all add up to? At worst, probably, an invitation to the less sophisticated users to over-interpret, to be misled into believing they have much more useful information than they actually possess, and to misclassify and to err in making educational decisions, especially about individual students. At best, another run-of-the-mill scholastic aptitude test series whose total score and language subscore correlate quite highly with standardized achievement tests and other tests of mental ability.

The CTMM was first published in 1936 and the current revisions (both Long Form and Short Form) bear close resemblance to their predecessors. Not only has the test format remained basically unchanged but the reported reliability and validity coefficients are of the same magnitude. Thus, past MMY reviews, especially those of the 1957 revisions, are still relevant.

Changes in the content and format of the 1963 revision do include one completely new subtest (Delayed Recall), and new names for some subtests (e.g., Number Concepts is now Numerical Values, Numerical Quantity has become Number Problems, and Verbal Concepts is called Verbal Comprehension). Further, nine subtests have been revised by replacing from 11 to 55 percent of their items with new items. Test 10, Immediate Recall, is essentially unchanged and the time limits for the total battery are the same as for the 1957 revision.

Since the 1963 Short Form consists of items drawn from the Long Form (only subtests "Rights and Lefts," "Manipulation of Areas," "Immediate Recall," and "Inferences" do not appear on the Short Form), Stanley's review of the Short Form in the Sixth MMY can be considered, in toto, appropriate to the Long Form. One additional comment appears in order: Given the social turmoil of the fifties and sixties it is surprising to observe the continuing content bias reflecting white, middle class values. For example, all the pictures of dwellings are of single family houses; not an apartment building is included. Moreover, the only apparent reference to a minority group depicts an Indian, attired in "traditional" costume and holding a spear! Even if such content selection does not differentially affect subjects' scores, it is perhaps time that major test publishers view their instruments as educational and social forces as well as psychometric devices.

The major technical changes in this revision, according to the Technical Report, include, "(1) scaling to the Stanford-Binet, Form L-M, 1960 Revision; (2) independent scaling of the Total, Language, and Non-Language I.Q.'s; (3) replacement of the Ratio I.Q. with the deviation I.Q.; and (4) extension of the I.Q. and M.A. tables to allow for direct look-up."

Moving to a deviation IQ places the CTMM, somewhat belatedly, in step with other major mental ability tests, while the IQ-MA arrangement is a convenience to the individual who desires both scores. The scaling issue is, however, a somewhat different matter. Given certain assumptions, the scaling procedure appears to be legitimate, but there is some question as to whether it is of any particular value to the test user. The authors apparently wanted their instrument to be viewed as a group-test equivalent of the Stanford-Binet. Thus, they first scaled the Short Form total score to the S-B, such that the Short Form IQ could be considered an estimate of an S-B IQ, and then scaled the Long Form to the Short Form. Finally, the various subscores were scaled to the total Long Form IQ. Just what is accomplished by all this is problematical. Moreover, it is doubtful that the average person who administers and interprets the test will be able to wade through the rather muddled description given of the scaling procedures with any degree of comprehension. Worst of all, the authors do not present any clear statement of their rationale for following these procedures nor how what they have done is to the benefit of the test interpreter.

NORMING. The standardization of the 1963 revision, if accomplished as described in the various California publications, appears to have been done with care. Classes from 253 schools, representing seven geographic regions and 49 states, comprised the sample. In addition, the cooperating schools were "urged" to take certain measures in order to insure comparable testing conditions, e.g., classes were to be excluded if they had recently taken similar tests, and testing was to be done during midweek. Unfortunately, no mention is made of the extent to which schools actually followed these directions or even if efforts were made to gather such information. Thus, the reader is left to make his own inferences as to what may have happened in various schools and, worse, to speculate about how different contingencies may have affected the standardization results. It would seem that a major test publisher could be expected to be quite specific about something as basic as standardization procedures.

RELIABILITY. With the exception of the K-R 21 reliability coefficients, *all* reliability and validity information presented in the Technical Report are based on the Short Form. One could reason that whatever is detected about the short form of a test will surely be as good or better for a longer version of the test. Nonetheless, some research data on the Long Form would be welcomed, especially since the L-F includes several components which are completely absent on the S-F. Furthermore, most of the studies with the S-F dealing with test-retest reliability or reporting correlations with other tests, except for the *California Achievement Tests* which was normed simultaneously with the CTMM, are based on relatively small samples (most of the N's range from 100–200). Thus, once again, the reader is left to his own devices to guess what the results might have been if the L-F were to be substituted for the S-F.

In any event, the K-R 21 coefficients are typical for tests of this type and similar to those reported for past revisions. Except for the very young ages, up to about 8, the total score reliabilities range from .93 to .96, those for the language section in the low .90's, and for the nonlanguage section in the high .80's. The factor scores, as expected, yield lower reliabilities, which are quite variable from level to level. These reliabilities are conspicuously low at the younger ages (several in the .40's and .50's), while the Spatial Relationship factor is low at just about every level (for example, with adults it is only .56). It should also be noted that, despite claims to the contrary, there is an element of speed present throughout the battery, i.e., each subtest has a time limit and the subjects are instructed to "work as fast as you can." Unfortunately, the effects of this speed factor are unknown, but, if anything, there would be a tendency to enhance these reliability coefficients.

A somewhat more encouraging picture, with notable exceptions, is presented in test-retest and adjacent test studies done with the Short Form over one year intervals. At about grade four and above (Levels 2 through 5) the total score and language section reliabilities tend to run in the mid to high .80's, with the nonlanguage section in the mid to high .70's. Below these ages, however, the reliabilities are shockingly low: of 9 coefficients, one is .39, three are in the .40's, two in the .50's, two in the .60's, and one at .70. Unfortunately, no data are presented for the factor scores.

One can only conclude, as have other reviewers, that little significance, if any, be attributed to the several subscores, with the exception of the language section, especially when dealing with individuals. Moreover, even the total scores and language scores are of questionable value for children under eight, and based on the data presented in the Technical Report, one would be tempted to recommend that Levels 0 and 1 *not* be given unless score interpretations are to be made by someone highly trained in measurement.

VALIDITY. Judged against the claims made for the CTMM in the publisher's manuals, the validity data presented are woefully inadequate. To cite but a few examples from the Guide to Interpretation: "The factor scores are useful in educational diagnosis and remedial instruction"; "When this procedure [profile analysis] is followed, the individual's unique pattern of mental functioning can be studied and the most appropriate actions can be taken in the instructional program"; "The CTMM provides information about the student's functional capacities that are basic to learning."

However, the only "validity" data included in any of the manuals are the now too familiar correlations with other tests: against the Stanford-Binet, the *California Achievement Tests* (CAT), and several group tests of mental ability. Interestingly enough, although the CTMM was originally designed to parallel the Stanford-Binet and, as indicated earlier, was even scaled to it, the correlations with this test tend to be the lowest of all reported (from .66 and .74). The highest correlations are with other group tests (mostly in the high .70's and .80's) and with the CAT (r's of .79, .81, .81, .84). With these correlations running so close to the reliabilities of the tests, one can only ask for the nth time what, if any, information is being added to our knowledge of human behavior or ability.

As far as the factor scores are concerned, the only validity correlations reported are with the various subsections of the CAT. However, in almost every possible instance (114 of 120 r's) the Language IQ correlates more highly with the subsections of the CAT than do the factor scores with the CAT. In addition, the Language IQ consistently correlates more highly with the CAT than does the Nonlanguage IQ (37 of 40 comparisons). In other words, it is difficult to see any particular advantage of using CTMM scores other than the Total and Language IQ's.

SUMMARY. As a simple, omnibus test of mental ability the CTMM is fairly comparable and probably on a par with so many other similar instruments. However, it is oversold in its various manuals and little if any use should be made of its various subscores or of the test as a whole with younger children. Adequate reliability data are lacking for the Long Form and there is simply a paucity of research evidence to support the claims made, explicitly and implicitly, in the manuals. Other than the fact that the Long Form should theoretically be somewhat more reliable than the Short Form, no persuasive case is made for using it in preference to more compact versions. The additional factor score provided by the L-F, Spatial Relationships, is not only of questionable value insofar as validity is concerned, but is singularly low in reliability.

Perhaps the most cogent comment about the CTMM was made by McNemar:[1] "the [CTMM]....serves as an illustration of factor icing a *g* cake * The advertising claims the measurement of not only factors but also *g*; not only *g* but also factors. This measurement absurdity is all too apt to go unrecognized by test users, and hence a sales advantage for the aptitude battery that produces both factor scores and an IQ."

For reviews by Frank S. Freeman and John E. Milholland of an earlier edition, see 5:314;

1 MCNEMAR, QUINN. "Lost: Our Intelligence? Why?" *Am Psychol* 19:871–82 D '64. *

for a review by Henry E. Garrett, see 3:223 (2 excerpts); for reviews by Raymond B. Cattell and F. Kuhlmann, see 2:1384 (1 excerpt); for reviews by W. D. Commins, Rudolf Pintner, and Arthur E. Traxler, see 1:1042 (1 excerpt). For reviews of the short form, see 6:443 (1 review), 5:313 (1 review), and 4:282 (1 excerpt).

[339]

*Canadian Academic Aptitude Test. Grades 8.5–9.0; 1959–68; CAAT; this test and tests 6:253 and 6:567 make up the *Canadian Test Battery*, grades 8–9; 3 scores: verbal, mathematical, non-verbal; 1 form; separate parts 1 ('62, 4 pages, verbal reasoning), 2 ('62, 4 pages, mathematical reasoning), 3 ('62, 6 pages, non-verbal reasoning, identical with test copyrighted in 1959); battery manual ('68, 5 pages); battery technical manual ('64, 59 pages); supplementary data ('68, 6 pages, identical with data copyrighted in 1963) for the battery; battery profile ('63, 1 page); separate answer sheets (Digitek) must be used; $1.75 per 25 tests; $3.50 per 50 answer sheets; 20¢ per hand scoring stencil; 20¢ per 15 battery profiles; 10¢ per battery manual; $1 per technical manual; 70¢ per specimen set; $3.25 per battery specimen set; postage extra; machine scoring service available from The Ontario Institute for Studies in Education; 30(40–45) minutes per part; Ontario Institute for Studies in Education; distributed by Guidance Centre. *

REFERENCES

1–2. See 6:445.
3. KHAN, S. B., AND ROBERTS, DENNIS M. "Relationships Among Study Habits and Attitudes, Aptitude and Grade 8 Achievement." *Ed & Psychol Meas* 29(4):951–5 w '69. * (PA 44:21525)

For reviews by Donald B. Black and George A. Ferguson, see 6:445.

[340]

★Canadian Cognitive Abilities Test. Grades kgn–1, 2–3; 1954–70; CCAT; adaptation of *Cognitive Abilities Test;* 2 levels; Form 1 ('70, 16 pages) for each level; manual ('70, 34 pages) for each level; Can $6.25 per 35 tests; $1.50 per specimen set; postage extra; original test by Robert L. Thorndike, Elizabeth Hagen, and Irving Lorge; adaptation by Edgar N. Wright; Thomas Nelson & Sons (Canada) Ltd. *
a) PRIMARY 1. Grades kgn–1; (45–55) minutes in 2 sessions.
b) PRIMARY 2. Grades 2–3; (55–60) minutes in 2 sessions.

[341]

★Canadian Lorge-Thorndike Intelligence Tests, Multi-Level Edition. Grades 3–9; 1954–67; CLTIT; adaptation of *Lorge-Thorndike Intelligence Tests, Multi-Level Edition;* 3 scores: verbal, non-verbal, composite; Form 1 ('67, 46 pages); Levels A (grade 3), B (4), C (5), D (6), E (7), F (8–9) in a single booklet; manual ('67, 84 pages); no norms or reliability data for composite score; separate answer sheets (MRC) must be used; Can 90¢ per test; $4 per 35 answer sheets for any one level; 60¢ per scoring stencil for any one level; $1.65 per manual; $3.25 per specimen set; postage extra; scoring service, 25¢ and over per test; 62(120) minutes in 2 sessions; original test by Irving Lorge, Robert L. Thorndike, and Elizabeth Hagen; adaptation by Edgar N. Wright; Thomas Nelson & Sons (Canada) Ltd. *

[342]

★The Carlton Intelligence Tests. Ages 10–12; 1962–65; CIT; 2 tests; 20p per specimen set of either test; postage extra; 10(15) minutes for practice test, 45(55) minutes for test; [W. K. Carlton]; University of London Press Ltd. *
a) TEST NO. 1. 1962; 1 form (16 pages); manual (11 pages); practice sheet (2 pages); 92½p per 20 tests; 30p per 20 practice sheets; 12½p per manual.
b) TEST NO. 2. 1965; 1 form (15 pages); manual (10 pages); practice sheet (2 pages); £1.05 per 20 tests; 25p per 20 practice sheets; 15p per manual.

STANLEY NISBET, *Professor of Education, University of Glasgow, Glasgow, Scotland.*

These two tests, originally designed to assist in the allocation of pupils to appropriate courses in the transition from primary to secondary education, contain most of the familiar types of intelligence test items (e.g., "odd man out," opposites, "is to....as," codes, anagrams, absurdities, missing elements, series) as well as a number of less common ones (e.g., "word ladders," interpreting simple tables of statistics). Each test includes a wide variety of verbal, numerical, spatial, alphabetical, and pictorial questions. Since the tests rest on such a broad base, the face validity is high.

In construction and standardisation procedures the tests are all that one could desire. Identical means (36) and standard deviations (20) were obtained for the two tests in the standardisation populations. These figures suggest a well constructed test with good discriminating power at all levels except the very lowest.

Each test is divided into two parts, A and B, the latter being "considerably more difficult" than A. No indication is given, however, as to whether the test user is to take any special account of this division; it is not suggested anywhere, for instance, that A and B could be used separately.

The only criticisms concern a few matters of detail: in one item, the opposite of "guess" is given as "prove." This seems dubious. At least three items are "dated": children can no longer be expected to know about half-crowns and furlongs, and some modern clocks do not have hands. Eight of the "always has" items are debatable. The instructions for subtest A-5 seem less clear than the fairly similar instructions for B-5. Similar criticisms may be made of a few other items.

A few items involve general knowledge as well as intelligence. The reviewer sees nothing wrong with this, but wonders if knowledge of the meaning of "mosque" and of the fact that hedgehogs hibernate or that most four legged animals can swim should be included in an intelligence test for 10–12 year olds.

To sum up, these are good tests and can be recommended as instruments of proven worth for measuring the general mental capacity of children between the ages of 10 and 12. They should be particularly efficient in the identification of academic potential among average and above-average children.

[343]

*Cognitive Abilities Test. Grades kgn–1, 2–3; 1954–68; CAT; revision of Levels 1 and 2 of still-in-print *Lorge-Thorndike Intelligence Tests;* 2 levels; $1.20 per specimen set, postage extra; Robert L. Thorndike, Elizabeth Hagen, and Irving Lorge; Houghton Mifflin Co. *
a) PRIMARY 1. Grades kgn–1; 2 editions; manual ('68, 34 pages) for each form; (45–55) minutes in 2 sessions.
1) *Hand Scorable Edition.* Forms 1, 2, ('68, 15 pages); $5.25 per 35 tests.
2) *Machine Scorable Edition.* Forms 1, 2, ('68, 16 pages); $9 per 35 tests; MRC scoring service, 45¢ and over per test.
b) PRIMARY 2. Grades 2–3; 2 editions; manual ('68, 34 pages) for each form; (55–60) minutes in 2 sessions.
1) *Hand Scorable Edition.* Forms 1, 2, ('68, 15 pages); $5.25 per 35 tests.
2) *Machine Scorable Edition.* Forms 1, 2, ('68, 16 pages); $9 per 35 tests; MRC scoring service, 45¢ and over per test.

MARCEL L. GOLDSCHMID, *Associate Professor of Psychology and Director, Centre for Learning and Development, McGill University, Montreal, Quebec, Canada.*

The CAT is part of an integrated series of intelligence tests. It can be used beginning in the second half of kindergarten through grade 3 and can be followed by the *Lorge-Thorndike Intelligence Tests, Multi-Level Edition,* which covers grades 3 through 13. The normative linking of the two tests makes it possible to obtain comparable test scores across the 14 grades.

The CAT can be given by teachers and scored by hand or machine and offers the further advantage of being designed for small group administration. The influence of reading competence is eliminated by the use of paced, oral, item-by-item directions. Unscored sample items, moreover, permit the child to get oriented to each of the four subtests. A shorter version of Primary 1 can be administered to children who are known to be slower than average in cognitive development. The deliberate overlap between the CAT and the Multi-Level Edition

provides flexibility in selecting the most suitable type of test for each group of children. For repeated testing of the same group of children, two equivalent forms are available.

Besides explicit test administration instructions, the manual offers useful suggestions and directions for selecting the proper test form, scheduling of the tests, general testing considerations, and use of the test results. The hand scoring is simple and objective.

The normative samples for the CAT (approximately 5,000 subjects in each of grades 1, 2, 3, and 4 and over 2,600 subjects in kindergarten) were drawn from a cross section of schools which were used in the Multi-Level Edition (180,000 pupils in 40 states). The means and standard deviations of the two tests were then equalized and the distribution of IQ's normalized. By using the tables in the manual, raw scores can easily be converted into deviation IQ's, which, in turn, can be converted into percentile ranks, stanines, or grade percentiles.

The reliability coefficients (K-R 20) are all around .90 at each grade level (based on samples of 300 for each). The reliability of the shortened version is only slightly lower.

Very sparse information about the validity of the CAT is reported. The CAT and Level A of the Multi-Level Edition were both given to 300 pupils in third grade. A factor analysis of these scores demonstrated that both the CAT and the L-T load heavily on a general reasoning factor (83 percent of the variance). Unfortunately, other than this bit of construct validity, no other validity data are contained in the manual. Neither are there data on the statistical relationship between the two "equivalent" forms.

In summary, the CAT is a well constructed and standardized test with excellent reliability and is based on representative and very substantial normative samples. It lends itself particularly well to the testing of large numbers of children, since it can be administered by teachers to groups and machine scored. Most regrettably, however, no concurrent or predictive validity data are presented in the manual. Since the CAT is normatively linked with the Multi-Level Edition of the *Lorge-Thorndike Intelligence Tests,* the potential CAT user is forced to search for indirect validity data in the manual of the Multi-Level Edition.

CAROL K. TITTLE, *Assistant Professor of Teacher Education, City University of New York, New York, New York.*

The *Cognitive Abilities Test* has four subtests: Oral Vocabulary; Relational Concepts (over, under, most, least, and so on); "Multimental" (identifying one picture in a set that does not belong); and Quantitative Concepts (find the square with three sticks). All instructions and questions are given orally, and responses are represented pictorially.

The *Cognitive Abilities Test* was standardized in January and February of 1968, using 45 of the 72 communities in the 1963 standardization of the *Lorge-Thorndike Intelligence Tests*. The manuals for the CAT give very limited descriptions of the norming sample and procedures. The manuals do promise a special study to check interpolated values in the norm tables from fall to winter and from winter to spring. For the early ages being tested here, there would seem to be a clear need to establish values for fall and spring on empirical data for the norms.

Scores provided are deviation IQ scores, with a mean of 100 and standard deviation of 16, and grade percentiles; in addition there are tables for converting DIQ's to percentile ranks and stanines. The use of intelligence test scores for pupils with varying social class and language backgrounds has been the subject of considerable debate. An up-to-date manual should provide norms, or discussion of the validity of scores, for special groups of pupils.

The reliability data presented were based on samples of 300 per grade from the standardization group. K-R 20, rather than an alternate forms method, was used to estimate the reliability. The reliability figures are satisfactory—.89 to .90. The section on cautions in interpreting and using the test results implies that the standard error of measurement is about 5 DIQ points. This section could discuss the standard error of measurement more explicitly and present the standard error of measurement for various score levels.

No data on validity are given, with the exception of a factor analysis of the CAT and Level A (grade 3) of the verbal and nonverbal tests of the L-T Multi-Level Edition. The factor analysis shows one main factor for the subtest scores of all three tests, labelled as a "general reasoning factor" by the authors.

The uses suggested for the test, for which validity should be demonstrated, are determining the "rate of introduction of new material for group activities"; "identifying individuals who need special attention"; "grouping within classrooms"; "selecting curriculum materials and learning tasks"; "conferring with parents on status and progress"; and "deciding about grade placement." Validity remains to be established for these uses.

Some evidence of the relationship of the earlier versions of the *Cognitive Abilities Test* to school achievement and reading achievement is available. These studies indicate at least moderate correlations with school achievement. The possible validity of the earlier L-T primary test in predicting reading achievement specifically also appears to be moderate. Users should assess the validity of the *Cognitive Abilities Test* for these purposes on an empirical basis in their own situation. Validity cannot be considered to be well demonstrated.

The authors are to be commended for the discussion which introduces the section on uses of the test. The first paragraphs point out the influence of informal experiences in development of the skills being measured. It is also noted that the skills measured by the test are in part *learned* skills and that low scores do *not* constitute "an excuse for passing the child by." This viewpoint is reiterated in the section providing cautions in interpreting and using the results of the test. The cautions note that the test measures the present status of a child, that test results for young children are relatively unstable, and that the test does not relate perfectly to school success.

For the test booklet available for review—Primary 1, Form 2—one comment can be made about the artwork: it does not represent minority groups satisfactorily where the pictures include people.

In summary, the *Cognitive Abilities Test,* Primary 1 and 2, is the downward extension of a widely used and well-constructed set of group intelligence tests. The reliability of the Primary tests is satisfactory; validity data are very limited. Some evidence from studies of the earlier Lorge-Thorndike indicates at least moderate correlations with school achievement and reading. Users will need to determine the validity of the CAT for their particular use of the scores.

J Ed Meas 6(2):123–4 su '69. Richard C. Cox. * there are two general problems which must be taken into account when using the CAT. The first is that this test demands, as do most tests intended for this age group, a certain amount of listening ability on the part of the test taker since the test is administered orally. Secondly, the test requires rather acute visual discrimination between multiple-choice answers which appear in the form of small pictures. These problems are not mentioned by the authors nor is the basis for item selection cited. For the most part, the directions are stated clearly and succinctly. One exception is that, if the directions are followed verbatim, grammatical errors such as "put your fingers on a.... apple" occur several times. * In general, the directions and scoring procedures are adequate. One minor criticism is that, when the CAT is scored by hand, there is no convenient place to record either total or subtest scores. * Standard errors, which may be useful for test interpretation, are not reported. In the Technical Considerations section of the examiners manual, the words "factor analysis" appear as a major heading in place of the more common "validity." This is the case since the only validity evidence presented is that from a factor analysis of data from the joint administration of the CAT and the Lorge-Thorndike Intelligence Tests, Multi-Level Edition, Level A in grade 3. This construct validation procedure seems to be rather narrow in scope and does not provide enough information for the reviewer to say much about validity. It does indicate, though, that the CAT does have some validity as a downward extension of the Lorge-Thorndike Intelligence Test. The norming procedure for the CAT seems well done in terms of both the numbers involved and the appropriateness of norm groups. I.Q. equivalents, percentile ranks and stanines of deviation I.Q.'s, and grade percentiles are clearly described and are easy to interpret using the tables provided in the manual. Also provided in the manual is a section entitled, "Using the Test Results." This may be a blessing or a Pandora's box for the potential user. The suggested uses are appropriate but are not to be blindly adopted by the naive test user. It is this reviewer's hope that persons desirous of using the results of the CAT in one of the ways suggested will also carefully read the following page in the manual which deals with cautions to be used in the interpretation of the test results. To summarize, the CAT is impressive with respect to the adequacy of directions, general test design, norm data, and other practical features. It is designed as a group test to measure cognitive ability at an early age, an area practically void of available standardized tests. Further data pertinent to the reliability and the validity of the test for certain purposes would be helpful for further evaluation.

[344]

***College Board Scholastic Aptitude Test.** Candidates for college entrance; 1926–71; SAT; tests administered each January, March, April, July, November, and December at centers established by the publisher; 2 scores: verbal, mathematical; descriptive booklet ('70, 55 pages); for additional information, see 663; examination fee, $5.75 per student; special editions available for the visually handicapped; 180 (240) minutes; program administered for the College Entrance Examination Board by Educational Testing Service. *

REFERENCES

1–22. See 4:285.
23–42. See 5:318.
43–121. See 6:449.
122. GIESSOW, FRED JUNIOR. *The Prediction of Success in First Year Natural Science Courses at Washington University.* Doctor's thesis, Washington University (St. Louis, Mo.), 1953. (*DA* 14:1046)
123. MARSH, FRANK EUGENE, JR. *An Analysis of Failure Among University Freshmen.* Doctor's thesis, Boston University (Boston, Mass.), 1959. (*DA* 20:2101)
124. BALLANTYNE, ROBERT HUBBARD. *An Analysis of Criteria for Selecting Freshmen Students for an Honors Program at Washington State University.* Doctor's thesis, Washington State University (Pullman, Wash.), 1962. (*DA* 23:2439)
125. QUILLER, GORDON FREDERICK. *A Study of College Predictors for First Year Students at Colorado State University.* Doctor's research study No. 1, Colorado State College (Greeley, Colo.), 1962. (*DA* 23:1253)
126. STEIGE, ROBERT. *A Differential Study of the Prognostic Value of Admission and Placement Criteria at the University of Colorado.* Doctor's thesis, University of Colorado (Boulder, Colo.), 1962. (*DA* 23:537)
127. TURRENTINE, EDGAR MAYER. *Predicting Success in Practice Teaching in Music.* Doctor's thesis, State University of Iowa (Iowa City, Iowa), 1962. (*DA* 23:2814)
128. CHASE, CLINTON I.; LUDLOW, H. GLENN; POMEROY, MARTHA C.; AND BARRITT, L. SPENCER. *Predicting Individual Course Success for Entering Freshmen.* Indiana Studies in Prediction No. 2. Bloomington, Ind.: Bureau of Educational Studies and Testing, Indiana University, 1963. Pp. i, 41. *
129. CHASE, CLINTON I.; LUDLOW, H. GLENN; POMEROY, MARTHA C.; AND BARRITT, L. SPENCER. *Predicting Success for University Freshmen.* Indiana Studies in Prediction No. 1. Bloomington, Ind.: Bureau of Educational Studies and Testing, Indiana University, 1963. Pp. vi, 47. *
130. CLARK, EUGENE WARREN. *An Evaluation of Predictive Criteria for a Group of High Ability College Freshmen.* Doctor's thesis, University of Denver (Denver, Colo.), 1963. (*DA* 25:957)
131. FINGER, JOHN A., AND SCHLESSER, GEORGE E. "Academic Performance of Public and Private School Students." *J Ed Psychol* 54:118–22 Ap '63. * (*PA* 37:8282)
132. LARE, JOAN HINCHMAN. *The Relationship of Ordinal Position and Sex of Sibling to Scholastic Aptitude Test Scores and the Academic Achievement of College Students From Two Child Families.* Doctor's thesis, Cornell University (Ithaca, N.Y.), 1963. (*DA* 24:275)
133. LEACH, ALICE REA. *Prediction of Academic Success in College Freshmen at the University of Denver.* Doctor's thesis, University of Denver (Denver, Colo.), 1963. (*DA* 24:5199)
134. NICHOLS, ROBERT C., AND HOLLAND, JOHN L. "Prediction of the First Year College Performance of High Aptitude Students." *Psychol Monogr* 77(7):1–29 '63. * (*PA* 38:4693)
135. RICHMAN, ELI. *College Admissions Based on S.A.T. Scores, 1962–1963.* [Chelsea, Mass.: the Author, School Department, 1963.] Pp. i, 63. *
136. RUSSELL, JAMES WILLIAM. *An Analysis of the Academic Performance of Transfer and Native Students and Their Major Fields in the College of Arts and Sciences at the University of*

Georgia. Doctor's thesis, University of Georgia (Athens, Ga.), 1963. (DA 25:1668)

137. THREATT, ROBERT. *A Study of Selected Characteristics and College Success of High- and Low-Achieving Negro Students on CEEB Scholastic Aptitude Test in Georgia.* Doctor's thesis, University of Oklahoma (Norman, Okla.), 1963. (DA 24:577)

138. AIKEN, LEWIS R., JR. "The Prediction of Academic Success and Early Attrition by Means of a Multiple-Choice Biographical Inventory." *Am Ed Res J* 1:127–35 Mr '64. * (PA 39:1692)

139. BACHMAN, JERALD G. "Prediction of Academic Achievement Using the Edwards Need Achievement Scale." *J Appl Psychol* 48:16–9 F '64. * (PA 38:9276)

140. BERKEY, ROSEMARY. *A Survey of Twelve High School Seniors Who Achieved Low Verbal Scores on the Scholastic Aptitude Test of the College Entrance Examination Boards.* Master's thesis, Glassboro State College (Glassboro, N.J.), 1964.

141. BOYDEN, BARTLETT W., AND HINDLE, PETER G. *How to Boost Your Marks in the S.A.T.* New York: Macfadden-Bartell Corporation, 1964. Pp. 143. *

142. CARLSMITH, LYN. "Effect of Early Father Absence on Scholastic Aptitude." *Harvard Ed R* 34:3–21 w '64. *

143. CHAUNCEY, HENRY. "What's Right With Testing." *Fla J Ed Res* 6:87–102 Ja '64. *

144. COLLEGE ENTRANCE EXAMINATION BOARD. *A Description of the College Board Scholastic Aptitude Test.* Princeton, N.J.: the Board, 1964. Pp. 55. *

145. COLLEGE ENTRANCE EXAMINATION BOARD. *Manual of Freshman Class Profiles, 1964 Edition.* Princeton, N.J.: the Board, 1964. Pp. xiv, 584. *

146. COOPER, CARL J. "Some Relationships Between Paired-Associates Learning and Foreign-Language Aptitude." *J Ed Psychol* 55:132–8 Je '64. * (PA 39:5823)

147. DIEPPA, JORGE J. "Developing the Spanish Version of the SAT." *Col Board R* 53:12–7 sp '64. *

148. FRENCH, JOHN W. "New Tests for Predicting the Performance of College Students With High-Level Aptitude." *J Ed Psychol* 55:185–94 Ag '64. * (PA 39:5979)

149. HART, MARCIA E., AND SHAY, CLAYTON T. "Relationship Between Physical Fitness and Academic Success." *Res Q* 35:443–5 O '64. * (PA 39:5971)

150. HILLS, JOHN R. "College Expectancy Tables for High School Counselors." *Personnel & Guid J* 42:479–83 Ja '64. *

151. HILLS, JOHN R. "Prediction of College Grades for All Public Colleges of a State." *J Ed Meas* 1:155–9 D '64. *

152. HILLS, JOHN R.; BUSH, MARILYN L.; AND KLOCK, JOSEPH A. "Predicting Grades Beyond the Freshman Year." *Col Board R* 54:23–5 f '64. *

153. HILLS, JOHN R.; KLOCK, JOSEPH A.; AND BUSH, MARILYN L. *Freshman Norms for the University System of Georgia, 1962–63.* Atlanta, Ga.: Office of Testing and Guidance, Regents of the University System of Georgia, March 1964. Pp. xi, 65. *

154. HILLS, JOHN R.; KLOCK, JOSEPH A.; AND BUSH, MARILYN L. "Scholastic Aptitude of an Entire State's Public College Students." *Col & Univ* 40:60–7 f '64. *

155. IVANOFF, JOHN M.; MALLOY, JOHN P.; AND ROSE, JANET R. "Achievement, Aptitude, and Biographical Measures as Predictors of Success in Nursing Training." *Ed & Psychol Meas* 24:389–91 su '64. * (PA 39:5972)

156. KAUFMAN, JAMES D., AND DEMPSTER, DENNIS. "Prediction of SAT Scores." *Personnel & Guid J* 42:1026–7 Je '64. * (PA 39:5069)

157. LINDQUIST, E. F. "Equating Scores on Non-Parallel Tests." *J Ed Meas* 1:5–9 Je '64. * (PA 39:7777)

158. McCORMICK, JAMES H., AND ASHER, WILLIAM. "Aspects of the High School Record Related to the First Semester College Grade Point Average." *Personnel & Guid J* 42:699–703 Mr '64. *

159. MARKS, EDMOND. *Nonadditive Effects in the Prediction of Academic Achievement.* Doctor's thesis, Pennsylvania State University (University Park, Pa.), 1964. (DA 25:6752)

160. MICHAEL, WILLIAM B.; BAKER, DAVID; AND JONES, ROBERT A. "A Note Concerning the Predictive Validities of Selected Cognitive and Non-Cognitive Measures for Freshman Students in a Liberal Arts College." *Ed & Psychol Meas* 24:373–5 su '64. * (PA 39:5984)

161. PAUL, GORDON L., AND ERIKSEN, CHARLES W. "Effects of Test Anxiety on 'Real-Life' Examinations." *J Personality* 32:480–94 S '64. * (PA 39:7961)

162. QUINLAN, CLAIRE A. *The Prediction of Freshman Academic Success at Colorado State College by Means of Selected Standardized Tests and Admission Data.* Doctor's research study No. 1, Colorado State College (Greeley, Colo.), 1964. (DA 25:5124)

163. SCHERER, GEORGE A. C., AND WERTHEIMER, MICHAEL. *A Psycholinguistic Experiment in Foreign-Language Teaching.* New York: McGraw-Hill Book Co., 1964. Pp. xiii, 256. *

164. SGAN, MATTHEW R. "An Alternative Approach to Scholastic Aptitude Tests as Predictors of Graduation Rank at Selective Colleges." *Ed & Psychol Meas* 24:347–52 su '64. * (PA 39:5986)

165. SMITH, PAUL M. "Some Implications for Freshman Orientation Activities With Negro College Students." *J Col Stud Personnel* 5:176–9+ Mr '64. *

166. VEAL, LELAND RAMON. *A Comparison of the Professional Growth of Student Teachers Under Two Different Time-Arrangements for Student Teaching at the Secondary Level.* Doctor's thesis, University of South Carolina (Columbia, S.C.), 1964. (DA 25:7104)

167. WALKER, PETER. *Is Either the SAT or the ACT a Superior Instrument for Predicting Academic Success at National College of Education.* Master's thesis, National College of Education (Evanston, Ill.), 1964.

168. WATLEY, DONIVAN J. "The Effectiveness of Intellectual and Non-Intellectual Factors in Predicting Achievement for Business Students." *J Ed Res* 57:402–7 Ap '64. *

169. WATLEY, DONIVAN J., AND MERWIN, JACK C. "The Effectiveness of Variables for Predicting Academic Achievement for Business Students." *J Exp Ed* 33:189–92 w '64. * (PA 39:8713)

170. WEBB, SAM C. "The Psychological Components of Scores for Two Tests of Report Writing Ability." *Ed & Psychol Meas* 24:31–46 sp '64. * (PA 39:1770)

171. ALTUS, WILLIAM D. "Birth Order and Scholastic Aptitude." *J Consult Psychol* 29:202–5 Je '65. * (PA 39:13030)

172. ANGOFF, WILLIAM H. "College Board SAT and the Superior Student." *Sup Stud* 7:10–5 Mr–Ap '65. *

173. BACHRACH, PAUL B., AND WEITZNER, MARTIN. "Factors Related to Academic Success in a College of Business Administration." *Psychol Sch* 2:156–61 Ap '65. *

174. BEHRING, DANIEL W. "Predicting College Achievement With an Activities-Preference Inventory." Abstract. *Proc Ann Conv Am Psychol Assn* 73:345–6 '65. * (PA 39:15182)

175. BIAGGIO, ANGELA M. B. *Relative Predictability of Freshman Grade-Point Averages From SAT Scores in Negro and White Southern Colleges.* Master's thesis, University of Wisconsin (Madison, Wis.), 1965.

176. BRADY, WILLIAM JOSEPH. *Twenty Quantitative Predictors of Academic Success in College as Measured by Grade Point Averages.* Doctor's thesis, University of Connecticut (Storrs, Conn.), 1965. (DA 26:5121)

177. CHANSKY, NORMAN M. "Aptitude, Personality, and Achievement in Six College Curricula." *Ed & Psychol Meas* 25:1117–24 w '65. * (PA 40:3564)

178. CHASE, CLINTON I. *The University Freshman Dropout.* Indiana University, Monograph of the Bureau of Educational Studies and Testing, Indiana Studies in Prediction, No. 6. Bloomington, Ind.: the Bureau, 1965. Pp. 36. *

179. COLLEGE ENTRANCE EXAMINATION BOARD. *Effects of Coaching on Scholastic Aptitude Test Scores.* Princeton, N.J.: the Board, 1965. Pp. 27. *

180. COSTELLO, JOHN JOSEPH. *A Study of the Relationship of College Board Scores and Physical Fitness to the Prediction of Academic Success in College.* Doctor's thesis, University of Connecticut (Storrs, Conn.), 1965. (DA 26:5150)

181. DYE, JAMES McKINLEY. *An Experimental Study in Selected Sectioning of Freshman English Composition Students.* Doctor's thesis, University of Georgia (Athens, Ga.), 1965. (DA 26:6466)

182. FINGER, JOHN A., AND SCHLESSER, GEORGE E. "Non-Intellective Predictors of Academic Success in School and College." *Sch R* 73:14–29 sp '65. * (PA 39:10832)

183. FLEMING, W. G. Chap. 5, "The Predictive Value of Scholastic Aptitude Scores," pp. 32–5. In his *Characteristics and Achievements of Students in Ontario Universities.* Atkinson Study of Utilization of Student Resources, Report No. 11. Toronto, Ont., Canada: Ontario Institute for Studies in Education, 1965. Pp. xiii, 197. *

184. GALLANT, THOMAS FRANCIS. *Academic Achievement of College Freshmen and Its Relationship to Selected Aspects of the Student's Background.* Doctor's thesis, Western Reserve University (Cleveland, Ohio), 1965. (DA 26:6468)

185. HAUN, KENNETH W. "Note on Prediction of Academic Performance From Personality Test Scores." *Psychol Rep* 16:294 F '65. * (PA 39:7687)

186. HEIL, LOUIS M. "Scholastic and Personality Variables Associated With Acceptance to and Success in the Brooklyn College Scholars' Program." *Sup Stud* 7:34–40 Mr–Ap '65. *

187. HERBSTRITT, RICHARD LLOYD. *The Identification of Potentially Successful Rejected College Applicants.* Doctor's thesis, Western Reserve University (Cleveland, Ohio), 1965. (DA 27:675A)

188. HILLS, JOHN R., AND KLOCK, JOSEPH A. "Predicting Grades for All Schools in a Large University." *Am Ed Res J* 2:145–50 My '65. *

189. HILLS, JOHN R.; KLOCK, JOSEPH A.; AND BUSH, MARILYN L. *Freshman Norms for the University System, 1963–64.* Atlanta, Ga.: Office of Testing and Guidance, Regents of the University System of Georgia, February 1965. Pp. xi, 65. *

190. HILLS, JOHN R.; KLOCK, JOSEPH A.; AND BUSH, MARILYN L. *Freshman Norms for the University System, 1964–65.* Atlanta, Ga.: Office of Testing and Guidance, Regents of the University System of Georgia, October 1965. Pp. xi, 68. *

191. HILLS, JOHN R.; KLOCK, JOSEPH A.; AND BUSH, MARILYN. "The Use of Academic Prediction Equations With Subsequent Classes." *Am Ed Res J* 2:203–6 N '65. *

192. IRVINE, DONALD W. "Estimated Grades and Freshman Achievement." *Voc Guid Q* 13:193–5 sp '65. * (PA 40:1949)

193. LEAVER, THOMAS EUGENE. *The Prediction of Academic*

Achievement of Freshman Business Students at Saint Joseph's College. Doctor's thesis, Temple University (Philadelphia, Pa.), 1965. (*DA* 26:1429)

194. LEMONS, CLIFTON DALE. *An Investigation of Relationships Between Mechanical Drawing Experience, Certain Measures of Academic Ability and Knowledge of Drawing Fundamentals to Determine Criteria for Assigning Students to Accelerated Sections of Engineering Drawing.* Doctor's thesis, Texas A & M University (College Station, Tex.), 1965. (*DA* 26:6533)

195. MCKELPIN, J. P. "Some Implications of the Intellectual Characteristics of Freshmen Entering a Liberal Arts College." *J Ed Meas* 2:161–6 D '65. *

196. MUNDAY, LEO. "Comparative Predictive Validities of the American College Tests and Two Other Scholastic Aptitude Tests." *ACT Res Rep* 6:2–14 Ag '65. *

197. PLAPP, JON M.; PSATHAS, GEORGE; AND CAPUTO, DANIEL V. "Intellective Predictors of Success in Nursing School." *Ed & Psychol Meas* 25:565–77 su '65. * (*PA* 39:15259)

198. ROBINSON, BEVERLY VICKERSTAFF. *Predicting College Grades on the Basis of College Entrance Examination Scores and Participation in Student Activities.* Doctor's thesis, University of Toledo (Toledo, Ohio), 1965. (*DA* 26:2550)

199. ROBINSON, FRANCES K. *An Investigation of the Value of the ACT Battery, the College Board Scholastic Aptitude Test, the Differential Aptitude Test Battery, and the University of Kansas Placement Battery as Predictors of University of Kansas Freshman Grades.* Master's thesis, University of Kansas (Lawrence, Kan.), 1965.

200. SASSENRATH, JULIUS M., AND PUGH, RICHARD. "Relationships Among CEEB Scholastic Aptitude Test and American College Test Scores and Grade Point Average." *J Ed Meas* 2:199–205 D '65. *

201. SKAGER, RODNEY W.; SCHULTZ, CHARLES B.; AND KLEIN, STEPHEN P. "Quality and Quantity of Accomplishments as Measures of Creativity." *J Ed Psychol* 56:31–9 F '65. * (*PA* 39:10180)

202. STAPLES, JOHN DIXON. *An Experimental Study to Identify the Basic Abilities Needed to Detect Typescript Errors With Implications for the Improvement of Instruction in Typewriting.* Doctor's thesis, University of North Dakota (Grand Forks, N.D.), 1965. (*DA* 27:1693A)

203. STARKMAN, STANLEY S. "The Effect of Training in Reading on Performance on a Scholastic Ability Test." *Psychol Sch* 2:137–40 Ap '65. *

204. STRICKER, GEORGE. "Intellective and Nonintellective Correlates of Grade-Point Average." Abstract. *Proc Ann Conv Am Psychol Assn* 73:305–6 '65. * (*PA* 39:16460)

205. WATLEY, DONIVAN J. "Personal Adjustment and Prediction of Academic Achievement." *J Appl Psychol* 49:20–3 F '65. * (*PA* 39:8598)

206. WHETSTONE, ROBERT DEAN. *A Tri-Group Prediction Paradigm for College Performance Based on Deviate High School Achievement.* Doctor's thesis, University of Denver (Denver, Colo.), 1965. (*DA* 26:884)

207. AIKEN, LEWIS R. "A Composite Normograph for Predicting Achievement in College." *J Ed Res* 60:127–9 N '66. *

208. BAER, DANIEL J. "Scholastic Aptitude and Smoking Attitude and Behavior of College Males." *J Psychol* 64:63–8 S '66. * (*PA* 40:12589)

209. BEHRING, DANIEL W. "Activities and Academic Achievement." *Personnel & Guid J* 44:734–7 Mr '66. * (*PA* 40:7199)

210. BELL, EVERETTE LYLE. *Factors Relating to Employment of Graduates of Des Moines Technical High School.* Doctor's thesis, Iowa State University (Ames, Iowa), 1966. (*DA* 27:892A)

211. CAMPBELL, JAMES PATRICK. *A Multivariate Analysis of the Relationship of Selected Academic Interest and Aptitude Variables in Choice of Major Field.* Doctor's thesis, Temple University (Philadelphia, Pa.), 1966. (*DA* 27:3663B)

212. CHASE, CLINTON I., AND BARRITT, L. SPENCER. "A Table of Concordance Between ACT and SAT." *J Col Stud Personnel* 7:105–8 Mr '66. * Comment by William H. Angoff and reply by the authors, 7:194–6 Jl '66. *

213. CRADDICK, RAY A. "Effect of Season of Birth on Achievement of College Students." *Psychol Rep* 18:329–30 F '66. * (*PA* 40:6625)

214. DICKEY, OUIDA WORD. *A Study of the Effects of Three Schedules of Reinforcement Upon Achievement and Retention in a Linear Program in College Business Mathematics.* Doctor's thesis, University of Georgia (Athens, Ga.), 1966. (*DA* 27:3363A)

215. FITZPATRICK, MARY REPARATRICE. *A Study of Cognitive Factors as Evidenced in the College Board SAT Scores of Seniors in a Suburban Catholic High School.* Doctor's thesis, Fordham University (New York, N.Y.), 1966. (*DA* 27:389A)

216. FLORA, LARRY DALE. *Predicting Academic Success at Lynchburg College From Multiple Correlational Analysis of Four Selected Predictor Variables.* Doctor's thesis, University of Virginia (Charlottesville, Va.), 1966. (*DA* 27:2276A) (Abstract: *Ed R* 4:53–5)

217. HALLADAY, ROY ELDON. *The Effect of Certain Subcultural Background Factors on the Prediction of Grades at the University of Michigan.* Doctor's thesis, Michigan State University (East Lansing, Mich.), 1966. (*DA* 27:2780A)

218. IRVINE, DONALD W. "Multiple Prediction of College Graduation From Pre-Admission Data." *J Exp Ed* 35:84–9 f '66. *

219. IVEY, ALLEN E.; PETERSON, FLOYD E.; AND TREBBE, E. STEWART. "The Personality Record as a Predictor of College Attrition: A Discriminant Analysis." *Col & Univ* 41:199–205 w '66. *

220. JACOBS, PAUL I. "Large Score Changes on the Scholastic Aptitude Test." *Personnel & Guid J* 45:150–6 O '66. * (*PA* 41:1004)

221. JEX, FRANK B. *Predicting Academic Success Beyond High School.* Salt Lake City, Utah: University of Utah Bookstore, 1966. Pp. vi, 41. *

222. JUDGE, ELLEN M. *A Comparison of One Non-Accelerated and Two Accelerated Mathematics Programs on Achievement Scores of the Scholastic Aptitude Tests.* Master's thesis, Marywood College (Scranton, Pa.), 1966.

223. KANTROWITZ, JUDY LEOPOLD. *The Effects of Crisis on Academic Achievement.* Doctor's thesis, Boston University (Boston, Mass.), 1966. (*DA* 27:1623B)

224. LINS, L. JOSEPH; ABELL, ALLAN P.; AND HUTCHINS, H. CLIFTON. "Relative Usefulness in Predicting Academic Success of the ACT, the SAT, and Some Other Variables." *J Exp Ed* 35:1–29 w '66. *

225. MALCOLM, RICHARD WARD. *An Analysis of Selected Conditional Admissions at the University of Southern California.* Doctor's thesis, University of Southern California (Los Angeles, Calif.), 1966. (*DA* 27:115A)

226. MEADOWS, MARK EUGENE. *A Comparative Study of Selected Characteristics of Counseled and Non-Counseled Students in a College Counseling Center.* Doctor's thesis, University of Georgia (Athens, Ga.), 1966. (*DA* 27:2404A)

227. NELSEN, EDWARD A., AND MACCOBY, ELEANOR E. "The Relationship Between Social Development and Differential Abilities on the Scholastic Aptitude Test." *Merrill-Palmer Q* 12:269–84 O '66. * (*PA* 41:5953)

228. O'ZEE, WILLIAM FREDERICK. *A Study of College Predictors for Opportunity Program Participants at Colorado State University.* Doctor's thesis, Colorado State College (Greeley, Colo.), 1966. (*DA* 27:3729A)

229. PRIEN, ERICH P., AND BOTWIN, DAVID E. "The Reliability and Correlates of an Achievement Index." *Ed & Psychol Meas* 26:1047–52 w '66. * (*PA* 41:4998)

230. ROWE, LAURA M. *The Predictive Value of the College Entrance Examination Board's Scholastic Aptitude Verbal Test Score and High School Index in Determining the Academic Performance of College Arts and Sciences Freshmen.* Master's thesis, American University (Washington, D.C.), 1966.

231. SASSENRATH, JULIUS M., AND PUGH, RICHARD. "Note: Relationships Among CEEB Scholastic Aptitude Test and American College Test Scores and Grade Point Average: A Replication." *J Ed Meas* 3:37–8 sp '66. *

232. SAUNDERS, H. REED. *A Comparison of Multiple Regression, Predictive Pattern and Bayes Techniques for the Prediction of College Grades.* Doctor's thesis, University of Wisconsin (Madison, Wis.), 1966. (*DA* 28:507A)

233. STOVALL, EULA MAE. *Sex Differences in Learning a Complex Motor Task.* Doctor's thesis, University of Southern California (Los Angeles, Calif.), 1966. (*DA* 26:7149)

234. SULLIVAN, GERTRUDE VERONICA. *A Study of Predictive Factors and the College Success of Above and Below 110 IQ Large-City Public School Graduates Attending Local Colleges and Universities.* Doctor's thesis, Temple University (Philadelphia, Pa.), 1966. (*DA* 27:889A)

235. TATHAM, CLIFFORD B., AND DOLE, ARTHUR A. "Academic Success of Foreign Undergraduates." *J Col Stud Personnel* 7:167–71 My '66. *

236. WEBB, SAM C. "Estimating Gains in Scholastic Aptitude Test Scores Attributable to Three Sources." *Ed & Psychol Meas* 26:633–41 au '66. *

237. *Manual of Freshman Class Profiles, 1967–69.* Princeton, N.J.: College Entrance Examination Board, 1967. Pp. xvi, 1242. *

238. *Normative Data for the 1965–66 Freshman Class, University System of Georgia.* Atlanta, Ga.: Regents of the University System of Georgia, December 1967. Pp. xi, 72. *

239. BENSON, PURNELL H. "Multiple-Regression Analysis of a Paired-Choice Division-of-Time Inventory in Relation to Grade-Point Average." *J Appl Psychol* 51:82–8 F '67. * (*PA* 41:4965)

240. BUTZOW, JOHN W., AND WILLIAMS, CLARENCE M. "College Freshman Achievement of Parochial and Public Secondary School Graduates." *J Ed Res* 60:215–7 Ja '67. *

241. CANNING, HELEN, AND MAYER, JEAN. "Obesity: An Influence on High School Performance?" *Am J Clin Nutr* 20:352–4 Ap '67. *

242. COFFMAN, WILLIAM E., AND PARRY, MARY ELLEN. "Effects of an Accelerated Reading Course on SAT-V Scores." *Personnel & Guid J* 46:292–6 N '67. * (*PA* 42:4481)

243. COLE, CHARLES W., AND MILLER, C. DEAN. "Relevance of Expressed Values to Academic Performance." *J Counsel Psychol* 14:272–6 My '67. * (*PA* 41:9363)

244. DOWD, ROBERT JOHN. *Divergent Thinking as a Factor*

Related to Achievement in College. Doctor's thesis, University of Connecticut (Storrs, Conn.), 1967. (*DA* 28:3993A)

245. FLOYD, WILLIAM A. "Longitudinal Study of the Scholastic Aptitude Test as a Predictor of College Success." *Sch Counselor* 14:138–42 Ja '67. *

246. FRIELDS, SUSAN IRENE. *A Comparison of the Relationships of the PSAT and SAT Test Scores for the Students of North Haven High School: 1965 and 1966.* Master's thesis, Southern Connecticut State College (New Haven, Conn.), 1967.

247. GALLESSICH, JUNE MARIE. *Factors Associated With Academic Success of Freshmen Engineering Students at the University of Texas.* Doctor's thesis, University of Texas (Austin, Tex.), 1967. (*DA* 28:1677A)

248. GARMS, JOE DEWAYNE. *Predicting Scholastic Achievement With Nonintellectual Variables.* Doctor's thesis, Texas Technological College (Lubbock, Tex.), 1967. (*DA* 28:3460B)

249. GERRY, ROBERT. *Computer-Learner Interaction in Problem Solving Tasks.* Doctor's thesis, University of Texas (Austin, Tex.), 1967. (*DA* 28:3997A)

250. HARRIS, JOHN, AND REITZEL, JOHN. "Negro Freshman Performance in a Predominantly Non-Negro University." *J Col Stud Personnel* 8:366–7 N 67. *

251. HILTON, THOMAS L., AND MYERS, ALBERT E. "Personal Background, Experience and School Achievement: An Investigation of the Contribution of Questionnaire Data to Academic Prediction." *J Ed Meas* 4:69–80 su '67. * (*PA* 42:4570)

252. JANSEN, DAVID G. "Verbal and Reading Skills of Students Participating in a University Reading and Study Skills Program." *J Col Stud Personnel* 8:181–4 My '67. *

253. KEENEN, CHARLES BENJAMIN. *Predicting Completion in a College of Liberal Arts by Content Analysis of the Candidate's Personal Application Statement.* Doctor's thesis, Boston University (Boston, Mass.), 1967. (*DA* 29:4285A)

254. KEESEE, CURTIS GORDON, JR. *The Relationship of Performance on the Scholastic Aptitude Test, the Meier Art Judgment Test, and the Graves Design Judgment Test to Successful Completion of Freshmen Commercial Art Courses.* Doctor's thesis, University of Virginia (Charlottesville, Va.), 1967. (*DA* 28:2516A) (Abstract: *Ed R* 5:58–60)

255. KENDRICK, S. A. "The Coming Segregation of Our Selective Colleges." *Col Board R* 66:6–13 w '67–68. *

256. KENDRICK, S. A. "When SAT Scores Go Down." *Col Board R* 64:5–11 su '67. *

257. LEATHERS, ROGER K. *A Study of the Relationships Between Physical Performance and Academic Achievement of Springfield College Students.* Doctor's thesis, Springfield College (Springfield, Mass.), 1967.

258. MAGOON, ROBERT ARNOLD. *The Prediction of Freshman Academic Performance in an Urban Southern College.* Doctor's thesis, University of Virginia (Charlottesville, Va.), 1967. (*DA* 28:3371A)

259. MEDNICK, MARTHA T., AND ANDREWS, FRANK M. "Creative Thinking and Level of Intelligence." *J Creative Behav* 1:428–31 f '67. *

260. PASSONS, WILLIAM R. "Predictive Validities of the ACT, SAT and High School Grades for First Semester GPA and Freshman Courses." *Ed & Psychol Meas* 27:1143–4 w '67. * (*PA* 42:9427)

261. PAYNE, DAVID A., AND VAUGHN, HAROLD A. "Forecasting Italian Language Proficiency of Culturally Immersed Students." *Mod Lang J* 51:3–6 Ja '67. *

262. RANGE, LEO HARRY. *A Comparison of ACT and SAT Standard Scores.* Master's thesis, St. Louis University (St. Louis, Mo.), 1967.

263. SACHTLEBEN, CLYDE CLINTON. *An Analysis of Selected Background Variables Which Affect Success in Physics in Liberal Arts Colleges.* Doctor's thesis, University of Iowa (Iowa City, Iowa), 1967. (*DA* 28:470A)

264. SASSENRATH, J. M. "Anxiety, Aptitude, Attitude, and Achievement." *Psychol Sch* 4:341–6 O '67. * (*PA* 42:2949)

265. STANLEY, J. C. "Further Evidence via the Analysis of Variance That Women Are More Predictable Academically Than Men." *Ont J Ed Res* 10:49–56 au '67. * (*PA* 42:6157)

266. STANLEY, JULIAN C., AND PORTER, ANDREW C. "Correlation of Scholastic Aptitude Test Score With College Grades for Negroes Versus Whites." *J Ed Meas* 4:199–218 w '67. * (*PA* 42:11210)

267. STEWART, CAROL J. *The Reliability and Validity of High School Grades and Scholastic Aptitude Test Scores for Predicting Freshman Success at Westminster College.* Master's thesis, University of Utah (Salt Lake City, Utah), 1967.

268. STIX, DANIEL L. "Discrepant Achievement in College as a Function of Anxiety and Repression." *Personnel & Guid J* 45:804–7 Ap '67. * (*PA* 41:12494)

269. SUTTER, EMILY MAY GEESEMAN. *Individual Differences and Social Conditions as They Affect Learning by Computer-Assisted Instruction.* Doctor's thesis, University of Texas (Austin, Tex.), 1967. (*DA* 28:4012A)

270. WALBERG, HERBERT J. "Scholastic Aptitude, the National Teacher Examinations, and Teaching Success." *J Ed Res* 61:129–31 N '67. *

271. WALTERS, NANCY ROCKHILL. *Predictive Characteristics of DePauw University Freshman Dropouts Over a Three Year Period.* Doctor's thesis, Indiana University (Bloomington, Ind.), 1967. (*DA* 28:3471A)

272. WEBB, SAM C. *The Relations of College Grades and Personal Qualities Considered Within Two Frames of Reference.* Multivariate Behavioral Research Monographs, No. 67-2. Ft. Worth, Tex.: Texas Christian University Press, 1967. Pp. 53. * (*PA* 42:9511)

273. WILLIAMS, RODNEY HOWE. *The Relationship Between the Vocational Development and Scholastic Achievement of Male College Students: A Correlational Analysis and Evaluation of the Relationship Between Scores of Vocational Maturity, Vocational Maladjustment, Intellectual Capacity, and Scholastic Index.* Doctor's thesis, New York University (New York, N.Y.), 1967. (*DA* 28:1318A)

274. WINDHOLZ, GEORGE, AND MCINTOSH, WILLIAM A. "Concurrent Validation of Guilford's Six Convergent Tests." *Ed & Psychol Meas* 27:393–400 su '67. * (*PA* 41:12843)

275. YEREMIAN, THAIS SHERMAN. *A Comparative Study of Divergent Thinking Ability and Academic Achievement of Students in the Honors Program at the University of Southern California.* Doctor's thesis, University of Southern California (Los Angeles, Calif.), 1967. (*DA* 28:109A)

276. ZIMMERMAN, WAYNE S., AND MICHAEL, WILLIAM B. "A Comparison of the Criterion-Related Validities of Three College Entrance Examinations With Different Content Emphases." *Ed & Psychol Meas* 27:407–12 su '67. * (*PA* 41:12845)

277. *Normative Data for the 1966–67 Freshman Class, University System of Georgia.* Atlanta, Ga.: Regents of the University System of Georgia, November 1968. Pp. xi, 84. *

278. AIKEN, LEWIS R., JR. "Three Alignment Charts for Use in Selective Admissions." *J Ed Res* 62:14–7 S '68. *

279. ANGOFF, WILLIAM H. "How We Calibrate College Board Scores." *Col Board R* 68:11–4 su '68. *

280. BEALS, ERNEST WESLEY. *Academic Characteristics and Academic Success Patterns of Community College Transfer Students at the University of Massachusetts.* Doctor's thesis, University of Massachusetts (Amherst, Mass.), 1968. (*DA* 29:2954A)

281. BROOKS, WINONA NOLAND. *Relationships of Variables Identified With Success in College Clothing Construction Courses: A View Toward Advanced Placement and Improved Learning.* Doctor's thesis, University of Southern California (Los Angeles, Calif.), 1968. (*DA* 29:1701A)

282. BUCKEYE, DONALD ANDREW. *The Effects of a Creative Classroom Environment on the Creative Ability of Prospective Elementary Mathematics Teachers.* Doctor's thesis, Indiana University (Bloomington, Ind.), 1968. (*DA* 29:1801A)

283. BUSZEK, BEATRICE R. "Differential Treatment of Test Scores." *Col & Univ* 43:294–307 sp '68. *

284. BUTLER, JOHN HARRISON. *Personality Factors as Correlates of Receptivity to Electronic Music.* Doctor's thesis, University of Georgia (Athens, Ga.), 1968. (*DA* 29:4514A)

285. CHASE, C. I.; PUGH, R. C.; AND LUDLOW, H. G. *Modern Language Placement: An Alternative to Testing.* Indiana University, Monograph of the Bureau of Educational Studies and Testing, Indiana Studies in Prediction, No. 10. Bloomington, Ind.: the Bureau, 1968. Pp. vii, 11. *

286. CLAWAR, HARRY J. "A Short Highly-Efficient Prediction of College Entrance Examination Board Scholastic Aptitude Test Performance." *Ed Rec B* 94:42–4 Jl '68. * (*PA* 44:21523)

287. CLEARY, T. ANNE. "Test Bias: Prediction of Grades of Negro and White Students in Integrated Colleges." *J Ed Meas* 5:115–24 su '68. *

288. CLEARY, T. ANNE, AND HILTON, THOMAS L. "An Investigation of Item Bias." *Ed & Psychol Meas* 28:61–75 sp '68. * (*PA* 42:11356)

289. COLGAN, RICHARD THOMAS. *A Longitudinal Study of the Relationship of Teacher Judgment Versus Objective Test Data With Respect to College Success.* Doctor's thesis, Southern Illinois University (Carbondale, Ill.), 1968. (*DA* 29:3413B)

290. COOK, RAYMOND L. *A Comparative Study of Scores on the CEEB Scholastic Aptitude Test Made by Graduates of Graded and Non-Graded High Schools.* Master's thesis, Stetson University (DeLand, Fla.), 1968.

291. CORSINI, RAYMOND J., AND BORGATTA, EDGAR F. "The Quick Number Test (QNT)." *J Exp Ed* 36:7–10 su '68. *

292. CROUCH, JOYCE G. *The Role of Sex, Anxiety and Independence as Moderator Variables in Achievement of College Freshmen.* Doctor's thesis, University of Tennessee (Knoxville, Tenn.), 1968. (*DA* 29:3827A)

293. DOERMANN, HUMPHREY. "Market for College Education." *Ed Rec* 49:49–57 w '68. *

294. DONNAN, HUGH. "Personality Factors Related to College Achievement and Attrition." *J Col Stud Personnel* 9:116–9 Mr '68. *

295. EVEN, ALEXANDER. *Patterns of Academic Achievement in Grade 12 Chemistry and Their Relationship to Personal Attitudinal and Environmental Factors.* Doctor's thesis, University of Toronto (Toronto, Ont., Canada), 1968. (*DAI* 31:1136A)

296. FLAUGHER, RONALD L., AND ROCK, DONALD A. "A Fixed Length Optimal Test Battery for Colleges Characterized by Diverse Aptitude Levels." *Am Ed Res J* 5:659–74 N '68. *

297. FLAUGHER, RONALD L.; MELTON, RICHARD S.; AND MYERS, CHARLES T. "Item Rearrangement Under Typical Test

Conditions." *Ed & Psychol Meas* 28:813–24 au '68. * (*PA* 43:4430)

298. FREMER, JOHN; COFFMAN, WILLIAM E.; AND TAYLOR, PHILIP H. "The College Board Scholastic Aptitude Test as a Predictor of Academic Achievement in Secondary Schools in England." *J Ed Meas* 5:235–41 f '68. * (*PA* 44:11411)

299. GAMBLE, KENNETH R., AND KELLNER, HAROLD. "Creative Functioning and Cognitive Regression." *J Pers & Social Psychol* 9:266–71 Jl '68. * (*PA* 42:13761)

300. GRAFF, ROBERT WALTER. *The Relationship of the Opinion, Attitude, and Interest Survey to College Achievement and Academic Adjustment Factors.* Doctor's thesis, State University of New York (Buffalo, N.Y.), 1968. (*DA* 29:2959A)

301. HAMM, BETTY HUGHIE. *A Study of Enrollee Characteristics in Schools of Nursing in Georgia.* Doctor's thesis, University of Georgia (Athens, Ga.), 1968. (*DA* 29:4324A)

302. HILLS, JOHN R., AND GLADNEY, MARILYN B. "Predicting Grades From Below Chance Test Scores." *J Ed Meas* 5:45–53 sp '68. *

303. HILLS, JOHN R., AND STANLEY, JULIAN C. "Prediction of Freshman Grades From SAT and From Level 4 of SCAT in Three Predominantly Negro State Colleges." Abstract. *Proc 76th Ann Conv Am Psychol Assn* 3:241–2 '68. *

304. HOWELL, JOHN J. "On the Meaning of SAT Scores Obtained by Foreign Students of Non-English Language Background." *Col & Univ* 43:225–32 w '68. *

305. HOYT, DONALD P. "Forecasting Academic Success in Specific Colleges." *ACT Res Rep* 27:1–52 Ag '68. *

306. JOHNSON, RICHARD W.; KFOCHAKIAN, SIMON V.; MORNINGSTAR, MONA; AND SOUTHWORTH, J. ALFRED. "Validation of Freshman Orientation Test Battery." *Ed & Psychol Meas* 28:437–40 su '68. * (*PA* 42:19274)

307. KIRK, CHARLES RICHARD. *The Suppression of Non-Valid Variance in Measures of Scholastic Aptitude as Predictors of Scholastic Achievement.* Doctor's thesis, Temple University (Philadelphia, Pa.), 1968. (*DA* 29:1835B)

308. KOVACS, ALBERTA ROSE. *Predicting Success in Three Selected Collegiate Schools of Nursing.* Doctor's thesis, Columbia University (New York, N.Y.), 1968. (*DAI* 31:266B)

309. LORD, FREDERIC M. "An Analysis of the Verbal Scholastic Aptitude Test Using Birnbaum's Three-Parameter Logistic Model." *Ed & Psychol Meas* 28:989–1020 w '68. * (*PA* 44:7266)

310. McENTIRE, EVALYN M. *The Relationship Between the Scores Made on the Florida State-Wide Twelfth Grade and the Scholastic Aptitude Test by Applicants to Stetson University in 1966 and 1967.* Master's thesis, Stetson University (DeLand, Fla.), 1968.

311. MANNING, WINTON H. "The Measurement of Intellectual Capacity and Performance." *J Negro Ed* 37:258–67 su '68. *

312. MARQUETTE, ALLAN J. *A Study of the Correlation Between the Scholastic Aptitude Test and the Grade Achievement of Majors in Mathematics at Central Connecticut State College.* Master's thesis, Central Connecticut State College (New Britain, Conn.), 1968.

313. MILLER, CAROL L.; FELDHUSEN, JOHN F.; AND ASHER, J. WILLIAM. "The Prediction of State Board Examination Scores of Graduates of an Associate Degree Program." *Nursing Res* 17:555+ N–D '68. *

314. MORGAN, LEWIS B. "The 'Calculated Risks': A Study of Success." *Col & Univ* 43:203–6 w '68. *

315. MUNDAY, LEO. "Correlations Between ACT and Other Predictors of Academic Success in College." *Col & Univ* 44:67–76 f '68. *

316. PERTUSIO, CAROLYN BOYER. *A Study of the Effects of a Seminar of Test-Taking Techniques on the College Board Scores of Palmyra Area High School Students.* Master's thesis, Millersville State College (Millersville, Pa.), 1968.

317. PUGH, RICHARD C., AND SASSENRATH, JULIUS M. "Comparable Scores for the CEEB Scholastic Aptitude Test and the American College Test Program." *Meas & Eval Guid* 1:103–9 su '68. * (*PA* 44:9266)

318. RECK, MARTIN. "The Prediction of Achievement in a College Science Curriculum." *Ed & Psychol Meas* 28:943–4 au '68. * (*PA* 43:4517)

319. ROBERTS, BRUCE BEN. *The Leader, Group, and Task Variables of Leader Selection in College.* Doctor's thesis, Claremont Graduate School (Claremont, Calif.), 1968. (*DA* 29:2360A)

320. SCHOEMER, JAMES R. "The College Pushout." *Personnel & Guid J* 46:677–80 Mr '68. * (*PA* 42:16005)

321. STIMSON, ROGER C., JR. "Factor Analytic Approach to the Structural Differentiation of Description." *J Counsel Psychol* 15:301–7 Jl '68. *

322. VAUGHAN, RICHARD P. "College Dropouts: Dismissed vs. Withdrew." *Personnel & Guid J* 46:685–9 Mr '68. * (*PA* 42:16144)

323. VELDMAN, DONALD J. "Effects of Sex, Aptitudes, and Attitudes on the Academic Achievement of College Freshmen." *J Ed Meas* 5:245–9 f '68. * (*PA* 44:11403)

324. WHITLA, DEAN K. Chap. 14, "Evaluation of Decision Making: A Study of College Admissions," pp. 456–90. In his *Handbook of Measurement and Assessment in Behavioral Sciences.* Reading, Mass.: Addison-Wesley Publishing Co., Inc., 1968. Pp. xx, 508. *

325. WILLINGHAM, WARREN W. "Validity of Several Methods of Expressing High School Achievement Level." *Col & Univ* 40:49–54 f '68. *

326. WOOD, DONALD A., AND LEBOLD, WILLIAM K. "Differential and Overall Prediction of Academic Success in Engineering: The Complementary Role of DAT, SAT and HSR." *Ed & Psychol Meas* 28:1223–8 w '68. * (*PA* 44:7339)

327. ZARFOSS, NORMA J. *The Effects of the Study of Latin on SAT Verbal Scores.* Master's thesis, Millersville State College (Millersville, Pa.), 1968.

328. *Normative Data for the 1967–68 Freshman Class, University System of Georgia.* Atlanta, Ga.: Regents of the University System of Georgia, May 1969. Pp. xi, 87. *

329. *Normative Data for the 1968–69 Freshman Class, University System of Georgia.* Atlanta, Ga.: Regents of the University System of Georgia, October 1969. Pp. xi, 87. *

330. ALKER, HENRY A. "Rationality and Achievement: A Comparison of the Atkinson-McClelland and Kogan-Wallach Formulations." *J Personality* 37(2):207–24 Je '69. *

331. ALKER, HENRY A.; CARLSON, JULIA A.; AND HERMANN, MARGARET G. "Multiple-Choice Questions and Student Characteristics." *J Ed Psychol* 60(3):231–43 Je '69. * (*PA* 43:13299)

332. ANDERSON, CARL EDWIN. *A Study of Selected Psycho-Social Correlates of College Student Protesters and Non-Protesters.* Doctor's thesis, University of Maryland (College Park, Md.), 1969. (*DAI* 30:606A)

333. BECHTOLD, DONALD WILLIAM. *Dynamic Structures of Occupational Choice of High School Seniors.* Doctor's thesis, Catholic University of America (Washington, D.C.), 1969. (*DAI* 30:2322A)

334. BEHLING, MARY ALICE. *The Development of a Screening Program for the Selection and Retention of Women Physical Education Major Students.* Doctor's thesis, Florida State University (Tallahassee, Fla.), 1969. (*DAI* 30:4258A)

335. BEHRING, DANIEL WILLIAM. *Adaptive Functioning: A Rationale for the Prediction of Achievement in Nursing Education.* Doctor's thesis, Ohio University (Athens, Ohio), 1969. (*DAI* 31:1065A)

336. BRAUN, JOHN ROBERT. *The BWWM Chemistry Placement Test as a Predictor of Achievement of General Chemistry Students.* Doctor's thesis, University of Georgia (Athens, Ga.), 1969. (*DAI* 30:5394B)

337. BRODY, ERNESS B. "Intellectual Ability, Social Desirability, and Differential Teacher Effectiveness." *J Exp Ed* 38(1):13–5 f '69. *

338. BUESCHER, RUTH MARIE. *The Relationship Between Selected Noncognitive Variables and Academic Achievement of College Women in Various Fields of Study.* Doctor's thesis, Fordham University (New York, N.Y.), 1969. (*DAI* 30:1858A)

339. BURGESS, THOMAS C. "Estimating Average Freshman Class Ability From Preliminary Information." *J Col Stud Personnel* 10(3):161–3 My '69. *

340. CASSEL, RUSSELL N., AND EICHSTEADT, ARDEN C. "Factorial Structure of CQT, ACT, and SAT Test Scores for 50 Available College Freshmen." *J Psychol* 71(2):199–204 Mr '69. * (*PA* 43:8675)

341. CHASTAIN, KENNETH. "Prediction of Success in Audio-Lingual and Cognitive Classes." *Lang Learning* 19(1–2):27–39 Je '69. *

342. CHERRY, ADA LOU. *A Comparison of Selected Characteristics of Graduated Students and Academically Disqualified Students Who Were Admitted With Warning to Ball State University Autumns, 1963 and 1964.* Doctor's thesis, Ball State University (Muncie, Ind.), 1969. (*DAI* 30:4217A)

343. CONLEY, HAROLD W. *The Analyses of the Academic Performance of "High Risk" and "Regular Admit" Negro Students Within a College Freshman Class.* Doctor's thesis, University of Connecticut (Storrs, Conn.), 1969. (*DAI* 30:577A)

344. DICKASON, DONALD G. "Predicting the Success of Freshman Engineers." *Personnel & Guid J* 47(10):1008–14 Je '69. * (*PA* 44:1369)

345. ESSER, BARBARA FELLER. *The Changing Relationship Between Verbal and Quantitative Aptitudes as Measured by the Scholastic Aptitude Test.* Doctor's thesis, Rutgers—The State University (New Brunswick, N.J.), 1969. (*DAI* 30:3780A)

346. EVANS, JAMES D. "The Relationships of Three Personality Scales to Grade Point Average and Verbal Ability in College Freshmen." *J Ed Res* 63(3):121–5 N '69. *

347. FLAUGHER, RONALD L., AND ROCK, DONALD A. "A Multiple Moderator Approach to the Identification of Over- and Underachievers." *J Ed Meas* 6(4):223–8 w '69. * (*PA* 44:17516)

348. HARVILLE, DENNIS L. "Early Identification of Potential Leaders." *J Col Stud Personnel* 10(4):333–5 S '69. *

349. HOWLETT, JOHN L. "A Study of Placement Methods for Entering College Freshmen in the Proper Mathematics Sequence at Michigan Technological University." *Math Teach* 62(8):651–9 D '69. *

350. JUDD, LARRY R., AND SMITH, CAROLYN. "Predicting

Success in the Basic College Speech Course." *Speech Teach* 18(1):13–7 Ja '69. *

351. KARAS, SHAWKY F. "Development of a Reduced Set of Composite Equations for Three Predictors." *Psychol Rep* 25(2):623–30 O '69. * (*PA* 44:5710)

352. KARLINS, MARVIN; SCHUERHOFF, CHARLES; AND KAPLAN, MARTIN. "Some Factors Related to Architectural Creativity in Graduating Architecture Students." *J General Psychol* 81(2):203–15 O '69. * (*PA* 44:6775)

353. LEE, ESSIE ELIZABETH. *The Examination and Evaluation of the Educational Experiences of "Risk Students" at an Urban Community College.* Doctor's thesis, Columbia University (New York, N.Y.), 1969. (*DAI* 30:3730A)

354. MAGRAB, PHYLLIS R. *Expectation-Press Congruence as a Psychological Variable in the Prediction of College Adaptation.* Doctor's thesis, University of Maryland (College Park, Md.), 1969. (*DAI* 30:5290A)

355. MILLER, DORIS METZGER, AND O'CONNOR, PATRICIA. "Achiever Personality and Academic Success Among Disadvantaged College Students." *J Social Issues* 25(3):103–16 su '69. *

356. NELSON, BRUCE EDWARD. *The Relationship of Mathematics in Oregon High Schools to Placement and Success in First-Year Mathematics at Oregon State University.* Doctor's thesis, Oregon State University (Corvallis, Ore.), 1969. (*DAI* 30:1401A)

357. NOTESTINE, EARL BRANDON. *A Comparative Study of Student Retention and Withdrawal in the School of Humanities, Social Science, and Education at Purdue University.* Doctor's thesis, Purdue University (Lafayette, Ind.), 1969. (*DAI* 30:1402A)

358. PREAS, NANCY BUSH. *A Study of the Relationship Between Selected Variables and Academic Achievement in a Community College.* Doctor's thesis, North Carolina State University (Raleigh, N.C.), 1969. (*DAI* 30:5245A)

359. PRICE, RICHARD LIONEL. *Scholastic Aptitude Test in Mathematics as a Predictor of Student Selection of Algebraic Versus Geometric Approaches to Problem Solving.* Doctor's thesis, Ohio State University (Columbus, Ohio), 1969. (*DAI* 30:4340A)

360. PUGH, RICHARD C.; HUTCHCRAFT, GILBERT; AND LUDLOW, H. GLENN. *An Analysis of Achievement Behavior in Selected Mathematics Courses.* Indiana Studies in Prediction No. 12. Bloomington, Ind.: Bureau of Educational Studies and Testing, Indiana University, August 1969. Pp. xiii, 42. *

361. REELING, PATRICIA ANN. *Undergraduate Female Students as Potential Recruits to the Library Profession.* Doctor's thesis, Columbia University (New York, N.Y.), 1969. (*DAI* 30:4470A)

362. ROBERTS, S. OLIVER; HORTON, CARRELL P.; AND ROBERTS, BARBARA T. "SAT Versus GRE Performance of Negro American College Students." Abstract. *Proc 77th Ann Conv Am Psychol Assn* 4(1):177–8 '69. * (*PA* 43:17912)

363. SHERRON, RONALD HOMER. *A Study of Academic and Nonacademic Predictors and Criteria of Success Among the Morehead Scholars at the University of North Carolina at Chapel Hill.* Doctor's thesis, University of North Carolina (Chapel Hill, N.C.), 1969. (*DAI* 30:3287A)

364. SIEGEL, ARTHUR I., AND PFEIFFER, MARK G. "Predicting Academic Success Through Application of Theory of Signal Detectability Variables." Abstract. *Proc 77th Ann Conv Am Psychol Assn* 4(1):145–6 '69. * (*PA* 43:17990)

365. SIEVEKING, NICHOLAS A., AND SAVITSKY, JEFFREY C. "Evaluation of an Achievement Test, Prediction of Grades, and Composition of Discussion Groups in College Chemistry." *J Res Sci Teach* 6(4):374–6 '69. *

366. SOCKLOFF, ALAN LEONARD. *The Analysis of Student Characteristics Associated With Grades for Varying Levels of College Freshman Grade Complexity.* Doctor's thesis, Emory University (Atlanta, Ga.), 1969. (*DAI* 31:903B)

367. SPIEGEL, JOSEPH A. *Test Score Performance on Irish and Italian College Freshmen.* Doctor's thesis, Rutgers—The State University (New Brunswick, N.J.), 1969. (*DAI* 30:3802A)

368. STONE, MICHAEL HORACE. *A Study of the Relationships Between Selected Variables and the Differential Academic Achievement of Freshmen in the University of Michigan School of Music.* Doctor's thesis, University of Michigan (Ann Arbor, Mich.), 1969. (*DAI* 30:1881A)

369. SZABO, MICHAEL. *The Relationship of Intellective, Personality, and Biographical Variables to Success and Its Prediction in an Independent Study Science Course at the College Level.* Doctor's thesis, Purdue University (Lafayette, Ind.), 1969. (*DAI* 30:4845A)

370. THOMAS, CHARLES LEO, AND STANLEY, JULIAN C. "Effectiveness of High School Grades for Predicting College Grades of Black Students: A Review and Discussion." *J Ed Meas* 6(4):203–15 w '69. * (*PA* 44:17514)

371. TOBIAS, SIGMUND. "Effect of Creativity, Response Mode, and Subject Matter Familiarity on Achievement From Programmed Instruction." *J Ed Psychol* 60(6):453–60 D '69. *

372. UTGARD, RUSSELL O. *Verbal Behavior of Recitation Teachers and Achievement of College Geology Students.* Doctor's thesis, Indiana University (Bloomington, Ind.), 1969. (*DAI* 30:4294A)

373. WATLEY, DONIVAN J. "Career Progress: A Longitudinal Study of Gifted Students." *J Counsel Psychol* 16(2):100–8 Mr '69. * (*PA* 43:10379)

374. WATSON, LARRY WAYNE. *The Relationship of the Mathematical Course Work of Teachers and the SAT-M Scores of Their Students.* Doctor's thesis, Duke University (Durham, N.C.), 1969. (*DAI* 30:2892A)

375. ZIMMERMAN, JOHN JAMES. *Relationships Among Scholastic Aptitude, Attitudes Toward Various Facets of College Life, and Academic Performance of Students at Lycoming College.* Doctor's thesis, Pennsylvania State University (University Park, Pa.), 1969. (*DAI* 30:4792A)

376. ADINOLFI, ALLEN A. "Characteristics of Highly Accepted, Highly Rejected, and Relatively Unknown University Freshmen." *J Counsel Psychol* 17(5):456–64 S '70. * (*PA* 45:2994)

377. BRODY, E. B. "The Effects of Creativity and Intelligence on Teacher Ratings." *Brit J Ed Psychol* 40(3):342–4 N '70. * (*PA* 45:7036)

378. BROTHERS, CASSANDRA THESAURUS. *The Construction, Validation, Analysis, Evaluation and Comparison of Scales for Predicting Academic Success in College.* Doctor's thesis, University of Houston (Houston, Tex.), 1970. (*DAI* 31:2953B)

379. BROWN, JANE LIGHTCAP, AND LIGHTSEY, RALPH. "Differential Predictive Validity of SAT Scores for Freshman College English." *Ed & Psychol Meas* 30(4):961–5 w '70. *

380. CAMPANILE, SALVATORE C. *Prediction of Academic Success and Description of Students in a Comprehensive Community College.* Doctor's thesis, Rutgers—The State University (New Brunswick, N.J.), 1970. (*DAI* 31:3331A)

381. CAMPBELL, DAVID P. "Report on Twenty Year Study of Dartmouth Freshmen Completing the Strong Vocational Interest Blank and Scholastic Aptitude Test." *Col & Univ* 45(4):585–605 su '70. *

382. CENTRA, JOHN A., AND LINN, ROBERT L. "On Interpreting Students' Perceptions of Their College Environments." *Meas & Eval Guid* 3(2):102–9 su '70. * (*PA* 45:1275)

383. CENTRA, JOHN A.; LINN, ROBERT L.; AND PARRY, MARY ELLEN. "Academic Growth in Predominantly Negro and Predominantly White Colleges." *Am Ed Res J* 7(1):83–98 Ja '70. *

384. CHASE, CLINTON I., AND HEMMETER, JOHN T. *A Characterization of Honors Students.* Indiana Studies in Prediction No. 14. Bloomington, Ind.: Bureau of Educational Studies and Testing, 1970. Pp. vii, 26. *

385. COLLEGE ENTRANCE EXAMINATION BOARD. *College Board Score Reports: A Guide for Counselors and Admissions Officers: Preliminary Scholastic Aptitude Test, Scholastic Aptitude Test, and Achievement Tests.* Princeton, N.J.: the Board, 1970. Pp. 37. *

386. COLLEGE ENTRANCE EXAMINATION BOARD, COMMISSION ON TESTS, DAVID V. TIEDEMAN, CHAIRMAN. *Report of the Commission on Tests: Vol. 1, Righting the Balance; Vol. 2, Briefs.* Princeton, N.J.: College Entrance Examination Board, 1970. Pp. xvi, 118; x, 194. *

387. COMBS, HARRISON TYLER, JR. *An Investigation of the Relationship Between the Academic Achievement Scale of the Strong Vocational Interest Blank and First Year Academic Achievement in College.* Doctor's thesis, University of South Carolina (Columbia, S.C.), 1970. (*DAI* 31:3262A)

388. DELAURETIS, ROBERT J.; LEBOLD, WILLIAM K.; AND MOLNAR, GEORGE E. "A Multiple-Regressional Analysis of the Complementary Roles of Cognitive and Noncognitive Measures of Engineering Behavior." Abstract. *Proc 78th Ann Conv Am Psychol Assn* 5(2):607–8 '70. * (*PA* 44:19532)

389. DOMINO, GEORGE. "Interactive Effects of Achievement Orientation and Teaching Style on Academic Achievement." *ACT Res Rep* 39:1–9 D '70. *

390. DUNN, DAVID CAMERON. *Scholastic Aptitude and Vocational Interest as Factors in the Selection of Entering Students in the School of Hotel Administration at Cornell University.* Doctor's thesis, Cornell University (Ithaca, N.Y.), 1970. (*DAI* 31:953A)

391. FRICKE, BENNO G. "Creative Writing Course Grades, OAIS Creative Personality Test Scores, and Other Assessment Measures." Abstract. *Proc 78th Ann Conv Am Psychol Assn* 5(2):617–8 '70. * (*PA* 44:19533)

392. FUJITA, GEORGE Y., AND O'REILLY, JOSEPH P. "A Two-Stage Sequential Strategy in the Placement of Students in an Undergraduate Curriculum." *J Res Math Ed* 1(4):241–50 N '70. *

393. HARTNETT, RODNEY T. "Differences in Selected Attitudes and College Orientations Between Black Students Attending Traditionally Negro and Traditionally White Institutions." Abstract. *Proc 78th Ann Conv Am Psychol Assn* 5(2):609–10 '70. * (*PA* 44:19340)

394. HIGHLEY, FRANK S. "Verbal Ability, Quantitative Ability, and the Rod-and-Frame Test." *Percept & Motor Skills* 30(3):95–8 Je '70. * (*PA* 44:15715)

395. HILLS, JOHN R., AND STANLEY, JULIAN C. "Easier Test Improves Prediction of Black Students' College Grades." *J Negro Ed* 39(4):320–4 f '70. * (*PA* 45:10957)

396. IHLANFELDT, WILLIAM IVAN. *Personal Characteristics of Satisfied and Non-Satisfied Northwestern University Students.* Doctor's thesis, Northwestern University (Evanston, Ill.), 1970. (*DAI* 31:3293A)

397. JONES, JOHN G., AND GRIENEEKS, LAURABETH. "Meas-

ures of Self-Perception as Predictors of Scholastic Achievement." *J Ed Res* 63(5):201–3 Ja '70. * *(PA* 46:5702)

398. JORDAN, MARY LOU, AND MICHAEL, WILLIAM B. "An Evaluation of the Resident Honors Program for High School Seniors at the University of Southern California 1961–1967." *Ed & Psychol Meas* 30(4):977–82 w '70. *

399. LeMAY, MORRIS. "Birth Order and Scholastic Aptitude and Achievement." Abstract. *J Consult & Clin Psychol* 34(2):287 Ap '70. * *(PA* 44:11388)

400. LIN, YI-GUANG, AND McKEACHIE, WILBERT J. "Aptitude, Anxiety, Study Habits, and Academic Achievement." *J Counsel Psychol* 17(4):306–9 Jl '70. * *(PA* 44:21601)

401. LYDEN, BARBARA A. *A Study of the Validity of SAT Scores in Mathematics Placement and the Effectiveness of Remedial Instruction for Students With Low SAT Scores.* Master's thesis, Virginia State College (Petersburg, Va.), 1970.

402. MAIER, NORMAN R. F., AND CASSELMAN, GERTRUDE G. "The SAT as a Measure of Problem-Solving Ability in Males and Females." *Psychol Rep* 26(3):927–39 Je '70. * *(PA* 45:1287)

403. NICHOLSON, EVERARD. *Final Report of the Study of Success and Admission Criteria for Potentially Successful Risks.* Providence, R.I.: Brown University, 1970. Pp. iv, 264. *

404. PUGH, RICHARD C., AND MORGAN, JAMES M. *Predicting Success for University Freshmen.* Indiana Studies in Prediction, No. 1, Supplement 3. Bloomington, Ind.: Bureau of Educational Studies and Testing, Indiana University, February 1970. Pp. 8. *

405. REINER, JOHN R. "Students' Academic Ability and Perceptions of College Environment." *J Exp Ed* 38(3):69–71 sp '70. *

406. ROCK, DONALD A.; CENTRA, JOHN A.; AND LINN, ROBERT L. "Relationships Between College Characteristics and Student Achievement." *Am Ed Res J* 7(1):109–21 Ja '70. *

407. SHERRON, RONALD H. "A Study of Academic and Nonacademic Predictors and Criteria of Success Among Scholarship Recipients." *J Exp Ed* 38(3):72–82 sp '70. *

408. SKINNER, SAMUEL BALLOU. *A Study of the Effect of the St. Andrews Presbyterian College Natural Science Course Upon Critical Thinking Ability.* Doctor's thesis, University of North Carolina (Chapel Hill, N.C.), 1970. *(DAI* 31:3984A)

409. STEININGER, MARION. "Aptitude, Dogmatism, and College Press as Codeterminants of Academic Achievement." *J Social Psychol* 80(2):229–30 Ap '70. * *(PA* 44:15462)

410. STRAHAN, ROBERT. "More on Correlates of Success in Undergraduate Statistics." Letter. *Am Psychologist* 25(12):1175–6 D '70. *

411. STROUP, ATLEE L. "The Prediction of Academic Performance From Personality and Aptitude Variables." *J Exp Ed* 38(3):83–6 sp '70. *

412. VROMAN, CLYDE, AND WILCOX, LEE. "Research on A.I.D. Sponsored Foreign Students." *Col & Univ* 45(4):717–23 su '70. *

413. WEISS, KENNETH P. "A Multi-Factor Admissions Predictive System." *Col & Univ* 45(2):203–10 w '70. *

414. WILLIS, CARL G., AND NICHOLSON, JAMES. "Series II SCAT as a College Aptitude Measure." *Ed & Psychol Meas* 30(4):971–5 w '70. *

415. ANGOFF, WILLIAM H., EDITOR. *The College Board Admissions Testing Program: A Technical Report on Research and Development Activities Relating to the Scholastic Aptitude Test and Achievement Tests.* New York: College Entrance Examination Board, 1971. Pp. xv, 181. *

416. DONLON, THOMAS F., AND ANGOFF, WILLIAM H. Chap. 2, "The Scholastic Aptitude Test," pp. 15–47. In *The College Board Admissions Testing Program,* see 415. *

417. FREMER, JOHN, AND CHANDLER, MARJORIE O. Chap. 6, "Special Studies," pp. 147–81. In *The College Board Admissions Testing Program,* see 415. *

418. SCHRADER, W. B. Chap. 5, "The Predictive Validity of College Board Admissions Tests," pp. 117–45. In *The College Board Admissions Testing Program,* see 415. *

419. SCHRADER, W. B., AND STEWART, E. ELIZABETH. Chap. 4, "Descriptive Statistics on College Board Candidates and Other Reference Groups," pp. 79–115. In *The College Board Admissions Testing Program,* see 415. *

PHILIP H. DuBois, *Professor of Psychology, Washington University, St. Louis, Missouri.*

The *College Board Scholastic Aptitude Test* probably is not the test that has been taken by the largest number of individuals in the history of testing. In respect to use, it is outstripped by the *Army General Classification Test,* the *Armed Forces Qualification Test,* and, perhaps, by one or more of the commercially available intelligence tests which date back 40 years or

more. In one respect, however, it is unquestionably outstanding. On no other test have there been expended so many man-years of planning, item writing, statistical analyses, and evaluation of its various forms.

Technically the SAT may be regarded as highly perfected—possibly reaching the pinnacle of the current state of the art of psychometrics. Actually it would be surprising if this were not so. Ever since the SAT was first administered in 1926, highly competent professional staffs have been available at all times to prepare new forms, being guided by objective findings on past administrations and on item analyses of experimental material.

Like many developments in measurement, the SAT is a direct descendant of the Army Alpha. The original plan was formulated by Robert M. Yerkes, Henry T. Moore, and Carl C. Brigham. Later Brigham became responsible for its development. A conscious effort was made to develop an instrument that would measure neither school achievement nor general mental alertness. With the passage of time, resemblance to its prototype lessened: subtests became fewer; speededness was reduced; and emphasis was placed upon two relatively homogeneous item types—verbal and mathematical. Currently the two subscores are referred to as SAT-V and SAT-M.

Even today, nearly three decades after Brigham's untimely death, the SAT continues a number of features which he initiated: (*a*) an attempt to measure "aptitude for college studies" rather than intelligence; (*b*) equating of numerous forms so that the predictive scores are stable irrespective of the time and place the student takes the test; (*c*) extensive and systematic use of item analysis; and (*d*) tryout of all new material before items are used operationally.

While the College Entrance Examination Board is responsible for the SAT, operations including test development, administration, score reports, and statistical analyses are carried out by the Educational Testing Service. The SAT is buttressed, of course, with not only an impressive array of managerial and psychometric talent but also the hardware (electronic scoring and computers) to make a magnificent program feasible. If only the hand methods used in the initial decade of the SAT were available now, the instrument either would be almost prohibitively expensive or supportive effort would have to be drastically reduced.

Items with known statistical characteristics are organized in sections requiring 30 or 45 minutes each for a total testing time of three hours. Within each block of items, arrangement is in terms of increasing difficulty, with "the mean difficulty of each block....equal to that of the test as a whole."

Test content is selected to avoid as far as possible inequities to any subclass of the intended population. The SAT-M requires as background only the mathematics taught in grades 1–9, while the SAT-V is related to social, political, scientific, artistic, philosophical, and literary areas. The earlier literary focus of the verbal items has been abandoned for a broader orientation, while the mathematical material now depends less on formal knowledge and more on "logical reasoning and....the perception of mathematical relationships."

As is well known, SAT scores are reported with mean 500 and standard deviation 100. It is not so well known that the standardization group consists of 10,654 students who took the test in April, 1941. Through somewhat involved methods, the various forms are equated accurately to one another and to the form yielding the initial norms.

Ask for any conventional statistic about the SAT and one can be practically certain that it will be available: reliabilities, validity coefficients, and item data. Not only are they available but they also reflect highly competent workmanship and are amazingly consistent from year to year, even though the program as a whole has undergone changes in conception and execution.

The internal consistency reliability estimates for 12 recent forms cluster closely around .91 and .90 for the verbal and mathematical scores, respectively; the parallel-form reliabilities average two points lower. In the 1950's the average correlation between the two parts was in the middle .50's; more recently, it has been in the high .60's, possibly reflecting a decreasing emphasis on specific knowledge in the two areas.

From the beginning, the SAT has been found to have reasonably good validities for predicting college achievement. Also it has been found consistently that the SAT increases the validity of the high school average or rank. Studies made in 1927 showed a median validity of the school record of .52, a median validity of the SAT of .34, and of the combination of both, .55.

For 38 years, most validity studies were made by participating colleges, but in 1964 the College Board Validity Study Service relieved the colleges of this chore.

Currently, typical validities are .39 for SAT-V, .33 for SAT-M, .55 for the high school record, with a multiple correlation of the order of .62. The picture today is not greatly changed from that in 1927 except that both SAT validities and school grade validities have increased, and the increment of the SAT over the high school record is a little greater than it was.

For schools of engineering, science, business, education, and liberal arts, the high school record is more valid than the SAT, but the SAT supplements the high school record with additional valid variance. Except in engineering, the SAT-V is generally more predictive than the SAT-M.

A somewhat surprising heritage from the past is the reliance on formulas for the correction of guessing. Although ETS has done some pertinent empirical studies, the studies seem to have been oriented more toward logical considerations and the effects of instructions on guessing behavior than toward validity. If wrong and right answers on the SAT measure different characteristics, this fact should be determinable in prediction studies. Few, if any, investigators have ever reported useful variance in the wrong answers on psychometric devices except in speeded perceptual tests. The trend in measurement generally, as in the SAT, has been away from speed, but the SAT has not followed the general trend toward exclusive reliance on the rights score.

The strategy of including in each SAT test booklet a number of "variant" items has been a long-standing practice. As far as the candidate is concerned, these variant items are indistinguishable from the operational items, which are exactly the same for all who take the SAT on a given day. On the other hand, in a given examination room the booklets may have 25 different sets of variant items, which are used later for equating forms and, after appropriate analyses, as operational material. This practice apparently has made possible great stability in test characteristics from form to form, as well as permitting incorporation of innovations after their probable effect has been ascertained.

The SAT is more of a system than a test. It is a system by which information of a defined type can be made available to college admissions officers. Security precautions in test development, printing, distribution, administration, and processing of results are such that the possibility of compromise is close to zero.

The SAT is not without its detractors, some of whom regard it as a "tool of the academic establishment." Of course it is! But it is a good tool, perhaps the best that can be devised with present psychometric technology. No attempt is made to adjust SAT scores for sex, socioeconomic status, race, or educational background. In this reviewer's opinion, such attempts would be difficult to justify. Adding substantially to the prediction of academic achievement as contrasted with the use of high school grades alone, the SAT has repeatedly proved its usefulness to colleges. It helps to pick those who fit in best in the program of a particular institution, and, of course, it can be supplemented with any other information that admissions officials may wish to use.

The question has arisen of whether or not it fits the needs of the students as well as those of the colleges and universities. No good end would be served by blunting this instrument. Certainly there are many aptitudes other than verbal and mathematical that some colleges might like to know about, such as musical, spatial, mechanical, and clerical abilities. College entrance examining could be broadened so that a profile of testable characteristics adequate for educational and vocational counseling would become available. The question is one of appropriate strategy, including how much testing should be required of all students; how much optional. The College Board already has an extensive program of achievement measurement which dates back to 1900, with frequent updating both in content and in measurement methods. Obviously the CEEB program could be broadened further. But even in a broadened program the present SAT measures would be important.

WIMBURN L. WALLACE, *Director, Professional Examinations Division, The Psychological Corporation, New York, New York.*

The SAT contains verbal ability and mathematical ability sections and yields separate scores in these two areas. Its purpose is to aid in assessing students' competence for satisfactory achievement in college, and it is designed to be effective over the full range of abilities of students applying for admission to colleges which run the gamut of academic standards. It is the most widely used collegiate entrance test; over one and one-half million candidates take it each year.

A long-overdue technical report has finally been prepared for the College Board Admissions Testing Program. A manuscript of that report plus a copy of Form RSA35 of the SAT provide the principal basis for this review. The report (*415*) is an excellent document, describing in detail and with candor most or all of the relevant information about the examinations.

Although there is a continuous program of development, standardization, and application of new parallel forms of the SAT, the content and format of the test have been essentially the same for a very long time. The verbal section (SAT-V) comprises 90 items in two separately timed parts for a total of 75 minutes, and the mathematics section (SAT-M) contains 60 items, also in two parts with a total time of 75 minutes. The reason for separately timed parts within the V and M sections is not evident. Both verbal parts contain some of each item type used, namely, sentence completions, antonyms, analogies, and reading comprehension. One of the mathematics parts is entirely general mathematics problems, while the other is about half general problems and half data sufficiency type items. Reference to the M section as "Arithmetic Reasoning" is somewhat misleading, since it contains a great deal of geometry and algebra. The mathematics problems are all of the conventional variety and show little or no influence of the terminology of the "new math"; this reviewer has no quarrel with that characteristic of the test. However, the items in the M section tend to be wordy, hence potentially introducing too great a verbal influence in a section intended to provide a reasonably independent dimension of assessment from that derived from the SAT-V.

All the items appearing in the SAT appear to be carefully constructed and edited. Items are always of the 5-option, multiple choice variety and are formula scored. The system of pretesting of items, analysis, and standardization of new forms exemplifies the most sophisticated procedures in modern psychometrics. Every step in the production of successive forms is no less than meticulous, and the methods of equating forms virtually guarantee parallelism of the highest order obtainable. Every form of the SAT includes about 30 minutes of experimental work devoted to items that are either being pretested or standardized.

The layout of the SAT test booklets is satisfactory but could be simplified in the interest of clarity. For instance, mathematics items might well be more precisely separated from each other and the options could be listed in a more consistent manner for easy reference and recognition. In the SAT-V there is a frequent shift of item type which does not seem entirely justifiable. The student would not have to change set so often if all the analogies were grouped together, all the antonyms, etc. In the same vein, a study should be made to ascertain whether fewer verbal item types would be as effective as the four now used.

The investigation of, or experimentation with, various and new test types for the SAT has been sporadic. There should be a sustained, regular effort toward new test development. The traditional test and item types are described historically and in great detail in the technical report, but the rationale for their persistence is somewhat thin. Internal validation is the main or only criterion for the survival of new items, whereas the use of an external criterion, e.g., college grades, would be a desirable supplementary or substitute means of identifying potentially powerful new items. When novel test types have been tried in the SAT program, careful statistical work has accompanied the effort, and appropriate validation studies carried out. However, the new types are usually discarded on the basis that they do not add sufficiently to the predictive effectiveness of the standard measures in the SAT to justify their permanent inclusion. Rarely does the question seem to be answered as to whether some combination of different tests would do a better job of predicting collegiate academic success than the traditional V and M measures. It is possible that the ultimate was reached decades ago in the practical, efficient, effective measurement of college potential by tests with the ingredients of the SAT; but it is discouraging to contemplate a permanent plateau in the state of the art.

Most of the psychometric characteristics of the SAT are above reproach. Internal consistency reliability coefficients are regularly about .91 for SAT-V and .90 for the SAT-M for recent forms. For those who prefer another method of estimating reliability, alternate-form coefficients of correlation are provided and closely substantiate the other data at levels of about .89 for SAT-V and .88 for SAT-M.

Many thousands of validity coefficients have been calculated between SAT scores and college grades. There is no meaningful way to summarize them briefly, since they are affected by the tremendous variety of the full spectrum of characteristics of American colleges and universities. Suffice it to say that the validities are as high as have been attained with any general testing instrument in comparable settings. The technical manual reports many illustrations of results of validity studies including those based on highly selective and least selective schools, specialized curricula, specific courses, classes with wide and with narrow dispersion of abilities, and other important categories. Extensive research has also been focused on the relative validities of the SAT for male versus female students and Negro versus white students. In neither of those sets of comparisons have any important differences been found. A common feature of many of the validity studies is the separate inclusion of high school record and College Board Achievement Tests as predictors of college grades. The increment in predictive effectiveness over the SAT alone is shown in these instances. Typically the high school record adds most, as might be expected, and the well-known importance of considering both types of predictors is given full support. A major shortcoming in otherwise commendably complete validation is the paucity of information on the relative weighting due the SAT-V and the SAT-M in predicting college success. Where multiple correlations are reported they usually include high school average, or achievement test scores, or both, but do not indicate the weights for V and M. The intercorrelation between V and M has been steadily and sharply increasing during the last 25 years to an average of .67 in 1969. The value of the separate scores needs concerted scrutiny in the light of this phenomenon.

Considerable attention has been given to such problems as concern about the effects of coaching, of practice and growth, and of fatigue and anxiety. Well-documented summaries of studies of these issues indicate insignificant improvement of scores by coaching and no deleterious effects from anxiety, but do show score changes over periods of time between testings. Although the changes over time are not surprising, extensive description of their magnitude and possible causes is provided.

Supplementary services and explanatory information for students, counselors, and admissions officers in connection with the SAT are quite appropriate to the purposes of the program. Among the special services offered at no cost to colleges, the Validity Study Service is a most valuable one in which test scores, high school grades, and other data are analyzed for their effectiveness in predicting success at the individual college. Every college participating in the SAT program should take advantage of this service, as it should indicate the appropriateness of the SAT for that school regardless of nationwide data.

The descriptive booklets are clear, straightforward explanations of the nature, purposes, content, limitations, and interpretation of the SAT. They constitute a happy balance between extremes of insufficient information and a plethora of printed matter. The typical user, be he the student, counselor, or administrator, can readily find in them answers to pertinent questions about the tests without the frustrations of verbosity in too many overlapping publications.

The supervisor's manual for administering the SAT is explicit and detailed to a fault. Although it is essential that testing conditions be as uniform as possible for all candidates, some brevity in the directions for the sake of clarity and emphasis might contribute toward that goal. However, it is evident that the huge task of organizing, administering, scoring, and reporting results for the SAT is consistently carried out with rigorous care and accuracy.

Comparison between the SAT and the American College Testing Program, the major alternative available, favors the SAT overall. Although validities against college achievement criteria are not strikingly different, the content mix, psychometric quality, and pertinent research efforts appear to be superior in the SAT. Ancillary services available with the two programs are comparable, but those with the SAT are the more succinct.

For reviews by John E. Bowers and Wayne S. Zimmerman of an earlier form, see 6:449; for a review by John T. Dailey, see 5:318; for a review by Frederick B. Davis, see 4:285.

[345]

*College Qualification Tests. Candidates for college entrance; 1955–61; CQT; 6 scores: verbal, numerical, information (science, social studies, total), total; Forms A ('56), B ('56), C ('59); 2 editions; revised manual ('61, 61 pages); distribution of Forms B and C restricted to colleges and universities; separate answer sheets (IBM 805, IBM 1230) must be used; 50¢ per manual, postage extra; George K. Bennett, Marjorie G. Bennett, Wimburn L. Wallace, and Alexander G. Wesman; Psychological Corporation. *
a) COMBINED BOOKLET EDITION. 14 pages; $5.50 per 25 tests; $3.90 per 50 IBM 805 answer sheets; $4.10 per 50 IBM 1230 answer sheets; 70¢ per set of IBM 805 hand scoring stencils; $1 per set of IBM 805 machine scoring stencils; 75¢ per set of IBM 1230 hand scoring stencils; 90¢ per specimen set; 80(105) minutes.
b) SEPARATE BOOKLET EDITION. $2.50 per 25 tests; $2 per 50 IBM 805 answer sheets; $1.20 per specimen set.
1) *Test V [Verbal].* 5 pages; 15(25) minutes.
2) *Test N [Numerical].* 6 pages; 35(45) minutes.
3) *Test I [Information].* 6 pages; 3 scores: science, social studies, total; 30(40) minutes.

REFERENCES

1–11. See 6:450.
12. HARTFORD, DONALD LEROY. *An Investigation of a Profile Method for Predicting College Grades From Scores of the College Qualification Tests.* Doctor's thesis, University of Kentucky (Lexington, Ky.), 1959. (*DA* 26:4373)
13. BUNGER, FRED ANTON. *Cultural Forces and Academic Success in College Freshmen.* Bulletin of the Bureau of School Service, College of Education, University of Kentucky, Vol. 33, No. 1. Lexington, Ky.: the Service, September 1960. Pp. 91. *
14. IKENBERRY, STANLEY O. "Factors in College Persistence." *J Counsel Psychol* 8:322–9 w '61. * (*PA* 37:3834)
15. COOPER, CARL J. "Some Relationships Between Paired-Associates Learning and Foreign-Language Aptitude." *J Ed Psychol* 55:132–8 Je '64. * (*PA* 39:5823)
16. JUOLA, ARVO E. "The Prediction of College Dropout From Freshman Level Ability Test Scores." *J Ed Meas* 1:35–7 Je '64.
17. BOYCE, RICHARD W., AND PAXSON, R. C. "The Predictive Validity of Eleven Tests at One State College." *Ed & Psychol Meas* 25:1143–7 w '65. * (*PA* 40:3563)
18. ELTON, CHARLES F. "A Comparative Study of Teacher Ratings, High School Average and Measures of Personality and Aptitude in Predicting College Success." *Psychol Sch* 2:47–52 Ja '65. *
19. LEHMANN, IRVIN J. "Curricular Differences in Selected Cognitive and Affective Characteristics." *J Ed Meas* 2:103–10 Je '65. * (*PA* 39:15160)
20. MCKAY, WILLIAM R. "Interpersonal Relationships, a Factor in Academic Success." *Calif J Ed Res* 16:189–96 S '65. * (*PA* 40:1943)
21. MILLS, DAVID H. "The Relationship of Abstraction to Selected Personality and Intellectual Variables." *Psychol* 2:10–5 N '65. * (*PA* 40:3091)
22. JUOLA, ARVO E. "Prediction of Successive Terms Performance in College From Tests and Grades." *Am Ed Res J* 3:191–7 My '66. *
23. KAFER, LOWELL GENE. *An Analysis of Selected Characteristics and Experiences of Freshman Students in the Michigan State University Justin Morrill College.* Doctor's thesis, Michigan State University (East Lansing, Mich.), 1966. (*DA* 27:4043A)
24. LINS, L. JOSEPH; ABELL, ALLAN P.; AND HUTCHINS, H. CLIFTON. "Relative Usefulness in Predicting Academic Success of the ACT, the SAT, and Some Other Variables." *J Exp Ed* 35:1–29 w '66. *
25. BAUER, ROGER; MEHRENS, WILLIAM A.; AND VINSONHALER, JOHN F. "Predicting Performance in a Computer Programming Course." *Ed & Psychol Meas* 28:1159–64 w '68. * (*PA* 44:7333)
26. BUSZEK, BEATRICE R. "Differential Treatment of Test Scores." *Col & Univ* 43:294–307 sp '68. *
27. CORSINI, RAYMOND J., AND BORGATTA, EDGAR F. "The Quick Number Test (QNT)." *J Exp Ed* 36:7–10 su '68. *
28. GREENLAND, THOMAS CHARLES. *Some Differential Relationships of Academic Ability and Personality Factors to Academic Status as Suggested by Inter-Institutional and Intra-Institutional Analyses of the Freshman Class at Four Campuses.* Doctor's thesis, University of Kentucky (Lexington, Ky.), 1968. (*DAI* 30:1921B)
29. LUEPTOW, LLOYD B. "Need for Achievement and Occupational Preferences: Some Operations With Value-Orientations as Intervening Variables in Need-Goal Relationships." *Sociometry* 31:304–12 S '68. *
30. CASSEL, RUSSELL N., AND EICHSTEADT, ARDEN C. "Fac-

torial Structure of CQT, ACT, and SAT Test Scores for 50 Available College Freshmen." *J Psychol* 71(2):199–204 Mr '69. * (*PA* 43:8675)

31. DREYER, DOROTHY E. *Listening Performance Related to Selected Academic and Psychological Measures.* Doctor's thesis, Michigan State University (East Lansing, Mich.), 1969. (*DAI* 30:5735B)

32. ELTON, CHARLES F. "Patterns of Change in Personality Test Scores." *J Counsel Psychol* 16(2):95–9 Mr '69. * (*PA* 43:10296)

33. JENKINS, NORMAN LEE. *An Analysis of the Relationship Between Academic Achievement and Selected Criteria for Junior College Freshmen in Terminal and Transfer Curricula.* Doctor's thesis, Purdue University (Lafayette, Ind.), 1969. (*DAI* 30:3728A)

34. JOHNSON, RICHARD J., AND LEONARD, LOUISE C. "Psychological Test Characteristics and Performance of Nursing Students." *Nursing Res* 19(2):147–50 Mr–Ap '70. *

35. VOHS, A. P. *A Study of First-Year Academic Performance as Related to Predicted Achievement of Freshmen Enrolled in Teacher Education at John Brown University, 1968–69.* Doctor's thesis, University of Arkansas (Fayetteville, Ark.), 1970. (*DAI* 31:2713A)

For reviews by Ralph F. Berdie and Warren G. Findley, see 6:450; for reviews by Gustav J. Froehlich, A. E. G. Pilliner, and David V. Tiedeman, see 5:320.

[346]

★**Cooperative Academic Ability Test.** Superior grade 12 students; 1963–64; AAT; also published in 1966 as Level 1 of *Cooperative School and College Ability Tests: Series 2,* Forms A and B; 3 scores: verbal, mathematical, total; Forms A, B, ('63, 7 pages); manual ('64, 16 pages); administration directions ('64, 1 page); separate answer sheets (Digitek, IBM 1230) must be used; no instructions on the use of specific answer sheets; $7 per 20 tests; $4 per 100 answer sheets; $1.25 per 10 IBM 1230 scoring stencils (answer pattern must be punched out locally); Digitek scoring stencils not available; $1 per manual; $2 per specimen set; cash orders postpaid; 40(50) minutes; Cooperative Tests and Services. *

REFERENCES

1. TRAXLER, ARTHUR E. "The New Cooperative Academic Aptitude Test Compared With the American Council Psychological Examination." *Ed Rec B* 85:55–64 F '64. *

2. CLAWAR, HARRY J. "A Short Highly-Efficient Prediction of College Entrance Examination Board Scholastic Aptitude Test Performance." *Ed Rec B* 94:42–4 Jl '68. * (*PA* 44:21523)

3. CONKLIN, R. C., AND OGSTON, D. G. "Prediction of Academic Success for Freshman at the University of Calgary." *Alberta J Ed Res* 14:185–92 S '68. * (*PA* 44:4244)

ERIC F. GARDNER, *Margaret O. Slocum Professor of Education and Psychology and Chairman, Department of Psychology; and Director, Psychological Services and Research Center; Syracuse University, Syracuse, New York.*

The *Cooperative Academic Ability Test* for superior grade 12 students was published in 1963–64 following a substantial amount of experimental work on the original SCAT series published in 1955–57. The AAT was designed to perform somewhat the same function as the SCAT but to require a much shorter total time for administration. Comments by previous MMY reviewers about the effectiveness of SCAT in achieving the purposes and objectives specified are appropriate for the AAT. The AAT in contrast to SCAT includes two item types and administrative parts as compared with four in SCAT, although three scores (verbal, mathematical, and total) are presented for each test. The AAT verbal items are of the analogy type which has been used in a number of other tests. The mathematical item type is a relatively unusual format and is intended to "place a minimum emphasis on reading, to require more resourcefulness and insight than straight computation problems, and to allow presentation of more items per unit of testing time....than most of the usual mathematical item types." No data are presented to support these claims. The format involves the presentation of pairs of quantitative expressions in parallel columns. The student is asked to select one of the following four options: (*a*) whether the quantity in column A is the greater, (*b*) whether the quantity in column B is the greater, (*c*) whether the two quantities are equal, or (*d*) whether the size relationship can not be determined from the information given.

The successful experience of ETS with the *Cooperative Academic Ability Test* caused them to completely revise SCAT in 1966. In this new revision the AAT was used as the highest level test in the battery and levels for lower grades with the same type of item format were constructed.

K-R 20 reliabilities range from .78 to .88 for the verbal portion, .86 to .92 for the mathematics portion, and .89 to .94 for the total test. Although these values are reasonably adequate, they (as the manual points out) were obtained for samples selected from several schools and as such are overestimates of what the reliability would be if they were obtained from a single class within a single school. To make matters worse these values are spuriously large also because they are based on *speeded* tests. In spite of the statement in the handbook that "Table 4 reveals that the Verbal sections of forms A and B are essentially unspeeded, while the Mathematical sections of both forms are characterized by a substantial amount of drop-out," it shows that only a little over half the students in each group completed the mathematical section and less than 75 percent of one group completed the verbal section. Although the manual suggests that test users should compute reliability coefficients for their own groups, it would have been more appropriate for the manual to present reliability coefficients more comparable to those needed by schools using the test.

The use of percentile bands rather than percentile points and the deficiencies in applying them to SCAT have been discussed in previous MMY reviews. In spite of the fact that the same difficulties are present in their application to the AAT, this reviewer is highly in favor of any device which will emphasize the need for the test user to consider errors of measurement and hence commends ETS for their presentation.

In addition to equating the two forms of the AAT with each other, the same procedure was used to equate the ACE (1948 College Edition) with the AAT. Comparable scores of this type have been requested by a number of test users. However, although the manual is careful to point out that the equating was done on a fairly large sample, the question of the extent to which the variables measured by the ACE and the AAT subtests are identical is not mentioned at all. Hence, the user, not receiving this kind of warning, may be under the impression that the corresponding scores given in the table actually represent identical performance. Caution should have been given that comparable scores on different instruments may not be entirely comparable with respect to content.

In general, the AAT is a test consisting of good items selected by appropriate experimental procedures and interpreted by a handbook which is well written.

WILLIAM B. MICHAEL, *Professor of Educational Psychology and Psychology, University of Southern California, Los Angeles, California.*

Published in 1963 to furnish measures of verbal and mathematical ability of those secondary school students of superior potential who are planning to attend college, the AAT requires only about 45 minutes of total administration time, yields in addition to a verbal score and mathematical score a total general ability score, possibly shows a relatively greater emphasis on power than on speed as compared with other well-known ability tests that have been prepared and distributed by ETS, utilizes a "number right" scoring procedure, and contains only two item types and two administrative sections (verbal and mathematics)—one item type per administrative section. The professional staff at ETS had apparently been so pleased with the initial outcomes of the AAT that in 1966 they incorporated the two AAT forms into the SCAT Series 2 for grade levels 12 through 14

and constructed a third parallel form as well. Thus to gain the maximum benefit from use of the AAT one needs to consult the 1967 handbook for SCAT Series 2, as this manual contains substantial new normative information as well as additional data on validity and reliability not reported in the 1964 handbook for the AAT.

The AAT and its incorporation within the SCAT Series 2 affords an attractive alternative to other commercially available instruments employed for college admissions and selection. With little or no loss in validity and reliability, the AAT requires only 40 minutes of working time and therefore only one class period for its administration.

This favorable state of affairs has been effected through the use of only two item types. Fifty 4-choice verbal analogy items have been employed to measure an examinee's understanding of words. It is apparent that each of these insightfully constructed and carefully pretested items demands a fine degree of discrimination on the part of the examinee. The other item type represented by 4-choice alternatives in the mathematics section constitutes an important innovation in test construction and probably a major breakthrough both in maximizing the reliability of a relatively short test in quantitative reasoning and in minimizing the amount of reading required. Given two columns, in which mathematical quantities—figural, symbolic, or semantic—are placed, the examinee must decide whether the quantity in column A is larger than that in column B, the quantity in column B is larger than the one in column A, the two quantities are equivalent, or that their relative magnitudes are indeterminate in light of the information presented. It goes almost without saying that the implications of this item format for tests of mathematical aptitude and achievement are great indeed.

The handbook for the AAT and especially the one for SCAT Series 2 are superior to most manuals. Based on large, carefully chosen representative samples of college-bound students, extensive normative data for each form are presented tabularly in raw scores and converted scores that are related to percentile bands—a concept which incidentally is quite clearly explained in the handbook. Scores can be readily equated from one test form to another in view of the application of quite precise equating procedures developed at ETS by Angoff, Lord, Tucker, and others. Substantial amounts of reliability data are also furnished, although the K-R 20 estimates may be slightly inflated in light of the somewhat speeded nature of the two tests—especially the mathematics forms.

In addition to showing what would be judged as satisfactory reliability characteristics, the test forms also compare favorably with other scales in criterion-related validity, although admittedly more data would be welcome. In a sample of 244 students the AAT and the SAT verbal sections showed validity coefficients of .49 and .57 respectively with normalized rank in class achievement. For the same criterion, the AAT and SAT mathematics parts yielded, respectively, validity coefficients of .50 and .48. Correlations between corresponding verbal and mathematics sections of the AAT and SAT were .83 and .86, respectively.

The reviewer has two major reservations regarding the AAT. First it would seem that the two subtests—especially the one in mathematics—are too highly speeded. The handbook for the SCAT Series 2 reports that only 54 percent of the examinees who took Form 1 reached the last test item, although 92 percent of them attained the three-quarters point. In the instance of the verbal part, the corresponding percentages were 77 and 98, respectively. An additional two minutes on the verbal subtest and another five minutes on the mathematics section would probably constitute an improvement that might well be reflected in a more positive attitude on the part of the examinees and perhaps in a higher degree of validity for the AAT—especially for students from culturally different backgrounds in which competitive activities involving clock watching are not strongly reinforced or rewarded. Even with an additional seven minutes for test taking, the total time of administration would not exceed 55 minutes.

The second concern relates to the need for a greater number of practice items at the beginning of each of the two test sections. Instead of the one practice item presented, four or five items would appear to be highly desirable. In taking one form of the AAT, the reviewer noted subjectively a practice effect after about the first six or seven questions in that he was able to work more and more rapidly, even though the items were becoming somewhat more difficult. Although it is true that an excellent study guide in the form of a one-sheet student

bulletin for SCAT Series 2 consisting of five verbal and 10 mathematics items is available, there is a substantial risk that not all potential examinees may gain access to the form in view of the frailties or even disinterest of certain counselors or test officers.

In summary, the AAT and its counterpart in SCAT Series 2 yield a highly economical yet comparatively reliable and valid estimate of academic potential in college for the superior high school junior or senior. The accompanying manuals rich in normative and other statistical data are competently prepared and highly readable, even for the counselor or admissions officer with somewhat limited training in measurement and evaluation. It is to be anticipated that the innovative format of the mathematics items as well as the general simplicity of the entire instrument will exert a substantial impact upon future test construction. In short, the AAT and SCAT Series 2 forms furnish a viable alternative to other commercially available ability tests of much greater length in the prediction of academic success for students entering institutions of higher learning.

J Ed Meas 3:81–3 sp '66. Kenneth D. Hopkins and Darrell L. Sander. * The test wisely does not presume to measure native intelligence, yet it does not offer tasks which generally duplicate those encountered in a school setting. * One of the most important features of the AAT is the relatively small amount of testing time required; the two twenty-minute segments of actual testing time are very attractive when compared to other competitive tests. It is unfortunate, however, that no provision is made for informing the examinees of the time allowance. Response style variance of the speed vs. accuracy might have been reduced by providing some basis for self-pacing. This factor takes on additional significance when one considers that on the average two and one-half items per minute must be answered in order to complete each test in the time allowed. About 81% of the normative sample attempted the last item on the verbal test, but only 52% on the mathematics test (even though the tests are described as "essentially unspeeded"). No correction for chance is employed, even though it seems to be a situation in which such an exploration is warranted. The logic favoring its use was apparently strong enough for Traxler....to recommend its use in independent schools even without empirical validation. The directions for administering and scoring are generally clear; however, some possible confusion could have been prevented by giving more orientation into the use of the new IBM 1230 answer sheets. Another minor point of confusion may result from the directions for both tests appearing prior to the initial (verbal) test. A suggestion that the test users develop their own local norms is quite appropriate in light of the limited information available. "The norms in this *AAT Handbook* are based on midyear performance of a representative group of high school seniors with two characteristics: they all intended to go to college and they are enrolled in high schools which send 75% or more of their graduates to college." No mention is made of what percent of the students in the schools would have "intended to go to college" if they had been asked near the middle of their senior year, a fact which introduced some ambiguity into the normative data. The term "representative" may be less appropriate than "restrictive," as only 52% (381 of 753) of the public secondary schools contacted in a related survey "produced usable response data," and of these only 9% (35 schools) had 75% or more of their graduating seniors attending college; and of these 9 (20%) did not participate in the norms testing program. The publishers are to be commended for the completeness with which they describe and report information about the tests even when it indicates certain limitations. A converted score scale is used with a mean of 150 and a standard deviation of 10 based on the senior norms sample. The rationale for this particular numerical base was not discussed. Percentile bands as well as mid-percentile ranks are given for the two tests as well as for the composite score. Negative skewing is present for all three distributions in the normative data. * This negative skewing suggests inadequate test ceiling for the select normative sample; the fact that the median scores were 65–70% of the total items on the two tests is also suggestive in this respect. The method of equating scores on Forms A and B appears satisfactory (using the ACE as a common equating test) although insufficiently described for the general test user. * All things considered, reliability seems quite satisfactory, especially in light of the limited testing time required. * Evidence for AAT's validity takes several forms. When correlating test scores from the normative

sample with subsequent rank in graduating class correlations of .52, .51, and .55 were obtained for the AAT verbal, math, and total scores respectively. These values compared favorably with the SAT and rank-in-class correlations. Also reported are correlation coefficients of .83 and .86 between corresponding AAT-SAT tests. The reason for the considerably higher values than those reported by Traxler (1964 .65 and .77) are not discussed. The variabilities of the samples on which these correlations were obtained were not reported, making interpretation very difficult. Traxler (1964) also found the AAT-ACE interrelationships to be approximately equal to the AAT-SAT correlations. He also noted the ACE and AAT correlations with the SAT did not differ substantially. SUMMARY. The AAT is a quickly administered and yet satisfactory reliable test of academic ability. It seems to compare favorably with its competitors in reliability and in validity, even though the amount of data on the latter for the AAT is as yet quite limited. It correlates substantially with the SAT, although its predictive validity for college success has as yet to be determined. The major deficiency seems to be in the rather unusually defined and select normative data which make individual interpretation difficult. For schools relying heavily on local norms, this, of course, is no problem.

[347]
*Cooperative School and College Ability Tests: Series 2. Grades 4–6, 7–9, 10–12, 12–14; 1955–70; SCAT; 3 scores: verbal, mathematical, total; 4 levels; handbook ('67, 54 pages); preliminary teacher's handbook for SCAT-STEP ('69, 48 pages); preliminary SCAT-STEP norms ('70, 64 pages); student bulletins for levels 1–3, 4, ('67, 2 pages); separate answer sheets (Digitek, Digitek-IBM 805, IBM 1230, SCRIBE) must be used; $7 per 20 tests; $4 per 100 answer sheets; $1.25 per 10 IBM scoring stencils (answer pattern must be punched out locally); Digitek and SCRIBE scoring stencils not available; $2 per handbook; $3 per 100 student bulletins; $3 per specimen set; SCRIBE scoring and statistical analysis service, 35¢ and over per test; 40(50) minutes; cash orders postpaid; Cooperative Tests and Services. *
a) LEVEL 4. Grades 4–6; Forms A ('66, 7 pages), B ('66, 8 pages).
b) LEVEL 3. Grades 7–9; Forms A, B, ('66, 7 pages).
c) LEVEL 2. Grades 10–12; Forms A, B, ('66, 8 pages).
d) LEVEL 1. Grades 12–14; Forms A, B, ('66, 7 pages, tests are identical to the tests copyrighted in 1963 under the title *Cooperative Academic Ability Tests*), C ('66, 8 pages); Form C available only by special arrangement for use with students in college. [The references which follow are for both editions of SCAT.]

REFERENCES

1–7. See 5:322.
8–71. See 6:452.

72. AMES, ROBERT. "Relationships Between Two Types of Verbal Ability." *Calif J Ed Res* 10:177–9+ S '59. * (*PA* 34:7344)

73. MALNIG, LAWRENCE R. *Differential Predictability of Academic Achievement From Aptitude Tests Administered Under Psychological Stress to Subjects With Varying Amounts of Anxiety.* Doctor's thesis, New York University (New York, N.Y.), 1959. (*DA* 20:3197)

74. STOKER, HOWARD W., AND KROPP, RUSSELL P. "The Predictive Validating and Factorial Content of the Florida State-Wide Ninth-Grade Testing Program Battery." *Fla J Ed Res* 2:105–14 Ja '60. *

75. LUNN, MERVEL SAMUEL, JR. *The Prediction of Success of Students Enrolled in Professional Education Courses at the University of Oklahoma.* Doctor's thesis, University of Oklahoma (Norman, Okla.), 1961. (*DA* 22:1490)

76. POLAND, HAROLD VINCENT. *The Relationship Between Self Concept and Supervisory and Peer Ratings of Success in Nurses' Training.* Doctor's thesis, Fordham University (New York, N.Y.), 1961. (*DA* 22:1260)

77. BROE, JOHN RICHARD. *Prediction of Success in Training Among Electronics Technicians.* Doctor's thesis, University of Southern California (Los Angeles, Calif.), 1962. (*DA* 23:2417)

78. DEHART, ARLA LANDO, JR. *Possible Selective Admissions Criteria for the California Public Junior College.* Doctor's thesis, Stanford University (Stanford, Calif.), 1962. (*DA* 22:4233)

79. OWEN, CRAMER. "An Investigation of Creative Potential at the Junior High Level." *Studies Art Ed* 3:16–33 sp '62. *

80. PERRY, JAMES OLDEN. *A Study of a Selective Set of Criteria for Determining Success in Secondary Student Teaching at Texas Southern University.* Doctor's thesis, University of Texas (Austin, Tex.), 1962. (*DA* 23:1617)

81. ANDERSON, RODNEY EARL. *A Comparison of the Performance of College Freshmen Participants and Non-Participants in an Honors Program on Four Psychological Measures.* Doctor's research study No. 1, Colorado State College (Greeley, Colo.), 1963. (*DA* 25:279)

82. BATES, CHARLES O. *A Study of Creative Potential as Found in Elementary Student Teachers.* Doctor's thesis, Ball State Teachers College (Muncie, Ind.), 1963. (*DA* 24:4561)

83. CRAWFORD, W. R., AND MOYEL, I. S. "Predicting Academic Achievement From Intelligence and Personality Data." *Fla J Ed Res* 5:19–28 Ja '63. *

84. DANIEL, KATHRYN LaVERNE BARCHARD. *A Study of Dropouts at the University of Alabama With Respect to Certain Academic and Personality Variables.* Doctor's thesis, University of Alabama (University, Ala.), 1963. (*DA* 25:1736)

85. DICK, WALTER. "Retention as a Function of Paired and Individual Use of Programed Instruction." *J Programed Instr* 2:17–23 f '63. * (*PA* 38:10409)

86. FORDHAM, SHELDON LeROY. *A Study of the Relationship of Selected Factors to Academic Success in Professional Physical Education at the University of Illinois (Chicago).* Doctor's thesis, Michigan State University (East Lansing, Mich.), 1963. (*DA* 25:270)

87. HILLIARD, ASA GRANT, III. *An Exploratory Study of Relationships Between Student Teacher Personality, Ability, Lower Division Grades, and the Student Teacher's Evaluation of Pupils.* Doctor's thesis, University of Denver (Denver, Colo.), 1963. (*DA* 24:5193)

88. HOOD, ALBERT B. "Predicting Achievement in Dental School." *J Dental Ed* 27:148–55 Je '63. *

89. REAMS, JAKE W. *The Relationship of Selected Factors to the Scholarship of Industrial Arts Teacher Education Students at Ball State Teachers College.* Doctor's thesis, Indiana University (Bloomington, Ind.), 1963. (*DA* 24:3222)

90. WILLIAMS, ROBERT A. *An Assessment of the Success of C Average High School Graduates in Grand Rapids Junior College.* Doctor's thesis, Michigan State University (East Lansing, Mich.), 1963. (*DA* 25:317)

91. ALLGOOD, EARL VANN. *Prediction of Academic Success of Freshman Students in Three Divisions at Virginia State College.* Doctor's thesis, Pennsylvania State University (University Park, Pa.), 1964. (*DA* 25:2303)

92. ATKINSON, BEA HENRIETTA. *The Relationship Between Problem-Solving Strategies and Measures of Convergent and Divergent Thinking in a Selected Group of Secondary School Pupils.* Doctor's thesis, University of Florida (Gainesville, Fla.), 1964. (*DA* 25:7070)

93. BONEY, JEW DON. *A Study of the Use of Intelligence, Aptitude, and Mental Ability Measures in Predicting the Academic Achievement of Negro Students in Secondary School.* Doctor's thesis, University of Texas (Austin, Tex.), 1964. (*DA* 25:5726)

94. BOYCE, RICHARD W. "The Prediction of Achievement in College Algebra." *Ed & Psychol Meas* 24:419–20 su '64. * (*PA* 39:5976)

95. BRODSKY, STANLEY LEON. *Language Patterns of Repressors and Sensitizers in Personal and Impersonal Descriptions.* Doctor's thesis, University of Florida (Gainesville, Fla.), 1964. (*DA* 25:4256)

96. BRODSKY, STANLEY MARTIN. *Predicting the Academic Competence of Students in Certain Technical Curricula at the New York City Community College of Applied Arts and Sciences After an Experimental, Preliminary, Remedial Semester.* Doctor's thesis, New York University (New York, N.Y.), 1964. (*DA* 25:928)

97. COOPER, LELAND ROSS. *The Relationship of Selected Factors to the Continuance of Junior College Graduates at Senior Institutions.* Doctor's thesis, University of Florida (Gainesville, Fla.), 1964. (*DA* 25:3924)

98. ENDLER, NORMAN S. "Factors Related to the Prediction of Academic Success." *Ont J Ed Res* 7:147–54 w '64–65. *

99. ENGEN, HAROLD BERNARD, JR. *Differential Prediction of Academic Success and Attrition-Survival of Entering Freshmen at the University of South Dakota.* Doctor's thesis, State University of South Dakota (Vermillion, S.D.), 1964. (*DA* 25:2847)

100. EVANS, RICHARD WILLIAM. *The School Counselor and Objective Measures as Predictors of High School Achievement and Relationship of Load to Achievement.* Doctor's thesis, Rutgers—The State University (New Brunswick, N.J.), 1964. (*DA* 25:2848)

101. GRIFFIN, WILLIAM MAXWELL. *A Study of the Relationship of Certain Characteristics of High School Seniors to Effectiveness in Independent Study.* Doctor's thesis, Syracuse University (Syracuse, N.Y.), 1964. (*DA* 25:5787)

102. GROSS, ARTHUR THOMAS. *A Study to Determine Relationships of Physical Fitness to Motor Educability, Scholastic Aptitude, and Scholastic Achievement of College Men.* Doctor's thesis, Louisiana State University (Baton Rouge, La.), 1964. (*DA* 25:5713)

103. HARE, ROBERT D. "Relationship of Level of Abstraction to Intelligence and Academic Performance." *Psychol Rep* 14:601–2 Ap '64. * (*PA* 39:1666)

104. HAUGEN, EARL STUART. *A Study of the Validity of the WAIS, SCAT, and STEP as Predictors of Success in College Mathematics.* Doctor's research study No. 1, Colorado State College (Greeley, Colo.), 1964. (*DA* 28:124A)

105. LONG, JOHN M. "Sex Differences in Academic Prediction Based on Scholastic, Personality and Interest Factors." *J Exp Ed* 32:239–48 sp '64. * (*PA* 39:6058)

106. McCORMICK, JAMES H., AND ASHER, WILLIAM. "Aspects of the High School Record Related to the First Semester College Grade Point Average." *Personnel & Guid J* 42:699–703 Mr '64. *

107. RITCHIE, RALPH WESTLEY, JR. *An Investigation of Factors Related to the Successful Completion of the Engineering Curriculum at California State Polytechnic College, Kellogg Campus.* Doctor's thesis, University of California (Los Angeles, Calif.), 1964. (*DA* 25:3446)

108. SHERMAN, VIVIAN MABEL STANLEY RUSHWORTH. *Personality Correlates of Differential Performance on Intelligence and Creativity Tests.* Doctor's thesis, Stanford University (Stanford, Calif.), 1964. (*DA* 25:4004)

109. STEWART, LAWRENCE H. "Factor Analysis of Nonoccupational Scales of the Strong Blank, Selected Personality Scales and the School and College Ability Test." *Calif J Ed Res* 15:136–41 My '64. * (*PA* 39:3201)

110. WAGNER, EDWIN E., AND SOBER, KATHRYN A. "Effectiveness of the Guilford-Zimmerman Temperament Survey as a Predictor of Scholastic Success in College." *J Counsel Psychol* 11:94–5 sp '64. *

111. WEBER, LOUISE A. *The Predictive Validity of the SCAT and the ACT at a Liberal Arts College for Women.* Master's thesis, John Carroll University (Cleveland, Ohio), 1964.

112. ACKERMAN, THOMAS J. *Language Laboratory Instruction and the Achievement of First-Year Students of Spanish in Florida.* Doctor's thesis, Florida State University (Tallahassee, Fla.), 1965. (*DA* 27:134A)

113. ANDERSON, HARRY E., AND BARRY, JOHN R. "Occupational Choices in Selected Health Professions." *Personnel & Guid J* 44:177–84 O '65. * (*PA* 40:3419)

114. BARGER, BEN, AND HALL, EVERETTE. "Relation of Expected College Activities to Ability and Achievement." *J Col Stud Personnel* 6:300–4 S '65. *

115. BLACK, HUBERT PERRY. *The Predictive Value of Selected Factors for Achievement of Lee College Freshmen.* Doctor's thesis, University of Tennessee (Knoxville, Tenn.), 1965. (*DA* 27:618A)

116. BOYCE, RICHARD W., AND PAXSON, R. C. "The Predictive Validity of Eleven Tests at One State College." *Ed & Psychol Meas* 25:1143–7 w '65. * (*PA* 40:3563)

117. CHAMBERS, JAY L.; BARGER, BEN; AND LIEBERMAN, LEWIS R. "Need Patterns and Abilities of College Dropouts." *Ed & Psychol Meas* 25:509–16 su '65. * (*PA* 39:16372)

118. DAVIS, LUTHER EDWARD, JR. *A Study of Selected Traits of St. Petersburg Junior College Students and Their Value in Predicting Academic Success in Certain Courses of Study at the Senior College Level.* Doctor's thesis, Auburn University (Auburn, Ala.), 1965. (*DA* 26:791)

119. DeSENA, PAUL A., AND WEBER, LOUISE ANN. "The Predictive Validity of the School College Ability Test (SCAT) and the American College Test (ACT) at a Liberal Arts College for Women." *Ed & Psychol Meas* 25:1149–51 w '65. * (*PA* 40:4603)

120. EDWARDS, MEREDITH PAYNE, AND TYLER, LEONA E. "Intelligence, Creativity, and Achievement in a Nonselective Public Junior High School." *J Ed Psychol* 56:96–9 Ap '65. * (*PA* 39:10171)

121. FELDHUSEN, JOHN F.; DENNY, TERRY; AND CONDON, CHARLES F. "Anxiety, Divergent Thinking, and Achievement." *J Ed Psychol* 56:40–5 F '65. * (*PA* 39:10771)

122. FOLDS, JONELL HEMPHILL. *A Comparison of the Recall of Test Scores and Change in Self-Concept of College Students Following Three Methods of Test Interpretation.* Doctor's thesis, University of Georgia (Athens, Ga.), 1965. (*DA* 26:2073)

123. FRANCIS, RICHARD LEE. *A Study of the Value of Selected Test Scores for Predicting Success in Analytic Geometry and Calculus.* Doctor's thesis, University of Missouri (Columbia, Mo.), 1965. (*DA* 26:7166)

124. GRIMSLEY, GLEN, AND SUMMERS, GEORGE W. "Selection Techniques for Pakistani Postgraduate Students of Business." *Ed & Psychol Meas* 25:1133–42 w '65. * (*PA* 40:4607)

125. HOLTBY, VANITA J. *A Set of Expectancy Tables for Use With SCAT-STEP Tests at Lewis and Clark Junior High School, Omaha, Nebraska.* Master's thesis, University of Kansas (Lawrence, Kan.), 1965.

126. KILPATRICK, ARNOLD ROY. *The Effectiveness of the School and College Ability Tests as a Predictor of Undergraduate Academic Achievement at Northeast Louisiana State College.* Doctor's thesis, Louisiana State University (Baton Rouge, La.), 1965. (*DA* 25:4380)

127. LEEP, ALBERT GENE. *Selected Pre-Service Measures as Predictors of First Year Teaching Performance of Elementary Teachers.* Doctor's thesis, Ball State Teachers College (Muncie, Ind.), 1965. (*DA* 26:3163)

128. LEUTENEGGER, RALPH R.; MUELLER, THEODORE H.; AND WERSHOW, IRVING R. "Auditory Factors in Foreign Language Acquisition." *Mod Lang J* 49:22–31 Ja '65. *

129. MORRIS, ROBERT O. *A Study of the Effects of Test Sequence on the Results of the SCAT-STEP Test Battery.* Master's thesis, University of Washington (Seattle, Wash.), 1965.

130. MUNDAY, LEO. "Comparative Predictive Validities of the American College Tests and Two Other Scholastic Aptitude Tests." *ACT Res Rep* 6:2–14 Ag '65. *

131. OTTE, HAROLD WILLIAM. *Comparisons of Abilities, Motivations, and Personality Traits of Continuing and Non-Continuing Freshmen in Colleges of the Lutheran Church—Missouri Synod.* Doctor's thesis, University of Colorado (Boulder, Colo.), 1965. (*DA* 26:6480)

132. POHLMAN, VERNON C. "The Inadequacy of Rank in High School Class as a Predictor of College Success." *Ill Sch Res* 2:16–9 O '65. *

133. PREDIGER, DALE J. "Prediction of Persistence in College." *J Counsel Psychol* 12:62–7 sp '65. * (*PA* 39:10725)

134. REILLY, HOWARD E. *A Comparative Analysis of Selected Characteristics of Admitted and Non-Admitted Students to the College of Education, Wayne State University.* Doctor's thesis, Wayne State University (Detroit, Mich.), 1965. (*DA* 27:988A)

135. SLAYTON, WILFRED GEORGE. *A Comparison of Successful and Unsuccessful Bible College Students With Respect to Selected Personality Factors.* Doctor's thesis, University of Arizona (Tucson, Ariz.), 1965. (*DA* 26:1487)

136. SMITH, ROBERT GOUGH. *An Evaluation of Selected Aspects of a Teacher Education Admissions Program.* Doctor's thesis, North Texas State University (Denton, Tex.), 1965. (*DA* 26:3771)

137. STONE, DONALD BRADFORD. *Predicting Student Retention and Withdrawal in a Selected State University College of New York.* Doctor's thesis, Cornell University (Ithaca, N.Y.), 1965. (*DA* 26:5184)

138. SWAN, ROBERT J., AND HOPKINS, KENNETH D. "An Investigation of Theoretical and Empirical Chance Scores on Selected Standardized Group Tests." *Calif J Ed Res* 16:34–41 Ja '65. * (*PA* 39:10156)

139. TULLY, G. EMERSON, AND HALL, BRUCE W. "Test-Retest Reliability of the School and College Ability Test." *J Ed Meas* 2:129 Je '65. *

140. WALLACH, MICHAEL A., AND KOGAN, NATHAN. *Modes of Thinking in Young Children: A Study of the Creativity-Intelligence Distinction,* pp. ix, 357. New York: Henry Holt & Winston, Inc., 1965. Pp. ix, 357. *

141. BELK, FLOYD EDMOND. *The Construction of a Simple Instrument to Predict Junior College Freshmen Attrition.* Doctor's thesis, Oklahoma State University (Stillwater, Okla.), 1966. (*DA* 27:4061A)

142. BONEY, J. DON. "Predicting the Academic Achievement of Secondary School Negro Students." *Personnel & Guid J* 44:700–3 Mr '66. * (*PA* 40:8064)

143. BRAY, DOUGLAS W., AND GRANT, DONALD L. "The Assessment Center in the Measurement of Potential for Business Management." *Psychol Monogr* 80(17):1–27 '66. * (*PA* 41:850)

144. BYLER, JESSE THOMAS. *The Relative Influence of Selected Variables in Determining Level of Vocational Preference.* Doctor's thesis, University of Virginia (Charlottesville, Va.), 1966. (*DA* 27:2385A) (Abstract: *Ed R* 4:56–8)

145. DENHAM, EDWARD CHAPLINE. *The Prediction of College Success With Biographical Data and Self-Ratings.* Doctor's thesis, University of Arkansas (Fayetteville, Ark.), 1966. (*DA* 27:599A)

146. DISTEFANO, M. K., JR., AND RICE, MARY L. "Predicting Academic Performance in a Small Southern College." *Ed & Psychol Meas* 26:487–9 su '66. * (*PA* 40:12758)

147. FOLDS, JONELL H., AND GAZDA, GEORGE M. "A Comparison of the Effectiveness and Efficiency of Three Methods of Test Interpretation." *J Counsel Psychol* 13:318–24 f '66. * (*PA* 40:12332)

148. FORD, ZANE BREWER. *Factors Related to Background of Senior Teacher Education Students Enrolled in Arkansas Institutions of Higher Education During the Academic Year 1964–65.* Doctor's thesis, University of Arkansas (Fayetteville, Ark.), 1966. (*DA* 27:627A)

149. FORREST, DONALD VINCENT. *A Comparative Study of Male Secondary School Underachievers Matriculating at the University of South Dakota.* Doctor's thesis, University of South Dakota (Vermillion, S.D.), 1966. (*DA* 27:671A)

150. FRIEDMAN, STUART M. *Predicting Students' Success in a Comprehensive Junior College.* Doctor's thesis, University of Southern California (Los Angeles, Calif.), 1966. (*DA* 26:7112)

151. GROSS, NATHAN. *English Grades as a Function of Intellectual Ability, Performance, and the Congruency of Teacher-Pupil Perceptions of Interpersonal Values.* Doctor's thesis, Harvard University (Cambridge, Mass.), 1966. (*DA* 28:123A)

152. GUILLIAMS, CLARK IRVIN. *Predicting Creative Productivity in College Classes Where Creative Thinking Is Emphasized.* Doctor's thesis, University of Arkansas (Fayetteville, Ark.), 1966. (*DA* 27:675A)

153. LEARD, JERRY LYNN. *A Statistical Study in the Building of Theoretically-Derived Equivalency Tables for Two Forms of the School and College Ability Test.* Master's thesis, University of Texas (Austin, Tex.), 1966.

154. LUNDSTEEN, SARA W., AND MICHAEL, WILLIAM B. "Validation of Three Tests of Cognitive Style in Verbalization for the Third and Sixth Grades." *Ed & Psychol Meas* 26:449–61 su '66. * (*PA* 40:12763)

155. LYON, JOHN THOMAS, JR. *An Experimental Investigation of the Relation Between Personality and Vocal Characteristics of Selected Beginning Adult Singers.* Doctor's thesis, Indiana University (Bloomington, Ind.), 1966. (*DA* 27:4285A)

156. MEANS, HESTER RICE. *An Analysis of the First Freshman Class of the DeKalb Junior College.* Doctor's thesis, University of Georgia (Athens, Ga.), 1966. (*DA* 27:1552A)

157. MILLER, WILLIAM EDGAR. *Factor Analytic Study of Perception of Self, Others, and the Environment.* Doctor's thesis, University of Kansas (Lawrence, Kan.), 1966. (*DA* 28:969A)

158. MORPER, JACK. *An Investigation of the Relationship of Certain Predictive Variables and Academic Achievement of Spanish-American and Anglo Pupils in Junior High School.* Doctor's thesis, Oklahoma State University (Stillwater, Okla.), 1966. (*DA* 27:4051A)

159. SCHUSLER, MARIAN M. "Prediction of Grades by Computer for High School Students: A Cross-Validation and Experimental Placement Study." *J Ed Data Processing* 3:97–110 su '66. *

160. STIVERS, EARL R. "A Study of Probationary Students at Manatee Junior College." *Fla J Ed Res* 8:81–91 Ja '66. *

161. SWANSON, JAMES R., AND TULLY, G. EMERSON. "Answer Sheet Format as a Variable in the Test Performance." *J Col Stud Personnel* 7:33–6 Ja '66. *

162. BRADLEY, R. C., AND MARTIN, BILLIE EDWARD. "A Study and Assessment of the Value of Selected Placement Tests for Predicting Achievement in Spanish, French, and German for First Semester Freshmen." *J Exp Ed* 36:50–4 w '67. *

163. CHABASSOL, DAVID J., AND THOMAS, DAVID C. "Anxiety, Aptitude, Achievement and Performance in Female Teachers." *Alberta J Ed Res* 13:291–4 D '67. * (*PA* 44:4218)

164. CLARKE, ROBERT B., AND GELATT, H. B. "Predicting Units Needed for College Entrance." *Personnel & Guid J* 46:275–82 N '67. * (*PA* 42:4512)

165. DANIEL, KATHRYN BARCHARD. "A Study of College Dropouts With Respect to Academic and Personality Variables." *J Ed Res* 60:230–5 Ja '67. *

166. FERRIS, MANFORD J. "Validity as a Function of Empirical Scaling of Test Items by a Logistic Model." *Ed & Psychol Meas* 27:829–35 w '67. * (*PA* 42:8091)

167. FOX, LOGAN JORDAN. *A Study of Relationships Between Grades and Measures of Scholastic Aptitude, Creativity, and Attitudes in Junior College Students.* Doctor's thesis, University of Southern California (Los Angeles, Calif.), 1967. (*DA* 28:4477A)

168. GOOLSBY, THOMAS M., JR. "Comparability and Validity of Three Forms of SCAT." *Ed & Psychol Meas* 27:1041–5 w '67. * (*PA* 42:9419)

169. GRECO, GERALDINE F. *A Study of STEP and SCAT as Predictors of School Achievement.* Master's thesis, Central Connecticut State College (New Britain, Conn.), 1967.

170. HILTON, THOMAS L., AND MYERS, ALBERT E. "Personal Background, Experience and School Achievement: An Investigation of the Contribution of Questionnaire Data to Academic Prediction." *J Ed Meas* 4:69–80 su '67. * (*PA* 42:4570)

171. INGRAM, JOHN ALLEN. *Factors Affecting the Success*

of Transfer Students at Drake University. Doctor's thesis, Iowa State University (Ames, Iowa), 1967. (*DA* 28:1341A)

172. LOHNES, PAUL R., AND McINTIRE, PAUL H. "Classification Validities of a Statewide 10th Grade Test Program." *Personnel & Guid J* 45:561-7 F '67. *

173. McGUIRE, DOUGLAS. *Multiple Discriminant Analysis of Test Scores and Biographical Data for the Description and Prediction of 12th Grade Educational Outcomes.* Doctor's thesis, University of Illinois (Urbana, Ill.), 1967. (*DA* 28:2987A)

174. MacNEIL, RONALD LAUCHLIN. *A Study of the Effectiveness of the SCAT and CTMM-SF to Predict First Semester Averages.* Master's thesis, St. Francis Xavier University (Antigonish, N.S., Canada), 1967.

175. MADAUS, GEORGE F. "Divergent Thinking and Intelligence: Another Look at a Controversial Question." *J Ed Meas* 4:227-35 w '67. * (*PA* 42:10584)

176. MASSAD, CAROLYN EMRICK. *A Comparative Study of Creativity, Language Aptitude, and Intelligence in Sixth-Grade Children From Low-Socioeconomic and Middle-Socioeconomic Levels.* Doctor's thesis, Kent State University (Kent, Ohio), 1967. (*DA* 29:4331A)

177. PATTERSON, BARBARA. *Comparison of Students From High and Low Socio-Economic Backgrounds Using Kuhlmann-Anderson and SCAT Total Test Scores.* Master's thesis, California State College (Hayward, Calif.), 1967.

178. TENOPYR, MARY L. "Social Intelligence and Academic Success." *Ed & Psychol Meas* 27:961-5 w '67. * (*PA* 42:9509)

179. TENOPYR, MARY L. "Symbolic Tests as Predictors of High-School Grades." *Ed & Psychol Meas* 27:385-391 su '67. * (*PA* 41:14227)

180. THACKER, JAMES HOSEA. *Pre-College Experience as Preparation for Success in a College of Agriculture.* Doctor's thesis, University of Missouri (Columbia, Mo.), 1967. (*DA* 28:3941B)

181. WARD, JAMES. "An Oblique Factorization of Wallach and Kogan's 'Creativity' Correlations." *Brit J Ed Psychol* 37:380-2 N '67. * (*PA* 42:4784)

182. BROWN, WILLIAM THOMAS. *Consideration of the Interrelationship of Five Aptitude and Achievement Factors in Successful Male Undergraduate Students at the University of Montana.* Doctor's thesis, University of Montana (Missoula, Mont.), 1968. (*DA* 29:3411A)

183. CAMERON, HOWARD K. "Nonintellectual Correlates of Academic Achievement." *J Negro Ed* 37:252-7 su '68. * (*PA* 45:7074)

184. CHABASSOL, DAVID J., AND THOMAS, DAVID C. "Anxiety, Aptitude, Achievement and Performance in Male Elementary Teachers." *Alberta J Ed Res* 14:233-7 D '68. * (*PA* 44:4219)

185. DAVIS, SAMUEL EUGENE. *Predicting Probable Failure in College-Level Music Theory Courses.* Doctor's thesis, University of Montana (Missoula, Mont.), 1968. (*DAI* 30:354A)

186. DIXON, PAUL W.; FUKUDA, NOBUKO K.; AND BERENS, ANNE E. "The Influence of Ethnic Grouping on SCAT, Teachers' Ratings, and Rank in High School Class." Abstract. *J Social Psychol* 75:285-6 Ag '68. * (*PA* 42:17056)

187. FARRAR, RONALD DOUGLAS. *The Non-Visa Foreign Student at Los Angeles City College: A Study of the Relation of Various Administrative and Academic Factors to the Immigrant Student.* Doctor's thesis, University of California (Los Angeles, Calif.), 1968. (*DAI* 30:487A)

188. FEE, FRANCIS. "An Alternative to Ward's Factor Analysis of Wallach and Kogan's 'Creativity' Correlations." Comment by James Ward. *Brit J Ed Psychol* 38:319-21 N '68. * (*PA* 43:6128)

189. FONTES, PATRICIA JOYCE. *The Effect of a Procedure for Simulating Norms for Newly Constructed Tests.* Doctor's thesis, Boston College (Chestnut Hill, Mass.), 1968. (*DAI* 30:57A)

190. GAGNI, ARSENIO OREVILLO. *The Differential Prediction of Selected Measurements in Ornamental Horticulture.* Doctor's thesis, Cornell University (Ithaca, N.Y.), 1968. (*DA* 29:4181A)

191. GINTHER, MARY LOU. *Relationships of Characteristics of Previous Education Obtained in Arkansas High Schools to Cumulative Grade-Point Averages of Seniors in the Various Undergraduate Colleges of the University of Arkansas in 1964-65.* Doctor's thesis, University of Arkansas (Fayetteville, Ark.), 1968. (*DA* 29:59A)

192. HARDESTY, D. L., AND JONES, W. S. "Characteristics of Judged High Potential Management Personnel—The Operations of an Industrial Assessment Center." *Personnel Psychol* 21:85-98 sp '68. * (*PA* 42:16197)

193. HEDLEY, CAROLYN NEAL. "Learning Relationship Differences and Curriculum Choice." *Improv Col & Univ Teach* 16:268-72 au '68. *

194. HEDLEY, CAROLYN NEAL. "The Relationship of Personality Factors to Scientific and Mathematical Ability Factors." *Sch Sci & Math* 68:265-71 Ap '68. *

195. HILLS, JOHN R., AND STANLEY, JULIAN C. "Prediction of Freshman Grades From SAT and From Level 4 of SCAT in Three Predominantly Negro State Colleges." Abstract. *Proc 76th Ann Conv Am Psychol Assn* 3:241-2 '68. *

196. HUTCHINS, BOB E. *The Relationship of Selected Factors to Performance of Teenage Teacher Aides in Eleven Ap-*

palachian School Districts. Doctor's thesis, Ohio University (Athens, Ohio), 1968. (*DA* 29:1041A)

197. KHAN, S. B. "The Relative Magnitude of Speed and Power in SCAT." *J Ed Meas* 5:327-9 w '68. * (*PA* 44:11222)

198. McGEE, JIM ED. *Selected Factors Associated With Success or Failure on the Junior English Examination at the University of Arkansas.* Doctor's thesis, University of Arkansas (Fayetteville, Ark.), 1968. (*DA* 29:99A)

199. MILLER, RICHARD HADDEN. *A Descriptive Study of the Relationship Between Potential and Performance of Freshman Students at the University of South Dakota.* Doctor's thesis, University of South Dakota (Vermillion, S.D.), 1968. (*DA* 29:2612A)

200. MUNDAY, LEO. "Correlations Between ACT and Other Predictors of Academic Success in College." *Col & Univ* 44:67-76 f '68. *

201. ORR, DAVID B., AND GRAHAM, WARREN R. "Development of a Listening Comprehension Test to Identify Educational Potential Among Disadvantaged Junior High School Students." *Am Ed Res J* 5:167-80 Mr '68. *

202. PRATT, MICHAEL, AND ALEAMONI, LAWRENCE M. *Predicting the Academic Performance of the Fall, 1967 Freshmen Engineering Students.* Research Report No. 277. Champaign, Ill.: Measurement and Research Division, Office of Instructional Resources, University of Illinois, 1968. Pp. 6. *

203. TSENG, MICHAEL. "Multiple Prediction of Programed Learning in Descriptive Statistics." *Proc W Va Acad Sci* 40:215-20 '68. *

204. VAN DERSLICE, JOHN FREDERICK. *The Educational, Social, and Economic Background of Engineering and Technical Students Analyzed for the Purpose of Establishing Profiles for Use in Counseling.* Doctor's thesis, Utah State University (Logan, Utah), 1968. (*DA* 29:1431A)

205. WILSON, ANAISE VICTORIANNE. *A Study of the Relationship of Selected Factors to the Academic Achievement of College Freshmen in the School of Education of Tuskegee Institute.* Doctor's thesis, New York University (New York, N.Y.), 1968. (*DAI* 30:144A)

206. AICHELE, DOUGLAS BRUCE. *Predicting Success in Basic Concepts of Modern Mathematics From Selected Test Scores and High School Measures.* Doctor's thesis, University of Missouri (Columbia, Mo.), 1969. (*DAI* 30:3623A)

207. CARVER, RONALD P. "Use of a Recently Developed Listening Comprehension Test to Investigate the Effect of Disadvantagement Upon Verbal Proficiency." *Am Ed Res J* 6(2):263-70 Mr '69. *

208. CUNNINGHAM, ROOSEVELT. *A Study to Determine Whether There Were Any Relationships Between High School Grade Point Averages and SCAT and STEP Tests.* Master's thesis, Virginia State College (Petersburg, Va.), 1969.

209. DE BERUFF, ELLEN. *The Prediction of Success in Master's and Doctoral Programs.* Doctor's thesis, University of Maryland (College Park, Md.), 1969. (*DAI* 31:1033A)

210. DIXON, PAUL W.; FUKUDA, NOBUKO K.; AND BERENS, ANNE E. "Teachers' Ratings, Sex, and SCAT as Predictors of Rank in High School Class." *J Exp Ed* 37(3):21-6 sp '69. *

211. DRUM, DAVID JOHN. *A Study of the Relationships Between Level of Development of Educational Interests and Academic Performance in First-Year College Students.* Doctor's thesis, American University (Washington, D.C.), 1969. (*DAI* 30:3317A)

212. FOLLMAN, JOHN; HERNANDEZ, DAVID; AND MILLER, WILLIAM. "Canonical Correlation of Scholastic Aptitude and Critical Thinking." *Psychol* 6(3):3-6 Ag '69. * (*PA* 44:2853)

213. FOLLMAN, JOHN; MILLER, WILLIAM; AND HERNANDEZ, DAVID. "Factor Analysis of Achievement, Scholastic Aptitude, and Critical Thinking Subtests." *J Exp Ed* 38(1):48-53 f '69. * (*PA* 45:10901)

214. FORD, ROBERT N.; BORGATTA, EDGAR F.; AND BOHRNSTEDT, GEORGE W. "Use of the Work Components Study With New College-Level Employees." *J Appl Psychol* 53(5):367-76 O '69. * (*PA* 44:1407)

215. FOSTER, GARRETT R. "An Analysis of Teacher Assigned Grades at Nova and Three Control Schools." *Fla J Ed Res* 11(1):1-24 Ja '69. *

216. GEORGE, WARREN EDWIN. *Significant Predictors for College Achievement in Specified Areas of Music Education and Identification of Potential Graduates.* Doctor's thesis, University of Kansas (Lawrence, Kan.), 1969. (*DA* 30:3040A)

217. GOOLSBY, THOMAS M., JR.; FRARY, ROBERT B.; AND LASCO, RICHARD A. "Selecting and Supplementing an Appropriate Achievement Battery for an Experimental School—A Factor Analytic Approach." *Ed & Psychol Meas* 29(2):403-8 su '69. * (*PA* 44:17319)

218. HAAKONSEN, HARRY OLAV. *An Investigation of the Relationships Between Selected Psychological Characteristics of Students and Performance in an Audio-Tutorial Genetics Program.* Doctor's thesis, Syracuse University (Syracuse, N.Y.), 1969. (*DAI* 31:63A)

219. HALL, LUCIEN TALMAGE, JR. *The Prediction of Success in Each of Six Four-Year Selections of Secondary Mathematics Courses.* Doctor's thesis, University of Virginia (Charlottesville, Va.), 1969. (*DAI* 30:4141A)

220. HARVEY, EVA DAVIS. *Relationships Between the National*

Teacher Examinations, Certain Variables, and Secondary Teacher Education Curricula. Doctor's thesis, North Texas State University (Denton, Tex.), 1969. (*DAI* 30:4852A)

221. HAYES, EDWARD MAJELLA. *The Relationship of Race and Sex to Academic Achievement in Selected Rural Elementary and High Schools Before and After Desegregation.* Doctor's thesis, University of Virginia (Charlottesville, Va.), 1969. (*DAI* 31:149A)

222. HINRICHS, J. R. "Comparison of 'Real Life' Assessments of Management Potential With Situational Exercises, Paper-and-Pencil Ability Tests, and Personality Inventories." *J Appl Psychol* 53(5):425–32 O '69. * (*PA* 44:1442)

223. HUSEMOLLER, KENNETH E. *The Prediction of Freshmen Academic Success at Eastern New Mexico University, Roswell, by Means of Selected Demographic and Standardized Tests Data.* Doctor's thesis, Colorado State College (Greeley, Colo.), 1969. (*DAI* 30:1467A)

224. IRVINE, S. H. "Factor Analysis of African Abilities and Attainments: Constructs Across Cultures." *Psychol B* 71(1):20–32 Ja '69. * (*PA* 43:7553)

225. KOOKER, EARL W., AND BELLAMY, ROY Q. "Some Psychometric Differences Between Graduates and Dropouts." *Psychol* 6(2):65–70 My '69. * (*PA* 43:14868)

226. LYONS, RICHARD ALAN, SR. *A Comparison of the Effect of Conceptually and Non-Conceptually Oriented Tests Upon Student Achievement and Attitude in Basic Electronics at the College Level.* Doctor's thesis, University of Missouri (Columbia, Mo.), 1969. (*DAI* 30:4254A)

227. MOTLEY, HESTER CHATTIN. *A Study of the Predictive Value of Certain Factors Related to Test Performance, Academic Achievement, and Educational Aspirations.* Doctor's thesis, American University (Washington, D.C.), 1969. (*DAI* 30:2807A)

228. PHILLIPS, RICHARD MARTIN. *A Multiple Regression Study of Academic Prediction at Gallaudet College.* Doctor's thesis, University of Maryland (College Park, Md.), 1969. (*DAI* 30:5257A)

229. RONAN, RICHARD JAMES. *A Study of the Relationships Between the Performance of College Freshmen in Mathematics and Selected Factors in Their Academic Background.* Doctor's thesis, University of New Mexico (Albuquerque, N.M.), 1969. (*DAI* 31:1694A)

230. SOURS, CHARLES F. RAY. *The Probability of Enrollment and Success of High School Seniors in an Industrial and Technical Teacher Education Program in the State of Arkansas.* Doctor's thesis, University of Arkansas (Fayetteville, Ark.), 1969. (*DAI* 30:1058A)

231. WEISGERBER, CHARLES A. *Psychological Assessment of Candidates for a Religious Order,* pp. 126–32. Chicago, Ill.: Loyola University Press, 1969. Pp. viii, 191. *

232. ALSPAUGH, CAROL ANN. *A Study of the Relationships Between Student Characteristics and Proficiency in Symbolic and Algebraic Computer Programming.* Doctor's thesis, University of Missouri (Columbia, Mo.), 1970. (*DAI* 31:4627B)

233. BOWERS, JOHN. "The Comparison of GPA Regression Equations for Regularly Admitted and Disadvantaged Freshmen at the University of Illinois." *J Ed Meas* 7(4):219–25 w '70. *

234. CARLETON, FREDERICK O. "Relationships Between Follow-Up Evaluations and Information Developed in a Management Assessment Center." Abstract. *Proc 78th Ann Conv Am Psychol Assn* 5(2):565–6 '70. * (*PA* 44:19655)

235. CROWELL, ORVILLE. *An Analysis of the Relationship of Measured Interests of Entering College Freshmen to Choice of Occupation Approximately Forty-Four Months Later.* Doctor's thesis, University of Arkansas (Fayetteville, Ark.), 1970. (*DAI* 31:2680A)

236. DIXON, PAUL W.; FUKUDA, NOBUKO K.; AND BERENS, ANNE E. "Cognitive and Personalogical Factor Patterns for Japanese-American High School Students in Hawaii." *Psychologia* 13(1):35–41 Mr '70. * (*PA* 45:8036)

237. DIXON, PAUL W.; FUKUDA, NOBUKO K.; AND BERENS, ANNE E. "Two-Factor Explanation of Post-High School Destinations in Hawaii." *J Exp Ed* 39(1):24–35 f '70. *

238. FARAGHER, JOHN P. *An Investigation of the Usefulness of the School and College Ability Tests as Utilized in the Tracking Process at Cleveland Heights High School.* Master's thesis, John Carroll University (Cleveland, Ohio), 1970.

239. FELDHUSEN, JOHN F.; TREFFINGER, DONALD J.; AND ELIAS, ROBERT M. "Prediction of Academic Achievement With Divergent and Convergent Thinking and Personality Variables." *Psychol Sch* 7(1):46–52 Ja '70. * (*PA* 44:11410)

240. FRANK, AUSTIN C., AND KIRK, BARBARA A. "Forestry Students Today." *Voc Guid Q* 19(2):110–26 D '70. *

241. GRANT, DONALD L., AND BRAY, DOUGLAS W. "Validation of Employment Tests for Telephone Company Installation and Repair Occupations." *J Appl Psychol* 54(1):7–14 F '70. *

242. GREEN, JOE L. *An Analysis of Factors Related to Academic Achievement in Introductory Geography at the University of Arkansas.* Doctor's thesis, University of Arkansas (Fayetteville, Ark.), 1970. (*DAI* 31:1510A)

243. HICKS, JACK M., AND WRIGHT, JOHN H. "Convergent-Discriminant Validation and Factor Analysis of Five Scales of Liberalism-Conservatism." *J Pers & Social Psychol* 14(2):114–20 F '70. * (*PA* 44:6741)

244. HILLS, JOHN R., AND STANLEY, JULIAN C. "Easier Test Improves Prediction of Black Students' College Grades." *J Negro Ed* 39(4):320–4 f '70. * (*PA* 45:10957)

245. KHAN, S. B. "Affective Correlates of Academic Achievement: A Longitudinal Study." *Meas & Eval Guid* 3(2):76–80 su '70. * (*PA* 45:1360)

246. KRANZLER, GERALD D. "Some Effects of Reporting Scholastic Aptitude Test Scores to High School Students." *Sch Counselor* 17(3):219–27 Ja '70. * (*PA* 44:21519)

247. LIBBY, WILLIAM L., JR. "Reaction Time and Remote Association in Talented Male Adolescents." *Develop Psychol* 3(3):285–97 N '70. * (*PA* 45:4001)

248. MILLER, BERNEICE BEADLES. *The Effects of Continuing or Changing Foreign Languages on Listening Comprehension and Selected Tests as Predictors of Success in Spanish or French at the Seventh-Grade Level.* Doctor's thesis, University of Oklahoma (Norman, Okla.), 1970. (*DAI* 31:2618A)

249. NASH, JOHN MORTON. *Prediction of Academic Achievement of Women at a Private Junior College Through Use of Certain Intellective and Family Relationships Measures.* Doctor's thesis, Boston University (Boston, Mass.), 1970. (*DAI* 31:2113A)

250. PACE, JESSE LEONARD, JR. *Relationships of the Dominant Value Constructs to Achieved Grade Point Averages of High and Low Ability Transfer Students in Two Age Groups at Phillips County Community College.* Doctor's thesis, University of Mississippi (University, Miss.), 1970. (*DAI* 31:1039A)

251. RARDIN, DONALD R., AND MOAN, CHARLES E. "Frustration Tolerance and College Grade Point Average." *Percept & Motor Skills* 31(3):1003–6 D '70. * (*PA* 46:1867)

252. RIECHARD, DONALD EDWARD. *The Acquisition of Selected Life-Science Concepts by Beginning Kindergarten Children From Three Different Community Settings.* Doctor's thesis, Ohio State University (Columbus, Ohio), 1970. (*DAI* 31:3366A)

253. ROSSMANN, JACK E., AND KIRK, BARBARA A. "Comparison of Counseling Seekers and Nonseekers." *J Counsel Psychol* 17(2):184–8 Mr '70. * (*PA* 44:9247)

254. ROSSMANN, JACK E., AND KIRK, BARBARA A. "Factors Related to Persistence and Withdrawal Among University Students." *J Counsel Psychol* 17(1):56–62 Ja '70. * (*PA* 44:5658)

255. SARUK, ALEC, AND GULUTSAN, METRO. "Academic Performance of Students and the Cultural Orientation of Their Parents." *Alberta J Ed Res* 16(3):189–95 S '70. * (*PA* 45:8988)

256. WEBB, JAMES BOYD. *A Comparative Study of the Relation of Broken Homes to the School Success of High School Students.* Doctor's thesis, George Washington University (Washington, D.C.), 1970. (*DAI* 31:3187A)

257. WILLIS, CARL G., AND NICHOLSON, JAMES. "Series II SCAT as a College Aptitude Measure." *Ed & Psychol Meas* 30(4):971–5 w '70. *

H. J. BUTCHER, *Professor of Educational Psychology, University of Sussex, Brighton, Sussex, England.*

This new and extended series of SCAT tests is designed to provide measures of basic verbal and mathematical ability for grades 4 to 14. The verbal and mathematical tests at each level consist, respectively, of verbal analogies and "quantitative comparisons." Item form in the verbal tests is uniform throughout, but varies quite widely in the quantitative tests. From inspection, both sections could be expected to have wide cross-cultural validity in all English-speaking countries in the sense that instructions and material contain little that is specific to American usage, although, of course, all the tables of norms are applicable only to the USA.

The tests are evidently the result of careful, scientific, and professionally expert construction. Items are generally ingenious, fair, and unambiguous, although an occasional diagram is misleadingly drawn. The handbook is in many ways a model of its kind and considerable pains have been taken to make it foolproof for the untrained administrator and to provide sufficient information for the expert psychometrist.

Details of how the tests should be given are clearly and briefly stated, and the main space is rightly given to score interpretation. Sufficient warning is provided about legitimate and illegitimate comparisons between different forms and levels and about the limitations of raw scores. For all forms and levels, tables are provided to enable the user easily to obtain first a converted score and then a percentile rank in terms of national norms. A welcome innovation is the provision of percentile bands extending one standard error of score above and below the percentile rank, this standard error being apparently derived, although this is not made quite explicit, from Kuder-Richardson coefficients. The percentile bands, besides giving the user a ready means of estimating the significance of differences between the scores of individuals and the differences between scores of one individual on different parts, also clearly indicate the varying precision of the tests for different levels of ability.

Selection of the national sample on which norms are based was thorough and professionally sophisticated. A probability sample was obtained of "all public school systems and church-related schools with an enrollment of at least 300 pupils," using the "probability proportional to size" method combined with systematic sampling through a list (with random start). Although this reviewer is not familiar enough with statistics of school size in the USA to estimate the proportion of schools thus excluded, it might be thought that the systematic exclusion of, e.g., small rural schools, would result in an upward bias of the resulting norms. Another possible source of bias is that, of 1,460 school superintendents selected in the sampling, only 835 agreed to participate. Again, the most plausible guess about the direction of such bias is that willingness to participate might be positively correlated with level of attainment in the system and thus raise the obtained norms to an unknown extent.

These speculative criticisms apart, the establishment of norms for SCAT was admirably done; also the handbook discussion of the separate components in the total error of measurement and of the factors determining their relative importance is thorough and instructive. Leaving aside possible error due to nonrandom sampling as discussed in the last paragraph,

sampling error has a negligible effect on the precision of the percentile norms relative to test unreliability, except at the extremes of the score distribution.

There are at least two parallel forms at each level. How parallel is parallel? The handbook goes into this quite deeply. It provides no between-forms correlations, but interpreting a rather complex series of inferences from the mean scores on the two forms of randomly divided classes leads to the conclusion that unwanted variance from between-forms differences is not large. The interpretation of the scores of individual students should not be affected, though care may be needed in interpreting small differences in the means of groups that have taken different forms of the test.

The handbook has little to say about speededness and nothing about its effect upon the size of the internal consistency coefficients and hence, presumably, upon the confidence intervals of the percentile ranks. The degree of speededness is not negligible, especially in the mathematical sections, since at three out of four levels 40 percent or more of the normative group failed to complete the test.

Predictive and concurrent validity, assessed by comparison with school and college grades and with other standard measures such as the SAT, appear adequate and fall within the expected range.

In sum, although further cumulative evidence about their properties is still desirable, these tests have all the appearance of being well engineered and quite well proven instruments.

Am Ed Res J 6 (2):306–9 Mr '69. Esin Kaya. In reviewing tests published by the Educational Testing Service one need not be concerned with whether or not the tests are reliable, the norms are based on representative samples, or the forms are adequately equated. Indeed, ETS can hardly be surpassed in efficiency and thoroughness in obtaining and reporting test data. The ....[test] under review....[reflects] this typical efficiency and thoroughness. * It is ironical, in a sense, that the thoroughness with which test development procedures and data are reported reveals certain test properties some of which may be construed as shortcomings. For example, both the normative data and a quick glance at the test content indicate that levels 1A and 2A of *SCAT Series II* overlap to a large extent. One is unable to determine the practical usefulness of having both levels. This problem of comparability of adjacent levels is augmented when one wants to measure gains of student groups who have scores near the top of any given level since the gains may not be validly measured because of difficulties in scaling the extreme scores on adjacent levels. Examination of the possible use of test results in the schools raises several more practical questions. Since the school practitioner is rarely aware of statistical subtleties, many of the technical cautions given by ETS are likely to go unnoticed by users of these tests *before* the decision is made to use them. Second, children in the extremes of the normative distributions frequently do not have their verbal and quantitative abilities differentiated. Rather, the data reported in the *Handbook* for *SCAT Series II* indicate that those groups who do well on quantitative tests also do well on verbal tests. The implication of this for the usefulness of administering both tests to all groups in the schools needs examination. Third, the predictive validity indices reported for *SCAT Series II* show a very large range so that the average r's, plus and minus one standard deviation, range from .18 to .84. When one notes, too, that midterm grades and cumulative grade point averages of the students were used as the validating criterion, the eternal question of the chicken or the egg applies. *

J Counsel Psychol 15:583–6 N '68. S. David Farr. * a set of tests covering the same range of grades and producing the same type of scores as the SCAT, but having shorter testing time, one less level, and different and more restricted item domains * The purpose of this series....is to produce scores useful in "comparing a student or class with other students or classes, comparing performance on the verbal and mathematical subtests, estimating growth of these basic skills over a period of time, and predicting success in related activities." The publisher has done a convincing job in terms of some of these objectives but has failed to produce useful information on others. * Each subtest consists of a single type of item—verbal analogies for the score labeled "verbal" and items demanding the judgment of relative magnitude of two stimuli for the "mathematical" score. * No rationale is presented for choosing these two item domains. As would be expected, the use of a single task leads to tests with high internal consistency coefficients in spite of relatively short testing times. Whether this narrow band-width high-fidelity approach produces a test which is also restricted in its range of applications cannot be determined from the data presented. * Although the handbook does not state the vocabulary level for the words used in the verbal analogies, it appears that at least for average and above average children the majority of the items pose a task of finding the relationships rather than of understanding the words used. The items which form Part II of each form and produce the mathematical score are of a less familiar sort. Each item presents two stimuli labeled A and B and the student is asked to judge whether the stimulus in Column A is greater, the stimulus in Column B is greater, the two parts are equal, or not enough information is given to decide. * Perhaps the primary question to be raised is whether all students in the range for which these tests are intended have an adequate concept of greater than and less than, in order that a lack in this concept should not interfere with the ability to make the keyed response when the rest of the task can be performed correctly. Evidence could undoubtedly be presented on this point, but CTD has not done so in the handbook. The format of the test booklets is good. Since the Part I directions are on the page facing the first 24 items of Part I, the perceptive student may use the time taken in giving directions to attempt the first few items of Part I, thereby giving him an advantage over the less test-wise student. The typeface used is small but clear. It is interesting to note that the text of the handbook is set in slightly larger type than the items of the test booklet, perhaps in regard for the older eyes which will be reading the handbook. The instructions are clearly and nicely stated. * The handbook accompanying the SCAT Series II is generally comprehensive (at least for a new test) and well written. * CTD probably should be complimented for inviting the criticism of reviewers by including discussion of certain topics for which they cannot yet provide adequate data, for example speededness * Three of the four objectives....deal at least in part with the description of individual differences, namely, the comparison of a student with other students, the comparison of performance on the verbal and mathematical subtests, and the estimation of growth in the basic skills represented by the items. SCAT Series II has achieved good accuracy for the first of these objectives, discrimination among students * As is typical, reliability information is provided for only one of the parallel forms, Form A. While one may question why CTD used shortcut procedures such as choosing small samples for the item statistics, and failing to study the reliability of Form B, there is no particular reason to expect that more elaborate or precise procedures would lead to different conclusions about the test. The publishers should be complimented for pointing out that since single school groups tend to be more homogeneous than the norm group, the within-school reliability will be somewhat less than that presented in the manual. * The second objective deals with the difference between verbal and mathematical scores for single students. The handbook provides an excellent discussion of the accuracy of such differences, at least to the extent of deciding whether differences are real. There is absolutely no data or even discussion, however, bearing on the meaning of such differences. Therefore, the discovery that a student is truly better in the verbal skills than in mathematical skills may be of little use. The third of the individual differences objectives has to do with estimating the growth of individuals. The handbook gives a minimum of information relevant to this objective. Short-term stability and practice-effect information are not presented. Concurrent interform correlations have been estimated from the correlation between part-class means on the two forms. This is inadequate, however, to deal with the problems of measuring growth. Interpretation of individual differences through relative position in a norm group has been well handled by the constructors of this series. A commendable job of national sampling has been done * Distinct advantages to placing the SCAT Series II on a scale that would enable the schools to "utilize data obtained on SCAT" (in some unspecified way) are implied on page 40 of the handbook, in spite of the fact that the importance of "lack of equivalence" is also noted on the same page. Granting the usefulness of such scaling, it appears that ETS has done a competent technical job. The reviewer feels, however, that the effort spent on scaling was misplaced, considering the minimal amount of data relevant to use of the test which had been assembled. * The question of speededness is discussed and the proportion of students in certain groups reaching the ¾ point and the last item of the test is reported. This is not the most relevant information, however, for determining whether a speed factor seriously affects relative position in the distribution of individual differences. * Evidence is presented which suggests that while students in modern math curricula score higher than those in traditional curricula, this phenomenon is approximately equal on the verbal and mathematical subtest. Some type of overall school differences seems a more reasonable hypothesis for explaining these data than does exposure to the modern math curriculum per se. The final technical topic is the formation of the total score. The definition of this score as the number right in the two subtests combined reflects a philosophy of defining a common domain of items rather than maintaining separate domains and combining scores in a way optimal to any given purpose. The fact that the correlations between the verbal and mathematical scores are substantially lower than the reliability of either part would support the reviewer's bias toward the latter philosophy rather than that adopted by CTD. USEFULNESS OF THE SERIES. Considering that the SCAT Series II "is intended primarily as a measure of a student's ability to succeed in future academic work," (Handbook, p. 41) only a trivial amount of relevant information is provided. * What is presented....tends to be concurrent correlations with marks and in some cases is based on the use of Level 1 outside of its recommended grade range. * The size of the coefficients suggests that the relationships between SCAT Series II and school marks are similar in strength to those found using other ability tests. However, the information is too skimpy to provide any real guidance in the use of this test. What, then, might the test user hope that ETS would make a serious attempt to provide in the future? While the benefits of local validity studies are not to be denied, it would seem that a responsible test publisher should provide some fairly specific predictive procedures for their tests. These are usually of two types. Regression data (not just correlation coefficients) are needed to predict relative position on some future measure, such as academic performance. On the other hand, to tell which of two or more clearly defined groups a student is more like, group distribution data, including covariance information, allows the description of similarity of a student to the various reference groups by multivariate classification procedures or some less formal process. The groups of interest may be academic groups, for example, college attenders versus non-college attenders or those attending various types of colleges, but the potential usefulness of abilities tests in career counseling should not be underestimated, as the ability tests are among the better discriminators among career groups. A third type of data helpful in both cases is the extent to which the information provided by the SCAT Series II duplicates that supplied by other typically available (or procurable) measures. Such information will allow a counselor to evaluate the wisdom of bringing additional data to bear on a particular question. Some of the data just described are impossible to develop during the few years taken to refine and produce this series. Those interested in mere description of individual differences can make use of the tests with the present data. Those interested in conducting research using the two domains represented will also find the present instrument useful. However, a user interested in prediction will have to either begin his own empirical investigation of the tests or wait until the publisher provides him with better information. It can be hoped that CTD will accept the responsibility to produce regression and group distribution data which will make the tests more useful. Scattered efforts of this type are represented in the supplements to the original SCAT Series. It is hoped by this reviewer that a more focused and well-planned program for developing the type of data described will be followed for Series II. SUMMARY. The present state of the SCAT Series II appears to reflect a philosophy by the publisher of providing a test which is technically excellent in terms of individual differences and letting the user generate his own data for the use of the test. The test is interesting in that of the two item domains represented, one is a well-established standard domain and the other appears to be a promising newer domain. The fidelity of the two part scores and total is acceptable and the norming processes commendable. It is hoped that the publisher will not take the short-sighted view that having done this much his job is finished. Only a well-considered program of studies, including substantial follow-up studies of students tested with appropriate levels of the series will turn SCAT Series II from an interesting, technically good test into a really useful instrument.

J Ed Meas 6(1):51–3 sp '69. Douglas McKie and Peggy Rae Koopman. Form IA and IB of

SCAT II originally appeared in 1964 as forms of the Cooperative Academic Ability Test, reviewed in the *Journal of Educational Measurement* by Hopkins and Sander (1966). These were renormed on a more representative sample in 1966, when the remaining forms were normed. SCAT Handbook II contains little indication of why SCAT II was developed, and what differences in philosophy guided the authors in changing the types of test tasks used. The most obvious reason is to provide a much shorter predictive instrument than SCAT I. * The SCAT II items appear slightly less school-specific and slightly more abstract than those of SCAT I. No explanation of a change from one item type in SCAT I to another in SCAT II appears in the Handbook II. In discussing the purpose of the test, Handbook II provides correlational evidence suggesting that the V and M scores of SCAT II may have more in common than have the V and Q scores of SCAT I. They are certainly not *purer* measures of these abilities. These correlations range from .68 (Grade 5) to .77 (Grade 11) in SCAT II, and .71 (Grade 5) through .61 (Grade 11) to .53 (Grade 13) in SCAT I. Somewhat disturbing is the fact that though, in the case of SCAT I, these measures become more independent with increased amounts of schooling, the dependence seems to *increase* for SCAT II. RELIABILITY. Reliability data on SCAT II, as for SCAT I, are obtained using KR 20. Coefficients range from .87 (Verbal, Form 2A) to .94 (Total Score, all forms) within grades. For the most part, they run higher than would be predicted by the Spearman-Brown formula for tests four-sevenths as long as the originals, so that in this respect, at least, the change in item type may have been beneficial. Within grades for a given school, however, the coefficients are reported to run .02 to .08 less than the above, presumably because of greater homogeneity. These reliabilities will tend to overestimate coefficients that take account of "occasions-variance," no measures for which are reported. Consequently, the standard error of measurement will be underestimated, and percentile bands used in norm tables will, as in SCAT I, be smaller than would otherwise be obtained. Not only that, but they will be smaller to a degree that is unknown but which varies with different forms and subtests-within-forms because of variable speeding. In this connection, the element of speed that was quite marked in SCAT I has been somewhat reduced, though the Handbook gives data showing that the mathematical subtests are still too long for a sizeable percentage of the students to complete in the time allotted. VALIDITY. Validity data on SCAT II are meager. At the grade 12 level, scores obtained in the Fall on the Cooperative Academic Ability Test (Forms 1A and 1B of SCAT II) were correlated against rank-in-graduating class. Coefficients obtained were .52, .51, and .56 for V, M, and T, respectively. * Also at the Grade 12 level, average *r*'s are quoted between scores on SCAT II, administered in the Fall, and midterm grades. They are .41 for V with English Composition, .46 for V with English (Literature plus Composition), .43 for M with Mathematics, and .59 for Total Score with G.P.A. These figures seem small for such a short period. * The most that can be said to date about SCAT II validities is that they are promising. For such a short instrument, they suggest that it is likely to be about as predictive as its longer predecessor (SCAT I). But the evidence for this conclusion is slender. More validity data are needed, particularly over longer time periods. No doubt they will soon begin to appear in the journals. SCAT II correlations with SAT scores are .83 (for V) and .86 (for M), compared with .86 (for SCAT I—V) and .78–.81 (for SCAT I—Q). Evidently, SCAT II should be useful to counselors who are asked questions like, "What are my chances on SAT?" However, the Handbook does not present either charts or expectancy tables from which probabilistic statements might be obtained. STANDARDIZATION AND NORMS. The norming....was conducted with the care typically associated with E.T.S. projects. Sampling was by grade, and an attempt was made to reflect percentages of students from each grade within regional areas. The attempt was not wholly successful because of unavoidable complications at the local level, but evidently the norm sample is fairly representative. No separate tables of norms are yet available for special groups like urban schools. However, considerable stress is placed upon the value of compiling local norms. Inspection of the tables of norms reveals that there is an element of negative skew in the score distributions for grades 8 to 12, with an accompanying lack of ceiling in some cases. The lack of ceiling is also apparent for one or two of the forms at lower levels. As in SCAT I, scores may be interpreted via "converted

scores," percentile ranks, or percentile bands (covering plus and minus 1 S.E.). The converted scores permit comparisons of performance across levels and forms, but not across subtests. For comparing individual scores or school averages with the appropriate norm group performance, percentile ranks or bands need to be used. An added convenience of the SCAT II norm tables that the SCAT I tables do not have is that one can enter the tables with the raw score instead of having first to obtain the converted score from another table. With regard to the precision of the norms, the authors carefully note that the accuracy of a P.R. for an individual depends primarily upon two sources of error: (*a*) the standard error of measurement of the test, and (*b*) the standard error of the mean of the norm group. They then note that the standard error of measurement indicates the extent to which the sample of items actually used in the test represents the universe of items that might have been included. This statement is true if KR 20 is used as a reliability measure in obtaining the standard error of measurement, as in fact it was. But the statement does not properly conform to the description on page nine of the Handbook as to what constitutes "error"—namely, "such extraneous factors as fatigue and practice" (commonly subsumed under some such label as "occasions-variance") as well as different samples of items. If this is what "error" is (and it surely should be), then an alternate forms reliability coefficient that takes account of occasions-variance as well as differences in item sampling is called for. It has already been noted that a consequence of failure to use such a reliability measure is that percentile bands are overly narrow. However, the practical difficulties of double testing on a large scale are well known. SUMMARY. In summary, the authors of SCAT II have produced a set of tests, each of which can be administered within a single class period. These relatively short tests have impressively high reliabilities. The validity data need considerable supplementing. College-level prediction is at present an unknown quantity, and little information is available about lower levels. What data are available, however, suggest that SCAT II can serve its predictive purposes well. Tables of norms have been carefully prepared, using scores that are comparable over different levels of schooling as well as conventional percentile ranks and bands. The tables are easily read and should prove serviceable to counselors, but norms for specially defined groups are not yet available.

For a review by Russel F. Green of the original 70 minute edition, see 6:452; for reviews by Frederick B. Davis, Hanford M. Fowler, and Julian C. Stanley, see 5:322.

[348]

★Dennis Test of Scholastic Aptitude. Grades 4–8, 5–8; DTSA; 1961–63; 2 levels labeled Forms 2, 3; no data on reliability; $2.50 per 35 tests; postpaid; specimen set not available; William H. Dennis; the Author. *
a) FORM 2. Grades 4–8; 1961–63; 1 form ('61, 2 pages); manual ('61, 6 pages); revised norms ('63, 2 pages); (40) minutes.
b) FORM 3. Grades 5–8; 1962; 1 form (2 pages); mimeographed temporary manual (11 pages); (35) minutes.

[349]

*Doppelt Mathematical Reasoning Test. Grades 16–17 and employees; 1954–68; DMRT; Form A ('54, 4 pages); revised manual ('68, 12 pages); bulletin of information ('70, 61 pages); guide for testing center operation ['64, 8 pages]; distribution restricted and test administered at specified licensed university centers; separate answer sheets (IBM 805-1230) must be used; scoring and reporting handled by the local center; examination fee to centers: $3 per examinee; fees to examinees are determined locally and include reporting of scores to the examinee and to 3 institutions or companies designated at the time of testing; additional score reports may be secured from the publisher at a fee of $1 each; 50(60) minutes; Jerome E. Doppelt; Psychological Corporation. *

REFERENCES

1–2. See 6:456.
3. HARDESTY, D. L., AND JONES, W. S. "Characteristics of Judged High Potential Management Personnel—The Operations of an Industrial Assessment Center." *Personnel Psychol* 21: 85–98 sp '68. * (*PA* 42:16197)
4. CARLETON, FREDERICK O. "Relationships Between Follow-Up Evaluations and Information Developed in a Management Assessment Center." Abstract. *Proc 78th Ann Conv Am Psychol Assn* 5(2):565–6 '70. * (*PA* 44:19655)

For a review by W. V. Clemans, see 6:456.

[350]

★Draw-A-Man Test for Indian Children. Ages 6–10; 1956–66; adaptation of *Goodenough Intelligence Test;* 1 form (no date, 1 page); manual ('66, 105 pages); Rs. 20 per manual and 20 tests, postage extra; (30) minutes; Pramila Phatak; distributed by Anand Agencies. *

REFERENCES

1. PHATAK, PRAMILA. "Application of Phatak's Draw-A-Man Scale for Indian Children of Gujarat." *Psychol Studies* 4:45–54 Jl '59. *
2. PHATAK, P. "Comparative Study of Revised Draw-A-Man Scale (Harris) and Phatak Draw-A-Man Scale for Indian Children." *Psychol Studies* 6:12–7 Jl '61. * (*PA* 38:2674)
3. PHATAK, P. "Sex Differences on Phatak's Draw-A-Man Scale." *Ed & Psychol R* 2:24–9 Ja '62. * (*PA* 37:7995)
4. MISRA, AJODHYA NATH. *To Work Out General Mental Ability Norms for Primary School Children Through Human Figure Drawings.* Doctor's thesis, University of Gorakhpur (Gorakhpur, India), 1966. (Abstract: *Indian Psychol R* 4: 161–2)

J Psychol Res 12:51 Ja '68. M. A. Faroqi. [Review of the manual.] Those familiar with the work of Dr. Phatak on development and standardization of the Draw-a-Man Test will welcome the present publication. It brings together all the information available on the test, some of it previously unpublished and some published in different journals. It gives detailed procedure for administering and scoring the test, provides carefully presented scoring exercises. * A book review perhaps is not the right place to evaluate the test as such. This is one of the small number of attempts to carry through a full programme of test development in this country. This is not just Goodenough test standardized for Indian children. A new conception of scoring has been evolved. The scale has a very satisfactory relationship with other tests and also good inter-observer agreement, which is the test of objectivity applied in such scoring situations. The assumptions and implications in developing separate norms for the five 'environmental levels' and the particular conception of 'environmental levels' employed here need careful examination. The present publication will serve as a useful starting point for research workers who need a simple, convenient intelligence test and are prepared to learn the scoring scheme.

[351]

★Gilliland Learning Potential Examination. Ages 6 and over; 1966; GLPE; an intelligence test "for use with remedial readers and the culturally disadvantaged"; 1 to 4 scores: total score for all subjects, non-reading-noncultural, predicted comprehension, and visual memory for subjects with reading problems; some subtests may be omitted in grades 3 and over to obtain a quick score and in grades 3 and under to obtain a primary score; 1 form (12 pages); manual (31 pages); norms booklet (12 pages); no data on reliability; 25¢ per test; 75¢ per set of keys, norms booklet, and manual (free with 50 or more tests); $1 per set of scoring templates; 75¢ per specimen set; postpaid; (40–50) minutes; Hap Gilliland; Montana Reading Clinic Publications. *

ALBERT J. HARRIS, *Emeritus Professor of Education, The City University of New York, New York, New York.*

This test is described by the author as an intelligence or scholastic aptitude test intended specifically for use with poor readers and "culturally handicapped" children. The test has not been fully standardized and is not recommended for use in its present state of development. Reasons for this statement are given below.

The test contains eight subtests. Test 1, Visual Memory, involves drawing from memory a series of designs held up by the examiner; it is not included in the total score, but used only to disclose an area of potential weakness. Test 2 is a symbol-substitution test called Symbolic Representation in which the symbols have some visual resemblance to the pictured objects they represent. In Test 3a the same symbols are employed and the task is to name them, in writing in group administration or orally in individual administration. In Test 3b, Symbol Interpretation, the task is to combine the sequence of symbols presented in Test 3a into a meaningful message. Tests 2 and 3 obviously were inspired by Indian picture writing. Test 4, called Relationships, is a pictorial analogies test. In Test 5, Listening Comprehension, a story about an Indian boy is read aloud by the examiner and 10 three-choice pictorial items test recall of details and comprehension. Test 6, Picture Completion, has an unusual format reminiscent of the old *Healy Pictorial Completion Test*, adapted to group testing; in each of 8 pictures, three or four white rectangles blot out parts of the picture, and the task is to select the correct choices from among 10 pictures and write their numbers in the correct spaces. Test 7, Information and Interests, uses a pictorial format in which 10 interest areas are sampled by five items each, using a picture matching form of response.

The test is intended to cover a wide range, ages 6 through 15. IQ norms are provided at six-month intervals, for a variety of scores: Total Score, NR (low reading or culturally different, omitting Tests 3b and 7), QS (quick scoring, based on the four subtests that are easiest to score), Pri (primary, omitting the two most difficult subtests), and PC (Predicted Comprehension, based on Tests 2 and 5 only). Norms are based on "2100 students in six western states." No information is given about sampling procedures used. There are also separate norms for Indian children based on 1250 cases. Time limits are quite short on some subtests, flexible on others.

Statistical information provided in the manual is far below expected standards. Absolutely no information of any kind is given concerning reliability. No information is given about item validity, correlations with achievement, or validation of the special scores provided. The manual provides one short paragraph on validity, which contains the following statement: "Statistical studies completed at the time of publication indicate a very high (above .80) correlation with the non-language portions of other highly regarded intelligence tests." If any further statistical work has been done on the test since its publication in 1966, the author did not supply information about it.

This test should be either further developed with the assistance of a competent statistician and testing specialist, or withdrawn from the market. At present it must be considered an experimental test not ready for general use, even with the populations for which the author intended it.

Howard B. Lyman, *Associate Professor of Psychology, University of Cincinnati, Cincinnati, Ohio.*

The GLPE is a test of intelligence emphasizing nonreading content, designed for individual or group administration, especially to Indians and other rural Americans age 6 and over.

Eight subtests combine in various ways to yield 1 to 4 intelligence scores, a visual memory score, and 10 interest scores. Visual Memory involves reproducing a design, exposed for five seconds, after a five-second delay. Symbolic Representation is a picture-symbol substitution task; Symbolic Identification involves symbol-picture substitution from memory of the previous test; Symbolic Interpretation demands translating the Identification task into a story. Relationship (only 10 items, but of 3 different types!) demands recognition of an association among drawings. In Listening Comprehension, the examinee selects drawings most closely related to a 200-word story that has been read to him. Picture Completion, similar to the classic *Healy Pictorial Completion Test,* has the examinee select drawings which fit appropriately into cutouts in a larger picture. In General Information and Interests, the examinee has 20 seconds to decide which sets of pictorial items seem easiest to him and then 10 minutes to select the answers in whatever order desired.

All subtests except Visual Memory contribute to Total. Dropping Symbolic Interpretation and General Information yields the "Non Reading and Non Cultural" score (sometimes NR, sometimes NR-NC, and probably the NC—explained nowhere—used in norms "for reservation Indians and other isolated rural groups"). Dropping (additionally) Symbol Identification and replacing General Information and Picture Completion yields the Quick Scoring score. Dropping Picture Completion and General Information while replacing Symbol Identification yields the Primary score "for children in grade 2 or below" (although norms are shown through age 15-11). The Predicted Comprehension score is the sum of Symbolic Representation and Picture Completion and "should be figured for all children whose noncultural IQ scores are 5 or more points higher than their total IQ scores and for all children who are suspected of having reading problems."

Visual Memory is treated separately. The test must be difficult to score reliably, but no evidence of scorer reliability is cited. The logic of some scoring is questionable: e.g., simple reversal of a figure sometimes gives less credit than does no drawing at all. Without explanation, the lowest-scoring 4% on single-year age norms are rated Critical; 4–12%, Problem Area; 12–25%, Low; and Upper 75%, Normal.

In addition, the rows of the General Information test are scored separately and used as guides to 10 "reading interest" areas. Here as elsewhere, the author places great faith in *face* validity.

Validity is dismissed with a single sentence: "Statistical studies completed at the time of publication indicate a very high (above .80) correlation with the nonlanguage portions of other [sic!] highly accepted intelligence tests." A letter from the author reveals that this was a single study with the nonverbal part of the *California Short-Form Test of Mental Maturity,* where a correlation of "+.8506" was found between mental ages on the CTMM and the GLPE; based on a combination of 18 third grade and 22 sixth grade pupils, even this one correlation coefficient is spurious because of the heterogeneity of the group. Other statistical data are completely missing as is any statement of how the IQ's were derived. There is no mention of mental ages (used in the one study). There is no discussion of preliminary research or the rationale of item content.

The norms were based on "2100 students in six western states." " 'Indian' scores were derived from 1250 rural and reservation Indians" in four northwestern states. It is uncertain whether the "2100 students" include the 1,250 Indians. No further information is given about the norms groups. Representativeness is doubtful, however, for there is at least one reversal in levels: slightly lower raw scores are needed for a given IQ at ages 12-6 through 12-11 than at ages 12-0 through 12-5.

The test booklet itself looks homemade. The drawings are rough and sometimes unclear. The booklet looks jumbled and crowded. The paper is not sufficiently opaque, for printing shows through on the opposite side of the sheet. This poor printing must be confusing on some tests (e.g., Visual Memory) and helpful on at least one other (Symbol Identification).

Gilliland's purpose of providing an intelligence test for rural and Indian youth is commendable. The test has some novel features, should be interesting to children, and does possess some face validity; but there is still much work that must be done on it. I suspect that, given some assistance (perhaps from a foundation or major test publisher), the author might be able to develop this instrument into a respectable test—especially if he could narrow his interest and concentrate on fewer scores. But in its present form, there is little to recommend it for use with Indians or anyone else.

[352]

Goodenough-Harris Drawing Test. Ages 3-15; 1926-63; GHDT; revision and extension of the *Goodenough Intelligence Test;* 1 form ('63, 4 pages); manual ('63, 80 pages, reprinted from *135* below); quality scale cards ('63, 24 cards); $3.90 per 35 tests; $2.90 per set of quality scale cards; $1.50 per manual; $5 per specimen set; postage extra; (10-15) minutes; Florence L. Goodenough and Dale B. Harris; Harcourt Brace Jovanovich, Inc. *

REFERENCES

1–60. See 4:292.
61–94. See 5:335.
95–137. See 6:460.
138. EARL, C. J. C. "The Human Figure Drawings of Adult Defectives." *J Mental Sci* 79:305-27 Ap '33. * (*PA* 8:5518)
139. HUNKIN, V. "Validation of the Goodenough Draw-A-Man Test for African Children." *J Social Res (Pretoria)* 1:52-63 Jl '50. * (*PA* 27:1181)
140. DÖRKEN, HERBERT, JR. "Personality Factors Associated With Paraplegia and Prolonged Hospitalization: A Clinical Note." *Can J Psychol* 5:134-7 S '51. * (*PA* 26:2922)
141. ANASTASI, ANNE, AND D'ANGELO, RITA Y. "A Comparison of Negro and White Preschool Children in Language Development and Goodenough Draw-A-Man IQ." *J Genetic Psychol* 81:147-65 D '52. * (*PA* 27:6492)
142. GOLDENBERG, SAMUEL. *Some Aspects of Diagnosis of Cerebral Damage in Children.* Doctor's thesis, University of Washington (Seattle, Wash.), 1953. (*DA* 13:1259)
143. DUNN, MICHAEL BUTLER. *Global Evaluation of Children's Drawings of "Person" and "Self."* Doctor's thesis, Columbia University (New York, N.Y.), 1955. (*DA* 15:1254)
144. DOWLEN, CAROLINE LAWTHER. *Parental Attitudes in Relation to Their Children's Social Acceptance, Intellectual Functioning Level and Emotional Adjustment.* Doctor's thesis, University of Houston (Houston, Tex.), 1956. (*DA* 16:2203)
145. VARVA, FRANK IRVIN. *An Investigation of the Effect of Auditory Deficiency Upon Performance With Special Reference to Concrete and Abstract Tasks.* Doctor's thesis, University of Pittsburgh (Pittsburgh, Pa.), 1956. (*DA* 16:2532)
146. WILSON, JOHN LEOD. *Changes in Brightness of Children, Age Three to Eleven, Living in a Low Socioeconomic Environment.* Doctor's thesis, Indiana University (Bloomington, Ind.), 1957. (*DA* 17:2211)
147. DENNIS, WAYNE. "Handwriting Conventions as Determinants of Human Figure Drawings." *J Consult Psychol* 22:293-5 Ag '58. * (*PA* 34:710)
148. ROBINAULT, ISABEL PICK. *Preschool Children's Accomplishments in Tactual and Visual Form Perception.* Doctor's thesis, Columbia University (New York, N.Y.), 1958. (*DA* 19:3219)
149. FULLER, CARL WELLINGTON. *A Study of the Growth and Organization of Certain Mental Abilities in Young Deaf Children.* Doctor's thesis, Northwestern University (Evanston, Ill.), 1959. (*DA* 20:2382)

150. HOZIER, ANN. "On the Breakdown of the Sense of Reality: A Study of Spatial Perception in Schizophrenia." *J Consult Psychol* 23:185–94 Je '59. * (*PA* 34:4680)

151. OGILVIE, DOUGLAS S. *A Pilot Study of an Extension of the Goodenough Draw-A-Man Test.* Master's thesis, Fordham University (New York, N.Y.), 1959.

152. SANTOS, BERTHA. *A Comparison of Memory and Learning Ability With Social Competence and Social Participation in Aged Senile Dements in a Mental Institution.* Doctor's thesis, New York University (New York, N.Y.), 1959. (*DA* 20:1441)

153. HOLDEN, RAYMOND HENRY. *Changes in Body Imagery of Physically Handicapped Children Due to Summer Camp Experience.* Doctor's thesis, Boston University (Boston, Mass.), 1960. (*DA* 21:3165)

154. LEVINSON, BORIS M. "A Comparative Study of the Verbal and Performance Ability of Monolingual and Bilingual Native Born Jewish Preschool Children of Traditional Parentage." *J Genetic Psychol* 97:93–112 S '60. * (*PA* 35:6190)

155. PHATAK, P. "A Study of the Revised Goodenough Scale With Reference to Artistic and Non-Artistic Drawings." *J Voc & Ed Guid* 7:35–40 Ag '60. * (*PA* 36:1HD35P)

156. COHEN, HASKEL. "Psychological Test Findings in Adolescents Having Ovarian Dysgenesis." *Psychosom Med* 24:249–56 Mr–Ap '62. * (*PA* 37:5107)

157. CORAH, NORMAN L., AND CORAH, PATRICIA LANEY. "A Study of Body Image in Children With Cleft Palate and Cleft Lip." *J Genetic Psychol* 103:133–7 S '63. * (*PA* 39:2414)

158. REDBIRD, HELEN MARIE. *A Study of the Intelligence of Children of Domestic Agricultural Migrant Workers in Colorado.* Doctor's thesis, University of Colorado (Boulder, Colo.), 1963. (*DA* 24:4486)

159. SINGER, MARGARET THALER. Chap. 12, "Personality Measurements in the Aged," pp. 217–49. In *Human Aging: A Biological and Behavioral Study.* Edited by James E. Birren, Robert N. Butler, Samuel W. Greenhouse, Louis Sokoloff, and Marian R. Yarrow. National Institute of Mental Health, Public Health Service Publication No. 986. Washington, D.C.: United States Government Printing Office, 1963. Pp. xiii, 328. * (*PA* 38:5821)

160. BALINKY, JEAN LAHN. *A Configurational Approach to the Prediction of Academic Achievement in First Grade.* Doctor's thesis, Rutgers—The State University (New Brunswick, N.J.), 1964. (*DA* 25:2844)

161. BRIGGS, PETER F., AND NELSON, SUSAN. "The Effect of Non-Dominant Hand Execution on the Goodenough Draw-A-Man Test." *J Clin Psychol* 20:496 O '64. * (*PA* 39:12277)

162. BROVERMAN, DONALD M. "Generality and Behavioral Correlates of Cognitive Styles." *J Consult Psychol* 28:487–500 D '64. * (*PA* 39:7680)

163. DANFORD, BART HARLAND. *Some Correlates of Two Brief Intelligence Tests Used by Pediatricians.* Doctor's thesis, University of Houston (Houston, Tex.), 1964. (*DA* 26:1772)

164. EASLEY, GLENN TRUETT. *The Draw-A-Man Test as an Index of Reading Readiness.* Doctor's thesis, Washington State University (Pullman, Wash.), 1964. (*DA* 25:2881)

165. FAHMY, MOSTAFA. "Initial Exploring of the Intelligence of Shilluk Children: Studies in the Southern Sudan." *Vita Hum* 7(3–4):164–77 '64. * (*PA* 39:7815)

166. FARRANT, ROLAND H. "The Intellective Abilities of Deaf and Hearing Children Compared by Factor Analyses." *Am Ann Deaf* 109:306–25 My '64. * (*PA* 39:2442)

167. GRINDER, ROBERT E.; SPOTTS, WENDY S.; AND CURTI, MARGARET WOOSTER. "Relationships Between Goodenough Draw-A-Man Test Performance and Skin Color Among Preadolescent Jamaican Children." *J Social Psychol* 62:181–8 Ap '64. * (*PA* 39:5121)

168. KENNEDY, WALLACE A., AND LINDNER, RONALD S. "A Normative Study of the Goodenough Draw-A-Man Test on Southeastern Negro Elementary School Children." *Child Develop* 35:33–62 Mr '64. * (*PA* 38:8425)

169. OUELLETTE, FLORIAN E. *The Administration of the Goodenough Draw-A-Man Test to Canadian Eskimos.* Master's thesis, University of Ottawa (Ottawa, Ont., Canada), 1964.

170. SHIPP, DONALD E., AND LOUDON, MARY LOU. "The Draw-A-Man Test and Achievement in the First Grade." *J Ed Res* 57:518–21 Jl–Ag '64. *

171. SILVER, ARCHIE A., AND HAGIN, ROSA A. "Specific Reading Ability: Follow-Up Studies." *Am J Orthopsychiatry* 34:95–102 Ja '64. * (*PA* 39:2863)

172. SWEENEY, NEIL R. "Reliability of Experienced and Inexperienced Scorers on Goodenough Draw-A-Man Test." *J Psychol* 57:281–7 Ap '64. * (*PA* 39:1763)

173. VANE, JULIA R., AND KESSLER, ROSALYN T. "The Goodenough Draw-A-Man Test: Long Term Reliability and Validity." *J Clin Psychol* 20:487–8 O '64. * (*PA* 39:12313)

174. WEST, PEGGY C. *An Experimental Study of Growth of Visual Perception in Educable Mentally Retarded Children Through Art Instruction as Indicated by Test-Retest of the Goodenough Draw-A-Man Test.* Master's thesis, East Tennessee State University (Johnson City, Tenn.), 1964.

175. ALZOBAIE, ABDUL JALIL. "The Validity of the Goodenough Draw-A-Man Test in Iraq." *J Exp Ed* 33:331–5 su '65. * (*PA* 39:12273)

176. BADRI, MALIK B. "Influence of Modernization on Goodenough Quotients of Sudanese Children." *Percept & Motor Skills* 20:931–2 Je '65. * (*PA* 39:15209)

177. BADRI, MALIK B. "The Use of Finger Drawing in Measuring the Goodenough Quotient of Culturally Deprived Sudanese Children." *J Psychol* 59:333–4 Mr '65. *

178. EKLUND, SUSAN, AND SCOTT, MYRTLE. "Effects of Bilingual Instruction on Test Response of Latin American Children." *Psychol Sch* 2:280 Jl '65. *

179. FUKADA, NAHIKO; VAHAR, MALL; AND HOLOWINSKY, IVAN Z. "Qualitative Interpretation of Draw-A-Person Reproductions by Japanese Children." *Training Sch B* 62:119–25 N '65. * (*PA* 40:2132)

180. KHATENA, JOE. *A Study of Comparative Performance on the Raven's Coloured Progressive Matrices and the Goodenough Draw-A-Man Test in Two Singapore Primary Schools.* Master's thesis, University of Singapore (Singapore, Malaysia), 1965.

181. KOPPITZ, ELIZABETH MUNSTERBERG. "A Comparison of Pencil and Crayon Drawings of Young Children." *J Clin Psychol* 21:191–4 Ap '65. * (*PA* 39:12393)

182. MEIER, JOHN HENRY. *An Exploratory Factor Analysis of Psychodiagnostic and Case Study Information From Children in Special Education Classes for the Educable Mentally Handicapped.* Doctor's thesis, University of Denver (Denver, Colo.), 1965. (*DA* 26:3153)

183. RAJALAKSHMI, R., AND JEEVES, M. A. "Discrimination Learning and Reversal Learning in Children as Related to Performance on Certain WISC Items and on the Goodenough Draw-A-Man Test." *J Genetic Psychol* 106:149–56 Mr '65. * (*PA* 39:11993)

184. RICHEY, MARJORIE H. "Qualitative Superiority of the 'Self' Figure in Children's Drawings." *J Clin Psychol* 21:59–61 Ja '65. * (*PA* 39:12402)

185. SCHULMAN, JEROME L.; KASPAR, JOSEPH C.; AND THRONE, FRANCES M. *Brain Damage and Behavior: A Clinical-Experimental Study.* Springfield, Ill.: Charles C Thomas, Publisher, 1965. Pp. ix, 164. *

186. STONE, PATRICIA A., AND ANSBACHER, HEINZ L. "Social Interest and Performance on the Goodenough-Harris Draw-A-Man Test." *J Indiv Psychol* 21:178–86 N '65. * (*PA* 40:2963)

187. THORPE, JOSEPH S. "A Cross-Cultural Study of Personality Development: Selection of Test Measures." *Congr Inter-Am Soc Psychol* 9(1964):242–9 ['65]. *

188. THRONE, FRANCES M.; KASPAR, JOSEPH C.; AND SCHULMAN, JEROME L. "The Peabody Picture Vocabulary Test in Comparison With Other Intelligence Tests and an Achievement Test in a Group of Mentally Retarded Boys." *Ed & Psychol Meas* 25:589–95 su '65. * (*PA* 39:16072)

189. ABERCROMBIE, M. L. J., AND TYSON, M. C. "Body Image and Draw-A-Man Test in Cerebral Palsy." *Develop Med & Child Neurol* 8:9–15 F '66. * (*PA* 40:6965)

190. ALEXANDER, DUANE; EHRHARDT, ANKE A.; AND MONEY, JOHN. "Defective Figure Drawing, Geometric and Human, in Turner's Syndrome." *J Nerv & Mental Dis* 142:161–7 F '66. * (*PA* 40:11185)

191. AURICCHIO, ELIZABETH WILLIAMS. "Comparison of Several Methods of Scoring Draw-A-Person Tests." *Percept & Motor Skills* 23:1124 D '66. * (*PA* 41:5981)

192. BRENNER, MAY WOOLF, AND GILLMAN, SELMA. "Visuomotor Ability in Schoolchildren: A Survey." *Develop Med & Child Neurol* 8:686–703 D '66. * (*PA* 41:4397)

193. CARKHUFF, ROBERT R. "Variations in Performance of Non-Institutionalized Retardates." *J Clin Psychol* 22:168–70 Ap '66. * (*PA* 40:8015)

194. DENNIS, WAYNE. "Goodenough Scores, Art Experience, and Modernization." *J Social Psychol* 68:211–28 Ap '66. * (*PA* 40:7590)

195. DODD, JOHN M., AND RANDALL, ROBERT R. "A Comparison of Negro Children's Drawings of a Man and a Woman." *J Negro Ed* 35:287–8 su '66. *

196. HILER, E. WESLEY. "Prognostic Indicators for Children in a Psychiatric Hospital." *J Consult Psychol* 30:169–71 Ap '66. * (*PA* 40:6773)

197. HIRSCHENFANG, SAMUEL; JARAMILLO, SELENE; AND BENTON, JOSEPH G. "Comparison of Scores on the Revised Stanford-Binet (L), Columbia Mental Maturity Scale (CMMS) and Goodenough Draw-A-Man Test of Children With Neurological Disorders." *Psychol Rep* 19:15–6 Ag '66. * (*PA* 40:12564)

198. KERNAN, JOHN S. "Test Age Equivalents for the Goodenough-Harris Drawing Scales." *Psychol Sch* 3:271-2 Jl '66. * (*PA* 41:1946)

199. McANINCH, MYRENE. "Body Image as Related to Perceptual-Cognitive-Motor Disabilities," pp. 137–70. In *Learning Disorders, Vol. 2.* Edited by Jerome Hellmuth. Seattle, Wash.: Special Child Publications, 1966. Pp. 422. *

200. MEDINNUS, GENE R.; BOBITT, DIANE; AND HULLETT, JACK. "Effects of Training on the Draw-A-Man Test." *J Exp Ed* 35:62–3 w '66. *

201. PAINTER, GENEVIEVE. "The Effect of a Rhythmic and Sensory Motor Activity Program on Perceptual Motor Spatial Abilities of Kindergarten Children." *Excep Children* 33:113–6 O '66. * (*PA* 41:800)

202. QUAST, WENTWORTH, AND IRETON, HAROLD. "Utility of the Goodenough Draw-A-Man Test as a Screening Device." *Percept & Motor Skills* 23:778 D '66. * (*PA* 41:7328)

203. ROBINSON, H. ALAN. "Reliability of Measures Related to Reading Success of Average, Disadvantaged, and Advan-

taged Kindergarten Children." Comments by Samuel Weintraub. *Read Teach* 20:203–9 D '66. * (*PA* 41:3344)

204. SELLS, S. B. *Evaluation of Psychological Measures Used in the Health Examination Survey of Children Ages 6–11*, pp. 34–53. Public Health Service Publication No. 1000, Series 2, No. 15. Washington, D.C.: United States Government Printing Office, March 1966. Pp. viii, 67. * (*PA* 40: 7217)

205. SILVERSTEIN, A. B. "Anxiety and the Quality of Human Figure Drawings." *Am J Mental Def* 70:607–8 Ja '66. * (*PA* 40:5889)

206. TAUBER, ROSALYN. "Identification of Potential Learning Disabilities." *Acad Ther Q* 2:116–9+ w '66–67. * (*PA* 41: 5004)

207. TAYLOR, JAMES B. "The Use of Human Figure Drawings With the Upper Level Mentally Retarded." *Am J Mental Def* 71:423–6 N '66. * (*PA* 41:1851)

208. WATKINS, DWIGHT G. *A Validity Study of the Goodenough-Harris Drawing Test (GHDT) in a School Setting.* Doctor's thesis, University of Cincinnati (Cincinnati, Ohio), 1966. (*DA* 27:2080A)

209. BRENNER, MAY WOOLF; GILLMAN, SELMA; ZANGWILL, O. L.; AND FARRELL, MARGARET. "Visuo-Motor Disability in School Children." *Brit Med J* 4:259–62 N 4 '67. *

210. BROMWICH, ROSE MEYER. *Some Correlates of Stimulus-Bound Versus Stimulus-Free Verbal Responses to Pictures by Young Negro Boys.* Doctor's thesis, University of California (Los Angeles, Calif.), 1967. (*DA* 28:1290A)

211. DATTA, LOIS-ELLIN. "Draw-A-Person Test as a Measure of Intelligence in Preschool Children From Very Low Income Families." *J Consult Psychol* 31:626–30 D '67. * (*PA* 42: 2561)

212. DUNN, JAMES A. "Inter- and Intra-Rater Reliability of the New Harris-Goodenough Draw-A-Man Test." *Percept & Motor Skills* 24:269–70 F '67. * (*PA* 41:8148)

213. DUNN, JAMES A. "Note on the Relation of Harris' Draw-A-Woman to WISC IQs." *Percept & Motor Skills* 24: 316 F '67. * (*PA* 41:8880)

214. DUNN, JAMES A. "Validity Coefficients for the New Harris-Goodenough Draw-A-Man Test." *Percept & Motor Skills* 24:299–301 F '67. * (*PA* 41:8149)

215. ETUK, ELIZABETH EME SAMSON. *The Development of Number Concepts: An Examination of Piaget's Theory With Yoruba-Speaking Nigerian Children.* Doctor's thesis, Columbia University (New York, N.Y.), 1967. (*DA* 28:1295A)

216. JOHNSON, DALE L.; JOHNSON, CARMEN A.; AND PRICE-WILLIAMS, DOUGLASS. "The Draw-A-Man Test and Raven Progressive Matrices Performance of Guatemalan Maya and Ladino Children." *Revista Interamericana de Psicología* 1:143–57 Je '67. * (*PA* 41:11919)

217. KHATENA, JOE, AND GOWAN, J. C. "Crosscultural Measurement of Intelligence With the DAM and CPM." *Gifted Child Q* 11:227–30 w '67. * (*PA* 42:7111)

218. LEPPKE, RONALD DEAN. *Perceptual Approaches for Disadvantaged Anglo- and Mexican-American Students.* Doctor's thesis, University of the Pacific (Stockton, Calif.), 1967. (*DA* 28:1302A)

219. MARSHALL, ANNE. *The Abilities and Attainments of Children Leaving Junior Training Centres.* London: National Association for Mental Health, 1967. Pp. i, 62. *

220. MASON, ANNE W. "Specific (Developmental) Dyslexia." *Develop Med & Child Neurol* 9:183–90 Ap '67. * (*PA* 41:14066)

221. MONEY, JOHN, AND WANG, CHRISTINE. "Human Figure Drawing: 2, Quality Comparisons in Gender-Identity Anomalies, Klinefelter's Syndrome and Precocious Puberty." *J Nerv & Mental Dis* 144:55–8 Ja '67. * (*PA* 41:12170)

222. MUZEKARI, LOUIS H. "Relationships Between the Goodenough DAM and Stanford-Binet in Negro and White Public School Children." *J Clin Psychol* 23:86–7 Ja '67. * (*PA* 41:6253)

223. OLIVIER, K., AND BARCLAY, A. "Stanford-Binet and Goodenough-Harris Test Performances of Head Start Children." *Psychol Rep* 20:1175–9 Je '67. * (*PA* 41:15275)

224. PANTHER, EDWARD E. "Prediction of First-Grade Reading Achievement." *El Sch J* 68:44–8 O '67. *

225. SAK, HELEN G.; SMITH, ALFRED A.; AND DAVIES, JOSEPH. "Psychometric Evaluation of Children With Familial Dysautonomia." *Am J Psychiatry* 124:682–7 N '67. * (*PA* 42:5959)

226. STEINMAN, WARREN M. "The Use of Ambiguous Stimuli to Predict General Competence." *J Sci Lab Denison Univ* 48:7–14 Je '67. * (*PA* 42:2590)

227. VANE, JULIA R. "An Evaluation of the Harris Revision of the Goodenough Draw-A-Man Test." *J Clin Psychol* 23:375–7 Jl '67. * (*PA* 41:14461)

228. VOGEL, FRANCIS XAVIER. *The Relationship of the Form of School Organization to Selected Classroom Behaviors of Pupils.* Doctor's thesis, Northwestern University (Evanston, Ill.), 1967. (*DA* 28:3957A)

229. WELLS, DONALD G., AND PEDRINI, DUILIO T. "Relationship Between the Stanford-Binet L-M and the Goodenough D-A-M." *Psychol Sch* 4:371–5 O '67. * (*PA* 42:2592)

230. WELLS, DONALD G., AND PEDRINI, DUILIO T. "Relationships Between the S-B L-M, G-H, and PPVT With In-

stitutionalized Retardates." *Am J Mental Def* 72:412–5 N '67. * (*PA* 42:7680)

231. YULE, WILLIAM; LOCKYER, LINDA; AND NOONE, AHILYA. "The Reliability and Validity of the Goodenough-Harris Drawing Test." *Brit J Ed Psychol* 37:110–1 F '67. *

232. ARMSTRONG, JUDITH GLANTZ. *Intellectual Competence and Coping Behavior in Preschool Children.* Doctor's thesis, University of California (Berkeley, Calif.), 1968. (*DA* 29: 4837B)

233. ARTH, ALFRED ARTHUR. *A Study of the Relationship Between Non-Completion and Intelligence Exhibited by Sixth Grade Elementary School Students.* Doctor's thesis, University of Oklahoma (Norman, Okla.), 1968. (*DA* 29:1666A)

234. BACH, LLOYD CARL. *A Comparison of Selected Psychological Tests Used With Trainable Mentally Retarded Children.* Doctor's thesis, University of South Dakota (Vermillion, S.D.), 1968. (*DA* 29:2990A)

235. BATLIN, R., AND KRAFT, IRVIN A. "Psycholinguistic Evaluation of Children Referred for Private Consultation to a Child Psychiatrist." *J Learn Dis* 1:600–5 O '68. * (*PA* 45: 2995)

236. BUCHANAN, BARBARA A. *Adolescent Human Figure Drawings Evaluated by the Goodenough-Harris Scoring Procedure Under Timed and Untimed Conditions.* Master's thesis, Pennsylvania State University (University Park, Pa.), 1968.

237. DE MOREAU, MARGARET, AND KOPPITZ, ELIZABETH M. "Relationship Between Goodenough Draw-A-Man Test IQ Scores and Koppitz Human Figure Drawing Scores." *Revista Interamericana de Psicología* 2:35–40 Mr '68. * (*PA* 42:13753)

238. FINE, MARVIN J., AND TRACY, D. B. "Performance of Normal and EMR Boys on the FRPV and GHDT." *Am J Mental Def* 72:648–52 Mr '68. * (*PA* 42:11049)

239. GADDES, W. H.; McKENZIE, AUDREY; AND BARNSLEY, ROGER. "Psychometric Intelligence and Spatial Imagery in Two Northwest Indian and Two White Groups of Children." *J Social Psychol* 75:35–42 Je '68. * (*PA* 42:13575)

240. GELLERT, ELIZABETH. "Comparison of Children's Self-Drawings With Their Drawings of Other Persons." *Percept & Motor Skills* 26:123–38 F '68. * (*PA* 42:10614)

241. GEORGAS, JAMES G., AND PAPADOPOULOU, ELLIE. "The Harris-Goodenough and the Developmental Form Sequence With Five-Year-Old Greek Children." *Percept & Motor Skills* 26:352–4 Ap '68. * (*PA* 42:11927)

242. HEPBURN, ANDREW W., AND DONNELLY, FRANK. "Psychometric Identification of Kindergarten Children With Visual Perceptual Impairment." *Excep Children* 34:708–9 My '68. *

243. KEOGH, BARBARA K. "The Copying Ability of Young Children." *Ed Res* 11:43–7 N '68. * (*PA* 45:6067)

244. KEOGH, BARBARA K., AND KEOGH, JACK F. "Pattern Walking: A Dimension of Visuomotor Performance." *Excep Children* 34:617–8 Ap '68. * (*PA* 42:17546)

245. KIRSCHNER, FREDERICK ERNST. *A Quasi-Experimental Study Using Human Figure Drawings for Predicting Intellectual Maturity in Kindergarten Children.* Doctor's thesis, University of Toledo (Toledo, Ohio), 1968. (*DA* 29:2566A)

246. KRAFT, MARCIA B. "The Face-Hand Test." *Develop Med & Child Neurol* 10:214–9 Ap '68. * (*PA* 42:13487)

247. KROP, HARRY D. "Education and the Self-Concept of the Mentally Retarded." *Training Sch B* 65:57–64 Ag '68. * (*PA* 44:4045)

248. LEVINE, HAROLD A., AND GROSS, MARILYN. "Suitability of the Harris Revision of the Goodenough Draw-A-Man Test for a Psychiatric Population." *J Clin Psychol* 24:350 Jl '68. * (*PA* 42:16415)

249. LEVY, IRWIN SAUL. *The Effect of Age as a Variable on the Scores of the Harris-Goodenough Drawing Test of Educable Retardates.* Doctor's thesis, University of North Carolina (Chapel Hill, N.C.), 1968. (*DA* 29:2123A)

250. LUONG, CORINA K. MONGCAL. *An Analysis of Factors Related to Difficulties in Learning and Adjustment Among Minority Group Children.* Doctor's thesis, Bryn Mawr College (Bryn Mawr, Pa.), 1968. (*DAI* 30:4795B)

251. McCLELLAN, DORINDA ANN. *Factors Which Are Predictive of Reading Success of Low-Socio-Economic Children in Selected First Grades.* Doctor's thesis, Oklahoma State University (Stillwater, Okla.), 1968. (*DAI* 30:933A)

252. MIEZITIS, SOLVEIGA AUSMA. *An Exploratory Study of Divergent Production in Preschoolers.* Doctor's thesis, University of Toronto (Toronto, Ont., Canada), 1968. (*DAI* 30: 589A)

253. MILLICHAP, J. GORDON; AYMAT, FERNANDO; STURGIS, LORETTA H.; LARSEN, KATHERINE W.; AND EGAN, ROSEMARY A. "Hyperkinetic Behavior and Learning Disorders: 3, Battery of Neuropsychological Tests in Controlled Trial of Methylphenidate." *Am J Dis Children* 116:235–44 S '68. * (*PA* 43:4123)

254. RAWL, MIRIAM FREEMAN. *A Study of the Relationship of Verbal Ability and Vocalization to Conceptual-Motor Tasks in Disadvantaged First-Grade Children.* Doctor's thesis, University of South Carolina (Columbia, S.C.), 1968. (*DAI* 30: 1028A)

255. ROBERTON, MARY ANN. *The Ability of Children Three, Five, and Seven Years of Age to Imitate Body Positions.* Master's thesis, University of California (Berkeley, Calif.), 1968.

256. ROBINSON, H. ALAN, AND HANSON, EARL. "Reliability

of Measures of Reading Achievement." *Read Teach* 21:307–13+ Ja '68. * (*PA* 42:17652)

257. STERNLOF, R. E.; PARKER, H. J.; AND McCOY, J. F. "Relationships Between the Goodenough DAM Test and the Columbia Mental Maturity Test for Negro and White Head-start Children." *Percept & Motor Skills* 27:424–6 O '68. *

258. STRÜMPFER, D. J. W., AND HUYSAMEN, G. K. "Correlates of the Communication Organ Score on the Harris-Goodenough Drawing Test." *J Indiv Psychol* 24:60–2 My '68. * (*PA* 42:12133)

259. STRÜMPFER, D. J. W., AND MIENIE, C. J. P. "A Validation of the Harris-Goodenough Test." *Brit J Ed Psychol* 38:96–100 F '68. * (*PA* 42:12134)

260. SUNDBERG, NORMAN, AND BALLINGER, THOMAS. "Nepalese Children's Cognitive Development as Revealed by Drawings of Man, Woman, and Self." *Child Develop* 39:969–85 S '68. * (*PA* 43:3765)

261. THOMPSON, CHARLES WILMER. *The Harris-Goodenough Draw-A-Man Test as a Predictor of Intelligence With Suspected Educable Retardates.* Doctor's thesis, University of North Carolina (Chapel Hill, N.C.), 1968. (*DA* 29:4339A)

262. BERKOWITZ, MICHAEL C. *A Revised Goodenough Draw-A-Man Test as a Measure of School Readiness.* Master's thesis, Kansas State Teachers College (Emporia, Kan.), 1969.

263. BEVAN, WILTSHIRE E., AND GRAY, JOHN E. "Draw-A-Man and Raven's Progressive Matrices (1938) Intelligence Test Performance of Reserve Indian Children." *Can J Behav Sci* 1(2):119–22 Ap '69. * (*PA* 44:12604)

264. BYRD, COLEEN, AND SPRINGFIELD, LYNN. "A Note on the Draw-A-Person Test With Adolescent Retardates." *Am J Mental Def* 73(4):578–9 Ja '69. * (*PA* 43:8571)

265. CAMPBELL, HENRY E. *The Influence of Motivation on Goodenough-Harris Intelligence Test Scores.* Master's thesis, Jersey City State College (Jersey City, N.J.), 1969.

266. DOKECKI, PAUL R.; FREDE, MARTHA C.; AND GAUTNEY, DONALD B. "Criterion, Construct, and Predictive Validities of the Wechsler Preschool and Primary Scale of Intelligence." Abstract. *Proc 77th Ann Conv Am Psychol Assn* 4(2):505–6 '69. * (*PA* 44:1253)

267. DUDEK, S. Z.; GOLDBERG, J. S.; LESTER, E. P.; AND HARRIS, B. R. "The Validity of Cognitive, Perceptual-Motor and Personality Variables for Prediction of Achievement in Grade 1 and Grade 2." *J Clin Psychol* 25(2):165–70 Ap '69. * (*PA* 43:14874)

268. HALL, JOSEPH CLARENCE. *A Comparative Study of Selected Measures of Intelligence as Predictors of First-Grade Reading Achievement in a Culturally Disadvantaged Population.* Doctor's thesis, Temple University (Philadelphia, Pa.), 1969. (*DAI* 31:1074A)

269. HENDERSON, NORMAN B.; GOFFENEY, BARBARA; AND BUTLER, BRUCE V. "Do Negro Children Project a Self-Image of Helplessness and Inadequacy in Drawing a Person?" Abstract. *Proc 77th Ann Conv Am Psychol Assn* 4(1):437–8 '69. * (*PA* 43:17226)

270. MALONEY, MICHAEL P., AND PAYNE, LAWRENCE E. "Validity of the Draw-A-Person Test as a Measure of Body Image." *Percept & Motor Skills* 29(1):119–22 Ag '69. * (*PA* 44:2366)

271. MINSKY, RAPHAEL. *An Investigation Into Children's Conceptualization of Proportionality as Expressed in Their Drawings of the Male Human Figure.* Doctor's thesis, University of Maryland (College Park, Md.), 1969. (*DAI* 31:1082A)

272. NASE, ROBERT R. *A Correlation Study of the Harris-Goodenough Draw-A-Man and the Wechsler Preschool and Primary Scale of Intelligence With Children Referred for Psychological Testing.* Master's thesis, Mankato State College (Mankato, Minn.), 1969.

273. NIELSEN, HELLE H., AND RINGE, KIRSTEN. "Visuo-Perceptive and Visuo-Motor Performance of Children With Reading Disabilities." *Scandinavian J Psychol* 10(4):225–31 '69. * (*PA* 44:9351)

274. ROCHE, DERMOT, AND ROCHE, P. J. D. "A Validity Study of the Goodenough-Harris Draw-A-Man Test." Abstract. *B Brit Psychol Soc* 22(76):215–6 Jl '69. *

275. VROEGH, KAREN, AND HANDRICH, MILLICENT. "The Validity of the Howard Maze Test as a Measure of Stimulus-Seeking in Preschool Children." *Ed & Psychol Meas* 29(2):495–502 su '69. * (*PA* 44:16395)

276. WATSON, BILLY LESLIE. *Field Dependence and Early Reading Achievement.* Doctor's thesis, University of California (Los Angeles, Calif.), 1969. (*DAI* 31:656A)

277. YATER, ALLAN C.; BARCLAY, ALLAN G.; AND McGILLIGAN, ROBERT. "Inter-Rater Reliability of Scoring Goodenough-Harris Drawings by Disadvantaged Preschool Children." *Percept & Motor Skills* 28(1):281–2 F '69. * (*PA* 43:11364)

278. YEN, SHERMAN M. Y. *A Comparative Study of Test Variability With Peabody Picture Vocabulary Test, Goodenough's Draw-A-Man Test, and Stanford-Binet Intelligence Scale as Intellectual Measurement With a Group of Urban Low Socio-Economic Status Pre-School Pupils.* Doctor's thesis, Catholic University of America (Washington, D.C.), 1969. (*DAI* 30:2625A)

279. CARLSON, JERRY S. "A Note on the Relationships Between the Draw-A-Man Test, the Progressive Matrices Test, and Conservation." *J Psychol* 74(2):231–5 Mr '70. * (*PA* 44:12310)

280. CUNDICK, BERT P. "Measures of Intelligence on Southwest Indian Students." *J Social Psychol* 81(2):151–6 Ag '70. * (*PA* 44:20655)

281. EYSENCK, SYBIL B. G.; RUSSELL, T.; AND EYSENCK, H. J. "Extraversion, Intelligence, and Ability to Draw a Person." *Percept & Motor Skills* 30(3):925–6 Je '70. * (*PA* 44:16371)

282. GAYTON, WILLIAM F. "Validity of the Harris Quality Scale With a Child Guidance Population." *Percept & Motor Skills* 31(1):17–8 Ag '70. * (*PA* 45:4532)

283. GAYTON, WILLIAM F.; BASSETT, JOHN E.; AND BISHOP, JOHN S. "The Harris Revision of the Goodenough Draw-A-Man Test: Suitability for a Retarded Population." *J Clin Psychol* 26(4):522–3 O '70. * (*PA* 45:4790)

284. HARCKHAM, LAURA D. *Prediction of Reading Achievement in Grades One, Two, Three, and Four Using Kindergarten Measures.* Doctor's thesis, Fordham University (New York, N.Y.), 1970. (*DAI* 31:3266A)

285. HARMAN, CHARLES E., AND RAYMOND, CHRISTOPHER S. "Computer Prediction of Chronic Psychiatric Patients." *J Nerv & Mental Dis* 150(6):490–503 Je '70. * (*PA* 45:8497)

286. INGRAM, T. T. S.; MASON, A. W.; AND BLACKBURN, I. "A Retrospective Study of 82 Children With Reading Disability." *Develop Med & Child Neurol* 12(3):271–81 Je '70. *

287. MERZ, WILLIAM ROBERT, SR. *A Factor Analysis of the Goodenough-Harris Drawing Test Across Four Ethnic Groups.* Doctor's thesis, University of New Mexico (Albuquerque, N.M.), 1970. (*DAI* 31:1627A)

288. NASH, HARVEY, AND HARRIS, DALE B. "Body Proportions in Children's Drawings of a Man." *J Genetic Psychol* 117(1):85–90 S '70. * (*PA* 45:2181)

289. PETRIE, RONALD GENE. *A Comparison of Verbal Responses of Anglo-Migrant and Anglo-Resident Children.* Doctor's thesis, Oregon State University (Corvallis, Ore.), 1970. (*DAI* 31:3181A)

290. ROCHE, DERMOT. "On the Concurrent Validity of the Goodenough-Harris Draw-A-Person Test." *Papers Psychol* 4(1–2):5–7 Ap–O '70. *

291. SAUNDERS, MAUDERIE HANCOCK, AND TESKA, PERCY T. "An Analysis of Cultural Differences on Certain Projective Techniques." *J Negro Ed* 39(2):109–15 sp '70. *

292. SINHA, M. "A Study of the Harris Revision of the Goodenough Draw-A-Man Test." Thesis abstract. *Brit J Ed Psychol* 40(2):221–2 Je '70. *

293. SPADAFORE, GERALD JOSEPH. *Differences in Learning Between Retardates and Nonretardates on the Draw-A-Man Test.* Doctor's thesis, University of Nebraska (Lincoln, Neb.), 1970. (*DAI* 31:1633A)

294. WERNER, EMMY E., AND MURALIDHARAN, RAJALAKSHMI. "Nutrition, Cognitive Status and Achievement Motivation of New Delhi Nursery School Children." *J Cross-Cultural Psychol* 1(3):271–81 S '70. * (*PA* 45:3803)

295. WILLIAMS, BARBARA KATHLEEN. *The Goodenough-Harris Draw-A-Man Test and Reflection-Impulsivity.* Master's thesis, University of Alberta (Edmonton, Alta., Canada), 1970.

ANNE ANASTASI, *Professor of Psychology and Chairman of the Department, Fordham University, New York, New York.*

Development of this revision and extension of the Goodenough Draw-A-Man test is described in detail in Harris' *Children's Drawings as Measures of Intellectual Maturity* (*135*). Part 2 of this book is reproduced in toto as a separately published manual for the convenience of test users. This manual, however, is concerned exclusively with instructions for administration, scoring, and use of norms. For any information on the construction and technical properties of the test, one must consult the original book, which also provides a comprehensive literature survey of the psychology of children's drawings, covering both empirical and theoretical publications and including the use of drawings not only as cognitive indicators but also as projective personality devices. Research on the Draw-A-Man, beginning with its first appearance in 1926, is reviewed in detail.

Like the original test, the present revision focuses on the child's accuracy of observation and on the development of conceptual thinking, rather than on artistic skill. The number of scorable items or points has been increased from 51 to 73. These items were selected from a pool of about 100 on the basis of age differentiation, relation to total scores on the provisional form, and relation to group intelligence test scores. Data for this purpose were obtained from 50 boys and 50 girls at each year of age from 6 to 15 years, drawn from a larger sample tested in rural and urban areas of Minnesota and Wisconsin and representative of the national distribution with regard to paternal occupation. The manual gives detailed instructions, with illustrations, for scoring the 73 points on an all-or-none basis. Raw scores are converted to standard scores with a mean of 100 and a standard deviation of 15. Norms were established on a new standardization sample of 2,975 children between the ages of 5 and 15 years, representative of the occupational distribution of the U.S. in 1950, and distributed among four major geographical areas. A table is provided for converting the standard scores to percentiles, although the limitations of percentile scores are noted and the use of standard scores is recommended.

In the present version of the test, the subject is also asked to draw a picture of a woman and of himself, in that order. The Woman scale is scored in terms of 71 items selected by the same procedures followed in developing the Man scale. Because the correlation of the Woman scale with the Man scale is about as high as the odd-even reliability of either scale alone, Harris recommends that their standard scores be averaged for higher reliability. The Self scale was included as a possible projective test of personality, but available findings from this application are not promising. Currently, the manual provides a qualitative checklist for assessing performance on this scale and comparing the Self drawing with the other two drawings. This checklist is presented as a subjective and thus far untested guide. It is also suggested that the Self scale be scored on the points of the Man or Woman scale (depending upon the subject's sex) and a standard score found from the corresponding normative table. The Self scale is offered principally as a device for further research.

In the new scale, as in the earlier version,

scorer reliabilities are usually over .90. In part, such interscorer agreement reflects the fullness of the scoring instructions and the care exercised in selecting items that can be scored with a minimum of uncertainty. Split-half reliabilities, found on the earlier form, are in the .70's and .80's. Retest reliabilities obtained with the earlier form over intervals as long as three months fall mostly in the .60's and .70's. Short-term fluctuations in performance are negligible as indicated by a study of the scores obtained on the revised form by kindergarten children given the test on each of ten consecutive school days. Examiner variance has proved insignificant, as has the effect of art training in school upon test scores. Judged artistic merit of the drawings, moreover, bears little or no relation to the point scores assigned to the drawings. Scores in the revised Man scale correspond closely to those obtained with the original version, the correlations ranging from .91 to .98 in homogeneous age groups.

An alternative way of evaluating performance on both Man and Woman scales utilizes the Quality scales. These scales substitute a simplified, global, qualitative assessment of the entire drawing for the detailed point scoring. The scorer simply chooses one of twelve sample drawings that most closely matches the performance level of the subject's product and assigns the scale value of that sample to the drawing. A separate quality scale is provided for the Man and Woman drawings. The scale drawings were selected by having judges assign specimen drawings to categories by the method of equal-appearing intervals, the specific procedures being quite similar to those followed by Thurstone in developing attitude scales. Interscorer reliabilities of the Quality scales are mostly in the .80's. Correlations of standard scores derived from Quality scale ratings and from point scores cluster closely in the .80's but tend to be lower at the upper ages. The Quality scales also show less age differentiation than the point scales at the upper ages.

Harris summarizes correlations obtained between the earlier Draw-A-Man test and the Stanford-Binet, WISC, WAIS, PMA, and a few other intelligence and special aptitude tests. Nearly all these correlations are significant and most are substantial. It should be noted, however, that several correlations between MA's of children ranging widely in age are cited with the sole comment that "As would be expected,

MA scores correlate more highly than IQ scores" (p. 99). The reader is not cautioned that these correlations are spuriously high and had better be ignored. The principal evidence for the validity of the test, of course, derives from the item analysis procedures followed in developing the scales. The effectiveness of the age differentiation criterion employed in item selection is reflected in the consistent and sharp rises in mean raw point scores between ages 5 and 14. From age 14 to 15 there is a decided leveling off in the scores of both sexes on both Man and Woman scales.

In summary, the original Draw-A-Man test has been updated, extended, and restandardized; the crude ratio IQ has been replaced with standard scores; and a parallel form has been developed in the Woman scale. Efforts to extend the scale chronologically into the adolescent years have failed. On theoretical grounds, Harris proposes that the child's drawings reveal his conceptual maturity but cease to show increments when the child moves from concrete concepts to higher-order abstractions and turns increasingly to more practiced and more suitable verbal modes of expression. Attempts to utilize children's drawings as a projective technique for the assessment of personality characteristics likewise proved fruitless. Both the specific research with the present drawing test and an analysis of the published literature on children's drawings led Harris to conclude that "consistent and reliable patterns having diagnostic significance for personality probably cannot be found in children's drawings" and that such drawings "primarily express cognitive processes."

JAMES A. DUNN, *Director, Developmental Systems Division, American Institutes for Research, Palo Alto, California.*

The Draw-A-Man test was originally published in 1926 by Florence Goodenough. Since that time it has enjoyed widespread popularity. Twenty years after its introduction, Louttit and Browne found it was the third most frequently used test in clinical psychology. Fifteen years later, in 1961, Sundberg found it still in the "top ten." This record is especially impressive considering that the instrument is appropriate for use only with children.

The test calls for the child to "make a picture of a man." This is a simple task which seldom takes more than five or ten minutes to admin-

ister. It may be administered either individually or to groups. If it is administered individually, it is often given as the first test in a battery because it is nonthreatening, quick, and often elicits interesting comments on the part of the subject. Scoring time is also on the order of ten minutes.

In 1963 Harris (*135*) published the results of an extensive revision of the Draw-A-Man test. First, Harris extensively redeveloped the Goodenough scoring criteria on a highly objective, empirical basis. (Anyone who has used the old version of the Goodenough readily appreciates the increased specificity that Harris brings to the scoring of the test.) Second, Harris devoted extensive effort to a new standardization of the test (the quality of the standardization far exceeds that of the original). Third, Harris converted the IQ computation from the old mental age/chronological age ratio concept to the deviation IQ concept. Fourth, Harris introduced a companion Draw-A-Woman test. Finally, Harris introduced a drawing quality score.

In addition to material improvement in the Draw-A-Man test (it should add another 20 years of life to the Goodenough procedure, even at today's obsolescence rate), Harris has given us an excellent review of the use of children's drawings as measures of intelligence and an example of scientific caution in making generalizations as to the effectiveness of the use of children's drawings in personality assessment.

It is at this point that the first criticism of the *Goodenough-Harris Drawing Test* can be made. Anyone contemplating using the test should not buy the examiner's kit alone. The manual provided is for administration and scoring only. It is not a manual in the sense of the *Standards for Educational and Psychological Tests and Manuals.* Thus, from a technical professional point of view, the manual is inadequate. Considerations of scale development, standardization, reliability, and validity are treated in part one of Harris's book, *Children's Drawings as a Measure of Intellectual Maturity,* rather than in the administration manual. To be sure, the manual cites the book and refers to it as the "basic reference for the use of the test," but it is this reviewer's opinion that the case for purchasing the book and considering *it* as the actual manual is not made forcefully enough.

There is one major problem that bothers this

reviewer: the manner in which reliability and validity for the new scales were handled. The case for the reliability and validity of the Drawing Test scales rests with their obvious similarity to the 1926 test. Harris' 1963 book refers almost exclusively to 1926 Draw-A-Man reliabilities and validities. The manual cites only one study, involving four small samples of 75 subjects each, in which the interscorer reliabilities for the new scales are reported; and only one study, on Canadian-Indian children, which reports correlations between the 1926 scale and the 1963 scale. These latter correlations are on the order of .91 to .98, the same range as for correlations between scorings of the same protocols by independent scorers.

While there is a lack of information about test-retest reliability and correlations with other IQ tests for the new scales, there is no lack of comparable information reported for the Goodenough Draw-A-Man. Harris very systematically, and conscientiously, reports these. Test-retest reliabilities are on the order of .60 to .70. Interscorer reliabilities are on the order of .80 to .96 and correlations with the Stanford-Binet are on the order of .36 to .65 (Goodenough reported correlations with the Binet on the order of .74).

No correlations with academic achievement were offered in *Children's Drawings* for either the 1926 or 1963 scales.

In short, in view of the excellent standardization of the new scales on 2,975 children "representative of the occupational distribution of the U.S. in 1950," one cannot help but wish that, at the same time, data offering comprehensive validation had been collected. Similarly, in view of the scholarship reflected in *Children's Drawings,* this reviewer also wishes that Harris had found time to include a capstone chapter in which to summarize his views on the theoretical relevance of the Draw-A-Man test, to discuss its implications for future conceptualizations of intelligence, and to comment on its relationship to such other instruments as the Binet, the Bender-Gestalt, and perhaps the Raven Matrices.

All things considered, this reviewer has used the Goodenough-Harris scale in the past, he will use it in the future, and he commends it to others for their use. It is hoped, however, that users of the scale will reflect seriously upon the sober, cautious, scientifically oriented interpretations offered by Harris in his book and consider them as models for their own behavior.

Brit J Ed Psychol 34:338 N '64. M. L. Kellmer Pringle. [Review of *Children's Drawings as Measures of Intellectual Maturity (135).*] * avowedly the work of a disciple rather than of a critic. The author has most ably met one of his aims, namely "to present a comprehensive survey of the literature on children's drawings in this country and abroad." * Since the presentation of past studies is, moreover, detailed enough to enable the researcher to make his own critical assessment, it is perhaps unreasonable to wish that the author had been more stringent in his evaluation of research designs, statistical methods and conclusions reached. It is probably more justified to regret that there are no suggestions for further research; for example, one would have thought there is a need for longitudinal studies of these revised and extended scales, all the more so in view of the lack of such studies with regard to Goodenough's original test. These criticisms, however, do not seriously detract from the great value of the book to the student of children's drawings, for whom it is likely to become a major source book. * Since the book provides both a comprehensive review of children's drawings and a fully illustrated and well-produced handbook for the revised and extended Draw-a-Man Test, its rather high cost seems justified.

Cont Psychol 11:28+ Ja '66. Marjorie P. Honzik. [Review of *Children's Drawings as Measures of Intellectual Maturity (135).*] This is a good book. Developmental and clinical psychologists may assign it to students without qualm or qualification. Its merits lie in the value of children's drawings in understanding cognitive development, in the comprehensive coverage of the literature and in the fact that it is theoretically eclectic and written with extraordinary care and thoughtfulness. * Goodenough wrote the first book on the *Measurement of Intelligence by Drawings* in 1926. For almost forty years Goodenough's volume has been in continuous use. Harris's book brings the technique up-to-date with alternate forms, a more exact method of scoring, and new norms based on a well selected sampling of children. Harris clearly and repeatedly points out that the "Draw-a-Man-Test" is primarily a test of conceptual and intellectual maturity. * This test yields many valuable and fascinating findings. *

The only criticism of this book is that it does not always convey the excitement inherent in a medium that can be used to assess individuality from the first to the last year of life. Here is a test that is pleasurable to the testee at most ages, takes relatively little time, yet yields estimates of cognitive development, can indicate brain impairment, and has been employed extensively as a personality and projective test. The fact that correlations have been low between drawings' scores and personality characteristics is not surprising. A drawing is a small sample of the child's creativity and there are no easily available truly comprehensive and valid measures of a child's personality. * Harris's book is basic and we are grateful to him for its excellence, but there is more gold in this mine of drawings, and it should stimulate further active research. We now need even more ideas, new perspectives and methods of analysis and, most of all, increasing sensitivity to this method of communication.

Ed & Psychol Meas 25:636–7 su '65. Carol Hunter. [Review of *Children's Drawings as Measures of Intellectual Maturity (135).*] * For the purposes of the school psychologist the "Quality" scale shows promise. One of the prime roles of schools today is prevention of school maladjustment. The Goodenough-Harris Drawing Test should be easily integrated with other screening tests into a battery which can be used to select children who should receive more detailed attention. Children can be quickly arranged in order of intellectual maturity in kindergarten and first grades when no group mental maturity test data are available. * School psychologists should find the Goodenough-Harris Drawing Test useful in screening primary children. Clinical psychologists should find the information provocative. One may hope that the ingenuity of psychologists is taxed in formulating experiments based on theories in order to clarify some of the issues which the author discussed.

J Proj Tech & Pers Assess 28:499–500 D '64. Adolph G. Woltmann. [Review of *Children's Drawings as Measures of Intellectual Maturity (135).*] Psychologists in the 1930's and 1940's used the Goodenough "Draw A Man" test as a very important addition to their test batteries for children. This simple, nonverbal test yielded an I.Q. which correlated closely with the Stanford Binet Measurement of Intelligence. Post War psychology saw the emergence of "projective tests." The intelligence quotient yielding "Draw A Man" test....published in 1926....became less prominent * Harris has rescued this test from falling into oblivion. This alone should earn him the gratitude of the psychological profession. Yet, he has done more than merely revising and bringing up to date the pioneer research of Florence Goodenough. He extended the original number of scorable items from 51 points to 73 points. He also worked out an analogous point scale for the drawing of a woman which contains 71 scorable items. He further added a "drawing of the self," reasoning that this would make possible a more valid projective device for the study of the emerging self concept. Goodenough's scoring instructions were purely descriptive. Harris supplemented this with numerous illustrations which show graphically what to score and what not. * Aside from the fact that Dr. Harris used more representative samples than were available to Goodenough in the early 1920's, he subjected his data to a painstaking statistical analysis which included, among other means of verification and validity, extensive retesting, agreements among independent judges and correlating his collected material statistically with other well known tests of intelligence. This book contains other features which make it a "must reading" for psychologists, regardless of whether they approach childhood academically or are engaged in the human interaction of clinical practice. * Post War psychologists, trained in the "projective hypothesis," may take issue with Harris' chapter on "Clinical and Projective Use of Children's Drawings." They may feel that the author is not sympathetic towards the large body of research papers that have accumulated in this area. Hammer's book on *The Clinical Application of Projective Drawings,* which contains a very comprehensive bibliography on the projective use of children's drawings up to 1957, is not mentioned although it was published 5 years prior to the volume under review. * Harris approaches his topic with the true spirit of the researcher. The original "Draw A Man" test contained 192 references. He retained 40 of these and added 426 references about studies published since 1926. The total bibliography of 466 entries comprises all that has been written about children's art in regard to theory, practice, application and statistical treatment. The book is highly recommended to all who, in one way or another, have contact with children, whether they be psychiatrists, psychologists, teachers or social workers. Researchers should find this well-printed and easily read book a gold mine for clues towards formulating new hypotheses. Dr. Harris is to be congratulated for having combined, in one volume, the revision of a test which has proven its worth and whose soundness in design and thinking will prevail. The profession is indebted to him for having tackled courageously, clarified and delineated this important aspect of child development.

Personnel & Guid J 43:830–1 Ap '65. Marvin S. Kaplan. [Review of *Children's Drawings as Measures of Intellectual Maturity* (135).] * this book....has much to recommend it beyond the presentation of a revised version of a useful test instrument. The book should be of great interest to anybody wishing to learn more about the literature, investigations and theories regarding children's thinking processes particularly as expressed through drawings. Harris comprehensively reviews the investigations regarding the projective uses of children's drawings and concludes that they have limited value in this regard. * Despite this quite skeptical conclusion regarding the use of children's drawings as measures of personality, Harris, as is the case with many of us, seems unable quite to accept the situation, i.e., that the drawing test evaluates primarily the ability to form concepts. He goes on to present us with a Guide for the Analysis of Self-Drawings. The Guide suggests the analysis of apparently idiosyncratic features and comparison with the like-sex and opposite-sex adult figures. He believes, however, that meaningful interpretations will be fairly obvious, "close to the surface" and interpretation does not require an elaborate theory of symbolism. * This is not only a much needed revision of the 1926 Goodenough Draw-A-Man Test but it is also a scholarly, comprehensive, carefully done survey of the literature on children's drawings. The test itself will be most useful to those working with elementary age children and will have only a limited applicability beyond the grade school level. The review of the literature and the theory should be fascinating to all who work with children and are interested in their thought processes.

Studies Art Ed 6:49–51 au '64. Mary J. Rouse. [Review of *Children's Drawings as Measures of Intellectual Maturity* (135).] * Harris' modest claim for his book is that it

is only an attempt to restandardize Florence Goodenough's earlier version of the "Draw-a-Man" test. Harris....has accomplished his task with efficiency. This, however, is not the whole story. Happily for art educators, his efforts have gone far beyond the minimum required for a test revision. For, along with the restandardization materials, he has included chapters which form the most interesting and complete compilation of research on children's drawings that this reviewer has yet seen. This collection is of such importance that every serious student of graphic expression must inevitably place Harris' book on his "required reading" list. These informative chapters cover several different, but related, topics: a historical survey of research studies concerning drawing which begins with information first published in 1885; a discussion of the non-intellective and cultural influences on graphic expression; a chapter that includes an exceedingly rich store of empirical studies; another that discusses every reputable drawing theory extant; and finally, a chapter that goes beyond the narrow confines of "drawing" and delves into the broader aspects of child art in general. Of interest, also, is the section containing the conclusions which Mr. Harris draws from the empirical evidence he has assembled. From the point of view of an art educator, one of the most important of these is his discussion of the three major stages which he believes occur in most children's drawings. * Harris' continued emphasis of the fundamental importance of the cognitive in shaping the child's drawing behavior may seem confusing to the teacher who has been trained to believe that only "self-expression" was of value to the younger child and that harmful effects would undoubtedly result from the imposition of any kind of cognitive training in art activities. His reasoning, however, based as it is on existing evidence, seems logical to this reviewer, who has long wondered why children could be (and indeed, must be) "trained" in every other area of the school curriculum but never, never, in ours. It seems clearly consistent with current psychological knowledge to suppose that the child can be helped to build up a "vocabulary" of visually-oriented concepts which he can utilize later, just as he can be helped to build a repertory of words which he will use later for more advanced purposes. Similarly, it seems logical to suppose that if the child does *not* build these kinds of concepts, he will not draw later, just as he will not read or write adequately (and creatively) if he has not had sufficient prior experience in reading and writing words. Mr. Harris' discussion of these three stages and their consequents could be regarded as a mandate for considerable restructuring of art education curricula. His conclusions suggest that the emphasis in the elementary grades ought to be on the development of enriched visually-oriented concepts in the child, with attention given to helping him to organize and communicate them more efficiently. Provided with such a rich foundation, the program in the secondary grades might then emphasize the aesthetic and expressive. * Harris discusses and compares the perceptual theories which have application to our understanding of graphic behavior, describing the Gestalt, the Organismic, and the Empiricist schools in a concise manner. * In summary, this book offers a wealth of invaluable information to the art educator who believes that educational objectives and philosophies must be formulated on the basis of empirical evidence. And, whether one agrees with them or not, Mr. Harris' own conclusions which he draws from this information are fresh and provocative. We must compliment him on his efforts, and hope that others in our field will act upon the stimulating and challenging leads which he has provided for us.

For a review by Naomi Stewart of the original edition, see 4:292.

[353]

*The Graduate Record Examinations Aptitude Test. Graduate school candidates; 1949–70; GREAT; 2 scores: verbal, quantitative; 8 current forms ('65–70, 32–40 pages) ; for more complete information, see 667; 180(200) minutes; Educational Testing Service. *

REFERENCES

1–2. See 4:293.
3–9. See 5:336.
10–26. See 6:461.
27. BAILLIE, GORDON STUART. *An Investigation of Objective Admission Variables as They Relate to Academic and Job Success in One Graduate Library Education Program.* Doctor's thesis, Washington University (St. Louis, Mo.), 1961. (*DA* 22:2804)
28. JOHNSON, BOBBY GENE. *The Prediction of Success in the Doctoral Program in the College of Education at the University of Houston on the Basis of Objective Test Scores and Quality-Point Averages.* Doctor's thesis, University of Houston (Houston, Tex.), 1963. (*DA* 24:4066)
29. TULLY, G. EMERSON, AND KING, F. J. "Comparative Performance of Florida Teachers on the Common Examinations of the National Teacher Examinations and the Aptitude Test of the Graduate Record Examinations." *Fla J Ed Res* 5:41–6 Ja '63. *
30. ZIMMERMAN, WILLIAM GEORGE, JR. *An Analysis of Selected Aspects of the Master of Education Program at the University of Miami.* Doctor's thesis, University of Miami (Coral Gables, Fla.), 1963. (*DA* 28:95A)
31. BURDICK, LOIS A. *Academic Performance of Graduate Students at Indiana State University as Related to the Graduate Record Examination Results.* Master's thesis, Indiana State College (Terre Haute, Ind.), 1964. (Abstract: *Teach Col J* 36:217–8)

32. NICHOLS, ROBERT C. "Effects of Various College Characteristics on Student Aptitude Test Scores." *J Ed Psychol* 55:45–54 F '64. * (*PA* 38:9269)
33. PONIATOWSKI, ROBERT A. *A Study of the Predictive Value of the Graduate Record Examination Aptitude Tests and Success in the Graduate Division of Rhode Island College.* Master's thesis, Rhode Island College (Providence, R.I.), 1964.
34. ROBERTSON, MALCOLM, AND HALL, EVERETT. "Predicting Success in Graduate Study." *J General Psychol* 71:359–65 O '64. * (*PA* 39:5997)
35. CREAGER, JOHN A. *Predicting Doctorate Attainment With GRE and Other Variables.* Technical Report No. 25. Washington, D.C.: National Academy of Sciences—National Research Council, November 1965. Pp. iv, 48. *
36. ELTON, CHARLES F. "The Use and Abuse of the Graduate Record Examination Area Tests." *Psychol Sch* 2:245–9 Jl '65. *
37. MADAUS, GEORGE F., AND WALSH, JOHN J. "Departmental Differentials in the Predictive Validity of the Graduate Record Examination Aptitude Tests." *Ed & Psychol Meas* 25:1105–10 w '65. * (*PA* 40:3580)
38. MOGHRABI, KAMEL M. *An Analysis of Factors That Influence the Degree of Success or Failure of Foreign Students at Texas A & M University.* Doctor's thesis, Texas A & M University (College Station, Tex.), 1966. (*DA* 27:3232A)
39. PALMER, ROBERT H. *A Statistical Analysis of the Graduate Record Examination and the Miller Analogies Test for Predicting Success in Graduate School at East Tennessee State University.* Master's thesis, East Tennessee State University (Johnson City, Tenn.), 1966.
40. RINDONE, RONALD. *Relationship of Graduate Aptitude Test Scores to Achievement in Industrial Arts.* Master's thesis, California State College (Long Beach, Calif.), 1966.
41. TUCKER, HARMON. *A Statistical Study to Determine the Relationship Between Scores of the Cooperative English Test and the Aptitude Sections of the Graduate Record Examinations.* Master's thesis, Stetson University (DeLand, Fla.), 1966.
42. BREIMEIER, KENNETH H. *Relationship Between Various Psychological Measures in Use at Theological Seminaries.* Comments by James E. Dittes. Occasional Papers No. 1. Washington, D.C.: Ministry Studies Board, 1967. Pp. iii, 59. *
43. CURETON, EDWARD E., AND SCOTT, THOMAS B. "Equivalent Scores for the Graduate Record Verbal and Miller Analogies Tests." *Ed & Psychol Meas* 27:611–5 au '67. * (*PA* 42:122)
44. STRICKER, GEORGE, AND HUBER, J. T. "The Graduate Record Examination and Undergraduate Grades as Predictors of Success in Graduate School." *J Ed Res* 60:466–8 Jl–Ag '67. *
45. WHITE, GORDON W. *A Predictive Validity Study of the Graduate Records Examinations Aptitude Test at the University of Iowa.* Master's thesis, University of Iowa (Iowa City, Iowa), 1967.
46. WHITELEY, JOHN M.; SPRINTHALL, NORMAN A.; MOSHER, RALPH L.; AND DONAGHY, ROLLA T. "Selection and Evaluation of Counselor Effectiveness." *J Counsel Psychol* 14:226–34 My '67. * (*PA* 41:9423)
47. ALEXAKOS, CONSTANTINE E. "The Graduate Record Examination: Aptitude Tests as Screening Devices for Students in the College of Human Resources and Education, West Virginia University." *Col & Univ* 43:342–7 sp '68. *
48. CARBONARI, JOSEPH PHILLIP, JR. *An Investigation of Residual Gain and Its Correlates.* Doctor's thesis, Northern Illinois University (DeKalb, Ill.), 1968. (*DA* 29:2559A)
49. COLVIN, GERALD FRANKLIN. *The Value of Selected Variables in Predicting Academic Success in Graduate Education at the University of Arkansas.* Doctor's thesis, University of Arkansas (Fayetteville, Ark.), 1968. (*DA* 29:55A)
50. NEWMAN, RICHARD I. "GRE Scores as Predictors of GPA for Psychology Graduate Students." *Ed & Psychol Meas* 28:433–6 su '68. * (*PA* 42:10277)
51. RICHTER, WALTER R. *The Graduate Record Examinations Aptitude Test and Success in Graduate Study in Business at San Diego State College.* Master's thesis, San Diego State College (San Diego, Calif.), 1968.
52. TOOKEY, MARY D. "Fathers' Occupations as Related to GRE Aptitude Test Scores of Eureka College Students." *Ill Sch Res* 4:22–6 My '68. *
53. WIGGINS, NANCY; BLACKBURN, MARGARET; AND HACKMAN, J. RICHARD. "Prediction of First-Year Graduate Success in Psychology." Abstract. *Proc 76th Ann Conv Am Psychol Assn* 3:237–8 '68. *
54. CHIMONIDES, STELIOS GEORGIOU. *Some Relationships Associated With Academic Success in Graduate Work at a Midwestern University.* Master's thesis, Western Michigan University (Kalamazoo, Mich.), 1969. (*Masters Abstracts* 7:200)
55. CIEBOTER, FRANK J. "Factors Related to the Performance of Foreign Graduate Students." *J Ed Res* 62(8):360–5 Ap '69. *
56. EWEN, ROBERT B. "The GRE Psychology Test as an Unobtrusive Measure of Motivation." *J Appl Psychol* 53(5):383–7 O '69. * (*PA* 44:1370)
57. FRANK, AUSTIN C., AND KIRK, BARBARA A. "Character-

istics and Attributes of Prospective City and Regional Planners." *J Col Stud Personnel* 10(4):317–23 S '69. *

58. GAB, DEL D. *Prediction of Success for Doctoral Students in Education at the University of North Dakota.* Doctor's thesis, University of North Dakota (Grand Forks, N.D.), 1969. (*DAI* 31:61A)

59. MEHRABIAN, ALBERT. "Undergraduate Ability Factors in Relationship to Graduate Performance." *Ed & Psychol Meas* 29(2):409–19 su '69. * (*PA* 44:17508)

60. RAWLS, JAMES R.; RAWLS, DONNA J.; AND HARRISON, C. WADE. "An Investigation of Success Predictors in Graduate School in Psychology." *J Psychol* 72(1):125–9 My '69. * (*PA* 43:16455)

61. ROBERTS, S. OLIVER; HORTON, CARRELL P.; AND ROBERTS, BARBARA T. "SAT Versus GRE Performance of Negro American College Students." Abstract. *Proc 77th Ann Conv Am Psychol Assn* 4(1):177–8 '69. * (*PA* 43:17912)

62. ROSCOE, JOHN T., AND HOUSTON, SAMUEL R. "The Predictive Validity of GRE Scores for a Doctoral Program in Education." *Ed & Psychol Meas* 29(2):507–9 su '69. * (*PA* 44:17512)

63. WIGGINS, NANCY; BLACKBURN, MARGARET; AND HACKMAN, J. RICHARD. "Prediction of First-Year Graduate Success in Psychology: Peer Ratings." *J Ed Res* 63(2):81–5 O '69. *

64. WILLIAMS, JOHN D., AND GAB, DEL. "Assessing the Doctoral Admission Policy." *Col Univ* 55(1):14–20 O '69. *

65. WOODARD, DUDLEY BLAKESLEE, JR. *Predicting Success in Graduate School From Biographical Data.* Doctor's thesis, Ohio University (Athens, Ohio), 1969. (*DAI* 31:170A)

66. HACKMAN, J. RICHARD; WIGGINS, NANCY; AND BASS, ALAN R. "Prediction of Long-Term Success in Doctoral Work in Psychology." *Ed & Psychol Meas* 30(2):365–74 su '70. * (*PA* 45:3060)

67. MEHRABIAN, ALBERT. "Ability Factors of Candidates for Graduate School." *Am Psychologist* 25(6):560–3 Je '70. *

68. STEIN, RITA F., AND GREEN, EDITH J. "The Graduate Record Examination as a Predictive Potential in the Nursing Major." *Nursing Res* 19(1):42–6 Ja–F '70. *

69. WILLIAMS, JOHN D.; HARLOW, STEVEN D.; AND GAB, DEL. "A Longitudinal Study Examining Prediction of Doctoral Success: Grade Point Average as Criterion, or Graduation vs. Non-Graduation as Criterion." *J Ed Res* 64(4):161–4 D '70. *

For reviews by Robert L. French and Warren W. Willingham of earlier forms, see 6:461; for a review by John T. Dailey, see 5:336; for reviews by J. P. Guilford and Carl I. Hovland, see 4:293. For reviews of the testing program, see 667 (1 review) and 5:601 (1 review).

[354]

★**Group Test 91.** Industrial applicants; 1949–68; verbal intelligence; 1 form ['49, 4 pages]; mimeographed manual ('68, 8 pages); instructions ('68, 1 page); 40p per 10 tests; 8p per single copy; 8p per key; 7p per instructions; 15p per manual; postpaid within U.K.; 15(25) minutes; National Institute of Industrial Psychology. *

[355]

*****Group Tests 70 and 70B.** Ages 15 and over; 1939–70; subtest of *N.I.I.P. Engineering Apprentice Selection Test Battery;* nonverbal intelligence; forms 70, 70B; booklet 70/1 ['50, 6 pages] is common to both forms; booklet 70/23 ['43, 15 pages] completes form 70; booklet 70/23B ['68, 15 pages] completes form 70B; mimeographed manual ('68, 10 pages); instructions ('68, 2 pages); mimeographed battery manual ['69, 19 pages, with 1970 revision]; 40p per 10 70/1 booklets; 8p per single copy; £1.50 per 10 70/23 or 70/23B booklets; 30p per single copy; 18p per scoring stencil; 7p per instructions; 15p per manual; 20p per battery manual; postpaid within U.K.; 18(35) minutes; National Institute of Industrial Psychology. *

REFERENCES

1–5. See 4:297.

6. MEHROTRA, S. N. "Predicting Intermediate Examination Success by Means of Psychological Tests: A Follow-Up Study." *J Voc & Ed Guid* 4:157–65 My '58. *

7. DHAR, CHANDRAKALA, AND MARR, EVELYN. "A Study of the Practice Effect of Taking Ravens Matrices on Performance on the N.I.I.P. Group Test 70/23 and of the N.I.I.P. on the

Ravens Matrices." *J Voc & Ed Guid* 5:187–9 My '59. * (*PA* 38:3188)

8. FRISBY, C. B.; VINCENT, D. F.; AND LANCASHIRE, RUTH. *Tests for Engineering Apprentices: A Validation Study.* National Institute of Industrial Psychology, Report 14. London: the Institute, 1959. Pp. iii, 24. *

9. JOG, R. N. "An Attempt to Predict Success at the 'First Year Engineering Examination.'" *J Voc & Ed Guid* 9:142–8 Ag '63. * (*PA* 38:6643)

10. JOG, R. N., AND AGA, H. "A Comparative Study of the Prediction of Academic Achievement of Engineering." *J Voc & Ed Guid* 12:45–50 My '66. *

For a review by George Westby of form 70, see 4:297.

[356]

★**Group Tests 72 and 73.** Industrial applicants; 1949–68; nonverbal intelligence; Group Tests 72 ['49, 12 pages], 73 ['50, 12 pages]; mimeographed manual ('68, 8 pages); instructions ('68, 2 pages); separate answer sheets must be used; £1.30 per 10 tests; 26p per single copy; 15p per 10 answer sheets; 15p per scoring stencil; 7p per instructions; 15p per manual; postpaid within U.K.; 15(30) minutes; National Institute of Industrial Psychology. *

REFERENCE

1. CASTLE, P. F. C., AND GARFORTH, F. I. DE LA P. "Selection, Training and Status of Supervisors: 1, Selection." *Occup Psychol* 25:109–23 Ap '51. * (*PA* 26:5858)

[357]

*****Group Tests 90A and 90B.** Ages 15 and over; 1950–70; subtest of *N.I.I.P. Engineering Apprentice Selection Test Battery;* verbal intelligence; forms 90A ['50, 12 pages], 90B ['57, 12 pages]; mimeographed manual ('68, 10 pages); instructions ('68, 2 pages); mimeographed battery manual ['69, 19 pages, with 1970 revision]; 60p per 10 tests; 12p per single copy; 12p per key; 7p per instructions; 15p per manual; 20p per battery manual; postpaid with U.K.; 20(30) minutes; National Institute of Industrial Psychology. *

REFERENCE

1. WILLIAMS, A. P. "The Selection of Maintenance Engineers for Data Processing Equipment." *Occup Psychol* 40:53–65 Ja–Ap '66. * (*PA* 41:851)

For a review by John Liggett of form 90A, see 5:340.

[358]

★**Illinois Index of Scholastic Aptitude.** Grades 9–12; 1966; IISA; 1 form (5 pages); manual (17 pages plus test); $8.50 per examiner's kit of 25 tests, key, and manual; $6.50 per 25 tests; $1 per key; $3 per manual; postpaid; 25(30) minutes; B. Everard Blanchard; Western Psychological Services. *

J. STANLEY AHMANN, *Professor of Psychology, Colorado State University, Fort Collins, Colorado.*

The *Illinois Index of Scholastic Aptitude* is a comparatively short group test designed for students in grades 9–12. It is intended to predict the probable success of high school students in four basic academic areas: English, social studies, science, and mathematics. In addition, the author believes that the IISA may be used for such purposes as (*a*) deciding if students are ready to begin the "regular" high school program, (*b*) deciding if preparatory work need be provided to students, and (c) scheduling classes by "ability grouping" techniques.

The content of the IISA is entirely verbal and is oriented toward formal education. Beyond a doubt, this test should be classified with the *CEEB Scholastic Aptitude Test* and with similar tests near the "crystallized achievement" end of the Cronbach spectrum for comparing tests of scholastic aptitude. Of the 108 items, 90 deal directly with vocabulary. They are four-option, multiple-choice items which require the selection of a synonym (55 items) or an antonym (35 items). The balance of the test (18 items) measures paragraph understanding. For each of six unrelated short paragraphs, three three-option, multiple choice items must be answered. The three parts are not separately timed; exactly 25 minutes is allowed for the entire test.

The development of the test is inadequately described. Evidently, many of the words for the vocabulary items were selected from the Declaration of Independence, the Gettysburg Address, and the Monroe Doctrine. No mention is made of any pretesting of these or of the paragraph understanding items. Item analysis data are not reported.

The sample of students used for standardizing the test is of questionable representativeness. Although the author's goal was to select a representative sample of high school students, examination of the list of participating high schools leads to the conclusion that he probably failed. For instance, of the 41 participating high schools, none is located in New York and only one in California. In contrast, five are Colorado schools. Furthermore, at least one-fourth of the 41 schools are private. Most significant of all, no description is given of the method by means of which the sample of schools was selected.

The number of students tested is comparatively small—only 1,850. Of these, 59 percent were students in the ninth and tenth grades. The proportions of male and female students are not given.

In view of the purposes of the IISA, the evidence concerning its validity is extremely limited. Amazingly, no evidence regarding predictive validity is reported. The degree of construct validity is represented by correlations with other common group mental ability tests. The largest correlation (.85) was found with the *California Test of Mental Maturity,* the lowest (.64) with the *Kuhlmann-Anderson*

Intelligence Test. Only split-half reliability coefficients are cited, varying from a low of .85 to a high of .90.

The author's suggestions for interpreting the IISA scores are unusual. Rather than convert the raw scores to standard scores or percentile ranks, he classifies them in terms of seven categories ranging from "exceptional" (93 through 108) to "poor" (0 through 30). No explanation is offered as to why the size of the categories varies so greatly, with two as small as 5 units and two as large as 31.

On balance, the IISA must be judged as anything but a strong competitor to the many verbal group mental ability tests now widely used in high schools. On the basis of the information provided in the manual, one must conclude that the IISA was developed in a somewhat casual manner and that it produces raw scores of largely uncertain value. This is not to say that the test is without promise. It is possible that further validation efforts may establish it as worthwhile for use in the high school. Much, much work needs to be done.

Davip A. Payne, *Professor of Educational Psychology and Curriculum and Supervision, The University of Georgia, Athens, Georgia.*

The evaluation of a test needs to be made against an authoritative and comprehensive set of criteria. Such a set of criteria can be found in the 1966 *Standards for Educational and Psychological Tests and Manuals.* Unfortunately, the IISA publication date is caught between the above Standards and the 1954 *Technical Recommendations for Psychological Tests and Diagnostic Techniques.* If the author and publisher cannot be held accountable for the letter of these standards, the spirit nevertheless applies.

ADMINISTRATION AND SCORING. Directions for administration, if one assumes appropriate motivational preparation for taking the test, are clear and concise. Examinees are allowed 25 minutes for the 90 four-choice, 18 three-choice, and 7 unscored sample items. There is no indication of how speed influences the scores.

VALIDITY. Beginning with the not unreasonable premise that vocabulary is the best single index of mental ability, at least as far as this concept is operationalized and employed in our tests and schools, the author describes the development of a verbal power test made up of word meaning (synonyms and antonyms) and paragraph understanding items. Content was drawn from English, social studies, mathematics and science. All vocabulary items were derived from the Declaration of Independence, the Gettysburg Address, and the Monroe Doctrine. It was assumed that such a procedure would help to insure common vocabulary background. No other specification of the domain being sampled is mentioned.

The manual claims that the test may be used (*a*) to determine readiness for high school, (*b*) to identify academic deficiencies, (*c*) to predict success in four academic areas, (*d*) for ability grouping, and (*e*) in research. Unfortunately no validity data directly related to these uses are reported. Indirect evidence in the form of correlations with six reputable group general intelligence tests is provided. These correlations ranged from .64 to .85, with a mean correlation of .74. It was apparently assumed that any validity evidenced by these instruments would by association be possessed by the IISA. Such an assumption is open to serious question. No responsive data in the form of IISA-achievement correlations, expectancy tables, group differences, or criterion-related or construct validating procedures are reported. There is also the implication that differential prediction is possible, but no data are presented to support this implication.

RELIABILITY. The assumption of content homogeneity is verified by corrected split-half correlations ranging from .85 to .90 for each of grades 9–12, with a mean of .87. The size of these coefficients is probably positively influenced by the large samples used, ranging from 350 to 600. Inasmuch as the uses suggested for the IISA include prediction, one would expect some indication of stability over time. No such data are reported. A commendable effort is made in reporting standard errors of measurement, as well as tabled confidence intervals. As commendable as this effort is, the probability interpretation for individual scores is open to question. Another interpretation not accepted by authorities is that the square root of a reliability coefficient (index of reliability) may be taken as evidence of validity.

INTERPRETATION OF SCORES. Scores are initially reported as raw scores. These can then be further classified into one of three "Ability Levels" (High, Medium, and Low) and then into two or three "Scholastic Aptitude Levels" within each of the ability levels.

No discussion of the derivation of these classifications is presented, nor is validity evidence included to support the verbal case-study-like descriptions of individuals classified into one of the seven aptitude levels. Some of these descriptions—when one considers we are talking here only of a total score on a single instrument—defy understanding. For example, an *exceptional* student "generally is an overachiever, strongly self-motivated, able and more than ready to follow directions, prompt in making decisions, punctual with assignments, and inclined to do more than is required of him/her."

The standardization details are fairly well explicated, but one wonders (*a*) how many schools, when invited to participate, declined, and (*b*) exactly how the data resulting from the administration of an experimental edition of the IISA to "varied ethnic groups" were used to reduce bias.

SUMMARY. The IISA, although beginning with some interesting assumptions and ideas, has probably been marketed too early. It is not yet ready for general consumption. At the very minimum, the IISA in its present form should be considered and labeled an "experimental edition." The chief shortcoming must be considered lack of relevant validity information, which is at least available for most of the potential competitors of the IISA.

[359]

*Lorge-Thorndike Intelligence Tests, College Edition. Grades 12–13; 1954–66; LTIT-H; Level H of the Multi-Level Edition (see 360); revision of still-in-print Level 5 (Grades 10–12), Separate Level Edition (see 6:467); 2 scores: verbal, nonverbal; Forms 1, 2, ('64, 23 pages); manual ('64, 32 pages); battery technical manual ('66, 33 pages); norms for grade 13 based upon 1954 testing with Level 5 of the separate level edition; separate answer sheets (IBM 1230, MRC) must be used; $6 per 35 tests; $8.55 per 100 MRC answer sheets and 3 group record sheets; $5.70 per 100 IBM answer sheets; 60¢ per MRC scoring stencil; $1.20 per set of IBM scoring stencils; 60¢ per manual; $1.20 per battery technical manual; $2.25 per specimen set; postage extra; MRC scoring service, 48¢ and over per test; 62(120) minutes; Irving Lorge, Robert L. Thorndike, and Elizabeth Hagen; Houghton Mifflin Co. *

ERIC F. GARDNER, *Margaret O. Slocum Professor of Education and Psychology and Chairman, Department of Psychology; and Director, Psychological Services and Research Center; Syracuse University, Syracuse, New York.*

This test is Level H of the *Lorge-Thorndike*

Intelligence Tests: Multi-Level Edition, which is an outgrowth and revision of the separate level edition of the LTIT published in 1954. These earlier tests were reviewed thoroughly and favorably in *The Fifth Mental Measurements Yearbook.*

The present tests contain the same rubrics, same item format, and in fact many of the same items as the earlier tests. The major change involves the adoption of the multi-level design and rescaling. The term "multi-level" signifies that for each subtest in the battery there is a graded series of items divided into eight different but overlapping scales in the grade range 3 through 13. Each higher level of a subtest is formed by dropping off one modular unit from the beginning of the next lower subtest and adding one at the upper end. Items are selected to show a progression in difficulty within a module and an overlapping in difficulty in successive modules. By combining modular structure with this type of graded item difficulty, the authors have produced a test in which at each level most of the items are in the immediate difficulty range and consequently are contributing most effectively to test discrimination. The relatively high average internal-consistency coefficients reported in the technical manual indicate the success of the authors, although the coefficients reported for the College Edition are the lowest of all eight levels.

Two types of norms are presented: intelligence quotient equivalents (deviation IQ's) and grade 12 percentile norms. No college norms are given.

The authors maintain that American colleges differ so widely in the intellectual selectivity of their input that no general "college norms" have much meaning. The reviewer concurs. The authors recommend that colleges devise local norms. The merit of the stress on local norms needs no comment, but advocating the construction of local norms does not satisfy the desire of the user for more adequate frames of reference. In view of the care with which the normative data for the lower levels have been collected and presented, it is unfortunate that the same concern was not shown for the College Edition. Data from a variety of colleges should be presented along with that of the basic group of 18-year-olds.

The manual reports odd-even reliability coefficients, based on a sample of 949 high school seniors drawn from a high school senior standardization group, of .93 for verbal and .90 for nonverbal. No reliability coefficients are reported for college groups, although such information is needed for a test advocated for college students.

The previous reviewers spoke well of the technical manual but indicated that additional validity studies would have been desirable. The authors have been greatly concerned about the validity of the revised tests and have presented worthwhile discussions and data about content, predictive, concurrent, and construct validity. These include correlations with achievement test batteries, and correlations with other aptitude tests such as the DAT, CEEB, and ACT. Correlations with academic grades are given for the lower levels but not for Level H. Such information from specific colleges would be useful. However, in general the sections in the technical manual on reliability and validity, which are well written and well illustrated, should be of real value to the user. This manual, overall, is far superior to its predecessor but gives the least information for the College Edition.

In an effort to furnish the much sought-after comparable scores on different aptitude tests, a table described as "Score Equivalents of Lorge-Thorndike Multi-Level IQ's in Terms of College Board and American College Testing Program Tests" is provided. This information is useful. However, the only warning given to the users about these scores is that the number of cases used in the equating procedure was small. Of greater concern is the implication that the three tests are measuring identical functions and hence, for example, a score on the quantitative portion of the SAT, which contains many data-sufficiency items, has the same meaning as a specific score on the Lorge-Thorndike. The fault is essentially the old one of assuming that all IQ's of a particular size are equivalent regardless of the specific intelligence test used.

In general, the favorable comments made by reviewers of the earlier Lorge-Thorndike are warranted. In fact, these are superior test batteries with superior ancillary materials and should have great value for the purposes defined by their authors. The major weakness is that the College Edition, which obviously is being recommended for college students, has minimum data on college students compared with the kinds supplied at the lower levels.

WILLIAM B. MICHAEL, *Professor of Educational Psychology and Psychology, University of Southern California, Los Angeles, California.*

The College Edition (Level H) is the most advanced of eight overlapping levels of the *Lorge-Thorndike Intelligence Tests* and is designed for superior students in grade 12 and students beginning college. It consists of a verbal battery (V) and a nonverbal battery (NV). The V battery requires 35 minutes of actual working time and is made up of five subtests: Vocabulary, Sentence Completion, Arithmetic Reasoning, Verbal Classification, and Verbal Analogies. The NV battery requires 27 minutes of working time and is made up of three subtests: Figure Classification, Number Series, and Figure Analogies.

The administration manual furnishes tables for converting the total raw scores on each battery (V and NV) into percentile ranks and deviation IQ's. In view of the correlation of .66 between the V and NV total scores on Level H (the correlations reported for the other levels were higher), one could argue against the value of providing separate V and NV IQ's. Whether the Arithmetic Reasoning subtest should have been included in the V battery is debatable, as the V scores could thereby be somewhat contaminated with nonverbal sources of factorial variance. It may well be, however, that a single general factor accounts for most of the reliable test-score variance—a hypothesis that is supported by one reported factor analysis of the intercorrelations of all eight subtests for a group of 250 sixth-grade pupils from the national standardization sample (see table 10 of the technical manual). Only one rotated factor could be clearly identified, and its loadings varied from .49 on the Arithmetic Reasoning subtest to .84 on the Figure Analogies subtest, the median loading being .69.

It is evident from an inspection of the items in the subtests and a study of the technical manual that great care was taken in the preparation and standardization of the 1964 Multi-Level Edition of the LTIT. For Level H, the average internal-consistency coefficient (biserial correlation) on the eight subtests varied from .41 to .56 for Form 1 and from .40 to .61 for Form 2. This is reflected in odd-even reliability estimates for Form 1 of .93 and .90 for the V and NV batteries (N = 949), respectively, and in corresponding alternate-form estimates (based on combined 1–2 and 2–1 sequences) of .90 and .92 for samples of 69 and 57 cases and of .83 and .83 for a sample of about 500 students. Reported at selected raw-score points, the standard errors of measurement for deviation IQ's varied from 3.9 to 4.6 on the V battery and from 4.0 to 5.1 on the NV battery. Thus it appears that the precision of the V and NV scores on Level H is relatively high and essentially comparable to that found in most major competitive instruments.

In the technical manual the authors argue for the validity of the LTIT in terms of (*a*) how well the items when logically viewed represent activities related to behavior that would be described as intelligent according to six enumerated criteria, (*b*) how accurately the LTIT battery scores predict performance on well-known standardized achievement tests as well as school grades, and (*c*) how clearly the LTIT signifies a construct largely in terms of its relationship with other measures designed to tap intelligence. Although the argument regarding construct validity seems somewhat weak, it is supported by correlations of the V battery scores with part scores on standardized achievement tests ranging roughly from .65 to .85 and with composite scores ranging from .79 to .90. The NV correlations were lower. Somewhat comparable ranges in correlation were found between the V and NV battery scores and scores on well-known measures of intelligence. Unfortunately, the findings cited for Level H are considerably less plentiful than those for the other levels. However, the general patterns of correlation are similar. It may be that the familiar "jangle fallacy" has shown itself again, as evidenced by high interrelationships between achievement and aptitude measures, which differ in name but not in function or process required.

Although, for the most part, the statistical data reported for Level H appear to indicate the adequacy of its reliability, validity, and norms (although deviation IQ's are based on 1954 normative data from only two educational institutions), the reviewer is concerned about the practicality of administering so many relatively short tests as well as with the seeming inconvenience of a working-time requirement of 35 and 27 minutes, respectively, for the V and NV batteries. Competing instruments, such as the *Academic Ability Test* in SCAT Series 2 for grades 12 through 14, that require only 45 minutes—or one class period—for administration may offer as useful information as does the LTIT.

Another concern relates to the appropriateness of several of the alternative answers in the Sentence Completion and Verbal Classification subtests. In many instances, a bright or an unusually creative person—especially one whose background differed from that found in the white middle-class culture—could defend his selection of an unkeyed answer. A careful review of these tests suggests that changes in societal expectations that have occurred in the past five years may have made some of the items inappropriate and possibly obsolete.

Despite the limitations that have been mentioned, the LTIT is a well-constructed, carefully normed instrument that is sufficiently reliable and valid to meet the needs of many school communities. One hopes that a shorter form will be built that could be administered in one class period, that an early revision will remove or revise certain items that may be ambiguous or at least suspect in an examinee's value expectations, and that forms for culturally different groups can be devised and separately normed —not an easy undertaking. Nevertheless, the LTIT compares favorably with other tests of general intelligence that are available from commercial publishers. The College Edition (Level H) should continue to make an important contribution to the counseling and placement of superior high school students who are seeking admission to college.

JOHN H. ROSENBACH, *Professor of Educational Psychology and Head of the Department, State University of New York at Albany, Albany, New York.*

The *Lorge-Thorndike Intelligence Tests* have gained the reputation of being among the better group tests of mental ability. Various reviewers have commented favorably on the development of the underlying constructs, the general design and construction of the tests, the ease of administration and scoring, the adequate standardization and norms, the satisfactory reliability, and, perhaps most significantly, the sophistication of the manuals. Unlike so many others, the authors present their case in a modest and reasonable way. Moreover, the sections on reliability and, especially, validity are not only informative but also a delight to read. Although brief, they could serve as helpful supplements for students enrolled in a basic tests and measurements course.

Unfortunately, despite the many positive features of the tests, there are some serious shortcomings associated with the edition under consideration here, Level H, for grade 12 and college. There are neither adequate validity data nor norms for this level, in contrast to the information presented for Levels A through G (grades 3 through 11 or 12). The most recent standardization of the tests—referred to as a Multi-Level Edition because of the overlapping nature of the items—was done in 1963. The sample consisted of *pupils* in grades 3 through 12; neither dropouts nor college students were included. Thus, the only published norms available to the user of Form H are those based on the performance of twelfth grade students. The authors suggest that these norms be used "only as rather general bench marks" and "that most colleges using the tests will want to develop their own tables of local norms."

Data bearing on the empirical validity of Form H are similarly limited. Correlations with the *Iowa Tests of Educational Development* and with the *Tests of Academic Progress* at grade 12 are high. In fact, the correlations between the verbal section of the L-T and the composite scores of these achievement tests are so high (*r*'s of .86, .90, and .895 based on N's of 138, 141, and 1,684, respectively) that one is led to suspect that the tests are measuring the same constructs. But this is certainly not a new or novel observation about mental ability and achievement tests.

Other "validity" data reported at grade 12 include correlations, within the typical range, with three other group intelligence tests (California, Kuhlmann-Anderson, and Otis), and with College Board and American College Testing Program scores. The CEEB and ACT data are based on extremely small N's (35 to 69) and narrowly selected samples; so much so, in fact, that Tables 24 (correlations) and 25 (score equivalents) of the Technical Manual, based on this material, appear virtually worthless. Their inclusion tends to mar the otherwise high quality of the manual.

No empirical information is presented for college-level students. The authors do state, however, that "experience with the items developed for Level H and tried out in several colleges and universities has indicated that the items discriminate well among individuals in college freshman groups."

An overall assessment of Level H leads one to mixed conclusions. The lack of appropriate norms and validity data is offset, in part, by the acknowledged overall quality of the items (content validity), satisfactory levels of reliability, and good performance characteristics of the lower level forms. Nonetheless, based on the information made available by the publisher, it would seem that this form has only limited applicability at the college level. The test user should be wary of making any other than the most general interpretations unless local norms and, hopefully, locally derived validity data are at his disposal.

[360]

*Lorge-Thorndike Intelligence Tests, Multi-Level Edition. Grades 3–13; 1954–66; LTIT; revision of Levels 3–5 of the still-in-print *Lorge-Thorndike Intelligence Tests* (see 6:467); 3 scores: verbal, nonverbal, composite; Forms 1, 2, ('64, 52 pages); overlapping Levels A (grade 3), B (4), C (5), D (6), E (7), F (8–9), G (10–11), H (12–13) in a single booklet; Level H available as a separate (see 359); manual ('64, 95 pages); technical manual ('66, 33 pages); no norms or reliability data for composite score; most data on validity based upon the earlier edition; separate answer sheets (Digitek, IBM 805, IBM 1230, MRC) must be used; 78¢ per test; $36 per 500 Digitek answer sheets; $4.80 per 100 IBM 805 answer sheets; $5.70 per 100 IBM 1230 answer sheets; $8.55 per 100 MRC answer sheets; Digitek scoring stencils not available; $1.20 per set of IBM scoring stencils; 60¢ per MRC scoring stencil; $1.20 per technical manual; $1.20 per manual; $3 per specimen set; postage extra; MRC scoring service, 24¢ and over per test; MRC scorable test booklet is available for Level A, Form 1 ($15 per 35 tests, 45¢ per directions, 45¢ and over per test for scoring service); 62(120) minutes; Irving Lorge, Robert L. Thorndike, and Elizabeth Hagen; Houghton Mifflin Co. *

REFERENCES

1–6. See 5:350.
7–17. See 6:467.
18. ROBERTS, DODD EDWARD. *Some Effects of an Oral-Visual Presentation of a Group Intelligence Test to Selected Seventh Grade Pupils Reading at Varying Levels.* Doctor's thesis, University of Missouri (Columbia, Mo.), 1958. (DA 19:1621)
19. BALOW, IRVING H. *The Relationship of Lateral Dominance Characteristics to Reading Achievement in the First Grade.* Doctor's thesis, University of Minnesota (Minneapolis, Minn.), 1959. (DA 20:2138)
20. GUNDERSEN, RICHARD OSCAR. *The Significance of Divergencies Between Verbal and Nonverbal Intelligence Scores.* Doctor's thesis, State University of Iowa (Iowa City, Iowa), 1959. (DA 20:2142)
21. FITZGERALD, LOUIS ALLEN. *Some Effects of Reading Ability on Group Intelligence Test Scores in the Intermediate Grades.* Doctor's thesis, State University of Iowa (Iowa City, Iowa), 1960. (DA 21:1844)
22. FISCHER, ROBERT FREDERICK. *Relationships Between School Achievement and the Verbal and Nonverbal Abilities of Children.* Doctor's thesis, University of Wisconsin (Madison, Wis.), 1961. (DA 21:3357)
23. HARMS, CALLIS R. *The Relationship Between Intelligence, Physical Growth, Socio-Economic Status, Social Acceptance and Academic Achievement in the Elementary School.* Doctor's thesis, Arizona State University (Tempe, Ariz.), 1961. (DA 22:2631)
24. BARRETT, THOMAS CLIFFORD. *The Relationship Between Selected Reading Readiness Measures of Visual Discrimination and First Grade Reading Achievement.* Doctor's thesis, University of Minnesota (Minneapolis, Minn.), 1962. (DA 24:193)
25. KATZENMEYER, WILLIAM GILBERT. *Social Interaction and Differences in Intelligence Test Performance of Negro and White Elementary School Pupils.* Doctor's thesis, Duke University (Durham, N.C.), 1962. (DA 24:1904)
26. MORTENSEN, JAMES BENSON. *A Study of Variables Related to First Grade Success in Selected Colorado School Districts.* Doctor's research study No. 1, Colorado State College (Greeley, Colo.), 1962. (DA 23:1236)
27. OLSON, D. R., AND MACARTHUR, R. S. "The Effect of Foreign Language Background on Intelligence Test Performance." *Alberta J Ed Res* 8:157–66 S '62. * (PA 37:8270)
28. ABDEL-GHAFFAR, ABDEL-SALAM ABDEL-KADER. *Relationships Between Selected Creativity Factors and Certain Non-Intellectual Factors Among High School Students.* Doctor's thesis, University of Denver (Denver, Colo.), 1963. (DA 25:1728)
29. MATTICK, WILLIAM E. "Predicting Success in the First Grade." *El Sch J* 63:273–6 F '63. *
30. SCHLUETER, MARY PETER. *The Role of Intelligence, Personality, and Selected Psychological Factors in Remedial Reading Progress.* Doctor's thesis, University of Rochester (Rochester, N.Y.), 1963. (DA 24:4088)
31. SONNEMAN, LAWRENCE J. *A Study of the Relationships Between Four Tests of Intelligence and One Test of Scholastic Achievement.* Doctor's thesis, State University of South Dakota (Vermillion, S.D.), 1963. (DA 24:4555)
32. DEMOPOULOS, CONSTANTINE GEORGE. *A Comparison of Verbal and Nonverbal IQ Scores of Negro School Children Using the Lorge-Thorndike Intelligence Test.* Master's thesis, Marshall University (Huntington, W.Va.), 1964.
33. DEUTSCH, MARTIN, AND BROWN, BERT. "Social Influences in Negro-White Intelligence Differences." *J Social Issues* 20:24–35 Ap '64. * (PA 39:4734)
34. EDWARDS, ALLEN JACK, AND KIRBY, M. ELSIE. "Predictive Efficiency of Intelligence Test Scores: Intelligence Quotients Obtained in Grade One and Achievement Test Scores Obtained in Grade Three." *Ed & Psychol Meas* 24:941–6 w '64. * (PA 39:8699)
35. JUNGEBLUT, ANN. "Some Further Data on the Lorge-Thorndike Intelligence Tests." *Ed Rec B* 85:69–71 F '64. *
36. KERFOOT, JAMES FLETCHER. *The Relationship of Selected Auditory and Visual Reading Readiness Measures to First Grade Reading Achievement and Second Grade Reading and Spelling Achievement.* Doctor's thesis, University of Minnesota (Minneapolis, Minn.), 1964. (DA 25:1747)
37. KLEIN, ROBERT A. *An Investigation of the Lorge-Thorndike Intelligence Test as an Instrument in the Prediction of Creativity in Elementary School Children.* Master's thesis, University of Tennessee (Knoxville, Tenn.), 1964.
38. SARASON, SEYMOUR B.; HILL, KENNEDY T.; AND ZIMBARDO, PHILIP G. "A Longitudinal Study of the Relation of Test Anxiety to Performance on Intelligence and Achievement Tests." *Monogr Soc Res Child Develop* 29(7):1–51 '64. * (PA 39:15263)
39. SHAFFER, RAYMOND GEORGE. *A Study of Four Group Intelligence Tests to Identify Ambiguous Pictures as a Factor Which Causes Some Children to Select Incorrect Answers.* Doctor's research study No. 1, Colorado State College (Greeley, Colo.), 1964. (DA 25:1014)
40. SHEA, CAROL ANN. *Visual Discrimination of Words as a Predictor of Reading Readiness.* Doctor's thesis, University of Connecticut (Storrs, Conn.), 1964. (DA 25:6321)
41. TAYLOR, ALTON L. "The Prediction of Success Using Programed Science Materials." *J Res Sci Ed* 2(1):58–59 '64. *
42. WEST, L. W., AND MACARTHUR, R. S. "An Evaluation of Selected Intelligence Tests for Two Samples of Metis and Indian Children." *Alberta J Ed Res* 10:17–27 Mr '64. * (PA 39:12328)
43. WILLIAMS, BENNIE LEE. *The Concurrent Validity of the Lorge-Thorndike Verbal and Nonverbal Intelligence Tests Among Negro Children.* Master's thesis, Marshall University (Huntington, W.Va.), 1964.
44. YAMAMOTO, KAORU. "Role of Creative Thinking and Intelligence in High School Achievement." *Psychol Rep* 14:783–9 Je '64. * (PA 39:5140)
45. BAILEY, RUBELLIA JOHNSON. *The Relationship of Educational Background, Socio-Economic Status, Level of Aspiration, and Intelligence to Success in Business Education.* Doctor's thesis, Temple University (Philadelphia, Pa.), 1965. (DA 26:1396)
46. CONSTANTINIDES, PANAYIOTES DEMOSTHENOUS. *The Relationship of Critical Thinking Ability to Intelligence, to Personality, and to Teacher Evaluation of Pupil Personality.* Doctor's thesis, University of Virginia (Charlottesville, Va.), 1965. (DA 26:5861) (Abstract: Ed R 3:43–5)
47. GLAD, JOAN ROGERS BOURNE. *Evaluation of the Remedial Reading Program in Utah Public Schools.* Doctor's thesis, University of Utah (Salt Lake City, Utah), 1965. (DA 26:5864)
48. KANGAS, RONALD D. "Factors Related to Success in 7th Grade Foreign Language Study." *Mod Lang J* 49:97–8 F '65. *
49. KARZEN, JUDITH MILLER; SUVETOR, HELENE; AND THOMPSON, GLEN. "Predicting First Grade Reading Achievement." *Ill Sch Res* 2:20–2 O '65. *

50. RAINEY, ROBERT G. "A Study of Four School-Ability Tests." *J Exp Ed* 33:305–19 su '65. * (*PA* 39:12306)

51. RAY, JOHN RICHARD. *The Predictive Value of Selected Factors for Achievement of Seventh Grade Pupils.* Doctor's thesis, University of Tennessee (Knoxville, Tenn.), 1965. (*DA* 26:4396)

52. SWAN, ROBERT J., AND HOPKINS, KENNETH D. "An Investigation of Theoretical and Empirical Chance Scores on Selected Standardized Group Tests." *Calif J Ed Res* 16:34–41 Ja '65. * (*PA* 39:10156)

53. YOLOYE, EMMANUEL AYOTUNDE. *The Performance of Bilingual Nigerian Students on Verbal and Nonverbal Tests of Intelligence.* Doctor's thesis, Columbia University (New York, N.Y.), 1965. (*DA* 26:4466)

54. DYKSTRA, ROBERT. "Auditory Discrimination Abilities and Beginning Reading Achievement." *Read Res Q* 1:5–34 sp '66. * (*PA* 40:11011)

55. EAGLE, NORMAN. "The Stability of Lorge-Thorndike IQ Scores Between Grades Three and Four and Grade Eight." *J Ed Res* 60:164–5 D '66. *

56. KANDEL, ARTHUR. *Discrepancies Between the Stanford-Binet and Three Group Tests of Intelligence in the Identification of Low I.Q. Children.* Doctor's thesis, Catholic University of America (Washington, D.C.), 1966. (*DA* 27:1659A)

57. KEACH, CHARLES CAMPBELL. *Discrepancies Between the Stanford-Binet and Three Group Tests of Intelligence in the Identification of High I.Q. Children.* Doctor's thesis, Catholic University of America (Washington, D.C.), 1966. (*DA* 27:1660A)

58. MORPER, JACK. *An Investigation of the Relationship of Certain Predictive Variables and Academic Achievement of Spanish-American and Anglo Pupils in Junior High School.* Doctor's thesis, Oklahoma State University (Stillwater, Okla.), 1966. (*DA* 27:4051A)

59. OHNMACHT, FRED W. "Achievement, Anxiety and Creative Thinking." *Am Ed Res J* 3:131–8 Mr '66. *

60. WARD, GEORGE, II. "Lorge-Thorndike Nonverbal IQ's and Verbal Achievement Tests Among a Group of Negro Pupils." *Proc W Va Acad Sci* 37:282–5 F '66. * (*PA* 40:8827)

61. BRENDEMUEHL, FRANK LOUIS. *The Influence of Reading Ability on the Validity of Group Non-Verbal Intelligence Tests.* Doctor's thesis, University of Minnesota (Minneapolis, Minn.), 1967. (*DA* 28:2088A)

62. CAVE, RICHARD LESTER. *A Factorial Comparison of Creativity and Intelligence.* Doctor's thesis, University of Tennessee (Knoxville, Tenn.), 1967. (*DA* 28:4293B)

63. CROPLEY, A. J. "Creativity, Intelligence, and Achievement." *Alberta J Ed Res* 13:51–8 Mr '67. * (*PA* 41:15253)

64. LANIER, PERRY EUGENE. *A Study of Creativity, Intelligence and Discovery Teaching as Related to Performance in Elementary School Mathematics.* Doctor's thesis, University of Oklahoma (Norman, Okla.), 1967. (*DA* 28:1004A)

65. McCOMAS, WILLIAM, AND WARD, GEORGE, II. "An Internal Factor Analysis of Lorge-Thorndike Scores of Negro Children." *Proc W Va Acad Sci* 39:59–61 '67. *

66. McCOMAS, WILLIAM C. *Structure and Function of the Lorge-Thorndike Intelligence Test When Used With Negro School Children.* Master's thesis, Marshall University (Huntington, W.Va.), 1967.

67. PANTHER, EDWARD E. "Prediction of First-Grade Reading Achievement." *El Sch J* 68:44–8 O '67. *

68. RICE, VICTOR. *An Appraisal of the Predictive Value of Patterns of Subtest Scores in Achievement Test Batteries.* Doctor's thesis, American University (Washington, D.C.), 1967. (*DA* 28:1267A)

69. ROBERTSON, JOHN W. *The Lorge-Thorndike Intelligence Tests as Predictors of Achievement in Remedial Reading Classes.* Master's thesis, University of Utah (Salt Lake City, Utah), 1967.

70. WARTENBERG, HERBERT. *The Relationship Between Success in Beginning Reading and Various Predictive Measures.* Doctor's thesis, Temple University (Philadelphia, Pa.), 1967. (*DA* 28:979A)

71. ALZOBAIE, ABDUL JALIL; METFESSEL, NEWTON S.; AND MICHAEL, WILLIAM B. "Alternative Approaches to Assessing the Intellectual Abilities of Youth From a Culture of Poverty." *Ed & Psychol Meas* 28:449–55 su '68. * (*PA* 42:19264)

72. BOERSMA, FREDERIC J., AND O'BRYAN, KENNETH. "An Investigation of the Relationship Between Creativity and Intelligence Under Two Conditions of Testing." *J Personality* 36: 341–8 S '68. * (*PA* 43:3993)

73. CICCHETTI, DOMENIC V., AND LERNER, EMANUEL. "Measures of Reliability and Validity of Verbal Intelligence Among Neuropsychiatric Patients." *J Abn Psychol* 73:420 O '68. * (*PA* 42:18084)

74. KAKKAR, S. B. "The Consistency of IQ Scores." *J Psychol Res* 12:111–3 S '68. *

75. KARNES, LUCIA ROONEY. *The Comparison of Scores of Eighth-Grade Reading and Nonreading Boys on the Lorge-Thorndike Tests, Wechsler Intelligence Scale for Children, the D 48 Test, and the Welsh Figure Preference Test, GW Scale.* Doctor's thesis, University of North Carolina (Chapel Hill, N.C.), 1968. (*DAI* 30:585A)

76. LEHRER, BARRY EUGENE. *An Investigation of the Role of Intellectual, Motivational, and Other Non-Intellectual Factors in the Prediction of Educational Achievement and Efficiency.* Doctor's thesis, University of Iowa (Iowa City, Iowa), 1968. (*DA* 29:3876A)

77. MACARTHUR, R. S. "Assessing Intellectual Potential of Native Canadian Pupils: A Summary." *Alberta J Ed Res* 14: 115–22 Je '68. * (*PA* 44:4170)

78. MACARTHUR, RUSSELL. "Some Differential Abilities of Northern Canadian Native Youth." *Int J Psychol* 3(1):43–50 '68. *

79. MANCOTT, ANATOL. "Prediction of Academic Achievement in a First Semester College Chemistry Course for Medical Laboratory Technologists." *Ed & Psychol Meas* 28:945–6 au '68. * (*PA* 43:4516)

80. RATTAN, M. S., AND MACARTHUR, R. S. "Longitudinal Prediction of School Achievement for Metis and Eskimo Pupils." *Alberta J Ed Res* 14:37–41 Mr '68. * (*PA* 44:4249)

81. ROSEN, CARL L., AND OHNMACHT, FRED. "Perception, Readiness, and Reading Achievement in First Grade." *Proc Ann Conv Int Read Assn* 12(4):33–9 '68. *

82. SATTABANASUK, THIRAPAN. *Junior High Student Performance and Related Student and Parent Characteristics.* Doctor's thesis, Colorado State University (Greeley, Colo.), 1968. (*DA* 29:1052A)

83. SHEA, CAROL ANN. "Visual Discrimination of Words and Reading Readiness." *Read Teach* 21:361–7 Ja '68. *

84. WESTON, LESLIE DONALD. *An Exploration of the Interrelationships Among Children's Arithmetic Achievement, Their Styles of Learning, Their Responsibility for Intellectual Academic Achievement, and Their Parents' Attitudes.* Doctor's thesis, Wayne State University (Detroit, Mich.), 1968. (*DAI* 30:1087A)

85. WOLF, WILLAVENE; KING, MARTHA L.; AND HUCK, CHARLOTTE S. "Teaching Critical Reading to Elementary School Children." *Reading Res Q* 3:435–98 su '68. *

86. BLAND, ROSA BEATRICE. *Relation of Auditory Discrimination to Reading Achievement.* Doctor's thesis, University of Virginia (Charlottesville, Va.), 1969. (*DAI* 31:1655A)

87. DUDEK, S. Z.; GOLDBERG, J. S.; LESTER, E. P.; AND HARRIS, B. R. "The Validity of Cognitive, Perceptual-Motor and Personality Variables for Prediction of Achievement in Grade 1 and Grade 2." *J Clin Psychol* 25(2):165–70 Ap '69. * (*PA* 43:14874)

88. DUDEK, S. Z.; LESTER, E. P.; GOLDBERG, J. S.; AND DYER, G. B. "Relationship of Piaget Measures to Standard Intelligence and Motor Scales." *Percept & Motor Skills* 28(2): 351–62 Ap '69. * (*PA* 43:15587)

89. FELTON, THOMAS A., JR. *Correlation Between Creativity as Measured by Torrance Tests of Creative Thinking Figural Forms A and B and Intelligence as Measured by the Lorge-Thorndike Intelligence Test of Fifty Sixth Grade Students.* Master's thesis, Old Dominion University (Norfolk, Va.), 1969.

90. HAYES, EDWARD MAJELLA. *The Relationship of Race and Sex to Academic Achievement in Selected Rural Elementary and High Schools Before and After Desegregation.* Doctor's thesis, University of Virginia (Charlottesville, Va.), 1969. (*DAI* 31:149A)

91. HIERONYMUS, A. N., AND STROUD, JAMES B. "Comparability of IQ Scores on Five Widely Used Intelligence Tests." *Meas & Eval Guid* 2(3):135–40 f '69. * (*PA* 44:13285)

92. LESSING, ELISE E., AND ZAGORIN, SUSAN W. "Correlation Between Lorge-Thorndike IQ and Factor B of the IPAT Children's Personality Questionnaire." *Psychol Rep* 24(2): 569–70 Ap '69. * (*PA* 43:15590)

93. MACARTHUR, RUSSELL S. "Some Cognitive Abilities of Eskimo, White, and Indian-Métis Pupils Aged 9 to 12 Years." *Can J Behav Sci* 1(1):50–9 Ja '69. * (*PA* 44:12319)

94. McCUTCHEON, NANCY SUSAN. *A Study of Relationships Among Creativity, Intelligence, and Test Anxiety of Middle-Class Fourth Grade Boys and Girls.* Doctor's thesis, University of South Carolina (Columbia, S.C.), 1969. (*DAI* 30:4833A)

95. MANCOTT, ANATOL. "Prediction of Performance in Chemistry." *Nursing Outl* 17(11):55 N '69. *

96. MEHRENS, WILLIAM A., AND LEHMANN, IRVIN J. *Standardized Tests in Education,* pp. 91–101. New York: Holt, Rinehart & Winston, Inc., 1969. Pp. xi, 323. *

97. MOTLEY, HESTER CHATTIN. *A Study of the Predictive Value of Certain Factors Related to Test Performance, Academic Achievement, and Educational Aspirations.* Doctor's thesis, American University (Washington, D.C.), 1969. (*DAI* 30:2807A)

98. NIKAS, GEORGE BILL. *Anxiety Levels of Upper-Middle and Upper-Lower Class First Grade Children Prior to and During Formal Reading Instruction.* Doctor's thesis, State University of New York (Buffalo, N.Y.), 1969. (*DAI* 30:2382A)

99. OAS, ROBERT T. *A Study of the Relationships of Students' Aptitude, Academic Achievement and Attitude Toward School for Selected School Populations.* Doctor's thesis, University of South Dakota (Vermillion, S.D.), 1969. (*DAI* 30:3644A)

100. RODGERS, DENIS CYRIL. *An Investigation of the Auditory Memory Abilities of Grade 2 Retarded-Underachieving Readers and Competent-Achieving Readers Under Conditions of Reinforcement and Non-Reinforcement.* Doctor's thesis,

University of Toronto (Toronto, Ont., Canada), 1969. (*DAI* 31:2196A)

101. SHIGAKI, IRENE SHIKIBU. *The Effects of Teacher Strength and Sensitivity and Pupil Intelligence and Creativity on the Production of Divergent Responses.* Doctor's thesis, Columbia University (New York, N.Y.), 1969. (*DAI* 30: 3864A)

102. TORRANCE, E. PAUL. "Prediction of Adult Creative Achievement Among High School Seniors." *Gifted Child Q* 13(4):223–9 w '69. * (*PA* 44:14620)

103. WESTPHAL, M. ELIZABETH; LEUTENEGGER, RALPH R.; AND WAGNER, DOROTHEA L. "Some Psycho-Acoustic and Intellectual Correlates of Achievement in German Language Learning of Junior High School Students." *Mod Lang J* 53(4):258–66 Ap '69. * (*PA* 44:21623)

104. YOUNG, WILLIAM THOMAS. *An Investigation of the Relative and Combined Power of Musical Aptitude, General Intelligence, and Academic Achievement Tests to Predict Musical Attainment.* Doctor's thesis, University of Iowa (Iowa City, Iowa), 1969. (*DAI* 30:758A)

105. ALLISON, DONALD E. "Test Anxiety, Stress, and Intelligence-Test Performance." *Can J Behav Sci* 2(1):26–37 Ja '70. * (*PA* 44:13275)

106. CALDWELL, JAMES R.; MICHAEL, WILLIAM B.; SCHRADER, DONALD R.; AND MEYERS, C. E. "Comparative Validities and Working Times for Composites of Structure-of-Intellect Tests and Algebra Grades and Composites of Traditional Test Measures and Algebra Grades in the Prediction of Success in Tenth-Grade Geometry." *Ed & Psychol Meas* 30(4):955–9 w '70. *

107. CANABAL, JUANA VILLANUEVA. *Comparison of Deaf and Normally Hearing Children on Analogy Items Under Different Methods of Instruction at Different Age Levels.* Doctor's thesis, St. John's University (Jamaica, N.Y.), 1970. (*DAI* 31: 3700B)

108. CAVE, RICHARD L. "A Combined Factor Analysis of Creativity and Intelligence." *Multiv Behav Res* 5(2):177–91 Ap '70. * (*PA* 44:16697)

109. LESTER, EVA P.; MUIR, R.; AND DUDEK, STEPHANIE Z. "Cognitive Structure and Achievement in the Young Child." *Can Psychiatric Assn J* 15(3):279–87 Je '70. * (*PA* 45:5058)

110. NYE, MAE REDDISH. *Changes in Lorge-Thorndike Scores and in Grade Point Averages Over Three Years.* Master's thesis, College of Idaho (Caldwell, Idaho), 1970.

111. SMITH, I. LEON. "IQ, Creativity, and the Taxonomy of Educational Objectives: Cognitive Domain." *J Exp Ed* 38(4):58–60 su '70. * (*PA* 46:5688)

112. WILLIS, JERRY. "Group Versus Individual Intelligence Tests in One Sample of Emotionally Disturbed Children." *Psychol Rep* 27(3):819–22 D '70. * (*PA* 45:10227)

CAROL K. TITTLE, *Assistant Professor of Teacher Education, City University of New York, New York, New York.*

The *Lorge-Thorndike Intelligence Tests* have been well received in previous reviews, and meet generally accepted standards for test construction and standardization procedures. Restandardization in 1963, administration of achievement tests to the same standardization sample, and the multi-level format are the main features to be noted in this revision. The revision for the multi-level edition includes about one-third new items; the major change is in the format and sequencing for the multi-level edition.

The standardization in 1963 was carried out with the *Iowa Tests of Basic Skills* (grades 3–8) and the *Tests of Academic Progress* (grades 9–12). The common standardization sample for both the intelligence and achievement tests will assist users in interpreting scores and making comparisons between the scores on the batteries. The standardization procedures appear in the main to have been carefully carried out; the problems encountered in participation (just over 50 percent of the first choice

units agreed to participate) and resulting statistical adjustments to the data are probably not uncommon to major test standardizations.

A major feature of the new edition is the multi-level arrangement. On first look at the test booklet, one is easily put off by the interruptions of the various start and stop statements for the different levels. However, it is likely that students adjust readily and probably do not experience difficulty because of the extraneous material.

The technical manual does not present adequate data, such as the item difficulty data, to support the arrangement of the modules of items for the multi-level arrangement. The items within a module are to show a progression in difficulty, but each new module is also to include items of lower difficulty to overlap with the preceding module. While the data is not given on distributions of item difficulties, the results of this type of scaling procedure seem to be satisfactory as nearly as can be inferred from the norm tables. Where some levels were administered a grade lower than that recommended, the norms tend to show small percentages of students down in the chance score area, when the actual score range used is considered (see data on Level C, for example). The tests appear to have considerable ceiling, since the number of items in the grade percentile norm tables is well under the total number of items in the verbal and nonverbal tests.

The tests are said to be primarily power tests. One study (66) found the tests to be too highly speeded to calculate internal consistency reliability coefficients for a sample of black students in grades 7–12. The manual should present data to show what effect time has on score distributions earned by subjects in the lower half of the distribution and for groups of special interest.

Reliability of the test is appropriately assessed with the alternate forms methods, and most data reported in the technical manual are developed by this method. The reliability coefficients are satisfactory, although the set of coefficients presented in Table 4 are on the low side (verbal battery .83 to .91, nonverbal battery .80 to .88, for different grades). The data for the standard error of measurement was based on the odd-even reliabilities and consequently may be slightly underestimated.

The inclusion of discussion on the standard error of measurement and the provision of the standard error of measurement in deviation IQ scores by raw score level (10 point intervals in raw scores) for both verbal and nonverbal tests is highly commended. The data allow the user to gain some understanding of the possible variability of scores, particularly at the extremes of the score distribution. The discussion and table should also be included in the administration manual, however, since many users of the test scores probably never see the technical manual, in contrast with the greater availability of the administration manual.

The data on practice effects are difficult to understand, particularly those for the nonverbal battery. Quite small effects were noted for the verbal battery, on a sample described as fairly sophisticated test takers. It is not clear exactly what is meant by the statement: "Some downward adjustment would need to be made in interpreting a retest" (i.e., since published norms are based upon an initial testing). A question can be raised concerning the amount of experience likely to have occurred within the standardization population, and how the user is to judge the amount of experience his pupils have had "with this type of test." Perhaps larger practice effects would have been noted on a random sample from the standardization group.

Content, predictive, and construct validity are discussed in the technical manual (labeled as representing, predicting, and signifying, respectively). Two of these areas will be considered here, predictive and construct, since the uses suggested for the test are: selecting curriculum materials and learning tasks (for students on the basis of the Lorge-Thorndike); comparing level of achievement and aptitude; formation of classroom groups by ability level; grouping within classroom; identifying students who may need special attention; reporting progress; counseling students; and vocational guidance.

Some correlations and related data are cited for the Lorge-Thorndike with achievement tests and school grades, but no specific data on the use of scores in grouping, identifying students who may need special attention, counseling and vocational guidance. The latter is particularly important, since the distinction between the verbal and nonverbal batteries implies that differences may have significance in relation to reading level, school achievement, or educational and vocational planning. There is indirect evidence on the latter in the correlations with the

Differential Aptitude Tests. These show higher correlations for the nonverbal IQ's with Space Relations, Abstract Reasoning, and Mechanical Reasoning.

Generally, the Lorge-Thorndike verbal and nonverbal tests provide relatively high correlations with tests of achievement (.60's to .70's, with some up to the .80's). The nonverbal typically provides the lower correlations within any set.

Two series of studies provide some data relevant to the use of the nonverbal score. In a group of studies of Eskimos and Indians, MacArthur and colleagues have found the nonverbal battery to compare favorably with the *Progressive Matrices* and other "culture reduced" tests in predicting school achievement (27, 42, 77, 78, 80). However, the MacArthur studies apparently did not include the L-T verbal, so direct comparisons cannot be made.

A series of studies by Ward and his students did use both the verbal and nonverbal tests with samples of black students. The nonverbal was found less effective in predicting school achievement, and Ward raised the question of the independence of the verbal and nonverbal in use with special populations, at least. Higher nonverbal IQ's were noted with increasing age, but were not more effective than the verbal IQ in predicting school achievement. Factor analytic studies also indicated one general factor. Ward's suggestion that the factor structure of the nonverbal be investigated seems reasonable (32, 43, 60, 65, 66). A study of the stability of verbal and nonverbal scores (grades 3 to 8) found the estimated true change for the nonverbal three times that for the verbal—indicating a greater instability in the nonverbal scores (55).

A study of Nigerian students also found the verbal and nonverbal correlated similarly with school marks. There was "no indication of the superiority of the verbal or nonverbal for educational guidance" (53). Lorge-Thorndike scores were not predictors of reading gains for elementary pupils in grades 2–6 in remedial reading classes (69).

Studies of construct validity cited included relationships with school achievement (as above) and with other tests that have acceptance as measures of intelligence. The most extensive study was conducted by Hieronymus and Stroud (91). In their study of the comparability of IQ's obtained from the Lorge-Thorndike and four other intelligence tests administered to pupils in Iowa in grades 4, 7, and 10, they note that the correlations were quite variable, and in most cases below the reliabilities of the test, indicating that the tests were measuring somewhat different traits. The nonverbal IQ scores of the L-T had lower correlations with the other intelligence test scores than the verbal. The Hieronymus and Stroud study also provides comparability data on the IQ's derived from the 1954 and 1963 editions of the Lorge-Thorndike. In their study the newer edition yielded slightly lower IQ's for the verbal score in grades 4, 7, and 10, and for the nonverbal in grades 7 and 10.

Other studies of the relationships of the L-T with IQ measures have been conducted by Rainey (50), Kandel (56), and Keach (57). In a study of 813 fourth grade pupils, 100 with Stanford-Binet IQ's below 75 were located; the *California Test of Mental Maturity* selected a higher percentage of those identified by the Stanford-Binet than did the L-T or Otis (56). A similar study with the 100 highest IQ children on the S-B found the L-T and the CTMM about equally satisfactory (57).

The Lorge-Thorndike IQ's correlate moderately to fairly highly with school achievement and with other IQ's derived from intelligence tests. The multi-level edition is a refinement and improvement over the earlier separate level edition. The issues raised in the review are intended to encourage further studies of this widely-used, well-constructed and presented series of tests.

For reviews by Frank S. Freeman, John E. Milholland, and D. A. Pidgeon of the Separate Level Edition, see 5:350.

[361]

*Lowry-Lucier Reasoning Test Combination.** Grades 5–16 and adults; 1956–65; LLRC; 3 scores: sequential relations, spatial relations, total; 2 tests; revised manual ('65, 15 pages); no data on reliability of subscores; tentative norms; $3.50 per 25 copies of either test; $6.50 per 25 sets of both tests; $1 per key; $1 per manual; postage extra; $5 per specimen set, postpaid; Ellsworth Lowry (test) and Omer Lucier; B. M. Farley. *

a) LOWRY-LUCIER REASONING TEST A. Sequential relations; LLRA; 1 form ('56, 3 pages); 15(20) minutes.

b) LOWRY-LUCIER REASONING TEST B. Spatial relations; LLRB; 1 form ('56, 3 pages); 20(25) minutes.

REFERENCES

1–6. See 6:468.
7. WALLACE, EDWIN C., JR. "The Selection and Training of Men and Women Programmers in a Bank." *Comput & Autom* 14:23–5 Ap '65. *

For reviews by Andrew R. Baggaley and Russel F. Green, see 6:468.

[362]

★**Mental Alertness.** Job applicants with 9–11, 12 or more years of education; 1945–62; 2 levels; no manual; no data on reliability and validity; R3.75 per 25 tests; 70c per key; sample copy available for inspection; postpaid within South Africa; Afrikaans edition available; National Institute for Personnel Research. *

a) TEST A/2. Job applicants with 9–11 years of education; Forms A/2/1 ('62, 8 pages), A/2/2 ['62, 8 pages]; norms ('57, 1 page); 30(35) minutes.

b) TEST A/1. Job applicants with 12 or more years of education; Forms A/1/1 ('62, 8 pages), A/1/2 ('61, 8 pages); norms ('57, 1 page); 35(40) minutes.

[363]

*Miller Analogies Test.** Candidates for graduate school; 1926–70; MAT; Forms J ('52, 4 pages), K ('59, 4 pages), M ('69, 4 pages), R ('50, 4 pages, formerly Form H); Forms J and R also published under the title *Advanced Personnel Test* for use in business; use of Form R restricted to retesting; revised manual ('70, 32 pages); bulletin of information ('70, 61 pages); guide for testing center operation ['64, 8 pages]; distribution restricted and test administered at specified licensed university centers; scoring and reporting handled by the local center; separate answer sheets (IBM 805-Digitek, IBM 1230) must be used; examination fee to centers: $3 per examinee; fees to examinees are determined locally and include reporting of scores to the examinee and to 3 institutions or companies designated at the time of testing; additional score reports may be secured from the publisher at a fee of $1 each; Braille and large type editions available; 50(55) minutes; W. S. Miller (test); Psychological Corporation. *

REFERENCES

1–16. See 4:304.
17–44. See 5:352.
45–70. See 6:472.
71. GLADING, JOHN CAMPBELL. *The Miller Analogies Test and Its Relationship to Other Tests and Scholastic Achievement at Springfield College.* Master's thesis, Springfield College (Springfield, Mass.), 1951.
72. HYMAN, SIDNEY ROBERT. *The Development of Criteria of Research Competence in Psychology and Their Prediction From Certain Intellectual and Achievement Measures.* Doctor's thesis, University of Pittsburgh (Pittsburgh, Pa.), 1954. (*DA* 14:2395)
73. BINFORD, MARJORIE LYNETTE. *A Study of the Relationship of Test Scores and Experience to Grades in a Graduate Engineering Program.* Master's thesis, George Washington University (Washington, D.C.), 1959.
74. BLATT, SIDNEY J., AND STEIN, MORRIS I. "Efficiency in Problem Solving." *J Psychol* 48:193–213 O '59. * (*PA* 35:4971)
75. ASHBROOK, JAMES BARBOUR. *Evaluating Seminary Students as Potential Ministers.* Master's thesis, Ohio State University (Columbus, Ohio), 1962.
76. ROSS, JOEL A. *Major Factors Related to Success in an M.A. Program in Psychology.* Master's thesis, Hofstra University (Hempstead, N.Y.), 1962.
77. BOONE, SAM W. *The Scholastic Achievement of Stetson University Freshmen Required to Take Remedial English.* Master's thesis, Stetson University (DeLand, Fla.), 1963.
78. LEHMKUHL, CARLTON BURDELL. *Test Performance Relationships Among Occupational Patterns of Educational Administration Program Graduates.* Doctor's thesis, University of Minnesota (Minneapolis, Minn.), 1963. (*DA* 24:4510)
79. CALLIS, ROBERT, AND PREDIGER, DALE J. "Predictors of Achievement in Counseling and Guidance Graduate Study." *Counselor Ed & Sup* 3:63–9 w '64. *
80. CAMPBELL, MARY LOU. *Verbal Analogies Tests: A Comparison of Vocabulary and Reasoning Components Using the Miller Analogies Test and the Concept Mastery Test.* Master's thesis, University of Utah (Salt Lake City, Utah), 1964.
81. DUNNETTE, MARVIN D.; WERNIMONT, PAUL; AND ABRAHAMS, NORMAN. "Further Research on Vocational Interest Differences Among Several Types of Engineers." *Personnel & Guid J* 42:484–93 Ja '64. * (*PA* 39:6040)
82. FEINBERG, ABRAHAM. *The Relative Efficiency of Several Variables Used in the Selection Process for Candidates in a*

Graduate Certification Program. Doctor's thesis, Rutgers—The State University (New Brunswick, N.J.), 1964. (*DA* 25:2871)
83. KOLTVEIT, THOMAS H. "A Critique of: A Comparison of Miller Analogies Test Scores, Undergraduate Grade Point Averages, and Faculty Ratings of Guidance Counselor Students." *Univ N Dak Col Ed Rec* 49:87–8 Mr '64. *
84. ROBERTSON, MALCOLM, AND HALL, EVERETT. "Predicting Success in Graduate Study." *J General Psychol* 71:359–65 O '64. * (*PA* 39:5997)
85. STERNAL, WILLIAM; CASH, W. LEVI, JR.; AND GADE, ELDON M. "A Comparison of Miller Analogies Test Scores, Undergraduate Grade Point Averages, and Faculty Ratings of Guidance Counselor Students." *Univ N Dak Col Ed Rec* 49: 75–6 F '64. *
86. BUTLER, MARJORIE JOHNSON. *Criteria for Creativity in Counseling.* Doctor's thesis, University of Pittsburgh (Pittsburgh, Pa.), 1965. (*DA* 27:977B)
87. LIEF, VICTOR F.; LIEF, HAROLD I.; AND YOUNG, KATHLEEN M. "Academic Success: Intelligence and Personality." *J Med Ed* 40:114–24 F '65. *
88. MONAHAN, RUSSELL D. *The Relationship Between the Miller Analogies Test and the Technical Vocabulary Test.* Master's thesis, University of Oregon (Eugene, Ore.), 1965.
89. AINSWORTH, L. L., AND FOX, A. M. "Prediction of Grades in Graduate Education Courses." *Ed & Psychol Meas* 26:499–500 su '66. *
90. BENTLEY, JOSEPH C. "Creativity and Academic Achievement." *J Ed Res* 59:269–72 F '66. * (*PA* 40:6631)
91. ECKHOFF, CONSTANCE M. "Predicting Graduate Success at Winona State College." *Ed & Psychol Meas* 26:483–5 su '66. * (*PA* 40:12759)
92. LANE, ROBERT G.; PENN, NOLAN E.; AND FISCHER, ROBERT F. "Miller Analogies Test: A Note on Permissive Retesting." *J Appl Psychol* 50:409–11 O '66. * (*PA* 40:13189)
93. MOORE, JAMES C. "The Relationship Between Time Taken to Complete the Example Questions and Raw Score on the Miller Analogies Test." *J Ed Meas* 3:175–7 su '66. *
94. PAYNE, DAVID A., AND TUTTLE, CYNTHIA E. "The Predictive Relationship of the Miller Analogies Test to Objective and Subjective Criteria of Success in a Graduate School of Education." *Ed & Psychol Meas* 26:427–30 su '66. * (*PA* 40:13534)
95. SCHOFIELD, WILLIAM, AND MERWIN, JACK C. "The Use of Scholastic Aptitude, Personality, and Interest Test Data in the Selection of Medical Students." *J Med Ed* 41:502–9 Je '66. *
96. THUMIN, FRED J., AND BOERNKE, CAROL. "Miller Analogies Test Performance as Related to Age, Sex, and Academic Field." *Psychol Rep* 19:751–4 D '66. * (*PA* 41:5005)
97. WARD, DOROTHY V. *The Prediction of Success in Graduate Education Based on Undergraduate Grade Point Averages and Miller Analogies Test Scores.* Master's thesis, Kent State University (Kent, Ohio), 1966.
98. WATLEY, DONIVAN J. "Counselor Variability in Making Accurate Predictions." *J Counsel Psychol* 13:53–62 sp '66. * (*PA* 40:5817)
99. CURETON, EDWARD E., AND SCOTT, THOMAS B. "Equivalent Scores for the Graduate Record Verbal and Miller Analogies Tests." *Ed & Psychol Meas* 27:611–5 au '67. * (*PA* 42:122)
100. JANSEN, DAVID G., AND JOHNSTON, FRED N. "Prediction of Graduate School Achievement." *J Col Stud Personnel* 8:296–9 S '67. *
101. MCGREEVY, C. PATRICK. "Factor Analysis of Measures Used in the Selection and Evaluation of Counselor Education Candidates." *J Counsel Psychol* 14:51–6 Ja '67. * (*PA* 41:3644)
102. MARASCUILO, LEONARD A., AND GILL, GARY. "Measurable Differences Between Successful and Unsuccessful Doctoral Students in Education." *Calif J Ed Res* 18:65–70 Mr '67. * (*PA* 41:9389)
103. SCHMITT, JOHN A. "A Note on the Miller Analogies Test and Selection of Graduate Students in Education." *J Teach Ed* 18:59–61 sp '67. *
104. SEIBEL, DEAN W. "Predicting the Classroom Behavior of Teachers." *J Exp Ed* 36:26–32 f '67. *
105. STORDAHL, KALMER E. "Predicting Grades in a Master's-Degree Program." *J Ed Meas* 4:119–22 su '67. *
106. WALLEN, NORMAN E., AND CAMPBELL, MARY LOU A. "Vocabulary and Non-verbal Reasoning Components of Verbal Analogies Tests (Miller Analogies Test and Concept Mastery Test)." *J Ed Res* 61:87–9 O '67. *
107. WHITELEY, JOHN M.; SPRINTHALL, NORMAN A.; MOSHER, RALPH L.; AND DONAGHY, ROLLA T. "Selection and Evaluation of Counselor Effectiveness." *J Counsel Psychol* 14:226–34 My.'67. * (*PA* 41:9423)
108. GRIMSRUD, RICHARD ARLO. *A Method for Predicting Success in a Counselor Education Training Program.* Doctor's thesis, University of Minnesota (Minneapolis, Minn.), 1968. (*DA* 29:2115A)
109. HARDESTY, D. L., AND JONES, W. S. "Characteristics of Judged High Potential Management Personnel—The Operations of an Industrial Assessment Center." *Personnel Psychol* 21:85–98 sp '68. * (*PA* 42:16197)
110. LAURENT, HARRY. Chap. 1, "Research on the Identification of Management Potential," pp. 1–34. In *Predicting Man-*

agerial Success. Edited by John A. Myers, Jr. Ann Arbor, Mich.: Foundation for Research on Human Behavior, April 1968. Pp. v, 173. *
111. MERLE, SHERMAN. *The Selection of Students at a Graduate School of Social Work: A Study of the Incremental Value of a Pre-Admission Interview, and the Use of the Undergraduate Grade Point Average and Miller Analogy Test in Identifying the Successful and Unsuccessful Student.* Doctor's thesis, Brandeis University (Waltham, Mass.), 1968. (*DA* 29:101A)
112. CARLSON, RAE. "Rorschach Prediction of Success in Clinical Training: A Second Look." *J Consult & Clin Psychol* 33(6):699–704 D '69. * (*PA* 44:3697)
113. DE BERUFF, ELLEN. *The Prediction of Success in Master's and Doctoral Programs.* Doctor's thesis, University of Maryland (College Park, Md.), 1969. (*DAI* 31:1033A)
114. DIGIORGIO, ANTHONY JOSEPH. *Discriminant Function Analysis of Measured Characteristics Among Committed Career Groups With Requisite Graduate Training.* Doctor's thesis, Purdue University (Lafayette, Ind.), 1969. (*DAI* 30:4769A)
115. EWEN, ROBERT B. "The GRE Psychology Test as an Unobtrusive Measure of Motivation." *J Appl Psychol* 53(5): 383–7 O '69. * (*PA* 44:1370)
116. GAB, DEL D. *Prediction of Success for Doctoral Students in Education at the University of North Dakota.* Doctor's thesis, University of North Dakota (Grand Forks, N.D.), 1969. (*DAI* 31:61A)
117. MEHRABIAN, ALBERT. "Undergraduate Ability Factors in Relationship to Graduate Performance." *Ed & Psychol Meas* 29(2):409 19 su '69. * (*PA* 44:17508)
118. POSTON, WILLIAM KENNETH, JR. *Educational Administrator Job Performance and Training Program Admission Criteria.* Doctor's thesis, Arizona State University (Tempe, Ariz.), 1969. (*DAI* 30:532A)
119. RAWLS, JAMES R.; RAWLS, DONNA J.; AND HARRISON, C. WADE. "An Investigation of Success Predictors in Graduate School in Psychology." *J Psychol* 72(1):125–9 My '69. * (*PA* 43:16455)
120. SMOLINSKY, MERVIN PHILIP. *An Empirical Study of a Method of Measuring a Criterion for Graduate Student Success.* Doctor's thesis, University of Pittsburgh (Pittsburgh, Pa.), 1969. (*DAI* 30:1879A)
121. WILLIAMS, JOHN D., AND GAB, DEL. "Assessing the Doctoral Admission Policy." *Col Ed Rec* 55(1):14–20 O '69. *
122. CARLETON, FREDERICK O. "Relationships Between Follow-Up Evaluations and Information Developed in a Management Assessment Center." Abstract. *Proc 78th Ann Conv Am Psychol Assn* 5(2):565–6 '70. * (*PA* 44:19655)
123. FERNANDES, LUCIA M. *The Miller Analogies Test as a Predictor of Success in the Graduate School of Education, University of Pittsburgh.* Master's thesis, University of Pittsburgh (Pittsburgh, Pa.), 1970.
124. MEHRABIAN, ALBERT. "Ability Factors of Candidates for Graduate School." *Am Psychologist* 25(6):560–3 Je '70. *
125. PRIEN, ERICH P. "Measuring Performance Criteria of Bank Tellers." *J Indus Psychol* 5(1):29–36 Mr '70. *
126. SMITH, I. LEON. "Associational Achievement, Aptitude, and Creativity." *Ed & Psychol Meas* 30(4):999–1000 w '70. *
127. WILLIAMS, JOHN D.; HARLOW, STEVEN D.; AND GAB, DEL. "A Longitudinal Study Examining Prediction of Doctoral Success: Grade Point Average as Criterion, or Graduation vs. Non-Graduation as Criterion." *J Ed Res* 64(4):161–4 D '70. *

For reviews by Lloyd G. Humphreys, William B. Schrader, and Warren W. Willingham of Forms H, J, K, and an earlier form, see 6:472; for a review by John T. Dailey, see 5:352; for reviews by J. P. Guilford and Carl I. Hovland, see 4:304.

[364]

*Moray House Intelligence Tests. Ages 8.5–10.5, 10–12, 10–12 of above average ability, 12–14.5, 13.5 and over; 1930–70; MHIT; 5 levels; distribution restricted to education authorities; 75p per 20 tests (except *a*, £1); 5p per single copy; 12½p per manual for any one form of any one test; postage extra; Department of Education, University of Edinburgh; University of London Press Ltd. *
a) MORAY HOUSE JUNIOR REASONING TEST FOR NINE YEAR OLDS. Ages 8.5–10.5; 1947–70; 4 forms: *Junior Reasoning Test 2* ['58], *3* ('69), *6, 7,* ('70), (12 pages); manual (dates same as for test, 12–19 pages) for each form; 45(104) minutes for form 2, 40(75) minutes for forms 3, 6, 7.

b) MORAY HOUSE VERBAL REASONING TEST. Ages 10–12; 1930–70; earlier forms called *Moray House Intelligence Tests;* 2–3 new forms issued annually; 19 forms currently available: forms 65 ['60], 66 ('69), 67 ('68), 68 ('68), 69 ['62], 70 ['62], 71 ['63], 72 ['63], 74 ('68), 75 ('68), 76 ('65), 77 ('68), 78 ('68), 79 ('68), 80 ('68), 82 ('69), 85 ('68), 86 ('69), 87 ('70), (8 pages); manual (dates same as for test, 12 pages) for each form; practice test (dates generally same as for test, 2 pages) for each form; 10(15) minutes for practice test, 45(50) minutes for test.

c) [MORAY HOUSE VERBAL REASONING TEST: VERNIER TEST 2.] Ages 10–12 of above average ability; 1954–57; a "slightly more difficult" test than the tests in *b* above; 1 form ['57, 8 pages]; manual ['57, 12 pages]; 45(50) minutes.

d) MORAY HOUSE VERBAL REASONING TEST (ADV.). Ages 12–14.5; 1940–68; forms 7 ('61, 8 pages), 9, 10, (68, 8 pages); manual (dates same as for test, 12 pages) for each form; practice tests 6 ['53, 2 pages, for form 7], 7 ['54, 2 pages, for forms 9–10]; 10(15) minutes for practice test, 45(50) minutes for test.

e) MORAY HOUSE ADULT INTELLIGENCE TEST I. Ages 13.5 and over; 1952; 1 form ['52, 8 pages]; manual ['52, 15 pages]; 45(50) minutes.

REFERENCES

1–2. See 3:241.
3–4. See 5:353.
5–17. See 6:474.
18. BOYNE, A. W., AND CLARK, J. R. "Secular Change in the Intelligence of 11-Year-Old Aberdeen Schoolchildren." *Hum Biol* 31:325–33 D '59. * (*PA* 35:690)
19. ENTWISTLE, N. J., AND WELSH, JENNIFER. "Correlates of School Attainment at Different Ability Levels." *Brit J Ed Psychol* 39(1):57–63 F '69. * (*PA* 43:17988)
20. McINTOSH, D. M., AND WALKER, D. A. "The O Grade of the Scottish Certificate of Education." *Brit J Ed Psychol* 40(2):179–99 Je '70. * (*PA* 44:21528)

For a review by Patrick Slater of earlier forms, see 3:241; for a review by C. Ebblewhite Smith, see 2:1409.

[365]

*New South African Group Test. Ages 8–11, 10–14, 13–17; 1931–65; NSAGT; 3 scores: verbal, nonverbal, total; 3 levels; preliminary manual ('65, 44 pages) for junior and senior levels; separate answer sheets (hand scorable, IBM 1230) must be used; R2 per 10 tests; R2.40 per 100 hand scorable answer sheets; R4 per 100 IBM 1230 answer sheets; 30c per hand scoring stencil; 60c per manual; postpaid within South Africa; specimen set free; Afrikaans edition available; 55(100) minutes; Human Sciences Research Council. *

a) JUNIOR. Ages 8–11; 1931–65; Forms J, K, ['65, 32 pages].
b) INTERMEDIATE. Ages 10–14; 1931–63; Form G ['63, 32 pages]; manual ['63, 19 pages].
c) SENIOR. Ages 13–17; 1931–65; Forms S, T, ['65, 32 pages].

REFERENCES

1. ELDER, C. M. "The Statistical Procedure Adopted in the Construction and Standardization of the New South African Group Test." *J Social Res (Pretoria)* 8:1–12 '57. * (*PA* 34:3630)
2. SUGARMAN, LOLA. "Alpha Rhythm, Perception and Intelligence." *J Nat Inst Personnel Res* 8:170–9 S '61. * (*PA* 36:4DG70S)
3. STRÜMPFER, D. J. W., AND MIENIE, C. J. P. "A Validation of the Harris-Goodenough Test." *Brit J Ed Psychol* 38:96–100 F '68. * (*PA* 42:12134)

[366]

★Non-Readers Intelligence Test. Ages 6–9 to 8–11; 1964; no reading by examinees; 1 form; manual (31 pages); 32½p per 20 answer sheets; 12½p per

scoring stencil; 25p per manual; postage extra; (60) minutes in 2 sessions; D. Young; University of London Press Ltd. *

[367]

*Non-Verbal Tests. Ages 8 to 11-0, 10 to 12-11, 10 to 15; 1947–65; 3 levels; postpaid within U.K.; published for the National Foundation for Educational Research in England and Wales; Ginn & Co. Ltd. *
a) NON-VERBAL TESTS 1–2. Ages 10 to 12-11; 1947–59; title on test is *A Scale of Non-Verbal Mental Ability;* 2 forms (12 pages); optional practice test ['50, 3 pages]; no data on validity; distribution restricted to directors of education; 7p per test; 4p per practice test; 15p per manual for either form; 10(15) minutes for practice test, 30(35) minutes for test.
1) *Non-Verbal Test 1.* 1947–59; 1 form ['49]; revised manual ('59, 20 pages); no norms for ages 12-0 to 12-11 for administration with practice test; Welsh edition ['54] available; J. W. Jenkins.
2) *Non-Verbal Test 2.* 1948–51; 1 form ['49]; manual ['51]; supplementary provisional norms ['51, for ages 10-3 to 11-2 only] for administration with practice test; D. M. Lee and J. W. Jenkins.
b) NON-VERBAL TEST DH. Ages 10 to 15; 1953–58; formerly called *Non-Verbal Test 3;* 1 form ['53, 28 pages]; may be administered as a short form for ages 10-6 to 12-0; revised manual ('58, 8 pages); no data on reliability; separate answer sheets must be used; 13p per test; 2p per answer sheet; 10p per manual and stencil; 50(60) minutes for full test, 35(45) minutes for short version; B. Calvert (test) and I. Macfarlane Smith (original manual).
c) NON-VERBAL TEST BD. Ages 8 to 11-0; 1953–65; formerly called *Non-Verbal Test 5;* 1 form ['53, 17 pages]; revised manual ('65, 15 pages); no data on validity; 10p per test; 10p per manual; 20(40) minutes; D. A. Pidgeon.

REFERENCES

1–3. See 4:307.
4. See 5:356.
5. See 6:479.
6. ENTWISTLE, N. J., AND WELSH, JENNIFER. "Correlates of School Attainment at Different Ability Levels." *Brit J Ed Psychol* 39(1):57–63 F '69. * (*PA* 43:17988)

For reviews by T. R. Miles and John Nisbet, see 6:479; for a review by Cyril A. Rogers, see 5:356; for a review by E. A. Peel of the original edition, see 4:307.

[368]

★OISE Picture Reasoning Test: Primary. Grades 1–2; 1969–70; PRT; replaces the *Group Test of Learning Capacity: Dominion Tests: Primary;* Forms A, B, ('69, 12 pages); manual ('70, 10 pages plus scoring keys); no data on reliability and validity; Can $4 per 20 tests and manual; $1 per specimen set; postage extra; 51(80) minutes; Ontario Institute for Studies in Education; distributed by Guidance Centre. *

[369]

★The Oregon Academic Ranking Test. Bright children grades 3–7; 1965; OART; for rapid identification of the top 3 percent; 9 scores: making sentences, making comparisons, numbers, secret words, working problems, reasoning, completing sentences, sayings, total; 1 form (4 pages); manual (16 pages plus test); no norms or reliability data for subscores; $7.50 per 25 tests and manual; $6.50 per 25 tests; $2 per manual; postpaid; (30–40) minutes; Charles H. Derthick; Western Psychological Services. *

ROBERT H. BAUERNFEIND, *Professor of Educational Psychology, Northern Illinois University, DeKalb, Illinois.*

The *Oregon Academic Ranking Test* was designed to identify the "exceptionally bright child"—the child who is talented in convergent skills (arithmetic and reading vocabulary) and who is also talented in divergent skills (using objects, completing sentences, and interpreting popular adages). This test, printed in a four-page folder, is divided into eight sections, each employing a different item type. Some sections are objectively scored and some subjectively scored. A perfect paper yields a score of 100 points.

I have mixed feelings about this test. The test questions are really very good—very clever, and they seem consistently relevant to the author's stated purposes. But after one praises the test questions, he finds that everything else is downhill.

The first fault involves format. The test materials have clearly been squeezed into a four-page format; the readability is quite poor, with small type and some line lengths exceeding seven inches; and, in the divergent sections, there is not nearly enough room for the handwriting of pupils in the elementary grades. In the very first test, the children are given only $\frac{3}{16}$ of an inch of vertical space between lines on which they are to write. This test is for third and fourth graders? Maybe children in Salem, Oregon, are taught differently. But children in my area stumbled badly in reading the test problems, and they could not print or write their answers within the confines imposed by the test publisher. (I doubt that the publisher's own art director can write or print the word "Thursday" in that little box in item 5-E!) Those who designed this format were terribly insensitive to their audience—i.e., children aged 8 to 13. On the criterion of format alone, I cannot recommend this test for use below the seventh grade.

The second fault is that the manual is misleading in several places. First, it implies that the exceptionally bright children are in the top three percent of some undefined group. Why the top three percent instead of any other percent? There is no discussion of this point anywhere in the manual. Three percent of what group? There is no discussion of this matter either. But raw scores corresponding to a 97th percentile are prominently printed on the front

cover of each test booklet. Where did these data come from? Well, they came from studies of children in Salem, Oregon, with an average N around 180 per grade. Since Salem is a large city, these children must have been selected in some manner. But the manual does not bother to mention the matter of selection.

If the manual had said, "Here's the story of how this test worked in one school system," that would be fine—interesting and professional. But when normative data from a single undefined group are printed on the front cover of every test booklet, the test reviewer simply must blow the whistle.

All technical data apparently are based on these same small undefined groups of children in Salem, Oregon. And these technical studies are largely meaningless. The reliability coefficients are irrelevant, since the stated purpose of the test is to select the top three percent of a school population. Thus, relevant data would show percentages of youngsters selected *both times* in test-retest studies. Under "validity," the manual shows three tables correlating OART with the Stanford-Binet. But on page 1 of the manual the author implies that OART is to measure something somewhat different from the Stanford-Binet. Do low correlations between the two tests then demonstrate the "validity" of OART? Well, maybe. But the author would have done much better by staying with his strong suit—content validity.

If asked to select the three percent most academically-talented pupils in a school district, I would give a general educational development test (such as the *Iowa Tests of Basic Skills*) districtwide for use with all pupils. Then I would list the top five or six percent on the total score and ask the teachers to select the final three percent by applying criteria of "divergent thinking" and "abstract reasoning."

In short, this is quite a good test except for its insensitive format, but it seems inefficient and unnecessary. It could be used with junior high pupils who like to write small, if the school personnel especially like the mix of item types. But they should make such a choice solely on the basis of the item mix. There are no statistical studies reported in the manual that are relevant or useful to anyone outside of Salem, Oregon.

[370]

*Otis-Lennon Mental Ability Test. Grades kgn, 1.0–1.5, 1.6–3.9, 4–6, 7–9, 10–12; 1936–70; OLMAT; revision of the still-in-print *Otis Quick-Scoring Men-*

tal Ability Tests; 2 forms; 6 levels; manual ('67, 23 pages) for grades 4 and over; technical handbook ('69, 52 pages); supplementary technical data report ('70, 2 pages); $2 per handbook; $2.25 per specimen set of any one level; postage extra; Arthur S. Otis and Roger T. Lennon; Harcourt Brace Jovanovich, Inc. *

a) PRIMARY 1. Kgn; 1967–69; Forms J ('67, 8 pages), K ('68, 8 pages); manual for Forms J ('67, 21 pages), K ('68, 21 pages); norms booklet for Forms J ('67, 4 pages), K ('68, 4 pages); $6.50 per 35 tests; scoring service, 90¢ per test; (30–35) minutes.

b) PRIMARY 2. Grades 1.0–1.5; 1967–69; 2 editions; Forms J ('67, 8 pages), K ('68, 8 pages); manual for Forms J ('67, 22 pages), K ('68, 22 pages); norms booklet for Forms J ('67, 4 pages), K ('68, 4 pages); (30–35) minutes.

  1) *Hand Scorable Edition.* $6.50 per 35 tests; scoring service, 90¢ per test.

  2) *Machine Scorable Edition.* $9 per 35 tests; MRC scoring service, 36¢ and over per test.

c) ELEMENTARY 1. Grades 1.6–3.9; 1936–69; 2 editions; Forms J ('67, 12 pages), K ('68, 12 pages); manual for Forms J ('67, 23 pages), K ('68, 23 pages); norms booklet for Forms J ('67, 6 pages), K ('68, 6 pages); (55–60) minutes.

  1) *Hand Scorable Edition.* $6.80 per 35 tests; scoring service, $1 per test.

  2) *Machine Scorable Edition.* $9.30 per 35 tests; MRC scoring service, 42¢ and over per test.

d) ELEMENTARY 2. Grades 4–6; 1936–69; Forms J ('67, 8 pages), K ('68, 8 pages); norms booklet for Forms J ('67, 6 pages), K ('68, 6 pages); $6.80 per 35 tests; separate answer sheets (Digitek, Harbor, IBM 805, IBM 1230) may be used; $2.80 per 35 Digitek or IBM 1230 answer sheets; $2.30 per 35 IBM 805 answer sheets; $3 per 100 Harbor answer cards; 70¢ per Digitek or IBM scoring stencil; Harbor or IBM scoring service, 21¢ and over per test; (45–50) minutes.

e) INTERMEDIATE. Grades 7–9; 1936–69; Forms J ('67, 8 pages), K ('68, 8 pages); norms booklet for Forms J ('67, 6 pages), K ('68, 6 pages); answer sheets, prices, and time same as for Elementary 2 level.

f) ADVANCED. Grades 10–12; 1936–69; Forms J ('67, 8 pages), K ('68, 8 pages); norms booklet for Forms J ('67, 6 pages), K ('68, 6 pages); answer sheets, prices, and time same as for Elementary 2 level.

REFERENCES

1. BURKHALTER, W. D., JR. *A Validation Study of the Otis-Lennon Mental Ability Test, Elementary 1 Level, Grade Three.* Doctor's thesis, University of Tulsa (Tulsa, Okla.), 1969. (*DAI* 30:1812A)
2. COX, OTIS. *Creative Thinking in a High School Experimental Humanities Program.* Doctor's thesis, University of Alabama (University, Ala.), 1969. (*DAI* 31:214A)
3. HANNA, GERALD S.; BLIGH, HAROLD F.; LENKE, JOANNE M.; AND ORLEANS, JOSEPH B. "Predicting Algebra Achievement With an Algebra Prognosis Test, IQs, Teacher Predictions, and Mathematics Grades." *Ed & Psychol Meas* 29(4): 903–7 w '69. * (*PA* 44:21615)
4. BREUER, CHARLES EDWARD, JR. *The Effect of Prejudice Upon Test Performance.* Doctor's thesis, University of South Carolina (Columbia, S.C.), 1970. (*DAI* 31:3259A)
5. COTLER, SHELDON, AND PALMER, RICHARD J. "The Relationships Among Sex, Sociometric, Self, and Test Anxiety Factors and the Academic Achievement of Elementary School Children." *Psychol Sch* 7(3):211–6 Jl '70. * (*PA* 45:5019)
6. SKRIPOL, JAMES N. *Correlation of the Otis-Lennon Intermediate and the Wechsler Intelligence Scale for Children.* Master's thesis, Springfield College (Springfield, Mass.), 1970.

JOHN E. MILHOLLAND, *Professor of Psychology, The University of Michigan, Ann Arbor, Michigan.*

The construction and norming of this test bespeaks adherence to the highest level of cur-

rent standards. Sophisticated authorship apparently backed by the publisher's determination to spare no effort or expense has resulted in a product of exceptional merit.

The rationale comes from Vernon's description of the structure of mental abilities, embodying two major divisions, verbal-educational and practical-mechanical, integrated into Spearman's *g.* The Otis-Lennon test aims to cover only the verbal-educational half of the structure.

The standardization sample was chosen to represent the country's educational system, not the population at large. Controls were applied for size of school, family income, educational level of adults, types of school (public, private, church-related), geographic location (all 50 states were represented) and quality of school in terms of educational achievement within its own system. At the kindergarten level, 5,379 pupils were tested; for grades 1–12 the samples per grade varied in size from 11,866 to 14,746. The technical handbook gives a thorough account of the norming operations and the results.

The question arises, however, to what purpose is all this effort expended? Just what is the value of national norms? Has one learned anything by discovering that a school pupil, a grade, or a system is this or that far above or below a nationwide norm figure? Does it help to guide instructional policy? One can, of course, make many kinds of predictions, with reasonable accuracy, from norm-referenced scores. But couldn't just as good a job be done with scaled scores? The College Board has been doing fairly well with this kind of mechanism for some years.

It would seem that local school problems can be best attacked through the use of local norms, and that the only really significant function served by norms is furnishing a scale. This function can certainly be carried out effectively without the elaborate structure of "representative" national norms.

Scores on the Otis-Lennon tests may be expressed as deviation IQ's and as age and grade percentile ranks and stanines. Users are gently urged to interpret scores in terms of stanines rather than IQ's, and this may be a sign of a healthy trend. Deviation IQ's are only transformed standard scores anyway, and the IQ unit implies a precision that is not justified. The standard errors of measurement, based on alternate-forms reliability estimates, for IQ's from the Otis-Lennon vary from 3.9 to 7.0 points.

In addition to reliability and validity data, information on reading proficiency level required, speededness, and practice effect is provided in the handbook. The three lower levels of the test require no reading, and median reading grade-level ratings for the other three are below the lowest grade for which the test is intended. A few items, however, were rated at reading difficulty levels higher than the highest grade for which the test is recommended.

A speededness study showed a gain of 2.9 IQ points under untimed conditions for the Advanced Level tests; gains at all other levels were less than 2 points. Mean practice effect gains for a 2-week interval ranged from 1 to 3.6 points of IQ, giving an average gain of 2.5 points for practice effect.

An alternate forms reliability estimate is given for each grade and for each age. Those for grades 4 and below range from .83 to .89; beyond grade 4 they are all above .90. Below age 10 the estimates go from .81 to .90; above that age they are all .90 or better. Standard errors of measurement average about 4.5 IQ points at ages 10 or above, around 6 points at the lower ages. An unusual feature is the provision of IQ standard errors by stanine level.

The discussion of validity is organized in accordance with the content, criterion-related, and construct categories of the 1966 *Standards for Educational and Psychological Tests and Manuals.* The validity research was wide-ranging, and abundant data are provided. The test correlates adequately with educational criteria and with other measures of general scholastic aptitude. The Otis-Lennon test should perform well the functions it is intended to serve. These explicitly do not include measuring innate learning potential, and in the manuals special caution is advised in interpreting results for children who do not have normal backgrounds and motivation.

J Counsel Psychol 17(1):91–2 Ja '70. Arthur E. Smith. * A number of changes from the previous Otis series reflect attention to recent research and currently recommended practices in test development. While the fundamental theory about intelligence remains the same (reliable measure of "g"), nearly all the items are new or revised. * Primary I and II, however, are identical except for method of scoring and recommended use. The former is suggested for students in the last half of kindergarten and the latter in the first half of Grade 1 or the last half for "slower, less mature first graders." This distinction is misleading and serves no good purpose. It is impossible, moreover, to follow the authors' recommendation to administer Primary I in two sittings on the same day separated by a lunch period since kindergartens are typically half-day sessions. * The format of the items is similar to that used in the previous tests with a smaller proportion of verbal items at the upper levels. * Time limits appear to be ample and the authors' claim of a power measure are substantiated except that the study on speededness was conducted with students who were "somewhat" superior to typical students. Speed is a greater factor among lower levels of ability and hence studies at these levels should be conducted by the publishers as soon as possible. The procedures used in the selection of items are appropriate. The care taken to reduce the effects of reading handicaps on the student's performance is commendable. The scoring directions are excellent, particularly for the early series. Methods of scoring are flexible and probably meet the needs of any user. Extensive care and planning are evident in choosing the sample for standardization. Intelligence or scholastic ability is highly correlated with socioeconomic level. In the new Otis-Lennon series, a comparison of median family income and education completed for sampled school systems and for adults in the general population were virtually identical. * Obviously, stability over time cannot be determined immediately for a new test such as this. The comparisons of scores obtained over a 1-year lapse look promising with correlation coefficients ranging from .80 to .94 (highest at upper levels). The comparisons appear to be based on above-average students and hence these should be replicated on a more typical population. Nevertheless, estimates of reliability using alternate forms and split-half techniques give the user assurance that the results can be used with reasonable confidence. Standard errors of measurement indicate that the results may be used in an appropriate manner. As the authors point out, however, some of the levels have insufficient "top" and "bottom." Judging the validity of the Otis-Lennon is preliminary. The authors discuss content, criterion related, and construct validity and present data which supports the use of the instrument.

Correlation coefficients with other measures are in the expected magnitudes and some indicate substantial relationships with composite or total scores. * The Otis-Lennon Tests can be a useful tool for teachers, administrators, and counselors. The same careful work which marked the previous tests of this nature are evident in the new series. Future research is needed to determine the adequacy of their sampling techniques and general usefulness of the test in predicting academic performance.

J Ed Meas 6(2):111-3 su '69. Arden Grotelueschen. * The test booklets are well organized and designed, and the ease with which the test may be administered and scored is a continued positive feature. Raw scores are easily convertible to various types of normative scores * The authors state that the Primary I level is a downward extension of the Alpha Test. More specifically, they claim that "The downward extension of the Otis-Lennon series to include a level especially designed for use with kindergarten pupils (Primary I) is a noteworthy addition." This reviewer has some serious reservations about this latter statement. First, it could be argued that the Primary I level is not in and of itself a distinct level, because every item of this level is identical to that contained in the Primary II level. Apparently, the authors felt justified in differentiating between the Primary I and Primary II levels on the basis of response mode alone. For example, at the Primary I level the pupil is required to circle the item option representing his choice; with the Primary II level the pupil shades in a small oval beneath his choice. A sampling of several 4-year-olds, by the reviewer, indicates no difference in their ability to complete either the response mode of the Primary I level or the response mode of the Primary II level. Second, the technical data provided for the Primary I level are neither as complete nor as acceptable as those provided for the other test levels. For example, no validity information is given other than that with the Quick-Scoring Alpha Test administered to kindergarten pupils, for which the Alpha is not recommended. Presumably, part of the incompleteness results from the assumption that evidence for Primary II is directly applicable to Primary I, an assumption which contradicts the fact that the two tests are defined as two distinct levels. In summary, it would appear that the Otis-Lennon should have been published as five levels with one Primary

level for kindergarten and first grade pupils. Also, validity data based on the performance of kindergarten pupils are lacking. The manual contains an excellent discussion of the use of the age and grade norms and the interpretation of test scores. In contrast, some sections of the Technical Data and Developmental Research parts of the manual lack specific information essential to test consumers. The most serious lack of data is that of validity. The authors intend well by stating that validity studies are being conducted and that the results will appear in a forthcoming Technical Handbook. * Information on the procedures for standardization, scaling and norming is presented in detail. Moreover, the procedures for each appear to have been carefully conceptualized and conducted. * Substantial evidence is provided to indicate that the Otis-Lennon is highly reliable. * The higher internal-consistency coefficients were assumed to have not been influenced by speed. This assumption was based on findings obtained from an experimental study designed to ascertain the effect of speed on test performance. The findings were interpreted to provide conclusive evidence that speed of responding had a negligible effect on test performance when administered within the specified time limits. Had the design of the study incorporated a group receiving the test under strictly power conditions, a more conclusive test of the effect of speed on test performance would have been ascertained. The authors should be applauded for facing up to an embarrassing situation— that of making explicit a rationale for a test which has been in existence for around 50 years. In the development of the rationale, it was reasoned that the Otis-Lennon series should continue to be a broadly based measure of general mental ability, defined more specifically as "verbal-educational *g*." * It would have been desirable if the authors had presented factor-analytic evidence to complement the logical claims for the test. The omission of a factor study, of available data, is of concern to this reviewer, especially since correlational evidence interpreted by the authors to support the construct validity of the test is inconclusive. For instance, the authors interpret the high correlations reported between the Otis-Lennon and various mental ability batteries as evidence for construct validity. No explanation is given, however, to account for similar high correlations reported between the Otis-Lennon and various achievement test scores. (The Otis-Lennon is not unique in this respect.) The high correlations, for example, between the Otis-Lennon and the *Iowa Tests of Basic Skills* composite score leaves only 5% of the nonerror variance unexplainable at the fifth and eighth grade levels, when both predictor and criterion are corrected for attenuation. This finding is not appreciably different than that observed between Forms J and K of the Otis-Lennon itself. Thus, the Otis-Lennon gives ample evidence for predicting scholastic success. However, without stronger evidence of construct validity, it may be concluded that the predictability of scholastic success is due to the fact that the Otis-Lennon is a direct measure of scholastic success. Stated more practically, present evidence indicates that schools with an achievement testing program may not be adding anything unique to the total testing program by using the Otis-Lennon as a measure of general mental ability. In summary, the Otis-Lennon is a marked improvement, both technically and substantively, over its immediate predecessor, the Otis Quick-Scoring series. Aside from the criticisms directed toward the test's purported construct validity and its downward extension, the Otis-Lennon is an outstanding test of its kind.

For reviews by D. Welty Lefever and Alfred Yates of the Otis Quick-Scoring Mental Ability Tests, *see 5:362; for a review by Frederic Kuder, see 3:249; for reviews by F. Kuhlmann and C. Spearman, see 2:1413; for reviews by Psyche Cattell and R. Pintner, see 1:1053 (2 excerpts).*

[371]

★**Pacific Reasoning Series Tests: Pacific Test Series.** Job applicants in Papua and New Guinea; 1962–68; PRST; Forms A, B, C, ('68, 4 pages); manual ('68, 29 pages); Aus 80¢ per 10 tests; $2.50 per manual; $2.80 per specimen set; postpaid within Australia; 45(50) minutes; I. G. Ord; Australian Council for Educational Research. *

REFERENCE

1. BENNETT, M. J. "Reasoning Test Response in Urban and Rural Fijian and Indian Groups in Fiji." *Austral Psychologist* 5(3):260–6 N '70. * (PA 46:5459)

[372]

★**Performance Alertness "PA" (With Pictures): Individual Placement Series.** Adults; 1961–66; Form C ('61, 4 pages); no specific manual; series manual ('66, 107 pages); separate answer sheets must be used; $12 per 20 tests; $4 per 100 answer sheets; 50¢ per scoring stencil; $2.50 per series manual; $3.75 per specimen set; cash orders postpaid; 12(17) minutes; J. H. Norman; Personnel Research Associates, Inc. *

JOEL T. CAMPBELL, *Senior Research Psychologist, Educational Testing Service, Princeton, New Jersey.*

This test is a 45-item measure of the ability to select rapidly the correct response to a set of incomplete drawings or diagrams. Of the 45 items, 23 are pictorial representations (scarecrow, man in a hospital bed, weight lifter, etc.), 17 are mosaic-type geometric patterns, and 5 are bar-chart type figures. The examinee is required to select the correct response to each item from a set of 120 possible choices. The correct response may be turned at a different angle. Since the 45 correct answers are scattered randomly through the 120 possible responses, the person taking the test must work very quickly to complete all items within the 12-minute time limit.

The fact that the 99th percentile for engineers includes scores from 36 to 45 is an indication that even persons of high ability are not likely to complete the test. No information is given on rationale for item development, nor are any item analysis data presented. Some of the pictorial items have a degree of cultural content which is probably not desirable—e.g., the shape of the devil's pitchfork.

Test-retest reliability with a six-month time interval is reported as .92 for a sample of 31 engineers. This level of reliability appears satisfactory, but the sample it is based on is quite small, particularly considering the number of cases in the norms tables. Validity coefficients are reported for five industrial jobs. The criterion was job performance, although there is no indication of how job performance was measured. The coefficient for production engineers is .02, but for the other four jobs, shop foremen, machinists, machine parts inspectors, and assemblers, the coefficients range from .34 to .45.

The manual also reports correlations with 5 other tests. The highest, .72, is with the "Army Beta Exam." The correlations with the *Army General Classification Test* and the *Tests of Mechanical Comprehension* are .51 and .45, respectively. *Performance Alertness* also correlates .60 with the Filing subtest of the Individual Placement Series, and −.43 with age. These latter correlations indicate that the test score is probably significantly influenced by perceptual speed.

Median scores are reported for 14 different

occupations, with N's ranging from 11 for tooling inspections to 41 for foremen. The median scores range from 14 for laborer to 26 for engineer, with a reasonable progression of scores corresponding to apparent job difficulty level in between.

Percentile score tables are based on over 7,000 industrial cases, with subgroupings reported for clerical workers, shop workers, engineers, and supervisors.

The manual states that "The [test] serves as an effective double check on the results of the Academic Alertness test, and is often a more accurate and suitable instrument for the individual who has been deprived of cultural and educational opportunities." This advice runs counter to the research findings that the largest minority group, Negroes, do relatively better on verbal tests than on tests in nonlanguage areas.[1] The fact that this test is highly speeded is probably additional reason not to use it with a disadvantaged group, unless the job for which selection is being done involves very highly speeded operations.

The test probably measures something useful to performance in some jobs which is not fully measured by a verbal or arithmetic test. If testing time were not a constraining factor, the reviewer would prefer to use the *Progressive Matrices* or the *Revised Minnesota Paper Form Board Test.*

[373]

*Personnel Tests for Industry. Trade school and adults; 1945–69; PTI; 3 tests; manual ('69, 23 pages) for *a* and *b;* 90¢ per specimen set including manual for *Oral Directions Test;* postage extra; Psychological Corporation. *

a) PTI-VERBAL TEST. 1952–69; PTI-V; Forms A, B, ('52, 3 pages), C, D, ('67, 3 pages); $3 per 25 tests; 5(15) minutes; Alexander G. Wesman.

b) PTI-NUMERICAL TEST. 1952–69; PTI-N; Forms A, B, ('52, 4 pages), C, D, ('67, 4 pages); $3 per 25 tests; 20(25) minutes; Jerome E. Doppelt.

c) PTI-ORAL DIRECTIONS TEST. 1945–54; ODT; 1 form; 2 formats: 33⅓ rpm record, 3¾ ips tape recording (or cassette); separate answer sheets must be used; preliminary manual ['54, 8 pages]; $12 per set of record, scoring key, 100 answer sheets, and manual; $12.50 ($13) per set of tape recording (cassette), scoring key, 100 answer sheets, and manual; $5 per 100 answer sheets; Spanish edition available on tape; (15) minutes; Charles R. Langmuir.

1 LESSER, GERALD S.; FIFER, GORDON; AND CLARK, DONALD H. "Mental Abilities of Children From Different Social-Class and Cultural Groups." *Monogr Soc Res Child Develop* 30(4): 1–115 '65. *
STODOLSKY, SUSAN S., AND LESSER, GERALD. "Learning Patterns in the Disadvantaged." *Harvard Ed Rev* 37:546–93 f '67. *
VERNON, PHILIP E. "Ability Factors and Environmental Influences." *Am Psychologist* 20:723–33 S '65. *

REFERENCES

1. See 4:309.
2. CAMPBELL, SAMUEL C. *An Evaluation of the Oral Directions Tests of General Intelligence as an Effective Predictor of On-the-Job Performance of "Blue Collar" Workers.* Master's thesis, Fordham University (New York, N.Y.), 1958.
3. HABER, WILFRED. *The Contribution of Selected Variables to Success or Failure in a Vocational Rehabilitation Evaluation.* Doctor's thesis, New York University (New York, N.Y.), 1959. (*DA* 20:4171)
4. WOLFE, RAYMOND N., AND DAVIS, JOHN A. "Use of the Oral Directions Test in a Domiciliary Setting." *J Gerontol* 19:349–51 Jl '64. *

For a review by Erwin K. Taylor, see 5:366; for reviews by Charles D. Flory, Irving Lorge, and William W. Turnbull of the Oral Directions Test, *see 3:245.*

[374]

*Picture Test A. Ages 7-0 to 8-1; 1955–70; PTA; formerly called *Picture Test 1* and, earlier, *Picture Intelligence Test 1;* 1 form ['70, 16 pages, identical with test published in 1955 except for title]; manual ('61, 8 pages, identical with 1955 manual); no data on validity; 8p per test; 7p per manual; postpaid within U.K.; 22(45) minutes; Joan E. Stuart; published for the National Foundation for Educational Research in England and Wales; Ginn & Co. Ltd. *

For reviews by Charlotte E. K. Banks and M. L. Kellmer Pringle, see 5:367.

[375]

*The Preliminary Scholastic Aptitude Test. Grades 11–12; 1959–70; PSAT; abbreviated adaptation of the *College Board Scholastic Aptitude Test* for guidance and scholarship testing; test last administered in 1970, this test and the *National Merit Scholarship Qualifying Test* will be replaced by a new test, PSAT/NMSQT, in fall 1971; 2 scores: verbal, mathematical; Forms SPT1 ('70, 18 pages), SPT2 ('70, 21 pages); supervisor's manual ('70, 24 pages); score report booklet for students ('70, 15 pages); score report booklet for counselors and admissions officers ('70, 38 pages); bulletin of information ('70, 31 pages); 120(140) minutes; program administered for the College Entrance Examination Board by Educational Testing Service. *

REFERENCES

1–2. See 6:487.
3. KAUFMANN, JAMES D., AND DEMPSTER, DENNIS. "Prediction of SAT Scores." *Personnel & Guid J* 42:1026–7 Je '64. * (*PA* 39:5069)
4. BRADY, WILLIAM JOSEPH. *Twenty Quantitative Predictors of Academic Success in College as Measured by Grade Point Averages.* Doctor's thesis, University of Connecticut (Storrs, Conn.), 1965. (*DA* 26:5121)
5. SEIBEL, DEAN W. "The Relationships of Some Academic Ability Characteristics of High School Seniors to College Attendance and Performance." *Col & Univ* 42:41–52 f '66. *
6. FRIELDS, SUSAN IRENE. *A Comparison of the Relationships of the PSAT and SAT Test Scores for the Students of North Haven High School: 1965 and 1966.* Master's thesis, Southern Connecticut State College (New Haven, Conn.), 1967.
7. HILTON, THOMAS L., AND MYERS, ALBERT E. "Personal Background, Experience and School Achievement: An Investigation of the Contribution of Questionnaire Data to Academic Prediction." *J Ed Meas* 4:69–80 su '67. * (*PA* 42:4570)
8. CLAWAR, HARRY J. "A Short Highly-Efficient Prediction of College Entrance Examination Board Scholastic Aptitude Test Performance." *Ed Rec B* 94:42–4 Jl '68. * (*PA* 44:21523)
9. CLEARY, T. ANNE, AND HILTON, THOMAS L. "An Investigation of Item Bias." *Ed & Psychol Meas* 28:61–75 sp '68. * (*PA* 42:11356)
10. HELM, CARL E., AND HARASYMIW, STEFAN J. "Computer-Based Verbal Score Reports for the Preliminary Scholastic Aptitude Test." *Meas & Eval Guid* 1:27–35 sp '68. * (*PA* 44:7264)

11. MANNING, WINTON H. "The Measurement of Intellectual Capacity and Performance." *J Negro Ed* 37:258–67 su '68. *
12. COLLEGE ENTRANCE EXAMINATION BOARD. *College Board Score Reports: A Guide for Counselors and Admissions Officers: Preliminary Scholastic Aptitude Test, Scholastic Aptitude Test, and Achievement Tests.* Princeton, N.J.: the Board, 1970. Pp. 37. *

For a review by Wayne S. Zimmerman of earlier forms, see 6:487.

[376]

*Progressive Matrices. Ages 5 and over; 1938–65; PM; 3 levels; postage extra; J. C. Raven; H. K. Lewis & Co. Ltd. (U.S. distributor: Psychological Corporation.) *
a) STANDARD PROGRESSIVE MATRICES. Ages 6 and over; 1938–60; manual also uses the title *Progressive Matrices (1938), 1956 Revision;* 1 form ('56, 62 pages, identical with test copyrighted in 1938 except for change in one item and order of items); revised manual ('60, 25 pages, identical with 1956 manual except for bibliography); no norms for individual administration for ages 14 and over; separate record forms or answer sheets must be used; 210s. ($14) per 25 (10) tests; 12s. 6d. ($2.40) per 50 record forms (answer sheets); 30s. (75¢) per scoring key (set of scoring key and manual); 3s. 6d. per manual; 25s. per specimen set including 5 copies of the complementary *Mill Hill Vocabulary Scale* ($2.85 per specimen set); (60) minutes.
b) COLOURED PROGRESSIVE MATRICES. Ages 5–11 and mental patients and senescents; 1947–63; individual for ages 5–6; 1 form ('56, 38 pages, subtest Sets A and B same as subtest Sets A and B of the *Standard Progressive Matrices* except for color); revised manual ('63, 43 pages, identical with 1958 and 1960 manuals except for bibliography and revision in norms tables); record booklet (no date); separate record forms or answer sheets must be used for group administration; 210s. ($14.50) per 25 (10) tests; 17s. 6d. ($2.40) per 50 record forms (answer sheets); 7s. 6d. ($1.10) per manual (set of scoring key and manual); 25s. per specimen set including 12 copies of the complementary *Crichton Vocabulary Scale* ($3 per specimen set); [30] minutes.
c) ADVANCED PROGRESSIVE MATRICES. Ages 11 and over; 1943–65; 2 editions; manual ('65, 28 pages); 12s. 6d. ($2.40) per 50 record forms (answer sheets) for both editions; 30s. per scoring key ($1 per set of scoring key and manual) for both editions; 7s. 6d. per manual; 42s. ($5) per specimen set for both editions.
1) *Progressive Matrices (1947): Set 1.* For use either as a practice test for Set 2 or as a rough screening test; 1 form ('47, 14 pages); 50s. ($4) per 25 (10) tests; (60¢ per single copy); (10) minutes.
2) *Advanced Progressive Matrices, Set 2: 1962 Revision.* For use either as "a test of intellectual capacity" when used without a time limit or as "a test of intellectual efficiency" when used with a time limit ("usually of 40 minutes"); 1 form ('62, 38 pages, a revision and abbreviation of the 1947 Set 2); no data on reliability and validity for revised form; estimated norms based on 1947 data; 340s. ($24) per 25 (10) tests; ($3 per single copy); [40] minutes.

REFERENCES

1–8. See 2:1417.
9–21. See 3:258.
22–53. See 4:314.
54–115. See 5:370.
116–193. See 6:490.
194. VARADACHAR, DORAISWAMY. *A Study of the Distribution of Intelligence Employing the Progressive Matrices.* Master's thesis, University of Mysore (Mysore, India), 1954.
195. VARVA, FRANK IRVIN. *An Investigation of the Effect of Auditory Deficiency Upon Performance With Special Reference to Concrete and Abstract Tasks.* Doctor's thesis, University of Pittsburgh (Pittsburgh, Pa.), 1956. (DA 16:2532)
196. STEPHENSON, GEORGE ROTHWELL. *Form Perception, Abstract Thinking and Intelligence Test Validity in Cerebral Palsy.* Doctor's thesis, Columbia University (New York, N.Y.), 1957. (DA 17:1600)
197. MEHROTRA, S. N. "Predicting Intermediate Examination Success by Means of Psychological Tests: A Follow-Up Study." *J Voc & Ed Guid* 4:157–65 My '58. *
198. DHAR, CHANDRAKALA, AND MARR, EVELYN. "A Study of the Practice Effect of Taking Ravens Matrices on Performance on the N.I.I.P. Group Test 70/23 and of the N.I.I.P. on the Ravens Matrices." *J Voc & Ed Guid* 5:187–9 My '59. * (PA 38:3188)
199. FULLER, CARL WELLINGTON. *A Study of the Growth and Organization of Certain Mental Abilities in Young Deaf Children.* Doctor's thesis, Northwestern University (Evanston, Ill.), 1959. (DA 20:2382)
200. RAAHEIM, KJELL. "The Ability to Name Functions for Common Objects." *Nordisk Psykologi* 11(5):215–24 '59. * (PA 34:5589)
201. RATH, R. "Standardization of Progressive Matrices Among College Students." *J Voc & Ed Guid* 5:167–71 My '59. * (PA 38:2675)
202. ROYO, D., AND MARTIN, F. "Standardized Psychometrical Tests Applied to the Analysis of the Effects of Anti-Convulsive Medication on the Intellectual Proficiency of Young Epileptics." *Epilepsia* 1:189–207 D '59. *
203. ESBENSHADE, ANN AUGUSTA. *Rigidity as a Function of Age and Intelligence.* Doctor's thesis, University of Pennsylvania (Philadelphia, Pa.), 1960. (DA 21:956)
204. GOETZINGER, C. P.; DIRKS, D. D.; AND BAER, C. J. "Auditory Discrimination and Visual Perception in Good and Poor Readers." *Ann Otol Rhinol & Laryngol* 69:121–36 Mr '60. *
205. LEVINSON, BORIS M. "A Comparative Study of the Verbal and Performance Ability of Monolingual and Bilingual Native Born Jewish Preschool Children of Traditional Parentage." *J Genetic Psychol* 97:93–112 S '60. * (PA 35:6190)
206. PHELPS, HENRY BEVERIDGE. *Conceptual Ability and the Perception of Interaction in Movement by Elderly Persons.* Doctor's thesis, Columbia University (New York, N.Y.), 1960. (DA 21:2007)
207. BANNISTER, D.; SLATER, PATRICK; AND RADZAN, M. "The Use of Cognitive Tests in Nursing Candidate Selection." *Occup Psychol* 36:75–8 Ja–Ap '62. *
208. FRISBY, C. B. "The Use of Cognitive Tests in Nursing Candidate Selection: A Comment." *Occup Psychol* 36:79–81 Ja–Ap '62. *
209. MONTGOMERY, G. W. G. "Predicting Success in Engineering." *Occup Psychol* 36:59–68 Ja–Ap '62. *
210. OLSON, D. R., AND MACARTHUR, R. S. "The Effect of Foreign Language Background on Intelligence Test Performance." *Alberta J Ed Res* 8:157–66 S '62. * (PA 37:8270)
211. ROSS, JEAN. "Predicting Practical Skill in Engineering Apprentices." *Occup Psychol* 36:69–74 Ja–Ap '62. *
212. TESI, GINO, AND YOUNG, H. BOUTOURLINE. "A Standardization of Raven's Progressive Matrices 1938 (Revised Order, 1956)." *Archivio di Psicologia, Neurologia e Psichiatria* 23:456–64 S–O '62. * (PA 37:4950)
213. BOTWINICK, JACK, AND BIRREN, JAMES E. Chap. 8, "Mental Abilities and Psychomotor Responses in Healthy Aged Men," pp. 97–108. In *Human Aging: A Biological and Behavioral Study.* Edited by James E. Birren, Robert N. Butler, Samuel W. Greenhouse, Louis Sokoloff, and Marian R. Yarrow. National Institute of Mental Health, Public Health Service Publication No. 986. Washington, D.C.: United States Government Printing Office, 1963. Pp. xiii, 328. * (PA 38:5821)
214. GIBBENS, T. C. N.; WITH THE ASSISTANCE OF A. MARRIAGE AND A. WALKER. *Psychiatric Studies of Borstal Lads,* pp. 143–84. London: Oxford University Press, 1963. Pp. vi, 230. *
215. MORRISON, MARY. "A Gaelic Translation of the Wechsler Intelligence Scale for Children." Undergraduate thesis abstract. *Brit J Ed Psychol* 33:89–90 F '63. *
216. YATES, AUBREY J. "A Further Study of Progressive Matrices (1947)." *Brit J Ed Psychol* 33:307–11 N '63. * (PA 38:8441)
217. ANDERSON, ROBERT ARNOLD. *Mathematical Student Achievement of Third Form (Ninth Grade) Students in London and St. Paul-Minneapolis Metropolitan Areas.* Doctor's thesis, University of Minnesota (Minneapolis, Minn.), 1964. (DA 25:5008)
218. BECK, ELIZABETH JOAN. *Relation Between Social Impact and Selected Intellectual Traits in Preadolescent Negro Boys.* Doctor's thesis, Fordham University (New York, N.Y.), 1964. (DA 25:1328)
219. BIRKEMEYER, FLORENCE. "The Relationship Between the Coloured Progressive Matrices and Individual Intelligence Tests." *Psychol Sch* 1:309–12 Jl '64. *
220. BRADLEY, BETTY HUNT. "Differential Responses in Perceptual Ability Among Mentally Retarded Brain-Injured Children." *J Ed Res* 57:421–4 Ap '64. *

221. EVANS, RAY B., AND MARMORSTON, JESSIE. "Scoring Raven's Coloured Progressive Matrices to Differentiate Brain Damage." *J Clin Psychol* 20:360–4 Jl '64. * (*PA* 39:10102)

222. FORBES, A. R. "An Item Analysis of the Advanced Matrices." *Brit J Ed Psychol* 34:223–36 N '64. * (*PA* 39: 7756)

223. FOULDS, G. A. "Organization and Hostility in the Thematic Apperception Test Stories of Schizophrenics." *Brit J Psychiatry* 110:64–6 Ja '64. * (*PA* 38:8870)

224. GILES, GEORGE C., JR. "Predictive Validity of Progressive Matrices and Two Other Nonlanguage Tests of Mental Ability." *J Ed Meas* 1:65–7 Je '64. * (*PA* 39:7757)

225. JAIN, K. S. PRABHACHANDRA. "An Organismic Study of Cognitive Errors." *Manas* 11(2):105–13 '64. * (*PA* 39: 7392)

226. KHATENA, JOE; KIANG, CHEW GUAN; AND GOWAN, J. C. "Reliability of Raven Progressive Matrices Test With Asian Children." *Ed Malaysia* 1(1):22 '64. *

227. KUNDU, RAMANATH, AND SEN (CHAKRABORTY), ANIMA. "Matrices Score With Time Limit and Without Time Limit and Its Relationship With Multiplication Score." *J Psychol Res* 8:120–3 S '64. * (*PA* 39:5073)

228. LARSON, KEITH HAROLD. *The Characteristics of Vocationally Successful Mentally Retarded Youth as Described by Two Types of Intelligence Tests.* Doctor's thesis, University of Oregon (Eugene, Ore.), 1964. (*DA* 25:2815)

229. LI, ANITA KING-FUN. "The Use of Ability Tests in Hong Kong." *Int J Exp Res Ed* 1(2):187–95 '64. *

230. MACARTHUR, R. S.; IRVINE, S. H.; AND BRIMBLE, A. R. *The Northern Rhodesia Mental Ability Survey 1963.* Rhodes-Livingstone Communication No. 27. Lusaka, Zambia: Rhodes-Livingstone Institute, 1964. Pp. ix, 100. *

231. MOGENSEN, ALAN. "Raven's Progressive Matrices in Twelve Pairs of Uniovular Twins Brought Up Apart." *Scandinavian J Psychol* 5(1):50–2 '64. * (*PA* 39:1787)

232. PHILLIPS, G. R. "A Study of Psychological Tests for the Selection of Trainee Nurses: 1, General Approach." *Personnel Prac B* 20:28–32 D '64. * (*PA* 39:10886)

233. TONN, MARTIN HELMUTH. *The Effect of Time in Mental Measurement.* Doctor's thesis, State University of Iowa (Iowa City, Iowa), 1964. (*DA* 25:5130)

234. WEST, L. W., AND MACARTHUR, R. S. "An Evaluation of Selected Intelligence Tests for Two Samples of Metis and Indian Children." *Alberta J Ed Res* 10:17–27 Mr '64. * (*PA* 39:12328)

235. WOLK, ROBERT L., AND RUSTIN, STANLEY L. "Psychologic Evaluation of Gerontologic Population: Comparison of Results With the Raven Progressive Matrices (1947) Versus the Wechsler Adult Intelligence Scale." *J Am Geriatrics Soc* 12:807–9 Ag '64. *

236. BIRKEMEYER, FLORENCE. "The Relationship Between Coloured Progressive Matrices and the Wechsler Intelligence Scale for Children." *Psychol Sch* 2:278–80 Jl '65. *

237. CASHDAN, ASHER. "Conditions Affecting Problem-Solving in the Mentally Subnormal." *Int Copenhagen Congr Sci Study Mental Retard* 1964:623–6 ['65]. *

238. DE RENZI, ENNIO, AND FAGLIONI, PIETRO. "The Comparative Efficiency of Intelligence and Vigilance Tests in Detecting Hemispheric Cerebral Damage." *Cortex* 1:410–33 Je–S '65. * (*PA* 40:1897)

239. GUPTA, KUNWAR PAL. *A Study of Two Non-Language Intelligence Tests With Deaf Subjects in the Intermediate and Advanced Departments of the Kansas School for the Deaf.* Master's thesis, University of Kansas (Lawrence, Kan.), 1965.

240. KAKKAR, ARUNA. "The Role of Intelligence in Adolescents' Adjustment." *Indian J Psychol* 40:179–84 D '65. * (*PA* 40:12179)

241. KEBBON, LARS. *The Structure of Abilities at Lower Levels of Intelligence: A Factor-Analytical Study.* Stockholm, Sweden: Skandinaviska Testförlaget AB, 1965. Pp. 112. *

242. KHATENA, J. "A Study on the Reliability of the Raven's Coloured Progressive Matrices 1947." *Ed J (Singapore)* 3:51–3 '65–66. *

243. KHATENA, JOE. *A Study of Comparative Performance on the Raven's Coloured Progressive Matrices and the Goodenough Draw-A-Man Test in Two Singapore Primary Schools.* Master's thesis, University of Singapore (Singapore, Malaysia), 1965.

244. KLEIN, JOSEPHINE. "Levels of Perceptual Organization and of Performance After Time for Reflection." *Brit J Ed Psychol* 35:60–2 F '65. * (*PA* 39:10820)

245. MCDONALD, RODERICK P. "Difficulty Factors and Non-Linear Factor Analysis." *Brit J Math & Stat Psychol* 18:11–23 My '65. * (*PA* 39:13277)

246. MAITRA, AMAL K. "An Examination of the Difficulty Index and Item Validity of Standard Progressive Matrices (1956) With Indian Data." *Indian J Psychol* 40:127–31 S '65. *

247. MEIER, JOHN HENRY. *An Exploratory Factor Analysis of Psychodiagnostic and Case Study Information From Children in Special Education Classes for the Educable Mentally Handicapped.* Doctor's thesis, University of Denver (Denver, Colo.), 1965. (*DA* 26:3153)

248. MUELLER, MAX W. *A Comparison of the Empirical Validity of Six Tests of Ability With Young Educable Retardates.* Institute of Mental Retardation and Intellectual Development, IMRID Behavioral Science Monograph No. 1. Nashville, Tenn.: Peabody College Bookstore, 1965. Pp. vii, 130. *

249. MUELLER, MAX WILLIAM. *A Comparison of the Empirical Validity of Six Tests of Ability With Educable Mental Retardates.* Doctor's thesis, George Peabody College for Teachers (Nashville, Tenn.), 1965. (*DA* 26:6853)

250. RICH, CHARLES C., AND ANDERSON, ROBERT P. "A Tactual Form of the Progressive Matrices for Use With Blind Children." *Personnel & Guid J* 43:912–9 My '65. * (*PA* 39: 15197)

251. SHANAN, JOEL, AND SHARON, MIRIAM. "Personality and Cognitive Functioning of Israeli Males During the Middle Years." *Hum Develop* 8(1):2–15 '65. * (*PA* 39:14799)

252. SHAW, C. NEIL. "An Investigation of Scores Earned by Adults on the Raven Progressive Matrices Test." *Fla J Ed Res* 7:40–4 Ja '65. *

253. WIRT, ROBERT. *Raven-Coloured Progressive Matrices, Metropolitan Readiness, and Detroit First Grade Intelligence Tests as Predictors of Achievement in Primary Grades.* Master's thesis, Central Washington College of Education (Ellensburg, Wash.), 1965.

254. BINGHAM, WILLIAM C.; BURKE, HENRY R.; AND MURRAY, STEWART. "Raven's Progressive Matrices: Construct Validity." *J Psychol* 62:205–9 Mr '66. * (*PA* 40:7203)

255. CANTWELL, ZITA M. "Relationships Between Scores on the Standard Progressive Matrices (1938) and on the D.48 Test of Non-Verbal Intelligence and 3 Measures of Academic Achievement." *J Exp Ed* 34:28–31 su '66. * (*PA* 40:11152)

256. COLONNA, A., AND FAGLIONI, P. "The Performance of Hemisphere-Damaged Patients on Spatial Intelligence Tests." *Cortex* 2:293–307 Ap '66. * (*PA* 41:4895)

257. FITCH, MICHAEL JOHN. *Verbal and Performance Test Scores in Bilingual Children.* Doctor's research study No. 1, Colorado State College (Greeley, Colo.), 1966. (*DA* 27:1654A)

258. FREYBERG, P. S. "The Efficacy of the Coloured Progressive Matrices as a Group Test With Young Children." *Brit J Ed Psychol* 36:171–7 Je '66. * (*PA* 40:9922)

259. GUPTA, G. C., AND GUPTA, SARLA. "Norms for Raven's Coloured Matrices." *Manas* 13(2):87–9 '66. *

260. IRVINE, S. H. "Towards a Rationale for Testing Attainments and Abilities in Africa." *Brit J Ed Psychol* 36:24–32 F '66. * (*PA* 40:6103)

261. JACOBS, PAUL I. "Programed Progressive Matrices." Abstract. *Proc 74th Ann Conv Am Psychol Assn* 1:263–4 '66. * (*PA* 41:6291)

262. JOHNSON, SONIA ANN HARRIS. *Some Selected Classroom Variables and Their Relationship to Mathematics Achievement in Central Minnesota and the Greater London Area.* Doctor's thesis, Rutgers—The State University (New Brunswick, N.J.), 1966. (*DA* 27:139A)

263. KILBURN, KENT L., AND SANDERSON, ROBERT E. "Predicting Success in a Vocational Rehabilitation Program With the Raven Coloured Progressive Matrices." *Ed & Psychol Meas* 26:1031–4 w '66. * (*PA* 41:4843)

264. KILBURN, KENT L.; SANDERSON, ROBERT E.; AND MELTON, KYLE. "Relation of the Raven Coloured Progressive Matrices to Two Measures of Verbal Ability in a Sample of Mildly Retarded Hospital Patients." *Psychol Rep* 19:731–4 D '66. * (*PA* 41:4915)

265. LEY, P.; SPELMAN, M. S.; DAVIES, ANN D. M.; AND RILEY, S. "The Relationships Between Intelligence, Anxiety, Neuroticism and Extraversion." *Brit J Ed Psychol* 36:185–91 Je '66. * (*PA* 40:10100)

266. MONTGOMERY, G. W. G. "The Relationship of Oral Skills to Manual Communication in Profoundly Deaf Students." *Am Ann Deaf* 111:557–65 S '66. * (*PA* 41:1800)

267. ORME, J. E. "Hypothetically True Norms for the Progressive Matrices Tests." *Hum Develop* 9(4):223–9 '66. * (*PA* 41:2872)

268. RADFORD, J. "Verbalisation Effects in a 'Non-Verbal' Intelligence Test." *Brit J Ed Psychol* 36:33–8 F '66. * (*PA* 40:6643)

269. SEMLER, IRA J., AND ISCOE, IRA. "Structure of Intelligence in Negro and White Children." *J Ed Psychol* 57:326–36 D '66. * (*PA* 41:1418)

270. SHANTZ, CAROLYN UHLINGER. *A Developmental Study of Piaget's Theory of Logical Multiplication.* Doctor's thesis, Purdue University (Lafayette, Ind.), 1966. (*DA* 27:603B)

271. SITKEI, E. GEORGE, AND MICHAEL, WILLIAM B. "Predictive Relationships Between Items on the Revised Stanford-Binet Intelligence Scale (SBIS), Form L-M, and Total Scores on Raven's Progressive Matrices (PM), Between Items on the PM and Total Scores on the SBIS, and Between Selected Items on the Two Scales." *Ed & Psychol Meas* 26:501–6 su '66. * (*PA* 40:12784)

272. WANG, FUNG YEE. "A Study in General Ability Testing in Hong Kong: The Application of Ravens Progressive Matrices (1938) as a Group Timed Test and Its Relations to Attainments in Four Academic Areas." *J Ed (Hong Kong)* 23:56–9 '66. *

273. WETHERICK, N. E. "The Responses of Normal Adult Subjects to the Matrices Test." *Brit J Psychol* 57:297–300 N '66. *

274. WILLIAMS, JANETTE R., AND WILCOCK, JOAN C. "An Alternative to the Binet Mental Age Score as a Criterion in

Discrimination Learning." *J Mental Def Res* 10:27–32 Mr '66. * *(PA 40:9420)*

275. YATES, AUBREY J. "Level, Speed and Personality Factors in the Intellectual Performance of Young Children." *Brit J Ed Psychol* 36:312–6 N '66. * *(PA 41:463)*

276. YATES, AUBREY J. "A Note on Progressive Matrices (1962)." *Austral J Psychol* 18:281–3 D '66. * *(PA 41:4571)*

277. YATES, AUBREY J. "The Relationship Between Level and Speed on Two Intelligence Tests." *Brit J Ed Psychol* 36:166–70 Je '66. * *(PA 40:9421)*

278. ANDERSON, HARRY E., JR.; KERN, FRANK E.; AND COOK, CHARLOTTE. "Correlational and Normative Data for the Progressive Matrices With Retarded Populations." *J Psychol* 67:221–5 N '67. * *(PA 42:1396)*

279. ARCHIBALD, Y. M.; WEPMAN, J. M.; AND JONES, L. V. "Nonverbal Cognitive Performance in Aphasic and Nonaphasic Brain-Damaged Patients." *Cortex* 3:275–94 S '67. * *(PA 42:9335)*

280. ARCHIBALD, Y. M.; WEPMAN, J. M.; AND JONES, L. V. "Performance on Nonverbal Cognitive Tests Following Unilateral Cortical Injury to the Right and Left Hemisphere." *J Nerv & Mental Dis* 145:25–36 Jl '67. * *(PA 42:4382)*

281. BANNISTER, D., AND PRESLY, A. S. "Test Selection of Overseas Nursing Candidates: A Cross Validation Study." *B Brit Psychol Soc* 20:21–4 Jl '67. *

282. BUDOFF, MILTON. "Learning Potential Among Institutionalized Young Adult Retardates." *Am J Mental Def* 72:404–11 N '67. * *(PA 42:7631)*

283. CANTWELL, ZITA M. "The Performance of American Pupils on the Coloured Progressive Matrices." *Brit J Ed Psychol* 37:389–90 N '67. * *(PA 42:5577)*

284. CATE, CLARENCE C. "Test Behavior of ESL Students." *Calif J Ed Res* 18:184–7 S '67. * *(PA 42:4480)*

285. FLEMING, JEAN McKEY. *Body Image and Learning of Deaf and Hearing Boys.* Doctor's thesis, University of Florida (Gainesville, Fla.), 1967. *(DA 29:144A)*

286. GANGULY, ARUN K. "An Experimental Study of the Variation in Concept Formation Ability of Young Adults Due to Socio-Economic Status." *Manas* 14:69–75 D '67. * *(PA 43:11098)*

287. GOETZINGER, CORNELIUS P.; WILLS, ROBERT C.; AND DEKKER, LYNN CROUTER. "Non-Language IQ Tests Used With Deaf Pupils." *Volta R* 69:500–6 O '67. *

288. HARFORD, THOMAS. "An Item Analysis of the Progressive Matrices Test for Samples of Male Schizophrenic Patients." *J Clin Psychol* 23:377–80 Jl '67. * *(PA 41:15268)*

289. HERON, ALASTAIR, AND CHOWN, SHEILA. *Age and Function.* London: J. & A. Churchill Ltd., 1967. Pp. x, 182. *

290. JOHNSON, DALE L.; JOHNSON, CARMEN A.; AND PRICE-WILLIAMS, DOUGLASS. "The Draw-A-Man Test and Raven Progressive Matrices Performance of Guatemalan Maya and Ladino Children." *Revista Interamericana de Psicología* 1:143–57 Je '67. * *(PA 41:11919)*

291. JURJEVICH, R. M. "Avoidable Errors on Raven Progressive Matrices and Psychopathological Indices." Abstract. *Psychol Rep* 21:364 O '67. *

292. JURJEVICH, R. M. "Intellectual Assessment With Gorham's Proverbs Test, Raven's Progressive Matrices, and WAIS." *Psychol Rep* 20:1285–6 Je '67. * *(PA 41:15271)*

293. KHATENA, J. "An Item Analysis of the Coloured Progressive Matrices With Asian Singapore Children." *Malaysian J Ed* 4:82–5 Je '67. *

294. KHATENA, JOE, AND GOWAN, J. C. "Crosscultural Measurement of Intelligence With the DAM and CPM." *Gifted Child Q* 11:227–30 w '67. * *(PA 42:7111)*

295. KLINGELHOFER, E. L. "Performance of Tanzanian Secondary School Pupils on the Raven Standard Progressive Matrices Test." *J Social Psychol* 72:205–15 Ag '67. * *(PA 41:15272)*

296. KUMAR, PRAMOD. "Intelligence and Student Leadership." *J Psychol Res* 11:45–8 My '67. * *(PA 42:7332)*

297. MAJUMDAR, P. K.; DASGUPTA, J.; BASU, K.; AND DUTTA, D. "On the Working of a Battery of Psychological Tests: Raven's Standard Progressive Matrices Test." *B Council Social & Psychol Res* 9:1–6 Jl '67. * *(PA 45:699)*

298. MANDEL, ROBERT. *A Study of the Performance of Disadvantaged Seventh Grade Males on the Colored Raven Progressive Matrices and the California Test of Mental Maturity.* Master's thesis, University of Tennessee (Knoxville, Tenn.), 1967.

299. MEARS, FREDERICK GARY. *Effects of Reward on the Raven Progressive Matrices With Normal and Retarded Children.* Master's thesis, Texas Christian University (Ft. Worth, Tex.), 1967.

300. NEWCOMB, WALDO BURKETT, JR. *Normal Achieving and Underachieving Hearing-Impaired Students' Performance on Raven's Progressive Matrices (1938) and the Hooper Visual Organization Test.* Master's thesis, University of Texas (Austin, Tex.), 1967.

301. NICKOLS, JOHN. "Structural Efficiency of the Raven Coloured Matrices." Abstract. *J Clin Psychol* 23:489 O '67. * *(PA 42:1414)*

302. RAFI, A. ABI. "The Progressive Matrices (1938) and the Dominoes (D48) Tests: A Cross-Cultural Study." *Brit J Ed Psychol* 37:117–9 F '67. *

303. SCHNELL, RICHARD R., AND DWARSHUIS, LOUIS. "Progressive Matrices—Scores and Time." *Ed & Psychol Meas* 27:485–7 su '67. * *(PA 41:13599)*

304. SEIDEL, H. E., JR.; BARKLEY, MARY JO; AND STITH, DORIS. "Evaluation of a Program for Project Head Start." *J Genetic Psychol* 110:185–97 Je '67. * *(PA 41:11718)*

305. SYDIAHA, DANIEL. "Prediction of WAIS IQ for Psychiatric Patients Using the Ammons' FRPV and Raven's Progressive Matrices." *Psychol Rep* 20:823–6 Je '67. * *(PA 41:13602)*

306. TAYLOR, A. J. W. "Prediction for Parole: A Pilot Study With Delinquent Girls." *Brit J Criminol* 7:418–24 O '67. *

307. TULLY, G. EMERSON. "Test-Retest Reliability of the Raven Progressive Matrices Test (Form 1938) and the California Test of Mental Maturity, Level 4 (S-F 1963)." *Fla J Ed Res* 9:67–74 Ja '67. *

308. ANDERSON, HARRY E., JR.; KERN, FRANK E.; AND COOK, CHARLOTTE. "Sex, Brain Damage, and Race Effects in the Progressive Matrices With Retarded Populations." *J Social Psychol* 76:207–11 D '68. * *(PA 43:4329)*

309. ARCHIBALD, Y. M., AND WEPMAN, J. M. "Language Disturbance and Nonverbal Cognitive Performance in Eight Patients Following Injury to the Right Hemisphere." *Brain* 91:117–30 Mr '68. * *(PA 42:19160)*

310. BLUMENKRANTZ, JACK; WILKIN, WENDELL R.; AND TUDDENHAM, READ D. "Relationships Between the Progressive Matrices and AGCT-3a Among Older Military Personnel." *Ed & Psychol Meas* 28:931–5 au '68. * *(PA 43:3317)*

311. CRICKMORE, LEON. "An Approach to the Measurement of Music Appreciation (II)." *J Res Music Ed* 16:291–301 w '68. * *(PA 43:8756)*

312. DAS, J. P., AND DUTTA, TAPATI. "Standardization of Coloured Progressive Matrices: Norms for 10, 11 and 12 Year Old School Children." *J Psychol Res* 12:143–8 S '68. *

313. DOMINO, GEORGE. "Culture-Free Tests and the Academic Achievement of Foreign Students." Abstract. *J Consult & Clin Psychol* 32:102 F '68. * *(PA 42:7843)*

314. ELKIN, LORNE. "Predicting Performance of the Mentally Retarded on Sheltered Workshop and Non-Institutional Jobs." *Am J Mental Def* 72:533–9 Ja '68. * *(PA 42:7638)*

315. FINNEY, BETTY JANE. *The Modification of Conceptual Tempo in Disadvantaged Boys.* Doctor's thesis, Case Western Reserve University (Cleveland, Ohio), 1968. *(DAI 30:3782A)*

316. FINNIE, FRANCES RUTH. *The Relationship Between Perceptual Field Articulation and Intellectual Functioning in Paranoid Male Schizophrenics.* Doctor's thesis, George Washington University (Washington, D.C.), 1968.

317. HARFORD, THOMAS. "An Item Analysis of the Progressive Matrices Test for Samples of Male Schizophrenic Patients." *J Clin Psychol* 24:204–7 Ap '68. * *(PA 42:12472)*

318. HUTCHINS, BOB E. *The Relationship of Selected Factors to Performance of Teenage Teacher Aides in Eleven Appalachian School Districts.* Doctor's thesis, Ohio University (Athens, Ohio), 1968. *(DA 29:1041A)*

319. JACOBS, PAUL I., AND VANDEVENTER, MARY. "Progressive Matrices: An Experimental, Developmental, Nonfactorial Analysis." *Percept & Motor Skills* 27:759–66 D '68. * *(PA 43:8354)*

320. KENCHAVEERAIAH, B., AND MENON, A. SREEKUMAR. "Relationship of Intelligence and Fluency Among Students." *Indian Psychol R* 4:123–5 Ja '68. * *(PA 43:11322)*

321. MACARTHUR, R. S. "Assessing Intellectual Potential of Native Canadian Pupils: A Summary." *Alberta J Ed Res* 14:115–22 Je '68. * *(PA 44:4170)*

322. MACARTHUR, RUSSELL. "Some Differential Abilities of Northern Canadian Native Youth." *Int J Psychol* 3(1):43–50 '68. *

323. MATTHEWS, CHARLES G.; CHUN, RAYMOND W. M.; GRABOW, JACK D.; AND THOMPSON, WAYNE H. "Psychological Sequelae in Children Following California Arboviros Encephalitis." *Neurol* 18:1023–30 O '68. * *(PA 43:5771)*

324. MEHROTRA, K. K. "The Relationship of the WISC to the Progressive Matrices." *J Psychol Res* 12:114–8 S '68. *

325. MEHROTRA, KRISHNA KANT. "A Comparative Study of WISC and Raven's Progressive Matrices." *Psychol Studies* 13:47–50 Ja '68. *

326. MUELLER, MAX W. "Validity of Six Tests of Ability With Educable Mental Retardates." *J Sch Psychol* 6:136–46 w '68. * *(PA 42:11152)*

327. MUNRO, HELLE. "Verbal Fluency in Test and Group Situations." *Brit J Proj Psychol & Pers Study* 13:25–9 Je '68. * *(PA 45:946)*

328. ORME, J. E. "A Comment on Estimating W.A.I.S. IQ From Progressive Matrices Scores." *J Clin Psychol* 24:94–5 Ja '68. *

329. PERIASWAMY, THIRU M. *Development of Norms for J. C. Raven's Intelligence Test on a Rural Sample.* Master's thesis, Meston Training College, University of Madras (Madras, India), 1968.

330. PHILLIPS, C. J., AND BANNON, W. J. "The Stanford-Binet, Form L-M, Third Revision: A Local English Study of Norms, Concurrent Validity and Social Differences." *Brit J Ed Psychol* 38:148–61 Je '68. * *(PA 42:17600)*

331. POTTASH, MYRA E. *An Evaluation of Raven's Progressive Matrices for the Measurement of Certain Ability,*

Achievement, and Personality Factors in Junior High School. Master's thesis, Bryn Mawr College (Bryn Mawr, Pa.), 1968.

332. RAO, S. NARAYANA, AND REDDY, I. K. S. "Development of Norms for the Raven's Coloured Progressive Matrices Test (Booklet Form) on Elementary School Children." *Psychol Studies* 13:105–7 Jl '68. *

333. RATTAN, M. S., AND MacARTHUR, R. S. "Longitudinal Prediction of School Achievement for Metis and Eskimo Pupils." *Alberta J Ed Res* 14:37–41 Mr '68. * *(PA* 44:4249)

334. SHEPPARD, CHARLES; FIORENTINO, DIANE; COLLINS, LOIS; AND MERLIS, SIDNEY. "Performance Errors on Ravens Progressive Matrices (1938) by Sociopathic and Schizotypic Personality Types." *Psychol Rep* 23:1043–6 D '68. * *(PA* 43: 8462)

335. SHEPPARD, CHARLES; FIORENTINO, DIANE; COLLINS, LOIS; AND MERLIS, SIDNEY. "Ravens Progressive Matrices (1938): Normative Data on Male Narcotic Addicts." *Psychol Rep* 23:343–8 O '68. * *(PA* 43:10036)

336. SINHA, UMA. "The Use of Raven's Progressive Matrices Test in India." *Indian Ed R* 3:75–88 Ja '68. * *(PA* 42:13757)

337. TAMHANKAR, V. S. "Norms for the X Grade on Advanced Progressive Matrices (1962) and Some Correlates of Intelligence." *J Psychol Res* 12:85–9 My '68. * *(PA* 43:5894)

338. TULKIN, STEVEN R., AND NEWBROUGH, J. R. "Social Class, Race, and Sex Differences on the Raven (1956) Standard Progressive Matrices." *J Consult & Clin Psychol* 32:400–6 Ag '68. * *(PA* 42:17225)

339. VEJLESKOV, HANS. "An Analysis of Raven Matrix Responses in Fifth Grade Children, 1." *Scandinavian J Psychol* 9(3):177–86 '68. * *(PA* 43:4018)

340. WATTIMENA, DANIEL MARCUS. *The Impact of Motivation on Intelligence.* Doctor's thesis, University of California (Berkeley, Calif.), 1968. *(DA* 29:3011A)

341. AFTANAS, M. S., AND ROYCE, J. R. "A Factor Analysis of Brain Damage Tests Administered to Normal Subjects With Factor Score Comparisons Across Ages." *Multiv Behav Res* 4(4):459–81 O '69. * *(PA* 44:11030)

342. ALMGREN, PER-ERIK; ANDERSSON, ALF L.; AND KULLBERG, GUNVOR. "Differences in Verbally Expressed Cognition Following Left and Right Ventrolateral Thalamotomy." *Scandinavian J Psychol* 10(4):243–9 '69. * *(PA* 44:9042)

343. BEVAN, WILTSHIRE E., AND GRAY, JOHN E. "Draw-A-Man and Raven's Progressive Matrices (1938) Intelligence Test Performance of Reserve Indian Children." *Can J Behav Sci* 1(2):119–22 Ap '69. * *(PA* 44:12604)

344. BLUE, ARTHUR WILLIAM. *Prediction of Learning Ability Across Cultures.* Doctor's thesis, Iowa State University (Ames, Iowa), 1969. *(DAI* 30:5220B)

345. BURKE, HENRY R., AND BINGHAM, WILLIAM C. "Raven's Progressive Matrices: More on Construct Validity." *J Psychol* 72(2):247–51 Jl '69. * *(PA* 44:71)

346. COSTA, LOUIS D.; VAUGHAN, HERBERT G., JR.; HORWITZ, MORTON; AND RITTER, WALTER. "Patterns of Behavioral Deficit Associated With Visual Spatial Neglect." *Cortex* 5(3):242–63 S '69. * *(PA* 44:13142)

347. EISENTHAL, SHERMAN, AND HARFORD, THOMAS. "Variation in the Form and Administration of Raven's Progressive Matrices Scale in a Neuropsychiatric Population." *Psychol Rep* 24(1):262 F '69. * *(PA* 43:13533)

348. FRACCHIA, JOHN F.; FIORENTINO, DIANE; SHEPPARD, CHARLES; AND MERLIS, SIDNEY. "A Comparison of Techniques for the Scoring of Avoidable Errors on the Raven Progressive Matrices." *J Psychol* 72(1):93–8 My '69. * *(PA* 43:15804)

349. FRANK, HARRY, AND FIEDLER, EDNA R. "A Multifactor Behavioral Approach to the Genetic-Etiological Diagnosis of Mental Retardation." *Multiv Behav Res* 4(2):131–45 Ap '69. * *(PA* 43:16258)

350. GOETZINGER, MADELON R., AND HOUCHINS, ROLLIE R. "The 1947 Colored Raven's Progressive Matrices With Deaf and Hearing Subjects." *Am Ann Deaf* 114(2):95–101 Mr '69. * *(PA* 43:11730)

351. HARFORD, THOMAS, AND EISENTHAL, SHERMAN. "An Item Analysis of the Progressive Matrices Test for a Sample of Hospitalized Schizophrenics." *J Clin Psychol* 25(2):185 Ap '69. * *(PA* 43:14468)

352. HWANG, CHIEN-HOU. "Parent-Child Resemblance in Psychological Characteristics." *Psychol & Ed* 3:29–36 D '69. *

353. IRVINE, S. H. "Factor Analysis of African Abilities and Attainments: Constructs Across Cultures." *Psychol B* 71(1):20–32 Ja '69. * *(PA* 43:7553)

354. IRVINE, SIDNEY H. "Figural Tests of Reasoning in Africa: Studies in the Use of Raven's Progressive Matrices Across Cultures." *Int J Psychol* 4(3):217–28 '69. * *(PA* 45:6334)

355. KINGSLEY, LEONARD. "Functioning of Acute and Chronic Schizophrenics on Measures of Abstract Reasoning." *J Clin Psychol* 25(2):144–7 Ap '69. * *(PA* 43:14470)

356. LANGE, UNA ANN. *Differential Performances of Minimally Brain-Damaged Boys and of Non-Brain-Damaged Boys on Selected Tests.* Doctor's thesis, University of Nebraska (Lincoln, Neb.), 1969. *(DAI* 30:2852A)

357. MacARTHUR, RUSSELL S. "Some Cognitive Abilities of Eskimo, White, and Indian-Métis Pupils Aged 9 to 12 years." *Can J Behav Sci* 1(1):50–9 Ja '69. * *(PA* 44:12319)

358. MACDONALD, H. A., AND NETHERTON, A. H. "Contribution of a Non-Verbal General Ability Test to the Educational Assessment of Pupils in the Cross-Cultural Setting of the Canadian North." *J Ed Res* 62(7):315–9 Mr '69. *

359. McNAMARA, J. REGIS; PORTERFIELD, CHARLES L.; AND MILLER, LAWRENCE E. "The Relationship of the Wechsler Preschool and Primary Scale of Intelligence With the Coloured Progressive Matrices (1956) and the Bender Gestalt Test." *J Clin Psychol* 25(1):65–8 Ja '69. * *(PA* 43:9766)

360. NICHOLSON, CHARLES L. "The Use of Four Screening Instruments." *Ann Inter Conf Assn Children Learn Dis* 6: 101–7 '69. *

361. OWENS, RICHARD THOMAS. *A Study of the Performance of Minimally Brain-Damaged and Emotionally Disturbed Boys on Six Selected Psychological Tests.* Doctor's thesis, University of Nebraska (Lincoln, Neb.), 1969. *(DAI* 31:383B)

362. PANDE, C. G., AND KOTHARI, S. "Field Dependence and the Raven's Progressive Matrices." *Psychologia* 12(1):49–51 Mr '69. *

363. PAYNE, J. F. "A Comparative Study of the Mental Ability of Seven- and Eight-Year-Old British and West Indian Children in a West Midland Town." *Brit J Ed Psychol* 39(3): 326–7 N '69. *

364. ROMNEY, DAVID. "The Validity of Certain Tests of Overinclusion." *Brit J Psychiatry* 115(522):591–2 My '69. * *(PA* 44:3689)

365. ROSENBERG, C. M. "Determinants of Psychiatric Illness in Young People." *Brit J Psychiatry* 115(525):907–15 Ag '69. * *(PA* 44:10505)

366. SHEPPARD, CHARLES; FIORENTINO, DIANE; COLLINS, LOIS; AND MERLIS, SIDNEY. "Further Study of Performance Errors on Ravens Progressive Matrices (1938)." *J Psychol* 71(1):127–32 Ja '69. * *(PA* 43:5430)

367. WOBER, MALLERY. "The Meaning and Stability of Raven's Matrices Test Among Africans." *Int J Psychol* 4(3): 229–35 '69. * *(PA* 45:6337)

368. CANABAL, JUANA VILLANUEVA. *Comparison of Deaf and Normally Hearing Children on Analogy Items Under Different Methods of Instruction at Different Age Levels.* Doctor's thesis, St. John's University (Jamaica, N.Y.), 1970. *(DAI* 31: 3700B)

369. CARLSON, JERRY S. "A Note on the Relationships Between the Draw-A-Man Test, the Progressive Matrices Test, and Conservation." *J Psychol* 74(2):231–5 Mr '70. * *(PA* 44:12310)

370. DAVIS, WILLIAM E.; DeWOLFE, ALAN S.; DIZZONNE, MICHAEL F.; AND AIR, DOROTHY HABERKAMP. "Relationship Between Schizophrenics' Premorbid History and Intelligence Test Performance." *Newsl Res Psychol* 12(4):5–6 N '70. *

371. FOULDS, G. A. "Progressive Matrices and the Mill Hill Vocabulary Scale as a Diagnostic Aid Among Psychiatric Patients." *Brit J Social & Clin Psychol* 9(1):80–2 F '70. *

372. FRACCHIA, JOHN; FIORENTINO, DIANE; SHEPPARD, CHARLES; AND MERLIS, SIDNEY. "Raven Progressive Matrices Avoidable Errors as a Measure of Psychopathological Ideational Influences Upon Reasoning Ability." *Psychol Rep* 26(2): 359–62 Ap '70. * *(PA* 44:21168)

373. FRACCHIA, JOHN; SHEPPARD, CHARLES; MERLIS, MICHAEL; AND MERLIS, SIDNEY. "Atypical Reasoning Errors in Sociopathic, Paranoid, and Schizophrenic Personality Types." *J Psychol* 76(1):91–5 S '70. * *(PA* 45:4560)

374. GIBSON, H. B., AND WEST, D. J. "Social and Intellectual Handicaps as Precursors of Early Delinquency." *Brit J Criminol* 10(1):21–32 Ja '70. * *(PA* 44:16949)

375. GROSVENOR, THEODORE. "Refractive State, Intelligence Test Scores, and Academic Ability." *Am J Optom* 47(5): 355–61 My '70. * *(PA* 46:4624)

376. HAZARI, ANANDI, AND THAKUR, GIRIDHAR P. "The Relation Between Manifest Anxiety and Intelligence." *J Ed & Psychol* 27(4):375–7 Ja '70. *

377. IRVING, DAVID J.; ROBINSON, R. A.; AND McADAM, W. "The Validity of Some Cognitive Tests in the Diagnosis of Dementia." *Brit J Psychiatry* 117(537):149–56 Ag '70. *

378. JACOBS, PAUL I., AND VANDEVENTER, MARY. "Information in Wrong Responses." *Psychol Rep* 26(1):311–5 F '70. * *(PA* 45:4253)

379. JOHNSON, JAMES E., AND OZIEL, LEON J. "An Item Analysis of the Raven Colored Progressive Matrices Test for Paranoid and Non-Paranoid Schizophrenic Patients." *J Clin Psychol* 26(3):357–9 Jl '70. * *(PA* 45:1054)

380. KEAR-COLWELL, J. J. "The B Factor Scale of the 16 PF as a Measure of Intelligence in Psychiatric Patients." *J Clin Psychol* 26(4):477–9 O '70. * *(PA* 45:4540)

381. KOTHARI, S. "Relationship Between the Progressive Matrices Tests and the Cancellation Task." *Psychol Studies* 15(1):59–61 Ja '70. *

382. NICHOLSON, CHARLES L. "Correlations Among CMMS, PPVT, and RCPM for Cerebral Palsied Children." *Percept & Motor Skills* 30(3):715–8 Je '70. * *(PA* 44:17151)

383. ORME, J. E. "A Practical Guide to Estimating Intelligence, Attainments and Intellectual Deficit." *Acta Psychologica* 32(2):145–61 Ap '70. * *(PA* 44:16684)

384. SCHUT, DIEN; BESIJN, J. W.; BOEKE, P. E.; AND ULEMAN, A. L. "Psychological Examination Before and After Stereotactic Operations in Parkinson Patients." *Psychiatria, Neurologia, Neurochirurgia* 73(5):375–86 S–O '70. *

385. SEIM, SOL. "The Teenagers Grow Up." *Int Congr Rorsch & Other Proj Tech* 7:387–98 '70. *

386. WARDER, JOHN; PRESLY, ALLAN S.; AND KIRK, JOAN. "Intelligence and Literacy in Prison and Hospital Populations." *Brit J Criminol* 10(3):286–7 Jl '70. * (*PA* 46:1469)

387. WEINGARTEN, GILAD, AND ALEXANDER, JOHN F. "Effects of Physical Exertion on Mental Performance of College Males of Different Physical Fitness Level." *Percept & Motor Skills* 31(2):371–8 O '70. * (*PA* 45:5441)

For a review by Morton Bortner, see 6:490; for reviews by Charlotte Banks, W. D. Wall, and George Westby, see 4:314; for reviews by Walter C. Shipley and David Wechsler of the 1938 edition, see 3:258; for a review by T. J. Keating, see 2:1417.

[377]

*Purdue Non-Language Personnel Test. Business and industry; 1957–69; PNPT; abbreviated revision of *Purdue Non-Language Test;* Forms A-S, B-S, ['69, 2 pages, all items taken from 1957 tests]; preliminary manual ('69, 4 pages); $4 per 25 tests, postage extra; 75¢ per specimen set, postpaid; 10(15) minutes; Joseph Tiffin; University Book Store. *

For reviews by John D. Hundleby and Benjamin Rosner of the earlier test, see 6:491.

[378]

★Quick Word Test. Grades 4–6, 7–12 and average adults, college and professional adults; 1957–67; QWT; 3 levels; manuals: elementary level ('67, 14 pages), levels 1 and 2 ('64, 14 pages), supplementary report ('67, 6 pages); 70¢ per scoring stencil; $1.50 per specimen set; postage extra; scoring service, 19¢ and over per test; (15–20) minutes; Edgar F. Borgatta and Raymond J. Corsini; Harcourt Brace Jovanovich, Inc. *

a) ELEMENTARY LEVEL. Grades 4–6; 1967; Form Am (1 page); $3 per 35 IBM 805/Digitek test-answer sheets; $3.30 per 35 IBM 1230 test-answer sheets.

b) LEVEL 1. Grades 7–12 and average adults; 1957–65; IBM 805 Forms Am, Bm, Cm, Dm, ('64, 1 page, identical with tests copyrighted 1957); IBM 1230 Forms Am ('64), Bm ('65), Cm ('65), Dm ('65), (1 page, identical with tests copyrighted 1957); Form Dm sales restricted; $3 per 35 IBM 805 test-answer sheets; $3.30 per 35 IBM 1230 test-answer sheets.

c) LEVEL 2. College and professional adults; 1957–65; IBM 805 Forms Am, Bm, ('64, 1 page, identical with tests copyrighted 1957); IBM 1230 Forms Am ('64), Bm ('65), (1 page, identical with tests copyrighted 1957); Form Bm sales restricted; prices same as for Level 1.

REFERENCES

1. BORGATTA, EDGAR F., AND CORSINI, RAYMOND J. "The Quick Word Test." *J Ed Res* 54:15–9 S '60. *

2. BORGATTA, EDGAR F., AND CORSINI, RAYMOND J. "The Quick Word Test (QWT) and the WAIS." *Psychol Rep* 6:201 Ap '60. * (*PA* 35:6397)

3. BORGATTA, EDGAR F., AND BOHRNSTEDT, GEORGE W. "Elementary Forms of the Quick Word Test." *J Exp Ed* 35:57–61 w '66. *

4. GROTELUESCHEN, ARDEN, AND KNOX, ALAN B. "Analysis of Quick Word Test as an Estimate of Adult Mental Ability." *J Ed Meas* 4:169–77 f '67. * (*PA* 42:3197)

5. GROTELUESCHEN, ARDEN, AND LYONS, THOMAS J. "Quick Word Test Validity With Adults." *Psychol Rep* 20:488–90 Ap '67. * (*PA* 41:8151)

6. REUBUSH, FAY JAYNES. *A Concurrent Validity Study of the Quick Word Test.* Doctor's thesis, University of Virginia (Charlottesville, Va.), 1967. (*DA* 28:2604A)

7. WESTBROOK, BERT W., AND SELLERS, JAMES R. "Critical Thinking, Intelligence, and Vocabulary." *Ed & Psychol Meas* 27:443–6 su '67. * (*PA* 41:13634)

8. GROTELUESCHEN, ARDEN, AND McQUARRIE, DUNCAN. "Cross-Validation of the Quick Word Test as an Estimator of Adult Mental Ability." *Adult Ed* 21(1):14–9 f '70. *

JUM C. NUNNALLY, *Professor of Psychology, Vanderbilt University, Nashville, Tennessee.*

The purpose of the QWT is to provide a quick, inexpensive, easily applied measure of general ability. It is based entirely on vocabulary items. The elementary form has 50 vocabulary items, and the other forms have 100 vocabulary items. The stem words for items were obtained by sampling the pages of dictionaries. Alternative response words were obtained from dictionary definitions. All stem words contain four letters, and all alternative choice words contain five letters. Numerous item analyses were undertaken to obtain words of moderate difficulty which correlated well with total test scores. Norms were obtained on large, representative groups of subjects at each age level.

Test manuals are clear and contain much useful information. Tables are presented for easily translating raw scores on the tests into percentiles and stanines. Impressive amounts of data are presented on various types of reliability and correlations with other measures of intelligence. Reliabilities in the neighborhood of .90 are reported for split-half and alternative form measures.

Because the original purpose for constructing the test was to obtain a quick estimate of general ability, it is important to inspect correlations between the test and established measures of intelligence. Numerous such correlations are reported in the test manuals, and many of them are surprisingly high. As an example, at the elementary level, the test correlates .86 with scores on the *Cooperative School and College Ability Test* and .84 with the *Lorge-Thorndike Intelligence Tests.*

The test is very simple to administer and score. All of the items are on a one-sided answer sheet. The test format is so simple to comprehend that directions to persons who are taking the test are adequately presented in a few short sentences on the answer sheet. Time for completing the test tends to vary between 10 minutes and less than 20, depending on the age level and differences among subjects in speed of work. Although the instructions urge the subject to work quickly, no time limit is put on the test. One would imagine that a very generous time limit for even the slowest of subjects would be 30 minutes. Thus, in that short amount of time, one can obtain much the same information that is obtained from some measures of general ability that are more time consuming, more expensive, and less simple to administer.

There are four important questions to ask about the QWT. First, why should one ever employ any other type of measure of general ability? If one is considering employing an instrument that is highly dependent on vocabulary scores, then in most cases (exceptions to be discussed later) one would be better off employing a simple vocabulary test like the *Quick Word Test*. For example, a correlation of .84 was found between scores on the QWT and scores on the *Wechsler Adult Intelligence Scale*. This is not much below the reliabilities of the two tests. The Wechsler test requires a highly expert professional examiner, and the test is much more expensive and time consuming to administer and score.

Before the answer to the first question lulls the reader into thinking that the millennium has been reached in the testing of general ability with very simple methods, however, we should ask a second question, one that is related to the first one: Can one measure general intelligence with simple vocabulary items? Such items are featured very prominently on the Wechsler scales and the Binet scales, and most group tests of intelligence also rely heavily on vocabulary items. However, on intuitive grounds and on the basis of a half century of factor analytic research, one could claim that a better measure of general ability could be obtained by mixing content from at least some other factors, in addition to verbal comprehension, particularly material from the general reasoning factor and the numerical facility factor. The latter would require a separate test with items like, "Which one of the following numbers is closest to 8.01?" The general reasoning factor, however, can be brought directly into the format of the vocabulary-type item by phrasing the items in terms of verbal analogies, which is done in some existing tests. This would make it more difficult to construct items, and such items might not be quite as simple for 4th grade children to understand; but bringing in the reasoning component logically would make a somewhat better measure of general ability than relying entirely on simple word knowledge, as is done in the QWT. However, to broaden the content

in such a way as to bring in more of the central factors in intellectual functioning would tend to destroy the original purpose of the test. The purpose was to provide a simple, economical, quick approximation of scores obtained on existing tests of general intelligence. The *Quick Word Test* does those things well.

The third question regarding the QWT is: In what ways would the test be most validly employed? The test probably would serve very well to (a) screen out individuals who needed more detailed interviewing and testing, e.g., transfer students from one school system to another, (b) help in the industrial selection of personnel, e.g., bank tellers and secretaries, (c) obtain a quick measure of general ability as part of experiments in psychology, sociology, and education, and (d) add to personnel folders in the many instances in which an approximate measure of general ability is useful, e.g., in prisons.

The fourth and final question is: When it is feasible to do so, when would it probably be better to employ some other types of instruments than a simple vocabulary test like the *Quick Word Test?* First, because no test forms are available below the 4th grade level, it is obvious that one would have to employ some other type of measure below that level. For most purposes in elementary education, it would be better to employ other types of instruments. For preschool children, it is better to rely on individual intelligence tests or "readiness tests" that emphasize the understanding of simple concepts. In the elementary grades, most important educational decisions (e.g., sectioning and promotion) are based on teacher-made tests and commercially distributed achievement tests. It is difficult to see how these and other decisions about students in the elementary grades would be materially enhanced by a simple vocabulary test. Second, instruments other than simple vocabulary tests are more useful in the testing of various atypical groups—the deaf, the blind, the mentally ill, recent immigrants, and various culturally disadvantaged groups in our society. With some of these groups it is best to employ individually administered intelligence tests; with others it is best to employ so-called "culture fair tests" that contain nonverbal reasoning items. Third, the test would not be highly useful in career guidance, such as in the advisement of senior high school students about choices of careers and higher education. In career guidance, one needs as much differential information as can be obtained about the individual's abilities, interests, personality characteristics, and other attributes. When it is done well, such career guidance should be based on multifactor batteries of ability tests and tests of other kinds.

To mention these and other limitations of the potential effectiveness of the *Quick Word Test* is not meant to be a general condemnation. The test was not designed to do those things. Rather, it was designed to provide an inexpensive, quick, easily applied approximation of what is measured by traditional measures of general intelligence, and it does these things surprisingly well.

J Counsel Psychol 12:436–7 w '65. Jack C. Merwin. * In general, the *Quick Word Test* appears to be about as economical an approach to measuring general ability as could be attempted. Reliability and normative information are satisfactory for such a new and short test. While the correlation with other general aptitude tests would indicate a need for greater caution in the use of equivalent raw scores with Level 2 than that probably needed with Level 1, the test seems capable of providing a relatively efficient estimate of performance on other general ability tests. The individual user will have to study the extent to which it can be used as a substitute for the other tests in predicting his unique criteria. He may also find norms developed on his unique groups of more value than those presented in the manual, as suggested by the authors.

J Ed Meas 2:257–8 D '65. Gilbert Sax and Ethel A. Oda. * Each word to be defined contains five letters. Four synonym alternatives are given for each word. Most of the options are well selected and clear. However, with a 15 minute time limit, defining words out of context may produce some confusion. * Directions for administering and scoring the QWT are simple and clear. * An examination of the mean Otis Gamma IQ scores obtained from the same students provides a useful estimate of the amount of bias present in the norming procedure. According to the QWT manual, the mean Otis IQ for ninth graders was 107.3. It is likely that the systematic elimination of all small schools was at least partially responsible for the over-selection of relatively bright examinees. * Percentile and stanine norms are also provided. The norms tables are extremely clear

and easy to use. * Alternate-form reliabilities have a median of .88, but are spuriously high inasmuch as data from two grades were combined. As a substitute for longer, more time consuming examinations, the QWT would seem to be able to provide reliable and useful information. Costs can also be reduced over other comparable types of tests because test items are printed directly on the answer sheet.

[379]

RBH Test of Learning Ability. Business and industry; 1947–63; TLA; 3 editions; directions (no date, 1 page) for each edition; 50¢ per key; $1.50 per manual; $1.50 per specimen set of any one edition; postage extra; Richardson, Bellows, Henry & Co., Inc. *

a) FORMS S AND T. Test ('47, 5 pages); manual ['63, 24 pages]; $4.50 per 25 tests; 15(20) minutes.

b) FORMS DS-12 AND DT-12. Identical with Forms S and T except for removal of directions from testing time; formerly titled *Test for Office Personnel;* test ('61, 5 pages, identical with 1947 tests); manual ['63, 27 pages, identical with manual for Forms S and T except for cover and 2 pages]; $4.50 per 25 tests; 12(20) minutes.

c) FORM ST. Consists of Forms S and T combined; test ('57, 8 pages); manual ['63, 8 pages]; $5.50 per 25 tests; 25(30) minutes.

REFERENCES

1–2. See 6:504.
3. ROSS, PAUL F., AND DUNFIELD, NEIL M. "Selecting Salesmen for an Oil Company." *Personnel Psychol* 17:75–84 sp '64. *
4. MOORE, CLAY L., JR.; MACNAUGHTON, JOHN F.; AND OSBURN, HOBART G. "Ethnic Differences Within an Industrial Selection Battery." *Personnel Psychol* 22(4):473–82 w '69. * (PA 44:13473)

ERWIN K. TAYLOR, *President, Personnel Research and Development Corporation, Cleveland, Ohio.*

Industrial test users constantly bring pressure on test publishers for tests with shorter and shorter time limits. RBH has responded to this pressure with this 12-minute spiral omnibus test (54 items) modeled after the 40-minute *Army General Classification Test* (150 items).

Manuals for Forms S and T are the same as for DS and DT except for the administration directions. The same norms are used for both tests since the difference in time limits, according to the publisher, has not changed the means or standard deviations to a substantial degree.

The manuals provide a wealth of normative, validity, and reliability data. A total of 16,993 male cases are reported. This population is broken into seven groups, varying in size from 48 technical and professional people to 10,576 industrial employees and applicants. Each of these seven groups is then further broken down into its component populations; means and standard deviations are provided for more than one hundred samples ranging in size from 5 to 1,500. A similarly bountiful list of relationships between Forms S and T and a large number of other tests, including personal background surveys, supervisory judgment tests, and personality tests are provided.

Female norms are based on a total of 6,386 cases, again divided into seven groups ranging in size from 67 statistical accounting and supply clerks to 3,550 miscellaneous or unspecified clerical applicants and employees. These are again broken down into the various specific populations of which the groups are constructed, with the N, mean, and standard deviation provided, and again a large number of correlations with a wide variety of other tests.

The reliability of the test is approximately .90 and is adequate for almost any purpose for which it is to be used. The manual also briefly describes about 20 validity studies conducted in 1963 or earlier and about 15 studies between 1967 and 1970. In those dated 1968 or later, both the N and the mean of minority group members are given in almost all cases. In one instance, a study of 64 office support personnel consisted of 27 minority and 37 nonminority group members. The test, validated against supervisory ratings, was in this small sample slightly more valid for the minority than for the nonminority group members.

The manuals mention that "The three types of items can be scored separately if desired." But they provide no rationale for doing so, nor do they provide normative, reliability, or validity data for the several item types separately.

Despite the test's reliability, we remain skeptical concerning the measurement of three intellectual variables (with 17 items for each) in 12 to 15 minutes. Considering the EEOC requirements for specific validity, we also question the value of an omnibus intelligence test. In the light of the Supreme Court decision in the Duke Power case, it seems that multiple factor tests are less likely to be acceptable to EEOC or OFCC than single factor tests validated against specific criteria. Sufficient short tests of verbal, numerical, and spatial ability exist to make these tests of questionable value.

[380]

RBH Test of Non-Verbal Reasoning. Business and industry; 1948–63; TNR; 1 form; 2 editions: long form ('48, 5 pages), short form ('50, 3 pages); catalog uses title *The RBH Non-Verbal Reasoning Test;* manual ['63, 10–11 pages] for each edition; directions (no date, 2 pages) for each edition; $4.50 per 25 tests of long form; $4 per 25 tests of short form 50¢ per key; $1.50 per manual for either edition $1.50 per specimen set of each edition; postage extra 10(15) minutes for short form, 15(20) minutes for long form; Richardson, Bellows, Henry & Co., Inc.

REFERENCES

1–3. See 6:505.
4. Moore, Clay L., Jr.; MacNaughton, John F.; and Osburn, Hobart G. "Ethnic Differences Within an Industrial Selection Battery." *Personnel Psychol* 22(4):473–82 w '69. (PA 44:13473)

Erwin K. Taylor, *President, Personnel Research and Development Corporation, Cleveland, Ohio.*

Like many tests from this publisher, these instruments were modeled, constructed and developed by the Personnel Research Section of the Adjutant General's Office during and shortly after World War II. The long form, composed of 50 items, has a 15-minute time limit, while the short form, with 24 items, has a 10-minute time limit.

The figures used in the items are all abstract and probably as "culture-free" as any that might be devised. Aside from the directions (which could be easily translated into any language), the test is essentially independent of the language of the subject. The understanding of certain concepts, such as symmetry, rectilinearity, and angular bifurcation is all that is essential to the solution of the problem.

The tests do not employ separate answer sheets, and thus can become rather costly in an extensive program. Separate answer sheets could, of course, be readily devised, but in a test as speeded as this, they would require renormalization. The typography of the test leaves something to be desired, and the test would be improved by better printing on more opaque stock.

While the test (except for the directions) is independent of language, this reviewer seriously questions whether this or any other paper-and-pencil test of this type, such as the *Minnesota Paper Form Board Test* or the *SRA Pictorial Reasoning Test,* is not really responded to by at least a large portion of a tested population in a verbal (but probably subvocal) fashion. Both forms correlate substantially (according to data provided in the manuals) with standard verbal intelligence tests. It might perhaps be more correct to name the test "Abstract Reasoning," as is done in the *Differential Aptitude Tests,* than to imply that, because the items are themselves nonverbal in construction, they are solved on a nonverbal basis.

The manuals give extensive normative data. For the long form, the total N is 3,118. This population includes 2,113 managers and executives in the largest single group. In the short form norms table, there are 5,499 cases. Here, however, the populations are primarily lower level: almost 3,000 are industrial applicants; another 1,000 clerical applicants and employees; and there are 1,345 mechanical and operating employees. Thus, the longer form appears to have been used with higher level employees and applicants than the shorter form. Each manual presents the N, mean, and standard deviation of each of the samples from which the norms categories were developed. The manuals also present numerous correlations with other tests. Separate norms are presented for female personnel.

Split-half reliability coefficients are .86 and .84 for the long and short forms, respectively. Five validity studies are reported for the long form. These are primarily at the managerial and executive levels and range in sample size from 28 to 443. In the former study, tests correlated .14 with a complex composite criterion. The highest correlation reported is .36. Eleven validity studies are reported for the shorter form, and these, generally speaking, deal with hourly workers and first-level supervisors. Validities range from lows of −.02, .03, .07, and .08 to a high of .38.

While no data with respect to the proportion of subjects who complete the test are provided, both forms seem to be too highly speeded (the longer form, ironically, being more so than the shorter). To complete the long form in 15 minutes, the subject must respond to three items per minute, while to complete the short form in ten minutes, 2.4 responses per minute are required. It is our feeling that a moderate extension of the time limit might render the test considerably more valid, particularly with lower socioeconomic level personnel.

These tests, along with the DAT abstract reasoning test and the *Minnesota Paper Form Board Test,* are probably as culture free as a pencil-and-paper test can be made. All of these are too highly speeded and would be more valid with more generous time limits, particularly for nonexempt positions. The RBH tests have the disadvantage of having the most complicated verbal directions and, simultaneously, the advantage of lower than usual opportunity for getting the correct answer by chance. Their industrial standardization is better than average, but they have not demonstrated consistent validity, particularly for nonexempt positions and for lower levels of supervision.

[381]

★SRA Pictorial Reasoning Test. Ages 14 and over; 1966–67; PRT; for use "with all major American subcultural groups"; 1 form ('66, 7 pages); preliminary manual ('67, 21 pages); $5.95 per 25 tests; 75¢ per manual; $1.25 per specimen set; postage extra; untimed (30–45) minutes or timed 15(20) minutes; Robert N. McMurry and Phyllis D. Arnold; Science Research Associates, Inc. *

RAYMOND A. KATZELL, *Professor of Psychology and Head of the Department, New York University, New York, New York.*

A consequence of recent heightened concern with social justice for disadvantaged minorities has been renewed attention to the equitability of tests for such populations. A long established approach to this kind of problem has been the attempt to develop culture free or culture fair tests. That strategy has not been pursued much in recent years, partly because cultural effects were not eliminated by the earlier attempts and partly because of the growing suspicion that culture free tests are likely also to be validity free.

The test under consideration represents a latter-day revival of the culture fair strategy in developing a test of general mental ability intended to be applicable to all major American subcultural groups. Like other attempts along these lines, it utilizes a type of subject matter believed to be relatively immune to cultural influences. In this instance, items entail reasoning with nonverbal, pictorial materials of the sort employed in the earlier *SRA Non-Verbal Form.* However, in addition to trying to control for cultural influences through the choice of test content, the authors also used the interesting idea of empirically identifying those 80 items which, from an edited pool of 270 experimental items, exhibited minimal differences in difficulty among seven subcultures while at the same time correlating with total score on the experimental test. The items constituting the test are reported as having lower inter-group variability in mean difficulty than did the experimental items. Emphasis on selecting items which minimize inter-group differences may have cost some internal consistency, since the K-R 20 reliability is .75 for a heterogeneous sample of 1,250 cases, and falls to the .60's in several culturally homogeneous groups. Reliability coefficients in this range call for the conventional note of tentativeness, especially in interpreting and acting upon scores of individuals.

The seven subcultures represented in the experimental and normative samples were described simply as urban whites from deprived areas of large cities, Appalachian whites, urban Negroes from deprived areas of large cities, rural Negroes from areas of the South, Spanish-speaking bilinguals, French-speaking bilinguals, and nonurban whites from rural, suburban, and smaller city areas, this last group bearing the anomalous label of "control group." The normative sample, consisting of 3,598 who took the test with a time limit and 1,250 who took it untimed, was composed of both male and female students whose ages ranged from 13 to 19 and whose completed schooling ranged from grades 8 through 12. Norms are provided in the manual for several breakdowns of the sample but there are none, inexplicably, by sex. Unfortunately, insufficient information is given about the seven subcultural groups to determine how comparable they were in other respects, such as age, education, whether the urban whites and blacks were from the same cities, or whether the Spanish-speaking group consisted of, say, rural Mexican-Americans or urban Puerto Ricans.

The remaining big question is, of course, to what extent the test is fair and valid among the several subcultures studied. As to fairness, the major evidence advanced in the manual is that the means and distributions of all seven cultural subgroups are "nearly the same." It would have been helpful had there been further statistical analysis of these data such as testing the hypothesis that the several group means and distributions are equivalent, or calculating what portion of score variance is accounted for by subculture. It might also have been instructive had the intergroup differences found with this test been compared with results obtained by using other mental ability tests with the same or similar groups. From the results presented it would appear that in a timed administration of the test, the disadvantaged groups typically obtained mean scores about half a standard deviation below the "control group," which is not a particularly unusual result for such comparisons. Under untimed administration, however, the means of most of the disadvantaged groups exceeded the "control group" by about one-third of a standard deviation.

The picture of the test's cultural fairness is further clouded by the aforementioned lack of information about the composition of the several subcultures which are compared. That 198 urban whites and 63 urban blacks obtained essentially the same mean scores on the untimed version of the test is of interest, but a conclusion regarding culture-fairness can hardly be drawn unless we can be sure of the comparability of the two samples in age, education, sex, and other relevant respects; no assurances of such comparability are provided in the manual.

But the most critical variable on which different cultural groups must be compared in order to assess a test's fairness is a relevant criterion of performance, such as success in school or work. A test on which two cultural groups attain the same mean score cannot be said to be fair if one group were to score significantly higher on such a criterion. Conversely, a test may be regarded as unfair only when there is a significantly different discrepancy in the test performance as compared to the criterion performance of two or more groups.[1] The manual is devoid of such comparisons involving criteria together with test performance.

Mention of criteria immediately raises the remaining big question, that of validity. The only test-criterion correlations presented are 49 which involve grades of one or another cultural subgroup in one or another school subject. Interestingly, the higher correlations are usually found with the control group, judged as closest to the mainstream of American culture. None of the correlations based on disadvantaged or minority groups appears to be significantly greater than zero, although here again the persistent failure of the manual to provide information on statistical significance requires the consumer to be his own statistician.

In brief, the method of construction gives reason to hope that the test *may* turn out to be useful in measuring "the learning potential of individuals from diverse backgrounds with reading difficulties, whose potential for training and employment cannot be reliably and validly measured by verbal instruments." The results reported in the manual do not dampen this hope, but they are too limited and imperfect to nurture it either. The test should therefore not be used for the stated purpose unless one is prepared

[1] KIRKPATRICK, JAMES J.; EWEN, ROBERT B.; BARRETT, RICHARD S.; AND KATZELL, RAYMOND A. *Testing and Fair Employment: Fairness and Validity of Personnel Tests for Different Ethnic Groups*, p. 7. New York: New York University Press, 1968. Pp. x, 145. *

to do further research on its fairness and validity in various subcultures.

JOHN E. MILHOLLAND, *Professor of Psychology, The University of Michigan, Ann Arbor, Michigan.*

Only a preliminary manual is available for this test, and it claims that the test

can be used to measure the learning potential of individuals from diverse backgrounds with reading difficulties, whose potential for training and employment cannot be reliably and validly measured by verbal instruments * The PRT is designed to be used as a general index of ability, measuring a person's potential to learn jobs independent of his background or culture * The PRT was expressly designed to yield comparable measurement across subcultures. * The PRT can be used as a placement instrument to measure the learning potential of dropouts, adults in basic education programs, or persons in remedial reading programs.

The support for the claims comes from the fact that one criterion of item selection was equal difficulty across samples from the following subpopulations: rural white, urban white, Appalachian, urban Negro, rural Negro, Spanish-speaking bilinguals, and French-speaking bilingual Canadians.

In order for the claim to be substantiated it would appear that one of two situations must be true: (*a*) The samples have been equated on some criterion of learning potential; or (*b*) The subculture populations have the same distribution of learning potential *and* the samples are representative of the populations. No evidence is given that either situation obtains and therefore this test should not be recommended for operational use.

The test consists of 80 sets of 5 pictures or designs; the task is to select the one that differs from the rest in some way in which the other four are alike. It can be given with a 15-minute time limit, or untimed. The untimed administration is recommended, since norms for the various subsamples are more alike in this mode. Hand scoring is convenient, consisting of counting the marks registered by carbon paper in squares corresponding to the keyed options.

Reliabilities (K-R 20) in the norm samples range from .59 to .83. Fourteen correlations with other tests are given, 11 of them based on "control group" samples consisting of nonurban whites. Six of them are with the *SRA Non-Verbal Form,* but the items in this instrument were a part of the pool from which the PRT items were chosen! These six correlations range from .37 to .75 and perhaps should be regarded

as reliability estimates. Their utility for this purpose, however, is diminished by the fact that every sample included individuals from grades 9 through 12. The other correlations are for single grade control group samples, with N's of 50 to 74. A number of correlations with school grades are also presented, but the authors quite rightly point out that conventional grades are unsuitable as criteria for this kind of a test.

The test was copyrighted in 1966, the preliminary manual in 1967, and here it is 1970. One suspects that no serious effort is going to be made to establish validity for the instrument.

J Ed Meas 6(1):41–3 sp '69. John L. Horn.
* intended to provide a measure of a general ability for which the averages across various ethnic and social groups in the U.S.A. and Canada are not notably different. As the authors state: "The PRT is designed to be used as a general index of ability, measuring a person's potential to learn jobs independent of his background or culture." This purpose makes the test vulnerable to criticisms that would not be directed at tests based upon less ambitious designs. * Because the test is based upon only one kind of task, a substantial proportion of the variation in test scores is likely to represent a test-specific factor—a factor which need not be integral to the concept of intelligence. Probably it is desirable to regard the test as a measure of a primary-level factor, cognition of classes, rather than as a measure of a general intellective ability. Some of the drawings are difficult to identify with certainty (e.g., two peppers (?), a watermelon, a pile of bricks, a tape measure) and in several such cases it is necessary to make proper identification of the depicted object in order to reason properly to obtain the correct answer. Also, to the reviewer it seems that some of the depicted objects would be unfamiliar to those for whom the test is intended (e.g., a microphone, snowshoes, comets (?), molded jello (?), different kinds of ships). To some extent, however, the method for selection of items obviates this criticism. Not obviated by the item-selection method, however, is the fact that several of the items have more than one answer-choice satisfying the conditions for a correct answer—e.g., in item 15, choice D represents the only animal that is clearly winged (one can't be sure about the insect of choice A), yet E, presumably the only legless animal (though one can't be sure about

this), is the one choice that is scored correct. This kind of problem arises with any ability test, of course; it may not be any more prevalent in this test than in others (the reviewer counted some 7 items for which this problem seemed to exist). In any case it no doubt produces some lowering of reliability and validity. * the test can be said to be self-administering only if subjects can read and understand such sentences as: "All four pictures except the phonograph are alike because they are musical instruments, and ONLY the phonograph repeats the sounds made by other instruments." * it is clear that one can find better tests than the PRT to predict academic performance. The test authors interpret the significant correlations between the PRT and the Nonverbal, Otis and DAT tests as supporting, or at least not overthrowing, an hypothesis that the PRT does, indeed, measure "learning potential." They imply that the low correlations between the PRT and measures of academic achievement indicate culture fairness. It is worth paying heed to the fact, however, that tests can show moderate correlation with so-called general ability tests and low correlation with academic performance and yet not be particularly culture fair, much less be measures of "learning potential." Fluency tests, for example, have these characteristics and yet are not regarded as culture fair. Low correlation with academic performance is by no means a necessary or sufficient indicator of culture fair measurement of "learning potential." SUMMARY. In the reviewer's opinion this test should be considered to be in an experimental stage of development. Institutional decisions should be based upon the use of this test only if additional research is done to establish the basis for the decision. Individual decisions based upon the use of this test should be made only with considerable caution and then only with the aid of a psychologist or educator who has a very good understanding of the measurement of human abilities.

[382]

★SRA Short Test of Educational Ability. Grades kgn–1, 2–3, 4–6, 7–8, 9–12; 1966–70; STEA; 2 editions; interpretive manual ('69, 9 pages); conversion tables ('70, 9 pages); approximately 80 per cent of the items in the series were taken from *SRA Primary Mental Abilities* and *SRA Tests of Educational Ability;* norms derived by equating with parent tests; 35¢ per interpretive manual; postage extra; Spanish edition available; Science Research Associates, Inc. *
a) HAND SCORED EDITION. Grades kgn–1, 2–3, 4–6, 7–8, 9–12; 5 levels in 3 booklets.

1) *Levels 1–2.* Grades kgn–1, 2–3; 2 overlapping levels in 1 booklet; 1 form ('66, 11 pages); manual ('66, 18 pages); $5.55 per 25 tests; $1.05 per specimen set; (30–40) minutes.
2) *Levels 3–4.* Grades 4–6, 7–8; 2 overlapping levels in 1 booklet; 1 form ('66, 7 pages, self-marking); manual ('66, 10 pages); $5.55 per 25 tests; $1.05 per specimen set; 20(30) minutes.
3) *Level 5.* Grades 9–12; 1 form ('66, 8 pages, self-marking); manual ('66, 8 pages); $4.80 per 25 tests; $1.05 per specimen set; 20(30) minutes.
b) MACHINE SCORABLE EDITION. Grades kgn–1, 2–3; 1 form ('66, 8 pages, NCS scorable); 2 levels; marking practice sheet ('66, 1 page); test materials and scoring service, 55¢ and over per test; specimen set not available; 30(40) minutes.
1) *Level 1.* Grades kgn–1; manual ('66, 14 pages).
2) *Level 2.* Grades 2–3; manual ('66, 13 pages).

REFERENCES

1. JONES, WILLIAM PAUL. *Predicting Academic Performance With the Short Test of Educational Ability Considering Social Class and Sex Differences.* Doctor's thesis, New Mexico State University (University Park, N.M.), 1968. (*DA* 29:3832A)
2. JONES, W. PAUL. "Sex Differences in Academic Prediction." *Meas & Eval Guid* 3(2):88–91 su '70. *

RUSSEL F. GREEN, *Research Consultant in Psychology and Education, Henrietta, New York.*

This test consists of five levels of increasing difficulty which are represented as spanning grades K through 12. The instructions are clearly written and seem to cover all details that might be needed. The format is easy to follow. The norms and conversion tables are well laid out and easy to follow.

Except for portions of Levels 1 and 5, the items used were taken from current editions of the *SRA Primary Mental Abilities* (PMA) or from the *SRA Tests of Educational Ability* (TEA). No standardization sample, as such, was used. Rather, these short forms were administered to students in six Chicago area schools, along with the PMA for grades K through 3 and the TEA for grades 4 through 11. IQ equivalents were then obtained by equating the STEA scores with the PMA and TEA scores using the equi-percentile method. The implication is that the norming of the STEA is equivalent to that of the PMA and the TEA.

Correlations between the STEA and PMA ranged from .53 to .78, averaging about .70. Correlations between the STEA and the TEA ranged from .54 to .82, averaging about .75. The implication here seems to be that the STEA is supposed to be valid for making the same kinds of predictions that the long forms (PMA and TEA) make. No other data relevant to validity are presented in the manual.

The STEA would appear to have quite limited usefulness and little reason for being published. There is a continuing desire on the part of educators to have tests which will provide valid predictors of academic achievement but which will not take much time away from instruction. This test represents another effort at developing a test which, presumably, is supposed to be better in some way than other tests on the market. No evidence that it is, is available. In fact, there are several shortcomings that the potential user should keep in mind.

First, the developers give no evidence that their choice of subtests or of items is the optimum set for the purpose. Developing such evidence would not have been difficult, and perhaps it was done; not mentioning it would represent a serious oversight.

Second, no evidence is presented to support the developers' claim that Levels 1 and 2 avoid "dependence on concurrent school achievement." Avoiding any items that depend on reading ability may accomplish this to some degree. There is substantial evidence, however, that avoiding verbal material is by no means a sufficient strategy for avoiding such dependence.

Third, the use of multiple choice items in a short-form test precludes the possibility of satisfactorily discriminating among students who are in the lower portion of the scale. *The mean for five-year olds on Level 1 is actually set at the theoretical chance score!* Hence for this test there probably is no discrimination at all in the entire lower two-thirds of the distribution. This situation improves somewhat at higher levels and ages but its discrimination is never satisfactory.

Fourth, added to the problem of poor discrimination among lower scores is the fact that the standard errors of measurement appear to be large (about 6.5) relative to the assumed standard deviations (16) for both Levels 1 and 2.

Fifth, the reliabilities of Levels 1 and 2 (.82 to .84) are too low for comfort if one wishes to make inferences about individuals. This probably is due to the chance element being so important in the lower half of the distributions.

Sixth, the IQ's obtained are too often poor estimates of the IQ's one would obtain from the longer, more reliable, more comprehensive versions from which these were constructed. The standard errors of estimate of predicting IQ's on the longer versions from the short forms are often more than one-half of the standard deviation.

CONCLUSION. It seems clear that the STEA fails in attempting to be a satisfactory short-form estimate of educational ability (aptitude). Its principal downfall can be traced to shortcomings inherent in the use of multiple choice items in short tests. If one is concerned only with differentiating among high aptitude students, the test might be suitable, but as age increases, the STEA becomes progressively more unsatisfactory for differentiating among the lower two-thirds to one-third of the students, depending on the level.

Educators, it seems, would be best advised to use long forms if their need is to make decisions about individual students in the lower one-third to two-thirds of the ability range.

As a short-form estimate to be used for some kinds of research on groups, Levels 2 through 5 probably would be quite satisfactory. One hesitates to recommend their use even for this purpose if the research is to depend on correlation estimates or covariance controls.

HENRY WEITZ, *Professor of Education and Director, Counseling Center, Duke University, Durham, North Carolina.*

The principal advantage claimed for the STEA is the limited time required for its administration. The 30 or so minutes required to administer most levels of the STEA represents an average of about half the time required for the *SRA Tests of Educational Ability* or the *SRA Primary Mental Abilities,* from which over 80 percent of the STEA items were drawn. This advantage was achieved at the cost of reduced reliability at some levels.

The test is said to be "designed to avoid reliance on achievement concepts and skills acquired in school" and, in the case of the first two levels, "or at home: the tests for Levels 1 and 2 do not, for example, require the pupil to read," while "the Level 3 and 4 tests....require only the simplest reading skills." The subtests of the first two levels, for example, purport to measure ability to identify cause and effect relationships, skill in simple problem solving, space visualization, pictorial vocabulary, and recognition of missing numbers in a series. Although these skills are rarely taught in the precise form in which they appear in the items, they do represent behavioral objectives of education at this level. Similar correspondence between skills measured by the test and educational objectives is found throughout the

STEA. And this is as it should be for a test designed to measure educational ability.

In the case of the Levels 1 and 2 tests, covering grades K-3, the split-half reliability coefficients reported, ranging from .82 to .84, represent a lower limit of usefulness for individual measurement. Split-half reliabilities for all other grades equal or exceed .90, which some will find acceptable for individual assessment. Slightly lower K-R 20's are also reported. Test-retest reliabilities would have been more meaningful.

Predictive validity data are not presently available, although the STEA is reported to correlate with the PMA and TEA. (The median correlation reported was .72, with correlations ranging from .53 to .82.) Thus it is difficult to say at this time how much, if any, this test can contribute to the management of the learning experiences of a student. The Interpretive Manual appropriately warns the prospective user that the test "should not be regarded as measuring all factors or processes usually associated with intelligence testing."

Conversions of raw scores to MA's and quotients for Levels 1 and 2 and to quotient scores, percentiles, and stanines for all levels are provided in the manuals. These norms were developed by an equi-percentile method relating the STEA raw scores to the raw scores of the parent test, the PMA or TEA. Hopefully, norms based on the STEA will be developed.

The STEA appears to be a moderately useful instrument for estimating educational ability if testing time is a crucial factor. Limited reliability and the lack of predictive validity information reduce its usefulness. Use of this instrument should be restricted to experimental administrations until local validity and reliability studies can be made or until the publishers provide adequate supporting information.

J Ed Meas 8(1):49–51 sp '71. Raynard J. Dooley. * Validity is mentioned only once: "Predictive validity is not available at this time." However, a concurrent type of validity is alluded to by establishing correlations between the STEA and the Primary Mental Abilities (PMA) or the STEA and the Tests of Educational Ability (TEA). The PMA and the TEA are parent tests of the STEA. The test publisher emphasizes these correlations by declaring: "The major value of the STEA lies in its....high correlation with existing tests that take somewhat longer to administer." But both the PMA and the TEA have had a weak validity history themselves, and the reported correlations are unimpressive when one considers the loss of content from the longer to the shorter form—from the PMA or the TEA to the STEA. * the entire process of relating the STEA to the PMA or the TEA can be called into question. First, the sample used to calibrate scores for the STEA were not equated with the anchor test norms (nor was matching intended by the test publisher). Second, the content of the tests was not similar even though the STEA was extracted from the PMA and TEA. Validity was sacrificed for reliability in the shorter form, as the test publisher apparently extracted only those items from the test that contributed the most to subtest score or total test score on the parent test. Content or factors of the parent test were not maintained in the shorter test * Third, the correlations, although high in the equating study, do not support the use of the equipercentile method. The correlations are spuriously high; identical items appear in both forms. The STEA illustrates the misuse of the split-half and the KR-20 formula in computing reliability. While reporting the upper level of the STEA to be somewhat speeded, the test publisher, nonetheless, employs these formulae in calculating the reliability coefficient. The STEA illustrates the inadequacies in measuring bright youngsters at grades 3, 6, and 8. Obviously, the bright youngsters tested with the STEA at their appropriate grade level would hit a ceiling at that level. But how does one identify a bright youngster: by school achievement, by previous test performance, or by intuition? Furthermore, should a 3-, 6-, or 8-grade student who reaches a ceiling at the appropriate grade level (assuming he is a student who has not been identified as bright before the test administration) be retested with the next level? The STEA manual answers neither question. Finally, are teachers who use this test willing to separate the bright youngsters from the group and test them separately, as is required in the STEA directions. The STEA illustrates an attempt to construct a test that avoids dependence on concurrent school achievement. However, the STEA was derived for most levels from the TEA. And the TEA was validated on common criterion measures such as grade point averages and achievement tests. The TEA score and, consequently, the STEA score are therefore estimates on ability derived from and predictive of formal educational encounters. Irrespective of STEA's claim that reading at the various levels is kept to a minimum, and omitted at the earlier levels, the parent test was originally related to school achievement criteria. Moreover, without further support for STEA, the claim of the test publisher appears unfounded. Summary. The test's strongest feaure is, of course, its brevity—administration time is only 30–35 minutes. The reliability coefficients are acceptable, ranging from .82 to .93. The test is easily scored, and converted scores are easily obtained in terms of quotients, mental ages, stanines, and percentiles. But validity information is nonexistent, except for what can be inferred from the equating study. However, the equating study in which the STEA scores were calibrated from the parent, reference test (either the PMA or the TEA) is a questionable approach. In conclusion, unless the person who uses the STEA is willing to do research on his own, the test has little to recommend its adoption.

J Ed Meas 8(1):51–2 sp '71. W. Paul Jones. [A rejoinder to the above review from the publisher.] * Dooley notes that "the PMA and TEA have had weak validity history themselves...." That point seems questionable to this writer. A review of TEA by Ahmann (1965) summarized that "the tests (TEA)....correlate very highly with common criterion measures such as grade point averages and achievement test scores." * The STEA is related to academic performance, because obviously an educational ability test without such relationship would be of little value. * Dooley's....key question seemed to be the lack of available data relating STEA scores to outside criteria. * Dooley....was correct in pointing out that the only validity information was that to be inferred from the parent instruments. * however, it should be noted that published data regarding the validity of STEA are now available * In summary, the STEA series seems to this writer to have attained the stated objective: to provide a reliable estimate of educational ability within a short administration time. Reliability coefficients are acceptable, and while there can probably never be "enough" validity data, the available data certainly suggest a significant relationship between STEA scores and academic performance criteria. Although a national standardization of STEA would certainly be preferable to the equated

norms, the generally accepted procedures used to calibrate STEA to the anchor tests should have resulted in useful norms conversions. The debt owed by STEA to the parent instruments in terms of content is obvious, but the publisher's statement that STEA does not measure all processes associated with intelligence testing is prudent. The objective of a short time limit for administration certainly precludes any objective of total factorial coverage. To suggest that the STEA has no faults is not the purpose of this reply. However, the data now available do suggest that for those test users desiring a useful estimate of educational ability with a minimal investment in testing time, the STEA series has much to offer.

[383]

*SRA Verbal Form. Grades 7–16 and adults; 1946–67; formerly called *SRA Verbal Classification Form;* abbreviated adaptation of *Thurstone Test of Mental Alertness* which is an abbreviated adaptation of *American Council on Education Psychological Examination for High School Students,* 1940 Edition; 3 scores: quantitative, linguistic, total; self-marking; Forms A ('47, 4 pages), B ('55, 4 pages); manual, third edition ('67, 10 pages); $5.95 per 25 tests; 40¢ per manual; $1.25 per specimen set; postage extra; 15(25) minutes; Thelma Gwinn Thurstone (test) and L. L. Thurstone (test); Science Research Associates, Inc. *

REFERENCES

1. GRIGG, AUSTIN E., AND FILER, ROBERT J. "Norms for Scientists and Engineers on SRA Verbal Test." *J Indus Psychol* 3:52–3 Je '65. *
2. PHILLIPS, RICHARD MARTIN. *A Multiple Regression Study of Academic Prediction at Gallaudet College.* Doctor's thesis, University of Maryland (College Park, Md.), 1969. (*DAI* 30:5257A)

For reviews by W. D. Commins and Willis C. Schaefer, see 4:319.

[384]

*Safran Culture Reduced Intelligence Test. Grades 1–6, 4 and over; 1960–69; SCRIT; separate answer sheets must be used; Can 2¢ per mimeographed answer sheet, postage extra; C. Safran; the Author. *

a) [SCALE 1.] Grades 1–6; 1960–66; 1 form ('60, 42 pages); mimeographed manual ('62, reprint of *1* below); mimeographed instructions for group administration in grades 1–3 ['65, 4 pages]; mimeographed instructions for individual administration ['61, 1 page]; mimeographed norms ['65, 2 pages] for grades 1 and 3 only; 40¢ per test; 10¢ per norms; 10¢ per manual; (30–45) minutes.

b) [REVISED SCALE 2.] Grades 4 and over; 1960–69; 1 form ['69, c1960, 26 pages, consisting of 21 of the 60 items from the 1960 edition]; mimeographed instructions for administration ['69, 1 page]; mimeographed introduction ['69, 3 pages]; no norms; 30¢ per test; 15(20) minutes.

REFERENCES

1. See 6:497.
2. WEST, L. W., AND MACARTHUR, R. S. "An Evaluation of Selected Intelligence Tests for Two Samples of Metis and Indian Children." *Alberta J Ed Res* 10:17–27 Mr '64. * (*PA* 39:12328)

3. FROST, BARRY P. "Intelligence, Manifest Anxiety and Scholastic Achievement." *Alberta J Ed Res* 11:167–75 S '65. * (*PA* 40:1948)
4. MACARTHUR, R. S. "Assessing Intellectual Potential of Native Canadian Pupils: A Summary." *Alberta J Ed Res* 14:115–22 Je '68. * (*PA* 44:4170)
5. MACARTHUR, RUSSELL. "Some Differential Abilities of Northern Canadian Native Youth." *Int J Psychol* 3(1):43–50 '68. *
6. RATTAN, M. S., AND MACARTHUR, R. S. "Longitudinal Prediction of School Achievement for Metis and Eskimo Pupils." *Alberta J Ed Res* 14:37–41 Mr '68. * (*PA* 44:4249)
7. SOLIS, MIGUELA M. "A Pilot Study of the SCRIT in the Philippines." *Alberta Psychologist* 8(4):8–31 Ja '68. *

LEE J. CRONBACH, *Vida Jacks Professor of Education, Stanford University, Stanford, California.*

SCRIT is in the figure analogies or figure series tradition. The 1969 revision consists of 21 items, each a brightly colored display of colored squares, circles, triangles, and other symbols. The examinee must induce a rule or pattern and select the figure, from 4 to 6 alternatives, that completes the pattern. Directions are somewhat complex, but the author expects the child to learn the rules of the game from the relatively easy items that begin the test. This revision is derived from a 60-item scale for grades 4–6, produced in 1960. A 36-item scale for the primary grades is still current.

SCRIT is in preliminary form and cannot be judged by the standards for a published test. Only bits and pieces of technical information are provided. The test should be regarded only as a set of items for possible use in research until norms and systematic information on validity are provided. A K-R 20 reliability of .76 (for sixth graders) indicates that SCRIT will function as a unit in a battery of tests but cannot be the sole basis for decisions.

SCRIT has been used in a number of studies in Alberta. These, in addition to the author's studies, provide scattered correlations of the 1960 forms with other measures. MacArthur finds SCRIT the near equal of *Progressive Matrices,* Lorge-Thorndike nonverbal sections, and a Cattell test, with respect to loading on a *g* factor. Safran reports correlations with teachers' marks of .43 to .78 for samples of unknown size and character. Apart from this the evidence is what one would expect for a short, internally consistent test with nonverbal displays that make strong demands on verbal mediation.

It is pointless to talk about "culture reduced" tests. Attending, encoding, and information-processing abilities, as well as the attitudes that go into successful test performance, are constructed through the child's interaction with his culture. The school psychologist should welcome tests that require little facility in any particular language. Such a test should not be rendered misleading by suggesting that it measures an inherited quality. Nor should psychologists abandon realism by arguing that on a truly valid test children from every subculture or Indian tribe will do equally well. Some cultures develop the skills and habits that make one capable at verbal reasoning about visual patterns, and some handicap the child in this regard. On the other hand, if there is any clearly intellectual task on which a disadvantaged minority has scores like those for the cultural majority, the school should strive to get equal educational results for those minority children.

Safran and MacArthur wisely emphasize that learning on a task like this takes place even in the few moments of the test itself. This thought should be pursued to its logical conclusion. The child who quickly gains insight into the task is exhibiting an easily-tapped readiness that is of undoubted significance. Perhaps many others could, by spending two weeks on practice exercises, greatly improve their scores and so earn a higher ranking in the group. The burden of proof is on those who contend that status at the beginning of the training period is a better index of educability than is performance at the end.

To defend a mental test simply on the ground that it manifestly requires reasoning and self-criticism is to evade the issue of relevance. A high score indicates a well-tuned mind, and if high-scoring children do poorly in school the school program is at fault. But what school program would be well suited to the child who scores high on SCRIT, Matrices, and similar tasks, while scoring at or below average on direct verbal tests? Until an investigator discovers the answer to this, and describes the successful instructional method so clearly that it can be used as a model, his test is of little use in education. Pointed questions are to be asked also about the child whose verbal reasoning is superior but whose SCRIT score is not. For some reason this child's intellectual skills are unbalanced, and a method of repairing the deficiency needs to be discovered. Predicting success in an established program is not a significant use for tests in education. When a society intends to educate everyone and can afford it, the educator has to plan alternative programs or instructional strategies, and tests have to have demonstrated relevance to the choice among the alternatives. This sort of relevance has never been demonstrated for group nonverbal tests. After half a century, such tests are still in the category of "promising."

[385]

*Scholastic Mental Ability Test. Grades kgn–1, 2–3, 4–5, 6–8; 1953–67; SMAT; various titles used by publisher; 1 form; 4 levels; statistical data ['62, 1 page] for grades 2–8; $5.95 per 35 tests, postage extra; 50¢ per specimen set of any one level, cash orders only; Oliver F. Anderhalter; Scholastic Testing Service, Inc. *
a) PRE-PRIMARY. Grades kgn–1; 1954–55; Form A ('55, 14 pages, identical to test copyrighted in 1954 except for format); revised manual ('55, 5 pages); no data on reliability and validity; (25–35) minutes.
b) PRIMARY. Grades 2–3; 1953–62; Form O ('61, 12 pages); manual ('62, 11 pages) with 1963 norms; (40–50) minutes.
c) ELEMENTARY. Grades 4–5; 1954–62; Form O ('61, 14 pages); manual ('62, 10 pages) with 1963 norms; separate answer sheets (Digitek) may be used; $5 per 50 answer sheets; $1.50 per school scoring kit; scoring service, 20¢ and over per test; (40–50) minutes.
d) ADVANCED. Grades 6–8; 1955–67; Form O ('61, 12 pages); 2 editions; prices same as for c; (40–50) minutes.
    1) Digitek Edition. 1955–67; manual ('67, 17 pages); separate answer sheets (Digitek) must be used.
    2) IBM 1230 Edition. 1955–66; manual ('66, 13 pages); separate answer sheets (IBM 1230) must be used.

For reviews by Walter N. Durost and Alexander G. Wesman of earlier editions, see 5:380.

[386]

*Schubert General Ability Battery. Grades 12–16 and adults; 1946–65; SGAB; 5 scores: vocabulary, analogies, arithmetic problems, syllogisms, total; 1 form ('65, 13 pages, identical with test copyrighted in 1946 except for revision of 4 items and omission of 3 items); manual ('65, 24 pages, identical with manual published in 1953 except for revised analogies norms for high school senior boys); 30¢ per test; $2 per manual; $3 per specimen set; postage extra; 16(25) or 32(40) minutes; Herman J. P. Schubert and Daniel S. P. Schubert (test); Herman J. P. Schubert. *

REFERENCE

1. NEIDT, CHARLES O., AND DREBUS, RICHARD W. "Characteristics Associated With the Creativity of Research Scientists in an Industrial Setting." J Indus Psychol 2:102–12 D '64. * (PA 40:11550)

For a review by William B. Schrader, see 5:382.

[387]

*Short Form Test of Academic Aptitude. Grades 1.5–2, 3–4, 5–6, 7–9, 9–12; 1936–70; SFTAA; revision of still-in-print California Test of Mental Maturity; 3 scores: language, nonlanguage, total; 1 form; 5 levels; preliminary interpretation guide ('70, 48 pages); technical bulletin ('70, 39 pages); individual record sheet ['70, 1 page]; optional tape recorded directions (3¾ ips) available for levels 2–5; no data on validity; separate answer sheets (CompuScan [NCS],

Digitek, IBM 1230, Scoreze) must be used for b1, c, d, and e; $3 per 100 individual record sheets; $1.50 per guide; $2.50 per technical bulletin; $6.50 per tape recording of any one level; postage extra; $1.30 per specimen set of any one level, postpaid; Elizabeth T. Sullivan, Willis W. Clark, and Ernest W. Tiegs; CTB/McGraw-Hill. *
a) LEVEL 1. Grades 1.5–2; 2 editions; manual ('70, 47 pages); 31(40) minutes.
    1) Hand Scorable Booklet. 1 form ['70, 13 pages]; $6.50 per 35 tests.
    2) CompuScan Machine Scorable Booklet. 1 form ('70, 12 pages); $8.50 per 35 tests; scoring service, 27¢ and over per test.
b) LEVEL 2. Grades 3–4; 2 editions; 38(45) minutes.
    1) Hand Scorable Booklet. 1 form ('70, 13 pages); manual ('70, 45 pages); $6.50 per 35 tests; $2.50 per 50 CompuScan, Digitek, or IBM answer sheets; $2.50 per 25 Scoreze answer sheets; $1 per set of IBM hand scoring stencils; CompuScan scoring service, 22¢ and over per test.
    2) CompuScan Machine Scorable Booklet. 1 form ('70, 12 pages); manual ('70, 51 pages); prices same as for a2.
c) LEVEL 3. Grades 5–6; 1 form ('70, 12 pages); manual ('70, 45 pages); $7.50 per 35 tests; remaining prices same as for b1; 38(45) minutes.
d) LEVEL 4. Grades 7–9; 1 form ('70, 16 pages); manual ('70, 47 pages); $7.50 per 35 tests; remaining prices same as for b1; 38(45) minutes.
e) LEVEL 5. Grades 9–12; 1 form ('70, 15 pages); manual ('70, 47 pages); $7.50 per 35 tests; remaining prices same as for b1; 38(45) minutes.

[388]

★Spiral Nines, Sixth Edition. Job applicants with 7–8 years of education; 1960–65; SN; also called Nines; Forms A, B, ('65, 15 pages); no manual; preliminary norms for Form A ('66), Form B norms ('65); no data on reliability and validity; separate answer sheets must be used; R17.85 per 25 tests; 75c per single copy; 40c per 25 answer sheets; 40c per scoring stencil; postpaid within South Africa; 60(70) minutes; National Institute for Personnel Research. *

REFERENCES

1. MACARTHUR, R. S.; IRVINE, S. H.; AND BRIMBLE, A. R. The Northern Rhodesia Mental Ability Survey 1963. Rhodes-Livingstone Communication No. 27. Lusaka, Zambia: Rhodes-Livingstone Institute, 1964. Pp. ix, 100. *
2. IRVINE, S. H. "Factor Analysis of African Abilities and Attainments: Constructs Across Cultures." Psychol B 71(1): 20–32 Ja '69. * (PA 43:7553)

[389]

★Test of Adult College Aptitude. Evening college entrants; 1966; TACA; 1 form (2 pages); mimeographed manual (14 pages); preliminary norms; 10¢ per IBM 1230 test-answer sheet, postpaid; specimen set free; (45) minutes; King M. Wientge and Philip H. DuBois; TACA Development Fund. *

KENNETH D. HOPKINS, Professor of Education and Director, Laboratory of Educational Research, University of Colorado, Boulder, Colorado.

PURPOSE. TACA has been designed to be a "brief measure of the learning potential of the adult who is considering entering a program of continuing education." It is to be used to obtain "an objective index of learning capacity," needed to advise prospective adult students.

TEST DEVELOPMENT AND DESIGN. TACA grew out of the authors' previous research pertaining to predicting the achievement (GPA) of adult students at Washington University. Part 1 consists of 22 biographical questions selected from a pool of "55 items of non-threatening nature ....on the basis of their contribution to the prediction of course grade." Part 2 contains 54 items (42 verbal and 12 numerical) that were selected from a pool of 100 items on the basis of a "difficulty analysis." All require the selection of the dissimilar option. The rationale for selecting the items on a difficulty rather than a discrimination criterion is unexplained.

The test is contained on both sides of a specially printed IBM 1230 form which serves as both booklet and answer sheet. The directions for administering and taking the test are both simple and straightforward but no directions are given regarding guessing. The simplicity of the test and the ease with which it can be administered and scored are appealing features. The 45 minutes for completion of the test is said to be adequate although no supporting data are provided on this point.

NORMS. "Preliminary norms" (percentile ranks) are based on a group described only as "329 students enrolled in....the evening division of Washington University." No information regarding age, sex, previous education or occupation are given, hence this reference group is so amorphous that it is little, if any, better than none at all. A "representative" norm group cannot be reasonably expected for such a new test, but the failure to describe the available sample on which the norms are based can be criticized —particularly when this information is a portion of the biographical items contained in Part 1 of the TACA!

RELIABILITY. The K-R 20 reliability estimates given for Part 2 of TACA for three samples are very high (.95–.96). No information is given on the mean number of items attempted, hence the influence of speed and guessing probably contributes to some unknown extent to these high values. It is this reviewer's opinion that although the time limits appear ample, the tendency of several examinees not to attempt several items (no directions are given regarding guessing) probably resulted in considerably inflated K-R 20 estimates.

No reliability information is given for Part 1: "since the material is heterogeneous, an internal measure of reliability is not appropriate."

Part 1 reliability is no doubt very high, yet Parts 1 and 2 correlate only meagerly (.29, .25, .17). The correlation between true scores on the two parts using the authors' data is estimated to be only .32, hardly a satisfactory relationship for justifying the combining of scores in Parts 1 and 2 into a single score. (Norms are given only for the total TACA score.)

The reliability data presented do not directly address the consistency of TACA *total* scores, the type of reliability information most important for the user. In addition, it is not clear from the manual whether or not the 249 students used for the item selection were a part of the 386 on whom the reliability estimates are based; if so, the estimates would be considerably and spuriously inflated. Standard errors of measurement are not given and cannot be estimated readily since a reliability estimate for total score is not provided.

VALIDITY. It is axiomatic that the validity of a test must always be viewed in relation to its function. The authors would be much less vulnerable to criticism if they purported solely a prognostic function for the test. But as a measure of "learning capacity," the TACA must be evaluated in terms of construct validity considerations (which of course subsumes predictive relationships). From a predictive standpoint, the TACA functioned reasonably satisfactorily (at least in a relative sense) for three samples of 100–150 students (r's of .28–.36 for single courses; r's of .38–.54 with cumulative GPA). It would appear, however, that since both parts are probably quite reliable and yet the entire correlation between them is low, a multiple regression approach could have meaningfully increased the validity coefficients.

As a measure of "learning potential," however, the TACA is grossly inadequate. A logical study of the items (vocabulary and arithmetic) suggests that they measure academic achievement far more than aptitude. But the most serious defect is the absence of any underlying rationale for "scoring" of biographical information (as "number right") and combining this "score" in an undifferentiated fashion with the score on Part 2. How can one justify (in terms of construct validity) the fact that an examinee's "learning potential," or "college aptitude" is 20 points (2σ!) less because he happens to be: a 24-year-old (not older), unmarried clerk with no dependents, who graduated below the top quarter in his high school class, who has less than 30 college hours, is taking the course at his employer's request, who says grades reflect his ability only most of the time (but not always), is not a member of any career organization or community group, who does not attend church weekly, is not a home owner, has attended only one art exhibit in the past year, rates himself as only an average reader, has not read more than 5 nonfiction books in the past year, and owns less than 50 books.

Since the test interpretation as normed is made from the sum of the two part scores, it is misleading to call TACA an aptitude test. Its prognostic function is, of course, another matter.

SUMMARY. The TACA is a test in an embryonic stage. Fragmentary norms are based on a group of unknown characteristics. The TACA appears to have satisfactory reliability although an undisclosed portion of this is probably the result of reliability response styles on which there are wide and reliable individual differences. The TACA may have promised a quick convenient *predictive* measure of GPA in adult education, but, in its present form, it appears to have little promise of attaining its purported objective as a measure of learning potential. The problems cited above lead to the conclusion that, while the test has merit from an administrative viewpoint, whether or not it is a usable tool for the counselor has not been demonstrated. With the present version, users of the test must be able and willing to develop their own norms, reliability and validity data.

[390]

★Test of Perceptual Organization. Ages 12 and over; 1967-69; TPO; formerly called *Test of Abstract Reasoning;* 1 form ('69, 3 pages); manual ('69, 12 pages); $6.50 per 25 tests; 50¢ per scoring stencil; $3 per manual; $3.75 per specimen set; cash orders postpaid; 10(15) minutes; William T. Martin; Psychologists and Educators Press. *

REFERENCE

1. MARTIN, WILLIAM T. "Analysis of the Abstracting Function in Reasoning Using an Experimental Test." *Psychol Rep* 21:593-8 O '67. * (PA 42:4815)

[391]

*Tests of General Ability: Inter-American Series. Preschool, grades kgn-1.5, 2-3, 4-6, 7-9, 10-13.5; 1961-67; TGA; revision of still-in-print *Tests of General Ability: Cooperative Inter-American Tests;* a series of parallel tests and manuals in English and Spanish; 6 levels; series manual ('67, 99 pages); series technical report ('67, 70 pages); tentative norms, publisher recommends use of local norms; $1 per manual; $1 per technical report; postage extra; 50¢ per specimen set of any one level except preschool, postpaid; Herschel T. Manuel; Guidance Testing Associates. *
a) PRESCHOOL LEVEL, EXPERIMENTAL EDITION. Ages 4-5; 1966-67; 3 scores: verbal-numerical, nonverbal, total; individual; 1 form ('66, 100 cards); English, Spanish, directions ('66, 12 pages); $5 per set of cards, English, Spanish directions, and record sheet; $4 per 100 record sheets; (40-50) minutes in 2 sessions.
b) LEVEL 1—PRIMARY. Grades kgn-1.5; 1962-67; 3 scores same as in *a;* 2 editions; 2 forms; pretest ['64, 4 pages] for use in teaching testing procedures to immature children; 3¢ per pretest.
1) *Regular Edition.* English Forms CE, DE, ('62, 11 pages); Spanish Forms CEs, DEs, ('62, 11 pages); English, Spanish, directions ['66, 11 pages]; $1.40 per 10 tests; (50-60) minutes in 2 sessions.
2) *Short Form.* English Forms CE-A, DE-A, ('63, 7 pages); Spanish Forms CEs-A, DEs-A, ('65, 7 pages); English, Spanish, directions ['66, 8 pages]; $1.20 per 10 tests; (40-50) minutes in 2 sessions.
c) LEVEL 2—PRIMARY. Grades 2-3; 1964-67; 3 scores same as in *a;* English Forms CE, DE, ('64, 12 pages); Spanish Forms CEs, DEs, ('65, 12 pages); English, Spanish, directions ['66, 11 pages]; $1.40 per 10 tests; (45-50) minutes.
d) LEVEL 3—ELEMENTARY. Grades 4-6; 1961-67; 4 scores: verbal, nonverbal, numerical, total; English Forms CE ('61, 15 pages), DE ('62, 15 pages); Spanish Forms CEs, DEs, ('62, 15 pages); English, Spanish, combined directions ['66, 7-8 pages] for Levels 3-5; separate answer sheets (IBM 805, IBM 1230) must be used for Levels 3-5; $1.60 per 10 tests; $5 per 100 answer sheets; 30¢ per IBM 805 scoring stencil; 15¢ per IBM 1230 scoring stencil; 52(65) minutes.
e) LEVEL 4—INTERMEDIATE. Grades 7-9; 1962-67; 4 scores same as in *d;* English Forms CE, DE, ('62, 15 pages); Spanish Forms CEs, DEs, ('62, 15 pages); remaining details same as for Level 3.
f) LEVEL 5—ADVANCED. Grades 10-13.5; 1962-67; 4 scores same as in *d;* English Forms CE, DE, ('62, 15 pages); Spanish Forms CEs, DEs, ('62, 15 pages); remaining details same as for Level 3.

REFERENCES

1-8. See 4:325.
9. MANUEL, HERSCHEL T. *The Preparation and Evaluation of Inter-Language Testing Materials.* Unpublished report to the U.S. Office of Education, Cooperative Research Project No. 681, University of Texas, 1963. Pp. vii, 112. * (ERIC ED 001 702)
10. MANUEL, HERSCHEL T. *Development of Inter-American Test Materials.* Unpublished report to the U.S. Office of Education, Cooperative Research Project No. 2621, University of Texas, December 1966. Pp. vii, 99. * (ERIC ED 010 670)

RUSSEL F. GREEN, *Research Consultant in Psychology and Education, Henrietta, New York.*

The objective of the author in preparing this test is a worthy one: to produce a new series of tests that will be parallel English and Spanish editions and which will yield "comparable" results when the Spanish edition is administered to Spanish-speaking people and the English edition is administered to English-speaking people. More narrowly, the objective was to select test items "common to the two cultures" and "of similar difficulty." The importance of the series lies primarily in the effort to produce parallel English and Spanish forms. This review is limited to an evaluation of this effort.

The tone of the author's writing is sincere, reasonable, and insightful. He is careful to write in language that persons with little background in testing should be able to understand. The author includes cautions concerning the interpretability of the test scores and especially the comparability of the scores obtained from the parallel English and Spanish versions.

Every item presented in one language is also presented in the parallel form of the other language. The tests consist of materials that are commonly found in tests of general ability. The language seems appropriate.

It is, of course, a difficult task to make a Spanish form acceptable to all Spanish-speaking subcultures. The solution adopted was to use rather formal Spanish that would be recognized as correct everywhere and to avoid local idioms or area usages. The result is that in almost every locality some items in the tests will sound a little strange to the examinee. This is unavoidable.

Many estimates of reliability are reported. The alternate-form reliabilities for the English total score range from .72 to .90 (median .80) and for the Spanish total score from .59 to .91 (median .88). Subtest reliabilities are, of course, somewhat lower. The verbal scores are a little more reliable than the nonverbal scores. This is a typical outcome for test materials of these kinds.

Quite a number of concurrent validity estimates are reported. These range from quite low to an occasional quite high correlation. Correlations with academic achievement, especially in reading, appear to average over .60 which seems quite good, especially in view of the apparently modest reliability of the tests.

No evidence is presented in the manuals that the parallel items are of equal difficulty in the two cultural settings. Many of them almost surely are not; nor is evidence presented that the distribution of difficulties of items is the same. The author states, "The Spanish items were administered to Spanish speaking children and the English items to English speaking children." The results were then compared for relative difficulty. Unfortunately, the groups to which the items were administered are not specified; the reader is expected to assume that the groups were equivalent in natural endowment and environmental advantages and that they would, therefore, have equivalent mastery of their native language and equivalent developmental histories such that the comparison of "relative difficulty" was valid. These are trou-

blesome assumptions; to make them about undescribed samples of children seems too much of an act of faith to ask of potential users. It seems highly likely that the items of the parallel forms are not parallel in difficulty; appropriate populations probably were not used. Defining such a Spanish-speaking population would be virtually impossible. Even if this could be done, inherent differences in the two languages would make it all but impossible to achieve equal difficulties of all items. There are many concepts that are more easily expressed in one language than in the other. The number of words needed to express many concepts differs. To some degree the conceptual worlds of the two language groups are different. To evolve truly parallel forms in the two languages would involve a whole series of progressive approximations from appropriate samples to be successful.

There are three tables presented (one being relevant to the *Tests of General Ability*) from which one could easily get the impression that *scores* on parallel English and Spanish forms were equivalent. The technical manual shows that the alternate forms in English and in Spanish have closely equivalent scores. By presenting both the English forms and the Spanish forms comparisons in the same table one can easily get the impression that the English and Spanish scores presented are also equivalent to each other. The fact that this is not so (except for carefully selected subsets of undefined students) can be verified by comparing the appropriate sections of this table with four other such tables. The comparison makes it clear that numerically similar scores derived from parallel forms from the two language groups are not equivalent.

In an effort to provide useful norms, the test developers have "equated" the *Tests of General Ability* with a large number of other tests. All this results in a rather confusing variety of "norms" from which it is hoped that a potential user can find a set which will suit his purpose. Much of this "equating" was done on small undefined samples and hence is of doubtful value. However, a few sets of the equivalents are probably quite useful, such as those involving Project Talent Tests and the *College Board Scholastic Aptitude Test*.

Tentative within-grade norms for an "islandwide administration of tests in Puerto Rico" are presented for "a limited sampling of pupils in the public schools." Even if these norms are adequate for Puerto Rico, they still would be of limited usefulness to other Spanish-speaking groups because of varying cultural emphasis in such areas as language development and usage. Good norms are not available for any Spanish-speaking area.

So this reviewer must close on a note of regret. The unique objectives have not been met. The tests are not adequate for cross-cultural research or comparisons. For that we must wait for a much more definitive test development and normative effort.

RICHARD E. SCHUTZ, *Director, Southwest Regional Laboratory for Educational Research and Development, Los Alamitos, California.*

The history of these tests is unique in the annals of American testing. From an individual perspective, the history reflects the personal pioneer efforts of a persevering author. From a societal perspective, the history reflects the attitude of American society toward ethnic minorities which, in retrospect, appears clearly tokenistic, but which was unrecognized as such at the time of the test's development.

The test development began in Puerto Rico in the early 1940's, sponsored by the Committee on Modern Languages of the American Council on Education, as a subordinate objective of an effort designed to teach English as a second language. The purpose was to develop measuring instruments "which will yield comparable results in....English and Spanish," to provide "comparable measures of ability....in the bilingual situation." While current linguistic knowledge makes it clear that this objective is both simplistic and chauvinistic, it remains the purpose of the tests in their present form.

The tests were published by the Educational Testing Service from 1950–1959 as the Cooperative Inter-American Tests. In 1959, three interrelated events stimulated further development activity. ETS discontinued distribution of the tests. A new nonprofit corporation was established in Texas by Herschel Manuel "specifically to assume responsibility for the tests." The U.S. Office of Education awarded a research contract to be directed by Manuel to the University of Texas to "provide means now lacking or imperfectly developed for comparing the abilities and educational achievements of different languages and cultures."

The spirit of both the times and the test series is reflected in the objectives of the research project:

(1) the improvement of international cooperation and communication in educational research and in the educative process; (2) provision of comparable measures of ability and achievement in the bilingual situation—for example, when a school is educating children of different home languages or when the ability of the same person in two languages needs to be estimated; (3) an increase of the supply of useful measuring instruments in each of the languages. * The use of the tests for communication across linguistic barriers and for comparison of ability in different languages will be greatly limited unless the Spanish tests are generally useful and widely used with Spanish-speaking children and the English tests with English-speaking children.

One result of the research effort was a revision and refinement of the 1950 series tests into Levels 1–5. USOE research support from 1964–1966 produced the Preschool Level tests and a large number of correlational analyses based on administration of various forms of the series with other commonly used test series. Although the examinee samples for these analyses are not well defined, the concurrently administered tests are all in English and the samples all appear to be from the United States. The objective of "international cooperation and communication" clearly lost a good deal in the translation from research proposal to project results.

While the history of the series is pertinent to the present prospective user, he is necessarily concerned with its current characteristics. These as well as the history are documented accurately and fairly in the manual and technical report, which are also relevant to the companion reading test in the Inter-American Series. A prime characteristic of each series, fully emphasized in the documentation, is that the tests are essentially unnormed. "The Inter-American Tests are recommended for use primarily with regional or local norms to be prepared by those who use the tests." A few norm tables are presented, and equivalent scores are given for several well known and well normed tests. However, the size and nature of the samples involved are such that the user would be foolhardy to disregard the publisher's advice on this matter. A user should be prepared to construct his own norms if he plans to use this series.

The obvious distinctive characteristic of the series is that forms are available in Spanish. This is true of both test booklets and directions for administration. At the Preschool Level through Level 2, this characteristic is a moot distinction for the test booklets, since all items are nonverbal. At the upper levels, the verbal items are Spanish-English translations. At all levels, the items and subtests have familiar analogs with other available tests; the series is neither more or less unique nor more or less culturally influenced than competing series.

Were any competing test publisher interested in converting an available English general ability test to Spanish, it would be possible to quickly generate a Spanish translation that would create a series with all of the distinguishing features of the Inter-American Series. This is not to suggest that any publisher should do such a translation. Quite the contrary, since the limitations of such a series would be patently obvious. Although the Inter-American Series test development has quite different historical antecedents, it incorporates the same patent limitations, even though the series was generated "the hard way."

The Spanish-speaking child in an English-speaking country unquestionably poses difficult and complex policy, pedagogic, and psychometric problems which include but are not restricted to those relevant to the English-speaking child. These problems, however, are likely to be obscured rather than ameliorated by use of the Spanish forms of the Inter-American Series. That is, test interpretations which treat the resulting scores in the same manner that one would treat the scores from an English mental ability test will almost certainly detract from rather than contribute to the enhancement of the potential of the examinee. Ethnic minority leaders who have in general opposed mental ability tests for ideologic rather than psychometric reasons should not be duped by the ostensible linguistic relevance of the series. Basically, the Spanish tests share the ideologic deficiencies reputed in English mental ability tests and add some severe psychometric limitations.

Regretfully, no stronger endorsement can be given either for the use of the Spanish forms of the tests in Spanish-speaking contexts or for the use of the English forms in either English-speaking or Spanish-speaking contexts. The goal of solving inter-American communication problems through the alchemy of comparable ability tests is a fanciful and outmoded ideal. The Inter-American Series tests are of and for a bygone era.

For reviews by Raleigh M. Drake and Walter N. Durost of the earlier edition, see 4:325.

[392]

*Thurstone Test of Mental Alertness.** Grades 9-12 and adults; 1943-68; TTMA; abbreviated adaptation of *American Council on Education Psychological Examination for High School Students,* 1940 Edition; for a shorter adaptation of this test, see *SRA Verbal Form;* 3 scores: quantitative, linguistic, total; Forms A ('52), B ('53), (9 pages, consumable booklet replacing original separate answer sheet edition); manual ('68, 16 pages); $5.95 per 25 tests; 40¢ per manual; $1.25 per specimen set; postage extra; 20(25) minutes; Thelma Gwinn Thurstone and L. L. Thurstone; Science Research Associates, Inc. *

REFERENCES

1-3. See 4:326.
4. PETERSON, FLOYD E. "Identification of Sub-Groups for Test Validation Research." *J Indus Psychol* 2:98-101 D '64. * (*PA* 40:10636)
5. VIVERS, BILLY B. *A Study of the Relationship Between Applicants Scores on the Thurstone Tests of Mental Alertness and the Allport, Vernon, Lindzey Study of Values and Subsequent Job Success as Psychiatric Aids.* Master's thesis, Kansas State College (Pittsburg, Kan.), 1965.
6. BENTZ, V. JON. Chap. 3, "The Sears Experience in the Investigation, Description and Prediction of Executive Behavior," pp. 59-152. In *Predicting Managerial Success.* Edited by John A. Myers, Jr. Ann Arbor, Mich.: Foundation for Research on Human Behavior, April 1968. Pp. v, 173. *
7. WHEELER, RICHARD WADE. *A Study of the Relationship Between Selected Interviewer Variables and the Interpretation of Interview Information.* Doctor's thesis, University of Houston (Houston, Tex.), 1969. (*DAI* 30:425B)

ROBERT D. NORTH, *Associate Director, Professional Examinations Division, The Psychological Corporation, New York, New York.*

Except for the addition of some new research and normative data to the manual, this test remains essentially unchanged from the 1952-53 edition. Each form of the test consists of 126 items of four types, arranged spirally and in order of difficulty. The seven items in each spiral segment occur in the following sequence: two same-opposites, one arithmetic reasoning (word-arithmetic problem), two definitions, and two number series. Although labelled a "test of mental alertness," it is actually a test of verbal and mathematical abilities.

Like its parent instrument, the time-honored *American Council on Education Psychological Examination,* this test yields separate linguistic (L) and quantitative (Q) scores, but unlike the ACE, the spiral arrangement of the items prevents separate timing of the sets of items that yield these scores. As a result, the interdependence of the two types of scores tends to be increased, since a student's hang-up on items of one type might keep him from progressing to some of the items of the other types that he could answer readily. Persistent students do not always heed the part of the directions stating: "Do not spend too much time on a single question."

The items are concise and are printed in easily readable type. In the case of the number series items—as well as the definition items, which call for identification of the correct response solely by its initial letter—traditional arguments about ambiguity or the justification of the keyed responses may be advanced.

Evidently the test is now going through a metamorphosis from the former reusable booklet style with "self-scoring" answer pads to a consumable booklet with an answer sheet, according to information given in the 1970 SRA catalog. The test booklets submitted for this review have a hybrid format, with the progressively narrowing columns of the step-down design being printed on full pages, flush right.

The percentile norms for high school students are based on the scores of 977 ninth grade students and 545 twelfth grade students "drawn in 1959 from four coeducational high schools representing diverse geographical areas of the country." Interpolated norms for the tenth and eleventh grades are also given. For a contemporary test of a major publisher, these school norms are scant.

Percentile norms are also presented for 15 categories of employees and job applicants, with the sizes of the norm groups ranging from 128 for secretaries to 4,447 for "Male Applicants with H.S. Education." The only information given about these norm groups is that they "are thought to be a cross section of most TMA takers." The publisher's advice that local norms should be developed for interpreting the test results might well be heeded.

Data given in the manual, based on a counterbalanced administration of the two forms to 202 twelfth graders in a 1962 study, indicate that Form A is somewhat easier than Form B, with the difference amounting to 3.8 total raw score points at the mean. This evidence should be taken into consideration in retesting situations, since a difference of about that magnitude corresponds to more than 10 percentile points in the 20–80 range of the twelfth grade norms. Correlations of equivalence between the two forms for the same 202 cases are reported as .79 for the L score, .81 for the Q score, and .85 for the total score.

Test-retest reliability coefficients over a 30-day interval for four groups of 55 to 89 twelfth grade students in two schools range from .84 to .96 for the part scores, and from .92 to .95 for the total score. As pointed out in the manual,

the memory effect involved in retesting with the same form after 30 days probably inflates these coefficients. Making some allowance for this effect, and also for the small sizes of the groups tested, the reviewer judges that the reliabilities nevertheless approach those of other current mental ability tests of similar length.

For student groups in the ninth and twelfth grades in one to four schools, the total scores have correlations of .40 to .77 (median, .64) with grade-point averages, .83 to .85 with *Iowa Tests of Educational Development* composite scores, and .71 to .73 with *SRA High School Placement Test* composite scores. These correlations are fairly typical of those yielded by creditable tests of verbal and mathematical abilities. No evidence is given of any differential validity for the L and Q scores for student groups.

At the adult level in the industrial area, correlations with the "verbal subtest of the *Wechsler Adult Intelligence Scale*" are given as .60 for the L score, .18 for the Q score, and .62 for the total score. Since means and standard deviations for this sample of 200 cases, with an age range of 22 to 70, are not reported, these correlations cannot be interpreted without ambiguity.

Some evidence of the validity of the test for certain business and industrial personnel uses is given in the form of correlations with supervisors' ratings and mean score differences between groups of employees rated "good" and "poor." The samples consist of 27 to 404 individuals in managerial, supervisory, sales, clerical, and bank-teller positions. Some of the correlations are impressive—ranging up to .63. Nevertheless, since job-success criteria are likely to vary greatly from one place of employment to another, the test user would be well advised to follow the manual's admonition to base his interpretation of the scores on his cumulative experience with the instrument.

On the whole, the *Thurstone Test of Mental Alertness* warrants consideration for use with high school students, employment applicants, or employees when a relatively quick measure of verbal and numerical abilities in combination is desired. Careful consideration should be given to the limitations of the normative and validity data, however, in choosing this test over such others as the *Cooperative School and College Ability Tests,* the *SRA Tests of Educational*

Ability, or the Verbal and Numerical subtests of the *Differential Aptitude Tests.*

For a review by Joshua A. Fishman, see 5:391; for reviews by Anne Anastasi and Emily T. Burr of an earlier edition, see 3:265.

[393]
★The Undergraduate Record Examinations: Aptitude Test. Grades 15–16; 1969–70; 2 scores: verbal, quantitative; Forms K-RUR1 ('69, 23 pages), RUR2 ('69, 22 pages); descriptive booklet ('70, 20 pages); for more complete information, see 671; 90(110) minutes; Educational Testing Service. *

For reviews of the testing program, see 671 (2 reviews).

[394]
The Verbal Power Test of Concept Equivalence. Ages 14 and over; 1959–63; VPTCE; Forms A, B, ('59, 2 pages) on a single sheet; manual ('63, 12 pages); $6 per set of 25 tests, key, and manual; $1.50 per manual; postpaid; (10–15) minutes; E. Francesco; Western Psychological Services. *

REFERENCES

1–3. See 6:508.

ERWIN K. TAYLOR, *President, Personnel Research and Development Corporation, Cleveland, Ohio.*

The title *Verbal Power Test of Concept Equivalence* is a rather grandiose name for what turns out to be a test of synonyms. The manual, published in 1963, provides little information with respect to the nature or philosophy of item construction; also, there are no data provided with respect to the kind of item analysis performed or the basis of item selection.

The manual stipulates that the test "requires fourth grade reading ability." While it is true that only four-letter words are used, many of them are so archaic and arcane as to make this statement patently ridiculous. Form A, for example, contains such terms as "ovum," "elan," "limn," "dyad," "cote," and "rive." To these Form B adds additionally such terms as "abet," "opus," "kris," "lode," "quay," "gaol," and others. It would strain fourth grade level readers to recognize that a "dirk" is equivalent to a "kris." One might even quarrel with some of the keying, such as giving "shed" and "emit" the same meaning. Similarly, "soar" and "rise" are keyed as synonyms, as are "norm" and "mode." Even "dear" and "high" are considered synonyms, as are "clay" and "mire." The correlation between the two forms of the test (printed on opposite sides of the same page) is quoted as .86 for a "slightly longer test form

than the present forms." Unidentified "between-test product-moment coefficients of correlation for Forms A and B" range from .61 to .94.

All of the "validity" data presented in the manual consist of correlations between the VPTCE and other intelligence tests, mostly from the 200 adult prisoners in a mid-Atlantic state prison. Unidentified additional studies from a variety of sources quote correlations between the test and the WAIS as ranging from .34 to .68. In the opinion of this reviewer, the VPTCE incorporates a high degree of cultural bias and offers little to the potential user that is not already available in comparable tests that are more highly standardized and better constructed; for example, the *Quick Word Test,* the verbal portions of the *Personnel Tests for Industry,* or the verbal comprehension test from the *Employee Aptitude Survey.* All three are equally short and can be administered as power tests (with the requisite restandardization) if so desired.

The VPTCE manual makes the usual suggestion (which few users are in a position to follow) that they construct their own norms. The norms in the manual are based on 1,096 subjects in five different groups. Four of these are academic, consisting of two populations (sophomores and seniors, respectively) from an unidentified Ivy League university, a population of freshmen from a Southwestern school of education, and a group of Eastern high school seniors. The only nonacademic population is an unselected group of prisoners in an "East Central" prison. Thus, with all of the types of populations for which normative data are presented, it is likely that more comprehensive and more adequately standardized measures of intelligence would be already available—making the administration of this device even less valuable than it would otherwise be.

It is indeed difficult for this reviewer to imagine a situation in which he would find it desirable to use the VPTCE in preference to any of the above-mentioned tests or short verbal tests available.

[395]
*Verbal Test (Adv.). Ages 12 to 13–11; 1954–67; 4 tests; practice test [dates same as for tests, 2 pages] for each test; no data on validity; distribution restricted to directors of education; 7p per test; 2p per practice test; 8p per manual for any one test except *d;* postpaid within U.K.; 10(15) minutes for practice test; D. A. Pidgeon (*a*); published for National Foundation for Educational Research in England and Wales; Ginn & Co. Ltd. *

a) VERBAL TEST (ADV.) 1. 1954–55; 1 form ['54, 10 pages]; manual ('55, 10 pages); 50(60) minutes.
b) VERBAL TEST (ADV.) 3. 1958; 1 form ['58, 11 pages]; manual ('58, 9 pages); 45(55) minutes.
c) VERBAL TEST (ADV.) 4. 1960; 1 form ['60, 11 pages]; manual ('60, 9 pages); 45(55) minutes.
d) VERBAL TEST (ADV.) 5. 1962–67; 1 form ['62, 11 pages]; mimeographed directions for administration ['62, 8 pages]; provisional norms ['67]; directions and norms free on request from NFER; 50(60) minutes.

For reviews by J. S. Lawes and John Nisbet of Tests 1–4, see 6:510.

[396]

*Verbal Tests BC, CD, C, and D. Ages 8-0 to 10-6, 9-0 to 11-6, 9-6 to 12-0; 1953–66; 3 levels; 5p per test; 7p per manual for Test BC or CD, 8p per manual for Test C or D; postpaid within U.K.; published for the National Foundation for Educational Research in England and Wales; Ginn & Co. Ltd. *
a) VERBAL TEST BC. Ages 8-0 to 10-6; 1953–62; formerly called *Primary Verbal Test 1;* adaptation of *A.C.E.R. Junior A Test* and *A.C.E.R. Junior B Test;* 1 form ['53, 8 pages]; revised manual ('62, 8 pages); 30(40) minutes; D. A. Pidgeon.
b) VERBAL TESTS CD AND C. Ages 9-0 to 11-6; 1959–66; 2 forms; 35(45) minutes.
  1) *Verbal Test CD.* Ages 9-0 to 11-6; formerly called *Primary Verbal Test 2;* 1 form ['59, 8 pages]; manual ['59, 7 pages]; Valerie Land.
  2) *Verbal Test C.* Ages 9-4 to 11-0; formerly called *Primary Verbal Test 2G;* 1 form ['65, 8 pages]; manual ['66, 9 pages].
c) VERBAL TEST D. Ages 9-6 to 12-0; 1962; formerly called *Primary Verbal Test 3;* 1 form ['62, 8 pages]; manual ['62, 11 pages]; 40(50) minutes; T. Neville Postlethwaite.

For reviews by John Nisbet and F. W. Warburton of a, see 5:369.

[397]

*Verbal Tests EF and GH. Ages 11.0–13.5, 13.5–15.0; 1960–66; 2 levels; 5p per test; 7p per manual for either level; postpaid within U.K.; Valerie Land and Olive Wood (*a*); published for the National Foundation for Educational Research in England and Wales; Ginn & Co. Ltd. *
a) VERBAL TEST EF. Ages 11.0–13.5; 1960; formerly called *Secondary Verbal Test 1;* 1 form ['60, 8 pages]; manual ['60, 7 pages]; 40(45) minutes.
b) VERBAL TEST GH. Ages 13.5–15.0; 1962–66; formerly called *Secondary Verbal Test 2;* 1 form ['62, 8 pages]; manual ['66, 7 pages]; 45(50) minutes.

For a review by Stanley Nisbet of a, see 6:499.

[398]

*Verbal Tests 14–21 and 69. Ages 10–12; 1951–70; 9 tests (8 pages); new test published annually; practice test (2 pages, dates same as for test) for each test; no data on validity; distribution restricted to directors of education; 5p per test; 2p per practice test; 8p per manual for any one test except *g2* and *h;* postpaid within U.K.; 10(15) minutes for practice test, 45(50) minutes for Tests 18–21, 50(55) minutes for Tests 14–17 and 69; published for the National Foundation for Educational Research in England and Wales; Ginn & Co. Ltd. *

a) VERBAL TEST 14. 1963–64; forms 14A, 14B, ['63]; manual ('64, 10 pages) for each form.
b) VERBAL TEST 15. 1964–65; forms 15A, 15B, ['64]; manual ('65, 10 pages) for each form.
c) VERBAL TEST 16. 1965–66; forms 16A, 16B, ['65]; manual ('66, 10 pages) for each form.
d) VERBAL TEST 17. 1966–67; forms 17A, 17B, ['66]; manual ('67, 10 pages) for each form.
e) VERBAL TEST 18. 1967–68; forms 18A, 18B, ['67]; manual ('68, 11 pages) for each form.
f) VERBAL TEST 19. 1968–69; forms 19A, 19B, ['68]; manual ('69, 11 pages) for each form.
g) VERBAL TESTS 20 AND 69. 1969–70; 2 editions.
  1) *Verbal Test 20.* 1969–70; forms 20A, 20B, ['69]; manual ('70, 11 pages) for each form.
  2) *Verbal Test 69.* 1969; multiple choice version of form 20A; 1 form ['69]; mimeographed instructions '69, 7 pages); provisional norms ['69, 2 pages]; no data on reliability; separate answer sheets (Parnall) must be used; 4p per answer sheet; 10p per scoring stencil; instructions and norms free on request from NFER.
h) VERBAL TEST 21. 1970; 1 form ['70]; mimeographed instructions (7 pages); no data on reliability; no norms; instructions free on request from NFER.

REFERENCE

1. See 6:511.

DAVID A. WALKER, *Formerly Director, The Scottish Council for Research in Education, Edinburgh, Scotland.* [Review of Tests 13–20.]

This series of tests is designed mainly to aid education authorities in England and Wales in allocating pupils to appropriate courses of secondary education. Each of the tests follows the same general pattern, there being 100 items in sections of six to eight items, each section preceded by instructions and an example.

All items are of the objective type and the answer keys provided in the manuals give the acceptable responses. The sections are separated only by the new instructions and an example; they bear no heading but cover the usual field of vocabulary, classification, analogies, coding, mixed sentences, and reasoning.

The manual which accompanies each test gives full instructions on administration, marking, and transformation of raw scores to standardised scores. It also contains a brief description of the method by which each test was constructed and the basis of standardisation. It is noticeable that the wording of the manuals is almost identical throughout the series, apart from the necessary changes in answer keys, in standardisation data and in conversion tables. This permanence of construction is possibly a reflection of the satisfaction expressed by the authorities using the tests over the years and their unwillingness to contemplate any radical changes.

There are several points which should be

noted about the standardisation of these tests. The numbers used are substantial, usually exceeding 10,000 for each test, but they are drawn from selected areas and usually from ages 10-2 to 11-5. No indication is given of the method of selecting the areas, but it seems almost certain that these were the areas using the test for allocating pupils to secondary schools. Many of the pupils taking the tests were probably highly motivated to obtain high scores and gain admission to grammar schools. If the norms obtained from these pupils are used for pupils who are not so highly motivated, the resulting scores may well be depressed by several points.

A factor operating in the opposite direction is the steady improvement of scores in tests of this type that has been shown over the years,[1] so that the norms especially for the earlier tests require adjustment. The norms for those aged 11-6 to 12-0 are obtained by extrapolation. Finally, the norms are given for boys and girls taken together, although the manual points out that girls, on average, score about three points higher than boys. The recommendation in the manual is that in an allocation procedure the two sexes be considered independently of each other.

No validity coefficients are given, the reader being referred to Yates and Pidgeon's *Admission to Grammar Schools* for evidence to support the claim that the validity of verbal tests as predictors of success in the grammar school has been firmly established from empirical evidence in follow-up studies. This was without doubt a justifiable claim in the days when the grammar school was the chosen method of educating the abler children of England and Wales. The position is constantly changing, however, as the number of schools described as comprehensive increases. What function would be served by tests of this type if the system became fully comprehensive? There is evidence that in that situation tests of this kind are still satisfactory predictors of success in the examinations that must be passed before entry is gained to academic courses in universities and similar institutions. It may well be that these tests will continue to be used by administrators and teachers to enable them to advise pupils and their parents on the selection of courses of study in the secondary school.

1 PILLINER, A. E. G.; SUTHERLAND, J.; AND TAYLOR, E. G. "Zero Error in Moray House Verbal Reasoning Tests." *Brit J Ed Psychol* 30:53–62 F '60. *

For a review by Arthur B. Royse of earlier tests, see 6:511.

[399]

★WLW Culture Fair Inventory. Job applicants; 1969; CFI; intelligence; 1 form (8 pages); preliminary manual (8 pages); reliability and validity data based upon earlier experimental forms; preliminary norms; $15 per set of 100 tests and manual, postpaid; specimen set not available; [30–45] minutes; Barbara O. Murray (test), Lynde C. Steckle (test), and Robert W. Henderson; William, Lynde & Williams. *

ARTHUR R. JENSEN, *Professor of Educational Psychology; and Research Psychologist, Institute of Human Learning; University of California, Berkeley, California.*

The *WLW Culture Fair Inventory* (CFI) is a nontimed, nonverbal test intended to eliminate verbal and other cultural effects. The 30 items comprising the test consist of figural materials involving logical-spatial relationships. There are five parts: (*a*) selection of the one figure in a set of five that is most different, (*b*) block counting, (*c*) selection of the fifth figure in a series, (*d*) paper form board-type items, (*e*) selection of a figure which completes a pattern (matrices). Each of these parts is preceded by printed instructions and two examples with the correct answers given.

Judging from inspection of the items and this reviewer's experience with a wide variety of psychometric tests, it is inferred that the CFI measures reasoning and spatial abilities, much the same abilities as are assessed by Cattell's *Culture Fair Intelligence Tests,* Raven's *Progressive Matrices,* and Domino's *D48 Test,* although the CFI appears to be more loaded on a spatial factor.

The test manual claims that the test should "be suitable for minority groups or 'hard-core' individuals in hiring situations." The test, however, appears to be too difficult for this population. The 50th percentile for college students is only 18 items correct (out of 30), and the median for Negro clerical workers is only 10 items correct; the 99th percentile for this group is only 20 items correct. It is this reviewer's prediction that culturally disadvantaged minority persons will average lower on this test, in relation to middle class whites, than on most other standard tests, especially verbal tests.

The test has at least three advantages: (*a*) it is "nonverbal" and eliminates or minimizes the influence of reading ability and formal education; (*b*) it presents a variety of figural subtests, so that its total score should not contain a factor specific to a particular form of figural test material such as Matrices; (c) it is untimed and is thus a power test, but this also may introduce personality factors into the score variance. (The reviewer found a correlation of −.45 between time taken on the *Progressive Matrices* and the extraversion scale of the *Eysenck Personality Inventory* when subjects had no time limit. The more extraverted subjects tend to get through faster or to give up sooner when the items increase in difficulty.) Raven's PM shares advantages *a* and *c*; Cattell's CFT shares advantages *a* and *b*.

Several criticisms can be made of the CFI: (a) Some of the items depend as much upon perceptual or visual acuity as much as upon reasoning ability. (b) The figural materials are not as clearly printed as those in the Cattell and Raven tests. (c) The test is too difficult for the general population, being more suited to college level persons. (d) There are no really easy items at the beginning of each subtest to permit the subject to catch on readily to what is required and to gain practice before he is confronted with the more difficult problems. The Cattell and Raven tests are superior in this respect.

Finally, the test manual is totally inadequate and makes it obvious that the test has been published and marketed much too prematurely. The manual contains virtually no helpful information. The "norms" of the CFI are based on 50 male and 50 female college students, and 24 Negro and 46 women applicants for clerical jobs in an insurance company! The intercorrelations among the five subtests are remarkably low, ranging from .29 to .55. No data are given concerning the test's reliability. Correlations with other intelligence tests are so low as to make one wonder what the CFI actually measures. Aside from these correlations suggesting very low concurrent validity, the manual gives no other evidence of the test's validity or usefulness.

In conclusion, there is no good reason to recommend this test in its present inadequate stage of development. Testers who are seeking a good nonverbal "culture fair" test of general intelligence are urged to consider Cattell's *Culture Fair Intelligence Tests* or Raven's *Progressive Matrices* (these tests come in different forms for various ages and populations). The construction of these alternative tests, the adequacy of their manuals, their normative data, and the research behind them are totally unmatched by the *WLW Culture Fair Inventory*.

JAMES E. KENNEDY, *Professor of Psychology, The University of Wisconsin, Madison, Wisconsin.*

This 30-item test, consisting of five varieties of pictorial problems, requires no writing and was designed for group administration with no time limit. The test manual does not say what the test purports to measure. Since most of the items were adapted from or modeled after items from standard intelligence tests, one can infer that it was probably intended to measure one or more aspects of nonverbal reasoning or intelligence.

The test was developed to meet the expressed need of industrial clients for "a culture fair test that would largely discount the influence of environment and education." Toward this end, the test is untimed and limited to nonverbal items which "most people have not encountered in their daily lives." It is said to be suitable for use with "minority groups or 'hard-core' individuals in hiring situations."

The test manual offers only a vague and clumsy description of how the test was developed. Using a sample of students in a small women's liberal arts college, some type of item analysis was performed on the nonverbal section of the WLW Mental Alertness Inventory, the *Culture Fair Intelligence Test,* and the *Chicago Non-Verbal Examination* as a basis for the selection of 70 items. In some fashion or other these 70 items were reduced to the 30 items comprising the current form of the test. Reference is made to adopting items from other tests as well, but there is no explanation. (The manual does not explain why the authors thought it advisable to use an item-analysis sample of college students to develop a test for "minority groups or 'hard-core' individuals.")

Norms are available on 50 male and 50 female college students and on 24 black and 46 white female applicants for entry clerical jobs at an insurance company. No further description of these groups, such as educational level, age, or socioeconomic status, is provided.

The manual also presents a hodgepodge of correlations between part scores on the *WLW Culture Fair Inventory* and part or whole scores on several other tests. Since the WLW scores used were based on the preliminary 70-item form of the test, these correlations have little relevance for the test being reviewed. No reliability estimates of the test are reported.

The manual reports a median score of 10 for the black applicants and 13 for the white applicants on this test and a median score of 20 for the blacks and 24 for the whites on the *Wonderlic Personnel Test*. While information of this kind is meaningless without a discussion of the comparability of these groups on other dimensions, it would not appear that this purportedly culture fair test operates differently from the Wonderlic, which makes no claims about culture fairness.

In summary, this test is not based on any stated theoretical grounds, the operations followed in its development are obscure, its reliability has not been estimated, and its validity has not been demonstrated nor even considered in the manual. The assumption that elimination of the time and verbal factor would "largely discount the influence of the environment and education" was at least naive, and, in my opinion, absurd. I know of no test that would serve the purpose for which this test was designed.

[400]

*Wesman Personnel Classification Test. Grades 8–16 and adults; 1946–65; WPCT; title on Forms A and B is *Personnel Classification Test;* 3 scores: verbal, numerical, total; Forms A ('46, 4 pages), B ('47, 4 pages), C ('64, 4 pages); revised manual ('65, 27 pages); $3 per 25 tests; 50¢ per specimen set; postage extra; 28(35) minutes; Alexander G. Wesman; Psychological Corporation. *

REFERENCES

1–3. See 4:331.
4–11. See 5:399.
12. ASH, PHILIP. "Validity Information Exchange, No. 13-05:D.O.T. Code 1-86.12, Salesmen, Typewriters." *Personnel Psychol* 13:454 w '60. *
13. ASH, PHILIP. "Validity Information Exchange, No. 13-06:D.O.T. Code 5-83.127, Typewriter Serviceman." *Personnel Psychol* 13:455 w '60. *
14. DUNNETTE, MARVIN D., AND KIRCHNER, WAYNE K. "Psychological Test Differences Between Industrial Salesmen and Retail Salesmen." *J Appl Psychol* 44:121–5 Ap '60. * (*PA* 35:4029)
15. VINCENT, NORMAN L., AND DUGAN, ROBERT D. "Validity Information Exchange, No. 15-03:D.O.T. Code 1-57.10, Salesman, Insurance." *Personnel Psychol* 15:223–5 su '62. *
16. DUNNETTE, MARVIN D.; WERNIMONT, PAUL; AND ABRAHAMS, NORMAN. "Further Research on Vocational Interest Differences Among Several Types of Engineers." *Personnel & Guid J* 42:484–93 Ja '64. * (*PA* 39:6040)
17. WELSCH, LAWRENCE A. *The Supervisor's Employee Appraisal Heuristic: The Contribution of Selected Measures of Employee Aptitude, Intelligence and Personality.* Doctor's thesis, University of Pittsburgh (Pittsburgh, Pa.), 1967. (*DA* 28:4321A)
18. PARRY, MARY ELLEN. "Ability of Psychologists to Estimate Validities of Personnel Tests." *Personnel Psychol* 21:139–47 su '68. * (*PA* 42:14727)

ARTHUR C. MACKINNEY, *Dean of Graduate Studies, Wright State University, Dayton, Ohio.*

Everyone has come to expect high quality from both Wesman and the Psychological Cor-

poration, and this test maintains the tradition. Overall, it appears to this reviewer to be an excellent example of a short, general-population-level, general intelligence test, composed of verbal and numerical subtests.

The verbal subtest is composed of 40 two-part analogy items arranged in increasing difficulty. The numerical subtest is composed of 20 items, mainly arithmetic, progressing from simple addition through more complex manipulations of fractions, square roots, and the like. Scores from both subtests are summed for a total score.

The manual is clear and well written, simple without being insulting. It is cautious and scholarly to an appropriate degree without compromising the obvious need for utility. Administration instructions are lucidly stated. Twenty-nine sets of norms are presented, encompassing many different occupational groups (ranging from "production workers" to "executive trainee" and "high level positions"), as well as several student groups (ranging from tenth grade students to college sophomores). Reliabilities (including the sub-score reliabilities), equivalence of forms, correlation between subtests and the influence of speed (negligible) are all within the acceptable range. Validity data of three general types are presented. First, correlations of this test with other tests give some good indication of the conceptual content being tapped. Second, the progression of mean scores across the occupational hierarchy is clearly demonstrated. Third, data from 12 concurrent validity studies show correlations primarily under .50. In general, these seem to follow the typical pattern of higher correlation for higher level jobs and for the more intellectual kinds of criteria. The user can be confident that the validity of this instrument will be no worse than that of similar tests, and probably better. In general, the use of this instrument seems indicated in those instances for which it was designed.

J Counsel Psychol 12:435–6 w '65. *Jack C. Merwin.* * Using two groups, one a high scoring group and one a lower scoring group, the proportion completing nine-tenths the items of each subtest in the stated time limits was calculated. * The proportion of the low scoring group completing nine-tenths of the numerical test, however, was only 43 per cent. The author interprets this as, "presumably a matter of running out of ability rather than out of time."

It is unfortunate that the low scoring group was not given additional time to finish so that this hypothesis could have been tested. It is encouraging to see a continuing updating of existing tests. Often the experience of various groups with a test over the years leads to identification of the real value of a test. The provision of a third form of this test is a significant addition. Inclusion of previous norms which have been in use along with the newer sets of norms should be helpful to the user. The new manual, with a relatively complete description of validity and reliability considerations, as well as data bearing on these considerations, is most readable. Study of the material presented in the revised manual by persons currently using the test should increase its value to them. This new material may also provide people who have previously considered the use of this test with new insights into its possibilities for their needs.

For reviews by John C. Flanagan and Erwin K. Taylor, see 4:331; see also 3:253 (1 excerpt).

[401]

Wonderlic Personnel Test. Adults; 1938-71; WPT; Forms D and F are adaptations of *Otis Self-Administering Tests of Mental Ability*, Higher Form; 14 forms (3 pages): Forms A, B, ('42), D ['38], F ('59, identical with undated form published in 1938), 1, 2, 4, 5, EM, ('59), APT, BPT, CPT, T-11, T-21, ('67); manual ('70, 19 pages); norms research report ('70, 264 looseleaf pages); norms summary ('70, 38 pages); minimum occupational scores monograph ('66, 64 pages, see p 96 below); position analysis reports ('71) for 34 positions: accountant (59 pages), accounting clerk (55 pages), administrator-executive (64 pages), bookkeeper (53 pages), cashier (51 pages), clerk-clerical (84 pages), computer operator (56 pages), custodian (57 pages), draftsman (57 pages), engineer (57 pages), file clerk (51 pages), foreman (58 pages), key punch operator (54 pages), lineman-utility (53 pages), maintenance (64 pages), manager-supervisor (83 pages), nurse's aide (56 pages), office-general (60 pages), police-patrolman (54 pages), programmer (53 pages), receptionist (52 pages), sales and service-customer service (62 pages), salesman-field representative (74 pages), secretary (61 pages), skilled labor and trades (85 pages), stenographer (58 pages), student-part time employee (54 pages), technician (67 pages), telephone operator (52 pages), teller (54 pages), typist (62 pages), unskilled labor (81 pages), warehouseman (59 pages), writer-news etc. (58 pages); no reliability data or norms for Forms D, F, BPT, CPT, T-11, and T-21; distribution of Forms EM, APT, BPT, and CPT restricted to employment agencies; distribution of Forms D, F, T-11, and T-21 restricted to users ordering 1,000 or more copies; $14.75 per 100 tests and manual, postage extra; $150 per norms report; $15 per norms summary; $7.50 per introductory package of 20 copies each of Forms 1 and 2, manual, and special reports; $5 per minimum occupational scores monograph; $15 to $12 per position analysis report; postpaid; 12(20) minutes; E. F. Wonderlic; E. F. Wonderlic & Associates, Inc. *

REFERENCES

1–2. See 2:1415.
3–9. See 3:269.
10–68. See 5:400.
69–85. See 6:513.
86. ROWE, FREDERICK B. *The Selection of Psychiatric Aides: Criterion Development and Prediction.* Doctor's thesis, University of Maryland (College Park, Md.), 1957. (*DA* 17:2674)
87. MAHONEY, T. A.; JERDEE, T. H.; AND NASH, A. N. "Predicting Managerial Effectiveness." *Personnel Psychol* 13: 147–63 su '60. * (*PA* 36:2LI47M)
88. MORRISON, WILLIAM E. *The Effectiveness of the Minnesota Clerical Test and the Wonderlic Personnel Test in the Selection of Clerk Typists and File Clerks.* Master's thesis, Springfield College (Springfield, Mass.), 1963.
89. HODGSON, RICHARD W. "Personality Appraisal of Technical and Professional Applicants." *Personnel Psychol* 17: 167–87 su '64. * (*PA* 39:6067)
90. HOSKINS, JOHN EMMETT. *A Study of Certain Characteristics Which Have Predictive Value for Vocational Adjustment in a Rehabilitation Workshop.* Doctor's thesis, Wayne State University (Detroit, Mich.), 1964. (*DA* 26:4797)
91. THUMIN, FRED J., AND WITTENBERG, ANGELA. "Personality as Related to Age and Mental Ability in Female Job Applicants." *J Gerontol* 20:105–7 Ja '65. *
92. JEX, FRANK B. *Predicting Academic Success Beyond High School.* Salt Lake City, Utah: University of Utah Bookstore, 1966. Pp. vi, 41. *
93. KEIM, LAWRENCE. *A Study of Psychometric Profile Patterns of Selected Associate Degree Technology Majors.* Doctor's thesis, Purdue University (Lafayette, Ind.), 1966. (*DA* 27: 2049A)
94. KOPFF, RICHARD GARMS. *Manager Performance as Related to Goal Setting, Intelligence, and Selected Personality Characteristics.* Doctor's thesis, Columbia University (New York, N.Y.), 1966. (*DA* 27:677A)
95. PENFIELD, ROBERT VERDON. *The Psychological Characteristics of Effective First-Line Managers.* Doctor's thesis, Cornell University (Ithaca, N.Y.), 1966. (*DA* 27:1610B)
96. WONDERLIC, E. F. *A Cooperative Research Study of Minimum Occupational Scores for the Wonderlic Personnel Test.* Northfield, Ill.: E. F. Wonderlic & Associates, Inc., 1966. Pp. 64. *
97. WONDERLIC, E. F. *A Selected, Annotated Bibliography for the Wonderlic Personnel Test.* Northfield, Ill.: E. F. Wonderlic & Associates, Inc., 1966. Pp. 104. *
98. SCHUH, ALLEN J. "Application Blank Items and Intelligence as Predictors of Turnover." *Personnel Psychol* 20:59–63 sp '67. * (*PA* 41:11002)
99. IRISH, THOMAS E. *An Evaluation of the Effectiveness of the Wonderlic Personnel Test, the Cleaver Self-Description, Previous Job Tenure, and Previous Insurance Selling Experience in the Successful Selection of Insurance Salesmen.* Master's thesis, Springfield College (Springfield, Mass.), 1968.
100. MITCHELL, M. D.; ALBRIGHT, L. E.; AND McMURRY, F. D. "Biracial Validation of Selection Procedures in a Large Southern Plant." Abstract. *Proc 76th Ann Conv Am Psychol Assn* 3:575–6 '68. *
101. PARRY, MARY ELLEN. "Ability of Psychologists to Estimate Validities of Personnel Tests." *Personnel Psychol* 21: 139–47 su '68. * (*PA* 42:14727)
102. RUDA, EDWARD, AND ALBRIGHT, LEWIS E. "Racial Differences on Selection Instruments Related to Subsequent Job Performance." *Personnel Psychol* 21:31–41 sp '68. * (*PA* 16233)
103. THUMIN, F., AND GOLDMAN, SUE. "Comparative Test Performance of Negro and White Job Applicants." *J Clin Psychol* 24:455–7 O '68. * (*PA* 43:4565)
104. BUTLER, PATRICK C., AND RUSMORE, JAY T. "Illumination Intensities and Test Performance." *Percept & Motor Skills* 29(2):653–4 O '69. * (*PA* 44:4167)
105. KARLINS, MARVIN; SCHUERHOFF, CHARLES; AND KAPLAN, MARTIN. "Some Factors Related to Architectural Creativity in Graduating Architecture Students." *J General Psychol* 81(2):203–15 O '69. * (*PA* 44:6775)
106. LORD, RAYMOND MORRISON. *Profile Patterns of Selected Business Majors as a Basis for Intra-Occupational Differentiation.* Doctor's thesis, Indiana University (Bloomington, Ind.), 1969. (*DAI* 30:551A)
107. RICHARDSON, BILLY K. *Prediction of Rehabilitation Counselor Effectiveness: The Relationship of Counselor Characteristics to Supervisors' Ratings.* Doctor's thesis, University of Iowa (Iowa City, Iowa), 1969. (*DAI* 30:3738A)
108. WILLE, GLENN R. *An Investigation of the Relationship Between the Wonderlic Personnel Test, Form I, and the General Clerical Test; the Relationship Between the Wonderlic Personnel Test, Form I, and Employee Job Performance.* Master's thesis, Wisconsin State University (Oshkosh, Wis.), 1969.
109. KEILLOR, JAMES SHERWOOD. *The Effects of Experimentally Induced Consciousness Expansion and Consciousness Control Upon Creativity and Intellectual Functioning.* Doctor's

thesis, Wayne State University (Detroit, Mich.), 1970. (*DAI* 31:4339B)

110. PRIEN, ERICH P. "Measuring Performance Criteria of Bank Tellers." *J Indus Psychol* 5(1):29–36 Mr '70. * (*PA* 45:7135)

111. RONAN, W. W. "Evaluation of Three Criteria of Management Performance." *J Indus Psychol* 5(1):18–28 Mr '70. * (*PA* 45:7148)

112. THUMIN, FRED J. "Comparative Study of Three Mental Ability Tests." *J Indus Psychol* 5(1):1–7 Mr '70. * (*PA* 45:7117)

113. WEVRICK, L. "Evaluation of the Personnel Test Battery," pp. 1–5. In *Applied Research in Public Personnel Administration*. By L. Wevrick and others. Personnel Report No. 702. Chicago, Ill.: Public Personnel Association, 1970. Pp. 29. *

ROBERT C. DROEGE, *Research Psychologist, Manpower Administration, U.S. Department of Labor, Washington, D.C.*

The WPT is a 12-minute test of general learning ability. Each form of the test has 50 verbal, numerical, and spatial test items arranged in spiral omnibus format. First published in 1938, the Wonderlic has been widely used in industry for screening applicants for jobs at various levels of complexity. The basic character of the test is unchanged since it was reviewed in *The Sixth Mental Measurements Yearbook*. But additional material has been published, including new test forms, an annotated bibliography, a publication of occupational cutoff scores in use, a performance norms report, and a revised manual.

The new forms are for employment agencies only (Forms APT, BPT, and CPT) or for users of 1,000 or more copies (Forms T-11 and T-21). The items were taken from forms previously published but still operational. Form APT consists of 25 items from Form A and 25 items from Form B. The other new forms each include items selected from all seven of the older forms.

A bibliography (97) of 361 entries relevant to the WPT is now available. Not all are references to occupational norming, occupational validation, and other research studies, but enough are to make this publication a useful one to those interested in the Wonderlic data base. Even more useful would be an organized presentation of the pertinent research findings. Development of this material would be a big undertaking, but a worthwhile one.

The Minimum Occupational Scores Monograph reports the practice of 703 firms in the use of minimum (and sometimes maximum) cutting scores for over 700 specific jobs. Most of the major and many minor occupations are represented, illustrating the widely held assumption in industry that the Wonderlic is applicable to the entire range of jobs, with their varying requirements of literacy skills, training time,

etc. Minimum scores range from 8 for janitors and other unskilled jobs to over 30 for some professional and managerial jobs. Convenient alphabetical listings of job titles with associated cutting scores invite potential users of the Wonderlic to make an immediate application to jobs in their own firms. It seems inevitable that this publication will be used for what it so obviously is—a means of selection of cutting scores to screen applicants for specific jobs. The fact is that no evidence is reported of validity underlying the use of any of these cutting scores by companies reporting them. The publication amounts to a guide to the use of a priori norms and cannot be justified.

Put together at considerable expense in both data collection and analysis (total cost estimated by the author at more than $500,000), the Norms Research Report is an example of the major accomplishments that can be achieved in developing a comprehensive data base for widely used tests such as the Wonderlic. Based on an analysis of data on 251,253 job applicants from 1,071 Wonderlic users, the report contains "performance norms" by age, sex, education, industry, geographic region, and position applied for. There are literally hundreds of tables and graphs in the ten sections of the report. For example, in section C "Test Scores by Education" there are 84 graphs showing the relationship between test scores and years of education for various age groups separately by sex and combined. And there is a table of means, standard deviations, and modes accompanying each graph. It is in this section of the report that the author tries to make a case for the validity of the test as a measure of "trainability" required both in school and on the job. Under this concept, proof of validity lies in the relationship between years of education and the Wonderlic test scores. (The correlations reported, however, are between years of education and *average* test scores for each of several age groups. These correlations are all .95 or above, considerably higher than would have been obtained if individual rather than average test scores had been used.) What the author is attempting to do is to make a virtue of what must be regarded as a severe limitation of general learning ability tests as screening instruments for jobs—their high relationships with educational achievement. For many jobs educational achievement is not a valid consideration and use of a test highly related to education leads to unfair discrimination against disadvantaged individuals. Twenty-eight alternate-form reliability coefficients, half of them .95 or higher, are presented. Detailed data on sample size and characteristics are shown for the various samples in the norms sections of the report, but none for the reliability samples. This is a curious omission in an otherwise detailed report.

The 1968 edition [1] of the manual is not much different from the previous editions, and this is too bad because it has the same serious defects. There still has been no attempt to meet the minimum requirements of the *Standards for Educational and Psychological Tests and Manuals.*

The reader of the manual is left with the impression that the validity of the test has been established for the entire range of occupations. The fact is that there are many studies which show that tests like the Wonderlic have no relevance for successful performance in many occupations. An example from occupational research with the *General Aptitude Test Battery* illustrates the point. Aptitude G (General Learning Ability) of the GATB has item content similar to that in the Wonderlic and studies have shown that the two measures correlate highly, indicating that they measure essentially the same abilities. Of the 413 occupational validation studies conducted with the GATB, as reported in the 1968 edition of the GATB manual, only 180 resulted in final selection test batteries that included Aptitude G. Thus, in less than half of the studies did Aptitude G contribute enough validity to enter into the final selection test battery established for the occupation.

There is evidence from the extensive bibliography on the Wonderlic that considerable occupational validation research has been conducted on this test, but the manual does not document it. It is time that a systematic effort was made to develop a comprehensive manual that will report the evidence of the extent to which the test does what the author states it does on page 4 of the 1968 (and 1961) edition of the manual: "This test has been shown to be a valid instrument in determining success on a number of different jobs. The number of questions right clearly distinguished between good and poor groups of employees differentiated on

1 At the time this review was being prepared, the 1970 manual was not available.—The Editor.

work records accumulated over a period of five years."

In summary, there is not nearly enough documented validation data to justify the current wide use of the *Wonderlic Personnel Test* in screening applicants for employment or candidates for promotion. Aptitude and intelligence tests are coming under increasing attack because of the possibility of unfair discrimination against minority groups in the application of the test results in selection. The Wonderlic is particularly vulnerable because of its known high relationship to formal education, the use of a priori norms, and the lack of documented evidence that it is a useful instrument in predicting success in many jobs. Unless the user first validates the test, preferably in combination with tests measuring other abilities, on a sample of his applicants or workers, he may find that he is in violation of Title VII of the Civil Rights Act of 1964. Companies considering the use of this test should first become familiar with the 1970 *Guidelines on Employee Selection Procedures,* published by the Equal Employment Opportunity Commission, Washington, D.C., and with the March 8, 1971 Supreme Court ruling in the case of Griggs, et al., vs. Duke Power Company.

JOHN P. FOLEY, JR., *President, J. P. Foley and Co., Inc., New York, New York.*

This well-known test continues to be widely used as a measure of adult intelligence in business and industry. As in the case of earlier forms, the more recent forms follow the same spiral omnibus pattern, with the 50 multiple choice items arranged in ascending order of difficulty. They are printed on the two inside pages of a four-page fold, the instructions, as well as sample and practice items, appearing on the first page. Although the test may be given with the work-limit method, i.e., unlimited time, most of the norms relate to a 12-minute time limit, which is satisfactory for most testing purposes. Scoring is done manually with strip keys and is simple and rapid. The test score is the number of items correct.

It is claimed that the first nine forms listed in the entry above "are equal and similar to a very high degree." Even so, it is admitted that "minor differences were observed in this study" and that "some of the test forms are more closely equated than others." A conversion table for the nine forms is provided on the same page of the manual, with the individual correction values ranging from $+3$ to -3. However, a request by this reviewer for reference to the raw data from which the suggested conversion values were obtained failed to elicit the desired information.

Norms for male and female high school and college graduates are presented in the 1968 manual,[1] as are other educational, age and sex norms. The "central tendency" (evidently the median) and the quartile range of scores obtained by professional and executive, managerial, clerical, sales, plant staff and line, and other groups are also reported. Minimum critical scores for a number of different occupations are suggested, although no supporting data are provided. Test users are advised to establish their own critical scores "since job titles are not completely descriptive," since they "vary from plant to plant even with the same organization," and since "the critical score....must be moved up or down, depending upon the available supply of applicants."

Claims for "good reliability" are made in the 1968 manual, as are claims for proven validity. Although high correlation coefficients are cited, the paucity of supporting information makes it difficult, if not impossible, to evaluate the studies underlying these claims. Moreover, a separate booklet titled "Summary of Experiences with the Wonderlic Personnel Test" is little more than a disorganized series of quoted passages from journal articles, textbooks, and other publications.

A 36-page norms booklet summarizes data from a more comprehensive study of 251,253 cases, a study designed "to up-date and re-verify the central tendency and the dispersion statistics affecting Personnel Placement and Selection" and "to provide the users of the Personnel Test with additional supportive statistics essential to the improved conduct of their testing programs." Original data were supplied by 1,071 participating business, industrial, and governmental organizations. The data presented relate to all forms of the test combined, and to a testing time of 12 minutes, no correction being made for age, form administered, or other factors. Among the data presented are tables showing distribution of scores by educational level and position applied for, as well as statistics relating to region, age, sex, and racial

grouping. Reliability coefficients are also presented, as are validity coefficients based on "the degree of covariance between years of education obtained and average test score achieved by level of education."

The *Wonderlic Personnel Test* is an appropriate screening device for use with clerical and other white-collar personnel. When combined with a clerical aptitude test, it constitutes an effective test battery for such an application. The availability of multiple forms is highly advantageous. Testing time and ease of administration represent favorable considerations. Moreover, the publisher is to be commended for recent efforts to accumulate normative information, as well as data relating to reliability and validity. And in the light of other materials available from the same publisher, it is implied that the test should form only one part of an overall selection or evaluation program, although this point is not always made explicit.

However, there is insufficient emphasis on the restricted applicability of the test, i.e., on the fact that it is most appropriate for a limited population, viz., white-collar employees. The widespread use and availability of the test tend to impair its effectiveness, although this limitation is to some extent mitigated by the multiple forms. More detailed percentile norms relating to occupational and other groups would be helpful, as would carefully designed and controlled validation studies. Much of the material in the manual and other supporting publications is loosely organized and presented. Just which test forms are available is not unequivocally stated. The term "central tendency" is not sufficiently explicit. A few passages in the manual are naive, such as the admonition: "In interpreting results, avoid trying to establish an I.Q. or any other psychological refinement. As a practical personnel man, you are interested *only* in finding the relationship of questions answered correctly." Some of the material in the supporting booklets is anecdotal in nature, consisting of little more than testimonials. And much of this material smacks too much of promotionalism, designed more to stimulate sale of the test than to provide relevant information. Lastly, there are signs of defensiveness, such as the reproduction of a letter from the president of the tabulating company which prepared the norms reports and the following statement contained in a letter from the publisher to this reviewer:

[1] At the time this review was being prepared, the 1970 manual was not available.—The Editor.

"Our construction methods have not and will not be published."

For reviews by N. M. Downie and Marvin D. Dunnette, see 6:513; for reviews by H. E. Brogden, Charles D. Flory, and Irving Lorge, see 3:269.

INDIVIDUAL

[402]

★**Bayley Scales of Infant Development.** Ages 2–30 months; 1969; BSID; 2 scores: mental, motor, plus 30 behavior ratings; the mental and motor scales "draw heavily upon" the *California First-Year Mental Scale,* the *California Preschool Mental Scale,* and the *California Infant Scale of Motor Development;* individual; 1 form; manual (185 pages); record booklets: mental scale (8 pages), motor scale (4 pages), infant behavior (6 pages); no data on validity of motor scale; no data on predictive validity of mental scale; $88 per set of testing materials including manual and 25 sets of record booklets; $3 per 25 mental scale record booklets; $2.25 per 25 motor scale or infant behavior record booklets; $5 per manual; (45–90) minutes for mental and motor scales; Nancy Bayley; Psychological Corporation. *

REFERENCES

1. BAYLEY, NANCY, AND SCHAEFER, EARL S. "Correlations of Maternal and Child Behaviors With the Development of Mental Abilities: Data From the Berkeley Growth Study." *Monogr Soc Res Child Develop* 29(6):1–8 '64. * (*PA* 39:11895)
2. PHATAK, PRAMILA; POFFENBERGER, THOMAS; PATEL, AN-JALI; AND BAROT, JYOTI. "Motor and Mental Development of Indian Infants of Ages 1 Month to 25 Months." *J Gujarat Res Soc* 27:106–13 Ap '65. *
3. COHEN, ABRAHAM I. "Hand Preference and Developmental Status of Infants." *J Genetic Psychol* 108:337–45 Je '66. * (*PA* 40:10986)
4. ESTES, BETSY, AND COMBS, ANN. "Perception of Quantity." *J Genetic Psychol* 108:333–6 Je '66. * (*PA* 40:11012)
5. KLATSKIN, ETHELYN H.; McGARRY, MARY E.; AND STEWARD, MARGARET S. "Variability in Developmental Test Patterns as a Sequel of Neonatal Stress." *Child Develop* 37: 819–26 D '66. * (*PA* 41:2668)
6. KOHEN-RAZ, REUVEN. "The Ring-Cube Test: A Brief Time Sampling Method for Assessing Primary Development of Coordinated Bilateral Grasp Responses in Infancy." *Percept & Motor Skills* 23:675–88 D '66. * (*PA* 41:7088)
7. WERNER, EMMY E., AND BAYLEY, NANCY. "The Reliability of Bayley's Revised Scale of Mental and Motor Development During the First Year of Life." *Child Develop* 37:39–50 Mr '66. * (*PA* 40:4770)
8. FRANCIS-WILLIAMS, JESSIE, AND YULE, WILLIAM. "The Bayley Infant Scales of Mental and Motor Development: An Exploratory Study With an English Sample." *Develop Med & Child Neurol* 9:391–401 Ag '67. * (*PA* 42:646)
9. KOHEN-RAZ, REUVEN. "Scalogram Analysis of Some Developmental Sequences of Infant Behavior as Measured by the Bayley Infant Scale of Mental Development." *Genetic Psychol Monogr* 76:3–21 Ag '67. * (*PA* 41:16466)
10. MENDELSON, MARTIN A. "Interdisciplinary Approach to the Study of the Exceptional Infant: A Large Scale Research Project," pp. 15–77. In *Exceptional Infant: The Normal Infant, Vol. 1.* Edited by Jerome Hellmuth. Seattle, Wash.: Special Child Publications, 1967. Pp. 568. *
11. ROBINSON, JOHN S., AND BAYLEY, NANCY. "Behavioral Criteria for Diagnosing Mental Retardation in the First Two Years of Life." Progress report. *Calif Mental Health Res Dig* 5:180–1 su '67. * (*PA* 42:2884)
12. GANNON, D. R. "Relationships Between 8-Mo. Performance on the Bayley Scales of Infant Development and 48-Mo. Intelligence and Concept Formation Scores." *Psychol Rep* 23:1199–205 D '68. * (*PA* 43:8104)
13. GERSON, ELAINE FREED. *Dimensions of Behavior in the First Half Year of Life and the Effect of Prenatal Parent Counseling.* Doctor's thesis, Pennsylvania State University (University Park, Pa.), 1968. (*DA* 29:4830B)
14. KOHEN-RAZ, REUVEN. "Mental and Motor Development of Kibbutz, Institutionalized, and Home-Reared Infants in Israel." *Child Develop* 39:489–504 Je '68. * (*PA* 42:13460)
15. GERSON, ELAINE F. "Dimensions of Infant Behavior in the First Six Months of Life." Abstract. *Proc 77th Ann Conv Am Psychol Assn* 4(1):269–70 '69. * (*PA* 43:17137)
16. CARR, JANET. "Mental and Motor Development in Young Mongol Children." *J Mental Def Res* 14(3):205–20 S '70. *
17. ERICKSON, MARILYN T.; JOHNSON, NANCY M.; AND CAMPBELL, FRANCES A. "Relationships Among Scores on Infant Tests for Children With Developmental Problems." *Am J Mental Def* 75(1):102–4 Jl '70. * (*PA* 45:926)
18. IRETON, HAROLD; THWING, EDWARD; AND GRAVEM, HOWARD. "Infant Mental Development and Neurological Status, Family Socioeconomic Status, and Intelligence at Age Four." *Child Develop* 41(4):937–45 D '70. * (*PA* 46:831)
19. MAN, EVELYN B.; ADELMAN, MAURICE; JONES, WALTER S.; AND LORD, ROBERT M., JR. "Development and BEI of Full-Term and Low-Birth-Weight Infants Through 18 Months." *Am J Dis Children* 119(4):298–307 Ap '70. * (*PA* 44:17246)
20. WILLERMAN, LEE; BROMAN, SARAH H.; AND FIEDLER, MIRIAM. "Infant Development, Preschool IQ, and Social Class." *Child Develop* 41(1):69–77 Mr '70. * (*PA* 44:8168)

ROBERTA R. COLLARD, *Assistant Professor of Human Development, University of Massachusetts, Amherst, Massachusetts.*

The *Bayley Scales of Infant Development* is a carefully standardized, well planned, and comprehensive measure of infant development from 2 months to 2½ years of age.

The BSID consists of three parts: a Mental Scale, a Motor Scale, and the Infant Behavior Record. The Mental Scale is made up of 163 items which measure responses to visual and auditory stimuli, manipulation and play with objects, and responses involving social interaction such as socialization and imitation. It also has items which measure discrimination of shapes, memory or object constancy, simple problem solving, and more abstract abilities such as naming objects, understanding prepositions, and the concept of the number one. The Motor Scale consists of 81 items which measure progressions of gross motor abilities such as sitting, standing, walking, and stair climbing as well as abilities involving finer motor coordination, such as those involved in grasping objects of various sizes. The Infant Behavior Record is a rating scale which measures various aspects of personality such as emotional and social behaviors, activity level, responses to objects, sensory areas of interest, and such ego functions as attention span, persistence, and endurance.

The BSID was designed to be used for both clinical and research purposes. The author states that the value of these scales in clinical practice does not lie in predicting a child's later abilities but in establishing his current developmental status in relation to others his age. These scales should prove useful in the recognition and diagnosis of sensory and neurological defects and emotional disturbances, and in indicating the possibility of environmental deficits. The value of the BSID as a research instrument lies in its careful standardization, high reliability, and broad coverage of many aspects of the behavior repertoire of infants, parts of which could be used as subscales in longitudinal studies.

The test materials are colorful, attractive, durable, washable, and have sufficient novelty to be intrinsically interesting to infants and young children and yet are similar to objects with which most subjects would be familiar. The use in the Motor Scale of heavy or bulky specially constructed stairs and a walking board may limit its use in some situations because of the difficulty of transporting these items.

The record forms include spaces for recording information about the child's health, prenatal or perinatal difficulties, educational and occupational level of parents, and family constellation.

The greatest advantage of the BSID over other tests of infant development lies in its excellent standardization. These scales were standardized on a sample of 1,262 infants and children, ranging from 2 to 30 months of age. The sample was selected to be representative of the U.S. population in terms of major geographic areas and residence (urban-rural) and was controlled for sex, race, and education of head of household. Only "normal" children living at home were included in the sample; prematures, institutional infants, and those from bilingual homes were excluded.

The split-half reliability coefficients reported for the 14 age groups range from .81 to .93 (median .88) on the Mental Scale and from .68 to .92 (median .84) on the Motor Scale.

To evaluate the neurological or mental developmental status of infants and young children, it is important to know the reliabilities of individual test items. The BSID items found to have high tester-observer and test-retest reliabilities are those having to do with eye-hand coordination directed toward a test object, those having to do with sustained attention toward a test object, those involving object constancy, and vocabulary items.

The validity of the Mental Scale was determined by correlating the scores of the two-year-olds in the standardization sample on this scale with their scores on the Stanford-Binet. The correlation was .57 over the 6-month age overlap of the two tests.

The directions in the manual are specific, clear, and logical. The items do not have to be given in a strict order but may be flexibly adapted to the infant's interest and state. Be-

haviors may be scored if they are observed before or after the administration of the test. Mother's reports of the occurrence of the behaviors tested are recorded and used in the evaluation of the adequacy of the test.

On the Mental Scale the 163 items are arranged in chronological order by tenths of months, and items are arranged in the same order in the manual. It is helpful that the items are also listed in categories or "situation codes" in which the same materials are used in different ways for different age levels. These categories are given letter names which appear near the items both in the manual and on the record forms. It would have been helpful if the age placement of the items had been listed after each item in the situation codes and if these categories were printed on the front and back of a cardboard card which could be consulted by the tester as the test is given. It is helpful that the pages in the manual for a particular scale are color coded to the record forms.

For one who is not familiar with infant tests (or even for one who is) the BSID is difficult to learn how to administer because of the overwhelming amount of information one must keep in mind while giving it. Not only does the large number of items in the scales make this difficult, but the variety of factors to remember in the instructions may make these scales seem formidable to an inexperienced tester. It is assumed that this difficulty would decrease for most testers with increasing practice and familiarity. Writing up detailed protocols of items and procedures before the first subjects in each age group are tested should prove helpful in learning how to administer these scales.

Scoring the BSID is straightforward and simple. The items are arranged by age level on the scoring forms, and each item passed is given a credit of one. Raw scores consist of each item passed plus the items below the basal level. Raw scores are easily changed to index scores by locating the former in the infant's age column in a table in the testing manual and finding the index score corresponding to the raw score on the same line.

An index score is a "normalized standard score" in which each infant is compared to others his age in the standardization sample. A Mental Development Index is derived from the Mental Scale, and a Psychomotor Development Index is based on the Motor Scale.

CONCLUSIONS. The *Bayley Scales of Infant Development* is the culmination of the development of mental and motor tests in the tradition of Binet and Gesell. The BSID is intermediate between the empirically constructed tests which sample the observed abilities of children in various situations and those tests which may be designed to measure specific mental processes such as memory, object constancy, generalization, learning to solve problems, or learning abstract language concepts. The BSID includes items involving these processes, but does not have sections which measure these processes specifically. Neither the Mental nor Motor Scale is designed to indicate specific neurological or sensory deficits nor is the Infant Behavior Record designed to indicate or measure kind or degree of emotional disturbance. However, because of the range of the items, the reliability of the scales, and their careful construction and standardization, the BSID is by far the best measure of infant development available today.

RAYMOND H. HOLDEN, *Professor of Psychology and Coordinator, Learning Center, Rhode Island College, Providence, Rhode Island.*

The *Bayley Scales of Infant Development* fills a long felt need for a well standardized and reliable instrument to assess the developmental progress of infants. Previous scales, based on test items formulated 20 to 40 years ago, utilized small samples of children of limited geographic and socioeconomic backgrounds. The present version of the BSID contains three parts: the Mental Scale, the Motor Scale, and the Infant Behavior Record.

The author states that "the indexes derived from the Mental and Motor Scales have limited value as predictors of later abilities, since rates of development for any given child in the first year or two of life may be highly variable over the course of a few months." According to the author, "the *primary* value of the development indexes is that they provide the basis for establishing a child's current status, and thus the extent of any deviation from normal expectancy."

Standardization was exceptionally well controlled. A stratified sample design was used, controlling "for sex and color within each age group, with further controls related to residence (urban-rural) and to education of the head of the household." The sample consisted of 1,262 children evenly distributed in age between 2 and 30 months.

The test materials are contained in a large black suitcase. The items have no particular standard place in the case; each repacking places them in a different location.

The manual presents detailed instructions to examiners on general testing considerations. One of the interesting rules stated is "Hurry yourself but do not hurry the child." Testing proceeds, like the Binet, from a basal level to the ceiling. The directions for administering are very clearly presented.

In summary, the *Bayley Scales of Infant Development* are well standardized developmental scales for infants and meet satisfactory standards of test reliability. The test is useful for the clinician and researcher alike.

Congratulations to Nancy Bayley and to the Psychological Corporation for the standards of scientific rigor provided in the standardization of this scale. It is a most useful and satisfactory addition to our test armamentarium in infancy and early childhood.

[403]

*Canadian Intelligence Test, 1966 Revision.** Ages 3–16; 1940–66; formerly called *Canadian Intelligence Examination;* a modification of the 1916 *Stanford Revision of the Binet-Simon Intelligence Scale;* individual; manual ('66, 86 pages); card book ('66, 31 pages); record booklet ('66, 8 pages); no data on reliability and validity; Can $2.50 per card book; $2 per 25 record booklets; $3.75 per manual; postage extra; specimen set available on 60 day approval; [60–75] minutes; Carman E. Stothers, Beverly R. Collier, James W. Covert, and James C. Williams; Ryerson Press. *

REFERENCE

1. See 3:272.

HUGH TAYLOR, *Assistant Professor of Education, University of Victoria, Victoria, British Columbia, Canada.*

The *Canadian Intelligence Test,* previously entitled the *Canadian Intelligence Examination,* is the second revision of a test originally published in 1940. It has a content and design similar to that of the Stanford-Binet. The test as a whole may be considered as measuring a highly verbal component of intelligence. Only a few items deal with the manipulation of materials. Beginning at Year 3, the test includes six or fewer items at each age level up to Year 14. Above Year 14 there are two levels entitled Young Adult 1 and Young Adult 2, each containing six items. This reviewer suspects that the average item is more difficult than that of the Stanford-Binet. Varying amounts of credit are assigned to each item passed and the resultant mental age score is used to calculate the traditional ratio intelligence quotient.

The 1966 revision of the test is a minor one. The content is basically the same as in previous editions. Three new words have replaced "copper," "outward," and "loiter" on the 55-word vocabulary test and two words have traded places at the 20th and 21st positions on the list. It would appear that these changes would have a very minor effect on scores, particularly at age 11 or over. The words in the vocabulary list seem to be free of any national bias when judged across the major English-speaking nations.

The testing materials—including the directions for administering, the card booklet, and the 8-page record form—are clearly written on high quality paper and well designed for effective use. Printing on each card page the year level for which it may be used would increase the efficient handling of the card booklet. Provision of a table for determining IQ scores or a mechanical IQ calculator would help the examiner avoid arithmetical errors as well as speed up and standardize the determination of the IQ score. A 2-page section in the manual entitled "Item Analysis of the Canadian Intelligence Test" does not contain any item analysis data. In fact, item difficulties and discrimination indices are not included in the test kit. A more appropriate title for the section would be "Content Outline of the Canadian Intelligence Test."

The *Canadian Intelligence Test* has only one form. The cost involved in developing an alternate form may not be desirable from the publisher's point of view. If this is the case, then a minimum substitute would be to provide the user with tables of score equivalents with other intelligence tests of parallel design.

Specific validity, reliability, and normative data for the 1966 revision are not included in the manual. There are general comments made relative to these concepts but the evidence cited is now over 30 years old! It is suggested that the publisher immediately proceed to re-norm this test, provide information on sex differences, produce current validity and reliability data as well as adopt the more prevalent deviation IQ score.

In summary, the *Canadian Intelligence Test* is simple in design, relatively easy to administer,

but lacking in empirical data for use in the meaningful interpretation of scores. The authors' suggested use of the test, namely in the training of teachers in individual test administration, might well be considered its only legitimate use at this stage in its development. No evidence is presented to suggest that this test may be used in making important clinical decisions related to intelligence.

For a review by Gwen F. Arnold of the 1947 edition, see 4:336; see also 3:272 (2 excerpts).

[404]

★**Cooperative Preschool Inventory, Revised Edition.** Disadvantaged children ages 3–6; 1965–70; CPI; achievement in areas necessary for success in school; individual; 1 form ('70, 4 pages); manual ('70, 13 pages); technical report ('70, 35 pages); the "national norms" are based on children enrolled in 11 Head Start Centers; $2.50 per 20 tests; $1 per technical report; $1 per manual; $2 per specimen set; cash orders postpaid; (15) minutes; Bettye M. Caldwell; Cooperative Tests and Services. *

REFERENCES

1. ALLERHAND, MELVIN E. "Effectiveness of Parents of Head Start Children as Administrators of Psychological Tests." *J Consult Psychol* 31:286–90 Je '67. * (*PA* 41:10474)
2. CALDWELL, BETTYE M. "Descriptive Evaluations of Child Development and of Developmental Settings." *Pediatrics* 40: 46–54 Jl '67. *
3. DATTA, LOIS-ELLIN. "Draw-A-Person Test as a Measure of Intelligence in Preschool Children From Very Low Income Families." *J Consult Psychol* 31:626–30 D '67. * (*PA* 42: 2561)
4. ASBURY, CHARLES ALEXANDER. *Factors Associated With Discrepant Achievement in Rural Economically Deprived White and Negro First Graders.* Doctor's thesis, University of North Carolina (Chapel Hill, N.C.), 1969. (*DAI* 31:208A)
5. HOWARD, MARSHALL J., JR.; HOOPS, H. RAY; AND Mc-KINNON, ARCHIE J. "Language Abilities of Children With Differing Socioeconomic Backgrounds." *J Learn Dis* 3(6): 328–35 Je '70. *

JOSEPH L. FRENCH, *Professor of Special Education and Educational Psychology and Head of the Department of Special Education, The Pennsylvania State University, University Park, Pennsylvania.*

"The *Cooperative Preschool Inventory* is a brief assessment and screening procedure designed for individual use with children in the age range of three-to-six years." While not an attempt to create a culture-fair instrument, the test was "developed to give a measure of achievement in areas regarded as necessary for success in school." The inventory comprises items of the "information" type and, to a lesser extent, items requiring ability to label quantities, identify serial positions, perceive shapes, and execute certain visual-motor basic drawing skills. It was anticipated that it would measure basic information children have about themselves, including their self-concept. A few easily obtained materials such as blank paper and crayons must be assembled locally prior to administration.

The revised 1970 edition contains 64 items scored as correct or incorrect and administered in 15 minutes. Responses are recorded in a four-page booklet in which the subjects may draw when necessary. Answers are found directly beneath the questions in the administrative manual. Internal design allows for administration by the child's own teacher, who is assumed to possess a minimal sophistication in measurement technique. Question and probe technique is similar to that of the Stanford-Binet. Periodically, however, the examiner is instructed to reinforce correct behavior. This revision includes minor changes in administrative procedure from the 1968 version which was known as the Standardization Edition. The final product is reduced considerably in length from the original 7-test inventory developed in 1965 by Bettye Caldwell during the original excitement surrounding the development of Project Head Start. Caldwell's inventory was designed for measuring a child's basic information vocabulary and number and space concepts prior to his enrolling in a Head Start program and at its conclusion. Subsequently, Donald Soule refined the scoring system and processed the data collected from the national field testing.

Standardization of the Revised Edition took place in 11 Head Start centers and the data are reported for those tested in English. Most of the technical data are available for the following age groups: 3-0 to 3-11, 4-0 to 4-5, 4-6 to 4-11, 5-0 to 5-5, 5-6 to 6-5. A larger number of subjects were tested at each level between ages 4-0 and 5-5 than at either extreme. Some regional normative data, based on 107 to 248 subjects per region at each age level, are available. Percentile ranks are available for each age group and for some regions.

K-R 20 reliability coefficients for the age groups range from .86 to .92. For the total standardization sample, the mean increases about four raw score points from one age group to another. The standard error of measurement for the age groups varies from 3.1 to 3.9.

The Stanford-Binet was used with 1,476 subjects during the standardization. Concurrent validity coefficients vary from .39 at age 3-0 to 3-11 to .65 at age 5-0 to 5-5. Additional data are expected to be reported in the professional press when the instrument becomes generally available.

Results from measurement of achievement before and after nursery school experiences were not available in the prepublication manual. Data indicating the power of the scores from this instrument to predict success in school were also unavailable. Analysis of the responses by the teacher may indicate some educational needs. Since its object is the identification of those individuals unprepared for traditional programs, studies which indicate the degree to which the items in the test are predictive of "success in school" will be of interest to many professionals concerned with child development.

J Ed Meas 6(1):33–5 sp '69. Dale Carlson. Referred to as the Cooperative Pre-school Inventory (CPSI) in the catalog, this little instrument sometimes carries the parenthetical subtitle, "Standardization Edition" or "Preliminary Version" to denote its embryonic if not germinal state of development. The publisher hopes to have a more complete edition out sometime in 1969. The catalog states that its purpose is to "provide an indication of a child's level of development prior to formal instruction in a variety of basic skills and concepts regarded as necessary for success in school." The author prefers to regard the CPSI as an achievement test which is sensitive to changes associated with educational intervention. Whether it is an achievement test or a readiness test as the catalog implies, the items are exceedingly similar to those of other preschool batteries. The test has a strong verbal emphasis, but is relatively light on tasks such as short-term memory, motor development, and visual perception. Only 4 of the 89 items tap the latter two functions. The four scales originated from a factor analysis of the initial test consisting of 161 items. Four factors emerged including one general factor which loaded on items requiring information from parents. Items from this factor were not included in the published edition. Instead, one factor was logically divided to yield scores for two of the four scales. On the Personal-Social Responsiveness variable, the items relating to the child's knowledge of his body actually loaded heavier on the discarded self-help factor. The items requiring the capacity to execute simple and complex directions are probably more deserving of the "activation" title than the scales which bear it. The second scale, Associative Vocabulary, is neither associative in any standard psychological sense, nor is it a vocabulary test. It has a few items of a motor-encoding variety, but is largely a test of information and comprehension in the Wechsler tradition. The Concept Activation-Numerical scale is clearly a measure of quantitative understanding and has several excellent items. The second part of that original factor, Concept Activation-Sensory, might better be called sensory-motor or perceptual motor. The manual is appropriately entitled, Directions for Administration and Scoring, for that is all it contains except for tables of norms and a three-page description of the test and its origin. No help is offered in the interpretation of scores in terms of meaning, applicability, or stability. Additional information in the technical report regarding reliability, relationships among sub-tests, and items statistics could easily have been included in the manual. This would have made a technical report unnecessary since the remainder of the technical report is devoted to what some would consider an irrelevant narrative of the details relating to the birth of the instrument and the convictions of the author. The instructions for administration are very explicit and complete. The general criteria for scoring are equally clear. The need for immediate feedback during administration is recognized and provided for by the placing of sample responses immediately following the question. The criteria for scoring appear to ensure objectivity, but no evidence on this dimension is provided. The claim is made for a total administration time of only fifteen minutes. This is probably an underestimate. * reports percentile conversion charts for ages 2-1 to 6-6 for both middle and lower class groups. These norms are based on a sample of 669. Although the schools from which the sample was drawn are listed, there is no mention of any scheme to ensure adequate sampling. The manual does faithfully point out, however, that 80% of the sample is from one city. The concept of presenting norms as a function of social class is appealing. No information is offered, however, regarding the criteria for placing children in either norm group; nor are such basic descriptive statistics as mean and standard deviation reported on either sample for any part of the test. * For the full-length experimental version the split half (odd-even) coefficient was .97. A coefficient of .95 is reported for the published edition. These were both computed on the initial standardization sample only. Is it possible that these coefficients are spuriously high? Inspection of the tests reveals clusters of items which are very similar in format. Although success on one item is not completely dependent upon success on other items, the items are probably so highly correlated that an odd-even coefficient could be seriously affected. These clusters are distributed throughout the test to contribute to the factor-based scores which are probably correlated, thereby compounding the problem. If not spuriously high, the reported coefficients probably approach upper-bound estimates. Coefficients which consider other sources of variance, such as time, are not reported. Separate reliability estimates of part scores are absent, as well as any discussion on the stability of part or whole scores in terms of standard error of measurement. No validity data are reported unless the factor analysis performed during the construction of the inventory would qualify as such. While this information helps to indicate what the test is measuring, the inclusion of some reference tests in the factor analysis would have buttressed the unstated construct validation claims. The only other evidence for construct validity, through a consideration of age differentiation, was also gathered during the process of building the instrument. A table showing the proportion of children passing each item at three age levels is not very reassuring. Many items show almost no differentiation and a few are actually negatively correlated with age. Unfortunately, there are no indications of the relationships between CPSI scores and other criteria, either concurrently with another preschool test, or predictively with such crucial variables as success in beginning reading. Focusing on the author's preference that it be considered an achievement test, the content validity picture is just as bleak. No attention is given to the definition of the universe of test behaviors which this test might represent, nor any assurance that items were systematically selected to assure representation. The qualities sought and probably captured in this instrument: speed and ease of administration, objectivity in scoring, and low cost, indicate the potential value of this instrument. However, a healthy skepticism is justified if not demanded in the use of this test which was hastily marketed with inadequate norms and meager reliability and validity data.

[405]

★**Denver Developmental Screening Test.** Ages 2 weeks to 6 years; 1968–70; DDST; 4 scores: gross motor, fine motor-adaptive, language, personal-social; individual; 1 form ('68, 2 pages and kit of small objects); manual, 1970 edition ('70, 65 pages); $1 per 100 tests; $6.25 per kit of objects; $1 per manual; cash orders (plus 5% for postage) only; [15–20] minutes; William K. Frankenburg and Josiah B. Dodds; Ladoca Project and Publishing Foundation, Inc. *

REFERENCES

1. FRANKENBURG, WILLIAM K., AND DODDS, JOSIAH B. "The Denver Developmental Screening Test." *J Pediatrics* 71:181–91 Ag '67. *
2. KOUPERNIK, CYRILLE. "The Denver Developmental Screening Test." *Develop Med & Child Neurol* 10:796–7 D '68. *
3. FRANKENBURG, WILLIAM K. "The Denver Developmental Screening Test." Reply by Cyrille Koupernik. *Develop Med & Child Neurol* 11(2):260–2 Ap '69. *
4. ROBISCHON, PAULETTE. *A Study of the Relationship Between Children's Developmental Level, Pica Practice, and Other Hand-Mouth Behavior.* Doctor's thesis, New York University (New York, N.Y.), 1970. (*DAI* 31:2786B)
5. SANDLER, LOUISE; VANCAMPEN, JACK; RATNER, GERALD; STAFFORD, CALVIN; AND WEISMAR, RICHARD. "Response of Urban Preschool Children to a Developmental Screening Test." *J Pediatrics* 77(7):775–81 N '70. *
6. SMITH, JOANN HORN. *A Study of the Relationship Between Dogmatic and Rigid Attitudes in the Mother and Early Developmental Progress in the Infant.* Doctor's thesis, New York University (New York, N.Y.), 1970. (*DAI* 31:4160B)

ALICE E. MORIARTY, *Senior Psychologist, The Menninger Foundation, Topeka, Kansas.*

Efforts to predict later intellectual functioning from measurement or observation of infant behavior have on the whole been disappointing. On the other hand, clinicians knowledgeable about infant behavior have documented qualitative differences in the range of behavior which discriminate between children who will later show neurological and intellectual deficits from those who will not. At the same time, increasing recognition of the importance of early development on later cognitive and affective functioning, along with needs for early diagnosis of delayed development or retardation in order to plan for effective care and treatment of deviant children, have pushed clinicians to formalize observations in normative sequences. One such effort with apparent promise is the *Denver Developmental Screening Test.*

Selecting 240 potentially discriminating items from 12 existing developmental and preschool tests, the authors, in a preliminary survey of 200 infants and preschool children, experimentally eliminated items felt to be ambiguous or insufficiently discriminating. From this survey, the authors culled 105 items which were administered to a standardization population of 1,036 children (543 males and 493 females) between the ages of 2 weeks and 6.4 years. Children who were adopted, premature, or known to be handicapped in any way were excluded from the sample, which quite closely approximated the ethnic and occupational groups of the population in the city of Denver according to the 1960 census. Computer calculations were then made of the age at which 25, 50, 75, and 90 percent of the sample passed each item. Though a relatively small number of children were retested by four separate examiners for reliability purposes, agreement between 90 and 100 percent on each of the items, arbitrarily assigned to the four measured areas of functioning (gross motor, fine motor-adaptive, language, and personal-social) appeared to justify the authors' claims for a high level of reliability in administration and scoring. Not made clear is why adaptive aspects of functioning were considered only in relation to motor functioning.

A parallel study of the correlation of the DDST scores with the Yale Developmental Examination yielded a correlation of .97, suggesting high validity, especially since there were few cases of discrepancy between the two tests in identifying normal and deviant children.

In our clinical use of the DDST, we have had some reason to question the circumscribed geographical selection of the sample and the applicability of norms in screening children from the lower socioeconomic groups, especially in the language area. Furthermore, even if the standardization sample is truly representative of the Denver population, we cannot automatically assume that the established norms are appropriate for assessment of individual minority group children outside of the population in the Denver area. Possible unfairness to minority group children could, of course, be stated as an objection leveled at almost all measurements of cognitive development and functioning in minority groups. To the extent that quantitative findings are assessed in the light of known deterrents to functioning and weighed against the observable assets in the child's style of functioning, these objections are reduced but not entirely eliminated. The authors' cautions against using the DDST as a diagnostic tool and their recommendations of close observation of qualitative aspects of test behavior in relation to motivation, dependency or hostility between mother and child, examiner-child interaction, and of the maintenance of optimal and standard testing conditions are therefore especially commendable.

With these reservations in mind and in the context of the purposes for which it was designed, the DDST is a practical, efficient, and dependable device. It is inexpensive, quick and easy to administer and evaluate with relatively little training or experience in testing. The manual is direct and clear, and scoring guides are explicit. The test seems to meet standards of reliability and validity for the purposes for which it was designed. The materials themselves are colorful and of inherent interest to young children. Furthermore, it has the advantage of providing graphic representation of passes and failures, allowing the examiner to look at the range of behavior in each infant, and to interpret meaningfully to parents the strengths and weaknesses in relative developmental pace in each of the areas assessed. This reviewer is impressed by the authors' continuing refinement of scoring techniques in a 1970 revision of the manual and by their awareness of the limits of the test's applicability and purposefulness.

In presenting the findings only in terms of developmental adequacy or inadequacy, the authors bypassed the question of relationship to later intelligence. It is likely, however, that the DDST is most useful in the intermediate range since there are relatively few items in the age range below three months, and there are many readily available and more clearly definitive diagnostic procedures, that is standard intelligence tests, for ages beyond four years. Within these limits, the DDST is a useful and acceptable screening device, particularly for those not specifically trained in test administration and evaluation. It is comparable to similar inventories, such as the *Developmental Screening Inventory,* based on the more extensive Gesell tests. In marginal or doubtful cases, it would seem important to remember the clinical need to look at the whole child in his specific environment. Specifically, one needs to keep in mind the effects of environmental experiences, such as the provision of opportunities for and freedom from deterrents to developmental progress, along with parental adequacy in reporting child behavior, and objective physical findings. For this purpose, the Hoopes Infant Rating Scale could serve as a useful extension of observed or reported functioning on the DDST items. With these reservations, this reviewer feels that the DDST, in the context of its stated aims to provide screening of developmental delay in young children, is an excellent addition to existing testing techniques.

EMMY E. WERNER, *Professor of Child Development and Research Child Psychologist, University of California, Davis, California.*

The DDST aims to be a simple, clinically useful tool for the detection of children with serious developmental delays for use by persons who have not had training in psychological testing. It evaluates four aspects of a child's functioning: gross motor, fine motor-adaptive, language, and personal-social development. More than 12 existing infant and preschool tests were surveyed to select 240 potential items which required no elaborate equipment and were easy to administer and score. After a pretest of 200 infants and preschool children, 105 items that best satisfied the above criteria were kept. The standardization group contained 1,036 normal children (543 M, 493 F) between the ages of 2 weeks and 6.4 years in Denver.

Test materials consist of a skein of red wool, a box of raisins, a rattle, a bottle, a bell, a tennis ball, and eight cubes. On the record form each test item in the four sectors is designated by a bar which indicates the ages at which 25, 50, 75, and 90 percent of the standardization population can perform the particular test item.

The results in each sector are categorized as normal, abnormal, and questionable. A child's performance in any sector is considered normal if he passes at least one item which is intersected by his age line and if he has no delays on any items in that sector (i.e., failure to perform any item passed by more than 90 percent of children his age). A child's performance in a sector is considered abnormal if he has two or more delays in that sector. It is considered questionable if he is delayed in just one item in each sector through which his age line passes.

The DDST is in use in Head Start programs, well-baby clinics and community health programs, and has gained popularity among pediatricians, medical students, and nonprofessional health workers. Although the authors, a pediatrician and a psychologist, state in the manual that the DDST was not designed to yield a developmental or mental age, or a developmental or intelligence quotient, this warning has not been heeded.

The test user should be aware of the following weaknesses of the DDST with regard to standardization, reliability, and validity. The norm group contains a significantly higher proportion of white children and of children whose fathers are in the professional, managerial, or sales occupation than the census distribution would warrant (*1*). The 105 items retained for the standardization were chosen on the basis of a pretest by four medical students. It is doubtful whether these students possessed the psychological training necessary to make such an examination meaningful.

Test-retest reliabilities and interexaminer reliabilities reported in the manual are based on extremely small samples of children (20 and 12, respectively), representing a wide age range, from 2 months to 5½ years. A more extensive tester-observer reliability study of 76 children, ranging in age from 4 to 77 months, and a test-retest reliability study (7 days apart) of 186 children between the ages of 1.5 and 76 months have been reported recently.[1] Mental ages were calculated for 13 age groups between 1.5 and 49 months, using the 50 percent pass method for each of the four sectors. Coefficients ranged between .66 and .93. Reliabilities were generally poor in the first and second years, but reached a more acceptable level in the third and fourth year. Of some concern is the fact that of the 28 items with the highest tester-observer and test-retest reliabilities, 17 could be passed by report of the mother, in contrast to only 5 of the 23 items with low tester-observer and test-retest reliabilities. The majority of the items on the DDST based on actual observations of the child's behavior had only low to moderate reliability. Thus the DDST seems to yield little more in the nature of reliable information than an interview with the mother, with the inherent distortion of developmental facts by recall.

The only preliminary validity study given in the 1968 manual is restricted to 18 children, ranging in age from 4 to 68 months who were given both the DDST and the Revised Yale Developmental Schedule (RYDS). Fifteen of the 18 children scored below 90 IQ on the RYDS. A correlation of .97 appears spuriously inflated, because the sample is small, skewed in the direction of abnormality, and encompasses a wide age range.

In a more extensive validity study,[2] 236 children were evaluated with the DDST and the following criterion tests: Stanford-Binet (N,

91; mean age, 52.5 months), RYDS (N, 64; mean age, 33 months), *Cattell Infant Intelligence Scale* (N, 50; mean age, 12.8 months) and *Bayley Scales of Infant Development* (N, 31; mean age, 6.2 months). Mental ages, mean DQ's/IQ's, and SD's on the criterion tests indicate that the majority of the children fell within the slow learner and mentally retarded range. Mental ages were obtained on the DDST by averaging scores for the four sectors and correlated with the scores on the criterion tests. Correlations ranged from .74 to .97. The agreement between the DDST and the criterion tests were compared in terms of co-positivity and co-negativity. The results of this analysis show a marked underselection by the DDST of children who received abnormal scores on the Bayley and Cattell tests. Seventy-one percent of the children called abnormal on the Bayley in the first year, and 43 percent of the children called abnormal on the Cattell in the second year were called normal on the DDST. Children over 30 months who were classified as abnormal on the RYDS and the Stanford-Binet were generally correctly identified on the DDST. There was a considerable overselection of normal children in the third year of life: 42 percent of normal children on the RYDS were called abnormal on the DDST. One wonders whether this may reflect on the insensitivity of untrained examiners to the period of negativism, shyness and distractibility that makes rapport with this age group a challenge to the most experienced tester.

In a report on the use of nonprofessional personnel for health screening of 298 Head Start children, comparisons were made between the referrals of health aides (mothers with less than high school education) and referrals made by psychologists and pediatricians.[3] Children whose scores the aides found to be below the 20th percentile on the DDST were compared with children scoring below IQ 80 on the Stanford-Binet. The aides referred only about half of the children below 80 IQ, and only one-fifth of the children identified by the pediatricians as having intellectual and developmental problems. The correlation between the aides' DDST scores and the psychologists' S-B scores for the same children was only .30.

1 FRANKENBURG, W. K.; CAMP, B. W.; VAN NATTA, P. A.; DE MERSSEMAN, J. A.; AND VORHESS, S. F. "Reliability of the Denver Developmental Screening Test." Unpublished paper.
2 FRANKENBURG, W. K.; CAMP, B. W.; AND VAN NATTA, P. A. "Validity of the Denver Developmental Screening Test." *Child Develop* 42(2):475-85 Je '71.

3 FURUNO, S., AND CONNOR, A. "Use of Non-Professional Personnel for Health Screening of Head Start Children." Unpublished paper presented at *Annual Meeting of the American Orthopsychiatric Association.* San Francisco, California, March, 1970.

SUMMARY. At a time of great interest in developmental screening for the sake of early intervention, the search for a foolproof, quick and easy screening instrument is bound to become popular. Already there are available variations of the DDST. The user of these screening tools needs to keep in mind that available evidence indicates that the DDST is not as reliable, valid, sensitive, and specific as its authors had hoped. Its use under the age of 30 months should be discouraged since it is of questionable reliability in the first two years of life and misses a high proportion of children identified by technically more superior tests, such as the Bayley and Cattell. In the third year of life, it tends to overselect normal children, possibly because of the difficulty of an inexperienced tester in establishing rapport with this age group. The DDST appears to be a fairly satisfactory screening tool at 4–4½ years of age, but even here its concurrent validity is lower than that of other screening tests, such as the *Peabody Picture Vocabulary Test.*

Most important, it needs to be kept in mind that a screening tool, even the simplest, is only as good as the sensitivity of its user to the behavior of young children. It is doubtful whether the authors' claim is justified that "in a few hours training almost any adult can administer this test competently."

[406]

*Detroit Tests of Learning Aptitude.** Ages 3 and over; 1935–68; DTLA; 20 scores: pictorial absurdities, verbal absurdities, pictorial opposites, verbal opposites, motor speed and precision, auditory attention span (for unrelated words, for related syllables), oral commissions, social adjustment A, visual attention span (for objects, for letters), orientation, free association, memory for designs, number ability, social adjustment B, broken pictures, oral directions, likenesses and differences, total; individual; 1 form; revised examiner's handbook ('67, 143 pages, with 1955 norms); supplement ('68, 15 pages); pictorial material ('58, 97 pages); revised record booklet ('59, 16 pages); no data on reliability for part scores; $3 per pictorial material; $5.90 per 35 record booklets; 30¢ per single copy; $4.45 per handbook; $1.20 per supplement; postage extra; (60–95) minutes; Harry J. Baker and Bernice Leland; Bobbs-Merrill Co., Inc. *

REFERENCES

1. See 3:275.
2. ASHLOCK, PATRICK ROBERT. *Visual Perception of Children in the Primary Grades and Its Relation to Reading Performance.* Doctor's thesis, University of Texas (Austin, Tex.), 1963. (DA 24:5186)
3. SANDSTEDT, BARBARA. "Relationship Between Memory Span and Intelligence of Severely Retarded Readers." *Read Teach* 17:246–50 Ja '64. *
4. ASHLOCK, PATRICK. "The Visual Perception of Children in the Primary Grades and Its Relation to Reading Performance." *Proc Ann Conv Int Read Assn* 10:331–3 '65. *
5. CHARRY, LAWRENCE BERNARD. *The Relationship Between Prereading and First Grade Reading Performances and Subsequent Achievement in Reading and Other Specified Areas.*

Doctor's thesis, Temple University (Philadelphia, Pa.), 1967. (DA 28:960A)
6. WARTENBERG, HERBERT. *The Relationship Between Success in Beginning Reading and Various Predictive Measures.* Doctor's thesis, Temple University (Philadelphia, Pa.), 1967. (DA 28:979A)
7. CHIAPPONE, ANTHONY D. "Use of the Detroit Tests of Learning Aptitude With EMR." *Excep Children* 35:240–1 N '68. * (PA 43:13075)
8. BANAS, NORMA, AND WILLS, I. H. "The Vulnerable Child and Prescriptive Teaching." *Acad Ther* 4(3):215–9 sp '69. * (PA 43:17927)
9. BRUININKS, ROBERT H. "Auditory and Visual Perceptual Skills Related to the Reading Performance of Disadvantaged Boys." *Percept & Motor Skills* 29(1):179–86 Ag '69. * (PA 44:2835)
10. NELSON, C. MICHAEL, AND HUDSON, FLOYD G. "Predicting the Reading Achievement of Junior High School EMR Children." *Am J Mental Def* 74(3):415–20 N '69. *
11. ENGELHARDT, GEORGE M. "Predicting Rehabilitation of Socially Maladjusted Boys." *J Counsel Psychol* 17(6):546–9 N '70. * (PA 45:2619)

For a review by F. L. Wells, see 3:275; for reviews by Anne Anastasi and Henry Feinberg of an earlier edition, see 1:1058 (1 excerpt).

[407]

★A Developmental Screening Inventory. Ages 1–18 months; 1966; DSI; consists of selected items from the *Gesell Developmental Schedules;* abnormal development; history and observation ratings in 5 areas: adaptive, gross motor, fine motor, language, personal-social; individual; 1 form ['66, 6 pages]; manual (15 pages, reprint of 1 below); no data on reliability; $4.50 per 25 tests, postpaid; sample test free; test materials must be assembled locally; (5–30) minutes; Hilda Knobloch, Benjamin Pasamanick, and Earl S. Sherard, Jr.; Hilda Knobloch. *

REFERENCE

1. KNOBLOCH, HILDA; PASAMANICK, BENJAMIN; AND SHERARD, EARL S., JR. "A Developmental Screening Inventory for Infants." *Pediatrics* 38(sup):1095–108 D '66. *

[408]

*English Picture Vocabulary Test. Ages 5-0 to 8-11, 7-0 to 11-11; 1962–66; EPVT; derived from *Peabody Picture Vocabulary Test;* individual for Test 1; 1 form; 2 levels: Test 1 ('62, 44 pages), Test 2 ('62, 47 pages); manual, second edition ('66, 44 pages, 39 of which are identical, including norms, with 1963 manual); separate answer sheets (for group administration, Test 2 only) or record sheets (for individual administration) must be used; £1.40 per set of 25 tests, 25 record sheets, 25 answer sheets, scoring stencil, and manual; 35p per 25 record sheets; 35p per 25 answer sheets; 5p per scoring stencil for answer sheets; 50p per manual; postage extra; specimen set not available; [15–45] minutes; M. A. Brimer and Lloyd M. Dunn; distributed by Educational Evaluation Enterprises. *

REFERENCES

1. MARSHALL, ANNE. *The Abilities and Attainments of Children Leaving Junior Training Centres.* London: National Association for Mental Health, 1967. Pp. i, 62. *
2. PHILLIPS, C. J., AND BANNON, W. J. "The Stanford-Binet, Form L-M, Third Revision: A Local English Study of Norms, Concurrent Validity and Social Differences." *Brit J Ed Psychol* 38:148–61 Je '68. * (PA 42:17000)
3. BRIMER, M. A. "Sex Differences in Listening Comprehension." Discussion by John B. Carroll. *J Res & Develop Ed* 3(1):72–81 f '69. *
4. WEDELL, K., AND HORNE, I. EDNA. "Some Aspects of Perceptuo-Motor Disability in 5½-Year-Old Children." *Brit J Ed Psychol* 39(2):174–82 Je '69. * (PA 44:6514)
5. O'KELLY, E. "A Method for Detecting Slow Learning Juniors." *Ed Res* 12(2):135–9 F '70. *

KENNETH LOVELL, *Professor of Educational Psychology, The Institute of Education, The University, Leeds, England.*

The purpose of this test is to assess the levels of listening vocabulary among children in the age range 5-0 to 11-11. The EPVT was derived from the *Peabody Picture Vocabulary Test* and depends upon it for some of the preparatory constructional data. In essence a page of four pictures together with a spoken word makes a test item and the child's task is to identify the picture to which the word refers. The booklets which contain the pictures are stoutly constructed and, of course, reusable. Moreover, the accompanying manual sets out clearly and fully the directions for administering and scoring the tests; although the manual itself could be improved from the point of view of format, size of print, and durability.

The standardisation was carried out in Wiltshire—a predominantly rural county. Care was taken to stratify the maintained schools within the county by type, locality, and size. However, whether it is possible to build a sample representative of the U.K. from within Wiltshire is a point which might be argued. Conversion tables give standardised scores at monthly intervals and the percentile equivalents for standardised scores are also given. The manual recommends the values of .88 and .92 be accepted as the reliabilities of Tests 1 and 2, respectively. There is a consistent difference in raw scores in favour of boys—a characteristic feature of many orally administered vocabulary tests—but no separate conversion tables for the sexes.

Test 2 is also now available in a group form which employs expendable booklets. The pictures are set out horizontally in fours, instead of in a 2 × 2 array as in the individual arrangements. The accompanying manual sets out fully and precisely the directions for administering and scoring the tests in the new format.

Here are tests which can be used to assess listening vocabulary regardless of reading ability, while handicapped pupils can take the test providing they can evoke some movement to indicate the correct picture. However, it should be noted that when testing pupils who are very backward in number work, group administration demands that a child recognise the number of the page when its number name is called, and in the group form he must recognise the row number when its name is announced.

The most difficult question concerns the validity of the EPVT. At present no evidence exists that it will give an understanding of reading difficulties and other verbal handicaps, as is claimed in the manual. In a study involving children between the ages 8-0 and 11-0, Test 2 is reported to correlate .61 with one of Schonell's reading comprehension tests, .76 with WISC Vocabulary, and .80 with Schonell's *Graded Word Reading Test*. In another study, a correlation of .82 was found with Stanford-Binet Vocabulary. These suggest that Test 2 does measure some function which is common to other tests of vocabulary, although little more than this can be said at present.

In summary, the EPVT is recommended as an orally administered vocabulary test suitable for normal and for many kinds of handicapped pupils. It compares favourably with any other test designed to measure difficulty of listening vocabulary.

For reviews by L. B. Birch and Philip M. Levy, see 6:520.

[409]

★**Haptic Intelligence Scale for Adult Blind.** Blind and partially sighted adults; 1964; HIS; 7 scores: digit symbol, block design, object assembly, object completion, pattern board, bead arithmetic, total; individual; 1 form; manual (45 pages); record form (4 pages); $175 per set of testing materials, manual, and 100 record forms; $7 per 100 record forms; $2.50 per manual; postage extra; (90–120) minutes; Harriett C. Shurrager and Phil S. Shurrager; Psychology Research. *

REFERENCES

1. WATSON, SHIRLEY B. *Development and Standardization of a Performance Scale for Adult Blind.* Doctor's thesis, Illinois Institute of Technology (Chicago, Ill.), 1956.
2. KAMIN, HERBERT SPENCER, JR. *Onset and Duration of Blindness: Affecters of Haptic Intelligence Scale Performance.* Doctor's thesis, Illinois Institute of Technology (Chicago, Ill.), 1964.
3. DAUTERMAN, WILLIAM L.; SHAPIRO, BERNICE; AND SUINN, RICHARD M. "Performance Tests of Intelligence for Blind Reviewed." *Int J Ed Blind* 17:8–16 O '67. *
4. EBER, HERBERT W. "The Factor Structure of the WAIS-Verbal and HIS-Test Combination." *J Ed Res* 61:27–8 S '67. *
5. GALLAGHER, PATRICIA. "A Correlation Study of Haptic Subtest Scores and Travel Rating Skills of Blind Adolescents." *New Outl Blind* 62:240–6 O '68. *
6. NADDEO, CANDICE L., AND CURTIS, W. SCOTT. "Some Effects of the Disorientation of Tactile-Kinesthesia." *Int J Ed Blind* 18:69–72 O '68. *
7. STREITFELD, JULIAN W., AND AVERY, CONSTANCE D. "The WAIS and HIS Tests as Predictors of Academic Achievement in a Residential School for the Blind." *Int J Ed Blind* 18:73–7 O '68. * (PA 43:10178)
8. AVERY, CONSTANCE D., AND STREITFELD, JULIAN W. "An Abbreviation of the Haptic Intelligence Scale for Clinical Use." *Ed Visually Handicapped* 1(2):37–40 My '69. * (PA 43:14459)
9. SAXON, JOHN P.; ALSTON, PAUL P.; AND PORTER, THOMAS L. "Comparison of Haptic Intelligence Scale and WAIS Scores in a Population of Blind Psychotics." *Rehabil Counsel B* 13(1):49–51 S '69. *

MARSHALL S. HISKEY, *Professor of Educational Psychology and Measurements and Director, Educational-Psychological Clinic, University of Nebraska, Lincoln, Nebraska.*

Based on the assumption that existing tests were neither designed for nor adapted to the blind and that certain facets of their intelligence were not assessed adequately by verbal tests, the *Haptic Intelligence Scale* was developed as a nonverbal test to measure the intelligence of blind adults. The authors stress that the scale should be used in conjunction with verbal tests of intelligence in order to provide a more comprehensive evaluation of blind persons.

Four of the five subtests of the original or experimental scale were modified adaptations of the performance scale of the WAIS. Since the intercorrelations of the subtests of the experimental scale suggested that a common factor was involved to a large degree, two additional tests which required somewhat less fine tactile discrimination and skillful manipulation of parts were devised and included in the final scale.

Since the scale was designed to be used in conjunction with the verbal scale of the WAIS, Wechsler's procedures were followed with respect to establishing age categories and with the statistical treatment of the data.

The subjects in the standardization sample were from four designated geographic regions within the United States. Visual acuity did not exceed 5/200 in the better eye with correction. Both whites and nonwhites were included in proportion to their population (1950 census reports) but for stated and justifiable reasons the sample was not stratified on the basis of occupation and education.

Since the standardization procedure and the analyses of data replicate the methods utilized by Wechsler, little will be stated on this subject. The 20–34 age group was used as the reference group since they obtained the highest scores. The distribution of scores was converted to a scale with a mean scaled score of 10 and a standard deviation of 3. Since scaled score values do not vary with age, it is possible to compare a subject's performance with the reference group but not with the group to which he belongs. Relative ratings within a group can be obtained by comparing the IQ's listed with the conversion tables for the particular age group.

A retest of 136 subjects after six months or more gave reliability coefficients varying from .70 to .81. Test-retest reliability for the sum of five subtests (Bead Arithmetic was omitted) was .91 (N, 124). Odd-even reliabilities varied from a low of .79 on Object Assembly to a high of .94 on Bead Arithmetic. The total HIS IQ's showed a split-half reliability of .95. When utilized with the adult blind (ages 20–34) the

HIS correlation with WAIS Verbal was .65.

Psychological examiners who are well versed in the administration and interpretation of the WAIS will have relatively little difficulty making the transition to the HIS. Due to the nature of the scale, the test materials are bulky. The materials are attractive and, in general, reveal fine craftsmanship. The manual is durable and contains a good review of the development and standardization of the scale as well as certain shortcomings, of which the authors are aware.

The test has some limitations when used with the partially sighted. Since it is based on a tactile approach even the slightest view of the materials would invalidate the subject's performance. Thus the partially-sighted person must wear a blindfold which often becomes irritating before the lengthy session is over. Likewise, there is the real question as to whether partially-sighted persons develop the tactile skills that were so much a part of the blind who were used in establishing the norms as the test was standardized.

In summary the *Haptic Intelligence Scale* is a nonverbal test patterned after the performance tests of the WAIS. The subtests are interesting and the blind enjoy them, but the administration time is rather long and perhaps should be divided in two sessions. The authors state that it is not a perfected test in its present form and should be administered and interpreted with caution. Its current value perhaps rests in the clinical clues it provides the trained psychologist. Users are cautioned that the HIS cannot be used with some blind persons of low ability or those who have psychological blockings. The obtained results correlate well with the WAIS but the authors stress that they in no way intend to imply that the HIS measures in the blind the same factors that the WAIS performance tests measure in the sighted. Nevertheless, it is a clinically useful instrument that should be valuable to those who work closely with the adult blind. A still greater service would have been rendered had the authors employed the same sample of blind adults to establish norms for the verbal scale of the WAIS.

[410]

Hiskey-Nebraska Test of Learning Aptitude. Ages 3–16 (deaf and hearing); 1941–66; HNTLA; revision of *Nebraska Test of Learning Aptitude;* individual; 1 form ('66); revised manual ('66, 70 pages); record booklet ['66, 4 pages]; completion of drawings sheet ['66, 2 pages]; $56 per set of testing materials,

25 record booklets, and 25 drawing sheets; $3 per 50 record booklets; $1.75 per 50 drawing sheets; postage extra; (45–60) minutes; Marshall S. Hiskey; the Author. *

REFERENCES

1–3. See 3:289.
4. See 4:353.
5–12. See 5:409.
13. KIRK, SAMUEL A., AND PERRY, JUNE. "A Comparative Study of the Ontario and Nebraska Tests for the Deaf." *Am Ann Deaf* 93:315–23 S '48. * (*PA* 23:1902)
14. MACPHERSON, JANE G., AND LANE, HELEN S. "A Comparison of Deaf and Hearing on the Hiskey Test and on Performance Scales." *Am Ann Deaf* 93:178–84 Mr '48. * (*PA* 22:5103)
15. VARVA, FRANK IRVIN. *An Investigation of the Effect of Auditory Deficiency Upon Performance With Special Reference to Concrete and Abstract Tasks.* Doctor's thesis, University of Pittsburgh (Pittsburgh, Pa.), 1956. (*DA* 16:2532)
16. MIRA, MARY P. "The Use of the Arthur Adaptation of the Leiter International Performance Scale and the Nebraska Test of Learning Aptitude with Preschool Deaf Children." *Am Ann Deaf* 107:224–8 Mr '62. * (*PA* 37:1617)
17. CASJENS, CLIFFORD CURTIS. *Performance of Brain-Injured and Non-Brain Injured Mentally Retarded Children on the Hiskey-Nebraska Test of Learning Aptitude.* Doctor's thesis, University of Nebraska (Lincoln, Neb.), 1965. (*DA* 26:2048)
18. GIANGRECO, C. JOSEPH. *The Hiskey-Nebraska Test of Learning Aptitude as a Predictor of Academic Achievement of Deaf Children.* Doctor's thesis, University of Nebraska (Lincoln, Neb.), 1965. (*DA* 26:155)
19. GENTILE, J. RONALD. "In Search of Research: Four Children's Tests." *J Sch Psychol* 5:1–13 au '66. * (*PA* 41:3335)
20. GIANGRECO, C. JOSEPH. "The Hiskey-Nebraska Test of Learning Aptitude (Revised) Compared to Several Achievement Tests." *Am Ann Deaf* 111:566–77 S '66. * (*PA* 41:999)
21. BACH, LLOYD CARL. *A Comparison of Selected Psychological Tests Used With Trainable Mentally Retarded Children.* Doctor's thesis, University of South Dakota (Vermillion, S.D.), 1968. (*DA* 29:2990A)
22. MORRIS, BERNIECE EVELYN JEPSEN VANCAMP. *Responses by Adult Retardates to Visual Stimuli of Variable Fidelity.* Doctor's thesis, University of Nebraska (Lincoln, Neb.), 1968. (*DA* 29:1788A)
23. MORRIS, GEORGE LEE, JR. *Effects of Variation in Fidelity Level of Visual Stimuli.* Doctor's thesis, University of Nebraska (Lincoln, Neb.), 1968. (*DA* 29:1788A)
24. PAUL, GERALD THOMAS. *The Relationship Between Prenatal and Perinatal Experiences and Intellectual, Perceptual-Motor, and Conceptual Functioning in Preschool Adopted Children.* Doctor's thesis, Temple University (Philadelphia, Pa.), 1968. (*DAI* 30:1364B)
25. HOWARD, JANE OSBURN. *A Comparison of the Revised Stanford-Binet Intelligence Scale, Form L-M, and the Nebraska Test of Learning Aptitude, 1966 Revision, With Groups of Mentally Retarded, Deaf, and Normal Children.* Doctor's thesis, University of New Mexico (Albuquerque, N.M.), 1969. (*DAI* 30:3322A)
26. LEWIS, JAMES F. *Differential Evaluation of Selected Tests When Utilized With Institutionalized and Non-Institutionalized Trainable Mentally Retarded.* Doctor's thesis, University of Nebraska (Lincoln, Neb.), 1969. (*DAI* 30:3793A)

T. ERNEST NEWLAND, *Professor of Educational Psychology, University of Illinois, Urbana, Illinois.*

This test is a revision of the 1941 *Nebraska Test of Learning Aptitude,* which came to be regarded by the author as useful with hearing children. With an added test, Spatial Reasoning, the test was administered to 1,107 deaf children and 1,101 hearing children from 2-6 years to 17-5 years in 10 states.

Understandably, the number of children in the standardization populations at each year level varies more for the deaf (25 to 106, median 71) than for the hearing (47 to 85, median 76). Parental occupational level sampling for the hearing population (no such data

on the deaf) corresponds closely to the U.S. census data. No breakdowns by race or sex are provided.

The total test age score is called "learning age" (LA) for deaf subjects and "mental age" for hearing subjects. Although the author recommends the use of age ratings, the deviation IQ may be computed for hearing children and "learning quotient" (LQ) for deaf children. The learning age is the median of the age scores on the subtests.

The split-half reliabilities reported (scores unspecified) are for wide-range populations: .95 for the deaf and .93 for the hearing in groups having an age range of 3 to 10; .92 and .90, respectively, in the range of 11 to 17. No other information is reported for these four groups.

The author presents four kinds of validity data: subtest intercorrelations, correlations between age ratings on the subtests and the median LA, correlations with the 1960 Stanford-Binet and the WISC for hearing children, and correlations with performance on achievement tests and teacher ratings for the deaf. For the deaf, subtest intercorrelations range from .33 to .74 (median .48) for the age range 3–10 and from .31 to .43 (median .37) for ages 11–17. For the hearing, the intercorrelations range from .32 to .78 (median .55) for ages 3–10 and .25 to .46 (median .34) for ages 11–17. The author reports a correlation of .86 (IQ's) with the S-B for 99 subjects ranging in age from 3 through 10 and a correlation of .78 for ages 11–17. For WISC, the correlation between IQ's is .82 on 52 subjects (age range 5–11) for the three groups.

It is this reviewer's opinion that, in spite of the absence of any discernable theory underlying the construction of the HNTLA, it does provide, at least in certain kinds of behavior samplings, a closer approximation to tapping the major psychological components necessary in the school learning of deaf children, especially the younger ones, than does, say, the WISC Performance test which is so widely used with deaf and seriously acoustically impaired children. The use of "learning ages" and "learning quotients" and the determination of the total test performance by taking the median subtest score are commendable. Test-retest information is needed, as is that on standard errors of measurement, at least for the year-age levels. The revised test is physically a distinct improvement over its predecessor in packaging and printing.

In spite of the impreciseness of much of the research cited in support of the HNTLA, this test is the most promising one available for assessing the "book learning" capability of deaf children. The behavior samplings in the areas of memory, picture identification, and picture association in particular have demonstrated relevance to the kinds of learning aptitude important in school work. The demands for testing time and highly technical test administration techniques are not great. Its nearest competitor is the *Leiter International Performance Scale*. More definitive research is needed, however, to demonstrate that the use of the HNTLA with hearing children can be as fruitful psycho-educationally over the age range claimed for it as is the Stanford-Binet or even the verbal portion of the WISC. For the lower portions of the HNTLA age range, the *Pictorial Test of Intelligence* appears to be a more promising test for use with hearing children.

For a review by William Sloan of an earlier edition, see 5:409; for a review by Mildred C. Templin, see 4:353.

[411]

Kahn Intelligence Tests: Experimental Form. Ages 1 month and over, particularly the verbally or culturally handicapped; 1960; KIT; uses same test objects as *Kahn Test of Symbol Arrangement;* main scale plus 6 optional scales: brief scale, concept formation, recall, motor coordination, scale for use with the deaf, scale for use with the blind; individual; 1 form (16 plastic objects); record form (4 pages); manual (34 pages, reprint of *2* below); $26 per set of testing materials including 50 record forms and manual; $2.50 per manual; cash orders postpaid; administration time not reported; Theodore C. Kahn; Psychological Test Specialists. *

REFERENCES

1–2. See 6:524.
3. KROSKE, WILLIAM H.; FRETWELL, LORETTA N.; AND CUPP, MARION E. "Comparison of the Kahn Intelligence Tests: Experimental Form, the Stanford-Binet and the WAIS for Familial Retardates." *Percept & Motor Skills* 21:428 O '65. * (PA 40:3310)
4. McDANIEL, ERNEST D., AND CARSE, WILLIAM T. "Validation of the Kahn Intelligence Tests." *Ed & Psychol Meas* 25:1153–6 w '65. * (PA 40:3581)
5. CARSE, WILLIAM T. "Further Validation of the Kahn Intelligence Tests." *Ed & Psychol Meas* 27:1055–60 w '67. * (PA 42:8935)
6. EPPLEY, EDWIN B. *A Validity Study Comparing the Main Scale of the Kahn Intelligence Test With the Wechsler Intelligence Scale for Children.* Master's thesis, Millersville State College (Millersville, Pa.), 1968.
7. ROFFMAN, PAMELA OLCOTT. *Validation of the Kahn Intelligence Tests: Experimental Form With Southeastern Second-Graders.* Master's thesis, University of Georgia (Athens, Ga.), 1968.
8. CHOVAN, WILLIAM L., AND HATHAWAY, MILDRED L. "The Performance of Two Culturally Divergent Groups of Children on a Culture-Free Test." Abstract. *J Sch Psychol* 8(1):66 '70. * (PA 44:10126)

MARJORIE P. HONZIK, *Lecturer in Psychology, and Research Psychologist, Institute of Human Development, University of California, Berkeley, California.*

The KIT is an age scale extending from 1 month to adulthood. The test materials consist of a felt strip (numbered from 1 to 15), and 16 small, flat, plastic objects (3 dogs, 3 hearts, 3 stars, 2 butterflies, an anchor, a cross, a parrot, a circle, and a segment of a circle). These materials vary in color and size as well as shape, and are intrinsically interesting to persons of all ages.

The test items for this age scale are patterned after those of the *Gesell Developmental Schedules* and the *Stanford-Binet Intelligence Scale*. Kahn's use of the plastic objects to test different age levels is ingenious. This test is weakest at the youngest age levels, where development is most rapid. There are only 6 test items covering the first 12 months of life, in contrast to 103 in the *Bayley Scales of Infant Development* and 55 in the *Cattell Infant Intelligence Scale*. The 6 items available for each of the second and third years are also too few for adequate testing. Six tests per year for the age period 4 to 14 should prove sufficient, especially after year 6.

The inadequacy of the test series for the first year is further indicated by the age placements. For example, item 1 of the scale is definitely much more difficult than item 2. The relative age placements of these items on the Bayley Scale are 3.3 months and .5 months, respectively. Also, first-year items 5 and 6 require manipulation of very small plastic objects which babies find difficult to manage. Most infants less than a year old would be frustrated by the problem of making a small flat plastic dog stand up and would probably brush the materials aside. The first-year scale should be either improved by adding more test items or deleted entirely. In its present form, it is worse than nothing, since it might suggest retardation where none exists.

Many of the concepts which are basic to the Stanford-Binet are used in the Kahn tests. Binet considered "following directions" an important aspect of intelligence. Success on many of the Kahn tests is highly dependent on attending to instructions. For example, at year 3–4, all six test items require that the child understand and comply with instructions: "Find me one just like it," "Put them together the way I had them," "Find something else that can run....fly," "Put one red thing in the box," and "Show me a bigger." This test depends heavily not only on verbal comprehension but also on verbal facility. Beginning at year 4–5, the child is asked to respond verbally to one or two items at most levels. The test instructions become rather complex and contrived at the older age levels and at times have a negative tone. For example, at year 13–14, the subject is asked not only which object is different from the others but is told *not* to judge "by what the object could stand for," nor by "thickness, thinness, or transparency."

Kahn's claim of freedom from cultural bias is not supported by McDaniel and Carse's study (*4*) of 50 children between the ages of 4 and 6. These children were tested on both the KIT and the Stanford-Binet. The KIT IQ's were more closely related to socioeconomic status than the S-B IQ's, suggesting that the KIT may be at least as culturally biased as the S-B, if not more so.

STANDARDIZATION. The age placement of test items is based on testing 40 adults and 297 children ranging in age from 1 month to 17 years. Item difficulty was determined by the responses of at least 10 children at each age level whose MA fell within that year level on the WISC, S-B, or Gesell. Clearly, KIT is not adequately standardized. Kahn considers these scales "frankly experimental."

RELIABILITY. Kahn reports a test-retest reliability of .94 based on the MA's of 23 children ranging in age from 1 to 14 years. It is difficult to understand why there is no correction for age, either by using IQ's or by partialling out chronological age.

VALIDITY. Kahn reports a validity coefficient of .75 based on a correlation of the MA's on the KIT and S-B for the same 23 children used in the reliability study. Fortunately, more adequate evaluations of the validity of this test are available. McDaniel and Carse (*4*) report a correlation of .83 between IQ's on the KIT and S-B for 50 children whose parents held predominantly managerial or professional positions. This coefficient suggests a high degree of comparability between the two scales. At the other end of the ability scale, Kroske and others (*3*) report the KIT IQ's for 34 cultural-familial retarded children living in an institution. The mean IQ of this group on the KIT was 43; on the S-B, 47; and on the WAIS, 56. The Kahn IQ correlated .62 with the S-B IQ and .51, .73, and .66 with the WAIS Verbal, Performance,

and the Full Scale, respectively, in spite of the restricted range of ability.

SUMMARY. The KIT consists of interesting test materials which yield information about the intellectual functioning of a child or adult. It should be used with extreme caution until adequately standardized. This test requires understanding of language but few verbal responses, and it is less culture free than the Binet tests. It is of little or no value as an infant test because of inadequate sampling of abilities. The test is worthy of consideration because it is intrinsically interesting, covers a wide age range, and correlates highly with the Binet and Wechsler scales in populations of both low and high ability. Also derived from this scale are shorter scales to estimate ability in areas of concept formation, recall, and motor coordination and special scales that can be administered by sign language and for testing the visually handicapped. The usefulness, reliability, and validity of these derived scales have not been determined.

[412]

★**New Guinea Performance Scales.** Pre-literates ages 17 and over; 1961–71; NGPS; based (except *f*) on the unpublished *PIR Test* used for screening for the Pacific Island Regiment; test (except *e*) is essentially the same as the *Queensland Test* except for minor differences in some of the testing materials and differences in administration, scoring, and norms population; 6 tests; 7 scores: cube imitation, bead threading, passalong, form assembly, observation, design construction, total; individual; 1 form; manual ('71, c1970, 274 pages, see *4* below); record form ('67, 2 pages); norms based on male Papuans and New Guineans; Aus $70 per set of testing materials; $9.50 (£2.75) per manual available from Jacaranda Press Pty Ltd. in Australia (Ginn & Co. Ltd. in Britain); postage extra; record form must be reproduced locally; (45–60) minutes; I. G. Ord; New Guinea Fund for Psychological Test Development. *
a) CUBE IMITATION TEST. An adaptation of Pintner's revision of the Knox test; (5) minutes.
b) BEAD THREADING TEST. (10) minutes.
c) PASSALONG TEST. Modification of a subtest of *Alexander Performance Scale;* test booklet title is *Passalong Test (New Guinea Version)*; 1 form ('61, 8 cards); (10–15) minutes.
d) FORM ASSEMBLY TEST. Single form, multiple form; (8–10) minutes.
e) OBSERVATION TEST (5–10) minutes.
f) DESIGN CONSTRUCTION TEST. Published separately as *Pacific Design Construction Test;* Form A ('65, 13 cards); (10–15) minutes.

REFERENCES
1. ORD, I. G. *Development of a Test of Cognitive Capacity for Indigenes of Papua-New Guinea.* Master's thesis, University of Queensland (Brisbane, Australia), 1959.
2. ORD, I. G. "The New Guinea Performance Scale and Its Educational Use." *Papua & New Guinea J Ed* 5:7–16 S '67. *
3. ORD, I. G. "The P.I.R. Test and Derivatives." *Austral Psychologist* 2:137–46 Mr '68. * (PA 42:18798)
4. ORD, I. G. *Mental Tests for Pre-Literates: Results Mainly*

From New Guinea Studies. London: Ginn & Co. Ltd., 1971 (c1970). Pp. xiii, 270. *

[413]

★**New South African Individual Scale.** Ages 6–17; 1964; NSAIS; 12 scores: verbal (vocabulary, comprehension, reasoning, problems, memory, total), nonverbal (pattern completion, blocks, absurdities, form board, total), total; both power and power-time scores are obtained for 4 subtests, the verbal and nonverbal test totals, and the overall total; individual; 1 form; preliminary manual in 3 booklets: background and standardisation (33 pages), instructions (27 pages), norms (50 pages); record booklet ['64, 4 pages]; R39 per set of testing materials and manual; R4 per 100 record booklets; R4 per 100 pattern completion practice sheets; R5 per set of manual booklets; postpaid within South Africa; Afrikaans edition available; (45–60) minutes; Human Sciences Research Council. *

REFERENCE

1. STRÜMPFER, D. J. W., AND MIENIE, C. J. P. "A Validation of the Harris-Goodenough Test." *Brit J Ed Psychol* 38: 96–100 F '68. * (*PA* 42:12134)

[414]

★**The Ohwaki-Kohs Tactile Block Design Intelligence Test for the Blind.** Blind ages 6 and over; 1965; OKTBD; record booklet title is *The Ohwaki-Kohs Tactile Block Design Intelligence Test;* adaptation of *Kohs' Block Design Test;* for American revision, see 427; individual; 1 form (blocks and design cards); record booklet (4 pages); manual (11 pages plus record booklet); norms based upon testing of Japanese subjects with Japanese edition first published in 1960; $47.50 per examiner's kit of testing materials, 25 record booklets, and manual; $42.50 per set of testing materials; $6.50 per 25 record booklets; $2.50 per manual; postpaid; administration time not reported; Yoshikazu Ohwaki; Western Psychological Services. *

REFERENCES

1. OHWAKI, YOSHIKAZU; TANNO, YUJI; OHWAKI, MIEKO; HARIU, TOHRU; HAYASAKA, KAZUKO; AND MIYAKE, KEIKO. "Construction of an Intelligence Test for the Blind (Ohwaki-Kohs Tactile-Block Intelligence Test)." *Tohuko Psychologica Folia* 18(2–4):45–65 '60. * (*PA* 34:8294)
2. BOZZO, MARIA TERESA, AND ZECCA, GRAZIELLA. "First Results of Applications on Italian Subjects of the Ohwaki-Kohs Intelligence Test for the Blind." *Psychologia* 7:121–3 Je '64. *
3. SUINN, RICHARD M. "The Ohwaki-Kohs Intelligence Test for the Blind: Standardization on American Adults." *Psychologia* 9:217–8 S '66. *
4. SUINN, RICHARD M.; DAUTERMAN, WILLIAM; AND SHAPIRO, BERNICE. "The Stanford Ohwaki-Kohs Tactile Block Design Intelligence Test for the Blind." *New Outl Blind* 60: 77–9 Mr '66. *

J Ed Meas 4:261–2 w '67. *Richard J. Rankin.* This test was developed in Japan with the current form basically an English translation. * The eleven page manual contains a relatively complete description of the test administration. Unfortunately there is little information about the normative sample, and the theoretical justification for use of a performance scale based on the single intellectual dimension tapped by block design is sketchy. The IQ is determined by summing the raw points obtained, converting to mental age, dividing by chronological age, and multiplying the result by 100. At age 13 and above, the mental age is divided by a correct

chronological age. Interestingly, the corrected chronological ages parallel exactly those presented in the 1937 Stanford Binet Manual. Since the S. B. adjustment was specific to that scale, it cannot be generalized as a constant chronological age correction table for performance scales. The disadvantages of the ratio IQ have been stressed many times in literature and the lack of a constant variation with age is well known. Indicative of the general quality of the manual, example C for computing the IQ is incorrect. Further confusion occurs on the test protocol where the steps for determining IQ read "Step 3 IQ equals C.A. in months over M.A. in months times 100." No statistical information concerning the mean score or the S.D. of scores is presented in the manual, however, an IQ distribution for 278 totally blind Japanese children is presented. The distribution is bimodal with peaks in the IQ range 65–74 and 125–134. The manual claims that the maximum obtainable raw score is 131 points, but in actuality the maximum obtainable score is 134 points. (Summation Column 6 of Protocol.) This error occurs in Table 2 of the manual and on the test protocol booklet. The norming group is not described. The assumption can be made that the norm data are based upon the scores of 278 totally blind persons ranging in age from 8 to 20 years. However, mental age equivalents are given down to year 5.3. If, indeed, the norms presented are a translation for use with American blind from a Japanese population, the cultural differences are so great as to cast severe doubt upon their usefulness. The validity data given for the O-KTBD is sketchy. Figure 2 of the manual describes a linear relationship between increasing O-KTBD score and increasing CA. This figure is based upon 243 cases with a CA range of 8 through 20 years. The fallacy of using increasing score with increasing age as a validity coefficient is obvious. The curve has the same general shape as a curve for increase in height over the same span of years. The relationship does not justify the statement "This finding does demonstrate a fairly high validity for the O-KTBD." * The reliability data presented on the O-KTBD are scanty. A test, re-test study, based upon 33 totally blind individuals ranging from age 8 to 20 made with a 3½ month interval, reported a reliability coefficient of .846. This is interpreted as an indication "that the O-KTBD as an intelligence test for the blind has a high reliability." The direct statement is made in the manual that the O-KTBD is applicable for use as an intelligence scale with children of normal intelligence and vision between 2 and 6 years. No norms are provided for youngsters in this age group, nor are the instructions clear as to how a child with normal vision is to be tested. The reviewer attempted to test several sighted children blind-folded and found that they were incapable of performing. It was thus determined that normal vision children should be tested in a non-blind-folded condition. Following the instructions of the manual, 26 children obtained from public schools and private kindergarten in Oklahoma ranging in age from 3.5 years to 8.0 years were given both the 1960 Form L-M Stanford Binet and the O-KTBD Intelligence Test. The tests were presented one week apart and were given in counterbalanced order. * The correlation between the IQ's yielded by the scale was .56. Discrepancies in the scores were spectacular. The mean IQ difference was 41.42 points, with a S.D. of the differences of 38.49 points. In 23 of the 26 cases the O-KTBD score was higher than the S.B. score. One 5-year, 10-months male achieved an S.B. IQ of 154 and an O-KTBD IQ of 34! The mean S.B. IQ of the validation group is 112.23 with a S.D. of 18.40. The mean O-KTBD IQ is 153.65 with a standard deviation of 45.78. It is emphatically recommended that the O-KTBD be used with neither blind nor sighted individuals until the severe defects in the test are eliminated.

[415]

★Pacific Design Construction Test. Illiterates and semiliterates in Papua and New Guinea; 1962–68; PDCT; based upon *Kohs' Block-Design Test* and block design subtest of *Wechsler Adult Intelligence Scale;* subtest of *New Guinea Performance Scales;* subtest (with minor modifications) of *Queensland Test* in which it is called *Pattern Matching Test;* individual; 1 form ('68, 13 design cards, 32 titles, and 5 tile trays); manual ('68, 29 pages); record form ('68, 1 page); norms based on natives of Papua and New Guinea; Aus $30 per set of testing materials and 10 record forms; 40¢ per 10 record forms; $1.50 per manual; postpaid within Australia; I. G. Ord; Australian Council for Educational Research. *

REFERENCES

1. ORD, I. G. *Development of a Test of Cognitive Capacity for Indigenes of Papua-New Guinea.* Master's thesis, University of Queensland (Brisbane, Australia), 1959.
2. KEARNEY, GEORGE E. "Cognitive Capacity Among the Orokaiva." *New Guinea Res B* 13:1–25 '66. *
3. ORD, I. G. *Mental Tests for Pre-Literates: Results Mainly From New Guinea Studies.* London: Ginn & Co. Ltd., 1971 (c1970). Pp. xiii, 270. *

[416]

★Pacific Infants Performance Scale. Ages 5.5–8; 1970; PIPS; preschool screening; revision of *Elementary Performance Scale* which was an adaptation of

3 subtests of the *New Guinea Performance Scales;* 4 scores: block tapping, bead threading, design making, total; individual; 1 form; manual (21 pages); reliability data for earlier edition only; no norms, authors recommend use of local norms; Aus $9.45 per set of testing materials; $1.20 per 100 record sheets; postage extra; specimen set not available; [20] minutes; I. G. Ord and J. Schofield; Jacaranda Press Pty Ltd. *

REFERENCE

1. ORD, I. G. *Mental Tests for Pre-Literates: Results Mainly From New Guinea Studies.* London: Ginn & Co. Ltd., 1971 (c1970). Pp. xiii, 270. *

[417]

*Peabody Picture Vocabulary Test. Ages 2.5–18; 1959–70; PPVT; individual; no reading by examinees; Forms A, B, ('59, 154 page picture booklet used with both forms); plastic edition of pictures also available; expanded manual ('65, 51 pages); individual record ('70, 4 pages) for each form; $10 per set of testing materials including 25 individual records for each form ($15 with set of plastic plates); $3 per 50 individual records; postage extra; (10–15) minutes; Lloyd M. Dunn; American Guidance Service, Inc. *

REFERENCES

1–21. See 6:530.
22. PATTERSON, HENRY J. *A Concurrent Validation of the Peabody Picture Vocabulary Test.* Doctor's thesis, Kansas State Teachers College (Emporia, Kan.), 1961.
23. TENHOFF, MARVIN LE ROY. *Conditions Associated With Readiness for School Entrance at Selected Ages.* Doctor's thesis, University of Minnesota (Minneapolis, Minn.), 1962. (*DA* 24:150)
24. GRAVES, GORDON R. *A Study of the Use of the Peabody Picture Vocabulary Test for Identifying Mentally Retarded Children, Using the Wechsler Intelligence Scale for Children as a Criterion.* Master's thesis, Fresno State College (Fresno, Calif.), 1963.
25. KRIPPNER, STANLEY. "Correlates of Reading Improvement." *J Develop Read* 7:29–39 au '63. *
26. ROOD, THOMAS M. *The Effectiveness of the Peabody Vocabulary Pictures Tests: A Study of Reliability and Validity.* Master's thesis, Western State College (Gunnison, Colo.), 1963.
27. WINSCHEL, JAMES FRANCIS. *Performance of Normal and Mentally Retarded Children on Selected Motor and Intellectual Tasks as a Function of Incentive Conditions.* Doctor's thesis, University of Pittsburgh (Pittsburgh, Pa.), 1963. (*DA* 25: 6443)
28. ALLEN, ROBERT M.; HAUPT, THOMAS D.; AND JONES, R. WAYNE. "A Suggested Use and Non-Use for the Peabody Picture Vocabulary Test With the Retarded Child." *Psychol Rep* 15:421–2 O '64. * (*PA* 39:5034)
29. DANFORD, BART HARLAND. *Some Correlates of Two Brief Intelligence Tests Used by Pediatricians.* Doctor's thesis, University of Houston (Houston, Tex.), 1964. (*DA* 26:1772)
30. FLOYD, WILLIAM A. "Aptitude Testing With Mental Patients." *Voc Guid Q* 12:203–6 sp '64. *
31. JACKSON, CECIL LEE. *Factor Structure of the Wechsler Intelligence Scale for Children and Selected Reference Tests at Pre-School Level and After First Grade: A Longitudinal Study.* Doctor's thesis, University of Georgia (Athens, Ga.), 1964. (*DA* 25:6052)
32. MARLEY, ALBERT D. *A Validity Study of the Columbia Mental Maturity Scale and the Peabody Picture Vocabulary Test, Using the Wechsler Intelligence Scale for Children as the Validating Criterion, With a Selected Sample of Educable Mentally Retarded Children.* Doctor's research study No. 1, Colorado State College (Greeley, Colo.), 1964. (*DA* 25:5386)
33. MATTHEWS, CHARLES G., AND MANNING, GEORGE C., JR. "Psychological Test Performances in Three Electroencephalographic Classifications of Mentally Retarded Subjects." *Am J Mental Def* 68:485–92 Ja '64. * (*PA* 39:2526)
34. NATION, JAMES EDWARD. *A Comparative Study of Comprehension and Usage Vocabularies of Normal and Cleft Palate Preschool Children.* Doctor's thesis, University of Wisconsin (Madison, Wis.), 1964. (*DA* 25:3747)
35. RUGG, ROGER H. *A Comparison of the Relative Effectiveness of the Peabody Picture Vocabulary Test and the Ammons Full Range Picture Vocabulary Test With Educable Mentally Retarded Children.* Master's thesis, Sacramento State College (Sacramento, Calif.), 1964.
36. SCHARF, MURRAY PATRICK. *The Performance of Twelve-Year-Old and Thirteen-Year-Old Children on the Peabody Picture Vocabulary Test.* Master's thesis, University of Saskatchewan (Saskatoon, Sask., Canada), 1964.

37. TUTTLE, LESTER EUGENE, JR. *The Comparative Effect on Intelligence Test Scores of Negro and White Children When Certain Verbal and Time Factors Are Varied.* Doctor's thesis, University of Florida (Gainesville, Fla.), 1964. (*DA* 25:7093)

38. BURNETT, ALASTAIR. "Comparison of the PPVT, Wechsler-Bellevue, and Stanford-Binet on Educable Retardates." *Am J Mental Def* 69:712–5 Mr '65. * (*PA* 39:12715)

39. CORWIN, BETTY JANE. "The Influence of Culture and Language on Performance of Individual Ability Tests." *J Sch Psychol* 3:41–7 sp '65. * (*PA* 39:15217)

40. EKLUND, SUSAN, AND SCOTT, MYRTLE. "Effects of Bilingual Instruction on Test Response of Latin American Children." *Psychol Sch* 2:280 Jl '65. *

41. GAGE, GERALD E., AND NAUMANN, THEODOR F. "Correlation of the Peabody Picture Vocabulary Test and the Wechsler Intelligence Scale for Children." *J Ed Res* 58:466–8 Jl–Ag '65. * (*PA* 40:422)

42. HAMMILL, DONALD, AND IRWIN, ORVIS C. "Peabody Picture Vocabulary Test as a Measure of Intelligence for Mentally Subnormal Children." *Training Sch B* 62:126–31 N '65. * (*PA* 40:2135)

43. HEDGER, MABLE F. Chap. 3, "An Analysis of Three Picture Vocabulary Tests for Use With the Deaf," pp. 12–9. In *Research Studies on the Psycholinguistic Behavior of Deaf Children.* Edited by Joseph Rosenstein and Walter H. MacGinitie. CEC Research Monograph, Series B, No. B-2. Washington, D.C.: Council for Exceptional Children, 1965. Pp. v, 40. *

44. HUGHES, ROBERT B., AND LESSLER, KEN. "A Comparison of WISC and Peabody Scores of Negro and White Rural School Children." *Am J Mental Def* 69:877–80 My '65. * (*PA* 39:12289)

45. IRWIN, ORVIS C., AND HAMMILL, DONALD D. "Effect of Type, Extent and Degree of Cerebral Palsy on Three Measures of Language." *Cereb Palsy J* 26:7–9 N–D '65. *

46. IRWIN, ORVIS C., AND HAMMILL, DONALD D. "Regional and Sex Differences in the Language of Cerebral Palsied Children." *Cereb Palsy J* 26:11–2 S–O '65. * (*PA* 40:1899)

47. IVANOFF, JOHN M., AND TEMPERO, HOWARD E. "Effectiveness of the Peabody Picture Vocabulary Test With Seventh-Grade Pupils." *J Ed Res* 58:412–5 My–Je '65. * (*PA* 39:15242)

48. KORST, JOSEPH W. *A Comparison of the Results Obtained for the Peabody Picture Vocabulary Test and the Leiter International Performance Scale With Children Having Functional Articulatory Disorders.* Master's thesis, Wichita State University (Wichita, Kan.), 1965.

49. MEIER, JOHN HENRY. *An Exploratory Factor Analysis of Psychodiagnostic and Case Study Information From Children in Special Education Classes for the Educable Mentally Handicapped.* Doctor's thesis, University of Denver (Denver, Colo.), 1965. (*DA* 26:3153)

50. MUELLER, MAX W. *A Comparison of the Empirical Validity of Six Tests of Ability With Young Educable Retardates.* Institute of Mental Retardation and Intellectual Development, IMRID Behavioral Science Monograph No. 1. Nashville, Tenn.: Peabody College Bookstore, 1965. Pp. vii, 130. *

51. MUELLER, MAX WILLIAM. *A Comparison of the Empirical Validity of Six Tests of Ability With Educable Mental Retardates.* Doctor's thesis, George Peabody College for Teachers (Nashville, Tenn.), 1965. (*DA* 26:6853)

52. SHANE, JAMES F. *Effectiveness of the Peabody Picture Vocabulary Test in Comparison to Wechsler Intelligence Scale for Children and Stanford-Binet Test Scores in Identification of Mentally Retarded and Gifted School Children.* Master's thesis, California State College (Long Beach, Calif.), 1965.

53. STRONG, ROBERT THOMAS, JR. *The Identification of Primary School Age Children With Learning Handicaps Associated With Minimal Brain Disorder.* Doctor's thesis, University of Utah (Salt Lake City, Utah), 1965. (*DA* 26:1489)

54. THRONE, FRANCES M.; KASPAR, JOSEPH C.; AND SCHULMAN, JEROME L. "The Peabody Picture Vocabulary Test in Comparison With Other Intelligence Tests and an Achievement Test in a Group of Mentally Retarded Boys." *Ed & Psychol Meas* 25:589–95 su '65. * (*PA* 39:16072)

55. CHILDERS, PERRY R. "Concurrent Validity of a Group Administered Peabody Picture Vocabulary Test." *J Ed Res* 60:92–3 O '66. *

56. EMERICK, LONNIE L. *An Evaluation of Three Psychological Variables in Tonic and Clonic Stutterers and in Non-stutterers.* Doctor's thesis, Michigan State University (East Lansing, Mich.), 1966. (*DA* 28:317A)

57. FARGO, GEORGE; CROWELL, DORIS; AND NOYES, MARY. "Screening for Learning Problems: A New Use for Educational Television." *Audio Vis Instr* 11:762+ N '66. *

58. HAMMILL, DONALD D., AND IRWIN, ORVIS C. "Relations Among Measures of Language of Cerebral Palsied and of Mentally Retarded Children." *Cereb Palsy J* 27:8–9 Ja–F '66. * (*PA* 40:5860)

59. IRWIN, ORVIS C. "A Comparison of the Vocabulary of Use and of Understanding by Mentally Retarded Children." *Cereb Palsy J* 27:8–10 N–D '66. * (*PA* 41:3239)

60. IRWIN, ORVIS C. "A Comparison of the Vocabulary of Use and of Understanding of Cerebral Palsied Children." *Cereb Palsy J* 27:7–11 My–Je '66. * (*PA* 40:10390)

61. IRWIN, ORVIS C. "A Language Test for Use With Cerebral Palsied Children." *Cereb Palsy J* 27:6–8 S–O '66. * (*PA* 41:1816)

62. IRWIN, ORVIS C. "The Relation of Vocabularies of Use and Understanding by Cerebral Palsied Children to Several Variables." *Cereb Palsy J* 27:3–4 Jl–Ag '66. * (*PA* 41:1818)

63. IRWIN, ORVIS C. "Vocabulary Ability of Two Samples of Cerebral Palsied Children." *Cereb Palsy J* 27:14–5 My–Je '66. *

64. IRWIN, ORVIS C., AND HAMMILL, DONALD D. "Effect of Type of Mental Retardation on Three Language Measures." *Cereb Palsy J* 27:9–10 Ja–F '66. * (*PA* 40:5881)

65. KAHN, HARRIS. "Evidence for Long-Term Reliability of the PPVT With Adolescent and Young Adult Retardates." *Am J Mental Def* 70:895–8 My '66. * (*PA* 40:9160)

66. KICKLIGHTER, RICHARD M. "Correlation of Peabody Picture Vocabulary Test Scores and Stanford-Binet Intelligence Scale, Form L-M Scores in an Educable Mentally Retarded Population." Abstract. *J Sch Psychol* 5:75–6 au '66. *

67. KILBURN, KENT L.; SANDERSON, ROBERT E.; AND MELTON, KYLE. "Relation of the Raven Coloured Progressive Matrices to Two Measures of Verbal Ability in a Sample of Mildly Retarded Hospital Patients." *Psychol Rep* 19:731–4 D '66. * (*PA* 41:4915)

68. KORST, JOSEPH W. "A Comparison of Results From the Peabody Vocabulary Test and Leiter International Performance Scale With Children Having Functional Articulatory Disorders." *Cereb Palsy J* 27:3–5 Ja–F '66. * (*PA* 40:5851)

69. LINDSEY, JAMES MORRISON. *The Factorial Organization of Intelligence in Children as Related to the Variables of Age, Sex and Subculture.* Doctor's thesis, University of Georgia (Athens, Ga.), 1966. (*DA* 27:3664B)

70. MAYANS, ANNA E. *Early Differential Prediction of First Grade Reading Achievement Among Three Culturally Different Kindergarten Groups.* Doctor's thesis, University of Cincinnati (Cincinnati, Ohio), 1966. (*DA* 27:2891A)

71. RICE, DON MARTIN, SR. *The Effects of Visual Perception Techniques With Cerebral Palsied Individuals Functioning at a Mentally Retarded Level.* Doctor's thesis, Colorado State College (Greeley, Colo.), 1966. (*DA* 27:3732A)

72. ROSENBERG, LEON A., AND STROUD, MICHAEL. "Limitations of Brief Intelligence Testing With Young Children." *Psychol Rep* 19:721–2 D '66. * (*PA* 41:4999)

73. SHAW, DALE J.; MATTHEWS, CHARLES G.; AND KLØVE, HALLGRIM. "The Equivalence of WISC and PPVT IQs." *Am J Mental Def* 70:601–4 Ja '66. * (*PA* 40:5454)

74. SHIPE, DOROTHY; CROMWELL, RUE L.; AND DUNN, LLOYD M. "Responses of Emotionally Disturbed and Nondisturbed Retardates to PPVT Items of Human Versus Nonhuman Content." *J Consult Psychol* 30:439–43 O '66. * (*PA* 40:13457)

75. SILBERBERG, NORMAN E., AND FELDT, LEONARD S. "The Peabody Picture Vocabulary Test as an IQ Screening Technique for Primary Grade Referral Cases." *J Sch Psychol* 5:21–30 au '66. * (*PA* 41:3345)

76. TAUBER, ROSALYN. "Identification of Potential Learning Disabilities." *Acad Ther Q* 2:116–9+ w '66–67. * (*PA* 41:5004)

77. TILLINGHAST, B. S., JR., AND RENZULLI, JOSEPH S. "Reliability of the Peabody Picture Vocabulary Test: A Preliminary Report." *Ed R* 4:1–6 '66. *

78. TUTTLE, LESTER EUGENE, JR. "The Comparative Effect on Intelligence Test Scores of Negro and Caucasian Children When Certain Verbal and Time Factors Are Varied by Use of the WISC, PPVT and CMMS." *Fla J Ed Res* 8:49–61 Ja '66. *

79. WARD, WILLIAM CORNELIUS, JR. *Creativity and Impulsivity in Kindergarten Children.* Doctor's thesis, Duke University (Durham, N.C.), 1966. (*DA* 27:2127B)

80. WHIPPLE, CLIFFORD I., AND MAIER, LOUISE JO. "Perceptual-Motor Maturation and Language Development in Young Children." *Percept & Motor Skills* 23:1208 D '66. * (*PA* 41:5794)

81. ALLERHAND, MELVIN E. "Effectiveness of Parents of Head Start Children as Administrators of Psychological Tests." *J Consult Psychol* 31:286–90 Je '67. * (*PA* 41:10474)

82. BASHAW, W. L., AND AYERS, JERRY B. "An Evaluation of the Norms and Reliability of the PPVT for Pre-School Subjects." *Ed & Psychol Meas* 27:1069–75 w '67. * (*PA* 42:9416)

83. BIGELOW, GORDON SHOEMAKER. *Global Versus Analytical Cognitive Style in Children as a Function of Age, Sex, and Intelligence.* Doctor's thesis, Brigham Young University (Provo, Utah), 1967. (*DA* 28:958A)

84. BROMWICH, ROSE MEYER. *Some Correlates of Stimulus-Bound Versus Stimulus-Free Verbal Responses to Pictures by Young Negro Boys.* Doctor's thesis, University of California (Los Angeles, Calif.), 1967. (*DA* 28:1290A)

85. BROWN, LOUIS F., AND RICE, JAMES A. "The Peabody Picture Vocabulary Test: Validity for EMRs." *Am J Mental Def* 71:901–3 My '67. * (*PA* 41:12378)

86. CARR, DONALD L.; BROWN, LOUIS F.; AND RICE, JAMES A. "The PPVT in the Assessment of Language Deficits." *Am J Mental Def* 71:937–40 My '67. * (*PA* 41:11915)

87. CORWIN, BETTY JANE. "The Relationship Between Read-

ing Achievement and Performance on Individual Ability Tests." Abstract. *J Sch Psychol* 5:156–7 w '67. * (*PA* 41:9386)

88. DATTA, LOIS-ELLIN. "Draw-A-Person Test as a Measure of Intelligence in Preschool Children From Very Low Income Families." *J Consult Psychol* 31:626–30 D '67. * (*PA* 42:2561)

89. DOCKRELL, W. B., AND BROSSEAU, J. F. "The Correlates of Second Language Learning by Young Children." *Alberta J Ed Res* 13:295–8 D '67. * (*PA* 44:3452)

90. FARGO, GEORGE A.; CROWELL, DORIS C.; NOYES, MARY H.; FUCHIGAMI, ROBERT Y.; GORDON, JOHN M.; AND DUNN-RANKIN, PETER. "Comparability of Group Television and Individual Administration of the Peabody Picture Vocabulary Test: Implications for Screening." *J Ed Psychol* 58:137–40 Je '67. * (*PA* 41:10445)

91. FULTON, ROBERT T. "Task Adaptation and Word Familiarity of W-22 Discrimination Lists With Retarded Children." *J Auditory Res* 7:353–8 O '67. *

92. GILMORE, STUART I., AND FAMILANT, ROSALEE P. "Race, Residence, Socioeconomic Status, and Responses to Articulation Test Stimuli." *Southern Speech J* 33:44–9 f '67. *

93. GRAUBARD, PAUL S. "The Use of the Peabody Picture Vocabulary Test in the Prediction and Assessment of Reading Disability in Disturbed Children." *J Ed Res* 61:3–5 S '67. *

94. GREEMORE, RUTH. *A Comparative Study on the Abstract and the Concrete Method of Teaching New Words to Mentally Retarded Children, Using the Peabody Picture Vocabulary Tests as an Instructional Tool.* Master's thesis, University of Kansas (Lawrence, Kan.), 1967.

95. HALE, JAMES ROY. *Peabody Picture Vocabulary Test: A Validity Study With Educable Mentally Retarded Children.* Master's thesis, University of Texas (Austin, Tex.), 1967.

96. HAMMILL, DONALD D., AND IRWIN, ORVIS C. "Factors Affecting Equivalency of PPVT and RSB When Used With Mentally Subnormal Children." *Am J Mental Def* 71:793–6 Mr '67. * (*PA* 41:8881)

97. HOWARD, JOYCE L., AND PLANT, WALTER T. "Psychometric Evaluation of an Operation Headstart Program." *J Genetic Psychol* 111:281–8 D '67. * (*PA* 42:6013)

98. IRWIN, ORVIS C. "Replications and Reliabilities of Four Speech Tests." *Cereb Palsy J* 28:5–6 My–Je '67. *

99. IRWIN, ORVIS C., AND KORST, JOSEPH W. "Comparison of Scores of Cerebral Palsied, Subnormal and Normal Children on Five Speech Tests." *Cereb Palsy J* 28:10–1 My–Je '67. *

100. IRWIN, ORVIS C., AND KORST, JOSEPH W. "Correlations Among Five Speech Tests and the WISC Verbal Scale." *Cereb Palsy J* 28:9–11 S–O '67. * (*PA* 42:3201)

101. IRWIN, ORVIS C., AND KORST, JOSEPH W. "Summary of Reliability Coefficients of Six Speech Tests for Use With Handicapped Children." *Cereb Palsy J* 28:6–7 Jl–Ag '67. *

102. KOH, TONG-HE, AND MADOW, ARNOLD A. "Relationship Between PPVT and Stanford-Binet Performance in Institutionalized Retardates." *Am J Mental Def* 72:108–13 Jl '67. * (*PA* 41:15728)

103. LAVITT, JERRY A. *A Comparative Evaluation of the Peabody Picture Vocabulary Test as a Measure of Ability for Children of Differing Reading Proficiency Levels.* Doctor's thesis, Oklahoma State University (Stillwater, Okla.), 1967. (*DA* 28:4877A)

104. LEPPKE, RONALD DEAN. *Perceptual Approaches for Disadvantaged Anglo- and Mexican-American Students.* Doctor's thesis, University of the Pacific (Stockton, Calif.), 1967. (*DA* 28:1302A)

105. LLOYD, LYLE L.; ROLLAND, JOHN C.; AND McMANIS, DONALD L. "Performance of Hearing Impaired and Normal Hearing Retardates on Selected Language Measures." *Am J Mental Def* 71:904–8 My '67. * (*PA* 41:12408)

106. MILGRAM, NORMAN A. "A Note on the PPVT in Mental Retardates." *Am J Mental Def* 72:496–7 N '67. * (*PA* 42:7658) See 147 for discussion of article.

107. MILGRAM, NORMAN A., AND OZER, MARK N. "Peabody Picture Vocabulary Test Scores of Preschool Children." *Psychol Rep* 20:779–84 Je '67. * (*PA* 41:13597)

108. NELSON, PIKE CORNELIUS. *A Statistical Analysis of San Diego Summer Head Start Children on Seven Variables.* Doctor's thesis, Colorado State College (Greeley, Colo.), 1967. (*DA* 28:3463B)

109. OSBORNE, R. T.; ANDERSON, HARRY E., JR.; AND BASHAW, W. L. "The Stability of the WISC Factor Structure at Three Age Levels." *Multiv Behav Res* 2:443–51 O '67. * (*PA* 42:6388)

110. PANTHER, EDWARD E. "Prediction of First-Grade Reading Achievement." *El Sch J* 68:44–8 O '67. *

111. RICE, JAMES A., AND BROWN, LOUIS F. "Validity of the Peabody Picture Vocabulary Test in a Sample of Low IQ Children." *Am J Mental Def* 71:602–3 Ja '67. * (*PA* 41:5960)

112. SILVERSTEIN, A. B., AND HILL, THOMAS VERNON. "Comparability of Three Picture Vocabulary Tests With Retarded School Children." *Training Sch B* 64:58–61 Ag '67. * (*PA* 42:1057)

113. SMITH, PETER BARKER, JR. *A Description of the Language Abilities of Institutionalized Phenylketonuric Individuals in the States of Washington, Oregon, Idaho, and Montana.*

Doctor's thesis, University of Washington (Seattle, Wash.), 1967. (*DA* 28:3917B)

114. SYDIAHA, DANIEL. "Prediction of WAIS IQ for Psychiatric Patients Using the Ammons' FRPV and Raven's Progressive Matrices." *Psychol Rep* 20:823–6 Je '67. * (*PA* 41:13602)

115. WEAVER, ANN SULLIVAN. *The Prediction of First Grade Reading Achievement in Culturally Disadvantaged Children.* Doctor's thesis, George Peabody College for Teachers (Nashville, Tenn.), 1967. (*DA* 28:3789A)

116. WELLS, DONALD G., AND PEDRINI, DUILIO T. "Relationships Between the S-B L-M, G-H, and PPVT With Institutionalized Retardates." *Am J Mental Def* 72:412–5 N '67. * (*PA* 42:7680)

117. ANDERSON, BEATRICE BETTY. *Evaluation of a Checklist to Measure Specific Reading Readiness Factors in Beginning First Grade Pupils.* Doctor's thesis, University of Maryland (College Park, Md.), 1968. (*DAI* 30:480A)

118. ANDERSON, DARRELL E., AND FLAX, MORTON L. "A Comparison of the Peabody Picture Vocabulary Test With the Wechsler Intelligence Scale for Children." *J Ed Res* 62:114–6 N '68. *

119. ANDO, KYOKO. "A Comparative Study of Peabody Picture Vocabulary Test and Wechsler Intelligence Scale for Children With a Group of Cerebral Palsied Children." *Cereb Palsy J* 29:7–9 My–Je '68. * (*PA* 42:15909)

120. BACH, LLOYD CARL. *A Comparison of Selected Psychological Tests Used With Trainable Mentally Retarded Children.* Doctor's thesis, University of South Dakota (Vermillion, S.D.), 1968. (*DA* 29:2990A)

121. BENGER, KATHLYN. "The Relationships of Perception, Personality, Intelligence, and Grade One Reading Achievement." *Proc Ann Conv Int Read Assn* 12(4):112–23 '68. *

122. BONNER, MARY WINSTEAD. *A Comparative Study of the Performance of Negro Seniors of Oklahoma City High Schools on the Wechsler Adult Intelligence Scale and the Peabody Picture Vocabulary Test.* Doctor's thesis, Oklahoma State University (Stillwater, Okla.), 1968. (*DAI* 30:921A)

123. BOROSAGE, VERA. *A Study of the Effect of Nursery School Experience on Intellectual Performance at Two Socio-Economic Levels.* Doctor's thesis, Michigan State University (East Lansing, Mich.), 1968. (*DA* 29:2993A)

124. CARTWRIGHT, G. PHILLIP. "A Note on the Use of the Peabody Picture Vocabulary Test With Disadvantaged Children." *J Ed Res* 61:285 F '68. *

125. COYLE, F. A., JR.; DANS, CLARICE; AND CORK, ELIZABETH. "Form Equivalence of the PPVT on Children in Speech Therapy." *Psychol Rep* 23:1002 D '68. * (*PA* 43:9037)

126. DEICH, RUTH F. "Correlations Between the PPVT and the CTMM." *Psychol Rep* 22:856 Je '68. * (*PA* 42:12982)

127. DiLORENZO, LOUIS T. "Effects of Year-Long Prekindergarten Programs on Intelligence and Language of Educationally Disadvantaged Children." *J Exp Ed* 36:36–42 sp '68. *

128. DiLORENZO, LOUIS T., AND BRADY, JAMES J. "Use of the Peabody Picture Vocabulary Test With Preschool Children." *Psychol Rep* 22:247–51 F '68. * (*PA* 42:10612)

129. ELKIN, LORNE. "Predicting Performance of the Mentally Retarded on Sheltered Workshop and Non-Institutional Jobs." *Am J Mental Def* 72:533–9 Ja '68. * (*PA* 42:7638)

130. ERNHART, CLAIRE B. "The Peabody Picture Vocabulary Test: Automated Application in a Statewide Psychiatric System." *Psychiatric Q Sup* 42(2):317–20 '68. * (*PA* 46:3313)

131. GARDNER, ANN M., AND BIRNBRAUER, J. S. "A Note on Possible Form Differences in the Peabody Picture Vocabulary Test." *Am J Mental Def* 73:86–7 Jl '68. * (*PA* 42:19184)

132. HAMMILL, DONALD D.; MYERS, PATRICIA I.; AND IRWIN, ORVIS C. "Certain Speech and Linguistic Abilities in Subclasses of Cerebral Palsy." *Percept & Motor Skills* 26:511–4 Ap '68. * (*PA* 42:12630)

133. HAYWOOD, H. CARL, AND HEAL, LAIRD W. "Retention of Learned Visual Associations as a Function of IQ and Learning Levels." *Am J Mental Def* 72:828–38 My '68. * (*PA* 42:14404)

134. JOHNSON, CAROLYNE MARGARET. *The Creative Thinking, Verbal Intelligence, and Creative Writing Ability of Young Gifted Children.* Doctor's thesis, Case Western Reserve University (Cleveland, Ohio), 1968. (*DA* 29:4187A)

135. KAPLAN, BURT EDWARD. *Psychophysiological and Cognitive Development in Children.* Doctor's thesis, Pennsylvania State University (University Park, Pa.), 1968. (*DA* 29:1859B)

136. KAUFMAN, HARVEY I., AND IVANOFF, JOHN M. "Evaluating the Mentally Retarded With the Peabody Picture Vocabulary Test." *Am J Mental Def* 73:396–8 N '68. * (*PA* 43:8590)

137. McARTHUR, CHARLES R., AND WAKEFIELD, HOMER E. "Validation of the PPVT With the Stanford-Binet-LM and the WISC on Educable Mental Retardates." *Am J Mental Def* 73:465–7 N '68. * (*PA* 43:8596)

138. McCLELLAN, DORINDA ANN. *Factors Which Are Predictive of Reading Success of Low-Socio-Economic Children in Selected First Grades.* Doctor's thesis, Oklahoma State University (Stillwater, Okla.), 1968. (*DAI* 30:933A)

139. MALERSTEIN, A. J., AND BELDEN, E. "WAIS, SILS,

and PPVT in Korsakoff's Syndrome." *Arch Gen Psychiatry* 19:743–50 D '68. * (*PA* 43:8472)

140. MAUSER, AUGUST JOHN. *First Grade Children's Comprehension of Oral Language in Sentences and Success in Beginning Reading Instruction.* Doctor's thesis, Indiana University (Bloomington, Ind.), 1968. (*DAI* 30:70A)

141. MIEZITIS, SOLVEIGA AUSMA. *An Exploratory Study of Divergent Production in Preschoolers.* Doctor's thesis, University of Toronto (Toronto, Ont., Canada), 1968. (*DAI* 30:589A)

142. MUELLER, MAX W. "Validity of Six Tests of Ability With Educable Mental Retardates." *J Sch Psychol* 6:136–46 w '68. * (*PA* 42:11152)

143. NESBITT, MARY CATHERINE. *Auding Achievement of First Grade Pupils Related to Selected Pupil Characteristics.* Doctor's thesis, University of Georgia (Athens, Ga.), 1968. (*DA* 29:2445A)

144. PLANT, WALTER T., AND SOUTHERN, MARA L. "First Grade Reading Achievement Predicted From WPPSI and Other Scores Obtained 18 Months Earlier." Abstract. *Proc 76th Ann Conv Am Psychol Assn* 3:593–4 '68. *

145. RAWL, MIRIAM FREEMAN. *A Study of the Relationship of Verbal Ability and Vocalization to Conceptual-Motor Tasks in Disadvantaged First-Grade Children.* Doctor's thesis, University of South Carolina (Columbia, S.C.), 1968. (*DAI* 30:1028A)

146. RENZULLI, JOSEPH S., AND PAULUS, DIETER H. "An Investigation of the Validity of the Order of Items on the Peabody Picture Vocabulary Test." Abstract. *AERA Paper Abstr* 1968:256–7 '68. *

147. RICE, JAMES A. "A Note on the Milgram Article." [see *106*] Reply by Norman A. Milgram. Letters. *Am J Mental Def* 73:520–1 N '68. *

148. RIEBER, MORTON, AND WOMACK, MARCELEETE. "The Intelligence of Preschool Children as Related to Ethnic and Demographic Variables." *Excep Children* 34:609–14 Ap '68. * (*PA* 42:17001)

149. STARK, JOEL; COHEN, SYLVIA; AND EISENSON, JON. "Performances of Aphasic Children on the PPVT and Auditory Decoding Tests." *J Spec Ed* 2:435–7 su–f '68. * (*PA* 43:10213)

150. STERNE, DAVID M. "Validity of the PPVT, Knox Cubes and ITPA With Aphasic Adults." Abstract. *Psychol Rep* 22:1014 Je '68. * (*PA* 42:12997)

151. TILLINGHAST, B. S., JR., AND RENZULLI, JOSEPH S. "Reliability of a Group Form of the Peabody Picture Vocabulary Test." *J Ed Res* 61:311–4 Mr '68. *

152. ZUNICH, M., AND TOLLEY, J. "Performance on the Peabody Picture Vocabulary Test and Stanford-Binet by Institutionalized Mentally Retarded Children." *Psychol Rep* 22:1212 Je '68. * (*PA* 42:19210)

153. ABRAMSON, THEODORE. "The Influence of Examiner Race on First-Grade and Kindergarten Subjects' Peabody Picture Vocabulary Test Scores." *J Ed Meas* 6(4):241–6 w '69. * (*PA* 44:17313)

154. ALLEN, ROBERT M. "The Developmental Test of Visual Perception and the Bender Gestalt Test Achievement of Educable Mental Retardate." *Training Sch B* 66(2):80–5 Ag '69. * (*PA* 44:4029)

155. ALLEN, ROBERT M. "The Mental Age—Visual Perception Issue Assessed." *Excep Children* 35(9):748–9 My '69. * (*PA* 44:19186)

156. ALLEN, ROBERT M., AND WALLACH, EDWARD S. "Word Recognition and Definition by Educable Retardates." *Am J Mental Def* 73(6):883–5 My '69. * (*PA* 43:13233)

157. ASBURY, CHARLES ALEXANDER. *Factors Associated With Discrepant Achievement in Rural Economically Deprived White and Negro First Graders.* Doctor's thesis, University of North Carolina (Chapel Hill, N.C.), 1969. (*DAI* 31:208A)

158. BAUMANN, KAREN SUZANN. *The Effects of an Educational Program on the Test Performance of Children With Psychoneurological Learning Disabilities.* Doctor's thesis, Oklahoma State University (Stillwater, Okla.), 1969. (*DAI* 31:3865A)

159. BECKER, JOHN T. *The Effect of Group Administration of Selected Individual Tests of Language, Visual Perception, and Auditory Perception to Kindergarten, First-, Second-, and Third-Grade Children.* Doctor's thesis, Catholic University of America (Washington, D.C.), 1969. (*DAI* 30:2367A)

160. BLUE, C. MILTON. "PPVT Temporal Stability and Alternate Form Reliability With the Trainable Mentally Retarded." *Am J Mental Def* 73(5):745–8 Mr '69. * (*PA* 43:10218)

161. COCHRAN, MALCOLM L., AND PEDRINI, DUILIO T. "The Concurrent Validity of the 1965 WRAT With Adult Retardates." *Am J Mental Def* 73(4):654–6 Ja '69. * (*PA* 43:8574)

162. CRAWFORD, VEDA B. *Relationships of Scores on the Wechsler Preschool and Primary Scale of Intelligence, the Stanford-Binet Intelligence Scale, Form LM, and the Peabody Picture Vocabulary Test, Form A.* Master's thesis, Bowling Green State University (Bowling Green, Ohio), 1969.

163. CURRY, DAL ROY. *The Effect of Two Types of Auditory Discrimination Training on Language Performance and Acquisition in a Culturally Deprived Preschool Population.*

Doctor's thesis, University of Kansas (Lawrence, Kan.), 1969. (*DAI* 30:5281A)

164. DiLORENZO, LOUIS T., AND BRADY, JAMES J. "Use of the Peabody Picture Vocabulary Test." *Training Sch B* 65(4):117–21 F '69. * (*PA* 44:4169)

165. DUNDORE, JAMES M., JR. *A Study of the Relationship Between Scores Earned on the Columbia Mental Maturity Scale and Peabody Picture Vocabulary Test and School Achievement of Culturally Disadvantaged Negro Children.* Master's thesis, Mississippi State University (State College, Miss.), 1969.

166. ELLIOTT, RAYMOND N., JR. "Comparative Study of the Pictorial Test of Intelligence and the Peabody Picture Vocabulary Test." *Psychol Rep* 25(2):528–30 O '69. * (*PA* 44:5541)

167. ENGLISH, RICHARD A., AND KIDDER, JACK W. "Note on Relationships Among Mental Ability Scores, Teacher's Rankings, and Rate of Acquisition for Four-Year-Old Kindergarteners." *Psychol Rep* 24(2):554 Ap '69. * (*PA* 43:15568)

168. GROPPER, ROBERT L. *Comprehension of Narrative Passages by Fourth-Grade Children as a Function of Listening Rate and Eleven Predictor Variables.* Doctor's thesis, George Peabody College for Teachers (Nashville, Tenn.), 1969. (*DAI* 30:4827A)

169. HALL, JOSEPH CLARENCE. *A Comparative Study of Selected Measures of Intelligence as Predictors of First-Grade Reading Achievement in a Culturally Disadvantaged Population.* Doctor's thesis, Temple University (Philadelphia, Pa.), 1969. (*DAI* 31:1074A)

170. KEIM, RICHARD PAUL. *Visual-Motor Training, Readiness, and Intelligence of Kindergarten Children.* Doctor's thesis, Temple University (Philadelphia, Pa.), 1969. (*DAI* 31:1076A)

171. KIRK, GIRVIN EATON. *The Performance of Advantaged and Disadvantaged Preschool Children on Tests of Picture-Phonemic Discrimination and Picture-Word Recognition Skills.* Doctor's thesis, University of Illinois (Urbana, Ill.), 1969. (*DAI* 30:930A)

172. KLAPPER, ZELDA S., AND BIRCH, HERBERT G. "Perceptual and Action Equivalence to Objects and Photographs in Children." *Percept & Motor Skills* 29(3):763–71 D '69. *

173. McCLARY, GEORGE OSCAR. *Cognitive and Affective Responses by Negro and White Children to Pictorial Stimuli.* Doctor's thesis, George Washington University (Washington, D.C.), 1969. (*DAI* 30:1901B)

174. MAZER, MARJORIE. *The Pre-School Inventory and the Peabody Picture Vocabulary Test With Preschool Children.* Master's thesis, Pennsylvania State University (University Park, Pa.), 1969.

175. MESSER, MICHAEL E., AND ALLEN, ROBERT M. "Verbal Recognition and Non-Verbal Reasoning of Retardates." *Percept & Motor Skills* 28(1):334 F '69. * (*PA* 43:11764)

176. MINSKY, RAPHAEL. *An Investigation Into Children's Conceptualization of Proportionality as Expressed in Their Drawings of the Male Human Figure.* Doctor's thesis, University of Maryland (College Park, Md.), 1969. (*DAI* 31:1082A)

177. MUELLER, MAX W. "Prediction of Achievement of Educable Mentally Retarded Children." *Am J Mental Def* 73(4):590–6 Ja '69. * (*PA* 43:8703)

178. NELSON, C. MICHAEL, AND HUDSON, FLOYD G. "Predicting the Reading Achievement of Junior High School EMR Children." *Am J Mental Def* 74(3):415–20 N '69. * (*PA* 44:3428)

179. NICHOLSON, CHARLES L. "The Use of Four Screening Instruments." *Ann Inter Conf Assn Children Learn Dis* 6:101–7 '69. *

180. OMER, JANE L. "Investigation of Speech Discrimination Ability of Children Selected for Learning Disability." *Kan Studies Ed* 19(3):25–8 Ag '69. *

181. RENZULLI, JOSEPH S., AND PAULUS, DIETER H. "A Cross-Validation Study of the Item Ordering of the Peabody Picture Vocabulary Test." *J Ed Meas* 6(1):15–20 sp '69. * (*PA* 44:15308)

182. SABATINO, DAVID A., AND BECKER, JOHN T. "Relations Among Five Basic Tests of Behavior." *Percept & Motor Skills* 29(2):487–90 O '69. * (*PA* 44:3428)

183. SHIPE, DOROTHY, AND MIEZITIS, SOLVEIGA. "A Pilot Study in the Diagnosis and Remediation of Special Learning Disabilities in Preschool Children." *J Learn Dis* 2(11):579–92 N '69. * (*PA* 46:7521)

184. SHOTWELL, ANNA M.; O'CONNOR, GAIL; GABET, YVONNE; AND DINGMAN, HARVEY F. "Relation of the Peabody Picture Vocabulary Test IQ to the Stanford-Binet IQ." *Am J Mental Def* 74(1):39–42 Jl '69. * (*PA* 43:17485)

185. STRANDBERG, T. E.; GRIFFITH, J.; AND MINER, L. "Child Language and Screening Intelligence." *J Commun Disorders* 2(3):268–72 Ag '69. * (*PA* 44:3464)

186. TEASDALE, G. R. "Validity of the PPVT as a Test of Language Ability With Lower SES Children." *Psychol Rep* 25(3):746 D '69. * (*PA* 44:17787)

187. WALKER, AUDREY JEAN MASSEY. *A Descriptive Study of the Oral Language Progress of Selected Disadvantaged and Advantaged Kindergarten Children.* Doctor's thesis, University of Georgia (Athens, Ga.), 1969. (*DAI* 30:5354A)

188. WILLIAMS, TANNIS M., AND FLEMING, JACK W. "Methodological Study of the Relationship Between Associative Fluency and Intelligence." *Develop Psychol* 1(2):155–62 Mr '69. * (*PA* 43:8146)

189. YEN, SHERMAN M. Y. *A Comparative Study of Test Variability With Peabody Picture Vocabulary Test, Goodenough's Draw-A-Man Test, and Stanford-Binet Intelligence Scale as Intellectual Measurement With a Group of Urban Low Socio-Economic Status Pre-School Pupils.* Doctor's thesis, Catholic University of America (Washington, D.C.), 1969. (*DAI* 30:2625A)

190. ALLEN, ROBERT M. "The PPVT Is Not a Test of Visual Perceptual Maturation." *Percept & Motor Skills* 31(1): 262 Ag '70. * (*PA* 45:3969)

191. ANASTASIOW, NICHOLAS J.; SIBLEY, SALLY A.; LEONHARDT, TERESA M.; AND BORICH, GARY D. "A Comparison of Guided Discovery, Discovery and Didactic Teaching of Math to Kindergarten Poverty Children." *Am Ed Res J* 7(4):493–510 N '70. *

192. ANDERSON, B. BETTY. "Classroom Diagnosis of Reading Readiness Factors." *J Learn Dis* 3(5):260–3 My '70. *

193. ARCHER, LORENE STURDIVANT. *The Effect of an Eight Weeks Summer Program on Preschool Readiness in Longview Public Schools.* Doctor's thesis, East Texas State University (Commerce, Tex.), 1970. (*DAI* 31:1987A)

194. BECK, RAY, AND TALKINGTON, LARRY W. "Frostig Training With Headstart Children." *Percept & Motor Skills* 30(2):521–2 Ap '70. * (*PA* 46:7765)

195. BONNER, MARY W., AND BELDEN, BERNARD R. "A Comparative Study of the Performance of Negro Seniors of Oklahoma City High Schools on the Wechsler Adult Intelligence Scale and the Peabody Picture Vocabulary Test." *J Negro Ed* 39(4):354–8 f '70. * (*PA* 45:10662)

196. BRUININKS, ROBERT H., AND FELDMAN, DAVID H. "Creativity, Intelligence, and Achievement Among Disadvantaged Children." *Psychol Sch* 7(3):260–4 Jl '70. * (*PA* 45:5015)

197. BRUININKS, ROBERT H., AND LUCKER, WILLIAM G. "Change and Stability in Correlations Between Intelligence and Reading Test Scores Among Disadvantaged Children." *J Read Behav* 2(4):295–305 f '70. * (*PA* 46:5700)

198. CALLAWAY, BYRON. "Factors Related to Reading of Children Referred to a University Reading Clinic," pp. 61–6. In *Reading Difficulties: Diagnosis, Correction, and Remediation.* Edited by William K. Durr. Newark, Del.: International Reading Association, 1970. Pp. vii, 276. *

199. COCHRAN, MALCOLM L. "A Profile of Psychological Test Scores for Retarded Adults." *Am J Mental Def* 74(4): 582–4 Ja '70. * (*PA* 44:11052)

200. COSTELLO, JOAN. "Effects of Pretesting and Examiner Characteristics on Test Performance of Young Disadvantaged Children." Abstract. *Proc 78th Ann Conv Am Psychol Assn* 5(1):309–10 '70. * (*PA* 44:18295)

201. CUNDICK, BERT P. "Measures of Intelligence on Southwest Indian Students." *J Social Psychol* 81(2):151–6 Ag '70. * (*PA* 44:20655)

202. ERNHART, CLAIRE B. "The Correlation of Peabody Picture Vocabulary and Wechsler Adult Intelligence Scale Scores for Adult Psychiatric Patients." *J Clin Psychol* 26(4):470–1 O '70. * (*PA* 45:4528)

203. FITZGERALD, BERNARD J.; PASEWARK, RICHARD A.; AND GLOECKLER, TED. "Use of the Peabody Picture Vocabulary Test With the Educationally Handicapped." *J Sch Psychol* 8(4): 296–300 '70. * (*PA* 46:1800)

204. GALLI, ANTHONY P. *Reliability of Measures From the Peabody Picture Vocabulary Test and Their Relation to Articulation.* Master's thesis, Sacramento State College (Sacramento, Calif.), 1970.

205. GARBER, MALCOLM, AND WARE, W. B. "Relationship Between Measures of Home Environment and Intelligence Scores." Abstract. *Proc 78th Ann Conv Am Psychol Assn* 5(2):64–8 '70. * (*PA* 44:18353)

206. GOLDSTEIN, LEO S.; COLLER, ALAN R.; DILL, JOHN; AND TILIS, HOWARD S. "The Effect of a Special Curriculum for Disadvantaged Children on Test-Retest Reliabilities of Three Standardized Instruments." *J Ed Meas* 7(3):171–4 f '70. * (*PA* 45:4917)

207. GOODGLASS, HAROLD; GLEASON, JEAN BERKO; AND HYDE, MARY R. "Some Dimensions of Auditory Language Comprehension in Aphasia." *J Speech & Hearing Res* 13(3):595–606 S '70. *

208. GROSSMAN, MARVIN. "Perceptual Style, Creativity, and Various Drawing Abilities." *Studies Art Ed* 11(2):51–4 w '70. *

209. HUBSCHMAN, EVA; POLIZZOTTO, EMILIA ANN; AND KALISKI, MYRA S. "Performance of Institutionalized Retardates on the PPVT and Two Editions of the ITPA." *Am J Mental Def* 74(4):579–80 Ja '70. * (*PA* 44:11063)

210. JOSELSON, MAURICE L. *The Role of Language Skills Within the Perspective of Other Psychosocial Factors in a Select Prison Population.* Doctor's thesis, University of Florida (Gainesville, Fla.), 1970. (*DAI* 31:4385B)

211. KAPLAN, BURT E. "Psychophysiological and Cognitive Development in Children: The Relationship of Skin Conductance and Heart Rate to Word Associations and Task Requirements." *Psychophysiol* 7(1):18–26 Jl '70. * (*PA* 45:6014)

212. LESSLER, KEN; SCHOENINGER, D. W.; AND BRIDGES, JUDITH S. "Prediction of First Grade Performance." *Percept & Motor Skills* 31(3):751–6 D '70. * (*PA* 45:10959)

213. LOCKYER, LINDA, AND RUTTER, MICHAEL. "A Five- to

Fifteen-Year Follow-Up Study of Infantile Psychosis: 4, Patterns of Cognitive Ability." *Brit J Social & Clin Psychol* 9(2): 152–63 Je '70. * (*PA* 44:16983)

214. MANDEL, ROBERT, AND McLEOD, PHILIP. "A Longitudinal Investigation of the Stability of IQ's on the Peabody Picture Vocabulary Test With High and Low Socioeconomic Subjects." *Excep Children* 37(4):300–1 D '70. *

215. NICHOLSON, CHARLES L. "Correlations Among CMMS, PPVT, and RCPM for Cerebral Palsied Children." *Percept & Motor Skills* 30(3):715–8 Je '70. * (*PA* 44:17151)

216. NURCOMBE, B., AND MOFFITT, P. "'Cultural Deprivation and Language Defect: Project Enrichment of Childhood." *Austral Psychologist* 5(3):249–59 N '70. * (*PA* 46:5744)

217. PALMER, FRANCIS H. "Socioeconomic Status and Intellective Performance Among Negro Preschool Boys." *Develop Psychol* 3(1):1–9 Jl '70. * (*PA* 44:16374)

218. POOL, DONALD A., AND BROWN, ROBERT. "The Peabody Picture Vocabulary Test as a Measure of General Adult Intelligence." *J Consult & Clin Psychol* 34(1):8–11 F '70. * (*PA* 44:6772)

219. RASKIN, LARRY M., AND FONG, LOUELLA J. "Temporal Stability of the PPVT in Normal and Educable-Retarded Children." *Psychol Rep* 26(2):547–9 Ap '70. * (*PA* 44:21438)

220. ROBERTS, ARTHUR JAMES. *The Relationship Between Kindergarten Experience and Fine-Muscle Eye-Hand Coordination Abilities of First Grade Children.* Doctor's thesis, Oregon State University (Corvallis, Ore.), 1970. (*DAI* 31:2019A)

221. UHL, NORMAN P., AND NURSS, JOANNE R. "Socio-Economic Level Styles in Solving Reading-Related Tasks." *Read Res Q* 5(3):452–85 sp '70. *

222. WOODY, ROBERT H., AND BILLY, HEIDI T. "Influencing the Intelligence Scores of Retarded and Nonretarded Boys With Clinical Suggestion." *Am J Clin Hyp* 12(4):268–71 Ap '70. * (*PA* 44:18849)

223. ZAESKE, ARNOLD. "The Validity of Predictive Index Tests in Predicting Reading Failure at the End of Grade One," pp. 28–33. In *Reading Difficulties: Diagnosis, Correction, and Remediation.* Edited by William K. Durr. Newark, Del.: International Reading Association, 1970. Pp. vii, 276. *

For reviews by Howard B. Lyman and Ellen V. Piers, see 6:530.

[418]

Pictorial Test of Intelligence. Ages 3–8; 1964; PTI; prepublication titles were *North Central Individual Test of Mental Ability* and *Pictorial Intelligence Test;* 7 scores: picture vocabulary, form discrimination, information and comprehension, similarities, size and number, immediate recall, total; individual; 1 form (54 stimulus cards and 137 response cards); may also be administered to 3- and 4-year-olds as a short form; manual (64 pages); record form (4 pages); no data on reliability of subscores; $33 per examiner's kit of test cards, 35 record forms, manual, and metal carrying case; $1.95 per 35 record forms; $3.60 per manual; postage extra; (45) minutes for full test; Joseph L. French; Houghton Mifflin Co. *

REFERENCES

1–2. See 6:531.

3. FRENCH, JOSEPH L., AND GREER, DONALD. "Effect of Test-Item Arrangement on Physiological and Psychological Behavior in Primary-School Children." *J Ed Meas* 1:151–3 D '64. * (*PA* 39:10105)

4. JENSON, G., III. *A Statistical Analysis of the Reliability and Validity of the Pictorial Test of Intelligence and the Stanford-Binet Intelligence Scale.* Master's thesis, University of Missouri (Columbia, Mo.), 1964.

5. MUELLER, MAX W. *A Comparison of the Empirical Validity of Six Tests of Ability With Young Educable Retardates.* Institute of Mental Retardation and Intellectual Development, IMRID Behavioral Science Monograph No. 1. Nashville, Tenn.: Peabody College Bookstore, 1965. Pp. vii, 130. *

6. MUELLER, MAX WILLIAM. *A Comparison of the Empirical Validity of Six Tests of Ability With Educable Mental Retardates.* Doctor's thesis, George Peabody College for Teachers (Nashville, Tenn.), 1965. (*DA* 26:6853)

7. GENTILE, J. RONALD. "In Search of Research: Four Children's Tests." *J Sch Psychol* 5:1–13 au '66. * (*PA* 41:3335)

8. HONSTEAD, CAROLE ANN. *Relationships Between Socioeconomic Level, Intelligence, and Piagetian Concept Attainment in Kindergarten Children.* Master's thesis, Iowa State University (Ames, Iowa), 1966.

9. HOWARD, JOYCE L., AND PLANT, WALTER T. "Psychometric Evaluation of an Operation Headstart Program." *J Genetic Psychol* 111:281–8 D '67. * (*PA* 42:6013)

10. PASEWARK, R. A.; SAWYER, R. N.; SMITH, E.; WASSERBERGER, M.; DELL, D.; BRITO, H.; AND LEE, R. "Concur-

rent Validity of the French Pictorial Test of Intelligence."
J Ed Res 61:179–83 D '67. *

11. BONFIELD, JOHN RONALD. *Predictors of Achievement for Educable Mentally Retarded Children.* Doctor's thesis, Pennsylvania State University (University Park, Pa.), 1968. (*DAI* 30:1009A)

12. MUELLER, MAX W. "Validity of Six Tests of Ability With Educable Mental Retardates." *J Sch Psychol* 6:136–46 w '68. * (*PA* 42:11152)

13. ORTIZ, KENNETH K. *A Concurrent Validation Study of a Spanish Version of the Pictorial Test of Intelligence and a Critical Analysis of the Use of the Wechsler Intelligence Scale for Children With Bilingual Mexican-American Children.* Master's thesis, California State College (Long Beach, Calif.), 1968.

14. PATTERSON, HENRY JAMES. *A Validation and Comparison of the Pictorial Test of Intelligence With the Stanford-Binet (L-M).* Doctor's thesis, University of Arizona (Tucson, Ariz.), 1968. (*DA* 29:485A)

15. PLANT, WALTER T., AND SOUTHERN, MARA L. "First Grade Reading Achievement Predicted From WPPSI and Other Scores Obtained 18 Months Earlier." Abstract. *Proc 76th Ann Conv Am Psychol Assn* 3:593–4 '68. *

16. SAWYER, R. N. "An Investigation of the Reliability of the French Pictorial Test of Intelligence." *J Ed Res* 61:211–4 Ja '68. *

17. VOGLER, JAMES DONALD. *The Influence of Ethnicity and Socioeconomic Status on the Pictorial Test of Intelligence.* Doctor's thesis, University of Arizona (Tucson, Ariz.), 1968. (*DA* 29:490A)

18. ELLIOTT, RAYMOND N., JR. "Comparative Study of the Pictorial Test of Intelligence and the Peabody Picture Vocabulary Test." *Psychol Rep* 25(2):528–30 O '69. * (*PA* 44:5541)

19. MUELLER, MAX W. "Prediction of Achievement of Educable Mentally Retarded Children." *Am J Mental Def* 73(4): 590–6 Ja '69. * (*PA* 43:8703)

PHILIP HIMELSTEIN, *Professor of Psychology and Head of the Department, The University of Texas at El Paso, El Paso, Texas.*

The PTI is a Binet type instrument which allows the subject to respond in a multiple choice fashion. The test requires only sufficient command of English to understand the simple instructions. Responses to the questions (e.g., "Find the one from which we tell the temperature") would usually take the form of pointing to one of four pictures on a test card. The drawings are spatially so arranged on the card that there could be little doubt of the subject's choices. The examiner merely records the position of the choice on an answer sheet by making a slash mark through the letter corresponding to the position on the card of the subject's choice. The total number of correct items (the raw score) is converted by table to MA units and to deviation IQ's.

While the PTI is presented as "a further development of Binet type scales," there are some dissimilarities to the Stanford-Binet. Items are not ordered according to mental age, but according to subtests, as in Wechsler scales. There are six subtests arranged in the order of difficulty. There is no base or ceiling to be obtained; instead, all items are administered (with a minor exception) regardless of the successes or failures of the subject. None of the subtests are timed. Finally, and most important for the test user, the PTI covers only the age

range of 3 to 8, while the Stanford-Binet tests children between the ages of 2 and 18.

Standardization, completed in 1962, was based on 1,830 children randomly selected to compare—by regional area, community size, and occupational level of father—with the 1960 census. The manual reports test-retest reliability coefficients ranging from .90 to .96 for time intervals of two to six weeks. K-R 20 reliability estimates from the standardization sample range from .87 to .93, with the lowest estimates at the upper and lower age limits of the test. Validity studies reported in the manual range in sample size from 9 to 32, rather inadequate for a test author's claim of validity.

While the test has not had adequate tryout by other investigators in the six years since it was published, a few studies are available. Sawyer (*16*) reports a test-retest reliability of .77 for kindergarten children with a 45-day interval and .88 for second graders with a 53-day interval. While the split-half reliabilities range from .95 to .98, the test-retest reliabilities seem woefully inadequate. Pasewark et al. (*10*) obtained a correlation of .75 between PTI and WISC IQ with a kindergarten sample and .71 with second grade children. With the S-B, Patterson (*14*) reported a correlation of .78 for randomly selected children (.38 and .65 for superior and retarded children, respectively). Mueller (*6*) obtained a correlation of .72 between PTI and S-B. Elliott (*18*) compared the PTI to another picture intelligence test, the PPVT, and, after relating the two tests to WRAT scores, concluded that "overall, the PTI appeared to be a more effective measure of intelligence in predicting class placement of institutionalized, educable mentally retarded students."

Some nine criticisms of the test are leveled by Pasewark et al. (*10*), including the restricted ages covered by the test and the increased testing time necessitated by the demand that all subjects, regardless of age, begin each subtest with the first item. There are suggestions in the published research that the test is least reliable at age 8, the highest age at which the test is used. The validity correlation reported would suggest that the PTI correlates about as well (in the .70's) with the S-B as the WISC does, and better than another picture test, the PPVT.

In sum, I can say that, like many other instruments, the PTI needs additional research. It does appear to have adequate validity so that it can be used with some confidence. Its application to the study of children with motor or speech handicaps would seem to be a special advantage.

T. ERNEST NEWLAND, *Professor of Educational Psychology, University of Illinois, Urbana, Illinois.*

The PTI differs from its preliminary edition, the NCITMA, by being standardized on a two-year wider age range, with two to three times more subjects at each level, and on subjects in 37 states (vs. two); by the exclusion of some of the old items and the addition of more difficult items; and by providing, within it, for a short form for use with three- and four-year-olds.

Test-retest reliabilities ranging from .90 to .94 are reported for groups of 25 to 31 children at year levels 5, 6, and 7. K-R 20 reliabilities range from .87 to .93.

The author presumes that content validity is apparent in the similarity between his test items and those of other "recognized tests of intelligence." No firm predictive validity data are presented, although the author does present rank correlations from .74 to .82, on from 9 to 11 cases, between scores (IQ's or MA's?) on the NCITMA and mean scores on three achievement tests (after 4 years). The author also reports rank correlations, for groups of 18 and 28, of .68 and .77 between his test (IQ's?) and two group intelligence tests administered three to five years later. Concurrent validity data are based on correlational studies of performances of three populations of no more than 32 subjects each: PTI with the 1960 Stanford-Binet, .72; with WISC (Full Scale IQ's?), .65; and with the *Columbia Mental Maturity Scale* (IQ's?), .53.

While terminological ambiguity hampers precise communication and rigorous evaluation, the PTI appears to be in the same "ball park" as the other tests cited, but who is on what base is not clear. Further skepticism regarding some of the statistics reported in the manual must be entertained, since the author points out that these analyses were made "before the standardization was complete." This reviewer has difficulty accepting the author's claim that the increase in PTI scores from lower to higher occupational levels is evidence of construct validity.

Sawyer (*16*) found split-half reliabilities quite in accord with those in the manual, but, on 52 kindergarten children, found a retest reliability of .77 and, on 38 second graders, one of .88. He observed that the subtest intercorrelations were "much higher than those reported in the manual." He regarded the effectiveness of PTI at the 8-year level as "subject to some doubt."

It is dangerous to generalize to the "normal" population the implications of the published research on the use of the PTI with retarded subjects. Correlations have been computed more in terms of psychometric curiosity than in terms of psychological inquiry. To correlate the PTI total results with the Stanford-Binet or with the WISC Verbal reflects good presumptive thinking, whereas to correlate PTI total results with the PPVT involves the tacit assumption that the two tests sample comparable forms of behavior.

If one desires to measure the learning aptitude of young children in a molar manner, particularly for ages 3–6, the PTI deserves serious consideration. To use it as though it could yield the same kind of psychological information as the PPVT, the Leiter, the Raven, or the CMMS would be a near-waste of examination time.

Because the response card is placed in a rack before the child, the test has considerable potential value in the cases of verbally constricted (or expressively impaired) children: the child merely needs to point to the desired response. With children with motor involvement of the arms or hands, the examiner can observe easily the eye movements of the child who has been instructed just to look at his "answer," since the spacing and location of the response elements on the cards make this quite feasible. When the short form is used, care should be taken to guard against positional perseveration in response. The response cards should be revised so that there is a more equitable distribution of the placement of the correct responses: 17 are at the bottom of the card, 23 are at the subject's right, 31 are at his left, and 26 are at the top. The answer sheet is easily used and scored, and is facilitative to a behavioral description of the subject in the test situation.

Even though the PTI is not truly based on a discernible psychological theory, as is true of the Stanford-Binet and many other individual tests of learning aptitude, and although rigorous research on it is yet to appear, the kinds of behavior samplings made constitute a composite that is plausibly relatable to the general cognitive demands in the school learning of children. Certainly, by virtue of the potential psychoeducational relevance of the variety of behaviors sampled and its broad standardization base, the PTI holds more promise as an individual learning aptitude test for young children than most other such tests recently released, including the *Wechsler Preschool and Primary Scale of Intelligence.*

[419]

*The Porteus Maze Test. Ages 3 and over; 1914–65; PMT; individual; 2 scores: quantitative, qualitative; 1 form; 3 editions and 2 supplements; no data on reliability; no adult norms; postage extra; Stanley D. Porteus. *

a) VINELAND REVISION. Ages 3 and over; 1914–24; 1 form ('21); 13 mazes: years 3–12, 14, adult 1, 2; manual ['24, 21 pages]; $19 per set of manual and 100 mazes of any one level; $1.35 per 100 copies of any one maze; (15–60) minutes; Stoelting Co.

b) VINELAND REVISION: NEW SERIES. Ages 3 and over; 1914–65; 1 form ('33); 12 mazes: years 3–12, 14, adult 1; combined manual ('65, 324 pages, see *143* below); $14.50 per set of 100 copies of each maze and pad of 100 scoring sheets; $1.60 per 100 mazes of any one level; $7.60 per manual; (15–60) minutes; Psychological Corporation.

c) PORTEUS MAZE EXTENSION. Ages 14 and over; 1953–65; for use only as a supplement to the *Vineland Revision: New Series;* 1 form ('53); 8 mazes: years 7–12, 14, adult; combined manual as in *b;* $10 per set of 100 copies of each maze and pad of 100 scoring sheets; $1.50 per 100 mazes of any one level; $7.60 per manual; (25) minutes; Psychological Corporation.

d) PORTEUS MAZE SUPPLEMENT. Ages 7 and over; 1959–65; a retesting series; 1 form ('59); 8 mazes: years 7–12, 14, adult; combined manual as in *b;* $9.50 per set of 100 copies of each maze; $1.70 per 100 mazes of any one level; $7.60 per manual; (25) minutes; Psychological Corporation.

e) BRITISH EDITION. Ages 3 and over; 1914–65; 1 form ('52, same as *Vineland Revision: New Series* copyrighted in 1933 except for format); 12 mazes: years 3–12, 14, adult 1; manual ('65, 324 pages, see *143* below); 35p per 100 mazes of any one level; 35p per 100 scoring sheets; 52½p per manual; [15–60] minutes; George G. Harrap & Co. Ltd.

REFERENCES

1–56. See 4:356.
57–84. See 5:412.
85–122. See 6:532.
123. EBERT, ELIZABETH, AND SIMMONS, KATHERINE. *The Brush Foundation Study of Child Growth and Development: 1, Psychometric Tests.* Monographs of the Society for Research in Child Development, Vol. 8, No. 2, Serial No. 35. Washington, D.C.: the Society, National Research Council, 1943. Pp. xiv, 113. * (*PA* 18:3322)
124. CROWN, SIDNEY. "An Experimental Study of Psychological Changes Following Prefrontal Lobotomy." *J General Psychol* 47:3–41 Jl '52. * (*PA* 27:6024)
125. GOLDENBERG, SAMUEL. *Some Aspects of Diagnosis of Cerebral Damage in Children.* Doctor's thesis, University of Washington (Seattle, Wash.), 1953. (*DA* 13:1259)
126. JUSTISS, WILL ALAN. *The Electroencephalogram of the Frontal Lobes and Abstract Behavior in Old Age.* Doctor's thesis, University of Florida (Gainesville, Fla.), 1957. (*DA* 18:308)
127. CRAWFORD, PAUL L. "The Relative Sensitivity of the LAIS, WAIS, and PM in Differentiating Between Psycho-

pathic and Psychotic Patients in a Mental Hospital." *Psychol Service Center J* 11(2):93–7 '59. * (*PA* 34:4374)
128. CRAWFORD, PAUL L. "The Statistical Significance of Difference in Performance on the Leiter Adult Intelligence Scale, the Wechsler Adult Intelligence Scale, and the Porteus Maze by a Heterogeneous Mental Hospital Population." *Psychol Service Center J* 11(2):89–92 '59. * (*PA* 34:4510)
129. FULLER, CARL WELLINGTON. *A Study of the Growth and Organization of Certain Mental Abilities in Young Deaf Children.* Doctor's thesis, Northwestern University (Evanston, Ill.), 1959. (*DA* 20:2382)
130. FOULDS, G. A. "Personality Traits and Neurotic Symptoms and Signs." *Brit J Med Psychol* 34:263–70 pt 4 '61. * (*PA* 37:1229)
131. GIBBENS, T. C. N.; WITH THE ASSISTANCE OF A. MARRIAGE AND A. WALKER. *Psychiatric Studies of Borstal Lads,* pp. 143–84. London: Oxford University Press, 1963. Pp. vi, 230. *
132. BROVERMAN, DONALD M. "Generality and Behavioral Correlates of Cognitive Styles." *J Consult Psychol* 28:487–500 D '64. * (*PA* 39:7680)
133. FAHMY, MOSTAFA. "Initial Exploring of the Intelligence of Shilluk Children: Studies in the Southern Sudan." *Vita Hum* 7(3–4):164–77 '64. * (*PA* 39:7815)
134. FOULDS, G. A., AND OWEN, ANNA. "Speed and Accuracy on Mazes in Relation to Diagnosis and Personality." *Brit J Social & Clin Psychol* 3:34–5 F '64. * (*PA* 38:8870)
135. WASSENAAR, G. M. C. "The Effect of General Anxiety as an Index of Lability on the Performance of Various Psychomotor Tasks." *J General Psychol* 71:351–7 O '64. * (*PA* 39:3667)
136. BLUMENKRANTZ, JACK; DAHLGREN, HELEN; AND BORUM, ELIZABETH. "An Abbreviated Scoring Method for Porteus Mazes." *Newsl Res Psychol* 7:19 F '65. *
137. CRAFT, MICHAEL. Chap. 3, "Diagnosis and Aetiology Illustrated by an Analysis of Admissions to a Psychopathic Unit," pp. 32–54. In *Ten Studies Into Psychopathic Personality: A Report to the Home Office and the Mental Health Research Fund.* Bristol, England: John Wright & Sons Ltd., 1965. Pp. 133. *
138. FELDMAN, RUTH CAMM. *A Study of Cognitive Style and Some Personality Variables in Relation to the Conceptual Performance of Emotionally Disturbed Adolescents.* Doctor's thesis, Temple University (Philadelphia, Pa.), 1965. (*DA* 26:1773)
139. FROST, BARRY P. "The Porteus Maze Test and Manual Proficiency." *Alberta J Ed Res* 11:17–20 Mr '65. * (*PA* 39:16418)
140. KAINER, ROCHELLE KRUGMAN. *The Porteus Maze Test and the Delay of Gratification.* Doctor's thesis, Columbia University (New York, N.Y.), 1965. (*DA* 26:4808)
141. LABARBA, RICHARD C. "Relation of Color Responses on the Rorschach to Qualitative Scores on the Porteus Maze Test." *Percept & Motor Skills* 21:61–2 Ag '65. * (*PA* 40:40)
142. PIERCE, ROBERT ALLYN. *Response Sets as Personality Variables: An Attempt at Validation.* Doctor's thesis, University of Rochester (Rochester, N.Y.), 1965. (*DA* 26:3490)
143. PORTEUS, STANLEY D. *Porteus Maze Test: Fifty Years' Application.* Palo Alto, Calif.: Pacific Books, Publishers, 1965. Pp. vii, 320. *
144. RILEY, J. E., AND ARMLIN, N. J. "The Dogmatism Scale and Flexibility in Maze Performance." *Percept & Motor Skills* 21:914 D '65. * (*PA* 40:4237)
145. ANDREWS, ROBERT SEWALL. *The Relationship Between Appropriateness of Emotional Response and Delay of Motor Behavior.* Doctor's thesis, Boston University (Boston, Mass.), 1966. (*DA* 27:1613B)
146. BARRY, JOHN R., AND FULKERSON, SAMUEL C. "Chronicity and the Prediction of Duration and Outcome of Hospitalization From Capacity Measures." *Psychiatric Q* 40:104–21 Ja '66. * (*PA* 40:6764)
147. ERIKSON, ROBERT V., AND ROBERTS, ALAN H. "A Comparison of Two Groups of Institutionalized Delinquents on Porteus Maze Test Performance." Abstract. *J Consult Psychol* 30:567 D '66. *
148. GAMBARO, SALVATORE, AND SCHELL, ROBERT E. "Prediction of the Employability of Students in a Special Education Work-Training Program Using the Porteus Maze Test and a Rating Scale of Personal Effectiveness." *Ed & Psychol Meas* 26:1021–9 w '66. * (*PA* 41:5012)
149. LEIBOWITZ, MARVIN. *Effects of Psychological Support on Test Performance of Four Types of Narcotic Addicts.* Doctor's thesis, New York University (New York, N.Y.), 1966. (*DA* 27:2873B)
150. MEIER, MANFRED J., AND RESCH, JOSEPH A. "Behavioral Correlates of Short-Term Change in Neurological Status Following Acute Onset of Cerebrovascular Symptomatology." *J Clin Psychol* 22:156–9 Ap '66. * (*PA* 40:8003)
151. RANKIN, R. J., AND THOMPSON, KENNETH. "A Factor Analytic Approach to Impulse as Measured by Arrow Dot I, Q, and SORT." *Percept & Motor Skills* 23:1239–45 D '66. * (*PA* 41:5262)
152. RANKIN, RICHARD, AND THOMPSON, KENNETH. "A Factorial Investigation of Scores on the Porteus Maze." *Percept & Motor Skills* 23:1255–60 D '66. * (*PA* 41:5263)

153. STERNE, DAVID M. "Use of the Porteus Mazes With Non-Retarded Adults." *Newsl Res Psychol* 8:51–3 My '66. *

154. BURNAND, G.; HUNTER, H.; AND HOGGART, K. "Some Psychological Test Characteristics of Klinefelter's Syndrome." *Brit J Psychiatry* 113:1091–6 O '67. * (*PA* 42:7632)

155. COOPER, G. DAVID; YORK, MICHAEL W.; DASTON, PAUL G.; AND ADAMS, HENRY B. "The Porteus Test and Various Measures of Intelligence With Southern Negro Adolescents." *Am J Mental Def* 71:787–92 Mr '67. * (*PA* 41:8879)

156. DAVID, KENNETH H. "Effect of Verbal Reinforcement on Porteus Maze Scores Among Australian Aborigine Children." *Percept & Motor Skills* 24:986 Je '67. *

157. DAVID, KENNETH H., AND BOCHNER, STEPHEN. "Teacher Ratings of IQ and Porteus Maze Scores of Pitjandjara Children." *Percept & Motor Skills* 25:639–40 O '67. * (*PA* 42:5578)

158. FISH, CAROLINE CHANDLER. *Impulsivity in Culturally Deprived Children.* Doctor's thesis, Boston University (Boston, Mass.), 1967. (*DA* 29:4322A)

159. MALMQUIST, CARL P.; KIRESUK, THOMAS J.; AND SPANO, ROBERT M. "Mothers With Multiple Illegitimacies." *Psychiatric Q* 41:339–54 Ap '67. * (*PA* 42:4189)

160. MEIER, M. J., AND STORY, J. L. "Selective Impairment of Porteus Maze Test Performance After Right Subthalamotomy." *Neuropsychologia* 5:181–9 My '67. * (*PA* 42:10045)

161. MEIER, MANFRED J., AND RESCH, JOSEPH A. "Behavioral Prediction of Short-Term Neurologic Change Following Acute Onset of Cerebrovascular Symptoms." *Mayo Clin Proc* 42:641–7 O '67. *

162. PORTEUS, S. D.; BOCHNER, S.; RUSSELL, J.; AND DAVID, KENNETH. "Age as a Factor in Australian Mentality." *Percept & Motor Skills* 25:3–16 Ag '67. * (*PA* 42:2563)

163. TILKER, HARVEY A., AND SCHELL, ROBERT E. "Concurrent Validity of the Porteus Maze Test: A Comparative Study of Regular and Educationally Handicapped High School Students." *Ed & Psychol Meas* 27:447–55 su '67. * (*PA* 41:12840)

164. BOURESTOM, NORMAN C., AND HOWARD, MARY T. "Behavioral Correlates of Recovery of Self-Care in Hemiplegic Patients." *Arch Phys Med & Rehabil* 49:449–54 Ag '68. *

165. GADDES, W. H.; McKENZIE, AUDREY; AND BARNSLEY, ROGER. "Psychometric Intelligence and Spatial Imagery in Two Northwest Indian and Two White Groups of Children." *J Social Psychol* 75:35–42 Je '68. * (*PA* 42:13575)

166. GILBERSTADT, HAROLD. "Relationships Among Scores of Tests Suitable for the Assessment of Adjustment and Intellectual Functioning." *J Gerontol* 23:483–7 O '68. *

167. LEFKOWITZ, MONROE M. "Nonintellective Components in the School Performance of Juvenile Delinquents." *Percept & Motor Skills* 26:1185–6 Je '68. * (*PA* 42:19246)

168. McALOON, FRANCIS WILLIAM. *The Inhibition Process, Stress, and Qualitative Performance on the Porteus Maze.* Doctor's thesis, Fordham University (New York, N.Y.), 1968. (*DA* 29:3089B)

169. MATTHEWS, CHARLES G.; CHUN, RAYMOND W. M.; GRABOW, JACK D.; AND THOMPSON, WAYNE H. "Psychological Sequelae in Children Following California Arboviros Encephalitis." *Neurology* 18:1023–30 O '68. * (*PA* 43:5771)

170. PALKES, HELEN; STEWART, MARK; AND KAHANA, BOAZ. "Porteus Maze Performance of Hyperactive Boys After Training in Self-Directed Verbal Commands." *Child Develop* 39:817–26 S '68. * (*PA* 43:3758)

171. PORTEUS, S. D. "New Applications of the Porteus Maze Tests." *Percept & Motor Skills* 26:787–98 Je '68. * (*PA* 42:14729)

172. ROBERTS, ALAN H., AND ERIKSON, ROBERT V. "Delay of Gratification, Porteus Maze Test Performance, and Behavioral Adjustment in a Delinquent Group." *J Abn Psychol* 73:449–53 O '68. * (*PA* 42:19056)

173. SCHALLING, DAISY, AND ROSÉN, ANNE-SOFIE. "Porteus Maze Differences Between Psychopathic and Non-Psychopathic Criminals." *Brit J Social & Clin Psychol* 7:224–8 S '68. * (*PA* 43:1115)

174. AFTANAS, M. S., AND ROYCE, J. R. "A Factor Analysis of Brain Damage Tests Administered to Normal Subjects With Factor Score Comparisons Across Ages." *Multiv Behav Res* 4(4):459–81 O '69. * (*PA* 44:11030)

175. COHEN, SHIRLEY. *Impulsivity in Low-Achieving and High-Achieving Lower Class Boys.* Doctor's thesis, Columbia University (New York, N.Y.), 1969. (*DAI* 30:4269A)

176. JARRAHI-ZADEH, ALI; KANE, F. J., JR.; VAN DE CASTLE, R. L.; LACHENBRUCH, P. A.; AND EWING, J. A. "Emotional and Cognitive Changes in Pregnancy and Early Puerperium." *Brit J Psychiatry* 115(524):797–805 Jl '69. * (*PA* 44:6605)

177. MEIER, MANFRED J., AND OKAYAMA, MASAHIRO. "Behavior Assessment." *Geriatrics* 24(11):95–110 N '69. *

178. PORTEUS, S. D. "The Porteus Maze and Clinical Psychology." *Prof Psychol* 1(1):52–4 N '69. * (*PA* 44:6833)

179. STERNE, DAVID M. "The Benton, Porteus and WAIS Digit Span Tests With Normal and Brain-Injured Subjects." *J Clin Psychol* 25(2):173–5 Ap '69. * (*PA* 43:14481)

180. TRAIL, BILLIE M. *Criminal Psychopathic vs Criminal Non-Psychopathic Scores on the Porteus Maze Test Series.* Master's thesis, Texas Woman's University (Denton, Tex.), 1969.

181. WHYBROW, P. C.; PRANGE, A. J., JR.; AND TREADWAY, C. R. "Mental Changes Accompanying Thyroid Gland Dysfunction: A Reappraisal Using Objective Psychological Measurement." *Arch Gen Psychiatry* 20(1):48–63 Ja '69. * (*PA* 43:11631)

182. COTLER, SHELDON, AND PALMER, RICHARD J. "The Effects of Test Anxiety, Sex of Subject, and Type of Verbal Reinforcement on Maze Performance of Elementary School Children." *J Personality* 38(2):216–34 Je '70. * (*PA* 44:17896)

183. LOOKER, ANDREW, AND CONNERS, C. KEITH. "Diphenylhydantoin in Children With Severe Temper Tantrums." *Arch Gen Psychiatry* 23(1):80–9 Jl '70. * (*PA* 44:18868)

184. MEIER, MANFRED J., AND MARTIN, WILLIAM E. "Intellectual Changes Associated With Levodopa Therapy." Letter. *J Am Med Assn* 213(3):465–6 Jl 20 '70. *

185. O'KEEFE, EDWARD JOHN. *Impulsivity and Its Relationship to Risk Taking.* Doctor's thesis, Fordham University (New York, N.Y.), 1970. (*DAI* 31:3000B)

186. QUERY, WILLIAM T. "A Comparative Study of the Relationship Between Need Affiliation and Need Achievement, and Success and Failure Among Indian and White Children." *Newsl Res Psychol* 12(2):95–6 My '70. *

187. ROSEN, MARVIN; KIVITZ, MARVIN S.; CLARK, GERALD R.; AND FLOOR, LUCRETIA. "Prediction of Postinstitutional Adjustment of Mentally Retarded Adults." *Am J Mental Def* 74(6):726–34 My '70. * (*PA* 44:17195)

188. SHARP, ELIZABETH YERXA. *The Relationship of Visual Closure to Speechreading Among Deaf Children.* Doctor's thesis, University of Arizona (Tucson, Ariz.), 1970. (*DAI* 31:2198A)

189. WERNER, EMMY E., AND MURALIDHARAN, RAJALAKSHMI. "Nutrition, Cognitive Status and Achievement Motivation of New Delhi Nursery School Children." *J Cross-Cultural Psychol* 1(3):271–81 S '70. * (*PA* 45:3803)

RICHARD F. DOCTER, *Professor of Psychology, San Fernando Valley State College, Northridge, California.*

The *Porteus Maze Test* is a performance test of intelligence yielding test age scores which may be converted into IQ estimates. In addition, by assigning various penalty scores to the subject's test-taking behavior regardless of his success in dealing with the mazes, a qualitative score (Q-score) is derived which has been shown to correlate with various indices of social adjustment and, especially, to differentiate delinquent youth from nondelinquents.

The materials consist of three different maze series: the Original or Vineland Series which is supposed to be given first, the Extension Series, and the Supplement Series. The latter two are intended as retest measures only. One of the nice things about this test is that almost everyone enjoys taking it. The mazes are seen by youngsters as puzzles similar to those they may have tried to do in comic books.

Porteus began the development of his test in 1914 and, like many other early test developers, his first concern was with the classification of mentally retarded youngsters and their assignment to a special school. There is considerable evidence from a variety of clinical settings spanning over half a century that the maze test can be a useful, sensitive, and powerful tool to assist in the differential assessment of both children and adults in the borderline range of intellectual endowment. This test, particularly when teamed with other measures of intelligence, often enhances the prediction of performance in training programs for mentally retarded children and for adults who might otherwise be considered untrainable. The test is entirely nonverbal, except for presentation of the instructions and even here it is possible to circumvent the use of spoken language.

TEST AGE SCORE. Porteus has long emphasized that maze solving requires planning capacity, foresight, and the ability to learn from experience. This may be true, but hard evidence to support the claim that this is what the mazes measure is difficult to come by. In general, the test author has been willing to accept as evidence of construct validity the results of many studies which show that maze scores correlate with ratings of social adjustment or trainability, often based on populations with borderline or low intelligence but these correlational studies do not prove what the maze test measures. At this point, the best we can say is that this test appears to have considerable face validity as a task requiring short term planning toward the solution of printed mazes; how this may generalize to other kinds of planning and learning essential to the solving of different kinds of problems remains to be seen. But there is no doubt that the mazes are indeed measuring intelligence. Numerous reports have been made showing the maze test age and various general intelligence tests as having correlations of from about .40 to .70. Thus, less than one-half of the variance of the maze test age score is accounted for by whatever it is that general intelligence tests are measuring. Since the maze test has been shown to detect performance changes following psychosurgery, while other tests including the Wechsler-Bellevue have failed to do so, it seems clear that maze solving calls for problem solving competencies not required by many other tests.

The test is disarming in its simplicity. To thread one's way through any but the most elementary of mazes it is necessary to perform some very complex behaviors. These include recognition of the goal (escape from the maze), identification of subgoals (landmarks along a successful track), short term memory for a preferred course of action, and, finally, carrying out one's plan without slipping into a blind alley. To better unravel maze-solving behavior, we shall have to learn more about individual differences in problem sets and in cognitive style, for it is the problem-attack strategy and the behavioral control essential to vicarious trial and error which are critical in maze solving. These are obviously very complex mental processes, and when combined with recognition that much learning goes on within the context of a single administration of a set of mazes, it is little wonder that no one has yet extracted the essence of what the maze test measures, at least not with the specificity and exactness that would be essential to consider the mazes a refined test.

The extension and supplement series were created to compensate for practice effects based on the original series, but their use in test-retest designs leaves many questions unanswered. A central difficulty is that while the group test age averages for the original and extension series are very similar, the correlation between scores on the two forms is only about .50. This similarity in group means is due mainly to the more difficult designs at the upper end of the extension series. This increase in difficulty has more of an effect on test age scores for subjects who have excelled on the original series than for those who did less well. In the absence of adequate evidence of high correlations among these three series, their application in test-retest designs does not appear justified.

THE Q-SCORE. The qualitative score is comprised of nine test performance characteristics (such as cutting corners, crossing lines, and lifting the pencil), none of which plays a direct part in the calculation of the test age score. The rationale for the Q-score is based on Porteus' observation that the test taking "style of response" was markedly different among various youngsters even when the test age score was held constant. He noted differences in "impulsiveness," carelessness in performance, and failure to follow the directions. While Porteus has termed this a "rough and ready" measure, it has consistently been shown to reflect differences between groups of delinquents and nondelinquents, and between other groups differing in social adjustment. The correlation between Q-score and various indices of intelligence has been shown to be in the range of about −.20 to −.40. While the reliability of scoring the qualitative errors tends to be very high (above .95), the test-retest correlation of the Q-score after a three-day interval was only .51 in a sample of psychiatric patients. A factor analysis of the Q-score revealed that about 70 percent of the variance of this measure is attributable to two errors: lift pencil and wavy lines. The subject who frequently lifts his pencil has either failed to learn the instructions or has failed to comply with them, while wavy lines reflect imprecision in motor performance. These two errors do not correlate with each other. Factor analytic evidence reveals that the Q-score should not be interpreted as indicative of a single trait such as "impulsivity" or impulse control. As with the test age score, the Q-score is deceptively simple, for it depends on the quality of attention and learning when the instructions are given, and on a multitude of personality and cognitive differences that can influence one's total style of response in maze solving behavior.

STANDARDIZATION. The trouble with the maze test is not that it lacks promise; the difficulty is that the standardization of the test was quite limited to begin with and is now long overdue for revision. Porteus' most recent book serves as the test manual, but it falls short of being satisfactory for this purpose. Its greatest fault is that standardization and validation data from previous studies have not been adequately pulled together and it is not possible for a maze test user to determine what subject samples were used in the establishment of norms. Other basic psychometric essentials, such as the standard deviation for test age scores by age level, are also missing. Far more would be accomplished by a thorough restandardization than would be lost by any possible test modification which would complicate the interpretation of existing maze test research.

After a lifetime of study with the maze test, Porteus, combining both the judgment of a sensitive clinician and extensive empirical data, is frank to admit that "the validation of the Maze Test is far less satisfactory than is desired." With this we must agree, for while there is much about the predictive validity of the test which is known, the full development of the test's potential has suffered from a lack of clearly focused validation research. If the mazes are to achieve the utilization that they may well deserve, the next step in their development would seem to be in pinning down more precisely those traits or abilities which appear to be uniquely measured by this test.

JOHN L. HORN, *Professor of Psychology, University of Denver, Denver, Colorado.*

In its basic form the Maze test of today differs little from the test first published in 1914. The test has a core set of 12 mazes and 2 extension forms, each consisting of 8 mazes. The extensions are graded in difficulty and standardized in a way designed to provide scores equivalent to the core series if they are given in a designated order. The purpose of this construction is to eliminate practice effects. This purpose is realized only to the extent that one can justify several rather strong assumptions about equality of units and change.

There is no manual for the test—at least, no manual of the kind recommended in *Standards for Educational and Psychological Tests and Manuals* (SEPTM). Instead, there is a book (*143*) which contains some of the information recommended in SEPTM. There is, however, no information on reliability, virtually no description of norms, and little indication of the qualifications required to administer and interpret the test, but there is an extended and lively discussion of the limitations of other tests and of the hazards of sampling and testing in Central Australia and South Africa. In conformance with SEPTM, the book deals rather fully (in a rambling and repetitious though entertaining way) with questions of validity, and there is a description of how the test is administered and scored.

The test is scored in three quite different ways to produce measurement of three distinct attributes. One scoring, recorded in mental age or test quotient units and here referred to as ability scores, indicates degree of success in solving the problems. A second scoring, producing a Q-score, indicates stylistic qualities and, loosely, the degree of sloppiness in pathway drawings. A third scoring provides what is called a Conformity-Variability score. It is important in evaluating results obtained with the Maze test to distinguish clearly between ability and qualitative scoring, for they are sometimes confused in writings about the test and yet the two appear to have quite different construct validities. The correlation between the two is about −.40.

The Maze ability scores have been found to correlate at well above the chance level with a variety of ability tests, both those comprised of one type of item (Block designs, Matrices) and omnibus measures of intelligence, such as the Binet and the Wechsler, in which several different kinds of items or subtests representing different primary abilities enter into the score. The test can be said to measure a process, or processes, involved in expressions of intelligence. Porteus has argued that this process is a capacity of foresight and planning which is measured also, but along with other things, in the tests with which the Maze is correlated.

The correlational evidence provides an indirect indication of the lower bound for the reliability of the Maze test. Since the test correlates about .75 with Knox Cubes, it can be reasoned that the reliability of the Maze is probably not less than .75.

The ability score has been found to correlate most highly with spatial tests such as Knox Cubes and Kohs Blocks. Such tests have been found to define a broad visual ability that can be distinguished from two equally broad intellectual factors referred to as fluid intelligence and crystallized intelligence.[1] Guilford [2] has classified Maze tests in the CFI (Cognition of Figural Implications) cell of the structure of intellect model.

Porteus finds that in a wide range of comparisons, males on the average obtain higher Maze scores than do females. This finding is consistent with several others showing differences in favor of males in tests involving figural content and calling for spatial-visualization ability. Nevertheless, these results should be tempered with an awareness that the sampling for males and females in most of the studies upon which the conclusion is based cannot be assumed to be equally representative and that, taken overall, the differences are not large.

Porteus bases a major part of his case for the usefulness of the Maze test on evidence relating test performance to effects produced by brain injuries. He suggests that the capacity measured by the Maze test is localized to a considerable extent in frontal lobe function. In keeping with the times, however, he also suggests that the midbrain reticular formation may govern Maze performance. Most of the relevant studies have been on the frontal lobes, in general, and leucotomy, in particular. The numbers of subjects in these studies were small and the experimental controls which might compensate for small N's were in all instances inadequate. The conclusions that can be drawn must therefore be regarded as tentative. Nevertheless, the

results from most of the studies [3] suggest that the ability measured by the Maze test is reduced by removal of frontal lobe tissue. There are a few results [4] indicating gains (not losses) in Maze performance following leucotomy, but these findings appear to be due in part to practice effect and in part to relief of a psychotic condition which severely hampered performance in the pretest.

The evidence thus supports the claim that the Maze test is sensitive to effects produced by the brain damage of prefrontal leucotomy. That this sensitivity is not associated exclusively with damage to the frontal lobes is indicated by the careful reviews of Hebb,[5] Meyer,[6] and Willett [7] and, more specifically and recently, by the findings of Brown and others,[8] Meier and Story (160), and Sterne (179). In the Brown and others study, for example, decrement in maze performance was found to be associated with temporal lobe surgery. Also, to acknowledge that the Maze test is "sensitive" to the effects produced by brain damage is not to imply that one can predict with high accuracy the loss to be incurred by any given individual. Averaging over the data provided by Crown,[9] King,[10] and Petrie,[11] the point biserial correlation, indicating the loss to be predicted from knowledge that the surgery has been performed, is only .29.

It is a bit misleading for Porteus to suggest that the Maze test alone among existing tests is sensitive to the effects produced by brain damage—that "losses after operation have been

3 CROWN, SIDNEY. "Psychological Changes Following Prefrontal Leucotomy: A Review." *J Mental Sci* 97:49-83 Ja '51. *
MEYER, V. Chap. 14, "Psychological Effects of Brain Change," pp. 529-65. In *Handbook of Abnormal Psychology: An Experimental Approach.* Edited by H. J. Eysenck. New York: Basic Books, Inc., Publishers, 1961. Pp. xvi, 816. *
WILLETT, R. A. Chap. 15, "The Effects of Psychosurgical Procedures on Behavior," pp. 566-610. In *Handbook of Abnormal Psychology: An Experimental Approach.* Edited by H. J. Eysenck. New York: Basic Books, Inc., Publishers, 1961. Pp. xvi, 816. *
4 JONES, ROBERT E. "Personality Changes in Psychotics Following Prefrontal Lobotomy." *J Abn & Social Psychol* 44:315-28 Jl '49. *
STRÖM-OLSEN, R.; LAST, S. L.; AND BRODY, M. B. "Results of Prefrontal Leucotomy in Thirty Cases of Mental Disorder." *J Mental Sci* 89:165-74 Ap '43. *
5 HEBB, D. O. "Man's Frontal Lobes: A Critical Review." *Arch Neurol & Psychiatry* 54:10-24 Jl '45. *
HEBB, D. O. *The Organization of Behavior: A Neuropsychological Theory.* New York: John Wiley & Sons, Inc., 1949. Pp. xix, 335. *
6 MEYER, op. cit.
7 WILLETT, op. cit.
8 BROWN, IAN A.; FRENCH, LYLE A.; OGLE, WILLIAM S.; AND JAHNSON, SHIRLEY. "Temporal Lobe Epilepsy: Its Clinical Manifestations and Surgical Treatment: A Preliminary Report, Part 1." *Medicine* 35:425-59 '56. *
9 CROWN, op. cit.
10 KING, HENRY EUGENE. Chap. 14, "Intellectual Function," pp. 178-207. In *Selective Partial Ablation of the Frontal Cortex.* Edited by Fred A. Mettler. New York: Paul B. Hoeber, Inc., 1949. Pp. xiv, 517. *
11 PETRIE, ASENATH. "Preliminary Report of Changes After Prefrontal Leucotomy." *J Mental Sci* 95:449-55 Ap '49. *

1 HORN, JOHN L. "The Organization of Abilities and the Development of Intelligence." *Psychol R* 75:242-59 My '68. *
HORN, JOHN L., AND CATTELL, RAYMOND B. "Refinement and Test of the Theory of Fluid and Crystallized General Intelligences." *J Ed Psychol* 57:253-70 O '66. *
2 GUILFORD, J. P. *The Nature of Human Intelligence.* New York: McGraw-Hill Book Co., Inc., 1967. Pp. xii, 538. *

inconsistent or slight except in the Maze." Porteus is correct in pointing out that omnibus tests of intelligence, such as the Binet and Wechsler, sometimes indicate little or no decrement when other tests, such as the Maze, show that there has been loss. This fact was emphasized by Hebb years ago. But a number of tests (such as Blocks, Matrices, Homographs, Associational Fluency, and Absurdities) are sensitive to this decrement—tests which require the subject to sustain attention in order to deduce complex and novel relations (and this may be at the core of capacity for planning). The Maze is apparently this kind of test, although the level of complexity of the most difficult items is relatively low. Indeed, it may be, as Robinson [12] suggested, that the Maze is mainly indicative of an ability, or inclination, to sustain attention, not a good measure of capacity for resolving complex relationships.

Related to these findings is a suggestion that relative to other tests which are sensitive to the effects of brain damage, there is, according to Porteus, a "greater resistance of Maze test performance to the inroads of old age." This is a particularly interesting conjecture in light of the evidence suggesting that "the inroads of old age" are, to a considerable extent, accumulations of brain injuries.[13] Unfortunately, there are few studies of aging in which the Maze test was used. In evaluating this evidence, one must wonder if the Maze test has sufficient ceiling to detect decline in persons who function at a relatively high level—say, above what is represented roughly by an IQ of 115. That this supposition has merit is suggested by unpublished results obtained by M. B. Jensen in 1961. These indicate decline in Maze performance between age 46 to 66 in adults who had had less than eight years of schooling, but not in adults whose formal education extended beyond the eighth grade. The results of a study by Porteus and others (162) are also consistent with this hypothesis.

A number of studies of relationships between Maze performance and the effects produced by

12 ROBINSON, MARY FRANCES. "What Price Lobotomy?" *J Abn & Social Psychol* 41:421-36 O '46. *
13 HORN, JOHN L. Chap. 16, "The Organization of Data on Life-Span Development of Human Abilities," pp. 423-66. In *Life-Span Developmental Psychology: Research and Theory.* Edited by L. R. Goulet and Paul B. Baltes. New York: Academic Press, Inc., 1970. Pp. 580.
HORN, JOHN L., AND CATTELL, RAYMOND B. "Age Differences in Fluid and Crystallized Intelligence." *Acta Psychologica* 26:107-29 Mr '67. *
HORN, JOHN L., AND CATTELL, RAYMOND B. "Age Differences in Primary Mental Abilities." *J Gerontol* 21:210-20 Ap '66. *

drugs suggest that agents which induce ataraxia, namely the phenothiazines (such as chlorpromazine, i.e., Thorazine) produce a decrement in Maze performance, whereas analeptic stimulants (such as phenidylate, i.e., ritalin) produce an increase in scores. Porteus interprets these findings as indicating that midbrain activating functions support a capacity to maintain attention, which in turn supports the planning that is required for successful performance on the Maze test.

Porteus originally developed the Maze test for the purpose of providing more accurate diagnosis of mental retardation than was provided by other tests. The results from no fewer than 10 studies have suggested that in samples of persons who score in the lower fourth of the distribution of scores obtained with omnibus tests of intelligence, the Maze test provides a useful guide for discriminating between persons who are able to manage their affairs and support themselves in the community and persons who are not thus capable. The studies suffer from a number of detracting limitations in design and analysis, and Porteus consistently fails either to acknowledge the limitations or to neutralize criticisms which follow from them. For example, Porteus gives no indication that he is aware of the arguments put against a posteriori matched-group designs. Nevertheless, the consistency of the findings in this area is impressive.

A few studies have directly attacked hypotheses stipulating that the Maze measures capacity or inclination to plan, exercise forethought, sustain attention, and delay gratification. For example, Kainer (140) found that children who delayed gratification scored higher on the Maze than children who did not, and that this relationship could not be entirely accounted for by differences in verbal comprehension. Palkes and others (170) showed that when a random set of hyperactive boys were trained to verbalize self-directed commands designed to alter a heedless, slapdash approach to tasks, they improved in their performance on the Maze Extension Series relative to another random set of hyperactive boys who were not given the training.

These kinds of results thus suggest that an interesting ability is measured, with a reliability of about .75 or better, using the Maze diagrams and the ability-scoring procedures which Porteus has recommended. The ability is probably best described as a capacity or inclination to sustain attention in the face of the difficulty involved in resolving moderately complex spatial relations. It is depressed by brain damage and treatments that induce ataraxia; it may be raised somewhat by treatment with central nervous system stimulants and training that teaches one to take a more considered, deliberate approach to intellectual tasks. The ability is important in distinguishing between persons of generally low intellectual ability who can and cannot take care of themselves in societies such as our own. The test appears to provide fairly accurate measurements among persons of generally low ability but may not have enough ceiling to discriminate finely among persons well above the average in general competence.

The qualitative score has been studied most fully for its relationship to delinquent, sociopathic, antisocial behavior and, in general, has been found to correlate with this kind of behavior, as well as with a variety of variables indicating extraversion, carelessness, impulsivity, a tendency to make errors, and a tendency to strive for speed rather than accuracy in ability tests (see Payne [14] for review). Thus, it would appear that the Q-score is mainly indicative of impulsivity or impetuousness— an inability or unwillingness to refrain from behaving in a hasty, slapdash manner.

The fact that the qualitative Maze score correlates about −.40 with the ability score indicates that some of the variance in what is interpreted as an ability to sustain attention may be due to the lack of impulse control which the qualitative score is assumed to measure. This suggests that for purposes of defining more clearly what the two scores measure, and in indicating the practical validities of the two scores, it will be useful to remove the variance in each score that can be accounted for by variance in the other. It is desirable, also, to obtain more precise information about the equivalency, reliability, and long-term stability of the qualitative and ability variables. More information on the factorial validity of the test would also be very useful.

The Maze test thus presents a paradox. On the one hand there is an accumulation of evidence indicating that it provides measurements of attributes which applied and clinical psy-

chologists are often called upon to measure. On the other hand, there is the sad fact that the norms and the information on reliability are not of a quality sufficient to justify using the test in individual diagnosis. The test and the test manual fall far short of meeting the standards recommended by the APA-AERA-NCME Committee on Test Standards. To make the test truly appropriate for use in situations where it has the greatest promise of being useful—in diagnosis of brain damage and identification of the adaptability of poorly acculturated persons—the applied and clinical psychologist must yet determine by his own research such items as: (a) the norms which apply in the population with which he is concerned, (b) whether or not the test reliability is sufficient for his purposes, and (c) the long-term practical predictions which the test can support.

Thus, sadly, after over 50 years of research on the Maze test, it must be concluded that the test can be recommended only for research purposes and applied work that is based upon additional research appropriate to a particular setting. Yet, paradoxical though it may seem, the evidence supports the hypothesis that the test measures an important attribute not measured by other popular devices and thus is one of the more interesting and promising tests now known to psychology. It is to be hoped that these qualities may yet provoke psychologists, as Louttit (4:356) suggested almost 20 years ago, "to establish it on a firm technical base."

Brit J Criminol 7:236–7 Ap '67. H. B. Gibson. [Review of the manual (*143*).] The Porteus Maze test has a special interest for criminologists because results obtained with it have a feature which has been shown to be discriminative of delinquent populations. This is the well-known qualitative score, which reflects the degree to which the task has been executed in an apparently slovenly manner. What components of behaviour this score really represents have never yet been fully determined. Indeed, neither have the implications of the Test Quotient (a cognitive measure like an I.Q.) ever been adequately determined scientifically, in spite of a number of attempts by distinguished research workers. The test is a triumph of empiricism. Professor Porteus, the innovator of half a century ago, has been

14 PAYNE, R. W. Chap. 6, "Cognitive Abnormalities," pp. 193–261. In *Handbook of Abnormal Psychology: An Experimental Approach.* Edited by H. J. Eysenck. New York: Basic Books, Inc., Publishers, 1961. Pp. xvi, 816. *

content to reiterate his opinions about what is supposedly measured, without showing great interest in research into the *mechanisms* involved, as distinct from what can be done with the test. Much of what appears in this book has been published before, but it is useful to have such an historical compendium. It was to Porteus' credit that in the early days of psychology he recognised the need for a test that was not heavily biased by verbal knowledge. For many years he waged a spirited campaign to show that his creation was a "better" test of intelligence than the Binet, and the whole story is now retold. Later on, he discovered the value of the qualitative score; still later, the use of the test in evaluating the effects of psychosurgery. The latest development is that Porteus has sought to invade the field of "projective" techniques with his Maze—there is nothing which cannot be attempted with it! This book contains a chapter wherein a most inappropriate comparison is made between the Rorschach and the Maze test. Many modern psychologists have come to the conclusion that the Rorschach test is a lot of nonsense anyway, and should be discreetly abandoned. It is a pity that the author of the Maze test, which has so much of scientific interest in it yet to be explored, should in his enthusiasm advocate it in a vague way as a competitor among the "projective devices." This book contains many curious data, anthropological and otherwise, gathered in the course of Porteus' indefatigable penetration of remote lands with his Maze. The Appendices contain normative data concerning the Test Quotient which recent studies have shown to be utterly inappropriate to two populations of modern British schoolchildren.

Brit J Psychol 57:470 N '66. D. C. Kendrick. [Review of the manual (*143*).] * traces the development of the Maze Test from its first uses with feeble-minded children in 1915 up to the production of a second parallel form of the test in 1959 * In his final chapter Porteus gives the latest instructions and scoring systems for the test, and the appendices contain all three forms of the test plus tables of test quotients and examples of scoring. Porteus considers his test to be one not only of intelligence but also one of foresight and planning. The main criticism of this book is that he fails to delineate in any clear fashion just what the test really is supposed to be measuring. There appears to be no extensive study reported in the literature

which answers this question. A wealth of studies is cited in the book purporting to show what the test measures, but they become a little confusing after a while. The book itself is written in a rather peculiar style. It is a mixture of the historical novel, test manual and social anthropological report, peppered with the most extraordinary passages of preaching and scolding. Many readers may find this quite irritating and distracting.

Cont Psychol 11:517–8 N '66. Laurance F. Shaffer. [Review of the manual (*143*).] For any psychological test to evoke wide use and new research after half a century is rare enough. Even more remarkable is the appearance of a new book about such a test written by its originator. The present volume shows that the Porteus Maze Test is still a vigorous youngster. The book digs into the past, as one would expect, but it also deals with some very present concerns and takes not a few glances into the future. * Two chapters are devoted to the author's remarkable expeditions to observe and test the primitive natives of Australia, with new data obtained in 1962. Another chapter summarizes many studies with the Mazes of members of other preliterate societies. This material makes splendidly interesting reading, but much of it is good travelogue with only incidental relevance to the psychology of individual differences. The primitive subjects tested with the Mazes have in most instances constituted samples of expediency (one cannot say of convenience!) whose degree of representativeness is unknown. That these persons tested below white standards on the Mazes was inevitable; it is remarkable that they were able to perform so alien a task at all. Although the norms obtained in the Caucasian culture are inapplicable, the raw scores of the preliterates are pure prime data of some interest. Differences between the performances of groups are generally interpreted in cultural terms with no evidence of "racial" bias. While the book contains much good and relevant evidence about the Maze Test, the reviewer cannot suppress the wish that the data and their presentation might have been better and more complete. In all too many instances the reader needs to know more in order to interpret findings intelligently. An example is the typical absence of data on the dispersion of scores in samples. One cannot compare correlation coefficients without knowing the variances of the groups on which they were determined. Another technical fault is the absence of any evidence about the reliability of the Maze Test. This lack must be forgiven for the original single form which was unsuited for repeated administration or for breaking into equivalent parts, but the development of the two new forms for retesting—the "Extension" and "Supplement"—surely could have provided useful evidence on test stability. Equally vexing is the absence of sufficient data on the standardization of the test and of the derivation of the Test Quotients. There is, for example, no way to learn what the standard deviation of a TQ is at various ages, an essential bit of information if one is to compare the Maze Test with other instruments which use quotients. The last section of the book is a satisfactory guide for the administration and scoring, both quantitative and qualitative, of the three forms of the Maze Test. It is the handbook that a user needs, and supersedes earlier versions. But, lacking the detailed technical and normative data about the test, it is not a Manual as that term is now understood. What kind of a judgment can one make of the Maze Test as a whole? In spite of the lack of some technical information usually deemed essential, and in spite of some faults in the reporting of earlier studies relevant to validity, the test holds up well. The reviewer expresses his bias that empirical evidence about the concurrent and predictive powers of a test stands higher in the hierarchy of values than evidence about internal characteristics and standardization. But it would be gratifying to have both varieties of knowledge about the test, and the reviewer hopes that Dr. Porteus will some day furnish the missing pieces.

Ed & Psychol Meas 26:511–4 su '66. William D. Altus. [Review of the manual (*143*).] Stanley Porteus' life by almost any standard has been a highly successful one. He was vouchsafed fairly early an original insight in psychometrics and has carefully nursed his brain child along for over fifty years of application, research, and controversy. * Porteus....has never been accorded adequate professional recognition among American psychologists, possibly because he was something of an Ausländer among the natives. It seems more probable, though, that his espousal of tests as a touchstone for evaluating racial differences in intelligence in the long dead controversies of a generation back had more to do with the lack of acceptance of his mazes and the claims he has made for

them. * For 20 years after its publication in 1916 the Stanford-Binet Intelligence Scale was accepted as the true measure of intelligence, against which any newcomer must be validated. Thus it can be seen that Porteus and his mazes gave many hostages to fortune while making a bid for professional recognition in the United States: Porteus was "foreign," he chose unpopular causes, and Terman's Stanford-Binet Intelligence Scale was already entrenched. Only through long life, energy, and persistence have these hostages been neutralized. This book tells the story—a successful one—of the tangled Odyssey of the mazes. * Porteus believed that the performance measure he invented in the maze test cut through the pitfalls of the purely verbal measure and got at some native aptitudes of a practical nature, especially of "planfullness." It has taken him a lifetime to document his original hunch, but he has done it in a number of specific ways. Aside from Porteus' own publications, one of the good early confirmations of the special extra quality to be found in the mazes but not in the Binet type test was a study of Poull and Montgomery in 1929. They gave the Stanford-Binet Intelligence Scale and the mazes to inmates of a youth facility on Randall's Island, New York, about one half of whom consisted of juvenile delinquents while the other half was relatively free of psychopathic tainting. Stanford-Binet Intelligence Scale showed no mean differences between the two groups; the mazes did—the juvenile delinquent group scoring nine points lower. Slowly here, more readily in England, the mazes began to be accepted as an adjunct test in the clinical armamentarium and increasingly often as the test of choice if the child or adult were non-English or nearly so. * The mazes would appear to measure something both quantitatively and qualitatively which discriminates against the impulsive individuals so frequently found among the delinquent and criminal. The Porteus Maze Test was found by Porteus and Peters, later by Landis and Zubin to be a sensitive measure of the cerebral insult of psychosurgery. Whereas the Wechsler-Bellevue Intelligence Scale showed no impairment subsequent to the operation, the mazes did. * Porteus also demonstrated from the beginning that the maze test is a measure much to be preferred to the traditional intelligence test when institutional groups—the feeble of mind, the criminal, or the delinquent—are to be sorted for training or treatment. * What has been reported makes it seem likely that the test is a valuable adjunct for the anthropologist to know about and to employ for research purposes in his investigations. * In 99 out of 105 studies Porteus has found the male to have a maze test mean superior to that of the female. Porteus does not exactly claim that this shows general male superiority of intelligence; he suggests that it probably represents inherent temperamental differences. Since he has so often equated temperamental differences with manifest intelligence, one wonders whether he does not feel about women's mental inferiority somewhat the way he did about the various non-Caucasian groups in Hawaii and their numerous crosses which he tested and found wanting a generation ago. One hastens to add that this claim is not made in this latest book of Porteus. It may be that he has succumbed to the Zeitgeist. It may also be that he feels it is better not to tilt at windmills without allies. We should be thankful to Porteus for his mazes and for his research. He is still a vigorous, undaunted sample of what originality, persistence, hard work, and long life can bring about. Let us hope that he brings us up-to-date once more when he reaches the century mark.

For reviews by C. M. Louttit and Gladys C. Schwesinger, see 4:356.

[420]

★Preschool Attainment Record, Research Edition. Ages 6 months to 7 years; 1966–67; PAR; 9 scores: ambulation, manipulation, rapport, communication, responsibility, information, ideation, creativity, total; individual; 1 form ('66, 5 pages plus profile); manual ['67, 24 pages plus test]; no data on reliability; no norms; $2.50 per 25 record blanks; $1.35 per manual; postage extra; $1.50 per specimen set, postpaid; [15–20] minutes; Edgar A. Doll; American Guidance Service, Inc. *

REFERENCES

1. Doll, Edgar A., and McKnight, Edward L. "A Preschool Educational Attainment Scale." *Cereb Palsy J* 26:3–5 Jl–Ag '65. * (PA 40:744)
2. Doll, Edgar A. "An Attainment Scale for Appraising Young Children With Expressive Handicaps." *Cereb Palsy J* 27:3–5 S–O '66. * (PA 41:1815)
3. Stedman, Donald J.; Clifford, Miriam; and Spitznagel, Anne. "A Comparison of Ratings of Mothers and Teachers on the Preschool Attainment Record of 17 Five Year Old Children." *Excep Children* 35(6):488–9 F '69. *
4. Blair, John R. "A Comparison of Mother and Teacher Ratings on the Preschool Attainment Record of Four Year Old Children." *Excep Children* 37(4):299–300 D '70. *
5. Owens, Earl P., and Bowling, Donald H. "Internal Consistency and Factor Structure of the Preschool Attainment Record." *Am J Mental Def* 75(2):170–1 S '70. * (PA 45:8814)

Roberta R. Collard, *Assistant Professor of Human Development, University of Massachusetts, Amherst, Massachusetts.*

The *Preschool Attainment Record* is an expansion of the early age levels of the *Vineland Social Maturity Scale* and is designed to measure the physical, social, mental, and language attainments of children from 6 months to 7 years. The purpose of the PAR is to determine the child's usual behavior in the areas tested rather than what he is able to do. Like the VSMS, the PAR is administered as a structured interview with an adult closely associated with the child to be evaluated, or on the basis of direct observation of the child's behavior by the examiner.

The test is divided into eight areas with 14 age items in each category: one item for each half-year interval up to 7 years. The eight areas are: Ambulation, Manipulation, Rapport, Communication, Responsibility, Information, Ideation, and Creativity. Items are arranged in order of increasing difficulty; for example, the category Ambulation includes a range of behavior items from "Sits unsupported" to "Rides play vehicles."

The scale is intended to be used to determine the developmental level of children for whom verbal intelligence tests are not appropriate; for example, children with sensory or neuromuscular impairments, speech or language disabilities, emotional disturbances, resistance to testing, and cultural differences. More specifically, it is well adapted for testing deaf, blind, or aphasic children; children with cerebral palsy, mental retardation, autism, or schizophrenia; and children whose development has been impaired by sensory or cultural deprivation or who do not speak English. It has the advantage over tests such as the Stanford-Binet of including motor skills, social competencies, and creativity, as well as intellectual abilities. The record blank includes spaces for a description of the child's socioeconomic and cultural-linguistic background and family constellation and for medical referral notes on disabilities or illnesses.

Items are scored +, −, or ± for pass, fail, and doubtful, respectively. To determine the raw score, each item passed is counted as one, and ± scores are given half credit. As there are 16 items per year, the Attainment Age is calculated by dividing the total score by 16, or the raw score could be multiplied by .75 to derive the month value.

The procedure of using precise numerical scoring may be open to criticism because of the possibility of subjectivity of the adult's report on the child and the impreciseness of the behavioral measures. However, if the test score is interpreted with these limitations in mind and the test results are used to note areas of difficulty and strengths in the child's development, the use of a precise score should not necessarily be misleading. Because of the unreliability of some of the items, such a criticism could be leveled at most developmental tests based on observation.

As Doll mentions in the manual, there is considerable overlap in the classification of the areas of behavior sampled by the PAR, particularly in the areas of Communication, Ideation, and Information. Although this problem cannot be completely surmounted, the logic of some of the classifications could be improved. For example, an item which involves adding amounts up to 10 and counting by 5's to 30 is included under Communication, while several levels of counting are included under Ideation. The area of Communication could best be called Language, because some of the items such as "Babbling" and "Imitation" are not, strictly speaking, Communication.

The instructions on the administration of the test are generally clear, but this reviewer would have appreciated a larger number of specific examples of good questions to be asked to elicit the information to be scored. Most of the definitions of the behaviors are clear, but some need examples for clarity. Also, some of the categories contain several behaviors, and it is not clearly stated whether the child must show *all* of these behaviors to pass the item completely.

I find the age placement of some of the items questionable as the behaviors are now defined. For example, play is arranged into six levels: from parallel play (age 3.0) to playing simple group table games (age 7.0). Although most of the age placements appear reasonable in terms of systematic observations reported in the literature, item 91, "Plays pretend" (which includes imaginative play and role play with leading or following in evidence) is given a mean of 6.0 years, which seems high to me, as I have observed such play to be almost universal after age 4½ in both upper middle class and Head Start children if they have had an opportunity to play with other children before. On the other hand, in the area of Creativity, item 48, "Dramatizes stories," which includes dressing up or acting out roles is placed at age 3.0 which seems low. Item 50, "Throws objects" (flings object nonrandomly with arm, hand, and wrist), is given an age mean of 3.5 years, whereas in the *Gesell Developmental Schedules* the age at which most children are expected to throw a ball in a particular direction is 21 months. To answer or score this item accurately would require careful observation of the child's method of throwing an object.

Some of the items under Rapport and Responsibility indicate a high value placed on conformity and obedience, such as "Minds" (age 2.0), "Complies" (age 2.5), "Cleans up" (age 5.0), "Helps" (age 5.5), "Conforms" (age 6.0), and "Observes routines" (age 7.0). A qualifying phrase such as "reasonably often" would give these items less of an authoritarian ring. I miss items under Rapport which would indicate whether or not the child has friends or shows empathy. Affectionate responses are placed in the category Information. I also miss items on moral development which would indicate degree of internalization of control versus impulsivity. There are few items indicating qualities of ego strength, such as confidence, self-esteem, frustration tolerance, persistence at tasks, foresight, and ability to find or accept substitute gratification or to delay gratification. The test includes few items on emotions, none on fears or on aggression toward persons.

Despite these omissions and within the limits of the areas covered, the PAR appears to be a good basic inventory of the behaviors of infants and young children, based on maturation and social expectations in American culture. As a scale which does not require language and includes motor and social as well as intellectual competencies, it should prove useful in evaluating the developmental strengths and weaknesses of young children with physical, emotional, or culturally-based developmental difficulties.

Psychol Rep 21:1029 D '67. C. H. Ammons. * assessment is much like that required on the Vineland Social Maturity Scale. Some item definitions are lacking in specificity. No normative data are presented. No reliability or validity information is reported.

[421]

★**Queensland Test.** Ages 7 and over; 1968–70; QT; based (except for pattern matching subtest) on the unpublished *PIR Test* used for screening for the Pacific Island Regiment; essentially the same as 5 of the 6 subtests in the *New Guinea Performance Scales* except for minor differences in some of the testing materials and differences in administration, scoring, and norms population; for the selection of subjects "likely to be able to learn rapidly the complex skills of westernized urbanized cultures from among groups who had had little contact with that culture"; administered by pantomime; 6 scores: *Knox Cube Test*, beads, modified *Passalong Test*, form assembly, pattern matching, total; individual; 1 form; manual ('70, 179 pages); record form ['68, 4 pages]; 3 sets of norms: Australian school children, aboriginal children with a medium amount of European contact, aboriginal children with low contact; Aus \$95 per set of testing materials, 50 record forms, and manual; \$3 per 50 record forms; \$7 per manual; postpaid within Australia; (45–65) minutes; D. W. McElwain, G. E. Kearney, and I. G. Ord (test and record form); Australian Council for Educational Research. *

REFERENCES

1. ORD, I. G. *Development of a Test of Cognitive Capacity for Indigenes of Papua-New Guinea.* Master's thesis, University of Queensland (Brisbane, Australia), 1959.
2. KEARNEY, GEORGE E. "Cognitive Capacity Among the Orokaiva." *New Guinea Res B* 13:1–25 '66. *
3. KEARNEY, JACQUELINE E. *A New Performance Scale of Cognitive Capacity for Use With Deaf Subjects.* Master's thesis, University of Queensland (Brisbane, Australia), 1967.
4. KEARNEY, GEORGE ENGLAND. *Some Aspects of the General Cognitive Ability of Various Groups of Aboriginal Australians as Assessed by the Queensland Test.* Doctor's thesis, University of Queensland (Brisbane, Australia), 1968.
5. ORD, I. G. "The P.I.R. Test and Derivatives." *Austral Psychologist* 2:137–46 Mr '68. * (*PA* 42:18-98)
6. KEARNEY, JACQUELINE E. "A New Performance Scale of Cognitive Capacity for Use With Deaf Subjects." *Am Ann Deaf* 114(1):2–14 Ja '69. * (*PA* 43:7197)
7. KEARNEY, JACQUELINE E. "Verbalization Tests." *Austral Psychologist* 5(2):164–76 Jl '70. * (*PA* 45:8719)

[422]

The Quick Test. Ages 2 and over; 1958–62; QT; picture vocabulary; individual; Forms 1, 2, 3, ('58, 1 card); provisional manual ('62, 54 pages, reprint of 2 below); instruction cardboard ('62, 1 page); item cardboard ('62, 1 page, includes words for all 3 forms); record-norms sheet ('62, 2 pages); norms for combinations of 2 or 3 forms also presented; \$8 per set of testing materials including all 3 forms, 100 record sheets, and manual; \$2.50 per manual; cash orders postpaid; specimen set not available (manual illustrates all materials); (3–10) minutes; R. B. Ammons and C. H. Ammons; Psychological Test Specialists. *

REFERENCES

1–3. See 6:534.
4. BIBB, JOHN JAMES, JR. *A Study of the Quick Test as a Screening Instrument for Educable Mentally Retarded Children.* Doctor's thesis, University of Virginia (Charlottesville, Va.), 1964. (*DA* 25:3386) (Abstract: *Ed R* 2:69–71)
5. METHVIN, MARILYN. "Quick Test Performances of Mentally Retarded Individuals." *Am J Mental Def* 68:540–2 Ja '64. *
6. CARLISLE, A. L. "Quick Test Performance by Institutional Retardates." *Psychol Rep* 17:489–90 O '65. * (*PA* 40:886)
7. DOYLE, EDWARD D. *A Comparison of IQ's on the WAIS and Q.T. With a Group of Spinal Cord Injury Patients.* Master's thesis, Loyola University (Chicago, Ill.), 1965.
8. OGILVIE, ROBERT D. "Correlations Between the Quick Test (QT) and the Wechsler Adult Intelligence Scale (WAIS) as Used in a Clinical Setting." *Psychol Rep* 16:497–8 Ap '65. * (*PA* 39:10081)
9. OTTO, WAYNE, AND McMENEMY, RICHARD A. "An Appraisal of the Ammons Quick Test in a Remedial Reading Program." *J Ed Meas* 2:193–8 D '65. * (*PA* 40:4769)
10. PLESS, I. BARRY; SNIDER, MARVIN; EATON, ANN E.; AND KEARSLEY, RICHARD B. "A Rapid Screening Test for Intelligence in Children: A Preliminary Report." *Am J Dis Children* 109:533–7 Je '65. * (*PA* 40:425)
11. WHITNEY, VIRGIL, AND METZGER, ROLLAND. "The Quick Test as an Intelligence Screening Device in a Large Scale Program of Employee Applicant Testing." *J Clin Psychol* 21:71–2 Ja '65. * (*PA* 39:12315)
12. ANDREWS, R. J., AND ANDERSON, J. "The Use of the Quick Test in a Number of Clinical and Routine Settings." *Austral Psychologist* 1:116–20 N '66. * (*PA* 42:3191)
13. ABIDIN, RICHARD R., JR., AND BYRNE, ALFRED V. "Quick Test Validation Study and Examination of Form Equivalency." *Psychol Rep* 20:735–9 Je '67. * (*PA* 41:13591)
14. COLE, SPURGEON, AND WILLIAMS, ROBERT. "The Quick Test as an Index of Intellectual Ability on a Negro Admission Ward." *Psychol Rep* 20:581–2 Ap '67. * (*PA* 41:8146)
15. KING, FRANCIS W. "Quick Test Inter-Form Reliability in Diverse Clinical Groups and the Effect of Age Correction Factor." *Psychol Rep* 20:193–4 F '67. * (*PA* 41:7502)
16. LAMP, ROBERT E., AND BARCLAY, A. "The Quick Test as a Screening Device for Intellectually Subnormal Children." *Psychol Rep* 20:763–6 Je '67. * (*PA* 41:13596)
17. MEDNICK, MARTHA T. "Relationship of the Ammons Quick Test of Intelligence to Other Ability Measures." *Psychol Rep* 20:523–6 Ap '67. * (*PA* 41:9390)
18. STEWART, HORACE; COLE, SPURGEON; AND WILLIAMS, ROBERT. "Relationship Between the QT and WAIS in a Restricted Clinical Sample." *Psychol Rep* 20:383–6 Ap '67. * (*PA* 41:9087)
19. WIRLS, CHARLES J., AND PLOTKIN, ROSALIE R. "Calculation of Quick Test IQs for Children With Mental Ages Seventeen and Above." *Psychol Rep* 20:603–5 Ap '67. * (*PA* 41:8172)
20. BONFIELD, JOHN RONALD. *Predictors of Achievement for Educable Mentally Retarded Children.* Doctor's thesis, Pennsylvania State University (University Park, Pa.), 1968. (*DAI* 30:1009A)
21. CONNOLLY, JOSEPH KENNETH. *The Discriminative Functions of Brief Tests With the Educable Mentally Retarded.* Doctor's thesis, Fordham University (New York, N.Y.), 1968. (*DA* 29:2997A)
22. COYLE, F. A., JR., AND ERDBERG, PHILIP. "Quick Test Administration With Mental Retardates." *Psychol Rep* 22:1091–2 Je '68. * (*PA* 42:18997)
23. FELDMAN, SOLOMON E. "Utility of Some Rapid Estimations of Intelligence in a College Population." *Psychol Rep* 22:23–6 F '68. * (*PA* 42:10572)
24. HOUSTON, CAMILLE, AND OTTO, WAYNE. "Poor Readers' Functioning on the WISC, Slosson Intelligence Test and Quick Test." Abstract. *AERA Paper Abstr* 1968:120-1 '68. *
25. HOUSTON, CAMILLE, AND OTTO, WAYNE. "Poor Readers' Functioning on the WISC, Slosson Intelligence Test and Quick Test." *J Ed Res* 62:15–9 D '68. *
26. LAMP, ROBERT E., AND BARCLAY, A. "Comparisons of Scores on Quick Test and Stanford-Binet, Form L-M, for Retarded Children." *Psychol Rep* 23:401–2 O '68. * (*PA* 43:10229)
27. LEVINE, NIRA R. *Validation of the Quick Test for an Elderly Population.* Doctor's thesis, University of Virginia (Charlottesville, Va.), 1969. (*DAI* 31:646A)
28. MEDNICK, MARTHA T. "The Validity of the Ammons' Quick Test of Intelligence." *Psychol Rep* 24(2):388–90 Ap '69. * (*PA* 43:15012)
29. QUATTLEBAUM, LAWRENCE F., AND WHITE, WILLIAM F. "Relationship Between Two Quick Screening Measures of Intelligence for Neuropsychiatric Patients." *Psychol Rep* 24(3):691–3 Je '69. * (*PA* 44:868)
30. QUATTLEBAUM, LAWRENCE F., AND WHITE, WILLIAM F. "Relationships Among the Quick Test, Two Measures of Psychomotor Functioning, and Age." *Percept & Motor Skills* 29(3):824–6 D '69. * (*PA* 46:5150)
31. STRANDBERG, T. E.; GRIFFITH, J.; AND MINER, L. "Child Language and Screening Intelligence." *J Commun Disorders* 2(3):268–72 Ag '69. * (*PA* 44:3464)
32. CULL, JOHN G., AND COLVIN, CRAIG R. "Correlation Between the Quick Test (QT) and the WAIS Verbal Scale in the Rehabilitation Setting." *Psychol Rep* 27(1):105–6 Ag '70. * (*PA* 45:6807)
33. DAVIS, WILLIAM E., AND DIZZONNE, MICHAEL F. "Relationship Between the QT and the WAIS." *Psychol Rep* 26(2):457–8 Ap '70. * (*PA* 44:21167)

Brit J Psychol 55:117 F '64. B. Semeonoff. * essentially a shortened version of the....*Full Range Picture Vocabulary Test* * Each of its three "forms" is represented by a card bearing four line drawings. The subject is required to say, for each of 50 words associated with a given card, which of the four pictures "best fits it." The purpose of the test is to provide a means of "quick screening of verbal intelligence in practical situations." Separate norms (in the form of "I.Q." conversions) are provided for each form separately, any pair, or all three together. The idea is an attractive one, but the material published is open to criticism. Three points, in order of increasing seriousness, are as follows: First, the drawings are crude—though seldom really ambiguous. Secondly, some of the attributions of meaning, and the cues on which they rest, are highly dubious. Thus, *celerity* is regarded as appropriate to a picture of a restaurant because the waitress is "bending over in her hurry." Again, in the same picture the diner very definitely looks *bovine*—another of the key words, for which the correct choice is a drawing showing a cow by a stream, because, the manual says, this "is the only drawing with a cow on it." Thirdly, and finally, the method seems positively to encourage acceptance of loose use of language. Whether this is inherent in the method would seem to rest on further experiment with better pictures. Here everything seems to have been sacrificed to convenience, and one cannot help feeling that the validities claimed for the test and its parent FRPV (which are considerable) must have been achieved in spite of rather than because of their characteristic features. *

Ed & Psychol Meas 25:268–71 sp '65. Peter F. Merenda. [Review of the Provisional Manual.] This excellent monograph....is....a provisional manual....[and]....a combination of *(a)* an exposition on the merits of brief screening devices for estimating a wide range of human intellectual abilities; *(b)* a plea to critics of short psychological tests to consider factors other than brevity in their evaluation of such instruments; and *(c)* a review and summary of the professional literature reporting a great scope of research findings with the *QT* and its parent test—*The Full-Range Picture Vocabulary Test (FRPV).* * the authors....maintain that they have found that reasonably intelligent adults with no formal training in testing can learn to administer the *QT* efficiently and that with some additional training such persons can be taught to interpret it adequately. They go on to say that it is better to train non-psychologists to administer and interpret these tests adequately rather than unrealistically to expect untrained persons to do absolutely no testing! In line with this reasoning, they have simplified the presentation of directions and materials in this manual. Such statements will undoubtedly elicit some strong negative reactions on the part of the authors' professional colleagues, but

this reviewer for one, on the basis of his own personal experiences, is willing to agree with Ammons and Ammons. * the controversial nature of the contents of much of this provisional manual for the *QT* is deemed inevitable. There will be those who will undoubtedly be greatly concerned about the brevity of the tests, the relatively small samples utilized in the normative, reliability, and validity research, and the rather high correlation coefficients reported which suggest spuriousness. To these critics, and to all users or potential users of the *QT,* this reviewer can only advise others to consult the basic research literature on the *QT* to which the authors make repeated reference in the monograph. Of course, this reviewer is not necessarily willing to accept all the findings reported in the monograph at face value. Nevertheless, the data and arguments presented by Ammons and Ammons are both impressive and seemingly convincing. Therefore, they cannot be blindly ignored! If the *QT* is only partly as good as the data and findings reported in this provisional manual seem to imply, then the authors will have made an outstanding and lasting contribution to the field of psychological testing. It is necessary, however, for the discriminating user and researcher to go beyond the data reported herein and, as the authors themselves suggest, conduct his own research with the *QT.*

For reviews by Boyd R. McCandless and Ellen V. Piers, see 6:534.

[423]
★**Ring and Peg Tests of Behavior Development.** Birth to age 6; 1958–64; RPTBD; experimental; 6 scores: ambulative, manipulative, communicative, social adaptive, emotive, total; individual; 1 form ('58); mimeographed revised manual ('64, 164 pages, identical with 1958 manual except for 9 pages of inserts); administration booklet ('64, 10 pages); $15 per kit including 10 scoring sheets, 10 administration booklets, manual, and set of manipulation objects; $6 per manual; cash orders postpaid; (20–50) minutes; Katharine M. Banham; Psychometric Affiliates. *

JANE V. HUNT, *Assistant Research Psychologist, Institute of Human Development, University of California, Berkeley, California.*

This infant and preschool scale contains items derived from a number of existing mental tests. Ten items and ten alternates are included at each age level. Age levels are divided into monthly intervals during the first year, bimonthly intervals during the second year, and six-month intervals from 2½ through 6 years.

An alternate item is included for each item of the scale, to be given and scored when the basic item is omitted or failed. Many of the alternates provide for the administration of the item by a familiar adult when the examiner cannot elicit the desired response; other alternates allow for varying the position of the stimulus, accepting alternative behaviors with test materials, providing different materials for the same task, or assessing completely different tasks. The test is scored either as a cumulative total score, yielding a behavior age and a ratio developmental quotient, or as a developmental profile of the five behavioral categories of the test. These categories (ambulative, manipulative, communicative, social adaptive, and emotive) are systematically represented by two items at each age level.

Reliability and validity studies with normal infants and children are essentially lacking. Scores on the Ring and Peg tests have been compared with scores on the *Cattell Infant Intelligence Scale* or on the *Stanford-Binet Intelligence Scale* for small groups of children at ages of approximately 7 months, 8 months, 4 years, and 5 years. These groups varied in size from 10 to 39 children; mean IQ for the groups ranged from 50 to 86. Split-half reliability (odd and even numbers) yielded rank difference coefficients of correlation of .95 or higher. Rank difference correlations between this test and the Cattell scale for the infant groups were .86 and .75. The correlation between the Ring and Peg tests and the Cattell scale for the four-year-olds was .73; the correlation between this test and the Stanford-Binet for the five-year-olds was .89.

Because of the lack of standardization on a representative sample of normal children, the RPTBD should be used as an experimental scale only and should not be used in lieu of a more reliable instrument. The behavioral subscales of the test are particularly experimental, as there are few items in each category at each level and because no evidence is presented to substantiate content validity. Item selection appears to have been made on an ad hoc basis, a method often debatable, particularly in the domains of social adaptive behavior and emotive behavior.

The author stresses the compact size of the test as an asset, but the advantage of compactness is offset by the extremely limited amount of material available to capture the interest of the child. Repeated presentation of the rings and pegs in different situations can lead either to diminished interest in the materials or to perseverative attempts to use the materials in a manner other than that desired at a given moment. For example, at the nine-month level the infant is expected to drop the peg and wait for the adult response, but at the ten-month level he is expected to hold two pegs and reach for a third. An infant tested on both items might elect to continue the first behavior when handed the same material again. Infants and young children sometimes display idiosyncratic preferences for, or rejection of, particular test materials. If the infant rejected either the pegs or rings of this test, test reliability would be considerably diminished. An additional drawback of the compact size of the test is the very fine, almost unreadable print used in the small administration booklet.

SUMMARY. This test is an unstandardized developmental scale which may be elected for research purposes but should not be used as a replacement for existing tests having known reliability. The systematic effort to include items from each of five behavioral categories at each age level is laudable, but the small number of such items at each age level and the ad hoc decisions of item selection make individual profile analyses extremely dubious. Research is needed to test the validity of the functional divisions of the test. The inclusion of an alternate for each item is novel but, again, research is needed to measure the effects of this innovative approach on test reliability.

EMMY E. WERNER, *Professor of Child Development and Research Child Psychologist, University of California, Davis, California.*

The *Ring and Peg Tests of Behavior Development* was published in experimental form in 1958 to serve the needs of clinical psychologists, psychiatrists, and pediatricians attached to child guidance clinics, hospitals, institutions for the mentally retarded, and traveling mental health clinics.

Test materials are inexpensive, simple, attractive to children, and less dependent on cultural opportunities than materials used in other preschool scales. They consist of pencil and paper, shoelaces, a handkerchief, a box, and a yellow (or blue) plastic pegbase with three blue (or yellow) pegs and eight graded rings to fit over them, four blue and four yellow.

Behavior subtests were selected on the basis of similarity to items of existing scales, including the Stanford-Binet, the Gesell, the California, Minnesota, Merrill-Palmer, Cattell, Northwestern, Buehler, Griffiths, and Vineland scales, with age placements taken from these scales. A thorough standardization on representative samples of children and a careful item analysis remain to be done.

A cursory examination of the age placement of the items in the five behavior categories suggests that some of the items in the section on ambulative development are now passed at an earlier age, as the 1969 revision of the *Bayley Scales of Infant Development* indicates. The same appears to hold for some of the items on social-adaptive development that were taken from the Vineland Scale. The section on manipulative development is excellent in its imaginative use of simple materials to test form-perception and eye-hand coordination. The section on communicative development has more detailed observations on early vocalizations than other infant and preschool scales. The predictive value of these items in forecasting later cognitive development ought to be explored. The section on emotive development (motivation, interest, drive) besides being probably the weakest, is difficult to differentiate from the other subscales.

Assets of the tests are: (*a*) the selection of test items that involve learning and problem solving with little dependence on cultural opportunities; (*b*) the imaginative use of simple materials; (*c*) clearly stated instructions that make allowance for alternate items; and (*d*) test items that can be administered as either an age scale or a point scale.

Data on the validity and reliability continue to be only preliminary in the 1964 manual. Preliminary studies of concurrent validity are based on correlations (ranging from .73 to .89) between behavior age scores on some small samples and scores on the *Cattell Infant Intelligence Scale* and the Stanford-Binet. Mean scores on the RPTBD are generally somewhat lower than mean scores on the Cattell and Stanford-Binet for the same children, but the variability of the scores is somewhat higher. Unfortunately, no additional validation studies have been undertaken since the publication of the revised manual in 1964.

SUMMARY. The Ring and Peg tests are still in experimental form, 12 years after their pub-

lication. It is hoped that, after a long period of neglect, the present surge of interest in the early diagnosis of developmental defects, especially among the culturally deprived, and in cross-cultural research with young children may lead to a rediscovery of this simple, imaginative, inexpensive, and reliable instrument that covers a wider range of behavior than most infant and preschool tests on the market. The real job of standardization and validation, however, remains to be done.

[424]

Slosson Intelligence Test. Ages 2 weeks and over; 1961–63; SIT; based in part upon *Stanford-Binet Intelligence Scale, Third Revision* and *Gesell Developmental Schedules;* individual; 1 form ('63); manual ('63, 43 pages, including test questions, sample score sheets, IQ finder, and other materials); score sheet ('63, 2 pages); IQ classification chart ('62, 2 pages); $3.75 per examiner's kit of manual, pad of 20 score sheets, and pad of 20 copies of the *Slosson Oral Reading Test;* $1 per additional pad of 20 score sheets; 75¢ per pad of 20 IQ classification charts; postpaid; (10–30) minutes; Richard L. Slosson; Slosson Educational Publications. *

REFERENCES

1. DELAPA, GIACINTO. *Correlates of Slosson Intelligence Test, Stanford Binet, Form L-M, and Achievement Indices.* Doctor's thesis, West Virginia University (Morgantown, W.Va.), 1967. (*DA* 28:3498A)
2. O'KEEFE, STEPHEN LOUIS. *An Inquiry Into the Use of the Slosson Intelligence Test With Fast Learning.* Master's thesis, Ohio State University (Columbus, Ohio), 1967.
3. AMES, LOUISE BATES. "Academic Progress in Negro Schools." *J Learn Dis* 1:570–7 O '68. * (*PA* 45:3029)
4. BONFIELD, JOHN RONALD. *Predictors of Achievement for Educable Mentally Retarded Children.* Doctor's thesis, Pennsylvania State University (University Park, Pa.), 1968. (*DAI* 30:1009A)
5. BURNS, LORNA M. *The Slosson Intelligence Test as a Pre-Screening Instrument With Potentially Gifted Children.* Master's thesis, Sacramento State College (Sacramento, Calif.), 1968.
6. DELAPA, GIACINTO. "The Slosson Intelligence Test: A Screening and Retesting Technique for Slow Learners." Abstract. *J Sch Psychol* 6:224–5 sp '68. *
7. DUGGAN, MARY DIONYSIA. *A Study of the Relation Between the Slosson Reading and Intelligence Tests and Other Standardized Tests at the Second Grade Level.* Master's thesis, Cardinal Stritch College (Milwaukee, Wis.), 1968.
8. FAGERT, CHARLES M. *The Relationship Between the Slosson Intelligence Test and the Wechsler Intelligence Scale for Children.* Master's thesis, Kent State University (Kent, Ohio), 1968.
9. HOUSTON, CAMILLE, AND OTTO, WAYNE. "Poor Readers' Functioning on the WISC, Slosson Intelligence Test and Quick Test." Abstract. *AERA Paper Abstr* 1968:120–1 '68. *
10. HOUSTON, CAMILLE, AND OTTO, WAYNE. "Poor Readers' Functioning on the WISC, Slosson Intelligence Test and Quick Test." *J Ed Res* 62:157–9 D '68. *
11. KEANY, MARY. *A Study of the Relation Between the Slosson Reading and Intelligence Tests and Other Standardized Tests at the Sixth Grade Level.* Master's thesis, Cardinal Stritch College (Milwaukee, Wis.), 1968.
12. MCRAE, J. *A Comparison of the Wechsler Preschool and Primary Scale of Intelligence With the Slosson Intelligence Test.* Master's thesis, Eastern Washington State College (Cheney, Wash.), 1968.
13. WHITACRE, ROGER L. *Use of the Slosson Intelligence Test With the Stanford-Binet, L-M, as a Screening Device for Slow Learner Placement.* Master's thesis, Bowling Green State University (Bowling Green, Ohio), 1968.
14. HAMMILL, DONALD. "The Slosson Intelligence Test as a Quick Estimate of Mental Ability." *J Sch Psychol* 7(4):33–7 '68–69 ['69]. * (*PA* 44:2794)
15. HUTTON, JERRY B. "Practice Effects on Intelligence and School Readiness Tests for Preschool Children." *Training Sch B* 65(4):130–4 F '69. * (*PA* 44:4229)
16. JONGEWARD, PAUL A. "A Validity Study of the Slosson Intelligence Test for Use With Educable Mentally Retarded

Students." *J Sch Psychol* 7(4):59–63 '68–69 ['69]. * (*PA* 44: 2702)

17. JONGEWARD, PAUL ALBERT. *A Validity Study of the Slosson Intelligence Test for Use With Educable Mentally Retarded Students.* Doctor's thesis, University of Oregon (Eugene, Ore.), 1969. (*DAI* 30:3323A)

18. KAUFMAN, HARVEY, AND IVANOFF, JOHN. "The Slosson Intelligence Test as a Screening Instrument With a Rehabilitation Population." *Excep Children* 35(9):745 My '69. * (*PA* 44:18977)

19. KILDUFF, CAROL T. *A Study of the Relation Between the Slosson Reading and Intelligence Tests and Other Standardized Tests at the Fourth Grade Level.* Master's thesis, Cardinal Stritch College (Milwaukee, Wis.), 1969.

20. NASH, MARY SAUNDERS. *The Development of Depth Perception in Intermediate Age Children.* Doctor's thesis, University of Kentucky (Lexington, Ky.), 1969. (*DAI* 30:3894B)

21. NICHOLSON, CHARLES L. "The Use of Four Screening Instruments." *Ann Inter Conf Assn Children Learn Dis* 6: 101–7 '69. *

22. O'NEILL, HUGH DANIEL, JR. *Partial Validation of the Slosson Intelligence Test.* Doctor's thesis, University of Oklahoma (Norman, Okla.), 1969. (*DAI* 30:3797A)

23. SHEPHERD, CLYDE W., JR. "Childhood Chronic Illness and Visual Motor Perceptual Development." *Excep Children* 36(1):39–42 S '69. * (*PA* 44:21470)

24. CARLISLE, A. LINDSAY; SHINEDLING, MARTIN M.; AND WEAVER, RICHARD. "Note on the Use of the Slosson Intelligence Test With Mentally Retarded Residents." *Psychol Rep* 26(3):865–6 Je '70. * (*PA* 45:1191)

25. GILLESPIE, PATRICIA HALL. *A Study of the Performance of Dyslexic and Normal Readers on the Slosson Intelligence Test for Children and Adults.* Doctor's thesis, West Virginia University (Morgantown, W.Va.), 1970. (*DAI* 31:2003A)

26. HAMMILL, DONALD D.; CRANDELL, JOHN M., JR.; AND COLARUSSO, RONALD. "The Slosson Intelligence Test Adapted for Visually Limited Children." *Excep Children* 36(7):535–6 Mr '70. *

27. HUTTON, JERRY BOB. *Relationships Between Preschool Screening Test Data and First Grade Academic Performance for Head Start Children.* Doctor's thesis, University of Houston (Houston, Tex.), 1970. (*DAI* 31:395B)

28. MEISSLER, GEORGE R. *A Correlation of the Slosson Intelligence Test and the Wechsler Intelligence Scale When Administered to Atypical Children.* Doctor's thesis, Catholic University of America (Washington, D.C.), 1970. (*DAI* 31:2191A)

29. NICHOLSON, CHARLES L. "Analysis of Functions of the Slosson Intelligence Test." *Percept & Motor Skills* 31(2): 627–31 O '70. * (*PA* 45:6336)

30. STUHLER, AGNES M. *An Experimental Study of the Relation Between the Slosson Reading and Intelligence Tests and Other Standardized Tests at the First Grade Level.* Master's thesis, Cardinal Stritch College (Milwaukee, Wis.), 1970.

31. SWANSON, MERLYN S., AND JACOBSON, ANITA. "Evaluation of the S.I.T. for Screening Children With Learning Disabilities." *J Learn Dis* 3(6):318–20 Je '70. * Reply by Richard L. Slosson. 3(9):466 S '70. *

PHILIP HIMELSTEIN, *Professor of Psychology and Head of the Department, The University of Texas at El Paso, El Paso, Texas.*

The *Slosson Intelligence Test* is a brief individual test of intelligence designed to be used by relatively untrained examiners as well as qualified professionals in working with both children and adults. Testing and scoring take from 10–30 minutes depending on how quickly the basal level (10 consecutive passes before the first error occurs) and the termination point (10 consecutive failures) are reached. Scoring is fairly objective and can be accomplished during testing without loss of rapport with the subject since each item is accompanied by the correct response.

The SIT is an adaptation of items from the Stanford-Binet, but with a lower base (2 weeks) and a higher ceiling (27 years) than the Binet. Many of the items in the lower age group are adapted from the *Gesell Develop-*

mental Schedules. In spite of the higher ceiling, the chronological age for purposes of calculating the IQ never exceeds 16 years, thus limiting the test for use with adults. Although the test is essentially adapted from and validated against the Stanford-Binet (Form L-M) the SIT continues to employ the ratio IQ. The test, therefore, has all of the problems of the ratio IQ, although this is apparently not recognized by the test author. Witness the following quotation from the test manual: "For validation purposes ....the Stanford-Binet, Form L-M has been used. Thus, while the SIT IQ's have a ratio basis—they have all of the advantages of the 'deviation IQ.'" Since one of the advantages of the deviation IQ is that the mean and standard deviation are the same for all age groups, Slosson can hardly claim to share in that advantage.

The manual has many serious deficiencies. One of these is the use of testimonials, often representing the worst of the advertising world. The back cover of the manual has tributes from unspecified authorities, such as "director of research in an institute of child development," "associate principal of a girl's senior high school," and "casework supervisor of a home for boys." Letters from school people endorsing the product are enclosed with the test material.

The manual describes the construction of the test itself in about 25 lines. The manual states that "only those items which produced favorable results were included." The criteria for retention or rejection of an item are not specified. Since Slosson has modeled his test after the Stanford-Binet, one might wonder if he has used the percent-pass at specific ages as the basis for including an item on the test. The standardization sample, children and adults from both rural and urban populations in New York State, is not well described. Departures from census data are not described, so that the age, sex, ethnic membership, educational, and socioeconomic characteristics of the standardization group are not indicated.

Validity studies in the manual leave much to be desired. Five studies, with N's ranging from 10 to 24, are devoted only to average differences between IQ's obtained on the SIT and the Stanford-Binet or Wechsler. One table, the only true validity study reported, shows correlations between SIT IQ and Stanford-Binet IQ for ages 4 to 17, and 18 years and older. N's for the age groups range from 23 to 71 and correlations range from .90 (age 4) to .98 (ages 6 and 7). Since items from the SIT at the ages reported are essentially adaptations from the Stanford-Binet, the correlations are spuriously high. A test-retest reliability coefficient ("within a period of two months") of .97 is reported in the manual.

Published validity studies provide a rather confusing picture of the worth of the SIT. Reported correlations between SIT and Wechsler Full Scale IQ's range from .54 to .93; between SIT and Stanford-Binet, from .76 to .90. As might be anticipated, those studies that do not unduly restrict the range of scores obtain correlations of respectable proportions. Kaufman and Ivanoff (*18*), employing a sample of 45 rehabilitation clients, obtained a product-moment correlation of .93 between SIT and WAIS Full Scale IQ, and .96 and .70 between SIT and Verbal and Performance IQ, respectively. Much lower correlations were obtained by Houston and Otto (*10*) and Jongeward (*16*) with the WISC. In the first study, a correlation of .60 was obtained between SIT and Full Scale IQ with a sample of 56 pupils with reading problems, with correlations of .64 and .42 for Verbal and Performance IQ's, respectively. Jongeward compared the SIT with both the WISC and Stanford-Binet with retarded children. Obtained product-moment correlations between SIT and WISC Full, Verbal, and Performance IQ's are as follows: .54, .85, and .20, in that order.

With the Stanford-Binet, Jongeward reported correlations of SIT and Stanford-Binet IQ of .76 and .81 with MA. De Lapa (*1*) reported correlations between SIT and Stanford-Binet for both educable retardates and regular class students. For the retardates, the obtained correlation was .60, raised to .79 when corrected for restriction of range. For the regular classroom students, the correlation was .90. These results would indicate that an examiner could substitute the SIT for the Binet with more confidence than when substituting for the WISC.

The SIT appears to be valuable as a quick screening device. Since inexperienced testers can administer this instrument quickly and accurately (*14*), it has much to recommend it as a preliminary screening procedure. However, the uncritical use of the SIT as a substitute for Wechsler or Binet instruments is ill advised.

Additional research with larger samples of more typical subjects is needed for this test.

JANE V. HUNT, *Assistant Research Psychologist, Institute of Human Development, University of California, Berkeley, California.*

This test is designed as "an individual screening instrument....for the use of school teachers, principals, guidance counselors, social workers, and other responsible persons." Considerable emphasis has been given to a format which is easily administered and scored. The manual is readable and explicit, standards for correct responses are unambiguous and instantly available during testing, and the method of scoring used is a multi-step procedure designed to augment scoring accuracy.

The author reports test-retest reliability of .97 within a two-month interval for a heterogeneous sample of 139 individuals from ages 4 to 50.

Comparability of IQ scores between SIT and Stanford-Binet was a goal of test construction. The author reports product moment correlations yielding correlations ranging from .90 to .98 at each age from 4 to 18 and above, derived from a heterogeneous population of 701 individuals. The sample includes both gifted and retarded children, which would inflate the magnitude of the correlation. Some unpublished studies report correlations of .91 for a group of 30 children with low-normal to superior intelligence, .89 for a group of slow learners with IQ's ranging from 50 to 80, and .91 for 72 boys with IQ range of 69 to 134. The goal of general comparability with Binet IQ seems to be met, despite the fact that the SIT yields a ratio IQ, and the Binet score is a deviation IQ.

TESTING ABOVE 4 YEARS. All questions are presented verbally and require spoken responses. Item content stresses mathematical reasoning, vocabulary, auditory memory, and information. An advantage of the test is that no time limits are imposed. The high ceiling makes the test sufficiently challenging for bright adolescents and adults.

PRESCHOOL TESTING. Between 2 to 4 years, the verbal format places heavy emphasis on language skills. With one exception, items measure or rely on achievements in language comprehension and speech. Test validity is dubious for children with delayed language development and for those whose environments do not include middle class language patterns. For this age group, the author makes no claim for predictive validity, and the only pretesting reported is the finding of a correlation of .93 with the Binet for a group of 16 "bright children" between 2 and 3 years of age.

INFANT TESTING. The infant portion of the test (0.5 to 24 months) is derived from items in the *Gesell Developmental Schedules* and uses the original Gesell age placements for these items. The author disavows the validity of the infant IQ, presumably as a predictive measure, but this test fails to meet essential requirements for evaluating current status of mental development in the infant. There are few items at each month's level and a large proportion of these assess postural control and locomotion. Age placements of items are often not in close agreement with contemporary standardization of the same items in the *Bayley Scales of Infant Development,* sometimes differing by as much as 3 or 4 months. The author reports a correlation of .70 with the *Cattell Infant Intelligence Scale* for 20 children under two years, age not otherwise specified.

SUMMARY. The SIT is designed to provide screening information and when used for this purpose can be a useful tool in selecting individuals for more comprehensive evaluation of mental ability. It is preferable to a group test, as the author indicates. The test is designed to be administered by persons who are not accustomed to interpreting test results. Extreme caution should be taken in relying on SIT test scores in situations where important diagnostic decisions are required, such as special class placements. As is the case with all short tests, the amount of information derived from the test is limited and the time spent with the child is brief. The ratio IQ is likely to be unstable in a given individual across age, and is more unstable for certain ages than for others. The heavy emphasis on language skills makes it a difficult test for children who, for cultural or individual reasons, have language problems. This disadvantage is accentuated at the preschool level. The infant portion of the test is less useful for screening purposes than is a test, such as the *Denver Developmental Screening Test,* which separates mental from motor development and which is standardized on contemporary infants.

[425]

Stanford-Binet Intelligence Scale, Third Revision. Ages 2 and over; 1916–64; S-B; a single-form combination of items selected from Forms L and M ('37) of still-in-print Second Revision; individual; Form L-M ('60); manual ('60, 374 pages, see 657a below); directions for administering ('64, 60 pages); record booklet ('60, 15 pages); record form ('60, 5 pages); $45 per set of test materials including manual (£9 without manual); $4.65 (£1) per 35 (25) record booklets; $2.55 (60p) per 35 (25) abbreviated record forms; $2.40 per directions for administering; $5.80 (£1.05) per manual; postage extra; (30–90) minutes; revised IQ tables by Samuel R. Pinneau; Lewis M. Terman and Maud A. Merrill; Houghton Mifflin Co. * (British edition: George G. Harrap & Co. Ltd.)

REFERENCES

1–134. See 2:1420.
135–351. See 3:292.
352–493. See 4:358.
494–620. See 5:413.
621–728. See 6:536.
729. EBERT, ELIZABETH, AND SIMMONS, KATHERINE. *The Brush Foundation Study of Child Growth and Development: 1, Psychometric Tests.* Monographs of the Society for Research in Child Development, Vol. 8, No. 2, Serial No. 35. Washington, D.C.: the Society, National Research Council, 1943. Pp. xiv, 113. * (PA 18:3322)
730. COLLINS, A. LOUISE, AND LENNOX, WILLIAM G. "The Intelligence of 300 Private Epileptic Patients." *Res Publ Assn Res Nerv & Mental Dis* 26:586–603 '47. *
731. KOLSTOE, OLIVER PAUL. *A Comparison of Mental Abilities of Bright and Dull Children Having the Same Mental Ages.* Doctor's thesis, State University of Iowa (Iowa City, Iowa), 1952. (DA 12:707)
732. ARMSTRONG, HUBERT COSLET. *The Relationship of the Auditory and Visual Vocabularies of Children.* Doctor's thesis, Stanford University (Stanford, Calif.), 1953. (DA 13:716)
733. GOLDENBERG, SAMUEL. *Some Aspects of Diagnosis of Cerebral Damage in Children.* Doctor's thesis, University of Washington (Seattle, Wash.), 1953. (DA 13:1259)
734. LEBERFELD, DORIS TREPEL. *An Investigation to Determine the Effect of Language and Speech Training on the Measurable Mental Abilities of Mentally Retarded Children.* Doctor's thesis, New York University (New York, N.Y.), 1953. (DA 14:735)
735. WELSH, GEORGE BYRON. *An Investigation of Some Predictive Factors in Auding Ability.* Doctor's thesis, University of Pittsburgh (Pittsburgh, Pa.), 1954. (DA 14:2407)
736. APGAR, VIRGINIA; GIRDANY, B. R.; McINTOSH, R.; AND TAYLOR, H. C., JR. "Neonatal Anoxia: 1, A Study of the Relation of Oxygenation at Birth to Intellectual Development." *Pediatrics* 15:6653–62 Je '55. *
737. WEINLANDER, MAX MARTIN. *Differential Rates of Mental Development in Children.* Doctor's thesis, University of Michigan (Ann Arbor, Mich.), 1955. (DA 15:1558)
738. LEHMANN, IRVIN JACK. *Rural-Urban Differences in Intelligence.* Doctor's thesis, University of Wisconsin (Madison, Wis.), 1957. (DA 17:1937)
739. TOMS, DOLORES CATHERINE. *Progress in Reading With Reference to the Quantitative Measurements of the Binet: A Study of Longitudinal Records.* Doctor's thesis, University of Michigan (Ann Arbor, Mich.), 1957. (DA 18:1725)
740. TRACHTMAN, GILBERT M. *Personality and Developmental Characteristics of Children Rated Most and Least Ready for First Grade by Their Kindergarten Teachers.* Doctor's thesis, New York University (New York, N.Y.), 1958. (DA 19:3028)
741. ALPER, ARTHUR E., AND HORNE, BETTY M. "Changes in IQ of a Group of Institutionalized Mental Defectives Over a Period of Two Decades." *Am J Mental Def* 64:472–5 N '59. * (PA 34:7994)
742. HOFFMAN, CARL BENTLEY. *The Relationship of Immediate Recall, Delayed Recall, and Incidental Memory to Problem-Solving Ability.* Doctor's thesis, University of Pennsylvania (Philadelphia, Pa.), 1960. (DA 21:813)
743. LEVINSON, BORIS M. "A Comparative Study of the Verbal and Performance Ability of Monolingual and Bilingual Native Born Jewish Preschool Children of Traditional Parentage." *J Genetic Psychol* 97:93–112 S '60. * (PA 35:6190)
744. BERNSTEIN, LEWIS. "Psychological Testing: 1, Intelligence Tests." *J Child Asth Res Inst & Hosp* 1:205–17 Je '61. *
745. HAAG, CARL HERBERT. *An Exploratory Study to Determine the Significance of Early Longitudinal Records of Ability and Achievement as Predictors of Academic Achievement in College.* Doctor's thesis, University of Michigan (Ann Arbor, Mich.), 1961. (DA 21:3702)
746. MORIARTY, ALICE. "Coping Patterns of Preschool Children in Response to Intelligence Test Demands." *Genetic Psychol Monogr* 64:3–127 Ag '61. * (PA 36:2FF03M)
747. NAKAMURA, HIROMU. "Nature of Institutionalized Adult Mongoloid Intelligence." *Am J Mental Def* 66:456–8 N '61. * (PA 36:4JI56N)
748. RICHARDS, BERNA FLANDERS. *A Predictive Longitudinal*

Study of Intellective and Non-Intellective Factors Affecting School Achievement of Gifted Children. Doctor's thesis, Ohio State University (Columbus, Ohio), 1961. (*DA* 22:3526)

749. SANDLER, ANNE-MARIE, AND SANDLER, JOSEPH. "Piaget's Approach to Problems of Intellectual Development." *Cereb Palsy B* 3(1):25–8 '61. * (*PA* 36:1FE25S)

750. SHECHTMAN, AUBREY M. *The Relationship of Variability in Children's Verbal and Non-Language Test Performance to Current and Later Behavioral Functions.* Doctor's thesis, University of Minnesota (Minneapolis, Minn.), 1961. (*DA* 22:2065)

751. TOUSSAINT, ISABELLA HASTIE. *Interrelationships of Reading, Listening, Arithmetic, and Intelligence and Their Implications.* Doctor's thesis, University of Pittsburgh (Pittsburgh, Pa.), 1961. (*DA* 22:819)

752. WITKIN, H. A.; DYKE, R. G.; FATERSON, H. F.; GOODENOUGH, D. R.; AND KARP, S. A. *Psychological Differentiation: Studies of Development.* New York: John Wiley & Sons, Inc., 1962. Pp. xii, 418. * (*PA* 37:819)

753. ABBOTT, ROBERT FRANKLIN. *The Prediction of First Grade Reading and Numbers Achievement by Means of Psychological Tests.* Doctor's thesis, University of Tennessee (Knoxville, Tenn.), 1963. (*DA* 25:1020)

754. DENUM, DONALD C. "The Use of the Stanford-Binet Intelligence Scale, Form L-M, 1960 Revision as a Criterion Instrument for Norming All Levels of the 1963 Revision of the California Test of Mental Maturity Series." *Yearb Nat Council Meas Ed* 20:50–3 '63. * (*PA* 38:8409)

755. GOULET, L. R., AND BARCLAY, A. "The Vineland Social Maturity Scale: Utility in Assessment of Binet MA." *Am J Mental Def* 67:916–21 My '63. * (*PA* 38:1273)

756. LEVINSON, ELIZABETH JOHNSON. *The Effects of Training in the Verbalization of Photoconcepts on Intelligence.* Doctor's thesis, University of Maine (Orono, Me.), 1963. (*DA* 26:1186)

757. REDBIRD, HELEN MARIE. *A Study of the Intelligence of Children of Domestic Agricultural Migrant Workers in Colorado.* Doctor's thesis, University of Colorado (Boulder, Colo.), 1963. (*DA* 24:4486)

758. ROTMAN, CHARLES B. *A Study of the Effect of Practice Upon Motor Skills of the Mentally Retarded.* Doctor's thesis, Boston University (Boston, Mass.), 1963. (*DA* 25:1755)

759. SONNEMAN, LAWRENCE J. *A Study of the Relationships Between Four Tests of Intelligence and One Test of Scholastic Achievement.* Doctor's thesis, State University of South Dakota (Vermillion, S.D.), 1963. (*DA* 24:4555)

760. SPIETH, PHILLIP EARL. *Intelligence as It Relates to Three Creativity Categories: Science, Art, and Literature.* Doctor's thesis, University of Michigan (Ann Arbor, Mich.), 1963. (*DA* 25:1759)

761. THOMPSON, MARY MARTHA. "Psychological Characteristics Relevant to the Education of the Pre-School Mongoloid Child." *Mental Retard* 1:148–51+ Je '63. * (*PA* 38:9243)

762. BIRKEMEYER, FLORENCE. "The Relationship Between the Coloured Progressive Matrices and Individual Intelligence Tests." *Psychol Sch* 1:309–12 Jl '64. *

763. CAPOBIANCO, R. J., AND KNOX, STANLEY. "IQ Estimates and the Index of Marital Integration." *Am J Mental Def* 68:718–21 My '64. * (*PA* 39:2322)

764. EARHART, RICHARD H., AND WARREN, SUE ALLEN. "Long Term Constancy of Binet IQ in Retardation." *Training Sch B* 61:109–15 N '64. * (*PA* 39:7753)

765. HAAN, NORMA. "The Relationship of Ego Functioning and Intelligence to Social Status and Social Mobility." *J Abn & Social Psychol* 69:594–605 D '64. * (*PA* 39:7560)

766. HUTTON, JERRY B. "A Comparison of Digit Repetition Scores on the WISC and Revised Binet, Form L-M." *J Clin Psychol* 20:364–6 Jl '64. * (*PA* 39:10124)

767. JENSON, G., III. *A Statistical Analysis of the Reliability and Validity of the Pictorial Test of Intelligence and the Stanford-Binet Intelligence Scale.* Master's thesis, University of Missouri (Columbia, Mo.), 1964.

768. LEVINE, DAVID, AND DYSINGER, DON W. "Patterns of Intellectual Performance and the Outcome of Institutionalization in the Mentally Retarded." *Am J Mental Def* 68:784–8 My '64. * (*PA* 39:2523)

769. LINDHOLM, BYRON W. "Changes in Conventional and Deviation IQ's." *J Ed Psychol* 55:110–3 Ap '64. * (*PA* 39:1749)

770. NUNNALLY, JUM C. *Educational Measurement and Evaluation*, pp. 251–7. New York: McGraw-Hill Book Co., Inc., 1964. Pp. xv, 440. *

771. PALMER, ALBERT B., JR. *Stanford-Binet Responses as a Function of Motivational Cue Properties of Items and of Children's Motivation.* Doctor's thesis, Southern Illinois University (Carbondale, Ill.), 1964. (*DA* 25:2615)

772. PHILLIPS, C. J., AND WHITE, R. R. "The Prediction of Educational Progress Among Cerebral Palsied Children." *Develop Med & Child Neurol* 6:167–74 Ap '64. * (*PA* 39:5648)

773. ROBECK, MILDRED C., AND WILSON, JOHN A. R. "Comparison of Binet and the Kindergarten Evaluation of Learning Potential." *Ed & Psychol Meas* 24:393–7 su '64. * (*PA* 39:5088)

774. SILVERSTEIN, A. B. "A Further Evaluation of Two Short Forms of the Stanford-Binet." *Calif Mental Health Res Dig* 2:15–6 au '64. *

775. TAVRIS, EDWARD. "An Attempt to Distinguish Between 'Successful' and 'Unsuccessful' Separation Groups in a Hospital for Mentally Retarded Patients." *Training Sch B* 60:184–91 F '64. * (*PA* 39:5488)

776. TIBER, NORMAN, AND KENNEDY, WALLACE A. "The Effects of Incentives on the Intelligence Test Performance of Different Social Groups." Abstract. *J Consult Psychol* 28:187 Ap '64. *

777. BEARD, R. M. "The Structure of Perception: A Factorial Study." *Brit J Ed Psychol* 35:210–22 Je '65. *

778. BURNETT, ALASTAIR. "Comparison of the PPVT, Wechsler-Bellevue, and Stanford-Binet on Educable Retardates." *Am J Mental Def* 69:712–5 Mr '65. * (*PA* 39:12715)

779. CASTELL, J. H. F., AND MITTLER, P. J. "Intelligence of Patients in Subnormality Hospitals: A Survey of Admissions in 1961." *Brit J Psychiatry* 111:219–25 Mr '65. * (*PA* 39:10453)

780. CHURCH, JANE CAROLYN. *A Short-Term Longitudinal Study of Factors Related to IQ Change in White Southern Rural Adolescents.* Doctor's thesis, University of North Carolina (Chapel Hill, N.C.), 1965. (*DA* 27:299B)

781. CIEUTAT, VICTOR J. "Examiner Differences With the Stanford-Binet IQ." *Percept & Motor Skills* 20:317–8 F '65. * (*PA* 39:10187)

782. CORDINER, MARIAN ESPACH. *A Comparative Study of the 1960 Stanford-Binet and the Wechsler Intelligence Scale for Children and Other Selected Variables.* Master's thesis, University of Utah (Salt Lake City, Utah), 1965.

783. DIBBLE, MARY F. *An Analysis of the Performance of Thirty-Three Retarded Readers on the Subtests of the Revised Stanford-Binet Intelligence Test, Form LM.* Master's thesis, University of Kansas (Lawrence, Kan.), 1965.

784. ESTES, BETSY WORTH. "Relationships Between the Otis, 1960 Stanford-Binet and WISC." *J Clin Psychol* 21:296–7 Jl '65. * (*PA* 39:15230)

785. GOLDSCHMID, MARCEL L., AND DOMINO, GEORGE. "Some Para-Diagnostic Implications of the IQ Among Mentally Retarded Patients." *Training Sch B* 61:178–83 F '65. * (*PA* 39:10586)

786. JENKINS, C. DAVID. "The Weight Discrimination Test as an Indicator of Brain Pathology." *J Clin Psychol* 21:76–7 Ja '65. * (*PA* 39:12699)

787. KABACK, GOLDIE RUTH. "A Comparison of WAIS, Binet, and WISC Test Results of Mentally Retarded Young Adults Born in New York City and Puerto Rico." *Training Sch B* 62:108–12 N '65. * (*PA* 40:2138)

788. KEBBON, LARS. *The Structure of Abilities at Lower Levels of Intelligence: A Factor-Analytical Study.* Stockholm, Sweden: Skandinaviska Testförlaget AB, 1965. Pp. 112. *

789. KROSKE, WILLIAM H.; FRETWELL, LORETTA N.; AND CUPP, MARION E. "Comparison of the Kahn Intelligence Tests: Experimental Form, the Stanford-Binet and the WAIS for Familial Retardates." *Percept & Motor Skills* 21:428 O '65. * (*PA* 40:3310)

790. LINDHOLM, BYRON W. "A Longitudinal Study of Deviation IQs and Grades in School." *J Ed Meas* 2:123–8 Je '65. * (*PA* 39:14710)

791. MEEKER, MARY. "A Procedure for Relating Stanford Binet Behavior Samplings to Guilford's Structure of the Intellect." *J Sch Psychol* 3:26–36 sp '65. * (*PA* 39:15303)

792. MEIER, JOHN HENRY. *An Exploratory Factor Analysis of Psychodiagnostic and Case Study Information From Children in Special Education Classes for the Educable Mentally Handicapped.* Doctor's thesis, University of Denver (Denver, Colo.), 1965. (*DA* 26:3153)

793. MITCHELL, ROBERT JEFFERY, SR. *An Experimental Study to Determine the Effects of Inhaling Pure Oxygen on I.Q.* Doctor's thesis, University of Oklahoma (Norman, Okla.), 1965. (*DA* 26:1188)

794. MUELLER, MAX W. *A Comparison of the Empirical Validity of Six Tests of Ability With Young Educable Retardates.* Institute of Mental Retardation and Intellectual Development, IMRID Behavioral Science Monograph No. 1. Nashville, Tenn.: Peabody College Bookstore, 1965. Pp. vii, 130. *

795. MUELLER, MAX WILLIAM. *A Comparison of the Empirical Validity of Six Tests of Ability With Educable Mental Retardates.* Doctor's thesis, George Peabody College for Teachers (Nashville, Tenn.), 1965. (*DA* 26:6853)

796. NAKAMURA, HIROMU. "An Inquiry Into Systematic Differences in the Abilities of Institutionalized Adult Mongoloids." *Am J Mental Def* 69:661–5 Mr '65. * (*PA* 39:12743)

797. SATTLER, JEROME M. "Analysis of Functions of the 1960 Stanford-Binet Intelligence Scale, Form L-M." *J Clin Psychol* 21:173–9 Ap '65. * (*PA* 39:12308)

798. SCHULMAN, JEROME L.; KASPAR, JOSEPH C.; AND THRONE, FRANCES M. *Brain Damage and Behavior: A Clinical-Experimental Study.* Springfield, Ill.: Charles C Thomas, Publisher, 1965. Pp. ix, 164. *

799. SHANE, JAMES F. *Effectiveness of the Peabody Picture Vocabulary Test in Comparison to Wechsler Intelligence Scale for Children and Stanford-Binet Test Scores in Identification of Mentally Retarded and Gifted School Children.* Master's thesis, California State College (Long Beach, Calif.), 1965.

800. SILVERSTEIN, A. B. "Comparison of Two Item-Classifi-

cation Schemes for the Stanford-Binet." *Psychol Rep* 17:964 D '65. * (*PA* 40:4219)

801. SMART, RUSSELL C. "The Changing Composition of 'Intelligence': A Replication of a Factor Analysis." *J Genetic Psychol* 107:111–6 S '65. * (*PA* 39:15308)

802. STERNLICHT, MANNY. "A Downward Application of the 1960 Revised Stanford-Binet With Retardates." *J Clin Psychol* 21:79 Ja '65. * (*PA* 39:12326)

803. WEISE, PHILLIP; MEYERS, C. E.; AND TUEL, JOHN K. "PMA Factors, Sex, and Teacher Nomination in Screening Kindergarten Gifted." *Ed & Psychol Meas* 25:597–603 su '65. * (*PA* 39:14718)

804. BARCLAY, A., AND CAROLAN, PATRICIA. "A Comparative Study of the Wechsler Intelligence Scale for Children and the Stanford-Binet Intelligence Scale, Form L-M." Abstract. *J Consult Psychol* 30:563 D '66. *

805. BLACK, D. B.; KATO, J. G.; AND WALKER, G. W. R. "A Study of Improvement in Mentally Retarded Children Accruing From Siccacell Therapy." *Am J Mental Def* 70:499–508 Ja '66. * (*PA* 40:5869)

806. BURSON, GERALD EDWARD. *A Comparative Study of the Effects of Programed Presentations of Selected Portions of the Stanford-Binet Intelligence Test on Student Examiners.* Doctor's thesis, Oklahoma State University (Stillwater, Okla.), 1966. (*DA* 27:4124A)

807. CHURCHILL, WILLIAM D., AND SMITH, STUART E. "The Relationship of the 1960 Revised Stanford-Binet Intelligence Scale to Intelligence and Achievement Test Scores Over a Three-Year Period." *Ed & Psychol Meas* 26:1015–20 w '66. * (*PA* 41:4567)

808. COLMAN, P. G. "A Comparative Study of the Test Performances of Brain-Injured Children." *S Afric Med J* 40:945–50 O 22 '66. *

809. HIMELSTEIN, PHILIP. "Research With the Stanford-Binet, Form L-M: The First Five Years." *Psychol B* 65:156–64 Mr '66. * (*PA* 40:4764)

810. HIRSCHENFANG, SAMUEL; JARAMILLO, SELENE; AND BENTON, JOSEPH G. "Comparison of Scores on the Revised Stanford-Binet (L), Columbia Mental Maturity Scale (CMMS) and Goodenough Draw-A-Man Test of Children With Neurological Disorders." *Psychol Rep* 19:15–6 Ag '66. * (*PA* 40:12564)

811. KANDEL, ARTHUR. *Discrepancies Between the Stanford-Binet and Three Group Tests of Intelligence in the Identification of Low I.Q. Children.* Doctor's thesis, Catholic University of America (Washington, D.C.), 1966. (*DA* 27:1659A)

812. KEACH, CHARLES CAMPBELL. *Discrepancies Between the Stanford-Binet and Three Group Tests of Intelligence in the Identification of High I.Q. Children.* Doctor's thesis, Catholic University of America (Washington, D.C.), 1966. (*DA* 27:1660A)

813. KICKLIGHTER, RICHARD M. "Correlation of Peabody Picture Vocabulary Test Scores and Stanford-Binet Intelligence Scale, Form L-M Scores in an Educable Mentally Retarded Population," Abstract. *J Sch Psychol* 5:75–6 au '66. *

814. KILBURN, KENT L.; SANDERSON, ROBERT E.; AND MELTON, KYLE. "Relation of the Raven Coloured Progressive Matrices to Two Measures of Verbal Ability in a Sample of Mildly Retarded Hospital Patients." *Psychol Rep* 19:731–4 D '66. * (*PA* 41:4915)

815. KIMBRELL, DON L. "Comparison of PPVT, FRPVT, RS-B, and Academic Achievement Scores Among Institutionalized Educable Mental Retardates." *Percept & Motor Skills* 23:1178 D '66. * (*PA* 41:6185)

816. LUSZKI, WALTER A. "Intellectual Functioning of Spastic Cerebral Palsied." *Cereb Palsy J* 27:7–9 Mr–Ap '66. * (*PA* 40:8010)

817. McKERRACHER, D. W., AND SCOTT, J. "I.Q. Scores and the Problem of Classification: A Comparison of the W.A.I.S. and S-B, Form L-M in a Group of Subnormal and Psychopathic Patients." *Brit J Psychiatry* 112:537–41 Je '66. * (*PA* 40:10101)

818. MATHENY, ADAM P., JR. "Improving Diagnostic Forecasts Made on a Developmental Scale." *Am J Mental Def* 71:371–5 N '66. * (*PA* 41:1706)

819. ROBERTS, DENNIS M. "Serial Position Effects in Two Stanford-Binet Subtests." *Psychol* 3:2–4 Ag '66. * (*PA* 40:12319)

820. ROSENBERG, LEON A., AND STROUD, MICHAEL. "Limitations of Brief Intelligence Testing With Young Children." *Psychol Rep* 19:721–2 D '66. * (*PA* 41:4999)

821. SATTLER, JEROME M. "Comments on Cieutat's 'Examiner Differences With the Stanford-Binet IQ.'" *Percept & Motor Skills* 22:612–4 Ap '66. * (*PA* 40:8270)

822. SATTLER, JEROME M. "Statistical Reanalysis of Canady's 'The Effect of "Rapport" on the I.Q.: A New Approach to the Problem of Racial Psychology.'" *Psychol Rep* 19:1203–6 D '66. * (*PA* 41:4444)

823. SIDERITS, MARY ANNE TERESA. *Indices of Change in the Cattell-Binet Ratings of Intellectually Sub-Average Children.* Doctor's thesis, University of Michigan (Ann Arbor, Mich.), 1966. (*DA* 27:2519B)

824. SILVERSTEIN, A. B. "A Further Evaluation of Two Short Forms of the Stanford-Binet." *Am J Mental Def* 70:928–9 My '66. * (*PA* 40:9174)

825. SILVERSTEIN, A. B. "Mental Growth in Mongolism." *Child Develop* 37:725–9 S '66. * (*PA* 40:12586)

826. SITKEI, E. GEORGE, AND MICHAEL, WILLIAM B. "Predictive Relationships Between Items on the Revised Stanford-Binet Intelligence Scale (SBIS), Form L-M, and Total Scores on Raven's Progressive Matrices (PM), Between Items on the PM and Total Scores on the SBIS, and Between Selected Items on the Two Scales." *Ed & Psychol Meas* 26:501–6 su '66. * (*PA* 40:12784)

827. SMITH, C. SIMPSON. "Changes in I.Q.'s of Educationally Subnormal Pupils: A Survey of West Riding Children." *Pub Health* 80:201–8 My '66. *

828. SMITH, HERBERT W.; MAY, W. THEODORE; AND LEBOVITZ, LEON. "Testing Experience and Stanford-Binet Scores." *J Ed Meas* 3:229–33 f '66. * (*PA* 41:11921)

829. STORMER, GEORGE EDWARD. *Dimensions of the Intellect Unmeasured by the Stanford-Binet.* Doctor's thesis, University of Illinois (Urbana, Ill.), 1966. (*DA* 27:2078A)

830. STOTT, LELAND H., AND BALL, RACHEL STUTSMAN. *Infant and Preschool Mental Tests: Review and Evaluation.* Monographs of the Society for Research in Child Development, Vol. 30, No. 3, Serial No. 101. Chicago, Ill.: University of Chicago Press, 1966. Pp. iv, 151. * (*PA* 40:7220)

831. VANE, JULIA R.; WEITZMAN, JONATHAN; AND APPLEBAUM, ADRIAN P. "Performance of Negro and White Children and Problem and Nonproblem Children on the Stanford Binet Scale." *J Clin Psychol* 22:431–5 O '66. * (*PA* 41:2875)

832. WALL, W. D., AND PRINGLE, M. L. KELLMER. "The Clinical Significance of Standard Score Discrepancies Between Intelligence and Social Competence." *Hum Develop* 9(3):121–51 '66. *

833. WILLIAMS, JANETTE R., AND WILCOCK, JOAN C. "An Alternative to the Binet Mental Age Score as a Criterion in Discrimination Learning." *J Mental Def Res* 10:27–32 Mr '66. * (*PA* 40:9420)

834. BUDOFF, MILTON. "Learning Potential Among Institutionalized Young Adult Retardates." *Am J Mental Def* 72:404–11 N '67. * (*PA* 42:7631)

835. CIEUTAT, VICTOR J., AND FLICK, GRAD L. "Examiner Differences Among Stanford-Binet Items." *Psychol Rep* 21:613–22 O '67. * (*PA* 42:4794)

836. DeLAPA, GIACINTO. *Correlates of Slosson Intelligence Test, Stanford Binet, Form L-M, and Achievement Indices.* Doctor's thesis, West Virginia University (Morgantown, W.Va.), 1967. (*DA* 28:3498A)

837. DOBSON, JAMES CLAYTON, JR. *Intellectual and Linguistic Development in Treated and Untreated Phenylketonuric Children.* Doctor's thesis, University of Southern California (Los Angeles, Calif.), 1967. (*DA* 28:1294A)

838. DUNN, JAMES A. "Validity Coefficients for the New Harris-Goodenough Draw-A-Man Test." *Percept & Motor Skills* 24:299–301 F '67. * (*PA* 41:8149)

839. EISENMAN, RUSSELL, AND ROBINSON, NANCY. "Complexity-Simplicity, Creativity, Intelligence and Other Correlates." *J Psychol* 67:331–4 N '67. * (*PA* 42:2567)

840. HAMMILL, DONALD D., AND IRWIN, ORVIS C. "Factors Affecting Equivalency of PPVT and RSB When Used With Mentally Subnormal Children." *Am J Mental Def* 71:793–6 Mr '67. * (*PA* 41:8881)

841. HOWARD, JOYCE L., AND PLANT, WALTER T. "Psychometric Evaluation of an Operation Headstart Program." *J Genetic Psychol* 111:281–8 D '67. * (*PA* 42:6013)

842. KLAPPER, ZELDA S., AND BIRCH, HERBERT G. "A Fourteen Year Follow-Up Study of Cerebral Palsy: Intellectual Changes and Stability." *Am J Orthopsychiatry* 37:540–7 Ap '67. *

843. KOH, TONG-HE, AND MADOW, ARNOLD A. "Relationship Between PPVT and Stanford-Binet Performances in Institutionalized Retardates." *Am J Mental Def* 72:108–13 Jl '67. * (*PA* 41:15728)

844. KOPPITZ, ELIZABETH MUNSTERBERG. "Expected and Exceptional Items on Human Figure Drawings and IQ Scores of Children Age 5 to 12." *J Clin Psychol* 23:81–3 Ja '67. * (*PA* 41:5985)

845. KUNDU, RAMANATH. "A Comparison of Stanford-Binet and Wechsler-Bellevue Scales." *Indian Psychol R* 3:114–8 Ja '67. * (*PA* 41:8901)

846. MARSHALL, ANNE. *The Abilities and Attainments of Children Leaving Junior Training Centres.* London: National Association for Mental Health, 1967. Pp. i, 62. *

847. MASON, ANNE W. "Specific (Developmental) Dyslexia." *Develop Med & Child Neurol* 9:183–90 Ap '67. * (*PA* 41:14066)

848. MILLER, BILLY. *A Comparison of the Columbia Mental Maturity Scale, the Leiter International Performance Scale, and the Wright Short Form of the Stanford Binet, Form L-M, With the Full Scale Stanford Binet, Form L-M, on a Group of Trainable Retardates.* Master's thesis, Central Missouri State College (Warrensburg, Mo.), 1967.

849. MISCEVICH, MADELEINE BECK. *Correlation of a Pre-School Test With the Stanford-Binet Intelligence Scale.* Master's thesis, Millersville State College (Millersville, Pa), 1967.

850. MOORE, TERENCE. "Language and Intelligence: A Longitudinal Study of the First Eight Years: Part 1, Patterns of Development in Boys and Girls." *Hum Develop* 10(2):88–106 '67. * (*PA* 41:7080)

851. MUZEKARI, LOUIS H. "Relationships Between the Good-enough DAM and Stanford-Binet in Negro and White Public School Children." *J Clin Psychol* 23:86–7 Ja '67. * (*PA* 41:6253)

852. OLIVIER, K., AND BARCLAY, A. "Stanford-Binet and Goodenough-Harris Test Performances of Head Start Children." *Psychol Rep* 20:1175–9 Je '67. * (*PA* 41:15275)

853. PICKLES, D. G. "Intelligence Tests and the Ascertainment of the Educationally Subnormal: A Comparative Study of the Stanford-Binet and Wechsler Intelligence Scales." *Pub Health* 81:133–44 Mr '67. *

854. RASOF, BEATRICE; LINDE, LEONARD M.; AND DUNN, OLIVE JEAN. "Intellectual Development in Children With Congenital Heart Disease." *Child Develop* 38:1043–53 D '67. * (*PA* 42:7687)

855. RUSSELL, CAROL A. *A Comparison of Performance on the Stanford-Binet Intelligence Scale, Form L-M, and the Wechsler Intelligence Scale for Children With Mentally Retarded Subjects.* Master's thesis, University of Utah (Salt Lake City, Utah), 1967.

856. SATTLER, JEROME M., AND THEYE, FRED. "Procedural, Situational, and Interpersonal Variables in Individual Intelligence Testing." *Psychol B* 68:347–60 N '67. * (*PA* 42:2564)

857. SEELYE, BARBARA JANE. *An Investigation of Language Development in Non-Institutionalized Mentally Retarded Children.* Doctor's thesis, University of Denver (Denver, Colo.), 1967. (*DA* 28:821A)

858. SHEVERBUSH, ROBERT L., JR. *An Analysis of Subtest Performance by Gifted Students on the Stanford-Binet Intelligence Scale (1960 Form L-M).* Doctor's thesis, Colorado State College (Greeley, Colo.), 1967. (*DA* 28:2568A)

859. SIGEL, IRVING; JARMAN, P.; AND HANESIAN, HELEN. "Styles of Categorization and Their Intellectual and Personality Correlation in Young Children." *Hum Develop* 10(1):1–7 '67. * (*PA* 41:7146)

860. SILBERBERG, NORMAN; IVERSEN, IVER; AND SILBERBERG, MARGARET. "Predicting End of First Grade Developmental Reading Test Scores From Gates Reading Readiness Test Scores Administered in Kindergarten." Abstract. *Proc 75th Ann Conv Am Psychol Assn* 2:291–2 '67. * (*PA* 41:14224)

861. SILVERSTEIN, A. B.; MOHAN, PHILIP J.; AND FRANKEN, ROBERT E. "A Problem-Solving Approach to the Assessment of Intellectual Functioning." *Training Sch B* 63:159–62 F '67. * (*PA* 41:9299)

862. SMITH, HERBERT W., AND MAY, W. THEODORE. "Individual Differences Among Inexperienced Psychological Examiners." *Psychol Rep* 20:759–62 Je '67. * (*PA* 41:13601)

863. WEAVER, ANN SULLIVAN. *The Prediction of First Grade Reading Achievement in Culturally Disadvantaged Children.* Doctor's thesis, George Peabody College for Teachers (Nashville, Tenn.), 1967. (*DA* 28:3789A)

864. WELLS, DONALD G., AND PEDRINI, DUILIO T. "Relationship Between the Stanford-Binet L-M and the Goodenough D.A-M." *Psychol Sch* 4:371–5 O '67. * (*PA* 42:2592)

865. WELLS, DONALD G., AND PEDRINI, DUILIO T. "Relationships Between the S-B L-M, G-H, and PPVT With Institutionalized Retardates." *Am J Mental Def* 72:412–5 N '67. * (*PA* 42:7680)

866. WELLS, DONALD G., AND PEDRINI, DUILIO T. "Where to Begin Testing on the 1960 Stanford-Binet L-M." *J Clin Psychol* 23:182–4 Ap '67. * (*PA* 41:8888)

867. WILLIAMS, JEROLD R. *A Correctional Study of Adult Comprehension Performance on the Stanford-Binet (1937) Form L Test and the Wechsler Adult Intelligence Scale.* Master's thesis, Illinois State University (Normal, Ill.), 1967.

868. YATES, LOUISE GRAHAM. *Comparative Intelligence of Negro and White Children From a Rural-Southern Culture.* Doctor's thesis, University of North Carolina (Chapel Hill, N.C.), 1967. (*DA* 28:4768B)

869. ANASTASI, ANNE. *Psychological Testing, Third Edition,* pp. 188–206. New York: Macmillan Co., 1968. Pp. xiii, 665. *

870. ANDERSON, CATHERINE J.; PORRATA, ELENA; LORE, JAMES; ALEXANDER, SHIRLEY; AND MERCER, MARGARET. "A Multidisciplinary Study of Psychogeriatric Patients." *Geriatrics* 23:105–13 F '68. * (*PA* 42:14051)

871. ARMSTRONG, JUDITH GLANTZ. *Intellectual Competence and Coping Behavior in Preschool Children.* Doctor's thesis, University of California (Berkeley, Calif.), 1968. (*DA* 29:4837B)

872. BACH, LLOYD CARL. *A Comparison of Selected Psychological Tests Used With Trainable Mentally Retarded Children.* Doctor's thesis, University of South Dakota (Vermillion, S.D.), 1968. (*DA* 29:2990A)

873. BATEMAN, BARBARA. " 'Clinically' Obtained IQs Versus 'Production Line' IQs in a Mentally Retarded Sample." *J Sch Psychol* 7(1):29–33 '68–69. * (*PA* 43:10217)

874. BAUGHMAN, E. EARL, AND DAHLSTROM, W. GRANT. *Negro and White Children: A Psychological Study in the Rural South,* pp. 38–48, passim. New York: Academic Press Inc., 1968. Pp. xx, 572. *

875. BENGER, KATHLYN. "The Relationships of Perception, Personality, Intelligence, and Grade One Reading Achievement." *Proc Ann Conv Int Read Assn* 12(4):112–23 '68. *

876. BONFIELD, JOHN RONALD. *Predictors of Achievement for Educable Mentally Retarded Children.* Doctor's thesis,

Pennsylvania State University (University Park, Pa.), 1968. (*DAI* 30:1009A)

877. BOROSAGE, VERA. *A Study of the Effect of Nursery School Experience on Intellectual Performance at Two Socio-Economic Levels.* Doctor's thesis, Michigan State University (East Lansing, Mich.), 1968. (*DA* 29:2993A)

878. BRITTAIN, MICHAEL. "A Comparative Study of the Use of the Wechsler Intelligence Scale for Children and the Stanford-Binet Intelligence Scale (Form L-M) With Eight-Year-Old Children." *Brit J Ed Psychol* 38:103–4 F '68. *

879. DiLORENZO, LOUIS T. "Effects of Year-Long Prekindergarten Programs on Intelligence and Language of Educationally Disadvantaged Children." *J Exp Ed* 36:36–42 sp '68. *

880. DiLORENZO, LOUIS T., AND BRADY, JAMES J. "Use of the Peabody Picture Vocabulary Test With Preschool Children." *Psychol Rep* 22:247–51 F '68. * (*PA* 42:10612)

881. DiLORENZO, LOUIS T., AND NAGLER, ERIC. "Examiner Differences on the Stanford-Binet." *Psychol Rep* 22:443–7 Ap '68. * (*PA* 42:11402)

882. EISENMAN, RUSSELL; PLATT, JEROME J.; AND DARBES, ALEX. "Creativity, Intelligence and Achievement." *Psychol Rep* 22:749–54 Je '68. * (*PA* 42:13739)

883. ERICKSON, MARILYN T. "The Predictive Validity of the Cattell Infant Intelligence Scale for Young Mentally Retarded Children." *Am J Mental Def* 72:728–33 Mr '68. * (*PA* 42:11047)

884. GANNON, D. R. "Relationships Between 8-Mo. Performance on the Bayley Scales of Infant Development and 48-Mo. Intelligence and Concept Formation Scores." *Psychol Rep* 23:1199–205 D '68. * (*PA* 43:8104)

885. HIMELSTEIN, PHILIP. "Use of the Stanford-Binet, Form LM, With Retardates: A Review of Recent Research." *Am J Mental Def* 72:691–9 Mr '68. * (*PA* 42:11054)

886. LAMP, ROBERT E., AND BARCLAY, A. "Comparisons of Scores on Quick Test and Stanford-Binet, Form L-M, for Retarded Children." *Psychol Rep* 23:401–2 O '68. * (*PA* 43:10229)

887. LARSEN, MARY RUTH JUHAN. *Item Performance of Five-Year-Old Georgia Subjects on the Stanford-Binet Form L-M Compared With the Standardization Sample.* Doctor's thesis, University of Georgia (Athens, Ga.), 1968. (*DA* 29:2529A)

888. LEVY, PHILIP. "Short-Term Tests: A Methodological Review." *Psychol B* 69:410–6 Je '68. * (*PA* 42:11410)

889. LUONG, CORINA K. MONGCAL. *An Analysis of Factors Related to Difficulties in Learning and Adjustment Among Minority Group Children.* Doctor's thesis, Bryn Mawr College (Bryn Mawr, Pa.), 1968. (*DAI* 30:4795B)

890. McARTHUR, CHARLES R., AND WAKEFIELD, HOMER E. "Validation of the PPVT With the Stanford-Binet-LM and the WISC on Educable Mental Retardates." *Am J Mental Def* 73:465–7 N '68. * (*PA* 43:8596)

891. MATTHEWS, CHARLES G.; CHUN, RAYMOND W. M.; GRABOW, JACK D.; AND THOMPSON, WAYNE H. "Psychological Sequelae in Children Following California Arboviros Encephalitis." *Neurol* 18:1023–30 O '68. * (*PA* 43:5771)

892. MIEZITIS, SOLVEIGA AUSMA. *An Exploratory Study of Divergent Production in Preschoolers.* Doctor's thesis, University of Toronto (Toronto, Ont., Canada), 1968. (*DAI* 30:589A)

893. MUELLER, MAX W. "Validity of Six Tests of Ability With Educable Mental Retardates." *J Sch Psychol* 6:136–46 w '68. * (*PA* 42:11152)

894. PATTERSON, HENRY JAMES. *A Validation and Comparison of the Pictorial Test of Intelligence With the Stanford-Binet (L-M).* Doctor's thesis, University of Arizona (Tucson, Ariz.), 1968. (*DA* 29:485A)

895. PHILLIPS, C. J., AND BANNON, W. J. "The Stanford-Binet, Form L-M, Third Revision: A Local English Study of Norms, Concurrent Validity and Social Differences." *Brit J Ed Psychol* 38:148–61 Je '68. * (*PA* 42:17000)

896. PLANT, WALTER T., AND SOUTHERN, MARA L. "First Grade Reading Achievement Predicted From WPPSI and Other Scores Obtained 18 Months Earlier." Abstract. *Proc 76th Ann Conv Am Psychol Assn* 3:593–4 '68. *

897. SCHREFFLER, ROY HOOVER. *Six Year Study of Three Groups of Students Screened for Sixth Grade Major Work Classes: Special and Regular Class Students of High Binet IQ, and Pseudogifted Students.* Doctor's thesis, Pennsylvania State University (University Park, Pa.), 1968. (*DA* 29:3473A)

898. SEKYRA, FRANCIS, III, AND ARNOULT, JOSEPH FRANCIS, III. "Negro Intellectual Assessment With Three Instruments Contrasting Caucasian and Negro Norms." *J Learn Dis* 1:564–9 O '68. * (*PA* 45:2174)

899. SHEVERBUSH, ROBERT L., JR. "An Analysis of Subtest Performance by Gifted Students on the Stanford-Binet Intelligence Scale (1960 Form L-M)." Abstract. *AERA Paper Abstr* 1968:324–5 '68. *

900. SHIPE, DOROTHY; VANDENBERG, STEVEN; AND WILLIAMS, R. D. BROOKE. "Neonatal Apgar Ratings as Related to Intelligence and Behavior in Preschool Children." *Child Develop* 39:861–6 S '68. * (*PA* 43:3762)

901. SULLIVAN, ROBYN A. *Adaptive Administration of the Stanford-Binet Intelligence Scale to Indian Children.* Master's thesis, Arizona State University (Tempe, Ariz.), 1968.

902. TUCHMAN, STEPHANIE B. *A Correlation Study of the*

Stanford-Binet and Academic Ability of Trainable Retarded Children. Master's thesis, Adelphi University (Garden City, N.Y.), 1968.

903. WHITACRE, ROGER L. Use of the Slosson Intelligence Test With the Stanford-Binet, L-M, as a Screening Device for Slow Learner Placement. Master's thesis, Bowling Green State University (Bowling Green, Ohio), 1968.

904. WHITE, LINDA ANN. A Comparative Study of the Performance of Negro Head Start Students on the Wechsler Preschool and Primary Scale of Intelligence, the Wechsler Intelligence Scale for Children, and the Stanford-Binet, Form L-M. Master's thesis, University of Texas (Austin, Tex.), 1968.

905. WISE, JAMES H. "Stick Copying of Designs by Preschool and Young School-Age Children." Percept & Motor Skills 27:1159–68 D '68. * (PA 43:9547)

906. ZIGLER, EDWARD, AND BUTTERFIELD, CARL C. "Motivational Aspects of Changes in IQ Test Performance of Culturally Deprived Nursery School Children." Child Develop 39:1–14 Mr '68. * (PA 42:10578)

907. ZUNICH, M., AND TOLLEY, J. "Performance on the Peabody Picture Vocabulary Test and Stanford-Binet by Institutionalized Mentally Retarded Children." Psychol Rep 22: 1212 Je '68. * (PA 42:19210)

908. BABSON, S. GORHAM, AND KANGAS, JOHN. "Preschool Intelligence of Undersized Term Infants." Am J Dis Children 117(5):553–7 My '69. * (PA 44:440)

909. BARABASZ, ARREED F. "Test-Retest Reliability of the Torrance Tests of Creative Thinking, and the Relationship Between Intelligence and Figural Creativity." Child Study Center B 5(4–5):73–4 S–N '69. * (PA 44:16369)

910. BARCLAY, ALLAN, AND YATER, ALLAN C. "Comparative Study of the Wechsler Preschool and Primary Scale of Intelligence and the Stanford-Binet Intelligence Scale, Form L-M, Among Culturally Deprived Children." Abstract. J Consult & Clin Psychol 33(2):257 Ap '69. * (PA 43:9734)

911. BRUININKS, ROBERT H. "Auditory and Visual Perceptual Skills Related to the Reading Performance of Disadvantaged Boys." Percept & Motor Skills 29(1):179–86 Ag '69. * (PA 44:2835)

912. BUNUAN, JOSEFINA S. Translation and Adaptation of the Stanford-Binet Intelligence Scale, Form L-M, for Filipino Children. Doctor's thesis, Boston University (Boston, Mass.), 1969. (DAI 31:377B)

913. COCHRAN, MALCOLM L., AND PEDRINI, DUILIO T. "The Concurrent Validity of the 1965 WRAT With Adult Retardates." Am J Mental Def 73(4):654–6 Ja '69. * (PA 43:8574)

914. CORNWELL, ANNE C., AND BIRCH, HERBERT C. "Psychological and Social Development in Home-Reared Children With Down's Syndrome (Mongolism)." Am J Mental Def 74(3):341–50 N '69. * (PA 44:5539)

915. CRAWFORD, VEDA B. Relationships of Scores on the Wechsler Preschool and Primary Scale of Intelligence, the Stanford-Binet Intelligence Scale, Form LM, and the Peabody Picture Vocabulary Test, Form A. Master's thesis, Bowling Green State University (Bowling Green, Ohio), 1969.

916. DiLORENZO, LOUIS T., AND BRADY, JAMES J. "Use of the Peabody Picture Vocabulary Test." Training Sch B 65(4): 117–21 F '69. * (PA 44:4169)

917. DOKECKI, PAUL R.; FREDE, MARTHA C.; AND GAUTNEY, DONALD B. "Criterion, Construct, and Predictive Validities of the Wechsler Preschool and Primary Scale of Intelligence." Abstract. Proc 77th Ann Conv Am Psychol Assn 4(2):505–6 '69. * (PA 44:1253)

918. DUFFETT, JOHN WARREN. The Influence of Stanford-Binet Items on Traditional Measures in Estimating First Grade Reading Success in a Selected Population. Doctor's thesis, University of Pittsburgh (Pittsburgh, Pa.), 1969. (DAI 31: 1683A)

919. ENGLISH, RICHARD A., AND KIDDER, JACK W. "Note on Relationships Among Mental Ability Scores, Teacher's Rankings, and Rate of Acquisition for Four-Year-Old Kindergartners." Psychol Rep 24(2):554 Ap '69. * (PA 43:15568)

920. FAGAN, JOEN; BROUGHTON, ELIZABETH; ALLEN, MILDRED; CLARK, BETTY; AND EMERSON, PATRICIA. "Comparison of the Binet and WPPSI With Lower-Class Five-Year-Olds." J Consult & Clin Psychol 33(5):607–9 O '69. * (PA 44: 2135)

921. GIOIOSO, JOSEPH V., AND ADERMAN, MORRIS. "The Combination Test as a Quick Screening Device to Differentiate Levels of Retardation." Psychol Rep 25(3):843–8 D '69. * (PA 44:18906)

922. HIRSHOREN, ALFRED. "A Comparison of the Predictive Validity of the Revised Stanford-Binet Intelligence Scale and the Illinois Test of Psycholinguistic Abilities." Excep Children 35(7):517–21 Mr '69. * (PA 44:17505)

923. HOWARD, JANE OSBURN. A Comparison of the Revised Stanford-Binet Intelligence Scale, Form L-M, and the Nebraska Test of Learning Aptitude, 1966 Revision, With Groups of Mentally Retarded, Deaf, and Normal Children. Doctor's thesis, University of New Mexico (Albuquerque, N. M.), 1969. (DAI 30:3322A)

924. JONGEWARD, PAUL A. "A Validity Study of the Slosson Intelligence Test for Use With Educable Mentally Retarded Students." J Sch Psychol 7(4):59–63 '68–69 ['69]. * (PA 44:2702)

925. JONGEWARD, PAUL ALBERT. A Validity Study of the Slosson Intelligence Test for Use With Educable Mentally Retarded Students. Doctor's thesis, University of Oregon (Eugene, Ore.), 1969. (DAI 30:3323A)

926. KAMII, CONSTANCE K., AND RADIN, NORMA L. "The Retardation of Disadvantaged Negro Preschoolers: Some Characteristics Found From an Item Analysis of the Stanford-Binet Test." Psychol Sch 6(3):283–8 Jl '69. * (PA 44:4040)

927. KEIM, RICHARD PAUL. Visual-Motor Training, Readiness, and Intelligence of Kindergarten Children. Doctor's thesis, Temple University (Philadelphia, Pa.), 1969. (DAI 31: 1076A)

928. KENNEDY, WALLACE A. "A Follow-Up Normative Study of Negro Intelligence and Achievement." Monogr Soc Res Child Develop 34(2):1–40 '69. * (PA 45:1350)

929. LEWIS, JAMES F. Differential Evaluation of Selected Tests When Utilized With Institutionalized and Non-Institutionalized Trainable Mentally Retarded. Doctor's thesis, University of Nebraska (Lincoln, Neb.), 1969. (DAI 30:3793A)

930. MASSARI, DAVID; HAYWEISER, LOIS; AND MEYER, WILLIAM J. "Activity Level and Intellectual Functioning in Deprived Preschool Children." Develop Psychol 1(3):286–90 My '69. * (PA 43:11105)

931. MAXWELL, JAMES. "Intelligence, Education and Fertility: A Comparison Between the 1932 and 1947 Scottish Surveys." J Biosocial Sci 1(3):247–71 Jl '69. * (PA 46:1184)

932. MEEKER, MARY NACOL. The Structure of Intellect: Its Interpretation and Uses, pp. 123–31. Columbus, Ohio: Charles E. Merrill Publishing Co., 1969. Pp. xix, 203. *

933. MUELLER, MAX W. "Prediction of Achievement of Educable Mentally Retarded Children." Am J Mental Def 73(4): 590–6 Ja '69. * (PA 43:8703)

934. NEEDHAM, WALTER E.; BRAY, PATRICK F.; WISER, WILMER C.; AND BECK, EDWARD C. "Intelligence and EEG Studies in Families With Idiopathic Epilepsy." J Am Med Assn 207(8):1497–501 F 24 '69. * (PA 44:21418)

935. RELLAS, ARCHIE J. "The Use of the Wechsler Preschool and Primary Scale (WPPSI) in the Early Identification of Gifted Students." Calif J Ed Res 20(3):117–9 My '69. * (PA 45:8921)

936. ROWLAND, MARY SARA. A Study of Cognitive Content in the Play Themes of Pre-School Children. Doctor's thesis, St. Louis University (St. Louis, Mo.), 1969. (DAI 30:3335A)

937. SHOTWELL, ANNA M.; O'CONNOR, GAIL; GABET, YVONNE; AND DINGMAN, HARVEY F. "Relation of the Peabody Picture Vocabulary Test IQ to the Stanford-Binet IQ." Am J Mental Def 74(1):39–42 Jl '69. * (PA 43:17485)

938. SILVERSTEIN, A. B. "Analysis of Two Item-Classification Schemes for the Stanford-Binet." Psychol Rep 24(2): 503–5 Ap '69. * (PA 43:16263)

939. SILVERSTEIN, A. B. "The Internal Consistency of the Stanford-Binet." Am J Mental Def 73(5):753–4 Mr '69. * (PA 43:10236)

940. TURNER, A. JACK, AND LAIR, CHARLES V. "The Use of Video Tape in Teaching and Evaluating Training of Individual Testing." J Clin Psychol 25(2):218–21 Ap '69. * (PA 43:13511)

941. YEN, SHERMAN M. Y. A Comparative Study of Test Variability With Peabody Picture Vocabulary Test, Goodenough's Draw-A-Man Test, and Stanford-Binet Intelligence Scale as Intellectual Measurement With a Group of Urban Low Socio-Economic Status Pre-School Pupils. Doctor's thesis, Catholic University of America (Washington, D.C.), 1969. (DAI 30:2625A)

942. ACHENBACH, THOMAS M. "Comparison of Stanford-Binet Performance of Nonretarded and Retarded Persons Matched for MA and Sex." Am J Mental Def 74(4):488–94 Ja '70. * (PA 44:11048)

943. ALPERN, GERALD D., AND KIMBERLIN, CAROLYN C. "Short Intelligence Test Ranging From Infancy Levels Through Childhood Levels for Use With the Retarded." Am J Mental Def 75(1):65–71 Jl '70. * (PA 45:1185)

944. BAYLEY, NANCY. Chap. 16, "Development of Mental Abilities," pp. 1163–209. In Carmichael's Manual of Child Psychology, Third Edition, Vol. 1. Edited by Paul H. Mussen. New York: John Wiley & Sons, Inc., 1970. Pp. xiii, 1519. *

945. BENNETT, DOROTHY KEMLER. The Tester and Intelligence Testing: An Examination of Protocol Interpretation. Doctor's thesis, Harvard University (Cambridge, Mass.), 1970. (DAI 31:2095A)

946. BERGER, M. "The Third Revision of the Stanford-Binet (Form L-M): Some Methodological Limitations and Their Practical Implications." B Brit Psychol Soc 23(78):17–26 Ja '70. * (PA 44:13629)

947. BLUM, JUNE E.; JARVIK, LISSY F.; AND CLARK, EDWARD T. "Rate of Change on Selective Tests of Intelligence: A Twenty-Year Longitudinal Study." J Gerontol 25(3):171–6 Jl '70. *

948. BRUININKS, ROBERT H., AND FELDMAN, DAVID H. "Creativity, Intelligence, and Achievement Among Disadvantaged Children." Psychol Sch 7(3):260–4 Jl '70. * (PA 45:5015)

949. BRUININKS, ROBERT H., AND LUCKER, WILLIAM G. "Change and Stability in Correlations Between Intelligence and Reading Test Scores Among Disadvantaged Children." J Read Behav 2(4):295–305 f '70. * (PA 46:5700)

950. BUTTERFIELD, EARL C., AND ZIGLER, EDWARD. "Pre-institutional Social Deprivation and IQ Changes Among Institutionalized Retarded Children." *J Abn Psychol* 75(1):83–9 F '70. * (*PA* 44:7155)

951. CALDWELL, MARK B., AND KNIGHT, DAVID. "The Effect of Negro and White Examiners on Negro Intelligence Test Performance." *J Negro Ed* 39(2):177–9 sp '70. * (*PA* 46:7443)

952. CALLAWAY, BYRON. "Factors Related to Reading of Children Referred to a University Reading Clinic," pp. 61–6. In *Reading Difficulties: Diagnosis, Correction, and Remediation.* Edited by William K. Durr. Newark, Del.: International Reading Association, 1970. Pp. vii, 276. *

953. COCHRAN, MALCOLM L. "A Profile of Psychological Test Scores for Retarded Adults." *Am J Mental Def* 74(4):582–4 Ja '70. * (*PA* 44:11052)

954. COSTELLO, JOAN, AND DICKIE, JOYCE. "Leiter and Stanford-Binet IQ's of Preschool Disadvantaged Children." Abstract. *Develop Psychol* 2(2):314 Mr '70. * (*PA* 44:6523)

955. CRANDALL, VIRGINIA C., AND BATTLE, ESTHER S. "The Antecedents and Adult Correlates of Academic and Intellectual Achievement." *Minn Symposia Child Psychol* 4:36–93 '70. *

956. DAVE, PRAFUL N. "Achievement Motivation and Risk-Taking in Kindergarten Children." *J Psychol Res* 14(1):7–13 Ja '70. *

957. DURKIN, DOLORES. "A Language Arts Program for Pre-First-Grade Children: Two-Year Achievement Report." *Read Res Q* 5(4):534–65 su '70. *

958. ENGELMANN, SIEGFRIED. "The Effectiveness of Direct Instruction on IQ Performance and Achievement in Reading and Arithmetic." *Disadvantaged Child* 3:339–61 '70. *

959. ESTES, ROBERT E., AND MORRIS, HUGHLETT L. "Relationship Among Intelligence, Speech Proficiency, and Hearing Sensitivity in Children With Cleft Palates." *Cleft Palate J* 7(9):763–73 Jl '70. *

960. FERINDEN, WILLIAM E., JR.; JACOBSON, SHERMAN; AND KOVALINSKY, THOMAS. *Educational Interpretation of the Stanford-Binet Intelligence Scale Form L-M and the Illinois Test of Psycholinguistic Abilities.* Linden, N.J.: Remediation Associates, Inc., 1970. Pp. 71. *

961. FISHER, MARY ANN, AND ZEAMAN, DAVID. "Growth and Decline of Retardate Intelligence." *Int R Res Mental Retard* 4:151–91 '70. *

962. FUTTERER, JAMES W. *An Investigation of the Relationship of the Wechsler Preschool and Primary Scale of Intelligence to the 1960 Revision of the Stanford-Binet Scale, Form L-M.* Master's thesis, Loyola University (Chicago, Ill.), 1970.

963. GAYTON, WILLIAM F. "Validity of the Harris Quality Scale With a Child Guidance Population." *Percept & Motor Skills* 31(1):17–8 Ag '70. * (*PA* 45:4532)

964. GOLDSTEIN, LEO S.; COLLER, ALAN R.; DILL, JOHN; AND TILIS, HOWARD S. "The Effect of a Special Curriculum for Disadvantaged Children on Test-Retest Reliabilities of Three Standardized Instruments." *J Ed Meas* 7(3):171–4 f '70. * (*PA* 45:4917)

965. HOFMEISTER, ALAN, AND ESPESETH, V. KNUTE. "Predicting Academic Achievement With TMR Adults and Teenagers." *Am J Mental Def* 75(1):105–7 Jl '70. *

966. HUMPHREYS, L. G. "Footnote to the Scottish Survey of Intelligence." *Brit J Ed Psychol* 40(1):72–4 F '70. * (*PA* 44:10411)

967. INGRAM, T. T. S.; MASON, A. W.; AND BLACKBURN, I. "A Retrospective Study of 82 Children With Reading Disability." *Develop Med & Child Neurol* 12(3):271–81 Je '70. *

968. IRETON, HAROLD; THWING, EDWARD; AND GRAVEM, HOWARD. "Infant Mental Development and Neurological Status, Family Socioeconomic Status, and Intelligence at Age Four." *Child Develop* 41(4):937–45 D '.0. * (*PA* 46:831)

969. KANGAS, JON ALAN. *Intelligence at Middle Age.* Doctor's thesis, Washington State University (Pullman, Wash.), 1970. (*DAI* 31:1520B)

970. KODMAN, FRANK, JR. "Effects of Preschool Enrichment on Intellectual Performance of Appalachian Children." *Excep Children* 36(7):503–7 Mr '71. * (*PA* 44:21495)

971. LARSEN, MARY JUHAN, AND ALLEN, JERRY C. "Effects of Certain Subject Variables on Stanford-Binet Item Performance of Five-Year-Old Children." *Psychol Rep* 26(3):975–84 Je '70. * (*PA* 45:517)

972. MEISSLER, GEORGE R. *A Correlation of the Slosson Intelligence Test and the Wechsler Intelligence Scale When Administered to Atypical Children.* Doctor's thesis, Catholic University of America (Washington, D.C.), 1970. (*DAI* 31:2191A)

973. MUMBAUER, CORINNE C., AND MILLER, J. O. "Socioeconomic Background and Cognitive Functioning in Preschool Children." *Child Develop* 41(2):471–80 Je '70. * (*PA* 44:14291)

974. NELSON, K. B., AND DEUTSCHBERGER, J. "Head Size at One Year as a Predictor of Four-Year IQ." *Develop Med & Child Neurol* 12(3):487–95 Je '70. * (*PA* 45:10490)

975. NICHOLSON, CHARLES L. "Analysis of Functions of the Slosson Intelligence Test." *Percept & Motor Skills* 31(2):627–31 O '70. * (*PA* 45:6336)

976. NURSS, JOANNE R. "A Diagnostic Comparison of Two Third Grade Reading Classes," pp. 42–54. In *Reading Difficulties: Diagnosis, Correction, and Remediation.* Edited by William

K. Durr. Newark, Del.: International Reading Association, 1970. Pp. vii, 276. *

977. PALMER, FRANCIS H. "Socioeconomic Status and Intellective Performance Among Negro Preschool Boys." *Develop Psychol* 3(1):1–9 Jl '70. * (*PA* 44:16374)

978. PEDRINI, DUILIO T. AND PEDRINI, LURA N. *The Pedrini Supplementary Aid to the Administration of the Stanford-Binet Intelligence Scale (Form L-M): A Handbook.* Los Angeles, Calif.: Western Psychological Services, 1970. Pp. iii, 50. *

979. RAMSEY, PHILLIP H., AND VANE, JULIA R. "A Factor Analytic Study of the Stanford Binet With Young Children." *J Sch Psychol* 8(4):278–84 '70. * (*PA* 46:1778)

980. REES, ANN H., AND PALMER, FRANCIS H. "Factors Related to Change in Mental Test Performance." *Develop Psychol Monogr* 3(2):1–57 S '70. * (*PA* 45:464)

981. SILVERSTEIN, A. B. "The Measurement of Intelligence." *Int R Res Mental Retard* 4:193–227 '70. *

982. TAYLOR, JOHN F.; WINSLOW, CHARLES N.; AND PAGE, HORACE A. "An MA Growth Curve for Institutionalized Mild and Moderate Retardates." *Am J Mental Def* 75(1):47–50 Jl '70. * (*PA* 45:1213)

983. WALKER, KENNETH P., AND GROSS, FREDERICK L. "I.Q. Stability Among Educable Mentally Retarded Children." *Training Sch B* 66(4):181–7 F '70. * (*PA* 44:13185)

984. WASHINGTON, ERNEST D., AND TESKA, JAMES A. "Relations Between the Wide Range Achievement Test, the California Achievement Tests, the Stanford-Binet, and the Illinois Test of Psycholinguistic Abilities." *Psychol Rep* 26(1):291–4 F '70. * (*PA* 45:4931)

985. WILLERMAN, LEE; BROMAN, SARAH H.; AND FIEDLER, MIRIAM. "Infant Development, Preschool IQ, and Social Class." *Child Develop* 41(1):69–77 Mr '70. * (*PA* 44:8168)

986. ZIMMERMAN, IRLA LEE, AND WOO-SAM, JAMES. "The Utility of the Wechsler Preschool and Primary Scale of Intelligence in the Public School." *J Clin Psychol* 26(4):472 '70. * (*PA* 45:6976)

DAVID FREIDES, *Associate Professor of Psychology, Emory University, Atlanta, Georgia.*

My comments in 1970 are not very different from those made by F. L. Wells 32 years ago in *The 1938 Mental Measurements Yearbook.* The Binet scales have been around a long time and their faults are well known.

In a simpler age, variations in accomplishment, especially in school performance, were explained by resort to the unitary concept of intelligence. This was measured by an instrument that yielded an index of underlying capability. The Stanford-Binet was the embodiment par excellence of this concept, the standard against which other instruments were evaluated. Unfortunately, if the score was low, the outlook was pessimistic: the explanation, hereditary. What could one do in the face of a fault in the biological past? Controversies raged (and still do) about the hereditary component of intelligence, while naive racial and hereditary concepts became part of the intellectual baggage in the field. Only recently has a sophisticated behavior genetics torn away the old naiveté and begun to show the inappropriateness of studying genic variations by examining so complexly determined a measure as IQ.

Meanwhile, many workers apparently disregarded unitary concepts and disdained pessimistic attitudes, with the result that a technology of (re)habilitation, (re)education, and (re)-motivation developed. A diversified evaluation, tapping different aspects of mental functioning and yielding indices of strength and weakness, had much greater utility than a singular index. Today, we remain a long way from systematic knowledge of the nature of intelligence and hence we still do not know exactly what to measure. But it is clear that this is the direction to go, which may explain why the Wechsler scales have largely superseded the Binet. Even when a Binet is used, patterns of successes and failures are analyzed and other tests are used to place the Binet result in perspective.

At present, no major, well standardized general intelligence test of the point scale type is available for children between 30 months, the ceiling of the *Bayley Scales of Infant Development,* and 48 months, the lowest age of the *Wechsler Preschool and Primary Scale of Intelligence.* Since tests are somewhat less reliable near the limits of the ages for which they were designed, the gap between these figures should be stretched some. But it is in filling this gap (especially along with the *Merrill-Palmer Scale of Mental Tests*) that the remaining utility of the Binet is found. Specifically to be avoided is its classic use in older cases of severe retardation in order to pinpoint levels of IQ below 50 or so. It is statistically meaningless to know that a subject is more than four or five standard deviations below the mean; however, the determination of a precise but meaningless number frequently precludes the search for behavioral potentials.

The *Stanford-Binet Intelligence Scale* is an old, old vehicle. It has led a distinguished life as a pioneer in the bootstrap operation that is the assessment enterprise. Its time is just about over. *Requiescat in pace.*

For a review by Elizabeth D. Fraser, see 6:536 (5 excerpts); for reviews by Mary R. Haworth and Norman D. Sundberg of the second edition, see 5:413; for a review by Boyd R. McCandless, see 4:358; see also 2:1420 (3 excerpts); for reviews by Francis N. Maxfield, J. W. M. Rothney, and F. L. Wells, see 1:1062.

[426]

★[Re Stanford-Binet Intelligence Scale] A Clinical Profile for the Stanford Binet Intelligence Scale (L-M). Ages 5 and over; 1965; title on profile is *A Profile for the Stanford Binet (L-M);* an item classification system for use by school psychologists in analyzing and reporting performance in 6 categories: general comprehension, visual-motor ability, arithmetic reasoning, memory and concentration, vocabulary and verbal fluency, judgment and reasoning; profile (2 pages); manual (4 pages); no data on reliability and validity of item classifications; $2.50 per 50 profiles; 50¢ per specimen set; postage extra; Robert E. Valett; Consulting Psychologists Press, Inc. *

[427]

★Stanford-Ohwaki-Kohs Block Design Intelligence Test for the Blind: American Revision of the Ohwaki-Kohs Test. Blind and partially sighted ages 16 and over; 1965–66; uses same testing materials as *The Ohwaki-Kohs Tactile Block Design Intelligence Test for the Blind;* individual; 1 form (blocks and design cards); record sheet (1 page); manual (18 pages plus record sheet); $47.50 per set of testing materials, 25 record sheets, and manual; $42.50 per set of testing materials; $12.50 per 100 record sheets; $3.50 per manual; postpaid; [60–120] minutes; Richard M. Suinn and William L. Dauterman; Western Psychological Services. *

[428]

★Vane Kindergarten Test. Ages 4-0 to 6-11; 1968; VKT; 4 scores: perceptual motor, vocabulary, drawing a man, total; individually administered in part; 1 form (1 page); manual (35 pages, reprint of *1* below); $3.50 per 50 tests; $4 per manual; postpaid; [30] minutes; Julia R. Vane; Clinical Psychology Publishing Co., Inc. *

REFERENCES
1. VANE, JULIA R. "The Vane Kindergarten Test." *J Clin Psychol* 24:121–54 Ap '68. * (*PA* 42:12096)
2. ELLERMAN, RICHARD A., AND WADLEY, JOYCE A. "A Readiness Experiment." *Read Teach* 23(6):556–8 Mr '70. *
3. WILLIS, DIANE JANICE. *Perceptual and Cognitive Performance of Children as Functions of Socio-Economic Class.* Doctor's thesis, University of Oklahoma (Norman, Okla.), 1970. (*DAI* 31:3045A)

DOROTHY H. EICHORN, *Research Psychologist and Administrator, Child Study Center, Institute of Human Development, University of California, Berkeley, California.*

The *Vane Kindergarten Test* utilizes three subtests and behavioral observations made during testing to assess "the intellectual and academic potential and behavior adjustment of young children." A rather unusual feature is the combination of group and individual testing. The Perceptual Motor subtest, in which the child makes three copies each of a box, a cross, and a hexagon, and the Man subtest (similar to the *Goodenough Intelligence Test* and the *Goodenough-Harris Drawing Test*), in which the child draws a man, are administered to a group. Then each child is tested individually for the 11-item Vocabulary subtest. Following the latter, the examiner notes on the test blank "behavior with respect to attention, ability to follow directions, self-control, cooperation, hand dominance and speech."

Tables for converting point scores to IQ are provided for each subtest for each month of age from 4-0 to 6-11. Full IQ is the average of the three subtest IQ's. For each subtest, mental age equivalents of point scores are also tabled so that ratio IQ's (mental age divided by chronological age) can be derived for children younger than 4-0 or older than 6-11.

All three subtests draw on classes of items widely used in tests for young children, and the empirical rationale for their selection is straightforward. Cited references indicate that form-copying skills are developmental in nature and related to success in reading and writing in the primary grades. The high correlation of vocabulary scores with total score on general tests of intelligence and with academic success is well known. In this particular test, the author considers the easier words to sample general information and the more difficult ones to require language facility as well as knowledge. A lengthy list of studies on the use of human figure drawing as an index of intelligence, adjustment, and future achievement of young children is provided.

Considerable effort was expended in the development and assessment of the VKT before its publication. A large variety of words (drawn from published lists and primary readers) and forms (recommended by teachers and psychologists working with young children) were first administered to "992 children, aged 5 to 10 years, in a lower middle class school district." Next a reduced number—15 words and 5 forms—were "given to 1809 children, aged 4 to 10 years, in a number of different school districts. Final selection of the items was then made." The methods used in item evaluation are not mentioned, except for the Man subtest. For this, rapidity and consistency of scoring by a number of examiners of varying experience, and comparability of correlation with the Stanford-Binet (.49) to that obtained with scoring by the Goodenough method (.52) were the criteria. The final standardization sample consisted of 400 children ages 4½ to 6 (the manual states that there were 100 of each sex at each half-year level, a seeming misprint) from the states of New York and New Jersey. The number of classrooms sampled, a factor which the literature suggests is as important as sample size, is not stated. Socioeconomic class was defined by father's occupational category. The VKT percentages of urban and of rural whites and the total of nonwhites are almost identical to those of the 1960 census. However, the sample contained very few nonwhite rural children and overly represented nonwhite urban

children in occupational categories IV through VIII. Norms for children younger or older than those in the standardization sample must be based on rescoring of tests from the pretest groups, a questionable procedure.

Intercorrelations among subtests range between .47 and .61. As would be expected from the averaging method for full IQ, the correlations of all subtests with full IQ are approximately the same, ranging from .78 to .86. Data on reliability come only from retests on very small groups—there is no alternate form of the VKT, and the brevity of the test contraindicates an odd-even assessment of reliability. Retesting of 14 kindergarten children after one week yielded high reliability coefficients: .97 for full IQ, .92 for the Man subtest, .82 for Perceptual Motor, and .81 for Vocabulary. Corresponding coefficients for 36 children tested in kindergarten in April and retested in the first grade the following October (at age levels in which the test is less discriminating) were .88, .79, .83, and .71. To assess the validity of full IQ's, correlations of the VKT with the Stanford-Binet were obtained in two samples. In one school district 212 children tested with the VKT in May of their kindergarten year were given the Binet sometime during the following two years. In another district the VKT was administered to 78 kindergarten children in October and the Binet was given in the same school year. Despite the temporal separations in testing, the correlation coefficient was about as high as would be expected under any circumstances (.76 for both samples), and the means on the two tests did not differ significantly.

The VKT is intended for use by school psychologists, not by teachers or other school personnel. This fact, of course, precludes its use in schools without psychological services. Among the advantages claimed for the VKT are "short administration time, simple directions, and rapid scoring," no disruption of school routine, and individual evaluation of "the influence of motivation, attention, perceptual motor skills or nonconforming behavior upon the test results." Although group tests require less time to administer, they do not offer the interpretative advantages of some individual contact.

For the most part, the directions for administration, both in terms of testing conditions and instructions to the children, and for scoring are clear and sufficiently detailed. Whether chronological age is to be calculated to the last month's birthdate or to nearest month is not specified. Minor perils in scoring are variations in point allotments. Some disruption of class routine must occur. Only 10 to 12 kindergarten children should be tested at one time; the others must be taken out of the room. An assistant is also recommended to supervise the remainder of the group while the examiner is administering vocabulary tests. The fact that the latter are likely to be given in a corner of the classroom introduces two possible problems: the child being tested may be disturbed by the other activities in the room, and children yet to take the Vocabulary may overhear responses. A further source of bias in Vocabulary scores, particularly with older or bright children, is the listing of the words on the same sheet on which the children copy forms. The compact record sheet is an advantage in many respects, but children who can already read may benefit from this exposure. Behavioral adjustment is evaluated from "signs" on the figure drawing and from observations during testing. Vane is careful to urge appropriate cautions in interpreting these data.

Although the VKT needs more extensive evaluation with broader and larger samples, it appears promising for its intended use. To date, reliability and validity coefficients are as good as those for any group test for young children, and relatively few are available. Among other group tests for this age range, only the *IPAT Culture Fair Intelligence Test* includes partial individual evaluation. If factor analyses justify the use of differential subtest scoring, such scores offer additional evaluative and predictive possibilities now paralleled probably only in the *California Short-Form Test of Mental Maturity*. Against these advantages must be weighed those of a series of graded tests by which to extend the age range covered, a characteristic of competing tests.

MARCEL L. GOLDSCHMID, *Associate Professor of Psychology and Director, Centre for Learning and Development, McGill University, Montreal, Quebec, Canada.*

The VKT may offer a considerable saving of time over conventional intelligence tests, since two of its three subtests, the Perceptual Motor and Draw A Man, can be administered to groups of children (8 to 12 at a time, depending on their age). The scoring also takes relatively little time, but it requires some judgment as to the quality of the response. Unfortunately, no interscorer reliability figures are presented for any of the three subtests. Given a random sample of examiners scoring the same set of VKT protocols, a considerable range of total scores might conceivably emerge.

A conversion table, broken down month by month from 4-0 to 6-11, shows the IQ equivalents of the total raw scores for each subtest. The total IQ is calculated by taking the average of the three subtest IQ's. The child's adjustment is evaluated on the basis of his total test behaviour and his draw-a-man performance. No quantitative measure is obtained, and no reliability or validity data (except for a handful of "successful" case studies) are provided for this assessment or for that of the child's perceptual motor development.

The norms are based on 400 subjects, a small and geographically unrepresentative sample (all subjects were from New York and New Jersey). The sample is, however, representative (for the U.S. as a whole) of different rural-urban, white-nonwhite, and occupational groups. Boys and girls did equally well, but white collar and white urban subjects obtained higher IQ's than blue collar and nonwhite subjects, respectively. (Unfortunately, no cross-tabulations were made in any of these comparisons.) Intercorrelations among the three subtests (.47 to .55) and for each subtest with the full test (.81 to .84) are satisfactory.

Test-retest reliability coefficients for the full test were .97 after one week and .88 after five months, but the samples were small and undefined in both cases.

Two separate samples (N's 212 and 78) were given both the VKT and the Stanford-Binet. In the first sample, the VKT was administered in kindergarten and the S-B in the following two years. In the second, the VKT was followed by the S-B later in the same year (kindergarten). Again the two samples are undefined with respect to sex, socioeconomic status, etc. No significant differences between the two means emerged for either sample and the correlation between the VKT and S-B was .76 in both cases. This correlation could conceivably be somewhat higher if both tests were given at the same time. It would have been very instructive to know the correlations between each VKT subtest and the S-B, since the correlation between S-B and full VKT approaches that between the VKT subtests and the full VKT. VKT IQ's obtained in kindergarten were also correlated with achievement deviations from grade expectations (as measured by the Stanford or California achievement tests) in first, second, and third grade. The coefficients were .59, .60, and .60, respectively. Thus it would appear possible to make reasonably good predictions about children's achievement in third grade based on their kindergarten VKT score.

The manual concludes with brief summaries of four illustrated case studies intended to "show that by utilizing the full IQ score and all other data derived from testing, a good picture of the child's functioning may be obtained." Such a small and highly selected sample can hardly be convincing. If such a claim is made, it would be desirable to support it with the results from other correlative studies or a predictive study of a larger and representative sample, particularly if the predictor variables are to include not only the VKT IQ scores but also quantified test behaviour and adjustment scores. The case studies do serve, however, the purpose of further illustrating the author's proposed scoring of entire VKT protocols. They also demonstrate the relatively curtailed range of possible scores, particularly at the lower end. The lowest Vocabulary IQ possible for a 4-year-old, for example, is 100 (if he can identify at least one word) or 0 (if he does not know any of the very short list of 11 words). (Note that the Vocabulary subtest does in fact have the lowest test-retest reliability, .71 after a 5-month interval.)

In summary, the VKT offers the advantages that part of the test can be administered to groups; the total IQ is a fair approximation of the Stanford-Binet IQ; it is reasonably well correlated with later achievement test scores; and it appears to have satisfactory reliability. On the other hand, the normative sample was small and geographically unrepresentative. The VKT, furthermore, requires a fair amount of judgment and experience (both with respect to administration and scoring). It is, in fact, meant to be administered by psychologists, rather than teachers.

[429]

Wechsler Adult Intelligence Scale. Ages 16 and over; 1939–55; WAIS; revision of Form 1 of *Wechsler-Bellevue Intelligence Scale;* individual; 14 scores: verbal (information, comprehension, arithmetic, similarities, digit span, vocabulary, total), performance (digit symbol, picture completion, block design, picture arrangement, object assembly, total), total; 1 form ['55]; manual ('55, 116 pages); record booklet ('55, 4 pages); supplementary record sheet ('55, 1 page); $26 per set of testing materials, 25 record booklets, and manual; $2.70 per 25 record booklets; $1 per 25 supplementary record sheets; $3.25 per manual; postage extra; Spanish edition ('68) available; (40–60) minutes; David Wechsler; Psychological Corporation. *

REFERENCES

1–42. See 5:414.
43–222. See 6:538.
223. STAKER, JAMES EDWARD. *A Study of Academically Successful Students in a Large Secondary School.* Doctor's thesis, Northwestern University (Evanston, Ill.), 1954. (*DA* 14:2280)
224. WAHLER, HARRY JOE. *Analysis of the Performance of Brain-Damaged Patients on a Memory-For-Designs Test.* Doctor's thesis, State University of Iowa (Iowa City, Iowa), 1954. (*DA* 14:2406)
225. WECHSLER, D. "The Measurement and Evaluation of Intelligence of Older Persons," pp. 275–9. In *Old Age in the Modern World: Report of the Third Congress of the International Association of Gerontology, London, 1954.* Edinburgh, Scotland: E. & S. Livingstone Ltd., 1955. Pp. vii, 647. *
226. KIRSCHNER, DAVID. *An Analysis of Certain Relationships Between "Abstract" and "Concrete" Attitude, Avoidance Behavior, and Stimulus Generalization.* Doctor's thesis, University of Pittsburgh (Pittsburgh, Pa.), 1957. (*DA* 17:2314)
227. DREWES, HENRY WALTER. *An Experimental Study of the Relationship Between Electroencephalographic Imagery Variables and Perceptual-Cognitive Processes.* Doctor's thesis, Cornell University (Ithaca, N.Y.), 1958. (*DA* 19:87)
228. ALPER, ARTHUR E., AND HORNE, BETTY M. "Changes in IQ of a Group of Institutionalized Mental Defectives Over a Period of Two Decades." *Am J Mental Def* 64:472–5 N '59. * (*PA* 34:7994)
229. CRAWFORD, PAUL L. "The Relative Sensitivity of the LAIS, WAIS, and PM in Differentiating Between Psychopathic and Psychotic Patients in a Mental Hospital." *Psychol Service Center J* 11(2):93–7 '59. * (*PA* 34:4374)
230. CRAWFORD, PAUL L. "The Statistical Significance of Differences in Performance on the Leiter Adult Intelligence Scale, the Wechsler Adult Intelligence Scale, and the Porteus Maze by a Heterogeneous Mental Hospital Population." *Psychol Service Center J* 11(2):89–92 '59. * (*PA* 34:4510)
231. FLEMING, JACK WAYNE. *The Relationships Among Psychometric, Experimental, and Observational Measures of Learning Ability in Institutional, Endogenous Mentally Retarded Persons.* Doctor's thesis, University of Colorado (Boulder, Colo.), 1959. (*DA* 20:4183)
232. KARLIN, ISAAC W.; EISENSON, JON; HIRSCHENFANG, SAMUEL; AND MILLER, MAURICE H. "A Multi-Evaluational Study of Aphasic and Non-Aphasic Right Hemiplegic Patients." *J Speech & Hearing Disorders* 24:369–79 N '59. * (*PA* 34:8078)
233. SANTOS, BERTHA. *A Comparison of Memory and Learning Ability With Social Competence and Social Participation in Aged Senile Dements in a Mental Institution.* Doctor's thesis, New York University (New York, N.Y.), 1959. (*DA* 20:1441)
234. KOROTKIN, ARTHUR LEWIS. *Perception and Intelligence: The Relationship of Certain Visual-Perceptual Skills With Intelligence, Age, and Sex.* Doctor's thesis, Temple University (Philadelphia, Pa.), 1960. (*DA* 21:1637)
235. NELSON, LOIS AUDREY. *A Study of Certain Cognitive Aspects of the Speech of Multiple Sclerotic Patients.* Doctor's thesis, University of Wisconsin (Madison, Wis.), 1960. (*DA* 21:1666)
236. WERTS, CHARLES EARL, JR. *Multidimensional Analysis of Psychological Constructs.* Doctor's thesis, University of Minnesota (Minneapolis, Minn.), 1960. (*DA* 21:2008)
237. BELL, ANNE, AND ZUBEK, JOHN P. "Effects of Deanol on the Intellectual Performance of Mental Defectives." *Can J Psychol* 15:172–5 S '61. * (*PA* 36:4J172B)
238. BERNSTEIN, LEWIS. "Psychological Testing: 1, Intelligence Tests." *J Child Asth Res Inst & Hosp* 1:205–17 Je '61. *
239. ILANIT, NATHAN. *Some Psychological Correlates of the Process-Reactive Concept of Schizophrenia.* Doctor's thesis, University of Southern California (Los Angeles, Calif.), 1961. (*DA* 21:3852)
240. GOUREVITCH, VIVIAN, AND FEFFER, MELVIN H. "A Study of Motivational Development." *J Genetic Psychol* 100:361–75 Je '62. * (*PA* 37:2891)
241. KOLE, DELBERT MERRILL. *A Study of Intellectual and Personality Characteristics of Medical Students.* Master's thesis, University of Oregon Medical School (Portland, Ore.), 1962.
242. MURDY, WILLIAM GEORGE, JR. *The Effect of Positive and Negative Administrations on Intelligence Test Performance.* Doctor's thesis, University of Florida (Gainesville, Fla.), 1962. (*DA* 23:1076)

243. NATHAN, PETER. *A Comparative Investigation of Conceptual Ability in Relation to Frustration Tolerance.* Doctor's thesis, Washington University (St. Louis, Mo.), 1962. (*DA* 24:394)

244. OBRIST, WALTER D.; BUSSE, EWALD W.; EISDORFER, CARL; AND KLEEMEIER, ROBERT W. "Relation of the Electroencephalogram to Intellectual Function in Senescence." *J Gerontol* 17:197–206 Ap '62. * (*PA* 37:2958)

245. WINER, DAVID. "The Relationship Among Intelligence, Emotional Stability, and Use of Auditory Cues by the Blind." *Am Found Blind Res B* 2:88–93 D '62. *

246. BERGER, LESLIE; BERNSTEIN, ALVIN; KLEIN, EDWARD; COHEN, JACOB; AND LUCAS, GERALD. "Effects of Aging and Pathology on the Factorial Structure of Intelligence." *Newsl Res Psychol* 5:35–6 Ag '63. * (*PA* 38:8442)

247. BERNSTEIN, ALVIN; KLEIN, EDWARD; BERGER, LESLIE; AND COHEN, JACOB. "The Influence of Institutionalization and Several Pre-Morbid and Demographic Variables on the Structure of Intelligence in Chronic Schizophrenics." *Newsl Res Psychol* 5:34–5 Ag '63. *

248. BIRREN, JAMES E.; BOTWINICK, JACK; WEISS, ALFRED D.; AND MORRISON, DONALD F. Chap. 10, "Interrelations of Mental and Perceptual Tests Given to Healthy Elderly Men," pp. 143–56. In *Human Aging: A Biological and Behavioral Study.* Edited by James E. Birren, Robert N. Butler, Samuel W. Greenhouse, Louise Sokoloff, and Marian R. Yarrow. National Institute of Mental Health, Public Health Service Publication No. 986. Washington, D.C.: United States Government Printing Office, 1963. Pp. xiii, 328. * (*PA* 38:5821)

249. BIRREN, JAMES E.; RIEGEL, KLAUS F.; AND MORRISON, DONALD F. Chap. 1, "Intellectual Capacities, Aging, and Man's Environment," pp. 9–44. In *Process of Aging: Social and Psychological Perspectives.* Edited by Richard H. Williams and others. New York: Atherton Press, 1963. Pp. xix, 587. *

250. BOTWINICK, JACK, AND BIRREN, JAMES E. Chap. 8, "Mental Abilities and Psychomotor Responses in Healthy Aged Men," pp. 97–108. In *Human Aging: A Biological and Behavioral Study.* Edited by James E. Birren, Robert N. Butler, Samuel W. Greenhouse, Louise Sokoloff, and Marian R. Yarrow. National Institute of Mental Health, Public Health Service Publication No. 986. Washington, D.C.: United States Government Printing Office, 1963. Pp. xiii, 328. * (*PA* 38:5821)

251. CAMPO, ROBERT ETTORE. *Clinical Versus Automated Administration of a Mental Test: A Study of Examiner Influence.* Doctor's thesis, University of Arizona (Tucson, Ariz.), 1963. (*DA* 25:285)

252. CANCRO, RALPH. *The Relation of Laterality of Brain Lesion to Intellectual Dysfunction.* Doctor's thesis, Columbia University (New York, N.Y.), 1963. (*DA* 24:2120)

253. DESROCHES, HARRY F.; BALLARD, H. TED; AND KIMBREALL, GORDON M. "Note on the Reliability of the WAIS Vocabulary Test in the Aged." *Newsl Res Psychol* 5:10 N '63. *

254. FLINN, DON E.; HARTMAN, BRYCE O.; POWELL, DOUGLAS H.; AND MCKENZIE, RICHARD E. "Psychiatric and Psychologic Evaluation," pp. 199–230. In *Aeromedical Evaluation for Space Pilots.* Edited by Lawrence E. Lamb. Brooks Air Force Base, Tex.: USAF School of Aerospace Medicine, July 1963. Pp. viii, 276. * (*PA* 38:4728)

255. GALLAHER, PHILLIP JAMES. *Effects of Increased Verbal Scale Difficulty and Failure on WAIS Digit Symbol Performance.* Doctor's thesis, University of Denver (Denver, Colo.), 1963. (*DA* 24:5544)

256. JENNINGS, WILLIAM G. "Psychologic Test Profiles of Special Groups." *Proc Ann Conf Air Force Clin Psychologists* 4:105–16 '63. *

257. KLETT, WILLIAM G. "An Analysis of Item Order in Seven Subtests of the Wechsler Adult Intelligence Scale." *Newsl Res Psychol* 5:30–2 N '63. *

258. MACKIE, JAMES BENJAMIN. *A Comparative Study of Brain Damaged and Normal Individuals on Tests of Intelligence, Perception and Rigidity.* Doctor's thesis, University of Utah (Salt Lake City, Utah), 1963. (*DA* 24:1700)

259. NICKOLS, JOHN. "Mental Deficit, Schizophrenia and the Benton Test." *J Nerv & Mental Dis* 136:279–82 Mr '63. * (*PA* 38:4615)

260. PARKER, ROLLAND S., AND DAVIDSON, NORMAN L. "A Comparison of Students of Nursing and Hospitalized Patients on Scores Derived From an Intelligence Test (WAIS)." *Psychiatric Q Sup* 37:298–306 pt 2 '63. * (*PA* 38:8431, 39:1789)

261. PASRICHA, PREM, AND PAGEDAR, RAJAMI M. "Adaptation of 'WAIS' to the Gujarati Population: Try-out With the School and College Population." *J Voc & Ed Guid* 9:174–84 N '63. * (*PA* 38:8432)

262. RUBIN, EDMUND JOSEPH. *Performance of Totally-Blind and Sighted Subjects on Tests of Abstraction.* Doctor's thesis, Fordham University (New York, N.Y.), 1963. (*DA* 24:2989)

263. SPIETH, PHILLIP EARL. *Intelligence as It Relates to Three Creativity Categories: Science, Art, and Literature.* Doctor's thesis, University of Michigan (Ann Arbor, Mich.), 1963. (*DA* 25:1759)

264. STEINER, FELIX. *Pictorial and Conceptual Thinking as Related to Personality.* Doctor's thesis, Yeshiva University (New York, N.Y.), 1963. (*DA* 25:2056)

265. WEBB, ALLEN P. "Some Issues Relating to the Validity of the WAIS in Assessing Mental Retardation," pp. 87–92. (*PA* 38:6075) In *Towards a Professional Identity in School Psychology.* California Association of School Psychologists and Psychometrists, Fourteenth Annual Conference, March 28–30, 1963. [Los Angeles, Calif.: the Association, 1963.] Pp. v, 97. * (*PA* 38:4904)

266. BERGER, LESLIE; BERNSTEIN, ALVIN; KLEIN, EDWARD; COHEN, JACOB; AND LUCAS, GERALD. "Effects of Aging and Pathology on the Factorial Structure of Intelligence." *J Consult Psychol* 28:199–207 Je '64. † (*PA* 39:4631)

267. BERMAN, ISAAC. *Wechsler Scores vs. Piaget Levels: A Study of the Cognitive Efficiency of Institutionalized Retardates.* Doctor's thesis, University of Southern California (Los Angeles, Calif.), 1964. (*DA* 25:2040)

268. BERMAN, ISAAC, AND RHONE, DORIS ELLEN. "Wechsler Scores VS. Piaget Levels: Cognitive Efficiency of Institutionalized Retardates." *Calif Mental Health Res Dig* 2:18 au '64. *

269. BEVERFELT, EVA; NYÅARD, MARIT; AND NORDVIK, HILMAR. "Factor Analysis of Wechsler Adult Intelligence Scale Performance of Elderly Norwegians." *J Gerontol* 19:49–53 Ja '64. *

270. BUTLER, ALFRED J., AND CONRAD, W. GLENN. "Psychological Correlates of Abnormal Electroencephalographic Patterns in Familial Retardates." *J Clin Psychol* 20:338–43 Jl '64. * (*PA* 39:10572)

271. DENNERLL, RAYMOND D. "Prediction of Unilateral Brain Dysfunction Using Wechsler Test Scores." *J Consult Psychol* 28:278–84 Je '64. * (*PA* 39:5618)

272. DENNERLL, RAYMOND D.; DEN BROEDER, JOAN; AND SOKOLV, SHERWIN L. "WISC and WAIS Factors in Children and Adults With Epilepsy." *J Clin Psychol* 20:236–40 Ap '64. * (*PA* 39:8347)

273. FEINBERG, M. R., AND PENZER, W. N. "Factor Analysis of a Sales Selection Battery." *Personnel Psychol* 17:319–24 au '64. * (*PA* 39:8794)

274. FISKE, DONALD W.; CARTWRIGHT, DESMOND S.; AND KIRTNER, WILLIAM L. "Are Psychotherapeutic Changes Predictable?" *J Abn & Social Psychol* 69:418–26 O '64. * (*PA* 39:8058)

275. FITZHUGH, KATHLEEN B., AND FITZHUGH, LOREN C. "WAIS Results for Ss With Longstanding, Chronic, Lateralized and Diffuse Cerebral Dysfunction." *Percept & Motor Skills* 19:735–9 D '64. * (*PA* 39:8353)

276. FITZHUGH, LOREN C., AND FITZHUGH, KATHLEEN B. "Relationships Between Wechsler-Bellevue Form I and WAIS Performances of Subjects With Longstanding Cerebral Dysfunction." *Percept & Motor Skills* 19:539–43 O '64. * (*PA* 39:8348)

277. FOGEL, MAX L. "The Intelligence Quotient as an Index of Brain Damage." *Am J Orthopsychiatry* 34:555–62 Ap '64. *

278. GENDEL, HOWARD, AND RICE, WARREN. "Correlation of the Kent EGY With WAIS IQ's and Scaled Scores." *Newsl Res Psychol* 6:43–4 Ag '64. *

279. GERDINE, PHILIP VAN HORN, JR. *Patterns of Ego Function in Psychophysiological Skin Disorders.* Doctor's thesis, Boston University (Boston, Mass.), 1964. (*DA* 25:3108)

280. GUYETTE, ANNA; WAPNER, SEYMOUR; WERNER, HEINZ; AND DAVIDSON, JOHN. "Some Aspects of Space Perception in Mental Retardates." *Am J Mental Def* 69:90–100 Jl '64. * (*PA* 39:2514)

281. HAUGEN, EARL STUART. *A Study of the Validity of the WAIS, SCAT, and STEP As Predictors of Success in College Mathematics.* Doctor's research study No. 1, Colorado State College (Greeley, Colo.), 1964. (*DA* 28:124A)

282. HUFF, FREDERICK WARE. *Reliability of Clinical, Psychological Judgment as a Function of Information Presentation and Response Classification.* Doctor's thesis, University of Georgia (Athens, Ga.), 1964. (*DA* 25:3110)

283. HUNT, WILLIAM A.; SCHWARTZ, MELVIN L.; AND WALKER, RONALD E. "The Correctness of Diagnostic Judgment as a Function of Diagnostic Bias and Population Base Rate." *J Clin Psychol* 20:143–5 Ja '64. * (*PA* 39:10278)

284. JASTAK, J. F., AND JASTAK, S. R. "Short Forms of the WAIS and WISC Vocabulary Subtests." *J Clin Psychol* 20:167–99 Ap '64. * (*PA* 39:7820)

285. JOHNSON, JAMES J. *The Significance of Verbal Sub-Test Discrepancies on the Wechsler Tests.* Master's thesis, Illinois State University (Normal, Ill.), 1964.

286. JURKO, M. F., AND ANDY, O. J. "Psychological Aspects of Diencephalotomy." *J Neurol Neurosurg & Psychiatry* 27:516–21 D '64. * (*PA* 39:9508)

287. KENDRICK, D. C. "Assessment of Pre-Morbid Intelligence of Elderly Patients With Diffuse Brain Pathology." *Psychol Rep* 15:188 Ag '64. * (*PA* 39:1389)

288. KETTELL, MARJORIE EDYTHE. *Integrity of Ego Processes in Aged Females.* Doctor's thesis, Boston University (Boston, Mass.), 1964. (*DA* 25:3111)

289. KRIPPNER, STANLEY. "The Relationship Between MMPI and WAIS Masculinity-Femininity Scores." *Personnel & Guid J* 42:695–8 Mr '64. * (*PA* 39:5072)

290. LADD, CLAYTON E. "WAIS Performances of Brain Damaged and Neurotic Patients." *J Clin Psychol* 20:114–7 Ja '64. * (*PA* 39:10132)

291. LASKY, JULIAN J. "Relationships Between Measures of Ego Strength, Intelligence and Anxiety." *Newsl Res Psychol* 6:52–3 My '64. *

292. LEVINSON, BORIS M. "The 'Beat' Phenomenon in Wechsler Tests." *J Clin Psychol* 20:118–20 Ja '64. * (*PA* 39:10133)

293. LEVINSON, BORIS M. "A Comparative Study of the WAIS Performance of Native-Born Negro and White Homeless." *J Genetic Psychol* 105:211–8 D '64. * (*PA* 39:7562)

294. LUSZKI, WALTER ALOISE. *Degree of Hearing Loss Related to Intelligence as Measured by the WAIS and WISC.* Doctor's thesis, University of Georgia (Athens, Ga.), 1964. (*DA* 25:3113)

295. MAJUMDAR, P. K. "Wechsler-Bellevue Adult Intelligence Scale in a Foreign Language." *B Council Social & Psychol Res* 3:11–6 Jl '64. * (*PA* 40:2872)

296. MATARAZZO, JOSEPH D.; ALLEN, BERNADENE V.; SASLOW, GEORGE; AND WIENS, ARTHUR N. "Characteristics of Successful Policemen and Firemen Applicants." *J Appl Psychol* 48:123–33 Ap '64. * (*PA* 39:6047)

297. MONEY, JOHN. "Two Cytogenetic Syndromes: Psychologic Comparisons: 1, Intelligence and Specific-Factor Quotients." *J Psychiatric Res* 2:223–31 O '64. * (*PA* 39:15981)

298. NUNNALLY, JUM C. *Educational Measurement and Evaluation,* pp. 257–62. New York: McGraw-Hill Book Co., 1964. Pp. xv, 440. *

299. OLSEN, INGER A., AND JORDHEIM, GERALD D. "Use of W.A.I.S. in a Student Counseling Center." *Personnel & Guid J* 42:500–3 Ja '64. * (*PA* 39:5512)

300. QUERESHI, MOHAMMED Y. "Maximum Versus Minimum Testing: A Problem in Individual Appraisal." *Univ N Dak Col Ed Rec* 49:89–92 Mr '64. *

301. SHAW, DALE JEAN. *An Analysis of Wechsler Adult Intelligence Scale Protocols of Students in a Midwestern University.* Doctor's thesis, Purdue University (Lafayette, Ind.), 1964. (*DA* 26:1175)

302. SWENSON, EDWIN WAYNE. *A Comparison of the Wechsler-Bellevue, Form I, and the Wechsler Adult Intelligence Scale for a Population of Average Intelligence.* Master's thesis, University of Utah (Salt Lake City, Utah), 1964.

303. TOLOR, ALEXANDER. "Abstract Ability in Organics and Schizophrenics." *J Proj Tech & Pers Assess* 28:357–62 S '64. * (*PA* 39:8520)

304. WALKER, RONALD E., AND SPENCE, JANET TAYLOR. "Relationship Between Digit Span and Anxiety." *J Consult Psychol* 28:220–3 Je '64. * (*PA* 39:5245)

305. WATSON, CHARLES GORDON. *Differences Between Brain-Damaged and Schizophrenic Patients in Three Aspects of Wechsler Adult Intelligence Scale Performance.* Doctor's thesis, University of Iowa (Iowa City, Iowa), 1964. (*DA* 25:1348)

306. WEBB, ALLEN P. "Some Issues Relating to the Validity of the WAIS in Assessing Mental Retardation." *Calif J Ed Res* 15:130–5 My '64. * (*PA* 39:5672)

307. WHEELER, LAWRENCE. "Complex Behavioral Indices Weighted by Linear Discriminant Functions for the Prediction of Cerebral Damage." *Percept & Motor Skills* 19:907–23 D '64. * (*PA* 39:8357)

308. WOLK, ROBERT L., AND RUSTIN, STANLEY L. "Psychologic Evaluation of Gerontologic Population: Comparison of Results With the Raven Progressive Matrices (1947) Versus the Wechsler Adult Intelligence Scale." *J Am Geriatrics Soc* 12:807–9 Ag '64. *

309. BERKOWITZ, BERNARD, AND GREEN, RUSSEL F. "Changes in Intellect With Age: 5, Differential Changes as Functions of Time Interval and Original Score." *J Genetic Psychol* 107:179–92 D '65. * (*PA* 40:5284)

310. BERNSTEIN, ALVIN S.; KLEIN, EDWARD B.; BERGER, LESLIE; AND COHEN, JACOB. "Relationship Between Institutionalization, Other Demographic Variables, and the Structure of Intelligence in Chronic Schizophrenics." *J Consult Psychol* 29:320–4 Ag '65. * (*PA* 39:16181)

311. BLATT, SIDNEY J.; ALLISON, JOEL; AND BAKER, BRUCE L. "The Wechsler Object Assembly Subtest and Bodily Concerns." *J Consult Psychol* 29:223–30 Je '65. * (*PA* 39:12225)

312. CARLISLE, A. L. "Quick Test Performance by Institutional Retardates." *Psychol Rep* 17:489–90 O '65. * (*PA* 40:886)

313. CASTELL, J. H. F., AND MITTLER, P. J. "Intelligence of Patients in Subnormality Hospitals: A Survey of Admissions in 1961." *Brit J Psychiatry* 111:219–25 Mr '65. * (*PA* 39:10453)

314. CONRY, ROBERT, AND PLANT, WALTER T. "*WAIS* and Group Test Predictions of an Academic Success Criterion: High School and College." *Ed & Psychol Meas* 25:493–500 su '65. * (*PA* 39:15216)

315. COSLETT, STEPHEN B. "The WAIS Masculinity-Femininity Index in a Paranoid Schizophrenic Population." *J Clin Psychol* 21:62 Ja '65. * (*PA* 39:12840)

316. CRAFT, MICHAEL. Chap. 3, "Diagnosis and Aetiology Illustrated by an Analysis of Admissions to a Psychopathic Unit," pp. 32–54. In *Ten Studies Into Psychopathic Personality: A Report to the Home Office and the Mental Health Research Fund.* Bristol, England: John Wright & Sons Ltd., 1965. Pp. 133. *

317. DE MILAN, JEAN. "Bilingualism and the Wechsler Vocabulary Scales." *J Clin Psychol* 21:298 Jl '65. * (*PA* 39:15346)

318. DOYLE, EDWARD D. *A Comparison of IQ's on the WAIS and Q.T. With a Group of Spinal Cord Injury Patients.* Master's thesis, Loyola University (Chicago, Ill.), 1965.

319. EDWARDS, HENRY P. *EEG and WAIS Intelligence in a Sample of Cultural-Familial Deficients.* Master's thesis, University of Ottawa (Ottawa, Ont., Canada), 1965.

320. FOGEL, MAX L. "The Proverbs Test in the Appraisal of Cerebral Disease." *J General Psychol* 72:269–75 Ap '65. * (*PA* 39:12281)

321. FOGEL, MAX L., AND BLUMKLOTZ, F. PETER. "Effects of Different Training Tasks on Digit Symbol Performance." *J Clin Psychol* 21:109–11 Ja '65. * (*PA* 39:12318)

322. GIBEAU, PHILIP JOSEPH. *Field Dependency and the Process-Reactive Dimension in Schizophrenia.* Doctor's thesis, Purdue University (Lafayette, Ind.), 1965. (*DA* 26:1775)

323. GREEN, HARRY BRUCE, JR. *A Statistical Comparison of the Wechsler Intelligence Scale for Children and the Wechsler Adult Intelligence Scale.* Doctor's thesis, University of Virginia (Charlottesville, Va.), 1965. (*DA* 26:5866) (Abstract: *Ed R* 3:61–3)

324. GREENWOOD, DENNIS I., AND TAYLOR, CHARLES. "Adaptive Testing in an Older Population." *J Psychol* 60:193–8 Jl '65. * (*PA* 40:32)

325. HALLENBECK, CHARLES E.; FINK, STEPHEN L.; AND GROSSMAN, JOEL S. "Measurement of Intellectual Inefficiency." *Psychol Rep* 17:339–49 O '65. * (*PA* 40:1590)

326. HAMLIN, ROY M., AND WARD, WILLIAM D. "Aging, Hospitalization, and Schizophrenic Intelligence." Abstract. *Proc Ann Conv Am Psychol Assn* 73:221–2 '65. * (*PA* 39:16202)

327. HASKELL, SIMON H. "The Use of the Shortened Form of the W.A.I.S. With Cerebral Palsied Adults." *Int Copenhagen Congr Sci Study Mental Retard* 1964:636–41 ['65]. *

328. HENNING, JOHN J. *Analysis of Examiner Variance on the Wechsler Adult Intelligence Scale.* Master's thesis, Loyola University (Chicago, Ill.), 1965.

329. HIMELSTEIN, PHILIP. "College Failure on the WAIS 'Population' Item." *Psychol Rep* 17:824 D '65. * (*PA* 40:4215)

330. HOLMES, DOUGLAS S.; ARMSTRONG, HUBERT E., JR.; JOHNSON, MONTY H.; AND RIES, HAROLD A. "Further Evaluation on an Abbreviated Form of the WAIS." *Psychol Rep* 16:1163–4 Je '65. * (*PA* 39:15238)

331. KABACK, GOLDIE RUTH. "A Comparison of WAIS, Binet, and WISC Test Results of Mentally Retarded Young Adults Born in New York City and Puerto Rico." *Training Sch B* 62:108–12 N '65. * (*PA* 40:2138)

332. KAHN, MARVIN W. "A Factor-Analytic Study of Personality, Intelligence, and History Characteristics of Murderers." Abstract. *Proc Ann Conv Am Psychol Assn* 73:227–8 '65. * (*PA* 39:16125)

333. KENNEDY, WALLACE A., AND WALSH, JOHN. "A Factor Analysis of Mathematical Giftedness." *Psychol Rep* 17:115–9 Ag '65. * (*PA* 40:1553)

334. KNOX, WILMA J. "The Effects of Alcoholic Overindulgence on Selected WAIS Sub-Test Scores in Domiciliary Members." *Newsl Res Psychol* 7:33–5 Ag '65. *

335. KOLE, DELBERT M., AND MATARAZZO, JOSEPH D. "Intellectual and Personality Characteristics of Two Classes of Medical Students." *J Med Ed* 40:1130–44 D '65. *

336. KRAMER, ERNEST, AND FRANCIS, PAUL S. "Errors in Intelligence Estimation With Short Forms of the WAIS." Abstract. *J Consult Psychol* 29:490 O '65. *

337. KRAUS, J. "Cattell Anxiety Scale Scores and WAIS Attainment in Three Groups of Psychiatric Patients." *Austral J Psychol* 17:229–32 D '65. * (*PA* 40:5451)

338. KRAUS, J. "Psychiatric Classification and Differential Value of WAIS Subtest Scores." *Austral J Psychol* 17:137–9 Ag '65. * (*PA* 40:894)

339. KRAUS, J., AND SELECKI, B. R. "Brain Atrophy and Assessment of Intellectual Deterioration on the Wechsler Adult Intelligence Scale." *J Nerv & Mental Dis* 141:119–22 Jl '65. * (*PA* 40:2468)

340. KROSKE, WILLIAM H.; FRETWELL, LORETTA N.; AND CUPP, MARION E. "Comparison of the Kahn Intelligence Tests: Experimental Form, the Stanford-Binet and the WAIS for Familial Retardates." *Percept & Motor Skills* 21:428 O '65. * (*PA* 40:3310)

341. LEVINSON, BORIS M. "Note on the Intelligence and WAIS Pattern of White First-Time Applicants for Shelter Care." *Psychol Rep* 16:524 Ap '65. * (*PA* 39:10602)

342. LUSZKI, WALTER A. "Hearing Loss and Intelligence Among Retardates." *Am J Mental Def* 70:93–101 Jl '65. * (*PA* 39:16056)

343. MCKEEVER, WALTER F.; MAY, PHILIP R. A.; AND TUMA, A. HUSSAIN. "Prognosis in Schizophrenia: Prediction of Length of Hospitalization From Psychological Test Variables." *J Clin Psychol* 21:214–21 Ap '65. * (*PA* 39:12856)

344. MEER, BERNARD, AND BAKER, JANET A. "Reliability of Measurements of Intellectual Functioning of Geriatric Patients." *J Gerontol* 20:410–4 Jl '65. *

345. NEWTON, G. MACKIE. "A Comparison of the Immediate Test and WAIS Verbal Scale in Vocational Rehabilitation Use." *J Clin Psychol* 21:300 Jl '65. * (*PA* 39:15368)

346. OGILVIE, ROBERT D. "Correlations Between the Quick Test (QT) and the Wechsler Adult Intelligence Scale (WAIS) as Used in a Clinical Setting." *Psychol Rep* 16:497–8 Ap '65. * (*PA* 39:10081)

347. PASRICHA, PREM, AND PAGEDAR, RAJANI M. "Item

Analysis of the Translation and Adaptation of WAIS for a Gujarati Speaking Population." *J Voc & Ed Guid* 11:12–7 F '65. * (*PA* 39:10243)

348. PETTIT, DONALD E. "A Note on the Satz-Mogel WAIS Abbreviation for Prison Populations." *Can J Correct* 7:111 Ja '65. *

349. PRADO, WILLIAM M., AND SCHNADT, FREDERICK. "Differences in WAIS—WB Functioning of Three Psychiatric Groups." *J Clin Psychol* 21:184–6 Ap '65. * (*PA* 39:12305)

350. RAMALINGASWAMI, PRABHA. "The Use of Block Design Test Among Illiterate Low Economic Group of People." *Indian J Psychol* 40:153–60 D '65. * (*PA* 40:11666)

351. SCHWARTZ, MARK S. "Relationships Between the Kent EGY and WAIS Scores, Functioning Levels and Subtests in a Veterans Neuropsychiatric Population." *Newsl Res Psychol* 7:8–9 My '65. *

352. SEGAL, STANLEY J.; NACHMANN, BARBARA; AND MOULTON, ROBERT. "The Wechsler Adult Intelligence Scale (WAIS) in the Counseling of Students With Learning Disorders." *Personnel & Guid J* 43:1018–23 Je '65. * (*PA* 39:16432)

353. SHAW, DALE J. "Sexual Bias in the WAIS." *J Consult Psychol* 29:590–1 D '65. * (*PA* 40:2874)

354. SMART, REGINALD G. "The Relationships Between Intellectual Deterioration, Extraversion and Neuroticism Among Chronic Alcoholics." *J Clin Psychol* 21:27–9 Ja '65. * (*PA* 39:12771)

355. SMITH, LAURENCE C., JR. "The Effects of Heat Stroke on Cognitive Functioning." *Proc Ann Conf Air Force Behav Sci* 11:130–42 Jl '65. *

356. STONE, LEROY A., AND RAMER, JOHN C. "Estimating WAIS IQ From Shipley Scale Scores: Another Cross-Validation." *J Clin Psychol* 21:297 Jl '65. * (*PA* 39:15276)

357. TEMMER, HELENA W. "Wechsler Intelligence Scores and Bender-Gestalt Performance in Adult Male Mental Defectives." *Am J Mental Def* 70:142–7 Jl '65. * (*PA* 39:16070)

358. WACHTEL, PAUL L., AND BLATT, SIDNEY J. "Energy Deployment and Achievement." *J Consult Psychol* 29:302–8 Ag '65. * (*PA* 39:16395)

359. WALKER, RONALD E.; HUNT, WILLIAM A.; AND SCHWARTZ, MELVIN L. "The Difficulty of WAIS Comprehension Scoring." *J Clin Psychol* 21:427–9 O '65. * (*PA* 40:1555)

360. WALKER, RONALD E.; NEILSEN, MARY KAY; AND NICOLAY, ROBERT C. "The Effects of Failure and Anxiety on Intelligence Test Performance." *J Clin Psychol* 21:400–2 O '65. * (*PA* 40:1556)

361. WATSON, CHARLES G. "Intratest Scatter in Hospitalized Brain-Damaged and Schizophrenic Patients." Abstract. *J Consult Psychol* 29:596 D '65. *

362. WATSON, CHARLES G. "WAIS Error Types in Schizophrenics and Organics." *Psychol Rep* 16:527–30 Ap '65. * (*PA* 39:10164)

363. WATSON, CHARLES G. "WAIS Profile Patterns of Hospitalized Brain-Damaged and Schizophrenic Patients." *J Clin Psychol* 21:294–5 Jl '65. * (*PA* 39:15377)

364. WHITE, J. GRAHAM, AND KNOX, S. J. "Some Psychological Correlates of Age and Dementia." *Brit J Social & Clin Psychol* 4:259–65 D '65. * (*PA* 40:4114)

365. WILLNER, ALLEN, AND REITZ, WILLARD. "Association as an Essential Variable in Tests of Abstract Reasoning." Abstract. *Proc Ann Conv Am Psychol Assn* 73:287–8 '65. * (*PA* 39:14009)

366. ZYTOWSKI, DONALD G., AND HUDSON, JACQUELINE. "The Validity of Split-Half Abbreviations of the WAIS." *J Clin Psychol* 21:292–4 Jl '65. * (*PA* 39:15284)

367. ABRAMS, STANLEY, AND NATHANSON, IRA A. "Intellectual Deficit in Schizophrenia: Stable or Progressive." *Dis Nerv System* 27:115–7 F '66. *

368. AFFLECK, D. CRAIG, AND FREDERICKSON, WILBUR K. "Testing Limits of WAIS Picture Arrangement Test." *Am J Mental Def* 70:605–6 Ja '66. * (*PA* 40:5863)

369. BERRY, ROSE AUERSPERG. *An Analysis of the Relationship Between Certain Variables of Students With Behavioral Disorders and Successful Completion of Vocational Training.* Doctor's thesis, University of Arkansas (Fayetteville, Ark.), 1966. (*DA* 27:1194A)

370. BINGHAM, WILLIAM C.; BURKE, HENRY R.; AND MURRAY, STEWART. "Raven's Progressive Matrices: Construct Validity." *J Psychol* 62:205–9 Mr '66. * (*PA* 40:7203)

371. BLATT, BENJAMIN, AND TSUSHIMA, WILLIAM. "A Psychological Study of Uremic Patients Being Considered for the Artificial Kidney Machine Programs (Hemodialysis)." *Newsl Res Psychol* 8:17–8 F '66. *

372. BLAZER, JOHN A. "Leg Position and Psychological Characteristics in Women." *Psychol* 3:5–12 Ag '66. * (*PA* 40:12361)

373. BOLTON, N.; BRITTON, P. G.; AND SAVAGE, R. D. "Some Normative Data on the WAIS and Its Indices in an Aged Population." *J Clin Psychol* 22:184–8 Ap '66. * (*PA* 40:7204)

374. BRITTON, P. G., AND SAVAGE, R. D. "A Short Form of the WAIS for Use With the Aged." *Brit J Psychiatry* 112:417–8 Ap '66. * (*PA* 40:9428)

375. CHANSKY, NORMAN M. "Measuring the Intelligence and Achievement of School Dropouts With the Benton Visual Retention Test." *Am J Mental Def* 71:191–5 S '66. * (*PA* 40:13186)

376. CRADDICK, RAY A. "WISC and WAIS IQs as a Func-

tion of Season of Birth." *Psychol Rep* 18:259–64 F '66. * (*PA* 40:6626)

377. DICKSTEIN, LOUIS S., AND BLATT, SIDNEY J. "Death Concern, Futurity, and Anticipation." *J Consult Psychol* 30:11–7 F '66. * (*PA* 40:4230)

378. DOHERTY, MARY AUSTIN, AND WALKER, RONALD E. "The Relationship of Personality Characteristics, Awareness, and Attitude in a Verbal Conditioning Situation." *J Personality* 34:504–16 D '66. *

379. EDWARDS, GENE A. "Anxiety Correlates of the Wechsler Adult Intelligence Scale." *Calif J Ed Res* 17:144–7 My '66. * (*PA* 40:10099)

380. FLYNN, WILLIAM F. "How Biased Was This Sample?" *Newsl Res Psychol* 8:45–7 N '66. *

381. FRIEDMAN, JOEL. *The Relationship Between Intelligence and Channel Capacity.* Doctor's thesis, Texas Technological College (Lubbock, Tex.), 1966. (*DA* 28:1191B)

382. GATHERCOLE, C. E. "I.Q. Scores and the Problem of Classification." Letter. *Brit J Psychiatry* 112:1181–2 N '66. *

383. GUERTIN, WILSON H.; LADD, CLAYTON E.; FRANK, GEORGE H.; RABIN, ALBERT I.; AND HIESTER, DOUGLAS S. "Research With the Wechsler Intelligence Scales for Adults: 1960–1965." *Psychol B* 66:385–409 N '66. * (*PA* 41:40)

384. HIGBEE, WALTER R. "Supervisors as Raters in the Assessment of Workshop Performance of Retarded Sheltered Employees." *Am J Mental Def* 71:447–50 N '66. * (*PA* 41:1838)

385. HIRSCHENFANG, SAMUEL, AND BENTON, JOSEPH G. "Note on Intellectual Changes in Multiple Sclerosis." *Percept & Motor Skills* 22:786 Je '66. * (*PA* 40:11405)

386. HOLDEN, RAYMOND H.; MENDELSON, MARTIN A.; AND DEVAULT, SPENCER. "Relationship of the WAIS to the SRA Non-Verbal Test Scores." *Psychol Rep* 19:987–90 D '66. * (*PA* 41:3721)

387. HOLMES, DOUGLAS S.; ARMSTRONG, HUBERT E., JR.; JOHNSON, MONTY H.; AND RIES, HAROLD A. "Validity and Clinical Utility of the Satz and Mogel Abbreviated Form of the WAIS." *Psychol Rep* 18:992–4 Je '66. * (*PA* 40:9435)

388. HOROWITZ, FRANCES DEGEN. "The Relationship Between Wechsler Intelligence Quotients and Parsons Language-Sample Scores of Mentally Retarded Children." *J Genetic Psychol* 108:59–63 Mr '66. * (*PA* 40:10400)

389. HUNT, WILLIAM A., AND WALKER, RONALD E. "Validity of Diagnostic Judgment as a Function of Amount of Test Information." *J Clin Psychol* 22:154–5 Ap '66. * (*PA* 40:7847)

390. HUNT, WILLIAM A.; QUAY, HERBERT C.; AND WALKER, RONALD E. "The Validity of Clinical Judgments of Asocial Tendency." *J Clin Psychol* 22:116–8 Ja '66. * (*PA* 40:4410)

391. JENNINGS, CHARLES L. "The Hewson Ratios Revisited via the WAIS." *Proc Ann Conf Air Force Behav Sci* 13:181–94 S '66. *

392. JOSLIN, HANNAH FAE. *Intelligence and Social Awareness: An Investigation of the Relationship Between Social Awareness, Planfullness and Performance on the Wechsler Picture Arrangement Subtests.* Doctor's thesis, New York University (New York, N.Y.), 1966. (*DA* 27:2871B)

393. KLØVE, H., AND MATTHEWS, C. G. "Psychometric and Adaptive Abilities in Epilepsy With Differential Etiology." *Epilepsia* 7:330–8 D '66. *

394. KRAUS, J. "On the Method of Indirect Assessment of Intellectual Impairment: A Modified WAIS Index." *J Clin Psychol* 22:66–9 Ja '66. * (*PA* 40:4216)

395. LEVINSON, BORIS M. "A Comparative Study of Northern and Southern Negro Homeless Men." *J Negro Ed* 35:144–50 sp '66. * (*PA* 44:10415)

396. LIBOWITZ, JUSTUS M. *The Effect of the Perceived Degree of Examiner Congruence Upon WAIS IQs.* Doctor's thesis, Yeshiva University (New York, N.Y.), 1966. (*DA* 28:1167B)

397. LUSZKI, MARGARET B.; DAWES, ROBYN M.; SCHULTZ, WILLIAM; AND LAYWELL, H. ROBERT. "A Study of an Abbreviated Form of the Wechsler Adult Intelligence Scale." *Newsl Res Psychol* 8:14–5 N '66. *

398. LUSZKI, WALTER A. "An Idiot Savant on the WAIS?" *Psychol Rep* 19:603–9 O '66. * (*PA* 41:719)

399. McKERRACHER, D. W., AND SCOTT, J. "I.Q. Scores and the Problem of Classification: A Comparison of the W.A.I.S. and S-B, Form L-M in a Group of Subnormal and Psychopathic Patients." *Brit J Psychiatry* 112:537–41 Je '66. * (*PA* 40:10101)

400. MATTHEWS, C. G.; SHAW, D. J.; AND KLØVE, H. "Psychological Test Performances in Neurologic and 'Pseudo-Neurologic' Subjects." *Cortex* 2:244–53 Ap '66. * (*PA* 41:672)

401. MEIER, MANFRED J., AND RESCH, JOSEPH A. "Behavioral Correlates of Short-Term Change in Neurological Status Following Acute Onset of Cerebrovascular Symptomatology." *J Clin Psychol* 22:156–9 Ap '66. * (*PA* 40:8003)

402. MILLS, DAVID H., AND TUCKER, LEDYARD R. "A Three-Mode Factor Analysis of Clinical Judgment of Schizophrenicity." *J Clin Psychol* 22:136–9 Ap '66. * (*PA* 40:7913)

403. MONROE, KENTON L. "Note on the Estimation of the WAIS Full Scale IQ." *J Clin Psychol* 22:79–81 Ja '66. * (*PA* 40:4217)

404. MORGAN, DONALD W. "WAIS 'Analytic Index' and Rehospitalization of Schizophrenic Servicemen." *J Consult Psychol* 30:267–9 Je '66. * (*PA* 40:9052)

405. NORMAN, RALPH D. "A Revised Deterioration Formula

for the Wechsler Adult Intelligence Scale." *J Clin Psychol* 22:287–94 Jl '66. * (*PA* 40:11293)

406. PAYNE, DAVID A., AND LEHMAN, IRVIN J. "A Brief WAIS Item Analysis." *J Clin Psychol* 22:296–7 Jl '66. * (*PA* 40:10635)

407. RADCLIFFE, J. A. "WAIS Factorial Structure and Factor Scores for Ages 18 to 54." *Austral J Psychol* 18:228–38 D '66. * (*PA* 41:3699)

408. REITZ, WILLARD E. "Association, Abstraction, and Intelligence." Abstract. *Proc 74th Ann Conv Am Psychol Assn* 1:239–40 '66. * (*PA* 41:5959)

409. RUSALEM, HERBERT; LIPTON, ROBERT; AND GOLDSAMT, MILTON. "Changes in Psychologic Test (WAIS) Scores of Older Disabled Persons During a Vocational Rehabilitation Program." *J Am Geriatrics Soc* 14:875–8 Ag '66. *

410. SANNITO, THOMAS C., AND HANNUM, THOMAS E. "Relationship Between the WAIS and Indices of Sociopathy in an Incarcerated Female Population." *J Res Crime & Del* 3:63–70 Ja '66. *

411. SAXE, ETTA LOU GLUCKSTEIN. *Intra-Test Scatter on the WAIS as a Diagnostic Sign: A Comparison of Schizophrenic, Neurotic, and Normal Groups.* Doctor's thesis, University of Michigan (Ann Arbor, Mich.), 1966. (*DA* 27:2517B)

412. SCHALON, CHARLES LAWRENCE. *Performance Following Failure Stress as a Function of Level of Self-Esteem.* Doctor's thesis, University of Iowa (Iowa City, Iowa), 1966. (*DA* 27:3296B)

413. SCHILL, THOMAS. "The Effects of MMPI Social Introversion on WAIS PA Performance." *J Clin Psychol* 22:72–4 Ja '66. * (*PA* 40:4239)

414. SCHWARTZ, MELVIN L. "The Scoring of WAIS Comprehension Responses by Experienced and Inexperienced Judges." *J Clin Psychol* 22:425–7 O '66. * (*PA* 41:2267)

415. SIMS, NEIL B., AND CLOWER, ROBERT P. "Correlation Between WAIS IQ's and 16 PF B Factor Scores of General Hospital Patients." *Newsl Res Psychol* 8:10–1 My '66. *

416. SMITH, AARON. "Talkers and Doers, or Education, Intelligence, and WAIS Verbal-Performance Ratios in Psychiatric Patients." Abstract. *Proc 74th Ann Conv Am Psychol Assn* 1:233–4 '66. * (*PA* 41:5975)

417. SPRAGUE, ROBERT L., AND QUAY, HERBERT C. "A Factor Analytic Study of the Responses of Mental Retardates on the WAIS." *Am J Mental Def* 70:595–600 Ja '66. * (*PA* 40:5891)

418. SPREEN, OTFRIED, AND ANDERSON, CHARLES W. G. "Sibling Relationship and Mental Deficiency Diagnosis as Reflected in Wechsler Test Patterns." *Am J Mental Def* 71:406–10 N '66. * (*PA* 41:1850)

419. STERNBERG, DAVID, AND SCHIFF, STANLEY. "Reality Checking Ability and Cognitive Functioning in Functional Psychiatric Disorders." *Psychiatric Q Sup* 40:306–14 pt 2 '66. * (*PA* 41:16823)

420. STERNE, DAVID M. "The Knox Cubes as a Test of Memory and Intelligence With Male Adults." *J Clin Psychol* 22:191–3 Ap '66. * (*PA* 40:7219)

421. TAYLOR, JAMES B. "The Use of Human Figure Drawings With the Upper Level Mentally Retarded." *Am J Mental Def* 71:423–6 N '66. * (*PA* 41:1851)

422. THOMAS, CHARLES A., JR. "The 'Yell Fire' Response as an Indicator of Impaired Impulse Control." *J Clin Psychol* 22:221–3 Ap '66. * (*PA* 40:7720)

423. THUNE, JEANNE; TINE, SEBASTIAN; AND CHERRY, NANCY. "Personality Characteristics of Successful Older Leaders." *J Gerontol* 21:463–70 Jl '66. *

424. VEALE, SARA OSTEEN. *Evaluating Two Approaches to Remedial Reading and Analyzing WAIS Profiles of Participants in DeKalb College.* Doctor's thesis, University of Georgia (Athens, Ga.), 1966. (*DA* 27:3325A)

425. VELLUTINO, FRANK R., AND HOGAN, TERRENCE P. "The Relationship Between the Ammons and WAIS Test Performances of Unselected Psychiatric Subjects." *J Clin Psychol* 22:69–71 Ja '66. * (*PA* 40:4221)

426. WATSON, CHARLES G. "Evidence on the Utilities of Three WAIS Short Forms." Abstract. *J Consult Psychol* 30:181 Ap '66. *

427. WEINER, IRVING B. *Psychodiagnosis in Schizophrenia.* New York: John Wiley & Sons, 1966. Pp. xiv, 573. * (*PA* 41:4753)

428. WILLNER, A. E., AND REITZ, W. E. "Association, Abstraction, and the Conceptual Organization of Recall: Implications for Clinical Tests." *J Abn Psychol* 71:315–27 O '66. * (*PA* 40:13178)

429. WILLNER, ALLEN E. "Associative Meaning and Vocabulary Tests." Abstract. *Proc 74th Ann Conv Am Psychol Assn* 1:241–2 '66. * (*PA* 41:5979)

430. WITKIN, HERMAN A.; FATERSON, HANNA F.; GOODENOUGH, DONALD R.; AND BIRNBAUM, JUDITH. "Cognitive Patterning in Mildly Retarded Boys." *Child Develop* 37:301–16 Je '66. * (*PA* 40:9184)

431. ABIDIN, RICHARD R., JR., AND BYRNE, ALFRED V. "Quick Test Validation Study and Examination of Form Equivalency." *Psychol Rep* 20:735–9 Je '67. * (*PA* 41:13591)

432. ANDERSON, HARRY E., JR.; KERN, FRANK E.; AND COOK, CHARLOTTE. "Correlational and Normative Data for the

Progressive Matrices With Retarded Populations." *J Psychol* 67:221–5 N '67. * (*PA* 42:1396)

433. BAER, P.; MERRYMAN, P.; AND GAITZ, C. "Performance Deficit Related to Chronic Brain Syndrome, Schizophrenia and Age." *Gerontologist* 7(3, pt 2):37 S '67. * (*PA* 41:16721)

434. BERKE, NORMAN DANIEL. *An Investigation of Adult Negro Illiteracy: Prediction of Reading Achievement and Description of Educational Characteristics of a Sample of City Core Adult Negro Illiterates.* Doctor's thesis, State University of New York (Buffalo, N.Y.), 1967. (*DA* 28:931A)

435. BLATT, SIDNEY J., AND QUINLAN, PAUL. "Punctual and Procrastinating Students: A Study of Temporal Parameters." *J Consult Psychol* 31:169–74 Ap '67. * (*PA* 41:7317)

436. BRIGHAM, BRUCE W. *A Study of the Reading Achievement and Certain Characteristics of Adult Males Convicted of Felonies.* Doctor's thesis, Temple University (Philadelphia, Pa.), 1967. (*DA* 28:4279B)

437. BRITTON, PETER G.; BERGMANN, KLAUS; KAY, DAVID W. K.; AND SAVAGE, R. DOUGLASS. "Mental State, Cognitive Functioning, Physical Health, and Social Class in the Community Aged." *J Gerontol* 22:517–21 O '67. *

438. BROWN, ORIL. "Relation of WAIS Verbal and Performance IQs for Four Psychiatric Conditions." *Psychol Rep* 20:1015–20 Je '67. * (*PA* 41:13951)

439. BUDOFF, MILTON. "Learning Potential Among Institutionalized Young Adult Retardates." *Am J Mental Def* 72:404–11 N '67. * (*PA* 42:7631)

440. BURNAND, G.; HUNTER, H.; AND HOGGART, K. "Some Psychological Test Characteristics of Klinefelter's Syndrome." *Brit J Psychiatry* 113:1091–6 O '67. * (*PA* 42:7632)

441. CATE, CLARENCE C. "Test Behavior of ESL Students." *Calif J Ed Res* 18:184–7 S '67. * (*PA* 42:4480)

442. de LINT, JAN. "Note on Birth Order and Intelligence Test Performance." *J Psychol* 66:15–7 My '67. * (*PA* 41:10444)

443. DICKSTEIN, LOUIS S., AND BLATT, SIDNEY J. "The WAIS Picture Arrangement Subtest as a Measure of Anticipation." *J Proj Tech & Pers Assess* 31:32–8 Je '67. * (*PA* 41:13613)

444. DOORBAR, RUTH RAE. "Psychological Testing of Transsexuals: A Brief Report of Results From the Wechsler Adult Intelligence Scale, the Thematic Apperception Test, and the House-Tree-Person Test." *Trans N Y Acad Sci* 29:455–62 F '67. * (*PA* 41:16827)

445. DOTY, BARBARA A. "Some Academic Characteristics of the Mature Coed." *J Ed Res* 61:163–5 D '67. *

446. DUKE, ROBERT B. "Intellectual Evaluation of Brain-Damaged Patients With a WAIS Short Form." Abstract. *Psychol Rep* 20:858 Je '67. *

447. EBER, HERBERT W. "The Factor Structure of the WAIS-Verbal and HIS-Test Combination." *J Ed Res* 61:27–8 S '67. *

448. GAMEWELL, JOYCE. *An Investigation of the Use of Two Instruments for Assessing Intellective and Nonintellective Aspects of Intelligence as Predictors of Post Degree Success of Psychology Graduate Students.* Doctor's thesis, Colorado State College (Greeley, Colo.), 1967. (*DA* 28:3022A)

449. GIBSON, JOHN, AND LIGHT, PHYLLIS. "Intelligence Among University Scientists." *Nature* 213:441–3 F 4 '67. * (*PA* 41:11916)

450. GILBERSTADT, HAROLD, AND SAKO, YOSHIO. "Intellectual and Personality Changes Following Open-Heart Surgery." *Arch Gen Psychiatry* 16:210–4 F '67. * (*PA* 41:7763)

451. GILMAN, ROBERT H. *A Study of Intellectual Change of Deaf Students as Measured by Standard Tests of Intelligence.* Master's thesis, Springfield College (Springfield, Mass.), 1967.

452. GOLDSTEIN, STEVEN G., AND LUNDY, CHARLES T. "Utilization of the Wechsler Adult Intelligence Scale (WAIS) in Predicting Success With Low Average High School Students." *Ed & Psychol Meas* 27:457–61 su '67. * (*PA* 41:14216)

453. GRISSO, J. THOMAS, AND MEADOW, ARNOLD. "Test Interference in a Rorschach-WAIS Administration Sequence." *J Consult Psychol* 31:382–6 Ag '67. * (*PA* 41:13617)

454. GROTELUESCHEN, ARDEN, AND LYONS, THOMAS J. "Quick Word Test Validity With Adults." *Psychol Rep* 20:488–90 Ap '67. * (*PA* 41:8151)

455. HARONIAN, FRANK, AND SAUNDERS, DAVID R. "Some Intellectual Correlates of Physique: A Review and a Study." *J Psychol Studies* 15:57–105 Je '67. *

456. HARWOOD, B. THOMAS. "Some Intellectual Correlates of Schizoid Indicators: WAIS and MMPI." Abstract. *J Consult Psychol* 31:218 Ap '67. *

457. HENNING, JOHN J., AND LEVY, RUSSELL H. "Verbal-Performance IQ Differences of White and Negro Delinquents on the WISC and WAIS." *J Clin Psychol* 23:164–8 Ap '67. * (*PA* 41:9127)

458. JONES, REGINALD L. "Validities of Short WAIS Batteries." Abstract. *J Consult Psychol* 31:103 F '67. *

459. JURJEVICH, R. M. "Intellectual Assessment With Gorham's Proverbs Test, Raven's Progressive Matrices, and WAIS." *Psychol Rep* 20:1285–6 Je '67. * (*PA* 41:15271)

460. KAUFMAN, HARVEY ISIDORE. *Cognitive and Noncognitive Indices of Employability in a Sampling of 17 to 21 Year Old Mentally Retarded Individuals.* Doctor's thesis, Marquette University (Milwaukee, Wis.), 1967. (*DA* 28:3027A)

461. KLAPPER, ZELDA S., AND BIRCH, HERBERT G. "A Fourteen Year Follow-Up Study of Cerebral Palsy: Intellectual Changes and Stability." *Am J Orthopsychiatry* 37:540–7 Ap '67. *

462. KRAUS, J., AND SELECKI, B. R. "Assessment of Laterality in Diffuse Cerebral Atrophy Using the WAIS." *J Clin Psychol* 23:91–2 Ja '67. * (*PA* 41:5958)

463. LABAK, ALEX S. *A Comparative Study of Three Short Individual Intelligence Tests, Using the Wechsler Adult Intelligence Scale as a Validating Criterion, With a Selected Group of Slow Learners.* Master's thesis, Moorehead State College (Moorehead, Minn.), 1967.

464. LASSMAN, FRANK M., AND ENGELBART, ELAINE S. "Methodology in Digit Memory Testing of College Students." *J Speech & Hearing Res* 10:268–76 Je '67. * (*PA* 41:15819)

465. LOWE, C. MARSHALL. "Prediction of Posthospital Work Adjustment by the Use of Psychological Tests." *J Counsel Psychol* 14:248–52 My '67. * (*PA* 41:9197)

466. LUSZKI, MARGARET B.; SCHULTZ, WILLIAM; LAYWELL, H. ROBERT; AND DAWES, ROBYN M. "A Study of an Abbreviated Form of the Wechsler Adult Intelligence Scale." *Newsl Res Psychol* 9:39–41 My '67. *

467. McCARTHY, DOROTHEA; SCHIRO, FREDERICK M.; AND SUDIMACK, JOHN P. "Comparison of WAIS M-F Index With Two Measures of Masculinity-Femininity." *J Consult Psychol* 31:639–40 D '67. * (*PA* 42:2587)

468. McDONALD, K. G., AND CROOKES, T. G. "The WAIS Picture Arrangement Test in British Psychiatric Patients." *Brit J Social & Clin Psychol* 6:72 F '67. *

469. MATTHEWS, C. G., AND KLØVE, H. "Differential Psychological Performances in Major Motor, Psychomotor, and Mixed Seizure Classifications of Known and Unknown Etiology." *Epilepsia* 8:117–28 Je '67. *

470. MONEY, JOHN, AND EPSTEIN, RALPH. "Verbal Aptitude in Eonism and Prepubertal Effeminacy—A Feminine Trait." *Dis Nerv System* 29:448–54 F '67. *

471. MURRAY, JOHN B. "College Students' IQs." *Psychol Rep* 20:743–7 Je '67. * (*PA* 41:13598)

472. NEWLAND, T. ERNEST, AND SMITH, PATRICIA A. "Statistically Significant Difference Between Subtest Scaled Scores on the WISC and the WAIS." *J Sch Psychol* 5:122–7 w '67. * (*PA* 41:8884)

473. OBERLEDER, MURIEL. "Adapting Current Psychological Techniques for Use in Testing the Aging." *Gerontologist* 7(3, pt 1):188–91 S '67. * (*PA* 42:3801)

474. OGDON, DONALD P. Section 2, "The Wechsler Scales," pp. 3–10, 75–7. In his *Psychodiagnostics and Personality Assessment: A Handbook.* Beverly Hills, Calif.: Western Psychological Services, 1967. Pp. v, 96. *

475. PAUL, MARY E. *The Effect of Stress on WAIS Digit Span, Digit Symbol and Picture Completion Performances.* Master's thesis, Loyola University (Chicago, Ill.), 1967.

476. REED, JAMES C., AND FITZHUGH, KATHLEEN B. "Factor Analysis of WB-1 and WAIS Scores of Patients With Chronic Cerebral Dysfunction." *Percept & Motor Skills* 25:517–21 O '67. * (*PA* 42:5964)

477. RHUDICK, P. J., AND GORDON, C. "Test-Retest IQ Changes in Bright Aging Individuals." Abstract. *Gerontologist* 7(3, pt 2):34 S '67. * (*PA* 41:16550)

478. RICHMAN, JOSEPH. "Reporting Diagnostic Test Results to Patients and Their Families." *J Proj Tech & Pers Assess* 31:62–70 Je '67. * (*PA* 41:13733)

479. ROSS, DONALD RUFUS. *Test Performance of Deaf Adults Under Two Modes of Test Administration.* Doctor's thesis, University of Arizona (Tucson, Ariz.), 1967. (*DA* 28:2992A)

480. ROSS, ROBERT T., AND MORLEDGE, JUNE. "Comparison of the WISC and WAIS at Chronological Age Sixteen." *J Consult Psychol* 31:331–2 Je '67. * (*PA* 41:10449)

481. RUBY, THOMAS M. *Performance on the Wechsler Adult Intelligence Scale by High and Low Anxious College Students.* Master's thesis, Southern Methodist University (Dallas, Tex.), 1967.

482. SATTLER, JEROME M., AND THEYE, FRED. "Procedural, Situational, and Interpersonal Variables in Individual Intelligence Testing." *Psychol B* 68:347–60 N '67. * (*PA* 42:2564)

483. SATZ, PAUL; RICHARD, WAYNE; AND DANIELS, AUBREY. "The Alteration of Intellectual Performance After Lateralized Brain-Injury in Man." *Psychon Sci* 7:369–70 Ap 5 '67. * (*PA* 41:8428)

484. SHAW, DALE J. "Estimating WAIS IQ From Progressive Matrices Scores." *J Clin Psychol* 23:184–5 Ap '67. * (*PA* 41:8886)

485. SHAW, DALE J. "Factor Analysis of the Collegiate WAIS." Abstract. *J Consult Psychol* 31:217 Ap '67. *

486. SILVERSTEIN, A. B. "A Short Short Form of the WISC and WAIS for Screening Purposes." *Psychol Rep* 20:682 Ap '67. * (*PA* 41:8164)

487. SILVERSTEIN, A. B. "Validity of WAIS Short Forms." *Psychol Rep* 20:37–8 F '67. * (*PA* 41:6463)

488. SINGH, UDAI PRATAP. "Intelligence in Criminals." *Indian J Social Work* 27:269–74 O '66. * (*PA* 41:4569) Reprinted 27:393–8 Ja '67. * (*PA* 41:9124)

489. SJOGREN, DOUGLAS D. "Achievement as a Function of Study Time." *Am Ed Res J* 4:337–43 N '67. * (*PA* 42:17816)

490. STEINBERG, MARVIN; SEGEL, RUEBEN H.; AND LEVINE, HARRY D. "Psychological Determinants of Academic Success:

A Pilot Study." *Ed & Psychol Meas* 27:413–22 su '67. * (*PA* 41:14226)

491. STEINMAN, WARREN M. "The Use of Ambiguous Stimuli to Predict General Competence." *J Sci Lab Denison Univ* 48:7–14 Je '67. * (*PA* 42:2590)

492. STEWART, HORACE; COLE, SPURGEON; AND WILLIAMS, ROBERT. "Relationship Between the QT and WAIS in a Restricted Clinical Sample." *Psychol Rep* 20:383–6 Ap '67. * (*PA* 41:9087)

493. STIER, SERENA AUSTER. *Developmental Attainment, Outcome and Symbolic Performance in Schizophrenia.* Doctor's thesis, University of California (Los Angeles, Calif.), 1967. (*DA* 28:4766B)

494. SUINN, RICHARD M.; DAUTERMAN, WILLIAM; AND SHAPIRO, BERNICE. "The WAIS as a Predictor of Educational and Occupational Achievement in the Adult Blind." *New Outl Blind* 61:41–3 F '67. *

495. SYDIAHA, DANIEL. "Prediction of WAIS IQ for Psychiatric Patients Using the Ammons' FRPV and Raven's Progressive Matrices." *Psychol Rep* 20:823–6 Je '67. * (*PA* 41:13602)

496. TELLEGEN, AUKE, AND BRIGGS, PETER F. "Old Wine in New Skins: Grouping Wechsler Subtests Into New Scales." *J Consult Psychol* 31:499–506 O '67. * (*PA* 41:16071)

497. TEMPLER, DONALD I. "Relation Between Immediate and Short-Term Memory and Clinical Implications." *Percept & Motor Skills* 24:1011–2 Je '67. * (*PA* 41:13086)

498. THALER, VICTOR HUGO. *Personality Dimensions Derived From Multiple Instruments.* Doctor's thesis, Columbia University (New York, N.Y.), 1967. (*DA* 28:509A)

499. TOOLSON, REX NOBLE. *An Investigation of the Relationship Between Measures of Intelligence and Season of Birth.* Doctor's thesis, Colorado State College (Greeley, Colo.), 1967. (*DA* 28:2572A)

500. WAGNER, RUDOLPH FRED. *An Explication of Gittinger's Internalizer-Externalizer Dimension by Factor Analysis Based Upon Related Personality Measures.* Doctor's thesis, George Washington University (Washington, D.C.), 1967.

501. WANG, H. A.; OBRIST, W. D.; AND BUSSE, E. W. "Electroencephalographic and Intellectual Changes in Healthy Elderly: A Longitudinal Study." Abstract. *Gerontologist* 7(3, pt 2):23 S '67. *

502. WILLIAMS, JEROLD R. *A Correctional Study of Adult Comprehension Performance on the Stanford-Binet (1937) Form L Test and the Wechsler Adult Intelligence Scale.* Master's thesis, Illinois State University (Normal, Ill.), 1967.

503. WILTBERGER, ARLENE CAMPBELL. *A Comparative Study of the Wechsler Intelligence Scale for Children and the Wechsler Adult Intelligence Scale With High IQ Level and Low IQ Level Subjects.* Master's thesis, Cornell University (Ithaca, N.Y.), 1967.

504. WINTER, GERALD DAVID. *Intelligence, Interest, and Personality Characteristics of a Selected Group of Students: A Description and Comparison of White and Negro Students in a Vocational Rehabilitation Administration Program in Bassick and Harding High Schools, Bridgeport, Connecticut.* Doctor's thesis, Columbia University (New York, N.Y.), 1967. (*DA* 28:4920A)

505. WIRLS, CHARLES J., AND PLOTKIN, ROSALIE R. "Calculation of Quick Test IQs for Children With Mental Ages Seventeen and Above." *Psychol Rep* 20:603–5 Ap '67. * (*PA* 41:8172)

506. WIRTH, GARY. *A Comparison of Wechsler Verbal, Performance and Full Scale IQ's for Schizophrenia, Anxiety Reaction, Psychoneurosis Brain Damage, and Mental Retardation.* Master's thesis, East Tennessee State University (Johnson City, Tenn.), 1967.

507. WOLFSON, WILLIAM, AND BACHELIS, LEONARD. "Time of Year as a Factor in Success on WAIS Items." *Psychol Rep* 21:268 Ag '67. *

508. ALLISON, JOEL; BLATT, SIDNEY J.; AND ZIMET, CARL N. Chap. 2, "The Wechsler Adult Intelligence Scale," pp. 20–88, passim. In their *Interpretation of Psychological Tests.* New York: Harper & Row, Publishers, Inc., 1968. Pp. x, 342. *

509. ANASTASI, ANNE. *Psychological Testing, Third Edition,* pp. 271–82. New York: Macmillan Co., 1968. Pp. xiii, 665. *

510. ANDERSON, CATHERINE J.; PORRATA, ELENA; LORE, JAMES; ALEXANDER, SHIRLEY; AND MERCER, MARGARET. "A Multidisciplinary Study of Psychogeriatric Patients." *Geriatrics* 23:105–13 F '68. * (*PA* 42:14051)

511. ANDERSON, HARRY E., JR.; KERN, FRANK E.; AND COOK, CHARLOTTE. "Sex, Brain Damage, and Race Effects in the Progressive Matrices With Retarded Populations." *J Social Psychol* 76:207–11 D '68. * (*PA* 43:4329)

512. AVERY, CONSTANCE. "A Psychological Study of Patients With Behavior Problems and 6 and 14 per Second Positive Spikes in Their Electroencephalograms." *J Clin Psychol* 24:171–3 Ap '68. * (*PA* 42:11777)

513. AX, ALBERT F., AND BAMFORD, JACQUELINE L. "Validation of a Psychophysiological Test of Aptitude for Learning Social Motives." *Psychophysiol* 5:316–32 S '68. * (*PA* 43:3943)

514. BARTZ, WAYNE R. "Relationship of WAIS, BETA and Shipley-Hartford Scores." *Psychol Rep* 22:676 Ap '68. * (*PA* 42:12089)

515. BAYLEY, NANCY. "Behavioral Correlates of Mental

Growth: Birth to Thirty-Six Years." *Am Psychologist* 23:1–17 Ja '68. * (*PA* 42:8705)

516. BAYLEY, NANCY. Chap. 9, "Cognition and Aging," pp. 97–119. In *Theory and Methods of Research on Aging.* Edited by K. Warner Schaie. Morgantown, W.Va.: West Virginia University, 1968. Pp. iv, 197. *

517. BIELEFELD, MARTIN OLIVER. *Prediction of Concept Attainment From the PAS.* Doctor's thesis, University of Missouri (Columbia, Mo.), 1968. (*DA* 29:3077B)

518. BLATT, SIDNEY J., AND ALLISON, JOEL. Chap. 14, "The Intelligence Test in Personality Assessment," pp. 421–60. In *Projective Techniques in Personality Assessment: A Modern Introduction.* Edited by A. I. Rabin. New York: Springer Publishing Co., Inc., 1968. Pp. x, 638. *

519. BONNER, MARY WINSTEAD. *A Comparative Study of the Performance of Negro Seniors of Oklahoma City High Schools on the Wechsler Adult Intelligence Scale and the Peabody Picture Vocabulary Test.* Doctor's thesis, Oklahoma State University (Stillwater, Okla.), 1968. (*DAI* 30:921A)

520. BOOR, MYRON, AND SCHILL, THOMAS. "Subtest Performance on the Wechsler Adult Intelligence Scale as a Function of Anxiety and Defensiveness." *Percept & Motor Skills* 27:33–4 Ag '68. * (*PA* 43:2609)

521. BOURESTOM, NORMAN C., AND HOWARD, MARY T. "Behavioral Correlates of Recovery of Self-Care in Hemiplegic Patients." *Arch Phys Med & Rehabil* 49:449–54 Ag '68. *

522. BROWN, FRED. "Applicability of the Jastak Short Form Revision of the WAIS Vocabulary Subtest to Psychiatric Patients." *J Clin Psychol* 24:454–5 O '68. * (*PA* 43:4145)

523. BURTON, D. A. "The Jastak Short Form WAIS Vocabulary Applied to a British Psychiatric Population." *J Clin Psychol* 24:345–7 Jl '68. * (*PA* 42:16404)

524. CARTWRIGHT, JERRY LEE. *A Comparison of a Generalized and a Differential Predictor of Risk Taking.* Doctor's thesis, University of Missouri (Columbia, Mo.), 1968. (*DA* 29:3077B)

525. CHABASSOL, DAVID J. "A Comparison of Measures of Masculinity-Femininity." *Meas & Eval Guid* 1:173–4 f '68. *

526. CLUM, GEORGE ARTHUR. *The Relationships Between Measures of Classical and Operant Conditioning, Psychiatric Diagnoses and Statistically Derived Classificatory Groups.* Doctor's thesis, St. John's University (Jamaica, N.Y.), 1968. (*DA* 29:3899B)

527. CONNOR, MARJORIE WELLS. *Learning Characteristics of Able Nonachievers in Audiolingual Foreign Language Classes.* Doctor's thesis, University of Cincinnati (Cincinnati, Ohio), 1968. (*DA* 29:1446A)

528. CRONHOLM, BÖRJE, AND SCHALLING, DAISY. "Cognitive Test Performances in Cerebrally Palsied Adults Without Mental Retardation." *Acta Psychiatrica Scandinavica* 44(1):37–50 '68. * (*PA* 43:2937)

529. DELUCA, JOSEPH. "Predicting the Full Scale WAIS IQ of Army Basic Trainees." *J Psychol* 68:83–6 Ja '68. * (*PA* 42:7326)

530. DESAI, ARVINDRAI N. "Behavioral Characteristics of Alcoholic Delinquents." *Indian J Appl Psychol* 5:54–61 Jl '68. *

531. DICKINSON, THOMAS C.; NEUBERT, JOAN; AND MCDERMOTT, DOROTHY. "Relationship of Scores on the Full-Range Picture Vocabulary Test and the Wechsler Adult Intelligence Scale in a Vocational Rehabilitation Setting." *Psychol Rep* 23:1263–6 D '68. (*PA* 43:8448)

532. DOMINO, GEORGE. "A Non-Verbal Measure of Intelligence for Totally Blind Adults." *New Outl Blind* 62:247–52 O '68. *

533. DUKE, ROBERT B.; BLOOR, BYRON M.; NUGENT, G. ROBERT; AND MAJZOUB, HISHAM S. "Changes in Performance on WAIS, Trail Making Test and Finger Tapping Test Associated With Carotid Artery Surgery." *Percept & Motor Skills* 26:399–404 Ap '68. * (*PA* 42:12653)

534. DUNN, JAMES A. "Anxiety, Stress, and the Performance of Complex Intellectual Tasks: A New Look at an Old Question." *J Consult & Clin Psychol* 32:669–73 D '68. * (*PA* 43:4014)

535. ELKIN, LORNE. "Predicting Performance of the Mentally Retarded on Sheltered Workshop and Non-Institutional Jobs." *Am J Mental Def* 72:533–9 Ja '68. * (*PA* 42:7638)

536. ERNHART, CLAIRE B. "The Peabody Picture Vocabulary Test: Automated Application in a Statewide Psychiatric System." *Psychiatric Q Sup* 42(2):317–20 '68. * (*PA* 46:3313)

537. FELDMAN, SOLOMON E. "Utility of Some Rapid Estimations of Intelligence in a College Population." *Psychol Rep* 22:23–6 F '68. * (*PA* 42:10572)

538. FINNIE, FRANCES RUTH. *The Relationship Between Perceptual Field Articulation and Intellectual Functioning in Paranoid Male Schizophrenics.* Doctor's thesis, George Washington University (Washington, D.C.), 1968.

539. FISHER, GARY. "Intellectual Impairment in a Patient With Hepatolenticular Degeneration (Wilson's Disease)." *J Mental Subnorm* 14:91–5 D '68. * (*PA* 44:2624)

540. FREEDMAN, SAUL. *The Relationship Between Selected Variables and Success in Transcribing Typing for Trainees Who Are Blind.* Doctor's thesis, New York University (New York, N.Y.), 1968. (*DA* 29:3000A)

541. FUNKHOUSER, THOMAS R. "Correlational Study of the

'Revised Beta Examination' in a Female Retarded Population." *Am J Mental Def* 72:875–8 My '68. * (*PA* 42:13754)

542. GALLAGHER, HELEN C. "Intelligence and Learning Structured Tasks." *Am J Occup Ther* 22:264–8 Jl-Ag '68. * (*PA* 43:2864)

543. GILBERSTADT, HAROLD. "Relationships Among Scores of Tests Suitable for the Assessment of Adjustment and Intellectual Functioning." *J Gerontol* 23:483–7 O '68. *

544. GONEN, JAY Y., AND BROWN, LOUIS. "'Role of Vocabulary in Deterioration and Restitution of Mental Functioning." Abstract. *Proc 76th Ann Conv Am Psychol Assn* 3:469–70 '68. *

545. GONEN, YECHIEL. "Does Vocabulary Resist Mental Deterioration?" *J Clin Psychol* 24:341–3 Jl '68. * (*PA* 42:17529)

546. HANNA, GERALD S.; HOUSE, BETTY; AND SALISBURY, LEE H. "WAIS Performance of Alaskan Native University Freshmen." *J Genetic Psychol* 112:57–61 Mr '68. * (*PA* 42:10574)

547. HOLMES, J. STEVEN. "Acute Psychiatric Patient Performance on the WAIS." *J Clin Psychol* 24:87–91 Ja '68. * (*PA* 42:8938)

548. HOLT, ROBERT R. "Concerning Scatter and the WAIS," pp. 161–71. In *Diagnostic Psychological Testing.* New York: International Universities Press, Inc., 1968. Pp. xi, 562. *

549. JACOBSON, LEONARD I.; ELENEWSKI, JEFFREY J.; LORDAHL, DANIEL S.; AND LIROFF, JEFFREY H. "Role of Creativity and Intelligence in Conceptualization." *J Pers & Social Psychol* 10:431–6 D '68. * (*PA* 43:6752)

550. KAHN, EDWIN, AND FISHER, CHARLES. "Individual Differences and Amount of Rapid Eye Movement Sleep in Aged Adulthood." Abstract. *Psychophysiology* 4:393–4 Ja '68. * (*PA* 42:15311)

551. KAHN, EDWIN, AND FISHER, CHARLES. "The Relationship of REM Sleep to Various Measures in the Aged." Abstract. *Psychophysiol* 5:228–9 S '68. * (*PA* 43:14153)

552. KAHN, MARVIN W. "Superior Performance IQ of Murderers as a Function of Overt Act or Diagnosis." *J Social Psychol* 76:113–6 O '68. * (*PA* 42:2823)

553. KASTL, ALBERT J.; DAROFF, ROBERT B.; AND BLOCKER, W. WEBSTER. "Psychological Testing of Cerebral Malaria Patients." *J Nerv & Mental Dis* 147:553–61 D '68. * (*PA* 43:14654)

554. KELLY, FRANCIS D. *An Investigation of the Performance of Schizophrenic Patients on the Picture Completion Subtest of the WAIS.* Master's thesis, Springfield College (Springfield, Mass.), 1968.

555. KNOX, ALAN B.; GROTELUESCHEN, ARDEN; AND SJORGREN, DOUGLAS D. "Adult Intelligence and Learning Ability." *Adult Ed* 18:188–96 sp '68. *

556. KRAUS, J., AND WALKER, WENDY. "A Pilot Study of Factors in WAIS 'Patterns' in Diffuse Brain Atrophy." *Am J Mental Def* 72:900–4 My '68. * (*PA* 42:14061)

557. LEVY, PHILIP. "Short-Form Tests: A Methodological Review." *Psychol B* 69:410–6 Je '68. * (*PA* 42:11410)

558. LEVY, RUSSELL H. "Group Administered Intelligence Tests Which Appropriately Reflect the Magnitude of Mental Retardation Among Wards of the Illinois Youth Commission." *J Correct Ed* 20:7–10 su '68. *

559. LEWIS, FARRELL W. *A Comparison of Wechsler Adult Intelligence Scale Scores of Dogmatic and Open-Minded Students.* Master's thesis, Brigham Young University (Provo, Utah), 1968.

560. LOGUE, VALENTINE; DURWARD, MARJORIE; PRATT, R. T. C.; PIERCY, MALCOLM; AND NIXON, W. L. B. "The Quality of Survival After Rupture of an Anterior Cerebral Aneurysm." *Brit J Psychiatry* 114:137–60 F '68. * (*PA* 42:8433)

561. LUND, RONALD DEAN. *Wechsler Subtest Patterns and Personality: An Application of Gittinger's Personality Assessment System to Verbal Activity, Self-Descriptions and Sociometric Choices.* Doctor's thesis, University of Colorado (Boulder, Colo.), 1968. (*DA* 29:3491B)

562. MCKERRACHER, D. W.; WATSON, R. A.; LITTLE, A. J.; AND WINTER, K. S. "Validation of a Short Form Estimation of W.A.I.S. in Subnormal and Psychopathic Patients." *J Mental Subnorm* 14:96–7 '68. * (*PA* 44:2530)

563. MCLELLAND, PAUL EUGENE. *A Comparative Study of the Reasoning Ability of Two Groups of Hearing Impaired Children in a Residential School.* Doctor's thesis, University of Virginia (Charlottesville, Va.), 1968. (*DA* 29:3005A)

564. MALERSTEIN, A. J., AND BELDEN, E. "WAIS, SILS, and PPVT in Korsakoff's Syndrome." *Arch Gen Psychiatry* 19:743–50 D '68. * (*PA* 43:8472)

565. MASSER, EDWARD V., AND ARNETTE, JOHNNY L. "The Use of the Satz-Mogel WAIS Short Form With Prison Inmates." *J Correct Ed* 20:7+ sp '68. *

566. MEIKLE, STEWART. "The Effect on Subtest Differences of Abbreviating the WAIS." *J Clin Psychol* 24:196–7 Ap '68. * (*PA* 42:12092)

567. MOORE, ANTHONY BRYAN. *Reasoning Ability and Verbal Proficiency in Deaf and Hearing Children.* Doctor's thesis, University of Massachusetts (Amherst, Mass.), 1968. (*DA* 29:4381B)

568. MOORE, WILLIAM BATEMAN. *Drawings of Human Figures in Relation to Psychopathology and Intellectual Function-*

ing. Doctor's thesis, George Washington University (Washington, D.C.), 1968. (*DA* 29:2657B)

569. MUSKERA, DAVID J. *The Effects of Verbal Reinforcement and Instructional Set on the Similarities Subtests of the WAIS.* Master's thesis, Marshall University (Huntington, W.Va.), 1968.

570. ORME, J. E. "A Comment on Estimating W.A.I.S. IQ From Progressive Matrices Scores." *J Clin Psychol* 24:94–5 Ja '68. *

571. PATRICK, JERRY H., AND OVERALL, JOHN E. "Validity of Beta IQ's for White Female Patients in a State Psychiatric Hospital." *J Clin Psychol* 24:343–5 Jl '68. * (*PA* 42:16422)

572. PEAK, DANIEL T. "Changes in Short-Term Memory in a Group of Aging Adults." *J Gerontol* 23:9–16 Ja '68. *

573. PELOSI, JOHN WILLIAM. *A Study of the Effects of Examiner Race, Sex, and Style on Test Responses of Negro Examinees.* Doctor's thesis, Syracuse University (Syracuse, N.Y.), 1968. (*DA* 29:4105A)

574. PIERCE, RICHARD M. "Comment on the Prediction of Posthospital Work Adjustment With Psychological Tests." *J Counsel Psychol* 15:386–7 Jl '68. * (*PA* 42:15539)

575. PIHL, ROBERT O. "The Degree of the Verbal-Performance Discrepancy on the WISC and the WAIS and Severity of EEG Abnormality in Epileptics." *J Clin Psychol* 24:418–20 O '68. * (*PA* 43:4327)

576. POLLACK, MAX; WOERNER, MARGARET G.; AND KLEIN, DONALD F. "IQ Differences Between Hospitalized Schizophrenic and Personality-Disorder Patients and Their Normal Siblings." Abstract. *Proc 76th Ann Conv Am Psychol Assn* 3:491–2 '68. *

577. PRICE, A. COOPER, AND GENTRY, WILLIAM D. "Schizophrenic Thought Process: Analysis of the WAIS." Abstract. *Psychol Rep* 22:1099–100 Jc '68. * (*PA* 42:19092)

578. QUERESHI, M. Y. "The Optimum Limits of Testing on the Wechsler Intelligence Scales." *Genetic Psychol Monogr* 78: 141–90 N '68. * (*PA* 43:4016)

579. QUERESHI, MOHAMMED Y. "The Comparability of WAIS and WISC Subtest Scores and *IQ* Estimates." *J Psychol* 68: 73–82 Ja '68. * (*PA* 42:7334)

580. ROSEN, MARVIN; STALLINGS, LINDA; FLOOR, LUCRETIA; AND NOWAKIWSKA, MYRA. "Reliability and Stability of Wechsler IQ Scores for Institutionalized Mental Subnormals." *Am J Mental Def* 73:218–25 S '68. * (*PA* 43:4352)

581. SAUNDERS, DAVID R., AND GITTINGER, JOHN W. "Patterns of Intellectual Functioning and Their Implications for the Dynamics of Behavior," pp. 377–90, discussion 403–18. In *The Role and Methodology of Classification in Psychiatry and Psychopathology.* Edited by Martin M. Katz and others. Public Health Service Publication No. 1584. Washington, D.C.: United States Government Printing Office, 1968. Pp. ix, 590. *

582. SAVAGE, R. D., AND BOLTON, N. "A Factor Analysis of Learning Impairment and Intellectual Deterioration in the Elderly." *J Genetic Psychol* 113:177–82 D '68. * (*PA* 43:4391)

583. SAVAGE, R. DOUGLASS, AND BRITTON, PETER G. "The Factorial Structure of the WAIS in an Aged Sample." *J Gerontol* 23:183–6 Ap '68. *

584. SCHILL, THOMAS; KAHN, MALCOLM; AND MUEHLEMAN, THOMAS. "Verbal Conditionability and Wechsler Picture Arrangement Scores." *J Consult & Clin Psychol* 32:718–21 D '68. * (*PA* 43:4037)

585. SCHILL, THOMAS; KAHN, MALCOLM; AND MEUHLEMAN, THOMAS. "WAIS PA Performance and Participation in Extracurricular Activities." *J Clin Psychol* 24:95–6 Ja '68. * (*PA* 42:8943)

586. SCHUCMAN, HELEN, AND THETFORD, WILLIAM N. "Expressed Symptoms and Personality Traits in Conversion Hysteria." *Psychol Rep* 23:231–43 Ag '68. * (*PA* 43:7148)

587. SCHWARTZ, MELVIN L.; DENNERLL, RAYMOND D.; AND LIN, YI-GUANG. "Neuropsychological and Psychosocial Predictors of Employability in Epilepsy." *J Clin Psychol* 24:174–7 Ap '68. * (*PA* 42:12633)

588. SEVERINSEN, K. NORMAN. "A.C.T., W.A.I.S. Test Scores and College Grades." *J Ed Meas* 5:161–2 su '68. *

589. SHERMAN, A. ROBERT, AND BLATT, SIDNEY J. "WAIS Digit Span, Digit Symbol, and Vocabulary Performance as a Function of Prior Experiences of Success and Failure." *J Consult & Clin Psychol* 32:407–12 Ag '68. * (*PA* 42:17224)

590. SILVERSTEIN, A. B. "Evaluation of a Split-Half Short Form of the WAIS." *Am J Mental Def* 72:389–40 My '68. * (*PA* 42:13756)

591. SILVERSTEIN, A. B. "Validity of a New Approach to the Design of WAIS, WISC, and WPPSI Short Forms." *J Consult & Clin Psychol* 32:478–9 Ag '68. * (*PA* 42:16432)

592. SILVERSTEIN, A. B. "Variance Components in Five Psychological Tests." *Psychol Rep* 23:141–2 Ag '68. * (*PA* 43: 6920)

593. SIMPSON, ROBERT LEE. *A Study of the Comparability of the WISC and the WAIS and the Factors Contributing to Their Differenecs.* Doctor's thesis, University of Southern California (Los Angeles, Calif.), 1968. (*DA* 29:1794A)

594. SINOWITZ, MELVIN, AND BROWN, FRED. "Wechsler's MF Score as an Indicator of Masculinity and Femininity in a Psychiatric Population." *J Clin Psychol* 24:92–4 Ja '68. *

595. SORENSEN, MOURITS A., AND CLIFTON, SILAS W. "Client Opinions of WAIS Interpretations." *Meas & Eval Guid* 1:168–72 f '68. * (*PA* 44:11281)

596. STEIN, HENRY. *Intellectual Functioning in Hospitalized Nonchronic Schizophrenic Patients: The Relationship of Early Characteristics to Adult I.Q.* Doctor's thesis, New York University (New York, N.Y.), 1968. (*DA* 29:488A)

597. STERNLICHT, MANNY; SIEGEL, LOUIS; AND DEUTSCH, MARTIN R. "WAIS Subtest Characteristics of Institutionalized Retardates." *Ed & Psychol Meas* 28:465–8 su '68. * (*PA* 42: 19207)

598. STRATTON, ALBERT J. "Validity of the SRA Non-Verbal Form for Adults." *Psychol Rep* 22:163–7 F '68. * (*PA* 42: 10577)

599. STREITFELD, JULIAN W., AND AVERY, CONSTANCE D. "The WAIS and HIS Tests as Predictors of Academic Achievement in a Residential School for the Blind." *Int J Ed Blind* 18:73–7 O '68. * (*PA* 43:10178)

600. WAGNER, NATHANIEL N. "The 'Intelligence' of Malaysian Medical Students." *Brit J Med Ed* 2:24–7 Mr '68. *

601. WATSON, CHARLES G., AND KLETT, WILLIAM G. "Prediction of WAIS IQ's From the Shipley-Hartford, the Army General Classification Test and the Revised Beta Examination." *J Clin Psychol* 24:338–41 Jl '68. * (*PA* 42:16437)

602. WHITE, J. G., AND PATTEN, MARY P. "Intellectual Performance, Activity Level, and Physical Health in Old Age." Discussion by D. B. Bromley. *Gerontologia Clinica* 10(3):157–73 '68. *

603. WILSON, JOHN D. "Predicting Student Performance in First Year Arts and Science." *Scottish Ed Studies* 1:68–74 My '68. *

604. ZUNG, WILLIAM W. K., AND GIANTURCO, JUDITH. "Further Validation of the Ohio Literacy Test: Correlation With the Wechsler Adult Intelligence Scale and Grade Achieved in School." *J Clin Psychol* 24:197–8 Ap '68. * (*PA* 42:12829)

605. ABRAM, HARRY S.; ALLAN, J. HAMILTON; HUGHES, DEANNA; SMITH, BURKE M.; HALL, WILLIAM E.; AND LEWIS, DAVID W. "A Multidisciplinary Computerized Approach to the Study of Adjustment to Lower Limb Amputation." *South Med J* 62(9):1072–6 S '69. *

606. ASSO, DOREEN. "W.A.I.S. Scores in a Group of Parkinson Patients." *Brit J Psychiatry* 115(522):555–6 My '69. * (*PA* 44:3963)

607. ASSO, DOREEN; CROWN, SIDNEY; RUSSELL, JOHN A.; AND LOGUE, VALENTINE. "Psychological Aspects of the Stereotactic Treatment of Parkinsonism." *Brit J Psychiatry* 115(522): 541–53 My '69. * (*PA* 44:3964)

608. BARCLAY, A.; FRIEDMAN, ELLEN C.; AND FIDEL, YILDIZ. "A Comparative Study of WISC and WAIS Performances and Score Patterns Among Institutionalized Retardates." *J Mental Def Res* 13(2):99–105 Je '69. * (*PA* 44:9089)

609. BASSETT, JOHN E., AND GAYTON, WILLIAM F. "The Use of Doppelt's Abbreviated Form of the WAIS With Mental Retardates." *J Clin Psychol* 25(3):276–7 Jl '69. * (*PA* 44:4030)

610. BURGESS, MICHAEL M., AND DUFFEY, MARGERY. "The Prediction of Success in a Collegiate Program of Nursing." *Nursing Res* 18(1):68–72 Ja–F '69. *

611. BURKE, HENRY R., AND BINGHAM, WILLIAM C. "Raven's Progressive Matrices: More on Construct Validity." *J Psychol* 72(2):247–51 Jl '69. * (*PA* 44:71)

612. CALLENS, CHARLOTTE J., AND MELTZER, MALCOLM L. "Effect of Intelligence, Anxiety, and Diagnosis on Arithmetic and Digit Span Performance on the WAIS." Abstract. *J Consult & Clin Psychol* 33(5):630 O '69. * (*PA* 44:2523)

613. CANTER, ARTHUR, AND STRAUMANIS, JOHN J. "Performance of Senile and Healthy Aged Persons on the BIP Bender Test." *Percept & Motor Skills* 28(3):695–8 Je '69. * (*PA* 43:17618)

614. COCHRAN, MALCOLM L., AND PEDRINI, DUILIO T. "The Concurrent Validity of the 1965 WRAT With Adult Retardates." *Am J Mental Def* 73(4):654–6 Ja '69. * (*PA* 43:8574)

615. COSTA, LOUIS D.; VAUGHAN, HERBERT G., JR.; HORWITZ, MORTON; AND RITTER, WALTER. "Patterns of Behavioral Deficit Associated With Visual Spatial Neglect." *Cortex* 5(3): 242–63 S '69. * (*PA* 44:13142)

616. CRAIG, ROBERT J. "An Illustration of the Wechsler Picture Arrangement Subtest as a Thematic Technique." *J Proj Tech & Pers Assess* 33(3):286–9 Je '69. * (*PA* 43:14311)

617. CRANDALL, FAYE ELIZABETH. *A Cross-Cultural Study of Ahtena Indian and Non-Indian High School Students in Alaska on Selected Value Orientations and Measured Intellectual Ability.* Doctor's thesis, Clark University (Worcester, Mass.), 1969. (*DAI* 31:214A)

618. DANA, JEAN M., AND DANA, RICHARD H. "Experimenter-Bias and the WAIS." *Percept & Motor Skills* 28(3):694 Je '69. * (*PA* 43:16652)

619. DAVIS, WILLIAM E. "Effect of Prior Failure on Subjects' WAIS Arithmetic Subtest Scores." *J Clin Psychol* 25(1): 72–3 Ja '69. * (*PA* 43:9760)

620. DAVIS, WILLIAM E.; PEACOCK, WILLIAM; FITZPATRICK, PHILIP; AND MULHERN, MICHAEL. "Examiner Differences, Prior Failure, and Subjects' WAIS Arithmetic Scores." *J Clin Psychol* 25(2):178–80 Ap '69. * (*PA* 43:14465)

621. DICKSTEIN, LOUIS S. "Prospective Span as a Cognitive Ability." *J Consult & Clin Psychol* 33(6):757–60 D '69. * (*PA* 44:3616)

622. ELWOOD, DAVID L. "Automation of Psychological Testing." *Am Psychologist* 24(3):28;–9 Mr '69. * (*PA* 44:3011)

623. Eme, Robert F., and Walker, Ronald E. "The WAIS as a Group Test of Intelligence." *J Clin Psychol* 25(3):277–8 Jl '69. * (*PA* 44:3618)

624. Fields, Francis R. J., and Whitmyre, John W. "Verbal and Performance Relationships With Respect to Laterality of Cerebral Involvement." *Dis Nerv System* 30(3):177–9 Mr '69. * (*PA* 44:1070)

625. Foster, Ashley. "The Use of Psychological Testing in Rehabilitation Planning for Alaskan Native People." *Austral Psychologist* 4(2–3):146–52 N '69. * (*PA* 46:5260)

626. Fox, Elizabeth, and Blatt, Sidney J. "An Attempt to Test Assumptions About Some Indications of Negativism on Psychological Tests." *J Consult & Clin Psychol* 33(3):365–6 Je '69. * (*PA* 43:12965)

627. Glick, Ira D., and Sternberg, David. "Performance I.Q. as Predictor of Hospital Treatment Outcome." *Comprehen Psychiatry* 10(5):365–8 S '69. * (*PA* 44:14863)

628. Goldfarb, William; Goldfarb, Nathan; and Pollack, Ruth C. "Changes in IQ of Schizophrenic Children During Residential Treatment." *Arch Gen Psychiatry* 21(6):673–90 D '69. * (*PA* 44:10887)

629. Green, Russel F. "Age-Intelligence Relationship Between Ages Sixteen and Sixty-Four: A Rising Trend." *Develop Psychol* 1(5):618–27 S '69. * (*PA* 43:11634)

630. Gressett, John D. "Prediction of Job Success Following Heart Attack." *Rehabil Counsel B* 13(1):10–4 S '69. *

631. Grossman, Joel Lawrence. *A Comparison of Cautious Behavior of Elderly and Young Persons on WAIS Subtest Performance.* Doctor's thesis, State University of New York (Buffalo, N.Y.), 1969. (*DAI* 30:2908B)

632. Herrans, Laura Leticia. *Sex Differences in the Spanish WAIS Scores.* Doctor's thesis, Catholic University of America (Washington, D.C.), 1969. (*DAI* 30:1432A)

633. Hodges, William F., and Spielberger, Charles D. "Digit Span: An Indicant of Trait or State Anxiety?" *J Consult & Clin Psychol* 33(4):430–4 Ag '69. * (*PA* 43:15857)

634. Hogan, Terrence P. "Relationship Between the Ammons IQ Norms and WAIS Test Performances of Psychiatric Subjects." *J Clin Psychol* 25(3):275–6 Jl '69. * (*PA* 44:3679)

635. Hollender, John W., and Broman, Harvey J. "Intellectual Assessment in a Disadvantaged Population." *Meas & Eval Guid* 2(1):19–24 sp '69. *

636. Holmes, Douglas S. "Note on Levy's Methodological Review of Studies on Short-Forms of the WAIS." *Psychol Rep* 24(1):49–50 F '69. * (*PA* 43:14312)

637. Jambor, K. L. "Cognitive Functioning in Multiple Sclerosis." *Brit J Psychiatry* 115(524):765–75 Jl '69. * (*PA* 44:7136)

638. Johnson, Dale T. "Introversion, Extraversion, and Social Intelligence: A Replication." *J Clin Psychol* 25(2):181–3 Ap '69. * (*PA* 43:14469)

639. Kahn, Edwin, and Fisher, Charles. "Some Correlates of Rapid Eye Movement Sleep in the Normal Aged Male." *J Nerv & Mental Dis* 148(5):495–505 My '69. * (*PA* 44:507)

640. Kanter, Harold M. *The Identification of Elements Which Contribute to Occupational Success and Failure of Adults Classified as Educable Mentally Retarded.* Doctor's thesis, Arizona State University (Tempe, Ariz.), 1969. (*DAI* 30:3790A)

641. Kaufman, Harvey, and Ivanoff, John. "The Slosson Intelligence Test as a Screening Instrument With a Rehabilitation Population." *Excep Children* 35(9):745 My '69. * (*PA* 44:18977)

642. Koestline, W. Charles, and Dent, Oran B. "Verbal Mediation in the WAIS Digit Symbol Subtest." *Psychol Rep* 25(2):377–8 O '69. * (*PA* 44:5156)

643. L'Abate, Luciano, and Gale, Elliot N. "Neurological Status and Psychological Functioning." *Percept & Motor Skills* 29(3):999–1007 D '69. * (*PA* 46:5330)

644. Levine, Nira R. *Validation of the Quick Test for an Elderly Population.* Doctor's thesis, University of Virginia (Charlottesville, Va.), 1969. (*DAI* 31:646A)

645. Levinson, Boris M. "Factor Scales in Evaluation of Intellectual Deficit." *Psychol Rep* 25(3):898 D '69. * (*PA* 44:18916)

646. Levy, Philip. "Short Forms of the WAIS: A Reply." *Psychol Rep* 24(2):654 Ap '69. * (*PA* 43:15807)

647. Love, Henry G. I. "Validity of the Doppelt Short Form WAIS in a Psychiatric Population." *Brit J Social & Clin Psychol* 8(2):185–6 Je '69. * (*PA* 43:15011)

648. McDonald, Carrick. "Clinical Heterogeneity in Senile Dementia." *Brit J Psychiatry* 115(520):267–71 Mr '69. * (*PA* 43:13272)

649. Mann, Edward T. "Male Drug Addiction and the Kahn Test of Symbol Arrangement." *Percept & Motor Skills* 29(3):875–80 D '69. * (*PA* 46:5154)

650. Meier, Manfred J., and Okayama, Masahiro. "Behavior Assessment." *Geriatrics* 24(11):95–110 N '69. *

651. Morris, Larry W., and Liebert, Robert M. "Effects of Anxiety on Timed and Untimed Intelligence Tests: Another Look." *J Consult & Clin Psychol* 33(2):240–4 Ap '69. * (*PA* 43:9768)

652. Moses, Joseph L. "Automation of Testing Procedures." Letter. *Am Psychologist* 24(12):1174 D '69. *

653. Nadel, Robert S. *Social Responsibility as a Criterion for the Prediction of Success of Volunteers: A Study of the Characteristics of People Who Volunteer to Serve.* Doctor's thesis, New York University (New York, N.Y.), 1969. (*DAI* 30:3549A)

654. Needham, Walter E.; Bray, Patrick F.; Wiser, Wilmer C.; and Beck, Edward C. "Intelligence and EEG Studies in Families With Idiopathic Epilepsy." *J Am Med Assn* 207(8):1497–501 F 24 '69. * (*PA* 44:21418)

655. Neuringer, Charles; Wheeler, Gayle R.; and Beardsley, James V. "Rating Diversity and Measures of Convergent and Divergent Intelligence." *J General Psychol* 80(1):73–9 Ja '69. * (*PA* 43:6919)

656. Orgass, B., and Poeck, K. "Assessment of Aphasia by Psychometric Methods." *Cortex* 5(4):317–30 D '69. * (*PA* 44:17125)

657. Palmore, Erdman B. "Physical, Mental, and Social Factors in Predicting Longevity." *Gerontologist* 9(2):103–8 su '69. * (*PA* 46:2787)

658. Parsons, Oscar A.; Vega, Arthur, Jr.; and Burn, Julian. "Different Psychological Effects of Lateralized Brain Damage." *J Consult & Clin Psychol* 33(5):551–7 O '69. * (*PA* 44:2695)

659. Phillips, Richard Martin. *A Multiple Regression Study of Academic Prediction at Gallaudet College.* Doctor's thesis, University of Maryland (College Park, Md.), 1969. (*DAI* 30:5257A)

660. Quattlebaum, Lawrence F., and White, William F. "Relationship Between Two Quick Screening Measures of Intelligence for Neuropsychiatric Patients." *Psychol Rep* 24(3):691–3 Je '69. * (*PA* 44:868)

661. Renear, Katherine Roberts. *Field Dependence and Parole Success.* Doctor's thesis, Claremont Graduate School (Claremont, Calif.), 1969. (*DAI* 30:56;8B)

662. Rosenquist, Carl M., and Megargee, Edwin I. *Delinquency in Three Cultures,* pp. 208–24. Austin, Tex.: University of Texas Press, 1969. Pp. xvi, 554. *

663–4. Rosicki, Maria. *A Comparison of the Critical Flicker Frequency and Other Perceptual Tasks in Mental Defectives and Normals.* Doctor's thesis, Fordham University (New York, N.Y.), 1969. (*DAI* 30:5697B)

665. Saber-Motamedi, Houshang. *A Comparison of Test Scores of Foreign College Students With American College Students on the Wechsler Adult Intelligence Scale at ETSU and Tusculum.* Master's thesis, East Tennessee State University (Johnson City, Tenn.), 1969.

666. San Diego, Ellinor Aguio. *A Comparison of M-F Scores of American and Philippine Ss on the WAIS and the MMPI.* Master's thesis, Loyola University (Chicago, Ill.), 1969.

667. Sattler, Jerome M.; Winget, Barbara M.; and Roth, Rosemary J. "Scoring Difficulty of WAIS and WISC Comprehension, Similarities, and Vocabulary Responses." *J Clin Psychol* 25(2):175–7 Ap '69. * (*PA* 43:14478)

668. Saxon, John P.; Alston, Paul P.; and Porter, Thomas L. "Comparison of Haptic Intelligence Scale and WAIS Scores in a Population of Blind Psychotics." *Rehabil Counsel B* 13(1):49–51 S '69. *

669. Schooler, Carmi, and Silverman, Julian. "Perceptual Styles and Their Correlates Among Schizophrenic Patients." *J Abn Psychol* 74(4):459–70 Ag '69. * (*PA* 43:16089)

670. Silverstein, A. B. "An Alternative Factor Analytic Solution for Wechsler's Intelligence Scales." *Ed & Psychol Meas* 29(4):763–7 w '69. * (*PA* 44:20972)

671. Silverstein, A. B., and Fisher, Gary. "WAIS Subtest Characteristics of Institutionalized Retardates." *Psychol Rep* 25(2):397–8 O '69. * (*PA* 44:5570)

672. Singer, Paul R. Chap. 9, "Psychological Testing: Thematic Apperception Test, Rorschach Test, and WAIS Vocabulary Scale," pp. 110–43. In *The Psychological World of the Teen-Ager: A Study of Normal Adolescent Boys.* By Daniel Offer and others. New York: Basic Books, Inc., Publishers, 1969. Pp. xiv, 286. *

673. Singh, Udai Pratap. "Movement From One's Own Position Towards a Group Norm as a Function of Intellect." *Psychol Studies* 14(2):88–93 Jl '69. *

674. Song, A. Y., and Song, R. H. "Prediction of Job Efficiency of Institutionalized Retardates in the Community." *Am J Mental Def* 73(4):567–71 Ja '69. * (*PA* 43:8603)

675. Sterne, David M. "The Benton, Porteus and WAIS Digit Span Tests With Normal and Brain-Injured Subjects." *J Clin Psychol* 25(2):173–5 Ap '69. * (*PA* 43:14481)

676. Stricker, George; Merbaum, Michael; and Tangeman, Paul. "WAIS Short Forms, Information Transmission and Approximations of Full Scale IQ." *J Clin Psychol* 25(2):170–2 Ap '69. * (*PA* 43:14482)

677. Templer, Donald I., and Hartlage, Lawrence C. "Physicians' I.Q. Estimates and Kent I.Q. Compared With WAIS I.Q." *J Clin Psychol* 25(1):74–5 Ja '69. * (*PA* 43:10025)

678. Vega, Arthur, Jr., and Parsons, Oscar A. "Relationship Between Sensory-Motor Deficits and WAIS Verbal and Performance Scores in Unilateral Brain Damage." *Cortex* 5(3):229–41 S '69. * (*PA* 44:13157)

679. Vitale, John H.; Steinhelber, John C.; Drake, William E., Jr.; and Dahlgren, Helen. "Psychological Dimensions of Cerebrovascular Insufficiency." *Percept & Motor Skills* 29(2):555–63 O '69. * (*PA* 44:3996)

680. Weinstock, Comilda Sundeen. *The Relations Be-*

tween Social Isolation, Social Cognition and Related Cognitive Skills in the Aged. Doctor's thesis, Columbia University (New York, N.Y.), 1969. (*DAI* 30:3376B)

681. WICKSTROM, MARGARET LEE. *The Relationship of Future Time Perspective to Rehabilitation Performance on a Leg Prosthesis.* Doctor's thesis, Columbia University (New York, N.Y.), 1969. (*DAI* 30:4802B)

682. WOLFF, RICHARD, AND WASDEN, RONALD. "Measured Intelligence and Estimates by Nursing Instructors and Nursing Students." *Psychol Rep* 25(1):77–8 Ag '69. * (*PA* 44:3622)

683. ADAR, LEA D. *An Investigation of the Relationship of Some Aspects of Frustration to Pulmonary Tuberculosis.* Doctor's thesis, New York University (New York, N.Y.), 1970. (*DAI* 31:4322B)

684. BEN-YISHAY, YEHUDA; DILLER, LEONARD; AND MANDLEBERG, IAN. "Ability to Profit From Cues as a Function of Initial Competence in Normal and Brain-Injured Adults: A Replication of Previous Findings." *J Abn Psychol* 76(3):378–9 D '70. * (*PA* 45:8763)

685. BEN-YISHAY, YEHUDA; DILLER, LEONARD; GERSTMAN, LOUIS; AND GORDON, WAYNE. "Relationship Between Initial Competence and Ability to Profit From Cues in Brain-Damaged Individuals." *J Abn Psychol* 75(3):248–59 Je '70. * (*PA* 44:15125)

686. BEN-YISHAY, YEHUDA; GERSTMAN, LOUIS; DILLER, LEONARD; AND HAAS, ALBERT. "Prediction of Rehabilitation Outcomes From Psychometric Parameters in Left Hemiplegics." *J Consult & Clin Psychol* 34(3):436–41 Je '70. * (*PA* 44:15081)

687. BERSOFF, DONALD N. "The Revised Deterioration Formula for the Wechsler Adult Intelligence Scale: A Test of Validity." *J Clin Psychol* 26(1):71–3 Ja '70. * (*PA* 44:10460)

688. BLATT, SIDNEY J.; BAKER, BRUCE L.; AND WEISS, JAY. "Wechsler Object Assembly Subtest and Bodily Concern: A Review and Replication." *J Consult & Clin Psychol* 34(2):269–74 Ap '70. * (*PA* 44:10408)

689. BONNER, MARY W., AND BELDEN, BERNARD R. "A Comparative Study of the Performance of Negro Seniors of Oklahoma City High Schools on the Wechsler Adult Intelligence Scale and the Peabody Picture Vocabulary Test." *J Negro Ed* 39(4):354–8 f '70. * (*PA* 45:10662)

690. BURGESS, MICHAEL M.; KODANAZ, ALTAN; AND ZIEGLER, DEWEY K. "Prediction of Brain Damage in a Neurological Population With Cerebrovascular Accidents." *Percept & Motor Skills* 31(2):595–601 O '70. * (*PA* 45:6841)

691. BURGESS, MICHAEL M.; KODANAZ, ALTAN; ZIEGLER, DEWEY; AND GREENBURG, HOWARD. "Prediction of Brain Damage in Two Clinical Populations." *Percept & Motor Skills* 30(2):523–32 Ap '70. * (*PA* 46:7299)

692. COCHRAN, MALCOLM L. "A Profile of Psychological Test Scores for Retarded Adults." *Am J Mental Def* 74(4):582–4 Ja '70. * (*PA* 44:11052)

693. COONS, W. H., AND PEACOCK, E. P. "Interpersonal Interaction and Personality Change in Group Psychotherapy." *Can Psychiatric Assn J* 15(4):347–55 Ag '70. * (*PA* 44:21108)

694. COOPER, GERTRUDE V. *Effects of Anxiety and Color Among Male and Female Subjects on the Block Design Subtest of the Wechsler Adult Intelligence Scale.* Doctor's thesis, American University (Washington, D.C.), 1970. (*DAI* 31:3701B)

695. CROOKES, T. G., AND PEARSON, P. R. "WAIS IQ, Sixteen PF B Score and Education." *J Clin Psychol* 26(3):348–9 Jl '70. * (*PA* 45:672)

696. CULL, JOHN G., AND COLVIN, CRAIG R. "Correlation Between the Quick Test (QT) and the WAIS Verbal Scale in the Rehabilitation Setting." *Psychol Rep* 27(1):105–6 Ag '70. * (*PA* 45:6807)

697. DAVIS, WILLIAM E., AND DIZZONNE, MICHAEL F. "Relationship Between the QT and the WAIS." *Psychol Rep* 26(2):457–8 Ap '70. * (*PA* 44:21167)

698. DAVIS, WILLIAM E.; DEWOLFE, ALAN S.; DIZZONNE, MICHAEL F.; AND AIR, DOROTHY HABERKAMP. "Relationship Between Schizophrenics' Premorbid History and Intelligence Test Performance." *Newsl Res Psychol* 12(4):5–6 N '70. *

699. DUNCAN, D. F. "LSD and Intelligence: An Exploratory Study." *Psychol* 7(2):6–7 My '70. * (*PA* 44:20905)

700. ELWOOD, DAVID L. "Automation of Testing Procedures: Elwood Replies to Moses." Letter. *Am Psychologist* 25(8):764–5 Ag '70. *

701. ERNHART, CLAIRE B. "The Correlation of Peabody Picture Vocabulary and Wechsler Adult Intelligence Scale Scores for Adult Psychiatric Patients." *J Clin Psychol* 26(4):470–1 O '70. * (*PA* 45:4528)

702. FERNALD, PETER S. "Consensus Intelligence Testing in Compatible and Incompatible Groups." *J Proj Tech & Pers Assess* 34(3):238–40 Je '70. * (*PA* 44:18690)

703. FRANK, GEORGE H. "The Measurement of Personality From the Wechsler Tests." *Prog Exp Pers Res* 5:169–94 '70. *

704. GOLDSTEIN, GERALD; NEURINGER, CHARLES; AND KLAPPERSACK, BERNARD. "Cognitive, Perceptual, and Motor Aspects of Field Dependency in Alcoholics." *J Genetic Psychol* 117(2):253–66 D '70. * (*PA* 45:6611)

705. GOLLAND, JEFFREY H.; HERRELL, JAMES M.; AND HAHN, MICHAEL. "Should WAIS Subjects Explain Picture Arrangement Stories?" *J Consult & Clin Psychol* 35(2):157–8 O '70. * (*PA* 45:4252)

706. GONEN, JAY Y. "The Use of Wechsler's Deterioration Quotient in Cases of Diffuse and Symmetrical Cerebral Atrophy." *J Clin Psychol* 26(2):174–7 Ap '70. * (*PA* 44:15117)

707. GREENBERG, IRWIN M. "Clinical Correlates of Fourteen- and Six-Cycles-Per-Second Positive EEG Spiking and Family Pathology." *J Abn Psychol* 76(3):403–12 D '70. * (*PA* 45:6649)

708. GROTELUESCHEN, ARDEN, AND MCQUARRIE, DUNCAN. "Cross-Validation of the Quick Word Test as an Estimator of Adult Mental Ability." *Adult Ed* 21(1):14–9 f '70. *

709. HANNON, JOHN E., AND KICKLIGHTER, RICHARD. "WAIS Versus WISC in Adolescents." *J Consult & Clin Psychol* 35(2):179–82 O '70. * (*PA* 45:2202)

710. HUSTMYER, FRANK E., JR. "Eye Movements, Intelligence and Field Dependency in Schizophrenics." *Percept & Motor Skills* 30(3):703–6 Je '70. * (*PA* 44:17000)

711. JORTNER, SIDNEY. "Overinclusion Responses to WAIS Similarities as Suggestive of Schizophrenia." *J Clin Psychol* 26(3):346–8 Jl '70. * (*PA* 45:1055)

712. KANGAS, JON ALAN. *Intelligence at Middle Age.* Doctor's thesis, Washington State University (Pullman, Wash.), 1970. (*DAI* 31:1520B)

713. KAPLAN, MARVIN L.; COLARELLI, NICK J.; GROSS, RUTH BRILL; LEVENTHAL, DONALD B.; AND SIEGAL, SAUL M. *The Structural Approach to Psychological Testing.* New York: Pergamon Press, Inc., 1970. Pp. xi, 195. *

714. KASSINOVE, HOWARD; ROSENBERG, EDWIN; AND TRUDEAU, PAUL. "Cross Validation of the Environmental Participation Index in a Group of Economically Deprived High School Students." *J Clin Psychol* 26(3):373–6 Jl '70. * (*PA* 45:575)

715. KAUFMAN, HARVEY I. "Diagnostic Indices of Employment With the Mentally Retarded." *Am J Mental Def* 74(6):777–9 My '70. * (*PA* 44:17178)

716. KLONOFF, HARRY; FEBIGER, CHRISTOPHER H.; AND HUTTON, GORDON H. "Neuropsychological Patterns in Chronic Schizophrenia." *J Nerv & Mental Dis* 150(4):291–300 Ap '70. * (*PA* 45:8632)

717. KNOX, WILMA J., AND GRIPPALDI, RICARDO. "High Levels of State or Trait Anxiety and Performance on Selected Verbal WAIS Subtests." *Psychol Rep* 27(2):375–9 O '70. * (*PA* 45:6319)

718. KUNCE, JOSEPH T., AND WORLEY, BERT. "Simplified Prediction of Occupational Adjustment of Distressed Clients." *J Counsel Psychol* 17(4):326–30 Jl '70. * (*PA* 44:21338)

719. LACKS, PATRICIA BRILLIANT, AND KEEFE, KATHRYN. "Relationships Among Education, the MMPI, and WAIS Measures of Psychopathology." *J Clin Psychol* 26(4):468–70 O '70. * (*PA* 45:4542)

720. LEWIS, WAYNE M. *A Study of the Relationship Between Personality and Intelligence.* Master's thesis, Springfield College (Springfield, Mass.), 1970.

721. LOOFT, WILLIAM R. "Note on WAIS Vocabulary Performance by Young and Old Adults." *Psychol Rep* 26(3):943–6 Je '70. * (*PA* 45:698)

722. LUSZKI, MARGARET BARRON; SCHULTZ, WILLIAM; LAYWELL, H. ROBERT; AND DAWES, ROBYN M. "Long Search for a Short WAIS: Stop Looking." *J Consult & Clin Psychol* 34(5):425–31 Je '70. * (*PA* 44:13631)

723. MCCARTHY, DOROTHEA; ANTHONY, ROBERT J.; AND DOMINO, GEORGE. "A Comparison of the CPI, Franck, MMPI, and WAIS Masculinity-Femininity Indexes." *J Consult & Clin Psychol* 35(3):414–6 D '70. * (*PA* 45:4284)

724. MACK, JAMES L. "A Comparative Study of Group Test Estimates of WAIS Verbal, Performance, and Full Scale IQs." *J Clin Psychol* 26(2):177–9 Ap '70. * (*PA* 44:14870)

725. MCKEE, JAMES LEE. *Intellectual and Behavioral Correlates of Chronic Exposure to Toxic Chemicals.* Doctor's thesis, University of Denver (Denver, Colo.), 1970. (*DAI* 31:4341B)

726. MALEY, ROBERT F. "The Relationship of Premorbid Social Activity Level of Psychiatric Patients to Test Performance on the WAIS and the MMPI." *J Clin Psychol* 26(1):75–6 Ja '70. * (*PA* 44:10494)

727. MATTHEWS, CHARLES G.; CLEELAND, CHARLES S.; AND HOPPER, CORNELIUS L. "Neuropsychological Patterns in Multiple Sclerosis." *Dis Nerv System* 31(3):161–70 Mr '70. * (*PA* 44:13128)

728. MEIER, MANFRED J., AND MARTIN, WILLIAM E. "Intellectual Changes Associated With Levodopa Therapy." Letter. *J Am Med Assn* 213(3):465–6 Jl 20 '70. *

729. PAULSON, MORRIS J., AND LIN, TIEN-TEH. "Age: The Neglected Variable in Constructing an Abbreviated WAIS." *J Clin Psychol* 26(3):336–43 Jl '70. * (*PA* 45:950)

730. PAULSON, MORRIS J., AND LIN, TIEN-TEH. "Predicting WAIS IQ From Shipley-Hartford Scores." *J Clin Psychol* 26(4):453–61 O '70. * (*PA* 45:4546)

731. PECK, DAVID F. "The Conversion of Progressive Matrices and Mill Hill Vocabulary Raw Scores Into Deviation IQ's." *J Clin Psychol* 26(1):67–70 Ja '70. * (*PA* 44:10420)

732. POOL, DONALD A., AND BROWN, ROBERT. "The Peabody Picture Vocabulary Test as a Measure of General Adult Intelligence." *J Consult & Clin Psychol* 34(1):8–11 F '70. * (*PA* 44:6772)

733. POWELL, BARBARA J. "Role of Verbal Intelligence in the Field Approach of Selected Groups of Psychotics." *J Abn Psychol* 76(1):47–9 Ag '70. * (*PA* 44:21246)

734. QURESHI, M. Y., AND MILLER, JEFFREY M. "The Comparability of the WAIS, WISC, and WBII." *J Ed Meas* 7(2):105–11 su '70. * (*PA* 44:18711)

735. QURESHI, M. Y., AND WIDLAK, FREDERIC W. "Perceptual Diversity as a Function of Intelligence." Abstract. *Proc 78th Ann Conv Am Psychol Assn* 5(1):379–80 '70. * (*PA* 44:18613)

736. ROCHESTER, DEAN E., AND BODWELL, AARON. "Beta-WAIS Comparisons for Illiterate and Indigent Male and Female Negroes." *Meas & Eval Guid* 3(3):164–8 f '70. * (*PA* 45:9974)

737. ROSEN, MARVIN; KIVITZ, MARVIN S.; CLARK, GERALD R.; AND FLOOR, LUCRETIA. "Prediction of Postinstitutional Adjustment of Mentally Retarded Adults." *Am J Mental Def* 74(6):726–34 My '70. * (*PA* 44:17195)

738. ROSENZWEIG, STANLEY P., AND HARFORD, THOMAS. "Correlates of the Psychotic Reaction Profile in an Outpatient Psychiatric Sample." *J Consult & Clin Psychol* 35(2):244–7 O '70. * (*PA* 45:4549)

739. RUBINO, CARL A. "Psychometric Procedures and the Detection and Exploration of Behavioral Deficits Due to Cerebral Dysfunction in Men." *Can Psychologist* 11(3):239–60 Jl '70. * (*PA* 44:21180)

740. RUSSELL, ELBERT W. "A WAIS Factor Analysis With Brain Damage Subjects Using Criterion Measures." *Newsl Res Psychol* 12(4):1–2 N '70. *

741. SAN DIEGO, ELLINOR A.; FOLEY, JEANNE M.; AND WALKER, RONALD E. "WAIS Scores for Highly Educated Young Adults From the Philippines and the United States." *Psychol Rep* 27(2):511–5 O '70. * (*PA* 45:6139)

742. SATTLER, JEROME M., AND WINGET, BARBARA M. "Intelligence Testing Procedures as Affected by Expectancy and IQ." *J Clin Psychol* 26(4):446–8 O '70. * (*PA* 45:4257)

743. SATTLER, JEROME M.; HILLIX, WILLIAM A.; AND NEHER, LINDA A. "Halo Effect in Examiner Scoring of Intelligence Test Responses." *J Consult & Clin Psychol* 34(2):172–6 Ap '70. * (*PA* 44:10422)

744. SCHUCMAN, HELEN, AND THETFORD, WILLIAM N. "A Comparison of Personality Traits in Ulcerative Colitis and Migraine Patients." *J Abn Psychol* 76(3):443–52 D '70. * (*PA* 45:6910)

745. SHIMKUNAS, ALGIMANTAS M. "Reciprocal Shifts in Schizophrenic Thought Processes." *J Abn Psychol* 76(3):423–6 D '70. * (*PA* 45:6724)

746. SHINN, STEVEN M. *A Comparative Investigation of Three Predictors of Academic Success at Springfield College.* Master's thesis, Springfield College (Springfield, Mass.), 1970. *

747. SILVERSTEIN, A. B. "The Measurement of Intelligence." *Int R Res Mental Retard* 4:193–227 '70. *

748. SILVERSTEIN, A. B. "Reappraisal of the Validity of a Short Short Form of Wechsler's Scales." *Psychol Rep* 26(2):559–61 Ap '70. * (*PA* 44:20973)

749. SILVERSTEIN, A. B. "Reappraisal of the Validity of WAIS, WISC, and WPPSI Short Forms." *J Consult & Clin Psychol* 34(1):12–4 F '70. * (*PA* 44:5886)

750. SIMPSON, ROBERT L. "Study of the Comparability of the WISC and the WAIS." *J Consult & Clin Psychol* 34(2):156–8 Ap '70. * (*PA* 44:10423)

751. SINGH, S. B., AND VIRMANI, VIMLA. "Differential WAIS Pattern Study in the Cases of General, Focal and Psychomotor Seizures." *Psychol Studies* 15(2):95–100 Jl '70. *

752. SMITH, HARRY ELMER. *The Beta-WAIS Relationship and the Intercorrelations Among Beta Subtests for a Youthful Offender Population.* Master's thesis, Millersville State College (Millersville, Pa.), 1970.

753. SOLTZ, WILLIAM HOWARD. *Comparative Study of Negro-White Differences on the MMPI and PAS.* Doctor's thesis, University of Missouri (Columbia, Mo.), 1970. (*DAI* 31:3009B)

754. TAYLOR, JOHN F. "Brief Note on Simplified Administration of the Object Assembly Subtest." *J Clin Psychol* 26(2):182 Ap '70. * (*PA* 44:14607)

755. THETFORD, WILLIAM N., AND SCHUCMAN, HELEN. "Conversion Reactions and Personality Traits." *Psychol Rep* 27(3):1005–6 D '70. * (*PA* 45:10346)

756. WALKER, KENNETH P., AND GROSS, FREDERICK L. "I.Q. Stability Among Educable Mentally Retarded Children." *Training Sch B* 66(4):181–7 F '70. * (*PA* 44:13185)

757. WALKER, RONALD E.; SANNITO, THOMAS C.; AND FIRETTO, ANTHONY C. "The Effect of Subjectively Reported Anxiety on Intelligence Test Performance." *Psychol Sch* 7(3):241–3 Jl '70. * (*PA* 45:4259)

758. WANG, H. SHAN; OBRIST, WALTER D.; AND BUSSE, EWALD W. "Neurophysiological Correlates of the Intellectual Function of Elderly Persons Living in the Community." *Am J Psychiatry* 126(9):1205–12 Mr '70. * (*PA* 44:14399)

759. WATKINS, JOHN T., AND KINZIE, WAYNE B. "Exaggerated Scatter and Less Reliable Profiles Produced by the Satz-Mogel Abbreviation of the WAIS." *J Clin Psychol* 26(3):343–5 Jl '70. * (*PA* 45:703)

760. WESSLER, RICHARD L. "Estimating IQ: Expertise or Examiner Effect?" *Percept & Motor Skills* 30(1):268 F '70. *

761. YOUNG, JOEL R. *A Study of WAIS Performance Varying Pretest Examiner-Subject Relationships.* Master's thesis, Springfield College (Springfield, Mass.), 1970.

762. ZIMMERMAN, S. F.; WHITMYRE, J. W.; AND FIELDS, F. R. J. "Factor Analytic Structure of the Wechsler Adult Intelligence Scale in Patients With Diffuse and Lateralized Cerebral Dysfunction." *J Clin Psychol* 26(4):462–5 O '70. * (*PA* 45:4776)

ALVIN G. BURSTEIN, *Professor and Chief, Division of Psychology, The University of Texas Medical School at San Antonio, San Antonio, Texas.*

The *Wechsler Adult Intelligence Scale* can be regarded as the psychological test apotheosized. In the two decades since its introduction as an updating of its prototype, the *Wechsler-Bellevue Intelligence Scale,* it has enjoyed unparalleled success. It is virtually impossible to imagine a setting in which the psychological testing of adults occurs in which the WAIS is not well known, just as it is virtually impossible to imagine a course in psychological testing which does not make liberal reference to this test.

Accordingly, no attempt will be made in this review to duplicate the readily available excellent descriptions of the history, development, and nature of the WAIS. Nor will an attempt be made to summarize fully the voluminous research efforts involving this test. The reader seeking such information will find it represented in previous editions of the *Mental Measurements Yearbook,* and in the work of Guertin and others (*154, 383*), as well as in a new review of the research literature scheduled for publication in 1972 (Guertin, private communication). The focus of this reviewer's concern will be rather to define some crucial questions regarding the clinical use of the WAIS and to review the recent literature in those specific areas.

Any evaluation of the clinical utility of the WAIS depends upon a clear understanding of the clinical concept of intelligence. Initially a clearly irreal construct intended as a mediating variable between the factors of test performance and school performance, the concept "intelligence" has undergone two important developments. The first is its assessment as a personality variable held in a kind of logical distinction from "dynamic" factors, and the second is its reification.

The urgency with which intelligence test scores are sought as things valuable in themselves by students, parents, and clinicians is familiar to anyone who has worked in counseling and laboratory school settings as well as to most people in many other clinical settings. The consumer not infrequently feels deprived if he is offered in place of the "real" score on the intelligence test a projected grade point average or other performance projection. This unhappy state of affairs, probably the joint product of poor consumer relations on the part of professional psychologists and the development of highly restricted and specialized notions of what human characteristics may be thought of as valuable, has reached a crescendo in the controversy surrounding the recent works of Jensen,[1] described in more detail below.

The tendency to regard intelligence as a personality variable to be distinguished from "dynamic" or "emotional" factors is embodied in the production of psychological reports by many generations of psychological diagnosticians in which these two variables are separately treated; the tendency is fostered by an unwitting commitment to the notion that feelings and thinking are somehow incompatible. Many able theoreticians, such as Schachtel,[2] have pointed out the limitations of such views, but their writing has done little to deflect the tendency for this distinction to be made.

Review of these general notions helps to define several crucial areas of research on the WAIS. The first comprises studies relating WAIS performance to sociocultural factors; the second, studies using the WAIS to predict specific areas of performance outside the school setting; and the third, work articulating theoretically the concept of intelligence and relating it to general personality theory.

The social developments of recent years, including the explosion of concern with minority civil rights and the rioting in and around black and white urban centers and university campuses, are considered by many to constitute a mandate for increased attention by the behavioral sciences to sociocultural issues. It is in that sense unfortunate that work relating sociocultural factors and WAIS performance is so scanty and of such poor quality. The tendency to use over-crude independent variables (e.g.,

black versus white, without regard for cultural characteristics) or to sample inadequately is one common defect; another is the tendency to design the studies as though variation from group to group in the configuration of scores were the primary interest rather than variation in the predictive meaning of scores. It is only in this latter sense that the issue of "cultural bias" has meaning. From the point of view of rhetoric and semantics, substituting the term "culturally specific validities" for the term "cultural bias" might help to sharpen the scientific issues involved.

Easily the most notorious controversy surrounding the cultural bias issue—though not involving the WAIS in particular—is that which ensued from the publication of Jensen's opinions that intelligence is largely genetically determined, and that remedial programs for the culturally deprived have been ill conceived to the extent that they depend on the assumption that cultural deprivation rather than genetic differences account for the differences in test and school performance. The polemic level to which some of the participants have sunk has obscured the highly specialized variable that Jensen is discussing and contributed to the unfortunate tendency to further reify the concept of "g." The central issue of the cultural specificity of the predictive validities of WAIS scores has simply not been dealt with adequately in the literature.

Turning from the confusions generated by the surplus meanings of the term intelligence, our attention is attracted to two areas of inquiry relative to the WAIS. The first deals with the predictive value of the WAIS performance relative to other specific performance, and the second deals with theoretical refinement and elaboration of the variable intelligence.

With respect to the first area, the classical target performance is, of course, academic success, and there is little reason to question the value of IQ scores in the prediction of academic success defined in the most generalized terms. However, when the type of academic performance is highly specific, there is room for considerable question. Although the number of recent studies is unfortunately small, the variability of WAIS scores among Oxford scientists (*449*) and the relative lack of success in relating IQ to success in specific curricular areas (*281, 452, 471, 527, 599*) suggest that

1 JENSEN, ARTHUR R. "How Much Can We Boost IQ and Scholastic Achievement?" *Harvard Ed R* 39(1):1–123 w '69. *
JENSEN, ARTHUR R. "Reducing the Heredity-Environment Uncertainty: A Reply." *Harvard Ed R* 39(3):449–83 su '69. *
KAGAN, JEROME S.; HUNT, J. McV.; CROW, JAMES F.; BERNREITER, CARL; ELKIND, DAVID; CRONBACH, LEE J.; AND BRAZZIEL, WILLIAM F. "Discussion: How Much Can We Boost IQ and Scholastic Achievement?" *Harvard Ed R* 39(2):273–356 sp '69. *
2 SCHACHTEL, ERNEST G. *Metamorphosis: On the Development of Affect, Perception, Attention, and Memory.* New York: Basic Books, Inc., Publishers, 1959. Pp. 344.

multiple factors, including nonintellectual ones, should be evaluated in such predictions.

The only nonacademic target performance given systematic attention in the current literature is employability. Here, if appropriate methodological cautions are invoked, as indicated by Kaufman (460) and Pierce (574), there is reason to believe that meaningful relationships with WAIS performance can be established. Then, too, as the population studied becomes more restricted and the employment behavior more highly specified, factors in addition to "g," or full scale IQ, score became increasingly relevant.

Overall, it seems that the use of WAIS performance to predict other concrete behaviors is an underworked area. For it to be explored fruitfully will require moving away from simplistic research designs utilizing IQ as the single, bipolar independent variable. Intelligence test performance itself is complex, and many aspects of it are potentially quantifiable; condensing the performance into a single score is inadequate.

Beyond relating intelligence test performance to subsequent behaviors of high pragmatic interest (e.g., school or job performance) is the goal of articulating theoretically the variable of intelligence by systematic exploration of patterns of test performance. Guilford's recent book,[3] though it does not focus on the WAIS, reflects an important and comprehensive effort in this direction. Recent factor analytic studies of the WAIS itself, such as Shaw's (485), confirm earlier studies identifying "verbal comprehension" and "perceptual organization" as general factors in WAIS performance. In addition, Shaw suggests the importance of motivational variables.

Other recent investigators have attempted to estimate, as reflected in WAIS performance, such variables as intellectual efficiency (325), nonintellective aspects of intelligence—described by Wechsler as such traits as persistence, zest, and desire to succeed—and to explore the substructure of the problem solving effort (429). The absolute incidence of such studies is small and none of the studies are definitive, but they represent an enormously exciting area of research.

The above work focuses on internal elaboration of the concept of intelligence; a convergent

scientific goal is pursued by researchers attempting to relate WAIS performance to motivational or other aspects of general personality. Perhaps the most ambitious such effort is the Gittinger Personality Assessment System, which is based upon WAIS performance. The details of Gittinger's system have not been widely available in literature, but three recent studies (517, 561, 586) indicate that the system, though highly complex, merits careful evaluation. In addition to the PAS anxiety, risk taking behavior (524), impulsivity (422), and future orientation (435, 443) have all been explored as relating to WAIS performance.

In general, the more carefully specified the personality variable, the more encouraging the research results. For example, relatively crude measures of anxiety yield less promising results than more sophisticated measures distinguishing between trait and state anxiety (633). Given that intellectual performance does not occur separately from motivational systems, and given the importance of such systems in determining human behavior, the importance of continued work in this area is clear.

In summary, I would hope that the utilization of the WAIS in basic personality research is considerably expanded, in part because of the clinical success of the test. Such utilization of the WAIS will be facilitated by abandoning the notion that the extended range of complex behaviors that constitute an individual's performance is best compressed into a single number. It will also require a commitment to the notion that intellectual activity is most productively viewed as one aspect of total psychological functioning, and should be assessed in the context of other relevant psychological factors.

HOWARD B. LYMAN, *Associate Professor of Psychology, University of Cincinnati, Cincinnati, Ohio.*

As Bayley and Guertin suggest in their earlier reviews (5:414), the WAIS is certainly the best of the adult individual tests of intelligence. It was carefully constructed and carefully standardized. The norms were intelligently conceived and meticulously developed. As Guertin suggested, this test has become *the* standard against which other adult tests can be compared.

But there is room for improvement. For example, Wechsler says nothing in the manual about his theory of intelligence—for anything about the meaning of intelligence one must

3 GUILFORD, J. P. *The Nature of Human Intelligence.* New York: McGraw-Hill Book Co., Inc., 1967. Pp. xii, 538. *

consult Wechsler's *The Measurement and Appraisal of Adult Intelligence* (*41*).

I wonder, too, whether the norms, based on tests given prior to 1955, are an honest reflection of the 1970's. After more than 15 years of extensive use, how much of the WAIS content is still unknown to mental hospital patients and to others who may have had several contacts with the test (e.g., in courts, psychiatric clinics, and the like)? All test publishers, of course, have a constant dilemma: whether to change items and improve a test or to make no changes and thereby take advantage of experience with proven items. Nevertheless, I think that most of us would be happier with some new content.

Some of the present items are in need of immediate change. For example: The scoring limits "130–190 million" for the population of the United States (Information, item 20) are unrealistic when the true population is in excess of 200 million. (I wonder whether some examiners actually use those limits shown in the manual—and fail subjects who give a close approximation of the present population.)

Other items seem more culture bound than necessary. Particularly for the foreign born, many of whom *do* take the WAIS, some of the information items seem particularly unfair (for example: identification of Longfellow or of Washington's birthdate). More satisfactory results probably could be obtained if greater attention were paid to the advisability of including items which rely so completely on American schooling.

In addition to the need for improvement and updating of items is the need for improvement in directions and in the format of both the manual and the record form. Particularly on the Vocabulary subtest are occasional subjects penalized. Directions tell the examiner to query further if "it is difficult to determine whether a subject does or does not know the meaning of a word." Obviously such a query may result in a clarification worth full credit (i.e., 2 points); however, a subject may receive only partial credit (1 point) for a clear, but not specific, definition. For example, "one of the seasons" is clearly a 1-point definition for *Winter;* therefore, an examiner should not query—despite the fact that the subject, if asked for more information, might give a 2-point response. My graduate students invariably report greater difficulty in scoring the WAIS

Vocabulary than they had (in an earlier course) in scoring the Stanford-Binet vocabulary items.

No set of scoring criteria and scoring samples can, of course, be sufficient to answer all questions; however, more attention should be given to the scoring samples to make them as helpful as possible—for Vocabulary and for the other subtests.

The manual is not conveniently arranged for the examiner. Scoring samples (for most subtests) are buried many pages away from the directions for administration. Certainly it would be easier for all examiners to have the samples immediately following the directions; conceivably, this latter arrangement could keep some examiners from making many mistakes in scoring.

The record form is economically arranged for saving paper, but not designed efficiently for the school or clinical psychologist who believes that he should make behavioral observations of the subject while testing. Available at extra cost is a supplementary sheet on which such observations may be made, but the standard record form contains barely enough space for the minimal recording of responses.

Several features of the record form for the *Wechsler Preschool and Primary Scale of Intelligence* should be used for the WAIS record form: (*a*) printing a statement of the number of successive failures needed for termination of a subtest; inasmuch as the directions for termination differ for the various subtests, even the skilled examiner can make mistakes; (*b*) printing a reminder about the need for (or acceptability of) further queries; and (*c*) allowing sufficient space for recording responses and for making behavioral observations.

Some examiners may memorize the standard layout of pieces for the Object Assembly subtest, but I usually have to check with the manual. Wouldn't it save many examiners a lot of fumbling if the directions told us to lay out the pieces *before testing* on separate sheets of cardboard? This procedure permits the examiner to review his layout without losing rapport with his subject or spoiling the pace of his testing.

It seems unfortunate that Wechsler and The Psychological Corporation neglect to give us any sort of bibliography, for there is an impressive list of works which might have been cited (see, for example, those listed above).

Nevertheless, the facts remain that the WAIS

is still the best we have, that clinical and school psychologists find the test very helpful, and that the standardization was very carefully done.

For reviews by Nancy Bayley and Wilson H. Guertin, see 5:414. For references to reviews of an earlier edition, see 6:539.

[430]
★[Re Wechsler Adult Intelligence Scale] Rhodes WAIS Scatter Profile. Ages 16 and over; 1971; a form for profiling WAIS scores; profile (2 pages); manual (4 pages); $4.50 per 50 profiles, postage extra; Fen Rhodes; Educational and Industrial Testing Service. *

[431]
Wechsler Intelligence Scale for Children. Ages 5–15; 1949; WISC; downward extension of Form 2 of *Wechsler-Bellevue Intelligence Scale;* 13–15 scores: verbal (information, comprehension, arithmetic, similarities, vocabulary, digit span [optional], total), performance (picture completion, picture arrangement, block design, object assembly, mazes [optional], coding, total), total; individual; 1 form; record booklet (6 pages, revised slightly in 1958 but dated 1949); manual (117 pages); $27.50 per set of testing materials, 25 record booklets, and manual; $2.75 per 25 record booklets; $1.35 per 25 WISC Maze Tests, an alternate subtest which may be used in place of Coding; $3.25 per manual; postage extra; Spanish edition available; (40–60) minutes; David Wechsler; Psychological Corporation. [Australian Edition. 1968; record booklet (8 pages); manual (93 pages); Aus $27.50 per set of testing materials; 90¢ per 10 record booklets; 45¢ per 10 WISC Maze Tests; $3.50 per manual; manual by J. A. Radcliffe and F. E. Trainer; Australian Council for Educational Research.] *

REFERENCES

1–22. See 4:363.
23–133. See 5:416.
134–288. See 6:540.
289. Kolstoe, Oliver Paul. *A Comparison of Mental Abilities of Bright and Dull Children Having the Same Mental Ages.* Doctor's thesis, State University of Iowa (Iowa City, Iowa), 1952. (*DA* 12:707)
290. Ellis, Earnest. *A Comparison of the Weschler Intelligence Scale for Children and the I.P.A.T. Free Intelligence Test.* Master's thesis, San Francisco State College (San Francisco, Calif.), 1953.
291. Goldenberg, Samuel. *Some Aspects of Diagnosis of Cerebral Damage in Children.* Doctor's thesis, University of Washington (Seattle, Wash.), 1953. (*DA* 13:1259)
292. Banaghan, William Francis. *A Study of Variability of Performance on the Wechsler Intelligence Scale for Children and Its Relationship to Diagnostic Categories.* Master's thesis, San Diego State College (San Diego, Calif.), 1955.
293. Coleman, Leonard. *An Investigation of the Relationship Between Categorizing Behavior and Intelligence in School Children.* Doctor's thesis, Michigan State University (East Lansing, Mich.), 1955. (*DA* 15:1648)
294. Morgan, Carl E. *Criteria for Diagnosis and Prediction in a Remedial Reading Program.* Doctor's thesis, University of Houston (Houston, Tex.), 1956. (*DA* 16:1507)
295. Morrison, Ernest Bruce. *A Comparison of Mental Abilities of Average-Bright and Dull Children With Comparable Mental Ages.* Doctor's thesis, State University of Iowa (Iowa City, Iowa), 1957. (*DA* 17:2922)
296. Patteson, Richard F. *A Longitudinal Analysis of the Relationship Between Growth Rate and Mental Development in Children Between the Ages of Four and Ten Years.* Doctor's thesis, Florida State University (Tallahassee, Fla.), 1958. (*DA* 18:1869)
297. Fleming, Jack Wayne. *The Relationships Among Psychometric, Experimental, and Observational Measures of Learning Ability in Institutional, Endogenous Mentally Retarded Persons.* Doctor's thesis, University of Colorado (Boulder, Colo.), 1959. (*DA* 20:4183)
298. Geuting, Mary P. *Validities of Abbreviated Scales of the Wechsler Intelligence Scale for Children.* Master's thesis, Fordham University (New York, N.Y.), 1959.
299. Hughes, Dorothy Hale. *A Study of Concept Formation in a Group of Superior, Average and Mentally Retarded Children of Similar Mental Age: A Comparison of the Concept Formation of Boys and Girls Whose Mental Ages Are Between 9-6 and 10-6, but Whose Intellectual Levels Vary From Superior to Mentally Retarded.* Doctor's thesis, New York University (New York, N.Y.), 1959. (*DA* 20:3378)
300. Bastendorf, William Leon. *Activation Level, as Measured by Palmer Conductance, and Intelligence in Children.* Doctor's thesis, Claremont Graduate School (Claremont, Calif.), 1960. (*DA* 21:3156)
301. Levinson, Boris M. "A Comparative Study of the Verbal and Performance Ability of Monolingual and Bilingual Native Born Jewish Preschool Children of Traditional Parentage." *J Genetic Psychol* 97:93–112 S '60. * (*PA* 35:6190)
302. Trapp, E. Philip, and Evans, Janet. "Functional Articulatory Defect and Performance on a Nonverbal Task." *J Speech & Hearing Disorders* 25:176–80 My '60. * (*PA* 35:6808)
303. Auria, Carl. *Differences in Specific Intellectual Functioning Among Children of the Same General Intellectual Ability but of Different Chronological Ages.* Doctor's thesis, University of Buffalo (Buffalo, N.Y.), 1961. (*DA* 22:2679)
304. Bernstein, Lewis. "Psychological Testing: 1, Intelligence Tests." *J Child Asth Res Inst & Hosp* 1:205–17 Je '61. *
305. Sosulski, Michael Carl. *A Validation of the Finley-Thompson Short Form of the WISC for the Educable Mentally Retarded.* Master's thesis, Assumption University of Windsor (Windsor, Ont., Canada), 1961.
306. Thompson, Bertha Boya. *The Relation of Auditory Discrimination and Intelligence Test Scores to Success in Primary Reading.* Doctor's thesis, Indiana University (Bloomington, Ind.), 1961. (*DA* 22:785)
307. Clements, Sam D., and Peters, John E. "Minimal Brain Dysfunction in the School-Age Child: Diagnosis and Treatment." *Arch Gen Psychiatry* 6:185–97 Mr '62. * (*PA* 37:3512)
308. Feldhusen, John F., and Klausmeier, Herbert J. "Anxiety, Intelligence, and Achievement in Children of Low, Average, and High Intelligence." *Child Develop* 33:403–9 Je '62. * (*PA* 37:3867)
309. Gourevitch, Vivian, and Feffer, Melvin H. "A Study of Motivational Development." *J Genetic Psychol* 100:361–75 Je '62. * (*PA* 37:2891)
310. Reger, Roger. "Brief Tests of Intelligence and Academic Achievement." *Psychol Rep* 11:82 Ag '62. * (*PA* 37:5654)
311. Safrin, Renate Kersten. *Differences in Visual Perception and in Visual-Motor Functioning Between Psychotic and Nonpsychotic Children.* Doctor's thesis, Columbia University (New York, N.Y.), 1962. (*DA* 23:1080)
312. Tanyzer, Harold Joseph. *The Relationship of Change in Reading Achievement to Change in Intelligence Among Retarded Readers.* Doctor's thesis, University of Connecticut (Storrs, Conn.), 1962. (*DA* 23:1612)
313. Witkin, H. A.; Dyke, R. G.; Faterson, H. F.; Goodenough, D. R.; and Karp, S. A. *Psychological Differentiation: Studies of Development.* New York: John Wiley & Sons, Inc., 1962. Pp. xii, 418. * (*PA* 37:819)
314. Anderson, Linnea Mae. *Factors Affecting High and Low Achievement Among Adolescents Enrolled in Special Classes for the Mentally Handicapped.* Doctor's thesis, Wayne State University (Detroit, Mich.), 1963. (*DA* 25:279)
315. Ashlock, Patrick Robert. *Visual Perception of Children in the Primary Grades and Its Relation to Reading Performance.* Doctor's thesis, University of Texas (Austin, Tex.), 1963. (*DA* 24:5186)
316. Converse, Harold Dale. *Screening for Non-Intellective Factors of Children With Emotional Handicaps.* Doctor's research study No. 1, Colorado State College (Greeley, Colo.), 1963. (*DA* 25:640)
317. Graves, Gordon R. *A Study of the Use of the Peabody Picture Vocabulary Test for Identifying Mentally Retarded Children, Using the Wechsler Intelligence Scale for Children as a Criterion.* Master's thesis, Fresno State College (Fresno, Calif.), 1963.
318. Koutstaal, Cornelis W. *A Relationship Between the Intelligence and the Speech of Deaf Children.* Master's thesis, Springfield College (Springfield, Mass.), 1963.
319. Krippner, Stanley. "Correlates of Reading Improvement." *J Develop Read* 7:29–39 au '63. *
320. McLean, Terry Keith. *A Comparison of the Subtest Performance of Two Groups of Retarded Readers With Like Groups of Non-Retarded Readers on the Wechsler Intelligence Scale for Children.* Doctor's thesis, University of Oregon (Eugene, Ore.), 1963. (*DA* 24:4800)
321. Morrison, Mary. "A Gaelic Translation of the Wechsler Intelligence Scale for Children." Undergraduate thesis abstract. *Brit J Ed Psychol* 33:89–90 F '63. *
322. O'Connell, April Welsh. *Sensori-Perceptual Differences Between Academically and Non-Academically Retarded Children.* Doctor's thesis, Ohio State University (Columbus, Ohio), 1963. (*DA* 24:4782)
323. Shohen, Samuel Sutland. *The Relationship Between*

Verbal Intelligence and Critical Reading Ability of Superior Readers. Doctor's thesis, Temple University (Philadelphia, Pa.), 1963. (*DA* 24:2979)

324. SONNEMAN, LAWRENCE J. *A Study of the Relationships Between Four Tests of Intelligence and One Test of Scholastic Achievement.* Doctor's thesis, State University of South Dakota (Vermillion, S.D.), 1963. (*DA* 24:4555)

325. WALKER, CARL. *The Relationship of Certain Selected Variables to First Grade Achievement.* Doctor's thesis, University of New Mexico (Albuquerque, N.M.), 1963. (*DA* 24:3242)

326. WEBB, ALLEN P. "Some Issues Relating to the Validity of the WAIS in Assessing Mental Retardation," pp. 87–92. (*PA* 38:6075) In *Towards a Professional Identity in School Psychology.* California Association of School Psychologists and Psychometrists, Fourteenth Annual Conference, March 28–30, 1963. [Los Angeles, Calif.: the Association, 1963.] Pp. v, 97. * (*PA* 38:4904)

327. WINSCHEL, JAMES FRANCIS. *Performance of Normal and Mentally Retarded Children on Selected Motor and Intellectual Tasks as a Function of Incentive Conditions.* Doctor's thesis, University of Pittsburgh (Pittsburgh, Pa.), 1963. (*DA* 25: 6443)

328. ABERCROMBIE, M. L. J., AND JONCKHEERE, J. "Visual, Perceptual and Visuomotor Impairment in Physically Handicapped Children: 5, Wechsler Intelligence Scale for Children." Discussion by M. L. J. Abercrombie. *Percept & Motor Skills* 18:574–82, 609–10 Ap '64. * (*PA* 39:5574)

329. AMES, LOUISE B., AND WALKER, RICHARD N. "Prediction of Later Reading Ability From Kindergarten Rorschach and IQ Scores." *J Ed Psychol* 55:309–13 D '64. * (*PA* 39:8662)

330. BAUMEISTER, ALFRED A. "Use of the WISC With Mental Retardates: A Review." *Am J Mental Def* 69:183–94 S '64. * (*PA* 39:5036)

331. BERMAN, ISAAC, AND RHONE, DORIS ELLEN. "Wechsler Scores vs. Piaget Levels: Cognitive Efficiency of Institutionalized Retardates." Abstract. *Calif Mental Health Res Dig* 2:18 au '64. * (*PA* 39:12712)

332. BIBB, JOHN JAMES, JR. *A Study of the Quick Test as a Screening Instrument for Educable Mentally Retarded Children.* Doctor's thesis, University of Virginia (Charlottesville, Va.), 1964. (*DA* 25:3386) (Abstract: *Ed R* 2:69–71)

333. BIRKEMEYER, FLORENCE. "The Relationship Between the Coloured Progressive Matrices and Individual Intelligence Tests." *Psychol Sch* 1:309–12 Jl '64. *

334. BUCHMAN, MARCIA D. *Speed of Response on the Wechsler Intelligence Scale for Children Under Varying Conditions of Test Administration.* Master's thesis, University of Chicago (Chicago, Ill.), 1964.

335. CROPLEY, A. J. "Differentiation of Abilities, Socioeconomic Status, and the WISC." *J Consult Psychol* 28:512–7 D '64. * (*PA* 39:7749)

336. DENNERLL, RAYMOND D.; DEN BROEDER, JOAN; AND SOKOLOV, SHERWIN L. "WISC and WAIS Factors in Children and Adults With Epilepsy." *J Clin Psychol* 20:236–40 Ap '64. * (*PA* 39:8347)

337. EISENMAN, RUSSELL, AND McBRIDE, JOHN W., JR. " 'Balls' on the WISC." *Psychol Rep* 14:266 F '64. * (*PA* 39:1725)

338. FROMMELT, LEO ALOIS. *An Analysis of the WISC Profiles of Successful and Unsuccessful Readers in the Elementary School.* Doctor's thesis, State University of South Dakota (Vermillion, S.D.), 1964. (*DA* 25:2849)

339. GARNER, EDITH H. *An Investigation of the Coding of the Wechsler Scales in Relation to Reading Achievement of the Mentally Retarded.* Master's thesis, Boston University (Boston, Mass.), 1964.

340. GROSSBERG, JOHN M. "A Comparison of the Full-Range Picture Vocabulary Test and WISC in Clinical Use." Abstract. *J Consult Psychol* 28:188 Ap '64. *

341. HOLROYD, JEAN COREY. *Neurological Implications of WISC Verbal-Performance Discrepancies in a Psychiatric Setting.* Doctor's thesis, University of Minnesota (Minneapolis, Minn.), 1964. (*DA* 25:2048)

342. HOPKINS, KENNETH D. "An Empirical Analysis of the Efficacy of the WISC in the Diagnosis of Organicity in Children of Normal Intelligence." *J Genetic Psychol* 105:163–72 S '64. * (*PA* 39:2466)

343. HUTTON, JERRY B. "A Comparison of Digit Repetition Scores on the WISC and Revised Binet, Form L-M." *J Clin Psychol* 20:364–6 Jl '64. * (*PA* 39:10124)

344. IRWIN, DALE ORVIS. *The Reliability and the Stability of the Wechsler Intelligence Scale for Children.* Doctor's thesis, State University of Iowa (Iowa City, Iowa), 1964. (*DA* 25:5018)

345. ISCOE, IRA, AND PIERCE-JONES, JOHN. "Divergent Thinking, Age, and Intelligence in White and Negro Children." *Child Develop* 35:785–97 S '64. * (*PA* 39:4589)

346. JACKSON, CECIL LEE. *Factor Structure of the Wechsler Intelligence Scale for Children and Selected Reference Tests at Pre-School Level and After First Grade: A Longitudinal Study.* Doctor's thesis, University of Georgia (Athens, Ga.), 1964. (*DA* 25:6052)

347. JASTAK, J. F., AND JASTAK, S. R. "Short Forms of the WAIS and WISC Vocabulary Subtests." *J Clin Psychol* 20: 167–99 Ap '64. * (*PA* 39:7820)

348. JENKIN, NOEL; SPIVACK, GEORGE; LEVINE, MURRAY; AND SAVAGE, WILLIAM. "Wechsler Profiles and Academic Achievement in Emotionally Disturbed Boys." Abstract. *J Consult Psychol* 28:290 Je '64. *

349. KAISER, MERLE DALLAS. *The Wechsler Intelligence Scale for Children as an Instrument for Diagnosing Sociopathy.* Doctor's thesis, Florida State University (Tallahassee, Fla.), 1964. (*DA* 25:2612)

350. KOOS, EUGENIA M. "Manifestations of Cerebral Dominance and Reading Retardation in Primary-Grade Children." *J Genetic Psychol* 104:155–65 Mr '64. * (*PA* 39:5940)

351. KRIPPNER, STANLEY. "Relationship Between Reading Improvement and Ten Selected Variables." *Percept & Motor Skills* 19:15–20 Ag '64. * (*PA* 39:5941)

352. KRIPPNER, STANLEY. "WISC Comprehension and Picture Arrangement Subtests as Measures of Social Competence." *J Clin Psychol* 20:366–7 Jl '64. * (*PA* 39:10130)

353. LARSON, KEITH HAROLD. *The Characteristics of Vocationally Successful Mentally Retarded Youth as Described by Two Types of Intelligence Tests.* Doctor's thesis, University of Oregon (Eugene, Ore.), 1964. (*DA* 25:2815)

354. LOVELL, K.; GRAY, E. A.; AND OLIVER, D. E. "A Further Study of Some Cognitive and Other Disabilities in Backward Readers of Average Nonverbal Reasoning Scores." *Brit J Ed Psychol* 34:275–9 N '64. * (*PA* 39:8668)

355. LUSIENSKI, DEAN RICHARD. *An Analysis of the Scores of Urban Negro Boys on the Wechsler Intelligence Scale for Children.* Doctor's thesis, University of Nebraska (Lincoln, Neb.), 1964. (*DA* 25:2854)

356. LUSZKI, WALTER ALOISE. *Degree of Hearing Loss Related to Intelligence as Measured by the WAIS and WISC.* Doctor's thesis, University of Georgia (Athens, Ga.), 1964. (*DA* 25:3113)

357. MAC VICAR, DONALD B. *A Study of Relationships Between WISC Subtest Scores and Reading Ability.* Master's thesis, Sacramento State College (Sacramento, Calif.), 1964.

358. MARLEY, ALBERT D. *A Validity Study of the Columbia Mental Maturity Scale and the Peabody Picture Vocabulary Test, Using the Wechsler Intelligence Scale for Children as the Validating Criterion, With a Selected Sample of Educable Mentally Retarded Children.* Doctor's research study No. 1, Colorado State College (Greeley, Colo.), 1964. (*DA* 25:5386)

359. MONEY, JOHN. "Two Cytogenetic Syndromes: Psychologic Comparisons: 1, Intelligence and Specific-Factor Quotients." *J Psychiatric Res* 2:223–31 O '64. * (*PA* 39:15981)

360. MUMPOWER, DANIEL L. "The Fallacy of the Short Form." *J Clin Psychol* 20:111–3 Ja '64. * (*PA* 39:10144)

361. NUNNALLY, JUM C. *Educational Measurement and Evaluation,* pp. 257–62. New York: McGraw-Hill Book Co., Inc., 1964. Pp. xv, 440. *

362. OSBORNE, R. TRAVIS. "WISC Factor Structure for Normal Negro Pre-School Children." *Psychol Rep* 15:543–8 O '64. * (*PA* 39:5133)

363. QUERESHI, MOHAMMED Y. "Maximum Versus Minimum Testing: A Problem in Individual Appraisal." *Univ N Dak Col Ed Rec* 49:89–92 Mr '64. *

364. ROBECK, MILDRED C. "Effects of Prolonged Reading Disability: A Preliminary Study." *Percept & Motor Skills* 19: 7–12 Ag '64. * (*PA* 39:5945)

365. ROBECK, MILDRED C. "Intellectual Strengths and Weakness Shown by Reading Clinic Subjects on the WISC." *J Develop Read* 7:120–9 w '64. *

366. SAFRIN, RENATE KERSTEN. "Differences in Visual Perception and in Visual-Motor Functioning Between Psychotic and Nonpsychotic Children." *J Consult Psychol* 28:41–5 F '64. * (*PA* 38:9025)

367. SANDSTEDT, BARBARA. "Relationship Between Memory Span and Intelligence of Severely Retarded Readers." *Read Teach* 17:246–50 Ja '64. *

368. SAWYER, RITA. *A Study of Discrimination by the Subtests of the Wechsler Intelligence Scale for Children Between Mildly Disabled and Severely Disabled Readers Diagnosed at the Syracuse Reading Center, September, 1958 to June, 1963.* Doctor's thesis, Syracuse University (Syracuse, N.Y.), 1964. (*DA* 26:2594)

369. SOLKOFF, NORMAN. "Frustration and WISC Coding Performance Among Brain-Injured Children." *Percept & Motor Skills* 18:54 F '64. * (*PA* 39:2482)

370. TUTT, MARY L. *A Comparison of the Wechsler Intelligence Scale for Children and the SRA Primary Mental Abilities Test.* Master's thesis, Northern Illinois University (DeKalb, Ill.), 1964.

371. TUTTLE, LESTER EUGENE, JR. *The Comparative Effect on Intelligence Test Scores of Negro and White Children When Certain Verbal and Time Factors Are Varied.* Doctor's thesis, University of Florida (Gainesville, Fla.), 1964. (*DA* 25:7093)

372. VIITAMÄKI, R. OLAVI. "A Psychological Follow-up Study: Psychoses in Childhood, Part 2." *Acta Psychiatrica Scandinavica Supplement* 174:33–93 '64. * (*PA* 39:8464)

373. WEBB, ALLEN P. "Some Issues Relating to the Validity of the WAIS in Assessing Mental Retardation." *Calif J Ed Res* 15:130–5 My '64. * (*PA* 39:5672)

374. WENDT, R. A., AND BURWELL, ELINOR. "Test Performance of Jewish Day-School Students." *J Genetic Psychol* 105:99–103 S '64. * (*PA* 39:1492)

375. WOODY, ROBERT HENLEY. *The Use of Electroencephalography and Mental Abilities Tests in the Diagnosis of Behavioral Problem Males.* Doctor's thesis, Michigan State University (East Lansing, Mich.), 1964. (*DA* 26:204)

376. ALLEN, ROBERT M.; HAUPT, THOMAS D.; AND JONES, R. WAYNE. "Visual Perceptual Abilities and Intelligence in Mental Retardates." *J Clin Psychol* 21:299–300 Jl '65. * (*PA* 39:16039)

377. ASHLOCK, PATRICK. "The Visual Perception of Children in the Primary Grades and Its Relation to Reading Performance." *Proc Ann Conv Int Read Assn* 10:331–3 '65. *

378. BIRKEMEYER, FLORENCE. "The Relationship Between Coloured Progressive Matrices and the Wechsler Intelligence Scale for Children." *Psychol Sch* 2:278–80 Jl '65. *

379. BLATT, SIDNEY J.; ALLISON, JOEL; AND BAKER, BRUCE L. "The Wechsler Object Assembly Subtest and Bodily Concerns." *J Consult Psychol* 29:223–30 Je '65. * (*PA* 39:12225)

380. CHURCHILL, JOHN A. "The Relationship Between Intelligence and Birth Weight in Twins." *Neurology* 15:341–7 Ap '65. * (*PA* 39:15288)

381. CLEMENTS, GLADYS R. "An Abbreviated Form of the Wechsler Intelligence Scale for Children." Abstract. *J Consult Psychol* 29:92 F '65. *

382. CORDINER, MARIAN ESPACH. *A Comparative Study of the 1960 Stanford-Binet and the Wechsler Intelligence Scale for Children and Other Selected Variables.* Master's thesis, University of Utah (Salt Lake City, Utah), 1965.

383. CORWIN, BETTY JANE. "The Influence of Culture and Language on Performance of Individual Ability Tests." *J Sch Psychol* 3:41–7 sp '65. * (*PA* 39:15217)

384. COYLE, F. A., JR. "Another Alternate Wording on the WISC." *Psychol Rep* 16:1276 Je '65. * (*PA* 39:15219)

385. DEAL, MARGARET. "A Summary of Research Concerning Patterns of WISC Sub-test Scores of Retarded Readers." *J Read Specialist* 4:101–11 My '65. *

386. DI NELLO, MARIO C. *WISC Subtest Patterns as Predictors of Reading Achievement of First Grade Boys.* Doctor's thesis, University of Iowa (Iowa City, Iowa), 1965. (*DA* 26:5862)

387. ESTES, BETSY WORTH. "Relationships Between the Otis, 1960 Stanford-Binet and WISC." *J Clin Psychol* 21:296–7 Jl '65. * (*PA* 39:15230)

388. FORD, JUNE BROOKS. *Identification of a Specific Language Disability (Dyslexia).* Doctor's thesis, University of Oklahoma (Norman, Okla.), 1965. (*DA* 26:1827)

389. FRANSELLA, FAY, AND GERVER, DAVID. "Multiple Regression Equations for Predicting Reading Age From Chronological Age and WISC Verbal I.Q." *Brit J Ed Psychol* 35:86–9 F '65. * (*PA* 39:10818)

390. FURTH, HANS G., AND MILGRAM, NORMAN A. "Verbal Factors in Performance on WISC Similarities." *J Clin Psychol* 21:424–7 O '65. * (*PA* 40:1414)

391. GAGE, GERALD E., AND NAUMANN, THEODOR F. "Correlation of the Peabody Picture Vocabulary Test and the Wechsler Intelligence Scale for Children." *J Ed Res* 58:466–8 Jl–Ag '65. * (*PA* 40:422)

392. GAINER, W. L. "The Ability of the WISC Subtests to Discriminate Between Boys and Girls Classified as Educable Mentally Retarded." *Calif J Ed Res* 16:85–92 Mr '65. * (*PA* 39:10106)

393. GARIBAY, CARMEN. *A Study of the Performance of Mexican-American Children on English and Spanish Versions of the Wechsler Intelligence Scale for Children.* Master's thesis, Fresno State College (Fresno, Calif.), 1965.

394. GILBERT, J. G., AND RUBIN, E. J. "Evaluating the Intellect of Blind Children: An Evaluation of the Relative Merits of the Hayes-Binet and the WISC in Examining the Intelligence of Blind Children." *New Outl Blind* 59:238–40 S '65. *

395. GOLEN, M. EVARISTA. *A Comparison of WISC and the PGS in Prediction of School Achievement.* Master's thesis, University of Detroit (Detroit, Mich.), 1965.

396. GREEN, HARRY BRUCE, JR. *A Statistical Comparison of the Wechsler Intelligence Scale for Children and the Wechsler Adult Intelligence Scale.* Doctor's thesis, University of Virginia (Charlottesville, Va.), 1965. (*DA* 26:5866) (Abstract: *Ed R* 3:61–3)

397. GREENMUN, RENNY. *Abbreviated Forms of the Wechsler Intelligence Scale for Children.* Master's thesis, Texas Christian University (Ft. Worth, Tex.), 1965.

398. HASKELL, SIMON H., AND HUGHES, V. A. "Some Observations on the Performance of Squinters and Non-Squinters on the Wechsler Intelligence Scale for Children." *Percept & Motor Skills* 21:107–12 Ag '65. * (*PA* 40:537)

399. HECHT, PATRICIA J., AND NEWLAND, T. ERNEST. "Learning Potential and Learning Achievement of Educationally Blind Third-Eighth Graders in a Residential School." *Int J Ed Blind* 15:33–8 My '65. * (*PA* 40:3386)

400. HOLROYD, JEAN, AND WRIGHT, FRANCIS. "Neurological Implications of WISC Verbal-Performance Discrepancies in a Psychiatric Setting." *J Consult Psychol* 29:206–12 Je '65. * (*PA* 42:2690)

401. HUGHES, ROBERT B., AND LESSLER, KEN. "A Comparison of WISC and Peabody Scores of Negro and White Rural School Children." *Am J Mental Def* 69:877–80 My '65. * (*PA* 39:12289)

402. KABACK, GOLDIE RUTH. "A Comparison of WAIS,

403. KRIEGMAN, LOIS S., AND KRIEGMAN, GEORGE. "The PaTE Report: A New Psychodynamic and Therapeutic Evaluative Procedure." *Psychiatric Q* 39:646–74 O '65. * (*PA* 40:3006)

404. LOPER, DORIS JEAN. *Auditory Discrimination, Intelligence, Achievement, and Background of Experience and Information in a Culturally Disadvantaged First-Grade Population.* Doctor's thesis, Temple University (Philadelphia, Pa.), 1965. (*DA* 26:5873)

405. LUSZKI, WALTER A. "Hearing Loss and Intelligence Among Retardates." *Am J Mental Def* 70:93–101 Jl '65. * (*PA* 39:16056)

406. McCAULEY, JOHN HOWARD, JR. *Rorschach, WISC, and ITBS Patterns of Nine-Year-Old School Boys With Labile and Stabile IQ Scores.* Doctor's thesis, University of Maryland (College Park, Md.), 1965. (*DA* 27:1663A)

407. McLEOD, J. "A Comparison of WISC Sub-Test Scores of Pre-Adolescent Successful and Unsuccessful Readers." *Austral J Psychol* 17:220–8 D '65. * (*PA* 40:5240)

408. McMULLEN, CATHERINE P. *WISC Profiles in Relation to Specific Aspects of Reading Disability.* Master's thesis, National College of Education (Evanston, Ill.), 1965.

409. MALIN, A. J. "An Indian Adaptation of the WISC." *J Voc & Ed Psychol* 10:128–31 N '65. * (*PA* 39:10136)

410. MASSEY, JAMES O. *WISC Scoring Supplement for the Wechsler Intelligence Scale for Children, Third Edition.* Palo Alto, Calif.: Consulting Psychologists Press, Inc., 1965. Pp. 46. *

411. MEIER, JOHN HENRY. *An Exploratory Factor Analysis of Psychodiagnostic and Case Study Information From Children in Special Education Classes for the Educable Mentally Handicapped.* Doctor's thesis, University of Denver (Denver, Colo.), 1965. (*DA* 26:3153)

412. MUEHL, SIEGMAR; KNOTT, JOHN R.; AND BENTON, ARTHUR L. "EEG Abnormality and Psychological Test Performance in Reading Disability." *Cortex* 1:434–40 Je–S '65. * (*PA* 40:1419)

413. NAAR, RAY. "A Note on the Intelligence of Delinquents in Richmond, Virginia." *Brit J Criminol* 5:82–5 Ja '65. *

414. OSBORNE, R. TRAVIS. "Factor Structure of the Wechsler Intelligence Scale for Children at Pre-School Level and After First Grade: A Longitudinal Analysis." *Psychol Rep* 16:637–44 Ap '65. * (*PA* 39:9799)

415. OTTO, WAYNE, AND McMENEMY, RICHARD A. "An Appraisal of the Ammons Quick Test in a Remedial Reading Program." *J Ed Meas* 2:193–8 D '65. * (*PA* 40:4769)

416. OWENS, KAYE DON. *A Comparison of the Behavioral Patterns of the Mentally Retarded and Average Children During the Administration of the Wechsler Intelligence Scale for Children.* Doctor's research study No. 1, Colorado State College (Greeley, Colo.), 1965. (*DA* 26:875)

417. PLESS, I. BARRY; SNIDER, MARVIN; EATON, ANN E.; AND KEARSLEY, RICHARD B. "A Rapid Screening Test for Intelligence in Children: A Preliminary Report." *Am J Dis Children* 109:533–7 Je '65. * (*PA* 40:425)

418. RAJALAKSHMI, R., AND JEEVES, M. A. "Discrimination Learning and Reversal Learning in Children as Related to Performance on Certain WISC Items and on the Goodenough Draw-A-Man Test." *J Genetic Psychol* 106:149–56 Mr '65. * (*PA* 39:11993)

419. RICH, CHARLES C., AND ANDERSON, ROBERT P. "A Tactual Form of the Progressive Matrices for Use With Blind Children." *Personnel & Guid J* 43:912–9 My '65. * (*PA* 39:15197)

420. SAWYER, RITA I. "Does the Wechsler Intelligence Scale for Children Discriminate Between Mildly and Severely Disabled Readers?" *El Sch J* 66:97–103 N '65. * (*PA* 40:2920)

421. SCHULMAN, JEROME L.; KASPAR, JOSEPH C.; AND THORNE, FRANCES M. *Brain Damage and Behavior: A Clinical-Experimental Study.* Springfield, Ill.: Charles C Thomas, Publisher, 1965. Pp. ix, 164. *

422. SHANE, JAMES F. *Effectiveness of the Peabody Picture Vocabulary Test in Comparison to Wechsler Intelligence Scale for Children and Stanford-Binet Test Scores in Identification of Mentally Retarded and Gifted School Children.* Master's thesis, California State College (Long Beach, Calif.), 1965.

423. SILBERBERG, NORMAN ESAU. *An Investigation to Identify Intellectual and Perceptual Correlates of Disability in Word Recognition.* Doctor's thesis, State University of Iowa (Iowa City, Iowa), 1965. (*DA* 26:878)

424. THORPE, JOSEPH S. "A Cross-Cultural Study of Personality Development: Selection of Test Measures." *Congr Inter-Am Soc Psychol* 9(1964):242–9 ['65].*

425. THRONE, FRANCES M.; KASPAR, JOSEPH C.; AND SCHULMAN, JEROME L. "The Peabody Picture Vocabulary Test in Comparison With Other Intelligence Tests and an Achievement Test in a Group of Mentally Retarded Boys." *Ed & Psychol Meas* 25:589–95 su '65. * (*PA* 39:16072)

426. UFFORD, MARY SOLANUS. *A Design and Application for the Evaluation of Effectiveness of Speech Therapy.* Doctor's thesis, Wayne State University (Detroit, Mich.), 1965. (*DAI* 30:3424B)

427. VANDERPOOL, JAMES. *An Investigation of the Potential*

Use of WISC Scores for Differential Diagnosis. Master's thesis, Loyola University (Chicago, Ill.), 1965.

428. WALLACH, MICHAEL A., AND KOGAN, NATHAN. *Modes of Thinking in Young Children: A Study of the Creativity-Intelligence Distinction,* pp. 25–65. New York: Henry Holt & Winston, Inc., 1965. Pp. ix, 357. *

429. WASSING, H. E. "Cognitive Functioning in Early Infantile Autism: An Examination of Four Cases by Means of the Wechsler Intelligence Scale for Children." *Acta Paedopsychiatrica* 32:122–35 Ap '65. * (*PA* 39:15376)

430. WECHSLER, DAVID, AND JAROS, EUGENIA. "Schizophrenic Patterns on the WISC." *J Clin Psychol* 21:288–91 Jl '65. * (*PA* 39:15378)

431. AHMAD, FARRUKH Z. "A Study of the Relationship Between Test Intelligence and Delinquency." *Psychologia* 9:24–6 Mr '66. * (*PA* 41:1729)

432. BARCLAY, A., AND CAROLAN, PATRICIA. "A Comparative Study of the Wechsler Intelligence Scale for Children and the Stanford-Binet Intelligence Scale, Form L-M." Abstract. *J Consult Psychol* 30:563 D '66. *

433. BAUMEISTER, ALFRED A., AND HAWKINS, WILLIAM F. "WISC Scores of Retardates in Relation to Learning Ability." *J Clin Psychol* 22:75–6 Ja '66. * (*PA* 40:4549)

434. BELMONT, LILLIAN, AND BIRCH, HERBERT G. "The Intellectual Profile of Retarded Readers." *Percept & Motor Skills* 22:787–816 Je '66. * (*PA* 40:11497)

435. BERG, VERNA. *The Effect of Timing on Performance on the Wechsler Intelligence Scale for Children.* Master's thesis, University of Utah (Salt Lake City, Utah), 1966.

436. BERLIN, MARTIN ALBERT. *The Use of a Modified Block Design Technique in the Assessment of Educability for Boys From Lower Socio-Economic Environments.* Doctor's thesis, Rutgers—The State University (New Brunswick, N.J.), 1966. (*DA* 27:4121A)

437. BRANSFORD, LOUIS ALEXANDER. *A Comparative Investigation of Verbal and Performance Intelligence Measures at Different Age Levels With Bilingual Spanish-Speaking Children in Special Classes for the Mentally Retarded.* Doctor's research study No. 1, Colorado State College (Greeley, Colo.), 1966. (*DA* 27:226-A)

438. BREESKIN, JOHN. *The Development of Time Estimation in Children.* Doctor's thesis, University of Texas (Austin, Tex.), 1966. (*DA* 27:3267B)

439. CAMP, BONNIE WEBB. "WISC Performance in Acting-Out and Delinquent Children With and Without EEG Abnormality." *J Consult Psychol* 30:350–3 Ag '66. * (*PA* 40:11181)

440. CRADDICK, RAY A. "WISC and WAIS IQs as a Function of Season of Birth." *Psychol Rep* 18:259–64 F '66. * (*PA* 40:6626)

441. DAVIS, LEO J., JR. "The Internal Consistency of the WISC With the Mentally Retarded." *Am J Mental Def* 70:714–6 Mr '66. * (*PA* 40:6972)

442. DWYER, ROBERT CORCORAN. *Development of Three Subtests of Verbal Intelligence for Use With Severely Response Handicapped Children.* Doctor's thesis, George Peabody College for Teachers (Nashville, Tenn.), 1966. (*DA* 27:3718A)

443. EGELAND, BYRON RICKER. *The Relationship of Intelligence, Visual-Motor Skills and Psycholinguistic Abilities With Achievement in the First Grade.* Doctor's thesis, University of Iowa (Iowa City, Iowa), 1966. (*DA* 27:388A)

444. EKWALL, ELDON EDWARD. *The Use of WISC Subtest Profiles in the Diagnosis of Reading Difficulties.* Doctor's thesis, University of Arizona (Tucson, Ariz.), 1966. (*DA* 27:950A)

445. EXNER, JOHN E., JR. "Variations in WISC Performances as Influenced by Differences in Pretest Rapport." *J General Psychol* 74:299–306 Ap '66. * (*PA* 40:7194)

446. FITCH, MICHAEL JOHN. *Verbal and Performance Test Scores in Bilingual Children.* Doctor's research study No. 1, Colorado State College (Greeley, Colo.), 1966. (*DA* 27:1654A)

447. FOLEY, MARY VENARD. *A Study of the Differences Between Boys and Girls, and Between Boys and Girls of Different IQ Levels, on a Certain Selection of Subtests of the Wechsler Intelligence Scale for Children.* Master's thesis, Cardinal Stritch College (Milwaukee, Wis.), 1966.

448. FULLER, GERALD B. "A Comparison of Intelligence and Perception in Emotionally Disturbed Children." *J Clin Psychol* 22:193–5 Ap '66. * (*PA* 40:7890)

449. HARTE, MARY LABOURE. *Anxiety and Defensiveness as Related to Measurable Intelligence and Scholastic Achievement of Selected Institutionalized Children.* Doctor's thesis, Fordham University (New York, N.Y.), 1966. (*DA* 27:2884A)

450. HOLTZMAN, WAYNE H. "Intelligence, Cognitive Style, and Personality: A Developmental Approach," pp. 1–32. In *Intelligence: Perspectives 1965: The Terman-Otis Memorial Lectures.* By Orville G. Brim, Jr., Richard S. Crutchfield, and Wayne H. Holtzman. New York: Harcourt Brace & World, Inc., 1966. Pp. x, 101. *

451. HOPKINS, KENNETH D., AND McGUIRE, LENORE. "Mental Measurement of the Blind: The Validity of the Wechsler Intelligence Scale for Children." *Int J Ed Blind* 15:65–73 My '66. * (*PA* 40:7985)

452. HOROWITZ, FRANCES DEGEN. "The Relationship Between Wechsler Intelligence Quotients and Parsons Language Sample Scores of Mentally Retarded Children." *J Genetic Psychol* 108:59–63 Mr '66. * (*PA* 40:10400)

453. IRWIN, DALE O. "Reliability of the Wechsler Intelligence Scale for Children." *J Ed Meas* 3:287–92 w '66. * (*PA* 41:11918)

454. KISSEL, STANLEY. "Juvenile Delinquency and Psychological Differentiation: Differences Between Social and Solitary Delinquents." *J Clin Psychol* 22:442 O '66. * (*PA* 41:3090)

455. KISSEL, STANLEY. "Schizophrenic Patterns on the WISC: A Missing Control." *J Clin Psychol* 22:201 Ap '66. * (*PA* 40:7910)

456. LAUER, BARBARA A. *The Relationship Between Creativity and Subtest Scores on the WISC.* Master's thesis, Kent State University (Kent, Ohio), 1966.

457. LERAND, LESLIE WAYNE. *Intelligence and Reading Level of Girls.* Doctor's research study No. 1, Colorado State College (Greeley, Colo.), 1966. (*DA* 27:2137B)

458. LINDSEY, JAMES MORRISON. *The Factorial Organization of Intelligence in Children as Related to the Variables of Age, Sex and Subculture.* Doctor's thesis, University of Georgia (Athens, Ga.), 1966. (*DA* 27:3664B)

459. McELHANEY, MARK LUCAS. *A Comparison of Temporal Lobe With Non-Temporal Lobe Brain Damage as Shown by Various Psychological Tests.* Doctor's thesis, University of Houston (Houston, Tex.), 1966. (*DA* 27:1625B)

460. McGRAW, JOSEPH J. *A Comparison of Mean Subtest Raw Scores on the Wechsler Intelligence Scale for Children of Regular and Over-Achieving Readers With Under-Achieving Readers.* Doctor's thesis, University of Oklahoma (Norman, Okla.), 1966. (*DA* 27:1552A)

461. McLEOD, JOHN. *Some Psychological and Psycholinguistic Aspects of Severe Reading Disability in Children.* Doctor's thesis, University of Queensland (Brisbane, Australia), 1966.

462. MONEY, JOHN, AND EHRHARDT, ANKE A. "Preservation of IQ in Hypoparathyroidism of Childhood." *Am J Mental Def* 71:237–43 S '66. * (*PA* 40:13235)

463. MORPER, JACK. *An Investigation of the Relationship of Certain Predictive Variables and Academic Achievement of Spanish-American and Anglo Pupils in Junior High School.* Doctor's thesis, Oklahoma State University (Stillwater, Okla.), 1966. (*DA* 27:4051A)

464. NICKOLS, JOHN, AND NICKOLS, MARCIA. "A Brief Arthur's Stencils Test, Form I." *J Clin Psychol* 22:436–8 O '66. * (*PA* 41:2263)

465. OSBORNE, R. T. "Stability of Factor Structure of the WISC for Normal Negro Children From Pre-School Level to First Grade." *Psychol Rep* 18:655–64 Ap '66. * (*PA* 40:8862)

466. REGER, ROGER. "WISC, WRAT, and CMAS Scores in Retarded Children." *Am J Mental Def* 70:717–21 Mr '66. * (*PA* 40:6987)

467. REID, WILLIAM R., AND SCHOER, LOWELL A. "Reading Achievement, Social-Class and Subtest Pattern on the WISC." *J Ed Res* 59:469–72 Jl-Ag '66. * (*PA* 41:11490)

468. SELLS, S. B. *Evaluation of Psychological Measures Used in the Health Examination Survey of Children Ages 6–11,* pp. 2–23. Public Health Service Publication No. 1000, Series 2, No. 15. Washington, D.C.: United States Government Printing Office, March 1966. Pp. viii, 67. * (*PA* 40:7217)

469. SEMLER, IRA J., AND ISCOE, IRA. "Structure of Intelligence in Negro and White Children." *J Ed Psychol* 57:326–36 D '66. * (*PA* 41:1418)

470. SHAW, DALE J.; MATTHEWS, CHARLES G.; AND KLØVE, HALLGRIM. "The Equivalence of WISC and PPVT IQs." *Am J Mental Def* 70:601–4 Ja '66. * (*PA* 40:5454)

471. SHEARER, PAUL D. *A Study of the Relationship Between the WISC and School Success of Emotionally Disturbed Children.* Master's thesis, University of Richmond (Richmond, Va.), 1966.

472. SILBERBERG, NORMAN E., AND FELDT, LEONARD S. "The Peabody Picture Vocabulary Test as an IQ Screening Technique for Primary Grade Referral Cases." *J Sch Psychol* 5:21–30 au '66. * (*PA* 41:3345)

473. SPREEN, OTFRIED, AND ANDERSON, CHARLES W. G. "Sibling Relationship and Mental Deficiency Diagnosis as Reflected in Wechsler Test Patterns." *Am J Mental Def* 71:406–10 N '66. * (*PA* 41:1850)

474. TEIGLAND, JOHN J.; WINKLER, RONALD C.; MUNGER, PAUL F.; AND KRANZLER, GERALD D. "Some Concomitants of Underachievement at the Elementary School Level." *Personnel & Guid J* 44:950–5 My '66. * (*PA* 40:10429)

475. TILLMAN, MURRAY HOWELL. *A Comparison of the Factor Structure of Blind and Normals on the Verbal WISC.* Doctor's thesis, University of Georgia (Athens, Ga.), 1966. (*DA* 27:3665B)

476-7. TUTTLE, LESTER EUGENE, JR. "The Comparative Effect on Intelligence Test Scores of Negro and Caucasian Children When Certain Verbal and Time Factors Are Varied by Use of the WISC, PPVT and CMMS." *Fla J Ed Res* 8:49–61 Ja '66. *

478. WISSER, ROBERT E. *The Relationship Between WISC Verbal-Performance Discrepancy and Degree of Delinquency.* Master's thesis, Springfield College (Springfield, Mass.), 1966.

479. WITKIN, HERMAN A.; FATERSON, HANNA F.; GOODENOUGH, DONALD R.; AND BIRNBAUM, JUDITH. "Cognitive Patterning in Mildly Retarded Boys." *Child Develop* 37:301–16 Je '66. * (*PA* 40:9184)

480. YUDIN, LEE WILLIAM. "An Abbreviated Form of the WISC for Use With Emotionally Disturbed Children." *J Consult Psychol* 30:272–5 Je '66. * (*PA* 40:8274)

481. ZEDLER, EMPRESS Y. "A Screening Scale for Children With High Risk of Neurological Impairment." *Ann Inter Conf Assn Children Learn Dis* 3:20–8 '66. *

482. ZLODY, RUDOLPH L., AND FITZGERALD, MARY CALLISTA. "WISC Scores Made by Children With Articulatory Speech Difficulties." *Cath Ed R* 64:551–4 N '66. *

483. ALPER, ARTHUR E. "An Analysis of the Wechsler Intelligence Scale for Children With Institutionalized Mental Retardates." *Am J Mental Def* 71:624–30 Ja '67. * (*PA* 41:6174)

484. BEAN, WILLIAM JAMES. *The Isolation of Some Psychometric Indices of Severe Reading Disability.* Doctor's thesis, Texas Technological College (Lubbock, Tex.), 1967. (*DA* 28:3012A)

485. BELMONT, IRA; BIRCH, HERBERT G.; AND BELMONT, LILLIAN. "The Organization of Intelligence Test Performance in Educable Mentally Subnormal Children." *Am J Mental Def* 71:969–76 My '67. * (*PA* 41:12371)

486. BIRCH, HERBERT G.; BELMONT, LILLIAN; BELMONT, IRA; AND TAFT, LAWRENCE T. "Brain Damage and Intelligence in Educable Mentally Subnormal Children." *J Nerv & Mental Dis* 144:247–57 Ap '67. * (*PA* 41:15702)

487. BORNSTEIN, ALAN VANDAM. *The Effects of Examiner Approval and Disapproval Upon the Performance of Subjects on the Performance Scale of the Wechsler Intelligence Scale for Children.* Doctor's thesis, Florida State University (Tallahassee, Fla.), 1967. (*DA* 28:3047B)

488. BRODT, AUDREY. *An Investigation of WISC Vocabulary Instructions.* Master's thesis, Loyola University (Chicago, Ill.), 1967.

489. BUTLER, KATHARINE GORRELL. *Psychogenic Articulation Disorders Related to Verbal Skills and Intelligence as Measured by the Wechsler Intelligence Scale for Children.* Doctor's thesis, Michigan State University (East Lansing, Mich.), 1967. (*DA* 28:4332B)

490. CATE, CLARENCE C. "Test Behavior of ESL Students." *Calif J Ed Res* 18:184–7 S '67. * (*PA* 42:4480)

491. CHANG, THOMAS M. C., AND CHANG, VIVIAN A. C. "Relation of Visual-Motor Skills and Reading Achievement in Primary-Grade Pupils of Superior Ability." *Percept & Motor Skills* 24:51–3 F '67. * (*PA* 41:8701)

492. CHARRY, LAWRENCE BERNARD. *The Relationship Between Prereading and First Grade Reading Performances and Subsequent Achievement in Reading and Other Specified Areas.* Doctor's thesis, Temple University (Philadelphia, Pa.), 1967. (*DA* 28:960A)

493. COLE, SPURGEON N.; WILLIAMS, ROBERT L.; NIX, ALICE P.; AND LITAKER, ROBERT G. "Validity of an Abbreviated WISC Scale for Retarded and Borderline Children." *Psychol Rep* 21:571–2 O '67. * (*PA* 42:4795)

494. CONKLIN, R. C., AND DOCKRELL, W. B. "The Predictive Validity and Stability of WISC Scores Over a Four Year Period." *Psychol Sch* 4:263–6 Jl '67. * (*PA* 41:15871)

495. CORWIN, BETTY JANE. "The Relationship Between Reading Achievement and Performance on Individual Ability Tests." Abstract. *J Sch Psychol* 5:156–7 w '67. * (*PA* 41:9386)

496. DAVIS, LEO J., JR., AND REITAN, RALPH M. "Dysphasia and Constructional Dyspraxia Items, and Wechsler Verbal and Performance IQs in Retardates." *Am J Mental Def* 71:604–8 Ja '67. * (*PA* 41:6179)

497. DEBRULER, RALPH MILES. *An Investigation of Relationships Between Subtest Scores on the Wechsler Intelligence Scale for Children and Reading Ability.* Doctor's thesis, University of Oregon (Eugene, Ore.). 1967. (*DA* 29:143A)

498. DUDEK, S. Z.; LESTER, L. P.; AND HARRIS, B. R. "Variability on Tests of Cognitive and Perceptual-Motor Development in Kindergarten Children." *J Clin Psychol* 23:461–4 O '67. * (*PA* 42:2400)

499. DUNN, JAMES A. "Note on the Relation of Harris' Draw-A-Woman to WISC IQs." *Percept & Motor Skills* 24:316 F '67. * (*PA* 41:8880)

500. DUNN, JAMES A. "Validity Coefficients for the New Harris-Goodenough Draw-A-Man Test." *Percept & Motor Skills* 24:299–301 F '67. * (*PA* 41:8149)

501. EGELAND, BYRON. "Influence of Examiner and Examinee Anxiety on WISC Performance." *Psychol Rep* 21:409–14 O '67. * (*PA* 42:6082)

502. ELITCHER, HELENE. *Children's Causal Thinking as a Function of Cognitive Style and Question Wording.* Doctor's thesis, New York University (New York, N.Y.), 1967. (*DA* 28:1294A)

503. ERIKSON, ROBERT V. "Abbreviated Form of the WISC: A Reevaluation." Abstract. *J Consult Psychol* 31:641 D '67. * (*PA* 42:2562)

504. FAST, ROBERT ERWIN. *The Effects of Verbal and Monetary Reward on the Individual Intelligence Test Performance of Children of Differing Socio-Economic Status.* Doctor's thesis, Rutgers—The State University (New Brunswick, N.J.), 1967. (*DA* 28:1703A)

505. FERNALD, PETER S., AND WISSER, ROBERT E. "Using WISC Verbal-Performance Discrepancy to Predict Degree of Acting Out." *J Clin Psychol* 23:92–3 Ja '67. * (*PA* 41:5957)

506. FLEMING, JEAN MCKEY. *Body Image and Learning of*

Deaf and Hearing Boys. Doctor's thesis, University of Florida (Gainesville, Fla.), 1967. (*DA* 29:144A)

507. FROSTIG, MARIANNE. "Testing as a Basis for Educational Therapy." *J Spec Ed* 2:15–34 f '67. * (*PA* 42:7770)

508. GALVAN, ROBERT ROGERS. *Bilingualism as It Relates to Intelligence Test Scores and School Achievement Among Culturally Deprived Spanish-American Children.* Doctor's thesis, East Texas State University (Commerce, Tex.), 1967. (*DA* 28:3021A)

509. GLASSER, ALAN J., AND ZIMMERMAN, IRLA LEE. *Clinical Interpretation of the Wechsler Intelligence Scale for Children (WISC).* New York: Grune & Stratton, Inc., 1967. Pp. v, 152. *

510. GRAUBARD, PAUL S. "The Use of the Peabody Picture Vocabulary Test in the Prediction and Assessment of Reading Disability in Disturbed Children." *J Ed Res* 61:3–5 S '67. *

511. HENNING, JOHN J., AND LEVY, RUSSELL H. "Verbal-Performance IQ Differences of White and Negro Delinquents on the WISC and WAIS." *J Clin Psychol* 23:164–8 Ap '67. * (*PA* 41:9127)

512. HERSHENSON, DAVID B. "Body-Image (Hand) and Arithmetic Ability." *Percept & Motor Skills* 25:967–8 D '67. * (*PA* 42:8994)

513. HOPKINS, KENNETH D., AND MCGUIRE, LENORE. "IQ Constancy and the Blind Child." *Int J Ed Blind* 16:113–4 My '67. * (*PA* 41:10945)

514. HUEFTLE, M. KEENE. *A Factor Analytic Study of the Frostig Developmental Test of Visual Perception, the Illinois Test of Psycholinguistic Abilities, and the Wechsler Intelligence Scale for Children.* Doctor's thesis, Colorado State College (Greeley, Colo.), 1967. (*DA* 28:2139B)

515. IRWIN, ORVIS C., AND KORST, JOSEPH W. "Correlations Among Five Speech Tests and the WISC Verbal Scale." *Cereb Palsy J* 28:9–11 S–O '67. * (*PA* 42:3201)

516. JACOBSON, FRANK N. "Differences on the WISC Digit Span Between Outpatient Clinic and Delinquent Boys." *Percept & Motor Skills* 25:840 D '67. * (*PA* 42:9160)

517. JONES, GENTRY THOMAS, JR. *An Experimental Investigation of Family Relationships Among Mental Retardates.* Doctor's thesis, University of Oklahoma (Norman, Okla.), 1967. (*DA* 27:4125B)

518. KOPPITZ, ELIZABETH MUNSTERBERG. "Expected and Exceptional Items on Human Figure Drawings and IQ Scores of Children Age 5 to 12." *J Clin Psychol* 23:81–3 Ja '67. * (*PA* 41:5985)

519. LAMP, ROBERT E., AND BARCLAY, A. "The Quick Test as a Screening Device for Intellectually Subnormal Children." *Psychol Rep* 20:63–6 Je '67. * (*PA* 41:13596)

520. LAVITT, JERRY A. *A Comparative Evaluation of the Peabody Picture Vocabulary Test as a Measure of Ability for Children of Differing Reading Proficiency Levels.* Doctor's thesis, Oklahoma State University (Stillwater, Okla.), 1967. (*DA* 28:4877A)

521. LOVELL, K., AND SHIELDS, J. B. "Some Aspects of a Study of the Gifted Child." *Brit J Ed Psychol* 37:201–8 Je '67. * (*PA* 41:15273)

522. MCLEOD, JOHN. "Some Psycholinguistic Correlates of Reading Disability in Young Children." *Read Res Q* 2:5–31 sp '67. * (*PA* 41:11883)

523. MILGRAM, NORMAN A. "A Note on the PPVT in Mental Retardates." *Am J Mental Def* 72:496–7 N '67. * (*PA* 42:7658)

524. MONEY, JOHN, AND EPSTEIN, RALPH. "Verbal Aptitude in Eonism and Prepubertal Effeminacy: A Feminine Trait." *Trans N Y Acad Sci* 29:448–54 F '67. * (*PA* 41:16833)

525. NALVEN, FREDRIC B. "Relationship Between Digit Span and Distractibility Ratings in Emotionally Disturbed Children." *J Clin Psychol* 23:466–7 O '67. * (*PA* 42:2731)

526. NAMY, ELMER. "Intellectual and Academic Characteristics of Fourth Grade Gifted and Pseudogifted Students." *Excep Children* 34:15–8 S '67. * (*PA* 41:17073)

527. NEUHAUS, MAURY. "Modifications in the Administration of the WISC Performance Subtests for Children With Profound Hearing Losses." *Excep Children* 33:573–4 Ap '67. * (*PA* 41:8883)

528. NEWLAND, T. ERNEST, AND SMITH, PATRICIA A. "Statistically Significant Difference Between Subtest Scaled Scores on the WISC and the WAIS." *J Sch Psychol* 5:122–7 w '67. * (*PA* 41:8884)

529. NICKOLS, JOHN. "Explorations on Productive Thinking Tasks for Group Testing." *Psychiatric Q Sup* 41:128–42 pt 1 '67. * (*PA* 44:8745)

530. OGDEN, DONALD P. Section 2, "The Wechsler Scales," pp. 3–10, 75–7. In his *Psychodiagnostics and Personality Assessment: A Handbook.* Beverly Hills, Calif.: Western Psychological Services, 1967. Pp. v, 96. *

531. OKI, TADAHIKO. "A Psychological Study of Early Childhood Neuroses." *B Osaka Med Sch Sup* 12:344–59 '67. *

532. OSBORNE, R. T., AND TILLMAN, M. H. "Normal and Retardate WISC Performance: An Analysis of the Stimulus Trace Theory." *Am J Mental Def* 72:257–61 S '67. * (*PA* 42:2882)

533. OSBORNE, R. T.; ANDERSON, HARRY E., JR.; AND BASHAW, W. L. "The Stability of the WISC Factor Structure at Three Age Levels." *Multiv Behav Res* 2:443–51 O '67. * (*PA* 42:6388)

534. OSBORNE, R. TRAVIS, AND LINDSEY, JAMES M. "A Longitudinal Investigation of Change in the Factorial Composition of Intelligence With Age in Young School Children." *J Genetic Psychol* 110:49–58 Mr '67. * (*PA* 41:7141)

535. OSMAN, HASSAN HAFEZ. *An Investigative Study in the Creative Thinking of Emotionally Disturbed Children in Special Classes.* Doctor's thesis, University of Kansas (Lawrence, Kan.), 1967. (*DA* 28:5210B)

536. PASEWARK, R. A.; SAWYER, R. N.; SMITH, E.; WASSERBERGER, M.; DELL, D.; BRITO, H.; AND LEE, R. "Concurrent Validity of the French Pictorial Test of Intelligence." *J Ed Res* 61:179–83 D '67. *

537. PICKLES, D. G. "Intelligence Tests and the Ascertainment of the Educationally Subnormal: A Comparative Study of the Stanford-Binet and Wechsler Intelligence Scales." *Pub Health* 81:133–44 Mr '67. *

538. REED, JAMES C. "Reading Achievement as Related to Differences Between WISC Verbal and Performance IQ's." *Child Develop* 38:835–40 S '67. * (*PA* 41:16696)

539. ROCKWELL, G. JAMES, JR. "WISC Object Assembly and Bodily Concern." Abstract. *J Consult Psychol* 31:221 Ap '67. *

540. ROSS, ROBERT T., AND MORLEDGE, JUNE. "Comparison of the WISC and WAIS at Chronological Age Sixteen." *J Consult Psychol* 31:331–2 Je '67. * (*PA* 41:10449)

541. RUSSELL, CAROL A. *A Comparison of Performance on the Stanford-Binet Intelligence Scale, Form L-M, and the Wechsler Intelligence Scale for Children With Mentally Retarded Subjects.* Master's thesis, University of Utah (Salt Lake City, Utah), 1967.

542. SAK, HELEN G.; SMITH, ALFRED A.; AND DAVIES, JOSEPH. "Psychometric Evaluation of Children With Familial Dysautonomia." *Am J Psychiatry* 124:682–7 N '67. * (*PA* 42:5959)

543. SATTLER, JEROME M., AND THEYE, FRED. "Procedural, Situational, and Interpersonal Variables in Individual Intelligence Testing." *Psychol B* 68:347–60 N '67. * (*PA* 42:2564)

544. SATZ, PAUL; VAN DE RIET, HANI; AND MOGEL, STEVE. "An Abbreviation of the WISC for Clinical Use." Abstract. *J Consult Psychol* 31:168 F '67. *

545. SCHUBERT, JOSEF. "Effect of Training on the Performance of the W.I.S.C. 'Block Design' Subtest." *Brit J Social & Clin Psychol* 6:144–9 Je '67. * (*PA* 41:13600)

546. SCOTTISH COUNCIL FOR RESEARCH IN EDUCATION. *The Scottish Standardisation of WISC.* Publications of the Scottish Council for Research in Education 55. London: University of London Press Ltd., 1967. Pp. 71. * (*PA* 39:15281)

547. SILVERSTEIN, A. B. "Estimating Full Scale IQs From WISC Short Forms." *Psychol Rep* 20:1264 Je '67. *

548. SILVERSTEIN, A. B. "A Short Short Form of the WISC and WAIS for Screening Purposes." *Psychol Rep* 20:682 Ap '67. * (*PA* 41:8164)

549. SILVERSTEIN, A. B. "Validity of WISC Short Forms at Three Age Levels." *J Consult Psychol* 31:635–6 D '67. * (*PA* 42:1415)

550. SILVERSTEIN, ARTHUR B. "Validity of WISC Short Forms at Three Age Levels." *Calif Mental Health Res Dig* 5:253–4 au '67. * (*PA* 42:138)

551. STEVENS, DOUGLAS A.; BOYDSTUN, JAMES A.; DYKMAN, ROSCOE A.; PETERS, JOHN E.; AND SINTON, DAVID W. "Presumed Minimal Brain Dysfunction in Children: Relationship to Performance on Selected Behavioral Tests." *Arch Gen Psychiatry* 16:281–5 Mr '67. * (*PA* 41:0252)

552. STONE, LEROY A. "The Devaluated Shilling and the WISC." *Psychol Rep* 20:280 F '67. * (*PA* 41:6466)

553. TAVA, EDWARD GERALD. *A Review of the Short Forms of the Wechsler Intelligence Scale for Children.* Master's thesis, Western Michigan University (Kalamazoo, Mich.), 1967. (*Masters Abstracts* 6:157)

554. TELLEGEN, AUKE, AND BRIGGS, PETER F. "Old Wine in New Skins: Grouping Wechsler Subtests Into New Scales." *J Consult Psychol* 31:499–506 O '67. * (*PA* 41:16071)

555. THORNTON, CARL L., AND BARRETT, GERALD V. "Psychological Differentiation and WISC 'Analytical IQ.' Methodological Note." *Percept & Motor Skills* 25:704 D '67. * (*PA* 42:8971)

556. TILLMAN, M. H. "The Performance of Blind and Sighted Children on the Wechsler Intelligence Scale for Children: Study 1." *Int J Ed Blind* 16:65–74 Mr '67. * (*PA* 41:10948)

557. TILLMAN, M. H. "The Performances of Blind and Sighted Children on the Wechsler Intelligence Scale for Children: Study 2." *Int J Ed Blind* 16:106–12 My '67. * (*PA* 41:10949)

558. TRIEGLAFF, ANNETTE L. *The Relationship Between the Wechsler Intelligence Scale for Children and Reading Scores for the Stanford Achievement Test.* Master's thesis, Sacramento State College (Sacramento, Calif.), 1967.

559. TURNER, R. K.; MATHEWS, A.; AND RACHMAN, S. "The Stability of the WISC in a Psychiatric Group." *Brit J Ed Psychol* 37:194–200 Je '67. * (*PA* 41:14459)

560. WARD, JAMES. "An Oblique Factorization of Wallach and Kogan's 'Creativity' Correlations." *Brit J Ed Psychol* 37:380–2 N '67. * (*PA* 42:4784)

561. WARRINGTON, ELIZABETH K. "The Incidence of Verbal Disability Associated With Retardation Reading." *Neuropsychologia* 5:175–9 My '67. * (*PA* 42:11212)

562. WILLERMAN, LEE, AND CHURCHILL, JOHN A. "Intelligence and Birth Weight in Identical Twins." *Child Develop* 38:623–9 S '67. * (*PA* 41:16697)

563. WILTBERGER, ARLENE CAMPBELL. *A Comparative Study of the Wechsler Intelligence Scale for Children and the Wechsler Adult Intelligence Scale With High IQ Level and Low IQ Level Subjects.* Master's thesis, Cornell University (Ithaca, N.Y.), 1967.

564. WOODY, ROBERT H. "Diagnosis of Behavioral Problem Children: Electroencephalography and Mental Abilities." *J Sch Psychol* 5:116–21 w '67. * (*PA* 41:9383)

565. YULE, WILLIAM. "Predicting Reading Ages on Neale's Analysis of Reading Ability." *Brit J Ed Psychol* 37:252–5 Je '67. * (*PA* 41:15822)

566. ANASTASI, ANNE. *Psychological Testing, Third Edition,* pp. 282–8. New York: Macmillan Co., 1968. Pp. xiii, 665. *

567. ANDERSON, DARRELL E., AND FLAX, MORTON L. "A Comparison of the Peabody Picture Vocabulary Test With the Wechsler Intelligence Scale for Children." *J Ed Res* 62:114–6 N '68. *

568. ANDO, KYOKO. "A Comparative Study of Peabody Picture Vocabulary Test and Wechsler Intelligence Scale for Children With a Group of Cerebral Palsied Children." *Cereb Palsy J* 29:7–9 My–Je '68. * (*PA* 42:15909)

569. ARMSTRONG, JUDITH GLANTZ. *Intellectual Competence and Coping Behavior in Preschool Children.* Doctor's thesis, University of California (Berkeley, Calif.), 1968. (*DA* 29:4837B)

570. BAE, AGNES Y. "Factors Influencing Vocational Efficiency of Institutionalized Retardates in Different Training Programs." *Am J Mental Def* 72:871–4 My '68. * (*PA* 42:14397)

571. BATTIN, R., AND KRAFT, IRVIN A. "Psycholinguistic Evaluation of Children Referred for Private Consultation to a Child Psychiatrist." *J Learn Dis* 1:600–5 O '68. * (*PA* 45:2995)

572. BECK, FRANCES. "Performance of Retarded Readers on Parts of the Wechsler Intelligence Scale for Children." *Sup Ed Monogr* 97:91–103 Ag '68. *

573. BOWLES, FRANK LOUIS. *Sub-Test Score Changes Over Twenty Months on the Wechsler Intelligence Scale for Children for White and Negro Special Education Students.* Doctor's thesis, University of Florida (Gainesville, Fla.), 1968. (*DAI* 30:54A)

574. BRITTAIN, MICHAEL. "A Comparative Study of the Use of the Wechsler Intelligence Scale for Children and the Stanford-Binet Intelligence Scale (Form L-M) With Eight-Year-Old Children." *Brit J Ed Psychol* 38:103–4 F '68. *

575. BRUNSON, FORREST WARD. *Comparative Ratings of Intelligence and of Achievement of Children From Low- and Middle-Socioeconomic Areas.* Doctor's thesis, University of Nebraska (Lincoln, Neb.), 1968. (*DA* 29:4318A)

576. BURCH, CHARLES WILLIAM. *Assessment Variables Relevant to the Referral and Placement of Pupils in Educationally Handicapped Classes.* Doctor's thesis, University of Southern California (Los Angeles, Calif.), 1968. (*DA* 29:2995A)

577. BURNES, DONNA KAY STANDLEY. *A Study of Relationships Between Measured Intelligence and Non-Intellective Factors for Children of Two Socioeconomic Groups and Races.* Doctor's thesis, Washington University (St. Louis, Mo.), 1968. (*DA* 29:4839B)

578. BUTTERFIELD, EARL C. "Stimulus Trace in the Mentally Retarded, Defect or Developmental Lag?" *J Abn Psychol* 73:358–62 Ag '68. * (*PA* 42:17539)

579. CACCAVO, EMIL. *The Listening Comprehension Level of an Informal Reading Inventory as a Predictor of Intelligence of Elementary School Children.* Doctor's thesis, New York University (New York, N.Y.), 1968. (*DAI* 30:164A)

580. CALDWELL, MARCUS B., AND SMITH, TIMOTHY A. "Intellectual Structure of Southern Negro Children." *Psychol Rep* 23:63–71 Ag '68. * (*PA* 43:6015)

581. CHAIN, RHODA U. *A Comparative Study of the Performance of Obese and Non-Obese Children on the Wechsler Intelligence Scale for Children.* Master's thesis, Southern Connecticut State College (New Haven, Conn.), 1968.

582. CHIAPPONE, ANTHONY D. "Use of the Detroit Tests of Learning Aptitude With EMR." *Excep Children* 35:240–1 N '68. * (*PA* 43:13075)

583. CHURCHILL, JOHN A.; WILLERMAN, LEE; GRISELL, JAMES; AND AYERS, MELVERN A. "Effect of Head Position at Birth on WISC Verbal and Performance IQ." *Psychol Rep* 23:495–8 O '68. * (*PA* 43:9492)

584. CONNOLLY, JOSEPH KENNETH. *The Discriminatory Functions of Brief Tests With the Educable Mentally Retarded.* Doctor's thesis, Fordham University (New York, N.Y.), 1968. (*DA* 29:2997A)

585. DAHLKE, ANITA B. *The Use of WISC Scores to Predict Reading Improvement After Remedial Tutoring.* Doctor's thesis, University of Florida (Gainesville, Fla.), 1968. (*DAI* 30:165A)

586. DUDEK, S. Z., AND LESTER, E. P. "The Good Child Facade in Chronic Underachievers." *Am J Orthopsychiatry* 38:153–60 Ja '68. * (*PA* 42:17778)

587. DUFF, MARIGENE MULLIGAN. *Language Functions in Children With Learning Disabilities.* Doctor's thesis, Northwestern University (Evanston, Ill.), 1968. (*DA* 29:3958B)

588. Eppley, Edwin B. *A Validity Study Comparing the Main Scale of the Kahn Intelligence Test With the Wechsler Intelligence Scale for Children.* Master's thesis, Millersville State College (Millersville, Pa.), 1968.

589. Fagert, Charles M. *The Relationship Between the Slosson Intelligence Test and the Wechsler Intelligence Scale for Children.* Master's thesis, Kent State University (Kent, Ohio), 1968.

590. Fee, Francis. "An Alternative to Ward's Factor Analysis of Wallach and Kogan's 'Creativity' Correlations." Comment by James Ward. *Brit J Ed Psychol* 38:319–21 N '68. * (*PA* 43:6128)

591. Fleeman, George W. *The Significance of Differences Between Non-Prorated and Prorated Scores for Verbal Performance and Full Scale I.Q.'s on the Wechsler Intelligence Scale for Children.* Master's thesis, East Tennessee State University (Johnson City, Tenn.), 1968.

592. Frostig, Marianne. "Testing as a Basis for Educational Therapy," pp. 64–86. In *Assessment of the Cerebral Palsied Child for Education.* Edited by James Loring. London: William Heinemann Ltd., 1968. Pp. vii, 112. *

593. Gaddes, W. H.; McKenzie, Audrey; and Barnsley, Roger. "Psychometric Intelligence and Spatial Imagery in Two Northwest Indian and Two White Groups of Children." *J Social Psychol* 75:35–42 Je '68. * (*PA* 42:13575)

594. Gardner, Riley W., and Moriarty, Alice. Chap. 8, "Individuality in Wechsler's Intelligence Scale for Children," pp. 129–33, passim. In their *Personality Development at Preadolescence: Explorations of Structure Formation,* see 595. *

595. Gardner, Riley W., and Moriarty, Alice. *Personality Development at Preadolescence: Explorations of Structure Formation.* Seattle, Wash.: University of Washington Press, 1968. Pp. xi, 344. *

596. Harris, A. J., and Lovinger, R. J. "Longitudinal Measures of the Intelligence of Disadvantaged Negro Adolescents." *Sch R* 76:60–6 Mr '68. * (*PA* 43:3138)

597. Holroyd, Jean. "When WISC Verbal IQ Is Low." *J Clin Psychol* 24:457 O '68. * (*PA* 43:3754)

598. Hommel, Ronald William. *An Index of Creativity as Derived From an Extended Form of Intelligence Testing.* Doctor's thesis, Rutgers—The State University (New Brunswick, N.J.), 1968. (*DA* 29:2618B)

599. Houston, Camille, and Otto, Wayne. "Poor Readers' Functioning on the WISC, Slosson Intelligence Test and Quick Test." Abstract. *AERA Paper Abstr* 1968:120–1 '68. *

600. Houston, Camille, and Otto, Wayne. "Poor Readers' Functioning on the WISC, Slosson Intelligence Test and Quick Test." *J Ed Res* 62:157–9 D '68. *

601. Ingham, J. G. "Comment on Effect of Training on the Performance of the WISC 'Block Design' Subtest by Josef Schubert." Reply by Josef Schubert. *Brit J Social & Clin Psychol* 7:149–50 Je '68. * (*PA* 42:16413, 16429)

602. Jackson, Elizabeth M. *The WISC Sub-Scores and Achievement in Reading Clinic.* Master's thesis, California State College (Long Beach, Calif.), 1968.

603. Kaspar, Joseph C.; Throne, Frances M.; and Schulman, Jerome L. "A Study of the Inter-Judge Reliability in Scoring the Responses of a Group of Mentally Retarded Boys to Three WISC Subscales." *Ed & Psychol Meas* 28:469–77 su '68. * (*PA* 42:18797)

604. Levy, Philip. "Short-Form Tests: A Methodological Review." *Psychol B* 69:410–6 Je '68. * (*PA* 42:11410)

605. Levy, Russell H. "Group Administered Intelligence Tests Which Appropriately Reflect the Magnitude of Mental Retardation Among Wards of the Illinois Youth Commission." *J Correct Ed* 20:7–10 su '68. *

606. Luong, Corina K. Mongcal. *An Analysis of Factors Related to Difficulties in Learning and Adjustment Among Minority Group Children.* Doctor's thesis, Bryn Mawr College (Bryn Mawr, Pa.), 1968. (*DAI* 30:4795B)

607. Lyle, J. G. "Errors of Retarded Readers on Block Designs." *Percept & Motor Skills* 26:1222 Je '68. * (*PA* 42:19419)

608. Lytton, H. "Some Psychological and Sociological Characteristics of 'Good' and 'Poor Achievers' (Boys) in Remedial Reading Groups." *Hum Develop* 11(4):260–76 '68. *

609. McArthur, Charles R., and Wakefield, Homer E. "Validation of the PPVT With the Stanford-Binet-LM and the WISC on Educable Mental Retardates." *Am J Mental Def* 73:465–7 N '68. * (*PA* 43:8596)

610. McKerracher, D. W., and Watson, R. A. "Validation of a Short Form WISC With Clinic Children." *Brit J Ed Psychol* 38:205–8 Je '68. * (*PA* 42:16418)

611. Matthews, Charles G.; Chun, Raymond W. M.; Grabow, Jack D.; and Thompson, Wayne H. "Psychological Sequelae in Children Following California Arboviros Encephalitis." *Neurology* 18:1023–30 O '68. * (*PA* 43:5771)

612. Mehrotra, K. K. "The Relationship of the WISC to the Progressive Matrices." *J Psychol Res* 12:114–8 S '68. *

613. Mehrotra, Krishna Kant. "A Comparative Study of WISC and Raven's Progressive Matrices." *Psychol Studies* 13:47–50 Ja '68. *

614. Miezitis, Solveiga Ausma. *An Exploratory Study of Divergent Production in Preschoolers.* Doctor's thesis, University of Toronto (Toronto, Ont., Canada), 1968. (*DAI* 30:589A)

615. Mordock, John B., and Bogan, Steve. "Wechsler Patterns and Symptomatic Behaviors of Children Diagnosed as Having Minimal Cerebral Dysfunction." Abstract. *Proc 76th Ann Conv Am Psychol Assn* 3:663–4 '68. *

616. Nalven, Frederic B., and Puleo, Vincent T. "Relationship Between Digit Span and Classroom Distractibility in Elementary School Children." *J Clin Psychol* 24:85–7 Ja '68. * (*PA* 42:9426)

617. Ortiz, Kenneth K. *A Concurrent Validation Study of a Spanish Version of the Pictorial Test of Intelligence and a Critical Analysis of the Use of the Wechsler Intelligence Scale for Children With Bilingual Mexican-American Children.* Master's thesis, California State College (Long Beach, Calif.), 1968.

618. Pedersen, Darhl M.; Shinedling, Martin M.; and Johnson, Dee L. "Effects of Sex of Examiner and Subject on Children's Quantitative Test Performance." *J Pers & Social Psychol* 10:251–4 N '68. * (*PA* 43:3760)

619. Pihl, Robert O. "The Degree of the Verbal-Performance Discrepancy on the WISC and the WAIS and Severity of EEG Abnormality in Epileptics." *J Clin Psychol* 24:418–20 O '68. * (*PA* 43:4327)

620. Qureshi, M. Y. "Intelligence Test Scores as a Function of Sex of Experimenter and Sex of Subject." *J Psychol* 69:277–84 Jl '68. * (*PA* 42:15462)

621. Qureshi, M. Y. "The Optimum Limits of Testing on the Wechsler Intelligence Scales." *Genetic Psychol Monogr* 78:141–90 N '68. * (*PA* 43:4016)

622. Qureshi, Mohammed Y. "The Comparability of WAIS and WISC Subtest Scores and IQ Estimates." *J Psychol* 68:73–82 Ja '68. * (*PA* 47:7334)

623. Qureshi, Mohammed Y. "The Internal Consistency of the WISC Scores for Ages 5 to 16." *J Clin Psychol* 24:192–5 Ap '68. * (*PA* 42:12093)

624. Qureshi, Mohammed Y. "Practice Effects on the WISC Subtest Scores and IQ Estimates." *J Clin Psychol* 24:79–85 Ja '68. * (*PA* 42:8942)

625. Rainwater, Harold G. "Reading Problem Indicators Among Children With Reading Problems." *Psychol* 5:81–3 N '68. *

626. Reed, James C. "Cognitive Factors Associated With Achievement in Reading at the Elementary Grades." Abstract. *AERA Paper Abstr* 1968:72 '68. *

627. Reid, Walter B.; Moore, Dana; and Alexander, Dwayne. "Abbreviated Form of the WISC for Use With Brain-Damaged and Mentally Retarded Children." Abstract. *J Consult & Clin Psychol* 32:236 Ap '68. * (*PA* 42:8103)

628. Rosen, Marvin; Stallings, Linda; Floor, Lucretia; and Nowakiwska, Myra. "Reliability and Stability of Wechsler IQ Scores for Institutionalized Mental Subnormals." *Am J Mental Def* 73:218–25 S '68. * (*PA* 43:4352)

629. Rymsza, Januszka Sofia De Lilio. *Factor Analysis of Measures of Divergent Thinking Obtained From the Children's Apperception Test and Measures of Intelligence Obtained From the Wechsler Intelligence Scale for Children.* Doctor's thesis, Florida State University (Tallahassee, Fla.), 1968. (*DAI* 30:831B)

630. Sabatino, David A.; assisted by R. L. Jones, Curtiss Brown, and W. M. Gibson. "The Relationship Between Twenty-Three Learning Disability Behavioral Variables," pp. 149–61. In *CEC Selected Convention Papers.* 46th Annual International Convention, 1968. Washington, D.C.: Council for Exceptional Children, [1968]. Pp. xii, 346. *

631. Sabatino, David A.; Wickham, William, Jr.; and Burnett, Calvin W. "The Psychoeducational Assessment of Learning Disabilities." *Cath Ed R* 66:327–41 My '68. *

632. Scallon, Richard J. *Field Articulation: A Study of the Perceptual Style of Enuretic Boys.* Doctor's thesis, St. John's University (Jamaica, N.Y.), 1968. (*DA* 29:4369B)

633. Sekyra, Francis, III, and Arnoult, Joseph Francis, III. "Negro Intellectual Assessment With Three Instruments Contrasting Caucasian and Negro Norms." *J Learn Dis* 1:564–9 O '68. * (*PA* 45:2174)

634. Silberberg, Norman, and Feldt, Leonard S. "Intellectual and Perceptual Correlates of Reading Disabilities." *J Sch Psychol* 6:237–45 su '68. * (*PA* 42:3033)

635. Silverstein, A. B. "Simple Summation vs Differential Weighting in the Construction of WISC Short Forms." *Psychol Rep* 23:960 D '68. * (*PA* 43:9743)

636. Silverstein, A. B. "Validity of a New Approach to the Design of WAIS, WISC, and WPPSI Short Forms." *J Consult & Clin Psychol* 32:478–9 Ag '68. * (*PA* 42:16432)

637. Silverstein, A. B. "Variance Components in Five Psychological Tests." *Psychol Rep* 23:141–2 Ag '68. * (*PA* 43:6920)

638. Silverstein, A. B. "WISC and WPPSI IQs for the Gifted." *Psychol Rep* 22:1168 Je '68. * (*PA* 42:18801)

639. Silverstein, A. B. "WISC Subtest Patterns of Retardates." *Psychol Rep* 23:1061–2 D '68. * (*PA* 43:8601)

640. Simpson, Robert Lee. *A Study of the Comparability of the WISC and the WAIS and the Factors Contributing to Their Differences.* Doctor's thesis, University of Southern California (Los Angeles, Calif.), 1968. (*DA* 29:1794A)

641. Slobodzian, Evelyn Birdsall. *The Relationship Between Certain Readiness Measures and Reading Achievement*

at Level One. Doctor's thesis, Temple University (Philadelphia, Pa.), 1968. (*DA* 29:1053A)

642. TILLMAN, M. H., AND BASHAW, W. L. "Multivariate Analysis of the WISC Scales for Blind and Sighted Children." *Psychol Rep* 23:523-6 O '68. * (*PA* 43:9745)

643. TOWNES, BRENDA, AND CHRIST, ADOLPHE E. "Psychological Testing: Its Usefulness in Teaching Psychotherapy and Psychodynamics to Medical Students." *Arch Gen Psychiatry* 19:487-90 O '68. * (*PA* 43:4068)

644. TOZIER, LEONARD LESLIE. *Modifications of the WISC Block Design Subtest.* Master's thesis, San Diego State College (San Diego, Calif.), 1968.

645. TYSON, MARTHA HARALSON. *The Effect of Prior Contact With the Examiner on the Wechsler Intelligence Scale for Children Scores of Third-Grade Children.* Doctor's thesis, University of Houston (Houston, Tex.), 1968. (*DA* 29:4372B)

646. VANCINI, JOHN PAUL. *The Stability and Utility of an Abbreviated Form of the WISC.* Doctor's thesis, University of Colorado (Boulder, Colo.), 1968. (*DA* 29:3499B)

647. WHITE, LINDA ANN. *A Comparative Study of the Performance of Negro Head Start Students on the Wechsler Preschool and Primary Scale of Intelligence, the Wechsler Intelligence Scale for Children, and the Stanford-Binet, Form L-M.* Master's thesis, University of Texas (Austin, Tex.), 1968.

648. WIDMAN, JOANNE B. *Wechsler Intelligence Scale for Children: A Study of Scores Obtained by Aleut Elementary School Students, St. Paul Island, Alaska.* Master's thesis, Pacific Lutheran University (Tacoma, Wash.), 1968.

649. WIENER, G.; RIDER, R. V.; OPPEL, W. C.; AND HARPER, P. A. "Correlates of Low Birth Weight: Psychological Status at Eight to Ten Years of Age." *Pediatric Res* 2:110-8 Mr '68. * (*PA* 42:15299)

650. WILLARD, LOUISA A. "A Comparison of Culture Fair Test Scores With Group and Individual Intelligence Test Scores of Disadvantaged Negro Children." *J Learn Dis* 1:584-9 O '68. * (*PA* 45:3968)

651. WOLF, CLIFTON W. *A Statistical Study of Specific Dyslexia-Characteristics and Syndrome Patterns.* Doctor's thesis, University of Houston (Houston, Tex.), 1968. (*DA* 29:2643B)

652. WOODY, ROBERT H. "Diagnosis of Behavioral Problem Children: Mental Abilities and Achievement." *J Sch Psychol* 6:111-6 w '68. * (*PA* 42:11148)

653. ZEDLER, EMPRESS Y. "Screening Underachieving Pupils for Risk of Neurological Impairment." *Learning Disorders* 3:249-74 '68. *

654. ABRAMS, STANLEY. "The Upper Weight Level Premature Child." *Dis Nerv System* 30(6):414-7 Je '69. * (*PA* 44:6420)

655. BANAS, NORMA, AND WILLS, I. H. "The Vulnerable Child and Prescriptive Teaching." *Acad Ther* 4(3):215-9 sp '69. * (*PA* 43:17927)

656. BARCLAY, A.; FRIEDMAN, ELLEN C.; AND FIDEL, YILDIZ. "A Comparative Study of WISC and WAIS Performances and Score Patterns Among Institutionalized Retardates." *J Mental Def Res* 13(2):99-105 Je '69. * (*PA* 44:9089)

657. BAUMANN, KAREN SUZANN. *The Effects of an Educational Program on the Test Performance of Children With Psychoneurological Learning Disabilities.* Doctor's thesis, Oklahoma State University (Stillwater, Okla.), 1969. (*DAI* 31:3865A)

658. BORTNER, MORTON, AND BIRCH, HERBERT G. "Patterns of Intellectual Ability in Emotionally Disturbed and Brain-Damaged Children." *J Spec Ed* 3(4):351-69 w '69. * (*PA* 44:14652)

659. BRODT, AUDREY M., AND WALKER, RONALD E. "Techniques of WISC Vocabulary Administration." *J Clin Psychol* 25(2):180-1 Ap '69. * (*PA* 43:14324)

660. BYRD, COLEEN, AND SPRINGFIELD, LYNN. "A Note on the Draw-A-Person Test With Adolescent Retardates." *Am J Mental Def* 73(4):578-9 Ja '69. * (*PA* 43:8571)

661. CANNON, THOMAS MILTON, JR. *The Wechsler Intelligence Scale for Children as a Prediction of Adjustment of First Grade Children.* Doctor's thesis, Texas Technological University (Lubbock, Tex.), 1969. (*DAI* 31:143A)

662. CHAWLA, TILAK R. "An Evaluative Study of New Culture-Free Intelligence Test (Kit:Exp)." *J Psychol Res* 13(2):74-6 My '69. * (*PA* 45:4248)

663. CRAWFORD, VEDA B. *Relationships of Scores on the Wechsler Preschool and Primary Scale of Intelligence, the Stanford-Binet Intelligence Scale, Form LM, and the Peabody Picture Vocabulary Test, Form A.* Master's thesis, Bowling Green State University (Bowling Green, Ohio), 1969.

664. CROCKETT, DAVID; KLONOFF, HARRY; AND BJERRING, JAMES. "Factor Analysis of Neuropsychological Tests." *Percept & Motor Skills* 29(3):791-802 D '69. * (*PA* 46:4665)

665. DE MARCO, WILLIAM. *The Scatter of Intellectual Abilities of the Hard of Hearing as Assessed by the Wechsler Intelligence Scale for Children.* Doctor's thesis, University of Illinois (Urbana, Ill.), 1969. (*DAI* 30:3383B)

666. DOUBROS, STEVE G., AND MASCARENHAS, JULIET. "Relations Among Wechsler Full-Scale Scores, Organicity-Sensitive Subtest Scores and Bender-Gestalt Errors Scores." *Percept & Motor Skills* 29(3):719-22 D '69. * (*PA* 46:4666)

667. DUDEK, S. Z.; GOLDBERG, J. S.; LESTER, E. P.; AND HARRIS, B. R. "The Validity of Cognitive, Perceptual-Motor and Personality Variables for Prediction of Achievement in Grade 1 and Grade 2." *J Clin Psychol* 25(2):165-70 Ap '69. * (*PA* 43:14874)

668. DUDEK, S. Z.; LESTER, E. P.; GOLDBERG, J. S.; AND DYER, G. B. "Relationship of Piaget Measures to Standard Intelligence and Motor Scales." *Percept & Motor Skills* 28(2):351-62 Ap '69. * (*PA* 43:15587)

669. EGELAND, BYRON. "Examiner Expectancy: Effects on the Scoring of the WISC." *Psychol Sch* 6(3):313-5 Jl '69. * (*PA* 44:3617)

670. ERTL, JOHN P., AND SCHAFER, EDWARD W. P. "Brain Response Correlates of Psychometric Intelligence." *Nature* 223(5204):421-2 Jl 26 '69. *

671. FEDIO, PAUL, AND MIRSKY, ALLAN F. "Selective Intellectual Deficits in Children with Temporal Lobe or Centrencephalic Epilepsy." *Neuropsychologia* 7(4):287-300 S '69. *

672. FERINDEN, WILLIAM E., JR.; JACOBSON, SHERMAN; AND KOVALINSKY, THOMAS. *Educational Interpretation of the Wechsler Intelligence Scale for Children (WISC).* Linden, N.J.: Remediation Associates, 1969. Pp. ii, 36. *

673. FLEMING, JUANITA WILSON. *The Interrelationship of Early Developmental Factors on the Academic Failure of Children.* Doctor's thesis, Catholic University of America (Washington, D.C.), 1969. (*DAI* 30:1429A)

674. FRIEDRICH, DOUGLAS; FULLER, GERALD B.; AND HAWKINS, WILLIAM F. "Relationship Between Perception (Input) and Execution (Output)." *Percept & Motor Skills* 29(3):923-34 D '69. * (*PA* 46:5346)

675. GIOIOSO, JOSEPH V., AND ADERMAN, MORRIS. "The Combination Test as a Quick Screening Device to Differentiate Levels of Retardation." *Psychol Rep* 25(3):843-8 D '69. * (*PA* 44:18906)

676. GOENS, BERT DOUGLAS. *Comparisons of the Wechsler Preschool and Primary Scale of Intelligence With the Wechsler Intelligence Scale for Children.* Master's thesis, Western Michigan University (Kalamazoo, Mich.), 1969. (*Masters Abstracts* 7:119)

677. HALL, LEON P., AND LaDRIERE, LaVERNE. "Patterns of Performance on WISC Similarities in Emotionally Disturbed and Brain-Damaged Children." *J Consult & Clin Psychol* 33(3):357-64 Je '69. * (*PA* 43:13078)

678. HEMBERGER, LANCE WARNER. *A Longitudinal Study of the Factorial Organization of Intelligence as Related to Socioeconomic Variables.* Doctor's thesis, University of Georgia (Athens, Ga.), 1969. (*DAI* 30:3321A)

679. HENDERSON, NORMAN B.; BUTLER, BRUCE V.; AND GOFFENEY, BARBARA. "Effectiveness of the WISC and Bender-Gestalt Test in Predicting Arithmetic and Reading Achievement for White and Nonwhite Children." *J Clin Psychol* 25(3):268-71 Jl '69. * (*PA* 44:4246)

680. HERRELL, JAMES M., AND GOLLAND, JEFFREY H. "Should WISC Subjects Explain Picture Arrangement Stories?" *J Consult & Clin Psychol* 33(6):761-2 D '69. * (*PA* 44:3678)

681. HEWITT, PATRICIA S., AND MASSEY, JAMES O. *Clinical Clues From the WISC, Wechsler Intelligence Scale for Children: With Special Sections on Testing Black and Spanish-Speaking Children.* Palo Alto, Calif.: Consulting Psychologists Press, Inc., 1969. Pp. 46. *

682. JOHNSON, CLIFFORD IVY. *An Analysis of the Predictive Validity of Selective Reading Readiness Factors to Third Grade Reading Achievement.* Doctor's thesis, University of Georgia (Athens, Ga.), 1969. (*DAI* 30:3363A)

683. JOHNSON, DONALD DAVID. *A Comparative Analysis of Special Education and Regular Program Students' Scores on Selected Subtests of the Wechsler Intelligence Scale for Children.* Doctor's thesis, New Mexico State University (University Park, N.M.), 1969. (*DAI* 30:3816A)

684. JONGEWARD, PAUL A. "A Validity Study of the Slosson Intelligence Test for Use With Educable Mentally Retarded Students." *J Sch Psychol* 7(4):59-63 '68-69 ['69]. * (*PA* 44:2702)

685. JONGEWARD, PAUL ALBERT. *A Validity Study of the Slosson Intelligence Test for Use With Educable Mentally Retarded Students.* Doctor's thesis, University of Oregon (Eugene, Ore.), 1969. (*DAI* 30:3323A)

686. KARP, STEPHEN A.; SILBERMAN, LESTER; AND WINTERS, STEPHEN. "Psychological Differentiation and Socioeconomic Status." *Percept & Motor Skills* 28(1):55-60 F '69. * (*PA* 43:11306)

687. KASS, CORRINE E. "Learning Disabilities." *R Ed Res* 39(1):71-82 F '69. * (*PA* 44:5671)

688. KEARNEY, JACQUELINE E. "A New Performance Scale of Cognitive Capacity for Use With Deaf Subjects." *Am Ann Deaf* 114(1):2-14 Ja '69. * (*PA* 43:7197)

689. LOCKYER, LINDA, AND RUTTER, MICHAEL. "A Five- to Fifteen-Year Follow-up Study of Infantile Psychosis: 3, Psychological Aspects." *Brit J Psychiatry* 115(525):865-82 Ag '69. * (*PA* 44:10847)

690. LYLE, J. G. "Reading Retardation and Reversal Tendency: A Factorial Study." *Child Develop* 40(3):833-43 S '69. * (*PA* 44:2706)

691. LYLE, J. G., AND GOYEN, JUDITH. "Performance of Retarded Readers on the WISC and Educational Tests." *J Abn Psychol* 74(1):105-12 F '69. * (*PA* 43:8790)

692. MARGACH, CHARLES, AND KERN, KATE CONDIT. "Visual

Impairment, Partial-Sight and the School Psychologist." *J Learn Dis* 2(8):407–14 Ag '69. * (*PA* 45:6995)

693. MARSDEN, GERALD, AND KALTER, NEIL. "Bodily Concerns and the WISC Object Assembly Subtest." *J Consult & Clin Psychol* 33(4):391–5 Ag '69. * (*PA* 43:15808)

694. MEEKER, MARY NACOL. *The Structure of Intellect: Its Interpretation and Uses*, pp. 132–46. Columbus, Ohio: Charles E. Merrill Publishing Co., 1969. Pp. xix, 203. *

695. MILLER, HAROLD R. "WISC Performance Under Incentive Conditions: Case Report." *Psychol Rep* 24(3):835–8 Je '69. * (*PA* 44:479)

696. NALVEN, FREDRIC B. "Classroom-Administered Digit Span and Distractibility Ratings for Elementary School Pupils." *Psychol Rep* 24(3):734 Je '69. * (*PA* 44:1222)

697. NALVEN, FREDRIC B., AND BIERBRYER, BRUCE. "Predicting Elementary School Children's Classroom Comprehension From Their WISC Results." *J Clin Psychol* 25(1):75–6 Ja '69. * (*PA* 43:10328)

698. NALVEN, FREDRIC B.; HOFMANN, LOUIS J.; AND BIERBRYER, BRUCE. "The Effects of Subjects' Age, Sex, Race, and Socioeconomic Status on Psychologists' Estimates of 'True IQ' From WISC Scores." *J Clin Psychol* 25(3):271–4 Jl '69. * (*PA* 44:3620)

699. NEEDHAM, WALTER E.; BRAY, PATRICK F.; WISER, WILMER C.; AND BECK, EDWARD C. "Intelligence and EEG Studies in Families With Idiopathic Epilepsy." *J Am Med Assn* 207(8):1497–501 F 24 '69. * (*PA* 44:21418)

700. NELSON, C. MICHAEL, AND HUDSON, FLOYD G. "Predicting the Reading Achievement of Junior High School EMR Children." *Am J Mental Def* 74(3):415–20 N '69. *

701. OAKLAND, JAMES A. "WISC Coding as a Measure of Motivation." *J Clin Psychol* 25(4):411–2 O '69. * (*PA* 44:10981)

702. O'NEILL, HUGH DANIEL, JR. *Partial Validation of the Slosson Intelligence Test*. Doctor's thesis, University of Oklahoma (Norman, Okla.), 1969. (*DAI* 30:3797A)

703. REED, JAMES C. "Children's Figure Drawing—A Clue to Reading Progress." *Read Teach* 23(2):132–6 N '69. * (*PA* 44:21620)

704. REED, JAMES C., AND REITAN, RALPH M. "Verbal and Performance Differences Among Brain-Injured Children With Lateralized Motor Deficits." *Percept & Motor Skills* 29(3):747–52 D '69. * (*PA* 46:5334)

705. REILLEY, ROBERT R. "Student Reactions to Use of Video Taped WISC Instruction." *Counselor Ed & Sup* 8(3):233–5 sp '69. *

706. RHODES, L. E.; DUSTMAN, R. E.; AND BECK, E. C. "The Visual Evoked Response: A Comparison of Bright and Dull Children." *Electroencephalography & Clin Neurophysiol* 27(4):364–72 O '69. * (*PA* 45:2142)

707. SABATINO, DAVID A., AND CRAMBLETT, HENRY. "A Longitudinal Study of Children With Learning Disabilities Subsequent to Hospitalization for Viral Encephalitis Part I." *J Learn Dis* 2(2):65–75 F '69. * (*PA* 45:6854)

708. SABATINO, DAVID A., AND CRAMBLETT, HENRY G. "A Longitudinal Study of Children With Learning Disabilities Subsequent to Hospitalization for Viral Encephalitis—Part II." *J Learn Dis* 2(3):124–35 Mr '69. * (*PA* 45:6855)

709. SATTLER, JEROME M. "Effects of Cues and Examiner Influence on Two Wechsler Subtests." *J Consult & Clin Psychol* 33(6):716–21 D '69. * (*PA* 44:4171)

710. SATTLER, JEROME M.; WINGET, BARBARA M.; AND ROTH, ROSEMARY J. "Scoring Difficulty of WAIS and WISC Comprehension, Similarities, and Vocabulary Responses." *J Clin Psychol* 25(2):175–7 Ap '69. * (*PA* 43:14478)

711. SCALLON, RICHARD J., AND HERRON, WILLIAM G. "Field Articulation of Enuretic Boys and Their Mothers." *Percept & Motor Skills* 28(2):407–13 Ap '69. * (*PA* 43:15604)

712. SILBERBERG, NORMAN E.; IVERSEN, IVER A.; AND SILBERBERG, MARGARET C. "A Model for Classifying Children According to Reading Level." *J Learn Dis* 2(12):634–43 D '69. *

713. SILVERSTEIN, A. B. "An Alternative Factor Analytic Solution for Wechsler's Intelligence Scales." *Ed & Psychol Meas* 29(4):763–7 w '69. * (*PA* 44:20972)

714. SIMON, WILLIAM E. "Expectancy Effects in the Scoring of Vocabulary Items: A Study of Scorer Bias." *J Ed Meas* 6(3):159–64 f '69. * (*PA* 44:13628)

715. SMITH, NATHANIEL CUTRIGHT, JR. *Factors Underlying WISC Performance in Juvenile Public Offenders*. Doctor's thesis, Ohio State University (Columbus, Ohio), 1969. (*DAI* 30:1888B)

716. SMITH, TIMOTHY A., AND CALDWELL, MARCUS B. "Intellectual Differences in Negro and White Mental Defectives." *Psychol Rep* 25(2):559–65 O '69. * (*PA* 44:5571)

717. SOLLEE, NATALIE DOSICK. *Verbal Competence and the Acquisition of Conservation*. Doctor's thesis, Boston University (Boston, Mass.), 1969. (*DAI* 30:2409B)

718. STRECKER, REBECCA V. *A Comparison of WISC Subtest Scores of Mentally Retarded Mexican-American and Caucasian Students*. Master's thesis, Chapman College (Orange, Calif.), 1969.

719. SWEET, ROGER CHARLES. *Variations in the Intelligence Test Performance of Lower-Class Children as a Function of Feedback or Monetary Reinforcement*. Doctor's thesis, University of Wisconsin (Madison, Wis.), 1969. (*DAI* 31:648A)

720. TALKINGTON, LARRY W., AND RIEKER, GRACE A. "A Short Form of the WISC for Use With the Mentally Retarded." *Psychol Rep* 25(2):461–2 O '69. * (*PA* 44:5574)

721. TALMADGE, MAX; HAYDEN, BENJAMIN S.; AND SCHIFF, DONALD. "Longitudinal Analysis of Intellectual and Educational Achievement Change in Culturally Deprived, Emotionally Disturbed Boys." *Percept & Motor Skills* 29(2):435–40 O '69. * (*PA* 44:3795)

722. TILLMAN, H. M., AND OSBORNE, R. T. "The Performance of Blind and Sighted Children on the Wechsler Intelligence Scale for Children: Interaction Effects." *Ed Visually Handicapped* 1(1):1–4 Mr '69. * (*PA* 43:13192)

723. TRAINER, F. E. *Australian Revision of the Wechsler Intelligence Scale for Children*. Master's thesis, University of Sydney (Sydney, N.S.W., Australia), 1969.

724. VANBRAMER, PETER J. *The Use of the Wechsler Intelligence Scale for Children in Selecting Students for Remedial Reading*. Master's thesis, Wisconsin State University (Platteville, Wis.), 1969.

725. WALLACE, GERALD. *A Study of the Relationship of Selected Visual Perceptual Capabilities and Intelligence to Achievement in Reading of Educable Mentally Retarded Children*. Doctor's thesis, University of Oregon (Eugene, Ore.), 1969. (*DAI* 30:3336A)

726. ALLOR, BARBARA A. *A Comparison of Good and Poor Readers on the Wechsler Intelligence Scale for Children at the Seventh Grade Level*. Master's thesis, Cardinal Stritch College (Milwaukee, Wis.), 1970.

727. BAIRD, ROBERT KAY. *A Comparison of the Performance of High and Low Sociometric Fourth Graders on Two Subtests of the Wechsler Intelligence Scale for Children*. Master's thesis, Brigham Young University (Provo, Utah), 1970.

728. BAR-OR, O.; SKINNER, J.; BERGSTEIN, V.; HAAS, J.; SHEARBURN, C.; AND BUSKIRK, E. Chap. 4, "Measures of Performance and Related Physiological Characteristics," pp. 47–73. In *Factors Related to the Speech-Hearing of Children of Below Normal Intelligence, see 787.* *

729. BARTON, BRENDA. *A Study of the Relationship Between School Anxiety and Performance on the Wechsler Intelligence Scale for Children*. Master's thesis, University of Texas (Austin, Tex.), 1970.

730. BLATT, SIDNEY J.; BAKER, BRUCE L.; AND WEISS, JAY. "Wechsler Object Assembly Subtest and Bodily Concern: A Review and Replication." *J Consult & Clin Psychol* 34(2):269–74 Ap '70. * (*PA* 44:10408)

731. BROCKWAY, ROBERT L. *Is There a Significant Difference Between the Verbal and Performance Scores of Juvenile Delinquents on the Wechsler Intelligence Scale for Children?* Master's thesis, Southern Connecticut State College (New Haven, Conn.), 1970.

732. BROWNE, DAUNA BELL, AND TIAHRT, HELEN GERTRUDE. *An Exploration of the Usefulness of Four Descriptive Clusters of Subtest Scores of the Wechsler Intelligence Scale for Children*. Doctor's thesis, University of Northern Colorado (Greeley, Colo.), 1970. (*DAI* 31:4983B)

733. BURNES, KAY. "Patterns of WISC Scores for Children of Two Socioeconomic Classes and Races." *Child Develop* 41(2):493–500 Je '70. * (*PA* 44:14344)

734. CHRISTIANSEN, TED, AND LIVERMORE, GARY. "A Comparison of Anglo-American and Spanish-American Children on the WISC." *J Social Psychol* 81(1):9–14 Je '70. * (*PA* 44:18706)

735. COYLE, F. A., JR., AND BELLAMY, EDWARD E. "Use of the California Abbreviated WISC With Institutionalized Retardates." *Am J Mental Def* 74(4):578 Ja '70. * (*PA* 44:11053)

736. CUNDICK, BERT P. "Measures of Intelligence on Southwest Indian Students." *J Social Psychol* 81(2):151–6 Ag '70. * (*PA* 44:20655)

737. EAVES, LINDA, AND KLONOFF, HARRY. "A Comparison of Blind and Sighted Children on a Tactual and Performance Test." *Excep Children* 37(4):269–73 D '70. *

738. EGELAND, BYRON; DI NELLO, MARIO; AND CARR, DONALD. "The Relationship of Intelligence, Visual-Motor, Psycholinguistic and Reading-Readiness Skills With Achievement." *Ed & Psychol Meas* 30(2):451–8 su '70. * (*PA* 45:3056)

739. ESTES, ROBERT E., AND MORRIS, HUGHLETT L. "Relationship Among Intelligence, Speech Proficiency, and Hearing Sensitivity in Children With Cleft Palates." *Cleft Palate J* 7(9):763–73 Jl '70. *

740. FITZGERALD, BERNARD J.; PASEWARK, RICHARD A.; AND GLOECKLER, TED. "Use of the Peabody Picture Vocabulary Test With the Educationally Handicapped." *J Sch Psychol* 8(4):296–300 '70. * (*PA* 46:1800)

741. FRETZ, BRUCE R. "Factor Structure of Intellectual, Visual Perception, and Visuomotor Performance of Poorly Coordinated Boys." *J Motor Behav* 2(2):69–78 Je '70. *

742. FRIEDMAN, RONALD. "The Reliability of the Wechsler Intelligence Scale for Children in a Group of Mentally Retarded Children." *J Clin Psychol* 26(2):181–2 Ap '70. * (*PA* 44:15147)

743. GARMS, JOE D. "A Validation Study of the Illinois Test of Psycholinguistic Abilities." *Psychol* 7(1):9–12 F '70. * (*PA* 44:13282)

744. GAYTON, WILLIAM F.; WILSON, WINSTON T.; AND BERNSTEIN, STEPHEN. "An Evaluation of an Abbreviated Form of

the WISC." *J Clin Psychol* 26(4):466–8 O '70. * (*PA* 45: 4533)

745. GILLINGHAM, WILLIAM HARVEY. *An Investigation of Examiner Influence on Wechsler Intelligence Scale for Children Scores.* Doctor's thesis, Michigan State University (East Lansing, Mich.), 1970. (*DAI* 31:2178A)

746. GRIMALDI, JOSEPH, JR. *A Factor Analytic Study of WISC Patterns in Children With CNS Dysfunction.* Doctor's thesis, St. John's University (Jamaica, N.Y.), 1970. (*DAI* 31: 3706B)

747. HAFNER, LAWRENCE E.; WEAVER, WENDELL W.; AND POWELL, KATHRYN. "Psychological and Perceptual Correlates of Reading Achievement Among Fourth Graders." *J Read Behav* 2(4):281–90 f '70. * (*PA* 46:5663)

748. HALL, LEON P., AND LA DRIERE, M. LaVERNE. "Evaluation of WISC Similarities Responses According to Cognitive Style and Error Analysis: A Comparative Study." *Psychol Sch* 26(1):175–80 F '70. * (*PA* 45:4537)

749. HANNON, JOHN E., AND KICKLIGHTER, RICHARD. "WAIS Versus WISC in Adolescents." *J Consult & Clin Psychol* 35(2):179–82 O '70. * (*PA* 45:2202)

750. HARRIS, HELENA. "Development of Moral Attitudes in White and Negro Boys." *Develop Psychol* 2(3):376–83 My '70. * (*PA* 44:12259)

751. HARTLAGE, LAWRENCE C. "Differential Diagnosis of Dyslexia, Minimal Brain Damage and Emotional Disturbances in Children." *Psychol Sch* 7(4):403–6 O '70. * (*PA* 46:1422)

752. HINE, W. D. "The Abilities of Partially Hearing Children." *Brit J Ed Psychol* 40(2):171–8 Je '70. * (*PA* 44:21362)

753. HINE, W. D. "Verbal Ability and Partial Hearing Loss." *Teach Deaf* 68(404):450–9 N '70. *

754. HIRSCH, ERNEST A. *The Troubled Adolescent: As He Emerges From Psychological Tests.* New York: International Universities Press, Inc., 1970. Pp. xv, 645. *

755. HUELSMAN, CHARLES B., JR. "The WISC Subtest Syndrome for Disabled Readers." *Percept & Motor Skills* 30(2): 535–50 Ap '70. * (*PA* 46:7506)

756. KRIPPNER, STANLEY. "Reading Improvement and Its Correlates." *Percept & Motor Skills* 31(3):727–31 D '70. * (*PA* 45:10694)

757. LESSING, ELISE E.; ZAGORIN, SUSAN W.; AND NELSON, DOROTHY. "WISC Subtest and IQ Score Correlates of Father Absence." *J Genetic Psychol* 117(2):181–95 D '70. * (*PA* 45:6017)

758. LESTER, EVA P.; MUIR, R.; AND DUDEK, STEPHANIE Z. "Cognitive Structure and Achievement in the Young Child." *Can Psychiatric Assn J* 15(3):279–87 Je '70. * (*PA* 45:5058)

759. LEWIS, FRANKLIN D.; BELL, D. BRUCE; AND ANDERSON, ROBERT P. "Reading Retardation: A Bi-Racial Comparison." *J Read* 13(6):433–6, 474–8 Mr '70. *

760. LOCKYER, LINDA, AND RUTTER, MICHAEL. "A Five- to Fifteen-Year Follow-Up Study of Infantile Psychosis: 4, Patterns of Cognitive Ability." *Brit J Social & Clin Psychol* 9(2): 152–63 Je '70. * (*PA* 44:16983)

761. LOVINGER, SOPHIE L. "Observation on the Arithmetic Subtest of the Wechsler Intelligence Scale for Children." Letter. *J Sch Psychol* 8(4):322 '70. *

762. McFIE, J., AND THOMPSON, J. A. "Intellectual Abilities of Immigrant Children." *Brit J Ed Psychol* 40(3):348–51 N '70. * (*PA* 45:7025)

763. MARSDEN, GERALD. "Intelligence and the Rorschach Whole Response." *J Proj Tech & Pers Assess* 34(6):470–6 D '70. * (*PA* 45:7873)

764. MAYCOCK, GEORGE ALBERT. *Emotional, Social, and Academic Adjustment of the Mentally Retarded as Related to Socio-Economic Level.* Doctor's thesis, Texas Technological University (Lubbock, Tex.), 1970. (*DAI* 31:3375A)

765. MILLER, CHARLES K.; CHANSKY, NORMAN M.; AND GREDLER, GILBERT R. "Rater Agreement on WISC Protocols." *Psychol Sch* 7(2):190–3 Ap '70. * (*PA* 45:700)

766. MOON, W. HAROLD, AND LAIR, CHARLES V. "Manifest Anxiety, Induced Anxiety and Digit Symbol Performance." *Psychol Rep* 26(3):947–50 Je '70. * (*PA* 45:134)

767. MUNZ, ADAM. *The Relationship Between Central Nervous System Functions and Verbal Communication.* Doctor's thesis, New York University (New York, N.Y.), 1970. (*DAI* 31:2193A)

768. NURSS, JOANNE R. "A Diagnostic Comparison of Two Third Grade Reading Classes," pp. 42–54. In *Reading Difficulties: Diagnosis, Correction, and Remediation.* Edited by William K. Durr. Newark, Del.: International Reading Association, 1970. Pp. vii, 276. *

769. ORPET, R. E., AND MYERS, C. E. "Discriminant Function Analysis of Conservation Stages by Structure of Intellect and Conceptual Style Variables." Abstract. *Proc 78th Ann Conv Am Psychol Assn* 5(1):279–80 '70. * (*PA* 44:18342)

770. POST, JOSEPH MARTIN. *The Effects of Vocalization on the Ability of Third Grade Students to Complete Selected Performance Subtests From the Wechsler Intelligence Scale for Children.* Doctor's thesis, University of South Carolina (Columbia, S.C.), 1970. (*DAI* 31:1579A)

771. QUERESHI, M. Y., AND MILLER, JEFFREY M. "The Comparability of the WAIS, WISC, and WBII." *J Ed Meas* 7(2):105–11 su '70. * (*PA* 44:18711)

772. QUERESHI, M. Y., AND WIDLAK, FREDERIC W. "Perceptual Diversity as a Function of Intelligence." Abstract.

Proc 78th Ann Conv Am Psychol Assn 5(1):379–80 '70. * (*PA* 44:18613)

773. QUERY, WILLIAM T. "A Comparative Study of the Relationship Between Need Affiliation and Need Achievement, and Success and Failure Among Indian and White Children." *Newsl Res Psychol* 12(2):95–6 My '70. *

774. REES, ANN H., AND PALMER, FRANCIS H. "Factors Related to Change in Mental Test Performance." *Develop Psychol Monogr* 3(2):1–57 S '70. * (*PA* 45:464)

775. RICE, DONALD B. "Learning Disabilities: An Investigation in Two Parts." *J Learn Dis* 3(3):149–55 Mr '70. *

776. ROSIER, F. N. G. "A Study of Juvenile Delinquents in a Remand Home." *Papers Psychol* 4(1–2):54–5 Ap–O '70. *

777. RUBINO, CARL A. "Psychometric Procedures and the Detection and Exploration of Behavioral Deficits Due to Cerebral Dysfunction in Man." *Can Psychologist* 11(3):239–60 Jl '70. * (*PA* 44:21180)

778. SABATINO, DAVID A., AND HAYDEN, DAVID L. "Information Processing Behaviors Related to Learning Disabilities and Educable Mental Retardation." *Excep Children* 37(1): 21–9 S '70. * (*PA* 46:5527)

779. SABATINO, DAVID A., AND HAYDEN, DAVID L. "Psycho-Educational Study of Selected Behavioral Variables With Children Failing the Elementary Grades." *J Exp Ed* 38(4): 40–57 su '70. * (*PA* 46:5680–1)

780. SABATINO, DAVID A., AND HAYDEN, DAVID L. "Variation in Information Processing Behaviors: As Related to Chronological Age Differences for Children Failing in the Elementary Grades." *J Learn Dis* 3(8):404–12 Ag '70. *

781. SATTLER, JEROME M.; HILLIX, WILLIAM A.; AND NEHER, LINDA A. "Halo Effect in Examiner Scoring of Intelligence Test Responses." *J Consult & Clin Psychol* 34(2): 172–6 Ap '70. * (*PA* 44:10422)

782. SCHOONOVER, SARAH M., AND HERTEL, RICHARD K. "Diagnostic Implications of WISC Scores." *Psychol Rep* 26(3): 967–73 Je '70. * (*PA* 45:956)

783. SCHWARTZ, MELVIN L., AND DENNERLL, RAYMOND D. "Neuropsychological Assessment of Children With, Without, and With Questionable Epileptogenic Dysfunction." *Percept & Motor Skills* 30(1):111–21 F '70. *

784. SCHWEBEL, ANDREW I., AND BERNSTEIN, ANDREW J. "The Effects of Impulsivity on the Performance of Lower-Class Children on Four WISC Tests." *Am J Orthopsychiatry* 40(4): 629–36 Jl '70. * (*PA* 45:7943)

785. SCOTT, RALPH; KELL, E. R.; AND SALISBURY, DONALD L. "Cognitive Profiles of 'Retarded' Children: A Survey of Inter- and Intra-child Differences." *Psychol Sch* 7(3):288–91 Jl '70. * (*PA* 45:4957)

786. SHATSWELL, DAVID WAYNE. *A WISC Profile of the Disabled Reader.* Master's thesis, Chico State College (Chico, Calif.), 1970.

787. SIEGENTHALER, BRUCE M., AND OTHERS. *Factors Related to the Speech-Hearing of Children of Below Normal Intelligence.* An unpublished report to the U.S. Office of Education, Project No. 8-0426, Pennsylvania State University, 1970. Pp. vi, 134. *

788. SILVERSTEIN, A. B. "The Measurement of Intelligence." *Int R Res Mental Retard* 4:193–227 '70. *

789. SILVERSTEIN, A. B. "Reappraisal of the Validity of a Short Short Form of Wechsler's Scales." *Psychol Rep* 26(2): 559–61 Ap '70. * (*PA* 44:20973)

790. SILVERSTEIN, A. B. "Reappraisal of the Validity of WAIS, WISC, and WPPSI Short Forms." *J Consult & Clin Psychol* 34(1):12–4 F '70. * (*PA* 44:5886)

791. SIMPSON, ROBERT L. "Reading Tests Versus Intelligence Tests as Predictors of High School Graduation." *Psychol Sch* 7(4):363–9 O '70. * (*PA* 46:1870)

792. SIMPSON, ROBERT L. "Study of the Comparability of the WISC and the WAIS." *J Consult & Clin Psychol* 34(2): 156–8 Ap '70. * (*PA* 44:10423)

793. SKRIPOL, JAMES N. *Correlation of the Otis-Lennon Intermediate and the Wechsler Intelligence Scale for Children.* Master's thesis, Springfield College (Springfield, Mass.), 1970.

794. SPREEN, OTFRIED, AND TRYK, H. EDWARD. "WISC Information Subtest in a Canadian Population." *Can J Behav Sci* 2(4):294–8 O '70. * (*PA* 45:4258)

795. STEWART, R. R.; WALKER, W.; AND SAVAGE, R. D. "A Developmental Study of Cognitive and Personality Characteristics Associated With Haemolytic Disease of the Newborn." *Develop Med & Child Neurol* 12(1):16–26 F '70. * (*PA* 44:17249)

796. SWANSON, MERLYN S., AND JACOBSON, ANITA. "Evaluation of the S.I.T. for Screening Children With Learning Disabilities." *J Learn Dis* 3(6):318–20 Je '70. *

797. TAYLOR, JOHN F. "Brief Note on Simplified Administration of the Object Assembly Subtest." *J Clin Psychol* 26(2):182 Ap '70. * (*PA* 44:14607)

798. THEYE, FRED W. "Violation of Standard Procedure on Wechsler Scales." *J Clin Psychol* 26(1):70–1 Ja '70. * (*PA* 44:10424)

799. THOMPSON, WILLIAM WARREN. "A Northern Iceland Standardization of the Vocabulary Subtest of the Wechsler Intelligence Scale for Children." *Papers Psychol* 4(1–2):28–30 Ap–O '70. *

800. VOGELSANG, MARCIA P. *The Performance of Culturally Deprived Negro Preschool Children on the Wechsler Preschool*

and Primary Scale of Intelligence. Master's thesis, Texas Woman's University (Denton, Tex.), 1970.

801. WAGNER, EDWIN E. "Results of Psychological Testing on a Child with Gilles De La Tourette's Disease." *J Clin Psychol* 26(1):52–7 Ja '70. * (PA 44:10955)

802. WAGONER, OMER LEON. *The Relation Between Reading Ability and Piaget's Developmental Stages as Determined by WISC Sub-Test Profiles.* Doctor's thesis, University of Michigan (Ann Arbor, Mich.), 1970. (*DAI* 31:3976A)

803. WALKER, KENNETH P., AND GROSS, FREDERICK L. "I.Q. Stability Among Educable Mentally Retarded Children." *Training Sch B* 66(4):181–7 F '70. (PA 44:13185)

804. WARD, BYRON J. "Two Measures of Reading Readiness and First Grade Reading Achievement." *Read Teach* 23(7): 637–9 Ap '70. * (PA 45:3070)

805. WEINBERG, SHEILA, AND RABINOWITZ, JOSHUA. "A Sex Difference in the Wechsler IQ Vocabulary Score as a Predictor of Strategy in a Probability-Learning Task Performed by Adolescents." *Develop Psychol* 3(2): 218–24 S '70. * (PA 44:20696)

806. WILLIS, JERRY. "Group Versus Individual Intelligence Tests in One Sample of Emotionally Disturbed Children." *Psychol Rep* 27(3):819–22 D '70. * (PA 45:10227)

807. WUSSLER, MARILYN, AND BARCLAY, A. "Cerebral Dominance, Psycholinguistic Skills and Reading Disability." *Percept & Motor Skills* 31(2):419–25 O '70. * (PA 45:4015)

DAVID FREIDES, *Associate Professor of Psychology, Emory University, Atlanta, Georgia.*

A twenty-second century museum devoted to intellectual history might include in a display of the beginnings of mental testing, three sets of Wechsler block design materials, from the set borrowed from Kohs (who borrowed from whom?) through the streamlined version found in the *Wechsler Preschool and Primary Scale of Intelligence.* The caption might explain that changes in the materials came about by trial and error and that although not much was known in the twentieth century about what was being measured, psychologists did the best they could and achieved a modicum of practical success.

This fantasy, and the knowledge that it took Wechsler and The Psychological Corporation 28 years and five test editions to simplify the blocks, militates against undue complacency when measuring intelligence. Our methods are quite primitive. We are working with an accumulated lore consisting of procedures that enable us to compare people but not to measure innate qualities or specified skills. The Wechsler tests represent the acme of such pragmatic accumulation.

The appeal of the Wechsler tests lies in their organized diversity. There are separate verbal and performance scales and individual subtests. Clinicians and learning disability specialists consider the pattern of strengths and deficits in formulating treatment plans. There is much art in this process and relatively little science. Research on score patterns has yielded no systematic confirmation and some work, especially on children, has even challenged the verbal-performance distinction. Nonetheless, the prac-

tice of distinguishing between the two persists, apparently because enough practical validation occurs to warrant its continuation in the absence of anything better. On the research side, the issue is certainly not yet settled. There is some evidence, for example, that the verbal and performance scales may be at least a preliminary way of approaching the knotty issue of lateral hemispheric differences in adults.

If we are to deal with present inadequacies in a fundamental way, new measurement concepts must be generated. There is promise of such development emerging from research in developmental psychology, neuropsychology, cognition, and information processing. But genuinely new instruments for general assessment are probably years away, while continuing widespread use of the Wechsler tests can be anticipated over the next two decades. This 21-year-old test is probably more directly instrumental in influencing life decisions on school age children than any other, yet the greatest part of its content was borrowed from a test for adults, Form 2 of the *Wechsler-Bellevue Intelligence Scale.* There is a need for revision and restandardization of the WISC now, and it can be accomplished without major theoretical innovation. Many obvious weaknesses can be corrected while retaining the same format. Since the publishers are planning a revision, due approximately in 1972, some suggestions follow:

a) A test covering age 30 months (the ceiling on the Bayley) to senility is both feasible and desirable. The *Wechsler Adult Intelligence Scale* (ages 16 and up) is now 15 years old and will soon need revising. Combining the accumulated lore from WAIS and WISC with that recently obtained in the standardization of the WPPSI would be most helpful to psychological assessment. There would be special advantages for longitudinal research, large gains in efficiency in educating psychologists and psychometricians, efficiencies in the economics of clinical practice, and technical advances contributing to the assessment of regressive and deficit conditions. Perhaps more importantly, such a test might help obliterate artificial distinctions between childhood and adulthood and would emphasize, instead, the continuity of development that is life but which eludes much clinical thinking.

b) Wechsler emphasizes that an IQ is no more than a score comparing a person with his peers. I wonder how much of his contribution is vitiated when the score attained is interpreted according to the table of intelligence classifications printed in all editions of his tests. The central group in the distribution is designated, appropriately, as average, a term whose meaning is essentially statistical, but adjacent groups are termed dull normal and bright normal. Granted that "normal" has a statistical meaning, it also has many other meanings, and these are frequently invidious and culture bound. Terms with less surplus meaning, possibly dull average and bright average, are much to be preferred.

c) Many of the Comprehension questions in the WISC are clearly inappropriate for children and should be replaced. Since appropriateness has been accomplished in excellent fashion on the WPPSI, it should present no difficulty here. However, care should be taken that revisions do not follow the example of the WAIS, where proverb interpretations were added to Comprehension, thereby mixing concept formation with practical judgment and muddling both.

d) WISC Comprehension also poses a methodological problem of some importance. Several items require the subject to give two correct answers spontaneously for full credit. This penalizes an individual who is content to provide a single answer to a single question while it rewards obsessive and talkative types. It confounds ability with response style. Although opportunity for the assessment of both skill and response style is needed, tests should be structured so that the two can be distinguished. It seems appropriate for intelligence tests to emphasize skill and ability and to de-emphasize response style. Once again, this has been accomplished in the WPPSI, where the examiner is instructed to request an additional response when it is not spontaneously given.

Criteria and procedure must vary from subtest to subtest, depending on what is being measured. For example, Vocabulary should be treated as a recognition task aimed at determining passive familiarity and/or understanding. To this end, the multiple choice synonym or antonym technique used in paper and pencil tests can be adapted to the individual testing situation. Or the method of requesting a definition can be retained with modification of follow-up questioning to get at the issue being assessed. For example, examiners can be allowed to ask for description of an object (How does it look? Describe it.) after the subject indicates that the word refers to the object.

This method contrasts with the noncommittal and awkward "Please explain a little more." (Incidentally, the introductory instruction on Vocabulary, "I want to see how many words you know," should be eliminated. It is threatening, unnecessary, and untrue.)

On the other hand, Similarities or other tests of concept formation might well be judged on the basis of the subject's production of categorizations, rather than merely on the recognition that a category is appropriate. Here the test construction problem is to find a means to be explicit about the level of categorization required for maximum credit. The WISC is imprecise. The question, "In what way are a plum and a peach alike?" is not specific as to the level of response desired. The responses "You eat both" and "Both are fruit" are equally true. It is not known whether a child who gives the former response could or could not have given the latter. Hence, it is not known whether conceptual style or conceptual ability is being assessed.

e) Wechsler's tests are compendia of previously studied materials, and the recent publication of the WPPSI indicates that he is prepared to borrow anew. The Geometric Designs of the WPPSI, borrowed from Bender (who borrowed from Wertheimer who borrowed from whom?), is an excellent choice and should certainly be represented in the WISC and also in the proposed lifetime test. Using scoring considerations and techniques advanced by Graham and Kendall (*Memory-for-Designs Test*), Beery and Buktenica (*Developmental Test of Visual-Motor Integration*), Fuller, (*Minnesota Percepto-Diagnostic Test*), and Koppitz (*Bender-Gestalt Test for Young Children*), it would be possible to devise a test of considerable range, even for adults.

f) The Picture Completion test, though showing up as a significant component of Witkin's field independence factor, is a rather banal and diagnostically unimportant test. I would substitute a test of figure-ground relationships such as the combination of overlapping figures and embedded figures contained in Ayres' *Southern California Figure-Ground Visual Perception Test* (borrowed from Witkin, borrowed from Gottschaldt, borrowed from whom?).

g) The Block Design test always shows up as a valuable assessment tool in both research and clinical work and should be retained, but two different kinds of errors appear at the easier levels: difficulty with spatial orientation and figure-ground confusion. It would be helpful to have more items explicitly designed to challenge each area of functioning.

h) There is no test of memory, verbal or nonverbal, in the Wechsler battery except perhaps the Digit Span. Schafer [1] and those in the Rapaport tradition borrowed the old Babcock-Levy Story Recall for this purpose. All studies indicate that Digit Span is the least reliable of the verbal subtests and in the WISC it was actually excluded from the computation of the norms. Although the Coding, or digit symbol, subtest in the Performance group is at times purported to reflect a memory factor, it is hardly a test of memory. I would suggest that Digit Span be replaced by a meaningful verbal memory test, made up of memory for phrases, sentences, and stories (like the Babcock-Levy or the *Wechsler Memory Scale*); and that Coding be replaced by a nonverbal recognition task involving figural identifications ranging from simple designs to faces.

i) Next to Digit Span, Arithmetic generally shows the least correlation with Verbal IQ. Neurological evidence and factor analysis both indicate independence in verbal and mathematical factors. In practice, results of the Arithmetic test have a nebulous significance. If they are inconsistent with other findings, the data are generally disregarded, perhaps because the test is just a collection of increasingly difficult arithmetical problems with no attention paid to the cognitive operations underlying this function. Pending the development of instruments which get at the structure of mathematical thinking, Arithmetic should be relegated to the status of a supplementary test, used in those instances when there is some special need for data in this area.

j) Wechsler uses Mazes (borrowed from Porteus who borrowed from whom?) as a supplementary test in the WISC and as a main test in the WPPSI. Its administration is somewhat cumbersome, but I favor its retention as a supplementary test on the WISC or the proposed lifetime test. It has a more promising research background (as a measure of planning, attention, and mental control) than many other procedures commonly in use.

k) Order of administration is least boring

---

1 SCHAFER, ROY. *The Clinical Application of Psychological Tests: Diagnostic Summaries and Case Studies.* The Menninger Foundation Monograph Series No. 6. New York: International Universities Press, Inc., 1948. Pp. 346. *

when Verbal and Performance tests are intermixed, as is done in the WPPSI.

l) Culture free tests and tests not favoring one social group over another may not be even theoretically attainable (the mind must grow on something and that, inevitably, is slanted culturally) and certainly will not be available in the near future. However, care can be exercised in the wording of items so as not to confound unduly the variables being measured with social class variables. "Why is it generally better to give money to an organized charity than to a street beggar?" is clearly inappropriate and "to pay bills by check [rather] than by cash" may be unsuitable for many adults, let alone children. Close scrutiny of the questions and careful consultation with experts in the various subcultures of the country is a sine qua non for the next revision.

To conclude, the WISC is currently the best available compendium of individually administered, subject comparison techniques purporting to measure intelligence. The test needs revision and restandardization, and the cumulation of available Wechsler lore should make possible a cradle-to-grave version that would be a real boon to clinical work and research.

R. T. OSBORNE, *Professor of Psychology and Director, Testing and Evaluation Center, The University of Georgia, Athens, Georgia.*

Despite the efforts of some well intentioned but misinformed school administrators, guidance counselors, and legislators to restrict the use of psychological tests in general and of intelligence tests in particular, the WISC has become of age and remains the individual intelligence test of choice for use with children in the 6 to 13 age range. For the WISC just to have survived the last six years in an atmosphere of test burnings, Congressional investigations, restrictive legislation, and claims that the IQ test is an instrument of subtle torture is no small accomplishment. For the WISC to have survived and grown in professional respect lends further support to Burstein's characterization of the WISC in *The Sixth Yearbook* as "a well standardized, stable instrument, correlating well with other tests of intelligence." There is nothing in the WISC literature of over 200 articles published since 1963 to suggest a substantial change in the earlier evaluation.

The four major WISC categories covered by Burstein, (*a*) reliability and validity, (*b*) derivatives of the WISC, including foreign translations, (c) psychopathological applications, and (d) nature and purpose of intelligence testing, will not be reviewed here. The interested reader should refer to *The Sixth Yearbook* and to the over 280 earlier references.

Burstein hopefully predicted that future research with the WISC would involve a broad-gauge application of the scale to total personality variables. In the opinion of this reviewer, Glasser and Zimmerman have made a significant effort to integrate intelligence and concepts of general personality in their manual, *Clinical Interpretations of the Wechsler Intelligence Scale for Children* (509). Using the broad base of 18 years of WISC research and their own clinical experiences, they have delineated certain examiner and child variables not ordinarily considered in the analysis of objective intelligence testing. The authors say "these qualitative factors permit valuable inferences to be drawn and can greatly enhance understanding of the individual child."

Space does not permit the discussion of the application of the WISC to special populations —retarded, blind, dyslexic, gifted, brain damaged, Negro, and other minority groups. Suffice it to say, little new knowledge has been added in these areas since 1963.

There are, however, some new and exciting WISC related investigations which may be of relevance to the growing body of knowledge linking genetics with behavior. Alexander and others,[1] Shaffer (242), and Money (359) have observed a specific cognitive deficit in gonadal aplasia (Turner's Syndrome) which may stem from an organic defect related to the chromosomal anomaly involved. It was noted that women with Turner's Syndrome and persons with lesions of the parietal lobes have similar impairments reflected in specific WISC factor patterns identified by Cohen (148) and confirmed by Osborne (414). There is evidence to suggest that the sex chromosome complement and related sex differences in biochemical processes may underlie sex differences in spatial and numerical abilities.

Both the WISC and WAIS have been used with encouraging results to evaluate electrophysiological correlates of intelligence. Correla-

tions as high as .70 between the Wechsler scales and the visually evoked response have been reported by Osborne,[2] Rhodes (806), and Vogel.[3]

The WISC design and standardization weaknesses recognized in earlier Yearbooks will hopefully be corrected in the revision of the scale tentatively scheduled for 1972. Misuses of the scale apparent to any first-day graduate student are another matter. Unfortunately, the weaknesses of misuse cannot be corrected in the next revision.

The WISC is a stable, general purpose, individual intelligence test and is a useful and valid measure of immediate or present mental functioning.

For a review by Alvin G. Burstein, see 6:540; for reviews by Elizabeth D. Fraser, Gerald R. Patterson, and Albert I. Rabin, see 5:416; for reviews by James M. Anderson, Harold A. Delp, and Boyd R. McCandless, see 4:363 (1 excerpt).

[432]

★[Re Wechsler Intelligence Scale for Children] California Abbreviated WISC. Educable mentally retarded ages 8–13.5, intellectually gifted elementary school children; 1966; CAW-MR, CAW-IG; consists of 5 subtests of *Wechsler Intelligence Scale for Children;* 6 scores: information, picture arrangement, picture completion, block design, coding (Form 1), similarities (Form 2), total; individual; 2 levels: Form 1 (4 pages) for the educable mentally retarded child, Form 2 (4 pages) for the intellectually gifted child; manual (12 pages plus tests); WISC testing materials must be used; $7 per examiner's kit of 10 sets of record booklets and manual; $6.50 per 25 record booklets; $3 per manual; postpaid; (20–30) minutes; Carmen J. Finley and Jack M. Thompson; Western Psychological Services. *

REFERENCE

1. COYLE, F. A., JR., AND BELLAMY, EDWARD E. "Use of the California Abbreviated WISC With Institutionalized Retardates." *Am J Mental Def* 74(4):578 Ja '70. * (PA 44: 11053)

A. B. SILVERSTEIN, *Research Specialist, Pacific State Hospital, Pomona, California.*

Developing short forms of Wechsler's tests has been a popular pastime of psychologists for years, but to the reviewer's knowledge, the CAW is the first of these to be published with a manual and protocol booklets of its own.

The CAW-MR was standardized on a sample of 309 educable mentally retarded children (IQ's 50–80) from California. The data for

1 ALEXANDER, DUANE, AND MONEY, JOHN. "Turner's Syndrome and Gerstmann's Syndrome: Neuropsychologic Comparisons." *Neuropsychologia* 4:265–73 Jl '66. *
ALEXANDER, DUANE; WALKER, H. T., JR.; AND MONEY, JOHN. "Studies in Direction Sense: 1, Turner's Syndrome." *Arch Gen Psychiatry* 10:337–9 Ap '64. *

2 OSBORNE, R. T. "Heritability Estimates for the Visual Evoked Response." *Life Sci* 9(9, pt 2):481–90 My 8 '70. *
3 VOGEL, WILLIAM, AND BROVERMAN, DONALD M. "Relationship Between EEG and Test Intelligence: A Critical Review." *Psychol B* 62:132–44 Ag '64. *

10 WISC subtests (Digit Span and Mazes omitted) were analyzed by the Wherry-Doolittle method, and the combination of five subtests having the highest multiple correlation with the Full Scale (R = .89) was selected. For a second sample, of 173 children, IQ's estimated on the basis of the original regression equation had a correlation of .86 with the IQ's actually obtained.

A similar, but not identical, procedure was used in the case of the CAW-IG, which was standardized on a sample of 400 intellectually gifted children (IQ's 125+), also from California. The same method was used to select the "best" combination of five subtests, but then the subtest scores were simply summed, not differentially weighted. The correlation between estimated and actual IQ's was .75 for the standardization sample, and .84 for a second sample of 151 children.

Even if one accepts the premise that developing a short form of the WISC is a worthwhile endeavor (not everyone would agree), a number of questions can be raised about the proper way of going about it.

How should the test be shortened? The two basic approaches are by reducing the number of subtests and by reducing the number of items within subtests. There is evidence, based on the WISC standardization data, that short forms developed by the second approach have validities—i.e., correlations with the Full Scale—which are comparable to those of short forms comprised of the best combination of five subtests. Moreover, advocates of this second approach point out that it does not sacrifice the variety of functions tapped by the Full Scale. Finley and Thompson cannot be faulted for proceeding as they have, but research is needed to compare the *external* validities of short forms developed by the two approaches.

Should subtest scores be differentially weighted? Most short forms involve only simple summation. Short forms that entail differential weighting will naturally afford something of an advantage, but the gain may not be worth the additional effort required. A re-analysis of the CAW standardization data shows that simple summation would reduce the validity of the CAW-MR by only .01, whereas differential weighting would increase the validity of the CAW-IG by .04. In the light of these findings, it is puzzling that Finley and Thompson elected to employ differential weighting for the CAW-MR and simple summation for the CAW-IG.

What is the appropriate standardization sample for a shortened test? Twenty years ago, McNemar argued convincingly for using the sample on which the test was originally standardized, rather than samples of exceptional children, adult schizophrenics, prisoners, student nurses, etc. For certain purposes, to be sure, it may be desirable to gather local data on special groups, but then one must question the propriety of publishing these data for general use. More specifically, are Finley and Thompson's findings on retarded and gifted children from California generalizable to children in other parts of the country?

How should validity be determined? When scores on a short form and those on the Full Scale are obtained from the same administration of the test, the resulting validity is spuriously high. In effect, this procedure implies that the subtests are all perfectly reliable, since those items passed on the Full Scale must also be passed on the short form. For the WISC standardization sample, the validities of the CAW-MR and the CAW-IG (using simple summation) are .94 and .95, respectively, but when allowance is made for subtest unreliability, the corresponding values drop to .88 and .90. The validities reported by Finley and Thompson would presumably drop similarly if subtest reliability were taken into account.

As alternatives to the CAW, the reviewer would recommend short forms based on available analyses of the WISC standardization data, or possibly short forms based on the analysis of one's own data on subjects of special interest.

[433]

★[Re Wechsler Intelligence Scale for Children] **Rhodes WISC Scatter Profile.** Ages 5-15; 1969; a form for profiling WISC scores; profile (2 pages); manual (4 pages); $4.50 per 50 profiles, postage extra; Fen Rhodes; Educational and Industrial Testing Service. *

[434]

★**Wechsler Preschool and Primary Scale of Intelligence.** Ages 4-6.5; 1967, c1949-67; WPPSI; 8 of the 11 tests provide the same measures as the *Wechsler Intelligence Scale for Children* and approximately ⅓ of the total number of items are essentially the same; 14 scores: verbal (information, vocabulary, arithmetic, similarities, comprehension, sentences-optional, total), performance (animal house, picture completion, mazes, geometric design, block design, total), total; individual; 1 form; manual (139 pages); record form (6 pages); $26 per set of testing materials including 50 geometric design sheets, 25 maze tests, 25 record forms, and manual; $2.50 per 25 record forms; $2.80 per 25 maze tests; $1.50 per 50 design sheets; $3.25 per manual; postage extra; (50–75) minutes; David Wechsler; Psychological Corporation.* (Australian edition: Australian Council for Educational Research.)

REFERENCES

1. SILVERSTEIN, A. B. "A Short Short Form of Wechsler's Scales for Screening Purposes." *Psychol Rep* 21:842 D '67. * (*PA* 42:7335)
2. BACH, LLOYD CARL. *A Comparison of Selected Psychological Tests Used With Trainable Mentally Retarded Children.* Doctor's thesis, University of South Dakota (Vermillion, S.D.), 1968. (*DA* 29:2990A)
3. BONFIELD, JOHN RONALD. *Predictors of Achievement for Educable Mentally Retarded Children.* Doctor's thesis, Pennsylvania State University (University Park, Pa.), 1968. (*DAI* 30:1009A)
4. CAMPANELLA, SAM. *The Validity and Use of the WPPSI in Predicting School Achievement.* Master's thesis, Utah State University (Logan, Utah), 1968.
5. FULLER, BARBARA L. *A Factor Analysis of the Wechsler Pre-School and Primary Scale of Intelligence.* Master's thesis, California State College (Long Beach, Calif.), 1968.
6. HERMAN, DAVID O. "A Study of Sex Differences on the Wechsler Preschool and Primary Scale of Intelligence." Abstract. *Proc 76th Ann Conv Am Psychol Assn* 3:455–6 '68. *
7. KNOLL, DONNA B. *A Comparison of the ABC Inventory and Wechsler Preschool and Primary Scale of Intelligence for Predicting Success in Kindergarten.* Master's thesis, Fort Hays Kansas State College (Hays, Kan.), 1968.
8. MCRAE, J. *A Comparison of the Wechsler Preschool and Primary Scale of Intelligence With the Slosson Intelligence Test.* Master's thesis, Eastern Washington State College (Cheney, Wash.), 1968.
9. PAUL, GERALD THOMAS. *The Relationship Between Prenatal and Perinatal Experiences and Intellectual, Perceptual-Motor, and Conceptual Functioning in Preschool Adopted Children.* Doctor's thesis, Temple University (Philadelphia, Pa.), 1968. (*DAI* 30:1364B)
10. PLANT, WALTER T., AND SOUTHERN, MARA L. "First Grade Reading Achievement Predicted From WPPSI and Other Scores Obtained 18 Months Earlier." Abstract. *Proc 76th Ann Conv Am Psychol Assn* 3:593–4 '68. *
11. RICHARDS, JOHN THOMAS. *The Effectiveness of the Wechsler Preschool and Primary Scale of Intelligence in the Identification of Mentally Retarded Children.* Doctor's thesis, University of Virginia (Charlottesville, Va.), 1968. (*DA* 29:3880A)
12. SILVERSTEIN, A. B. "Validity of a New Approach to the Design of WAIS, WISC, and WPPSI Short Forms." *J Consult & Clin Psychol* 32:478–9 Ag '68. * (*PA* 42:16432)
13. SILVERSTEIN, A. B. "Validity of WPPSI Short Forms." *J Consult & Clin Psychol* 32:229–30 Ap '68. * (*PA* 42:8108)
14. SILVERSTEIN, A. B. "Variance Components in Five Psychological Tests." *Psychol Rep* 23:141–2 Ag '68. * (*PA* 43:6920)
15. SILVERSTEIN, A. B. "WISC and WPPSI IQs for the Gifted." *Psychol Rep* 22:1168 Je '68. * (*PA* 42:1880)
16. SILVERSTEIN, A. B. "WPPSI IQs for the Mentally Retarded." *Am J Mental Def* 73:446 N '68. * (*PA* 43:8602)
17. SMITH, RALPH A. *Abbreviated Forms of the Wechsler Preschool and Primary Scale of Intelligence for a Kindergarten Population.* Master's thesis, Fort Hays Kansas State College (Hays, Kan.), 1968.
18. WHITE, LINDA ANN. *A Comparative Study of the Performance of Negro Head Start Students on the Wechsler Preschool and Primary Scale of Intelligence, the Wechsler Intelligence Scale for Children, and the Stanford-Binet, Form L-M.* Master's thesis, University of Texas (Austin, Tex.), 1968.
19. BARCLAY, ALLAN, AND YATER, ALLAN C. "Comparative Study of the Wechsler Preschool and Primary Scale of Intelligence and the Stanford-Binet Intelligence Scale, Form L-M, Among Culturally Deprived Children." Abstract. *J Consult & Clin Psychol* 33(2):257 Ap '69. * (*PA* 43:9734)
20. BRITTAIN, MICHAEL. "The WPPSI: A Midlands Study." *Brit J Ed Psychol* 39(1):14–7 F '69. * (*PA* 43:17903)
21. BRUDENELL, GERALD ALFRED. *Predicting Achievement of Head Start Children Using Personal, Testing, and Rating Data.* Doctor's thesis, Colorado State College (Greeley, Colo.), 1969. (*DAI* 30:4269A)
22. CURRY, DAL ROY. *The Effect of Two Types of Auditory Discrimination Training on Language Performance and Acquisition in a Culturally Deprived Preschool Population.* Doctor's thesis, University of Kansas (Lawrence, Kan.), 1969. (*DAI* 30:5281A)
23. DIENSTAG, ROBERT. *The Efficacy of the Wechsler Preschool and Primary Scale of Intelligence in Diagnosing Minimal Cerebral Dysfunction.* Master's thesis, California State College (Long Beach, Calif.), 1969.
24. DOKECKI, PAUL R.; FREDE, MARTHA C.; AND GAUTNEY, DONALD B. "Criterion, Construct, and Predictive Validities of the Wechsler Preschool and Primary Scale of Intelligence." Abstract. *Proc 77th Ann Conv Am Psychol Assn* 4(2):505–6 '69. * (*PA* 44:1253)
25. FAGAN, JOEN; BROUGHTON, ELIZABETH; ALLEN, MILDRED; CLARK, BETTY; AND EMERSON, PATRICIA. "Comparison of the Binet and WPPSI With Lower-Class Five-Year-Olds." *J Consult & Clin Psychol* 33(5):607–9 O '69. * (*PA* 44:2135)
26. GARVER, SHERRY A. *A Comparison of the Verbal IQ Scores of the Wechsler Preschool and Primary Scale of Intelligence and the Wechsler Intelligence Scale for Children at the Kindergarten Level.* Master's thesis, Wisconsin State University (River Falls, Wis.), 1969.
27. GOENS, BERT DOUGLAS. *Comparisons of the Wechsler Preschool and Primary Scale of Intelligence With the Wechsler Intelligence Scale for Children.* Master's thesis, Western Michigan University (Kalamazoo, Mich.), 1969. (*Masters Abstracts* 7:119)
28. GREEN, REGINA MIRIAM. *The Relationship of Nutritional States, Performance I.Q. and Self Concept in 4–6 Year Old Inner City Children.* Doctor's thesis, University of Maryland (College Park, Md.), 1969. (*DAI* 31:2085B)
29. KAVAJECZ, LEONARD GARY. *A Study of Results on the Wechsler Preschool and Primary Scale of Intelligence of Inadequate Readers.* Doctor's thesis, Colorado State College (Greeley, Colo.), 1969. (*DAI* 30:4143A)
30. KREBS, ELEONORE GOODLIN. *The Wechsler Preschool and Primary Scale of Intelligence and Prediction of Reading Achievement in First Grade.* Doctor's thesis, Rutgers—The State University (New Brunswick, N.J.), 1969. (*DAI* 30:4279A)
31. LICHTMAN, MARILYN VICKMAN. *Intelligence, Creativity, and Language: An Examination of the Interrelationships of Three Variables Among Preschool, Disadvantaged Negro Children.* Doctor's thesis, George Washington University (Washington, D.C.), 1969. (*DAI* 31:1625A)
32. LIVO, NORMA JOAN. *The Degree of Relationship Among a Number of Readiness Factors and Success in Beginning Reading.* Doctor's thesis, University of Pittsburgh (Pittsburgh, Pa.), 1969. (*DAI* 30:2379A)
33. MCNAMARA, J. REGIS; PORTERFIELD, CHARLES L.; AND MILLER, LAWRENCE E. "The Relationship of the Wechsler Preschool and Primary Scale of Intelligence With the Coloured Progressive Matrices (1956) and the Bender Gestalt Test." *J Clin Psychol* 25(1):65–8 Ja '69. * (*PA* 43:9766)
34. MEEKER, MARY NACOL. *The Structure of Intellect: Its Interpretation and Uses,* pp. 132–46. Columbus, Ohio: Charles E. Merrill Publishing Co., 1969. Pp. xix, 203. *
35. MILLIREN, ALAN P., AND NEWLAND, T. ERNEST. "Statistically Significant Differences Between Subtest Scaled Scores for the WPPSI." *J Sch Psychol* 7(3):16–9 '68–69 ['69]. * (*PA* 44:2188)
36. NASE, ROBERT R. *A Correlation Study of the Harris-Goodenough Draw-A-Man and the Wechsler Preschool and Primary Scale of Intelligence With Children Referred for Psychological Testing.* Master's thesis, Mankato State College (Mankato, Minn.), 1969.
37. RELLAS, ARCHIE J. "The Use of the Wechsler Preschool and Primary Scale (WPPSI) in the Early Identification of Gifted Students." *Calif J Ed Res* 20(3):117–9 My '69. * (*PA* 45:8921)
38. SHIPE, DOROTHY, AND MIEZITIS, SOLVEIGA. "A Pilot Study in the Diagnosis and Remediation of Special Learning Disabilities in Preschool Children." *J Learn Dis* 2(11):579–92 N '69. * (*PA* 46:7521)
39. SILVERSTEIN, A. B. "An Alternative Factor Analytic Solution for Wechsler's Intelligence Scales." *Ed & Psychol Meas* 29(4):763–7 w '69. * (*PA* 44:20972)
40. VINGOE, FRANK J.; BIRNEY, S. DARYL; AND KORDINAK, S. THOMAS. "Note on Psychological Screening of Preschool Children." *Percept & Motor Skills* 29(2):661–2 O '69. * (*PA* 44:4182)
41. YULE, W.; BERGER, M.; BUTLER, S.; NEWHAM, V.; AND TIZARD, J. "The WPPSI: An Empirical Evaluation With a British Sample." *Brit J Ed Psychol* 39(1):1–13 F '69. * (*PA* 43:17914)
42. CUNDICK, BERT P. "Measures of Intelligence on Southwest Indian Students." *J Social Psychol* 81(2):151–6 Ag '70. * (*PA* 44:20655)
43. DELANEY, RICHARD J. *Short Forms of the WPPSI for Screening and Research.* Master's thesis, Loyola University (Chicago, Ill.), 1970.
44. FUTTERER, JAMES W. *An Investigation of the Relationship of the Wechsler Preschool and Primary Scale of Intelligence to the 1960 Revision of the Stanford-Binet Scale, Form L-M.* Master's thesis, Loyola University (Chicago, Ill.), 1970.
45. GRAHAM, GERALDINE AGNES. *The Effects of Material and Social Incentives on the Performance on Intelligence Test Tasks by Lower Class and Middle Class Negro Preschool Children.* Doctor's thesis, George Washington University (Washington, D.C.), 1970. (*DAI* 31:4311B)
46. HANDLEY, WILLIAM B. *A Validity and Reliability Study of the Wechsler Preschool and Primary Scale of Intelligence Using Six Year Old Children.* Master's thesis, University of Saskatchewan (Saskatoon, Sask., Canada), 1970.
47. JONES, ELOISE LORRAINE HARRIS. *The Effects of a Language Development Program on the Psycholinguistic Abili-*

ties and IQ of a Group of Preschool Disadvantaged Children. Doctor's thesis, University of Arkansas (Fayetteville, Ark.), 1970. *(DAI* 31:2761A)

48. NURCOMBE, B., AND MOFFITT, P. "Cultural Deprivation and Language Defect: Project Enrichment of Childhood." *Austral Psychologist* 5(3):249–59 N '70. * *(PA* 46:5744)

49. O'KEEFE, GERALD S. *The Factorial Structure of the Wechsler Preschool and Primary Scale of Intelligence.* Master's thesis, Loyola University (Chicago, Ill.), 1970.

50. RICHARDS, JOHN T. "Internal Consistency of the WPPSI With the Mentally Retarded." *Am J Mental Def* 74(4):581–2 Ja '70. * *(PA* 44:11072)

51. SILVERSTEIN, A. B. "Reappraisal of the Validity of a Short Short Form of Wechsler's Scales." *Psychol Rep* 26(2): 559–61 Ap '70. * *(PA* 44:20973)

52. SILVERSTEIN, A. B. "Reappraisal of the Validity of WAIS, WISC, and WPPSI Short Forms." *J Consult & Clin Psychol* 34(1):12–4 F '70. *

53. TAYLOR, VERA COOK. *An Evaluation of Three Compensatory Education Kindergarten Programs.* Doctor's thesis, University of Southern California (Los Angeles, Calif.), 1970. *(DAI* 31:2749A)

54. WASIK, JOHN L., AND WASIK, BARBARA H. "A Note on Use of the WPPSI in Evaluating Intervention Programs." *Meas & Eval Guid* 3(1):54–6 sp '70. * *(PA* 45:2958)

55. WORKS, MARIAN NEWMAN. *Some Variables Involved in the Reading Process.* Doctor's thesis, University of Oklahoma (Norman, Okla.), 1970. *(DAI* 31:2765AAA)

56. ZIMMERMAN, IRLA LEE, AND WOO-SAM, JAMES. "The Utility of the Wechsler Preschool and Primary Scale of Intelligence in the Public School." *J Clin Psychol* 26(4):472 O '70. * *(PA* 45:6976)

DOROTHY H. EICHORN, *Research Psychologist and Administrator, Child Study Center, Institute of Human Development, University of California, Berkeley, California.*

In composition and in both positive and negative characteristics, the youngest member of the family of Wechsler scales strongly resembles its older siblings. All five of the regular verbal subtests and three of the five performance subtests are downward extensions of like-named subtests of the WISC. The new supplementary verbal test (Sentences) is in lieu of the Digit Span subtest of the WISC and WAIS, and Animal House (one of the two new performance subtests) is analogous to Coding in the older scales. Geometric Design, the other new performance subtest, involves copying forms (circle, square, etc.), an item long popular on tests for young children.

Among the desirable traits of the WPPSI are the usual advantages of point scales over age scales (comparison of an individual only with his age peers, equality of means and standard deviations across ages, less variation in administration time, and avoidance of terminating the test with a long succession of failures), compact and attractive test materials, standardization closely approximating the American Psychological Association standards, and reliabilities satisfactorily high for individual evaluation.

Less satisfactory traits require more extended comment. The only validity data reported in the manual were obtained by administering the WPPSI, *Stanford-Binet Intelligence Scale,*

Peabody Picture Vocabulary Test, and the *Pictorial Test of Intelligence* to 98 children aged 5 to 6 years from a single school district. Although the means of the various tests were all within four points of one another (highest on the S-B), the correlations with the WPPSI Full Scale IQ ranged from .58 (PPVT) to .75 (S-B). Almost all studies appearing since the publication of the manual report higher mean scores on the Stanford-Binet than on the WPPSI (*19, 24, 25, 37*). This direction of the difference was found for culturally disadvantaged as well as advantaged and gifted groups. Correlations between the WPPSI and the S-B were about of the order reported in the WPPSI manual, supporting Wechsler's comment that the tests are not interchangeable. In general, the correlations with the Stanford-Binet are higher for the Verbal than for the Performance IQ of the WPPSI. Correlations of WPPSI IQ's and subtest scores with a number of other tests have also been reported. With the exception of the *SRA Primary Mental Abilities,* correlations were lower than those of the WPPSI with the S-B. Predictive validity, as assessed by later performance on achievement tests, appears to be better for the WPPSI than for the Stanford-Binet, Peabody, Bender-Gestalt, and Draw-a-Person (*10, 24*).

Most of the reliabilities reported in the manual are based on corrected split-half correlations. Odd-even correlations of a comparably high order have been reported for a random sample of 60 5½-year-olds from Nottingham, England (*20*) and 40 mentally retarded children from a clinic in the southern U.S. (*50*). Except for the Animal House subtest, for which reliability was calculated from an immediate retest, the only test-retest reliabilities presented in the manual are correlations of .86, .89, and .92 for the Verbal, Performance, and Full Scales IQ's, respectively, obtained from a sample of 50 children aged about 5½ years and retested after an average of 11 weeks. Substantiation of these estimates, as well as item-rater reliabilities for subtests requiring examiner discretion in scoring, are needed.

A format of subtest scores and separate verbal and performance IQ's offers temptations for overinterpretation. Although factor analyses and analyses of variance components (*14, 24, 39*) contraindicate pattern analysis of subtest scores, they do suggest the existence of two major factors in the WPPSI (as in the WISC and WAIS). Interpretation of Verbal-Performance differences must, however, be tempered by the finding of discrepancies much greater than those observed in the standardization sample by several investigators (*20, 24, 41*).

Queries of experienced examiners and a review of the literature to date on the WPPSI revealed several recurrent complaints. A minor annoyance, also characteristic of the WISC and WAIS, is the use in the vocabulary subtests of words which have homonyms (e.g., fur) or near-homonyms (e.g., gamble). Other irritants are the necessity for interrupting the child after error on the mazes, asking for additional reasons on some items, and the obviousness of failure—all of which were seen as making discomfort for the child. Disconcerting to examiners were the subjectivity of scoring of a number of subtests and changes in materials or directions for administration within subtests. More major complaints concerned the length of the test and limited degree to which it extended the age range downward from the WISC. Although administration time does vary less than that for the Stanford-Binet, many testers find the WPPSI unduly long for preschool children. This problem was not often reported to be serious with children of five years or over, but even for children of this age, needs for rapid screening have precipitated a rash of short forms. Reviewers of the WISC noted its limited sensitivity and discrimination at its lower age limit. This fact and the desirability of having a point scale of intelligence for children younger than five made for eager anticipation of the WPPSI. Unfortunately, it suffers from the same sorts of limitations with respect to age and ability. The youngest age for which norms are given is 3 years, 10 months, 16 days. A child can receive a scaled score greater than zero without passing a single item, and gifted children may earn a sum of scaled scores higher than those for which IQ equivalents are tabled.

In view of the fact that much of the pressure for a downward extension of the WISC arose from programs of early educational intervention, most of which enroll children by at least three years of age, the relatively high "bottom". of the WPPSI and the length of administration time are disappointing restrictions on its utility. On the other hand, some of a generally good thing is better than none. For the age and ability range covered the WPPSI is the best standardized and most up-to-date individual test available.

A. B. SILVERSTEIN, *Research Specialist, Pacific State Hospital, Pomona, California.*

Although it is a separate and distinct test, the WPPSI bears such a strong family resemblance to the WISC that it appears reasonable to appraise the new test by comparing and contrasting it with its older "sibling."

ORGANIZATION. The WPPSI contains 11 subtests, 6 verbal and 5 performance. Except for Sentences, which replaces Digit Span as the supplementary subtest, the names of the verbal subtests are the same as those on the WISC, and they incorporate many of the same items. Modifications in the performance scale are more extensive: Animal House and Geometric Design replace Picture Arrangement, Object Assembly, and Coding, and there is no supplementary subtest, Mazes having been promoted to regular status. These changes are intended to increase the suitability of the test for younger children, and Wechsler suggests that the WPPSI be used in place of the WISC at age levels where the two tests overlap.

STANDARDIZATION. "The WPPSI was standardized on a sample of 100 boys and 100 girls in each of six age groups, ranging by half-years from 4 through 6.5." As with the WISC, the sample was stratified with respect to geographic region, urban-rural residence, and father's occupation, but on the basis of the 1960 census, rather than that of 1940. A noteworthy innovation was the stratification of the WPPSI sample with respect to color (white versus nonwhite). In general, the data reported in the manual support the representativeness of the sample.

ADMINISTRATION AND SCORING. In contrast to the WISC, the WPPSI is administered with the verbal and performance subtests intermixed, a procedure which should facilitate the use of the test with younger children. The examiner is free, however, to change the prescribed order to meet the needs of the testing situation.

The procedures for translating raw scores to scaled scores and converting sums of scaled scores to IQ's are identical to those for the WISC, and the same methods are used to obtain "equivalent MAs" (or "test ages"). Although the scaled scores on both tests have the same means and standard deviations, their possible range on the WPPSI is from 1 to 19, whereas on the WISC it is from 0 to 20. Thus, a child of 4 with a raw score of zero on every subtest should receive a total of 32 scaled score points, and a Full Scale IQ of 51. However, Wechsler recommends that IQ's not be calculated unless a child obtains raw scores greater than zero on at least two verbal and two performance subtests.

As on the WISC, if only four subtests are given on either scale, proration must be used to calculate the IQ's. However, if Sentences is administered in addition to the other verbal subtests, it is *not* used in calculating the IQ's. This represents an improvement over the WISC procedure, where proration is used when six subtests are given on either scale.

PSYCHOMETRIC PROPERTIES. Split-half reliabilities are reported at each age level for every subtest except Animal House, for which test-retest reliabilities are given. (In the WISC manual, reliabilities are reported at only three "representative" age levels.) The average reliabilities of six of the eight subtests which are common to both tests are higher for the WPPSI than for the WISC. The average reliabilities of the Verbal, Performance, and Full Scale IQ's on the WPPSI are .94, .93, and .96, respectively; the corresponding values on the WISC are .94, .88, and .94.

In addition to the reliability data given for the standardization sample, data on stability are reported for an independent sample of 50 children. With a mean retest interval of approximately 11 weeks, the reliabilities of individual subtests ranged from .60 to .93. The reliabilities of the Verbal, Performance, and Full Scale IQ's were .86, .88, and .91, respectively. On almost every subtest, the mean scaled score was higher on the second testing than on the first; the Verbal, Performance, and Full Scale IQ's rose 3.0, 6.6, and 3.6 points, respectively. No comparable data are given in the WISC manual.

Data on the correlations with three other intelligence tests are reported from a special study of 98 children. The correlations between the Full Scale IQ and IQ's on the *Stanford-Binet Intelligence Scale,* the *Peabody Picture Vocabulary Test,* and the *Pictorial Test of Intelligence* were .75, .58, and .64, respectively. The correlation with the Stanford-Binet is in the range usually reported between the WISC and the Stanford-Binet (although again, no comparable data are given in the WISC manual), and, as is also found with the WISC, the Verbal IQ correlated more highly with the

Stanford-Binet than did the Performance IQ. The *greatest* difference between the mean Full Scale IQ and the mean IQ on any of the other three tests was less than 2 points.

One feature of the WPPSI manual which does not appear in the WISC manual is a table showing the critical values of differences between scaled scores on all possible pairs of subtests. A similar table shows the critical values of differences between Verbal and Performance IQ's. Since the manual does not state what interpretations are intended for the scores on individual subtests, or even for the IQ's on the two scales, it is not clear what use the examiner is to make of these data.

SUMMARY. Test users who prefer the WISC to the Stanford-Binet will be pleased to have a highly similar test designed especially for use with younger children. Those who prefer the Stanford-Binet to the WISC will presumably see no reason to switch to the WPPSI.

J Ed Meas 5:347–8 w '68. O. A. Oldridge and E. E. Allison. * An improvement over the WISC in the norms and hence usefulness of the WPPSI results from the inclusion of non-whites (14%) in the standardization sample. This seems particularly important since extensive use will be made of this instrument in the assessment of the mental ability of non-whites in pre-school situations. * The WPPSI, like the WISC, appears to suffer from inadequate floor to differentiate abilities at the lower end of the scale. A four-year-old making no correct responses would obtain a Verbal I.Q. of 56, Performance I.Q. of 57, and Full-Scale I.Q. of 53. Although the manual's recommendation that no I.Q.'s be computed unless the child obtains a raw score greater than zero on two of the Verbal tests and two of the Performance tests, its usefulness for differentiating among the moderately to severely retarded is absent. The manual suggests the tests may be too difficult for four-year-olds with I.Q.'s below 75. This rules out 5% of the four-year-old population (as reported in Table 6) and would seem to cast considerable doubt upon the test's value for this group of children at a very critical point. This deficiency would have been avoided if a few more very easy items had been included in each subtest. Verbal-Performance and subtest differences necessary for significance at the 15% level of confidence are included to reduce the common tendency toward type-I errors in interpretation. Since the common minimum acceptable confidence levels are 5% and 1%, it would have been valuable to have included subtest difference values for those levels. The manual reports that obtained differences of approximately three points (one standard deviation) between scaled scores on any pair of tests are significant at the 15% level, but a difference of at least 4 is needed to be significant at the 5% level and slightly more than 5 to be significant at the 1% level. The manual gives extensive reliability figures. Odd-even reliability coefficients appear to be quite substantial for the Verbal (.89 to .90), Performance (.84 to .91), and Full-Scale I.Q.'s (.92 to .94) but somewhat less so for the subtest scores (.62 to .88). These values are inflated to the extent that certain pupils could correctly answer items after the cut-off criterion had been reached for each subtest. No data are given as to whether the cut-off criteria were determined empirically or intuitively. The inclusions of retest reliabilities is a helpful addition. Stability coefficients over a three month period for fifty five-year-olds were .86, .89, and .92 for Verbal, Performance, and Full-Scale I.Q. scores, respectively. The subtest reliabilities were considerably lower, with ten of the eleven yielding coefficients of less than .8, five of these below .7, suggesting that the cut-off scoring did not result in inflated odd-even reliability coefficients for the subtests. The reliability of the Verbal, Performance, and Full-Scale I.Q.'s are satisfactory, but the subtests are not sufficiently stable to be of much value for individual use. McNemar's (1956, p. 127) statement regarding the WAIS is also relevant to the WPPSI: "....the author of the WAIS has attempted an impossible task; the construction of a scale to measure general (global) intelligence which at the same time will provide differences among subtests which are of a diagnostic value." Only the global objective appears to be well-achieved. Valuable concurrent validity data are also included which show the expected substantial relationship (r = .76) between the WPPSI-Verbal and the Stanford-Binet (Form L-M) for approximately 100 five- to six-year-olds. The less-than-normal variability (S = 12.8) for this sample makes the estimate conservative. The long administration time necessary for some children is also a concern to the reviewers. In many cases, especially with the younger or with "handicapped" children, the test requires two sessions. The ex-

tent to which this break affects the normative data and thus affects the validity of the results is uncertain; the manual only states that some children will need two sessions for the test. In the standardization sample it was found that about 10% of those tested needed one and one-half hours or more to complete the test. Summary: The WPPSI is a carefully developed and well standardized instrument of general intelligence that warrants widespread acceptance, although the value of subtest scores for individual use remains yet to be established.

Psychol Rep 21:1029 D '67. C. H. Ammons. * items are interesting and materials are satisfactorily sturdy * The sample of 600 boys and 600 girls seems adequately controlled for obvious factors judging from the data presented in the manual. Reliability estimates range from .71 to .94 depending on the subtest and age group, but SE_m varies sufficiently to require caution in comparing profiles of groups or points within profiles. * *Much* research is called for as the variance of WPPSI scores is not currently adequately accounted for. Tabled summaries and score equivalents in the manual will be useful in that undertaking as well as in clinical assessments.

SPECIFIC

[435]

*Closure Flexibility (Concealed Figures).** Industrial employees; 1956-65; CF; revision of *Gottschaldt Figures;* formerly called *Concealed Figures: A Test of Flexibility of Closure;* Form A ('56, 8 pages); manual ('65, 20 pages, identical—including norms—with manual published in 1963); norms for males only; $4 per 20 tests, postage extra; $2 per specimen set, postpaid; 10(15) minutes; L. L. Thurstone (test), T. E. Jeffrey (test), and Manpower Research and Development Division, Industrial Relations Center, University of Chicago (manual); the Center. *

REFERENCES

1-4. See 6:545.
5. UHLMANN, FRANK WALTER. *Retention of Anxiety Material as a Function of Cognitive Style.* Doctor's thesis, Wayne State University (Detroit, Mich.), 1962. (*DA* 28:5196B)
6. DAUGHERTY, ROBERT ALTON. *Perceiving One's Own Performance Level as a Function of Cognitive Control and Motivation.* Doctor's thesis, Wayne State University (Detroit, Mich.), 1963. (*DA* 29:405B)
7. LEWIN, PAUL B. *Validity of Thurstone's Test of Closure Flexibility to Predict Student Teaching Effectiveness.* Master's thesis, East Tennessee State University (Johnson City, Tenn.), 1966.
8. MANGAN, GORDON L. "Studies of the Relationship Between Neo-Pavlovian Properties of Higher Nervous Activity and Western Personality Dimensions: 4, A Factor Analytic Study of Extraversion and Flexibility, and the Sensitivity and Mobility of the Nervous System." *J Exp Res Personality* 2:124-7 My '67. * (*PA* 41:11908)
9. OHNMACHT, FRED W. "Factorial Invariance of the Teacher Characteristics Schedule and Measures of Two Cognitive Styles." *J Psychol* 69:193-9 Jl '68. * (*PA* 42:15472)
10. STEINMETZ, ANDRÉS. *Perceptual Style and Response to*

Single Concept Science Films. Doctor's thesis, Indiana University (Bloomington, Ind.), 1968. (*DAI* 30:504A)

11. BAEHR, MELANY E.; FURCON, JOHN E.; AND FROEMEL, ERNEST C. *Psychological Assessment of Patrolman Qualifications in Relation to Field Performance.* Washington, D.C.: United States Government Printing Office, 1969. Pp. vii, 246. *

12. GARDNER, RILEY W., AND LOHRENZ, LEANDER J. "Some Old and New Group Tests for the Study of Cognitive Controls and Intellectual Abilities." *Percept & Motor Skills* 29(3):935–50 D '69. * (*PA* 46:4981)

13. SCHEIBNER, RUTH MARTIN. *Field Dependence-Independence as a Basic Variable in the Measurement of Interest and Personality.* Doctor's thesis, Temple University (Philadelphia, Pa.), 1969. (*DAI* 30:3375B)

For a review by Leona E. Tyler, see 6:545.

[436]

*Closure Speed (Gestalt Completion). Industrial employees; 1956–66; formerly called *Gestalt Completion: A Test of Speed of Closure;* Form A ('56, 3 pages); revised manual ('66, 18 pages); norms for males only; $3 per 20 tests, postage extra; $2 per specimen set, postpaid; 3(8) minutes; L. L. Thurstone (test), T. E. Jeffrey (test), and Norman J. Kantor (manual); Industrial Relations Center, University of Chicago. *

REFERENCES

1–3. See 6:546.

4. BAEHR, MELANY E.; FURCON, JOHN E.; AND FROEMEL, ERNEST C. *Psychological Assessment of Patrolman Qualifications in Relation to Field Performance.* Washington, D.C.: United States Government Printing Office, 1969. Pp. vii, 246. *

5. SANDERS, JAY W., AND COSCARELLI, JANET E. "The Relationship of Visual Synthesis Skill to Lipreading." *Am Ann Deaf* 115(1):23–6 Ja '70. * (*PA* 44:10988)

For a review by Leona E. Tyler, see 6:546.

[437]

★Concept Assessment Kit—Conservation. Ages 4–7; 1968; CAKC; individual; 2 tests; manual (16 pages plus record forms); $23.50 per kit of testing materials, 1 copy of each record form, and manual; $1.25 per manual; postage extra; Marcel L. Goldschmid and Peter M. Bentler; Educational and Industrial Testing Service. *

a) FORMS A AND B. 13 scores: 2 scores (behavior, explanation) in each of 6 areas (2-dimensional space, number, substance, continuous quantity, weight, discontinuous quantity), total; Forms A, B, (4 pages); $4 per 25 record forms; (15–20) minutes.

b) FORM C. 13 scores: 2 scores (behavior, explanation) in area (3 scores) and length (3 scores), total; Form C (2 pages); $3.50 per 25 record forms; (10–15) minutes.

REFERENCES

1. GOLDSCHMID, MARCEL L. "Different Types of Conservation and Nonconservation and Their Relation to Age, Sex, IQ, MA, and Vocabulary." *Child Develop* 38:1229–46 D '67. * (*PA* 42:7086)

2. GOLDSCHMID, MARCEL L. "The Relation of Conservation to Emotional and Environmental Aspects of Development." *Child Develop* 39:579–89 Je '68. *

3. GOLDSCHMID, MARCEL L., AND BENTLER, P. M. "The Dimensions and Measurement of Conservation." *Child Develop* 39:787–802 S '68. * (*PA* 43:3774)

4. BAKER, EUGENE AUSTIN. *Conservation and Two Related Cognitive Functions.* Doctor's thesis, University of Missouri (Columbia, Mo.), 1970. (*DAI* 31:4965B)

5. BENTLER, P. M. "Evidence Regarding Stages in the Development of Conservation." *Percept & Motor Skills* 31(3):855–9 D '70. * (*PA* 45:9648)

J. DOUGLAS AYERS, *Professor of Education, University of Victoria, Victoria, British Columbia, Canada.*

The *Concept Assessment Kit—Conservation* is designed to assess young children's attainment of the principles involved in comprehending conservation. As such, it is a type of intelligence test, limited to a narrow age range and to conservation tasks and excluding such other important Piagetian concepts as seriation, classification, and transitivity. As with all Piagetian scales, the focus is on measuring optimal performance of the process aspect of intelligence rather than maximum performance of the content component (e.g., number of synonyms recognized).

Forms A and B are parallel tests composed of a series of tasks that present the child with two objects or sets of objects that are the same with respect to amount of matter of a given type: particled material (discontinuous quantity), plastic material (substance), blocks of solid material (two-dimensional space), liquid (continuous quantity), pieces (number), and weight. In Form C the objects are the same with respect to length or area. One object or set of objects is then changed spatially or in shape and the child is asked, e.g., "Is there as much corn in *this* glass as in *that* one, or does one have more in it?" If the child answers "the same," he gets one point for behavior. He is then asked "Why?" to measure comprehension. An adequate explanation adds another point for that task.

The three forms were determined primarily by multidimensional homogeneity scaling of an initial battery consisting of three to seven tasks representing each of 10 types of conservation. The battery, containing 44 behavior items and 43 explanation items, was administered in two 45-minute sessions to 142 children in kindergarten, first, and second grades. Three dimensions, or factors, emerged for explanation. A general dimension, amount of matter, included the six types of conservation in the two parallel forms, A and B. Form C was composed of two minor dimensions, length and area.

That the six types of conservation in Forms A and B are unidimensional is not surprising. Five of the tasks obviously involve conservation of amount or quantity. The sixth task, weight conservation, as used in Forms A and B, involves balls of Playdoh of the same amount as well as same weight, making a quantity interpretation possible.

In addition to dimensionality, other criteria governing final selection of tasks for the scales are reported as high internal consistency, reliability, and between-forms reliability. Because all statistics are based on the complete range of grades, they are spuriously high, but it might be argued that no real harm is done except to give an unrealistic impression of the characteristics of the tryout battery. This would be true if the tryout were used only for item selection, but most of the reliability and validity data reported in the manual are based on the initial tryout and not on the final scales. Also, several of the tables fail to indicate that the data are based on the tryouts and the discussion implies that Forms A, B, and C are separate entities and not purely hypothetical tests that require cross-validation. The manual also fails to report that the content of several of the tasks was changed between the tryout and the final scales.

The manual states that norms are based on 560 children tested individually with either Forms A and C, or B and C, from 20 schools, day care centers, and Head Start centers in the Los Angeles area. The schools were selected to represent the entire spectrum of socioeconomic status and race, but the sample is said to be biased slightly toward lower-middle-class children. The only norms reported are percentile ranks, and these, together with means and standard deviations, are provided for a confusing variety of age ranges. But for the critical ages $5\frac{1}{2}$ to $7\frac{1}{2}$, the norms for Forms A and B are based on too few children, approximately 75 of each sex for each form. Also, there is no mention of the limitations of percentile ranks and the dangers of overinterpretation. Despite the higher reported reliability, the standard error is $1\frac{1}{4}$ points on a 12-item test.

The data also reveal that the test is difficult for children below age $6\frac{1}{2}$. For example, in the $5\frac{1}{2}$ to $6\frac{1}{2}$ age range, the expected chance score on Form A is equivalent to a percentile rank of 69, and in the 4 to $5\frac{1}{2}$ age range, in which the percentile norms are the same for each half-year age, the expected chance score on Form A is equivalent to a percentile rank of 94. To administer these scales routinely to children under the age of $5\frac{1}{2}$, when only two or three percent will obtain a score of 4 in 12, is futile. The normative data, as well as general experience, indicate that the age range should be $5\frac{1}{2}$ to $7\frac{1}{2}$, rather than the recommended 4 to 7.

For a test of 12 items at these grade levels the K-R 20, parallel-form, and retest reliabilities are very high, typically .94 or .95, but they are based on a three-grade spread instead of single age groups.

Content validity was established by multi-dimensional homogeneity scaling of the tryout battery and was confirmed in the standardization. Adequate predictive and concurrent validity data are also provided.

The authors are to be commended for developing a record form that contains all of the essential directions in a very convenient format. The directions for each task are separated into five columns: pictorial illustration, specific procedures, verbal instructions and questions, recording of responses, and score. Such a format is very efficient because the examiner quickly learns the procedures but has the verbal instructions and questions column as a guide for uniform administration. He is further assisted by the italicizing and indenting of each instruction and question. Two other points warrant approval. Because the correct answer to all conservation questions is "the same," the authors have included two tasks that require a "more" answer, in order to ensure that there will be no response set. Also, in agreement with research findings, manipulation of materials by children is minimized.

The authors have diligently pursued procedures that would ensure uniform administration, yet the question remains, have they established psychometric standardization? For example, there has been little or no attempt to control the situational variables, particularly form and style of questioning and comprehension of instructions. In traditional testing, understanding of directions is controlled by sample and practice exercises, especially with unfamiliar tasks and in the primary grades. It would seem essential to provide the equivalent for Piagetian tasks. This criticism is aimed not only at this instrument, but at nearly all Piagetian measurement procedures. Administering Piagetian tasks in a uniform fashion does not necessarily ensure standardization in the psychometric sense.

The authors have apparently given considerable thought to the questioning techniques; the critical question for each task uses the phrase "as much _____," rather than the more usual, "Is there the same amount of _____, or ...." The new wording may be preferable, particularly for inexperienced administrators, as there is no chance of indicating the correct answer by inflection. On the other hand, it precludes the use of the more precise term "amount." The effect of these and other variations in wording may be minimal, especially with older children, but because each task is really measured with a single item, it is essential that conditions be such as to ensure optimal performance. As yet, very little research has been done on the effects of varying questioning techniques with Piagetian tasks.

There are also several specific criticisms of the questioning techniques. For two-dimensional space and for number tasks, the children are asked if the amounts in the two objects are the same to begin with, but in all other tasks they are told that the amounts are the same. The former would seem to be preferable because it eliminates extra verbiage and does not suggest the answer. There is also no apparent reason for including extraneous running commentary, such as, "See, I am making this ball into a hotdog." This can only tend to make conditions less standard.

In summary, the authors have assembled three scales that have clear directions; attractive, well-organized format; together with considerable data on homogeneity, reliability, and validity. However, they have failed to provide essential details of test development and to include cautionary statements regarding norms and their interpretation.

As this is a first-of-its-kind instrument, measuring a single Piagetian task in the 4 to 7 age range (this reviewer, however, recommends that its use be limited to ages 5½ to 7½), and as our knowledge of measurement techniques in this area is not fully developed, the *Concept Assessment Kit—Conservation* must be considered essentially experimental.

J Ed Meas 6(4):263–6 w '69. Rheta DeVries and Lawrence Kohlberg. * is directed toward providing a measure of conservation as an indicator of cognitive change from the prelogical mode of thought to the concrete operational mode which Piaget found to occur roughly at about age seven or eight years. * In summary, effort aimed toward providing test materials and procedures for assessment of qualitative aspects of intellectual functions which differ from the traditional psychometrically assessed functions is to be applauded. However, it must be cautioned that the Concept Assessment Kit—Conservation provides only a limited measure of conservation and cannot be used alone to establish the presence of concrete operational thought. While it may be a desirable goal to de-

part from Piaget's clinical method of assessing the presence of conservation and to develop a more standardized technique, the challenge lies in preserving the opportunity for expression of subtleties in thinking which frequently do not appear with more limited procedures. The inclusion of standard probes and ceiling-level items would help to make the instrument under review less equivocal on individual assessment. If the realization of the goal of a satisfactory standardized measure of Piagetian cognitive development is possible at all, continued research is necessary to establish just how much and what kind of test procedures constitute a minimal requirement. [See original review for critical comments not excerpted.]

J Ed Meas 6(4):266–9 w '69. Vernon C. Hall and Michael Mery. * The tasks involving types of conservation are taken from a specific theory (Piaget's), but the procedures, scoring, and even the purpose of the test (as understood by the present authors) seem unrelated to this theory. * In many ways, then, the test resembles the conventional intelligence test which was noted by Goldschmid and Bentler as inappropriate, *i.e.*, numerical scores which give no obvious indication as to how they came about. The general issue, as we see it, is how to specify the abilities required to conserve and the assessment techniques, including criteria, which follow from that specification. In any future revision of the test under review, we would suggest incorporating many diverse procedures in the attempt to provide sufficient *standardized* data of a diagnostic nature in order to attempt to specify the subject's (or subjects') developmental level in terms of Piagetian theory. Such procedures might include counter-suggestion, extinction, standardized probing, etc. We would also suggest changing the scoring procedure. As the test now stands, one point is given for a correct answer and one for a correct explanation regardless of the skill the item is testing. This leads to problems in interpreting a score based upon, for example, different combinations of correct answers across tasks and/or correct items and explanations combined within and across tasks. As is the case with most intelligence tests, it is difficult to determine how a subtest or a combined score was achieved. Another issue in current conservation research concerns the antecedents necessary for conservation to take place. It is probably not reasonable to expect a child to conserve successfully without first determining whether he knows the adult meaning of important terms, *e.g.*, same, different, longer, etc. It is also important that we learn more about the relationship between meaning of these terms for children and conservation behavior * Goldschmid and Bentler recognize this difficulty as seen by their suggestion that *S*s under four years of age not be given the test because "part of the difficulty appears to be related to the children's lack of understanding of relational terms such as 'more' or 'same.'" In their procedures, however, they simply have the Examiner state the relationship between the objects rather than assessing the *S*s' use of relevant terms. We would prefer to see such an assessment as an integral part of the instrument. Turning to item format we find problems which in themselves might serve to influence results. We would think that including items which begin with different amounts as well as the same amount (included in the test to guard against a response set of saying "same" every time) should be included in all types of conservation assessed. Part of being a conserver is to understand that if two objects originally have different amounts of "something," changing an irrelevant dimension does not change this relationship. Finally, the verbal instructions remain constant throughout the test. In all questions the ending phrase is "or does one have more?" By varying this wording across items, it would have been possible to determine if the subject was being led by the experimenter and in what way. Additional problems tend to follow from the general issues already discussed. For instance, why are item difficulties based on a total sample of different aged subjects relevant? Why did the authors include correlations between academic achievement and total test scores? Although the correlations are substantial, a Piagetian would neither be surprised nor view the information as particularly relevant. In summary, we view the attempt at standardizing procedures in conservation research as being laudable. We feel, however, that such an instrument must recognize that measurement procedures are influenced by the purpose for which they are going to be used. We have raised only a few of what we feel to be important issues in the validation of Piaget's theory in general and conservation specifically which should influence measurement procedures. Goldschmid and Bentler seemingly did not find these issues sufficiently important

and thus will probably find limited circulation for their test. [See original review for critical comments not excerpted.]

Prof Psychol 1(5):491–3 f '70. Charles D. Smock. * provides, at best, a limited measure of conservation. It is not recommended to establish either the presence of generalized concrete operational thought nor for conservation in a particular content area. The Kit can be very useful in providing the novice an opportunity to gain experience in the Piagetian approach and the demonstration of the subtleties involved in children's thinking. However, the realization of the goal for standardized measure of an important aspect of cognitive development à la Piaget will require a more thorough analytical and empirical inquiry into the theory and the invention of procedures that constitute minimal requirements for testing that theory.

[438]

★**Fret Continuation Test, I.B.P. Edition 1968.** Semiliterate adults; 1966–69; perceptual analysis; no reading by examinees; 1 form ('66, 14 pages); manual ('69, 17 pages, English and Venda); no data on validity; R3.60 per 25 tests; 16c per single copy; R2 per manual; postpaid within South Africa; (25–30) minutes; G. V. Grant (manual); National Institute for Personnel Research. *

[439]

★**Fret Repetition Test, I.B.P. Edition 1968.** Illiterate adults; 1966–69; perceptual analysis; 1 form ('66, 16 pages); manual ('69, 16 pages, English and Venda); no data on validity; R4 per 25 tests; 16c per single copy; R2 per manual; postpaid within South Africa; (20–25) minutes; G. V. Grant (manual); National Institute for Personnel Research. *

[440]

*****Hidden Figures Test.** Grades 6–16; 1962–63; HFT; for research use only; flexibility of closure; 2 tests; no data on reliability and validity; no norms; cash orders postpaid; Educational Testing Service. *
a) FORM CF-1. 1962–63; 1 form ('62, 5 pages); no specific manual; combined manual ('63, 126 pages) for this and other tests in 6:551; 20¢ per test; $2.40 per manual; 20(25) minutes; manual by John W. French, Ruth B. Ekstrom, and Leighton B. Price.
b) FORM 5. 1962; 1 form (33 pages); no manual; 75¢ per test; scoring key not available; 10(15) minutes.

REFERENCES

1. RICHARDS, JAMES M., JR.; CLINE, VICTOR B.; AND NEEDHAM, WALTER E. "Creativity Tests and Teacher and Self Judgments of Originality." *J Exp Ed* 32:281–5 sp '64. * (*PA* 39:5135)
2. ANDERSON, C. C., AND CROPLEY, A. J. "Some Correlates of Originality." *Austral J Psychol* 18:218–27 D '66. * (*PA* 41:4572)
3. BECKERLE, GERALD PAUL. *Behavioral Traits Related to Psychological Differentiation in Pre-Adolescent Boys.* Doctor's thesis, Michigan State University (East Lansing, Mich.), 1966. (*DA* 28:336B)
4. CROPLEY, A. J. "Creativity and Intelligence." *Brit J Ed Psychol* 36:259–66 N '66. * (*PA* 41:5˜3)
5. ACKER, MARY BRYANT. *The Relation of Achievement Need, Time Perspective, and Field Articulation to Academic Performance.* Doctor's thesis, University of California (Berkeley, Calif.), 1967. (*DA* 29:1492B)
6. BRIGHAM, BRUCE W. *A Study of the Reading Achievement and Certain Characteristics of Adult Males Convicted of*

Felonies. Doctor's thesis, Temple University (Philadelphia, Pa.), 1967. (*DA* 28:4279B)

7. CROPLEY, A. J. "Creativity, Intelligence, and Achievement." *Alberta J Ed Res* 13:51–8 Mr '67. * (*PA* 41:15253)

8. DAVIS, JON KENT. *Concept Identification as a Function of Cognitive Style, Complexity, and Training Procedures.* Doctor's thesis, University of Wisconsin (Madison, Wis.), 1967. (*DA* 28:4476A)

9. FREDRICK, WAYNE CLARENCE. *Information Processing and Concept Learning at Grades Six, Eight, and Ten as a Function of Cognitive Styles.* Doctor's thesis, University of Wisconsin (Madison, Wis.), 1967. (*DA* 28:4478A)

10. BARRETT, GERALD V.; CABE, PATRICK A.; AND THORNTON, CARL L. "Relation Between Hidden Figures Test and Rod and Frame Test Measures of Perceptual Style." *Ed & Psychol Meas* 28:551–4 su '68. * (*PA* 42:18139)

11. BOERSMA, FREDERIC J. "Test-Retest Reliability of the Cf-1 Hidden Figures Test." *Ed & Psychol Meas* 28:555–9 su '68. * (*PA* 42:18083)

12. BRYAN, VINCENT. *The Experimental Induction of Stress in Relation to Field Articulation.* Doctor's thesis, Yeshiva University (New York, N.Y.), 1968. (*DAI* 30:1354B)

13. FARR, ROBERTA SIEGEL. *Personality Variables and Problem Solving Performance: An Investigation of the Relationships Between Field-Dependence-Independence, Sex-Role Identification, Problem Difficulty and Problem Solving Performance.* Doctor's thesis, New York University (New York, N.Y.), 1968. (*DA* 29:2561A)

14. WERBEL, STEPHEN A. *Response to Loss and Its Relation to Personality Measures.* Doctor's thesis, University of Kansas (Lawrence, Kan.), 1968. (*DA* 29:2213B)

15. BARRETT, GERALD V.; THORNTON, CARL L.; AND CABE, PATRICK A. "Relation Between Embedded Figures Test Performance and Simulator Behavior." *J Appl Psychol* 53(3):253–4 Je '69. * (*PA* 43:11980)

16. BARTELT, CLAUDIA ANN. *The Relation Between Field Articulation, Locus of Control and Subjective Probability of Success.* Doctor's thesis, University of California (Berkeley, Calif.), 1969. (*DAI* 31:1571A)

17. BRINTON, GEORGE, AND ROULEAU, ROBERT A. "Automating the Hidden and Embedded Figures Tests." *Percept & Motor Skills* 29(2):401–2 O '69. * (*PA* 44:3652)

18. CONKLIN, R. C., AND ZINGLE, H. W. "Counsellor Sensitivity and Cognitive Style." *West Psychologist* 1(1):19–28 S '69. * (*PA* 45:8948)

19. DUVALL, NANCY SHERMAN. *Field Articulation and the Repression-Sensitization Dimension in Perception and Memory.* Doctor's thesis, University of North Carolina (Chapel Hill, N.C.), 1969. (*DAI* 30:3864B)

20. ERGINEL, ADNAN. *The Relation of Cognitive Style and Intelligence to Achievement and Errors in Thinking.* Doctor's thesis, Lehigh University (Bethlehem, Pa.), 1969. (*DAI* 31:216A)

21. HUCKABEE, MALCOM W. "Personality and Academic Aptitude Correlates of Cognitive Control Principles." *South J Ed Res* 3(1):1–9 Ja '69. *

22. TITUS, H. EDWIN. "Prediction of Supervisory Success by Use of Standard Psychological Tests." *J Psychol* 72(1):35–40 My '69. * (*PA* 43:16503)

23. BARRETT, GERALD V.; THORNTON, CARL L.; AND CABE, PATRICK A. "Cue Conflict Related to Perceptual Style." *J Appl Psychol* 54(3):258–64 Je '70. * (*PA* 44:11696)

24. CREGO, CLYDE A. "A Pattern Analytic Approach to the Measure of Modes of Expression of Psychological Differentiation." *J Abn Psychol* 76(2):194–8 O '70. * (*PA* 45:4277)

25. DAVIS, J. KENT, AND KLAUSMEIER, HERBERT J. "Cognitive Style and Concept Identification as a Function of Complexity and Training Procedures." *J Ed Psychol* 61(6):423–30 D '70. * (*PA* 45:7431)

26. GRUENFELD, LEOPOLD W., AND WEISSENBERG, PETER. "Field Independence and Articulation of Sources of Job Satisfaction." *J Appl Psychol* 54(5):424–6 O '70. * (*PA* 45:3159)

27. KAZELSKIS, RICHARD. "Field Independence and the Free-Recall of Nonsense Syllables." *Percept & Motor Skills* 31(2):351–4 O '70. * (*PA* 45:6317)

28. McWHINNIE, HAROLD J. "A Third Study of Some Relationships Between Creativity and Perception in 6th Grade Children." *Calif J Ed Res* 21(1):35–42 Ja '70. *

29. MAUSNER, BERNARD, AND GRAHAM, JUDITH. "Field Dependence and Prior Reinforcement as Determinants of Social Interaction in Judgment." *J Pers & Social Psychol* 16(3):486–93 N '70. * (*PA* 45:4127)

30. OHNMACHT, FRED W.; WEAVER, WENDELL W.; AND KOHLER, EMMETT T. "Cloze and Closure: A Factorial Study." *J Psychol* 74(2):205–17 Mr '70. * (*PA* 44:12542)

31. SHARP, ELIZABETH YERXA. *The Relationship of Visual Closure to Speechreading Among Deaf Children.* Doctor's thesis, University of Arizona (Tucson, Ariz.), 1970. (*DAI* 31:2198A)

[441]

★**Higgins-Wertman Test: Threshold of Visual Closure.** Ages 5–15; 1968; manual title is *Visual Closure Assessment;* 6 scores: initial closure, final closure, number of responses prior to final closure (whole

and detail), perseveration, impotence; Forms 1, 2, (23 scales in separate 14–22 page booklets, 11 scales per form plus alternate scale); mimeographed manual (139 pages); $65 per set of both forms; $5.25 per 25 record blanks of each form; $7.50 per manual; postpaid; (30) minutes; Conwell Higgins and Howard Wertman; Higgins-Wertman Associates. *

REFERENCE

1. RUSCH, REUBEN R. "Reliability of the Higgins-Wertman Test of Visual Closure." *Percept & Motor Skills* 30(3):879–85 Je '70. * (*PA* 44:17513)

[442]

Illinois Test of Psycholinguistic Abilities, Revised Edition. Ages 2–10; 1961–68; ITPA; 11–13 scores: auditory reception, visual reception, visual sequential memory, auditory association, auditory sequential memory, visual association, visual closure, verbal expression, grammatic closure, manual expression, auditory closure (optional), sound blending (optional), total; individual; 1 form ('68); manual ('68, 134 pages); record form ['68, 16 pages]; visual closure picture strips ['68, 5 pages]; $43.50 per set of testing materials, carrying case, 25 record forms, and 25 sets of picture strips; $7.75 per 25 record forms and sets of picture strips; $5.75 per manual; cash orders from individuals; (45–60) minutes; Samuel A. Kirk, James J. McCarthy, and Winifred D. Kirk; University of Illinois Press. *

REFERENCES

1–22. See 6:549.

23. OLSON, JAMES L. "Deaf and Sensory Aphasic Children." *Excep Children* 27:422–4 Ap '61. * (*PA* 36:4JD220)

24. BATEMAN, BARBARA DEE. *Reading and Psycholinguistic Processes of Partially Sighted Children.* Doctor's thesis, University of Illinois (Urbana, Ill.), 1962. (*DA* 23:2416)

25. KASS, CORRINE EVELYN. *Some Psychological Correlates of Severe Reading Disability (Dyslexia).* Doctor's thesis, University of Illinois (Urbana, Ill.), 1962. (*DA* 23:2421)

26. SMITH, JAMES OTTO. *Effects of a Group Language Development Program Upon the Psycholinguistic Abilities of Educable Mental Retardates.* Doctor's thesis, George Peabody College for Teachers (Nashville, Tenn.), 1962. (*DA* 23:3821)

27. BATEMAN, BARBARA D. *Reading and Psycholinguistic Processes of Partially Seeing Children.* CEC Research Monograph, Series A, No. 5. Washington, D.C.: Council for Exceptional Children, National Education Association, 1963. Pp. v, 46. *

28. FERRIER, ELMER EARL. *An Investigation of Psycholinguistic Factors Associated With Functional Defects of Articulation.* Doctor's thesis, University of Illinois (Urbana, Ill.), 1963. (*DA* 25:290)

29. HAMLIN, CAROLYN S. *A Study Using the Illinois Test of Psycholinguistic Abilities in the Determination of the Language Abilities of Hearing Impaired Children.* Master's thesis, University of Kansas (Lawrence, Kan.), 1963.

30. McCARTHY, JAMES J., AND KIRK, SAMUEL A. *The Construction, Standardization and Statistical Characteristics of the Illinois Test of Psycholinguistic Abilities.* [Urbana, Ill.: University of Illinois Press], 1963. Pp. vii, 90. *

31. MIRON, MURRAY S. Appendix B, "A Psycholinguistic Analysis of Some Frequently Used Tests for Aphasia," pp. 176–99. In *Approaches to the Study of Aphasia: A Report of an Interdisciplinary Conference on Aphasia.* Edited by Charles E. Osgood and Murray S. Miron. Urbana, Ill.: University of Illinois Press, 1963. Pp. vii, 210. * (*PA* 38:4504)

32. MUELLER, MAX W. "Peabody College Research on the Illinois Test of Psycholinguistic Abilities," pp. 183–7. In *Selected Convention Papers: 41st Annual CEC Convention, Philadelphia, Pennsylvania, 1963.* Washington, D.C.: Council for Exceptional Children, National Education Association, [1963]. Pp. iv, 235. *

33. BLESSING, KENNETH RICHARD. *An Investigation of a Psycholinguistic Deficit in Educable Mentally Retarded Children: Detection, Remediation and Related Variables.* Doctor's thesis, University of Wisconsin (Madison, Wis.), 1964. (*DA* 25:2372)

34. CARR, DONALD LEE. *The Concept Formation and Psycholinguistic Abilities of Normal and Mentally Retarded Children of Comparable Mental Age.* Doctor's thesis, State University of Iowa (Iowa City, Iowa), 1964. (*DA* 25:997)

35. GUNZBURG. H. C. "The Reliability of a Test of Psycholinguistic Abilities (I.T.P.A.) in a Population of Young Male Subnormals." *J Mental Subnorm* 10:101–12 D '64. * (*PA* 39:10116)

36. HASTEROK, GERALD S. "The Training of Mentally Re-

tarded Children With Sense Modality Disabilities," pp. 128–31. In *Inspection and Introspection of Special Education*. Selected Convention Papers, 42nd Annual CEC Convention, 1964. Washington, D.C.: Council for Exceptional Children, [1964]. Pp. v, 288. *

37. KENNEY, ELEANORE T. "The Small Classroom—A Developmental Idiosyncratic Approach to Learning and Behavioral Disorders in Children of Normal Intelligence," pp. 208–16. In *Inspection and Introspection of Special Education*. Selected Convention Papers, 42nd Annual CEC Convention, 1964. Washington, D.C.: Council for Exceptional Children, [1964]. Pp. v, 288. *

38. MCCARTHY, JAMES J. "The Importance of Linguistic Ability in the Mentally Retarded." *Mental Retard* 2:90–6 Ap '64. *

39. MCCARTHY, JAMES J. "The Use and Usefulness of the ITPA," pp. 195–202. In *Inspection and Introspection of Special Education*. Selected Convention Papers, 42nd Annual CEC Convention, 1964. Washington, D.C.: Council for Exceptional Children, [1964]. Pp. v, 288. *

40. MCCARTHY, JAMES J., AND OLSON, JAMES L. *Validity Studies on the Illinois Test of Psycholinguistic Abilities*. [Urbana, Ill.: University of Illinois Press], 1964. Pp. viii, 106. *

41. MCLEOD, J. "The Search for Measurable Intellectual Causes of Reading Disability." *Slow Learning Child* 11:80–94 Jl '64. * (*PA* 39:16413)

42. MUELLER, MAX W. "Comparison of Psycholinguistic Patterns of Gifted and Retarded Children," pp. 143–9. In *Inspection and Introspection of Special Education*. Selected Convention Papers, 42nd Annual CEC Convention, 1964. Washington, D.C.: Council for Exceptional Children, [1964]. Pp. v, 288. *

43. MUELLER, MAX W. "Language Profiles of Mentally Retarded Children," pp. 149–53. In *Inspection and Introspection of Special Education*. Selected Convention Papers, 42nd Annual CEC Convention, 1964. Washington, D.C.: Council for Exceptional Children, [1964]. Pp. v, 288. *

44. MUELLER, MAX W., AND WEAVER, S. JOSEPH. "Psycholinguistic Abilities of Institutionalized and Non-Institutionalized Trainable Mental Retardates." *Am J Mental Def* 68:775–83 My '64. * (*PA* 39:2529)

45. OUTRIDGE, MARGARET. "Psycholinguistic Abilities of Five Children Attending Baroona Opportunity School." *Spec Sch B* 6:8–21 My '64. *

46. RAGLAND, GILBERT GRAY. *The Performance of Educable Mentally Handicapped Students of Differing Reading Ability on the Illinois Test of Psycholinguistic Abilities*. Doctor's thesis, University of Virginia (Charlottesville, Va.), 1964. (*DA* 25:3407)

47. RAYNOR, JUDITH E. *Effect of an Immediate Visual Memory Factor in the Visual Decoding Subtest of the Illinois Test of Psycholinguistic Abilities*. Master's thesis, University of Washington (Seattle, Wash.), 1964.

48. STRUNK, DEFOREST LIVINGSTON, II. *An Analysis of the Psycholinguistic Abilities of a Selected Group of Mongoloids*. Doctor's thesis, University of Virginia (Charlottesville, Va.), 1964. (*DA* 26:203) (Abstract: *Ed R* 3:46–8)

49. WELSH, JOAN B. *Differences in Language Performance as Measured by the Illinois Test of Psycholinguistic Abilities Among Groups of Children With Severe Language Disorders: Deaf Children and Brain Injured Deaf Children*. Master's thesis, University of Pittsburgh (Pittsburgh, Pa.), 1964.

50. WISEMAN, DOUGLAS E. "Program Planning for Retarded Children With Psycholinguistic Abilities," pp. 241–52. In *Inspection and Introspection of Special Education*. Selected Convention Papers, 42nd Annual CEC Convention, 1964. Washington, D.C.: Council for Exceptional Children, [1964]. Pp. v, 288. *

51. BATEMAN, BARBARA. *The Illinois Test of Psycholinguistic Abilities in Current Research: Summary of Studies*. [Urbana, Ill.: University of Illinois Press], 1965. Pp. iii, 43. *

52. BATEMAN, BARBARA. "The Role of the ITPA in Differential Diagnosis and Program Planning for Mentally Retarded." *Am J Orthopsychiatry* 35:465–72 Ap '65. * (*PA* 39:10088)

53. BATEMAN, BARBARA, AND WETHERELL, JANIS. "Psycholinguistic Aspects of Mental Retardation." *Mental Retard* 3:8–13 Ap '65. * (*PA* 39:10569)

54. BILOVSKY, DAVID, AND SHORE, JACK. "The ITPA and Down's Syndrome: An Exploratory Study." *Am J Mental Def* 70:78–82 Jl '65. * (*PA* 39:16042)

55. ENSMINGER, E. EUGENE, AND SMITH, JAMES O. "Language Development and the ITPA." *Training Sch B* 62:97–107 N '65. * (*PA* 40:3301)

56. ESPESETH, VERNON KNUTE. *An Investigation of Visual Sequential Memory in the Deaf Child*. Doctor's thesis, University of Wisconsin (Madison, Wis.), 1965. (*DA* 26:5288)

57. FORD, JUNE BROOKS. *Identification of a Specific Language Disability (Dyslexia)*. Doctor's thesis, University of Oklahoma (Norman, Okla.), 1965. (*DA* 26:1827)

58. GRAUBARD, PAUL STUART. *Psycholinguistic Correlates of Reading Disability in Disturbed Children*. Doctor's thesis, Yeshiva University (New York, N.Y.), 1965. (*DA* 26:3172)

59. HARRIES, W. T. *The Illinois Test of Psycholinguistic Abilities (ITPA): An Appraisal*. Australian Council for Educational Research, Memorandum No. 1. Victoria, Australia: the Council, January 1965. Pp. ii, 19. *

60. MCCARTHY, JAMES J. "Notes on the Validity of the ITPA." *Mental Retard* 3:25–6 Ap '65. * (*PA* 39:10139)

61. MCCARTHY, JEANNE MCRAE. *Patterns of Psycholinguistic Development of Mongoloid and Non-Mongoloid Severely Retarded Children*. Doctor's thesis, University of Illinois (Urbana, Ill.), 1965. (*DA* 26:872)

62. MCLEOD, JOHN. *Some Psychological and Psycholinguistic Aspects of Severe Reading Disability in Children*. Doctor's thesis, University of Queensland (Brisbane, Australia), 1965.

63. MILLS, ESTHER BROWNELL. *Relationships Between Psycholinguistic Abilities of Educable Mentally Retarded Pupils and the Effectiveness of Four Instructional Approaches in the Language Arts*. Doctor's thesis, University of Maryland (College Park, Md.), 1965. (*DA* 27:145A)

64. MUELLER, MAX W. "Comparison of Psycholinguistic Patterns of Gifted and Retarded Children." *J Sch Psychol* 3:18–25 sp '65. * (*PA* 39:15126)

65. MUELLER, MAX W. *A Comparison of the Empirical Validity of Six Tests of Ability With Young Educable Retardates*. Institute of Mental Retardation and Intellectual Development, IMRID Behavioral Science Monograph No. 1. Nashville, Tenn.: Peabody College Bookstore, 1965. Pp. vii, 130. *

66. MUELLER, MAX WILLIAM. *A Comparison of the Empirical Validity of Six Tests of Ability With Educable Mental Retardates*. Doctor's thesis, George Peabody College for Teachers (Nashville, Tenn.), 1965. (*DA* 26:6853)

67. MYERS, PATRICIA. "A Study of Language Disabilities in Cerebral Palsied Children." *J Speech & Hearing Res* 8:129–36 Je '65. * (*PA* 39:15127)

68. OLSON, JAMES L.; HAHN, HANS R.; AND HERMANN, ANITA L. "Psycholinguistic Curriculum." *Mental Retard* 3:14–9 Ap '65. *

69. OUTRIDGE, MARGARET. "Psycholinguistic Abilities of Five Children Attending a Brisbane Opportunity School." *Slow Learning Child* 11:165–74 Mr '65. * (*PA* 39:12997)

70. PURKHISER, CAROL ANNE. *A Comparative Investigation of the Verbal Behavior and Psycholinguistic Abilities of a Group of Hydrocephalic Children and Their Matched Controls*. Doctor's thesis, Northwestern University (Evanston, Ill.), 1965. (*DA* 26:3538)

71. RADUS, LIBBY. *Dysphasia: Musical Perception as a Stimulus in Communication*. Doctor's thesis, University of Florida (Gainesville, Fla.), 1965. (*DA* 26:6230)

72. RANTUCCI, DORIS A. *A Correlation Study of the Visual and Auditory Subtests of the Detroit Tests of Learning Aptitudes With the Illinois Tests of Psycholinguistic Abilities*. Master's thesis, University of Kansas (Lawrence, Kan.), 1965.

73. STRONG, ROBERT THOMAS, JR. *The Identification of Primary School Age Children With Learning Handicaps Associated With Minimal Brain Disorder*. Doctor's thesis, University of Utah (Salt Lake City, Utah), 1965. (*DA* 26:1489)

74. VEST, MARY LOU R. *The Determination of Some Variables Which Are Related to the Auditory Decoding Subtest of the Illinois Test of Psycholinguistic Abilities*. Master's thesis, University of Kansas (Lawrence, Kan.), 1965.

75. WISEMAN, DOUGLAS EDMUND. *The Effects of an Individualized Remedial Program on Mentally Retarded Children With Psycholinguistic Disabilities*. Doctor's thesis, University of Illinois (Urbana, Ill.), 1965. (*DA* 26:5143)

76. BATEMAN, BARBARA. "The Application of Language and Communication Models in Programs for the Trainable Retarded," pp. 45–9. In *Special Education: Strategies for Educational Progress*. Selected Convention Papers, 44th Annual CEC Convention, 1966. Washington, D.C.: Council for Exceptional Children, [1966]. Pp. viii, 259. *

77. BRADLEY, BETTY HUNT; MAURER, RUTH; AND HUNDZIAK, MARCEL. "A Study of the Effectiveness of Milieu Therapy and Language Training for the Mentally Retarded." *Excep Children* 33:143–50 N '66. * (*PA* 41:1824)

78. CRIPE, ANTJE G., AND WILSON, BETTY ANN. "Auditory and Visual Learning Related to ITPA Sensory Channels," pp. 153–6. In *Special Education: Strategies for Educational Progress*. Selected Convention Papers, 44th Annual CEC Convention, 1966. Washington, D.C.: Council for Exceptional Children, [1966]. Pp. viii, 259. *

79. CRIPE, ANTJE GREEN. *Auditory and Visual Learning Related to ITPA Sensory Channels*. Doctor's thesis, Purdue University (Lafayette, Ind.), 1966. (*DA* 27:635B)

80. DILLON, EDWARD JOSEPH. *An Investigation of Basic Psycholinguistic and Reading Abilities Among the Cerebral Palsied*. Doctor's thesis, Temple University (Philadelphia, Pa.), 1966. (*DA* 27:949A)

81. EGELAND, BYRON RICKER. *The Relationship of Intelligence, Visual-Motor Skills and Psycholinguistic Abilities With Achievement in the First Grade*. Doctor's thesis, University of Iowa (Iowa City, Iowa), 1966. (*DA* 27:388A)

82. FERRIER, E. E. "An Investigation of the ITPA Performance of Children With Functional Defects of Articulation." *Excep Children* 32:625–9 My '66. * (*PA* 40:7992)

83. GENTILE, J. RONALD. "In Search of Research: Four Children's Tests." *J Sch Psychol* 5:1–13 au '66. * (*PA* 41:3335)

84. HART, N. W. M.; SEARLE, E. B.; AND PHILLIPS, B. "The Use of I.T.P.A. and an Associated Language Program

With Partially Sighted Children." *Spec Sch B* 8:16–24 Ag '66. *

85. HORNER, RALPH D. *A Comparison of the Illinois Test of Psycholinguistic Abilities and the Parsons Language Sample in Assessing the Linguistic Abilities of Institutionalized Mentally Retarded Children.* Master's thesis, Kansas State College (Pittsburg, Kan.), 1966.

86. JOHNSON, GLEN BROOKS. *A Comparison of Scores Earned by Certain Groups of Residential School Deaf Children and the Standardization Sample of the Illinois Test of Psycholinguistic Abilities on Four Selected Subtests.* Doctor's thesis, University of Oregon (Eugene, Ore.), 1966. (*DA* 27:3723A)

87. KASS, CORRINE E. "Psycholinguistic Disabilities of Children With Reading Problems." *Excep Children* 32:533–9 Ap '66. * (*PA* 40:6515)

88. KIRK, SAMUEL A. *The Diagnosis and Remediation of Psycholinguistic Disabilities.* Urbana, Ill.: University of Illinois Press, 1966. Pp. x, 250. *

89. KIRK, SAMUEL A., AND MCLEOD, JOHN. "Research Studies in Psycholinguistic Disabilities," pp. 173–84. In *Special Education: Strategies for Educational Progress.* Selected Convention Papers, 44th Annual CEC Convention, 1966. Washington, D.C.: Council for Exceptional Children, [1966]. Pp. viii, 259. *

90. MCLEOD, JOHN. "Psychological and Psycholinguistic Aspects of Severe Reading Disability in Children: Some Experimental Studies." *Ann Inter Conf Assn Children Learn Dis* 3:186–205 '66. *

91. PAINTER, GENEVIEVE. "The Effect of a Rhythmic and Sensory Motor Activity Program on Perceptual Motor Spatial Abilities of Kindergarten Children." *Excep Children* 33:113–6 O '66. * (*PA* 41:800)

92. RAGLAND, GILBERT. "Performance of Educable Mentally Handicapped Students of Differing Reading Ability on the ITPA," pp. 69–72. In *Special Education: Strategies for Educational Progress.* Selected Convention Papers, 44th Annual CEC Convention, 1966. Washington, D.C.: Council for Exceptional Children, [1966]. Pp. viii, 259. *

93. ROBERTS, LAURENCE H. *A Study of the Value of the American Council on Education Psychological Examinations for Predicting Student Achievement in an Independent School.* Master's thesis, Trinity College (Hartford, Conn.), 1966.

94. SPICKER, HOWARD H. "The Remediation of Language Deficiencies of Educable Mentally Retarded Children." *Ed & Train Mental Retard* 1:137–40 O '66. *

95. STARK, JOEL. "Performance of Aphasic Children on the ITPA." *Excep Children* 33:153–8 N '66. * (*PA* 41:1203)

96. STEARNS, KEITH EUGENE. *Experimental Group Language Development for Psycho-Socially Deprived Preschool Children.* Doctor's thesis, Indiana University (Bloomington, Ind.), 1966. (*DA* 27:2078A)

97. SUMNER, JOSEPH WILLIAM. *A Comparison of Some Psycholinguistic Abilities of Educable Mentally Retarded Readers and Non-Readers.* Doctor's thesis, University of North Carolina (Chapel Hill, N.C.), 1966. (*DA* 27:2411A)

98. SWEARENGEN, MARY-B MOSLEY. *The Psycholinguistic Abilities of Beginning First-Grade Children and Their Relationship to Reading Achievement.* Doctor's thesis, University of New Mexico (Albuquerque, N.M.), 1966. (*DA* 27:1808A)

99. TUBBS, VIRGINIA K. "Types of Linguistic Disability in Psychotic Children." *J Mental Def Res* 10:230–40 S '66. * (*PA* 41:4792)

100. WEBER, MARYLOU ADAM. *The Motor Behavior Characteristics of Children With Operant Language Disorder.* Doctor's thesis, University of Arizona (Tucson, Ariz.), 1966. (*DA* 27:2381A)

101. ANDERSON, GLADYS L., AND MAGARY, JAMES F. "The Illinois Test of Psycholinguistic Abilities and the School Psychologist," pp. 342–54. In *School Psychological Services: In Theory and Practice: A Handbook.* Edited by James F. Magary. Englewood Cliffs, N.J.: Prentice Hall, Inc., 1967. Pp. xxi, 774. *

102. BATEMAN, BARBARA. "A Reference Line for Use With the ITPA." *J Sch Psychol* 5:128–35 w '67. * (*PA* 41:8715)

103. BROWN, LOUIS F., AND RICE, JAMES A. "Psycholinguistic Differentiation of Low IQ Children." *Mental Retard* 5:16–20 F '67. * (*PA* 41:7730)

104. CANNON, BONNIE G. *A Comparative Study of ITPA Verbal Scores With the Verbal Behavior of Children in a Child-Child Interaction.* Master's thesis, Utah State University (Logan, Utah), 1967.

105. CARR, DONALD L.; BROWN, LOUIS F.; AND RICE, JAMES A. "The PPVT in the Assessment of Language Deficits." *Am J Mental Def* 71:937–40 My '67. * (*PA* 41:11915)

106. CAWLEY, JOHN F. "Psycholinguistic Characteristics of Preschool Children." *Training Sch B* 64:95–101 N '67. * (*PA* 42:5385)

107. DICKSON, STANLEY. "Clinical Judgement of Language Delay and ITPA Measurements." *J Commun Disorders* 1:35–40 My '67. * (*PA* 41:17014)

108. DOBSON, JAMES CLAYTON, JR. *Intellectual and Linguistic Development in Treated and Untreated Phenylketonuric Children.* Doctor's thesis, University of Southern California (Los Angeles, Calif.), 1967. (*DA* 28:1294A)

109. FROSTIG, MARIANNE. "Testing as a Basis for Educational Therapy." *J Spec Ed* 2:15–34 f '67. * (*PA* 42:7770)

110. GRAUBARD, PAUL S. "Psycholinguistic Correlates of Reading Disability in Disturbed Delinquent Children." *J Spec Ed* 1:363–8 su '67. * (*PA* 42:4503)

111. GRAUBARD, PAUL S. "The Use of the Peabody Picture Vocabulary Test in the Prediction and Assessment of Reading Disability in Disturbed Children." *J Ed Res* 61:3–5 S '67. *

112. HAMALUK, OREST J. *The Effectiveness of the Illinois Test of Psycholinguistic Abilities in Predicting Reading Achievement.* Master's thesis, University of Alberta (Edmonton, Alta., Canada), 1967.

113. HIRSHOREN, ALFRED. *The Prognostic and Diagnostic Utility and the Stability of the Illinois Test of Psycholinguistic Abilities.* Doctor's thesis, University of Illinois (Urbana, Ill.), 1967. (*DA* 28:3026A)

114. HORNER, R. DON. "A Factor Analysis Comparison of the ITPA and PLS With Mentally Retarded Children." *Excep Children* 34:183–9 N '67. * (*PA* 42:9359)

115. HUEFTLE, M. KEENE. *A Factor Analytic Study of the Frostig Developmental Test of Visual Perception, the Illinois Test of Psycholinguistic Abilities, and the Wechsler Intelligence Scale for Children.* Doctor's thesis, Colorado State College (Greeley, Colo.), 1967. (*DA* 28:2139B)

116. KING, JOHN D., AND MASAT, LARRY J. "Implications of the Illinois Test of Psycholinguistic Abilities for Teachers of Educable Mentally Retarded Children." *Ed & Train Mental Retard* 2:107–11 O '67. *

117. MCLEOD, JOHN. "Some Perceptual Factors Related to Childhood Dyslexia." *Slow Learning Child* 14:5–12 Jl '67. * (*PA* 42:569)

118. MCLEOD, JOHN. "Some Psycholinguistic Correlates of Reading Disability in Young Children." *Read Res Q* 2:5–31 sp '67. * (*PA* 41:11883)

119. MATHEWS, PAULA R. *A Study of the Concurrent and Diagnostic Validity of the Illinois Test of Psycholinguistic Abilities.* Master's thesis, Utah State University (Logan, Utah), 1967.

120. MESSINEO, JOSEPH F. *The Environmental Utilization of Psycholinguistic Abilities of Disadvantaged Slow Learners in Relation to the Ecology of Test Intelligence.* Doctor's thesis, University of Rochester (Rochester, N.Y.), 1967. (*DA* 28:4006A)

121. MINSKOFF, JOSEPH GERALD. *A Psycholinguistic Approach to Remediation With the Retarded-Disturbed.* Doctor's thesis, Yeshiva University (New York, N.Y.), 1967. (*DA* 28:1625A)

122. MITCHELL, RUTH SMITH. *A Study of the Effects of Specific Language Training on Psycholinguistic Scores of Headstart Pupils.* Doctor's thesis, Florida State University (Tallahassee, Fla.), 1967. (*DA* 28:1709A)

123. NELSON, CHARLES DONALD. *Comparison of Sensory Modality Differences in Children With Communication Disorders.* Doctor's thesis, University of Washington (Seattle, Wash.), 1967. (*DA* 28:1921A)

124. QUERESHI, MOHAMMED Y. "Patterns of Psycholinguistic Development During Early and Middle Childhood." *Ed & Psychol Meas* 27:353–65 su '67. * (*PA* 41:13420)

125. RECHNER, JOAN, AND WILSON, BETTY ANN. "Relation of Speech Sound Discrimination and Selected Language Skills." *J Commun Disorders* 1:26–30 My '67. * (*PA* 41:16658)

126. RICE, JAMES A. "The ITPA: A Note on Critical Evaluations." Letter. *Excep Children* 34:71–2 S '67. *

127. ROBERTS, THOMAS GENE. *An Investigation of Language Abilities and Their Relation to School Achievement in Educable Mentally Retarded Children.* Doctor's thesis, University of North Carolina (Chapel Hill, N.C.), 1967. (*DA* 28:3037A)

128. SCHWARTZ, SOL; DEUTSCH, CYNTHIA P.; AND WEISSMANN, ANN. "Language Development in Two Groups of Socially Disadvantaged Young Children." *Psychol Rep* 21:169–78 Ag '67. * (*PA* 42:2381)

129. SEELYE, BARBARA JANE. *An Investigation of Language Development in Non-Institutionalized Mentally Retarded Children.* Doctor's thesis, University of Denver (Denver, Colo.), 1967. (*DA* 28:821A)

130. SILVERSTEIN, A. B. "Variance Components in the Illinois Test of Psycholinguistic Abilities." *Percept & Motor Skills* 24:1315–6 Je '67. * (*PA* 41:14455)

131. SMITH, HERBERT W., AND MAY, W. THEODORE. "Individual Differences Among Inexperienced Psychological Examiners." *Psychol Rep* 20:759–62 Je '67. * (*PA* 41:13601)

132. SMITH, HERBERT W., AND MAY, W. THEODORE. "Influence of the Examiner on the ITPA Scores of Negro Children." *Psychol Rep* 20:499–502 Ap '67. * (*PA* 41:8862)

133. SMITH, PETER BARKER, JR. *A Description of the Language Abilities of Institutionalized Phenylketonuric Individuals in the States of Washington, Oregon, Idaho, and Montana.* Doctor's thesis, University of Washington (Seattle, Wash.), 1967. (*DA* 28:3917B)

134. STARK, JOEL. "A Comparison of the Performance of Aphasic Children on Three Sequencing Tests." *J Commun Disorders* 1:31–4 My '67. * (*PA* 41:17016)

135. TOBACK, CHARLES. *Speech Intelligibility of Congenitally Deaf Children as Related to Intelligence and Language Ability.* Doctor's thesis, New York University (New York, N.Y.), 1967. (*DA* 28:4395A)

136. WARDEN, PAUL G. *The Validity of the Illinois Test of*

Psycholinguistic Abilities as a Predictor of Academic Achievement of First Grade Students. Master's thesis, Kent State University (Kent, Ohio), 1967.

137. WEAVER, ANN SULLIVAN. *The Prediction of First Grade Reading Achievement in Culturally Disadvantaged Children.* Doctor's thesis, George Peabody College for Teachers (Nashville, Tenn.), 1967. *(DA* 28:3789A)

138. WEAVER, S. JOSEPH, AND WEAVER, ANN. "Psycholinguistic Abilities of Culturally Deprived Negro Children." *Am J Mental Def* 72:190–7 S '67. * *(PA* 42:2536)

139. WEENER, PAUL; BARRITT, LOREN S.; AND SEMMEL, MELVYN I. "A Critical Evaluation of the Illinois Test of Psycholinguistic Abilities," pp. 373–80. Response by James J. McCarthy, pp. 380–2. Reply by authors, pp. 382–4. *Excep Children* 33:373–84 F '67. * *(PA* 41:5282, 41:5278, 41:5283)

140. WISLAND, MILTON V., AND MANY, WESLEY. "A Study of the Stability of the Illinois Test of Psycholinguistic Abilities." *Ed & Psychol Meas* 27:367–70 su '67. * *(PA* 41:12844)

141. BACH, LLOYD CARL. *A Comparison of Selected Psychological Tests Used With Trainable Mentally Retarded Children.* Doctor's thesis, University of South Dakota (Vermillion, S.D.), 1968. *(DA* 29:2990A)

142. BATEMAN, BARBARA. "The Efficacy of an Auditory and a Visual Method of First Grade Reading Instruction With Auditory and Visual Learners." *Proc Ann Conv Int Read Assn* 12(4):105–12 '68. *

143. BATEMAN, BARBARA. *Interpretation of the 1961 Illinois Test of Psycholinguistic Abilities: With Reproductions of Original Profiles.* Seattle, Wash.: Special Child Publications, 1968. Pp. 108. *

144. BATTIN, R., AND KRAFT, IRVIN A. "Psycholinguistic Evaluation of Children Referred for Private Consultation to a Child Psychiatrist." *J Learn Dis* 1:600–5 O '68. * *(PA* 45:2995)

145. BLOUNT, WILLIAM R. "Language and the More Severely Retarded: A Review." *Am J Mental Def* 73:21–9 Jl '68. * *(PA* 42:19171)

146. BONFIELD, JOHN RONALD. *Predictors of Achievement for Educable Mentally Retarded Children.* Doctor's thesis, Pennsylvania State University (University Park, Pa.), 1968. *(DAI* 30:1009A)

147. COHEN, LINDA. *Performance of Cleft Palate Children on the Illinois Test of Psycholinguistic Abilities.* Master's thesis, Queens College (Flushing, N.Y.), 1968.

148. ETIENNE, JERALD FRANCIS. *The Relationship Between Language and Employment of Caucasian, Negroid, and Spanish-American Male Educable Mentally Retarded Adults.* Doctor's thesis, Colorado State College (Greeley, Colo.), 1968. *(DA* 29:1037A)

149. FOX, FRANK HEWITT. *A Description of Language and Perceptual Function of Culturally Deprived Children.* Doctor's thesis, University of Wisconsin (Madison, Wis.), 1968. *(DA* 29:4323A)

150. FROSTIG, MARIANNE. "Testing as a Basis for Educational Therapy," pp. 64–86. In *Assessment of the Cerebral Palsied Child for Education.* Edited by James Loring. London: William Heinemann Ltd., 1968. Pp. vii, 112. *

151. FROSTIG, MARIANNE, AND MASLOW, PHYLLIS. "Language Training: A Form of Ability Training." *J Learn Dis* 1:105–15 F '68. * *(PA* 44:5680)

152. GATES, MAXINE FULLER. *A Comparison of the Learning Characteristics of Hyperactive and Hypoactive Children With Related Central Nervous System Dysfunctions.* Doctor's thesis, Ohio State University (Columbus, Ohio), 1968. *(DAI* 30:166A)

153. GELHART, ROBERT PRESTON. *Auditory Discrimination in the Educable Mentally Retarded.* Doctor's thesis, University of Southern California (Los Angeles, Calif.), 1968. *(DA* 29:833A)

154. GENTILE, LOUIS ANDREW. *An Investigation of the Relationship Between the Reflective-Impulsivity Cognitive Dimension and Psycholinguistic Abilities.* Doctor's thesis, University of Maryland (College Park, Md.), 1968. *(DA* 29:1449A)

155. HEPBURN, ANDREW WATSON. *The Performance of Normal Children of Differing Reading Ability on the Illinois Test of Psycholinguistic Abilities.* Doctor's thesis, University of Minnesota (Minneapolis, Minn.), 1968. *(DA* 29:2116A)

156. HURLEY, OLIVER L. "Perceptual Integration and Reading Problems." *Excep Children* 35:207–15 N '68. * *(PA* 43:13365)

157. JOYNT, DENIS, AND CAMBOURNE, BRIAN. "Psycholinguistic Development and the Control of Behaviour." *Brit J Ed Psychol* 38:249–60 N '68. * *(PA* 43:6747)

158. KASS, CORRINE E. "The Psycholinguistic Abilities of Retarded Readers." *Kan Studies Ed* 18:35–47 Ap '68. *

159. KIRK, SAMUEL A. "Illinois Test of Psycholinguistic Abilities: Its Origin and Implications." *Learning Disorders* 3:395–427 '68. *

160. LUONG, CORINA K. MONGCAL. *An Analysis of Factors Related to Difficulties in Learning and Adjustment Among Minority Group Children.* Doctor's thesis. Bryn Mawr College (Bryn Mawr, Pa.), 1968. *(DAI* 30:4795B)

161. MASSENGILL, JANET. *A Comparison of the Performance of Aphasic and Nonaphasic Male Adults of the Illinois Test of Psycholinguistic Abilities and the Minnesota Test for Differen-*

tial Diagnosis of Aphasia. Master's thesis, East Tennessee State University (Johnson City, Tenn.), 1968.

162. MOULIN, EUGENE KARL. *The Effects of Client-Centered Group Counseling Utilizing Play Media on the Intelligence, Achievements, and Psycholinguistic Abilities of Underachieving Primary School Children.* Doctor's thesis, University of Toledo (Toledo, Ohio), 1968. *(DA* 29:1425A)

163. MUELLER, MAX W. "Validity of Six Tests of Ability With Educable Mental Retardates." *J Sch Psychol* 6:136–46 w '68. * *(PA* 42:11152)

164. NORTH, GEORGE E. "The Illinois Test of Psycholinguistic Abilities (ITPA) Before and After a Poverty Area Program." *J Ed Res* 62:93 O '68. *

165. OGLAND, VANETTA SUYDAM. *Performance of Special Class Educable Mentally Retarded Children on the ITPA and Other Language Measures as a Function of Selected Variables.* Doctor's thesis, University of Minnesota (Minneapolis, Minn.), 1968. *(DAI* 30:174A)

166. O'GRADY, DONALD JOHN. *Psycholinguistic Abilities in Primary School Age Children With Learning Disabilities.* Doctor's thesis, University of Cincinnati (Cincinnati, Ohio), 1968. *(DA* 29:1848B)

167. PHILLIPS, C. J. "The Illinois Test of Psycholinguistic Abilities: A Report on Its Use With English Children and a Comment on the Psychological Sequelae of Low Birth-Weight." *Brit J Dis Commun* 3:143–9 O '68. * *(PA* 45:9681)

168. SIGEL, IRVING E., AND PERRY, CERETA. "Psycholinguistic Diversity Among 'Culturally Deprived' Children." *Am J Orthopsychiatry* 38:122–6 Ja '68. * *(PA* 42:17002)

169. SILVERSTEIN, A. B. "Variance Components in Five Psychological Tests." *Psychol Rep* 23:141–2 Ag '68. * *(PA* 43:6920)

170. SLOBODZIAN, EVELYN BIRDSALL. *The Relationship Between Certain Readiness Measures and Reading Achievement at Level One.* Doctor's thesis, Temple University (Philadelphia, Pa.), 1968. *(DA* 29:1053A)

171. SMITH, ROBERT M., AND McWILLIAMS, BETTY JANE. "Psycholinguistic Abilities of Children With Clefts." *Cleft Palate J* 5:238–49 Jl '68. *

172. SMITH, ROBERT M., AND McWILLIAMS, BETTY JANE. "Psycholinguistic Considerations in the Management of Children With Cleft Palate." *J Speech & Hearing Disorders* 33:26–33 F '68. * *(PA* 42:9321)

173. STARK, JOEL; COHEN, SYLVIA; AND EISENSON, JON. "Performances of Aphasic Children on the PPVT and Auditory Decoding Tests." *J Spec Ed* 2:435–7 su-f '68. * *(PA* 43:10213)

174. STEPHENSON, BOBBY LYNN. *A Study of Sex and Race Variables and Psycholinguistic Abilities of Lower Socioeconomic Status First Grade Children.* Doctor's thesis, University of Alabama (University, Ala.), 1968. *(DA* 29:3475A)

175. STERNE, DAVID M. "Validity of the PPVT, Knox Cubes and ITPA With Aphasic Adults." Abstract. *Psychol Rep* 22:1014 Je '68. * *(PA* 42:12997)

176. WEBB, PATRICIA KIMBERLEY. *A Comparison of the Psycholinguistic Abilities of Anglo-American, Negro, and Latin-American Lower-Class Preschool Children.* Doctor's thesis, North Texas State University (Denton, Tex.), 1968. *(DA* 29:3351A)

177. WISEMAN, DOUGLAS E. "The ITPA and Remediation." *Ann Inter Conf Assn Children Learn Dis* 5:81–7 '68. *

178. ASTILL, DOLORES ELLEN. *Visual Memory Deficits and Reading Disabilities.* Doctor's thesis, University of Utah (Salt Lake City, Utah), 1969. *(DAI* 30:3310A)

179. AYRES, A. JEAN. "Deficits in Sensory Integration in Educationally Handicapped Children." *J Learn Dis* 2(3):160–8 Mr '69. * *(PA* 45:6978)

180. BAKER, GEORGIA ANN PITCHER. *The Efficiency of Diagnostic, Readiness, and Achievement Instruments as Predictors of Language Arts Achievement: A Longitudinal Study From Kindergarten Through Second Grade.* Doctor's thesis, Purdue University (Lafayette, Ind.), 1969. *(DAI* 30:3624A)

181. BANAS, NORMA, AND WILLS, I. H. "The Vulnerable Child and Prescriptive Teaching." *Acad Ther* 4(3):215–9 sp '69. * *(PA* 43:17927)

182. BANNATYNE, ALEX D. "A Comparison of Visuo-Spatial and Visuo-Motor Memory for Designs and Their Relationship to Other Sensori-Motor and Psycholinguistic Variables." *J Learn Dis* 2(9):451–66 S '69. * *(PA* 45:6004)

183. BANNATYNE, ALEX D., AND WICHIARAJOTE, PENNY. "Hemispheric Dominance, Handedness, Mirror Imaging, and Auditory Sequencing." *Excep Children* 36(1):27–36 S '69. * *(PA* 44:20147)

184. BANNATYNE, ALEX D., AND WICHIARAJOTE, PENNY. "Relationships Between Written Spelling, Motor Functioning and Sequencing Skills." *J Learn Dis* 2(1):4–16 Ja '69. * *(PA* 45:7915)

185. BRUININKS, ROBERT H. "Auditory and Visual Perceptual Skills Related to the Reading Performance of Disadvantaged Boys." *Percept & Motor Skills* 29(1):179–86 Ag '69. * *(PA* 44:2835)

186. CRITTENDEN, JERRY BLICKMAN. *An Empirical Investigation of the Behavioral Dimensions of Four Tests of Learning Disabilities.* Doctor's thesis, Michigan State University (East Lansing, Mich.), 1969. *(DAI* 30:5310A)

187. DUGGER, JAMES G. "The ITPA as a Diagnostic Instru-

ment for Reading Disability Problems in Mental Deficiency." *Psychol* 6(4):47–51 N '69. * (*PA* 44:9122)

188. EFRON, MARVIN. *The Influence of Communication Ability on the Incidence of Over-Referral in the Use of the School Vision Tester.* Doctor's thesis, University of South Carolina (Columbia, S.C.), 1969. (*DAI* 30:4825A)

189. ESPESETH, V. K. "An Investigation of Visual-Sequential Memory in Deaf Children." *Am Ann Deaf* 114(4):786–9 S '69. * (*PA* 44:7120)

190. EVANS, DAVID. "The Assessment of Language Abilities in Subnormal Children With Special Reference to the Illinois Test of Psycholinguistic Abilities." *Med Officer* 122(17):219–22 O 24 '69. *

191. GERBER, SANFORD E., AND HERTEL, CHRISTINA G. "Language Deficiency of Disadvantaged Children." *J Speech & Hearing Res* 12(2):270–80 Je '69. *

192. GOLDEN, NANCY E., AND STEINER, SHARON R. "Auditory and Visual Functions in Good and Poor Readers." *J Learn Dis* 2(9):476–81 S '69. * (*PA* 45:6066)

193. GORDON, SUSAN B. *The Relationship Between the English Language Abilities and Home Language Experiences of First-Grade Children, From Three Ethnic Groups, of Varying Socioeconomic Status and Varying Degrees of Bilingualism.* Doctor's thesis, University of New Mexico (Albuquerque, N.M.), 1969. (*DAI* 31:2252A)

194. HATCH, ERIC J. *A Stability and Validity Study of the Illinois Test of Psycholinguistic Abilities With Educable Mental Retardates.* Master's thesis, Pennsylvania State University (University Park, Pa.), 1969.

195. HIRSHOREN, ALFRED. "A Comparison of the Predictive Validity of the Revised Stanford-Binet Intelligence Scale and the Illinois Test of Psycholinguistic Abilities." *Excep Children* 35(7):517–21 Mr '69. * (*PA* 44:17505)

196. KASTNER, SHELDON B. "Reversal Shifts and Problem-Solving Abilities at Ages 4–7." *Genetic Psychol Monogr* 79(2): 211–49 My '69. * (*PA* 43:15589)

197. KUSKE, IRWIN I., JR. *Psycholinguistic Abilities of Sioux Indian Children.* Doctor's thesis, University of South Dakota (Vermillion, S.D.), 1969. (*DAI* 30:4280A)

198. LOMBARDI, THOMAS PHILIP. *Psycholinguistic Abilities of Papago Indian Children.* Doctor's thesis, University of Arizona (Tucson, Ariz.), 1969. (*DAI* 30:1891A)

199. LUCAS, MARILYN STEUDE. *The ITPA and the Coding Process in Mental Retardates.* Doctor's thesis, Ohio State University (Columbus, Ohio), 1969. (*DAI* 30:3374B)

200. MACIONE, JOSEPH R. *Psychological Correlates of Reading Disability as Defined by the Illinois Test of Psycholinguistic Abilities.* Doctor's thesis, University of South Dakota (Vermillion, S.D.), 1969. (*DAI* 30:3817A)

201. MANN, LESTER. "Are We Fractionating Too Much?" *Acad Ther* 5(2):85–91 w '69–70 ['69]. * (*PA* 44:15347)

202. MEYERS, C. E. "What the ITPA Measures: A Synthesis of Factor Studies of the 1961 Edition." *Ed & Psychol Meas* 29(4):867–76 w '69. * (*PA* 44:20897)

203. MITTLER, PETER. "Genetic Aspects of Psycholinguistic Abilities." *J Child Psychol & Psychiatry* 10(3):165–76 N '69. * (*PA* 44:8198)

204. MUELLER, MAX W. "Prediction of Achievement of Educable Mentally Retarded Children." *Am J Mental Def* 73(4): 590–6 Ja '69. * (*PA* 43:8703)

205. OKADA, DORIS MAMIYA. *The Effects of Perceptual and Perceptual-Motor Training on the Visual Perception, Auditory Perception, and Language Performance of Institutionalized Educable Mental Retardates.* Doctor's thesis, New York University (New York, N.Y.), 1969. (*DAI* 30:2857A)

206. PARASKEVOPOULOS, JOHN N., AND KIRK, SAMUEL A. *The Development and Psychometric Characteristics of the Revised Illinois Test of Psycholinguistics.* Urbana, Ill.: University of Illinois Press, 1969. Pp. x, 243. *

207. PEROZZI, JOSEPH ANTHONY. *The Relationship Between Speech Sound Discrimination Skills and Language Abilities of Kindergarten Children.* Doctor's thesis, University of Washington (Seattle, Wash.), 1969. (*DAI* 30:5278B)

208. RICE, JAMES A. "Confusion in Laterality: A Validity Study With Bright and Dull Children." *J Learn Dis* 2(7): 368–73 Jl '69. * (*PA* 45:6889)

209. RYCKMAN, DAVID B., AND WIEGERINK, RONALD. "The Factors of the Illinois Test of Psycholinguistic Abilities: A Comparison of 18 Factor Analyses." *Excep Children* 36(2): 107–13 O '69. * (*PA* 44:19766)

210. SCHILLER, JEROME J., AND DEIGNAN, MARGARET C. "An Approach to Diagnosis and Remediation of Learning Disabilities." *J Learn Dis* 2(10):508–19 O '69. * (*PA* 45:7011)

211. SEARS, CHARLES RICHARDS. *A Comparison of the Basic Language Concepts and Psycholinguistic Abilities of Second Grade Boys Who Demonstrate Average and Below Average Levels of Reading Achievement.* Doctor's thesis, Colorado State College (Greeley, Colo.), 1969. (*DAI* 30:1758A)

212. SHIPE, DOROTHY, AND MIEZITIS, SOLVEIGA. "A Pilot Study in the Diagnosis and Remediation of Special Learning Disabilities in Preschool Children." *J Learn Dis* 2(11):579–92 N '69. * (*PA* 46:7521)

213. SIMMONS, HELEN. *Decision Strategy as a Function of Sensory Modality.* Doctor's thesis, University of Oregon (Eugene, Ore.), 1969. (*DAI* 31:1089A)

214. SMITH, CAROLYN MEREDITH. *The Relationship of Read-*

ing Method and Reading Achievement to ITPA Sensory Modalities. Doctor's thesis, University of Georgia (Athens, Ga.), 1969. (*DAI* 30:2916A)

215. TESKA, JAMES ALLEN. *Success and Failure in Five Different Programs of Preschool Intervention With Culturally Disadvantaged Children.* Doctor's thesis, University of Illinois (Urbana, Ill.), 1969. (*DAI* 30:2917A)

216. WISLAND, MILTON, AND MANY, WESLEY A. "A Factorial Study of the Illinois Test of Psycholinguistic Abilities With Children Having Above Average Intelligence." *Ed & Psychol Meas* 29(2):367–76 su '69. * (*PA* 44:17341)

217. BRICKMAN, LILLIAN. *A Study of Anxiety and Performance on the ITPA by Children With Minimal Cerebral Dysfunction.* Master's thesis, California State College (Long Beach, Calif.), 1970.

218. BROCHU, EDITH WILLIAMSON. *A Study of Selected Communication Abilities of Boys in All-Male and Traditional Kindergarten and First Grade Classes.* Doctor's thesis, University of Northern Colorado (Greeley, Colo.), 1970. (*DAI* 31:4031A)

219. BRUININKS, ROBERT H.; LUCKER, WILLIAM G.; AND GROPPER, ROBERT L. "Psycholinguistic Abilities of Good and Poor Reading Disadvantaged First-Graders." *El Sch J* 70(7): 378–86 Ap '70. *

220. CHOVAN, WILLIAM L. "Vocal Mediating Responses in Short-Term Memory of Severely and Profoundly Deaf Children." *Percept & Motor Skills* 31(2):539–44 O '70. * (*PA* 45:6826)

221. CLARK, ALICE, AND FOSTER, JAMES. "Objective Measures and Occupational Success." *Mental Retard* 8(4):41–4 Ag '70. *

222. DURKIN, DOLORES. "A Language Arts Program for Pre-First-Grade Children: Two-Year Achievement Report." *Read Res Q* 5(4):534–65 su '70. *

223. EGELAND, BYRON; DI NELLO, MARIO; AND CARR, DONALD. "The Relationship of Intelligence, Visual-Motor, Psycholinguistic and Reading-Readiness Skills With Achievement." *Ed & Psychol Meas* 30(2):451–8 su '70. * (*PA* 45:3056)

224. FERINDEN, WILLIAM E., JR.; JACOBSON, SHERMAN; AND KOVALINSKY, THOMAS. *Educational Interpretation of the Stanford-Binet Intelligence Scale Form L-M and the Illinois Test of Psycholinguistic Abilities.* Linden, N.J.: Remediation Associates, Inc., 1970. Pp. 71. *

225. FLYNN, PAULINE T., AND BYRNE, MARGARET C. "Relationship Between Reading and Selected Auditory Abilities of Third-Grade Children." *J Speech & Hearing Res* 13(4): 731–40 D '70. *

226. GARMS, JOE D. "A Validation Study of the Illinois Test of Psycholinguistic Abilities." *Psychol* 7(1):9–12 F '70. * (*PA* 44:13282)

227. GOODSTEIN, H. A.; WHITNEY, G.; AND CAWLEY, J. F. "Prediction of Perceptual Reading Disability Among Disadvantaged Children in the Second Grade." *Read Teach* 24(1): 23–8 O '70. * (*PA* 45:10955)

228. HOFMEISTER, ALAN, AND ESPESETH, V. KNUTE. "Predicting Academic Achievement With TMR Adults and Teenagers." *Am J Mental Def* 75(1):105–7 Jl '70. *

229. HOWARD, MARSHALL J., JR.; HOOPS, H. RAY; AND MCKINNON, ARCHIE J. "Language Abilities of Children With Differing Socioeconomic Backgrounds." *J Learn Dis* 3(6):328–35 Je '70. *

230. HUBSCHMAN, EVA; POLIZZOTTO, EMILIE ANN; AND KALISKI, MYRA S. "Performance of Institutionalized Retardates on the PPVT and Two Editions of the ITPA." *Am J Mental Def* 74(4):579–80 Ja '70. * (*PA* 44:11063)

231. JONES, ELOISE LORRAINE HARRISS. *The Effects of a Language Development Program on the Psycholinguistic Abilities and IQ of a Group of Preschool Disadvantaged Children.* Doctor's thesis, University of Arkansas (Fayetteville, Ark.), 1970. (*DAI* 31:2761A)

232. JOSELSON, MAURICE L. *The Role of Language Skills Within the Perspective of Other Psychosocial Factors in a Select Prison Population.* Doctor's thesis, University of Florida (Gainesville, Fla.), 1970. (*DAI* 31:4385B)

233. KARR, SHARON KAY STUDER. *Differences in Psycholinguistic Abilities and Intellectual Maturity Among Sierra Leonean Children From Four Cultural Systems of Varying Degrees of Modernization.* Doctor's thesis, Southern Illinois University (Carbondale, Ill.), 1970. (*DAI* 31:3958A)

234. LEEDS, DONALD S. "Illinois Test of Psycholinguistic Abilities: Summary of Research and Commentary." *J Read Specialist* 9(4):169–83 My '70. *

235. LEVENTHAL, DONALD S., AND STEDMAN, DONALD J. "A Factor Analytic Study of the Illinois Test of Psycholinguistic Abilities." *J Clin Psychol* 26(4):473–7 O '70. * (*PA* 45:4923)

236. LOKERSON, JEAN ELIZABETH. *An Investigation of Visual Perception and the Psycholinguistic Process: The Comparative Performance of First Grade Boys on the Illinois Test of Psycholinguistic Abilities Adapted for Visual-Perceptual Impairment.* Doctor's thesis, University of Maryland (College Park, Md.), 1970. (*DAI* 31:3992A)

237. LOMBARDI, THOMAS P. "Psycholinguistic Abilities of Papago Indian School Children." *Excep Children* 36(7):485–93 Mr '70. * (*PA* 44:21498)

238. MITTLER, P., AND WARD, J. "The Use of the Illinois Test of Psycholinguistic Abilities on British Four-Year-Old

Children: A Normative and Factorial Study." *Brit J Ed Psychol* 40(1):43–53 F '70. * (*PA* 44:11226)

239. MITTLER, P.; WARD, J.; AND MARINOSSON, GRETAR. "Suggestions for Re-Wording of Items From the Revised Edition of the Illinois Test of Psycholinguistic Abilities for Use With British Children." *Brit J Ed Psychol* 40(1):53–4 F '70. *

240. MOULIN, EUGENE K. "The Effects of Client-Centered Group Counseling Using Play Media on the Intelligence, Achievement, and Psycholinguistic Abilities of Underachieving Primary School Children." *El Sch Guid & Counsel* 5(2):85–98 D '70. *

241. NURCOMBE, B., AND MOFFITT, P. "Cultural Deprivation and Language Defect: Project Enrichment of Childhood." *Austral Psychologist* 5(3):249–59 N '70. * (*PA* 46:5744)

242. NURSS, JOANNE R. "A Diagnostic Comparison of Two Third Grade Reading Classes," pp. 42–54. In *Reading Difficulties: Diagnosis, Correction, and Remediation.* Edited by William K. Durr. Newark, Del.: International Reading Association, 1970. Pp. vii, 276. *

243. ORPET, R. E., AND MYERS, C. E. "Discriminant Function Analysis of Conservation Stages by Structure of Intellect and Conceptual Style Variables." Abstract. *Proc 78th Ann Conv Am Psychol Assn* 5(1):279–80 '70. * (*PA* 44:18342)

244. RICE, JAMES A., AND DOUGHTIE, EUGENE B. "IQ and the ITPA Classification Versus Diagnosis." *J Learn Dis* 3(9):471–4 S '70. *

245. SABATINO, DAVID A., AND HAYDEN, DAVID L. "Information Processing Behaviors Related to Learning Disabilities and Educable Mental Retardation." *Excep Children* 37(1):21–9 S '70. * (*PA* 46:5527)

246. SABATINO, DAVID A., AND HAYDEN, DAVID L. "Psycho-Educational Study of Selected Behavioral Variables With Children Failing the Elementary Grades." *J Exp Ed* 38(4):40–57 su '70. * (*PA* 46:5680–1)

247. SABATINO, DAVID A., AND HAYDEN, DAVID L. "Variation in Information Processing Behaviors: As Related to Chronological Age Differences for Children Failing in the Elementary Grades." *J Learn Dis* 3(8):404–12 Ag '70. *

248. ST. GEORGE, ROSS. "The Psycholinguistic Abilities of Children From Different Ethnic Backgrounds." *Austral J Psychol* 22(1):85–9 Ap '70. * (*PA* 45:4053)

249. SEVERSON, ROGER A., AND GUEST, KRISTIN E. Chap. 15. "Toward the Standardized Assessment of the Language of Disadvantaged Children," pp. 309–34. In *Language and Poverty: Perspectives on a Theme.* Edited by Frederick Williams. Chicago, Ill.: Markham Publishing Co., 1970. Pp. xii, 459. *

250. SHARP, ELIZABETH YERXA. *The Relationship of Visual Closure to Speechreading Among Deaf Children.* Doctor's thesis, University of Arizona (Tucson, Ariz.), 1970. (*DAI* 31:2198A)

251. SLOBODZIAN, EVELYN B. "Use of the Illinois Test of Psycholinguistic Abilities as a Readiness Measure," pp. 43–8. In *Reading Diagnosis and Evaluation.* Edited by Dorothy L. De Boer. Newark, Del.: International Reading Association, 1970. Pp. vi, 138. *

252. SMITH, JOAN MELVIN. *Utilization of the Illinois Test of Psycholinguistic Abilities With Educationally Handicapped Children.* Doctor's thesis, University of the Pacific (Stockton, Calif.), 1970. (*DAI* 31:3973A)

253. TEN BRINK, TERRY D. "Critique of Hirshoren's ITPA Validity Study." Reply by Alfred Hirshoren. *Excep Children* 36(5):351–6 Ja '70. *

254. UHL, NORMAN P., AND NURSS, JOANNE R. "Socio-Economic Level Styles in Solving Reading-Related Tasks." *Read Res Q* 5(3):452–85 sp '70. *

255. WADDELL, KATHLEEN J., AND CAHOON, DELWIN D. "Comments on the Use of the Illinois Test of Psycholinguistic Abilities With Culturally Deprived Children in the Rural South." *Percept & Motor Skills* 31(1):56–8 Ag '70. * (*PA* 45:3967)

256. WASHINGTON, ERNEST D., AND TESKA, JAMES A. "Relations Between the Wide Range Achievement Test, the California Achievement Tests, the Stanford-Binet, and the Illinois Test of Psycholinguistic Abilities." *Psychol Rep* 26(1):291–4 F '70. * (*PA* 45:4931)

257. WEYCHERT, MARIE C. *The Utilization of Illinois Test of Psycholinguistic Abilities Profiles to Provide a Structured, Language Oriented Curriculum for Mentally Retarded Children.* Master's thesis, Cardinal Stritch College (Milwaukee, Wis.), 1970.

258. WISEMAN, DOUGLAS E. "Remedial Education: Global or Learning-Disability Approach?" *Acad Ther* 5(3):165–75 sp '70. * (*PA* 44:19423)

259. WORKS, MARIAN NEWMAN. *Some Variables Involved in the Reading Process.* Doctor's thesis, University of Oklahoma (Norman, Okla.), 1970. (*DAI* 31:2765AAA)

260. WUSSLER, MARILYN, AND BARCLAY, A. "Cerebral Dominance, Psycholinguistic Skills and Reading Disability." *Percept & Motor Skills* 31(2):419–25 O '70. * (*PA* 45:4015)

261. ZBINDEN, WILLIAM ROSS. *Psycholinguistic and Perceptual Correlates of Spelling in Educable Mentally Handicapped Children.* Doctor's thesis, University of Illinois (Urbana, Ill.), 1970. (*DAI* 31:2765AAA)

JOHN B. CARROLL, *Senior Research Psychologist, Educational Testing Service, Princeton, New Jersey.*

It requires some stretching of meaning to call the ITPA a measure of "psycholinguistic abilities." The interdisciplinary field of psycholinguistics studies the role of natural language systems in human communication and thinking—in particular, the way in which individuals acquire and use such systems. Only about half of the subtests in the ITPA clearly involve a natural language system, i.e., English; the remainder of the tests are essentially "nonlanguage" tests that could be performed, conceivably, by individuals who had never acquired any language system at all, and with appropriate translation of instructions, they could be performed by non-English speakers. In the construction and development of this test, a "psycholinguistic ability" was apparently viewed as any ability that reflects or involves some kind of "communicative" transaction between the individual and his environment, whether or not this transaction requires the use of symbols in a particular language such as English. But by this definition, almost any testable cognitive ability could be regarded as "psycholinguistic." The title of the ITPA is a misnomer, and users should be cautioned to look carefully at the true nature of the test, which might less misleadingly have been named something like the "Illinois Diagnostic Test of Cognitive Functioning."

From the present title, a potential user might feel justified in expecting it to cover such language skills as reading, writing, and spelling. Actually, tests of these skills were deliberately excluded from the battery, since the authors' intention was to measure basic cognitive skills that are not usually attained through schooling.

The confusion that the test engenders about what kinds of abilities are "psycholinguistic" is aggravated when a user of the test claims that the difficulties it reveals are "psycholinguistic in nature," as Ferrier (*82*) did in a report on his use of the test with a group of children with "functional defects of articulation."

If the ITPA were truly a test of psycholinguistic abilities, it would limit its attention to language functions, but it would provide information on a much wider range of such functions, with considerably more detail and precision.

The authors' original purpose was to develop a diagnostic test of a variety of basic mental functions that might be relevant in the analysis of intellectual deficits exhibited in cases of mental retardation, "learning disability," and the like. They were convinced that tests of global intelligence such as the Stanford-Binet or the WISC do not provide sufficient diagnostic information. To develop the experimental version of the test, they made use of a model of the communication process that had been proposed by C. E. Osgood, a psycholinguist on the University of Illinois faculty. The model purported to analyze the individual's communication with the environment and with other individuals in terms of *channels, levels of organization,* and *processes. Channels* referred to auditory, visual, tactual, and other sensory modalities (on the receptive side), and to vocal and motor classes of responses (on the output side). Three *levels of organization* were postulated: a "projection" level, dealing primarily with physiological processes; an integrative or "automatic" level, mediating the habitual processing of symbols and response chains; and a "representational" level, dealing with the meanings of stimuli. *Processes* included decoding and encoding of symbols and the finding of associations among stimuli. The ITPA's authors considered the possibility of constructing tests for 48 possible combinations of channels, levels, and processes suggested by the Osgood model, but found it impracticable to do so. The experimental version of the ITPA comprised nine tests designed to tap what were considered to be the more important of these combinations—primarily, combinations that would contrast the "representational" and the "automatic" levels, "auditory-vocal" and "visual-motor" channels, and (at the "representational" level) "decoding," "associational," and "encoding" processes. It was intended in this way to measure nine more or less independent abilities. The Revised Edition retains the basic plan of the experimental edition but adds a test of one "new" ability, Visual Closure (to measure "visual-motor automatic function"), and two further tests claimed to measure "auditory-vocal automatic functions."

The ITPA's model of cognitive function invites comparison with Guilford's "structure of intellect" model. The pitfalls of model-making are starkly illustrated by this comparison, for there is little coincidence between the models. Possibly Guilford's "operations" correspond in a limited way to Osgood's "processes," if we assume that "cognition" corresponds to "de-

coding" and that "convergent production" and "divergent production" are types of "encoding." There seems to be nothing in the ITPA model that would correspond to Guilford's "contents" and "products." But Guilford's model is largely an arbitrary construction, and if the abilities tested at different intersections of his model are truly independent, it cannot be firmly supported even by factor-analytic evidence. The logic by which the authors of the ITPA expected the tests at the intersections of *their* model to be independent is certainly not clear. One would think that they ought to expect, for example, that all tests measuring the "representational" level would have at least some covariance on this account. This possibility has now been recognized by those associated with the development of the revised edition (*206*).

Fortunately, factor-analytic studies (mainly for the experimental version) that enable one to appraise the validity of some aspects of the ITPA cognitive model are available. One must, however, largely discount the numerous studies that have factor-analyzed the ITPA with little or no use of external reference tests, for such studies would automatically fail to identify unique abilities in the separate tests. Silverstein (*130, 169*) has reported that the nine tests in the experimental edition have considerable variance in common; this is also apparent from inspection of correlation matrices presented by the test authors. Meyers (*202*) attempted to synthesize the factor analyses of the experimental edition of the ITPA and reported that it appears to measure "six separate and established abilities, and possibly a seventh." Meyers suggested how these factors might be labeled according to Guilford's system. He also discussed the extent to which the factor-analytic results seem to provide confirmation of the postulated model of communicative abilities. While separation by "channel" does occur, the "representational" level is identified mainly with the well-known verbal comprehension factor. The concept of an "automatic" level is not well supported, and the notion of different "processes" is "completely unsubstantiated," according to Meyers, who further states that the "sequential" tests are just tests of "short-term memory."

Probably the most useful factorial study of the ITPA is that by Uhl and Nurss (*254*), which used a large number of reference tests and which was able to identify only three or four interpretable factors in the 1961 version. These factors were: (a) a factor of "vocabulary," which for upper-middle-class children was significantly tapped by at least six of the nine tests, but which split into "expressive" and "receptive" verbal factors for lower-class children; (b) an "immediate memory span" factor, present for both upper-middle- and lower-class children; and (c) a factor of "auditory processing," which was found only in the data for lower-class children. Uhl and Nurss interpreted this last factor as representing the extent to which the children understood the dialect of the examiner.

A casual inspection of the subtests will reinforce the conclusion that many of them, even the "non-language" ones, measure a "vocabulary" factor, or rather, a factor having to do with the range of cultural experiences to which the child has been exposed—cultural experiences symbolized by *words* in some tests and by *pictures* and visual symbols in others. For example, in the Auditory Reception test of the Revised Edition, the child may be asked such questions (orally) as "Do bugles camouflage?" or "Do meteorites collide?" (meteorites *do* collide, according to the answer key, although I have never heard of their colliding with each other). In Visual Association, the child may be shown an item requiring him to make an association between a microscope and a telescope. In Visual Reception, he may have to associate a picture of a regular table-top pencil sharpener with the miniature variety one can put in one's purse, or an ordinary screwdriver with the automatic type one can insert in the chuck of an electric hand drill. It seems hardly necessary to point out that such items involve quite specific knowledges that can be expected only of children who have had wide cultural experiences.

It is somewhat ironic, however, that in a test of "psycholinguistic abilities" the test on Verbal Expression, scored as directed in the manual, affords little information on the expressive linguistic development of the child. Scoring of this test focuses on the number of ideas within certain restricted types that are present in the child's talk when he is asked to "tell about" a few simple objects. There is, for example, no scoring for mean length of utterance in morphemes, a measure that has been found to be highly indicative of level of linguistic development. Whether the score on the test of Gram-

matic Closure is an adequate substitute for such a measure is not indicated.

To a degree, then, the ITPA may be regarded as just another test of a limited number of intellectual abilities—verbal comprehension and general information, immediate memory span, and perhaps special capacities in the visual and auditory perceptual domains, as well as a special kind of expressive verbal fluency. The precise factorial composition of the Revised Edition is still to be explored, but it is likely to contain few surprises. Although the test was intended as a "diagnostic" instrument, the manual gives directions for computing and interpreting scaled scores based on an unweighted sum of the subtest scores. These scaled scores generally have correlations in the .80's with the Stanford-Binet MA or similar measures, according to several studies (e.g., *256*). The considerably lower correlations with Stanford-Binet MA's reported by the test authors are for highly restricted ranges in terms of ability and age.

It would seem that much care and effort were expended in construction and refining the test materials. Technical characteristics such as reliability seem to be highly satisfactory. However, the ITPA is a fairly complicated battery to administer. Despite the many improvements in the Revised Edition to facilitate administration, one finds it hard to believe that the battery can typically be given in 45, or even 60, minutes, as claimed by the authors. Several studies of the experimental edition (*55, 131, 132*) suggest that there can be fairly wide variation in scores due to examiner differences. Whether the ITPA is more sensitive to examiner differences than other individually administered clinical instruments is an open question.

It has already been noted in the literature (*139*) that the standardization procedures adopted by the test authors were somewhat unusual and possibly open to question. For both the Experimental Edition and the Revised Edition, the standardization samples consisted of groups of "normal," "average" children. The authors justified their procedure by saying that they desired a reference group against which deficits of learning disability and mental retardate cases could be evaluated. For the Revised Edition, the norm group comprised 962 children (about 120 children in each of eight age-groups) who were carefully screened to have "average" intelligence (IQ 84 to 116), to be from schools with achievements in a "middle range" in middle-class communities, and to be free from physical handicaps, emotional disturbances, etc. Only 4 percent were Negro; all samples were from medium-sized cities or towns in the Midwest. There is a distinct possibility that the normative sample had average IQ's below the average for the populations from which the samples were drawn.

There may be some merit in the authors' standardization procedures, but those procedures can be criticized on the ground that the norms do not include data on groups of children representative of the "learning disability" and mental retardate populations for which the test was presumably designed. It has been left to other investigators to collect such norms, but the available literature contains few, if any, studies of respectably large groups of systematically selected "learning disability" cases. A user of the ITPA should not be surprised if he finds that on a given subtest a particular child scores at or below the lowest possible score in the norms given for "average" children. He would probably be justified in concluding that the child is in some way deviant from "average" children, but he would still not know how to relate the score to those typically obtained by "learning disability" cases, mental retardates, etc.

If the use of the ITPA were to be restricted to certain types of learning disability cases, the authors' standardization procedures might be regarded as acceptable. There is, however, a serious issue latent in the fact that nowhere in the materials accompanying the test do the authors make a clear and explicit statement concerning the types of populations for which the test is designed. They make vague references to "learning disabilities" and mental retardation, but one gathers that the kinds of cases they are referring to are those that are found with significant frequency in middle-class, white, English-speaking communities, not only in the Midwest, of course, but throughout the country. At least, their selection of norm groups from such communities suggests such an interpretation. It would appear, however, from studies reported in the literature, that by far the greatest use of the ITPA has been in the assessment of the "psycholinguistic" abilities of lower-class children, particularly from minority groups— Blacks, Chicanos, and even Papago Indians. The test has also been applied to adolescent and adult mental retardates. Little justification for

such uses is to be found in the standardization of the test. If fault is to be found, at least some of it must be attributed to the authors for not making suitable cautionary statements regarding the use of the test with lower-class and minority groups. From an inspection of test content and in view of a number of research studies, one can raise serious questions concerning the validity of the test for such groups.

Consider, first, the fact that the test is replete with materials that are characteristic of middle-class culture—pictures of electric mixers, violins, tennis rackets, and motor-driven hand tools, and words like *cosmetics, meteorite, beverage,* and *architect.* Consider also the fact that several of the tests require the child to exhibit his familiarity with, or his ability to conform to, the lexical and grammatical norms of "standard" American English (as opposed to the many varieties of "nonstandard" or "substandard" English). Consider the fact that Uhr and Nurss's study suggested that the "auditory" factors in the test might be associated more with the child's ability to understand the dialect of the examiner than with any defect of auditory perception. Howard, Hoops, and McKinnon (*229*) have made pointed criticism of the test on the grounds that the scoring often unjustly penalizes the child who happens to have been reared in a community with nonstandard speech patterns. For such cases, low ITPA scores cannot be interpreted as necessarily reflecting any real intellectual deficit, unless one believes in the discredited notion that nonstandard speech patterns betoken faulty intellectual functioning. Consider also the fact that Verbal Expression (Vocal Encoding in the experimental edition) —a test requiring the child to "talk about" each of a series of such objects as a wooden block, an envelope, etc.—is very likely to "tongue-tie" a child from a lower-class environment when he is confronted with a strange and (possibly) ethnically-different examiner. The sociolinguist William Labov [1] has dramatically illustrated how such children can be highly verbal and fluent when they are observed in a situation which is less unnatural to them than a test. Severson and Guest (*249*) have written a particularly valuable discussion of the limitations of the ITPA when it is used with disadvantaged children.

[1] LABOV, WILLIAM. Chap. 9, "The Logic of Nonstandard English," pp. 153–89. In *Language and Poverty: Perspectives on a Theme.* Edited by Frederick Williams. Chicago, Ill.: Markham Publishing Co., 1970. Pp. xii, 459. *

Thus, the use of the ITPA in evaluating the effects of language programs for the disadvantaged is highly questionable, unless one views the purpose of such testing as that of finding out how much these programs advance the child towards certain middle-class language norms. And even if that is the purpose, the ITPA is hardly adequate for the task. One doubts that the test can be used to assess progress of these groups in "intellectual functioning" per se because the cultural element is too dominant. Much caution must be urged in interpreting the results of studies that have used the ITPA with lower-class minority groups.

If we must doubt the validity of the ITPA for children from lower socioeconomic classes or from nonstandard language backgrounds, we may nevertheless inquire into its validity and usefulness for the types of children for whom it was designed. The "average" middle-class children in the norms groups exhibited considerable variability in performance. The test authors display data based on the norms groups (206, Table 7-6) showing that differences among subtest scores are in general highly reliable, a finding that supports the notion that the test shows promise for diagnostic use. Kirk (88) has published a number of case studies showing how "psycholinguistic disabilities" can be diagnosed by the test in its experimental form; presumably the Revised Edition would be useful in similar ways. He also illustrates a variety of remedial techniques, including programmed instruction, whose use would be indicated by certain profiles of subtest scores. Nevertheless, there are few systematic studies in the literature concerning the effectiveness of remedial procedures selected in accordance with test results. Weener, Barritt, and Semmel (139) pointed to the need for "evidence....to show how subscale performance is related to educationally relevant behaviors." Ferrier (82), working with functional disorders of articulation, complained that the remedial procedures that would be suggested by test performances "would, in most cases, bear little resemblance to what is usually considered speech therapy." Ogland (165), studying educable mental retardates, found that the test showed no significant differences between subjects with and without language training, but Okada (205) found the ITPA was useful in measuring the effects of certain kinds of perceptual training.

Studies are divided on the usefulness of the test in prediction or diagnosis of reading disabilities. Some favorable evidence is presented by Bateman (27), Kass (87), and Macione (200). (Macione's study is one of the few that concerns the Revised Edition.) However, Sears (211) found no significant differences between average and disabled readers in any of the ITPA skill areas, and Smith (214) found no interaction between reading method and "auditory" vs. "visual" types as identified by the test.

Reviewing the material on the use of the test in diagnosis and remediation, one gets the impression that its main contribution might be to differentiate deficits in the "auditory" and "visual" areas, with secondary values in cases of poor verbal expression. The authors have an obligation to report further research supporting the usefulness of the ITPA for the major purpose for which it was designed—diagnosis and remediation. As matters stand, it is difficult to see wherein the ITPA represents a diagnostic instrument that is markedly superior to other tests of this genre, such as the Stanford-Binet and the WISC—tests that are more extensively standardized and in general, one would judge, more appealing to children.

CLINTON I. CHASE, *Professor of Educational Psychology and Chairman of the Department; and Director, Bureau of Educational Studies and Testing; Indiana University, Bloomington, Indiana.*

The ITPA departs from the standard kit of individual tests in the psychometrist's cabinet in that it is not intended to be an intelligence test and it emphasizes intraindividual, rather than interindividual, differences. It is a test of language, perception, and short-term memory abilities. Since so many school learning problems are tied to these skills, this test presents a unique tool for diagnosing school learning difficulties. The test also has the desirable quality of being based on a reasonably well developed psycholinguistic theory, Charles Osgood's model. This theory describes the receptive process for language; the organizing process—which deals with the internal manipulation of percepts, concepts, and symbols; and the expressive process. The ITPA attempts to assess quality of performance within each of these three processes. Visual and auditory channels of input, and vocal and motor channels of output provide the bases for assessment.

The 1968 ITPA departs from the 1961 edition primarily in that the revised edition attempts to tease out the assessment of processes into more specific operations. Therefore, 12 subscales are included in the test, whereas the 1961 edition had only 9. The new tests are designed primarily to extend the assessment of the child's ability to put bits of a communication together into an organized whole. These new tests include a test of Visual Closure, Auditory Closure, and Sound Blending. The last two subtests are for optional use.

Since the test is designed to identify departures from "normal," the standardization population included only children who demonstrated average intellectual functioning, average school achievement, average personal-social adjustment, who had sensory-motor integrity, and who came from predominantly English-speaking homes. Therefore, norms are available for average children alone and run from ages 2 to 10. The children tested for normative data came from five Midwestern towns of moderate size. A wider sample of children probably would have been desirable, including both large metropolitan and clearly rural areas.

The standardization sample was also from homes slightly above the national average in income and education, with middle occupational levels slightly overrepresented at the expense of lower levels. The sample clearly underrepresents Negroes, and the number of Spanish-American children is not reported. In addition, it is interesting to note that almost none of the preschool children screened were rejected from the normative group, whereas more than half of the school-age children screened were rejected. One wonders if the character of preschool norms, compared to norms on older children, is influenced by this factor.

In the collection of normative data, 17 examiners were employed. Only three of these were male. Noting differences in responses obtained by different examiners on individual tests, one may wonder if the disproportionately large number of female examiners influenced the normative data.

Since the profile of tests is designed to be diagnostic, subtest reliabilities and intercorrelations are especially important. Because the standardization sample for the ITPA is limited to "normal" children, an obvious restriction in range of scores must occur. Since this typically results in lower reliabilities, the authors have reported both the obtained reliabilities and esti-

mates of the reliabilities for "the full range of intelligence." There are 12 subtests and a composite at each of eight age levels, resulting in 104 internal consistency coefficients. Of the 104 uncorrected reliabilities, 51 fall below .80, 23 below .70, and 15 above .90. The corresponding numbers for the corrected-for-range estimates are 15, 6, and 40, respectively. The tests appear to be reasonably reliable at each age level, with Visual Closure and Auditory Closure the least reliable subtests in the battery. Visual Closure reliabilities range from .49 to .71 (corrected estimates, .67 to .83). The Auditory Closure data are only slightly better.

As a measure of stability, a retest of the ITPA was conducted after a five- to six-month interval for three age groups (71 4-year-olds, 55 6-year-olds, and 72 8-year-olds). The retest reliabilities for the 12 subtests range from .12 to .86, with median .50; the corrected-for-range estimates range from .28 to .90, with median .71. The retest correlations for the Composite score are .83, .70, and .70, respectively, for the three age groups.

If a test such as the ITPA is going to be diagnostic, the differences between pairs of scores in a child's profile must be stable. The authors report median reliabilities of the differences among all subtest pairs, ranging from .57 to .88, with median .74; the corrected-for-range reliabilities range from .67 to .91, with median .81. Score profiles appear to be moderately stable.

Several types of validity data are available that fit the construct on which the ITPA was based. The tests correlate poorly with social class and poorly with Stanford-Binet scores. However, a substantial amount of validity information still must be collected before hard data can be presented to define the behaviors associated with performance on each of the subtests in the ITPA.

In summary, the revised ITPA allows the examiner to assess psycholinguistic behavior in more detail than the earlier edition, and does it with moderate reliability and with a fairly stable profile of scores. However, scores hold up only fairly well with time. Further, the standardization group has a "middle America" bias, with minority groups clearly underrepresented. Much research is still needed before confident statements can be made concerning validity. Nevertheless, the test has been carefully constructed and goes far toward extending the psychometrist's ability to diagnose learning difficulties effectively.

[443]

★[Re Illinois Test of Psycholinguistic Abilities] A Filmed Demonstration of the ITPA. 1969; black and white 16 mm. instructional sound film demonstrating the administration of the ITPA; $360 per film, cash orders postpaid; rental fee, $12 (available from University of Illinois Visual Aids Service); running time, 43 minutes; University of Illinois Press.

Except Children 36(8):631 Ap '70. Don Mahler. Of all the new tests introduced during the Decade of the 60's (to borrow a current popular phrase) and used by special educators, the Illinois Test of Psycholinguistic Abilities certainly must be one of the most popular. Experienced administrators of individual tests probably can teach themselves the ITPA in a reasonably short time without this film, but its use should shorten the learning period as well as result in a more standardized administration. For the neophyte, the film should provide an invaluable introduction and supplement to the manual. The film itself is simple in format. Mrs. Kirk administers the test to a young boy while Dr. Samuel Kirk provides occasional narration. Some items of the ITPA have been eliminated in order to reduce the overall length, but all of the subtests are included. This reviewer is mindful of the problems inherent in making a testing film but would like to offer a few comments. Using other camera angles—perhaps one from the right to show more of John's expressions and another to illustrate the actual scoring more clearly—would provide more visual interest as well as more information to the student examiner. A brief guide addressed specifically to some of the questions apt to be generated by the contents would be helpful. This latter comment arises because about half way through the film the examinee shows signs of tiredness/anxiety and near the end he appears to be saying, "Let's stop. I've had enough." Several natural questions arise. For example, Do the authors of the ITPA feel this is significant in this instance? How might the examiner deal with it? Was the filming session a major contributing factor? In the reviewer's opinion, the film should be shown only after the viewer has read the manual and has developed some familiarity with the test materials. Maximum benefits will be obtained from two viewings, with the second broken into segments for discussion purposes if used in a training class.

[444]

*Perceptual Speed (Identical Forms). Grades 9–16 and industrial employees; 1956–66; 1 form ('56, 8 pages); revised manual ('66, 20 pages); norms for males only; $4 per 20 tests, postage extra; $2 per specimen set, postpaid; 5(10) minutes; L. L. Thurstone (test), T. E. Jeffrey (test), and Norman J. Kantor (manual); Industrial Relations Center, University of Chicago. *

REFERENCES

1. BOND, GUY L., AND DYKSTRA, ROBERT. "The Cooperative Research Program in First-Grade Reading Instruction." *Read Res Q* 2:5–142 su '67. * (*PA* 42:4557)
2. BAEHR, MELANY E.; FURCON, JOHN E.; AND FROEMEL, ERNEST C. *Psychological Assessment of Patrolman Qualifications in Relation to Field Performance.* Washington, D.C.: United States Government Printing Office, 1969. Pp. vii, 246. *

For a review by Leroy Wolins, see 6:556.

[445]

★Remote Associates Test. College and adults; 1967, c1959–67; RAT; "ability to think creatively"; Forms 1 ('67, 4 pages), 2 ('67, 4 pages, "in an experimental stage"); manual ('67, 17 pages); $3.60 per 35 tests; 60¢ per manual; $1.20 per specimen set; postage extra; 40(45) minutes; Sarnoff A. Mednick and Martha T. Mednick; Houghton Mifflin Co. *

REFERENCES

1. ANDREWS, FRANK MEREDITH. *Creativity and the Scientist.* Doctor's thesis, University of Michigan (Ann Arbor, Mich.), 1962. (*DA* 23:3524)
2. MEDNICK, SARNOFF A. "The Associative Basis of the Creative Process." *Psychol R* 69:220–32 My '62. * (*PA* 37:6161)
3. MEDNICK, SARNOFF A., AND MEDNICK, MARTHA T. "A Theory and Test of Creative Thought," pp. 40–7. (*PA* 37:4961) In *Industrial and Business Psychology.* Proceedings of the XIV International Congress of Applied Psychology, Vol. 5. Copenhagen, Denmark: Munksgaard Ltd., 1962. Pp. 229. *
4. JENKINS, ADELBERT HOWARD. *Tolerance for Unrealistic Experience as a Cognitive Control.* Doctor's thesis, University of Michigan (Ann Arbor, Mich.), 1963. (*DA* 24:834)
5. LAHN, MARION. *Some Effects of Conflict on Creative Thinking.* Doctor's thesis, University of Michigan (Ann Arbor, Mich.), 1963. (*DA* 24:835)
6. MEDNICK, MARTHA T. "Research Creativity in Psychology Graduate Students." *J Consult Psychol* 27:265–6 Je '63. * (*PA* 38:958)
7. WALKER, HOWARD EDGAR. *Relationships Between Predicted School Behavior and Measures of Creative Potential.* Doctor's thesis, University of Michigan (Ann Arbor, Mich.), 1963. (*DA* 24:636)
8. WHITTEMORE, ROBERT GEORGE, JR. *Modification of Originality Responses in Academically Talented, Male University Freshmen.* Doctor's thesis, Arizona State University (Tempe, Ariz.), 1963. (*DA* 25:6403)
9. DATTA, LOIS-ELLIN. "A Note on the Remote Associates Test, United States Culture, and Creativity." *J Appl Psychol* 48:184–5 Je '64. * (*PA* 39:6064)
10. DATTA, LOIS-ELLIN. "Remote Associates Test as a Predictor of Creativity in Engineers." *J Appl Psychol* 48:183 Je '64. * (*PA* 39:6063)
11. EASTERBROOK, CAROLYN M. *Pursuit of a Quest: Mortalities Along the Way. A Study of a Selected Group of Variables Relative to the Holding Power of the Art Teaching Profession.* Doctor's thesis, Wayne State University (Detroit, Mich.), 1964. (*DA* 26:4478)
12. FLEISCHER, GERALD. *The Effects of Anxiety Upon Tests of Creativity.* Doctor's thesis, State University of New York (Buffalo, N.Y.), 1964. (*DA* 25:5372)
13. GINSBURG, GERALD PHILLIP. *Creative Potential and Childhood Antecedents.* Doctor's thesis, University of Michigan (Ann Arbor, Mich.), 1964. (*DA* 25:3725)
14. MALTZMAN, IRVING; BELLONI, MARIGOLD; AND FISHBEIN, MARTIN. "Experimental Studies of Associative Variables in Originality." *Psychol Monogr* 78(3):1–21 '64. * (*PA* 39:1785)
15. MEDNICK, MARTHA T.; MEDNICK, SARNOFF A.; AND JUNG, CHARLES C. "Continual Association as a Function of Level of Creativity and Type of Verbal Stimulus." *J Abn & Social Psychol* 69:511–5 N '64. * (*PA* 39:7824)
16. MEDNICK, MARTHA T.; MEDNICK, SARNOFF A.; AND MEDNICK, EDWARD V. "Incubation of Creative Performance and Specific Associative Priming." *J Abn & Social Psychol* 69:84–8 Jl '64. * (*PA* 39:1786)
17. RAINWATER, JANETTE MUNKITTRICK. *Effects of Set on*

Problem Solving in Subjects of Varying Levels of Assessed Creativity. Doctor's thesis, University of California (Berkeley, Calif.), 1964. (*DA* 25:6753)

18. WHITE, LOUISE ELIZABETH. *Creativity as a Function of Feelings of Self Worth.* Doctor's thesis, Vanderbilt University (Nashville, Tenn.), 1964. (*DA* 25:2619)

19. ANDREWS, FRANK M. "Factors Affecting the Manifestation of Creative Ability by Scientists." *J Personality* 33:140–52 Mr '65. * (*PA* 39:10168)

20. BUTLER, MARJORIE JOHNSON. *Criteria for Creativity in Counseling.* Doctor's thesis, University of Pittsburgh (Pittsburgh, Pa.), 1965. (*DA* 27:977B)

21. CASTIGLIONE, LAWRENCE VIRGIL. *The Relation of Intelligence to Selected Measures of Creativity.* Doctor's thesis, New York University (New York, N.Y.), 1965. (*DA* 27:1278B)

22. FLEISCHER, GERALD, AND COHEN, IRA S. "The Relationship Between Test Anxiety and Tests of Creativity." Abstract. *Proc Ann Conv Am Psychol Assn* 73:311–2 '65. * (*PA* 39:15458)

23. FREEDMAN, JONATHAN L. "Increasing Creativity by Free-Association Training." *J Exp Psychol* 69:89–91 Ja '65. * (*PA* 39:7816)

24. GRISWOLD, BARBARA BALLENGEE. *Context Effects in Paired Associate Learning as a Function of Associative Strength and Level of Assessed Creativity.* Doctor's thesis, University of California (Berkeley, Calif.), 1965. (*DA* 26:4062)

25. YAHAV, AVIVA LEVY. *Associative Processes, Environmental Stimuli, and the Remote Associates Test of Creativity.* Doctor's thesis, University of California (Berkeley, Calif.), 1965. (*DA* 26:7443)

26. ANDERSON, C. C., AND CROPLEY, A. J. "Some Correlates of Originality." *Austral J Psychol* 18:218–27 D '66. * (*PA* 41:4572)

27. CROPLEY, A. J. "Creativity and Intelligence." *Brit J Ed Psychol* 36:259–66 N '66. * (*PA* 41:573)

28. DANKS, JOSEPH H., AND GLUCKSBERG, SAM. "Asymmetric Transfer Between the Remote Associates Test and Functional Fixedness." *Psychol Rep* 19:682 D '66. * (*PA* 41:3939)

29. GANTZ, BENJAMIN SOULÉ, JR. *Predicting and Training Originality.* Doctor's thesis, Claremont Graduate School (Claremont, Calif.), 1966. (*DA* 28:1225B)

30. GUILLIAMS, CLARK IRVIN. *Predicting Creative Productivity in College Classes Where Creative Thinking Is Emphasized.* Doctor's thesis, University of Arkansas (Fayetteville, Ark.), 1966. (*DA* 27:675A)

31. HIGGINS, JERRY. "A Further Study of Correlates of the Remote Associates Test of Creativity." *Psychol* 3:18–20 F '66. * (*PA* 40:6634)

32. LUCAS, FRANCES H., AND DANA, RICHARD H. "Creativity and Allocentric Perception." *Percept & Motor Skills* 22:431–7 Ap '66. * (*PA* 40:8858)

33. MENDELSOHN, GERALD A., AND GRISWOLD, BARBARA B. "Assessed Creative Potential, Vocabulary Level, and Sex as Predictors of the Use of Incidental Cues in Verbal Problem Solving." *J Pers & Social Psychol* 4:423–31 O '66. * (*PA* 40:12919)

34. PELZ, DONALD C., AND ANDREWS, FRANK M. Chap. 9, "Creativity," pp. 154–73. In their *Scientists in Organizations: Productive Climates for Research and Development.* New York: John Wiley & Sons, Inc., 1966. Pp. xiii, 318. *

35. PERKINS, STANLEY ARTHUR. *A Comparative Analysis of the Congruence of High Creative and Low Creative High School Students.* Doctor's thesis, University of Oregon (Eugene, Ore.), 1966. (*DA* 27:2074A)

36. TAFT, RONALD, AND ROSSITER, JOHN R. "The Remote Associates Test: Divergent or Convergent Thinking?" *Psychol Rep* 19:1313–4 D '66. * (*PA* 41:3947)

37. ZOOB, INA. *Some Variables of Creativity as Measured by the Remote Associates Test.* Doctor's thesis, Adelphi University (Garden City, N.Y.), 1966.

38. ARVIDSON, ROBERT MANFRED. *False Recognition Produced by Implicit Associative Responses as a Function of Performance on the Remote Associates Test.* Doctor's thesis, University of Nevada (Reno, Nev.), 1967. (*DA* 28:4277B)

39. DAMM, VERNON JOHN. *The Relation of Ego-Strength to Creativity and Intelligence in High School Students.* Doctor's thesis, University of Oregon (Eugene, Ore.), 1967. (*DA* 28:3016A)

40. FLANAGAN, MARIE L., AND GALLUP, HOWARD F. "Creativity Training." *Psychol Rep* 21:934 D '67. * (*PA* 42:7336)

41. HIGGINS, JERRY. "Creativity in Comic Strip Authors." *J Creative Behav* 1:366–9 f '67. *

42. HIGGINS, JERRY, AND DOLBY, LISE-LOTTE LEHD. "Creativity and Mediated Association: A Construct Validation Study of the RAT." *Ed & Psychol Meas* 27:1011–4 w '67. * (*PA* 42:8098)

43. JACOBY, JACOB. "Open-Mindedness and Creativity." *Psychol Rep* 20:822 Je '67. *

44. KARLINS, MARVIN. "Conceptual Complexity and Remote-Associative Proficiency as Creativity Variables in a Complex Problem-Solving Task." *J Pers & Social Psychol* 6:264–78 Jl '67. * (*PA* 41:11922)

45. LUCAS, FRANCES HOWERTON. *Conceptual Complexity and the Facilitation and Inhibition of Creative Behavior.* Doctor's thesis, West Virginia University (Morgantown, W.Va.), 1967. (*DA* 28:5194B)

46. LYNCH, MERVIN D., AND KAYS, DAN. "Effects on Journalistic Performance of Creativity and Task Dispersion." *Journalism Q* 44:508–12 au '67. * (*PA* 42:750)

47. LYNCH, MERVIN D., AND SWINK, ELEANOR. "Some Effects of Priming, Incubation and Creative Aptitude on Journalism Performance." *J Commun* 17:372–82 D '67. * (*PA* 42:7339)

48. MEDNICK, MARTHA T., AND ANDREWS, FRANK M. "Creative Thinking and Level of Intelligence." *J Creative Behav* 1:428–31 f '67. *

49. TAFT, RONALD. "Predicting School Examination Results by Tests of Intelligence and Creativity." *Austral J Ed* 11:126–33 Je '67. * (*PA* 42:1189)

50. TORTORELLA, WILLIAM MICHAEL. *The Effects of a Stressful Situation on a Creative Task.* Doctor's thesis, Fordham University (New York, N.Y.), 1967. (*DA* 28:1214B)

51. ARVIDSON, ROBERT M. "Performance of Canadian Students on the Remote Associates Test." *J Social Psychol* 76:133–4 O '68. * (*PA* 43:2561)

52. BECICA, BOZA. *A Comparison of Selected Characteristics of Students With Higher Grades in Their Foreign Language Courses Than in Their Nonlanguage Courses.* Doctor's thesis, University of Texas (Austin, Tex.), 1968. (*DA* 29:4315A)

53. BERMAN, JOAN RONNIE. *Abstractness, Creativity, and Anxiety in Verbal Learning.* Doctor's thesis, Northwestern University (Evanston, Ill.), 1968. (*DA* 29:4838B)

54. BONE, RONALD N., AND CORLETT, FAITH. "Brief Report: Frequency of Dream Recall, Creativity, and a Control for Anxiety." *Psychol Rep* 22:1355–6 Je '68. * (*PA* 42:18193)

55. CRAVER, ANN APRIL. *Convergent and Divergent Creative Thinking as a Function of Stimulation.* Doctor's thesis, University of Georgia (Athens, Ga.), 1968. (*DA* 29:4842B)

56. GAMBLE, KENNETH R., AND KELLNER, HAROLD. "Creative Functioning and Cognitive Regression." *J Pers & Social Psychol* 9:266–71 Jl '68. * (*PA* 42:13761)

57. GINSBURG, GERALD P., AND WHITTEMORE, ROBERT G. "Creativity and Verbal Ability: A Direct Examination of Their Relationship." *Brit J Ed Psychol* 38:133–9 Je '68. * (*PA* 42:17230)

58. HAM, DON GAY. *Performance, Goal and Role Ambiguity.* Doctor's thesis, Colorado State University (Ft. Collins, Colo.), 1968. (*DAI* 30:826A)

59. JACOBSON, LEONARD I.; ELENEWSKI, JEFFREY J.; LORDAHL, DANIEL S.; AND LIROFF, JEFFREY H. "Role of Creativity and Intelligence in Conceptualization." *J Pers & Social Psychol* 10:431–6 D '68. * (*PA* 43:6752)

60. JACOBY, JACOB. "Creative Ability of Task-Oriented Versus Person-Oriented Leaders." *J Creative Behav* 2:249–53 f '68. * (*PA* 43:14232)

61. JOHNSON, DAVID ARIO. *The Relationship Between Remote Associational Ability and Dogmatism.* Master's thesis, Ohio State University (Columbus, Ohio), 1968.

62. LAUGHLIN, PATRICK R.; DOHERTY, MARY A.; AND DUNN, RALPH F. "Intentional and Incidental Concept Formation as a Function of Motivation, Creativity, Intelligence, and Sex." *J Pers & Social Psychol* 8:401–9 Ap '68. * (*PA* 42:8397)

63. McGAUGHEY, MARILYN VANCE. *The Formation of Learning Sets as a Function of Creativity and Intelligence in Adolescent Females.* Doctor's thesis, University of Georgia (Athens, Ga.), 1968. (*DA* 29:3090B)

64. MEDNICK, SARNOFF A. "The Remote Associates Test." *J Creative Behav* 2:213–4 su '68. * (*PA* 43:5354)

65. SCHLICHT, WILLIAM J., JR.; ANDERSON, DERWYN L.; HELIN, WILLIAM C.; HIPPE, DOUGLAS L.; LISTIAK, RICHARD L.; MOSER, RICHARD J.; AND WALKER, JAMES L. "Creativity and Intelligence: Further Findings." *J Clin Psychol* 24:458 O '68. * (*PA* 43:4025)

66. SHRY, STEPHEN ALLEN, JR. *The Relation of Creativity in College Students to Attention Cues.* Doctor's thesis, Oklahoma State University (Stillwater, Okla.), 1968. (*DAI* 30:1368B)

67. STOCK, WILLIAM H., JR. *Some Psychological and Physiological Factors Affecting Excellence in Acting.* Doctor's thesis, Michigan State University (East Lansing, Mich.), 1968. (*DA* 29:3716A)

68. ABNEY, CLAIRE WINSOME. *A Comparative Study of Creative Thinking Ability in Three Student Groups at the University of Arkansas as Measured by the Remote Associates Test.* Doctor's thesis, University of Arkansas (Fayetteville, Ark.), 1969. (*DAI* 30:2717A)

69. ANTELL, MAXINE JOAN. *The Effect of Priming and the Subliminal Presentation of Sexual and Aggressive Stimuli on Tests of Creativity.* Doctor's thesis, New York University (New York, N.Y.), 1969. (*DAI* 30:3859B)

70. BURGESS, MICHAEL M., AND DUFFEY, MARGERY. "The Prediction of Success in a Collegiate Program of Nursing." *Nursing Res* 18(1):68–72 Ja–F '69. *

71. CICIRELLI, VICTOR G. "University Supervisors' Creative Ability and Their Appraisal of Student Teachers' Classroom Performance: An Exploratory Study." *J Ed Res* 62(8):375–81 Ap '69.

72. DAY, H. I., AND LANGEVIN, R. "Curiosity and Intelligence: Two Necessary Conditions for a High Level of Creativity." *J Spec Ed* 3(3):263–8 f '69. * (*PA* 44:14614)

73. GOODMAN, P.; FURCON, J.; AND ROSE, J. "Examination of Some Measures of Creative Ability by the Multitrait-Multimethod Matrix." *J Appl Psychol* 53(3):240–3 Je '69. * (*PA* 43:11327)

74. HAAG, RICHARD A., AND DAVID, KENNETH H. "The Latent Dimensionality of Several Measures of Creativity." *J General Psychol* 80(2):279–85 Ap '69. * (*PA* 43:11328)

75. HOOD, RALPH W., JR. "On Creativity as Defined by the Remote Associates Test." *Psychol Rep* 24(3):914 Je '69. * (*PA* 44:657)

76. HOOD, RALPH W., JR., AND GINSBURG, G. P. "Cultural Availability: An Associative Characteristic of Remote Associates Test Items." *Psychol Rep* 25(2):443–6 O '69. * (*PA* 44:5176)

77. KARLINS, MARVIN; SCHUERHOFF, CHARLES; AND KAPLAN, MARTIN. "Some Factors Related to Architectural Creativity in Graduating Architecture Students." *J General Psychol* 81(2):203–15 O '69. * (*PA* 44:6775)

78. KROP, HARRY D.; ALEGRE, CECILIA E.; AND WILLIAMS, CARL D. "Effect of Induced Stress on Convergent and Divergent Thinking." *Psychol Rep* 24(3):895–8 Je '69. * (*PA* 44:218)

79. MEDNICK, MARTHA T., AND HALPERN, SHARON K. "Comparison of Two Administration Times for the Remote Associates Test." *Psychol Rep* 24(2):507–10 Ap '69. * (*PA* 43:15002)

80. MEDNICK, SARNOFF A. "Reply to Hood's 'On Creativity as Defined by the Remote Associates Test.'" *Psychol Rep* 25(1):194 Ag '69. * (*PA* 44:3626)

81. OLCZAK, PAUL V., AND KAPLAN, MARTIN F. "Originality and Rate of Response in Association as a Function of Associative Gradient." *Am J Psychol* 82(2):157–67 Je '69. * (*PA* 43:15754)

82. SIMON, LAURENCE RALPH. *Incidental Stimulation and Problem Solving.* Doctor's thesis, New York University (New York, N.Y.), 1969. (*DAI* 30:3877B)

83. TOBIAS, SIGMUND. "Effect of Creativity, Response Mode, and Subject Matter Familiarity on Achievement From Programmed Instruction." *J Ed Psychol* 60(6):453–60 D '69. *

84. ANDREWS, FRANK M., AND GORDON, GERALD. "Social and Organizational Factors Affecting Innovation in Research." Abstract. *Proc 78th Ann Conv Am Psychol Assn* 5(2):589–90 '70. * (*PA* 44:19654)

85. BADER, LAWRENCE JOSEPH. *The Effects of Task-Taking Atmosphere, Level of Creativity and Field-Independence on Creative Production.* Doctor's thesis, Boston University (Boston, Mass.), 1970. (*DAI* 31:2974B)

86. BRODY, E. B. "The Effects of Creativity and Intelligence on Teacher Ratings." *Brit J Ed Psychol* 40(3):342–4 N '70. * (*PA* 45:7036)

87. CICIRELLI, VICTOR G., AND CICIRELLI, JEAN S. "Counselors' Creative Ability and Attitude in Relation to Counseling Behavior With Disadvantaged Counselees." *J Counsel Psychol* 17(2):177–83 Mr '70. * (*PA* 44:8550)

88. DAMM, VERNON J. "Creativity and Intelligence: Research Implications for Equal Emphasis in High School." *Excep Children* 36(8):565–9 Ap '70. * (*PA* 46:1754)

89. GINSBURG, G. P., AND HOOD, RALPH W., JR. "Associative Clustering and Performance on the Remote Associates Test." *J Exp Res Personality* 4(3):1–5 Je '70. * (*PA* 44:16689)

90. GINSBURG, G. P., AND HOOD, RALPH W., JR. "Water Jar and Remote Associates Test Performances: An Associative Clustering Interpretation." *J Exp Res Personality* 4(4):286–90 O '70. * (*PA* 45:6348)

91. HARRIS, RICHARD, AND HALL, ALFRED E. "Creativity and the Need for Associative Novelty." *Can J Psychol* 24(2):90–7 Ap '70. * (*PA* 46:1190)

92. HOOD, RALPH W., JR., AND GINSBURG, G. P. "Connotative Similarity of Remote Associates Test Items as a Function of Their Cultural Availability." *Psychol Rep* 27(1):127–30 Ag '70. * (*PA* 45:6339)

93. HOOD, RALPH W., JR., AND GINSBURG, G. P. "Cultural Availability: A Cross-Culturally Stable Determinant of Performance on Remote Associates Test Items." *Psychol Rep* 26(3):755–8 Je '70. * (*PA* 45:5–4)

94. KEILLOR, JAMES SHERWOOD. *The Effects of Experimentally Induced Consciousness Expansion and Consciousness Control Upon Creativity and Intellectual Functioning.* Doctor's thesis, Wayne State University (Detroit, Mich.), 1970. (*DAI* 31:4339B)

95. LIBBY, WILLIAM L., JR. "Reaction Time and Remote Association in Talented Male Adolescents." *Develop Psychol* 3(3):285–97 N '70. * (*PA* 45:4001)

96. MEDNICK, MARTHA T., AND SILBER, DAVID E. "Comparison of Two Administration Times for the Remote Associates Test: An Attempt at Partial Replication." *Psychol Rep* 27(2):474 O '70. * (*PA* 45:5271)

97. MENDELSOHN, GERALD A., AND GALL, MEREDITH D. "Personality Variables and the Effectiveness of Techniques to Facilitate Creative Problem Solving." *J Pers & Social Psychol* 16(2):346–51 O '70. * (*PA* 45:2395)

98. SMITH, I. LEON. "Associational Achievement, Aptitude, and Creativity." *Ed & Psychol Meas* 30(4):999–1000 w '70. *

99. TREADWELL, YVONNE. "Humor and Creativity." *Psychol Rep* 26(1):55–8 F '70. * (*PA* 45:4271)

100. WARDESKA, BRENDA C. *Psychological Needs as Measured by the Edwards Personal Preference Schedule of High Scorers Versus Low Scorers on the Remote Associates Test (A Test of Creativity).* Master's thesis, East Tennessee State University (Johnson City, Tenn.), 1970.

LEONARD L. BAIRD, *Research Psychologist, Educational Testing Service, Princeton, New Jersey.*

This test stems directly from Mednick's (*2*) theory of creativity. He assumes that in connection with a stimulus, each person has a hierarchy of potential responses. The responses have different probabilities of being elicited, ranging from the most accessible response to the least accessible. There are, thus, gradients of probability of responses, some steep, some flat. The original person is thought to have flatter gradients, so he is more likely to give associative responses of lower probability when presented with a stimulus. These responses of lower probability may include some that are unusual but appropriate; in other words, a creative response. Thus, in the manual the authors define the creative thinking process as "the forming of associative elements into new combinations which either meet specified requirements or are in some way useful. The more mutually remote the elements of the new combination, the more creative the process or solution."

This conception of creative thinking led directly to the *Remote Associates Test*. The task provides sets of three stimulus words from realms of meaning that are remote from one another, and asks the subject to find another word that can be associated with them all in a meaningful way. Words were chosen because they are a universal part of the culture. An attempt was made to use common words as stimuli, using the Thorndike-Lorge Word Count to check the familiarity of the words. The answers came from low probability responses to words in the norms for the *Kent-Rosanoff Word Association Test*. For example, the common word stimuli are "cookies, sixteen, heart." These words were given as rare responses to the Kent-Rosanoff stimulus word "sweet," which is now the answer to the item. The content of the test consists of similar groups of three words, for which the subject must find another word that will connect with all of them. The final items were selected by typical item selection techniques. (An additional form, Form 2, is available on an experimental basis. The items for this form were selected by similar tech-

niques, but items that were highly related to intelligence were rejected.)

NORMS, INTERPRETATION, AND RELIABILITY. Norms and percentile equivalency tables are provided for a number of college student groups, for one group of psychology graduate students, and for a group of research scientists. Means and standard deviations are also given for certain IBM professional groups. These are clearly presented. High scores are interpreted as indicating creative capacity.

The test is supposed to be a power test but has a 40-minute time limit. The manual states that additional time does not result in significant changes in score rank.

Odd-even reliability estimates for Form I are given for two student groups; they are .91 and .92. The correlation between forms is .81.

VALIDITY. The manual properly devotes much of its text to consideration of the validity of the test. The most important task of any test of creativity is to demonstrate that it has useful power to predict real-life creative accomplishment. The manual summarizes validity studies under several headings: ratings of individuals, ratings of products, other associative measures, and measures of intelligence, achievement, and personality. This review will use these same rubrics, but include research not available when the manual was written.

Ratings of Individuals. The manual reports substantial correlations between RAT scores and creativity ratings of architecture students, psychology graduate students, and "scientists in a chemical firm." However, Datta (9), Pelz and Andrews (34), and Goodman, Furcon, and Rose (73) found no relation between ratings of creativity and the RAT in samples of research scientists and engineers. Karlins and others (77) found no relation between the RAT and ratings of the creativity of graduating architecture students and no relation to architecture school grades.

Ratings of Products. In some small samples of scientists and engineers the manual reports some moderate relations between the RAT and such accomplishments as winning contracts, winning suggestion awards, and obtaining patents. On the other hand, Pelz and Andrews report almost no significant relations between the RAT and such criteria as number of papers and patents, reports, overall contribution, and usefulness in samples of scientists and engineers

(and as many relations were negative as positive).

Other Associative Measures. Most of the studies in the manual report correlations from .31 to .44 between the RAT and verbal fluency tasks such as making as many four letter words as possible from the word *generation.* However, Higgins and Dolby (42) and Jacobson and others (59) report low or no relation between the RAT and tasks requiring mediated association. In addition, Haag and David (74), Goodman, Furcon, and Rose (73), and Taft and Rossiter (36) report no or very low relations between the RAT and certain tests from the Guilford battery. The former study also found no relation with the *AC Test of Creative Ability* or with self-ratings. Other studies have found no relations between the RAT and classical problem solving tasks such as Duncher's Candle Problem (28, 44, 73).

Relations to Academic Aptitude. The manual reports correlations of about .40 between the present version of the test and various measures of academic aptitude. Ginzburg and Whittemore (57), Cropley (27), Taft and Rossiter (36), and Karlins and others (77) found that the RAT and academic ability are moderately (.40 to .60) related, even at high levels of ability. (However, the RAT does not seem to be related to grades.) In addition, some factor analytic studies (27, 36, 74) found that the RAT did not have high loadings on creativity or flexibility factors, but did have loadings on "intelligence factors." Thus the RAT seems to be measuring verbal intelligence, in addition to whatever else it measures. Furthermore, as Cronbach[1] has pointed out, even if there were less overlap with tests of verbal intelligence, we would still need to know if the RAT accomplishes something that conventional reasoning tests cannot.

SUMMARY EVALUATION. The RAT may be criticized on three grounds: (*a*) the evidence for its validity in predicting real-life accomplishments and creativity ratings is mixed; in studies reported since the manual was written, it seems to have little predictive power; (*b*) it seems to have little relation to other measures of creativity or problem solving; and (*c*) much of what it measures seems to be academic or verbal intelligence. On the other hand, the test has the advantage of being a clear-cut extension

1 CRONBACH, LEE J. *Essentials of Psychological Testing,* *Third Edition.* New York: Harper & Row, Publishers, Inc., 1970. Pp. xxx, 752. *

of a theory of creativity, and criteria of real-life creativity are difficult to construct. The effort to build another version of the test that is unrelated to verbal intelligence is, on the current evidence, commendable. While the present version would not be recommended as a device to select potentially creative students or personnel, it may be useful in studies of the nature of the creative process. It may be hoped that the authors will succeed in their efforts to develop a version of the test unrelated to verbal intelligence.

GEORGE K. BENNETT, *Formerly President, The Psychological Corporation, New York, New York.*

The two college and adult forms consist of 30 items each and the score is the number of items correctly answered. Means and standard deviations are reported for more than 4,000 students and a few hundred "research scientists" and IBM employees. Odd-even reliability coefficients of .91 and .92 are reported for two groups of undergraduates. These appear to be remarkably high values for a 30-item power test.

In several studies a positive relationship is reported between the RAT score and one or another index of purported creativity. In each instance the number of subjects is small. In one larger study, no relationship was observed with supervisors' ratings for 214 research scientists and engineers working in government laboratories.

The introductory section of the manual states that "The Remote Associates Test is a measure of the ability to think creatively." This theme is then developed with the aid of quotations from and references to Einstein, Coleridge, André Breton, Poincaré, the British associationists, Freud, Hollingsworth, and Binet. This reviewer hesitates to offer a critical comment regarding a product carrying the real or implied endorsement of so distinguished a group of sponsors but is nevertheless impelled to voice his own opinion. This test samples a kind of verbal facility akin to that required for success in crossword puzzles and the word games found in the daily newspapers. To the extent that cleverness of a verbal sort and knowledge of the clichés which pervade our culture are of significance, the *Remote Associates Test* may have some value. The reviewer does not disparage virtuosity in the manipulation of these symbols but does question the judgment of persons who attempt to equate this characteristic with the sort of creativity which has meaning beyond the construction of advertising jingles.

PHILIP E. VERNON, *Professor of Educational Psychology, The University of Calgary, Calgary, Alberta, Canada.*

The Mednicks' *Remote Associates Test* might appear to be based on a sounder and more carefully argued psychological theory than most tests in the creativity area, notably the numerous divergent thinking tests. As pointed out in the manual, many of the accounts by artists and scientists of their creative processes involve seeing relations between remote ideas. At the same time the authors do not make exaggerated claims for the test, stating merely that it measures "an ability fundamental to the creative thinking process" by asking the subjects "to form associative elements into new combinations by providing mediating connective links." The advocates of divergent tests, however, would probably reply that any test whose items depend on finding the one right answer, this answer either chosen from Kent-Rosanoff association lists or thought up by the authors, is antithetical to truly creative thinking. And the discovery of an associate which is common to three words (e.g., *cheese* as an associate with *mouse, sharp,* and *blue*) cannot really be regarded as bearing much resemblance to the way the creative artist or scientist works.

But the authors do not rely solely on theoretical arguments. They collected some striking empirical evidence of validity before publishing, despite the difficulties of arriving at good criteria. The test has correlated to a promising extent with ratings of architectural design students and graduate psychology students, and with job level of industrial chemists; also with the numbers of research proposals by scientists which won contracts, and with award-winning suggestions among IBM technicians. There is also some overlapping with divergent measures, such as an anagrams test. Subsequent users, however, seldom seem to get as good results, and there is no doubt that the test is fairly heavily weighted with verbal intelligence as measured by the *Miller Analogies Test* or the *Concept Mastery Test.* The list of group means quoted in the manual shows graduate psychology students scoring highest, then honours students and professional research scientists, followed by female then male freshmen, and the least educated IBM technicians at the bottom. However the test is not merely one of verbal achievement, since correlations with grades tend to be negative, and there is other construct validity evidence.

In the present writer's view, the test probably measures a rather specialized verbal skill, similar to that involved in finding anagrams or doing crossword puzzles. Indeed one might make as good a case that grasping unusual associations is elicited by difficult crossword clues, as the Mednicks' case for their type of item. Nevertheless the decision to publish the test was entirely justifiable, since questions regarding its validity can only be answered by more extensive research in more varied contexts.

Most work, including the standardization data on over 4,000 college students and over 500 adults, has been done with Form 1. The experimental Form 2 should be interesting in so far as its items have been selected to minimize strong verbal intelligence correlations. Odd-even reliabilities average close to .90, and though the correlation between Forms 1 and 2 is only .81 in a group of 61 undergraduates, this may reflect the rather different procedures for selecting items. The manual is extremely clearly written. The sample items in the test instructions, however, are perhaps rather difficult for subjects who are not well above average in verbal abilities. It would be interesting to see how much scores would rise with further practice on relatively simple items (as they do in crossword solving).

[446]

*The Rutgers Drawing Test. Ages 4–6, 6–9; 1952–69; RDT; 2 levels labeled forms; 6¢ per test; $1 per manual for each level; $1 per specimen set of either level; postage extra; (5–10) minutes; Anna Spiesman Starr; the Author. *
a) FORM A. Ages 4–6; 1952–68; test ['52, 1 page]; revised manual ('68, 35 pages); record sheet ['66, 2 pages]; no data on reliability; 3¢ per record sheet.
b) FORM B. Ages 6–9; 1959–69; test ('59, 1 page); mimeographed manual ('69, 54 pages).

REFERENCES

1–2. See 6:559.
3. STEVENS, MARGARET CLARK. A Drawing Test for the Preschool Child. Master's thesis, Rutgers—The State University (New Brunswick, N.J.), 1937.
4. BALINKY, JEAN LAHN. A Configurational Approach to the Prediction of Academic Achievement in First Grade. Doctor's thesis, Rutgers—The State University (New Brunswick, N.J.), 1964. (DA 25:2844)
5. DUDEK, S. Z.; LESTER, L. P.; AND HARRIS, B. R. "Variability on Tests of Cognitive and Perceptual-Motor Development in Kindergarten Children." J Clin Psychol 23:461–4 O '67. * (PA 42:2400)
6. PANTHER, EDWARD E. "Prediction of First-Grade Reading Achievement." El Sch J 68:44–8 O '67. *
7. YUDIN, LEE WILLIAM. "The Rutgers Drawing Test and Intelligence: A Preliminary Comparative Study." Percept & Motor Skills 24:1038 Je '67. *
8. DUDEK, S. Z.; GOLDBERG, J. S.; LESTER, E. P.; AND HARRIS, B. R. "The Validity of Cognitive, Perceptual-Motor and Personality Variables for Prediction of Achievement in Grade 1 and Grade 2." J Clin Psychol 25(2):165–70 Ap '69. * (PA 43:14874)

MELVYN I. SEMMEL, Professor of Special Education, Indiana University, Bloomington, Indiana.

The Rutgers Drawing Test is a nonverbal copying test which was constructed in order to provide "a non-verbal test of increasing difficulty to tap such abilities as perception of form and space, analysis of design in reproduction, motor coordination, critical attention and a demonstration of how the child revealed his personality strength in attacking a new and unfamiliar problem." It is essentially a test of visuomotor ability. Form A requires a child to copy a series of 14 two-dimensional geometric and bilaterally symmetrical designs of increasing complexity and difficulty. Two practice figures are also included. The figures, drawn to scale, are arranged on a simple record form with space provided beneath each figure for the child's copy. There is no time limit for individual drawings. Some of the designs had appeared as subtests in other test batteries and served as guideposts in assembling Form A of the RDT. The test is given individually, but the author claims that it may also be used as a group test using essentially the same directions.

Form B was designed as an upward extension of Form A. The 16 designs of Form B are more difficult and complex. Both forms are simple to administer and require only an average of five minutes for completion. Separate manuals are presented for each form. However, there is needless repetition of identical information in the two manuals. A single manual for both forms would be more efficient.

A relatively objective though crude scoring key is presented. Performance is scored in terms of the correctness of reproduction. The scoring norms of Form A provide "drawing ages" in months. Form B gives only drawing scores. Subjectivity in scoring borderline drawings appears to be a potential problem, particularly with respect to the atypical response.

Form A was standardized on a sample of 1,428 children between the ages of 4 and 7, while Form B was standardized on a sample of 2,074 children from age 6 through 9. Both samples consisted mainly of children examined at the Rutgers Clinic. Selection of the standardization samples is inadequately described. There is no information reported regarding distributions with respect to sex, age, socioeconomic status, or intelligence. The total sample, though extensive, is too homogeneous to ensure desirable representativeness of norms. Test users may find local norms more suitable for their own purposes than the RDT norms. Revision of the RDT norms on the basis of a more representative sample would be desirable.

No reliability data are provided for Form A. However, data are presented which suggest that Form A is reasonably stable within each six month interval. Furthermore, scorer reliability of Form A appears satisfactory. Retest reliability of Form B based on a sample of children in grades 2 and 3 tested one week apart was relatively low, .79. Retest reliability for a group of 7-year-olds was also low, .69.

Only scattered studies of validity are available for Form A. For nonretarded children between the ages of 4 and 7, the drawing scores show a regular increase with age and a fairly high correlation (.72) with Stanford-Binet mental ages between the ages of 3 and 6 years. For moderately retarded children under 12 a moderate correlation (.61) between the S-B and drawing scores is reported. A correlation of .70 was obtained between S-B IQ and Rutgers Drawing IQ. These correlations may be regarded as a measure of concurrent validity for Form A. Data are provided from a pilot study with kindergarten children which suggest that the test may be a good predictor of reading achievement in the primary grades. However, the analysis was based on a small sample and needs further verification.

Continuing research on predictive validity for both test forms with different samples and ages, and against other criteria is required. Furthermore, comparisons of normal children with children labeled as retarded, emotionally disturbed, or neurologically impaired will provide meaningful information concerning the diagnostic validity of the RDT, and its feasibility in detecting serious forms of perceptual motor performance.

When used as an individual test, the RDT provides an opportunity for the experienced clinician to observe qualitative data and the child's manner in attacking problems. In fact the author states that this may be the test's greatest value.

In summary, the RDT appears to have promise as a rapid performance test of perceptual motor ability and as a screening device for detecting serious forms of visuomotor handicaps. The test appears to display acceptable reliability and validity with younger children (ages 4–7); however, the data are relatively meager. Continuing research on empirical reliability and validity for different samples and ages is required. The normative data are rather restricted and require extension and revision on a more representative sample. Hence, they are of limited use. Experienced clinicians may find the test a help in making subjective observations of perceptual-motor dysfunction or emotional disturbance. The test may be useful in establishing initial rapport in testing non-English speaking, culturally deprived, preschool, or speech-impaired children. The RDT may provide supplemental information to the Bender-Gestalt and the Frostig tests. It should be classified as a structured clinical tool with data too incomplete to warrant its use as a standardized psychometric tool.

[447]

★Symbol Series Test: I.B.P. Edition, 1968. Illiterate and semi-literate adults; 1969; abstract reasoning; 1 form (2 pages); manual (20 pages, English and Venda); no data on validity; R1.25 per 25 tests; 5c per single copy; 50c per demonstration poster; R2 per manual; postpaid within South Africa; (45–65) minutes; G. V. Grant; National Institute for Personnel Research. *

[448]

★Torrance Tests of Creative Thinking, Research Edition. Kgn through graduate school; 1966; TTCT; revision of *Minnesota Tests of Creative Thinking;* 2 forms; 2 tests; technical manual (95 pages); scoring worksheet (1 page) for each test; $5 per 25 sets of test and scoring worksheet; $1 per technical manual; $3 per specimen set; postpaid; scoring service, $1.30 per verbal or figural test; E. Paul Torrance; Personnel Press, Inc. *
a) VERBAL TEST. Test booklet title is *Thinking Creatively With Words;* 3 scores: fluency, flexibility, originality; individual in grades kgn–3; Forms A, B, (15 pages); directions manual (53 pages, minor revisions 1968) for each form; $7.50 per examiner's kit of reusable toys and pictures; 45(60) minutes.
b) FIGURAL TEST. Test booklet title is *Thinking Creatively With Pictures;* 4 scores: fluency, flexibility, originality, elaboration; Forms A (8 pages), B (7 pages); Form A directions manual (43 pages, minor revisions 1970), Form B directions manual (42 pages, minor revisions 1968); 30(45) minutes.

REFERENCES

1. TORRANCE, E. PAUL. "Explorations in Creative Thinking in the Early School Years: A Progress Report." *Univ Utah Res Conf Identif Creat Sci Talent* 3:58–71 '59. *
2. HENRICKSON, PAUL R., AND TORRANCE, E. PAUL. "Some Implications for Art Education From the Minnesota Tests of Creative Thinking." *Studies Art Ed* 2:36–44 sp '61. *
3. HART, ANN M. *A Study of Creative Thinking and Its*

Relation to Nursing. Doctor's thesis, Indiana University (Bloomington, Ind.), 1962. (*DA* 23:4323)

4. PHATAK, PRAMILA. "Exploratory Study of Creativity and Intelligence and Scholastic Achievement." *Psychol Studies* 7:1–9 Ja '62. * (*PA* 37:2013)

5. RAY, PHILIP BOND. *A Descriptive Study of Certain Characteristics of "High Creative" Freshman Arts College Students as Compared With "High Academic Potential" Students.* Doctor's thesis, University of Minnesota (Minneapolis, Minn.), 1962. (*DA* 24:1924)

6. TORRANCE, E. PAUL. *Guiding Creative Talent,* pp. 44–64, 213–54. Englewood Cliffs, N.J.: Prentice-Hall, Inc., 1962. Pp. xi, 278. *

7. ANDERSON, RODNEY EARL. *A Comparison of the Performance of College Freshmen Participants and Non-Participants in an Honors Program on Four Psychological Measures.* Doctor's research study No. 1, Colorado State College (Greeley, Colo.), 1963. (*DA* 25:279)

8. BLOCKHUS, WANDA ALEXANDER. *Creativity and Money Management Understandings.* Doctor's thesis, University of Minnesota (Minneapolis, Minn.), 1963. (*DA* 25:2373)

9. EVEN, ROBERT LAWRENCE. *An Experimental Study of the Comparative Effect of Selected Art Experiences on the Creative Performance and Attitudes of Academically Superior Students.* Doctor's thesis, University of Minnesota (Minneapolis, Minn.), 1963. (*DA* 24:4470)

10. JOHNSON, RICHARD THEODORE. *The Growth of Creative Thinking Abilities in Western Samoa.* Doctor's thesis, University of Minnesota (Minneapolis, Minn.), 1963. (*DA* 24:1922)

11. KETCHERSIDE, WILLIAM JOSEPH. *Creative and Adjustive Factors Involved in Educational Development Beyond Expectancy.* Doctor's thesis, University of Missouri (Columbia, Mo.), 1963. (*DA* 24:4545)

12. LUCHT, WAYNE EDWARD. *Creativity: A Study of Relationships.* Doctor's thesis, State University of Iowa (Iowa City, Iowa), 1963. (*DA* 24:4085)

13. McELVAIN, JUDITH L.; FRETWELL, LORETTA N.; AND LEWIS, ROLAND B. "Relationships Between Creativity and Teacher Variability." *Psychol Rep* 13:186 Ag '63. * (*PA* 38:6665)

14. ROUGHTON, EDGAR LEROY. *Creativity as a Factor in Reading Achievement.* Doctor's thesis, University of South Carolina (Columbia, S.C.), 1963. (*DA* 25:1012)

15. ROUSE, SUE THOMPSON. *Effects of a Training Program on the Productive Thinking of Educable Mental Retardates.* Doctor's thesis, George Peabody College for Teachers (Nashville, Tenn.), 1963. (*DA* 25:1053)

16. WODTKE, KENNETH HENRY. *A Study of the Reliability and Validity of Creativity Tests at the Elementary School Level.* Doctor's thesis, University of Utah (Salt Lake City, Utah), 1963. (*DA* 24:4091)

17. BECK, ELIZABETH JOAN. *Relation Between Social Impact and Selected Intellectual Traits in Preadolescent Negro Boys.* Doctor's thesis, Fordham University (New York, N.Y.), 1964. (*DA* 25:1328)

18. BISH, GERTRUDE GANTZ. *A Study of the Relationships of Intelligence, Achievement, Creativity, Anxiety, and Confidence Among Intermediate Grade Pupils in a Suburban Area Elementary School.* Doctor's thesis, George Washington University (Washington, D.C.), 1964.

19. CICIRELLI, VICTOR GEORGE. *The Relationship Between Measures of Creativity, IQ, and Academic Achievement; Interaction and Threshold Effects.* Doctor's thesis, University of Michigan (Ann Arbor, Mich.), 1964. (*DA* 25:3388)

20. DEVER, WAYMAN TODD. *The Relationship Between the Creative Thinking Ability of Selected Fourth Graders and Parental Attitudes.* Doctor's thesis, North Texas State University (Denton, Tex.), 1964. (*DA* 25:3390)

21. DUKES, BEN MARSHALL. *Anxiety, Self Concept, Reading Achievement, and Creative Thinking in Four Socio-Economic Status Levels.* Doctor's thesis, University of Alabama (University, Ala.), 1964. (*DA* 25:7076)

22. ELLINGER, BERNICE DEES. *The Home Environment and the Creative Thinking Ability of Children.* Doctor's thesis, Ohio State University (Columbus, Ohio), 1964. (*DA* 25:6308)

23. GOLDMAN, R. J. "The Minnesota Tests of Creative Thinking." *Ed Res* 7:3–14 N '64. * (*PA* 39:10114)

24. HANSON, DORIS ELIZABETH. *Home Economists in Overseas Work.* Doctor's thesis, Columbia University (New York, N.Y.), 1964. (*DA* 26:346)

25. HAVEN, GEORGE A., JR. *Creative Thought, Productivity, and the Self-Concept.* Doctor's thesis, University of Minnesota (Minneapolis, Minn.), 1964. (*DA* 25:2030)

26. MEARIG, JUDITH SUZANNE. *Fluency and Dependency as Predictors of Sex Differences in Ability and Achievement.* Doctor's thesis, University of Michigan (Ann Arbor, Mich.), 1964. (*DA* 25:3401)

27. OWENS, RICHARD E. *The Relationship of Creative Thinking Ability to Extreme Over and Underachievement.* Doctor's thesis, Colorado State College (Greeley, Colo.), 1964. (*DA* 25:5122)

28. POGUE, BETTY CASKEY. *An Exploration of the Interrelationship Among Creativity, Self-Esteem and Race.* Doctor's thesis, Ball State Teachers College (Muncie, Ind.), 1964. (*DA* 26:3155)

29. RAGOUZIS, PERRY NICHOLAS. *An Experimental Study of the Effects of Non-Grading of Student Art Products on Selected Aspects of Creativity, Personality Adjustment and Art Quality in Art Education Courses for Elementary School Teachers.* Doctor's thesis, University of Minnesota (Minneapolis, Minn.), 1964. (*DA* 26:877)

30. RAMBO, FLORENCE LASSETER. *Pupil Characteristics Related to Creativity.* Doctor's thesis, University of Georgia (Athens, Ga.), 1964. (*DA* 25:2857)

31. SMITH, ROBERT HOUSTON. *A Study of Pre-Adolescent Boys Demonstrating Varying Levels of Creativity With Regard to Their Social Adjustment, Peer Acceptance and Academically Related Behavior.* Doctor's thesis, North Texas State University (Denton, Tex.), 1964. (*DA* 25:4553)

32. TRUE, SALLY RALSTON. *A Study of the Relation of General Semantics and Creativity.* Doctor's thesis, University of Wisconsin (Madison, Wis.), 1964. (*DA* 25:2390)

33. WALLACE, HAROLD RONALD. *Creative Thinking: A Factor in the Performance of Industrial Salesmen.* Doctor's thesis, University of Minnesota (Minneapolis, Minn.), 1964. (*DA* 26:4463)

34. WODTKE, KENNETH H. "Some Data on the Reliability and Validity of Creativity Tests at the Elementary School Level." *Ed & Psychol Meas* 24:399–408 su '64. * (*PA* 39:5110)

35. YAMAMOTO, KAORU. "Evaluation of Some Creativity Measures in a High School With Peer Nominations as Criteria." *J Psychol* 58:285–93 O '64. * (*PA* 39:5138)

36. YAMAMOTO, KAORU. *Experimental Scoring Manuals for Minnesota Tests of Creative Thinking and Writing.* Kent State University, Bureau of Educational Research, Research Monograph Series, No. 1. Kent, Ohio: the Bureau, May 1964. Pp. 160. *

37. YAMAMOTO, KAORU. "Role of Creative Thinking and Intelligence in High School Achievement." *Psychol Rep* 14:783–9 Je '64. * (*PA* 39:5140)

38. YEE, GEORGE FONG. *The Influences of Problem-Solving Instruction and Personal-Social Adjustment Upon Creativity Test Scores of Twelfth Grade Students.* Doctor's thesis, Pennsylvania State University (University Park, Pa.), 1964. (*DA* 26:916)

39. CICIRELLI, VICTOR G. "Form of the Relationship Between Creativity, IQ, and Academic Achievement." *J Ed Psychol* 56:303–8 D '65. * (*PA* 40:3373)

40. DAUW, DEAN CHARLES. *Life Experiences, Vocational Needs and Choices of Original Thinkers and Good Elaborators.* Doctor's thesis, University of Minnesota (Minneapolis, Minn.), 1965. (*DA* 26:5223)

41. DAVIS, O. L., JR., AND YAMAMOTO, KAORU. "Creative Thinking and Achievement Item Responses of Elementary School Pupils: A Preliminary Investigation." *J Peabody Ed* 42:349–55 My '65. *

42. EASTWOOD, GORDON R. "Divergent Thinking and Academic Success." *Ont J Ed Res* 7:241–54 sp '65. * (*PA* 39:16453)

43. GOWAN, J. C., AND TORRANCE, E. P. "An Intercultural Study of Non-Verbal Ideational Fluency." *Gifted Child Q* 9:13–5+ sp '65. * (*PA* 39:12005)

44. HADLEY, DONALD JAMES. *Experimental Relationships Between Creativity and Anxiety.* Doctor's thesis, University of Michigan (Ann Arbor, Mich.), 1965. (*DA* 26:2586)

45. KELLY, GEORGE RICHARD. *Creativity, School Attitude, and Intelligence Relationships in Grades: Four, Six, and Eight.* Doctor's thesis, University of New Mexico (Albuquerque, N.M.), 1965. (*DA* 25:6390)

46. KELSON, FLORENCE. *An Assessment of Creativity in the Retarded Child.* Doctor's thesis, Yeshiva University (New York, N.Y.), 1965. (*DA* 26:3478)

47. KIRSH, JACK LORIN. *Relationship Between Certain Teacher Personality Traits and Background Experiences and Teacher Preference for Working With Children Who Exhibit a High Degree of Originality.* Doctor's thesis, University of Florida (Gainesville, Fla.), 1965. (*DA* 27:704A)

48. PALERMO, RICHARD RANDOLPH. *A Study of the Relationship of Students' Descriptions of Teachers' Styles of Teaching and Teachers' Creativity.* Doctor's thesis, Western Reserve University (Cleveland, Ohio), 1965. (*DA* 27:130A)

49. PATON, CORA LOUISE. *Divergent Thinking and Language Enrichment of Nursery School Children.* Doctor's thesis, Florida State University (Tallahassee, Fla.), 1965. (*DA* 26:4456)

50. RODERICK, JAMES LEROY. *An Investigation of Selected Factors of the Creative Thinking Ability of Music Majors in a Teacher Training Program.* Doctor's thesis, University of Illinois (Urbana, Ill.), 1965. (*DA* 26:409)

51. ROUSE, SUE T. "Effects of a Training Program on the Productive Thinking of Educable Mental Retardates." *Am J Mental Def* 69:666–73 Mr '65. * (*PA* 39:13001)

52. SCOTT, LEON EDWARD. *Underachievers as Contrasted to Overachievers With Respect to Creative Ability, Achievement Motivation, Self-Control, and Parental Aspirations.* Doctor's thesis, University of Nebraska (Lincoln, Neb.), 1965. (*DA* 26:5881)

53. SHELDON, MARGARET JEAN REED. *A Statistical Study of the Reliability of a Single Paper and Pencil Test of Creativity.* Master's thesis, American University (Washington, D.C.), 1965. (*Masters Abstracts* 5:4)

54. Torrance, E. Paul. "Scientific Views of Creativity and Factors Affecting Its Growth." *Daedalus* 94:663–81 su '65. *

55. Torrance, E. Paul, and Dauw, Dean C. "Aspirations and Dreams of Three Groups of Creatively Gifted High School Seniors and a Comparable Unselected Group." *Gifted Child Q* 9:177–82 w '65. * (*PA* 40:5281)

56. Tucker, Casey Allen. *Creativity and Its Relationship to Success in College as Measured by the Grade Point Average.* Doctor's research study No. 1, Colorado State College (Greeley, Colo.), 1965. (*DA* 26:5275)

57. Van Pelt, Bobby Newell. *A Study of Creativity and Other Selected Variables as Related to Academic Achievement in the Upper Elementary Grades.* Doctor's thesis, University of New Mexico (Albuquerque, N.M.), 1965. (*DA* 26:5884)

58. Yamamoto, Kaoru. "Effects of Restriction of Range and Test Unreliability on Correlation Between Measures of Intelligence and Creative Thinking." *Brit J Ed Psychol* 35:300–5 N '65. * (*PA* 40:2876)

59. Carey, Joseph Edward. *The Relationship Between Creative Thinking Ability, Intellectual Ability, Educational Achievement, and Writing Ability of Sixth Grade Children.* Doctor's thesis, Indiana University (Bloomington, Ind.), 1966. (*DA* 27:2095A)

60. Cicirelli, Victor G. "Vocational Aspirations and Creativity." *J Ed Res* 60:68–70 O '66. *

61. Collins, Dwane R.; Collins, Myrtle T.; and Leton, Donald A. "The Effects of the Flight Technique of Teaching on Creativity Scores." *J Exp Ed* 34:32–7 su '66. * (*PA* 40: 11154)

62. Dauw, Dean C. "Career Choices of High and Low Creative Thinkers." *Voc Guid Q* 15:135–40 D '66. * (*PA* 41: 12658)

63. Dauw, Dean C. "Life Experiences of Original Thinkers and Good Elaborators." *Excep Children* 32:433–40 F '66. * (*PA* 40:6632)

64. Dauw, Dean C. "Personality Self-Descriptions of Original Thinkers and Good Elaborators." *Psychol Sch* 3:78–9 Ja '66. *

65. Dauw, Dean C. "Scholastic Aptitudes and Vocational Needs of Original Thinkers and Good Elaborators." *Personnel & Guid J* 45:171–5 O '66. *

66. Davis, Donald Jack. *The Effects of Two Methods of Teaching Art Upon Creative Thinking, Art Attitudes, and Aesthetic Quality of Art Products in Beginning College Art Students.* Doctor's thesis, University of Minnesota (Minneapolis, Minn.), 1966. (*DA* 27:2272A)

67. Duenk, Lester G. "A Study of the Concurrent Validity of the Minnesota Tests of Creative Thinking for Eighth Grade Industrial Arts Students." *J Indus Teach Ed* 3:30–5 sp '66. *

68. Duenk, Lester Gerald. *A Study of the Concurrent Validity of the Minnesota Tests of Creative Thinking, Abbr. Form VII, for Eighth Grade Industrial Arts Students.* Doctor's thesis, University of Minnesota (Minneapolis, Minn.), 1966. (*DA* 27:1653A)

69. Fuqua, Norman Vince. *An Analysis of the Relationships and Differences Among Measures of Creative Thinking and Selected Other Factors in Educable and Less Educable Groups of Negro Children.* Doctor's thesis, Wayne State University (Detroit, Mich.), 1966. (*DA* 27:2314A)

70. Grover, Burton L. "Prediction of Achievement in Divergent and Convergent Learning Situations." *J Ed Res* 59: 402–5 My–Je '66. * (*PA* 40:11488)

71. Guth, Robert Otto. *Creativity, Competitive Drive, and Interest Patterns Associated With Success in a Program for Academically Talented High School Students.* Doctor's thesis, Temple University (Philadelphia, Pa.), 1966. (*DA* 27:3692A)

72. Hamby, Trudy M. *An Investigation of the Relationship Between Teacher Structuring and Change in Children's Creative Performance and Self-Ideal Self Reports.* Doctor's thesis, University of Maryland (College Park, Md.), 1966. (*DA* 27: 993A)

73. Huguelet, Patricia Williams. *A Perceptual Approach to the Creative Process.* Doctor's thesis, University of Michigan (Ann Arbor, Mich.), 1966. (*DA* 27:2069A)

74. Laynor, Harold Arthur. *Some Indicators of Levels of Creativity in Eighth Grade Pupils (A Comparison of Artwork Judgment and Teacher Choice With Selected Tests From the Minnesota Creativity Test Battery).* Doctor's thesis, State University of New York (Albany, N.Y.), 1966. (*DA* 27:4047A)

75. MacDougall, Mary Julia. *Relationship of Critical Reading and Creative Thinking Abilities in Children.* Doctor's thesis, Ohio State University (Columbus, Ohio), 1966. (*DA* 27:3779A)

76. Mayhon, Woodrow G. *The Relationship of Creativity to Achievement and Other Student Variables.* Doctor's thesis, University of New Mexico (Albuquerque, N.M.), 1966. (*DA* 27: 1713A)

77. Olson, David R.; Rumley, Evelyn; Reardon, Barbara; and Gill, Mary Jane. "Creativity and Social Acceptability." *Can Ed & Res Dig* 6:205–8 S '66. *

78. Perry, Joyce Marlene. *Correlates of Teacher Prediction for Student Success Six Years Beyond Sixth Grade.* Doctor's thesis, University of Illinois (Urbana, Ill.), 1966. (*DA* 27: 2012A)

79. Smith, David Lyle. *An Exploratory Study of a Means for Assessing Both Creativity and Conformity of First Graders.* Doctor's thesis, Michigan State University (East Lansing, Mich.), 1966. (*DA* 28:158A)

80. Stafford, Richard Lindsay. *The Effects of Creativity and Intelligence on Information Seeking Strategies Used in a Problem Solving Task by Sixth Grade Boys.* Doctor's thesis, University of Houston (Houston, Tex.), 1966. (*DA* 27:973B)

81. Torrance, E. Paul, and Dauw, Dean C. "Attitude Patterns of Creatively Gifted High School Seniors." *Gifted Child Q* 10:53–7 su '66. * (*PA* 41:788)

82. True, Sally. "A Study of the Relation of General Semantics and Creativity." *J Exp Ed* 34:34–40 sp '66. * (*PA* 40:8079)

83. Wirth, Janina Wirpsa. *Relationships Between Teacher Opinions of Disadvantaged Children and Measures of Selected Characteristics of These Children.* Doctor's thesis, University of Florida (Gainesville, Fla.), 1966. (*DA* 27:1290A)

84. Yamamoto, Kaoru, and Chimbidis, Maria E. "Achievement, Intelligence, and Creative Thinking in Fifth Grade Children: A Correlational Study." *Merrill-Palmer Q* 12:233–41 Jl '66. * (*PA* 41:5818)

85. Yamamoto, Kaoru, and Frengel, Barbara A. "An Exploratory Component Analysis of the Minnesota Tests of Creative Thinking." *Calif J Ed Res* 17:220–9 S '66. * (*PA* 41: 28-8)

86. Bellin, Adelaida Peinado. *Creative Thinking Ability and Its Relationship to Reading Comprehension and Intelligence of Fourth Grade Pupils.* Doctor's thesis, University of Minnesota (Minneapolis, Minn.), 1967. (*DA* 28:2429A)

87. Benton, John Eldon. *A Study of the Relationship of Openness and Drive to Creativity.* Doctor's thesis, Arizona State University (Tempe, Ariz.), 1967. (*DA* 28:995A)

88. Bilon, Louisa Russell. *Improving Children's Creative Thinking Through Group Discussion Treatment of Mothers: An Experimental Study of the Impact of Group Discussion on Maternal Attitudes and on Children's Creative Thinking.* Doctor's thesis, George Washington University (Washington, D.C.), 1967. (*DA* 28:2618B)

89. Broome, Lillian Wisler. *The Effect of Teachers' Creativity on Children's Learning.* Doctor's thesis, Temple University (Philadelphia, Pa.), 1967. (*DA* 28:4040A)

90. Cawley, John F., and Chase, Donna V. "Productive Thinking in Retarded and Non-Retarded Children." *Brit J Ed Psychol* 37:356–60 N '67. * (*PA* 42:5977)

91. Cummings, Susan Pauline Noll. *Curiosity as a Measure of Cortical Potential.* Doctor's thesis, Arizona State University (Tempe, Ariz.), 1967. (*DA* 28:1323A)

92. Dauw, Dean C. "Vocational Interests of Highly Creative Computer Personnel." *Personnel J* 46:653–9 N '67. * (*PA* 42:4632)

93. Fletcher, Kenneth Richard. *Congruence of Self and Ideal-Self in Original and Non-Original High School Seniors.* Doctor's thesis, University of Minnesota (Minneapolis, Minn.), 1967. (*DA* 28:4907A)

94. Gensemer, Ira Bennett. *A Study of Psychometric Measures of Creativity and Their Relationship to Field-Dependency, Teacher Proficiency and Attitudes.* Doctor's thesis, Temple University (Philadelphia, Pa.), 1967. (*DA* 29:1128A)

95. Goldman, R. J., and Clarke, D. F. "The Minnesota Tests of Creative Thinking—A Note on Scorer Reliability in Follow-Up Studies With English Primary School Children." *Brit J Ed Psychol* 37:115–7 F '67. *

96. Hahn, Marshall Sterling. *The Influence of Creativity on the Effectiveness of Two Methods of Instruction.* Doctor's thesis, University of Minnesota (Minneapolis, Minn.), 1967. (*DA* 28:2895A)

97. Henson, James Pinkney. *The Creative Thinking Abilities of Elementary Students in Public and Parochial Schools.* Doctor's thesis, Indiana University (Bloomington, Ind.), 1967. (*DA* 28:2094A)

98. Hine, Willa Wasson. *An Evaluation of Creativity as a Factor in the Development of Problems for Some School Children.* Doctor's thesis, University of Denver (Denver, Colo.), 1967. (*DA* 28:4875A)

99. Irons, Jerry Lee. *Creative Thinking Abilities of Rural and Urban Elementary School Students.* Doctor's thesis, East Texas State University (Commerce, Tex.), 1967. (*DA* 28: 2897A)

100. Jennings, Betty Lea. *A Comparison of Creative and Non-Creative Pre-Service Teachers on Scholastic Aptitude, Academic Achievement, Personality, and Item Sorts on Behavioral Classroom Situation Variables.* Doctor's thesis, University of Oklahoma (Norman, Okla.), 1967. (*DA* 28:987A)

101. Johnson, Jennings Oliver. *The Relationship Between Science Achievement and Selected Student Characteristics.* Doctor's thesis, University of Minnesota (Minneapolis, Minn.), 1967. (*DA* 28:2029A)

102. Karioth, Emil Joseph. *Creative Dramatics as an Aid in Developing Creative Thinking Abilities.* Doctor's thesis, University of Minnesota (Minneapolis, Minn.), 1967. (*DA* 28: 5180A)

103. Kuo, You-Yuh. *A Comparative Study of Creative Thinking Between Delinquent Boys and Non-Delinquent Boys.* Doctor's thesis, University of Maryland (College Park, Md.), 1967. (*DA* 28:1166B)

104. Kuo, You-Yuh. "Creative Thinking: Delinquent vs. Nondelinquent Boys." *J Creative Behav* 1:411–8 f '67. *

105. LANIER, PERRY EUGENE. *A Study of Creativity, Intelligence and Discovery Teaching as Related to Performance in Elementary School Mathematics.* Doctor's thesis, University of Oklahoma (Norman, Okla.), 1967. (*DA* 28:1004A)

106. McDANIEL, SARAH W. "Counselor Selection: An Evaluation of Instruments." *Counselor Ed & Sup* 6:142–4 w '67. *

107. MACKLER, BERNARD, AND SHONTZ, FRANKLIN C. "Characteristics of Responses to Tests of Creativity." *J Clin Psychol* 23:73–80 Ja '67. * (*PA* 41:5961)

108. MADAUS, GEORGE F. "A Cross-Cultural Comparison of the Factor Structure of Selected Tests of Divergent Thinking." *J Social Psychol* 73:13–21 O '67. * (*PA* 42:650)

109. MADAUS, GEORGE F. "Divergent Thinking and Intelligence: Another Look at a Controversial Question." *J Ed Meas* 4:227–35 w '67. * (*PA* 42:10584)

110. MERRYMAN, EDWARD PAUL. *An Analysis of Open-Closed-Mindedness and Selected Variables as Predictors of Creativity.* Doctor's thesis, Ball State University (Muncie, Ind.), 1967. (*DA* 28:1303A)

111. MIDDENTS, GERALD JOHN. *The Relationship of Creativity and Anxiety.* Doctor's thesis, University of Minnesota (Minneapolis, Minn.), 1967. (*DA* 28:2562A)

112. MITCHELL, BRUCE MARVIN. *An Assessment of Changes in Creativity Factors of Elementary School Children Involved in a Creativity Project.* Doctor's thesis, University of Denver (Denver, Colo.), 1967. (*DA* 28:3376A)

113. MOSS, JEROME, JR., AND DUENK, LESTER G. "Estimating the Concurrent Validity of the Minnesota Tests of Creative Thinking." *Am Ed Res J* 4:387–96 N '67. * (*PA* 42:16421)

114. NEAL, JOYCE A. *A Study of the Creative Ability of Mental Retardates Compared With That of Normal and Gifted Pupils Through Use of the Minnesota Tests of Creative Thinking and Writing.* Master's thesis, University of Louisville (Louisville, Ky.), 1967.

115. OSMAN, HASSAN HAFEZ. *An Investigative Study in the Creative Thinking of Emotionally Disturbed Children in Special Classes.* Doctor's thesis, University of Kansas (Lawrence, Kan.), 1967. (*DA* 28:5210B)

116. PHILIPP, JOAN ALICE. *The Comparison of Motor Creativity With Figural and Verbal Creativity, and Selected Motor Skills.* Doctor's thesis, University of Michigan (Ann Arbor, Mich.), 1967. (*DA* 28:4899A)

117. PLOGMAN, BERNARD EDWARD. *The Creative Relationship Between Art Teachers and Their Ninth Grade Art Students in Art Room Practices, Personality and Pencil Drawing in Catholic Schools.* Doctor's thesis, University of Cincinnati (Cincinnati, Ohio), 1967. (*DA* 28:3534A)

118. POPE, ALLEN LAWRENCE. *An Exploratory Study of Certain Aspects of the Personal-Social Relations of the Highly Creative Student as Compared to the Academically-Intelligent Student.* Doctor's thesis, University of Montana (Missoula, Mont.), 1967. (*DA* 28:1629A)

119. RODERICK, JESSIE ALICE. *Some Relationships Between Creativity and the Reading Preferences and Choices of a Group of Sixth Graders.* Doctor's thesis, Temple University (Philadelphia, Pa.), 1967. (*DA* 28:1012A)

120. ROGERS, DONALD WESLEY. *A Comparison of Selected Art Abilities of Elementary School Students From Varying Socioeconomic Levels.* Doctor's thesis, University of Connecticut (Storrs, Conn.), 1967. (*DA* 28:3381A)

121. SOLIMAN, ABDALLA MAHMOUD. *A Study of the Relationships Between Creativity, Social Class, Social Mobility, and Vocational Goals of High School Seniors.* Doctor's thesis, University of Minnesota (Minneapolis, Minn.), 1967. (*DA* 28:3518A)

122. STUBBINGS, JOHN ROBERT, JR. *A Comparison of the Torrance Tests of Creative Thinking and Guilford's Measures of Creative Ability on Sex, Cognitive, and Personality Variables.* Doctor's thesis, University of Virginia (Charlottesville, Va.), 1967. (*DA* 28:4496A)

123. TORRANCE, E. PAUL. "The Minnesota Studies of Creative Behavior: National and International Extensions." *J Creative Behav* 1:137–54 sp '67. * (*PA* 41:15284)

124. WEBER, WILFORD ALEXANDER. *Teacher Behavior and Pupil Creativity.* Doctor's thesis, Temple University (Philadelphia, Pa.), 1967. (*DA* 29:159A)

125. AMRAM, FRED M., AND WILLIAMS, FRANK E. "Creative Thinking Skills and Personality Traits: A Study of Their Relationship Among Young Adults." *J Nat Assn Women Deans & Counselors* 31:176–81 su '68. *

126. ARASTEH, JOSEPHINE D. "Creativity and Related Processes in the Young Child: A Review of the Literature." *J Genetic Psychol* 112:77–108 Mr '68. * (*PA* 42:10353)

127. BELEFF, NICHOLAS. *An Experiment to Increase Ideational Fluency Gain Scores of Ninth Grade Students Through Brainstorming and Questioning Methods, Developmental Exercises, and Social Studies Content.* Doctor's thesis, Indiana University (Bloomington, Ind.), 1968. (*DA* 29:1668A)

128. BOERSMA, FREDERIC J., AND O'BRYAN, KENNETH. "An Investigation of the Relationship Between Creativity and Intelligence Under Two Conditions of Testing." *J Personality* 36:341–8 S '68. * (*PA* 43:3993)

129. BRADFIELD, ROBERT HARRISON. *Divergent and Convergent Thinking: Achievement Motivated Processes.* Doctor's thesis, University of California (Berkeley, Calif.), 1968. (*DA* 29:4272A)

130. BREWTON, BARNEY CAMBON. *Relationships of Sex-Role Identification and Conformity to Creative Thinking.* Doctor's thesis, University of Georgia (Athens, Ga.), 1968. (*DAI* 30:828B)

131. BURKE, BARBARA PATRICIA. *An Exploratory Study of the Relationships Among Third Grade Negro Children's Self-Concept Creativity and Intelligence and Teachers' Perceptions of Those Relationships.* Doctor's thesis, Wayne State University (Detroit, Mich.), 1968. (*DAI* 30:1327A)

132. CALVERT, JOHN F. *An Exploration of Some of the Relationships Between Sense of Humor and Creativity in Children.* Doctor's thesis, Syracuse University (Syracuse, N.Y.), 1968. (*DA* 29:1494B)

133. COONE, JIM GARON. *A Cross-Cultural Study of Sex Differences in the Development of Selected Creative Thinking Abilities.* Doctor's thesis, University of Georgia (Athens, Ga.), 1968. (*DA* 29:4828B)

134. COVINGTON, NEIL RONALD. *Creativity in Culturally Deprived Adolescent Boys.* Doctor's thesis, Florida State University (Tallahassee, Fla.), 1968. (*DA* 29:1608A)

135. DAUW, DEAN C. "Creativity Research on Actuaries." *J Creative Behav* 2:274–80 f '68. * (*PA* 43:14316)

136. FREYERMUTH, ROBERT ALLAN. *A Comparison of the Effects of Various Preschool Experiences Upon the Imaginative Visual Expression of Five-Year-Olds.* Doctor's thesis, University of Miami (Coral Gables, Fla.), 1968. (*DA* 29:2603A)

137. GALLAGHER, MARIE SPELLMAN. *A Comparative Study of the Most Creative and Least Creative Student in Grades 4–8 at the Boston School for the Deaf, Randolph, Massachusetts.* Doctor's thesis, Boston College (Chestnut Hill, Mass.), 1968. (*DAI* 30:130A)

138. GLASS, GENE V. "Correlations With Products of Variables: Statistical Formulation and Implications for Methodology." *Am Ed Res J* 5:721–8 N '68. *

139. HATFIELD, ROBERT C. *A Study of the Relationships of Selected Components of Creativity, Cognitive Style, and Self-Concept Identified in a Random Sample of Twelfth Grade Students in One High School With Their Learning of Selected Information in the Social Studies.* Doctor's thesis, Wayne State University (Detroit, Mich.), 1968. (*DAI* 30:1334A)

140. HOLMAN, EUGENE RILEY. *An Experimental Investigation Designed to Enhance the Creative Potential and Teaching Ability of Students Majoring in Elementary Education.* Doctor's thesis, Brigham Young University (Provo, Utah), 1968. (*DA* 29:1165A)

141. INGMIRE, BRUCE DOUGLAS. *Relationships Between Creativity Scores and Leadership Behavior in a Group of High School Seniors.* Doctor's thesis, Arizona State University (Tempe, Ariz.), 1968. (*DA* 29:1365A)

142. IRVINE, FLEET RAYMOND. *A Study of Creative Thinking Ability, and Its Relationship to Psychomotor Ability, Mechanical Reasoning Ability, and Vocational Aptitude of Selected High School Industrial Arts Students.* Doctor's thesis, Utah State University (Logan, Utah), 1968. (*DA* 29:1768A)

143. JOHNSON, CAROLYNE MARGARET. *The Creative Thinking, Verbal Intelligence, and Creative Writing Ability of Young Gifted Children.* Doctor's thesis, Case Western Reserve University (Cleveland, Ohio), 1968. (*DA* 29:4187A)

144. KERNALEGUEN, ANNE PAULE. *Creativity Level, Perceptual Style and Peer Perception of Attitudes Towards Clothing.* Doctor's thesis, Utah State University (Logan, Utah), 1968. (*DA* 29:2960B)

145. MANY, WESLEY A., AND ELLIS, JOSEPH R. "Relationships Between Creativity and Report of Self-Concept of Ability for Upper Elementary School Children." *Ill Sch Res* 5:11–5 N '68. *

146. O'ROURKE, RICHARD HUGH. *A Study of the Creative Thinking Abilities, Attitudes, and Achievement of Academically Talented Students in the Honors Program and Regular Classes at Cooley High School, 1962–65.* Doctor's thesis, Wayne State University (Detroit, Mich.), 1968. (*DAI* 30:962A)

147. PANG, HENRY, AND HORROCKS, CAROL. "An Exploratory Study of Creativity in Deaf Children." *Percept & Motor Skills* 27:844–6 D '68. * (*PA* 43:8551)

148. PAULUS, DIETER H., AND RENZULLI, JOSEPH S. "Scoring Creativity Tests by Computer." *Gifted Child Q* 12:79–83 su '68. *

149. RAINA, M. K. "A Study Into the Effect of Competition on Creativity." *Gifted Child Q* 12:217–20 w '68. * (*PA* 43:14318)

150. RITTMAYER, JANE FOEHL. *Relationships Among High Verbal, High Non-Verbal and High Total Creativity Scores and Intelligence, Academic Achievement, Socio-Economic Status and Teacher Judgements.* Doctor's thesis, Rutgers—The State University (New Brunswick, N.J.), 1968. (*DA* 28:4913A)

151. RODERICK, JESSIE A. "Some Relationships Between Creativity and the Reading Preferences and Choices of a Group of Sixth Graders." *Ed Leadership* 26:49–52 O '68. *

152. SCHMIDT, RUSSELL HARRIS. *A Comparative Study of Students, Teachers, and Scientists as Judges of Science Fair Projects.* Doctor's thesis, University of Florida (Gainesville, Fla.), 1968. (*DAI* 30:224A)

153. SHAPIRO, R. J. *Creative Research Scientists.* Psychologica Africana Monograph Supplement No. 4. Johannesburg, South Africa: National Institute for Personnel Research, 1968. Pp. 180. *

154. SHELDON, ERIC. *Parental Child-Rearing Attitudes and Their Relationship to Cognitive Functioning of Their Pre-Adolescent Sons.* Doctor's thesis, Syracuse University (Syracuse, N.Y.), 1968. (*DA* 29:4370B)

155. SOLOMON, ANITA OSTRIN. *A Comparative Analysis of Creative and Intelligent Behavior of Elementary School Children With Different Socio-Economic Backgrounds.* Doctor's thesis, American University (Washington, D.C.), 1968. (*DA* 29:1457A)

156. STEINMETZ, CLOYD S. "Creativity Training: A Testing Program That Became a Sales Training Program." *J Creative Behav* 2:179–86 su '68. * (*PA* 43:6028)

157. THOMPSON, RICHARD ARLEN. *An Evaluation of a Two-Week Workshop in Education (Exploring Creativity).* Doctor's thesis, Ball State University (Muncie, Ind.), 1968. (*DA* 29:1470A)

158. TIBBETTS, JOHN WESLEY. *Relationships of Creativity to Socioeconomic Status, Race, Sex, IQ, Age and Grade-Point Average in an Adolescent Population.* Doctor's thesis, University of Southern California (Los Angeles, Calif.), 1968. (*DA* 29:1174A)

159. TORRANCE, E. PAUL. Chap. 7, "The Measurement of Creative Behavior in Children," pp. 199–222; comments by William J. Tisdall and Charles E. Bish. In *Productive Thinking in Education.* Edited by Mary Jane Aschner and Charles E. Bish. Washington, D.C.: National Education Association, 1968. Pp. x, 349. *

160. TORRANCE, E. PAUL. "Examples and Rationales of Test Tasks for Assessing Creative Abilities." *J Creative Behav* 2: 165–78 su '68. * (*PA* 43:5166)

161. TORRANCE, E. PAUL. "A Longitudinal Examination of the Fourth Grade Slump in Creativity." *Gifted Child Q* 12: 195–9 w '68. * (*PA* 43:14129)

162. TORRANCE, E. PAUL. *Minnesota Studies of Creative Behavior, 1958–1966.* Greensboro, N.C.: Creativity Research Institute of The Richardson Foundation, Inc., February 1968. Pp. i, 63. *

163. TORRANCE, E. PAUL, AND FORTSON, LAURA R. "Creativity Among Young Children and the Creative-Aesthetic Approach." *Ed* 89:27–30 S–O '68. *

164. TRYK, H. EDWARD. "The Torrance Tests of Creative Thinking," pp. 44–9. In *Advances in Psychological Assessment, Vol. I.* Edited by Paul McReynolds. Palo Alto, Calif.: Science & Behavior Books, Inc., 1968. Pp. xiii, 336. *

165. ALIOTTI, NICHOLAS CASPER. *The Effects of Warm-Up Activities on the Verbal Creative Thinking Abilities of Disadvantaged First Grade Children.* Doctor's thesis, University of Georgia (Athens, Ga.), 1969. (*DAI* 30:5275A)

166. BAHLKE, SUSAN JOYCE MOORE. *Componential Evaluation of Creativity Instructional Materials.* Doctor's thesis, Purdue University (Lafayette, Ind.), 1969. (*DAI* 30:1426A)

167. BARABASZ, ARREED F. "Test-Retest Reliability of the Torrance Tests of Creative Thinking, and the Relationship Between Intelligence and Figural Creativity." *Child Study Center B* 5(4–5):73–4 S–N '69. * (*PA* 44:16369)

168. BOLTON, SHIRLEY L. "An Introductory Study of Art as Creative Learning for the Rural Culturally Disadvantaged." *Studies Art Ed* 10:50–6 w '69. *

169. BOWERS, JOHN. "Interactive Effects of Creativity and IQ on Ninth-Grade Achievement." *J Ed Meas* 6(3):173–7 f '69. * (*PA* 44:15469)

170. CICIRELLI, VICTOR G. "University Supervisors' Creative Ability and Their Appraisal of Student Teachers' Classroom Performance: An Exploratory Study." *J Ed Res* 62(8): 375–81 Ap '69. *

171. COX, OTIS. *Creative Thinking in a High School Experimental Humanities Program.* Doctor's thesis, University of Alabama (University, Ala.), 1969. (*DAI* 31:214A)

172. DACEY, J.; MADAUS, G.; AND ALLEN, A. "The Relationship of Creativity and Intelligence in Irish Adolescents." *Brit J Ed Psychol* 39(3):261–6 N '69. * (*PA* 44:8234)

173. DAVIS, DONALD JACK. "The Effects of Depth and Breadth Methods of Art Instruction Upon Creative Thinking, Art Attitudes, and Aesthetic Quality of Art Products in Beginning College Students." *Studies Art Ed* 10(2):27–40 w '69. *

174. DENT, PAULA ANN. *Creativity in Inner-City Children, in Relation to Aptitude, Achievement, and Background.* Doctor's thesis, Wayne State University (Detroit, Mich.), 1969. (*DAI* 31:1682A)

175. ELSOM, BILLY FRED. *Creative Ability and Perceived Parent-Child Relations.* Doctor's thesis, North Texas State University (Denton, Tex.), 1969. (*DAI* 31:59A)

176. FELTON, THOMAS A., JR. *Correlation Between Creativity as Measured by Torrance Tests of Creative Thinking Figural Forms A and B and Intelligence as Measured by the Lorge-Thorndike Intelligence Test of Fifty Sixth Grade Students.* Master's thesis, Old Dominion University (Norfolk, Va.), 1969.

177. FRICK, RALPH CARL. *An Inquiry Into Certain Aspects of Intuition.* Doctor's thesis, Northern Illinois University (DeKalb, Ill.), 1969. (*DAI* 30:2376A)

178. GROSSMAN, MARVIN JAY. *Developing Aesthetic and Creative Visual Abilities in Kindergarten Children Through a Structured Developmental Art Program.* Doctor's thesis, University of Georgia (Athens, Ga.), 1969. (*DAI* 30:3375A)

179. HILLERY, MILTON C. *The Effects of Lack of Formal School Experience on Performance on Tests of Creative Thinking.* Doctor's thesis, Michigan State University (East Lansing, Mich.), 1969. (*DAI* 30:2376A)

180. JOHNSON, JENNINGS O. "The Relationship Between Science Achievement and Selected Student Characteristics." *Sci Ed* 53(4):307–18 O '69. *

181. JUFFER, VIRGINIA MAHANNAH. *Socialization of Children With Varying Levels of Originality: An Analysis of Parent-Child Interaction.* Doctor's thesis, Iowa State University (Ames, Iowa), 1969. (*DAI* 30:1253A)

182. KALTSOUNIS, BILL. *Factors Related to Creative Thinking Among Deaf and Hearing Children.* Doctor's thesis, University of Georgia (Athens, Ga.), 1969. (*DAI* 30:3324A)

183. KALTSOUNIS, BILL. "Impact of Instruction on Development of Deaf Children's Originality of Thinking." *Percept & Motor Skills* 29(1):298 Ag '69. * (*PA* 44:2802)

184. KOBAYASHI, MICHAEL JUNICHI. *Relationships of Intelligence and Creativity to Anxiety and Extroversion-Introversion in Ninth Grade Japanese Boys.* Doctor's thesis, Boston College (Chestnut Hill, Mass.), 1969. (*DAI* 30:3730A)

185. LICHTMAN, MARILYN VICKMAN. *Intelligence, Creativity, and Language: An Examination of the Interrelationships of Three Variables Among Preschool, Disadvantaged Negro Children.* Doctor's thesis, George Washington University (Washington, D.C.), 1969. (*DAI* 31:1625A)

186. McCORMACK, ALAN JOSEPH. *The Effect of Selected Teaching Methods on Creative Thinking, Self-Evaluation, and Achievement of Students Enrolled in an Elementary Science Education Methods Course.* Doctor's thesis, Colorado State College (Greeley, Colo.), 1969. (*DAI* 30:4311A)

187. McCUTCHEON, NANCY SUSAN. *A Study of Relationships Among Creativity, Intelligence, and Test Anxiety of Middle-Class Fourth Grade Boys and Girls.* Doctor's thesis, University of South Carolina (Columbia, S.C.), 1969. (*DAI* 30: 4833A)

188. McWHINNIE, HAROLD J. "Some Relationships Between Creativity and Perception in Fourth Grade Children." *Acta Psychologica* 31(2):169–75 Ag '69. * (*PA* 44:14345)

189. MIDDLETON, FRANCES TALLULAH. *Creative Thinking Abilities of Selected Sixth-Grade Children.* Doctor's thesis, University of Georgia (Athens, Ga.), 1969. (*DAI* 30:5348A)

190. NUTTALL, ENA VAZQUEZ. *Creativity in Boys: A Study of the Influence of Social Background, Educational Achievement, and Parental Attitudes on the Creative Behavior of Ten Year Old Boys.* Doctor's thesis, Boston University (Boston, Mass.), 1969. (*DAI* 31:231A)

191. ORLANDI, LISANIO ROBERT. *Social Class and Subcultural Patterns of Performance in Divergent Thinking of Students in Urban Elementary Schools.* Doctor's thesis, Boston College (Chestnut Hill, Mass.), 1969. (*DAI* 30:4282A)

192. PHILIPP, JOAN A. "Comparison of Motor Creativity With Figural and Verbal Creativity, and Selected Motor Skills." *Res Q* 40(1):163–73 Mr '69. *

193. POLLERT, LESLIE H.; FELDHUSEN, JOHN F.; VAN MONDFRANS, ADRIAN P.; AND TREFFINGER, DONALD J. "Role of Memory in Divergent Thinking." *Psychol Rep* 25(1):151–6 Ag '69. * (*PA* 44:3471)

194. PORTER, CHARLES MACK. *Figures of Speech, Divergent Thinking, and Activation Theory.* Doctor's thesis, North Texas State University (Denton, Tex.), 1969. (*DAI* 30:2384A)

195. RAINA, M. K. "A Study of Sex Differences in Creativity in India." *J Creative Behav* 3(2):111–4 sp '69. *

196. SHERWOOD, DAVID WILLIAM. *The Differential Effects of Assessment Context and Scoring Method on Creativity Performance in Children.* Doctor's thesis, Duke University (Durham, N.C.), 1969. (*DAI* 30:1888B)

197. SHIGAKI, IRENE SHIKIBU. *The Effects of Teacher Strength and Sensitivity and Pupil Intelligence and Creativity on the Production of Divergent Responses.* Doctor's thesis, Columbia University (New York, N.Y.), 1969. (*DAI* 30: 3864A)

198. SMITH, GEORGE PRITCHY. *The Relationships Among Selected Variables of Creative Thinking and Visual, Auditory, and Tactual Sensory Perception.* Doctor's thesis, North Texas State University (Denton, Tex.), 1969. (*DAI* 30:4839A)

199. SPRINGER, THOMAS A. *An Experimental Study of the Effects of Group Counseling Upon the Creative Thinking of Selected Senior High School Students.* Doctor's thesis, Ball State University (Muncie, Ind.), 1969. (*DAI* 31:165A)

200. STEVENS, JOHN CULVER. *A Study of the Relationships Between Field Independence, Dogmatism, and Creativity in Rural Seventh Grade Students.* Doctor's thesis, University of Georgia (Athens, Ga.), 1969. (*DAI* 30:2863A)

201. STIMELING, WILLIAM F. *An Investigation of the Relationship of Selected Attributes of Creativity and Success Evaluations of Indiana Public School Superintendents.* Doctor's thesis, Indiana University (Bloomington, Ind.), 1969. (*DAI* 30:4746A)

202. TORRANCE, E. PAUL. "Curiosity of Gifted Children and Performance on Timed and Untimed Tests of Creativity." *Gifted Child Q* 13(3):155–8 au '69. * (*PA* 44:12332)

203. TORRANCE, E. PAUL. "Prediction of Adult Creative Achievement Among High School Seniors." *Gifted Child Q* 13(4):223–9 w '69. * (*PA* 44:14620)

204. TORRANCE, E. PAUL, AND ALIOTTI, NICHOLAS C. "Sex

Differences in Levels of Performance and Test-Retest Reliability on the Torrance Tests of Creative Thinking Ability." *J Creative Behav* 3(1):52–7 w '69. *

205. WALKER, PERRY CRANE. *A Study of Creativity Among Mexican School Children.* Doctor's thesis, University of Georgia (Athens, Ga.), 1969. (*DAI* 31:650A)

206. WELTNER, WILLIAM HAROLD. *Evaluations by Teacher Educators of Observable Behavior Characteristics Used to Predict Creative Teaching Potential of Elementary Education Student Teachers.* Doctor's thesis, Ball State University (Muncie, Ind.), 1969. (*DAI* 31:1128A)

207. WOOD, REBECCA HOLCOMBE. *Three Environmental Press Variables and Their Relationship to Coping Behavior and Creativity in Children.* Doctor's thesis, University of Alabama (University, Ala.), 1969. (*DAI* 30:5306A)

208. BACHTOLD, LOUISE M., AND WERNER, EMMY E. "An Evaluation of Teaching Creative Skills to Gifted Children in Grades 5 and 6." *J Ed Res* 63(6):253–6 F '70. * (*PA* 46:5761)

209. BADER, LAWRENCE JOSEPH. *The Effects of Task-Taking Atmosphere, Level of Creativity and Field-Independence on Creative Production.* Doctor's thesis, Boston University (Boston, Mass.), 1970. (*DAI* 31:2974B)

210. BAILEY, JUNE T.; MCDONALD, FREDERICK J.; AND CLAUS, KAREN E. "Evaluation of the Development of Creative Behavior in an Experimental Nursing Program." *Nursing Res* 19(2):100–8 Mr–Ap '70. *

211. BARRISH, BERNARD. *Inductive Versus Deductive Teaching Strategies With High and Low Divergent Thinkers.* Doctor's thesis, Stanford University (Stanford, Calif.), 1970. (*DAI* 31:4029A)

212. BRUININKS, ROBERT H., AND FELDMAN, DAVID H. "Creativity, Intelligence, and Achievement Among Disadvantaged Children." *Psychol Sch* 7(3):260–4 Jl '70. * (*PA* 45:5015)

213. BURSTINER, IRVING. *Effects of a Workshop in Creative Thinking for Secondary School Department Chairmen—On Their Perceptions of Supervisory Activities, on Problem-Solving, and on Creativity Test Scores.* Doctor's thesis, St. John's University (Jamaica, N.Y.), 1970. (*DAI* 31:3197A)

214. CAVE, RICHARD L. "A Combined Factor Analysis of Creativity and Intelligence." *Multiv Behav Res* 5(2):177–91 Ap '70. * (*PA* 44:16697)

215. CICIRELLI, VICTOR G., AND CICIRELLI, JEAN S. "Counselors' Creative Ability and Attitude in Relation to Counseling Behavior With Disadvantaged Counselees." *J Counsel Psychol* 17(2):177–83 Mr '70. * (*PA* 44:8550)

216. CLARK, PHILIP M., AND MIRELS, HERBERT L. "Fluency as a Pervasive Element in the Measurement of Creativity." *J Ed Meas* 7(2):83–6 su '70. * (*PA* 44:19354)

217. DEWING, K. "Some Correlates of Creativity Test Performance in Seventh Grade Children." *Austral J Psychol* 22(3):269–76 D '70. * (*PA* 46:889)

218. DEWING, KATHLEEN. "The Reliability and Validity of Selected Tests of Creative Thinking in a Sample of Seventh-Grade West Australian Children." *Brit J Ed Psychol* 40(1):35–42 F '70. * (*PA* 44:10128)

219. GROSSMAN, MARVIN. "Perceptual Style, Creativity, and Various Drawing Abilities." *Studies Art Ed* 11(2):51–4 w '70. *

220. HARVEY, O. J.; HOFFMEISTER, JAMES K.; COATES, CAROLIE; AND WHITE, B. JACK. "A Partial Evaluation of Torrance's Tests of Creativity." *Am Ed Res J* 7(3):359–72 My '70. *

221. HURLEY, JOHN DONALD. *The Relationship of Dogmatism With Two Measures of Originality.* Doctor's thesis, Boston University (Boston, Mass.), 1970. (*DAI* 31:2183A)

222. JONES, JOAN C. *A Study of the Effect of a Teaching Strategy in Divergent Thinking Upon the Behavior of Student-Teachers and the Children They Teach.* Doctor's thesis, Boston University (Boston, Mass.), 1970. (*DAI* 31:2231A)

223. KALTSOUNIS, BILL. "Comparative Study of Creativity in Deaf and Hearing Children." *Child Study J* 1(1):11–9 f '70. *

224. KALTSOUNIS, BILL. "Differences in Verbal Creative Thinking Abilities Between Deaf and Hearing Children." *Psychol Rep* 26(3):727–33 Je '70. * (*PA* 45:1133)

225. KALTSOUNIS, BILL. "Intellectual Functioning of Deaf Children." *Percept & Motor Skills* 30(1):49–50 F '70. *

226. KARIOTH, JOSEPH. "Creative Dramatics as Aid in Developing Creative Thinking Abilities." *Speech Teach* 19(4):301–9 N '70. *

227. KEENAN, JUNE F. *The Relationship of Certain Socio-Cultural and Community Factors Among Sixth Grade Students to Creativity in Art.* Doctor's thesis, North Texas State University (Denton, Tex.), 1970. (*DAI* 31:3782A)

228. LANDRY, RICHARD GEORGE. *The Relationship of Second Language Learning to Divergent Thinking Abilities of Students in Urban Schools.* Doctor's thesis, Boston College (Chestnut Hill, Mass.), 1970. (*DAI* 31:2615A)

229. LINDSEY, JAMES F., AND HICKS, DAVID. "A Note on Teaching for Creativity." *Calif J Ed Res* 21(2):84–7 Mr '70. *

230. MCWHINNIE, HAROLD J. "A Third Study of Some Relationships Between Creativity and Perception in 6th Grade Children." *Calif J Ed Res* 21(1):35–42 Ja '70. *

231. MARTIN, FELIX. "Questioning Skills Among Advantaged and Disadvantaged Children in First Grade." *Psychol Rep* 27(2):617–8 O '70. * (*PA* 45:6068)

232. PAULUS, DIETER H. "Are Sub-Tests of the Torrance Test Independent?" Abstract. *Am Ed Res Assn 1970 Ann Meeting Abstr* 2:42–3 '70. *

233. PESCI, MICHAEL LINDEN. *Psychological Differences Between Research, Development and Product Engineers and Their Implications for Placement Decisions.* Doctor's thesis, University of Minnesota (Minneapolis, Minn.), 1970. (*DAI* 31:3048B)

234. RAIA, JAMES R., AND OSIPOW, SAMUEL H. "Creative Thinking Ability and Susceptibility to Persuasion." *J Social Psychol* 82(2):181–6 D '70. * (*PA* 45:6341)

235. RAINA, MAHARAJ K. "Creative, Critical and Power Motivations of High and Low Creative Students." *J Psychol Res* 14(3):107–12 S '70. *

236. RAINA, MAHARAJ K. "Creativity and Teaching Success." *Psychol Rep* 26(1):70 F '70. * (*PA* 45:5001)

237. RAINA, MAHARAJ K. "A Study of Creativity in Teachers." *Psychol Studies* 15(1):28–33 Ja '70. *

238. RAPPEL, DOROTHY. *Teacher-Pupil Interaction at the Elementary Grade Level and Pupil Creativity.* Doctor's thesis, Catholic University of America (Washington, D.C.), 1970. (*DAI* 31:2965B)

239. TORRANCE, E. PAUL. "Influence of Dyadic Interaction on Creative Functioning." *Psychol Rep* 26(2):391–4 Ap '70. * (*PA* 44:20849)

240. TORRANCE, E. PAUL; GOWAN, JOHN C.; WU, JING-JYI; AND ALIOTTI, NICHOLAS C. "Creative Functioning of Monolingual and Bilingual Children in Singapore." *J Ed Psychol* 61(1):72–5 F '70. * (*PA* 44:6532)

241. TREFFINGER, DONALD J., AND RIPPLE, RICHARD E. "Teachers' Ratings of Pupil Creativity." *Child Study J* 1(1):5–10 f '70. *

242. TREFFINGER, DONALD J.; FELDHUSEN, JOHN F.; AND THOMAS, SUSAN BAHLKE. "Relationship Between Teachers' Divergent Thinking Abilities and Their Ratings of Pupils' Creative Thinking Abilities." *Meas & Eval Guid* 3(3):169–76 f '70. * (*PA* 45:10616)

243. BATES, OPAL ELAINE. *The Correlation of Children's Perception of Locus of Control to Originality in Selected Groups of Sixth Grade Children.* Doctor's thesis, Oregon State University (Corvallis, Ore.), 1971. (*DAI* 31:3865A)

LEONARD L. BAIRD, *Research Psychologist, Educational Testing Service, Princeton, New Jersey.*

The *Torrance Tests of Creative Thinking* were designed to measure four aspects of "creative thinking"—fluency, flexibility, originality, and elaboration. Two scores for each aspect are provided—verbal and figural (although norms are not provided for the verbal elaboration scores). The author and publisher recommend that the TTCT be used in research studies of cognitive functioning, individualized instruction, remedial programs, and new educational programs, but also suggest its use for assessing individual students' potentials.

ADMINISTRATION AND SCORING. The manual and administration guide provide clear, detailed and comprehensive directions for administering and scoring the TTCT. The TTCT can be administered individually or in groups. Three figural tests can be given in 30 minutes of testing time, with additional time required for instructions. Seven verbal tasks require 45 minutes of testing time. Since the subjects give free responses to semistructured tasks, the test must be scored by hand. The guides for scoring are quite clear, and the manual discusses scoring errors to avoid. While a rationale is provided for each scale, no empirical evidence of the development of the scoring methods is discussed, with the exception of the originality scale. (The originality scale is based on the statistical rarity of the responses.) A scorer requires some training and experience with the instrument. The reported correlations between scores of inexperienced and experienced scorers are generally in the high 90's, ranging from .66 to .99. However, the inter-scorer agreement among inexperienced scorers (such as some school teachers) will probably be lower. The manual and scoring guide do not provide estimates of the time needed to score each test, but it appears that scoring a test would take a considerable time, even for an experienced scorer. (A scoring service is available through the publisher.)

CONTENT. While the manual includes a sentence that the tests attempt to assess "these test activities in terms of Guilford's divergent thinking factors," no evidence is provided for any relation with Guilford's model, and no effort is made to seek logical connections with Guilford's work. (No correlations of the TTCT with the Guilford battery are reported.) In general the tests seem to be derived from Torrance's long thinking about creativity and tend to be eclectic, rather than based on a systematic theory of creativity. They may be best interpreted as an attempt to measure certain particular aspects of creativity, and not as an attempt to measure all of the important dimensions of creative thinking. Some of the rationales given for the scales are rather vague and discursive. The relation between a scale score and the interpretation provided for the score in some cases seems to be based more on the rationale for the scale than on the evidence provided for it.

RELIABILITY. Creative thinking may be influenced by personality and situational variables, so, as the manual points out, "it is to be expected that motivational conditions affect test-retest reliability" and that motivational aspects are probably controlled more adequately in research studies than in normative studies. Thus, test-retest reliabilities range from .50 to .93 over one- to two-week periods, and from .35 to .73 over three-year periods. Although the reliability studies of the TTCT are well summarized in the manual, many of the studies used only one or a few scales. These studies are not fully reported, so it is difficult to assess them in some cases. However, the diversity of studies and samples suggests that the scales have adequate reliability.

VALIDITY. The manual summarizes more than 50 studies of the validity of the test. The majority of the studies concerned with construct validity are studies of the personalities of high and low scorers. Many of these studies utilize extreme groups without any information about students in the middle; others use designs that compare "creatives" with an "unselected" sample. In spite of these weak designs and many results that show only slight relations, the studies do suggest that the test does measure behaviors consistent with the literature on creative behavior.

In a section on concurrent validity, the TTCT seems to have only slight relations to peer nominations and low relations to teacher nominations. The TTCT seems to be related to both academic intelligence and educational achievement test scores, both in the studies reported in the manual and in subsequent work. This last fact leads to some question about the extent to which the TTCT scales are saturated with general academic aptitude.

The manual partially reports only one study of predictive validity. This same study is the only one involving criteria of *real-life* creative accomplishment. (There is a great difference between a measure of "Planfulness" and actually having "had scientific or scholarly paper published in a scientific or professional journal.") This leads to two criticisms of the TTCT. First, there needs to be much more work examining the predictive validity of the test. Second, the TTCT needs to be firmly linked to reality by showing that it predicts socially valuable creative behavior. It may be that a student could think of many unusual ways to improve a toy in the testing situation but make no original and useful contributions in real-life situations. While the studies in the manual suggest that there could be some predictive validity, the relation remains to be established. And, ultimately, without considerable work on the validity of the test for predicting real-life creativity, it is difficult to evaluate the utility of the test or to compare it with other tests.

NORMS AND INTERPRETATION. Means and standard deviations are provided for a number of samples, most somewhat restricted. The basic groups used for the two main score conversion tables are 118 fifth graders in St. Croix, Wisconsin, and 108 seventh graders. (These identifications are tentative, because the manual is not as clear as it might be about these groups.) No other conversion tables are provided, and the scores are converted into T scores, but not to centile ranks or other scales. Of course, one could construct his own conversion tables from the means and standard deviations of other groups, as the manual suggests. The means and standard deviations for the groups used for the conversion tables sometimes vary considerably from the means and standard deviations reported in the manual for other fifth and seventh grade groups. For example, on one scale the mean of the fifth graders in one sample is at the 90th percentile of the one used for the tables. Thus, any interpretation of a score must be quite tentative, at best. Although this would seem to be a major limitation, the manual states, "The author and publisher will continue to accumulate comparison group norms on a variety of kinds of populations ranging from kindergarten through graduate school. There is no plan at the present time to compile what might be called 'children-in-general' type norms." Thus, the norms will apparently continue to be based on restricted, available samples. This tends to make any interpretation of the scores, even in research projects, very tentative. The interpretations provided for the scale scores are clear, but seem to go beyond the evidence presented in the manual.

The scales are supposed to measure independent traits, but the intercorrelations presented in the manual, as well as some factor-analytic evidence (e.g., *232*), suggest that there is a great deal of overlap in the scales.

The manual provides a good deal of information about the studies using the test, but in many places the writing seems to be straining to be persuasive. In a few places, reliance seems to be placed on the "author's belief." There are also occasional arguments with critics. The general format of the manual could be much improved.

SUMMARY EVALUATION. The TTCT seems to be useful as a basis for further research into the nature and nurture of creativity. The work already done with the TTCT has made a considerable contribution to the literature on creative behavior. However, without better norms, studies of predictive validity, and anchoring of the test to real-life creative behavior, the TTCT should probably be used for assessment of an individual's creative potential only with great caution. If the author and publisher could make these changes, as well as other improvements promised in the manual, the test could be a powerful and useful tool for research and practice, thus joining Torrance's other significant contributions to our understanding of creativity.

ROBERT L. THORNDIKE, *Professor of Psychology and Education, Teachers College, Columbia University, New York, New York.*

There seems little question that "creativity" is one of the "in" things in psychology of 1970. Thus, whereas the number of references under this heading in the *Psychological Abstracts* of 1949 was 7 out of 6,530, or 1.1 per 1,000, in 1969 the number was 218 out of 18,068, or 12.1 per 1,000. The curve during this period was positively accelerated and need be extrapolated only about another 20 years for the topic to take over the PA completely.

It is natural, therefore, that the period should have yielded creativity tests. Whereas Guilford's tests were embedded in his larger Structure of Intellect, being primarily measures of various cells in the slab labelled "divergent thinking," Torrance's tests stand as a single and separate publication.

Torrance's tests are of two main types, tests involving words (semantic material, in Guilford's terms) and tests involving pictorial material (figural content). The several verbal subtests appear in one booklet, and the several pictorial in another. Two forms of each are available. It is claimed that either the verbal or the pictorial test can be used from kindergarten through graduate school, though data on reliability and validity are typically limited to elementary and secondary school students. Rather full manuals are provided to guide both the administration and the scoring of the tests.

From each of his tests Torrance extracts scores for fluency, flexibility, originality, and elaboration. Fluency is simply the number of relevant responses given; flexibility is the number of different categories of response; originality is a sum of credits where some routine responses count zero, less common responses get a unit score, and, in some cases, responses too infrequent to be on the list in the manual get a credit of two; and the elaboration score is a count of the additional details used in each response totaled over responses. It is not surprising, under these circumstances, that the fluency, flexibility, and originality scores tend to be highly correlated, since all are accumulated over the same set of responses given by the examinee. Harvey and others (*220*), working with the seven subtests of the verbal test, found the average correlation of the different traits within a single subtest to be .54, while the average correlation for a single trait over the different subtests was .50 for fluency, .32 for flexibility, and .25 for originality. In another study (*19*), the following intercorrelations were obtained among the verbal tests: .79 between fluency and flexibility, .80 between fluency and originality, and .74 between flexibility and originality. The corresponding correlations reported for the figural tests are .77, .68, and .66. An average of the correlations of verbal with pictorial scores gave the following: same trait correlated across tests, .44; different traits correlated across tests, .40. Thus, the evidence of consistently different meaning for the fluency, flexibility, and originality scores is almost vanishingly small.

Results such as these raise serious question as to whether any attention should be paid to the separate scores on each form of the test, or whether a single score for the verbal and one for the pictorial would be more appropriate. The author gives no clear guidance on this point. Scoring and norms emphasize the separate scores, but much of the research on validity of the instrument seems to use a total score as a variable, or contrasting groups formed on the basis of a total score. Unless adequate evidence is provided that the separate scores are accomplishing measurement of really different attributes, and this seems unlikely, it would seem better to think of each test as yielding a single total score. It would be desirable that some uniform way of arriving at that score be specified in the scoring guide, so that comparable results might be obtained from one user to another.

Scores on flexibility and originality are so contaminated by the basic fluency component that it is difficult to interpret data on the reliability of either scoring or performance for the flexibility and originality components, after basic fluency of responding has been partialed out. A total score apparently would have fairly adequate alternate-forms reliability—perhaps .85 to .90 for the verbal test and .70 to .80 for the figural test.

The author reports a variety of interesting correlates of scores on one or another of the tests that have gone into the battery. Many of the studies relate to component subtests or to earlier versions of the material, so it is somewhat difficult to pull together a coherent picture of the validity of the instrument in its current published form. However, it should be recognized that the author presents the tests to potential users as a "research edition." Hopefully, their existence in a standard format will lead to a more coherent body of research that will provide systematic information both on their internal structure and their external correlates, so that the would-be user can better judge to what extent they merit their somewhat ambitious title.

Am Ed Res J 5:272–81 Mr '68. Michael A. Wallach. By publishing the *Torrance Tests of Creative Thinking* as a commercial undertaking, the author of these materials is recommending their use as a standard set of assessment procedures that are different from intelligence tests but that, like intelligence tests, will help teachers sift out more from less talented students. * Although called a "research edition," advertising matter presents the tests, together with a series of workbooks and phonograph records, as "a complete program in creative development." The intent, then, is to make available for general use instruments that are presumed to be not just tests of intelligence but tests of creative thinking. Torrance gives a definition of creativity that indicates concern for assessing problem-solving in a general sense. * Effective dealing with the environment, the hallmark of intelligence as generally defined, thus represents the core of Torrance's construal of creative thinking. * The crucial issue....in evaluating the Torrance tests is, of course, their psychological meaning. * the Torrance instruments themselves correlate substantially with intelligence * Rather than viewing peer judgments for fluency as validation for fluency scores from the creativity tests, or peer judgments for flexibility as validation for flexibility scores from the creativity tests, in the manner suggested by Torrance, we have to entertain seriously the more parsimonious hypothesis that general intelligence alone accounts for the degree to which the peer judgments correlate with Torrance scores. * One is led to suspect....that whatever small degree of enhanced predictability of academic achievement comes about from adding the Torrance tests as a predictor arises not because a new cognitive domain of "creativity" in thinking is being sampled but rather because these tests offer an alternate measure of general intelligence. * In sum, we have been able to find little evidence in support of an interpretation of the Torrance tests that would construe them as "creative thinking" rather than simply as "thinking." * that the Torrance tests seem to be functioning essentially as a battery of general intelligence assessors should come as no surprise in the light of the Torrance definition of creative thinking * this definition is quite close to the traditional conception of intelligence, including everything, say, that Wechsler's definition of general intelligence includes, with the addition of greater specific emphasis upon hypothesis-search activities in seeking problem solutions * We turn, finally, to the question of recommending the applied use of the Torrance tests. It is evident that we feel extreme caution is necessary. Most of the scoring practices commented upon in the Technical Manual seem to yield results that are hard to distinguish from assessment of general intelligence. At least no convincing empirical separability from intelligence has yet been demonstrated. If we view the Torrance materials as a possible supplement to intelligence testing, it is not evident that one will obtain results that differ clearly from what can be obtained by spending an equivalent amount of time with additional assessors of general intelligence. While the Torrance battery may function as a substitute for a general intelligence test, the user can be misled by the creativity label into believing that he is assessing something different from intelligence as usually defined. The consequence, ironically enough, is that the students of high intelligence will also be identified as creative. Such considerations are by no means intended to imply, of course, that one should be satisfied with general intelligence as a definition of talent. On the contrary, the importance of moving away from a uni-dimensional conception of talent centered upon general intelligence has in recent years become increasingly apparent. Furthermore, the Torrance materials for assessing fluency may represent an approach that has the potential for defining a considerably different kind of talent than is caught in the net of the general intelligence concept, but this would constitute a very different kind of emphasis than the Torrance battery provides. Efforts to determine the usefulness of fluency levels in selection are certainly needed. While publication of the *Torrance Tests of Creative Thinking* may encourage such efforts, we are left with the nagging suspicion

that the major effect of the tests will be to give intelligence assessment a more fashionable name. [See original review for additional comments not excerpted.]

J Counsel Psychol 15:297–8 My '68. John L. Holland. * Because a subject gives free responses to several semistructured tasks, the scoring must be done by hand. A "Directions Manual and Scoring Guide" is provided for each form of the verbal and figural batteries (Forms A and B). These guides are unusually clear, complete, and explicit. Many test authors will find them helpful models. The specific origin of the interpretation of a person's responses is not always clear. Except for the originality scales, all keys or scoring guides were evolved rationally during the long period of the tests' development. Torrance provides an extensive rationale for each scale, but no empirical evidence about scale development except for the originality scales. These scales were developed by categorizing statistically rare responses as "original." More information about scoring is contained in the "Norms-Technical Manual." That publication suggests that interscorer reliability is usually above .90 for individual scales scored by elementary teachers. Other studies with similar reliabilities are alluded to but not reported. These interscorer reliabilities are impressive, but more explicit reporting and more evidence are desirable. The normative information is helpful, although much more information for larger, clearly defined populations is needed. On the other hand, there is enough information to distinguish high, middle, and low scores for a wide range of age groups. A related, interpretative section is less satisfactory. The relationship between the interpretation of a scale score and the evidence for the meaning of that score appears to rest more on its rationale than the evidence. Despite extensive work, much more is required to clarify and substantiate the scale interpretations. The evidence for the test-retest and equivalent-forms reliability of the Torrance batteries is more extensive and satisfactory. In 15 studies using equivalent forms or time intervals from 1 week to 3 years, the majority of reliability coefficients exceeded .70. Although these studies are not fully reported, the diversity of samples and time intervals strongly suggests that the TTCT scales have useful reliability. The validity of the TTCT rests on more than 50 investigations using samples of children, adolescents, and adults.

Of these, only one incompletely reported study is concerned with the predictive validity of the tests. Most investigations are concerned with construct and concurrent validities. An inordinate number of these validation studies capitalize on extreme group comparisons without any information about the excluded middle; many others use weak designs—"creative" versus "unselected" sample, simple matching of controls and "creatives." Despite these gross statistical deficiencies and weak designs, most of the evidence seems internally consistent and generally consistent with the literature of creative behavior. The failure to deal with external predictive validity remains a serious deficiency. It is quite possible that a subject can give many unusual uses for a brick or a cardboard box, but fail to perform originally in real-life situations. Unless tests like the TTCT are tied to reality by studies of their external validity, it will never be known whether high scores identify original people or crazy bricklayers and packers. The current evidence about the TTCT *implies* that it may have some predictive validity, but explicit evidence is needed about its ability to forecast socially relevant creative behavior. It would also be helpful to know more about the relationships between the TTCT scales and other common measures of originality or creative behavior. Normally, the writing, printing, and format of a test manual do not warrant comment. In this instance, Torrance's valuable substantive contributions are blurred by a dull, sometimes ugly and hard-to-read layout and typography. But, more important, the writing of the manual is poor, containing intrusive arguments with critics, promises of things to come, and excessive persuasion. And, although I enjoyed Torrance's encounters with critics (there should be a 1-month open season for this kind of activity), these, and other intrusions, make it difficult to quickly locate and interpret the guts of the evidence about the tests. At this time, the TTCT appear to have useful reliability and validity for research purposes. If they can be linked both to other common tests of originality and to criteria of greater social relevance, they will become powerful and valuable tools for research and practice. I wonder, however, if it might be more helpful, in education at least, to sensitize teachers to original behavior and its development rather than to have teachers use a somewhat laborious technique to find out who is "creative." In several publications for teachers, Torrance himself has already demonstrated how. Whatever the eventual uses of the TTCT, Torrance has made a large, substantive contribution to our knowledge of creative imagination.

J Ed Meas 4:191–2 f '67. Ralph Hoepfner. * an early attempt to measure an area of individual differences about which much more needs to be learned, and as such, is designed to be used for research purposes, and not for counseling or guiding the lives of people. With this in mind, it is surprising that the manual for this test so persistently underplays an objective scientific appraisal in favor of a sales pitch. *Interpretation.* Information supporting the values and interpretations of the tests is extensive and easily understood. Test-score interpretations are explained clearly in the manual and are simplified in scoring forms, but the names applied to the scores for tests may be open to misinterpretation. Different names imply different concepts, but different test scores don't necessarily imply different independent trait standings. As the intercorrelations among the test scores amply indicate, there is a great deal of overlap and nonindependence in each of the test scores. *Scoring.* The test manual is most comprehensive with regard to the administration of the tests (maintaining appropriate tone and intent) and in the necessarily complex scoring procedures, which are clearly detailed and based upon rational analysis of responses. The necessary training for scorers is described, and the reported inter-scorer reliabilities (.76 to .99; most in the high .90's) is evidence of the care taken in the training of scorers. But scorer training cannot be expected to be of so high a standard for all novices who will use these tests, and therefore inter-scorer agreement may be expected to be of a much lower level. Although there is no estimate of time required to score a test battery, one may assume that it will be a long affair. *Content.* The eight possible scores....purport to measure eight aspects of creative thinking, but the universe of behavior described as creative thinking is considerably larger. The manual readily admits to this inadequate coverage, which is, incidentally, not due entirely to the state of our knowledge. The logical basis of trait coverage stresses the complexity of creative thinking, but the scores are supposed to reflect unitary factor-like traits.

Further, the scores are supposed to be free from technical or subject-matter content (which they must surely be) and are also supposed to be appropriate to all age levels (regardless of the fact that one's educated psychological intuition, supported by the age-norm data, would strongly disagree). *Validity and Reliability.* The predictive ability of the tests is quite in line with other, unpublished, measures of creative potential—low. The relationships of the TTCT performance to other constructs which one might hypothesize to be related to creative potential, experimental measures of "preferred ways of learning," "long-range aspirations," or "attitude patterns," add a great deal of interest to these tests, but do fail to strongly anchor the test score meanings more firmly into the concept of creative potential. Because creative thinking, as measured, may take into account the influences of many personality and situational variables that fluctuate, we might expect the stability of test scores to suffer. They do. Test-retest reliabilities ranged from .71 to .93 over two-week intervals, and from .35 to .73 over three-year intervals. Although the studies on the reliability of the TTCT are well summarized, as are those concerned with test validity, the summaries do not contain the descriptive statistics, like means and standard deviations, necessary to make generalizations or to measure the comparability of forms or the absolute constancy of scores. *Norms.* Raw scores from the tests are to be converted to T-scores, but such a scale is not converted to centile ranks, or any other well-known scales. The scales and normative data were gathered on rather restricted samples, presumably on the basis of availability only, which may make generalizations, even for research purposes, somewhat ill-advised. * these tests do not measure up to the level of "format" quality one would expect as a product from a major publishing house and prominent psychologist and educator. Although the TTCT may have significance as a stimulant to further research, one certainly hopes that the author's and publisher's promise of major improvements will be actualized as soon as possible, so that the revision may offer theoretical, scientific, and practical values not yet incorporated into this bold venture into the mystery of creativity.

MATHEMATICS

REVIEWS BY *W. L. Bashaw, E. G. Begle, James Braswell, James R. Caldwell, L. Ray Carry, John Cook, M. Vere DeVault, Gerald L. Ericksen, Mary O. Folsom, Robert A. Forsyth, Cyril J. Hoyt, Carl J. Huberty, Dorothy L. Jones, Jeremy Kilpatrick, William E. Kline, Peter A. Lappan, Jr., J. S. Lawes, John W. Lombard, Kenneth Lovell, Arthur Mittman, Sheldon S. Myers, Thomas C. O'Brien, Alan R. Osborne, Len Pikaart, Lynnette B. Plumlee, Jack Price, C. Alan Riedesel, G. Edith Robinson, W. Todd Rogers, Thomas A. Romberg, Evan D. Shull, Leslie P. Steffe, Marilyn N. Suydam, Kenneth J. Travers, Harold C. Trimble, J. R. Jefferson Wadkins, John Wagner, Willard G. Warrington, Carl G. Willis, James W. Wilson, and Blaine R. Worthen.*

[449]

★ACT Mathematics Placement Examination. College entrants; 1968, c1965-68; MPE; 6 scores: algebra (intermediate, college, total), trigonometry, total, special topics; Form A (16 pages); manual (38 pages); supervisor's manual ['68, 7 pages]; publisher recommends use of local norms; separate answer sheets (Digitek, IBM 805, IBM 1230) or cards (MRC) must be used; $25 per 25 sets of test and answer sheet or card; $1.25 per 25 additional answer sheets; postpaid; specimen set available upon request; MRC scoring service, 50¢ per student; 100(110) minutes; manuals by Linda R. Shevel and Douglas R. Whitney; American College Testing Program. *

REFERENCE

1. SHEVEL, LINDA R., AND WHITNEY, DOUGLAS R. "Predictive Validity of the Mathematics Placement Examination." *Ed & Psychol Meas* 29(4):895-901 w '69. * (PA 44:21621)

WILLIAM E. KLINE, *Director of Test Development, CTB/McGraw-Hill, Monterey, California.*

The *ACT Mathematics Placement Examination* was developed to assist colleges in placing entering students in the mathematics classes most appropriate for their ability and preparation.

The test is divided into two separately timed parts of 50 minutes each, with 40 items in Part 1 and 35 items in Part 2. Each part contains some items in each of the four categories for which scores are available: intermediate algebra, college algebra, trigonometry, and "special topics." This last category includes some geometry items as well as items on set theory, numeration in bases other than ten, and domain and range of functions. The manual lists the content categories of the items with the numbers of items in each category. The distribution of items seems very reasonable; it reflects the emphasis to be found in currently popular textbooks. Some users may prefer a little more of the language of the "modern" mathematics; some may feel that the topic of exponents has been overly stressed.

Although the manual states that the test is "designed to measure knowledge of techniques and achievement in computational skills rather than memorization of formulas," this reviewer found, in solving many of the trigonometry problems, that without having many of the formulas memorized, he would have been hard pressed for time if he had derived each formula before using it.

Items, in general, are well constructed and carefully edited. Answer choices, although arranged in logical order within each item, are sometimes in order of increasing value and at other times in order of decreasing value. The test's directions tell the examinee to pay no attention to the suggested answers until he has obtained his own answer. However, in some problems it is impossible to arrive at the correct answer without using the answer choices. Of the 75 problems, 36 include in the stem, "which of the following," where "following" refers to the answer choices.

In place of national norms, the manual reports means and standard deviations of the raw score distributions, for subtests and total score, at many colleges. The wide range of these means emphasizes the need for local norms. Suggestions are provided in the manual for using this test for the first time. Each user is advised to prepare, from the data obtained in the first year's testing, his own cutting scores or regression formulas for subsequent use.

Many users will find that weighted combinations of the part scores will be more useful for placement than the total score. Experience has shown the test to be most useful for predicting success in the highest-level freshman mathematics courses, in analytic geometry, and in calculus. The intermediate algebra score may be found useful at some institutions for placement in the low-level, terminal, or remedial courses. Some schools, with high school grades and aptitude scores available for their entrants, may very well decide that any increased efficiency in prediction resulting from the use of this test is not worth the time, money, and effort involved in administering it.

The manual reports the K-R 21 reliability estimates for the part scores as .44 (for the 9-item Special Topics), .51, .59, and .75; for the total score the reliability is .81. No evidence is provided on the test's speededness. This reviewer needed almost twice as long to do Part 2 as Part 1. Because there is also no evidence provided for the difficulty of the items, one cannot estimate the power or speed components.

The test is easy to administer and score. It can be administered in two sessions, although this is not suggested in the supervisor's manual. Students are advised to answer all questions, because the raw score is the number of items answered correctly. However, no warning is provided in the directions when the time limit is nearly reached. In a room without a wall clock, students without a watch are at a disadvantage. Because the items that make up the part scores are intermingled throughout the test, scoring by hand is a bit tedious, but not complex.

The test booklet's format is both tasteful and functional. The type style, type size, and spacing make it a very legible instrument. It is designed to be consumable, because it provides space for the examinee to do his figuring in the booklet. However, users could provide scratch paper for the examinee and use the booklet several times.

Any college that is not happy with its current procedures for placing students in freshman mathematics courses would be well advised to try the *ACT Mathematics Placement Examination,* as well as other measures of achievement in secondary school mathematics—but only if it has a reliable criterion against which to judge the test's effectiveness!

[450]

★**Advanced Mathematics (Including Trigonometry): Minnesota High School Achievement Examinations.** High school; 1969-71; new or revised form issued each May; Form EH Rev. ('71, 5 pages); no specific manual; series manual ('71, 16 pages); no data on reliability; 15¢ per test; separate answer sheets (IBM 1230) may be used; 10¢ per answer sheet including scoring service; $1 per series manual; postage extra; $1.10 per specimen set, postpaid; 60(65) minutes; edited by V. L. Lohmann; American Guidance Service, Inc. *

[451]

*Advanced Placement Examination in Mathematics.** High school students desiring credit for college level courses or admission to advanced courses; 1954–70; Forms RBP ('69, 24–25 pages), SBP ('70, 31–33 pages) in 2 booklets (objective, essay); 2 levels; for more complete information, see 662; 180(200) minutes; program administered for the College Entrance Examination Board by Educational Testing Service. *
a) CALCULUS AB. Equivalent of 1 semester college calculus.
b) CALCULUS BC. Equivalent of 1 year college calculus.

REFERENCES

1–4. See 6:570.
5. RALSTON, NANCY CAROLINE. *A Study of the Advanced Placement Program in the Cincinnati Public Schools.* Doctor's thesis, Indiana University (Bloomington, Ind.), 1961. (DA 22:3074)
6. FRANCIS, RICHARD L. "A Placement Study in Analytic Geometry and Calculus." *Ed & Psychol Meas* 26:1041–6 w '66. * (PA 41:5028)

For a review by Paul L. Dressel of an earlier form, see 5:419. For a review of the testing program, see 662.

[452]

★**Basic Mathematics Tests.** Ages 9-0 to 10-6, 10-0 to 12-6, 12-0 to 14-6; 1969–70; 3 levels; no data on reliability; instructions for administration and norms for c free on request from NFER; postpaid within U.K.; (50–60) minutes; published for the National Foundation for Educational Research in England and Wales; Ginn & Co. Ltd. *
a) BASIC MATHEMATICS TEST C. Ages 9-0 to 10-6; 1970; 1 form ['70, 8 pages]; mimeographed instructions ('70, 5 pages); no norms; 5p per test.
b) BASIC MATHEMATICS TEST DE. Ages 10-0 to 12-6; 1969; 1 form ['69, 12 pages]; mimeographed instructions ('69, 6 pages); no norms; 7p per test.
c) BASIC MATHEMATICS TEST FG. Ages 12-0 to 14-6; 1969; 1 form ['69, 12 pages]; mimeographed instructions ('69, 7 pages); provisional norms ('69, 1 page) for ages 12-9 to 13-8 only; 7p per test.

[453]

★**Bristol Achievement Tests: Mathematics.** Ages 8-0 to 9-11, 9-0 to 10-11, 10-0 to 11-11, 11-0 to 12-11, 12-0 to 13-11; 1969; 6 scores: number, reasoning, space, measurement, arithmetic laws and processes, total; Forms A, B, ['69, 8 pages]; 5 levels; administrative manual ['69, 8 pages] for each level; battery interpretive manual (78 pages); battery profile ['69, 2 pages] for each form; £1.90 per 25 tests; £1 per 25 profiles; 60p per teacher's set (without interpretive manual) of any one level (must be purchased to obtain administrative manual and keys); 75p per interpretive manual; postage extra; 55(60) minutes; Alan Brimer; Thomas Nelson & Sons Ltd. *

KENNETH LOVELL, *Professor of Educational Psychology, The Institute of Education, The University, Leeds, England.*

These tests are said to assess attainment in those skills most emphasized in modern British curriculum development programmes. In selecting the level of test, one must pay attention to both chronological age and the length of time the pupil has been in school, with the latter

criterion taking precedence over the former. Thus, strictly, Level 1 should be used with second-year junior school pupils, and Level 5 in the second year of the British secondary school.

Both the Administrative Manual for each level and the Interpretive Manual for the battery (the other tests in the battery cover English and study skills), are well written documents which concisely convey much useful information. In the latter manual are adequate details on the construction of the tests and sections dealing with the principles of mental measurement and standard error of measurement which may be of help to many test users. This manual also includes tables for converting raw scores to standardized scores for the tests at each level. The Administrative Manuals also set out sufficient detail concerning the general character and psychometric properties of the tests at each level, give clear guidance for administering and marking the tests, and include well set-out conversion tables for each form of the test.

In addition to the standardized scores for each two-month age group, percentile equivalents for standardized scores are provided. Also given are decile scores and their standard score equivalents for each of the five parts at each age level and for each form. Armed with these data, and with the aid of the Interpretive Manual, the user can complete the profile card provided at each level, so that a pupil's relative standing on each of the five parts at each level can be seen. Moreover, the manual gives tables from which one can easily and quickly compute the error limits of the decile scores.

The standardization sample was taken from schools "selected in England and Wales which in terms of their type, urban-rural character and their size would represent a national sample of children throughout England and Wales." No further details of the schools and their backgrounds or situations are given. The numbers of pupils on which the standardized scores were calculated ranged from 1,072 at Level 5 to 1,265 at Level 3. There were roughly equal numbers of boys and girls at each age level except at Level 3, where there were 796 boys as against 469 girls. At Levels 2, 3, and 5 there are significant sex differences, favourable to the boys, in respect to the raw scores obtained on both forms of the test, although separate conversion tables are not provided for the sexes. However, a standardized score is available, for a given raw score, for any child within a level regardless of his age.

The total score reliabilities based upon parallel forms given within a two-week period varied from .92 to .94 and may be regarded as satisfactory. Naturally the part scores have lower reliabilities, ranging from .63 to .89.

In general, the tests are well presented. The print is of a suitable size, the layout is clear, and there are only a few points to note. In Level 3, Form A, item 99, the lines separating numerator and denominator have been omitted; and in Level 5, Form A, item 100, and in Form B, item 96, the indices are badly positioned. But British users should note that in the few examples involving money, pounds, shillings, and pence are the units used, while most of the examples involving measurement use imperial and not metric units.

It is argued in the Interpretive Manual that the given account of curriculum sampling and test construction testifies to the rational validity of the tests, but there are no data bearing on the relationship between performance on these tests and other criteria. Test users will have their own views on what they regard as good curriculum sampling. While agreeing with much of the Interpretive Manual, the reviewer questions two points. Although the use of the "domino" form of testing for conservation of number through unprovoked correspondence is entirely suitable at Level 1, to continue to use this type of item at each level to Level 4 is to exclude more useful items. In addition, the items in Part 3 of the tests are rather limited in nature and exclude questions involving, say, geometrical transformations.

In summary, it may be said that, apart from a few blemishes, this very useful test may be recommended. This and the other tests which make up the *Bristol Achievement Tests* provide the only battery of its kind constructed for use in the U.K. Such ground would have to be tested at the different age levels by using a number of unrelated tests if this battery were not employed.

For a review of the complete battery, see 4.

[454]

★**CLEP Subject Examination in College Algebra and Trigonometry.** 1 semester or equivalent; 1968–70; for college accreditation of nontraditional study, advanced placement, or assessment of educational achievement; tests administered monthly at regional centers throughout the United States; tests also available for institutional testing at any time; Form RCT1 ('68, 21 pages); for program accessories, see 664; rental and scoring fee, $5 per student; postpaid; 90(95) minutes; program administered for the College Entrance Examination Board by Educational Testing Service. *

CARL G. WILLIS, *Assistant Director, University Testing and Counseling Service, University of Missouri, Columbia, Missouri.*

The *CLEP Subject Examination in College Algebra and Trigonometry* is one of a number of subject matter instruments which are available to complement five general, or common, examinations. The general examinations have a format similar to the older college-level GED. Available informational pamphlets on the CLEP program claim that these tests can be implemented for almost all purposes and all people. Although suggestions for many uses are presented, little actual research evidence is given. One pamphlet indicates that the tests are available for institutional testing at any time; however, all subject exams must be returned to ETS for scoring. This could lessen their utility, especially when score reports are needed quickly for institutional decisions.

To insure measurement of appropriate content and skill areas, the construction of this examination was guided by a panel of college and university mathematicians, allegedly knowledgeable of college algebra and trigonometry. The exam was designed to be an end-of-course test "intended to serve colleges and universities that want to measure individual achievement" in this particular subject. ETS test development specialists worked with the expert panel in the preparation and evaluation of test questions. This same expert panel reviewed the final edition of the test before it was made available for use. Because of this concern, there is good assurance that the most important content and skill areas are measured by the examination.

Several questionable procedures were followed in readying the algebra-trigonometry examination for general use. A heavy reliance on the competence of test construction specialists resulted in the construction of only 90 items. This implies or assumes that all items are satisfactory and can be used in total for the 90-item test. There was no tryout of the test to locate faulty items before the norming took place. This procedure allowed a small number of items to be included which do not significantly contribute to the total test score. If an excess of test items had been included in a tryout, perhaps these nonrelevant questions could have been eliminated.

The data for concurrent validity appear adequate. There were 33 colleges and universities in the normative population and 3,734 students who were completing a college course in algebra-trigonometry. Unfortunately, despite this base, the test user is not provided data concerning predictive validity, i.e., the relationship of a test score and a grade in the next mathematics course. No indications are provided regarding the relative success of students completing a college algebra-trigonometry course and those taking the same CLEP exam when they take the next higher level mathematics course. In fact, there are no validity data available to aid the test user in determining the applicability of this examination to any of the suggested purposes described by the test publisher.

In describing the test, CEEB indicates that "although there is a wide variation in the difficulty of individual questions on the test, most are intended to be of only moderate difficulty." Yet statistical data based on the results of the normative population show that approximately 10 percent of the students attempted only three-fourths of the items. A large majority of the students did not complete or attempt all items on both sections of the two available test forms. This, according to CEEB, is probably related both to insufficient time and to the high difficulty level of the test items. The mean raw scores on the two test forms, after correction for guessing, are 30 and 26, probably somewhat low for a 90-item test. Scores more to the middle of the possible score range would seem more desirable.

Considering the various factors relevant to test usage, the *CLEP Subject Examination in College Algebra and Trigonometry* is a well planned and constructed instrument for assessing end-of-course achievement and/or nontraditional learning. One of the strongest reasons for its use is its wide acceptance by many colleges and universities as part of their advanced credit programs. The test construction additions suggested above would add to the quality of the examination. An option to allow local scoring of subject tests would provide flexibility to the user of the CLEP.

For reviews of the testing program, see 664 (3 reviews).

[455]

California Achievement Tests: Mathematics, 1970 Edition. Grades 1.5–2, 2–4, 4–6, 6–9, 9–12; 1933–70; previous edition (see 6:564 and 6:616) still available; 3 scores: computation, concepts and problems, total; 1 form; 5 levels; for battery manuals and accessories, see 5; separate answer sheets (CompuScan [NCS], Digitek, IBM 1230) may be used in grades 4–12; postage extra; original edition by Ernest W. Tiegs and Willis W. Clark; CTB/McGraw-Hill.*

a) LEVEL 1. Grades 1.5–2; Form A ('70, 7 pages); $5 per 35 tests; $2.45 per specimen set, postpaid; 31(50) minutes.

b) LEVEL 2. Grades 2–4; Form A ('70, 7 pages); prices same as for level 1; 48(69) minutes.

c) LEVEL 3. Grades 4–6; Form A ('70, 19 pages); $6 per 35 tests; $2.50 per 50 answer sheets; $1 per IBM hand scoring stencil; $2 per specimen set, postpaid; CompuScan scoring service, 22¢ and over per test; 64(85) minutes.

d) LEVEL 4. Grades 6–9; Form A ('70, 17 pages); prices same as for level 3; 51(70) minutes.

e) LEVEL 5. Grades 9–12; Form A ('70, 17 pages); prices same as for level 3; 56(75) minutes.

REFERENCES

1. GUILER, W. S. "Computational Weaknesses of College Freshmen." *J Am Assn Col Reg* 20:367–82 Ap '45. * (*PA* 19:2750)
2. BONNER, LEON WILLIAM. *Factors Associated With the Academic Achievement of Freshmen Students at a Southern Agricultural College.* Doctor's thesis, Pennsylvania State University (State College, Pa.), 1956. (*DA* 17:266)
3. PETA, STEPHEN BENJAMIN. "An Evaluation of Arithmetical Competence in the Junior High Schools of Lethbridge." *Alberta J Ed Res* 2:114–28 Je '56. *
4. RUSCH, CARROLL ERNEST. *An Analysis of Arithmetic Achievement in Grades Four, Six, and Eight.* Doctor's thesis, University of Wisconsin (Madison, Wis.), 1957. (*DA* 17:2217)
5. KRATTIGER, JOHN TRUBERT. *An Evaluation of the Freshman Testing Program of Southeastern State College of Oklahoma.* Doctor's thesis, University of Oklahoma (Norman, Okla.), 1958. (*DA* 19:718)
6. HANEY, RUSSELL; MICHAEL, WILLIAM B.; AND JONES, ROBERT A. "Identification of Aptitude and Achievement Factors in the Prediction of the Success of Nursing Trainees." *Ed & Psychol Meas* 19:645–7 w '59. * (*PA* 34:6164)
7. MICHAEL, WILLIAM B.; JONES, ROBERT A.; AND HANEY, RUSSELL. "The Development and Validation of a Test Battery for Selection of Student Nurses." *Ed & Psychol Meas* 19:641–3 w '59. * (*PA* 34:6171)
8. HANEY, RUSSELL; MICHAEL, WILLIAM B.; JONES, ROBERT A.; AND GADDIS, L. WESLEY. "Cognitive and Non-Cognitive Predictors of Achievement in Student Nursing." *Ed & Psychol Meas* 20:387–9 su '60. * (*PA* 35:7120)
9. ANDERSON, HARRY E., JR. "The Prediction of Reading and Language From the California Tests." *Ed & Psychol Meas* 21:1035–6 w '61. *
10. ANDERSON, HARRY E., JR. "A Study of Language and Nonlanguage Achievement." *Ed & Psychol Meas* 21:1037–8 w '61. *
11. MICHAEL, WILLIAM B.; JONES, ROBERT A.; GETTINGER, TED, JR.; HODGES, JOHN D., JR.; KOLESNIK, PETER E.; AND SEPPALA, JAMES. "The Prediction of Success in Selected Courses in a Teacher Training Program From Scores in Achievement Tests and From Ratings on a Scale of Directed Teaching Performance." *Ed & Psychol Meas* 21:995–9 w '61. *
12. CANISIA, M. "Mathematical Ability as Related to Reasoning and Use of Symbols." *Ed & Psychol Meas* 22:105–27 sp '62. * (*PA* 37:1212)
13. HANEY, RUSSELL; MICHAEL, WILLIAM B.; AND GERSHON, ARTHUR. "Achievement, Aptitude, and Personality Measures as Predictors of Success in Nursing Training." *Ed & Psychol Meas* 22:389–92 su '62. * (*PA* 37:3869)
14. BALDAUF, ROBERT J. "Predicting Success in Eighth Grade Algebra." *Psychol Rep* 12:810 Je '63. * (*PA* 38:6580)
15. MICHAEL, WILLIAM B.; HANEY, RUSSELL; AND GERSHON, ARTHUR. "Intellective and Non-Intellective Predictors of Success in Nursing Training." *Ed & Psychol Meas* 23:817–21 w '63. *
16. RILEY, MARY FELICITAS. *An Analysis of Timed and Untimed Test Scores of Subjects From Two Different Arithmetic Curricula.* Doctor's thesis, Fordham University (New York, N.Y.), 1963. (*DA* 25:2354)
17. HOPKINS, KENNETH D. "Extrinsic Reliability: Estimating and Attenuating Variance From Response Styles, Chance,

and Other Irrelevant Sources." *Ed & Psychol Meas* 24:271–81 su '64. * (*PA* 39:3152)

18. OSBORNE, R. T. "Cultural Bias of Psychological Test Items." *Mankind Q* 4:134–7 Ja–Mr '64. *

19. HUNGERMAN, ANN DOROTHY. *A Study of the Achievement and Attitude of Sixth-Grade Pupils in Conventional and Contemporary Mathematics Programs.* Doctor's thesis, University of Michigan (Ann Arbor, Mich.), 1965. (*DA* 27:414A)

20. MICHAEL, WILLIAM B.; HANEY, RUSSELL; AND BROWN, STEPHEN W. "The Predictive Validity of a Battery of Diversified Measures Relative to Success in Student Nursing." *Ed & Psychol Meas* 25:579–84 su '65. * (*PA* 39:15247)

21. DELIBERTY, WILLIAM F. *The California Arithmetic Test as a Predictor for Selecting 9th Grade Algebra Students.* Master's thesis, Millersville State College (Millersville, Pa.), 1966.

22. GALLIAN, RICHARD DONALD. *A Content Validation Study of the Arithmetic Test Items of Four Arithmetic Achievement Tests Compared With the Content of Six Arithmetic Series at the Intermediate Level.* Doctor's thesis, University of Missouri (Columbia, Mo.), 1967. (*DA* 28:3361A)

23. LOVETT, CARL JAMES. *An Analysis of the Relationship of Several Variables to Achievement in First Year Algebra.* Doctor's thesis, University of Texas (Austin, Tex.), 1969. (*DAI* 30:1470A)

24. MOORE, CLAY L., JR.; MACNAUGHTON, JOHN F.; AND OSBURN, HOBART G. "Ethnic Differences Within an Industrial Selection Battery." *Personnel Psychol* 22(4):473–82 w '69. * (*PA* 44:13473)

25. MARS, PAUL ARNE. *High School Geometry Achievement as Related to Reading Achievement, Arithmetic Achievement, and General Intelligence in the Public Schools of Lincoln, Nebraska.* Doctor's thesis, University of Nebraska (Lincoln, Neb.), 1970. (*DAI* 31:1691A)

For a review by Robert D. North of an earlier edition, see 5:468; for a review by Robert L. Burch of the tests for grades 1–9, see 4:411; for reviews by C. L. Thiele and Harry Grove Wheat, see 2:1459; for a review by William A. Brownell, see 1:893. For reviews of earlier editions of the complete battery, see 6:3 (2 reviews), 5:2 (1 review), 4:2 (3 reviews), 3:15 (1 review), 2:1193 (2 reviews), and 1:876 (1 review, 1 excerpt).

[456]

*College Board Achievement Test in Mathematics, Level 1. Candidates for college entrance; 1901–71; test administered each January, March, May, July, and December at centers established by the publisher; for more complete information, see 663; 60(80) minutes; program administered for the College Entrance Examination Board by Educational Testing Service. *

REFERENCES

1. BURGESS, THOMAS C. "Estimating Average Freshman Class Ability From Preliminary Information." *J Col Stud Personnel* 10(3):161–3 My '69. *

2. NELSON, BRUCE EDWARD. *The Relationship of Mathematics in Oregon High Schools to Placement and Success in First-Year Mathematics at Oregon State University.* Doctor's thesis, Oregon State University (Corvallis, Ore.), 1969. (*DAI* 30:1401A)

3. PUGH, RICHARD C.; HUTCHCRAFT, GILBERT; AND LUDLOW, H. GLENN. *An Analysis of Achievement Behavior in Selected Mathematics Courses.* Indiana Studies in Prediction No. 12. Bloomington, Ind.: Bureau of Educational Studies and Testing, Indiana University, August 1969. Pp. xiii, 42. *

4. STOVER, DONALD W. "Pretesting for the College Boards." *Math Teach* 62(7):537–41 N '69. *

[457]

*College Board Achievement Test in Mathematics, Level 2. Candidates for college entrance; 1901–71; test administered each January, May, and December at centers established by the publisher; for more complete information, see 663; 60(80) minutes; program administered for the College Entrance Examination Board by Educational Testing Service. *

REFERENCE

1. STOVER, DONALD W. "Pretesting for the College Boards." *Math Teach* 62(7):537–41 N '69. *

[458]

*College Placement Test in Advanced Mathematics. Entering college freshmen; 1962–70, c1957–70; CPTAM; irregularly scheduled reprintings of inactive forms of *College Board Achievement Test in Advanced Mathematics;* Forms KPL1 ['62, reprint of 1957 test], LPL ['63, reprint of 1958 test] in a single booklet (19 pages); for more complete information, see program entry (665); 60(70) minutes; program administered for the College Entrance Examination Board by Educational Testing Service. *

For a review by Saunders Mac Lane of Form KPL1 (formerly FAC), see 6:568; for a review by Paul L. Dressel of earlier forms, see 4:367. For a review of the testing program, see 665.

[459]

*College Placement Test in Intermediate Mathematics. Entering college freshmen; 1962–70, c1956–70; CPTIM; irregularly scheduled reprintings of inactive forms of *College Board Achievement Test in Intermediate Mathematics;* Forms KPL1 ['62, reprint of 1956 test], KPL2 ['62, reprint of 1957 test] in a single booklet (20 pages); for more complete information, see program entry (665); 60(70) minutes; program administered for the College Entrance Examination Board by Educational Testing Service. *

For a review by Paul L. Dressel of earlier forms, see 6:569; for a review by Paul J. Blommers, see 4:368. For a review of the testing program, see 665.

[460]

★College Placement Test in Mathematics, Level 1. Entering college freshmen; 1964–70; CPTM; irregularly scheduled reprintings of inactive forms of *College Board Achievement Test in Mathematics, Level 1;* Forms NPL ('65), OPL ['66, reprint of 1965 test] in a single booklet (19 pages); for more complete information, see program entry (665); 60(70) minutes; program administered for the College Entrance Examination Board by Educational Testing Service. *

For a review of the testing program, see 665.

[461]

★College Placement Test in Mathematics, Level 2. Entering college freshmen; 1965–70; CPTM; irregularly scheduled reprintings of inactive forms of *College Board Achievement Test in Mathematics, Level 2;* Form OPL ['66, reprint of 1965 test, 11 pages]; for more complete information, see program entry (665); 60(70) minutes; program administered for the College Entrance Examination Board by Educational Testing Service. *

For a review of the testing program, see 665.

[462]

★Contemporary Mathematics Test: Advanced (Senior High). Grades 9–12; 1965–66; for all tests in the series, see 464; developed to supplement the arithmetic tests of the *California Achievement Tests;* Forms W, X, ('65, 12 pages); no specific manual; series manual, revised ('66, 14 pages); series technical report ('66, 30 pages); IBM 1230 directions ('65, 4 pages); $5.50 per 35 tests; separate answer sheets (IBM 1230) may be used; $2.50 per 50 answer sheets; $1 per scoring stencil; $1 per technical report; 15¢ per IBM directions; postage extra; $2 per specimen set of any one level, postpaid; scoring service, 22¢ and over per test; 45(50) minutes; CTB/McGraw-Hill. *

JEREMY KILPATRICK, *Associate Professor of Mathematics, Teachers College, Columbia University, New York, New York.*

This test, devised as a supplement to the *California Mathematics Test,* is the product of an attempt to accommodate the necessarily laggard processes of standardized test construction to a changing mathematics curriculum. Teachers of "traditional" mathematics are apparently supposed to use the *California Mathematics Test* alone; teachers of "contemporary" mathematics are apparently supposed to use both tests. Although this arrangement has spared the publisher from withdrawing the earlier test from the market, it reflects a distorted view of recent reforms in school mathematics. Particularly at the secondary school level, the new mathematics curricula are more than just additions to existing courses; they represent a fundamental reorientation of instructional goals. Truly contemporary mathematics tests ought to mirror this change in goals. The *Contemporary Mathematics Test: Advanced (Senior High)* does not.

The test consists of 56 three- and four-choice items. It is divided into two parts, for administration in two sessions if necessary, but it yields only a single score. Content categories (with the number of items per form in parentheses) are properties of numbers (7), mathematical structures (8), systems of numeration (3), nature and structure of proof (6), ratio and proportion (3), mathematical sentences (8), geometry (13), and variables, functions, and graphs (8). One of the criteria of item selection was that "no item was retained which was passed by more than 60 percent of the students in traditional mathematics classes." Whether or not this criterion is the cause, the test is heavy with items on modern terminology, such as "closure" and "commutativity." The attempt to be mathematically contemporary has led in some instances to awkward circumlocutions, such as "If $f(x) = \sqrt{3 - x}$ is a real number, which of the values given below are numbers of the domain of the function?" Only a few items, mostly on functions, require the student to apply

his knowledge. (One item in Form X, in which base six numerals are used to number the pages in a book, takes a prize for inanity.) Most of the items in both forms, especially those in Part One, deal with content taught in junior high school programs.

About one-fifth of the items offer the unfortunate three answer choices: "true under *all* circumstances," "impossible to tell," and "false under *all* circumstances." Such items are susceptible to response sets. Furthermore, they can be confusing, since "impossible to tell," although used as shorthand for "neither true nor false under all circumstances," implies the stronger condition that one cannot give a rule describing the circumstances under which the statement is true. A student who sees that it *is* possible to tell when a given statement is true and when it is false may balk at marking "impossible to tell."

Since the manual provides little descriptive information on the test itself and almost nothing on the test development procedures, the test user must turn to the technical report for this information. The report claims that the test is essentially a power test. It was tried out with maximum and minimum time limits before the final time limit was set. However, since 56 items have to be completed in 45 minutes and since the 99th percentile is at 40 and 42 items for the fall and the spring, respectively, the test appears to be speeded.

The two forms are closely equivalent, both in content and in difficulty. Alternate-forms reliabilities averaged .61 over seven days and .90 over 180 days. K-R 20 reliabilities are reported as .85 for Form W and .89 for Form X.

The technical report discusses various steps taken during the development of the test to strengthen content validity, such as using classroom teachers as item writers and representatives of experimental mathematics curriculum projects as reviewers. Results of a factorial analysis of variance, in which ability level was significantly (.01 level) related to test scores but sex, test form, and geographic area were not, are presented as evidence for validity.

Norms giving percentile rank, standard scores, and stanines for fall and spring administrations are provided in the manual. A single set of norms is meant to apply across grades 9 to 12. Since the norming sample consisted of tenth and eleventh graders only (the number at each grade is not given), the norms may be inappropriate for ninth and twelfth graders. Apparently ninth graders were to have been included in the norming sample, but only a few students, of high ability, were available. Nonetheless, "after careful study," according to the manual, "it was concluded that the norms as presented....are appropriate for students in grades 9–12 who meet the specifications for the....test: students who have had (or are completing) at least two years of contemporary mathematics, one of which is contemporary algebra." We are not told what this "careful study" consisted of.

Some of the test items could have used further editing, but as a whole the test is attractively packaged and appears easy to administer. The technical report candidly discusses some of the problems of updating mathematics achievement tests and stresses the tentative nature of the norms, with a plea for local experimentation and local norms, where necessary.

Although the test is designed as a supplement to another test, it is, for reasons of convenience, likely to be used alone. In fact, it apparently was used alone in the norming studies, since no data are given on the relationship between the two tests. It is not clear what this test measures, apart from knowledge of modern terminology, that the earlier test does not. Studies of the relationship between the two tests and their relationship to outside criteria are needed to enable test users to judge if it is worthwhile to give both tests.

In sum, the test seems most useful as part of a larger battery that would sample a broader range of instructional goals. Users should recognize the limitations of both the test content and the norms. Used alone, the test is likely to be inadequate either for program evaluation or for assessing students' progress in high school mathematics courses.

J. R. JEFFERSON WADKINS, *Associate Examiner in Mathematics, Educational Testing Service, Princeton, New Jersey.*

"The Contemporary Mathematics Test series is designed to assess knowledge of concepts unique to the several most widely taught modern mathematics programs"—so says the publisher's catalogue. There can be little doubt that there are many teachers and administrators involved in modernized mathematics programs who thirst for an opportunity to evaluate their efforts objectively by testing their students' understanding and knowledge of important mathematical concepts and then comparing the results of such tests with some established norms. It is clear that much time and effort were expended in establishing norms for this series once the test was developed. One can only wonder why more time and effort were not expended on the development of high quality test questions.

The Advanced (Senior High) test does concern itself with topics that are, for the most part, unique to newer, nontraditional math programs. (The two most prominent exceptions involve (a) direct and inverse variation—not phrased in terms of functions, and (b) use of such phraseology as "y as a function of x." It is difficult to see how such questions could be included in an examination intended to test concepts "unique to the several most widely taught modern mathematics programs." While such material does form a part of some modern programs, it is much more prevalent in traditional presentations.) There are, however, few questions which test anything deeper than terminology, symbolism, and certain textbook conventions. One item type (described later) that is used repeatedly has an inherent logical flaw. The questions on logic and proof are shallow and artificial; some are incorrect; and virtually all are loosely phrased. In general, the quality of language used throughout the test would possibly be excusable in courses where precision of language receives little attention, but in a standardized test of contemporary mathematics at the secondary school level, a test that might be looked upon as a desirable standard by some students—and even teachers—who stand in awe of the printed word, such atrocious use of language borders on criminal neglect.

Typical of the careless wording of questions is item 5, Part I of Form W:

> The statement below is false.
>   Joe is slow and Pete is quick.
> Which of the following sentences is/are logically equivalent to the statement above?
>   I. Joe is not slow and Pete is not quick.
>   II. Joe is not slow or Pete is not quick.
>   III. Joe is quick and Pete is slow.
>   a. II only
>   b. I and III
>   c. II and III
>   d. I, II, and III

If "the statement above" refers to "Joe is slow and Pete is quick," the correct answer is "none."

If "the statement above" refers to "The statement below is false," then the correct answer is (a) as intended, but the logic is less than straightforward; and use of "the statement above" to refer to the penultimate statement calls into question the meaning of "The statement below." It would seem that the intention was to ask for a statement equivalent to "It is false that 'Joe is slow and Pete is quick.'"

Another item on logic having a clear-cut logical flaw is item 11 of Part 1, Form X. The question is asked as to which one of four statements "denies" a given statement. The intention was obviously to ask for the negation of the given statement. However, one would be hard pressed to explain why two other choices are not correct answers when each implies that the given statement is false. It would hardly be appropriate to claim that "Everybody should know that 'denies' means. . . ."

There is an item type used 11 times in Form W and 12 times in Form X that is truly exasperating. The choices for these items are:

    T. True under *all* circumstances
    ? Impossible to tell
    F. False under *all* circumstances

Ignoring the more subtle difficulties of the meaning of "*all* circumstances," one finds that the objects under consideration are sometimes single statements, more frequently conclusions of statements, and occasionally series of statements. The only indication as to which is intended is the answer key given in the manual. The single-statement items are maddening in that "under *all* circumstances" is irrelevant; the conclusions-of-statements items will worry anyone who has learned that there are negations to if-then statements as well as negations to conclusions; and any teacher who has been careful to point out the difference between "truth" and "validity" in logic will cringe at the series-of-statements questions in this format.

There is scarcely an item in either form which could not be advantageously rephrased. Minor annoyances such as indefinite antecedents, inappropriate labels, ambiguous phraseology, inconsistent conventions in figures, and less-than-universal conventions used without explanation are understandable and excusable in a classroom test where the students are accustomed to individual idiosyncracies of the teacher and where the teacher is available for explanations during the test period. Even in a standardized test, a few such irritations are to be expected, but these forms are so filled with such vexations that one must continually ask the question, "Should I answer this on the basis of what it actually says, or shall I try to guess what the testmaker meant to say?"

The technical report informs us that classroom teachers wrote the questions for these tests and that each question was reviewed by not less than four and sometimes as many as eight "professional experts in the field of contemporary mathematics"—experts representing the various contemporary mathematics programs. One can only wonder how much effect these reviews could possibly have had on the final form in which these questions appear. It would seem to have been more preferable to have had one competent mathematician who would give each question a thorough, nit-picking review and who would have veto power over any wording which might offend him. Granted that precise language can be—and often is—obtuse, careful mathematical language is an ideal that should be compromised in standardized tests only with the greatest reluctance. The tendency to shrug off picayune criticisms of language can only lead to an atmosphere of review in which items which are incorrect by any standards are bound to slip by. In addition to the items already mentioned, and in addition to many items in both forms for which one could give a fairly good argument that there is no correct answer given or that there is more than one correct answer, Form X contains three questions which have flaws regardless of how the wording is interpreted:

Item 7 of Part 1 asks for the value of $\sqrt{x^2}$. The intended key is "$|x|$," but who can deny that $\sqrt{x^2}$ is either x or $-x$? One of the other available choices is $\pm x$.

Item 22 of Part 1 seems intended to ask if it is true that there exist x, y in a certain set for which $x \boxed{F} y = y \boxed{F} x$. The answer is "No" unless $x = y$, a picayunish eventuality not eliminated by the wording of the question but ignored by the intended answer, "False under *all* circumstances."

Item 16 of Part 2 has no correct answer among the choices. The question is in essence: For all real numbers a and b with $a < b$ and for all $c > 0$, what is the order relationship between $\frac{a}{b}$ and $\frac{a+c}{b+c}$? (We will ignore such bothersome cases as when b = o or when b + c = o.) Now $-3 < -2$ and $\dfrac{-3}{-2} < \dfrac{-3+1}{-2+1}$, but $\dfrac{-3}{-2} > \dfrac{-3+3}{-2+3}$. None of the choices offered covers this eventuality. The intended answer would lead one to believe that if a < b and c > o, then $\dfrac{a}{b} < \dfrac{a+c}{b+c}$.

In summary, there seem to be few advantages to using these tests in preference to tests made up by the individual teacher or supervisor; and there are many disadvantages, not the least of which is the danger of interpreting the results as being—in any sense –a "truc" indication of the quality of instruction in a given program or the degree to which "important" mathematical concepts of nontraditional presentations receive proper emphasis in that program. It is quite probable that these CMT (Advanced) tests will suffice to separate a class into two groups—those who have a knowledge of basic terminology and symbolism, and those who do not; however, the individual classroom teacher could undoubtedly prepare a much more relevant test if this is to be the only criterion. Such a teacher-made test would probably do a better job of ranking the students within each group than would the CMT (Advanced) test because the students with a deeper understanding of concepts will undoubtedly be bothered by many things on the standardized test—things which the more naive or more cavalier student will simply ignore. Long before taking the teacher-made tests, the better students will have accustomed themselves to idiosyncratic ambiguities of individual teachers.

It is possible that there may be individual programs in which "new" mathematics subject matter—such as that of sets, logic, axioms, number bases—is taught without emphasis upon careful language or without the careful nurturing of an appreciation of mathematics in and of itself. In such cases, these standardized tests might well be valid instruments to measure achievement in proportion to other such programs. A perusal of the test by the teacher or supervisor could indicate if such is the case. Again, the danger would be in judging the results as an indication of the relative value of the program or of the relative abilities of individual students to pursue further mathematical activities.

For excerpts from reviews of the series, see 464 (2 excerpts).

[463]

★**Contemporary Mathematics Test: Elementary and Junior High.** Grades 3-4, 5-6, 7-9; 1965-66; for all tests in the series, see 464; developed to supplement the arithmetic tests of the *California Achievement Tests;* 2 forms; 3 levels; no specific manual; series manual, revised ('66, 14 pages); series technical report ('66, 30 pages); IBM 1230 directions ('65, 4 pages); $5.50 per 35 tests; separate answer sheets (IBM 1230) may be used; $2.50 per 50 answer sheets; $1 per scoring stencil; $1 per technical report; 15¢ per IBM directions; postage extra; $2 per specimen set of any one level, postpaid; scoring service, 22¢ and over per test; CTB/McGraw-Hill. *
a) LOWER ELEMENTARY LEVEL. Grades 3-4; Forms W, X, ('65, 12 pages); practice exercises ('64, 2 pages) for IBM answer sheets; $3 per 100 practice exercises; 35(40) minutes.
b) UPPER ELEMENTARY LEVEL. Grades 5-6; Forms W, X, ('65, 12 pages); 35(40) minutes.
c) JUNIOR HIGH SCHOOL LEVEL. Grades 7-9; Forms W, X, ('65, 11 pages); 40(45) minutes.

REFERENCE

1. HUNGERMAN, ANN DOROTHY. *A Study of the Achievement and Attitude of Sixth-Grade Pupils in Conventional and Contemporary Mathematics Programs.* Doctor's thesis, University of Michigan (Ann Arbor, Mich.), 1965. (*DA* 27:414A)

E. G. BEGLE, *Professor of Mathematics Education, Stanford University, Stanford, California.*

These tests were designed to measure the extent to which students have acquired a grasp of certain mathematical topics which are included in contemporary mathematics programs but do not appear in traditional mathematics programs. In order to make sure that the final versions of these tests would concentrate on contemporary mathematics, the authors eliminated any item in the first experimental edition if it was passed by more than 60 percent of the tryout students who were in traditional mathematics classes. Thus, these tests should be looked at as supplements to, rather than replacements for, previously developed tests.

When the construction of these tests was started in 1963, there were a large number of contemporary mathematics programs that had recently been constructed or were being developed. Potential items were reviewed by experts in mathematics education in an attempt to eliminate those not equally appropriate for students in all the new programs.

A technical report contains a full account of the development of these tests, of the size and nature of the norming sample, and of the relevant statistics.

Although each test booklet contains two parts, only a single score is obtained—the total number of correct responses. Tables provided in the manual convert the total raw score into a percentile rank, a standard score, or a stanine—for either spring or fall administrations.

Reliabilities (K-R 20) for the individual elementary forms range from .72 to .84, and for the junior high school forms from .84 to .87. A variety of other statistical analyses are reported, including 7-day and 180-day test-retest reliability coefficients.

It is clear that in the development of these tests, all the proper steps were taken and all the proper procedures were followed. Nevertheless, the results are less than satisfactory. There are three reasons for this.

The first is that the objectives of mathematics education change. Certain topics which were considered important in 1963 are now (1970) considered less important. Examples are sets and non-decimal number bases. For present purposes these topics are overrepresented in these tests.

The second reason is that some of the items in these tests are technically poor. One item is miskeyed, some items have more than one correct answer, other items use terminology or notation or grammatical constructions which are not standard in contemporary mathematics programs. Most, but not all, of these poor items appear in the junior high school forms.

The major problem is the norms. The average number of years of exposure to contemporary mathematics programs for the norming sample in 1965 was probably considerably less than for today's students, because contemporary mathematics programs are much more widely used today. Since the tests are deliberately biased against traditional programs, one would expect that today's students would score higher than did the norming group. On the other hand, as is discussed at some length in the technical report, it was still the tendency in 1965 to restrict the use of contemporary mathematics programs to the more able students. Hence it is likely that the norming population was higher in ability than the present contemporary mathematics population, which would argue that the norms might be too high. How important these two factors actually are, and whether they might cancel each other out, is, of course, unknown. But the fact remains that national norms established in 1965 are of dubious validity after five years of continued change in the schools.

Prospective users of these tests are advised to examine them carefully to see if they are really relevant to the contemporary mathematics program in use and are advised also to consider the possibility of developing local norms.

THOMAS C. O'BRIEN, *Associate Professor of Education, Southern Illinois University, Edwardsville, Illinois.*

This test was designed "to be used in addition to the *California Achievement Tests*" in order to obtain an estimate of the extent to which the student has acquired knowledge and understanding of the subject matter of contemporary mathematics programs.

It is a bias of this reviewer that tests of this sort should be of some usefulness to the teacher. They should tell him something about his class and, it is hoped, about its individual members. Further, they should tell him something *important* about the mathematical abilities of the class or individual students whose "knowledge" is measured.

The *Contemporary Mathematics Test* fails in both respects. It is limited, in general, to measuring children's recall of definitions, notation, and conventions; in those rare instances in which any sort of relational or productive activity is involved, it is the product rather than the process with which the test item is concerned. (What information useful for further teacher action lies in the fact that a student answered "8" to "$21 + 7 = 20 + \square$"? Did the child compute 28 and then ask himself, "What number do I add to 20 to get 28?" Or did he employ associativity straightaway?) Worse, even when important ideas are involved, no suggestion is made that teachers might profitably interview students to gain further information about the state of their knowledge. No suggestion is made that an item analysis might be useful. Further, the manual does not suggest follow-up items, an especially useful feature in tests such as these, in which a small number of items are used to cover a large number of topics. A single item on proportionality—$14/7 = 28/n$, for example —gives relatively little information about children's achievement in this area since the research shows that a ratio of 2 to 1 is a very special case of proportionality so far as the growth of this concept in children is concerned.

Several ambiguities appear in the test. For example, only one of three correct answers is keyed for "Which number sentence shows that subtraction will undo addition?" "$4 + 3 - 3 = 4$," "$5 - 3 = 2$," "$(5 - 4) + 4 = 5$," "$4 + 3

= 12 − 5," and it is conceivable that a case could be built for the fourth choice. Similarly, "(a + b) + 9 □ (a +b) · 9. Which symbol should go in the box to make the sentence true? (a and b ≠ o) a. <, b. >, c. = d. None of these" seems to be both ambiguous and too difficult for upper elementary students. Just what does this item test?

Administration of this test seems to be adequately described in the test manual, save for some awkward reading of optional instructions depending upon whether a test is to be administered in one or two sittings and whether it is to be machine scored or hand scored. According to the manual, machine scoring—for what it is worth—is available from the publisher.

Several issues may be of interest concerning the published norms. One is that the norms were obtained in 1965 and thus the present user would be comparing his students with students in what might have been very different circumstances. Second, the technical report points out that the norming sample may not have been representative of the population in terms of IQ, mathematics abilities, and in planning for future action, save in the most global way. The use of a single score for a student or a class is a pseudo-mathematization of the actual state of affairs. Even if this were not so, it is not clear to this reviewer just what an overall class mean or an individual score of x, corresponding to y percentile, a z standard score, and a k stanine, tells a teacher about the state of knowledge of his student(s) in a particular area or about any future action he might take.

In short, this test measures the worst of what was regarded as "modern mathematics." For the teacher interested in the status and development of mathematical activity in children, it is of very little value.

For excerpts from reviews of the series, see 464.

[464]

★**Contemporary Mathematics Tests.** Grades 3–4, 5–6, 7–9, 9–12, 8–9; 1965–66; CMT; for additional information and reviews, see the separate test entries; CTB/McGraw-Hill. *
a) ELEMENTARY AND JUNIOR HIGH. Grades 3–4, 5–6, 7–9. See 463.
b) ADVANCED (SENIOR HIGH). Grades 9–12. See 462.
c) ALGEBRA. 1 year grades 8–9. See 499.

J Ed Meas 4:123–4 su '67. *Fred M. Smith.* * Since the test is designed as a supplement to the....[California Achievement Test], data indi-

cating the comparability of scores between it and the CAT would greatly enhance its use. None, however, are available at the present time. Nor is any information presented on specific uses for which the test is intended. * On page 5 of the manual, the examiner is advised that the parts are not to be timed separately, but on the next page he is instructed to say at the end of one-half the allotted time, "Everyone should now begin Part Two if you have not already done so. You have approximately....minutes to finish the test." Is this just a suggestion to the students, or is everyone *required* to begin Part Two when the call is made? If a student finishes before time is called, may he go back and work on Part One? He may not do so if the test is administered in two sittings, but nothing is said about this when the test is administered in one sitting. A definite improvement over the CAT is the absence of a diagnostic profile based on part scores composed of too few items for acceptable reliability. Kuder-Richardson 20 reliability coefficients based on total scores are not as high as would be desirable, ranging from .70 to .87. * this....[manual] is rather brief giving only a superficial description of the test, directions for administration and scoring, and the norms tables. More complete data are promised in the technical report, but schools are asked to buy the test on the basis of the description furnished in the manual. This departure from past practice is disappointing. * Several test publishers have begun to include tables of specifications in their achievement test manuals to aid teachers in determining content validity and in using the test. This highly desirable practice, if used here, would certainly add to the value of the CMT. Another question also arises with any test which purports to measure outcomes common to all programs in contemporary mathematics. If a test attempts to measure that which is common to all programs, can it be completely valid for any one program? What about the relative performance of groups pursuing different programs? Data concerning this are sorely needed, before a great deal of use can be made of the test. * The general impression one receives from a review of this test is one of haste rather than thoroughness in its preparation. After data from further research and refinement are supplied, the CMT may prove to be as good a test as any in this particular area of mathematics. Any final statement of its quality will have to be withheld at the present time, however.

J Ed Meas 5:349–51 w '68. Thomas A. Romberg. One of the major problems in the now decade-old mathematics curriculum revolution has been the lack of appropriate assessment devices for measuring the effectiveness of modern mathematics programs. The Contemporary Mathematics Test Series (CMT) was designed with this in mind. One can only applaud attempts to develop such long needed tests. However, for this series there was a big difference between expectations and actual test content. The reviewer was hoping to find these tests filled with creative problems assessing the varied performance expectations of the modern programs. Instead, he found mundane vocabulary and symbolism items measuring only the lowest and least interesting changes in behavior anticipated in the curriculum revolution. In defense of the publishers, these were my expectations, not theirs, for they clearly indicate the purpose for developing these tests was to yield estimates of *knowledge* and *understanding* of subject matter common to the several programs in contemporary mathematics. After studying these tests the reviewer is concerned that others with similar expectations to his will naively use these tests to measure overall achievement in modern courses rather than measuring only the use of unique symbols and terminology which is such a small part of contemporary mathematics programs. * For the CMT Series what is to be measured is "understanding of concepts and skills pertinent to solving problems in areas of 1. structure in number, and 2. special mathematical devices" (p. 8). Content validity was obtained by defining four categories under each area. Some reservations about the adequacy of this domain of items is in order. For example, in the lower elementary form it would seem inappropriate that four out of thirty items be on even-odd numbers or five out of thirty items be on reading graphs and tables. Likewise, across forms it seems inappropriate to ask so many questions (27) on other number bases. But, much more serious validity problems arise from the terms "understanding of concepts" and "pertinent to solving problems"—their statements of *why* the test was developed. "To understand" does not denote behavior. It can only be inferred from other behaviors. This implies a network of behaviors which operationalize understanding. Since no network is

specified, no definitive demonstration of construct validity is possible. An alternative is to accept the battery as an operational definition of understanding. This I am unwilling to do for the items fail to fit any hierarchy of behaviors. For I would interpret "understanding" to include knowledge, comprehension, and ability to use a concept. To substantiate this point, the categories of Bloom's taxonomy were used as a rough indication of levels and the items of one form of each level were categorized by the reviewer. Of thirty items in the Lower Elementary Level, 27 were categorized at the first two levels, only three at the third level, and none at the higher cognitive levels. The same pattern for the remaining tests were observed, although perhaps not quite as dramatically. Only the Algebra Test has even a representative proportion of items at the application level. However, even this test had half of the items rated below the application level and only three above that level. For all five tests, only seven items were categorized above application. "Pertinent to solving problems" implies that performance on this test is a good predictor of ability to solve problems. No evidence for this assertion is presented. It is questionable whether scores on these tests would be any better as predictors of problem solving ability than I.Q. scores or computation scores. Hence, predictive validity has not been established. The individual population for each test is not specified except to say they should have been in contemporary programs at specific grades. It is not clear, except for the Algebra Test, whether any of the content is covered in the specified grades. In particular, it is not clear who the Advanced Senior High Form is designed for since most of the items were contained in earlier forms. Apparently it is for students who have been through some modern program but who have not had algebra, geometry, advanced algebra, etc., since no knowledge of these subjects is required. Taken together the reviewer doubts that these tests are valid measures for the purposes stated. At best, these tests could be used as measures of a very narrow range of achievement (knowledge of terminology and symbolism). However, to compound the problem, because different modern texts use different terms and symbols, the authors have tried to compromise in many places and have ended with inexact terminology or symbolism, depending upon different texts. However, in each case the intended meaning should be clear to the students. It would seem that items at this level could be better written for particular standard textbooks. * The authors....are to be commended for the care in which they developed reliability information and the norming data on these tests. The comparable background of students taking each form are carefully reported. * The format of these tests is attractive although changes in number of distractors and changes in indicator for the distractors from numbers to letters and back might be confusing. In addition, some figures were hard to read causing difficulty in determining which answer is required. *Summary.* The real problem with these tests is not in their content or in their reliability but in their likely use by schools as overall achievement measures for contemporary mathematics programs. One must not confuse success on this kind of test with knowledge of mathematics, or ability to do mathematics. It is unfortunate that with all of the care that has gone into the development of this series more time was not taken to conceptualize behaviors more broadly. If achievement as defined by these tests is considered as success in modern programs, then the overall purposes of the revolution have not been met.

[465]

Cooperative Mathematics Tests. Grades 7-8, 7-9, 8-9, 10-12, high school and college; 1962-65; CMT; 9 tests; for additional information and reviews, see the separate test entries; Cooperative Tests and Services. *
a) STRUCTURE OF THE NUMBER SYSTEM. Grades 7-8. See 466.
b) ARITHMETIC. Grades 7-9. See 515.
c) ALGEBRA I AND II. Grades 8-9, 10-12. See 500.
d) GEOMETRY. Grades 10-12. See 533.
e) TRIGONOMETRY. High school and college. See 543.
f) ALGEBRA III. High school and college. See 501.
g) ANALYTIC GEOMETRY. High school and college. See 532.
h) CALCULUS. High school and college. See 531.

J Counsel Psychol 12:105–6 sp '65. Jack C. Merwin. * This test series is characterized by obvious care in test planning and item contruction, generally pleasing format and provision of extensive statistical information; characteristics it shares with the series it replaces. School systems which used the earlier series should find that the corresponding replacements in this new series will meet their needs equally well. * The *Handbook* for the series includes technical information and aids for interpreting scores, but makes no mention of administration and

scoring procedures. * No concurrent validity evidence is provided to show the extent of correlation with corresponding tests in the old series. However, a table for equating scaled scores from the old series to the converted scores of the new series appears in the *Handbook*. This would indicate that such information could be made available and it would be of value particularly for schools which must replace the older series in their testing program. * Based on percent answering the last item and percent reaching the three-quarter point of each test on each form, the section in the *Handbook* on speededness concludes that, "Algebra I is the only test of the series for which speededness can be regarded as relatively unimportant; all other tests exhibiting speededness characteristics to some degree." This leads to the unstated conclusion that this speededness will have in some degree spuriously inflated the reliability coefficients reported and somewhat spuriously lowered the resulting standard errors of measurement. * Statistical weighting of scores was accomplished in an attempt to make adjustments for proportions of urban and non-urban students, size of schools, and proportion of public, Roman Catholic and independent school students. This is probably as much statistical adjustment as is practical and still leaves geographical representation somewhat less than desirable as indicated by tables provided. Statistical procedures of adjusting norms are at best make-shift measures. * The norms....are probably as good a set of norms as could be offered under the circumstances described in the *Handbook*. * According to the *Handbook*, the percentile band can be interpreted as including scores such that the chances are two to one that the interpreter is correct in assuming that the student's actual standing is in that range. * In a section following the discussion of percentile bands entitled, "Meaningful Interpretations," the qualification of "the chances are two to one" seems to have been ignored. In citing an example of a girl whose percentile band is from 75 to 93, the interpretation given is that "this means that only 7 percent of the students in the norms group clearly rank higher than Barbara, while 75 percent of the students clearly rank lower. Barbara is in the top quarter of the group on this test." Going on to compare Barbara's percentile band with another student's percentile band of 36 to 66, the *Handbook* states that "therefore, the conclusion that Barbara's standing in the national norms group is higher than Ted's standing is justified." This suggested means of interpretation unjustifiably implies that the "actual standing" of each individual student falls within the band obtained. In the section suggesting the value of and procedures for developing and using locally constructed norms, a table for developing percentile bands appears to gloss over the differences in standard errors of measurement for the various tests and their different forms. However, the units suggested will, in general, provide conservative sets of limits. The *Handbook* notes that a special pamphlet entitled "Constructing and Using Local Norms" is available upon request from the publisher. It is to be recommended that a school system not attempt to use the percentile band approach as described in the *Handbook* without first consulting this pamphlet. CONCLUSION. This series of mathematics tests continues a series of end-of-course achievement examinations which reflect careful attention to curriculum sampling, item construction, and statistical treatment of scores. This reviewer recommends more cautious interpretation of percentile bands and differences in percentile bands than those used in the example found in the *Handbook,* suggests that the national norms might well be used exclusively, even by urban high schools, and believes that schools which have used earlier editions of the Cooperative Mathematics Test will find that these tests will continue to meet their needs.

J Ed Meas 2:223–30 D '65. John R. Hills. * Here are course-oriented mathematics tests of apparently excellent quality with the comprehensive test manual that we now expect from ETS. The content of the items is carefully described, the forms are carefully matched, the norms are carefully developed and described, and more detail is provided than most users will have learned to expect from anyone. There is only one major flaw which disturbs the reviewer; no predictive, concurrent, or construct validity information of any kind are presented in the manual. * modernization is most evident in the manual and in the test on Structure of the Number System. The nature of most of the items in the other tests appears to be not especially different from the traditional test items in algebra, geometry, trigonometry, analytic geometry, and calculus. * The reviewer would need to see additional data to be convinced that the tests do indeed measure ability

to reason with insight, and it appears to him that a substantial part of success in many of the tests will depend on factual recall of the vocabulary and symbol systems of the subject under examination. * A series of tables in the handbook presents for each test and each of its forms a tabulation showing the content measured by each item, the correct response to each item, and the percent of correct responses to each item by one or more appropriate groups of examinees. These tables should be exceedingly welcome and helpful; they are quite revealing. * study of the item content classification tables reveals such things as the fact that on this Algebra I test, more of the items have lower percent-correct values for ninth graders than for eighth graders. This seems surprising until one realizes that probably only the most able of eighth graders are introduced to Algebra. * It is indeed surprising to observe that, in general, the college students in the norms groups had more difficulty with these tests than did the high-school students, and that the SCAT Q means for college students taking mathematics courses were lower than the SCAT Q means for high school students taking mathematics courses, but such appears to be the case. Examinees will be pleased to learn that they rank higher when compared with college students than when compared with high school students. * The quality of materials and workmanship is excellent. The test booklets are on substantial white paper; the type is clear and easy to read. There is no impression of either crowding or waste of space. * The Handbook ....is well written, with its only flaw being a tendency of the writers to ignore implications of their data that are significant for the total educational enterprise. One wonders at times whether they failed to note some of the details of their data, whether they decided not to disseminate new research findings in a test manual, or whether they doubted that their findings were generalizable. If the last is the case, then the use of these data for norms would also have to come under scrutiny. * differences [between education and engineering students] were not found in the norms of the new Cooperative Mathematics series. One wonders whether there has been a radical and marked change in the aptitude of education majors in the last few years, whether the education majors who are to be found in mathematics courses in college are a markedly unrepresentative group of education majors, or whether something went wrong in the norming or in the data analysis for the Cooperative Mathematics Test. It would help if the publisher had said something about such findings of general educational interest. * The manual....is an excellent technical product. * The norms provide an important and helpful feature in that they include a report of the mean SCAT Quantitative scores for each of the norms groups. This is especially important as one realizes from their examination that these means are exceedingly high. Students of mathematics are apparently highly select on SCAT Quantitative. For only one part of the entire norms group was the SCAT Q mean near the fiftieth percentile on the national normative data. That part was the ninth-graders taking arithmetic. * [otherwise] the SCAT Q means seem to range from the seventieth percentile on up to the mean SCAT Q of high-school students taking calculus which was the ninety-nine and three tenths percentile, a very able group indeed! It will be exceedingly important that the users of this series of tests keep in mind the relationship between the publisher's norms and the level of quantitative aptitude of the students the publisher found taking these mathematics courses. * There is a possible bias in the norms in that many of the sample of schools did not participate in the testing, did not have students in the designated courses (e.g., algebra in the eighth grade), or incurred irregularities in the test administration. The sample was not stratified by geographic region; the mountain states and the southern states are generally rather seriously under-represented in the secondary-school norms, but the northeast is under-represented and the southeast is over-represented in the college norms. * Except for these geographical problems, and the fact that no mention is made of race so that the reader cannot tell to what extent it was properly reflected in the data, the norming seems to be of excellent quality. * The greatest weakness of this battery is its lack of data on concurrent and predictive validity. The publisher seems to excuse this on the ground that content validity is of primary importance, and content validity has been attended to exceedingly well. However, the person who might want to use the Cooperative Algebra I test to decide whether a person could reasonably move on to the second course in algebra, or who wanted to know whether an individual or group knew enough trigonom-

etry so that trig would not pose a problem for the analytic geometry or calculus teacher, will have no data on the basis of which to evaluate these tests. The potential user who might be objective enough to ask just how well the scores on these tests do agree with teacher grades in the subjects in some appropriate sample of classes will also be without any semblance of an attempt to provide information. It seems to the reviewer inexcusable that so much effort and such sophistication should have gone into everything else, with not even a nod to statistical evidence of validity. The validity section of the technical report is only four sentences long! One can't decide whether to be nonplussed, appalled, or underwhelmed; it is simply unbelievable that a matter of such importance could be overlooked or shrugged aside. Can a test developed at great expense over a period of years be placed on the market by a reputable agency without any evidence that in any situation, anywhere, its scores have been shown to be associated with anything? Worse than that, with all the repeated test administrations for norming, equating, and all else that has gone into the preparation of this battery, and the associated opportunity to develop a magnificent construct-validity network, did no one ever think to collect the grades in associated classes of even a single teacher? Or were such data collected but the results found to be unpromising? The thought is scarcely charitable, but what is one to think? The least that can be said is that the user will have to find out for himself whether there is any chance that scores from these tests will be of any value to him. Just looking at the items, the reviewer does, however, remain willing to bet that for many purposes good levels of predictive, concurrent, and construct validity will be found. *Summary.* The new Cooperative Mathematics Tests appear to be a carefully developed modernization and extension of the earlier subject-matter mathematics tests of this publisher. They are the product of years of painstaking, sophisticated, and expensive work. They should be very useful to teachers who want an objective, external evaluation of mathematics achievement at any level from arithmetic through the calculus. * [See original review for additional critical comments not excerpted.]

[466]

*Cooperative Mathematics Tests: Structure of the Number System.** Grades 7–8; 1963–65; for all tests in the series, see 465; Forms A, B, ('63, 6 pages); no specific manual; series manual ('64, 79 pages); student bulletin ('65, 2 pages); separate answer sheets (Digitek, IBM 805, IBM 1230, SCRIBE) must be used; $6 per 20 tests; $4 per 100 answer sheets; $1.25 per 10 IBM hand scoring stencils (answer pattern must be punched out locally); Digitek scoring stencils not available; $2 per series manual; $3 per 100 student bulletins; $3 per specimen set of the series; cash orders postpaid; SCRIBE scoring and statistical analysis service, 35¢ per test; 40(45) minutes; Cooperative Tests and Services. *

M. Vere DeVault, *Professor of Education, The University of Wisconsin, Madison, Wisconsin.*

The *Structure of the Number System* was designed to measure achievement of junior high school students in modern mathematics classes. Norms for the test were established using students in special modern mathematics programs, such as the School Mathematics Study Group program. Although a single raw score is obtained from the test, the 40 items for Form A (the number of items in each classification is not the same in each of Forms A and B) are reported in the following classifications: arithmetic judgment, 6; commutative, associative, and distributive laws, 6; closure, 2; inverses and identities, 1; properties of integers, 3; place value, 2; factors, divisors, and multiples, 8; prime numbers, 1; number lines, 2; zero denominator, 1; number systems (bases other than 10), 6; modular arithmetic, 1; and Roman numerals, 1.

The handbook for the Cooperative Mathematics Tests states that "Content validity is best insured by entrusting test construction to persons well-qualified to judge the relationship of test content to teaching objectives." The details of test construction are included in the handbook and the identified item authors are well qualified. The question of validity must be considered both in terms of the content of the items and the manner in which that content is presented through the item. Many of the objectives of modern mathematics instruction are related to understanding and application, not content per se. The items appear to be creatively constructed in ways which emphasize the measurement of the student's understanding. The range of content covered by the 40 items appears excellent, the one exception which might be taken being the limited attention given the rational numbers. The focus of the test appears to be on the integers. It must be said, however, that even though no special classification of

content related to the rational numbers is identified, a total of 13 items in the two forms of the test derive responses from or make applications to rational number contexts.

The norming data for the test were obtained from 21 and 17 schools, respectively, for grades 7 and 8. From 245 to 285 students were used in the norming of each form of the test in each grade. Mean scores for the tests ranged from 15.6 to 20.7 (39 to 52 percent). K-R 20 reliabilities ranged from .82 to .86, and correlations with the SCAT quantitative test ranged from .61 to .68. Mean biserial correlations between individual items and total scores ranged from .43 to .50.

In summary, it seems that the content has been appropriately identified and items have been carefully prepared for the purpose of measuring junior high school students' understandings of modern mathematics content relative to the number system. The handbook clearly presents appropriate data concerning the nature of item and test characteristics. The handbook appears to be complete in regard to directions for both administering and interpreting the results of the test.

Leslie P. Steffe, *Associate Professor of Mathematics Education, University of Georgia, Athens, Georgia.*

Each form of the *Structure of the Number System* contains 40 multiple choice items with five choices per item. Achievement is assessed by utilizing 13 "content classifications": arithmetic judgment; commutative, associative, and distributive laws; closure; inverses and identities; properties of integers; place value; factors, divisors, and multiples; prime numbers; number lines; zero denominator; number systems (bases other than 10); modular arithmetic; and Roman numerals. These content classifications are consistent with objectives of present-day grade 7 and 8 mathematics programs.

Because the series handbook does not contain much information concerning each test in the series, it is difficult to ascertain just what content the test was designed to measure. If the test was designed to measure achievement in major content areas of a seventh or eighth grade modern mathematics class, as one would be led to believe from the handbook, then the content classifications are not exhaustive enough (e.g., no geometry content classification is included). On the other hand, if the test was designed to measure only structural aspects of the real number system, as one would be led to believe from the test's title and the publisher's catalog, then the content classifications "arithmetic judgment," "modular arithmetic," and those involving numeration are not appropriate. These five content classifications are represented by 16 items in Form A and 14 in Form B. Test users, then, must look carefully at the content classifications and items to ascertain what is being measured and not misinterpret test scores as reflecting general achievement in a "typical" seventh or eighth grade modern mathematics program nor as reflecting knowledge of just structural aspects of the real number system.

The careful test development procedures employed by CTS minimize ambiguity of test items. There are, however, two items with at least two possible choices and one item with an ambiguous stem. The items in the former category (34, Form A and 35, Form B) involve judgments of the truth value of choices in the item, based on the conditions stipulated in the item stem. Not enough information is provided in the stem to ascertain whether a statement is to be judged "true" only if it is always true or whether a statement can be judged "true" if it is sometimes true. The item (24, Form B) in the latter category involves an illustration of a "proof" of the distributive principle using dots. It is not clear just what axiom system the item writer assumed. Even if such an axiom system were clear, the illustration is oversimplified and does not illustrate complexities involved. No serious ambiguities were noted in the way the other items were written.

The handbook is generally done well. Test usages, however, are discussed for the series and not for the specific tests. Because content classifications for *Structure of the Number System* are not exhaustive, individual test scores may not give parents a realistic estimate of a student's proficiency in mathematics, as suggested. Moreover, because no information is given concerning predictive validity, suggested general usages involving decisions regarding a student's vocational or academic choices, prediction of future mathematics achievement, or how students are grouped and treated for instruction are at least tenuous.

The national norms were developed by testing only students enrolled in modern mathematics courses at the end of the school year. Substantial K-R 20 reliability coefficients (ranging from .82 to .86) were obtained from subsamples selected randomly from the norms groups. In addition, the items discriminate well between high and low scorers. Average biserial correlations (a measure of item discrimination) between item scores and total test scores ranged from .43 to .50.

A substantial number of children did not finish the test. Only 60 to 77 percent (a function of test form and grade) answered the last item, while 91 to 98 percent reached the three-quarter point. Speededness, then, contributed to the generally increasing difficulty of the items. Item information (especially information from the last one-fourth of the items) must be used cautiously in end-of-the-year curriculum evaluation and in making post hoc instructional decisions, because item difficulty may be a function of speededness as well as of achievement. If item information is used for diagnostic purposes, the user should consult suggested procedures in the handbook and be cautious about over-interpreting the results.

In summary, the items are a major strength of the test. Within constraints noted, mathematics teachers in grades 7 and 8, principals, or supervisors of those grades can obtain useful items for diagnosis of student strengths or weaknesses within instructional contexts, as well as make profitable end-of-the-year comparisons of individual test scores with the norms group. If the test is used in measuring end-of-the-year mathematics achievement for structural aspects of the real number system, the discussion concerning content classifications should be noted. A weakness of the handbook is that recommendations are not given concerning specific uses of each test of the series. General usages that are suggested are not always supported by accompanying statistics for specific tests.

For excerpts from reviews of the series, see 465.

[467]

*ERB Mathematics Tests, Experimental Form. High school; 1961–69; 4 tests; no manual; norms ('68, c1969, 1 page) for Tests 1, 3, and 4 for independent school students only; no data on reliability; nonmember schools must use scoring service; separate answer sheets (IBM 805) must be used; $3.10 per 10 tests; 80¢ per 10 answer sheets; 28¢ per scoring stencil; $5 per norms; $3 per specimen set of any one test; postage extra; machine scoring service, 85¢ and over per test; hand scoring service, $1.10 and over per test; 40(45) minutes; Subcommittee on Mathematics Tests; Educational Records Bureau. *

a) TEST I: ANALYTICAL GEOMETRY TEST. Grades 11–12; 1961–69; 1 form ('61, 5 pages).

b) TEST 2: SETS, EQUATIONS, INEQUALITIES, AND NUMBER CONCEPTS. Grades 9–12; 1961; 1 form ('61, 5 pages); no norms.

c) TEST 3: PROBABILITY AND STATISTICS. Grade 12; 1961–69; 1 form ('61, 6 pages).

d) TEST 4: INTRODUCTORY CALCULUS. Grade 12; 1961–69; 1 form ('61, 5 pages).

REFERENCES

1–2. See 6:574.

[468]

★ERB Modern Mathematics Test. Grades 7–8; 1965–67; Forms L ('65, 12 pages), M ('66, 10 pages); no manual; norms: Forms L ('67, 1 page), M ('66, 1 page), for independent school students only; no data on reliability; nonmember schools must use scoring service; separate answer sheets (IBM 1230) must be used; $3.10 per 10 tests; 80¢ per 10 answer sheets; 28¢ per scoring stencil; $5 per norms; $3 per specimen set; postage extra; scoring service, $1 and over per test; 80(90) minutes; William S. Litterick, Frederic Bonan, Edwin C. Douglas, Foye Perry, Reinhoud H. van der Linde, and Frederick Watson; Educational Records Bureau. *

REFERENCE

1. LITTERICK, WILLIAM S. "Observations on the New ERB Mathematics Tests." *Ed Rec B* 88:62–3 Jl '65. *

[469]

*The Graduate Record Examinations Advanced Mathematics Test. Graduate school candidates; 1939–70; 6 current forms ('66–70, 32–40 pages); descriptive booklet ('70, 7 pages); for more complete information, see 667; 180(200) minutes; Educational Testing Service. *

REFERENCE

1. See 5:427.

For a review by Paul C. Rosenbloom of earlier forms, see 6:578; for a review by Eric F. Gardner, see 5:427. For reviews of the testing program, see 667 (1 review) and 5:601 (1 review).

[470]

★Mathematics Attainment Tests C1 and C3. Ages 9-3 to 10-8; 1965–69; 2 tests; reliability data and norms based on pre-decimalization and metrication edition published in 1965–66; 5p per test; 7p per manual; postpaid within U.K.; (50–60) minutes; published for the National Foundation for Educational Research in England and Wales; Ginn & Co. Ltd. *

a) MATHEMATICS ATTAINMENT TEST C1. 1965–69; formerly called *Junior Mathematics Test C1;* 1 form ['69, 8 pages]; manual ['69, 8 pages].

b) MATHEMATICS ATTAINMENT TEST C3. 1966–69; formerly called *Junior Mathematics Test C3;* 1 form ['69, 8 pages]; manual ['69, 8 pages].

JOHN COOK, *Educational Psychologist, Buryfields Clinic, Guildford, Surrey, England.*

These tests were devised by two separate groups of teachers to estimate the progress in mathematics of children in their third year of the junior school. Open tests for use by teachers, they can, for practical purposes, be considered as parallel, for both cover similar areas and are of much the same order of difficulty. Setting out to examine children's knowledge and understanding of mathematics rather than purely mechanical skills, the tests limit computation. There are 50 questions, with no time limit, and although the manual estimates that most children will be finished in 50 minutes, some would be expected to take more than an hour.

The content seems a reasonable compromise between traditional and modern approaches to mathematics but, necessarily, it will not be readily acceptable to those who are heavily committed to one or other of these views. In these times of rapid change in the mathematics content of a junior school course, it is unlikely that any one test would be acceptable to everybody. Going beyond traditional arithmetic, these tests include questions on graphs, simple geometry, bases, series and number patterns, fractions, arithmetical processes and equations. All relevant questions, with one exception on Test C1, have been altered to meet the requirements of decimalisation and metrication. The reviewer would have expected that when adapting C1 to meet these new circumstances, the authors would have taken the opportunity to include the standard abbreviation for new pence, as they have done on C3. C1, too, still has a question about pecks, bushels and quarters.

The layout for each of the seven quarto sides which comprise both tests is excellent, interestingly and clearly presented to appeal to junior school children. There is enough space for working for all but the child who never has enough space. Most of the questions are open ended but there are several of the multiple choice type. Some other questions are divided into two or more parts and it seems unfortunate that although many children may correctly complete these questions no allowance may be made for a partially correct answer. If no allowance is to be made for partially correct answers, it might be well not to include questions of this type. Other problems in C3 are presented side by side and may well be omitted unintentionally by some children, especially those who are anxious to complete the test. The language throughout is clear and understandable by most third year children. Care must be taken, however, when administering to the poorer readers, for they may well find the language too difficult, especially when the manual explicitly states that no questions may be answered during testing.

The instructions for administration in the manual are set out in clear detail and are easily understood.

Both C1 and C3 were standardised on large numbers of children. Each of the standardisation samples consisted of all children in their third year of the junior school within each of the two areas chosen. Both of these areas are in the Southeast of England (a socially and culturally good area), so caution must be used in any nonlocal interpretation. The raw scores are converted into standardised scores with a mean of 100 and a standard deviation of 15, easily read from the conversion table given in the manual.

In both tests about 20 percent of the questions have been altered since standardisation to allow for the appropriate decimal and metric alternatives. This throws considerable doubt on the results obtained and the manual rightly gives a clear warning in heavy type to regard the standardisation with caution.

In conclusion, these are two thoughtfully prepared tests for use by teachers in schools in assessing the mathematical progress of third year junior school children. They are carefully devised to appeal to children but many slow children or poor readers may find them heavy going. The reviewer warmly recommends their use by teachers, providing that urgent steps are taken for their restandardisation necessitated by the inclusion of 20 percent of new material.

[471]

★**Mathematics Attainment Tests DE1 and DE2.**
Ages 10–12; 1966–70; 2 tests; 5p per test; postpaid within U.K.; (50–60) minutes; published for the National Foundation for Educational Research in England and Wales; Ginn & Co. Ltd. *
a) MATHEMATICS ATTAINMENT TEST DE1. 1966–70; modification of *Mathematics Test 17;* 1 form ['70, 8 pages, essentially the same as former test published in 1966 except for revision of 12 items for metrication and decimalization]; manual ('70, 11 pages); reliability data and norms based on 1966 version; 8p per manual.
b) MATHEMATICS ATTAINMENT TEST DE2. 1967–70; formerly called *Intermediate Mathematics Test 1;* 1 form ['70, 8 pages, identical with test published in 1969 except for title]; manual ['70, 8 pages]; 13p per manual.

[472]

★**Mathematics Attainment Tests (Oral).** Ages 7-0 to 8-6, 8-6 to 9-8; 1965–70; 2 levels; 5p per test; postpaid within U.K.; published for the National Foundation for Educational Research in England and Wales; Ginn & Co. Ltd. *
a) MATHEMATICS ATTAINMENT TEST A (ORAL). Ages

7-0 to 8-6; 1969–70;· formerly called *Junior Mathematics Test A1;* 1 form ['69, 8 pages]; mimeographed instructions ['69, 10 pages]; provisional norms ('70, 3 pages); no data on reliability; instructions and norms free on request from NFER; (40–45) minutes.
b) MATHEMATICS ATTAINMENT TEST B (ORAL). Ages 8-6 to 9-8; 1965–69; formerly called *Junior Mathematics Test B1;* 1 form ['69, 8 pages]; manual ['69, 16 pages]; reliability data and norms based on predecimalization and metrication edition published in 1965; 10p per manual; (45–50) minutes.

JOHN COOK, *Educational Psychologist, Buryfields Clinic, Guildford, Surrey, England.* [Review of Test B1.]

This test was constructed by a panel of teachers in order to examine the mathematical experience and understanding of children in the second year of the junior school. Since this test of arithmetical understanding was developed originally to try to compensate for the disadvantages that poor readers must face when attempting an arithmetic test, the items are presented orally. In this way the confounding factor of the degree of literacy of the child is kept to a minimum.

Traditional arithmetic skills are tested, largely associated with the four rules of number, but there are also questions on a bar chart, pictorial fractions, area, and volume. Little attempt has been made to broaden the test's scope by introducing topics from recent developments in mathematics. One or two concepts from modern mathematics could have been introduced with advantage, to give the test a more mathematical, rather than arithmetical, bias. As the trend towards introducing modern mathematics in the junior school continues, teachers looking for a test are increasingly likely to favour one with some new content. Care has been taken to convert to the relevant metric and decimal alternatives and to introduce the abbreviations for the new decimal currency.

The six quarto sides of the test are clearly laid out but are perhaps a little too cramped. It might have been as well to expand to the seventh side (now blank) to give the extra space.

There are several questions in which a child has to be correct on two items before a mark may be credited. Either questions of this type should not have been included or some allowance for partial credit should have been made.

The manual is clear and concise, with the oral instructions to be read by the administrator in a form readily understandable by children.

The manual also reports the research project

which led to the production of this test. Groups of good and poor readers were given an oral and non-oral version. All children showed a significant increase in score when orally tested, but the increase for poor readers was nearly three times that made by the good readers. A discussion of the reasons for these results could usefully have been attempted. Some doubt is thrown on the reliability of this study when the figures quoted are investigated. The children scoring in the top quarter of the *Sentence Reading Test 1* increased their mean mathematics score from 42.5 to 45.5. This is not unreasonable in isolation, but this reviewer finds it difficult to understand when there are only 42 questions comprising the test and only one mark is given per correct answer.

The test was standardised on 5,422 children. The area from which the sample was drawn is largely rural, so some care must be taken when making any national interpretation. The raw scores are converted into standardised scores with a mean of 100 and a standard deviation of 15. There are separate tables for boys and girls. The discrimination is fine, one unit of raw score being equal to one unit of standardised score over most of the range.

Nearly 20 percent of the questions have been changed since standardisation to allow for the appropriate decimal and metric alternatives. This suggests that there is considerable doubt about the results obtained, and the manual rightly gives a clear warning in heavy type to regard the standardisation with caution.

In conclusion, this orally presented test of arithmetic skills and experience for children in their second year of the junior school is designed to overcome the problem that poor readers face when attempting an arithmetic test in the usual way. The test is good as far as it goes, but the scope could usefully be broadened, especially by the incorporation of material from modern trends in mathematics. The inclusion of 20 percent new material, together with the smallish standardisation sample, means that the results obtained must be regarded with some caution.

[473]

*Mathematics: Minnesota High School Achievement Examinations.** Grades 7, 8, 9; 1955–71; new or revised form issued each May; Form EH Rev.; 3 levels: grade 7 ['71, c1968, 4 pages], grade 8 ('71, 4 pages), grade 9 ('71, 6 pages); no specific manual; series manual ('71, 16 pages); no data on reliability; 15¢ per test; separate answer sheets (IBM 1230) may be used; 10¢ per answer sheet including scoring service; $1 per series manual; postage extra; $1.10 per specimen set, postpaid; 60(65) minutes; edited by V. L. Lohmann; American Guidance Service, Inc. *

For a review by Gerald L. Ericksen of an earlier form of the test for grade 9, see 6:577.

[474]

*Mathematics Test (Adv.).** Ages 12-0 to 13-11; 1954–67; 4 tests; distribution restricted to directors of education; postpaid within U.K.; 50(55) minutes; published for the National Foundation for Educational Research in England and Wales; Ginn & Co. Ltd. *
a) ARITHMETIC TEST (ADV.) 1. 1954–57; test ['54, 8 pages]; manual ('57, 8 pages); 5p per test; 7p per manual; D. A. Pidgeon.
b) MATHEMATICS TEST (ADV.) 3. 1958; test ['58, 12 pages]; manual (9 pages); 7p per test; 8p per manual.
c) MATHEMATICS TEST (ADV.) 4. 1960; 1 form ['60, 12 pages]; manual (9 pages); 7p per test; 8p per manual.
d) MATHEMATICS TEST (ADV.) 5. 1962–67; 1 form ['62, 12 pages]; mimeographed directions for administration ['62, 10 pages]; provisional norms ['67, 1 page]; 7p per test; directions and norms free on request from NFER.

For a review by Kenneth Lovell of Tests 1–4, see 6:585.

[475]

★**Mathematics Test: Content Evaluation Series.** Grades 7–9; 1969; Form 1 (8 pages); manual (14 pages); series technical manual (21 pages); separate answer sheets (MRC) must be used; $7.20 per 35 tests; $4.20 per 35 answer sheets; 60¢ per hand scoring stencil; 39¢ per manual; 90¢ per technical manual; $1.35 per specimen set of series; postage extra; scoring service, 27¢ per test; 40(50) minutes; Gilbert Ulmer; Houghton Mifflin Co. *

ROBERT A. FORSYTH, *Assistant Professor of Education, The University of Iowa, Iowa City, Iowa.*

This test is one of six tests in the Content Evaluation Series. Each test was developed "as an end-of-year achievement test to assess the progress made in its subject matter area by students in grades 7, 8, and 9."

The most important characteristic of any end-of-year achievement test is its content validity. As the publisher states, *"Content Validity is the measure of how well the content of the test samples the subject matter to be tested* [italics added]. The authors of the Content Evaluation Series, as specialists and teachers in each of their own fields, analyzed the leading textbooks and courses of study for content and weighting in the construction of tables of specifications for each of the tests. These tables were then examined by curriculum experts to determine proper content and balance. Items were then constructed to meet these specifications; the implementation of the table of specifications was presented to curriculum experts to insure the proper fulfillment of the requirements of the table of specifications."

The procedure described above is certainly a commendable attempt to insure the content validity of the test. However, one wonders whether any procedure could lead to a valid end-of-year achievement test for three grades when the final form of the test consists of only 44 items. It is difficult to imagine that a 44-item test adequately samples enough behaviors in any of the three grades to be considered an appropriate end-of-year achievement test for any grade. This inadequacy of sampling seems most obvious when the test is viewed as a test for a ninth grade algebra class. This attempt to cover three grades also has led to a relatively difficult test for seventh grade students. The mean raw score for the grade 7 standardization group was 15.4. Thus, the average item difficulty was 35 percent. In ninth grade, the average item difficulty was 50 percent.

Although some criterion related validity evidence is reported for several of the other tests, the validity of the math test rests solely on content validity considerations. The publisher does indicate, however, that future editions will present additional criterion related data. These future data may provide some support for the validity of the math test.

In addition to these concerns about content validity, one other factor indirectly related to the validity of the test scores must be mentioned. The test has the following distribution of correct answers: 3 A's; 21 B's; 12 C's; 5 D's; and 3 E's. Thus, 33 out of 44 items (75 percent) of the items have B or C as the correct answer. (If a seventh grade student marks all B's, his percentile rank is 80.) Furthermore, of the last 14 items (where guessing may be occurring, particularly for 7th graders), 9 B's, 3 C's, and 2 D's make up the correct responses. A much more reasonable distribution of correct responses would be preferred.

The Technical Manual is well written and provides much of the necessary data for judging the merits of the test. However, the "Use and Interpretation" section contains several statements that imply uses for the tests which would seem difficult to justify. For example, the following statement is made: "Administrators must be sure that teachers are aware that these standardized tests are essentially diagnostic in nature, whether the diagnosis is for individual students, the whole student body or curricular analysis." From a measurement viewpoint, this statement is questionable. As far as individual students are concerned, this reviewer sees no possibility of using this test as a diagnostic device. Most of the content categories contain a very limited number of items. (According to the author's classification, 17 out of the 22 content categories have 3 or fewer items.) Thus, the reliability of the individual scores for these categories would be too low to make any judgment on the basis of these data alone. Even for relatively large groups of students, considerable care and corroboration would be necessary before any diagnosis was undertaken.

In general, the technical aspects of the test construction were carefully done. Extensive item tryouts were undertaken. The standardization sample was selected in accordance with the model developed for the Project Talent survey. The test was standardized on more than 3,000 students in each of the three grades. The split-half reliabilities range from .79 (grade 7) to .90 (grade 9). The time limit of 40 minutes seems adequate; thus, the split-half procedure would not lead to markedly inflated reliabilities. Since no parallel forms exist, parallel forms reliabilities could not be obtained.

In summary, the construction of the *Mathematics Test: Content Evaluation Series* followed all the usual rules of good achievement test construction; however, the validity of the test for its intended purpose—measurement of end-of-year achievement in grades 7, 8, and 9—is still open to question.

[476]

★A Mathematics Test for Grades Four, Five and Six. Grades 4–6; 1969; 13 scores: numeration systems, set terminology, mathematical structure, addition and subtraction, multiplication, division, common fractions, decimal fractions and per cent, measurements, geometry, problems, graphs and scales, total; 1 form (8 pages); manual (8 pages); separate answer sheets (IBM 805) must be used; $6 per 25 tests; $4 per 100 answer sheets; $1 per specimen set (must be purchased to obtain manual and scoring key); cash orders postpaid; (120–180) minutes in 2 sessions; Stanley J. LeJeune; Psychometric Affiliates. *

ARTHUR MITTMAN, *Professor of Education and Chairman, Department of Educational Psychology, University of Oregon, Eugene, Oregon.*

This test represents an attempt to provide an achievement test for mathematics that is compatible with modern mathematics curricula for grades 4–6. It is based on the material presented in the texts published by six different companies. The prospective user is encouraged to review the test item by item to determine the content validity for his purposes. Also, extreme caution should be exercised if the subtests are to be used for diagnostic purposes, as suggested by the author. Some of the subtests are very short and lack the reliability necessary to be of value for diagnosis and prescription for individual students.

Several things about the test and the manual demand comment. The manual is inadequate in content and format. As an example, in the section "Directions to the Teacher," the teacher is told that two hours should be set aside for the test, not more than one hour on each of two days. The passage goes on to say that it may be possible that more than two hours will be needed. The reviewer took the test and concludes that considerably more time will be necessary for most students in grades 4–6. This opinion is corroborated by the actual average testing time for the standardization group reported in a later section of the manual.

The directions for administration are ambiguous and incomplete, and should be reviewed and revised. This revision might, in turn, invalidate the norms and reliability data reported in the manual. Percentile ranks are provided for each of the three grades but no information is offered as to the time of year the tests were administered. No other statistics are given to describe the performance of the norm group. Also, no information is given as to the size of the norming sample or the population it represents. The norming group's mean IQ was 102 and the teachers judged 74 percent of the sample to be middle class and 26 percent from the lower socioeconomic class. What this means is not clarified nor is information given as to the geographic location of the schools, the number of school districts involved, or the number of classes represented within each grade.

Within-grade reliabilities are reported for each subtest and the total test. The reliability of the total score seems reasonable and adequate for a test of 110 items in mathematics for most fourth, fifth, and sixth grade populations. At the same time, the reported reliabilities may be spurious since they were determined by the split-half technique. Since item characteristic information is missing, it is difficult to assess the effect, if any, which the use of this technique may have had on the estimates. As more evidence is assembled, the manual should be expanded and made more complete following the *Standards for Educational and Psychological Tests and Manuals*.

The test items themselves are in general well conceived and ask significant questions. Several of them could use editing to improve the quality and remove ambiguity. For example, item 73 reads, "Which one is another name for 55%?" In some items the responses could be arranged in order of magnitude that would minimize confusion that arises when the fourth largest is in the second position. One item has two correct responses, another has no correct answer, one is incorrectly keyed, and some have questionable best answers. The test format is seriously in need of attention. Figures that are to be used in a subsequent problem are inappropriately placed and in many instances of a low quality, which may introduce an unwanted extraneous factor. For a test intended for commercial distribution, it is below par in format.

Concern must be expressed for the appropriateness of all the items for all the grades. Because of the multitude of topics covered by the test, it is questionable whether many of the items would be understood by fourth and fifth grade students. It may be a discouraging experience for the younger students to be asked to attempt all of the items when expectation must be low. Since the test is divided into subtests and administered accordingly, the possibility of a teacher's selecting parts is not precluded. However, no mention or suggestion of the use of this prerogative is made in the manual. Likewise, the normative data provided could not be of use under those conditions. Perhaps the usefulness of the instrument would be enhanced if information were provided for use in this manner.

In summary, it must be said that the test is an attempt to fulfill a need. Colleagues in the area of elementary mathematics education attest to this. It is worthy of a sound salvage operation, but until that is performed, this test cannot be recommended for purchase or widespread use.

[477]

★Mathematics Test: McGraw-Hill Basic Skill System. Grades 11–14; 1970; also called *MHBSS Mathematics Test;* although designed for use with the MHBSS instructional program, the test may be used independently; 4 scores: arithmetic, elementary algebra, intermediate algebra, total; Forms A, B, (14 pages); manual (31 pages); separate answer sheets (Digitek, IBM 1230, Scoreze) must be used; $6 per 25 tests; $2.50 per 50 IBM or Digitek answer sheets; $3 per 25 Scoreze answer sheets; $1 per IBM or Digitek scoring stencil; postage extra; $1.25 per specimen set, postpaid; IBM scoring service, 25¢ and over per test ($20 minimum); 42(52) minutes; McGraw-Hill Book Co., Inc. *

JAMES BRASWELL, *Associate Examiner in Mathematics, Educational Testing Service, Princeton, New Jersey.*

Each form of the MHBSS Mathematics Test contains items covering arithmetic, elementary algebra, and intermediate algebra. A separate score is reported for each part as well as for the test as a whole. The test contains no items relating to geometry, trigonometry, or calculus. The test can be used in a number of ways: (*a*) at the end of algebra I for guidance relating to algebra II or geometry; (*b*) at the end of algebra I or algebra II as a modest measure of achievement; and (*c*) by two-year and four-year colleges to channel students into appropriate remedial courses. Since the test is not comprehensive of the high school mathematics program, it is not appropriate for seniors taking four years of mathematics or promising juniors who contemplate a fourth year of mathematics.

The topics from arithmetic and algebra appearing on the test are, with a couple of exceptions, traditional in nature and straightforward to solve. A comprehensive table in the manual outlines the concept tested by each item. The item difficulties provided are based on a sample composed of freshmen and sophomores in four-year colleges, two-year college students, and college-bound high school juniors and seniors. A glance at the item difficulties in relation to particular items leads one to believe that the norming group was not typical of college or college-bound students, but was somewhat below average. However, the test is intended as a diagnostic instrument for students who are likely below average in achievement. This reviewer does not necessarily consider the atypical norming group a weakness.

Almost every item is presented in clear and simple language with consistent editorial style. Item 38 on Form A has an obvious typographical error ("property" was printed instead of "proper") and item 39 would be better were each *number line* labeled. Item 50 on Form B confuses *rational number* with *integer.* Other than these three points, all items appear to be quite sound.

The items sample a wide variety of content (basic skills) from arithmetic and algebra. The only topics that may have been overtested were factoring and simplifying polynomial expressions. The concept of significant figures tested by item 13, Form A does not seem worthy of being tested. Item 60 on Form A is much more difficult than it should have been due to the inclusion of "none of these" as an option. The question is:

Which one of the following is equal to $(a + b)^0$?

F $a + b$
G $a^0 + b^0$
H 0
J x^0
K   None of these

The student is likely to reason that $(a + b)^0 = 1$, and when 1 is not among the choices given he may respond "K." Only 14 percent of the norming group got this item correct. If K had been another plausible distractor (for example, $a + b^0$), the student would be more inclined to look for an alternate expression for 1, namely x^0. Item 56 on Form B is parallel to the item above, but avoids using "none of these" as an option. The result is that 46 percent answered it correctly.

Comprehensive norms are provided for three groups: freshmen in four-year colleges, first-year students in two-year colleges, and college-bound high school juniors and seniors. A list of schools that participated in the norming process is provided in the manual. The authors suggest that schools may wish to prepare local norms due to the wide differences that exist among schools. The prepared norms are, however, clearly presented and easy to follow. One interesting conclusion that can be drawn from the norms tables is that the high school group was by far the best.

The test is likely to be most valid when used to evaluate achievement on MHBSS materials. However, the basic skills tested are by no means unique to MHBSS and the test may be useful in both high school and college as a diagnostic and achievement measure in basic arithmetic and algebra. The prospective user is advised to examine the test thoroughly to see if the skills tested are consistent with the intended purpose. One should not expect the test to be a valid measure for any mathematics outside the domain of arithmetic and algebra. Moreover, it appears that the test would be more useful in guidance and placement than as a comprehensive test of achievement in arithmetic and algebra.

Reliabilities were computed from a sample that included approximately equal numbers of students from the three groups described above. For Form A the reliability was .94 and for Form B it was .95. Both are quite high. No reliabilities are reported for part scores.

SUMMARY. The MHBSS Mathematics Test is a well-documented test covering a variety of basic skills in arithmetic and algebra. Although some modern terminology is used, the test is for the most part traditional. While the principal purpose of the test is to function with the MHBSS package, the test may be a useful guidance tool in high schools and colleges. In college the test could be used to place students in need of remedial instruction and subsequently to assess their progress.

CARL J. HUBERTY, *Assistant Professor of Education, University of Georgia, Athens, Georgia.*

The main purpose of this test is to measure the individual student's "general level of competence in the mathematics that is prerequisite to participating in college-level courses in mathematics." To accomplish this diagnostic function, the authors have included 20 items from each of three content areas: arithmetic, elementary algebra, and intermediate algebra. The test was designed to be "complementary with, but not restricted to," the MHBSS learning materials.

A crucial characteristic of an instrument of this kind is content validity. As stated in the Guide to MHBSS, contents of all tests and learning materials in the system were drawn mostly from "beginning texts in college subject-matter fields." The initial pool of items for this particular test was considered a sample from a universe that was "defined as all of the mathematics problems for which instruction for solving is provided in the three mathematical texts" of the MHBSS and which covered the aforementioned areas. This pool was prepared by CTB/McGraw-Hill staff members and edited by the author of the three levels of instructional materials. Item characteristics such as discrimination and difficulty indices and distracter effectiveness were considered in the final item construction. In the judgment of this reviewer, most of the items require little more than recall and algebraic manipulative skills, i.e., "algo-

rithmic thinking"; comprehension is called for only in a limited number of items. The authors further state that the test is designed to be "diagnostic only in a general way. A low score implies a need for remedial work." It appears that this instrument would do nothing more than determine those students who do *not* know some basic mathematical definitions and algorithms. It may be argued that having such knowledge would hardly indicate that the prerequisites to participating in college-level mathematics courses are met. It does not seem necessary to use a standardized test to gain such information.

In the standardization the test was administered to "samples of students like those for whom the tests are designed." Three reference groups were determined: (*a*) "freshmen (and a few sophomores) in four-year colleges or universities," (*b*) "first-year students in two-year colleges," and (*c*) "college-bound high school juniors and seniors." The sampling units were colleges and high schools in four geographic areas of the United States that were "willing to participate" in the norming. The month and year in which the norm testing took place, as well as the number of sampling units used, are not reported. The sample sizes are not adequate; they range from 270 to 657. Based on these small numbers, two norm tables are given. The first table converts raw scores for each part score and for the total score to standard scores and stanines. The reference group(s) used to obtain this table is (are) not indicated. The second table converts raw scores for each part score and for the total score to percentile ranks for each reference group. Because of the scanty information given, interpretive information obtained by the use of the norm tables would be of little value.

Reliability coefficients (K-R 20) are given for part scores as well as for total scores for each form. The coefficients range from .82 to .89 for the part scores. For the total test, the K-R 20 for Form A is .94 and for Form B, .95. Item difficulties are also reported. Because the total norming group was used in determining the above statistics, the reliability coefficients are probably spurious, being inflated by the heterogeneity of the reference groups. Thus, the reported coefficients, as well as the item difficulties, are relatively valueless.

Using the reported table of specifications as a criterion, the two forms appear to be parallel

—more so, in fact, than might be expected if the items were randomly selected from a universe of items in each classification category. It appears as though items for one of the forms were developed from the other form. If a coefficient of correlation between scores on the two forms had been reported (data were not available at the time of manual printing), it would be expected to be quite (spuriously) high.

The item construction leaves something to be desired. As mentioned previously, the thought processes expected of the examinee are at a low level. Also, inconsistencies in the stems of the multiple choice items appear frequently. For example, in four items in Form A, the examinee is requested to use the equals relation in four different ways; namely, the examinee is asked to find a number that (a) is equal to, (b) is the same as, (c) is equivalent to, and (d) has a simpler name for, the given arithmetic expressions. In some items the examinee is asked to "solve" an open sentence, in others to find "a solution set for" an open sentence, and in still others to find "the value of" a symbol in an open sentence. To select the correct alternative on a few items, it is necessary to have knowledge of more than one concept—that of equation solving and that of distance along the number line. Why the examinee misses these items is, therefore, unknown. In item 25, Form B, the examinee is asked to solve a pair of equations. No distracter is a solution for the first equation and not the second; it seems desirable to have such a distracter.

SUMMARY. This test may be considered an integral part of the measurement-diagnosis-instruction-evaluation sequence in the MHBSS. Unless this test is used to accompany the MHBSS learning materials (a review of which is not at all intended here), its use cannot be recommended. Regardless, there is some doubt whether or not this test serves its intended purpose. The overabundance of poorly constructed items and the insufficient norming information also reflect its inadequacy. The advantages of standardized tests over those constructed locally are not apparent in this test.

[478]

*Mathematics Tests 20–21. Ages 10-0 to 12-0; 1951–70; 2 tests; distribution restricted to directors of education; 7p per test; postpaid within U.K.; 45(50) minutes; published for the National Foundation for Educational Research in England and Wales; Ginn & Co. Ltd. *

$a)$ MATHEMATICS TEST 20. 1969–70; 1 form ['69, 12 pages]; manual ('70, 12 pages); 8p per manual.
$b)$ MATHEMATICS TEST 21. 1970; 1 form ['70, 12 pages]; mimeographed instructions (6 pages); no data on reliability; no norms; instructions free on request from NFER.

REFERENCE

1. See 6:614.

[479]

*Metropolitan Achievement Tests: High School Mathematics Tests. Grades 9–13; 1962–64; catalog uses the title *Metropolitan High School Mathematics Test;* subtest of *Metropolitan Achievement Tests: High School Battery;* 2 scores: computation and concepts, analysis and problem solving; Forms Am ('62, 7 pages), Bm ('63, 7 pages); manual ('64, 22 pages); for battery accessories, see 15; separate answer sheets (Digitek, Harbor, IBM 805, IBM 1230) must be used; $5.90 per 35 tests; $2.30 per 35 IBM 805 answer sheets; $2.80 per 35 Digitek or IBM 1230 answer sheets; $3 per 100 Harbor answer cards; 70¢ per Digitek or IBM scoring stencil; $1.25 per specimen set; postage extra; Harbor or IBM scoring service, 19¢ and over per test; 72(86) minutes; Walter N. Durost, William H. Evans, James D. Leake, Howard A. Bowman, Clarke Cosgrove, and John G. Read; Harcourt Brace Jovanovich, Inc. *

JEREMY KILPATRICK, *Associate Professor of Mathematics, Teachers College, Columbia University, New York, New York.*

Since high school students take a variety of mathematics courses and since the mathematics curriculum in most high schools has been changing over the past two decades, to define a body of content called "high school mathematics" is a tall order. The authors of the *Metropolitan High School Mathematics Test* attempted the job by reviewing "expert pronouncements" on instructional goals, current research on skills, "representative courses of study, and several widely used textbooks." They drew up a blueprint for each of the two tests that specified the objectives and the content topics to be covered, with an indication of the relative emphasis each objective or topic was to receive. Unfortunately, these blueprints are not available to the test user. He must infer what the test authors mean by "high school mathematics" from a content description, a content outline, and the tests themselves.

Apparently the test authors conceive of high school mathematics as consisting primarily of arithmetic, with some elementary notions from algebra and geometry. Most of the test items treat topics that are commonly introduced in junior high or elementary school, and none goes beyond what might be covered in a conventional ninth-grade general mathematics course.

Should one, then, expect performance on the tests to increase with grade level? According to the manual, "the ability of an item to distinguish between students at successive grade levels" was one of the criteria of item selection. In the item analysis samples, there was a modest increase in mean scores each year from grade 9 to 12, which was probably attributable mostly to a handful of items testing concepts from algebra and geometry that would become increasingly familiar to students in college preparatory courses. The differences in mean scores between adjacent grades, however, were never more than one standard error of measurement, and frequently they were much less.

The content description given in the manual is misleading. Test 1, Mathematical Computation and Concepts, contains 35 four-choice items that allegedly measure "both understanding and skill in handling fundamental operations with whole numbers, common fractions, decimals, and per cents; number theory and definitions; measurement and estimation; algebraic functions and relationships; geometric relationships; and combinations and permutations." The actual coverage is neither so broad nor so deep as this list implies. Arithmetic (especially operations with decimals) and algebra are best represented, although the algebra never gets much beyond simple linear equations and the products of binomials. Number theory, measurement, and estimation are tested with only one or two items apiece in each form. Combinations and permutations are represented in Form Bm by a single item on the notation for combinations. Quite a few items might be classed as measuring skills in arithmetic operations, but closer examination reveals that in many cases either additional concepts are demanded or the choices given allow the student to eliminate alternatives without carrying out the complete calculation.

Test 2, Mathematical Analysis and Problem Solving, contains 30 four-choice items that are supposed to measure "ability to apply mathematical principles and relationships to solution of problems involving basic arithmetic processes, practical mathematics, graphs, algebraic functions and relationships, trigonometric functions, geometric relationships, ratio and proportion, and probability." Here again the description is deceptive. There are no items on probability in either form, and only by the most generous interpretation of the categories can one come up with more than one or two items from geometry and trigonometry. The greatest emphasis is on basic arithmetic processes and on "practical mathematics," that is, items on income tax, interest, bank accounts, etc. that require calculations with decimals and percents.

The content outline, published as a separate booklet, gives a clearer picture of the tests' content than does the manual. In the outline, the test items are classified according to the topic being measured. Although many of these classifications are debatable, the content outline documents an imbalance in content between the two forms: Form Am has more items than Form Bm on common fractions and on algebraic expressions and fewer items on decimal fractions and on money, interest, and discounts. About one-third of the items in each form have rather exact parallels in the other form (with essentially only the numbers changed), which might be expected to yield a practice effect, but alternate forms data in the manual show that this effect is negligible.

Test 2 is relatively unreliable for an achievement test, with K-R 20 reliabilities ranging from .70 to .84, split-half reliabilities from .76 to .92, and alternate-forms reliabilities in the low .80's. All but one of the 11 corresponding reliability coefficients for Test 1 are higher, typically by at least .05. The correlation of .67 between the two tests suggests that they could be combined to yield a more reliable scale, but normative data for the total score are not provided.

Neither test contains items reflecting topics introduced into the secondary mathematics curriculum in the past two decades. Both tests emphasize factual knowledge and the ability to perform simple manipulations, thereby neglecting knowledge of principles and the ability to analyze non-routine situations. Students in modern mathematics programs will probably not be at much of a disadvantage on these tests (although they may not have mastered such arcana as angular minutes and seconds), but neither will they be able to exhibit much of what they may know.

The format of the tests is attractive; the manual is clear and, except for details of test development and item analysis, reasonably comprehensive. Separate norms are provided for college preparatory students, although these are the students for whom the tests are probably least appropriate. Additional data on the tests are available on request from the publisher, including norms for junior college freshmen.

The *Metropolitan High School Mathematics*

Tests can be used to measure certain restricted components of the secondary mathematics curriculum—mainly the content associated with courses in general mathematics. Since a good many high school mathematics courses today go well beyond this content, however, the tests are likely to be useless either for appraising students' progress in a given program of instruction or for judging the effectiveness of the program itself. Potential users should consider whether tests would be more appropriate for their purposes.

LEN PIKAART, *Professor of Mathematics Education, University of Georgia, Athens, Georgia.*

The *Metropolitan High School Mathematics Test* consists of two subtests: Test 1, Mathematical Computation and Concepts, and Test 2, Mathematical Analysis and Problem Solving. The three stated uses of the derived scores on these tests are student guidance, instructional and curricular analysis, and administrative evaluation of instructional goals. Although the authors point out that other reliable information must be employed in conjunction with scores on these tests, a review of the content of the tests, of validity procedures, and of reliability measures leads to a conclusion that the tests may yield only measures of traditional mathematics knowledge and skills for beginning algebra students. Use of the tests for students in the upper three grade levels in high school, particularly for those in contemporary mathematics programs, is questionable.

The inherent danger in developing a test which is based on content validity only is that reviewers and users may not agree with the authors' choice of representative items. In examining both forms of this test with the authors' content specifications in mind, several disappointing weaknesses were discovered. In Test 1, Form Am, no items involving permutations or combinations were found, while one question on Form Bm asked "Which of the following has a value of 10? [e] $(5)_3$, [f] $\binom{5}{3}$, [g] $(5)^3$, [h] $5!$" and thus used the binomial coefficient notation. The only number theory item on Form Am involved knowing that the quotient of any nonzero number divided by itself is one, and the only geometry items were exercises in computing the perimeter of a parallelogram and the area of a circle. Also, a problem like, "The

product of 62.4 and .34 is" appears to be designed as an estimation problem because the four choices are, "[a] 2.1216, [b] 212.16, [c] 21.216, and [d] 21,216." However, the directions advise the student, "As soon as you figure out the answer to an example, look at the four answers given beneath the example." Thus, only "test sophisticated" students would respond to this item as a problem in estimation.

In Test 2, no items involving probability were found. The only trigonometry problem on Form Am required the student to know the definition of the cosine and to determine the hypotenuse of a 45° right triangle, given one leg and $\cos 45 = .7071$. (Of course a student could opt to use the Pythagorean Theorem.) On Form Bm, no problem would reasonably be solved by employing a trigonometric function. Although the authors claim that "computational demands are held to the lowest level possible," problems which contradicted this were found on both forms. For example, one problem requires the examinee to calculate the following batting averages and select the largest: 16/61, 15/50, 20/48, 15/35. Even a student very adept at estimation would likely have to carry out the division in the last two cases.

The tests heavily emphasize ratio, proportion, decimals, percent, and algebra. For this reason, the tests appear to be measures of learning and retaining eighth and ninth grade general mathematics and elementary algebra. The authors' apparent disregard of curriculum revisions in the last two decades is also disappointing. For example, items were not found which emphasize understanding the structure of number systems, and geometry learnings appear to be envisioned as simply the ability to apply measurement formulas. Dressel, in a review of the entire high school battery (6:15), noted the small influence of mathematics curriculum revision in these tests. He also pointed out how the authors' validation technique of selecting items which distinguished between students at successive grade levels can easily lead to the construction of a test composed of many elementary items and few from advanced study.

An original pool of items was administered to students in 10 school systems in 7 states. The results were subjected to item analysis and discrimination analysis to develop equivalent forms which discriminate between grade levels and meet the authors' standards. The revised tests were administered again in four of the

New England school systems which participated in the first testing. The purpose of this testing was to develop conversion tables for each form from the raw score distribution to a normalized standard score distribution with a mean of 50 and a standard deviation of 15.

Finally, the standardization was completed by administering the tests to 31,000 students in 29 school systems in 19 states. Percentile rank and stanine norm tables were developed for both an "Age-Controlled" group and a "College Preparatory" group. The age-controlled group for a grade level is defined to be those students who are in an age-grade placement which is the "18-month range including the greatest percent of students in the grade." The use of age-controlled norms permits comparing student scores to those who are "at-grade-for-age," but the age-controlled sample seems to differ from the total sample by very little—approximately 1.5 mean Otis IQ points in favor of the age-controlled sample.

K-R 20, split-half, and alternate-form reliabilities are reported. The reliability estimates for Test 1 are satisfactory (K-R range of .80 to .89 for grades 9–12, and split-half range of .80 to .89 for grades 10–11 combined). The Test 2 reliability estimates are low compared to other standardized tests (K-R range of .77 to .78 on Form Am and .70 to .84 on Form Bm for grades 9–12, split-half range of .83–.87 on Form Am and .76 to .92 on Form Bm, for grades 10–11 combined). Two estimates of alternate-form reliabilities are acceptable for Test 1 (.87 to .90), but barely acceptable for Test 2 (.80 to .82). Reliability estimates for Form Bm are more variable than Form Am. As noted by Dressel (6:15), the reliability of Test 2 could be improved if more than 30 items were included.

SUMMARY. The two mathematics tests reviewed are of limited use. Perusal of the items indicates that emphasis has been placed on the content of eighth and ninth grade general mathematics and elementary algebra. Although grade norms have been carefully developed, the tests are not deemed representative of contemporary high school mathematics programs. The emphasis on algebra must cause a serious discrimination against general mathematics students.

The *Stanford High School Numerical Competence Test* presents a more valid sampling of computational skills and is more current in terms of curriculum, less laborious, and shorter.

For reviews of the complete battery, see 15 (2 reviews) and 6:15 (3 reviews).

[480]

*Metropolitan Achievement Tests: Mathematics Tests. Grades 3.5–4.9, 5.0–6.9, 7.0–9.5; 1932–71; 4 scores: computation, concepts, problem solving, total; 3 levels; Form F ('70, 8 pages); battery teacher's handbook ('71, 16–17 pages) for each level; $6.50 per 35 tests; 70¢ per set of hand scoring stencils; 50¢ per battery handbook; $2 per battery specimen set of any one level; postage extra; Walter N. Durost, Harold H. Bixler, J. Wayne Wrightstone, George A. Prescott, and Irving H. Balow; Harcourt Brace Jovanovich, Inc. *

a) ELEMENTARY MATHEMATICS TESTS. Grades 3.5–4.9; 1937–71; directions ('70, 9 pages); scoring service, $1.25 and over per test; 90(110) minutes in 3 sessions.
b) INTERMEDIATE MATHEMATICS TESTS. Grades 5.0–6.9; 1932–71; directions ('71, 12 pages); separate answer sheets (Digitek, IBM 805, IBM 1230, MRC) may be used; $2.80 per 35 Digitek or IBM 1230 answer sheets; $2.50 per 35 MRC answer sheets; $2.30 per 35 IBM 805 answer sheets; 80¢ per Digitek or IBM scoring stencil; MRC scoring service, 23¢ and over per test; IBM scoring service, 50¢ and over per test; 85(105) minutes in 2 sessions.
c) ADVANCED MATHEMATICS TESTS. Grades 7.0–9.5; rest of information same as for intermediate level.

REFERENCES

1. See 6:627.
2. BRENNAN, JOSEPH T., JR. *Estimating Expected Reading Achievement in the Junior High School.* Doctor's thesis, University of Pittsburgh (Pittsburgh, Pa.), 1966. (*DA* 27:4033A)
3. GALLIAN, RICHARD DONALD. *A Content Validation Study of the Arithmetic Test Items of Four Arithmetic Achievement Tests Compared With the Content of Six Arithmetic Series at the Intermediate Level.* Doctor's thesis, University of Missouri (Columbia, Mo.), 1967. (*DA* 28:3361A)
4. STILGEBAUER, LARRY K. *A Study of Selected Data in Predicting Success in Ninth Grade Mathematics at Jefferson Junior High School, Mattoon, Illinois.* Master's thesis, Eastern Illinois University (Charleston, Ill.), 1967.
5. WALKER, CHARLES EVERETT. *The Effect of Variations in Test Administration Conditions on Arithmetic Test Performance.* Doctor's thesis, University of Rochester (Rochester, N.Y.), 1969. (*DAI* 31:242A)

For reviews by O. F. Anderhalter and E. W. Hamilton of an earlier edition, see 6:627; for a review by Robert L. Burch, see 4:416; for reviews by Peter L. Spencer and Harry Grove Wheat, see 2:1458.1; for reviews by Foster E. Grossnickle and Guy M. Wilson, see 1:892. For reviews of an earlier edition of the complete battery, see 6:15 (3 reviews), 4:18 (1 review), 2:1189 (2 reviews), and 1:874 (3 reviews).

[481]

★Modern Mathematics Supplement to the Iowa Tests of Basic Skills. Grades 3–9; 1968; MMS; 6 overlapping levels (grades 3, 4, 5, 6, 7, 8–9) in a single booklet; 1 form ('68, 15 pages, labeled Test X); manual ('68, 22 pages); answers must be recorded on the battery MRC answer sheet if used as a supplement to the ITBS or if scoring is to be done locally, otherwise on a MRC answer card; $6.15 per 35 tests; $3.90 per 100 battery answer sheets; 90¢ per set of scoring stencils for answer sheets; $3 per 100 answer cards; 90¢ per specimen set; postage extra; scoring service, 12¢ per test; 30(40) minutes; E. F. Lindquist, A. N. Hieronymus, and H. D. Hoover; Houghton Mifflin Co. *

E. G. BEGLE, *Professor of Mathematics Education, Stanford University, Stanford, California.*

The MMS can be considered an updated version of the Arithmetic Concepts test (AC) in the *Iowa Tests of Basic Skills.* As the authors point out in the manual, the Arithmetic Concepts test, which was standardized in 1963, was constructed during the middle of the period when a number of curriculum projects were producing new elementary school mathematics series and before much agreement had been reached on the many experimental procedures then being tried.

Before items for this test were constructed, the leading texts copyrighted since 1963 were carefully examined. Before the final form was put together, the five leading textbook series at that time were examined from the point of view of the content classification system used in the Arithmetic Concepts test. While there was, of course, variation from text series to text series in the distribution of emphasis on various topics, this test was constructed to approximate closely the average distribution over these five texts.

In comparing the coverage of the MMS with that of AC, the following differences were noted: about a third of the items in AC are devoted to measurement (including currency); in the MMS less than 10 percent of the items are devoted to measurement. A substantial number of items in the MMS involve open mathematical sentences; none of these appears in AC. Similarly, items on number lines, inequalities, and structural properties of number systems are included in MMS but not in AC. The AC contains 12 items testing students' understanding of arithmetic algorithms, while the MMS contains only one. Finally, the MMS contains five times as many geometry items as does AC.

The format for the MMS is quite similar to that of AC in that there is overlap between the tests for different grades. Thus, for example, the last 15 items for grade 3 are the first 15 for grade 4. However, in the MMS the items for grades 3 through 6 are separate from those for grades 7 through 9.

Tables are provided in the manual for converting raw scores into grade-equivalent scores, and also into percentile ranks for the beginning, the middle, or the end of the year. These grade-equivalent scores and percentile ranks were computed from the distribution of raw scores obtained by a large norming sample in the

spring of 1968. The sample had been chosen so as to represent the national distribution of textbook usage in the 1967–68 school year. The reliability coefficients range from .87 to .91.

At the time the norming scores were obtained, one form of the Arithmetic Concepts test was also administered, thus making it possible to obtain correlations between the AC and the MMS. The correlation for grade 3 was .75, and for each of the other grades between .82 and .87.

The manual states that the new mathematics programs developed during the first half of the 1960's "did not differ greatly in objectives from those of the 1950's, but the methods and materials that were accomplishing the objectives were, in many instances, dramatically different." This statement is only partially true. Most of the objectives of the 1950's have been retained, but some new ones have been added. The differences between the AC and the MMS listed above, with the exception of the decrease in the number of items on comprehension of algorithms, all reflect new objectives of our mathematics programs. Consequently, the MMS is, on the whole, a more useful test for today than is the AC and could well be substituted for the AC in the *Iowa Tests of Basic Skills.*

THOMAS C. O'BRIEN, *Associate Professor of Education, Southern Illinois University, Edwardsville, Illinois.*

These tests were designed to measure children's abilities to handle mathematics questions related to "current objectives, content, placement, and emphasis" in grades 3–9. In general, they deal with issues of importance in such areas as equations and inequalities, and numeration and number systems without the undue attention so often given low level issues such as definitions, notation, and conventions. The test items do not deal only with the mathematical ideas introduced since 1958; rather some old and some recently introduced ideas are covered with nomenclature tending toward that which is currently used. Relatively few computation items are included in these tests, though principles of computation are treated in various items. The MMS consists of six overlapping levels presented in one test booklet.

Results of tests such as these should give information upon which teachers can base further action. The test manual is helpful in classifying items according to content and in recommending the use of item analysis to obtain further information about specific difficulties. Unfortunately, item analysis is restricted to determining the percentage of pupils in a class who answer an item correctly. No suggestion is made that an examination of pupils' actual responses, individually or classwide, might yield useful information about the process—rather than merely the product—of children's thinking. The manual is helpful in recommending follow-up testing using teacher made tests or tests supplied with mathematics textbooks. It does not, however, recommend administration of certain items in free response form, or on-the-spot or follow-up interviews of children, to probe further the nature of their thinking. Of what use is it to know that a child or a class has a weakness in "Measurement—Length" or "Numeration and Number Systems—Counting"? How is one to know the process that produced a response to "Which of the following is *not* equivalent to 8×9? 1) 7×10; 2) 6×12; 3) 9×8; 4) 2×36"?

Further, some items are misclassified in the manual. It is not at all clear why the item "In the numeral 5764, what digit is second from the right?" should be classified under numeration and the item "Karen's little brother is 3 feet tall. How many inches tall is he?" should be classified as measurement.

In general, the test items are unambiguous, save for those which involve interpretation of Venn diagrams. The instructions for administration, too, are relatively straightforward. It is not certain, however, that young children would ably deal with the format and compactness of the computer card which is used for machine scoring. Machine scoring, potentially useful from this reviewer's standpoint only if it gives a frequency count for each choice in each item, is available.

Substantial attention was given by the testmakers to the grade placement of topics and items, though the test manual wisely suggests that items at a particular level may not have a perfect fit with a certain class's instructional background; hence, a mismatch in a few items can be costly in terms of a grade equivalent or a percentile score.

Normative data were obtained from some 600 pupils per grade in 14 school systems enrolled in the Iowa Basic Skills Testing Program. Some evidence of the representativeness of the sample is given by the fact that the seven basal texts used in the schools accounted for about 90 percent of adoptions in grades K-8 in the United States. Since the tests were administered in May 1968 and since all but one of the school systems had been using the then-current text series for at least two years, the results obtained seem less likely to have been influenced by the vagaries so common at an earlier time, when "modern mathematics" was new to most schools. How the normative data apply to the growing proportion of classrooms in which textbooks are playing a diminished role, however, is unknown.

Split-half reliabilities based on the equating sample range from .87 to .91, and correlation coefficients between these tests and the Arithmetic Concepts tests in the *Iowa Tests of Basic Skills* range from .75 to .87. The manual provides standard errors of measurement for various raw score ranges, accompanied, as a bonus, by an explanation of standard error in terms teachers can use.

Raw scores may be interpreted in terms of grade-equivalent scores, percentile ranks, or stanines from straightforward tables in the manual. The bias of this reviewer, however, is that one bit of data—a percentile score for a class or a student, for example—is virtually no information, save in the most global sense, in terms of future teacher action. As the manual quite rightly suggests, the test involves only a small sample of items in each particular area; there may be cases in which the grade-level correspondence is poor, and a child's performance is a function of his particular motivation, attentiveness, and particular state of physical and emotional health at the time of testing. Further, the test norms are based on a small number of school systems about which only 1968 textbook use is known. Just what does a single bit of derived data tell a teacher about the quality and quantity of mathematical knowledge of a child or a class, and what inferences may be drawn for future teacher action?

In general, this test is one of the more competent of its kind in terms of item quality and ease of administration. Very highly regarded by this reviewer is the text of the manual, which gives the impression that this test is an aid, not the ultimate answer, in the assessment of children's mathematical achievement.

[482]

★**Moray House Mathematics Tests.** Ages 8.5–10.5, 10–12; 1964–70; 2 levels; distribution restricted to education authorities; 75p per 20 tests; 12½p per manual; postage extra; 45(50) minutes; Godfrey Thomson Unit, University of Edinburgh; University of London Press Ltd. *

a) MORAY HOUSE JUNIOR MATHEMATICS TEST. Ages 8.5–10.5; 1964–70; forms 1, 2, ('70, 11 pages); manual ('70, 12 pages) for each form.

b) MORAY HOUSE MATHEMATICS TEST. Ages 10–12; 1964–69; forms 3, 3A, ('66, 8 pages) in one booklet, 4 ('69, 8 pages), 4A ('66, 8 pages) in one booklet; manual (dates same as for tests, 11 pages) for each form.

[483]

★N.B. Mathematics Tests. Standards 7–8 (ages 14–15); 1967; NBMT; 7 tests; preliminary manual (18 pages); separate answer sheets (IBM 1230) must be used; R1 per 10 tests; R4 per 100 answer sheets; 30c per set of scoring stencils; 60c per manual; postpaid within South Africa; specimen set not available (sample copy of test free); Afrikaans edition available; Human Sciences Research Council. *

a) ALGEBRA. Forms C ['67, 8 pages], D ['67, 9 pages]; 40(45) minutes.

b) ALGEBRA: FUNDAMENTAL CONCEPTS. 1 form ['67, 6 pages]; 25(30) minutes.

c) ALGEBRA: BASIC COMPUTATIONS. Forms A, B, ['67, 7 pages]; 25(30) minutes.

d) ALGEBRA: EQUATIONS. 1 form ['67, 8 pages]; 30(35) minutes.

e) ALGEBRA: PROBLEMS. 1 form ['67, 8 pages]; 35(40) minutes.

f) ALGEBRA: FACTORS. 1 form ['67, 7 pages]; 25(30) minutes.

g) GEOMETRY AND GRAPHS. Forms A ['67, 13 pages], B ['67, 11 pages]; 30(35) minutes.

[484]

*National Teacher Examinations: Mathematics. College seniors and teachers; 1940–70; Forms K-ONT ('69, 14 pages), RNT ('69, 16 pages), SNT1 ('70, 15 pages), SNT2 ('70, 18 pages); descriptive booklet ('70, 8 pages); for more complete information, see 582; 120(165) minutes; Educational Testing Service. *

For a review by Paul Blommers of earlier forms, see 6:583. For reviews of the testing program, see 582 (2 reviews), 6:700 (1 review), 5:538 (3 reviews), and 4:802 (1 review).

[485]

★SRA Modern Math Understanding Test. Grades 4–9; 1966–68; MMUT; 8 scores: foundations of mathematics, arithmetic operations, geometry and measurement, knowledge and computation, elementary understanding, problem solving and application, structure and generalization, total (only total score if locally scored); Forms C, D, ('66, 11 pages); 3 levels: blue (grades 4–6), green (grades 6–8), and red (grades 8–9) in a single booklet; directions for administration ('66, 2 pages); interpretive guide ('67, 47 pages); technical report ('68, 29 pages); norms booklet ('66, 8 pages); separate answer sheets (DocuTran) must be used; $1.05 per specimen set, postage extra; 45(55) minutes; Science Research Associates, Inc. *

a) SRA SCORED. Rental and scoring service, 55¢ and over per student.

b) LOCALLY SCORED. $7.20 per 25 tests; $9.30 per 100 answer sheets; 55¢ per scoring stencil; $1.50 per set of interpretive materials (interpretive guide and technical report).

ARTHUR MITTMAN, *Professor of Education and Chairman, Department of Educational Psychology, University of Oregon, Eugene, Oregon.*

In both a very adequate Technical Report and a carefully prepared Interpretive Guide, the test is described as sampling "the common core of concepts and goals of modern mathematics instruction. Constructed independently of any particular instructional programs, it can be used to measure student achievement and improvement regardless of the specific textbooks or instructional materials a school has adopted." A review of the procedures followed in the test's development substantiates this claim in that accepted practices were followed with respect to statements of objectives, determination of content, item writing, tryout of items and final item selection. Similarly, the format of the test, clarity of instructions, manuals, and printing are generally of good quality and could serve as models for measurement classes.

As true as the foregoing may be, it does not preclude the possibility of certain problems arising in the use of the test. Multilevel features of any test are obtained at a price. If the tests, for example, are to serve grades 4, 5, and 6, as the Blue Level of this test is intended to do, the difficulty level will vary from grade to grade. This is necessarily so if the test is to measure achievement and improvement from one grade to the next. Thus, the average item difficulty for the lowest grade, in this instance grade 4, is likely to approach the level of chance. In fact, the technical manual reports an average item difficulty of .30 for grade 4 based upon a sample of students from a suburban Chicago school district. The expected chance score on a 4-response multiple choice item is .25. Furthermore, the mean of 15.7 for the middle of grade 4 is only 3.7 points higher than the expected chance score of 12. To interpret the performance of a class as reflecting normal progress if its mean score is near the expected chance score is questionable at best and not too reassuring to the teacher.

The situation is not as critical for grade 6 of the Green Level (intended for grades 6, 7, and 8) or for grade 8 of the Red Level (designed for grades 8 and 9). In any case, the prospective user should go through the test item by item and consider the appropriateness of the test for the population in question. As stated earlier, the items of this test are of a high quality and ask significant questions, but they may be difficult for certain populations.

There is no doubt, in this reviewer's opinion, that the better students would view these tests as fair and challenging and attack them with a favorable attitude. On the other hand, less competent pupils might consider the exercise very discouraging. The measures that would result from the latter situation could have little interpretive value.

The effect of the difficulty level of the test is undoubtedly reflected in the reliabilities (.72 and .73 for Forms C and D, respectively) reported for grade 4. Reliabilities for all grades and levels range from .72 to .78 with median .80. These coefficients tend to be on the low side for a 48-item test in mathematics.

One of the perils of testing that arise in the electronic age is the tendency to report subtest scores for groupings of items by areas of content and class of objectives. The danger lies in the tendency to suggest using scores from a small group of items, classified as homogeneous with respect to some variable, for diagnosis. If the users of this test elect to buy the scoring service with the tests, they will receive a report providing seven subtest scores plus the total score for each student. This, in itself, is not bad but the interpretive manual suggests that these subscores may be used "to decide where the students' strong points are and where they seem to be weaker, and to undertake enrichment or remediation where it is most needed." Furthermore, class average scores in each area are reported and classified as "Hi," "Av," or "Lo" as compared to the top 23%, middle 54%, or lower 23% of the norming population. Since each of the seven subscores on Form C are reported to correlate .71 or more with the total score in grade 4 and .81 or more in grade 9, can much be gained for diagnostic purposes from subtest scores? It should be noted that the ease with which computers can provide an abundance of subtest scores is not directly proportional to the ease of interpreting the data they produce.

The *SRA Modern Math Understanding Test* is undoubtedly one of the most carefully constructed tests, if not the best available, for the intended purpose. It must be emphasized that this test should be selected for use only in those instances in which it fits the needs of the curriculum being studied and the population being served. Interpretation of subtest scores without other evidence for diagnostic purposes should be avoided. If used in this fashion and under these conditions the test can serve a useful function in the schools. In view of the fact that the modern math curriculum has been in the schools for several years, it is time tests are available to measure achievement in this area.

LESLIE P. STEFFE, *Associate Professor of Mathematics Education, University of Georgia, Athens, Georgia.*

According to the manual, this test was constructed independently of any instructional program and "can be used to measure student achievement and improvement regardless of the specific textbooks....a school has adopted." Items were categorized within grade level by utilizing a two-dimensional matrix with dimensions of mathematical content and facets of mathematical understanding. Content categories include foundations of mathematics, arithmetic operations, and geometry and measurement; and facets of mathematical understanding include knowledge and computation, elementary understanding, problem solving and applications, and structure and generalization.

The Technical Report and Interpretive Guide are lacking in what this reviewer considers necessary information. Item classification in the two-dimensional matrix was judgmental because "each item was reviewed several times by a number of mathematics educators." No indices are given, however, to indicate degree of consistency among judges. In view of the lack of such indices, an examination of the item classification was conducted. It was clear that a substantial number of items could be placed justifiably in more than one cell. By necessity, then, extent of agreement among judges needs to be known before the instrument is construed as valid by the test user. The Interpretive Guide does give a detailed explanation of the scales used (grade equivalents, percentiles, and stanines) in establishing national school norms. The within-grade K-R 20 reliabilities range from .73 to .88, with median .84, for Form C and from .72 to .82, with median .79, for Form D. They were based on data from a Chicago suburban school district but there is no indication of how the district was chosen. Standard errors of measurement, standard deviations, and means are included. In view of suggested uses of the test, which include selecting students for advanced placement and establishing homogeneous grouping for instruction, relevant criterion-related validity coefficients should have been presented. Since such correlations are not presented, the suggested recommendations are at best tenuous.

Even though the NMUT is timed, the authors consider it to emphasize power more than speed and the alloted time is considered generous. No information is supplied, however, to indicate if speededness is actually a factor influencing test scores (such as number of students finishing the three-quarter point or information on individual item difficulties). Even if speededness is not a factor, no information is supplied as to whether students are encouraged to guess. This apparent lack of directions may introduce unnecessary variability in test scores.

Relationships which may exist between the four facets of mathematical understanding and Bloom's *Taxonomy of Educational Objectives* are not made explicit, even though the test authors indicate indebtedness to the taxonomy. Moreover, there is no discussion as to how particular facets of mathematical understanding used may be related to other existing taxonomies in mathematics education. However, data are presented concerning interrelationships among facets of mathematical understanding, along with interrelationships among content categories. Intercorrelations within grade 4 range from .31 to .49, with median .37, among facets of mathematical understanding and from .42 to .48, with median .45, among content categories, which indicates the subparts of the test are not measuring the same thing for that grade. The results for grade 9 are not as clear-cut. Intercorrelations range from .39 to .68, with median .57, for facets of mathematical understanding and .48 to .68, with median .58, for content categories. Because the greatest correlations of the latter two ranges approach the reliabilities, the distinctiveness of the subparts is not as well supported for grade 9 as for grade 4.

The items generally appear to be unambiguous and differ enough on the two forms to justify the use of two forms. Even though no correlations are reported between the forms and no information is reported on stability of scores over time, distributions of the scores of the two forms are reported to be nearly identical. The mathematical terminology used in the items is consistent with most present-day mathematics programs, but no indication is given as to the reading level at which categories of items were written. Given that a child can read the items, some items clearly can be answered correctly by employing processes other than those which the item writer assumed necessary (excluding random processes). As examples, one item involving brackets and parentheses could be correctly answered by misapplication (or nonapplication) of the distributive property. Other items involving geometrical content could be correctly answered by visual inspection rather than by logical reasoning.

The test is exceedingly difficult for all the grades for which each level was primarily designed. With four-response items scored number right, the expected chance score in terms of percentages is 25. When expressed as a percentage of possible score, the national medians for midyear testing are approximately as follows: 28, 38, and 51 for grades 4, 5, and 6, using the Blue Level; 32, 41, and 47 for grades 6, 7, and 8, using the Green Level; and 31 and 37 for grades 8 and 9, using the Red Level. Each of these percentages may be converted to the estimated percentage of items known by subtracting one-third of the percentage of wrong answers. The corrected percentages range from 4 to 35, with median 17.

Test users can obtain subtest scores from the central scoring and reporting service of SRA in two formats. Whether these subtest scores can be used to plan "enrichment or remediation" for individuals or groups is questionable from two points of view. First, because the tests are exceedingly difficult, any interpretation that students need remediation or enrichment based on a comparison to the national sample or on a comparison to other criteria may be quite misleading. Other measures of mathematics achievement may give radically different results. Second, because substantial correlations exist among subtests in some cases, just what differential mathematics instruction should be planned on the basis of subtest scores is obscured.

In summary, the weaknesses of the test outweigh the strengths. A major goal of mathematics instruction has always been to build in school children confidence that they can do and enjoy mathematics. Subjecting them to an achievement test which is known to be exceedingly difficult is not consistent with such a goal. The difficulty of the test, along with the other weaknesses discussed, provides sufficient reason for not using it with the populations for which it was intended. Restricted usages such as identification of superior mathematics students from selected populations, however, do seem feasible.

[486]

*Sanders-Schrader General Mathematics Test. 1, 2 semesters high school and college; 1962–64; first published 1962–63 in the Every Pupil Scholarship Test series; Forms A, B, ('64, 2 pages) ; 2 levels labeled Tests 1, 2; manual ('64, 3 pages) ; $1.75 per 25 tests, postage extra ; 75¢ per specimen set, postpaid ; 40(45) minutes ; H. Eugene Schrader and M. W. Sanders; Data Processing and Educational Measurement Center. *

[487]

★Senior Mathematics Test. Technical college entrants; 1963–66; 1 form ['63, 8 pages] ; mimeographed manual ['66, 5 pages] ; norms ('66, 4 pages) ; 5p per test, postpaid within U.K.; manual and norms free on request from NFER; 45(50) minutes; published for the National Foundation for Educational Research in England and Wales; Ginn & Co. Ltd. *

[488]

★Stanford Achievement Test: High School Mathematics Test. Grades 9–12; 1965–66; catalog uses the title *Stanford High School Mathematics Test;* subtest of *Stanford Achievement Test: High School Basic Battery;* 2 scores: Part A (basic), total (basic and advanced) ; Part A is for all students in grades 9–12, Part B is only for students enrolled in 3rd and 4th year advanced mathematics courses; Forms W, X, ('65, 7 pages) ; no specific manual ; battery manual ('65, 48 pages) ; supplementary directions ('66, 4 pages) for each type of answer sheet ; separate answer sheets (IBM 805, IBM 1230) must be used; $8.20 per 35 tests ; $2.30 per 35 IBM 805 answer sheets ; $2.80 per 35 IBM 1230 answer sheets ; 70¢ per scoring stencil ; $1.20 per battery manual ; $2 per specimen set; postage extra ; scoring service, 19¢ and over per test ; 40(45) minutes per part ; Eric F. Gardner, Jack C. Merwin, Robert Callis, and Richard Madden ; Harcourt Brace Jovanovich, Inc. *

JAMES BRASWELL, *Associate Examiner in Mathematics, Educational Testing Service, Princeton, New Jersey.*

This fairly comprehensive test samples a variety of topics covered during the high school years. The two forms, W and X (a third form, S, is available for larger studies), are essentially parallel and each contains a total of 74 four-choice items. The test is separated into two 40-minute sections. Part A contains 40 items that are typically covered during the first three years of high school. Part B contains 34 items which sample content that the student is more likely to encounter during the junior and senior years. Normative data are available for Part A and the total test, but not for Part B alone.

The 74 items on each form cover topics mainly from algebra and geometry. A few items sample content from other areas, with trigonometry receiving surprisingly light coverage.

The number of problems devoted to each area is : algebra, 42 ; geometry, 15 ; probability and statistics, 4 ; trigonometry, 2 ; matrices and determinants, 2 ; vectors, 2 ; arithmetic, 2 ; graphs, 2 ; functional notation, 2 ; and logic, 1. The accompanying manual includes a more detailed description of content for each form. Fourteen of the 42 algebra items test the student's ability to solve equations or substitute numbers in a given equation. Some algebra items are redundant (for example, compare items 30 and 40 on Form X). Each of the geometry items, as well as those in the miscellaneous categories, seems to test a unique aspect of the mathematics curriculum.

Most items fall in the lower to middle level of Bloom's Taxonomy. A few items require synthesis of knowledge, but the more insightful applications of mathematics are rare. Item 37 on Form X is a pleasant exception.

With a few exceptions, the problems are presented in clear and unambiguous language. This is not surprising, as the pretest phase described in the manual seems quite thorough. Item 65 on Form W and item 67 on Form X, however, are unnecessarily complicated and they could be confusing. Item 17 on Form X may not have a key. A strange answer is offered to another problem, "The sum of the angles of a right triangle must be" and the key was not 180°, but "less than 360°."

The manual contains a complete description of how the test was developed, the standardization procedure, and the norming process. Normative information is furnished for each of grades 9–12. One table relates raw scores to standard scores and other tables relate standard scores to both the stanine scale and percentile ranks for each grade. There is a table which gives the item difficulty (percent responding correctly) for each item, by form, for all grades. Several of the items show low, nearly constant, difficulty across all years. Such items might not be appropriate for the group.

The validity of the test rests in part on the authority of the subject matter experts and consultants who helped plan and write the test. The prospective user of this test is advised to examine the test carefully to see if its content is consistent with the objectives of the high school's mathematics program. Since the test contains only two trigonometry items, the potential user should not expect the test to yield a valid measure of achievement in trigonometry.

JAMES W. WILSON, *Associate Professor of Mathematics Education and Head of the Department, University of Georgia, Athens, Georgia.*

This test, one of ten in the *Stanford Achievement Test: High School Battery,* is printed in a separate booklet to permit its use independent of the total battery. There is no separate manual, however, and the user interested only in the mathematics tests will be forced to sift through a lot of extraneous information in the manual. A separate manual for the mathematics test would be an asset.

The discussion in the manual of the test development procedures is too general to give any clue about the type of mathematics program the test items might sample. Here again, a separate manual would have made possible the discussion of the specific procedures and problems of the mathematics test development.

The manual provides an outline of the mathematics covered in the test: numbers, 18 items; powers and roots, 5 items; primes and factors, 3 items; equations and functions, 16 items; geometry and trigonometry, 20 items; sets, 4 items; statistics, 4 items; and miscellaneous, 4 items. The larger sets of items are further identified by finer content distinctions. This outline, however, does not adequately describe the mathematics in the test. Nor, on the other hand, does it describe the school mathematics program for which the test might be appropriate.

The general test development procedures cannot be faulted. The norms and norming procedures are well described. The quality of the items from a tests-and-measurement point of view appears to be fairly good. The quality of the items as judged by the mathematics content is subject to some criticism.

For example, one item in Form W has the symbols,

$$\left\{ \left. \left| \begin{array}{c} x \\ y \end{array} \right| \begin{array}{c} \leqq 5 \\ \leqq 5 \end{array} \right. \right\}$$

as one distractor. Mathematically, this is a meaningless mess and has no place in a published test. On another question the student is presented the "infinite decimal" 1.232323.... and asked to select an expression that represents the same number. Unless the student has been exposed to a particular nonstandard algorithm for converting a repeating decimal to a fraction, he is unlikely to recognize $-22 + 23 \times$

[100/99] as the correct answer except by the elimination of the other three distractors. In some contemporary mathematics programs, the term "infinite decimal" would be confusing to students. It is, however, clear in the item context that a repeating decimal is identified.

There is a confusion between a *numeration* system and a *number* system. Item 68, Form W has two correct answers because of the confusion. (There is a "binary system" for which the theorem "pq = 0 implies p = 0 or q = 0" does not hold; it also does not hold for a "modulo 12 system.")

There are several other questionable bits of mathematics in the test items. Item 31, Form X, presents triangle ABC with exterior angle BCQ (figure provided). Then item 32 refers back to item 31 and has a distractor concerning the "triangle QCB." Obviously Q, C, and B do form a triangle, but it is not relevant to this question and is possibly confusing. In some items there appears "the solution set (or truth set)" and in others—in the same test form—it is "the truth set (or solution set)." Why not be consistent? The representation of sample spaces utilizes a notation that will not be familiar to all students who have studied probability. Item 61, Form X, tries to use "$+$" and "$\times$" to mean addition and multiplication of real numbers in one situation and "union and set intersection" in another. First, the question is of dubious value. But, more important, most secondary school students will not have used "$+$" and "$\times$" for set union and set intersection. Item 62, Form X, has a typographical error using lower case "y" rather than uppercase "Y" in the *correct* (?) response. Some items ask the student to select a "correct theorem." For some students, a proposition to be proved is a conjecture; it becomes a theorem only after it has been proved. The idea of an "incorrect theorem" would be meaningless. The items concerning "infinity" in Euclidean geometry would be very questionable for some mathematics curricula.

Perhaps the goal of the test is to be challenged. Can one mathematics test be responsive to the whole range of mathematics instruction at the high school level? Can it reflect the curricula in use in contemporary comprehensive high schools? This test was developed in the early 1960's during a period of rapid change in school mathematics. While it may represent a measure of broad mathematical development, it does not reflect contemporary programs of the 1970's. Therefore, its use for measuring the achievement of students in specific courses is seriously questioned.

The manual presents some suggested uses of the test battery. It seems to me that the primary justification for the use of this mathematics test is as part of the total battery.

Even with the concerns that I have stated for the mathematics content of this test, I feel it has better content validity for the comprehensive range of mathematics achievement than other available tests such as *Contemporary Mathematics Test: Advanced (Senior High), Metropolitan Achievement Tests: High School Mathematics Tests,* or *Test of Academic Progress: Mathematics.* For the purpose of obtaining a general index of mathematics achievement, from among these tests my choice would be either the Stanford or the TAP tests. The choice between these two mathematics tests would be determined by whether the other parts of the test battery were to be used.

For reviews of the complete battery, see 27 (2 reviews).

[489]

★Stanford Achievement Test: High School Numerical Competence Test. Grades 9–12; 1965–66; catalog uses the title *Stanford High School Numerical Competence Test;* subtest of *Stanford Achievement Test: High School Basic Battery;* Forms W, X, ('65, 4 pages); no specific manual; battery manual ('65, 48 pages); supplementary directions ('66, 4 pages) for each type of answer sheet; separate answer sheets (IBM 805, IBM 1230) must be used; $8.20 per 35 tests; $2.30 per 35 IBM 805 answer sheets; $2.80 per 35 IBM 1230 answer sheets; 70¢ per scoring stencil; $1.20 per battery manual; $2 per specimen set; postage extra; scoring service, 19¢ and over per test; 40(45) minutes; Eric F. Gardner, Jack C. Merwin, Robert Callis, and Richard Madden; Harcourt Brace Jovanovich, Inc. *

SHELDON S. MYERS, *Chairman, Mathematics Department, Educational Testing Service, Princeton, New Jersey.*

The Numerical Competence Test is more than a test of computational skill. Besides measuring arithmetic computation with fractions, decimals, and percents, it includes questions on data interpretation, ratio and proportion, denominate numbers, simple equations, exponents, and numeration systems involving new symbols. Aside from the questions on numeration systems, the questions are fairly traditional in language and symbolism. This test should be quite fair for a wide variety of curricular groups.

In both forms, the questions are of consistently high quality. The vocabulary is appropriate and the language clear and concise. A careful examination of each question in both forms reveals only one or two that might have some faults. The question on pacing off steps in Form X appears to be a little less airtight than the one in Form W. In Form X, the question states what a step averages. Presumably some steps are greater and some less than this. One has to assume in the question that the average will be achieved in only six steps. This similar question in the other form is a little more explicit on this point. Towards the end of each form there is a set of items on a strange and unfamiliar numeration system with new symbols which enhances the interest and variety of the forms. This reviewer found one of these items in each form to be rather time consuming since one had to grope toward the desired form of the answer.

The manual deals with all of the tests in the battery and constitutes as remarkable and thorough an effort in this direction as has been produced by any test maker. This battery seems to have been prepared with about as much statistical care as is possible with modern measurement technology. From the preparation and repeated tryout and revision of items to the careful statistical selection and sampling of the schools for standardization, to the use of an anchor test for control, to the study of grade-to-grade increases of means, to the factor analysis of the battery in order to give more meaning to validity, to the equating of forms, to the presentation of numerous interpretive graphs and tables, to detailed item-by-item content description, to detailed item difficulties for each form for each of four grade levels for each item —the manual is a most comprehensive presentation of information about the battery. While there are a number of parts of the manual that could be understood only by measurement experts, there are also large and significant portions of direct value to the average classroom teacher. The section "Use of Test Results" is particularly helpful to the teacher. Administrative, instructional, and counseling uses are discussed separately. Adequate precautions on the use and comparison of scores are given.

In summary, this well-made test with reliabilities at or near .90 should prove useful in assessing numerical competence for general education in a wide variety of schools.

LEN PIKAART, *Professor of Mathematics Education, University of Georgia, Athens, Georgia.*

The High School Numerical Competence Test of the *Stanford Achievement Test: High School Basic Battery* is a reasonably brief and accurate test of numerical competence. The battery manual describes this test as "designed to measure general mathematical competence, emphasizing arithmetical and numerical concepts. It is assumed that this competence is an integral part of general education and is basic preparation for more advanced study in mathematics." This stated philosophy is operational in that two other tests in the battery are designed to measure: mathematical ability in elementary algebra and geometry; and advanced algebra, trigonometry, and other selected concepts. The reviewer heartily endorses the scheme of designing specific tests for different types of mathematical learnings and encourages even more refinement in testing cognitive achievement in mathematics.[1]

The test is brief and very easy to administer. The manual which describes the development, standardization, and other characteristics of the test encompasses the whole high school battery. As the numerical competence test may be used separately, the publisher is encouraged to provide a separate manual, uncluttered by information about other tests, which would specifically describe the characteristics of this test.

The content description (with the number of items on Form W in parentheses) follows: basic arithmetical processes (12); percent, ratio, and proportion (10); measurement (4); powers and roots (2); graphs and tables (6); symbols, terms, numerals, and numbers (6); and relationships (5). As is to be expected, most of the items are standard calculation exercises and short word-problems. A few, e.g. "If $264 \div 6 = 40 + n$, $n = $," might appear to be more suitable for students who have completed algebra, but these items are all phrased in such a way as to be deemed appropriate for any student in a contemporary secondary school.

A small number of items appear weak. The reviewer objects to a problem which asks the examinee to carry out four or five division exercises of the type, $68/420$. Three items on each form involve a 3-symbol number code. The

difficulty measures of these items are similar and it appears that the only justification for three such problems, in lieu of one, is to increase the split-half reliability of the test. Also, two items on each form are problems in bases other than ten. Ability to answer these would depend heavily on the student's exposure to nondecimal systems. The authors claim that the test is a power test and so the very low difficulty (proportion of students answering the item correctly) of an item on base four (.07 to .11) may indicate that the item is inappropriate for many students. Finally, items like "5 times (2 pounds, 7 ounces) = " appear to test knowledge of conversion tables and not numerical competence.

The publisher's description of the test development and standardization covers the whole high school battery and therefore will not be reviewed here. All raw scores must be converted to standard scores which have a mean of 50 and a standard deviation of 10. Standard scores can then be converted to percentile ranks or stanines within grade levels. These scores then can be compared to the total standardization population or to the college preparatory standardization population. Raw score increases of means between successive grade levels are only approximately two points, which indicates that only a small difference exists between grade levels. However, this also implies that the test is a satisfactory measure of general computational ability and insensitive to students' programs of study.

Content validity only is reported by the publisher. Research concerning the usefulness of a numerical competency score is clearly in order. Both split-half and K-R 20 reliabilities are reported. In general, the reliabilities, ranging between .89 and .91, are satisfactory. Alternate-form reliabilities would be of interest, but are not reported.

As previously noted, the publisher commendably provides difficulty estimates for each item at each grade level 9–12. Also, factor analysis of the whole high school battery at each grade level indicates the existence of three factors. However, the loadings for numerical competence are low, e.g., at grade 9, only .51, .44, and .44 on verbal-language, science-technology, and mathematics, respectively. The mathematics factor is heavily loaded with the mathematics test—Part A and total mathematics. Because

1 For a discussion and example of such refinement, see BEGLE, EDWARD G., AND WILSON, JAMES W. "Evaluation of Mathematics Programs," pp. 367–404. In *Mathematics Education: 69th Yearbook of the National Society for the Study of Education, Part I.* Chicago, Ill.: University of Chicago Press, 1970. Pp. xi, 467. *

over half of the total mathematics test consists of Part A, the mathematics factor was certain to emerge and have low loadings on all other tests. That numerical competence is the next highest loading on this factor implies that there may well be a genuine mathematics factor, but the authors are advised to conduct the analysis correctly!

SUMMARY. This test appears to be a brief and reasonable test of numerical competency. It is easy to administer and score. Items, for the most part, are well chosen and well written. The *Stanford High School Numerical Competency Test* is favored by this reviewer over the *Metropolitan High School Mathematics Test* in providing a measure of general computational ability.

For reviews of the complete battery, see 27 (2 reviews).

[490]

★**Stanford Modern Mathematics Concepts Test.** Grades 5.5–6.9, 7.0–9.5; 1965; test booklet title is *Stanford Achievement Test: Modern Mathematics Concepts Test;* Forms W, X, (4 pages); 2 levels: intermediate 2, advanced; manual (8 pages) for each level; supplementary directions (1–2 pages) for each type of answer sheet; $5.80 per 35 tests; separate answer sheets (Digitek-IBM 805, IBM 1230, Harbor) may be used; $2.30 per 35 Digitek-IBM 805 answer sheets; $2.80 per 35 IBM 1230 answer sheets; $3 per 100 Harbor answer cards; 70¢ per IBM scoring stencil; $1.50 per specimen set; postage extra; scoring service, 19¢ and over per test; 50(58) minutes; Truman L. Kelley, Richard Madden, Eric F. Gardner, and Herbert C. Rudman; Harcourt Brace Jovanovich, Inc. *

REFERENCES

1. WOODWARD, JEAN W. *Identification of Mathematical Concepts Causing Learning Difficulties to Fifth-Grade Students.* Doctor's thesis, University of Houston (Houston, Tex.), 1967. (*DA* 28:2467A)
2. QUALLS, LULA JANE. *Effects of Review and Cueing on Elementary School Teachers' Performance on a Standardized Mathematics Test.* Doctor's thesis, University of Tennessee (Knoxville, Tenn.), 1969. (*DAI* 30:4693A)
3. ERICKSON, BARNEY LEE. *Effects of a College Mathematics Sequence Upon the Attitudes and Achievement in Mathematics of Prospective Elementary School Teachers.* Doctor's thesis, Utah State University (Logan, Utah), 1970. (*DAI* 30:5337A)

JAMES R. CALDWELL, *Counselor, Alhambra High School, Alhambra; Visiting Assistant Professor of Educational Psychology, University of Southern California, Los Angeles; California.*

The authors designed the test "to provide a measure of the current objectives of modern mathematics programs," placing particular emphasis on such factors as curriculum improvement. Yet because of the omission of pertinent information, there is little evidence that these goals have been adequately achieved.

Although an arithmetic achievement test should necessarily encompass a broad range of objectives, the manual fails to list any objectives specifically. Without a list to delineate which "current objectives" should receive priority, effective curriculum improvement becomes difficult. The "Item Content Outline" included in the manual is helpful in this respect, but limited. This outline places each test item into one of ten general categories. Some items overlap two or more categories.

While the authors report that an extensive review of existing modern mathematics programs and relevant textbooks was used to develop the test, they fail to include specific references. Not even the most important of the relevant textbooks and syllabi are identified. The authors state that throughout the test development process, "reliance was placed on the judgment of subject-matter specialists in modern mathematics." Again, they omit such pertinent information as the qualifications and professional experience of the specialists, the specific instructions under which they made their decisions, and the extent of agreement among independent judgments. Such information could help explain, for instance, why more emphasis was placed on "sets" in the intermediate tests than in the advanced forms. This reviewer does commend, however, the increased emphasis placed on "factors and primes" in the advanced tests.

While data are provided to account for the test's reliability, more information could have been offered. The range of reliability correlation coefficients calculated by the split-half method is .81 to .91 for both ability levels. The corresponding K-R 20 reliabilities range from .82 to .92. Although two forms are available at each ability level, the authors fail to include alternate-form reliability coefficients, as well as means and variances for each test.

Significant facts were omitted in the manual's discussion of the norm group. Initially a questionnaire was sent to "a sample of" school systems. The method of selecting this sample, its size, and the geographical locations and type of school systems contacted, is not reported, nor is information regarding the percentage of responses and possible biases due to the subsample of questionnaires returned. The manual notes that nine school systems from seven different states comprise the final norm group. Because little information is furnished on specific characteristics of the norm group, it is difficult to ascertain the type of student for whom the test is appropriate. The authors admit that the standardization group was "somewhat above average in ability" but they do not report new empirically derived norms. Rather, they state that the norms have been adjusted to be comparable with norms for the *Stanford Achievement Test.* Had they identified or explained the equating procedure in some detail, the adequacy of this process would have been easier to assess. Additional handicaps in arriving at the type of student appropriate for this test come from a lack of demographic information of distributions of the norm subjects with respect to sex, minority group membership, and socioeconomical levels.

As mentioned previously, limited evidence for content validity is presented in the manual. Moreover, the evidence presented for other types of validity is also limited. Specific references of independent follow-up studies of criterion-related validity is lacking. However, the authors do furnish validity information of a sort in terms of a table of correlations between this test, the *Stanford Achievement Test: Arithmetic Tests,* and the *Otis Quick-Scoring Mental Ability Test.*

It is possible that certain directions for administering the tests could have an adverse effect on highly anxious, poorly motivated, or low ability students. Blunt and authoritarian sentences like "Write your first and last names here. Do it as quickly as you can," and "After you have begun, you must not ask questions," could have a detrimental effect on some students. This is especially true since the time limits do not appear ample for the lower ability range of pupils. The time allowed for this test is 50 minutes, plus 8 minutes for the actual mechanics of administration. Consequently, the test could not be administered in a typical class period. This time requirement could create awkward administrative problems for a test which hardly justifies involving two class periods. Furthermore, the present format does not readily lend itself to division into two separate testing sessions.

In this reviewer's judgment, the actual test items, on the whole, are excellent. The tests, particularly the advanced forms, appear challenging for many typical seventh and eighth graders, but they may be a bit too difficult in some cases. Problems dealing with geometric

concepts, symbolism, number relationships and bases, and the use of the literal element, appear to be relatively difficult items for students at these grade levels, especially within the imposed time limits.

There are, however, a few test items which need revision. For a more expedient evaluation of this aspect of the test, references will be made to the W forms only. For example, item 1, advanced level, implies a definition of a cone that is unacceptable if one uses the precise terminology of modern mathematics. It states that a cone is "a solid which has a point at one end and a circle at the other end." The in-between portion is neglected entirely in this definition. Because a cone may be too difficult to define accurately at this level, it might have been more advisable to select a figure with an easier definition. Item 5 of the same test— "Which of these could be used as a divisor and not change a dividend?"—should be rephrased. (Do the authors mean quotient, rather than dividend?) Item 1 of the lower level test could be stated with less colloquial vagueness and more mathematical precision if instead of "any number minus zero is always....(b) that number," it read, "if you subtract zero from a number, the result is....(b) that number." Item 28 of this test could have more than one correct response. To the question, "In which of these sentences will you *add* to find the final value of *w*?" the following answers are plausible: (g) $4 = w - 6$ (add a positive 6 to each member) and (f) $9 = w + 3$ (add negative 3 to each member). Item 35, "A set of numbers is 'closed' for an operation when....(b) no more numbers are needed for the operation," could be challenged for its accuracy. It is the set that is closed, not the operation. Item 39 of the same test should also be rephrased. It reads, "A piece of paper is 1 ft. $1\frac{1}{4}$ in. long. The unit of measure used is." Obviously there are two units of measure referred to in the stem of the question, and a refinement of the item seems in order.

In conclusion, this test offers many challenging items, although some ambiguous ones are in need of editing and revision. Information regarding reliability, validity, and norms is not altogether satisfactory or sufficiently comprehensive. Troublesome factors exist in the tenor of the directions and in time requirements for administration. In view of these limitations the teacher might be well advised to consider alternative tests or approaches to the evaluation of success in modern mathematics at the elementary and junior high school levels.

J Ed Meas 3:331–4 w '66. B. R. Hopkins. * attempts to provide a measure of achievement for pupils in modern mathematics courses in grades 5 through 9.1. An efficient instrument designed for this purpose is presently needed as an aid in pupil guidance and curricular evaluation. The publishers are to be commended for their effort in this direction. * The general suggestions for administering the instrument are helpful and the directions for its administration are clear. An item-by-content outline is given which classifies the items into ten categories. Such could be an aid to diagnosing a class' or teacher's problem areas. Unfortunately no item statistics are presented to give further assistance in this task. * These data [on reliability] are judged to be insufficient since no data are presented to indicate the extent to which these coefficients are spuriously inflated due to the speededness of the test. In addition, the coefficients are somewhat liberal due to an extension in the range brought about by pooling the three administrations of the test for each grade level. That is, the October 1, March 1, and June 1 results are combined for the purpose of computing the reliability coefficients. Had the coefficients been computed for each administration of the test they would have been more appropriate and realistic. No mention as to the form on which the reliability data were obtained is made; more seriously, both forms use the same norm conversion tables. No data are provided to illustrate the degree to which the forms are equivalent in difficulty. * Several subject-matter specialists edited and reviewed all of the tests, and teacher reactions were sought. The relevant professional experience and qualifications of these specialists are not reported, nor are data presented to indicate the extent of their agreement. * The MMCT manual is grossly deficient in describing the sample on which the norms were derived. Strangely however the discussion of the norm group is preceded by the statement, "Therefore, the norm group must be described accurately and in detail, especially with respect to the amount of modern mathematics studied by pupils in the norm group." One wonders why such excellent advice was not heeded. No indication is given of the geographical regions sampled or the size, ethnic,

or socio-economic characteristics of the nine participating school systems. * Approximately 80 percent of the MMCT norm group is above the Otis median. Since the MMCT norm group is selective in this regard, it probably is also non-representative in other related characteristics such as reading skills, socio-economic status, attitude toward school, and degree of parental involvement. In addition, no information on the degree of selectivity introduced by the non-cooperating schools is given, which is apt to be substantial since only schools which returned a questionnaire were included in the sample. The nine undescribed school systems from seven unmentioned states introduces much ambiguity into the interpretation of normative data. * The norms presented in the manual have been adjusted to render them more comparable to the norms for the *Stanford Achievement Test* (SAT). "....the ability level of the standardization group was equated for ability with the standardization group for *Stanford Achievement Test.*" The details of the adjustment, the dependent variable(s) used in the regression equation, the tenability of the required assumptions, and the magnitude of the adjustments are omitted. It seems likely that the Otis IQ was the measure upon which the adjustment was made. An adjustment based upon a differential Otis IQ of approximately 10 points necessitates a careful scrutiny of the IQ X MMCT distribution for precise linearity. Two other unanswered questions of importance are (1) were both the SAT and MMCT norm groups administered the same instrument to assess ability, and (2) were the time intervals between the testings the same for both groups? Both issues would seriously attenuate the accuracy of any adjusting procedure. A more serious omission concerns the mathematical background of the participating pupils. "The major requirement for inclusion of a school system in the norm group was that the system had a *recognized* modern mathematics program in effect for a *reasonable* length of time in each of the grades (5–9) being tested." (Italics by reviewer.) This statement gives rise to several important but unanswered questions. Which are the "recognized" programs? Presumably the SMSG regular and UICSM texts are among the recognized programs. Does the SMSG-M text or the Ball State Teachers College program qualify? Which program approaches were actually included in the standardization sample? What is the breakdown by percentage of pupils for the various approaches involved? What constitutes a "reasonable" length of time? The group average was three years in a modern mathematics program. Did "reasonable" include a 2–8 year span in modern math background? These questions are especially relevant since they are needed to ascertain whether a given school district could be considered as a member of the population for which the norms apply. No empirical evidence is given to support the claim that "no one approach to modern mathematics is specifically favored." A table of means, standard deviations, and ability levels for the various approaches sampled would have been extremely reassuring to the skeptical. Another severe inadequacy of the MMCT manual is its deficient treatment of the relationship of MMCT test scores with years of background in the study of modern mathematics. It does not seem reasonable to suppose that students with a modern math background of two years perform as well as students with 4–8 years of study. The comparability of such groups cannot be assumed but must rest upon empirical verification. Of great interest and desirability would be a 2-way table (program type-by-years of study) indicating means, standard deviations, and ability levels for the doubly classified groups. Such a table would enable a prospective MMCT user to more readily ascertain the applicability of the instrument for his school district and also to enhance the interpretability of a test score. No data are given to insure the equivalence of scores obtained when using IBM answer sheets, MRC Harbor Cards, or booklet marking. Also no mention is made as to which method(s) was used in the standardization procedures. The interpretation of a MMCT score is vulnerable with respect to the gambling response set. No mention is made of any attempt to minimize or compensate for this set to guess either through explicit directions or by employing a correction formula. A group of beginning fifth grade "gamblers," *without the benefit of a test booklet,* would have an expected mean raw score of 13.5 which is converted to the 23rd percentile or stanine 4. The middle two-thirds of the gambling pupils would be expected to have percentile ranks between 6 and 46, and 95% between 2 and 64 without the benefit of any knowledge of the test content. With possible chance scores of this magnitude interpretation is severely hampered, particularly

with respect to the below-average pupil. The authors' statement concerning stanine norms: "Therefore, a pupil's achievement in various areas as expressed in stanine terms is an accurate portrayal of relative strengths and weaknesses," could be misleading to the uninstructed test consumer. One standard error of measurement added to some raw scores would increase the stanine value by two. A 95% confidence band could include as many as 6 stanine scores. *Summary.* The number and importance of the unreported and/or unknown considerations concerning reliability, validity, standardization, and interpretation lead the reviewer to consider the MMCT of uncertain value. With additional information and/or more adequate norming and standardization procedures, the instrument could prove to be a helpful tool for the purposes for which it is designed. A school district would be well advised to establish local norms for all its tests, but especially for the MMCT. Comparison of such norms would provide more meaningful information than could be obtained from a single set of norms.

[491]

★**Tests of Academic Progress: Mathematics.** Grades 9–12; 1964–66; Form 1 ('64, 15 pages); 4 levels (grades 9, 10, 11, 12) in a single booklet; no specific manual; battery teacher's manual ('64, 62 pages); battery manual for administrators, supervisors, and counselors ('65, 45 pages); battery norms booklet for IQ levels ('66, 26 pages); separate answer cards (MRC) must be used; 30¢ per test; $3 per 100 MRC answer cards; MRC keys not available; scoring service, 27¢ per test; $1.20 per battery teacher's manual; 96¢ per battery administrator's manual; 60¢ per battery norms booklet; $3 per specimen set of the complete battery; postage extra; 60(70) minutes; Dale P. Scannell and Gilbert Ulmer; Houghton Mifflin Co.*

REFERENCE

1. GOOLSBY, THOMAS M., JR. "The Appropriateness of the Tests of Academic Progress for an Experimental School." *Ed & Psychol Meas* 30(4):967–70 w '70. *

CARL J. HUBERTY, *Assistant Professor of Education, University of Georgia, Athens, Georgia.*

This test is one of six in the complete TAP battery. It is a multilevel test for grades 9–12 and consists of 102 multiple choice items, 51 items for each grade level: 1–51 for grade 9, 18–68 for grade 10, 35–85 for grade 11, and 52–102 for grade 12.

The mathematics test, as well as each of the other five in the battery, "was designed to measure the extent to which the objectives of [each] basic area of high school instruction have been achieved." It is also stated in the manuals that "the tests were constructed according to specifications reflecting currently accepted curriculum practices and were then reviewed by subject-matter specialists." It must be assumed, then, that the reference group for this test is made up of schools that, in 1963–64, incorporated acceptable mathematics curricula and courses of study. In selecting a test such as this, it would be helpful to have more information concerning the types of curricula and courses of study on which the norm data were based.

From the manuals it is most difficult to assess the validity of this test. Only content validity is touched upon, and even this aspect of validity is foggy, since the relevant professional experience and qualifications of the specialists employed are not reported. However, the teacher's manual does present a Content and Skill Outline, according to which the items are classified. There are appropriate decreases and increases in the numbers of items in each of the six categories (arithmetic, algebra, geometry, structure, properties of relations and functions, other topics) as one progresses from grade 9 to grade 12. For example, in Form 1 there are 25 "arithmetic" items for grade 9 and only seven for grade 12; there are no items pertaining to "properties of relations and functions" in the grade 9 test, but there are seven in the grade 12 test. The proportions of the 102 items in the respective categories in Form 2 are not at all similar to those for Form 1. A simple table depicting these differences would be informative for the consumer. In the classification, starred items were judged "likely to require the conscious application of basic mathematical principles." Such items are distributed quite well over grades, the only exception being that for grade 12 there are 9 items in Form 1 and 12 in Form 2. It is explicitly stated that the scores "should be quite predictive of success in colleges," but no evidence of such implied criterion-related validity is stated or cited. Upon contacting the publisher about data that were to be "published in technical reports and supplements as they become available," which would possibly reflect evidence of concurrent or predictive validity, the reviewer learned that only limited, inconclusive results were available.

The standardization data were obtained in the fall of 1963 for Form 1. The sampling plan appears quite good; however, the characteristics of the reference group employed are not clearly identified. The standardization sample was to represent the national population with respect to intelligence; however, information sufficient to judge representativeness is lacking. The sample is also said to have been stratified with respect to socioeconomic characteristics, but no details are indicated. Before referring to norm tables—group or individual—the consumer must ask if the reference group represents the unit of concern. From the information given, it would be most difficult to answer such a question. Norms for both school averages and individual performance are presented for each grade and for three test times (beginning, middle, and end of the year). Although three sets of norms are available for each grade, it is stated that the lone standardization sample was tested only at the beginning of the school year. Tables convert raw scores to standard scores (obtained by an equi-percentile method) for each grade and each form. Conversion of standard scores to percentile ranks is accomplished by going from marginal column entries (standard scores) to the table proper (percentile ranks) for school averages, but in the reverse direction for individual scores. Such inconsistency in tables may be confusing for some consumers. The authors indicate cautions in the interpretation of scores with respect to "national" norm data, and they emphasize the importance of local norms. Local norms may be obtained as part of an optional machine scoring service.

A supplementary manual is available in which percentile norms for IQ levels are reported. These norms are based on eight verbal IQ levels as measured by the *Lorge-Thorndike Intelligence Tests*. Mean sample size with respect to grade was over 2,000; however, the number of students in each IQ level is not reported.

Although two forms are available, complete normative data are given only for Form 1. Equivalence of the two forms is not obvious; no statistical evidence of such equivalence is reported, and, as mentioned earlier, the numbers of items in the classification categories for each grade for the two forms are quite different.

Reliability data (for Form 1) are quite impressive; coefficients, based on a split-test procedure, range from .85 to .92. Standard errors of measurement—both over the complete range of test scores and for average percentile ranks (in varying intervals)—are also presented, along with standard deviations. In all tables the standard errors and standard deviations are given in both raw score and standard score (mean of 50 and standard deviation of 10) units for all four grades. As the authors obligingly report, had an equivalent forms approach been used, the reliability probably would have been somewhat lower and the standard errors somewhat higher. Data which might reflect the speededness of the test are not given. The norms do indicate, however, that the test is either quite difficult or speeded, since a raw score of 30 (out of 51) attained at the end of the year by a ninth grader would place him at the 90th percentile. A score of 35 similarly places a twelfth grader.

The format of the test is good and the items are very well written. Some users may be bothered by the preponderance of the "none of the above" alternative—in 85 of the 102 items in Form 1. The inclusion of this alternative may be considered good practice, but its effectiveness as a "distractor" in this test is open to question. The proportion of individuals in the norming sample selecting the five alternatives is not given. On Form 1, only three out of the 85 items have "none of the above" as the correct answer. Other item characteristics, such as difficulty and discrimination indices, are also not reported. The appropriateness of this test as an end-of-year examination for tenth graders may be in doubt since only six out of the 51 items are classified as "geometry" items. A possible exception to the otherwise excellent item construction may be found by examining items 61 and 62. In item 61 the expression $(x - 3)(x + 5)$ is used in the stem, whereas $(x - 5)(x + 3)$ appears in the stem of item 62. The great similarity of symbols may interfere with the different processes which the examinee is asked to use in the two items.

Administration and scoring are straightforward, although the total administration time of 70–75 minutes may prove inconvenient in schools with 55-minute class periods.

In summary, this test, because of its 1963 normative data and content and the absence of concrete evidence of validity, can be recommended for use only if the consumer fully realizes its limitations. Despite the standardization shortcomings, individual teachers might react favorably to the blend of well constructed items dealing with both traditional and modern mathematics and to its multilevel character.

J. R. Jefferson Wadkins, *Associate Examiner in Mathematics, Educational Testing Service, Princeton, New Jersey.*

As an attempt to provide a valid test of achievement in secondary school mathematics for a sizable majority of the secondary school population in the United States, this test is quite successful. According to the manual for administrators the test is intended to be "neither traditional nor extremely modern. Approximately 50 per cent of the items are quite traditional; approximately 40 per cent embody the spirit of new mathematics without using new terminology; and 10 per cent use terminology that has been introduced into secondary-school mathematics in the past ten years." In my opinion, Form 1 is considerably more traditional than the manual would have us believe, but it is a very good traditional test. I found two items (out of 102 in Form 1) with serious mathematical errors. It is probable, however, that few, if any, students will be troubled by either of these items because the traditional nature of the test as a whole requires the student to make many "obvious," but unstated, assumptions. In such a context, therefore, he probably will not be bothered by loose or ambiguous terminology, even though he may have had excellent courses in which such looseness would have been reprehensible.

Each of the first two parts for grades 9 and 10 have 24 "word problems," i.e., questions in which the candidate must set up one or two equations, or inequalities, appropriate to the situation described. Grade 11 has 19 such items and grade 12 has 16. It is this emphasis that gives the test its more traditional flavor and sets the tone in which the candidate will approach the test as a whole. The items for grades 9 and 10 that are intended as "modern" are rather straightforward questions involving bases for systems of numeration or involving axioms for number systems. There are only a few questions on geometry in the parts for grades 9 and 10, and these are appropriate for the grade levels. The parts for grades 11 and 12 have considerable emphasis on Euclidean and analytic geometry, as would be expected. The terminology for geometry is quite neutral, and the wording is relatively tight and unambiguous, although the stickler for purity of language can find points to quibble over here and there—but, again, the tone of the test as a whole is such that the conscientious student will have few problems in deciding exactly what the intention of the questions is. For a detailed outline of the content of each form, the prospective user should consult the teacher's manual which contains a content classification for all questions on both forms. Most teachers will consider these classifications to be as accurate as any other except their own.

My harshest criticism of the test is that the bright student will find it rather dull and deficient in questions that reward ingenuity. The student who dislikes translating "real life" situations into algebraic language may also react so negatively that his score may not indicate in any way his mathematical abilities and achievements. On the other hand, this emphasis on "word problems" tends to neutralize the differences in measurement between "modern" and "traditional" methods of teaching that might otherwise occur; i.e., "word problems" are applications of the mathematics learned by either method and the only advantage will be to those who have achieved better results as far as applications to "real life" situations are concerned—or to those who have had courses in which the primary emphasis has been upon such "word problems." While I would scarcely recommend such application as the ultimate goal of secondary school mathematics teaching, it does have its place and it does form a common part of all secondary school curriculums.

In summary, TAP Mathematics is a good instrument for obtaining a measure of class achievement in mathematics, although it could well be misleading in individual cases for reasons already outlined. It is usually preferable for a test to be designed specifically for a particular program; however, this test could be used with some confidence in a variety of secondary school mathematics curriculums if national norms are desirable. The ambiguities in the questions will undoubtedly not bother the vast majority of conscientious students.

For a review of the complete battery, see 31.

[492]

★**Tests of Achievement in Basic Skills: Mathematics, Level C.** Grades 7–9; 1970–71; TABSM; test consists of 64 items each of which is designed to measure a particular objective; 4 scores: arithmetic skills, geometric concepts, modern mathematics concepts, total; Forms 1, 2, ('70, 7 pages); manual ('71, 13 pages); technical supplement ('71, 26 pages); norms for part and total scores consist of means and variances; item norms consist of percentages of tryout population answering a given item correctly; re-

liability data for total score only; separate answer sheets (Digitek) must be used; $7.50 per 35 tests; $2.75 per 35 answer sheets; $1.50 per set of hand scoring stencils; $2.25 per specimen set; postage extra; scoring service, 35¢ per test; [40–60] minutes; Robert R. Knapp (manual) and James C. Young; Educational and Industrial Testing Service. *

REFERENCE

1. YOUNG, JAMES C.; KNAPP, ROBERT R.; AND MICHAEL, WILLIAM B. "The Validity of the Tests of Achievement in Basic Skills for Predicting Achievement in General Mathematics and Algebra." *Ed & Psychol Meas* 30(4):951–4 w '70. *

[493]

★**Tests of Basic Experiences: Mathematics.** Prekgn–kgn, kgn–grade 1; 1970–71; 1 form; Levels K ('70, 34 pages), L ('70, 18 pages); for battery manual and accessories, see 33; $9 per 30 tests, postage extra; scoring service, $1.20 per test; (25) minutes; Margaret H. Moss; CTB/McGraw-Hill. *

For a review of the complete battery, see 33.

[494]

★**The Undergraduate Record Examinations: Mathematics Tests.** College; 1969–70; 5 tests: 1 field test, 4 modular tests; descriptive booklet ('70, 24 pages); for more complete information, see 671; Educational Testing Service. *
a) MATHEMATICS TEST. Forms RUR ('69, 17 pages), SUR ('70, 18 pages); 120(140) minutes.
b) MODULAR TESTS DESIGNED TO COMPLEMENT THE TWO-HOUR MATHEMATICS TEST. 45(55) minutes.
   1) *Abstract Algebra.* Forms K-RUR, K2-RUR, ('69, 14 pages).
   2) *Linear Algebra.* Form RUR ('69, 14 pages).
   3) *Real Analysis 1.* Form RUR ('69, 17 pages).
   4) *Real Analysis 2.* Form RUR ('69, 16 pages).

L. RAY CARRY, *Assistant Professor of Mathematics Education and Mathematics, The University of Texas, Austin, Texas.*

The items in these five mathematics tests are imaginative and have obviously been developed with great care. Many of the items require an insightful ability both to choose and apply correct procedures. This latter characteristic enhances one's confidence in the test as a predictor of success in graduate work.

The extensive statistical information made available includes individual score reports, frequency distributions of scaled scores by tested groups, and, on an optional basis, group item summaries. These data could be particularly useful for evaluating the effectiveness of a program relative to a specific college's objectives. In addition, the scaled scores for the mathematics test are statistical estimates of scaled scores for the *Graduate Record Examinations Advanced Mathematics Test.* Unfortunately, information is not available as to the level of accuracy which can be attached to these estimates, and, furthermore, the norming sample is not representative of all colleges and universities in the country. It is composed mainly of small (1,000–3,000 students) liberal arts colleges. Whether the student populations from a user college would differ from the norming sample one cannot say, but it is a reasonable possibility.

MATHEMATICS TEST. Each form is a 60-item test intended to assess the knowledge and ability of a mathematics major who has completed undergraduate work. Each form samples pre-calculus mathematics, manipulative techniques of calculus, theoretical aspects of calculus, sequences and series, linear algebra, abstract algebra, and miscellaneous analysis. About 75 percent of the items deal with analysis concepts and about 25 percent deal with algebraic concepts. The two forms appear to be parallel both in content and difficulty.

Some cautionary remarks are in order. First, the tests have reported reliabilities of .85 (the manual is not clear whether this figure applies to both forms). This is a good reliability for any mathematics test that is not homogeneous in content, but scores on the test should not be trusted to the extent that they become sole criteria for counseling students to enter graduate school. Second, the tests sample only certain content areas of analysis and algebra, omitting completely such topics as probability, statistics, and geometry (except analytic geometry). Although the tested content may be most relevant for predicting successful graduate study in mathematics, it omits much that is important in undergraduate mathematics.

In summary, the test should be very useful for evaluating the effectiveness of college mathematics programs in terms of the content tested. The limitations in content of the test restrict its usefulness for comprehensive evaluation of total programs. When used in connection with undergraduate grade point average and other predictive criteria, the test should be very helpful in counseling individual students concerning graduate study in mathematics. However, the test score should not be used as a sole criterion.

ABSTRACT ALGEBRA. This is a good 40-item test covering topics from groups, rings, and fields. Approximately half of the items deal with group theory, the remainder with rings and fields. The content represents what would likely be taught in a one-year upper level undergraduate course in abstract algebra. From relatively simple items about groups, the test progresses to include items concerning quotient groups, ideals, and polynomials over a field. The reliability is reported as .82, a little low for sensitive differentiation between students.

LINEAR ALGEBRA. This well-designed 40-item test includes 16 items on matrix theory, 12 on vector spaces, 12 on linear transformations, 7 on matrix manipulation, and 2 considered miscellaneous. (Some items are classified in two categories.) The content sampled is about what may be expected from a one-semester course in linear algebra taught at an advanced undergraduate level. Reliability is reported as .68. This figure is quite low for tests that are to be used for assessing individual student achievement. It is probably adequate for test use in evaluating group performance.

REAL ANALYSIS I. This is a 40-item test covering single variable calculus, multivariable calculus, sequences and series, questions related to specific functions, and theoretical questions. The content suggests an advanced course in applications of calculus. Some of the concepts tested include gradient, Jacobian, vector inner product, and partial derivative of a function of two real variables. The items are good and sample the intended content representatively. The reported reliability is .76, too low for using the test to make critical decisions concerning individuals, but again adequate for evaluating group performance.

REAL ANALYSIS 2. This 40-item test covers topics from foundations of number systems, metric topology, functions on metric spaces, sequences and series of function, differentiation, and integration. A few concepts which are tested include the notions of countability, compactness, uniform continuity, Lebesque measure, Dedekind cut, complete ordered field, and Cauchy sequence. The test covers very well the content of a one-year introductory course in real analysis, approximately fitting the description of Mathematics 11 and 12 from recommendations of the Committee on the Undergraduate Program in Mathematics. No norming data or reliability estimates are available for this test.

SUMMARY. The *Undergraduate Record Examinations: Mathematics Tests* represent the first available set of instruments that can profitably be used by college and university departments of mathematics for program evaluation. The modular tests can be used to pinpoint areas of strength and weakness. Of particular value in this regard is the availability of group performance data on an item-by-item basis.

Although the reviewer has made a few criticisms—e.g., a nonrepresentative norming sample and some slightly low reliabilities—he views this battery of tests as a welcome addition to available mathematics tests and considers the tests extremely well designed. There remains, however, one concern that demands the attention of the user. The battery should not be taken as testing comprehensively all important undergraduate mathematics content. It probably does test the content that is most important relative to preparation for graduate study in mathematics, but no part of the battery covers content that the Committee on the Undergraduate Program in Mathematics identifies as Mathematics 7 (Probability and Statistics), Mathematics 8 (Numerical Analysis), Mathematics 9 (Geometry or Differential Geometry), or Mathematics 10 (Applied Mathematics).

For reviews of the testing program, see 671.

[495]

★**Wisconsin Contemporary Test of Elementary Mathematics.** Grades 3-4, 5-6; 1967-68; WCTEM; 3 scores: facts, concepts, total; Forms A, B; 2 levels: grades 3-4 ('67, 10 pages), 5-6 ('67, 12 pages); manual ('68, 35 pages); $4.75 per 25 tests; separate answer sheets (Digitek-IBM 805, IBM 1230) may be used; $3 per 50 answer sheets; 75¢ per scoring stencil; $1 per specimen set; postpaid; Digitek-IBM 805 scoring service, 12¢ and over per test; 50(60-75) minutes; M. Vere DeVault, Elizabeth Fennema, K. Allen Neufeld, and Lewis B. Smith; Personnel Press, Inc. *

MARILYN N. SUYDAM, *Associate Professor of Education, The Pennsylvania State University, University Park, Pennsylvania.*

The WCTEM is designed as a "test whose content focuses on those mathematical facts and concepts....introduced into elementary mathematics curricula and texts primarily since 1962." Actually, between one-third and one-half of the 52 items for grades 3-4 and of the 60 items for grades 5-6 measure topics also found in pre-1962 texts. The WCTEM does assess "modern" content, using contemporary terminology and symbolism, to a greater extent than most current tests, however. Because the manual considers in detail the procedures used to establish content validity, one is more inclined to be critical of statements like the one quoted above than if the concern had not been so evident.

The WCTEM is suggested for independent use or "as a supplement to a traditional test."

Since there is no problem-solving section, independent use would not assess the full scope of the mathematics program.

The content of all the test items was compared with the content of one "extremely modern" and two "modern" texts. While this is a laudable (though limited) attempt to quantify content validity, a discussion of the two types of texts does not adequately describe them. Moreover, that the two forms have "comparable content validity" for the modern texts is not wholly supported by the data; e.g., in grade 5, the percentages of agreement between test and text are 75 and 77 for Form A and 83 and 90 for Form B. Later study of the equivalency of forms during norming indicated the need for separate norms tables in grades 3-4, though a single table can be used at grades 5-6.

How school personnel could classify their own program to determine how well the test will assess it, is unclear. Either identification of test items applicable to various texts or a list showing the content of each item would be helpful. Telling the sixth grade teacher that if he judges his program to be modern, then "about 88-90% of the items on Test A measure directly the content of his course" is rather misleading.

Accepted norm-test development criteria and procedures were followed and are concisely explained. Norm revision every two years and content revision every four years, if completed as anticipated, should extend usefulness.

Each test is divided into two equal parts, facts and concepts. The difference between types of items on the subtests, while defined, is not always apparent. Correlations between subtest and total scores range from .82 to .95, with median .92; and between subtests from .54 to .79, with median .67. These are high; the manual acknowledges that "the extent to which the two subtests measure distinctly different" aspects is yet unclear.

Correlations (based on very small samples) between total scores on the WCTEM and the combined score on the Arithmetic Concepts and Problem Solving sections of the *Iowa Tests of Basic Skills* average .75. Thus, there is "some difference" in what is being tested, but a later statement that "on the whole a different set of content" is being measured does not seem justified. If the test is to be useful as a supplement, this correlation should be lower. Mean correlations between subtests are correspondingly high, averaging .65, also indicative that some content from WCTEM subtests is measured by each ITBS subtest.

Studies indicate that the reliability of the WCTEM is high. Internal consistency of Form A was estimated (K-R 20) for samples of over 300 pupils at each grade. Correlations ranged from .88 to .91 for the total test. Data from two geographically different groups, each with approximately 200 pupils per grade, indicated coefficients (Hoyt's method) of .85 to .89.

To speed preparation, norms were built with data from actual users, since there is (uncited) "evidence from the field" that users of modern textbooks are characterized by higher-than-average socioeconomic level, per pupil costs, and student ability. Characteristics of the norm groups are presented, but it is difficult to judge how appropriate the norms are for specific groups.

The test is easily administered, with very explicit directions for administration, scoring, and using norms tables. Suggestions for using test results in instruction are discussed in some detail. Booklets are easy to use, with items generally well-spaced.

With the overall time limit, the first part may be basically untimed while pressure mounts on the last half. Error variance could be increased by directions to work quickly, guessing if necessary. The 60–75 minute sitting seems long, particularly for third graders, on a test which has two parts.

Even though some details need further consideration by authors and publishers, the WCTEM is basically a well constructed test. If the content validity is determined to be appropriate for a given situation, then the WCTEM, supplemented by a problem solving section, should be useful in measuring the achievement of pupils using contemporary textbooks.

J Ed Meas 6(2):125–6 su '69. Robert A. Smith. * attractively designed and easily administered. It is a reasonably priced short test that is administered in one sitting. Printing, paper, and other physical characteristics of the test are of excellent quality. * Pupils are encouraged "to finish all the questions before time is called, even if you have to guess at some." This attempt to minimize the gambling response set variance, when coupled with a 10 minute warning, could conceivably increase

error variance due to random marking, particularly for the second half of the test. * The composition of the schools in the norming group is detailed in terms of socioeconomic level, location, student ability, and size. Unfortunately, there is no indication if any of these factors differentially influenced the norms. A discussion of the effects of the factors would have been most helpful in assisting the user to judge the degree of "fit" between his pupils and the norm groups. Kuder-Richardson Formula 20 was used to provide estimates of internal consistency, since "WCTEM is essentially a work-limit test." No data are presented to substantiate the assertion. The particular method of administering the test—no common starting time for the second half—could cause the second half of the test and the entire test to be a time limit test. * The test is designed to focus "on those mathematical facts and concepts which have been introduced into elementary mathematics curriculum and texts primarily since 1962." An examination of the items in one test (Form A Grades 3–4) indicated that 14 of the 26 items in Part I and 10 of the 26 items in Part II were covered in pre-1962 textbooks. Since the test is designed for use as an index of pupil accomplishment in contemporary mathematics or as a supplement to a traditional test, it would have been most helpful to identify test items applicable to the various modern texts so the content validity could be measured by the local school district. A mean correlation of .75 with the Iowa Test of Basic Skills (ITBS) is offered as evidence that "the WCTEM test measures something different than the ITBS and other tests of traditional arithmetic." In light of the avowed purpose (as a supplement to a traditional test) of the test, it would seem this correlation should be considerably lower. The absence of a problem solving test would make it difficult to use this test for its second stated purpose (as an overall index of pupil accomplishment in mathematics). A division between mathematics facts and concepts is admittedly arbitrary and in the context of the present test seems unnecessary. SUMMARY. Major problems are encountered regarding the validity of this test for its avowed purposes. * a problem solving section and identification of items specific to post 1962 mathematics texts are needed. The test does meet an operational definition of validity and in this context has much to recommend its usage for evaluating levels of group accomplishment.

ALGEBRA

[496]

*Algebra Tests. High school; 1933–70; 3 levels; no manual; no data on reliability; no norms; $1 per 10 tests, postpaid; 25¢ per single copy, cash orders only; 50(55) minutes; Robert J. Bryant; High School Testing Service, Purdue University. *
a) ALGEBRA TEST, FIRST SEMESTER. 1933–70; 1 form ('70, 5 pages).
b) ALGEBRA TEST, SECOND SEMESTER. 1933–70; 1 form ('70, 5 pages).
c) ALGEBRA, THIRD YEAR. 1934–70; 1 form ('70, 8 pages).

[497]

*Blyth Second-Year Algebra Test, Revised Edition. Grades 9–12; 1953–66; Forms E, F, ('66, 8 pages); manual ('66, 18 pages); $8.70 per 35 tests; $1 per key; separate answer sheets (Digitek-IBM 805, IBM 1230) may be used; $2.30 per 35 Digitek-IBM 805 answer sheets; $2.80 per 35 IBM 1230 answer sheets; 70¢ per scoring stencil; $1.50 per specimen set; postage extra; scoring service, 19¢ and over per test; 40(50) minutes; M. Isobel Blyth; Harcourt Brace Jovanovich, Inc. *

PETER A. LAPPAN, JR., *Professor of Mathematics, Michigan State University, East Lansing, Michigan.*

Each form of the *Blyth Second-Year Algebra Test* consists of 50 questions in a 5-option multiple choice format. The test covers the basic content of second year algebra courses as taught with a "modern" flavor. The individual questions are worded in such a way as to be fair to almost all pupils with a moderate exposure to "modern mathematics," regardless of the particular text used. The questions, both individually and as a whole, emphasize understanding rather than manipulative skill, although the ability to manipulate algebraic symbols is certainly measured by a reasonable number of questions. The time of 40 minutes allowed for the test would seem adequate for a pupil to read and answer all the questions within his ability at a not too hurried pace. The instructions in the manual for administering and scoring the test are complete and straightforward.

This test is well conceived and well constructed. Every major topic that could reasonably be expected to receive any emphasis in the second year of algebra is adequately covered. The questions range over a wide variety of difficulty levels, but there are not a great many

questions to challenge the very best students. The questions as a whole can be expected to maintain the pupils' interest. Many of the questions focus on an intermediate step in the solution process, rather than on the final answer, and this seems to be a reasonable method of testing understanding of the underlying concepts. None of the questions involves a detailed computation—and the total absence of such questions is a weakness of the test—but there is sufficient emphasis on basic computations of all varieties to provide a reasonable measure of computational skill.

An interesting feature of the test is the answer choice "DK," meaning "Don't Know," appearing as the fifth choice of each question. The advertised reason for including this choice is to provide a response indicating that the pupil knows he is unable to solve the problem. (In most multiple choice tests, the pupil who knows he is unable to solve the problem can either not respond at all or else make a wild guess.) In theory, the DK choice should minimize the effects of wild guessing, since the pupil is instructed to make the DK choice rather than make a wild guess among the other four choices. The manual suggests that the DK response worked well in tryouts and claims that it should minimize the effects of wild guessing. But it should be apparent that the pupil who marks the DK response cannot possibly expect to increase his score, while the pupil who makes a wild guess among the other four choices has a positive expectation of increasing his score, which is the total number of correct answers. Thus, the effectiveness of the DK response might depend upon the general classroom atmosphere and the importance placed by the pupils upon obtaining the highest possible score. There seems a danger here of creating a situation in which dishonesty might be profitable. If wild guessing were considered a serious threat to the value of the scores, it might have been better and fairer either to introduce some correction factor (such as a penalty for incorrect answers) or else simply to encourage wild guessing for those questions for which the pupil had inadequate knowledge. The reviewer considers the DK choice as a noble but ill-conceived device which should have little, if any, bearing on the effectiveness of the test.

Regardless of the wisdom of using the DK choice, the reviewer is somewhat disappointed that no instructions are provided for use of the DK choice as a diagnostic tool. It would be very valuable to a teacher to be aware of those questions which his pupils were, by their own admission, unable to handle. If the test were administered under conditions which encouraged all pupils to use the DK-response honestly—most pupils probably would do so anyway, without any unusual encouragement—the information theoretically made available would be put in a form that the teacher could interpret. Probably a simple tally of the number of DK responses for each question would be the most useful single statistic relating to the DK response, and this could be obtained very quickly and easily. Armed with this tally, the teacher could then probe further and perhaps pinpoint the sources of difficulty.

There are a few flaws in the makeup of the test, most notably that the figures are quite small and sometimes not very clear as to intent; in one case the figure is inaccurate enough to raise doubts about the correct answer. Although a moderate amount of editing could improve future editions of this test, the flaws detected by this reviewer are quite minor and do not detract from a very good job of test construction.

The manual contains much statistical information that a teacher with minimal training might realistically be expected to use. In particular, there appears a brief summary of the item analysis from the 1965 norming population. A careful examination of this item analysis will reveal that very similar questions on the two forms sometimes give quite different results. A further examination suggests that the positioning of these questions on the test contributes to this difference, with later questions being more difficult than similar earlier ones. Although teachers may find these item analyses a useful guide, care should be taken in drawing firm conclusions from a comparison of the performance of a particular class with the published item analysis.

This test accomplishes its objective very well and is to be recommended for use as an end-of-course examination for second-year algebra classes. It should be emphasized that it measures basic understanding and so may not be an adequate measure of topics given special emphasis by a specific text or teacher. Thus, it is probably appropriate not as a final examination on which a pupil's grade should be based but rather as a supplementary examination. Al-

though it is to be hoped that teachers would not teach toward any specific test, the teacher who teaches toward this test will at least be aiming his students in the right general direction, both in content and in spirit, toward the kind of mathematics they should be learning.

G. EDITH ROBINSON, *Associate Professor of Mathematics, The University of Georgia, Athens, Georgia.*
According to the manual, this test

is designed to measure what is currently being taught in algebra at the tenth grade level * the appropriateness of each objective measured by the test was determined according to the frequency of its inclusion in current mathematics-education materials. Widely-used textbooks of various publishers, representative courses of study, publications of educational and mathematical associations, recommendations by notable experts in the field of mathematics, and pronouncements of professional committees and commissions were all taken into consideration in the selection of objectives and in the writing of items to measure those objectives.

Thus any criticism of this test would appear to be wholesale criticism of some 15 years of curricular reform in high school algebra. Be that as it may, the test is essentially one of facts and skills. As with any standardized test, a school can administer it and determine how the scores of its students compare with those of students throughout the United States on the same test.

The authors make no claim that the test measures what *ought* to be taught in second year high school algebra. About 40 percent of the items on each form cover such "new" topics as sets and the properties of number systems, but as already indicated, the items are cast in terms of facts or skills. Thus, for example, the student is asked to identify "$x + 7 = 7 + x$" as an instance of the commutative, associative, transitive, or distributive property (or to reply that he doesn't know).

There are items on graphs, absolute value, determinants, complex numbers, arithmetic and geometric progressions, factoring, quadratic equations, and powers and exponents. A few verbal problems are also included. There are some inequalities to solve, and some literal equations. Absent are questions requiring anything but the most elementary deductions and questions using quantifiers. Thus, in one item the student is to select the expression equal to a given one, when, in fact, for different replacements of the variable, any one of the foils *could* equal the given expression. Probably most students would know which is the "right" answer, but it seems to this reviewer that including the phrase, "for all real replacements of *a* and *b*" would make the item more appropriate for students whose algebra preparation has included some attention to precision of language.

One of the distinctive features of the test is the inclusion of a "Don't Know" foil for each item. According to the manual, experimental subjects did make increasing use of this choice as item difficulty increased. Since the elimination of guessing reduces the probability that a correct answer is obtained accidentally, it seems reasonable to suppose that this gives a fairer assessment of a student's achievement in the areas measured by this test.

In summary, this is a test of facts and skills, the content covering both traditional second year algebra and some "modern" topics. The questions require little thought on the part of the student, and, as advised by the authors in the manual, a school desiring an achievement test for second year algebra must assess the test's validity in terms of the goals it has set for its own algebra program.

For reviews by Paul Blommers and Myron F. Rosskopf of the original edition, see 5:443.

[498]

★**CLEP Subject Examination in College Algebra.** 1 semester or equivalent; 1968–70; for college accreditation of nontraditional study, advanced placement, or assessment of educational achievement; 2 parallel editions: 90 and 45 minute tests; for program accessories, see 664; program administered for the College Entrance Examination Board by Educational Testing Service. *
a) 90 MINUTE EDITION. Tests administered monthly at regional centers throughout the United States; tests also available for institutional testing at any time; Form RCT1 ('68, 23 pages); separate answer sheets (SCRIBE) must be used; rental and scoring fee, $5 per student; 90(95) minutes.
b) 45 MINUTE EDITION. Available only for institutional testing; Forms QSL1 ('68, 11 pages), QSL2 ('68, 12 pages); separate answer sheets (Digitek-IBM 805, IBM 1230) must be used; rental fee, 75¢ per student; scoring service not available; 45(50) minutes.

For reviews of the testing program, see 664 (3 reviews).

[499]

★**Contemporary Mathematics Test: Algebra.** 1 year grades 8–9; 1965–66; for all tests in the series, see 464; developed to supplement the *California Achievement Tests*; Forms W, X, ('65, 11 pages); no specific manual; series manual, revised ('66, 14 pages); series technical report ('66, 30 pages); IBM 1230 directions ('65, 4 pages); $5.50 per 35 tests; separate answer sheets (IBM 1230) may be used; $2.50 per 50 answer sheets; $1 per scoring stencil;

$1 per technical report; 15¢ per IBM directions; postage extra; $2 per specimen set of any one level, postpaid; scoring service, 22¢ and over per test; 45(50) minutes; CTB/McGraw-Hill. *

PETER A. LAPPAN, JR., *Professor of Mathematics, Michigan State University, East Lansing, Michigan.*

The advertised purpose of the test is "to assess knowledge of concepts unique to the several most widely taught modern mathematics programs." Each form of the test consists of 54 questions in a 3- and 4-response multiple choice format. These questions are separately numbered over two parts, with the first part containing 29 questions concentrating on "Algebraic Expressions and Operations" and the second part containing 25 questions concentrating on "Structure, Sentences, and Functions." The parts are not timed or scored separately. Information concerning norms obtained in 1965 is supplied in the manual, with more detailed statistical data given in the technical report.

Unfortunately, the test does not live up to its stated purpose for a variety of reasons, the most prominent of which is that those persons most influential in the construction of the test do not seem to have been conversant with the spirit of "modern mathematics." "Modern mathematics" attempts to stress understanding rather than rote learning. In doing so, it introduces a vocabulary in order to state, and aid in the understanding of, the concepts considered. The teacher or testmaker who is not aware of the spirit of "modern mathematics" can easily make the error of stressing vocabulary rather than concept, and stressing memory rather than understanding. Those who constructed this test seem to have made this error. The test puts a heavy stress on vocabulary and very rarely gets at the concepts which are supposed to be clarified by the vocabulary. The questions individually and as a whole fail to measure understanding.

Although the manual suggests that this test should be used in conjunction with the *California Achievement Tests* for an adequate coverage of both modern and traditional materials, some traditional material is covered in this test. However, the questions of a more traditional nature are all fairly straightforward, with no elaborate or multi-step reasoning involved. Certain topics, such as completing the square and situations in which a solution set is the empty set or the universal set, are overemphasized, while story problems are conspicuous by their almost total absence. As noted above, the questions involving modern mathematics are generally superficial and directed more toward recall than understanding.

In addition to the difficulties arising from a lack of a feel for modern mathematics, numerous flaws in test construction also exist. The wording in a great majority of the questions is ill-chosen, with several instances of grammatical or typographical errors. There is one question (Form X, Part 2, item 3) having no correct answer choice listed, and there are numerous questions where the wording is sufficiently ambiguous that the pupil must read the mind of the testmaker to determine the choice to be scored as correct. In a few cases, the answer choices are listed in a deceptive order; in one blatant instance, the answer choices are figures numbered in the reverse order of their appearance. That this was apparently done to make the same key work for both forms is not a valid excuse for such lack of consideration for the pupil.

The questions dealing with the topic of "proof and the nature of proof" are especially poor questions. In most cases the wording is sloppy and the question is unclear, even though a pupil of average ability could probably realize the intent of the test maker. For example, one particularly bad question appearing on Form W reads: "Some Happies have six toes. Bongo has seven toes. Therefore, Bongo is not a Happy." The answer choices are: "1. True under *all* circumstances. 2. Impossible to tell. 3. False under *all* circumstances." Despite the fact that no instructions or guidelines are given as to what question is asked—the "question" consists of three declarative sentences—it is probably obvious to a majority of pupils that the question intends to ask whether the statement "Bongo is not a Happy" is true or false, assuming that the first two statements are true. However, a second legitimate question a reasonable person might ask is whether the entire syllogism is true (valid reasoning) or false (invalid reasoning), and this question has a much different answer. The wording of the answer choices indicates some confusion about the meaning of the words "true" and "false" in the testmakers' minds. It should further be noted that these same answer choices appear verbatim in five questions on each form of the test.

The reviewer cannot recommend that this test be used in any school under any conceivable circumstances, with the possible exception of using it as an example of what not to do in the construction of a test. It is difficult to believe that the elaborate procedures described in the Technical Report for developing and trying out the test could result in such a weak product. The only conclusions possible are that those responsible were either spectacularly careless or unfamiliar with sound test construction techniques.

SHELDON S. MYERS, *Chairman, Mathematics Department, Educational Testing Service, Princeton, New Jersey.*

This test contains a rather wide sampling of such contemporary topics as set language and notations, the field properties of the real number system, absolute value, inequalities, the number line, functional notation, and propositional logic. Thus, it lives up to the label "contemporary" in its title more than many so-called contemporary tests in recent years. The test seems to be reasonably fair for the variety of contemporary programs now in existence.

A comparison of the two forms shows that, except for a few common questions, they are parallel in difficulty and topical coverage but not in actual questions. They could therefore be used in pretesting and posttesting situations without undue practice effects.

The test is moderate in difficulty and seems to be adjusted to average classes taking contemporary algebra rather than to more able advanced placement groups. Part 1 in each of the two forms of the test largely measures straightforward knowledge and routine manipulation, while Part 2 seems to contain more applications and questions on reasoning with concepts.

The technical report is thorough and well done, although the average teacher will probably not be able to understand all of the technical statistics that it contains. The technical report indicates that the algebra forms were carefully developed with respect to sampling the content of modern programs, pretesting of questions, statistical and sampling procedures in norming and standardizing. There seems to be a reasonable awareness of the shifting, changing nature of the curriculum and sound advice is offered teachers in the use of the normative data.

However, with the obviously expensive care

taken in the statistical procedures for the development of the test, it is regrettable that serious errors appear in the final tests. In spite of four to eight evaluations by professional experts, it appears that the questions were not subjected to at least one highly critical, high-level, mathematical review. A glaring example of what such a review should catch is the question which asks which property is demonstrated by a certain expression. The intended answer is "the associative property in multiplication" but, clearly, "the identity element in multiplication" is also a possible answer and is listed among the choices. The difficulty arises from the fact that the expression as presented goes too far and includes the step $\frac{2}{11} \cdot 11 = 2$. Another question asks that a polynomial be "factored over the integer," instead of "factored over the integers."

For six questions in Form X and five questions in Form W, the following three-choice format is used: (1) True under *all* circumstances; (2) Impossible to tell; (3) False under *all* circumstances. Serious logical difficulties arise in the attempt to standardize these choices for these different questions. Sometimes it is not clear what is meant by "circumstances." For some kinds of statements, a single exception or counter-example makes (3) the correct answer; for other kinds of statements, the exceptions make (2) the correct answer. This reviewer recommends that this standard format be abandoned and the choices worded to fit closely the particular statement being considered.

While there exists a rationale for alternating the choice labels "a, b, c, d" with "e, f, g, h" from item to item, it becomes difficult to justify mixing a third set of labels "1, 2, 3, 4" at irregular intervals.

The K-R 21 reliabilities of .80 and .81 appear to be correct, especially since the tests are power, rather than speeded, tests. These reliabilities are about what one would expect to get with 50-item tests with wide variety of content given to what the technical report implies were selected, somewhat homogeneous groups. On the basis of these reliabilities the test can be useful for group comparisons and curricular assessments. They would have to be used with more caution and with an eye on the standard error of measurement when used for individual comparisons.

In conclusion, this reviewer finds the test to be a very promising, forward-looking examination which, in spite of a few technical and substantive errors, should prove useful in group evaluations of contemporary algebra.

For excerpts from reviews of the series, see 464.

[500]

*Cooperative Mathematics Tests: Algebra I and II. Grades 8–9, 10–12; 1962–65; for all tests in the series, see 465; Forms A, B, ('62, 7 pages); 2 levels; no specific manual; series manual ('64, 79 pages); student bulletin ('65, 2 pages) for each test; separate answer sheets (Digitek, IBM 805, IBM 1230, SCRIBE) must be used; $6 per 20 tests; $4 per 100 answer sheets; $1.25 per 10 IBM hand scoring stencils (answer pattern must be punched out locally); Digitek scoring stencils not available; $2 per series manual; $3 per 100 student bulletins; $3 per specimen set of the series; cash orders postpaid; SCRIBE scoring and statistical analysis service, 35¢ per test; 40(45) minutes; Cooperative Tests and Services. *
a) ALGEBRA I. 1 semester grades 8–9.
b) ALGEBRA II. Grades 10–12.

REFERENCES

1. ALI, MD. BASHARAT. *To Establish the Feasibility of Using Translated and Adapted Versions of an American-Made Mathematics Achievement Test in East Pakistan.* Doctor's research study No. 1, Colorado State College (Greeley, Colo.), 1964. (*DA* 28:115A)
2. LOVFTT, CARL JAMES. *An Analysis of the Relationship of Several Variables to Achievement in First Year Algebra.* Doctor's thesis, University of Texas (Austin, Tex.), 1969. (*DAI* 30:1470A)
3. CALDWELL, JAMES R.; MICHAEL, WILLIAM B.; SCHRADER, DONALD R.; AND MEYERS, C. E. "Comparative Validities and Working Times for Composites of Structure-of-Intellect Tests and Algebra Grades and Composites of Traditional Test Measures and Algebra Grades in the Prediction of Success in Tenth-Grade Geometry." *Ed & Psychol Meas* 30(4):955–9 w '70. *
4. MORGAN, WILLIAM P. "Prediction of Success in Junior College Mathematics." *Math Teach* 63(3):260–3 Mr '70. *

KENNETH J. TRAVERS, *Associate Professor of Mathematics Education, University of Illinois, Urbana, Illinois.*

These relatively short tests (40 items) appear to achieve to a commendable degree the stated aim for each test in the series, that, "Where possible, many of the newer trends and emphases in mathematics are represented in the tests, but content has been selected carefully to ensure the appropriateness of the tests for most students."

ALGEBRA I. The content classification of the items as reported in the manual was found by this reviewer to be a fairly accurate reflection of the kind and difficulty level of topics in current first courses in high school algebra. K-R 20 reliabilities based on randomly selected subsamples of size 300 for each form and separately for eighth and ninth grades are between .84 and .86. Speededness data on these same samples reveal that more than 97 percent of the students answered 30 of the 40 items while 82 to 91 percent answered all. It seems reasonable to eliminate speed as an important factor for these tests.

The items are clearly stated and generally unambiguous. One exception is an item referring to *"the square root"* (italics added) of a number, expecting, apparently, the positive square root. Common usage appears to prefer *"a square root,"* making it clear that either the positive or negative root is acceptable.

A more important comment concerning the quality of the items has to do with the level of cognitive behavior (in the sense of Bloom and his taxonomy) which each samples. By and large, the items would seem to require thinking at lower levels, such as comprehension or knowledge, rather than at the higher levels of analysis or synthesis.

Norms are provided for a highly representative national sample (126 high schools, drawn from public, Roman Catholic, and independent institutions in 36 states). Urban norms are drawn from schools in the national sample located in cities of at least 100,000 in population. The test developers are to be commended for their care in constructing the norms to represent accurately schools of various types (public, private) and sizes.

Caution should be exercised by persons interpreting the test results for eighth grade students. Apparently, as is pointed out in the manual, the norming sample of eighth grade was very capable, and in many cases performed better than the ninth grade group. This is not surprising, since we might expect that schools offering algebra earlier than the usual pattern would offer it primarily to the most able students.

ALGEBRA II. Prospective users of this test will find that the items adequately sample topics dealt with in at least the first semester of second-year algebra courses currently being taught. But, in some cases, this test will offer inadequate coverage since topics such as trigonometry, determinants, and properties of polynomials, which are recently more common in algebra II classes, are deferred until subsequent tests in this series (viz., trigonometry and algebra III).

As in the Algebra I test, the test items here do not often sample cognitive behavior above the comprehension or application stage. Those who would wish a model which is helpful in describing and testing higher levels of mathematical thought (so commonly pleaded for by contemporary mathematics educators) will be interested in the work of Avital.[1]

One category in the content classification for the items, that of "solution of quadratic equations and inequalities," did not help this reviewer in obtaining a true picture of the test's coverage. The difficulty is that on the surface these important concepts receive but limited sampling (1 item so categorized in Form A, 2 in Form B). Sampling is found to be more thorough, however, when additional items are found in other classifications (particularly, "solution of systems of equations and inequalities" and "properties of quadratic functions").

The K-R 20 reliabilities, based on randomly selected subsamples of size 300 for grades 10 through 12, are .84 and .89 for Forms A and B, respectively. Speededness data on these same samples indicate that while over 95 percent of the students answered 30 of the 40 items, only between 68 and 71 percent of the students completed the tests. Therefore, speededness does appear to be a factor which may influence the scores.

GENERAL COMMENTS. Overall, these tests are well constructed, easy to administer, and should meet the needs of educators having a wide variety of testing objectives. The manual is thorough, precise, and informative. Objections previously raised (see 6:594) concerning inadequacies of the normative data in earlier versions of the manual have now been met to a large extent. Since only illustrative data are provided for suburban schools, it is hoped that complete normative information for these schools will soon be available.

Illustrative uses of test scores (such as employment of item information by teachers to assess the progress of students in their own classes) are given in the manual, together with difficulty levels of the items for random samples of students in the national norms groups. Although individual item discrimination indices are not reported, means and standard deviations of the distribution of these indices are provided.

A feature of the series which should serve to reduce anxiety arising from anticipation of the tests is a student bulletin. This short, well-worded statement gives a brief explanation of the nature of the tests and provides sample items to be attempted.

1 AVITAL, SHMUEL M., AND SHETTLEWORTH, SARA J. *Objectives for Mathematics Learning: Some Ideas for the Teacher.* Ontario Institute for Studies in Education, Bulletin No. 3. Toronto, Canada: the Institute, 1968. Pp. vii, 57. *

For a review by Paul Blommers, see 6:594. For excerpts from reviews of the series, see 465 (2 excerpts).

[501]
Cooperative Mathematics Tests: Algebra III.
High school and college; 1963–65; for all tests in the series, see 465; Forms A, B, ('63, 7 pages); no specific manual; series manual ('64, 79 pages); student bulletin ('65, 2 pages); separate answer sheets (Digitek, IBM 805, IBM 1230, SCRIBE) must be used; $6 per 20 tests; $4 per 100 answer sheets; $1.25 per 10 IBM hand scoring stencils (answer pattern must be punched out locally); Digitek scoring stencils not available; $2 per series manual; $3 per 100 student bulletins; $3 per specimen set of the series; cash orders postpaid; SCRIBE scoring and statistical analysis service, 35¢ per test; 40(45) minutes; Cooperative Tests and Services. *

JAMES R. CALDWELL, *Counselor, Alhambra High School, Alhambra; and Visiting Professor of Educational Psychology, University of Southern California, Los Angeles; California.*

This test was designed to measure "understanding and achievement in advanced secondary school or college algebra." The test items were constructed to assess performance in terms of an individual's grasp of the basic concepts, skills, and unifying principles.

The catalog reports that in this test, "traditional topics are combined with more contemporary material such as inequalities and functional notation." The authors fail to describe adequately, however, the similarities and differences between "traditional" and "contemporary" college algebra. When the reviewer consulted chairmen of mathematics departments from three Southern California high schools, most had difficulty in articulating the differences between these two approaches. Therefore, a more adequate coverage of this issue could prove profitable for both the test publisher and the test user. The department chairmen independently agreed that basically the test reflected a traditional curriculum and approach.

From the above discussions and personal investigations, this reviewer attempted to determine how this test tended to differ from a modern curriculum and approach. Modern curricula that pursue all levels of mathematics from a field-system approach stress that Algebra III is a way of thinking as well as a way of computing problems. More emphasis is placed on logical and analytical thinking. As well as being required to compute a reasonably complex problem using logarithms, for example, students would have to understand the meaning of a logarithm in greater depth than a traditional approach would develop. Some modern curricula approach college algebra as a course in fundamental concepts of analysis. Teachers who subscribe to these modern curricula may need an alternative test, or at least supplementary test items, which could better assess some of these modern trends.

Rather than prescribe a particular curriculum, the authors note that the test samples "widely-shared elements of existing curricula." The included item classification table categorizes each test item into one of 16 broad topical headings. In both forms, two of these categories contain only one item each, while six other categories each contain only two items. Consequently, the test might prove misleading when a teacher attempts to determine which of the broad categories are troublesome for individual pupils or classes. Extreme caution should be observed in generalizing from one or two items to a broad category of concepts and principles.

Throughout the development phase of the test, the authors explain, carefully devised procedures were followed to ensure maximum content validity. Additional validity information was supplied through the inclusion of correlation coefficients between the Algebra III test and the quantitative score on the *School and College Ability Test.* The usefulness of this test would be further enhanced if research were carried out in three other areas. Independent follow-up studies of criterion-related validity would be helpful. Since Algebra III is one of a set of sequential tests with one common manual, programmers could benefit by knowing to what degree a student's performance on the Algebra II Test predicts his success on the Algebra III Test. The extent of success in analytic geometry predicted by the Algebra III Test scores would also be useful. Since a related research problem involves multiple predictors, placement would benefit from knowledge of the likelihood of the Algebra III Test scores raising a multiple validity coefficient when combined with variables like grades, CEEB scores, and IQ scores to predict success in analytic geometry, for example. The manual does not offer expectancy tables for Algebra III taken singly or combined with other variables.

While the authors report K-R 20 reliabilities of .84 and .80 for both forms, they fail to include alternate-form reliability. Information on the test's general variance, based on a time interval between the two testing sessions, would prove valuable in estimating score variance due to relatively permanent abilities and habits. This would also provide information on the effect of speededness on the reported K-R 20 co-efficients. The authors admit that in the Co-operative Mathematics Series, the Algebra I Test is the only one "for which speededness can be regarded as relatively unimportant." Of the Algebra III college norm sample, only 48.9 and 51.1 percent answered the last item on the two forms of the test. Only 85.1 and 88.4 percent of the norm group reached the test's three-quarter point. Understandably, the authors admit that "it is not possible with the available data to isolate the uncontaminated effect of speededness."

An outstanding feature in the technical report is the adequacy of normative information. In addition to high school norms and national college norms, norms are supplied for three major fields of college study: education, liberal arts, and engineering. This information allows the test interpreter to compare a student's score with scores from students in the national college norm group or with students from each of the three fields of study. Additional evidence of the outstanding treatment and development of normative data includes the selection of representative samples of students in independent, public, and Roman Catholic schools; the identification of specific schools and states for each norm sample; and the availability of a separate ETS publication informing how to construct and interpret local norms. One omission the reviewer noted was the lack of demographic information concerning the norm subjects' distribution with respect to sex and minority group membership. A rationale supporting the selection of the three specific college major fields as norm subgroups, to the exclusion of others, would have been helpful. A mathematics non-engineering norm group, for instance, may have performance characteristics different from the engineering subgroup.

The manual's directions for interpretation of test scores are excellent. The norms tables present both raw scores and converted scores, the raw scores having been equated statistically and transformed to a common score scale so that both Algebra III forms are relatively comparable. The norms tables express percentile ranks both as mid-percentile ranks and percentile bands, which increases the probability of accurate score interpretations.

In conclusion, Algebra III is probably superior to any other existing college algebra test. The norm information and directions for score interpretation are excellent. The test could be more beneficial, however, with the inclusion of more information regarding "traditional" and "modern" curricula as well as follow-up studies on criterion-related validity. Improvements could be made by placing more emphasis on analytical thinking, and by having a greater number of test items included in some of the 16 broad categories. Perhaps some consideration should be given to adding a second part, which would be similar to the format of the geometry test in the Cooperative Mathematics Tests series.

WILLARD G. WARRINGTON, *Director, Office of Evaluation Services, Michigan State University, East Lansing, Michigan.*

In the early 1960's the Cooperative Test Division (CTD) developed a new series of tests in mathematics. This new series covers areas previously tested and, in addition, introduces tests for several new areas of mathematics at both the high school and college levels. Algebra III is one of these tests. CTD materials describe this new test as follows: "Measures understanding and achievement in advanced secondary or college algebra courses." Since these same materials describe the CTD Algebra II test as being designed to "sample the concepts and skills that students would be expected to have mastered by the end of a second course in algebra," it is not completely clear precisely what level of content is being covered in the Algebra III test. In the reviewer's opinion, this test might be most appropriate at the high school level for end-of-course testing for fourth year or advanced honors mathematics courses. However, since most such courses also introduce students to concepts dealing with trigonometry, analytic geometry, and even calculus, the Algebra III test should not be the only test used to determine course outcomes. Potential users of this test at the high school level should examine it carefully to determine if the test measures objectives for which they are teaching.

As is typical of most of the CTD tests, the format of the booklets is attractive and well done and the items appear to have been carefully prepared and edited. All items are of the 5-

response, multiple choice type. Students are told to make the best guess possible and that their score will be the number of correct answers marked. The test contains only 40 items but a surprising array of the more advanced topics of algebra are covered. A deliberate attempt has been made to develop items that would be appropriate for *both* traditional and modern approaches to algebra. Like most compromises, this solution is not ideal but students from either program should do well on the test if they thoroughly understand the fundamental concepts and principles of algebra.

There seems to have been a deliberate attempt to minimize the verbal aspects of the tests, since most items are stated in as few words as possible. In fact, in the opinion of the reviewer, this skimpiness of words tends to make the test somewhat pedantic and unexciting. A few word or situation-type problems might make the test more interesting although this would add to the problem of time, which will be discussed below.

While the items are cryptic and precise they do test more than simple recall and computational ability. For most questions, translation or application of mathematical principles is necessary to arrive at the correct responses.

Two forms of the tests are provided and the data presented indicate that these two forms are reasonably parallel. While there is considerable variation in the item content and format between the two forms, there is probably enough similarity to cause worry about practice effects. For example, item 25 in Form A and item 31 in Form B are so nearly alike and so unique that carry-over is almost certain to occur.

I am genuinely concerned about the 40-minute time limit for each of the 40-item forms of the tests. One-a-minute items are appropriate for many content areas, but mathematics items, particularly those that require some thought and some computation or manipulation, often do not fall into this category. It should be pointed out that the publishers, too, are concerned about this aspect of their test. They present data indicating that only half of the students in a particular administration answered the last item of the test. There should have been fewer items or a more generous time limit for both forms of this test.

Among the support materials for this test is a 77-page handbook which provides directions for administration and scoring, and normative and technical data for *all* nine CTD mathe-

matics tests. The format of the handbook is excellent and the material is generally of high quality. This reviewer is particularly pleased to see less emphasis on national and regional norms and more emphasis on the importance and interpretation of local norms. Reference is made to a pamphlet entitled "Constructing and Using Local Norms" as being available from CTD. While the reviewer knows that this is a useful document, it would seem preferable to have some descriptive information in the handbook on how to develop local norms. One strong point in the handbook, so often lacking in test materials, is the section stressing the importance and use of item response data. Since more and more schools have access to scoring equipment, this positive emphasis on the significance of item analysis is most appropriate.

The technical data in the handbook pertaining directly to the Algebra III tests is limited but minimally adequate. National high school and college norms are presented separately but are based on only 813 and 1,008 students, respectively, from 35 high schools and 49 colleges. A useful table that allows for the comparison of scores from earlier versions of CTD mathematics tests with those from the new series is provided. Such data are vital if on-going testing programs are to have any continuity. The K-R 20 reliabilities of .80 and .84 seem reasonable for a 40-item test in this area, although due to the possible speeded nature of the test, some test-retest reliability data should have been included.

No validity data are provided except correlations of .58 and .60 with the SCAT-Q. The case for validity rests solely upon the publisher's claim for content validity. This claim is established on the basis of the rather elaborate system of involving testing, curriculum and subject matter experts in the development of the test over a three year period. While the publisher is to be commended for the care taken in developing this test, it does seem that an organization of the status of CTD might have included some predictive validity, such as correlations with grades in mathematics or with success in academic areas requiring mathematics achievement at this level. However, the reviewer does approve of the cautionary statement in the handbook which recommends "that each test user make an individual judgment of content validity with respect to his own course content and educational aims."

In summary, this reviewer sees the CTD Algebra III test as an acceptable measuring instrument for evaluating achievement in algebra at the first course level in college or at the advanced or fourth year level in high school. The test format is good, the items are carefully constructed, the coverage is adequate although somewhat traditional and the supporting materials are of high quality. The statistical data are rather limited but acceptable considering the rather specific area that is being tested and the emphasis upon the importance of locally developed data for maximum interpretation of the test results.

For excerpts from reviews of the series, see 465 (2 excerpts).

[502]

★**ERB Modern Elementary Algebra Test.** Grades 8–9; 1965–67; Forms L ('65, 12 pages), M ('66, 8 pages); no manual; norms: Forms L ('67, 1 page), M ('66, 1 page), for independent school students only; no data on reliability; nonmember schools must use scoring service; separate answer sheets (IBM 1230) must be used; $3.10 per 10 tests; 80¢ per 10 answer sheets; 28¢ per scoring stencil; $5 per norms; $3 per specimen set; postage extra; scoring service, $1 and over per test; 80(90) minutes; Frederic Bonan, Philip Avirett, Karl S. Kalman, Stephen S. Ober, Foye Perry, Randolph Stone, Reinhoud H. van der Linde, and Frederick Watson; Educational Records Bureau. *

REFERENCE

1. LITTERICK, WILLIAM S. "Observations on the New ERB Mathematics Tests." *Ed Rec B* 88:62–3 Jl '65. *

[503]

★**ERB Modern Second Year Algebra Test.** High school; 1968–69; Forms X ('68, 8 pages), Y ('69, 5 pages); no manual; norms ('69, 1 page) for independent school students only; no data on reliability; nonmember schools must use scoring service; separate answer sheets (IBM 1230) must be used; $3.10 per 10 tests; 80¢ per 10 answer sheets; 28¢ per scoring stencil; $5 per norms; $3 per specimen set; postage extra; scoring service, $1 and over per test; 80(90) minutes; Frederic P. Bonan, Philip Avirett, Karl S. Kalman (Form X), Stephen S. Ober, Foye Perry, Randolph Stone, Reinhoud H. van der Linde (Form X), Frederick Watson, and Arthur Weeks (Form Y); Educational Records Bureau. *

[504]

*****Elementary Algebra: Minnesota High School Achievement Examinations.** High school; 1955–71; new or revised form issued each May; Form EH Rev. ('71, 5 pages); no specific manual; series manual ('71, 16 pages); no data on reliability; 15¢ per test; separate answer sheets (IBM 1230) may be used; 10¢ per answer sheet including scoring service; $1 per series manual; postage extra; $1.10 per specimen set, postpaid; 60(65) minutes; edited by V. L. Lohmann; American Guidance Service, Inc. *

For a review by Lynnette B. Plumlee of earlier forms, see 5:448.

[505]

*****Iowa Algebra Aptitude Test, Third Edition.** Grade 8; 1931–69; IAAT; 1 form ('67, 8 pages); manual ('69, 15 pages); $6.50 per 35 tests; 50¢ per key; separate answer sheets (IBM 805, IBM 1230) may be used; 6¢ per answer sheet; 30¢ per scoring stencil; 40¢ per manual; 75¢ per specimen set; postage extra; 40(45–50) minutes; H. A. Greene and Darrell Sabers; Bureau of Educational Research and Service. *

REFERENCES

1. See 2:1441.
2–3. See 3:327.
4. KEARNEY, CHARLES PHILLIP. *A Comparative Study of the Predictive Efficiency of the Iowa Algebra Aptitude Test and the Portland Prognostic Test.* Master's thesis, University of Portland (Portland, Ore.), 1960.
5. McCABE, MARTHA S. *An Analysis of the Effectiveness of the Iowa Algebra Aptitude Test in Selecting Students for an Accelerated Mathematics Program.* Master's thesis, University of South Carolina (Columbia, S.C.), 1963.
6. COFFIE, FRAZIER L. *The Iowa Algebra Aptitude Test Administered in the 8th Grade as a Predictor of Success in High School Mathematics, Geometry and Above.* Master's thesis, Drake University (Des Moines, Iowa), 1966.
7. HULLING, ROBERT H. *Predictive Validity of the Iowa Algebra Aptitude Test at Stilwell Junior High School, West Des Moines, Iowa.* Master's thesis, Drake University (Des Moines, Iowa), 1966.
8. SABERS, DARRELL LEE. *A Study of the Predictive Validity of the Iowa Algebra Aptitude Test for Prognosis in Ninth Grade Modern Mathematics and Traditional Algebra.* Doctor's thesis, University of Iowa (Iowa City, Iowa), 1967. (*DA* 28:2919A)
9. SABERS, DARRELL L., AND FELDT, LEONARD S. "An Empirical Study of the Effect of the Correction for Chance Success on the Reliability and Validity of an Aptitude Test." *J Ed Meas* 5:251–8 f '68. * (*PA* 44:11233)
10. SABERS, DARRELL L., AND FELDT, LEONARD S. "The Predictive Validity of the Iowa Algebra Aptitude Test for Achievement in Modern Mathematics and Algebra." *Ed & Psychol Meas* 28:901–7 au '68. * (*PA* 43:4435)
11. LIPPINCOTT, WILLIAM R. *Use of the Iowa Algebra Aptitude Test in Predicting Achievement in Ninth Grade Algebra in Sac County Public Schools.* Master's thesis, Iowa State University (Ames, Iowa), 1969.

W. L. BASHAW, *Professor of Educational Psychology, University of Georgia, Athens, Georgia.*

The procedure used in preparing this major revision is well described. It is based on an item analysis of the earlier version, conducted on 1,130 subjects during 1962 and 1963. The new test has one entirely new section—Lessons—which consists of items like those in the *Orleans-Hanna Algebra Prognosis Test.* There are four lessons to be studied. Each is followed by three to five questions based on the lesson. The original Arithmetic subtest was deleted entirely. (The review by Drake in *The Second Yearbook* criticized the Iowa as having too much arithmetic.) One subtest, Dependence and Variation, is unchanged. The other two subtests, Open Phrases (formerly Abstract Computation) and Sequences, are slightly revised.

The general format of the test is adequate. The Lessons subtest is cramped and could be improved by spreading it out over more pages. It is difficult to read, but the difficulty does not appear to be serious enough to prevent its use.

Validity and reliability information is inadequate. All validity data are based on Iowa school children; however, the Iowa samples are described fairly well and validity coefficients are reported for 18 different samples. Validity information is separated into that from algebra classes and that from modern mathematics classes, a feature that competitors are urged to adopt. The overall predictive validity of the test using an achievement test criterion was .78 for modern mathematics and .74 for algebra. Similar coefficients for predicting teacher grades were .69 and .64, respectively.

Split-half reliabilities of .94 and .93 are reported for total scores for the validation and norm groups. Speededness is discounted, since 90 percent of the students finished within the time limits.

Norms are reported separately for Iowa children and for a national sample. Iowa norms are divided into "all students," algebra students, and modern mathematics students. Percentiles only are reported for these groups. The user might be confused to see that the median for "all students" is lower than that for either subgroup. Perhaps this confusion would be removed if the tables gave sample sizes for each of the three columns instead of reporting only the overall sample size. The column "all students" includes students who took the Iowa test but elected neither algebra nor modern mathematics. Such students generally include the lower scoring students. This data breakdown was made clear in the discussion of validity and reliability but needs to be clarified again in the section on norms.

The national norms are largely unidentified. The authors state that no claims are made that the norm tables are representative. The percentile and stanine norms given are not identified by the type of mathematics course as they are with the Iowa norms.

A discussion of the value of local norms and local expectancy tables and an adequate discussion of the construction of expectancy tables are presented.

In general, this appears to be a good test. Its primary limitation is the absence of data on well defined samples of children. Users who are willing to compare their children to those in Iowa, or who are willing to study local validity and reliability and build local norms, might choose to use the IAAT as a predictor of algebra achievement.

CYRIL J. HOYT, *Professor of Educational Psychology, University of Minnesota, Minneapolis, Minnesota.*

This test is composed of 80 multiple choice items divided into four subtests, or parts, separately timed and using 14, 12, 10, and 4 minutes. Part 1 contains 34 sequences of numbers or algebraic terms for each of which the student is directed to select the next term from among four suggested responses. Part 2 presents four simple "lessons," each followed by three to five items testing the student's comprehension of the lesson. These "lessons" describe such procedures as evaluating a two-row determinant and performing addition of vectors. Part 3, Open Phrases, consists of 20 simple examples of translating verbal statements into algebraic symbols, such as, "Indicate the number of cents in m dimes and 2 pennies" and "How many hours will it take a person to go m miles, if he goes r miles in one hour?" Part 4, Dependence and Variation, presents 10 formulas solved for X in terms of two or three other literal numbers. The items ask the student to decide the effect on X of making verbally specified changes in one or more of the other literal numbers.

The format and printing of the test and answer sheets are excellent. The manual is very well done and contains much pertinent information which users need.

Some students may be unduly confused by the use of exponents in Part 1, though an understanding of exponents is not necessary for making the correct selection. Another matter of symbols used in this test, which users must be careful that all students understand, is that a times b or 5 times a can be expressed as ab or $5a$. This understanding is important in Part 3 especially.

The manual states "that 90 per cent or more of the pupils had finished each subtest when time was called. The average number of items omitted was less than four items per pupil for the total test." These observations do not jibe with this reviewer's experience. Prospective users should be aware of the importance of speed in influencing the scores on this test.

Evidence presented indicates that the total score on this test has sufficiently high reliability when the specified time limits are used. The manual also gives the standard errors of measurement for raw scores of different magnitudes. This information is helpful for a user, though he is not informed regarding the quantities or sources of the data from which these estimates were made.

The authors point out that in a school which has a substantial battery of achievement tests, the improvement in prediction made by adding this test may be considered a "luxury item" which may have its chief value in its face validity, especially in helping to convince over-ambitious parents to reconsider the advisability of certain students' choosing mathematics courses.

Percentile and stanine norms are presented for two markedly differing groups of eighth grade pupils. The first consists of 9,270 pupils tested between January 15th and April 15 in 40 school systems (names listed) reasonably well distributed geographically but excluding large cities. The second group consists of 1,363 pupils from 15 selected Iowa school systems tested in May. Criterion data were obtained from 613 of this latter group who took a ninth grade course in modern mathematics and 380 who completed one in regular algebra. The "national norm" and the Iowa group differed so greatly in their IAAT scores that users must recognize that the validation data reported for these Iowa schools may not be generalizable to their situation.

Expectancy tables for these two Iowa groups, modern mathematics and algebra, are given for five levels of scores on the IAAT. These data indicate that this test score could be a useful source of predictive information in the schools in this Iowa sample.

J Ed Meas 7(2):137-8 su '70. Russell A. Chadbourn. * The authors admit that a school which had available scores on a test battery such as the Iowa Test of Basic Skills would gain very little in predictive accuracy by using the IAAT. However, use of the IAAT for placement would probably be more acceptable to parents and students because of face validity. * An examination of the test questions reveals use of symbols and terminology which may be unfamiliar to a potentially successful algebra student. Although words such as product, quotient, even, integer and term may be common to all eighth graders, the symbol ab to represent $a \times b$ is probably not. Yet, 17 out of 20 questions in part III and 3 questions in part I used this concept, while one question in Part I used the same symbol to mean a pair of consecutive alphabetic characters. A similar objection applies to the five questions in part I which involve exponents. Although an understanding of exponents is not necessary to answer the problems, their presence might arouse anxiety in some students. The directions for part IV define X, y, m and s as counting numbers, while questions 5, 7, and 9 give rise to likely fractional or negative values of X. This difficulty could be eliminated by *not* defining X as a counting number. Two other minor points—the answer to the sample question in part I is given in such circular fashion that it seems unlikely to be of much help as an example, and part II, Lesson 1 has a format different enough from other sections to be momentarily disconcerting. The manual is, in general, well done with the test user being cautioned to consider also other factors from the student's record rather than placing total reliance on the test score. The manual also recommends that subscores not be used for diagnostic purposes. However, in the section on interpretation of results insufficient stress was placed on the fact that the extreme inequality of the Iowa group and the national group made the printed expectancy table inappropriate for most groups. In summary, the Iowa Algebra Aptitude Test's face validity and ease of administration and scoring would please counselors and teachers. Once local norms were developed it could be a useful tool in student placement within the mathematics program.

For reviews by Harold Gulliksen and Emma Spaney of an earlier edition, see 4:393; for a review by David Segel, see 3:327; for reviews by Richard M. Drake and M. W. Richardson, see 2:1441.

[506]

★Kepner Mid-Year Algebra Achievement Tests. 1 semester high school; 1969; KMAAT; 1 form (6 pages); manual (9 pages); separate answer sheets (IBM 1230) must be used; $6.50 per 35 tests; $18.50 per 100 answer sheets; 6¢ per scoring stencil; 40¢ per manual; 75¢ per specimen set; postage extra; 50(55) minutes; Henry S. Kepner, Jr. and Darrell Sabers; Bureau of Educational Research and Service. *

GERALD L. ERICKSEN, *Professor of Psychology and Head of the Department, St. Olaf College, Northfield, Minnesota.*

The publisher's catalog states that this test is "designed to measure the important objectives of both regular algebra and modern mathematics * no emphasis is placed on knowledge of modern vocabulary."

A major difficulty in evaluating the KMAAT lies in the wide range of topics, as well as the depth of coverage, which may be emphasized in the introduction to algebra during the first half year. It is essential, as acknowledged in the test manual, that "the mathematics staff of a particular school must judge test validity in terms of the local program." Nevertheless, consideration of certain general characteristics of the KMAAT may aid the teacher seeking a midyear algebra test.

Certainly a student lacking the minimum essentials of algebra covered in either a modern or a traditional curriculum would be identified by the KMAAT, which is easy both to administer (most students should finish the test within the allotted 50 minutes) and to score. The problem seems to be one of the diagnostic value of the test in planning for further specific remedial work for these students.

The KMAAT emphasizes primarily the minimum essentials of solving single and paired first-degree equations, including the translation of word problems. Secondarily, the polynomial operations of addition, subtraction, and simplification—as well as simple binomial multiplication and factoring—are included. Operations requiring a knowledge of some of the rules of signs, exponents, and inequalities are also tested.

The items are carefully selected. The teacher following a more traditional curriculum should find the KMAAT useful for a midyear evaluation of the above areas. However, the potential user should also be aware that the test does not assess knowledge of absolute value, method of approximating square roots, graphing, mixture and investment problems, or reciprocals. The teacher may also wish for a more explicit testing of the relationship of base, power, and exponent.

The shortcomings of the KMAAT appear to be greatest for the teacher interested in assessing students' appreciation of certain concepts basic to the more modern curricula. Omissions include (a) an intuitive understanding of nearly all the basic axioms involving closure, associativity, commutativity, etc. underlying an algebraic group or field; (b) logical reasoning involving, for example, the connectives "and," "or," "if, then," "if and only if" underlying the nature of algebraic proofs; (c) distinction of the properties distinguishing the natural, rational and real number systems; (d) the definition of inequality and the related proper-

ties necessary to define a complete ordered field; (e) a number line; and (f) number base systems.

SUMMARY. Mechanically, the KMAAT is simple to administer and has an easy-to-read format with carefully thought-out questions having a reported reliability coefficient of .89. One question (item 20), however, does have an arrangement that may easily be misread due to the placement of the letter "a" in the algebraic statement. Three or four other questions are apt to be missed because of mechanical errors, such as giving an incorrect sign, rather than because of a basic misunderstanding of the underlying concept. There are no alternate forms available. The KMAAT should be most useful for identifying, in a general way, those students deficient in the minimum essentials of a traditional first-year algebra curriculum. It will be less useful for providing a systematic diagnosis of specific gaps in intuitive understandings required for later work in algebra involving the field axioms, logical proofs, and properties of different number systems.

J Ed Meas 8(2):139–40 su '71. Arthur Mittman. Mid-year or one semester, two, three and even one and one-half semester algebra achievement tests have been in print for many years. The mid-year variety merits consideration from the standpoint that if it reveals that certain instructional objectives have not been realized up to that point in time, time remains in the school year to alter instructional plans to care for this deficit. * the Kepner test has been designed for norm reference use as well. Whether or not it can serve this dual role must be examined. The behaviors elicited by the items were categorized as belonging either to fundamental operations, concepts, or problem solving. Each item, as well as the behavior it elicits, can then be assigned a given content area. The manual gives the per cents of the norming sample ($n = 2728$) that selected each response to each item. Thus it is possible for the instructor to compare the performance of his class on each item with that of the norming sample. However, if the teacher wishes to use the results of the item analysis for diagnostic purposes, it is incumbent upon him to decide if the quality and quantity of the items classified by content and objective suffice for that purpose. * The reported reliability of the total test score is .89 * The reliability for subsets of items varying in size from one to six obviously would be much smaller. However, it is feasible to assume diagnosis is possible if test scores are used along with other evidence the teacher has collected. * Turning to the use of the test for norm referencing commendation without reservation is in order. * it is reasonable to consider the norming sample as representative of the population of ninth grade algebra students. At the same time, no claim can be made that the norms would be appropriate for schools which require all ninth grade students to enroll in algebra. * An effort has been made to explain the true score concept, but it would be advisable for the teacher interested in employing confidence bands to consult the school or district measurement specialist to avoid misinterpretation or misuse. Another interpretative aid is an expectancy table using the IATT as a predictor. This is a laudable aspect, but again help may be needed if optimal and appropriate use is to be made from it. Finally, a school means norm table is included, which should be of special interest to the school administrator. The explanation for its use is adequate. In summary, the test has been carefully planned and should be of value both for the purpose of making mid-year evaluation and for providing normative data. The manual is a model in honesty and completeness and should be of great help in realizing the full value of the test. The time limits seem appropriate and the directions for administration are simple and unambiguous.

[507]

*Lankton First-Year Algebra Test, Revised Edition. Grades 8–12; 1950–65; Forms E, F, ('65, 8 pages) ; manual ('65, 18 pages) ; no norms for grade 8; $8.70 per 35 tests; $1 per key; separate answer sheets (Digitek-IBM 805, IBM 1230) may be used; $2.30 per 35 Digitek-IBM 805 answer sheets ; $2.80 per 35 IBM 1230 answer sheets ; 70¢ per scoring stencil ; $1.50 per specimen set; postage extra; scoring service, 19¢ and over per test; 40(50) minutes; Robert S. Lankton; Harcourt Brace Jovanovich, Inc. *

REFERENCES

1. See 4:394.
2. SOMMERFELD, ROY E., AND TRACY, NEAL H. "A Study of Selected Predictors of Success in Second-Year Algebra in High School." H Sch J 46:234–40 Ap '63. *
3. DIRR, PIERRE MARIE. Intellectual Variables in Achievement in Modern Algebra. Doctor's thesis, Catholic University of America (Washington, D.C.), 1966. (DA 27:2873A)
4. CALDWELL, JAMES R.; MICHAEL, WILLIAM B.; SCHRADER, DONALD R.; AND MEYERS, C. E. "Comparative Validities and Working Times for Composites of Structure-of-Intellect Tests and Algebra Grades and Composites of Traditional Test Measures and Algebra Grades in the Prediction of Success in Tenth-Grade Geometry." Ed & Psychol Meas 30(4):955–9 w '70. *

LYNNETTE B. PLUMLEE, formerly Director of Test Development, Educational Testing Service, Princeton, New Jersey.

This test is an effort to provide a single measure of the attainment of "important objectives in....first-year high school algebra as typically taught in grade 9." Content was based on an analysis of textbooks, representative courses of study, and other relevant sources.

The objective of serving the users of all major first-year algebra texts is ambitious, especially if one includes the integrated mathematics content for the ninth grade level. With the current variation among texts, the potential user must judge from his own review of the test content whether it is sufficiently pertinent to his course objectives. The publisher encourages supplementing the test as necessary with locally made tests covering other topics of importance in the user's curriculum. If the purpose is to test the student's comprehension of the material covered in a particular course, supplementary material may well be needed. If the purpose is to compare understanding of typical topics by a given group of students with that by students elsewhere in the country without concern for complete coverage, the present test may suffice.

The publisher recognizes curricular differences by providing some separate statistics for modern algebra and for traditional algebra students, including means, standard deviations, and correlations with the Otis Quick-Scoring Mental Ability Tests, but does not provide separate norms. The classification as "modern" or "traditional" was left to the participating school and hence is not clearly defined. The manual suggests that the higher levels of achievement by the modern curriculum group "may be due, in part, to their higher levels of mental ability." However, data provided in the manual suggest that as a group modern students perform substantially better relative to their Otis IQ scores than do traditional students taking this test.

Some questions have probably been made unnecessarily difficult for the traditional student by the use of such terms as "solution set," which may discourage the timid student unfamiliar with the term from attempting an item which he is quite capable of solving. Separate item analysis data are not available for the traditional and modern students, and thus it is difficult to evaluate the seriousness of this disadvantage. A few items may be easier for traditional than for modern students. Separate item analyses for students in the two curricula would also help to indicate whether specific items are functioning less effectively for one group than for the other.

The content analysis provided in the manual may be of some help in evaluating test emphasis relative to the user's course, but it is probably too generalized (only 5 classifications on each axis) for judging adequacy of coverage for the course. There appears to be some duplication of content at the expense of omitted concepts, but the items in general appear to be nonroutine.

The two 110-item tryout forms of the test were administered alternately to 5,040 first-year algebra students in 28 public high schools whose characteristics are specified by city size and by state. On the basis of the tryout, they were shortened to two 50-item final forms and re-scored for standardization purposes. It is not clear how test statistics and form equivalence may have been affected by selecting items from a somewhat speeded test (75 percent completion) and then rescoring the same answer sheets to obtain final norms for a shortened test presumed to allow most students to finish. (No subsequent check has been made on the equivalence of the two forms.)

Normative data include both percentiles and standard scores for the total population sample. The standard scores are based on conversion to a scale which is intended to permit comparisons across tests in different areas. Performance of each achievement test population sample on the Otis tests is used as a basis for placing different tests on the same scale. Since publication of the manual in 1965, additional normative data for modern curriculum students have been obtained. These data had raised the median of the total group from 20.5 to 26.2 as of May 1968. The traditional group constituted two-thirds of the 1965 standardization sample, compared with one-fourth of the total 1968 sample. A traditional student who performed at the mean of the traditional group in the standardization sample would be approximately at the 45th percentile on the 1965 norms and at the 26th percentile on the 1968 norms. A modern student at the 1965 mean for modern students would be at the 71st and 47th percentiles, respectively, on the two norms.

It is possible that the new samples have correspondingly higher scores on the Otis and that the conversion to standard scores would be unchanged if computed again on recent data, but supplementary reports giving the new percentile ranks do not provide data on either Otis

or standard scores. New data are sufficiently different to suggest the advisability of a new conversion study. It would appear that the user should be very careful to adhere to one set of norms if scores are to be compared over different administrations. Separate norms for traditional and modern curriculum students should be provided as long as the test is designed to be used with both types of curriculum. A comparison of traditional curriculum norms scores against those for modern curriculum may be worthwhile as one basis for judging the initial handicap of the traditional student who transfers into a modern curriculum program where he is in competition with students from a modern background.

The manual provides suitable cautions regarding the interpretation of test results and encourages the user to develop local norms. Extensive instruction in the interpretation of test results is generally helpful. However, this reviewer feels that some of the discussion, such as that relating achievement score expectations to Otis scores, may be oversimplified and thus lead the statistically unsophisticated user to errors in interpretation. The inclusion of item analysis data for both forms is commendable, although a breakdown by curriculum would be helpful.

Use of the same scoring key for the two forms could present a problem in situations where one wishes to substitute another form because of loss of security.

In conclusion, items appear to test understanding rather than rote learning, but the test may fail to sample all areas of some curricula because of the goal of serving both traditional and modern programs. Normative data should be used with caution.

KENNETH J. TRAVERS, *Associate Professor of Mathematics Education, University of Illinois, Urbana, Illinois.*

In spite of the terminology and notation problems which have accompanied the emergence of rather diverse curriculum development projects in school mathematics, this test appears to sample adequately the major concepts in first-year algebra. It is probably true, as the author states, that "the test is useful....in most high school algebra classes where either traditional or modern approaches to the teaching of algebra are being used." There also appears to be a predominance of questions dealing with solution sets and graphing. While this balance is undoubtedly to the liking of many, others will object to the comparatively light sampling of such topics as rate problems and solution of quadratics. Furthermore, while the test has sufficient coverage of the sharp inequality ("strictly less than"), considerably fewer items deal with the blunt inequality ("less than or equal to").

The test has many desirable features. It is easy to read, the questions are well spaced, and the answers are easy to key. Directions are clear.

The test manual is informative, well prepared and useful. Especially noteworthy is the taxonomy of test items reported in two dimensions: content (topic) and objectives (number, set, operation, structure, relation). This classification enables the user to determine quickly the extent to which the test's objectives appropriately sample his own. The taxonomy further reveals that on the content dimension, the two forms of the test are fairly comparable.

A further extremely informative and useful feature of the manual is the reporting of individual item characteristics (difficulty level and discrimination index). This information will be particularly welcomed by those interested in program planning and evaluation and those doing individual diagnosis on a limited basis. Tables are provided to convert raw scores to standard scores which would be expected to be obtained by a population having Otis IQ scores of mean 105 and standard deviation 12. This provision is an interesting one and doubtless points very clearly to the caution with which one must interpret normed scores. But the usefulness of these transformed scores for making inferences concerning a particular person in a particular school setting is somewhat problematic.

There is some question as to the adequacy of the standardization sample. For example, no differentiation is made between urban and suburban school samples, even though differences in performance of these groups are universally accepted. Furthermore, only public high schools are represented. Certainly, for the populations sampled (28 public high schools in 16 states) the test was relatively difficult (levels of .435 for Form E and .409 for Form F). Information concerning standard error of measurement is incomplete. Speededness data for the tests are not reported.

In the present revision of the test, the addition of the guessing distracter "Don't Know" in an attempt to minimize contamination of scores by wild guessing surely raises other psychometric questions. As Chauncey (see 6:598) has noted concerning the use of "none of these answers" as a choice, such a distracter may also have the effect of attracting "good students making trivial clerical errors" when "otherwise they might be led to recheck their work." The present reviewer further suspects that brighter students, at least, would quickly surmise that the probability of gaining points by choosing a "Don't Know" response is rather low and could easily revert to wild guessing among the four remaining answers in any case.

Overall, however, the test is a useful instrument with many desirable psychometric properties and reflects adequately current trends in curriculum.

For a review by Emma Spaney of the original edition, see 5:451; for a review by Stanley Clark, see 4:394.

[508]

*Lee Test of Algebraic Ability, Revised.** Grades 7–8; 1930–64; TAA; identical with the 1930 edition except for adaptation to machine scoring; 1 form ('64, 10 pages); manual ('64, 18 pages); publisher recommends use of local norms; $4.40 per 35 tests; separate answer sheets (IBM 1230) may be used; $2 per 35 answer sheets; 50¢ per scoring stencil; 75¢ per specimen set; postage extra; 25(35) minutes; J. Murray Lee; Bobbs-Merrill Co., Inc. *

REFERENCES

1. See 2:1443.
2. GROTHUS, JOSEPH ROBERT. *A Prognostic Comparison of the Validity of the Lee Test of Algebraic Ability and Subsequent Grades Received.* Master's thesis, Chapman College (Orange, Calif.), 1964.
3. STILGEBAUER, LARRY K. *A Study of Selected Data in Predicting Success in Ninth Grade Mathematics at Jefferson Junior High School, Mattoon, Illinois.* Master's thesis, Eastern Illinois University (Charleston, Ill.), 1967.

W. L. BASHAW, *Professor of Educational Psychology, University of Georgia, Athens, Georgia.*

When this test was originally published 40 years ago, three of the four subtests were made up of short-answer items and one of multiple choice items. The only change in the 1964 revision is that all items have been recast into multiple choice form. Foils for the new edition were chosen from among the wrong answers most frequently given on the 1930 edition.

The test administrator must warn examinees about an error on the answer sheet; hyphens instead of colons are used in the examples given for the analogies test. This will create confusion for students who expect samples to be similar to test items.

In the analogy section, correct solutions sometimes cannot be found without distracter analysis. For example, the answer for "2:8:: 4:?" could reasonably be 10, 16, or 64. One must search the distracters to determine the intended answer. Solutions should be independent of the choice of distracters. In the formulas section, the use of a slash notation for a division operator is ambiguous in one item and in one example.

The manual fails to meet the minimal expectations of the APA guidelines for test manuals. Reliability data consist of two split-half coefficients. No information is given as to the data gathering procedure or the characteristics of the two samples. Validity data are presented for 13 different samples ranging in size from 16 to 138. Coefficients of predictive validity for heterogeneous classes were reasonably high— ranging from .21 to .73, with median .54. There is little information on the characteristics of these validation samples, although the author does distinguish first-semester-grade predictive validities from second-semester-grade predictive validities. Advice on cutting scores is made on the basis of validity data. A good discussion is presented on the construction of local scattergrams.

Norms are inadequate for a test that has been used so long. The author does present data for seventh grade and eighth grade students, but both sets of data are small (N = 470 and 677, respectively). The seventh grade mean is incorrectly reported to be 39.0; it should be 28.9. The manual states that "a standard score of 50 is equivalent to a percentile rank of 50, the average of the norm sample." This is true for the eighth grade only; in the seventh grade a standard score of 50 is equivalent to a percentile rank of 58.

It is this reviewer's opinion that considerably more effort should be given to the development of norms and technical data. Moreover, some attention must be given to the curriculum developments in mathematics during the 1960's.

CYRIL J. HOYT, *Professor of Educational Psychology, University of Minnesota, Minneapolis, Minnesota.*

This test is composed of four subtests: arithmetic problems, analogies, number series, and formulas—taking 7, 5, 7 and 6 minutes, respec-

tively, of student work time. The time allowed is so limited that the scores are highly dependent on speed. This fact makes the split-half reliability data reported inappropriate. The items in each subtest appear to be arranged in order of difficulty, though the manual does not report any item difficulty or item analysis data. Furthermore, since the manual does not indicate the standard deviation in the sample for which the reliability is reported, the standard error of measurement cannot be determined by the prospective user until he collects his data.

The decision to use the particular four subtests chosen was based upon a multiple correlation study on data collected in the Los Angeles schools in 1928. This study tried nine predictor tests, which were correlated with an algebra achievement examination given at the end of the first semester. Since considerable revision in the mathematics curriculums has occurred in the past 30 years in many American schools, it is doubtful that the results of this study are likely to be pertinent in modern schools.

Three tables based upon 85 students in one school are used to illustrate how to build an expectancy table on the basis of grades earned by students who have previously taken the ability test. The manual does not caution the builder of local expectancy tables against basing his percentages on small numbers in the row totals. This problem of obtaining adequately large numbers is one which will trouble most builders of local expectancy tables.

Very inadequate predictive validity information is presented in the manual. Predictive validity correlation coefficients are given for nine selected classes. When first semester grades were used as the criterion, these correlations ranged from .21 to .67, with median .54; with second semester grades from .43 to .73, with median .57.

The test format has certain inadequacies which detract from the test's usefulness. The response choices in the analogies subtest are spread out across the whole width of the eight-inch page. The manner of designating fractions in the choices in the number series subtest is not consistent.

The manual has a serious omission in the directions for administration. The signal "Go" is omitted from the directions for the first subtest, with the result that the signal for pupils to begin and for timing of the seven minutes is not given. This lack of the signal "Go" is likely to confuse students, especially since the time limits are so important in determining the test score.

Tables 6, 7, and 8, showing the raw score distributions for an eighth grade group of 677 and a seventh grade group of 470, designate the mean incorrectly for the seventh grade group. Percentile norms and normalized standard scores are reported for these two groups, hopefully with more accuracy in arithmetic than that for the computation of the mean.

The manual emphasizes that the test assesses "algebraic ability" rather than general ability or mathematical ability. However, evidence that the construct "algebraic ability" exists separately from mathematical ability is not presented or considered. In this reviewer's judgment, scores on this test have a heavy component closely associated with other speeded tests of the kind found in general scholastic ability tests.

Since this test was revised in 1964, the publisher should have provided supplementary information on the omissions and errors in the manual. This test is not recommended for use as it is presently published.

J Counsel Psychol 13:248–9 su '66. William Mehrens. * The manual contains no reference to either content or construct validity, with the exception of a brief statement listed under "the special advantages of the test" which states that the test, "....covers only algebraic instead of general mathematical ability." These constructs are given no elaboration in the manual and the distinction is not obvious. For a critical reader to agree that the four subtests included in this test do cover only algebraic instead of general mathematical ability, further development of the distinction between these constructs would be of value. * The author also gives as evidence of validity the fact that in selecting students for *8th* grade algebra one school chose, out of an original group of 330 students, 19 students who scored above 40 on the test. Of these, 5 received A's, 10 B's and 4 C's, with no D's or F's. Without information on the grading policy of the school or what the other students *would have achieved,* it is uncertain why the author reports this under the validity section of his manual. As presented it should not be taken as an indication of validity. The author makes the point under the validity section that each

school should develop its own predictive tables. It is interesting that, although he indicates that there is no doubt a sex factor operating in the prediction, he does not suggest that separate expectancy tables be built for boys and girls. * A standard error of measurement is not reported, nor can it be obtained or estimated, since no information is given concerning the variability of the groups on which the reliability coefficients were computed. In fact, it is not even known for sure that the groups were either seventh or eighth graders; no information other than size is reported. * Another "special advantage of the test" (other than the one mentioned under validity) suggested by the author deserves specific comment. This is the statement that: "The test is given before the student begins the study of algebra." Modern mathematics curriculums being advocated and taught throughout the country often begin the study of algebra long before the eighth or ninth grade. It is quite surprising, in fact, that a 1930 test revised in 1964 does not mention the changing mathematics curriculum and how these changes may affect the type and level of test questions that may indeed predict success in an 8th or 9th grade algebra class. * While the meager predictive validity data reported indicates that the test may have some merit, there are several serious omissions in the information provided * Examples of the limitations are as follows: (1) No indication concerning the type of item analysis (if any) that accompanied the revision. (2) No report on the standard error of measurement or the variability of the group on whom the reliability is computed. (3) No discussion concerning the reasons behind the statement that this is a measure of algebraic instead of general mathematical ability. (4) Very limited normative data. (5) Very limited predictive validity data. While the test may indeed be worthwhile, the preparation of the manual leaves much to be desired. The saving grace....is that the author strongly suggests that each school must make its own validity studies on the test. The reviewer agrees completely with this statement. If empirical studies within a school indicate improved prediction by using this test, over and above the best efforts without it, it could be helpful. In the final analysis, *all* tests should be validated within the particular locale of the user.

For a review by S. S. Wilks, see 2:1443.

[509]
★**Mid-Year Algebra Test.** High school; 1968; Form A (8 pages); manual (15 pages); $7.70 per 35 tests; separate answer sheets (Digitek-IBM 805, IBM 1230) may be used; $2.30 per 35 Digitek-IBM 805 answer sheets; $2.80 per 35 IBM 1230 answer sheets; 70¢ per scoring stencil; $1.50 per specimen set; postage extra; scoring service, 19¢ and over per test; 40(50) minutes; Harcourt Brace Jovanovich, Inc. *

GERALD L. ERICKSEN, *Professor of Psychology and Head of the Department, St. Olaf College, Northfield, Minnesota.*

The *Mid-Year Algebra Test* "reflects recent trends in the mathematics curriculum and contains a representative sample of the content currently being studied during the first semester of a first year algebra course." It will, however, be necessary for the mathematics staff to judge test validity locally in view of the wide range of topics that may be emphasized during the first semester of a first year algebra course.

The MYAT content is generally appropriate for most introductory algebra curricula, although the first year student in a "traditional" course may be at a slight disadvantage when confronted with the few questions emphasizing sets and solution sets.

TRADITIONAL CURRICULUM. The teacher should find the coverage of single and paired linear equations adequate for both numerically presented problems and "verbal" problems concerning rates and mixtures. The graphic interpretation of linear relationships receives much less emphasis. The basic operations with monomials, including averaging and the rules governing exponents, are well covered. Furthermore, the test items involving binomials and trinomials should permit the teacher to identify a student having difficulty with elementary polynomial multiplication, division, simplification, or factoring. Finally, the teacher of traditional algebra will find the questions dealing with the properties of the real number system helpful in identifying a lack of understanding of such concepts as algebraic or absolute value, a number line, or the transformation principles used in generating equivalent equations. The potential user should, at the same time, be aware that number base systems and approximating square roots are topics not included and that the properties of an inequality are only sampled.

MODERN CURRICULUM. Any student who has had an adequate introduction to modern mathematics should have little difficulty with either the items related to the axioms of an algebraic

group or to the distinguishing characteristic of the rational number system. Specifically, however, although closure and associativity, as well as sets and deductive reasoning, are necessary concepts to be mastered by the modern mathematics student, they are not sufficient for developing an understanding of algebraic groups and fields or of the logical nature of algebraic proofs. Perhaps justifiably in a midyear test, the MYAT does not adequately test for such logical reasoning as is required for later mathematical proofs involving compound sentences with the associated connectives "and," "or," "if, then," and "if and only if." The MYAT, then, does provide a measure of a selected few minimum essentials of a modern mathematics curriculum. Whether this sampling is adequate for discriminating among students or isolating specific difficulties of the better student in the modern curriculum is open to question.

TECHNICAL CHARACTERISTICS. The MYAT manual is carefully written and informative. The test itself is easy to administer and to score, either manually or by machine, with an easy-to-follow test format for the student. While there is only one test form available, separate normative data are provided for a shorter version of the test including 14 percent fewer items. The manual presents data indicating that "over 25% of the students in the Mid-Year Test standardization sample omitted items 44 through 50." Hence, the below average student may well feel rushed in an allotted time of 45–50 minutes. Consequently, such a student is likely to make hurried computational errors, which is unfortunate in view of the purpose of a midyear algebra test. In using the test results for "guidance and instructional purposes," the teacher should take into account the possibility of such errors.

SUMMARY. The MYAT merits consideration by the teacher seeking a standardized test of general concepts of introductory work in algebra. The stated test objectives appear to have been reached and the teacher emphasizing some of the "recent developments" of algebra should find the MYAT more satisfactory, in terms of both the language used and the content, than the traditionally oriented *Kepner Mid-Year Algebra Achievement Tests.*

[510]
***Orleans-Hanna Algebra Prognosis Test.** Grades 7–11; 1928–69; OHAPT; revison of *Orleans Algebra Prognosis Test;* 1 form ('68, 11 pages); manual ('68,

19 pages); norms for grade 7 ('69, 2 pages); separate answer sheets (Digitek, IBM 805, IBM 1230) must be used; $8.70 per 35 tests; $2.30 per 35 IBM 805 answer sheets; $2.80 per 35 Digitek or IBM 1230 answer sheets; 70¢ per scoring stencil; $1.50 per specimen set; postage extra; grade 7 norms free on request from publisher; IBM scoring service, 19¢ and over per test; 40(55–60) minutes; Joseph B. Orleans and Gerald S. Hanna; Harcourt Brace Jovanovich, Inc. *

REFERENCES

1–4. See 2:1444.
5. See 4:396.
6. HINES, ALAN C. *The Prediction of Success in Algebra by the Orleans Algebra Prognosis Test as Affected by a Modern Mathematics Curriculum.* Master's thesis, Mankato State College (Mankato, Minn.), 1965.
7. KATZ, EDWARD M. *A Study to Assess the Value of the Orleans Algebra Prognosis Test to the North Thurston School District.* Master's thesis, Pacific Lutheran University (Tacoma, Wash.), 1967.
8. HANNA, GERALD S.; BLIGH, HAROLD F.; LENKE, JOANNE M.; AND ORLEANS, JOSEPH B. "Predicting Algebra Achievement With an Algebra Prognosis Test, IQS, Teacher Predictions, and Mathematics Grades." *Ed & Psychol Meas* 29(4):903–7 w '69. * (PA 44:21615)

W. L. BASHAW, *Professor of Educational Psychology, University of Georgia, Athens, Georgia.*

New users of the Orleans-Hanna will probably believe that it is based on a new and ingenious concept in testing for the purpose of predicting learning. They will be surprised to learn that the item type in the 1968 revision was used in the original 1928 version. The items consist of sets of questions which correspond to an instructional lesson. The student studies a lesson, then answers questions about the lesson. The concept is analogous to modern mini-courses used in teacher education. It has been used in one subscale of a recent revision of a competitor—the *Iowa Algebra Aptitude Test.* It is a feature that could profitably be borrowed for learning-aptitude tests in other areas.

Major new features include excellent supporting documents for machine scoring, a very good and readable manual, some "new math" items, and a questionnaire section. Individual lessons are no longer separately timed.

Students are asked to answer five "questionnaire items." It is stated that the purpose of these questions is to assist in student counseling and grouping. However, the items are included in the total test score. They consist of self-report questions concerning previous grades in mathematics, science, English, and social studies and an estimate of the expected algebra grade. These questionnaire items are scored according to the following point system: A = 4, B = 3, C = 2, D = 1, E = 0, and F = 0. The points are added and the sum is doubled. The final questionnaire total is added to the number of questions answered correctly in the examination section. The administrator and the person scoring papers must take extreme caution that these questionnaire items are correctly filled out, since multiple marks are required of the examinee. (He makes five marks for an A, four for a B, etc.) Questionnaire scores range from 0 (all E's or F's) to 40 (all A's). Since there are 58 questions on the exam itself, the questionnaire items are weighted heavily. Student faking or poor memory can affect the questionnaire scores drastically.

Little evidence of the worth of the questionnaire data is presented. These questions correlate .63 with the test score and .84 with the total score. The number of correct responses to regular test questions correlates .95 with the total score. These correlations are based on the norms sample of 5,833 students. Thus, there is some good evidence that the regular test questions alone can do the job of both together. Unfortunately, norms are based only on total scores. The reviewer recommends that separate norms be established for test scores that do not involve the questionnaire items due to the expected difficulties in accurately responding to it. Presently, students who do not complete the questionnaire correctly cannot have their scores interpreted. Moreover, multiple regression equations between the two sections and various criteria could be presented in defense of the weighting system that is used. Moreover, evidence could be presented concerning the typical accuracy with which students report earned grades.

In general, this appears to be an excellent instrument. Norms are established on a reasonably large sample and some major characteristics of the norm group are reported. Item data are reported as well (but not for the questionnaire items). Predictive validities are high (.39 to .82, median .71) and are reported for both mid-year and full-year algebra performance. There is a good discussion on the construction of local norms and on the estimation of local validity. All reliability data are based on test-retest estimation procedures with a two-week time interval, hence avoiding the spurious effect of speededness that is typically ignored in tests of this type. Coefficients range from .91 to .96 for total scores and .89 to .95 for questionnaire items.

CYRIL J. HOYT, *Professor of Educational Psychology, University of Minnesota, Minneapolis, Minnesota.*

This test contains 58 work-sample items in multiple choice form, divided into 10 tests of 5 or 6 items each. Each test is preceded by "lesson" material explaining and illustrating the principles required for answering the test items. For slow readers and somewhat inept students the 40-minute time limit seems to the reviewer not to provide sufficient time to show their power. A recent study (8) indicates that the score on this section of the OHAPT correlated .82 with Otis-Lennon IQ's for a group of 310 students.

The lesson materials seem well chosen for an earlier day but it is hard for this reviewer to visualize an eighth grade mathematics course in which some, if not most, of the material has not been introduced. The "lessons" deal with the following: substitution of numerical values in monomials and in binomials, additive combining of two or more signed numbers and of the absolute values of such; combining similar and dissimilar terms; recognizing appropriate literal expressions for verbal ones, such as "the number of yards in a street n feet long" and ten more than a number x; recognizing illustrations of the use of the associative or commutative principles in addition and multiplication. The raw score on the test is found by giving one point for each correctly answered test item and adding this sum to the student's report of his "most recent report-card grade in each of four subject areas (mathematics, science, English, and social studies) and the grade he thinks he would earn in an algebra course."

The student reports of grades, or the questionnaire items, are completed with 10–15 additional minutes of student time. Examination of the data shows that "questionnaire" and "work sample" scores correlate .63, which indicates that a somewhat different ability is being measured by the two test parts. However, predictive validity studies (8) show that when teachers' grades (at end of first or second semester) are used as criteria, the inclusion of the "questionnaire items score" raises the prognostic correlations from .63 to .68 for first semester and from .62 to .66 for second semester. When the *Lankton First-Year Algebra Test* score was used as a criterion, however, the "work sample" item correlation was .80 as compared to .78

for the total score predictive validity. Thus, the reviewer concludes that if a prospective user is concerned more with predicting students' ability to achieve high algebra achievement test scores (such as for college or senior high admissions test), he might prefer to use only the prognostic test score on the work-sample items. If teachers' grades are the criterion of concern, there seems to be a slight advantage to using the total score on both parts of the test, since the total score reflects within it some aspects of grade-getting ability which is not identical with the ability to respond correctly to an achievement test.

The test manual contains percentile rank and stanine norms for 5,109 eighth grade students completing eighth grade mathematics. A second norm table is given for that subgroup of 2,860 who enrolled in first year algebra. These two are the only norm tables given, even though the advertising indicates the test is appropriate for grades 8–11. The norms were based on data from 25 school systems reasonably well distributed geographically but somewhat deficient in representing systems (*a*) with less than 1,200 student enrollment and (*b*) those classified in the lowest 20 percent on socioeconomic status.

The test manual shows four expectancy tables based on 518 to 637 students for whom the particular criterion data were available from six school systems. Though these numbers of students seem sizable, the expectancy tables contain inadequate frequencies in low-scoring categories. For example, for midyear testing some of the expected percentages are based on frequencies of 4, 19, and 25. The reader cannot have much confidence in percentages based on such small frequencies. Table I shows that of 109 students earning OHAPT raw scores of 40 or lower, 41 percent received failing midsemester grades (i.e., F) and 41 percent received D, the lowest passing grade. Of the 528 with OHAPT scores 41 and higher, only 3 percent received failing grades and 15 percent received D.

Validity results as good as these are highly commendable and compel the reviewer to suggest that the test be recommended for the purpose of advising eighth grade students concerning their likelihood of success in a first-year algebra course. This recommendation is based on the assumption that the schools used were not atypical of the population of concern to the prospective user.

For reviews by Harold Gulliksen and Emma Spaney of an earlier edition, see 4:396; for a review by S. S. Wilks, see 2:1444.

[511]

*Tucker-Sanders First Year Algebra Test. 1, 2 semesters high school; 1962–64; first published 1962–63 in the Every Pupil Scholarship Test series; Forms A, B, ('64); 2 levels labeled Tests 1 (2 pages), 2 (4 pages); manual ('64, 4 pages); $1.75 per 25 tests, postage extra; 75¢ per specimen set, postpaid; 40(45) minutes; Charles B. Tucker and M. W. Sanders; Data Processing and Educational Measurement Center. *

ARITHMETIC

[512]

*Arithmetic Fundamentals Test. High school; 1944–70; Forms A ('70, 7 pages), B ('70, 6 pages), essentially the same as forms issued in 1944 except for 5 items; no manual; no data on reliability; no norms; $1 per 10 tests, postpaid; 25¢ per single copy, cash orders only; 50(55) minutes; original test by Doyle T. French and Albert R. Mahin, revision by Robert J. Bryant; High School Testing Service, Purdue University. *

[513]

Bobbs-Merrill Arithmetic Achievement Tests. Grades 1, 2, 3, 4, 5, 6, 7, 8–9; 1963; 3 scores: concepts and problems, computation, total; 2 forms; 8 levels; no data on reliability of subscores; separate answer sheets (IBM 805) must be used in grades 4–9; $3.80 per 35 tests of levels 1, 2, or 3; $4.10 per 35 tests of levels 4, 5, or 6; $4.60 per 35 tests of levels 7 or 8; $1.25 per set of scoring stencils for levels 1 or 2; $1.75 per set of scoring stencils for level 3; $2.05 per 35 answer sheets for levels 4–8; 35¢ per scoring stencil; 60¢ per specimen set of any one level; $4.20 per specimen set of all levels; postage extra; William E. Kline and Harry J. Baker; Bobbs-Merrill Co., Inc. *
a) LEVEL 1. Grade 1; Forms A, B, (4 pages); manual (11 pages) for each form; (50–65) minutes in 2 sessions.
b) LEVEL 2. Grade 2; Forms A, B, (4 pages); manual (11 pages) for each form; (50–65) minutes in 2 sessions.
c) LEVEL 3. Grade 3; Forms A, B, (7 pages); manual (12 pages); 40(45) minutes in 2 sessions.
d) LEVEL 4. Grade 4; Forms A, B, (8 pages); combined manual (17 pages) for levels 4–6; 50(55) minutes.
e) LEVEL 5. Grade 5; Forms A, B, (11 pages); combined manual (17 pages) for levels 4–6; 50(55) minutes.
f) LEVEL 6. Grade 6; details same as for level 5.
g) LEVEL 7. Grade 7; Forms A, B, (11 pages); combined manual (17 pages) for levels 7–8; 60(65) minutes.
h) LEVEL 8. Grades 8–9; Forms A, B, (12 pages); combined manual (17 pages) for levels 7–8; 60(65) minutes.

C. ALAN RIEDESEL, *Professor of Education, Georgia State University, Atlanta, Georgia.*

These tests form a series of measures of arithmetic achievement in grades one through nine. They purport to reflect the recent major changes in the mathematics curriculum often referred to as the "new mathematics." There are two subtests at each level: one is designed to measure knowledge of concepts taught and the ability to solve word problems using the concepts, and the second to test computational skill.

At the primary level the wording of many of the "concept" items is ambiguous. For example, first grade children are told, "The two words are 'Yard' and 'Inch.' Put an X on the one that is longer." Since both words, *yard* and *inch,* are the same length (four letters), the task is quite confusing. Children who have been taught to differentiate between ideas and the words used to express ideas may have difficulty with the items. Other items ask children to "Put an X on the number that is the same as the word." This also might cause difficulty. In contrast to the "concept" items, the word problems (to be read to the children) at the primary level are excellent.

At the upper grade level there are fewer poor "concept" items. The word problem items remain well above average. The computational items are routine and appear to be no better nor worse than similar items on other tests.

The manual suggests, "Each prospective user of a Bobbs-Merrill Arithmetic Test is urged to study the test, item by item, to determine to what extent the items of the test are successful in sampling the objectives of the course for which the test is being considered." Certainly this is sound advice.

In addition to this face validity suggestion, concurrent validity is developed by correlation coefficients which were obtained between the raw score of the Bobbs-Merrill tests and the total grade equivalents of the arithmetic test of the *Iowa Tests of Basic Skills* (at Levels 3, 4, 5, 6, 7, and 8). Such a procedure is to be questioned since the Iowa tests do not have a computation section. One wonders why the authors have written a mathematics achievement test if they feel that the Iowa test measures the content appropriately.

At Levels 1 and 2 the same procedure is followed using the *California Arithmetic Test* as the yardstick. Although the California test does have a computation section, the use of it as a criterion for concurrent validity is still to be questioned.

The split-half reliability correlation coefficients are typical of those found in the majority of standardized mathematics tests. The standard errors of measurement are very respectable.

After a reasonable pilot test, the published version of the tests was administered to 4,000 students of Baltimore County, Maryland, and Southfield and Lathrup Village, in Michigan. If one considers that there are two forms at each of eight levels, this means that there were approximately 250 subjects for each test. Certainly the representativeness of this group of students is to be questioned. Considering the great variability in achievement from city to city and state to state, a much more scientifically drawn sample should have been used.

If the test is used, the norms should be carefully studied. In an attempt at developing national norms all students in the Bobbs-Merrill sampling took either the California (Levels 1 and 2) or the Iowa (Levels 3, 4, 5, 6, 7, and 8) tests at the same grade level. Then a "equipercentile equating technique" was used to equate the raw scores on each of the two parts of the Bobbs-Merrill with the California or the Iowa. Such a procedure raises the question, "Why the Bobbs-Merrill?" when it seems to rely on either the California or the Iowa for its documentation.

The tests have fine manuals. They are concisely written and the sections for administration, scoring, and interpretation are very well done. There are good, short discussions of grade equivalents and percentiles which should help the teacher overcome typical misconceptions.

In summary, the tests have good and bad items (of particular merit are the primary problem solving items). The sampling of items is reasonable for most textbooks and curricula currently used. There are very few items which call for higher level thought processes. The standardization procedures leave much to be desired. The manuals are well written and contain excellent suggestions for test use. The *Bobbs-Merrill Arithmetic Achievement Tests* are average tests of mathematics achievement. If careful study of the items reveals a one-to-one correspondence between the test items and the major mathematical achievement objectives of a school district, the tests should prove satisfactory.

[514]

★**Comprehensive Tests of Basic Skills: Arithmetic.** Grades 2.5-4, 4-6, 6-8, 8-12; 1968-70; 4 scores: computation, concepts, applications, total; 2 forms; 4 levels; for battery manuals and accessories, see 9; separate answer sheets (CompuScan [NCS], Digitek, IBM 1230, Scoreze) must be used for levels 2-4; postage extra; $1.75 per specimen set of any one level, postpaid; CTB/McGraw-Hill. *
a) LEVEL 1. Grades 2.5-4; Forms Q ('68, 10 pages), R ('69, 10 pages) ; $5.35 per 35 tests; 79(95) minutes.
b) LEVEL 2. Grades 4-6; Forms Q ('68, 14 pages), R ('69, 13 pages) ; $5.75 per 35 tests; $2.50 per 50 Digitek or IBM answer sheets; $3 per 50 CompuScan answer sheets; $2.75 per 25 Scoreze answer sheets; $1 per IBM hand scoring stencil; CompuScan scoring service, 17¢ and over per test; 73(93) minutes.
c) LEVEL 3. Grades 6-8; Forms Q ('68, 13 pages), R ('69, 13 pages) ; prices same as for level 2; 69(89) minutes.
d) LEVEL 4. Grades 8-12; Forms Q ('68, 13 pages), R ('69, 13 pages) ; prices same as for level 2; 65(85) minutes.

JACK PRICE, *Director, Curriculum Coordination Section, Department of Education, San Diego County, San Diego, California.*

CTB/McGraw-Hill has done an excellent job in developing the technical aspects of the *Comprehensive Test of Basic Skills: Arithmetic.* The Technical Report, examiner's manuals, and Test Coordinator's Handbook tell almost more than one cares to know about the design and construction of the tests. Detailed information on reliability, validity, and on three different norm samples is simply but copiously presented. In addition to nationwide norms, large city and Catholic school norms are also available.

The arithmetic tests are Tests 6, 7, and 8 of the complete CTBS battery. Test 6 is called Computation; Test 7, Concepts; and Test 8, Applications. The computation tests are made up essentially of items which deal with the fundamental operations of addition, subtraction, multiplication, and division. They seem appropriate for the particular grade levels. There are two nearly identical forms of each test at each level. Additionally, nearly identical items appear in adjoining levels. Since the levels overlap, this is to be expected.

For the low ability reader, Tests 7 and 8 leave much to be desired. The "applications" of Test 8 turn out to be the same tired word problems that have troubled students for years. Tests 7 and 8 present problems which seldom reach beyond knowledge or comprehension level. For those who can read, the problems present no challenge; for those who cannot, they become linguistic hurdles rather than mathematics problems. The Level 1 test items in a hand scorable form have the added disadvantage of being crowded together, making them confusing as well as difficult to read.

The fact that these tests are still called "arithmetic" while most teachers and textbook publishers have moved to "mathematics" is perhaps symbolic of the kinds of problems required in Tests 7 and 8.

The thinking student will also experience difficulty with Tests 7 and 8 if he has a tendency to read too much into test items. For example, in both forms of Level 3, Test 8, an item like this is found: "X has $\frac{1}{2}$ of a cake and Y has $\frac{1}{4}$ of a cake. How much more cake does X have than Y?" Students taking both forms of Level 1, Test 7, are asked: "What goes in the box: $3 + 4 = \square + 2$?" At Level 2 the students are asked that as well as "Which pair of numbers, if put in the box, *would make the sentence true?*" [Italics added.] Students who have worked with true and false sentences will be needlessly confused.

In summary, the entire set of arithmetic tests appears to be no better and no worse than similar tests on the market. Test 6, Computation, gives sufficient items (60 at Level 1, 48 at Levels 2–4) and is well enough normed to provide some useful data on achievement of skills in basic operations. Tests 7 and 8 cannot be as highly recommended. A potential user should carefully consider whether these tests measure the objectives of his own mathematics program. One could only wish that the great pain taken with the technical aspects could have been reflected in the original construction of Tests 7 and 8.

C. ALAN RIEDESEL, *Professor of Education, Georgia State University, Atlanta, Georgia.*

The items of this arithmetic test are representative of a middle-of-the-road new mathematics curriculum.

Although the computational items break no new ground in the measurement of computational skill, they should be adequate for measurement of the typical computational skills taught in most schools.

The concept items tend to be slanted too much toward factual knowledge. However, to their credit, they are designed to measure concepts, not vocabulary alone, in contrast with many current mathematics tests which measure the vocabulary of contemporary mathematics without measuring the concepts.

The applications section (problem solving) is representative but rather routine. There are a few ambiguous problems, such as, "On a map 1 inch = 50 miles. How far is $3\frac{1}{2}$ inches on the map?" While most children will interpret the question in the manner the authors had in mind, a reasonable answer might be $3\frac{1}{2}$ inches. However, it should be noted that items such as this are few in number. The reading skill required for Level 1 could easily cause problems for many second and third graders. Care should be taken to insure that limited reading skill is not interpreted as lack of mathematical understanding.

Although content validity is reported to be the most important type of validity for this test, little actual information is given on the curricular emphasis taken or the procedures used to insure items representative of a wide range of mathematics curricula. This does not mean that such procedures were not properly employed. However, the technical report could and should have been more explicit about the curricular selection of items. The classification, writing, editing, and tryout of items appear to have been very carefully handled.

To obtain interform reliability, Forms Q and R were administered to students in two school districts at an interval of approximately six weeks. The correlation coefficients are not as high as one would hope. They range from a low of .65 at grade 3 on applications to a high of .91 at grade 7 on computation.

The K-R 20 reliability coefficients for subtests are satisfactory, ranging from a low of .79 for problem solving to a high of .96 for computation. The K-R 20 reliabilities for total scores, ranging from .94 to .96, are quite satisfactory.

The selection of a standardization group of 170,000 students was carefully planned. Consideration was given to school district enrollment, educational-economic index, and geographic region.

The careful examiner can gain a great deal of insight into the procedures used in developing the battery by a study of the comprehensive manual and technical report.

In summary, the Comprehensive breaks no new ground in mathematics testing. The tests are carefully developed measures of the standard variety. The norms are carefully developed and care was taken in reporting a wide variety of tryout data. The tests merit consideration for a school district looking for a "workhorse" type test of mathematics achievement in the conventional sense.

For reviews of the complete battery, see 9 (2 reviews, 3 excerpts).

[515]

*Cooperative Mathematics Tests: Arithmetic.
Grades 7–9; 1962–65; for all tests in the series, see 465; Forms A, B, C, ('62, 8 pages); no specific manual; series manual ('64, 79 pages); student bulletin ('65, 2 pages); separate answer sheets (Digitek, IBM 805, IBM 1230, SCRIBE) must be used; $6 per 20 tests; $4 per 100 answer sheets; $1.25 per 10 IBM hand scoring stencils (answer pattern must be punched out locally); Digitek scoring stencils not available; $2 per series manual; $3 per 100 student bulletins; $3 per specimen set of the series; cash orders postpaid; SCRIBE scoring and statistical analysis service, 35¢ per test; 40(45) minutes; Cooperative Tests and Services. *

REFERENCES

1. ALI, MD. BASHARAT. *To Establish the Feasibility of Using Translated and Adapted Versions of an American-Made Mathematics Achievement Test in East Pakistan.* Doctor's research study No. 1, Colorado State College (Greeley, Colo.), 1964. (*DA* 28:115A)
2. CAHEN, LEONARD S.; ROMBERG, THOMAS A.; AND ZWIRNER, WALTER. "The Estimation of Mean Achievement Scores for Schools by the Item-Sampling Technique." *Ed & Psychol Meas* 30(1):41–60 sp '70. * (*PA* 44:17766)

ALAN R. OSBORNE, *Associate Professor of Mathematics Education, The Ohio State University, Columbus, Ohio.*

The *Cooperative Mathematics Tests: Arithmetic* is designed to measure achievement for grades 7, 8, and 9. Although cast in language appropriate to most currently used junior high school texts, the tests are *not* comprehensive in that achievement of geometrical content, for example, is not measured and only a limited number of items may be construed as application problems. A premium is placed on the measurement of processes which call on a combination of ideas and skills to produce the answer. Computational skill is implicit in many items but is not the primary objective to be measured. The scope of arithmetical concepts tested is as comprehensive as that of most competitive tests.

The tests were begun in 1958 to accommodate the changes evident in junior high school curricula. In May 1960, pretests developed by leaders in mathematics and mathematics education were administered. Initial responses indicated the pretests possessed surface validity but the test designers had been "too optimistic about the mathematical training of American students." Subsequent revision resulted in the three forms of the test published in 1962. The writer would hope that the "too optimistic" judgment would be a function of introducing new curricula and that renorming of the test would establish this.

There is some variation in the topics stressed from one form of the test to another. For example, Form B possesses three more items concerned with operations on the whole numbers than Form A. Unlike the other forms, Form C contains no items on estimation. Although the norms equate the tests statistically, teachers and school systems should examine the forms of the tests in terms of their intended use. There also appears to be some variation from form to form in terms of speededness. Specific diagnostic or predictive uses of the tests should, therefore, depend upon the form selected.

Generally, items were thoughtfully constructed. The distracters are well selected. Some teachers might quarrel with the questions concerned with denominate numbers in the context of ratio. Is the ratio of 1 quart to 5 gallons 1 to 5 or 1 to 20? Some teachers desire students to evaluate the context of usage of the ratio before making conversion to the same unit. In Form C a hint for this type of item is given by the use of boldface type in the stem. This is not the case in comparable items in Form A. There are very few linguistic errors in the items. Notable exceptions which might, for example, penalize the bright student are: (*a*) The value of a number may be changed by performing an operation on it (Form A, item 33). (*b*) Item 40, Form C offers two correct distracters for students who have worked with negative numbers. (*c*) Purists might complain that there exists no symbol of operation between the 2 and the $\frac{3}{4}$ in the number $2\frac{3}{4}$, though an operation may be inferred.

Norms are provided for the nation generally and for urban schools particularly. Randomized procedures were used to select public, private, and parochial schools in a manner which was balanced geographically. The grade 9 norms are restricted to arithmetic classes rather than the total grade 9 population. Measures of reliability, discrimination, and so forth are provided by randomly selected subpopulations of 300 students for each grade level for each of the three 50-item forms. Reliabilities range from .86 to .91 when determined by K-R 20. The Handbook provides scale-score conversion pairings between forms as well as percentile rankings and confidence bands. Item content classification, item difficulty, and correlations with the SCAT-Q are provided.

ETS is to be complimented for its attempt to provide sound instruction for the appropriate use of standardized tests in the Handbook. Indeed, the limitations on the use of such tests receive more careful attention than do the potentials.

The tests will clearly need revision as the "modern" curriculum becomes better established than it was at the time of test design. They are thorough tests of arithmetical content but are not comprehensive tests of the intuitive geometric and algebraic content of current junior high school curricula. It is almost impossible for a 50-item test to be sufficiently comprehensive to encompass the new standard content of junior high school mathematics. Perhaps the test should be extended in time and number of items to be more congruent with current curricula.

For a review by O. F. Anderhalter, see 6:607. For excerpts from reviews of the series, see 465 (2 excerpts).

[516]

*Diagnostic Fractions Test 3. Ages 7–11; 1957–66; 1 form ('57, 8 pages); no specific manual; series manual ('66, 26 pages); no data on reliability; no norms; 5p per test, postage extra; Aus 75¢ per manual, postpaid within Australia; [30–45] minutes; E. W. Seville; James Nisbet & Co. Ltd. (test), Australian Council for Educational Research (manual). *

[517]

*Diagnostic Number Tests 1–2. Ages 8–11, 9–12; 1951–66; formerly called *Diagnostic Arithmetic Tests 1–2*; 2 tests; manual ('66, 22 pages); no data on reliability; no norms; Aus 50¢ per 10 tests; 75¢ per manual; $2.30 per specimen set; postpaid within Australia; E. W. Seville; Australian Council for Educational Research. *
a) TEST 1. Ages 8–11; 1 form ['66, 4 pages, identical with the 1951 edition]; 75¢ per set of scoring stencils; [20–30] minutes.
b) TEST 2. Ages 9–12; 1 form ['66, 3 pages, identical with the 1951 edition]; 60¢ per set of scoring stencils; [30–40] minutes.

[518]

★ERB Modern Arithmetic Test. Grades 5–6; 1969–70; Form B ('70, 7 pages); no manual; no data on reliability; no norms; nonmember schools must use scoring service; separate answer sheets (IBM 1230) must be used; $5 per 10 tests; 80¢ per 10 answer sheets; 28¢ per scoring stencil; $3 per specimen set; postage extra; scoring service, 55¢ and over per test; 40(45) minutes; Frederic P. Bonan, Philip Avirett, Stephen S. Ober, Foye Perry, Randolph Stone, Frederick Watson, and Arthur Weeks; Educational Records Bureau. *

[519]

*Emporia Arithmetic Tests. Grades 1, 2–3, 4–6, 7–8; 1962–64; first published 1962–63 in the Every Pupil Scholarship Test series; Forms A, B, ('64, 4 pages); 2 levels labeled tests 1, 2; manual for grades 2–8 ('64, 4 pages); $1.75 per 25 tests, postage extra; 75¢ per specimen set of any one level, postpaid; Ieleen Engelson (manual, *d*), Ruth Otterstrom (manual, *c*),

Patricia M. Pease (manual, *a, b*), and M. W. Sanders; Data Processing and Educational Measurement Center. *
a) EMPORIA PRIMARY ARITHMETIC TEST. I, 2 semesters in grade 1; manual ('64, 3 pages); directions for administration (no date, 2 pages); (60) minutes.
b) EMPORIA ELEMENTARY ARITHMETIC TEST. I, 2 semesters in grades 2–3; directions for administration (no date, 1 page); (60) minutes.
c) EMPORIA INTERMEDIATE ARITHMETIC TEST. I, 2 semesters in grades 4–6; 50(60) minutes.
d) EMPORIA JUNIOR HIGH SCHOOL ARITHMETIC TEST. I, 2 semesters in grades 7–8; 50(60) minutes.

MARILYN N. SUYDAM, *Associate Professor of Education, The Pennsylvania State University, University Park, Pennsylvania.*

This set of tests is designed as a survey of skills in arithmetic computation and problem solving. It is claimed that a "high degree of validity is assured" since each item was "carefully selected and checked against reputable criteria, such as courses of study, textbooks, word lists, criticisms of teachers and supervisors, and analyses of pupils' test papers." It is apparent from a scrutiny of the tests that this validity pertains to "traditional" content rather than "modern."

The manual of directions is concise, so concise that it is hardly helpful. Too little information on construction and too little data on reliability and norms are provided. It would seem more appropriate for 1930, as would the format and appearance of the tests. Only those who wish to make no attempt to measure newer content or to measure beyond the facts and skills level should use these tests.

PRIMARY TESTS. Split-half reliabilities range from .88 to .90, with number of pupils ranging from 1,027 to 1,867.

A sheet of directions for administering the test reflects little of the explicitness expected for a standardized test. The teacher "should use her own discretion" in deciding how long pupils should be "actively engaged in working parts of the test."

The placement of scoring directions on the key is confusing. (All tests must be hand scored.) The number of points for items varies, making the recording of scores difficult. Some answers on the key are not correctly given; e.g., "2 or two" when both are required. Format of the tests, and, in particular, type size and spacing, might make both use and scoring difficult.

Interpretation of results "is accomplished by use of table of percentile norms." Aside from the "number of cases," no information on the derivation of these norms is included. Results are to be used to "motivate pupils to put forth greater zeal in learning," in assigning term marks or determining promotion, and for diagnostic uses. One sentence is particularly confusing: "Since the test is divided into three distinct parts, it is possible to discover on which particular type of reading function a pupil may have his weakness." The three parts are not evident; the reference to reading leads one to believe these are directions for another test. At any rate, even an "alert teacher" will hardly find this sufficient to "apply remedies to aid the pupil to overcome his difficulties." Equivalent forms are provided to aid in measuring gains. The forms are so closely parallel, however, that learning from the test would most probably be a factor in the scores.

Specific instructions are given for translating scores into marks; e.g., "Give A for percentile score of 90 or higher." How these are derived or whether they are appropriate to all schools is not considered.

ELEMENTARY, INTERMEDIATE, AND JUNIOR HIGH TESTS. An identical manual (cover, one page of instructions, two pages of norms) accompanies all three sets of tests. Norms were computed from the scores of more than 44,000 pupils, with approximately 1,000 to 1,900 pupils in each grade using each form. Tables of percentile norms are given for each form and level for grades 2–8. This is very compact—and confusing, especially since possible scores range from 80 to 150.

Reliability coefficients (split-half) are estimated to be from .87 to .92. "Special directions" for the elementary tests are attached to the key; like those on the primary tests, these are very general (e.g., at the teacher's discretion, "a problem too advanced" may be omitted). No special directions are provided for either the intermediate or junior high levels, though on each there is need to time subsections. Print size at these levels decreases; it is difficult to "make answers stand out clearly." Scoring is somewhat confusing. Interpretation of results is related only to converting scores to percentiles and school marks.

For specific survey information, the Emporia tests might be useful, but their content should be carefully studied by potential users to ascertain applicability.

BLAINE R. WORTHEN, *Co-director, Laboratory of Educational Research, University of Colorado, Boulder, Colorado.*

The content of these tests is appropriate for their designated grade levels if traditional arithmetic skills are to be assessed. Recognition and counting skills, knowledge of order relationships and place value, and use of algorithms are emphasized throughout. Although problem-solving skills are given increasing emphasis in the intermediate and junior high tests, no attempt has been made to measure mathematical concepts, generalizations, and understandings more typical of contemporary arithmetic programs. For example, pupils in modern mathematics curricula might experience difficulty with persistent use of the term "number" to refer to numerals.

Each of the four tests comprises four purportedly equivalent forms, but no evidence is provided to support this claim.

TEST USE. Several serious inadequacies limit the use of these tests. First, the instructions for administration are vague and virtually preclude standardization of testing procedures. For the primary test, the teacher is asked to read aloud the instructions for each question. At the elementary level, written instructions are included, but the teacher is permitted to read aloud any part of the test where written instructions, statements, or story problems appear. At both these levels, specific directions to pupils are sometimes imprecise or misleading. For example, the instruction, "Draw a line joining each group of dots with a word which tells how many dots there are in the group," is given for an item which contains *no* words, only numerals. How much time should be spent on each item and the amount of additional oral clarification are left to the discretion of the teacher, thus allowing wide differences in test administration procedures and difficulties in establishing meaningful norms.

The intermediate and junior high tests are each divided into three timed sections. Although no explicit directions are given, it appears that pupils who complete a section before the time expires are not expected to go on then to the next section. However, the format does not prevent pupils from studying portions of the next section that appear on the same page as the ends of previous sections.

The format is sometimes cramped; for example, primary grade pupils are told to "Draw six boats" within a small square that would provide a challenge even for adults with normal hand-eye coordination.

The tests are hand scored, with a separate answer key for each form. The keys are cumbersome to use and scorers will probably depend on recall on at least the more simple tests rather than continue to look back and forth between test and answer key. More serious, there are several errors in the keys. For example, "6" is given as the response to the item, "Three threes are _____." The answer to "62 + 27" is listed as 189. In another item, one option ($\frac{5}{6}$) is keyed as correct but another ($\frac{15}{18}$) is equally correct in the absence of specific instructions directing pupils to express fractions in simplest form.

TEST INTERPRETATION. Tables of percentile norms are provided, but no description of the norm groups is given, other than their size. In the absence of data on the type of pupils included, geographical distribution of the samples, and conditions under which the norm data were collected, the norms have little utility. They become even more meaningless when one recalls the lack of carefully standardized procedures for administering the tests.

The suggestion is made that the percentile scores be used to translate test scores into school marks. Distributions of letter grades and percentage marks are provided, based on a normal curve for the normed group. The teacher is told to give an A to a pupil whose percentile score is 90 or higher, B for a percentile score of 75 to 89, C for one of 25 to 74, and so on. Such suggestions exhibit shocking naiveté. It is difficult to conceive of any situation where it would be appropriate to use norms from an unknown group as a basis for assigning school marks. It is easier to conceive of a situation where all pupils in a group of "slow learners" receive marks of F or D despite a possible range of 24 percentile points in their distribution of scores. Such a technique is patently indefensible.

TECHNICAL CONSIDERATIONS. Very little useful technical information is presented in the 3- to 4-page manual that accompanies each test. Although the authors state that each item was carefully selected and checked against reputable criteria, thus assuring a "high degree of validity," no description of the courses of study or textbooks sampled or of the qualifications and interrater reliabilities of the judges are pro-

vided. Data on item difficulties and discrimination are also lacking, as are means and standard deviations for each form and intercorrelations among the four forms of each test. Unfortunately, the above information cannot be provided by the test publisher (personal letter, June 1970).

The reported reliabilities for each form of each test were determined by an unidentified split-half method. Although the values range between .87 and .92, these are likely to be at least somewhat spurious because of the effect of speededness on this type of reliability estimate. The severely speeded tests at grades 4–6 and 7–8 and the overall time limit allotted for administration of the primary and elementary tests have not been adequately considered in this attempt to estimate reliability. Standard errors of measurement and standard deviations of scores that might have supplemented the reliability estimates are lacking.

It is suggested in the manual that equivalent forms of the test are provided to facilitate retesting; however, no evidence of between-form test reliability is provided.

SUMMARY. The *Emporia Arithmetic Tests* have very little to offer. Their content makes them unsuitable for use in other than strictly traditional arithmetic programs. Even in such programs, other arithmetic tests that reflect traditional content and are designed for approximately the same grade levels could be used with a much greater degree of confidence and the results would be much more interpretable. Either the *SRA Achievement Series: Arithmetic* or the *Metropolitan Achievement Tests: Arithmetic* is far superior as a measure of traditional arithmetic content. By contrast to the careful developmental work evident in the above tests, the *Emporia Arithmetic Tests* appear to have been hurriedly thrown together. An enormous amount of work would be necessary before they could be viewed as a serious competitor in this area of testing. Imprecision and vagueness in instructions need to be eliminated; serious errors must be removed, and more care and thought given to accuracy and detail throughout. Test development and norming procedures must be adequately described and better evidence of reliability and validity must be presented. Until these steps are taken, this reviewer strongly advises against the use of these tests.

[520]
Manchester Mechanical Arithmetic Test (Sen.)
1. Ages 13.5–15; 1959; MMAT; 1 form (10 pages);
manual (8 pages); 75p per 20 tests; 10p per manual;
15p per specimen set; postage extra; 60(65) minutes;
Jack Wrigley (test) and Stephen Wiseman; University of London Press Ltd. *

J. S. LAWES, *Principal Lecturer in Education, Westminster College, North Hinksey, Oxford, England.*

Inspection of this test suggests that within its 60 questions the four basic arithmetic processes are covered adequately, although the manual contains no indication of any tryout or item analysis procedures undertaken to establish the suitability of the items. The questions are well spaced on the pages of the booklet and sufficient space is some way provided for any working required, but it is not always clear where the answer should be written and in some cases the answer space is removed from the question. The presentation of some questions might be improved to avoid possible difficulties. For example, on the page which contains a number of algebraic expressions, the values to be substituted are printed within and as part of the first of four questions, all of which require the use of these values; if the number of the first question (52) had been printed just one line lower, then the fact that the values applied to all four questions would be clear. Again, question 47 states simply "5% of £250," yet every other question contains an instruction such as "Change into" or "Find." Question 27 prices eggs at 2s. 6d. per dozen; with today's rapid changes in prices such questions soon become unrealistic and could well be avoided.

The manual contains clear instructions for the administration and marking of the test. It also contains two erratum slips. One, which is firmly attached to the appropriate page, corrects the answer given for one of the questions! The other is a loose slip and therefore easily lost. It directs the attention of the reader to the small print at the foot of the back page of the test booklet. If this includes the words "Third impression 1964" then three other answers in the key must be altered. As the three questions concerned contain farthings in the original printing one must assume that in later printings these items were modified. It would be a simple matter to state this on the slip and to attach the slip firmly to the manual.

The test is well standardised on a complete age group of 6,679 boys and 6,763 girls aged

14.1 to 15.0. Tables extending down to 13.6 are provided to convert raw scores to standardised scores. Separate tables are given for boys and girls "since the performance of boys and girls tends to differ on tests of arithmetic" but no indication is given of the nature and size of the differences found in the standardisation population. Reliability has been assessed on adequate samples using split-half, internal consistency, and test-retest methods. Values of .97, .96, and .95, respectively, are quoted.

This test was designed to fill a gap in the lists of tests available in England for the 14 to 15 age group. In the decade since it was first published many changes have taken place in mathematics courses, but where schools still follow syllabuses for which the content of this test is appropriate then the test might well be used, for it is reliable and well standardised on a large urban population. Many test users will now be looking away from the traditional forms and hoping for tests appropriate in content to the new mathematics and tests which assess understanding of mathematical concepts. This is where the gaps in the lists of tests now appear.

[521]
***Moray House Arithmetic Test 43.** Ages 10–12;
1935–69; 1 form ('69, 8 pages); manual ('69, 12 pages); distribution restricted to education authorities; 75p per 20 tests; 5p per single copy; 12½p per manual; postage extra; 45(55) minutes; Godfrey Thomson Unit for Educational Research, University of Edinburgh; University of London Press Ltd. *

REFERENCES
1–9. See 6:628.

For a review by John Cohen of earlier forms, see 3:346.

[522]
★Number Test DE. Ages 10.5–12.5; 1965; formerly called *Number Test 1;* 1 form ['65, 8 pages]; manual ['65, 12 pages]; 5p per test; 8p per manual; postpaid within U.K.; (50–60) minutes; E. L. Barnard; published for the National Foundation for Educational Research in England and Wales; Ginn & Co. Ltd. *

[523]
RBH Arithmetic Fundamentals Test. Business and industry; 1951–63; Forms 1 ('51, 5 pages), 2 ('59, 5 pages); manual ['63, 10 pages]; directions (no date, 2 pages); $4.50 per 25 tests; 50¢ per key; $1.50 per manual; $1.50 per specimen set; postage extra; 20(25) minutes; Richardson, Bellows, Henry & Co., Inc. *

JOHN W. LOMBARD, *Director, Guidance Department, Science Research Associates, Inc., Chicago, Illinois.*

Although the manual does not state the purpose of the test, it may be inferred that it is intended for use in screening applicants and classifying employees in basic industrial jobs.

The 42 items are all basic arithmetic; the most complex item deals with fundamental operations using simple fractions. Of the 63 studies reported in the manual, approximately a fifth show mean scores of 35 or higher, indicating that the test may be too easy to differentiate among subjects with more than minimal arithmetic skills. The publisher acknowledges this limitation in the manual. No description of test development procedures is given.

The test appears easy to administer and score. No guidelines, however, are given for scoring equivalent answers ($^{25}\!/_{12}$ rather than $2\frac{1}{12}$, for example), a shortcoming which could perplex a test-scoring clerk.

Three reliability studies are reported, but they are all split-half, and no speededness data or backup descriptive statistics are given. The validity studies reported give correlations of test scores with supervisors' ratings, and these average in the low .20's. The usefulness of this type of statistic for a test designed for selection and placement of individuals is obviously questionable.

The two forms of the test are parallel in content but no data are reported on equating, intercorrelations, or equivalence. The statement is made in the manual that "comparability studies have indicated that data can be combined for normative purposes," but no such studies are described.

The page of scoring directions states that "norms developed on local populations are always of most value." This is true, of course, but it does not relieve the publisher of his responsibilities. This test has been available for approximately 20 years. If after that length of time the manual cannot be more specific in answering questions about how, why, when, and with whom the test should be used or describe more appropriate validity studies, then the test cannot be recommended for continued use.

[524]

*The RBH Arithmetic Reasoning Test. Business and industry; 1948–63; forms 1, 2, ('61, 5 pages); manual ['63, 13 pages]; directions (no date, 2 pages); no data on reliability for form 2; no norms for form 2, publisher recommends use of local norms; $4.50 per 25 tests; 50¢ per scoring key; $1.50 per manual; $1.50 per specimen set; postage extra; 15(20) minutes; Richardson, Bellows, Henry & Co., Inc. *

JOHN W. LOMBARD, Director, Guidance Department, Science Research Associates, Inc., Chicago, Illinois.

There was an era when it was fashionable for a management consulting firm, if hired to establish a program for selection, classification, and promotion of blue-collar employees, to administer large numbers of short, separate tests and to attempt to develop guidelines for their use alone or in combination. It was obviously convenient if the tests were developed by the consulting firm. Since the tests were used by the firm for specific purposes, there was little need for norms, guidelines for use, and other information and data helpful to general users. A cynic might argue that a complete test manual would make the consulting firm unnecessary, since the customer could use the tests effectively by himself.

The RBH Arithmetic Reasoning Test is a test from this mold. The test itself consists of 25 arithmetic "word problems," with a 15-minute time limit. No description of test development procedures is given. No data on speededness are shown, though the only reliabilities reported are split-half, and the instructions to examinees state that they are not expected to finish in the allotted time. Because the test items are word problems, there is undoubtedly a significant reading component reflected in the test scores, but no judgments about the influence of this variable can be made on the basis of information in the manual. The claim is made that the test is useful with a wide range of employees, from clerks to executives, but the reported studies show the test is probably too easy for groups with more than minimal arithmetical proficiency.

There are two forms of the test but all data reported are for Form 1 and no evidence of equivalence of forms is given. All validity studies (undated) reported give correlations of test scores with various criteria, usually supervisor's rankings. The best of these correlations are moderate, which emphasizes not only the need to develop local norms but also the need for information about the appropriate test population. Can it be used with high school dropouts? Minority groups? Poor readers or non-English-trained individuals?

In summary, the RBH Arithmetic Reasoning Test is an organized collection of 25 test items. Without the management consultants, however, one is in the dark about why or with whom to use it, or how to use the results appropriately.

[525]

RBH Shop Arithmetic Test. Industry; 1948–63; Forms 1 ('48, 5 pages), 2 ('51, 5 pages) ; Form 2 is a slightly easier form rather than a parallel form; manual ['63, 12 pages] ; directions sheet (no date, 2 pages) ; norms for males only; $4.50 per 25 tests; 50¢ per key; $1.50 per manual; $1.50 per specimen set; postage extra; 15(20) minutes; Richardson, Bellows, Henry & Co., Inc. *

REFERENCES

1–2. See 6:636.

JOHN W. LOMBARD, *Director, Guidance Department, Science Research Associates, Inc., Chicago, Illinois.*

There is little that can be said favorably about this test. Each form contains 20 arithmetic word problems that *appear* to be typical shop problems. However, closer examination of Form 1 reveals that knowledge of geometric principles, such as "a line segment parallel to the base of a triangle and equal to one-half of it bisects the altitude," is necessary to answer a problem. The datedness of the test is seen in an item that has a worker earning 86 cents an hour.

By putting the items in a word-problem setting with a 15-minute time limit, the authors introduce a reading factor into the scores, but at no time is mention made of its significance. However, Form 1 correlates .74 with the language score of the *California Test of Mental Maturity.* No speededness data are reported.

In the studies users have reported, the group means range from a high of 15 for managers to a low of 5 for a sample of process employees. This indicates that the test is useful for only certain classifications of employees, but without more adequate explanations of the samples studied, the user would have to determine the test's appropriateness on a trial-and-error basis.

No test construction rationale or procedure is given, and it is not clear whether the two forms were deliberately or accidentally made nonparallel.

The usual correlation studies of test scores and supervisors' ratings are reported as validity studies, with the usual low to modest correlations resulting. The value of such studies for a test to use in hiring, reclassifying, or promoting individuals is questionable. Model studies of test scores and attrition, expectancy of success, or individual predictions would be more helpful for users developing local norms.

The relations between this test, the *RBH Arithmetic Fundamentals Test,* and the *RBH Arithmetic Reasoning Test* are nowhere explained. Why are three overlapping tests offered? What are their intercorrelations? For what situations is each recommended?

This test cannot be recommended for use in its present state. There are too many unanswered questions about its rationale, reading level, speededness, appropriateness with various groups, and validity in situations most closely related to its probable use.

[526]

*****SRA Achievement Series: Arithmetic.** Grades 1–2, 2–4, 4–9; 1954–69; 4 scores: concepts, reasoning, computation, total ; 2 forms ; 5 levels in 3 booklets ; no specific manual ; for series manuals and accessories, see 18; postage extra; Louis P. Thorpe, D. Welty Lefever, and Robert A. Naslund; Science Research Associates, Inc. *

a) HAND SCORED EDITION. Grades 1–2, 2–4; 1955–68; test booklet title is *Let's Figure This Out;* 2 levels.

1) *Grades 1–2.* 1958–68; Forms C, D, ('63, 21 pages) ; $4.35 per 25 tests; 105(155) minutes in 3 sessions.

2) *Grades 2–4.* 1955–68; Forms C, D, ('63, 21 pages) ; $3.75 per 25 tests; 110(160) minutes in 3 sessions.

b) MULTILEVEL EDITION. Grades 4–9; 1963–69; Forms C, D, ('63, 31 pages) ; 3 levels: blue (grades 4.5–6.5), green (grades 6.5–8.5), and red (grades 8.5–9) in a single booklet; separate series answer sheets (Digitek, DocuTran, IBM 805, IBM 1230) must be used; $8.70 per 25 tests; $9.30 per 100 DocuTran answer sheets; 110(141) minutes in 2 sessions.

REFERENCES

1. See 6:632.
2. RILEY, MARY FELICITAS. *An Analysis of Timed and Untimed Test Scores of Subjects From Two Different Arithmetic Curricula.* Doctor's thesis, Fordham University (New York, N.Y.), 1963. (*DA* 25:2354)
3. HOPKINS, KENNETH D. "Extrinsic Reliability: Estimating and Attenuating Variance From Response Styles, Chance, and Other Irrelevant Sources." *Ed & Psychol Meas* 24:271–81 su '64. * (*PA* 39:3152)
4. ANASTASIOW, NICHOLAS J. "Fourth Through Sixth Grade Student Performance Differences on STEP and SRA Achievement Tests." *Meas & Eval Guid* 2(3):149–52 f '69. * (*PA* 44:13276)

MARY O. FOLSOM, *Professor of Education, University of Miami, Coral Gables, Florida.*

The concepts tested in grades 1 and 2 include recognition and writing of numerals, place value, the meaning of numbers, unit fractions, and simple measurements. In grades 2–4 the meaning of operations, understanding of "borrowing" and "carrying," and inequalities are included. In both cases items dealing with the recognition of the number of a set from drawings, the recognition of simple geometric figures and their regions, and the use of the number line would strengthen this section of the battery. The Multilevel Edition includes 47 items at each level. The questions vary in difficulty from the simple recognition of an improper fraction to the understanding that the corresponding angles of parallel lines cut by a transversal are congruent. The various topics of traditional arithmetic are covered, as well as topics from business arithmetic and some of the properties of real numbers, i.e., identifying elements for addition and multiplication.

The reasoning sections at all levels have the same format as that used in the previous edition. Data are given and a number of questions refer to this information. While the format does require the ability to reason and organize material, the constant need to refer back to the original data to answer as many as eight problems might be questioned. In addition, a premium is placed on reading ability as early as grade 2 in the level for grades 2–4.

These tests are heavy on computation items: 38 to 42 percent in grades 1–2, 44 to 49 percent in grades 2–4, and 34 percent in grades 4–9. Since children are notoriously poor at copying from the chalkboard or book, the reviewer wonders how many children err because they copy digits incorrectly.

The within-grades reliabilities (K-R 20) are all .90 or higher; the subtest reliabilities range from .70 to .96, with median .86.

The content validity of these tests for a particular school system can be determined only by a detailed examination of the tests themselves. For those school systems which prefer an emphasis on mathematical ideas rather than computation and which do not wish children to be handicapped by lack of reading ability, the mathematics subtest in the *Cooperative Primary Tests* for grades 1–3 might well be considered.

For a review by E. W. Hamilton of earlier forms, see 6:632; for reviews by Robert D. North and J. Fred Weaver, see 5:483. For reviews of the complete battery, see 18 (2 reviews), 6:21 (1 review), and 5:21 (2 reviews).

[527]

*Stanford Achievement Test: Arithmetic Tests.** Grades 4.0–5.4, 5.5–6.9, 7.0–9.9; 1923–68; catalog uses the title *Stanford Arithmetic Tests;* 3 scores: computation, concepts, applications; Forms W, X, ('64, 8 pages); 3 levels; battery technical supplement ('66, 55 pages); expected grade score tables ('68, 10 pages) based on *Otis-Lennon Mental Ability Test* available on request; supplementary directions ['64–66, 1–2 pages] for each type of answer sheet; $6 per 35 tests; 60¢ per key; separate answer sheets (Digitek, Harbor, IBM 805, IBM 1230) may be used; $2.30 per 35 IBM 805 answer sheets; $2.80 per 35 Digitek or

IBM 1230 answer sheets; $3 per 100 Harbor answer cards; 70¢ per Digitek or IBM scoring stencil; $2 per technical supplement; $1.75 per specimen set of any one level; postage extra; Harbor or IBM scoring service, 19¢ and over per test; Braille and large type editions available from American Printing House for the Blind; Truman L. Kelley, Richard Madden, Eric F. Gardner, and Herbert C. Rudman; Harcourt Brace Jovanovich, Inc. *
a) INTERMEDIATE 1. Grades 4.0–5.4; manual ('64, 8 pages); 85(95) minutes in 2 sessions.
b) INTERMEDIATE 2. Grades 5.5–6.9; manual ('64, 10 pages); 87(95) minutes in 2 sessions.
c) ADVANCED. Grades 7.0–9.9; manual ('64, 10 pages); 87(95) minutes in 2 sessions.

REFERENCES

1–7. See 6:637.
8. LONG, JOHN ADAM, JR. *Some Aspects of an Oral-Visual Presentation of an Achievement Test to Educable, Mentally Retarded Pupils.* Doctor's thesis, Pennsylvania State University (University Park, Pa.), 1962. (*DA* 23:3728)
9. RILEY, MARY FELICITAS. *An Analysis of Timed and Untimed Test Scores of Subjects From Two Different Arithmetic Curricula.* Doctor's thesis, Fordham University (New York, N.Y.), 1963. (*DA* 25:2354)
10. NAMKIN, SIDNEY. *The Stability of Achievement Test Scores: A Longitudinal Study of the Reading and Arithmetic Subtests of the Stanford Achievement Test.* Doctor's thesis, Rutgers—The State University (New Brunswick, N.J.), 1966. (*DA* 27:398A)
11. GALLIAN, RICHARD DONALD. *A Content Validation Study of the Arithmetic Test Items of Four Arithmetic Achievement Tests Compared With the Content of Six Arithmetic Series at the Intermediate Level.* Doctor's thesis, University of Missouri (Columbia, Mo.), 1967. (*DA* 28:3361A)
12. COHEN, JERRY MARVIN. *A Study of the Validity of the Predictor Variables Used for Determining the Admission of Ninth Grade Students to the College Preparatory and Vocational-Technical Curricula in the Tenth Grade of the Baltimore City Public Schools.* Doctor's thesis, George Washington University (Washington, D.C.), 1969. (*DAI* 30:1328A)
13. SLOCUM, THOMAS J., AND LIEBERMAN, MARCUS. "Investigation of Low Scores on Standardized Arithmetic Computation Tests." *Ill Sch Res* 5(2):7–9 F '69. *

HAROLD C. TRIMBLE, *Professor of Mathematics Education, The Ohio State University, Columbus, Ohio.*

As one might expect in the fourth extensive revision of a battery of tests made after nearly 50 years of experience gained in extensive use, these tests do superbly well what they claim to do. The 1964 edition avoids some of the criticisms properly made of the 1953 edition. The "reasoning" score of the 1953 forms becomes the "concepts" and "applications" scores of the 1964 form. The new categories are more homogeneous and better defined than was the previous single category. Some test items which reflect the newer trends in arithmetic programs have been included under each of the three categories of computation, concepts, and applications.

Although the tests are best suited to a traditional program in arithmetic, there is no reason why students in contemporary programs should be confused by the items. There are, to be sure, exceptions. For example, some of today's students will be surprised to be asked to recognize the "commutative property of numbers" (item

30, Form X, Advanced) in contrast, say, to the commutative property of addition. But even when the language of the items is not quite in the accepted mathematical idiom, it should be clearly understood by well taught children who have studied from the newer textbook series.

Researchers seeking a kind of common denominator for arithmetic programs throughout the United States will do well to consider these tests. The 55-page technical supplement is excellent. Well constructed norms enable the user to place a student by grade level, with a good data base up to 9 years, 6 months. Moreover, percentile scores are converted to stanine scores which are easily found for students at numerous stages in the school grade structure. Thus a student may be placed among his grade-level peers as being from 0 to 4 equal steps above or below the normal 5 of the stanine scale. And even this does not exhaust the possibilities. By combining a student's scores on the Otis IQ test with his scores on the appropriate arithmetic test one can compare achievement level with capacity to learn.

What, then, are the limitations?

First, the tests do not touch upon many commonly taught topics. The number line with its extension to the Cartesian plane is almost entirely absent. Students are asked to perform arithmetical calculations, but there is almost no attention to the why's of the algorithms. It seems evident that teachers using any of the current arithmetic texts will need to supplement these tests with items designed to sample topics emphasized in their materials but not touched upon in these tests. Teacher-made tests or tests prepared by textbook publishers are still needed to achieve curricular validity in a contemporary testing program.

Second, the usual precautions must be taken in interpreting test results. For example, the "computation" score may well be more a function of speed than of ability to perform calculations that are entirely correct. Some teachers will be willing to settle in an age of computers for a lower level of computational skill, provided that understanding is adequate for a high level of accuracy of calculation even though it is performed at a slower rate. Are the "concepts" emphasized in the tests the concepts about which a teacher is most concerned? Only a careful analysis of teacher objectives and of test items will provide answers to this question. Are the "applications" appropriate as to scope and level of difficulty? Again, the teacher should react to the test items as such rather than to the word applications.

Third, experience would indicate that test results are frequently misused. Researchers seize upon such statistically immaculate scores as these tests provide. Often they forget the source of these numbers and use them to "prove" the superiority of program A over program B. Teachers become smug when their classes beat the norms; or they despair of students who fall below the median. Principals and supervisors often overinterpret the scores by approving or disapproving the performance of a teacher or the success of an instructional program. In this connection one should keep in mind the many and diverse factors that common sense would suggest as potentially significant in influencing scores on such tests. It is quite possible to teach for the test, especially when the test has been used year after year. Thus students may achieve spuriously high scores that do not reflect their true level of achievement. Moreover, students do have bad days; some students get their answers in the wrong place on the answer sheet; some students mark at random; etc.

In summary, this reviewer is much impressed by these tests and by the supporting materials that the publisher provides. At the same time, he is mindful that results of standardized tests have been taken at face value, overinterpreted, and used inappropriately in the past. It will be especially tempting to forget the limitations of these tests. They do what they do so well that users may be prone to credit them with doing other things they make no claim of doing.

For a review by C. Alan Riedesel of an earlier edition, see 6:637; for a review by Robert L. Burch, see 4:419. For reviews of the complete battery, see 25 (1 excerpt), 6:26 (1 review, 1 excerpt), 5:25 (1 review), 4:25 (2 reviews), and 3:18 (2 reviews).

[528]

★**Stanford Diagnostic Arithmetic Test.** Grades 2.5-4.5, 4.5-8.5; 1966-68; SDAT; Forms W ('66, 8 pages), X ('68, 8 pages); 2 levels; $7.90 per 35 tests; 50¢ per key; $1.75 per specimen set of either level; postage extra; scoring service, $2 per test; Leslie S. Beatty, Richard Madden, and Eric F. Gardner; Harcourt Brace Jovanovich, Inc. *
a) LEVEL I. Grades 2.5-4.5; 13 scores grouped in 3 categories: concepts (counting, operations, decimal place value, total), computation (A—addition, B—subtraction, C—multiplication, D—division, A + B for grade 3 or A + B + C + D for grade 4), number

facts (addition, subtraction, multiplication, division); manual ('66, 38 pages); 170(205) minutes in 6 sessions.

b) LEVEL 2. Grades 4.5–8.5; 16 scores grouped in 5 categories: concepts (number system and operations, decimal place value, total), computation (addition and subtraction, multiplication, division, total), common fractions (understanding, computation, total), decimal fractions and percent, number facts (addition, subtraction, multiplication, division, carrying); manual ('66, 42 pages); 210(250) minutes in 7 sessions.

W. TODD ROGERS, *Fellow, Laboratory of Educational Research, University of Colorado, Boulder, Colorado.*

According to the manual for administering and interpreting the *Stanford Diagnostic Arithmetic Test,* the SDAT "is designed to diagnose specific weaknesses in working with numbers." Specifically, the focus is on an understanding of properties of the number system and on computation. Other areas of arithmetic, such as geometry, measurement, and problem solving, are not tested. The test has two levels, with two forms at each level. Designed for group administration and easily scored by hand, it can be used for either individual or class diagnosis. A pupil profile is included on the front of each test booklet, and a class record and class analysis chart are provided. The test manual contains norms, interpretations of several sample pupil profiles and one class analysis record, and suggestions for remedial instruction.

TEST DEVELOPMENT. An item analysis was performed, but no summary data on item difficulties and discriminations are provided. The item analysis data were obtained not only for the total item analysis sample but also for the upper and lower 27 percent of that group. Consideration of these two subgroups is not only outmoded in the age of computers but also inappropriate for this type of test, for which the distributions are not necessarily normal. No details are provided regarding the bases for identifying items that did not function as intended; neither is the method described which was used to assign retained items to the final two forms. Means and standard deviations for the subtests and tests for each form, and the correlations between corresponding subtests of each form are not reported, although they would have been most helpful. Although the item analysis sample was large (approximately 15,000) and was selected from seven school systems in five states, no descriptive information is provided about this sample (e.g., age, sex, mental ability, type of curriculum, and geo-graphical distribution). Such data are necessary before one can determine whether the item analysis sample is representative of the population for which the authors intended the test.

STANDARDIZATION. Percentile and stanine norms are reported for all scores except for the Number Facts subtests and for the Division subtest in grades 2.5–3.5. The norm data were obtained at the beginning of October in keeping with the recommendation that the test be used early in an instructional sequence. For each grade level, norm samples of 100 were selected. These samples were selected from approximately 8,000 pupils in four school districts to duplicate the national norm group for the *Stanford Achievement Test: Arithmetic Computation.* The method described in the manual of selecting the norm groups is not strictly random; therefore, the obtained norms are subject to bias through nonrandomization. Use of an equi-percentile procedure to obtain the norm groups would have avoided this problem. The extent to which the SDAT norm samples represent the national school population is not defined. Statements describing the communities in terms of median family income, educational level of adults, and the curriculum in effect in the schools represented in the norm samples are given, but no data to support these statements are included. No other information necessary when describing norm samples (e.g., sex, age, mental ability, race, and size of school) is presented.

Pupils taking Form X served as the basic norm group. The norms for Form W were developed in terms of Form X, using an equi-percentile procedure. This commendable procedure minimizes the lack of comparability between norms for the two forms.

The stanine transformation seems inappropriate for this type of test, since the distribution of raw scores is not necessarily normal. The imprecision of the stanine scale does not contribute to the identification of individual weaknesses, the stated purpose of the test. (It is possible for pupils to earn stanine scores which differ by two stanines when their performance on the test varies slightly, while other students whose performance varies much more will be assigned to adjacent stanines.) Grade score norms were developed for the Concept and Computation total scores. These norms, included to represent the pupils' overall level of performance, serve no diagnostic function. Norms are reported as letter grades (A, B, C) for the Number Facts subtests. Not a common type of norm, these ratings seem appropriate for the distributions of raw scores obtained.

RELIABILITY. Split-half reliability coefficients and the corresponding errors of measurement (in raw score units) are reported at each grade level for the subtest and test scores on Form W, but not on Form X. Calculation of errors of measurement in the norm units would have been helpful. The reported reliabilities range between .89 and .98 for total scores, and .82 and .95 for the Concept, Common Fractions, and Decimal Fractions and Per Cent subtests. Several of the Computation subtests have reliabilities in the .70's. In two instances, reliabilities of .57 and .60—much too low for a diagnostic test—are reported. While the tests, which are timed, are not designed as speed tests, evidence relating the extent of speededness should be included when using a split-half method for computing reliabilities. Unfortunately, although equivalent forms were available, equivalent form reliabilities are not reported. The equivalent forms procedure constitutes a more demanding test of an instrument's precision and as such is more suitable for a test with a stated diagnostic purpose.

It is reported in the manual that maximum reliability is provided at the lower levels of performance for most distributions, but no data are provided indicating variation in reliabilities and errors of measurement by score level. The inclusion of the reliabilities of difference scores, or the minimum significant differences between pairs of scores, would have been helpful to aid in the interpretation of student profiles.

VALIDITY. The content validity of the test is described in terms of an item content outline for each level. Correlations between the subtests and tests of the SDAT and the three arithmetic tests of the Stanford Achievement Test, obtained on pupils in the Form W norm groups, are reported for each grade level. The majority of the correlations are high; most of the low correlations are based on markedly skewed distributions, which prevent a high correlation. It would appear, on the basis of these data, that the SDAT is suitable for achievement testing at these grade levels. As stated in the manual, no direct evidence of diagnostic validity is provided. Intercorrelations among the SDAT subtests, Form W, are reported at each grade

level. As is the case for the correlations between SAT and SDAT, the majority of the correlations among the SDAT subtests are high, while the few remaining correlations are based on markedly skewed distributions. Therefore, it is not clear that the subtests are even measuring unique numerical concepts or computational skills.

EVALUATION. The legitimacy of the SDAT as a diagnostic test is not clear. Little research on the effectiveness of group diagnostic tests in arithmetic has been reported. The manual states, "It is hoped that SDAT will contribute to the development of research on diagnostic validity." At present it would seem that this test should be reserved for research use only.

[529]
★Watson Number-Readiness Test, Fifth Edition. Grades kgn–1 ; 1963 ; 6 scores: subjective test (teacher's ratings of social, emotional, and psychological readiness, total), objective test, total; 1 form (4 pages) ; manual (12 pages) ; no data on reliability and validity ; no description of norms population ; Can $1.50 per 25 tests ; 25¢ per manual ; 35¢ per specimen set ; postage extra ; [20–25] minutes ; G. Milton Watson and others ; Book Society of Canada Ltd. *

CALCULUS

[530]
★CLEP Subject Examination in Introductory Calculus. 1 year or equivalent ; 1964–70 ; for college accreditation of nontraditional study, advanced placement, or assessment of educational achievement ; tests administered monthly at regional centers throughout the United States ; tests also available for institutional testing at any time ; Form MCT ('64, 13 pages) ; optional essay supplement: Form MCT-A ('64, 2 pages) ; for program accessories, see 664 ; rental and scoring fee, $5 per student ; postpaid ; essay supplement scored by the college ; 90(95) minutes, same for essay supplement ; program administered for the College Entrance Examination Board by Educational Testing Service. *

For reviews of the testing program, see 664 (3 reviews).

[531]
*Cooperative Mathematics Tests: Calculus. High school and college ; 1963–65 ; for all tests in the series, see 465 ; Forms A, B, ('63, 10 pages) ; no specific manual ; series manual ('64, 79 pages) ; student bulletin ('65, 2 pages) ; separate answer sheets (Digitek, IBM 805, IBM 1230, SCRIBE) must be used ; $6 per 20 tests ; $4 per 100 answer sheets ; $1.25 per 10 IBM hand scoring stencils (answer pattern must be punched out locally) ; Digitek scoring stencils not available ; $2 per series manual ; $3 per 100 student bulletins ; $3 per specimen set of the series ; cash orders postpaid ; SCRIBE scoring and statistical analysis service, 35¢ per test ; 80(92) minutes ; Cooperative Tests and Services. *

WILLIAM E. KLINE, *Director of Test Development, CTB/McGraw-Hill, Monterey, California.*

The calculus test of the *Cooperative Mathematics Tests* provides a reliable score that is valid for measuring achievement at the conclusion of one year's formal study of calculus in many high schools and colleges. Of the 60 items, about 20 percent are devoted to analytic geometry; the rest are aimed at measuring the understanding of calculus concepts and at applying them. Emphasis is on the understanding and application, with factual recall and computation minimized.

The Handbook (a manual for all of the *Cooperative Mathematics Tests*) provides classification for all items. The difference in the classification of items for the two forms is minimal. There are many pairs of items, one in each form, that are identical except for numerical values, signs, or functions. The topics in the classification are those included in most first-year calculus courses and are weighted closely to the relative emphasis on the topics found in the popular textbooks. Although the forms are very similar in content, there is evidence that Form B provides greater variance than Form A and thus permits both a lower floor and higher ceiling.

The items are well constructed and edited. This reviewer found only two, both in Form A, that were faulty. One item asks for a numerical answer "approximately." The keyed answer contains three significant digits but differs by 20 percent from the exact numerical value of the problem's solution. Another weakly constructed item asks the examinee which of three mathematical sentences is true. The examinee who can correctly determine that the first sentence of a set is not true can, upon inspecting the five answer choices, select the right answer without looking at the second and third sentences.

Norms are provided for five national reference groups: high school, colleges of education, engineering, and liberal arts, and total college. All groups were tested in the closing weeks of a one-year calculus course. Of these groups, the high school students performed best. The surprise to this reviewer was the poor performance of the engineering school group, below that of the liberal arts group. All participants in each norming group also took the quantitative part of the *Cooperative School and College Ability Test.* Their mean performance, reported in the Handbook, provides the user with an anchor against which he can compare the "ability" of his group with that of the norm group. However, the correlation coefficient between SCAT-Q and the calculus test for college students is about .40.

Although Tucker's method, used for equating the two forms, provided the common converted score scale, many users would like to see correlation coefficients between the two forms. These are not reported in the Handbook. Internal consistency is evidenced by the K-R 20 coefficients of .87 and .84 for Forms A and B, respectively, in the testing of college students. The mean biserial correlations (item versus total score) were .44 and .41 for the two forms; the standard deviation for the frequency distributions of both was .12.

Both forms are speeded. About 50 percent of the college norm group finished Form B; about 60 percent finished Form A. However, the test items are relatively difficult, which makes it hard to isolate the uncontaminated effect of speededness. The effect of the speededness is probably minimal.

The test is simple to administer. It consists of two parts, each 40 minutes in length, so that it can be given in two sessions. The Handbook does not provide detailed directions for administering the second part, but any experienced teacher or examiner can easily improvise these directions with little chance of significantly affecting student performance or the usefulness of the norms. The Handbook, too, could have aided the user more if it had been more specific in outlining the role of the proctor during a testing session. Any number of the *Cooperative Mathematics Tests* can be administered in the same testing session. Many secondary schools will be pleased that, with one set of directions, they can give algebra, geometry, trigonometry, and calculus tests simultaneously.

The test is easy to score. The raw score is merely the number of right responses. The examinees are advised of this at the start of the test and are informed of the time limit. Unfortunately, the student without a watch in a room without a wall clock is at a disadvantage, because he is given no warning near the time limit.

The calculus test, like other ETS tests, gives the appearance of having been produced inexpensively. At the same time, it is most functional and legible. One minor criticism can be made of its numerical fractions used in the answer choices : the size of the numerals and the spacing and aligning of the fractions often cause them to be confused with whole numbers.

The Handbook provides some helpful suggestions for using item information from the test by program evaluators, curriculum planners, and teachers. In fact, these sections of the Handbook are applicable to most, if not all, standardized achievement tests. They point up the need to relate the test, item by item, to curricular objectives.

This reviewer, in conclusion, knows of no standardized test designed to measure achievement at the close of a year's course in calculus that is better than the *Cooperative Mathematics Tests: Calculus*.

G. Edith Robinson, *Associate Professor of Mathematics, University of Georgia, Athens, Georgia.*

The series manual states : "Achievement is assessed in terms of students' comprehension of the basic concepts, techniques and unifying principles in each content area." This criterion appears to have been successfully met in the case of the calculus test. In the opinion of this reviewer, the student who has a good grasp of first-year college calculus should score well; the student whose comprehension is good, but who operates at a slower pace, will do less well. Most severely penalized will be the student who attempts to memorize his way through the course or whose only achievement is skill in the techniques of differentiation and integration. Most items require application or interpretation of principles ; and for those demanding recall, the foils provided incorporate enough similarity to confuse the student with little or no understanding. On the other hand, in many cases in which knowledge of facts would be an advantage timewise, correct answers can be reasoned out by the thoughtful student.

Both forms provide a balance between theory (ideas of continuity, limit, etc.) and application (area, slope of tangent, etc.) and include a few items on such topics as parametric equations and polar coordinates. A specific item content classification is given in the series manual.

The series manual gives a table of national college norms for comparison purposes, including a breakdown of the colleges as "Education," "Liberal Arts," and "Engineering." Norms are

also given for high school, but are based on a small sample (168) drawn from nine schools. This is probably no great drawback, for the test, although appropriate for a high school offering a good college-level calculus course, is certainly not appropriate when a mediocre-to-poor course is offered. In the former case, the school would probably wish to examine college norms ; in the latter case, examination of the test itself should preclude its use.

SUMMARY. This is a good achievement test for a beginning college course in calculus ; it is not recommended for high schools offering an "introduction" to the calculus.

For excerpts from reviews of the series, see 465 (2 excerpts).

GEOMETRY

[532]

★**Cooperative Mathematics Tests: Analytic Geometry.** High school and college ; 1963–65 ; for all tests in the series, see 465 ; Forms A, B, ('63, 6 pages) ; no specific manual ; series manual ('64, 79 pages) ; student bulletin ('65, 2 pages) ; separate answer sheets (Digitek, IBM 805, IBM 1230, SCRIBE) must be used ; $6 per 20 tests ; $4 per 100 answer sheets ; $1.25 per 10 IBM hand scoring stencils (answer pattern must be punched out locally) ; Digitek scoring stencils not available ; $2 per series manual ; $3 per 100 student bulletins ; $3 per specimen set of the series ; cash orders postpaid ; SCRIBE scoring and statistical analysis service, 35¢ and over per test ; 40(45) minutes ; Cooperative Tests and Services. *

L. Ray Carry, *Assistant Professor of Mathematics Education and Mathematics, The University of Texas, Austin, Texas.*

Each form is a 35-item, 40-minute test intended to measure knowledge of the content of a one-semester course in analytic geometry or of the analytic geometry content of a combined course in analytic geometry and calculus.

The items in this test sample almost all of the important content from analytic geometry. In terms of the raw score distribution for the norming sample, the two forms are closely parallel in difficulty and this has been achieved without undue similarity of items across forms. This latter fact is particularly desirable for course evaluations in which one form may be used as a pre-measure and the other as a post-measure.

Although this reviewer considers the tests to be of high quality relative to most standardized mathematics tests, he also feels that the publisher should be more cautious in the representations of the tests to the consumer. Almost all of the items from both forms measure either recall of concepts or routine application of procedures that one can reasonably expect to be taught and practiced in an analytic geometry course. This appears to be in conflict with the claim that "ability to apply understanding of mathematical ideas to new situations and to reason with insight are emphasized." Since mathematics tests that do meet the above claim are exceedingly rare, this is not a serious criticism of the test but rather a call for a more objective description to the consumer.

One criticism is related to the composition of the norming sample. According to the manual, only 22 secondary schools belong to the sample and data for these schools were not used in reporting test reliability. The remainder of the sample is composed of 49 colleges, heavily weighted by junior colleges and small liberal arts colleges. The reviewer does not feel that this sample is representative of the total population for which the test is intended.

Finally, the tests are not as high in reliability as one would desire. The K-R 20 reliabilities (computed with the college sample only) are .79 (Form A) and .77 (Form B). The latter is the lowest reliability coefficient reported for any of the 33 Cooperative mathematics tests. Although reliability estimates in this range are undoubtedly adequate for decisions to be based on group data such as course evaluations, one should exercise caution when using the tests for making decisions about individual students.

In summary, these tests are probably the best available for the content of analytic geometry. But they measure primarily knowledge of facts and procedures rather than the ability to "reason with insight." There is some question about the applicability of the norms for students in very large colleges and universities. Finally, their reliability is low enough to raise some doubt about their use for evaluating differences between individual students.

For excerpts from reviews of the series, see 465 (2 excerpts).

[533]

Cooperative Mathematics Tests: Geometry. Grades 10–12; 1962–65; 2 scores: Part I (Euclidean geometry), total; for all tests in the series, see 465; Forms A, B, ('62, 16 pages); no specific manual; series manual ('64, 79 pages); student bulletin ('65, 2 pages); separate answer sheets (Digitek, IBM 805,

IBM 1230, SCRIBE) must be used; $6 per 20 tests; $4 per 100 answer sheets; $1.25 per 10 IBM hand scoring stencils (answer pattern must be punched out locally); Digitek scoring stencils not available; $2 per series manual; $3 per 100 student bulletins; $3 per specimen set of the series; cash orders postpaid; SCRIBE scoring and statistical analysis service, 35¢ per test; 80(92) minutes; Cooperative Tests and Services. *

REFERENCES

1. See 6:645.
2. ALI, MD. BASHARAT. *To Establish the Feasibility of Using Translated and Adapted Versions of an American-Made Mathematics Achievement Test in East Pakistan.* Doctor's research study No. 1, Colorado State College (Greeley, Colo.), 1964. (*DA* 28:115A)
3. NORTH, ROBERT D. "Geometry Test Results of Tenth-Grade Pupils in the ERB Public School Norms Project, 1964." *Ed Rec B* 87:57–9 F '65. *

EVAN D. SHULL, *Coordinator of Mathematics, Township High School District 214, Mount Prospect, Illinois.*

The apparent intent of these geometry tests is to measure the standard Euclidean geometry program of schools in terms of concepts, proofs, spatial reasoning, and "advanced understandings." Either of the two forms of the test meets these stated objectives. Both forms are divided into two parts, with the first part concentrating on direct application of geometric facts and the second part being more reasoning or problem-solving oriented. The items in both sections of the two forms are five-option multiple choice in nature and provide an adequate range of difficulty.

A comprehensive handbook is provided with the testing program. Within the handbook are directions for administering, scoring, and interpreting scores; technical data on the construction and norming of the tests; and a variety of tables (some useful and some superfluous). The handbook is applicable to the complete Cooperative Mathematics Series, so any person using only one of the tests, say the geometry test, has to sort out of this conglomeration that which is useful to him. Nevertheless, much of the material in the handbook could be useful and might give some direction toward the developing of a testing program. More specifically, there are tables in the handbook which allow a tester to compare results on this test with results on older forms of the geometry test. There is also a chart which will help the tester to use this instrument as a diagnostic test as well as an achievement test. Of course, there are the usual national norming tables and a number of correlation tables for this test and others constructed by Educational Testing Service.

Each of the two parts of the test is to be completed in 40 minutes, and it will probably take the average student about all of the allotted time to finish. There are a variety of answer sheets available, some of them quite confusing. It would be well for the tester to examine the different types of answer sheets available for the test before he orders them in quantity. It would also be wise for him to take the test himself before he administers it to students, because several of the questions might need some interpretation; thus, any ambiguities could be avoided. This comment is not meant to imply a frequent occurrence of poor items because either form of the test, in general, is an acceptable choice for group or individual achievement or diagnostic testing.

In summary, this geometry test is an adequate instrument to use for testing students in a traditional Euclidean geometry program. The test package provides versatility by being somewhat diagnostic as well as being able to measure achievement. For the school with a limited testing program, its multi-purposed possibilities make the test a desirable choice.

For excerpts from reviews of the series, see 465 (2 excerpts).

[534]
*Geometry: Minnesota High School Achievement Examinations. High school; 1952–71; new or revised form issued each May; Form EH Rev. ('71, 4 pages); no specific manual; series manual ('71, 16 pages); no data on reliability; 15¢ per test; separate answer sheets (IBM 1230) may be used; 10¢ per answer sheet including scoring service; $1 per series manual; postage extra; $1.10 per specimen set, postpaid; 60(65) minutes; edited by V. L. Lohmann; American Guidance Service, Inc. *

For a review by Harold P. Fawcett of an earlier form, see 5:495.

[535]
*Geometry Test. 1, 2 semesters high school; 1933–70; formerly called *Plane Geometry Test;* 2 levels; no manual; no data on reliability; no norms; $1 per 10 tests, postpaid; 25¢ per single copy, cash orders only; 50(55) minutes; Robert J. Bryant; High School Testing Service, Purdue University. *
a) FIRST SEMESTER. 1 form ('70, 7 pages).
b) SECOND SEMESTER. 1 form ('70, 8 pages).

[536]
★Howell Geometry Test. Grades 9–12; 1969; HGT; Forms A (8 pages), B (7 pages); manual (16 pages); $8.70 per 35 tests; $1 per key; separate answer sheets (Digitek-IBM 805, IBM 1230) may be used; $2.30 per 35 Digitek-IBM 805 answer sheets; $2.80 per 35 IBM 1230 answer sheets; 70¢ per scoring stencil; $1.50 per specimen set; postage extra; scoring service, 19¢ and over per test; 40(50) minutes; Edgar N. Howell; Harcourt Brace Jovanovich, Inc. *

DOROTHY L. JONES, *Assistant Professor of Education, University of Pennsylvania, Philadelphia, Pennsylvania.*

This test should be well received by teachers of geometry for one major reason—all items employ the language and symbolism appearing in most modern geometry books. Likewise, the content of a modern geometry course appears fairly well represented among the 45 items making up each form of the test.

The manual also stands out as an example of what a good test manual should contain. Test users are becoming sophisticated with respect to measurement procedures and this manual attempts to acknowledge that fact. It includes a rather thorough classification of items according to nine content areas and three cognitive categories and describes the development of the test, including item analysis and standardization procedures.

Although it is claimed that the test was constructed in accordance with the recommendations given in *Standards for Educational and Psychological Tests and Manuals,* in actuality there is a very serious departure. The manual reports that "From the 100 items in each experimental form, 45 were selected for each of the final forms. All answer sheets were then rescored on the basis of the items chosen for the shortened format. Percentile ranks, stanines, and relevant normative statistics as reported in this *Manual* were then derived." The Standards recommend: "If a short form of the test is prepared by reducing the number of items or organizing a portion of the test into a separate form, new evidence should be obtained and reported for that shorter test." Obviously, the statistical results and all norms given in the manual are relevant to scores based on the selected 45 items of the final form only for testees who have experienced all 100 items.

The section of the manual concerned with the interpretation of test results is good; percentile ranks, stanines, and standard scores are briefly but adequately described, enabling most test users to apply the information when using the accompanying tables for raw score conversions.

The approach taken in the validity and reliability section of the manual was encouraging; however, the author failed to develop it into its full potential. A split-half reliability coefficient of .82 is reported for each form. How worthwhile these statistics are is problematic since they were computed from results of 45 items selected out of the 100 answered by the 7,163 students in the norming population. A discussion of the importance and appropriate use of the standard error of measurement was also begun but dropped abruptly. The statement that "the standard error of measurement is particularly useful when comparisons are made between raw scores or standard scores earned by different individuals" was never developed; instead, four sentences later there appears the following concluding remark: "Detailed explanations and formulas for the standard error of difference scores are given in many elementary measurement or statistics texts."

The nature of the two forms of the test was not made explicit in the manual. Comparison of the items in the two forms of the test suggests that they may not have been drawn randomly from a larger pool of acceptable items. In fact, items seem to have been purposely matched in format and specific content. This type of situation leads to correlated errors of measurement between items belonging to different forms of the test and limits the usefulness of the two tests as parallel forms. However, the second form certainly may be used as a replacement exam for students who missed taking the first form.

All items are multiple choice, having four solution alternatives and a fifth, DK, for "don't know." The last option is considered a "guessing distracter." Although the test author claims that a subsequent analysis of the DK responses supported the guessing-distracter role, it is possible that the above-average geometry student might use it inappropriately, not because of insufficient knowledge, but rather because of his vast store of knowledge coupled with a poorly written question. Fortunately, this type of ambiguity is rare, but use of a DK alternative presupposes masterly written items.

On the whole, items are concise, lucid, and unambiguous. Some of the questions are dependent on visual acuity even though the testee is warned: "On those questions for which figures have been drawn, you may assume that the indicated points lie on the lines as drawn in the figure. You may *not* assume, however, that measures are necessarily equal or that lines, line segments, and rays are necessarily parallel or perpendicular"; yet, solutions to item 2 in Form A and its correspondent, item 7 in Form B, are based precisely on observation of the figures' "suggested" appearance.

In summary, the *Howell Geometry Test* is composed of well-constructed items which correspond fairly adequately to the content of a modern geometry course and is recommended as an instrument for measuring achievement in geometry. The format of the manual is definitely geared in the right direction, but at this writing inadequate standardization procedures stand out as the test's major weakness.

JOHN WAGNER, *Professor of Mathematics, Michigan State University, East Lansing, Michigan.*

Both the Directions to Students and the manual are concise, straightforward, and non-ambiguous.

In the main, the content coverage of the test reflects the newer curriculum aspects of school geometry. In particular, the modern terminology of geometry is adequately reflected in the test items. The material also maintains a reasonable balance between the traditional aspects of geometry and the newer ideas. This is especially seen in the inclusion of some cogent items in coordinate geometry. However, space or solid geometry is sadly relegated to a subsidiary position; as a matter of fact, three-dimensional geometry is not even present. Material on techniques of proof or postulational systems is certainly not a strong point.

Each form, containing only 45 items, gives little expanse to cover adequately the full range of school geometry; consequently, the coverage is rather thin.

The geographic range of the standardization sample and depth of the item analysis appear adequate.

In summary, the manual appears more than adequate for administration and for meaningful interpretation. The test itself is average—not too good and not too bad. The coverage is somewhat hurried and thin. The coverage is adequate to the extent that the test encompasses the scope of most texts in the field, with a severe weakness in the areas of solid geometry and concepts of proof. Overall, the test is not the best of its kind, being overshadowed by the *Cooperative Mathematics Tests: Geometry.* However, it is recommended for use in that, with the defects above noted, it will key the examiner in on the status of the group effort of the concerned students.

[537]

*Iowa Geometry Aptitude Test, Third Edition.
High school; 1935–69; IGAT; revision of *Iowa Plane Geometry Aptitude Test;* 1 form ('69, 8 pages); manual ('69, 11 pages); separate answer sheets (IBM 1230) must be used; $6.50 per 35 tests; 6¢ per answer sheet; 30¢ per scoring stencil; 40¢ per manual; 75¢ per specimen set; postage extra; 50(55) minutes; James Maxey and Darrell Sabers; Bureau of Educational Research and Service. *

REFERENCES

1. HANNA, GERALD STANLEY. *An Investigation of Selected Ability, Aptitude, Interest, and Personality Characteristics Relevant to Success in High School Geometry.* Doctor's thesis, University of Southern California (Los Angeles, Calif.), 1965. (DA 26:3152)
2. HANNA, GERALD S. "An Empirical Comparison of Three Geometry Aptitude Tests." *Sch Sci & Math* 68:8–10 Ja '68. *

LYNNETTE B. PLUMLEE, *Formerly Director of Test Development, Educational Testing Service, Princeton, New Jersey.*

The Third Edition of this test is an extensive revision of the 1942 edition. Parts which proved no longer valid as indicators of success in geometry were deleted, and new material which correlated well with marks in geometry was incorporated. Previous marks in mathematics, science, and English, as reported by the student, and the mark he expects in geometry have been included in the determination of the total IGAT score. Little information is available on the procedures used in hypothesizing or developing new materials. Nor is evidence provided that the predictive value of the total score is greater than that of marks alone.

Validity data are provided for the total test score against first-semester geometry marks as a criterion (.68 for the validation sample of 343 on which part weights were based and .66 for the crossvalidation sample of 193). The publisher advises the user to conduct his own validity study since results may not be generalizable. It would be helpful to see validity data separately for marks, test items, and combined score. The user should have such information, preferably for his own population and criterion, in order to make a sound judgment as to whether the test score adds enough to prediction over use of marks alone to warrant the time and cost of testing. (See related comments in my review of the *Orleans-Hanna Geometry Prognosis Test.*) The potential user should of course consider the test's effectiveness for the group with which he presumably is most concerned, those who perform substantially better or worse in geometry than they have in previous mathematics.

The reviewer would also like to see an investigation of the need for a geometry aptitude test for students of those "modern" or "integrated" mathematics courses in which an effort has been made to introduce at an earlier level the kind of mathematical thinking and understanding required for success in geometry. An analysis of validity separately for traditional and modern curriculum students, as well as item analysis data for the different population samples, would be helpful in determining usefulness for different curricula. By the same token, validity data obtained by the user for his own population should be used with caution in considering students transferring from a different curriculum, unless such transfers are considered as a separate group in making the study.

The items generally seem clear and the test is not highly speeded (90 percent of the experimental population answered the last items in each part of the test). The format and typography are good. The option "Not given" is used with most items, but it appears to have been used with caution. The items in Part 1 are largely nonroutine and varied. However, Part 2, a test of cube visualization, places heavy weight on apparently homogeneous content and a student could miss several items for the same error. One would prefer to see more visualization situations with fewer items on each. The directions for Part 2 may be confusing to some students. Although the students are told to use scratch paper in the general instructions by the administrator, Part 2 directions state, "This is a test of your ability to picture a geometrical figure in your mind," and the student may believe scratch paper is not to be used for Part 2. The publisher plans to eliminate the phrase "in your mind" in reprinting, but users of the earlier printing may wish to make certain that all students have the same understanding of the instructions.

Percentile norms are provided for the score on the test items and also for the composite (total) IGAT score. Standard and probable errors of measurement are provided only for the score on the test items. Explanations of statistical data are good as far as they go. The standard error of measurement is discussed helpfully and at some length, but for the person who needs this discussion it may not be obvious that there is another source of error, that due to less than perfect correlation between the test and the criterion. However, the discussion of expectancy tables should help the user make sound judgments if the recommendation to prepare local tables is followed.

In conclusion, this reviewer prefers the content of this test to others reviewed which have the same purpose but would like more evidence on the effectiveness of Part 2. Also, data have not been provided by the publisher to demonstrate experimentally the value of the test beyond that of available nontest predictors.

For a review by Philip H. DuBois of an earlier edition, see 3:360; for reviews by Edward E. Cureton and Charles C. Weidemann, see 2:1469.

[538]

★Mid-Year Geometry Test. High school; 1968; Form A (8 pages); manual (14 pages); $7.70 per 35 tests; separate answer sheets (Digitek-IBM 805, IBM 1230) may be used; $2.30 per 35 Digitek-IBM 805 answer sheets; $2.80 per 35 IBM 1230 answer sheets; 70¢ per scoring key; $1.50 per specimen set; postage extra; scoring service, 19¢ and over per test; 40(45) minutes; Harcourt Brace Jovanovich, Inc. *

EVAN D. SHULL, *Coordinator of Mathematics, Township High School District 214, Mount Prospect, Illinois.*

The *Mid-Year Geometry Test* is a 50-item test best used after one semester of a relatively modern geometry course. Some items are multiple choice, some are true-false, and others are mixed in nature. The difficulty of the items varies but is somewhat on the easy side. There are at least two trick questions which have no place in a serious test. Nevertheless, the variety of question formats makes it interesting to take.

The manual provided with the test is adequate. Besides the usual norming data, it provides a table of discrimination values of each item and gives an indication of the difficulty of each item. The concept or concepts being tested by each item are also presented.

In summation, the *Mid-Year Geometry Test* is an interesting and adequate test for checking student progress after a one semester geometry course having a "modern flavor." Though 2 of the 50 items are inappropriate, this test should be as useful as most other midyear tests. However, if the geometry course being taught is quite traditional, the teacher should look for a different instrument.

[539]

*Orleans-Hanna Geometry Prognosis Test. Grades 8–11; 1929–68; OHGPT; revision of *Orleans Geometry Prognosis Test;* 1 form ('68, 14 pages); manual ('68, 18 pages); separate answer sheets (Digitek, IBM 805, IBM 1230) must be used; $8.70 per

35 tests; $2.30 per 35 IBM 805 answer sheets; $2.80 per 35 Digitek or IBM 1230 answer sheets; 70¢ per scoring stencil; $1.50 per specimen set; postage extra; IBM scoring service, 19¢ and over per test; 40(55–60) minutes; Joseph B. Orleans and Gerald S. Hanna; Harcourt Brace Jovanovich, Inc. *

REFERENCES

1–3. See 2:1471.
4–5. See 4:427.
6. HANNA, GERALD S. "An Empirical Comparison of Three Geometry Aptitude Tests." *Sch Sci & Math* 68:8–10 Ja '68. *
7. HANNA, GERALD S., AND ROSCOE, JOHN T. "The Contribution of Work-Sample Test Items, Past Grades, and Student-Predicted Grades to the Prediction of Geometry Enrollment." *Ed & Psychol Meas* 29(4):909–13 w '69. * (PA 44: 21616)
8. CALDWELL, JAMES R.; MICHAEL, WILLIAM B.; SCHRADER, DONALD R.; AND MEYERS, C. E. "Comparative Validities and Working Times for Composites of Structure-of-Intellect Tests and Algebra Grades and Composites of Traditional Test Measures and Algebra Grades in the Prediction of Success in Tenth-Grade Geometry." *Ed & Psychol Meas* 30(4):955–9 w '70. *
9. HANNA, GERALD S., AND LENKE, JOANNE M. "Moderator Variables in Predicting Geometry Success." *Sch Sci & Math* 70(4):299–302 Ap '70. *

LYNNETTE B. PLUMLEE, *formerly Director of Test Development, Educational Testing Service, Princeton, New Jersey.*

This test is designed to assist in guiding students concerning probable success in geometry and to assist in sectioning geometry classes.

The test consists of two parts: a set of test questions and a "questionnaire," each with a maximum score of 40 points. The questionnaire concerns past course marks in four subjects and the grade the student expects in geometry. A work-sample approach is used in the test section: five lessons are provided, each followed by questions which test understanding and application of the lesson. The lessons are primarily concerned with definitions and simple concepts; the questions test the ability to apply these in reading and working with diagrams. Few questions appear to require insights beyond such application.

Normative data are provided for 3,525 students completing first year algebra and 2,218 completing algebra and enrolled in geometry. The total group is described relative to geographical area, school district size, and socioeconomic status. The manual provides expectancy tables for predicting midyear and final course grades and corresponding test scores for an experimental population, but it also encourages the user to develop his own local tables.

Extensive research appears to have been done in developing the test. Considerable data relevant to development, evaluation, and standardization are provided in the manual and in subsequent reports. Content was reportedly based on a review of research literature regarding factors related to students' success in learning geometry and on factor analysis studies by one of the authors; however, it is not clear how items were developed to measure the ascertained factors and there is no evidence that the final test was analyzed to determine whether content objectives were achieved.

Of most importance in evaluating a prognosis test is whether use of the test improves judgment regarding future performance. Data on the relative contributions of student-reported grades and of the work sample test were provided by the publisher. The population consisted of 745 first year algebra students in seven states. Validity data are based on 387 to 482 of this sample, depending on the criterion. Although findings could have been influenced by partial differences in population, the work sample test appeared to be a clearly better predictor of midyear and final *test scores* than the questionnaire (validity coefficients of .60 and .63 for the work sample, compared to .41 and .39 for the questionnaire). However, the questionnaire seemed to be a better predictor of midyear and final geometry *grades* than the work sample (coefficients of .67 and .68, compared to .42 and .47). The combined score added little or nothing to prediction of either criterion. Use of multiple regression analysis and assigning best weights improved prediction of both grade and test criteria, but such use would necessitate using different weights depending on the criterion to be used, and the publisher felt this was not warranted by the gain. The potential user is advised to make his own study of predictive value for his own criterion before deciding whether the cost and time of testing are warranted. He should prepare his own expectancy tables (separately for grades, if grades are used as criteria) and study these to ascertain the probability of students at various critical levels achieving according to expectation.

Another question of interest to present geometry teachers is whether the test is equally predictive for students in modern and traditional curricula and whether students from the two curricula can be compared using the same norms. Norms are available for the total standardization groups only. However, some clue is available from a table in the manual which provides validity data separately for seven school systems. Systems 2 and 3, reportedly following a traditional geometry curriculum, do not differ consistently from the other systems (reportedly modern) in mean, standard devia-

tion, or correlation with the criterion. Within each system the test seems to function satisfactorily as a predictor. However, for those who may be comparing students from different systems it should be noted that much of the lesson material is covered in earlier years of at least some modern mathematics courses, and a student from such a course can answer many or most questions without use of the lessons. In fact, the use of the work sample approach in a speeded test may be open to question when substantial differences in prior mathematics experience exist among those to be tested. The test is intentionally speeded, with less than 70 percent of the standardization sample completing it. The counselor who uses the test results should therefore bear in mind the possible advantage time-wise to the modern curriculum student who is covering familiar material in the lessons. Separate statistics on completion for the two groups would be helpful, as would a comparison study which more adequately controls ability and curriculum differences.

The inclusion of item analysis data is commendable, although a breakdown by curriculum group would be useful.

In general, I prefer the content of the *Iowa Geometry Aptitude Test* (with the reservations noted in my review of that test) and the higher reported completion rate, but validity coefficients reported by the two publishers are similar, and lack of statistical data, especially on the IGAT, makes an adequate comparison of usefulness difficult. The potential user should compare the content of these tests with his course content. He should make his own study to determine whether any geometry aptitude test helps predict geometry grades of his students.

For reviews by Edward E. Cureton and Charles C. Weidemann of the original edition, see 2:1471.

[540]

Plane Geometry: National Achievement Tests. High school; 1958–70; Forms A ('70, 4 pages, identical with test copyrighted in 1958 except for cover page and format), B ('59, 8 pages); no specific manual; combined manual ['58, 12 pages] for this test and tests 6:600, 6:653, and 6:656; $6 per 25 tests; $4 per 100 key-class record sheets; $1 per specimen set; cash orders postpaid; 40(45) minutes; Ray Webb and Julius H. Hlavaty; Psychometric Affiliates. *

DOROTHY L. JONES, *Assistant Professor of Education, University of Pennsylvania, Philadelphia, Pennsylvania.*

Each form consists of 48 multiple choice items couched in the traditional language and symbolism of geometry of the pre-1960 era. This is not necessarily a fault since there are still students being taught with the "old texts" as course guidelines. However, this fact should be made clear in the test description with an expressed discouragement of its use for students who have studied the modern symbolism.

The items, while generally unambiguous, do appear to be verbally cumbersome and in need of rewriting. For example, consider item 17 of Form A: "One diagonal of a square is 14 inches. The number of square inches in the area of the square is (a) 49 sq. in. (b) 98 sq. in. (c) 196 sq. in. (d) $49\sqrt{2}$ sq. in. (e) none of these answers." Obviously the redundancy is unnecessary, and, in fact, since so many questions reflect this tendency, it is possible that a significant portion of the test's variance may be attributable to a speed of reading factor. Many of the stems consist of a sentence followed by either a question or an incomplete statement; most of these stems should have been simplified and written more concisely. Ambiguities in items tend to slow the better geometry student who would lose testing time in their resolution, while the average or below average geometry student would be totally unaware of them. For example, part of one item reads, "The whole secant is 28 inches long" when a *segment* of the secant is meant.

Although many of the items appear to be computational, closer examination reveals that both depth and breadth of knowledge in plane geometry are necessary for successful answering. Again, the items are geared toward content emphasized in the "older" texts. There are no questions on coordinate geometry, but in general the major topics of a plane geometry course appear to be well covered. Many of the questions demand that the examinee perceive underlying relationships and apply one or more geometric truths to arrive at the solution. It would have been extremely desirable to report difficulty indices in the manual for all items.

Probably the most serious drawback of this test is the limited, if not inadequate, information provided in the manual. The manual states: "Each item of the test in the original form and also in the final form was analyzed and difficulty and validity indices were computed," but actual indices were not reported nor was the notion of validity developed beyond that brief mention. The split-half reliabilities of .85 and .86 might be overestimated since the tests appear to be speeded.

Examination of Forms A and B reveal a serious deficiency in the procedures used in constructing equivalent forms. More than half the items of one form were matched to items in the other form. Numbers were changed in computational problems, or the nature of inequalities was reversed, but on the whole, the items measure the same specific content. "This procedure [according to Cureton [1]] can never be justified where a major objective is construction of *equivalent* forms, because of the impossible requirement that every individual pair of items so allocated must have equal indices of discrimination. If two items are judged to be too much alike to be included in the same form, they are certainly too much alike to be included in two equivalent or even parallel forms."

Percentile norms for both raw scores and scores corrected for guessing are provided but no adequate description of the groups on which these norms and other statistical data were based is given. Not even the testing date of the norming groups is reported.

There is no question but that this test needs to be updated. Items not only need rewriting, but also should be checked against the content of a modern plane geometry course. The manual is practically useless in its present form.

[541]

*Tucker-Sanders Plane Geometry Test. 1, 2 semesters high school; 1962-64; first published 1962-63 in the Every Pupil Scholarship Test series; Forms A, B, ('64, 8 pages); 2 levels labeled Tests 1, 2; manual ('64, 3 pages); $1.75 per 25 tests, postage extra; 75¢ per specimen set, postpaid; 40(45) minutes; Charles B. Tucker and M. W. Sanders; Data Processing and Educational Measurement Center. *

TRIGONOMETRY

[542]

★CLEP Subject Examination in Trigonometry. 1 semester or equivalent; 1968-70; for college accreditation of nontraditional study, advanced placement, or assessment of educational achievement; 2 parallel editions: 90 and 45 minute tests; for program accessories, see 664; program administered for the College Entrance Examination Board by Educational Testing Service. *

a) 90 MINUTE EDITION. Tests administered monthly at

1 CURETON, EDWARD E. "The Definition and Estimation of Test Reliability." *Ed & Psychol Meas* 18:715-38 w '58. *

regional centers throughout the United States; tests also available for institutional testing at any time; Form RCT1 ('68, 20 pages); separate answer sheets (SCRIBE) must be used; rental and scoring fee, $5 per student; 90(95) minutes.

b) 45 MINUTE EDITION. Available only for institutional testing; Forms QSL1 ('68, 12 pages), QSL4 ('68, 11 pages); separate answer sheets (Digitek-IBM 805, IBM 1230) must be used; rental fee, 75¢ per student; scoring service not available; 45(50) minutes.

For reviews of the testing program, see 664 (3 reviews).

[543]

*Cooperative Mathematics Tests: Trigonometry. High school and college; 1962-65; for all tests in the series, see 465; Forms A, B, ('62, 7 pages); no specific manual; series manual ('64, 79 pages); student bulletin ('65, 2 pages); separate answer sheets (Digitek, IBM 805, IBM 1230, SCRIBE) must be used; $6 per 20 tests; $4 per 100 answer sheets; $1.25 per 10 IBM hand scoring stencils (answer pattern must be punched out locally); Digitek scoring stencils not available; $2 per series manual; $3 per 100 student bulletins; $3 per specimen set of the series; cash orders postpaid; SCRIBE scoring and statistical analysis service, 35¢ per test; 40(45) minutes; Cooperative Tests and Services. *

THOMAS A. ROMBERG, *Associate Professor of Education and Associate Director, Wisconsin Research and Development Center for Cognitive Learning, The University of Wisconsin, Madison, Wisconsin.*

In 1958, concurrent with the ferment of change in mathematics curricula, Educational Testing Service began initial planning for a new cooperative mathematics series. One eventual product of that development was the *Cooperative Mathematics Test—Trigonometry,* copyrighted in 1962 with norms developed in 1961, 1962, and 1963. Is this test, which is one of the few tests available on trigonometry, still valid and reliable today? That is the question faced in this review.

The materials provided are of an extremely high quality. The tests are attractive. The manual for administering the test is exceptionally well written. The directions for administration are clear and concise and should be understandable to any potential user. The technical data presented in the manual are easy to interpret. A high school or college teacher should be able to administer the test, score it, and interpret the results with ease.

This test is designed as a sample of performance related to skills in trigonometry. The content selection for the test is well documented. A content categorization scheme is presented and specific items for each form are related to this content scheme. A rationale for both the scheme and the percentage of items in each category is given. However, the content of trigonometry in today's high school or college courses is not quite that of this test. The test does have broad scope; it has questions on radians, inverse functions, solving triangles, and graphs. But today's trigonometry teacher looking for items on the use of DeMoivre's theorem or complex numbers will be generally disappointed. Today's students should be able to solve a relatively simple equation like $z^4 + p = 0$ (p = positive integer) and be able to express and recognize the solution in standard form $E^{i\theta}$. Other minor omissions of items which instructors may look for include a graph where the amplitude is not 1 or a graph where the argument is of the form, $x + q\pi$ (q = rational). The emphasis of this test seems to be on the results of a trigonometric formula and not derivations or applications of such a formula. None of the items includes work on trigonometric identities.

More seriously, there seems to be no awareness on the part of the test writers that trigonometry is an excellent model for other mathematical methods, that there are techniques ubiquitous to mathematics, and that these are the trigonometric interpretations of general mathematical processes. For example, inverse functions are included but there is no question on how inverses behave. Period is examined but not periodicity. Radians need to be computed, but there are no questions on why radians are used. Interpolation needs to be done, but no mention is made of how good an approximation this is or even if it is an approximation.

In spite of these negative comments about content, the test is well constructed and includes many very clever items. Most of the questions have both sophisticated and unsophisticated methods of solution. Also, many questions actually coordinate more than one concept.

K-R 20 reliabilities of Forms A and B are reported as .80 and .83 for high school and .78 and .80 for college students. However, these coefficients are undoubtedly spuriously high due to the speededness of the tests. On Form A, only a third of the college students reached the last item; their average percentage of correct answers to the last 11 items was only 12 percent. The test is hard; mean values range from 14.81 to 16.25 for the different groups out of a 40-item test with standard deviations of about

6. Thus, the test can be summarized as difficult with a high spurious reliability caused by considerable speededness. Comparability of forms has been carefully checked out. No alternate-form reliabilities are reported.

The scales for reporting scores are carefully described and the norming procedure appears to be quite adequate. However, for someone to use the norms now would be difficult. Mathematics courses which include trigonometry, at both high school and college level, are quite different from those of 10 years ago when the test was being developed. Persons intending to use this test as a means of assessing performance in trigonometry should take this into consideration.

Of the tests that are currently available for assessing performance in trigonometry, this is probably the best one. Its content, although not particularly modern, is adequate. Many of the items are excellent, but a user should be cautioned that (*a*) some areas of content currently covered in trigonometry courses are not adequately covered, (*b*) the statistical characteristics of the test indicate that it is hard and speeded, and (*c*) the norms are probably no longer appropriate.

For excerpts from reviews of the series, see 465.

[544]

*Trigonometry: Minnesota High School Achievement Examinations.** High school; 1961–71; new or revised form issued each May; Form EH Rev. ['71, c1968, 4 pages]; no specific manual; series manual ('71, 16 pages); no data on reliability; 15¢ per test; separate answer sheets (IBM 1230) may be used; 10¢ per answer sheet including scoring service; $1 per series manual; postage extra; $1.10 per specimen set, postpaid; 60(65) minutes; edited by V. L. Lohmann; American Guidance Service, Inc. *